The Indispensable PC Hardware Book

Your Hardware Questions Answered

SECOND EDITION

Hans-Peter Messmer

ADDISON-WESLEY
PUBLISHING
COMPANY

Wokingham, England • Reading, Massachusetts • Menlo Park, California • New York
Don Mills, Ontario • Amsterdam • Bonn • Sydney • Singapore
Tokyo • Madrid • San Juan • Milan • Paris • Mexico City • Seoul • Taipei

The programs in this book have been included for their instructional value. They have been tested with care but are not guaranteed for any particular purpose. The publisher does not offer any warranties or representations, nor does it accept any liabilities with respect to the programs.

Many of the designations used by manufacturers and sellers to distinguish their products are claimed as trademarks. Addison-Wesley has made every attempt to supply trademark information about manufacturers and their products mentioned in this book. A list of the trademark designations and their owners appears on page XXIV.

Cover designed by Chris Eley
and printed by The Riverside Printing Co. (Reading) Ltd.
Typeset by someTimes GmbH, Munich.
Printed in the United States of America.

First edition published 1993. Reprinted 1994.
Second edition printed 1995. Reprinted 1995.

ISBN 0-201-87697-3

British Library Cataloguing in Publication Data
A catalogue record for this book is available from the British Library.

Library of Congress Cataloging in Publication Data
Messmer. Hans-Peter.
[PC-Hardwarebuch. English]
The indispensable PC hardware book : your hardware questions answered / Hans-Peter Messmer. – 2nd ed.
p. cm.
Translation of: PC-Hardwarebuch.
Includes index.
ISBN 0–201–87697–3
1. Computer input-output equipment. 2. Microcomputers.
I. Title.
TK7887.5.M4613 1995 94–25279
004.165–dc20 CIP

Contents

Introduction XXIII

Part 1: Basics 1

1	**Main Components**	**1**
1.1	The Computer and Peripherals	1
1.2	Inside the Personal Computer	2
1.2.1	How to Open the Case	2
1.2.2	Data Flow inside the PC	6
1.2.3	The Motherboard	7
1.2.4	Graphics Adapters and Monitors	11
1.2.5	Drive Controllers, Floppy and Hard Disk Drives	14
1.2.6	Streamers and Other Drives	16
1.2.7	Parallel Interfaces and Printers	18
1.2.8	Serial Interfaces and Modems	20
1.2.9	Network Adapters and LANs	22
1.2.10	CMOS RAM and Real-Time Clock	24
1.2.11	Keyboard	26
1.2.12	Mice and other Rodents	27
1.2.13	The Power Supply	29
1.3	Documentation	30
1.4	Taking Care of Data and Users	31
1.5	Operating System, BIOS and Memory Organization	32

Part 2: Processor and Memory 39

2	**Intel's Microprocessor for Beginners – The i386**	**39**
2.1	The Field-Effect Transistor	39
2.2	Basics of Machine Related Information Representation	42
2.2.1	Decimal and Binary System	43
2.2.2	ASCII Code	44
2.2.3	Negative Integers and Two's Complement	44
2.2.4	Hexadecimal Numbers	45
2.2.5	BCD Numbers	46
2.2.6	Little Endian Format and Intel Notation	47
2.3	The CPU as the Kernel of all Computers	47
2.4	Pre-Summary: Processors, Bus Widths and other Characteristics from PC to EISA and Local Bus	49
2.5	The i386 Microprocessor	50
2.5.1	General Structure of the i386	51
2.5.2	CPU, Main Memory and Segmentation in Real Mode	52
2.6	General-Purpose and Segment Registers	55

2.7 The Flags 60
2.8 Control and Memory Management Registers 63
2.8.1 Control Registers 63
2.8.2 Debug Registers 65
2.8.3 Memory Management Registers 67
2.9 The CPU Bus as the Connection to the Outside World 68

3 Logical Memory Addressing and Memory Access 69
3.1 Code Segment and Instruction Pointer 69
3.2 Stack Segment and Stack Pointer 71
3.3 Data Segment DS and Addressing 72
3.4 Addressing Schemes and Instruction Encoding 73
3.4.1 Mnemonics and the Assembler 73
3.4.2 Addressing Schemes 74
3.4.3 Instruction Encoding 76
3.4.4 Reading Instructions and Prefetching 77
3.5 i386 Real Mode, High-Memory Area and HIMEM.SYS 79
3.6 Interrupts and Exceptions 80
3.6.1 Software Interrupts 81
3.6.2 Hardware Interrupts 83
3.6.3 Exceptions 84
3.7 i386 Protected Mode 86
3.7.1 Segment Selectors, Segment Descriptors and Privilege Levels 87
3.7.2 Global and Local Descriptor Tables 92
3.7.3 Segment Descriptor Cache Registers 95
3.7.4 Switching into Protected Mode 96
3.7.5 Memory Addressing in Protected Mode 97
3.7.6 Segment and Access Types 98
3.7.7 Control Transfer and Call Gates 102
3.7.8 Interrupt Descriptor Table 106
3.7.9 Multitasking, TSS and Task Gates 107
3.7.10 I/O Address Space Protection via the IOPL Flag 111
3.7.11 I/O Address Space Protection via the I/O Permission Bit Map 112
3.7.12 Protected Mode Exceptions 114
3.7.13 Summary of Protection Mechanisms in Protected Mode 115
3.7.14 BIOS Access to Extended Memory 115
3.7.15 Interface to Hardware in Protected Mode – the ABIOS 115
3.8 Paging 118
3.8.1 Logical, Linear, Physical Addresses and Paging 119
3.8.2 Page Directory, Page Tables, Page Frames and the CR3 Register 120
3.8.3 Paging Exceptions 125
3.8.4 Test Registers TR6 and TR7 for Checking the TLB 125
3.9 i386 Virtual 8086 Mode – Myth and Reality 127
3.9.1 Virtual Machines and Virtual 8086 Monitors 128
3.9.2 Addresses in Virtual 8086 Mode 128

3.9.3 Entering and Leaving Virtual 8086 Mode 129
3.9.4 Tasks in Virtual 8086 Mode 130
3.9.5 Paging and Virtual 8086 Mode 134

4 Physical Memory Addressing and Memory Access 136
4.1 i386 Pin Connections 136
4.2 Physical Memory Access 140
4.2.1 Signal Path Between CPU and Memory 140
4.2.2 Bus Cycle for Read Access 142
4.2.3 Bus Cycle for Write Access 144
4.2.4 Wait States 145
4.2.5 Address Pipelining or Pipelined Addressing 147
4.2.6 Double Word Boundary 148
4.2.7 Special Bus Cycles 150
4.2.8 Flexible i386 Bus – 16-bit Data Bus and Write Data Duplication 151
4.3 I/O Address Space and Peripherals 152
4.3.1 I/O Addressing 153
4.3.2 I/O Cycles 154

5 Processor Reset and the i386 Internal Self-Test 155

6 Basics: Logic Gates and Microprogramming – Two Basic Elements of a Processor 157
6.1 AND and OR Gates as Basic Logical Elements 157
6.2 CMOS Inverters as Low-power Elements 158
6.3 An Example: 1-Bit Adder 161
6.4 Microencoding of Machine Code Instructions 162

7 Calculating Semiconductor – The i387 Mathematical Coprocessor 167
7.1 Number Excursion – The Representation of Floating-Point Numbers 167
7.1.1 Scientific Notation and Biased Exponent 167
7.1.2 The Standard – IEEE Formats 169
7.1.3 BASIC Programmers Pay Attention – The MSBIN Format 172
7.2 Functional Expansion and Performance Gain 173
7.3 i387 Number Formats and Floating-point Instructions 174
7.4 i387 Pinout and Signals 176
7.5 Structure and Function of the i387 180
7.6 i387 Exceptions 185
7.7 The Protected Mode and Memory Images of Instruction and Data Pointers 187
7.8 i387 Memory Cycles and Communication Between the i386 and the i387 189
7.9 i386/i387 System Configuration 190
7.10 i387 Reset 191

8	**i386 Processor Derivatives**	**192**
8.1	Cutting Down – The SX Variants of the Processors	192
8.2	386SL Chip Set – A Two-Chip AT	194
8.2.1	Internal Structure of the 386SL and 82360SL	194
8.2.2	Terminals and Signals	196
8.3	Processor Confusion by i386 Clones	203
8.3.1	AMD Processors	204
8.3.2	Chips & Technologies Processors	206
8.3.3	Cyrix CPUs	209
8.3.4	IBM – For Members Only	210
9	**Caching – Cooperation with High Speed Memories**	**211**
9.1	Cache Principle and Cache Strategies	211
9.2	Cache Organization and Associative Memory (CAM)	214
9.3	Cache Hit Determination	217
9.4	Replacement Strategies	218
9.5	On-Chip and Second-Level Caches	220
9.6	Cache Consistency and the MESI Protocol	221
9.6.1	The Four MESI States	221
9.6.2	MESI State Transitions	222
9.6.3	L2-Cache Subsystems and MESI Cache Consistency Protocol	225
10	**Performance Enhancement – The i486**	**227**
10.1	i486 Pins and Signals	227
10.2	i486 Internal Structure	233
10.3	A Star is Born – RISC Principles on a Hardware and Software Level	235
10.3.1	Surprising Results – Less is More	236
10.3.2	RISC Characteristics at a Hardware Level	237
10.3.3	RISC Characteristics at a Software Level	242
10.4	i486 Pipeline	245
10.5	i486 On-Chip Cache	247
10.6	i486 and i386/i387 – Differences and Similarities	249
10.6.1	Differences in Register Structures	249
10.6.2	Differences in Memory Management	251
10.6.3	i486 Reset	252
10.6.4	i486 Real Mode	252
10.6.5	i486 Protected Mode	253
10.6.6	i486 Virtual 8086 Mode	253
10.6.7	Integer Core and Floating-Point Unit	253
10.6.8	FPU Exceptions	254
10.6.9	Translation Lookaside Buffer (TLB)	254
10.7	i486 Bus	254
10.7.1	Burst Cycles	255
10.7.2	Special Cycles	256
10.7.3	Invalidation Cycles	257
10.8	Test Functions	257

10.8.1	Internal Self-Test BIST	258
10.8.2	Testing the TLB	258
10.8.3	Testing the On-Chip Cache	259
10.8.4	Tristate Test Mode	261
10.8.5	JTAG Boundary Scan Test	261
10.9	i486 I/O Address Space	266
11	**i486 Cut-down Versions, Overdrives, Upgrades and Clones**	**267**
11.1	i486SX and i487SX – First Reduce, Then Upgrade	267
11.1.1	i486SX – More Than an i386	267
11.1.2	Clock Frequencies	270
11.1.3	i487SX – i486SX Upgrade	270
11.2	486DX2 Processors with Internal Frequency Doubling	273
11.2.1	The Clock Frequencies Problem	273
11.2.2	The Solution – Internal Frequency Doubling	274
11.2.3	So What's the Gain?	275
11.2.4	Clock Statements	276
11.2.5	Upgrading and Overdrives	276
11.3	Low-power Versions of i486DX/SX	279
11.4	The i486DX4	280
11.4.1	Pin Connections	281
11.4.2	New Flags, Control Registers and Extensions to the Virtual 8086 Mode	283
11.4.3	i486DX4 Identification with CPUID	284
11.4.4	Power Saving Features	285
11.4.5	i486DX4 JTAG Boundary Scan Test	286
11.5	The SL Enhanced i486	287
11.5.1	SL Enhanced i486DX with 1x-clock	287
11.5.2	SL Enhanced i486DX2 with 1/2x-clock	288
11.5.3	SL Enhanced i486SX with 1x-clock	288
11.5.4	SL Enhanced i486DX with 2x-clock	289
11.5.5	SL Enhanced i486SX with 2x-clock	289
11.5.6	i486SL Identification with CPUID	289
11.6	i486 Clones	290
11.6.1	AMD Clones	290
11.6.2	Cyrix Clones	294
11.6.3	IBM's Blue Lightning	294
12	**At Present, Land's End – The 110 MIPS RISC Superscalar Pentium**	**295**
12.1	Pins and Signals	296
12.2	Internal Pentium Structure	307
12.2.1	The Integer Pipelines u and v	309
12.2.2	Instruction Pairing Inside the Integer Pipelines	312
12.2.3	The Floating-point Pipeline	315
12.2.4	Instruction Serialization	317
12.2.5	Dynamic Branch Prediction	318
12.2.6	Pentium On-Chip Caches	320

12.3 Pentium Compatibility and New Pentium Features 325
12.3.1 Extensions to the Pentium Registers 325
12.3.2 Model-Specific Registers 326
12.3.3 Pentium Real Mode 327
12.3.4 Pentium Protected Mode 328
12.3.5 Pentium Virtual 8086 Mode 328
12.3.6 Paging on the Pentium 329
12.3.7 Debug Extensions 331
12.3.8 Pentium Reset, Pentium Initialization and Self-Test 332
12.3.9 CPU Identification with CPUID 334
12.4 Pentium Bus 335
12.4.1 Single Transfer Cycles 336
12.4.2 Burst Cycles 336
12.4.3 Pentium Address Pipelining 339
12.4.4 Special Bus Cycles 340
12.4.5 Inquiry Cycles and Internal Snooping 341
12.4.6 Internal Pentium Bus Buffers 341
12.5 Pentium System Management Mode 342
12.5.1 System Management Mode Interrupt SMI 342
12.5.2 SMM RAM Structure 343
12.5.3 Program Execution in System Management Mode 345
12.5.4 Return from System Management Mode 345
12.6 Code Optimization with Performance Monitoring 345
12.6.1 Hardware Elements for Performance Monitoring 346
12.6.2 Access via the Test Access Port 346
12.7 Pentium Test Functions 347
12.7.1 Pentium JTAG Boundary Scan Test 347
12.7.2 Detection of Internal Errors 348
12.7.3 Detection of Bus Interface Errors 348
12.7.4 Execution Tracing 349
12.7.5 Hardware Debug Support and Probe Mode 350
12.7.6 Machine Check Exception 351
12.8 Pentium I/O Address Space 351
12.9 L2-Cache Subsystem 82496/82491 for the Pentium 351

13 Compatibility Downwards – The 80286 354
13.1 80286 Connections and Signals 354
13.2 80286 Registers 358
13.3 80286 Protected Mode 358
13.3.1 80286 Memory Management Registers 358
13.3.2 80286 Segment Descriptors 358
13.3.3 80286 Segment and Access Types 359
13.3.4 Multitasking, 80286 TSS and 80286 Task Gate 360
13.3.5 80286 Protection for I/O Address Space 362
13.4 80286 Bus Cycles and Pipelining 362

13.5 Word Boundaries 363
13.6 80286 Reset 364

14 The 80287 – Mathematical Assistant in Protected Mode 365
14.1 80287 Connections and Signals 366
14.2 80287 Structure and Functioning 369
14.3 80287 Reset 369
14.4 80287 Exceptions 370
14.5 Communication Between CPU and 80287 370
14.6 80286/80287 System Configuration 371

15 Everything Began with the Ancestor 8086 372
15.1 8086 Pins and Signals 372
15.2 8086 Operating Modes and the 8288 Bus Controller 376
15.3 8086 Real Mode 377
15.4 Memory Access 377
15.5 Word Boundary 380
15.6 Access to the I/O Address Space 380
15.7 8086 Reset 381
15.8 The 8088 382
15.9 The 80186/88 383

16 Our Mathematical Grandmother – The MathCo 8087 385
16.1 8087 Number Formats and Numerical Instruction Set 385
16.2 8087 Pins and Signals 385
16.3 8087 Structure and Functioning 388
16.4 8087 Memory Cycles 389
16.5 8086/8087 System Configuration 390

17 Memory Chips 392
17.1 Small and Cheap – DRAM 392
17.1.1 Structure and Operation Principle 394
17.1.2 Reading and Writing Data 395
17.1.3 Semiconductor Layer Structure 400
17.1.4 DRAM Refresh 402
17.1.5 DRAM Chip Organization 404
17.1.6 Fast Operating Modes of DRAM Chips 405
17.1.7 SIMM and SIP 410
17.2 A Didactical Example for Intelligent Memory Controllers – The 82C212 Page/Interleave Memory Controller 412
17.2.1 Terminals and Signals 413
17.2.2 Internal 82C212 Structure 419
17.2.3 Shadow RAM and BIOS 421
17.2.4 Expanded Memory and Memory Mapping 424
17.2.5 82C212 Configuration Registers 427
17.3 Fast and Expensive – SRAM 434
17.3.1 The Flip-Flop 434

17.3.2 Access to SRAM Memory Cells 436
17.3.3 Typical SRAM – The Intel 51258 437
17.4 Long-Term Memory – ROM, EPROM and other PROMs 438
17.4.1 ROM 438
17.4.2 EPROM 439
17.4.3 EEPROM 441
17.5 Silicon Hard Disks – Flash Memories 443

Part 3: Personal Computer Architectures and Bus Systems 449

18 The 8-Bit PC/XT Architecture 449
18.1 The Components and their Cooperation 449
18.2 DMA Architecture 454
18.2.1 8-Bit Channels 455
18.2.2 Memory Refresh 457
18.2.3 Memory–Memory Transfer 457
18.3 I/O Channel and Bus Slots 457

19 16-Bit AT Architecture 461
19.1 Components and Their Cooperation 461
19.2 DMA Architecture 467
19.2.1 8-Bit and 16-Bit Channels 467
19.2.2 Memory Refresh 469
19.2.3 Memory–Memory Transfers 469
19.3 I/O Channel and Bus Slots 470
19.4 AT Bus Frequencies and the ISA Bus 474

20 32-Bit EISA Architecture 476
20.1 EISA Bus Structure 477
20.2 Bus Arbitration 479
20.3 DMA Architecture 480
20.4 Interrupt Subsystem 482
20.5 EISA Timer and Fail-Safe Timer 484
20.6 I/O Address Space 484
20.7 CMOS-RAM 485
20.8 EISA Adapters and Automatic Configuration 488
20.9 EISA Slot 489
20.10 EISA Signals 491

21 32-Bit Microchannel – Revolution 494
21.1 MCA Bus Structure 494
21.2 Bus Arbitration 496
21.3 Memory System 498
21.4 DMA 499
21.5 Interrupts 499
21.6 MCA Timer and Fail-Safe Timer 499

21.7	I/O Ports and I/O Address Space	500
21.8	MCA Adapters and Automatic Configuration	501
21.9	On-Board VGA and External Graphics Adapters	504
21.10	PS/2 Model 30	505
21.11	The MCA Slot	505
21.12	MCA Signals	507
22	**32 Bits and More – The Local Bus**	**512**
22.1	Peripheral Component Interconnect (PCI)	513
22.1.1	PCI Bus Structure	513
22.1.2	Bus Cycles	516
22.1.3	Bus Arbitration	521
22.1.4	DMA	522
22.1.5	Interrupts	522
22.1.6	I/O Address Space	523
22.1.7	Configuration Address Space	525
22.1.8	PCI-Specific BIOS Routines	530
22.1.9	PCI Slots	532
22.1.10	PCI Adapters	535
22.1.11	PCI Signals	535
22.2	VESA Local Bus VLB	540
22.2.1	VLB Bus Structure	540
22.2.2	Bus Cycles	542
22.2.3	Bus Arbitration	546
22.2.4	DMA	547
22.2.5	Interrupts	547
22.2.6	I/O Address Space	549
22.2.7	VLB Slots	549
22.2.8	VLB Adapters	549
22.2.9	VLB Signals	550
22.3	Typical Local Bus Units	554
22.4	Bottlenecks in Local Bus Systems	554
Part 4:	**Support Chips – Nothing Runs Without Us**	**557**
23	**Hardware Interrupts and the 8259A Programmable Interrupt Controller**	**557**
23.1	Interrupt-Driven Data Exchange and Polling	557
23.2	8259A Connections and Signals	559
23.3	Internal Structure and Interrupt Acknowledge Sequence	560
23.4	Cascading	563
23.5	Initialization and Programming	565
23.6	Masking the NMI	573
23.7	Remarks About Powerful Multiprocessor Interrupt Subsystems	575
23.7.1	APIC 82489DX Structure and Function	576
23.7.2	Multi-APIC Systems and the ICC Bus	577

24	**8253/8254 Programmable Interval Timer**	**579**
24.1	Structure and Functioning of the PIT 8253/8254	579
24.2	8253/8254 Terminals and Signals	581
24.3	Programming the 8253/8254	582
24.4	Writing Count Values	583
24.5	Reading Count Values	584
24.6	8253/8254 Counting Modes	588
24.7	System Clock	592
24.8	Memory Refresh	594
24.9	The Speaker	596
24.10	Failsafe Timer	596
25	**DMA Chip 8237A – A Detour Highway in the PC**	**598**
25.1	Direct Memory Access with Peripherals and Memory	598
25.2	Standard 8237A DMA Chip	599
25.2.1	8237A Connections and Signals	599
25.2.2	Internal Structure and Operation Modes of the 8237A	603
25.2.3	Programming the 8237A	612
25.2.4	Example: Initialize DMA 1, Channel 2 for Floppy Data Transfer	619
25.2.5	DMA Cycles in Protected and Virtual 8086 Mode	620
26	**Other Peripheral Chips and Components**	**622**
26.1	About Tones and Sounds – The Speaker	622
26.1.1	Direct Activation via the 8253/8254 PIT	624
26.1.2	Periodic Activation by the CPU	626
26.2	The 8255 Programmable Peripheral Interface	628
26.2.1	PPI 8255 Terminals and Signals	628
26.2.2	8255 PPI Structure and Operating Modes	630
26.2.3	Programming the 8255 PPI	632
26.2.4	Port Assignment in the PC/XT	633
26.3	CMOS RAM and Real-Time Clock	636
26.3.1	MC146818 Structure and Programming	637
26.3.2	Access via the BIOS	647
26.3.3	Access via Address and Data Register	647
26.3.4	Extended CMOS RAM	648
Part 5:	**Mass Storage**	**651**
27	**Floppies and Floppy Drives**	**651**
27.1	Ferromagnetism and Induction – The Basis of Magnetic Data Recording	651
27.1.1	Diamagnetism and Paramagnetism	651
27.1.2	Ferromagnetism	652
27.1.3	Induction	654
27.2	Structure and Functioning of Floppies and Floppy Drives	655
27.3	Physical Organization of Floppies	660
27.4	Logical Organization of Floppies and Hard Disks with DOS	663

27.4.1	Logical Sectors	664
27.4.2	The Partition	664
27.4.3	The Boot Sector	668
27.4.4	The Root Directory	670
27.4.5	The Subdirectories	674
27.4.6	The File Allocation Table (FAT)	675
27.4.7	The Files	679
27.4.8	DOS Version Differences	681
27.4.9	Other File Systems	682
27.5	System Configuration PC-Controller-Drive	683
27.5.1	Controllers and Drives	684
27.5.2	Drive Configuration	686
27.6	Recording Formats and CRC	689
27.6.1	Sector Layout	689
27.6.2	FM and MFM	691
27.6.3	CRC – Nothing Can Hide From Me	694
27.6.4	For Freaks Only – Some Amazing Features of CRC Codes	699
27.7	Programming Floppy Drives – Access Levels and Compatibility	702
27.7.1	Application Programs	702
27.7.2	High-Level Languages and Operating Systems	702
27.7.3	BIOS and Registers	704
27.8	Programming Floppy Drives – Access via DOS	705
27.9	Programming Floppy Drives – Access via BIOS Interrupt INT 13h	709
27.10	Programming Floppy Drives – Direct Access via Registers	713
27.10.1	Structure and Functioning of a Floppy Controller	713
27.10.2	Configuration of a PC Floppy Controller	715
27.10.3	Floppy Controller Registers	716
27.10.4	Floppy Controller Commands and Command Phases	720
27.10.5	Specify Drive Parameters	728
27.10.6	Error Recovery Strategy	730
28	**Hard Disk Drives**	**731**
28.1	Structure and Functioning of Hard Disk Drives	732
28.1.1	The Head-Disk Assembly (HDA)	732
28.1.2	Interleaving	742
28.1.3	Controller and Interfaces	744
28.1.4	Capacity, Data Transfer Rate and Reliability	747
28.1.5	BIOS Configuration	753
28.2	Recording Formats, Low-Level Formatting and Bad-Sector Mapping	754
28.2.1	MFM and RLL	754
28.2.2	High-Level Formatting of Hard Disks with FORMAT	757
28.2.3	Low-Level Formatting and Bad-Sector Mapping	758
28.2.4	Error Recovery Strategies	763
28.2.5	Autoconfiguration	765
28.3	Integrating Exotic Drives and Translating	766

28.3.1 BIOS Interrupt 13h, Function 09h – Set Drive Parameters 766
28.3.2 BIOS Extensions and Booting 768
28.3.3 Translating and Zone Recording 771
28.4 Access via DOS and the BIOS 773
28.4.1 DOS Interrupts 25h and 26h 773
28.4.2 Hard Disk Functions of BIOS Interrupt 13h 776
28.5 ST412/506 and ESDI 780
28.5.1 ST412/506 Interfaces and the Connection Between Drive and Controller 780
28.5.2 Connecting and Configuring ST412/506 Hard Disk Drives 783
28.5.3 The ESDI Interface 783
28.5.4 ESDI Commands and Configuration Data 787
28.5.5 Connecting and Configuring ESDI Hard Disk Drives 789
28.6 Drives with IDE, AT Bus or ATA Interface 790
28.6.1 The Physical CPU-Drive Interface 791
28.6.2 Features of IDE Hard Disk Drives 794
28.6.3 The AT Task File 795
28.6.4 IDE Interface Programming and Command Phases 800
28.6.5 Enhanced IDE 804
28.7 SCSI 805
28.7.1 SCSI Bus and Connection to the PC 806
28.7.2 Memory-Mapped I/O and SCSI Task File of Host Adapters ST01 and ST02 815
28.7.3 Programming and Command Phases 820
28.7.4 ASPI 825
28.7.5 Other Standardized SCSI Programming Interfaces 828
28.7.6 Different SCSI Standards 830
28.8 Optical Mass Storage 832
28.8.1 CD-ROM 833
28.8.2 WORM 835
28.8.3 Magneto-Optical Drives 835

Part 6: Externals and Peripherals 839

29 Interfaces – Connection to the Outside World 839
29.1 Parallel Interface 839
29.1.1 Printing 839
29.1.2 Printing Via DOS 840
29.1.3 Printing Via BIOS Interrupt INT 17h 842
29.1.4 Structure, Function and Connection to Printers 844
29.1.5 Programming the Registers Directly 847
29.1.6 More About LPTx – LPTx General Interface Assignment 850
29.2 Serial Interface 853
29.2.1 Serial and Asynchronous Data Transfer 853
29.2.2 RS-232C Interface 857
29.2.3 Connection to Printers and the Zeromodem 864
29.2.4 Access Via DOS 867

29.2.5	Access Via the BIOS	868
29.2.6	The UART 8250/16450/16550	871
29.3	Other Interfaces	889
29.3.1	IBM Adapter for Computer Games	889
29.3.2	Network Adapters	893
29.3.3	Datanets, Packet Switching and PAD Adapters	894
29.3.4	Fax Adapter Cards	896
29.4	Small but Universal – PCMCIA	896
29.4.1	Structure and Function	897
29.4.2	PCMCIA Contacts	899
29.4.3	Access with Socket Services of INT 1ah, Functions 80h–ffh	902
29.4.4	Access Through PCMCIA Controller Registers – An Example	904
30	**Local Area Networks and Network Adapters**	**910**
30.1	Network Topologies	910
30.1.1	Bus Topology	910
30.1.2	Ring Topology	912
30.1.3	Star Topology	912
30.2	Access Procedure	913
30.2.1	CSMA/CD	913
30.2.2	Token Passing	914
30.2.3	Token Bus	914
30.3	Ethernet	915
30.3.1	Thick Ethernet	915
30.3.2	CheaperNet or Thin Ethernet	916
30.4	Token Ring	916
30.5	FDDI	918
31	**Keyboards and Mice**	**919**
31.1	The Keyboard	919
31.1.1	Structure and Functioning of Intelligent and Less Intelligent Keyboards	920
31.1.2	Scan codes – A Keyboard Map	921
31.1.3	Keyboard Access Via DOS	925
31.1.4	Keyboard Access Via the BIOS	926
31.1.5	Programming the Keyboard Directly via Ports	932
31.2	Mice and Other Rodents	943
31.2.1	Structure and Function	943
31.2.2	Mouse Driver and Mouse Interface	944
31.2.3	Programming the Mouse	946
31.2.4	The PS/2 Mouse	948
31.3	Trackball	952
31.4	Digitizer or Graph Tablet	953
32	**Graphics Adapters**	**954**
32.1	Displaying Images on a Monitor and the General Structure of Graphics Adapters	954
32.2	Screen Modes and the 6845 Graphics Controller	957

32.2.1	6845 Video Controller	958
32.2.2	Character Generation in Text Mode	960
32.2.3	Character Generation and Free Graphics in Graphics Mode	962
32.2.4	General Video RAM Organization and Structure	963
32.2.5	The Hercules Card and Programming the 6845	967
32.3	Most Important Adapter Types and Their Characteristics	976
32.3.1	MDA – Everthing is Very Grey	977
32.3.2	CGA – It's Getting to Be Coloured	978
32.3.3	Hercules – The Non-Fitting Standard	979
32.3.4	EGA – More Colours and a Higher Resolution	980
32.3.5	VGA – Colours and More Colours	985
32.3.6	VESA SVGA – High-Resolution Standard	988
32.3.7	8514/A and Windows Accelerator – One More Window	989
32.3.8	TIGA – Bigger, Better, Faster	990
32.4	Accessing the Screen via DOS	992
32.5	Accessing the Screen Via the BIOS	993
32.5.1	Graphics Routines of Standard BIOS	994
32.5.2	Trouble Support – The EGA and VGA BIOS	995
32.5.3	Standard Extension – VESA SVGA BIOS	1000
32.6	Help for Self-Help – Accessing the Video Memory Directly	1001
32.6.1	MDA	1002
32.6.2	CGA	1002
32.6.3	Hercules Graphics Card	1004
32.6.4	EGA	1005
32.6.5	VGA	1008
32.6.6	SVGA	1009
32.6.7	Accelerators	1011
32.6.8	Summary	1011
32.7	Graphics Processor Versus Local Bus	1011
33	**Multimedia**	**1014**
33.1	Technological Background	1014
33.2	Programming	1018
33.3	An Example: The FM Channels of SoundBlaster	1019
33.3.1	Sound with Nine Channels	1020
33.3.2	Sound with Six Channels and Five Percussions	1025
	Appendices	**1027**
A	**ASCII and Scan Codes**	**1027**
A.1	ASCII Code	1027
A.2	Scan Codes UK	1030
A.3	Scan Codes USA	1032

B	**80x86 Processor Machine Instructions**	**1034**
B.1	8086/88	1034
B.2	80186/88	1039
B.3	80286	1039
B.4	i386	1040
B.5	i486	1042
B.6	Pentium	1043
B.7	Pentium Instruction Pairing Rules	1043
C	**80x87 Processor Machine Instructions**	**1045**
C.1	8087	1045
C.2	80287	1049
C.3	80287XL and i387/i387SX	1049
C.4	i486	1050
C.5	Pentium	1050
D	**Interrupts**	**1051**
D.1	PC Hardware Interrupts	1051
D.2	PC Software Interrupts	1051
D.3	80x86 Exceptions	1052
E	**BIOS Clock Interrupt 1ah and Functions 83h/86h of INT 15h**	**1054**
E.1	BIOS Interrupt INT 1ah	1054
E.2	Wait Functions 83h and 86h of BIOS Interrupt INT 15h	1056
F	**BIOS Interrupt INT 13h**	**1058**
F.1	The Functions	1058
F.2	Error Codes	1068
F.3	Hard Disk Drive Parameter Table	1069
F.4	Format Buffer	1069
F.5	Floppy Disk Parameter Table	1070
G	**Floppy Disk Controllers**	**1071**
G.1	The Commands	1071
G.1.1	List of Valid Commands	1071
G.1.2	Data Transfer Commands	1072
G.1.3	Control Commands	1078
G.1.4	Extended Commands	1082
G.2	Status Registers ST0 to ST3	1085
H	**Hard Disk Drive Controllers**	**1089**
H.1	The IDE Interface Commands	1089
H.1.1	Summary of the Listed Commands	1090
H.1.2	Required Commands	1090
H.1.3	Optional Commands	1100
H.1.4	Optional IDE Commands	1103
H.2	SCSI Commands	1104
H.2.1	Summary of Listed Commands	1105

H.2.2	6-Byte Commands	1107
H.2.3	10-Byte Commands	1121
H.2.4	Status Key	1132
H.2.5	Additional Status Codes	1132
H.3	ASPI Programming Interface	1134
H.3.1	ASPI Functions	1134
H.3.2	SCSI Request Block	1135
H.3.3	ASPI Status Codes	1138
I	**Access to Interfaces**	**1139**
I.1	Parallel Interface	1139
I.1.1	DOS Functions	1139
I.1.2	BIOS Functions	1140
I.1.3	Printer Status Byte	1141
I.2	Serial Interface	1141
I.2.1	DOS Functions	1141
I.2.2	BIOS Functions	1142
I.2.3	Transmit Status	1145
I.2.4	Modem Status	1145
I.2.5	Parameter Byte	1146
I.2.6	Modem Control Register	1146
J	**Keyboard and Mouse Access**	**1147**
J.1	The Keyboard	1147
J.1.1	DOS Functions	1147
J.1.2	BIOS Interrupt INT 16h	1149
J.1.3	BIOS Interrupt INT 15h	1151
J.1.4	First Shift Status Byte	1152
J.1.5	Second Shift Status Byte	1152
J.2	Mouse Interrupt 33h	1152
J.2.1	Functions of INT 33h	1153
J.2.2	Button Byte	1158
J.3	PS/2 Mouse Support via BIOS Interrupt INT 15h, Function c2h	1158
J.3.1	Subfunctions of INT 15h, Function c2h	1158
J.3.2	Status Byte	1161
J.3.3	Mouse Packet on the Stack	1161
K	**Access to Graphics Adapters**	**1162**
K.1	DOS Functions	1162
K.2	BIOS Interrupt INT 10h – Standard Functions of the System BIOS	1163
K.3	BIOS Interrupt INT 10h – Additional Functions of the EGA/VGA BIOS	1170
K.4	BIOS Interrupt INT 10h – Additional SVGA BIOS Functions	1187
L	**Functions 87h and 89h of Interrupt 15h**	**1193**

M PCMCIA Socket Services **1195**
M.1 Function Groups 1195
M.2 The Functions 1196
M.3 Error Codes 1211
M.4 PCMCIA Card Services Summarized 1212
M.4.1 Card Services Functions 1212
M.4.2 Events 1214
M.4.3 Error Codes 1214

Glossary **1217**

Index **1269**

Introduction

Dear Reader,

Thank you for consulting this introduction. As a long preface is a waste of time, I just want to give you a short glance at the contents of the revised and extended second edition of this – what I hope to be – Indispensable PC Hardware Book.

Who should read this book

This book aims to address a wide range of people who are interested in knowing more about the inner workings of a personal computer. Even beginners should not shy away from the extensive number of pages – they will be introduced gradually to the subject from a basic level of knowledge in Part 1. This book is for:

- everybody who wants to or who has to understand the structure and functioning of a personal computer, either as a professional or as a private user;
- programmers who want to access hardware components at a very low level;
- users who want to upgrade their PCs and who would like to understand what they are about to do;
- dealers who wish to advise their customers well;

and last but not least,

- curious people who want to look somewhat beyond the horizon and hear about the ideas behind such magic words as, for example, «protected and virtual 8086 mode» or the methods of packing hundreds of Mbytes into a pocket-sized box called HDD.

The indispensable contents of this book

The book is divided into six major parts which are self-contained and can be used independently.

Part 1, Basics, introduces the subject of personal computer hardware and takes a short tour through all the major components, so that beginners are prepared for the following more demanding parts.

Part 2, which includes Chapters 2 to 17, presents the motherboard components, that is, the Intel microprocessors from the ancestor 8086 up to the i486DX4 and Pentium as well as memory chips. They form the heart and brain of a PC. Part 2 focuses on the technology and the ideas behind these chips.

Part 3, including Chapters 18 to 22, introduces you to the various PC architectures. All bus systems from the legendary PC/XT up to EISA, microchannel and the modern VLB and PCI local buses are detailed.

Part 4, encompassing Chapters 23 to 26, provides extensive information about the support chips present in all PCs. You will learn why they are necessary and how to program them.

Part 5, including Chapters 27 and 28, is dedicated to mass storage. Floppy drives as well as hard disks and optical drives are discussed. Modern recording and reliable encoding techniques are presented and widely used drive interfaces are included, for example SCSI I/II/III and (Enhanced) IDE.

Part 6, comprising Chapters 29 to 33, presents interfaces, keyboards and mice as well as modern graphics adapters and multimedia. The structure, functioning and programming – indispensable in the case of interfaces – of these components are discussed. The chapter on multimedia introduces you to the ideas behind this keyword.

The extensive appendices provide a lot of practical information, especially for programmers. They can use Appendices E to M as a programming manual for DOS, BIOS and register-programmed functions.

Finally, the Glossary is a small but nevertheless comprehensive computer encyclopedia which explains most terms and concepts related to personal computer hardware.

Acknowledgements

This book is the result of a lot of work – not only by the author but also by many other people whom I would like to thank very warmly. In particular, Nicky Jaeger looked after me and the manuscript at all times. I also have to thank Jeremy Thompson and Annette Abel for carefully copy-editing and proofreading the manuscript. Moreover, I would like to thank all the companies and people who assisted me in writing the book by providing written or verbal information.

Hans-Peter Messmer
Bonn, April 1995

Part 1
Basics

This chapter outlines the basic components of a Personal Computer and various related peripherals as an introduction to the PC world. Though intended for beginners, advanced users would also be better prepared for the later and more technically demanding parts of the book.

1 Main Components

1.1 The Computer and Peripherals

Personal Computer (PC), by definition, means that users actually work with their own «personal» computer. This usually means IBM-compatible computers using the DOS, OS/2 or Windows (NT) operating system. Mainframe users may wonder what the difference is between a PC and a *terminal*: after all, a terminal also has a monitor, a keyboard and a small case like the PC, and looks much the same as that shown in Figure 1.1. Where there is a difference is that the PC contains a small but complete computer, with a processor (hidden behind the names 8086/8088, 80286 or i486, for example) and a floppy disk drive. This computer carries out data processing on its own, that is, it can process files, do mathematical calculations, and much more besides. On the other hand, a terminal only establishes a connection to the actual computer (the mainframe). The terminal can't carry out data processing on its own, being more a monitor with poor input and output capabilities that can be located up to a few kilometres away from the actual computer. That a small PC is less powerful than a mainframe occupying a whole building seems obvious (although this has changed with the introduction of the Pentium), but that is only true today. One of the first computers (called *ENIAC*, developed between 1943 and 1946, which worked with tubes instead of transistors) occupied a large building, and consumed so much electricity that the whole data processing institute could be heated by the dissipated power! Nevertheless, ENIAC was far less powerful than today's PCs.

Because PCs have to serve only one user, while mainframes are usually connected to more than 100 users (who are *logged in* to the mainframe), the lack of data processing performance in the PC is thus reduced, especially when using powerful Intel processors. Another feature of PCs (or microcomputers in general) is their excellent graphics capabilities, which are a necessary prerequisite for user-friendly and graphics-oriented programs like Microsoft's Windows. In this respect, the PC is superior to its «big brother».

Figure 1.1 shows a basic PC workstation. The hub, of course, is the PC, where you find not only the above-mentioned processor but one or more floppy disk drives, hard drives, interfaces and other devices. These are dealt with in some detail in Section 1.2. Because you can't enter commands into the actual PC, or receive data from it, a *keyboard* (for entering commands and data) and a *monitor* (for data output) are also present. High quality computer monitors are far more powerful (and therefore much more expensive) than a TV.

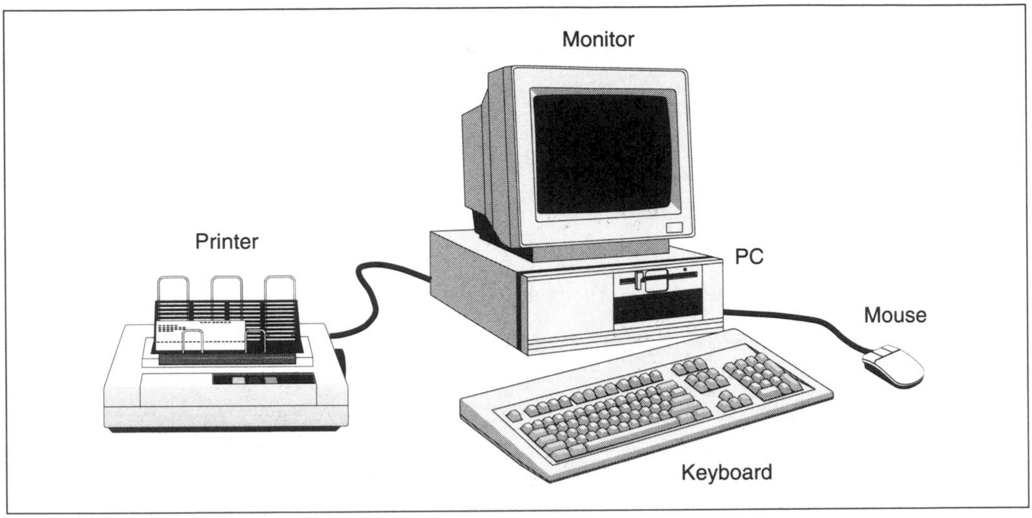

Figure 1.1: Basic PC equipment.

With this equipment you can start work: for example, entering text files, doing mathematical calculations, or playing computer games. To use the PC's graphics capabilities (with Windows, for example) a *mouse* is usually needed. In this book, «PC» always means the sum total of these components, because without a keyboard and a monitor you can't control the machine.

For printing text files, of course, you need a printer. By using various *interfaces* you can connect additional *peripherals* like a *plotter* (for drawing plans with coloured pencils) or a *modem* (for worldwide data communication). «Peripherals» means all those units located outside the PC's case.

1.2 Inside the Personal Computer

This chapter deals with the various components of a PC, starting with basic definitions of concepts like the motherboard, the controller etc; their functions are outlined. Also, an overall picture of the interworkings between individual components is given.

1.2.1 How to Open the Case

To work with a PC or to understand how it works, you don't, of course, need to open the case. But I think there are a lot of curious users who will soon want to look inside. The following gives some tips on doing this, while trying to avoid burnt-out electric components and rather unpleasant electric shocks. To open the case you'll need a screwdriver and some common sense.

It is best to use a magnetic screwdriver because, in my own experience, one or more screws will inevitably fall into the case. With a magnetic screwdriver you can get them out quite easily.

You may have heard that magnetic objects should never be placed near a PC. I would like to comment on this:

- the Earth has a magnetic field;
- if you scratch your disk with a sharp object you do so at your own risk; it doesn't matter whether it is a knitting needle, a hammer or a magnetic screwdriver;
- opening a hard disk drive means losing the data simply because of the dust that is always present in the air; whether the hard disk is disturbed magnetically afterwards is completely insignificant;
- the distance between the read/write heads and the disk surface is less than about 1 μm.

In principle, the Earth's magnetic field is shielded by the PC's metal case, but as soon as you remove the cover the magnetic field penetrates all the components. As all electronic and magnetic components are exposed to the Earth's magnetic field when the computer is assembled, this obviously can't have an adverse influence. Floppy and hard disks are coated with a thin magnetizing layer: if someone deliberately scratches off this coating, he really doesn't know what he is doing. The data medium of the hard disk drives is enclosed in a case so that dust particles in the air don't act as a sort of scouring powder. Therefore, the hard disk is destroyed not by magnetic but by mechanical action. Whether you are additionally damaging the still present magnetic pattern with a magnetic object after the mechanical destruction of the data medium would seem to be unimportant.

Finally, the distance between the read/write heads and the data medium is less than about 1 μm. Because of the protective envelope the closest you can bring the screwdriver to the data medium of a floppy disk is one millimetre away at most. That is one thousandth of the head-data medium distance. According to magnetostatic laws, the strength of the magnetic field decreases in proportion to the square of the distance. This means that the screwdriver must have a local field strength which is one millionth of the field of the read/write head. Perhaps someone could show me this monster of a screwdriver with its superconducting magnet! In the case of hard disk drives, this ratio is much greater because of the additional separation provided by the drive's case.

The dangers of mechanical destruction are clearly far more likely. I always use a magnetic screwdriver because I always lose a screw in the case, and because of the danger of a short circuit caused either by the screw or by a rash action after having tried to get the screw out.

Advice: **If your case is sealed and there is a notice advising that breaking the seal will invalidate the warranty, you should open the case only after having contacted your dealer.**

Figure 1.2 shows three examples of PC cases (two desktops and one tower), which are the most common types.

If you are one of those lucky PC buyers who got a technical reference book or at least a user handbook when you bought your PC, you should have a look at this handbook first to find out how to open the case. If you've found this information, then follow the manual and ignore the next paragraph.

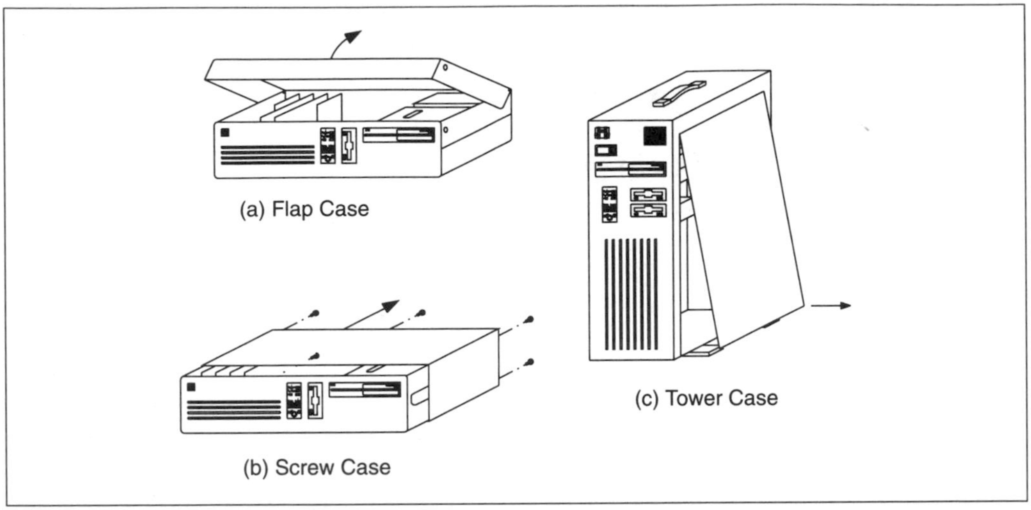

Figure 1.2: Cases. (a) flap case, (b) normal desktop case, (c) tower for a PC with extensive drives and adapter cards.

Advice: **Unplug all cables going into the PC before opening the case. If you damage a cable with your screwdriver an unpleasant electric shock may be the result. However, even if you have unplugged your PC, you should still be careful not to damage any cables or circuit boards.**

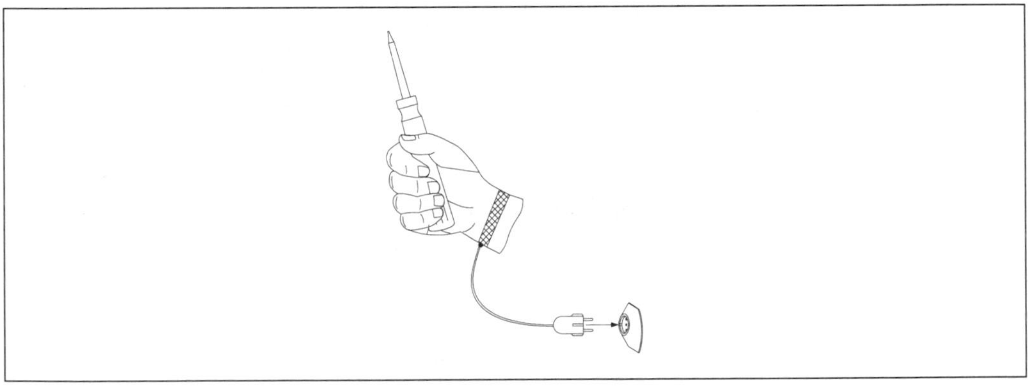

Figure 1.3: Earthing bracelet. This bracelet is inserted into a electric socket that is earthed so that charges can flow away from the user.

Figure 1.2a shows a case with a flap cover. To open the case you must press the buttons on each side and flip the cover off. If the case is screwed on, you'll have to remove the screws located at the sides and then flip away the cover. On the desktop case (Figure 1.2b), several screws are located on the back. Only remove those screws arranged at regular intervals from the edge of the case. Sometimes, the power supply and other peripherals are fixed onto the back with screws, so don't unscrew these by mistake.

Tower cases (shown in Figure 1.2c) usually have a side that can simply be removed, as it is held only by sheet springs. If you can't see any screws, try removing the side with some force (don't be too violent!).

Take Care Against Electric Shocks

Remember that inside the PC most parts are sensitive. You may have had a slight electric shock after getting out of your car or walking over a carpet. This is because you have been charged with *frictional electricity*. Most electronic circuits in a PC would not survive a discharge of such *static electricity*. Therefore, don't touch any internal components if you are not discharged completely.

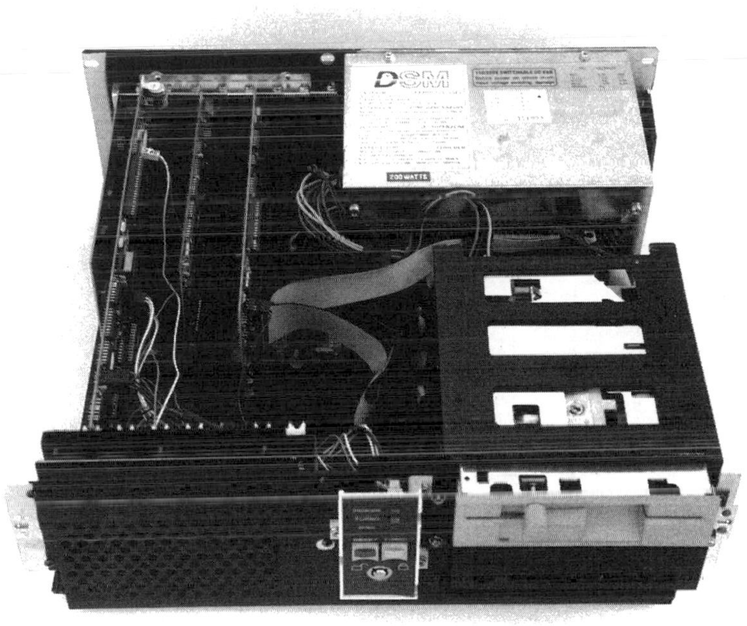

Figure 1.4: The interior of a PC, showing a typical interior with various adapter cards and drives.

But now you have a dilemma: either unplug the computer and risk «flash-overs» caused by static electricity, destroying the computer's circuits, or keep the PC plugged in and risk an electric shock. The best solution is to buy an earthing bracelet (see Figure 1.3). You are thus always earthed and no static electricity can accumulate. Otherwise, plug your computer into an electric socket protected by a circuit-breaker and avoid using both hands simultaneously so that no current path between hand-heart-hand can occur. Before picking up circuit boards you should always touch the case of your power supply to discharge yourself. If you want to examine boards with electronic circuitry more closely and you take the boards out, only handle them by their edges.

Inside the PC there are various circuit boards (see Figure 1.4). With some imagination you can also locate the components in an exotic-looking PC. To find out whether a certain board is a controller, a parallel or serial interface or a graphics adapter, it is best to investigate which devices the board is connected to. The individual components are presented below in greater detail.

1.2.2 Data Flow inside the PC

Personal Computers, like other computers, are used for *electronic data processing* (*EDP*). For this, data must be input into the PC, and the PC has to supply (the resulting) data. Between input and output, a varying amount of data processing takes place using a *program*. Figure 1.5 shows a typical PC with the most important functional units necessary for data processing.

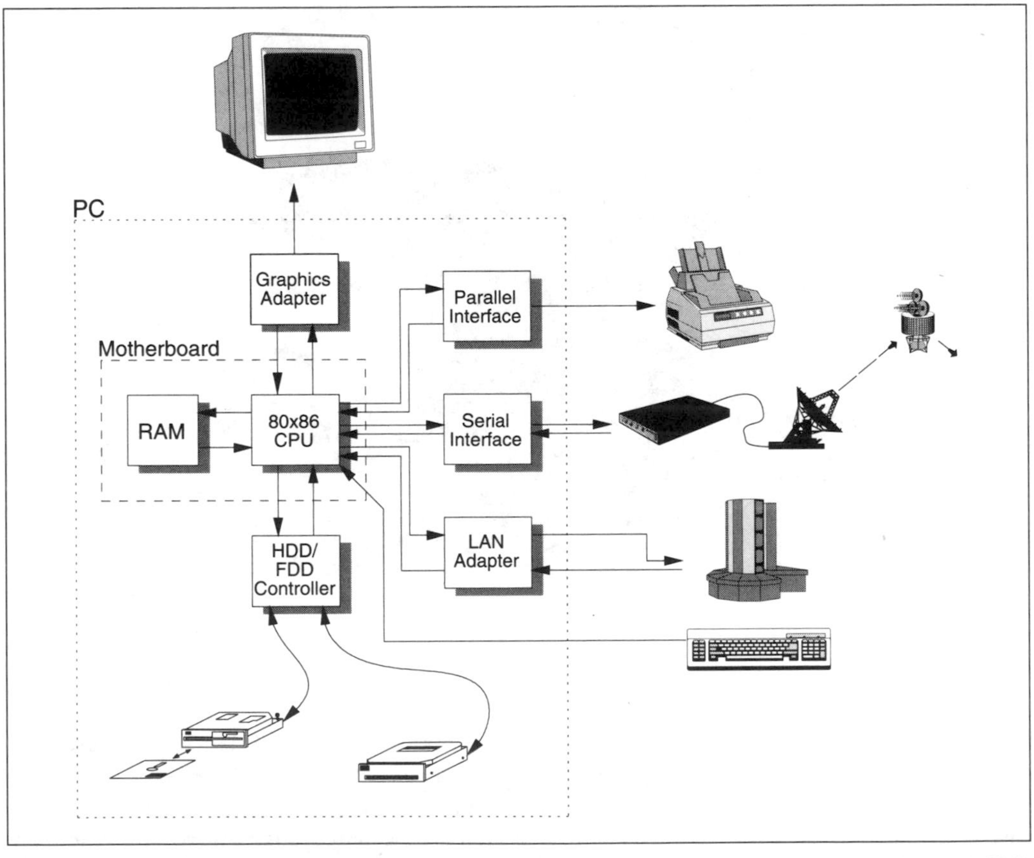

Figure 1.5: Block diagram of a PC with peripherals. The arrows indicate the direction of the data flow. The 80x86 CPU and the RAM are located on the motherboard. All parts surrounded by the broken line are normally inside the PC case.

The main part is the processor, also called the 80x86 Central Processing Unit (*CPU*) (x is a dummy variable from «#» to «4» or Pentium to denote the 8086/8088, 80186, 80286, i386, i486, Pentium family of Intel processors used in IBM-compatible PCs). Because of the large number of incoming and outgoing arrows, it can be seen that this processor represents (so to speak) the heart of the computer, in which all data processing events take place. Immediately next to the CPU is the *main memory*, or Random Access Memory (RAM) that the CPU uses to store or read intermediate results of the data processing or programs to/from. The CPU and RAM are the main components of the *motherboard*. The processor is connected to the keyboard, with which you enter data (text, for example) or commands (DIR, for example). To display such inputs visually, the CPU is further connected to a *graphics adapter*, which accepts the data to display, and processes it so it can be displayed on the monitor. At this point I want to mention that a computer doesn't necessarily need a monitor to output data; the monitor mainly supports the user. There are a lot of computers (the engine control Motronic, for example) that are very powerful, but which have neither a keyboard nor a monitor. In this case, the computer is usually called a *process computer*. To read more extensive datasets, or to store them for a longer time, *floppy* and *hard disk drives* are included. The processor may read data from them or write data to them with a *controller*. This is necessary because (apart from CMOS-RAM and the main memory of some laptops) all RAMs lose their contents when the PC is powered down. All data stored in that memory is thus irrevocably lost.

Nearly all PCs have at least one *parallel interface* (called PRN, LPT1, LPT2 or LPT3 under DOS) to which a printer may be connected, and at least one *serial interface* (called COM1–COM4 under DOS). The serial interface is also often called the *communication interface* because a modem can be connected to it, and with an appropriate program you can exchange data with other computers via public telephone or data networks. For example, it is possible to access a database in another country via satellite. In this way, your tiny (and seemingly unimportant) PC becomes a member of an international data network. (You can see what unexpected possibilities a PC offers beyond computer games!) Many PCs also have a *network adapter*, with which you embed your computer into a *local area network (LAN)*, that is, you may exchange data with another or several computers that are also equipped with a network adapter. Nevertheless, the other computer does not also have to be a PC. With your network adapter and appropriate software you may easily access a supercomputer and start to work on it.

1.2.3 The Motherboard

As the name implies, the motherboard is the heart of your PC, on which all components that are absolutely necessary are located. Figure 1.6 shows a typical motherboard, though the layout of motherboards may vary considerably. You can see the motherboard and several *slots* into which the circuit boards of the graphics adapter and the interfaces are located (the slots are often called *bus slots*). If your motherboard has such bus slots but no further electronic components, you have a PC with a so-called *modular board*. The motherboard in a modular PC is divided into a *bus board* (which has the slots) and a separate *processor board*. The latter is inserted into a slot in the same way as all the other boards, but its internal structure is the same as the motherboard described below. Figure 1.7 shows the motherboard in diagrammatic form.

Figure 1.6: The motherboard comprises all the central parts of a Personal Computer such as, for example, the CPU, main memory and extension slots for additional adapter cards.

As mentioned earlier, the 80x86 processor is the central unit of the board. It executes all the data processing, that is, numbers are added, subtracted, multiplied or divided, logic operations with two items are executed (logical AND, for example) and therefore their relations (equal, above, below, etc.) are determined, or data is input and output. For extensive mathematical operations such as, for example, the calculation of the tangent of two real numbers with very high accuracy, a mathematical *coprocessor* or *processor extension* is available. Intel calls the coprocessors belonging to the 80x86-family 80x87, for example, the 80287 is the coprocessor for the 80286 chip. Other companies also supply mathematical coprocessors (Weitek, Cyrix).

Usually, PCs are not equipped with a coprocessor when shipped, only with a socket for it. You can buy the corresponding chip afterwards and put it into this socket. The 80x86 automatically recognizes whether a coprocessor is present, and transfers the corresponding commands to it; the 80x87 then calculates the requested mathematical value. Coprocessors may calculate the tangent of an arc up to 100 times more quickly than «normal» processors. So if you are doing extensive mathematical applications (like, for example, three-dimensional computer graphics or CAD) this gives an enormous advantage.

Another important motherboard component is the main memory or RAM. Usually, the RAM is divided into several *banks*, though recently it has been made up of memory modules (SIMM or SIP). Each bank has to be fully equipped with memory chips, meaning that the main memory may only be extended bank-by-bank – the memory of a partially equipped bank will not be recognized by the PC. The lowest value for the main memory size of an AT today is 4 Mbytes; fully equipped 386 and 486 PCs have at least 16 Mbytes of RAM. The CPU stores data and intermediate results, as well as programs, in its memory and reads them later. For this, the processor has to tell the memory which data it wants to read (for example). This is done by an *address*, which is something like the house number of the data unit requested. Transferring this address to the memory is carried out by an *address bus*, and the transfer of the data by a *data bus*. Generally, in computer terms a *bus* means a number of lines through which data and signals are transferred. Therefore, the address bus consists of several lines, in the PC generally 20 (PC/XT), 24 (AT) or 32 (i386, i486, Pentium) lines.

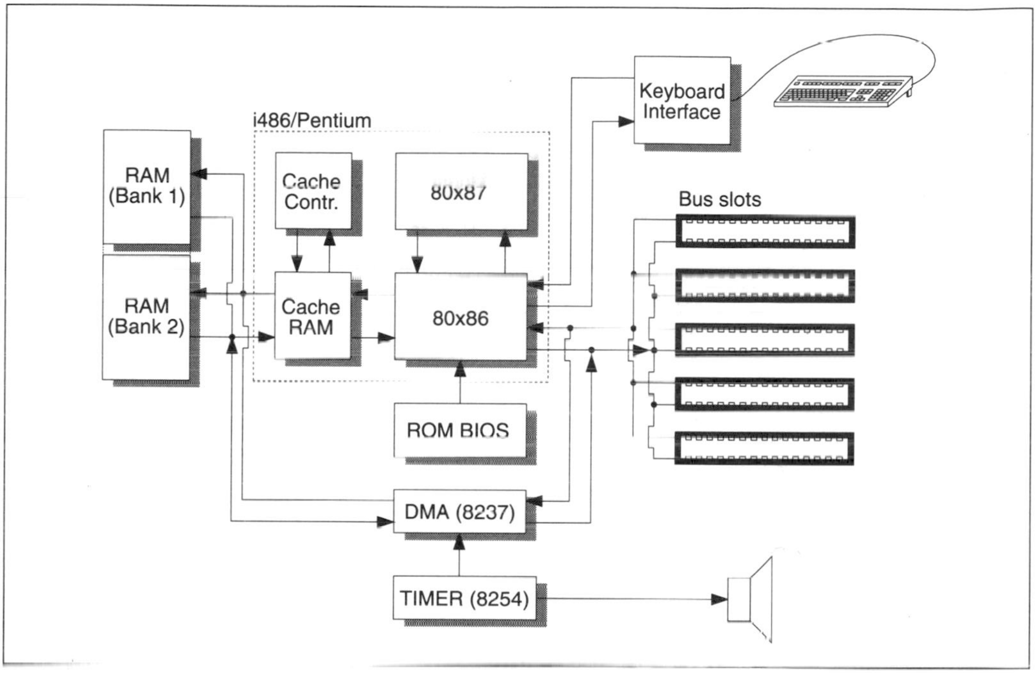

Figure 1.7: Diagram of a motherboard. The diagram shows the typical structure of a motherboard. The central part is the CPU 80x86. The CPU can be associated with an 80x87 coprocessor for mathematical applications and a cache controller and cache RAM to enhance performance. The i486 or Pentium integrates all these parts on a single chip. Additionally, on the motherboard there are the memory (RAM), the ROM BIOS, the 8237 and 8254 support chips, a keyboard interface, and the bus slots.

In the context of main memory you will often hear the expression *access time*. This is the time period between the CPU's command to the memory that data should be read and these data being transferred to the processor. Modern memory chips have an access time of about 60–100 ns, which for humans is a minute time period (batting the eyelid takes at least one 100th of a second, that is, 100 000 * 100 ns), but not so for modern computers with a high clock frequency. Actually, the access time is one of the most important restrictions on the operational speed of a PC. Therefore, powerful and fast-clocked computers (25 MHz and above) have a so-called *cache* or *cache memory*. Usually, this cache is significantly smaller than the main memory, but much faster (with an access time of 15–25 ns). The cache holds data that is frequently accessed by the CPU so it is available to the processor more quickly. The CPU, therefore, doesn't have to wait for its relatively slow main memory. If the CPU reads data out of main memory, the cache controller first checks to see whether this data is held in the cache memory. If it is, the data is immediately transferred to the CPU; otherwise, the cache controller reads the data from the main memory and transfers it to the processor simultaneously. If the CPU wants to write data it is written into the cache memory at a high speed. Later, the cache controller writes it into the main memory. You sometimes demonstrate similar behaviour yourself; for example, if you are programming some routines you take off the shelf those documents that you are likely to need. In this case, your desk is the cache memory and you are the cache controller. When a problem arises you take additional documents off the shelf and put them on your desk. If the desk is full (the cache memory is exhausted) you put those documents you are unlikely to need back on the shelf. Other documents that you need may then be placed on your desk. In these circumstances it is important that the cache memory is *transparent* to the processor, that is, the CPU doesn't recognize that a fast cache memory is installed between itself and the main memory. In other words, the processor operates as if no cache memory were present. On the new and powerful 80x86 family processors, the processor, coprocessor, cache memory and a cache controller are integrated on a single chip to form the i486 or Pentium.

The motherboard also includes a *Read Only Memory* (*ROM*). Located on this chip are the programs and data that the PC needs at power-up (because it loses the contents of its main memory when it is powered down). The processor reads these programs and executes them at power-up. In the ROM there are also various support routines for accessing the keyboard, graphics adapter, etc. – known collectively as the *ROM-BIOS*. If you enter data via the keyboard, the keyboard interface communicates directly with the processor (for advanced readers, it issues a hardware interrupt; see Chapter 23), and informs it that a character has been input. The CPU can then read and process that character.

As mentioned above, data is exchanged via the address and data buses. To control the data transfer processes, additional control signals are required; for example, the CPU must tell the memory whether data should be read or written. This is carried out by a so-called *write-enable* signal, for which one bus line is reserved. Because of the various signals, the slot has, for example, 62 contacts for the XT bus (the XT's system bus) and 98 contacts for the AT bus. (Note that the bus slots therefore have different lengths.) The lines for the control signals are guided in parallel to the address and data buses and lead to the bus slots. The data bus, address bus and all the control lines are known as the *system bus*, which ensures that all inserted adapter cards are informed about all the operations taking place in the PC.

For example, a memory expansion card may be inserted in one bus slot. The CPU accesses the memory on this adapter card in the same way as it accesses the memory on the motherboard. Therefore, the bus slots must have all the signals necessary to control the PC components (and this expansion card, for example, is one of them). Theoretically, it does not matter into which free slot an adapter card is inserted, as long as all the contacts fit into the bus slot. In practice (especially if you are using a low quality motherboard or adapter card), an adapter card may only run correctly in a certain bus slot, as it is only in this bus slot that all the bus signals arrive at the appropriate time. Frequently, extensive amounts of data must be transferred from a hard or floppy disk into the main memory, as is the case when a text is loaded into a word processor, for example. For such minor tasks an 80x86 processor is too valuable a chip, because it can carry out far more complex operations than this. For this reason, the motherboard has one (PC/XT) or two (AT) chips optimized for data transfer within the computer – the *Direct Memory Access*

(*DMA*) *chips*. They are connected to the main memory and the data bus, and to certain control lines that are part of the bus slots. Using these control lines, the DMA chips can be activated to carry out data transfer from a hard disk into main memory, for example, at a very high speed. In this process the CPU is bypassed and is not allocated the data transfer operation.

You have probably realized that your PC can also be used as a clock, telling the date and time (DOS commands DATE and TIME). To implement this function a *timer chip* is present, which periodically tells the processor that the DOS-internal clock has to be updated. (This chip also controls memory refresh and the speaker.) In a *Dynamic RAM (DRAM)*, the information stored vanishes as time passes (typically within a period of 10 ms to 1 s). To avoid this, the DRAM has to be periodically refreshed to regenerate the memory contents. DRAMs are used in the PC as main memory. Bus slots are vitally important in making PCs flexible. Besides the standard plug-in graphics adapters, controllers, etc., you can also insert other adapters, such as a voice synthesizer to program spoken output on your PC. This might be a first step towards a *multimedia PC*.

1.2.4 Graphics Adapters and Monitors

For a user, an essential part of a PC is the monitor, as well as the accompanying graphics or display adapter card. Strictly speaking, a graphics adapter is electronic circuitry for displaying graphics. A display adapter is the generic term, and it also includes electronic devices that can only display text (that is, no free lines, circles etc.), though because text adapters are no longer used in PCs, this strict distinction has vanished. The graphics adapter is usually constructed as a plug-in card for a bus slot. Figure 1.8 shows a VGA adapter card.

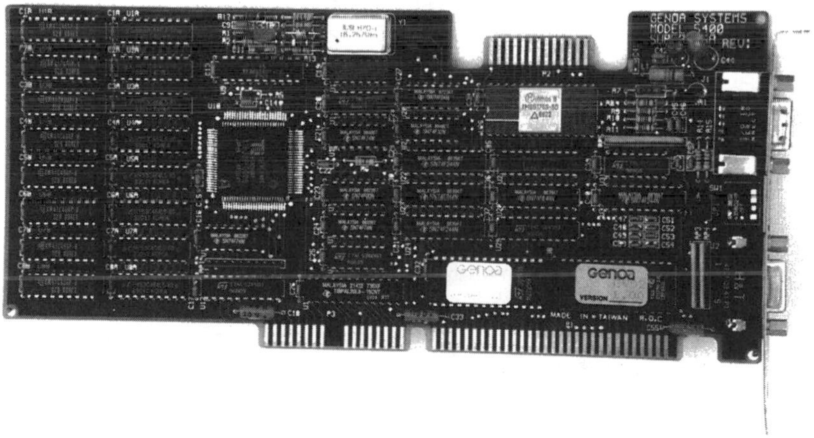

Figure 1.8: A typical VGA adapter card for displaying text and graphics on-screen.

Although it is possible to run a PC without a monitor and to output directly to a printer, this is a painstaking process. If graphics are to be printed, a dot matrix printer is usually occupied for several minutes, and a laser printer will be tied up for many seconds. Moreover, in the age of the «paperless office» it is inappropriate to output all draft documents to paper immediately. Therefore the monitor, with its short response time and the vibrancy of its displayed data, is far better as an output medium. If, for example, a line has to be inserted into a drawing, only this new line has to be formed, not the whole displayed image. Under DOS, the monitor and the keyboard are regarded as a single entity because of their special usage as standard input/output devices, and are thus called the console (DOS-unit CON).

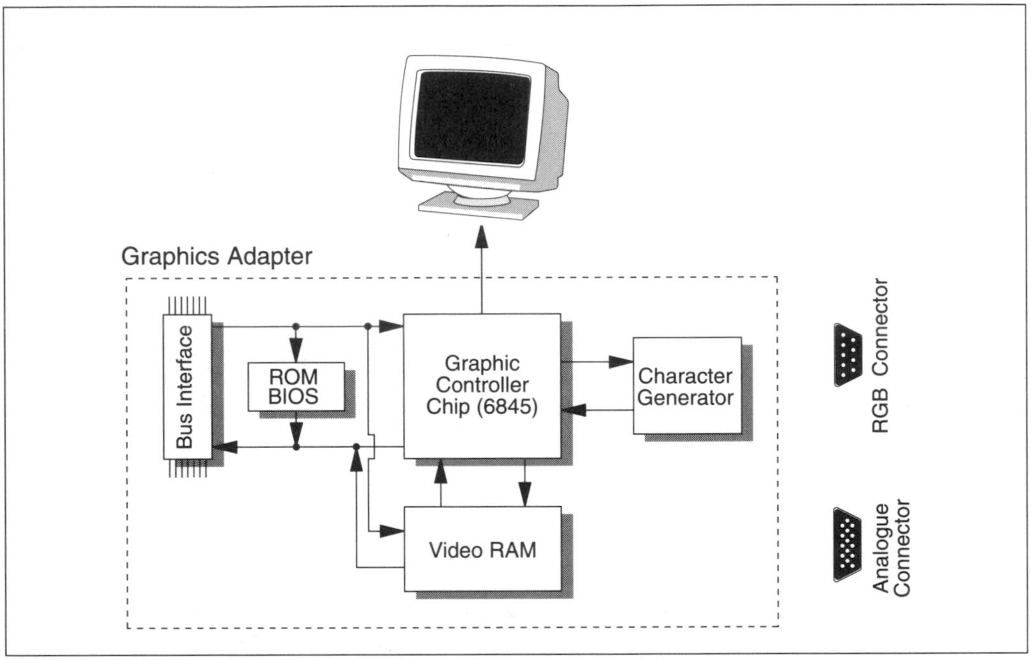

Figure 1.9: Graphics adapter. The central part is a graphics control chip, which controls the character generator and the video RAM. The CPU can access the control chip and the video RAM via the bus interface.

The hub of a graphics adapter is the *graphics control chip*, for example a Motorola 6845 (Figure 1.9). You'll find this, or a compatible and more developed chip, on many adapters. It is responsible for driving the monitor, that is, supplying pulses for horizontal and vertical retraces, displaying the cursor, controlling the number of text lines and columns, as well as the display of text and graphics. The picture on the monitor is written by an electron beam similar to that in a TV, which scans the screen line by line. If the beam reaches the lower right corner, it returns to the upper left corner, that is, a new page.

The graphics adapter has two operation modes: text and graphics. Characters are displayed as a fixed pattern of points, graphics as a free pattern. If a certain character is to be displayed in *text mode*, the CPU need pass only the number or *code* of this character to the graphics control chip. The *video RAM* holds data (codes) that determine the character to be displayed on-screen. The job of the *character generator* is to convert this code into a corresponding pattern of pixels so that the character can be displayed on-screen by the graphics control chip. On the other hand, in *graphics mode* the video RAM is read out directly and the character generator is not enabled. Therefore, far more complex «patterns» (i.e. graphics) may be displayed.

The data for the screen contents is written into the video RAM by the CPU. The CPU may also read data out of the video RAM, for example to determine the character at a certain location on-screen. For this the graphics adapter has a bus interface, which detects whether data for the graphics adapter is present on the system bus. Via the bus interface, the CPU can write data into the video RAM which, for example, is displayed as text on-screen. On the other hand, the CPU may read data about to be overwritten by a new window under MS-Windows and store it in main memory. It is thus possible to restore the original state by retransferring, after closing the window, the data stored in main memory back into the video RAM. Moreover, the graphics control chip can be reprogrammed via the bus interface so that, for example, instead of the usual 25 lines and 80 columns each, a new mode with 60 lines and 132 columns each is displayed.

Because reprogramming the graphics control chip from a standard mode to the mode mentioned above is dependent upon the particular hardware on the graphics adapter, high-resolution EGA and VGA adapter cards have their own BIOS. This is located in a ROM, and supports the ROM-BIOS on the motherboard. It includes routines to switch between different display modes (modern graphics adapters may have up to 80 different such modes), to set points with a certain colour at a certain location on the screen, or to use various pages in video memory. For this, the CPU on the motherboard calls the corresponding program in the ROM-BIOS of the graphics adapter via the bus interface.

On the back of the graphics adapter there are usually one or more jacks. Connectors for monochrome and RGB monitors (*red-green-blue*) have two rows of holes; connectors for analogue monitors have three rows. Monochrome and RGB monitors are driven by digital signals so that a maximum of 16 different colours may be displayed simultaneously: two each for red, green and blue, and an additional intensity signal (high, low). Therefore, $2^4=16$ different signal combinations are possible. With an EGA adapter card, these 16 colours may be chosen from a *palette* containing 64 colours. This means that only 16 of these 64 colours can be displayed simultaneously. The VGA card and other new adapters drive an analogue monitor with an analogue signal. In principle, any number of colours may now be displayed simultaneously, but for technical reasons the VGA standard limits them to 256 simultaneously displayable colours. The 256 colours may be selected from a palette of 262144 (64 red$*$64 green$*$64 blue) different colours. Extremely high-resolution graphics adapters with a resolution of 1280$*$1024 points drive the correspondingly more powerful monitors by an analogue signal, which is transmitted via a BNC cable. The cable is shielded against external influences so that the driving signals are not disturbed and the cable doesn't act as an antenna and influence other equipment. Some graphics adapters have all three jacks. On the Hercules and other compatible graphics cards, a parallel interface is integrated onto the adapter card. You will see this if a jack for connecting a printer with a parallel interface is present. Figure 1.15 shows the layout of the parallel interface jack.

1.2.5 Drive Controllers, Floppy and Hard Disk Drives

As already mentioned, the main disadvantage of main memory is the volatility of the stored data. When the PC is switched off, or if the power supply is interrupted, all the data is lost. Therefore, RAM is unsuitable for long-term data storage. For this reason, magnetic memories were developed very early on. Before the invention and the triumphant progress of semiconductor memories and integrated memory chips, even main memory consisted of magnetic drums. Later, these drums were replaced by magnetic core memories, tiny magnetic rings through which run read and write wires. In the PC field, floppy disks and hard disk drives are now generally established (see Figure 1.10).

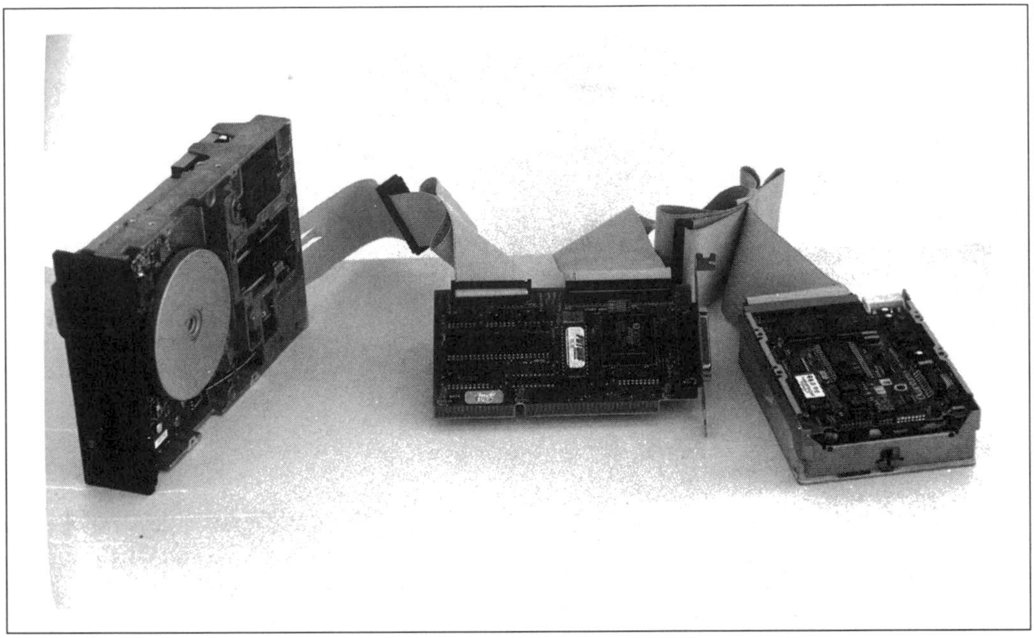

Figure 1.10: A typical floppy drive, hard disk drive and combicontroller.

Floppy disk drives belong to the group of drives with so-called *removable data volume*, because different floppies (data volumes) can be inserted into a single drive and removed later. The actual floppy disk is a circular and flexible disk, coated with a magnetic material and housed in a protective envelope (see Figure 1.11).

For IBM-compatible PCs, floppy disks 5¼" and 3½" in diameter are available. The smaller 3½" floppies are enclosed in a hard plastic case, and are inserted together with the case into the drive, which writes data to it or reads data from it. On 5¼" floppy drives, the drive flap must be locked down as otherwise no data can be read or written; 3½" drives automatically lock the floppy disk in place. On the other hand, on *hard disk drives* or *hard disks* the data volume cannot be removed; it is fixed in the drive. Furthermore, the data volumes are no longer flexible, but stiff («hard») disks. Typically, a hard disk holds 100 times more data than a floppy disk.

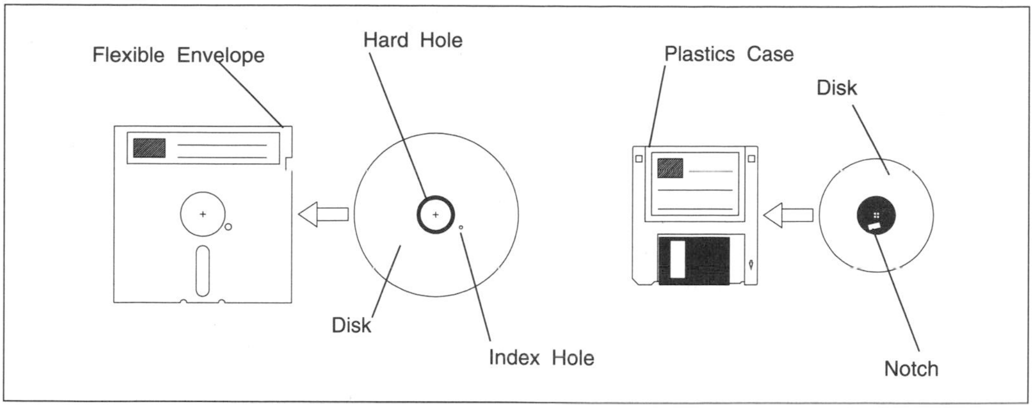

Figure 1.11: Floppy disks. Presently for the PC, 5 1/4" floppy disks in a flexible envelope with capacities of 360 kbytes and 1.2 Mbytes as well as 3 1/2" floppy disks in hard plastic cases with capacities of 720 kbytes and 1.44 Mbytes are available.

Floppy and hard disk drives are also used in other computers, such as the Apple Macintosh, Commodore Amiga, or mainframes. Therefore, the technique of floppy and hard disk drives is completely independent of the technology of a PC. To read and write data with the CPU on the motherboard, it is necessary to control the drives. For this, a *controller* is inserted into one bus slot to control the floppy and hard disk drives, and to transfer data between the drive and main memory. Figure 1.12 shows a block diagram of a controller.

The controller is the link between the CPU and the drives. For this reason it has two interfaces: the bus interface (which we met in the section on graphics adapters) for data exchange with the CPU; and one interface for every floppy or hard disk drive. Today's PCs usually have a *combicontroller*, with which two or more floppy drives and two hard disk drives can be connected. The combicontroller has its own microprocessor, with programs stored in ROM to control the electronic components on the controller card. To avoid any confusion, I must emphasize that this microprocessor is not identical to the 80x86 CPU on the motherboard, but is sited independently on the controller. Therefore, the controller is actually a small and independent computer (a further example of a computer without a monitor), to which the CPU on the motherboard supplies «commands» via the bus interface. Similarly, you enter commands for the CPU via the keyboard (interface). We shall meet this idea of independent, small computers that support the central processor on the motherboard again, hence the name *Central* Processor Unit. The microprocessor now controls data flow between the bus and drive interfaces by driving the programmable storage controller and the data synchronizer appropriately. On floppy and hard disks, the data is held in a form that is especially suited for data recording on these magnetic data carriers. For processing in a PC this form is, however, completely unsuitable. Therefore, the data synchronizer carries out a conversion between these two incompatible formats. The programmable storage controller controls the read and write operations, and checks the read data for correctness.

To use and control the drives effectively, many controllers have their own ROM-BIOS. As for the ROM-BIOS on a graphics adapter, this ROM-BIOS holds several routines for accessing the hard disk controller. The control routines for the floppy drives are already located in the ROM-

BIOS on the motherboard – do not confuse this ROM-BIOS with the ROM code. The routines in the ROM code control the microprocessor on the controller and cannot be accessed by the CPU on the motherboard, whereas the routines in the ROM-BIOS on the controller *support* the CPU on the motherboard.

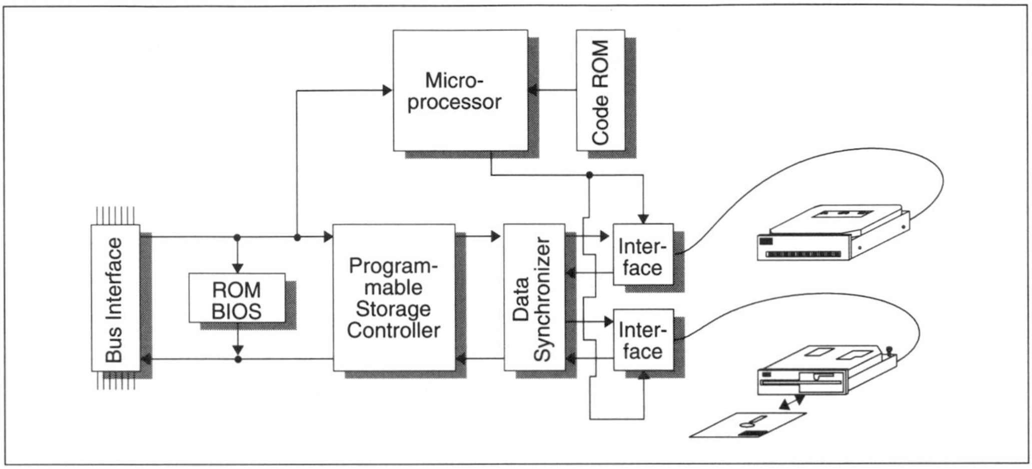

Figure 1.12: A controller and drives. The controller's microprocessor controls the components according to the microprogram in the ROM code. Data is transferred beween the drive and controller via an interface.

With intelligent drives like the AT bus, SCSI or ESDI, the controller is fixed to the drive so that drive and controller together form an entity. Therefore, instead of a controller being inserted into a bus slot, there is a *host adapter* in the slot; this host adapter establishes a connection between the system bus and the controller. Usually, the host adapter has its own BIOS. In the mainframe field, the actual computer is called «the host», and the user is connected to the host via a terminal.

Because a standard controller can be connected to many different drives, the controller has to be constructed in a very general and simple way. A controller that is fixed to a certain drive, however, may be adapted specially to that drive. Because of the low prices of today's electronic components, using a fixed controller (which requires one controller per drive) influences the overall price only a little.

Some host adapters or controller cards have a jack on the reverse to connect an external drive. SCSI adapters often have an additional jack on the back which directly connects to the internal SCSI bus; thus external SCSI units may also be connected, for example, an external streamer drive can be used.

1.2.6 Streamers and Other Drives

Data backup is enormously important for users. Using floppy disks means spending a lot of time on data backups because floppy drives are slow compared to hard disk drives; also, the capacity of a floppy disk is roughly 100 times smaller than that of hard disks – to back up a hard disk of about 100 Mbytes capacity you would need 100 floppy disks. It is particularly frustrating because almost every minute the filled floppy disk has to be removed and a new one inserted!

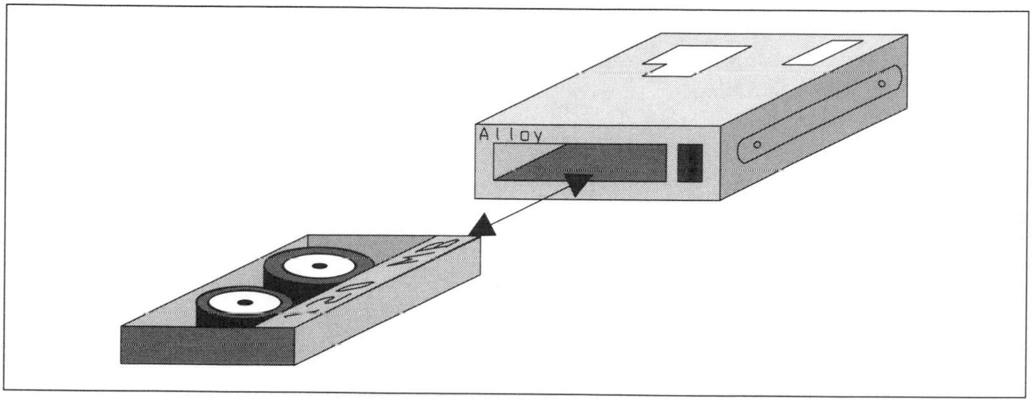

Figure 1.13: Streamer drive and cartridge. In the PC domain, tape drives are used in the form of cartridge drives. Such streamer cartridges have a capacity of up to 250 Mbytes.

To overcome this restriction, and so that a qualified programmer is not occupied as a sort of «disk jockey», streamer drives (*streamers*) were developed (see Figure 1.13). As the name indicates, a regular streaming of data from the hard or floppy drives to a magnetic tape enclosed in a streamer cartridge takes place. Magnetic tapes have been unbeatable up to now in view of their simple handling, insensitivity, storage capacity and price, so they are well-suited for data backup. The tapes used have an enormous storage capacity (up to 250 Mbytes) and are enclosed in a highly accurate case. This virtually guarantees that the read/write head will be able to locate the data tracks again later. Simple streamer drives may be connected to a floppy disk controller. Very powerful streamers with a higher data transfer rate, on the other hand, have their own controller, which is inserted into a bus slot and controlled by the accompanying software, or have a SCSI interface. With such a system, a medium-sized hard disk can be backed up in less than 15 minutes.

In recent years, many other drive types and corresponding data carriers have come onto the market, largely optical data volumes. They allow an even greater enhancement of storage capacity compared to high density hard disks. For distributing huge and unchangeable data sets (like databases, program libraries, etc.), *CD-ROM* is especially well-suited. The name is derived from the well-known CD player (Compact Disc), but instead of music signals, data is transferred to the PC. In principle this is the same, as music can also be regarded as a data set. With only one of these shiny CD-ROM disks, data that would normally occupy a large pack of floppy disks can be shipped. The CD-ROM drive scans the surface of the disk with a laser beam and converts the back-scattered laser light into a data stream. Depending on the technical design, CD-ROM drives can be connected to existing floppy disk controllers or have a separate controller that has to be inserted into a bus slot.

One big disadvantage with CD-ROMs is that data can be read but not modified. Progress towards «real» optical data recording is offered by WORMs (Write Once, Read Many). In such drives, data may be written onto an optical disk once and read an infinite number of times afterwards. If a data record is to be modified it must be written in the modified form at another, free location. The original data remains on the disk but will be ignored. You can imagine that the disk will fill within a short time, and will have to be replaced quite soon. If we consider the development of hard drives (the first 10 Mbyte hard disk for the XT was extraordinarily expensive), we can expect cheap optical data carriers that will be freely erasable and writeable to arrive within the next few years.

One relic of the PC's ancient past should be mentioned: the cassette recorder. The first PC was delivered by IBM in 1980 without a floppy drive but with a cassette recorder! This, of course, had a specially adapted interface so that the CPU could read and write data. When loading a program from the cassette recorder, which today's hard drives carry out within a second, the user could go out for a cup of coffee. Not least because of this, office work today has become much more hectic....

Obviously the bus slots allow an enormous flexibility of expansion for your PC. In principle, such seemingly exotic components as magnetic bubble or holographic memories can also be embedded into your PC – but by doing this you would already be crossing into the next century.

1.2.7 Parallel Interfaces and Printers

A PC is equipped with at least one parallel interface, which may be located on the monochrome or Hercules graphics card (see Section 1.2.4) or on a separate interface adapter card (see Figure 1.14). On a separate interface adapter card, in most cases, you'll find an additional serial interface.

Via the system bus, data is transmitted in units of one (PC/XT), two (AT bus) or four bytes (EISA bus, 32-bit microchannel, Local Bus). The bus interface (see Figure 1.15) of a parallel interface is therefore always one byte (or eight bits) wide. This means that one byte (or eight bits) are transferred to the interface at a time (also true for graphics adapters, hard disk controllers, serial interfaces, etc.). They are supplied with data in units of one byte. In the case of a graphics adapter for the 32-bit EISA bus, for example, four such units may be transferred *simultaneously*. On the other hand, a graphics adapter for the 8-bit XT bus must be supplied with four such units *in succession*.

The I/O-chip on the interface card accepts these eight bits together and transfers them together, (that is, in parallel) to the connected device (usually a printer) so that eight data lines are present. Besides this data byte, control signals are also transmitted to indicate whether the data has arrived. Up to 100 kbytes of data can thus be transferred every second if the parallel interface and connected peripheral hardware is correctly adapted. On the interface is a jack with 25 holes, which supply signals according to the *Centronics standard*. The standard actually claims 36 contacts, but the PC occupies only 25: the remaining 11 were not used by IBM, and are therefore omitted. Because all manufacturers orient to «Big Blue», in time this has led to a «reduced» standard with only 25 contacts.

You should be able to recognize a parallel interface by this jack, if in doubt. The disadvantage of the Centronics standard is that cables with individual shielded wires are not used. The maximum distance between the PC and printer is therefore limited to about 5 m. Of particular importance is that the data is exchanged via *handshaking*, that is, the receiver confirms the reception of every data byte, and a clock signal (*strobe*) is transmitted together with the data signals.

Figure 1.14: Typical interface adapter card on which a parallel interface and a serial interface are integrated.

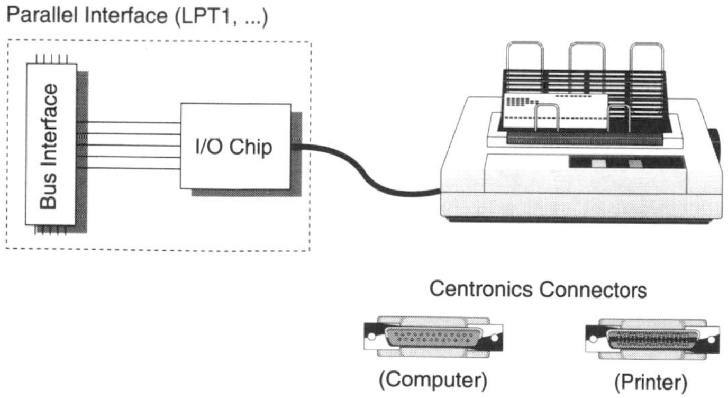

Figure 1.15: A parallel interface card has an I/O chip or an equivalent circuit that transmits or receives data at the contacts of the Centronics connector to or from a printer.

The printer accepts the transmitted data and prints the corresponding text or graphics. In doing this, it generally responds to certain data patterns in the received data stream. In particular, it checks whether so-called «printer control characters» or «escape sequences» are included, which indicate a control command for the printer. The printer then reacts accordingly. For example, the character sequence 0dh 0ah means a carriage return and line feed (*CR* = ***C**arriage **R**eturn*, *LF* = ***L**ine **F**eed*).

Other peripherals may also be connected to a parallel interface, assuming that the receiving interface satisfies the Centronics standard. Usually, the parallel interface only supplies data, but doesn't receive any. Actually, the older I/O-chips of parallel interfaces are unable to receive data, but more recently, versions of these chips can receive data, and it is thus possible to exchange data between computers via the parallel interface (and suitable software). IBM uses this method in its PS/2 series to transfer data between computer systems with 5¼" and 3½" floppy disk drives, because their floppy formats are wholly incompatible.

1.2.8 Serial Interfaces and Modems

As well as a parallel interface, a PC usually has one or more serial interfaces. These are integrated on an interface adapter card together with a parallel interface (see Figure 1.14). Figure 1.16 shows a diagram of a serial interface.

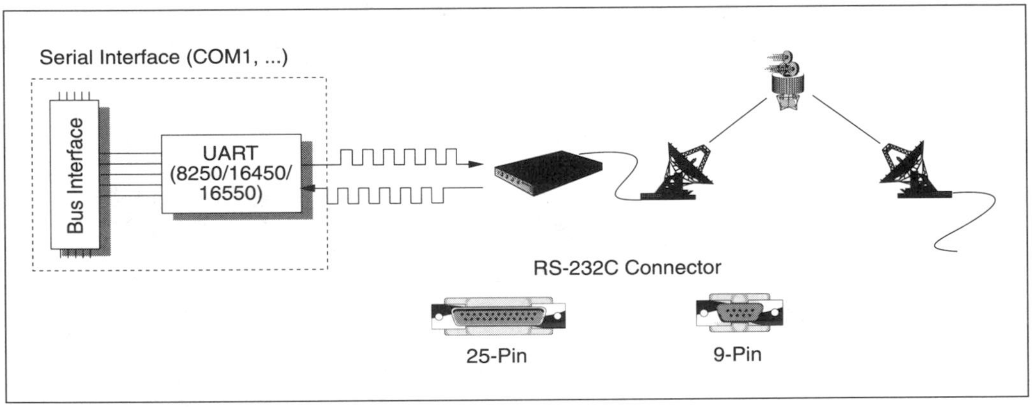

Figure 1.16: The serial interface largely consists of a UART, which executes the transformation to or from serial data. With a serial interface a modem for data communications can be connected, for example. The PC has a serial port with nine or 25 contacts.

The central component is a so-called UART. Older PC/XTs have an 8250 chip; the AT has the more advanced 16450. Via the bus interface, the CPU on the motherboard may access the UART and read or transmit data. In the case of a serial interface, like the parallel interface, data is transferred to the bus interface, and from there to the UART, in units of one byte. Unlike the parallel interface, however, the UART doesn't transfer the data to the peripheral in a parallel way, but converts each byte into a serial stream of individual bits. This stream is transmitted via a single data line, not eight as is the case for the parallel interface. Moreover, the UART adds additional bits, if necessary: start, stop and parity bits. A data packet consisting of eight data bits and the additional UART control bits is thus formed. The number of signal changes per second is called the *baud rate*. The parity bit serves as a simple validity check for the transmitted data. In this way, much longer distances compared to the parallel interface are possible (up to 100 m without signal amplification). Moreover, the cable between the serial interface and any peripheral is more convenient, as only one data line is present. However, the transfer rate is therefore lower (in a PC up to 115 200 baud). Unlike connection via the parallel interface, no synchronization signal is transmitted.

Serial interfaces in PCs conform to the *RS232C standard*, which defines the layout and meaning of the connections, and which requires 25 contacts. However, serial interfaces in PCs only occupy 14 at most, even if the corresponding plug has 25 pins. Additionally, a reduced version with only nine pins exists, but this is sufficient only for use in PCs defined by IBM. Note that the contacts on the reverse of the interface adapter card are, unlike the parallel interface, formed into a plug (that is, there are pins, not holes). You can thus easily tell serial and parallel interfaces apart.

One feature of UART, and therefore of the serial interface, is that the transmission and reception of data may take place asynchronously. If data is arriving, the UART is activated without intervention from the CPU, and it accepts the data. Afterwards, it tells the processor that data has been received and is to be transferred to the CPU. If you connect a modem to your serial interface (also called the communications interface, COM), you can exchange data with other computers of any size via the public telephone or data networks (your friend's PC, or the computing centre of a database service provider, for example). Your PC then behaves like a terminal that may be up to 20 000 km (or taking into account satellite transmissions, up to 100 000 km) away from the actual computer. In this case, data is sent to the UART by the CPU in your PC. The UART converts it into a serial bit stream and transfers the stream to the modem. In the modem a carrier signal is modulated and transmitted via the telephone network and satellite to another modem, which is connected to the destination computer. That modem demodulates the signal (hence the name modem, MOdulator/DEModulator), extracts the data, and transfers it as a serial bit stream to the UART of the destination computer. The UART accepts this bit stream, converts it into one byte, and transfers that byte to the destination computer's CPU. If that computer is to supply data to your PC, the process works in the opposite direction. This only works, of course, if the transmission parameters (baud rate, number and values of start, stop and parity bits) of your serial interface and the destination computer coincide.

Because data reception may take place asynchronously (that is, the UART need not know that data is arriving at 15:01 GMT), a communications program may run in the background. Therefore, you may, for example, input text while your PC is transmitting a message or receiving an image. Using the serial interface, a simple local area network can be made to exchange small amounts of data among several PCs. This method is popular for transferring data between laptops and «normal» PCs (Laplink, for example, does this).

I should mention that a serial interface often connects a mouse, trackball or a joystick to the PC. If the user changes the position of these devices they output a serial data stream to the UART, like a modem. The UART accepts it and supplies the data byte to the CPU. Because of the rather long distances (compared to the parallel interface) that can be spanned with a serial interface, devices in another room or even another building may be driven. Nevertheless, the data transmission is very reliable, especially at low baud rates.

1.2.9 Network Adapters and LANs

The basic concept of the PC was to put an individual computer at every user's disposal. At that time (planning started in the mid 1970s), the PC was (according to today's standards) very expensive, and a method of mass storage of extensive databases beyond most users' means. This led to typically only one computer being present in an office, and much work was done manually or with a typewriter. Problems of data exchange could not arise because all data were managed on this single computer. As the price of PC hardware rapidly decreased and very powerful programs for word processing, databases, etc., appeared, the PC replaced manual work and typewriters more and more, leading to the introduction of innovative methods (like, for example, CAD in the field of architecture or engineering). According to Figure 1.1, every user would get their own printer and modem. That is, of course, a pure waste of resources, as a laser printer, for example, is more expensive today than the PC (and out of order for more than 90% of the time!) Moreover, the data cannot be managed centrally, resulting in data chaos. As a pure typewriter, a PC is far too good. Instead, its use for data processing and data exchange with other PCs is unavoidable.

For this reason, local area networks (LANs) are being used more and more. As the name implies, computers are networked locally (within a room, building or area) so that data (text files, database records, sales numbers, etc.) may be interchanged among individual PCs. The central part of a LAN is the *server* (see Figure 1.17).

The counterpart of a LAN is – what else – a *wide area network* (WAN). Computers are thus networked over long distances, for instance, the new passenger booking system AMADEUS with which you can reserve airline tickets all over the world. The AMADEUS computer centre is located in Erding, near Munich, with network nodes on all five continents.

On the server, all data which is accessible by more than one user is managed centrally. For this, the server has a high-capacity hard disk drive on which to hold all the data. Via cables and network adapters, data may be transferred from the server to the *netnodes*, that is, the PCs connected to the server, and vice versa. Moreover, a data exchange among the individual netnodes is also possible. Therefore, it is no longer necessary to copy the data onto a floppy disk, carry the floppy disk to the destination PC, and restore the data there. With a network, data can be transmitted from your workstation to one or more destinations, as over a pneumatic dispatch system. You can also fetch data from another netnode via the server. Unlike working on a PC, which doesn't usually have any password protection against illegal access, in a network you need an access entitlement to be able to read or write certain data.

One particular advantage of the network as compared to a terminal is when the central computer (here the server) fails: with a terminal you are brought to a complete standstill, but as a user in a LAN you can go on working with your own, local PC. A further advantage is that on the server, all common data is managed centrally (and is backed up in one go there). Your personal data stock is at your disposal on your own PC. Therefore, a maximum of data security (by central management and backup) and, on the other hand, a maximum of flexibility, is possible. Usually, all netmembers share one or more printers so that considerable savings are possible, and the printer works to capacity. You may also exchange data via the server, so only one telephone line is required.

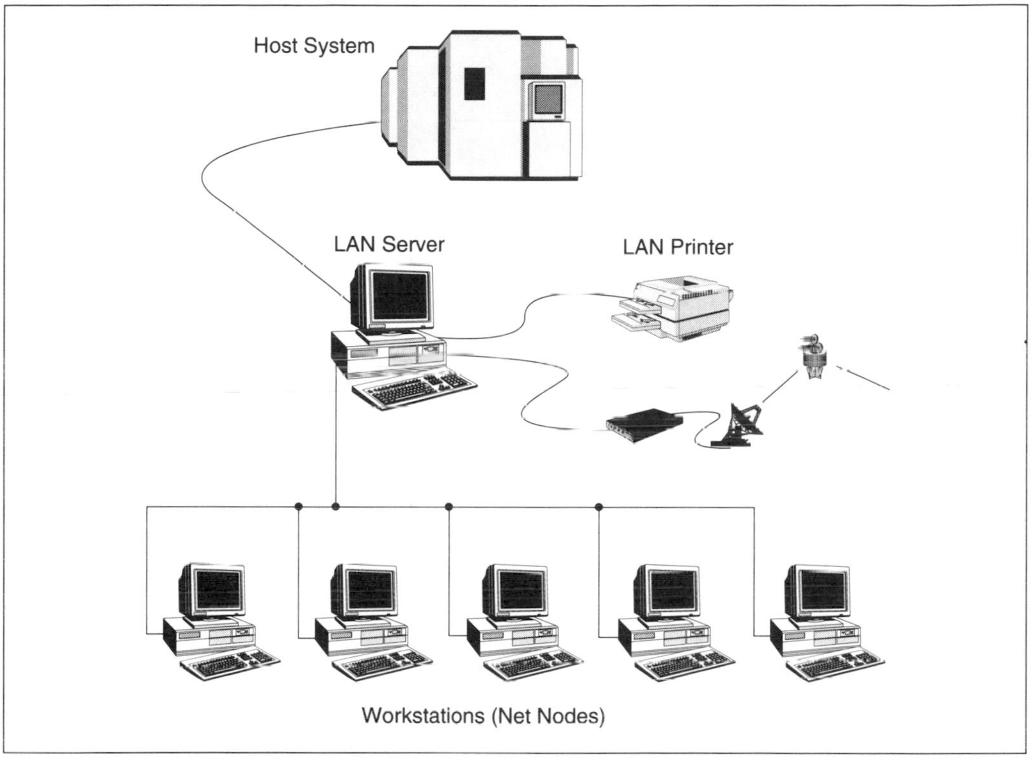

Figure 1.17: Structure of a local area network. LANs are locally bounded. The central part of a LAN is a server, which manages all the common data of all the network nodes, and establishes connections to peripherals or other computers.

Like a controller (see Figure 1.12), a network adapter also has two interfaces: one bus interface for connection to the PC's CPU, and a network interface for accessing the network (see Figure 1.18). Like any other extension adapter card (graphics adapter, controller), the network adapter may be inserted into any free bus slot.

The CPU on the motherboard transfers data and commands to the I/O chip or buffer memory on the network adapter card via the bus interface. This I/O chip converts the data into a form that is adapted for transmission via the network, and it supplies the data to the network interface. The network now transfers the data to the intended computer (server or netnode). If, on the other hand, a command for transmitting data to the server or a netnode arrives at the I/O chip, the command is placed into the buffer memory and the CPU is informed about it at a suitable time.

The CPU interrupts the ongoing process (the calculation of a mathematical expression, for example), carries out the requested enquiry, and then restarts the interrupted process. If the bus interface for a PC on the network adapter card is replaced by an interface for another kind of computer (a UNIX machine, for example) and you insert this newly setup adapter card in the other computer, very different computers may be networked. Any computer can thus be accessed via a network adapter, as is the case with a serial interface and a modem. Because network adapters are much more powerful (the data throughput is up to 100 times higher), the data is much faster.

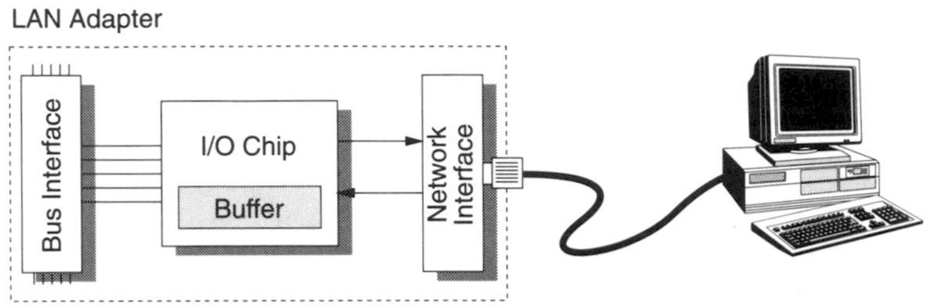

Figure 1.18: A network adapter card has a (more or less) complicated I/O chip, which normally has a buffer in which to temporarily store incoming or outgoing data. The network interface depends on the network used, e.g. Ethernet or Token Ring.

1.2.10 CMOS RAM and Real-Time Clock

From the previous sections you can see that a PC may be equipped with an endless variety of expansion adapters such as graphics adapters, hard disk controllers, interfaces, etc. If the computer is switched off, the PC loses its memory, and therefore doesn't know what components are installed. At power-up, all drives and components must be initialized, that is, set to a defined start-up state. You can imagine that there is a significant difference as to whether a 10 Mbytes or 300 Mbytes hard disk drive, or a main memory with 256 kbytes or 8 Mbytes, is present at initialization.

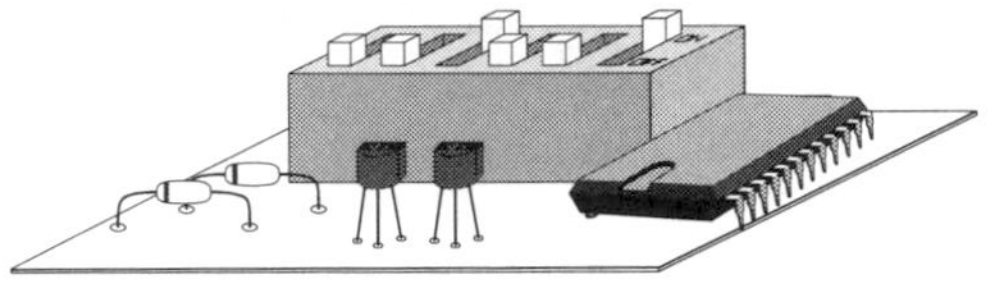

Figure 1.19: DIP switches. On adapter cards or the motherboard you often find small DIP switches. These are used to configure the adapter card or the motherboard.

In the first PCs and XTs the configuration could be set by different positions of so-called *DIP switches* (see Figure 1.19). At power-up, the processor reads the switch positions and determines which drives are installed and how much main memory is available. Because these switches are located on the motherboard, they are often hidden by expansion adapter cards, so it is difficult to make new settings.

Beginning with the AT, this information was then held by a chip on the motherboard, the *CMOS RAM* (see Figure 1.6). The feature of this chip is that it needs relatively little power compared with other memory chips. In ATs and all newer IBM-compatibles, a battery or accumulator is present to supply power to this CMOS RAM (see Figure 1.20).

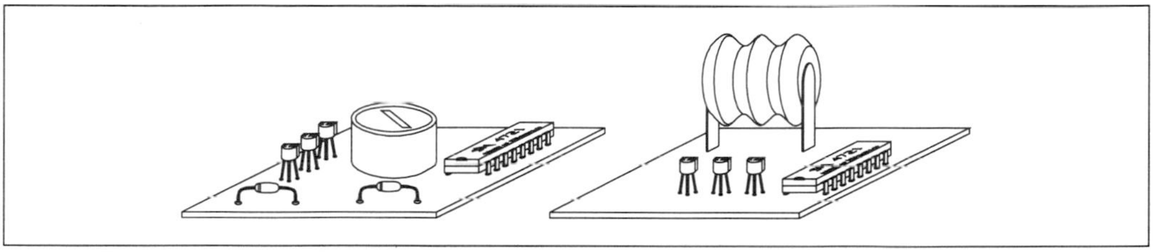

Figure 1.20: Battery and accumulator. Today's PCs generally have a battery or an accumulator to back up the configuration data of the CMOS RAM when the PC is switched off, and to periodically update the internal real-time clock.

But the CMOS chip has another function: it includes a *real-time clock* (see Figure 1.21). When the PC is switched off (or even unplugged) this clock is powered by the battery or accumulator, and is therefore able to update time and date independently. Today you don't have to provide the time or date at power-up, as the computer reads the CMOS RAM (where, in addition to the configuration data, the time and date are stored), and sets the DOS-internal system clock automatically. A correct system time is necessary because DOS appends a time mark to all files, indicating the time and date of the last file change. Backup programs like BACKUP may use this mark to determine which data to back up.

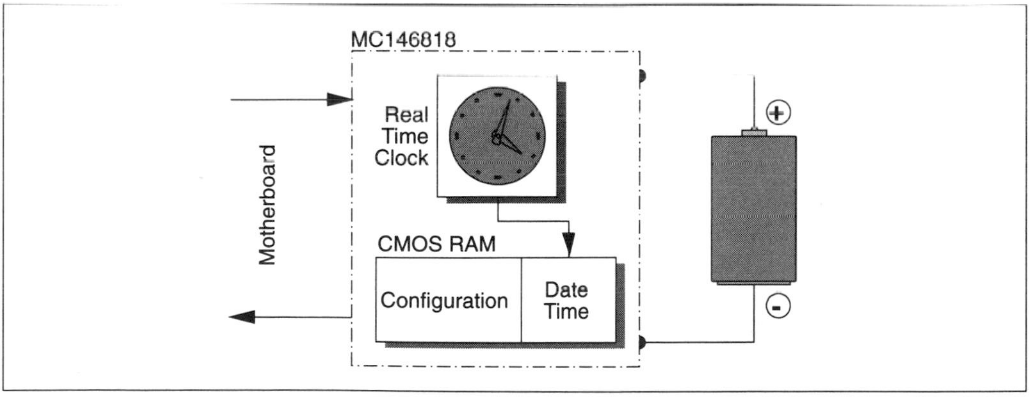

Figure 1.21: CMOS RAM and real-time clock. The PC has an MC146818 chip which has a real-time clock and a battery buffered CMOS RAM in which to store the configuration data.

The CMOS RAM and real-time clock are integrated on a single chip, Motorola's MC146818 or compatible. The CMOS RAM usually has 64 bytes, and works for two or three years with one battery.

1.2.11 Keyboard

The keyboard has remained the most important input device despite advances in graphics-oriented user shells (such as Windows or SAA standards). Figure 1.22 shows an opened MF II keyboard.

Figure 1.22: An opened MF II keyboard. You can see the keyboard chip, the scan matrix and the small switches at the crossings of the matrix.

Like the controller, the keyboard is also a small «computer» specialized for the conversion of key hits into a bit stream (Figure 1.23).

The main part of the keyboard is a microprocessor (8042 for PC/XT and 8048 for AT and MF II keyboards). This supervises the so-called *scan matrix* of the keyboard, which is made up of crossing lines each connected to the keyboard processor. At the crossing points, small switches are located, and on every switch a key is fixed. If you press a key the switch closes a contact between the crossing lines of the scan matrix. Now the microprocessor can determine the coordinates of the pressed switch, and therefore the activated key. This is done in the form of a *scan code*, which is transmitted via a buffer to the keyboard interface on the motherboard; thus the CPU knows which key has been pressed. Conversion of the scan code into the correspon-ding character (letter A in Figure 1.23) is carried out by a program called the *keyboard driver* (in the case of DOS, keyb.com). Using this method, a lot of different keyboard layouts may be realized: without needing to change the keyboard hardware, and especially the scan matrix, keyboards for various languages can be realized simply by adjusting the keyboard driver for the language concerned. With DOS you may choose American (US), British (UK), German (GR), etc. keyboards.

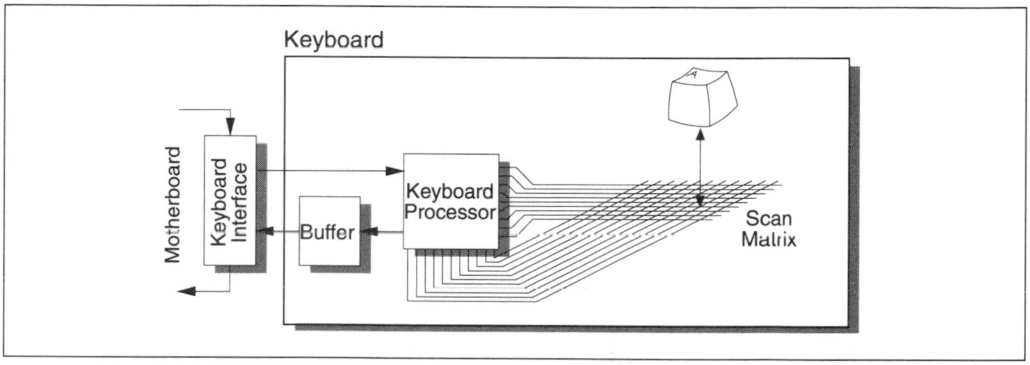

Figure 1.23: The keyboard has a keyboard processor to supervise the scan matrix, and a buffer in which to store the characters. The characters are transferred to the keyboard interface on the motherboard. Programmable keyboards can also receive data from the motherboard.

1.2.12 Mice and other Rodents

With the advance of graphic-oriented user shells, so-called *pointing devices* have become more important. For the operation of many programs (Windows) they are very useful or even necessary (for example, AutoCAD). The oldest pointing device is the *mouse,* so called because of its plump body and long tail. Usually, a mouse is connected to the serial interface of the PC, but there are versions with their own adapter card for a bus slot, so-called *bus mice*. Originally, Microsoft planned three buttons for the mouse, but only two were used. Therefore, many mice have only two buttons. Well-known compatible mice are manufactured by Genius, Logitech and other companies.

The mouse is of no use on its own: to move the *mouse pointer* (usually an arrow or rectangle on-screen), every mouse needs (like the trackball or tablet) a program called a *mouse driver*. This converts the signals from the mouse into commands for the CPU on the motherboard. The CPU then drives the graphics adapter so that the pointer is actually moved. As you may already have seen from looking at the outside, the mouse includes a gummed ball. Figure 1.24 shows the inside of a mouse.

The ball is in contact with two small rollers. When you move the mouse the ball is rotated, and the movement transmitted to the rollers. At the other end of the roller axis a disk with small holes located at regular distances is fixed. On both sides of the disk there is a transmitter and a receiver photosensor assembly. When the rollers are rotated by the ball, the disk interrupts the photosensor assembly and opens it, depending on whether a hole in the disk is located between the transmitter and receiver of the photosensor assembly. The number of such interruptions is proportional to the number of ball rotations, and therefore to the distance the mouse is moved. Because the two rollers are located perpendicular to each other (thus constituting a Cartesian coordinate system), any oblique movement of the mouse is converted into two numbers by the mouse's electronic controls. These describe the number of interruptions and openings of the photosensor assembly for both disks, thus the mouse knows exactly how far it has been moved. Now the values are transmitted via the cable to the serial interface, which then transfers the values received to the CPU.

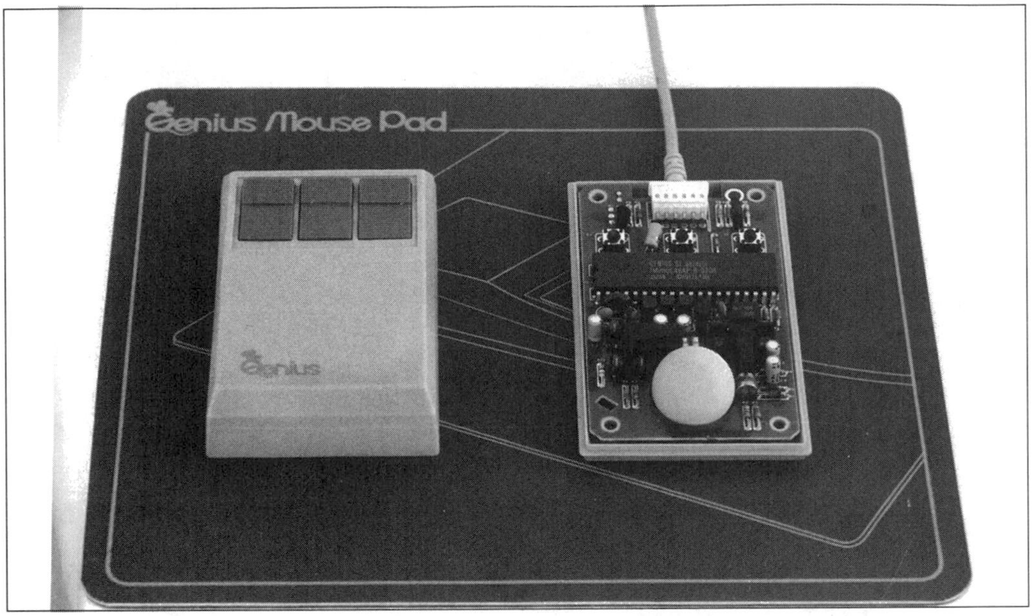

Figure 1.24: An opened mouse, with the ball and photosensor assembly for sensing movement.

In addition to this kind of mouse there are «tailless» mice that transmit the signal via an infrared signal (similar to the remote control of a TV) to a receiver. The receiver is connected to the serial interface or an adapter card. Moreover, *optical mice* have recently come onto the market. These don't have a ball, but determine the direction and amount of movement using the pattern on a special *mouse pad* on which they are moved. In contrast to the rollers of a conventional mouse, the sensors necessary for this don't wear out, and because of the loss of the iron ball they are lighter. The optical pattern is converted into a number by the mouse's electronics, which represent the direction and the amount of movement. This conversion is rather complicated, and requires more expensive electronic equipment, therefore optical mice are, unfortunately, far more expensive than mechanical ones. If you put a mouse onto its «back» you virtually get a *trackball*. Actually, the interior of a trackball is very similar to that of a mouse, but in general the ball is considerably larger. You can rotate this ball in different directions with your fingers, and thus move the mouse pointer on the screen. In some keyboards and notebooks the trackball has already been integrated. For professional CAD and graphics applications a *tablet* is recommended. Here, conversion of the sledge movement into pointer movement onscreen is executed purely by electronics. Below the surface of the tablet there is a matrix made of wires through which run current pulses. These pulses are detected by the magnifying glass and delivered to the PC. The advantage of this matrix is the very high resolution. A high-quality mouse reaches up to 400 dots per inch (dpi); a tablet, on the other hand, reaches 1000 dpi. Because the CPU knows exactly where each pulse is at what time, the CPU can determine the exact position of the magnifying glass on the tablet using the time at which the magnifying glass supplies a pulse. Unlike the mouse, which may be placed anywhere on the desk and only returns the direction and the amount of its movement, the tablet returns the absolute position (or coordinates). Usually, a tablet is divided into a central part, which serves as a drawing area and a peripheral part, where symbol fields are located. The symbol fields depend on the application (AutoCAD, for example). If you click on a point in the drawing area, AutoCAD draws a point. If, on the other hand, you click a symbol field in the peripheral area, AutoCAD executes a certain command (which is symbolized by the field). There are further pointing devices such as the *joystick*, with which you may move a pointer on-screen similar to the mouse. Another, older pointing device is the so-called *light pen*. This takes the form of a pencil with which you can «press» certain optical keys or draw lines on the screen. The light pen works in a similar way to a tablet, but here no electrical pulses run through a wire matrix. Instead, the light pen detects the light-up of the screen at that position where the electron beam of the monitor hits the screen surface. Therefore, the light pen (or better, the graphics adapter) can determine its location (line, column) on the screen. As a user, you do not recognize the light-up as the eye is too slow.

1.2.13 The Power Supply

Of course, the components described above have to be supplied with energy in some way. Therefore, the power supply is explained here in brief. Figure 1.25 shows a standard power supply. (Depending on the computer manufacturer, there are many different shapes, of course.)

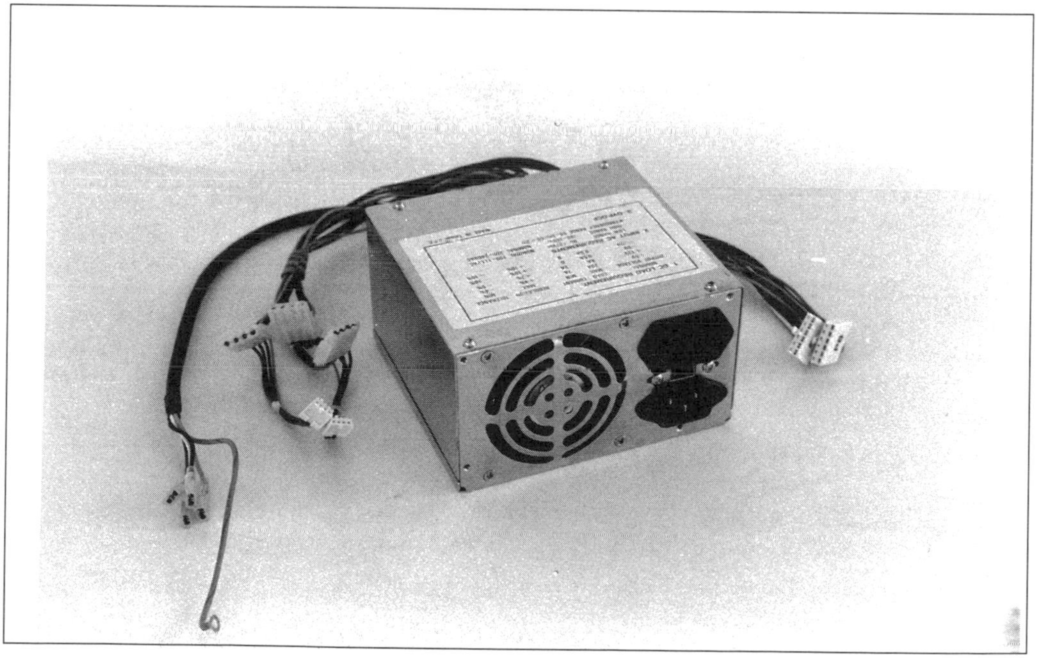

Figure 1.25: The power supply.

Usually, the power supply has one or two plugs for the motherboard, through which the motherboard is supplied with the necessary power. Adapter cards connected and inserted into the bus slots are usually supplied via the bus slots. Because the floppy and hard disk drives require far more current (power dissipation of 10–30 W each), the power supply additionally has up to four equal wire groups with appropriate plugs for the drives. Power supplies also include a thin wire with a further plug for the motherboard, through which the so-called *power-good signal* is transmitted to an electronic switch on the motherboard. The signal indicates that all necessary voltages are stable after power-up. A low voltage may lead to undefined states in initialization of the memory chips or the CPU, and therefore to disastrous failures. Thus, the electronic switch releases the 80x86 processor only if the power supply signals a stable voltage with the power-good signal. Not until then does the CPU call the BIOS to initialize all chips and boot the PC. The usual supply voltages in a PC are ±5 V and ±12 V. Some power supplies also include a socket for inserting the monitor power cable, but bigger monitors with a correspondingly higher power dissipation are usually plugged into their own socket.

1.3 Documentation

A very poor aspect of Personal Computers, especially of compatible products bought from the smaller shops, is usually the low-quality documentation. As a respectable PC user you have, of course, got a licensed operating system (MS-DOS, PC-DOS or DR-DOS, in most cases). Along with this licence you normally get a detailed description of the system commands and, in most cases, a BASIC interpreter or compiler (like GWBASIC, BASICA or Quick Basic). Any hints about which of all the plugs and sockets is the serial interface, or where the main switch of your computer is located (don't laugh, the main switch can be hidden very efficiently) are missing in most manuals.

Therefore, you should make sure that you invest in an additional *user manual*, besides all the DOS manuals, which covers the following information:

- care and transportation of your PC;
- diagnostics software and instructions;
- memory expansion and installation capabilities;
- type and resolution of the graphics adapter;
- type of connectable monitors;
- number and type of hard disk drive(s), and installation;
- number and type of floppy drives;
- opening the case and exchanging adapter cards;
- number and location of interfaces;
- type and layout of the keyboard;
- setting the clock frequency;
- calling the SETUP program and adjusting the system configuration.

IBM and some other manufacturers usually deliver such a manual along with their products, but with most of the cheaper products you rarely get any technical information about what you are buying. Also, some howlers seem to be unavoidable when translating manuals from Chinese into English. Also, dig a little deeper when you are buying expansion devices (another hard disk, more powerful graphics adapter, etc.), and ask for documentation. If, when you've installed the new device, the PC stops working, this information may be invaluable. For example, interface adapter cards installed later have to be configured according to the number and type of the previously installed adapters. Without documentation you will not be able to locate the jumpers for the configuration setting.

Further, the manual should include information on diagnostics software. This may detect the reason for failure in the case of technical failures and, for example, checks whether the hard disk controller is working correctly. Because this diagnostics software is dependent on the hardware, only the hardware manufacturer's software is useful.

A *technical reference* is beyond the scope of a user manual. In a technical reference, details are listed (in varying degrees of quality) that are of interest to programmers, for example. Only renowned PC manufacturers deliver such a technical reference, though, unfortunately, you may often only understand its contents when you already know the facts.

Essential documentation which must accompany your PC includes:

- operating system manual;
- interpreter manual;
- user manual with diagnostics software;
- technical reference manual.

1.4 Taking Care of Data and Users

Personal Computers are sensitive devices. It is obvious that you shouldn't leave your PC or printer in the rain, expose it to enormous heat, or play football with it. Yet water and other liquids, such as coffee or orange juice, may lead to a short circuit. A glass of orange juice tipped over the keyboard makes all the keys sticky. If such a mishap has happened, switch off the PC immediately and remove the liquid straight away with absorbent fabric. Rinse with distilled water if necessary.

Put on an earthing bracelet when opening the case (see Section 1.2.1) or discharge yourself by touching the power supply. This, of course, also holds if you want to insert memory chips, for example. Avoid touching the connections and pins as far as possible.

Shocks of all kinds are dangerous for the read/write heads, and the data media of floppy and hard disk drives. If you want to ship your PC, use the head parking of your hard disk drive. Today, nearly all hard disk drives have an *autopark* function, where the heads are automatically moved to a safe parking location upon power down. But be careful; older hard disks don't have this function. Whether your hard disk drive implements such a function and which precautions have to be taken should be listed in the user manual. Utilities are available for hard disk drives without autopark functions that «park» the read/write heads manually at a certain track. These programs are usually called something like *park.exe* or *diskpark.exe*. Call the appropriate program in advance of each move. You can protect 5¼" disk drives by inserting a specially-shaped piece of cardboard (usually delivered with the drive), and locking it in. If necessary, you can use an unused floppy disk instead of cardboard. No special transport protection is required for 3½" drives.

Handle all floppies with care. Labels must be written before they are stuck onto the envelope. If the label is already stuck on the floppy disk, only use a felt pen, never a ballpoint pen as the hard steel ball damages the surface of the disk. There is a slit in 5¼" floppy disks through which the disk surface is exposed. Never touch this magnetic surface as dust and fat particles may be deposited and damage the surface, thus destroying the data. Because of their plastic case, the newer 3½" floppy disks are more stable and have a metal lock. If you move it aside, the floppy disk is exposed. In this case, never touch the surface.

Many users don't pay attention to an important point – data backup. This may have disastrous consequences. Like all other preventive actions, data backup is tiresome and the catastrophe may possibly never happen. As a private computer user usually it is only private data, computer games or some smaller programs that are lost, but bigger engineers' offices and legal chambers, for example, are controlled more and more by computers and the information they store. A complete loss may lead directly to ruin, or at least several months of data recovery. For small amounts of information, floppy disks are adequate, but large amounts of data should be managed centrally and periodically backed up by a powerful backup system, such as a streamer with appropriate software. Attention should also be given to some rare dangers such as fire. All the backup copies in the office are of no value if they burn along with the original data, or if they are destroyed by water damage. Therefore, important information should not only be backed up regularly, but also stored in another safe place. These hints, incidentally, evolve from experience.

Besides physical data damage (by fire, wear or negligence), logical damage may also arise. This is the product of incorrectly working hardware, user faults or malicious damage. If your PC is telling you that it is full of water but you didn't actually spill your coffee, it is probably infected by a computer virus. Some viruses are very dangerous and may destroy all your data within a few seconds. If you are only using licensed software from respectable suppliers, the probability of infecting your computer with a virus is very low. However, if you are using the one-hundredth unlicensed copy from a copying freak, such damage can't be excluded. Even so, in this case backups and some expert knowledge are usually enough to restore the data.

1.5 Operating System, BIOS and Memory Organization

The previous sections demonstrate that a PC may include a multitude of hardware components. In most cases, a user is not interested in all the details of their hard disk drive and how it is controlled by the hard disk controller. Instead, he or she uses an application program (such as CorelDRAW!) and wants to save data (drawings, in this case) as well as reread, alter or print them, if necessary. Figure 1.26 shows the different levels for accessing your PC's hardware.

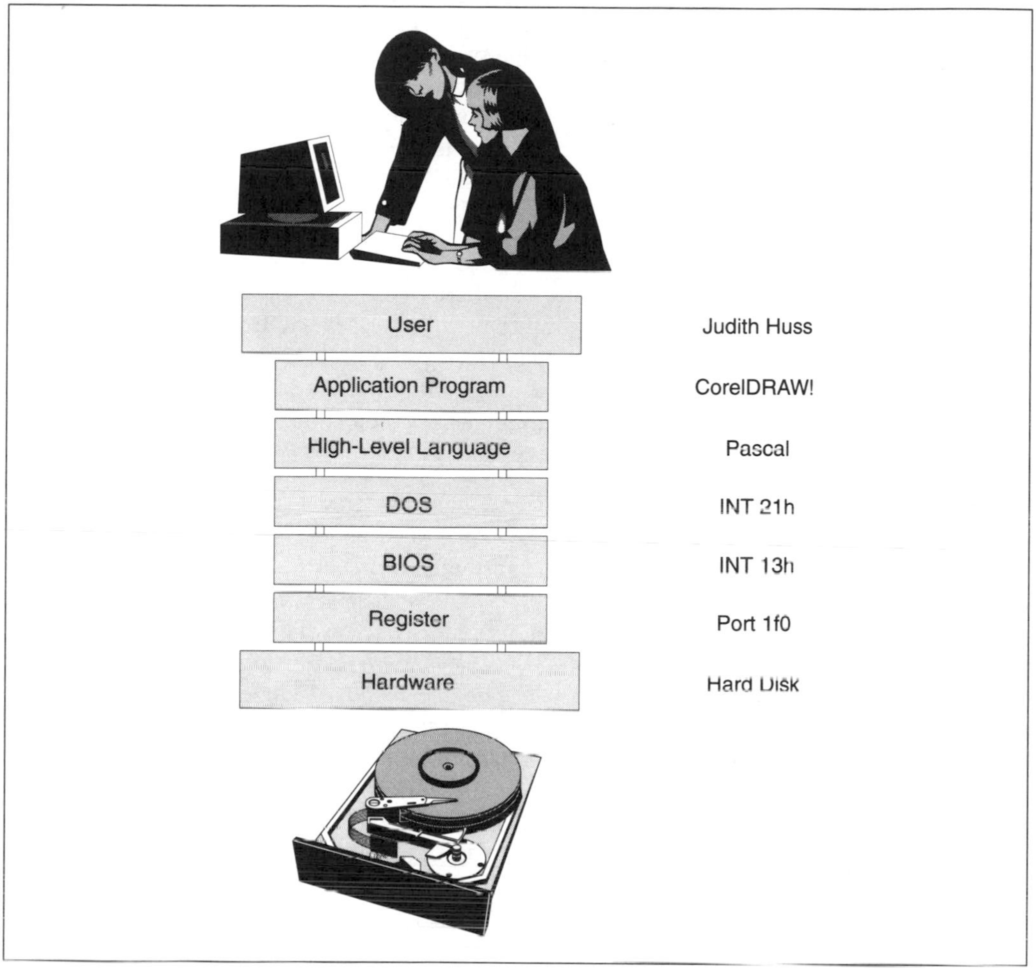

Figure 1.26: Different access levels. On the left are shown the different access levels between user and hardware. On the right is an example for each level. The top level is the application, which is the interface to the user. The bottom level is the registers that directly control the hardware.

Application programs are usually programmed with the help of high-level languages (C, BASIC, Pascal and COBOL, for example). Characteristic of high-level languages are commands adapted to human thinking, which may be used for searching and opening files and transferring parts (records) of them into memory. Skilful programming of the application hides this process behind a menu entry like *open file*. To do this, most high-level languages incorporate commands (or library routines) such as OPEN file FOR INPUT AS #1 in BASIC. One main feature of high-level languages is that they are portable, meaning that Pascal on a PC scarcely differs from Pascal on a supercomputer (the hardware is very different, of course). This is possible because an *operating system* (here DOS) supplies certain functions that make up the interface to the drives and the data on the volume. Thus, the program (or the user) doesn't need to locate the individual data on the volume, or read one or more records into memory. Instead, the operating system returns the requested data to the application (and therefore to the user) after a system call (here a command to DOS). Moreover, the operating system allows input and output of data through the parallel and serial interfaces, and displays text and graphics on the screen. It manages main memory and allocates part of it to application programs. Therefore, the system controls and supervises the operation of the whole computer. For these tasks, the «tiny» operating system DOS for your PC doesn't differ significantly from a big operating system (VMS, for example) for a mainframe. In a mainframe, the operating system also controls the computer, allocates memory, processor and other system elements to application programs, etc.

All of these tasks are carried out by DOS in the background. If your *autoexec.bat* contains a line that automatically calls an application program you will never be confronted with the *prompt* C:>. Instead, the input mask or shell of the application program is loaded immediately. Many users confuse the C:> command and commands like DIR, CHDIR and DEL with the operating system or DOS. The prompt, as well as the internal DOS commands are, in fact, part of the *command interpreter* or *user shell*. Figure 1.27 shows a diagram of DOS components.

The «real» DOS with its interfaces to hardware and the management of memory, interfaces, etc. is located in the bottom two parts. Microsoft calls them IO.SYS and MSDOS.SYS (IBM IBMBIOS.SYS and IBMDOS.SYS). The lowest, and therefore the most hardware-oriented, level is IO.SYS. Here the routines for accessing the BIOS and registers are located. The interfaces that are important for programmers and application programs, such as file opening, byte output via the parallel interface, etc., are integrated in MSDOS.SYS. These instructions are converted into a command sequence for IO.SYS, therefore it is possible to adapt DOS to various hardware environments simply by changing the hardware-oriented IO.SYS part. Thus, the manufacturers of PCs have the opportunity to choose different technical solutions. By adapting IO.SYS accordingly, DOS (MSDOS.SYS) is then able to access this different hardware in exactly the same way as an original IBM PC because IO.SYS converts all instructions into correct commands for the different hardware. However, the passion of the Taiwanese for copying has made the adaptation of IO.SYS unnecessary, as at least 99.9999% of the hardware functions have been copied. Therefore, no different registers or additional instructions are needed.

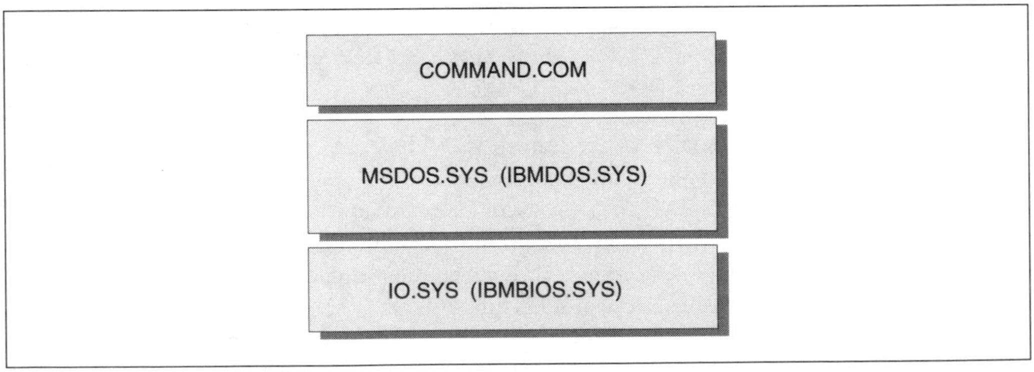

Figure 1.27: The DOS components. DOS consists of three parts: the most user-oriented is COMMAND.COM; the most hardware-oriented IO.SYS.

For a user, the command interpreter is of great importance. In DOS its name is *COMMAND.COM*. This program displays the prompt (typically C:>), accepts your commands (DIR, COPY, etc.), or loads and calls programs. Within the command interpreter the so-called *internal DOS commands* are incorporated. If you issue such a command (for example, DIR), COMMAND.COM executes an internal routine (which, for example, executes a system call to read the directory of the floppy or hard disk). On the other hand, the *external DOS commands* are present as autonomous and complete programs that are loaded and executed, as are all other application programs (Word, for example), by COMMAND.COM. Unlike IO.SYS and MSDOS.SYS, COMMAND.COM may be replaced by another command interpreter (by means of the CONFIG.SYS command SHELL=...). This again emphasizes that DOS is made up of the files IO.SYS and MSDOS.SYS, or IBMBIOS.SYS and IBMDOS.SYS. They are located in the root directory as hidden files. With a suitable utility (such as Norton Utilities or PCTools) which locates hidden files, you should be able to track them down.

DOS, in turn, uses the BIOS to access certain hardware components. Usually, the BIOS supplies programs for accessing drives, the graphics adapter and parallel/serial interfaces on a physical (that is, hardware) level. Now you can see a distinct hierarchy: the menu item *open file* with CorelDRAW! is converted by the high-level language (at compile time) into system calls to DOS (at runtime), where DOS in turn internally converts these calls and uses BIOS programs to execute the menu item. In turn, the BIOS accesses the hardware by so-called *registers*. Registers are certain interfaces that are directly assigned to hardware. Commands that directly control the hardware operation are placed in registers. For example, the DMA chip, timer chip, graphics controller chip and drive controllers are accessed via registers. By using appropriate values, data exchange, the sound of a certain frequency, or various line frequencies on the monitor may be set. The address, size and meaning of the registers are, of course, largely dependent on the hardware. The job of the BIOS is to convert a defined function call into a corresponding command sequence for the registers concerned. Thus, the hierarchical concept of Figure 1.19 can be understood: if you program an application by directly accessing registers, the resulting program code can be executed only on a certain PC, and is therefore completely incompatible with other machines because the manufacturer is, in principle, free to choose any address and meaning for the registers. However, the access hierarchy, with its exactly defined interfaces between the different levels, allows (from the viewpoint of the application) a floppy drive with a 360 kbytes capacity to be accessed in the same way as a modern hard disk with a capacity of several gigabytes. BIOS and IO.SYS execute the necessary adapations to the physical drive. That the internal conversion of the menu item *open file* is very different for these two cases seems to be natural.

It should be noted that with the aid of hardware-oriented high-level languages like C, for example (and nowadays even with Pascal or BASIC), you have the opportunity to access the BIOS and registers of a PC directly. Direct access to the BIOS in particular became established with graphics applications or tools such as Norton Utilities or PCTools. Programmers want to speed up the performance of their programs and use the graphics capabilities of a PC (DOS doesn't incorporate any system call to output a graphics point on-screen, for example). As can be seen from Figure 1.26, you move around the operating system. In a PC with DOS this is not critical, because you are always working alone and only one application is running at a time. DOS is a *singletasking operating system*. More powerful computer systems (i386/i486/Pentium

PCs with OS/2 , UNIX or Windows NT also belong to this group), on the other hand, run with a *multitasking operating system*. Popular resident programs such as the external DOS command PRINT or Borland's Sidekick occupy a position somewhere in the middle. PRINT prints files independent of the actual application running but, in contrast to a background program in a multitasking environment, the activation of PRINT is not carried out by the operating system (DOS) but by the periodic timer interrupt. PRINT intercepts this interrupt to activate *itself* for a certain self-defined time period. In contrast, with a multitasking operating system, all the applications residing in memory are activated by the *operating system* for a time period defined by the system. Thus, with OS/2 you can print a text while your CAD application is calculating the reinforcement of a house in the background and you are editing a letter in the foreground. Therefore, it is obvious that a multitasking system cannot allow any bypassing. In this case, there may be events running in the computer that are not controlled by (and therefore hidden from) the operating system. Actually, memory resident programs like PRINT and Sidekick for DOS give the user some feeling of a multitasking environment.

A serious disadvantage of DOS is the so-called 640 kbytes boundary. This means that for all programs (including the operating system) only 640 kbytes are available at most. The reason is not some problem with space for memory chips or that memory is very expensive above 640 kbytes, but the *memory organization* defined by the designers of DOS (see Figure 1.28 for a description of this organization).

You can see that the first 640 kbytes (addresses 0000h to 9999h) are reserved for programs. In the lowest parts reside interrupt vectors, BIOS and DOS data areas, IO.SYS, MSDOS.SYS, drivers and the resident part of COMMAND.COM. The *application programs area* (reserved for programs like Word or CorelDRAW!) runs on from this. At the upper end the transient part of COMMAND.COM overlaps with the application program area. To use memory as efficiently as possible, COMMAND.COM is divided into two parts: the resident part holds the routines that are, for example, necessary to load the transient part after completion or abortion of an application; the transient part holds the internal commands like DIR and COPY that are not necessary during execution of the application program, and which thus may be overwritten. Resident means that the corresponding code remains in memory even when the application is loaded: the code will not be overwritten under any circumstances; transient means that the corresponding program code can be overwritten to enhance the memory space for the application's code and data. Starting with DOS 4.0, you may determine the occupation of the first 640 kbytes by system and application programs, drivers, buffers, etc. using the command MEM /PROGRAM or MEM /DEBUG.

Above the 640 kbyte boundary are the 128 kbytes of the video RAM (see also Figure 1.9). The next 128 kbytes are reserved for BIOS extensions on graphics adapters and controllers (see also Figures 1.9 and 1.12). Above this there are 128 kbytes for the system BIOS on the motherboard (see Figure 1.7). In the original IBM PC, the ROM BASIC is also integrated into this area. All memory areas in total give a memory of 1 Mbyte.

The first two processors (8088 and 8086) had 20 lines for the address bus, and they could address a maximum of 2^{20} = 1 Mbyte. Therefore, an *address space* (the number of addressable bytes) of 1 Mbyte was assumed and divided in the way described above. This separation was completely arbitrary, but you should notice that the first PC was delivered with 64 kbytes (!) of main memory. The reservation of the lower 640 kbytes for application programs and DOS (with 16 kbytes at that time) seemed as if it would be enough to last for decades. The designers of DOS were caught completely unawares by later developments in computing, and therefore we are now struggling with this 640 kbyte boundary in the era of cheap and high-capacity memory chips.

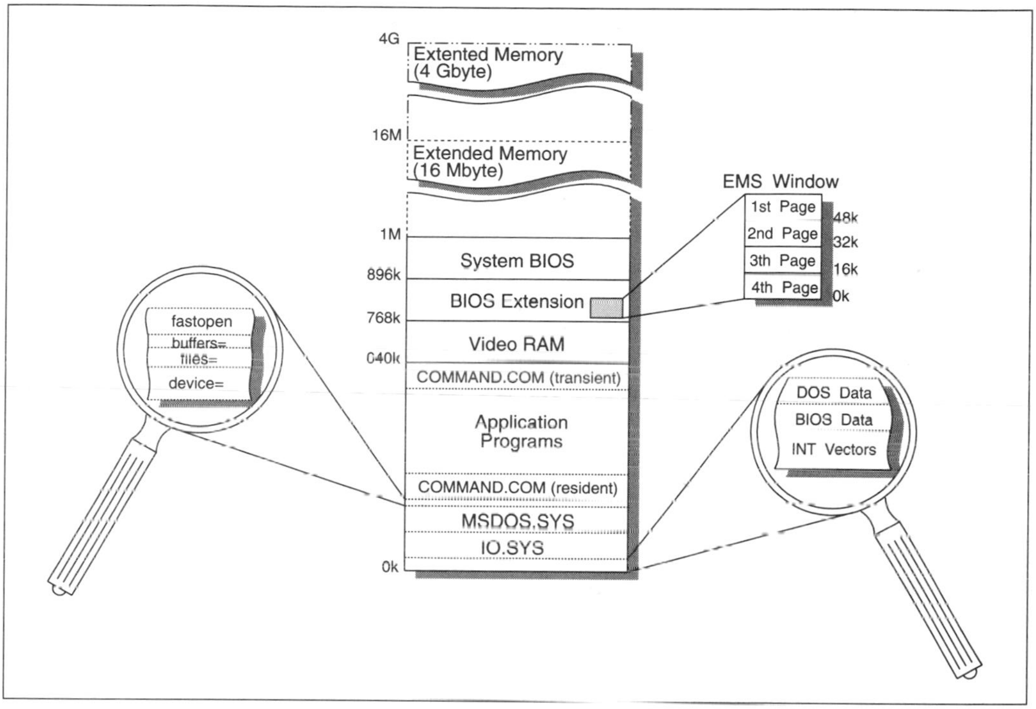

Figure 1.28: DOS memory organization. With DOS the first 640 kbytes are reserved for the operating system and application programs. Above the first 640 kbytes there is the video RAM, and starting from 768 kbytes there follow various (and optional) BIOS extensions. Above 1 Mbyte extended memory starts, which can be up to 4 Gbyte on an i386, i486 or Pentium.

In particular, it is worth noting that the individual areas of the memory organization need not be completely filled. For example, it is possible to limit the main memory (the reserved lower 640 kbytes) to 256 kbytes instead of using the full 640 kbytes. That doesn't change the address A000h of the video memory in any way. The 384 kbytes in between remain empty and virtually constitute a «hole» in the address space. In the same way, the amount of the reserved areas for video RAM and ROM BIOS actually used has no influence on their location in the address space.

Unfortunately, because of the concept of the PC (and DOS), it is impossible to fill these holes with additional RAM. The CPU may not be able to access the corresponding memory chips, therefore all DOS programs are limited to a size of 640 kbytes less the memory area occupied by the system. Meanwhile DOS, together with all its drivers (for printer, screen, mouse, etc.) occupies a large amount of memory, so that less and less memory remains for application programs. Version 5.0 together with at least an 80286 chip offers progress to some extent. Here a large part of DOS is moved to the HIMEM area or extended/expanded memory. Application programs then have the opportunity to use a «fabulous» 620 kbytes of memory.

In the application area, the called program is stored and may itself request memory for its own purposes, for example to load a text file into memory. As the extent of the text file can't be foreseen at programming time, memory is assigned dynamically. This means that the application has to inform DOS how much memory is needed for the text file, and DOS assigns it to the application. That is the reason why some programs display the message *Not enough memory!*, although enough memory was available for loading the program. A request to DOS to provide additional memory for the text file can't be fulfilled by the operating system if there is too little memory available.

An important advance with the AT – or better, the 80286 processor and higher – is that the 80286, with its 24 address lines, can now address 16 Mbytes of memory (and the i386/i486/Pentium with 32 address lines can address 4 Gbytes). But this only works in the so-called *protected mode*. Memory above 1 Mbyte is called extended memory, and may be accessed by an 80286/i386/i486/Pentium processor in protected mode only. This advanced protected mode is wholly incompatible with DOS. To retain compatibility, even the i386, i486 and Pentium are operated in *real mode*. Here they can only address 1 Mbyte of memory, even though 32 address lines are present. Therefore, PCs with i386, i486 or Pentium processors are also subject to the 640 kbyte boundary for application programs. However, Windows and OS/2 successfully attempt to break through this barricade. Switching between real and protected mode is possible to allow access to extended memory for at least a certain time. This method is used by programs like RAMDRIVE.SYS or VDISK.SYS for virtual drives. Another possibility is that a 64 kbyte region of memory may be inserted into free memory above the 640 kbyte boundary (into a hole in the address space); this region constitutes a so-called *window* into a much larger memory (up to 8 Mbytes). This large memory is called expanded memory, or EMS memory. By means of appropriate commands to registers on an EMS memory expansion adapter, the window (which consists of four partial windows) may be moved within the EMS memory. Therefore, the 8 Mbytes are available in sections of 64 kbytes (or 4 *16 kbytes) each. Details about real and protected mode, as well as extended and expanded memory, are given later.

Part 2
Processor and Memory

The processor and memory, together with the support chips, are usually the main components of the motherboard. It is these components that make up the actual computer. Important units such as hard disk drives and interfaces are already known as peripherals. It is only because the integration of electronic elements is so advanced today that the motherboard doesn't seem to be as important as it should. Before the integration of a million elements on a finger-nail sized chip was possible, the «motherboard» occupied a whole room! Therefore, it isn't surprising that discussing the motherboard will take up a large part of this book. I will start with the heart and brain of the computer – processor and memory.

Some remarks about the processor names are in order: from the 8086/88 up to the 80386 they follow the convention 80x86. Accordingly, the coprocessors are called 80x87 in general, and 8087, 80287 and 80387 specifically. After releasing the 80386 chip, Intel changed this naming convention slightly. Now the CPUs are denoted as i386 (or 386 for short), i486, etc., and the coprocessors as i387, i487, etc. In the following, I will use the terms 8086/88 to 80286, and i386, i486 for the CPUs, as well as 8087, 80287 and i387 for the coprocessors.

2 Intel's Microprocessor for Beginners – The i386

The processor – often also called the CPU – is the heart or brain of a PC. In the processor, data processing takes place, which requires at least a minimum of intelligence. All other, sometimes rather complicated, chips are simply slaves of the processor which, together with the memory chips, is one of the highest integrated elements in a PC. If you look at the mass market for powerful general-purpose microprocessors, you will find there are two different processor families in the CPU industry. They are the 80x86 family from Intel and the 68000 series from Motorola. The former are installed in IBM-compatible Personal Computers; the 68000 series are largely used in Apple Macintosh machines, which are the biggest competitor to IBM compatible PCs. It's a shame that both families are not compatible; the way in which instructions are given internally, the language in which the instructions are given, how the addresses are allocated in the memory (RAM) and the I/O address areas are entirely different. But let us first turn to the unavoidable basics for understanding these seemingly very intelligent chips.

2.1 The Field-Effect Transistor

For highly integrated circuits such as microprocessors or memory chips, the MOS Field-Effect Transistor (MOSFET) is particularly suitable. It is small and easy to manufacture, yet has a very low power consumption, which is the difference between supplied power (from a battery, for example) and the power output by the circuit (for operating a light bulb, for example). This difference is entirely converted into heat, and heats up the circuit. With one million tiny transistors which each consume only 1/100 000 Watt, the overall power consumption has already reached 10 W. Note that it is not primarily a high current that destroys the circuit, but the heating caused by an excessively high current which burns the elements. Figure 2.1a shows an n-channel MOSFET.

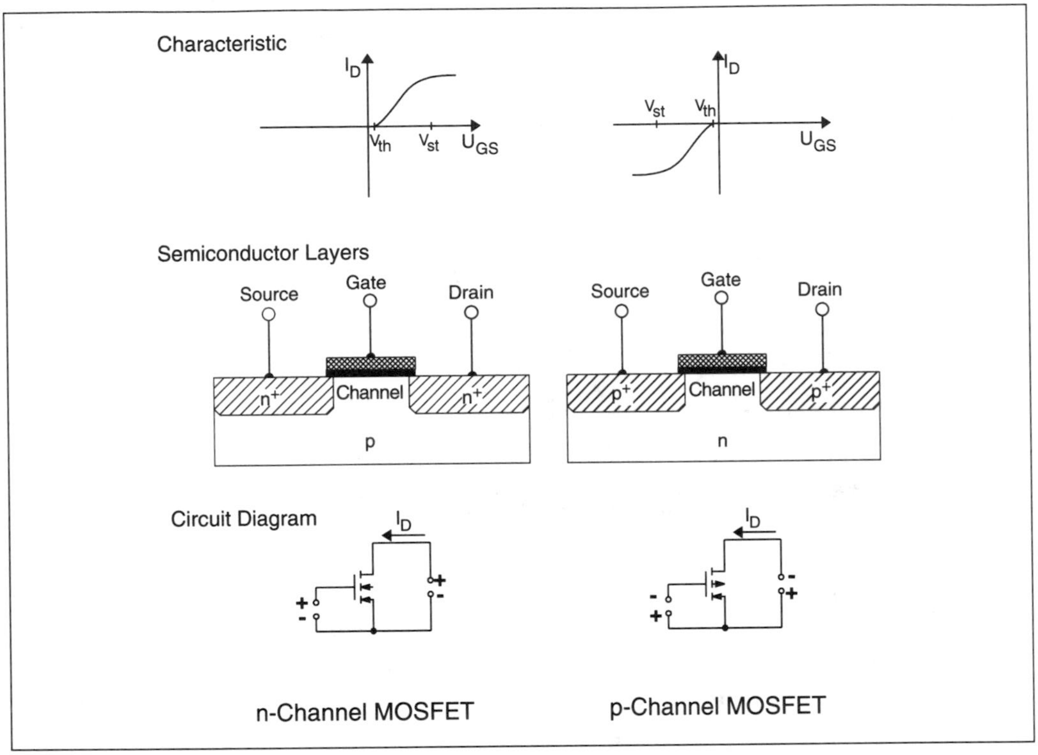

Figure 2.1a: n-channel field-effect transistor; Figure 2.1b: p-channel field-effect transistor. The characteristics of n-channel and p-channel transistors are complementary to each other. A field-effect transistor comprises two doped regions called source and drain in a lightly doped substrate. The conductivity of the channel between source and drain is altered by means of the gate voltage.

The n-channel MOSFET consists of a p-doped silicon substrate in which two n^+-doped regions are formed, called *source* and *drain*. The distance between source and drain in an IC is usually about 0.5–5 μm. P-doping means that the substrate accommodates more positively charged ions than negatively charged electrons as charge carriers for the current flow inside the substrate. This is achieved by implanting *impurities*. These atoms have less (p-doping with boron, etc.) or more (n-doping with phosphorous, arsenic, etc.) electrons compared to a silicon atom. The «+» indicates that the corresponding regions are highly doped (have a high concentration of these impurities). Between the two regions the so-called *channel* is located. The conductivity of the channel (and therefore the resistance of the MOSFET) is controlled by a *gate* formed of metal or polycristalline silicon, which is separated (and thus isolated) from the substrate by an oxide layer. Reading from top to bottom, the layer sequence reads metal–oxide–semiconductor; that is where the name MOS transistor comes from. If a control voltage is applied to the gate, free charge carriers arise through something like a «sucking effect». The higher the voltage, the more charge carriers are available, that is, the lower is the resistance of the channel. Note that transistor is the abbreviation of *tran*sfer re*sistor*. If a voltage U_{GS} is applied between the source and drain, then the current I_D (and therefore also the voltage output by the MOSFET) is governed by the gate voltage. The current flow does not start until the threshold voltage V_{th} has been exceeded. If the saturation value V_{st} is reached, current through the MOSFET no longer rises, even if the voltage U_{GS} between the gate and source rises further. The MOSFET operates in the saturation region. The currently described MOSFET is, more exactly, called an n-channel enhancement-type field-effect transistor (see Figure 2.1a).

In the same way, a p-channel enhancement-type MOSFET may be constructed by exchanging the n- and p-layers (see Figure 2.1b). A significant difference between them is the opposite course of the conductivity with the voltage U_{GS} between the gate and source: a rising U_{GS} means a rise in conductivity for an n-channel MOSFET, but the decline of the conductivity for a p-channel MOSFET to zero. Pictorially, the gate voltage drives the charge carriers out of the channel and thus increases its resistance.

According to individual characteristics, it is apparent that from the threshold voltage V_{th} up to the saturation voltage V_{st}, a linear dependency between the applied voltage and the current through the MOSFET (and therefore the voltage output by the MOSFET) appears. The MOSFET is operated in this proportional region if it is installed in an *analogue* circuit. This is, for example, the case for a radio or TV receiver. Here an indefinite number of intermediate levels between minimum and maximum values (minimum and maximum loudness of music, for example) is possible. But because the current through the MOSFET (and thus its resistance) can only be determined down to a certain finite precision, the intermediate levels are smudged. Therefore, no exact value of an intermediate level can be indicated, only its range.

In a *digital circuit*, however, the MOSFET is operated in a completely different way. Here the voltage U_{GS} between the gate and source is either below (or in the region of) the threshold voltage V_{th} or above (or in the region of) the saturation voltage V_{st}. Thus, two stable and unambiguous states of the transistor are defined: the off- and on-states, respectively. In the off-state, the MOSFET is completely turned off (has an indefinite resistance value), and a maximum voltage occurs between the source and the drain. In the on-state, the MOSFET leads the maximum current (has a resistance value of zero) and the voltage between the source and drain is minimal (equal to the threshold voltage V_{th}). Therefore, the transistor is used as a switch with two switching positions (on/off). For logic circuits, the existence of clearly defined and stable switching positions is essential because logic doesn't allow any woolly terms such as maybe, nearly, etc. With two clearly defined and distinguishable switching positions (and therefore output currents and voltages), we get digital circuits with dual or binary (that is, two-valued) logic.

To complete the picture, I want to mention that in very fast circuits (supercomputers, for example) a substrate made of gallium-arsenide (GaAs) instead of silicon is used. Moreover, sometimes bipolar transistors are also used in ECL or BiCMOS circuits to enhance the operation speed. However, this is achieved with the disadvantage of having a power consumption three times that of a pure CMOS circuit. Applications of these technologies are the Pentium (BiCMOS) and the R6000 (ECL), for example. Further, in the context of so-called *fuzzy logic*, ambiguous terms like nearly, possible, etc. are also allowed. Up to now, this logic has mainly been of interest in research, but some minor applications, such as in the field of autofocus cameras, are already on the market. In the original field of data processing, this logic is not used in applications yet. The on/off logic states of a MOS transistor are converted using corresponding biasing voltages, resistance combinations, etc. to certain voltage values. In Table 2.1, the voltages for logical «1» and logical «0» for the NMOS and CMOS family, as well as for three additional bipolar families, are given.

Family	U_0 [V]	U_1 [V]
NMOS	−1...+1	5...10
CMOS	1...2	4...15
TTL	0...0.5	2.5...5
ECL	ca. 3	4...5
IIL	ca. 1	2...5

NMOS: logic with n-channel MOS transistors
CMOS: logic with complementary MOS transistors
TTL: (bipolar) transistor–transistor logic
ECL: (bipolar) emitter-coupled logic
IIL: (bipolar) integrated injection logic

Table 2.1: Logic levels of different logic families

2.2 Basics of Machine-Related Information Representation

An essential point in the last section was that a transistor in digital circuits (including the processors, memory, controllers etc. of your PC) is only operated in the on and off states. Thus, it seems natural to use a binary (two-valued) information representation in which each kind of information must be expressed by a series of on/off states, or 1/0.

At first glance this seems to be somewhat abstract. However, we are daily confronted with this process of information representation, but have adapted to it over the years so that it is no longer apparent to us. For example, in this book information about PC hardware is given in the form of a series of letters and punctuation marks. The only difference is that 26 different letters (a to z) and six punctuation marks (.,:;?!) are available. The electronic chips in your PC know only the on/off states, or 1/0; this means that letters and punctuation marks have to be converted to 1/0 states. This conversion is done by means of a *code*. If you look at the following line

5 ٥

you assume that it means two completely different things: first the number five and then a donut-like symbol. Depending on your viewpoint, this may be false. The donut is the Arabic symbol for the digit 5. Therefore, the two symbols *mean* the same, but the item is *represented* differently. This also remains true with a secret code. The encoded text means the same as it did prior to encoding, but the representation has completely changed and the text is meaningless for most people. Of course, in the field of computers different codes also exist (and are used). The most common code (and in the case of a PC the only one used) is *ASCII*, which assigns certain characters a number (namely the code).

2.2.1 Decimal and Binary System

As well as characters, numbers must also be represented in some way. Don't confuse the terms digit and number: a digit is one of the symbols 0–9, but a number denotes a value. The *decimal numbers* familiar to us are represented by the digits 0 to 9 (ten, therefore decimal numbers). In other words, ten different states 0–9 can be distinguished, but in the case of a computer only two such states are available: 0 and 1. To understand the number representation in a computer we have to analyse the interpretation of a decimal number first. Our number system is also called a *positional system* because every position of a decimal number corresponds to a certain value. Generally the rightmost (first) position represents the value 1, the second position the value 10, the third position the value 100, etc. The number of such values per position is expressed by the corresponding digit.

Example:

```
The interpretation of the number 318 is
3 x 100 + 1 x 10 + 8 x 1
or expressed by powers
3 x 10² + 1 x 10¹ + 8 x 10⁰
```

This scheme may be extended to any number of an arbitrarily high value, of course. The «ten» represents the *base* of the number system and is equal to the number of distinguishable digits. In a computer, on the other hand, only two such digits are available for the base. Therefore the «ten» has to be replaced by «two». This directly leads to the *binary* or *dual system*. Numbers in the binary system are characterized by the suffix b:

Example:

```
The number 100111110b means
1x2⁸+0x2⁷+0x2⁶+1x2⁵+1x2⁴+1x2³+1x2²+1x2¹+0x2⁰
or in more detail
1x256+0x128+0x64+1x32+1x16+1x8+1x4+1x2+0x1 = 318
```

Thus we get two different representations of the decimal value 318: 318 in the decimal system and 100111110b in the binary or dual system. As for decimal numbers, the binary scheme can be extended to any number of an arbitrarily high value. However, you can immediately see a big disadvantage of the binary system as compared to the decimal system: the numbers become «longer», that is, you need more room to write them down.

In computing it became established to bundle eight such digits or *bits* (abbreviation for *binary digit*) into one *byte*. Half a byte, or four bits, is called a *nibble*; two bytes are called a *word*; and four bytes are called a *double word*. With one byte a total of $2^8=256$ different numbers between 0 and 255 can be represented. By grouping several bytes, numbers with higher values may also be represented. For example, the bundling of two bytes to one word leads to numbers in the range 0–65 535 (2^{16}–1). They are called *unsigned integers* (abbreviated to *unsigned*). A double word with four bytes may express numbers from 0–4 294 967 295 (2^{32}–1). This grouping leads to *unsigned long integers* (abbreviated to *unsigned long*).

2.2.2 ASCII Code

With the ASCII code, every one of these 256 different values of 1 byte is assigned a character; in other words, 256 chosen symbols are enumerated. Strictly speaking, the ASCII code only defines 128 characters; the first 32 are so-called *control characters* used to give messages concerning the transmitted data to the receiver. For example, the control character ^D (EOT=End Of Transmission) indicates the end of the current data transfer. But in the field of PCs, the *extended ASCII code* (introduced by IBM) has become firmly established. Here, even codes 128–255 are occupied by fixed characters. Furthermore, the first 32 codes (0–31) are assigned certain symbols. Appendix A gives a table with the symbols, characters and codes for the extended ASCII code according to IBM. It should be mentioned that the assignment of numbers and characters has been done completely arbitrarily. Beyond some practical considerations (you unavoidably need letters and digits), there is no particular reason why, for example, code 65 is assigned to uppercase A:

Example:

```
ASCII code 65:           uppercase A
(ext.) ASCII code 203:   graphics symbol ╦
ASCII code 10 (LF):      control code for line feed
```

You can see that ASCII is very useful for representing text files (actually, text files are often called ASCII files). If you compose a chain of several continuous ASCII codes or, in other words, a chain of characters, you get a *string*. Because strings (which may correspond to a sentence, for example) may be of different lengths, usually the length of the string concerned must be specified. In BASIC this is done by a string descriptor which has, as one entry, the length of the string belonging to the descriptor. With DOS and some programming languages (C, for example), every string is terminated by ASCII code 0 (zero). Such a string is also called an *ASCIIZ string*. Besides the ASCII code there are, of course, other codes. Of importance for mainframes in particular is the so-called *EBCDIC code*, mainly used by IBM for its mainframes. Naturally, every user may construct his own code and may, for example, assign the letter A the code 1. By doing this, however, all compatibility is lost.

2.2.3 Negative Integers and Two's Complement

As well as the positive integers in arithmetic, negative integers are also of significance. One may think of introducing negative integers simply by a preceding bit that indicates whether the sign is positive (sign bit = 1) or negative (sign bit = 0). But in the field of computers, another representation has been established for practical reasons, the so-called two's complement representation (also written 2' complement representation). A negative integer is represented by replacing all 0s by 1s and all 1s by 0s in the corresponding positive number (forming the complement), and adding the value 1 to the complement's result:

Example:

```
positive integer 256:  0000 0001 0000 0000b
negative integer -256:
complement              1111 1110 1111 1111b
add one               +                   1b
result                  1111 1111 0000 0000b
```

Note that *signed integers* (abbreviated to *integer*) may have values in the range –32 768 (-2^{15}) to 32767 ($2^{15}-1$). If the high-order (leftmost) bit is equal to 1, the signed integer represented is negative. The interpretation of signed integers is very different from the interpretation of unsigned integers:

Example:

```
binary number 1111 1111 1111 1111b
interpretation as an unsigned integer:
1x2^15+1x2^14+...+1x2^1+1x2^0 = 65,535
interpretation as a signed integer:
high-order bit equals 1, therefore the number is negative;
thus the procedure of the example mentioned above has to be inverted:
binary              1111 1111 1111 1111b
subtract one        1111 1111 1111 1110b
complement          0000 0000 0000 0001b
result                                 -1
```

Actually, in the two's complement representation of signed integers, something like a sign is present (the most significant bit). But the rest of the number must not be interpreted as the absolute value of the number (in the example mentioned above this would lead to the value –32,766). The two's complement representation is applied in exactly the same way to signed long integers. Thus they have a range of values between –2,147,483,648 (-2^{31}) and +2,147,483,647 ($2^{31}-1$). The reason for using the two's complement representation for negative numbers is that the subtraction of a number (the subtrahend) from another number (the minuend) can be accomplished by the addition of the two's complement of the subtrahend and the minuend. A possible carry is ignored. Strictly mathematical (in an axiomatic sense), this also holds in a similar form for normal addition: the subtraction of a number is put down to the addition of its *inverse* (*represented* as –number). Therefore the subtraction rule for binary numbers is:

minuend – subtrahend = minuend + two's complement(subtrahend)

Example:

```
      calculate difference 15 - 1
             15d = 0000 0000 0000 1111b
              1d = 0000 0000 0000 0001b
  2'complement(1d) = 1111 1111 1111 1111b
  therefore 15 - 1 = 0000 0000 0000 1111b
                    +1111 1111 1111 1111b
                   1 0000 0000 0000 1110b
  the leading 1 (carry) is ignored: thus the result is
0000 0000 0000 1110b or 14 decimal.
```

2.2.4 Hexadecimal Numbers

The representation of numbers by a series of 0s and 1s is rather tedious, and with a longer series you may soon lose track of your position. Therefore, it has become established practice to group four bits (one nibble), which means the introduction of a number system with the base 16, because four bits may represent 16 digits (0–15). Thus, the nibble constitutes the base of the *hexadecimal system*. All information units (byte, word, double word) are multiples of one nibble. Because our familiar decimal system only knows digits 0–9, symbols for the new hexadecimal digits «10» to «15» must be added. Usually, the (uppercase or lowercase) letters a (10) to f (15) are used for this. To characterize a hexadecimal number an *h* or *H* (for hexadecimal) is added on (as in 2Fh, for example) or a *0x* is put in front (0x2F in C, for example). Conversion to the decimal system is carried out analogously to the conversion of binary numbers, only the base is now 16 instead of 2:

Example:

```
unsigned decimal integer  65,535
binary number             1111 1111 1111 1111b
hexadecimal number        ffffh
```

Example:

```
hexadecimal number        9BE7h
binary number             1001 1011 1110 0111b
decimal number            9x16³+11x16²+14x16¹+7x16⁰
                          = 39,911 (unsigned integer) or
                          = -25,625 (signed integer)
```

You therefore get a more compact notation without losing the reference to computer hardware (which can only «think» in 0s and 1s) because each digit of a hexadecimal number may be represented by a nibble (four bits, half a byte). Thus, a hexadecimal number can be readily converted into a binary number (and therefore into the contents of a register, for example). Note that a hexadecimal number, like its binary counterpart, is unsigned. No minus sign exists, and only the interpretation of a binary or hexadecimal number can decide whether the number is positive or negative. Actually, the common decimal number system has something like an 11th digit in addition to 0–9, the sign «–», to distinguish positive and negative values.

2.2.5 BCD Numbers

Another important representation of numbers is given by the *binary coded decimals* (abbreviated to *BCD* or *BCD numbers*). With these numbers, the value of a byte represents the corresponding decimal digit:

Example:

```
decimal number 28
BCD               0000 0010  0000 1000

The first byte 0000 0010 indicates the digit 2 and
the second byte 0000 1000 the digit 8.
```

One advantage of the binary coded decimals is that no conversion between decimal and binary numbers is necessary, as each digit is represented by its own byte. Note that the bytes indicate the *binary value* of the digits, and not their ASCII or EBCDIC codes. The main disadvantage is obvious: with one byte, 256 different numbers (or digits) can be represented, but BCDs only use ten of them. To reduce this wastefulness, *packed BCDs* are often used. Here, each nibble of a byte represents a digit.

Example:

```
decimal number 28 (compare to the example above)
packed BCD     0010 1000

The first nibble 0010 of the byte indicates the
digit 2 and the second nibble 1000 the digit 8.
```

Note that in the case of packed BCDs, the nibbles also represent the binary value of the corresponding digit. With one byte, 100 numbers (0–99) can be represented here. The interpretation of a byte as a (packed) binary coded decimal leads, of course, to a completely different value compared to interpretation as an unsigned binary number (40 in the example).

Further different interpretations of bytes, words and other information units also exist. Of particular importance are the *instruction codes* for a processor, composed of one or more bytes which instruct the processor to execute a certain process (transfer data, compare, add, etc.). You can see that a few «bare» bytes may, depending on their interpretation, have very different meanings and consequences.

2.2.6 Little Endian Format and Intel Notation

Intel's processors use the *little endian format*, meaning that a word or double word always starts with the low-order byte and ends with the high-order byte. In other words, the high-byte of a multiple-byte unit is stored at a higher address than the low-order byte. When writing a word or double word we write the high-order byte at the leftmost position and the low-order byte at the rightmost. But storage addresses increase from left to right, therefore the 80x86 processors seemingly exchange the individual bytes compared to the «natural order» in words or double words. Because the processor stores data in the same way as in main memory and on disk, they are also exchanged there (you may confirm this with the hex editor of Norton Utilities or PCTools). This only has consequences if the word or double word represents a number and you want to split it up into the individual digits, because the order then becomes important (remember that all number systems used are positional systems):

Example: `the hexadecimal word 1234h (decimal 4660) is stored in memory and on disk as 3412h;`
`the hexadecimal double word 12345678h (decimal 405 419 896) is stored as 78563412h.`

In contrast, with *big endian format* a word or double word always starts with the high-order and ends with the low-order byte. In other words, the high-byte of a multiple-byte unit is stored at a lower address than the low-order byte. Motorola's 68000 family uses the big endian format.

2.3 The CPU as the Kernel of all Computers

The 80x86 as the CPU is the most essential part of a PC. In the 80x86, all logical and arithmetic operations are executed. In general, the processor reads data from memory, processes it in a way defined by an instruction, and writes the result into memory again. The following briefly describes the general structure of a microprocessor. The Pentium chip is shown in Figure 2.2.

To execute the above-mentioned logical and arithmetic operations (processes), a microprocessor has (see Figure 2.3) a *Bus Unit* (*BU*), an *Instruction Unit* (*IU*), an *Execution Unit* (*EU*) as well as an *Addressing Unit* (*AU*). Among other things, the bus unit includes a so-called *prefetch queue*. The execution unit is responsible for the data processing (add, compare, etc.), and for this purpose has a Control Unit (*CU*), an *Arithmetic and Logical Unit* (*ALU*), and various registers. Frequently, the addressing unit incorporates a *memory management unit (MMU)*. In the i386, for example, the MMU comprises a *segmentation unit (SU)* and a *paging unit (PU)*.

Figure 2.2: Pentium, currently the most powerful member of the 80x86 family. It integrates a high-performance CPU, coprocessor and two caches on a single chip.

The bus unit establishes the connection to the outside world, that is, the data, address, and control bus. It fetches instructions from memory into the prefetch queue which, in turn, transfers them to the instruction unit. The IU then controls the execution unit so that the instructions fetched are actually executed by the ALU. Here, the control unit supervises the registers as well as the ALU to ensure trouble-free execution.

With the data bus, the microprocessor can read data out of or write data into memory. The memory location to read or write is accessed by an *address*. The processor calculates the address in the addressing unit, and supplies it via the address bus. Reading and writing is carried out via the bus unit. For this, the BU outputs the address and supplies the data to write, or fetches the data to read. The memory is addressed in the same way to fetch an instruction. In contrast, the data read (the instructions) are transferred into the prefetch queue, not into one or more of the registers in the execution unit, as is the case in normal data reading. The instruction unit reads the instruction from the prefetch queue, decodes it, and transfers the decoded instruction to the execution unit.

An essential point here is that instructions and data reside in the same memory. This means that there is no strict separation of instruction and data memory: each memory chip may serve as a data as well as an instruction memory. This is not obvious. The Z4 of Konrad Zuse (the first free-programmable electro-mechanical computer for numerical applications) had a program and a data memory that were strictly separate. In the instruction memory only instructions (and in the data memory only data) could be stored. Later, the mathematician John von Neumann developed the concept of mixed data and program memory.

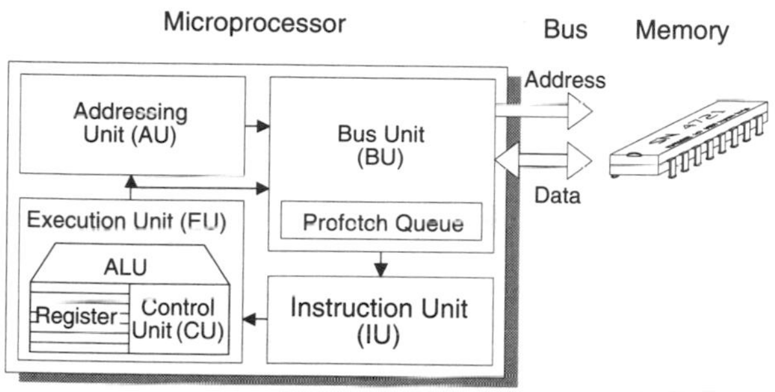

Figure 2.3: Structure of a microprocessor. A microprocessor comprises a bus interface with a prefetch queue for reading and writing data and instructions, an instruction unit for controlling the execution unit with its registers, and an addressing unit for generating memory and I/O addresses.

2.4 Pre-Summary: Processors, Bus Widths and other Characteristics from PC to EISA and Local Bus

Table 2.2 gives an overview of the use of 80x86 processors in various PCs. The table lists processor type, internal register width, width of address and data bus, maximum address space, and those PCs that use the processor concerned.

Processor	Register width	Address bus	Data bus	Address space	Clock frequency	Used in
8088	16 bits	20 bits	8 bits	1 Mbyte	6..10 MHz	PC
8086	16 bits	20 bits	16 bits	1 Mbyte	6..10 MHz	XT,PS/2
80188	16 bits	20 bits	8 bits	1 Mbyte	6..16 MHz	–1)
80186	16 bits	20 bits	16 bits	1 Mbyte	6..16 MHz	–1)
80286	16 bits	24 bits	16 bits	16 Mbyte	12..20 MHz	AT,XT286, PS/2
i386SX	32 bits	24 bits	16 bits	16 Mbyte	16..25 MHz	AT, PS/2
i386DX	32 bits	32 bits	32 bits	4 Gbyte	16..40 MHz	AT, PS/2, EISA
i486	32 bits	32 bits	32 bits	4 Gbyte	25..50 MHz	AT, PS/2, EISA, PCI, VLB
i486DX2	32 bits	32 bits	32 bits	4 Gbyte	50..66 MHz	AT, PS/2, EISA, PCI, VLB
i486SX/i487SX	32 bits	32 bits	32 bits	4 Gbyte	25 MHz	AT, PS/2, EISA
Pentium	32 bits	32 bits	64 bits	4 Gbyte	60..99 MHz	AT, PS/2, EISA, PCI, VLB

1) Hardly used in PCs.
PCI: PCI local bus systems
VLB: VESA local bus systems

Table 2.2: Characteristics of the various processors

2.5 The i386 Microprocessor

For a short time the i386 was the king of PC processors; 32-bit technology was then reserved for very expensive workstations. But this has changed dramatically within only a few years. Today, the i386 is virtually the beginner's desktop PC, and is, moreover, a necessity if using graphic-oriented operating systems or GUIs (graphical user interfaces) such as Windows (NT) and OS/2. Therefore, I will use the i386 as the gateway to processor hardware.

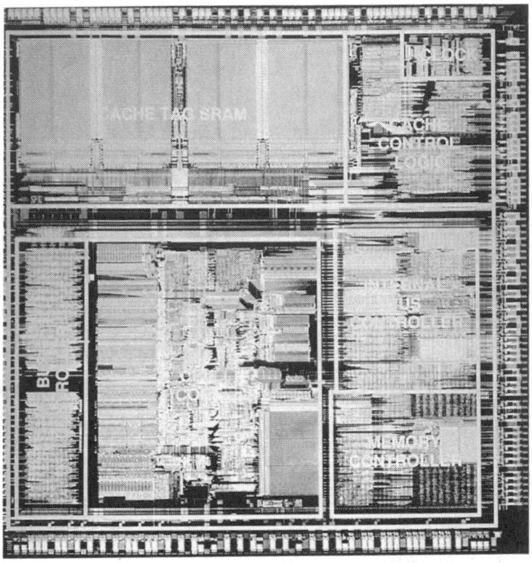

Figure 2.4: The i386 CPU as part of the i386SL (Photo: Intel GmbH (Deutschland)). Intel's i386 family is integrated as the CPU core in the i386SL, and is supported by various peripheral logic circuits (AT bus controller, memory controller, cache) which previously had been separate chips.

A short list of key features of the i386:

- 32-bit general-purpose and offset register,
- 16-byte prefetch queue,
- Memory Management Unit (MMU) with a segmentation and Paging Unit (PU),
- 32-bit data and address bus,
- 4 Gbyte physical address,
- 64 Tbyte virtual address,
- 64 kbyte 8-, 16- or 32-bit ports,
- implementation of real, protected and virtual 8086 mode.

Before things become too abstract, Figure 2.4 shows a die photo of the 386SL which includes the i386 as the CPU core. Section 8.2 details the 386SL chip set.

2.5.1 General Structure of the i386

The i386 also follows the general structure of other microprocessors, as shown in Figure 2.3. Besides the control unit it has several registers. Additionally, several registers for memory management are available which are, however, important only in protected mode. Figure 2.5 shows all the implemented registers.

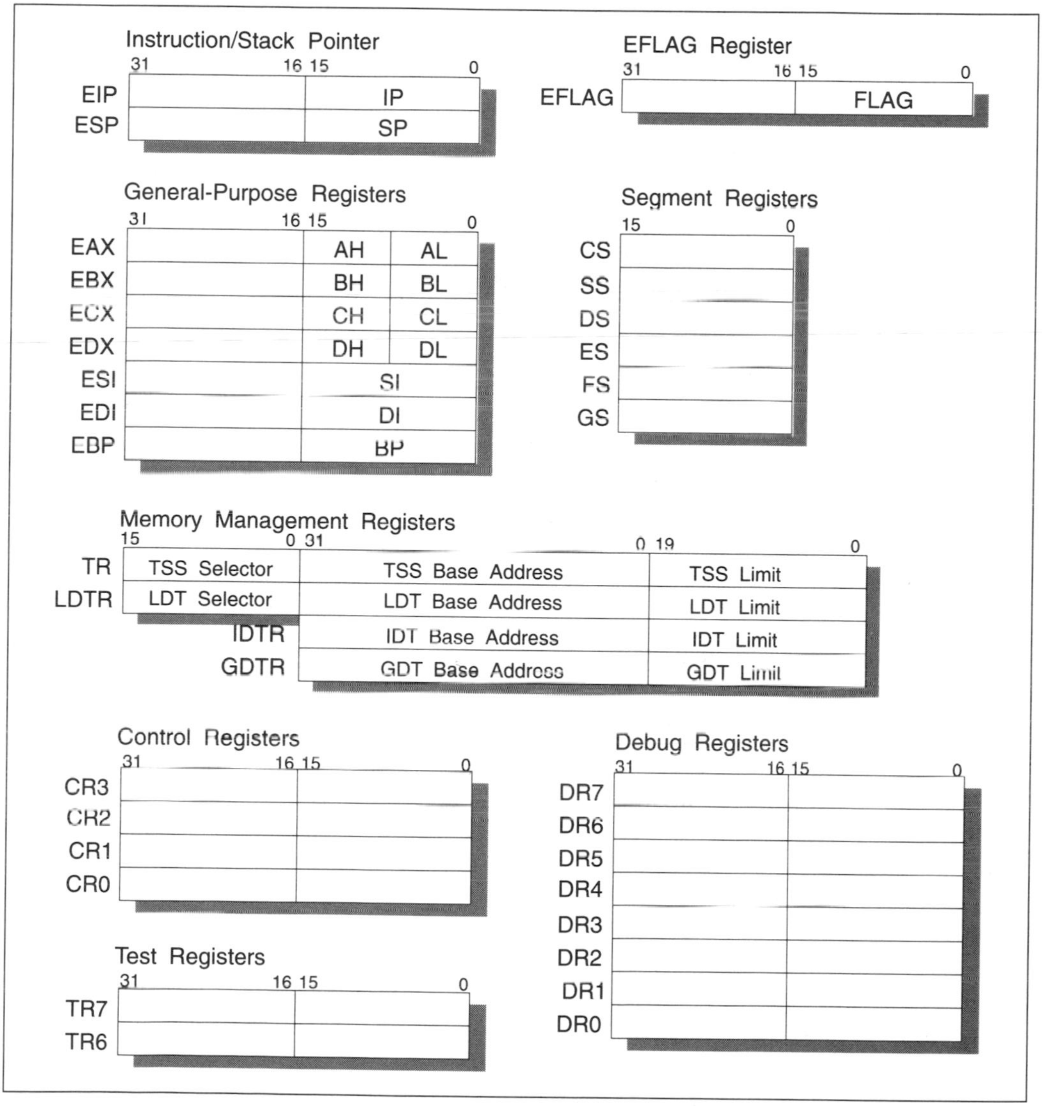

Figure 2.5: i386 processor registers. The general-purpose registers of the i386 are 32 bits wide, but can also be accessed as 16-bit or 8-bit registers. Additionally, there are six segment registers and an instruction pointer, which addresses the instruction to be executed next, as well as a flag register storing the current processor status flags and various control and test registers.

First the i386 registers are discussed, which can already be used in real mode. Of course, the processor has a lot of internal registers, for example for storing temporary results. They are, however, not accessible to the programmer, and will therefore not be discussed here. Only the segment descriptor cache register is detailed further in connection with the protected mode.

The general-purpose registers serve as fast CPU-internal data storage. The execution unit reads values from one or more of these registers, supplies them to the ALU to manipulate them, and finally, writes back the result into one or more registers. That is an example of a register–register operation, because registers are both the source and destination of the processed data. Additionally, the i386 can fetch and store data as the source and destination, respectively, directly from or to memory using memory–memory, register–memory, or memory–register operations. In addition to the general-purpose registers, there are segment registers for memory management, control registers and various other registers.

The i386 reads data from memory, or writes it into memory, through its 32-bit data bus. The location in the memory is determined by a 32-bit address, which is calculated with the help of the addressing unit and output to the memory subsystem via the 32-bit address bus. The address calculation is, depending upon the i386 operation mode (real, protected or virtual 8086 mode), more or less complicated; details are given about this later in the chapter. The read and write process is carried out, as is usual for microprocessors, through the bus unit. For that purpose, the BU provides the address and eventually the value of the data to write, or fetches the value from memory according to the address. In the same way, the i386 accesses the memory to fetch instructions. This *instruction fetch* is, however, not issued by an explicit read instruction; the BU does this automatically. The read data, that is, the instruction, is not transferred into a register in the execution unit, but into the prefetch queue. In a later step, the instruction unit reads the instruction from the prefetch queue, decodes it, and transfers this decoded instruction to its execution unit.

Instructions and data are located in the same physical memory, as is usual today. In the case of the 80x86 family (and therefore in the case of the i386, too), this physical memory is logically divided into several portions (the so-called *segments*) which hold program code or data.

2.5.2 CPU, Main Memory and Segmentation in Real Mode

The 8086, as the first 80x86 CPU, already divided the available memory into *segments*. Later CPUs, from the 80286 to the Pentium, do exactly the same. As the 8086 has only 20 address lines compared to the 32 of the i386, it can only address a maximum of 2^{20} bytes (1 Mbyte) of memory. This is why the *physical address space* is a maximum of 1 Mbyte. Each of the general-purpose registers in a 16-bit 8086 processor (at the time, almost a sensation in comparison to its 8-bit 8080 predecessor) is still only 16-bit, and can therefore only address a maximum of 2^{16} bytes (64 kbytes).

The 8086 divides the physical address area into 64k segments with a capacity of 64 kbytes each. In a segment, the position of a byte is given by an *offset*. Offsets are stored in the general-purpose registers. The segments are controlled by the segment registers CS to ES (two additional segment registers FS and GS are installed in the i386). The CPU uses a so-called segment offset pair to access the memory. The segment of a specific memory object (byte, word, double word, etc.) is indicated by the segment register, the offset in that segment by the general-purpose register.

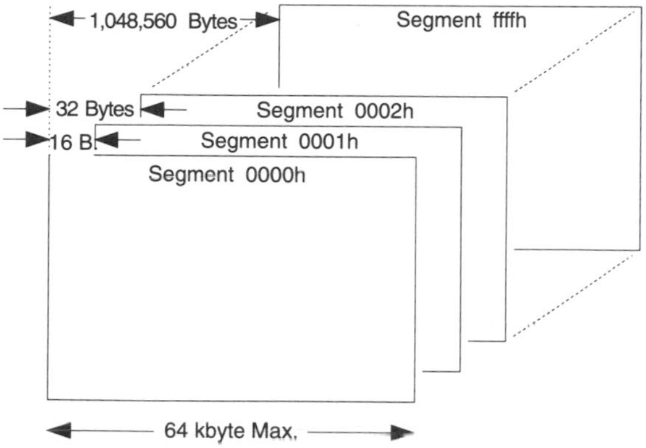

Figure 2.6: Segment interleaving. The 8086 divides the address space of 1 Mbyte into 64k segments of 64 kbytes each. By doing this, successive segments are shifted by 16 bytes and overlap at regular intervals of 16 bytes – they are interleaved.

The 16-bit segment register can address segments like the 16-bit offset register of the 8086; each segment contains 64 kbytes (64k = 65 536). The theoretically possible address space is therefore 64k * 64 kbytes = 4 Gbytes. This is not possible with the 20-bit address bus of the 8086, as it is only capable of addressing 1 Mbyte. The segments are spaced 16 bytes apart (see Figure 2.6). When the value of a segment register is increased by 1, the segment simply moves 16 bytes, not 64 kbytes. In comparison, when the offset register is increased by one, the memory object only moves one position (1 byte). A change in the segment register value causes a significantly larger (16 times) result than a change in the offset register value. This is a characteristic of *real mode*. The 8086 can only work in real mode, whereas the i386 only operates in real mode after it is switched on, or after a processor reset. It can, however, be switched into real mode with a specific instruction during protected or virtual 8086 mode. The addresses are then calculated differently. (More details are given later.)

The address of an object in real mode is calculated with a simple formula:

16 * Segment + Offset

or similarly

10h * Segment + Offset

Simply stated, this means that the segment register is shifted four bits to the left and the offset is added. The four bits that were not affected by the shifting of the segment register are set to zero. The addressing unit carries out this shift and performs the addition process: after the segment address has been moved four bits to the left, an adder in the address unit adds the new segment address and the offset to calculate the *linear address* (see Figure 2.7).

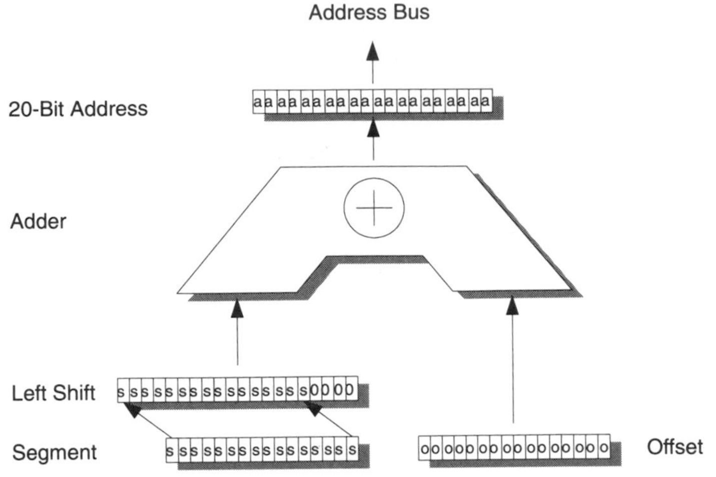

Figure 2.7: Combination of segment address and offset in real mode. In real mode the addressing unit shifts the segment register value left by four bits, thus multiplying the segment value by 16, and adds the offset. The result is a 20-bit address.

The segment and offset are normally given in the hexadecimal *segment:offset* format.

Example:

```
1F36:0A5D means segment 1F36, offset 0A5D;
according to the above formula the linear address is:
1F36h * 16 + 0A5Dh = 7990 * 16 + 2653 = 130,493

Alternatively we can use the segment shift by four bits:
1F360h + 0A5Dh = 1FDBDh = 130,493
```

Note that the two different segment offset pairs in real mode can give the same memory address (this is not possible in protected mode for a number of different reasons).

Example:

```
1FB1:02AD means segment 1FB1, Offset 02AD; thus we get for the address:
1FB1h * 16 + 02ADh = 8113 * 16 + 685 = 130,493
```

As already explained, this method of address calculation is a characteristic of real mode, or even of the 8086. In the protected mode of the considerably newer 80286, the segment and offset are entirely separate. The segment register has a different use, and there is no simple formula like that mentioned above. Therefore, the 80286 has a maximum *logical address space* of 1 Gbyte, and the i386 can have up to 64 Tbytes for each task (program). This logical address space is, however, restricted by the segmentation logic of the 80286 to a maximum *physical address space* of 16 Mbytes because of its 24 address lines ($2^{24}=16$M). In the i386, 4 Gbytes are available. Note, however, that the actual memory capability of a computer is often considerably less than this maximum value.

The *virtual 8086 mode*, implemented in the i386, is a substantial innovation for the running of real mode programs in the multitasking environment of the protected mode. In this mode, the i386 calculates the addresses using the previously described formula of the real mode, whereby access to the memory and peripherals is monitored and protected from unauthorized and incorrect instructions by the same mechanism that is characteristic of protected mode. More details on this are included in Section 2.8.

2.6 General-Purpose and Segment Registers

The general-purpose registers in the i386 are 32-bit because of the need for compatibility with their 16-bit 8086/186/286 predecessors. They can also be used as 16- or 8-bit registers. Figure 2.5 has already shown all the registers in the i386. The registers for memory management are used in protected mode. As an introduction, I would first like to discuss the most important registers in the i386 that are already used in real mode. These are the general-purpose and segment registers, the flag register and the CR0 control register. The lower value word of the CR0 control register is already implemented in the 80286 as the *Machine Status Word* (*MSW*), which regulates the switching into protected mode and contains the status information necessary for protected mode operation.

The i386 has seven general-purpose registers (EAX to EBP), six segment registers (CS to GS), an instruction pointer (EIP), a stack pointer (ESP), and a flag register (EFLAG). The general-purpose registers, instruction pointer, stack pointer and the flag register are all 32-bit, whereas the segment register is only 16-bit. Due to the 32-bit maximum size of the general-purpose register, the i386 can have offsets of 32-bit, such as 0 to 4G–1. Segments can also be considerably greater with an i386 than is possible with an 8086, but that's not surprising for a fourth generation chip. With all 32-bit registers, it is also possible to communicate with only the two lower byte values. They are marked as AX to DI (general-purpose registers), IP (instruction pointer), SP (Stack Pointer), and FLAG (flag register). The lower value word of the four general-purpose registers (AX to DX) can be sub-divided even further into two register bytes, namely AH and AL for the AX register. Therefore, the i386 can also process single data bytes.

The EAX register, with the sub-divisions AX, AH and AL, is used as a special so-called *accumulator*. The most quickly executing and most highly optimized instructions are available to EAX (and the sub-divisions AX and AH, AL). The ECX (or CX) register is mainly used as a count register during programming and the execution of loops. Every loop pass reduces the value in CX by 1, until CX reaches a value of zero. Table 2.3 shows the conventional designations of the registers and their main uses.

Register 32-bit	16-bit	8-bit	Name	Task
EAX	AX	AH, AL	accumulator	multiplication/division, I/O, fast shifts
EBX	BX	BH, BL	base register	pointer to base address in data segment
ECX	CX	CH, CL	count register	count value for repetitions, shifts, rotates
EDX	DX	DH, DL	data register	multiplication, division, I/O

Table 2.3: i386 registers and their uses

Register 32-bit	16-bit	8-bit	Name	Task
EBP	BP		base pointer	pointer to base address in stack segment
ESI	SI		source index	source string and index pointer
EDI	DI		destination index	destination string and index pointer
ESP	SP		stack pointer	stack pointer
	CS		code segment	segment of instructions
	DS		data segment	standard segment of data
	SS		stack segment	segment of stack
	ES		extra segment	freely usable segment
	FS		extra segment	freely usable segment
	GS		extra segment	freely usable segment
EIP	IP		instruction pointer	offset of instructions
EFLAG	FLAG		flags	indicators for processor status and operation results

Table 2.3: cont.

The i386 32-bit processor is the successor to the 16-bit CPU 80286, and is fully compatible with it. It is necessary for the 32-bit registers of the i386 to communicate with 16-bit registers, and so the 32-bit registers are designated with an E (Extended) at the beginning. In comparison, the 80286 possesses only the usual AX register, etc. Use of the 32- or 16-bit i386 register depends upon the operating mode, which can be selected. This subject will be explained further later.

A further quality of the i386 is its *backwards compatibility* with all previous 80x86 microprocessors, including the 8086 and the 80286. Therefore, the i386 can do everything that its predecessors are capable of. In the following, the general-purpose and segment registers are described in more detail.

Accumulator EAX

The accumulator is used mainly as a temporary storage area for data and for holding operands. This special use of the accumulator is historically so because microprocessors originally had only one register (the accumulator), and so only one operation could be executed. An example would be the addition (accumulation) of values. It is only in the past ten years that microprocessors have had many registers – SPARC-RISC CPUs can have up to 2048 registers. The i386 accumulator still has its uses, as many instructions are optimized for it with respect to execution speed. By accessing the accumulator, the instructions are executed faster than if, for example, the EBX register was used. In addition, some register instructions are only valid for the accumulator. An example of this would be the input/output of data to and from ports.

In a multiplication, the accumulator contains one of the factors in advance of execution, and part of or the complete result afterwards. In a division, the accumulator stores the whole or part of the divisor before the division, and the quotient afterwards. If data has to be input or output via an I/O port, the accumulator accepts the incoming data or holds the data to be output, respectively.

The 32-bit accumulator (EAX) can be reduced to a 16-bit (AX) accumulator. Additionally, it can be divided into two 8-bit sub-accumulators, the high value accumulator byte AH from AX and the low value accumulator byte AL from AX. The reason is that in the former 16-bit 8086 to 80286 processors, the accumulator AX was divided into the two sub-accumulators AH (high-order byte of AX) and AL (low-order byte of AX).

Example:

```
OUT 70h, al        ; the value in the accumulator;
                   ; al is output via port 70h
```

Base Register EBX

The base register is used to store a value temporarily, or as a pointer to the start of a data object (e.g. the start of an array) by indirect addressing. You will learn more about types of addresses in Section 3.4. The 32-bit register can also be reduced to a 16-bit register (BX), and further reduced to the 8-bit BL and BH registers.

Example:

```
MOV ecx, [ebx]   ; load 32-bit count register ECX with the value
                 ; which is stored at the base address EBX
```

Count Register ECX

The conventional use of the count register is to determine the number of loop, string instruction (REP) or shifting and rotation (SHL, ROL, etc.) repetitions. After completion of the loop (e.g. after the loop instruction), the value in ECX is reduced by one. You can also use ECX or CX as a standard general-purpose register in which to store data temporarily. Furthermore, the 32-bit ECX register can be reduced to a 16-bit CX register, and further sub-divided into two 8-bit CL and CH registers.

Example:

```
MOV ecx, 10h      ; load ecx with 10h
start:            ; define beginning of loop
  OUT 70h, al     ; output al via port 70h
LOOP start        ; 16 repetitions (until ecx is equal 0)
```

Data Register EDX

The EDX data register is normally used for the temporary storage of data. The EDX and DX registers have an important task during data input and output to and from ports: EDX contains the I/O address (from 0 to 65 535) of the respective port. Only with the help of the EDX data register is it possible to communicate with I/O addresses greater than 255. The 32-bit EDX register can also be divided into a 16-bit DX register and further sub-divided into two 8-bit DL and DH registers.

Example:

```
MUL ebx ; multiplication of EBX with EAX (implicitly)
        ; after the multiplication DX:AX holds the product
        ; (high-order word in DX, low-order word in AX)
```

Base Pointer EBP

Although the base pointer may be used in the same way as the EBX, ECX or EDX registers for temporary data storage, it is most powerful when used as a pointer. In this case, BP usually serves as a pointer to the base of a stack frame, and is employed to access the procedure arguments. For this purpose, the stack segment (SS) is assumed to be the assigned segment register, that is, a memory access always uses the pair SS:BP. With a so-called *segment override*, however, the SS can be replaced by any other segment, for example the ES segment.

Example: procedure call with BP as stack frame base (MASM 5.0)

```
         PUSH sum1           ; push first summand onto stack
         PUSH sum2           ; push second summand onto stack
         PUSH sum3           ; push third summand onto stack
         CALL addition       ; add up all three
         .
addition PROC NEAR           ; near-call with four bytes for old eip as return address
         PUSH ebp            ; save base pointer
         MOV  ebp, esp       ; move stack pointer into base pointer; esp points to old
                             ; base pointer bp on the stack; sum1, sum2, sum3 are
                             ; local variables
         MOV  eax, [ebp+8]   ; load sum1 into eax
         ADD  eax, [ebp+12]  ; add sum2 to sum1 in eax
         ADD  eax, [ebp+16]  ; add sum3 to sum1+sum2 in eax
         POP  ebp            ; restore old base pointer
         RET                 ; return
addition ENDP
```

Source Index ESI

As for EBP, the source index ESI may also be used for temporary data storage, or as a pointer. In most cases, SI is used as the index of a data object within an array or similar structure, whose base is usually defined by the base register EBX. In string instructions, ESI points to single bytes, words or double words within the source string. Repeated execution (with REP) automatically decrements or increments SI, depending on the direction flag. A MOVS instruction with a REP prefix is the fastest way of transferring data between two memory locations via the processor.

Example: display string «abcdefghij» underlined on a monochrome monitor with MOVSD

```
string   DB   20 DUP ('a☺b☺c☺d☺e☺f☺g☺h☺i☺j☺')
                               ; provide string to move (☺ = ASCII code 1
                               ; is the attribute for underlining)
         MOV  eax, @data       ; load 16-bit data segment of buffer string into ax
         MOV  ds, eax          ; adjust ds to data segment of string
         MOV  eax, b800h       ; move segment of monochrome video RAM to ax
         MOV  es, eax          ; load video segment into extra segment es
         CLD                   ; ascending order
         MOV  ecx, 4           ; transfer 5 words of 4 bytes (2 characters + 2 attributes)
         MOV  esi, OFFSET string ; load address of string into source index
         MOV  edi, 00h         ; display string in upper left corner of monitor
                               ; (corresponding offset 0 in video RAM)
         REP  MOVSD            ; transfer a double word four times
```

With REP MOVSD edi and esi are incremented by four after each double-word transfer and point to the next double word in the string.

Destination Index EDI

The destination index is the partner of the ESI source index. The EDI can be used for temporary data storage or, like the ESI, as a pointer, but at the end of an operation. In string instructions, the EDI indicates bytes, words or double words in the string. The EDI is automatically incremented or decreased (depending on the value of the direction flag) when instructions using the REP prefix are used.

Example: `see source index.`

A further group of registers are the so-called *segment registers*. The i386 has six of them, CS, DS, SS, ES, FS and GS. The extra registers FS and GS are not included in the i386's 16-bit predecessors, the 8086 and 80286. In contrast to the general-purpose registers, the segment registers were not increased to 32-bit when converted from the 80286 to the i386. They have 16 bits each.

Code Segment CS

The code segment builds a data block for holding the instructions and addressed data. The instructions contained in the segment are addressed via the Extended Instruction Pointer (EIP). This does not change the content of the CS. Only a far call (or far jump) and an INT can automatically change the CS content. In protected mode, the i386 automatically checks the contents of the segment register during a change to make sure that the applicable task can access the new segment.

Data Segment DS

The data segment usually contains the data for the active program. To be exact, the DS is the standard data segment – many instructions (such as MOV) use only this data segment to address data in the memory using an offset. The i386 can only change this setting with a so-called *segment override* using another (extra) segment. By using DS as a standard data segment, the program code is more compact, because not every applicable data segment is given for each instruction.

Stack Segment SS

The stack segment contains data that can be addressed with stack instructions such as PUSH, POP, PUSHALL, etc. The stack forms a special section in the memory, normally used for a CPU return address. Additionally, the so-called *local variables* or *local data* of procedures are normally stored on the stack. When a procedure is finished, the segment will be overwritten by a new procedure. The stack instructions use the value of SS to store data on, or read data from the stack. Note that the storing of data on the stack (e.g. with the instruction PUSH EAX) automatically results in the reduction of the ESP stack pointer, corresponding to the size of the stored data. In this way, the PUSH EAX instruction *reduces* the value of ESP by four. Consequently, the stack «grows» from higher to lower memory addresses.

Extra Segments ES, FS and GS

The extra segments and their registers are mainly used for string instructions. ES, FS and GS can also be used to address data not contained in the standard data segment (DS) because of the segment override facility. DOS and the BIOS of Personal Computers frequently use ES to pass the segment of a string when calling a function. For example, a buffer must be supplied before INT 13h; function 02h can be called to read one or more sectors from disk. The buffer's segment is passed in the ES register.

The six segment registers play a considerable part in all three operating modes of the i386 for organizing and addressing the memory. You will find more information about the logical addressing of the memory in Chapter 3.

2.7 The Flags

In advance of conditional jumps or branches that are necessary for the logical structure of a program, a logical comparison of two quantities (the checking of a condition) is usually processed, as the word «condition» implies.

These instructions, at the processor level, are comparable to the BASIC instructions GOTO... or IF...THEN GOTO.... The flag register is of greater importance in this context; the specific flags are set (flag equal to 1) or reset (flag equal to 0) depending on the result of the comparison. In addition, some instructions (such as ADC – addition and carry) set and reset specific flags. The i386 flags are shown in Figure 2.8. They are known as EFlags because only the lower value 16-bit flags were available to the 8086.

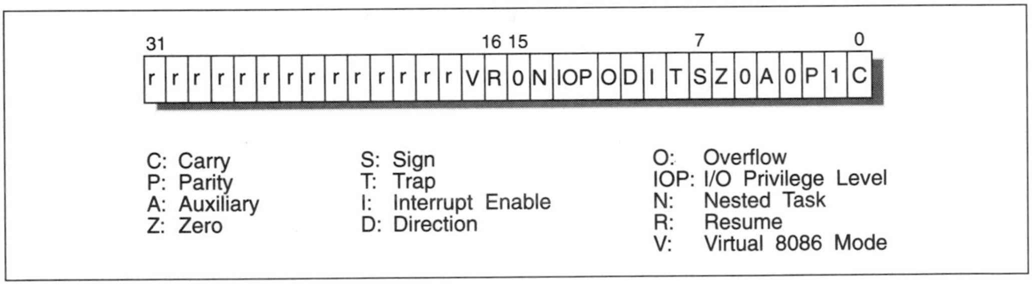

Figure 2.8: The EFlags of the i386. The i386 microprocessor comprises several flags which indicate the result of the previous operation or the current processor status. With the new operation modes of the i386, the number of flags has also increased compared to the 8086.

In the following, each separate i386 flag is explained. The processor that first implemented each flag is given in parentheses.

Carry (8086)

Carry is set if an operation produces a carry or a borrow for the destination operand. This is the case during a 32-bit addition if the sum of two 32-bit numbers produces a result of more than

4G–1. Carry is set by the STC (Set Carry) instruction, reset by the CLC (Clear Carry) instruction, and complemented with the CMC (Complement Carry) instruction.

Parity (8086)

Parity is set if the result of an operation produces an even number of set bits. Parity is set by the processor.

Auxiliary Carry (8086)

The auxiliary carry flag is used, and set by arithmetic operations on BCD values, if an operation produces a carry or borrow for the four least significant bits of an operand (the BCD values only use the lower four bits of a byte; see Section 2.2.5).

Zero (8086)

Zero is set by the processor if the result of an operation is zero. An example of this would be the subtraction of two numbers with the same value, or the bit logic AND with a value of zero.

Sign (8086)

Sign is equal to the most significant bit of the result (0 = positive result, 1 = negative result) of an operation, and so is only important for negative numbers. When the difference between two numbers is negative, the sign is set to 1 by the processor. This is how two numbers can be compared with each other.

Trap (8086)

When trap is set, the processor issues an interrupt 1 after every step. Trap belongs to the exceptions class. Real-mode debuggers mainly use trap to carry out a program step-by-step. They use the interrupt to check the individual steps of a program. Trap cannot be set or reset by a specific instruction. This is only possible, in a roundabout way, with the use of the PUSHF (put the flags onto the stack) and POPF (write the flags on the stack back to the flag register) instructions. PUSHF puts the flags onto the stack where they are manipulated. The altered flags, i.e. after setting trap, are then written back to the flag register by the POPF instruction.

Interrupt Enable (8086)

When interrupt enable is set, the processor accepts hardware interrupt requests, i.e. it reacts to an active signal at the INTR input. This leads to an INTA sequence with the PIC 8259A. In contrast to trap, this flag can be set and reset with specific instructions (CLI clears the flag and STI sets it). Interrupts must be blocked for applications that do not allow interrupts. An excessively long interruption can cause problems for real-time applications (it is possible for received bytes to be lost at the serial port interface). Normally, the operating system should change this flag. This applies mainly to the multitasking environment.

Direction (8086)

Direction determines the direction of string instructions (e.g. MOVS). When the direction flag is set, strings can be copied from higher to lower addresses, or from lower to higher addresses. It is possible to set the direction flag with the STD instruction and to reset it with the CLD instruction.

Overflow (8086)

The i386 sets the overflow flag if the result of an operation is too large or too small for the format of its destination. For example, the addition of two 16-bit numbers may produces a value that cannot be written to a 16-bit destination register.

I/O Protection Level (80286)

This 2-bit flag defines the minimum protection level required for input and output operations in protected mode, and is managed by the operating system (OS/2, UNIX, etc.). This is discussed in some detail in Section 3.7.10. In real mode, this flag has no meaning.

Nested Task (80286)

Nested task is used in protected mode to supervise the chaining of interrupted and reactivated tasks, and is managed by the operating system (OS/2, UNIX, etc.). A set NT flag indicates that at least one task switch occurred, and an inactive TSS is present in memory. Some detailed information for technophiles is given in Section 3.7.9.

In the i386, two additional flag registers are included for the newly implemented debugger support and the innovative virtual 8086 mode. These additional flags follow.

Resume (i386)

The resume flag controls the restarting of a task after a breakpoint interrupt through the debug register of the i386. When resume is set, the i386 debug tasks are temporarily disabled. This means that the task can be resumed at the breakpoint, without a new debug exception error occurring (the i386 would otherwise go into a breakpoint exception/resume loop when it encountered a breakpoint).

Virtual 8086 Mode (i386)

To switch the i386 into virtual 8086 mode, the operating system must set the VM flag. This is only possible in protected mode and through a gate. You will find more on this theme in Section 2.8. When virtual 8086 mode is set, the i386 (and naturally also the Pentium) operates in virtual mode. The i386 can then execute the simple 8086 real mode address calculations, and so can run real mode applications (for example, DOS programs). This all happens contrary to real mode in a protected environment. Together with active paging, the i386 can in principle execute many 8086 tasks in parallel, that is, it executes protected multitasking of programs that were originally designed for use in an unprotected single tasking environment. Alternatively, you could say that an i386 operating in 8086 virtual mode with active paging (and a considerably more complicated operating system) is equivalent to many 8086 processors. When the VM flag is reset, the i386 will operate in the normal protected mode. In real mode, the VM flag has no use (and therefore no effect).

The special significance of the flag register derives from the fact that all instructions for specific branches check various combinations of the flags to a greater or lesser degree; the flags are set or reset by the processor as a result of the normal predetermined comparison instructions.

Example: `if the value in register AX is equal to 5, the program shall branch to HOLDRIUM:`

```
CMP ax, 5       ; compare register AX with value 5
JZ HOLDRIUM     ; jump to HOLDRIUM
```

First, the processor carries out the comparison CMP ax, 5 and sets the applicable flags. In this example, 5 is subtracted from the value of the AX register and the zero flag is set if the result is equal to zero (AX contains the value 5). If, however, AX is greater than 5 (the result of the subtraction is greater than zero), the i386 resets the sign and zero flags (sign = 0, zero = 0). If AX is smaller than 5 (the result of the subtraction is less than zero), zero is set to 0 and sign is set to 1 (negative result).

Some branch instructions (such as JBE – jump if below or equal) test several flags simultaneously (in this example, sign and zero) to determine if the jump conditions have been met. The flags also indicate additional information about the condition of the processor (trap, interrupt enable, direction, resume, virtual 8086 mode), the active tasks (I/O protection level, nested task), or the result of an operation (carry, parity, auxiliary carry, zero, sign, overflow).

2.8 Control and Memory Management Registers

The i386 contains four separate control registers and four memory management registers for the protected mode, and eight debug registers. The control and debug registers are all 32-bit.

2.8.1 Control Registers

Figure 2.9 shows control registers CR0 to CR3.

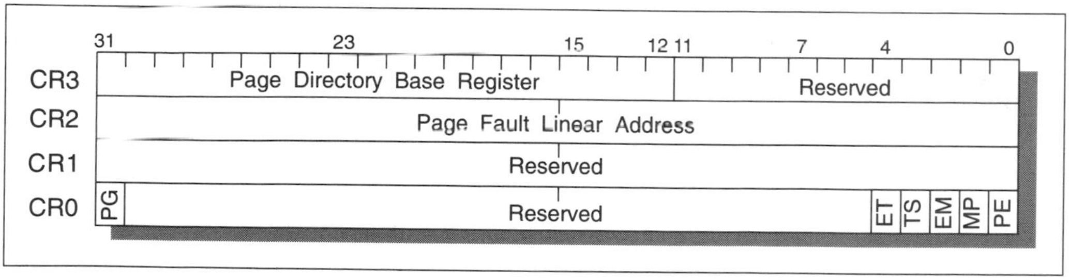

Figure 2.9: i386 control registers.

The *Machine Status Word (MSW)*, known from the 80286 for supporting 16-bit protected mode, is located in the lower value word of the CR0 control register. The TS, EM, MP and PE bits are the same as in the 80286. On compatibility grounds, the lower value MSW word of the CR0 register continues to use the 80286 instructions LMSW (Load MSW) and SMSW (store MSW). Naturally, the paging bit is no longer used. Next we want to look at the CR0 control register with regard to the protected mode and the paging function of the i386. The processor that first implemented each bit is given in parentheses.

PE (Protection Enable; 80286)

If the PE-bit is set, the i386 switches into protected mode. With the 80286 it was only possible to return to real mode with a processor reset or a triple fault; with the i386, it is possible with an instruction that resets the PE bit. Only the operating system is allowed to do this, otherwise an exception occurs.

MP (Monitor Coprocessor; 80286)

If the MP-bit is set, a WAIT instruction can produce a «no coprocessor available» exception leading to an interrupt 7.

EM (Coprocessor Emulation; 80286)

A set EM-bit tells the i386 that all coprocessor functions will be emulated by software; this means that there will be no transfer of data between the CPU and the coprocessor. In place of this, the i386 issues an exception 7 for every coprocessor ESC instruction. The applicable instruction is then handled by the integer arithmetic of the i386. An example would be where a logarithm is not calculated by the operation of the i387, but taken from the mathematical function library.

TS (Task Switched; 80286)

If this bit is set, a task switch has occurred; the i386, operating in protected mode, has used at least one task gate. The TS-bit is important to determine whether the coprocessor is processing an instruction for the old task, or already working on the newly activated task. As some complicated i387 instructions need up to 1000 clock cycles, it is possible that the i386 CPU has switched to a new task, executed it, and then switched back to the old task, before the coprocessor has carried out its instruction. This is the case if the newly activated task wishes to execute a disk access. After a few instructions to set the floppy controller, the applicable ABIOS function, as a multistage routine, will normally return to the interrupted task because the positioning of the head takes a long time. This reduces the chances of blocking the processor. The initialization of the ABIOS function needs considerably fewer clock cycles, and so it is quite possible that the coprocessor has not finished a complicated instruction before the applicable task has been newly activated.

The four previous bits in the CR0 register are already implemented in the 80286 MSW. In the i386, a single additional bit is included for activating and deactivating the paging unit.

ET (Extension Type; i386)

The ET-bit determines whether the installed coprocessor is an i387 (ET = 1) or an 80287 (ET = 0). The i386 can cooperate with both of them because the interface and the data transfer protocol is identical. However, the data bus width is less for the 80287. Accordingly, more I/O cycles must be carried out by the i386 and the 80287 to exchange code and data.

PG (Paging Enable; i386)

With the PG-bit, it is possible to enable (PG = 1) or disable (PG = 0) the Paging Unit (PG) in the memory management unit of the i386. When the PU is disabled, the i386 will not perform any address translations. The linear address automatically allocates the physical address of the memory object after the addition of offset and segment base, as does the i386, which physically addresses the memory through its address lines. With an enabled paging unit, the i386, in addition to the segmenting (which is already difficult enough), performs a further address translation to obtain the physical address from the linear address. Paging can only be used in protected mode. You will find more on this in Section 3.8.

There are two special instructions for MSW access, namely LMSW and SMSW. However, if it is necessary to access the PG-bit of the CR0 register or the CR1–CR3 registers, the four control registers in the i386 have to be addressed with the MOV instruction. The LMSW and SMSW instructions are, more or less, a form of sub-instruction of the MOV CR0, value instruction, or MOV value, CR0 respectively.

Example: `The i386 shall be switched into Protected Mode by setting the PE bit in CR0.`

```
1st possibility:   MOV CR0, 0001h ; set PE bit by MOV instruction with 32 bit operand;
2nd possibility:   LMSW 01h       ; set PE bit by LMSW instruction with 16-bit operand.
```

An i386 with an activated paging unit deposits the 20 most significant bits of the page directory address into the CR3 control register; i.e. the page table in order of importance. If a page error occurs during execution of an instruction, the i386 stores the linear address that caused the page error in the CR2 register. You will find more about the page directory, page table and page error in Section 3.8.

2.8.2 Debug Registers

Debugging in a multitasking environment is a very difficult matter because a program has to be checked while breakpoints, changes in registers and other influences on the debugger are being executed. Real mode debuggers frequently write bytes to specific breakpoints with the code 11001100 for the INT 3 instruction. When the program reaches such a breakpoint, the processor produces an interrupt 3, which the debugger intercepts. To continue the program execution, the debugger overwrites the code 11001100 with the byte previously located at the applicable breakpoint.

In the protected mode of the i386 this is no longer possible, as it is in principle impossible to write to the code segments. The debugger can neither replace the old byte with the opcode 11001100 of INT 3, nor undo the replacement in order to continue with the program execution without producing a protection error. A further serious disadvantage of the real mode strategy is that it is not possible to access a specific data area. For determining wild pointers in a program (an oft occurring bug, especially in C programs), this would be a great advantage. An i386 in protected mode usually operates in a multitasking environment, where other tasks besides the debugger are also active. This is why the debugger must be considerably more aware of what possible direct influence it can have on the computer (including the consequences of overwriting specific program code). Therefore, hardware support for the debugger is necessary.

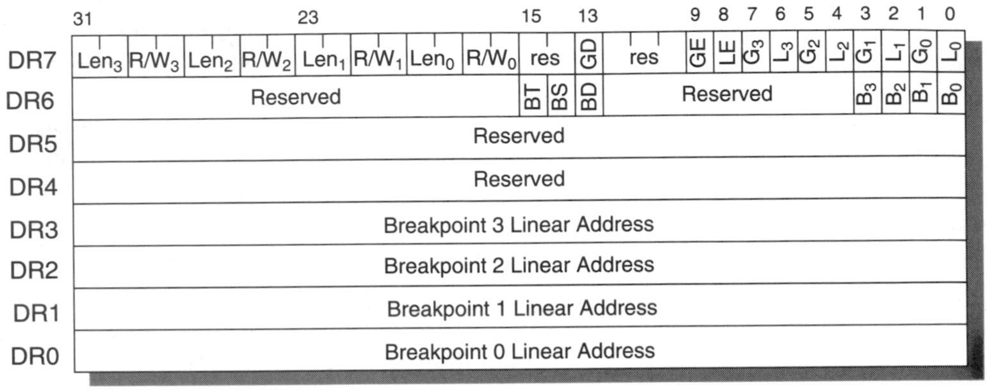

Len_3–Len0:	Breakpoint Size 00=1 Byte 01=2 Bytes 10=Invalid 11=4 Bytes
R/W_3–R/W0:	Breakpoint Memory Access 00=Code Execution 01=Data Write 10=Invalid 11=Data Read or Write, No Code Fetch
GD:	Global Detection of Debug Register Accesses 1=Enabled 0=Disabled
GE, LE:	Global, Local Data Breakpoint Precision 1=Enabled 0=Disabled
G_3–G0:	Global Breakpoint Enable 1=Global Enable 0=Global Disable
L_3–L_0:	Local Breakpoint Enable 1=Local Enable 0=Local Disable
BT:	Debug Trap Because of Task Switch 1=Exception 1 Because of Task Switch 0=Other Source
BS:	Debug Trap Because of Single Step 1=Exception 1 Because of Single Step 0=Other Source
BD:	Debug Fault Because of Access to Debug Register (if GD=1) 1=Exception 1 Because of Access 0=Other Source
B_3–B0:	Debug Exception Because of Breakpoint 3 to 0 1=Breakpoint Triggered Debug Exception 0=Other Breakpoint Triggered Debug Exception

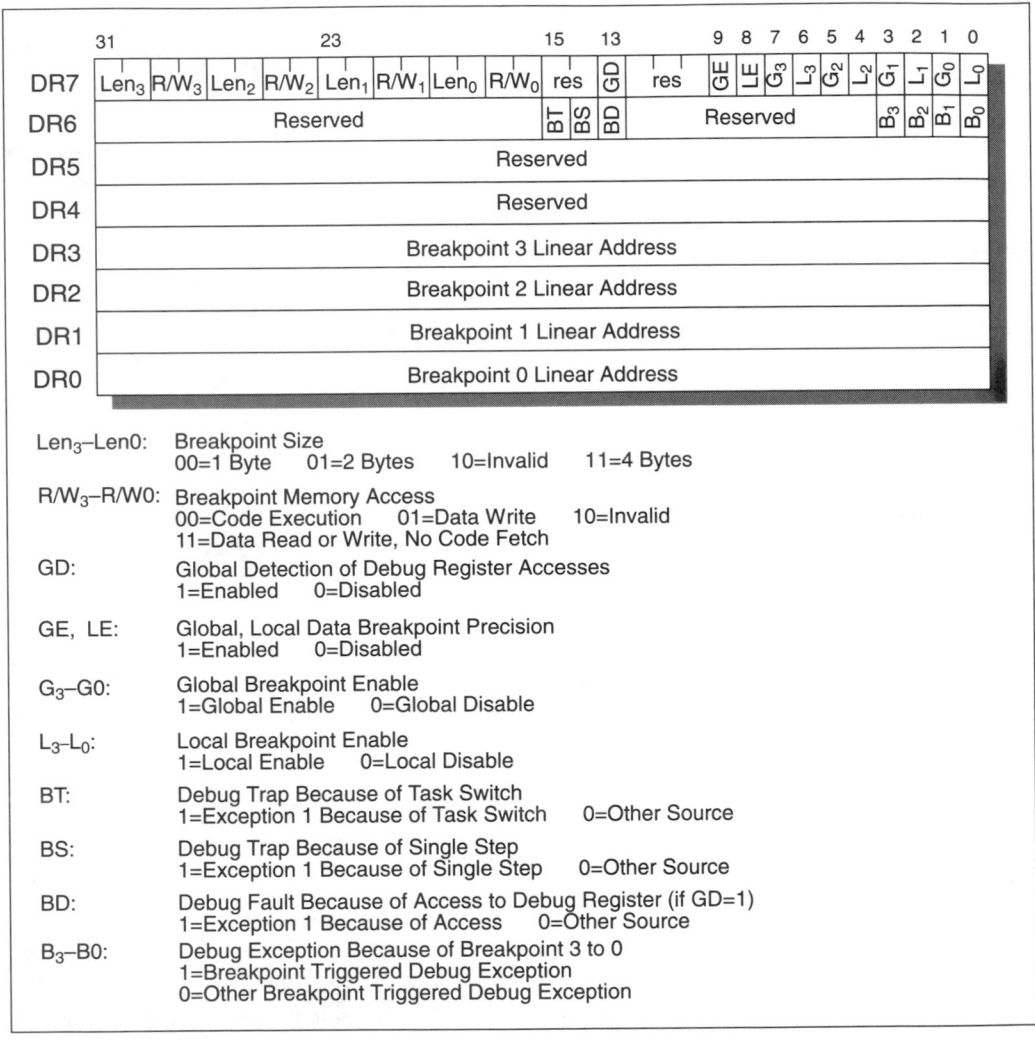

Figure 2.10: i386 debug registers.

In the i386, this is achieved with eight debug registers (DR0 to DR7), each of 32-bits. They support the debugger in protected or virtual 8086 mode at a hardware level. Figure 2.10 shows the structure of the debug register.

In the following, the register entries are briefly explained. If you need more information about this specialized hardware aspect of the i386, please refer to a more specific programming handbook for the i386.

With the help of the debug register, it is possible to define four breakpoints. That is not many, in comparison to the many breakpoints of CodeView or Turbo Debugger, but they do have it easier in real mode. The linear addresses (the address after the addition of offset and segment base, but without paging) of the four chosen breakpoints are stored in the debug address registers (DR0 to DR3). The debug registers DR4 and DR5 are reserved for future use.

The entries in the debug status registers DR6 and DR7 control the behaviour of the i386 by arriving at each breakpoint separately. The entries R/W_0 to R/W_3 define each breakpoint independently, when the i386 executes a debug exception causing an interrupt 1. It is possible to choose between executing an instruction, data reading or data writing. The last two possibilities allow the access of data to be monitored. In contrast, breakpoints in real mode debuggers are usually only used for executing instructions because the code 11001100 for the INT 3 instruction must be used. Only with complicated additional adapter cards is it possible to monitor data areas. This is already implemented in the i386 processor chip.

In the same way, entries LEN_0 to LEN_3 define the size of the breakpoint area separately for each breakpoint. The breakpoints can be globally activated with the G_0 and G_3 bits. The i386 then issues a debug exception if any task references the specific memory area. That is an advantage when several tasks have to be checked in a multitasking environment. The breakpoints are locally activated with the bits L_0 to L_3. The i386 will then produce a debug exception if a specified task (usually the task in the debugger) references the specific memory area. The four inputs GD, BT, BS and BD are used to control the restart after a debug exception and analyse the cause.

2.8.3 Memory Management Registers

Besides the control and debug registers, the i386 has four memory management registers (Figure 2.11). They operate as memory managers, and divide the memory into segments during protected mode. I therefore wish to discuss them in connection with segmenting in protected mode, in Section 3.7.

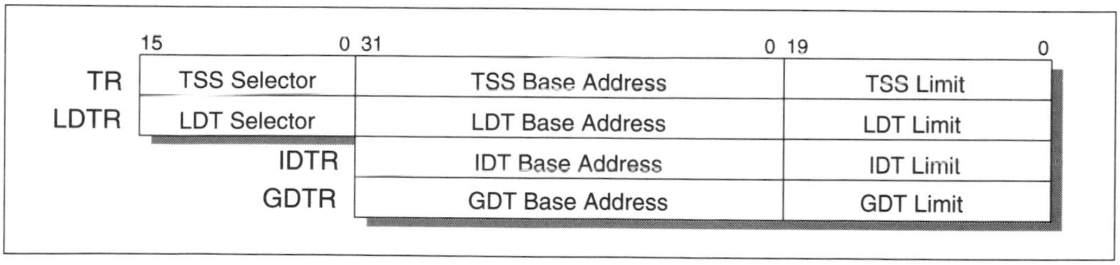

Figure 2.11: i386 memory management registers.

At this point, to round things off, I would like to mention the test registers TR6 and TR7. Their purpose is to test the internal buffer of the Translation Lookaside Buffers (TLB) which is used for the caching of page table entries when the paging unit is enabled (see Section 3.8 for more information).

2.9 The CPU Bus as the Connection to the Outside World

The registers mentioned previously are integrated into the processor. The i386 alone can do nothing because there are no connections to the other important parts of the computer, notably the CPU bus. It is nothing more than a collection of wires and accompanying driver circuits that provide a connection to main memory and the other elements such as the control registers, etc. The bus is usually divided into a data bus, for the transfer of data between the i386 and main memory, an address bus (whose signals specify which data should be addressed), and a control bus, for transferring the required control signals to control the data transfer. The i386 has a 32-bit data bus, and so can displace four bytes at a time. The data is addressed through a 32-bit address bus, so that $2^{32}=4\,G$ data units can be transferred. The byte is commonly used as a data unit. The address bus can therefore address 4 Gbytes of data. In addition, the i386 can send or receive a total of 17 control signals using a 17-bit control bus.

3 Logical Memory Addressing and Memory Access

This chapter deals with the logical addressing of the memory. For this, it will be necessary to thoroughly examine the segmented memory organization and the applicable registers. In addition, memory addressing depends upon the active operating mode such as real, protected or virtual 8086 mode, and whether or not the paging unit is active.

3.1 Code Segment and Instruction Pointer

As explained previously, the processor fetches instructions from memory and then executes them, to run a program. The code segment and the instruction pointer form the basis for this automatic reading. The code segment sets the segment for the next instruction; the instruction pointer gives the offset for the next instruction to be read. The value or register pair, code segment: instruction pointer, thus defines the next instruction in memory to be executed. The processor can then read and carry out the instruction. The code of the instruction tells the processor how many bytes it must read in, so that the whole instruction is contained in the processor. Instructions for the 80x86 are between 1 and 15 bytes long.

When the instruction is executed, the instruction counter is incremented by the number of bytes contained in the executed instruction. With a short 2-byte instruction, the instruction counter is increased by two, and the code segment:instruction counter pair then refers to the next instruction to be executed. The next instruction is read and executed in the same way. Subsequently, the processor increments the instruction counter again. The reading and incrementing are both carried out by the processor completely independently. No action from the control program or user is necessary. Once activated, the CPU will continuously read in and execute instructions.

The prefetch queue and bus interface play an important role in instruction fetching. As stated earlier, the instruction is first read into the prefetch queue, which then passes it on to the instruction unit. If, after the instruction bytes have been passed to the control unit, there are as many bytes free in the prefetch queue as the processor data bus is wide, the bus interface will read the applicable number of bytes from the memory into the prefetch queue. For example, the i386 has a four byte (32-bit) data bus. It will, therefore, independently read in four bytes when four bytes are free in the prefetch queue. In this way, the processor uses the data bus optimally: when the i386 carries out an instruction that does not cause an immediate memory access (for example, the addition of two registers), the bus interface can load the prefetch queue without hindering the currently active instruction. Immediately after an instruction has been executed, the next instruction is available, and so need not be read from the memory. Obviously, a memory access due to an active instruction (for example, after the use of MOV, register, memory) has priority over the reloading of the prefetch queue. Parallel to the execution of the currently active instruction and the reloading of the prefetch queue, the instruction unit decodes the next instruction and prepares it for the EU and for execution. The execution unit carries out the instruction in a specific number of clock cycles. Simple instructions such as CLC need two clock cycles, whereas complicated instructions such as a task switch via a gate in protected mode need more than 300.

Therefore, we get a uniform instruction flow from the memory to the processor. In other words, a program is sequentially executed. Today, the intention is to perform as many independent steps as possible, in parallel, in order to increase the capabilities of the computer. The Pentium chip can use three independent pipelines for parallel processing.

The uniform flow of instructions can be constantly interrupted and redirected by conditional and unconditional jumps and branches. This is very important for the logical construction of a program, because a computer should frequently perform different things, depending on the specific instructions. To carry out a jump or a branch (which is nothing more than a jump under specific conditions), only the value of the instruction pointer and, if necessary, the code segment must be changed. With a so-called near call or near jump, the code segment remains unchanged – only the new value of the EIP is loaded. The instruction flow is also located in the same segment. With a far call or jump, in comparison, the code segment is also changed and a so-called *intersegment call* or *intersegment jump* is executed. The processor refers to a different segment for the program execution. Additionally, with this sort of jump, the prefetch queue is emptied so that the bytes that have been read in are not included with the new instruction.

Example: The value in the code segment register CS is equal to 24d5, the value of the instruction pointer is equal to 0108. Thus the next instruction is located at address 24d5:0108. The code at this address is 8cc0. The control unit CU decodes this 2-byte code and determines the instruction

```
MOV EAX, ES
```

It should therefore transfer the value of the extra segment ES into the 32-bit accumulator register EAX. After execution of this instruction, the value of the instruction pointer is increased by two because MOV EAX, ES is a two byte instruction. The value of EIP is then 10a0, the value of the code segment CS remains unchanged.

Example: The value of the code segment is equal to 80b8, the value of the instruction pointer is equal to 019d. Thus the next instruction is located at address 80b8:019d. The code at this address is 7506. The control unit CU decodes this code and determines the instruction

```
JNZ 01a5
```

This is a conditional branch (*J*ump if *N*ot *Z*ero) to the instruction with the address 01a5. Here, the code segment is not changed, even when the jump condition is fulfilled and the processor executes a jump. Usually, a comparison of two values occurs before such a branch occurs. The processor sets or resets specific flags depending on the result of the comparison. The flags are also necessary for the logical flow of a program.

If the result of the comparison is «not equal zero», the program will branch: the instruction pointer IP is loaded with the value 01a5 and the i386 continues at the address 80b8:01a5. If, on the other hand, the result of the comparison is «equal zero», no jump occurs and the instruction continues in the usual way, i.e. the instruction pointer EIP simply increases by two to 019f, because JNZ 01a5 is a two byte instruction. Note that the 1-byte jump address 06 in the opcode 7506 is relative to the instruction pointer EIP after the loading of the 2-byte opcode. From this, the target address for the example is calculated as 019d (old EIP value) + 2 (2-byte instruction) + 06 (jump width) which gives 01a5.

The 32-bit instruction pointer EIP allows programs of up to 4 Gbytes, whereas its 16-bit 80286 predecessor only allowed programs of up to 64 kbytes, with the use of the 16-bit offset register. With a change in the code segment possible through the use of a specialized instruction (the loading of CS with a specific value), larger programs are possible. Note that the code segment can be changed, but not the instruction pointer. There is no direct loading instruction for the EIP. The value in the instruction pointer can only be changed with a conditional or unconditional jump (or call) to another program. Far calls and far jumps automatically influence the value in the code segment CS.

The i386 instruction set, with 206 instructions and additional instruction variations, is very extensive with respect to the register width and its addressing methods – a true CISC device. A complete discussion of all instructions would therefore go far beyond the scope of this (hardware) book. However, you will find in Appendix B a list of the 80x86 instruction set. Extensive descriptions should be given in good books dealing with assembler programming, or in the original Intel manuals.

3.2 Stack Segment and Stack Pointer

Of some importance are the stack segment and accompanying stack pointer. Usually, every program has its own stack segment, where the value of a register or a memory word can be stored with PUSH. The flags may be pushed onto the stack with PUSHF, and the general-purpose registers with PUSHA (80186 and higher). With POP, POPF and POPA (80186 and higher) the corresponding data can be retrieved from the stack.

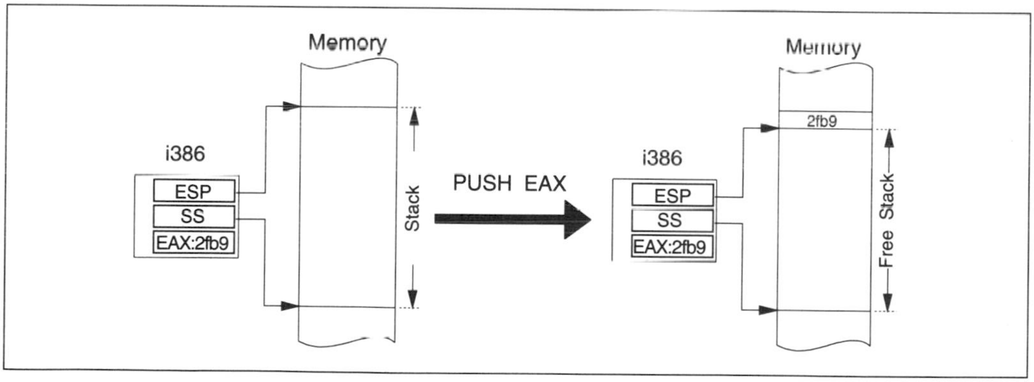

Figure 3.1: Stack and stack pointer. The i386 uses the stack mainly as temporary storage for return addresses or register values. PUSH EAX saves the accumulator value EAX on the stack. Simultaneously, the stack pointer is decremented by four. Thus the stack grows downwards, that is, towards lower addresses.

Note that the value of the stack pointer ESP reduces as the stack grows (Figure 3.1). If data is stored on the stack, the value of ESP is reduced by four, because a complete double word (four bytes) is always written to the stack. When the i386 operates in 16-bit mode, naturally only two bytes are written to the stack, and the value of ESP is only reduced by two with every PUSH. This also applies to the 16-bit 8086 and 80286 predecessors. If the stack is empty, the stack pointer contains its largest possible value. After the word has been stored, the stack pointer indicates the last stored word on the stack. A PUSH instruction first increases the value of the stack pointer ESP, then the register or memory value is stored on the stack.

Because of the downward growth of the stack, a stack overflow can easily be detected: if ESP=0 the stack is full, and application programs that regularly check the stack display the message *stack overflow!* Usually, programmers reserve sufficient memory area for the stack (a sufficiently high value of ESP to start with) so that such a stack overflow will only arise because of a programming error or faulty program use. In protected mode the processor's hardware (starting with the 80286) checks whether a stack overflow has occurred, thus a very fast check is possible without any program overhead for software check routines.

The stack may be used as a temporary memory for data that is difficult to access without PUSH and POP (the trap flag, for example). On the whole, though, the stack is used to pass parameters to procedures and subroutines. For this purpose, the calling program pushes the parameters to be passed onto the stack using one or more PUSH instructions. The called procedure fetches these parameters with one or more POP instructions, or by addressing with the base pointer EBP. Further, the called procedure stores its local variables on the stack. Depending on the programming language, the called procedure or the calling program cleans up the stack on its return from the subroutine, that is, it restores the stack state before the call. Thus, the parameters and local temporary variables stored on the stack are destroyed with the next procedure or subroutine call.

Most BIOS routines don't have their own stack, but use the stack of the calling program. On the other hand, DOS uses three internal stacks in total for its functions. The way in which 80x86 processors execute a PUSH ESP instruction (that is, the stack pointer itself is pushed onto the stack) is quite different from the 8086/88 and all the other 80x86 processors:

- The 8086/88 updates SP first (decreases SP by two) and copies the value of SP onto the stack afterwards.
- Starting with the 80186/88, (E)SP is copied onto the stack first and then updated (decreased by two or four).

3.3 Data Segment DS and Addressing

Next to the code and stack segment registers, the data segment register DS also has a special use. It is important when an instruction reads data from or writes data to the memory, that is, when memory operands are necessary. The offset of the memory operand is usually contained in a general-purpose register and the DS:offset pair refers to the applicable value. The DS data segment register is normally used as an offset-associated segment register. When it is necessary to read or write a value into another segment, either the segment register DS must be loaded with the value of the new segment or a segment prefix must be used so that the data register DS is replaced with one of the extra segment registers ES to GS. More on this subject follows.

The data of the code segment will only be executable and (at most) readable. Overwriting code unavoidably means crashing the program. Execute-only data may be fetched into the prefetch queue, but not into general-purpose or segment registers, therefore a program cannot use it in the sense of data that is processed.

The use of different segments for code, stack and data allows the separation of the different sections of a program. The protected mode makes intensive use of this to avoid any erroneous overwriting of code by a program error (a main cause of crashed programs). Of course, all segment registers may hold the same value. In this case, no separation of code, stack and data occurs. The COM-programs of DOS are structured like this. COM-programs are relics from the days of CP/M, which was an operating system (control program) for simple 8-bit processors. COM-programs don't support a memory divided into segments, so segment registers in COM-programs have no meaning. The program deals only with offsets, and all segment registers hold the same value, thus the address space for code and data is limited to 64 kbytes (one 8086 segment) in total.

3.4 Addressing Schemes and Instruction Encoding

In the previous section, instructions such as JNZ, MOV and CALL were discussed. However, when a program requires a specialized editor or the DOS instruction TYPE, such codes are not used. JNZ, MOV, etc. are called *mnemonic codes* or *mnemonics* for short. These short names only serve as support for the programmer and repeat the operation of the applicable instruction in a shorter form (compared to a home-made C routine with the name _lets_fetch_data_now).

3.4.1 Mnemonics and the Assembler

An *assembler* understands these mnemonic codes and translates them into *machine code* instructions for the processor. Machine code instructions are (naturally) a series of zeros and ones contained in one or more bytes. The instruction TYPE, as a «text indicator», interprets all of the codes as ASCII characters which produces apparently confused nonsense. For example, if TYPE is used in conjunction with the previously used mnemonic code JNZ 2a51, the screen will show: *Q.

However, with an assembler a lot of other things can also be simplified. For example, many assemblers can process macros (hence the name *macro-assembler*), carry out various addressing schemes, and access variables, jump targets (JNZ proceed_here) and procedures (CALL sub_routine) in a symbolic way. The assembler then converts these instructions into corresponding machine instructions. An assembler is the closest you can get to the hardware when writing programs; you can influence hardware directly at the register level. Programs written in assembler are usually very compact and extremely fast (important for real-time applications for machine control). Pure programming in machine language doesn't lead to any further control over the microprocessor, but only makes the matter more difficult and error-prone.

In all further descriptions of machine instructions, I use the mnemonic codes and elements of assembler programming (for example, symbolic jump targets or names of procedures). In

Appendix B there is a list of the 80x86 instructions, which you are advised to study to get an appreciation of what your processor can do.

3.4.2 Addressing Schemes

If a register such as the accumulator EAX is loaded with a value through the use of MOV EAX, three possibilities can be used:

- **Immediate Operand: MOV EAX, 6a02h**
  The accumulator register EAX is loaded with the value 6a02h. This value was written explicitly by the programmer and is part of the program code; this means that it appears as a part of the instruction stream that is loaded by the bus interface into the prefetch queue. The corresponding segment is the code segment CS, not the data segment DS or an extra segment. The control unit, however, passes it on to the EAX register and not to the execution unit, as it would for a instruction.

- **Register Operand: MOV EAX, EBX**
  The register EAX is loaded with the value in the register EBX. As in the above example, EAX is a register operand (the destination operand). Here the source operand is also a register (EBX).

- **Memory Operand: MOV EAX, mem32**
  In place of mem32, the assembler must insert the *effective address* of the symbolic operand mem32. If the effective address is already known by the assembler, representing static size, it inserts the unchanged value during the assembling procedure. In this case, mem32 is a so-called *direct memory operand*. Usually, such direct memory operands in a macro-assembler are indicated with a symbol (such as *array*). If the effective address is dynamic (if the address can change at run time, for example, a register with a previously unknown value), then the CPU calculates the effective address at run time. In this case, mem32 is an *indirect memory operand*.
  The effective address is understood to mean the offset of an operand contained in the chosen segment (usually DS). The effective address can be constructed of up to four elements.

- **Displacement: MOV EAX, array [0]**
  The first element of the array is loaded into the accumulator. *Array[0]* is a symbolic designation, showing how a macro-assembler can operate to make the work of a programmer easier. In an assembled program, there is a number in place of *array[0]*, that indicates the address of the symbolic *array[0]*. If, for example, the address of array [0] is 0f2h, the instruction would be MOV EAX, [0f2h]. Don't confuse this with an immediate operand: with a displacement, the value gives the applicable address and not the value itself. In our example, the value in the DS segment with an offset of 0f2h is loaded, and not the value 0f2h itself.

- **Base Register: MOV EAX, [EBX]**
  The instruction loads the operand in the DS segment with the offset given by the value in the register BX, into the accumulator. If, for example, EBX contains the value 0f2h, this instruction is equivalent to the previous example MOV EAX array[0]. The main logical diffe-

rence between [EBX] and array[0] is that the value of BX can be dynamically changed during program execution, while array[0] is a fixed and constant value throughout. With the dynamic changing of EBX, it is possible to use multiple loops for accessing the complete array, similar to the BASIC instruction FOR I=1 TO 9 ... NEXT I. The base registers are EBX and EBP.

- **Index Register: MOV EAX, [ESI]**
  In this base form, the use of the index register has the same rules as the use of the base registers. Additionally, the index register has another possibility, the assignment of a scaling factor. The index registers are ESI and EDI.

- **Scaling Factor MOV EAX, [ESI*4]**
  To calculate the effective address for this example, the value of the ESI index register is multiplied by four. With this example, it is possible to index array elements by four. The i386 carries out the scaling (or multiplication) with a factor greater than 1, without support. The values 1, 2, 4 and 8 can be used as scaling factors. Scaling factors introduced for addressing were in the i386. The 8086 and 80286 have to operate without scaling factors.

Displacement, base registers, index registers and scaling factors can be used in any combination. In this way, very complicated and multidimensional addresses can be defined, such as those necessary for array elements.

Example: An array with 10 elements is given which defines various bodies, each element has a structure of height:width:depth:cross-section. The partial elements height etc. each comprise 1 byte. The array starts at 0c224h. The following program fragment loads the depths into the accumulator EAX:

```
MOV EBX, 0c224h          ; load base address into EBX
MOV ESI, nr              ; load element number into ESI
MOV EAX, [EBX+ESI*4+2]   ; load depth (displacement 2 from start element)
                         ; of element nr (element size = 4 bytes, thus scaling 4)
                         ; of array (starting at base address in EBX) into
                         ; accumulator EAX
```

In the previous example, the i386 normally uses the DS segment register (or SS where EBP is the base register). The i386 also has the three extra segment registers ES to GS and the code segment register CS. Instead of DS and SS, these segment registers may be used if, for example, the value of ES or CS is loaded into the DS or SS register. Another possibility for using ES for a data access is a *segment override*. The assembler recognizes such an override, where the identification of the applicable segment in the memory operand is separated by a colon from the remainder of the operand. If, in the above example, it is necessary to address a field in a segment that will be defined by the value in the ES segment register, the instruction MOV EAX, ES:[EBX+ESI*4+2] must be used. Such a segment override is advantageous if a segment is only to be addressed infrequently. If, on the other hand, a series of instructions access the ES segment, it is better to load the value from ES into DS. The value of ES can then be accessed from DS and the processor does not need to perform an ES override.

3.4.3 Instruction Encoding

In the displacement section, I briefly explained that in the given example, the assembler converts the instruction MOV EAX, array[0] to MOV EAX, 02fh. But how does the i386 know that 02fh represents a displacement (an address) and not a value, where the value in the address DS:02fh and not the value 02fh itself should be loaded into the AX register? The key to this is contained in the encoding of the instruction.

The processor does not understand symbolic instructions such as MOV AX, ES:[BX+SI*4+2] (with this, ASCII encoding would also be far too extravagant), only bytes or series of bytes. An assembler or compiler converts symbolic instructions into a long series of bytes. For this, every instruction is divided into four main parts:

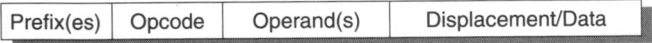

Prefix(es)	Opcode	Operand(s)	Displacement/Data

The most important part is the so-called *opcode* (operation code). It consists of one or two bytes and describes the instruction in simple terms. If the first byte is 00001111b, the opcode consists of two bytes. If the first byte starts with the bit sequence 11011 (27 in decimal corresponding to ESC), the instruction is an instruction for the mathematic coprocessor (the i387). Simple instructions without operands such as CLC (clear carry flag=reset carry flag) consist of only 1-byte opcodes. Complex instructions with prefixes and many operands/displacements/data can, in the i386, consist of up to 15 bytes. The opcode contains information pertaining to the prefix, operand and displacement/data of the instruction, as necessary. The two least significant bits of the opcode frequently indicate the direction of data transfer (register to register/memory or memory to register) as with the use of 8-/16- or 8-/32-bit operands (for example, AL, AX or EAX).

The field *operand(s)* defines which register uses which direct or indirect memory operands. The field *displacement/data* indicates a displacement or an immediate operand which is already known at assemble time.

The Instruction Unit (IU) knows if a MOV instruction with a displacement or an immediate operand is necessary with the different opcodes. The IU then controls the Execution Unit (EU) accordingly, so that a MOV instruction with a displacement or an immediate operand is executed. With a displacement, the EU tells the addressing unit to load the value in the address DS:02fh from the memory into the accumulator through the bus interface. If 02fh is an immediate operand, the i386 loads the value 02fh from the prefetch queue into EAX as part of an instruction. In the first case, an additional memory access is necessary, whereas the EU processes an immediate operand at once.

If, with the displacement of an operand, it is necessary to use the offset address 02fh in the extra segment ES, FS or GS in place of the normal data segment DS, a *prefix* is attached to the instruction code instead of using an additional opcode. This segment override prefix causes an extra segment (which may also be CS or SS) to override the standard data segment DS. Table 3.1 shows all the valid segment override prefixes for the i386.

Segment	Prefix
CS	00101110 (2eh)
DS	00111110 (3eh)
SS	00110110 (36h)
ES	00100110 (26h)
FS	01100100 (64h)
GS	01100101 (65h)

Table 3.1: Segment override prefixes

There are other prefixes in addition to these segment override prefixes. They are used for repeating string operations (with REP), the control of the bus (with LOCK), and the changing of operands (16 or 32-bit) and address sizes (16 or 32-bit). The advantage of a prefix over an additional opcode lies in the fact that prefixes are only added when an instruction requires it. In comparison, the size of the code for each instruction would be increased if its opcode always included information that is only required occasionally. Thus, either the length of the opcode or its complexity would be increased. Using prefixes when required uses less memory space, and the programs are more compact. Disregarding extensive memory accesses, instructions using the segment override prefix in instruction fetching, where the standard data segment DS is replaced by another segment (ES, FS, GS, SS or CS), are carried out in the same amount of time. With the constant and automatic reloading of the prefetch queue in the background, the additional memory access caused by the prefix only seldom slows down the operating speed, for example, when the prefetch queue is reset after a jump or a function call.

Assemblers recognize automatically from designations such as EAX or ES: the operand size required for the segment to be used and the corresponding opcode, operand(s) and displacement/data. They also insert the necessary prefix. Programming with a powerful assembler and the very extensive instruction set of the 80x86 processors sometimes gives the feeling of dealing with a high-level language.

3.4.4 Reading Instructions and Prefetching

As mentioned at the start, the prefetch queue has the purpose of relieving the bus system, because the prefetcher is constantly reading new instruction bytes as soon as enough space becomes available in the prefetch queue. A double word is always read if four bytes are free in the queue when using a 32-bit system. This automatic instruction fetching is linear, which means that the prefetcher commences with a start address and always reads the following double word. It thus ignores any jumps and branches. For a conditional jump this is correct, as the processor has to evaluate the jump condition first. This may, however, occur a significant time after fetching the jump instruction. The situation is different for unconditional branches and subroutine calls: they are always executed, of course. Actually, the hardware engineers who design high-end processors (the Pentium, for example) include many strategies to force the prefetcher to continue the instruction fetching according to the branch instructions. One magic topic would be *branch prediction*. More about this in Chapter 12 about the Pentium.

Let's go back to the instruction prefetching. Normally, as the prefetcher usually accesses double words at addresses that are multiples of four, the bus interface usually fetches a complete double word at a double word address. The only exception is when a CALL or jump instruction branches to a memory address that is not a double-word address. In this case, the prefetcher reads one to three bytes via the bus unit until a double word is reached. Subsequently, a complete 32-bit double word with a double-word address is always read (as long as four bytes are free in the prefetch queue).

Memory accesses obtained as the result of machine code instructions, for example MOV reg, mem have, of course, priority over instruction fetching. When the i386 executes such an instruction, the prefetch queue has to wait. When executing instructions without memory access, for example ADD reg, reg and the internal execution of an instruction in a phase that does not require memory accesses, the prefetcher can read a double word into the prefetch queue without interruption, and without the need to disturb the performance of instructions in the i386. This ensures a maximum throughput of the memory bus as well as a (nearly) always full prefetch queue.

The i386 stops prefetching if the Instruction Unit (IU) records a CALL or jump instruction and actually assigns the call or jump (that is, the call or jump condition is achieved). In this instance, the i386 empties its prefetch queue, invalidates the already decoded instructions in the instruction Unit IU, and commences the jump address by reading the new instructions. Prefetching is then executed linearly until a further CALL or jump instruction is executed. The same applies, of course, to RET and IRET instructions. The problem is that the next instruction not only has to be read, but also decoded. Note that i386 instructions can contain 15 bytes, so up to four bus cycles can be necessary in order to read an instruction. These cycles are additional to the time needed for decoding and execution. The execution time given in manuals always refers only to the execution time itself, therefore they are only valid if the instruction has been fully read and decoded. In most cases, prefetching makes sure that instructions are ready for execution. If you can imagine what it would be like without prefetching, where for every instruction the instruction reading and decoding time was apparent, then you will quickly realize the performance advantage that prefetching achieves.

The control unit must wait for a long period for the next decoded instruction after a jump or procedure call to an address that is outside the previously read code area. If the jump target is still within the queue and the instruction contains very few bytes, resulting in it being fully read, then all that remains is for it to be decoded. The instruction reading cycle is dropped. Where no jump is to be executed (because the jump conditions, for example JNE, are not fulfilled), the i386 continues without delay.

If you examine a complicated program using a debugger, you will realize that it is teeming with JUMPs and CALLs. For example, a compiler converts many of the C language CASE statements into a number of conditional JUMPs. If the target address is outside the area covered by the prefetch queue, the i386 has to start the instruction fetching and decoding from the beginning. Converting source code into an unfavourable sequence of JUMP instructions can badly affect the execution time of a program. Assembler programmers should take note of this. Unfortunately, optimizing compilers from well-known manufacturers are also known to skip willingly outside the prefetch boundaries, and sometimes without good reason.

3.5 i386 Real Mode, High-Memory Area and HIMEM.SYS

On compatibility grounds, the i386 can operate in real mode in addition to the more modern protected and virtual 8086 modes. In this mode, it forms linear addresses in the same way as the 8086, with the multiplication of the segment register value by 16 and the addition of the offset (Figure 2.7). With the 8086, the addresses are strictly limited to 1 Mbyte because the 20-bit adder in the addressing unit only has a 20-bit bus. Because both the segment and the offset registers have a width of 16 bits, their maximum value equals ffffh. When adding the segment ffffh and the offset ffffh in real mode to form a physical address, we get the following value:

```
  segment (*2⁴)    ffff0h
 +offset            ffffh
 ------------------------
 phys. address    10ffefh
```

Because the 8086/88 has only a 20-bit address bus and therefore only a 20-bit adder in the addressing unit AU, the leading «1» is ignored as a carry. The remaining physical address is ffefh which lies in the first 64 kbyte segment of the address space. A so-called *wrap-around* occurs.

With the i386, the limit of 20 bits naturally does not apply, as it has a 32-bit adder with a 32-bit address bus located in the addressing unit and can, therefore, produce 32-bit addresses. Thus the leading «1» is not ignored as a carry. Instead, 21 address lines are activated and the i386 operates with a «limited» 21-bit address bus. Therefore, bytes with addresses 10000h to 10ffefh in extended memory can be accessed. The 1 Mbyte-barrier in real mode is broken by fff0h (65,520) bytes or almost 64 kbytes (Figure 3.2). This memory area is called the *High Memory Area*, which can be used by DOS and real mode applications as a 10%-extension beyond the 640 kbyte base memory. Typically, parts of DOS and drivers are located there. Of course, the output of the address 10ffefh does not correspond to a «real» 21-bit address bus, because with 21 address bits all bytes between 00000h and 1fffffh can be accessed.

The HIMEM.SYS device driver is provided from DOS 4.00 onwards to access these first 64 kbytes beyond the 1 Mbyte-boundary in real mode under clearly defined circumstances. Because device drivers such as SMARTDRV.SYS and RAMDRIVE.SYS also use this memory area, a collision may occur if HIMEM.SYS is not installed. Another problem arises with certain MS-DOS versions: some internal and non-documented functions rely on the wrap-around of the 8086/88. In an i386 this, of course, never happens. To deceive the i386, the address line A20 carrying the 21st address bit is forced to low (0) by an external gate. In this way, the wrap-around of the 8086 is emulated. In the AT the gate is mainly controlled by the keyboard controller under supervision of the HIMEM.SYS driver (see Section 31.1.5).

Among other things, HIMEM.SYS is responsible for ensuring that only in an intended access to the first 64 kbytes of extended memory is the A20 address line activated. In all other cases, A20 is disabled by HIMEM.SYS to emulate a wrap-around in the processor. SMARTDRV.SYS and RAMDRIVE.SYS, however, use the protected mode to access extended memory, but this must not collide with the data within the first 64 kbytes of the high memory area. In protected mode, all 32 address lines are available with no restrictions. Further, certain HIMEM.SYS functions may be used to access extended memory in protected mode.

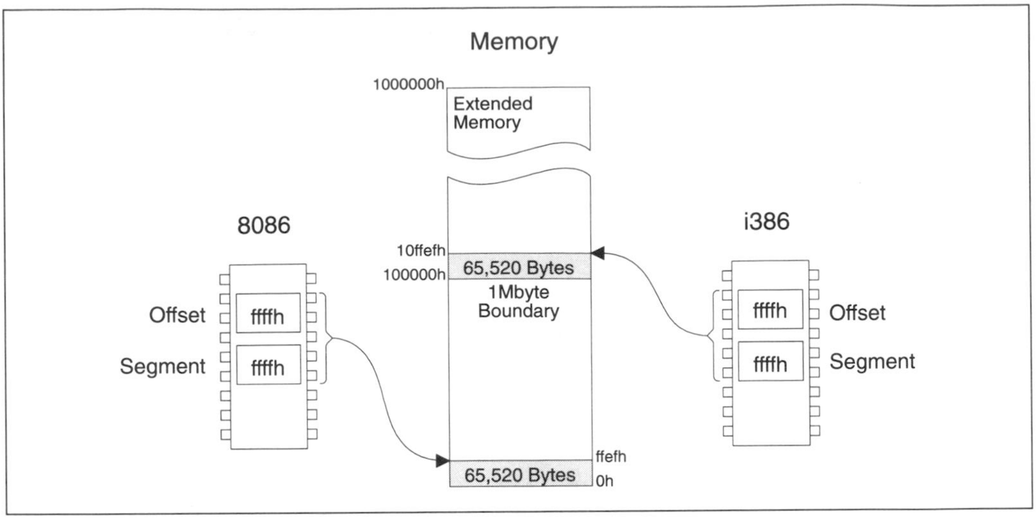

Figure 3.2: Breakthrough of the 1Mbyte barrier in real mode. In real mode, when the value of a segment register is multiplied by 16 and the offset is added, the result may be above 1Mbyte. Because of the 32 address lines of the i386 (unlike the 8086 20-bit address bus), this address above 1Mbyte is actually output.

The address generation in the real mode of the i386 is different to the 8086 and 80286 in another way. With its 32-bit offset register and help from address prefixes, the i386 can actually produce 32-bit addresses. If the content of a 32-bit offset register is used as an address and the value of the effective address is over ffffh, the i386 produces a so-called pseudo-protection exception without an error code, which leads to an interrupt 12 or 13 (see the next chapter). In this way, a halt is called to the production of linear addresses beyond 10ffefh (it's a shame, otherwise the complete i386 address space of 4Gbytes would be available in place of a meagre 1Mbyte).

In real mode, all of the instructions specific to protected mode such as LLDT (load local descriptor table – a data structure that is only available in protected mode) are as useless as the unnecessary opcodes.

I would like to mention that besides the high memory area there also exists a so-called *Upper Memory Area* – DOS users are naturally very inventive in finding in their 8 Mbyte PCs some additional 64 kbytes or sometimes 128 kbytes of storage. The real mode address area between 640 k and 1 M reserved for ROM extensions is, however, only very rarely actually occupied by such ROMs. Modern memory controllers are able to remap some RAM onto that ROM area if no ROM is installed there. Thus, the processor is able in real mode to access some more kbytes.

3.6 Interrupts and Exceptions

From the combined efforts of the bus interface, prefetch queue, execution unit, etc. of the processor, it is easy to see that the processor can carry out instructions endlessly. As soon as an instruction has been executed, the next one is loaded and executed. Even if it appears that the computer is inactive, ready for you to type in an instruction (such as DIR, for example), it does not mean that it has stopped working, only to start again when instructed to. Many more routines run in the background, such as to check the keyboard to determine whether a character has been typed in. Thus, a program loop is carried out. Only notebooks with power management actually stop the processor from functioning after a specific time without an instruction. The first key press reactivates the CPU immediately.

To interrupt the processor in its never-ending execution of these instructions, a so-called *interrupt* is issued. For example, a periodic interrupt (the timer interrupt) is used to activate the resident program PRINT regularly for a short time. For the 80x86 256 different interrupts (0–255) are available in total. Intel has reserved the first 32 interrupts for exclusive use by the processor, but this unfortunately didn't stop IBM from placing all hardware interrupts and the interrupts of the PC BIOS in exactly this region. I cannot see any real reason for this, and it may give rise to some strange consequences. If you are checking the index into an array against the array boundaries by means of the BOUND instruction on an AT and the index is outside, then the 80286 issues an exception which corresponds to interrupt 5. Therefore, your AT starts to print the screen. You may test this if you like with DEBUG by explicitly writing the opcode of BOUND into memory and loading the necessary registers with values that lead to an index outside the array boundaries. With G for Go you issue the index check, and as a consequence a usually unwanted screen print is produced. You'll be reassured to learn that printing via the PrtScrn key is carried out according to a completely different principle. PrtScrn therefore also works on a PC/XT, which only incorporates an 8086/88 and doesn't yet know the instruction BOUND.

Depending on the source of an interrupt, one can distinguish three categories:

- software interrupts,
- hardware interrupts,
- exceptions.

3.6.1 Software Interrupts

Software interrupts are initiated with an INT instruction. For example, the instruction INT 10h issues the interrupt with the hex number 10h. Figure 3.3 shows the procedure for carrying out an interrupt in real mode.

In the real mode address space of the i386, 1024 (1k) bytes are reserved for the interrupt vector table. This table contains an *interrupt vector* for each of the 256 possible interrupts. In the 8086, the position of this table was pre-set by the hardware. The i386 in real mode manages this itself and is a little more flexible. From all memory management registers (see Figure 2.11) the Interrupt Descriptor Table Register (IDTR) is already valid in real mode. It stores the base address and the limit of the real mode descriptor table. After a processor reset, the IDTR is normally loaded with the value 00000000h for the base and 03ffh for the limit. This corresponds exactly to a 1 kbyte table of segment 0000h and offset 0000h. Through the two i386 instructions LIDT (Load IDTR) and SIDT (store IDTR), it is possible to change the base and limit values, and so to change the table size and to move it to a different position in the real mode address space.

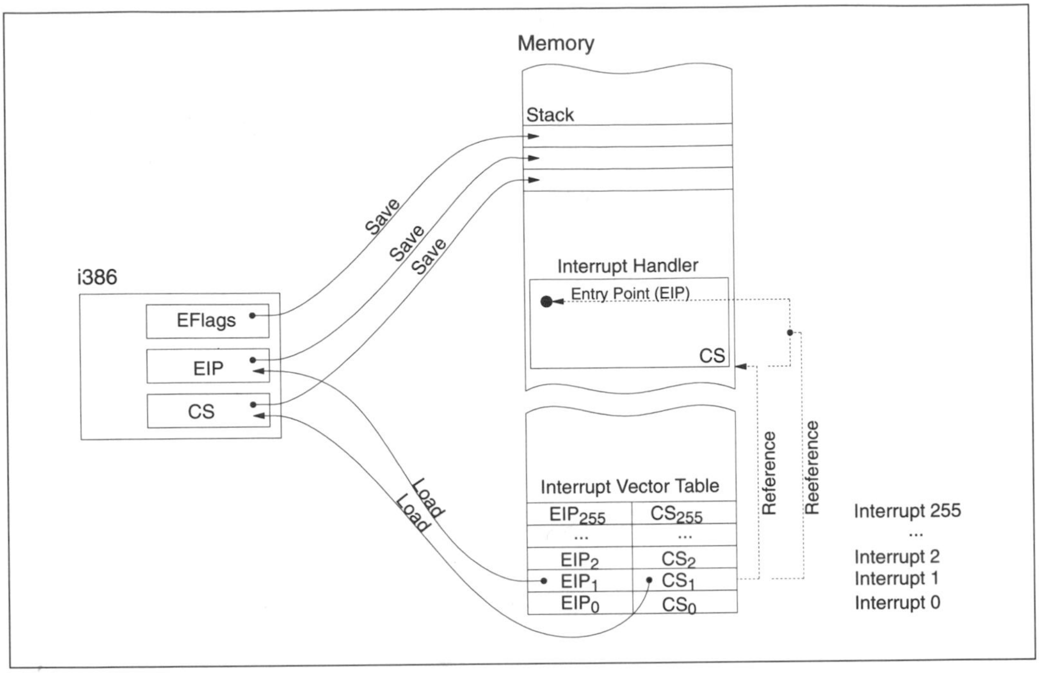

Figure 3.3: Interrupts in real mode. When an interrupt is issued to the i386 the processor automatically transfers the current flags, the instruction pointer EIP and the code segment CS onto the stack. The interrupt number is internally multiplied by four and then provides the offset in segment 00h where the interrupt vector for handling the interrupt is located. An interrupt vector is an address in segment:offset format which represents the entry point of the applicable handler. The i386 loads EIP and CS with the values in the table.

Note, however, that the table can record all of the vectors for all of the possible interrupts, otherwise an exception 8 would result (see below).

Every interrupt vector in real mode consists of four bytes and gives the jump address of the *interrupt handler* for the particular interrupt in segment:offset format. As the interrupts usually only have one cause (such as the request of an operating system function or receipt of data at the serial interface, etc.), the interrupt handler handles the interrupt in the applicable way. For example, it carries out the operating system function or receives the character. Through the replacement of the handler, the interrupt can simply take on another function.

The coordination of interrupts and interrupt vectors is accomplished on a one-to-one basis; this means that the interrupt 0 is assigned the interrupt vector 0 (at the address 0000:0000) and the interrupt 1 is assigned the interrupt vector 1 (at the address 0000:0004), etc. The i386 only has to multiply the number of the interrupt by 4 to establish the offset of the interrupt vector in segment 0000h. The overwriting of the interrupt vector table with incorrect values has a catastrophic effect on the i386. The next interrupt will not be able to find the applicable jump address, causing the computer to crash.

When an interrupt occurs, the i386 automatically carries out the following procedure (see Figure 3.3), without any further input from the program:

- The i386 puts the EFlags CS and EIP – in this sequence – onto the stack (naturally only the flags CS and IP in 16-bit mode);
- the interrupt and the trap flag are reset;
- the i386 addresses the interrupt vector in the interrupt vector table corresponding to the number of the interrupt and loads EIP (or IP in 16-bit mode) and CS from the table.

CS:EIP of the interrupt vector gives the entry point of the interrupt handler. In this way, the processor continues its work with the interrupt handler. The return to the current program occurs with an IRET.

Example: `INT 10h`

```
The processor saves the current flags, CS and EIP on the stack, clears the interrupt and trap
flags and reads the interrupt vector at location 0000:0040. The two bytes at 0000:0040 are
loaded into EIP, the two bytes at 0000:0042 into CS (note the Intel format low–high).
```

Note that the i386, in 32-bit mode, loads the offset value of the handler into EIP, but the offset in the interrupt vector table is only 16-bit due to the need for compatibility with the 16-bit 8086 and 80286 predecessors of the i386. The two most significant bytes in EIP are simply filled with the value 0000h.

The encoding of an INT instruction is also interesting:

INT 3

11001100

INT 0..2, 4..255

11001101	vvvvvvvv

11001100 and 11001101 represent the opcode, *vvvvvvvv* indicates the number of the interrupt. Thus the INT 3 instruction consists of only one byte. You will find more about this interrupt in the exceptions section. For all other interrupt instructions, only one immediate addressing is possible; this means that the number of the interrupt vector is part of the instruction. In this way, the number of the interrupt cannot be held in a register or memory operand.

Software interrupts are synchronized with program execution; this means that every time the program gets to the point where there is an INT instruction, an interrupt is issued. This is very different to hardware interrupts and exceptions.

3.6.2 Hardware Interrupts

As the name suggests, these interrupts are set by hardware components (timer interrupts, for example, by the timer component), or by peripheral devices such as a hard disk. There are two basic types of hardware interrupts: *Non Maskable Interrupts (NMI)* and (maskable) *interrupt requests (IRQ)*. For handling such IRQs the interrupt controller 8259A plays an important role (see Section 25.1). It manages several interrupt requests and passes them on to the processor depending on their priority.

When the computer issues an NMI, the NMI pin of the processor (Pin B8 in the i386) receives an active signal. The i386 finishes the current instruction and immediately afterwards carries out an interrupt 2 in exactly the same way as before. An NMI in the PC is, generally, the result of a serious hardware problem, such as a memory parity error or a erroneous bus arbitration. The computer displays a message like

Parity Error at xxxx:xxxx

xxxx:xxxx indicates the byte with the parity error. An NMI is different in that it cannot be suppressed (or masked as its name suggests). An NMI always pushes its way to the forefront. As it normally indicates a serious failure, this is understandable and also correct. A computer with incorrectly functioning hardware must be prevented from destroying data.

Interrupt requests, on the other hand, can be masked with a reset interrupt flag IE. In real mode, this can be accomplished with the CLI instruction. All interrupt requests at the INTR connection (pin B7) are ignored. The opposite STI instruction reactivates these interrupts. Note that the software instruction INT xx specifically carries out a CLI; this means it blocks all interrupt requests. It is, therefore, necessary to carry out an STI to reactivate the interrupt requests after an INT instruction, otherwise the computer would be deaf. Interrupt requests are usually issued by a peripheral device. An example would be where the serial interface informs the i386 that it has just received a character. The course of such an interrupt is detailed in Section 23.1.

Hardware interrupt requests are managed by the interrupt controller. When it receives a signal from a unit to indicate that the unit has requested an interrupt, the interrupt controller sends the interrupt request signal (IRQ) to the INTR input (pin B7) of the i386. If the processor can handle the interrupt (IE is set), the i386 sends the confirmation signal $\overline{\text{INTA}}$ (interrupt acknowledge) by setting each of the control signals $M/\overline{IO}$ $D/\overline{C}$ and $W/\overline{R}$ to a low level (see Chapter 4.1). During an INTA cycle, the interrupt controller delivers the number of the active interrupt. The processor continues in the same way as explained previously, and addresses the applicable interrupt handler.

Hardware interrupts (NMI and IRQ) are, contrary to software interrupts, asynchronous to the program execution. This is understandable because, for example, a parity error does not always occur at the same program execution point. Also, the hard disk needs a certain amount of time, depending on the initial location of the read/write heads, before data can be transferred to the processor. This makes the detection of program errors very difficult if they only occur in connection with hardware interrupts.

3.6.3 Exceptions

We have already learned about two sources of interrupts; a third originates in the processor itself. Interrupts produced by the i386 are known as *exceptions*. The production of an exception corresponds to that of a software interrupt. This means that an interrupt whose number is set by the i386 itself is issued. The cause of an exception is generally an internal processor error caused by system software that can no longer be handled by the processor alone.

Exceptions are distinguished according to three classes: faults, traps and aborts. In the following I will discuss the characteristics of these three classes.

- Fault: a fault issues an exception prior to completing the instruction. The saved EIP value then points to the instruction that led to the exception. By loading the saved EIP value (for example, with IRET) the i386 is able to re-execute the instruction, hopefully without issuing an exception again. One example of a fault is the exception *segment not present*. The i386 has the ability to reload the segment and attempt another access.

- Trap: a trap issues an exception after completing an instruction execution. Thus the saved EIP value points to the instruction immediately following the instruction that gave rise to the exception. The instruction is therefore not re-executed again. Traps are useful if the instruction has been executed correctly, but the program should be interrupted nevertheless, for example, in the case of debugger breakpoints. Here the instructions should be executed, and the debugger only checks the register contents, etc. Re-executing the corresponding instruction would lead to a faulty instruction flow.
- Abort: unlike faults and traps, an abort does not always indicate the address of the error. Therefore, recovering program execution after an abort is not always possible. Aborts are only used to indicate very serious failures, such as hardware failures or invalid system tables.

Most of the exceptions are used when the i386 operates in protected mode. In real mode, only the following exceptions are used:

- Division by 0 (exception 0): if, with the instruction DIV or IDIV, the devisor equals zero, then the result of the operation is not mathematically defined and the i386 cannot reply. The ALU of the i386 would need an indefinitely long time to calculate such a quotient. When a division has not finished within a specific number of clock cycles, the control unit interprets this as a division by zero and issues interrupt 0.
- Single Step (exception 1): if the trap flag is set, the i386 issues an interrupt 1 after each separate step. The trap flag is automatically reset by the i386 when an interrupt is issued so that the processor can continue with the interrupt routine. Debuggers mostly use the trap flag and intercept the interrupt so that the program can be carried out step-by-step.
- Breakpoint (exception 3): in the i386, a breakpoint exception can occur in two different ways. The i386 contains an internal debug register which assists the i386 in issuing an interrupt 3 under specific circumstances. Additionally, a debugger can set a breakpoint in place of an instruction, in which the instruction (or its first byte) is overwritten with the opcode 11001100 for the INT 3 instruction. When the program reaches this point, the i386 issues an interrupt 3 and the program is interrupted. To continue the program, the debugger overwrites the opcode 11001100 with the byte existing previously at this location and carries out an IRET. Naturally the i386 can also use the INT 3 instruction to issue a software interrupt 3. This also applies to all of the other exceptions, except that there is no reason for the subsequent interrupt as the source of the interrupt lies in a processor error and not in an explicit software interrupt.
- Overflow with INTO (exception 4): if the overflow flag is set and the INTO instruction is sent, the processor produces an interrupt 4.
- BOUND (exception 5): the i386 will issue an interrupt 5 if an index into a field is checked with the BOUND instruction and is found to lie outside the boundaries of the field.

- Invalid opcode (exception 6): if the instruction unit comes across an opcode without an associated instruction, the processor will issue interrupt 6. The causes of invalid opcodes are mostly incorrect assemblers or compilers, or a program error that causes a jump to a position that does not contain an opcode, but a data word that the instruction unit interprets as an opcode.
- No coprocessor available (exception 7): if the instruction unit receives an opcode for a coprocessor instruction (an ESC instruction) and there is no coprocessor installed, the i386 issues an interrupt 7.
- IDT limit too small (exception 8): if the limit of the IDT is too small for the vector of the interrupt, the i386 issues an interrupt 8. This is often the case when a program has read and incorrectly changed the IDT.
- Stack Exception (exception 12): the stack pointer ESP delivers a higher value than ffffh for the stack access. This can occur because ESP represents a 32-bit register and its value is not restricted to 1M. The i386 then issues an interrupt 12 to stop the allocation of linear addresses above 10ffefh in real mode.
- General protection error (exception 13): a 32-bit offset register delivers a larger effective address than ffffh for a memory access. As for the stack pointer ESP, the allocation of linear addresses above 10ffefh in real mode is stopped; in this case the i386 issues an interrupt 13.
- Coprocessor error (exception 16): an error occurs in the coprocessor and the i386 is alerted with an active $\overline{\text{ERROR}}$ signal. The result is an interrupt 16.

Note that the interrupt 02h is associated with an NMI. Additionally, the exceptions 8, 12, 13 and 16 are not implemented in the 8086 as no IDT or 32-bit register is present, and the 8087 can issue an interrupt directly without going through the CPU when there is a coprocessor error.

3.7 i386 Protected Mode

The *Protected Virtual Address Mode* (or *Protected Mode*) was originally implemented in the 80286 to protect (as its name suggests) the different tasks in a multitasking operating system from invalid or incorrect accesses. For this purpose, the i386 hardware checks all accesses of a program to data and code and provides access rights for such accesses with four *privilege levels*. Thus, data and code are protected and a complete system crash of the PC is impossible.

The access checks in protected mode provide hardware support for *multitasking operating systems* such as OS/2, UNIX and Windows NT. In a multitasking operating system environment, several programs (tasks) run concurrently (in parallel). Strictly speaking, the individual tasks are activated periodically by the operating system, are executed for a short time period, and are interrupted again by the operating system. Then the system activates another task. Unlike the TSR (Terminate and Stay Resident) programs of MS-DOS (PRINT, for example), the programs are activated by the operating system. TSR programs, on the other hand, activate themselves, usually by intercepting the periodic timer interrupt. Thus, a multitasking operating system often switches between the individual tasks within a short time (that is, a *task switch* is carried out), and users have the impression that the programs are running in parallel. With the i386 hardware support in protected mode, these task switches may be carried out both quickly and efficiently.

Another essential difference between protected and real mode is the different way in which linear addresses for a memory object are calculated in protected mode. The following section details the special characteristics of the protected mode.

3.7.1 Segment Selectors, Segment Descriptors and Privilege Levels

As previously described, in real mode the addressing unit of the i386 simply multiplies the value of the segment register by 16 to determine the base address of the applicable segment. The address contained in such a 64 kbyte segment is then given by the offset. In protected mode, the values in the segment registers are interpreted very differently; they represent so-called *selectors* and not base addresses. Figure 3.4 shows the organization of such a segment selector.

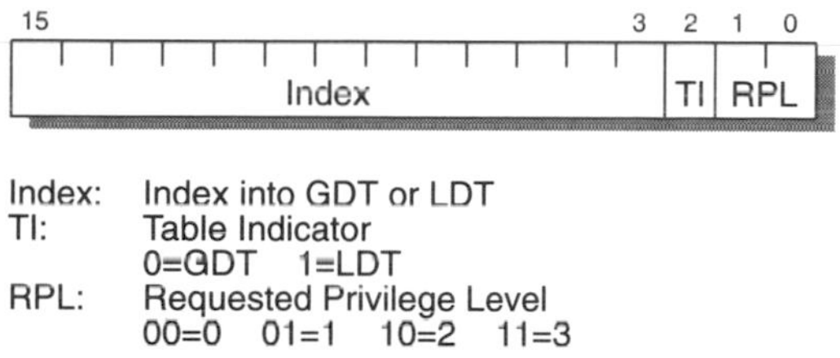

Figure 3.4: Structure of a segment selector.

As in real mode, the selector is 16 bits long and is stored in a 16-bit segment register. The two least significant bits 0 and 1 specify the *Requested Privilege Level (RPL)* that a program can access the segment from here we are first confronted with an access check of the protected mode. The value of the RPL field in the segment selector of the code segment CS is known as the *Current Privilege Level (CPL)*. This refers to the privilege level of the currently active program. The active program can access data segments that have a privilege level the same as or higher than the CPL. The value of RPL can also be larger than the value of CPL, meaning that the segment set by the selector is accessed with a lower privilege level. The larger of the CPL and RPL values defines the *Effective Privilege Level (EPL)* of the task. The i386 has in total four privilege levels (PL) 0 to 3. Note that 0 is the highest and 3 is the lowest privilege level – a higher value indicates a lower privilege level, and vice versa. An RPL of 0 does not restrict the privilege level of a task at all, whereas a selector with RPL 3 can only access segments that have a privilege level of 3 independently of the CPL.

Programs with lower privilege levels (a higher CPL) can only access a segment with a higher privilege level (lower CPL) in strictly defined circumstances. For this, the i386 uses so-called *gates* to «open the door» to segments with higher privileges. In this way, the i386 hardware implements a method of protection within the task through the use of the different privilege levels. Figure 3.5 graphically shows the four privilege level concept.

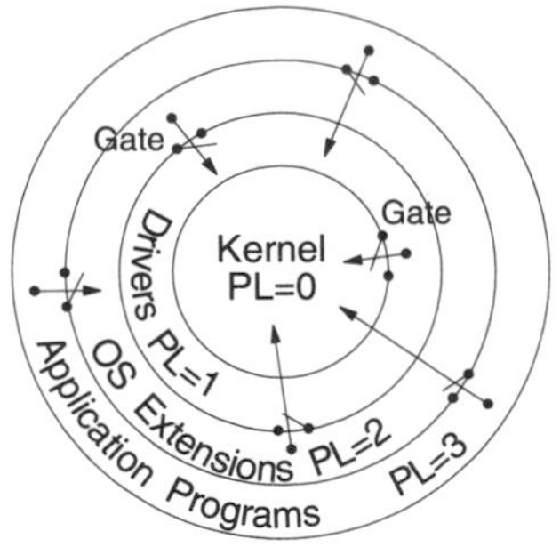

Figure 3.5: The concept of the four privilege levels in the i386.

Usually, the critical part or the *kernel* of the operating system has the highest privilege level 0. The kernel comprises at least the routines for memory management, executing task switches, handling critical errors, etc. Many instructions that directly influence the status of the processor or computer (for example, LGDT (load global descriptor table) or LMSW (load MSW)) may be executed in protected mode only by a program with a privilege level 0. This avoids application programs destroying the operating system because of a program bug, or a hacker obtaining uncontrollable access to data.

Operating systems not only manage the computer but also supply certain functions for data management, character output, etc. In the PC this is done by the interrupt 21h, for example, the so-called *DOS function interrupt*. Such *operating system functions* usually run at PL = 1. Also, unit and device drivers (for example, for accessing interfaces and drives) often run at this level. Less critical operating system functions such as the support of a graphics-oriented user shell may be assigned level 2.

The lowest privilege level is assigned to *application programs* because they only use the computer, and don't control it. Because of the low level (high PL), the data and codes of the operating system and other programs are protected against program errors. For example, with MS-DOS a program error that erroneously overwrites the interrupt vector table leads to a complete system crash. In protected mode the operating system reacts by displaying an error message and aborting only the erroneous program. All other tasks stay running with no further destruction or influence. Therefore, bugs (that is, program errors) may be detected more easily. However, this is only true if the operating system (OS/2, for example) is error-free. Unfortunately, this is by no means a matter of course, because multitasking operating systems are very complex.

In the following explanation, the task concept occurs often. First, a few words are in order to explain this concept. A task includes the applicable program (such as Word) and data (or text), as well as the necessary system functions (for example, data management at the hard disk level). Under Windows, for example, it is possible to start Word for Windows and load text ready for processing. To edit an additional text file in parallel, it is possible to load the additional file into Word and to switch between the two Word windows. In this way, two texts are loaded into one program, and Word and the two texts together form a *single* task. Another possibility for editing the second text is to start Word for Windows again. Windows accomplishes this with an additional window. The second text file is then loaded into the most recently started Word. In this case also it is possible to switch between the two windows. The main difference from the first example is that now two programs have been started, that is, two initializations of Word with a text file loaded into each. Each program, together with its corresponding text, is a task. Even though the program is the same in both cases, the PC runs *two* tasks.

The i386 provides a separate stack for every privilege level (PL = 0 to PL = 3) of a task. For the previous example, there would be a stack available for the application Word (PL = 3), the functions of the user interface (PL = 2), the operating system functions for data management (PL = 1) and the kernel (PL = 0).

For a controlled program access to data and code in segments with a higher privilege level, gates are available. The gates supply maximum protection against unauthorized accesses to another's data and programs. If, for example, an application program uses operating system functions to open or close files – thus the application accesses another's functions – the gates ensure that the access is carried out without any faults. If the application program were to attempt to call the functions with an incorrect entry address, unpredictable behaviour of the computer would be likely to occur. Therefore, the gates define (what else) «gates» through which the application program has access to the operating system or other routines.

Bit 2 in the segment register (Figure 3.4) specifies, as the so-called *table indicator (TI)*, whether the global (TI = 0) or the local (TI = 1) descriptor table for the location of the segment in the memory should be used. These two tables are decisive for segmenting the memory in protected mode. In protected mode, the i386 uses the segment selector in the segment register as an index for the global or local descriptor tables.

The *global descriptor table* is a list in the memory that describes the segment sizes and addresses in memory in the form of *segment descriptors*. The construction of such a segment descriptor is shown in Figure 3.6. Every descriptor contains eight bytes. This descriptor table is called global because it describes the segments that are usually available for all tasks (when they have access to the privilege levels and applicable gates). The *local descriptor table* is a list of similarly constructed segment descriptors. In contrast to the global descriptor table, the local descriptor table is only available to the currently active task, i.e. when the task changes, the local descriptor table also changes.

The 32 *base* bits of the segment descriptor specify the start address of the segment in the memory (see Figure 3.7). These 32 bits of the base address correspond to the 32 address lines of the i386. In protected mode, addressing can be performed using these 2^{32} bytes or 4 Gbytes. The base entry of the segment descriptor specifies the start address of the applicable segment in this very large address space. Figure 3.7 shows how the segment descriptor sets the start of the segment. Note that the i386 recognizes – according to the entry 00000000 in the field base 31..24 – that an 80286 segment descriptor is present. The 80286, as a 16-bit processor with a 24-bit data bus, does not use the base bits 31–24 because they can never be output. Further details concerning the differences between protected mode for the 80286 and the i386 are discussed in Section 16.2.

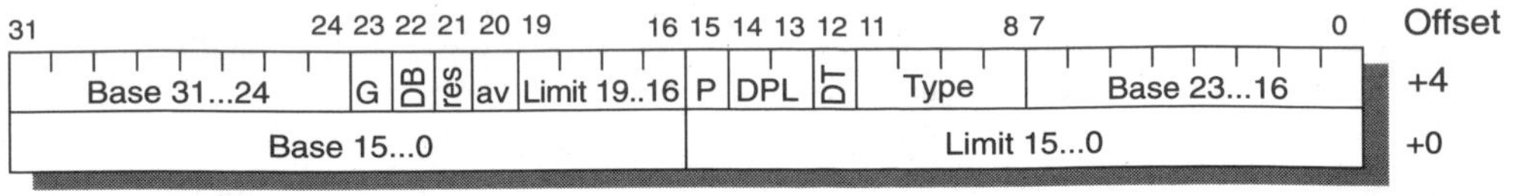

Base 31...24, Base 23...16, Base 15...0: Segment Base
Limit 19...16, Limit 15...0: Segment Limit
G: Granularity
0=Byte Granularity 1=Page Granularity
DB: Segment Size (Default/Big)
0=16-Bit Operands/Addresses (Default) 1=32-Bit Operands/Addresses (Big)
res: Reserved
av: Available for Operating System
P: Segment Present
0=Segment Not in Memory 1=Segment in Memory
DPL: Descriptor Privilege Level
00=0 01=1 10=2 11=3
DT: Descriptor Type
0=System Segment 1=Application Segment
Type: Type of System or Application Segment

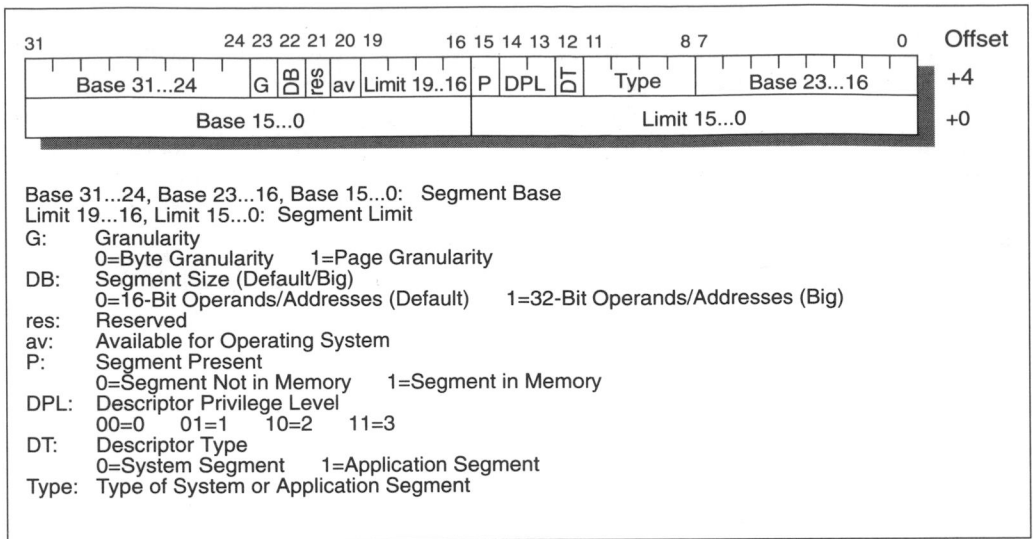

Figure 3.6: Format of the i386 segment descriptor.

In real mode, each segment is defined as being 64 kbytes in size, even if only a small amount of data is actually stored in a segment. The setting of the distance between the segments to 16 bytes makes certain that a maximum of 15 bytes are lost (or empty). The uncoupling of the segment in protected mode changes this completely, because, depending upon the selector value in the segment register, sequential segments should on no account be physically stored in the memory sequentially. Every segment descriptor therefore refers to an entry *limit* in the least significant byte of the descriptor, in order to actually define the size of the segment (Figure 3.7). Through the 20 bits of the entry limit, segments in protected mode are possible up to a maximum of 1 Mbyte with byte granularity, and 4 Gbytes with page granularity. The actual segment limit (or size) of the segment described by the descriptor depends on the granularity bit G as well as on the 20-bit entry limit. Note that in the i386, a page is 4 kbytes (=4096 bytes) in size.

Example:
```
limit=1000, G=0:  segment limit 1000 bytes
limit=1000, G=1:  segment limit 1000*4kbyte=4,096,000 bytes
```

The full address area of the 32-bit offset register comes only from the page granularity. In this case, the smallest assignment unit for a segment is 4 kbytes in size. This means that the memory is sectioned into portions of 4 kbytes. This is only suitable for larger systems; for PC users, segments of 1 Mbyte are most suitable so that the memory can be used more beneficially. OS/2 and Windows NT use a so-called *flat memory model*, in which a single 4 Gbyte segment contains all tasks. This means that segmentation is almost irrelevant. In its place, memory sections in pages are used as a further protection mechanism (see Section 3.8).

The *DT*-bit in the segment descriptor defines the type of descriptor. If DT equals 0, the descriptor describes a system segment, otherwise it describes an application segment. The *type* field indicates the type and *DPL* the privilege level (from 1 to 3) of the applicable segment. DPL is also known as the descriptor privilege level. Finally, the *P*-bit indicates whether the segment is actually located in the memory.

The *av*-bit in the segment descriptor is for the use of the operating system or user. The i386 does not use it, and Intel has not reserved it for future use.

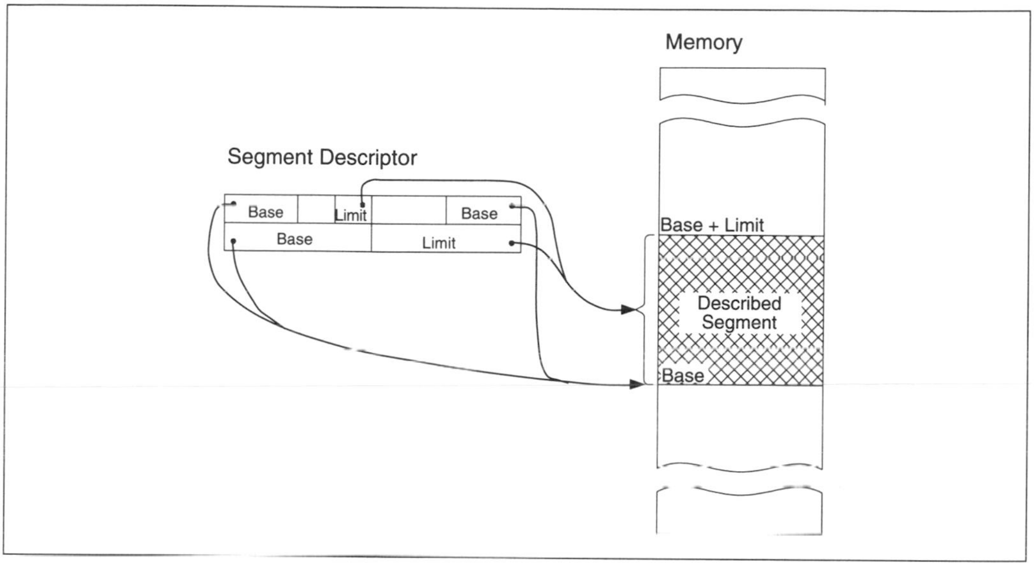

Figure 3.7: Segment descriptor base and limit. In protected mode a segment descriptor defines a segment: the base address indicates the physical start of the segment in memory, the limit its size.

You will recall that the 32-bit offset registers EAX, etc. can be reduced to 16-bit and also further to 8-bit registers. Additionally, every program code that was developed for the 8086 and 80286 16-bit processors requires 16-bit addresses. On compatibility grounds, the i386 must also be able to use such addresses in addition to new 32-bit program code. For this reason, the *DB*-bit is important. It indicates whether the i386 should use 16- or 32-bit operands for the segment if it is a data segment, and whether 16- or 32-bit addresses should be used for a code segment. If DB = 0, the i386 uses 16-bit operands or 16-bit addresses. Note that the DB-bit equals 0 for standard values given for an 80286 segment descriptor. The 80286 code can, therefore, be carried over to the 32-bit architecture of the i386 without a problem, as all operands and addresses are normally handled as 16-bit. Also, the other 80286 standard values use the 16-bit architecture with 24-bit address bus calculation.

With a reset DB-bit, operands and addresses can be expanded to 32-bit for specific instructions with the so-called *operand size prefix 66h* and the *address size prefix 67h*. The operand size prefix sets the size using the DB-bit of the applicable *data* segment, the address size prefix sets the size using the DB-bit of the applicable *code* segment. With a reset DB-bit (DB = 0), the applicable segment normally uses 16-bit operands and 16-bit addresses. The prefix instructs the i386 to use 32-bit operands or 32-bit addresses in place of the standard 16-bit. If, on the other hand, the DB-bit is set, the segment uses the standard 32-bit. An operand or address prefix forces the i386 to use a 16-bit operand or a 16-bit address, respectively, in place of 32-bit. The great advantage of using the DB-bit and prefixes is that the i386 does not need different opcodes for similar instructions such as MOV ax, mem16 and MOV eax and mem32 that are sometimes 16-bit and sometimes 32-bit. This reduces the number of opcodes necessary for the implementation of an extensive instruction set and also the average encoding complexity. These prefixes lead to a more compact program in exactly the same way as segment override prefixes.

Example: The opcode for the two instructions MOV eax, [01h] and MOV ax, [01h] is 10111000 in both cases. The i386 distinguishes them according to the DB bit and operand size prefix. It is assumed that the DB bit in the code segment descriptor is cleared, i.e. the i386 uses 16-bit displacements as a standard. With a cleared DB bit in the data segment descriptor an assembler has to insert the operand size prefix 66h in front of the opcode in the first case. We get the following instruction encoding:

```
MOV eax, 01h:    66 b8 00 01 (The instruction transfers the 32-bit value at offset 01h into the
32-bit accumulator eax.)
MOV ax, 01h:        b8 00 01 (The instruction transfers the 16-bit value at offset 01h into the
16-bit accumulator eax.)
```

If DB is set in the corresponding data segment descriptor then, in the second case, the assembler inserts the operand size prefix 66h in front of the opcode because the i386 now uses 32-bit quantities as a standard. The encodings are:

```
MOV eax, 01h:       b8 00 01 (The instruction transfers the 32-bit value at offset 01h into the
32-bit accumulator eax.)
MOV ax, 01h:     66 b8 00 01 (The instruction transfers the 16-bit value at offset 01h into the
16-bit accumulator eax.)
```

3.7.2 Global and Local Descriptor Tables

For managing the local and global descriptor tables, as well as the interrupt descriptor table (which will be detailed below) and the tasks, the i386 implements five registers, shown in Figure 3.8. These are the control register CR0 and the following four memory management registers: Task Register (TR), Local Descriptor Table Register (LDTR), Global Descriptor Table Register (GDTR) and Interrupt Descriptor Table Register (IDTR).

The index or higher-value 13 bits of the segment selector (Figure 3.4) specify the number of the segment descriptor in the descriptor table that describes the applicable segment. With these 13 bits, a maximum of 8192 different indices are possible, so that the global and local descriptor tables can each contain a maximum of 8192 entries of 8 bytes, or a total of 64 kbytes. In this way, each table describes up to 8192 different segments. The construction and size of the segment descriptors for the Local Descriptor Table (LDT) and the Global Descriptor Table (GDT) are identical. The Table Indicator (TI) in the selector indicates whether the segment selector is contained in a segment register of the GDT or the LDT. If the i386 wishes to access an entry in the GDT or the LDT, it multiplies the index value of the selector by 8 (the number of bytes in each descriptor) and adds the result to the base address of the corresponding descriptor table.

The least significant word of the control register is known in the 80286 as the Machine Status Word (MSW), and can also be addressed in the i386 in this way on compatibility grounds. The most significant PG-bit activates or deactivates the paging unit (see Section 3.8). The use of the bits in control register CR0 was discussed previously (see Section 2.8.1) in connection with the control registers.

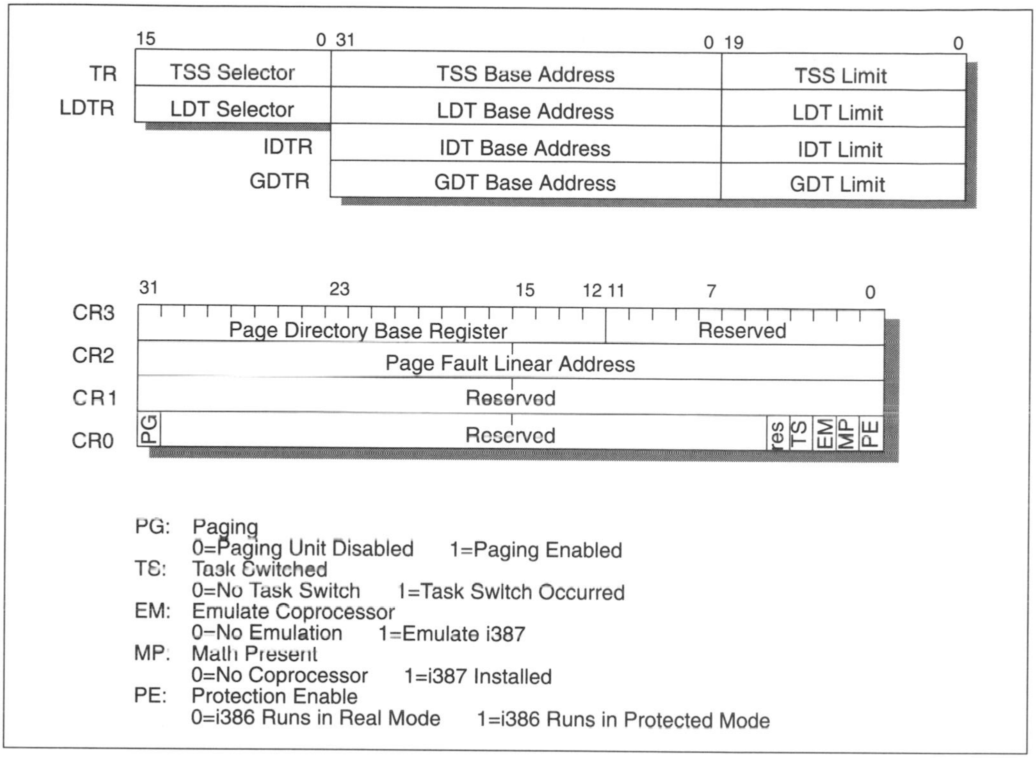

Figure 3.8: Memory management and control registers for i386 protected mode.

The PE-bit (protection enable) is of special importance for the protected mode. When set to 1, the i386 immediately switches into protected mode. It can be reset with the MOV CR0, xxxxxxxx xxxxxxxx xxxxxxxx xxxxxxx0b instruction, a processor reset, or an i386 triple fault.

The base address of the global and local descriptor tables is stored in the GDT and LDT registers respectively. These registers are loaded with the applicable values by the load routine of the operating system (GDTR) or by the operating system itself (LDTR). In contrast to the LDT, the zero entry (beginning with the base address of the GDT) of the GDT cannot be used. Any write to the zero entry leads directly to the exception «general protection error». In this way, a non-initialized GDTR is prevented from being used.

A special feature of GDT is that the i386 uses it for building up the complete segment and, therefore, the whole memory management. In the GDTR (see Figure 3.8) the processor stores both the base address and the limit (the size of GDT in bytes) of the global descriptor table – the GDTR thus refers to the GDT in the memory. In contrast, the i386 manages the local descriptor table dynamically, as many LDTs are possible (compared to only one possible GDT). For every local descriptor table, there is an entry in the GDT. In this way, the LDTs are managed similarly to segments (Figure 3.9). The GDTR therefore contains a *segment descriptor,* but the LDTR contains a *segment selector.*

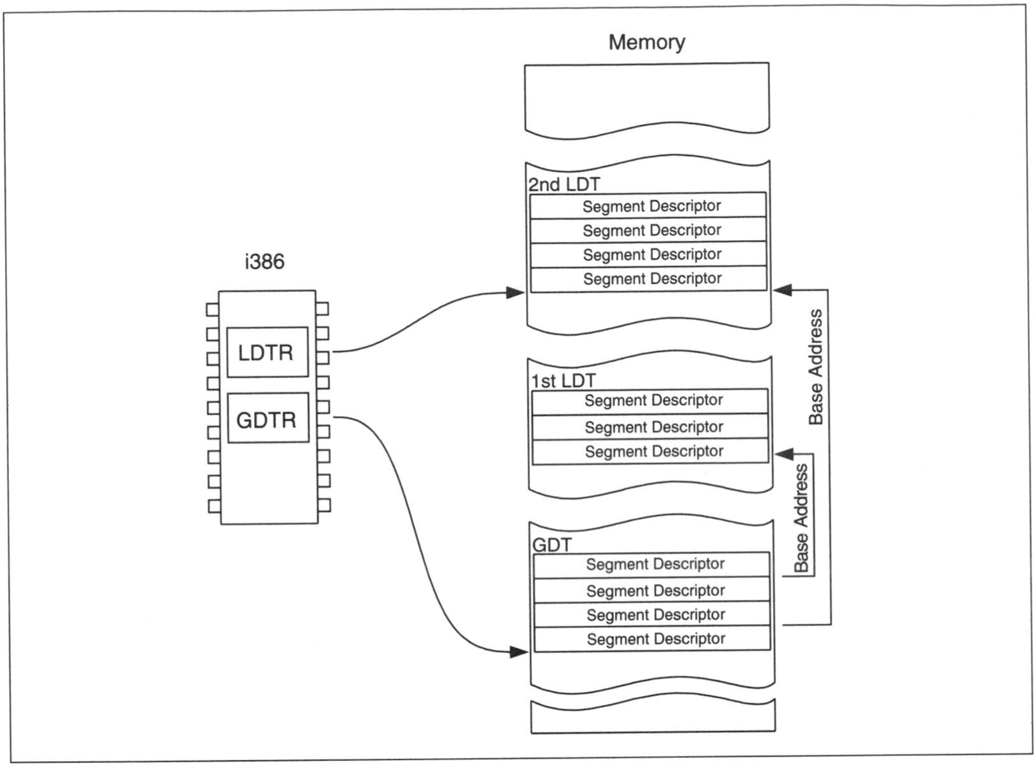

Figure 3.9: Global and local descriptor tables. The i386 GDTR points to the GDT in memory which may hold segment descriptors for various LDTs. The LDTR then indicates (similar to a segment selector) the number of the segment descriptor in the GDT, which in turn defines the corresponding LDT.

The GDTR can be loaded with the segment *descriptor* mem64 by the LGDT mem64 instruction. The operating system loader must carry out this step before the i386 can be switched into protected mode. If it is not performed, the memory management will not function correctly. In contrast, the LDTR is loaded with a segment *selector* by the LLDT reg16 or LLDT mem16 instruction. The segment selector sets the applicable entry in the global descriptor table that contains the descriptor for the required local descriptor table. The management of the descriptor tables is controlled by the operating system (OS/2, Windows NT, etc.) – the application programmer cannot influence this process. In protected mode, the instruction to load the descriptor table registers LDTR and GDTR must be initiated by a task with a privilege level of 0, usually the kernel of the operating system. This is not surprising, as memory management is also the responsibility of the operating system. All attempts to change the descriptor table registers by an application with PL = 3 cause the exception «general protection error» and the interrupt 0dh.

For each task, the operating system delivers the global and also a local descriptor table. This is advantageous in that segments that are used by a number of tasks (for example, a segment with an operating system function) are stored in the GDT, and the segments that are used by the current task (such as program code or program data), are stored in the LDT. In this way, different tasks can be isolated from one another. Each task can use a maximum of two complete descriptor tables, containing up to 8192 entries, where the zero entry in the GDT is not used. This leads to a maximum of 16 383 segments. Every segment in the i386 can contain up to 1 Mbyte (granularity bit equals zero) or 4 Gbytes (G-bit set). This produces a maximum *logical* or *virtual address space* of 16 Gbytes or 64 Tbytes respectively for each task. In the latter case, this is an immense size. If a bit is represented in terms of approximately 10 mg of rice , 64 Tbytes with eight bits each would equate to more than 5 billion (US: trillion) tonnes (5 000 000 000 000 t) of rice. At the present rate of world rice consumption, that would be enough for one thousand years.

But even with byte granularity and a virtual address space of only 16 Gbytes it is impossible to hold all segments in memory. If a segment is stored, for example, by the operating system on a hard disk, then it sets the P-bit in the segment descriptor of the corresponding descriptor table LDT or GDT to a value of 0. If the processor attempts to access this segment, then the hardware issues an exception «segment not available», i.e. interrupt 0bh.

The interrupt handler called can then reload the applicable segment into memory, usually after it has removed a different segment from the memory and stored it externally. The i386 hardware supports this *swapping* process in that exceptions are generated. The actual loading and external storage of segments must be performed by the operating system. The i386 only provides the trigger (the exception) for the process. The large virtual address space is then a physical combination of the small internal main memory (the RAM chips) and a large external mass storage (hard disk).

3.7.3 Segment Descriptor Cache Registers

If, in protected mode, the i386 loads a segment selector into a segment register, the i386 hardware automatically and independently checks whether or not the active task should be allowed to access the newly loaded segment. For a positive result of this check, it is essential that the value of the effective privilege level EPL of the task is lower than or equal to the descriptor privilege level DPL of the loaded segment. If this is not the case, the i386 issues the exception «general protection error» to stop the illegal access. If the access is valid, the processor loads the base address and the limit of the selector designated segment into the applicable *segment descriptor cache register* (Figure 3.10). Because of the intensive access checks and the loading of the cache register, instructions that alter a segment register in protected mode require many more clock cycles than in real mode. This is because the cache register must not only be loaded with a 16-bit selector, but also with an additional 64-bit descriptor. For example, Intel states that the instruction LDS esi, fpointer (load the far pointer fpointer in the register pair DS:ESI) requires seven clock cycles in real mode, and in comparison, 22 clock cycles in protected mode.

In protected mode, every segment register is assigned such a segment descriptor cache register. The cache register is only used internally in the i386 – programmers have no access to it. For every instruction that changes a segment register entry, the processor automatically reads (i.e. without further software instructions) the limit, base address and the access privilege bit for the segment, from the GDT or LDT respectively, into the relevant cache register. This multiple memory access automatically activates the LOCK signal of the i386. The purpose of the cache register is that, following the address calculation of an operand and the verification of the access privilege, the i386 does not need to access an entry in the descriptor table in the memory, as it can access the data in an internal processor register with much greater speed. In the following description of the i386 and its operating modes, I will always mention «segment descriptor in the GDT or LDT», but remember that the i386 only addresses the GDT and LDT respectively during the first descriptor access. Subsequently, the internal cache register is always used in their place.

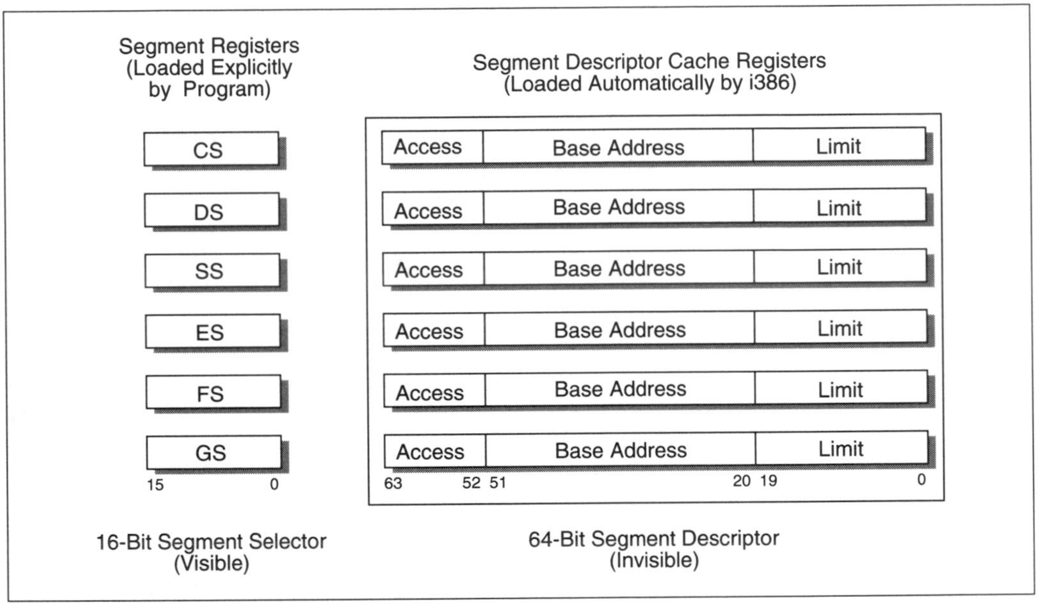

Figure 3.10: The segment descriptor cache registers.

3.7.4 Switching into Protected Mode

Should a switch into protected mode occur, the operating system or the ROM BIOS must assemble the required tables in the memory and, at least, initialize the GDTR and IDTR registers with the appropriate values. When this has taken place, the system, or the ROM BIOS, sets the PE-bit in the CR0 control register with the MOV CR0, value instruction. The i386 then switches into protected mode. With the personal computer, it is also possible to switch the i386 into protected mode using the 89h function of the INT 15h interrupt. Due to the need for compatibility with the 80286, the i386 can also be switched into protected mode with the 80286 LMSW (Load Machine Status Word) instruction. Note that LMSW only addresses the least significant word of the CR0 control register. In contrast to the MOV CR0, value, for example, it cannot activate the paging.

The i386 can leave protected mode by a simple method, in that a task with PL = 0 (the highest privilege level) can reset the PE-bit with a MOV CR0, value instruction. The i386 then immediately switches back into real mode. In the 80286, this is unfortunately not possible. Once switched into protected mode, the PE-bit of the 80286 can no longer be reset in order to switch the 80286 back into real mode. The reason for this is probably that Intel could not imagine how anyone (namely DOS) could ignore the innovative protected mode. In the 80286, the real mode should only perform the necessary preparation to enable switching into protected mode. A return from protected mode into real mode seems absurd (it is, if you compare the physical real mode address space of 1 Mbyte to the 4 Gbytes of protected mode). First the compatibility principle, and then the market significance of DOS, forced Intel to include a way of returning from protected mode into real mode (and here all DOS users sweat, despite memory expansion, etc. even today!).

3.7.5 Memory Addressing in Protected Mode

In real mode, the determination of the linear address of an object is quite simple: the addressing unit multiplies the value of the corresponding segment register by a factor of 16, and then adds the offset. Protected mode, in comparison, requires considerably more steps (see also Figure 3.11).

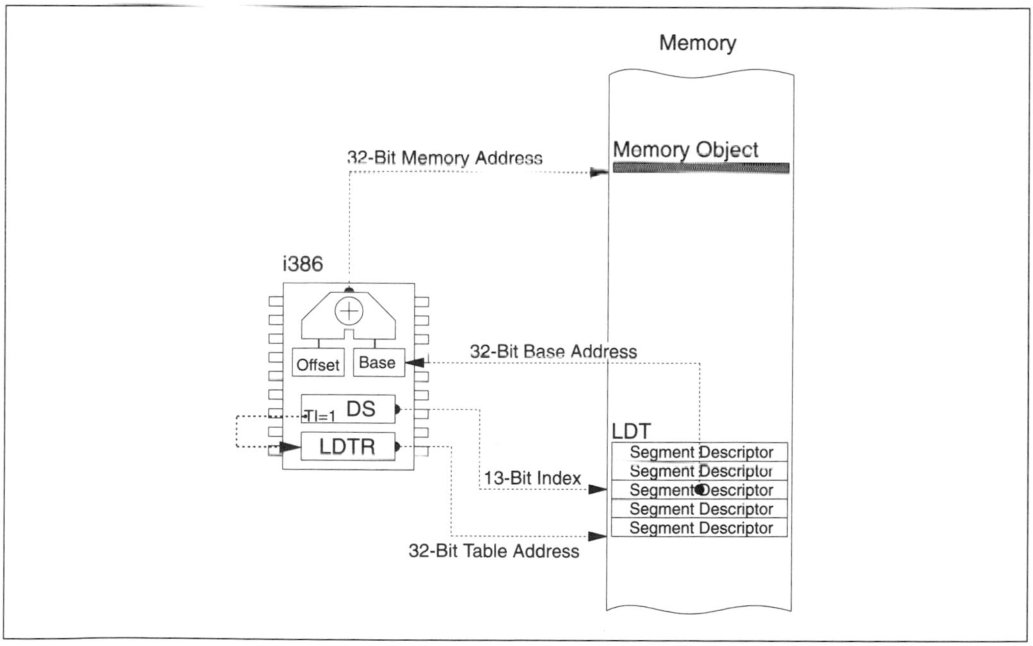

Figure 3.11: Determining a memory address in protected mode.

- With the aid of the segment selector in the applicable segment register, the i386 determines whether the global or the local descriptor table should be used for the access.
- The base address of the global or local descriptor table is determined with the help of the GDTR or LDTR memory management registers, respectively.
- The i386 multiplies the index entry in the segment selector by 8, and adds the result to the base address of the descriptor table.
- With the help of the segment descriptor (8 byte) in the addressed descriptor table, the base address and the limit of the segment are now determined.
- The address adder in the addressing unit of the i386 adds this base address and the offset; furthermore, the i386 checks that the obtained value is less than the limit of the applicable segment; if that is not the case, the processor issues the «general protection fault» exception and the corresponding 0dh interrupt.
- Thus, the determined address represents the linear (and without paging, also the physical) address of the object.

Here, the advantages of the segment descriptor cache register are again clear: mostly with the addressing of an object, the descriptor need not actually be read in as mentioned previously. Often, after the first access to the segment, the required values are already stored in the cache registers. All later accesses can use this on-chip value.

The method described indicates the logical way in which the i386 determines linear (or even physical) addresses. All checks run parallel to the calculation; additionally, after the first access, all important data is already contained in the cache registers. Perhaps somewhat surprisingly, this complicated calculation and check procedure does not result in a loss of performance (in protected mode, the i386 uses a large quantity of additional transistors for this purpose), in comparison to the simple address calculation in real mode. Apart from the instructions that explicitly or implicitly load a new segment descriptor, and so invalidate the applicable entry in the segment descriptor cache register, all memory accesses in protected and real mode are executed at the same speed.

3.7.6 Segment and Access Types

When discussing the segment descriptors in Section 3.7.1 I have only briefly indicated some of the bit fields. Referring to Figure 3.6, I want to detail their meaning now.

The *DT*-bit, just as the four typ bits in the segment descriptor, give the type and rights of an access to the described segment. If DT (*descriptor type*) is set (DT=1), then the described segment is an *application segment*, that is, the segment contains program code or program data. In addition to applications, system routines used for managing the computer down to the kernel level of the operating system also belong to such programs. In comparison, the *system segments* and *gates* (DT=0) describe reserved data structures used to control and monitor a number of parallel running tasks in the computer, or for the call of procedures and jumps to segments with a different privilege level.

Application Segments

If DT=1, the segment is handled like an application segment, so the *type* field in the segment descriptor has the following composition:

Bit	11	10	9	8
Meaning	EXE	E/C	W/R	A

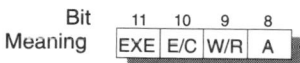

Table 3.2 contains all of the possible combinations of the EXE, E/C, W/R and A-bits and their applicable meaning.

Type	EXE	Content	E	W	A	Meaning
0	0	Data	0	0	0	read only
1	0	Data	0	0	1	read only, accessed
2	0	Data	0	1	0	read/write
3	0	Data	0	1	1	read/write, accessed
4	0	Data	1	0	0	read only, expand down
5	0	Data	1	0	1	read only, expand down, accessed
6	0	Data	1	1	0	read/write, expand down
7	0	Data	1	1	1	read/write, expand down, accessed
8	1	Code	0	0	0	execute only
9	1	Code	0	0	1	execute only, accessed
10	1	Code	0	1	0	execute/read
11	1	Code	0	1	1	execute/read, accessed
12	1	Code	1	0	0	execute only, conforming
13	1	Code	1	0	1	execute only, conforming, accessed
14	1	Code	1	1	0	execute/read, conforming
15	1	Code	1	1	1	execute/read, conforming, accessed

Table 3.2: Application segment types (DT=1)

If the term *data* is interpreted in a wide sense, then any set of information is meant that has a certain meaning. In this sense, programs are also data because they represent (of course) a set of information (a bit sequence) that has a meaning (namely, what the computer has to do). That this kind of information is not always obvious to us is immaterial in this respect.

But in a narrower sense, one distinguishes between data and programs: data is information that has to be processed; programs, on the other hand, are the tools that process the data. The main difference between these two categories is that the data set «program» is usually not changed during the course of program execution, but data should be processed and altered. This differentiation of «data» is also reflected in the segment descriptors: there are executable (that is, program) as well as non-executable (that is, data) segments. This difference is marked by the bit *EXE*: if EXE is equal to 1 then it is a program segment.

Implicitly, data segments are always characterized as readable, but they may only be written if the bit *W* (*write*) is set. A write attempt to a segment with a write bit cleared (W=0) issues an exception «general protection error», and therefore an interrupt 0dh. Stack segments must thus always be marked as writeable (W=1) because the stack is periodically written by PUSH and read by POP. Data segments may differ in the direction in which they «grow». If the *E* (*expand-*

down) bit is set, the segment grows downwards, otherwise it grows upwards. The interpretation of the limit differs in these two cases. With a segment growing upwards (E = 0) the offset must always be smaller than or equal to the limit. On the other hand, with a segment growing downwards (E = 1), the offset must always exhibit a value above the limit. If these conditions are not fulfilled, the i386 issues an exception «general protection error», and therefore an interrupt 0dh. One example of a segment growing downwards is the stack segment, because the stack grows downwards during an expansion (a PUSH instruction) by the decremented stack pointer (ESP). Most other segments, however, grow upwards.

If the i386 accesses data or code in a segment, it automatically sets the *A (accessed)* bit in the applicable descriptor. The operating system can then ascertain which segments are frequently accessed. This is important, to implement swapping of segments. The swap routine of the operating system resets the accessed bits of the loaded segments at regular intervals. Every later access to a segment then sets the A-bit again. Through a periodic evaluation of the set and reset A-bits, the system can determine which segments are frequently, and which segments are infrequently, addressed. The swap routine gives preference to the least used segments, and stores them externally, in order to keep the number of required swaps to a minimum. A similar strategy occurs in the *demand paging* that is supported by the paging unit of the i386. More of this later.

In contrast to data segments, program segments are always implicitly identified as not writeable (read only). The i386 should never attempt a write access to such a code segment, as the «general protection error» exception would be the result. This is part of the protection philosophy of the protected mode, and is used for protection against program errors. A frequent cause of system crashes, in DOS programs, for example, are bugs that overwrite program code. The chances of this occurring are reduced by the write protection of code segments. However, sometimes it is necessary to overwrite code or immediate operands (which are part of the instruction flow and, for this reason, of code segments) during the execution of a program. For this purpose, the implementation of the protected mode allows a data and a code segment to overlap. For example, a segment can be identified as a code segment when a second segment, with the same base and the same limit, is defined as a data segment. In this roundabout way, with the help of a so-called *alias* and the data segment, the i386 can overwrite code. Naturally, this is not without danger because, in principle, the same source of errors mentioned previously can occur.

Through the setting of the *R (Read)* bit in the segment descriptor of a code segment (R = 1), the segment is not only carried out (that is, read from the bus interface, exclusively into the prefetch queue), but a task can, with the help of a MOV instruction, also transfer data from this code segment into a general-purpose register. This is necessary when data (such as immediate operands or tables) is embedded in program segments. Above all, the ROM BIOS of a PC frequently contains embedded tables for the hard disk type, base addresses of the monitor memory, etc., that must be read by the start program of the BIOS when the PC is switched on. If a table is only to be read, it is possible to save a difficult and error-prone alias through the use of the R-bit. The value in the code segment is then only read and not written. In this way, a program crash due to the overwriting of code is prevented.

The segment descriptor has an accessed bit for a code segment, in the same way as for a data segment. Thus, code segments can also be stored in an external memory object through the use of the swap routine. In place of the expand down bit (E-bit) of data segment descriptors, the code segment descriptor provides the *C (Conforming)* bit. Program segments identified as conforming can also be addressed directly by code segments with lower privileges, without the need for a difficult roundabout way through a gate. Typically, all functions of the operating system (such as library and coding functions) that do not use a protected part of the system elements are placed in conforming segments. Thus, applications can access a few critical functions without needing to pass through a call gate.

System Segments

The i386 has three basic types of system segments (Table 3.3), namely a *Task State Segment (TSS), Local Descriptor Table (LDT)* and *Gate*. They are used for memory management (LDT) and the calling of tasks and procedures. If DT is reset (DT=0), a system descriptor describes a system segment. The i386 then interprets the value in the *type* field of the descriptor as shown in Table 3.3. For example, if a local descriptor table is described by a system segment descriptor, the typ field refers to entry 2 (0010b). In addition to the system segments, gates also exist.

Type	Meaning	
0	reserved	
1	available 80286 TSS	System segment
2	LDT	System segment
3	active 80286 TSS	System segment
4	80286 Call Gate	Gate
5	Task Gate (80286+i386)	Gate
6	80286 Interrupt Gate	Gate
7	80286 Trap Gate	Gate
8	reserved	
9	available i386 TSS	System segment
10	reserved	
11	active i386 TSS	System segment
12	i386 Call Gate	Gate
13	reserved	
14	i386 Interrupt Gate	Gate
15	i386 Trap Gate	Gate

Table 3.3: System segment and gate types (DT=0)

Table 3.3 clearly shows that most of the gates and the task state segments for the 80286 and the i386 are different. The cause is the 32-bit architecture of the i386, which in comparison to the 80286 has, for example, 32-bit offsets and permits 32-bit stack values. Due to the need for compatibility, the i386 can use the 80286 system segments with no problems. Naturally, this is not the case in reverse. The TSS defines the condition of an active (busy) or interrupted (available) task; in the i386, it is mainly for the hardware support of multitasking operating systems. Note that TSS and LDT descriptors are only permissible in the GDT as entries, and are not allowed into the LDT. Further TSS and gate details are included below.

The base address entry of a system segment descriptor for an LDT defines the start of the table in the memory, as is the case for a «normal» segment. As the LDT consists of entries each containing eight bytes, the entry limit in the system segment descriptor is the corresponding factor of eight.

In protected mode, the i386 uses so-called *gates* to control task access to data and code in segments with a higher privilege level. The gates implement a substantial protection against unauthorized or incorrect accesses to foreign data and programs. If an application requires operating system functions (for example, to open or close files), then the gates guarantee that the access is error-free, otherwise an exception would be produced. The application cannot bypass the protection mechanism without alerting the operating system. DOS, in comparison, is completely blind. An incorrect access does not necessarily cause an immediately obvious problem in the computer. It is usually only apparent after the system has already crashed. This sometimes makes the debugging of real mode applications quite complicated. If an application attempts to call a function with an incorrect jump address, it is retained by the computer as unforeseeable. In protected mode, the gates define the access to foreign routines for applications. You will learn more about gates in the next section.

3.7.7 Control Transfer and Call Gates

A near call or a near jump transfers control to a procedure or an instruction that is located in the same segment as the CALL or JMP instruction. Such a transfer only changes the value of the instruction pointer EIP, and the i386 simply checks whether EIP exceeds the limit of the segment. If the offset lies within the correct area, the call or jump is carried out, otherwise, the i386 sends out the usual «general protection error» exception.

Tasks, however, are rarely made up of only one code segment. Many code segments are usually present. An access to a code segment other than the active one causes, for example, a far call, a far jump or an interrupt. In all three cases, the current segment selector in the code segment register is replaced by a new one. In real mode, such an *intersegment call* simply loads the instruction pointer EIP and the code segment CS with the appropriate new values that give the entry point of the routine. Naturally, this is not so easy in protected mode; the loading of a code segment requires an extensive check procedure.

For a far call or a far jump three different possibilities are available:

- If the target segment of the call or jump has the same Privilege Level (PL) as the segment from which the call originates, then the i386 carries out the far call by directly loading the target segment selector into the code segment CS. In this case, the i386 simply checks whether the new value in the instruction pointer EIP exceeds the set area of the limit entry in the target segment, and whether the typ of the target segment (EXE=0 or 1) is consistent with the call.
- If the target segment is indicated as conforming, and its privilege level is higher than that of the initial segment, then the far call is carried out in the same way as described for the previous example. The i386 then carries out the code in the conforming segment with a privilege level (CPL) that corresponds to the lower privilege level of the called segment, and

not to the higher privilege level of the conforming segment. This prevents programs with lower privilege levels from obtaining higher privilege levels through the back-door use of a conforming segment, and so from achieving accesses to protected system areas.

- If the target segment has a different privilege level to the initial segment, and it is not identified as conforming, the far call can only be accomplished through the use of a call gate.

In the first two cases, the i386 simply loads the target segment selector into the CS register, loads the instruction pointer value into EIP, and then executes the program. This is similar (with the exception of checking) to a far call or far jump in real mode. In the latter case, on the other hand, the segment selector of the target segment for the far call or far jump doesn't point first to the target segment itself but to a so-called *call gate*.

The handling of interrupts is generally an inherent and also critical function of the operating system kernel, because interrupts immediately affect the computer. Therefore, an interrupt call usually results in a change of the privilege level (for example, when an application with PL=3 is stopped with an interrupt, and an interrupt handler in the kernel with PL=0 is called). The interrupt must use an interrupt or trap gate to activate the interrupt handler (see below). I will explain the use of task gates in the multitasking section.

The call, interrupt and trap gates permit jumping to a routine in another segment with a different privilege level. Gates are defined by the DT=0 bit in the segment descriptor, and a value of the type field from 4 to 7 and from 12 to 15. They are also part of the system segments. Table 3.3 shows all of the gate descriptors that are valid for the i386.

The organization of i386 *gate descriptors* is represented in Figure 3.12. Call gates are not only used to call procedures using a far call, but also for all unconditional and conditional jump instructions using a far jump. Call gates can be used in local and the global descriptor tables, but not in the interrupt descriptor table. Here, only trap and task gates are allowed.

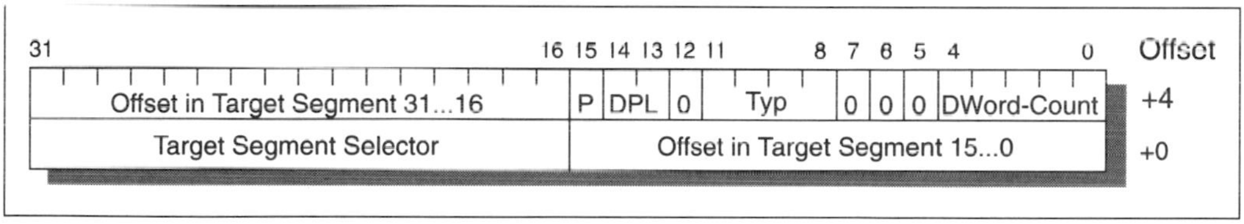

Figure 3.12: Format of an i386 gate descriptor.

As Figure 3.12 clearly shows, the organization of a gate descriptor is very different to that of a «normal» segment descriptor. For example, the base address of the segment is missing. In its place, a 5-bit field *DWord count* is provided, and the bits from 5 to 7 in the second descriptor double word are set to 0. Additionally, the second word is reserved for a segment selector. It defines the target segment for the far call or far jump and, together with the offset in the least significant and most significant word, gives the jump address. To actually allocate the jump address in the i386, a further descriptor access is necessary. The gate finally contains only the target segment selector, not its linear address. In this way, the i386 grabs two segment descriptors (Figure 3.13) for a far call or a far jump through a call gate. The first access loads the gate descriptor, and the second then loads the base address of the applicable segment. The addressing unit of the i386 adds this base address of the target segment, set by the segment selector in the gate descriptor, to the offset given by the gate descriptor. The resulting value represents the jump address.

With an entry in the type field, the i386 knows whether the target segment selector for the CS register of a far call or a far jump directly represents a code segment or a gate descriptor. In the first case, the processor checks whether the direct call is permitted (such as whether or not the target segment is identified as conforming), and depending on this, whether it should be carried out or an exception produced. In the latter case, in comparison, it first loads the segment descriptor given by the call gate.

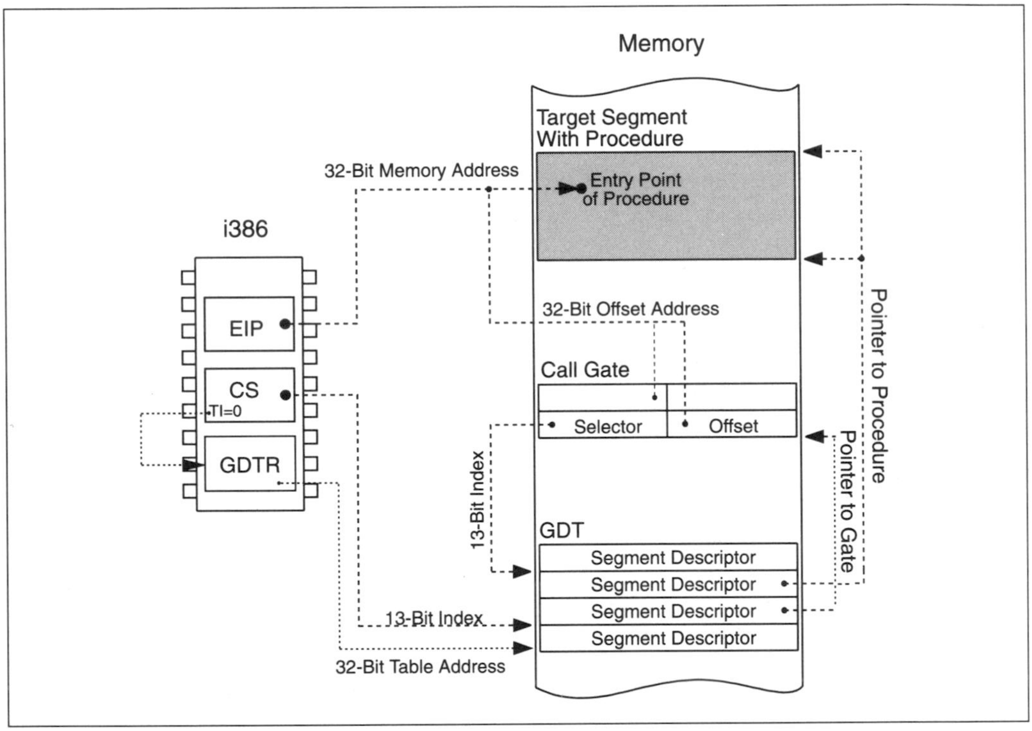

Figure 3.13: Far call via a gate and a segment descriptor.

The meaning and purpose of this strategy lies in the fact that a gate defines an exact and correct jump point, so that the applicable code cannot give an incorrect call or jump target. This is especially important if the code calls operating system functions. An incorrect jump point in these routines normally leads to a total system crash; an incorrect gate, on the other hand, only causes the loss of the task and the production of an error message.

I have already mentioned that each task of the four different privilege levels has its own stack. Naturally, data must be transferred between these tasks frequently, so that the code of a different level has access to the data of the called code. For this access, the system or the compiler/assembler carries the number of double words (each of four bytes) to be copied, in the field Dword count. With a call to the call gate, the i386 automatically transfers these words from the stack of the calling to the stack of the called procedure. With these five bits, a maximum of 31 double words (that is, 124 bytes) can be transferred. This should be sufficient for the transfer of parameters; if not, it is possible to construct a far pointer to transfer a data structure containing the required parameters.

Due to compatibility, the i386 can also use 80286 gates. The 80286 gates are only different in that bits 31 to 16 are reserved (equal 0) for the target offset of the call or jump, and that the Dword count field does not indicate double words but normal 16-bit words. The reason for this restriction is the 16-bit architecture of the 80286. If the i386 comes across an 80286 gate, it interprets the DWord count field as a word count, and only copies the corresponding number of words (each of 16 bits). Obviously, the i386 also checks the access privileges for a call through a gate. The following privilege levels are used in this checking:

- CPL;
- RPL of the segment selector for the call gate;
- DPL of the gate descriptor;
- DPL of the segment descriptor for the target segment of the call or jump.

The DPL entry of the gate descriptor sets which privilege level should be used for the gate. Gates are used, for example, to transfer control at the highest privileged levels (e.g. the operating system) or code of the same privilege level. In the latter case, this is not absolutely necessary (it is also possible directly, as explained previously), but always possible. Note that only call instructions, and not jump instructions, can use gates to call routines with a lower privilege level (higher PL). Jump instructions, can only use call gates for a control transfer to a code segment with the same privilege level, or to a conforming segment with the same or a higher privilege level. For a jump instruction to a segment that is not identified as conforming, the different privilege levels must fulfil the following conditions:

- The value of the Effective Privilege Level (which is the maximum of CPL and RPL) must be smaller than, or the same as, the DPL value of the gate descriptor.
- The DPL of the target segment descriptor must be the same as the CPL of the applicable program.

In comparison, for the execution of a CALL or a jump instruction to a conforming segment, the following conditions must be met:

- The value of the Effective Privilege Level (which is the maximum of CPL and RPL) must be smaller than, or the same as, the DPL value of the gate descriptor.
- The DPL value of the target segment descriptor must be less than or equal to the CPL value of the applicable program.

For a call through a call gate of a procedure with a higher privilege level, the i386 does the following:

- The CPL value is changed so that it reflects the new privilege level.
- The i386 transfers control to the called procedure or the addressed data.
- In place of the previously used stack, the stack of the new privilege level is used.

In this way, the stacks of all privilege levels are defined in the Task State Segment (TSS) of the relevant tasks (see the next section).

Perhaps I should stress here that all of these extensive checks are carried out by the i386 *automatically and independently*, without the corresponding presence of a software instruction in the instruction flow. In place of these software instructions, extensive microprograms stored in the microcode ROM of the i386 monitor on-line all accesses in protected mode.

3.7.8 Interrupt Descriptor Table

In addition to the registers for the global and local descriptor tables and the task register, the i386 has a further register for the *interrupt descriptor table* (*IDT*; Figure 3.14). In real mode, the 1024 (1k) least significant bytes of the address space are reserved for the 256 entries of the interrupt vector table, corresponding to the 256 interrupts of the i386. Every table entry contains the jump address (target) of the applicable interrupt handler in the segment:offset format.

Also in protected mode, the 256 i386 interrupts from 0 to 255 are available. Contrary to real mode, the interrupt handlers are no longer addressed with a double word in the segment:offset format, but through a gate. Only task, interrupt and trap gates are permitted as entries in the IDT, and every entry contains eight instead of four bytes. To even things up, through the entry limit in the IDTR (Figure 3.14), the actual size requirements of the interrupt descriptor table can be adapted. If, for example, a system only requires the 64 interrupts from 0 to 63, an IDT with 64 entries of eight bytes is sufficient (that is, 512 bytes). If an interrupt is issued for which there is no longer an entry in the IDT (in this case, for example, an INT 64), the i386 switches into shutdown mode and signals this through the corresponding level of the signals COD/$\overline{\text{INTA}}$, M/$\overline{\text{IO}}$, $\overline{\text{S1}}$, $\overline{\text{S0}}$ and A1 (see Section 4.1). Because the IDTR indicates both the IDT limit and the IDT base address, the table can be located anywhere in memory (Figure 3.14).

Before the i386 can be switched into protected mode, the initialization program that runs in real mode must compose the IDT as well as the GDT, and load the base address and limit into the IDTR. If this does not occur, the system will crash with an almost 100% certainty, before the IDT can be made available in protected mode. The initialization table refers somewhere (exactly where it is not possible to say) for each exception and interrupt, or issues a further exception error that cannot be handled. When switched on, or when the processor is reset, the i386 loads a value of 000000h for the base address, and 03ffh for the limit, from the IDTR. These values correspond to the reserved area for the interrupt vector table in real mode.

The interrupt, trap and task gates have the same composition as a call gate (Figure 3.12). Only the Dword count entry has no use. Interrupt and trap gates define entry points in a handler, through the offset and segment selector entries, in the same way as the call gate. The segment selector, like the call gate, refers to the applicable segment descriptor in the LDT or GDT that contains the base address of the corresponding segment. In this way, the entry point of the interrupt handler is clear and correctly defined. Interrupt and trap gates differ in that an interrupt call through an interrupt gate resets the IE and T flags; the trap gate, on the other hand, does not.

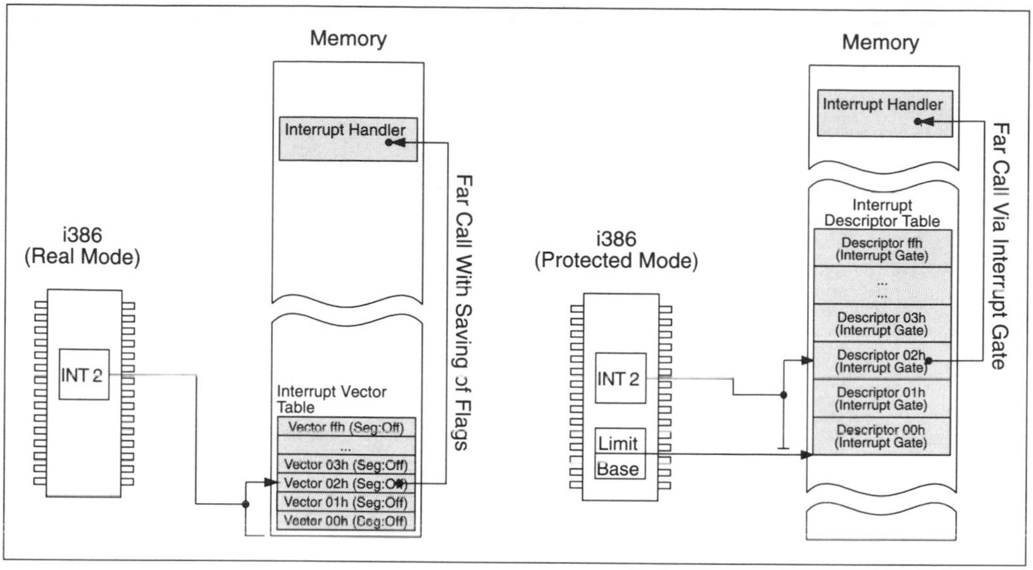

Figure 3.14: Interrupt tables in real and protected mode. In real mode the interrupt number is simply multiplied by four to evaluate the offset in the segment 00h where the applicable interrupt vector is stored. In protected mode the IDTR points to a descriptor table which holds the gates to the corresponding interrupt handlers.

In the following section I will explain what the i386 does if it meets a task gate during the execution of an interrupt, CALL or jump instruction.

3.7.9 Multitasking, TSS and Task Gates

The protection functions of the i386, above all, have an overriding purpose, namely the support of a multitasking operating system through i386 hardware. With an efficient PC system, a number of tasks should, more or less, run in parallel. Actually, a processor only appears to execute tasks in parallel; the separate tasks are only carried out for a short time, and then interrupted; after another short period they are restarted again at the same point. To achieve this, the condition of the task at the point of interruption must be completely protected, otherwise the task will not be restarted at the same position or under the conditions present at the time of the interruption.

A similar, if also clearer and simpler operation already occurs under MS-DOS. If a hardware interrupt occurs, such as a timer interrupt, for example, then the processor saves all registers on the stack, the interrupt is executed, and all of the registers are again loaded with the old values from the stack. With this, it is very important that the CS:EIP register pair is saved, because it gives the position in the program where it has been interrupted.

It is no doubt sensible, due to the extensive protection functions of the i386 and the requirements of a number of tasks running in parallel, not just to save only the two CS and EIP registers. Much more about this is provided in the subsequently described system segment, with «Task State Segment», or TSS for short. It represents a complete segment that is exclusively used for storing the condition of a task. Figure 3.15 shows the composition of the TSS.

31 ... 16	15 ... 0	Offset
I/O Map Base	0 0 0 0 0 0 0 0 0 0 0 0 0 0 0 T	+100 (64h)
0 0 0 0 0 0 0 0 0 0 0 0 0 0 0 0	Task LDT Selector	+96 (60h)
0 0 0 0 0 0 0 0 0 0 0 0 0 0 0 0	GS Selector	+92 (5ch)
0 0 0 0 0 0 0 0 0 0 0 0 0 0 0 0	FS Selector	+88 (58h)
0 0 0 0 0 0 0 0 0 0 0 0 0 0 0 0	DS Selector	+84 (54h)
0 0 0 0 0 0 0 0 0 0 0 0 0 0 0 0	SS Selector	+80 (50h)
0 0 0 0 0 0 0 0 0 0 0 0 0 0 0 0	CS Selector	+76 (4ch)
0 0 0 0 0 0 0 0 0 0 0 0 0 0 0 0	ES Selector	+72 (48h)
EDI		+68 (44h)
ESI		+64 (40h)
EBP		+60 (3ch)
ESP		+56 (38h)
EBX		+52 (34h)
EDX		+48 (30h)
ECX		+44 (2ch)
EAX		+40 (28h)
EFLAG		+36 (24h)
EIP		+32 (20h)
CR3 (PDBR)		+28 (1ch)
0 0 0 0 0 0 0 0 0 0 0 0 0 0 0 0	SS for CPL2	+24 (18h)
ESP for CPL2		+20 (14h)
0 0 0 0 0 0 0 0 0 0 0 0 0 0 0 0	SS for CPL1	+16 (10h)
ESP for CPL1		+12 (0ch)
0 0 0 0 0 0 0 0 0 0 0 0 0 0 0 0	SS for CPL0	+8 (08h)
ESP for CPL0		+4 (04h)
0 0 0 0 0 0 0 0 0 0 0 0 0 0 0 0	Back Link to Previous TSS	+0 (00h)

Figure 3.15: i386 task state segment (TSS).

In addition to the usual offset and segment registers in the TSS, there is also the ESP pointer and segment SS for the stacks of the different privilege levels, the selector for the local descriptor table (LDT) used by the task, and the saved CR3 register which gives the base address of the page directory for the described task (see Section 3.8). The *I/O map base* entry gives the address of an I/O map which is used together with the IOPL flag for the protection of the I/O address space in protected mode. You will find more concerning this subject later. The *back link* field contains a segment selector that refers to the TSS of the previous interrupted task. The entry is only valid if the *NT*-bit (Nested Task) in the EFlag register is set. If the T-bit (debug trap bit) is set and there is a task switch (for example, when the TSS is loaded), the i386 produces a debug exception and the corresponding interrupt 1.

If the corresponding TSS descriptor in the LDT or GDT refers to the value 1 in the typ field (80286 compatible TSS) or the value 9 (i386 TSS), the TSS described by the descriptor is available. The task described by the TSS can be started. If an entry 3 is located in the typ field (80286 compatible TSS) or 11 (i386 TSS), the TSS is identified as active (busy). A task described by such a TSS is active and need not be expressly activated. That aside, it must not be activated, because the stored TSS still contains the old values. In principle, contrary to procedures, tasks are not re-entrant. First, when the current (active) task is interrupted (to activate another task, for instance), the i386 saves all the current values of the active task in the corresponding TSS, and then loads the values of the task to be started into the segment, offset and control registers. This occurs entirely *automatically*, without the further influence of software.

How then, does the i386 know when to interrupt a task, and which new task it should reactivate, that is, what forms the trigger for a task switch? The key lies in the task gates. Figure 3.16 shows the construction of such a task gate. Note that there is no difference between the structure of the task gates for the 80286 and the i386, contrary to the other gates and system segments.

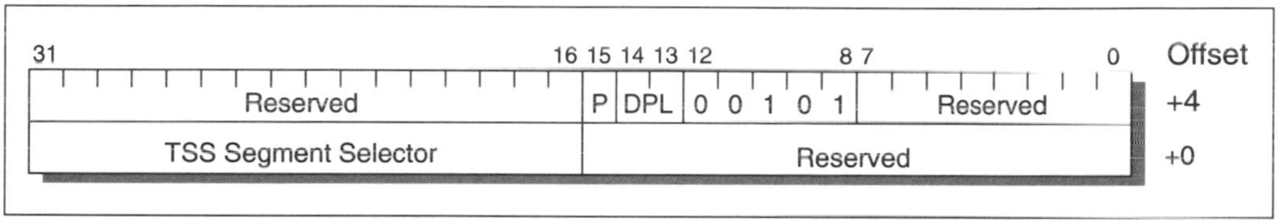

Figure 3.16: Task gate descriptor.

The TSS segment selector in the task gate refers to the segment descriptor that is described by the TSS of the activated task. If the i386 encounters a task gate during the execution of a CALL instruction, a jump instruction or an interrupt, then it carries out a so-called *task switch*. The i386 stores the condition of the currently active task into the TSS set by the TR task register (Figure 3.8), and writes the value 1 (80286 compatible TSS) or 9 (i386 TSS) into the type field of the applicable TSS descriptor. In this way, the TSS is identified as an available TSS. Finally, the i386 loads the new TSS segment selector from the task gate descriptor into the task register and reads in the base address, limit, and access privileges of the task gate descriptor from the LDT or GDT (depending on which table of the segment selector is referred to in the task gate). To conclude the task switch, the processor identifies the applicable TSS descriptor in the type field as busy, that is, it writes the value 3 (80286 compatible TSS) or 11 (i386 TSS) into this field. Finally, the i386 loads the values for the segments and offsets stored in the new TSS into the corresponding register. The CS:EIP register pair now points to the instruction of the newly activated task that was interrupted previously; its execution is then continued from the point of interruption. Figure 3.17 shows the four ways in which a task switch can be initiated, and the processes by which the i386 accomplishes them. Tasks called for the first time – that is, tasks that are newly loaded – are activated by the i386 in the same way. Here, the CS:EIP register pair refer to the start instruction of the program, and not to the instruction at the point of interruption.

Example: The active task is the word processor Word, which is currently performing page formatting. Now a timer interrupt occurs. During the processing of the corresponding interrupt handler, the i386 encounters a task gate which points to dBase. The i386 suspends executing Word by saving all registers in the TSS of Word. Afterwards it loads all necessary data from the dBase TSS and restarts this earlier suspended task. After a short time another timer interrupt occurs. But now dBase is suspended, and instead the C compiler is activated. This permanent suspending and restarting of tasks is carried out continuously and very quickly.

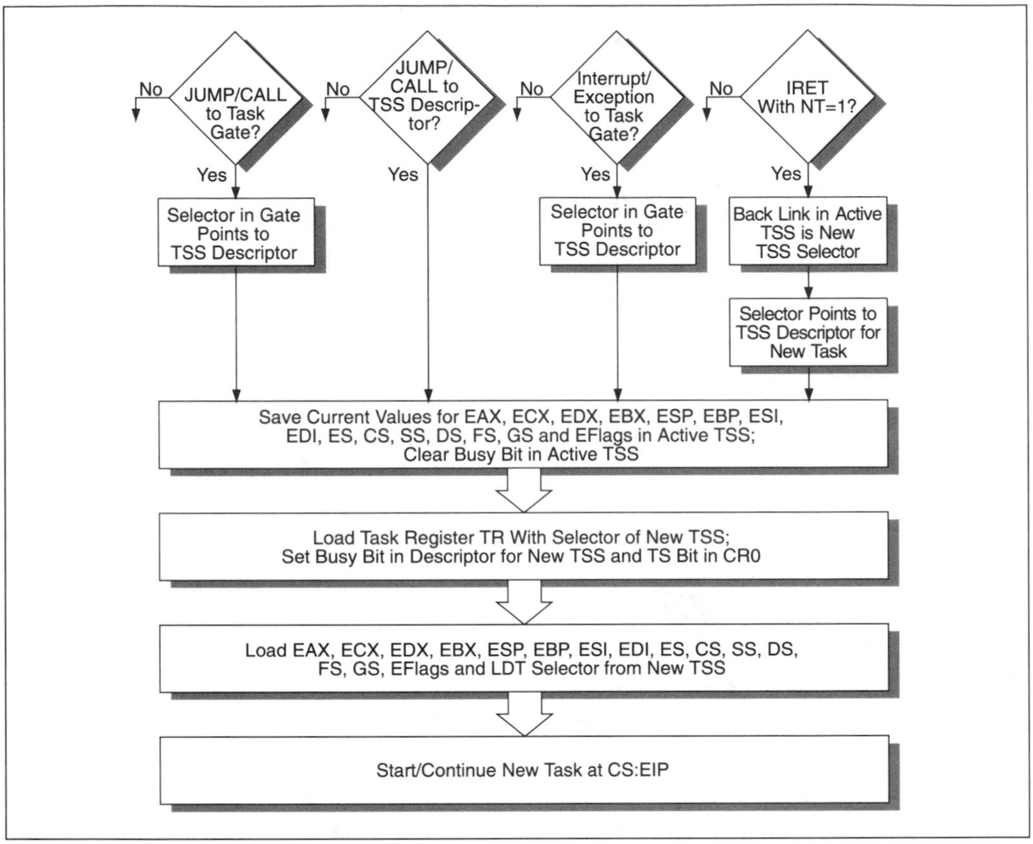

Figure 3.17: Issuing and executing a task switch. The i386 executes a task switch if a JUMP or CALL instruction encounters a task gate or a TSS descriptor, an interrupt or an exception hits a task gate, or if an IRET instruction occurs with a set NT bit.

When a new task is started, the operating system provides a new TSS for this task. A multitasking operating system is quite complicated, and must be able to carry out very complex operations quickly. OS/2, UNIX and Windows NT are examples of multitasking operating systems (or operating system extensions), and, to a lesser extent, also normal Windows (in which the tasks themselves decide when to pass control to another task, that is, when to permit a task switch). Multitasking operating systems are very effectively supported by the i386: the operating system only has to provide a task gate, a TSS descriptor and a TSS for the task switch. The i386 saves the old contents of the registers and loads the new values independently and automatically. No software instruction to the operating system is necessary: during a task switch, the i386 saves the 104 bytes of the old TSS and loads the 104 bytes of the new TSS completely independently.

It is the operating system's responsibility to allocate a suitable amount of processor time to each of the separate tasks. The control of task switches can only be achieved by the operating system; the programs themselves are unable to influence the process in a true multitasking operating system such as OS/2 or Windows NT. Windows (without NT) is significantly different. Here, the Windows application (and not Windows as the operating system extension) decides when to transfer control to another task (another application or Windows itself). A very uncomfortable effect is that a PC running Windows seems to ignore or to respond quite late to intended task switch requests (via Ctrl-ESC, for example). «Real» multitasking operating systems, on the other hand, carry out a so-called *preemptive multitasking*; Windows, however, has *non-preemptive multitasking*.

Now an important warning: the well-known and popular DOS operating system doesn't use any of the functions indicated above. Also, the SMARTDRV.SYS and RAMDRIVE.SYS drivers only build up one GDT and one IDT to move byte groups between the lower 1 Mbyte of memory and extended memory. Task switches and the extensive and very useful access checks are not used in any form.

Besides these checks and special properties when calling procedures, or during the course of switching between several tasks, a system programmer has to pay attention to many other restrictions and precautions. It is now possible to program a fully functional operating system that uses all the features of the 80286. This subject could fill two books with no problem: I want to be content with this basic course. In the next section, only the protection strategies for the second 80286 address space (namely, the access checks for the I/O address space) are described.

3.7.10 I/O Address Space Protection via the IOPL Flag

In general, the i386 communicates with the registers in external hardware components (such as the hard disk controller or the control register of the DMA chip) through the I/O ports. However, control and monitoring of the hardware is the responsibility of the operating system alone. For this it mainly uses drivers with the privilege level PL=1. The I/O address range is thus also included in the access protection area in protected mode. Ports, however, are not addressed with the help of a segment register, and so this form of access protection is not available here.

The i386 accomplishes the protection of the I/O address space with two completely different strategies: the IOPL flag in the flag register (Figure 2.8), and additionally, the I/O permission bit map in the Task State Segment (TSS). First, the IOPL flag.

The value of the IOPL flag is set by the minimum privilege level that a code segment must refer to, to access the address space, i.e. CPL ≤ IOPL. If the CPL value of the active task is greater (that is, it has a lower privilege level), the IN, OUT, INS and OUTS I/O instructions lead to the already well-known «general protection error» exception. Rational applications running under a rational operating system carry out such accesses exclusively through the operating system. A few rational applications under an irrational operating system (such as DOS) do this directly, in some cases to increase the performance, and in other cases to enable communication with specific components. In addition to the above-mentioned immediate I/O instructions, the CLI and

STI instructions also depend upon the IOPL flag. The six instructions together are known as *IOPL sensitive* instructions, in that the value of the IOPL flag has an influence on their execution.

The grounds for this restriction become clear immediately if we consider the following situation: a system function reads, for example, a data set from the hard disk, and is interrupted by a task switch, and the newly activated task then immediately communicates with the control register in the controller using an I/O instruction. If, in protected mode, the second immediate access to the control register was not strictly forestalled by the protection of the I/O space using an exception, the system routine interrupted by the task switch would be in a completely different condition after its reactivation. The PC ignores or, worse, deletes such data.

There is no explicit instruction available for changing the IOPL flag (such as CLI or STI for the interrupt flag). This is only possible in the i386 with the POPF (POP flags) and the PUSHF (PUSH flags) instructions. These two instructions are, however, privileged; they can only be executed in a code segment with the highest privilege level of CPL=0. This is usually reserved for the operating system kernel – applications, therefore, cannot change the IOPL flag. When this is attempted, the processor issues (once again) the «general protection error» exception. The flags are part of the TSS and so can be different from task to task. It is possible that one task has access to part of the I/O address space, but another task has not.

This global security strategy for the I/O address space using the IOPL flag is already implemented in the 80286. Additionally, the i386 can individually protect the ports. This protection strategy for the ports is implemented in particular with regard to the virtual 8086 mode.

3.7.11 I/O Address Space Protection via the I/O Permission Bit Map

In addition to the global protection through the IOPL flag, the i386 has a further protection mechanism for accesses to the I/O address space, namely the so-called *I/O permission bit map*. It is part of the TSS of the respective task, so that different tasks can refer to different I/O permission bit maps. The *I/O map base* entry in the TSS descriptor gives the offset within the TSS where the corresponding I/O permission bit map begins. It stretches to the end of the TSS, as it defines the limit entry of the i386 TSS descriptor. Therefore, the I/O permission bit map need not begin immediately after the entries for the register in the TSS. Moreover, an almost arbitrary sized area can lie between the I/O map base entry and the start of the I/O permission bit map; this space can be used by the operating system for storing information. Figure 3.18 schematically shows the I/O permission bit map in the i386 TSS. Note that the most significant byte of the map (the byte immediately before the end of the TSS) must have the value 11111111b (ffh). Only an i386 TSS can be used for the I/O permission bit map; an 80286 TSS cannot be used as it has no I/O map base entry.

A valid I/O permission bit map is present if the I/O map base is contained in the TSS. If the value indicates a base outside the TSS, the i386 ignores all of the checks that are associated with the I/O permission bit map. In that case, access protection for the I/O address space is only accomplished with the IOPL flag.

The I/O permission bit map is an access protection of the second level: if the value of the CPL and IOPL for the active task permits an access to the I/O address space, the i386 additionally examines the I/O permission bit map to determine whether the required port can actually be addressed. The basis for this is the one-to-one association between the I/O address and the corresponding bit in the map. This means that the port with the address 0 is associated with the bit contained in the map that has an offset of 0, and the port with the address 1 is associated with the bit that has an offset of 1, etc. When the bit in the map corresponding to the port is set (equals 1), and there is an access to the applicable port, the i386 issues the «general protection error» exception. If this bit is reset, the processor continues with the I/O operation.

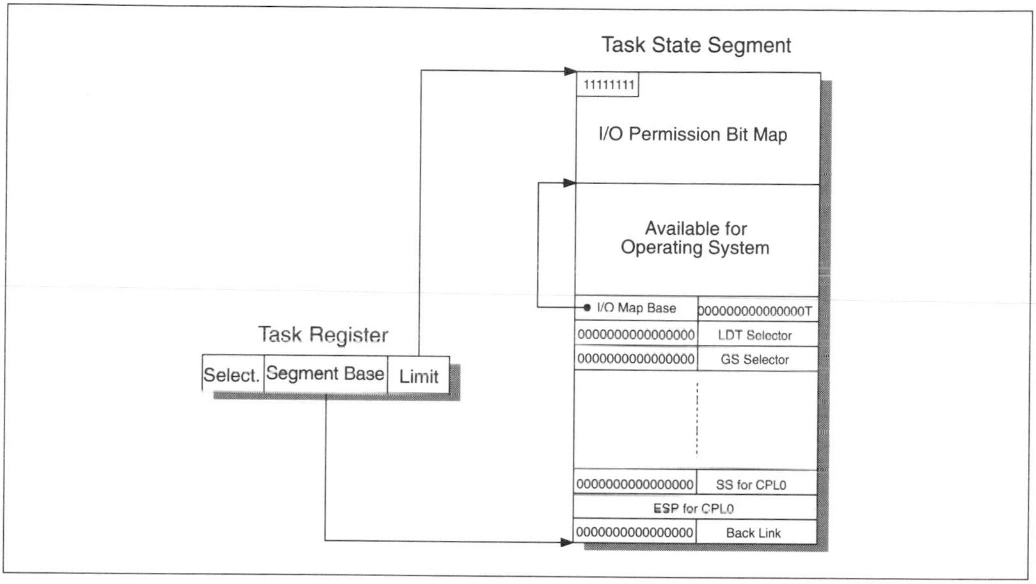

Figure 3.18: The I/O permission bit map in the i386 TSS. The i386 protects the I/O address space not only by means of the IOPL flag in a global manner, but additionally via the I/O permission bit map which is stored in the i386 TSS. A set bit protects the corresponding port and gives rise to an exception if an unauthorized access attempt occurs.

The length of the map sets the additional number of protected ports. It is, therefore, not necessary for the I/O permission bit map to cover all of the available I/O addresses. All of the ports that are not included in the map are automatically assigned a set bit. An access to a port that is not included in the map automatically produces an exception. In an ISA PC, it is sufficient, for example, to protect the 3ffh least significant ports using a map. An access to ports with a higher address can only mean a program error, because beyond these I/O addresses, no more physical ports are available. The i386 automatically issues an exception. You can again see that the protection mechanism of the protected mode not only protects programs and the system, but it also offers a substantially simpler method for localizing bugs. To protect the complete I/O address space with its 64k 8-bit ports, a total of (64k ports)/(8 bits for every byte) + (8-bit 11111111), that is, 8193 bytes are necessary.

A 16-bit port has two, and a 32-bit port has four, sequential bits assigned to it. Only if both, or all four, respectively, assigned bits are simultaneously reset can the i386 perform an I/O operation. If only one of the bits equals 1, the processor issues an exception.

Example:

```
The bit map is          11111111 11001101 00110000 11010100
                        end of the map          map

1st case: 8-bit ports
locked ports        2, 4, 6, 7, 12, 13, 16, 18, 19, 22, 23
unlocked ports      0, 1, 3, 5, 8, 9, 10, 11, 14, 15, 17, 20, 21
2nd case: 16-Bit-Ports
locked ports        2, 4, 6, 12, 16, 18, 22
unlocked ports      0, 8, 10, 14, 20
3rd case:
locked ports        0, 8, 12, 16, 20
unlocked port       8
The 8-bit, 16-bit and 32-bit ports can also, of course, be mixed depending on the register
width of the I/O device at the corresponding address.
```

I would like to mention at this point that the i386 does not use the IOPL flag in virtual 8086 mode; it achieves protection of the I/O address space exclusively through the I/O permission bit map. In this way, the i386 can emulate the characteristics of the 8086, for an 8086 program that runs in virtual 8086 mode, under a protected mode operating system. The I/O permission bit map is especially implemented with regard to the virtual 8086 mode.

3.7.12 Protected Mode Exceptions

In protected mode, in comparison to real mode, more exceptions are implemented, whose main purpose is to indicate error conditions. The reason for these new exceptions lies in the additional checks required for protected mode. The following list contains the new exceptions:

- Double fault (exception 8): If two exceptions occur, one after the other (e.g. an exception occurring when the handler is called after a previous exception), before the first can be handled, and it is not possible for the i386 to carry out both of the exceptions, then the i386 issues an interrupt 8. In this case, the i386 cannot always handle both exceptions sequentially, if both in each case represent an exception 0 (division by 0), 9 (coprocessor segment overflow), 10 (invalid task state segment), 11 (segment not available), 12 (stack exception) or 13 (general protection error). For example, if exceptions 11 and 13 occur, an exception 8 is produced.
- Coprocessor segment overflow (exception 9): if a part of a coprocessor operand is protected or not available, the i386 issues an interrupt 9.
- Invalid task state segment (exception 10): every task switch with an invalid TSS produces an interrupt 10 (0ah). The reason for this is an inconsistency in the TSS (e.g. the segment indicated by CS cannot be carried out, or a selector exceeds the applicable table limit).
- Segment not available (exception 11): if the i386 attempts to access a segment that is not available in the memory, that is, the present bit is reset in the corresponding descriptor, then the i386 issues an interrupt 11 (0bh).
- Stack exception (exception 12): if an instruction attempts to exceed the stack segment limit, or the segment indicated by SS is not available in the memory (for example, after a task switch), then the i386 issues an interrupt 12 (0ch).

- General protection error (exception 13): if the protection rules in the protected mode of the i386 are violated, and the cause cannot be associated with one of the exceptions 8–12, then interrupt 13 (0dh) is the result.
- Coprocessor error (exception 16): if the coprocessor functions are not emulated by a software library in the i386 (the EM-bit in the CR0 control register equals 0), and the i386 has an active signal from the coprocessor at the $\overline{\text{ERROR}}$ pin (a low level signal), then the i386 sends out an interrupt 16 (10h). The active $\overline{\text{ERROR}}$ signal indicates an error condition in the coprocessor (for example, an underflow or an overflow).

3.7.13 Summary of Protection Mechanisms in Protected Mode

The protection mechanisms in the protected mode of the i386 apply mainly to instructions that read and control the condition of the CPU, or that access code and data segments. In this way, incorrect or inadequate instructions that crash the system or block the CPU should be prevented (such as an erroneously placed HLT instruction). In addition, protected mode should prevent data and code segments from being used incorrectly and, thereby, affecting the system integrity. For this purpose, the i386 implements three groups of protection mechanisms:

- Restricted usage of segments: for example, code segments, in principle, cannot be written to, and data segments can only be written to if the write bit (bit W) is set. Accessible segments are written to through the GDT or LDT; all other segments cannot be reached by the task.
- Restricted access to segments: the different privilege levels, and the use of CPL, DPL, EPL and RPL, restrict the access of programs with a specific privilege level (CPL, RPL and EPL) to data and code of other segments (DPL). Permitted call-up mechanisms (call gate, etc.) are the only possible exceptions).
- Privileged instructions: instructions that immediately influence the condition of the CPU (such as LGDT and LLDT), or that change the descriptor tables, can only be executed by tasks with CPL or IOPL values of a higher privilege level.

In protected mode, if one of these protection mechanisms is violated, the i386 immediately issues an error exception.

3.7.14 BIOS Access to Extended Memory

The AT BIOS has two functions, 87h and 89h of interrupt INT 15h, for moving data blocks between the first 1 Mbyte of memory and extended memory and for switching the processor into protected mode. The functions are described in Appendix L, together with the call formats. Additionally, the HIMEM.SYS driver is available as a programming interface.

3.7.15 Interface to Hardware in Protected Mode – the ABIOS

All routines of the conventional Personal Computer BIOS are programmed in real mode, and therefore cannot be used by the i386 in protected mode. Moreover, the BIOS was designed for a single tasking operating system, so that every BIOS call must be completed before the BIOS routine returns control to the calling task. Thus the BIOS processes a call in one stage (also called *single-staged processing*). For fast executable functions such as reading the internal system clock, this is of no importance. But in a multitasking environment, processes that have to wait for the reaction of a rather slow hardware device (for example, the floppy drive) lock the PC. The time necessary to start the drive motors alone is nearly infinitely long for a fast-clocked i386. The *ABIOS* (*advanced BIOS*) has to solve these problems, and to implement an interface to hardware for a multitasking operating system in protected mode. For calls that may last for a longer time, the ABIOS implements a so-called *multistaged processing*. Figure 3.19 shows a comparison of the various processing models for the conventional BIOS (also called *CBIOS*) and for the ABIOS.

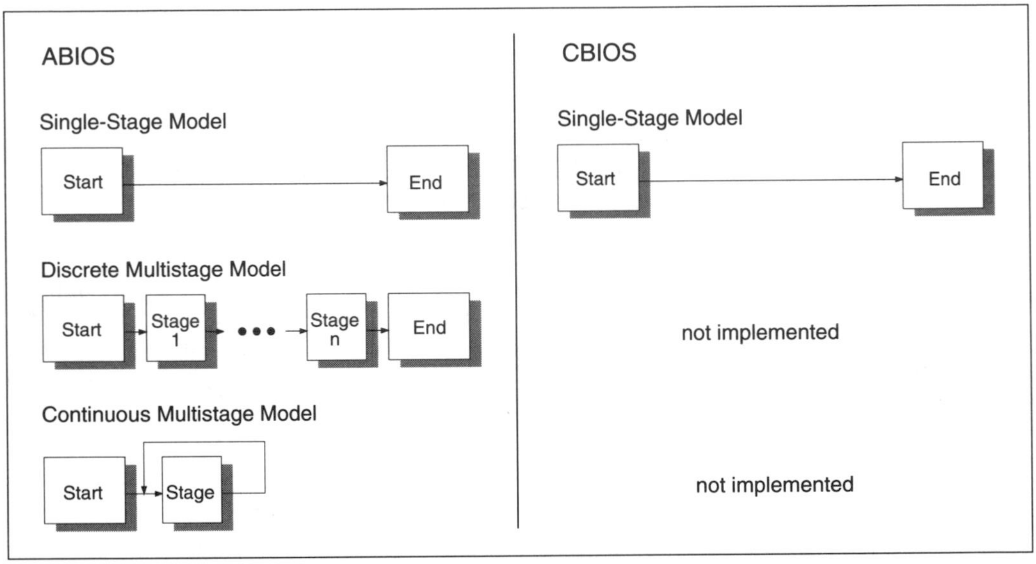

Figure 3.19: Processing models of CBIOS and ABIOS.

The CBIOS only implements the already mentioned single-staged model in the form of a *call-processing-return*. The call of a CBIOS function dedicates the CPU to the processing of this call. Only hardware interrupts are serviced. The ABIOS only uses the single-staged model for functions that can be completed at once, such as reading the internal system clock (here only an immediately executable memory access to the data structure of the system clock is necessary).

All other ABIOS calls proceed according to a discrete or continuous multistaged model, where each stage can be executed at once. All necessary wait processes are carried out between the individual stages, thus the CPU is not locked. For example, during an access to the hard disk, in one stage the seek instructions for the read/write heads are transferred to the controller. Then the ABIOS immediately returns control so that the CPU is available for another task. Once the drive has positioned the heads correctly, the controller issues an interrupt and the next stage of the ABIOS function is called. This example shows how the individual stages are called, that is, how the multistaged functions are driven. One possibility is a hardware interrupt that the accessed device issues if it is ready for the next function stage (floppy and hard disk drives, for example). Another possibility is the activation of individual stages after the lapse of a predefined time period (time period driven function). One example of this would be writing of the complete VGA colour register block, where only one register block is written during each stage.

Continuous multistaged functions are different from discrete ones in that after completing a stage, the same stage is called again in the next activation of the function. Thus, the continuous multistaged function is never terminated, it is always in a request state. Both multistaged models are only implemented by the ABIOS. The CBIOS only supports the single-staged model.

Every multistaged ABIOS function consists of three routines: a start routine, an interrupt routine and a time-out routine. The start routine is called if the corresponding function is started. The hardware interrupts assigned to the various stages, or the lapse of a predefined time period, activates the interrupt routine. A hardware time-out in interrupt-driven functions calls the time-out routine. The ABIOS usually supports 16 devices and units that are defined by a corresponding ID number. Table 3.4 lists these devices and units. Additionally, the ABIOS uses the ID=0 for internal function calls.

ID	Device/service	ID	Device/service
00h	internal ABIOS functions	0ah	NMI
01h	floppy drive	0bh	mouse
02h	hard disk drive	0ch–0dh	reserved
03h	graphics adapter	0eh	CMOS RAM
04h	keyboard	0fh	DMA
05h	parallel interface	10h	POS
06h	serial interface	11h	error tracking
07h	system clock	12h–15h	reserved
08h	real-time clock	16h	keyboard lock
09h	system functions	17h–ffffh	reserved

Table 3.4: Devices and units supported by the ABIOS

The call of ABIOS services is no longer carried out by registers, as was the case with the CBIOS. Instead, the ABIOS uses four data structures: a function transfer table, a device block, a common data area and a request block. Every ABIOS service is assigned a *function transfer table,* which includes a table of pointers to the start, interrupt and time-out routines assigned to the ABIOS service. Additionally, it holds a table of pointers to the beginning of the individual functions of the ABIOS service. An ABIOS service is assigned a *unit block* corresponding to the serviced physical device that holds the interrupt and arbitration level of the hardware device, and other important information. In the *common data area* a table of pointers to the function transfer table and the device block of each ABIOS service is stored. Such a pointer pair in the table is identified by a unique ID. During ABIOS initialization, the logical IDs are assigned. Calling programs use the logical IDs as an index to the common data area to call ABIOS services and functions. All function transfer tables, all device blocks and the common data area are generated and initialized during ABIOS initialization.

The *request block* constitutes the interface between the calling task and an ABIOS function. All input and output parameters are transferred via this data structure (for example, the logical ID, the function number, or the return code). Before a task can start an ABIOS function, it has to initialize the request block. The request block remains in memory until the call is completed, thus the request block takes over the job of the CPU registers for parameter passing (as is the case with the CBIOS). Table 3.5 lists the correspondences between ABIOS and CBIOS.

Process	ABIOS	CBIOS
parameter passing	request block	CPU registers
identification of the BIOS service by number	logical ID	interrupt
location of the BIOS service by vector table	logical ID as an index into common data area	interrupt
location of the BIOS function table	vector in the function transfer table	internal jump into CBIOS code

Table 3.5: Correspondences between ABIOS and CBIOS

Every ABIOS service has nine standard functions (see Table 3.6). The other numbers are available for device-dependent functions.

Number	Function
00h	standard interrupt handler
01h	return logical ID
02h	reserved
03h	read device parameters
04h	set device parameters
05h	reset / initialize
06h	activate
07h	deactivate
08h	read
09h	write

Table 3.6: ABIOS standard functions

After the calling task has initialized the request block, it can call the intended ABIOS function and pass control to the ABIOS. The actual call is then (for example, with OS/2) executed by the operating system function ABIOSCommonEntry or ABIOSCall. Readers interested in details on ABIOS should consult a programmer's reference for OS/2 (or another operating system) which uses the ABIOS.

3.8 Paging

A further essential component of the i386 is the paging unit located in the memory management unit. Its connection with paging and the new possibilities it introduces, with respect to the virtual 8086 mode, are detailed in the next section.

3.8.1 Logical, Linear, Physical Addresses and Paging

With its 32-bit offset registers and 16-bit segment registers the i386 has a logical address space of 64 Tbytes per task. Because the base address in the segment descriptors is 32 bits wide, these 64 Tbytes are mapped to an address space with 4 Gbytes at most. The combination of the segment's base address and the offset within the segment in the address adder leads to a so-called *linear address*. This means that the address indicates the address of a memory object in a linear fashion. Thus, with a larger address you find the memory object higher up in memory. The segment number, that is, the segment selector, doesn't indicate linearity. A selector larger in value may directly point to a segment at the lowest segment address. Mapping the 64 Tbytes onto the 4 Gbytes is possible because not all segments of the 64 Tbytes must be actually present (P bit of the segment descriptors). The rest may, for example, be swapped onto a (really very large) hard disk.

If all 32 i386 address lines are used, this linear 32-bit address can be converted to a *physical address*, which in turn has 32 bits. Then, each address in the logical address space of 4 Gbytes corresponds to a memory object in one of these countless memory chips – countless because to realize a physical memory of 4 Gbytes, without taking into account the chips for the parity bits, 8192 (!) 1 Mbyte memory chips are necessary. The chips alone weigh about 40 kg (at 5g/chip) and cost (even with a bulk discount) about $50,000. No computer, except for massively parallel computers like the Connection Machine with its 65536 processors, comes into such a category. For a PC, such storage is nonsense (even with Windows and OS/2). Typical i386 PCs are presently equipped with 4 Mbytes or 16 Mbytes at most. This is not very much for extensive database applications, DTP or powerful graphics programs. Such memories may generate data amounts internally that exceed the computer's available main memory.

We have already met one possibility of enlarging the virtual address space beyond the actual physical memory during the discussion on protected mode and the segment descriptors connected to it. In the segment descriptors a P (present) bit is available which indicates whether the segment is actually in memory. If the processor attempts to access a segment whose P bit is cleared (that is, the intended segment is not in memory), the «segment not present» exception is issued. Now the operating system can load the segment concerned into memory, and give the instruction the chance to access the segment again. It is therefore possible to generate more segments for a program than may simultaneously fit into the memory. The swapped segments are only loaded if needed. If not enough space is available in memory, one or more other segments must be swapped to make memory available for the newly read segment.

But now new problems arise. The data may only be swapped and loaded segment-by-segment. Further, the size of the segments corresponds to the size of the data structures they hold. The data segment for an extensive drawing or the code segment of a powerful program module may be very large. On the other hand, the data segment that contains the address text for a letter, or a code segment that holds a simple procedure, is usually very small. If a large segment is now to be loaded from the hard disk into memory, then possibly numerous small segments must be swapped. This is becoming very awkward, particularly if only one byte or word has to be accessed in the loaded segment, but then immediately afterwards an access to the code or data in one of the segments just swapped out takes place. The segment just loaded must be swapped out again and the required code or data segment reloaded. If the program now needs more data from the data segment that has just been swapped out, then everything has to be carried out again from the beginning, etc. You can see what this means in the case of a 1 Mbyte database segment: a long coffee break!

Another problem arises with a low memory configuration: for the database segment there remains only that memory which has been left unused by the operating system, drivers, system tables and at least one code segment of the current program. If the swapped segment is larger than this remaining memory, it is impossible to read the whole segment into memory.

Thus the operating system has to do a lot of things: determine what segment it is best to swap, whether the now available memory is sufficient, eventually swap another segment, etc. The swapping process is very slow. By now, though, you have surely guessed that a better method exists: *paging*. Because all segments must be present in the physical memory, which is usually much smaller than 4 Gbytes, the base addresses of all the segments are also within the address space of the physical memory. With a main memory of, for example, 4 Mbytes, all base addresses are lower than 4 Mbytes, that is, the complete linear address space between 4 Mbytes and 4 Gbytes is not used. In other words, about 99.9% of the linear address space remains unused. A lot of memory for many, many segments!

Paging maps a very large linear address space onto the much smaller physical address space of main memory, as well as the large address space of external mass storage (usually a hard disk). Hard disks, though, rarely have a capacity that corresponds to the i386 virtual address space. This mapping is carried out in «portions» of a fixed size called *pages*. In the case of the i386, a page size of 4 kbytes is defined (this size is fixed by processor hardware and cannot be altered). Thus the complete linear address space consists of one million pages. In most cases, only a few of them are occupied by data. The occupied pages are either in memory or swapped to the hard disk. Whether the i386 actually uses this paging mechanism is determined by the PG bit in the CR0 register. If the PG bit is set then paging is carried out; otherwise it is not. Because the operating system must manage and eventually swap or reload the pages, it is not sufficient to simply set the PG bit. The i386 hardware only supports paging analogous to the protection and task switch mechanisms. The operating system must intercept the paging exceptions and service them accordingly, look for the swapped pages, reload them, etc.

Thus a double address mapping is carried out in the i386. The segment and offset (virtual address) of a memory object are combined to form a linear address in the linear 4 Gbytes address space corresponding to one million pages. Then, these one million pages corresponding to the linear address are converted into a physical address or an exception «page not present» is issued so that the page concerned can be loaded.

3.8.2 Page Directory, Page Tables, Page Frames and the CR3 Register

To determine a linear address from a segment and an offset, one needs information as to where the segment concerned begins. This information is stored in the descriptor tables. Two levels of such tables exist: the global descriptor table (GDT) forms the «root directory», where the local descriptor tables (LDT) may appear as «subdirectories». The address of the descriptor tables is stored in the GDTR and LDTR, respectively. With the information held, segment and offset can be combined into a linear 32-bit address, which is used unaltered as the physical address. For example, for a PC with an i386 processor and 4 Mbytes of main storage space, the segment starts at 1b0000h and the offset is d23a0h. The linear address is thus 2823a0h. The byte with the number 2 630 560 or 0000 0000 0010 1000 0010 0011 1010 0000b decimal is addressed. Since the main storage area is limited to 4 Mbytes, the ten most significant bits are always equal to 0, that is, the address will always read 0000 0000 00xx xxxx xxxx xxxx xxxx xxxx, where x is equal to the binary number 1 or 0. In a similar manner to the representation of segment and offset in the form of a linear address, the implementation of mapping a linear address onto a physical address is carried out. This is achieved using a two-level directory and a register, which in turn defines a sort of «main directory». A table defines the mapping between linear and physical addresses. For this, a special interpretation of the linear address is required (Figure 3.20).

With an activated paging unit, the ten most significant bits of the linear address indicate the number of the applicable page tables in the page directory; this corresponds to the current linear address. The ten bits that follow define the page number of the established page table. Subsequently, the 12 least significant bits indicate in the usual manner the offset within the defined page. The 12 bits are sufficient for this task, because a page only consists of $2^{12}=4096$ bytes. However, a segment requires a 32-bit offset. A linear address is represented by a physical address, which is specified by *DIR* for a page table, by *page* for a page within the page table and, finally, by *offset* to indicate an offset in the given page (Figure 3.21). This can be interpreted in another way. Paging remaps the 20 most significant address bits onto new values, whereas the 12 least significant address bits are taken over, unchanged, as an offset.

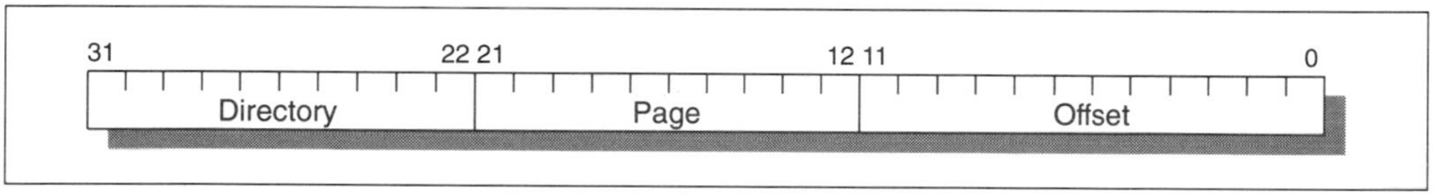

Figure 3.20: Interpreting the linear address with active paging.

It is easy to understand the reasoning behind having two such page table levels. Each page table entry comprises four bytes (Figure 3.22). If every page (of 4 kbytes) of the linear address space of 4 Gbytes (equivalent to one million pages) was represented by a single page table in the memory, this would on its own require 4 Mbytes just for the page tables! The creation of a second–level makes it possible to administer page tables of a lower level as if they were themselves pages. They are similar to a normal page in that they are only 4 kbytes. With the assistance of the operating system, the i386 loads and unloads second-level page tables like normal pages. It is only the 4 kbyte page directory that must be constantly maintained in the memory. Its base address is saved by the CR3 register.

Both the page directory and the second–level page tables each have 1 024 (1k) page table entries, each with a length of 4 bytes. Figure 3.22 shows the structure of such a page table entry.

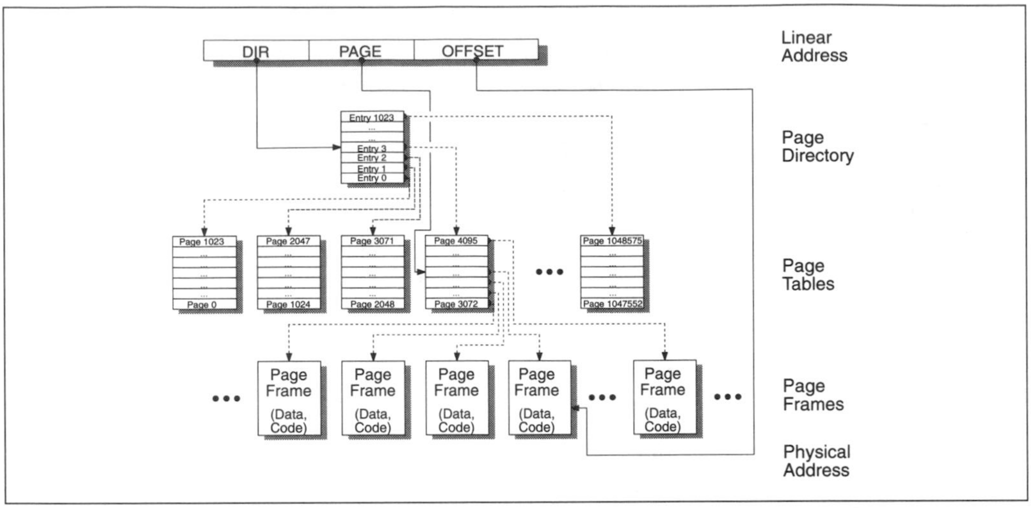

Figure 3.21: Mapping of a linear address onto a physical address with active paging. After combining segment and offset into a linear address, the resulting linear address is split into a 10-bit page directory address, a 10-bit page address and a 12-bit offset, if paging is enabled. Every page comprises 4 kbytes, thus the full address space is divided into 4 kbyte blocks.

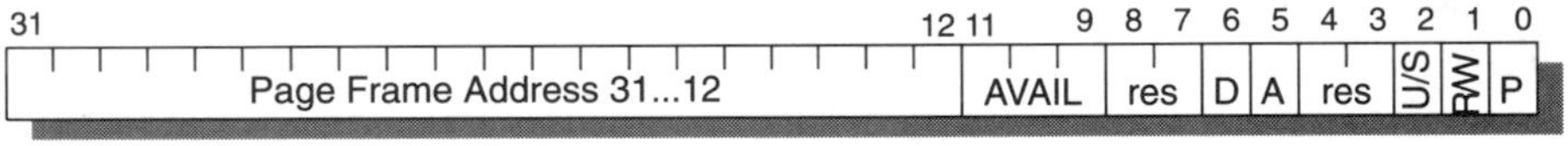


```
Page Frame Address: address bits 31...12 of the page frame
AVAIL:  available for the operating system
D:   dirty
   0=page has not yet been overwritten   1=page has been overwritten
A:   accessed
   0=page has not yet been accessed      1=page has already been accessed
U/S: page access level (user/supervisor)
   0=supervisor (CPL=0..2)               1=user (CPL=3)
R/W: write protection (read/write)
   0=page is read-only                   1=page can be written to
P:   page present
   0=page is swapped                     1=page resides in memory
res: reserved (equal 0)
```

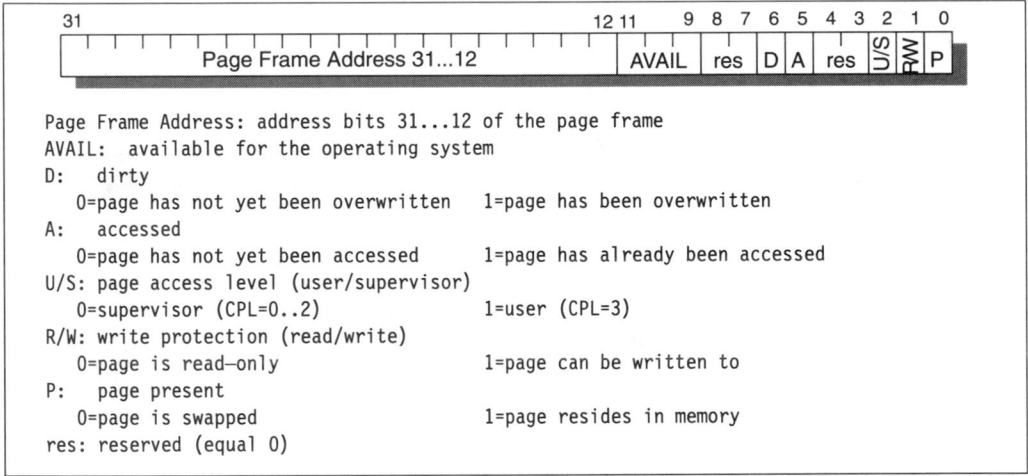

Figure 3.22: The structure of a page table entry.

The *P*-bit (page present) indicates whether the respective page is in memory (P=1) or stored outside (P=0). In the latter case, the remaining 31 bits of the page table entry contain information with regard to where the page is located on the hard disk or other memory medium. Therefore, the entries that follow it have no meaning.

If the page is in memory (P=1), the 20 high-order bits define the address of the *page frame*. A page frame is a memory area the size of a page (4 kbytes) that holds the data of a page. The addresses of such page frames are always multiples of 4096 (1000h): 0, 4096, 8192, ... or 0000h,

1000h, 2000h, ... You are free to imagine this pictorially as a «frame» (of a picture, for example). In the same way, a sheet («page») with information may be inserted into a frame; the paging mechanism inserts pages with various contents into the page frames. The frames remain the same (and are located on the same wall, to follow the metaphor through), but the information has changed.

The paging mechanism therefore replaces the 20 high-order address bits in the physical 32-bit address by these 20 bits of the page frame address. The 12 least significant bits of the physical address indicate the offest of the memory object within that page. The 12 low-order bits in the page table entry, on the other hand, serve to manage the page. If paging is active, the i386 combines the 20 page frame address bits and the 12 offset bits of the linear address into a physical 32-bit address. If the page is swapped (P=0) the i386 issues a «page fault» exception corresponding to interrupt 0eh. Now the paging routine of the operating system can load the required page into a free or freed page frame.

This loading and unloading of pages, triggered by the page fault exception, also occurs if a memory object such as a double word no longer fits on one page and is split over two pages.

Example: a double word (4 bytes) at offset fffdh (decimal 4094). The two low-order bytes of the double word are stored in the two high-order bytes of the page. But the two high-order bytes of the double word are already held by another page which, moreover, may be swapped.

In general, the 32-bit i386 processor constantly addresses the physical double-word addresses 0, 4, 8, etc. If a double word does not commence at a double word boundary, the i386 has to execute two memory accesses, each of which starts with a double word. In the example given, the last four bytes of the first page are addressed, in which the two least significant bytes of the double word are found. Subsequently, the processor accesses the first four bytes of the next page. This is loaded if it is not currently in memory. Thus, the processor can address the two most significant values of the double word. The 4 kbyte size of the page does not cause any problems. In the worst case, two page fault exceptions are issued and two pages are loaded into memory.

The advantages compared to swapping complete segments are obvious. The smaller sections with 4 kbytes each can be reloaded or stored very quickly. Further, programs usually access data that is quite close together. Even with the rather small page size of 4 kbytes compared with the linear address space of 4 Gbytes (a factor of one million), the probability is high that the intended data is already present in memory. For large segments, only those parts that are currently processed or executed must be loaded. A complete swapping and immediate reloading, as described above, does not occur with paging. The computer therefore runs much faster.

One could be of the opinion that the new address conversion that is necessary with paging, in addition to forming the linear address from the segment and offset, may lead to delays for address determination. This is not true in most cases, however. The i386 contains a cache memory where the most recently used page table entries are stored. This cache memory is called the *translation lookaside buffer* (*TLB*). Only if a page table entry is to be used that is not present in the TLB, and thus has to be reloaded from memory, is the address translation delayed by the memory access. But if the page table with the entry is swapped onto disk, the access takes much more time because the page table first has to be loaded into memory, and its entry must be read into the processor. Using intelligent algorithms in the operating system for managing page tables and their entries, this case rarely occurs and there are only a few delays. The gain of a very large linear address space compared to a small physical one by means of paging is really very significant.

For the management of pages and the second-order page tables, several bits are reserved in the page table entries (see Figure 3.22). If the processor has accessed a page once (that is, if it reads or writes data), the *A* (accessed) bit in the corresponding page table entry is set. If the operating system regularly clears these A bits it may determine which pages are used often. Thus it only swaps the less used pages to cause as few read and write accesses of the hard disk drive as possible. Therefore, paging runs with hardly any delay.

The *D* (dirty) bit characterizes pages whose contents have been altered, that is, overwritten. If this bit is cleared the page need not be written onto disk when swapped, because there is still an unaltered former copy of that page on the disk. If the D bit is set, however, the operating system detects a change of data and writes (as well as information for relocating the page on disk) the data of the page itself onto the disk.

As is the case for segments, pages can also be protected against an access by programs. Unlike the segments (where four privilege levels 0–3 are available), the protection mechanism for pages only implements two levels: user and supervisor. Programs with privilege levels CPL=0 to CPL=2 (that is, operating system, device drivers and operating system extensions) use the supervisor level. Application programs, on the other hand, usually have the user privilege level. The privilege level of pages is indicated by the *U/S* (user/supervisor) bit, therefore U/S=0 holds for operating system, system software, etc. (CPL=0, 1, 2) and U/S=1 holds for application code and data (CPL=3).

With the *R/W* (read/write) bit, pages are marked as read-only (R/W=0) or as readable and writeable (R/W=1). A violation (for example, a write access to a read-only page (R/W=0), leads to a «page fault» exception. On the other hand, the segmenting mechanism protects the data on a segment basis when in protected mode. A violation of the paging protection mechanism, such as an attempt to write to a read-only page (R/W=0) or using user access on a supervisor page, leads to «Page Fault», and the associated interrupt 0eh. The three *AVAIL*-bits are available to the operating system for page management. All other bits are reserved.

In the i386, segmenting and paging produce duplicate address conversions. Segmenting produces the base address of the segment from the virtual address in the segment:offset format with the help of the descriptor tables and the segment descriptors and, with the addition of the offset, forms the linear address in the large linear address space. Paging converts this linear address into a physical address of the usually much smaller physical address space or to a «Page Fault» exception. This procedure is shown in Figure 3.23. In most cases, the i386 can execute this conversion without a time delay, due to the segment descriptor cache register and the translation lookaside buffer.

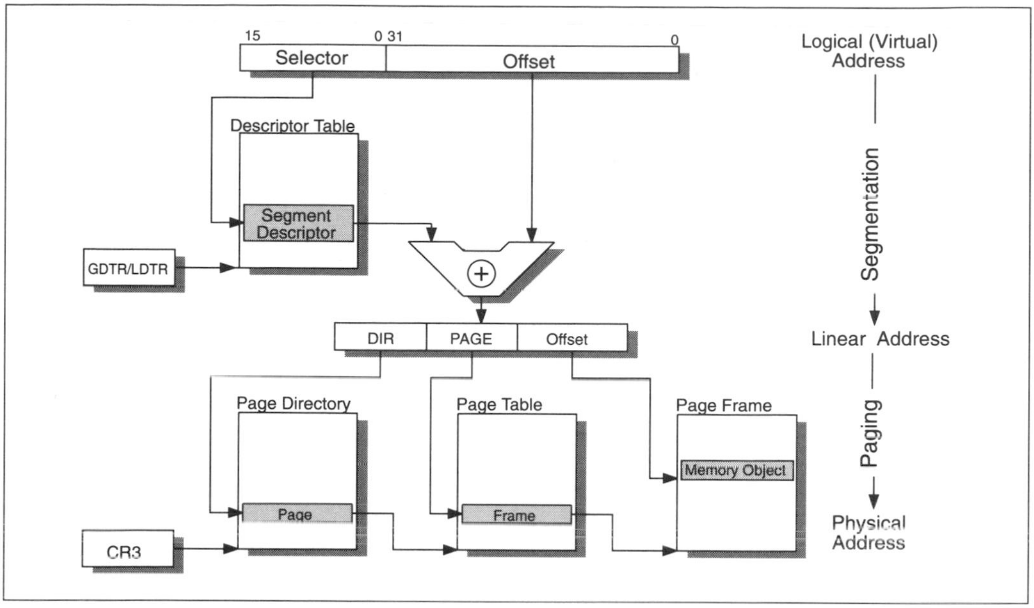

Figure 3.23: The double address translation with segmentation and paging.

3.8.3 Paging Exceptions

In addition to the previously mentioned exceptions, paging can lead to a further exception, namely:

- Page Fault (exception 14): if, during the conversion of a linear to a physical address, the paging unit determines that the required page table or the page itself is externally stored, or if the task that wishes to read the data in a page is only running at the user level but is, however, identified as being at the supervisor level, then the i386 issues an interrupt 14 (0eh). The operating system can load the respective page or page table into memory, or can register an access error.

3.8.4 Test Registers TR6 and TR7 for Checking the TLB

Because the two test registers TR6 and TR7 (Figure 2.5) are only implemented for testing the TLB, I would like to discuss them here in connection with the TLB itself. If you are a little unsure about cache memory, then at this stage you should refer to Chapter 10.

The TLB is implemented as a 4-way set-associative memory, and uses a random replacement strategy. It is an integrated part of the i386 chip, and does not require any external SRAM memory. Like other cache memories, each entry in the set 0–3 consists of the 24-bit tag and the actual 12-bit cache data. Each set comprises of eight entries, therefore the TLB can accept 32 entries, giving a total size equivalent to 144 bytes. 32 entries for each 4kbyte page mean that the TLB manages 128 kbytes of memory. Each 24-bit tag stores the 20 most significant bits of the linear address (the DIR and page part), a validity bit and three attribute bits. The data entry contains the 12 most significant value bits of the associated physical address.

If the physical address of the page format is already stored in the TLB when a page table access occurs, the i386 uses it internally, to produce physical 32-bit addresses. Otherwise, the processor has to first read the page table entry. Intel specify a 98% TLB hit rate, that is, 98% of all memory accesses for code and data refer to a page whose frame address is already contained in the TLB. Stated differently, in 98% of all cases paging does not slow down code and data accesses.

The i386 has two test registers for testing the translation lookaside buffers, these being the test instruction register TR6 and the test data register TR7. Figure 3.24 shows their structure.

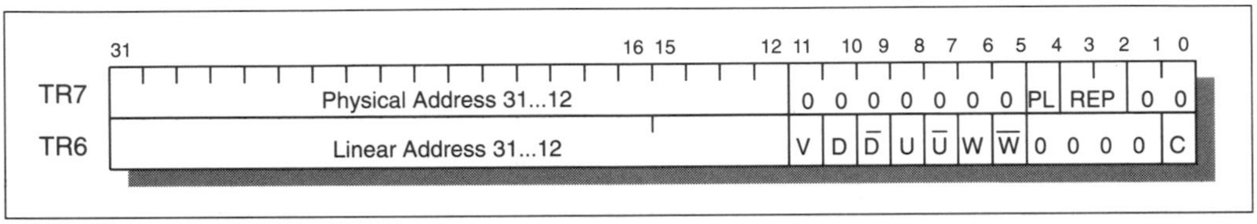

Figure 3.24: Structure of the test registers TR6 and TR7.

To test the TLB, you must first disable paging, that is, the i386 must not perform any paging. The TLB test is sub-divided into two procedures: writing entries to the TLB, and reading TLB entries (performing a TLB Lookup). The following text explains, in more detail, the test register entries.

The *C*-bit in the test instruction register indicates whether a write to the TLB (C=0) or TLB lookup (C=1) will be executed.

The *linear address* represents the TLB tag field. A TLB entry is attached to these linear addresses during a write to the TLB, and the contents of TR6 and TR7 are transferred to the attached entry. During a TLB lookup, the test logic checks whether these linear addresses and the attribute bits agree with a TLB entry. If this is the case, then the remaining fields of TR6 and the test register TR7 are loaded from the confirmed entry into the TLB.

During a write to the TLB, the physical address is transferred into the TLB entry that corresponds to the linear address. During a TLB lookup, the test logic loads this TR7 field with the value stored in the TLB.

The meaning of *PL* varies depending on C. If a TLB entry is written (C=0) and if PL=1, then the TLB associated block to be written is determined by REP. If, however, PL is reset (PL=0), an internal pointer in the paging unit selects the TLB block to be written. For a TLB lookup (C=1), the PL value specifies whether the lookup has led to a hit (PL=1) or not (PL=0).

V is the TLB entry validity bit. A V-bit that is set shows that an entry is valid; a V-bit that has been reset shows that the entry is invalid. The remaining TR6 register bits correspond to the attribute bits of a page table entry. D, $\overline{D}$ represents the dirty bit, U, $\overline{U}$ the user/supervisor bit and W, $\overline{W}$ the write protection bit for the (or from the) corresponding TLB entry. The three bits are given in normal and complementary form (Table 3.7). In this way, for table lookups for example, it is possible to instruct the test logic to ignore the value of the bit during a lookup (if both are set, the logic will always agree). If both the attribute bit and its complement are set (=1), then the logic will always produce a hit for the corresponding attribute. In other words, the attribute value in this case is insignificant.

D,U,W	$\overline{D},\overline{U},\overline{W}$	Effects on TLB-Lookup	Value in TLB after Write
0	0	always miss for D, U, W	D, U, W undefined
0	1	hit for D, U, W=0	D, U, W set (=1)
1	0	hit for D, U, W=1	D, U, W cleared (=0)
1	1	always hit for D, U, W	D, U, W undefined

Table 3.7: Effects of the complementary bit pairs

Testing of the TLB is achieved by read and write (TLB lookup) of the TR6 and TR7 test registers. To set a TLB entry for a test, you must first load TR7 with the values for the physical address, PL=1 and REP. Subsequently, you have to write suitable values for the linear address and the attributes to TR6, and erase the instruction bit C. To perform a TLB lookup (that is, reading of a TLB entry), you must load TR6 with the necessary linear address and set C. Subsequently, you have to read both test registers TR6 and TR7. The PL-bit indicates whether the result is a hit (PL=1) or not (PL=0). In the first instance, the values in the test register reflect the content of the respective TLB entry. However, if no hit occurs, the values are invalid.

3.9 i386 Virtual 8086 Mode – Myth and Reality

With the i386 a new operating mode was introduced which, as was the case for the 80286 protected mode, led to some confusion and a few myths. In the following sections I want to clarify the virtual mode. Together with the paging mechanisms, extensive capabilities for multitasking are available even for programs that are actually unable to use multitasking (what a contradiction!).

The incentive for the implementation of the virtual mode came from the enormous variety of programs for PCs running under MS-DOS, which is a purely real mode operating system. Remember also that powerful i486 PCs with MS-DOS always operate in real mode, and therefore use only the first of all the 4096 Mbytes of the 32-bit address space. Moreover, neither the extensive protection mechanisms of the protected mode nor the i386 paging mechanisms are used. Therefore, the virtual mode now enables the execution of unaltered real mode applications, as well as the use of protected mode protection mechanisms. The *virtual 8086 tasks* may run in parallel with other virtual 8086 tasks or i386 tasks, that is, *multitasking* with programs not designed for multitasking is taking place. 8086 programs running with MS-DOS are not designed for multitasking because DOS as the operating system is *not re-entrant*. If a DOS function is interrupted by an interrupt, which in turn calls a DOS function, then the PC frequently crashes because after an IRET the original stack is destroyed. Because of this, the programming of resident (TSR) programs is very complicated. By means of the virtual mode and paging these problems can be avoided. The virtual 8086 mode is, for example, used by the DOS windows under Windows or OS/2. Alternatively, it is possible to use a proper protected mode operating system with the corresponding protected mode applications (for example, OS/2 and a database programmed for OS/2 right from the start).

3.9.1 Virtual Machines and Virtual 8086 Monitors

In virtual mode the i386 hardware and the *virtual 8086 monitor* constitute a so-called *virtual machine*. The virtual machine gives the program or user the impression that a complete computer is dedicated to its use alone, even if it is only a member in a multiuser environment. The complete computer, for example, has its own hard disk, its own tape drive, or its own set of files and programs. Actually, the system may generate and manage many of these virtual machines. The system divides the physically present hard disk into sections each dedicated to one of the virtual machines. Thus, the user has the impression that he/she is in possession of a complete hard disk.

With a multiuser system such as UNIX/XENIX, many users can work on the computer. But every user has the impression that he/she is currently the only one. A mainframe succeeds with more than 1000 (!) such users. In a single-user system with multitasking such as OS/2, virtual machines are not generated for several *users*. Instead, the system generates its own virtual machine for each *task*. Because virtual machines are only serviced for a short time period, multitasking occurs. Thus, for example, a compiler, the printer spooler and an editor may run in parallel. Windows/386 and Windows 3.0 (and higher) on an i386, as well as the 32-bit version of OS/2, use such virtual machines on the basis of the virtual 8086 mode to execute real mode applications in parallel.

Just a few more words on the virtual 8086 monitor. This monitor, of course, has nothing to do with the screen, but represents a system program (typically a part of the operating system kernel) that is used to produce and manage (thus monitor) the virtual 8086 tasks. The i386 hardware uses a TSS to produce a set of virtual i386 registers. Further to this, a virtual memory is formed corresponding to the first Mbyte of the linear address space. A real mode program then has the impression that a normal 8086 is available. The processor then carries out physical instructions that affect these virtual registers and the virtual address space of the task. The purpose of the virtual 8086 monitor is essentially to supervise the external interfaces of the virtual machine, that is, of the virtual 8086 task. The interfaces are formed from interrupts, exceptions and I/O instructions, through which the virtual 8086 task can logically communicate with the other parts of the system. The exceptions and interrupts take on the role of physical interfaces (e.g. the control registers) in a normal 8086 PC. The monitor makes sure that the virtual 8086 machine fits into the extensive i386 system in protected mode, as a separate task without the possibility of interfering with other tasks, or with the i386 operating system itself.

3.9.2 Addresses in Virtual 8086 Mode

The main incompatibility between real and protected mode is the different address determination methods. In real mode the value of the segment register is simply multiplied by 16. In protected mode, however, the segment register is used as an index to a table, where the «real» address of the segment is stored. Therefore, it is impossible, for example, to determine the linear address of a memory object immediately from the segment and offset register values. However, many real mode programs do exactly that, and thus make it impossible to execute them in protected mode properly.

If the i386 is in virtual 8086 mode and has to run 8086 programs, it must calculate the linear address of an object in the same way as the 8086 in real mode due to the reasons stated above. Thus, in virtual 8086 mode, the i386 produces the linear address of an object by multiplying the value of the applicable segment register by 16 and then adding the offset as in real mode. There is, however, a difference between the 8086 and the i386 in that the i386 makes use of 32-bit offset registers and the 8086 does not. Virtual 8086 tasks can produce linear 32-bit addresses through the use of an address size prefix. If the value in an i386 offset register in virtual 8086 mode exceeds 65 535 or ffffh, the i386 issues a pseudo protection exception, in that it generates the exception 0ch or 0dh but not the error code. As in the normal real mode, the combination of a segment ffffh with an offset of ffffh in virtual 8086 mode leads to an address 10ffefh which is beyond the first Mbyte in the real mode address space. The i386 can then break through the 1Mbyte barrier of real mode by almost 64 kbytes also in virtual 8086 mode.

3.9.3 Entering and Leaving Virtual 8086 Mode

The i386 can be easily switched into virtual 8086 mode, the *VM (virtual mode)* flag in the EFlag register is simply set. Note that additionally, the i386 must already be working in protected mode. A direct jump from real into virtual 8086 mode is not possible. The VM flag can only be set by code with the privilege level 0 (the operating system kernel), a task switch through an i386 TSS, or an IRET instruction that collects the EFlags with a set VM-bit from the stack. A task switch automatically loads the EFlags from the TSS of the newly started task. In this way, it is not necessary for the operating system itself to decide at each task switch whether the newly started task should be carried out in protected or virtual 8086 mode.

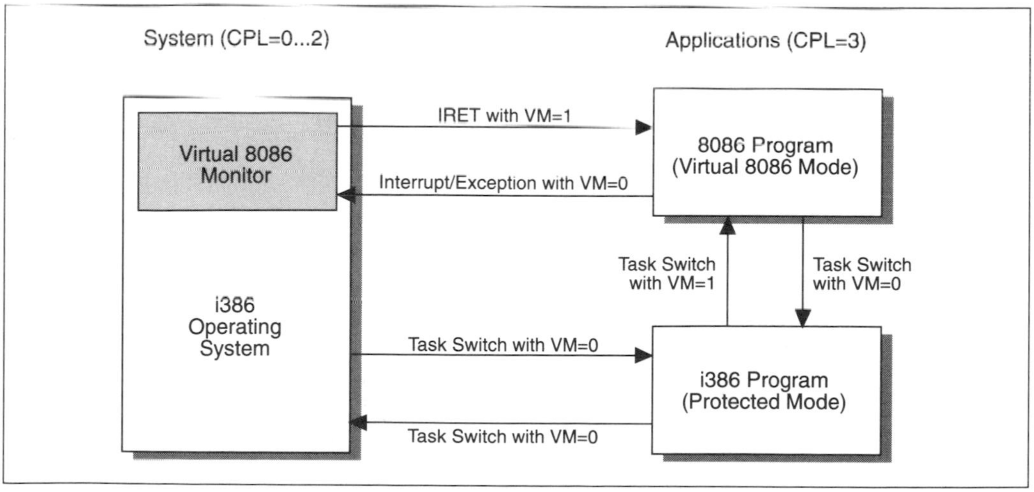

Figure 3.25: Entering and leaving virtual 8086 mode.

Moreover, since the TSS of the operating system makes this decision only when the TSS for the task is created, it is necessary to set the EFlag entry, thus ensuring that the task will always be carried out in virtual 8086 mode. An 80286 TSS, on the other hand, cannot change the most significant word in the EFlag register containing the VM flag, because of the reduction of the flag entry to 16-bit.

The i386 quits virtual 8086 mode when the VM flag is reset. This is possible through the use of an i386 TSS or an interrupt, that is, an exception that refers to a trap or an interrupt gate. The i386 then returns to the normal protected mode, in order to carry out other protected mode tasks. This is more clearly illustrated in Figure 3.25.

In virtual 8086 mode all 8086 registers are available and are expanded to 32-bit (through the use of a preceding E). Additionally, the new i386 registers such as FS, GS, the debug register etc. are available. Further to this, a virtual 8086 task can use the new instructions that were implemented in the 80186/286/386 such as BOUND, LSS, etc. Even though the mode is called virtual 8086 mode, it would be more accurate to call it virtual i386 real mode.

3.9.4 Tasks in Virtual 8086 Mode

In addition to the hardware platform of the i386, it is necessary to use a number of software components to assemble a virtual machine that can execute an 8086 program in virtual 8086 mode. These are:

- the 8086 program itself (real mode),
- the virtual 8086 monitor (protected mode),
- operating system functions for the 8086 program (real or protected mode).

You can see that the i386 hardware only supports the virtual tasks; on its own it is not sufficient. The same applies to the normal protected mode. The i386 hardware supports a multitasking operating system through the use of automatic access checks, etc. in protected mode. That on its own is not sufficient, but enables a lot more work to be done by the system programmer to set up a stable system. Without protected mode, a multitasking operating system would still be possible in principle, but, without the hardware support, it would be much harder to program and keep stable (and it's better to say nothing at all about the performance).

Let us look at the example of an editor for MS-DOS; this is an 8086 program. The virtual 8086 monitor is part of the protected mode operating system for the i386, because the monitor directly affects the system (for example, through the memory management). Further, the editor needs operating system functions to open and close files which, up to now, have been carried out by DOS.

The three parts together form a *virtual 8086 task*. It is managed by an i386 TSS. In this way, it is possible to call the virtual 8086 task like any other, and specifically for the protected mode formulated task, through a task switch and the i386 TSS. The 8086 program can be embedded in a multitasking environment.

The virtual 8086 monitor runs in protected mode with the privilege level PL=0 and contains routines for loading the 8086 programs and for handling interrupts and exceptions. In comparison, an actual 8086 program has a privilege level of CPL=3 (after all, it is only an application). In virtual 8086 mode, the first 10fff0h bytes of the i386 linear address space (from 4 Gbytes equals 100 000 000h) are used by the 8086 program, as in real mode. Addresses outside this area cannot be used by the 8086 program. The addresses beyond 10ffefh are available to the virtual 8086 monitor, the i386 operating system and other software.

The virtual 8086 task is now only missing the normal operating system functions of the 8086 operating system (in our case, above all, those of INT 21h). For the implementation of this, there are two strategies:

- The 8086 operating system runs as part of the 8086 program, that is, the 8086 program and MS-DOS form a unit. In this way, all of the necessary operating system functions are available.
- The i386 operating system emulates the 8086 operating system.

The advantage of the first option is that the previous real mode operating system can be used in a nearly unaltered form. Every virtual 8086 task has its own MS-DOS copy (or the copy of another real mode operating system) exclusively dedicated to it. Several different operating systems may therefore run in an i386 machine: the overall i386 operating system for protected mode programs as well as the various 8086 operating systems for 8086 programs in virtual 8086 mode. But there remains a serious problem: the operating system functions of MS-DOS and other systems are called by means of interrupts; and interrupt handlers are very critical sections of the *i386* operating system, which runs in protected mode. The way in which the problem is solved is described below.

If several virtual 8086 tasks are to run in parallel, their coordination is easier if we use the second option above. In this case, the real mode operating system of the 8086 tasks is emulated by calls to the i386 operating system in most cases.

In protected mode, the I/O instructions are sensitive as to the value of the IOPL flag. A value of CPL above IOPL gives rise to an exception. In virtual 8086 mode, these I/O instructions are not sensitive to the IOPL flag, however. Protection of the I/O address space is carried only by means of the I/O permission bit map. Instead, the instructions PUSHF, POPF, INTn, IRET, CLI and STI now respond to the IOPL value, as the instructions PUSHF, POPF, CLI and STI may alter flags. In the wider i386 environment, with possibly several virtual 8086 and protected mode tasks running, changing flags is the job of either the virtual 8086 monitor or the i386 operating system alone – and not the responsibility of antiquated and inferior MS-DOS programs.

Because of the dependency of the INTn and IRET instructions on IOPL, the virtual 8086 monitor may intercept operating system calls from the 8086 program via interrupts. If the value of IOPL is lower than 3 (that is, lower than the CPL of the 8086 program), the monitor intercepts the interrupt. If the 8086 operating system is part of the 8086 program, the monitor hands the interrupt over to it. Call and result may eventually be adapted to the i386 environment. Alternatively, the monitor may emulate the function of the 8086 operating system concerned directly. Remember, however, that interrupts in real and protected mode appear very different.

The 8086 program is usually written for an 8086 processor (or an i386 in real mode). The virtual 8086 task uses an interrupt vector table in real mode form with the interrupt vectors in the CS:IP format. The table begins at the linear address 0000h and contains 1 kbyte. Also, in virtual 8086 mode, the i386 does not use these real mode tables directly; first it uses an INT instruction of the 8086 program to call the corresponding handler of the i386 operating system through the IDT. It then quits the virtual 8086 mode. The flow of an interrupt in virtual 8086 mode can be seen in Figure 3.26.

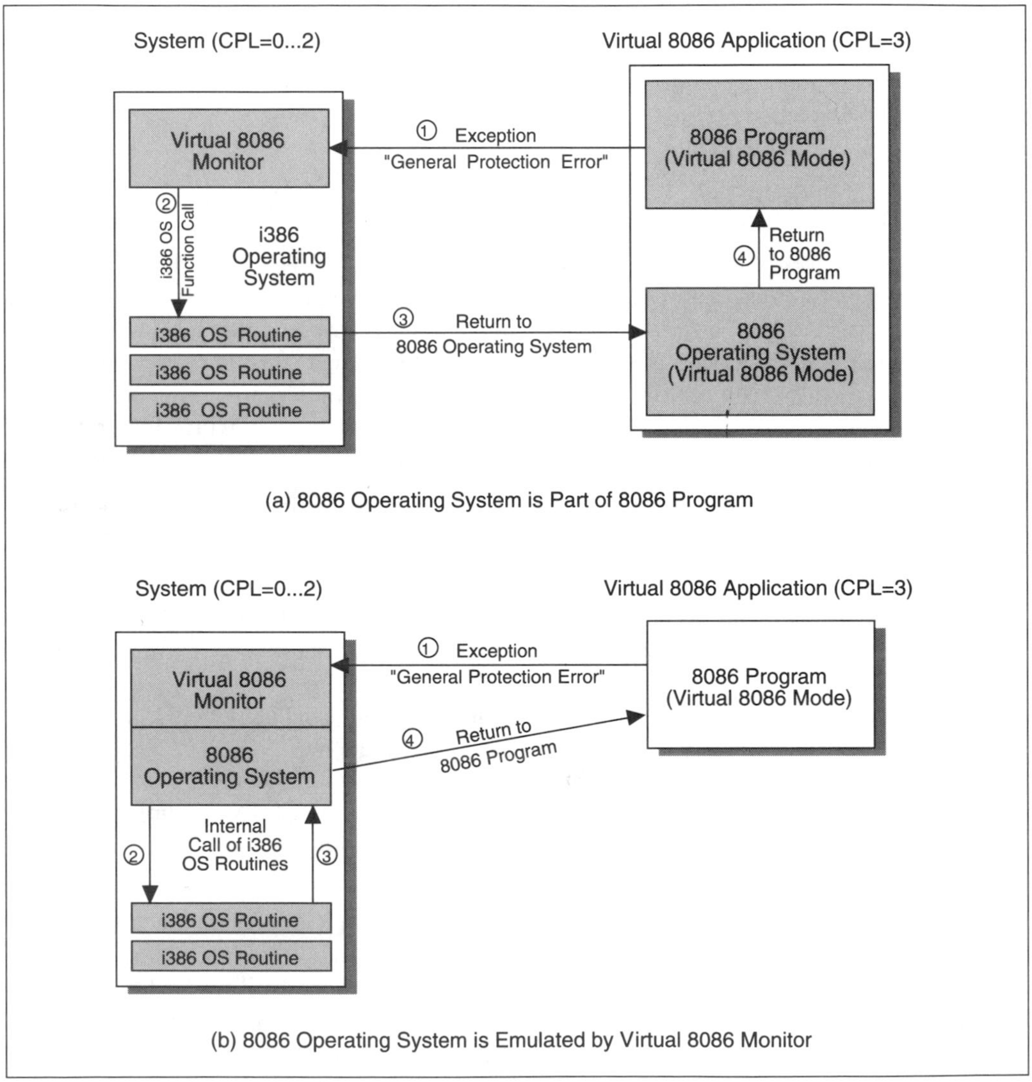

Figure 3.26: The course of interrupts in virtual 8086 mode.

As usual with an interrupt, the i386 stores the EFlags on the stack. Thus, the called handler knows by means of the stored flag whether or not the VM flag was set at the time of the interrupt, that is, whether or not the interrupt stopped a virtual 8086 task. If VM is set, the interrupt handler passes control to the virtual 8086 monitor. The monitor itself can handle the interrupt or again pass control to the interrupt handler of the 8086 program. For this purpose, the monitor checks the interrupt vector table of the interrupted 8086 task, to determine the entry point of the real mode interrupt handler. Through an IRET instruction (with the privilege level PL=0 of the monitor), the i386 switches back into virtual 8086 mode and calls the handler. After the real mode interrupt handler has finished, the completed IRET instruction of the real mode handler is sent again to the virtual 8086 monitor. After it has prepared the stacks for the return, a further IRET is issued. In this way, the i386 restarts the virtual 8086 program that was stopped by the interrupt. The interrupt is served in this roundabout way through the IDT monitor handler from the real mode handler of the 8086 task. As you can clearly see, it forces an interrupt to use a very extensive and, therefore, protracted procedure. In the Pentium, the process is more optimized.

Many MS-DOS programs set and clear the IE interrupt flag, to control the operation of hardware interrupts in critical code sections. The i386 operating system, which is responsible for the whole machine, cannot tolerate such interference. It is the responsibility of the operating system alone to decide whether a hardware interrupt request should be serviced immediately, after a short time, or not at all. In virtual 8086 mode, there are also the PUSHF, POPF, CLI and STI instructions that depend upon the IOPL, as they can directly (CLI and STI), or indirectly (PUSHF and POPF) change the IE flag. The monitor intercepts these instructions and processes them in such a way that they are compatible with the whole i386 system. The reason for the interference of the monitor when an IOPL dependent instruction is issued by an 8086 program is clear: the 8086 program is under the impression that these instructions should be executed as in real mode.

A further critical area for multitasking systems are the I/O ports, because with their help, the processor can access the registers of hardware components. Here also, the i386 operating system cannot tolerate interference from an 8086 program in virtual 8086 mode. Many real mode programs, unfortunately, access the I/O ports directly; under MS-DOS, this is no great problem, the PC crashes regularly anyway. Under a multitasking system, on the other hand, most programs can only do this in a roundabout way through the operating system so that accesses to the I/O ports are coordinated. After all, a task containing errors should not affect other tasks, or other users in a multi-user system. In virtual mode, the I/O port access problem does not exist, as the system protects the critical ports through the use of the I/O permission bit map and not the IOPL flag. The I/O instructions are no longer IOPL sensitive even though the i386 is running in protected mode. In this way, the virtual 8086 monitor can, in one respect, permit an 8086 program to directly access critical I/O ports. If, for example, an 8086 program targets a plug-in board programmed for controlling a robot, the registers would not be used by another program, and so for this port a conflict would never occur – the roundabout way through the i386 operating system would only cause delays and would not provide any additional protection. With the help of the permission bit map, however, critical ports such as the registers of a monitor screen control chip or a hard disk controller are protected against unauthorized and possibly erroneous accesses. The virtual 8086 monitor intercepts such accesses and handles them accordingly.

3.9.5 Paging and Virtual 8086 Mode

As long as only one task is running, no problems arise concerning the use of main memory. The first 10fff0h bytes of the linear address space are reserved for the virtual 8086 task. The operating system and all other tasks occupy the addresses above. But what happens with the video memory? Many 8086 programs directly write into the video RAM to speed up text and graphics output, and they prefer to do this from the upper left to the lower right corner for the whole screen. If several tasks running in parallel output data onto the screen, a hopeless confusion is the result. This is especially true if some of these tasks output data in text mode and others output it in graphics mode (and, very likely, using various graphics modes). These problems led to the development of the Presentation Manager for OS/2 and Windows, which supplies a unique interface to the screen for all programs. An older 8086 program, of course, doesn't know anything about this.

The solution for this problem is paging; the address space reserved for the video RAM (see Figure 1.29) can be mapped to a video buffer in main memory. This video buffer forms a «virtual» screen. Then the virtual 8086 monitor can decide which data in the video buffer is actually transferred to which location in the real video RAM. It is thus possible to assign an 8086 program a window on the screen for data output. For this purpose, the data need not even be available in the same form. The virtual 8086 monitor, for example, may convert the data delivered by the 8086 program in text mode into a graphics representation suitable for output in a Windows window or OS/2 Presentation Manager window.

In most cases, 8086 programs don't occupy all the memory that is available with MS-DOS. Thus, a further advantage of paging even with only one virtual 8086 task is that the unoccupied sections of the 10fff0h bytes can be used by other tasks. Without paging, the memory chips at the free locations are not filled with data, yet are unavailable for the storage of data and code for other tasks. As already mentioned, the 8086 program of a virtual 8086 task occupies the lower 10fff0h bytes of *linear address space*. If several virtual 8086 tasks run in parallel they must be swapped completely during a task switch to avoid collision of the address and data of the various tasks. The only option to solve these problems is the i386 paging mechanism.

Each of the various virtual 8086 tasks must map the lower 10fff0h bytes of linear address space to different physical address spaces. This can be achieved by different page table entries for the first 10fff0h bytes corresponding to 272 pages with 4 kbytes each for the individual virtual 8086 tasks. Thus the individual virtual 8086 tasks, and therefore also the 8086 programs, are isolated. Additionally, the other advantages of paging, for example, a large virtual address space and protection of the pages, can be used. If the 8086 programs do not alter the 8086 operating system (that is, they don't overwrite its code), then several 8086 programs may share one copy of the 8086 operating system and the ROM code. The program code always remains the same, but the differences of the 8086 operating systems for the individual tasks are only the different values of registers CS, EIP, SS, SP, DS, etc. These register values are stored in the TSS of the individual virtual 8086 tasks, and therefore define the state of the codes for the individual tasks without the need for several operating system codes. Therefore, a very economical use of the available memory is possible.

In the case of a bug in an 8086 program, it is possible that the 8086 operating system has been overwritten erroneously. Thus, an error in one program also affects the execution of another. This is a clear violation of the i386's protection philosophy! It can be avoided by marking the pages for the 8086 operating system in the page table as read-only (R/W=0) so that any write attempt leads to an exception. If the attempt is a legal update of an 8086 operating system table, the monitor can carry out this job. If an illegal attempt to write occurs, the monitor aborts the 8086 program. Program errors can therefore be detected very quickly.

Destruction caused by overwriting the 8086 program or the 8086 operating system which is exclusively dedicated to the task concerned is not very serious. Only the erroneous program crashes. The virtual 8086 monitor, on the other hand, remains operable if one of the following precautions has been observed.

- The first 10fff0h bytes of the linear address space are exclusively reserved for the 8086 program and the 8086 operating system. Addresses beyond this section cannot be generated without issuing an exception. i386 protected mode applications and system routines are always loaded beyond the address 10fff0h.
- The pages of the virtual 8086 monitor are identified in the respective page table as being supervisor pages (U/S=0). As the 8086 program of virtual 8086 tasks always runs with CPL=3, i.e. the user level, it cannot, therefore, overwrite the virtual 8086 monitor. Such an attempt will lead to an exception, which stops the monitor, to interrupt the erroneous 8086 program.

Do not expect too much from the 8086 compatibility of OS/2 or Windows. The problem with real mode applications under DOS is quite simply that many programmers apply their skills and knowledge to out-trick DOS to obtain the maximum possible performance from a PC. Thus, such programs, for example, read the interrupt vector table and sometimes jump directly to the entry point of the handler, or they overwrite an interrupt vector directly using a MOV instruction instead of using a much slower DOS function call. Such contrived strategies do improve performance under DOS, but at the same time the i386 operating system or the virtual 8086 monitor is being regularly out-smarted. The PC itself is unwilling to execute such «expert programs» for compatibility. In spite of this, the virtual 8086 mode is a powerful instrument, particularly when used together with the paging mechanism of the i386, for embedding older real mode programs in a multitasking environment.

4 Physical Memory Addressing and Memory Access

The memory addressing described previously is of a purely logical nature. You can force the i386, for example, with the instructions MOV reg, mem or MOV mem, reg to access the memory. Besides the memory space, the i386 (and, of course, all other 80x86 processors) have a so-called I/O address space which is accessed by means of the machine instructions IN, OUT, etc. via *ports* in quantities of one byte, word or double word. More details about this in Section 4.3. In reality, to read and write data, the i386 must be able to transmit and receive various control signals and, of course, it also needs power for its circuitry.

4.1 i386 Pin Connections

The i386 control signals and supply voltages are exchanged and received over a total of 124 pins. The i386 is supplied as a *Pin Grid Array (PGA)* package with 132 interface pins. Due to the advances in integrating electronic circuits, the terminals of a chip often need more space than the chip itself. On its underside, the PGA has a corresponding number of contact pins. What is difficult to imagine is that the chip interfaces require more space than the i386 chip itself. Figure 4.1 schematically shows the i386 pinout.

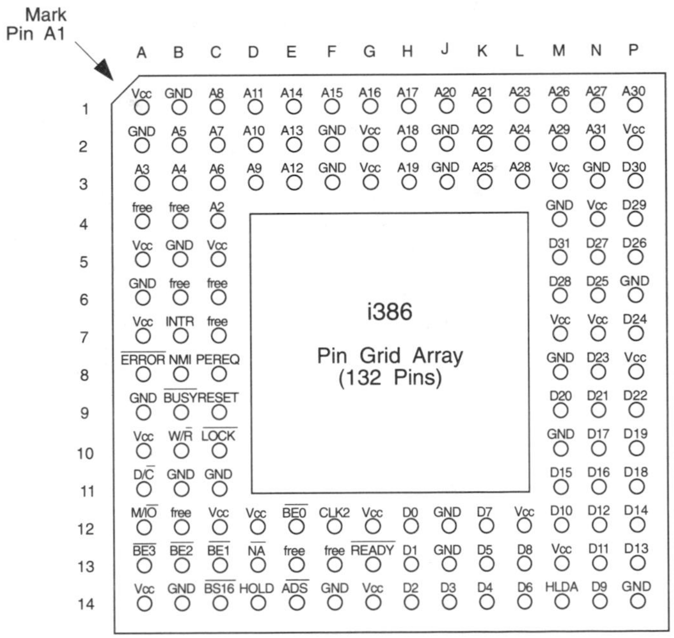

Figure 4.1: The i386 pinout.

In the following, I would like to introduce the i386 interfaces and signals. Using these, the i386 is able to communicate with its environment, that is, the main memory, various controllers and drivers. In the following list, the «I» indicates that the i386 receives (input) a signal at the respective pin, and «O» that a signal is transmitted (output) from the respective pin. A logical high level is usually equal to Vcc (i.e. +5 V), a logical low level equal to GND (0V). LV-models (for Low-Voltage) require only 3.3 V for Vcc. That reduces the power consumption by about 50%. A signal without an overline (such as Signal) is active when high. This means that when it is at a high level, the signal has the specified effect, or indicates at high level the required status. An overlined signal (such as $\overline{\text{Signal}}$) is active when low. In microelectronics, inverted signals are identified using either an overline ($\overline{\text{Signal}}$), a diagonal stroke before (/Signal), a star afterwards (Signal*), or the hash sign afterwards (Signal#). The pins are alphabetically listed.

A31–A2 (O)

Pins A3, B3–B2, C4–C1, D3–D1, E3–E1, F1, G1, H3–H1, J1, K1–K3, L1–L3, M1–M2, N1–N2, P1

The 30 pins produce outputs for the 30 most significant bits of the 32-bit address bus. The two least significant address bits A1 and A0 can be determined via the signals at pins $\overline{\text{BE0}}$–$\overline{\text{BE3}}$.

$\overline{\text{ADS}}$ (O)

Pin E14

As a result of a low level for the address status signal at this pin, the i386 shows that the pins W/$\overline{\text{R}}$, D/$\overline{\text{C}}$ and M/$\overline{\text{IO}}$ are currently providing valid signals for defining the bus cycle and the pins BE0–BE3 and A31–A2 are outputting valid address signals. Normally, when there is a high level at the $\overline{\text{ADS}}$ pin, the aforementioned pins will only transfer non-defined signals.

$\overline{\text{BE3}}$–$\overline{\text{BE0}}$ (O)

Pins A13, B13, C13, E12

The byte enable signals at these four pins indicate, during the current bus cycle, which byte groups of the 32-bit data bus are actually transferring valid data. $\overline{\text{BE0}}$ corresponds to the least significant data byte D0–D7, $\overline{\text{BE3}}$ to the most significant data byte D24–D31. Only combinations of $\overline{\text{BEx}}$ such that there is no inactive $\overline{\text{BEx}}$ between two active $\overline{\text{BEx}}$'s are possible. If the i386 transfers, for example, a word (2 bytes) via pins D23–D8, then it sets $\overline{\text{BE2}}$ and $\overline{\text{BE1}}$ to low (equivalent to active) and $\overline{\text{BE3}}$ and $\overline{\text{BE0}}$ to high (inactive). Thus, $\overline{\text{BE0}}$–$\overline{\text{BE3}}$ determine, in a long-winded way, both of the least significant address bits A1 and A0.

$\overline{\text{BS16}}$ (I)

Pin C14

If an external driver or an external logic transmits a low level signal to this pin (bus size 16), then the i386 will operate its data bus at 16 instead of the usual 32 bits. Thus, the i386 can be directly integrated into a system that only has a 16-bit data bus. In this instance, it operates in the same way as an i386SX. No additional external components are necessary to reduce the data bus width to 16-bits, that is, to split a 32-bit value into two 16-bit values or to join two 16-bit values to give one 32-bit value. This is done automatically by the i386. The 8086 and 80286, for example, require an 8/16-bit converter to allow processor accesses to the 8-bit PC/XT slot.

$\overline{\text{BUSY}}$, $\overline{\text{ERROR}}$ (I, I)
Pins B9, A8

Via this pin, a coprocessor (normally an i387 or other compatible chip) can inform the i386 of its current status. If $\overline{\text{BUSY}}$ is active, then the coprocessor is, at that moment, working with an instruction and cannot accept any further instructions. If the $\overline{\text{ERROR}}$ signal is at a low level (active), the i386 produces a coprocessor interrupt, if it executes certain ESC instructions or a WAIT instruction.

CLK2 (I)
Pin F12

This pin receives the clock signal of an external oscillator. Internally, the i386 divides the clock signal CLK2 by two, to create the effective processor clock (PCLK). Therefore, CLK2 is double the size of the processor clock (hence, the «2»). All clock data and data of the clock cycle for the execution of an instruction relate to the processor clock PCLK.

D31–D0 (I/O)
Pins H12–H14, J14, K14–K12, L14–L13, M12–M11, M9, M6, M5, N14–N8, N6, N5, P13–P9, P7, P5–P3

These 32 pins form the i386 bidirectional 32-bit data bus for the input and output of data. The data bus can be configured as a 32-bit or 16-bit data bus by a high or low level signal at the $\overline{\text{BS16}}$ input. During write operations in 16-bit data mode, the i386 operates using all 32 signals.

HOLD, HLDA (I, O)
Pins D14, M14

The two bus hold request and bus hold acknowledge pins serve the purpose of bus arbitration, that is, for the controlled transfer of control of the local bus between differing local bus masters. If another bus master wishes to take control, it sends a high level signal to the i386 HOLD input. If the control transfer is not internally locked by an active $\overline{\text{LOCK}}$ or the executing of an instruction, then the i386 sends the high level HLDA signal. This is an indication for the requesting bus master that it can take over control of the local bus, but to do so it must first produce the necessary bus control signals. The new bus master maintains the HOLD signal active until it wishes to (or must) return control of the local bus. Subsequently, it deactivates the HOLD signal, and once again the i386 resumes control of the local bus.

INTR (I)
Pin B7

On completion of each instruction, the i386 senses the signal status at this pin. A high level indicates that an interrupt request exists from a hardware unit. Erasing the IE interrupt flag suppresses this strobe, and with it the masking of all hardware interrupt requests.

$\overline{\text{LOCK}}$ (O)
Pin C10

When $\overline{\text{LOCK}}$ is active, that is, a low level signal at this pin, the i386 will not transfer control of the local bus to another bus master, which requests control by means of HOLD. Subsequently, the i386 executes a locked bus cycle and does not react to the HOLD request with an acknowledge (HLDA).

M/$\overline{\text{IO}}$, D/$\overline{\text{C}}$, W/$\overline{\text{R}}$ (O, O, O)
Pins A12, A11, B10

The type of current bus cycle is determined by the signals Memory/$\overline{\text{IO}}$, Data/$\overline{\text{Control}}$, Write/$\overline{\text{Read}}$ at these pins. The possible signal combinations have the following meaning:

(000) Interrupt acknowledge sequence
(001) Invalid
(010) Reading from an I/O port
(011) Writing to an I/O port
(100) Reading an instruction from memory (instruction prefetching)
(101) HALT, if $\overline{\text{BE0}}$=$\overline{\text{BE1}}$=$\overline{\text{BE3}}$=high, $\overline{\text{BE2}}$=low or shutdown, if $\overline{\text{BE0}}$=low, $\overline{\text{BE1}}$=$\overline{\text{BE2}}$=$\overline{\text{BE3}}$=high
(110) Reading data from memory
(111) Writing data to memory

$\overline{\text{NA}}$ (I)
Pin D13

The next address signal has the purpose of implementing address pipelining. The address decoding system of the computer indicates, by means of a low level signal at this pin, that it is ready to receive the new values $\overline{\text{BE0}}$–$\overline{\text{BE3}}$, A2–A31, W/$\overline{\text{R}}$, D/$\overline{\text{C}}$, and M/$\overline{\text{IO}}$ for decoding. Thus, the next bus cycle commences before the present bus cycle is completed by a READY signal, and the i386 performs address pipelining.

NMI (I)
Pin B8

If this pin receives a high level signal, then the i386 issues an interrupt 2, which in contrast to INTR cannot be masked by the interrupt flag, thus it is a non-maskable interrupt (NMI). On completion of the currently running instruction and under all conditions, the i386 suspends the program execution and attends to the interrupt.

PEREQ (I)
Pin C8

An active processor extension request signal at this pin indicates to the i386 that the coprocessor wishes to transfer data to the i386. As the i387 has no memory management and paging unit, the i386 must effect all i387 memory accesses to control access authorization and perform paging.

$\overline{\text{READY}}$ (I)
Pin G13

The signal at this pin indicates whether the addressed peripheral device, for example the main storage area or an I/O device, has completed the necessary access ($\overline{\text{READY}}$=low) or whether it requires more time ($\overline{\text{READY}}$=high). Memory components or peripheral devices that react too slowly to the i386 clock rate tell the i386 to insert one or more wait cycles (wait states), using the

$\overline{READY}$ signal. Thus, the i386 waits until the addressed device has completed the access. A wait state is one processor clock cycle, or two CLK2 clock cycles long.

RESET (I)
Pin C9

If an external unit transmits a high level signal to this pin for at least 15 CLK2 clock cycles, then the i386 will cancel all of its activities and perform an internal processor RESET.

Vcc (I)

Pins A1, A5, A7, A10, A14, C5, C12, D12, G2–G3, G12, G14, L12, M3, M7, M13, N4, N7, P2, P8

These pins are fed with the supply voltage (normally +5 V) to supply the i386 with power.

GND
Pins A2, A6, A9, B1, B5, B11, B14, C11, F2–F3, F14, J2–J3, J12–J13, M4, M8, M10, N3, P6, P14

These pins are connected to ground (normally 0 V).

Free
Pins A4, B4, B6, B12, C6–C7, E13, F13

These pins should always be maintained in a free (not connected) condition.

4.2 Physical Memory Access

In Chapter 3 we only encountered how the i386, with the assistance of its segment and offset registers, logically organizes and addresses data. In reality, to read data from or to write data to the memory, the i386 has to physically address the memory (using the address bus) and transfer the data (via its data bus). Such a bus cycle, whereby data is read or written, follows a definite and strictly defined sequence of address, data and control signals. In addition, the i386 provides its address pins A31–A2 and $\overline{BE3}$–$\overline{BE0}$ with the physical address of the memory object on completion of segmentation and paging, via the addressing unit and the bus interface.

4.2.1 Signal Path Between CPU and Memory

For the correct operation of data transfers, the i386 signals are not normally used directly for the control of the memory or the system bus. Instead, an additional bus controller is usually available, which makes all bus signals available to the memory device with sufficient strength. The bus controller also serves to implement the MULTIBUS bus design, in order to make possible a so-called *multiprocessor operation* of many processors. Today, the bus controller is, together with the address and data buffers and additional control circuitry, the main part of a highly integrated system controller. It embraces the functions of earlier support chips, for example the DMA chip 8237, the programmable interval timer 8253/8254 and the programmable interrupt controller 8259. Their logical structure, and how they appear to the programmer at a register level, remain the same. Thus, all further explanations (including Part 4 which describes support chips) are still valid. However, at this point, I do not wish to go into any further depth regarding i386 support chips. Figure 4.2 shows the principal signal paths between the processor and the memory.

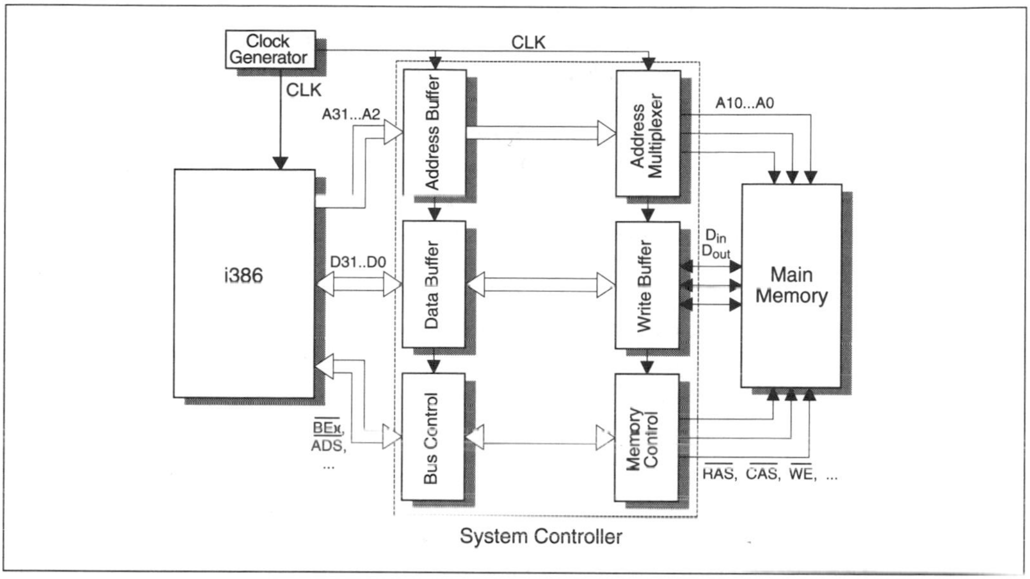

Figure 4.2: The path between processor and main memory. Usually the processor does not access the memory directly. Instead a bus controller for generating the necessary control signals for the bus and various buffers for temporary storage and amplifying the data and address signals are provided between the i386 and the RAM. The memory controller drives the main memory, so that it outputs correct data or writes it to the appropriate location. The buffer and control elements shown as individual components in the figure are today usually part of one single, highly integrated system controller.

If the i386 wishes to read data from memory, it transmits an address to the *address buffer*, via its address bus. If the $\overline{ADS}$ signal is active, the address buffer accepts the address bits and locks them. At this point, $\overline{BE0}$–$\overline{BE3}$ define which data bus line should actually transfer the data. To address the correct word in the main storage area, an *address multiplexer* is available; it selects the chosen word from the main memory with the assistance of the *memory controller*. The data that has been read is then transferred from the main memory to the memory buffer. Subsequently, the *memory buffer* transfers the data to the *data buffer*, from which the i386 can read the data. The diagram shown represents a memory system without a cache. The memory and data buffers can also be one and the same, to prevent an extra transfer from the memory to the data buffer from occurring. Such matters are entirely dependent upon the individual design of the motherboard. The developer has almost total freedom, because the layout is transparent for software. Data transfer is only achieved by electrical signals, and not by software instructions.

The coordination of all these processes (that is, driving the buffer and control circuits) is carried out using the clock signal from the clock generator. Without this signal, complete chaos would arise, and correct data transfer would be impossible. However, the clock signals lead to correct execution, and give the individual circuits enough time to fulfil their tasks. If the clock frequency is increased, at some time a point is reached where one or more circuits is unable to keep up, and completely unpredictable values are read. The computer crashes.

Perhaps you have wondered why the upper 384 kbytes of main memory (with a total of 1 Mbyte) don't start immediately above the lower 640 kbytes but instead continue above 1 Mbyte? Of course, you have inserted memory chips without leaving any «hole» between 640 k and 1 M. The memory chips are correctly located side-by-side. The address multiplexer is responsible for managing this «hole» in the address space. It passes all accesses to the lower 640 kbytes of main memory to the inserted chips, but an access to the section between 640 kbytes and 1 Mbyte is handled according to the mapping shown in Figure 1.28. Thus, the address multiplexer (or an equivalent chip), for example, accesses the video RAM in the graphics adapter if a write to address B800:0210 occurs. Similarly, accesses to the ROM chips of the BIOS, to the extension adapters for networks, and to others are also diverted. For an address above 1 M, the address multiplexer again accesses the main memory chips on the motherboard. This assignment is wired and can be programmed with modern memory controllers (see Section 17.2), but has nothing to do with the logical mapping of the address space in the segmentation and paging unit.

As you can see in Figure 4.2, data and control bus signals can be transferred/communicated in both directions. Thus, a bidirectional bus is created. Primarily, the control bus carries $\overline{\text{READY}}$ and the various signals for the definition of the current bus cycle (M/$\overline{\text{IO}}$, D/$\overline{\text{C}}$, W/$\overline{\text{R}}$). In contrast, the i386 transmits addresses, but of course never reads them. Therefore, this part of the system bus is unidirectional.

4.2.2 Bus Cycle for Read Access

In Figure 4.3 you can see the waveform of the most important system bus signals for reading data. The i386 can execute an access either with or without pipelined addressing; the deciding factor is the level of the $\overline{\text{NA}}$ signal.

The following signals are essential for reading data without address pipelining and waitstates:

- the external clock signal CLK2 from the clock generator,
- the address and status signals $\overline{\text{BE0}}$–$\overline{\text{BE3}}$, A2–A31 and $\overline{\text{ADS}}$ from the processor,
- the $\overline{\text{NA}}$ signal from the system controller for the control of the address pipelines,
- the data signals D0–D31 from memory, and
- the $\overline{\text{READY}}$ signal, to indicate completion of data reading.

The typical i386 bus cycle, shown in Figure 3.3, for reading data from memory without waitstates, requires at least four clock cycles at CLK2, which is equivalent to two processor clock cycles PCLK. Thus, an i386 at 40 MHz can execute 20 million bus cycles per second. Theoretically, using a 32-bit data bus, the i386 reaches a transfer rate of 80 Mbytes per second.

Each bus cycle is divided into two parts, T1 and T2. T1 identifies the so-called *status cycle* and T2 the *command cycle*. Both cycles are either exactly one processor clock cycle (PCLK) long, or exactly two system clock cycles (CLK2) long. During the T1 status cycle, the control and address signals are transmitted and, additionally during the writing of data, the data signals D31 to D0 are transmitted. The $\overline{NA}$ signal is produced by the system controller and is used to control the address pipelines. An active $\overline{NA}$ signal (low level) instructs the i386 to make the address for the subsequent bus cycle available to the system controller prior to completion of the current cycle. More detail is contained in the following.

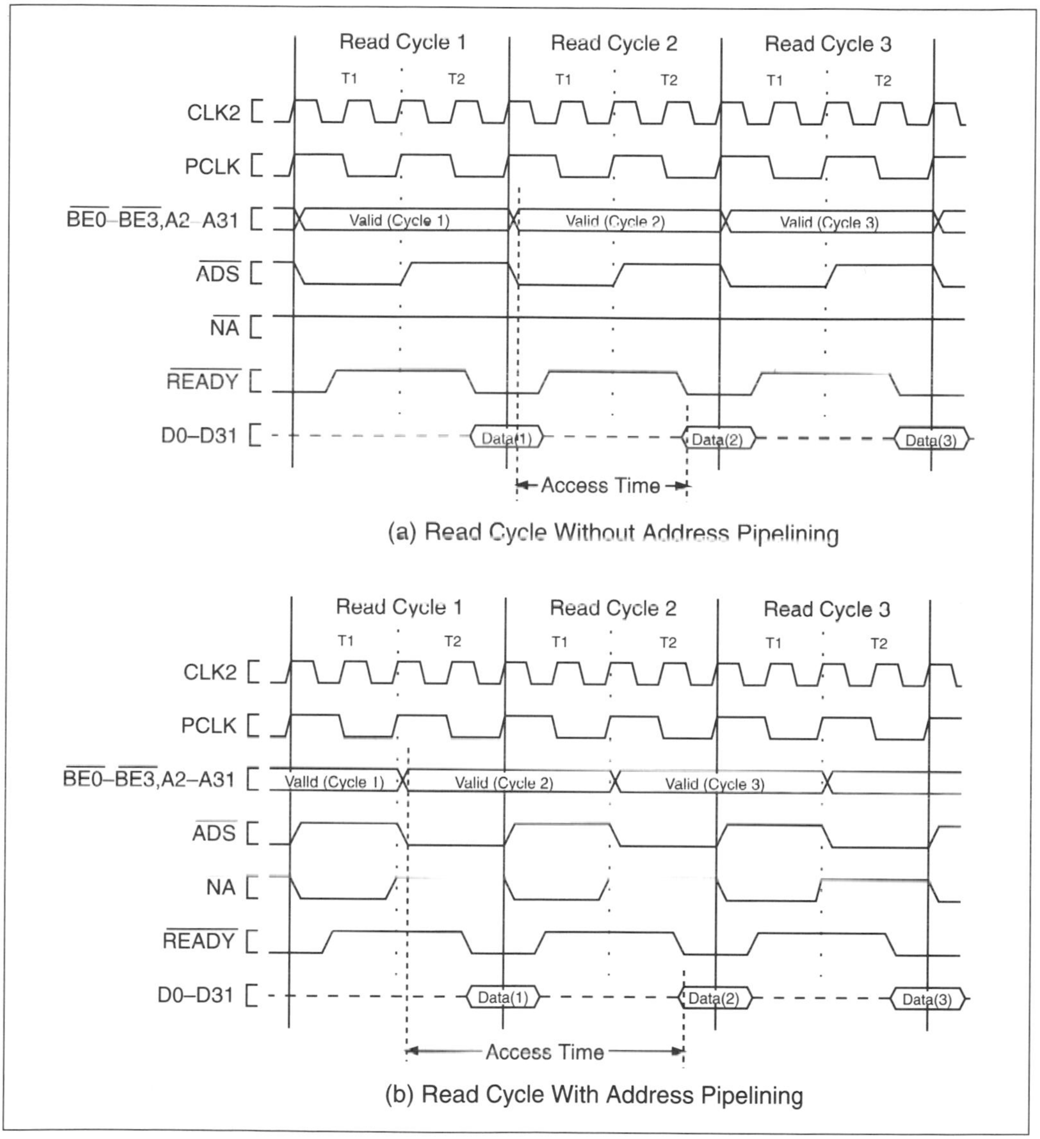

Figure 4.3: i386 read cycles with and without address pipelining. The i386 is able to operate without (a) or with (b) pipelined addressing in a selectable manner. First the processor outputs the address and waits for the data from main memory. The access time is the time interval between the output of the address by the i386 and the return of the data from main memory.

The address signals A31 to A2 define the address of a memory double word. The $\overline{\text{BE0–BE3}}$ signals specify whether an individual byte, a word or a double word should be read, and determine which bytes are valid within the addressed double word. The i386 $\overline{\text{ADS}}$ indicates that the address and control signals are valid. The reading process is thus started, and the $\overline{\text{READY}}$ signal rises to a high level. It only drops back down to a low level once the memory has transferred the required data to the data buffer. The memory controller initiates an internal read process of the main memory, and the address multiplexer addresses the corresponding data in the main memory.

During the course of the T2 bus cycle, the memory (or some other peripheral device) executes the i386 read requirements, transfers the data bytes that have been read to the data buffers, and sets $\overline{\text{READY}}$ to low, to indicate the internal reading process. The data buffer amplifies and locks the data. Subsequently, the i386 reads the data from the data buffer and completes the bus cycle.

On completion of the T2 cycle, the system bus returns to the start condition. It is now possible to commence a new read or write process. If no data transfer is to take place, the bus remains in an idle condition until such time as the i386, using the corresponding control signals, indicates that it again wishes to read or write data.

Figure 4.3 also shows the *memory access time,* that is, the time that has elapsed before the memory has answered a read request with a data output. The access time is the time difference between the input of a valid address signal to memory and the output of valid data from memory.

The circuitry clock frequency and reaction times between the processor and the main memory are fixed by the electronic design of the computer. Therefore, the memory must adjust itself to the required access time, and not the CPU. From Figure 4.3 you can see that the memory access time, without waitstates, may amount to a maximum of three clock cycles (CLK2), or one and a half processor clock cycles (PCLK), that is, the time difference from the address output to the data validity at the bus. Added to this are the signal transmission times in the buffer circuits, which in practice means that the time available for the memory component access is actually shorter. If the memory chip can not fulfil this requirement, the i386 must wait. This is controlled by the $\overline{\text{READY}}$ signal.

4.2.3 Bus Cycle for Write Access

Similar processes apply for writing data to memory as for reading data from memory. Figure 4.4 shows the most important signals for an i386 write cycle without address pipelining.

Using the control signal W/$\overline{\text{R}}$ with a high level (here, «W» is decisive, not «R»), the i386 indicates to the addressing and memory device that it wishes to write to memory. First, at the start of T1 the processor transmits the address to the address bus and, additionally, at the end of the first T1 CLK2 cycle the write data to the data bus. Using an active $\overline{\text{ADS}}$, the data buffer accepts the write data and transfers it to the memory buffer. At the same time, the memory controller controls the main memory, to address the internal memory cells and to execute the internal write procedure.

If the memory subsystem has completed the internal write process, the memory controller pulls the $\overline{\text{READY}}$ signal to a low level so as to inform the processor of the execution of the write access. The i386 completes the write process by deactivating the buffer and resetting the system bus to the start condition.

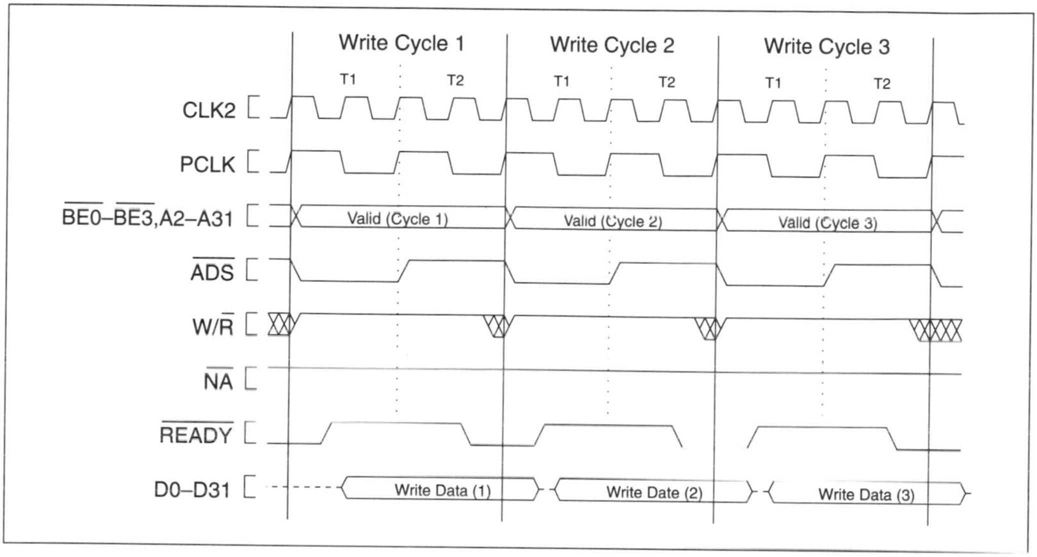

Figure 4.4: i386 write cycles without address pipelining. Unlike a read cycle, in a write cycle the i386 not only provides the memory address, but also the write data a short time afterwards.

Even when writing, the $\overline{\text{READY}}$ signal produces a flexible reaction to delays in the addressed memory, in that the memory requests wait cycles. More about this in the next section.

4.2.4 Wait States

If the memory or peripheral device cannot conclude a read or write request within the two T1 and T2 cycles, then the memory controller (or more generally, the controller of the addressed unit) holds the $\overline{\text{READY}}$ signal at high level. This indicates to the i386 that it should implement another T2 instruction cycle to give the memory or peripheral device more time to conform to the request. This is known as a *Wait cycle* or a *Wait state*. If, on completion of the additional T2, the $\overline{\text{READY}}$ signal is still at a high level, then the processor inserts another wait cycle (and another, and another and so on). Figure 4.5 shows a write bus cycle with one wait state (or wait cycle).

In the illustration, the nth bus cycle leads to a wait cycle, the $(n+1)^{th}$, however, does not. The i386 maintains the write data active until the end of the first system clock CLK2 after the last T2 of the current bus cycle. If two bus cycles follow immediately after each other, this means that the write data is active until, at least, the end of the first system clock CLK2 of the *next* bus cycle.

Of course, the number of wait cycles for writing data can differ to that for reading data. DRAM main memories can, in fact, write data quicker than they can read it. The reason for this is that when writing, it is sufficient to transfer the memory controller address and the value of the data byte. The memory controller executes the write process independently using the stored data from the data or the memory buffer, while the i386 can devote itself to another process, and does not have to wait for the conclusion of the write process resulting from a slow memory device. In contrast, when reading, the CPU has no other choice but to wait for the completion of the internal reading process in the main storage area. Prior to this, no other data will be available.

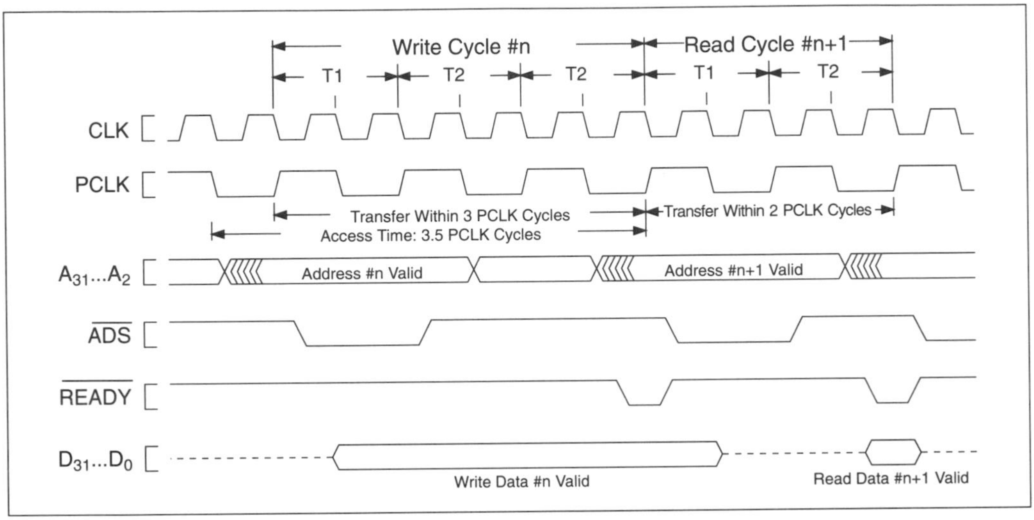

Figure 4.5: i386 write bus cycle with one wait state. The i386 inserts one or more wait states if the accessed device is not able to follow the fast clocked i386 and does not activate the $\overline{READY}$ signal (with a low level) in time.

The number of wait cycles can also depend upon the location of the memory. The main storage area on the motherboard operates with far fewer wait states than, for example, the video RAM on a graphics adapter, which in a PC is also a part of the i386 address space. Anything up to ten wait states can occur in this case. The cause of this is not an incorrectly chosen memory chip, but the low clock rate of 8 MHz for the connection between the plug-in board and the adapter (the i386 can run at up to 40 MHz). Furthermore, the video RAM is not always accessible in many graphic adapters, thus further delays occur.

The quantity of wait states was previously determined by the board design, or could be ascertained by a jumper, depending on how fast the installed memory chips were. In those days, the memory controller reacted in a standard manner with a predetermined delay of the $\overline{READY}$ signal. Today this process is out of date. Modern and efficient concepts such as cache memory and page interleaved memory use principles of statistics, therefore a flexible output of the $\overline{READY}$ signal is required, as the exact quantity of wait cycles for an individual memory access cannot be predicted. This requires a flexible quantity of wait cycles in relation to the actual installation. Therefore, with fast clocked 40 MHz i386 PCs, no wait cycle is necessary, for example, during access to the main memory. An access to the normal main storage area would typically require two wait cycles.

4.2.5 Address Pipelining or Pipelined Addressing

To execute memory and port accesses as quickly as possible, pipelining is supported by the i386 bus interface (Figure 4.3b). In the illustration you can see that the i386 transmits the address signal for the next bus cycle prior to the end of the current bus cycle. This is possible because the processor only has to make the address of the memory position to be addressed available in the status cycle. By the activation of $\overline{ADS}$, the signals are transferred to the address buffer and decoded using the address decoder. In this case, it is important that the decoder completes its operation, that is, decoding of an address, before the memory accepts data (write) or transfers data to the processor (read). During the time that the main memory is internally reading (or writing to) the chosen memory position, the addressing logic in the associated processor-memory connection is almost redundant while waiting for the next address to be decoded. In the same sense, the data transfer logic is not active if the address decoder is decoding the next address.

The i386 can transfer the next address to the decoder at the same time that the data transfer logic is still busy with data reading or writing. Thus, the decoder logic and address buffer can work in advance. Subsequent accesses are interlocked: the addressing logic receives the new address one processor clock cycle prior to the end of the current bus cycle. In this way, consecutive bus cycles require three clock cycles, but the effective time is reduced to two PCLK cycles as a result of interlinking the bus cycles. This interlinking, or overlapping, of input and output data and addresses of consecutive bus cycles is known as *pipelined addressing* or *address pipelining*. The signals flow continuously as if in a pipeline. Figure 4.6 shows this overlapping of bus cycles.

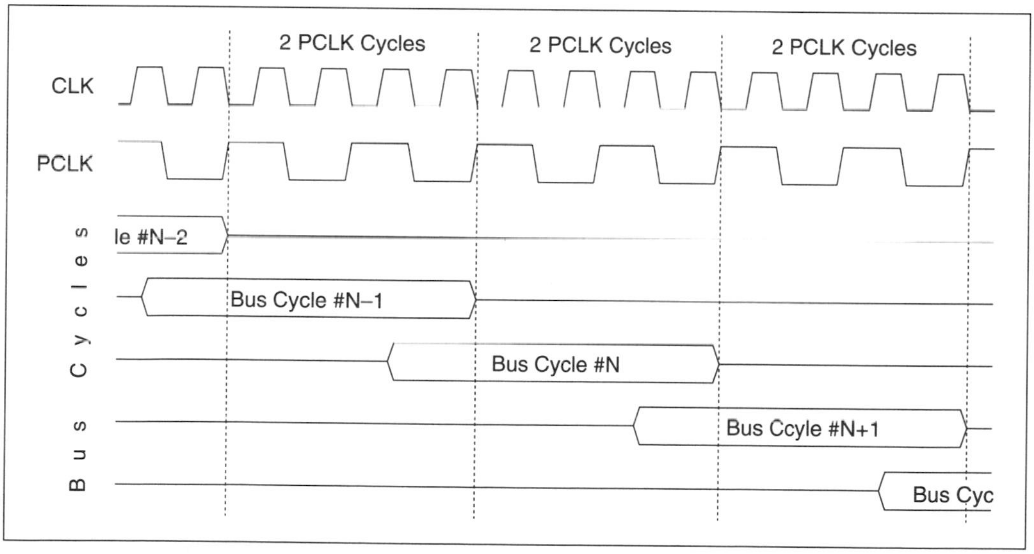

Figure 4.6: Pipelined addressing on the i386. With active pipelined addressing the i386 outputs the following address before the current bus cycle has terminated. Thus, the addressed device is able to decode the new address while the previous data is still being transferred.

Pipelined addressing is only an advantage if several memory accesses are to be executed one after the other. During the first access, the i386 has to start the pipelining by producing the address of the first access. This is similar to the production line at a car factory: several hours pass before the first car can be assembled and eventually leave the production line. Once the production line (or the «vehicle pipeline») is full, a new car will leave the assembly area every couple of minutes. Pipelined addressing is particularly advantageous for extensive memory accessing, such as occurs with a task switch or when loading the processor cache register in protected mode.

The i386 piplined addressing is controlled by the (external) control signal $\overline{NA}$. The system designer is thus free to choose between addressing with or without address pipelining. A special feature is that during i386 operation, the choice can be almost on-line, individual for each bus cycle. Thus, the i386 can be switched between an access, either with or without address pipelining (Figure 4.3).

Without address pipelining, the $\overline{NA}$ signal is always high, that is, inactive. At the start of a read cycle, the address signals $\overline{BE0}$–$\overline{BE3}$ and A31–A2 are output, and these remain valid until the end of the respective read cycle. The interval between address signal output and the transfer of data (the access time) is approximately three CLK2 cycles.

The i386 only performs address pipelining if $\overline{NA}$ is pulled down to a low level in time by the memory addressing logic. The i386 then, during the second half of the preceding bus cycle, produces the necessary address signals. In this instance, the interval between the output of the address and the receipt of the data lasts five CLK2 cycles. Therefore, for accesses, two more CLK2 cycles or an internal processor clock PCLK are available without a reduction in the data transfer rate between the CPU and memory. Put another way, during memory access, the number of wait cycles can be reduced by one, or other slower components could be used, without an increase in the number of wait states.

Address pipelining is, therefore, very advantageous for accessing slower memory components. Address pipelining is generally used by the i386 for the addressing of slower DRAM components. No address pipelining is necessary if a cache memory is available with a very short access time, as the SRAM components of the cache are quick enough to provide data without address pipelining and with 0 wait cycles.

Pipelining was first implemented with the 80286 (although not in such a flexible way as in the i386). The first 80x86 processor, the 8086, was not able to carry this out as, unlike the 80286, it has a combined address/data bus. Thus, during the later data transfer phase the bus is occupied by this data, and cannot be used for an early transfer of the following address.

4.2.6 Double Word Boundary

The i386 represents a 32-bit processor with a 32-bit data bus, thus the main memory is normally organized as a physical 32-bit memory (a 16-bit organization, as with the 80286, would halve the bus bandwidth). This means that the i386 always physically addresses the byte addresses 0, 4, 8, ..., 4G–4. In fact, logically, double words (32-bit) can start at an address that is not a multiple of four. However, the double word cannot be physically read from or written to such an address in one attempt. If a double word is to be stored at or read from an address that does not represent a double word address, the i386 bus interface splits the double word access into two accesses. The first access reads or writes the least significant part of the double word; the second accesses the most significant part. Such a double word part is between one and three bytes long (four bytes would, of course, be a double word access at a double word address).

This process is totally transparent to the software, that is, the hardware is responsible for the division and double memory access without the influence of software. Thus the programmer can sort data into a preferential form without having to worry about double word boundaries.

During the two-part access, the memory is physically addressed by the double word addresses 0, 4, etc., but is only read or written according to the setting of bytes $\overline{BE0}$–$\overline{BE3}$. Furthermore, the i386 can also read and write individual bytes or 16-bit words. A single access is all that is required, providing that a 16-bit data word does not cross a double word boundary.

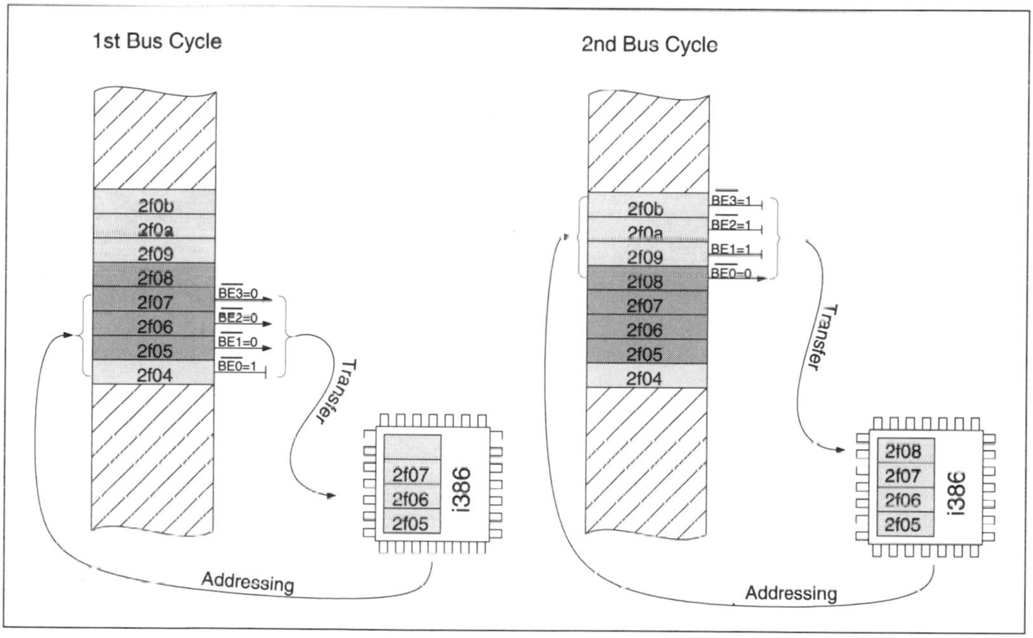

Figure 4.7: Access to a double word that does not begin at a double word boundary. As the memory of the 32-bit processor i386 is organized in 32-bit portions, the i386 cannot access directly double words that do not start at double word boundaries. Instead, the i386 has to split such an access into two successive accesses. In both accesses a whole double word is addressed, but only the required one to three bytes are actually fetched and combined into one single 32-bit double word. The i386 bus interface carries out the two accesses automatically.

Figure 4.7 represents a read access. The bus interface executes an access twice when accessing the word with the odd address 2f05h. Initially, the three bytes with the addresses 2f05h, 2f06h and 2f07h are read. This occurs as a result of the processor producing the 2f04h address, and simultaneously setting the byte enable signals as shown: $\overline{BE0}=1$, $\overline{BE1}=0$, $\overline{BE2}=0$, $\overline{BE3}=0$. The three least significant bytes of the double word are thus read to the address 2f05h. Immediately after this, the CPU provides the 2f08h address and simultaneously sets $\overline{BE0}=0$, $\overline{BE1}=1$, $\overline{BE2}=1$,

$\overline{\text{BE3}}$=1. The most significant byte is therefore read to the address 2f08h. The bus interface combines the first three bytes and the last byte read into a double word at the address 2f05h. Thus, by using a double access, the i386 has addressed a double word that does not start at a double word address. To write a word to such an address, the same process is run in reverse.

Bytes with the address *4n* (n=0 to G=1) are always carried over the data bus lines D7 to D0, and bytes with the address *4n+1* via D15 to D8. The same applies for bytes with the address *4n+2*, which always use the lines D23 to D16, and bytes with the address *4n+3*, which use lines D31 to D24. Something similar also applies to ports.

Generally, during both part accesses, the memory controller executes a complete 32-bit access and can, in each case, also output all 32-bits to the data bus. However, either the system controller or the i386 will accept only the bytes for which $\overline{\text{BEx}}$ (x=0–3) is at a low level.

It is clear that reading or writing a double word from/to an address that is not a multiple of four always requires two bus cycles, whereas accessing a double word at a double word address only requires one bus cycle. Therefore, it is advantageous, even when unnecessary, always to sort the data in memory so that double words start at a double word address and the normal 16-bit words do not cross double word boundaries.

This procedure only applies to data. The prefetch queue always reads the code in double word portions, which start at a double word address. For this reason, the prefetch queue is only refilled if it has at least four bytes free. To reach a double word address, the processor, if required, reads one to three bytes first.

4.2.7 Special Bus Cycles

In addition to the three «normal» bus cycles for reading and writing data, and the passive bus cycle (if neither the prefetch queue has to be loaded, nor the instruction that has just been executed requires a memory or I/O access), there are also the shutdown and halt cycles. These are given by the combination (101) of the M/$\overline{\text{IO}}$, D/$\overline{\text{C}}$, W/$\overline{\text{R}}$ signals and differentiated by levels of $\overline{\text{BE0}}$–$\overline{\text{BE3}}$. The shutdown cycle ($\overline{\text{BE0}}$=0, $\overline{\text{BE1}}$=$\overline{\text{BE2}}$=$\overline{\text{BE3}}$=1) takes place if, during execution of an instruction, several exceptions occur and the processor is overloaded. To cope with this, the processor goes «on strike». The halt condition ($\overline{\text{BE0}}$=$\overline{\text{BE1}}$=$\overline{\text{BE3}}$=1, $\overline{\text{BE2}}$=0) can be initiated by the HLT instruction. In this instance, the processor is stopped and does not execute any further instructions. Table 4.1 summarizes the special cycles. Note that special cycles must be acknowledged by the system with $\overline{\text{READY}}$ in the same way as normal bus cycles.

$\overline{\text{BE3}}$	$\overline{\text{BE2}}$	$\overline{\text{BE1}}$	$\overline{\text{BE0}}$	**Special cycle**
1	0	1	1	halt cycle
1	1	1	0	shutdown cycle

Table 4.1: i386 special cycles (signals M/$\overline{\text{IO}}$=1, D/$\overline{\text{C}}$=0, W/$\overline{\text{R}}$=1)

If the hardware IRQs are enabled, then the IE flag is set, and the processor can be forced to leave the halt condition by initiating an IRQ. For example, in the PC, such an IRQ can be activated by touching the keyboard. The shutdown condition is not affected by this; the processor ignores the demand.

To end the shutdown condition, either an NMI or a processor reset must be initiated. Both of these also end the halt condition. The difference between them is that the NMI does not change the processor mode. If, prior to shutdown, the i386 was running in protected mode, then, after an NMI, it is returned to protected mode and the interrupt handler 2 corresponding to NMI is started. In contrast to this, a processor reset returns the i386 to real mode, and the i386 begins program execution with CS=f000h, EIP=0000fff0h and the activated address lines A31–A20.

Shutdown only occurs as the result of a very serious problem, the cause of which is most likely to be an extensive hardware error function. Such a serious error function can be caused by, for example, power failure, lightning strike or chip destruction. Most often, as the result of an external initiation of an NMI or reset, the processor starts a so-called *recovery routine* in order to save what is possible. Application programmers are hardly ever confronted with this problem. Recovery and handling routines for a shutdown status are part of the operating system.

4.2.8 Flexible i386 Bus – 16-bit Data Bus and Write Data Duplication

When the 32-bit data bus was introduced with the i386, 32-bit peripheral chips were either very expensive or did not exist. That is why Intel included a very flexible data bus with the i386, which can be run using either the 16-bit width or the full 32-bit width. Thus, the i386 can be integrated into a 16-bit system and make use of the 16-bit peripheral chips, if it can be justified. Today, however, little use is made of this. As a result of the flexible construction of the buses, the i386 can be connected directly to a 16-bit data bus and simultaneously to a 32-bit data bus. This is because the switch-over does not occur through wiring, but instead is flexible for each bus cycle. Therefore, it is possible, for example, for the i386 to use a 32-bit data bus for main storage area access, and a 16-bit data bus for accessing the I/O address space or ISA bus slots.

If the pin $\overline{\text{BS16}}$ is fed with the low level signal, then the current bus cycle is restricted to the 16 bits between D15–D0. Bytes addressed via $\overline{\text{BE2}}$ and $\overline{\text{BE3}}$, which apply to the most significant 16 bits D31–D16, are internally transferred by the i386 to the least significant bits D15–D0 in a suitable manner. If values greater than 16 bits are to be transferred, then the i386 will independently execute several bus cycles, one after the other, until the data transfer has been completed.

A further special feature of the i386 for increasing system throughput is the automatic duplication of write data. Using the signals $\overline{\text{BE0}}$–$\overline{\text{BE3}}$, the processor determines which 8-bit groups of its 32-bit data bus will transfer valid data. If the i386 implements a bus cycle for writing data, in which the written data only occurs at the most significant word (D31–D16), that is, only $\overline{\text{BE2}}$ and $\overline{\text{BE3}}$ are active, then the i386 automatically produces the same data on the least significant half (D15–D0) of the data bus. Using this principle, the throughput of a system with a 16-bit data bus can be increased independently of $\overline{\text{BS16}}$. This is because the 16/32-bit converter of the 16-bit bus system must first transfer the data bytes from the most significant half to the data bytes of the least significant half. This transfer is no longer necessary as the data is automatically duplicated; the bus system is, therefore, more efficient. If the written data is only output on the least significant half (D15–D0) of the data bus, then there will be no written data duplication to the most significant half. Table 4.2 shows the relationship between the signals $\overline{BE0}$–$\overline{BE3}$ and written data duplication.

$\overline{BE3}$	$\overline{BE2}$	$\overline{BE1}$	$\overline{BE0}$	D31–D24	D23–D16	D15–D8	D7–D0	Duplication
0	0	0	0	B31–B24	B23–B16	B15–B8	B7–B0	no
0	0	0	1	B23–B16	B15–B8	B7–B0	undef.	no
0	0	1	1	B15–B8	B7–B0	B15–B8	B7–B0	yes
0	1	1	1	B7–B0	undef.	B7–B0	undef.	yes
1	1	1	0	undef.	undef.	undef.	B7–B0	no
1	1	0	0	undef.	undef.	B15–B8	B7–B0	no
1	0	0	0	undef.	B23–B16	B15–B8	B7–B0	no
1	1	0	1	undef.	undef.	B7–B0	undef.	no
1	0	0	1	undef.	B15–B8	B7–B0	undef.	no
1	0	1	1	undef.	B7–B0	undef.	B7–B0	yes

B31–B24: write data bits 31–24 B23–B16: write data bits 23–16 undef.: values are undefined
B15–B8: write data bits 15–8 B7–B0: write data bits 7–0

Table 4.2: Write data duplication on the i386

4.3 I/O Address Space and Peripherals

So far, we have only learned about logical addressing of the memory using offset and segment and physical addressing with the assistance of the 32-bit address bus. For example, the memory is addressed with the instructions MOV reg, mem or MOV mem, reg. In addition to the memory area, the i386 has a so-called *I/O address space,* which can be accessed with the machine instructions IN, OUT, etc. via ports. Altogether, the i386 can address 65356 (=64k) 8-bit ports using the addresses 0 to 65535; 32768 (=32k) 16-bit ports using the addresses 0, 2, 4, ..., 65532, 65534; or 16348 (=16k) 32-bit ports 0, 4, ..., 65532. A mixture of 8-bit, 16-bit and 32-bit ports is also possible. The respective 8-bit equivalent, however, must not exceed 64k. Thus, the i386 has two totally separate address spaces: the memory and the I/O space, both of which are addressed via the data and address bus. A memory access is differentiated from an I/O access by the M/$\overline{IO}$ control signal. The I/O address space can only be addressed logically with the help of the accumulator; the memory, on the other hand, can be addressed by all registers. Additionally, the segment registers for the I/O address space have no significance. It can be said that the 64k port represents its own segment, which is addressed by IN and OUT. Common IBM-compatible PCs only use the lower 1024 (1k) ports between 0 and 3ffh. EISA, microchannel and local bus PCs expand the I/O address area.

The ports and the I/O address space are mostly used for addressing *registers* in peripheral devices. The IN and OUT instructions (and variations) make direct contact between the processor accumulator and the peripheral device register, and transfer data between them. This means that when the i386 executes an *I/O mapped I/O* (or *I/O mapped Input/Output*), the registers are located in the I/O-address space, in contrast to the so-called *memory mapped I/O,* where the peripheral device registers are located in the conventional memory address space. They are addressed with the normal memory instructions, for example, MOV mem, reg. A suitable decoder and controller logic then accesses a register instead of a memory cell.

4.3.1 I/O Addressing

If the i386 wishes to address a port, then it produces the low level $M/\overline{IO}$ output signal. The system controller recognizes that an access to the I/O address space should be executed. Additionally, via $W/\overline{R}$, the transfer direction is determined i386 → port ($W/\overline{R}=1$) or port → i386 ($W/\overline{R}=0$). Writing data to a port, or reading data from a port is performed in the same manner as writing and reading data to and from the memory. Figure 4.8 shows the path for the data transfer between processor and ports.

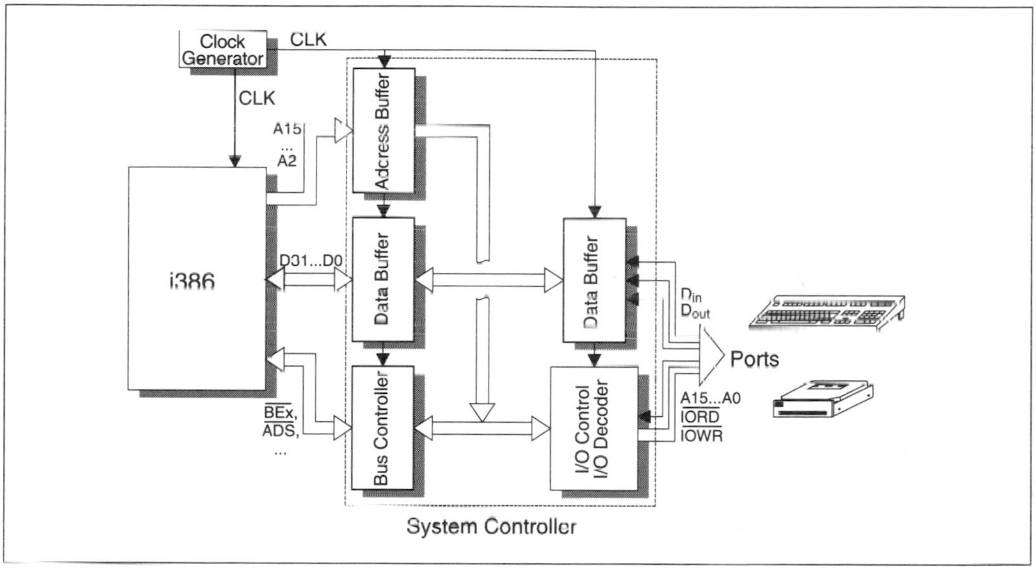

Figure 4.8: The path between processor and ports. Usually the processor does not access the I/O address space directly, but instead via a bus controller, as is the case for main memory, too. The bus controller generates the necessary control signals for the bus and various buffers for temporary storage and amplifying the data and address signals. These intermediate circuits are today integrated into one single system controller.

Like the reading and writing of data from and to the main memory, the CPU gives an address to the address buffer and controls the bus controller using the status signals $M/\overline{IO}$, $D/\overline{C}$ and $W/\overline{R}$. If data is to be transferred to a port (with OUT), the i386 provides additional information. The bus controller logic recognizes from the $M/\overline{IO}$ control signal that an access of the I/O-address space and not the memory should take place. Thus, instead of the memory controller, the I/O controller is activated, which decodes the address signal from the address buffer and addresses the appropriate port. This applies in most cases to a register in a peripheral device (for instance, keyboard or hard disk) or in a hardware component (for example, the mode controller register in a DMA chip). Thus, data can be transferred between the processor and a register in the I/O address space of the PC. The i386 can address a maximum of 64k 8-bit ports, such that the 16 most significant lines A31–A16 are always at a low level for access to a port.

4.3.2 I/O Cycles

Figure 4.9 shows the bus cycle for a write access to the I/O address space. A comparison with Figure 4.3 shows that the bus cycle and the associated signals agree, with the exception of M/$\overline{\text{IO}}$, with which a write access to the memory is made.

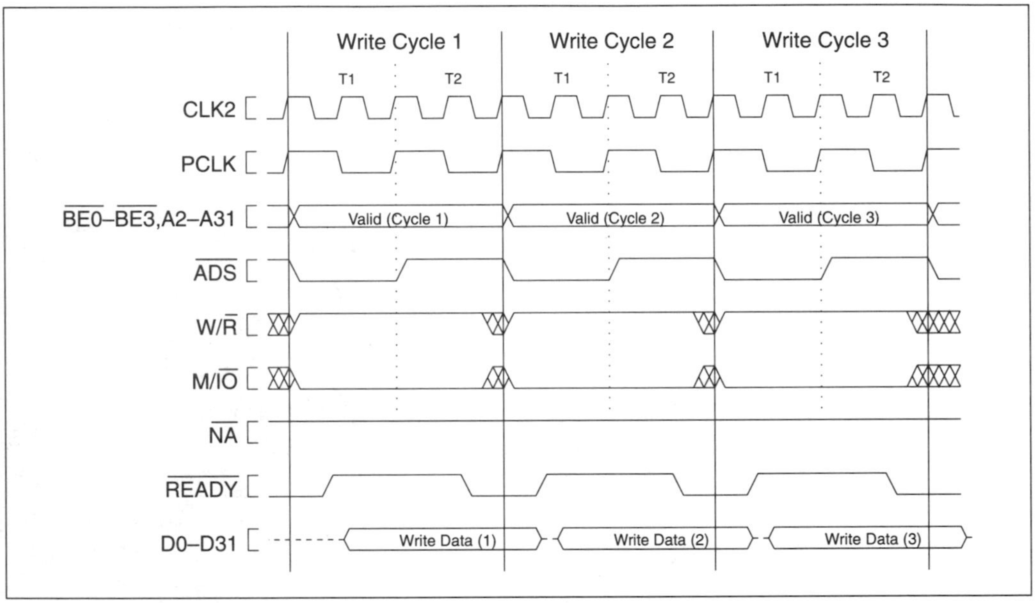

Figure 4.9: i386 bus cycle for a write access to the I/O address space.

As ports refer mostly to control and status registers of hardware components, which moreover (for example, in a PC) are frequently placed on a slower plug-in board in a bus slot, the i386 frequently inserts more wait cycles for port accesses than for memory accesses. For this reason, the device being addressed also uses the $\overline{\text{READY}}$ signal to request additional wait cycles from the CPU. This, of course, increases the I/O access time. Otherwise, there is no difference to a memory cycle, except for the fact that other buffers and decoders are addressed.

5 Processor Reset and the i386 Internal Self-Test

The i386 initiates a reset, in that the system controller feeds a high level signal for at least 15 CLK2 clock cycles to the RESET pin. If the signal subsequently returns to a low level, the i386 carries out an internal initialization. During this operation, the registers are loaded with the values shown in Table 5.1.

Register	Value
EFlag	uuuuuuuu uuuuuu00 00000000 00000010 = uuuu0002h
CR0	0uuuuuuu uuuuuuuu uuuuuuuu uuuu0000 = uuuuuuu0h
EIP	00000000 00000000 11111111 11110000 = 0000fff0h
CS	11110000 00000000 = f000h*)
DS	00000000 00000000 = 0000h
SS	00000000 00000000 = 0000h
ES	00000000 00000000 = 0000h
FS	00000000 00000000 = 0000h
GS	00000000 00000000 = 0000h
EDX	processor identification
all others	uuuuuuuu uuuuuuuu uuuuuuuu uuuuuuuu = uuuuuuuuh

u: undefined
*) base address = ffff0000h, limit = ffffh (segment descriptor cache register)

Table 5.1: i386 register contents after a processor reset

The i386 starts operation in real mode. As shown in Table 5.1, the pair CS:EIP contains f000:0000fff000 after the internal initialization of the memory address. In reality, however, the i386 produces the physical address fffffff0h because the 12 most significant lines A31–A20 of the address bus are held at a high level (due to the value ffff0000h for the base address of the code segment in the segment descriptor cache register). That is 16 bytes less than the absolute end of the physical address space. Additionally, the machine status word is loaded with fff0h. The GDTR, LDTR, IDTR and the task register have no influence.

After the first JMP or CALL instruction outside the segment limit (that is, after an inter-segment jump or call), the address lines A31–A20 drop to low level. The associated CS change invalidates the entries in the segment descriptor cache register, and the i386 now loads and handles the segment values strictly in accordance with the rules of real mode. The i386 can then only address objects below 1 M. After the first code segment change, the address fffffff0h is no longer available, unless another processor RESET is carried out.

The entry point of the BIOS start routine is usually found at the initial address fffffff0h. As only 16 bytes are available from fffffff0h to the addressing limit ffffffffh (equivalent to 4Gbyte), one of the first instructions is usually a jump instruction (JMP) to the «real» entry point. This jump instruction does not have to go beyond the segment limit, that is, it is not connected with a change of CS. Despite the JMP instruction, the complete BIOS can remain at the top end of the 4 Gbyte address space.

With a PC, the processor reset (also known as a *cold boot*), is released by operating the network switch (switching on) or the reset button, but not by the well-known three-finger-touch Ctr-Alt-Del. This only causes a *warm boot*, where DOS issues an INT 19 interrupt, but does not have a reset effect on the processor. The INT 19h only reloads the operating system; there is no check on the condition of the hardware components such as memory, interrupt controller, etc. You can recognize a cold boot from the memory check: the memory addresses are counted up. In a warm boot this time consuming test is bypassed.

Because of the value 1234h at memory address 0040:0072h the start routine is able to determine whether a cold or warm boot is in progress. If the value 1234h is stored at this address then a warm boot has to be executed. All other values indicate a cold boot. The probability that at power-on (that is, completely random values in memory) the word 1234h is present at this location is 1 to 65536. Statistically speaking, you have to switch your PC on and off 65536 times before the BIOS interprets a cold boot as a warm boot. If you need one minute for one cold boot then you will be occupied for 45 days and nights switching your PC on and off to provoke one such mistake. Thus, the security «built-in» is statistically more than enough. But what are statistics? If you are playing a lottery and you do one lottery every minute then it will take nearly 27 (!) years to get six correct numbers. Nevertheless, every week several people succeed in doing this, and among them are some who are not yet 27 years old! That's statistics.

With a reset, the i386 can also be made to perform an internal self-test. This occurs when the $\overline{\text{BUSY}}$ pin remains at a low level for at least eight CLK2 clock cycles, before and after the falling edge of the reset signal. The self-test checks the i386 microcode ROM as well as a large part of the logic circuitry. To execute the self-test, the i386 requires approximately 2^{19} clock cycles, equivalent to approximately 15 ms for a 33 MHz i386. If the self-test does not detect any errors, then the i386 puts the value of 0 into the EAX register. Each non-zero value indicates that there is an internal processor error – the chip is faulty. Additionally, the DX register receives a 16-bit processor identification number with the value of 03xxh. The most significant byte 03h indicates that it is dealing with an i386, the eight xx bits represent the i386 version. Normally xx increases with new versions (for instance, the cut-down version of the i386, the i386SX, has the version number 2).

6 Basics: Logic Gates and Microprogramming – Two Basic Elements of a Processor

Today, microprocessors, and especially memory chips, are the most complex of all integrated circuits. They are constructed from the smallest possible electronic components. We already know the most important of these: the MOS Field Effect Transistor (MOSFET). But one such element is not sufficient for complex logic operations. A large quantity (for example, 3 million in the Pentium) of such MOSFETs are connected to set up the required logic circuitry. Examples are AND gates and full adders. I want to discuss some more or less complicated gates in Sections 6.1–6.3. Additionally, the individual functional groups of a processor need an exactly balanced control. How the i386 and typically all CISC processors solve this problem will be detailed in Section 6.4.

6.1 AND and OR Gates as Basic Logical Elements

In this section, I would like to introduce the two most basic elements of logic circuits, the AND and OR gates. They implement the abstract AND and OR combination of two quantities I_1 and I_2 by means of an electronic circuit and two signals, and generate an output quantity O, which in turn is expressed as a signal (or to be more exact, its level), too. Table 6.1 shows the truth tables for the AND and OR combinations.

I_1	I_2	AND value O	OR value O
0	0	0	0
0	1	0	1
1	0	0	1
1	1	1	1

Table 6.1: Truth table for AND and OR combination

The OR operation is in fact a representation of the mathematical OR, and is not to be confused with the colloquial either–or. This is implemented by the XOR operation. Many logic operations are constructed from the AND and OR operations. AND and OR take over the role of 0 and 1 from the Natural Numbers.

In the following, I have assumed that the logic 1 is represented by a high level signal and logic 0 by a low level signal. A circuit must be constructed for the AND operation, such that only two high level signals at both I_1 and I_2 inputs produce a high level signal at output O, whereas an OR operation, that has a high level signal at one of the I_1 or I_2 inputs produces a high level signal at output O. In Figure 6.1 you can see a simplified implementation of this requirement using MOSFETs.

The two n-channel MOSFETs Tr_1 and Tr_2 (referred to in Figure 6.1a) only switch the supply current Vcc through to output O if both I_1 and I_2 input signals are at a high level, that is, logic 1. If either one of the I_1 or I_2 input signals is equivalent to 0, then one of the transistors Tr_1 or Tr_2

closes, and the output O produces a low level signal representing the logical 0. Thus, the circuit shown in Figure 6.1a implements an AND operation for input signals I_1 and I_2. The symbol shown above the circuit diagram in the illustration is a standard symbol used to represent an AND gate as a functional unit in logic circuit diagrams.

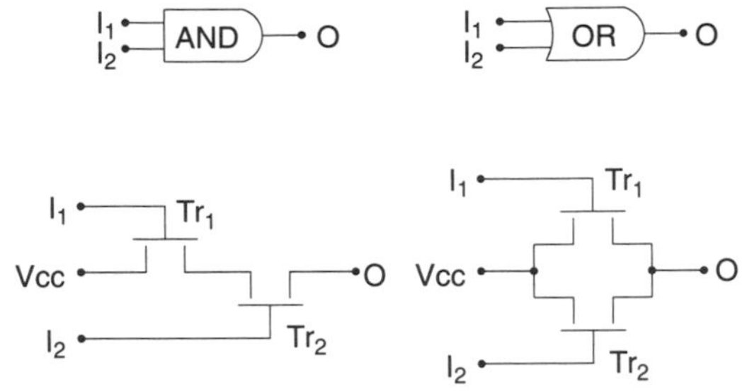

Figure 6.1: Implementing AND (a) and OR (b) with MOSFETs.

Figure 6.1b shows the implementation of an OR gate from the two n-channel MOSFETs Tr_1 and Tr_2. In this case, it is enough for one of the two MOSFETs to be switched on so as to provide output O with a high level signal. Therefore, it is sufficient that I_1 or I_2 is on a high level. The symbol given is that of the standard symbol as used for an OR gate in logic circuit diagrams.

The logic gates represented are 2-input AND and 2-input OR gates, respectively. Without any problems, the circuits can be extended to n-input AND and n-input OR gates. This is done simply by inserting and connecting n MOSFETs in series (AND) or in parallel (OR) between Vcc and output O.

6.2 CMOS Inverters as Low-power Elements

The above MOS transistor has, when compared to a bipolar transistor (the conductivity of which is not controlled by a gate *voltage*, but instead by a base *current*), a very small power consumption. Currently, however, with the integration of many millions of transistors on one chip (newest generation 16 Mbit DRAM memory chips contain more than 16 million transistors and 16 million capacitors), the power consumption is quite considerable. Therefore, there is a further requirement to reduce the power consumption. To fulfil this requirement, the CMOS technique is employed, its basic element being that of a *CMOS inverter*. A CMOS inverter is simply achieved from the parallel switching of a p-channel and an n-channel MOSFET, as shown in Figure 6.2.

Both MOSFETs are connected in series between ground and the supply voltage (Vcc). The MOSFET gate is isolated from the substrate, and thus from the source and drain, by a thin layer of oxide, thus preventing a current flow through the gate. It is necessary, for the current to flow from Vcc to GND, that both transistors are simultaneously conductive. Only then will a current path between ground and supply voltage exist. As the characteristics in Figures 2.1a and 2.1b (see Chapter 2) show, there is no overlapping of the conductivity from p-channel and n-channel

MOSFETs. Therefore, one of the two MOSFETs is always OFF, and there will never be a current flow. If the voltage U_I is adequately positive (greater than the threshold voltage V_{thn} of the n-channel MOSFET Tr_n) at input I, then the n-channel MOSFET conducts, and the p-channel MOSFET Tr_p is closed. With adequate negative voltage U_I (less than the voltage threshold V_{thn} of the p-channel MOSFET Tr_p), the p-channel MOSFET is conductive and the n-channel MOSFET is closed. Both transistors are off between V_{thn} and V_{thp}.

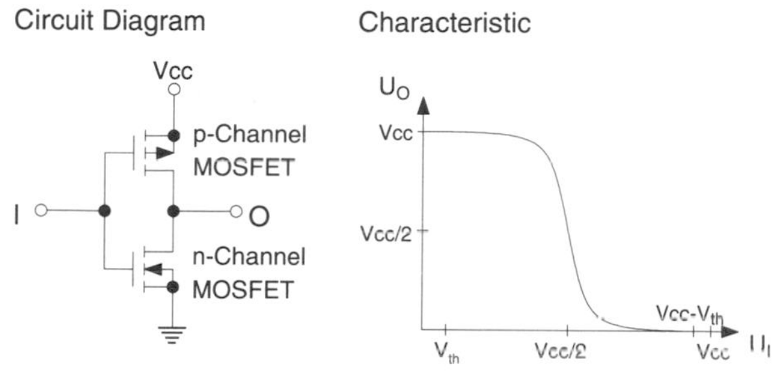

Figure 6.2: The CMOS inverter. A CMOS inverter consists of two MOSFETs, with opposite conductivity, which are connected between ground and Vcc. A characteristic curve with a sharp transition can thus be obtained.

It is decisive for use in (digital) computer technics that the *voltage* U_O at the output O is changed according to the variation of the input voltage U_I in a range between the supply voltage Vcc and ground. MOSFETs are not controlled by the gate current but the gate voltage. You can use the voltage U_O delivered at the output O to control MOSFETs in succeeding stages of the logic circuitry. Thus, signals (or data) are processed:

- If U_I is sufficiently negative, then Tr_p conducts and Tr_n is closed, output O is connected to Vcc, and the CMOS inverter produces a logic 1 (or logic 0 with negative logic).
- If U_I is sufficiently positive, then in this case Tr_n conducts and Tr_p is closed, output O is connected to ground, and the CMOS inverter produces a logic 0 (or logic 1 with negative logic).

As the characteristic curve in Figure 6.2 shows, due to the extremely sharp transition between Vcc and ground, the CMOS inverter almost perfectly accomplishes the requirements with two clearly defined and separate logic conditions. Also, as CMOS elements require very little *power consumption* when compared to normal MOS chips, then we are hypothetically killing two birds with one stone. A current will only flow by switching over the output voltage between Vcc and ground, in order to charge or discharge the respective layers of the CMOS transistor to their respective capacities. CMOS elements have a small *static power consumption*, which is mainly caused by a current leakage, which in turn is caused by the gate oxidation layer (which is never absolute). Additionally, there is a *dynamic power consumption* caused by a toggle in the voltage U_O at output O as a result of a change in the input voltage U_I. Since, with every toggle, the semiconductor layers are charged and discharged, the dynamic power input is proportional to the toggle frequency (P~v). CMOS elements (for example, the i387) with a fast clock speed therefore require more current than those with a slow clock speed. This has a useful purpose in application to a Notebook computer, as when it is in Power-down mode the clock frequency is reduced to zero. This only leaves the very small static power consumption. Energy saving can amount to as much as 99.99% (this is not a printing error).

A serious problem in realizing ever higher integration densities (and thus, for example, higher memory chip capacities) is additional to the miniaturization of the elements: the increase of the power consumption. The size and therefore the power consumption of the individual elements on the chip decreases, but as the number of these elements rises enormously, we have a higher power consumption in the end (for example, an i386 consumes about 3 W, but the Pentium, despite the most modern technology, 13 W). The power consumed is nearly all converted into heat and warms up the chip. The real workaholics, and thus also current eaters, are the coprocessors. You can easily burn your fingers on an intensively used coprocessor. The powerful i387 implemented using the CMOS technique consumes only 1.5 W; that is only about half compared to that of its ancestor, the 8087, with its 2.5 W – a clear hint of the modest power consumption of CMOS chips.

If the heat produced cannot be dissipated, the chip gets into a muddle because of calculation errors caused by overheated transistors. The computer crashes and is inoperable until it cools down. A further temperature increase may finally result in damaged semiconductor layers, and therefore a damaged chip. For this reason, all highly integrated processors, starting with the i386 and i387, are implemented using the CMOS technique. With the conventional NMOS technique, the i387 in particular would be more of a radiator than a coprocessor!

As Goethe once said, where there is light, there is also shadow. Of course CMOS technology does have a disadvantage; a CMOS inverter always has to have two MOSFETs, whereas a MOS transistor only requires one (namely, itself). In comparison, the integration density of CMOS inverters is smaller than that of MOS transistors. By a clever arrangement of the different layers on the substrate, almost the same quantity can be obtained. It is only the extent of the technology required that is greater. Moreover, CMOS elements do not alter their switching state as fast as bipolar transistors. The Pentium (and some other extremely fast clocked CPUs such as the MIPS R6000) deviate from the pure CISC implementation due to the high speed. To stand the enormous clock rates they are partially (Pentium: BiCMOS) or completely (R6000: ECL) realized with bipolar transistors. This enhances the performance, but again makes cooling a problem of central importance. The CPUs of supercomputers are therefore sometimes cooled by liquid nitrogen (for example, the ETA computers of Control Data).

Another hint on how to identify CMOS components: the CMOS processor derivatives or other logic chips have a «C» in their type names, for example 80C286 or 80C287 instead of 80286 and 80287, respectively. These CMOS chips consume only one third of the power compared to the usual chips. Generally, you can expect a CMOS chip if the type name includes a «C». The opposite, however, does not necessarily apply: no «C» – for example, there is no iC386 – does not necessarily mean today that the chip has been manufactured with conventional n-MOS or p-MOS technology.

6.3 An Example: 1-Bit Adder

In the following, I would like to introduce the use of AND, OR and XOR gates, using the example of a 1-bit adder with carry. It has the function of adding pairs of binary numbers. Figure 6.3 shows the combination of AND, OR and XOR gates for determining the sum and carry which result from two summands A_X and B_X as well as an original carry C_X.

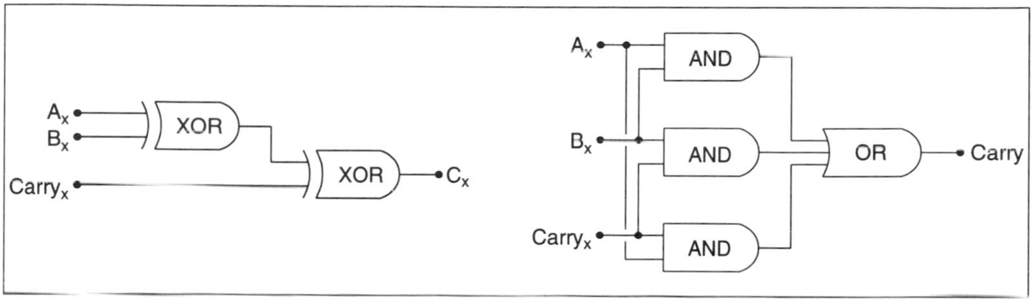

Figure 6.3: 1-bit adder with carry.

For determining the sum, the two summand bits A_X und B_X are fed to an XOR gate. The output signal of the first XOR gate, together with the carry bit $Carry_X$ of a preceding stage, is then passed to a second XOR gate. The resulting output signal produces the corresponding total bit C_X.

The carry bit can be determined by, for example, three AND gates which ascertain whether or not at least two of the fed bits A_X, B_X and $Carry_X$ are equal to 1, and the combination of the outputs from the AND gates in an OR gate. If you analyse the circuit logic, you end up with the combinations in Table 6.2.

A_X 1st Summand	B_X 2nd Summand	$Carry_X$ From Previous Stage	C_X Result	Carry
0	0	0	0	0
0	0	1	1	0
0	1	0	1	0
0	1	1	0	1
1	0	0	1	0
1	0	1	0	1
1	1	0	0	1
1	1	1	1	1

Table 6.2: Combining summand and carry bits in the 1-bit adder

For a 32-bit full adder you «only» need to connect 32 of these 1-bit adders in series, and to connect each carry output with the corresponding carry input of the succeeding adder.

6.4 Microencoding of Machine Code Instructions

We have already come across the mnemonics and encoding of instructions and addressing in Chapter 3. The i386 (and many other processors) have to process these encoded bit streams internally to execute the required instructions with the necessary data. Further, the huge number of internal circuits require an exact balance of their functions. In this respect, we will learn about the fundamental characteristics of CISC processors, in fact, the *microencoding* of machine instructions.

You can see from Figure 2.3 and associated text that the instructions are read into a prefetch queue. An attached decoding unit then decodes them. With microprogrammed processors, an instruction is not executed directly, but is available, in a *microcode ROM* within the processor, as a *microprogram*. Figure 6.4 schematically shows the basic concept.

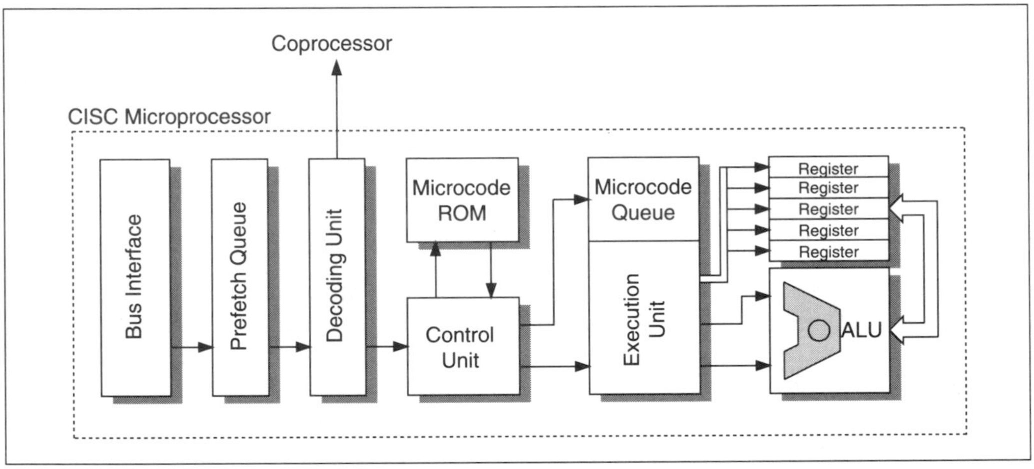

Figure 6.4: The concept of microprogramming. With microprogramming the processor fetches the instructions via the bus interface into a prefetch queue, which in turn transfers them to a decoding unit. The decoding unit decomposes a machine instruction into a number of elementary microinstructions and applies them to a microcode queue. The microinstructions are transferred from the microcode queue to the control and execution unit so that the ALU and registers are driven accordingly.

The processor decoding unit must, therefore, decode the instruction, that is, split it into the actual instruction, the type of address, extent and type of relevant register, etc. All of this information is contained in the opcode, prefix operand and displacement/data. The control unit calls the relevant microprograms to execute the instructions with the help of the ALU, register, etc. It becomes apparent that the decoding process and the preparation for executing the microprograms require a specific amount of time. The decoding time can, therefore, be equal in length to, or even longer than, the execution time of the instruction itself. Thus, the execution time of an instruction consists of the decoding time plus the execution time. (Note that the execution times given in the processor manuals usually indicate the pure execution time, that is, the instruction must already be decoded.) In addition to relieving the bus interface, the prefetch queue plays a further important role. As it already contains the next available instructions, prior to executing the current instructions, the decoding unit can stock up work in advance by decoding the next instruction and preparing it for execution in the control unit while the execution unit is still busy processing the current instruction. Thus, an extensive prefetch queue enhances the processor's performance. That is one reason why the i486, with its 32-byte queue, executes faster than the i386 with a prefetch queue of only 16 bytes. If you can imagine what it would be like without prefetching, where for every instruction the instruction reading and decoding time was apparent, then you will quickly realize the performance advantage that prefetching achieves.

This all works well as long as the prefetch queue is constantly topped up at the same speed at which the processor executes the instructions. With a jump or procedure call that exceeds the boundaries of the prefetch queue (this is very often the case), the processor must empty its prefetch queue and start again by reading the new instruction byte at the target address. This, of course, also applies to RET and IRET instructions. The problem is that the next instruction not only has to be read but also decoded. If the jump target is still within the queue and if the instruction comprises only a few bytes so that it has already been completely fetched, then it only needs to be decoded. The instruction fetch cycle is obsolete. If no jump is executed (because, for example, a JNE is not fulfilled) then the processor carries on without any interruption.

If you examine a complicated program using a debugger, you will realize that it is teeming with JUMPs and CALLs. For example, a compiler converts many of the C language CASE statements into a number of conditional JUMPs. If the target address is outside the area covered by the prefetch queue, then the i386 has to start instruction fetching and decoding from the beginning. Converting the source code into an unfavourable sequence of JUMP instructions can badly affect the execution time of a program. Assembler programmers should take note of this. Unfortunately, optimizing compilers from well-known manufacturers are also known to skip willingly outside the prefetch boundaries, and sometimes without good reason.

In the following, I would like to briefly present the steps for the MOVS/MOVSB/MOVSW /MOVSD (move data from string to string) instruction. This instruction is one of the most powerful i386 machine code instructions, and is typical of a CISC processor. Intel specify the following i386 operations for the instruction:

```
IF (instruction = MOVSD) OR (double word operand available)
  THEN Operand size <– 32;
  ELSE Operand size <– 16;
FI;

IF address size = 16
  THEN SI=SourceIndex and DI=DestinationIndex;
  ELSE ESI=SourceIndex and EDI=DestinationIndex;
FI;

IF Operation of byte–type
  THEN
    [DestinationIndex] <– [SourceIndex];
    IF DF=0
      THEN IncDec <– 1
```

```
      ELSE IncDec <— -1
    FI;
  ELSE
    IF Operand size = 16
      THEN
        [DestinationIndex] <— [SourceIndex];
        IF DF=0
          THEN IncDec <— 2
          ELSE IncDec <— -2
        FI;
      ELSE
        [DestinationIndex] <— [SourceIndex];
        IF DF=0
          THEN IncDec <— 4
          ELSE IncDec <— -4
        FI;
    FI;
FI;

SourceIndex <— SourceIndex + IncDec
DestinationIndex <— DestinationIndex + IncDec
```

The individual operations are represented by matching microcodes in the microcode ROM and are executed by the Execution Unit (EU) with the assistance of logic gates, the ALU and bus interface. You can see that a considerable number of internal microinstructions are executed for the instruction MOVSx. Intel specify that the execution time of the instruction is eight processor clock cycles PCLK. If the instruction is repeatedly executed with a prefix of REPxx, then the first execution of MOVSx requires eight clock cycles, but each subsequent execution only requires four. The complete IF-THEN-ELSE-FI block is only required at the start, to determine the operands, addresses and IncDec quantities. Each following run just transfers data from the source to the destination. For this, four processor clock cycles are required (including the test for completion of all repetitions).

A very complex circuit would be necessary to implement this operation as hardwired logic. On the other hand, however, the microcodes repeatedly access the same hardware logic elements. The execution unit has a micro instruction pointer analogous to the EIP instruction pointer of the «entire processor», which addresses the microinstructions in the microprogram memory. The complexity of the MOVSx instruction is due to the binary encoding in the microcode ROM, and not circuit layout. Similar aspects also led to the general development of microprocessors or free programmable computers. Also in this case, the one-off fixed and relatively simple circuit structure is repeatedly used by a program, which is stored in memory. It would be possible, in principle, to implement a complex word processor (for example, Word, AmiPro) by hardwired logic purely in hardware. The technical difficulties would unfortunately be enormous. I am sure that you can imagine that considerably more components would be required, more even than the Pentium has. Instead, it is better to transfer the complexity of the word processor into a program memory where the individual instructions can be stored in coded form. A further advantage is that the content of the memory can be altered much faster and easier than a circuit.

One disadvantage of microencoding can be seen immediately: the execution speed is much slower than that of direct hardware implementation. One reason for this is, that many individual steps and individual decisions are necessary (and thus many clock cycles), whereas a pure hardware implementation disposes of the whole instruction in one go.

Microprogramming has developed over a period of time, and has many advantages. For instance, for a very compact instruction code, the size of the instructions and, thus, the memory requirement is small. You can get 256 different instruction codes in one byte, if each modification of the type of address, register concerned, etc. is regarded as an individual instruction. In the early 1960s, the core storage (made of ferromagnetic rings), which in those days was the write and read memory, was the most expensive and, unfortunately, also the slowest component of a computer, having a typical average access time of 1 μs. Today, a good DRAM will achieve 0.060 μs and a fast SRAM approximately 0.012 μs. However, in those days ROMs could be realized with an access time of 100 ns to 200 ns, and, moreover, were considerably cheaper than the core memories. For a single access of the write or read memory, the processor could execute between five and ten ROM accesses. Put another way: while the prefetcher is reading an instruction code from the write/read memory, the processor is capable of internally extracting and executing between five and ten microinstructions from the microcode ROM. Even in those days, microencoding had a minimal effect on reducing the speed of instruction execution.

Due to the high cost and sluggishness of the core memories, it was necessary to reduce the load of program code on the write/read memory. The alternative was to load the complex program code into the cheaper and faster (Microcode) ROM in the processor. This resulted in microprogramming. Of course, in the 1960s there were no microprocessors, just enormous processor cards. Even since the introduction of microprocessors, the concept of microprogramming has not changed. Today, the majority of microprocessors (with the exception of pure RISC implementations) are still microencoded. The Pentium is no exception. The fact is that the majority of commonly used and relatively simple instructions are available in hardwired form, but the complex instructions such as MOVSx as mentioned previously are still microencoded.

An additional advantage of microprogramming is that, in simple terms, compatibility can be achieved with earlier processors. All that is required is to maintain the old code and implement it with additional instructions for the newer, more efficient processors. To that end, the microcode ROM in the processor is simply enlarged and the microcodes of the new instructions are also stored. Thus, in theory, a new generation of processors is created. It is, therefore, hardly surprising that the higher family members of the different processor families have an ever increasing number of powerful instructions, thereby leading to the evolution of CISCs. The present culmination of this development is the i486 from Intel (the Pentium implements many more RISC principles) and the 68040 from Motorola.

At the end of the 1970s, the relationship between the access time of the internal microcode ROM and the external main memory slowly but surely reversed. The slower core storage was replaced completely by semiconductor memories as the result of great advances in memory technology. Today, due to the high integration, mainly in memory chips, and the resulting reduction in price, processors are far more costly than memory, and whether the instruction code is compact or not no longer has any bearing.

The concept of microprogramming can be likened, to some extent, to a simple BASIC interpreter. In the interpreter, the instruction is split into its component parts, that is, interpreted, and then executed in accordance with the decoded component parts. But microprogramming does not know powerful instructions such as GWBASIC, nor can instructions be nested, for example PRINT(STRLEN("ww"+A$+STRING(20, "q"))+9).

The equivalent for the hardwired instructions in RISC processors would be a compiled program. Here, instructions would be immediately executed without the influence of higher level (Interpreter and Microcode) programs. I am sure that you are aware of the difference in speed between an interpreted and a compiled BASIC program. It is no great shock that RISC processors carry out instructions much faster than CISC processors. A realistic factor of three or even four can be applied to comparable processors. To achieve this, though, other criteria are also necessary, for example, pipelined execution of machine instructions, at best in several independent pipelines. But the huge number of MS-DOS programs for the Intel world will ensure the on-going success of Personal Computers for a long time to come – despite the power of modern RISC concepts.

Here I would like to summarize the main characteristics of CISC microprocessors:

- extensive (complex) instructions,
- complex and efficient machine instructions,
- microencoding of the machine instructions,
- extensive addressing capabilities for memory operations,
- relatively few, but very useful registers.

The modern RISC processors change all the points listed in a more or less drastic way. In anticipation, I have listed the corresponding basics of RISCs:

- reduced instruction set,
- less complex and simple instructions,
- hardwired control unit and, thus, hardwired machine instructions,
- few addressing schemes for memory operands with only two basic instructions, LOAD and STORE,
- many symmetric registers which are organized in a register file.

7 Calculating Semiconductor – The i387 Mathematical Coprocessor

Coprocessors produce an increase in performance aimed at certain types of applications. Generally speaking, a coprocessor is a mathematical coprocessor which supports the CPU in calculating complicated mathematical expressions using floating-point arithmetic at the hardware level. The i387 is the mathematical coprocessor for the i386. Let's turn first to some more basics about the representation of floating-point numbers and their formats.

7.1 Number Excursion – The Representation of Floating-Point Numbers

In Section 2.2 we discussed the internal representation of positive and negative integers, as well as binary coded decimals. But for extensive mathematical calculations, broken numbers like 1/4 or –0.06215, or mixed numbers like –1 5/7 or 19456.208, are missing.

7.1.1 Scientific Notation and Biased Exponent

The basis for the representation of such numbers in a computer is so-called *scientific notation* or *floating-point representation*. In this (decimal) notation, every number different from zero is represented by a signed number between 1 and 10 (the *mantissa* ±M) and a power to the *base* B with a value of 10 with a signed *exponent* ±E:

$$\text{number} = \pm M * B^{\pm E}$$

At first glance this seems to be pure mathematics. To calm you down, I therefore want to give a brief example with the numbers mentioned above.

Example: scientific notation with decimal base 10

$1/4 = 0.25 = 2.5 * 0.1 = 2.5 * 10^{-1}$	mantissa 2.5, base 10, exponent –1
$-0.06215 = -6.215 * 0.01 = -6.215 * 10^{-2}$	mantissa –6.215, base 10, exponent –2
$-1\ 5/7 = -1.71428... = -1.71428 * 1 = -1.71428 * 10^{0}$	mantissa –1.71428, base 10, exponent 0
$19456.208 = 1.9456208 * 10.000 = 1.9456208 * 10^{4}$	mantissa 1.9456208, base 10, exponent 4

Now the reason for the name floating-point representation also becomes apparent. The point is moved until the mantissa has one digit before and the rest of the digits after the decimal point. The number's value is maintained by increasing or decreasing the exponent accordingly. Unlike so-called fixed-point numbers, the position of the decimal point is (as the name already implies) fixed. In today's computers, usually only floating-point numbers are used. But with the third number in the above example, you can see the disadvantage of scientific notation. A number that is not representable as a finite decimal fraction (and all broken numbers whose divisor is not a pure product of 2s and 5s belong to this group) is simply «cut off» after a certain number of digits. In the example, –1 5/7 is not simply equal to –1.71428 but must be infinitely continued with the periodical digit sequence 5714.... On the other hand, 1/4 can be represented exactly because the divisor 4 is equal to 2*2 and therefore a pure product of only 2s. Of course, you have neither a pencil and paper nor the time to write down an infinite digit series, which, in most cases, would be pointless anyway. Instead, we are content with a finite number of mantissa digits. The number of these mantissa digits is called the *precision*. In the example, therefore, the numbers have a precision of two, four, six and eight decimal digits, respectively.

For a better understanding of broken numbers in a PC we should first analyse the interpretation of a number in floating-point notation, as we did previously for the integers. The integer decimal 2806 was interpreted as $2*10^3+8*10^2+0*10^1+6*10^0$. In the case of the floating-point number $6.215*10^{-2}$, we proceed in a similar way:

$$6.215*10^{-2} = [6*10^0+2*10^{-1}+1*10^{-2}+5*10^{-3}]*10^{-2}$$
$$= [6*1+2*0.1+1*0.01+5*0.001]*0.01 = 0.06215$$
or
$$= 6*10^{-2}+2*10^{-3}+1*10^{-4}+5*10^{-5}$$
$$= 6*0.01+2*0.001+1*0.0001+5*0.00001 = 0.06215$$

You can see that the interpretations are similar. The value of each digit decreases from left to right by one power of ten. One starts with the value given by the exponent. The same applies for floating-point numbers with a value greater than 1.

$$1.9456208*10^4 = [1*10^0+9*10^{-1}+4*10^{-2}+5*10^{-3}+6*10^{-4}+2*10^{-5}+0*10^{-6}+8*10^{-7}]*10^4$$
$$= [1*1+9*0.1+4*0.01+5*0.001+6*0.0001+2*0.00001+0*0.000001+8*0.0000001]*10000$$
$$= 19456.208$$
or
$$= 1*10^4+9*10^3+4*10^2+5*10^1+6*10^0+2*10^{-1}+0*10^{-2}+8*10^{-3}$$
$$= 10,000+9,000+400+50+6+0.2+0.00+0.008 = 19456.208$$

Floating-point numbers are represented in a computer in a similar way, except the «2» corresponding to the binary system replaces the «10» of the decimal system.

Example: $1.1011001*2^{10011}$ in the binary system means
$$[1*2^0+1*2^{-1}+0*2^{-2}+1*2^{-3}+1*2^{-4}+0*2^{-5}+0*2^{-6}+1*2^{-7}]*2^{19}$$
$$=[1*1+1*0.5+0*0.25+1*0.125+1*0.0625+0*0.03125+0*0.015625+1*0.0078125]*524,288$$
$$= [1.6953125]*524,288 = 888,832$$
In "normal" binary representation this would be 888,832 = 1101 1001 0000 0000 0000b.

The example illustrates the principle of the representation of floating-point numbers in the binary system, but negative numbers and numbers with a negative exponent (that is, numbers below 1) are not covered completely. Generally, the scientific notation is number $= \pm \text{mantissa}*\text{base}^{\pm\text{exponent}}$. Therefore, two negative numbers are possible. For the representation of negative numbers we have (according to Section 2.2.3) two possibilities: sign bit and 2'complement representation.

Although the 2'complement representation turned out to be very advantageous, another method is used in the representation of floating-point numbers. For the mantissa a sign bit is used, and for the exponent a so-called *biased exponent* is employed. Thus, a floating-point number in the binary system has the following form:

$$\text{number} = \pm\text{mantissa} * 2^{\text{exponent}-\text{bias}}$$

The sign ± of the mantissa is indicated by a sign bit and a fixed bias value is subtracted from the indicated exponent.

Example:

```
floating-point representation with bias 127 of number 888,832:
1.1011001*2^10010010
value in "normal" representation therefore:
1.1011001*2^(10010010-1111111)=1.1011001*2^10011
```

As you can see, the result coincides with the example mentioned above.

The fact that the two binary floating-point numbers $1.1011001*2^{10010010}$ and $1.1011001*2^{10011}$ indicate the same value is a further example that not only is the digit sequence essential but so too is its interpretation. Of course, you can introduce a self-made «John-Smith-representation» of binary floating-point numbers by, for example, using 2'complement for the mantissa as well as for the exponent. Your imagination can run riot here, but whether the result is, first, sensible, second, useful and, third, generally acknowledged is another matter.

The implementation of floating-point arithmetic by electronic circuitry is far more complicated than that of integers. For example, two floating-point numbers cannot be added without a further investigation, because possibly their exponents do not coincide. The CPU must first check the exponents and equalize them, before the also adapted mantissas can be added. For that reason, the electronic circuitry for floating-point arithmetic is frequently formed on a separate coprocessor. The i386 only has an ALU for integer arithmetic, not one for floating-point operations. That is provided by the i387 coprocessor.

7.1.2 The Standard – IEEE Formats

As is the case for integers and long integers, for floating-point numbers you have to reserve a certain number of bits. In principle, you are free to choose an «odd» number of bits for a floating-point number, for example 43 bits. However, to enable binary floating-point numbers to be exchanged easily between different platforms, one generally uses the so-called *IEEE formats* today. Nearly all compilers and computers use this standard. Only Microsoft's BASIC interpreters traditionally use Microsoft's own format, the Microsoft binary format (MSBIN).

In the following sections, these representation standards are discussed in detail. Figure 7.1 shows the IEEE formats for the number types short real, long real and temporary real. They occupy 32, 64 and 80 bits, respectively, and all use a biased exponent.

The values represented by the IEEE formats are, in general:

$$\text{value} = (-1)^S * (1 + M1*2^{-1} + M2*2^{-2} + \ldots + M23/M52/M63*2^{-23/52/63}) * 2^{E7/E10/E14\ldots E1E0-127}$$

The short real format actually has a 24-bit mantissa but integrates only 23 of these bits into the four bytes of the defined format. Where is bit M0 of the mantissa? The answer is simple but inspired. It was mentioned above that in scientific notation a number between 1 and 10 is always in front of the decimal point. This representation is called *normalized* representation. If one does the same with binary floating-point numbers, the number 1 should be in front of the point because only 0 and 1 are available in binary. 0 does not apply, as by decreasing the exponent the point is moved through the number until a 1 is in front.

Short Real (32 Bits)
Range of Value $1.18 * 10^{-38} < |x| < 3.40 * 10^{+38}$, Precision 24 Bits

S: Sign Bit (1=Mantissa Negative, 0=Mantissa Positive)
$E_7 \ldots E_0$: Exponent (8 Bits, Bias 127)
$M_1 \ldots M_{23}$: Mantissa (23 Bits Plus Implicit M0=1)

Long Real (64 Bits)
Range of Value $2.23 * 10^{-308} < |x| < 1.79 * 10^{+308}$, Precision 53 Bits

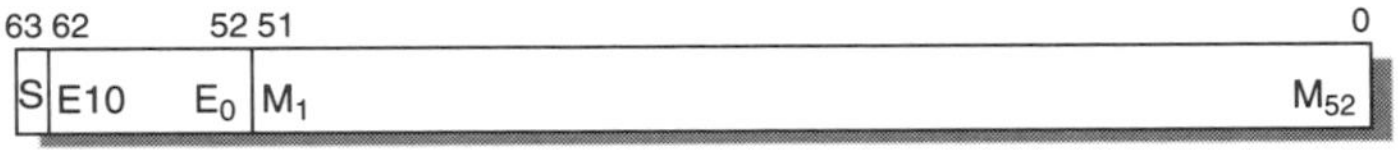

S: Sign Bit (1=Mantissa Negative, 0=Mantissa Positive)
$E_{10} \ldots E_0$: Exponent (11 Bits, Bias 1023)
$M_1 \ldots M_{52}$: Mantissa (52 Bits Plus Implicit M0=1)

Temporary Real (80 Bits)
Range of Value $3.37 * 10^{-4932} < |x| < 1.18 * 10^{+4932}$, Precision 64 Bits

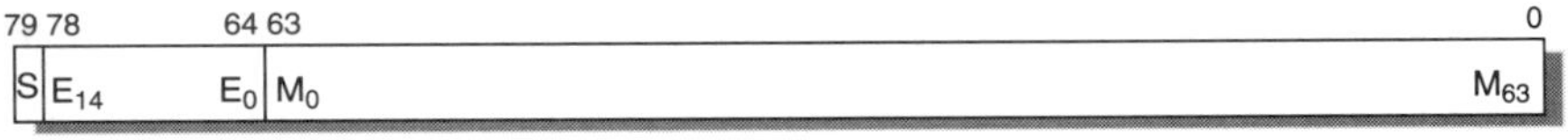

S: Sign Bit (1=Mantissa Negative, 0=Mantissa Positive)
$E_{14} \ldots E_0$: Exponent (15 Bits, Bias 16.383)
$M_0 \ldots M_{63}$: Mantissa (64 Bits)

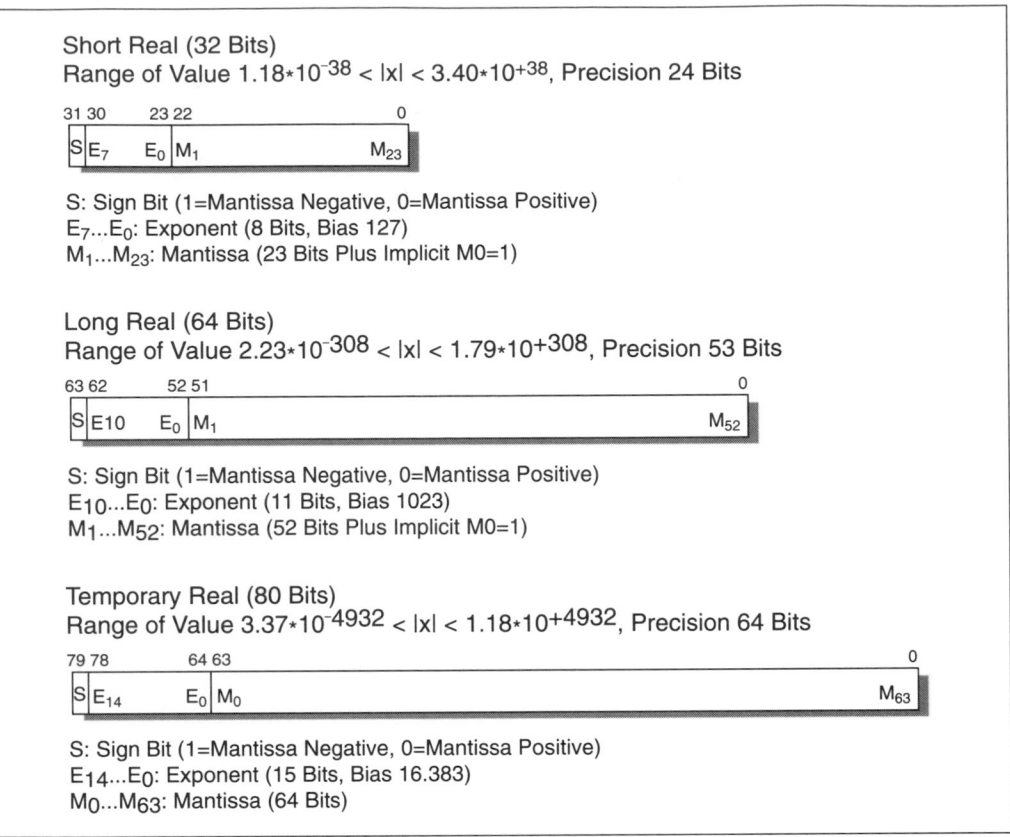

Figure 7.1: IEEE formats for short real, long real and temporary real.

Example: $0.001011 * 2^{01101}$
Move point until 1 is in front
-> $0.1011 * 2^{01100}$ -> $1.011 * 2^{01011}$
in normalized form therefore the number is $1.011 * 2^{01011}$

Therefore, in normalized representation *every* floating-point number starts with a 1. The IEEE format only uses normalized floating-point numbers so that the first digit M0 of the mantissa (that is, the digit before the point) is always equal to 1. It need not be integrated into the number explicitly but is implicitly known to be 1. Thus, the stored mantissa indicates only the digit after the point. Bits 23–30 hold the biased exponent: to get the «real» exponent you must subtract the value 127 from the stored exponent. Values smaller than 127 lead to negative exponents, and therefore represent numbers smaller than 1. The choice of 127 as the bias is arbitrary, but with 127 the exponent 0 for the number 1 is between the highest and the lowest possible exponents in the IEEE format. Finally, the S bit indicates the sign of the whole number.

Example: `70.457 = 7.0457 * 10^1 in short real format is:`

```
428ce9fc = 0100 0010 1000 1100 1110 1001 1111 1100b
           |    |__| |___________________________|
           |      |                |
           |      |                +--mantissa: 2^-4+2^-5+2^-8+2^-9+2^-10+2^-12+2^-15
           |      |                             +2^-16+2^-17+2^-18+2^-19+2^-20+2^-21 = 0.1008906
           |      |                             add the implicit 1: 1.1008906
           |      +-----------------------exponent: 133-bias(127) = 6
           +------------------------------sign: 0 = positive number
Therefore the number is +1.1008906*2^6 = +1.1008906*64 = 70.457
```

The same applies to the long real format. Bits 0–51 hold the mantissa digits after the decimal point. Here, too, the M0 bit is always equal to 1, and the format is therefore normalized. Together with the biased exponent, which is enhanced to 11 bits and has a bias value of 1023, the range of values is much larger than with the short real format. For most applications the long real format is enough. Even with the short real format, the ratio of the highest and the smallest possible values is much larger than the ratio between the size of the universe and that of an atom. And the precision of nearly 16 decimals in the long real format exceeds the experimental accuracy of all known constants of nature.

The values 255 and 2048 for the biased exponent in the short and long real formats are reserved by definition. A floating-point number with these exponents is called *NAN* (not a number) and is not regarded as a number. Coprocessors or software emulations of coprocessors report an error message if such a number occurs, or process a predefined number instead.

Coprocessors such as Intel's 80x87 family (and software emulations of coprocessors) often use the temporary real format with a width of 80 bits. This format does not need to be normalized. The M0 bit of the mantissa is actually stored in the format, and is not presupposed implicitly to be 1. The range of values and precision of this format are enormous. With the 80 bits of the temporary real format, $2^{80} = 1.2 * 10^{24}$ different numbers can be represented. Even a very fast PC that can load one million different numbers in the temporary real format per second into the coprocessor would need more than 30 billion years to read every possible number – that is, twice the age of the universe. The 80 bits should also be enough for very ambitious programmers.

But now something confusing seems to occur: a positive and a negative zero (that is, two zeros). Mathematically speaking, this is nonsense; there is *exactly one* and only one zero (moreover, with no + or – sign). The reason for the sudden existence of two zeros is that the floating-point formats and coprocessors define numbers by way of their *representation*, but in mathematics numbers are defined abstractly by way of their *properties*. Both the long and the short real formats hold a sign bit. If all other 31 bits are equal to 0, then obviously the number 0 will be represented. However, because of the sign bit two representations seem to be possible: +0 with the sign bit cleared and –0 with sign bit set. The same also applies for the other floating point formats. It becomes even more complicated with floating-point numbers in normalized form. Here, the leading 1 of the mantissa is never stored. But how can one know whether the short real number 00000000h really has the value zero, or whether it is, by way of the implicit M0 = 1, the value $1*2^{-127}$?

The only way out of this is a strict definition: for a floating-point number in normalized form with the smallest possible exponent, the mantissa must be also equal to 0. Then the number represents the value 0. If, on the other hand, the exponent has the smallest possible value and the mantissa is not equal to 0, then it is presupposed that the mantissa is not in normalized but in «real» representation. This leads to a number that may be represented in the intended format only by gradual underflow. The number is too small for normalized representation, but can still be represented if the normalization is cancelled and leading zeros are allowed. However, in this way the precision is degraded.

Example: `00000001h`

```
Sign 0b       -> positive number
Biased exponent 0000 0000b -> exponent -127, therefore no normalization of the mantissa
Mantissa 000 0000 0000 0000 0000 0001 = 2^-22
Value of the not-normalized number: mantissa * 2^Exponent = 2^-22 * 2^-127 = 2^-149 = 1.4012985 * 10^-45
But in normalized representation the end is already reached with 00800000h=1*2^-126=1.1754944 *
10^-38.
```

7.1.3 BASIC Programmers Pay Attention – The MSBIN Format

Besides the IEEE format, the MSBIN format is also of some importance because the BASIC interpreters GWBASIC and BASICA of Microsoft and IBM, respectively, use this format for the internal representation of floating-point numbers. Figure 7.2 shows the MSBIN format of floating-point numbers.

The bias value in the MSBIN format is 129 compared to 127 in the IEEE format. The values represented by the MSBIN formats are, in general:

$$value = (-1)^S * (1 + M1*2^{-1} + M2*2^{-2} + \ldots + M23/M55*2^{-23/55}) * 2^{E7\ldots E0-129}$$

The long real format has nearly twice the precision, but no more extensive a range of values than the short real format. As some compensation, the precision is three bits higher than that of the IEEE long real format. Converting MSBIN's long real format to IEEE's long real format is always possible, but the reverse is only possible if the absolute value of the number in the IEEE format doesn't exceed $1.7 * 10^{38}$ and doesn't fall below $3.0 * 10^{-39}$.

All real formats require extensive calculation capabilities because real numbers must first be separated into their parts: sign, exponent and mantissa. Thereafter exponent and mantissa are calculated separately, and the result is combined into a new real number. Therefore, it is better to use long integers instead of real numbers even if a coprocessor is installed. This is especially advantageous for financial applications: it is faster to calculate the amount of money with long integers in units of cents or pennies (or even a hundredth of them) instead of employing real numbers. The result is converted into dollars or pounds sterling for display at the end by dividing by 100 or 10000.

The length and structure of the real formats are dependent upon the computer employed. If you are writing assembler programs for real formats, or if you want to manipulate individual bits and bytes of a real number, then be aware that the Intel processors store the bytes in little endian format.

Example: `70.457=428ce9fch (IEEE short real format) is stored in memory as fce98c42h.`

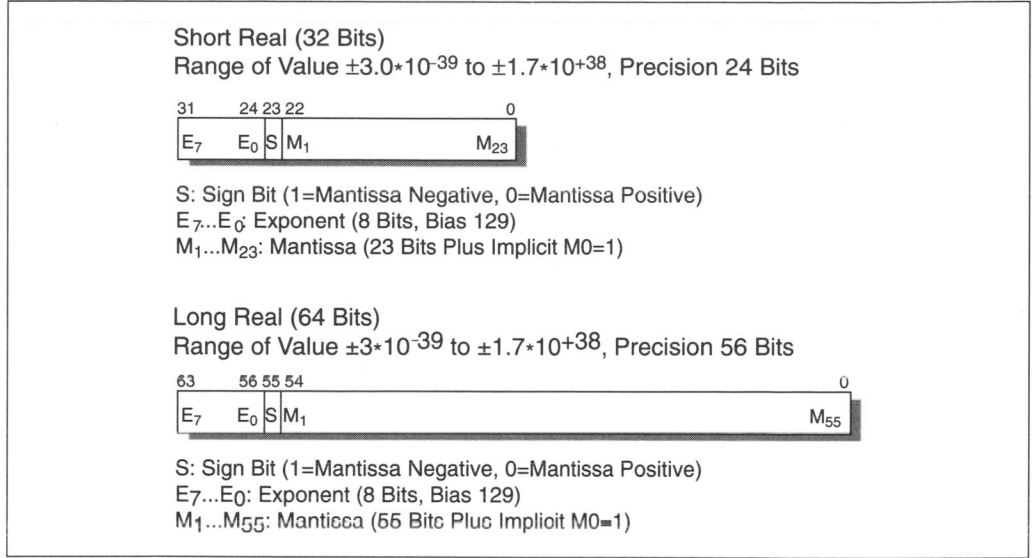

Short Real (32 Bits)
Range of Value $\pm 3.0*10^{-39}$ to $\pm 1.7*10^{+38}$, Precision 24 Bits

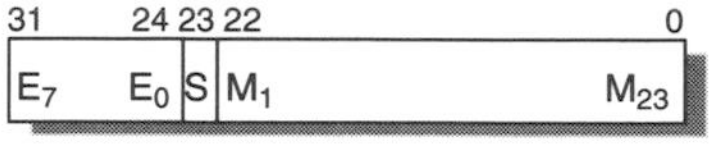

S: Sign Bit (1=Mantissa Negative, 0=Mantissa Positive)
$E_7...E_0$: Exponent (8 Bits, Bias 129)
$M_1...M_{23}$: Mantissa (23 Bits Plus Implicit M0=1)

Long Real (64 Bits)
Range of Value $\pm 3*10^{-39}$ to $\pm 1.7*10^{+38}$, Precision 56 Bits

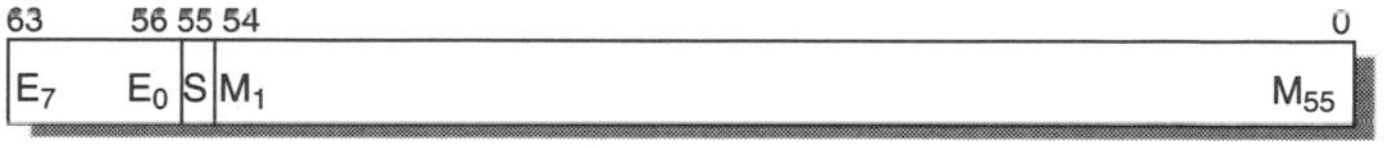

S: Sign Bit (1=Mantissa Negative, 0=Mantissa Positive)
$E_7...E_0$: Exponent (8 Bits, Bias 129)
$M_1...M_{55}$: Mantissa (55 Bits Plus Implicit M0=1)

Figure 7.2: MSBIN formats for short real and long real.

7.2 Functional Expansion and Performance Gain

The four basic types of arithmetic using integers are already integrated with the i386. The entire mathematical structure is based upon the use of integers, from the smallest of operations such as one times one, to transcendental logarithms. In principle, the i386 can execute all mathematical calculations on its own. Nevertheless, the i387 supports the i386 when calculating mathematical expressions with floating-point numbers. These include addition, subtraction, multiplication and division of floating-point numbers, the evaluation of square roots and logarithms etc. For the i387, all i386 addressing schemes for memory operands are available. Programs that carry out the functions of the mathematical coprocessor i387 in the same way, and provide the same results, are identified as being *software emulations* of the i387. By the implementation of these functions at a hardware level instead of software level, the i387 floating-point calculations are executed at a much higher speed. Table 7.1 shows the gain in performance.

As you can see, the increase in speed lies somewhere between 50 and 500 times faster. Application programs, such as CAD or numerical control of machinery and robots, which require the intensive use of mathematical calculations using floating-point numbers, would be executed at a much faster rate when using a coprocessor. The factors of 50 to 500 only refer to the mathematical calculations themselves. To a large extent, application programs must also be able to perform other functions such as the input and output of data, user guidance etc. When considering all factors, it is realistic to say that speed will be increased by a factor of between two and ten times. On the one hand, for the representation of a circle using a CAD program, a coprocessor will help with the necessary calculation of the points of the circle. On the other hand, the points of the circle must also be shown on the monitor. The i387 does not assist the CPU in accessing the video memory.

Floating-point operation	i387	Emulation on the i386
addition/subtraction	0.7	125
multiplication (single precision)	0.9	125
division	2.6	250
square root	3.5	1500
tangent	9.8	1000
exponentiation	9.6	1350
load (double precision)	0.9	100
store (double precision)	1.6	130

For the emulation typical average values are given; more or less effective programming using i386 instructions may increase or decrease the values.

Table 7.1: Floating-point calculations on the i387 and i386 (execution times in μs at 33 MHz clock rate)

The concept of coprocessors is not just limited to the expansion of the CPU to handle decimal values. For example, there are also I/O coprocessors, like the 82389, which support the exchange of data between the i386 and the system bus. Generally speaking, every coprocessor, which has a specific task in supporting the CPU, is designated as a coprocessor. Examples of these are used for mathematical, I/O graphics and other applications. Coprocessors are often referred to as a processor extension, which is more of an appropriate definition because the coprocessors extend the function of the CPU.

7.3 i387 Number Formats and Floating-point Instructions

In addition to logic operations, the i386 can also perform arithmetical operations and supports the following number formats:

- signed and unsigned integers (16-bit),
- signed and unsigned long integers (32-bit),
- packed and non-packed binary coded decimal numbers (8-, 16-bit).

The i386 can only emulate floating-point arithmetic, treating it internally as if it were a chain of characters. The coprocessor emulation program then separates the 32-, 64- or 80-bit floating-point number into its constituent parts, sign, mantissa and exponent, then processes them separately using the four basic types of arithmetic available. Finally the emulation program formulates the result into a chain of characters in floating-point arithmetic format.

As a mathematical coprocessor, the i387 directly processes the floating-point arithmetic without the requirement of separating the sign, mantissa and exponent. The i387 also goes a step further, by internally interpreting all numbers, from integers with a length of 16-bit to temporary real floating-point numbers, as 80-bit floating-point numbers in temporary real format, in accordance with the IEEE standard representation. Figure 7.3 shows all of the number formats supported by the i387.

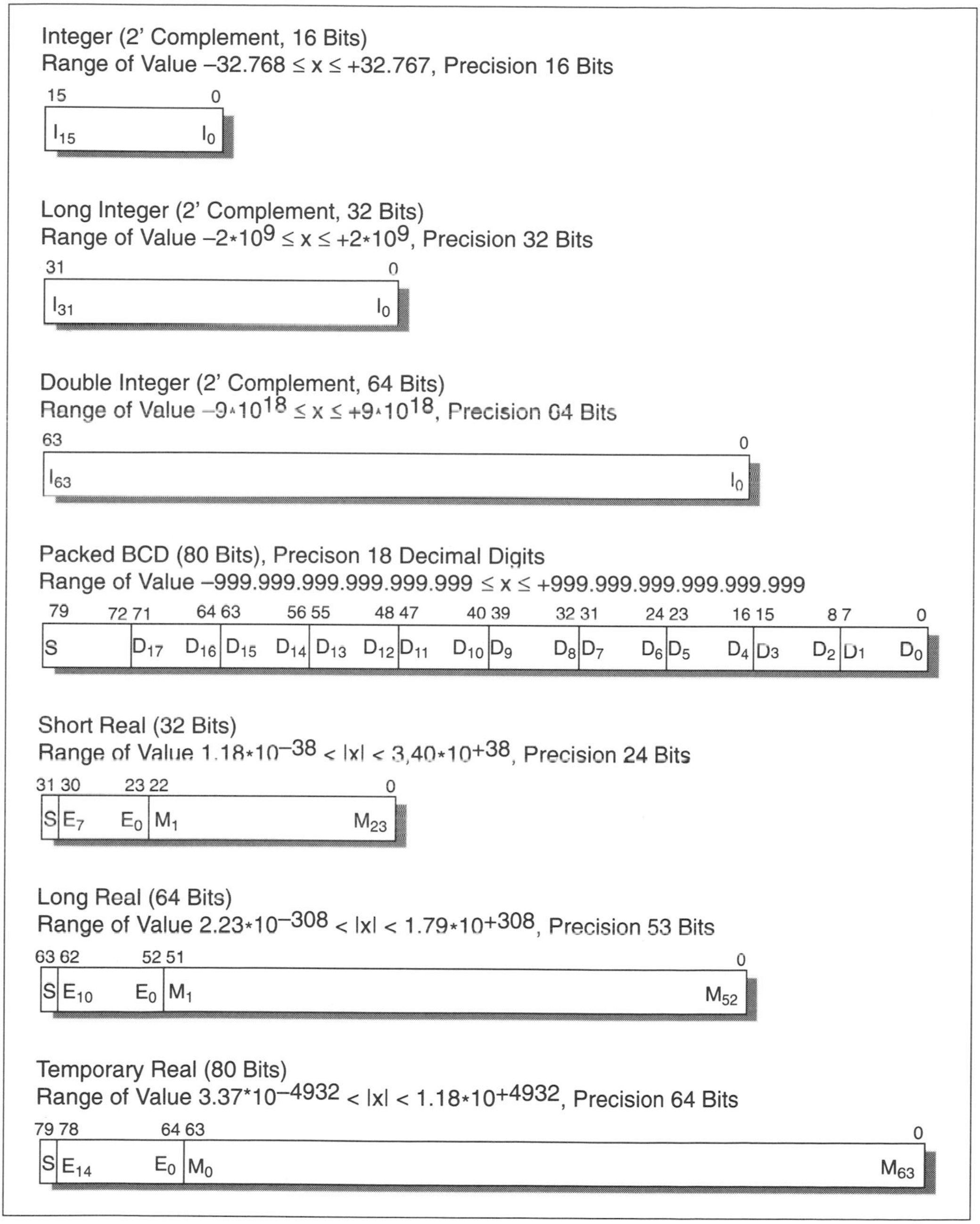

Figure 7.3: i387 number formats.

From the list of i387 instructions (see Appendix C), there are two instructions, *Load* and *Store*, which have special importance for the management of number formats. Using the load instruction, a number from one of the formats shown in Figure 7.3 is loaded into one of the i387 registers, and at the same time converted into the 80-bit temporary real format. Using this number format, the i387 executes all the necessary calculations, from simple comparisons to complicated logarithms or tangent calculations. The store instruction is the counterpart to load: it stores a number located in the i387 in temporary real format in one of the formats shown in Figure 7.3. For this, the i387 again carries out the conversion automatically. The formats shown in Figure 7.3 are the formats supported by the i387 for conversion, and not the internal representation.

You are probably aware that converting number formats is complicated and time consuming. For example, it takes up to 53 clock cycles to load a 16-bit integer from memory into the i387, and for the associated format conversion. In the case of a BCD number, this process can take up to 97 clock cycles. The unloading takes even longer. For simple calculations such as addition, subtraction and multiplication using floating-point numbers, the additional workload necessary to convert the format is greater than the advantage gained from processing floating-point numbers in the i387. For this reason, many applications use i386 software emulation for floating-point arithmetic, and only access the coprocessor when dealing with long and complicated calculations such as logarithms, as the coprocessor can execute these tasks much more quickly. Simple spreadsheet calculations such as the creation of totals and average values for a column or a row are often executed at the same speed with or without a coprocessor. On the other hand, three-dimensional CAD applications often require trigonometric functions such as sine and tangent, in order to calculate projections onto a particular plane. You can calculate the sine of a (floating-point) value of x using the following equation:

$$\text{sine } x = x - x^3/3! + x^5/5! - x^7/7! +- \ldots \quad (3!=1*2*3=6,\ 5!=1*2*3*4*5=120 \text{ etc.})$$

Depending upon the value of x, more or less $x^n/n!$ places are required to determine the value of sine x with sufficient accuracy. As you can see from the formula, a considerable number of extensive arithmetic floating-point multiplications and floating-point divisions are necessary to calculate the potential x^n. Considerable time is required by the i386 using software emulation, whereas the i387 can use its calculating ability to the full.

When looking at the i387 instructions a little more closely, it becomes apparent that the i387 does not recognize machine code instructions in order to transfer data from its register into a register of the i386. For example, you cannot shift a 32-bit integer from the i387 into the accumulator EAX of the i386. The data transfer takes place via the main storage area, thus making it slow. This is due to the need always to have two memory accesses and a format conversion. This is also the reason why simple calculations with floating-point arithmetic can be executed at the same speed using an i386 with an optimized emulator as with an i387.

7.4 i387 Pinout and Signals

The i387 has 68 pins for the transfer of input and output signals and supply currents. It comes in a 68-pin PGA. Figure 7.4 schematically shows the pinout.

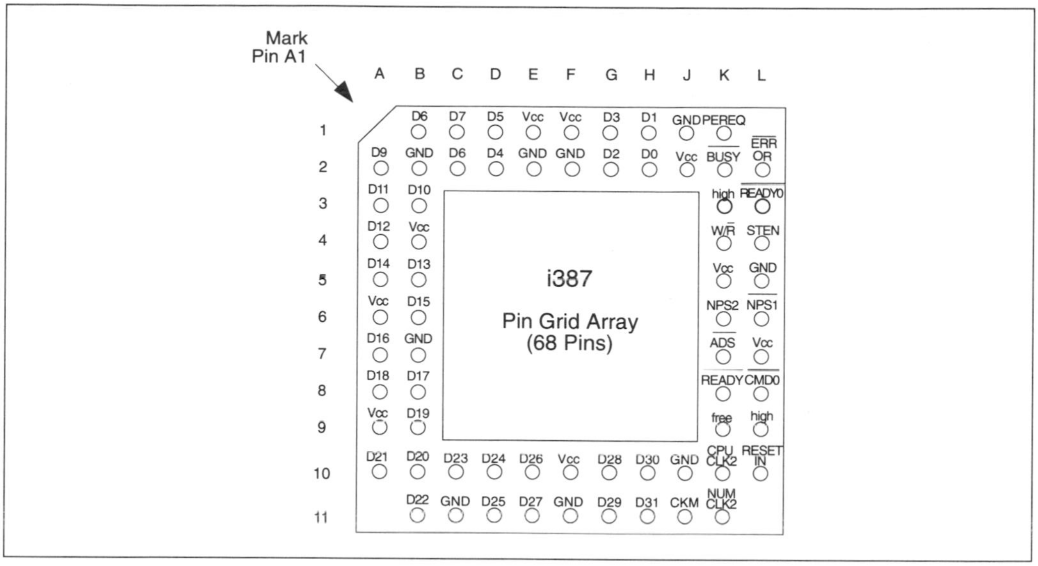

Figure 7.4: i387 pinout. The i387 is usually shipped in a 68-pin PGA.

In comparison to the i386, which has 132 pins, the i387 only has 68. The reason for this is that the i387 does not have an address bus, because the i386 undertakes all of the addressing tasks. This in turn results in some of the bus control signals being omitted. In the following, I will explain the remaining pins and signals. The «I» in the following list indicates that the i387 receives a signal at the corresponding pin; the «O» indicates that the i387 passes a signal to its respective pin. The pins are listed alpha numerically.

$\overline{\text{ADS}}$ (I)
Pin K7

The i386 signal address strobe specifies together with $\overline{\text{READY}}$ when the i387 bus controller can read the W/$\overline{\text{R}}$ signal and the chip selection signal from the CPU. The i387 $\overline{\text{ADS}}$ pin is normally connected to the i386 $\overline{\text{ADS}}$ pin.

$\overline{\text{BUSY}}$ (O)
Pin K2

If this signal is low level, then the i387 executes an ESC instruction.

CKM (I)
Pin J11

When this pin is supplied with a high level signal, the i387 operates in synchronized mode. This means that all components are operated by CPUCLK2, which also clocks the i386. When CKM is connected to ground, only the bus controller uses the external processor clock CLK2; all other components are clocked by NUMCLK2. In this case, an external clock generator is necessary for the i387.

$\overline{\text{CMDO}}$ (I)
Pin L8

The instruction signal indicates, during a read cycle, whether the control or status register ($\overline{\text{CMD0}}$ at low level, therefore active) or the data register ($\overline{\text{CMD0}}$ at high level, therefore inactive) will be read by the i386. If, during a write cycle, $\overline{\text{CMD0}}$ is active, the i386 will transfer an ESC opcode; otherwise, it transfers a data value.

CPUCLK2 (I)
Pin K10

The external CPU clock signal CLK2 is supplied to this pin. The i387 uses CLK2 for the internal time harmonization of its bus controller logic. If CKM is high level, then the i387 is synchronized with the CPU. The other components are also clocked with this signal.

D31–DO (I/O)
Pins A2–A5, A7–A8, A10, B1, B3, B5–B6, B8–B11, C1–C2, C10, D1–D2, D10–D11, E10–E11, G1–G2, G10–G11, H1–H2, H10–H11

These 32 pins form the bidirectional data bus for data exchange between the CPU and the coprocessor.

$\overline{\text{ERROR}}$ (O)
Pin L2

When $\overline{\text{ERROR}}$ is active, this pin provides a low level signal as a non-maskable interrupt has been issued in the i387. Thus, $\overline{\text{ERROR}}$ states the condition of bit ES in the status register.

$\overline{\text{NPS1}}$, NPS2 (I)
Pins L6, K6

If both numeric processor select signals are active, then $\overline{\text{NPS1}}$ is at a low level and NPS2 at a high level. In this state, the i386 records an ESC instruction and activates the i387, so that the instruction can be transferred and executed. $\overline{\text{NPS1}}$ is normally connected to the i386 M/$\overline{\text{IO}}$ pin so that the i387 can only be activated for I/O cycles. NPS2 is normally connected to the most significant address bit A31 so that the i387 can recognize I/O cycles.

NUMCLK2 (I)
Pin K11

If CKM is at a low level, then the i387 runs in an asynchronous mode using the input signal to clock all components, with the exception of the bus controller, which is always run synchronized. The relationship between NUMCLK2 and CPUCLK2 must be between 0.625 and 1.400.

PEREQ (O)
Pin K1

An active processor extension request signal, that is, a high level signal, indicates to the i386 that the i387 is either waiting for data from the CPU or is ready to transfer data to the CPU. Once all of the bytes have been transferred, the i387 deactivates the signal, to inform the i386 that the complete data transfer has taken place.

$\overline{\text{READY}}$ (I)
Pin K8

This pin receives the same signal as the $\overline{\text{READY}}$ pin of the i386, that is, it indicates whether the present bus cycle can be finished or whether the addressed unit requires more time. The i387 itself does not access the main memory or carry out I/O cycles (with the exception of data exchange with the CPU). The $\overline{\text{READY}}$ signal makes it possible for the i387 bus unit to observe all bus activities.

$\overline{\text{READYO}}$ (O)
Pin L3

The i387 activates the signal ready output to this pin so that, after two clock cycles, write cycles can be finished, and after three clock cycles, read cycles can be finished. $\overline{\text{READYO}}$ is sent, when an i387 bus cycle has finished, as long as there are no additional wait cycles. This is necessary because different ESC instructions require different times in advance of, during or after the transfer of operands.

$\overline{\text{RESETIN}}$ (I)
Pin L10

A low-level signal at this pin has the effect of an i387 internal reset. It breaks off all instructions and adopts a defined condition. For this to occur, $\overline{\text{RESETIN}}$ has to remain at a high level for a minimum of 40 NUMCLK 2 cycles.

STEN (I)
Pin L4

The purpose of the status enable signal is for the selection of the coprocessor chip. When STEN is active, the i387 reacts to address signals M/$\overline{\text{IO}}$, A31, A2, W/$\overline{\text{R}}$, $\overline{\text{ADS}}$ etc. from the i386. The following meanings apply to the combination (STEN $\overline{\text{NPS1}}$ NPS2 $\overline{\text{CMDO}}$ W/$\overline{\text{R}}$) of coprocessor control signals:

(0xxxx) i387 not selected
(11xxx) i387 not selected
(1x0xx) i387 not selected
(10100) the i386 reads a control or status word from the i387
(10101) the i386 writes an opcode into the i387
(10110) the i386 reads data from the i387
(10111) the i386 writes data to the i387

W/$\overline{\text{R}}$ (I)
Pin K4

The level of this signal determines whether the current I/O cycle with the i386 represents a write (W/$\overline{\text{R}}$ high level) or read cycle (W/$\overline{\text{R}}$ low level).

Vcc (I)

Pins A6, A9, B4, E1, F1, F10, J2, K5, L7

To supply the i387 with current, these pins are provided with the supply voltage (normally +5 V).

GND

Pins B2, B7, C11, E2, F2, F11, J1, J10, L5

These pins are connected to ground (normally 0 V).

high

Pins K3, L9

Both of these pins are pulled to a high level by means of a resistor, or are connected to Vcc.

free

Pin K9

This pin is not connected to an element or to a potential. It is floating.

7.5 Structure and Function of the i387

The i387 makes additional registers, data types and instructions available to the CPU. This happens as a result of defined cooperation between the i386 and the i387 at the hardware level. For the programmer, assembler or machine code programmer, the combination of i386/i387 appears as one single processor, the difference being that together they have a much higher capacity for performing mathematical calculations at speed than an i386 on its own. The i386/i387 combination can also be described as one processor on two chips. Figure 7.5 shows the internal structure of the i387.

The i387 is divided into two main functional groups, the *Control Unit (CU)* and *Numeric Unit (NU)*. The numeric unit performs the mathematical calculations; the control unit reads and decodes the instructions, reads and writes memory operands using the i386, and executes the control instructions. The CU can dedicate itself to synchronization with the CPU, while the NU executes the difficult numeric work.

On mathematical grounds, the exponent and mantissa of a floating-point number are subjected to differing operations for calculation. For example, the multiplication of two floating-point numbers $\pm M1 * B^{\pm E1}$ and $\pm M2 * B^{\pm E2}$ leads to the addition of the exponents and multiplication of the mantissas. Thus, the result is

$$\pm M1 * B^{\pm E1} * \pm M2 * B^{\pm E2} = (\pm M1 * \pm M2) * B^{(\pm E1 + \pm E2)}$$

Therefore, the arithmetic logic unit of the NU is separated into exponential and mantissa parts. The interface between these two parts has the function of normalizing the result by increasing or reducing the exponent.

The i386 and i387 coprocessor differ significantly in their instructions: the i387 cannot process any i386 instructions, and vice versa. One might expect that now there are two different instruction streams, one with instructions for the CPU and the other with (mathematical) instructions for the coprocessor. This is, however, not the case. Instead, the instructions for the two processors are mixed in a single instruction stream. Coprocessor instructions are essentially different from i386 instructions in that they always start with the bit sequence 11011 (= 27) and are identified as *ESC instructions* whereas i386 instructions and prefixes start with a bit sequence other than 11011.

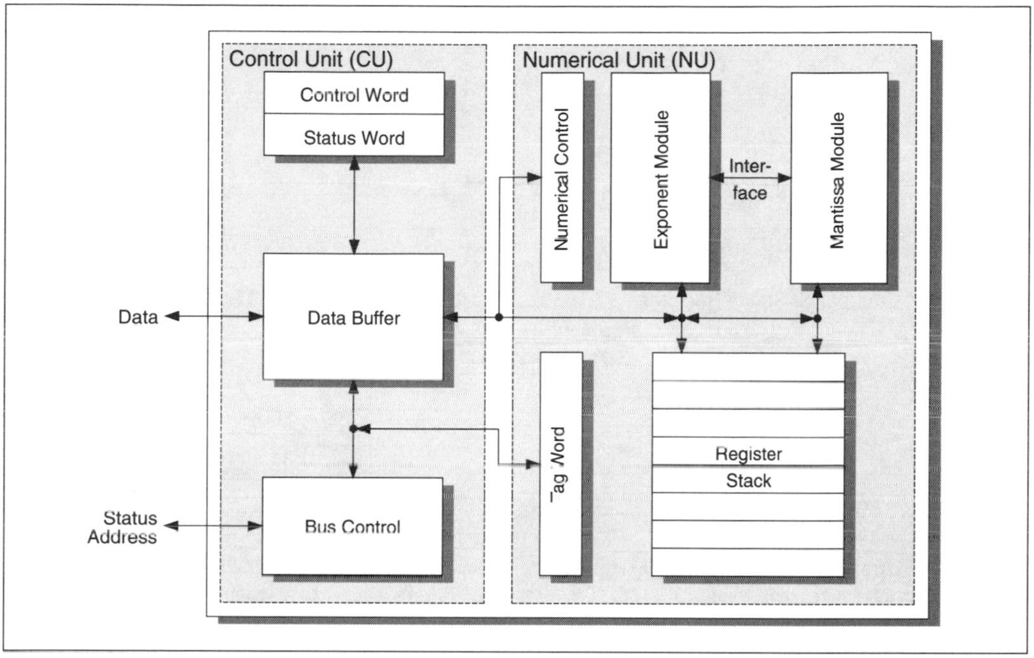

Figure 7.5: Internal i387 structure. The i387 has a control unit for driving the bus and for controlling the numeric unit. The numeric unit carries out all calculations with floating-point numbers in an exponent and a mantissa module. Unlike the i386, the i387 has a register stack instead of discrete registers.

There are many individual general-purpose registers (EAX, EBX, etc.), as well as segment registers (CS, DS and SS), which are available for access in the i386. The i387, though, has a register stack containing eight 80-bit registers (R1 to R8), as well as various control and status registers (Figure 7.6).

Each of the eight data registers is sub-divided into three bit groups corresponding to the temporary real format. The eight data registers are organized as a stack and not as individual registers. The 3-bit field (TOP) in the status word (Figure 7.7) shows the current «Top» register. TOP has similar qualities and tasks to those of the i386 stack pointer ESP. These can, via i387 instructions such as FLD (floating load and push) and FSTP (floating store and pop), which are similar to the i386 instructions PUSH and POP, reduce TOP by 1 and place a value in its respective register, or increase TOP by 1 and take off the applicable stack register. As with the i386, the stack increases downwards to registers with smaller numbers. Most coprocessor instructions implicitly address the top register in the stack, that is, the register whose number is stored in the TOP field of the status register. You can also explicitly specify a register with many i387 instructions. Note that the explicitly specified register is not absolute but relative to TOP.

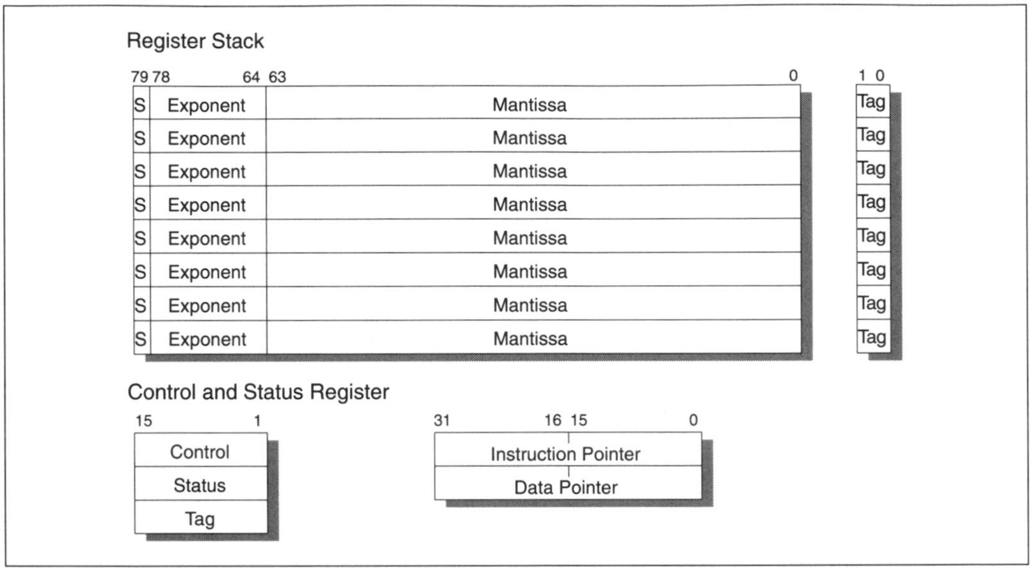

Figure 7.6: i387 internal registers.

Example: `FLD st(3)` addresses the third register, but which of the registers R0 to R7 is actually accessed depends upon TOP. If, for example, TOP is equal to 5 then register 2 is accessed. If TOP is equal to 1, then FLD st(3) means an invalid operation, as register R(−2) does not exist. The i387 reports an error.

Within the i387, the data transfer between registers R0 and R7 is very fast because the coprocessor has an 84-bit path and within the i387 itself no format transfer is necessary.

Information relating to the current condition of the i387 is held in the status word. The coprocessor can write the status word to memory using the instructions FSTSW/FNSTSW (store status word). It is then that the i386 can examine the status word to determine, for example, the cause of an exception.

The i387 *B*-bit is only partly available due to compatibility with the 8087, and is always equal to the ES-bit. On no account does B produce any data with regard to the condition of the numeric unit and therefore the pin $\overline{\text{BUSY}}$.

The i387 error status is indicated by the new *ES*-bit. If ES is set, then an unmasked exception has occurred, the cause of which is given by bits SP to IE. Bit SP is used to differentiate between invalid operations caused by register stack under- or overflow and invalid operations with other causes. If *SP* is set and an under- or overflow of the stack register has occurred, then due to bit *C1*, it is possible to differentiate between an overflow (C1=1) and an underflow (C1=0).

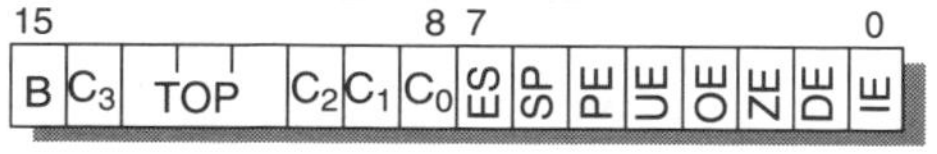

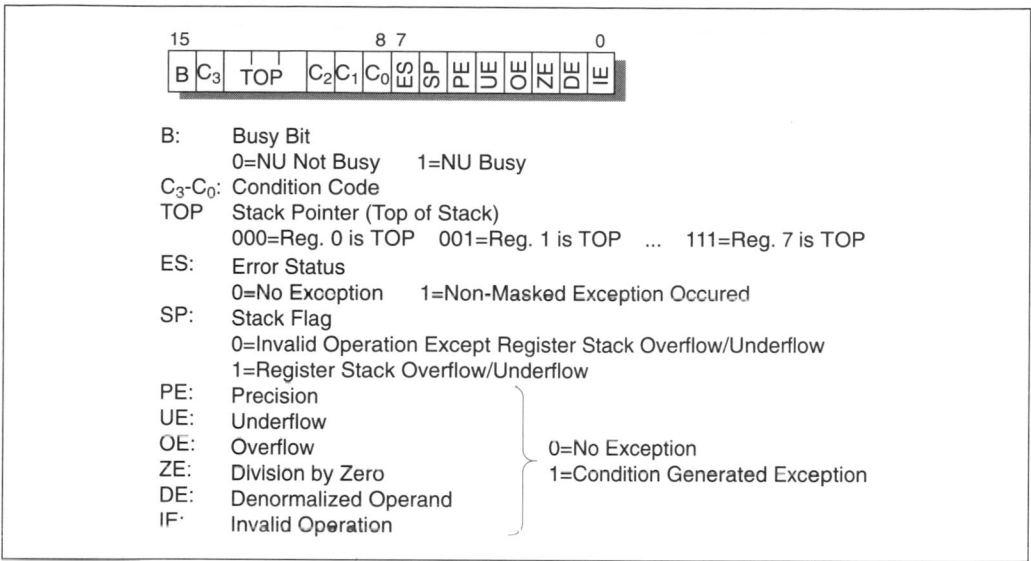

B: Busy Bit
0=NU Not Busy   1=NU Busy
C_3-C_0: Condition Code
TOP Stack Pointer (Top of Stack)
000=Reg. 0 is TOP   001=Reg. 1 is TOP   ...   111=Reg. 7 is TOP
ES: Error Status
0=No Exception   1=Non-Masked Exception Occured
SP: Stack Flag
0=Invalid Operation Except Register Stack Overflow/Underflow
1=Register Stack Overflow/Underflow
PE: Precision
UE: Underflow
OE: Overflow
ZE: Division by Zero
DE: Denormalized Operand
IE: Invalid Operation
(PE–IE:) 0=No Exception
1=Condition Generated Exception

Figure 7.7: i387 status word format.

For an interpretation of the condition codes *C3–C0* of a comparison or similar operation, refer to Table 7.2. These are similar to the flags of the i386. Note that in this relationship, the i387 operates with two zeros. A detailed explanation of all condition codes is detailed in the Pentium section of this book. I would also like to refer those interested to an i387 Programmer's Manual. The three TOP bits form the stack pointer for the registers R7 to R0 located at the top.

Instruction Type	C3	C2	C1	C0	Meaning
	0	0	x	0	TOP > operand (instruction FTST)
compare	0	0	x	1	TOP < operand (instruction FTST)
test	1	0	x	0	TOP = operand (instruction FTST)
	1	1	x	1	TOP cannot be compared
investigate	0	0	0	0	valid, positive, denormalized
	0	0	0	1	invalid, positive, exponent–0 (+NAN)
	0	0	1	0	valid, negative, denormalized
	0	0	1	1	invalid, negative, exponent=0 (–NAN)
	0	1	0	0	valid, positive, normalized
	0	1	0	1	infinite, positive (+∞)
	0	1	1	0	valid, negative, normalized
	0	1	1	1	infinite, negative (-∞)
	1	0	0	0	zero, positive (+0)
	1	0	0	1	not used

Table 7.2: i387 condition codes

Instruction Type	C3	C2	C1	C0	Meaning
	1	0	1	0	zero, negative (-0)
	1	0	1	1	not used
	1	1	0	0	invalid, positive, exponent=0 (+ denormalized)
	1	1	0	1	not used
	1	1	1	0	invalid, negative, exponent=0 (– denormalized)
	1	1	1	1	not used

Table 7.2: cont.

Under certain circumstances the i387 produces a coprocessor exception. These exceptions can be individually masked. What is more, you can determine different modes for rounding and precision. The control word is used for this purpose, the structure of which you can see in Figure 7.8.

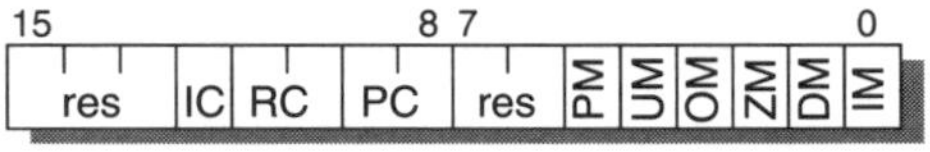

IC: No Meaning (Only for Compatibility with 8087/80287:
0=projective (∞), 1=affine (±∞)
RC: Rounding
00=to Nearest Value 01=to Lower (to ±∞)
10=to Higher (+∞) 11=Cut-Off (to 0)
PC: Precision
00=24 Bits 01=Reserved 10=53 Bits 11=64 Bits
PM: Precision
UM: Underflow
OM: Overflow
ZM: Division by Zero
DM: Denormalized Operand
IM: Invalid Operation
(PM–IM: 0=Exception Masked, 1=Exception Enabled)
rs: Reserved

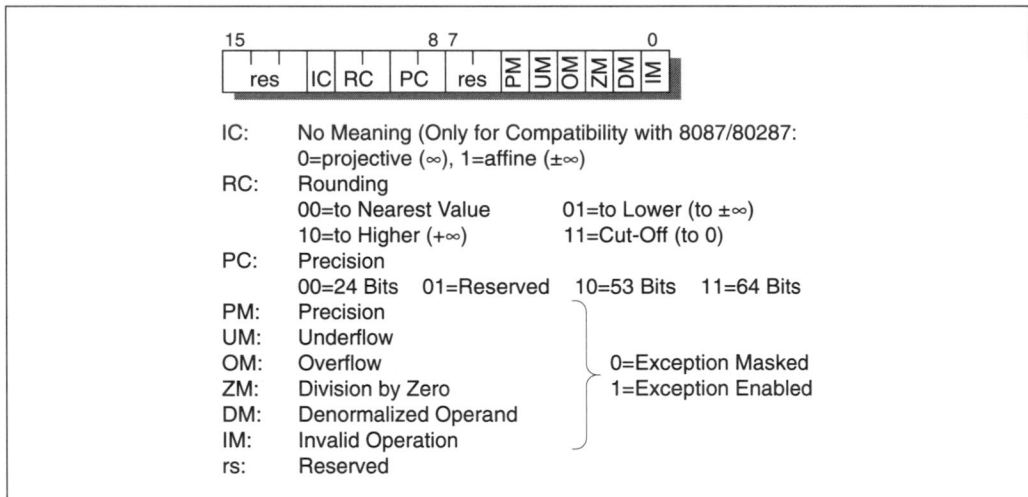

Figure 7.8: Format of the i387 control word.

I want to mention that the i387, unlike the 8087, is only able to issue an interrupt indirectly via the $\overline{\text{ERROR}}$ signal and the i386. It indicates an error to the CPU by means of $\overline{\text{ERROR}}$. Then the CPU may generate an interrupt. For the 8087, however, the coprocessor itself can issue an interrupt. The interrupt mask bit M of the 8087 therefore has no meaning and is not used by the i387.

In the i387, the *IC*-bit has no purpose when handling infinite quantities, because the i387 complies strictly with the IEEE standard when handling floating-point numbers. On the grounds of compatibility with the 8087 and 80287, the IC-bit is available but has no effect. The i387 always handles countless dimensions in the affine sense of ±∞, even if you set IC to 0. The term «infinite» must be used with care, because in a strict mathematical sense no infinite quantities exist, only quantities which are *not limited* upwardly (+∞) or downwardly (–∞), or

Riemann's far-point. The two *RC*-bits control the rounding in the defined way. The accuracy of the i387 calculations is set by the PC-bits, to achieve compatibility with older coprocessors from the 8-bit era. *PC* only has an effect on the result of the ADD, SUB, MUL, DIV and SQRT instructions.

The remaining control word bits *PM, UM, OM, ZM, DM,* and *IM* control the generation of an exception and the resulting interrupt. Altogether, the i387 uses six different exceptions. You can mask the exceptions individually using bits PM, UM, OM, ZM, DM and IM; the coprocessor then executes a standard routine to deal with the respective error using a so-called standard on-chip exception handler. This is an integral part of the chip. The reasons for each exception, as well as the corresponding standard handler, are detailed in Section 7.6.

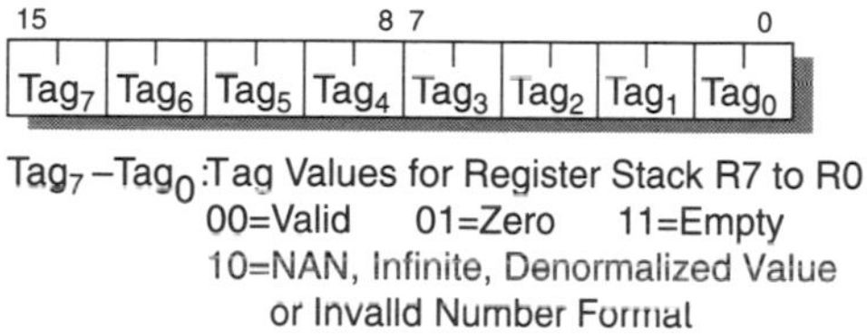

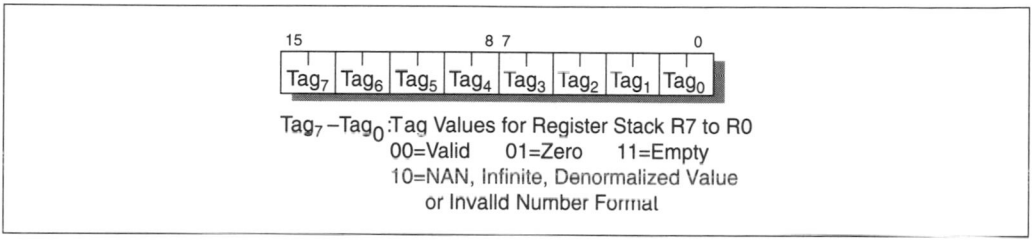

Figure 7.9: i387 tag word format.

There is a further status register available in the i387, the *tag word*. Its construction is shown in Figure 7.9. Tag_7–Tag_0 contain information which identifies the contents of the eight data registers R7–R0. The coprocessor uses this information to perform certain operations at an increased speed. Using this process, the i387 can very quickly determine empty and non-empty stack registers, or determine certain values such as NAN, infinity, etc., without the need to decode the value from the respective register. Using the FSTENV/FNSTENV (store environment state) instructions, you can store the tag word in memory and examine it with the CPU.

7.6 i387 Exceptions

The following list shows the cause of each exception as well as the respective standard handler. For an unmasked exception, the applicable bits are set in the status word (Figure 7.7).

- Precision (PE, PM): the result of an operation cannot be represented exactly in the determined format. The coprocessor continues its task without further action if the bit is PM.

- Underflow (UE, UM): the result is not zero, but too small to represent in a determined format. If UM is equal to 1, the 387 cancels the normalization of the result and displaces the leading 1 in the mantissa to the right until the exponent conforms to the chosen format. Each displacement to the right results in a division of the mantissa by 2, therefore the value of the exponent must be increased by 1. This process is known as a *gradual underflow*.

- Overflow (OE, EM): the result is too large for the determined format. If the exception is masked, the i387 produces a code internally for the value $\pm\infty$, and uses this for further operation.
- Division by zero (ZE, ZM): the divisor was equal to zero, the dividend other than zero. On mathematical grounds, the result is not definable (thus not equal to $\pm\infty$). Undefined things are difficult to work with. The i387 produces an encoding for $\pm\infty$ internally for masked exceptions.
- Denormalized operand (DE, DM): at least one operand, or the result of the operation, cannot be represented in normalized form (having the smallest possible exponent with a mantissa different to zero). If DM=1, then the i387 continues to operate with the denormalized number without any further action.
- Invalid operation (IE, IM): either an overflow or an underflow of the register stack has taken place (PUSH on a full register stack or POP on an empty register stack). Either an undefined mathematical operation such as $0 \div 0$, $\infty \div \infty$ or $\infty - \infty$ should be executed, or a NAN value used as an operand. The i387 produces either a predetermined NAN value or outputs a NAN value as a result for a masked exception.

On the 8087 a non-masked exception generates an interrupt directly. For this purpose, the 8087 has an INT pin whose signal may issue a hardware interrupt. In protected mode interrupts are quite uncomfortable and, thus, are part of the operating system or at least part of system-near code. The i387 has only an $\overline{\text{ERROR}}$ pin which can indicate an exception in the coprocessor to the CPU, but cannot directly issue an interrupt. The active $\overline{\text{ERROR}}$ signal generates an i386-exception 16 (coprocessor error).

In this way, the i387 exceptions can also use the protection mechanism of protected mode intended for interrupts. Additionally, there are the three exceptions, 7, 9 and 13, for the handling of errors which occur in the i387 but are recognized and processed by the i386. In the following, all the exceptions that occur in connection with the i387 are listed.

- Exception 7 (no coprocessor available): the EM bit (coprocessor emulation) or the TS bit (Task Switch) is set in the CPU, and during execution of instructions the CPU receives an ESC instruction. If EM=1 the coprocessor instruction must be emulated by software, and the interrupt handler must execute the emulation itself or call the appropriate software. If TS=1 an ESC or WAIT instruction will cause this interrupt to be generated, indicating that the current coprocessor context may not correspond to the actual task. The operating system must resolve this situation.
- Exception 9 (coprocessor segment overflow): in protected mode, an operand spans an address space that is not covered by the segment of the operand, or the operand lies partly at the extreme top/bottom of the segment and partly elsewhere (that is, the operand contains a wrap-around).
- Exception 13 (general protection error): in protected mode, part of the first word or double word of a numerical operand is located outside the segment.

- Exception 16 (coprocessor error): the previously executed numerical instruction caused a non-maskable exception. Only ESC and WAIT instructions can generate this interrupt. Therefore, an i387 internal exception can only issue an interrupt at the *next* coprocessor or WAIT instruction.

The previous numeric instruction leads to a non-masked exception, whereby its address and the operand address are stored in the instruction and data pointer register. Only ESC and WAIT instructions may issue that interrupt. Thus, on the i387 an exception will not give rise to an interrupt until the *next* coprocessor or WAIT instruction. Depending on the application, as well as on the type and number of loaded tasks, a considerable time period may elapse before the coprocessor error generates an interrupt. Conversely, the 8087 issues an interrupt immediately after the occurrence of an exception.

If exceptions are masked in the control register then the i387 executes a standard on-chip exception handler. Note that the i387 knows only affine infinite quantities (±∞) and not projective ones (∞). Infinite results due to a division by zero or an overflow therefore always have a sign. On the 8087 and 80287 the result of the on-chip handler can also be a projective infinite quantity without a sign, depending on the IC bit in the control register.

7.7 The Protected Mode and Memory Images of Instruction and Data Pointers

If the coprocessor executes a numerical instruction, the i387 stores the control, status and tag words. Additionally, there are two registers available in the i386 which contain the instruction and a possible operand address. If a coprocessor exception occurs, and if the i387 generates an interrupt as a result of this, then using the FSTENV/FNSTENV instruction the handler can store the environment in the memory and subsequently determine the cause of the exception. The handling of a coprocessor error is thus greatly eased.

The memory representation is differentiated depending on whether protected or real mode is active, and whether the i387 is currently operating with 16- or 32-bit operands and offsets. The different formats are shown in Figure 7.10.

From the opcode only the three bits $I_0..I_2$ of the first opcode byte, as well as the second opcode byte $I_{15}..I_8$ are stored in the field $opcode_{10..0}$. Because all coprocessor opcodes begin with the 5-bit combination 11011b (equal to ESC), the five opcode bits $I_7..I_3$ need not be saved – they are known implicitly. Note that the three bits of the first opcode byte are stored in the three high-order bits of the opcode field.

Using the FSETPM (floating set protected mode) instruction, the i387 can be switched into protected mode, then using the FRSTPM (floating return from protected mode) instruction it can be switched back to real mode. The i387 FSETPM is implemented only for compatibility with the 80287. The i387 treats the coprocessor instructions identically in both real and protected modes, because the memory management unit is a part of the i386; the i387 is thus not required to perform addressing and access checks. The instruction codes and operands are transferred to the i387 after the CPU has addressed the memory and read the data. In the 80287, the registers for operands and instruction addresses are available in the coprocessor, which in reality means that the 80287 must know whether an address is to be executed in protected or in real mode. Otherwise, in the case of an exception, the pointer is stored in an incorrect format. Thus, the i387 continues to support the FSETPM instruction by ignoring it, but at the same time it does not produce an «invalid opcode» error message.

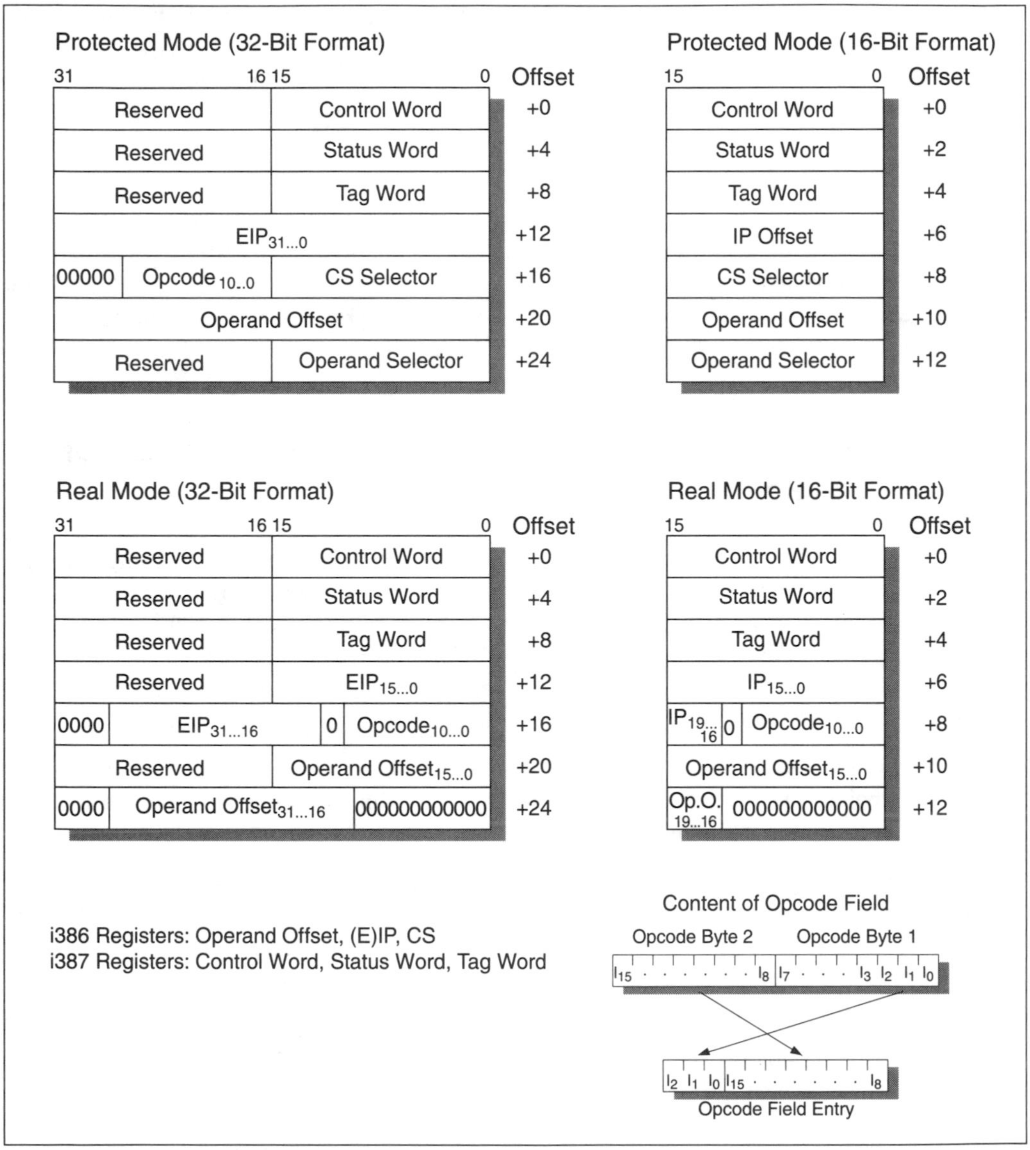

Figure 7.10: Memory images of instruction and data pointers.

7.8 i387 Memory Cycles and Communication Between the i386 and the i387

From the pinout (Figure 7.4) it is apparent that the i387 is unable to address the memory itself (a non-addressing bus emanates from the i387). Like the i386 instructions, i387 instructions can contain a memory operand, for example, the STORE array (ebx) instruction. The i387 itself does not access memory; instead, it uses the i386 to load and store instruction codes and operands. Therefore, all data passes through the i386 memory management unit, so the i387 has available all the advantages of protected mode, virtual 8086 mode and paging.

The i387 is always supplied with the external CPU clock signal CLK2 for clocking the bus interface, so the bus interface is always synchronized with the CPU. Communication between i386 and i387 takes place over I/O bus cycles. The control unit, or more precisely the bus interface of the control unit, behaves like a special I/O unit with respect to the i386. If the CPU recognizes an ESC instruction from the flow of instruction code to be written to the prefetch queue, then the i386 automatically executes an I/O bus cycle, to transfer the opcode to the coprocessor. The i387 supports data transfer between the processor and the coprocessor using bus cycles, both with and without address pipelining, which pass through reserved I/O ports. The port addresses used are outside the normal I/O address space. See Table 7.3, where you will find the I/O addresses used by the i386, and the respective registers with which the processor can communicate via the applicable port.

i386 I/O Port	i387 Register
800000f8h	opcode register
800000fch	operand register

Table 7.3: Coprocessor port addresses

You can see from the leading «8» that the i386 activates the address line A31, to make contact with the coprocessor. For accesses to the normal I/O address space, only the 16 least significant address bits are available, that is A15–A2 and $\overline{BE3}$–$\overline{BE0}$. Both ports are 32-bit ports because the data transfer between the CPU and the coprocessor takes place through the i386 32-bit local bus. Also, the complete data transfer between the memory and coprocessor takes place over the three coprocessor ports. The addressing is carried out in the i386 memory management unit:

- Reading of data: the i386 addresses the memory and reads the addressed data or loads code via a memory read cycle. Subsequently, it transfers the data or ESC instruction code to an I/O bus cycle via the i387 coprocessor ports.
- Writing of data: the CPU reads the data from an I/O cycle via the i387 coprocessor ports. Then the i386 addresses the memory and, via a normal memory write cycle, writes the data to memory.

Thus, two complete bus cycles are always necessary for the i387 LOAD and STORE instructions: one for data transfer between the CPU and coprocessor, the other for i386 memory access. This is another reason why simple floating-point instructions can be executed much quicker when using an emulator.

If the i386 wants to carry out a data transfer such as the transfer of the opcode of an ESC instruction, the CPU starts an I/O bus cycle for communication with the i387 by activating the two coprocessor signals $\overline{\text{NPS1}}$ and NPS2. Then the i387 investigates the signals at the $\overline{\text{CMD0}}$ and W/$\overline{\text{R}}$ pins to determine the direction of the data transfer (to the CPU and from the CPU, respectively), and to prepare the internal data buffers for output or input of data. If the coprocessor is ready for the data transfer it activates the PEREQ signal. The CPU carries out, on the one hand, the transfer between coprocessor and i386 and, on the other, the transfer between memory and CPU. If all data has been transferred the i386 reacts with a PEACK, the i387 deactivates the PEREQ signal and the data transfer between memory and coprocessor or between coprocessor and memory is completed. Alternatively, the i387 can request a memory cycle by activating the PEREQ signal. The i386 recognizes this and responds accordingly.

7.9 i386/i387 System Configuration

Figure 7.11 shows a schematic diagram of the i386/i387 system configuration. Asynchronous operation of CPU and coprocessor is possible because the i387 (unlike the 8087, for example) cannot control the local bus itself. All opcodes and data are transferred by the i386. The i387 uses its data bus only for that process.

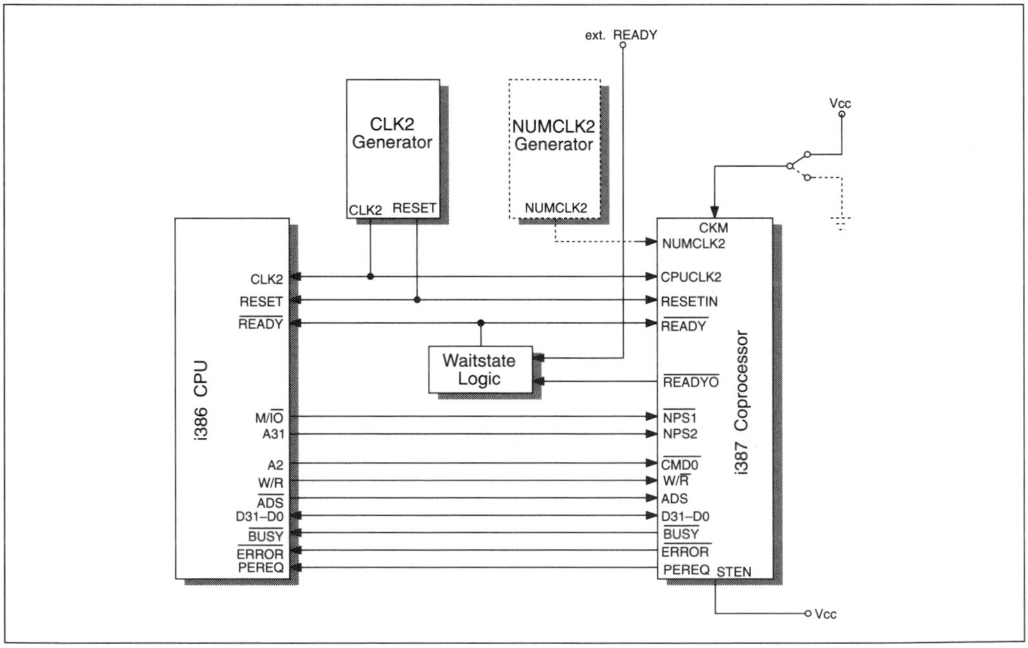

Figure 7.11: i386/i387 system configuration.

The processor addresses the i387 via the signals $M/\overline{IO}$, A2, $W/\overline{R}$, $\overline{ADS}$ and A31, the most significant address bit. The data transfer takes place over the 32-bit data bus D31–D0. The STEN pin is constantly supplied with the supply voltage to activate the coprocessor. The waitstate logic produces wait cycles for the CPU, and for this it uses the coprocessor $\overline{READYO}$ signal along with other $\overline{READY}$ signals from, for example, peripheral equipment or slower memory components. Because the i386 and i387 operate asynchronously, the i387 may be clocked by its own clock generator.

If an error or exception occurs during the course of a numeric calculation in the coprocessor, such as an overflow or underflow, the i387 activates its $\overline{ERROR}$ output to issue an interrupt in the i386. You can see that the i387, unlike the first 80x87 coprocessor – the 8087 – may not operate as a bus master: the HOLD/HLDA pins for the transfer of bus control are not implemented. Thus, the i387 is conceived of more as a «processor extension» than the 8086/87.

7.10 i387 Reset

The i387 performs an internal initialization when it is reset. This occurs as the result of a transition of the signal at the RESETIN pin from a low to a high level, and subsequently maintaining the signal at a low level for at least 40 NUMCLK2 cycles. For this, the i387 requires 50 NUMCLK2 cycles, during which it cannot accept any external instructions. The instruction FNINIT (coprocessor initialization) also puts the i387 internally back into a clearly defined start condition. Table 7.4 shows the different register values after execution of a RESET or FNINIT instruction.

Register	Value	Meaning
control word	37fh	all exceptions are masked, precision 64 bits, rounding to nearest value
status word	xy00h[1)]	all exceptions cleared, TOP=000b[2)], condition code undefined, B=0
tag word	ffffh	all registers are empty

1) $x=0$ or $x=4$, $0 \le y \le 7$

2) TOP points to register 7 (111b) after the first PUSH instruction, the stack grows downwards.

Table 7.4: i387 register contents after a Reset/FNINIT

8 i386 Processor Derivatives and Clones

The above discussion dealt with the «pure» i386, that is, the *i386DX*. It has – as a brief reminder – a 32-bit data bus and a 32-bit address bus. Internally, it has only a complete CPU core, but neither a cache nor a floating-point unit. Starting with this i386 implementation, several derivatives have been developed, including the i386SX with a limited bus (16-bit data bus, 24-bit address bus) as an entry-level i386, and the 386SL chip set with an integrated cache and peripheral controller (ISA bus, memory controller) for installation in Notebook computers. The following sections discuss these two i386 Intel derivatives, as well as cloned 386 CPUs. «Clone» only refers to the logical and functional structure of the processors, not the actual internal electronic structures. These are (with some limitations as far as microcode is concerned), at the circuit and manufacturing level, entirely new developments.

8.1 Cutting Down – The SX Variants of the Processors

Shortly after introducing the i386 and i387 32-bit processors, Intel developed two «cut down» variants of these chips: the i386SX and the accompanying i387SX coprocessor. Internally they are identical to their big brothers, with the exception of an altered bus unit. Thus the i386SX can run in real, protected and virtual 8086 modes; it comprises the same control, debug and test registers, and carries out demand paging if the paging unit is active. Internally, it has the same 32-bit registers as the i386, and can thus manage a virtual address space of 64 Tbytes per task, and may also execute 32-bit instructions. Moreover, the prefetch queue with its 16 bytes is the same size as in the i386. The i387 recognizes the same instructions, has the same registers, and exchanges data with the CPU in the same way as the i387. Table 8.1 lists the main differences, which exclusively refer to the address space and data bus.

	i386/i387	**i386SX/i387SX**
Address bus	32 bits	24 bits
Physical address space	4 Gbytes	16 Mbytes
I/O address space	64 kbytes	64 kbytes
Coprocessor port	800000fxh	8000fxh
Data bus	32 bits	16 bits
Data transfer rate*)	80 Mbytes/s	25 Mbytes/s
Max. clock speed	40 MHz	25 MHz

*) at max. clock speed with zero wait states.

Table 8.1: SX processor model differences

You can see that the «normal» processor variants are far more powerful. The i386 is currently available with clock frequencies up to 40 MHz, compared to 25 MHz for the i386SX. Together with a data bus that is twice as wide, the fastest i386 is therefore able to transfer nearly four times more data than the fastest i386SX. While the physical address space of 4 Gbytes seemed as if it would be enough for decades, there are already PCs on the market that have a main memory of 16 Mbytes, that is, the maximum for the i386SX. Because such a large storage capacity is only necessary for a very powerful system (EISA, OS/2), and a complete i386 is usually employed, this disadvantage is only of a theoretical nature.

PCs, and especially Notebooks with an i386SX base, have been developed successfully because all the innovative features of paging and the virtual 8086 mode are available to the user, but the system hardware, because of the smaller bus width, is easier and therefore cheaper. Only a 16-bit data bus and a 24-bit address bus are needed on the motherboard, as was already the case for a normal 80286 AT. Thus, the i386SX and its derivatives are very useful for compact Notebooks. However, using paging and the virtual 8086 mode, more advantages (together with innovative programs such as Windows or OS/2) are available with the i386SX compared to the 80286. An i386SX-based PC is therefore a good compromise between power and money.

The i386SX comes in a plastic quad flatpack package (PQFP) with 100 pins, and the i387SX in a PLCC package with 68 pins. Figure 8.1 shows the pin assignments of these two SX chips.

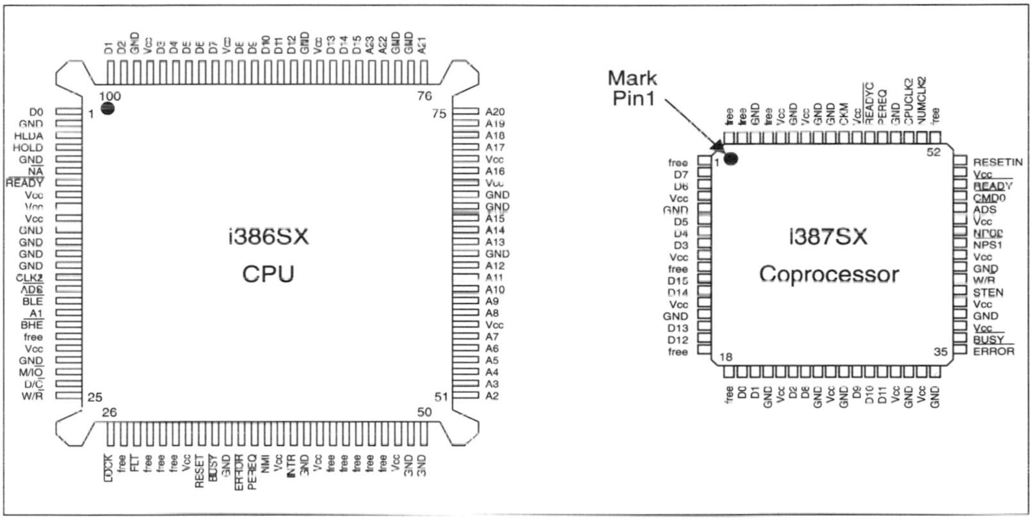

Figure 8.1: i386SX and i387SX terminals. With the SX variants (that is, the i386SX and i387SX) the external data bus is only 16 bits wide, although the data is processed internally with 32 bits, as is the case for the i386/i387. Because of the address bus reduction to 24 address lines, the i386SX/i387SX physical address space comprises only 16 Mbytes, compared to 4 Gbytes.

It is immediately noticeable that these processors have fewer connections when compared to their counterparts. In the following, the altered pins and signals that are not self-explanatory are briefly discussed.

$\overline{BHE}$, $\overline{BLE}$ (O)
Pins 19, 17

These bus high enable and bus low enable signals indicate which part (low-order and/or high-order) of the data bus supplies or accepts valid data. On an i386 this job is carried out by the pins $\overline{BE0}$–$\overline{BE3}$.

$\overline{\text{FLT}}$ (O)
Pin 28

An active signal at this float pin (that is, a low-level signal) forces all i387SX pins that are able to output signals into an inactive state. This signal is largely applied for test purposes.

As for the i386, the i386SX can also carry out an internal self-test. It is issued in the same way and lasts for about 2^{20} clock cycles, that is, about 30 ms with a 20 MHz i386SX. After the self-test the DX register contains a signature byte. The eight high-order bits have the value 23h. The «3» characterizes the i386 family and the «2» indicates that this is the second member of the family, that is, the i386SX. The low-order byte indicates the i386SX version number.

The i386SX and i387SX cooperate in the same way as the i386 and i387, thus the i386SX accesses the coprocessor with reserved I/O ports located outside the normal I/O address space. But because the i386SX has only 24 address lines instead of 32, the address line A23 instead of A31 is now activated. The I/O addresses for communication between CPU and coprocessor therefore comprise only three bytes (Table 8.2). The transfer protocol is the same as for the i386/i387 combination, but the data transfer for 32-bit operands lasts longer as more bus cycles must be carried out because of the 16-bit data bus.

i386SX I/O port	i387SX register
8000f8h	opcode register
8000fch	operand register
8000feh*)	operand register

*) used during the second bus cycle in a 32-bit operand transfer.

Table 8.2: Coprocessor port addresses

8.2 386SL Chip Set – A Two-Chip AT

The steadily increasing integration density of transistors and other electronic elements not only refers to RAM chips or the CPU (the number of integrated transistors rose from the 30000 on an 8086 up to more than three million (!) for the P5 or Pentium). Another trend is that more and more single elements (for example, DMA controller, interrupt controller, timer, etc.) are integrated on one or two chips. PCs are therefore not only getting more compact, but the power consumption has also decreased significantly; an obvious advantage for Notebooks. The provisional summit of this development is Intel's 386SL chip set, which has the CPU chip 386SL and the I/O subsystem 82360SL, and integrates nearly all CPU, support and peripheral chips on these two chips.

8.2.1 Internal Structure of the 386SL and 82360SL

Figure 8.2 schematically shows the internal structure of the 386SL and 82360SL.

The 386SL integrates an improved i386 CPU core, a cache controller and tag RAM, an ISA bus controller and a memory controller on a single chip. The CPU core is implemented in a static design, and may be clocked down to 0 MHz to save power. Presently, the 386SL is available in two versions for clock frequencies of 20 MHz and 25 MHz. The cache interface may be directly connected to a 16, 32 or 64 kbyte cache. The cache organization is programmable as direct mapped, 2- or 4-way set associative. The 20 MHz version may also be delivered without a cache controller and tag RAM.

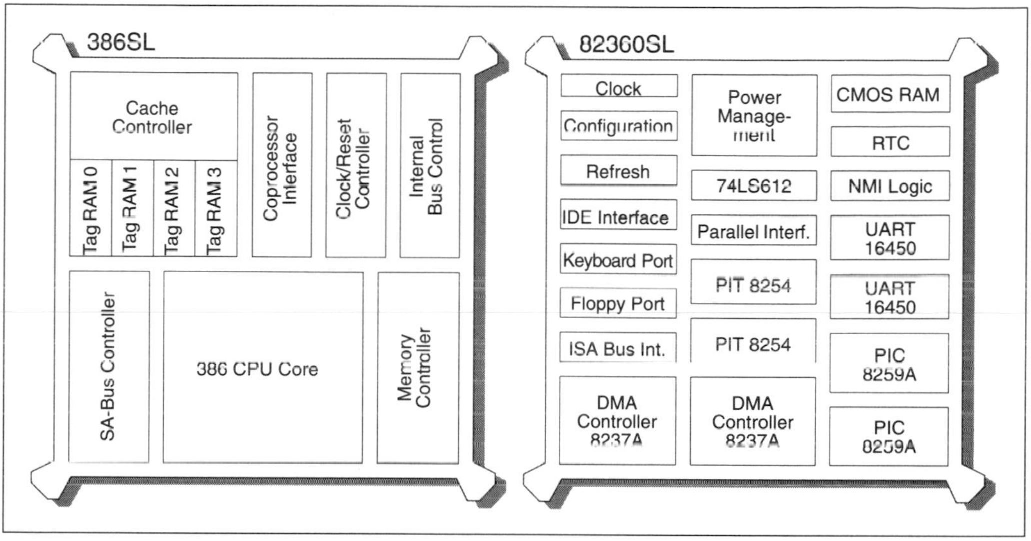

Figure 8.2: Internal structure of the 386SL and 82360SL.

The memory controller accesses the main memory via a 24-bit address bus and a 16-bit data bus. To its environment, the 386SL CPU therefore behaves like an i386SX. Main memory can be organized with one-, two- or four-way interleaving, and the number of wait states is programmable in the 386SL. Additionally, the memory controller incorporates an EMS logic, which implements LIM-EMS 4.0. The controller may also carry out ROM BIOS shadowing. An external shadow logic is not required – the ISA bus controller generates all necessary signals for the ISA bus. In the 386SL sufficiently powerful driver circuits are integrated for this purpose so that no external buffers and drivers are necessary. This significantly simplifies the design of a PC. Additionally, a *peripheral interface bus (PI bus)* is implemented. The 386SL may exchange data with fast peripherals (for example, the integrated 82370SL VGA controller) or flash memories by means of this bus. For controlling the PI bus the pins (and signals) PCMD, PM/$\overline{\text{IO}}$, $\overline{\text{PRDY}}$, $\overline{\text{PSTART}}$ and PW/$\overline{\text{R}}$ are implemented.

For a lower power consumption the 386SL can operate in *power management mode* in which, for example, the 386SL clock frequency can be decreased, or even switched off. The power management is carried out by a non-maskable interrupt SMI of a higher priority. The handler of this interrupt is located in its own system power management RAM, which is separate from the ordinary main memory. The 386SL may access this memory only by means of the $\overline{\text{SMRAMCS}}$

signal. Thus, this concept is similar to that which AMD and Chips & Technologies follow with their low-power versions of the i386 (see Section 8.3).

On the 82360SL a real-time clock, a CMOS RAM, two 8254 timers with three channels each, two 8237A DMA controllers with improved page register 74LS612, a bidirectional parallel interface, two 8259A interrupt controllers, two serial interfaces (a UART 16450 and a support interface for a floppy controller), a keyboard controller and an IDE interface are integrated. Of significance is the additional power management control. This always activates only the currently driven unit, and thus reduces the power consumption significantly. Instead of the internal real-time clock, an external clock may also be used.

The 386SL chip set is already prepared for the integration of a VGA, and the 386SL outputs a special interface signal $\overline{\text{VGACS}}$ when it accesses the address space where the VGA is usually located. With the 386SL and 82360SL chips, some DRAMs and a high-integrated graphics controller (for example, the 82370SL VGA controller) you can build a complete AT. Thus the PW (Personal Workstation) on your wrist would seem to be only a short time away.

8.2.2 Terminals and Signals

To avoid repetition and to save space, the connections and signals of the 386SL and 82360SL are discussed group by group.

386SL

Figure 8.3 shows the pin assignment of the 386SL in a PQFP with 196 pins. Additionally, the 386SL is also availabe in a pin grid array package with 227 connections.

CA15–CA1, CD15–CD0, $\overline{\text{CCSH}}$, $\overline{\text{CCSL}}$, $\overline{\text{COE}}$, $\overline{\text{CWE}}$ (O, I/O, O, O, O, O)
Pins 160–162, 164, 166–176; 177–178, 180, 182–194; 6; 195; 159; 158

(Cache Address, Cache Data, Cache Chip Select High Byte, Cache Chip Select Low Byte, Cache Output Enable, Cache Write Enable).

These 34 connections form the cache bus to the cache SRAM.

CMUX0–CMUX 14 (O; CMUX12–CMUX13: I/O)
Pins 100–111, 127–128, 14
(CPU Multiplexed Bus)

These 15 connections form the memory control bus and supply the CAS, RAS, and parity signals if the main memory is implemented with DRAMs. If the main memory consists of SRAM chips only, CMUX0–CMUX14 provide the control signals for the SRAM chips.

$\overline{\text{BUSY}}$, $\overline{\text{NPXRDY}}$, $\overline{\text{NPXCLK}}$, $\overline{\text{NPXADS}}$, $\overline{\text{ERROR}}$, NPXRESET, NPXW/$\overline{\text{R}}$, PEREQ (I, I, O, O, I, O, O, I)
Pins 150, 153, 157, 154, 152, 156, 155, 149
(Busy, NPX Ready, NPX Clock, NPX Address Strobe, NPX Error, NPX Reset, NPX Write/Read, Processor Extension Request)

These eight signals constitute the coprocessor interface to an i387SX.

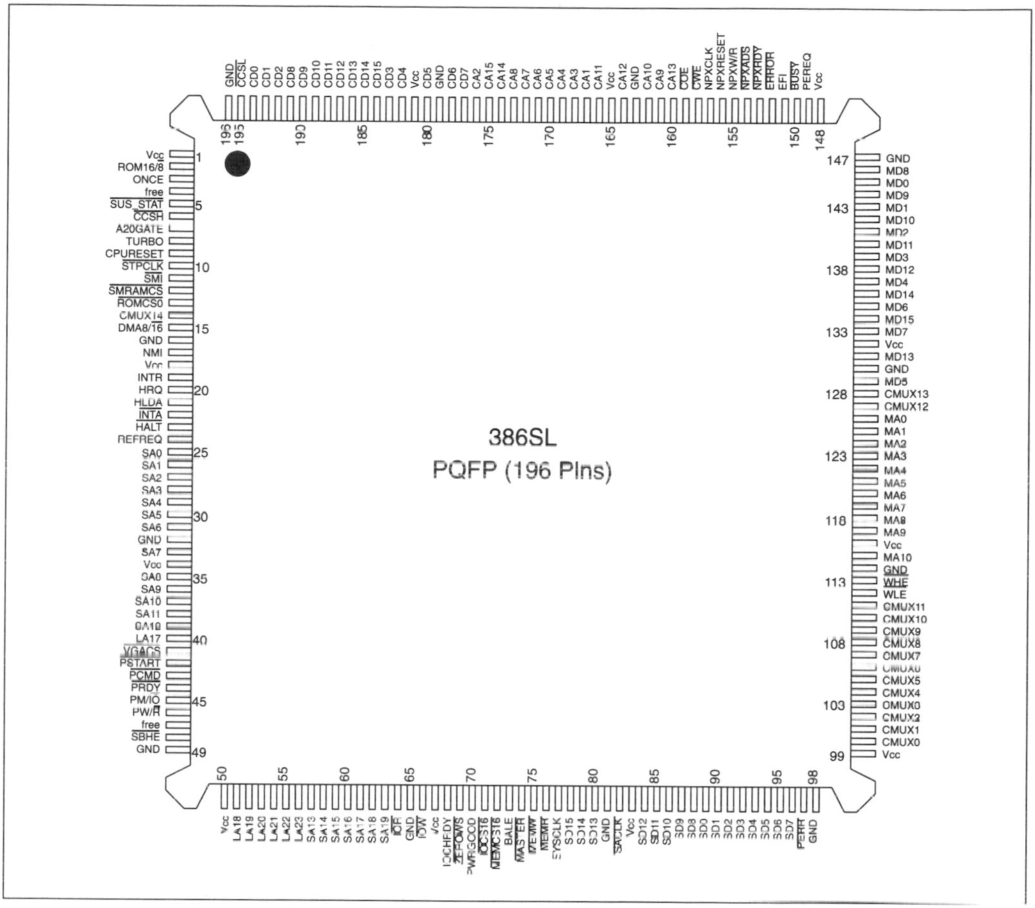

Figure 8.3: Pin assignment of the 386SL in PQFP.

BALE, HLDA, HRQ, IOCHRDY, IOCS16, IOR, IOW, LA23–LA17, MASTER, MEMCS16, MEMR, MEMW, SA19–SA0, SBHE, SD15–SD0, ZEROWS (O, O, I, I/O, I/O, I/O, I/O, I/O, I, I/O, I/O, I/O, I/O, (SA17–SA19: O), I/O, I/O, I)
Pins 73; 21; 20; 68; 71; 64; 66; 40, 51–56; 74; 72; 76; 75; 25–31, 33, 35–39, 57–63; 48; 78–80, 84–96; 69

(Bus Address Latch Enable, Hold Acknowledge, Hold Request, I/O Channel Ready, I/O Chip Select 16, I/O Read, I/O Write, Latchable Address, ISA Master, Memory Chip Select 16, Memory Read, Memory Write, System Address, System Byte High Enable, System Data, Zero Wait States)

These 56 connections form the ISA bus interface of the 386SL.

MA10–MA0, MD15–MD0, PERR, WHE, WLE (O, I/O, O, O, O)
Pins 115, 117–126; 129, 131, 133–146; 97; 113; 112

(Memory Address, Memory Data, Parity Error, Write High Enable, Write Low Enable)

These 30 connections constitute the local memory bus between the CPU and main memory.

A20GATE, CPURESET, DMA8/$\overline{16}$, $\overline{\text{HALT}}$, $\overline{\text{INTA}}$, INTR, NMI, $\overline{\text{ONCE}}$ (I, I, I, O, O, I, I, I)
Pins 7, 9, 15, 23, 22, 19, 17, 3

(Address Line 20 Gate, CPU Reset, DMA Width 8/16, CPU HALT, Interrupt Acknowledge Sequence, Interrupt Request, Non-Maskable Interrupt, On-Board Circuit Emulation)

These eight pins accept various control signals for the CPU.

EFI (I)
Pin 151
(External Frequency Input)

The clock frequency supplied is divided by two inside the 386SL, and then used as the internal processor clock.

PCMD, PM/$\overline{\text{IO}}$, $\overline{\text{PRDY}}$, $\overline{\text{PSTART}}$, PW/$\overline{\text{R}}$ (O, O, I, O, O)
Pins 43, 45, 44, 42, 46
(PI-Bus Command, PI-Bus Memory/IO, PI-Bus Ready, PI-Bus Start, PI-Bus Write/Read)

These five connections form the control bus for PI cycles.

PWRGOOD (I)
Pin 70
(Power Good)

A high-level signal indicates a sufficient power supply.

REFREQ (I)
Pin 24
(Refresh Request)

A high-level signal indicates that the 386SL should issue a refresh cycle for main memory.

ROM16/$\overline{8}$, $\overline{\text{ROMCS0}}$ (I, O)
Pins 2, 13
(ROM-Size 16/8, ROM Chip Select 0)

These two connections provide the signals for accessing the ROM BIOS.

$\overline{\text{SMI}}$, $\overline{\text{SMRAMCS}}$, $\overline{\text{STPCLK}}$, $\overline{\text{SUS\_STAT}}$ (I, O, I, I)
Pins 11, 12, 10, 5
(System Power Management Interrupt, System Power Management RAM Chip Select, Stop Clock, Suspend Status)

These signals implement the system's power management.

ISACLK2 (I)
Pin 82
(ISA Clock Two)

This connection is supplied twice with the frequency of the ISA bus (usually 16 MHz).

SYSCLK (O)
Pin 77
(System Clock)

This pin provides the ISA system clock (usually 8 MHz), that is, half the frequency of the ISACLK2 signal.

TURBO (I)
Pin 8

A high level signal forces the 386SL to run at maximum clock rate.

$\overline{\text{VGACS}}$ (O)
Pin 41
(VGA Chip Select)

The 386SL outputs a low-level signal if it accesses the VGA address space.

82360SL

Figure 8.4 shows the pin assignment of the 82360SL in a PQFP with 196 terminals.

A20GATE, CPURESET, DMA8/$\overline{\text{16}}$, $\overline{\text{HALT}}$, $\overline{\text{INTA}}$, INTR, NMI, $\overline{\text{ONCE}}$ (O, O, O, I, I, O, O, I)
Pins 135, 141, 136, 133, 134, 139, 140, 195

(Address Line 20 Gate, CPU Reset, DMA Width 8/16, CPU HALT, Interrupt Acknowledge Sequence, Interrupt Request, Non-Maskable Interrupt, On-Board Circuit Emulation)

These eight connections provide or accept various control signals for or from the CPU.

BALE, AEN, DACK7–5, DACK3–0, DRQ7–5, DRQ3–0, HLDA, HRQ, $\overline{\text{IOCHCK}}$, IOCHRDY, $\overline{\text{IOCS16}}$, $\overline{\text{IOR}}$, $\overline{\text{IOW}}$, IRQ15, IRQ14, IRQ12–IRQ9, IRQ7–IRQ3, IRQ1, LA23–LA17, $\overline{\text{MASTER}}$, $\overline{\text{MEMR}}$, $\overline{\text{MEMW}}$, OSC, $\overline{\text{REFRESH}}$, RESETDRV, SA16–SA0, $\overline{\text{SBHE}}$, SD7–SD0, $\overline{\text{SMEMR}}$/$\overline{\text{LOMEM}}$, $\overline{\text{SMEMW}}$, TC, $\overline{\text{ZEROWS}}$ (I, O, O, O, I, I, O, I, I/O, I, I/O, I/O, I, I, I, I, I, I/O, I, I/O, I/O, O, I/O, O, I/O, O, I/O, O, O, O, O)

Pins 97; 37, 91, 87, 89; 42, 44, 59, 79; 88, 90, 92; 43, 45, 85, 194; 137; 138; 193; 36; 192; 41; 40; 77; 78; 74–76, 100; 48, 51–54; 61; 63–64, 69–73; 95; 80; 86; 115; 46; 107; 14–15, 17, 19–31, 33; 62; 6–13; 39; 60; 35

(Bus Address Latch Enable, Address Enabled, DMA Acknowledge, DMA Request, Hold Acknowledge, Hold Request, I/O Channel Check, I/O Channel Ready, I/O Chip Select 16, I/O Read, I/O Write, Interrupt Request, Latchable Address, ISA Master, Memory Read, Memory Write, Oscillator, System Refresh, Reset Drive, System Address, System Byte High Enable, System Data, System Memory Read, System Memory Write, Terminal Count, Zero Wait States)

These connections constitute the ISA bus interface of the 82360SL.

BATTDEAD, BATTLOW, BATTWARN (I, I, I)
Pins 188, 187, 189
(Battery Dead, Battery Low, Battery Warning)

These three signals inform the 82360SL of the current power status of the battery or accumulator.

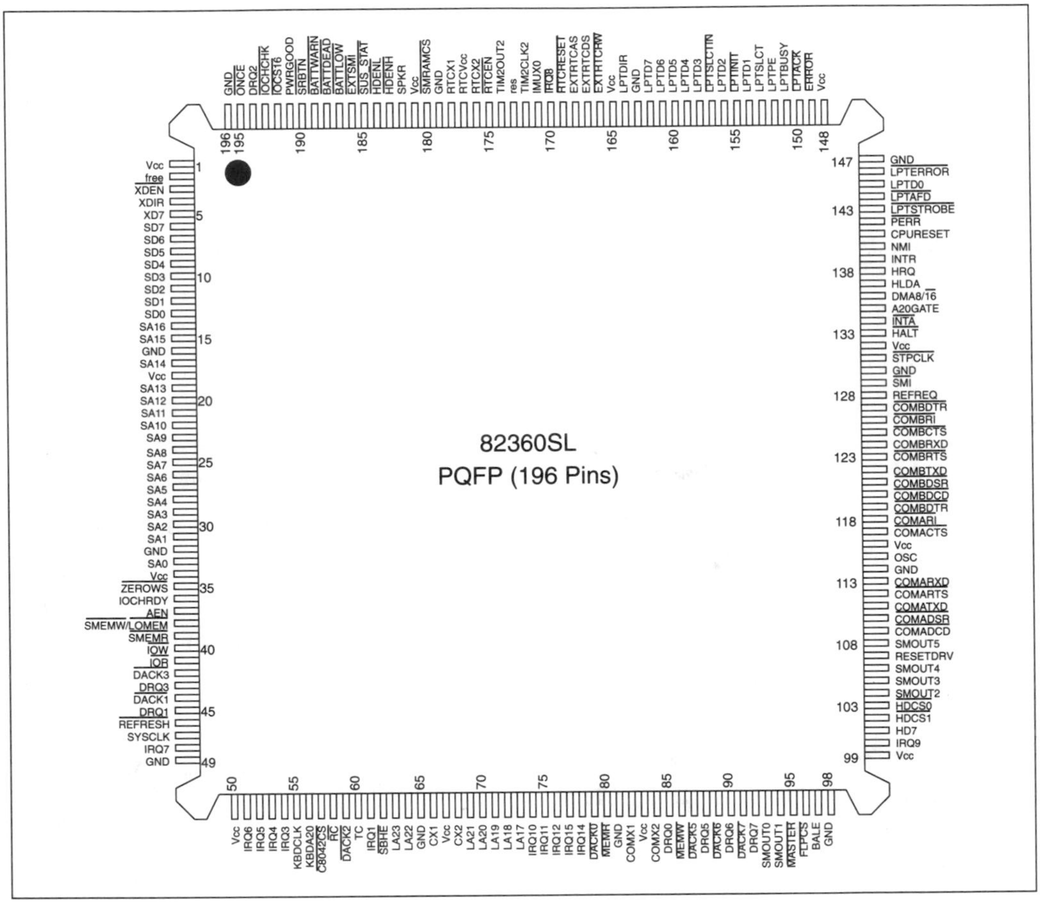

Figure 8.4: Pin assignment for the 82360SL in a PQFP.

PERR, RC, REFREQ (I, I, O)
Pins 142, 58, 128
(Parity Error, Reset CPU, Refresh Request)

These connections directly accept signals from the CPU or provide them to the CPU.

PWRGOOD (I)
Pin 191
(Power Good)

A high-level signal indicates a sufficient power supply.

RTCEN (I)
Pin 175
(RTC Enable)

If this pin is provided with a low-level signal, the 82360SL enables the internal clock; otherwise it enables an external real-time clock.

RTCRESET, RTCVCC, RTCX1, RTCX2 (I, I, I, O)
Pins 169, 177, 178, 176
(RTC Reset, RTC Vcc, RTC External Crystal Oscillator)

These four connections drive the internal real-time clock.

SPKR (O)
Pin 182
(Speaker Output)

This connection supplies the signal for the speaker.

SYSCLK (I)
Pin 47
(System Clock)

The pin supplies the ISA system clock (usually 8 MHz), that is, half the frequency of the ISACLK2 signal.

SMI, SMOUT0–SMOUT5, SMRAMCS, SRBTN, STPCLK, SUS_STAT (O, O, I, I, O, O)
Pins 129; 93–94, 104–106, 108; 180; 190; 131; 185
(System Power Management Interrupt, System Management Output Control, System Power Management RAM Chip Select, Suspend/Resume Button, Stop Clock, Suspend Status)

These signals implement the system's power management.

FLPCS (O)
Pin 96
(Floppy Chip Select)

This pin provides a signal with a low level if the CPU accesses a floppy controller port.

HD7, HDCS1–HDCS0, HDENL, HDENH (I/O, O, O, O)
Pins 101, 102–103, 184, 183
(Hard Disk Bus Data 7, Hard Disk Chip Select, Hard Disk Buffer Enable Low, Hard Disk Buffer Enable High)

These five connections form the control bus of the IDE interface.

IMUX0 (I)
Pin 171
(Input Multiplex)

This pin may be provided with an input signal for the gate input of timer 2 or an external audio signal for the speaker.

IRQ8, EXTRTCAS, EXTRTCDS, EXTRTCRW (I, O, O, O)
Pins 170, 168, 167, 166
(Interrupt Request 8, External RTC Address Strobe, External RTC Data Strobe, External RTC Read/Write)

These connections form the interface to an external real-time clock.

EXTSMI (I)
Pin 186
(External System Management Interrupt Request)

A low-level potential causes an SMI request.

C8042CS, KBDA20, KBDCLK (O, I, O)
Pins 57, 56, 55
(Keyboard Controller 8042 Chip Select, Keyboard A20 Gate, Keyboard Clock)

These connections constitute the interface for driving the keyboard controller.

COMACTS, COMADCD, COMADSR, COMADTR, COMARXD, COMARI, COMARTS, COMATXD (I, I, I, O, I, I, O, O)
Pins 117, 109, 110, 119, 113, 118, 112, 111
(COM A Clear to Send, COM A Data Carrier Detect, COM A Data Set Ready, COM A Data Terminal Ready, COM A Received Data, COM A Ring Indicator, COM A Request to Send, COM A Transmit Data)

These eight connections implement the first serial interface in the 82360SL.

COMBCTS, COMBDCD, COMBDSR, COMBDTR, COMBRXD, COMBRI, COMBRTS, COMBTXD (I, I, I, O, I, I, O, O)
Pins 125, 120, 121, 127, 124, 126, 123, 122
(COM B Clear to Send, COM B Data Carrier Detect, COM B Data Set Ready, COM B Data Terminal Ready, COM B Received Data, COM B Ring Indicator, COM B Request to Send, COM B Transmit Data)

These eight connections implement the second serial interface in the 82360SL.

COMX1, COMX2 (I, O)
Pins 82, 84
(COM External Oscillator)

These pins must be connected to a 1.8432 MHz oscillator, and supply the base clock for the two UARTs.

CX1, CX2 (I, O)
Pins 66, 68
(Crystal External Oscillator)

These pins must be connected to a 14.31818 MHz oscillator. After a division by 12, they provide the base clock for the timers.

$\overline{\mathrm{ERROR}}$ (I)
Pin 149
(NPX Error)

This signal indicates a coprocessor error.

$\overline{\mathrm{LPTACK}}$, $\overline{\mathrm{LPTAFD}}$, LPTBUSY, LPTD7–LPTD0, LPTDIR, $\overline{\mathrm{LPTERROR}}$, $\overline{\mathrm{LPTINIT}}$, LPTPE, LPTSLCT, $\overline{\mathrm{LPTSLCTIN}}$, $\overline{\mathrm{LPTSTROBE}}$ (I, O, I, I/O, O, I, O, I, I, O, O)
Pins 150; 144; 151; 145, 154, 156, 158–162; 164; 146; 155; 152; 153; 157; 143
(LPT Acknowledge, LPT Auto Line Feed, LPT Busy, LPT Data, LPT Direction, LPT Error, LPT Initialization, LPT Paper End, LPT Selected, LPT Select In, LPT Strobe)

These 18 connections implement the parallel interface.

TIM2CLK2 (I)
Pin 172
(Timer 2 Clock 2)

This pin is provided with the clock signal for timer 2, channel 2.

TIM2OUT2 (O)
Pin 174
(Timer 2 Output 2)

This connection supplies the output signal of timer 2, channel 2.

XD7 (I/O)
Pin 5
(X-Bus Data)

This pin forms bit 7 of the X-bus.

$\overline{\mathrm{XDEN}}$, XDIR (O, O)
Pins 3, 4
(X-Bus Data Enable, X-Bus Data Direction)

These two connections provide control signals for the X-bus.

8.3 Processor Confusion by i386 Clones

The passion for copying that has hit the PC market, and which is the reason for the enormous drop in prices over the past ten years, does not exclude the heart of a PC. Only a few years ago, Intel more or less held the CPU monopoly, but today enormous competition is taking place (at least up to the i386 level) even there. It is not only coprocessors that are now manufactured by competitors, but also the CPUs.

Users are happy with this, as prices seem to be in endless decline, and the CPU clones are not only equal to the Intel models, but often do better in terms of performance and power consumption. At this time there are three main microelectronics firms manufacturing i386-compatible processors: AMD (Advanced Micro Devices); Chips & Technologies; and Cyrix. The most important i386 clones are briefly discussed below.

8.3.1 AMD Processors

AMD is currently the most important manufacturer in the i386 market segment other than Intel. AMD processors are not only cheaper, but in most cases also faster and, especially, far more power efficient than Intel's models. These chip types are particularly suitable for Notebooooks. Currently, AMD offers three different DX models with a complete 32-bit data bus, as well as three SX models with a 16-bit data and a 24-bit address bus.

Am386DX/Am386SX

The Am386DX is an i386DX-compatible processor available for clock frequencies from 20 MHz up to 40 MHz, that is, its clock rate and therefore the performance can be up to 20% higher than the original i386. The Am386SX is the well-known cut-down version, and has only a 16-bit data and a 24-bit address bus. Both processor types are strictly orientated to the Intel models, and have no significant differences in comparison. They come in a 132-pin PGA or a 132-terminal PQFP (Am386DX) and a 100-terminal PQFP (Am386SX), respectively.

Am386DXL/Am386SXL

The i386DX and i386SX-compatible processors, respectively, are implemented with a special power-saving design (the «L» in the processor name means low power). The Am386DXL/SXL consumes about 40% less power than the comparable Intel models. The DXL type may be clocked with between 20 and 40 MHz, and the SXL model with 25 MHz at most.

The main feature of the Am386DXL/Am386SXL is the static design of its circuits. The clock rate may thus be decreased to 0 MHz, that is, the clock signal can effectively be switched off. The processor does not lose its register contents in this case. With a dynamic circuit design, on the other hand, the clock frequency may not fall below a minimum value without causing a processor malfunction. If the external clock signal is switched off, then, for example, the DXL processor draws a current of only about 0.02 mA compared to 275 mA at 33 MHz. This means a reduction in power consumption by a factor of 10000 (!). Battery-operated notebooks are very happy with this. Using the static processor design, a standby mode can readily be implemented. The BIOS need not save the processor registers, but can just switch off the clock signal after the lapse of a usually programmable time period within which no key press or other action has taken place. If, for example, you then press a key to reactivate the PC, the standby logic releases the clock signal. Then the CPU again operates without the need for the BIOS to restore the registers' contents. This simplifies the implemention of a power-saving standby mode significantly. The Am386DXL comes in a 132-pin PGA or a 132-terminal PQFP, the Am386SXL in a 100-terminal PQFP.

Am386DXLV/Am386SXLV

The Am386DXLV/Am386SXLV is directed uncompromisingly towards low power consumption. It operates with a supply voltage of only 3.3 V compared to the 5 V of an Am386DX/Am386DXL (hence, the LV, for low voltage). The power consumption of CMOS chips is proportional to the square of the supply voltage. By decreasing the supply voltage to 3.3 V, 50% of the power is saved. But at 3.3 V the chip may only be operated up to 25 MHz; to use the maximum 33 MHz a supply voltage of 5 V is necessary. The Am386DXLV/SXLV, too, is implemented in an entirely static design. Thus the external processor clock may be switched off and the Am386DXLV, for example, needs only 0.01 mA compared to 135 mA at 25 MHz.

The Am386DXLV comes in a 132-terminal PQFP, the Am386SXLV in a 100-terminal PQFP. The terminals (except those for system management mode, etc.) provide and accept, respectively, the same signals as the Intel models. The following lists the additional signals and the assigned terminals.

$\overline{\text{FLT}}$ (I)
Pin 54 (Am386DXLV), 28 (Am386SXLV)

If a low-level signal is applied to the float pin, the Am386DXLV/SXLV floats all its bidirectional and output terminals.

$\overline{\text{IIBEN}}$ (I)
Pin 58 (Am386DXLV), 29 (Am386SXLV)

If an active low-level signal is supplied to this I/O instruction break input, the Am386DXLV/SXLV suspends instruction execution until it receives an active signal at its $\overline{\text{READY}}$ input. Upon this it executes the next instruction. This function is mostly used in connection with system management mode. The Am386DXLV/SXLV can give a device accessed through an I/O port and currently in a power-down mode (such as a «sleeping» interface) the opportunity to reactivate itself. This reactivation process may take many more clock cycles than a usual I/O access with wait states.

$\overline{\text{SMI}}$, $\overline{\text{SMIADS}}$, $\overline{\text{SMIRDY}}$ (I/O, O, I)
Pins 59, 37, 36 (Am386DXLV), 43, 31, 30 (Am386SXLV)

These three terminals form the interface to the system management mode (SMM). If a low-level signal is applied to the SMI (system management interrupt) input, an interrupt with a higher priority than even the NMI occurs. The Am386DXLV/SXLV calls the SMI handler and addresses a certain memory area. The SMI address status signal $\overline{\text{SMIADS}}$ corresponds to the $\overline{\text{ADS}}$ signal during normal operation and indicates a valid bus cycle. Finally, the SMI ready signal $\overline{\text{SMIRDY}}$ determines the completion of a bus cycle in SMM; it has the same job as $\overline{\text{READY}}$ in normal operation mode.

AMD System Management Mode

AMD has additionally implemented a so-called *system management mode (SMM)* with the Am386DXLV/SXLV to control the power consumption independently of the operating mode and operating environment. For this purpose, the Am386DXLV/SXLV recognizes a *system management interrupt (SMI)*, which has an even higher priority than the NMI. Further, an additional address space of 1 Mbyte, which is separate from ordinary main memory, is available for system management mode. The SMI is issued by a signal with a low level at the $\overline{\text{SMI}}$ pin, or by setting a certain bit in the debug register 7 and executing opcode f1h. In both cases, the Am386DXLV/SXLV issues something like a major NMI, stores the current operating state of the processor at address 0006:9999 to 0006:00c8 and 0006:0100 to 0006:0124 in the SMM memory, eventually returns to real mode, and starts execution of the SMI handler at address ffff:fff0. Now all memory accesses refer only to SMM memory. The processor indicates this by the signals $\overline{\text{SMIADS}}$ and $\overline{\text{SMIRDY}}$. I/O accesses via instructions such as IN or OUT are still directed to the normal I/O address space.

To return from SMM mode to the interrupted task, and to restore the original processor state, the register pair ES:EDI must be loaded with the far address 0006:0000. Execution of the 32-bit opcode 0fh 07h then restores the processor state from the data held in SMM memory.

8.3.2 Chips & Technologies Processors

C & T became famous with its NEAT chip set for AT-compatible PCs. Meanwhile, C & T also manufacture complete (and, compared with Intel models, more powerful) CPUs. These are the 38605DX, 38605SX, 38600DX and 38600SX processors, which are together called Super386. Unfortunately, C&T has discontinued Super386 production in the meantime.

38600DX/38600SX

An i386DX and i386SX-compatible processor, respectively, with SuperState V mode in power-saving CMOS design. The 38600SX has only a 16-bit data and a 24-bit address bus. Unlike the 38605DX/38605SX, neither an instruction cache nor the SuperState V mode are implemented.

The 38600DX comes in a 132-pin PGA. The terminals (except those for configuring CLKIN as a 1x- or 2x-clock) provide and accept, respectively, the same signals as the Intel models. USE2x has the same meaning as in the 38605DX.

38605DX/38605SX

An i386 and i386SX-compatible processor, respectively, with an internal 512-byte instruction cache and SuperState V mode in power-saving CMOS design. The 38605SX has only a 16-bit data and a 24-bit address bus.

The 38605DX comes in a 144-pin PGA. The terminals (except the new ones for SuperState V mode and controlling the on-chip cache) provide and accept, respectively, the same signals as the Intel models. The following lists the additional signals and the assigned terminals.

$\overline{\text{AADS}}$ (O)
Pin P15

When this alternate address space pin provides a low-level signal, the 38605DX carries out an access to the alternate address space in SuperState V mode.

$\overline{\text{ANMI}}$ (I)
Pin N15

If an active low-level signal is applied to this alternate NMI pin, the 38605DX/SX issues an alternate NMI, having a higher priority than even the normal NMI, and enters SuperState V mode.

$\overline{\text{A20M}}$ (I)
Pin M15

If this address 20 mask pin is driven to a low level, the 38605DX/SX masks the address bit A20 internally before every memory access. Thus, it emulates the 8086 address wrap-around.

$\overline{\text{EADS}}$ (I)
Pin A15

If an active low-level signal is supplied this external address pin, an external busmaster has applied a valid address to its address pins. The 38605DX/SX uses this address for an internal cache invalidation.

$\overline{\text{FLUSH}}$ (I)
Pin B15

When $\overline{\text{FLUSH}}$ is activated by a low-level signal, the 38605DX/SX invalidates the content of its instruction cache.

$\overline{\text{KEN}}$ (I)
Pin C15

Through this cache enable terminal $\overline{\text{KEN}}$, the 38605DX/SX determines whether the current read cycle is cachable, that is, whether the addressed memory area can be transferred into the cache. If that is possible, the current read access is enlarged to a cache line fill cycle, that is, a complete cache line is read into the on-chip cache. With $\overline{\text{KEN}}$, certain address areas can be protected from caching by hardware.

USE2X (I)
Pin P8

An active high-level signal at this terminal indicates to the 38605DX/SX that it receives a clock signal at its CLKIN pin whose frequency is double the internal processor clock. The 38605DX/SX must divide the clock by two (like the i386). With a low USE2X level, however, the 38605DX/SX uses the external CLKIN clock as processor clock PCLK without any further processing.

SuperState V Mode

The two 38605DX/SX processors implement an advanced operating mode, the so-called *SuperState V mode*. This mode has an even higher privilege level than the protected mode, and implements system management functions such as driving external devices for reducing power consumption, for backing up data in advance of power-down, etc. These functions are especially valuable for Notebooks.

In SuperState V mode the processor does not access ordinary main memory, but a separate memory area. Thus, normally running tasks and those tasks in protected mode are not affected; ordinary main memory and the memory area for the system management functions are separate from one another. This is achieved by means of two additional pins marked as free on the Intel CPUs: $\overline{\text{ANMI}}$ (alternate NMI, pin N15) and $\overline{\text{AADS}}$ (alternate address space, pin P15). A low level signal at $\overline{\text{ANMI}}$ issues an NMI with an even higher priority than an ordinary NMI, and switches the 3860xDX/SX into SuperState V mode. Then the processor informs the bus controller by an active (that is, low level) $\overline{\text{AADS}}$ signal that it is attempting to access the alternate memory which is completely dedicated to the SuperState V mode. Here, for example, the handler for the ANMI may be located, which shuts down external devices or even the CPU to save power.

To activate SuperState V mode there are three options:

- Activation of the $\overline{\text{ANMI}}$ signal; the CPU issues an ANMI.
- Setting the I/O trap bit in the configuration register; every I/O access to a port switches the CPU to SuperState V mode.
- Explicitly by executing the new instruction *AENTER* (enter SuperState V mode).

The 3860xDX/SX processors may be supplied with the single (CLK1X) or double (CLK2X) clock signal by the clock signal generator. To distinguish it, the processor has the USE2X connection (pin P8). In the first case, the internal processor clock PCLK coincides with the clock signal CLK1X from the generator, and USE2X is on a low level. In the second case, the CPU divides the applied clock signal internally by two, as is the case with the original Intel i386, to generate the processor clock PCLK. USE2X is on a high level for this purpose.

The 05 models of the 386xxDX/SX CPUs additionally implement an internal instruction cache with 512 bytes. That is not as much as on the i486, and the data cache is also missing, but the performance is nevertheless enhanced. Further, the 05 models have an $\overline{\text{A20M}}$ (address 20 mask, pin M15) connection. If an external logic applies a signal with a low level, then the processor masks the address line A20 internally, and thus emulates a wrap-around at address 1 M if it addresses its internal cache. The 386xxDX CPUs may be clocked up to 40 MHz, that is, 20% higher than an original Intel i386.

A special feature of the Super386 architecture is the implementation of two instruction pipelines. Instruction pipelining, which is analagous to address pipelining, but refers to the execution of instructions in the CPU and not the execution of bus cycles, is discussed in Section 10.3.2. For readers already familiar with instruction pipelining, I will summarize the main characteristics of the Super386 pipelines in brief. Two pipelines are implemented in the Super386, but they cannot operate in parallel; thus, unlike the Pentium, the Super386 is not a superscalar. The first, the I-pipeline, comprises three stages and executes CPU instructions (instruction pipe). The first D-stage decodes the instruction, the second E-stage executes it, and the last W-stage writes the result into the destination operand. The instruction decoder is implemented in hardware, that is, it doesn't need any microcode for decoding. This reduces the usually rather complex decoding process for most instructions to one clock cycle. This particularly accelerates jump instructions and procedure calls when the 12-byte prefetch queue of the Super386 is cancelled, and new instructions must be fetched and decoded before processing can continue. The M-pipeline carries out memory accesses (memory pipe) and has two stages. The first translates linear to physical addresses and determines whether they coincide with debug breakpoints. The second stage executes the access and drives the bus interface for that purpose.

The pipelines are not microencoded but controlled by hardware. This enhances the Super386 performance. Together with the instruction cache, a performance increase of about 30% compared to the Intel and AMD CPUs is possible. Moreover, instruction pipelining is not carried out in Intel CPUs earlier than the i486. Thus, the Super386 already implements 486 technologies. The same applies, by the way, to Cyrix' 386, but Cyrix was more courageous and named its half 386/half 486 chip 486DLC/SLC (which readily gave rise to certain discussions!).

8.3.3 Cyrix CPUs

Until now, Cyrix has largely been known for its fast 80x87 coprocessors, but it has tried to get a slice of the CPU cake. The result of these efforts is the 486DLC with a 32-bit data and a 32-bit address bus, as well as the 486SLC with a 16-bit data and a 24-bit address bus. Despite the name 486, these CPUs are more of an i386 than a real Intel i486, so they are discussed in connection with the i386. The following reasons justify this opinion:

- The 486DLC/SLC has an internal 1 kbyte cache; the original i486, however, has an 8 kbyte on-chip cache. Compared to an i386, even such a small cache speeds up program execution significantly.
- Neither the 486DLC nor the 486SLC has an on-chip coprocessor; it must be added externally with an i387 (or compatible Cyrix chip, of course). To be fair, it must be said that the i486SX also lacks the floating-point unit.
- The «SX» Cyrix 486 model has, like an i386SX, only a 16-bit data bus and a 24-bit address bus. That is very small for a 486 chip; thus, the 486SLC is, despite the «486», more suited to Notebooks.
- The burst mode for quickly filling the on-chip cache is not supported by the Cyrix 486DLC/SLC; therefore, cache line fills are significantly slower.

A further disadvantage of the 486DLC/SLC, namely the lack of inquiry cycles for the on-chip cache to establish cache consistency spanning several 486DLC/SLC CPUs, seems to be of a more theoretical nature. For such a multiprocessor system requiring considerable safeguards to be carried out by the operating system, an engineer would surely use the presently most advanced high-end processor, such as the Pentium or the PowerPC. All the overhead of distributing the tasks over several 486DLC/SLC CPUs can be saved when only one Pentium is installed (which runs two pipelines up to 99 MHz).

The properties listed above, which argue against the term 486, are compensated for by some pure 486 characteristics, and even some improvements compared to the original Intel 486. These are:

- All instructions are executed in a pipeline, as is the case for the «real» i486. That is an important characteristic for the partial application of RISC technologies in the i486, to which instruction pipelining also belongs.
- The 486DLC/SLC supports all i486 instructions, that is, the new i486 instructions for controlling the on-chip cache.
- The Cyrix CPUs have a fast hardware multiplier which executes integer multiplications even faster than the original i486.

Whether you agree with the above-mentioned arguments for or against calling it a 486 – and thus consider the denotion 486DLC/SLC, especially in the case of the 486DLC, to be justified or not – is up to you. In either case, the Cyrix CPUs are significantly more powerful than the Intel (or AMD) 386 chips, but cannot reach the real 486 CPUs in user-typical applications. A value-for-money PC based on the 486DLC is surely a good investment if you don't need high-end performance under all circumstances.

Be careful when buying a 486 Notebook. You can often determine only after a close look whether a real i486 or a 486DLC/SLC is installed. The 486DLC and i387 combination is nearly as powerful as an i486, however.

8.3.4 IBM – For Members Only

IBM did not want to get behind the times, so they launched an i386-compatible processor with the name 386SLC. The 386SLC has an internal 8 kbyte cache and is implemented in a power-saving static design. At present, the 386SLC is not freely available on the market, as IBM uses it exclusively for its own products.

9 Caching – Cooperation with High Speed Memories

Fast clocked processors naturally require fast memory with short access times. What is the use of a 40 Mhz CPU if it has to insert five or more wait states for every memory access? Today's DRAM chips have standard access times of 60–100 ns. This is even worse for the 40 MHz clock rate, especially when you look at the considerably longer cycle time of the DRAMs. Also the page and static column modes and memory organization are insufficient, although they can reduce the access time to 35 ns. SRAM components with a typical access time of 15–25 ns offer a way out. For supercomputers there are high-end SRAMs using bipolar or ECL technology with an access time of not more than 12 ns. For comparison: in 12 ns, a commercial aircraft flying at 850 km/h would only move 0.003 mm, or a tenth of the diameter of a hair. SRAM chips are unfortunately very expensive, and are larger than DRAMs.

9.1 Cache Principle and Cache Strategies

A cache attempts to combine the advantages of quick SRAMs with the cheapness of DRAMs, to achieve the most effective memory system. You can see the cache principle in Figure 9.1.

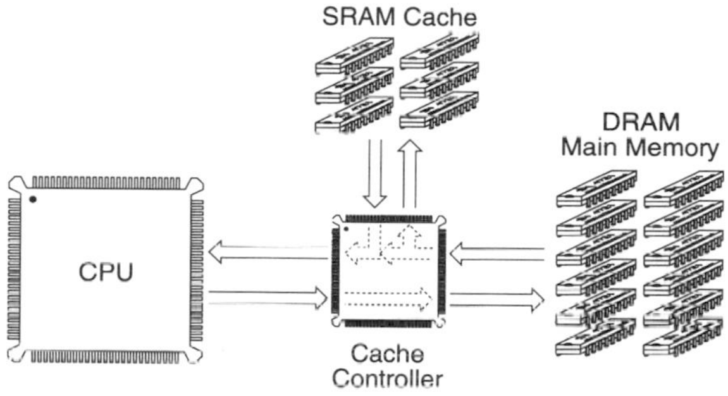

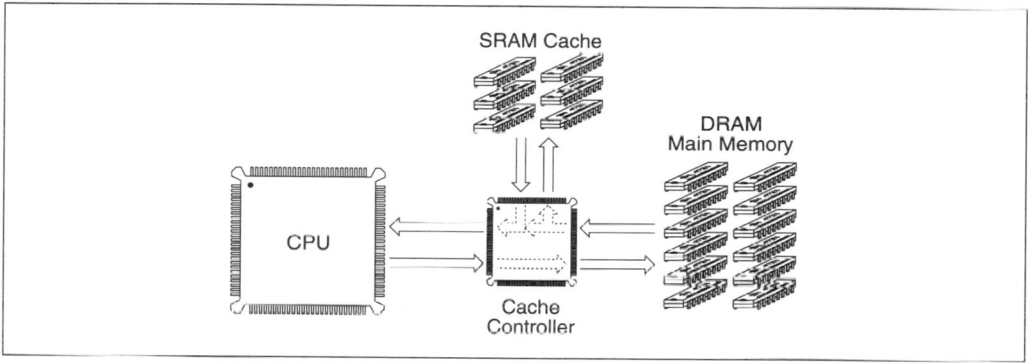

Figure 9.1: The cache principle. Between the CPU and the main memory DRAM a fast cache SRAM is provided. It holds the frequently accessed data and delivers it very quickly. The process is controlled by a cache controller which may implement various write strategies, such as write-through or write-back.

A cache unit is inserted between the CPU and main memory; it consists of a cache controller and a cache SRAM. They can be included on the same chip as the CPU (on-chip cache) or can exist as a separate component. There are also mixes (such as the 386SL), whereby the cache controller is included on the CPU chip and the actual cache memory is formed by external SRAM chips. The cache memory is, with its 128–512 kbytes, typically between ten and a thousand times smaller than the main memory.

As most successive memory accesses affect only a small address area, the most frequently addressed data is held in a small high-speed memory – the cache. The advantage with this is a very much reduced access time, which, added up over the many closely packed memory accesses, produces a considerable increase in speed. The data and code that is not currently required can be stored in the slower main memory without greatly slowing down program execution. The cache principle of using a small SRAM cache memory and a large but slower DRAM main memory combines the speed advantages of SRAM chips with the lower cost of DRAMs.

When the CPU reads data, it sends out the corresponding memory address, as usual. However, here the cache controller is located between the processor and the main memory address. It determines whether the requested data is available in the SRAM cache. If this is the case, it is known as a *cache hit*. On the other hand, if the data is only available in the main memory, it is known as a *cache miss*. In the first case, the cache controller reads the data from the quicker cache memory and passes it on to the CPU. This usually takes place without wait states, that is, with the maximum bus speed. The read access is intercepted by the cache and the main memory knows nothing about it.

On the other hand, if a cache miss occurs, the cache controller must first read the data from the main memory, thus the read access is switched through to the main memory. As this usually takes longer, an appropriate number of wait states are required; the cache controller disables the ready (or an equivalent) signal so that the CPU inserts wait states. The cache controller addresses the main memory simultaneously. The internal organization of most caches means that when a cache miss occurs, not only the requested data bytes but also a complete *cache line* is read from the main memory into the SRAM cache. This operation is known as a *cache line fill*. For this, it is possible that changed data must first be stored in the main memory, before the new data in the cache line can be read into the SRAM cache. The cache controller is intelligent enough to independently perform bus cycles for writing and reading data to or from the main memory, respectively. The data bytes addressed by the CPU are immediately passed on by the cache controller, that is, before transfer of the whole cache line is completed.

Cache lines are typically 16 or 32 bytes in size, because the data and program codes, as already explained, are formed into blocks and, therefore, it is quite likely that the next access will require a value contained in the same cache line. This increases the hit rate. Additionally, most cache controllers implement a so-called *burst mode*, through which a complete data block is read that contains more bytes than the data bus is wide (whereby multiple bus cycles are required to read in the complete block). The burst mode almost doubles the bus transfer rate, so that a complete cache line can be read much quicker than a single value. Thus, the organization of caches into cache lines increases the system performance.

If, on the other hand, the CPU writes data, the cache controller determines whether the data is also located in the SRAM cache. If this is the case, the data from the CPU is written to the SRAM cache. There are three different strategies for the further operation of the cache controller: write-through, write-back (also known as copy-back) and write-allocate. The first two strategies affect a cache hit, the last a cache miss.

The simplest case is the *write-through strategy*, which is implemented in most caches. A write operation from the CPU always leads to the transfer of data to the main memory, even with a cache hit; all write operations are switched through to the main memory. Naturally, this also involves writing to and updating the applicable entry in the cache. Write-through has the disadvantage that all write operations must also be switched through to the much slower main memory. Without further measures this would, in principle, switch off the cache for write operations, and an unjustifiably long write access time would be the result. For this reason, write-through caches use fast write buffers, which buffer the write accesses. However, depending on its size, this is only possible until the buffer is full. Thus, multiple write accesses invariably lead to wait states. On the other hand, the write-through strategy in a multiprocessor system automatically ensures main memory consistency, because all updates are switched through to the main memory. The cache consistency, however, is not so safe in a multiprocessor system. It is possible that a different CPU has overwritten the main memory; the cache of a different CPU would know nothing of this. Only an inquiry cycle can re-establish the consistency.

A *write-back cache* collects all write operations and only updates the cache entry, and not the content of the main memory. Only after an explicit instruction is the changed cache line copied to the main memory, to update the information there. In the Pentium, this instruction can be initiated by software, for example through the WBINVD instruction (write-back and invalidate data cache), through a hardware signal such as $\overline{\text{FLUSH}}$, for example, implicitly as the result of a cache miss, where one cache line is exchanged with another (see below), or through an internal or external inquiry cycle. The disadvantage of the write-back cache is that the exchanging of cache lines takes longer, because the data must first be written to memory before the new data can be read into the cache. However, this disadvantage is usually more than made up for by the fact that the previous write accesses need not be switched through to the slower main memory.

The two cache strategies described do not, however, make clear the behaviour when a cache miss occurs during a write operation, that is, the required address is not located in the cache. If the cache implements a *write-allocate strategy*, then the cache controller fills the cache space for a cache line with the data for the address to be written. Usually, the data is first written through to the main memory; the cache controller then reads into the cache the applicable cache line with the entry to be updated. Because the data is initially written through, the CPU can immediately restart the program execution. The cache controller independently performs the write-allocate in parallel to the CPU operation. In the worst case, it must first write a changed cache line to the main memory before it can use the cache line for the new data. For this reason, and because of the complicated cache implementation, most caches do not use a write-allocate strategy. Write accesses that lead to a cache miss are simply switched through to the main memory and are ignored by the cache.

If other processors or system components have access to the main memory, as is the case, for example, with the DMA controller, and the main memory can be overwritten, the cache controller must inform the applicable SRAM that the data is invalid if the data in the main memory changes. Such an operation is known as a *cache invalidation*. If the cache controller implements a write-back strategy and, with a cache hit, only writes data from the CPU to its SRAM cache, the cache content must be transferred to the main memory under specific conditions. This applies, for example, when the DMA chip should transfer data from the main memory to a peripheral unit, but the current values are only stored in an SRAM cache. This type of operation is known as a *cache flush*.

Software caches implemented on your PC will have similar properties. DOS, for example, uses internal buffers for floppy and hard disk accesses. You may define the number of such internal buffers by means of the CONFIG.SYS command BUFFERS. These buffers serve as a cache between CPU, main memory and the floppy or hard disk controller. They don't use a write-through strategy, so that in a system crash some data which has not yet been written to disk may be present in the buffer. Only once the file concerned is closed, or the buffer is required for another file or record, does DOS actually write the buffer contents onto disk. With the functions 0dh, 5d01h and 68h of INT 21h you can force DOS to carry out a cache flush. Most software caches for hard disks (for example, former versions of SMARTDRV that emulate a cache for hard disk accesses) in main memory, on the other hand, use a write-through strategy. All write processes are thus handed over to disk, but a read only accesses the copy in main memory. Newer versions of SMARTDRV.SYS use the write-back strategy. In this case, write accesses to disk are carried out at a later time as soon as the write-back can be carried out without affecting other programs.

9.2 Cache Organization and Associative Memory (CAM)

In this section, I would like to explain the different types of cache organization, and also associated concepts such as direct-mapped, 4-way, tag and associative memory. The best way to describe such things is to use an example; for this purpose, in the following description I assume that the cache has been constructed for an i386. Its size should be 16 kbytes and a cache line should contain 16 bytes.

The cache controller internally splits the 32-bit address from the i386 into a 20-bit tag address A31–A12, an 8-bit set address A11–A4 and a 2-bit double word address A3–A2 (corresponding to a 4-bit byte address) (Figure 9.2). A cache entry consists of a cache directory entry and the corresponding cache memory entry. The cache directory contains information such as what data is stored in the cache; the actual data itself is stored in the cache memory entry. The cache directory can be stored internally in the cache controller, or in an external SRAM. For this reason, most cache systems require more SRAM chips than is actually necessary according to their memory capacity. This is because one or more SRAM chips must store the cache directory, while the others store the actual data. For a 4-way cache, the cache directory entry contains a 20-bit tag address for each way and also, typically, a write protection bit, a valid bit, and three LRU-bits (*L*ast *R*ecently *U*sed), which are used together for all ways. The cache memory entry, that is, the corresponding cache line, is 16 bytes long as per the above assumptions, and so contains four double words each of 32-bits (the width of the i386 data bus).

In the following section, I would briefly like to explain the important concepts that often occur in connection with caches.

Tag

The tag is an element of the cache directory entry. With its help, the cache controller determines whether a cache hit or a cache miss has occurred. The tag stores the tag address, namely the address bits A31–A12 of the corresponding cache line (cache memory entry). The tag address is only valid with a set valid bit, otherwise it or the cache line contains incorrect values. For example, after a cache flush the valid bits of all cache lines are reset, and in this way all entries are identified as invalid. If the write protection bit is set, then the corresponding cache line cannot be overwritten. This is necessary, for example, so that a cache line fill can be completed without interruption, and so that a cache line fill cycle does not overwrite data that has already been changed by the CPU before the cache line is contained completely within the SRAM cache.

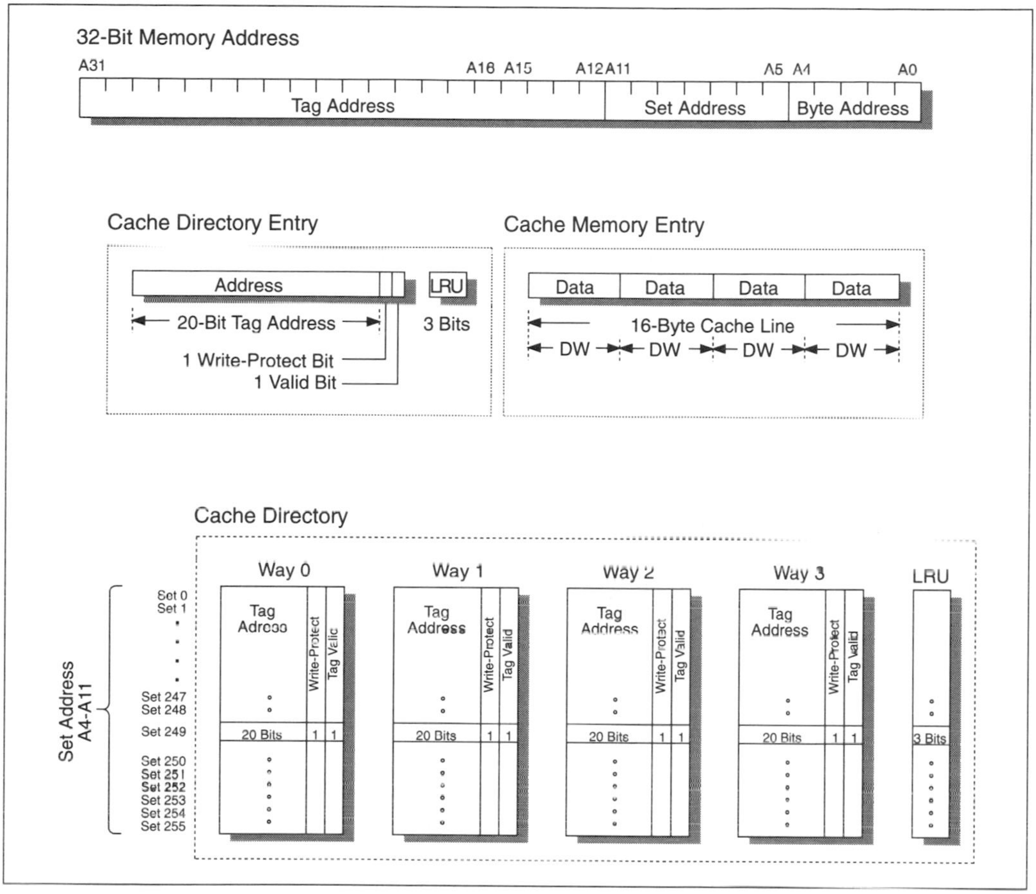

Figure 9.2: Memory address, cache entry and 2-way cache directory.

Set

Every tag and the corresponding cache line are elements of the set. The 8-bit set address A11–A4 defines the required set from 256 possibilities. Thus, in principle, a set is composed of a cache directory entry and the corresponding cache memory entry together, for each way.

Way

The way concept indicates the associativity of the cache system. For a given set address, the tag addresses of all ways are simultaneously compared with the tag part of the address given out by the CPU, in order to ascertain whether it is a cache hit or a cache miss. The example is of a 4-way set associative cache, that is, it has four ways. Thus, a data group that corresponds to a cache line can be stored in the cache at four different positions. Each way in the example cache contains 256 sets with a cache line size of 16 bytes each. This, according to the formula: capacity = ways x sets x cache line size, gives the stated 16 kbyte cache memory. A set entry for the four ways together is assigned a 3-bit LRU entry; the cache controller uses these bits to determine which of the four cache lines should be replaced after a cache miss. There are a number of different algorithms for this.

Note that in this context, the memory address at the top of Figure 9.2 contains no entry for the way. With the way, the associativity comes into play. A *direct-mapped cache* only has one way, thus, it is not associative; a data group can – if stored in the cache – only be stored at one position in the cache, subject to the 12 least significant bits. As an example, the data corresponding to the binary address xxxx xxxx xxxx xxxx xxxx ssss sssx xxxxb would always be stored in the set sssssss. The entry previously stored here must be replaced by the new one. In a 4-way set-associative cache, the data corresponding to the binary address xxxx xxxx xxxx xxxx xxxx ssss sssx xxxxb would also always be stored in the set sssssss. Here, however, four ways are available for every set, and so it is not absolutely necessary to overwrite the previous entry. If a cache line in another way is free, then the cache controller can store the data in the free way. This increases the hit rate of the cache, as here four entries are available for the same set address. 8-way set-associative caches have a correspondingly higher hit rate, but the technical complexity is also increased. The frequently implemented 2-way set-associative caches, on the contrary, have a significantly reduced hit rate, but the logic required for determining cache hits is considerably smaller. Thus, the operating speed increases. They are especially used for very fast caches (for example, the Pentium on-chip caches).

Cache Line

The cache line forms the complete data portion that is exchanged between the cache and the main memory. In a cache line, the double word for the 32-bit data bus is given by the address bits A3–A2. A cache line is either completely valid or completely invalid; it cannot be partially valid. Even when the CPU only wishes to read one byte, all 16 bytes of the applicable cache line must be stored in the SRAM cache, otherwise a cache miss will occur. The cache line forms the actual cache memory; the cache directory is used only for its management. Cache lines usually contain more data than it is possible to transfer in a single bus cycle. For this reason, most cache controllers implement a burst mode, in which pre-set address sequences enable data to be transferred more quickly through the bus. This is very simple for cache line fills or for writing back cache lines, because they always represent a continuous and aligned address area.

Content Addressable Memory

The associative memory concept often appears in connection with caches. It is also known as a *Content Addressable Memory* or *CAM*. This identifies its principle of operation. Usually, data in a memory is explicitly communicated with through its address. In an associative memory, however, this is achieved through a part of the data itself stored in memory – hence, the name CAM. To read information from the CAM, a section of the information in question is input into the CAM; this should agree with a section of information already stored. If this is the case, the CAM returns all the information associated with that section; in other words, it «completes» the section. As the section of information input to the CAM is only part of the information content, it is possible that sections of other information also match, and thus are also returned. The result can be ambiguous, but this should not be surprising with associations – you yourself may associate «Sea» with many things, such as holidays, beaches, swimming, sunburn, etc. If there is no agreement at all with the data stored, then the CAM will not return any data. This is as it is in real life: a sensible association with avfjnweflkad is, at least, difficult.

A cache performs associative addressing set by set, thus the association takes place in both ways. The addressing of the set, however, is explicitly given by the set address A5–A11. The information section for the associative addressing is given by the tag address in the set. This tag address is compared to the tag addresses A12–A31 from the CPU. If they agree, the cache controller associates the whole applicable cache entry, that is, the complete cache line that belongs to the corresponding way of the set with the correct tag address. More about that in the following.

9.3 Cache Hit Determination

In Figure 9.3 you can see the determination of a cache hit or cache miss schematically for the case of a 4-way set-associative cache with a 16 kbyte memory capacity.

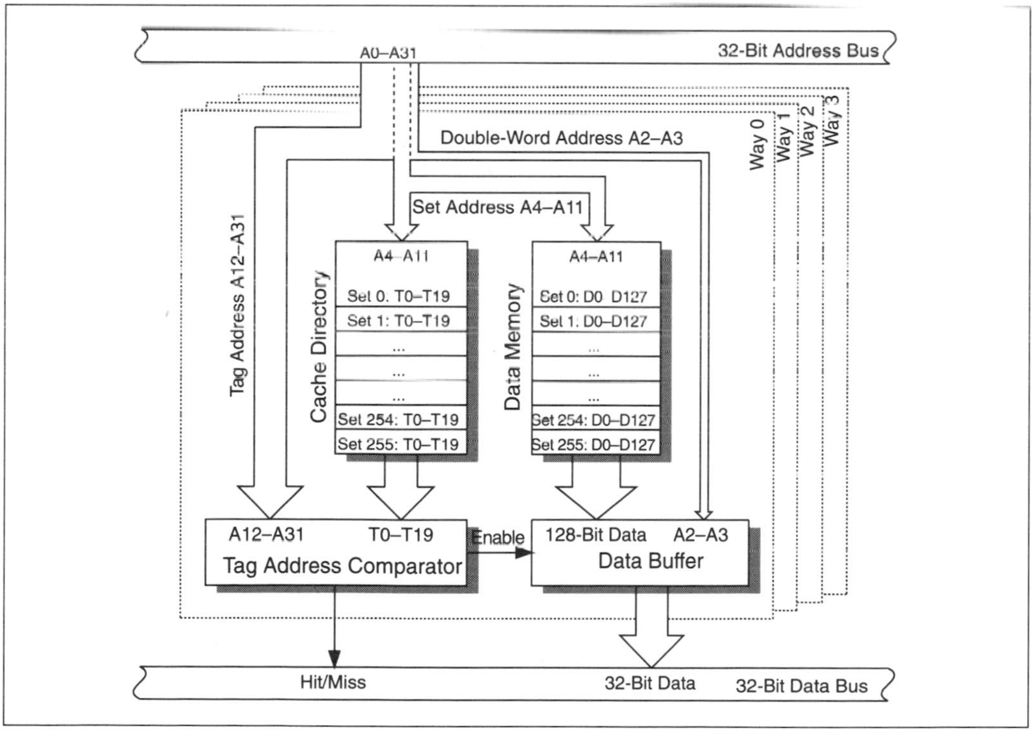

Figure 9.3: Determining cache hits.

The CPU puts the 32-bit address of the data to be read onto the address bus; this is taken by the cache controller and split, as shown in Figure 9.3, into the tag, set and byte addresses. The tag address is immediately passed on to the tag address comparator. The controller uses the set address A4–A11 to choose a set in the cache directory for every way 0 to 3, and to send out the tag address for the set to the tag address comparator. The cache controller transfers the cache line corresponding to the set given in the 128-bit data buffer from the SRAM data memory. The data buffer selects a double word from the cache line through the double word address A2–A3.

The tag address comparator compares the tag address from the CPU with the tag address from the cache directory. If the two agree, it activates the enable signal to the data buffer, and the data is then available. If the two tag addresses are different, the output is blocked and a cache miss is indicated by the hit/miss signal. The cache controller must then address the main memory to transfer the data to the CPU and to begin the cache line fill. The selection and comparison operations described are performed in the same way for all four ways. Thus, among other things, four comparators, four data buffers, etc. are required. The quantity increases as the associativity increases, that is, grows in line with the number of ways. Therefore, the direct-mapped caches are the simplest, the sometimes used 8-way set-associative caches are the most complicated. If the tag address from the CPU agrees with a tag address in any one of the different ways, a cache hit results, otherwise a cache miss.

The 20-bit tag address divides the 4 Gbyte address space of the i386 into 2^{20} cache pages, each of 4 kbytes. Through the 256 sets, a page is further divided into 16 byte cache lines. Each of the four ways uses 256 of these cache lines.

Naturally, there are types other than the 4-way set-associative cache described. In a 2-way set-associative cache, for example, there are only the ways 0 and 1. A direct-mapped cache, on the other hand, only contains a single way. Naturally, the number of sets need not be restricted to 256. For example, a typical L2-cache with a 512 kbyte memory capacity, organized as a 2-way set-associative cache with a cache line size of 64 bytes, will have a total of 8192 sets (which is typical for a 64-bit data bus between cache and main memory). With this structure, the address partitioning is different to that shown in Figure 9.2: the byte address A5–A0 is extended to six bits ($2^6=64$), the set address contains the 13 address bits A18–A6, and the tag address, the 13 most significant address bits A31–A19.

For the implementation of a large cache, external SRAMs are used both for the tag and the data memory. As is apparent from Figure 9.3, the tags must be available much earlier than the data because the tag data additionally needs to be compared in the comparator with the tag part of the CPU address. Therefore, you may frequently find one or two SRAM chips with a very short access time (about 15 ns) and many others with a longer access time (about 20 ns) in your motherboard. The SRAMs with the short access time hold the tag values, the SRAMs with the longer access time the cache data.

9.4 Replacement Strategies

The cache controller uses the LRU bits assigned to a set of cache lines (Figure 9.2) for marking the last addressed (most recently accessed) way of the set. A possible LRU strategy is the following: if the last access was to way 0 or way 1, the controller sets the LRU bit B0. For an access to way 0, bit B1 is set; for addressing way 1, B1 is cleared. If the last access was to way 2 or way 3, the controller clears bit B0. For an access to way 2 the LRU bit B2 is set; for addressing way 3, B2 is cleared. The LRU bits are updated upon every cache access and cleared upon each cache reset or cache flush.

If a cache miss now occurs during the course of a data read, the cache controller replaces a cache line by the cache line containing the data read. To find out which cache line should be replaced, the controller carries out the following pseudo-LRU strategy, which is shown in Figure 9.4.

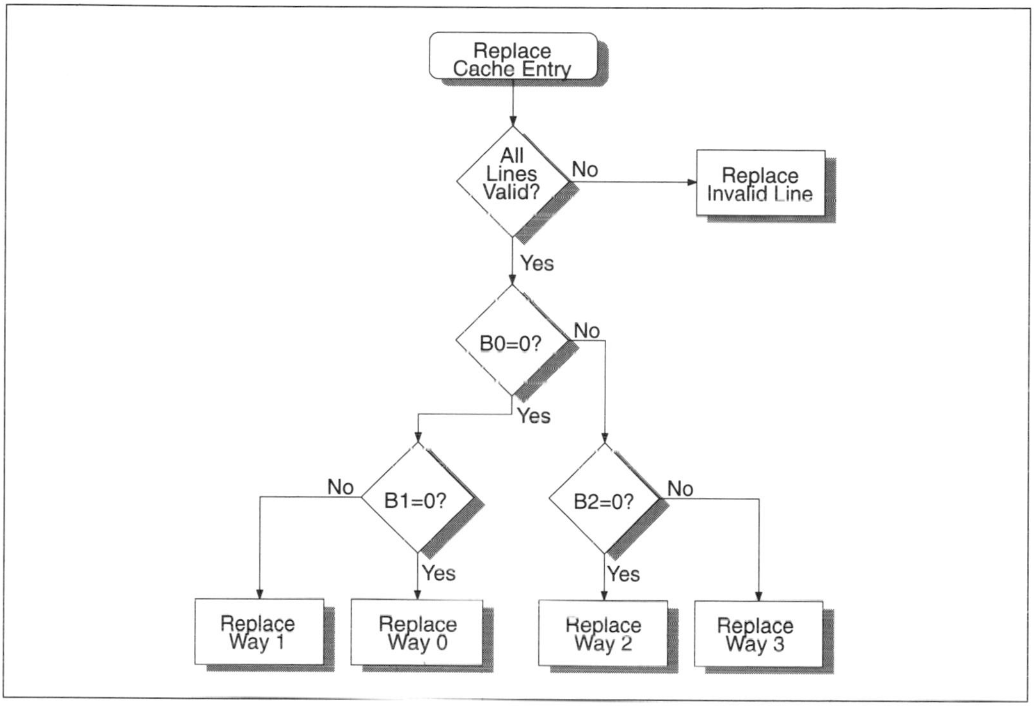

Figure 9.4: Pseudo LRU replacement strategy.

Using B0 the cache controller determines which pair of ways 0 and 1 or ways 2 and 3 have not been accessed for the longest time. Then, the controller (with the help of B1 or B2) determines which of the two assigned cache lines hasn't been accessed for the greatest time, and marks that line as replaceable. The cache controller now reads one cache line from main memory and writes it into the SRAM, overwriting the cache line that has been marked as replaceable by the pseudo LRU algorithm; it performs a cache line fill.

With the LRU strategy, the cache line of a set in the ways that is not the least recently accessed is overwritten by a new one. It is possible to use only one LRU bit whose value indicates which cache line has been used last. In a direct-mapped cache the LRU strategy does not apply as only one way exists and, thus, the cache controller does not need any assistance for determining the line to replace.

In addition to the LRU strategy, the cache controller can also exchange the cache lines randomly. This is known as *random replacement*. The frequency of accesses to the individual cache lines then has no influence on their «permanence» in the cache. Comprehensive statistical analyses have shown that there is very little difference between the efficiency of an LRU and a random replacement algorithm. Due to the fact that it is less complex, the random replacement algorithm is easier to implement and it also works quicker, because it does not require conditional operations.

The definition and implementation of the replacement strategy relies solely on the judgement of the cache system designer. Which cache construction and replacement strategy is chosen can depend on the application, the cache size and the materials (financially) available.

9.5 On-Chip and Second-Level Caches

As already mentioned in Section 8.3, C&T's 38605DX/SX and Cyrix' 486DLC/SLC have a cache which is integrated on the processor chip itself. The i486 also has an *on-chip cache*, or *L1-cache* for short, with a capacity of 8 kbytes. At first glance this seems to be too small; nevertheless, these small caches lead to quite a significant performance increase, especially for fetching CPU code. Besides the on-chip cache, an external cache can also be present. Common motherboards typically have a cache memory with 128–512 kbytes, called a *second-level cache*, or *L2-cache* for short. If the CPU is unable to locate the required data in its internal cache, it looks in the external cache memory as a second step, that is, the L2-cache controller first searches the L2-cache before the read request, in the case of a cache miss, is switched through to main memory. The external second-level cache may, in principle, be expanded to any size. The external cache controller must obviously be able to handle such a cache memory. The actual main memory is then located «behind» the second cache stage.

The i486 on-chip cache, for example, is organized as a 4-way set-associative cache. It has four ways with 128 sets (or cache lines), each holding 16 bytes, thus providing the 8 kbytes of memory mentioned above. One main difference between an on-chip and a second-level cache is that the CPU can read data from the on-chip cache usually in a single clock cycle. An access to the second-level cache, on the other hand, has to carry out a normal bus cycle, which lasts at least two clock cycles. Thus an access to the on-chip cache is significantly faster. For pure CPU and memory benchmarks such as the Landmark Test, the activation of the on-chip cache increases the displayed performance by a factor of four. In practice, the on-chip cache is effective to this extent only for sequential read accesses. For data spread over an area of more than the storage capacity of the L1-cache, the gain is not so high. Iterating mathematical calculations which are largely based on joined and frequently executed program loops are strongly accelerated by this; database accesses, on the other hand, are not.

One line of the on-chip cache is always filled by a burst cycle if the main memory can do this; external bus cycles are shortened by this (burst mode is discussed in Section 10.7.1). On the other hand, not every cache controller is designed for such a compressed bus cycle. The 485-TurboCache can execute such a cycle, others cannot. Stated briefly, the i486, the 38605DX/SX and the 486DLC/SLC operate much faster than the i386/i387 combination without a cache, if the current code and data are located within an area loaded into the on-chip cache. A significant performance deterioration occurs if code and data are spread to such an extent that they can no longer be held in the second-level cache. Then the CPU has to carry out a longer bus cycle. Finally, another significant jump to a longer execution time occurs if the second-level cache can no longer hold the data, and the CPU must carry out an ordinary main memory access. Even advanced concepts such as paging and interleaving are slow compared to the on-chip cache of a 50 MHz i486 (but they're real missiles compared to the 250 ns DRAMs from the PC's Stone Age!)

9.6 Cache Consistency and the MESI Protocol

A major problem occurs as soon as two caches are available in a system. They can be, for example, an on-chip cache and an external L2-cache, or two CPUs each with an on-chip cache. The basic difficulty lies in the fact that the consistency of the data in the two different caches must be assured. That means that every read access to a memory address always provides the most up-to-date data at that address. For example, the second CPU is not allowed to overwrite a common memory location without informing the other. The cache consistency problem thus particularly appears in multiprocessor systems. I want to discuss the MESI basics here because they are closely related to caches in general, and also several i386s with external caches can be connected to one single multiprocessor system. For supporting cache consistency on a hardware level the MESI protocol for cache lines has been defined. It was first implemented in the Pentium, so I will discuss the implementation of the protocol in that section.

9.6.1 The Four MESI States

The MESI protocol gives every cache line one of four states which are managed by the two MESI-bits. MESI is an abbreviation of Modified, Exclusive, Shared, Invalid. The four terms also identify the four possible states of a cache line. The state of a cache line can be changed by the processor itself (through read and write operations, and through internal snooping), and also by external logic units, such as other processors or an L2-cache controller (through external snooping). But first, the four MESI states; at any given time, a cache line will have any one of four states:

- **Modified M:** the data of a cache line that is marked as modified is only available in a single cache of the complete system. The line can be read and written to without the need for a write access through an external bus. Note that the actual value need not necessarily also be located in the main memory.
- **Exclusive E:** an exclusive cache line, like the M cache line, is stored in only one of the caches in a system; however, it is not changed by a write access, that is, modified. Thus, the values are identical to those in the main memory. As an exclusive cache line is only stored in a single cache, it can be read and overwritten without the need for an external bus cycle. After an overwrite, the cache line is identified as modified.
- **Shared S:** a shared cache line can also be stored in other caches in the system; it is – as the name suggests – shared with a number of other caches. A shared cache line always contains

the most up-to-date value; in this way, read accesses are always serviced by the cache. Write accesses to a shared cache line are always switched through to the external data bus independently of the cache strategy (write through, write back), so that the shared cache lines in the other caches are invalidated. The address given out during the bus cycle is used as an external inquiry cycle for invalidating the cache lines in the other caches. At the same time, the content of the main memory is also updated. The write operation in the local cache itself only updates the content of the cache; it is not invalidated.

- **Invalid I**: a cache line marked as invalid is logically not available in the cache. The cause could be that the cache line itself is empty or contains an invalid entry, that is, not updated. Invalid or empty tag entries also cause cache lines to be marked as invalid. Every access to an invalid cache line leads to a cache miss. In the case of a read access, the cache controller normally initiates a cache line fill (if the line can be cached and its transfer into the cache is not blocked). A write access, however, is switched through to the external bus as a write-through. The MESI protocol will not provide a write-allocate. Table 9.1 lists the MESI states and also their causes and effects.

MESI state	Cache line valid?	Values in memory are	Is there a copy in another cache?	Write access refers to[1)]
M	yes	invalid	no	cache
E	yes	valid	no	cache
S	yes	valid	possibly	cache/memory subsystem
I	no	unknown	possibly	memory subsystem

[1)] memory subsystem means main memory or L2-cache

Table 9.1: The four MESI states

The definitions of the four MESI states clearly show that the MESI protocol has been developed for a write-back cache without a write-allocate strategy for write misses. To be able to use the MESI protocol for a write-through cache, all valid cache lines must be held in the shared state; the modified and exclusive states cannot occur. In accordance with the MESI protocol, all write accesses must then be switched through to the external bus. Stated differently, the cache performs a write-through strategy. Note that the MESI protocol is only employed in memory cycles and not in I/O or special cycles. These cycles are directly switched through to the external bus, so that the cache is not affected. The write-through strategy is, above all, necessary for accesses to the video RAM of graphic adapters; after all, changes should also be immediately shown on the monitor and not just stored (invisibly) in the cache.

9.6.2 MESI State Transitions

The state of a cache line can change in a read access, a write access or an inquiry cycle (snooping). The following rules apply to the transition of the various states into another state. They are given separately for the three types of access; Figure 9.5 shows the corresponding transition diagram.

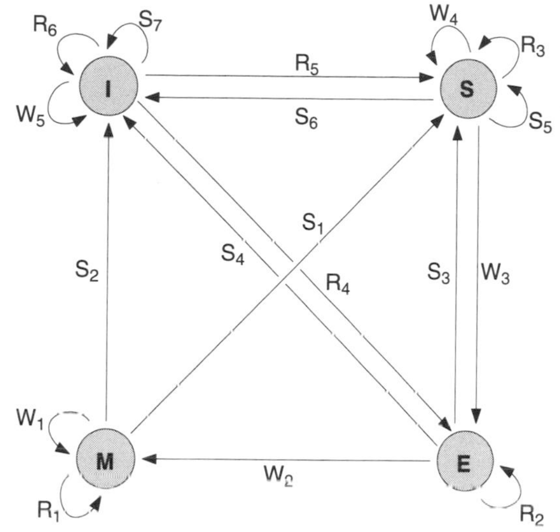

Figure 9.5: Transitions of the MESI states into another state.

Read Accesses

M to M (R_1): the read access has led to a hit, the data is available in the cache and is transferred to the CPU.

E to E (R_2): as above, the read access has led to a hit, the data is available in the cache and is transferred to the CPU.

S to S (R_3): the read access has led to a hit, the data is available in the cache and is transferred to the CPU. Summed up, it is clear that according to the cache principle, a cache hit has no influence on the state of the cache, or the stored data during a read access.

I to E (R_4): the read access has led to a miss, the data is not stored in the cache. The cache controller sends out an external read cycle in order to read the data. As the cache line is in the exclusive state at the end, the addressed data must be cachable, so that the cache controller can execute a line fill, and a write-back strategy must be implemented for it.

I to S (R_5): as above, the read access has led to a miss, the data is not stored in the cache. Here also, the cache controller sends out a cache line fill in order to read the data. As the cache line is in the shared state at the end, the addressed data must be cachable, so that the cache controller can execute a cache fill, and a write-through strategy must be implemented for it.

I to I (R_6): the read access has led to a miss, the data is not stored in the cache. However, the cache controller cannot execute a line fill in order to load the cache line. Thus, it remains invalid.

Write Accesses

M to M (W_1): the write access has led to a hit, the data is available in the cache and so is updated. According to the MESI protocol, this relates to a write-back cache, so that no write-back cycle is sent through the external bus.

E to M (W_2): as above, the write access has led to a hit, whereby the cache line was not previously overwritten. The cache controller then overwrites the cache line and annotates it as modified. According to the MESI protocol, this case also relates to a write-back cache, so that no write-back cycle is sent through the external bus.

S to E (W_3): the write access has produced a cache hit. As the original line is marked as shared, it could also be stored in other caches. According to the MESI protocol, this entry must be invalidated, and so the cache controller sends a write cycle through the external bus. Thus, the line is now only stored in the local cache; due to the write-through cycle, the entry in the main memory is also updated. The cache line can then be identified as exclusive.

S to S (W_4): here also, the write access has produced a cache hit. However, W4 relates to a write-through cache. For this reason, all subsequent write accesses are switched through to the bus, that is, the write-through strategy is also actually implemented, and the cache line remains identified as shared.

I to I (W_5): the write access has led to a miss, the data is not stored in memory. The MESI protocol does not include a write-allocate strategy. For this reason, the missing entry is not loaded into the cache from the main memory. The cache line remains invalid.

Snooping

M to S (S_1): the inquiry cycle has hit a modified cache line; it should not be invalidated. Despite this, the applicable cache line is written back to the main memory.

M to I (S_2): as above, the inquiry cycle has reached a modified cache line, which here should be invalidated. The applicable cache line is written back to the main memory.

E to S (S_3): the inquiry cycle has hit a cache line marked as exclusive. It has not been modified and so need not to be written back to the main memory. This transition serves to transfer a line previously located in only one cache, additionally into another cache. The cache line is then no longer exclusive; it must be marked as shared.

E to I (S_4): as in S3, the inquiry cycle has reached a cache line marked as exclusive. It also has not been modified and so need not be written back to the main memory. S4 also serves to transfer a line previously located in only one cache, additionally into another cache. Contrary to the previous transition, the cache line is invalidated, so that it is available in a different cache as an exclusive cache line.

S to S (S_5): the inquiry cycle has reached a cache line that is marked as shared. This interaction only informs the system that the applicable cache line is available in the cache. No bus activity results.

S to I (S_6): the inquiry cycle has reached a cache line marked as shared. It has not been modified and so need not be written back to the main memory during the subsequent invalidation. The external controller performing the inquiry then knows that its copy has been updated.

I to I (S_7): the inquiry cycle has found a cache line that is marked as invalid, that is, it does not contain valid data. No bus activity results; the controller performing the inquiry can ignore the content of the local cache for the applicable cache line.

9.6.3 L2-Cache Subsystems and MESI Cache Consistency Protocol

Usually, on-chip caches are rather small (between 512 bytes and 16 kbytes), so that for fast CPUs in many cases there is an external L2-cache. The size for typical L2-caches for Personal Computers is 128 kbytes to 512 kbytes, that is, ten to a hundred times more. We are confronted now with a multi-cache system and the MESI protocols can be applied. The system, consisting of the CPU and the L2-cache, delivers the cache consistency through so-called *inclusion*. What is meant by this is that all addresses in the CPU on-chip cache are also available in the L2-cache (of course this does not apply in reverse, as the L2-cache is larger than the L1-cache). Note that in a write-back cache this does not necessarily imply that the data at these addresses is the same, that is, the CPU caches can have more up-to-date values than the L2-cache. Figure 9.6 shows the inclusion schematic.

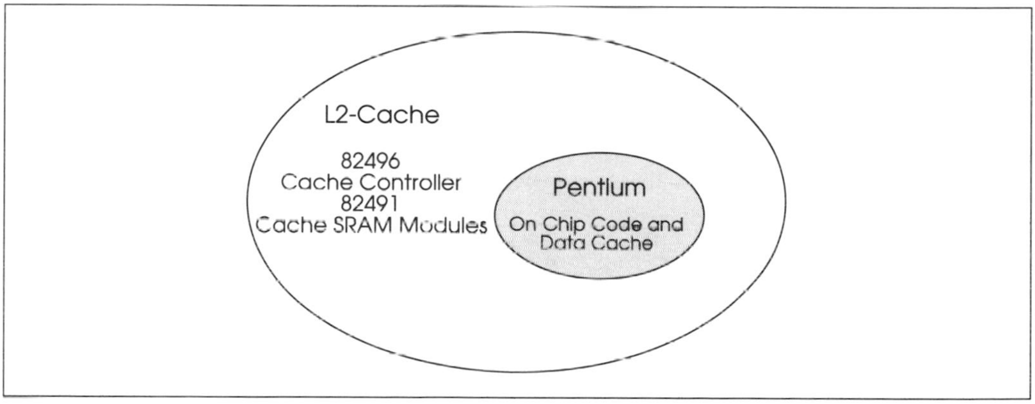

Figure 9.6: Cache consistency by inclusion. All addresses in the Pentium on-chip caches are also present in the L2-cache.

The transfer of data between the CPU cache and the main memory takes place over the L2-cache, so that the MESI protocol is also fully valid via the three stages L1-cache, L2-cache and the main memory. To this end, the MESI state of an L2-cache line always runs one step in front of the MESI state of the corresponding L1-cache line in the on-chip cache (in accordance with Table 9.1 and the MESI transition diagram in Figure 9.5).

The inclusion of the on-chip caches is realized by inquiry and back invalidation cycles as well as a *write once policy*. In the following I shall explain these terms.

The L2-cache controller establishes, during an inquiry cycle of the L2-cache on the L1-cache, whether a certain cache line in the on-chip cache is available, and whether the line is changed. That corresponds to a cache inquiry hit to a modified line. In the latter case, the CPU writes back the modified line into the L2-cache, and thus carries out a write-back cycle to the L2-cache. The line in the L2-cache is therefore updated. If the L2-cache controller which drives the inquiry cycle additionally requests a back invalidation cycle, then the snoop access leads to the invalidation of the hit line. Its state changes to invalid. Inquiry and back invalidation cycles by the L2-cache controller are driven to the CPU with on-chip cache in the following cases to ensure cache consistency:

- An external snoop, which is issued by the bus activity of another bus master (that is, another processor in a multiprocessor system), has hit an M-line in the L2-cache.
- A cache flush, from an external control signal (usually $\overline{\text{FLUSH}}$), refers to a modified line.
- A line should be replaced in the L2-cache, thus, a cache line fill is executed. If the same line is also available in the L1-cache, then it must be replaced, or at least invalidated.

Additionally, the write once policy has the task of ensuring that the L2-cache controller is always aware of the modified lines in the on-chip cache. The L2-cache controller can only allow the on-chip cache to change a cache line into the exclusive state if the same cache line is also available in the L2-cache subsystem in the modified state. Thus, the affected cache line must be changed in the L2-cache from the exclusive to the modified state, or it must already be in the modified state. As a result of the inclusions principle, each exclusive line in the L1-cache is available as a modified line in the L2-cache. This causes the L2-cache controller to execute an inquiry cycle to the L1-cache for each write-back cycle, irrespective of the cause of this cycle, in order to first write back the possibly modified line (if the L1-cache uses a write-back strategy) to the L2-cache and then to the main memory. Thus, the requirement for cache consistency is guaranteed, not only for an individual L1-cache/L2-cache/main memory configuration, but also for a multiprocessor system with several such units.

The Pentium, as a processor which is designed for multiprocessing right from the start, and which contains two independent on-chip caches for data and code (L1-caches) together with the 82496/82491 cache subsystem (L2-cache), supports such an inclusion, and therefore cache consistency is implemented at the hardware level. That is not the case for the i486 and the associated 485-TurboCache. Here a considerable amount of additional data or some software is necessary.

10 Performance Enhancement – The i486

A very powerful member of Intel's 80x86 series is the i486. On one chip, the i486 integrates an improved i386 CPU, an improved coprocessor compared to the i387, and a cache controller including 8 kbytes of cache memory. The i486 can be obtained with 25 to 50 MHz clock frequencies, or even 100 MHz in the i486DX4. Using the 32-bit data bus, it is possible to transfer data at a rate of up to 160 Mbyte/s in burst mode. Unlike the i386, the i486 executes frequently used instructions (such as MOV, for example) within a single clock cycle. The i486 is thus about three times as fast as an i386 clocked with the same frequency. The number of elements used in its construction, though, is enormous: the i486 integrates more than one million transistors on a finger-nail sized semiconductor chip, nearly 50 times more than its ancestor the 8086.

In some respects, the i486 represents a hybrid between CISC and RISC processors. The regularly used instructions (for example, MOV), are hardwired in RISC fashion and, therefore, executed extremely fast. In comparison, complex and less regularly used instructions are available in microencoded form. A sequence of simple instructions can, therefore, be quicker than a complex instruction with the same effect. The instructions are executed in a five-stage pipeline. The hardwiring of some instructions, and also the partial use of RISC technology, is not always visible.

Of course, the i486 is entirely downward compatible with the i386/i387 combination. It understands the same instructions and data types, runs in real, protected and virtual 8086 modes, and carries out memory segmentation and demand paging in the same way. Because the coprocessor is integrated on the same chip as the CPU, data exchange between them also runs more quickly. The i486 can therefore be seen as the ideal candidate for intensive mathematical applications such as CAD and computer graphics.

Yet a comment has to be made about the most powerful i386 successor being used in combination with the world's most widely used operating system: DOS running on the i486 is about the same as a supertanker with an outboard motor (presently, I am thinking about a comparison for the Pentium and DOS). Figure 10.1 shows a photo of the i486 die.

10.1 i486 Pins and Signals

The many different components of the i486 must be supplied with a stable operating current. This takes place through a total of 24 Vcc and 28 GND pins. Thus, together with the 116 signal pins, the i486 has 168 pins; it is concealed in a pin grid array housing containing the 168 pins. Figure 10.2 schematically shows the i486 pins.

In the following section, I would like to list the pins of the i486. Pins and signals already implemented in the i386/387 are only briefly detailed. Refer to the applicable chapter for more information.

Figure 10.1: The i486 die.

A31–A2 (O; A31–A4: I/O)
Pins P2–P3, Q1, Q3–Q14, R1–R2, R5, R7, R12–R13, R15, S1–S3, S5, S7, S13, S15–S16

These 30 pins constitute the 30 most significant bits of the 32-bit address bus. The two least significant address bits A1 and A0 can be determined from the signals at the pins $\overline{BE0}$–$\overline{BE3}$. The 28 most significant address bits A31–A4 can also be used as input terminals for the cache inquiry cycle.

$\overline{A20M}$ (I)
Pin D15

If this address 20 mask pin is at low level, the i486 internally masks the address bit A20 before every memory access. Thus, it emulates the address wrap-around of the 8086; for this reason, $\overline{A20M}$ must only be activated in real mode.

$\overline{ADS}$ (O)
Pin S17

The address status signal at this pin indicates that the i486 outputs valid bus control signals W/$\overline{R}$, D/$\overline{C}$, and M/$\overline{IO}$ and valid address signals that can be used and decoded by other devices.

AHOLD (I)
Pin A17

If an external device sends a high level signal to this address hold pin, a different bus controller can access the i486 through the address bus, to carry out a cache invalidation in the i486. This, for example, is necessary for cache consistency in conjunction with an L2-cache or a multiprocessor system. When AHOLD is active, the i486 does not use its address bus and waits for an external address; all other bus signals continue to be active.

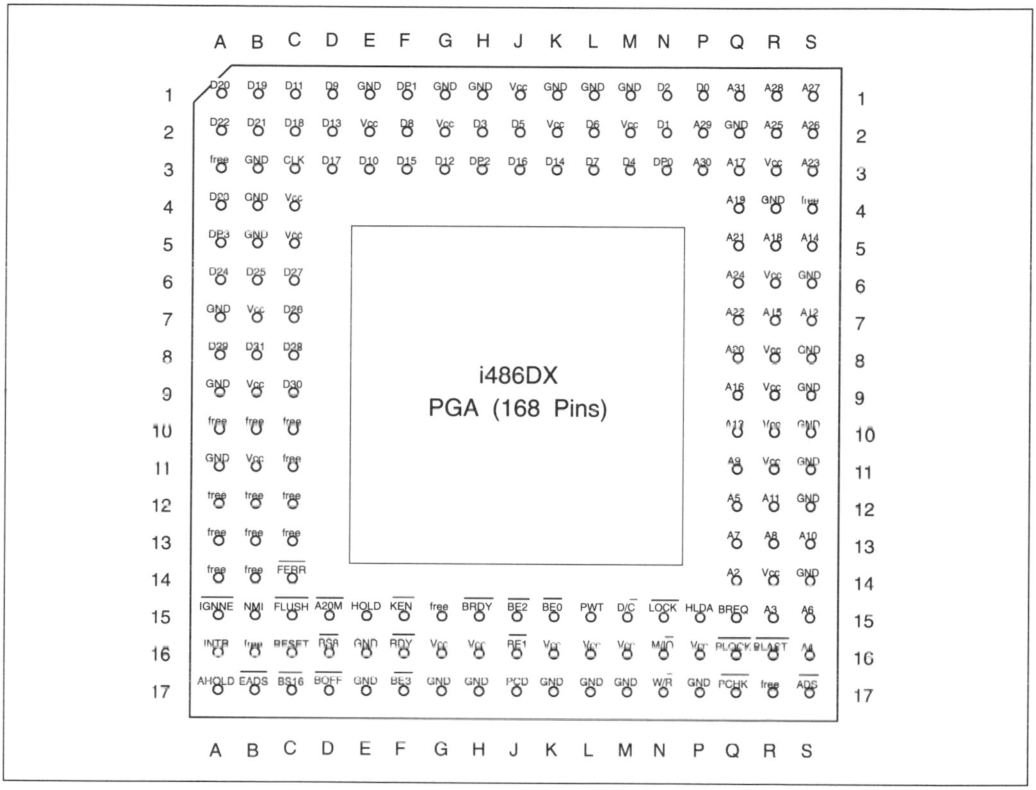

Figure 10.2: The i486 pinout.

$\overline{\text{BE0–BE3}}$ (O)
Pins F17, J15–J16, K15

As in the i386, these four byte enable signals indicate which bytes of the 32-bit data bus are active in the current bus cycle.

$\overline{\text{BLAST}}$ (O)
Pin R16

The burst last signal $\overline{\text{BLAST}}$ indicates that the current burst cycle will finish with the next $\overline{\text{BRDY}}$ signal.

$\overline{\text{BOFF}}$ (I)
Pin D17

If the backoff pin receives a low level signal, the i486 will deactivate its bus with the next clock cycle.

$\overline{\text{BRDY}}$ (I)
Pin H15

The burst ready signal $\overline{\text{BRDY}}$ has the same significance during the burst cycle as the $\overline{\text{RDY}}$ signal has during a normal bus cycle, that is, during a burst cycle, the addressed system has sent data across the data bus or has received data from it.

BREQ (O)
Pin Q15

This bus request signal indicates that the i486 has internally requested the bus.

$\overline{\text{BS16}}$, $\overline{\text{BS8}}$ (I, I)
Pins C17, D16

If one of these bus size pins receives a signal with a low level, the i486 operates its data bus with a width of 16 or 8-bits respectively, instead of the usual 32-bits. The bus interface then automatically carries out the corresponding number of bus cycles to transfer, for example, a double word with 32-bits. Thus, the i486 can be directly connected to a system that has only a 16- or 8-bit data bus. The bus width can be altered for each bus cycle. In this way, for example, it is possible to communicate with both the 32-bit main storage area and the 16-bit I/O address space without an external 32/16-bit converter.

CLK (I)
Pin C3

The external clock signal is received at this pin. Unlike the i386, the i486 does not divide the external processor clock cycle by two; instead, it uses the signal as an internal processor clock without changing it.

D31–D0 (I, O)
Pins A1–A2, A4, A6, A8, B1–B2, B6, B8, C1–C2, C6–C9, D1–D3, E3, F2–F3, G3, H2, J2–J3, K3, L2–L3, M3, N1–N2, P1

These 32 terminals form the bidirectional 32-bit data bus of the i486 for data input and output. The data bus can also be configured as a 16- or 8-bit data bus through the use of the $\overline{\text{BS16}}$ and $\overline{\text{BS8}}$ signals respectively. The signals at the pins $\overline{\text{BE0}}$–$\overline{\text{BE3}}$ indicate which bytes of the data bus are active for data transfer.

DP0–DP3 (I, O)
Pins A5, F1, H3, N3

The i486 supports the generation of parity for the data bus, that is, for every write cycle and for every byte of the data bus D31–D0, the processor sends out a parity bit DP3–DP0 so that even parity is achieved. With every reading of data, the system must send a signal to the data parity pin DP3–DP0 to ensure even parity. If the external device does not support this parity function, DP0–DP3 should be held at Vcc. Signals sent during the reading of data do not have an immediate effect on the execution of the program; if parity is lost, only the PCHK signal is activated, so that, for example, the program execution can be stopped by a hardware interrupt.

$\overline{\text{EADS}}$ (I)
Pin B17

If the external address pin receives an active signal, that is, a signal with a low level, the i486 knows that an external bus controller has sent a valid address to the address pins A31–A2. The i486 uses this address for an internal cache invalidation.

$\overline{\text{FERR}}$ (O)
Pins C14

When an error occurs in the internal floating-point unit of the i486, the processor activates this floating-point error signal. $\overline{\text{FERR}}$ is similar to the $\overline{\text{ERROR}}$ signal of the i387.

$\overline{\text{FLUSH}}$ (I)
Pin C15

If the external system activates the cache flush signal $\overline{\text{FLUSH}}$, the i486 writes the complete contents of the cache to memory, that is, it carries out a cache flush.

HOLD, HLDA (I, O)
Pins E15, P15

The bus hold request and bus hold acknowledge signals at these pins are generally used for bus arbitration, that is, they transfer the control of the local bus between the different bus controllers.

$\overline{\text{IGNNE}}$ (I)
Pin A15

If this ignore numeric error terminal receives a low level, that is, active signal, the i486 will ignore the numerical error and will execute all of the instructions that do not require the floating-point unit. $\overline{\text{FERR}}$ is simply activated. If the NE-bit is set in the control register CR0, $\overline{\text{IGNNE}}$ has no effect.

INTR (I)
Pin A16

The interrupt controller can issue a hardware interrupt request through the INTR pin. A reset interrupt flag IE will prevent (mask) the recognizing of INTR.

$\overline{\text{KEN}}$ (I)
Pin F15

Through the cache enable signal, the i486 determines whether the current cycle can be cached, thus, whether the addressed address area can be transferred to the cache. If this is the case, the processor extends the current read access to a cache line fill cycle, that is, the i486 automatically reads a complete cache line into its on-chip cache. Using $\overline{\text{KEN}}$, specific address areas with respect to hardware can be protected from caching.

$\overline{\text{LOCK}}$ (O)
Pin N15

If LOCK is active (low level), the i486 will not pass control of the local bus to a different bus controller if it receives a HOLD bus request signal. Additionally, it will not send out an HLDA acknowledge.

M/$\overline{\text{IO}}$, D/$\overline{\text{C}}$, W/$\overline{\text{R}}$ (O, O, O)
Pins N16, M15, N17

Memory/IO, data/control and write/read signals at these pins define the actual bus cycle. The following combinations are possible:

(000) Interrupt acknowledge sequence
(001) STOP/special bus cycle[1)]
(010) Reading from an I/O port
(011) Writing to an I/O port
(100) Reading an instruction from memory (prefetching)
(101) Reserved
(110) Reading data from memory
(111) Writing data to memory

1) $\overline{\text{BE3}}$=0, $\overline{\text{BE2}}$=$\overline{\text{BE1}}$=$\overline{\text{BE0}}$=1: write-back cycle
$\overline{\text{BE2}}$=0, $\overline{\text{BE3}}$=$\overline{\text{BE1}}$=$\overline{\text{BE0}}$=1: halt cycle
$\overline{\text{BE1}}$=0, $\overline{\text{BE3}}$=$\overline{\text{BE2}}$=$\overline{\text{BE0}}$=1: flush cycle
$\overline{\text{BE0}}$=0, $\overline{\text{BE3}}$=$\overline{\text{BE2}}$=$\overline{\text{BE1}}$=1: shutdown cycle

NMI (I)
Pin B15

The changing of the signal at this pin from a low level to a high level causes an interrupt 2, even with a reset IE flag. The i486 interrupts the execution of the program after the completion of the current instruction and calls the applicable handler.

$\overline{\text{PCHK}}$ (O)
Pin Q17

After data has been read, the i486 sends out a signal through this parity check pin to indicate whether the transferred data and the parity bit were at parity. If $\overline{\text{PCHK}}$ is at a low level, the i486 has identified a parity error.

$\overline{\text{PLOCK}}$ (O)
Pin Q16

With an active pseudo lock signal, the i486 indicates that the current data transfer requires more than one bus cycle. This is the case, for example, when reading segment descriptors with a length of more than 64-bits from a descriptor table or for a cache line fill of the on-chip cache.

PWT, PCD (O, O)
Pin L15, J17

These two signals, page write-through and page cache disable, indicate the condition of the page attribute bits PWT and PCD in the page table entry or the page directory entry. If paging is not active, or the current cycle requires no paging, PWT and PCD give the status of the PWT and PCD-bits respectively, in the control register CR3.

$\overline{\text{RDY}}$ (I)
Pin F16

If the non-burst ready signal is active, that is, at a low level, the addressed system (memory, I/O register) has already sent data through the bus or read data from the bus.

RESET (I)
Pin C16

If this input is at a high level for a minimum of 15 CLK cycles, the i486 immediately stops its current task and carries out a processor reset.

Vcc (I)
Pins B7, B9, B11, C4–C5, E2, E16, G2, G16, H16, J1, K2, K16, L16, M2, M16, P16, R3, R6, R8–R11, R14
These pins receive the supply voltage (usually +5 V).

GND
Pins A7, A9, A11, B3–B5, E1, E17, G1, G17, H1, H17, K1, K17, L1, L17, M1, M17, P17, Q2, R4, S6, S8–S12, S14.
These pins are connected to ground (usually 0 V).

Free
Pins A3, A10, A12–A14, B10, B12–B14, B16, C10–C13, G15, R17, S4
These pins are floating.

10.2 i486 Internal Structure

Because three processors were integrated onto a single chip (CPU, coprocessor and cache controller), the internal structure of the i486 became more complicated than the i386. Therefore, the i486 structure is briefly explained below (and shown in Figure 10.3).

Connection to the rest of the (computer) world is established by the bus unit: it accepts or supplies data via the D31–D0 data bus, addresses the two address spaces via the A31–A2, $\overline{\text{BE3}}$–$\overline{\text{BE0}}$ address bus, and supplies information concerning the i486's state, or accepts instructions from outside via the control bus. The bus unit is directly connected to the cache unit. The integrated 8 kbyte cache buffers data as well as instructions, and delivers them to the registers, ALU, floating-point unit or the prefetcher. Unlike the memory cycles for an external *second-level cache*, an access to the internal cache is carried out within a single bus cycle. For external cache memories, on the other hand, two bus cycles are required. Although the internal cache is rather small with its 8 kbyte capacity, this leads to a very significant increase in performance.

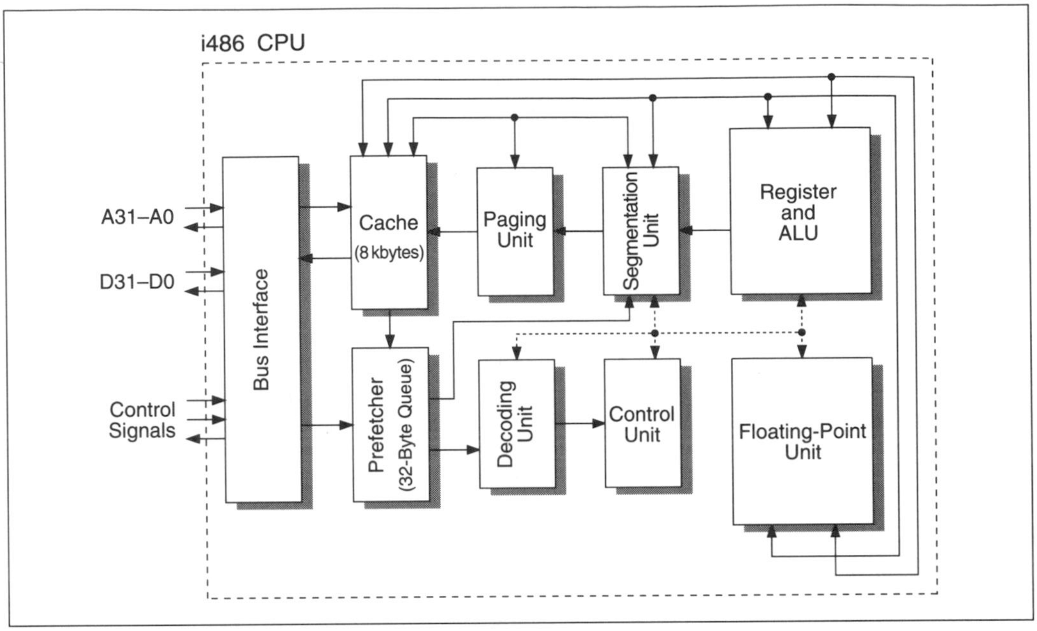

Figure 10.3: i486 internal structure. On a single chip, the i486 integrates not only an improved CPU, but also a more powerful version of the i387, a cache controller, and an 8 kbyte cache. The prefetch queue grew to 32 bytes.

If data or instructions not buffered in the cache have to be read from memory, the registers or the prefetcher directly access the bus unit. This may happen if very scattered data has to be processed, or if a jump instruction to an address far away is executed.

After the cache, the paths of the data and instruction codes separate. The data bytes are passed on to the registers or floating-point unit, while the instruction bytes are sent to the prefetch queue which, in the i486, consists of 32 bytes. The decoding unit decodes all instructions in the prefetch queue, then passes them on to the control unit which controls the registers, ALU, segmentation unit and the floating-point unit. The decoder and the execution unit are part of the five stage i486 pipeline, which I will explain later. Many instructions pass through the partially hardwired control unit of the i486 and are carried out immediately, that is, they are not processed by a microprogram. The prefetcher separates immediate operands or displacements in the instruction flow and passes them on to the ALU or addressing unit, which consists of the paging and the segmentation unit, as applicable.

The data bytes that have been read are transferred to the segmentation unit, the registers, the ALU or the floating-point unit and are processed. The two 32-bit data buses together form the internal 64-bit data bus for the transfer of data between the CPU core, corresponding to the i386, and the floating-point unit, corresponding to the i387. Unlike the i386/i387 combination, no I/O bus cycles are necessary for the transfer of opcodes and data between the CPU and the coprocessor; in addition, the data transfer occurs internally with a width of 64-bits compared to the 32-bit data bus of the i386/i387. This, of course, makes a noticeable difference to the execution speed of floating-point instructions, and enables the i486 to process ESC instructions considerably quicker than the i386/i387 combination.

For address evaluation the i486, like all other members of the 80x86 family, uses a segment and an offset register. In the segmentation unit the contents of the two registers are combined into a linear address. In protected mode the segmentation unit simultaneously carries out the relevant protection checks to ensure protection of the individual tasks and the system. If paging is active then the linear address evaluated in the segmentation unit is further translated into a physical address by the paging unit. Without paging, the linear address is identical to the physical address. The bus unit then supplies the physical address, and eventually the data to be written, or fetches the addressed data. The i486 also has four write buffers. If the i486 bus is currently not available – for example, because the i486 is currently carrying out a cache line fill – the processor writes the data into a write buffer first. The buffers may be filled at a rate of one write process per clock cycle. The data is put into the four buffers in the order in which it is output by the i486. If the bus becomes available later, the write buffers transfer the data to the bus on their own. If, on the other hand, the i486 bus is immediately available in a write process, the write buffers are bypassed and the write data is directly transferred to the bus. If the write process leads to a cache hit, the data is stored in the on-chip cache in both cases.

Additionally, the i486 may alter the order of bus unit read and write accesses to further increase performance. This is the case if all write accesses waiting in the write buffers for execution are cache hits and the read access is a cache miss. Then the i486 carries out the read access first, followed by the write accesses. This is possible because the read access does not reference a memory location that has to be updated by one of these write accesses first. Thus the write buffers enhance the performance of the i486 bus for several successive write accesses. If the bus is unavailable for a short time then the CPU need not wait, but simply writes the data into the buffers. The i386, on the other hand, implements no write buffers; the bus access may be delayed, and the i386 performance thus degraded.

Additionally, the i486 has a cache line fill buffer with a width of 128 bits or 16 bytes. If a cache line has to be reloaded after a cache miss, the bus interface does not write the 4-byte portions into the applicable cache line immediately. Instead they are written into the cache line fill buffer. Not until this buffer is filled, that is, the complete cache line has been read from the external memory, does the control logic transfer the content of the cache line fill buffer into the corresponding cache line in one step. It was mentioned above that the i486 has a five-stage instruction pipeline. It performs the instructions and is a characteristic element of RISC processors. In the following, I would like to describe this «magic» abbreviation.

10.3 A Star is Born – RISC Principles on a Hardware and Software Level

The abbreviations RISC and CISC stand for *reduced instruction set computer* and *complex instruction set computer*, respectively. The latter refers to microprocessors such as Intel's 80x86 family or Motorola's 68000 generation, which is used (besides others) in Apple Macintosh computers.

Characteristic of CISC processors is their extensive instruction set of more than 300 machine instructions, the complex addressing schemes, and the *microencoding* of the processor instructions. In contrast, RISC processors such as Intel's i860, the MIPS R2000, R3000 and R4000 and the SPARC processors have a significantly reduced instruction set.

10.3.1 Surprising Results – Less is More

From Section 6.4, we already know that in the i386 the instructions are read into the prefetch queue and are decoded by the decoding unit. Each instruction is not immediately executable but is available as a so-called *microprogram* in a ROM within the processor. This is a significant characteristic of CISCs. Without microprogramming, neither the extensive instruction set nor the complex addressing schemes were possible.

Another reason for the microprogramming concept was the significantly shorter access time of the processor ROM containing the microcodes compared with that of the very expensive core memory. The advances in memory technology, and especially the transition from core to today's semiconductor memories, has reversed this relationship. Due to the enormous integration of memory chips and the accompanying decline in prices, today processors are much more expensive than memory, and it is no longer important whether the instruction code is very or somewhat less compact. In the mid-1970s, IBM performed a detailed statistical investigation, whose unexpected but impressive results led to the development of RISCs:

- In a typical CISC processor program, approximately 20% of the instructions take up 80% of program time.
- In some cases, the execution of a sequence of simple instructions runs quicker than a single complex machine code instruction that has the same effect.

In the first instance, the result is due to the different, but in principle, simple tasks executed by the computer. The complex instructions are aimed mainly at a very small number of highly complex tasks that seldom occur. In addition, the programmer's familiarity with simple instructions must be considered. Furthermore, programs have an extensive number of branches (some statistics show figures of up to 30% of program code for jumps, calls etc.). Thus, the very simple MOV, TEST and branch instructions make up the majority of the machine code instructions that are used.

The decoding time is mainly responsible for the second result. The instruction execution time issued by processor manufacturers is only valid for instructions that have been decoded and are already available for execution; the decoding time is not taken into consideration. The decoding of very complex instructions can take a long time, whereas many simple instructions can be decoded much more quickly, and in many circumstances can be used to perform the same task.

When looking at the first result a little more closely, the most obvious solution is to reduce the quantity of instructions down to the necessary 20%, and to optimize them such that they can be executed in the shortest possible time. Considerations such as this led to the concept of RISC processors, which are no longer microencoded, but instead execute each instruction by hardwired logic without the need to access a microprogram. Therefore, most instructions can be completed within a single clock cycle. Using an i386, the instruction MOV reg, reg requires two clock cycles, whereas the i486 only requires one.

In some respects, the i486 represents a hybrid between CISC and RISC processors. The regularly used instructions (for example, MOV), are hardwired in RISC fashion and, therefore, executed extremely fast. In comparison, complex and less regularly used instructions are available in microencoded form. If you are programming specifically for the i486, you should consider whether a sequence of simple instructions might be quicker than a complex instruction with the same effect.

10.3.2 RISC Characteristics at a Hardware Level

The RISC concepts of the individual manufacturers are, naturally, slightly different. However, many of the essential points are similar, such as:

- reduction of the instruction set;
- instruction pipelining: the interleaved execution of many instructions;
- load/store architecture: only the load and store instructions have access to memory, all others work with the internal processor registers;
- unity of RISC processors and compilers: the compiler is no longer developed for a specific chip, but instead, at the outset, the compiler is developed in conjunction with the chip to produce one unit;
- a modified register concept; in some RISC processors, for a fast subroutine call, the registers are no longer managed as ax, bx, etc. but exist in the form of a variable window which allows a «look» at certain register files.

Reduced Instruction Set and Hardwired Instructions

Closely related to the abbreviation RISC is the reduction of the almost unlimited instruction set of highly complex CISCs. One of the first prototypes that implemented the RISC concept, the *RISC-I*, had 31 instructions, whereas its successor, the *RISC-II*, had 39. The simplicity of the processor structure is shown by the reduced number of integrated transistors: in the RISC-II there are only 41 000 (in comparison to more than one million in the i486 and three million in the Pentium). What is also interesting is that the RISC prototypes already had an additional on-chip cache, which was larger than the actual processor. In the i486 the supporting units for the processor take up more space on the processor chip than the highly efficient CPU itself.

One additional very important characteristic is that the instructions (or put somewhat better: the hardwired Control Unit CU) are hardwired. This means that in a RISC processor, the Execution Unit EU is no longer controlled by the CU with the assistance of extensive microcodes. Instead, the whole operation is achieved in the form of hardwired logic. This greatly accelerates the execution of an instruction.

For example, in a CISC the complexity of a multiplication instruction is located in a very extensive microcode which controls the ALU. For a RISC CPU the chip designers put the complexity in a complicated hardware multiplier. Typically, in a CISC CPU multiplications are carried out by many additions and shifts, whereas a RISC multiplier performs that operation in one or two (dependent on the precision) passes. Due to the reduced number of machine instructions, there is now enough space on the chip for implementing such highly complex circuitries.

Instruction Pipelining

The execution structure of an instruction is, as a result of the basic microprocessor working principles, the same for the majority of machine code instructions. The following steps must be carried out:

- read the instruction from memory (instruction fetching);
- decode the instruction (decoding phase);
- where necessary, fetch operand(s) (operand fetching phase);
- execute the instruction (execution phase);
- write back the result (write-back phase).

The instruction is decoded during the decoding phase and, in most cases, the operand addresses are determined. In a CISC processor this instruction step is performed by the bus interface and the prefetcher as soon as there is enough space in the prefetch queue. Even the second step, the decoding of the instruction, is executed in the decoding unit prior to the instruction execution itself, thus the decoded microcode is available in the microcode queue. The remaining three steps are executed by microcode in the Execution Unit (EU) under the control of the CU. In normal circumstances, a single clock cycle is not sufficient, or the clock cycle must be very long, that is, the clock frequency is very low.

Machine instructions are very well suited for pipelined execution. For comparison, let us look at address pipelining, which we have already met. In one complete bus cycle there are at least two very independent sequential processes: memory addressing and data transfer. Pipelined addressing now means that the addressing phase of the following bus cycle overlaps with the data transfer phase of the current bus cycle. Application of this principle to instruction pipelining means that the above-mentioned five basic phases for successive instructions are each shifted by one stage relative to one another.

Decisive for the result of instruction pipelining is not that an instruction is *executed* within a cycle, but instead, that an instruction is *completed* for every cycle. What at first appears as linguistically subtle, has enormous consequences. Here, each executable instruction is divided into a set number of sub-steps, such that the processor executes every sub-step in a single stage of a pipeline in one single clock cycle. Thus, the intended aim is achieved: single cycle machine instructions. This means that ideally, each machine code instruction is executed within one processor clock cycle, or, put another way: only one clock cycle per instruction is necessary, thus Clocks Per Instruction (CPI) = 1. This is shown graphically in Figure 10.4.

As you can clearly see from the figure, the processor commences with the execution of the nth instruction, as soon as the $(n-1)^{th}$ instruction has left the first pipeline stage. In other words, the controller unit starts the instruction fetching phase for the nth instruction as soon as the $(n-1)^{th}$ instruction enters the decoding phase. In the given example of a five-stage pipeline, under ideal circumstances, five instructions can be found in different execution phases. It can be optimistically assumed that a processor clock cycle (PCLK) is necessary per instruction phase and, therefore, an instruction is always executed within five clock cycles. As there are five instructions simultaneously in the pipeline, which are each displaced by one clock cycle (PCLK), an instruction result is available from the pipeline for each clock cycle (that is, each step contains an instruction in differing stages). Normally, a register is situated between the individual pipeline steps; it serves as the output register for the preceding pipeline step and, at the same time, as the input register for the following pipeline step.

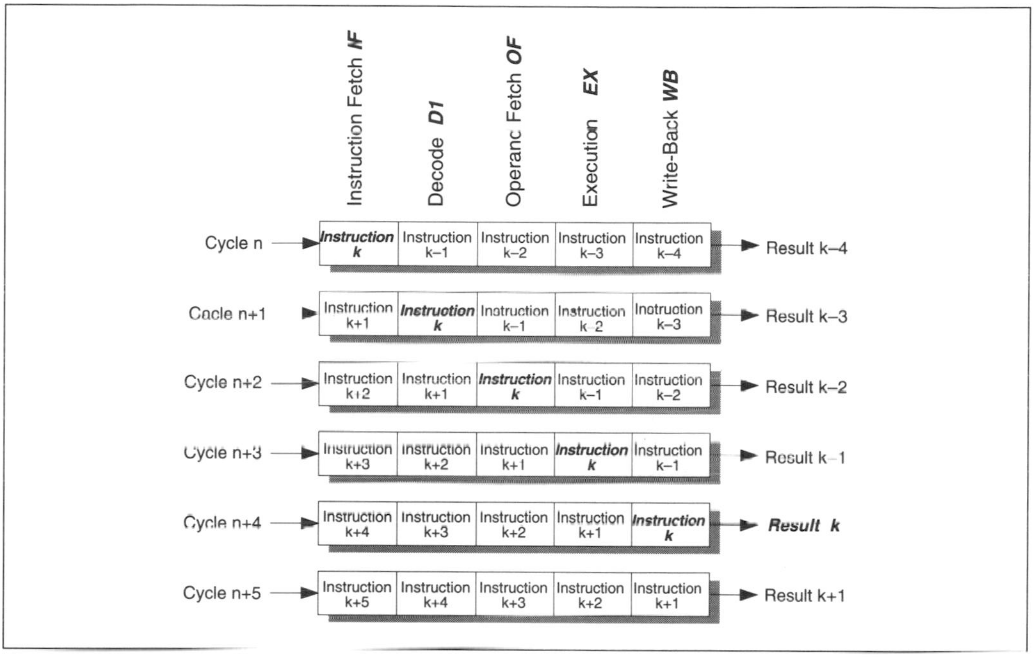

Figure 10.4: Instruction pipelining. Every instruction is broken down into partial steps for execution in the five-stage pipeline. The partial steps are executed within one single clock cycle. Thus, for example, the instruction k needs five cycles to complete. But at the pipeline output an instruction result is available with each clock cycle.

In comparison, without pipelining (as is normally the case with CISC processors), only the nth instruction is started, thus the instruction fetching phase of the nth instruction only starts after the (n–1)th instruction is completed, thus after five clock cycles. Ideally, the overlapping of the instructions alone leads to increase in speed by a factor of five (!) without the need of increasing the clock frequency.

The five-stage pipeline represented in Figure 10.4 is just an example. With some processors, the phases are combined into one single phase; for example, the decoding phase and the operand fetching phase (which is closely linked to the decoding phase) may be executed in a single pipeline stage. The result would be a four-stage pipeline. On the other hand, the individual instruction phases can be sub-divided even further, until each element has its own subphase, thus, through simplicity, very quick pipeline stages can be implemented. Such a strategy leads to a *superpipelined architecture* with many pipeline stages (ten or more). The Alpha can achieve its 150 MHz speed only with the use of such superpipelined architecture.

Another possibility for increasing the performance of a RISC microprocessor is the integration of many pipelines operating in parallel. With this method, the result is a *superscalar*. One example is the Pentium with two parallel operating integer pipelines. I am sure you can imagine that, with this, the complexity of coordinating the components with one another is increased still further. Here, not only the individual pipeline stages have to co-operate, but also the different pipelines themselves.

Pipeline Interlocks

You can recognize one serious problem for the implementation of instruction pipelining, for example, with the two following instructions

```
ADD eax, [ebx+ecx]
MOV edx, [eax+ecx]
```

The value of the eax register for the address calculation of the second operand in the MOV instruction is only known after the execution phase of the ADD instruction. On the other hand, the MOV instruction can already be found in the decoding phase, where the operand addresses [eax + ecx] are generated, while the ADD instruction is still in the execution phase. At this time, the decoding phase cannot determine the operand address. The RISC CPU control unit must recognize such *pipeline interlocks*, and react accordingly. The problem always appears when a following instruction n+1 (or n+2) in an earlier pipeline stage needs the result of the instruction n from a later stage.

The simplest solution is to delay the operand calculation in the decoding phase by one clock cycle. The Berkeley concept uses *scoreboarding* to deal with this pipeline obstruction. For this, a bit is attached to each processor register. For machine instructions that refer to a processor register, the bit is initially set by the control unit to show that the register value is not yet defined. The bit is only removed, if the register is written to during the execution phase and its new content is valid. If a subsequent instruction wishes to use the register as an operand source, it checks whether the scoreboarding bit is set, that is, the content is undefined. If this is the case, then the control unit holds back the execution of the new instruction until the storage stage writes to the register and resets the associated scoreboarding bit.

Another possibility is offered by optimized compilers. They can simply insert NOPs (No-Operation Opcodes) or restructure the program code so that obstacles never occur. In this example, it is apparent from the start that RISC hardware and software form a unit.

Register dependencies can be weakened by so-called *register bypassing*. This, for example, causes the ALU to supply the result of the ADD instruction at the same time as the last pipeline stage (write-back of the instruction result) and the input to the ALU. In this way, the ALU result is available to the following instruction earlier, and the operand fetching phase is no longer applicable. Such coordination of the pipeline stages is, of course, very complicated, and there is an additional increase in the hardware work load. The technology of bypassing and forwarding generally saves register read and write access, which do not contain logical operations.

There is a direct escalation of the problems with pipeline interlocks in superscalar processors: in this case, data dependencies do not just occur between individual stages of one pipeline, they also occur between the stages of different pipelines. On these grounds, the Pentium only uses its pipelines in parallel for so-called «simple» instructions, which reduce the probability of data dependencies right from the start.

If a memory operand occurs in the instruction, the CPU has to fetch the operand from the cache, or worse, from main memory. Even an access to the extremely fast on-chip cache requires a clock cycle. However, if the operand has to be fetched from the slower DRAM main memory, several additional clock cycles are necessary. The continued transfer of the instruction from the operand fetch stage to the execution stage then has to be delayed accordingly. Alternatively, the processor can execute NOPs. Program execution is slowed down by both processes.

Pure RISC implementation has a load/store architecture in which only the two Load and Store instructions have access to memory. In comparison, all other instructions (for example, ADD or MOV) refer to internal processor registers (instructions such as ADD reg, mem are, therefore, not possible). Even the load/store architecture leads to delayed loads, not just instructions with extensive addressing like the instruction ADD eax, [ebx + ecx] mentioned earlier.

The Horizontal Machine Code Format

Few and simple instructions and, in particular, the customary RISC load/store architecture enable a horizontal machine code format and a unified length of machine instruction. This means that the individual positions in the opcode (nearly) always have the same meaning. This greatly reduces the amount of decoding, therefore the decoding phase can be reduced and the pipeline decoding stages can be simplified. For example, the i860 normally uses a 32-bit instruction format with predetermined segregation in the individual fields.

In comparison, CISCs generally use a vertical machine code format, which distinguishes itself by its compactness and powerful coding. The result is that the opcodes have differing lengths (with an i386, between one byte for NOP and a maximum of 15 bytes). This is especially true of the x86 processors, with their prefixes and their various addressing formats. The decoding of such highly coded instruction formats can only be performed with the help of microcode, because the necessary decoding circuitry would be too complicated.

Register Files

I have already mentioned that fast processors are slowed down by memory accesses. In particular, the slow main memory should be accessed as little as possible. In other words, many operands must be stored in the processor itself. This requires a large number of processor registers. It is better to turn disadvantages into advantages and, thus, throw out the old concept of general-purpose registers used in CISCs (originally just a continuation of the limited integration possibilities from 20 years ago).

Modern RISC CPUs therefore have register files. Typically, they comprise between 32 and 2048 (or even more) registers with uniform qualities. There is no special register available (like, for example, ECX in the i386 for counting loops). A simple general-purpose register file is the simplest register structure for a RISC processor (Figure 10.5a). It consists of 32 registers in a stack, similar to the eight floating-point registers FP(0) to FP(7) that we learnt about previously in the i387. RISC processors using the Stanford concept (for example, R2000 to R6000) generally work with such a register file.

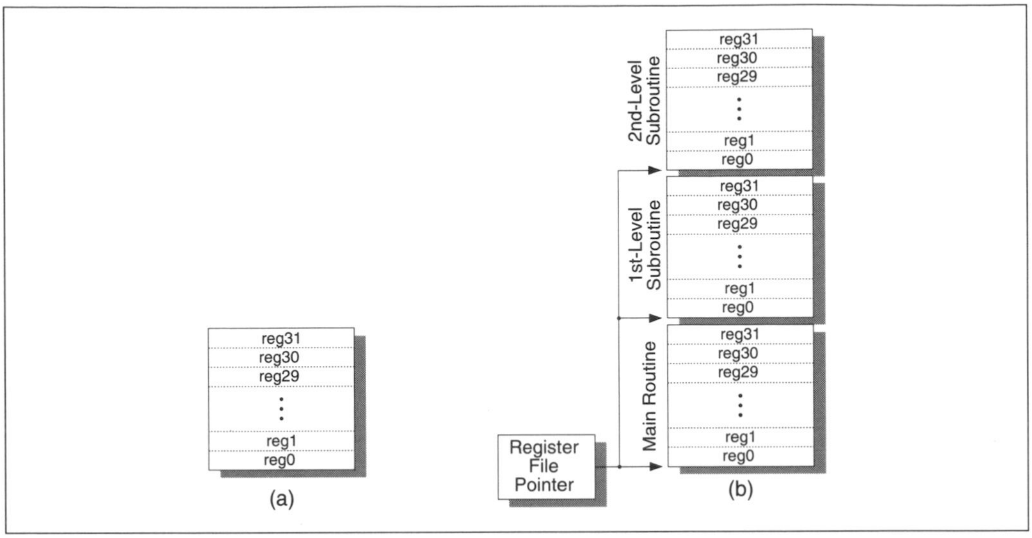

Figure 10.5: Various register file structures. (a) Simple register file (MIPS, R2000, R3000), (b) several logical register files for each nesting level; one physical register file.

To overcome the problem of saving complete register files when a subroutine is called, some RISC CPUs implement so-called *multiple register files*. Each sub-section of these multiple register files contains its own complete logical register file, managed by a *register file pointer* (Figure 10.5b). When a CALL occurs, the register file pointer is simply switched one file further (upwards) and then points to a register file that is currently not in use; this is then assigned to the called subroutine. In this way, the storing of register values in memory for a CALL becomes unnecessary. If a RETURN from the subroutine causes a return to the called program, then the CPU simply switches the register file pointer back by one, and the program can then, once again, «see» the old register values.

The register file concept can be expanded further. For example, there are partially overlapping register files within a multi-register file. Thus, the input parameters for a subroutine are stored in the physically identical registers of the calling routine as the output parameters. Moreover, in principle, there can be several multi-register files which are, for instance, attached to different tasks. With an increasing number of registers the diffentiation between register file and data cache vanishes more and more.

10.3.3 RISC Characteristics at a Software Level

RISC machines, for the implementation of high level language architecture, require the support of an optimized compiler in order to achieve a high efficiency of any sort. First, in this case, the assembler plays almost no part at all, because the code optimization for an instruction pipeline is very difficult and can hardly be achieved by an assembler programmer. Developing optimized code would require many test runs under various circumstances. Without high level languages, an application programmer has to concentrate on the technical details, such as the pipelines and their interlocks – a very extensive and, therefore, error-prone task.

RISC Processor and Compiler as an Undividable Unit

An important characteristic of the RISC concept is the unit of processor and compiler. Until recently, it was normal for one development team to develop the processor and for another to be responsible for the compiler and system software. The dialogue between processor and software took place via a defined interface, that of the processor instruction set. Today's RISC concepts create a single unit right from the start. The RISC chip only contains instructions that reduce the work of the compiler and accelerate program execution. The homogeneity of the compiler and processor enables considerably more effective program optimization using the compiler than is possible with commercial CISC processors and a thrown-in compiler.

The early synchronization of hardware development and the machine code instruction set is absolutely necessary because of the hardwiring of the control unit. A change to the instruction set, or even a single machine code instruction, requires a total redesign of the control unit – a rather extensive enterprise. In comparison, the microcode in the microencoded units of the CISC processor can, even after development of the hardware, be changed within certain limits so that the content of the microcode ROM is suitably matched. For example, a few new instructions can be inserted, or already implemented instructions can be modified, without the need to change the control unit of the CPU extensively.

Delayed Jump, Delayed Branch and Delay Slots

Jump and branch instructions constitute a large number of the machine code instructions (according to investigations, approximately 30%). They have an undesirable effect on instruction pipelining. The instruction fetching phase takes place in the first pipeline stage, and the current instruction pointer value determines the address of the instruction to be fetched. If a jump or branch occurs, that is, if a branch instruction leads to a new instruction address, then the new value for the instruction pointer is only known after the execution phase. This is identified as a *delayed jump* or *delayed branch,* because the jump or branch is executed with a delay. While the jump or branch instruction was passing through the pipeline, many more new instructions were being loaded into the pipeline. This does not cause a problem if the processor does not execute the jump, because the program execution is continued sequentially. This, of course, is not the case if the jump or branch is actually executed. Depending on the length of the pipeline, the processor has already partially executed a number of instructions which, due to the branch, should not actually have been executed. This can lead to further problems. For example, if the instruction that follows the jump instruction is already in the execution phase, possible changes could occur to processor flags or other things, because during the write-back phase of the jump instruction the value of the instruction pointer is changed. Therefore, the control unit must ensure that such effects do not occur, and that once the jump instruction is executed the pipeline is flushed. Alternatively, the compiler can insert one or more NOP instructions directly after the jump instruction; these have no effect. This process is schematically shown in Figure 10.6.

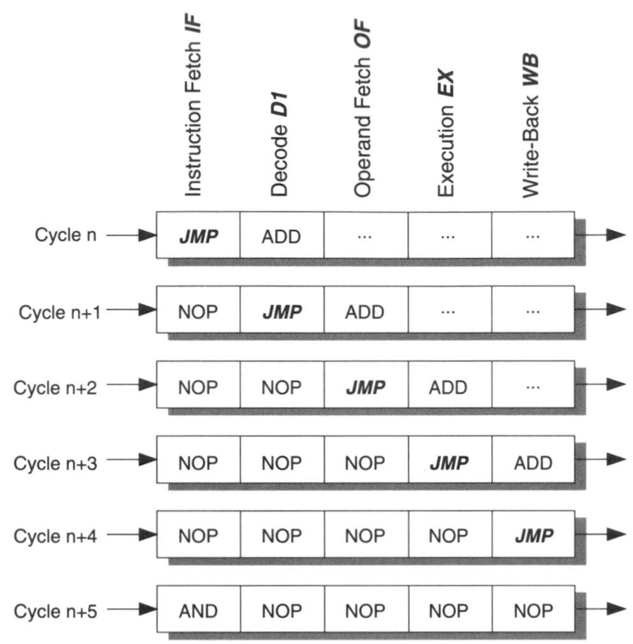

Figure 10.6: Delayed branch with inserted NOPs. Without pipelining and delayed branch the processor would continue execution with the first instruction at the jump target (here: AND) immediately after the branch instruction. Because of instruction pipelining, several NOPs have to be inserted after the JMP instruction (four NOPs with the five-stage pipeline) so that the processor does not provide any incorrect result. Not before cycle n+4 does the processor carry out the write-back of the operation result, that is, it writes the instruction pointer with the jump target address. Therefore, instruction AND at the target address cannot occur before cycle n+5.

Note that the NOPs are in the sequential control flow and not in the jump target. This means that the NOPs are almost always executed completely, independently of whether or not the jump is actually executed.

A better method is to rearrange the code generated, so that the processor can execute useful instructions instead of NOPs, without producing nonsense. The positions where previously the NOPs were located are identified as being *branch delay slots,* in which the compiler can insert other instructions. This again emphasizes that RISCs require a much more elaborate cooperation between hardware and software than was necessary when using CISC processors (although even there a more or less intelligent reordering of jump instructions may affect the performance significantly, due to the prefetch queue and instruction decoding). If compiler and CPU are not synchronized then a performance decrease of 50% or more can appear. For that reason, the Pentium implements many support functions so that software companies can design compilers and applications providing the best possible performance. Among these support functions, performance monitoring is the most important. This allows you to determine cache hit rates, the frequency of interlocks and many other things.

10.4 i486 Pipeline

The different CPU units of the i486 can, in a sense, operate in parallel, in that during the execution of an instruction the next instruction can be decoded and the instruction following that can be fetched. The i486 pipeline is, therefore, more of a relatively loose connection between the separate functional units than the closely coupled model shown in Figure 10.4. One cause of this is the very different complexity and execution time of the separate instructions (which is reflected in the large difference in workload required for decoding). Through the parallel operation of the prefetcher, decoder, and execution unit as well as a register write stage, instruction pipelining is performed. A «true» RISC pipeline, that is, a pipeline with closely joined stages, is first realized in the Pentium. In Figure 10.7 you can see the functional structure of the i486 pipeline.

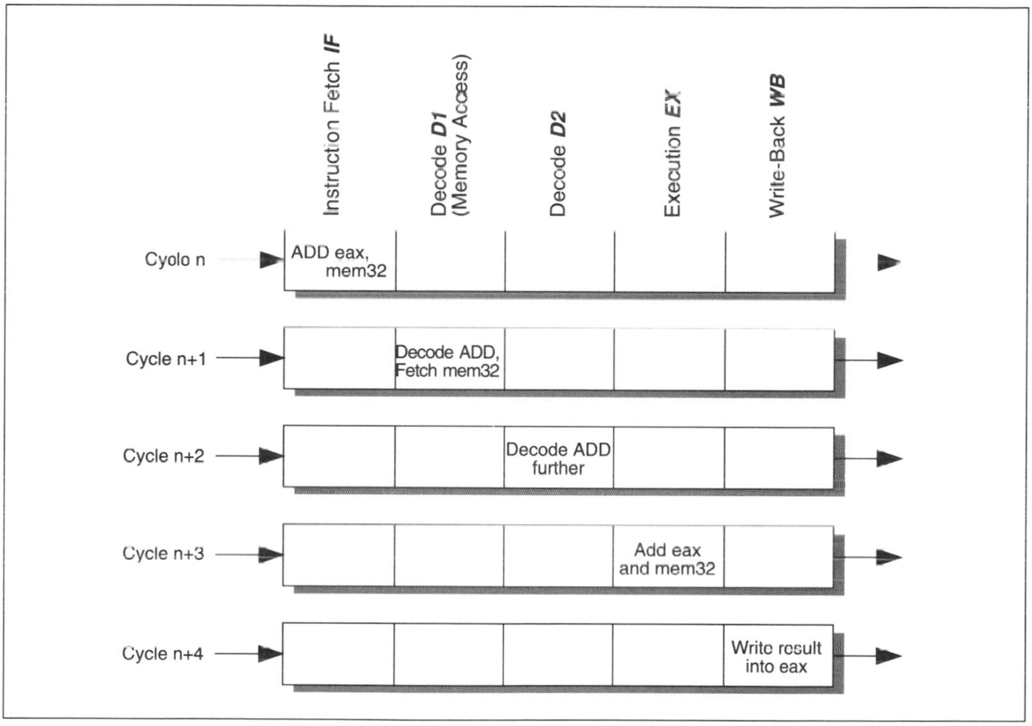

Figure 10.7: Structure of the i486 pipeline. The i486 pipeline comprises one prefetch, two decoding, one execution and one write-back stage. The figure shows, as an example, the execution of an ADD eax, mem32 instruction.

The first stage in the pipeline – the prefetch stage – reads 16-byte instruction blocks from memory into the prefetch queue and, simultaneously, into the on-chip cache. For this, the i486 can use the burst mode (see Section 10.6). In total, the prefetch queue has enough room for two such 16 byte units; it contains 32 bytes, and so is twice the size of that in the i386.

The decoding unit forms the second and third stages in the i486 pipeline. It converts simple machine instructions directly into control instructions for the control unit, and more complex machine instructions into microcode jump addresses. In the latter case, the microcode is transferred to the control unit where it controls the execution of the instruction. The fact that the first decoding stage can instigate a memory access has a considerable effect on the performance of the pipeline. The decoding stages one and two correspond to the decode and operand fetch stages in the true RISC pipeline model shown in Figure 10.4.

The two-stage decoding is necessary due to the complex CISC instructions of the i486; it does, however, also produce considerable increases in performance when memory operands must be loaded. In this case, the first decoding stage sends out a memory access. If the operand is located in the on-chip cache, it can be read from the on-chip cache in one clock cycle, during which the instruction is processed in the second decoding stage. The memory operand is, therefore, available during the execution phase of the instruction without hindering the pipeline. This is true for the combination of a load instruction (MOV eax, mem32) and a subsequent instruction that uses or affects the loaded operand (such as ADD eax, ebx). The ADD instruction is immediately available for the operand mem32 loaded into the accumulator EAX. This is also true if the ADD instruction contains a memory operand similar to the example shown in Figure 10.7. In this way, the i486 pipeline supports effective program code that already exists, but which is not optimized for the pipelining of instructions, for example, through the rearranging of code and delayed load. In addition to the register–register instruction MOV eax, ebx, the memory–register instruction MOV eax, mem32 is also executed in only one clock cycle.

During the execution step, the control unit interprets the control signals or the microcode jump addresses and controls the ALU, floating-point unit or other logic element of the i486 in order to carry out the instruction. This can take one or more clock cycles, depending on the instruction. The execution of the subsequent already decoded instruction is delayed until the current instruction has been fully executed.

The last pipeline stage writes the result of the instruction into the target register (if the instruction has specified a register as the target) or a temporary register for the output back to memory (if the instruction specified a memory operand as the target).

The i486 recognizes exceptions and software interrupts as soon as the corresponding instruction is executed in the execution stage of the pipeline. All instructions that are already in one of the following stages are completed; all instructions in the prefetch and decode stage, on the contrary, are invalidated. In the unpipelined i386 the processor doesn't need to invalidate any instruction.

On the other hand, external hardware interrupt requests are asynchronous and are triggered by a signal with the corresponding level at an interrupt input. For this, it is necessary for the i486 to continually check the actual interrupt input. This always occurs when a new instruction is loaded into the execution stage EX. As with a software interrupt or an exception, the i486 completes all instructions that are located in a subsequent pipeline stage, and the instructions in the prefetch and the decoding stage are invalidated. The interrupt is handled when the preceding instructions have been completed. Instructions that remain in the EX stage for more than one cycle, and also pipeline stalls, cause a delay in the recognition of the interrupt. This is similar to the i386 without instruction pipelining. The i386 checks the interrupt inputs when it has executed an instruction. Due to the large variation in execution times of the various micro-encoded instructions, the average interrupt delay time is clearly more than one processor clock cycle. In real mode, as previously in the i386, the first 1024 (1k) bytes are reserved for the interrupt vector table. The i486 manages these tables, also in real mode, through the Interrupt Descriptor Table Register (IDTR). It stores the base address and the limit of the real mode descriptor table. After a processor reset, the IDTR is loaded with the value 00000000h for the base and 03ffh for the limit. This corresponds exactly to a 1 kbyte table in segment 0000h at offset 0000h. With the help of the two LIDT (load IDTR) and SIDT (store IDTR) instructions you can change this value and store the table with a different size, at a different position in the real mode address space. Note that the table can also store all of the vectors for the interrupts that can possibly occur. Otherwise, an exception 8 (double fault) is the result.

10.5 i486 On-Chip Cache

As already mentioned, the i486 chip holds an 8 kbyte cache for code and data. It is 4-way set-associative, and comprises 128 sets at a cache line size of 16 bytes. In burst mode, one cache line can be read within four contiguous transfer cycles via the 32-bit data bus, or written back into memory.

Cache flushes can be issued by external hardware and software instructions. If a low-level signal is present at the FLUSH pin, a hardware initiated cache flush is performed. The i486 writes all modified lines back into memory and generates a flush acknowledge cycle. For a cache flush by software there are the two instructions, INVD (*Inv*alidate *D*ata Cache) and WBINVD (*W*rite *B*ack and *Inv*alidate *D*ata Cache). In both cases, the i486 generates a flush special cycle to indicate the invalidation.

The cache doesn't support the MESI protocol with its four states but invalidation cycles via the signals AHOLD and EADS (Section 10.6.3). For the i486 cache the hardware implements only a write-through strategy. Replacement of cache lines in the on-chip cache is carried out using a pseudo LRU algorithm which is shown in Figure 9.4. Figure 10.8 shows the structure of the tag and memory entries for the on-chip cache.

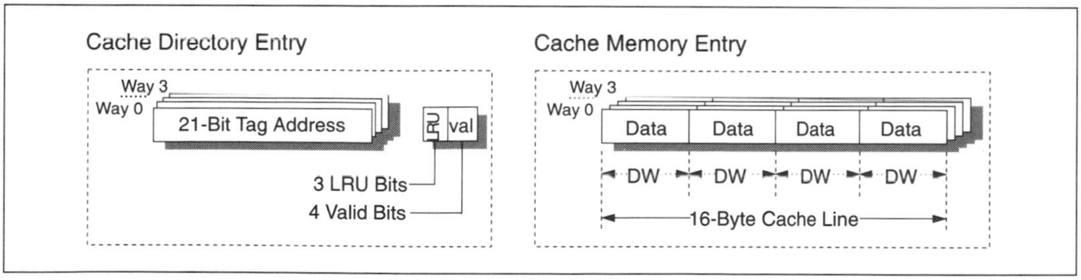

Figure 10.8: Tag and memory entries for the i486 cache.

The on-chip cache can be enabled or disabled by setting or clearing the CD bit in the CR0 control register. The structure of this control register CR0 is shown in Figure 10.9. Bits which are significant for the cache are shaded.

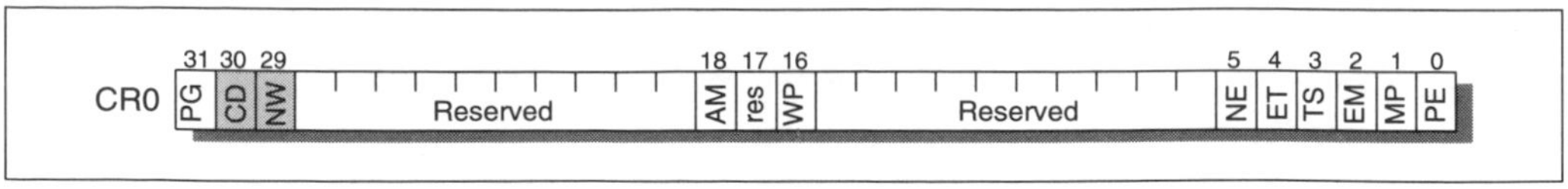

Figure 10.9: Control register CR0.

The effects of the four possible combinations of both control bits for the i486 on-chip cache are summarized in the following.

CD=0, NW=0

Read accesses are dealt with by the cache when a hit occurs. Misses initiate a cache line fill, if the values are cachable ($\overline{KEN}$ at a low level). Thus, the on-chip cache is fully enabled. Independent of a cache hit, for write accesses the i486 always generates an external write cycle. Thus, the cache operates using a write-through strategy.

CD=0, NW=1

This bit combination is invalid.

CD=1, NW=0

Read accesses are dealt with by the cache when a hit occurs. Misses do not initiate a cache line fill, because the cache is disabled by CD=1. Write data always appears on the external bus.

CD=1, NW=1

Read accesses are dealt with by the cache when a hit occurs. Misses do not initiate a cache line fill, because the cache, as above, is disabled by CD=1. Write accesses may update the cache and are switched through to the external bus.

You can see that the CD bit only disables cache line fills but not the cache function itself. If the on-chip cache should actually be disabled, you must additionally issue a cache flush. Then, all entries are invalidated and therefore no cache hits can occur. CD=1 blocks the otherwise generated line fills.

With the two new bits, PCD and PWT, in the page directory entry or page table entry you can define individual pages as cachable or non-cachable. For that the paging unit PU must be enabled. Also, in control register CR3 two such entries are available for the page directory. In Figure 10.10 you can see the structure of the entries – the bits which are important for the caching function are shaded.

If the *PCD*-bit is reset, the page data can be transferred to the on-chip cache, that is, a cache line fill is executed, if $\overline{KEN}$ is at a low level, too. If, on the other hand, the PCD-bit is set (equals 1), then no data of the written page can be loaded into the cache, even if there is nothing to stop it from the hardware side (low level $\overline{KEN}$ signal). If the PWT-bit equals 0, that is, reset, then the cache should use a write-back strategy for the data of the page. If *PWT* is set (equals 1), then the page requires a write-through strategy. Naturally, the value of PWT has no effect if no caching is necessary for the page, or the hardware (as in the i486) implements a write-through strategy. During a memory access, the effective values of PCD and PWT are given by the PCD and PWT pins, respectively. If an L2-cache is available, the signals can be used to individually match an applicable cache strategy to the current memory access.

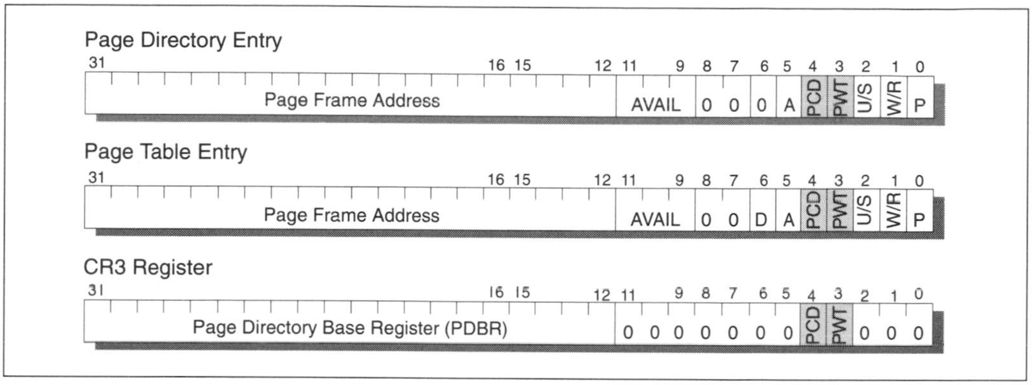

Figure 10.10: Page directory entry, page table entry and control register CR3.

10.6 i486 and i386/i387 – Differences and Similarities

As a member of the 80x86 family, the i486 is downward-compatible with the i386/i387 combination. In the following sections only the main differences between the two are compared, and new internals introduced.

10.6.1 Differences in Register Structures

The EFlag register of the i486 (Figure 10.11) has been expanded to include the *AC*, or *Alignment Check*, flag. The alignment check is implemented in the i486 so that misaligned accesses to memory can be identified.

```
AC: Alignment Check        O:  Overflow           S: Sign
V:  Virtual 8086 Mode      D:  Direction          Z: Zero
R:  Resume                 I:  Interrupt Enable   A: Auxiliary Carry
N:  Nested Task            TF: Trap               P: Parity
IOPL: I/O Privilege Level                         C: Carry
```

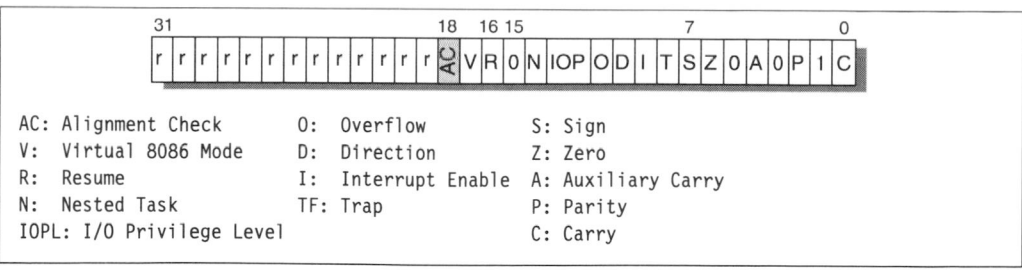

Figure 10.11: i486 eflag register.

If the AC flag is set, the i486 generates an exception and the corresponding interrupt 17 if an alignment error occurs. The alignment check only affects programs with a privilege level of 3; a misalignment in programs with privilege levels 0–2 is ignored. Alignment errors occur with word accesses to uneven addresses, double word accesses to addresses that are not a multiple of four, or 8 byte accesses to addresses that are not multiples of eight. All other flags are unchanged in comparison to the i386.

In addition to supporting caching, control register CR0 has other roles. Therefore, it has five new bits (including the caching control bits). Figure 10.12 shows the new structure of control register CR0. All new bits are shaded.

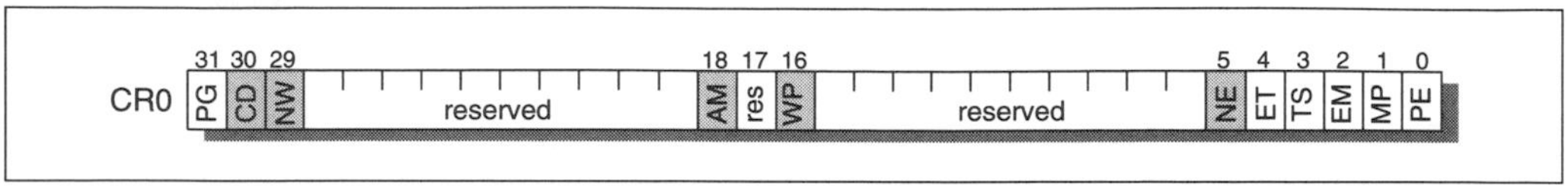

Figure 10.12: Control register CR0.

As already explained in Section 10.5, bits *CD* and *NW* control the operating mode of the i486 on-chip cache, therefore details are not repeated here.

With the *AM* bit it is possible to define whether the AC bit in the EFlag register can issue an alignment exception. A set AM bit allows exceptions, and a cleared one masks the AC flag, thus the AM bit has a higher priority than the AC flag.

With the *WP* bit it is possible to protect pages marked as read-only in the page table entry against overwriting by a supervisor, that is, a program with a privilege level of 0–2. With the i386, on the other hand, read-only pages can always be overwritten by a supervisor. The more restricted protection mechanism (by segmentation in the protected mode) is not affected by this. It still has a higher priority. With the WP bit, segment areas can be protected against overwriting. The protection mechanisms of the protected mode, however, protect complete segments and not just parts of them. This is very important for operating systems with «flat» memory models (for example, UNIX), because these systems use only a single segment. On an i386/i486, this segment can comprise 4 Gbytes of memory. With the WP bit it is possible to emulate the segment-by-segment protection of the segmented memory model.

The *NE* bit controls the behaviour of the i486 when a non-masked numerics exception occurs. If NE is set then the exception is handled by means of interrupt 10h and the i486 issues an interrupt 10h. With a cleared NE bit, the exception is serviced with an external hardware interrupt, ensuring compatibility with DOS systems. For this purpose, the i486 recognizes the $\overline{\text{IGNNE}}$ and $\overline{\text{FERR}}$ signals. If an inactive (high-level) signal is applied to the $\overline{\text{IGNNE}}$ input of the i486, then the processor activates the $\overline{\text{FERR}}$ signal if a numeric error occurs. An external interrupt controller may receive the signal and issue a hardware interrupt request to the i486. During the course of its acknowledgement, the controller supplies the i486 with the handler address. In PCs, $\overline{\text{FERR}}$ is identical to IRQ13 and an interrupt 75h is issued. The LMSW instruction, supported by the i486 for compatibility reasons, does not alter the NE bit.This doesn't apply to the i386 because the NE bit wasn't implemented until the i486. The *ET* bit (Extension Type) which could be altered in the i386 and which indicated the coprocessor (i387, ET=1; 80287, ET=0), is hardwired in the i486 to a value of 1. The i486 has an on-chip coprocessor which functionally corresponds to the i387.

10.6.2 Differences in Memory Management

In the i486, the structure of the page table entry also reflects the caching through the use of two new bits. In Figure 10.13 you can see the format of an i486 page table entry. The additional bits compared to the i486 are shaded.

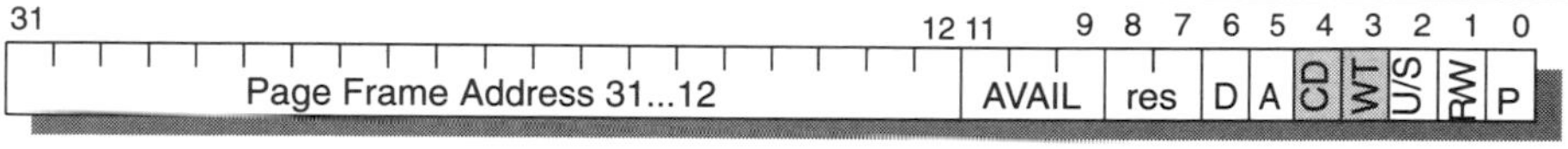

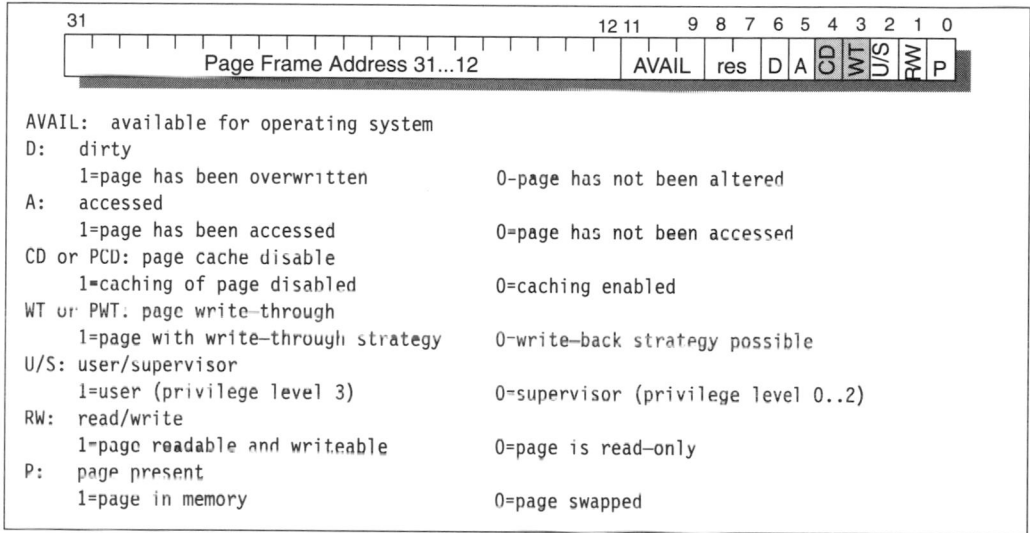

```
AVAIL:  available for operating system
D:      dirty
        1=page has been overwritten          0=page has not been altered
A:      accessed
        1=page has been accessed             0=page has not been accessed
CD or PCD: page cache disable
        1=caching of page disabled           0=caching enabled
WT or PWT: page write-through
        1=page with write-through strategy   0=write-back strategy possible
U/S: user/supervisor
        1=user (privilege level 3)           0=supervisor (privilege level 0..2)
RW:     read/write
        1=page readable and writeable        0=page is read-only
P:      page present
        1=page in memory                     0=page swapped
```

Figure 10.13: i486 page table entry.

The two new PCD and PWT-bits define the cache strategy individually for each page. A set *PCD* bit prevents data in a page from being transferred to the on-chip cache. A reset PCD bit, on the other hand, permits the caching of data located in the applicable page. If *PWT* is set, the i486 uses a write-through strategy for the applicable page. If PWT equals 0, then if a write hit occurs, the data is only written to the cache and not to the main storage area. You will also find these two new bits in the CR3 control register (Figure 10.12), where they have the same meaning. However, in the control register, they apply to the page directory entry and not to the page table entry.

If the i486 accesses a page in the external memory, it sends signals to the PWT and PCD pins, which correspond to the bits PWT and PCD in the page table entry or page table directory. When paging is enabled, if the PE-bit in the control register CR0 equals 0, PCD and PWT are taken as 0 independently of their actual value in CR3.

In addition to test registers TR6 and TR7 in the i386 for testing the translation lookaside buffer, the i486 has three additional test registers, TR3 to TR5. They serve for testing the i486 on-chip cache.

10.6.3 i486 Reset

Like the i386, with a reset the i486 can be made to perform an internal self-test. This occurs when the AHOLD pin remains at a high level for two clock cycles, before and after the activation of the reset signal. The self-test checks the CPU logic as well as the on-chip cache and the floating-point unit. After completion, the high-order DX-byte contains the value 04h (for i486) and the low byte contains the version number. As was the case in the i386, the i486 also starts operation at the address fffffff0h. After the first intersegment jump or call, the address lines A31–A20 drop to low level, and the i486 addresses in real mode only the first Mbyte of its address space. Table 10.1 summarizes the initialization values after a reset.

Register	Value
EFlag	uuuuuuuu uuuuuu00 00000000 00000010 = uuuu0002h
CR0	0uuuuuuu uuuuuuuu uuuuuuuu uuuu0000 = uuuuuuu0h
EIP	00000000 00000000 11111111 11110000 = 0000fff0h
CS	11110000 00000000 = f000h[1]
DS	00000000 00000000 = 0000h
SS	00000000 00000000 = 0000h
ES	00000000 00000000 = 0000h
FS	00000000 00000000 = 0000h
GS	00000000 00000000 = 0000h
EDX	00000000 00000000 00000100 version = 000004xxh
all others	uuuuuuuu uuuuuuuu uuuuuuuu uuuuuuuu = uuuuuuuuh

[1] base address = ffff0000h, limit = ffffh (segment descriptor cache register).
u: undefined

i387-FPU:

control word	37fh	all exceptions masked, precision 64 bits, rounding to nearest
status word	xy00h[1]	all exceptions cleared, TOP=000b[2], condition code undefined, B=0
tag word	ffffh	all registers empty

[1] $x = 0$ or $x = 4$, $0 \le y \le 7$
[2] TOP points to register 7 (111b) after the first PUSH instruction, the stack grows downward.

Table 10.1: i486 register contents after a processor reset

10.6.4 i486 Real Mode

The real mode of the i486 is entirely compatible with that in the i386. For the calculation of linear and, at the same time, physical addresses, the i486 shifts the value in a segment register by four bit positions to the left and, as usual, adds the offset or the effective address. This produces physical addresses between 000000h and 10ffefh. Even though the offset register contains 32 bits, you cannot generate offset values greater than ffffh without causing an interrupt 12 (0ch) or 13 (0dh). Also in the i486, the address space in real mode is limited to just over 1 Mbyte. All other characteristics of the i386 real mode also apply to the i486 real mode. You will find more details in Chapter 3.

10.6.5 i486 Protected Mode

Also, the protected mode of the i486 is compatible with the protected mode of the i386. The use of segment register values as segment selectors and the interpretation of segment descriptors remain unchanged. The i486 protected mode can effectively support multitasking operating systems in exactly the same way as that of the i386. The complete physical 32-bit address space with a 4 Gbyte capacity is accessible. The memory of the i486 is managed with the help of the memory management registers GDTR, LDTR, IDTR and TR. Protected mode is discussed in Section 3.7.

10.6.6 i486 Virtual 8086 Mode

The virtual 8086 mode of the i486 is identical to the virtual 8086 mode of the i386. It has a great importance for DOS compatibility boxes of the OS/2 and Windows NT operating systems, and also for the operating system extension Windows. In this way, the performance should be increased. The main problem is, as in the i386, that DOS programs very often issue interrupts to call operating system functions. The handling of such interrupts in a real mode manner, but under the protected mode monitor in virtual 8086 mode, takes a long time. The main reason for this is the lengthy switching between the virtual 8086 program, the virtual 8086 monitor and the emulation routines for the required operating system functions. Only the Pentium implements a so-called «virtual interrupt» for accelerating the interrupt handling in virtual 8086 mode.

10.6.7 Integer Core and Floating-Point Unit

Between the i386 and i387, data and opcodes must be exchanged through the usual I/O bus cycles. This takes a considerable time, because every bus cycle lasts two CLK cycles, and only 32 bits can be transferred via the bus. This restriction is obsolete in the i486. Due to the on-chip floating-point unit, no bus cycles are necessary for a data exchange between the CPU core and the floating-point unit. Moreover, whole operands and opcodes are transferred in one operation, even if they are larger than 32 bits. This is achieved by a wide internal data bus, and its effect is especially noticeable with simple instructions such as FADD or FSUB with a memory operand. Here, all the bus cycles previously necessary for transferring the operand to the coprocessor are obsolete. For an i386/i387 these transfer cycles sometimes require more time than the actual floating-point calculation itself.

The i486 FPU has an improved hardware multiplier which is able to process eight bits in one clock cycle (the i387 can handle only two). Note that even the i486 multiplier is not a full multiplier, because only subgroups and not all operand bits are processed in one instance. Therefore, the i486 multiplier requires the assistance of microcode (as do many other components, too). Although the floating-point unit and the integer core both access the same microcode ROM, and thus interfere with each other, the floating-point instructions can be executed in parallel to the CPU core instructions once started.

The on-chip cache also contributes to performance enhancement compared to the i386/i387. Due to the rather poor register set of only eight floating-point registers, the operand must be frequently stored in or read from memory. Therefore, the significantly faster cache accesses accelerate the floating-point calculations.

10.6.8 FPU Exceptions

Unlike the i386/i387 combination the i486 doesn't generate an exception 9 (coprocessor segment overflow). Instead it uses the more general exception 13, indicating a general protection fault. It is issued when an operand spans an address area in protected mode which is not covered by the operand's segment. This is similar to the fault condition for exception 9. Because in the i486 the CPU and FPU are no longer separate, the distinction between exception 9 (which originates in the i387 FPU) and exception 13 (which is issued by the i386 CPU) is no longer applicable.

10.6.9 Translation Lookaside Buffer (TLB)

As in the i386, the i486 TLB is organized as a four-way set-associative memory, and uses a pseudo LRU replacement strategy in the same way as the on-chip cache (the i386, on the contrary, uses a random replacement strategy). Each set comprises eight entries, thus the complete TLB can accommodate in its four sets a total of 32 entries. The tag part consists of a 17-bit tag together with the four page protection bits valid (V), user/supervisor (U/S), read/write (R/W) and dirty (D). The data part of an entry holds the 20 bits of the physical address and the two page attributes PCD and PWT. Like the on-chip cache, one LRU entry is formed for the four ways. It consists of the three LRU bits L_0 to L_2. The entries are replaced using the pseudo LRU replacement strategy shown in Figure 9.4 when a page access leads to a TLB miss. Due to the somewhat altered TLB structure (especially in view of the pseudo LRU replacement strategy instead of the random strategy), test registers TR6 and TR7 for testing the TLB, as well as the testing procedure itself, are changed. More details about this in Section 10.8.2.

10.7 i486 Bus

The i486 has a very flexible bus in view of its size and cycle behaviour. The data bus can be operated with a width of 8, 16 and 32 bits by the $\overline{BS8}$ and $\overline{BS16}$ signals. The bus width can be defined separately and independently for every cycle, and need not be predefined at the time of system design. Thus the i486 can cooperate flexibly with memories and peripherals of various widths. Note that there is no $\overline{NA}$ terminal (Next Address) for controlling an eventual address pipelining. The i486 does not perform such bus cycles. However, the new burst mode increases the transfer rate significantly. Burst mode and address pipelining have now been combined in the Pentium.

10.7.1 Burst Cycles

For the transfer of large amounts of data, the i486 implements a new bus mode called *burst mode*. In normal mode one bus cycle without wait states lasts two clock cycles, as is the case for the i386. Therefore, the i486 can read or write one quantity within two processor clock cycles. In burst mode the time necessary for transferring one quantity is reduced to one clock cycle, thus the transfer rate is doubled. The burst mode is subject to some restrictions, though, and is therefore not always applicable.

A burst cycle is started by a first normal memory access which lasts for two clock cycles. With an inactive $\overline{\text{BLAST}}$ during the second clock cycle, the i486 indicates that it wants to execute a burst cycle. If the addressed system is able to carry out a burst cycle it reacts by activating the $\overline{\text{BRDY}}$ signal. All further accesses then last for only one clock cycle. To terminate the burst cycle, the i486 activates the $\overline{\text{BLAST}}$ signal in the final access, showing that the last value of the current burst cycle is transferred with the next $\overline{\text{BRDY}}$ or $\overline{\text{RDY}}$. Figure 10.14 shows a signal diagram for a 2-1-1-1 burst.

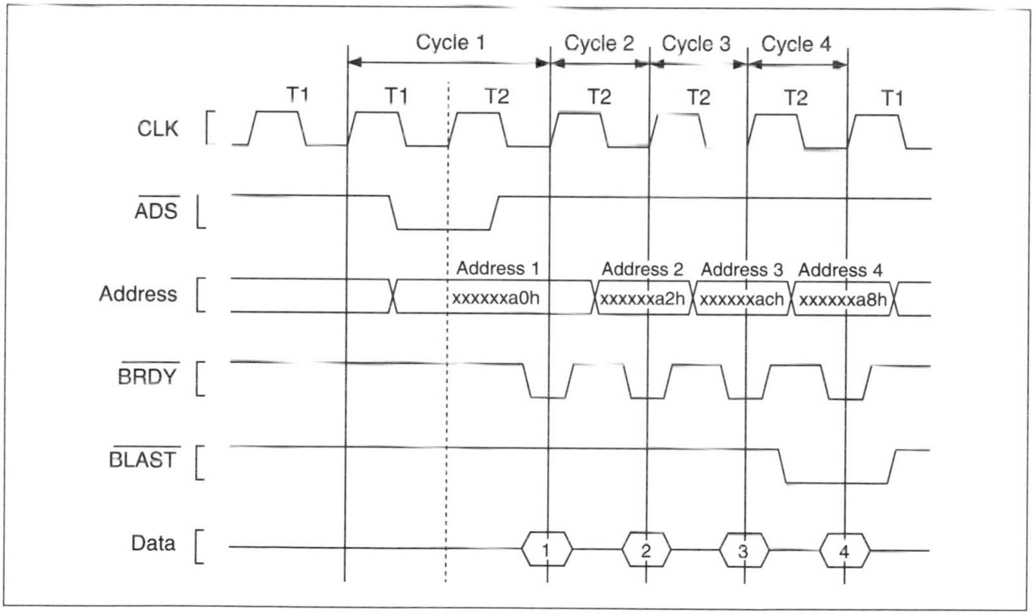

Figure 10.14: In i486 burst mode the bus cycle for a 16-byte address area is shortened from two to one processor clock cycle; only the first access needs two clock cycles. Thus, one line of the internal cache can be filled very quickly, namely within five instead of eight PCLK cycles. The cycle shown is also called 2-1-1-1 burst.

The burst cycle is restricted in that the amount of data to be transferred within one burst cycle must fall into a single 16-byte area which starts at a 16-byte boundary, that is, their addresses must be in the range xxxxxxx0h to xxxxxxxfh (xxxxxxx = 0000000h to fffffffh). This corresponds to a cache line in the internal cache memory. If the required data goes beyond this address area, then the burst cycle must be split into two cycles. Because of this address area restriction, only the A2, A3 and $\overline{\text{BE0}}$–$\overline{\text{BE3}}$ address signals change during a burst cycle; all other relevant signals like A31–A4, $M/\overline{IO}$, $D/\overline{C}$ and $W/\overline{R}$ remain the same. The addressed external system is thus able to determine the address of the succeeding transfers easily and efficiently. The decode overhead is therefore reduced, and only one clock cycle is required.

The name 2-1-1-1 burst comes from the fact that the first bus cycle lasts two PCLK cycles but the following three only last one clock cycle each. If additional wait states are necessary the numbers increase accordingly. For example, a 3-2-2-2 burst means that for every individual access there is one additional wait cycle.

The burst cycle is particularly suited to filling a cache line which comprises exactly 16 bytes and starts at a 16-byte boundary, or loading a TSS during the course of a task switch, as well as for descriptors. Unfortunately, write cycles can only be carried out in burst mode up to 32 bits. If the full width of the i486 data bus (32 bits) is used, then no advantages result from the burst mode for a data write. Only if the data bus is set to a width of 8 or 16 bits by means of the $\overline{BS8}$ and $\overline{BS16}$ signals is the write operation carried out faster in burst mode.

Thus, 16 bytes at most can be read in burst mode. With a data bus width of 32 bits, four read cycles are required in total. In burst mode the i486 needs $2 + 3 = 5$ clock cycles for this. The transfer rate of 16 bytes within five clock cycles on a 50 MHz i486 corresponds to a burst transfer rate of 160 Mbyte/s. However, when looking at this huge number, note that this rate is only valid for 0.1 μs and, moreover, may only be achieved for read accesses. For a data write without wait states, the transfer rate reaches 100 Mbyte/s. This is, nevertheless, a remarkable value. Fast hard disk drives, on the other hand, allow only a transfer rate of about 2–4 Mbyte/s. Thus, the processor bus is not the bottleneck in the system; the (unfortunately very effective) breaks are located elsewhere. (These bottlenecks are discussed later.)

10.7.2 Special Cycles

In addition to the shutdown and halt special cycles known already from the i386, the i486 has two more special cycles which apply to the cache. These are the so-called «flush» and «write-back» cycles. In general, special cycles are indicated by the combination (001) of the signals $M/\overline{IO}$, $D/\overline{C}$, $W/\overline{R}$ and differentiated by the levels of $\overline{BE0}$–$\overline{BE3}$. Table 10.2 lists the various levels. Special cycles must be acknowledged by the system as usual bus cycles with a low-level $\overline{RDY}$ or $\overline{BRDY}$.

The i486 issues a *flush special cycle* (1101) if it has executed an INVD (invalidate cache) or WBINVD (write-back and invalidate cache). Note that in the case of WBINVD, the i486 firstly executes a write-back cycle and then finally sends out a flush cycle. The flush special cycle only shows that the internal cache has been invalidated. It does not indicate whether the changed data has also been written back. The external system can use the flush special cycle, for example, to send out a cache flush for the L2-cache also, if one is available. Without this special cycle, the external system could otherwise not differentiate between a cache flush with a write-back of the modified cache lines through WBINVD, and a normal write-back. Although the i486 on-chip cache implements a write-through strategy and therefore INVD and WBINVD have the same effect on the L1-cache (only an invalidation), the write-back special cycle explained in the following informs a write-back L2-cache whether an INVD or WBINVD is executed by the i486.

$\overline{BE3}$	$\overline{BE2}$	$\overline{BE1}$	$\overline{BE0}$	Special cycle
0	1	1	1	write-back
1	0	1	1	halt
1	1	0	1	flush
1	1	1	0	shutdown

Table 10.2: i486 special bus cycles (signals $M/\overline{IO}$, $D/\overline{C}$, $W/\overline{R}$=0,0,1)

The i486 sends out a *write-back special cycle* (0111), only after a WBINVD instruction has been executed. In this way, it indicates that all modified cache lines in the on-chip cache have been written back to the main memory or to an intermediate second-level cache (note that this does not apply to the write-through L1-cache of the i486). The system can use the write-back special cycle, for example, to finally write back all modified cache lines in the L2-cache to the main memory. Immediately after a write-back special cycle, the i486 sends out an additional flush cycle.

10.7.3 Invalidation Cycles

Inquiry cycles are used for ensuring the consistency of the i486 on-chip cache and an external L2-cache or main memory, when another busmaster may access the L2-cache or main memory without using the i486. If the external busmaster overwrites an entry there which is also used by the i486 on-chip cache, then the L1-cache entry is no longer up to date. The corresponding cache line must be invalidated. For this purpose, the external busmaster (or system controller) drives an invalidation cycle by activating the AHOLD signal first. The i486 switches the address terminals A31–A4 into a state which enables the input of an external address. A3 and A2 are not required because the 16-byte cache line must be replaced as a whole, and can therefore be addressed at a 16-byte boundary. Immediately afterwards, the address of the applicable memory location is applied and $\overline{EADS}$ is enabled. The i486 then fetches the supplied address.

In such an externally initiated inquiry cycle, as in normal memory accesses, the tag logic of the on-chip cache checks whether the address is located in the tag memory and, thus, whether the corresponding value is available in the on-chip cache. In an inquiry cycle, the address originates in the external logic; in a normal memory cycle, on the other hand, it originates from the CPU core. In both cases, the address comparator compares the cache control, tag and transferred addresses to determine either a hit or a miss. If a hit has occurred, the i486 invalidates the corresponding cache line. An explicit write-back process is not necessary because, due to the fixed write-through strategy, all write accesses are switched through to the L2-cache or main memory. The invalidation should only avoid the on-chip cache being referenced for read accesses and provided with an out-dated value.

10.8 Test Functions

All i486 models have some in-built test functions, such as the internal self-test BIST (built-in self-test), testing of the TLB, checking the on-chip cache and, for the DX/50 MHz and all SX and DX2/DX4 derivatives, the JTAG boundary scan test. More about this in the following.

10.8.1 Internal Self-Test BIST

The internal self-test is activated when a high level signal is applied to the AHOLD input for at least two CLK cycles before and after the reset signal again returns to a low level after being activated. The self-test lasts about 2^{20} CLK cycles. This corresponds to 32 ms at 33 MHz. The BIST tests the internal logic, the microcode ROM, the on-chip cache and the TLB. The i486 stores the BIST result in the EAX register. A value of 00000000h indicates an error-free completion, all other values a functional error – the chip is unusable. Additionally, the value 04h in the high-order DX byte identifies the processor as being an i486.

10.8.2 Testing the TLB

For testing the TLB the test registers TR6 and TR7 are implemented, as in the i386. Because of the changed TLB structure they deviate from those in the i386. Figure 10.15 shows the TR6 and TR7 registers.

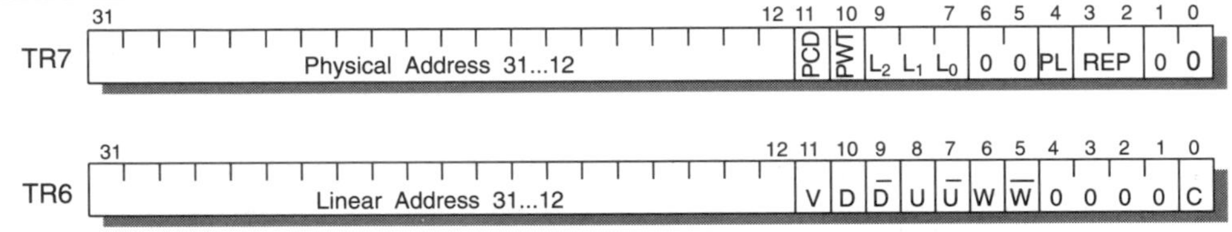

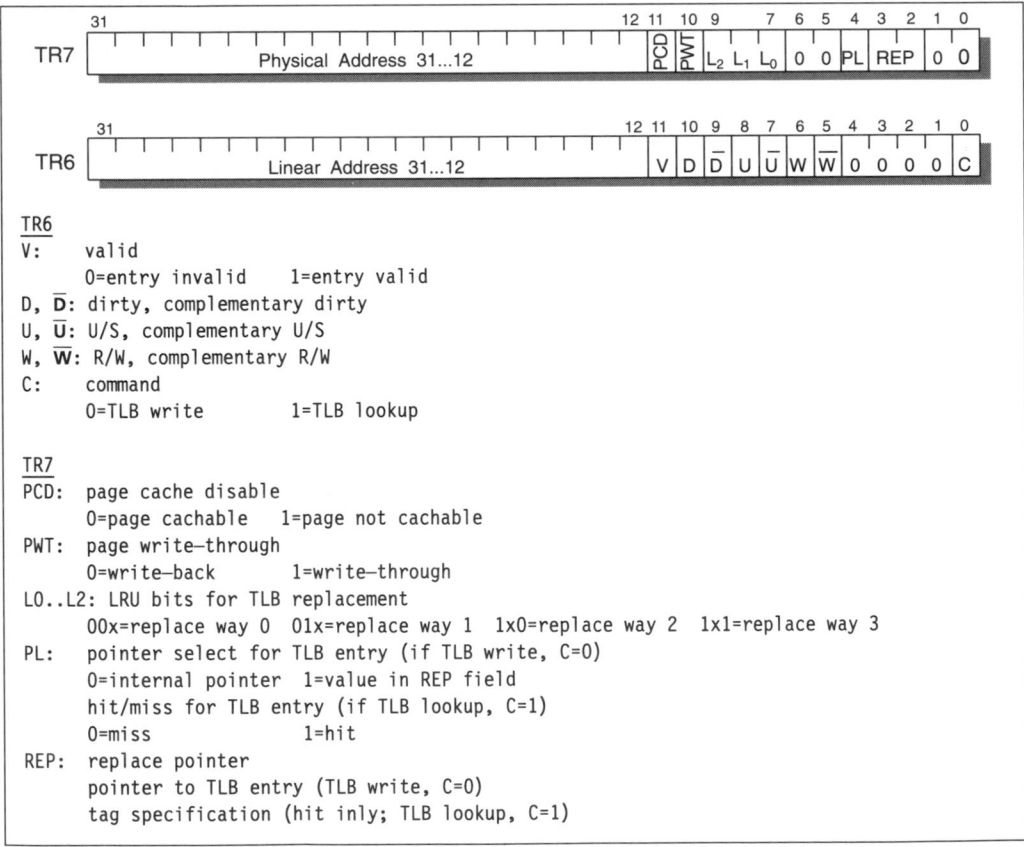

TR6
V: valid
  0=entry invalid 1=entry valid
D, $\overline{D}$: dirty, complementary dirty
U, $\overline{U}$: U/S, complementary U/S
W, $\overline{W}$: R/W, complementary R/W
C: command
  0=TLB write 1=TLB lookup

TR7
PCD: page cache disable
  0=page cachable 1=page not cachable
PWT: page write–through
  0=write–back 1=write–through
L0..L2: LRU bits for TLB replacement
  00x=replace way 0 01x=replace way 1 1x0=replace way 2 1x1=replace way 3
PL: pointer select for TLB entry (if TLB write, C=0)
  0=internal pointer 1=value in REP field
  hit/miss for TLB entry (if TLB lookup, C=1)
  0=miss 1=hit
REP: replace pointer
  pointer to TLB entry (TLB write, C=0)
  tag specification (hit inly; TLB lookup, C=1)

Figure 10.15: Structure of test registers TR6 and TR7.

The structure of the TR6 test command register has not changed, whereas the test data register TR7 reflects the altered TLB structure. The *PCD* and *PWT* bits hold the page attributes, and $L_2..L_0$ are the three LRU bits. All other positions remain unchanged. TR6 and TR7 are written and read by the instructions MOV TR6/TR7, reg and MOV reg, TR6/TR7, respectively. The TLB testing is sub-divided into two processes as usual: writing entries into the TLB and reading TLB entries (TLB lookup). To test the TLB you must disable the paging unit, that is, the i486 must not perform any paging process. As in the i386, here also, the *C*-Bit in the test command register specifies whether a TLB write (C=0) or a TLB lookup (C=1) should be performed. The three LRU bits have a meaning only for TLB lookups. They indicate the current LRU status in the corresponding set.

The *linear address* represents the TLB tag field. A TLB entry is attached to these linear addresses during a write to the TLB, and the contents of TR6 and TR7 are transferred to the attached entry. During a TLB lookup, the test logic checks whether these linear addresses and the attribute bits agree with a TLB entry. If this is the case, then the remaining fields of TR6 and the test register TR7 are loaded from the confirmed entry into the TLB.

During a write to the TLB, the *physical address* is transferred into the TLB entry that corresponds to the linear address. During a TLB lookup, the test logic loads this TR7 field with the value stored in the TLB.

The meaning of *PL* varies depending on C. If a TLB entry is written (C=0) and if PL=1, then the TLB associative block to be written is determined by REP. If PL is reset (PL=0), an internal pointer in the paging unit selects the TLB block to be written. For a TLB lookup (C=1), the PL value specifies whether the lookup has led to a hit (PL=1) or not (PL=0).

The five attribute bits V, D, $\overline{D}$, U, $\overline{U}$ and W, $\overline{W}$ have the same meaning as in the i386 (Table 3.7). Note that an access to the TLB command register TR6 triggers the TLB test procedure. For a TLB write (C=0) immediately afterwards, the content of TR7 is transferred to the TLB. For TLB lookup (C=1) the applicable positions are moved to TR7. If you perform a TLB write, you must therefore load the TLB test data register TR7 first. Otherwise, old, and therefore in most cases, wrong, values are supplied to the TLB.

10.8.3 Testing the On-Chip Cache

For testing the on-chip cache, the i486 implements the test registers TR3–TR5. Figure 10.16 shows this structure. The test procedure itself is similar to that for testing the TLB.

Writing a 16-byte cache line is performed in the same way as a cache line fill, through the line fill buffer. For this purpose you must supply four times four bytes via the cache test data register TR3. The i486 then replaces a cache line by the content of the line fill buffer. In a similar way, you may read a cache line through the test register TR3 as four times 4-byte data. This is performed by means of a cache read buffer. Thus, the test data register TR3 does not access the cache immediately but through the two mentioned buffers. Note that you must always read or write the complete buffer, that is, four 32-bit accesses are always required. The two *DW*-bits in the cache test control register TR5 specify the double word within the 16-byte cache line and the 16-byte cache buffer, respectively, which is accessed.

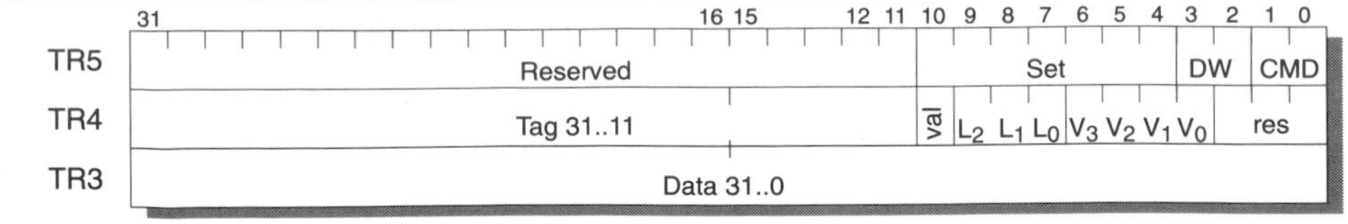


```
TR4
V:  valid
    0=cache entry invalid    1=cache entry valid
L0..L2: LRU bits for cache entry replacement
    00x=replace way 0  01x=replace way 1  1x0=replace way 2  1x1=replace way 3
V0..V3: valid bits for ways 0 to 3
    0=way invalid       1=way valid

TR5
DW: line buffer access: double-word group within the cache line
    00=bits 0..31   01=bits 32..63   10=bits 64..95   11=bits 96..127
    read/write cache:
    00=way 0   01=way 1   10=way 2   11=way 3
CMD: test command
    00=line buffer access   01=write test   10=read test   11=cache flush
```

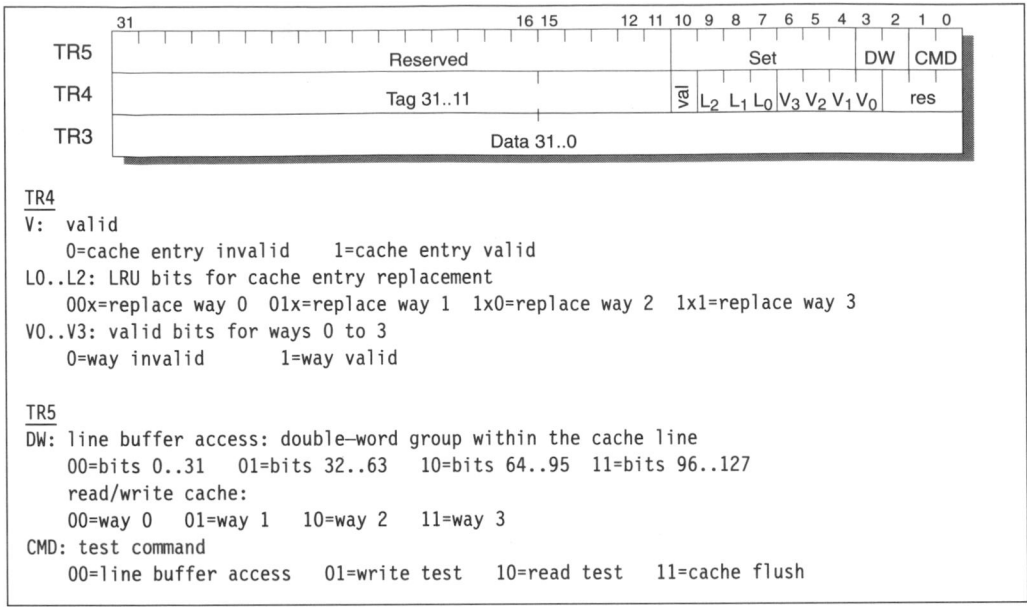

Figure 10.16: Structure of cache test registers TR3–TR5.

The cache test status register TR4 contains the 21-bit tag address as well as the valid bit *val* for the accessed entry. Additionally there are the three LRU bits L_2–L_0 and the four valid bits V_3–V_0 for the set entry which spans all four ways. The cache test control register TR5 determines not only the double word to be accessed (by means of DW) but also the process (via *CMD*) to be performed. The seven set select bits specify the addressed set. In the following, I will discuss the five possible operations in brief.

Cache Buffer Access

For writing the line fill buffer you must first write the test control register TR5 with an entry CMD=00b and the double word DW which is to be transferred into the line fill buffer later. Here the set entry has no meaning, thus the test control logic is prepared for an access to the line fill buffer. If you now write a value into the test data register TR3 by means of the MOV TR3, reg instruction, the value is transferred to the location in the line fill buffer specified by DW.

You may read a 32-bit double word from the cache read buffer by writing the test register TR5 with a value CMD=00b and specifying with DW the double word to be accessed. With a MOV reg, TR3 instruction which reads the test data register TR3, the 32 bits of the addressed double word in the cache read buffer are transferred into the test data register and further to the destination register reg.

Thus, read and write accesses to the cache buffer are distinguished by a read or write access to the test data register TR3. Note that for the two following processes, cache write and cache read, four accesses to the cache buffer are always required for filling the line fill buffer or emptying the cache read buffer completely.

Cache Write Access

First, four write accesses to the line fill buffer are necessary to fill it with the values for the intended cache line. Afterwards the line must be actually transferred into the cache. This is achieved as follows. TR4 is loaded with the 21-bit tag and the intended valid bits for the cache entry. Afterwards you write the test control register TR5 with MOV TR5, reg while the CMD field has a value of 01b, and the fields set and DW specify the set address and the way within the set, respectively. The write access to TR5 then automatically issues a transfer from the line buffer into the cache. The internal LRU logic of the on-chip cache updates the LRU bits with its own. You may read and check them, for example, using the following process.

Cache Read Access

The reading of a cache line is also a two-stage process. First, the intended cache line must be transferred from the cache into the cache read buffer. This is carried out by the MOV TR5, reg instruction. In reg you must provide a value with CMD=10b and corresponding entries for set and DW, which define the set to be read and the way within that set, respectively. Afterwards TR4 holds the 21-bit tag from the cache directory of the on-chip cache, as well as the allocated three LRU bits L_2–L_0 and valid bits V_3–V_0 for the four ways of the addressed set. At the same time, the cache line is transferred into the cache read buffer and is accessible via TR3. By reading TR4 once and accessing TR3 four times, you are thus able to extract all of the information which is available for the defined cache line.

Cache Flush

When you load the test command register TR5 with a value CMD=11b, the i486 issues an internal cache flush. It invalidates all cache entries (that is, all cache lines) by clearing the LRU and valid bits. Note that the data and tag entries themselves are not cleared; they remain unchanged, but are not used for normal cache operation. Unlike a cache flush with the INVD and WBINVD instructions, here the i486 does not drive any flush special cycle into the bus. External components are not informed about the invalidation.

10.8.4 Tristate Test Mode

The tristate test mode serves for implementing hardware checks for complete boards. For that purpose, the i486 floats all output and bidirectional terminals so that the motherboard cannot receive any signals from the processor. The high-level test logic is then able to carry out the necessary hardware tests and locate any malfunctions more easily. The i486 leaves the tristate test mode immediately after a reset is initiated (by an active RESET signal).

10.8.5 JTAG Boundary Scan Test

In addition to the test modes described previously, the 50 MHz i486 contains a so-called «boundary scan» test, in accordance with the IEEE 1149.1 standard. The first i486 chips lack this powerful diagnostic function. However, computer users cannot really use it. All i486DX2 and i486SX

CPUs, which came onto the market much later, implement this JTAG test right from the start. Therefore, I want to discuss the boundary scan test in general here. The explanations are valid for all processors from the i486SX up to the Pentium. Deviations in some details are listed in connection with the individual processors.

Hardware manufacturers have, with the boundary scan test, a powerful tool for externally checking the processor's logic units and their circuits by software, even after completion of manufacture and their inclusion in the computer. Extensive diagnostics can be carried out. The JTAG test is supported by the TCK (test clock), TDI (Test Data Input), TDO (Test Data Output), TMS (Test Mode Select) and, in some processors, also by the $\overline{\text{TRST}}$ (test reset) pins. Note that TRST is not available for all processors. The i486SX and i486DX2 have to work without it, whereas the Pentium has a TRST pin. Internally, the i486 has a boundary scan register and a JTAG logic, which is accessed through the Test Access Port, TAP. The test must be performed by external logic, which uses the JTAG test bus with the TCK, TDI, TDO, TMS and (optional) $\overline{\text{TRST}}$ pins. In the following I will summarize the JTAG terminals in brief.

TCK (I)
Pin A3

This test clock pin is sent a test clock signal for the boundary scan test. Synchronized with this clock signal, test data and also status information is input and output.

TDI (I)
Pin A14

The Test Data Input (TDI) pin is sent TAP (Test Access Port) instructions and data serially synchronized with TCK. The instructions and data are necessary for the boundary scan test.

TDO (I)
Pin B16

From the Test Data Output (TDO) pin, instructions and result data from the boundary scan test is sent out. It is serially synchronized with TCK.

TMS (I)
Pin B14

If this test mode select pin receives a high level signal, the test access port sends out the JTAG test logic for the boundary test scan. If TMS remains at a high level for five TCK cycles or more, then it restarts the test logic independent of the currently active condition.

$\overline{\text{TRST}}$ (I, Pentium only)

This pin is implemented in the Pentium only. To complete the picture, I want to present it here. An active signal with a low level at this test reset pin initializes the boundary scan test logic.

As Figure 10.17 shows, a boundary scan register and a JTAG logic, or a TAP controller which is accessed through the Test Access Port TAP, is available on the i486 chip. The test must be performed by an external logic, which uses the JTAG test bus with the TCK, TDI, TDO and TMS pins. Note that the chip integrates the actual i486 processor and, additionally, the JTAG logic.

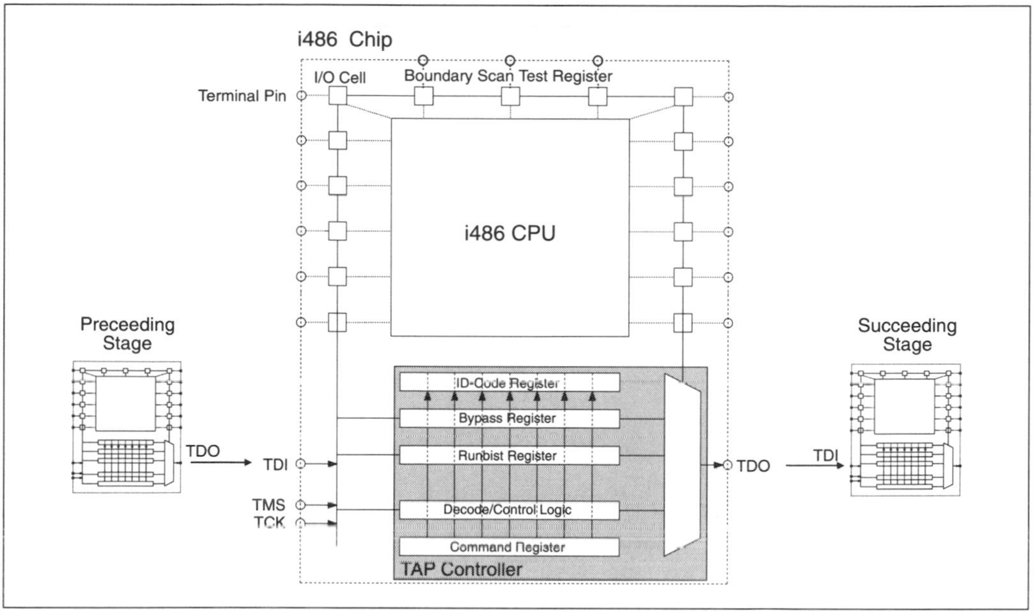

Figure 10.17: i486 TAP structure. The input TDI and output TDO can be connected to the output of a circuit in a preceding stage and the input of a circuit in a successive stage, respectively.

The scanning path is located between the input pin TDI and the output pin TDO. A 1-bit shift register is provided for each pin, through which all applicable inputs and outputs from the i486 flow. If TAP control is not active, these registers pass on the supplied data to the corresponding pin, or to the i486, without change. If JTAG mode is active, the 1-bit shift registers are configured as input or output cells. The input cells intercept the values at the corresponding input pins and store them. No further influence on the i486 takes place, because the i486 does not support the INTEST instruction of JTAG. Active output cells, on the other hand, store the value which then appears at the corresponding pin.

The shift registers are not only connected to the input/output pins of the i486, they are also connected to each other; in this way, they form a pathway between TDI and TDO. Additionally, there are control cells at many positions. Data in the 1-bit shift registers is moved from TDI to TDO every TCK cycle, without being changed during the process. The name boundary scan should now also be clear: through the shift registers located at the «boundary», the «boundary values» of the i486 are scanned and sent out through TDO. All of the 1-bit shift registers, or input/output and control cells joined together, form the so-called boundary scan register. The control cells determine the transfer direction for bidirectional pins (such as D31–D0, for example), or cut off the output pin (such as $\overline{ADS}$, for example), that is, they go into a tristate condition. A «1» in the corresponding control cell defines the applicable bidirectional pin as an input and so cuts off the output pin. A «0» selects the bidirectional pin as an output and so activates the output pin. The control signals always work in conjunction with a group of pins. Table 10.3 lists the control cells and their corresponding groups.

Control cell	Pin group
ABUSCTL	A31–A2
WRCTL	D31–D0, DP3–DP0
BUSCTL	$\overline{ADS}$, $\overline{BE3}$–$\overline{BE0}$, $\overline{BLAST}$, $\overline{PLOCK}$, $\overline{LOCK}$, W/$\overline{R}$, M/$\overline{IO}$, D/$\overline{C}$, PWT, PCD
MISCCTL	$\overline{PCHK}$, HLDA, BREQ, $\overline{FERR}$

Table 10.3: JTAG control cells and assigned pin groups for the i486DX

The boundary scan path is gone through as follows (note the control cell xxxCTL):

TDI→WRCTL→ABUSCTL→BUSCTL→MISCCTL→$\overline{ADS}$→$\overline{BLAST}$→$\overline{PLOCK}$→$\overline{LOCK}$→$\overline{PCHK}$→$\overline{BRDY}$→$\overline{BOFF}$→$\overline{BS16}$→$\overline{BS8}$→$\overline{RDY}$→$\overline{KEN}$→HOLD→AHOLD→CLK→HLDA→W/$\overline{R}$→BREQ→$\overline{BE0}$→$\overline{BE1}$→$\overline{BE2}$→$\overline{BE3}$→M/$\overline{IO}$→D/$\overline{C}$→PWT→PCD→$\overline{EADS}$→$\overline{A20M}$→RESET→$\overline{FLUSH}$→INTR→NMI→$\overline{FERR}$→$\overline{IGNNE}$→D31→D30→D29→D28→D27→D26→D25→D24→DP3→D23→D22→D21→D20→D19→D18→D17→D16→DP2→D15→D14→D13→D12→D11→D10→D9→D8→DP1→D7→D6→D5→D4→D3→D2→D1→D0→DP0→A31→A30→A29→A28→A27→A26→A25→A24→A23→A22→A21→A20→A19→A18→A17→A16→A15→A14→A13→A12→A11→A10→A9→A8→A7→A6→res→A5→A4→A3→A2→TDO

Other important JTAG registers include the bypass, the ID code, the runbist and the instruction registers. The most significant bits of all registers are connected with TDI and the least significant bits with TDO. The bypass register, like the other cells, is a 1-bit write register and is used to «short circuit» TDI and TDO. After the corresponding BYPASS instruction to the TAP controller, only a single TCK cycle is necessary in order to send a given value from TDI to TDO, instead of the usual 105 CLK cycles. The bypass register is initialized with a «0» (which then represents the first value given to TDO). The ID code register stores 32-bit identification information for examining the chip. In the case of the i486DX, the following contents apply: Bit 0=1, bits 1 to 11=manufacturer (Intel=09h), bits 12 to 27=part number (0410h for series Ax, 0411h for series Bx), bits 28 to 31=version (00h). The 32-bit i486DX ID code is thus 00410013h (series Ax) and 00411013 (series Bx), respectively.

The runbist register stores the 1-bit test result after an internal self-test. A successful test stores the value 0. Any other value indicates that the i486 is damaged to some extent. The boundary scan test is executed with the help of a defined test instruction set, which currently contains five instructions. The nine most significant bits of the 13-bit instruction register are reserved. The four least significant bits store the corresponding instruction bit for the five EXTEST, IDCODE, RUNBIST, SAMPLE-PRELOAD and BYPASS instructions. They are listed in the following section, together with their 4-bit opcodes.

- EXTEST (opcode xx0h): this instruction tests the external circuits of the i486 (or the chip generally using the JTAG test). For this, the i486 sends out from output pins the values stored in the individual cells of the boundary scan register, and reads the values sent to the i486's input pins into the corresponding cells. Bidirectional pins are handled as input or output pins, depending on the value in the control cell. Note that the data sent to the input pins, and which is read into the cells, is not transferred to the i486. Thus, it has no influence whatsoever on the behaviour of the i486. The i486 must be reset after an EXTEST instruction.
- SAMPLE/PRELOAD (opcode xx1h): depending on the condition of the TAP controller, this instruction scans the condition of the input/output pins of the i486, or establishes data for the output pins. In capture DR condition (see below), the values that are sent out by the i486 to the output pins, and the values received by the i486 at the input pins, are transferred to

the cells of the boundary scan register and can then be read from TDO. In update DR condition, this instruction establishes the data that the i486 chip sends out from its output pins to the board on which it is mounted, using an EXTEST instruction.

- IDCODE (opcode xx2h): this instruction connects the ID code register with TDI and TDO. Through the switching (toggling) of TCK, the ID code is then given out through TDO, and can be used by the external test logic. After an initialization or a i486 reset, the instruction register contains the opcode for IDCODE.
- RUNBIST (opcode xx7h): this instruction connects the runbist register to TDO and loads the value «1». Then, the Built-In Self Test (BIST) is activated. If the test is successful, it overwrites the «1» in the runbist register with a «0». When BIST has been completed, after approximately 1.2 million processor clock cycles (not TCK cycles), the test value can be read through TDO.
- BYPASS (opcode xxfh): this instruction connects the bypass register with TDI and TDO, and breaks the connection between TDI/TDO and the boundary scan register. In this way, the data input to TDI is sent out to TDO, unchanged, after only one TCK cycle. BYPASS is used for implementing checks for complex circuits, if individual components must be tested without being removed from the circuit. This naturally assumes that all components to be tested support the JTAG test. Thus, the TDI input of the i486 can, for example, be connected with the TDO output of a different component, and the TDO output with the TDI input of another chip. In this way, it is possible to form very long scan paths over a complete board.
- PRIVATE: all other opcodes are reserved and can be used by the chip manufacturer for its own purposes. Generally, they have no effect; they are more or less NOPs.

In addition to the test data, the instructions are also serially sent to the i486 through the input pin TDI. The clock signal at the TCK pin is used for this purpose. Therefore, the TAP controller must be aware of which register (for example, boundary scan register, instruction register, etc.) the input data bits have been defined for. For this purpose, a clearly defined condition sequence for the TAP controller has been implemented. Starting with the reset condition, which the TAP controller receives after the activation of $\overline{\text{TRST}}$ (Pentium only) or of TMS for a minimum of five TCK cycles, the different controller conditions are executed in a set sequence, depending on the different combinations of TMS and TCK. For this, TCK is used as the driving clock cycle and TMS as the branch signal, which selects the different branches of the condition diagram. These conditions also include the capture DR and update DR conditions described above. They affect the data transfer from TDI to TDO through the boundary scan register. The instruction register is loaded when the TAP controller is located in the instruction branch of the condition diagram. Thus, the tester (an external logic for performing the JTAG test) must define the transfer sequence of the serial test data exactly, and must also include the activation of the TMS and TCK signals. A far from trivial task.

Upon completion of a test, instruction result data is available in a result register. It can be accessed via the output terminal TDO. The external busmaster can check this result data and determine whether the i486 is operating correctly. Manufacturers also perform tests similar to the JTAG for DRAM and SRAM chips, to check whether the chips operate correctly, or contain faults after their manufacture. For this purpose, different data is serially sent to the on-chip test control, and is written to the memory cells as a test sample. Finally, the data is read back by the on-chip test control, in order to determine whether or not it has been changed. Many chip faults can only be discovered by specific data patterns.

The external addressing of individual memory cells and an external data comparison would take far too long. For this reason, most modern chips perform this check internally. Like the JTAG test, the extensive test data is very quickly input serially through a specific pin, and only the result data – chip o.k. or not – is then output through a pin.

10.9 i486 I/O Address Space

The i486 I/O address space comprises 64k 8-bit ports, 32k 16-bit ports, 16k 32-bit ports or an equivalent mix of them, as in the i386. Also, the i486 indicates an I/O bus cycle by an $M/\overline{IO}$ signal with low level. For compatibility reasons, the port addresses 0f8h to 0ffh are reserved, as in the i386 (or 80286). However, they are no longer used for communication between CPU and coprocessor because the floating-point unit is already integrated on the chip. I/O accesses are switched through to the bus under all circumstances; they are not intercepted by the cache. This applies to read and write accesses. Additionally, I/O write accesses are not buffered in the i486 write buffers. The i486 accomplishes all addressing and protection of the I/O address space in protected mode via the IOPL flag and the I/O permission bit map in the same way as the i386. For details, refer to Sections 3.7.10 and 3.7.11.

11 i486 Cut-down Versions, Overdrives, Upgrades and Clones

The SX and clone game which began with the i386 has been continued with the i486. Additionally, Intel introduced a new upgrade concept with overdrives, whereby unexperienced users and sales people would have the opportunity to enhance the performance of their PCs easily.

11.1 i486SX and i487SX – First Reduce, Then Upgrade

The «cut-down» concept familiar to us from the i386SX has also been continued with the i486. Intel has introduced an i486SX together with its i487SX coprocessor onto the market. For a certain time the i486SX was very popular, especially for Notebooks. However, with falling CPU prices, users preferred to buy a «real» i486 right from the start – the i486DX. What especially characterizes the i487SX as an upgrade instead of a coprocessor will be discussed in the following sections.

11.1.1 i486SX – More Than an i386

Shortly after having presented the i486, Intel introduced a «light» version similar to the i386: the i486SX. Because only a few PC users are involved in highly mathematical applications like CAD or solving differential equations, the integrated coprocessor is unnecessary for most users, and only has the effect of increasing the PC's price. Thus Intel left out the coprocessor in the i486SX, but all the other features which characterize the i486 compared to the i386 (on chip cache, RISC core, etc.) have been kept. The result is a very fast processor which can equal the i486 in normal applications (at the same clock rate, of course). Only in intensive mathematical applications is the i486SX significantly slower. This can be solved by additionally using the i487SX «coprocessor». The quote marks already indicate that the i487SX may not be classified as a pure member of the 80x87 family. Moreover, with the i487SX Intel introduced the concept of so-called *upgrades* which not only deliver a further coprocessor, but also enhance the performance of the CPU itself. Further details concerning this are given later. Note that unlike in the i386SX, neither the data nor the address bus has been reduced in the i486SX. Both are implemented with the full DX width of 32 bits.

I would further like to mention that the first i486SX CPUs nevertheless integrated the coprocessor on their chip. It was only disabled by a gate. Experienced SX users could remove the gate with a small drill so that afterwards a full i486DX was available. This has changed in the meantime. All of today's i486SXs lack the coprocessor. You will doubtless ask yourself why such a partially disabled i486DX was sold more cheaply than an i486SX, although the technical burden did not decrease compared to an i486DX. Here we meet again the unfathomable marketing ploys of hardware manufacturers. The reason for simply inserting a gate instead of actually removing the coprocessor was simply that the mask and process for producing the i486DX were already available, and inserting a gate meant an inexpensive change in the production process. Moreover, Intel was able to put the i486SX onto the market at once. A new layout together with the necessary mask would have been time-consuming and expensive. These were made up one year later.

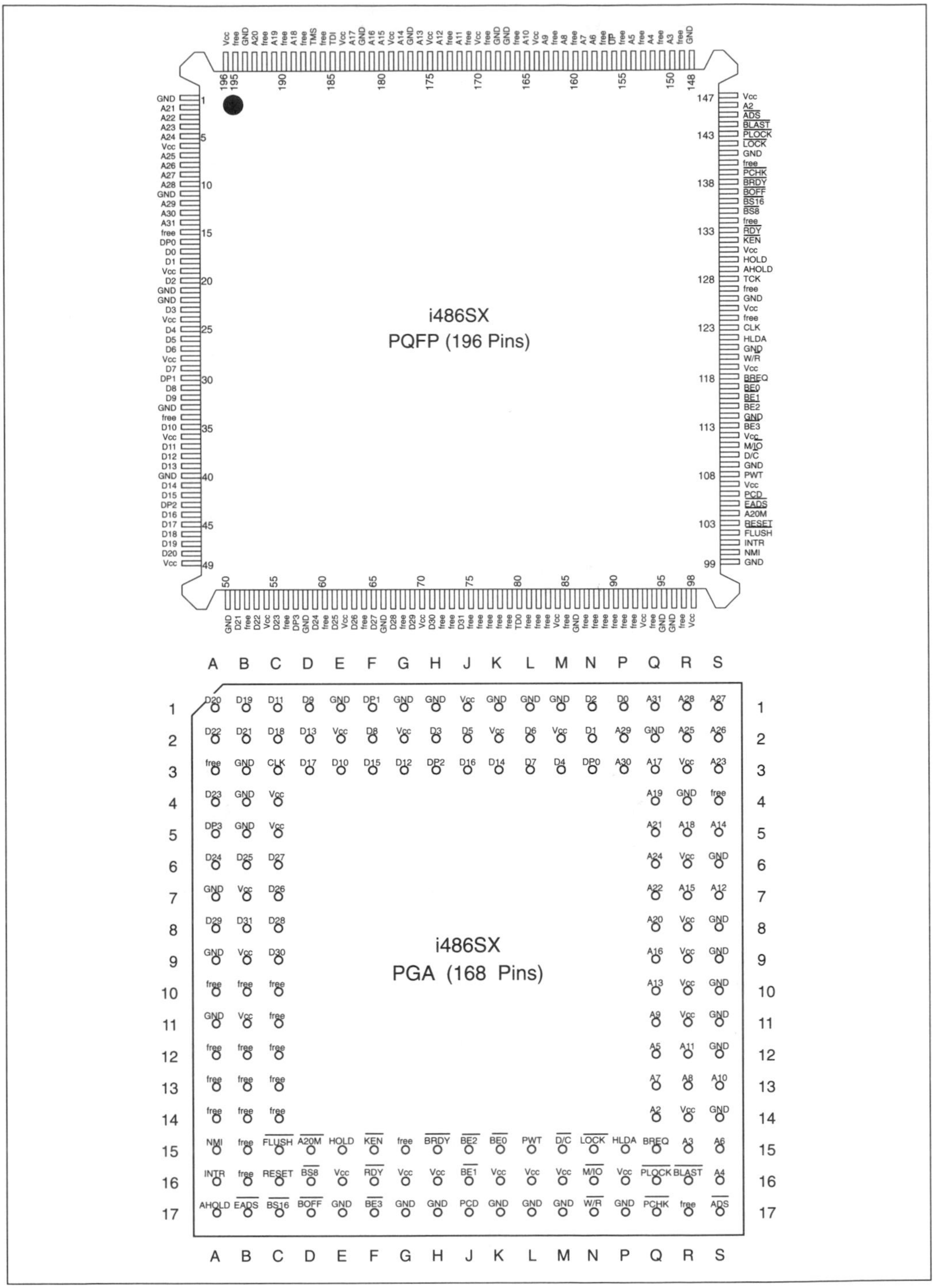

Figure 11.1: i486SX in PGA and PQFP packages.

Package Types

The i486SX comes in two different package types: a pin grid array with 168 pins, and a plastic quad flat package (PQFP) with 196 terminals. Figure 11.1 shows the layout of these two packages.

Besides the five new terminals, the PQFP version of the i486SX implements the following additional features:

- JTAG boundary scan test (not implemented in the PGA model),
- lower power consumption by an improved CMOS design,
- power-down mode which reduces the power consumption from about 500 to 50 mA.

In the following, the five additional terminals of the PQFP version are discussed. The other pins are already known from the i486DX. The most important is the $\overline{\text{UP}}$ pin, which is intended for upgrade support by an i487SX.

$\overline{\text{UP}}$ (I)
Pin 156

If this Update Present connection is supplied with a low-level signal, the i486SX cuts off all inputs and outputs and enters a power-down mode with significantly reduced power consumption. In other words, the i486SX is more or less disabled.

TCK, TDI, TDO, TMS (I, I, O, I)
Pins 128, 185, 80, 187
These are the four connections for the JTAG boundary scan test. Note that there is no $\overline{\text{TRST}}$ pin.

The JTAG Boundary Scan Test

In the i486SX a JTAG boundary scan test has been implemented which follows the principles discussed in Section 10.8.5. Thus, in the following I will only list the control cells (Table 11.1) and the scan path followed. Neither the i486SX in the PGA nor the i486SX implements such a JTAG test.

Control cell	Pin group
ABUSCTL	A31–A2
WRCTL	D31–D0, DP3–DP0
BUSCTL	$\overline{\text{ADS}}$, $\overline{\text{BE3}}$–$\overline{\text{BE0}}$, $\overline{\text{BLAST}}$, $\overline{\text{PLOCK}}$, $\overline{\text{LOCK}}$, W/$\overline{\text{R}}$, M/$\overline{\text{IO}}$, D/$\overline{\text{C}}$, PWT, PCD
MISCCTL	$\overline{\text{PCHK}}$, HLDA, BREQ, $\overline{\text{FERR}}$

Table 11.1: JTAG control cells and assigned pin groups for the i486SX

The boundary scan path is gone through, including the control cells xxxCTL, as follows:

TDI→WRCTL→ABUSCTL→BUSCTL→MISCCTL→$\overline{\text{ADS}}$→$\overline{\text{BLAST}}$→$\overline{\text{PLOCK}}$→$\overline{\text{LOCK}}$→$\overline{\text{PCHK}}$→$\overline{\text{BRDY}}$→$\overline{\text{BOFF}}$→$\overline{\text{BS16}}$→$\overline{\text{BS8}}$→$\overline{\text{RDY}}$→$\overline{\text{KEN}}$→HOLD→AHOLD→CLK→HLDA→W/$\overline{\text{R}}$→BREQ→$\overline{\text{BE0}}$→$\overline{\text{BE1}}$→$\overline{\text{BE2}}$→$\overline{\text{BE3}}$→M/$\overline{\text{IO}}$→D/$\overline{\text{C}}$→PWT→PCD→$\overline{\text{EADS}}$→$\overline{\text{A20M}}$→RESET→$\overline{\text{FLUSH}}$→INTR→NMI→res→res→D31→D30→D29→D28→D27→D26→D25→D24→DP3→D23→D22→D21→D20→D19→D18→D17→D16→DP2→D15→D14→D13→D12→D11→D10→D9→D8→DP1→D7→D6→D5→D4→D3→D2→D1→D0→DP0→A31→A30→A29→A28→A27→A26→A25→A24→A23→A22→A21→A20→A19→A18→A17→A16→A15→A14→A13→A12→A11→A10→A9→A8→A7→A6→$\overline{\text{UP}}$→A5→A4→A3→A2→TDO

After a self-test, which is issued by the JTAG command RUNBIST, the ID code register stores 32-bit identification information for the examined chip. In the case of the i486SX, the following contents apply: Bit 0=1, bits 1 to 11=manufacturer (Intel=09h), bits 12 to 27=part number (0427h), bits 28 to 31=version (00h). The 32-bit i486SX ID code is thus 00427013h.

11.1.2 Clock Frequencies

One disadvantage of the SX as compared to the i486DX is the lower clock frequency. The i486SX comes with 25 MHz at most, and the processor accordingly operates far slower. The performance reduction is only a consequence of the lower clock frequency, though, and not of a less effective SX chip construction.

Some manufacturers check CPU chips to see whether they can also stand a higher clock frequency. This is often the case, therefore i486SX boards up to clock frequencies of 33 MHz are available. Technically speaking, the DX and SX chip models do not differ much; they are manufactured at the same scale and with a comparable layout. The manufacturing tolerances are simply more generous with the SX, and thus their manufacture is easier and cheaper, leading to a higher production yield. A processor that malfunctions at 25 MHz but runs correctly at 20 MHz would be no good as a DX model, but leaves the plant as a checked 20 MHz SX chip.

As 33 MHz i486 chips exist, it might be possible, of course, that among a number of technologically equivalent i486SX chips there is one which has been manufactured just as well as the more critical i486DX by chance, and is also running at 33 MHz without any malfunction. For example, the 60 ns model DRAM chips do not differ from their 100 ns counterparts in either technology or manufacturing methods. With the 60 ns models, every manufacturing step is carried out in the best possible way. During the course of manufacturing the 100 ns chip, there may have been a misalignment of a photo mask by 100 nm. Following completion of manufacturing, a check is made to establish at which clock frequency the chip runs without problems, and the chip is then specified accordingly. The best ones get the *-60* stamp, the less well manufactured (but fully operable at lower clock frequencies) get the *-100* stamp. However, a problem with the increased clock frequencies is that for CMOS chips (to which all i486 chips, independent of SX or DX, belong) the power consumption is proportional to the operating frequency. Therefore, the current drain is about 35% higher at 33 MHz than at 25 MHz. The faster clocked chip heats up to a higher temperature. In some extreme cases, it can malfunction because of overheating, or its lifetime is reduced drastically. Pay attention to a good cooling system, best achieved in the case of a CPU by a temperature sink.

11.1.3 i487SX – i486SX Upgrade

Starting with the i487SX, Intel introduced the upgrading concept. Until now the 80x87 coprocessors have only been a numerical extension of the 80x86 CPUs, and have been accessed in I/O cycles via reserved ports. With the i487SX this has changed completely. The i487SX is not only a numerical coprocessor, but also a complete i486 CPU with an addressing unit, bus unit, CPU core, cache and, of course, a numerical unit. Thus, the i487SX can be compared to a low-clocked i486DX. It is available for clock frequencies between 16 and 25 MHz, and is shipped in a pin grid array package with 169 pins. The only difference from the i486DX is the additional encoding pin and the reservation of pin B14 for the $\overline{MP}$ (math present) signal. Figure 11.2 shows the pin assignment of the i487SX.

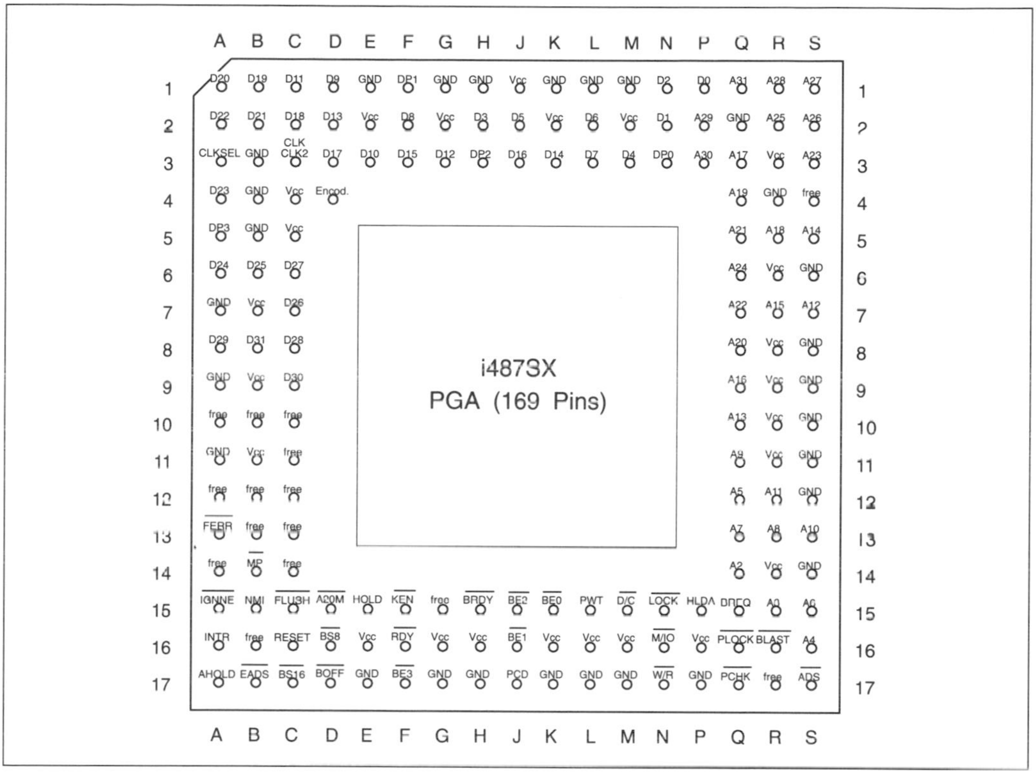

Figure 11.2: i487SX pin assignment.

Now the upgrade principle becomes clear. Not only is the numerical coprocessor delivered, as has been the case up to now, but the upgrades additionally integrate a powerful CPU. Thus the performance enhancement is not limited to new instructions and data formats, as is the case with the numerical 80x87 coprocessors, but the CPU itself is replaced by a more powerful CPU core integrated on the upgrade. The upgrade processor only has to inform the previous CPU that it is now present. This is carried out in the i487SX by means of the additional $\overline{MP}$ signal, indicating that an upgrade is present that now takes over all functions of the previous CPU. The old CPU is not actually necessary any more: upgrading is thus, more or less, a replacement of the old CPU by a new one without the need to remove the previous CPU. The 169th pin, D4, serves for encoding so that the i487SX may not be inserted into the upgrade socket with a wrong orientation. Intel has implemented this pin because, according to the new strategy, the general public should be able to carry out upgrading without major problems.

For combining the i486SX in the PQFP package and 196 pins with the i487SX in the PGA, connection of the CPU and upgrade is very simple (see Figure 11.3a). The $\overline{MP}$ outputs of the i487SX must be connected to the UP input of the i486SX. The i487SX outputs a low-level signal at the MP which informs the UP input of the i486SX that an upgrade is present. The i486SX then cuts off all its connections to the bus and enters a power-down mode to save power. The i486SX now draws only 50 mA instead of 500 mA, and the heat dissipation is accordingly less. The connection MP of the i487SX is pulled to a high level by means of internal resistors in the i486SX. Therefore, the i486SX operates normally without an i487SX. However, with an inserted i487SX the signal UP is stronger, and it pulls MP to low. Without an i487SX the FERR signal is always kept on a high level by means of a resistor which is connected to the supply voltage Vcc. In this case, FERR thus indicates that no floating-point error has occurred. However, an i487SX present is able to drive FERR to low.

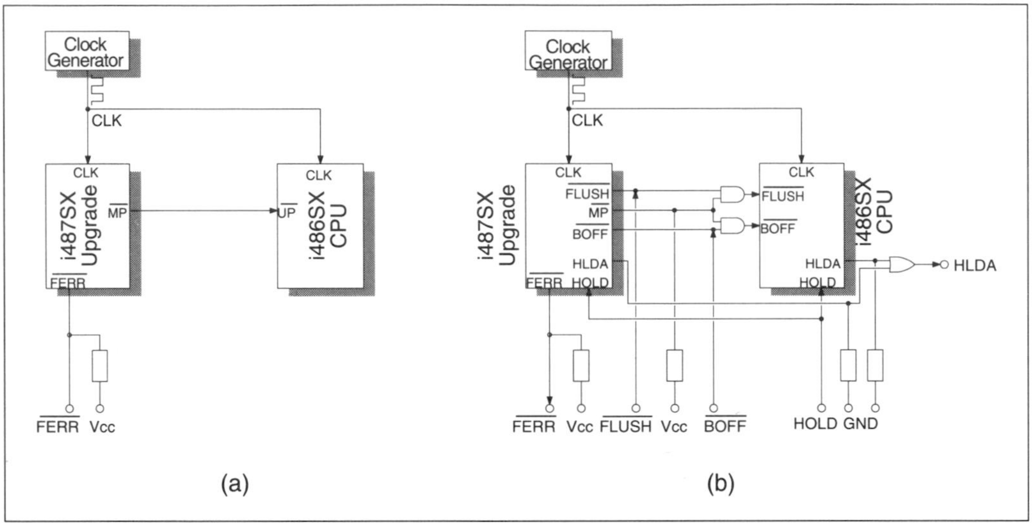

Figure 11.3: i486SX and i487SX upgrade connection. (a) i486SX in PQFP, (b) i486SX in PGA.

The circuitry gets significantly more complicated if an i486SX in the PGA package with 168 pins is used. This model has no input UP, so the i487SX can't tell the i486SX of its presence. Moreover, this i486SX model implements no power-down mode. The i486SX thus draws 500 mA even with an upgrade present, although it makes no contribution to the computer's performance but waits for activation *ad infinitum*. Because of the missing UP input, we have to apply a trick to separate the i486SX from the bus. This is carried out via the BOFF connection. Additionally, an active FLUSH signal for the i486SX causes it to write back its internal cache into memory to avoid data being lost immediately after a reset or the PC's power-on. The BOFF and FLUSH pins are driven by the MP output of the i487SX. Because BOFF may also be activated by an external logic in normal i486SX operation, the i486SX is not able to determine with BOFF whether an upgrade is present or if an external logic is the source of BOFF. Thus, an eventually present power-down mode would not give rise to any advantages. With an active BOFF the i486SX lowers the power consumption by no more than 20%, because all input and output buffers for the pins are deactivated. To ensure normal operation of the i486SX without an upgrade, and that the bus arbitration and signal generation for floating-point errors with and without upgrade are carried out correctly, two additional AND gates and one OR gate are required.

A special feature of the i487SX is that it can be operated by a 1x- or a 2x-clock. The 1x-clock is the standard and is used for upgrading a conventional i486SX. The 2x-clock, on the other hand, is for supporting a low-power i486SX (see Section 11.3). The clock selection is carried out via CLKSEL (pin A3). A high-level CLKSEL pulse after power-on selects a CLK2 clock, that is, the i487SX divides the external clock frequency by two to generate the internal processor clock. If CLKSEL is constantly held on a low level, the i487SX uses the external clock immediately as the internal processor clock.

11.2 486DX2 Processors with Internal Frequency Doubling

Besides a variety of CPUs released in a variety of guises, recently Intel has presented the i486DX2 CPU with internal frequency doubling. In particular, the i486DX2-66 with (today) a tolerable external 33 MHz but a fast internal 66 MHz was (and is) very successful. The features, advantages and disadvantages of the DX2 compared to the DX are discussed in the following sections.

11.2.1 The Clock Frequencies Problem

The permanently rising CPU clock frequencies lead to two major problems. The emission of electromagnetic waves is proportional to the fourth power of the frequency. This means that for a 40 MHz i386 with an 80 MHz external clock, the emission became 80000 times (!) larger than in the original PC with its 4.77 MHz clock. First, this requires an effective shielding of the motherboard against the environment, because otherwise you would not be able to listen to the radio any more! But much more serious are the consequences for the components in the PC or on the motherboard itself. If the resistors and capacities of the elements (and at such frequencies, also, a cable with a length of 2 cm plays an important role) are not harmonized perfectly, then signal reflexions or dampings occur which make reliable operation of the computer impossible. Therefore, with the i486 Intel decided to equalize the internal processor clock and the external clock signal. This is called a 1x-clock. The i386, on the other hand, has been externally supplied with the double processor clock frequency. The i386 then divides the external clock CLK internally by two to generate the processor clock – it is supplied with a 2x-clock. With the 50 MHz i486, even with this technique we are at a critical limit again, and if development is to go on in the same way 100 Mhz will soon be reached with a 1x-clock, too.

A further effect of these high clock rates is that the signal propagation times on the motherboard between, for example, the CPU and various buffers and drivers to the main memory are going to reach the cycle time of the clock signal even with very fast components. Even fast SRAM caches get out of step beyond 50 MHz. Only the highest quality SRAM chip (with prohibitive PC prices) allows access times down to 12 ns, corresponding to a clock frequency of 80 MHz. But these specifications are estimated very optimistically. If one adds the signal propagation delays between the CPU and SRAM via various buffers, drivers and the cache controller, then about 33 MHz to 50 MHz without wait states may be achieved. Not to talk about DRAMs....

11.2.2 The Solution – Internal Frequency Doubling

To avoid the problems indicated above, Intel had a simple but very effective idea: internal frequency doubling. This means that the i486DX2 (the «2» stands for doubling) internally doubles the supplied clock signal – a 33 MHz i486DX2 internally becomes a 66 MHz i486DX. All internal units of the CPU such as, for example, the ALU, decoding unit, floating-point unit, segmentation unit and access to the 8 kbyte cache run at twice the speed. With the 33 MHz i486DX2 this leads to 66 MHz, therefore. Only the bus unit runs from the external clock because the rest of the motherboard has to be protected from the higher clock according to this principle. Thus the i486DX2 (to keep the previous notation) is clocked by a 1/2x-clock.

Doubling the clock frequency inside the processor may be achieved easily, for example, by using a switching element which is triggered by every edge of the external clock signal CLK, independently of whether the edge is rising or falling. The switching element must only be designed in a manner such that it already changes its state in advance of the next edge. For this purpose, a monostable multivibrator can be used. By choosing appropriate resistors and capacitors, the internal frequency doubling can be carried out easily. The generated signal then synchronizes an internal PLL (phase locked loop) circuitry which provides the actual processor clock. Figure 11.4 illustrates this method.

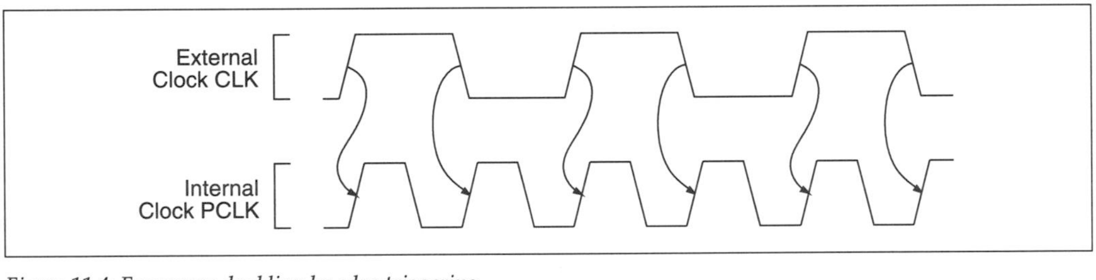

Figure 11.4: Frequency doubling by edge triggering.

Fortunately, the internally doubled clock does not give rise to the same problems as on the motherboard. For this the connections within the processor are much too short, and therefore they cannot function as antennas. With the conductor paths on the motherboard this appears to be completely different, of course.

From the outside the i486DX2 hardly differs from a normal i486DX. Figure 11.5 shows its pin assignment. The DX2 is currently available for internal clock frequencies of 50 and 66 MHz, and the external clock is 25 and 33 MHz, respectively. Thus the clock rates indicated on the chips refer to the *internal* clock frequency.

All i486DX2 chips implement a boundary scan test (see Section 10.8.5). For this, the PGA comprises the four test pins TDI, TDO, TCK and TMS. Additionally, every i486DX2 is prepared so that it can accept a replacement upgrade in the future. Therefore, a connection $\overline{\text{UP}}$ (pin C11) is also present.

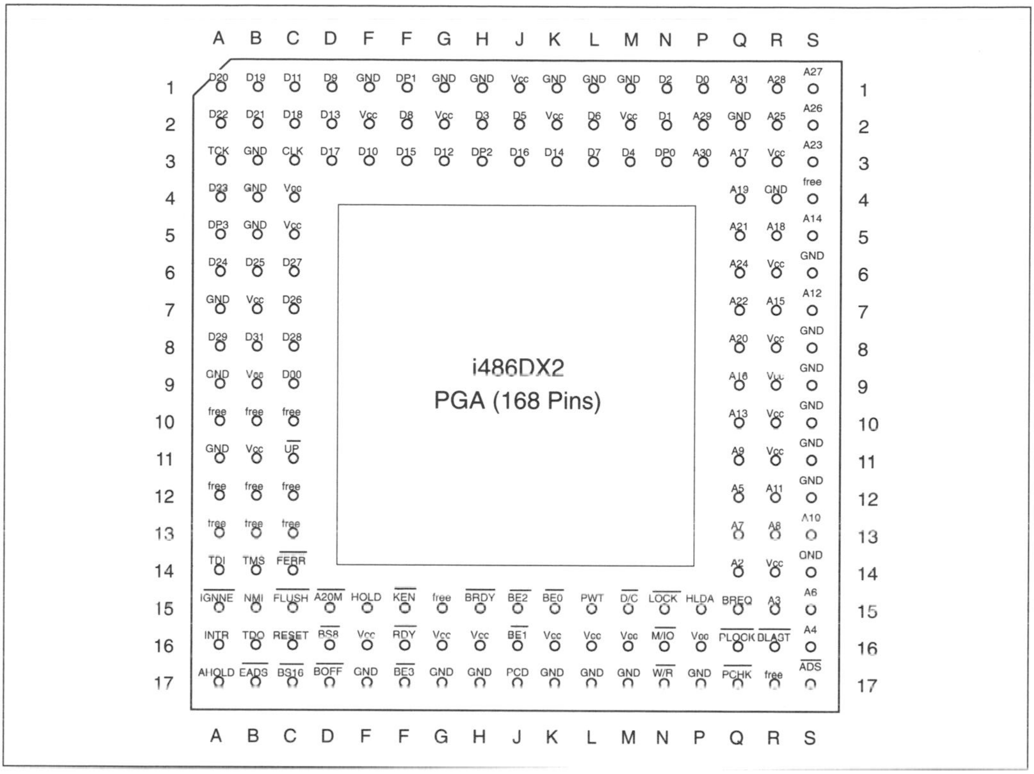

Figure 11.5: i486DX2 pin assignment.

11.2.3 So What's the Gain?

By means of the doubled frequency of the logic units, with the exception of the bus unit all instructions are executed twice as quickly as in an i486DX which is externally clocked with the same frequency – if the data and instructions are available in time. This is fulfilled if the data required is present in a processor register or in the on-chip cache. Every access to an external memory (also to a second-level cache) slows down program execution because of the slower clocked bus unit. The access is further slowed down by the large access time if the DRAM main memory is involved. On the other hand, programs with many iteration steps such as, for example, certain mathematical applications which frequently access a small data and code area, make full use of the doubled processor clock. The 50 MHz i486DX CPU (with full external 50 MHz) carries out an access to the fast second-level cache, for example, for line fills of the internal cache significantly faster than the 50 MHz i486DX2 processor (with external 25 MHz). But for an access to main memory with the slow DRAM chips, it makes virtually no difference whether the processor is running with external 25 or 50 MHz. The bottleneck is located at the DRAM chips, and a «real» 50 MHz i486DX then only inserts more wait cycles.

Thus the internal frequency doubling has some major advantages. For example, it is possible to equip an existing and well-operating 33 MHz board with an i486DX2 CPU. The performance of the PC is thus enhanced significantly without any change of motherboard. This leads directly to the overdrives and the upgrade concept. Moreover, the internal frequency doubling will enable even higher frequencies in future. Instead of the 50 MHz i486DX CPU a (future) 100 MHz i486DX2 may be employed. The required motherboard can be taken over from the 50 MHz i486DX without any alterations. Another possibility is, for example, to triple the internal clock. The DX4 and IBM's Blue Lightning are doing that, reaching 100 MHz. Thus, the internal instruction execution in the single i486 pipeline is nearly as fast as that in the two parallel Pentium pipelines (because not all instructions can be paired and executed in parallel). But the Pentium shows the big advantages of an external 64-bit data bus, a more powerful burst cycle, etc. so that its performance is, nevertheless, higher.

11.2.4 Clock Statements

As already mentioned, the clock statements on the processor chips always refer to the internal processor clock rate. At this time, 50 MHz i486DX and 50 MHz i486DX2 models are available on the market. Because of the double external clock rate, the DX version is somewhat faster than its DX2 counterpart. Therefore, always ask whether a DX or DX2 processor is installed. It gets even more complicated because of the huge number of i386 clones which are coming onto the market now. Remember that Cyrix' 486DLC is not a real i486. To clarify the situation, always ask for detailed and correct information from your dealer, or consult the accompanying manual.

11.2.5 Upgrading and Overdrives

As already mentioned, the i487SX was Intel's first upgrade and referred to the i486SX. Starting with the i486DX2 CPU, Intel is continuing to upgrade as a new strategy for performance enhancement. Up to the i386, the only possibility for increasing processing power was to install an additional coprocessor. But this chip only speeds up floating-point operations; increasing the clock frequency was impossible. This has changed completely with the DX2. The so-called *overdrives* consist of an i486DX2 with the same external clock frequency as the previous processor (unlike the usual DX2 CPUs, the overdrives do not implement a boundary scan test), but by means of internal frequency doubling the processor's performance increases by 100% without the need to alter anything on the motherboard. The overdrives are inserted into an upgrade socket similar to a coprocessor but, unlike the coprocessor, they replace the previous CPU completely. Thus the CPU is disabled, and waits for its reactivation *ad infinitum*. Consequently, Intel has defined an upgrade socket for the upgrade processors. Figure 11.6 shows its layout.

Note that Figure 11.6 shows the top view of the socket, in the same way as it is seen on the motherboard. The pin assignment of the processors, on the other hand, always refers to a «pin look», that is, a view from below.

The overdrives are available in two basic forms, dependent on whether an upgrade socket is present or not. For an i486SX or i486DX with an upgrade socket there are overdrives based on the i486DX2 in a 169-pin PGA. Its pin layout corresponds to that of the i487SX. The 169th pin,

D4, serves for coding to avoid an erroneous insertion of the chip. Thus, for the upgrading you only need to insert the overdrive into the socket. These 169-pin overdrives come with 20 MHz, 25 MHz and 33 MHz (external), where the 20 MHz version supports both the 16 MHz and 20 MHz i486SX or i486DX. Of course, you may use the i487SX upgrade. Here only the coprocessor is provided additionally, but the processor clock is not increased, unlike the overdrives.

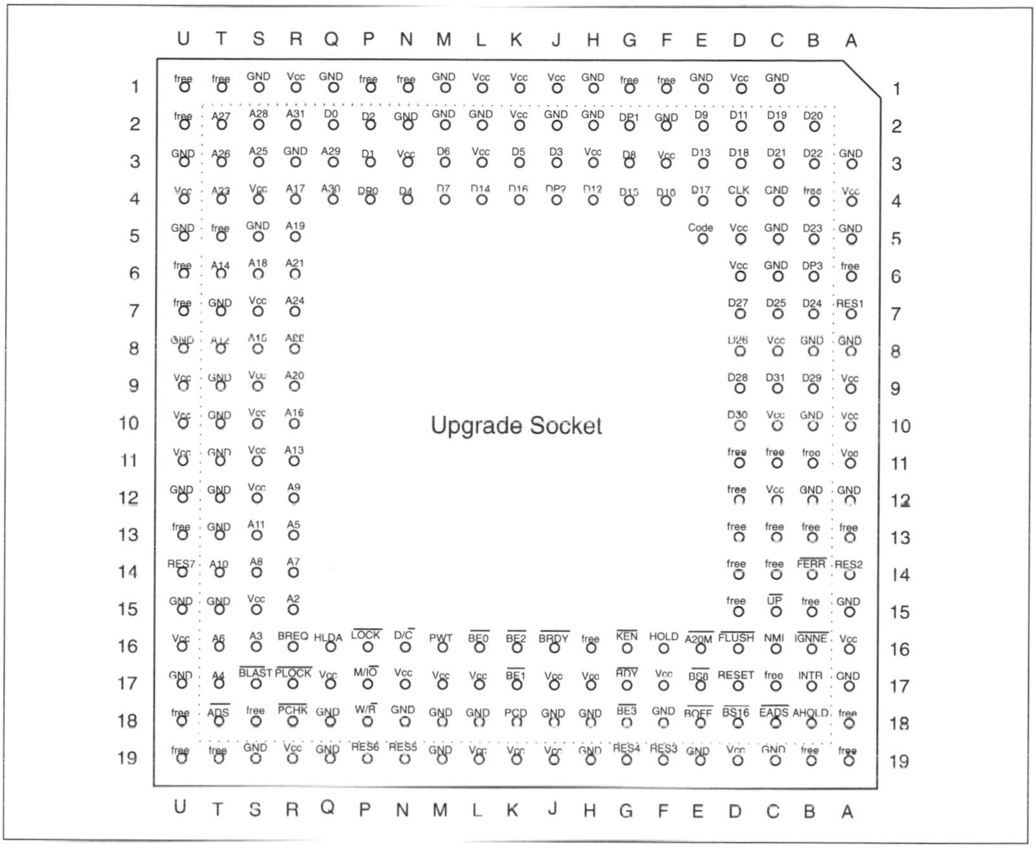

Figure 11.6: Upgrade socket layout.

But you can also upgrade an i486DX system without an upgrade socket by an overdrive. However, for that it is necessary to remove the old CPU and to replace it by a 168-pin PGA overdrive. In principle, this overdrive is nothing more than a usual i496DX2 with an i486DX pinout, i.e. this i486DX2 has neither pins for the boundary scan test nor a $\overline{\text{UP}}$ (moreover, $\overline{\text{UP}}$ is not necessary as the old CPU has to be removed). This overdrive comes with 25 MHz and 33 MHz (external).

It is not only the older i486DX CPUs that can be replaced by an internally higher clocked i486DX2, but also the i486DX2 processors themselves. Possible upgrades are, for example, the Pentium overdrive. For that purpose the upgrade socket has four pin rows on all four sides. The outer row is reserved for the additional terminals of an overdrive on the base of the Pentium, for example, for implementing a write-back cache and inquiry cycles according to the MESI protocol. Besides some connections for the supply voltage Vcc and ground GND, seven terminals RES1 to RES7 are formed. The socket contacts for an i486DX2 overdrive are included in Figure 11.6 within a broken line. Usually, the i486SX and i486DX systems (not DX2) are shipped with an upgrade socket which includes only the inner three pin rows.

Also, untrained users should be able to carry out upgrading, hence the socket has an encoding mechanism which prevents incorrect insertion of the upgrade processor (contact holes A1, A2 and B1 are missing), thus it is impossible to insert an upgrade incorrectly. Contact hole E5 *(encoding)* is present for compatibility with the i487SX, but newer upgrades no longer use it. As an end-user product, the overdrives (except the 20 MHz model) are already provided with a heat sink, so the user no longer needs to take account of the cooling as well as the correct mounting of such a heat sink.

Processor	**Model**	**DH**	**DL**
i486SX	A0	04h	20h
i486SX	B0	04h	22h
i486SX	cA0	04h	27h
i486SX	cB0	04h	28h
i487SX	A0	04h	20h
i487SX	B0	04h	21h
i486DX	B3	04h	01h
i486DX	B4	04h	01h
i486DX	B5	04h	01h
i486DX	B6	04h	01h
i486DX	C0	04h	02h
i486DX	C1	04h	03h
i486DX	D0	04h	04h
i486DX	cA2	04h	10h
i486DX	cA3	04h	10h
i486DX	cB0	04h	11h
i486DX	cB1	04h	11h
overdrive for SX/DX	A2	04h	32h
overdrive for SX/DX	B1	04h	33h
i486DX2	A	04h	32h
i486DX2	B	04h	33h
i486DX4	A	04h	80h
overdrive for DX2		15h	30h–3fh

Table 11.2: i486 identification codes

Another problem is the considerable force required to insert the many upgrade or overdrive pins into a socket. The contact holes must fasten securely on the processor pins to ensure a good contact, and to avoid corrosion by the penetration of humidity or oxygen. The force required may reach 500–800N (110 to 180 lbs). Additional to the problem of generating such forces (a person with less than 1700 lbs might have some problems) there is the danger of damaging the chip or board. Thus, the upgrade socket is usually implemented as a zero insertion force (ZIF) socket to reduce the insertion force to zero. Once the chip has been installed you can turn a clamp to lock the socket and ensure a good contact to the pins.

Because all i486DX2 processors are prepared for upgrading, they have a connection $\overline{UP}$ (upgrade present, pin C11). If an upgrade is present it applies a low-level signal to the $\overline{UP}$ connection of the previous CPU to indicate that an upgrade processor is now taking over the data processing. The i486DX2 then enters power-down mode, cuts off all its outputs from the bus, and deactivates the internal function units: the power consumption thus reduces by 90%.

To complete the picture I shall list the various identification codes which are passed by the i486DX/SX, i487SX and overdrives in the DX register after a reset. You will find them in table 11.2. The BIOS (or a self-made routine) is then able to determine the processor type.

11.3 Low-power Versions of i486DX/SX

Not even Intel could avoid the trend towards microprocessors with a lower power consumption. The corresponding i386 clones from AMD were, in this respect, very successful, especially when installed in Notebooks. Intel has now also developed power saving i486DX and i486SX processors which, contrary to the AMD clones, continue to use 5 V in place of the usual 3.3 V for low-power versions. At full operating frequency, these processors continue to have the same power consumption. However, contrary to conventional i486DX/SXs, the clock frequency can be dynamically reduced, that is, without predetermined graduations at an arbitrary rate, to 2 MHz. The i486 then requires only 150 mA instead of 700 mA (i486DX–25 Mhz). In addition, the low-power versions are more tolerant with respect to fluctuations in the supply voltage, as is the case when the battery requires recharging; Vcc can vary from 5 V by up to 10% (normally ±5%). The power saving reduction of CLK thus ensures that the low-power versions are again supplied with a 2x-clock cycle (as in the i386 and 80286), that is, the external clock frequency is twice as high as the internal processor clock speed. The low-power i486DX comes with a processor clock speed of 25 MHz (corresponding to an external speed of 50 MHz). The low-power i486SX can have 16 MHz, 20 MHz or 25 MHz (corresponding to 32 MHz, 40 MHz or 50 MHz, respectively).

The low-power 486DX is, as usual, delivered in a 168 pin PGA, and the low-power 486SX is delivered in a 168 pin PGA or a 196 pin PQFP. The internal layout and interface schematic are identical to the other i486DX and i486SX variants, with the exception of the external 2x-clock speed (only the PQFP version of the low-power i486SX also offers a boundary scan test). Only the CLK pin (C3 in the i486DX, C3 in the i486SX/PGA and 123 in the i486SX/PQFP, respectively) is supplied with the 2x-clock speed, and so here is identified as the CLK2 pin. In addition, the CLKSEL pin is also provided, which activates the 2x-clock speed through a short pulse when the computer is switched on. Subsequently, CLKSEL must be kept at a low level. CLKSEL is used mainly for defining the phase of CLK2 during power-up, as all bus cycles are relative to the first two CLK2 cycles of a processor clock cycle. Without the exact phase definition through CLKSEL, external components could otherwise not determine the phase. For the low-power versions, CLKSEL is assigned to pin A3 (i486DX), A3 (i486SX/PGA) and 127 (i486SX/PQFP), respectively. Note that A3 in the conventional i486DX–50 MHz is used by TCK for the boundary scan test. In addition, a system based on a low-power i486DX/SX cannot operate in conjunction with an overdrive DX2 (should *low-power* refer not only to the power consumption, but also to the calculating performance?).

The only possibility for increasing the performance is through the use of the i487SX. It can operate with either a 1x- or a 2x-clock speed (see Section 11.1.3). The clock speed can be selected. For combination with a low-power i486SX, the CLKSEL connection (pin A3) of the i487SX must be sent an impulse with a high level during power-up. The i487SX then divides the external clock frequency by two to produce the internal processor clock speed.

You will perhaps be asking yourself why the low-power versions have gone back to a 2x-clock speed, even though higher clock frequencies mostly mean a higher power consumption. The reason for this is that it is simpler to dynamically change the clock frequency within a wide range than to complicate matters by electronically switching the processor (for example, the register). Every microprocessor contains a complicated internal clock signal generator, which produces multiple internal control signals with differing phases and frequencies for the individual components from the clock signal supplied (for example, a source register must be signalled earlier than a target register). This means that the clock signal generator must have a very exact internal definition, because only a single cycle or a maximum of two flanks (rising/falling) are available. With a 2x-clock speed, two cycles or four flanks are now available, the definition is simpler and, therefore, so is the scalability of the operating frequency. Note, however, that the low-power versions from Intel only achieve a power saving with a lower clock frequency, that is, in wait mode. When the processor is operating, it requires exactly the same amount of power as the conventional model. The 3.3 V examples, on the other hand, also save power in full operation because the power consumption *P* of a CMOS chip is approximately proportional to the square of the supply voltage *U*, and is proportional to the clock frequency (simply a result of the Ohms Law $U=R*I$ and so $P=U^2/R$ if you consider the processor as a resistor *R*).

In addition to the previously described low-power versions of the i486DX and i486SX, which operate with 5 V and only reduce their power consumption at a reduced clock frequency, there is now also a 3.3 V version of the i486SX. It operates at 16 MHz, 20 MHz or 25 MHz, and requires a maximum current of 340 mA at 25 MHz – almost 50% less (in comparison, the normal i486SX–25 MHz uses 630 mA). The 3.3 V i486SX is only delivered in a 196 pin PQFP, and is fully pin and function compatible with the normal i486SX.

11.4 The i486DX4

After IBM had paraded its clock tripled Blue Lightning and, similarly, AMD had caught up the Intel 486s with its Am486DX2-66, something was expected from Intel to fill the performance gap between the Am486DX/2 or i486DX2 and the Pentium. The high speed i486, originally known in the technical press as the DX3, was finally released to the general public in March 1994. Its external clock speed can be selected as either double or triple and, in addition, it can operate with a 2½-times clock speed. The main differences between the i486DX4 and its i486 predecessors are listed below:

- 25 MHz, 33 MHz or 50 MHz external clock speed and 75 MHz, 83 MHz or 100 MHz internal,
- 80 Mbyte/s, 106 Mbyte/s or 160 Mbyte/s burst bus,
- 4-way set-associative 16 kbyte on-chip cache with a write-through strategy,

- BiCMOS technology for high clock speeds and low power consumption,
- 3 W to 5 W power consumption due to the 3.3 V operating voltage,
- an improved hardware integer multiplier with integer multiplications increased by a factor of 5.

The main difference to existing i486 models is the new PLL oscillator on the i486DX4 chip. It can selectively increase the external clock frequency by two, two and a half or three times, that is, the i486DX4 operates with a 1/2x, 2/5x or 1/3x clock speed, respectively. This processor has a new system management mode similar to that known from the Pentium (see Section 12.5). In addition, through two steps – the stop clock mode and switching off external clock signals – the power consumption can be considerably reduced in a wait condition (from 1450 mA at 100 MHz, through 100 mA to approximately 1 mA). Furthermore, a JTAG boundary scan test is implemented. The on-chip cache of the i486DX4, with its 16 kbyte storage capacity, is twice as large as those of the previous i486s, but the organizational structure is unchanged. Compared to that in the i486DX and i486DX2, the improved integer multiplier increases the most frequently occurring integer multiplications by an additional factor of 5. All other functions are identical to those of the previous i486 versions.

11.4.1 Pin Connections

The i486DX4 is delivered with two different housing variations: in a pin grid array with 168 pins and, additionally, in a Surface-mounted Quad Flat Package (SQFP) with 208 pins. You can see the layout of the PGA in Figure 11.7.

In addition to the previously known pins of the i486DX, the i486DX4 contains a few additional pins which are used for controlling the new functions. I would briefly like to detail them in the following section. The other pins are already known from the i486DX/SX or i486DX2.

CLKMUL (I)
Pin R17

The signal sent to the clock multiplier pin during a reset sets the multiplication rate of the internal PLL oscillator as compared to the external clock CLK. If CLKMUL is at a low level, then the PLL oscillator doubles the external clock (the i486DX4 operates with a ½ clock speed); if, on the other hand, CLKMUL is at a high level or the pin is floating, then CLK is tripled (the i486DX4 operates with a $^1/_3$ clock speed). Finally, CLKMUL can also be connected with BREQ; it then runs internally with 2½ times the external clock speed and the i486DX4 operates with a $^2/_5$ clock speed.

SRESET (I)
Pin C10

If the soft reset pin is sent a signal with a high level, the i486DX4 carries out an internal initialisation (reset). Contrary to the activation of RESET (pin C16), the SMBASE register for system management mode is not reset.

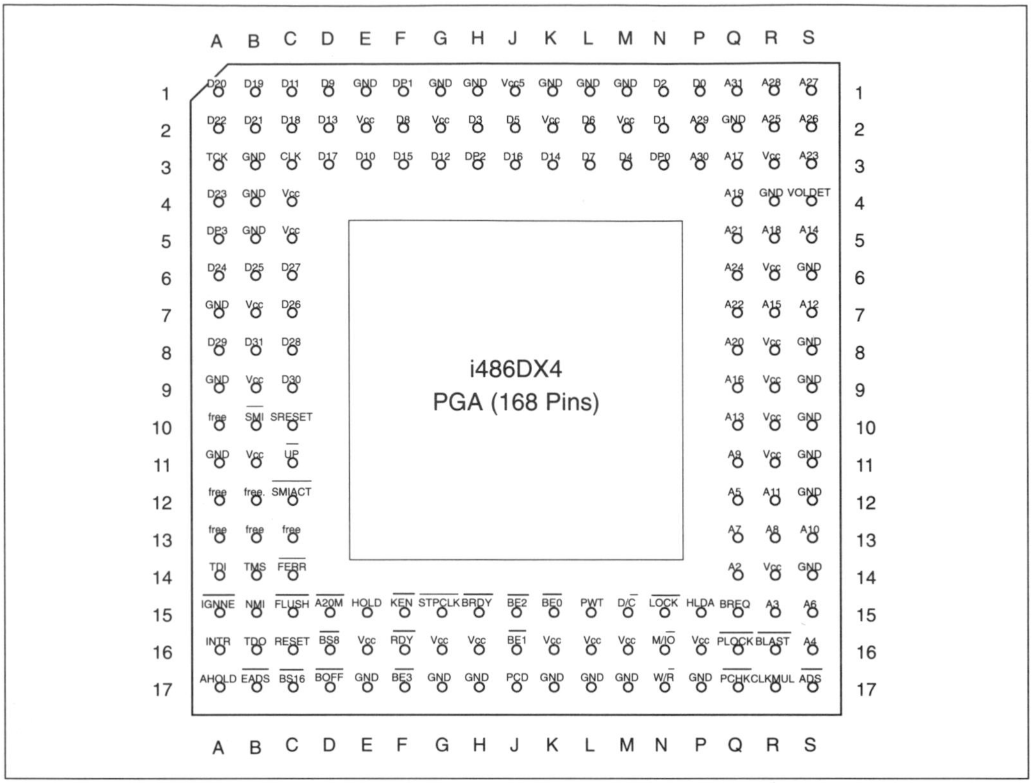

Figure 11.7: i486DX4 pinout.

$\overline{\text{STPCLK}}$ (I)
Pin G15

If the stop clock input pin receives a signal with a high level, the i486DX4 then stops its PLL oscillator, that is, the internal circuits are no longer clocked. $\overline{\text{STPCLK}}$ is implemented as an interrupt with the lowest priority. Before the oscillator is stopped, the processor firstly completes all pending instructions. Finally, it sends out a stop grant special cycle on the bus: $M/\overline{IO}=D/\overline{C}=0$, $W/\overline{R}=1$, A31–A5 = A3–A2 = 0, A4 = 1, $\overline{BE3}$–$\overline{BE0}$ = 1011b.

VOLDET (O)
Pin S4

Through the voltage detect signal at this pin, the external system logic can differentiate between a i486DX4 processor operating with 3.3 V and a 5 V i486DX: a low VOLDET signal indicates a 3.3 V i486DX4. This pin connection is not included in the SQFP version of the i486DX4.

n.c.
Pins A10, A12–A13, B12–B13

These pins are identified as *not connected* and are internally free; however, they are reserved by Intel for future versions of the i486DX4 CPU.

Vcc5 (I)
Pin J1

The 5 V reference voltage pin is supplied with a 5V reference signal if signals with more than 3.3 V are sent from the system logic to one or more i486DX4 pins. If the board is provided with true 3.3 V logic, then Vcc5 is held at 3.3 V.

$\overline{\text{SMI}}$, $\overline{\text{SMIACT}}$ (I, O)
Pins B10, C12

The two system management interrupt and system management interrupt active pins form the interface for the System Management Mode (SMM). It was implemented in the Pentium first and transferred to the i486DX4 later. You will find a more thorough explanation of the SMM in Section 12.5.

11.4.2 New Flags, Control Registers and Extensions to the Virtual 8086 Mode

The EFlag register in the i486DX4 has been extended by three additional flags, and so now contains the EFlag structure of the Pentium. The new flags reflect the extensions to virtual 8086 mode and the identification of the CPU type. You can see the EFlags in Figure 11.8. The three new flags are shown and have the same function as in the Pentium. For this, refer to Section 12.3.1.

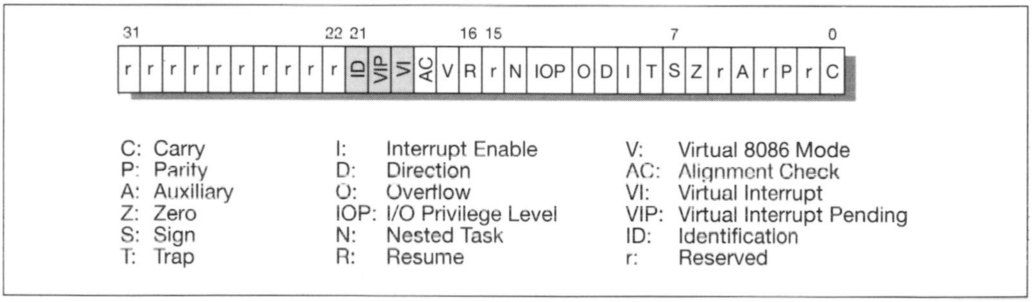

Figure 11.8: New flags of the i486DX4.

The virtual interrupt flag *VI* is a virtual copy of IE for sending out interrupts in virtual 8086 mode. In a similar way, the virtual interrupt pending flag *VIP* also supports tasks in virtual 8086 mode, to make a virtual IE flag available. Both flags should increase the speed of interrupt execution in virtual 8086 mode. Consequently, the i486DX4 implements the same extensions to virtual 8086 mode as in the Pentium. You will find the corresponding details in Section 12.3.5. As a final innovation, an identification flag *ID* is provided in the EFlag register, which indicates whether the processor supports the CPUID instruction for its identification. If you can set and reset the ID flag, then CPUID is correctly executed, and supplies information concerning the type and capabilities of the processor.

The i486DX4 has been extended by control register CR4, which controls activation of the virtual flags. The four control registers CR0–CR3 remain unchanged compared to those in the conventional i486. You can see the structure of the new control register CR4 in Figure 11.9.

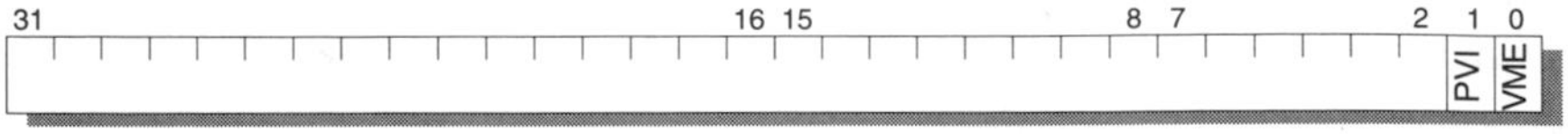

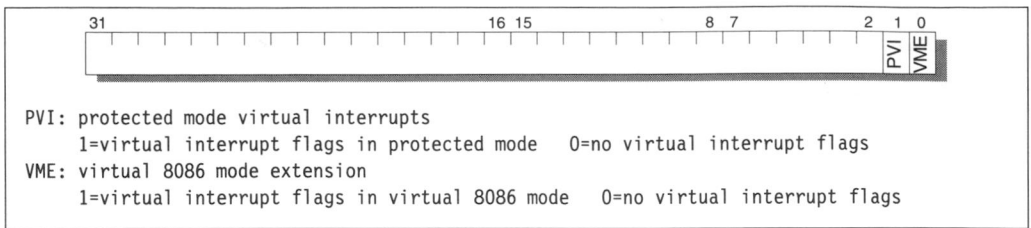

```
PVI: protected mode virtual interrupts
     1=virtual interrupt flags in protected mode    0=no virtual interrupt flags
VME: virtual 8086 mode extension
     1=virtual interrupt flags in virtual 8086 mode    0=no virtual interrupt flags
```

Figure 11.9: Control register CR4.

A set virtual 8086 mode extension bit *VME* activates the supporting of virtual interrupt flags in virtual 8086 mode. In this way, the interrupts are performed quicker to increase the performance in virtual 8086 mode. The virtual 8086 monitor must then no longer be called, and all of the associated task switches (Figure 3.25) are unnecessary. The protected mode virtual interrupt bit *PVI* has a similar task in protected mode to the VME bit in virtual 8086 mode, that is, a set PVI bit activates the supporting of virtual interrupt flags in protected mode. In this way, programs designed for execution with CPL=0 can, under certain circumstances, also be performed with CPL=3.

11.4.3 i486DX4 Identification with CPUID

Intel included a long-standing request from programmers in the Pentium, namely the wish for a simple method of identifying the CPU, and this possibility is now also implemented in the i486DX4. The new *CPUID* instruction from the Pentium removes this identification problem in only a few CLK clock cycles, even a long time after the boot sequence where the CPU type is determined by the BIOS.

Before you can execute the CPUID instruction, you must first determine whether the CPU supports this instruction. If not, the processor will send out an *invalid opcode* exception. For this reason, Intel has provided the *ID* flag in the EFlag register. If you can set and reset the ID flag, then the installed processor supports the CPUID instruction.

In addition to identification of the i486DX4, CPUID also delivers information about which special functions are supported. To perform CPU identification, you must first load the value 0 into the EAX register and then issue the CPUID instruction. The processor will then send back the highest identification level in EAX which it supports (currently level 1). The three registers EBX, ECX and EDX, in that sequence, contain a 12-byte identification in ASCII format: "GenuineIntel". If you then load the EAX register with the value 01h and issue the CPUID instruction again, the i486DX4 returns an identification value to the EAX register. The EDX register contains additional information concerning which special functions are supported. In Table 11.3 you will find the call and returned values of CPUID.

Register	Call value	Returned value
EAX	00h	01h (max. identification level)
EBX		"Genu"
ECX		"inel"
EDX		"ntel"
EAX	01h	Identification value1)
EBX		Reserved (=0000h)
ECX		Reserved (=0000h)
EDX		Feature Flags2)

1)

Bits 31–16: Reserved (= 00h)
Bits 15–12: 0000b
Bits 11–8: Processor family(0100b = 04h for i486DX)
Bits 7–4: Model number (1000b = 08h for DX4)
Bits 3–0: Version

2)

Bits 31–2: Reserved (= 0000h)
Bit 1: Implemented special functions
Bit 0: On-chip floating-point unit (1 = On-chip FPU, 0 – no on-chip FPU)

Table 11.3: Call and return values of CPUID

When CPUID is called with an EAX parameter greater than 1, the i486DX4 returns the value 0000h to each of the four registers EAX, EBX, ECX and EDX.

11.4.4 Power Saving Features

There are a number of features implemented in the i486DX4 for saving power. This begins with the supply voltage of only 3.3 V compared to the standard 5 V. Because the power consumption is proportional to the square of the supply voltage, the reduction to 3.3 V alone gives a power saving of approximately 50%. Other power saving functions (also useful for other purposes) include system management mode and the two-stepped variable processor clock speed.

System Management Mode

The system management mode of the i486DX4 is identical to that of the Pentium. Refer to Section 12.5 for further information concerning SMM.

Stop Clock Mode

For installation in portable Notebooks or green PCs, the switching off or slowing down of the processor clock signal offers a further power saving possibility. In this way, a 3.3 V i486DX4 requires no more power than a conventional i486DX. Switching off the processor clock signal is achieved in two steps: stop clock mode and switching off the external clock signal. The power consumption is considerably reduced in this wait condition (from 1450 mA at 100 MHz through 100 mA to approximately 1 mA). By activation of the stop clock signals $\overline{STPCLK}$, the processor is instructed to complete the instructions currently being performed and to empty its pipelines. Finally, it sends out a *stop grant* special cycle on the bus. The stop grant special cycle is identified by the following signal conditions: M/$\overline{\text{IO}}$=D/$\overline{\text{C}}$=0, W/$\overline{\text{R}}$=1, A31–A5=A3–A2=0, A4=1, $\overline{\text{BE3}}$–$\overline{\text{BE0}}$=1011b. It must be confirmed by the system with either a $\overline{\text{RDY}}$ or a $\overline{\text{BRDY}}$. The PLL oscillator continues to operate; the functions of the internal processor clock signal from the PLL oscillator to the actual processor, however, are blocked. In this way, the power consumption sinks from a typical 1450 mA (at 100 MHz) to 100 mA, that is, 1350 mA are normally used by the processor. $\overline{\text{STPCLK}}$ is implemented as an interrupt, and so only occurs at instruction limits. Thus, there can be a delay of a few clock cycles before the i486DX4 actually reacts to $\overline{\text{STPCLK}}$. In addition, $\overline{\text{STPCLK}}$ contains the lowest priority of all possible interrupts:

Interrupt	Priority
RESET/SRESET	highest
$\overline{\text{FLUSH}}$	|
$\overline{\text{SMI}}$	|
NMI	|
INTR	|
$\overline{\text{STPCLK}}$	lowest

The external system logic can recognize the stop grant special cycle and then also switch off the external clock signal CLK. This is the second stage of stop clock mode, which reduces the power consumption still further by around 99% to approximately 1 mA. In total, the i486DX4 requires less than a thousandth of the normal power in this *stop clock* condition. The processor can be immediately switched back from the stop grant condition to its normal operating condition by a high level $\overline{\text{STPCLK}}$ signal (hence the deactivation of the signal). This is not possible in the stop clock condition. First, the external clock signal CLK must be sent for a minimum of 1 ms to stabilize the PLL oscillator. Only then will the i486DX4 return to the stop grant condition (but without sending out a stop grant special cycle), that is, the PLL oscillator delivers a stable processor clock signal, but its output remains blocked. Therefore, by deactivating $\overline{\text{STPCLK}}$, the i486DX4 can be returned to its normal operating condition quickly.

11.4.5 i486DX4 JTAG Boundary Scan Test

The i486DX4 includes the previously described JTAG boundary scan test (see Section 10.8.5). For this reason, I shall only detail the control cells (see Table 11.4) and the scan path.

Control cell	**Pin groups**
ABUSCTL	A31–A2
WRCTL	D31–D0, DP3–DP0
BUSCTL	$\overline{\text{ADS}}$, $\overline{\text{BLAST}}$, $\overline{\text{PLOCK}}$, $\overline{\text{LOCK}}$, W/$\overline{\text{R}}$, $\overline{\text{BE3}}$–$\overline{\text{BE0}}$, M/$\overline{\text{IO}}$, D/$\overline{\text{C}}$, PWT, PCD
MISCCTL	$\overline{\text{PCHK}}$, HLDA, BREQ, $\overline{\text{FERR}}$

Table 11.4: JTAG control cells and corresponding pin groups for the i486DX4

The boundary scan path comprising of the control cells xxxCTL is performed in the following sequence:

TDI→WRCTL→ABUSCTL→BUSCTL→MISCCTL→$\overline{ADS}$→$\overline{BLAST}$→$\overline{PLOCK}$→$\overline{LOCK}$→$\overline{PCHK}$→$\overline{BRDY}$→$\overline{BOFF}$→$\overline{BS16}$→$\overline{BS8}$→
CLKMUL→$\overline{RDY}$→$\overline{KEN}$→HOLD→AHOLD→CLK→HLDA→W/$\overline{R}$→BREQ→$\overline{BE0}$→$\overline{BE1}$→$\overline{BE2}$→$\overline{BE3}$→M/$\overline{IO}$→D/$\overline{C}$→PWT→PCD→$\overline{EADS}$→
$\overline{A20M}$→RESET→$\overline{FLUSH}$→INTR→NMI→SRESET→$\overline{SMIACT}$→$\overline{SMI}$→$\overline{FERR}$→$\overline{IGNNE}$→$\overline{STPCLK}$→D31→D30→D29→D28→D27→
D26→D25→D24→DP3→D23→D22→D21→D20→D19→D18→D17→D16→DP2→D15→D14→D13→D12→D11→D10→D9→
D8→DP1→D7→D6→D5→D4→D3→D2→D1→D0→DP0→A31→A30→A29→A28→A27→A26→A25→A24→A23→A22→A21→
A20→A19→A18→A17→A16→A15→A14→A13→A12→A11→A10→A9→A8→A7→A6→UP→A5→A4→A3→A2→TDO

After a self-test, which is initiated by the JTAG instruction RUNBIST, the ID code register stores the 32-bit identification information for the chip in question. In the case of the i486DX4, it has the following structure: bit 0=1, bit 1...11=manufacturer (Intel=09h), bit 12...27=part number (0427h; bit 12..16=model: 01000b, bit 17..20=family: 0100b, bit 21..26=architecture: 000001b, bit 27=voltage: 0=5 V, 1=3 V), bit 28...31=version (xxh). The 32-bit i486DX4 ID code is thus x8288013h.

11.5 The SL Enhanced i486

The all round requirement for power saving CPUs for both portable and stationary Personal Computers has forced Intel into developing an especially low-power version of the 486: the SL enhanced i486. Here, contrary to the i386SL, SL does not mean that an i486 processor has been assembled together with other parts (such as an ISA bus and a DRAM controller) to form a highly integrated component. The i486SL (as abbreviated) instead represents a conventional i486DX or i486SX with all of its usual features such as an 8 kbyte on-chip cache, but in addition it has a number of power saving features. The SL enhanced i486 comes in the following variations:

- SL enhanced i486DX with 1x-clock speed for 3.3 V (33 MHz) and 5 V (33 MHz, 50 MHz),
- SL enhanced i486DX2 with ½x-clock speed for 3.3 V (40 MHz) and 5 V (50 MHz, 66 MHz),
- SL Enhanced i486SX with 1x-clock speed for 3.3 V and 5 V (25 MHz, 33 MHz),
- SL Enhanced i486DX with 2x-clock speed for 3.3 V and 5 V (33 MHz),
- SL Enhanced i486SX with 2x-clock speed for 3.3 V and 5 V (25 MHz, 33 MHz).

All versions can be obtained as either 3.3 V or 5 V. The 3.3 V variants have an approximately 50% lower power consumption, but only the 5 V CPUs achieve the highest clock frequencies. All versions are available in a 196 pin PQFP, a 168 pin PGA or a 208 pin SQFP. The following section details the different characteristics of the SL variants.

11.5.1 SL Enhanced i486DX with 1x-clock

Contrary to the normal i486DX, the SL Enhanced i486DX contains a $\overline{STPCLK}$ input (PQFP: pin 75, PGA: pin G15, SQFP: pin 73) to activate the *stop grant mode* and *stop clock mode*, as known from the i486DX4. Here, I would like to explain these two modes only briefly; you will find more details in Section 11.4.4. By the activation of the stop clock signal $\overline{STPCLK}$, the processor is instructed to complete the current instructions and to empty its pipelines. A stop grant special cycle is then sent on the bus (M/$\overline{IO}$=D/$\overline{C}$=0, W/$\overline{R}$=1, A31–A5=A3–A2=0, A4=1, $\overline{BE3}$–$\overline{BE0}$=1011b). In a stop grant condition, the PLL oscillator continues to operate, but the output of the internal processor clock signal from the PLL oscillator is blocked and the power consumption sinks to between 20 and 55 mA. The external system logic can recognize the stop grant special cycle and then also switch off the external clock signal CLK. This is the stop clock condition, and the power consumption sinks again to between 100 and 200 μA.

Furthermore, an *auto halt power-down mode* is implemented: after execution of a HALT instruction, the i486SL automatically enters this mode and then only uses between 20 and 55 mA, exactly the same as in the stop grant mode.

Finally, *System Management Mode* (*SMM*) is implemented. After activation of $\overline{\text{SMI}}$, the i486SL stores a register dump in SMM RAM. The interface to SMM is formed by the two new pins $\overline{\text{SMI}}$ (PQFP: pin 85, PGA: pin B10, SQFP: pin 65) and $\overline{\text{SMIACT}}$ (PQFP: pin 92, PGA: pin B10, SQFP: pin 59) for all i486SLs.

Similar to the i486DX4, all i486SLs also include a *soft reset* through activation of the SRESET input (PQFP: pin 94, PGA: pin C10, SQFP: pin 58). In this way, the i486SL internally performs an initialization (reset). Contrary to the activation of RESET, the SMBASE register for system management mode is not reset.

In all other functions, the SL Enhanced i486DX with a 1x-clock speed is identical to the conventional i486DX. In particular, it is supplied with a 1x-clock signal, that is, the external clock frequency is identical to the processor clock speed.

11.5.2 SL Enhanced i486DX2 with 1/2x-clock

The SL Enhanced i486DX2 includes the same power saving features as the SL Enhanced i486DX, thus in stop grant, stop clock, auto halt power-down and system management modes, a soft reset is also possible. In addition, an *auto idle power-down mode* is also available. If the CPU is waiting for $\overline{\text{RDY}}$ or $\overline{\text{BRDY}}$ from the addressed memory or an I/O subsystem, it halves the internal clock frequency, making it the same as the external CLK clock frequency. This is possible because the bus interface always runs with CLK and not PCLK=2*CLK. In this way, 50% of the power is saved. Intel has stated that in a typical example with an average taken over a long period of time, a total power saving of 10% is likely.

In all other functions, the SL Enhanced i486DX2 is compatible with the conventional i486DX2. In particular, it is supplied with a ½x-clock signal, that is, the processor internally doubles the external clock frequency, to feed the processor kernel.

11.5.3 SL Enhanced i486SX with 1x-clock

Here little more needs to be said, apart from that the SL Enhanced i486SX with 1x-clock speed implements the same power saving features as the SL Enhanced i486DX, thus stop grant, stop clock, auto halt power-down and system management modes, and also a soft reset, are available. The auto idle power-down mode is, of course, unavailable. In all other functions, the SL Enhanced i486SX (as expected) is compatible with the conventional i486SX. In particular, it is supplied with a 1x-clock signal, that is, the processor operates internally with the same frequency as that externally supplied.

11.5.4 SL Enhanced i486DX with 2x-clock

The SL Enhanced i486DX2 with a 2x-clock speed is supplied with an external CLK2 clock signal which has a frequency double that of the internal processor clock speed; the processor operates in a similar way to the low-power versions examined in Section 11.3. However, no CLKSEL pin (low-power i486SX/DX: PQFP pin 127) is provided. The internal switching of the clock signal is not necessary due to the 2x external clock speed. In addition, the clock frequency can be dynamically varied between 2 MHz and the maximum operating frequency without having to remove the PLL oscillator from the cycle. Only if CLK2 is to be completely switched off (thus 0 MHz supplied) is it necessary to activate $\overline{\text{STPCLK}}$. The other functions such as stop grant, stop clock, auto halt power-down and system management mode are identical to those in the SL Enhanced i486DX with a 1x-clock speed. This also applies to the usual i486DX features such as the on-chip cache and instruction pipelining.

11.5.5 SL Enhanced i486SX with 2x-clock

Very briefly, the SL Enhanced i486SX with 2x-clock speed is an SL Enhanced i486SX which operates with an external CLK2 clock signal whose frequency is twice that of the internal processor clock speed. This processor also operates similar to the low-power versions from Section 11.3, where no CLKSEL pin is available. The clock frequency can be dynamically varied between 2 MHz and the maximum operating frequency. Here, only if CLK2 should be completely switched off (thus 0 MHz supplied) is it necessary to activate $\overline{\text{STPCLK}}$. The other functions such as stop grant, stop clock, auto halt power-down and system management mode are identical to those in the SL Enhanced i486SX with a 1x-clock speed.

11.5.6 i486SL Identification with CPUID

In addition to the i486DX4 and the Pentium, the SL Enhanced i486 chip can also identify the CPU using the CPUID instruction. Before initiating the CPUID instruction you must first determine whether the CPU actually supports this instruction. Otherwise, the processor will issue an *invalid opcode* exception. For this reason, Intel has included in the EFlag register the same *ID* flag known from the i486DX4 (bit 21 in the EFlag register, see Figure 11.8). If you can set and reset the ID flag, then the installed processor supports the CPUID instruction.

To perform CPU identification, you must first load the value 0 into the EAX register and then initiate the CPUID instruction. The i486SL processor then sends back to EAX the highest identification level that it supports (currently level 1). The three registers EBX, ECX and EDX, in that sequence, contain a 12-byte identification in ASCII format: «GenuineIntel». If you then load the value 01h into EAX and repeat the CPUID instruction, the i486SL sends back an identification value to the EAX register. The register EDX contains additional information concerning which special functions are supported. In Table 11.5 you will find the call and returned values from CPUID.

Register	Call value	Returned value
EAX	00h	01h (max. identification level)
EBX		"Genu"
ECX		"inel"
EDX		"ntel"
EAX	01h	Identification value[1)]
EBX		Reserved (=0000h)
ECX		Reserved (=0000h)
EDX		Feature Flags[2)]

1)
Bits 31–16: Reserved (= 00h)
Bits 15–12: 0000b
Bits 11–8: Processor family (0100b = 04h for i486)
Bits 7–4: Model number (0001b = 01h for DX, 0010b = 02h for SX, 0011b = 03h for DX2)
Bits 3–0: Version

2)
Bits 31–2: Reserved (= 0000h)
Bit 1: Implemented special functions
Bit 0: On-chip floating-point unit (1 = On-chip FPU , 0 = no on-chip FPU)

Table 11.5: Call and return values of CPUID

For a CPUID call with an EAX parameter greater than 1, the i486SL sends back the value 0000h to each of the four registers EAX, EBX, ECX and EDX.

11.6 i486 Clones

After the great success of Intel's competitors in producing 386 clones and the enormous significance of the 486 market (Intel is currently producing an unbelievable yield on its turnover), it is not surprising that AMD, Cyrix and IBM are also bringing i486 compatible microprocessors onto the market. In the following section, I would briefly like to describe the most important 486 clones. Due to the legal battles which often take place between so-called «friendly» companies (production cooperation agreements), it is quite possible that one or more processors may have been withdrawn from the market and replaced with other models by the time you read this book.

11.6.1 AMD Clones

Here, as in the i386, I begin with Intel's main rival, AMD. Officially, the two CPU manufacturers are at war with each other, but the data sheets that AMD provides are very similar and, in some cases, like photocopies of Intel's originals (it is probably to do with the use of Intel microcode in AMD processors, so that the relevant data sheets may also be copied). Currently, AMD is offering three different DX versions and two SX versions.

Am486DX/Am486SX

These processors are i486DX and i486SX compatible processors, respectively; each can be delivered with a clock frequency of 33 MHz or 40 MHz. The Am486SX, as expected, is the lower specification SX version, and does not contain a coprocessor. Both processors are strictly oriented to the equivalent Intel model, and so, in comparison, contain no great differences. The only differences are that a JTAG boundary scan test is included in all Am486DX models, and the clock frequency of the Am486SX at a maximum of 40 MHz exceeds the Intel upper limit of 33 Mhz by 25%. Both are delivered in a 168 pin PGA with i486DX and i486SX compatible pin layouts, respectively. The power consumption is also as high as in the Intel models.

Am486DXLV/Am486SXLV

These i486DX/i486SX compatible processors, respectively, are specially designed for saving power. They operate with a supply voltage of only 3.0 V to 3.6 V (usually 3.3 V) compared to the 5 V of the Am486DX/Am486DXL – hence the LV identification, for Low Voltage. As the power consumption of CMOS chips, as explained previously, is proportional to the square of the operating voltage, the Am486DXLV/SXLV has a power saving of more than 60%. The current used at 33 MHz is only 425 mA compared to 700 mA used in the Am486DX/SX. The reduction of the supply voltage to 3.3 V also produces a reduction in power consumption (P=U*I). Thus, the Am486DXLV/SXLV only uses 1.5 W instead of the 4.5 W used in the Am486DX/SX.

The Am486DXLV/SXLV, as previously in the Am386DXLV/Am386SXLV, is implemented entirely statically. In this way, the clock frequency can be reduced to 0 MHz, that is, the clock signal is practically switched off, without causing the processor to lose the contents of its registers or to leave the cycle. Like the low-power 486s from Intel, the Am486DXLV/SXLV is also supplied with a 2x-clock speed up to a maximum of 66 MHz (corresponding to a processor clock speed of 33 MHz). If the external clock signal is switched off, that is, reduced to 0 MHz, then the DXLV/SXLV processor requires far less power – approximately a magnitude of three less (a factor of 1000).

Both Am486 variants implement a JTAG boundary scan test and also a system management mode, like that already known from the Am386DXLV/SXLV. The Am486DXLV and the Am486SXLV are supplied in a 196 pin PQFP. The pin connections of the Am486SXLV are compatible with an i486SX in a PQFP, only in addition the three pins 82 ($\overline{\text{SMI}}$), 134 ($\overline{\text{SMIRDY}}$) and 140 ($\overline{\text{SMIADS}}$) in the Am486SXLV are used for the control signals of system management mode. These three pins form the interface to System Management Mode (SMM). The pin layout of the Am486DXLV is identical to that of the Am486SXLV (and thus the i486SX), only in addition pins 77 ($\overline{\text{IGNNE}}$) and 81 ($\overline{\text{FERR}}$) are used by signals from the on-chip coprocessor.

Am486DX2

Like Intel, AMD also has an internally clock-doubled 486 in its range, the Am486DX2-50 with an internal 50 MHz. Like the i486DX2 or i486DX, it is supplied in a 168 pin PGA, and is pin compatible with the i486DX2 or i486DX-50; the only difference between these two Intel CPUs is that the pin C11 in the i486DX2 is used by the $\overline{\text{UP}}$ signal and is free in the i486DX-50. The

Am486DX2 can tolerate both uses (thus, with and without $\overline{\text{UP}}$). Like its model, the Am486DX2 supports the JTAG boundary scan test.

AMD System Management Mode

The following pins are provided in the Am486DXLV/SXLV for system management mode:

$\overline{\text{SMI}}$, $\overline{\text{SMIADS}}$, $\overline{\text{SMIRDY}}$ (I/O, O, I)
Pins 82, 140, 134

These three pins form the interface to System Management Mode (SMM). If a low level signal is sent to the System Management Interrupt ($\overline{\text{SMI}}$) input, then it leads to an interrupt with a higher priority than an NMI has. The Am486DXLV/SXLV calls the SMI handler and addresses a special memory area. The SMI address status signal $\overline{\text{SMIADS}}$ corresponds to the $\overline{\text{ADS}}$ signal in normal operating mode and indicates valid bus cycles. Finally, the SMI ready signal $\overline{\text{SMIRDY}}$ indicates the completion of a bus cycle in SMM, thus its task is analogous to $\overline{\text{RDY}}$ in normal operating mode.

Memory accesses in SMM are indicated by an active $\overline{\text{SMIADS}}$ signal. The external system *can* use this address strobe signal to address an other-than-usual area of the memory but, naturally, *need not* necessarily do so. Thus, it depends upon whether the system designer wishes to take advantage of the protection and separation function of SMM. On the other hand, however, all I/O accesses via IN or OUT, for example, activate the $\overline{\text{ADS}}$ signal and are switched through to the usual I/O address area.

Typical applications for SMM are the power management functions for the partial or complete switching off of individual components in a power saving green PC (starting with the monitor or hard disk, through to the processor and main memory itself). Naturally, the SMM RAM can also be used for other purposes, such as storing restart routines after serious computer system errors. All accesses using an active $\overline{\text{SMIADS}}$ are not cachable, that is, the SMM RAM is not subject to caching in the on-chip cache of the Am486DXLV/SXLV. The SMM instruction UMOV determines the interface between normal and SMM RAM. If the processor is operating in system management mode, then you can use UMOV to transfer data between a CPU register and the normal RAM (UMOV activates $\overline{\text{ADS}}$ instead of $\overline{\text{SMIADS}}$ and senses $\overline{\text{RDY}}$ in place of $\overline{\text{SMIRDY}}$). In normal mode, UMOV permits an access to the SMM RAM, thus it activates $\overline{\text{SMIADS}}$ instead of $\overline{\text{ADS}}$. Furthermore, the instruction RES4 is provided for SMM, which can also be performed only in SMM (in normal operation it initiates an *invalid opcode* exception). SMM is exited with RES4. The following operations take place in system management mode.

- System management mode is initiated by an active signal at the $\overline{\text{SMI}}$ input or an explicit SMI instruction. The Am486DXLV/SXLV indicates this with an impulse at the $\overline{\text{SMIADS}}$ pin and then by sending out the $\overline{\text{SMI}}$ signal, NMI and INTR are blocked.
- The processor starts to save its current operating condition in SMM RAM (thus, with the help of $\overline{\text{SMIADS}}$ and $\overline{\text{SMIRDY}}$) at the physical addresses 60000h-601a7h. You can see the layout of the processor status report in Table 11.6. Note that the registers DR0 to DR3, CR2 and CR3, and also TR6 and TR7 are not saved.

Address	Content	Address	Content	Address	Content
6000:0000	CR0	6000:0058	TSS base	6000:00ac	SS base
6000:0004	EFlag	6000:005c	TSS limit	6000:00b0	SS limit
6000:0008	EIP	6000:0060	Reserved	6000:00b4	CS attribute
6000:000c	EDI	6000:0064	IDT base	6000:00b8	CS base
6000:0010	ESI	6000:0068	IDT limit	6000:00bc	CS limit
6000:0014	EBP	6000:006c	Reserved	6000:00c0	ES attribute
6000:0018	ESP	6000:0070	GDT base	6000:00c4	SS base
6000:001c	EBX	6000:0074	GDT limit	6000:00c8	ES limit
6000:0020	EDX	6000:0078	LDT attribute	6000:0100	
6000:0024	ECX	6000:007c	LDT base	6000:....	Temporary register
6000:0028	EAX	6000:0080	LDT limit	6000:0124	
6000:002c	DR6	6000:0084	GS attribute	6000:0128	Old EIP
6000:0030	DR7	6000:0088	GS base	6000:012c	
6000:0034	TR	6000:008c	GS limit	6000:....	Reserved
6000:0038	LDT	6000:0090	FS attribute	6000:0148	
6000:003c	GS	6000:0094	FS base	6000:014c	
6000:0040	FS	6000:0098	FS limit	6000:0150	Unused
6000:0044	DS	6000:009c	DS attribute	6000:0150	
6000:0048	SS	6000:00a0	DS base	6000:0154	
6000:004c	CS	6000:00a4	DS limit	6000:....	FPU
6000:0050	ES	6000:00a8	SS attribute	6000:01a4	
6000:0054	TSS attribute				

Table 11.6: Register dump of the Am486DXLV/SXLV

- The Am486DXLV/SXLV initializes its internal processor register as if it were reset, that is, it switches into real mode independently of the previous operating mode (real, protected or virtual 8086) and loads EIP with fff0h and CS with ffffh.

- The execution of the SMM program after an SMI now starts at ffff:fff0 in exactly the same way as after a processor reset. However, as in normal mode, it is possible to switch into protected or virtual 8086 mode, only here $\overline{\text{SMIADS}}$ in place of $\overline{\text{ADS}}$ is used for addressing the SMM RAM. The system tables for protected mode must, therefore, be located in SMM RAM; the full 4 Gbyte address area is then available (even though this may be a little excessive for system management). Through UMOV, conventional RAM as well as SMI RAM can be used for data accesses, but not for instruction fetching. I/O accesses with IN or OUT are switched through to the usual I/O address area; there is no SMM I/O area.

- To return to the interrupted task from SMM mode and to restore the original state of the processor from the processor status report (Table 11.6), the register pair ES:EDI must point to the physical address 60000h. The execution of the 32-bit opcodes 0fh and 07h for the instruction RES4 then restores the state of the processor from the data stored in the SMM memory (however, the register values at the addresses 6000:0120h to 6000:0144h are not rewritten). A further method of leaving SMM is, naturally, through a processor reset. In most cases, this is not satisfactory because the processor should restart operation at the point where it was interrupted by the SMI.

11.6.2 Cyrix Clones

In addition to the 486SLC and 486DLC clones which tended towards the i386, Cyrix now also has a truly i486SX compatible chip in its product range, the Cx486S. As the Cx486S-40 it operates at 40 MHz, or as the internally clock-doubled Cx486S2/50 at 50 MHz, and executes instructions in a pipeline. The instruction pipelining, however, is not as effective for all instructions as in the i486 or Am486; some instructions require one clock cycle more. Thanks to a purely hardware implemented integer multiplication unit, however, the Cyrix SX and DX achieve a seven times greater multiplication speed than the microencoded multipliers of the Am486 or i486, for example. Either the i486/Am486 or the Cyrix is quicker, depending on the application or benchmark test. A cache of 2 kbytes capacity with a selectable write-back strategy is integrated onto the chip. The i486SX compatible Cyrix chip does not include an on-chip coprocessor; the Cx487S is delivered separately. Contrary to the i487SX, the Cx487S is a true coprocessor and not an upgrade, thus it does not completely replace the CPU. The Cyrix processors are available as either 5 V or 3.3 V (up to 33 MHz). In addition, an i486DX compatible chip with an integrated coprocessor and an 8 kbyte cache, usual in the i486, has also been promised. As with all modern power saving microprocessors, the Cyrix processors also include a system management mode.

11.6.3 IBM's Blue Lightning

The personal computer and its microprocessor, not that long ago seen by proper computer manufacturers as an immature toy, have developed into competitors to the established mainframes in a very short time. Even giant IBM is not unaffected by this development. On the other hand, IBM's decade-long experience (and that of DEC) with complex systems at both hardware and software levels is the basic reason that Big Blue has also been forging ahead. The result is the 486DLC3 also known as the *Blue Lightning*. The 3 indicates that it, like the i486DX3, operates internally with a tripled clock frequency and, in this way, achieves 100 MHz. The 486DLC3 includes a 16 kbyte cache (i486DX: 8 kbyte), which operates using write allocation. Thus, a cache miss during writing, like a cache miss during reading, initiates a cache line fill. An on-chip coprocessor, on the other hand, is not included. Unfortunately, the Blue Lightning is internally based mainly on the i386 processor kernel without instruction pipelining. This gives it a distinct disadvantage in the execution time of machine instructions. For example, the instruction MOV reg, reg requires two processor clock cycles instead of only one in the i486. Accesses to the on-chip cache (cache hits) also require two clock cycles instead of one, and so take twice as long. However, a special feature accelerates the 486DLC compared to the i486: the microcode of the 486DLC3, as far as possible, combines each of four individual 8-bit shifts of a REP MOVSB (with respect to bytes, the shifting of string data) after an alignment at a 32-bit limit, into a single 32-bit MOV. The bus transfer rate for extensive accesses (for example to the video RAM) is increased considerably. The reduction of the operating voltage to 3.3 V and a system management mode contribute to power saving – the 486DLC3 uses 3.6 W. In addition to the 486DLC3 there is also the 486SLC2, which operates internally with only a doubled clock frequency (like the i486DX2 or Am486DX2); otherwise it is almost identical to the 486DLC3. However, do not confuse the IBM 486DLC and 486SLC chips with the CPUs from Cyrix with the same name.

12 At Present, Land's End – The 110 MIPS RISC Superscalar Pentium

The i486's successor was surrounded by secrecy for a long time, beginning with its name, and continuing with some very speculative properties of the P5 (as it was called for some time). In the following sections, the features of this superscalar are examined to open a window onto RISC technologies that give rise to an instruction throughput of 112 MIPS compared to the 54 MIPS of an i486DX2-66. The term «RISC» is not fully justified as the Pentium (of course) is completely i486-compatible, and thus has to deal with more than 400 i486 machine instructions.

First, I would like to present the characteristic features of the Pentium:

- two integer pipelines and a floating-point pipeline (superscalar architecture);
- dynamic branch prediction;
- separate data and code caches each with 8 kbytes, write-back strategy and supporting the MESI cache consistency protocol;
- external 64-bit data bus with pipelined burst mode for quicker cache line fills and write-backs up to 528 million bytes/s;
- execution tracing for external monitoring of internal command execution;
- system management mode for implementing power saving functions;
- performance monitoring for the optimization of code sequences.

Figure 12.1 is a photograph of an unbonded Pentium chip in which the separate elements can be clearly seen. Regular structures represent memory, such as the two caches, the TLBs and the branch trace buffer. The chip shown has more than three million transistors.

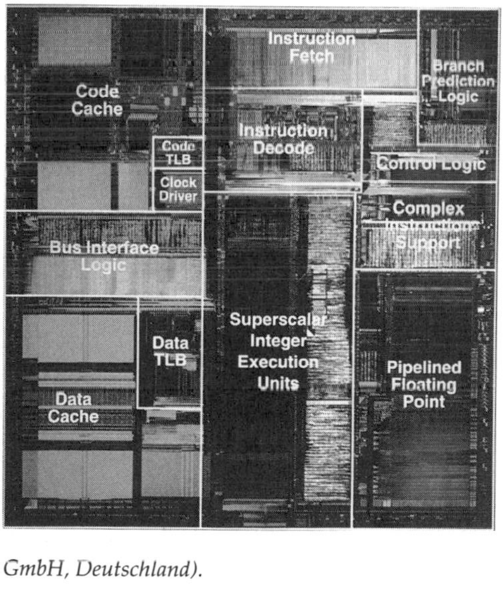

Figure 12.1: Pentium die (Intel GmbH, Deutschland).

12.1 Pins and Signals

Because of its 64-bit data bus, the Pentium requires an additional pin row and is shipped in a pin grid array package with 273 pins, of which 267 are used. The current consumption of more than 3 A at 66 MHz is handled by 50 Vcc and 49 GND terminals for supplying the current and partially draining the resulting heat of 13 W. The rest is transferred to the environment by a big heat sink. Figure 12.2 schematically shows the pinout of the Pentium.

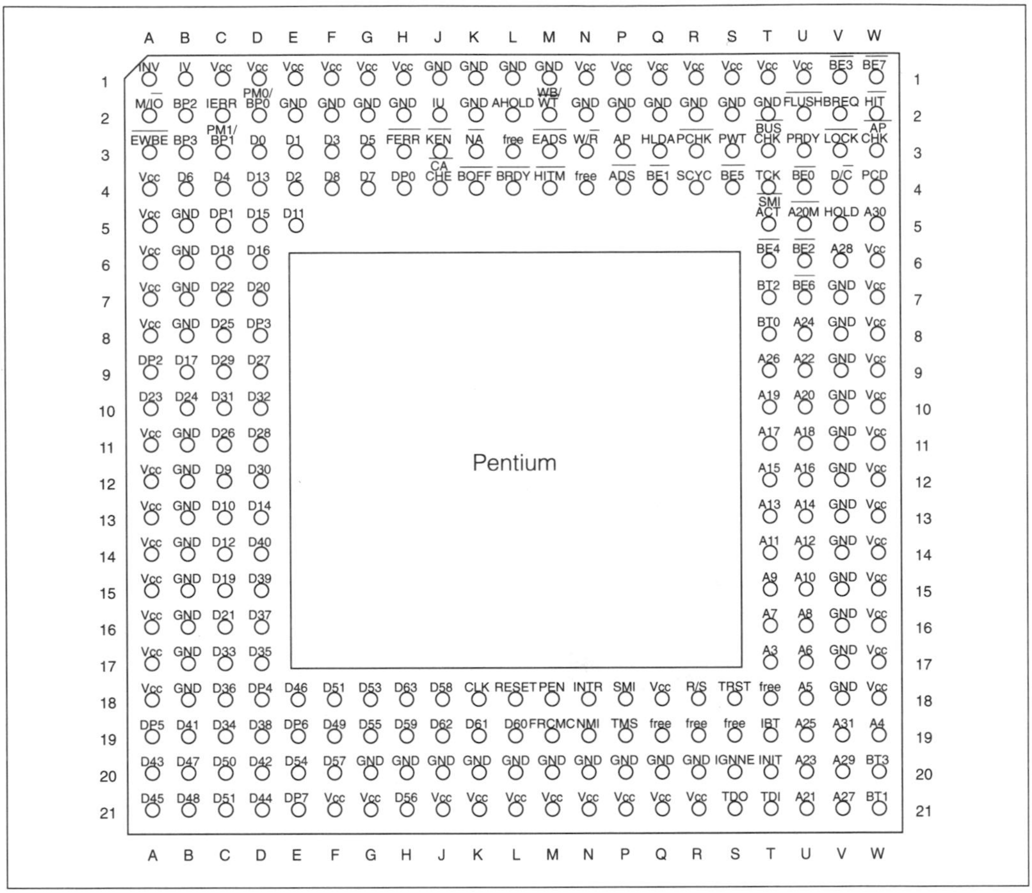

Figure 12.2: Pentium pinout.

The following presents the large number of pins, and explains the input and output signals. The sequence is given in alphabetical order.

$\overline{\text{A20M}}$ (I)
Pin U5

If this address 20 mask pin is at a low level, then before every memory access the Pentium internally masks the address bit A20. This also affects all accesses (look-ups) to the two internal cache memories. In this way, the Pentium emulates the wrap-around of the 8086 at address 1M. $\overline{\text{A20M}}$ must only be activated in real mode.

A31–A3 (O; A31–A5: I/O)
Pins T9–T17, U8–U21, V6, V19–V21, W5, W19

These 29 pins provide the 29 most significant bits of the 32-bit address for write and read operations. The three least significant address bits A0 to A2 are coded by the eight byte enable signals $\overline{\text{BE0}}$–$\overline{\text{BE7}}$. In an inquiry cycle, the external logic uses the 27 signals A31–A5 to transfer the inquiry address to the Pentium.

$\overline{\textbf{ADS}}$ (O)
Pin P4

A low level address status signal at this pin indicates that the Pentium has started a new bus cycle, that the pins W/$\overline{\text{R}}$, D/$\overline{\text{C}}$, and M/$\overline{\text{IO}}$ give valid signals for the definition of the bus cycle, and that the pins $\overline{\text{BE0}}$–$\overline{\text{BE7}}$ and also A31–A3 give valid address signals.

AHOLD (I)
Pin L2

If a high level signal is applied to this address hold pin, the Pentium does not drive its address bus (A31–A3, BT3–BT0 and AP) and prepares it for an input operation. An external busmaster can then access the address bus of the Pentium, to perform an inquiry cycle. All other signals remain active, so that data for previously sent bus cycles can still be transferred.

AP (I/O)
Pin P3

In addition to parity formation for the data bus, the Pentium also supports parity formation for the address bus. Contrary to DP7–DP0, AP is given out for the complete 29-bit address bus part A31–A3. For every write cycle, the Pentium sends out the AP parity bit so that parity is achieved. When reading data, the system must send a signal to the AP pin that causes even parity (for A31–A3 and AP). Systems that do not support this parity function mostly fix AP at Vcc or GND. In a read operation, the AP associated signal does not influence the program execution; the Pentium reacts to an address parity error only by activating $\overline{\text{APCHK}}$ two CLK cycles after the activation of $\overline{\text{EADS}}$ by the interrogating subsystem.

$\overline{\textbf{APCHK}}$ (O)
Pin W3

After reading in an external address during an inquiry cycle, the Pentium sends out a signal through the address parity check pin that indicates whether the transferred address bits A31–A3 and the address parity bit AP are consistent. If $\overline{\text{APCHK}}$ is at a low level, then an address parity error has occurred. The system need not necessarily serve or use $\overline{\text{APCHK}}$ or the other parity checking signals.

$\overline{\mathrm{BE7}}$–$\overline{\mathrm{BE0}}$ (O)
Pins U4, U6–U7, Q4, S4, T6, V1, W1

These (byte enable) signals indicate which byte group of the 64-bit data bus will actually transfer data in the current bus cycle. $\overline{\mathrm{BE0}}$ corresponds to the least significant data byte D7–D0, $\overline{\mathrm{BE7}}$ corresponds to the most significant data byte D63–D56. During a cachable read cycle, all data lines must be used with a valid data signal independently of $\overline{\mathrm{BEx}}$ values because, in principle, the Pentium carries out a cache line fill for such read accesses.

$\overline{\mathrm{BOFF}}$ (I)
Pin K4

If the backoff pin receives a signal with a low level, the Pentium disables its bus. It disconnects nearly all pins and suspends all currently running bus cycles. After the deactivation of $\overline{\mathrm{BOFF}}$, the Pentium restarts the interrupted bus cycle anew, in that all necessary address, data and control signals for the interrupted cycle are given out again, that is, it starts the interrupted bus cycle again from the beginning.

BP3–BP2, PM1/BP1–PM0/BP0 (O)
Pins B2–B3, C3, D2

The breakpoint pins BP3–BP0 correspond to the debug registers DR3–DR0. If a breakpoint occurs for one of the registers, the Pentium enables the corresponding BPx signal. Through the two bits PB1 and PB0 in the debug mode control register DR4, you can set whether PM1/PB1 or PM0/PB0, respectively, should be used as a breakpoint pin (PBx=1), or for performance monitoring. BP3–BP0 enable breakpoint hits to be instantaneously seized by external hardware. Otherwise, an internal breakpoint interception only runs after a delay, because the Pentium must first internally produce the corresponding exception and jump to the handler using a relatively long-winded interrupt call.

$\overline{\mathrm{BRDY}}$ (I)
Pin L4

The burst ready signal at this pin indicates whether the addressed peripheral system, for example the main memory or an I/O device, has already completed the requested access ($\overline{\mathrm{BRDY}}$=low), or requires more time ($\overline{\mathrm{BRDY}}$=high). As is the case for all other 80x86 CPUs, the ready signal causes the Pentium to insert one or more wait states if the addressed unit is unable to respond in time. Unlike the i486, the Pentium does not differentiate between a usual ready and a burst ready signal. $\overline{\mathrm{BRDY}}$ refers both to burst cycles (which are only possible for a memory access) and to single transfer and I/O cycles.

BREQ (O)
Pin V2

Through the bus request signal BREQ, the Pentium indicates that it has requested the internal bus. It is possible that the Pentium cannot use the bus at this moment (due to an active AHOLD, HOLD or $\overline{\mathrm{BOFF}}$ signal). Despite this, BREQ is still sent out and can be used by the bus operation logic to give the Pentium priority after the deactivation of AHOLD, HOLD or $\overline{\mathrm{BOFF}}$. This is required especially in multimaster systems (for instance, a Pentium and busmaster DMA or several CPUs).

BT3–BT0 (O)
Pins T7–T8, W20–W21

The three branch trace signals BT2–BT0 give the bits A2–A0 the linear branch address (the other address bits through A31–A3) during a branch trace message cycle, BT3 defines the standard operand size. If BT3 is active (high level), then the standard operand size is 32-bit, otherwise it is 16-bit. A set ET-bit in the test register TR12 instructs the Pentium to execute such a branch trace message cycle and to send out the signals BT3–BT0 for every activation of IBT.

$\overline{\mathrm{BUSCHK}}$ (I)
Pin T3

An active bus check signal informs the Pentium about an incomplete bus cycle, that is, the cycle was finished, but the subsystem could not correctly execute the cycle (data read, data write, or other access, etc.) as instructed by the Pentium. In this case, the Pentium stores the addresses and values according to the control signals in the machine check register. A set MCE-bit in the CR4 control register then leads to a machine check exception corresponding to interrupt 18 (12h).

$\overline{\mathrm{CACHE}}$ (O)
Pin J4

An active CACHE signal indicates that the current memory cycle sent by the Pentium is internally cachable. If the Pentium initiates a memory read cycle or an instruction fetching cycle and $\overline{\mathrm{CACHE}}$ is active (at a low level), then the Pentium extends the memory read cycle to a cache line fill in burst mode, providing the addressed memory subsystem activates $\overline{\mathrm{KEN}}$, and in this way informs the subsystem that the required data or codes are cachable. If $\overline{\mathrm{KEN}}$ remains inactive, then despite an active $\overline{\mathrm{CACHE}}$, the Pentium will not perform a cache line fill. The cause can be, for example, that with a memory mapped I/O a control register is located at the addressed memory position. An inactive $\overline{\mathrm{CACHE}}$ signal, independently of the $\overline{\mathrm{KEN}}$ signal level, always leads to a single transfer without internal caching of the transferred data or code bytes. If $\overline{\mathrm{CACHE}}$ is activated by the Pentium for a write cycle, then it executes a write-back of a cache line in burst mode. Write-throughs to the external memory are executed with an inactive $\overline{\mathrm{CACHE}}$. These are write operations that lead to a cache miss in the on-chip data cache. The Pentium does not execute a cache line fill for such write cache misses. The $\overline{\mathrm{CACHE}}$ signal could also be described as a burst instruction signal, because an active $\overline{\mathrm{CACHE}}$ signal with a low level always results in a burst mode and the transfer of 32 bytes of code or data. In principle, I/O cycles are not cachable, because usually a control or status register is lurking behind the addressed port.

CLK (I)
Pin K18

The clock signal is sent to this pin which the Pentium uses unchanged as the internal processor clock signal PLCK.

D63–D0 (I/O)

Pins A10, A20–A21, B9–B10, B19–B21, C4, C6–C21, D3–D7, D9–D17, D19–D21, E3–E5, E18, E20, F3–F4, F18–F20, G3, G18–G19, H18–H19, H21, J18–J19, K19, L19

These 64 pins form the bidirectional 64-bit data bus for the input and output of data. Thus, the Pentium data bus is double the width of that in the i486. This, above all, increases the speed with which the two internal caches are filled or written back. During a data read operation, the data at these pins is taken as soon as the $\overline{\text{BRDY}}$ signal is active.

D/$\overline{\text{C}}$, M/$\overline{\text{IO}}$, W/$\overline{\text{R}}$, (O, O, O)

Pins V4, A2, N3

The data/control (1=data cycle, 0=instruction/special cycle), memory/IO (1=memory cycle, 0=I/O cycle) and write/read (1=write cycle, 0=read cycle) signals at these pins set the current bus cycle type. The possible signal combinations have the following meanings:

```
(000) interrupt acknowledge sequence
(001) special cycle

BE7=BE6=BE5=BE4=BE3=BE2=BE1=1, BE0=0: Shutdown
BE7=BE6=BE5=BE4=BE3=BE2=BE0=1, BE1=0: Internal cache flush (INVD, WBINVD)
BE7=BE6=BE5=BE4=BE3=BE1=BE0=1, BE2=0: Stop
BE7=BE6=BE5=BE4=BE2=BE1=BE0=1, BE3=0: Write-back cycle (WBINVD)
BE7=BE6=BE5=BE3=BE2=BE1=BE0=1, BE4=0: Flush acknowledge
BE7=BE6=BE4=BE3=BE2=BE1=BE0=1, BE5=0: Branch trace message cycle

(010) reading from an I/O port
(011) writing to an I/O port
(100) instruction fetching
(101) invalid
(110) reading of data from memory
(111) writing of data to memory
```

DP7–DP0 (I/O)

Pins A9, A19, C5, D8, D18, E19, H4

The Pentium supports the formation of parity for the data bus, that is, it sends out the parity bit DP7–DP0 for every byte of the data bus D63–D0 during every write cycle, so that even parity is achieved. When reading data, the system must send signals to the pins DP7–DP0 that will give an even parity. Systems that do not support this parity function mostly fix DP7–DP0 at Vcc or GND. The signals sent to the pins during a read operation do not influence the program execution, if $\overline{\text{PEN}}$ is not simultaneously active, that is, at a low level. With an active $\overline{\text{PEN}}$, the addresses in the applicable read cycle, and the type of cycle, are stored in the MCA and MCT registers, respectively. Through a set MCE-bit in CR4, the Pentium sends out a machine check exception corresponding to interrupt 18 (12h). If $\overline{\text{PEN}}$ is not active, the only reaction of the Pentium to a data parity error is the activation of the $\overline{\text{PCHK}}$ signal.

$\overline{\text{EADS}}$ (I)

Pin M3

An active low level signal at this external address pin indicates to the Pentium that an external bus controller has sent a valid address to its address pins and drives an inquiry cycle.

$\overline{\text{EWBE}}$ (I)
Pin A3

An active low level signal at this external write buffer empty pin informs the Pentium that the external system (such as a second–level cache) is ready to take write data from the Pentium. If, on the other hand, $\overline{\text{EWBE}}$ is inactive (at a high level), the system must first execute an additional write cycle before the Pentium can proceed with transferring data. Only when $\overline{\text{EWBE}}$ is again active can the Pentium continue with the write operation.

$\overline{\text{FERR}}$ (O)
Pin H3

This pin sends out an active signal with a low level if a non-masked exception occurs in the floating-point unit of the Pentium. In this way, the Pentium can be built into a personal computer that can, for reasons of compatibility, issue a coprocessor interrupt in order to indicate such a coprocessor error.

$\overline{\text{FLUSH}}$ (I)
Pin U2

If the cache flush pin receives a $\overline{\text{FLUSH}}$ signal with a low level, then the Pentium writes back to memory all changed cache lines of the on-chip data cache and invalidates both on-chip caches (data and code cache). It carries out a cache flush. After completion of the cache flush, the Pentium initiates a flush acknowledge cycle (see D/$\overline{\text{C}}$, M/$\overline{\text{IO}}$ and W/R).

$\overline{\text{FRCMC}}$ (I)
Pin M19

The signal at this functional redundancy checking master/checker input indicates to the Pentium during a reset and its subsequent initialization whether it should operate as a master or a checker. As a master (high level $\overline{\text{FRCMC}}$), the Pentium controls the bus according to the usual bus protocol (for example, it activates the address and control signals). In checker mode, on the other hand, the Pentium determines the signal level at all output (O) pins (with the exception of $\overline{\text{IERR}}$ and TDO) and compares them with internal values. $\overline{\text{IERR}}$ is activated if the signal levels are not the same as the internal values. Two Pentium CPUs can thus check one another.

$\overline{\text{HIT}}$ (O)
Pin W2

The $\overline{\text{HIT}}$ signal indicates the result of an inquiry cycle. If a hit occurs in the on-chip data or instruction cache, the Pentium drives the $\overline{\text{HIT}}$ signal to a low level. If a miss occurs, the pin sends out a low level signal.

$\overline{\text{HITM}}$ (O)
Pin M4

The hit modified line signal, similar to $\overline{\text{HIT}}$, indicates the result of an inquiry cycle. If a changed line in the on-chip data cache is referenced, the Pentium activates the $\overline{\text{HITM}}$ signal at a low level. The external system can then use $\overline{\text{HITM}}$ during bus arbitration to prevent a different bus controller from using the applicable data before the Pentium has written back the content of the changed line to memory.

HOLD, HLDA (I, O)
Pins V5, Q3

The two bus hold request and bus hold acknowledge pins are used as usual for bus arbitration. If a different busmaster wishes to have control, it sends a high level signal to the HOLD input of the Pentium. If the control transfer is not internally blocked by an active $\overline{\text{LOCK}}$ signal, or the current operation of an instruction, then the Pentium reacts with an active HLDA signal. The new busmaster keeps the HOLD signal active until it wishes to hand back control of the local bus (or until it must). It will then deactivate the HOLD signal, and the Pentium then retakes control. HOLD and HLDA play an important bus arbitration role in EISA and microchannel systems.

IBT (O)
Pin T19

The instruction branch taken pin gives out a signal with a high level if the Pentium internally executes a branch. With a set ET-bit in the control register TR12, the Pentium will additionally execute a branch taken message cycle.

$\overline{\text{IERR}}$ (O)
Pin C2

An active internal error signal with a low level at this pin indicates an internal error in the Pentium. This could be a parity error when reading internal data fields. A Pentium, working as a master, then activates IERR and goes into a shutdown condition. In checker mode, $\overline{\text{IERR}}$ is activated if the received value at the output pins does not agree with the internally calculated value.

$\overline{\text{IGNNE}}$ (I)
Pin S20

If this ignore numeric error pin receives a low level signal and the NE-bit in the control register CR0 is reset (thus, equals 0), then the Pentium will ignore numerical errors (exceptions) and continue to execute floating-point instructions. Despite this, $\overline{\text{FERR}}$ is activated. If $\overline{\text{IGNNE}}$ is at a high level (thus, inactive) and the next floating-point instruction is a FINIT, FCLEX, FSTENV, FSAVE, FSTSW, FSRCW, FENI, FDIDI or FSETPM, then the Pentium executes the new instruction instead of the exception. If $\overline{\text{IGNNE}}$ is at a high level, and the subsequent instruction is other than one of those above, then the Pentium stops the instruction execution and then waits for an external interrupt. If the NE-bit in the control register CR0 is set, then $\overline{\text{IGNNE}}$ has no effect.

INIT (I)
Pin T20

A signal with a high level at this initialization pin for a minimum of two CLK clock cycles sets the Pentium into a defined initial start condition in a similar way to a reset. However, contrary to a reset, the internal caches, write buffers, model registers and floating-point registers are not reset, but retain their values. In addition to a reset and changing the value of the PE-bit in control register CR0, INIT also enables another possibility: to switch the Pentium back into real mode. In this way, driver programs that were developed for the 80286 and only switch back into real mode when reset operate in the Pentium at a much higher speed (but who would want to do that?). With a reset instruction from a keyboard controller, a corresponding external logic uses the INIT input in place of the reset input. In this way, a complicated and lengthy reset is avoided and the Pentium again runs in 80286 compatible real mode after only two clock cycles.

INTR (I)
Pin N18

A high level signal at this interrupt terminal indicates that an interrupt request from a hardware unit exists. If the interrupt flag IE in the EFlag register is set, then the processor completes the active instruction and afterwards immediately executes an INTA cycle to read the applicable interrupt number from the interrupt controller. Dependent on the operating mode the Pentium then calls the corresponding handler via the interrupt vector table (real mode) or the interrupt descriptor table (protected mode). By resetting the IE flag, the checking of INTR can be suppressed and, in this way, hardware interrupt requests can be masked.

INV (I)
Pin A1

During an inquiry cycle, a high level invalidation request signal at this pin leads to the invalidation of the applicable cache line, if a hit occurs (it is marked as invalid). A low level marks the cache line as shared if a hit occurs. If no hit occurs, INV has no effect. Upon an active $\overline{\text{EADS}}$ signal, the addresses are transferred at A31–A5.

IU (O)
Pin J2

If the Pentium has completed an instruction in the u-pipeline, for a CLK cycle, it sends out a signal with a high level from this instruction/u-pipeline pin.

IV (O)
Pin B1

If the Pentium has completed an instruction in the v-pipeline, for a CLK cycle it sends out a signal with a high level from this instruction/v-pipeline pin. IU and IV are used for externally monitoring the pipeline activity.

$\overline{\text{KEN}}$ (I)
Pin J3

Through $\overline{\text{KEN}}$ (cache enable), the Pentium determines whether the current cycle is «cachable», and thus whether the addressed address area can be transferred to the cache. If that is the case, and if the Pentium has sent out a cachable cycle (thus, $\overline{\text{CACHE}}$ is active), then the current read access is expanded to a cache line fill cycle. The Pentium will then read a complete cache line f 32 bytes into one of its two on-chip caches. As $\overline{\text{KEN}}$ information originates in a memory subsystem, specific address areas of hardware devices can be protected from caching by $\overline{\text{KEN}}$.

$\overline{\text{LOCK}}$ (O)
Pin V3

With an active $\overline{\text{LOCK}}$, and thus a low level signal at this pin, the Pentium will not pass control of the local bus to another bus controller which requests control using HOLD. Thus, it executes a locked bus cycle and does not respond to a HOLD request with an acknowledge (HLDA).

$\overline{\text{NA}}$ (I)
Pin D13

The next address signal is used for the implementation and control of address pipelining. The address decoder system of the computer indicates with a low level signal at this pin that the new values for $\overline{\text{BE0}}$–$\overline{\text{BE7}}$, A3–A31, W/$\overline{\text{R}}$, D/$\overline{\text{C}}$ and M/$\overline{\text{IO}}$ can be transferred to the decoder before the current cycle is completed. In this way, the next bus cycle has already begun before the current bus cycle ends with a $\overline{\text{BRDY}}$ signal. The Pentium carries out address pipelining, in that it begins the applicable bus cycle two CLK cycles after activation of $\overline{\text{NA}}$. $\overline{\text{NA}}$ is latched in the processor and is activated with the next clock cycle; the Pentium «notes» it as a type of pipeline request.

NMI (I)
Pin N19

If this pin receives a signal with a high level, then the Pentium issues an interrupt 2 which, contrary to INTR, cannot be masked by the interrupt flag IE. Thus, it is the well-known non-maskable interrupt. After the completion of the current instruction, the Pentium, in all conditions, stops the program execution and attends to the interrupt. Note that contrary to INTR, no INTA sequence is executed because the vector is hardwired to «2».

PCD, PWT (O, O)
Pins W4, S3

The page cache disable signal at this pin indicates the value of the PCD-bit in the CR3 control register, the page table entry, or the page directory entry for the current page. Thus, at this pin, the Pentium delivers external caching information on a page basis. The page write-through signal at this pin indicates the value of the page write-through bit PWT in the CR3 control register, the page table entry or the page directory entry for the current page. Thus, at this pin, the Pentium delivers external write-back or write-through information on a page basis.

$\overline{\text{PCHK}}$ (O)
Pin R3

After reading the data, the Pentium gives out a signal through the parity check pin that indicates whether the transferred data bits D63–D0 and the parity bits DP7–DP0 are consistent. Only the data bytes explicitly identified as active with $\overline{\text{BEx}}$ are checked. If $\overline{\text{PCHK}}$ is low, then a parity error has occurred. $\overline{\text{PCHK}}$ is given out by the addressed subsystem two CLK cycles after the activation of $\overline{\text{BRDY}}$, and remains active for one CLK cycle. The system need not necessarily supply or use $\overline{\text{PCHK}}$ or any of the other parity checking signals.

$\overline{\text{PEN}}$ (I)
Pin M18

Together with the MCE-bit in the CR4 control register, the signal at this parity enable pin defines whether the Pentium should send out a machine check exception corresponding to interrupt 18 (12h) if a data parity error occurs (for D63–D0, DP7–DP0) during a read cycle. With an active $\overline{\text{PEN}}$, the Pentium stores the address bits and the values of the bus control signals in the machine check registers. If the MCE-bit is also set, then the Pentium sends out a machine check exception.

PRDY (O)
Pin U3

A signal with a high level at this probe ready pin indicates that the Pentium has gone into probe mode as a reaction to a low level R/$\overline{\text{S}}$ signal. PRDY is used for the implementation of the new Intel debug ports, through which a debugger can be supported by external hardware.

PWT (O)
Pin S3

In a bus cycle that does not support paging, even though paging is active, PWT indicates the value of the PWT-bit in the CR3 control register. With disabled paging, the Pentium always gives out a low level signal at PWT.

RESET (I)
Pin L18

If this pin receives a high level signal for a minimum of 15 CLK cycles, then the Pentium completely stops what it is doing and carries out an internal processor reset. Additionally, all caches are invalidated (changed cache lines are not written back). The Pentium checks the signals at $\overline{\text{FLUSH}}$, $\overline{\text{FRCMC}}$ and INIT to determine the operating condition after such a reset.

R/$\overline{\text{S}}$ (I)
Pin R18

A signal with a low level at this resume/stop pin interrupts the currently running program execution. The Pentium restarts the instruction execution when the signal changes to high level.

SCYC (O)
Pin R4

With a 16- or 32-bit access straddling a double word boundary, or a 64-bit access straddling a quad word boundary (a so-called misaligned access), the Pentium must carry out two memory accesses to read in, or to write, words, double words or quad words, respectively. With two sequential locked cycles ($\overline{\text{LOCK}}$ at a low level), for example a locked read-modify-write cycle, then four accesses are required. The Pentium then gives out an active split cycle signal at the SCYC pin to indicate that more than two locked bus cycles will follow. In the example given, four locked cycles are necessary, two for reading and two for writing. Such locked read-modify-write cycles are performed to ensure data integrity in a multi-bus controller system, that is, the Pentium reads, modifies and writes a data unit (such as a variable), without another bus controller having permission to access the data using HOLD and the subsequent bus arbitration.

$\overline{\text{SMI}}$ (I)
Pin P18

An active low level signal at this input for a minimum of two CLK cycles causes the Pentium to activate the $\overline{\text{SMIACT}}$ signal, if it reaches an instruction boundary. In addition, it waits initially for the completion of all write cycles and the activation of $\overline{\text{EWBE}}$. The Pentium then stores the register values in the SMRAM (System Management RAM), and branches to the SMM (System Management Mode) handler to carry out the necessary functions. An RSM (resume from system management mode) instruction reloads the register values from the SMRAM back into the Pentium and enables the processor to resume the interrupted program.

$\overline{\text{SMIACT}}$ (O)
Pin T5

An active low level signal at this system management interrupt active pin indicates to the system that the Pentium is currently running in system management mode and only accesses the SMRAM.

TCK (I)
Pin T4

This test clock pin is sent a test clock signal for the boundary scan test.

TDI (I)
Pin T21

The Test Data Input (TDI) pin is sent TAP (Test Access Port) instructions and data serially synchronized with TCK.

TDO (I)
Pin S21

From the Test Data Output (TDO) pin, instructions and result data from the boundary scan test are sent out. It is serially synchronized with TCK.

TMS (I)
Pin P19

If this test mode select pin receives a high level signal, the test access port sends out the JTAG test logic for the boundary test scan. If TMS remains at a high level for five TCK cycles or more, then it restarts the test logic independent of the currently active condition.

$\overline{\text{TRST}}$ (I)
Pin S18

An active signal with a low level at this test reset pin initializes the boundary scan test logic.

WB/$\overline{\text{WT}}$ (I)
Pin M2

A signal with a high level at this write-back/write-through pin defines the corresponding cache line as write-back, or otherwise write-through, during a memory access. In this way, the cache lines can be individually configured as write-back or write-through. WB/WT, together with PWT is necessary for implementation of the MESI protocol.

Free
Pins L3, N4, Q19, R19, S19, T18

These pins should always be held in a free (floating) condition. If a second-level cache is available with an 82496 cache controller, pins L3 ($\overline{\text{BRDYC}}$) and N4 ($\overline{\text{ADSC}}$) serve as pins between the Pentium and the cache controller.

Vcc (I)

Pins A4–A8, A11–A18, C1, D1, E1, F1, F21, G1, G21, H1, J21, K21, L21, M21, N1, N21, P1, P21, Q1, Q18, Q21, R1, R21, S1, T1, U1, W6–W18

These pins receive the supply voltage (usually +5 V) to supply the Pentium with current. Up to 3.2 A flows through Vcc (hence a 64 mA maximum for each pin).

GND (I)

Pins B5–B8, B11–B18, E2, F2, G2, G20, H2, H20, J1, J20, K1–K2, K20, L1, L20, M1, M20, N2, N20, P2, P20, Q2, Q20, R2, R20, S2, T2, V7–V18

Theses pins are connected to ground (usually 0 V).

12.2 Internal Pentium Structure

Although the Pentium has a 64-bit data bus it is a 32-bit processor, like its i386 and i486 predecessors. The data bus serves the on-chip caches directly, and the 32-bit processor register indirectly. The internal data paths of the Pentium are between 128 and 256 bits wide, so that the transfer of data and codes can be carried out very quickly. Figure 12.3 is a block diagram of the Pentium.

The bus interface, through the external 64-bit data bus and the 32-bit address bus, provides a connection to the outside world. Both on-chip caches are directly connected to the bus interface. Contrary to the i486, two separate and independent 8 kbyte caches for code and data are provided. Because of the data bus enhanced to 64 bits, the cache line size is 32 bytes. Each cache is connected to its own Translation Lookaside Buffer (TLB). In addition to the standard 4 kbyte pages, 4 Mbyte pages are provided for the support of larger systems with a linear memory model. The caches use physical addresses; the data cache can work with both write-through and write-back strategies as necessary. (Code cannot be overwritten in protected mode – the only reasonable operating mode of the Pentium – thus, no write-back strategy is implemented for the code cache.) Details of the caches are discussed in Section 12.2.6.

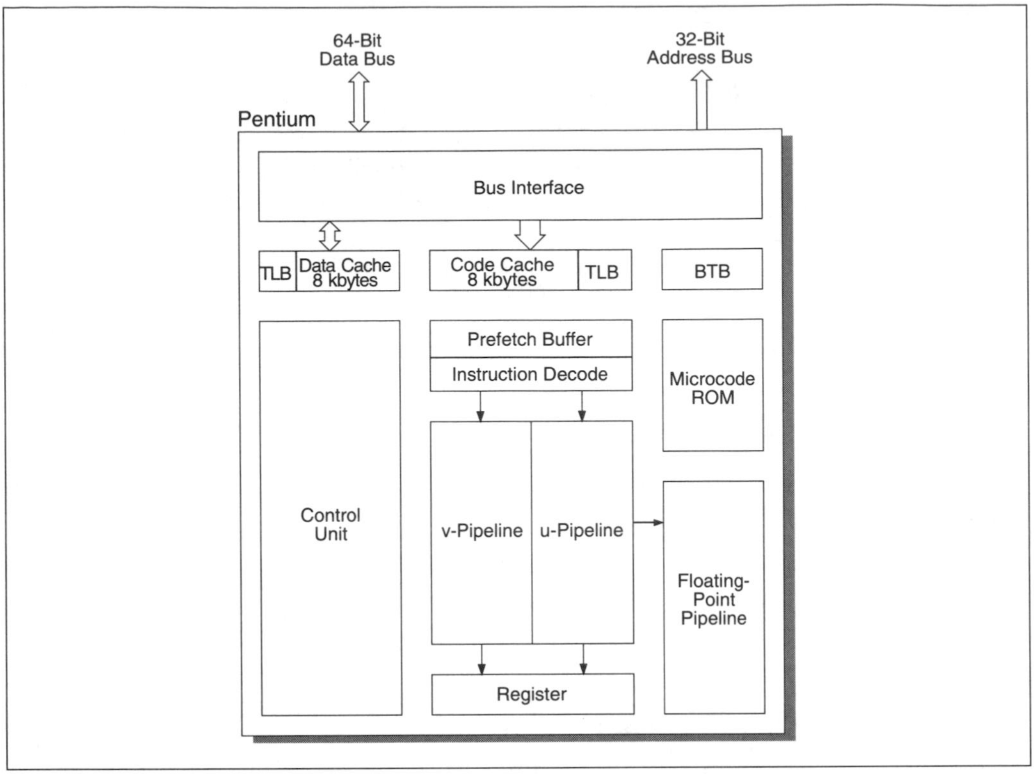

Figure 12.3: Pentium block diagram.

The control unit controls the five-stage integer pipelines u and v, and the eight-stage floating-point pipeline. In this case, the term «integer» refers to all commands that do not contain floating-point operations. That also includes jump instructions. As a superscalar the Pentium executes an instruction in the u-pipeline and another (called *simple*) in the v-pipeline simultaneously. Under the right conditions, the Pentium can thus execute two integer commands in a single clock cycle. Under certain conditions, the integer and floating-point pipelines can also work in parallel. In comparison to an i486DX of a similar clock speed, the Pentium FPU executes floating-point commands up to ten times more quickly. This is achieved through the integration of a hardware multiplier and divider, and also through the implementation of quicker algorithms for the microcoded floating-point commands. The two pipelines are supplied with codes by two independent 32-byte prefetch buffers. Only in this way is it possible to have overlapping instruction execution in the two pipelines. The pipelines are detailed in Sections 12.2.1 to 12.2.4.

The branch prediction logic gives the Pentium an essential advantage for the handling of branches, which can cause considerable delays. It consists of a control unit and a Branch Trace Buffer (BTB). In this way, the branch prediction logic can reliably predict branches, and can considerably accelerate program execution.

As an x86 and x87 compatible microprocessor, the Pentium must, naturally, support all commands of the microcoded i386 and i387 processors. This is not possible using the hardwired control unit, especially when considering the very complex commands and functions of protected mode, task switches and the transcendental functions of the floating-point unit. For this reason, the Pentium does not operate with pure hardwired instructions, but contains microcode in a support unit ready for these complex functions. The microcode is constructed in such a way that it can use both pipelines of the Pentium at the same time. Thus, even microcoded commands in the Pentium run much quicker than in the i486. Simpler functions, on the other hand, such as all ALU functions, are performed by the hardwired logic in accordance with the RISC principle.

12.2.1 The Integer Pipelines u and v

As with the i486, the Pentium also uses RISC concepts to increase performance. One such concept is the implementation of instruction pipelining. While the i486 only contained a single instruction pipeline, the Pentium can call on two integer pipelines, known as the u- and the v-pipelines. Under certain conditions, they can operate in parallel and execute so-called «paired instructions». Additionally there is a floating-point unit, which will be discussed separately.

Pipeline Structure

The two Pentium pipelines each contain five stages for instruction execution, namely instruction fetch (IF), decoding 1 (D1), decoding 2 (D2), execution (EX) with ALU and cache accesses, and also register write-back (WB). The u-pipeline can carry out all instructions of the x86 architecture including existing complex instructions in microcode. The v-pipeline, on the other hand, is only used for so-called «simple integer instructions» and the FPU instruction FXCHG. The grouping of instructions into instruction pairs, and their parallel execution in both of the pipelines, must conform to certain rules; these are explained in Section 12.2.2. Figure 12.4 shows the basic structure of the two five-stage integer pipelines. Under ideal circumstances, for each cycle, two results leave the pipelines.

The first *instruction prefetch stage IF* collects two instructions (one for each pipeline) from the on-chip code cache (cache hit) or from an external storage device (cache miss). The prefetch buffers work together with the Branch Target Buffer (BTB) to implement the dynamic branch prediction. You will find more on dynamic branch prediction in Section 12.2.5. The currently active prefetch buffer reads the instructions in a predefined sequence, and then passes them on to the decoders until they reach a branch (JMP, Jcc) or a call (CALL) instruction. At this point, the branch prediction logic becomes active, and with the help of the stored entry in the branch target buffer, predicts whether the branch will actually be carried out (*taken branch*) or whether the instruction flow will be sequentially continued (*not taken branch*).

In the case of a taken branch, the currently active prefetch buffer is disabled, and the other prefetch buffer starts fetching instructions at the position where the BTB predicted. Thus, instruction fetching is continued as if the branch will actually be executed. Note that at this point in time, it is not yet known whether the branch will actually be carried out. The compare instructions necessary for the decision, etc. find themselves in the pipeline at various stages of completion. As we know from astrology and fortune-telling, predictions have the property of sometimes being false. If the prediction is later found to be false, the Pentium pipeline is emptied, thus the incorrectly carried out instruction is deleted and the other prefetch buffer continues the prefetching at the correct address.

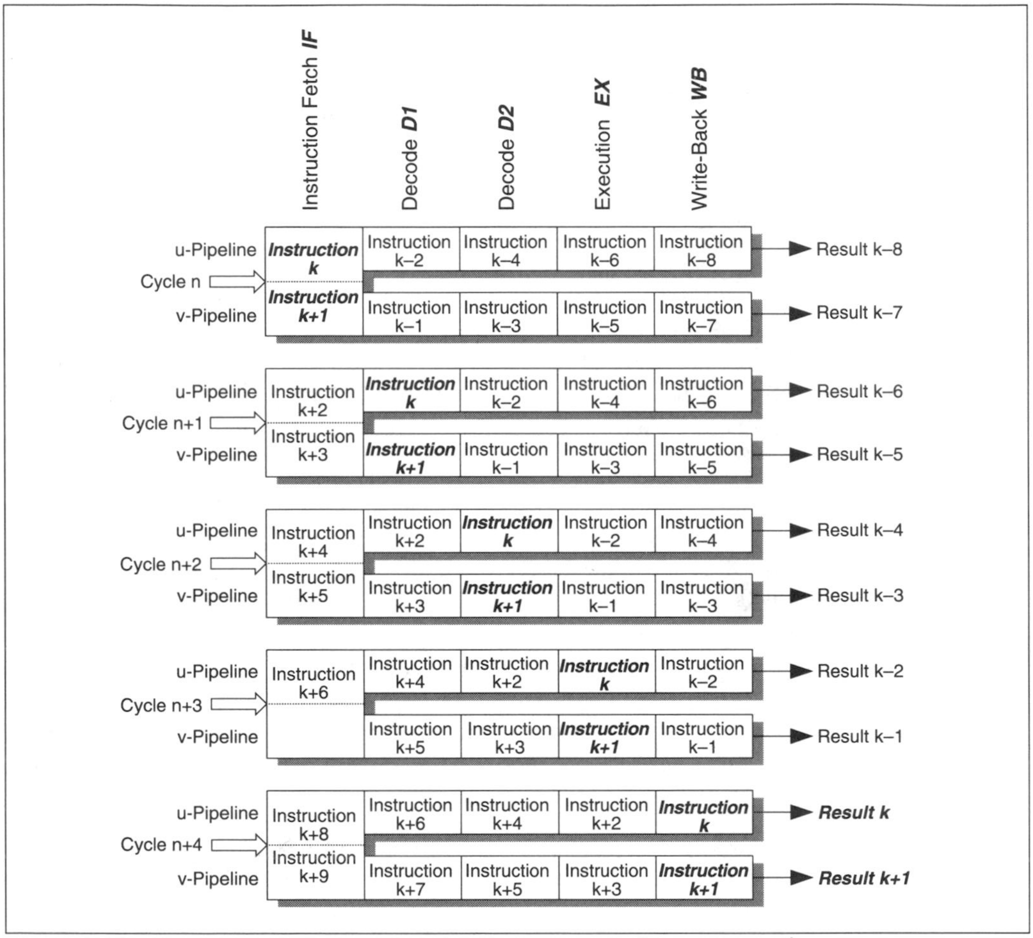

Figure 12.4: The two integer pipelines u and v. The figure shows the five-stage structure of the two integer pipelines. It is assumed that the instruction pairing is possible for every two instructions, and therefore in each clock cycle. Thus, with every clock two results leave the pipelines.

The second stage of the Pentium pipeline, the *first decoding stage D1*, consists of two parallel working decoders; they both perform first-stage decoding of the instructions passed on from the instruction prefetch stage. This first D1 stage also determines whether the two *k* and *k+1* instructions can be paired and, thus, whether the instructions can be executed, in parallel, in the u- and v-pipelines.

The instruction decoding stage D1 also decodes instruction prefixes and passes them on to the u-pipeline. The pairing rules prevent prefixes, apart from the 2-byte opcode prefix 0fh for the

Jcc instruction, from being passed through the v-pipeline. For each prefix, a processor clock cycle is necessary, so that every prefix delays the execution of the proper instruction in the u-pipeline by one cycle. After all prefixes have been loaded into the u-pipeline, the proper instruction code is transferred, which then enables it to be paired with another instruction.

The *second instruction decoding stage D2* forms the third stage of the Pentium pipeline. It determines operand addresses. Also, instructions with an immediate operand and a displacement (such as ADD [array], 08h), and instructions with base and simultaneous index addressing (like MOV dword ptr [ebp][edi], value), can be executed in the D2 stage in a single clock cycle. The i486 requires two clock cycles for this.

The *execution stage EX*, as the fourth pipeline stage, deals with all ALU and cache accesses required to perform ALU operations and to load memory operands from the cache. Instructions with an ALU and a cache access, such as ADD eax, mem32 (ALU access: ADD, cache access: mem32) require more than one clock cycle in this stage. The execution stage also checks branch predictions which have been carried out in the D1 stage. Note that conditional jumps in the v-pipeline are first verified in the WB stage.

The last *write-back stage WB* writes back the instruction results into the destination registers. In this way, the instruction execution is completed. Additionally, branch predictions for conditional jumps of the v-pipeline are checked for correctness.

Instruction Pipelining and Interrupts

Exceptions and software interrupts are recognized by the Pentium when the corresponding instruction is executed in the execution stage of the pipeline. All instructions already located in the following pipeline stages are completed. Instructions in the prefetch and decoding stages, on the other hand, are deleted. Thus, the interrupt behaviour of the Pentium is similar to that in the i486.

On the other hand, external hardware interrupt requests are asynchronous, and are triggered by a signal with the corresponding level at an interrupt input. For this, it is necessary for the Pentium to continually check the actual interrupt input. This always occurs when a new instruction is loaded into the execution stage EX. As with a software interrupt or an exception, the Pentium completes all instructions that are located in subsequent pipeline stages, and the instructions in the prefetch and the decoding stage are deleted. Through the superscalar architecture of the Pentium, it is possible that two instructions are located, in parallel, in the u- and v-pipelines when an interrupt occurs. The interrupt is handled when the instructions in both of the pipelines have been completed. You can stop the scanning of the INTR input by resetting the IE interrupt flag; the Pentium then only recognizes the Non Maskable Interrupt (NMI). In addition to the hardware interrupts known from the i386, the signals $R/\overline{S}$, $\overline{FLUSH}$, $\overline{SMI}$ and INIT are also implemented as interrupts. This means that the activation of these signals will, possibly, not lead to the immediate interruption of the program execution. The difference between the i386 without a pipeline, and the superscalar Pentium, is that in the Pentium, an interrupt is recognized even though the previous instruction has not yet been completed (however, this does not necessarily give rise to an immediate response). The i386, on the other hand, finishes every instruction in its entirety before it checks whether there is an interrupt request.

If a number of interrupt requests occur simultaneously, then the Pentium handles them in accordance with the following priorities:

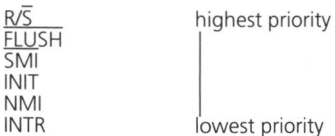

R/$\overline{S}$	highest priority
$\overline{FLUSH}$	
SMI	
INIT	
NMI	
INTR	lowest priority

You will find a complete list of all Pentium exceptions in Appendix D.3.

The exceptions can occur as traps or faults; the saved instruction address then refers either to the instruction immediately following the error (trap) or to the instruction itself (fault). The abort 08h (double fault) switches the Pentium, like its protected mode predecessors 80286 to i486, into shutdown mode, which it can only leave after an NMI or a reset.

12.2.2 Instruction Pairing Inside the Integer Pipelines

For the simultaneous execution of two integer instructions, the Pentium uses the mechanism of instruction pairing. In the instruction flow, the instruction of an instruction pair that is loaded into the v-pipeline immediately follows the instruction loaded into the u-pipeline; it is in fact a pair, and not just two instructions, that is executed. A very important feature of the Pentium is that the Pentium carries out this instruction pairing automatically and independently. With many other superscalars (such as the i960 and the i860, for example), the compiler must specifically call for parallel processing in the pipelines. The Pentium, in comparison, requires neither software control instructions nor specific dual instructions to use the superscalar architecture. This is also necessary with respect to compatibility with the Pentium's x86 predecessors, because they only contained a microencoded control unit (8086 to i386), or only one pipeline (i486), so that instructions could not be executed in parallel. Instruction pairing and the parallel execution of two instructions in the superscalar architecture of the Pentium is thus entirely transparent to the programmer. Naturally, this in no way means that the correspondingly adapted encoding, and the sequence of the instructions, does not play an important part in increasing the performance. Even slight changes in the code sequence to avoid register dependency can produce substantial increases in the performance. But now first to the basic rules according to which the Pentium assembles sequential instructions into pairs.

Pairing Rules

Instruction pairing is governed by six rules. Rules seldom exist without exceptions (as these examples confirm), and it is not astonishing that the rules are not strictly observed all the time.

Rule 1

Both instructions of a pair must be simple. The simple instructions of the Pentium are entirely hardwired; in no way are inputs of microcode from the microcode ROM necessary. In this way they can normally be executed in a single clock cycle. The simple instructions include (ALU indicates any arithmetic or logical instruction, such as ADD or AND, for example):

```
MOV reg, reg/mem/imm        DEC reg/mem
MOV mem, reg/imm           PUSH reg/mem
ALU reg, reg/mem/imm        POP reg/mem
ALU mem, reg/imm            LEA reg, mem
INC reg/mem                 JMP/Jcc NEAR/CALL
NOP
```

Rule 2

Unconditional jumps JMP, conditional jumps *Jcc near* and function calls can only be paired if they occur as the second instruction in a pair, that is, loaded into the v-pipeline.

Rule 3

Shifting by one position (SAL/SAR/SHL/SHR reg/mem, 1) or an immediate operand (SAL/SAR/SHL/SHR reg/mem,imm) and rotations by one position (RCL/RCR/ROL/ROR reg/mem, 1) must occur as the first instruction in an instruction pair, that is, they must only be loaded into the u-pipeline.

Rule 4

No register dependencies must occur between the instructions in an instruction pair. They generate an interlock and stall the pipeline accordingly. This cancels the advantage of instruction pairing.

Note that such register dependencies, which make instruction pairing impossible, are not restricted to an explicit register dependency alone. Moreover, indirect or implicit dependencies can also occur, if registers or flags are affected, that are not explicitly given in the instruction.

Rule 5

Instructions with a prefix (such as the segment override, the LOCK or the repeat prefix), can only occur in the u-pipeline. The only exception is the 0fh prefix which indicates a 2-byte opcode. 0fh can occur in connection with a conditional branch Jcc, and is the only prefix that can be loaded into the v-pipeline. Only in this way is it possible for conditional jumps to obey rule 2.

Rule 6

The two instructions executed in parallel must not simultaneously refer to a displacement and an immediate operand. This occurs, for example, in the following instruction: ADD array[02h],08h. In this case, array[02h] represents the displacement and 08h the immediate operand.

Figure 12.5 shows an example of a realistic instruction execution in the two integer pipelines, when instruction pairing is sometimes possible and sometimes does not fulfil the pairing rules.

Deviations

The exceptions which prove the rules 1–6 are summarized in the following.

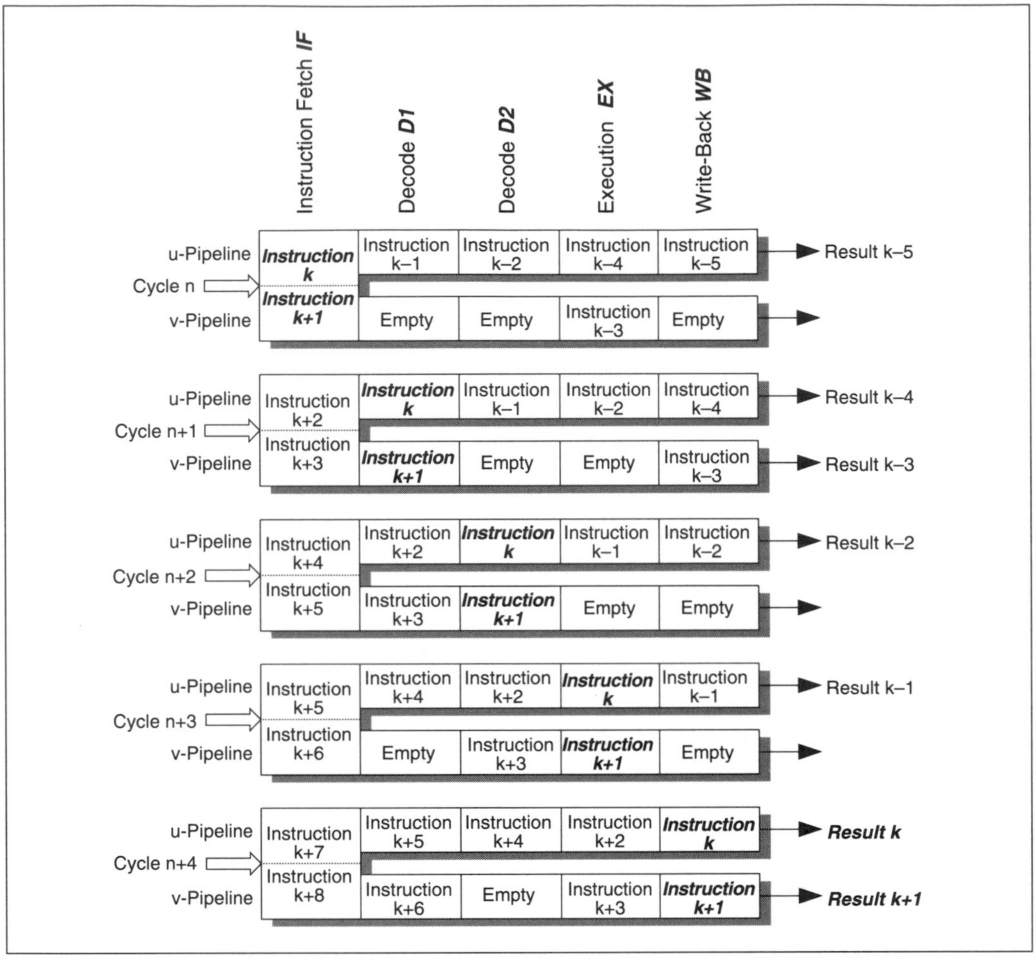

Figure 12.5: Instruction execution in the two integer pipelines u and v. In the example shown, instruction pairing is not always possible. The instructions k–4 and k–3, k and k+1, k+2 and k03 as well as k+5 and k+6 can be paired. The instructions k–5, k–2, k–1 and k+4 can only be executed individually. The result flow «splutters».

Deviation from Rule 1

The simple instructions ALU reg,mem and ALU mem,reg require two and three clock cycles respectively, and therefore deviate from the requirement of 1-cycle instructions.

Deviation from Rule 4

Comparison and branch instructions can be paired. This occurs very often because, in general, a comparison precedes a conditional branch. Above all, especially in programs that are not optimized for the pipelined processing of instructions, these two instructions immediately follow each other. Therefore, it is important that the two instructions can be paired, in order to increase the performance of the Pentium. Fortunately, this is possible without causing problems, because conditional branches are controlled by branch prediction, which takes place in the instruction fetch stage and is thus carried out prior to the production of the jump condition; the jump is executed (taken branch) or not executed (not taken branch) independently of the jump condition. The actual jump is only executed after the verification in the EX or WB stages as applicable, if the jump condition has already been evaluated.

Implicit Instruction Pairing by CISC Microcode

If we look at instruction pairing as the parallel operation of both pipelines, something like implicit instruction pairing is done by the CISC microcode. As I have already mentioned, the complex instructions (for example, string operations, task switch algorithms, ENTER, LOOP etc.) are microencoded. They are stored in a microcode ROM in the form of a series of micro instructions. The Pentium microcodes have been optimized for the superscalar architecture and use both pipelines in parallel as far as possible. REP MOVSD can be considered as a repeated series of elementary instructions which are executed by the microcode in the pipelines in parallel – a type of implicit instruction pairing. By the way, for microcode there is an optimization level available (namely the individual elements of the u- and v-pipelines) which is not accessable even for an optimizing compiler. This, too, contributes to a significantly enhanced throughput and compatibility. The main obstacles in the way of a pure RISC Pentium are in fact the complex CISC instructions which appear in already existing programs. Existing microcode either cannot, or can only with a considerable amount of work, be mapped onto a completely different instruction set. Thus, it is better to keep the CISC instructions and to pack the optimization into the newly designed chip. The optimization can be carried out completely transparently for existing software without any need to decrease compatibility. Of course, this is not as successful as the request for unified hardware and software right from the start, which is significant for RISCs. Nevertheless, the performance gain in the Pentium is impressive.

12.2.3 The Floating-point Pipeline

In addition to the two integer pipelines, the Pentium also contains a floating-point unit, which executes floating-point instructions in a pipelined manner.

Structure of the Floating-point Pipeline

The floating-point pipeline contains eight stages, with the first five stages IF to WB being shared with the u-pipeline. The pairing rules prevent the parallel execution of integer and floating-point instructions. Only the FXCHG instruction, which exchanges two elements of the register stack in the floating-point unit, can be executed simultaneously with another floating-point instruction in the v-pipeline. In Figure 12.6, you can see a schematic representation of the structure of the floating-point unit.

As the pairing of integer and floating-point instructions is not possible due to the pairing rules, the u- and the floating-point pipelines can share the first five pipeline stages. In this way, the floating-point pipeline uses the WB stage of the u-pipeline as its first execution stage, which likewise performs write operations. The destination is, however, not an integer register but the register stack FP(0) to FP(7) of the floating-point unit. A significant difference between the Pentium and the i486 is that, in addition to an adder, a multiplier and a divider are also included in the hardware, in order to accelerate floating-point multiplications and divisions. The remaining elements of the Pentium floating-point unit are more or less identical to those in the i486; for example, a register stack with eight 80-bit registers which store floating-point numbers in the temporary real format is available.

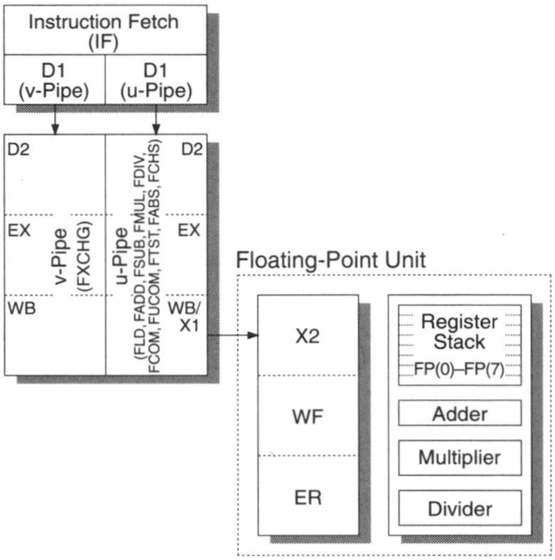

Figure 12.6: The structure of the Pentium floating-point unit. The floating-point unit implements a pipeline with eight stages. It shares the first five stages with the u-pipeline.

The first stage IF, as previously explained, reads in the instruction and passes it on to the first decoding stage D1. The second decoding stage D2 produces the operand addresses (for example, for the instruction FLD mem_real). In the EX stage, the data cache and the register operand are read, and in the case of an FSTORE instruction, data in the internal 80-bit representation is converted into the representation of the memory target. The last X1 stage, shared with the u-pipeline, handles floating-point instructions in a similar, but not identical way to integer instructions. For the u-pipeline, X1 represents the register write stage WB. X1, as the first FP execution stage, has a similar function in the floating-point pipeline: an operand read from the data cache or memory is converted into the temporary real format and is written to one of the registers in the register stack FP(0) to FP(7).

In addition to this, the X1 stage has the additional task of identifying so-called *safe instructions;* this is also known as *Safe Instruction Recognition* (*SIR*). Safe instructions do not cause an overflow, underflow or exception through an inaccuracy. Additionally, they can handle masked exceptions internally (for example, provide a value of 0 in the case of an underflow). If the current instruction is recognized as safe, then the subsequent floating-point instruction – providing that there is one at hand – leaves the EX stage and enters the X1 stage as soon as the previous instruction has proceeded to the second execution stage X2. If it is not certain that the current instruction is safe, then the subsequent instruction in the EX stage is held up, and thus so is the complete pipeline, until the current instruction has left the last ER stage without producing an error.

The three stages that follow are only implemented in the floating-point pipeline, and are totally independent from the u-pipeline. The second FP execution stage X2 performs the actual execution of the floating-point instruction. Finally, the eighth and last *ER* stage of the floating-point pipeline deals with errors that may occur and updates the status word accordingly.

Instruction Pairing

Floating-point instructions can be paired to execute two instructions at the same time. They are, however, considerably more restrictive, because «full» floating-point instructions require stages IF to X1 of the u-pipeline and X2 to ER of the floating-point pipeline, of which only one of each is available. Only the instruction FXCHG for exchanging two register values on the register stack FP(0) to FP(7) can, in certain circumstances, be executed in the v-pipeline, in parallel to another floating-point instruction. With only eight floating-point registers FP(0) to FP(7), stack overflows can quickly occur. To prevent this, and also to be able to use lower lying register values, for example as source operands, the value in TOP must be exchanged frequently with other register values. The FXCHG instruction serves this purpose. Its simple structure makes the FXCHG instruction an ideal candidate for instruction pairing. The following rules apply.

Rule 1

A floating-point instruction can only be paired with an FXCHG instruction; other pairings of floating-point instructions with each other are not possible

Rule 2

Only the following floating-point instructions can be paired with the FXCHG instruction:

- FLD memreal32/memreal64/ST(i);
- all types (normal, integer, with or without POP) of the instructions FADD, FSUB, FMUL, FDIV, FCOM, FUCOM, FTST, FABS and FCHS.

Rule 3

All instructions that neither represent an FXCHG instruction nor belong to the instruction group defined in rule 2 are processed as single instructions in the u-pipeline. They cannot be paired with a simple instruction in the v-pipeline because they themselves are not simple instructions (violation of rule 1 for integer instruction pairings).

Rule 4

The FXCHG instruction must be the second of the pair, that is, it must be loaded into the v-pipeline. If the subsequent instruction is other than FXCHG, then it is executed as a separate instruction in the u-pipeline, that is, not paired.

12.2.4 Instruction Serialization

For many situations and instructions, it is essential that an instruction is completed before the next instruction is transferred for execution into the Pentium pipeline. An example of this is the OUT instruction, which switches an external gate for the address line A20 to emulate the stone-age-like address wrap-around of the 8086. This switching informs the Pentium through the A20M signal that it also masks the address line A20 for internal accesses to the on-chip cache. If the instruction following the OUT instruction does not switch into, or switches back from, the wrap-around condition, then pipelined instruction execution can lead to problems. The OUT instruction is first executed in the EX stage and, in this way, an I/O bus cycle to the A20 gate is executed. The subsequent instruction finds itself in the second decoding stage D2, and so has already been read in and partly decoded. For this reason, the instruction fetching for the instruction is not influenced by the switching of the gate, and so, possibly, an incorrect instruction has been collected.

The problem described above can be solved through *serializing the instruction execution*. This means that the next instruction is only loaded into the first pipeline stage when the current instruction has been fully completed and has left the last stage. Additionally, serializing causes an emptying of the prefetch queue. It is carried out when the Pentium executes one of the following (serialization) instructions:

- MOV control register/debug register (except for CR0);
- INVD, INVLPG, WBINVD;
- IRET, IRETD;
- LGDT, LLDT, LIDT, LTR;
- CPUID;
- RSM, WRMSR.

Above all, the CPUID instruction is useful for serialization because it can be carried out at every protection level without causing a protection exception and, additionally, it in no way influences control registers and EFlags; only the four general-purpose registers EAX, EBX, ECX and EDX are overwritten with an identification code. The i486 implicitly performs a serialization as soon as a jump or a branch instruction occurs.

12.2.5 Dynamic Branch Prediction

Jumps and branches have slowed down program execution significantly in modern microprocessors for a long time. Thus, it is not astonishing that the hardware engineers are looking for appropriate solutions. One idea can be found in the Pentium: branch prediction logic, which in most cases can avoid prefetch delays. By the way, branch prediction is not a monopoly of Intel chips. It is included in various forms in many modern RISC chips, such as DEC's Alpha or Motorola's PowerPC. RISC CPUs suffer greatly from branch delays because of the instruction pipelining.

Structure and Functionality of Branch Prediction Logic

Branch prediction logic consists of a control unit and the *branch trace buffer* or *branch target buffer* (BTB). The BTB represents a type of cache with a total of 256 entries, whose tags contains the addresses of instructions that immediately precede the branch instruction, that is, not that of the branch instruction itself. Furthermore, as an actual cache entry it contains the target address of the jump and also history bits that deliver statistical information about the frequency of the current branch. In this respect, an executed branch is known as a *taken branch* and a non-executed branch is known as a *not-taken branch*. The dynamic branch prediction predicts the branches according to the instructions that the Pentium has executed previously, thus the Pentium «learns».

The prefetch buffer and BTB work together to fetch the most likely instruction after a jump. Note that the Pentium supplies the address of the instruction in the D1 decoding stage to the BTB, that is, the EIP address of the instruction that precedes a jump instruction, and not the EIP address of the jump instruction itself. With a BTB hit, the branch prediction logic delivers the address of the jump target instruction, as the instruction fetch address, to the IF stage of the pipeline. If many branch instructions occur in a program, the BTB, like all caches, will at some point become full; then BTB misses also occur for branch instructions. A BTB miss is handled as a not-taken branch. The dynamic BTB algorithms of the Pentium independently take care of the reloading of new branch instructions, and the «noting» of the most likely branch target. In this way, branch prediction logic can reliably predict the branches.

Usually, preceding a conditional branch, a comparison of two numbers occurs, for example, either explicitly through CMP or implicitly through SUB. The execution of this comparison takes place in the fourth EX stage, and the writing of the EFlag register takes place in the fifth WB stage. At this point, the subsequent CMP instruction is already in the second decoding stage D2 or the execution stage. In the case of an instruction pairing, it can even be in the same stage as the comparison instruction. The prediction for unconditional jumps (using JMP) and conditional jumps (using Jcc) of the u-pipeline, and for calls (using CALL), can first be checked in the execution stage EX. For conditional jumps of the v-pipeline, the prediction can first be checked in the register write stage WB.

If the prediction is shown to be correct, as is nearly always the case with unconditional jumps and procedure calls (only incorrect or old BTB entries from a different task can change this), then all instructions loaded into the pipeline after the jump instruction are correct, and the pipeline operation is continued without interruption. Thus, if the prediction is correct, branches and calls are executed within a single clock cycle, and in accordance with the pairing rules, in parallel to other instructions. If, in the EX or WB stages, the prediction is found to be incorrect, then the Pentium empties the pipeline and tells the instruction fetching stage to fetch the instruction at the correct address. Finally, the pipeline restarts operations in the normal way. The dynamic algorithms can, however, generally avoid such situations with the history bit.

Effects of Branch Prediction – An Example

Even in the i486, the effects of executed branches (taken branches) are noticeable. They delay the instruction execution quite considerably. As a short explanation, I would like to discuss the following example. The init_loop is important in the example, as it is run a hundred times for field initialization.

Example: `initialize array with 100 double words 00000000h.`

```
mov edx, 00000000h  ; load initialize value into edx
lea eax, array      ; store start address of array in eax
mov ecx, eax+396    ; load address of last field element into ecx
init_loop:          ; beginning of initializing loop
  mov [eax], edx    ; set field element to 00000000h
  add eax, 04h      ; next field element
  cmp eax, ecx      ; determine whether last address has been reached, i.e. whether eax-exc>0
  jbe init_loop     ; loop again, if last address has not yet been reached
```

In the i486, the instructions MOV, ADD, CMP and JBE are executed sequentially, because only one pipeline is available. The first three instructions each require only one clock cycle. The conditional jump JBE is executed 99 times and needs three clock cycles on the i486. So in the i486, six cycles are required for each loop.

This is different in the Pentium. Here, the four loop instructions can be paired:

```
u-pipeline        v-pipeline

mov [eax], edx    add eax, 04h
cmp eax, ecx      jbe init_loop
```

The first line with MOV and ADD is executed in one cycle. If it establishes the branch prediction for JBE as correct, then the second line is also executed in only one cycle. Thus, in total, only two clock cycles are required to complete the operation of the loop. This is three times quicker than with the i486 (and 6.5 times quicker compared to the i386). Note that the higher Pentium clock rate (except the DX2/66 and DX4) enhances the performance further.

A false prediction by the BTB logic would cause a delay in the execution of four clock cycles, because the JBE instruction is located in the v-pipeline and is not verified before the WB stage. Due to operation of the initialization loop a hundred times, the BTB logic learns fairly quickly that a taken branch is correct. Only for the first loop is it likely that the BTB logic will produce an erroneous branch prediction, because as yet the BTB has no «experience» with the outcome of the CMP and JBE instructions. Also, it is quite likely that the BTB will predict an erroneous branch for the last loop operation, because of the history bits and the previous 99 taken branches. Thus, branch prediction gives a great advantage when frequently repeated loops are required, as is often the case with the implementation of algorithms employed in the calculation of mathematical expressions, or with visualization of processor results.

12.2.6 Pentium On-Chip Caches

As already mentioned, there are two separate and independent 8 kbyte caches for code and data. In this way, no collisions are possible between instruction prefetching and data accesses occurring in one of the pipeline stages; the data and code caches work in parallel, and can be addressed simultaneously. Each cache is laid out as 2-way set-associative (i486: 4-way set-associative), each cache line is 32 bytes long (i486: 16 bytes) giving a total of 128 sets. In burst mode a cache line can be read or written back via the 64-bit data bus within four transfer cycles.

For cache flushes through software, the two instructions INVD (invalidate data cache) and WBINVD (write-back and invalidate data cache) are available as in the i486. In both cases the Pentium sends a flush special cycle through the bus to indicate that invalidation has been executed. For the WBINVD, first a write-back special cycle is driven and then a flush special cycle is sent through the bus.

On-Chip Code and Data Caches

The data cache fully supports the MESI protocol with its four states. In this way, the write-through or write-back strategy of the data cache, according to the MESI protocol, can be set individually for each 32 byte cache line using the shared state. The code cache cannot be written to – except, of course, through an automatic reloading during instruction fetching – and so only supports the shared and invalid states. Together with the setting of individual pages as cachable or not cachable through the PCD and PWT-bits in the page directory or page table entry, by resetting and setting the CD-bit in the CR0 control register the two caches can be enabled or disabled. The replacement strategy and the MESI protocol are implemented as fixed parts of the hardware, so no software is necessary for managing the caches.

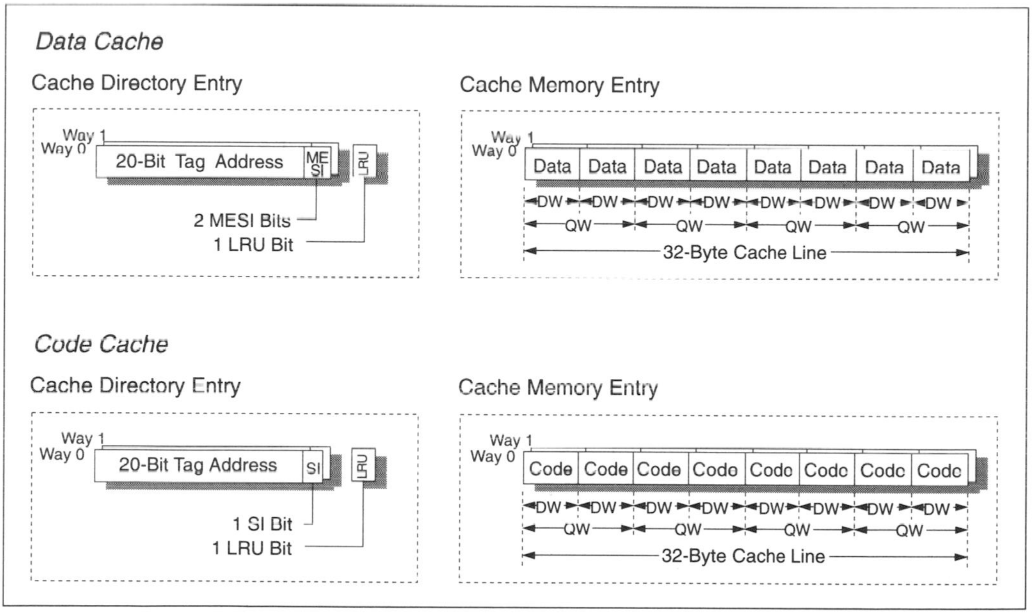

Figure 12.7: Tag and memory entries of the Pentium caches.

The replacement of cache lines in the two on-chip caches is accomplished through an LRU algorithm that replaces the least used entry in the two ways by the new data. For implementation of the LRU algorithm, every set contains an LRU-bit that points to the least frequently used entry. Additionally, every tag also requires information about the current MESI state of the applicable line. In the data cache, this is achieved by two MESI-bits that codify in binary the four possible MESI states: modified, exclusive, shared and invalid. As the code cache only supports the shared and invalid states, one MESI-bit is sufficient. Figure 12.7 shows the structure of the tag and memory entries for both on-chip caches.

Translation Lookaside Buffers

As is apparent from Figure 12.1, every cache has its own Translation Lookaside Buffer (TLB). The caches use physical addresses, that is, the conversion of the linear address into the corresponding physical address must be accomplished before access to the cache.

Two TLBs are assigned to the data cache: the first is for managing the standard 4 kbyte pages, and the second is for the newly implemented 4 Mbyte pages. The first TLB has the capacity for 64 entries and is laid out as a 4-way set-associative cache with 16 sets. The second TLB is also a 4-way set-associative cache, but it only has eight entries.

The code cache has only one TLB, which is used for both the standard 4 kbyte pages and the new 4 Mbyte pages. It has a capacity of 32 entries, and is configured as a 4-way set-associative cache. Thus, the code cache TLB is much smaller than the data cache TLB (which you can also clearly see from Figure 12.1). Code accesses are executed because of the linear instruction flow in a more continuous way compared to data accesses. Thus, the code cache TLB does not require as many entries to achieve just as good a hit rate (typically 99% or more, according to Intel).

Operating Modes and Registers for Controlling On-Chip Caches

Activation of the on-chip cache and the cache strategy therein is mainly set by the CR0 control register, as in the i486. You can see its structure in Figure 12.8.

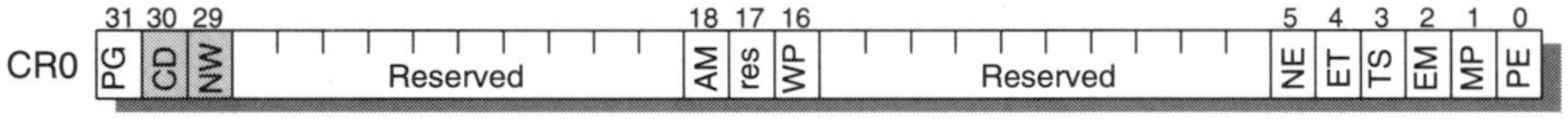

CD: cache disable
0=on-chip caches enabled 1=on-chip caches disabled
NW: not write-through
0=write-through strategy for data cache 1=write-back strategy for data cache

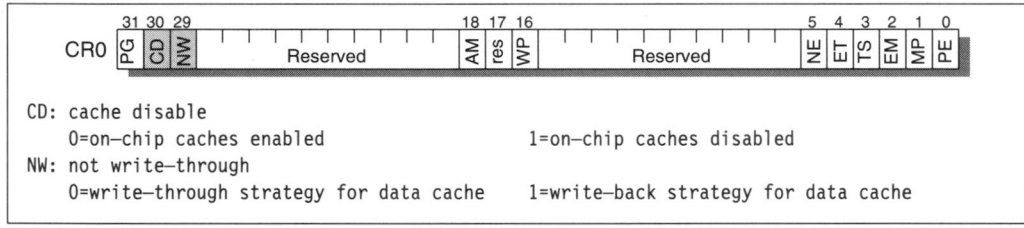

Figure 12.8: Structure of control register CR0.

The bits CD (Cache Disable) and NW (Not Write-through) influence the on-chip caches. The effects of the four possible combinations of the two control bits are given in the following.

CD=0, NW=0

Read accesses are dealt with by the applicable cache when a hit occurs in a code or data cache. Misses initiate a cache line fill if the values are cachable ($\overline{KEN}$ at a low level); the loaded cache line is then stored in the exclusive or shared state, depending on the external signal WB/$\overline{WT}$. Thus, the on-chip caches are fully enabled. Only during a hit to a shared cache line or a miss is an external write bus cycle initiated. Thus, the cache operates using a write-back strategy according to the MESI protocol. Finally, the on-chip caches support inquiry cycles and the corresponding invalidations.

CD=0, NW=1

This bit combination is invalid. The Pentium issues a general protection fault corresponding to the interrupt 0dh.

CD=1, NW=0

Read accesses are dealt with by the applicable cache when a hit occurs in a code or data cache. Misses do not initiate a cache line fill, because the cache is disabled by CD=1. Write accesses update the data cache when a hit occurs. The data to be written only additionally appears on the external bus if a hit to a shared cache line or a miss occurs. The write-back strategy is set by NW=0, even if cache line fills are disabled. Even though the caches are in fact disabled, they still support inquiry cycles and the corresponding invalidations.

CD=1, NW=1

Read accesses are dealt with by each cache when a hit occurs. Misses do not initiate a cache line fill, because the cache, as above, is disabled by CD=1. Write accesses update the data cache when a hit occurs, but due to NW=1 are never switched through to the external bus. For a write miss, the write access is switched through to the external bus. The caches support neither inquiry cycles nor invalidations.

From the description you can see that the CD-bit only disables cache line fills, but not the cache function as a whole. If you wish to actually disable the on-chip caches, you must additionally issue a cache flush. Through this, all entries are invalidated and no more cache hits can occur. CD=1 disables the otherwise generated line fills.

The MESI transitions and the results of inquiry cycles in the Pentium are controlled and given respectively, by a number of different signals. Table 12.1 lists the input or output signals. The transition diagram has already been shown in Figure 9.5.

Transition	**Signal**
Read access	
M → M (R_1)	none
E → E (R_2)	none
S → S (R_3)	none
I → E (R_4)	$\overline{\text{CACHE}}$=0, $\overline{\text{KEN}}$=0, WB/$\overline{\text{WT}}$=1, PWT=0
I → S (R_5)	$\overline{\text{CACHE}}$=0, $\overline{\text{KEN}}$=0, WB/$\overline{\text{WT}}$=0 or $\overline{\text{CACHE}}$=0, $\overline{\text{KEN}}$=0, PWT=1
I → I (R_6)	$\overline{\text{CACHE}}$=1 or $\overline{\text{KEN}}$=1
Write access	
M → M (W_1)	none
E → M (W_2)	none
S → E (W_3)	PWT=0, WB/$\overline{\text{WT}}$=1
S → S (W_4)	PWT=0, WB/$\overline{\text{WT}}$=0 or PWT=1
I → I (W_5)	none

Transition	Signal
Inquiry cycle	
M → S (S_1)	INV=0, $\overline{HIT}$=0, $\overline{HITM}$=0
M → I (S_2)	INV=1, $\overline{HIT}$=0, $\overline{HITM}$=0
E → S (S_3)	INV=0, $\overline{HIT}$=0
E → I (S_4)	INV=1, $\overline{HIT}$=0
S → S (S_5)	INV=0, $\overline{HIT}$=0
S → I (S_6)	INV=1, $\overline{HIT}$=0
I → I (S_7)	INV=0, $\overline{HIT}$=1 or INV=1, $\overline{HIT}$=1

Table 12.1: Pentium signals for MESI transitions and inquiry cycles

R_4 to R_6 (Figure 9.5) are controlled in the Pentium by the $\overline{KEN}$ signal (for cachable data) and the WT/$\overline{WB}$ signal (for the write-through or write-back cache strategies).

Caching at a Page Level

In addition to the individual definitions of the cache strategy and activation of the cache at a cache line level, with an active Paging Unit (PU) it is also possible to influence caching at a page level in the same way as in the i486. Bits PCD (Page Cache Disable) and PWT (Page Write Through) are used for this. They are included in the page directory and the page table entry, and control the activation of caching (PCD) and the cache strategy (PWT), respectively. Figure 12.9 shows the structure of the entries.

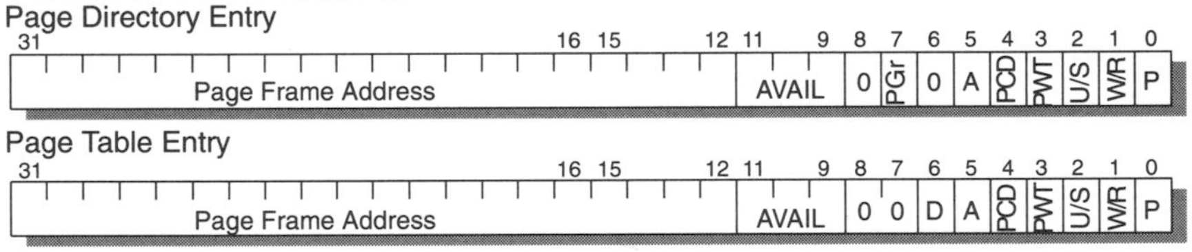

PCD: page cache disable
 0=page cachable 1=page not cachable
PWT: page write-through
 0=page uses write-back strategy 1=page uses write-through strategy

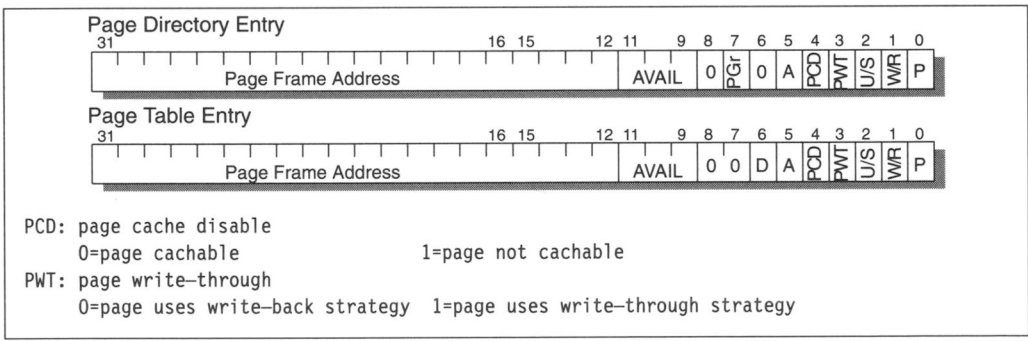

Figure 12.9: Page directory and page table entries.

If the PCD-bit is reset, the page data can be transferred to the on-chip cache, that is, a cache line fill is executed, if $\overline{KEN}$ is also at a low level. If, on the other hand, the PCD-bit is set (equals 1), then no data of the written page can be loaded into the cache, even if there is nothing to stop it from the hardware side (low level $\overline{KEN}$ signal). If the PWT-bit equals 0, that is, reset, then the cache should use a write-back strategy for the data of the page. If PWT is set (equals 1), then the page requires a write-through strategy. Naturally, the value of PWT has no effect if no caching is necessary for the page. During a memory access, the effective values of PCD and PWT are given by the PCD and PWT pins of the Pentium, respectively. If an L2-cache is available, the signals can be used to individually match an applicable cache strategy to the current memory access.

12.3 Pentium Compatibility and New Pentium Features

In this section, I will discuss the compatibility between the Pentium and its predecessors, i386 and i486. If it is not explicitly indicated that there is a difference between the Pentium and these two processors, then all explanations for the i386 and i486 are also valid for the Pentium. This particularly applies to the protected mode mechanisms.

12.3.1 Extensions to the Pentium Registers

This section briefly introduces the register extensions in the Pentium. There are some additional bits and newly implemented test and control registers. Except for CR4 and TR12, all the registers have already been implemented in the i386 and i486.

Pentium EFlags

In the Pentium, the EFlag register has been enlarged by three additional flags. These refer to the Pentium enhancements for virtual 8086 mode and identification of the CPU type. The three new EFlags flags are shaded in Figure 12.10.

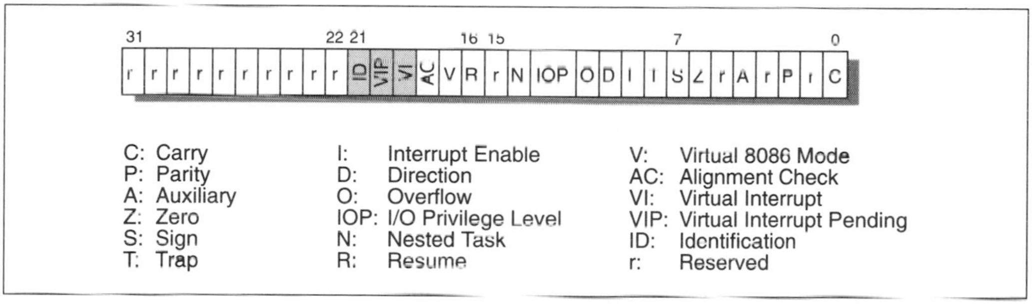

Figure 12.10: Pentium EFlags.

The virtual interrupt flag *VI* flag is a virtual version of IE for issuing interrupts in virtual 8086 mode. In a similar way, the virtual interrupt pending flag *VIP* also supports tasks in virtual 8086 mode to provide a virtual IE flag. In this way, interrupts in virtual 8086 mode are accelerated considerably. Further details about Pentium enhancements to the virtual 8086 mode are discussed in Section 12.3.5. As a final new element in the EFlag register there is an identification flag *ID*, which indicates whether the processor supports the CPUID instruction for its identification. If you can set and reset the ID flag, then CPUID will be correctly carried out, and will deliver information concerning the type and functional capabilities of the processor.

Control Register CR4

The Pentium has been extended by a control register CR4. This register controls the Pentium extensions for virtual 8086 mode, debugger support and the enhanced 4 Mbyte pages. The four control registers CR0 to CR3 remain unchanged. Figure 12.11 shows the structure of the new control register CR4.

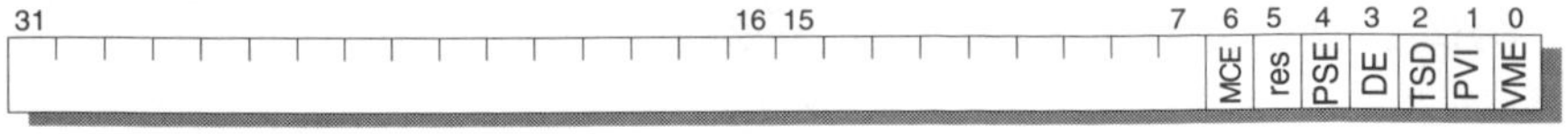


```
MCE: machine check enable
     1=machine check exception enabled        0=machine check exception disabled
PSE: page size extension
     1=4Mbyte pages                           0=4kbyte pages
DE:  debugging extension
     1=breakpoints also for I/O space         0=breakpoint for memory space only
TSD: time stamp disable
     1=RDTSC only with CPL=0                  0=RDTSC also with CPL=3..1
PVI: protected mode virtual interrupts
     1=virtual interrupt flags in protected mode     0=no virtual interrupt flags
VME: virtual 8086 mode extension
     1=virtual interrupt flags in virtual 8086 mode  0=no virtual interrupt flags
```

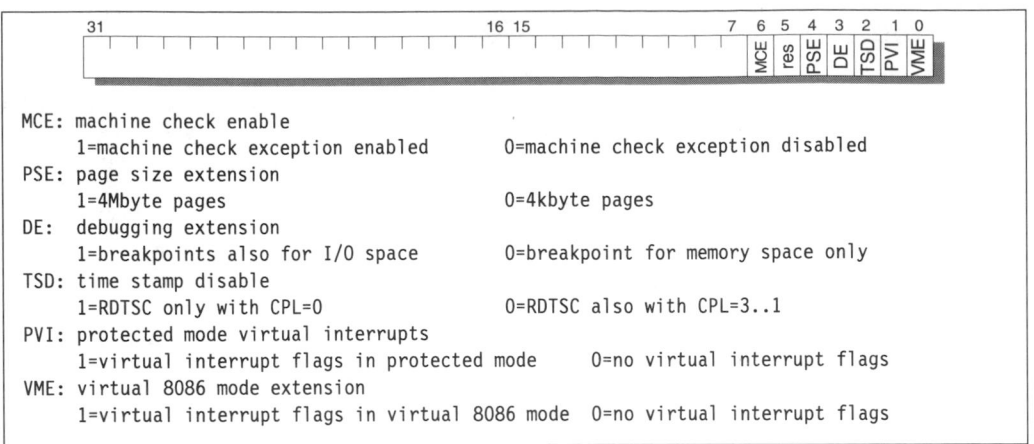

Figure 12.11: CR4 control register.

The control register CR4 implements six new control bits for supporting virtual 8086 mode and other new features.

A set virtual 8086 mode extension bit *VME* enables the support of virtual interrupt flags in virtual 8086 mode. In this way, interrupts are executed more quickly, and performance in virtual 8086 mode increases. The virtual 8086 monitor is then no longer required. The associated task switches (Figure 3.25) are unnecessary.

The protected mode virtual interrupt bit *PVI* has, in protected mode, a similar purpose to the VME-bit in virtual 8086 mode. A set PVI-bit enables the supporting of virtual interrupt flags in protected mode. In this way, programs that were originally designed for execution with CPL=0 can, under certain circumstances, be executed with CPL=3. By setting the time stamp disable bit *TSD*, the RDTSC instruction, which reads the value of the time stamp counter, becomes a so-called «privileged instruction». It can then only be executed with CPL=0 without generating a protection exception. If you also want to cover the I/O address space with breakpoints, you must set the debugging extension bit *DE*. The Pentium then interprets the 10b combination of the R/Wx-bits (invalid in the i386/i486) as a breakpoint for I/O write and I/O read accesses. Additionally, with the help of the page size extension bit PSE, you can set the size of a page. A set PSE-bit sets the page size at 4 Mbytes; with a reset PSE-bit, the PU will use the standard and i386/i486-compatible page size of 4 kbytes. Finally, by setting the machine check enable bit *MCE*, you enable the machine check exception (more on this subject in Section 12.7.6).

12.3.2 Model-Specific Registers

With Pentium, Intel has introduced the concept of «model-specific registers». To this group belong the machine check address register, the machine check type register, test registers TR1 to TR12, the time stamp counter, the control/event select register, and the two counters 0 and 1. For accesses to these registers, two new instructions RDMSR (read model-specific register) and WRMSR (write model-specific register) have been implemented. They have the formats shown in Table 12.2.

Register	Call value	Return value
RDMSR		
EAX		MSR content (low-order double word)
ECX	MSR number	
EDX		MSR content (high-order double word)
WRMSR		
EAX	MSR content (low-order double word)	
ECX	MSR number	
EDX	MSR content (high-order double word)	

MSR: model-specific register

Table 12.2: Format of instructions RDMSR and WRMSR

The three model-specific registers have the MSR numbers shown in Table 12.3.

Model-specific register	MSR number	Used for
Machine Check Address Register	00h	physical address of erroneous bus cycle
Machine Check Type Register	01h	type of erroneous bus cycle
TR12	0eh	control register for branch trace message special cycle
Time Stamp Counter	10h	read/write of internal 64-bit counter

Table 12.3: Model-specific register numbers

The other MISR numbers are reserved by Intel for test registers TR1 to TR11, as well as for the control and status registers of the performance monitoring feature. They are regarded by Intel as confidential (at least at the time of publishing this book). In most cases you can get some information about them directly from Intel, but you (like the author) are not allowed to republish it. Therefore, you will only find some of the model-specific registers in Table 12.3.

Intel's model-specific registers are used in this way only in the Pentium. In future processors of the 80x86 family and in Pentium derivatives such as the Pentium overdrive etc., they will possibly no longer be implemented, or at least not in the same way. All model-specific registers are 64-bits wide. In addition to Intel's intention to summarize such different registers as the test registers and various counters which are of partial importance only for a certain processor type under one single name, there is another reason for the concept of model-specific registers. In the Pentium, their number has been increased to such an extent that the processor is simply running out of opcodes for the former access scheme, for example with MOV CR0, reg or MOV reg, TR6. Thus, it is better to implement the two instructions RDMSR and WRMSR together with an indication of the model-specific register in form of a 32-bit number.

12.3.3 Pentium Real Mode

The real mode of the Pentium is compatible with that in the i386 or i486. For the calculation of linear and, at the same time, physical addresses, the Pentium shifts the value in a segment register by four bit positions to the left and, as usual, adds the offset or the effective address.

This produces physical addresses between 000000h and 10ffefh. Even though the offset register contains 32 bits, you cannot generate offset values greater than ffffh without causing an interrupt 12 (Och) or 13 (0dh). All other characteristics of the i386 real mode also apply to the Pentium real mode. You will find more details in Chapter 3.

12.3.4 Pentium Protected Mode

Also, the protected mode of Pentium is compatible with the protected mode of the i386/i486. The use of segment register values as segment selectors and the interpretation of segment descriptors remains unchanged. The complete physical 32-bit address space with a 4 Gbyte capacity is accessible. The memory of the Pentium is managed with the help of the memory management registers GDTR, LDTR, IDTR and TR. Protected mode is discussed in Section 3.7.

12.3.5 Pentium Virtual 8086 Mode

The virtual 8086 mode of the Pentium has been expanded due to its importance for DOS compatibility with the OS/2 and Windows NT operating systems, and also due to the operating system extension Windows. In this way, the performance should be increased. The main problem was that up until the i486, DOS programs often issued interrupts to call operating system functions. The handling of such interrupts in a real mode manner, but under the protected mode monitor in virtual 8086 mode, takes a long time. The main reason for this is the lengthy switching between the virtual 8086 program, the virtual 8086 monitor and the emulation routines for the required operating system functions, which are mostly carried out via task switches. They generate enormous data traffic (172 bytes in two TSSs per task switch) compared to the simple saving and restoring of ten bytes (EIP, CS, EFlags).

For enabling and controlling the Pentium virtual 8086 mode, the EFlag register and the new control register CR4 are implemented. You enable the address translation according to the virtual 8086 mode by setting the *VM*-flag in the EFlag register. With a cleared *VME*-bit in CR4, the Pentium virtual 8086 mode is just the same as in the i386/i486. By setting VME you are able to activate the new virtual 8086 functions of the Pentium. The bits *VIP* and *VI* now also have a meaning: VI is a virtual image of the usual interrupt flag; and a set VIP bit enables virtual interrupt flags for 8086 programs in virtual 8086 mode. Details of this are discussed in the following.

i386/i486 Compatible Pentium Virtual 8086 Mode

If the VME-bit in the CR4 control register is reset (equal to 0) then the virtual 8086 mode of the Pentium is compatible with the virtual 8086 mode of the i386 and i486. The two flags VIP (Virtual Interrupt Pending) and VI (Virtual Interrupt) in the EFlag register have no meaning and are not used. The handling of interrupts and exceptions in virtual 8086 mode, and especially switching between the 8086 program, virtual 8086 monitor and the protected mode operating system as represented in Figure 3.25, is performed in exactly the same way as in the i386/i486.

Extensions to Pentium Virtual 8086 Mode

Most information concerning the Pentium's extensions to virtual 8086 mode is, unfortunately, a closely guarded Intel secret (at least at the time of publishing this book). For this reason, only a brief overview of the new functions can be given.

The extensions of the Pentium for the virtual 8086 mode mainly affect the management of virtual interrupts through the virtual interrupt flag VIF and the virtual interrupt pending flag VIP in the EFlag register. Additionally, it is possible to redirect interrupts in virtual 8086 mode (thus, 8086-type interrupts) with the help of a so-called *redirection bit map*. You can also use the concept of virtual interrupts in normal protected mode. For this purpose, the EFlag register contains the protected mode virtual interrupt flag PVI.

Software interrupts, above all, represent a considerable problem in virtual 8086 mode. On the one hand, 8086 DOS programs can only communicate with DOS functions if INT 21h is called. On the other hand, the handling of interrupts was originally the responsibility of the operating system, or in this case, the virtual 8086 monitor. The redirection bit map enables the Pentium to redirect a software interrupt of the virtual 8086 task directly to the real mode interrupt handler. The interrupt handler is given at segment 0:offset 0 in the interrupt vector table of the virtual 8086 task.

The execution of some instructions depends in the virtual 8086 mode upon the value of the IOPL flag. These so-called «IOPL sensitive instructions» include CLI, STI, PUSHF, POPF, INTn and IRET. These instructions influence the condition of the processor and, therefore, the behaviour of the system, but they occur frequently in real mode applications.

An IOPL value of less than 3 causes an exception 0dh if one of these instructions occurs and no virtual 8086 mode extensions have been enabled. INTn and IRET can be handled by the redirection bit map. Only the four instructions CLI, STI, PUSHF and POPF remain. The virtual 8086 extensions of the Pentium now include a virtual interrupt flag VIF, and also a virtual interrupt pending flag VIP for the virtual 8086 mode, so that instructions which change the value of the interrupt flag IF (thus, CLI, STI, PUSHF and POPF), do not necessarily cause an exception which the virtual 8086 monitor will intercept.

The handling of hardware interrupts when the virtual 8086 extensions are active is a two-step operation. The interrupt initiated by the activation of the INTR input calls a protected mode interrupt handler through a gate; the handler deals with the interrupt accordingly, and sets the VIP flag on the stack. The interrupt handler is left and the interrupted 8086 program is resumed with an IRET. We again find ourselves in virtual 8086 mode. Here, the Pentium reacts to a VIP flag in a similar way to a hardware signal at the INTR input. CLI, STI, PUSHF and POPF only influence the masking of interrupts locally for the virtual 8086 task, and not globally for the whole system.

12.3.6 Paging on the Pentium

The paging function of the Pentium, compared to the i386 and i486, contains a new feature. In addition to the standard 4 kbyte pages, pages of 4 Mbytes are also possible in the Pentium. The cache strategy of the on-chip caches can be separately set for each page, as in the i486. At a hardware level, this is accomplished with the WB/$\overline{WT}$ signal through software with the PWT-bit in the page table entry. In this way, it is possible to choose either a write-through strategy (WB/$\overline{WT}$ at a low level, or PWT equals 1), or a write-back strategy (WB/$\overline{WT}$ at a high level, or PWT equals 0). In the following section, I only wish to explain the paging differences between the Pentium and the i386 and i486. You will find details concerning the general principles in Sections 3.8 and 10.6.

4 kbyte and 4 Mbyte Pages

For managing the «large» 4 Mbyte pages, the new SIZ-bit is provided in the page directory entry. Figure 12.12 shows the structure of the page directory and page table entries. Bit positions which have already been discussed in Sections 3.8.2 and 10.6.2 are not repeated here.

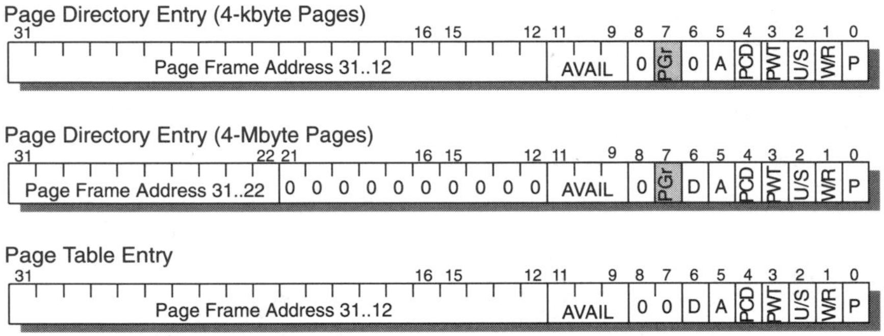

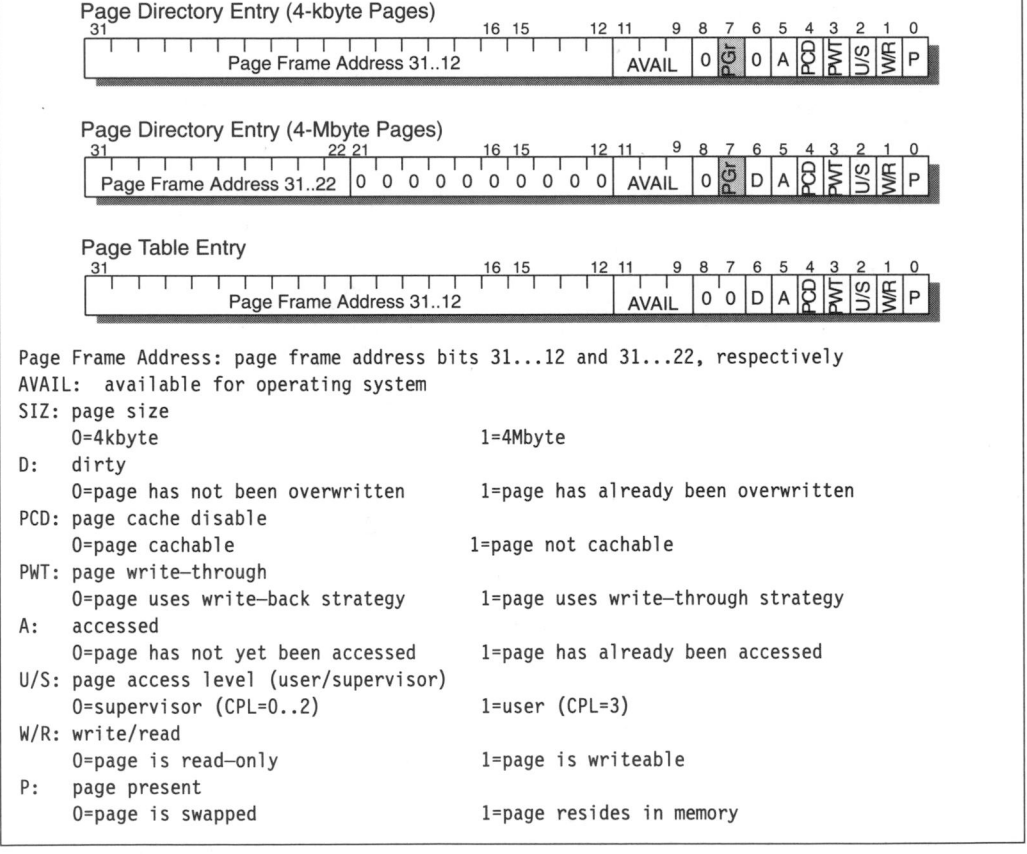

```
Page Frame Address: page frame address bits 31...12 and 31...22, respectively
AVAIL:  available for operating system
SIZ: page size
     0=4kbyte                          1=4Mbyte
D:   dirty
     0=page has not been overwritten   1=page has already been overwritten
PCD: page cache disable
     0=page cachable                  1=page not cachable
PWT: page write-through
     0=page uses write-back strategy   1=page uses write-through strategy
A:   accessed
     0=page has not yet been accessed  1=page has already been accessed
U/S: page access level (user/supervisor)
     0=supervisor (CPL=0..2)           1=user (CPL=3)
W/R: write/read
     0=page is read-only               1=page is writeable
P:   page present
     0=page is swapped                 1=page resides in memory
```

Figure 12.12: Page directory and page table entries.

The *SIZ*-bit indicates the actual size of the applicable page. Pages of 4 Mbytes can only occur in the page directory, and are only managed by the page directory entry; page table entries are thus only relevant to 4 kbyte pages. A set SIZ-bit defines a page size as 4 Mbytes of memory capacity. The page directory entry then contains the ten most significant bits of the correspon-ding page frame address in bits 31 to 22; bits 21 to 12 equal 0 (for a 4 kbyte page, these positions contain an additional ten bits for the *page frame address*). Additionally, the dirty bit must be defined here, because the page directory entry points directly to a page and the page content could have changed. For page directory entries which manage second-order page tables, the D-bit is not implemented thus bit 6 always equals 0. In the TLB of the on-chip data cache, eight separate entries are provided exclusively for the 4 Mbyte pages. On the other hand, the TLB of the on-chip code cache does not differentiate between 4 kbyte and 4 Mbyte pages.

The interpretation of the linear address, as compared to that for 4 kbyte pages, has been changed for the 4 Mbyte pages. The pages now begin at a 4 Mbyte boundary, but within a page an object is addressed with 22 offset bits (2^{22}=4M). The previously used 10-bit page table and 12-bit offset entries are combined into a single 22-bit offset. Figure 12.13 shows a comparative representation of both the 4 kbyte and 4 Mbyte page interpretations.

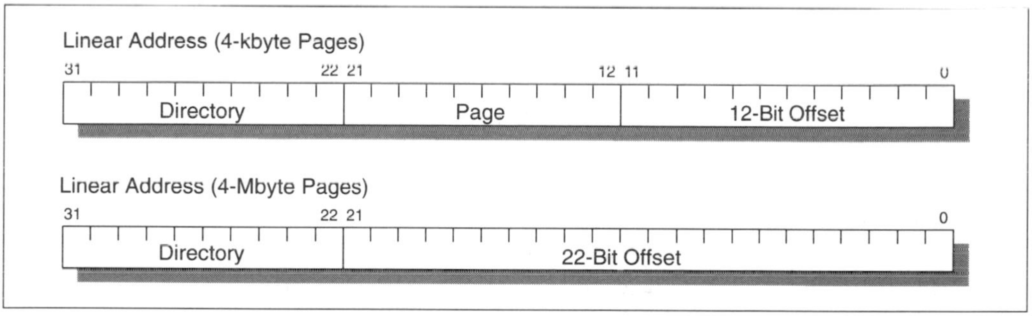

Figure 12.13: The interpretation of a linear address when paging is enabled for 4 kbyte and 4 Mbyte pages.

Paging Control Register

Control registers CR0 and CR2–CR4, already shown in Figure 12.11, are important for the paging function. The *PG*-bit in the CR0 control register enables (PG=1) or disables (PG=0) the paging unit of the Pentium, as in the i386/i486. You can use the possibility of 4 Mbyte pages by means of the PSE-bit in CR4. Only then has the SIZ entry in the page directory entry any meaning. A set PSE-bit enables 4 Mbyte pages. With a cleared *PSE*-bit, the PU uses only the standard pages of 4 kbytes each.

12.3.7 Debug Extensions

As in the i386 and i486, the Pentium contains eight debug registers DR0–DR7, each 32 bits wide and supporting debuggers at a hardware level in both protected and virtual 8086 modes. Their structure has already been described in Section 2.8.2, and shown in Figure 2.10. Only the R/W_x-bits are extended by the 10b combination. You enable the 10b combination by setting the DE-bit in the CR4 control register. In the i386 and i486, this combination was reserved, that is, invalid. An R/W_x-bit value of 10b also enables the corresponding breakpoint for I/O read and I/O write accesses. In the i386 and i486 (or the Pentium with a cleared DE-bit), only the memory area can be observed through the debug registers. For the R/W_x-bits, the following interpretations can occur if the DE-bit in the CR4 control register equals 1:

00b: Stop only for instruction execution (instruction fetching);
01b: Stop only for data write accesses to memory;
10b: Stop for I/O read and I/O write accesses;
11b: Stop only for data read or write accesses to memory, not code fetches.

12.3.8 Pentium Reset, Pentium Initialization and Self-Test

In addition to the reset through an active RESET signal, the Pentium can also execute a true initialization. The processor initialization is issued if a signal with a high level is received at the T20 INIT pin for a minimum of two CLK cycles have elapsed. A reset, on the contrary, is not recognized before 15 CLK cycles have elapsed. An init resets the Pentium into real mode and initializes the segment and offset registers; additionally, the TLBs and the BTB are invalidated. The internal caches, write buffers, model registers and floating-point registers, however, are not reset. Instead, they maintain their values. INIT serves as a quick way of resetting the Pentium into real mode by means of external hardware (for instance, the keyboard controller of the AT) in place of a privileged MOV CR0, value instruction, for resetting the PE-bit. Further internal tests are not carried out; this is the job of a reset.

An extensive reset of the Pentium is issued by a high level signal at the RESET pin. If the signal then returns to a low level, the Pentium checks the signal levels at the $\overline{\text{FLUSH}}$, $\overline{\text{FRCMC}}$ and INIT pins to determine the operating condition and the checks necessary, and also to carry out an internal initialization. The Pentium can execute a check through the internal self-test BIST (Built-In Self Test), the functional redundancy checking, or the tristate test mode. Table 12.4 lists the signal combinations which give rise to the various tests.

INIT	**$\overline{\text{FLUSH}}$**	**$\overline{\text{FRMC}}$**	**Issued test**
1	–	–	internal self-test BIST
0	–	0	functional redundancy checking
0	0	–	tristate test mode

Table 12.4: Pentium tests

The internal self-test takes approximately 2^{19} CLK cycles; at 66 MHz this corresponds to approximately 8 ms. Without BIST, the Pentium is ready for operation after 150–200 CLK cycles, thus after approximately 3 μs. The BIST's responsibility is to check the microcode ROM, internal logic fields (PLAs), caches, TLBs and the BTB. The Pentium stores the result of the BIST check in the EAX register. A value of 00000000h indicates an error-free BIST conclusion; a value other than zero indicates an error, and the chip is then unusable. The Pentium activates the $\overline{\text{IERR}}$ signal if it discovers an internal parity error; it then goes into a shutdown condition.

With the functional redundancy checking (FRC) the Pentium can check a second Pentium. In FRC mode, with the exception of $\overline{\text{IERR}}$ and TDO, the Pentium stops sending signals through its output pins, and instead checks the level of the signals received. If the thus determined levels do not agree with those calculated internally, the Pentium activates the $\overline{IERR}$ signal to indicate the fault externally. Through functional redundancy checking, for example, the individual processors in a multiprocessor system can be mutually checked. The tristate test mode is used for checking complete boards. In tristate mode the Pentium disconnects all output and bidirectional connections. The high level test logic can then execute a hardware check more easily, and locate any possible errors more simply. A reset, and also an initialization through INIT, resets the value of certain registers. Table 12.5 indicates the corresponding values for the individual registers.

Register	Reset Value	Initialization Value
(ALU/integer)		
EAX	00000000h	00000000h
EBX, ECX	00000000h	00000000h
EDX	identific. [1]	identific. [1]
EBP, ESP	00000000h	00000000h
ESI, EDI	00000000h	00000000h
EIP	0000fff0h	0000fff0h
CS	f000h [2]	f000h [2]
DS, ES, FS, GS	0000h [3]	0000h [3]
SS	0000h [3]	0000h [3]
EFLAG	00000002h	00000002h
CR0	00000000h	[4]
CR2, CR3, CR4	00000000h	00000000h
LDTR, TR	00000000h [4]	00000000h [5]
GDTR, IDTR	00000000h [5]	00000000h [6]
DR0–DR3	00000000h	00000000h
DR6	ffff0ff0h	ffff0ff0h
DR7	00000400h	00000400h
TR12	00000000h	00000000h
all others	nnnnnnnnh	nnnnnnnnh
(FPU)		
control word	0040h	uuuuh
status word	0000h	uuuuh
tag word	5555h	uuuuh
FIP, FEA, FOP	00000000h	uuuuuuuuh
FCS, FDS	0000h	uuuuh
FSTACK	0000000000h	uuuuuuuuuuh
caches	nnnnnnnnnnn	uuuuuuuuuuu
cache TLBs	nnnnnnnnnnn	nnnnnnnnnnn
BTB, SDC	nnnnnnnnnnn	nnnnnnnnnnn

n: not defined
u: unchanged
[1] processor identification number 00000500h + model
[2] base address = ffff0000h, limit = ffffh (segment descriptor cache register)
[3] base address = 00000000h, limit = ffffh (segment descriptor cache register)
[4] CD, CW unchanged, bit 4 = 1, all others = 0
[5] selector = 0000h, base address = 00000000h, limit = ffffh
[6] base address = 00000000h, limit = ffffh

Table 12.5: Pentium register contents after a reset or init

Like the i386, the Pentium also restarts operations in real mode after a reset or init. The CS:EIP pair points to the memory address f000:0000fff0. Additionally, the 12 most significant address lines A31–A20 are held at a high level. After the first JMP or CALL instruction over a segment limit, the address lines A31–A20 return to a low level, and the Pentium only addresses objects within 1M.

The Pentium loads the IDTR with the values 00000000h for the base and 03ffh for the limit after a processor reset. These values correspond to the reserved area for the interrupt vector table in real mode. It is possible for the two LIDT (load IDTR) and SIDT (store IDTR) instructions to change these values and, in this way, the interrupt vector table used by the Pentium in real mode can be shifted to any other position in the real mode address space.

12.3.9 CPU Identification with CPUID

With the Pentium, Intel has satisfied an old request, namely the possibility of simply identifying the CPU on which the present program is being executed. Until the i486 this was only possible by means of an extensive procedure, which checked the abilities of the processor and, thus, determined the processor type (as in the i386 the AC flag is not implemented and therefore cannot be changed, of course, but this is possible in the i486). With the help of the BIST, starting with the i386, determining the processor type is not very complicated for the BIOS. But this is only executed immediately after a reset so that a program cannot access the BIST result later. The new *CPUID* instruction of the Pentium now solves the identification problem unambiguously within a few CLK cycles.

Before you can execute the CPUID instruction you must first determine whether the CPU actually supports this instruction. If not, the processor produces an invalid opcode exception. For this reason, Intel has implemented a new flag in the EFlag register, the *ID* flag. If a task can set and reset the ID flag, then the installed processor supports the CPUID instruction. The CPUID instruction, in addition to identifying the Pentium, also delivers information concerning which special features are supported. To carry out CPU identification, you must first load the value 0 into the EAX register, and then issue the CPUID instruction. The Pentium then returns in EAX the highest identification level that it supports. This is currently only level 1. The three EBX, ECX and EDX registers, in that sequence, contain a 12-byte identification in ASCII format: «GenuineIntel».

Future Pentiums, and possible clones from other manufacturers, may return a different character string. If you load the EAX register with a value of 01h and afterwards issue the CPUID instruction again, the Pentium returns an identification value similar to the identification information in the ID-code register of the TAP controller. The register DX contains additional information regarding which functions are supported. You will find the call and return values of CPUID in Table 12.6.

Register	Call Value	Return value
EAX	00h	01h (max. identification level)
EBX		«Genu»
ECX		«inel»
EDX		«ntel»
EAX	01h	identification value[1)]
EBX		reserved (=0)
ECX		reserved (=0)
EDX		feature flags[2)]

1)

bits 31..12	reserved (= 00h)
bits 11..8	processor family (05h for Pentium)
bits 7...4	model (01h for ordinary Pentium)
bits 3...0	revision

2)

bits 31..9:	reserved (= 00h)
bit 8:	CMPXCHG8B (1 = implemented, 0 – not implemented)
bit 7:	machine check exception (1 = implemented, 0 = not implemented)
bit 6:	reserved
bit 5..1:	implemented special functions
bit 0:	on-chip FPU (1 = yes, 0 = no)

Table 12.6: Call and return values of CPUID

12.4 Pentium Bus

The three pipelines of the Pentium achieve an instruction throughput which would overwhelm a simple memory bus. Thus, the Pentium bus is aligned with a quick second-level cache. Frequently required instructions and data are held ready in the two on-chip caches. For connection to the second-level cache (L2-cache), the Pentium's data bus has been widened to 64-bits, so the on-chip caches can be reloaded and written back with sufficient speed.

Despite this, the Pentium can also address individual bytes, words or double words through byte enable signals $\overline{BE7}$–$\overline{BE0}$. Every bus cycle addresses memory through A31–A3 at quad word boundaries, thus in multiples of 8 (0, 8, 16 etc.). Accesses to memory objects which span such a boundary (so-called *misaligned accesses*) are split into two consecutive accesses by the Pentium.

The Pentium tries to carry out memory accesses as cache line fills or write-backs as far as possible. Only accesses to the I/O address space and non-cachable areas in the memory address space (such as register addresses for memory mapped I/O) are carried out as single transfer cycles. The single transfer cycles described in Section 12.4.1 are more or less the exception. The burst mode, already known from the i486, has been extended to the writing of data (the i486 allows only burst read accesses). Together with the improved address pipelining, the maximum data transfer rate has been increased to 528 million bytes (at 66 MHz).

Contrary to memory accesses, accesses to the I/O address area have not been widened to 64-bit. The maximum width here is only 32-bit, as in the i386 or i486 case. The reason for this is that I/O accesses, in principle, do not pass through the on-chip data cache; instead, they are directly «switched through» from a 32-bit register to the bus. Of course, the Pentium can also address 8- or 16-bit ports. The I/O subsystem must decode port address bits A2–A0 from the byte enable signals $\overline{\text{BE7}}$–$\overline{\text{BE0}}$.

12.4.1 Single Transfer Cycles

The single transfer read and single transfer write cycles are the two simplest memory access cycles of the Pentium. During execution, data of 8-, 16-, 32- or 64-bits in size is transferred from memory to the Pentium, or from the Pentium to memory, respectively. Such Pentium bus cycles are not much different from those in the i386 or i486, despite the larger width of data bus. For a single transfer it holds $\overline{\text{CACHE}}$ on a high level to indicate that no line fill should be carried out.

Single transfer write cycles in the Pentium are also not very different from those in the i386 or i486. The $\overline{\text{CACHE}}$ signal is again inactive. Additionally, the Pentium supplies write data and the required parity bits.

In single transfer mode (read and write), a data transfer without wait states requires at least two CLK cycles. With a data bus width of 64-bits, this leads to a maximum data transfer rate of 264 million bytes/s. This can be doubled in pipelined burst mode to 528 Miobytes/s or 504 MBytes/s.

12.4.2 Burst Cycles

For the transfer of larger quantities of data, the Pentium implements a burst mode similar to that in the i486, but unlike the i486, the Pentium burst mode can also be used for write-back cycles. For the write-through cache of the i486 this is not necessary, because each write access is switched through to the memory subsystem. But there are other differences, too. In principle, all cachable read cycles and all write-back cycles are carried out in burst mode. By the extension of the data bus to 64 bits, in a burst cycle 32 bytes are transferred with four bus cycles. They are contiguous, and are aligned to 32-byte boundaries (this corresponds to a cache line of the two on-chip caches).

A burst cache is started as in the i486, by a normal memory access which lasts for two clock cycles. Figure 12.14 shows the flow of the most important signals for a burst read cycle.

For a burst read cycle, the $\overline{\text{CACHE}}$ signal from the Pentium and the $\overline{\text{KEN}}$ signal from the memory subsystem also play an important role. The Pentium indicates to the subsystem, through an active $\overline{\text{CACHE}}$ signal with a low level, that it wants to transfer the addressed object into the on-chip cache. If the $\overline{\text{KEN}}$ signal delivered by the memory subsystem is active, then the Pentium independently and automatically extends the single transfer to a cache line fill to store a complete data block with the addressed object in the on-chip cache.

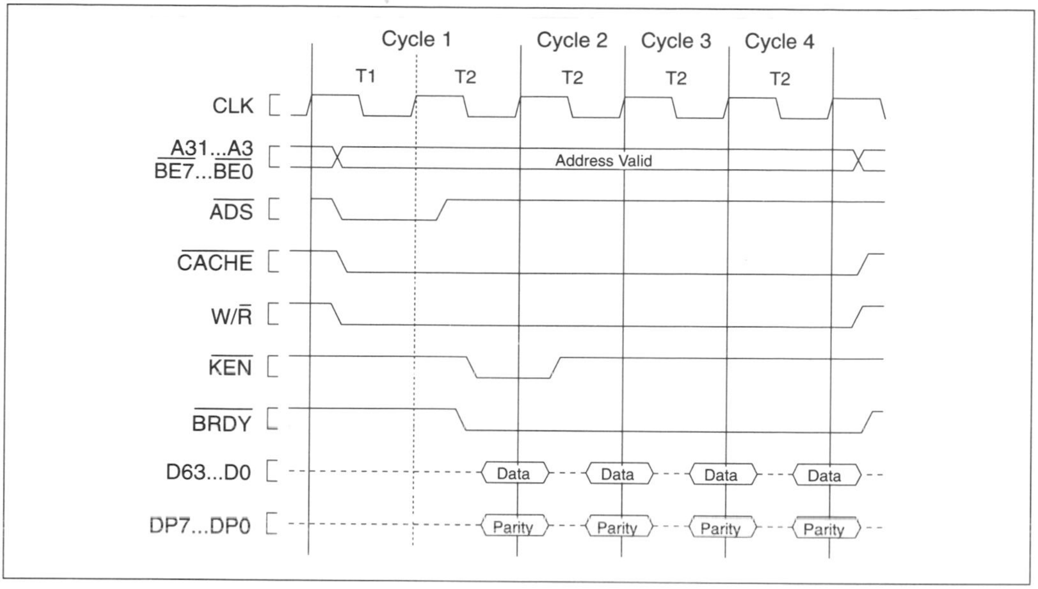

Figure 12.14: Burst read cycle without wait states and pipelining. In burst mode, the bus cycle for a 32-byte address area is reduced from two processor clock cycles to one cycle starting with the second access. Thus, a cache line of the internal caches can be filled very quickly. The cycle shown is a 2-1-1-1 burst.

As already mentioned, a burst cycle is limited to an address area which begins at a 32-byte boundary. With the first output address, therefore, the three other burst addresses are also implicitly known. The subsystem can independently calculate the other three burst addresses, without the need to decode further address signals from the Pentium. This is much faster, and enables the bus cycle to be reduced to one clock cycle. The Pentium only sends the address and $\overline{BEx}$ signals during the first cycle; they are not changed during the subsequent three bus cycles (the i486, on the contrary, addresses the data within the 16-byte group further via the address signals A3–A2 and $\overline{BE3}$–$\overline{BE0}$).

In the Pentium the address sequence in burst mode is fixed dependent on the first address. This is necessary because the first address given out by the Pentium need not necessarily define a 32-byte boundary; it can lie anywhere in the address space. During the course of the first transfer cycle, $\overline{KEN}$ determines whether a single or burst transfer should be carried out. But then the first quad-word has already been transferred. The fixed address sequence shown in Table 12.7 is not cyclic, but has been chosen to support 2-way interleaving of DRAM memory.

First address output by the Pentium	Second address	Third address	Last address
0h	8h	10h	18h
8h	0h	18h	10h
10h	18h	0h	8h
18h	10h	8h	0h

Table 12.7: Address sequence for burst read cycles

After decoding the start address, the external memory subsystem calculates the sequence of the addresses given, and then follows the sequence when memory is addressed. The Pentium receives the data without sending out any more addresses, and then distributes the data delivered by the subsystem according to the quad word entries in the applicable cache line. In the i486, a burst cycle is explicitly initiated by a $\overline{BLAST}$ signal (which is not available in the Pentium) during the first cycle. $\overline{KEN}$ alone is not sufficient for a burst cycle. Moreover, a burst transfer for the i486 always starts at a 16-byte boundary.

The write-back cache of the Pentium requires that burst mode can also be used for write transfers. In Figure 12.15 you can see the signal flow for such a write burst transfer.

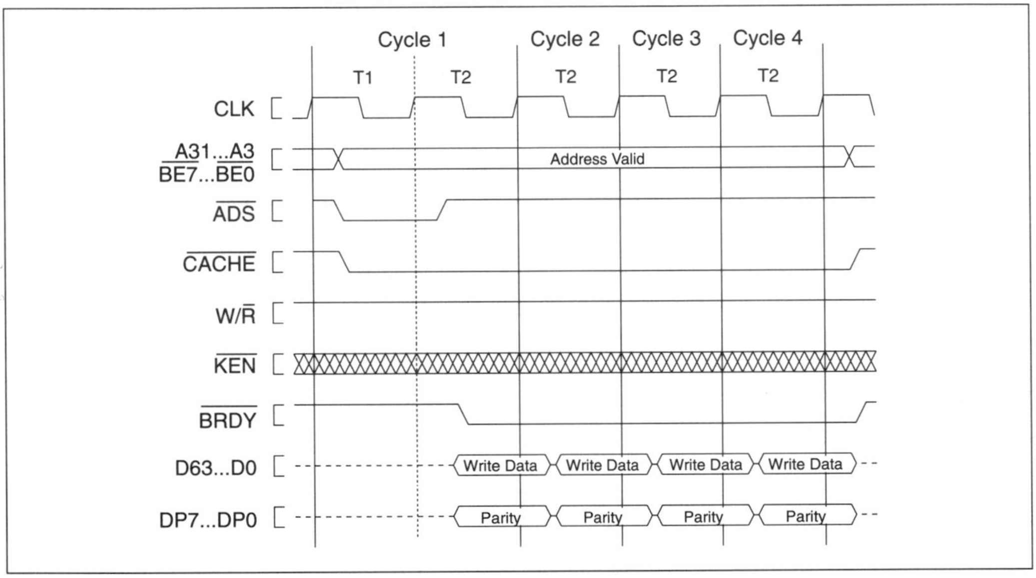

Figure 12.15: Burst write cycle without wait states and pipelining. The Pentium uses the burst write cycle to carry out a cache line write-back. The cycle shown is a 2-1-1-1 burst.

As you can see, the signal flow is nearly identical to that for a burst read cycle. Only the $W/\overline{R}$ signal is different, in that it is at a high level to indicate the write transfer. In addition, $\overline{KEN}$ is ignored because all data available in the on-chip cache is obviously cachable. A burst write cycle is always a write-back cycle for a modified line in the data cache.

Because, for burst write cycles which are exclusively the consequence of cache line write-backs, the first address sent out always defines a 32-byte boundary, there is only the first address sequence of Table 12.7, that is, 0h → 8h → 10h → 18h.

Thus, a burst cycle can read in or can write a maximum of 32 bytes, which requires a total of four bus cycles. In a 2-1-1-1 burst the Pentium needs 2+3=5 clock cycles. 32 bytes every five clock cycles of 16 ns in the 66 MHz Pentium corresponds to a burst transfer rate of approximately 403 Mbytes/s (or 422 million bytes/s). Address pipelining (described in Section 12.4.3) can also reduce the first burst bus cycle to a single CLK cycle; then only four clock cycles are necessary. The transfer rate increases to 504 Mbytes/s or 528 million bytes/s.

Wait states can also be inserted in burst mode (through $\overline{BRDY}$), if the memory subsystem cannot follow quickly enough. Such an access is known as a «slow burst cycle», and can give rise, for example, to a 3-2-2-2 burst.

12.4.3 Pentium Address Pipelining

The Pentium implements address pipelining to further increase the data throughput and its bus bandwidth, which in principle is already known from the 80286. The Pentium can «note» two pending bus cycles, and with the help of address pipelining it can execute them consecutively. Instruction execution in the CPU pipelines and, for instance, cache line fills or write-backs will be decoupled as far as possible.

A special feature of Pentium address pipelining is that the first bus cycle in burst mode can also be reduced to a single clock cycle, whereby the data transfer rate increases by an additional 25% to 504 Mbytes/s, or 528 million bytes/s. Figure 12.16 shows two consecutive cache line fills in burst mode with active address pipelining.

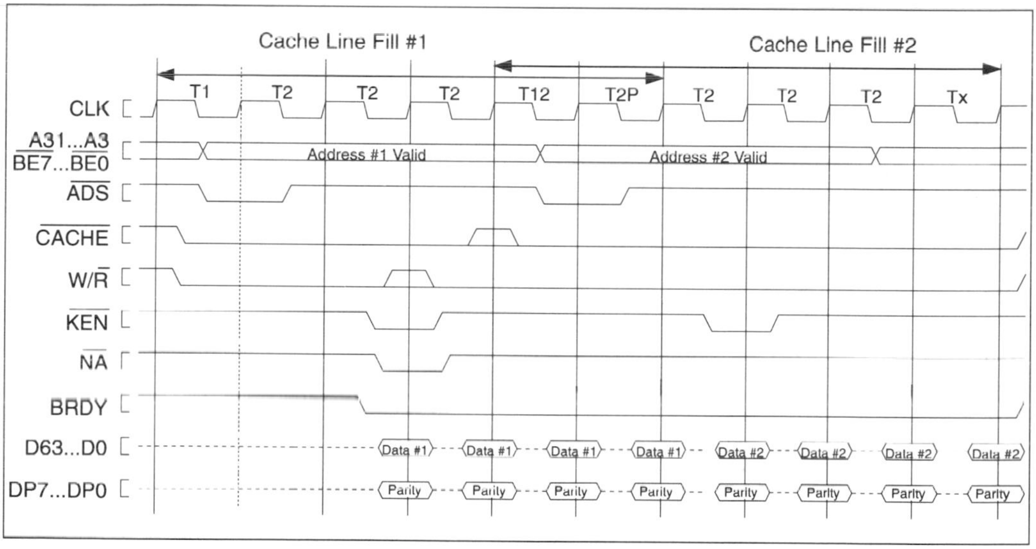

Figure 12.16: Pipelined cache line fills in burst mode without wait states. The figure shows two successive cache line fills. By means of address pipelining, the second cache line fill overlaps the first one, and the data transfer can be carried out within four CLK cycles.

As in the i386, address pipelining is controlled by the $\overline{NA}$ (Next Address) signal. If the subsystem addressed has decoded this address, and is ready to take the next cache line fill address for decoding, it sends an active $\overline{NA}$ signal to the Pentium. The subsystem can then decode the new address, while the third data transfer of the previous burst is still in progress. Immediately after the transfer of the last eight bytes from cache line fill #1, the memory subsystem delivers the data (and the parity) for cache line fill #2, so that a CLK cycle is saved. Two or more such bursts can then be executed consecutively, for example, if a task switch is executed where a complete TSS must be saved and a new one loaded. A slow 4-1-1-1 burst, for example, therefore only affects the first burst access. The addressing phase of all successive bursts overlaps with the data phase of the preceding burst. Thus, three of the four addressing cycles are carried out in advance, so that only one cycle remains (3+1=4). Also, burst write cycles and single transfers can use address pipelining.

The Pentium monitors how many $\overline{BRDY}$ signals have been returned and, therefore, knows which burst is currently being executed. A maximum of two bus cycles (single transfers, burst transfers) can be active at any one time.

12.4.4 Special Bus Cycles

The Pentium can also, apart from data transfer cycles, drive special cycles onto the bus to indicate certain internal processor operations. A special cycle takes place if the Pentium sends out the $D/\overline{C}$ and $M/\overline{IO}$ signals at a low level and the $W/\overline{R}$ signal at a high level. Compared to the i486, two additonal cycles are provided. Table 12.8 summarizes all six special cycles.

$\overline{BE7}$	$\overline{BE6}$	$\overline{BE5}$	$\overline{BE4}$	$\overline{BE3}$	$\overline{BE2}$	$\overline{BE1}$	$\overline{BE0}$	Special Cycle	Reason
1	1	1	1	1	1	1	0	shutdown	triple fault, parity error
1	1	1	1	1	1	0	1	flush	INVD, WBINVD
1	1	1	1	1	0	1	1	halt	HLT instruction
1	1	1	1	0	1	1	1	write-back	WBINVD instruction
1	1	1	0	1	1	1	1	flush acknowledge	$\overline{FLUSH}$ signal
1	1	0	1	1	1	1	1	branch trace message	taken branch

1 = high signal level, 0 = low signal level

Table 12.8: Pentium special cycles ($D/\overline{C}=M/\overline{IO}=0$, $W/\overline{R}=1$)

The external system must also confirm such a special cycle as a normal bus cycle by activating $\overline{BRDY}$. The following section briefly discusses the meaning and cause of the two new special cycles.

A new special cycle that refers to the writing back and invalidation of the on-chip data cache is the *flush acknowledge special cycle* (11101111). The Pentium sends this special cycle through the bus if an external unit (such as the system controller) has applied an active signal with a low level to the $\overline{FLUSH}$ input, to initiate a write-back and a cache invalidation, and the Pentium has executed these operations. In this way, the system controller can differentiate between a cache flush through software (an INVD or WBINVD), and a cache flush through hardware (an active $\overline{FLUSH}$ signal). The flush acknowledge cycle, like the write-back special cycle, indicates a write-back *and* invalidation of the cache lines. The flush special cycle, on the other hand, only indicates an invalidation.

The Pentium issues a *branch trace message special cycle* (11011111) if the ETE-bit (Execution Tracing Enable) is set in the TR12 test register, and the Pentium has executed a branch immediately beforehand. During the branch trace message special cycle, the Pentium sends out the linear address of the branch target to its address pins A31–A3 and the branch target pins BT2–BT0. Additionally, through the BT3 signal, it indicates whether the standard operand size is 32 bits (BT3=high level), or 16 bits (BT3=low level). The branch trace message special cycle is part of execution tracing.

12.4.5 Inquiry Cycles and Internal Snooping

Inquiry cycles are used for the implementation of the MESI protocol for multiprocessor systems. In this way, it is possible for an external unit to determine whether the data at a specific address is stored in the on-chip cache of the Pentium. Additionally, the external unit can invalidate the stored data and, thus, the whole corresponding cache line.

For an inquiry cycle, the external unit first activates the AHOLD signal. After two CLK cycles, it transfers the (physical) address of the data to be inquired to the Pentium through A31–A5. A4 and A3 are ignored, because a complete cache line is always addressed in an inquiry cycle. Upon an active $\overline{\text{EADS}}$, the Pentium fetches the address supplied as the inquiry address. In addition, the INV signal must also be sent. In the case of an inquiry or inquiry hit, it indicates whether the applicable cache line should be marked as invalidated (INV=1) or shared (INV=0). INV has no effect for inquiry misses.

In an externally initiated inquiry cycle, as in normal memory accesses, the tag logic of the on-chip cache checks whether the address is located in the tag memory. If a hit has occurred in the code or data cache, the Pentium sends out an active signal with a low level from the $\overline{\text{HIT}}$ pin. If a miss occurs, the $\overline{\text{HIT}}$ output sends out a signal with a high level. If a hit for a modified cache line is at hand (which is only possible for the data cache), then the Pentium activates its $\overline{\text{HITM}}$ (hit modified) output. In this case the Pentium writes back the applicable line to memory. Thus it issues a burst write-back cycle. In this way, it is ensured that the inquiring system contains the latest data.

In addition to this externally (through $\overline{\text{EADS}}$) initiated inquiry cycle, there is also internal snooping, mainly used for checking the consistency of the two independent on-chip caches. Above all, in real mode, the same data can be available in both the code and data caches as an indirect result of prefetching. Internal snooping can occur in the following cases:

- the CPU core of the Pentium accesses the code cache, and this access results in a miss,
- the CPU core accesses the data cache, and this access leads to a cache miss (read access), or a write-through (write access) to the L2-cache or the main memory,
- the A- or D-bit (accessed and dirty bit, respectively) of a page table or page directory entry has been overwritten as the result of an access or a change to the corresponding page.

12.4.6 Internal Pentium Bus Buffers

To ease the burden of the external bus and to prevent unnecessary wait states if the bus is currently occupied, the Pentium (like the i486) includes a number of internal buffers.

The bus interface of the Pentium contains two 64-bit write buffers, where each buffer is assigned to one of the two pipelines, u or v. They should prevent the Pentium pipelines from breaking if the external bus is not immediately available. This can occur if a cache line fill or a simultaneous memory access of both pipelines is currently in progress. Note that only memory write accesses are temporarily stored in the write buffers, but not write accesses to the I/O address space.

In addition to the 64-bit write buffers, the Pentium contains three 32-byte write-back buffers which are available for each of the possible causes of a cache line write-back. Thus, each of these buffers encompasses a complete cache line and supports the Pentium during write-backs of cache lines in the on-chip data cache.

Further, the Pentium contains two line fill buffers. They are each 32 bytes wide (one cache line) and assigned to the data and code caches, respectively. If the Pentium reads a complete cache line, during a burst cycle, into the on-chip data or code cache, then the bus interface does not successively fill the on-chip cache with the transferred 8-byte groups. Instead, it first transfers them to the corresponding line fill buffer. Only when all 32 bytes of the applicable cache line have been stored in the line fill buffer is the complete cache line transferred to the code or data cache.

12.5 Pentium System Management Mode

Not only for portable computers has power consumption become an important criterion. So-called *Green PCs* should have a very low power consumption in idle mode. Then it is unnecessary to switch them on and off all the time. Especially with Windows and several SCSI adapters the boot process takes a considerable time. The 66MHz Pentium, with its typical power consumption of between 13W and 16W, is not exactly designed to be power saving equipment. Reducing the current draw is therefore one main aim of Pentium's new system management mode SMM. An advantageous side-effect is the hardwired separate address SMM area where, for example, recovery routines can be stored. In the following sections I will discuss these new Pentium functions in brief.

12.5.1 System Management Mode Interrupt SMI

The Pentium includes two interfaces for system management mode, namely $\overline{\text{SMI}}$ (input) and $\overline{\text{SMIACT}}$ (output). The Pentium goes into SMM as soon as it receives an active SMI signal with a low level at its $\overline{\text{SMI}}$ input. The Pentium may leave SMM only with an explicit RSM (resume from system management mode) instruction. The SMI is implemented as an interrupt, that is, it is only recognized at instruction boundaries. Only R/$\overline{\text{S}}$ and $\overline{\text{FLUSH}}$, which are conceptualized as interrupts, have a higher priority than $\overline{\text{SMI}}$.

Register	Value
EAX, EBX, ECX, EDX,	undefined
EBP, ESI, EDI	undefined
EFlag	00000002h
EIP	00008000h
CS	3000h (base address=30000h)
DS, ES, FS, GS, SS	0000h (base address=00000000h, limit=ffffffffh, standard size=16 bits)
CR0	PE=EM=TS=PG=0, others unchanged
CR4	00000000h
DR6	undefined
DR7	00000400h
GDTR, LDTR, IDTR, TR	undefined

Table 12.9: SMM initialization values

After capturing an active $\overline{\text{SMI}}$ signal, the Pentium first waits for the execution of all memory operations and the activation of $\overline{\text{EWBE}}$. Then, it sends out an active signal with a low level from the $\overline{\text{SMIACT}}$ output for as long as it remains in SMM. Immediately afterwards, the Pentium stores its current register values in memory (starting at the physical address 3ffa8h), and initializes its registers for system management mode according to Table 12.9.

12.5.2 SMM RAM Structure

For the system management mode, it is intended that battery-buffered SRAM chips are mapped into the address space between 30000h and 3ffffh. They use the normally present DRAM memory addresses. For this purpose, the external hardware can use the $\overline{\text{SMIACT}}$ signal, for example, as a chip select signal and, thus, address the SRAM chips ($\overline{\text{SMIACT}}$ at a low level), or the normal main memory ($\overline{\text{SMIACT}}$ at a high level). With $\overline{\text{SMIACT}}$, SMM memory and normal memory are strictly separated (this is, of course, entirely optional; the external hardware may simply ignore the $\overline{\text{SMIACT}}$ signal). Generally, the SMM RAM is mapped onto the physical 4 Gbyte Pentium address space, as shown in Figure 12.17. This structure is implemented in the Pentium hardware.

The lower 32 kbytes between addresses 30000h and 37fffh are optional. At address 3000:8000h is the entry point of the SMM handler which the Pentium accesses upon every SMI. The 32256 bytes between 3000:8000h and 3000:fdffh are available for the code and data of the SMI handler. Located here are, for example, the complete routines for saving the contents of memory to disk, or for deactivating individual components. Note that the Pentium can also produce addresses outside the 64 kbyte SMM RAM; then, in system management mode, it can also access data outside the area reserved for SMM.

The CPU register dump is also attached to the handler area in SMM RAM; it consists of 512 bytes. When the SMI signal is activated and system management mode is entered, the Pentium automatically, that is, without any further influence from software (with the exception of the Pentium's microcode), stores into this area all register values that are necessary for the restoration of its original condition. In this way, after an RSM instruction, the Pentium can continue on from the point at which it was interrupted by the system management interrupt.

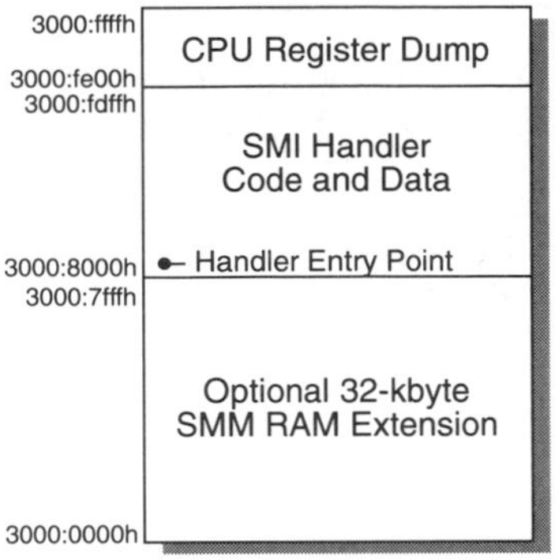

Figure 12.17: Logical structure of SMM RAM.

Table 12.10 shows the organization of the register dump in SMM RAM. Note that the offsets are relative to the segment 3000h.

Offset	Register content	Offset	Register content
fffch	CR0	ffc4h	TR
fff8h	CR3	ffc0h	LDTR
fff4h	EFlag	ffbch	GS
fff0h	EIP	ffb8h	FS
ffech	EDI	ffb4h	DS
ffe8h	ESI	ffb0h	SS
ffe4h	EBP	ffach	CS
ffe0h	ESP	ffa8h	ES
ffdch	EBX	ff04h–ffa7h	reserved
ffd8h	EDX	ff02h	halt auto restart
ffd4h	ECX	ff00h	I/O-trap restart
ffd0h	EAX	fefch	SMM identification
ffcch	DR6	fef8h	register dump base
ffc8h	DR7	fe00h–fef7h	reserved

Table 12.10: Pentium register dump in SMM RAM

In addition to the saved registers in the register dump, you will also find the four control fields, halt auto restart, I/O trap restart, SMM identification and register dump base.

A value of 1 in the *halt auto restart* entry (offset ff02f) indicates that the Pentium was in a halt condition when the SMI occurred. You may clear halt auto restart so that the Pentium continues program execution beyond the HLT instruction upon leaving the SMM. It is possible that the SMI interrupts an I/O instruction. If you write a value of ffffh into the *I/O trap restart* entry (offset ff00h), the Pentium carries out the interrupted I/O instruction again after a return through an RSM. The entry *SMM identification* (offset fefch) indicates the revision level and the functional capabilities of the implemented system management mode.

The Pentium contains an internal register in which the base address for the register dump is stored. It is initialized to a value of 30000h. The current value is stored in the *register dump base* entry (offset fef8h) when system management mode is entered and, from there, reloaded into the register after an RSM. You can change the value in this entry in SMM RAM and, thus, alter the SMM RAM base in the 4 Gbyte address space. The new value is not active until the next SMI. An init does not reset the register dump base; this is only possible by a reset (or another explicit overwrite).

12.5.3 Program Execution in System Management Mode

As is apparent from Table 12.9, the Pentium automatically resets the PE-bit and the PG-bit so that it now operates in SMM in an extended real mode. The only difference to the conventional real mode is that the SMM address space is not limited to 1 Mbyte, but the offset registers can use their full 32-bit width. Operating in SMM, the Pentium recognizes a $\overline{FLUSH}$ and carries out a cache flush. Not until the Pentium has left the SMM again are the NMI and INIT serviced.

Generally, SMM uses 16-bit operands and 16-bit addresses. However, you can use prefixes to generate 32-bit operands and 32-bit addresses. Note that with the segment registers alone you can only produce addresses within the first Mbyte of memory (the 16-bit segment values are simply shifted by four bits). Only the 32-bit offset registers allow 32-bit addresses up to 4G–1.

12.5.4 Return from System Management Mode

The Pentium only leaves system management mode after an explicit RSM (resume from system management mode) instruction. The deactivation of the $\overline{SMI}$ input signal, however, does not set the Pentium back into the condition it was in before interruption. Note that the RSM instruction is only valid in SMM; in all other modes it leads to an invalid opcode exception. Pay attention when manipulating the register dump in SMM RAM that no inconsistent values are written, otherwise a shutdown is the result.

12.6 Code Optimization with Performance Monitoring

Unfortunately, Intel has kept many details of performance monitoring under lock and key. Here also, for this reason, only a brief overview of the corresponding functions can be given.

Performance monitoring enables a number of parameters to be determined exactly, which provide a vital contribution to the overall performance of a Pentium system. These include, for example, the hit rate of the on-chip cache, the number and length of pipeline stalls, and also the hit rates in the TLB and BTB. They greatly depend upon the quality of the program code produced, and so performance monitoring represents a useful tool for compiler developers and system programmers for producing the most effective code for the Pentium. This clearly points to the fact that the superscalar architecture of the Pentium, despite compatibility targeted branch prediction, can only be used to the full if the code has been optimally tuned to the Pentium's hardware elements. This is nothing more than an unerring indication of the use of RISC concepts.

12.6.1 Hardware Elements for Performance Monitoring

For the implementation of performance monitoring, the Pentium contains the already mentioned Time Stamp Counter (TSC), two programmable event counters CTR0 and CTR1, two pins PM0/BP0 and PM1/BP1 which are associated with the two event counters, and a Control/Event Select Register (CESR).

As a single element, TSC can be addressed by an executable instruction at user level, namely RDTSC (read time stamp counter) if the TSD-bit in the CR4 control register is reset (CPL=0 is required for TSD=1). All other registers are only accessible through the RDMSR and WRMSR instructions. You can also access TSC with RDMSR and WRMSR.

The Time Stamp Counter (TSC) is a 64-bit wide counter that is triggered by processor clock signals and is incremented at every cycle (at 66 MHz it will take $2^{64}*16$ ns = $2.8*10^{11}$ s or almost 9000 years for TSC to overflow; a 32-bit counter, on the other hand, would be exhausted after only a minute). By reading the time counter, for example, before and after execution of a procedure, you can very precisely determine the time required for the procedure based on the processor cycle time.

The two programmable 40-bit event counters CTR0 and CTR1 can be individually assigned to different events. These two counters are directly connected to the two pins PM0/BP0 and PM1/BP1 which, when configured as performance monitoring interfaces, send out signals through the debug mode control register. They then indicate the current activity of the counter. They observe, for example, events such as TLB hits and TLB misses, hits and misses to lines in the on-chip data cache, snoop cycles, BTB hits or erroneous predictions, etc. All in all, you could say that with performance monitoring, almost all operations can be evaluated in respect of duration and frequency. This gives useful information about the efficiency of code produced by a compiler or programmed (assembled) by hand.

12.6.2 Access via the Test Access Port

I have already explained that the performance monitoring registers can also be accessed through the TAP. For supporting performance monitoring a probe data register is implemented in the TAP controller. The JTAG logic operates in parallel to the Pentium CPU and, therefore, does not disturb the program's execution. Accesses to the performance monitoring register, with the help of the RDMSR, WRMSR, and also RDTSC instructions, on the other hand, are part of the instruction flow and must be performed by the interrogating Pentium CPU itself. The main advantage in using the RDMSR and WRMSR instructions is that performance monitoring can be carried out purely on a software basis and, thus, without additional hardware. To implement an access through the TAP, on the other hand, is not quite so simple, as external hardware is required. To compensate, other TAP functions are also available.

12.7 Pentium Test Functions

The Pentium implements several functions for recognizing certain malfunctions. They refer to internal functional units such as the microcode ROM, the bus interface with address and data bus and the JTAG boundary scan test.

12.7.1 Pentium JTAG Boundary Scan Test

The Pentium implements a boundary scan test, in accordance with the IEEE 1149.1 standard. This permits external checking of the Pentium's logic units and their circuits, even after completion of manufacture and their inclusion in the computer. In addition, the Pentium can be explicitly instructed to perform the internal self-test BIST. All explanations of Section 10.8.5 are still valid, therefore I will only discuss the differences in the Pentium's JTAG compared to the JTAG in the i486.

For the Pentium's JTAG there is an additional TRST terminal. An active low-level signal at this test reset pin resets and initializes the boundary scan test logic. As usual, the scan path is located between the input terminal TDI and the output terminal TDO.

In addition to the cells assigned to the Pentium terminals, there are five control cells. The control cells determine the transfer direction for bidirectional pins (such as D63–D0, for example), or cut off output pins (such as ADS, for example). Table 12.11 lists the control cells.

Control cell	Pin group
DISABUS	A31–A3, AP, BT3–BT0
DISBUS	ADS, BE7–BE0, CACHE, SCYC, M/IO, D/C, W/R, PWT, PCD, LOCK
DISMISC	BREQ, APCHK, SMIACT, PRDY, IU, IV, IBT, BP3, BP2, PM1/BP1, PM0, BP0, FERR, HITM, HIT, PCHK, HLDA
DISFRC	IERR
DISWR	D63–D0, DP7–DP0

Note: DIS stands for disable as a «1» disables the corresponding output.

Table 12.11: JTAG control cells and assigned pin groups

The boundary scan path is gone through in the following way (note the control cell DISxxx):

TDI→free→free→free→RESET→FRCMC→PEN→R/S→NMI→INTR→IGNNE→SMI→INIT→free→CLK→free→A3→A4→A5→A6→A7→A8→A9→A10→A11→A12→A13→A14→A15→A16→A17→A18→A19→A20→A21→A22→A23→A24→A25→A26→A27→A28→A29→A30→A31→BT0→DISABUS→BT1→BT2→BT3→BE7→BE6→BE5→BE4→BE3→BE2→BE1→BE0→SCYC→D/C→PWT→PCD→W/R→ADS→ADSC→PRDY→AP→LOCK→HLDA→APCHK→PCHK→HIT→HITM→DISBUS→BREQ→SMIACT→A20M→FLUSH→HOLD→WB/WT→EWBE→EADS→BUSCHK→AHOLD→BRDYC→BRDY→KEN→NA→INV→BOFF→IU→IV→CACHE→M/IO→BP3→BP2→PM1/BP1→PM0/BP0→DISMISC→FERR→IERR→DISFRC→DP0→D0→D1→D2→D3→D4→D5→D6→D7→DP1→D8→D9→D10→D11→D12→D13→D14→D15→DP2→D16→D17→D18→D19→D20→D21→D22→D23→DP3→D24→D25→

D26→D27→D28→D29→D30→D31→DP4→D32→D33→D34→D35→D36→DISWR→D37→D38→D39→DP5→D40→D41→
D42→D43→D44→D45→D46→D47→DP6→D48→D49→D50→D51→D52→D53→D54→D55→DP7→D56→D57→D58→D59→
D60→D61→D62→D63→IBT→TDO

The ID code register stores 32-bit identification information in the Pentium with the following content: Bit 0=1, bits 1 to 11=manufacturer (Intel=09h), bits 12 to 27=part number (bits 12 to 16=model 01h, that is, DX; bits 17 to 20=generation 05h, that is, Pentium; bits 21 to 27=type 01h, that is, CPU), bits 28 to 31=version (not defined in the Pentium). The 32-bit Pentium ID code is thus x02a1013h (x=undefined).

12.7.2 Detection of Internal Errors

To ensure operative reliability, the Pentium continuously carries out a parity check of the following memory fields:

- data/code cache memory entry,
- data/code cache tag entry,
- data/code TLB memory entry,
- data/code TLB tag entry,
- microcode ROM.

This parity check is completely transparent. Only when the error detection logic discovers a parity fault does the Pentium send out an active signal from its $\overline{\text{IERR}}$ output and go into shutdown mode.

12.7.3 Detection of Bus Interface Errors

In addition to the internal parity check, the Pentium can also check the parity of the external data and address buses. For this purpose, in addition to the actual data and address bus interfaces D63–D0 and A31–A3 respectively, it also contains eight data bus parity interfaces DP7–DP0 and an address parity pin AP. Additionally, it can also identify general bus faults.

Data Parity Fault

During a write cycle (single or burst), in addition to the data at pins D63–D0, the Pentium also provides eight parity bits DP7–DP0 so that for every data byte even parity is achieved. The external system can use the parity information to check the inner consistency of the data.

In a read cycle, the external system can transfer the parity information together with the data bytes. The Pentium checks the resulting parity and sends out the corresponding signal from the $\overline{\text{PCHK}}$ pin. A low level indicates a parity error. Only if an active $\overline{\text{PEN}}$ signal with a low level is applied does the Pentium store the physical address in the Machine Check Address (MCA) register and store the type of cycle that caused the parity fault in the Machine Check Type (MCT) register. You can see the structure of the machine check type register in Figure 12.18.

If the CHK-bit is set, then bits *LOCK*, $M/\overline{IO}$, $D/\overline{C}$ and $W/\overline{R}$ indicate the type of cycle and the machine check address MCA register contains the physical fault address. Note that a set LOCKbit indicates an active, that is, a low level $\overline{LOCK}$ signal. If the MCE-bit in the new CR4 control register is also set, then the processor also issues the machine check exception corresponding to interrupt 18 (12h).

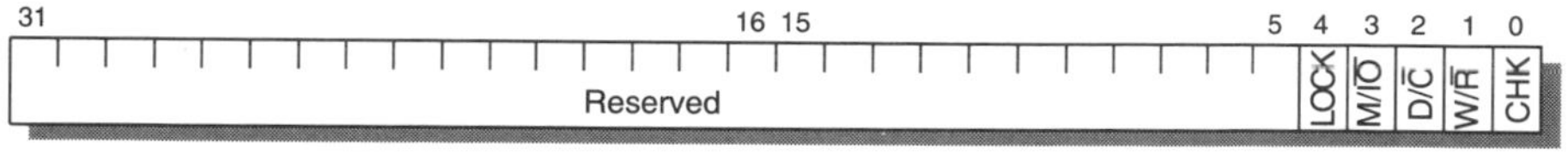

LOCK: LOCK State
0=LOCK Disabled (high) 1=LOCK Enabled (low)
M/$\overline{IO}$: Cycle Type
0=I/O Cycle 1=Memory Cycle
D/$\overline{C}$: Cycle Type
0=Command Cycle 1=Data Cycle
W/$\overline{R}$: Cycle Type
0=Read Cycle 1=Write Cycle
CHK: Check Status
0=MCT and MCA Registers Invalid 1=Register Contents Valid

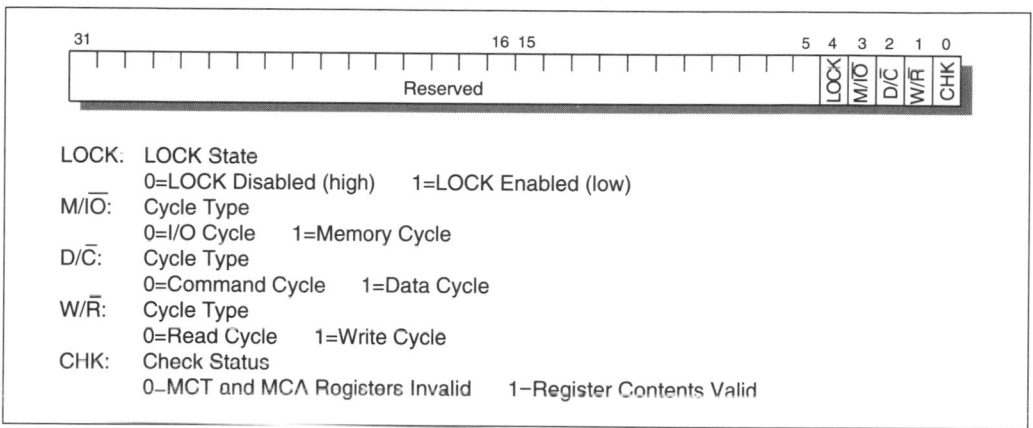

Figure 12.18: The machine check type register.

Address Parity Error

Except for inquiry cycles, the address bus always outputs an address. Thus, the Pentium does not perform an address parity check, but it does produce an address parity bit at AP so that even parity occurs. Note that only address bits A31–A5 are used in the calculation of parity; A4 and A3 are ignored. In an inquiry cycle, however, the Pentium checks the parity of the address bits; it now receives address signals. The inquiring system delivers the inquiry address at A31–A5 (corresponding to a cache line) and, additionally, a parity bit at AP. If the Pentium detects an address parity fault, it activates its $\overline{APCHK}$ (address parity check) output. Contrary to a data parity fault, an address parity fault has no further effect on the behaviour of the Pentium. The external system can use $\overline{APCHK}$ or simply ignore it.

12.7.4 Execution Tracing

With program execution tracing an external system can monitor the internal program execution in the Pentium. Execution tracing is a new function of the Pentium. The processor indicates with the signals IU, IV and IBT, and also the branch trace special cycle, when the u- or v-pipeline has completed an instruction, or when a branch has been carried out. The signals IU, IV and IBT are given out by the Pentium without further programming. However, the branch trace message special cycle must be enabled with the tracing bit TR in the test register TR12 (Figure 12.19).

If an instruction in the u-pipeline has left the last stage, then the Pentium sends out an active signal with a high level from its IU pin. The same applies to the v-pipeline. Table 12.12 lists all possible combinations of the IU, IV and IBT signals. In addition to conditional and unconditional jumps, taken branches also include procedure calls (CALLs), interrupts, RETs and IRETs, and also certain segment descriptor load operations, serialization instructions and most exceptions.

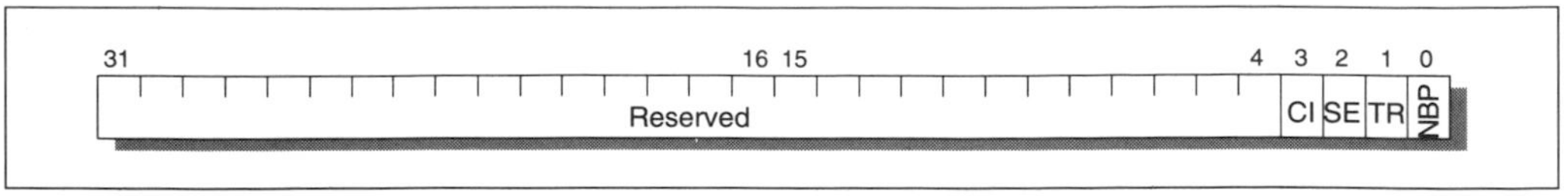

Figure 12.19: Control register TR12.

For the complete picture at this point, I would briefly like to repeat the signals and data given out by the Pentium during a branch trace message cycle:

$\overline{BE7}$ = $\overline{BE6}$=$\overline{BE4}$=$\overline{BE3}$=$\overline{BE2}$=$\overline{BE1}$=$\overline{BE0}$=1;$\overline{BE5}$=0
D/$\overline{C}$=M/$\overline{IO}$=0,W/$\overline{R}$=1)

```
A31–A3:      bits 31..3 of branch target linear address
BT2–BT0:     bits 2..0 of branch target linear address
BT3:         1=standard operand size 32 bits; 0=standard operand size 16 bits
```

IU	IV	IBT	
0	0	0	instruction not completed (at least the u-pipeline contains a not-completed instruction)
0	0	1	invalid
0	1	0	invalid
0	1	1	invalid
1	0	0	u-pipeline has completed an instruction other than a branch
1	0	1	an instruction completed in the u-pipeline led to a branch
1	1	0	u-pipeline and v-pipeline each completed an instruction other than a branch
1	1	1	u-pipeline and v-pipeline each completed an instruction; the instruction in the v-pipeline led to a branch

Table 12.12: IU, IV and IBT during execution tracing

12.7.5 Hardware Debug Support and Probe Mode

In Sections 2.8 and 10.3.7 you have already learnt part of the way in which the Pentium supports hardware debugging. However, this only concerns the supporting of a debugging program, thus of software, through the debug registers of the Pentium. These functions have not been provided for supporting hardware which directly accesses the Pentium's registers and directly monitors the program execution. For this purpose, the new probe mode has been implemented together with the debug port. The debug port comprises the signals INIT, DBRESET, RESET, $\overline{SMIACT}$, R/$\overline{S}$, SYSR/$\overline{S}$, PRDY, TDI, TDO, TMS, TCLK, $\overline{TRST}$, $\overline{DBINST}$ and $\overline{BSEN}$. Using these signals, the external hardware debugger can directly affect the instruction execution in the Pentium (for example, stopping program execution by activating R/$\overline{S}$).

In probe mode, only the normal CPU activity is shut down; inquiry cycles are still supported. The probe register of the TAP controller can be addressed, and the different internal Pentium registers can be read and changed through the boundary scan path. Thus, the TAP control is not influenced by an R/$\overline{S}$ signal. After the corresponding configuration, probe mode can also be enabled by a debug exception in place of the applicable interrupt. In this way, extensive examinations are possible into the behaviour of the Pentium and programs, and this even bypasses the processor and all protections to give you immediate access to the registers.

12.7.6 Machine Check Exception

When compared to the i486, the Pentium includes a new exception, the *machine check exception*, which leads to an interrupt 18 (12h). Note that this exception is only active if you set the MCE-bit (Machine Check Enable) in the CR4 control register. Otherwise, the Pentium ignores any exception conditions that occur. Note that in the personal computer, this interrupt 18 is assigned a BIOS function which determines the actual memory size.

After a reset, the MCE-bit in the CR4 control register is reset, thus the Pentium does not generally send out a machine check exception. The 64-bit machine check address register stores the actual physical address given out on the address bus when an MCE exception occurs; the 64-bit machine check type register stores the type of active bus cycle. The structure of the machine check type registers is shown in Figure 12.18.

12.8 Pentium I/O Address Space

The address space of the Pentium includes 64k 8 bit ports, 32k 16-bit ports and 16k 32-bit ports, or an equivalent mix of them. Accesses to the I/O address space are accomplished with a maximum width of 32 bits, and the remaining 32 bits of the 64-bit Pentium data bus are then unused. The Pentium bypasses the cache for I/O accesses; they are directly sent to the bus. I/O write accesses are also not temporarily stored in the write buffers. The addressing of the I/O ports and the protection of the I/O address space in protected mode using the IOPL flag and the I/O permission bit map is executed in the Pentium in exactly the same way as in the i386 and i486. The relevant details are contained in Sections 3.7.10 and 3.7.11.

12.9 L2-Cache Subsystem 82496/82491 for the Pentium

Intel had a special cache controller developed for the Pentium, the 82496, which, together with the cache SRAM modules, can create an L2-cache. In Figure 12.20 you can see the structure of the L2-cache with an 82496 cache controller and several 82491 cache SRAM modules.

For an L2-cache, the cache controller and the SRAM modules are located between the Pentium, the memory bus and the memory controller, which controls the DRAMs of the main memory. The necessary address, data and control signals are transferred between the components over a total of six channels. The interfaces between these components are optimized for the chip set consisting of the Pentium CPU, 82496 cache controller, 82491 cache SRAM and the memory system. As usual, the 82496 checks all memory accesses from the CPU, the Pentium here. In addition, it either makes the data available from the 82491 SRAM modules, or controls the memory bus and the memory controller, to read the data from the main memory if a cache miss occurs. The 82496 is additionally responsible for the implementation and execution of the MESI protocol, so as to attain cache consistency over several such L2-caches.

The 82496 for the Pentium is an improved version of the i486 82495DX cache controller. It can be configured as an L2-cache with a 256 kbyte or 512 kbyte memory capacity. The 82496 operates fixed with 2-way set-associative cache architecture and supports cache line sizes of 32, 64 and 128 bytes. In contrast to Pentium on-chip caches, the 82496 also supports write allocation. The cache SRAM modules 82491 implement the data memory for the L2-cache subsystem. They each have a memory capacity of 32 kbyte or 256 kbits, respectively, and an internal logic, thus they are more than just pure SRAM chips.

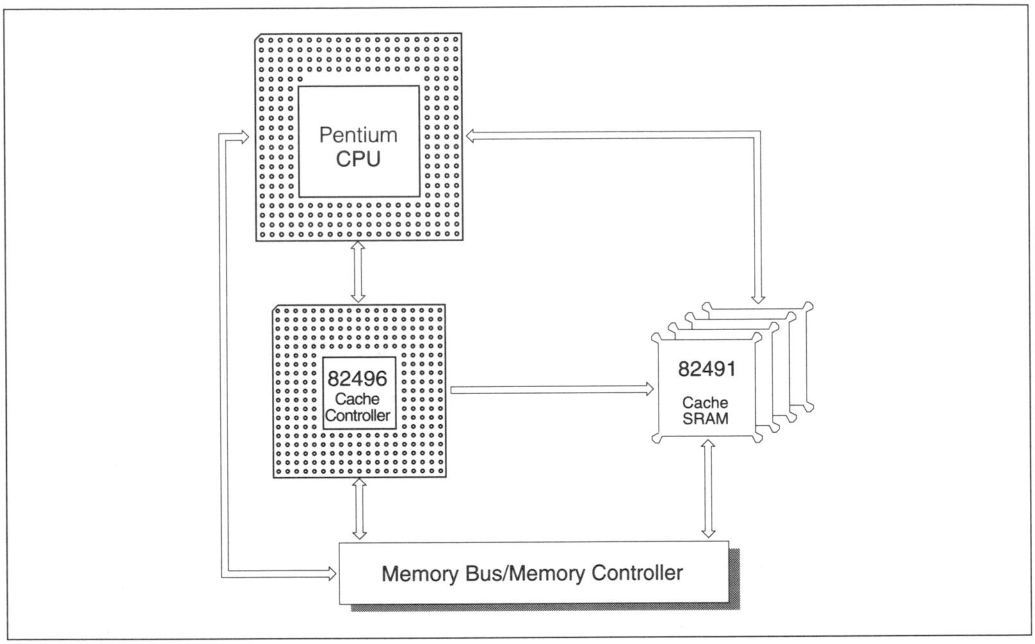

Figure 12.20: L2-cache with an 82496 cache controller and several cache SRAM modules 82491.

The 82496 also supports *cache sectoring*. Generally, with cache sectoring, several cache lines are combined into one cache sector. Sectors with only one or two cache lines are included in the case of the 82496.

Finally, a few observations with regard to the increase in performance in connection with an L2-cache. The obtainable performance is dependent on many parameters. The number of write accesses is clearly reduced by the write-back strategy. An L2-cache configured as write-back delivers a performance increase of 30% in comparison to an L2-cache with a write-through strategy. If the L1-cache is also configured as write-back, a further increase of only 5% can be expected. The reason is obvious: in most cases, no wait cycles are necessary for a Pentium write access to the L2-cache; on the other hand, this is not the case for a write access of the 82496

66 MHz L2-cache controller to DRAM main memory. Tests show, in typical application programs, that cache association plays a large role. A direct-mapped cache is approximately 15% slower than a 2-way set-associative cache. Surprisingly, the size of cache plays a much smaller role than would perhaps be thought: the transition from a 128 kbyte to a 256 kbyte cache produces a 4–5% increase, a further increase to 512 kbytes a meagre 2–2.5%. The greatest significance for an increase in performance is as a result of the two Pentium on-chip caches, when compared to the i486. The result implies that a moderate L2-cache brings with it an obvious, but not miraculous performance improvement. In comparison, money would be better spent on a good PCI graphics adapter and a fast hard disk controller than on the expensive SRAM modules to extend the L2-cache.

13 Compatibility Downwards – The 80286

While the 80286, like its 8086 and 8088 predecessors, is only a 16-bit processor with 16-bit registers, its main innovation is the protected virtual address mode, or *protected mode* for short. Although it is not apparent from the outside, Intel has integrated an enormous variety of functions so that the access checks of protected mode are carried out without delay. Compared to the i386, the 80286 not only lacks the 32-bit registers, but also the paging unit and the virtual 8086 mode.

The 80286 has a 24-bit address bus and a 16-bit data bus. Thus 16 Mbytes of memory can be addressed in protected mode. In real mode, the 80286 just works like a fast 8086. The higher execution speed is the result of the higher processor clock frequency (newer types reach up to 25 MHz) and the optimized electronic circuitry in the instruction, execution and addressing units, so that fewer clock cycles are required for executing an instruction. Also, a bus cycle which can read and write data significantly faster than in the 8086 enhances the 80286's performance compared to the 8086. The 80286 is entirely microencoded; RISC elements are not present. The 80286 I/O address space comprises 64k 8-bit ports at addresses 0–65 535, or 32k 16-bit ports with addresses 0, 2, 4, ..., 65532, 65534, or an equivalent mixture of 8-bit and 16-bit ports until 64k is reached.

13.1 80286 Connections and Signals

The 80286 comes in two different packages: a *plastic leaded chip carrier (PLCC)* or a *pin grid array (PGA)*. The internal structure of the processor is identical in both cases; only the sockets into which it is inserted differ in shape and contact assignment. Because of the higher pin density, the pin grid package is smaller. Figure 13.1 shows the 80286 pinout.

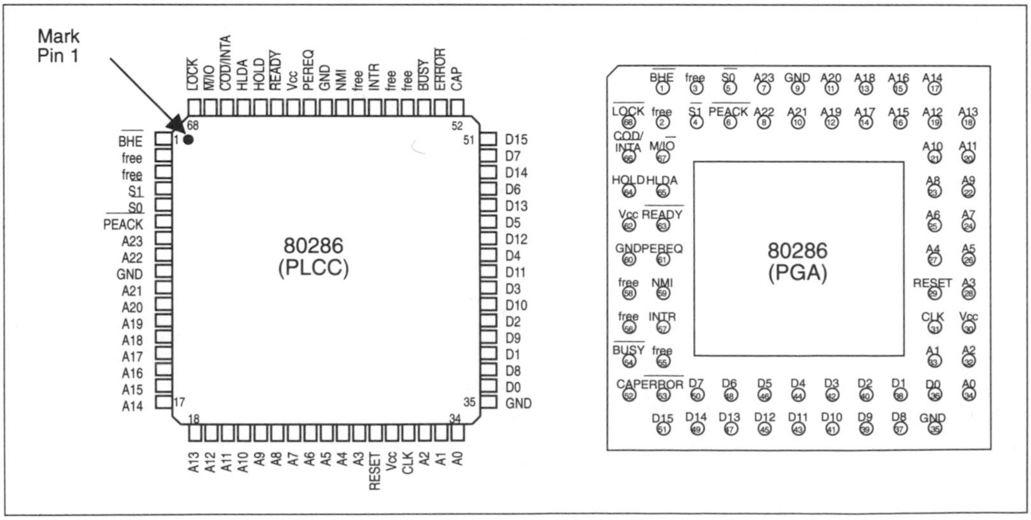

Figure 13.1: 80286 pinout. The 80286 comes in a PLCC or a PGA package with 68 contacts.

The following discusses only the 80286 terminals. Pins and signals which are also implemented in the i386 are only listed in brief. Details are given in the relevant chapter.

A24–A0 (O)
Pins 7, 8, 10–28, 32–34

These 24 terminals form the 24-bit address bus.

$\overline{\text{BHE}}$ (O)
Pin 1

The bus high enable signal at this pin indicates, together with A0, whether a complete word or only one byte is transferred on the high-order and low-order part of the data bus, respectively. If $\overline{\text{BHE}}$ provides an active (low-level) signal the high-order part of the data bus transfers a byte. For ($\overline{\text{BHE}}$, A0) the following meanings apply:

```
(00) one word (2 bytes) is transferred via D15-D0;
(01) one byte is transferred on D15-D8 from/to an odd byte address;
(10) one byte is transferred on D7-D0 from/to an even byte address;
(11) invalid.
```

$\overline{\text{BUSY}}$, $\overline{\text{ERROR}}$ (I, I)
Pins 54, 53

These signals inform the 80286 about the current coprocessor status. If $\overline{\text{BUSY}}$ is active the coprocessor is executing an instruction. The 80286 operation is stopped for some ESC instructions, as is the case for an active WAIT instruction. If the signal $\overline{\text{ERROR}}$ is active the 80286 issues a coprocessor interrupt when it executes certain ESC instructions or a WAIT instruction.

CAP (I)
Pin 52

Between this connection and ground (0 V) a capacitor with a capacity of 0.047 μF must be connected to correctly operate the internal bias generator of the 80286.

CLK (I)
Pin 31

This pin receives the clock signal. Internally, the 80286 divides CLK by two, in order to create the effective processor clock (PCLK). Therefore the 80286 is supplied with a 2x-clock in the same way as the i386.

COD/$\overline{\text{INTA}}$, M/$\overline{\text{IO}}$, $\overline{\text{S1}}$, $\overline{\text{S0}}$ (O, O, O, O)
Pins 66, 67, 4, 5

These signals define the status of the active bus cycle. The combinations (COD/$\overline{\text{INTA}}$, M/$\overline{\text{IO}}$, $\overline{\text{S1}}$, $\overline{\text{S0}}$) have the following meaning:

(0000) INTA sequence;
(0100) halt for A1 = 1, shutdown for A1 = 0;
(0101) data is read from memory;
(0110) data is written into memory;

(1001) an I/O port is read;
(1010) an I/O port is written;
(1101) instruction prefetching.

All other combinations are invalid.

D15–D0 (I/O)
Pins 36–51

These 16 pins form the 80286 bidirectional data bus.

HOLD, HLDA (I, O)
Pins 64, 65

These signals serve for switching the local bus among various busmasters. If another busmaster wants to take control of the local bus, it issues a request signal via the HOLD pin to the 80286. If the 80286 can release control, it outputs an acknowledge signal via the HLDA pin. Thus the requesting processor takes control of the local bus until it deactivates the signal to the HOLD input of the 80286 again. Now the 80286 deactivates HLDA and takes control of the local bus once more.

INTR (I)
Pin 57

Via the INTR pin, an interrupt controller can issue a hardware interrupt. The strobing of INTR is blocked (masked) by a cleared interrupt INTR flag IE.

$\overline{\text{LOCK}}$ (O)
Pin 68

When $\overline{\text{LOCK}}$ is active, that is, there is a low level signal at this pin, the 80286 will not transfer control of the local bus to another busmaster, which requests control by means of HOLD. It does not respond to the HOLD request with an acknowledge (HLDA).

NMI (I)
Pin 59

A transition of the signal at this pin from a low to a high level issues an interrupt 2. The 80286 suspends program execution and attends to the interrupt.

PEREQ, $\overline{\text{PEACK}}$ (I, O)
Pins 61, 6

If the coprocessor 80287 attempts to read data from or write data into memory, it activates the processor extension request signal PEREQ. As soon as the 80286 has transferred the data from or to memory, it applies an active processor extension acknowledge signal $\overline{\text{PEACK}}$ to the 80287.

$\overline{\text{READY}}$ (I)
Pin 63

The signal at this pin indicates whether the addressed peripheral device, for example the main memory or an I/O device, has completed the access ($\overline{\text{READY}}$ on a low level) or whether it re-

quires more time ($\overline{READY}$ on a high level). Thus, the 80286 is able to insert wait states in the same way as the i386.

RESET (I)
Pin 29

If this input is on a high level for at least 16 CLK cycles, the 80286 aborts the present operation and executes a processor reset.

Vcc (I)
Pins 30, 62

These pins are fed with the supply voltage (normally +5 V).

GND
Pins 9, 35, 60

These pins are connected to ground (normally 0 V).

Free
Pins 2, 3, 55, 56, 58

These pins should always be maintained in a free (not connected) condition.

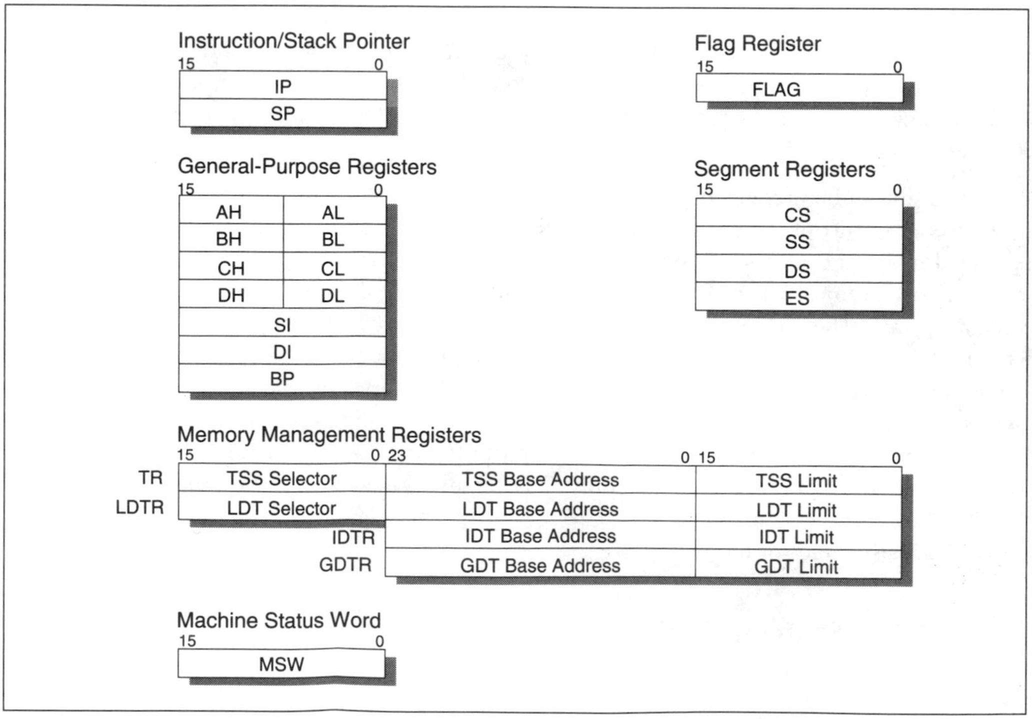

Figure 13.2: The 80286 registers.

13.2 80286 Registers

All general-purpose registers encompass 16 bits in the 80286. If you restrict yourself to registers without a preceding E when looking at Figure 2.5, you get all 80286 general-purpose registers. These are the AX, BX, CX, DX, SI, DI and BP registers. Additionally, the instruction pointer IP, stack pointer SP and the flags are implemented. The 80286 has neither the debug, control nor test registers which are present in the i386. Only the machine status word as a part of CR0 is already implemented here. Figure 13.2 summarizes the 80286 registers.

13.3 80286 Protected Mode

As far as its function is concerned, the 80286 protected mode is identical to that in the i386, but it cannot be surprising that all register and descriptor structures are directed to the 16-bit architecture of the 80286, as the i386 and thus also the i386 protected mode are a later enhancement to the earlier 80286. The following sections are therefore restricted mainly to the differences and limitations as compared to the i386 protected mode.

13.3.1 80286 Memory Management Registers

For the protected mode, the 80286 has five registers: the machine status word (MSW), the task register (TR), and the registers for the local descriptor table (LDT), interrupt descriptor table (IDT), and global descriptor table (GDT). They are shown in Figure 13.2 together with the other 80286 registers.

Because of the 16-bit architecture of the 80286, the machine status word only comprises 16 bits. In the i386 it is part of the control register CR0 (Figure 3.8). If the 80286 has been switched to protected mode, it can be switched back into real mode only by a processor reset. That calls the initialization routine, and the processor once again runs in real mode. This is, of course, a time-consuming task. The AT's ROM BIOS recognizes by a shutdown status entry in the CMOS RAM whether the PC must be booted, or whether only the processor must be switched back into real mode. The entries in the four descriptor and task registers are also adapted to the 80286 architecture. The base address encompasses 24 bits according to the 24-bit address bus, and the limit entry encompasses only 16 bits because of the 16-bit offset registers here. With an 80286, the segments may comprise 64 kbytes only. The segment selectors are the same as in the i386; the i386's segment registers are also only 16 bits wide. The segment selector structure shown in Figure 3.4 is also valid for the 80286.

13.3.2 80286 Segment Descriptors

The 80286 segment descriptors must reflect the 16-bit structure of the 80286. For example, 32-bit base entries are impossible because of the 24-bit address bus. Figure 13.3 shows the 80286 segment descriptor structure; it encompasses (with great foresight) eight bytes as in the i386.

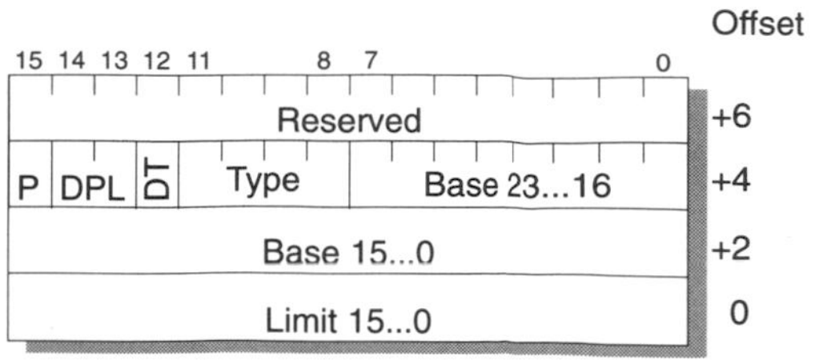

Figure 13.3: Structure of an 80286 segment descriptor.

The 24 base bits indicate the starting address of the segment in memory and correspond to the 24 80286 address lines. Therefore, the 80286 can address 2^{24} bytes or 16 Mbytes in protected mode. The 16 bits of the limit entry give the size of the segment in bytes, so that in protected mode, segments with 64 kbytes are also possible. As no granularity bit is available, larger segments cannot be constructed, but this is impossible in any case because of the 16-bit offsets. The *DT* bit indicates the descriptor type. The *type* field defines the segment type, and *DPL* the accompanying privilege level (from 0 up to 3). Finally the *P* bit is an indicator of whether the segment is actually in memory or not. These entries are also present in the i386 segment descriptor.

The two most significant bytes are reserved. In an i386 segment descriptor the granularity bit G, the segment size bit DB, the missing eight base bits 31–24 for a 32-bit base address and the four limit bits 19–16 for the 20-bit limit in an i386 are located there. For compatibility with the i386 and later processors, you should always set the two high-order bytes equal to 0. Then the DB-bit is always equal to 0, and the 80286 code can be ported without any problem to the 32-bit architecture of the i386, because all operands and addresses are handled as 16-bit quantities.

13.3.3 80286 Segment and Access Types

For the 80286, two segment tyes are available: application and system segments. The DT-bit and the four type bits in the segment descriptor determine the type and rights of access to the segment described. If DT is equal to 1, an application segment is indicated, otherwise a system segment.

Application Segments

The definition of application segments is the same as for the i386; the *type* field in the segment descriptor has the following structure:

Bit:	11	10	9	8
Meaning:	EXE	E/C	W/R	A

The classification of all fields and the assigned application segments is summarized in Table 3.2 (Section 3.7.6). Thus, for application segments, there is no difference between the 80286 and the i386. This is, however, not the case for the system segments.

System Segments and Gates

The 80286 knows a total of seven system segment types (Table 13.1). The task state segments (TSS) define the state of active or suspended (available) tasks. Also in the 80286, TSS and LDT descriptors, as system segments, are only allowed in the GDT. The four gates serve for a well-defined control transfer between tasks of different privilege levels, as in the i386.

Type	Meaning	Type
1	available 80286 TSS	system segment
2	LDT	system segment
3	active 80286 TSS	system segment
4	80286 call gate	gate
5	task gate	gate
6	80286 interrupt gate	gate
7	80286 trap gate	gate

Table 13.1: 80286 system segment types (DT=0)

All other values valid for the i386 are invalid here.

The structure of the *gate descriptors* for the 80286 is shown in Figure 13.4. Call gates are, however, not only used for procedure calls, but also for all conditional and unconditional jumps; they can occur in the local or global descriptor table, but not in the interrupt descriptor table. There, only interrupt, trap, and task gates are allowed.

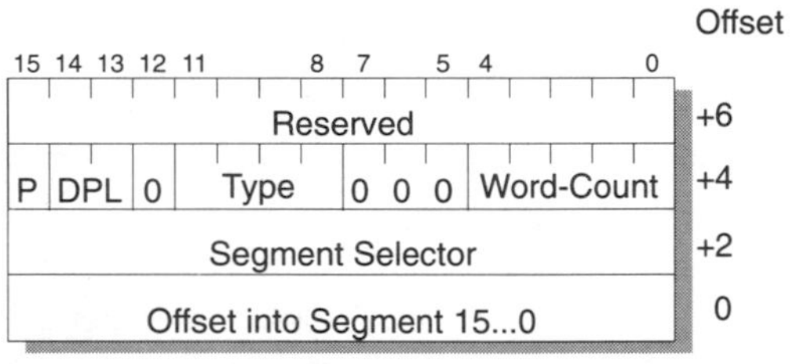

Figure 13.4: 80286 gate descriptor.

The 80286 gates differ from i386 gates in that bits 31–16 for the jump target offset are not present, and the *word count* field indicates not double but simple 16-bit words. The reason for these limitations is, once again, the 16-bit architecture of the 80286. On compatibility grounds, the i386 can also process 80286 gates. When the i386 encounters an 80286 gate, it interprets the dword count field as a word count and copies only an applicable number of words (of 16 bits each).

13.3.4 Multitasking, 80286 TSS and 80286 Task Gate

The 80286 protected mode also serves to support multitasking systems. For this purpose, a task state segment is adopted in the 80286 architecture; its structure is shown in Figure 13.5.

It is not surprising that the 80286 TSS is smaller than its i386 counterpart, as only 16-bit registers must be saved. Nevertheless, two important differences are apparent: the entries for an I/O map base and CR3, as well as the T-bit, are missing.

The 80286 protects its I/O address space only through the IOPL flag; an I/O map is not present, as it was not implemented until the i386. Moreover, the 80286 has no paging unit, thus the page directory base entry in the (also unimplemented) control register CR3 has no meaning. For the 80286, it is not intended that a task switch (that is, upon loading a new TSS) should issue a debug exception corresponding to interrupt 1. The debug registers required for that are missing.

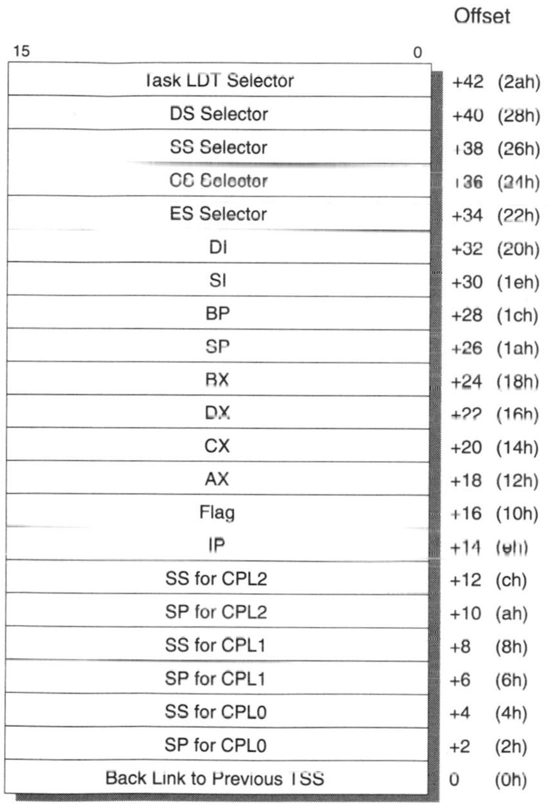
Offset
15
0
Task LDT Selector +42 (2ah)
DS Selector +40 (28h)
SS Selector +38 (26h)
CS Selector +36 (24h)
ES Selector +34 (22h)
DI +32 (20h)
SI +30 (1eh)
BP +28 (1ch)
SP +26 (1ah)
BX +24 (18h)
DX +22 (16h)
CX +20 (14h)
AX +18 (12h)
Flag +16 (10h)
IP +14 (eh)
SS for CPL2 +12 (ch)
SP for CPL2 +10 (ah)
SS for CPL1 +8 (8h)
SP for CPL1 +6 (6h)
SS for CPL0 +4 (4h)
SP for CPL0 +2 (2h)
Back Link to Previous TSS 0 (0h)

Figure 13.5: 80286 task state segment (TSS).

The task gate for an 80286 and an i386 does not differ; only the TSS segment selector is stored in the task gate descriptor, and the selector structure did not change between the 80286 and the i386. The function of the task state segments and the task gates for switching between various tasks is identical to that in the i386. All processes discussed there are, in principle (after adaptation to the 16-bit architecture of the 80286), still valid.

13.3.5 80286 Protection for I/O Address Space

As already mentioned, the I/O ports are protected in the 80286 only with the IOPL flag in the flag register. The value of the IOPL flag indicates, as usual, the minimum privilege level necessary for a code segment to access the I/O address space, that is, CPL ≤ IOPL must be fulfilled. If the CPL of the current task is higher (lower privilege level), the IOPL-sensitive instructions IN, OUT, INS, OUTS, CLI and STI give rise to the «general protection error».

Thus, the 80286 implements only a strategy of global I/O address space protection through the IOPL flag. Additional individal protection of the ports with an I/O map as in the i386, is not available. But this is understandable, since the I/O map has been mainly implemented for supporting the virtual 8086 mode.

13.4 80286 Bus Cycles and Pipelining

The 80286 bus cycle hardly differs from that in the i386; only some other control signals are driven which, after decoding, have the same effects. Among these are, for example, the address signals A23–A0 and the $\overline{\text{BHE}}$ signal. In the i386, the two address signals, A1 and A0, are missing, and must be decoded with the help of the $\overline{\text{BEx}}$ signals. The 80286 bus cycle lasts, without wait cycles, for two PCLK cycles; this corresponds to four CLK cycles. A 10 MHz 80286 can thus carry out 5 million bus cycles per second, corresponding to a transfer rate of 10 Mbytes/s.

If the memory or peripheral cannot execute the read or write request in time, it holds the $\overline{\text{READY}}$ signal on a high level, as in the i386. This signals to the 80286 that it should insert a wait cycle to give the memory or peripheral more time to complete the pending cycle.

Special Cycles

In addition to the three «normal» bus cycles for reading and writing data and the passive bus cycle (when neither the prefetch queue must be refilled nor the presently executed instruction requires a memory or I/O access), the 80286 implements two special cycles: Shutdown and Halt. These are indicated by the combination (0100) of the COD/$\overline{\text{INTA}}$, M/$\overline{\text{IO}}$, $\overline{\text{S1}}$, $\overline{\text{S0}}$ signals, and distinguished by the value of A1. The shutdown cycle is driven when several exceptions occur during the execution of an instruction, and the processor is overtaxed by them. The halt state can be entered by a HLT instruction. In this case also, the processor is stopped and does not carry out further instructions. Table 13.2 summarizes the special cycles. Note that special cycles must be acknowledged by $\overline{\text{READY}}$, too.

A1	Special cycle
1	Halt
0	Shutdown

Table 13.2: 80286 special cycles (COD/$\overline{\text{INTA}}$ = 0, M/$\overline{\text{IO}}$ = 1, $\overline{\text{S1}}$ = $\overline{\text{S0}}$ = 0)

If the hardware IRQs are enabled (that is, the IE flag is set), the processor can be forced to leave the halt state by issuing a hardware IRQ. In the PC, such an IRQ is activated, for example, by pressing a key on the keyboard. The shutdown state is not affected by that; the processor simply ignores the request.

To terminate the shutdown state, you must issue either an NMI or a processor reset. These also terminate the halt state. The difference between them is that the NMI does not change the processor mode: if the 80286 is operating in protected mode before shutdown, the operation is continued in protected mode again after an NMI, and the interrupt handler 2 corresponding to the NMI is addressed. On the other hand, a reset always switches the processor into real mode, and the 80286 starts program execution at CS=f000h, IP=fff0h, and additionally address lines A23–A20 are activated.

Pipelining

To carry out an access to memory or ports at the fastest speed, the 80286 bus interface supports address pipelining. Unlike the i386, no $\overline{\text{NA}}$ signal (next address) is implemented for that purpose; the 80286 always carries out pipelined addressing. Thus, the external decoding system must be prepared for pipelined accesses. The 80286 already transfers the new address to the decoding logic one processor clock cycle PCLK before the termination of the current bus cycle. In fact, the succeeding bus cycles last for three bus cycles, but by using bus cycle interleaving through pipelining the effective period is reduced to only two cycles.

13.5 Word Boundaries

As is the case with the other 80x86 processors, the 80286 can also address memory byte by byte, although it has a 16-bit data bus. Thus we are confronted with the problem of word boundaries here. During an access to a 16-bit word at an odd address, the 80286 has to execute two bus cycles. This is carried out in the same way as with the i386, when that processor accesses a double word which is not aligned at a double word boundary. Similarly, the 80286 carries out this double access on its own, so that misalignments are completely transparent to software. The bus unit combines the two bytes read into one word (reading) or divides the word to be written into two bytes (writing).

Bytes with an even address are transferred via lines D7–D0 of the data bus, and bytes with an odd address via lines D15–D8. If a word with an even address is to be transferred, the 80286 uses data pins D15–D0 and completes the transfer within one bus cycle. Oddly addressed words are transferred within two bus cycles, where the first access is carried out via D15–D8 (byte with an odd address) and the second access via D7–D0 (byte with an even address).

During the two byte accesses, memory is physically addressed in even-numbered portions, but only the required byte is fetched. The processor informs the memory controller of this using $\overline{\text{BHE}}$ and A0 (the least significant address bit). Thus, an individual byte (low or high) at an even address 0, 2, ... ($\overline{\text{BHE}}$=1, A0=0) or an odd address 1, 3, ... ($\overline{\text{BHE}}$=0, A0=1) may be read or written.

Note that the prefetch queue in the 80286 always fetches the code in portions of 16-bit words, which start at even storage addresses. Because of this, the prefetch queue is reloaded only if at least two bytes are free. To get even storage addresses the processor may need to read one single byte first.

13.6 80286 Reset

An 80286 reset is issued if the system controller supplies a high-level signal to the RESET pin for at least 16 CLK cycles. If the signal returns to a low level afterwards, the 80286 carries out an internal initialization, during which the registers are loaded with the values indicated in Table 13.3.

Register	Value
Flag	00000000 00000010 = 0002h
IP	11111111 11110000 = fff0h
CS	11110000 00000000 = f000h[1)]
DS	00000000 00000000 = 0000h
SS	00000000 00000000 = 0000h
ES	00000000 00000000 = 0000h
MSW	11111111 11110000 = fff0h[2)]
all others	uuuuuuuu uuuuuuuu = uuuuh

u: undefined
1) base address = ff0000h, limit = ffffh (segment descriptor cache register)
2) PE = MP = EM = RS = 0, all reserved are equal to 1

Table 13.3: 80286 register contents after a reset

After a reset, the 80286 always starts operation in real mode (PE=0 in the machine status word). The GDTR, LDTR, IDTR and the task register have no meaning, thus for the moment, the 80286 starts instruction execution like the 8086. Moreover, after a reset the four most significant address lines A23–A20 are activated because the CS base entry in the segment descriptor cache register is set to ff0000h. The 80286 begins program execution at the physical 24-bit address fffff0h (16 bytes below 16 Mbytes). The four address lines A23–A29 are disabled as soon as the code segment CS has been altered (for example, by a far jump). The entry point of the start-up BIOS is, therefore, located at the upper end of the 80286 physical address space. After the first code segment change, this point cannot be reached again. In contrast to the i386 and its successors, no routines for an internal self-test are implemented.

14 The 80287 – Mathematical Assistant in Protected Mode

The 80287 is available in two versions: as a «bare» 80287 and as the more developed 80287XL. The 80287 is hardly more than an 8087 because its numeric unit has been transferred from the 8087 without any significant change. Thus the 80287 doesn't calculate any faster than its 8087 predecessor. Only the control unit has been adapted to the special data transfer protocol between CPU and coprocessor, because all data runs through the memory management unit in the 80286 in the same way as in the i386/i387 combination. That is necessary because memory addressing in protected mode may lead to many more problems and errors, such as an access denial for a task, than is the case in real mode. The 8087, on the contrary, is able to address the memory on its own.

The more advanced 80287XL also implements, in addition to a better numeric unit for faster execution of mathematical calculations, all the new functions of the i387, and strictly implements the new IEEE standard for handling roundings and infinite values. The interface to the 80286, however, remains the same. (If 80287 is indicated in the following, all the facts apply to both the 80287 and the 80287XL. If 80287XL is stated explicitly, only this enhanced coprocessor is concerned.)

Like the i387, the 80287 doesn't carry out any access to memory. With the 80286/287 combination the 80286 not only determines the memory address, but also executes all necessary accesses to memory. Therefore, all data runs through the memory management unit in the 80286. The 80287 supports the same number formats as the i387 (Figure 7.3), and represents all numbers internally in the temporary real format with 80 bits. As for the i387, all numbers are converted according to whether they are read by a load or written by a store instruction.

As mentioned above, the 80286 divides the clock signal CLK supplied by two to generate the internal processor clock. The 80287 behaves in a similar way, but here the clock signal CLK is divided by three. Thus the 80287 runs at only two-thirds of the CPU's speed. Therefore, the oft-complained-of clock reduction is not the result of a lower external clock frequency, but is built into the 80287. Remember that the numeric unit does not differ from that in an 8087, and originally the 8087 cooperated with a 4.77 MHz 8086 CPU. The jump up to 12.5 MHz, at which a normal 80286 operates without any problems, is very large. Intel's engineers were careful not to destroy their «old» 8087 in the new-look 80287.

The division by three may be cancelled in principle by fixing the CKM pin (see next section) on Vcc (high). Then the 80287 uses the external clock signal CLK directly without any division, but this option is for combination with another CPU and not with an 80286. In the PC the CKM pin is always low, and the external clock signal CLK is always divided by three if you insert an 80287 into the coprocessor socket on your motherboard. As is the case with the 80286, all specifications of the 80287 clock frequency apply to the effective frequency after the division by three. Thus, in a 10 MHz AT you need a coprocessor with an indicated clock frequency of $2/3*10$ MHz = 6.67 MHz.

One possibility to increase the clock frequency of the coprocessor is the installation of a so-called «piggyback board». Usually, this board is inserted into the 80287 socket on the motherboard, and has its own oscillator and an 82284 clock signal generator with a higher frequency, as well as the 80287 coprocessor. If you install a piggyback board with a 10 Mhz 80287 and a clock signal generator with 30 MHz in a 10 MHz AT, then both the CPU and the coprocessor will run at an effective processor clock of 10 MHz.

The 80287XL, as a further development of the 80287, takes a more direct and better route. Unlike the normal 80287, in the 80287XL the external clock CLK is divided not by three but by two to generate the effective coprocessor clock, as is the case in the 80286. That is possible because the electronic components in the 80287XL are far more powerful. You can never install a 10 MHz 80287XL in an 80287 piggyback board with a 30 MHz oscillator. The effective clock frequency of 15 MHz greatly exceeds the specification of 10 Mhz, and the 80287XL no longer operates correctly, or may be damaged.

14.1 80287 Connections and Signals

The 80287 comes in a 40-pin DIP or a 44-pin PLCC package. Figure 14.1 shows the pin assignment of the 80287.

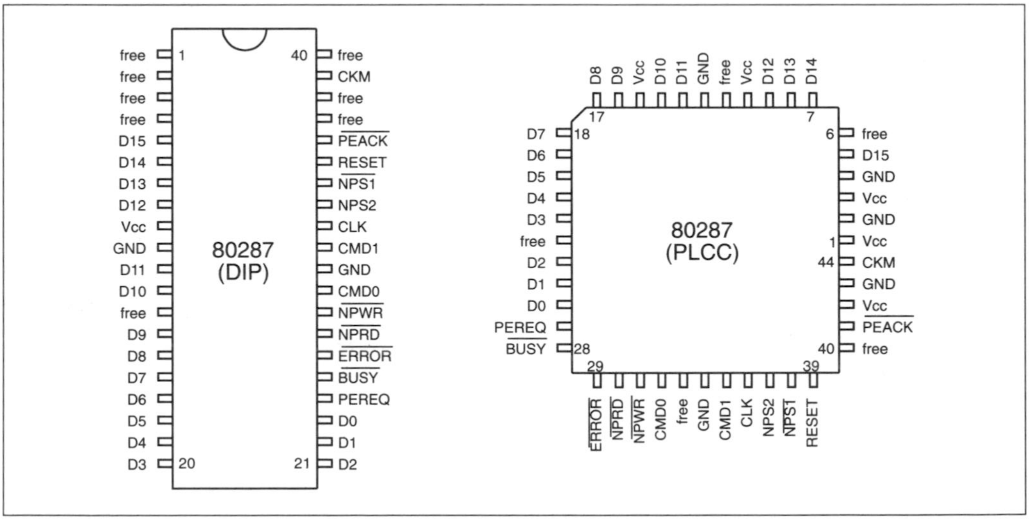

Figure 14.1: 80287 pin assignment.

In the following, only the new 80287 connections and signals or the altered ones compared to the i387 are discussed in detail.

$\overline{\text{BUSY}}$ (O)
Pin (DIP) 25
Pin (PLCC) 28
If this signal is high the 80287 is currently executing an ESC instruction.

CKM (I)
Pin (DIP) 39
Pin (PLCC) 44

Usually, this clocking mode pin is fixed (by soldering) on Vcc (+5 V) or GND (0 V). In the former case, the 80287 uses the external clock signal CLK directly without any division. In the latter case, the 80287 divides CLK by three, and the 80287XL by two, to generate the effective processor clock.

CLK (I)
Pin (DIP) 32
Pin (PLCC) 36

This pin is supplied with the clock signal. The 80287 divides CLK, depending upon the CKM level, by three (80287) or two (80287XL), or uses CLK directly.

CMD0, CMD1 (I, I)
Pins (DIP) 29, 31
Pins (PLCC) 32, 35

Together with pins $\overline{\text{NPS1}}$, NPS2, $\overline{\text{NPRD}}$ and $\overline{\text{NPWR}}$, the CPU can control the coprocessor's operation by these command select signals. For the combinations (NPS1 NPS2 CMD0 CMD1 $\overline{\text{NPRD}}$ $\overline{\text{NPWR}}$) the following meanings apply:

(x0xxxx) 80287 not activated;
(1xxxxx) 80287 not activated;
(010010) opcode is transferred to the 80287;
(010001) 80287 transfers control or status word to the CPU;
(011001) 80287 transfers data to the CPU;
(011010) CPU transfers data to the 80287;
(010110) exception pointer is written;
(010101) reserved;
(011101) reserved;
(011110) reserved.

D15–D0 (I/O)
Pins (DIP) 5–8, 11, 12, 14–23
Pins (PLCC) 5, 7–9, 13, 14, 16–22, 24–26

These 16 connections form the bidirectional 16-bit data bus for data exchange between the 80286 CPU and 80287 coprocessor.

$\overline{\text{ERROR}}$ (O)
Pin (DIP) 26
Pin (PLCC) 29

If $\overline{\text{ERROR}}$ is active (that is, low), a non-masked exception has occurred. Thus, $\overline{\text{ERROR}}$ indicates the value of the ES bit in the status register (see below).

$\overline{\text{NPRD}}$ (I)
Pin (DIP) 27
Pin (PLCC) 30

If the signal at this numeric processor read pin is low (active) then data may be transferred from coprocessor to CPU. For this purpose, the signals $\overline{\text{NPS1}}$ and NPS2 must additionally be active. Otherwise, $\overline{\text{NPRD}}$ will be ignored.

$\overline{\text{NPS2}}$, NPS1 (I, I)
Pins (DIP) 33, 34
Pins (PLCC) 37, 38

If both numeric processor select signals are active ($\overline{\text{NPS2}}$=0, NPS1=1), the 80286 has detected an ESC instruction, and it activates the 80287 to execute the instruction.

$\overline{\text{NPWR}}$ (I)
Pin (DIP) 28
Pin (PLCC) 31

If the numeric processor write signal at this pin is low (active), then data may be transferred from the CPU to the coprocessor. For this purpose, signals $\overline{\text{NPS1}}$ and NPS2 must additionally be active. Otherwise, $\overline{\text{NPRW}}$ will be ignored.

$\overline{\text{PEACK}}$ (I)
Pin (DIP) 36
Pin (PLCC) 41

If the 80287 is executing a coprocessor instruction (that is, an ESC instruction), and if it activates the PEREQ signal to supply data to or to accept data from the CPU, then the 80286 responds with a processor extension acknowledge signal ($\overline{\text{PEACK}}$) to inform the coprocessor that the request has been acknowledged and the data transfer is in progress.

PEREQ (O)
Pin (DIP) 24
Pin (PLCC) 27

If PEREQ is active (that is, the processor extension request pin is on a high level potential), the 80287 informs the 80286 that it can accept data from or may supply data to the CPU. If all data have been transferred, the 80287 disables the signal PEREQ again.

RESET (I)
Pin (DIP) 35
Pin (PLCC) 39

If this input is on a high-level potential for at least four CLK cycles, the 80287 carries out a coprocessor reset.

Vcc (I)
Pin (DIP) 9
Pins (PLCC) 1, 3, 10, 15, 42
These pins are fed with the supply voltage (usually +5 V).

GND (I)
Pins (DIP) 10, 30
Pins (PLCC) 2, 12, 34, 43

These pins are connected to ground (normally 0 V).

14.2 80287 Structure and Functioning

The internal 80287 structure is very similar to that of the i387. To be compatible with the 8087, the 80287 supports the same ESC instructions, and the 80287XL further supports the new i387 instructions. Also, the 80287 implements a register stack with eight 80-bit registers, which are accessed and managed in the same way as with an i387. Additionally, a status, control and tag word are implemented. The status word differs only slightly from that of the i387; the control and tag words remained the same. The memory images of instruction and data pointers can be present only in 16-bit format, and are, therefore, identical to the 16-bit and 16-bit protected mode format, respectively, in the i387; they are shown in Figure 7.10 (see Chapter 7).

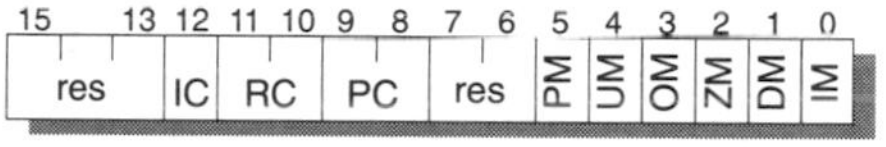

Figure 14.2: 80287 control word format.

Therefore, the following discusses only the difference between the 80287 and the i387 control word.

In Figure 14.2 you can see the format of the 80287 control word. The 80287XL control word is the same as that in the i387; the *IC* bit is without any meaning there because the IEEE standard demands an affine sense ±∞ for infinite values. IC can be set and cleared, but has no effect. However, in the 80287 (without XL), the *IC* bit for the handling of infinite quantities has the same meaning as in the 8087. The 80287 can process infinite quantities in a projective sense as ∞ (IC = 0), or in an affine sense as ±∞ (IC = 1), dependent upon your choice.

14.3 80287 Reset

After an 80287 reset which is issued by a high-level signal at the RESET pin lasting for at least four 80287 CLK cycles, the coprocessor executes an internal reset. For the reset the 80287 needs 25 CLK cycles, during which time it is unable to accept external instructions. Thus, the CPU has to wait for at least 25 coprocessor clock cycles after a coprocessor reset before it may hand over the first opcode. Also, the instruction FNINIT (initialize coprocessor) resets the 80287 internally into a strictly defined state. After the coprocessor reset, the 80287 should always be initialized with an FNINIT instruction. For the current 80287 types this is not absolutely necessary, but Intel recommends it to ensure compatibility with future versions. Table 14.1 lists the values of various 80287 registers after a reset or an FNINIT instruction.

Register	Value	Interpretation
Control word	37fh	all exceptions masked, precision 64 bits, rounding to next value
Status word	xy00h[1]	all exceptions cleared, TOP=000b[2], condition code undefined, B=0
Tag word	ffffh	all registers empty

[1] x = 0 or x = 4, 0 ≤ y ≤ 7
[2] after the first PUSH instruction, TOP points to register 7 (111b), thus the stack is growing downwards

Table 14.1: Register values after RESET/FNINIT

14.4 80287 Exceptions

To complete the picture, the following summarizes all exceptions which refer to the 80287 and 80287XL directly or indirectly. A detailed discussion of their sources is given in Section 7.6:

- exception 7 (no coprocessor available),
- exception 9 (coprocessor segment overflow),
- exception 13 (general protection error),
- exception 16 (coprocessor error).

14.5 Communication Between CPU and 80287

As is the case with the i387, the 80287 cannot address the memory on its own. For every memory acess, it depends upon the 80286, and communicates with the CPU through reserved ports in the same way as the i387. The 80286 carries out all necessary memory accesses. Therefore, all data runs through the 80286 memory management unit so that the 80287, too, can take advantage of the protected mode.

The 80286 and the 80287 are in special tune with each other: to reach a very fast data exchange via the ports, this I/O bus cycle is carried out without wait states. Table 14.2 indicates the I/O addresses used by the 80286 and the assigned 80287 registers with which the processor communicates through the respective port.

I/O Address	80287 Register
0f8h	opcode register
0fch	operand register

Table 14.2: 80287 port addresses

Through these coprocessor ports, all data exchanges between memory and coprocessor are carried out. The corresponding process is discussed in Section 7.8.

14.6 80286/80287 System Configuration

Figure 14.3 shows the typical connection of the 80287 coprocessor and 80286 CPU. By means of data pins D15–D0, both access the same local bus but the addressing and therefore the output of the address signals A23–A0 is only carried out by the CPU 80286. With the configuration indicated, both CPU and coprocessor receive the same clock signal from the same 82284 clock generator. Because 80287 and 80286 run asynchronously, the 80287 may also be clocked by a separate clock generator, which does not need to be an 82284.

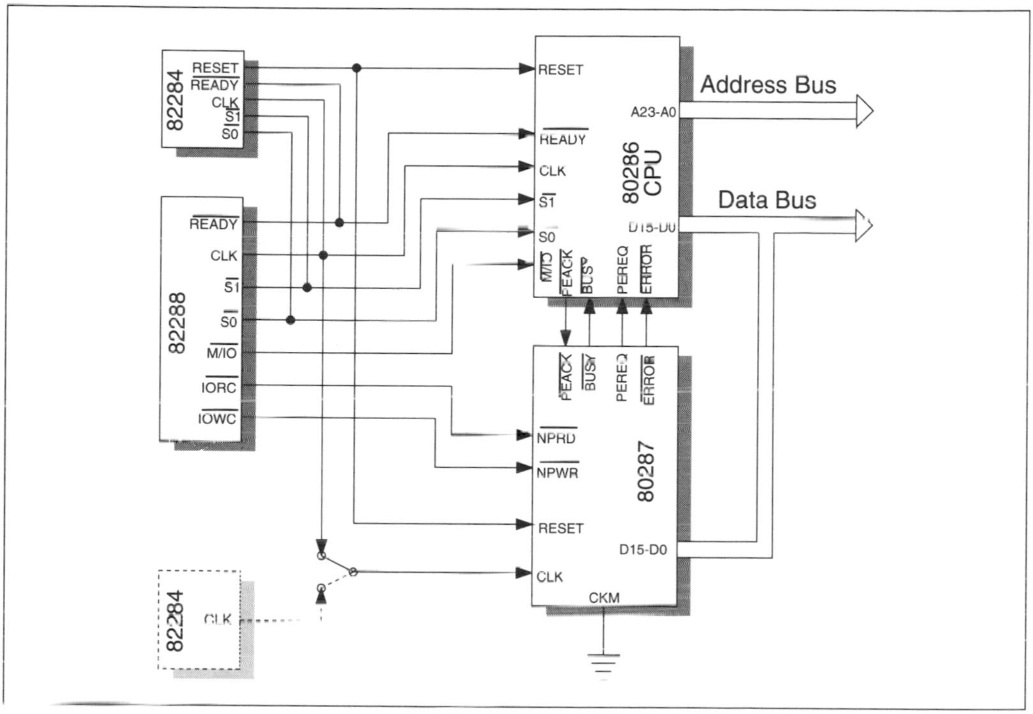

Figure 14.3: 80286/80287 system configuration. The 80287 harmonizes best with the 80286 and can therefore be connected to the 80286 without any problem. Unlike the 8086/8087 combination, the 80287 runs asynchronous to the CPU, and thus can be clocked by a separate clock generator.

An asynchronous operation of CPU and coprocessor is possible because, unlike the 8087, the 80287 is unable to control the local bus on its own. Instead, it receives all instruction code and data from the 80286. For this purpose the 80287 has a data bus which establishes the connection between CPU and coprocessor. The connections $\overline{\text{ERROR}}$, $\overline{\text{BUSY}}$, PEREQ, $\overline{\text{PEACK}}$, $\overline{\text{NPRD}}$, $\overline{\text{NPWR}}$, NPS2, $\overline{\text{NPS1}}$, CMD0 and CMD1 form a control bus for the 80287, which controls the data transfer from and to the CPU.

If an error or an exception occurs in the coprocessor during a numeric calculation (for example, an overflow or an underflow), then the 80287 activates its $\overline{\text{ERROR}}$ output to issue an interrupt in the 80286, whereas the 8087 requests a hardware interrupt using a dedicated INT pin.

15 Everything Began with the Ancestor 8086

The 8086 was presented as the successor to the widely used 8080 8-bit processor, and with its 16-bit architecture it was as sensational as the i386 proved to be ten years later. The instruction set for the 8086 encompassed 123 instructions. Among them are such powerful commands as the transfer of a complete string with the source and destination indexes, the subroutine call through CALL, and the explicit call of a software interrupt with INT. Therefore, I don't want to let this Pentium ancestor go by the board. Moreover, I'm sure that some readers will have an XT old-timer, which is based on the 8086, in a corner of their room. An 8086/88 derivative, the 80186/88, is widely used even today for hard disk controllers. Two 8086 features are the multiplexed data/address bus and the maximum and minimum operating modes. Intel gave up both with the 80286 because they represent relics from the time of simple 8-bit processors.

15.1 8086 Pins and Signals

The following explains the connections of the 8086 and the meanings of the corresponding signals. First, we cover the pins, which have the same meaning both in maximum and minimum mode. Figure 15.1 shows the 8086 pinout; it comes in a 40-pin DIP package.

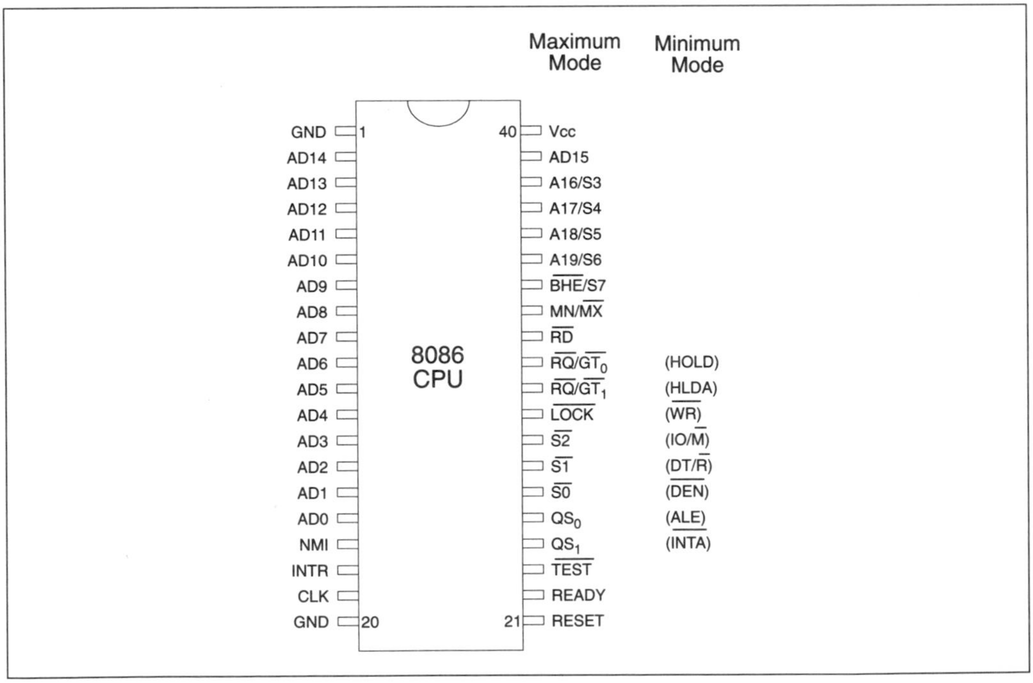

Figure 15.1: 8086 pinout. The 8086 comes in a standard DIP package with 40 pins. Some connections provide different signals in minimum and maximum mode.

AD15–AD0 (I/O)
Pins 2–16, 39

These 16 connections form the 16 data bits when the 8086 is reading or writing data as well as the lower 16 address bits when the 8086 is addressing memory or peripherals. The address signals are always supplied first and at a later time the data signals are output or read. Therefore these 16 pins form a *time-divisionally multiplexed* address and data bus.

A19–A16/S6–S3 (O)
Pins 35–38

These four pins form the four high-order bits of the address bus as well as four status signals which indicate the processor's current activity. Thus, these four lines form a time-divisionally multiplexed address and control bus. If the pins supply status information, S5 (pin 36) indicates the value of the interrupt flag in the processor's flag register, and S4/S3 indicate the segment register that is used for the access, according to the following list:

A17/S4	A16/S3	Register for data access
0	0	ES
0	1	SS
1	0	CS or none
1	1	DS

S5 = status of the IE flag (interrupt enable)
S6 = 0 (low) always

$\overline{\text{BHE}}$/S7 (O)
Pin 34

This bus high enable signal indicates whether a whole word (2 bytes) or only one byte is transferred. For the combination ($\overline{\text{BHE}}$/S7, A0) the following meanings hold:

(00) one complete word (2 bytes) is transferred via D15–D0;
(01) one byte on D15–D8 is transferred from/to an odd byte address;
(10) one byte on D7–D0 is transferred from/to an even byte address;
(11) invalid

CLK (I)
Pin 19

CLK is the clock signal for the processor and the bus controller. The 8086 uses it without any further division.

INTR (I)
Pin 18

This interrupt pin is checked after completion of each instruction to determine whether an interrupt request from a hardware unit is pending. This check may be masked by a cleared interrupt flag.

MN/$\overline{\text{MX}}$ (I)
Pin 33

The signal at this minimum/maximum pin determines the operating mode. If MN/$\overline{\text{MX}}$ is grounded, the 8086 is running in maximum mode. If the pin is fixed to Vcc the 8086 is operating in minimum mode.

NMI (I)
Pin 17

A change of this signal from low to high causes an interrupt 2. This interrupt cannot be masked by the interrupt flag. The interrupt is executed immediately after completion of the current instruction.

RD (O)
Pin 32

An active read signal with a high level indicates that the processor is reading data from memory or from an I/O register. For RD=0 the 8086 is writing data.

READY (I)
Pin 22

If the accessed memory or peripheral has completed the data transfer from or to the memory or peripheral, READY is set high to indicate that state to the processor. Therefore, slow memory chips or peripherals can cause the processor to insert wait states. Note that READY is an active-high signal in the 8086.

RESET (I)
Pin 21

If this input is high for at least four clock cycles, the processor aborts its operation immediately and executes a processor reset as soon as the RESET signal becomes low again. All internal registers are set to a defined value, and the processor starts execution at address 0f000:fff0.

$\overline{\text{TEST}}$ (I)
Pin 23

This input is continuously checked by the WAIT instruction. If the level of $\overline{\text{TEST}}$ is low, the processor continues to execute the program. Otherwise, it executes dummy cycles until $\overline{\text{TEST}}$ is low. Thus, the processor can be stopped, by means of the WAIT instruction, until the coprocessor has completed a calculation, without locking out hardware interrupt requests via the INTR terminal.

Vcc (I)
Pin 40
This pin is supplied with the supply voltage of +5 V.

GND
Pins 1, 20

These pins are grounded (usually 0 V).

The following signals and pin assignments are valid for maximum mode only.

$\overline{S2}$, $\overline{S1}$, $\overline{S0}$ (O, O, O)
Pins 26–28

The 8288 bus controller uses these three control signals to generate all necessary memory and I/O control signals that control a read or write access to memory or I/O space. For the combinations ($\overline{S2}$, $\overline{S1}$, $\overline{S0}$) the following interpretations hold:

```
(000) INTA sequence;
(001) an I/O port is read;
(010) an I/O port is written;
(011) HALT condition;
(100) instruction fetching;
(101) data is read from memory;
(110) data is written into memory;
(111) passive state.
```

$\overline{RQ}/\overline{GT0}$, $\overline{RQ}/\overline{GT1}$ (I/O, I/O)
Pins 30, 31

These request/grant signals serve for switching the local bus between various busmasters. The $\overline{RQ}/\overline{GT0}$ connection has a higher priority than $\overline{RQ}/\overline{GT1}$. If another processor wants to get control of the local bus, it outputs a request signal via $\overline{RQ}/\overline{GTx}$ (x=0,1) to the currently active processor (current busmaster). If the addressed processor can release control (after completing its own instructions) it supplies an acknowledge signal via the same $\overline{RQ}/\overline{GTx}$ pin. Thus, the requesting processor takes control of the local bus. Beginning with the 80286, the HOLD/HLDA signals carry out this task.

$\overline{LOCK}$ (O)
Pin 29

If $\overline{LOCK}$ is active (that is, low) the processor may not release the local bus to another processor. The 8086 doesn't respond to a request via $\overline{RQ}/\overline{GTx}$ with an acknowledge. Using the LOCK instruction, the $\overline{LOCK}$ signal may be activated explicitly. Some memory-critical instructions such as XCHG activate the $\overline{LOCK}$ signal on their own.

QS1, QS0 (O, O)
Pins 24, 25

These queue status signals indicate the status of the prefetch queue. Thus, the internal prefetch queue of the 8086 can be seen externally. For the possible combinations (QS1, QS0) the following interpretations hold:

```
(00) the prefetch queue is not active;
(01) the first byte of the opcode in the prefetch queue is processed;
(10) the prefetch queue is cancelled;
(11) the next byte of the opcode in the prefetch queue is processed.
```

The following signals and pin assignments are valid for minimum mode only.

ALE (O)
Pin 25
This address latch enable signal activates the address buffer. The buffer then accepts the address supplied by the processor and latches onto it. Thus, throughout the whole bus cycle the address is available and will not be altered until a new ALE signal is active.

DEN (O)
Pin 26
If this data enable pin is low, data is written into the external data buffer and latched there.

DT/$\overline{\text{R}}$ (O)
Pin 27
If this data transmit/receive pin is high then data is written; if it is low then data is read. Therefore, DT/$\overline{\text{R}}$ indicates the direction of the data transfer on the bus.

HOLD, HLDA (I, O)
Pins 31, 30
These signals serve for switching the local bus among various busmasters. If another busmaster wants to take control of the local bus, it issues a request signal via the HOLD pin to the 8086. If the 8086 can release control, it outputs an acknowledge signal via the HLDA pin. Thus the requesting processor takes control of the local bus until it deactivates the signal to the HOLD input of the 8086 again. Now the 8086 deactivates HLDA and takes control of the local bus once more.

INTA (O)
Pin 24
Confirms the acknowledge of a hardware interrupt request.

M/$\overline{\text{IO}}$, W/$\overline{\text{R}}$ (O, O)
Pins 28, 29
These memory/IO and write/read signals define the type of the current bus cycle. The possible combinations have the following meanings:

```
(00) an I/O port is read;
(01) an I/O port is written;
(10) data is read from memory;
(11) data is written into memory.
```

15.2 8086 Operating Modes and the 8288 Bus Controller

One characteristic of the 8086 and 8088 compared to other 80x86 processors is that they can be operated in *maximum* or *minimum mode*. Selection is carried out by the MN/$\overline{\text{MX}}$ pin 33. If it is fixed at the supply voltage Vcc of +5 V, the 8086/88 operates in maximum mode. If it is grounded (0 V, GND), the 8086/88 runs in minimum mode. Because the structure of a computer is very different, depending upon the operation mode of the processor, this pin is usually soldered to one of these two potentials at the time of the computer's manufacture. In PCs with the 8088 processor (and the XT with the 8086 processor) the CPU always operates in maximum mode, but in other computers that use an 8086/88 the processor may be running in minimum mode.

The difference between minimum and maximum mode is how the bus is driven. In minimum mode, the 8086/88 generates the necessary control signal for the bus on its own. In maximum mode, it only outputs status signals to the accompanying *bus controller*. The bus controller interprets these status signals and generates the necessary signals for the bus. The predecessors of the 8086/88 were the simpler 8-bit processors (for example, the 8080), which generated the bus signals themselves. These chips were built into simple computers (compared to today's state-of-the-art) without much extension capability and poor memory size. Therefore, the chips didn't need to supply high currents for driving the individual components, which is why no additional bus controller was necessary. With an 8086/88 in minimum mode, a very compact computer is possible.

The flexible and more extensive design of the PC, however, requires an additional bus controller to supply all bus signals with the necessary power. Further, Intel (the processor family manufacturer) introduced a new bus design called MULTIBUS, which enables the cooperation of several processors – so-called *multiprocessing*. This is, however, not used in the PC (with the exception of an additional coprocessor).

15.3 8086 Real Mode

The real mode is the only addressing of which the 8086 is capable. Because the first IBM Personal Computer was equipped with the 8086 and 8088, respectively, the real mode represents the base of DOS up to the Pentium. For forming a physical address, the 8086 shifts the segment register value by four bits as usual (multiplies the value by 16) and adds the offset stored in a general purpose register. The result is a «real» 20-bit address, because the 8086 has only a 20-bit address bus. If 16*segment+offset is beyond the value of fffffh, a wrap-around to 00000h occurs. Addresses beyond fffffh, thus, cannot be generated, unlike in the 80286 and above; the 1M-barrier is never broken through.

15.4 Memory Access

As already mentioned in Section 15.1, the 8086 has a multiplexed data and address bus; the respective lines are used for data and address transfer. In the case of a write access, address and write data would collide. The 8086 bus cycle, therefore, must deviate from that of the later processors. Figure 15.2 shows the course of the main signals on the system bus for reading and writing data.

For this memory access, four signals are essential:

- the clock signal CLK from the clock generator,
- address and status signals ADDR/Status from the processor,

- address and data signals ADDR/DATA from the processor and memory, and
- the READY signal to indicate the completion of data reading.

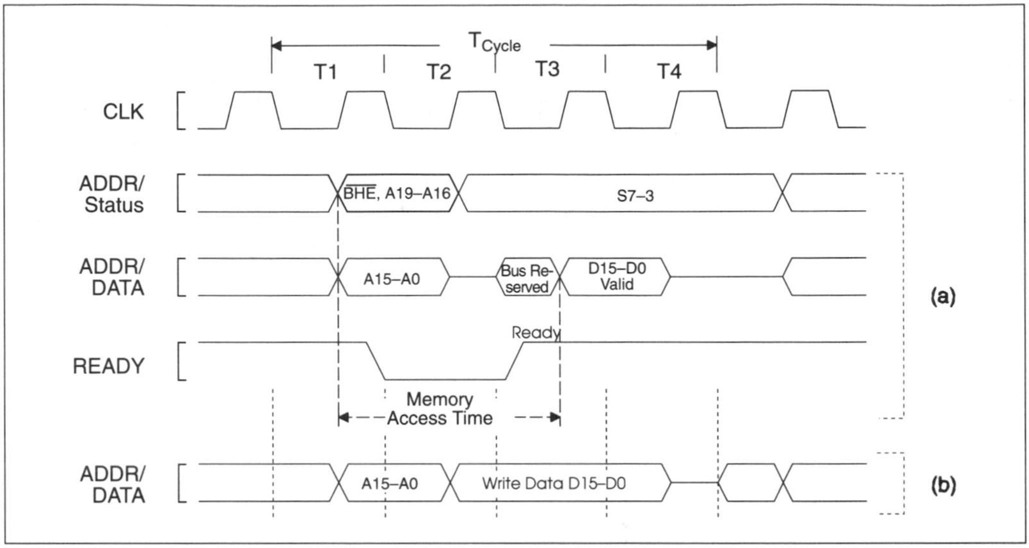

Figure 15.2: 8086 bus cycle. (a) Memory read without wait cycles: the 8086 outputs the address and waits for the data from main memory. (b) Memory write without wait cycles: the processor outputs the address and immediately afterwards the data. Both bus cycles are completed after four clock cycles; no wait cycle T_{wait} is inserted.

A bus cycle is divided into four parts comprising one clock cycle each: T1 to T4. Beginning with the 80286, the bus cycle has been shortened to two processor clock cycles. In cycle T1 the 8086 outputs the address of the data to be read. This data is transferred to the processor during the course of cycles T3 and T4. In cycle T2 the transfer direction of the bus is inverted. In the following, these four cycles are explained in more detail because they deviate significantly from the cycles of all later processors. The reason is the multiplexed data/address bus.

T1

The processor outputs control signals $\overline{S2}$–$\overline{S0}$ to the bus controller, which in turn activates the address and data buffers. Afterwards, the address of the required data is supplied by pins A0–A19 and fetched into the address buffer. The $\overline{BHE}$ signal indicates whether a whole word or only one byte is read. Therefore, the read process has been started and the READY signal drops to low. The memory controller starts an internal read process of the main memory. This addressing and reading process needs some time.

T2

Now an inversion of the transmission direction on the bus takes place. Up to now the processor has supplied an address, but now it fetches data. For this purpose, the lines $\overline{BHE}$ and A19–A16 are switched by the processor in such a way that they output the corresponding status information. The combined address/data bus of the pins A15–A0 is switched from address bus mode to data bus mode.

T3

Now the data transfer cycle begins. First, the data bus (ADDR/DATA) is reserved for the data transfer from memory. The bus waits until the data is supplied. In this state D15–D0 are not yet valid, and the status signals S7–S3 are output. When the memory has completed its internal read process and has transferred the data to the memory buffer, the memory controller raises the READY signal to high. The data signals at the 8086 pins D15–D0 are thus valid, and the processor starts to fetch data.

T4

The processor finishes the read-in process after the half clock cycle. The buffers are disabled but the processor continues to output the status signals S7–S3. After the end of cycle T4, the system bus is again in the initial state. Now a further read or write process may be started. If no data has to be transferred the bus remains in a standby state until the processor again signals that data should be read or written.

The access time of the memory chips in a PC and XT may last two clock cycles at most; this is the period between the supply of a valid address and the delivery of the data to the bus. Because the signal propagation times in the buffer circuits supervene, in practice only memory chips whose access time is about half of this memory access time may be used. In a 4.77 MHz PC, memory chips with an access time of 200 ns could therefore be employed. For comparison: modern DRAMs achieve access times of 30 ns to 35 ns in page or static column mode.

Because the 8086 needs at least four clock cycles for every bus cycle, a 10 MHz XT can carry out 2.5 million bus cycles per second. Together with the 16-bit data bus, this leads to a transfer rate of 5 MBytes/s. The first PC with its 4.77 MHz 8088 with 8-bit data bus achieved only 1.1 Mbyte/s (compare that to the 504 Mbytes/s of a 66 MHz Pentium in pipelined burst mode). Today, even low quality hard disk drives are faster.

Address pipelining is not possible in the 8086 because it has a combined data/address bus, and the ADx pins are always occupied by an address or data. Therefore, the 8086 cannot provide the address for the following bus cycle while the current data transfer is still in progress.

If the CPU is writing data into memory without wait states, similar processes are carried out. In Figure 15.2b only the behaviour of the ADDR/DATA signal is shown, because all other signals are the same as in the case of data reading.

T1

All processes are identical to those indicated above, and only the bus controller is affected by the fact that data is to be written. Accordingly, it prepares the buffers and the memory controller for a data write.

T2

The direction of the combined address/data bus (ADDR/DATA) need not be switched because both the address and the data have to be output. Therefore, immediately after supplying the address the processor may output the data to be written to the data buffer in T2.

T3

If the main memory has completed its internal write process the memory controller raises the READY signal to indicate completion to the processor.

T4

The processor terminates the write process. The buffers are disabled but the processor continues to supply the status signals S7–S3. After the end of cycle T4, the system bus is again available for the next bus cycle.

The READY signal enables a flexible response to delays in the accessed memory. The 8086 then inserts wait cycles between T3 and T4 until READY reaches a high level.

15.5 Word Boundary

Because the 8086 is a 16-bit processor with a 16-bit data bus, main memory is physically organized as a 16-bit memory as with an 80286. This means that the 8086 always accesses the memory physically at the byte addresses 0, 2, 4, ..., 1048574. Logically, data words (16 bits) may start at odd addresses, but physically the word at the odd address can't be accessed all at once. If a word is to be stored at or read from an odd address, the bus unit of the 8086 divides this word access into two separate byte accesses. This process is entirely transparent for software, that is, the hardware carries out the separation and the double memory access without any intervention from the software. Thus, the programmer may arrange data in any form without taking word boundaries into account.

During the two separate byte accesses, memory is physically addressed in even-numbered portions, but only the required byte is fetched. The processor informs the memory controller of this using $\overline{BHE}$ and A0 (the least significant address bit). Thus, an individual byte (low or high) at an even address 0, 2, ... ($\overline{BHE}$=1, A0=0) or an odd address 1, 3, ... ($\overline{BHE}$=0, A0=1) may be read or written. The same applies for $\overline{BHE}$ and A0, of course, in cases where only a single byte is to be read (MOV al, [bx], for example) or written.

You can see that reading or writing one word at an odd address requires two bus cycles. In contrast to this, reading or writing one word at an even address lasts for only one bus cycle. Therefore, it is advantageous (but not necessary, as mentioned above) to arrange data words at even storage addresses. Incidentally, these explanations only apply to data words. The prefetch queue always fetches the code in portions of one word, which start at even storage addresses. Because of this, the prefetch queue is reloaded only if at least two bytes are free. To get even storage addresses the processor may need to read one single byte, for example, because of a jump or call with an odd target address.

15.6 Access to the I/O Address Space

If the 8086 wants to access a port, it activates control signals $\overline{S2}$–$\overline{S0}$ accordingly:

$\overline{S2}$=0, $\overline{S1}$=0, $\overline{S0}$=1: the 8086 reads an I/O port;
$\overline{S2}$=0, $\overline{S1}$=1, $\overline{S0}$=0: the 8086 writes an I/O port.

Writing data to a port or reading data from a port is carried out in the same way as writing data into or reading data from memory.

As is the case in reading and writing data from and into memory, the CPU outputs an address to the address buffer and drives the bus controller by means of the status signals. If data has to be transmitted to a port (OUT), the processor additionally outputs data to the data buffer during the T2 cycle. With the control signals, the logic on the motherboard recognizes that an access to the I/O address space and not the memory is required. Therefore, the I/O controller is activated instead of the memory controller. The I/O controller decodes the address signal from the address buffer and accesses the corresponding port. Usually, this port is assigned a register in a peripheral (keyboard or hard disk drive, for example), or in a hardware chip (mode control register in a DMA chip, for example). Thus, data may be exchanged between the processor and a register in the I/O address space of the PC. Because the 8086 can access 64 k ports at most, the four high-order address lines A_{19}–A_{16} are low during access to ports. Further, in the PC, the address lines A_{15}–A_{10}=0 because only the first 1024 ports are used.

The bus cycle and the accompanying signals are the same as in Figure 15.2. Again, the READY signal is used to insert wait cycles as required. This is necessary, in particular, because access to registers in a chip in a peripheral (hard disk controller, for example) is usually much slower than access to main memory.

15.7 8086 Reset

An 8086 reset is issued by setting the RESET pin high for at least four clock cycles. Once the signal has returned to low, the processor carries out an internal initialization. During the course of this initialization the registers are loaded wih the values indicated in Table 15.1.

After the internal initialization, the CS:IP pair points to the memory address f000:fff0 or, combined, ffff0h. At this location the entry point to the start routine of the BIOS is usually present. Because only 16 bytes are available between ffff0h and the addressing limit fffffh (=1 Mbyte), one of the first instructions is usually an unconditional jump (JMP) to the «real» target address. Now the BIOS boots the PC.

Register	Value
flag	0002h
IP	fff0h
CS	f000h
DS	0000h
ES	0000h
SS	0000h

Table 15.1: Register values after a processor RESET

15.8 The 8088

The 8088 is something like a «cut down» form of the 8086. Its internal structure with a bus unit, instruction unit, etc. is nearly identical to that of the 8086. Further, the 8088 has the same instruction set, knows the same addressing schemes, and handles segments and offsets in the same way as the 8086. Like its «big brother», the 8088 is also a 16-bit processor, that is, it processes data with a maximum width of 16 bits (one word).

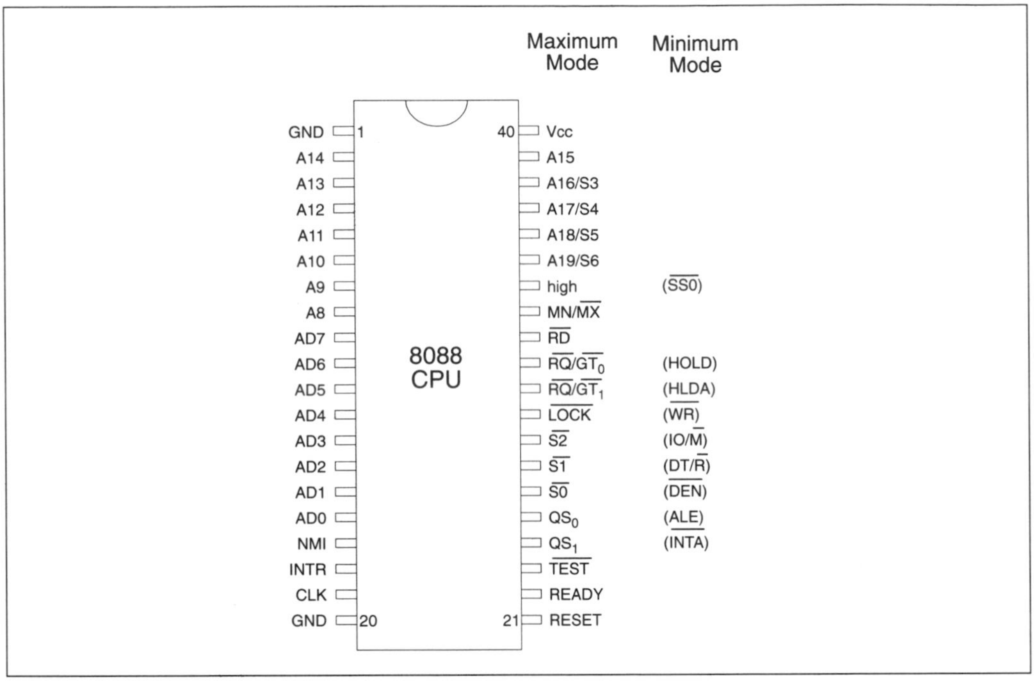

Figure 15.3: 8088 pin assignment. The 8088 comes in a standard DIP package with 40 pins. Some terminals supply different signals in maximum and minimum mode.

The only difference from the 8086 is that the 8088 has only an 8-bit data bus (see Figure 15.3). Remember that the 8086 implements a 16-bit data bus. Because only one byte at a time can be transferred via an 8-bit data bus, the 8088 has to access memory or a port twice when it is reading or writing a 16-bit word.

Example: `During the course of executing an instruction MOV ax, [bx] the 8088 accesses the memory twice to load the word at offset [bx] into the 16-bit accumulator ax.`

This twice repeated access is completely transparent for software, that is, the bus unit automatically accesses the memory or port twice if a whole word has to be transferred. Therefore, all discussions concerning the word boundary in connection with the 8086 are irrelevant. Independent of whether the data word begins at an odd or an even address, two bus cycles are always required to transfer one 16-bit word. The bus cycles are executed in the same way as for the 8086.

Compared to the 8086, all instructions that involve the transfer of a 16-bit word last at least four clock cycles longer (corresponding to a bus cycle without wait states). Thus, the 8088 processes data more slowly, on average.

Example: `MOV ax, [bx]` needs at least four additional clock cycles compared to the 8086; `MOV al, [bx]`, on the other hand, needs an equal number of cycles because only one byte is transferred from memory into the 8-bit accumulator.

Another difference from the 8086 processor is that the prefetch queue of the 8088 has only four bytes (compared to six bytes in the 8086). Because of the 8-bit data bus, the prefetch queue is reloaded if only one byte is free (two bytes with the 8086). The smaller prefetch queue and the slower data transfer may therefore give rise to the processing speed of the processor being limited not by the internal program execution but by the speed with which the prefetch queue is reloaded. If several instructions that can be executed in a few clock cycles (for example, CLC, AND, CBW) occur in succession, then the processor has already completed the instruction after two clock cycles. But the bus unit needs at least four clock cycles to reload the prefetch queue. Therefore, the processor has to wait for the bus unit to fetch the next instruction.

The development of an 8086 with an 8 bit data bus (namely the 8088) has historical reasons. When the 8086 came onto the market in the mid-1970s to replace the 8-bit processors common at that time, hardly any support chips with a data width of 16 bits were available, or they were very expensive. Moreover, the construction of a board with a full 16-bit data bus is far more costly than a board with only an 8-bit data bus. For example, all data buffers must have a double capacity. To give an 8086 the chance to use the existing 8-bit technology further, the 16-bit data buffer was integrated onto the processor chip. Now the processor appeared to be an 8-bit processor – hence the 8088! Before you dismiss this solution as nonsense, be aware of the extremely fast development in computer technology during the past 15 years. The whole PC world was steamrollered by this development. The results are (among others) the 640 kbyte boundary of MS-DOS, the 8-bit DMA chips in an AT, and an i486 running in real mode.

15.9 The 80186/88

To complete the picture, I want to briefly mention the successor of the 8086/88, the 80186/88. The relationship between the 80186 and 80188 is the same as for the 8086 and 8088, the only difference being that the 80186 has a 16-bit and the 80188 only has an 8-bit data bus. However, the 80186/88 is not just a microprocessor. Intel additionally integrated an interrupt controller, a DMA controller and a timer onto this single chip. Therefore, the 80186/88 is more of an integrated microcontroller. The instruction set has been expanded compared to the 8086/88 and some instructions are optimized so that an 80186/88 is about 25% faster than an equivalent 8086/88. The new 80186/88 instructions are listed in Appendix B.2. As is the case for the 8086/88, the 80186/88 also operates in real mode only, and has an address space of 1 Mbyte. It was not until the 80286 that protected mode was introduced and the address space extended to 16 Mbytes.

The main disadvantage of using the 80186/88 in a PC is that the register addresses of interrupt, DMA and timer chip are entirely incompatible with the corresponding register addresses in the

PC. Therefore, integration of the 80186/88 would only be possible with additional and extensive decode logic. Because of this, the 80186/88 is hardly ever used in PC/XTs or compatibles. Instead, most manufacturers use the much more powerful 80286. As a stand-alone microprocessor on adapter cards for PCs (for example, facsimile adapters), the 80186/88 is, nevertheless, popular. Incompatibilities between the 8086/88 and the other support chips do not play a role here.

Integrated microcontrollers or chip sets such as the 80186/88 are becoming more and more popular, especially for very compact Notebooks. It was only with these integrated solutions that the development of Laptops and Notebook Computers became possible. Leading this field at the moment is Intel's 386SL together with the accompanying I/O subsystem, the 82360SL. The 386SL integrates an i386 CPU, a cache controller and tag RAM, an ISA bus controller and a memory controller on a single chip. On the 82360SL I/O subsystem are integrated a real-time clock, two timers with three channels each, a memory decoder, two DMA controllers, a parallel interface, two interrupt controllers and two serial interfaces. The two 386SL and 82360 SL chips together with some DRAMs make up a complete AT.

16 Our Mathematical Grandmother – The MathCo 8087

The four basic arithmetical operations with integers are already integrated on the 8086/88. It is not surprising that the 8086/88 can handle neither floating-point numbers nor transcendental functions; this is carried out by the mathematical coprocessor 8087. It can enhance the performance up to a factor of 100, when compared to software emulations. Additionally, the 8087 supports an 8086/88 CPU in maximum mode with 68 new mnemonics.

16.1 8087 Number Formats and Numerical Instruction Set

As a mathematical coprocessor, the 8087 can process floating-point numbers directly. In the same way as the 80286 and its successors, the 8087 represents all numbers in the temporary real format according to the IEEE standard. Figure 7.3 (Chapter 7) shows the number formats that are supported by the 8087. Unfortunately, the 8087 does not implement the IEEE standard for floating-point numbers in a very strict way (not very surprising – the 8087 was available before the standard). The 8087 numeric instruction set is slightly smaller than that for an i387 or 80287XL; for example, the FSETPM (set protected mode) instruction is (of course) missing. Further, no functions for evaluating sine and cosine are available. But they can be constructed with the help of the tangent. A detailed list of all 8087 instructions is given in Appendix C.1.

16.2 8087 Pins and Signals

Like the 8086/88, the 8087 has 40 pins in all for inputting and outputting signals and supply voltages. Usually, the 8087 comes in a 40-pin DIP package. Figure 16.1 shows the pin assignment of the 8087.

AD15–AD0 (I/O)
Pins 39, 2–16

These 16 connections form the 16 data bits when the 8087 is reading or writing data, as well as the lower 16 address bits for addressing memory. As is the case with the 8086, these 16 pins form a time-divisionally multiplexed address and data bus.

A19–A16/S6–S3 (I/O)
Pins 35–38

These four pins form the four high-order bits of the address bus, as well as four status signals, and form a time-divisionally multiplexed address and control bus. During bus cycles controlled by the 8087, the S6, S4 and S3 signals are reserved and held on a high level. Additionally, S5 is then always low. If the 8086/88 is controlling the bus then the 8087 observes the CPU activity using the signals at pins S6 to S3.

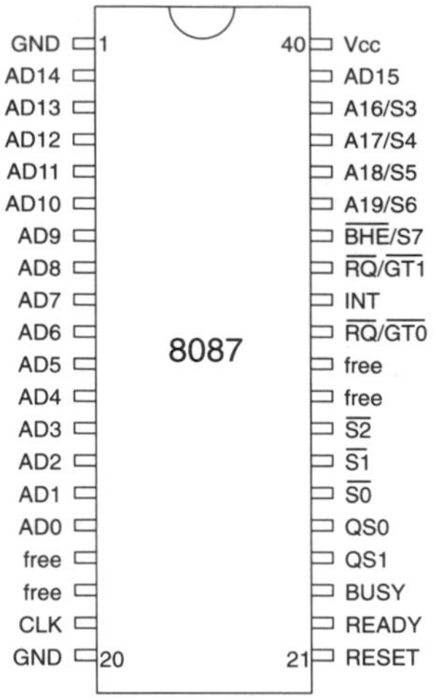

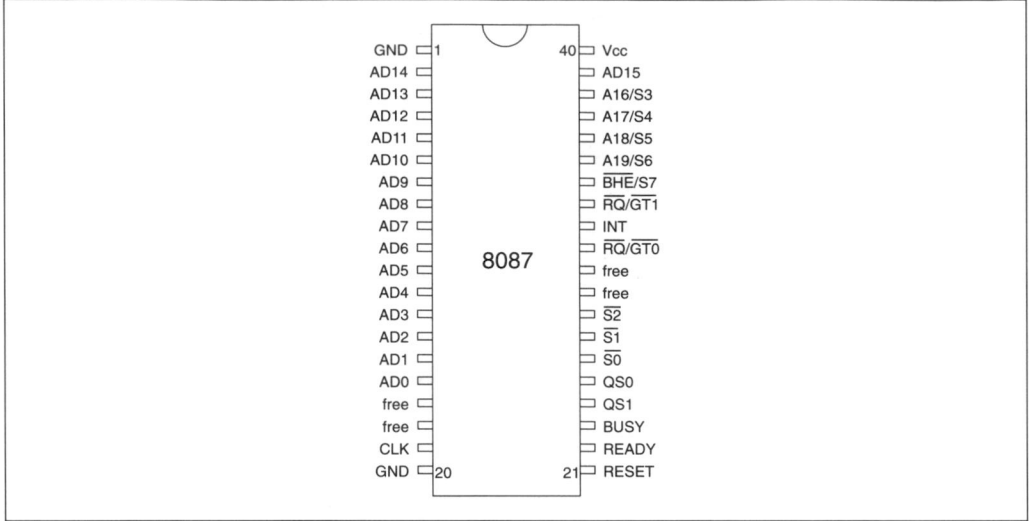

Figure 16.1: 8087 pin assignment. The 8087 comes in a standard DIP package comprising 40 pins.

$\overline{\text{BHE}}$/S7 (I/O)
Pin 34

This bus high enable signal indicates whether a byte is transferred on the high-order part AD15-AD8 of the data bus. When the 8086/88 is in control of the bus the 8087 observes the signal at pin S7 supplied by the CPU.

BUSY (O)
Pin 23

If the signal at this pin is high then the 8087 is currently executing a numerical instruction. Usually, BUSY is connected to the $\overline{\text{TEST}}$ pin of the 8086/88. The CPU checks the $\overline{\text{TEST}}$ pin and therefore the BUSY signal to determine the completion of a numerical instruction.

CLK (I)
Pin 19

CLK is the clock signal for the 8087.

INT (O)
Pin 32

The signal output at this pin indicates that during the execution of a numerical instruction in the 8087, a non-maskable exception has occurred, for example an overflow. The output of the signal can be suppressed by interrupt masking in the 8087.

QS1, QS0 (I, I)
Pins 24, 25

The signals at these pins indicate the status of the prefetch queue in the 8086/88. Thus, the 8087 can observe the CPU's prefetch queue. For (QS1, QS0) the following interpretations hold:

```
(00) the prefetch queue is not active;
(01) the first byte of the opcode in the prefetch queue is processed;
(10) the prefetch queue is cancelled;
(11) a next byte of the opcode in the prefetch queue is processed.
```

READY (I)
Pin 22

The addressed memory confirms the completion of a data transfer from or to memory with a high-level signal at READY. Therefore, like the 8086/88, the 8087 can also insert wait cycles if the memory doesn't respond quickly enough to an access.

RESET (I)
Pin 21

If this input is high for at least four clock cycles, the 8087 aborts its operation immediately and carries out a processor reset.

$\overline{RQ}/\overline{GT0}$ (I/O)
Pin 31

The 8087 uses this pin to get control of the local bus from the 8086/88 so as to execute its own memory cycles. $\overline{RQ}/\overline{GT0}$ is connected to the CPU's $\overline{RQ}/\overline{GT1}$ pin. Normally, the 8086/88 is in control of the bus to read instructions and data. If the 8087 accesses the memory because of a LOAD or STORE instruction, it takes over control of the local bus. Therefore, both the 8086/88 and the 8087 can act as a local busmaster.

$\overline{RQ}/\overline{GT1}$ (I/O)
Pin 33
This pin may be used by another local busmaster to get control of the local bus from the 8087.

$\overline{S2}$, $\overline{S1}$, $\overline{S0}$ (I/O)
Pins 28–26

These three control signals indicate the current bus cycle. For the combinations ($\overline{S2}$, $\overline{S1}$, $\overline{S0}$) the following interpretations hold for bus cycles controlled by the 8087:

```
(0xx) invalid;
(100) invalid;
(101) data is read from memory;
(110) data is written into memory;
(111) passive state.
```

If the 8086/88 is controlling the bus, the 8087 observes the CPU activity using the signals at pins $\overline{S2}$ to $\overline{S0}$.

Vcc (I)
Pin 40
This pin is supplied with the supply voltage of +5 V.

GND
Pins 1, 20
These pins are grounded (usually at 0 V).

16.3 8087 Structure and Functioning

The control unit largely comprises a unit for bus control, data buffers, and a prefetch queue. The prefetch queue is identical to that in the 8086/88 in a double sense:

- It has the same length. Immediately after a processor reset the 8087 checks by means of the $\overline{BHE}$/S7 signal whether it is connected to an 8086 or 8088. The 8087 adjusts the length of its prefetch queue according to the length in the 8086 (six bytes) or 8088 (four bytes), respectively.
- The prefetch queue contains the same instructions. By synchronous operation of the 8086/88 and 8087, the same bytes (and therefore also the same instructions) are present in the prefetch queues of both CPU and coprocessor.

Thus, the CU of the coprocessor attends the data bus synchronously to and concurrently with the CPU and fetches instructions to decode. Like the other 80x87 coprocessors, the 8087 also has a status, control and tag word, as well as a register stack with eight 80-bit FP-registers. Additionally, the two registers for instruction and data pointers are implemented.

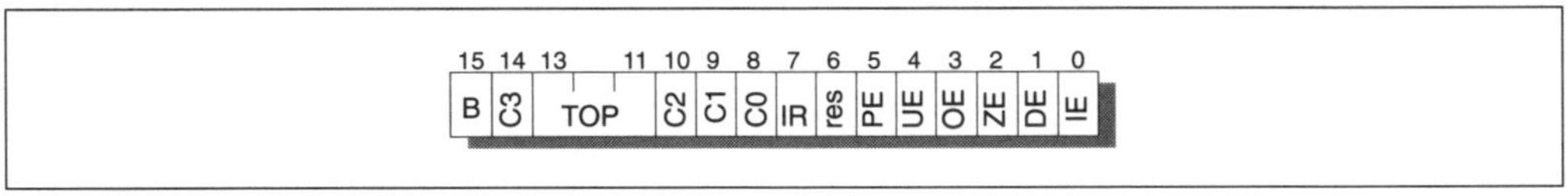

Figure 16.2: 8087 status word.

The status word format is shown in Figure 16.2. If bit *B* is set the numerical unit NU is occupied by a calculation or has issued an interrupt that hasn't yet been serviced completely. If the *IR* bit is set, a non-maskable exception has occurred and the 8087 has activated its INT output. In the PC/XT an NMI is issued. (Beginning with the 80287, IR has been replaced by ES=error status.) The meaning of the remaining bits *C3–C0, TOP, PE, UE, OE, ZE, DE* and *IE* is the same as for the 80287.

The 8087 generates an exception under various circumstances, but some exceptions may be masked. Further, you are free to define various modes for rounding, precision and the representation of infinite values. For this purpose, the 8087 has a control word, shown in Figure 16.3.

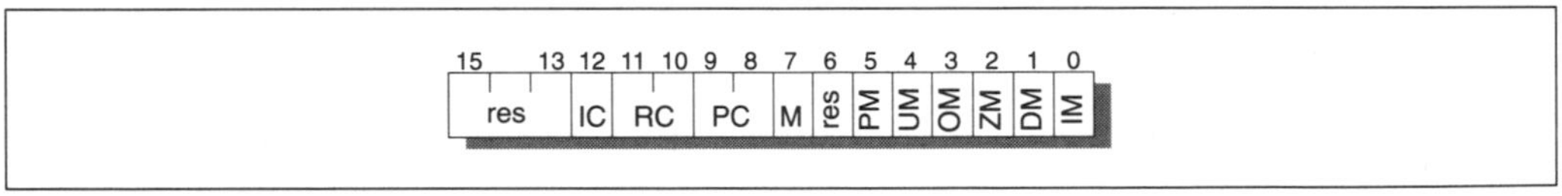

Figure 16.3: 8087 control word.

The *IC* bit controls the processing of infinite values. Projective infinity leads to only one value, namely ∞. If you set IC equal to 0, then the 8087 operates with affine infinity, and two infinite values +∞ and -∞ are possible. Beginning with the 80287XL, the IC bit is only present on compatibility grounds because the IEEE standard allows affine infinity only. With the *M* bit, you can mask interrupts globally, in which case the 8087 ignores all exceptions and doesn't execute an on-chip exception handler. This capability has also been removed with the 80287. The function of the remaining bits *PM, UM, OM, ZM, DM* and *IM* is the same as in the i387 (Section 7.5).

You will find the 8087 tag word in Section 7.5; it is identical to that in the i387. Moreover, the memory images of the instruction and data pointers match those for the 16-bit real format in the i387. They are shown in Figure 7.10.

16.4 8087 Memory Cycles

An interesting difference between the 8087 and all later 80x87 models occurs in the memory access: the 8087 can access memory on its own; there are no I/O cycles between CPU and coprocessor.

The 8086/88 distinguishes instructions with memory access from pure arithmetical instructions handed by the 8087. The CPU calculates the operand address according to the addressing scheme indicated, and then the 8086/88 executes a *dummy read cycle*. This cycle differs from a normal read cycle only in that the CPU ignores the data supplied by the memory. If the CPU recognizes a coprocessor instruction without a memory operand, it continues with the next instruction after the 8087 has signalled via its BUSY pin that it has completed the current instruction.

The 8087 also behaves differently for instructions with and without a memory operand. In the first case, it simply executes an instruction such as FSQRT (square root of a floating-point number). For an instruction with a memory operand it uses the 8086/88 dummy read cycle in the following way:

- Fetching an operand from memory: the 8087 reads the address supplied by the CPU in the dummy read cycle via the address bus and stores it in an internal temporary register. Then the 8087 reads the data word that is put onto the data bus by the memory. If the operand is longer than the data word transferred within this read cycle, the 8087 requests control of the local bus from the 8086/88. Now the 8087 carries out one or more succeeding read cycles on its own. The coprocessor uses the memory address fetched during the course of the dummy read cycle and increments it until the whole memory operand is read. For example, in the case of the 8088/87 combination, eight memory read cycles are necessary to read a floating-point number in long real format. Afterwards, the 8087 releases control of the local bus to the 8086/88 again.
- Writing an operand into memory: in this case the coprocessor also fetches the address output by the CPU in a dummy read cycle, but ignores the memory data appearing on the data bus. Afterwards, the 8087 takes over control of the local bus and writes the operand into memory, starting with the fetched address, in one or more write cycles.

Because of the dummy read cycle the 8087 doesn't need its own addressing unit to determine the effective address of the operand with segment, offset and displacement. This is advantageous because the 8087, with its 75000 transistors, integrates far more components on a single chip compared to the 28000 transistors of the 8086/88, and space is at a premium (remember that the 8087 was born in the 1970s).

The 8087 also uses the 8086/88 addressing unit if new instructions have to be fetched into the prefetch queue. The CPU addresses the memory to load one or two bytes into the prefetch queue. These instruction bytes appear on the data bus. The processor status signals keep the 8087 informed about the prefetch processes, and it monitors the bus. If the instruction bytes from memory appear on the data bus, the 8087 (and also the 8086/88, of course) loads them into the prefetch queue.

For the data transfer between memory and coprocessor, no additional I/O bus cycles between CPU and 8087 are necessary. Therefore, the LOAD and STORE instructions require more time on an 80287. Don't be surprised if, for pure mathematical applications, a 10 MHz XT with an 8087 coprocessor is nearly as fast as a 10 MHz AT with an 80287. The 80287 (without XL) runs only at two-thirds of the CPU speed, thus at 6.67 MHz. Moreover, it requires the additional I/O bus cycles between CPU and 80287 when accessing memory. However, the 80286/80287 combination cancels this disadvantage with a more effective bus cycle lasting for only two clock cycles per data transfer at zero wait states, compared to the four clock cycles of the 8086/8087 combination. In the end, both systems give about the same performance.

16.5 8086/8087 System Configuration

Figure 16.4 shows typical wiring of the 8087 coprocessor and CPU 8086/88. As they are busmasters, both chips access the same local bus which is connected to memory, the I/O address space and the bus slots via the 8288 bus controller. The 8086/88 and the 8087 read and decode the same instruction stream at the same speed, thus they operate *synchronously* and are supplied with the same clock signal (CLK) by the 8284 clock generator. All higher coprocessors, however, such as the 80287, i387, etc., run asynchronously to the CPU. For synchronous operation of the 8086/88 and 8087, the 8087 must always know the current state of the 8086/88.

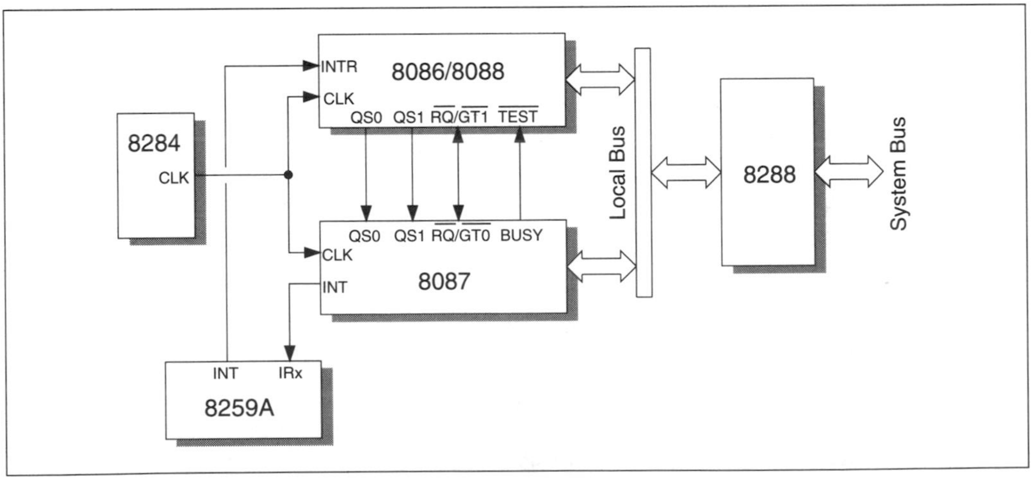

Figure 16.4: 8086/8087 system configuration. The 8087 harmonizes especially well with the 8086/88, and can therefore be connected to the 8086/88 without difficulties. The 8087 uses the same bus controller, the same clock generator, and the same interrupt controller as the CPU.

The 8087 can process its instructions independently of the CPU. Even concurrent (parallel) execution of instructions is possible, but here the problem of resynchronization arises after completion of the coprocessor instruction. After decoding the current ESC instruction, the 8086/88 would prefer to execute the next instruction at once, but cannot do so because the CPU has to wait for the coprocessor. Because of this, the BUSY pin of the 8087 is connected to the $\overline{\text{TEST}}$ pin of the 8086/88. When the coprocessor executes an instruction it activates the BUSY signal. When it has completed the instruction, it deactivates the signal. The WAIT instruction of the 8086/88 causes the CPU to check the $\overline{\text{TEST}}$ pin continuously to observe the BUSY state of the coprocessor. Only when the 8087 has deactivated BUSY to signal to the 8086/88 that the current instruction is completed and the 8087 is ready to accept further numeric instructions does the CPU continue with the next instruction. Via the QS0 and QS1 pins, the 8087 detects the status of the 8086/88's prefetch queue to observe the CPU's operation. Thus, the 8086/88 and 8087 always operate synchronously.

If an error or an exception occurs during a numerical calculation in the coprocessor, such as overflow or underflow, the 8087 activates its INT output to issue a hardware interrupt request to the CPU. Usually, the INT signal of the 8087 is managed by an interrupt controller (the 8259A, for example) and then applied to the 8086/88. But the PC/XT does it in another way: the 8087 hardware interrupt request is supplied to the NMI input of the 8086/88. The PC/XT has only one 8259A PIC and must therefore save IRQ channels. Note that besides the coprocessor interrupt, an error on an extension adapter or a memory parity error may also issue an NMI corresponding to interrupt 2. Thus, the interrupt handler must be able to locate the source of an NMI.

Figure 16.4 demonstrates that both the 8086/88 and the 8087 can access the local bus, to read data from memory, for example. 8086/88 instructions such as MOV reg, mem or the LOAD instruction of the 8087 carry out a memory access. Thus there are two busmasters, each using the local bus independently. A simultaneous access of the local bus by the CPU and coprocessor would give rise to a conflict between them, with disastrous consequences. Therefore, only one of these two processors may control the local bus, and the transfer of control between them must be carried out in a strictly defined way. Because of this, the $\overline{\text{RQ}}/\overline{\text{GT1}}$ pins of the 8086/88 and $\overline{\text{RQ}}/\overline{\text{GT0}}$ pins of the 8087 are connected. From the description above you can see that these pins serve to request and grant local bus control. The 8087 uses the $\overline{\text{RQ}}/\overline{\text{GT0}}$ pin to get control of the local bus for data transfers to and from memory. The $\overline{\text{RQ}}/\overline{\text{GT1}}$ pin is available for other busmasters, for example the I/O 8299 coprocessor. Therefore, CPU and coprocessor may alternate in controlling the local bus. The 8087 bus structure and its bus control signals are equivalent to those of the 8086/88.

17 Memory Chips

Virtually no other computer element has been the subject of such almost suicidal competition between the world's leading microelectronic giants over the past ten years as memory chips. At the beginning of the PC-era 64 kbit chips and 16 kbit chips were considered to be high-tech. But today in our PCs, 4 Mbit chips are used, and 64 Mbit chips are already running in several laboratories.

Note that the storage capacity of memory chips is always indicated in bits and not in bytes. Today's most common 4 Mbyte memory chip is therefore able to hold four million bits, or 512 kbytes. For a main memory of 4 Mbytes, eight of these chips (plus one for parity) are thus required.

The technological problems of manufacturing such highly-integrated electronic elements are enormous. The typical structure size is only about 1 μm, and with the 64 Mbyte chip they will be even less (about 0.3 μm). Human hairs are at least 20 times thicker. Moreover, all transistors and other elements must operate correctly (and at enormous speed); after all, on a 64 Mbyte chip there are more than 200 million (!) transistors, capacitors and resistors. If only one of these elements is faulty, then the chip is worthless (but manufacturers have integrated redundant circuits to repair minor malfunctions that will then only affect the overall access time). Thus, it is not surprising that the development of these tiny and quite cheap chips costs several hundred million dollars.

For the construction of highly integrated memory chips the concept of dynamic RAM (DRAM) is generally accepted today. If only the access speed is in question (for example, for fast cache memories), then static RAM (SRAM) is used. But both memory types have the disadvantage that they lose their ability to remember as soon as the power supply is switched off or fails. They store information in a volatile manner. For the boot routines and the PC BIOS, therefore, only a few types of ROM are applicable. These memories also hold the stored information after a power-down. They store information in a non-volatile manner, but their contents may not be altered, or at least only with some difficulty.

17.1 Small and Cheap – DRAM

The name dynamic RAM (or DRAM) comes from the operation principle of these memory chips. They represent the stored information by charges in a capacitor. However, all capacitors have the disadvantageous characteristic of losing their charge with the lapse of time, so the chip loses the stored information. To avoid this the information must be refreshed periodically or «dynamically», that is, the capacitor is recharged according to the information held. Figure 17.1 shows the pin assignment of a 4 Mbyte chip as an example. Compared with the processors, we only have to discuss a few pins here.

A10–A0 (I)
Pins 5–9, 11–16
These eleven pins are supplied with the row and column address of the memory cell.

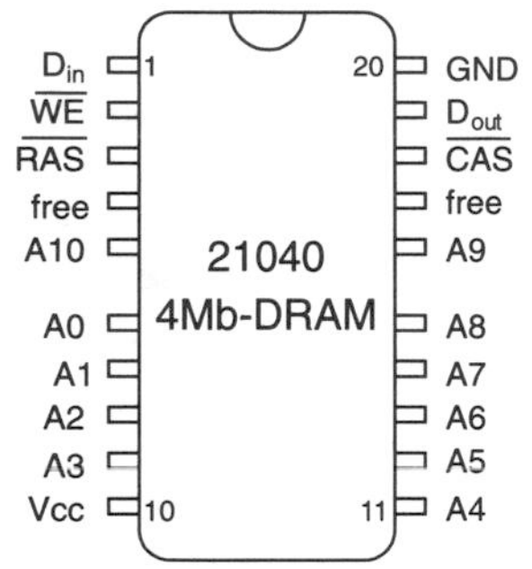

Figure 17.1: Pin assignment of a 4 Mbyte chip.

$\overline{\text{CAS}}$ (I)
Pin 18

If this column address strobe pin is low the DRAM accepts the supplied address and uses it as a column address.

Din (I)
Pin 1
This pin is supplied with the write data during a write process.

Dout (O)
Pin 19
This pin provides read data during a read process.

$\overline{\text{RAS}}$ (I)
Pin 3

(Row Address Strobe) If this pin is low the DRAM accepts the supplied address and uses it as a row address.

WE (I)
Pin 2

(Write Enable) If the signal at this pin is low the DRAM carries out a write operation otherwise data is read from the addressed memory cell and output.

Vcc (I)
Pin 10
The supply voltage (usually +5 V) is applied to this pin.

GND
Pin 20
The ground potential (usually 0 V) is applied to this pin.

17.1.1 Structure and Operation Principle

For data storage, reading the information, and the internal management of the DRAM, several functional groups are necessary. Figure 17.2 shows a typical block diagram of a dynamic RAM.

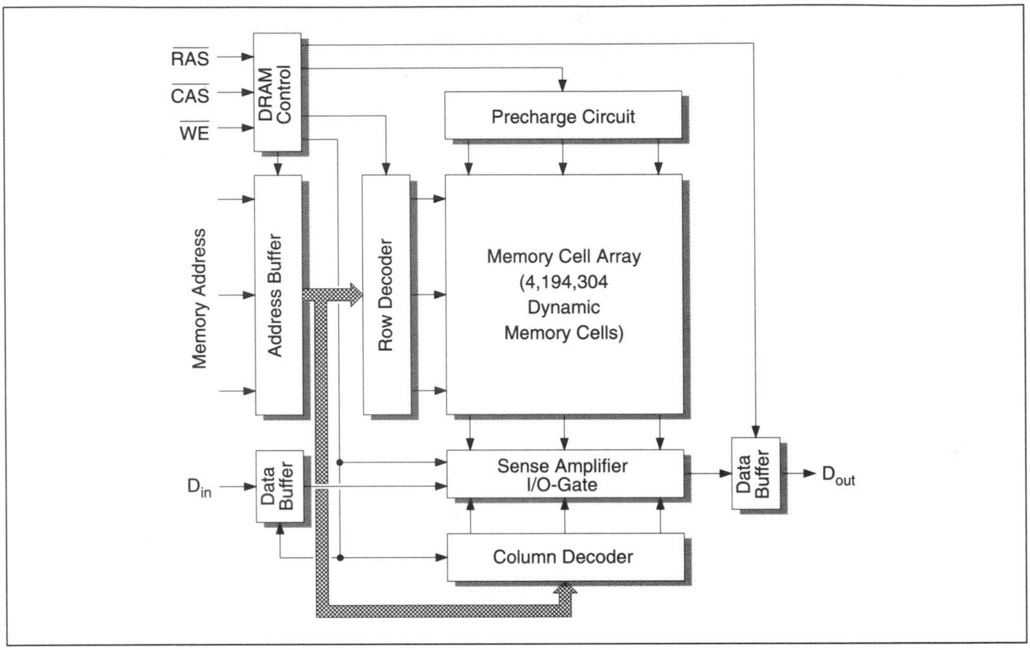

Figure 17.2: Block diagram of a dynamic RAM. The memory cells are arranged in a matrix, the so-called memory cell array. The address buffer sequentially accepts the row and column addresses and transmits them to the row and column decoder, respectively. The decoders drive internal signal lines and gates so that the data of the addressed memory cell is transmitted to the data buffer after a short time period to be output.

The central part of the DRAM is the *memory cell array*. Usually, a bit is stored in an individually addressable unit memory cell (see Figure 17.3), which is arranged together with many others in the form of a matrix with rows and columns. A 4 Mbyte chip has 4194304 memory cells arranged in a matrix of, for example, 2048 rows and 2048 columns. By specifying the row and column number, a memory cell is unambiguously determined.

The address buffer accepts the memory address output by the external memory controller according to the CPU's address. For this purpose, the address is divided into two parts, a row and a column address. These two addresses are read into the address buffer in succession: this process is called *multiplexing*. The reason for this division is obvious: to address one cell in a 4 Mbyte chip with 2048 rows and 2048 columns, 22 address bits are required in total (11 for the row and 11 for the column). If all address bits are to be transferred at once, 22 address pins would also be required. Thus the chip package becomes very large. Moreover, a large address buffer would be necessary. For high integration, it is disadvantageous if all element groups that establish a connection to their surroundings (for example, the address or data buffer) have to be powerful and therefore occupy a comparably large area, because only then can they supply enough current for driving external chips such as the memory controller or external data buffers.

Thus it is better to transfer the memory address in two portions. Generally, the address buffer first reads the row address and then the column address. This address multiplexing is controlled by the $\overline{RAS}$ and $\overline{CAS}$ control signals. If the memory controller passes a row address then it simultaneously activates the $\overline{RAS}$ signal, that is, it lowers the level of $\overline{RAS}$ to low. $\overline{RAS}$ *(row address strobe)* informs the DRAM chip that the supplied address is a row address. Now the DRAM control activates the address buffer to fetch the address and transfers it to the row decoder, which in turn decodes this address. If the memory controller later supplies the column address then it activates the $\overline{CAS}$ *(column address strobe)* signal. Thus the DRAM control recognizes that the address now represents a column address, and activates the address buffer again. The address buffer accepts the supplied address and transfers it to the column decoder. The duration of the $\overline{RAS}$ and $\overline{CAS}$ signals as well as their interval (the so-called *RAS–CAS delay*) must fulfil the requirements of the DRAM chip.

The memory cell thus addressed outputs the stored data, which is amplified by a sense amplifier and transferred to a data output buffer by an I/O gate. The buffer finally supplies the information as read data D_{out} via the data pins of the memory chip.

If data is to be read the memory controller activates the $\overline{WE}$ signal for *write enable* and applies the write data D_{in} to the data input buffer. Via the I/O gate and a sense amplifier, the information is amplified, transferred to the addressed memory cell, and stored. The precharge circuit serves to support the sense amplifier (described later).

Thus the PC's memory controller carries out three different jobs: dividing the address from the CPU into a row and a column address that are supplied in succession, activating the signals $\overline{RAS}$, $\overline{CAS}$ and $\overline{WE}$ correctly, and transferring and accepting the write and read data, respectively. Moreover, advanced memory concepts such as interleaving and page mode request wait cycles flexibly, and the memory controller must prepare the addressed memory chips accordingly (more about this subject later). The raw address and data signal from the CPU is not suitable for the memory, thus the memory controller is an essential element of the PC's memory subsystem.

17.1.2 Reading and Writing Data

The 1-transistor-1-capacitor cell is mainly established as the common unit memory cell today. Figure 17.3 shows the structure of such a unit memory cell and the I/O peripherals required to read and write data.

The unit memory cell has a capacitor which holds the data in the form of electrical charges, and an access transistor which serves as a switch for selecting the capacitor. The transistor's gate is connected to the word line WLx. The memory cell array accommodates as many word lines WL1 to WLn as rows are formed.

Besides the word lines the memory cell array also comprises so-called bit line pairs BL, $\overline{BL}$. The number of these bit line pairs is equal to the number of columns in the memory cell array. The bit lines are alternately connected to the sources of the access transistors. Finally, the unit memory cell is the capacitor which constitutes the actual memory element of the cell. One of its electrodes is connected to the drain of the corresponding access transistor, and the other is earthed.

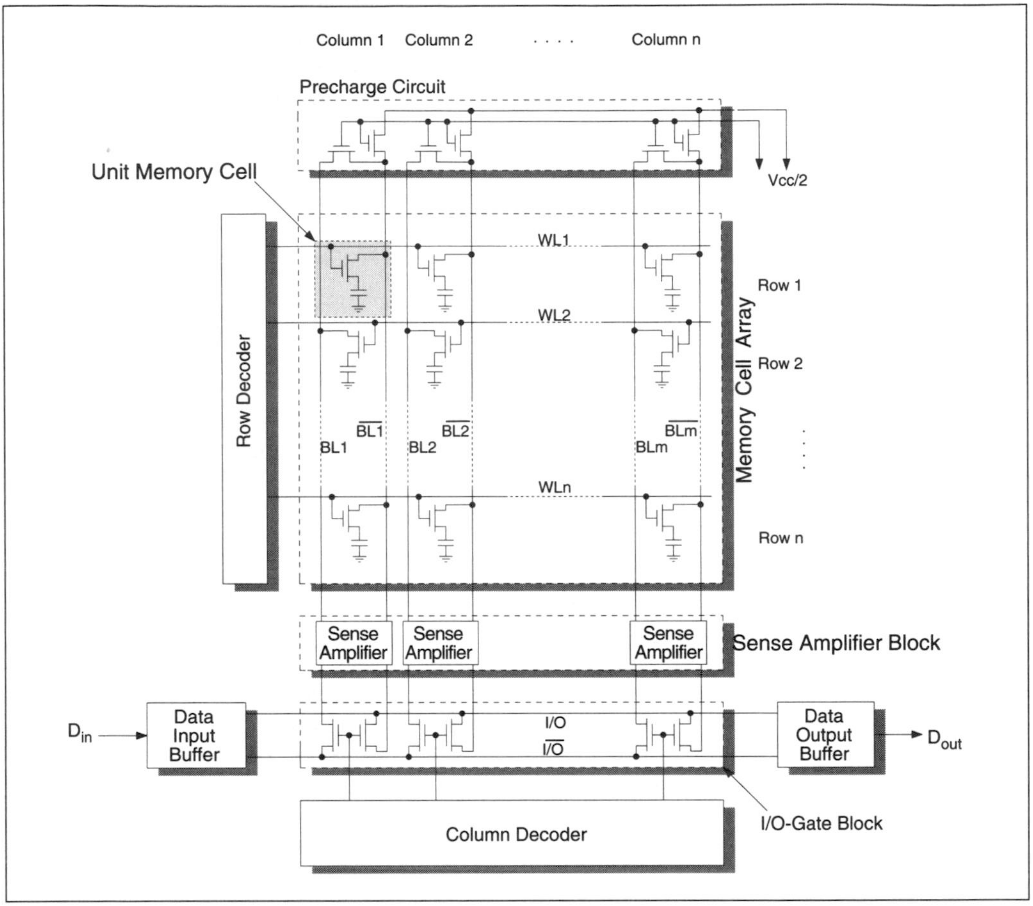

Figure 17.3: Memory cell array and I/O peripherals. The unit memory cell for holding one bit comprises a capacitor and a transistor. The word lines turn on the access transistors of a row and the column decoder selects a bit line pair. The data of a memory cell is thus transmitted onto the I/O line pair and afterwards to the data output buffer.

The regular arrangement of access transistors, capacitors, word lines and bit line pairs is repeated until the chip's capacity is reached. Thus, for a 1 Mbyte memory chip, 4194304 access transistors, 4194304 storage capacitors, 2048 word lines and 2048 bit line pairs are formed.

Of particular significance for detecting memory data during the course of a read operation is the precharge circuit. In advance of a memory controller access and the activation of a word line (which is directly connected to this access), the precharge circuit charges all bit line pairs up to half of the supply potential, that is, Vcc/2. Additionally, the bit line pairs are short-circuited by a transistor so that they are each at an equal potential. If this equalizing and precharging process is completed, then the precharge circuit is again deactivated. The time required for precharging and equalizing is called the *RAS precharge time*. Only once this process is finished can the chip carry out an access to its memory cells. Figure 17.4 shows the course of the potential on a bit line pair during a data read.

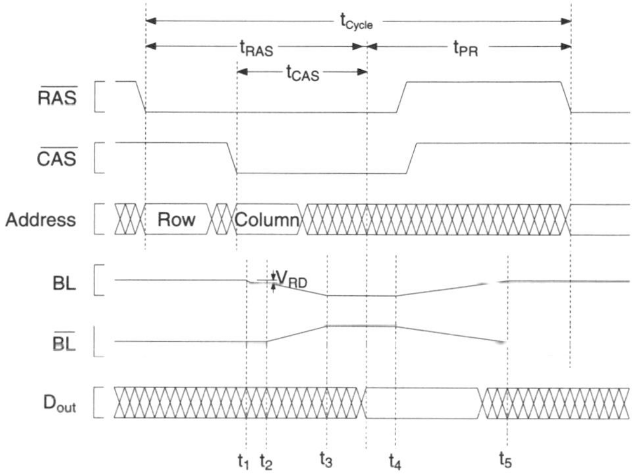

Figure 17.4: Potential course for a data read. After the access transistor has been turned on, a tiny potential charge V_{RD}, which depends on the stored value, appears on the corresponding bit line. The potential difference is amplified by the sense amplifier so that the read data becomes available after a short delay.

When the memory controller addresses a memory cell within the chip the controller first supplies the row address signal, which is accepted by the address buffer and transferred to the row decoder. At this time the two bit lines of a pair have the same potential Vcc/2. The row decoder decodes the row address signal and activates the word line corresponding to the decoded row address. Now all the access transistors connected to this word line are switched on. The charges of all the storage capacitors of the addressed row flow onto the corresponding bit line (time t_1 in Figure 17.4). In the 4 Mbyte chip concerned, 2048 access transistors are thus turned on and the charges of 2048 storage capacitors flow onto the 2048 bit line pairs.

The problem, particularly with today's highly integrated memory chips, is that the capacity of the storage capacitors is far less than the capacity of the bit lines connected to them by the access transistors. Thus the potential of the bit line changes only slightly, typically by ±100 mV (t_2). If the storage capacitor was empty, then the potential of the bit line slightly decreases; if charged then the potential increases. The sense amplifier activated by the DRAM control amplifies the potential difference on the two bit lines of the pair. In the first case, it draws the potential of the bit line connected to the storage capacitor down to ground and raises the potential of the other bit line up to Vcc (t_3). In the second case, the opposite happens – the bit line connected to the storage capacitor is raised to Vcc and the other bit line decreased to ground.

Without precharging and potential equalization by the precharge circuit, the sense amplifier would need to amplify the absolute potential of the bit line. But because the potential change is only about 100 mV, this amplifying process would be much less stable and therefore more likely to fail, compared to the difference forming of the two bit lines. Here the dynamic range is ±100 mV, that is, 200 mV in total. Thus the precharge circuit enhances reliability.

Each of the 2048 sense amplifiers supplies the amplified storage signal at its output and applies the signal to the I/O gate block. This block has gate circuits with two gate transistors, each controlled by the column decoder. The column decoder decodes the applied column address signal (which is applied after the row address signal), and activates exactly one gate. This means that the data of only one sense amplifier is transmitted onto the I/O line pair I/O, $\overline{\text{I/O}}$ and transferred to the output data buffer. Only now, and thus much later than the row address, does the column address become important. Multiplexing of the row and column address therefore has no adverse effect, as one might expect at a first glance.

The output data buffer amplifies the data signal again and outputs it as output data D_{out}. At the same time, the potentials of the bit line pairs are on a low or a high level according to the data in the memory cell that is connected to the selected word line. Thus they correspond to the stored data. As the access transistors remain on by the activated word line, the read-out data is written back into the memory cells of one row. The reading of a single memory cell therefore simultaneously leads to a refreshing of the whole line. The time period between applying the row address and outputting the data D_{out} via the data output buffer is called *RAS access time* t_{RAS}, or *access time*. The much shorter *CAS access time* t_{CAS} is significant for certain high-speed modes. This access time characterizes the time period between supplying the column address and outputting the data D_{out}. Both access times are illustrated in Figure 17.4.

After completing the data output the row and column decoders as well as the sense amplifiers are disabled again, and the gates in the I/O gate block are switched off. At that time the bit lines are still on the potentials according to the read data. The refreshed memory cells are disconnected from the bit lines by the disabled word line, and the access transistors thus switched off. Now the DRAM control activates the precharge circuit (t_4), which lowers and increases, respectively, the potentials of the bit lines to Vcc/2 and equalizes them again (t_5). After stabilization of the whole DRAM circuitry, the chip is ready for another memory cycle. The necessary time period between stabilization of the output data and supply of a new row address and activation of $\overline{\text{RAS}}$ is called *recovery time* or *RAS precharge time* t_{RP} (Figure 17.4).

The total of RAS precharge time and access time leads to the *cycle time* t_{cycle}. Generally, the RAS precharge time lasts about 80% of the access time, so that the cycle time is about 1.8 times more than the access time. Thus, a DRAM with an access time of 100 ns has a cycle time of 180 ns. Not until this 180 ns has elapsed may a new access to memory be carried out. Therefore, the time period between two successive memory accesses is not determined by the short access time but by the nearly double cycle time of 180 ns. If one adds the signal propagation delays between CPU and memory on the motherboard of about 20 ns, then an 80286 CPU with an access time of two processor clock cycles may not exceed a clock rate of 10 MHz, otherwise one or more wait states must be inserted. Advanced memory concepts such as interleaving trick the RAS precharge time so that in most cases only the access time is decisive. In page mode or static column mode, even the shortest CAS access time determines the access rate. (More about these subjects in Section 17.1.6.)

The data write is carried out in nearly the same way as data reading. At first the memory control supplies the row address signal upon an active $\overline{RAS}$. Simultaneously, it enables the control signal $\overline{WE}$ to inform the DRAM that it should carry out a data write. The data D_{in} to write is supplied to the data input buffer, amplified and transferred onto the I/O line pair I/O, $\overline{I/O}$. The data output buffer is not activated for the data write.

The row decoder decodes the row address signal and activates the corresponding word line. As is the case for data reading, here also the access transistors are turned on and they transfer the stored charges onto the bit line pairs BLx, $\overline{BLx}$. Afterwards, the memory controller activates the $\overline{CAS}$ signal and applies the column address via the address buffer to the column decoder. It decodes the address and switches on a single transfer gate through which the data from the I/O line pair is transmitted to the corresponding sense amplifier. This sense amplifier amplifies the data signal and raises or lowers the potentials of the bit lines in the pair concerned according to the value «1» or «0» of the write data. As the signal from the data input buffer is stronger than that from the memory cell concerned, the amplification of the write data gains the upper hand. The potential on the bit line pair of the selected memory cell reflects the value of the write data. All other sense amplifiers amplify the data held in the memory cells so that after a short time potentials are present on all bit line pairs that correspond to the unchanged data and the new write data, respectively.

These potentials are fetched as corresponding charges into the storage capacitors. Afterwards, the DRAM controller deactivates the row decoder, the column decoder and the data input buffer. The capacitors of the memory cells are disconnected from the bit lines and the write process is completed. As was the case for the data read, the precharge circuit sets the bit line pairs to a potential level Vcc/2 again, and the DRAM is ready for another memory cycle.

Besides the memory cell with one access transistor and one storage capacitor, there are other cell types with several transistors or capacitors. The structure of such cells is much more complicated, of course, and the integration of its elements gets more difficult because of their higher number. Such memory types are therefore mainly used for specific applications, for example, a so-called dual-port RAM where the memory cells have a transistor for reading and another transistor for writing data so that data can be read and written simultaneously. This is advantageous, for example, for video memories because the CPU can write data into the video RAM to set up an image without the need to wait for a release of the memory. On the other hand, the graphics hardware may continuously read out the memory to drive the monitor. For this purpose, VRAM chips have a parallel random access port used by the CPU for writing data into the video memory and, further, a very fast serial output port that clocks out a plurality of bits, for example a whole memory row. The monitor driver circuit can thus be supplied very quickly and continuously with image data. The CRT controller need not address the video memory periodically to read every image byte, and the CPU need not wait for a horizontal or vertical retrace until it is allowed to read or write video data.

Instead of the precharge circuit, other methods can also be employed. For example, it is possible to install a dummy cell for every column in the memory cell array that holds only half of that charge which corresponds to a «1». Practically, this cell holds the value «1/2». The sense amplifiers then compare the potential read from the addressed memory cell with the potential of the dummy cell. The effect is similar to that of the precharge circuit. Also, here a difference and no absolute value is amplified.

It is not necessary to structure the memory cell array in a square form with an equal number of rows and columns and to use a symmetrical design with 2048 rows and 2048 columns. The designers have complete freedom in this respect. Internally, 4 Mbyte chips often have 1024 rows and 4096 columns simply because the chip is longer than it is wide. In this case, one of the supplied row address bits is used as an additional (that is, 12th) column address bit internally. The ten row address bits select one of $2^{10}=1024$ rows, but the 12 column address bits select one of $2^{12}=4096$ columns. In high-capacity memory chips the memory cell array is also often divided into two or more subarrays. In a 4 Mbyte chip eight subarrays with 512 rows and 1024 columns may be present, for example. One or more row address bits are then used as the subarray address; the remaining row and column address bits then only select a row or column within the selected subarray.

The word and bit lines thus get shorter and the signals become stronger. But as a disadvantage, the number of sense amplifiers and I/O gates increases. Such methods are usual, particularly in the new highly-integrated DRAMs, because with the cells always getting smaller and smaller and therefore the capacitors of less capacity, the long bit lines «eat» the signal before it can reach the sense amplifier. Which concept a manufacturer implements for the various chips cannot be recognized from the outside. Moreover, these concepts are often kept secret so that competitors don't get an insight into their rivals' technologies.

17.1.3 Semiconductor Layer Structure

The following sections present the usual concepts for implementing DRAM memory cells. Integrated circuits are formed by layers of various materials on a single substrate. Figure 17.5 is a sectional view through such a layer structure of a simple DRAM memory cell with a plane capacitor. In the lower part of the figure, a circuit diagram of the memory cell is additionally illustrated.

The actual memory cell is formed between the field oxide films on the left and right sides. The field oxides separate and isolate the individual memory cells. The gate and the two n-doped regions source and drain constitute the access transistor of the memory cell. The gate is separated from the p-substrate by a so-called gate isolation or gate oxide film, and controls the conductivity of the channel between source and drain. The capacitor in its simplest configuration is formed by an electrode which is grounded. The electrode is separated by a dielectric isolation film from the p-substrate in the same way as the gate, so that the charge storage takes place below the isolation layer in the substrate. To simplify the interconnection of the memory cells as far as possible, the gate simultaneously forms a section of the word line and the drain is part of the bit line. If the word line W is selected by the row decoder, then the electric field below the gate that is part of the word line lowers the resistance value of the channel between source and drain. Capacitor charges may thus flow away through the source–channel–drain path to the bit line BL, which is connected to the n-drain. They generate a data signal on the bit line pair BL, $\overline{BL}$, which in turn is sensed and amplified by the sense amplifier.

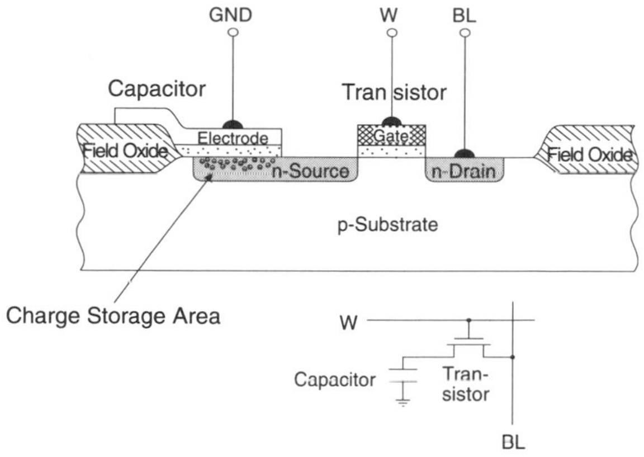

Figure 17.5: A typical DRAM cell. The access transistor of the DRAM cell generally consists of a MOS transistor. The gate of the transistor simultaneously forms the word line, and the drain is connected to the bit line. Charges that represent the stored information are held in the substrate in the region below the electrode.

A problem arising in connection with the higher integration of the memory cells is that the size of the capacitor, and thus its capacity, decreases. Therefore, fewer and fewer charges can be stored between electrode and substrate. The data signals during a data read become too weak to ensure reliable operation of the DRAM. With the latest 4 Mbit chip the engineers therefore went over to a three-dimensional memory cell structure. One of the concepts used is shown in Figure 17.6, namely the DRAM memory cell with trench capacitor.

In this memory cell type the information charges are no longer stored simply between two plane capacitor electrodes, but the capacitor has been enlarged into the depth of the substrate. The facing area of the two capacitor electrodes thus becomes much larger than is possible with an ordinary plane capacitor. The memory cell can be miniaturized and the integration density enlarged without decreasing the amount of charge held in the storage capacitor. The read-out signals are strong enough and the DRAM chip also operates very reliably at higher integration densities.

Unfortunately, the technical problems of manufacturing such tiny trenches are enormous. We must handle trench widths of about 1 μm at a depth of 3–4 μm here. For manufacturing such small trenches completely new etching techniques had to be developed which are anisotropic, and therefore etch more in depth than in width. It was two years before this technology was reliably available. Also, doping the source and drain regions as well as the dielectric layer between the two capacitor electrodes is very difficult. Thus it is not surprising that only a few big companies in the world with enormous financial resources are able to manufacture these memory chips.

To enhance the integration density of memory chips, other methods are also possible and applied, for example folded bit line structures, shared sense amplifiers, and stacked capacitors. Lack of space prohibits an explanation of all these methods, but it is obvious that the memory chips which appear to be so simple from the outside accommodate many high-tech elements and methods. Without them, projects such as the 64 Mbit chip could not be realized.

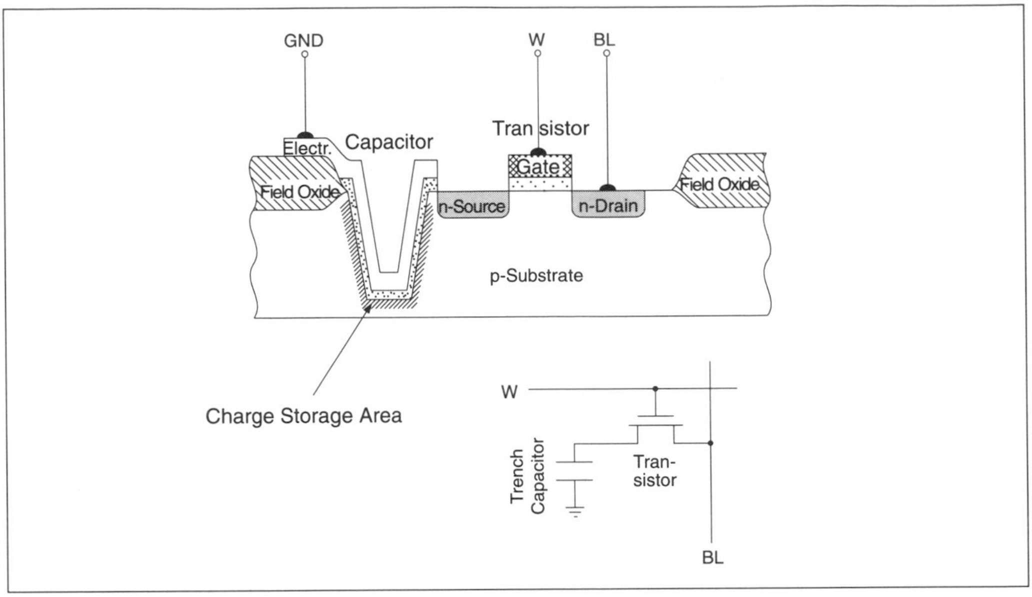

Figure 17.6: Trench capacitor for highest integration densities. To enhance the electrode area of the storage capacitor, the capacitor is built into the depth of the substrate. Thus the memory cells can move closer together without decreasing the stored charge per cell.

17.1.4 DRAM Refresh

From Figure 17.5 you already know that the data is stored in the form of electrical charges in a tiny capacitor. As is true for all technical equipment, this capacitor is not perfect, that is, it discharges over the course of time via the access transistor and its dieletric layer. Thus the stored charges and therefore also the data held get lost. The capacitor must be recharged periodically. Remember that during the course of a memory read or write a refresh of the memory cells within the addressed row is automatically carried out. Normal DRAMs must be refreshed every 1–16 ms, depending upon the type. Currently, three refresh methods are employed: RAS-only refresh; CAS-before-RAS refresh and hidden refresh. Figure 17.7 shows the course of the signals involved during these refresh types.

RAS-Only Refresh

The simplest and most used method for refreshing a memory cell is to carry out a dummy read cycle. For this cycle the $\overline{\text{RAS}}$ signal is activated and a row address (the so-called *refresh address*) is applied to the DRAM, but the $\overline{\text{CAS}}$ signal remains disabled. The DRAM thus internally reads one row onto the bit line pairs and amplifies the read data. But because of the disabled $\overline{\text{CAS}}$ signal they are not transferred to the I/O line pair and thus not to the data output buffer. To refresh the whole memory an external logic or the processor itself must supply all the row addresses in succession. This refresh type is called *RAS-only refresh*. The disadvantage of this outdated refresh method is that an external logic, or at least a program, is necessary to carry out the DRAM refresh. In the PC this is done by channel 0 of the 8237 DMA chip, which is periodically activated by counter 1 of the 8253/8254 timer chip and issues a dummy read cycle. In a RAS-only refresh, several refresh cycles can be executed successively if the CPU or refresh control drives the DRAM chip accordingly.

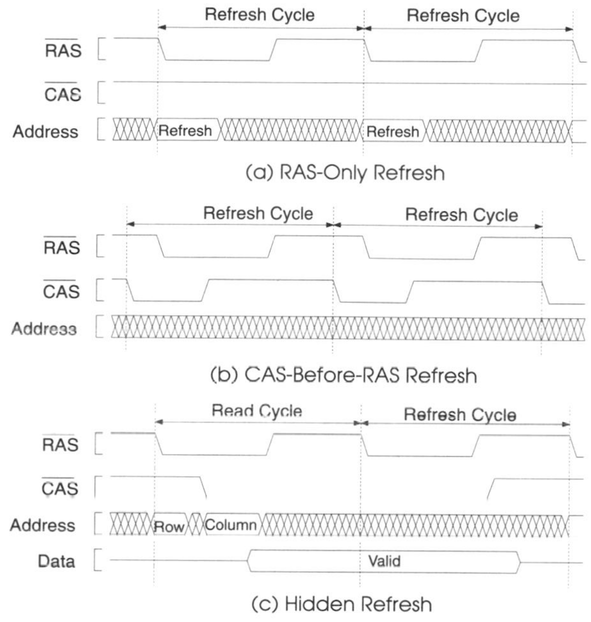

Figure 17.7: Three refresh types. (a) RAS-only refresh; (b) CAS-before-RAS refresh; (c) hidden refresh.

CAS-Before-RAS Refresh

Most modern DRAM chips additionally implement one or more internal refresh modes. The most important is the so-called *CAS-before-RAS refresh*. For this purpose, the DRAM chip has its own refresh logic with an address counter. For a CAS-before-RAS refresh, *CAS* is held low for a certain time period before *RAS* also drops (thus CAS-before-RAS). The on-chip refresh (that is, the internal refresh logic) is thus activated, and the refresh logic carries out an automatic internal refresh. The refresh address is generated internally by the address counter and the refresh logic, and need not be supplied externally. After every CAS-before-RAS refresh cycle, the internal address counter is incremented so that it indicates the new address to refresh. Thus it is sufficient if the memory controller «bumps» the DRAM from time to time to issue a refresh cycle. With the CAS-before-RAS refresh, several refresh cycles can also be executed in succession.

Hidden Refresh

Another elegant option is the *hidden refresh*. Here the actual refresh cycle is more or less «hidden» behind a normal read access. During a hidden refresh the $\overline{CAS}$ signal is further held on a low level, and only the $\overline{\text{RAS}}$ signal is switched. The data read during the read cycle remains valid even while the refresh cycle is in progress. Because the time required for a refresh cycle is usually shorter than the read cycle, this refresh type saves some time. For the hidden refresh, too, the address counter in the DRAM generates the refresh address. The row and column addresses shown in Figure 17.7 refer only to the read cycle. If the $\overline{\text{CAS}}$ signal remains on a low level for a sufficiently long time, then several refresh cycles can be carried out in succession. For this it is only necessary to switch the $\overline{\text{RAS}}$ signal frequently between low and high. New motherboards with the programmable NEAT chips often implement the option of refreshing the DRAM memory with CAS-before-RAS or hidden refresh instead of the detour via the DMA and timer chip. This is usually faster and more effective. You should use this option, which comes directly from the field of mainframes and workstations, to free your PC from unnecessary and time-consuming DMA cycles.

17.1.5 DRAM Chip Organization

Let us look at a 16-bit graphics adapter equipped with 1 Mbyte chips. As every memory chip has one data pin, 16 chips are required in all to serve the data bus width of 16 bits. But these 16 1 Mbyte chips lead to a video memory of 2 Mbytes; that is too much for an ordinary VGA. If you want to equip your VGA with «only» 512 kbytes (not too long ago this was actually the maximum) you only need four 1 Mbyte chips. But the problem now is that you may only implement a 4-bit data bus to the video memory with these chips. With the continual development of larger and larger memory chips, various forms of organization have been established. The 1 Mbyte chip mentioned above with its one data pin has a so-called *1Mword * 1bit organization*. This means that the memory chip comprises 1 M words with a width of one bit each, that is, has exactly one data pin. Another widely used organizational form for a 1 Mbyte chip is the *256kword * 4bit organization*. These chips then have 256 k words with a width of four bits each. The storage capacity is 1 Mbit here, too. Thus the first number always indicates the number of words and the second the number of bits per word. Unlike the 1M*1-chip, the 256k*4-chip has four data pins because in a memory access one word is always output or read. To realize the above-indicated video RAM with 512 kbytes capacity, you therefore need four 1 Mbit chips with the 256k*4 organization. As every chip has four data pins, the data bus is 16 bits wide and the 16-bit graphics adapter is fully used. Figure 17.8 shows the pin assignment of a 256k*4-chip. Unlike the 1M*1 DRAM of Figure 17.1, four bidirectional data input/output pins D0–D3 are present. The signal at the new connection $\overline{\text{OE}}$ (output enable) instructs the DRAM's data buffer to output data at the pins D0–D3 ($\overline{\text{OE}}$ low) or to accept them from the data pins D0–D3 ($\overline{\text{OE}}$ high).

Besides the 256k*4-chip there is also a 64k*4-chip with a storage capacity of 256 kbits, often used in graphics adapters of less than 512 kbytes of video-RAM, as well as a 1M*4-chip with a capacity of 4 Mbits, which you meet in high-capacity SIMM or SIP modules. These chips all have four data pins that always input or output a data word of four pins with every memory access. Thus the chip has four data input and output buffers. Moreover, the memory array of these chips is divided into at least four subarrays, which are usually assigned to one data pin each. The data may only be input and output word by word, that is, in this case in groups of four bits each.

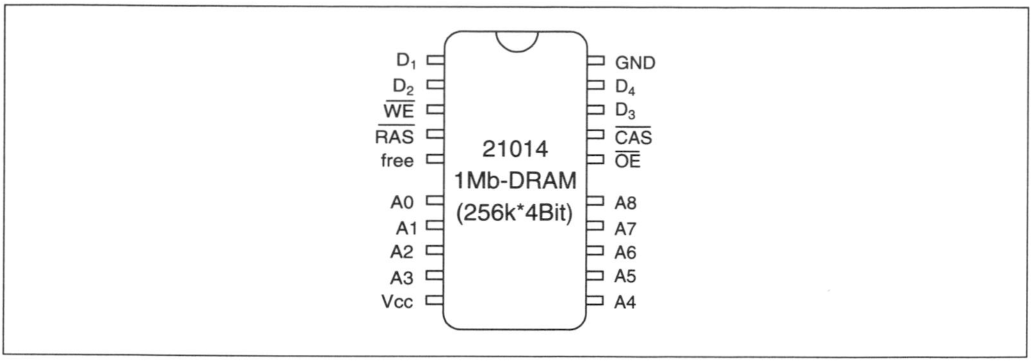

*Figure 17.8: Pin assignment for a 256k*4-chip.*

17.1.6 Fast Operating Modes of DRAM Chips

A further feature of modern memory chips is the possibility of carrying out one or more column modes to reduce the access time. The best known is the *page mode*. What is actually behind this often quoted catchword (and the less well-known static-column, nibble and serial modes) is discussed in the following sections. Figure 17.9 shows the behaviour of the most important memory signals if the chip carries out one of these high-speed modes in a read access. For comparison, in Figure 17.9a you can also see the signal's course in the conventional mode.

Page Mode

Section 17.1.2 mentioned that during the course of an access to a unit memory cell in the memory chip, the row address is input first with an active $\overline{\text{RAS}}$ signal, and then the column address with an active $\overline{\text{CAS}}$ signal. Additionally, internally all memory cells of the addressed row are read onto the corresponding bit line pair. If the successive memory access refers to a memory cell in the same row but another column (that is, the row address remains the same and only the column address has changed), then it is not necessary to input and decode the row address again. In page mode, therefore, only the column address is changed, but the row address remains the same. Thus, one page corresponds exactly to one row in the memory cell array. (You will find the signal's course in page mode shown in Figure 17.9b.)

To start the read access the memory controller first activates the $\overline{\text{RAS}}$ signal as usual, and passes the row address. The address is transferred to the row decoder, decoded, and the corresponding word line is selected. Now the memory controller activates the $\overline{\text{CAS}}$ signal and passes the column address of the intended memory cell. The column decoder decodes this address and transfers the corresponding value from the addressed bit line pair to the data output buffer. In normal mode, the DRAM controller would now deactivate both the $\overline{\text{RAS}}$ and $\overline{\text{CAS}}$ signals, and the access would be completed.

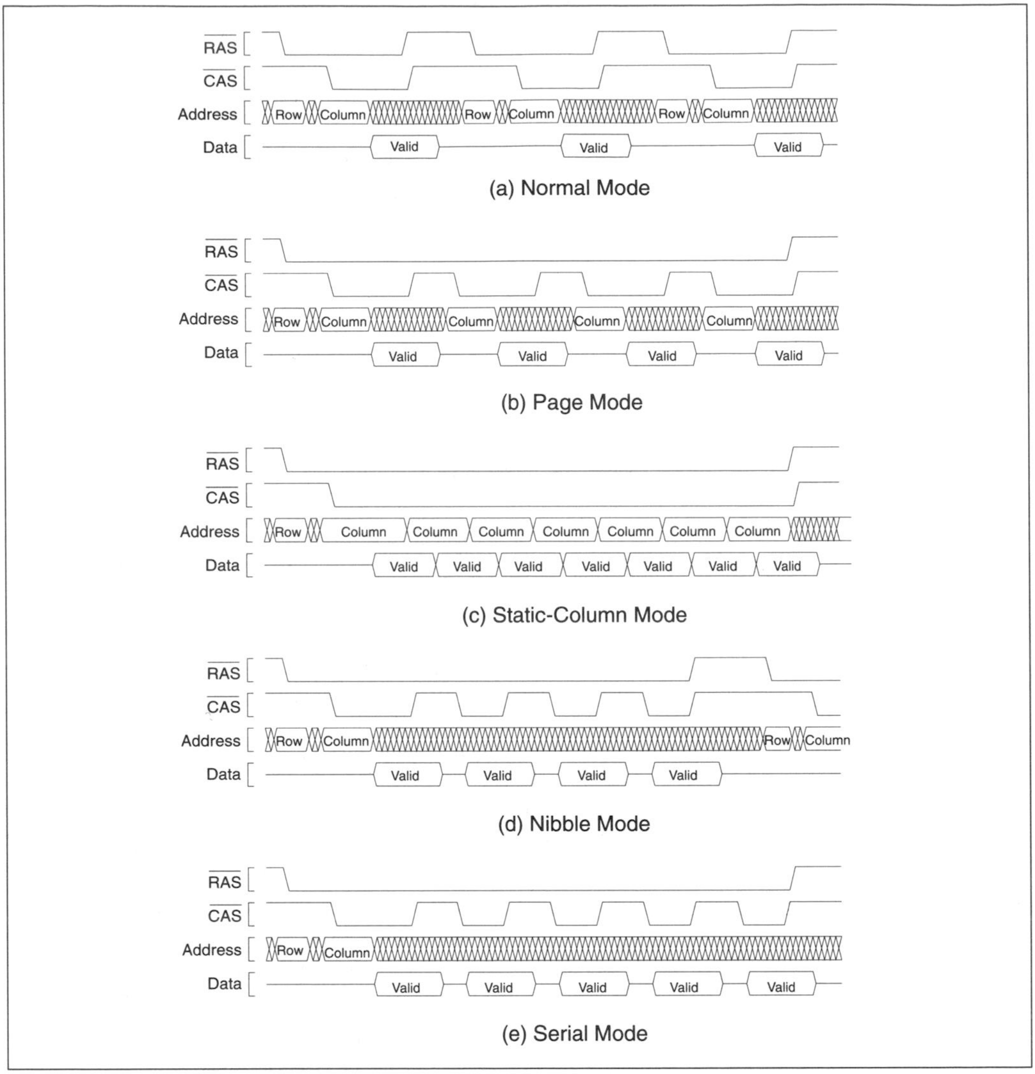

Figure 17.9: Signals during a read access in various DRAM operating modes.

If the memory controller, however, accesses in page mode a memory cell in the same row of the DRAM (that is, within the same page), then it doesn't deactivate the $\overline{RAS}$ signal but continues to hold the signal at an active low level. Instead, only the $\overline{CAS}$ signal is disabled for a short time, and then reactivated to inform the DRAM control that the already decoded row address is still valid and only a column address is being newly supplied. All access transistors connected to the word line concerned thus also remain turned on, and all data read-out onto the bit line pairs is held stable by the sense amplifiers. The new column address is decoded in the column decoder, which turns on a corresponding transfer gate. Thus, the $\overline{RAS}$ precharge time as well as the transfer and decoding of the row address is inapplicable for the second and all succeeding accesses to memory cells of the same row in page mode. Only the column address is passed and decoded. In page mode the access time is about 50% and the cycle time up to even 70% shorter than in normal mode. This, of course, applies only for the second and all successive accesses. However, because of stability, the time period during which the $\overline{RAS}$ signal remains active may not last for an unlimited time. Typically, 200 accesses within the same page can be carried out before the memory controller has to deactivate the $\overline{RAS}$ signal for one cycle.

However, operation in page mode is not limited to data reading only: data may be written in page mode, or read and write operations within one page can be mixed. The DRAM need not leave page mode for this purpose. In a 1 Mbyte chip with a memory cell array of 1024 rows and 1024 columns, one page comprises at least 1024 memory cells. If the main memory is implemented with a width of 32 bits (that is, 32 1 Mbyte chips are present), then one main memory page holds 4 kbytes. As the instruction code and most data tend to form blocks, and the processor rarely accesses data that is more than 4 kbytes away from the just accessed value, the page mode can be used very efficiently to reduce the access and cycle times of the memory chips. But if the CPU addresses a memory cell in another row (that is, another page), then the DRAM must leave page mode and the $\overline{RAS}$ precharge time makes a significant difference. The same applies, of course, if the $\overline{RAS}$ signal is disabled by the memory controller after the maximum active period.

Static-Column Mode

Strongly related to the page mode is the static-column mode (Figure 17.9c). Here the $\overline{CAS}$ signal is no longer switched to inform the chip that a new column address is applied. Instead, only the column address supplied changes, and $\overline{CAS}$ remains unaltered on a low level. The DRAM control is intelligent enough to detect the column address change after a short reaction time without the switching of $\overline{CAS}$. This additionally saves part of the $\overline{CAS}$ switch and reaction time. Thus the static-column mode is even faster than the page mode. But here also the $\overline{RAS}$ and $\overline{CAS}$ signals may not remain at a low level for an unlimited time. Inside the chip only the corresponding gates are switched through to the output buffer. In static-column mode, therefore, all memory cells of one row are accessible randomly. But DRAM chips with the static-column mode are quite rare on the market, and are little used in the field of PCs. Some IBM PS/2 models, though, use static-column chips instead of DRAMs with page mode.

Nibble Mode

The nibble mode is a very simple form of serial mode. By switching $\overline{CAS}$ four times, four data bits are clocked-out from an addressed row (one nibble is equal to four bits, or half a byte). The first data bit is designated by the applied column address, and the three others immediately follow this address. Internally, a DRAM chip with the nibble mode has a 4-bit data buffer in most cases, which accommodates the four bits and shifts them, clocked by the $\overline{CAS}$ signal, successively to the output buffer. This is carried out very quickly because all four addressed (one explicitly and three implicitly) data bits are transferred into the intermediate buffer all at once. The three successive bits need only be shifted, not read again. DRAM chips with the nibble mode are rarely used in the PC field.

Serial Mode

The serial mode may be regarded as an extended nibble mode. Also in this case, the data bits within one row are clocked out by switching $\overline{CAS}$. Unlike the nibble mode, the number of $\overline{CAS}$ switches (and thus the number of data bits) is not limited to four. Instead, in principle a whole row can be output serially. Thus, the internal organization of the chip plays an important role here, because one row may comprise, for example, 1024 or 2048 columns in a 1 Mbit chip. The row and column addresses supplied characterize only the beginning of the access. With every switching of $\overline{CAS}$ the DRAM chip counts up the column address internally and automatically. The serial mode is mainly an advantage for reading video memories or filling a cache line, as the read accesses by the CRT or the cache controller are of a serial nature over large address areas.

Interleaving

Another possibility to avoid delays because of the $\overline{RAS}$ precharge time is memory interleaving. For this purpose, memory is divided into several banks interleaved with a certain ratio. This is explained in connection with a 2-way interleaved memory for an i386 CPU. For example, because of the 32-bit i386 address bus, the memory is also organized with a width of 32 bits. With 2-way interleaving, memory is divided into two banks that are each 32 bits wide. All data with even double–word addresses is located in bank 0 and all data with odd double-word addresses in bank 1. For a sequential access to memory executed, for example, by the i386 prefetcher, the two banks are therefore accessed alternately. This means that the RAS precharge time of one bank overlaps the access time of the other bank. Stated differently: bank 0 is precharged while the CPU accesses bank 1, and vice versa. Figure 17.10 shows this, together with the relevant signals.

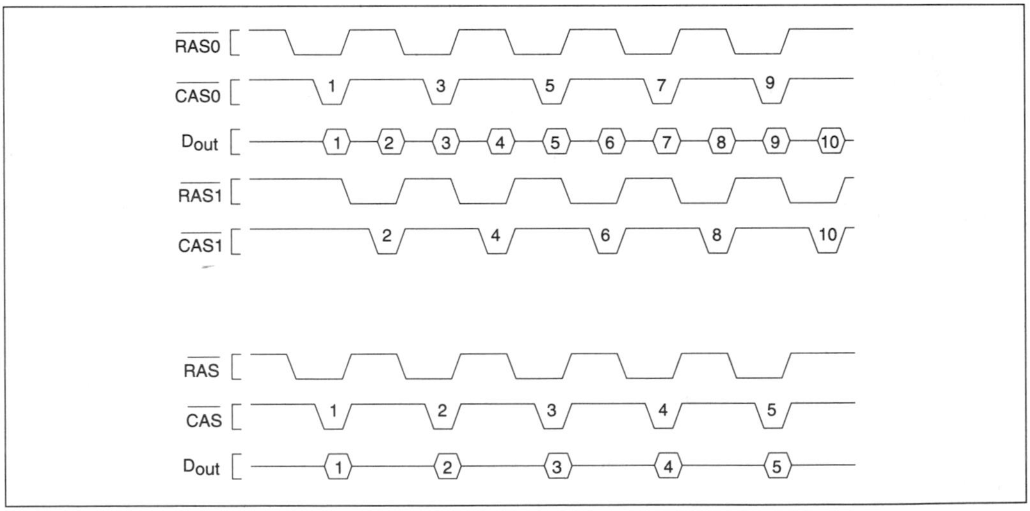

Figure 17.10: 2-way interleaving. By means of interleaving the RAS precharge time is avoided when accessing the two memory banks alternately. Therefore, only the access time of the chip is important, not the cycle time. Without interleaving, on the other hand, the nearly double cycle time is dominant so that repetitive accesses to memory are delayed.

As only the access time and not the cycle time is significant for the CPU access rate, here the access rate can be doubled. Thus the effective access time for several successive memory accesses is halved. In the lower part of Figure 17.10 the same process without interleaving is shown. You can clearly see the difference.

3-way and 4-way interleaving is carried out according to the same principle, but memory is divided into three and four banks respectively, here, and the $\overline{RAS}$ and $\overline{CAS}$ shifts are only one third or one fourth of the time compared with half of the normal cycle time. Many NEAT boards allow custom setup of the interleaving factor. If your memory chips have four banks in total, you may choose either 2-way or 4-way interleaving. In the first case, two banks are always combined into one group; in the latter case, each bank is accessed individually.

So far I have described the concepts of page mode and interleaving in connection with a read access. But for data writing the same principles apply, of course. Moreover, read and write accesses can be mixed. The page mode does not need to be left, nor is interleaving without any value.

To use the advantages of both interleaving and page mode, many storage chips are now configured as paged/interleaved memory. Figure 17.11 shows the course of the $\overline{RAS}$ and $\overline{CAS}$ signals, as well as the output data, for a 2-way interleaved configuration with page mode.

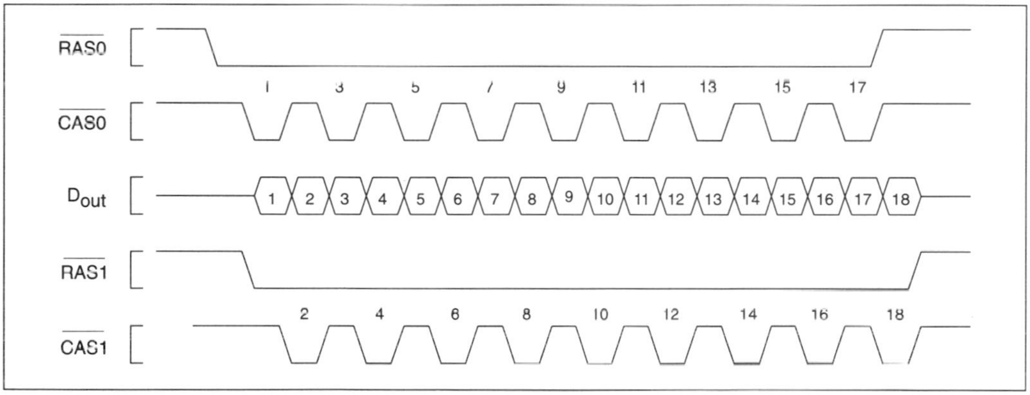

Figure 17.11: 2-way interleaving with page mode. In interleaving with page mode, successive pages are located in different banks so that a page change is executed more quickly.

As you can see, the $\overline{CAS1}$ signal is phase-shifted by 180° compared to $\overline{CAS0}$. Thus, bank 0 accepts column addresses, decodes them and supplies data, while for bank 1 the strobe signal $\overline{CAS1}$ is disabled to change the column address, and vice versa. The access rate is thus further increased compared to conventional interleaving or page mode. With conventional interleaving the DRAMs are interleaved according to the width of memory word by word or double word by double word. In page/interleaving this is done page by page. If a $\overline{RAS}$ precharge cycle is required during a page change, the access to the other bank is carried out with a probability of 50%. Thus, interleaving is effective in a way similar to conventional memory operation.

However, the page mode and interleaving are not always successful, unfortunately. As mentioned, it is necessary that the memory accesses are carried out for the same page. A page change gives rise to a $\overline{\text{RAS}}$ precharge time, and thus delays the memory access. In the same way, to gain an advantage from interleaving it is required that the accesses with a 32-bit data bus are alternately carried out for odd and even double-word addresses, or alternately for odd and even word addresses in the case of a 16-bit data bus. If the CPU twice accesses an odd or even double-word or word address one after the other, in this case $\overline{\text{RAS}}$ precharge time is also required. Fortunately, program code and data tend to form blocks. Moreover, prefetching is executed sequentially so that page mode and interleaving significantly increase the memory access rate in most cases – but not always.

The hit rate is typically about 80% with page/interleaving. A very intelligent memory controller is required for this, which must be able to detect in page mode whether an access occurs within the same page, or with interleaving whether the other bank has to be accessed. If this condition is not fulfilled, the memory controller must flexibly insert wait states until the DRAMs have responded and output the required data or accepted the data supplied. Such powerful memory controllers are rather complicated, but interesting (from a technical viewpoint). Therefore, a typical member, the 82C212 for the 80286 CPU, is discussed below.

17.1.7 SIMM and SIP

Today, compact memory modules such as SIMM and SIP are often used instead of single chips. These modules have a standard width of nine bits, with the relevant number (*1 or *4-chips) allocated to reach the indicated storage capacity (1 Mbyte, for example). Thus, a 1M*9-module may comprise nine 1 Mbyte chips with the organization 1M*1, or two 4 Mbyte chips with the organization 1M*4 for data as well as one 1 Mb chip with the organization 1M*1 for parity information. The SIMM or SIP modules must be inserted into the intended sockets of the banks. Internally the modules are often combined pair by pair or four by four to realize a main memory with a data width of 16 or 32 bits.

Figure 17.12 shows a 4 Mbyte SIMM and a 4 Mbyte SIP module and the connection of the nine 4 Mbit*1 chips to a nine bit wide module. SIMM modules have a contact strip similar to the adapter cards for the bus slots; SIP modules are equipped with pins that must be inserted into corresponding holes.

The following sections briefly discuss the terminals of the SIMM and SIP modules.

A0–A10 (I)
Connections 4–5, 7–8, 11–12, 14–15, 17–19
These eleven connections are supplied with the row and column addresses.

$\overline{\text{CAS}}$ (I)
Connection 2
This column address strobe connection is supplied with the column address strobe signal from the memory controller for the eight data chips.

$\overline{\text{CAS8}}$ (I)
Connection 28
The signal at this connection activates the 9th DRAM chip with the parity information.

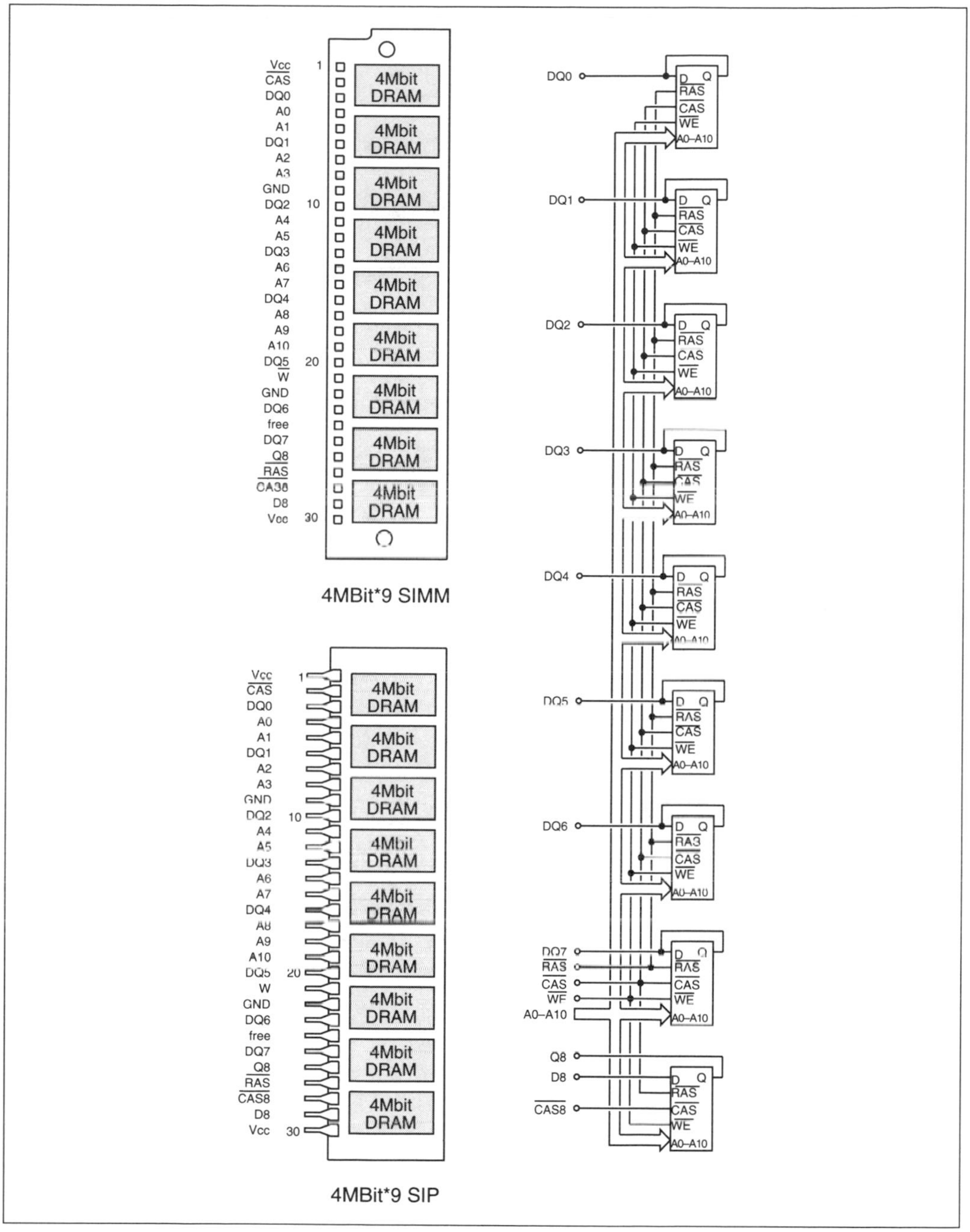

Figure 17.12: SIMM and SIP.

D8 (I)
Connection 29
Via this connection, the module accepts the parity bit for the 9th chip during the course of a data write.

DQ0–DQ7 (I(O)
Connections 3, 6, 10, 13, 16, 20, 23, 25
Via these connections, the data for the eight data DRAMs are supplied or provided.

Q8 (O)
Connection 26
The connection supplies the 9th DRAM chip signal containing the parity information.

$\overline{RAS}$ (I)
Connection 27
Via this row address strobe connection, the row address strobe signal for all nine DRAM chips is supplied.

$\overline{WE}$ (I)
Connection 21

If data must be written into the chips, the memory controller activates the $\overline{WE}$ signal. With a high level, data is read from the DRAM chips.

Vcc (I)
Connections 1, 30
These two connections are supplied with the supply voltage.

GND
Connection 9, 22
These two connections are grounded.

17.2 A Didactical Example for Intelligent Memory Controllers – The 82C212 Page/Interleave Memory Controller

The following section may appear quite out-dated for many readers – the principal functioning of modern DRAM memory controllers will be discussed with a chip designed for the 80286. However, as a didactical example, the 82C212 is very well suited because it has all major functions, and its structure is nevertheless easily comprehensible. The function, pinout and internal structure of DRAM controllers for the i386/i486 or Pentium are, in principle, identical to the discussed 82C212; only the data and address bus, as well as the register widths, must be scaled accordingly. Of course, there is a register compatibility neither between the 82C212 and, for example, the i386/i486 controllers, nor between the i386/i486 controllers themselves. They are very specialized hardware components or chip sets, and every manufacturer can do (and is doing) what they want. Thus, the BIOS setup program for the various chip sets and motherboards must be adapted for each hardware platform. Even as a system programmer, you will hardly recognize the differences (except if you are writing performance optimizing programs), and as an application programmer you will probably see no difference at all; memory controllers are entirely transparent to software. But now let's turn to the 82C212.

Besides the generation of various chip signals such as $\overline{RAS}$, $\overline{CAS}$ and $\overline{WE}$, the 82C212 has the job of carrying out a page mode access with interleaving, of remapping the address space between 640 kbytes and 1 Mbyte to extended memory, of enabling shadowing of ROM BIOS code into the faster RAM, and of quickly switching the 80286 between protected and real modes.

17.2.1 Terminals and Signals

The 82C212 comes in a PLCC package with 84 terminals. Their configuration is shown in Figure 17.13.

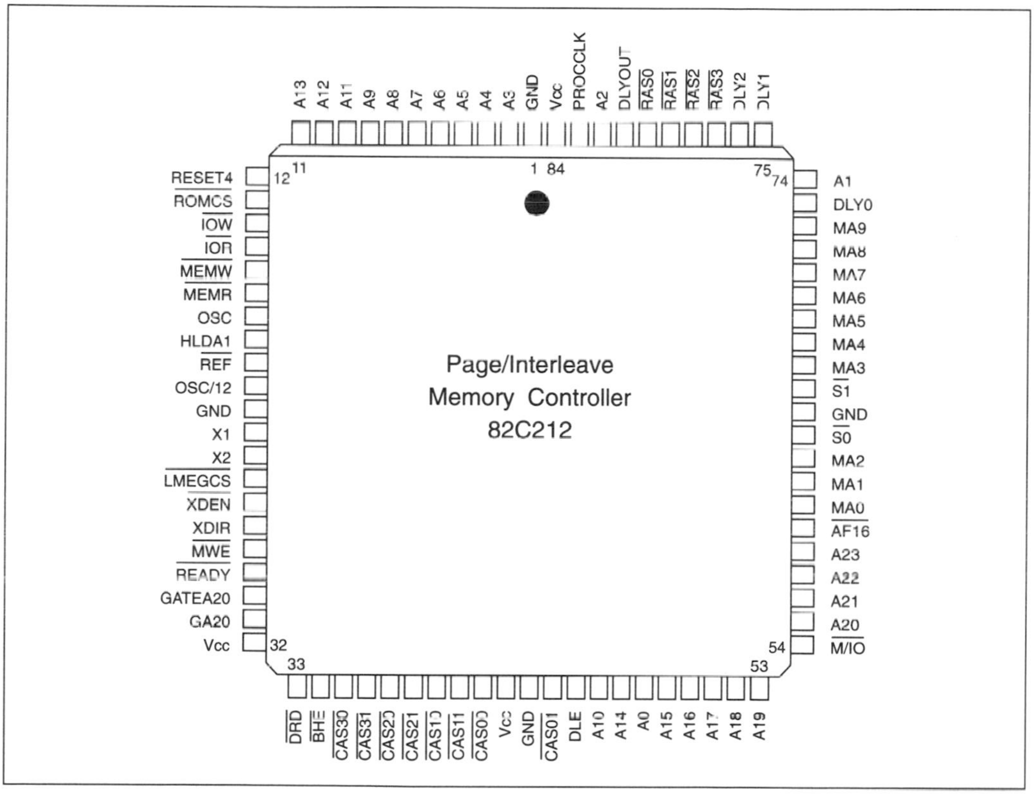

Figure 17.13: 82C212 connections. The 82C212 belongs to the modern memory controllers that support page mode and interleaving. Furthermore, the 82C212 generates the refresh addresses for the DRAM chips autonomously.

The 82C212 can serve four DRAM banks with a width of 16 data bits plus two parity bits in total. The storage capacity that the 82C212 can manage is four banks with 4 Mbytes each. This 16 Mbytes of memory is the maximum physical memory for the 80286. For an i386/i486 or Pentium with a 32-bit address bus and a 32-bit or 64-bit data bus, respectively, the banks have, of course, a width of 32 bits plus 4 parity bits and 64 bits plus 8 parity bits, respectively. A motherboard with these 32-bit processors usually incorporates a DRAM controller which can access at least 32 Mbytes, but in most cases 128 Mbytes and more of on-board memory. Nevertheless, the organization and structure are, in principle, the same as for the 82C212.

The following sections briefly describe the signals and pins of the 82C212.

A23–A0 (I)
Pins 2–11, 46–53, 58–55, 74, 82

These 24 pins are supplied with the address of the local CPU bus to address this memory. The 82C212 generates row and column addresses for the DRAM and EPROM chips from these signals.

$\overline{\text{AF16}}$ (O)
Pin 59

The 82C212 outpts a low-level signal via this pin during the course of accesses to local memory. If the CPU accesses ports or memory chips located on expansion adapters, this pin is on a high level.

$\overline{\text{BHE}}$ (I)
Pin 34

The CPU applies a low-level signal to the byte high enable pin to transfer data on the high-order byte of the data bus.

$\overline{\text{CAS00}}$–$\overline{\text{CAS31}}$ (O)
Pins 35–41, 44

The 82C212 outputs a column address strobe signal $\overline{\text{CASx0}}$ (x=0,1,2,3) to select the DRAMs with the low-order data byte of bank x. Similarly, $\overline{\text{CASx1}}$ accesses the DRAMs with the high-order data byte.

DLE (O)
Pin 45

If the 82C212 activates this data latch enable signal, the local memory buffer is enabled to accept and latch data.

DLY0–DLY2 (I)
Pins 73, 75, 76

The delay circuit outputs signals to the 82C212 using these three delay input pins to generate the DRAM control signals.

DLYOUT (O)
Pin 81

Via this delay line out pin the 82C212 outputs a signal to a delay circuit to generate the DRAM control signals.

$\overline{\text{DRD}}$ (O)
Pin 33

With an active data read signal $\overline{\text{DRD}}$ (that is, the signal is on a low level), data is transferred from the memory bus to the local bus of the CPU. If $\overline{\text{DRD}}$ is on a high level, data transfer occurs in the opposite direction.

GA20, GATEA20 (O, I)
Pins 31, 30

With the gated address line A20 signal applied to the pin GA20, external hardware may control the masking of address line A20 to emulate a wrap-around at 1 M. Thus, strict compatibility with the 8086/88 in real mode is possible. If the gate address A20 signal GATEA20 is at a low level, then address line A20 is masked, a wrap-around at 1 M occurs, and GA20 is low. If GATEA20 is at a high level, the 82C212 transfers the signal on line A20 to GA20.

HLDA1 (I)
Pin 19

If a high-level hold acknowledge 1 signal is applied to this pin, the 82C212 generates $\overline{\text{RAS}}$ and $\overline{\text{CAS}}$ signals for DMA bus cycles.

$\overline{\text{IOR}}$ (I)
Pin 15
A low-level I/O read signal at this pin informs the 82C212 that an I/O read cycle is in progress.

$\overline{\text{IOW}}$ (I)
Pin 14
A low-level I/O write signal at this pin indicates an I/O write cycle.

$\overline{\text{LMEGCS}}$ (O)
Pin 25

If the CPU is accessing the least significant Mbyte of memory, or if a refresh cycle is carried out, then the 82C212 activates this low meg memory chip select signal.

MA0–MA9 (O; MA0–MA7: I/O)
Pins 60–62, 66–72

Via these multiplexed DRAM address pins, the 82C212 supplies the multiplexed row and column addresses that are applied to the DRAM chips. Together with the bank selection signals $\overline{\text{RAS0}}$–$\overline{\text{RAS3}}$ and $\overline{\text{CAS00}}$–$\overline{\text{CAS31}}$ and a 16-bit memory organization, 16 Mbytes of memory can thus be accessed in four banks of 4 Mbytes each. Additionally, the pins MA0–MA7 serve as a bidirectional 8-bit data bus for an access to the internal 82C212 registers.

$\overline{\text{MEMR}}$ (I)
Pin 17

A low-level memory read signal at this pin informs the 82C212 that a memory read cycle must be carried out.

$\overline{\text{MEMW}}$ (I)
Pin 16

A low-level memory write signal at this pin informs the 82C212 that a memory write cycle must be executed.

M/$\overline{\text{IO}}$ (I)
Pin 54

This memory/IO pin is supplied with the M/$\overline{\text{IO}}$ signal from the CPU so that the 82C212 can distinguish between memory cycles and I/O cycles.

$\overline{\text{MWE}}$ (O)
Pin 28

To carry out a write process in the addressed DRAMs, the 82C212 activates this memory write enable signal. $\overline{\text{MWE}}$ is connected to the $\overline{\text{WE}}$ pin of the DRAM chips.

OSC (O)
Pin 18

This pin outputs the oscillator clock signal with a frequency of 14.31818 MHz, which is generated by the crystal between X1 and X2.

OSC/12 (O)
Pin 21

This pin supplies a frequency of CLK/12. The OSC/12 signal with a frequency of 1.19381 MHz is used internally to disable the $\overline{\text{RAS}}$ signal after the maximum active time in page mode of about 10 μs.

PROCCLK (I)
Pin 83

This processor clock pin is supplied with the processor clock signal from the 82C211 system controller.

$\overline{\text{RAS3}}$–$\overline{\text{RAS0}}$ (O)
Pins 77–80

Via these row address strobe pins, the 82C212 supplies the $\overline{\text{RAS}}$ signals for the DRAM chips in the four banks that the controller can serve at most. One of the banks is thus enabled for an access.

$\overline{\text{READY}}$ (O)
Pin 29

If the addressed memory has completed the data read or write then the 82C212 outputs a low-level signal at this pin. Thus the CPU can flexibly insert wait cycles if, for example, the memory has to change the page or, despite interleaving, a $\overline{\text{RAS}}$ precharge cycle is required.

$\overline{\text{REF}}$ (I)
Pin 20

A low-level signal at this refresh pin issues a refresh cycle for the DRAMs.

RESET4 (I)
Pin 12

If a high-level signal is applied to this pin, the 82C212 configuration registers are reset to predefined standard values.

$\overline{\text{ROMCS}}$ (O)
Pin 13

If the 82C212 accesses an EPROM it activates the ROM chip select signal $\overline{\text{ROMCS}}$ to prepare the EPROM for a data output.

$\overline{\text{S1}}$, $\overline{\text{S0}}$ (I, I)
Pins 65, 63

The 80286 status signals are applied to these two pins. The 82C212 observes them to detect the beginning of a bus cycle.

X1, X2 (I)
Pins 23, 24

These two pins are connected to a crystal oscillator, which usually generates a frequency of 14318180 Hz.

$\overline{\text{XDEN}}$ (O)
Pin 26

During an I/O access to ports 22h and 23h, the memory controller outputs low-level X-data buffer enable signals to enable the buffers for data transfer. Using ports 22h and 23h the CPU can access the index and data register inside the 82C212.

XDIR (I)
Pin 27

The signal at this X-bus direction pin determines the data transfer direction between 82C212 and CPU for an access to the ports 22h and 23h.

Vcc (I)
Pins 32, 42, 84
The supply voltage is applied to these pins (usually +5 V).

GND
Pins 1, 22, 43, 64
These pins are grounded (usually 0 V).

After briefly listing the confusingly large number of signals, let us now turn to the actual application of the 82C212. Figure 17.14 shows the DRAM organization of the four banks with a width of 18 bits each. 16 bits are reserved for data and two bits for the parity of the low-order and high-order 8-bit groups. If 1 Mbyte chips are used for main memory then each bank may comprise up to 4 Mbytes of RAM. Thus, the maximum main memory can be 16 Mbytes in all. If you employ 256 kbit chips, each bank can only hold 1 Mbyte, so the memory can only be equipped up to 4 Mbytes. Today, the banks are mainly formed by SIMM or SIP modules.

Usual sizes are 1 Mbyte or 4 Mbyte memory capacity at a data width of nine bits (eight data bits plus one parity bit) or 36 bits (32 data bits plus 4 parity bits, 4 Mbyte modules only).

Instead of the memory chips with 256k*1 or 1M*1 organization, 256k*4 or 1M*4 DRAMs can also be used. Now 18 chips are no longer required for every bank, only four plus two 256k*1 or 1M*1 chips to realize the width of 18 bits. Without interleaving you may equip the various banks with any DRAM chips. With 2-way interleaving the equipment within a bank pair must be equal, that is, banks 0 and 1 as well as banks 2 and 3 must be identically equipped.

But you are free, for example, to use 256 kbit DRAMs for banks 0 and 1 and 1 Mbit chips for banks 2 and 3. For 4-way interleaving, all the four banks must be identically equipped. Higher interleaving factors are not possible with four banks, and also not useful as a performance increase is not possible any more, and the control gets only more complicated.

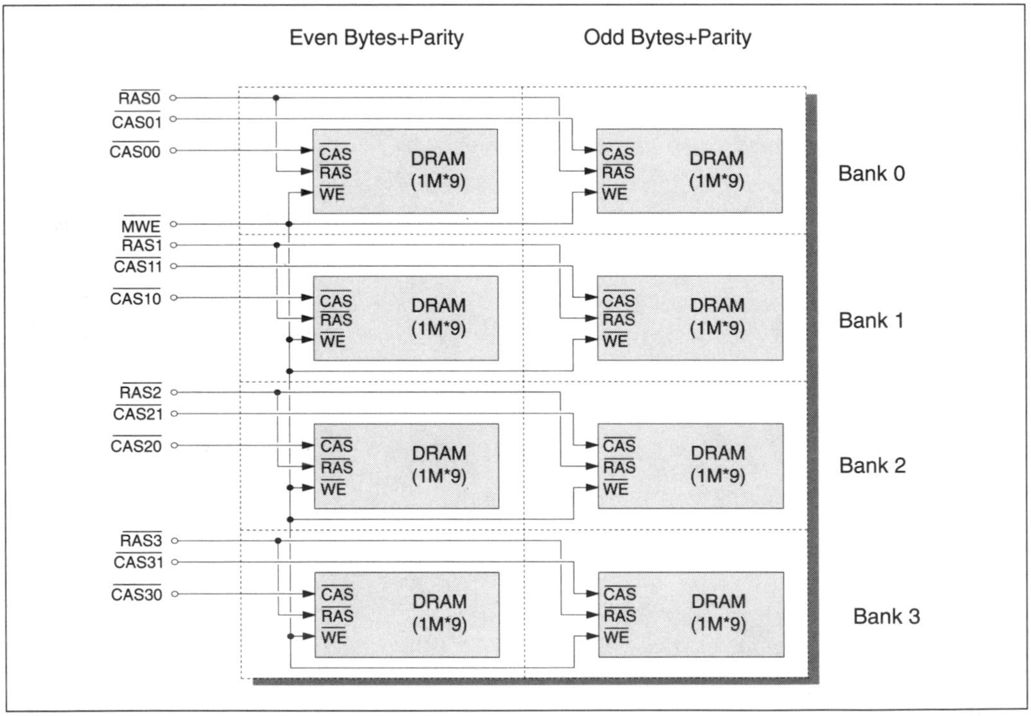

Figure 17.14: 82C212 DRAM organization. Here the DRAM is divided into four banks at most so that 4-way interleaving is possible.

17.2.2 Internal 82C212 Structure

The signals indicated above control the 82C212 memory controller and are generated by it, respectively. Figure 17.15 shows its internal structure.

The oscillator circuit uses a 14.31818 MHz crystal to generate the OSC and OSC/12 signals. The 82C212 uses the OSC/12 clock with 1.19381 MHz to disable the $\overline{\text{RASx}}$ signal in page mode if the maximum active time period of 10 μs of each bank has elapsed.

The DRAM and EPROM control logic generate the $\overline{\text{RAS}}$, $\overline{\text{CAS}}$ and $\overline{\text{MWE}}$ signals for DRAM accesses, as well as the $\overline{\text{ROMCS}}$ signal for activating the EPROM chips containing the boot and BIOS code. You may program the control logic for different numbers of wait states for DRAM or EPROM accesses by writing the intended value into the wait state register (see below). The control logic module then activates a $\overline{\text{READY}}$ signal for the CPU after completing the memory access concerned. If the access is delayed by a $\overline{\text{RAS}}$ precharge time (a page change is required, for example), then $\overline{\text{READY}}$ is not activated until more than these programmed wait cycles have elapsed. The system control module generates the signals $\overline{\text{XDEN}}$, DLE, $\overline{\text{DRD}}$ and $\overline{\text{AF16}}$ so the CPU can access the internal 82C212 registers.

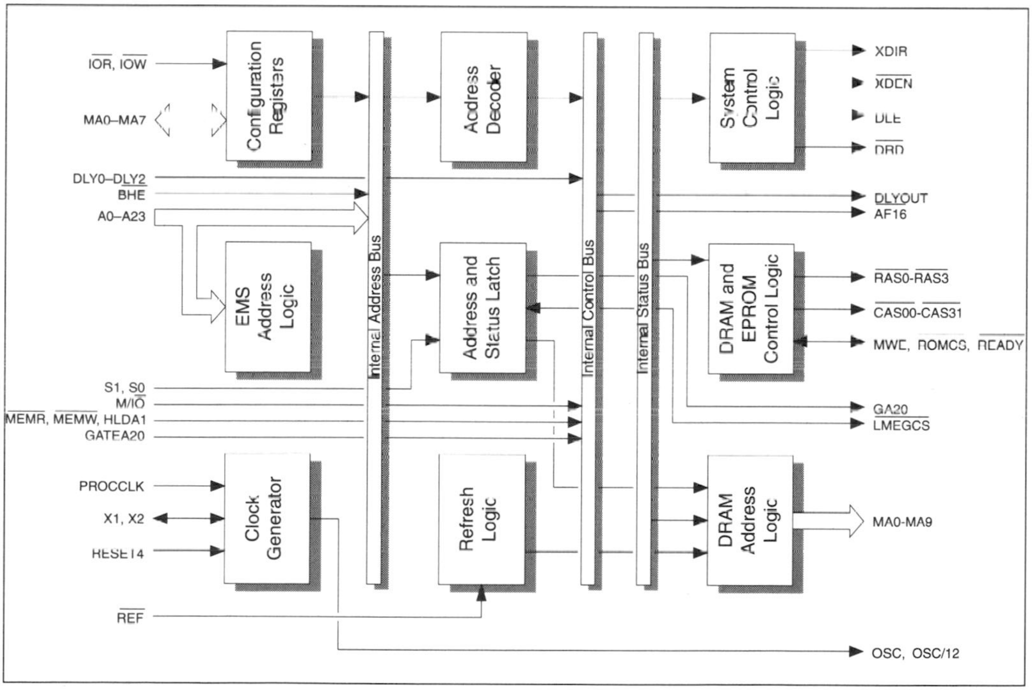

Figure 17.15: Internal 82C212 structure.

Other system and memory controllers (for example, the CS82310 from Chips & Technologies) additionally enable the setup of the RAS/CAS delay, that is, the time period between the activation of $\overline{\text{RAS}}$ upon the transfer of the row address, and the activation of $\overline{\text{CAS}}$ upon the transfer of the row address, or the definition of the $\overline{\text{RAS}}$ pulse length for row decoding. Further, you may define a different number of wait cycles for read and write accesses, where a write usually requires fewer wait cycles. The reason is that many memory controllers have a fast write buffer where the CPU deposits the write data. Afterwards, the controller actually drives a write access to the DRAMs; this strategy is called *write-posting*. If several write accesses occur one after the other so that the write buffer is not always available at once, the controller simply activates the READY signal later, and the CPU inserts additional wait cycles.

To refresh the memory chips the memory controller has its an own refresh logic, which is driven by another member of the 82Cxxx chip set, the 82C211 system controller. For this purpose, the 82C211 activates the $\overline{\text{REF}}$ signal and outputs the refresh address via address lines A0–A9. The remaining 14 address signals A10–A23 are ignored. Thus with fully equipped memory the refresh is always carried in groups of 2^{14} = 16kbytes. If less memory is installed, the block size of simultaneously refreshed cells decreases accordingly. The 82C212 outputs the refresh addresses via address lines MA0–MA9 to the DRAM chips, and issues a refresh by means of the $\overline{\text{RASx}}$ signals without activating the column addresses and the $\overline{\text{CASx}}$ signal. Internally, one memory cell row is selected within each DRAM chip, the stored data is read out onto the bit line pairs, and the sense amplifiers are activated, but the amplified data signals are not transferred through the transfer gates to the data output buffer. Thus, the refresh operation usually runs more quickly than a normal data read.

It is apparent from the above discussion that the 82C212 carries out a RAS-only refresh according to the original AT. For this, a HOLD/HLDA arbitration is necessary to prevent the CPU from accessing the DRAM main memory while the refresh is in progress. Especially for systems with fast caches, this is disadvantageous because the cache with its SRAMs doesn't need any refresh, and the CPU can read data from or write data into the cache with no problem while a DRAM row is refreshed. With a modern DRAM controller, you can therefore often select the refresh type; for example, hidden instead of RAS-only refresh. As the refresh is hidden behind a usual memory access, the only effect is that the DRAM chip is available slightly later for the subsequent access, that is, the cycle time is slightly longer. However, neither a HOLD/HLDA sequence is necessary nor does the refresh address need to be provided externally. Eventually, the DRAM controller services an access request by the CPU with a small delay, that is, the READY signal is returned a little later, and the CPU inserts one or more wait states. Hidden instead of RAS-only refresh enhances the DRAM subsystem performance by some 5%–10%.

When refreshing a large main memory, there is another problem: the memory chips draw a significant current upon activation and the refresh of internal rows. In some cases this may give rise to spikes on the lines to memory, and provoke data errors or inadequate reactions of, for example, buffers, latches or even the CPU. Memory controllers for large systems therefore use *RAS staggering* during refresh, that is, the $\overline{\text{RAS}}$ signals for different banks or modules are activated one after another with a small delay (3–10 ns). Thus, always only one bank or one module draws a high activation current; the otherwise significant power consumption peak is wider and, therefore, less high. Spikes on the lines are prevented.

Besides the modules already mentioned, the 82C212 additionally implements a memory mapping logic and accompanying registers. As you know, the address area between 640 k and 1 M is reserved for ROM chips with BIOS routines. If you have 1 Mbyte of memory installed, for example with four 256k*9 SIMMs, then the addresses from 0 bytes to 1 Mbyte are contiguous, but simultaneously the area between 640 kbytes and 1 Mbyte is reserved for ROM chips. To avoid any address conflict the addresses between 640 k and 1 M of RAM must be masked off, and 384 kbytes of RAM memory get lost. Thus, the memory controller carries out a so-called *memory mapping*. The 384 kbytes of RAM memory between 640 kbytes and 1 Mbyte are thus mapped onto the addresses between 1 M and 1.384 M. This process is shown in Figure 17.16.

Thus RAM accesses with addresses between 0 and 640 k proceed unaltered. If the address is in the range between 640 k and 1 M, the memory controller accesses the ROM chips. After addresses beyond 1 M, the memory controller accesses the 384 high-order kbytes of the 1 Mbyte RAM, thus these 384 kbytes of RAM are already in extended memory.

Another feature of modern memory controllers (and therefore also of the 82C212) is shadowing ROM data in the faster RAM, or alternatively the possibility of configuring the main memory above 1 M as extended or expanded memory, or as a mixture. More about this subject in the next two sections.

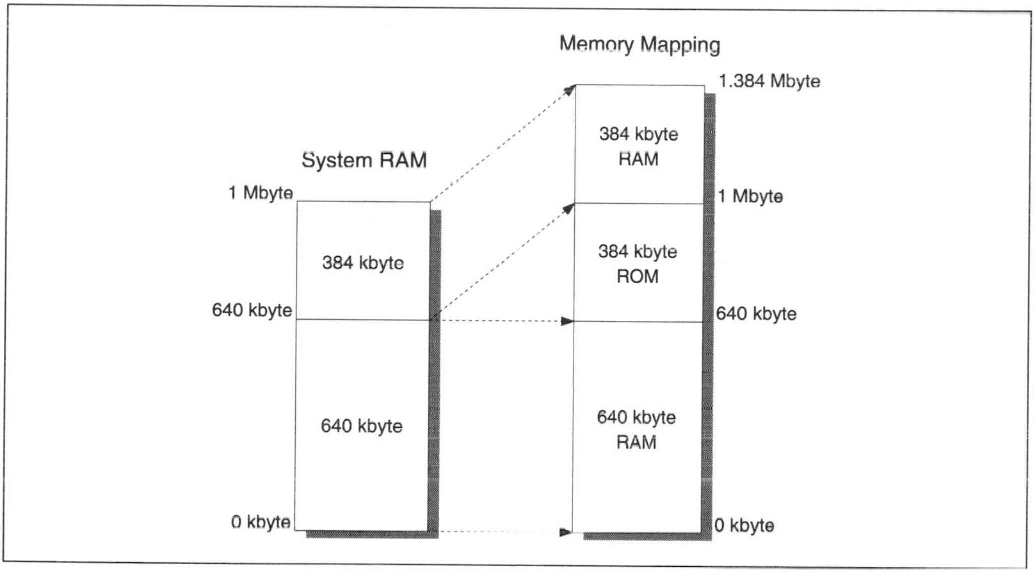

Figure 17.16: RAM memory mapping. The 82C212 can divide a physical memory of 1 Mbyte into a section of 640 kbytes between 0 k and 640 k, and a section of 384 kbytes above 1 M. The «hole» in between is filled with ROM.

17.2.3 Shadow RAM and BIOS

One disadvantage of ROM chips compared to DRAM or SRAM is the significantly longer access time. Today, DRAM chips with access times of about 70 ns and SRAM chips with access times below 25 ns are usual. But EPROMs and other ROM types need up to 200 ns before the addressed data is available. That is an important disadvantage, because extensive BIOS routines for access to floppy and hard disk drives or the graphics adapters are located in the slower ROM. Moreover, these routines are frequently called by the operating system or application programs, and thus slow down program execution. What better solution than to move code and data from the slow ROM into the faster main memory? This process is supported by shadowing. The performance increase when BIOS routines are called can be up to 400%. Generally, the better the RAM chips and the slower the ROM the higher is the performance increase. To move the ROM data into the RAM, two things are necessary:

- software that transfers the data from ROM to RAM;
- a memory controller that maps the ROM address space onto the RAM area to which the ROM data have been moved.

The former is carried out by the BIOS during the course of the PC's boot process. The processor simply reads the whole ROM and transfers the read data into the RAM area, which is then mapped onto the addresses of the original ROM address space by the memory controller. Then, ROM code and ROM data are still located at the same physical address. But now RAM instead of ROM chips are accessed, so no address alteration within the ROM code is required. For this purpose, the 82C212 has several registers through which the address «bending» can be carried out (more about this subject later). If more than 1 Mbyte of RAM is installed and shadowing is not active, the 82C212 maps RAM and ROM in the way illustrated in Figure 17.17.

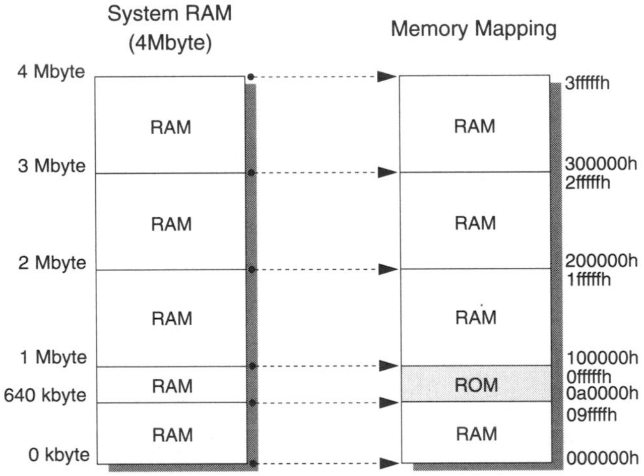

Figure 17.17: Memory mapping with more than 1 Mbyte without shadowing. Without shadowing the RAM section between 640 k and 1 M is masked off, because the ROM chips are located at these addresses.

You can see that with addresses between 640 k and 1 M, the ROM chips are still accessed. Moreover, the higher 384 kbytes of RAM memory are lost because they cannot be mapped onto the area between 1 Mbyte and 1.384 Mbytes without overlapping the installed memory between 1 M and 2 M. If shadowing is enabled, a completely different situation arises. The corresponding memory mapping is shown in Figure 17.18.

The shadow RAM is located in the address space between 640 k and 1 M; the ROM chips are completely masked off from the address space. If an application such as Word attempts to access the hard disk via BIOS interrupt 13h to read data, the CPU no longer addresses the code in ROM, but that transferred into shadow RAM. To avoid a computer crash during a BIOS call, all data needs to be transferred from the ROM to the RAM chips, of course, because application programs and the system cannot now access the ROM chips. Only a direct and therefore hardware-dependent programming of the 82C212 registers can still access the ROM.

With most memory controllers you can move individual sections of ROM address space into the shadow RAM. Thus, it is not absolutely necessary to move all the 384 kbytes reserved for the ROM BIOS between 640 k and 1 M to the shadow RAM all at once. You may, for example, move the BIOS area between C0000h and C8000h, which is reserved for the EGA and VGA BIOS, to the shadow RAM to speed up picture setup. On the other hand, it is sometimes impossible to map certain parts of the ROM address space. This especially applies to SCSI host adapters, which carry out a so-called *memory mapped I/O* for data transfer between PC and SCSI bus. Modern cache controllers or chip sets can also lock some abitrarily chosen memory areas for caching. The addresses lie in the area between 0a0000h and 0fffffh (that is, between 640 k and 1 M) in most cases; usually, the video RAM and the ROMs are located there.

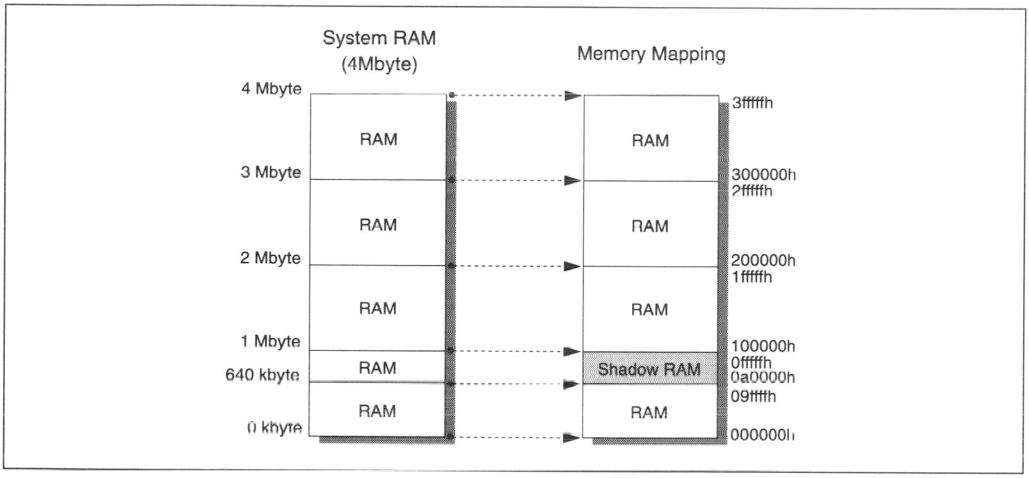

Figure 17.18: Memory mapping with shadowing enabled. With shadowing enabled the content of the ROMs between 640 k and 1 M is copied into the corresponding RAM section. Afterwards, the ROM chips between 640 k and 1 M are masked off.

With normal XT and AT hard disk drives, sectors are read into a buffer on the controller that cannot be accessed via the normal address space. The CPU is only able to address the read data via a register port, and to transfer it into main memory. Alternatively, the data can be transferred by the DMA controller. The code in the expansion ROM on the controller adapter can be readily mapped onto the shadow RAM with no problem, because no write accesses are carried out into the ROM memory on the controller. Instead, the data is transferred directly into the main memory, whose addresses don't fall into the range between 640 k and 1 M. Thus, memory mapping for the shadow RAM plays no role in this case.

The situation is different again for SCSI adapters with memory mapped I/O. In the address range between 640 k and 1 M, which is reserved for the ROM BIOS, these adapters usually have a small RAM memory. The SCSI bus writes the data from the hard disk drive into this RAM section. The advantage is that the data is immediately transferred by the controller into the memory address space, and no additional transfer via register ports or the DMA chips is required. With shadowing this gives rise to a disaster: as the small RAM is located in the ROM address space, the RAM of the SCSI host adapter is also masked off, and the startup routine of the BIOS transfers only the data present in the host adapter RAM into the shadow RAM before the controller enables shadowing. If a sector of the SCSI hard disk is to be read later, then the code is executed correctly, but the SCSI hard disk still transfers the read data into the RAM on the host adapter; its addresses, however, are masked off as a part of the ROM address space. The connection between SCSI bus and the RAM on the SCSI host adapter is wired, and therefore nothing can be remapped. The SCSI bus writes into the adapter RAM, but the CPU accesses the remapped address, which still contains the data that was transferred there during the course of the shadow RAM activation process. No matter which sector is read, the CPU always finds the same data. In a favourable case the BIOS issues an error message, for example «bad track 0», because the data transferred into the shadow RAM doesn't lead to a consistent partition table. In the worst case, the BIOS interprets this «table» and carries out unpredictable processes. Therefore, you should never map the address area of a SCSI host adapter that uses memory mapped I/O into the shadow RAM.

17.2.4 Expanded Memory and Memory Mapping

Besides extended memory there is another memory type that can be used by DOS for expanding the normal base memory of 640 kbytes – the so-called *expanded memory*. Figure 17.19 shows the principle of this storage.

Expanded memory inserts a so-called EMS window with a maximum size of 64 kbytes into the first Mbyte of the real mode address space of the 80x86 CPU. EMS is the abbreviation for *Expanded Memory Specification* or *Expanded Memory System*. The start address and size of this window can be chosen by means of jumpers, or via the BIOS setup program. In most cases, the area between 640 k and 1 M that is reserved for ROM chips is not entirely occupied, so it is useful to put the EMS window into this area. But you have to be sure that the entire memory section occupied by the EMS window is really free, otherwise address conflicts occur and the PC crashes.

The EMS window is divided into four pages, with 16 kbytes at most, which are contiguous in the address space. The start address of each page can be defined by software commands that control the logic of expanded memory by means of a driver so that the four pages with 16 kbytes each can be moved within the much larger physical expanded memory. By definition, a maximum physical memory of 8 Mbytes is available for expanded memory. The principles of EMS are rather old, and were already being used more than 15 years ago on the CP/M machines with their 8-bit processors. Lotus, Intel and Microsoft decided some years ago to set up a strictly defined standard for the software control of expanded memory. The result is *LIM-EMS* (Lotus Intel Microsoft expanded memory specification). Today, LIM-EMS 4.0 is the *de facto* standard for expanded memory systems. The hardware forming the base and the manner in which the pages in the large physical memory are inserted into the EMS window between 640 k and 1 M (that is, how the address translation is carried out) is completely hidden from the programmer who wants to use expanded memory. Together with the EMS hardware, the manufacturer delivers a driver whose software interface corresponds to LIM-EMS, and whose hardware interface is directed to the electronics used.

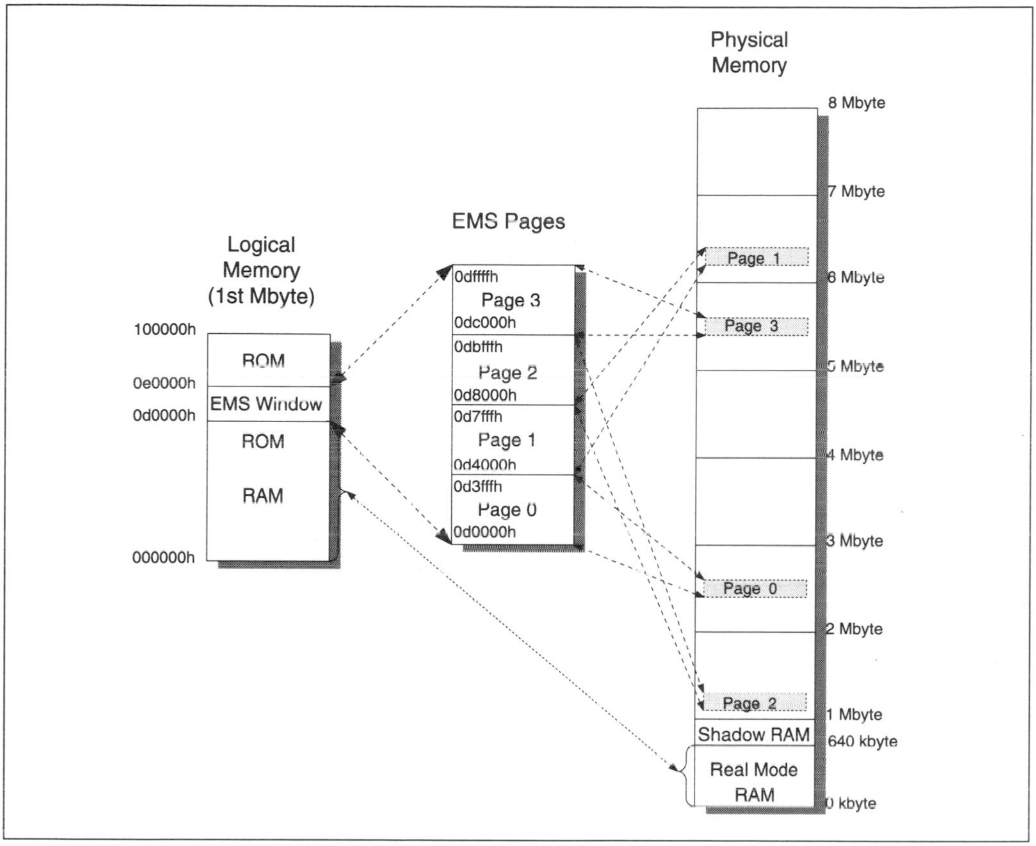

Figure 17.19: Expanded memory and memory mapping with the 82C212.

Earlier EMS systems were mainly implemented using an EMS adapter card in a bus slot. The start address of the EMS window can then be defined by means of jumpers. The EMS driver accesses the address transformation logic on the adapter card using reserved port addresses in most cases, so that, for example, the address 0d0000h (which corresponds to the first EMS page) is mapped onto the address 620000h (which is far beyond the 20-bit address space of the 8086 or the later processors in real mode, and is above 6 M). Modern memory controllers (including the 82C212) can configure the physically available main memory beyond the 1 Mbyte border as either extended or expanded memory, or as a mixture of them both. In EMS mode the 82C212 uses the EMS translation registers to remap the address bits A14–A22. You may usually choose the mode and set up the size of these two memory types using the BIOS setup program. Figure 17.19 shows a physical on-board memory of 8 Mbytes, whose first Mbyte is used as real mode RAM with 640 kbytes and as shadow RAM for ROM with 384 kbytes at most. This part of main memory is thus not available for expanded memory, but only the remaining 7 Mbytes. Analogous to an EMS memory expansion adapter with separate address translation logic, the 82C212's internal EMS logic remaps the pages of the EMS window onto these seven Mbytes. With the configuration registers, the internal EMS logic of the 82C212 can be programmed according to the EMS window's start address (0d0000h in the example), as well as the address of the EMS pages in main memory.

Today, the mapping discussed for inserting EMS windows into the address space between 640 k and 1 M is carried out only in very few cases by hardware. Instead, the EMS drivers for i386 PCs and above make use of the paging mechanism for remapping a 16-kbyte address area beyond 1 M to an address in low memory. However, this does not change the logical structure of expanded memory at all.

For addressing the physical 8 Mbyte memory of Figure 17.19, 23 address bits are required. For expanded memory the restriction to 20 address bits is bypassed by dividing the 23-bit address into two subaddresses comprising 20 bits at most. This is, on the one hand, the start address of the EMS page concerned in the physical memory. For this, nine address bits are required, as expanded memory is divided into «segments» of 16 kbytes each. On the other hand, within such a «segment» a 14-bit offset is formed. I have used the expression «segment» to indicate the analogy to the 80x86 segment and offset registers. If you load a segment register with a certain value then you need only an offset register later to access all objects within the segment concerned. After addressing an object in another segment you must reload the offset *and* the segment register with new values. A similar case arises with the EMS windows and expanded memory. To map an EMS page into expanded memory you need to write the 9-bit number (segment address) of the corresponding 16 kbyte block in expanded memory into an EMS table. If only objects within this EMS page are accessed it is sufficient to alter the 14-bit offset, but because the EMS page has to be inserted in 16 kbyte steps into the 20-bit address space of the 80x86 running in real mode, the 80x86 additionally needs to know the number of the 16 kbyte block in memory between 0 and 1024kbytes that holds the EMS page. For this purpose, six address bits are required. Thus the 80x86 needs its complete 20-bit address bus to determine the 16 kbyte block of the EMS page on the one hand, and to access objects within this page with a 14-bit offset on the other. Not until the EMS page must be moved in expanded memory (that is, another 16 kbyte block is selected) has the 80x86 to alter the 9-bit block address with the EMS driver. Afterwards, the 14-bit offset is again sufficient to address objects within the thus defined EMS page.

One characteristic of expanded memory compared with extended memory is that processors with a small address bus can also access a large memory. The 8-bit 8080 (Intel) or Z80 (Zilog) processors which played an important role in the CP/M era have only a 16-bit address bus, and can therefore only address 64 kbytes of memory. By means of the «detour» via expanded memory they can, in principle, address a memory of any size. For this, only a programmable address translation logic is required, and eventually the output of a «larger» address by repeatedly activating the 16-bit address bus.

Another advantage compared to extended memory is that the 80x86 need not be switched into protected mode to activate the complete address bus with a width of more than 20 bits. Starting with the i386, this is not important because these processors can clear the PM flag in the CR0 control register to reset the processor to real mode immediately. With an 80286 more problems occur, as a return to real mode is only possible via a time-consuming processor reset. If the expanded memory is realized using an intelligent memory controller in the fast on-board memory instead of on a slow adapter card, then on an 80286 the addressing of expanded memory can eventually be much faster than using extended memory. This especially applies if small amounts of data are to be accessed. Another advantage of expanded memory is that it can accommodate not only data code but also program code. The EMS pages are actually accessed in the processor's real mode so that the address interpretation need not be altered. The 80x86 can execute the real mode code without any change. If, on the other hand, program code needs to be stored in extended memory, the codes must be retransferred into the real mode address space and the CPU must be switched back to real mode to execute the program; otherwise the CPU has to execute the code in protected mode. That would involve generating the program for protected mode and a mixture of real mode and protected mode code. DOS is completely overstretched with this job. Only Windows and OS/2 use this method in some way.

17.2.5 82C212 Configuration Registers

To complete this DRAM controller example, I will discuss the 82C212 registers in brief. You can program the 82C212 with these 12 configuration registers. To limit the number of 82C212 ports, the memory controller uses an indexing scheme. You first have to write the index of the register to be programmed into the index register port 022h. Afterwards, you write or read the value to or from the data register port 023h. Table 17.1 lists all registers and their corresponding indices. Note that the implementation and structure of control registers is usually highly dependent upon the controller model and its manufacturer. Normally the memory controllers are register-incompatible with one another.

Register	Index
Version	064h
ROM configuration	065h
Memory enable 1	066h
Memory enable 2	067h
Memory enable 3	068h
Memory enable 4	069h
Bank 0/1 enable	06ah
DRAM configuration	06bh
Bank 2/3 enable	06ch
EMS base register	06dh
EMS address extension	06eh
Miscellaneous	06fh
Index register port:	022h
Data register port:	023h

Table 17.1: Register ports and register indices

The version register (index 064h) contains information concerning the type and version of the memory controller used. The registers with indices 065h to 069h shadow ROM data. The bank enable registers (index 06ah, 06ch) and the DRAM configuration register give some information about the type and number of memory chips installed. The two EMS registers (index 06dh, 06eh) manage expanded memory in main memory, and the miscellaneous register holds values for various 82C212 configuration setups.

Example: `read version registers.`

```
OUT 022h, 064h  ; pass index 064h of version registers to index register port
IN al, 023h     ; read contents of version register into accumulator al
```

Also, if you want to access the same configuration register twice you always have to output the index to the index register port first before you can write data into or read data from the data register port. The following discusses the various registers in more detail.

The version register (Figure 17.20) contains a value that identifies the 82C212 to the system or BIOS. If the *ID* bit is cleared then it is an 82C212. *Ver* holds the version of the memory controller. All other bits are reserved, and must be initialized to 0 at power-up.

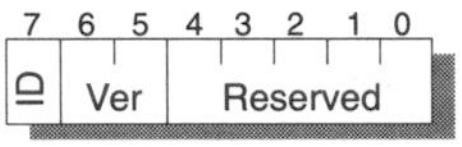

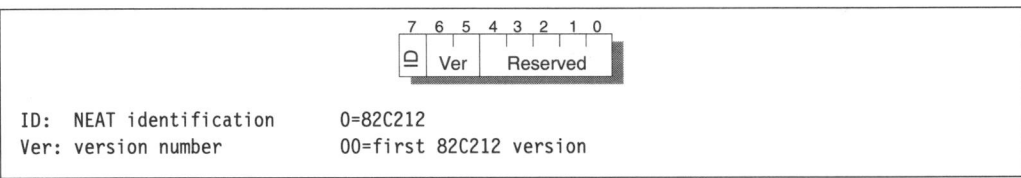

```
ID:  NEAT identification        0=82C212
Ver: version number             00=first 82C212 version
```

Figure 17.20: Version register (index 064h).

Using the ROM configuration register (Figure 17.21) you can activate the ROM in address space 0c0000h to 0fffffh in 64 kbyte blocks and prepare them for shadowing. If you clear one of the *Shadow* bits, the corresponding ROM area is activated. If the corresponding bit is set, the 82C212 outputs no $\overline{ROMCS}$ (ROM chip select) signal and the memory controller accesses no ROM chips within the address area concerned, thus a shadowing in RAM can be carried out. At power-up the least significant Shadow bit is cleared and no shadowing is enabled for the ROM BIOS between 0f0000h and 0fffffh. The remaining three Shadow bits are initialized to 1, however.

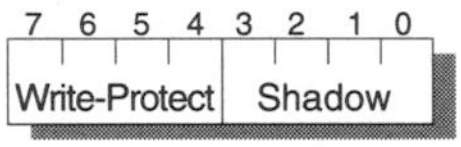


```
Write-Protect: write protection for shadow RAM at addresses
         1xxx=0c0000h-0cffffh   x1xx=0d0000h-0dffffh
         xx1x=0e0000h-0effffh  xxx1=0f0000h-0fffffh
         0=read and write (standard)    1=read only
Shadow: shadow enable for ROM addresses
         1xxx=0c0000h-0cffffh   x1xx=0d0000h-0dffffh
         xx1x=0e0000h-0effffh   xxx1=0f0000h-0fffffh
         0=ROM active    1=shadowing enabled
```

Figure 17.21: ROM configuration register (index 065h).

Write accesses to ROM chips are insignificant for the crash reliability of your PC because their contents can't be altered. This situation changes if shadowing is enabled. Now all ROM data is present in a readable and writeable RAM. A program error that leads, for example, to an invalid pointer causing a write access to an address between 0c0000h and 0fffffh overwrites BIOS code and a future call of BIOS routines may therefore lead to a system crash. Thus the 82C212 enables a write protection for the 64 kbyte segments between 0c0000h and 0fffffh in shadow RAM. You can activate this write protection using the *Write-Protect* bits. If one of these bits is set then the corresponding shadow RAM area is protected against any overwrite. The 82C212 does not pass write accesses to the DRAM chips.

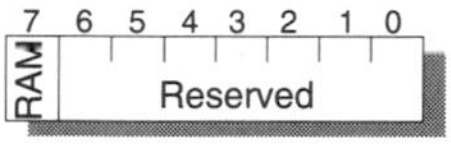


```
RAM:  RAM between 512 kbytes and 640 kbytes
      0=address section in I/O channel    1=address section on system board
res:  reserved  (initialize res=0)
```

Figure 17.22: Memory enable register 1 (Index 066h).

The memory enable register 1 (Figure 17.22) controls the management of memory between 512 and 640 kbytes.

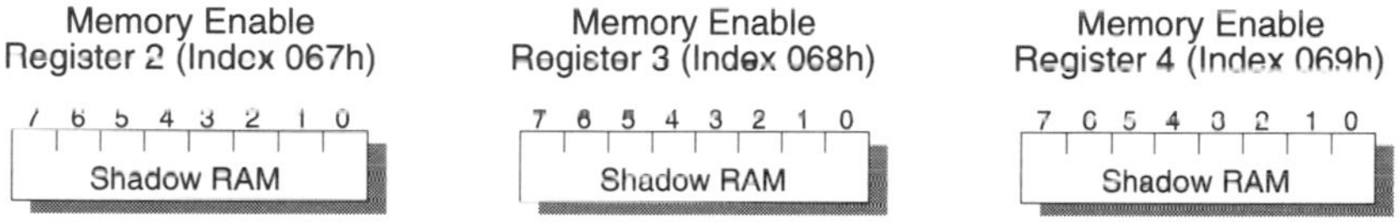


```
Shadow RAM: shadow RAM enable
            0=shadow RAM disabled       1=shadow RAM enabled

Memory Enable Register 2
1xxxxxxx=0ac000h–0affffh   x1xxxxxx=0a8000h–0abfffh
xx1xxxxx=0a4000h–0a7fffh   xxx1xxxx=0a0000h–0a3fffh
xxxx1xxx=0bc000h–0bffffh   xxxxx1xx=0b8000h–0bbfffh
xxxxxx1x=0b4000h–0b7fffh   xxxxxxx1=0b0000h–0b3fffh

Memory Enable Register 3
1xxxxxxx=0dc000h–0dffffh   x1xxxxxx=0d8000h–0dbfffh
xx1xxxxx=0d4000h–0d7fffh   xxx1xxxx=0d0000h–0d3fffh
xxxx1xxx=0cc000h–0cffffh   xxxxx1xx=0c8000h–0cbfffh
xxxxxx1x=0c4000h–0c7fffh   xxxxxxx1=0c0000h–0c3fffh

Memory Enable Register 4
1xxxxxxx=0fc000h–0fffffh   x1xxxxxx=0f8000h–0fbfffh
xx1xxxxx=0f4000h–0f7fffh   xxx1xxxx=0f0000h–0f3fffh
xxxx1xxx=0ec000h–0effffh   xxxxx1xx=0e8000h–0ebfffh
xxxxxx1x=0e4000h–0e7fffh   xxxxxxx1=0e0000h–0e3fffh
```

Figure 17.23: Memory enable registers for shadow RAM (index 067h, 068h, 069h).

If the *RAM* bit is cleared, the address section concerned is present in the I/O channel (that is, in an area not managed by the 82C212). This may be an adapter card in a bus slot. If the RAM bit is set, the accompanying memory chips are installed in a bank accessed by the 82C212, and the memory controller also generates the DRAM control signals for this address area. The *res* bits are reserved, and are initialized to 0 by the 82C212 at power-up.

With the memory enable registers 2, 3 and 4 (Figure 17.23) you may control the shadowing of the address area between 0a0000h and 0fffffh in units of 16 kbyte blocks. For this purpose, however, it is necessary that the SHx bit of the corresponding ROM address section that is subject to shadowing is set in the ROM configuration register (index 065h); otherwise, the 82C212 does not output the ROM activation signal $\overline{ROMCS}$. If one of the *Shadow RAM* bits is set then all accesses to the corresponding 16 kbyte block are diverted to shadow RAM. Note, though, that the BIOS or you as the programmer are responsible for transferring all the data of the ROM chips into the shadow RAM *before* enabling the shadowing.

Using memory enable register 2 you may also move address areas into the shadow RAM that correspond to the video RAM of the graphics adapters. If you do this, the CPU writes all graphics data into the shadow RAM instead of the video RAM; the graphics adapter, however, continues to access the video RAM and not the shadow RAM. The monitor seems to be dead, although the CPU actually updates its contents. All these accesses, though, are diverted to the shadow RAM, and get lost.

```
Bank 0/1 Enable Register
DRAM: type of installed DRAM chips
      00=no chips                    01=256 kbit and 64 kbit chips for 640 kbyte main memory
      10=256 kbit chips (standard)   11=1 Mbit chips
NRB:  number of used banks
          0=one bank, no interleaving  1=two banks

Bank 2/3 Enable Register
DRAM: type of installed DRAM chips
      00=no chips                    01=reserved
      10=256 kbit chips (standard)   11=1 Mbit chips
NRB:  number of used banks
      0=one bank, no interleaving   1=two banks
4-W:  page/interleave mode
      0=2-way interleaving     1=4-way interleaving (standard)
```

Figure 17.24: Bank enable registers (index 06ah, 06ch).

Using the two bank enable registers (Figure 17.24) you specify for the 82C212 which chips are installed, how many banks are used, as well as whether and eventually which type of interleaving is to be carried out. Register programming is usually carried out by the BIOS during the course of the boot precedure according to the configuration information that you have written with the BIOS setup program.

The *DRAM* bits characterize the type of DRAM chips installed. Note that only for bank 1 are 64 kbit chips allowed to exhaust the maximum real mode main memory of 640 kbytes. The *NRB* bit indicates the number of used banks for the bank pair 0/1 or 2/3 concerned. If only one bank is so equipped, then the 82C212 can't carry out interleaving, of course. In the bank-2/3-enable register, the *4-W* bit is additionally available, with which you can choose between 2-way and 4-way interleaving; 4-way interleaving is only possible, however, if all four banks are equipped with identical DRAM chips.

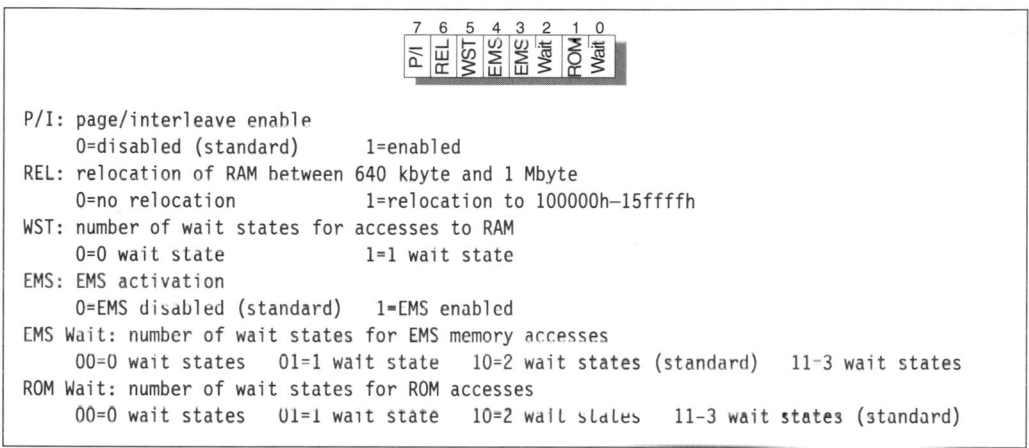

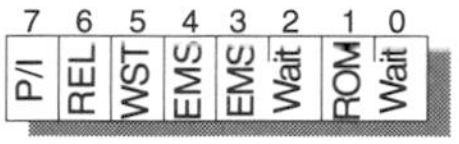


```
P/I: page/interleave enable
     0=disabled (standard)      1=enabled
REL: relocation of RAM between 640 kbyte and 1 Mbyte
     0=no relocation            1=relocation to 100000h-15ffffh
WST: number of wait states for accesses to RAM
     0=0 wait state             1=1 wait state
EMS: EMS activation
     0=EMS disabled (standard)   1=EMS enabled
EMS Wait: number of wait states for EMS memory accesses
     00=0 wait states   01=1 wait state   10=2 wait states (standard)   11=3 wait states
ROM Wait: number of wait states for ROM accesses
     00=0 wait states   01=1 wait state   10=2 wait states   11=3 wait states (standard)
```

Figure 17.25: DRAM configuration register (index 06bh)

The DRAM configuration register (Figure 17.25) controls the management of the installed DRAM memory. With the *P/I* bit you can disable (P/I=0) or enable (P/I=1) the page/interleave mode. The *REL* bit controls the relocation of the RAM between 640 kbytes and 1 Mbyte. If REL is equal to 0, the 82C212 doesn't carry out a relocation, the RAM section is masked off and is only available as shadow RAM. If the main memory only has up to 1 Mbyte, it is better to map the RAM between 640 kbytes and 1 Mbyte onto the address area 1 Mbyte to 1.384 Mbyte. Thus, 384 kbytes of extended memory is available. With the *WST* bit you can control the number of wait states that the 82C212 inserts as standard for an access to RAM.

Instead of extended memory you may also configure the RAM memory above 640 kbyte as either expanded memory or a mixture of extended and expanded memory. As standard the 82C212 manages the memory above 640 kbytes as extended memory if the section between 640 kbytes and 1 Mbyte is not used as shadow RAM. With the *EMS* bit you may also configure the RAM memory or a part of it as expanded memory. The *EMS Wait* bits determine the number of wait states that the CPU then inserts for an access to EMS memory. The *ROM Wait* bits define the number of wait cycles for ROM accesses. As ROM chips are usually much slower than DRAMs, the 82C212 standard value at power-up is three wait states.

Using the EMS base register (Figure 17.26) you can define the base address of the EMS windows. The *EMS Base* bits indicate the address of the first EMS window; all others follow at intervals of 16 kbytes. With the *I/O Base* bits you may determine the I/O base address of the EMS page register. (Details are described below.)

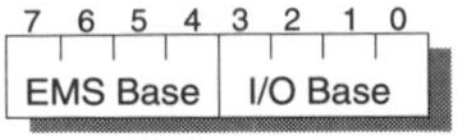


```
EMS Base: base address of EMS window
          0000=0c0000h   0001=0c4000h   0010=0c8000h   0011=0cc000h   0100=0d0000h
          0101=0d4000h   0110=0d8000h   0111=0dc000h   1000=0e0000h   1xxx=reserved
I/O Base: I/O base address of EMS page registers
          0000=0208h/0209h   0001=0218h/0219h   0101=0258h/0259h   0110=0268h/0269h
          1010=02a8h/02a9h   1011=02b8h/02b9h   1110=02e8h/02e9h
```

Figure 17.26: EMS base address register (index 06dh).

The four bit pairs *EMSx* (x=0,1,2,3) determine in which Mbyte the corresponding EMS page x starts (Figure 17.27). Thus, the bit pairs constitute the address bits A22 and A21.

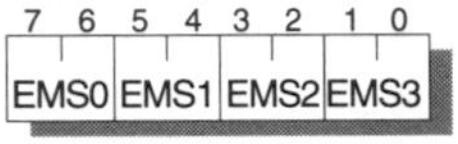


```
EMS0: extension bits for EMS page 0
EMS1: extension bits for EMS page 1
EMS2: extension bits for EMS page 2
EMS3: extension bits for EMS page 3
      00=0 Mbyte to 2 Mbyte (000000h ... 1fffffh) 01=2 Mbyte to 4 Mbyte (200000h ... 3fffffh)
      10=4 Mbyte to 6 Mbyte (400000h ... 5fffffh) 11=6 Mbyte to 8 Mbyte (600000h ... 7fffffh)
```

Figure 17.27: EMS extension register (index 06eh).

The three *EMS Size* bits specify the size of the EMS memory (Figure 17.28). The value 000 applies only to a memory provision of 1 Mbyte if the 384 kbytes above the real mode RAM of 640 kbytes is configured as expanded instead of extended memory. With the *RAS* bit you can activate the 82C212 RAS time-out counter which disables the $\overline{RAS}$ signal after the maximum active time in page mode to issue a $\overline{RAS}$ precharge cycle. The *GA20* bit controls the A20 address line for strict 8086 compatibility. If GA20 is cleared then the A20 address bit is transferred to the GA20 terminal of the 82C212. If, on the other hand, GA20 is set, the GA20 terminal always outputs a value of 0, thus a wrap-around at 1 Mbyte occurs.

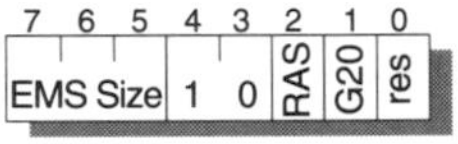


```
EMS Size: size of EMS memory
          000=<1 Mbyte   001=1 Mbyte   010=2 Mbyte   011=3 Mbyte   ...   111=7 Mbyte
RAS: RAS time-out counter for page mode
     0=deactivated (standard)   1=active
G20: GA20 control
     0=A20 transmitted to GA20   1=GA20 always low (standard)
res: reserved (res=0)
```

Figure 17.28: Miscellaneous register (index 06fh).

For the address of the EMS pages in expanded memory only the two bits Px1, Px0 in the EMS extension register (Figure 17.27) have been available up to now. Seven further address bits can be read or written via the EMS page register. Table 17.2 lists the addresses of the EMS page register for the four EMS pages.

Page	Address
0	002x8h/002x9h
1	042x8h/042x9h
2	082x8h/082x9h
3	0c2x8h/0c2x9h

x = 0, 1, 5, 6, a, b, e

Table 17.2: EMS page registers

The value of x and therefore the I/O base address is defined in the EMS base register (Figure 17.26). Table 17.3 lists the assignment of the bits in the EMS page register and the address bits A14–A20. Address bits A21 and A22 are already defined by the EMS extension register. Together, only those nine address bits required to define the address of a 16 kbyte block within 8 Mbytes of expanded memory are available.

Data bit	Meaning
0	A14
1	A15
2	A16
3	A17
4	A18
5	A19
6	A20
7	0 = page disabled 1 = page enabled

Table 17.3: Entries in the EMS page register

If you set data bit 7 in one of the four EMS page registers to 0, the page is disabled and is no longer available for mapping into expanded memory.

Example: `EMS page 1 shall begin at address 05a4000h in expanded memory`

```
OUT 022h, 06eh    ; address EMS extension register via index register
IN al, 023h       ; read old value via data port into accumulator al
AND al, 0c0h      ; clear P11, P10 for page 1, I/O base address at 0208h
OR al, 020h       ; set P11=1, P10=0, because address is between 4 Mbyte and 6 Mbyte
OUT 022h, 06eh    ; address EMS extension register via index register
OUT 023h, al      ; write EMS extension register
OUT 04208h, 0a9h  ; write EMS page register, page 1 enabled
```

17.3 Fast and Expensive – SRAM

In the following sections we shall examine the «racehorse» of memory chips – the SRAM. In the SRAM the information is no longer stored in the form of charges in a capacitor, but held in the state of a so-called flip-flop. Such a flip-flop has two stable states that can be switched by a strong external signal (the word flip-flop itself should tell you what's meant). Figure 17.29 shows the structure of a memory cell in an SRAM.

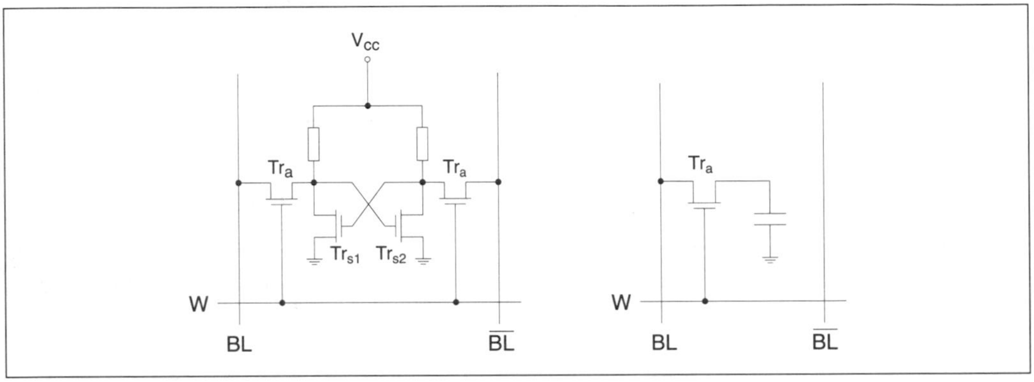

Figure 17.29: SRAM memory cell. The SRAM memory cell (left) generally consists of a flip-flop, the circuit condition of which represents the stored value. In a DRAM memory cell (right), on the other hand, the information is stored in the form of electrical charges in a capacitor.

You can see immediately that the SRAM cell structure is far more complicated than that of a DRAM memory cell, illustrated on the right of Figure 17.29. While the DRAM cell consists only of an access transistor Tr_a and a capacitor holding the charges according to the stored data, in a typical SRAM cell two access transistors Tr_a and a flip-flop with two memory transistors Tr_s as well as two load elements are formed. Thus the integration of the SRAM memory cell is only possible with a much higher technical effort. Therefore, SRAM chips are more expensive, and usually have less storage capacity than DRAM chips. For this reason, SRAMs are mainly used for fast and small cache memories while DRAM chips form the large and slow main memory. High-quality SRAM chips for fast-clocked RISC machines or supercomputers achieve access times of no more than 12 ns. In a PC in most cases chips with access times of 15–25 ns are used, depending on the clock rate and their use as tag or data storage.

17.3.1 The Flip-Flop

Now we turn to the flip-flop to get an understanding of the functioning of an SRAM memory cell. Figure 17.30 shows the structure of a flip-flop.

The flip-flop is also called a *bistable multivibrator* because it can be switched between two stable internal states by external signals. The occurrence of two stable states gives rise to something like hysteresis in the flip-flop's characteristic. The higher the hysteresis the stronger is the stability of the states, and the more powerful the external signal must be to switch the flip-flop.

The simple flip-flop of Figure 17.30 consists of two feedback-coupled NMOS transistors Tr_1 and Tr_2, as well as two load elements R_1 and R_2. Feedback means that the source of Tr_1 is connected to the gate of Tr_2 and vice versa. At all outputs Q and $\overline{Q}$ two stable states may then occur. If Tr_1 is turned on then in the left branch of the flip-flop the overall voltage drops at the resistor R_1 and the output Q is grounded (low). The gate of transistor Tr_2 is therefore also supplied with a low-level voltage. Tr_2 is then turned off, and in the left branch the complete voltage drops at transistor Tr_2. Thus output $\overline{Q}$ is on a high-level of Vcc.

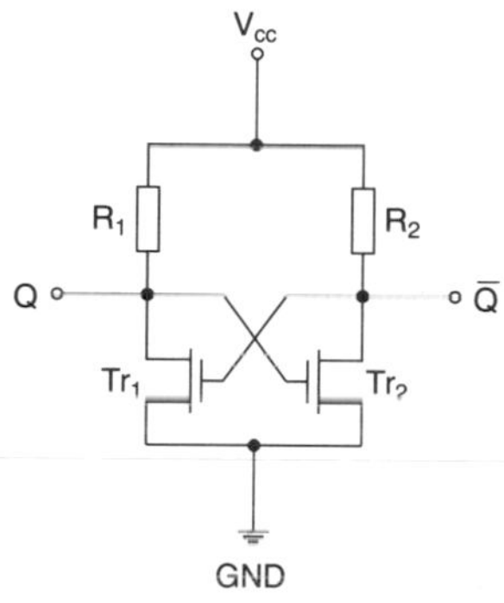

Figure 17.30: The flip-flop comprises two transistors Tr_1, Tr_2 and two load resistors R_1, R_2.

If, on the other hand, Tr_1 is turned off, then the complete voltage in the left flip-flop branch drops at transistor Tr_1 and the output Q is equal to Vcc (high). Therefore, a high voltage is applied to the gate of transistor Tr_2, thus Tr_2 is turned on and in the right branch the complete voltage drops at resistor R_2. The output $\overline{Q}$ is therefore grounded (low).

On the other hand, the outputs Q and $\overline{Q}$ can also be used as inputs to set up the flip-flop state, that is, switching the state of transistors Tr_1 and Tr_2 on and off. The setup of this state is equal to the storing of one bit, because the flip-flop stably supplies, for example, at output $\overline{Q}$ a high- or low-level signal.

The programming of a flip-flop state is briefly explained now with reference to an example. If transistor Tr_1 is switched on then output Q supplies a low-level signal, transistor Tr_2 is turned off, and output $\overline{Q}$ supplies a high-level signal. Every transistor has a certain resistance value even in the on state, that is, the so-called on-state resistance. The flip-flop's load elements R_1 and R_2 have a much higher resistance value than the on-state resistance of transistors Tr_1 and Tr_2. Thus, despite the on-state resistance of Tr_1 and the accompanying voltage drop, the voltage at output Q is small enough to represent a low level and, on the other hand, a voltage is applied to the gate of transistor Tr_2 which turns off Tr_2. If the value of R_1 is, for example, nine times larger than the on-state resistance of Tr_1, then 90% of the voltage Vcc drops at R_1 and only 10% at Tr_1. That's sufficient to keep the output Q at a low level and Tr_2 turned off.

To switch the state, the connection Q (which is simultaneously an output and an input) must be supplied with a signal that is so strong that the transistor turned on is unable to lead this signal to ground completely because of its on-state resistance. Thus a signal is applied to the gate of transistor Tr_2 which gives rise to a slight on-state of Tr_2. Therefore, the voltage at $\overline{Q}$ slightly decreases because of the lower voltage drop at Tr_2. This lower voltage than previously is simultaneously applied to the gate of Tr_1 so that its conductivity is somewhat degraded and the voltage drop at Tr_1 increases. By means of the feedback to the gate of Tr_2, transistor Tr_2 is further turned on and the process works itself up. During the course of this process, transistor Tr_1 turns off and transistor Tr_2 switches through more and more so that the flip-flop finally «flips» (or flops?); thus the name flip-flop. If the signal at input Q is switched off, then the output Q supplies a high-level signal and the complementary output $\overline{Q}$ a low-level signal; the flip-flop state has been altered. In other words: a new bit was written-in or programmed.

For the flip-flop's stability the ratio of the resistance values of the load elements R_1 and R_2 and the on-state resistances of the transistors Tr_1 and Tr_2 are decisive. The higher the load resistances compared to the on-state resistances, the more stable the stored states are. But it is also more difficult, then, to switch the flip-flop states. The flip-flop responds inertly to the programming signal supplied. If the resistance ratio is small then the flip-flop stability is lower. Yet the switching can be carried out more easily and therefore more quickly. The designer of a flip-flop always treads a thin line between stability and operation speed.

If connection Q is supplied with a signal of the same level as it has just output, the new signal has no influence on the flip-flop state. If you write the same value that is already there into a memory cell, then there is, of course, no consequence for the stored value. You can also program a flip-flop by applying a signal to the complementary connection $\overline{Q}$, which is complementary to the bit to program. Thus flip-flops are well suited as storage elements, and they are widely used, for example, in latch circuits, shift registers, etc.

In the simple flip-flop described above a new bit is always stored when the connection Q or $\overline{Q}$ is supplied with an external signal. For the clocked elements in computers this is not very favourable, because at certain times an unpredictable and invalid signal may occur on the signal lines. Therefore, clocked flip-flops are mainly used in computers. They accept the applied bit signals only if the clock signal is valid simultaneously. Such flip-flops have one or more additional access transistors controlled by the clock signal, and which transmit the applied write signal only upon an active clock signal for a store operation by the flip-flop.

Unlike the storage capacitors in DRAM memory cells, the flip-flop cells supply a much stronger data signal as transistors Tr_1 and Tr_2 are already present in the memory cell, which amplify the signal and are thus able to drive the bit lines. In a DRAM cell, however, only the tiny charge of a capacitor is transferred onto the bit line without any amplification, thus the signal is very weak. Accordingly, in a DRAM signal amplification by the sense amplifiers needs more time, and the access time is longer. For addressing memory flip-flops in an SRAM, additional access transistors for the individual flip-flop cells, address decoders, etc. are required, as is the case in a DRAM.

17.3.2 Access to SRAM Memory Cells

In an SRAM the unit memory cells are also arranged in a matrix of rows and columns, which are selected by a row and column decoder, respectively. As is the case for the DRAM, the gates of the access transistors Tr_a are connected to the word line W and the sources are connected to the bit line pair BL, $\overline{BL}$ (Figure 17.30).

If data has to be read from such a memory cell, then the row decoder activates the corresponding word line W. The two access transistors Tr_a turn on and connect the memory flip-flop with the bit line pair BL, $\overline{BL}$. Thus the two outputs Q and $\overline{Q}$ of the flip-flop are connected to the bit lines, and the signals are transmitted to the sense amplifier at the end of the bit line pair. Unlike the DRAM, these two memory transistors Tr_s in the flip-flop provide a very strong signal as they are amplifying elements on their own. The sense amplifier amplifies the potential difference on the bit line pair BL, $\overline{BL}$. Because of the large potential difference, this amplifying process is carried out much faster than in a DRAM (typically within 10 ns or less), so the SRAM chip needs the column address much earlier if the access time is not to be degraded. SRAM chips therefore don't carry out multiplexing of row and column addresses. Instead, the row and column address signals are provided simultaneously. The SRAM divides the address into a row and column part internally only. After stabilization of the data the column decoder selects the corresponding column (that is, the corresponding bit line pair BL, $\overline{BL}$) and outputs a data signal to the data output buffer, and thus to the external circuitry.

The data write proceeds in the opposite way. Via the data input buffer and the column decoder, the write data is applied to the corresponding sense amplifier. At the same time, the row decoder activates a word line W and turns on the access transistors Tr_a. As in the course of data reading, the flip-flop tries to output the stored data onto the bit line pair BL, $\overline{BL}$. However, the sense amplifier is stronger than the storage transistors Tr_s, and supplies the bit lines BL, $\overline{BL}$ with a signal that corresponds to the write data. Therefore, the flip-flop switches according to the new write data, or keeps the already stored value depending upon whether the write data coincides with the stored data or not.

Unlike the DRAM, no lasting RAS/CAS recovery times are necessary. The indicated access time is usually equal to the SRAM's cycle time. Advanced DRAM memory concepts such as page mode, static-column mode or interleaving have no advantages for SRAMs because of the lack of address multiplexing and RAS recovery times. SRAM chips always run in «normal mode», in which both row and column address are supplied.

17.3.3 Typical SRAM – The Intel 51258

The memory controller for SRAM chips is quite simple because row and column addresses are supplied simultaneously. Because of the missing address multiplexing, more pins are required and the SRAM packages are larger than comparable DRAM chips. Further, SRAM chips don't use any high-speed operating modes (for example, page mode or static-column mode). Internal driving of the memory cells is thus easier. Because of the static design memory, a refresh is unnecessary. The state of the memory flip-flops is kept as long as the SRAM chip is supplied with power. This simplifies the peripheral circuitry of the SRAM chips when compared to that of the DRAM chips, and compensates for the disadvantage of the much more complicated memory cell structure, to a certain degree. Nevertheless, the integration density of DRAM chips is about four times larger than that of SRAM chips using the same technology. Figure 17.31 shows the pin assignment of a typical SRAM chip – Intel's 51258.

The 51258 has a storage capacity of 256 kbits with an organization of 64kword*4bit. Thus for addressing, the 64kword 16 address pins A15–A0 are required, because the SRAM doesn't carry out any address multiplexing. The 4-bit data is applied to or delivered by the 51258 via four data pins D3–D0. As is the case for DRAM chips, the further connections $\overline{CS}$ (chip select) and $\overline{WE}$ (write enable) are present to enable the SRAM chip ($\overline{CS}$=low) or to carry out a data write ($\overline{WE}$=low). $\overline{CS}$ instructs the SRAM to accept the supplied address, and to address its memory cell array. $\overline{RAS}$ and $\overline{CAS}$ are missing here, of course, so that $\overline{CS}$ has to carry out this triggering. If the 51258 is to be used for the cache memory of an i386 or i486, then at least eight of these chips must be installed to service the data bus with a width of 32 bits. The storage capacity of this cache memory then has 256 kbytes, sufficient for a medium-sized workstation. Because of the larger number of address pins, SRAM packages are usually much bigger than DRAM chips. Don't be surprised, therefore, if you find real SRAM memory blocks instead of tiny chips in your PC.

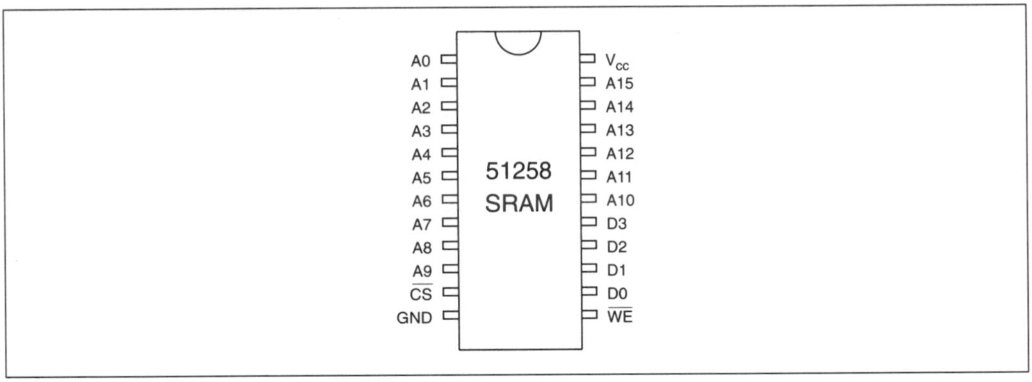

Figure 17.31: Pin assignment of a typical SRAM chip.

17.4 Long-Term Memory – ROM, EPROM and other PROMs

The disadvantage of all the memory elements discussed above is the volatility of the stored data; once switched off they lose their memory. DRAM and SRAM chips are therefore unsuitable for PC startup routines that carry out the boot process. Instead so-called *ROM* chips are employed. The storage data is written once into the ROM in a non-volatile way so that it is held all the time.

17.4.1 ROM

In ROM chips the information is not present in the form of charges, as in DRAMs, or as an alterable circuit state of electronic elements, as in SRAMs, but generally as a fixed wiring state of the elements. Often, switching elements are used that are connected between a word and a bit line, and whose switching state (on, off) is fixed.

«Pure» ROM is very rare today. In these chips the data to be stored has already been taken into account in advance of manufacturing. The data is integrated into the circuit design as either present or missing connections of nodes within the chip's circuitry. A very compact circuit design can thus be achieved, as the circuit can be optimized in view of the information to be stored. This can be carried out only at the expense of flexibility, because the change of only a single bit requires an alteration of the complete circuit.

For this reason, only programmable ROM *(PROM* for short) is used today. In these chips the information needs to be «burnt in» by the user, or at least following the last manufacturing step. In the latter case, the chip is called a *mask ROM* because programming in these ROM chips is carried out by means of a mask. Also, all other layers for gate, source and drain regions of transistors, conductive layers for word and bit lines, etc. are manufactured using such masks. The last mask then contains the connection information according to the data to be stored. Thus the manufacturing steps up until the last masks are the same for all ROMs, and independent of the information to be stored. Different data only needs to be handled by a single different mask. This is a significant advance compared to pure ROM.

Such mask-programmable ROMs are advantageous if a large number of identical ROM chips with the same information are to be manufactured. The main effort is in the design and manufacture of the programming mask; the production of the last layer for the ROM chips is easy. The same applies, for example, to the printing of a book: the most extensive work is in the manufacture of the printing plate. Whether 100 or 10000 copies are to be printed is irrelevant (apart from the paper required).

The main disadvantage of mask-programmed ROMs is that the programming can be carried out only at the manufacturer's site. As you may know, the manufacturing process must be carried out in clean-rooms. The computer shop around the corner, though, which readily programs the newest BIOS version for you, cannot do this. Thus, for ROMs required only in small quantities the electrically programmable ROMs dominate.

17.4.2 EPROM

In an electrically programmable ROM (EPROM) data is written (as the name indicates) in an electrical manner, but unlike DRAMs and SRAMs, this data is stored in a non-volatile fashion. One method for achieving non-volatility is to burn a fusable link between the word and bit line. During programming a much stronger current pulse is supplied than in the future normal operating mode. As in an ordinary fuse, the pulse burns the connection between word and bit line so that they are now disconnected, and the stored value is equal to «0». All non-burned fusable links represent a «1» and data according to the open or closed connections between word and bit line is stored. The generation and supply of such strong pulses can also be carried out by the user with a so-called programmer. The chip has already been mounted in a package and therefore no further manufacturing steps are required. The storage content cannot be altered afterwards, that is, such PROMs are *one time programmable* only and, thus, called *OTPs*.

Another possibility for the non-volatile storage of data is the use of a storage transistor with a so-called *floating gate*. This gate is located between the actual control gate and the substrate, and (unlike the control gate) is not connected to word, bit or other lines; it «floats» (that is, its potential has no defined value). In most cases, control and floating gate consist of the same material, for example polycrystalline silicon, which is a reasonably good conductor. Figure 17.32 is a sectional view through such a storage transistor.

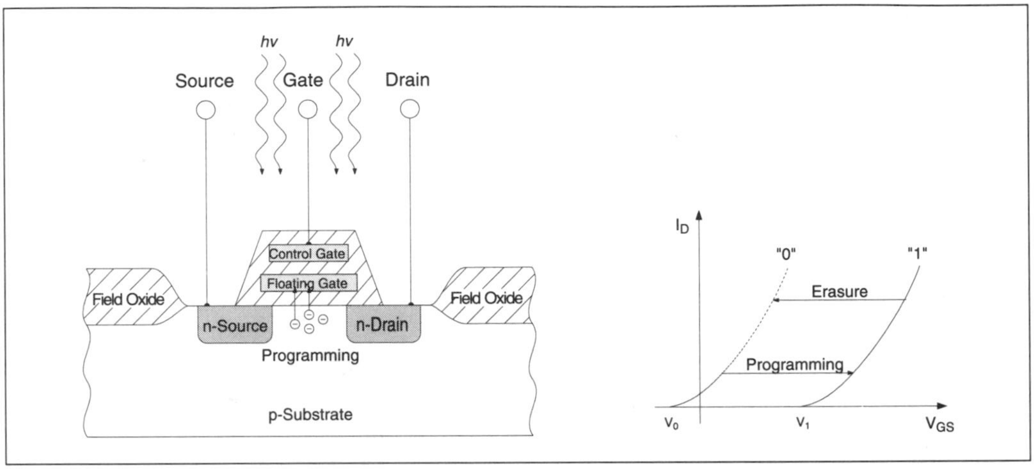

Figure 17.32: Storage transistor with floating gate. The charges in the floating gate determine the stored value.

In memory cells with a storage transistor, the gate is usually connected to a word line, the drain to a bit line, and the source to a reference potential (Vcc, for example). In the above-mentioned ROM chips, the connection between word and bit line was realized by a simple conductor bridge, but now the storage transistor takes over this job. With the word line activated, a normal MOS transistor without a floating gate would always connect the bit line via drain, channel and source to Vcc. Storage of any values is not yet carried out by this, but here the state of the floating gate leaves permanent information on the memory cell. If the floating gate is neutral (that is, no charges are stored), then it has no influence on the electrical field that the control gate generates in the channel region between source and drain. The storage transistor operates as a normal MOS transistor, and applies the reference potential to the bit line as soon as the word line is activated.

The situation changes completely, though, if the floating gate holds electrons, that is, is charged with negative charges. The electric charges in the floating gate shield the field of the control gate and generate an electrical field in the channel region which is opposite to the field of an active control gate (the control gate is supplied with a positive voltage). Thus an activated word line cannot generate a sufficiently strong field with the control gate to turn on the transistors. The bit line is not supplied with the reference potential, and the storage transistor stores the value «0». Only with a much higher control gate potential can the storage transistor be turned on, that is, if the field of the control gate is strong enough to compensate the field of the floating gate, and to make the channel between source and drain conductive. Thus the electric charge in the floating gate shifts the storage transistor's characteristic, and therefore also the threshold voltage, to higher values (Figure 17.32).

Loading the floating gate with electrons can be carried out by a pure electric pulse. As the floating gate is completely embedded in an isolating layer, and has no connection to other elements, the charges are held there for a long time (at least ten years). This long lifetime (and the well-isolated connections to it) is, of course, an obstacle to charging the floating gate. To program a «0» a pulse lasting 50 ms with a voltage of 20 V is applied between word and bit line, that is, between gate and drain. Thus, in the channel region fast (hot) charge carriers (electrons) are generated that have enough energy to pass the isolation region between substrate and floating gate. They accumulate in the floating gate and are held there after the programming pulse has been switched off, as the floating gate is isolated and the electrons do not have enough energy after cooling to get over the isolation layer again. Thus, the isolation layer is impermeable only to low-energy cold electrons. High-energy electrons can penetrate the isolation layer, but without destroying it. This type of storage transistor is also called *FAMOST (floating gate avalanche injection MOS transistor)*.

The programming time of 50 ms is very long compared to the 70 ns of modern DRAMs, or even to the 20 ns of SRAM chips. But with a shorter programming time not enough electrons would be collected in the floating gate to achieve the intended effect. Remedial action might be taken by means of a higher programming voltage, but then there would be the danger of damaging the isolation layer and destroying the chip. For the timing and strength of the write pulses, therefore, a so-called *PROM programmer* is available. This is a small piece of equipment into which you may insert the PROM chips and which carries out the PROM chip programming according to your write data.

You might expect that the floating gate can be discharged and thus the data can be erased by reversing the polarity of the programming pulse. But this is not true, as in this case hot electrons are also generated in the substrate and not in the floating gate. To erase the data the ROM chip must be exposed to UV radiation. The electrons in the floating gate absorb the rays and thus take in energy. They get «hot», and can leave the floating gate in the same way as they previously got in. If the chip package is equipped with a UV-permeable quartz window then we get a so-called *EPROM* (*Erasable PROM*). You may have already seen such chips. Through the quartz window you have a clear view of the actual chip and the bonding wires; other silicon chips are usually hidden in black or brown packages. After irradiating for about 20 minutes, all charge carriers are removed from the floating gate and the EPROM chip can be programmed again.

17.4.3 EEPROM

A quartz glass window and a UV lamp for clearing data are extensive (and also expensive) equipment for erasing EPROM chips. It would better and much easier if the chip could be cleared in the same way as it was programmed, by means of an electrical pulse. Fortunately, memory chip techniques have made considerable progress during the past few years, and now supply inexpensive *EEPROMs* (*electrically erasable PROM*) as well. Figure 17.33 shows a sectional view through the storage transistor of such an EEPROM.

Loading the floating gate with electrons (that is, the programming of the memory cell) is carried out in the same way as in an EPROM: by means of a relatively long (50 ms) voltage pulse of

+20 V between gate and drain high-energy charge, carriers are generated in the substrate which penetrate the gate oxide and accumulate in the floating gate. The positive potential of +20 V during programming «draws up» the negative electrons from the substrate into the floating gate. To clear the EEPROM the thin tunnel oxide film between a region of the floating gate extending downwards in direction to the substrate and the drain is important. Because of basic physical laws, isolation layers are never isolated perfectly. Instead, charge carriers can penetrate the isolation layer (with a low probability). The probability gets higher the less the thickness of the isolation layer and the higher the voltage between the two electrodes on the two sides of the layer.

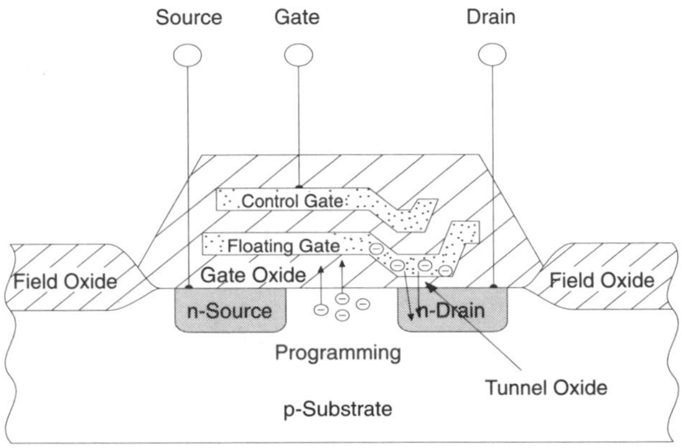

Figure 17.33: EEPROM storage transistor. In an EEPROM the charges in the floating gate can be removed by means of an electrical pulse.

For discharging the floating gate an inverse voltage is applied between gate and drain, that is, the drain is on a potential of +20 V against the gate. Thus the negative electrons in the floating gate are drawn to the drain through the thin tunnel oxide, and the stored data is thus erased. It is important to ensure that this charge drawing does not last too long, as otherwise too many electrons are drawn out of the floating gate and the gate is then charged positively. The transistor's characteristic is thus shifted to the left too much, and the threshold voltage is lowered too far, so that normal operation of the storage transistor becomes impossible.

A word about the storage capacities and access times of ROM chips. Because of the enormous advance in integrating electronic circuits, ROM chips with a capacity of 1 Mbit are not unusual today. On modern motherboards you will usually see only a single EPROM or EEPROM chip. The access times are between 120 ns and 250 ns in most cases, and thus are much longer than those of DRAMs or even SRAMs. You should move frequently used BIOS routines held in ROM into the faster RAM by shadowing if your PC can do this. Only the POST and boot routines must be held in ROM, as they initialize and boot the PC. The BIOS routines are needed later for supporting the operating system and application programs, therefore they may also be loaded externally, for example from a floppy disk. OS/2 currently follows this procedure. As most BIOS variants in the PC are only suited for operation in real mode, but OS/2 (except for its loading routines) runs in protected mode, all the BIOS routines in ROM are unusable. Only the advanced BIOS of some PS/2 models accommodates a protected mode BIOS. For PCs without advanced BIOS, all BIOS routines for protected mode must therefore be loaded from disk. The OS/2 that is currently freely available on the market strictly (100%) orients to IBM hardware; one reason why OS/2 has more compatibility problems than DOS.

17.5 Silicon Hard Disks – Flash Memories

In the past few years a new type of non-volatile memory has come onto the market, frequently used in small portable computers as a substitute for floppy and hard disk drives – so-called flash memories. The structure of their memory cells is fundamentally the same as that of EEPROMs (Figure 17.33); only the tunnel oxide is thinner than in an EEPROM memory cell. Therefore, they need an erase and programming voltage of only 12 V so that 10000 program and erase cycles can be carried out without any problems. Despite the memory cell array, several additional control circuits and registers are formed in a flash memory, and the program and erase operations are carried out in a somewhat different way. Flash memories may thus be programmed nearly as flexibly as DRAMs or SRAMs, while they don't lose the data held. Figure 17.34 shows a block diagram of the internal flash memory structure.

The central part of the flash memory is the memory cell array, which comprises FAMOST memory cells as described in Section 17.4. The cells are addressed by an address buffer, which accepts the address signals and transfers them to the row and column decoders, respectively. Flash memories, like SRAM chips, don't carry out address multiplexing. The row and column decoders select one word line and one or more bit line pairs as in a conventional memory chip. The read data is externally output via a data input/output buffer or written into the addressed memory cell by this buffer via an I/O gate.

It is important that the read process is carried out with the usual MOS voltage of 5 V, but for programming and erasing the memory cells a higher voltage V_{pp} of 12 V is required. To program a memory cell the flash control applies a short voltage pulse of typically 10 μs and 12 V. This leads to an avalanche breakthrough in the memory transistor, which loads the floating gate. A 1 Mbit flash memory can be programmed within about 2 s, but unlike the conventional EEPROM, erasure is carried out chip by chip. In a erasure process the flash control applies an erasure pulse to the whole memory cell array by the erasure voltage switch, so that all memory cells are erased. For an EEPROM the EEPROM programmer, on the other hand, carries out erasure cell by cell. The erase time for the whole flash memory is about 1 s. There are also variants of this memory available that can be erased page by page, that is, one complete row of memory cells is always erased. Moreover, some flash memories generate the programming and erasing voltage internally. A boosting circuitry boosts the normal operation voltage of 5 V through charge pumping up to 12 V. The programming and erasing rate of these flash memories is limited by the boosting performance of that circuitry; thus, usually lower than the rate of flash memories with an external programming and erasing voltage. As some compensation, they do not require a second supply voltage.

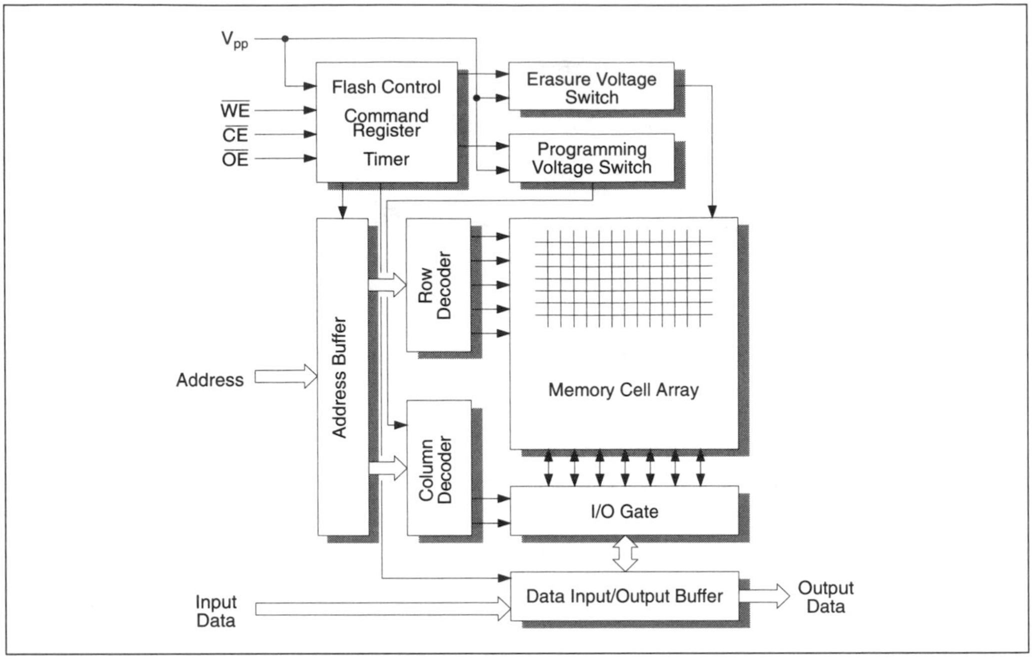

Figure 17.34: Block diagram of a flash memory.

The read, program and erase processes are controlled by means of 2-byte instructions, which the external microprocessor writes to the instruction register of the flash control. Also, for this the high voltage V_{pp} of 12 V is necessary. For a typical flash memory the following instructions are available:

- Read memory: the flash memory supplies data via the data pins.
- Read identifier code: the flash memory supplies a code at the data pins, which indicates the type and version of the chip.
- Setup erase/erase: prepares the flash memory for an erase process and carries out the erasure.
- Erase-verify: erases all memory cells and verifies this process.
- Setup program/program: prepares the programming of individual memory cells and carries out this process.
- Program-verify: executes the programming and verifies this process.
- Reset: resets the flash memory to a defined initial state.

Thus flash memories have a more extensive functionality than normal EEPROMs, and are a virtually autonomous memory subsystem. For example, unlike conventional EEPROMs they can be programmed and erased while installed in the computer. Some models even generate the high voltage V_{pp} from the supply voltage of 5 V internally. With an EEPROM you need dedicated peripheral equipment (the EEPROM programmer), and the chips must be removed from the computer in advance of programming or erasure. The so-called *flash BIOS* makes use of that. With ordinary ROM chips these must be removed for a BIOS update, and replaced by new ones (PROM and EPROM), or they must be reprogrammed with the new BIOS data in an external programmer (EEPROM). With a flash BIOS this is far easier: you simply start the necessary software, and the flash EPROM is internally erased by an erase or erase-verify command. Afterwards, the setup software transfers the new BIOS bytes (data and code) to the flash chip and writes them with a program or program-verify command into the flash memory.

Flash memories are mainly used as a substitute for floppy and low-capacity hard disk drives in portable computers, but also for a variety of chip cards. Because of advances in integrating electronic elements, the chips are very small and have a very low power consumption. In the non-selected state the flash chip enters a standby mode where the power consumption is again drastically reduced. Hard disks, on the other hand, require relatively large, «current-eating» electric motors to rotate the storage medium and the head actuator. *Solid state hard disks* on a base of flash memories are therefore more favourable, in terms of power consumption as well as cost, up to a size of several Mbytes. You will find them mainly as so-called *memory cards*. Compared with battery-buffered SRAM solutions, their inherent non-volatility is a big advantage. There is no battery to fail and cause a data loss. The storage time of information in a flash memory is at least ten years, and typically 100 years. Over this time period, hard disks or floppies will become demagnetized.

Flash memories are mainly used in fields where a power failure would give rise to disastrous consequences, or where the operating conditions are very rough. Hard disk drives are very sensitive to shocks and floppies to mechanical damage or humidity. Flash memories, sealed in a stable package with no mechanical movable parts, are immune to such external influences. Table 17.4 compares some values for ordinary hard disks and mass storages based on flash memories.

	Hard disk	**Flash memory**
Access time	24 ms	0 ms
Track-track-positioning	5 ms	0 ms
Data transfer rate	1 Mbyte/s	16 Mbytes/s
Writing a 10 kbyte block	46 ms	0.6 ms

Table 17.4: Hard disks and flash memories

You can see that inertia as well as transfer rate are far better for a flash memory. However, one disadvantage for its use as mass storage is that flash memories can usually only be erased chip by chip or page by page. This may give rise to problems if, for example, one sector of a file or a directory entry is to be updated. The driver for mass storages on a flash memory base must take this into account.

Figure 17.35 shows the pin assignment of a typical flash memory, the Intel 28F010, with a storage capacity of 128kword*8bit (1 Mbit in all). It has an access time of 120 ns, and is therefore as fast as older DRAM chips.

The chip comes in the familiar DIP or PLCC packages, but you may also find a special occupation-area-saving version in a *TSOP* (*thin small outline package*), which is only 1.2 mm thick. Small and handy memory cards can thus be constructed. Most pins and signals are self-evident; the following only presents the most important ones.

A0–A16 (I)
Pins 2–12, 23, 25–29 (DIP, PLCC)
Pins 1–5, 10–20, 31 (TSOP)

These 17 pins are supplied with the address for accessing the 128 k words. No address multiplexing is carried out.

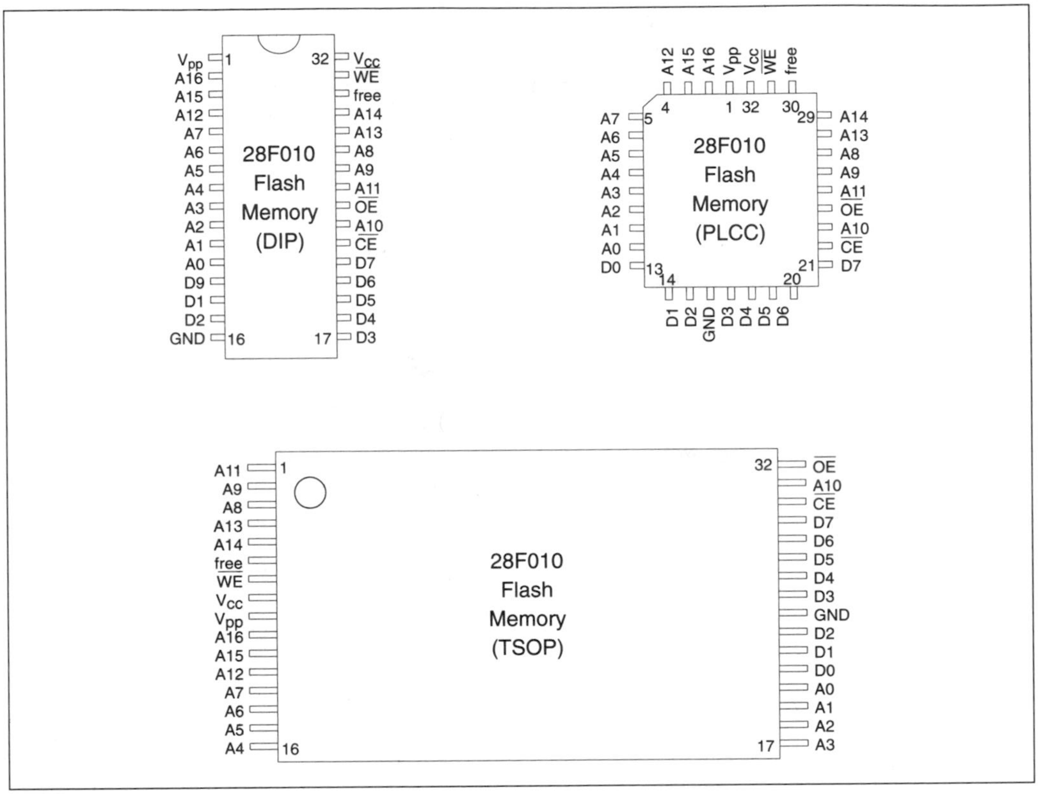

Figure 17.35: The 28F010 flash memory.

$\overline{\text{CE}}$ (I)
Pin 22 (DIP, PLCC)
Pin 30 (TSOP)

If the signal at this chip enable pin is high, the flash chip is activated and leaves the standby mode.

D0–D7 (I/O)
Pins 13–15, 17–21 (DIP, PLCC)
Pins 21–23, 25–29 (TSOP)

These pins supply the read data or accept the data for programming.

$\overline{OE}$ (I)
Pin 24 (DIP, PLCC)
Pin 32 (TSOP)

If the output enable signal $\overline{OE}$ is low the chip outputs data.

$\overline{WE}$ (I)
Pin 31 (DIP, PLCC)
Pin 7 (TSOP)

If the write enable signal at $\overline{WE}$ is on a low level, commands can be written into the instruction register and the memory cells.

V_{PP} (I)
Pin 1 (DIP, PLCC)
Pin 9 (TSOP)

This pin is supplied with the erase and program voltage (12 V) for writing the instruction register, for erasing the complete memory cell array, or for programming individual bytes in the memory cell array.

Part 3
Personal Computer Architectures and Bus Systems

The two components discussed so far, microprocessor and memory, are not yet enough to build a complete computer. These components are the heart and brain of the machines but some more «organs» (to continue the biological theme) are still necessary. Their number, tasks and connections are the actual implementation of a *computer architecture*. For example, drives and the graphics adapter must be accessed, and the interrupts issued by them should be handled accordingly by the processor–memory system. A major – and for the enormously successful IBM-compatible Personal Computer, decisive – property is the very flexible bus system with the expansion bus (or slot). The simple installation of a variety of LAN, graphics and other adapters is only then possible. For that reason, Part 3 is dedicated to the structure (and architecture) of the various «classes» of Personal Computers and their accompanying bus systems.

You can, of course, combine the chips described earlier, and those described later, and construct a robot or a laser printer controller, for example; one advantage of microprocessors is their flexibility. You may also meet the chips described in this book in other products, such as in your washing machine or in an aeroplane. But let us now turn to the actual architecture of the PC/XT.

18 The 8-Bit PC/XT Architecture

The PC/XT was the first IBM Personal Computer. For today's demands it would not be sufficient even for simple computer games; its 8-bit architecture is far out-dated. Nevertheless, many components have survived from the PC/XT decade up to the i486 and Pentium machines, for example, the 8237A DMA chips or the PIC 8259A. Their logical structure still determines the behaviour of the most advanced chip set. I will discuss the PC/XT structure mainly for reasons of completeness.

18.1 The Components and their Cooperation

Figure 18.1 shows a block diagram of a PC/XT. If you have looked in vain for the chip names indicated in the figure on your motherboard, this doesn't mean that you didn't buy a PC! Instead, the chips will have been provided by a third-party manufacturer, or the functions of several chips integrated into a single chip. But the functional construction, and therefore the architecture, remains the same. Therefore, I only want to describe the basic configuration.

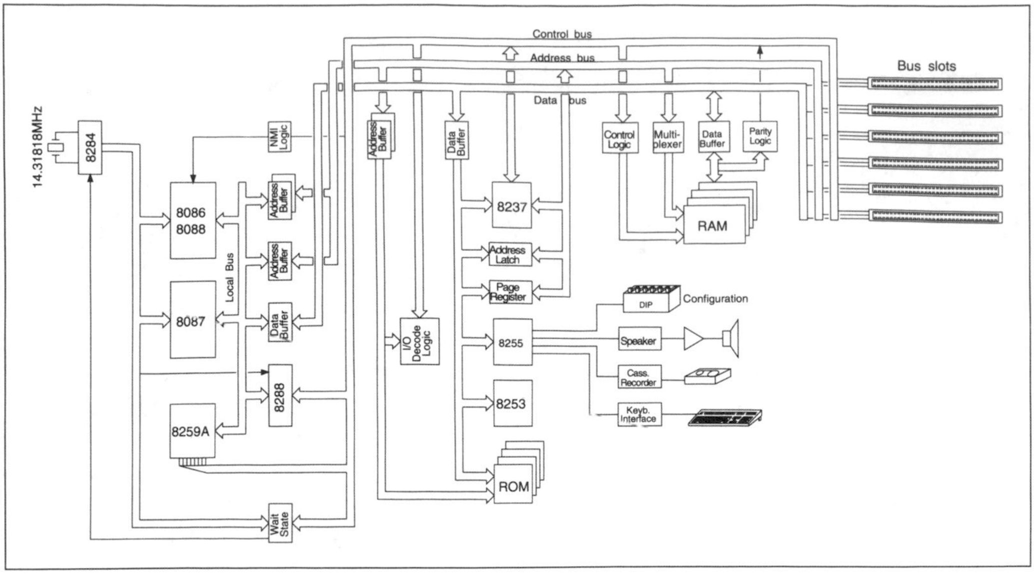

Figure 18.1: The PC/XT architecture.

The central part is of course the processor. In a PC you will find an 8088 and in an XT the 8086. For a short time, an XT/286 was also on the market with the newer and more powerful 80286, but it did not have any other modification. This XT/286 was soon replaced by the more powerful and modern AT.

In addition to the 8086/88, a mathematical 8087 coprocessor can be installed, or at least a socket for it may be present on the motherboard. An 8284 clock generator generates the system clock, and in the first PC was supplied with a crystal signal of 14318180 Hz. The 8284 divides this frequency by three to generate the effective system clock of 4.77 MHz. In more modern turbo-PC/XTs an oscillator with a higher frequency is present, which enables a system clock of 8 MHz or even 10 MHz. Further, an NEC CPU called V30 or V20 may be present instead of the 8086/88. The V30 and V20 are faster and have a slightly extended instruction set compared to the 8086/88, but are entirely downwards compatible with the Intel CPUs. The enhanced instruction set is of no use in a PC, as it can't be used for compatibility reasons.

A further essential component of the computer is the main memory. The processor is connected to it via the data, address and control buses. The CPU addresses the memory by means of the address bus, controls the data transfer with the control bus, and transfers the data via the data bus. The necessary control signals are generated by the 8288 bus controller according to instructions from the 8086/88. In order to carry out data exchange in as error-free and orderly a way as possible, the signals are buffered and amplified in various address and data buffer circuits.

In the PC/XT four different address buses can be distinguished:

- local address bus: comprises the 20 address signals from the 8086/88. External address buffers and address latches separate the local bus from the system address bus.

- system address bus: this is the main PC/XT address bus and represents the latched version of the local address bus. The signal for latching the address signals on the local address bus into the latches for the system address bus is ALE. In the PC/XT the system address bus leads to the bus slots.
- memory address bus: this is only implemented on the motherboard, and represents the multiplexed version of the system address bus. Via the memory address bus, the row and column addresses are successively applied to the DRAM chips (see Chapter 17).
- X-address bus: this is separated from the system bus by buffers and drivers, and serves to address the I/O units and the ROM BIOS on the motherboard. These may, for example, be the registers of the interrupt controller, the timer or an on-board floppy controller. I/O ports and BIOS extensions on expansion adapters are accessed by the system address bus.

Besides the four address buses there are four different data buses:

- local data bus: comprises the 16 or eight data signals from the 8086/88. Additionally, a bus logic is necessary to distinguish byte and word accesses. External data buffers and data latches separate the local data bus from the system data bus. In the PC the local data bus is eight bits wide, and in the XT it is 16 bits wide.
- system data bus: is the latched version of the local data bus in the PC/XT, and has eight bits in the PC and 16 bits in the XT. One byte of the system data bus leads to the bus slots.
- memory data bus: this is only present on the motherboard, and establishes the connection between main memory and the system data bus. In the PC the memory data bus is eight bits wide, and in the XT it is 16 bits wide.
- X-data bus: this is separated from the system bus by buffers and drivers and accesses I/O units and the ROM BIOS on the motherboard. I/O ports and BIOS extensions on expansion adapters are accessed by the system data bus.

As already mentioned, the difference between the 8086 and the 8088 is the different width of their data buses. The 8086 has a 16-bit data bus, but the 8088 only has an 8-bit one. Therefore, in the PC the data bus on the motherboard for an access to main memory is only eight bits wide, but in an XT it is 16 bits wide. Besides the main memory on the motherboard, the CPU can also access chips on the adapter cards in the bus slots. A more detailed explanation of the structure and functioning of the bus slots is given below. Here, I only want to mention that all essential signals of the system bus lead to the bus slots, for example address, data and certain control signals necessary to integrate the adapter cards into the PC system.

In this respect, it is also important that in an XT the data bus is guided into the bus slots with only eight bits. In a 16-bit access via the complete 16-bit data bus of the 8086, an 8/16-converter must carry out the separation of one 16-bit quantity into two 8-bit quantities, or has to combine two 8-bit quantities into one 16-bit quantity. On the XT motherboard this is not necessary. The memory access is always carried out with the full width of 16 bits. On an XT this has, of course, enormous consequences for accesses to on-board memory on the one hand and to memory on an adapter card which is located in one of the bus slots on the other. Because of the limited 8-bit width for accesses to memory on the adapter card, less data is transferred each time. Thus, the data transfer rate is smaller. If 16-bit values are to be transferred then these values must be separated into two 8-bit values, or they must be combined from them. This takes some time, and the access time for accessing the memory expansion adapter card increases further compared to the on-board memory. This is especially noticeable on a turbo XT. The ancestor PC only ran at 4.77 MHz; with this clock rate the bus slots and inserted adapter cards don't have any problem in following the clock, but with the 10 MHz turbo clock this is not the case. In most cases, the slow bus slots are run at only half the turbo clock speed, that is, 5 MHz. An access to expansion memory on the adapter card is therefore slower in two ways: the 8/16-bit conversion lasts one bus cycle, and halving the bus frequency decreases the transfer rate further. Therefore, you should always choose to expand the on-board memory as long as the motherboard can accommodate additional memory chips. That is especially true for fast-clocked i386 and i486 computers. Even in these PCs, the bus slots run at 8 MHz at most. What a shock for the proud owners of a 50 MHz computer! Some PCs have a dedicated memory slot besides the normal bus slots. Special memory adapter cards may be inserted into these memory slots to run at a higher frequency than the bus slots.

To decode the processor's addresses in a memory access, the PC/XT includes an address multiplexer. Together with the memory buffer, it drives the memory chips on the motherboard. The check logic for memory parity issues an NMI if the data doesn't conform to the additionally held parity bit at the time of data reading. The parity check is carried out on a byte basis, that is, each individually addressable byte in main memory is assigned a parity bit. When you extend your storage, therefore, you not only have to insert the «actual» memory chips, but also an additional chip for every eight memory chips. This 9th chip holds the corresponding parity bits. Generally, the memory is divided into *banks* which must always be completely filled. How many chips correspond to a bank depends on the number of data pins that one chip has for outputting or inputting data.

The older 64 kbit or 256 kbit chips usually have only one data pin. If memory is organized in eight bits, as is the case for a PC (that is, if it has an 8-bit data bus), then one bank is usually made up of eight memory chips plus one chip for parity. The reason is that in a read or write access, one byte is always transferred at a time, and therefore eight data connections are necessary. With a 16-bit organization, 18 chips (16 data chips plus two parity chips) are required. If you don't fill a bank completely then the address multiplexer accesses «nothing» for one or more bits, and the PC unavoidably crashes. However, do not mix these «expansion banks» with the banks of an interleaved memory organization. Because of the low PC/XT clock rates, an interleaved access to the main memory is unnecessary. Modern DRAMs can handle 10 MHz without any problem; the banks need not be interleaved. An expansion bank only determines the smallest unit by which you may expand the memory.

The PC/XT also has a ROM, where code and data for the boot-up process and the PC's BIOS routines are stored. The 8086/88 accesses the BIOS in ROM in the same way as it does with main memory. Wait cycles during an access to main memory, ROM or the I/O address space are generated by the wait state logic.

For supporting CPU and peripherals an 8259A Programmable Interrupt Controller (PIC) is present in the PC/XT. It manages external hardware interrupts from peripherals such as the hard disk controller or timer chip. The 8259A has eight input channels connected to a chip, each of which may issue an interrupt request. In the PC these channels are called IRQ0–IRQ7. Table 18.1 shows the assignment of interrupt channel IRQx and the corresponding peripheral or support chip. How the 8259A works and how you may program it is explained in Chapter 23.

Channel	Interrupt	Used by
NMI	02h	parity, 8087 fault
IRQ0	08h	channel 0 of timer 8253
IRQ1	09h	keyboard
IRQ2	0ah	reserved
IRQ3	0bh	COM2
IRQ4	0ch	COM1
IRQ5	0dh	hard disk controller
IRQ6	0eh	floppy disk controller
IRQ7	0fh	LPT1

Table 18.1: Hardware interrupt channels

Another support chip is also present, the 8253 programmable interval timer (PIT) (or timer chip). It has three individually programmable counters in all (see Table 18.2). Counter 0 is used in the PC/XT to update the internal system clock periodically. For this purpose, this counter is connected to IRQ0 of the PIC. The hardware interrupt issued in this way updates the internal clock. This clock may be read or written using the DOS commands TIME and DATE. Counter 1 together with the DMA chip carries out the memory refresh, and counter 2 generates a tone frequency for the speaker. In Chapter 24, details on the operation modes and programming of the PIT 8253 and speaker are given.

Channel	Used by
0	internal system clock (IRQ0)
1	memory refresh
2	speaker frequency

Table 18.2: PC/XT timer channel

The keyboard is connected to the PC/XT's system bus by an 8255 programmable peripheral interface (PPI) (see Section 26.2). With the same chip, the BIOS can check the system configuration, which is set by DIP switches. But newer turbo XTs, like the AT, have a real-time clock and a CMOS RAM, which holds all necessary configuration data. Thus, DIP switches are no longer necessary. However, the PC/XT accesses the keyboard through the 8255. Also connected to the PPI are the speaker and the cassette logic for driving the cassette drive. Using the 8255, the speaker is either enabled or disconnected (the cassette drive is only of historical importance today).

The whole PC is powered by a power supply that outputs voltages of –12 V, –5 V, 0 V, +5 V and +12 V. The adapter cards in the bus slots are usually powered by corresponding contacts in the bus slots. Only «current eaters», for example FileCards with integrated hard disk drives, must be directly connected to the power supply.

As hardware components, the support chips mentioned above are accessed via ports in the I/O address space. Thus, the PC/XT uses *I/O mapped input/output (I/O)*. Table 18.3 shows the port addresses of the most important hardware components in the PC/XT.

Port address	Used by
000h–00fh	DMA chip 8237A
020h–021h	PIC 8259A
040h–043h	PIT 8253
060h–063h	PPI 8255
080h–083h	DMA page register
0a0h–0afh	NMI mask register
0c0h–0cfh	reserved
0e0h–0efh	reserved
100h–1ffh	unused
200h–20fh	game adapter
210h–217h	extension unit
220h–24fh	reserved
278h–27fh	parallel printer
2f0h–2f7h	reserved
2f8h–2ffh	COM2
300h–31fh	prototype adapter
320h–32fh	hard disk controller
378h–37fh	parallel interface
380h–38fh	SDLC adapter
3a0h–3afh	reserved
3b0h–3bfh	monochrome adapter/parallel interface
3c0h–3cfh	EGA
3d0h–3dfh	CGA
3e0h–3e7h	reserved
3f0h–3f7h	floppy disk controller
3f8h–3ffh	COM1

Table 18.3: PC/XT port addresses

The registers of hardware components on adapter cards that are inserted into the bus slots (for example, the UART on the serial interface adapter or the 6845 on the graphics adapter) are also accessed via port addresses. The PC/XT hands over all accesses to the I/O address space to the bus slots in the same way as for accesses to memory on adapter cards. Note that any address, no matter whether in the memory or I/O address space, may only be assigned a single component. If you assign the same I/O address to, for example, the UART registers of COM1 and COM2, the chips disturb each other because they respond to the CPU's instructions (nearly) at the same time. Thus the interfaces don't work at all, or at least not correctly.

18.2 DMA Architecture

To complete the picture, I will explain in advance the DMA architecture of the PC/XT (the pins and signals of the 8237A, as well as the terms «page register», etc. are detailed in Chapter 25).

Besides the processor, there is another chip able to carry out memory and I/O accesses: the 8237A DMA chip. It enables fast data transfer between main memory and I/O units such as the floppy controller. Unlike the 8086/88, the 8237A cannot process data but only transfer it (at high speed). The 8237A has four separately programmable transfer channels, used as indicated in Table 18.4.

Channel	Used by
0	memory refresh
1	SDLC adapter
2	floppy disk controller
3	hard disk controller

Table 18.4: PC/XT DMA channels

Channel 0 is reserved for memory refresh, and is activated periodically by the 8253A PIT to carry out a dummy access to memory. The memory chips are thus refreshed. The remaining three channels are available for data transfer. If, for example, the hard disk controller has read one sector then it activates channel 3 of the 8237A and hands the data transfer over to it without any intervention from the CPU. Besides the 8086/88 CPU, the 8237A is another, independent chip for carrying out bus cycles; thus it is a *busmaster* – but with a limited function. The function, programming and transfer protocol of the DMA chip are described in Chapter 25. The CPU and DMA chip are located on the motherboard. The PC/XT bus doesn't support external busmasters that may be located on an adapter card in a bus slot. It would be useful, for example, if the processor of a network adapter could access the main memory independently and without intervention from the motherboard's CPU to deliver data to the network, or to transfer data from the network into main memory. But in a PC/XT (and also in an AT), the adapter must issue a hardware interrupt to indicate the required data transfer to the CPU. Then the CPU carries out this transfer. With the advent of EISA and the microchannel, though, busmasters may be located on an external adapter card. They are then able to control the EISA bus or the microchannel on their own.

18.2.1 8-Bit Channels

From Table 18.4 it is apparent that the 8237A mainly serves for a data transfer between main memory and an I/O device in a bus slot. As the PC/XT slots only encompass eight bits, only an 8-bit transfer takes place – the PC/XT has only 8-bit DMA channels.

Because of the 8088 processor the PC has only an 8-bit data bus and a 20-bit address bus, thus a DMA page register with a width of only four bits is required in the PC (their I/O addresses are listed in Table 18.5). The eight address bits from the 8237A plus eight address bits from the DMA address latch plus four bits from the page register together form a 20-bit address for the PC/XT address space. As an 8-bit chip, the 8237A is perfectly designed for the 8088. Because of the 8-bit data bus only 8-bit DMA channels are possible. During the course of a read transfer the 8237A provides the memory address and activates the $\overline{MEMR}$ signal to read a data byte from memory onto the 8-bit data bus. Afterwards, it enables the $\overline{IOW}$ signal so the peripheral can accept the data byte. A write transfer proceeds in exactly the opposite direction: the 8237A outputs the memory address and activates the $\overline{IOR}$ signal to read out a data byte from the peripheral's I/O register onto the 8-bit data bus. Afterwards, it enables the $\overline{MEMW}$ signal so that the memory can fetch the data byte.

Port	Page register
87h	channel 0
83h	channel 1*)
81h	channel 2
82h	channel 3

*) simultaneously channel 0

Table 18.5: I/O addresses of the PC/XT page registers

Note that in the PC/XT, channels 0 and 1 are assigned the same physical page register. You access the same physical page register through the two different I/O addresses 87h and 83h. In the AT, the page register for channel 4 – which serves only for cascading – holds the page address for the memory refresh.

On the XT the situation becomes more ponderous and complex. Because of the 8086 the XT has a 16-bit data bus internally. As is the case on the PC, the only DMA chip present is designed for 8-bit channels to 8-bit peripherals. Only 8-bit devices can be installed into the XT bus slot anyway, as the data bus only leads into them with 8 bits. But because of the 16-bit data bus of the 8086, memory is organized as 16-bit storage. This means that on the low-order data bus byte D0–D7 only data bytes with an even address (and on the high-order data bus byte D8–D15 only data bytes with an odd address) appear.

If the 8237A continuously counts up or down the source address during the course of a read transfer, the intended data byte appears on memory bus lines D0–D7 if an even address is supplied, and on lines D8–D15 if an odd address is output. Thus, an additional logic is required to transfer the data byte with an odd address onto data bus lines D0–D7 so that an 8-bit peripheral with an even I/O address can fetch it. At the same time, the memory only outputs the data byte with an odd address without driving the lines D0–D7. In the same way as for a peripheral with an odd I/O address, an additional logic is required to transfer the data byte with an even address onto lines D8–D15, so that the 8-bit peripheral can actually fetch it. A similar problem arises with the 8086 if it attempts to read a date byte with an odd address from or write a date byte with an odd address to the memory. The 8086 manages this by means of the control signal $\overline{BHE}$ which, together with the least significant address bit A0, disables the upper or lower half of the data bus.

The 8237A, on the other hand, continuously increments or decrements the target address in memory during the course of a write transfer, and the data byte from the 8-bit peripheral always appears on the same data bus bits. With an even target address the data byte needs to appear on the low-order part D0–D7 of the memory bus; with an odd address, however, it appears on the high-order part D8–D15 of the memory bus so that the memory can write the data byte upon activation of the $\overline{MEMW}$ signal to the memory location intended.

18.2.2 Memory Refresh

Channel 0 is dedicated to memory refresh. For refresh purposes, counter 1 of the 8253/8254 PIT operates in mode 3 (square-wave generator) with a count value 18 (12h). Only the low-order counter byte is loaded (RW1=0, RW0=1), that is, the PIT generates a square wave with a frequency of 1.19318 MHz/18=66288 Hz. Counter 1 therefore issues a DREQ every 15 μs for a dummy transfer, which refreshes the DRAMs. Channel 0 of the 8237A is programmed in single transfer mode with a read transfer for this purpose. During the course of the dummy cycle, the DMA chip reads data from the memory onto the data bus, whereby the address buffers, address decoders and sense amplifiers in the memory chips are enabled. This automatically leads to the refresh of one memory cell row. But the data is not fetched by a peripheral, as no device has issued a DREQ0 and would be able to respond to $\overline{\text{DACK0}}$, $\overline{\text{MEMR}}$ and $\overline{\text{IOW}}$. The data therefore disappears upon the next bus cycle. Because all these control signals lead into the bus slots and are thus also available for the adapter cards, the dummy cycle may also refresh the memory on expansion adapters (for example, graphics adapters). Only adapters with their own refresh logic generate refresh cycles on their own.

The PIT defines the refresh time by means of the periodic square-wave signal. The DMA chip is used to generate the refresh address and the control signals for reading the main memory. The startup routine of the BIOS usually loads the count register with a suitable count value, and sets channel 0 to single transfer mode and autoinitialization. Thus every request via channel 1 of the PIT issues exactly one transfer, increments the refresh address, and decrements the count register. If the count register reaches the value ffffh, then a TC occurs and channel 0 of the DMA controller is automatically initialized. The refresh process starts from the beginning again.

18.2.3 Memory–Memory Transfer

On each of the channels a page register is allocated. IBM, though, has implemented a common page register for channels 0 and 1 in the PC/XT. Therefore, memory–memory transfer is only possible within a single DMA page of 64 kbytes, as only channels 0 and 1 can carry out this transfer and have to share one register on the PC/XT. Note that channel 0 is further occupied by the memory refresh. Before you issue a memory–memory transfer within the 64 kbyte page you must, therefore, disable the memory refresh. And don't forget to reprogram channel 0 after the transfer for the refresh again. Additionally, the refresh may only be interrupted for a short time period (less than 1 ms) by the memory–memory transfer, because otherwise the DRAM «forgets» data. Summarized, these are all requirements that make the memory–memory transfer through the 8237A quite inconvenient.

18.3 I/O Channel and Bus Slots

Most of the PC/XT system bus leads into the bus slots, all of which have the same structure. Theoretically, it doesn't matter into which slot you insert your brand-new adapter card, but in practice some adjoining adapter cards may disturb each other, so you may have to insert one adapter into another slot. During bus cycles that only refer to components on the motherboard, the slots are usually cut off from the system bus to minimize the load on the driver circuits, and to avoid any noise induced by the slots. Using the bus slot contacts, a PC/XT may be configured very flexibly. The inserted adapter cards behave like components that have been integrated onto the motherboard. Figure 18.2 shows the structure and contact assignment of a bus slot.

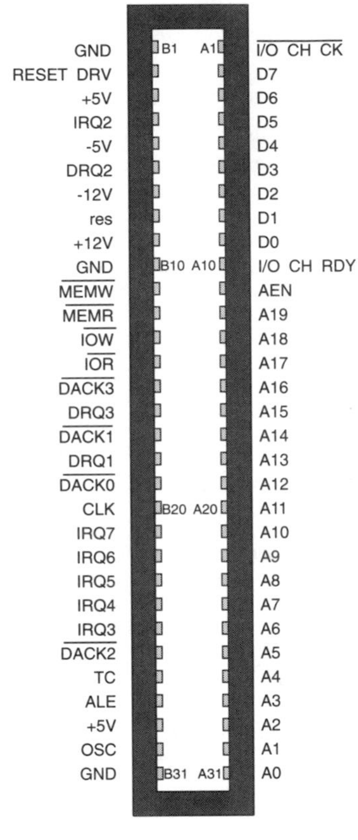

Figure 18.2: The PC/XT bus slot is laid out for an external 8-bit data bus, and has 62 contacts.

The following sections discuss the contacts and the meaning of the supplied or accepted signals.

A19–A0 (O)
Terminals A12–A31

These contacts form the 20-bit address bus of the PC/XT, and either indicate the state of the 8086/88 address signals directly, or are generated by DMA address logic.

AEN (O)
Terminal A11

If the address enable signal at this contact is active the DMA controller is controlling the bus for a data transfer. The processor and other peripherals are cut off from the bus.

ALE (O)
Terminal B28
The address latch enable signal ALE is generated by the 8288 bus controller, and indicates that valid address signals are present on the bus. Adapter cards may now decode these signals.

CLK (O)
Terminal B20
CLK is the system clock of the PC/XT. In the first PC, OSC was divided by three to generate the system clock with a frequency of 4.77 MHz.

D7–D0 (I/O)
Terminals A2–A9
These signals form an 8-bit data bus for data transfer from or to adapter cards.

$\overline{\text{DACK3}}$–$\overline{\text{DACK0}}$ (I)
Terminals B15, B17, B19, B26
These four DMA acknowledge contacts are used for acknowledging DMA requests DRQ3 to DRQ1, and for the memory refresh (DACK0). Once a DRQx request has been acknowledged by the corresponding DACKx, the data transfer via the corresponding DMA channel may take place.

DRQ3–DRQ1 (I)
Terminals B6, B16, B18
With these DMA request contacts a peripheral on an adapter card indicates to the motherboard system that it wants to transfer data via one of the three DMA channels. Channel 0 of the DMA chip is connected on the motherboard with channel 1 of the timer chip to periodically carry out memory refresh. Therefore, DRQ0 doesn't lead to the bus slots. Lines DRQ3 to DRQ1 must be held active until the corresponding DACK signal also becomes active; otherwise the DMA request is ignored.

$\overline{\text{I/O CH CK}}$ (I)
Terminal A1
With this I/O channel check contact the adapter cards flag errors to the motherboard to indicate, for example, a parity error on a memory expansion board, or a general error on an adapter card. An active $\overline{\text{I/O CH CK}}$ signal (that is, a low level signal) issues an NMI corresponding to interrupt 2 in the PC/XT.

I/O CH RDY (I)
Terminal A10
The I/O channel ready contact receives the ready signal from addressed units on an adapter card. If I/O CH RDY is low, the processor or DMA chip extends the bus cycle by inserting one or more wait states.

$\overline{\text{IOR}}$ (O)
Terminal B14
The I/O read signal at this contact indicates that the processor or the DMA controller wants to read data, and the addressed peripheral should supply data onto the data bus. An active $\overline{\text{IOR}}$

corresponds to an active $\overline{IORC}$ of the 8288 bus controller, which indicates a read access to the I/O address space.

$\overline{IOW}$ (O)
Terminal B13

The I/O write signal at this contact indicates that the processor or the DMA controller wants to write data, and that the addressed peripheral should take the data off the data bus. An active $\overline{IOW}$ corresponds to the active $\overline{IOWC}$ of the 8288 bus controller, which indicates a write access to the I/O address space.

IRQ2–IRQ7 (I)
Terminals B4, B21–B25

These contacts transmit the hardware interrupt requests corresponding to channels IRQ2–IRQ7 to the PIC on the motherboard. For example, the hard disk controller activates IRQ5 after reading data from the disk into an internal buffer. The IRQ0 and IRQ1 lines are assigned channel 0 of the timer chip and the keyboard, respectively. Therefore, they do not need to be integrated into the bus slots.

$\overline{MEMR}$ (O)
Terminal B12

By an active memory read signal $\overline{MEMR}$ (that is, a low level signal), the motherboard tells the adapter cards that the processor or DMA controller wants to read data from main memory. An active $\overline{MEMR}$ corresponds to the active $\overline{MRDC}$ of the 8288 bus controller, which indicates a read access to memory address space.

$\overline{MEMW}$ (O)
Terminal B11

By an active memory write signal $\overline{MEMW}$ (that is, a low level signal), the motherboard tells the adapter cards that the processor or DMA controller wants to write data into main memory. An active $\overline{MEMW}$ corresponds to the active $\overline{MWTC}$ of the 8288 bus controller, which indicates a write access to memory address space.

OSC (O)
Terminal B30
This contact supplies the oscillator's clock signal of 14318180 Hz.

RESET DRV (O)
Terminal B2
This contact supplies a reset signal to reset the whole system at power-up or during a hardware reset.

T/C (O)
Terminal B27

If the counter of a DMA channel has reached its final value, the DMA transfer is complete and the terminal count terminal T/C supplies a pulse to indicate the end of the DMA cycle.

19 16-Bit AT Architecture

There are no major differences between a PC and an AT, except that the PC with its 8088 processor only has an 8-bit data bus internally on the motherboard. On the other hand, the XT data bus internally comprises 16 bits. But in both PCs only 8 bits lead into the bus slots. Also, the internal structure is the same as far as the number and connections of the support chips 8237A, 8259A, 8253, etc. are concerned. Compared to the XT, the AT is a significant advance (AT actually means *advanced technology*), and its architecture is quite different from that of the PC/XT. The following sections briefly present these main differences.

19.1 Components and Their Cooperation

Figure 19.1 gives a block diagram of an AT. In most of today's ATs or AT-compatibles, several chips are integrated into one single chip, but the functional groups remain the same. Therefore, you may not find any of the chips shown in Figure 19.1. If you look at the data sheet of your motherboard, though, you will recognize that in chip X the functions of, for example, the two interrupt controllers, etc. have been integrated. It is the aim of Figure 19.1 to represent the functional structure of the AT as it was originally realized by individual chips, before the development of large-scale integration technology.

Here, the central part is also the processor. In the AT you will find the 80286, with 24 address lines. Thus, the AT may have 16 Mbytes of memory at most. Further, with the 80286 the AT can operate in protected mode to run with advanced operating systems like OS/2 or UNIX. The A20 address line is controlled by the 8042 keyboard controller. It can be locked so that the 80286 in real mode strictly addresses only the lowest 1 Mbyte of memory, and carries out a wrap-around like the 8086/88. Unfortunately, some DOS-internal functions dating from the PC's Stone Age rely on this wrap-around, but compatibility with the Stone Age may be, in my opinion, a matter of taste.

In addition to the 80286, the 80287 mathematical coprocessor can be installed. Normally, there is at least one socket for it present on the motherboard. The system clock is supplied by the 82284 clock generator, which is the successor of the PC/XT's 8284. The first AT ran with an effective processor clock of 6 MHz, so that the clock generator had to supply twice this frequency (12 MHz). The processor clock frequency was increased up to a giant 8 MHz with the AT03 model. Meanwhile, there are 80286 CPUs on the market (Harris or AMD, for example) which run with an effective processor clock of up to 25 MHz. But the support chips and the AT bus are nowhere near this frequency, so wait states are often required.

A further component of the AT (as in every computer) is the main memory. The processor is connected to it by means of data, address and control buses, as is the case in the PC/XT. The CPU addresses the memory via a 24-bit address bus, controls the data transfer with the control bus, and transfers the data via a 16-bit data bus. The necessary control signals are generated by the 82288 bus controller, which is the successor of the PC/XT's 8288, and which is dedicated to the 80286. To carry out the data exchange in as error-free and orderly a manner as possible, the signals are buffered and amplified in various address and data buffers.

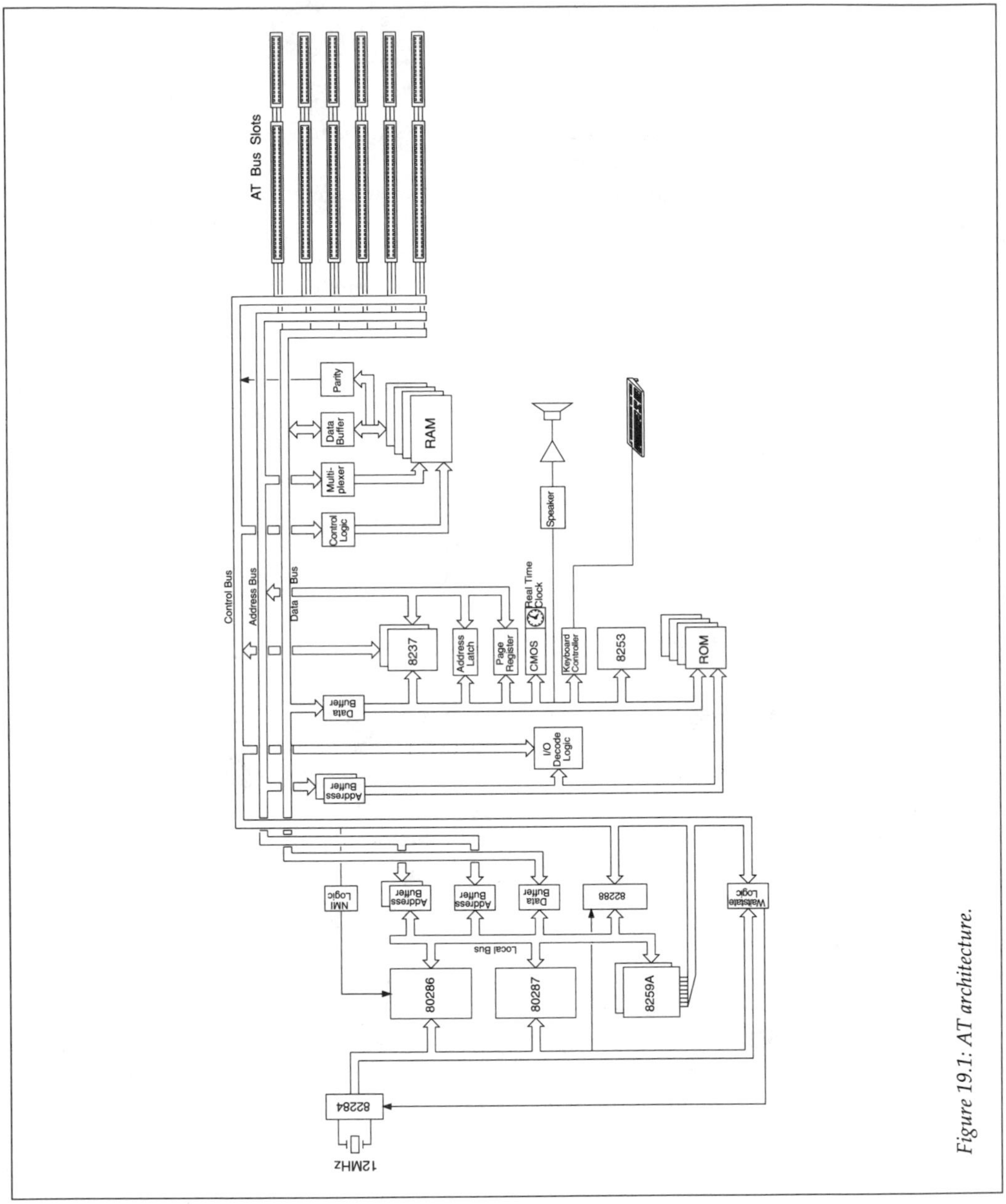

Figure 19.1: AT architecture.

In the AT and all its successors up to the EISA PC, five different address buses can be distinguished:

- Local address bus: comprises the 24 address signals from the 80286. External address buffers and address latches separate the local bus from the system address bus.

- System address bus: as is the case for the PC/XT, this bus is the main address bus and represents the latched version of bits A0 to A19 of the local address bus. Thus the system address bus in the AT is a 20-bit address bus. The signal for latching the address signals on the local address bus into the latches for the system address bus is ALE. In the AT, the system address bus is led to the bus slots as A0 to A19.

- Memory address bus: this address bus is only present on the motherboard, and represents the multiplexed version of the system address bus. Via the memory address bus, the row and column addresses are sucessively applied to the DRAM chips (see Chapter 6).

- X-address bus: this bus is separated from the system bus by buffers and drivers, and serves to address the I/O units and the ROM BIOS on the motherboard. These may, for example, be registers of the interrupt controllers, the timer or an on-board floppy controller. On the other hand, I/O ports and ROM BIOS on extension adapters are accessed by the system address bus.

- L-address bus: this bus comprises the seven high-order (L=large) and non-latched address bits A17–A23 of the local address bus. It leads into the AT slots as LA17–LA23.

Besides these, there are four different data buses implemented in the AT:

- Local data bus: comprises the 16 data signals from the 80286. Additionally, a bus logic is necessary to distinguish byte and word accesses. External data buffers and data latches separate the local data bus from the system data bus.

- System data bus: this is the latched version of the local data bus in the AT, and it is 16 bits wide. The system data bus leads into the bus slots.

- Memory data bus: this data bus is only present on the motherboard, and establishes the connection between main memory and the system data bus.

- X-data bus: this bus is separated from the system bus by buffers and drivers, and accesses I/O units and the ROM BIOS on the motherboard. I/O ports and BIOS extensions on extension adapters are accessed by the system data bus.

Besides the main memory on the motherboard the CPU can also access chips on the adapter cards in the bus slots. A more detailed explanation of the construction and function of the AT slots is given below. Unlike the XT, the data bus leads into the bus slots with the full width of 16 bits. The additional control and data signals are located in a new slot section with 38 contacts. However, older XT adapters with an 8-bit data bus can also be inserted into the AT slots by means of the two new control signals *MEM CS16* and $\overline{\text{I/O CS16}}$. The bus logic automatically recognizes whether a 16-bit AT or an 8-bit PC/XT adapter is present in the bus slot. An 8/16-bit converter carries out the necessary division of 16-bit quantities into two 8-bit quantities, and vice versa. Like the PC/XT bus, the AT or ISA bus also supports only the CPU and the DMA chips on the motherboard as busmasters which can arbitrate directly, without using a DMA channel. On external adapter cards in the bus slots, no busmaster may operate and control the AT bus. The arbitration is carried out only indirectly, via a DMA channel, and not directly by a master request. It was not until EISA and the microchannel that such busmasters could also operate from peripheral adapter cards.

The first AT model ran at a processor clock of only 6 MHz. The bus slots and the inserted extension adapters have no problem in following the clock, but the situation is different with a turbo clock of, for example, 16 MHz. The inert bus slots then usually run with only half the turbo clock, that is, 8 MHz. Problems mainly arise with «half»-turbo clocks of 10 MHz or 12.5 MHz. In most cases, the bus slots also run at this frequency, but only very high quality adapters support 10 MHz or even 12.5 MHz. The consequence is frequent system crashes, especially if the PC has been running for a long time and the warmer chips of the peripheral adapters can no longer follow the clock. Meanwhile, the ISA standard (which corresponds to the AT bus in most respects) requires a clock frequency for the bus slots of 8.33 MHz at most. Even adapter cards that could run more quickly are supplied in ATs which strictly implement this standard, with only 8.33 MHz.

Unlike the bus slots, the main memory on the motherboard runs with the full processor clock, even if this is 25 MHz. The main memory controller may advise the CPU at most to insert wait cycles if the RAM chips are too slow. But advanced memory concepts such as paging or interleaving (see Chapter 17) shorten the memory access times. Thus, an access to memory expansions on adapter cards is much slower than an access to the on-board memory (remember this if you want to extend your memory). You should always prefer an extension of the on-board memory as long as the motherboard can integrate more chips. This applies particularly to very fast-clocked i386 and i486 models. Some PCs have a special *memory slot* besides the normal bus slots into which special memory adapter cards may be inserted, largely running with the full CPU clock so that no delays occur compared to the on-board memory.

To decode the processor's addresses in a memory access, the AT also has an address multiplexer. Together with the memory buffer, it drives the memory chips on the motherboard. The check logic for memory parity issues an NMI if the data does not conform with the additionally held parity bit at the time of data reading. Also, additional memory on an adapter card may issue this memory parity error. Other sources for an NMI in an AT may be errors on an adapter card, indicated by $\overline{\text{I/O CH CK}}$. In the PC/XT the memory refresh was carried out only via channel 0 of the DMA chip. This channel is activated periodically by channel 1 of the timer chip. In the AT, the refresh interval is further defined by channel 1 of the timer chip, but the refresh itself is usually carried out by a dedicated refresh logic driven by the timer channel 1. Thus, channel 0 would normally be available, but certain manufacturers do use it further for refresh. For this purpose, the lines $\overline{\text{DACK0}}$ and $\overline{\text{REF}}$ lead into the AT slots (see below).

Like the PC/XT, the AT also has a ROM for holding boot code and data and the AT's BIOS routines. Unlike the 8086/88, in the PC/XT the AT's 80286 may also be operated in protected mode. These two operation modes are completely incompatible, which is, unfortunately, bad news for the BIOS: BIOS routines in real mode cannot be used by the 80286 in protected mode. Only the original AT, or other manufacturers' ATs, incorporate an *advanced BIOS*, which holds the corresponding routines for protected mode. The advanced BIOS is located in the address space just below 16 Mbytes. If you buy a freely available version of OS/2 then usually the disks not only hold the operating system, but also the BIOS for protected mode. Thus, during the OS/2 boot process not only the operating system is loaded, but also the BIOS for protected mode. The BIOS routines present in ROM are only used for booting as long as the 80286 is not switched to protected mode.

For supporting the CPU and peripherals, the AT also has several support chips. Instead of one 8259A programmable interrupt controller (PIC), two are present in an AT: one *master PIC* and one *slave PIC*. The INTRPT output of the slave is connected to the master's IR2 input, thus the two PICs are cascaded. Therefore, 15 instead of eight IRQ levels are available in the AT. Table 19.1 shows the assignment of the interrupt channels IRQx to the various peripherals or support chips. Besides the IRQs, the NMI also is listed as a hardware interrupt, but the NMI directly influences the CPU, and no 8259A PIC is used for this purpose. Section 23 describes how the 8259A operates and how it may be programmed.

Channel	Interrupt	Used by
NMI	02h	parity, error on extension card, memory refresh
IRQ0	08h	channel 0 of timer 8253
IRQ1	09h	keyboard
IRQ2	0ah	cascade from slave PIC
IRQ3	0bh	COM2
IRQ4	0ch	COM1
IRQ5	0dh	LPT2
IRQ6	0eh	floppy disk controller
IRQ7	0fh	LPT1
IRQ8	0fh	real time clock
IRQ9	0fh	redirection to IRQ2
IRQ10	0fh	reserved
IRQ11	0fh	reserved
IRQ12	0fh	reserved
IRQ13	0fh	coprocessor 80287
IRQ14	0fh	hard disk controller
IRQ15	0fh	reserved

Table 19.1: AT hardware interrupt channels

Besides the PICs, a 8253/8254 programmable interval timer (PIT), or for short, timer chip, is present. The 8254 is the more developed successor to the 8253 but has the same function set. It includes three individually programmable counters (see Table 19.2). Counter 0 is used for periodically updating the internal system clock, as is the case in the PC/XT, and is connected to the IRQ0 of the master PIC. The hardware interrupt issued thus updates the internal clock, which can be checked by means of the DOS commands TIME and DATE. Timer 1 periodically activates the memory refresh, which is indicated by an active signal $\overline{REF}$ in the AT bus slot. Counter 2 generates the tone frequency for the speaker. In Section 24 some details about the operation modes and the programming of the 8253 PIT and the speaker are given.

Channel	Used by
0	internal system clock (IRQ0)
1	memory refresh
2	speaker frequency

Table 19.2: AT timer channels

Unlike the PC/XT, the more modern and programmable keyboard of the AT is connected by a keyboard controller to the AT system bus. In the PC/XT, an 8255 programmable peripheral interface (PPI) was included for this purpose. The functions of the AT keyboard and its successor, the MF II keyboard, may be programmed (details are discussed in Section 31.1).

Instead of the DIP switches you will find a CMOS RAM in the AT. The CMOS RAM holds the system configuration and supplies it at power-up. EISA and microchannel further extend this concept: here you may even set up the DMA and IRQ channels used by EISA or microchannel adapters by means of an interactive program. These setups are stored in an extended CMOS RAM, and no jumpers need to be altered (after deinstalling all adapters to expose the motherboard...). Together with the CMOS RAM, a real-time clock is integrated which periodically updates date and time, even if the PC is switched off. The two DOS commands DATE and TIME are no longer necessary at power-up for setting the current date and time. They are mainly used for checking these values.

The whole AT is powered in the same way as the PC/XT, by means of a power supply that supplies voltages of –12 V, –5 V, 0 V, +5 V and +12 V. In the AT, too, the adapter cards in the bus slots are usually powered by corresponding contacts in the bus slots. Only «current eaters» like FileCards with integrated hard disk drives must be directly connected to the power supply. As hardware components, the support chips mentioned are accessed via ports in the I/O address space. Thus, the AT as well as the PC/XT uses *I/O mapped input/output (I/O)*. Table 19.3 shows the port addresses of the most important hardware components in the AT.

Port address	Used by
000h–00fh	1st DMA chip 8237A
020h–021h	1st PIC 8259A
040h–043h	PIT 8253
060h–063h	keyboard controller 8042
070h–071h	real-time clock
080h–083h	DMA page register
0a0h–0afh	2nd PIC 8259A
0c0h–0cfh	2nd DMA chip 8237A
0e0h–0efh	reserved
0f0h–0ffh	reserved for coprocessor 80287
100h–1ffh	available
200h–20fh	game adapter
210h–217h	reserved
220h–26fh	available
278h–27fh	2nd parallel interface
2b0h–2dfh	EGA
2f8h–2ffh	COM2
300h–31fh	prototype adapter
320h–32fh	available
378h–37fh	1st parallel interface
380h–38fh	SDLC adapter
3a0h–3afh	reserved
3b0h–3bfh	monochrome adapter/parallel interface
3c0h–3cfh	EGA

Table 19.3: AT port addresses

Port address	Used by
3d0h–3dfh	CGA
3e0h–3e7h	reserved
3f0h–3f7h	floppy disk controller
3f8h–3ffh	COM1

Table 19.3: cont.

Besides the 80286, ATs often also include an i386 or i486 processor, seldom a Pentium. With these processors, the on-board data and address buses (the memory address bus, for example) are usually 32 or 64 bits wide, but only 24 address lines and 16 data lines lead into the bus slots, as is the case for an original AT. The conversion to 32-bit or 64-bit quantities is carried out by special swappers and buffers. In principle, the architecture of these i386, i486 or Pentium ATs therefore doesn't differ from that of a conventional AT. Only the internal address and data buses may be adapted accordingly. The AT or ISA bus (as it is called in its strictly defined form) is very popular as an additional standard expansion bus for VLB and PCI systems. Thus, modern and very powerful graphics and drive host adapters can be integrated into the system. On the other hand, cheap and readily available ISA adapters (for example, parallel and serial interfaces, games adapters, etc.) can also be used.

19.2 DMA Architecture

As already done for the PC/XT, I will also discuss the AT's DMA subsystem in connection with the bus architecture. DMA basics are detailed in Chapter 25.

19.2.1 8-Bit and 16-Bit Channels

For memory and I/O accesses without any intervention from the CPU, the AT has two 8237A DMA chips which are cascaded so that seven DMA channels are available. For that purpose an 8237A is operated as a master, and is connected to the CPU. The HRQ and HLDA terminals of the slave DMA are connected to channel 0 of the master DMA so that slave channels 0–3 have a higher priority than the three remaining master DMA channels. Channels 0–3 of the master are usually called the AT's DMA channels 4–7. The four slave DMA channels serve 8-bit peripherals, and the other channels 5–7 are implemented for 16-bit devices. The use of the separately programmable transfer channels is listed in Table 19.4.

Channel 0 is reserved for memory refresh, although in most ATs their own refresh logic is present for the refresh process. The remaining three 8-bit channels are available for an 8-bit data transfer. Usually, the DMA chips run with a much lower clock frequency than the CPU. The frequency is typically about 5 MHz (even in cases where the CPU is clocked with 25 MHz). Some ATs enable a DMA frequency of up to 7 MHz, not very exciting compared to the CPU clock. Thus it is not surprising that most AT hard disk controllers do not transfer data by DMA but by means of programmed I/O, because the 80286 runs much faster than an 8086/88 and the DMA chips. But the 16-bit hard disk controllers are sometimes served by one of the DMA channels 5–7. Because of its 16 Mbyte address space, the AT has an 8-bit page register (PC/XT: 4-bit page register) to generate a 24-bit address together with the two 8-bit addresses from the 8237A and the DMA address latch.

Channel	Used by	Width
0	reserved (memory refresh)	8 bits
1	SDLC adapter/tape drive	8 bits
2	floppy disk controller	8 bits
3	reserved	8 bits
4	cascade DMA1→DMA2	–
5	reserved	16 bits
6	reserved	16 bits
7	reserved	16 bits

Table 19.4: AT DMA channels

The functioning of the AT DMA is, in principle, the same as in the PC/XT; however, 24-bit addresses can be generated, and 16-bit channels are available. During the course of a read transfer the 8237A provides the memory address and activates the $\overline{MEMR}$ signal to read a data word from memory onto the 16-bit data bus. Afterwards, it enables the $\overline{IOW}$ signal so the peripheral can accept one (8-bit channel) or two (16-bit channel) data bytes. A write transfer proceeds in exactly the opposite direction: the 8237A outputs the memory address and activates the $\overline{IOR}$ signal to read out one or two data bytes from the peripheral's I/O register onto the 16-bit data bus. Afterwards, it enables the $\overline{MEMW}$ signal so that the memory can fetch the data byte(s). For that purpose, the system controller must be able to recognize whether an 8-bit or 16-bit DMA channel is used and generate signals according to $\overline{BHE}$ and A0.

With an 80286 the data from the 8-bit peripheral must be put onto or taken off the low-order or high-order part of the data bus (depending on the storage address). The situation becomes even more ponderous with PCs that have an i386 or i486 chip (or even a Pentium). They usually implement main memory with a 32-bit or 64-bit organization. Here, according to the storage address, one of the now four or eight data bus bytes is responsible for fetching or providing the 8-bit data from or to the peripheral. An additional logic that decodes the two or three least-significant address bits from the DMA chip can easily carry out the transfer.

The three free channels of the new second DMA chip in the AT are already designed for serving 16-bit peripherals. This can be, for example, a 16-bit controller for hard disk drives. Although the 8237A is only an 8-bit chip, it can carry out a 16-bit or even a 32-bit transfer between peripherals and main memory. How the DMA controller carries out this, at first glance impossible, job is described below.

The descriptions up to now have shown that the internal temporary 8-bit register of the 8237A doesn't play any role in data transfer between peripherals and memory (it is only important for memory–memory transfers). The transfer target receives the data from the source directly via the data bus. The only problem left is that the 8237A address register provides byte addresses and no word addresses. But if the coupling of address bits A0–A15 from the 8237A and the DMA address latch to the system address bus is shifted by one, which corresponds to a multiplication by a factor of two, and address bit A0 of the system bus is always set to 0, then the 8237A will generate word addresses. This also applies to the 16-bit DMA channels in the AT. A0 is always equal to 0 here. The 8237A and the DMA address latch provide address bits A1–A16, and the DMA page register supplies address bits A17–A23. Therefore, one DMA page of the 16-bit channels now has 128 kbytes instead of 64 kbytes and the data transfer is carried out in 16-bit sections. Transferring the data bytes onto the low-order or high-order part of the data bus according to an even or an odd address is unnecessary.

Only on systems with a 32-bit data bus do the words need to be transferred by an additional 16/32-bit logic onto the low-order or high-order data bus word, according to whether their addresses represent double-word boundaries. This is carried out analogously to the transfer of 8-bit quantities on the XT.

For a data transfer between memory and peripherals (the main job of DMA), it is insignificant, therefore, as to whether an 8- or 32-bit chip is present. The shifting of the address bits supplied by the 8237A by one or two places leads to 16- or even 32-bit addresses. Unfortunately, the transfer can then only start and end at word or double-word boundaries, and the transferred quantities are limited to multiples of 16 or 32 bits. If a peripheral supplies, for example, 513 bytes, this may give rise to some difficulties. EISA therefore implements a 32-bit DMA controller which also runs somewhat faster than 4.77 MHz.

19.2.2 Memory Refresh

Channel 0 is dedicated to memory refresh. In modern ATs and other computers with intelligent DRAM controllers, the memory refresh need not be carried out by a DMA cycle; instead, the DRAM controller or even the DRAM chips themselves do this on receipt of a trigger signal from the PIT. The PIT defines the refresh time by means of the periodic square-wave signal. The DMA chip is used to generate the refresh address and the control signals for reading the main memory (if the memory controller or even the DRAM chips themselves are doing that). Modern memory controllers handle these processes on their own. Channel 0 of the 8237A is no longer required for memory refresh. On such motherboards you would therefore be able to use channel 0 together with channel 1 for a memory–memory transfer. However, the AT architecture thwarts your plans again.

19.2.3 Memory–Memory Transfers

On each of the channels a page register is allocated, whose addresses are listed in Table 19.5. IBM, though, has implemented a common page register for channels 0 and 1 in the PC/XT, as already mentioned. Therefore, memory–memory transfer was only possible within a single DMA page of 64 kbytes, as only channels 0 and 1 can carry out this transfer, and they have to share one register on the PC/XT.

On the AT also, no memory–memory transfer is possible for the following reasons: DMA channel 4, corresponding to the master's channel 0, is blocked by cascading from the slave DMA. Thus the master DMA chip is not available for a memory–memory transfer. Only the slave DMA remains, but here also the problems are nearly insurmountable. On the AT and compatibles the memory refresh is no longer carried out by a DMA cycle, so channel 0 would then be free for a memory–memory transfer.

Port	Page register
87h	channel 0
83h	channel 1
81h	channel 2
82h	channel 3
8fh	channel 4 (refresh)
8bh	channel 5
89h	channel 6
8ah	channel 7

Table 19.5: I/O addresses of the AT page registers

But for the memory–memory transfer, the internal temporary register of the 8237A is also involved – and this is only eight bits wide. Thus, 16-bit data on the 16-bit data bus cannot be temporarily stored; for this a 16-bit DMA chip would be required. If we restrict all memory–memory transfers to 8-bit transfers, then the data byte can be temporarily stored, but depending upon an even or odd source address, the byte appears on the low- or high-order part of the data bus. After temporary storage the data byte must be output by the 8237A, again depending on an even or odd target address onto the low- or high-order part of the data bus. This is possible in principle by using a corresponding external logic, but is quite complicated and expensive. Therefore, the AT and i386/i486 motherboards generally don't implement memory–memory transfer. It could be worse, because the REP MOVS instruction moves data on an 80286 in 16-bit units and on an i386/i486 even in 32-bit units very quickly. The much higher CPU clock rate additionally enhances the effect. IBM has probably implemented the second DMA chip only because some peripherals might request a 16-bit DMA channel for data transfer. Note that the XT carries out the transfer of sector data from or to the hard disk (originally a job of the DMA) via a DMA channel but the AT employs PIO for this. Only EISA and PS/2 still use DMA for this job.

19.3 I/O Channel and Bus Slots

Similar to the PC/XT, here also a main part of the system bus leads into the bus slots. The AT bus slots incorporate 36 new contacts, compared to the XT bus slot, to integrate the additional address, data, DMA and IRQ lines. Thus, 98 contacts are present in total. The additional AT contacts are included in a separate section, which is always arranged immediately behind the slot with the conventional XT contacts. Usually, each AT or AT-compatible has several pure XT and several pure AT slots with corresponding contacts. Also, it is completely insignificant (in theory) into which slot you insert an adapter card in the AT. You only have to ensure that you really do insert an AT adapter (discernible by the additional contacts on the bottom) into an AT slot and not into an XT slot. Figure 19.2 shows the structure and assignment of an AT bus slot.

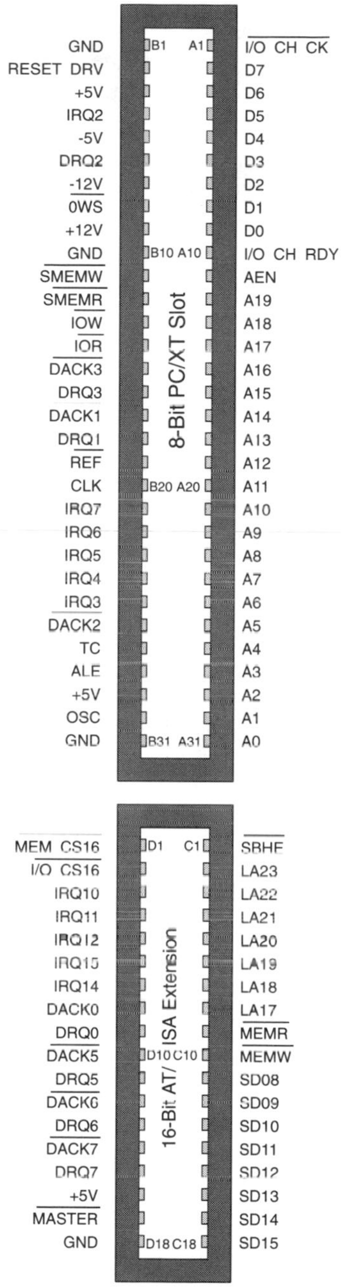

Figure 19.2: The AT bus slot comprises a separate section with 38 new contacts for the extension up to 16 bits.

In the following sections only the new contacts and the meaning of the supplied or accepted signals are presented. The assignment of the XT part of an AT slot (with the exception of the $\overline{\text{0WS}}$ and $\overline{\text{REF}}$ contacts) is given in Section 18.3. $\overline{\text{0WS}}$ has been added instead of the reserved XT bus contact B8 to service fast peripherals without wait cycles. Because the AT bus and ISA can support busmasters on external adapters up to a certain point, all connections are bidirectional. To show the data and signal flow more precisely, I have assumed for the transfer directions indicated that the CPU (or another device on the motherboard) represents the current busmaster. Anyway, there are virtually no AT adapters with a busmaster device.

$\overline{\text{0WS}}$ (I; PC/XT slot)
Terminal B8

The signal from a peripheral indicates that the unit is running quickly enough to be serviced without wait cycles.

$\overline{\text{DACK0}}$, $\overline{\text{DACK5}}$–$\overline{\text{DACK7}}$ (O)
Terminals D8, D10, D12, D14

These four DMA acknowledge contacts are used for the acknowledgement of the DMA requests DRQ0 and DRQ5-DRQ7. Compared to the XT, $\overline{\text{DACK0}}$ has been replaced by $\overline{\text{REFR}}$ because the memory refresh is carried out via $\overline{\text{REFR}}$ in the AT.

DRQ0, DRQ5–DRQ7 (I)
Terminals D9, D11, D13, D15

With these DMA request contacts a peripheral on an adapter card may tell the system on the motherboard that it wants to transfer data via a DMA channel. Channel 0 of the first DMA chip is designed for an 8-bit transfer, the three additional channels 5–7, on the other hand, for 16-bit transfers. Channel 4 is used for cascading the two DMA chips.

$\overline{\text{I/O CS16}}$ (I)
Terminal D2

The signal at this contact has a similar meaning to MEM CS16. $\overline{\text{I/O CS16}}$ applies to I/O ports and not memory addresses.

IRQ10–IRQ12, IRQ14, IRQ15 (I)
Terminals D3–D7

These contacts transmit the hardware interrupt requests according to the channels IRQ10–IRQ12 and IRQ14, IRQ15 to the slave PIC on the motherboard. IRQ13 in the AT is reserved for the 80287 coprocessor, which is located on the motherboard. Therefore, this signal doesn't lead into the bus slots.

LA17–LA23 (O)
Terminals C2–C8

The large address contacts supply the seven high-order bits of the CPU address bus. Compared to the normal address contacts A0–A19 of the conventional XT bus, the signals at these contacts are valid much earlier, and may be decoded half a bus clock cycle in advance of the address bits A0–A19. Note that LA17–LA19 and A17–A19 overlap in their meaning. This is necessary because the signals on A17–A19 are latched and therefore delayed. But for a return of the signals $\overline{\text{MEM CS16}}$ and $\overline{\text{I/O CS16}}$ in time, it is required that address signals A17–A19 are also available very early.

$\overline{\text{MASTER}}$ (I)
Terminal D17

The signal at this contact serves for bus arbitration. Thus, busmasters on adapter cards have the opportunity to control the system bus. For this purpose they must activate $\overline{\text{MASTER}}$ (that is, supply a low level signal). In the AT the integration of a busmaster is carried out by an assigned DMA channel. Via this channel the busmaster outputs a DRQx signal. The DMA chip cuts the CPU off the bus using HRQ and HLDA, and activates the $\overline{\text{DACKx}}$ assigned to the busmaster. The busmaster responds with an active $\overline{\text{MASTER}}$ signal and thus takes over control of the bus.

$\overline{\text{MEM CS16}}$ (I)
Terminal D1

A peripheral adapter card must return a valid $\overline{\text{MEM CS16}}$ signal in time if it wants to be serviced with a data bus width of 16 bits. Using $\overline{\text{MEM CS16}}$, therefore, 8-bit and 16-bit adapters may be inserted into an AT slot without any problem. The AT bus logic recognizes whether the adapter must be accessed with 8- or 16-bits.

$\overline{\text{MEMR}}$ (O)
Terminal C9

An active memory read signal $\overline{\text{MEMR}}$ (that is, a low level) signal indicates that the processor or DMA controller wants to read data from memory with an address between 0 M and 16 M. On the other hand, the $\overline{\text{SMEMR}}$ signal in the XT slot only applies to the address space between 0 M and 1 M. With an address below 1 M, $\overline{\text{MEMR}}$ is inactive (that is, high).

$\overline{\text{MEMW}}$ (O)
Terminal C10

An active memory write signal $\overline{\text{MEMW}}$ (that is, a low level signal) indicates that the processor or DMA controller wants to write data into memory with an address between 0 M and 16 M. On the other hand, the $\overline{\text{SMEMW}}$ signal in the XT slot only applies to the address space between 0 M and 1 M. With an address below 1 M, $\overline{\text{MEMW}}$ is inactive (that is, high).

$\overline{\text{REF}}$ (O; PC/XT slot)
Terminal B19

The refresh signal at this contact indicates that the memory refresh on the motherboard is in progress. Thus, peripherals may also carry out a memory refresh simultaneously with the motherboard.

$\overline{\text{SBHE}}$ (O)
Terminal C1

If data is output onto or read from the high-byte SD8–SD15 of the data bus by the CPU or another chip, then the system bus high enable signal $\overline{\text{SBHE}}$ is active and has a low level.

SD8–SD15 (I/O)
Terminal C11–C18
These eight system data contacts form the high-order byte of the 16-bit address bus in the AT.

$\overline{\text{SMEMR}}$ (O; PC/XT slot)
Terminal B12

An active S-memory read signal $\overline{\text{SMEMR}}$ (that is, low level) signal indicates that the processor or DMA controller wants to read data from memory with an address between 0 M and 1 M. On the other hand, the $\overline{\text{MEMR}}$ signal in the AT extension applies to the address space between 0 M and 16 M. With an address above 1 M, $\overline{\text{SMEMR}}$ is inactive (that is, high).

$\overline{\text{SMEMW}}$ (O; PC/XT slot)
Terminal B11

An active memory write signal $\overline{\text{MEMW}}$ (that is, a low level signal) indicates that the processor or DMA controller wants to write data into memory with an address between 0 M and 1 M. On the other hand, the $\overline{\text{MEMW}}$ signal in the AT extension only applies to the address space between 0 M and 1 M. With an address above 1 M, $\overline{\text{SMEMW}}$ is inactive (that is, high).

19.4 AT Bus Frequencies and the ISA Bus

The concept and architecture of the AT have been very successful during the past few years. This makes it worse that no strictly defined standard for the bus system has actually existed. That became especially clear as the clock frequencies were increased more and more, and therefore problems with the signal timing became heavier. IBM never specified the AT bus in a clear and unambiguous way. All standards in this field are therefore rather woolly. For IBM that was not very serious, because Big Blue went over to the PS/2 series before its AT products exceeded the 8 MHz barrier. It was only after this barrier was broken that users of AT compatibles had to deal with bus problems. I have already mentioned that the bus slots run at 8.33 MHz at most, even in a 25 MHz AT. Before the AT manufacturers agreed to this strict definition, every manufacturer chose their own standard – not very pleasant for AT users. The consequence was that in many older turbo-ATs the bus as well as the CPU ran at 10 MHz or even 12.5 MHz. Such frequencies are only handled by a very few adapter cards. They cannot follow the clock, especially if the chips get warm after a certain time. A warmer chip usually has a lower operating speed, even if only by a few nanoseconds. This is enough, though, and the computer crashes. Things get even more confusing if we remember that the 8237A DMA chips and the 8259A PICs run at 5 MHz at most. Even the faster types only reach 8 MHz. Moreover, the timer chip is operated at 1.193180 MHz, namely 1/4 of the PC/XT base clock of 4.77 MHz, even in a 50 MHz i486 PC. That some misalignments and therefore unnecessary wait cycles occur with a CPU clock of 25 MHz, a bus frequency of 10 MHz, a DMA frequency of 5 MHz and a timer frequency of 1.19 MHz seems to be obvious.

Seven years after presenting the AT the computer industry has become reconciled to a clearer, but unfortunately not very strict, standard for the AT bus. The result now is the *ISA bus* which is about 99% compatible with the AT bus in the original IBM AT. ISA is the abbreviation for

Industrial Standard Architecture. Thus, ISA will really define an obligatory bus standard for all AT manufacturers.

This standard specifies that the bus slots should run at 8.33 MHz at most. If a 33 MHz i386 wants to access the video RAM, it must insert a lot of wait states. A reading bus cycle, for example, needs two bus cycles, but one bus clock cycle lasts four CPU clock cycles so that eight CPU clock cycles are necessary. If the memory on the graphics adapter has an (optimistic) access time of 80 ns, about five wait cycles are additionally necessary (the cycle time of a 80 ns DRAM lasts for about 150 ns, and the cycle time of the CPU clock is 30 ns; this leads to five wait cycles). If the two CPU cycles are subtracted, which a memory access always needs, then even with the optimum cooperation of a graphics adapter and a bus, eleven (!) wait states are necessary. Drivers, buffers etc. connected in between and misalignments may readily increase this value up to 20 wait cycles. The transfer rate with an ISA bus width of 16 bits is decreased to 3 Mbytes/s compared to a memory transfer rate of 66 Mbytes/s. A Windows window of 640*512 pixels with 256 colours is filled within 100 ms; a time period which is clearly recognized by the eye. No wonder that even 33 MHz i486 ATs do not always operate brilliantly with Windows. The enormous number of wait cycles during reads and writes from and to video RAM slows down the high-performance microprocessor. Whether the CPU needs some additional cycles for calculating a straight line is thus of secondary importance. Only special motherboards and graphics adapters where the video memory is (more or less) directly connected to the memory bus or a fast local bus, and not accessed indirectly via the ISA bus, may solve this problem.

The bus frequency is generated by dividing the CPU clock, thus the ISA bus largely runs synchronously to the CPU. This is different, for example, from the microchannel, which uses its own clock generator for the bus so that the microchannel runs asynchronously to the CPU. The ISA bus also operates asynchronous cycles, for example if a DMA chip that runs at 5 MHz initiates a bus cycle. The big disadvantage of synchronous ISA cycles is that a whole clock cycle is lost as soon as an adapter becomes too slow even for only a few nanoseconds. Therefore, EISA enables the stretching of such cycles to avoid unnecessary wait states. Actually, a bus is much more than a slot on a motherboard.

Besides the layout of the bus slots and the signal levels, the ISA standard also defines the time period for the rise and fall of the address, data and control signals. But these properties are only important for developers of motherboards and adapter cards, therefore a vast number of signal diagrams and exact definitions are not given here. Signal freaks should consult the original ISA specification.

20 32-Bit EISA Architecture – Evolution

The introduction of the i386 and i486 32-bit microprocessors with full 32-bit data bus and 32-bit address bus also required an extension of the ISA bus. This bus was implemented for the 80286, with its 16-bit address bus and 16 Mbyte address space only. Not only is the small width of the bus system outdated today, but so are the antiquated 8-bit 8237A DMA chips, with their limitation to 64 kbyte blocks, and the rather user-unfriendly adapter configuration (using jumpers and DIP switches). Another serious contradiction between the very powerful 32-bit processors and the «tired» 8-bit AT concept is the lack of supporting busmasters on external adapter cards.

Two completely different solutions for these problems are established today: IBM's microchannel for PS/2, and EISA, which has been developed by a group of leading manufacturers of IBM-compatible PCs. IBM has gone down a completely different road with its microchannel, not only because of the new geometric layout of the bus slots, but also with the architecture implemented. Moreover, IBM has denied the microchannel to other manufacturers by means of patents and other protective rights. This is a consequence of the fact that these other clone manufacturers had previously got a large part of the PC market. As IBM is rather miserly with issuing licences, the microchannel is no longer the completely open architecture that users and manufacturers have been accustomed to with the PC/XT/AT. Together with the significantly larger functionality of the microchannel, one may speak of a radical reorganization or indeed view of the microchannel as a revolutionary step towards real 32-bit systems.

EISA, on the other hand, tries to take a route that might be called «evolutionary». The maxim of EISA is the possibility of integrating ISA components into the EISA system without any problems. This requires an identical geometry for the adapter cards and, therefore, unfortunately also the integration of obsolete concepts for the EISA's ISA part. With this concept, 16-bit ISA components can be integrated in an EISA system with no problems, but you don't then have any advantage. Under these conditions the EISA bus operates more or less identically to the conventional ISA bus. Only 16- and 32-bit EISA components really take advantage of the EISA bus system, using, for example, burst cycles or 32-bit DMA. The EISA bus is capable of a data transfer rate of up to 33 Mbytes/s, compared to 8.33 Mbytes/s with an ISA bus.

In view of the technical structure, EISA is more complicated than the microchannel because it not only needs to carry out EISA bus cycles, but for compatibility reasons also ISA cycles. This applies, for example, to DMA, where the EISA system must decide whether an 8237A-compatible DMA cycle (with its known disadvantages) or a full 32-bit EISA DMA cycle has to be executed. The hardware must be able to carry out both, and thus is, of course, rather complicated. In this aspect, the microchannel has an easier life; it frees itself from the outdated PC/XT/AT concepts, and starts from a new beginning. This restriction to a new beginning makes the microchannel less complicated. However, stronger competition in the field of EISA has surely led to cheaper EISA chips, even though their technology is more complex. Additionally, as the user you have the advantage that older ISA components may also be used initially. Later you can integrate more powerful EISA peripherals. In view of the speedy development, though, who is going to use his old hard disk controller or 8-bit graphics adapter with 128 kbytes of memory when buying a computer of the latest generation?

Therefore, the more straightforward concept is surely the microchannel, which frees itself from the old traditions; but because of IBM's restrictive policy, it has been almost exclusively dedicated to IBM products up to now. On a BIOS, operating system or application level you don't notice whether you are working with an EISA or microchannel PC. Only system programmers and bit freaks have to deal with their differences.

20.1 EISA Bus Structure

The name EISA, as an abbreviation for *extended ISA*, already indicates the evolutionary concept of this 32-bit extension for the AT bus. ISA components may be used in an EISA system with no alterations. Pure EISA adapters inform the EISA system (by means of the $\overline{EX32}$ and $\overline{EX16}$ signals) that they are EISA components with the extended functions which are provided for EISA. Internally, EISA machines differ drastically from their ISA predecessors in many aspects, discussed in the following sections. Figure 20.1 shows a schematic block diagram of the EISA architecture.

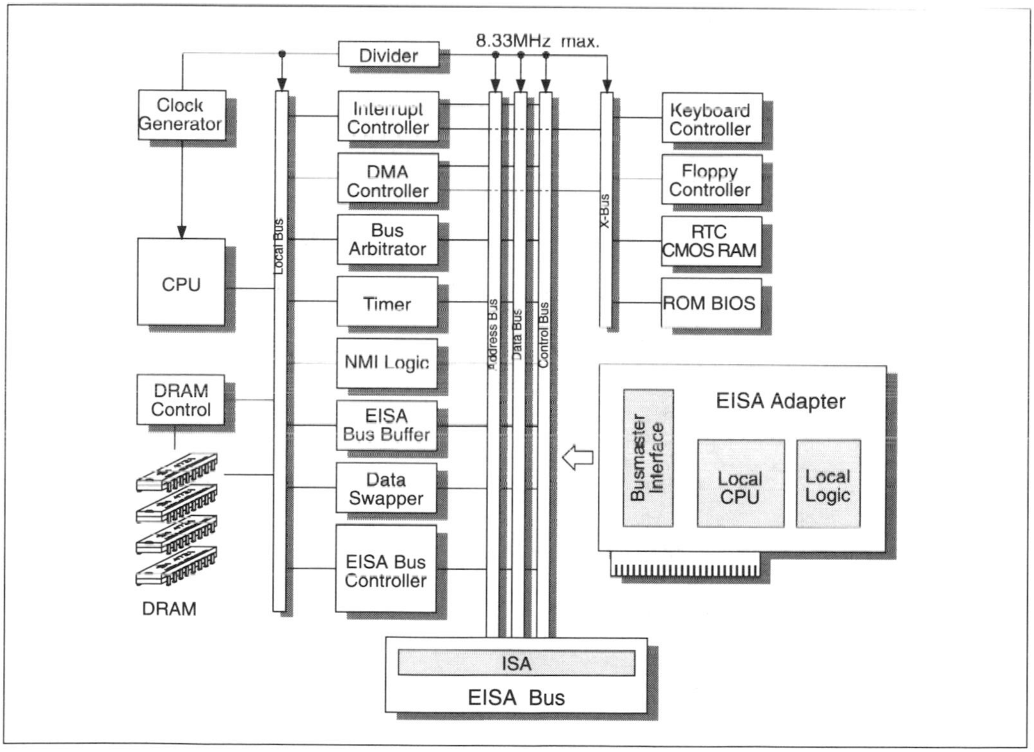

Figure 20.1: EISA architecture.

The clock generator supplies both the CPU and, after division of the frequency in the frequency divider, the EISA bus with a clock signal. Thus the EISA bus is a synchronous bus system, because the CPU and EISA bus are supplied by the same clock signal source, and are thus running synchronously. The maximum frequency of the EISA bus is 8.33 MHz. This clock rate determines the access of the CPU to all external units. On the other hand, the i386/i486/Pentium may access the main memory at the full clock frequency (with possible wait states). The EISA bus buffer provides for a controlled data transfer between the local bus and the EISA bus.

The heart of an EISA bus is the EISA bus controller. It distinguishes between EISA and ISA bus cycles, supplies all the required ISA and EISA bus signals, executes normal and burst cycles, and carries out the entire bus control operation in the EISA PC. Together with the data swapper, it divides 32-bit quantities into 8- or 16-bit portions for 8- and 16-bit peripherals, or recombines such portions into a 32-bit quantity. That is necessary, for example, if you insert a 16-bit ISA adapter into an EISA slot. The EISA maxim of compatibility then requires that the EISA logic accesses the ISA adapter without any problem.

EISA adapter cards with their own busmaster have a busmaster interface which enables a local CPU (the busmaster) to control the EISA bus. Thus, EISA is an important step towards a multiprocessor environment. Moreover, the arbitration logic and the altered assignment of DMA and interrupt channels already supports multitasking operating systems on a hardware level. It would be a pity to waste an i486 or Pentium on DOS alone. Presently, there is an EISA chip set from Intel on the market that integrates the interrupt controller, DMA controller, bus arbitrator, timer and the NMI logic on a single chip: the 82357 ISP (integrated system peripheral). The bus controller is available as the 82358 EBC (EISA bus controller). The EISA bus can carry out various bus cycles:

- standard bus cycle,
- burst cycle,
- bus cycle with BCLK stretching, and
- enhanced master burst cycles EMB-66 and EMB-133.

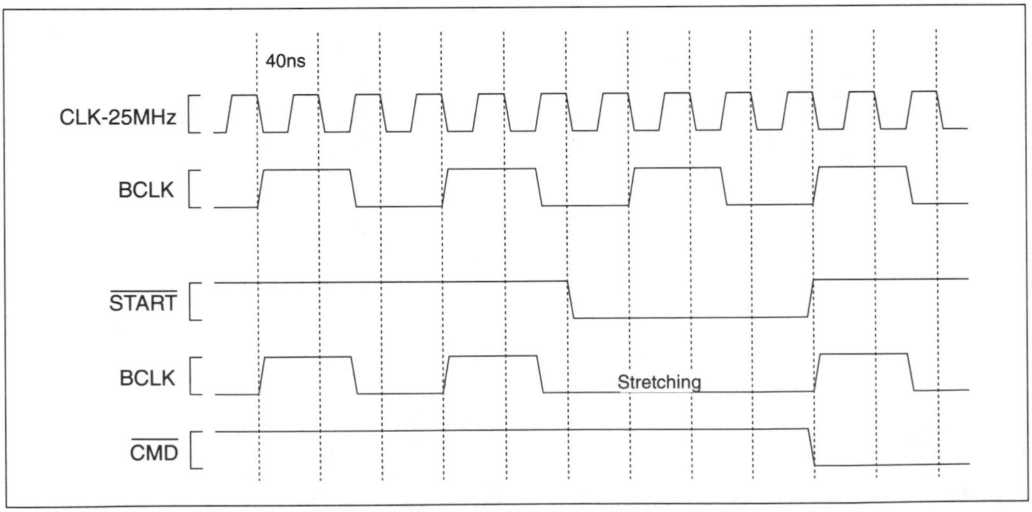

Figure 20.2: BCLK stretching. By means of stretching one half cycle of the bus clock BCLK, the bus clock can be resynchronized with slower operating devices more quickly.

The standard bus cycle is a normal i386 bus cycle, at least as far as the course of the participating address, data and control signals are concerned. As the EISA bus is running with a bus clock of at most 8.33 MHz, even with slow-clocked i386 CPUs a lot of CPU wait cycles are necessary. The standard bus cycle requires two BCLK cycles for transferring at most one quantity of 32 bits. The burst cycle is the same as the i486 burst cycle, but here the bus clock BCLK instead of the processor clock PCLK is decisive. A real novelty is the bus cycle with BCLK stretching. The EISA bus controller is able to stretch one half cycle of BCLK to service slower devices at best, and to restore synchronization with the CPU clock again. Figure 20.2 illustrates this: the CPU frequency is 25 MHz, and the bus frequency BCLK is generated by dividing by three, so it is therefore 8.33 MHz. A half cycle of BCLK is stretched under two circumstances:

- synchronization of the rising BCLK edge with the falling edge of $\overline{CMD}$ if the busmaster on the motherboard addresses an EISA or ISA slave;
- synchronization of the rising BCLK edge with the falling edge of $\overline{CMD}$ if an ISA master addresses an EISA slave.

By stretching BCLK, an EISA or ISA slave can be better integrated into an EISA system, as with the AT. The number of clock cycles for slower peripherals is reduced, and the system throughput is enhanced.

The advance of VLB and PCI is also reflected by the EISA specification. The EISA interest group has recently defined a new *enhanced master burst* cycle which should increase the transfer rate up to 66 Mbyte/s (EMB-66) or even 133 Mbyte/s (EMB-133). To achieve that, a data transfer is no longer only triggered by the ascending BCLK edge. Additionally, both the ascending and the descending BCLK edges can issue a data transfer. Thus, the transfer rate is doubled, while the bus frequency remains unchanged at a maximum of 8.33 MHz for compatibility reasons. Together with a data bus width of 32 bits, this leads to a transfer rate of 66 Mbytes/s. To reach the mentioned 133 Mbytes/s, additionally the 32-bit address part of the EISA bus is used for the data transfer, as this part is unused during the data transfer phase in burst mode. Therefore, the data bus width increases to 64 bits.

20.2 Bus Arbitration

A significant advance compared to the ISA bus is *bus arbitration*. This means that an external microprocessor on an EISA adapter card can also completely control the bus, and may therefore access the system's main memory, the hard disk and all other system components on its own, without the need of support by the CPU. This is necessary for a powerful multiprocessor operation if, for example, the 82596 LAN controller wants to access main memory and the hard disk. Such external *EISA busmasters* can request control of the bus by the EISA $\overline{MREQ}$ (master request) signal from the host CPU on the motherboard. The host CPU is the standard busmaster in this case.

The release of the bus control to an external busmaster on an adapter card was also possible with the AT, but in the AT this takes place via a DMA channel, and a powerful arbitration for several external busmasters is impossible in practice. The PC/XT and AT were only conceived of as single processor machines. Arbitration in the AT can only be a last resort, therefore. An efficient and fair arbitration model is not implemented.

On the other hand, for releasing the EISA bus to various busmasters EISA uses an arbitration model with three levels: DMA/refresh (highest level); CPU/master; other masters (lowest level). On each level several masters may be present. Within the level concerned the bus is switched in a rotating order. Refreshing the memory has the highest priority, because a lock of the refresh by another master would lead to a data loss in DRAM, and therefore to a crash of the whole system. If the refresh control requests the bus via an arbitration, it always gets control after a short reaction time period. All other busmasters have to wait until the current refresh cycle is completed.

EISA busmasters don't have to worry about refreshing the main memory on the motherboard. This is carried out by a dedicated refresh logic. On the other hand, in the AT the pseudo-ISA busmasters on an ISA adapter must also control the memory refresh if they are in control of the bus.

With the EISA busmaster status register, EISA implements the possibility of determining the last active busmaster. This is important, for example, for an NMI handler which, after a time-out error for the EISA bus, must evaluate which busmaster has operated erroneously. Figure 20.3 shows the structure of this register. Note that a zero value indicates the slot with the last active busmaster.

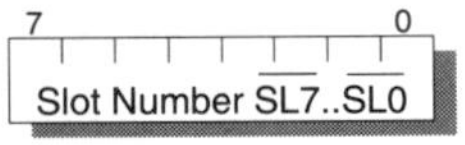

$\overline{SL0}$... $\overline{SL7}$: Slot containing the last active busmaster
$\overline{SLx}$=0: Slot x contains last active busmaster

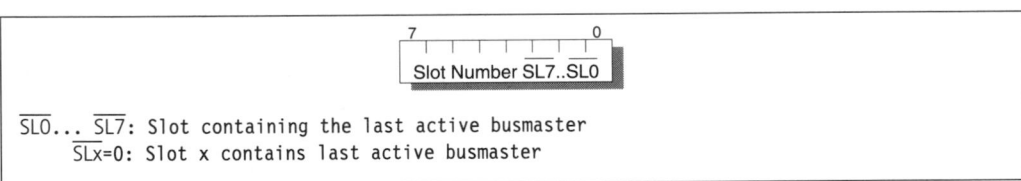

Figure 20.3: EISA busmaster status register (Port 464h).

20.3 DMA Architecture

The DMA system has also been improved significantly compared to the AT bus. Not only is the complete 32-bit address space available for *every* DMA transfer (the AT bus allows only 64 or 128 kbyte blocks), but three new DMA operation modes with improved data throughput have also been implemented: DMA types A, B and C. The previous mode is now called the *compatible mode*. In this mode, the addresses are generated at the same clock cycles with an identical clock length, as on the ISA bus (that is, as was the case with the 8237A).

The new EISA DMA operating type A, on the other hand, shortens the memory phase of the DMA transfer, but the I/O phase remains equal. Thus, one DMA cycle is carried out within six BCLK cycles, and the maximum data throughput reaches 5.56 Mbyte/s. Most ISA devices can be operated on an EISA system with type A without causing a malfunction. With the DMA type B, the I/O cycle also needs less time so that only four BCLK cycles are necessary for one DMA transfer. The data throughput is 8.33 Mbytes/s at the most. Type B is supported by only a few

ISA devices. Finally, only EISA devices that support burst cycles are able to follow burst type C. Here, one DMA transfer is executed within a single BCLK cycle. With DMA burst type C, DMA transfer rates of up to 33 Mbytes/s can be achieved if the full 32-bit width of the EISA data bus is used. This is the maximum transfer rate for the EISA bus. EISA DMA modes A to C support an 8-, 16- and 32-bit data transfer. The transfer of data read or data write from/to hard disks by means of DMA is again becoming interesting with EISA.

To address the 32-bit address space two page registers are available with EISA: the low- and high-page registers. Their addresses are listed in Table 20.1. The low-page register is completely compatible with the conventional DMA page register, known from the AT. The high-page register supplies the high-order address byte A31–A24, and often serves to distinguish ISA and EISA DMA cycles: if the high-page register is not initialized in advance of a DMA transfer, an ISA DMA cycle has to be executed which is compatible with the 8237A chip. Once the high-page register has also been initialized, the DMA control is really operating in EISA mode and the complete 32-bit address space is available. The EISA DMA chip increases or decreases the whole 32-bit address. Therefore (theoretically), a complete 4 Gbyte block can be transferred. In 8237A-compatible mode, on the other hand, only the current address register with a width of 16 bits is altered, so that only a 64 or 128 kbyte block can be moved.

Channel	Low-page register	High-page register
0	87h	487h
1	83h	483h
2	81h	481h
3	82h	482h
4	8fh	48fh
5	8bh	48bh
6	89h	489h
7	8ah	48ah

Table 20.1: I/O addresses of EISA page registers

With EISA the service of the DMA channels is no longer carried out according to a scheme with fixed priorities, but distributed over three levels. Within each level the channels are allocated according to a rotating scheme. This avoids the case where one peripheral with a high DMA priority locks out other devices with lower priorities by frequent DMA requests. This might be possible, for example, if a task services a communications port where external requests are arriving continuously, but another task with a lower DMA priority accesses the hard disk. The frequent requests lock out the task which attempts to read data from the hard disk. Thus the more elaborate DMA hierarchy (as compared to the AT) supports multitasking operating systems where several tasks are competing for the DMA channels – more or less a protection of minorities in the PC. Also, the microchannel follows a similar strategy.

EISA implements seven DMA channels in total, which may be programmed to serve 8-, 16- or 32-bit devices. The control of channels 0–7 for an ISA-compatible or real EISA transfer is carried out with the two extended mode registers. They are write-only, and are located at I/O addresses 40bh (channels 0–3) and 4d6h (channels 4–7), respectively. Figure 20.4 shows the structure of these registers.

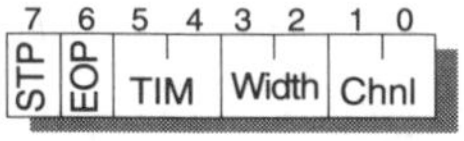

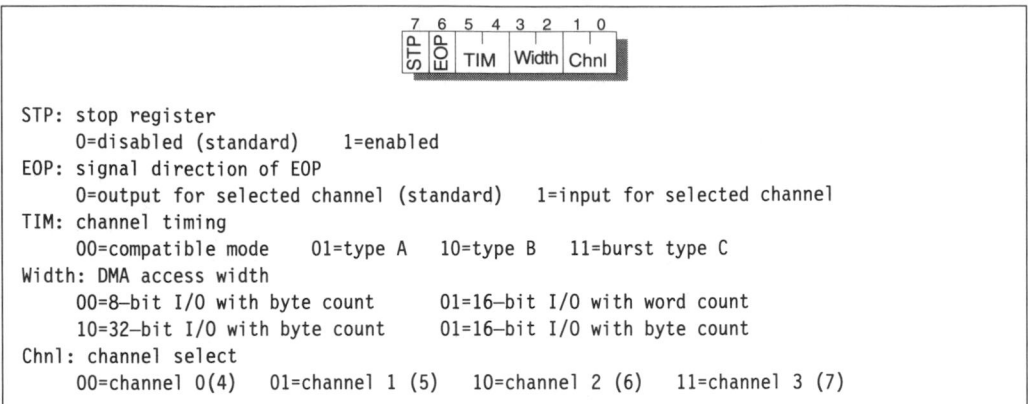

```
STP: stop register
     0=disabled (standard)    1=enabled
EOP: signal direction of EOP
     0=output for selected channel (standard)   1=input for selected channel
TIM: channel timing
     00=compatible mode    01=type A    10=type B    11=burst type C
Width: DMA access width
     00=8-bit I/O with byte count      01=16-bit I/O with word count
     10=32-bit I/O with byte count     01=16-bit I/O with byte count
Chnl: channel select
     00=channel 0(4)   01=channel 1 (5)    10=channel 2 (6)    11=channel 3 (7)
```

Figure 20.4: Extended mode register (channels 0–3: port 40bh; channels 4–7: port 4d6h).

Through the *STP* bit you activate the EISA extension for a DMA buffer structure in the main memory from where data is sequentially read or stored. Usually this feature is not used, and STP equals 0. The *EOP* bit determines the direction of the EOP signal for the selected channel. In the PC/XT/AT, EOP was configured as output. EISA additionally allows EOP from an external device (for example, a communication interface). The *TIM* entry defines the transfer mode, *Width* the access width of the DMA channel, and the counting mode. A value of 00b corresponds to the 8-bit DMA channels of the PC/XT/AT, and a value of 01b to the 16-bit AT channels. Thus, for Width=01b the output address is shifted by one bit to address 16-bit words. The address generated internally in the word count register is incremented only by one upon each transfer. Through the shifted address, however, this means an incrementation by two. On the other hand, for Width=10b, the word count register is incremented by two upon every transfer. Finally, the DMA controller increments the address by four when 32-bit I/O with byte count is selected. The two *Channel* bits determine for which of the eight channels 0–7 the other entries are valid.

20.4 Interrupt Subsystem

As is the case with ISA, EISA also implements 15 interrupt levels which are managed by the EISA interrupt controller. Table 20.2 lists the typical assignment of these IRQ channels.

Channel	Priority	Assigned to	Interrupt vector
IRQ0	1	timer 0, internal system clock	08h
IRQ1	2	keyboard	09h
IRQ2	–	cascading according to the second PIC in the AT	0ah
IRQ3	11	COM2	73h
IRQ4	12	COM1	74h

Table 20.2: EISA IRQ channels

Channel	Priority	Assigned to	Interrupt vector
IRQ5	13	LPT2	75h
IRQ6	14	floppy controller	76h
IRQ7	15	LPT1	77h
IRQ8	3	real time clock	0bh
IRQ9	4	unused	0ch
IRQ10	5	unused	0dh
IRQ11	6	unused	0eh
IRQ12	7	unused	0fh
IRQ13	8	coprocessor	70h
IRQ14	9	hard disk controller	71h
IRQ15	10	unused	72h

Table 20.2: cont.

For compatibility reasons, IRQ2 is occupied by cascading. The EISA interrupt controller behaves in the same way as the two cascaded 8259A PICs in the AT. Thus you have to output a double EOI to master and slave for the IRQ8–IRQ15 channels to terminate a hardware interrupt. Unlike the AT, the interrupt channels assigned to EISA adapters may also operate with level instead of edge triggering. The level of an IRQ line above a certain threshold level issues an interrupt request in this case, and not the rise itself. It is therefore possible for several sources to share an IRQ. If one source is serviced the corresponding IRQ remains active and shows that a further device on the same IRQ line requests an interrupt. This means that in principle any number of devices may request an interrupt. Unlike the PC/XT and the AT, a line is no longer reserved for a single device. In the case of the three serial interfaces COM1, COM2, COM3, for example, previously only COM1 and COM2 could issue an interrupt via IRQ4 and IRQ3, while COM3 could only be operated with polling.

The PIC 8259A in the PC/XT and AT can also operate with level triggering. Upon initialization, however, you must decide whether *all* interrupts should be detected by level or edge triggering. An individual choice is not possible there; EISA permits this by means of the control register for level/edge triggering (Figure 20.5).

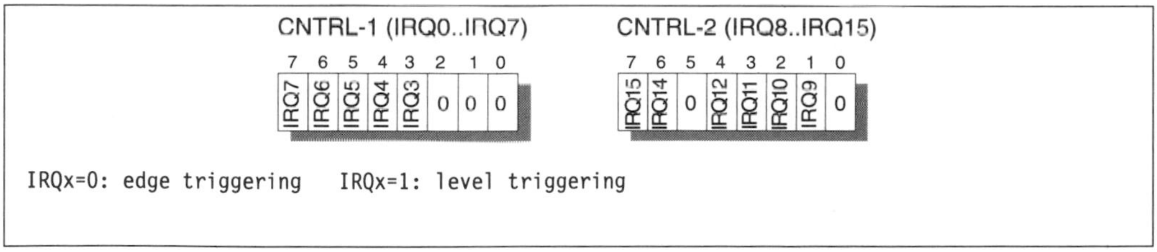

Figure 20.5: Control register for level/edge triggering (IRQ 0–7: port 4d0h; IRQ 8–15: port 4d1h).

Entries for IRQ0–IRQ2, IRQ8 and IRQ13 are missing because they refer to devices integrated on the motherboard (see Table 20.2). Note that only interrupts that service an EISA device may operate with level triggering. If you use an ISA adapter, the interrupt assigned to it must be programmed as edge triggered for compatibility reasons.

To complete the picture, I should mention that you can issue an NMI via software by writing an arbitrary value to the 8-bit port 462h. Do not confuse that with the INT 02h instruction which also leads to an interrupt 02h. Writing to the port 462h supplies the processor with an active NMI signal externally and, thus, simulates a hardware-issued non-maskable interrupt.

20.5 EISA Timer and Fail-Safe Timer

The EISA timer comprises six channels in total, and is equivalent to and register-compatible with two 8254 chips. The first three channels 0–2 are reserved for the internal system clock, the memory refresh, and tone generation for the speaker, as was the case with the AT. One of the remaining three timers is used as a failsafe or watchdog timer. Generally, this is timer 3, that is, counter 0 of the second 8254. It issues an NMI if a certain time period has elapsed. This prevents an external busmaster from keeping control of the bus too long and blocking necessary interrupts or memory refresh. If an external busmaster keeps control of the EISA bus too long, in contradiction to the bus arbitration rules, this indicates a hardware malfunction or the crash of the external busmaster. The failsafe timer then issues an NMI, and the arbitration logic returns control to the CPU so that it may service the NMI. You may access the first timer via the I/O addresses 40h to 43h, and the second timer through 48h to 4bh.

20.6 I/O Address Space

With EISA, the support and controller chips are also accessed via ports. Table 20.3 lists the new I/O address areas for EISA. Unlike ISA, the individual EISA slots, and therefore also the inserted EISA adapters, can be addressed individually. Internal registers on the EISA adapters therefore have different base addresses 1000–8000h. This is important so that EISA adapters can be automatically configured without DIP switches. The high-order byte of the I/O address is decoded by the I/O address logic of the motherboard, which uses it to drive the expansion slot concerned. The address decoder on the expansion adapters then only decodes the low-order address bytes further. Thus, an ISA adapter which knows only a 10-bit I/O address can also be inserted into an EISA slot without any problems.

I/O address	Meaning
0000h ... 00ffh	ISA motherboard
0100h ... 03ffh	ISA expansion adapter
0400h ... 04ffh	reserved for controllers on the EISA motherboard
0800h ... 08ffh	reserved for EISA motherboard
0c00h ... 0cffh	reserved for EISA motherboard
1000h ... 1fffh	expansion slot 1
2000h ... 2fffh	expansion slot 2
3000h ... 3fffh	expansion slot 3
4000h ... 4fffh	expansion slot 4
5000h ... 5fffh	expansion slot 5

Table 20.3: EISA port addresses

I/O address	Meaning
6000h ... 6fffh	expansion slot 6
7000h ... 7fffh	expansion slot 7
8000h ... 8fffh	expansion slot 8
9000h ... 9fffh	reserved for additional expansion slots*)

*) Most EISA PCs have only eight expansion slots.

Table 20.3: cont.

20.7 CMOS-RAM

With EISA adapter cards the IRQ used, as well as the DMA channels, are programmable. The configuration information is stored in the extended CMOS RAM. EISA specifically extends the CMOS RAM by 4 kbytes for this purpose. Special installation programs provide support when configuring the EISA adapters, and automatically write data into the extended EISA CMOS RAM. Typical information is which I/O ports are used by the adapter, which IRQ and DMA channels are assigned to the adapter, etc. This EISA system information can be retrieved by means of several functions of INT 15h. They are listed in the following.

- **INT 15h, Function d8h, Subfunction AL=00h – Access to EISA System Information, Read Slot Info**

This function returns information pertaining to the adapter in a certain slot.

Register	Call value	Return value
AH	d8h	error code1)
AL	00h/80h2)	vendor byte3)
BH		utility revision (high)
BL		utility revision (low)
CH		check sum configuration file (MSB)
CL	Slot (0–63)	check sum configuration file (LSB)
DH		number of device functions
DL		function information
SI:DI		compressed vendor ID
Carry		error if <> 0

1) see Table 20.4.
2) 00h=CS with 16-bit addressing; 80h=CS with 32-bit addressing
3) Bit 7=1:multiple ID present
Bit 6: product ID
Bit 5..4: device/slot type (00=slot, 01=embedded device, 10=virtual device, 11=reserved)
Bit 3..0: multiple ID (0000=no multiple ID, 0001=first multiple ID, ..., 1111=15th multiple ID)

– INT 15h, Function d8h, Subfunction AL=01h – Access to EISA System Information, Read Function Info

This function returns 320 information bytes in an info table pertaining to the indicated function in a certain slot. The calling program must provide a sufficiently large buffer for the info table.

Register	Call value	Return value
AH	d8h	error code[1)]
AL	01h/81h[2)]	
CH	function (0–n–1)	
CL	slot (0–63)	
[E]SI	offset info table[3)]	offset info table[3)]
DS	segment info table[3)]	segment info table[3)]
Carry		error if <> 0

[1)] see Table 20.4.

[2)] 01h=CS with 16-bit addressing; 81h=CS with 32-bit addressing

[3)] information table:

Offset	Size	Entry
00h	2 words	compressed ID (bits 0..1 and 13–15=character 2, bits 2..6=character 1, bit 7=reserved, bits 8..12=character 3, bits 16–19, 20–23, 28–31=first, second and third digit of product number, bits 24..27=revision number)
04h	1 word	ID and slot info (bit 7=1:multiple ID present, Bit 6: ID readable, bits 5..4: 00=slot, 01=embedded device, 10=virtual device, 11=reserved, bits 3..0: 0000=no multiple ID, 0001=first multiple ID, ..., 1111=15th multiple ID, bit 8=1/0: EISA ENABLE supported/not supported, bit 9=1/0: EISA IOCHKERR supported/not supported, bits 10..14=reserved, bit 15=1/0: configuration incomplete/complete
06h	1 word	revision number of configuration file
08h	13 words	select (byte 0=first select, byte 1=second select, ..., Byte 25=26th select)
22h	1 byte	type of following function info (bit 0=type/subtype, bit 1=memory, Bit 2=interrupt, bit 3=DMA, bit 4=port address area, bit 5=port initialization, bit 6=free entry, bit 7=1/0: function disabled/enabled)
23h	80 bytes	type/subtype as ASCII string
73h	63 bytes	memory configuration (bit 0=1/0: RAM/ROM, bit 1=1/0: not cachable/cachable, bit 2=reserved, bit 3..4=memory type (00=system, 01=expanded, 10=virtual, 11=else), bit 5=1/0: shared/non-shared memory, bit 6=reserved, bit 7=1/0=more entries/last entry, bits 8..9=data access size (00=byte, 01=word, 10=dword, 11=reserved), bits 10..11=decode size (00=20, 01=24, 10=32 bits, 11=reserved), bits 12..15=reserved, bits 8–31=memory start address/100h, bits 32–47=memory size/400h; max. eight identical 7-byte entries follow)
b2h	14 bytes	interrupt configuration (bits 0..3=interrupt no.. 0h..0fh, bit 4=reserved, bit 5=1/0: level/edge triggered, bit 6=1/0=shared/non-shared, bit 7=1/0: more entries/last entry; max. six identical 2-byte entries follow)
c0h	4 words	DMA configuration (bits 0..2=channel no. 0..7, bits 3–5=reserved, bit 6=1/0: shared/non-shared, bit 7=1/0: more entries/last entry, bits 8..9=reserved, bits 10..11=transfer size (00=8, 01=16, 10=32 bits, 11=reserved), bits 12..13=clocking (00=ISA compatible, 01=type A, 10=type B, 11=burst type C), bits 14..15=reserved; max. three identical 2-byte entries follow)
c8h	60 bytes	I/O port info (bits 0..4=number of successive ports minus 1, bit 5=reserved, bit 6=1/0: shared/non-shared, bit 7=1/0: more entries/last entry, bits 8..23=port address; max. 19 identical 3-byte entries follow)

104h	60 bytes	initialization info (bits 0..1=access type (00=byte, 01=word, 10=dword, 11=reserved), bit 2=1/0: port write with/without mask, bits 3..6=reserved, bit 7=1/0: more entries/last entry, bits 8..23=port address; if bit 2=0 (no mask): byte 3 or bytes 3..4 or bytes 3..6=value; if bit 2=1 (mask): byte 4 or bytes 5..6 or bytes 7..10=mask; max. seven identical 4-byte, 5-byte, 7-byte or 11-byte entries follow)
or after the first 115 bytes (free entry):		
073h	205 bytes	205 free data bytes

- **INT 15h, Function d8h, Subfunction AL=02h – Access to EISA System Information, Erase Configuration RAM**

This function erases the CMOS RAM by writing a value of 0 to all addresses.

Register	Call value	Return value
AH	d8h	error code1)
AL	02h/82h2)	
BH	utility revision (high)	
BL	utility revision (low)	
Carry		error if <> 0

1) see Table 20.4

2) 02h=CS with 16-bit addressing; 88h=CS with 32-bit addressing

- **INT 15h, Function d8h, Subfunction AL=03h – Access to EISA System Information, Write Configuration**

This function writes configuration values from a table of the calling program into the CMOS RAM. Additionally, a new checksum is calculated and written to the appropriate location, although you must also specify a correct value. The function must be called successively for every slot present in the system, even if no adapter is installed (the passed values must be set to 0).

Register	Call value	Return value
AH	d8h	error code1)
AL	03h	
CX	byte length of table	
[E]SI	offset of table2)	
DS	segment of table 2)	
Carry		error if <> 0

1) see Table 20.4

2) information table (the structure of the individual entries is the same as that of the information table of subfunction 01h):

Size	Entry
2 words	compressed ID
1 word	ID and slot info
1 word	revision number of configuration file
1 word	function length (this entry and the checksum do not contribute to the function length!)

2–26 bytes	select
1 byte	type of function info
2–80 bytes	type/subtype as ASCII string
7–63 bytes	memory configuration
2–14 bytes	interrupt configuration
1–4 words	DMA configuration
3–60 bytes	I/O port info
4–60 bytes	initialization info
1 word	checksum
or after the first 115 bytes (free entry):	
205 bytes	205 free data bytes

Error code	**Meaning**
00h	no error
80h	invalid slot number
81h	invalid function number
82h	extended CMOS RAM damaged
83h	slot doesn't contain any adapter
84h	error upon writing into extended CMOS RAM
85h	CMOS RAM full
86h	invalid BIOS call
87h	invalid system configuration

Table 20.4: Error codes for INT 15h, function d8h

20.8 EISA Adapters and Automatic Configuration

On EISA adapters you will look in vain for DIP switches, which sometimes made configuring ISA adapters appear like gambling, with an unpredictable result. EISA solves the configuration problem much more efficiently: every EISA adapter comes with a floppy disk holding a *configuration file (CFG)*. The CFG stores the system elements of the EISA PC used, such as, for example, the assigned IRQ and DMA channels. This information is used by a configuration utility which is delivered together with each EISA PC to configure both the adapter and PC correctly. Additionally, the utility is intelligent enough to detect access conflicts and to react appropriately. Examples of this are address conflicts between two adapters whose address areas overlap, at least partially. This may occur with interfaces whose register addresses are equal, or with identical ROM base addresses of the SCSI host and VGA graphics adapters. Such address conflicts are the main reason why an AT refuses to run after installing and configuring the brand-new VGA adapter.

The CFG file was part of the EISA concept from the start. All the firms involved in EISA agreed to a standard for the file format, so incompatibilities do not arise here. The name of every CFG file must obey the following rule: !hhhpppp.CFG; where hhh is an abbreviation for the manufacturer, and pppp is a product identification. The CFG files themselves are pure ASCII files, and use a language with strictly defined commands that recall the CONFIG.SYS of MS-DOS. Examples of CFG commands are: *NAME = ???, SLOT = ???, BUSMASTER = value?,*

COMMENTS = text. Manufacturers can determine all the important parameters for their EISA adapters by using the CFG commands, so that the configuration utility need only read the CFG file to configure the EISA PC correctly with details of the newly installed adapter. The user does not need detailed knowledge of occupied addresses, DMA channels, etc. and the typical cow-at-a-five-barred-gate feeling of untrained users can thus be avoided. The configuration data is stored in the extended CMOS RAM, and the EISA PC boots without additional configuration next time. If the configuration data in the CMOS RAM gets lost, for example, through a battery power-break, then you need simply start the configuration utility and reconfigure the system again using the CFG files for all installed adapters.

Besides the CFG files, EISA has another concept for supporting configuration, the so-called *overlay files (OVL)*. They supplement the configuration language on the level of the configuration utility, and contain instructions in a format that looks like a mixture of C and Assembler. By means of the OVL files, a very exotic EISA adapter can be integrated into an EISA system automatically. The OVL files are in about the same relationship to the configuration utility as a ROM extension is to the system ROM of the motherboard, and they extend the CFG language by new commands. An OVL file is integrated into a CFG file by means of an INCLUDE command, for example, INCLUDE=«super_ad.ovl».

20.9 EISA Slot

For extension of the ISA bus up to 32 bits, EISA additionally implements 90 new contacts. Presently, only 16 of them are used for data lines, 23 for address lines, and 16 for control and status lines. In addition to the 98 ISA contacts already present, these 90 new contacts would lead to a huge EISA contact strip on the motherboard (probably bigger than the motherboard itself). The microchannel solves this problem by miniaturizing the contacts and the distance between them, thus making the microchannel plug-incompatible. But EISA was launched to enable an integration of the previous ISA components without any problem. This, of course, means that the geometry of the EISA slots is harmonized with the existing ISA adapters. The members of the EISA group negotiated these obstacles elegantly by implementing a second layer of contacts in the EISA plug which is shifted against the previous ISA contacts so that only EISA adapters can reach them. ISA adapter cards do not short-circuit the contacts because an ISA adapter cannot penetrate deep enough into the EISA slot. Thus an EISA slot is quite compact for the enormous number of contacts and, moreover, completely compatible with the ISA adapter cards which have only one contact layer. Figure 20.6 schematically shows the structure of an EISA slot and the assignment of the corresponding contacts.

The signals listed on the outer sides of the figure are the new EISA signals which are supplied or accepted by the lower-lying contacts. By means of the shifted arrangement of the EISA contacts, 38 instead of 36 new contacts have been added to the previous ISA extension. Thus the EISA slot comprises 188 contacts. The encoding barriers in the slots prevent an EISA adapter card from being inserted wrongly, or an EISA card from penetrating too deep into the slot and short-circuiting the EISA contacts.

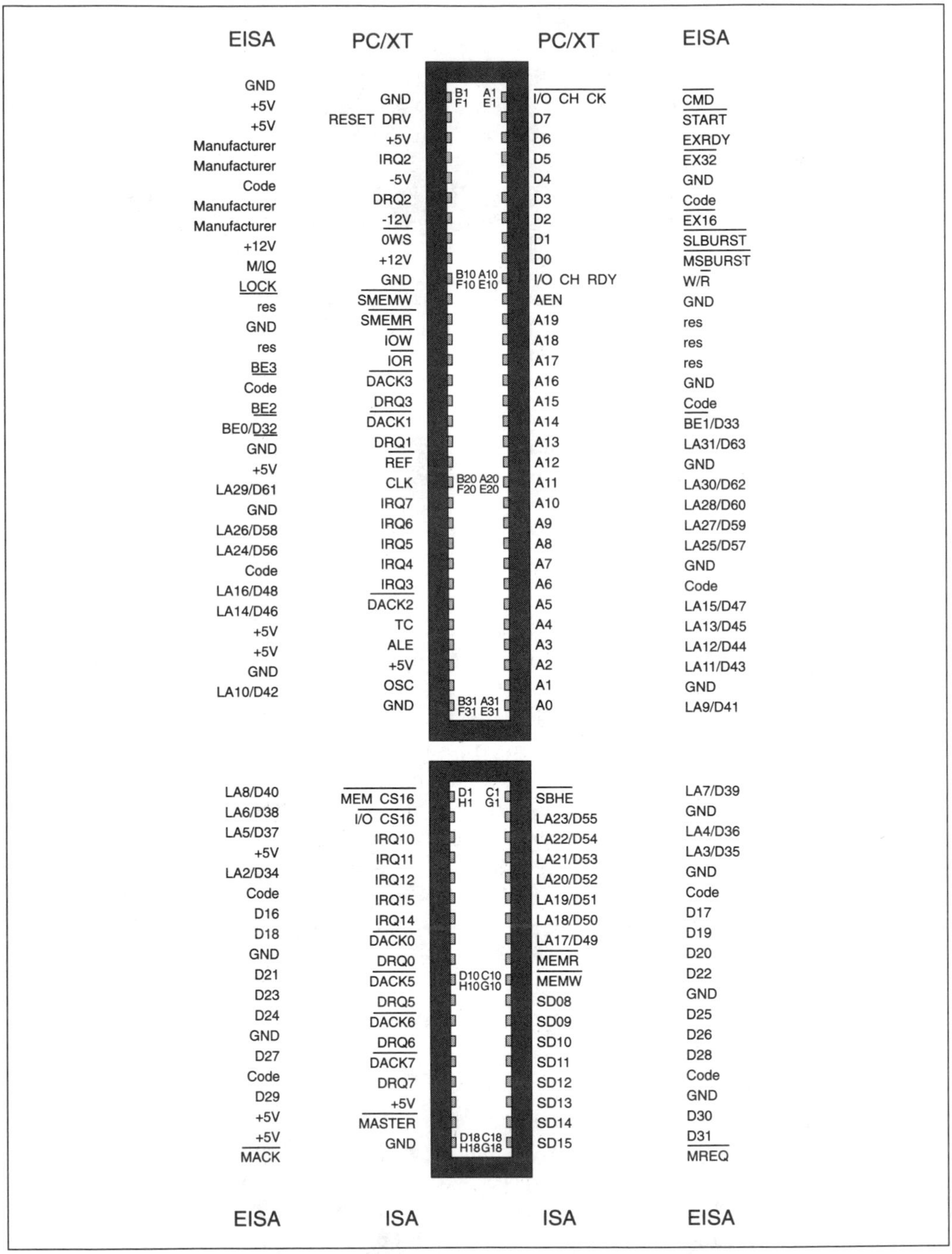

Figure 20.6: The EISA slot has lower and shifted contacts for the extension to 32 bits. Thus the slot size remains the same as for the ISA bus. Address connections assigned twice are used in an EMB cycle for the data transfer.

Four of these contacts are available to each manufacturer for their own purposes. Using these, a manufacturer can develop a specially adapted adapter card for applications that need signals that go beyond the EISA specification. Such adapters are, of course, no longer completely EISA compatible. On the other hand, though, the manufacturer is not restricted too much in his freedom to develop certain adapters.

20.10 EISA Signals

In the following sections the new EISA contacts are discussed, as well as the meaning of the supplied or delivered signals. The ISA part's assignment of an EISA slot can be found in Section 19.3. The ISA contacts CLK and ALE are indicated by BCLK and BALE here, as is usual for EISA. Because EISA supports busmasters on external adapters without any restriction, all connections are bidirectional. To show the data and signal flow more precisely, I have assumed for the transfer directions indicated that the CPU (or another device on the motherboard) represents the current busmaster.

BALE (O; ISA)
Terminal B28
The address latch enable signal BALE is generated by the bus controller and indicates that valid address signals are present on the I/O channel. The adapters can then decode the address.

BCLK (O; ISA)
Terminal B20
BCLK is the bus clock signal for the EISA bus, and is generated by dividing the CPU frequency so that BCLK has a frequency of 8.33 MHz at most. BCLK determines the data transfer rate. In burst mode or EISA DMA mode C, the transfer rate reaches up to 33.3 Mbyte/s (8.33 MHz*32 bits).

$\overline{\text{BE0}}$–$\overline{\text{BE3}}$
Terminals E17, F15, F17–F18
These four byte enable signals indicate on which byte of the 32-bit data bus data is transferred. Therefore, they correspond to the A0 and A1 address bits. The signals come directly from the CPU. $\overline{\text{BE0}}$ refers to the least-significant byte D0–D7 of the data bus, $\overline{\text{BE3}}$ to the most-significant byte D24–D31.

$\overline{\text{CMD}}$
Terminal E1
This command signal serves for clock harmonization within an EISA bus cycle by stretching a bus clock cycle BCLK appropriately. $\overline{\text{CMD}}$ is generated by the EISA bus control for all EISA bus cycles.

Cod.
Bridges E6, E16, E25, F6, F16, F25, G6, G15, H6, H16
The coding bridges prevent an ISA adapter penetrating too deep into an EISA slot and, thus, short-circuiting or damaging the lower EISA contacts.

D16–D31
Terminals G7–G10, G12–G14, G17–G18, H7–H8, H10–H12, H14, H16
These 16 bits form the high-order word of the 32-bit EISA data bus. The 16 low-order bits are transferred via the ISA bus section.

$\overline{\text{EX16}}$
Terminal E7
An EISA slave activates the $\overline{\text{EX16}}$ signal if it can run with a 16-bit data bus only (that is, is an EISA 16-bit device). The EISA bus controller then accesses the device via D0–D15 with a width of 16 bits. The EISA bus controller also divides all 32-bit quantities from the CPU into 16-bit portions, and combines 16-bit portions from the EISA slave into a 32-bit quantity for the CPU, respectively.

$\overline{\text{EX32}}$
Terminal E4
An EISA slave activates the $\overline{\text{EX32}}$ signal if it can run with a 32-bit data bus (that is, is an EISA 32-bit device). The EISA bus controller then accesses the device via D0–D31 with a width of 32 bits.

EXRDY
Terminal E3
An active EISA ready signal EXRDY indicates that the addressed EISA device may complete the current bus cycle. EXRDY serves to insert wait states into an EISA bus cycle.

LA2–LA16, LA24–LA31
Terminals E18, E20–E23, E26–E29, E31, F21, F23–F24, F26–F27, F31, G1, G3–G4, H1–H3, H5
The large address signals LA2–LA16 correspond to the A2–A16 signals of the ISA bus, but they are valid earlier because, unlike the A2–A16 signals, they are not latched and thus delayed. LA24–LA31 is the high-order address byte of the 32-bit EISA data bus. Together with the non-latched ISA address signals LA17–LA23, the LA2–LA16 and LA24–LA31 signals form the address bus for fast EISA bus cycles. ISA bus cycles, on the other hand, use the latched (and therefore slower) address signals A0–A16. In EISA bus cycles, the two low-order address bits corresponding to A0 and A1 are decoded from the four bits $\overline{\text{BE0}}$–$\overline{\text{BE3}}$.

$\overline{\text{LOCK}}$
Terminal F11
This locked cycle signal is active (low) if a busmaster on the motherboard carries out a locked bus cycle with an EISA slave. Using this, the busmaster has the exclusive access right to memory as long as $\overline{\text{LOCK}}$ is active. Other chips such as, for example, DMA cannot use the memory during this time period.

M/$\overline{\text{IO}}$
Terminal F10
This signal serves to distinguish memory and I/O EISA bus cycles.

Manufacturer (I/O)
Terminals F4–F5, F7–F8
These connections can be used by EISA OEMs for their own purposes.

$\overline{\text{MACK}}$

Terminal H19

The system arbitrator responds with a master acknowledge signal $\overline{\text{MACK}}$ to a $\overline{\text{MREQ}}$ from an external busmaster to pass over control of the EISA bus.

$\overline{\text{MREQ}}$

Terminal G19

An external device activates the master request signal $\overline{\text{MREQ}}$ to take over control of the EISA bus as a busmaster. The system arbitrator detects $\overline{\text{MREQ}}$ and passes control if no other master is active. Normally, the CPU on the motherboard is the active busmaster.

$\overline{\text{MSBURST}}$

Terminal E9

An EISA master activates the master burst signal $\overline{\text{MSBURST}}$ to inform the EISA bus controller that the master can carry out the next bus cycle as a burst cycle. The bus transfer rate is thus doubled. This is particularly advantageous for cache line fills and DMA transfers.

$\overline{\text{SLBURST}}$

Terminal E8

An EISA slave activates the slave burst signal $\overline{\text{SLBURST}}$ to inform the bus controller that it can follow a burst cycle. Typical EISA slaves that activate $\overline{\text{SLBURST}}$ are fast 32-bit main memories.

$\overline{\text{START}}$

Terminal E2

This signal serves for clock signal coordination at the beginning of an EISA bus cycle. $\overline{\text{START}}$ indicates the beginning of a cycle on the local bus.

W/$\overline{\text{R}}$

Terminal E10

The signal serves to distinguish write and read EISA bus cycles.

D32–D63 (I/O; corresponding to $\overline{\text{BE0}}$, $\overline{\text{BE1}}$, LA2–LA31)

Terminals C2–C8, E17–E18, E20–E23, E26–E29, E31, F18, F21, F23–F24, F26–F27, F31, G1, G3–G4, H1–H3, H5

In an enhanced master burst the 30 address terminals LA2–LA31 and the two byte enable terminals $\overline{\text{BE0}}$ and $\overline{\text{BE1}}$ transfer the 32 high-order data bits of a 64-bit data quantity.

All other contacts are reserved (res), are grounded (GND), or transfer supply voltages for chips (+5 V, –5 V) and interfaces or drives (+12 V, –12 V).

21 32-Bit Microchannel – Revolution

Together with its new generation of PCs, the PS/2, IBM also implemented a new bus system and a new PC architecture, the *microchannel.* In view of its geometry as well as its logical concept, this bus is a radical departure from the AT bus, which had been very successful up until that time. Hardware compatibility to previous PC models is no longer kept, but there are some good reasons for this: the AT bus was only designed for 16-bit processors, but the new i386 and i486 CPUs run with 32 bits. Furthermore, because of its edge triggered interrupts, the AT bus is directed to singletasking operating systems such as DOS. The aim when designing the PS/2, on the other hand, was to go over to multitasking systems, particularly OS/2. Therefore, the problems are similar to those already mentioned in connection with EISA. It is also interesting that the microchannel was presented much earlier than EISA. EISA was supposedly designed as a reaction to the microchannel, so as not to leave the 32-bit market all to IBM. Identical problems often lead to similar solutions, thus it is perhaps not surprising that the microchannel (apart from the completely incompatible bus slot) does not differ radically from EISA. After all, at the operating system level, and especially at the application level, complete compatibility with the AT must be achieved. Programs that do not explicitly refer to the hardware registers also run on the PS/2 without any problems, and with no noticeable difference for the users.

21.1 MCA Bus Structure

Figure 21.1 shows a schematic block diagram of the microchannel architecture (MCA). A significant difference from EISA is the separate system clock which supplies a frequency of 10 MHz at most for all microchannel components. Only the local bus between the CPU and the memory operates faster to carry out data accesses of the CPU to main memory at a maximum speed. Thus the microchannel is an *asynchronous bus system*; the CPU is clocked by its own CPU clock. The microchannel was initially introduced with three different bus cycles:

- standard bus cycle,
- synchronous extended bus cycle, and
- asynchronous extended bus cycle.

The standard bus cycle corresponds to a conventional CPU bus cycle at 10 MHz with no wait cycles. In an extended bus cycle the device addressed inserts wait states by means of the *CHRDY* signal. If CHRDY becomes active synchronous to the data half-cycle of the MCA bus cycle, this is called a synchronous extended bus cycle, otherwise it is an asynchronous extended bus cycle. CHRDY refers to the bus clock of 10 MHz but not to the CPU clock, which may be much higher, especially with i386 or i486 processors. Because of their high clock rates, i386 and i486 always insert several CPU wait cycles which are controlled by the bus controller using the READY processor signal. One MCA bus cycle without wait cycles lasts for two bus clock cycles with 100 ns each. Thus the microchannel is presently conceived for a maximum data transfer rate of 20 Mbytes/s. The data transfer rate can be slightly increased by the so-called *matched-memory cycles*. These are only implemented with the 16 MHz model 80, and are controlled by the $\overline{\text{MMC}}$ and $\overline{\text{MMCR}}$ signals. To carry out a matched-memory cycle the bus controller of the motherboard activates the $\overline{\text{MMC}}$ (matched-memory cycle) signal. If the addressed device responds with an active $\overline{\text{MMCR}}$ (matched-memory cycle return), the bus controller shortens the cycle time of the MCA bus clock to 93.75 ns. $\overline{\text{ADL}}$ and $\overline{\text{CMD}}$ are not generated here, but $\overline{\text{MMCCMD}}$ is. Because of the shorter cycle time, a data transfer rate of at most 21.4 Mbytes/s is possible; this is an incredible increase of 7%.

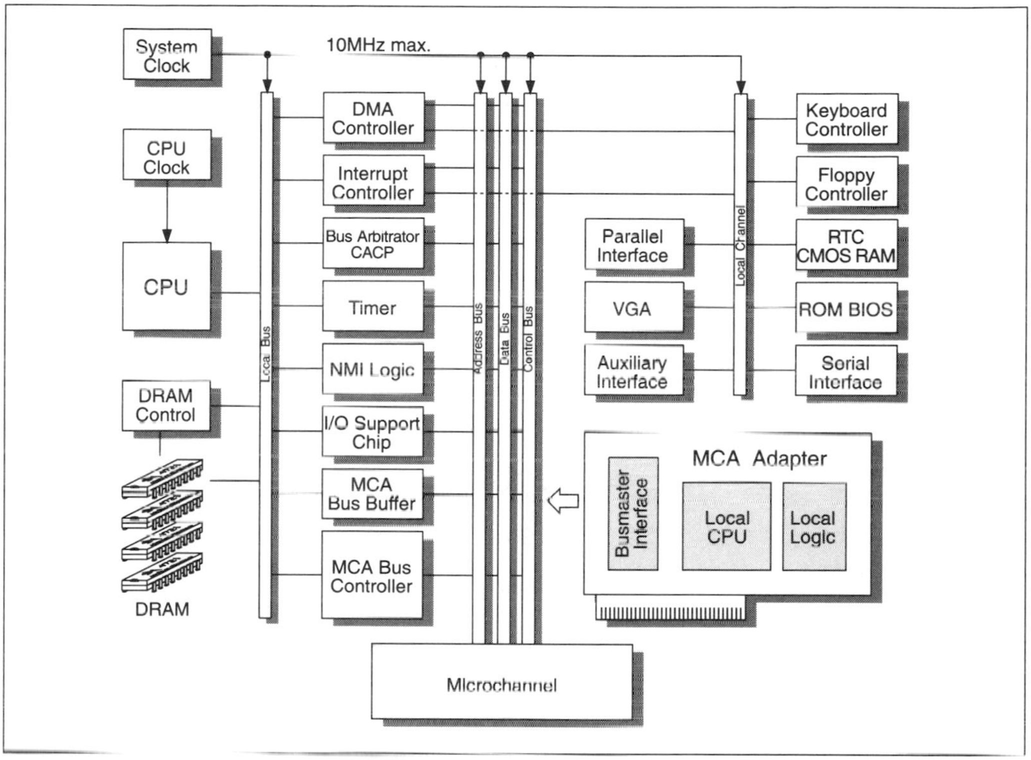

Figure 21.1: The MCA architecture.

No wonder, then, that IBM mothballed the matched-memory cycle, and developed the *streaming data procedure (SDP)* concept. Presently, three such SDPs have been designed:

- 32-bit SDP,
- 64-bit SDP, and
- extended 64-bit SDP.

IBM uses the microchannel not only in its PS/2 series but also in much more powerful RISC System/6000 workstations with a basis of RISC processors with the POWER architecture (**P**erformance **O**ptimization **W**ith **E**nhanced **R**ISC).

In view of the signal course, the 32-bit SDP coincides with the i486 burst mode. To request a 32-bit SDP the busmaster deactivates the $\overline{\text{BLAST}}$ signal. The device addressed responds with a $\overline{\text{BRDY}}$ to indicate that it is able to carry out 32-bit burst mode. With the 32-bit SDP four bytes are transferred within a single MCA bus clock cycle. Using this the data transfer rate increases to 40 Mbytes/s for a short time. This is even more than the 33 Mbytes/s for the EISA burst mode.

A further enhancement is possible with the 64-bit SDP. Here, only during the first bus cycle is the address output. The addressed device accepts and stores it. Afterwards, the data is transferred not only via the 32-bit data bus, but also via the 32-bit address bus, that is, with a width of 64 bits or 8 bytes in total. The device addressed comprises an address counter that counts up with each 64-bit SDP automatically. It therefore only needs the start address. With the 64-bit SDP a data transfer rate of 80 Mbytes/s can be achieved. The extended 64-bit SDP is even more powerful. Here the bus cycle is reduced from 100 ns down to 50 ns, but the transfer itself is identical to that of a normal 64-bit SDP. The data transfer rate doubles to 160 Mbytes/s, that is, a medium-sized hard disk could be read within one second.

21.2 Bus Arbitration

Like EISA, the MCA also supports external busmasters on adapter cards. Including the CPU, up to 16 different busmasters can be integrated. For this purpose, IBM implemented a dedicated chip, the so-called *central arbitration control point* (*CACP*), which carries out the bus arbitration and passes control to a busmaster. With the MCA the motherboard's CPU, the refresh logic, the DMA controller and external busmasters on adapter cards can operate as busmasters. Table 21.1 shows the priorities assigned to these busmasters.

Priority	**Device**
–2d	memory refresh
–1d	NMI
00h	DMA channel 0*)
01h	DMA channel
02h	DMA channel
03h	DMA channel
04h	DMA channel 0*)
05h	DMA channel
06h	DMA channel
07h	DMA channel
08h	available for external busmaster
09h	available for external busmaster
0ah	available for external busmaster
0bh	available for external busmaster
0ch	available for external busmaster
0dh	available for external busmaster
0eh	available for external busmaster
0fh	CPU on the motherboard

*) Priority can be programmed freely.

Table 21.1: Arbitration priorities in the PS/2

The –2 priority of the memory refresh means that the arbitration logic always passes control of the bus if a refresh is requested. The memory refresh is located on the motherboard and drives the arbitration logic by an internal *refresh request* signal. The next lower priority, –1, of the NMI is also processed internally. The source of an NMI is usually an error on an adapter card, a time-out in connection with bus arbitration, or another serious malfunction. The NMI may only be serviced by the CPU on the motherboard. However, for this the CPU needs to be in control of the system bus, because the program code of the accompanying interrupt handler 2 must be read from memory. Therefore, an NMI always forces the CACP to snatch away the system bus from another active busmaster, and to pass control to the CPU.

The lowest priority 0fh of the CPU means that the CPU on the motherboard is always in control of the system bus if no other busmaster requests bus control. No arbitration signal line is necessary for this. Instead, the CACP automatically assigns the CPU control by means of the HOLD and HLDA processor signals, in this case.

All other busmasters can request control of the bus via the $\overline{\text{PREEMPT}}$ signal. Then, by means of ARB0–ARB3, the bus arbitration passes control to one of the requesting busmasters according to a strategy using a largely equal treatment. For this, the following steps are carried out:

- The busmasters that want to take over control of the system bus set $\overline{\text{PREEMPT}}$ to a low level.
- The CACP activates ARB/$\overline{\text{GNT}}$ to indicate that an arbitration cycle is in progress.
- Each of the requesting busmasters outputs its priority code via ARB0–ARB3, and compares its code with the code on ARB0–ARB3, which consists of the priority code of all the requesting busmasters.
- If its priority code is lower then it deactivates its code on ARB0–ARB3 and rules itself out of the competition, but continues to drive $\overline{\text{PREEMPT}}$ to indicate that it wants to take over control in a later arbitration cycle.
- After a certain time period (in the PS/2 300 ns are usually available for this purpose), only the highest priority code is still present on ARB0–ARB3.
- The CACP pulls ARB/$\overline{\text{GNT}}$ down to a low level to indicate that the bus control has passed to a new busmaster (GNT=grant) whose priority code is present on ARB0–ARB3.
- The new busmaster deactivates its $\overline{\text{PREEMPT}}$ signal. All other busmasters which were unable to take over control continue to drive $\overline{\text{PREEMPT}}$ to a low level.
- Now the new busmaster can control the bus for one bus cycle.
- Burst busmasters that want to transfer a whole data block and are allowed to keep control of the system bus for at most 7.8 μs (the maximum allocation time for external busmasters) are an exception to this rule. Such busmasters activate the $\overline{\text{BURST}}$ signal to inform the CACP that an arbitration cycle shall not be carried out for every bus cycle. But if $\overline{\text{PREEMPT}}$ or a refresh request is active, an arbitration cycle is executed nevertheless. Thus, $\overline{\text{BURST}}$ only has an effect if the current burst busmaster is the only one requesting control of the system bus.
- Afterwards, the CACP releases control to the CPU or starts a further arbitration cycle if $\overline{\text{PREEMPT}}$ is driven low by another busmaster.

Every busmaster adapter has a local bus arbitrator which drives the adapter card's $\overline{\text{PREEMPT}}$ and ARB0–ARB3, and compares the priority code of the busmaster adapter with the overall code ARB0–ARB3.

If the busmaster does not release control after 7.8 μs, the CACP interprets this as a malfunction. It disconnects the busmaster from the bus, passes control to the CPU, and issues an NMI.

The CACP can be programmed via the arbitration register at I/O address 090h (Figure 21.2).

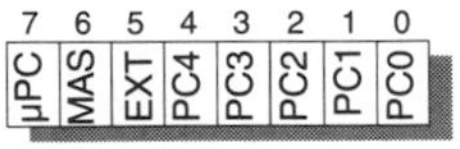


```
µPC: CPU cycles during arbitration cycle
     1=yes    0=no (standard)
MAS: mask
     1=ARB//GNT always high   0=normal arbitration
EXT: extended arbitration cycle
     1=600ns  0=300ns
PC4–PC0: reading=priority code of the busmaster that won the last arbitration
         writing=not defined, always equal 0
```

Figure 21.2: Arbitration register (Port 090h).

If you set bit *µPC* equal to 1, the CPU on the motherboard executes further bus cycles, for example to fetch instructions while the CACP carries out an arbitration cycle. For the bus arbitration only the lines $\overline{\text{PREEMPT}}$ and ARB0–ARB3 are required, which are not used during a CPU bus cycle. Therefore, the two cycles do not affect each other. If *MAS* is set the CACP always drives the ARB/$\overline{\text{GNT}}$ signal high, that is, always indicates an arbitration cycle. As long as MAS is set, only the CPU is in control of the system bus, and all other busmasters are locked out. By means of *EXT*, the arbitration cycle can be enhanced from the standard 300 ns up to 600 ns. This is advantageous if slow devices are present in the system. Finally, the five bits *PC4–PC0* indicate the priority code of the device that last won the bus arbitration. When writing into the register, bits PC4–PC0 have no meaning and should always be set equal to 0.

21.3 Memory System

The PS/2 memory system has also been improved with the development of the microchannel. If the startup routine of the PC detects a defect in main memory, the memory is reconfigured in 64 kbyte blocks so that eventually a continuous and error-free main memory again becomes available. The block with the defect is logically moved to the upper end of the main memory and locked against access. If such a defect occurs in the lower address area in an AT, the whole of the main memory from the defective address upwards becomes unusable.

For the PS/2 models 70 and 80, two memory configuration registers at the port addresses e0h and e1h are additionally available. Using these ports, the division of the first Mbyte in RAM can be controlled so that, for example, the ROM BIOS is moved into the faster RAM (shadowing), or the memory is divided to be as RAM-saving as possible (split-memory option). These possibilities are not discussed here in detail because these setups can usually be done with the help of the extended PS/2 setup during the course of the boot process.

21.4 DMA

In terms of their functions, the microchannel's support chips differ very little from their EISA counterparts, but they are completely harmonized with this new and advanced bus system. Thus, for example, the DMA controller always carries out a 32-bit DMA transfer for the complete address space if a 32-bit microchannel is present. There is no 8237A-compatible DMA transfer. Moreover, the microchannel architecture allows all eight DMA channels to be active simultaneously. Thus, MCA is really well suited for multitasking operating systems.

Originally, in the PS/2 only a 16-bit DMA controller was intended, which could only serve the first 16 Mbytes of memory. Here again you can see the enormously fast development in the field of microelectronics. Although the microchannel and the PS/2 were intended as a new standard to replace the AT and last for years, the 16 Mbytes (which seemed astronomically large a few years ago) are no longer enough, since memory-eaters like OS/2 and Windows have appeared. Modern motherboards can usually be equipped with 32 Mbytes or even 64 Mbytes of memory.

21.5 Interrupts

As well as the bus system and the DMA controller, the interrupt controller was also harmonized with the new architecture. All interrupts are level-trigger invoked only. With EISA, on the other hand, interrupts can be level- or edge-triggered so that an ISA adapter can be operated as the serial interface adapter, which operates exclusively with edge-triggering in an EISA slot. Because of the level-triggering used in MCA, various sources can share one interrupt line IRQx. Additionally, level-triggering is less susceptible to interference, as a noise pulse only leads to a very short voltage rise but level-triggering requires a lasting high level. For the microchannel, 255 different hardware interrupts are possible; the AT allows only 15. The assignment of the IRQ lines and the correspondence of hardware interrupt and interrupt vector coincides with that in the AT and EISA.

21.6 MCA Timer and Fail-Safe Timer

The MCA timer comprises four channels in total, and is equivalent to an 8254 chip with four counters. The first three channels 0–2 are occupied by the internal system clock, memory refresh and tone generation for the speaker, as is the case in the AT. The fourth timer is used as a fail-safe or watchdog timer in the same sense as for EISA. It issues an NMI if a certain time period has elapsed, thus preventing an external busmaster from keeping control too long and blocking necessary interrupts or the memory refresh. If an external busmaster retains control of the MCA bus for too long, and thereby violates the bus arbitration rules, this indicates a hardware error or the crash of an external busmaster. Then the fail-safe timer issues an NMI and the arbitration logic releases control to the CPU again so that it can handle the NMI.

On the PC/XT/AT, timer 1 for memory refresh is programmable, but on the PS/2 it is not. IBM thus wants to avoid nosy users who like to experiment with changing the refresh rate and crashing the PC because of too few refresh cycles. Programmers can access the timer via port 041h, but passing new values doesn't have any effect on its behaviour.

21.7 I/O Ports and I/O Address Space

As for EISA, in the PS/2 the support and controller chips are also accessed via ports. Table 21.2 lists the new I/O address areas for MCA. Unlike ISA, the MCA slots, and therefore also the inserted MCA adapters, can be addressed individually. To do this, however, you must explicitly activate a slot for a setup. This is necessary to configure MCA adapters with no DIP switches automatically.

Address	Meaning
000h–01fh	master DMA
020h–021h	master 8259A
040h–043h	timer 1
044h–047h	fail-safe timer
060h–064h	keyboard/mouse controller
070h–071h	real-time clock/CMOS RAM
074h–076h	extended CMOS RAM
080h–08fh	DMA page register
090h	CACP
091h	feedback register
092h	system control port A
096h	adapter activation/setup register
0a0h–0afh	slave 8259A
0c0h–0dfh	slave DMA
0e0h–0efh	memory configuration register
0f0h–0ffh	coprocessor
100h–107h	POS registers 0 to 7
200h–20fh	game adapter
210h–217h	reserved
220h–26fh	available
278h–27fh	2nd parallel interface
2b0h–2dfh	EGA
2f8h–2ffh	COM2
300h–31fh	prototype adapter
320h–32fh	available
378h–37fh	1st parallel interface
380h–38fh	SDLC adapter
3a0h–3afh	reserved
3b0h–3b3h	monochrome adapter
3b4h–3bah	VGA
3bch–3beh	parallel interface
3c0h–3dfh	EGA/VGA
3e0h–3e7h	reserved
3f0h–3f7h	floppy controller
3f8h–3ffh	COM1

Table 21.2: MCA port addresses

21.8 MCA Adapters and Automatic Configuration

There is also a significant advantage here compared to the old AT concept, that of the automatic identification of an adapter by the system. Microchannel adapters, like their EISA counterparts, are no longer configured by jumpers. This can instead be carried out in a dialogue with the accompanying system software. For this purpose, IBM assigns every adapter an identification number which can be read and analysed by the system. Also, third-party manufacturers get an identification number for their MCA products which is centrally managed by IBM. The configuration information is stored in an extended CMOS RAM (as is the case with EISA). Additionally, you may activate or disable individual MCA slots, thus a defective or suspicious adapter can be disabled until the maintenance technician arrives, without the need to open the PC and remove the adapter. This also allows you to operate two adapters alternately, which normally disturb each other, without pottering around the PC all the time.

To achieve these advantages, all MCA adapters and the MCA motherboard hold so-called *programmable option select (POS) registers*. They always occupy the I/O address area 0100h to 0107h. Table 21.3 lists the registers.

Number	I/O address	Meaning
0	0100h	adapter identification ID (low-byte)
1	0101h	adapter identification ID (high-byte)
2	0102h	option byte 1
3	0103h	option byte 2
4	0104h	option byte 3
5	0105h	option byte 4
6	0106h	sub-address extension (low-byte)
7	0107h	sub-address extension (high-byte)

Table 21.3: POS registers.

During the boot process the POST routine of the BIOS reads the adapter identification ID and compares it with the configuration data which is held in the CMOS RAM. The adapter identification ID is awarded centrally by IBM, that is, IBM assigns every manufacturer of an MCA adapter such a number for the product concerned. The four option bytes are available for the adapter manufacturer to configure the inserted adapter and thus fulfil the functions of the former DIP switches. If the four option bytes are insufficient, the manufacturer may implement an additional configuration register on the adapter card. They are accessed by means of the two sub-address extension registers.

Three bits in the POS registers are predefined, and are listed in Table 21.4. By means of the bit *adapter activation* in the POS register 2, the adapter concerned can be disabled or activated. If it is disabled the system behaves as if the adapter were not present. Therefore it is possible, for example, to alternately operate two different graphics adapters with overlapping address areas in a PS/2. Their addresses do not then disturb each other. If a hardware error occurs on an adapter which leads to an NMI, then bit 7 in POS register 5 is set to 0 and the adapter generates an active $\overline{CHCK}$ signal. If additional status information is available in POS registers 6 and 7, the adapter also sets bit 6 to a value of 0. The remaining bits are freely available for implementing software option switches which replace the previous DIP switches.

POS register	Bit	Meaning
2	0	adapter enable
5	6	status for channel check available
5	7	channel check active

Table 21.4: Reserved POS register bits

The POS registers are present at the same address on all adapters and the motherboard, thus access conflicts seem to be preprogrammed. To avoid this, two additional registers are implemented, the adapter activation/setup register at I/O address 096h, and the motherboard activation/setup register at I/O address 094h.

Each adapter can be operated in two different modes:

- Active mode: the POS registers are not accessible and the adapter is operating normally. You may access the ordinary control registers (the DAC colour register on a VGA, for example).
- Setup mode: here only the POS registers are accessible, not the ordinary control registers.

Using the adapter activation/setup register you may activate a slot and thus an adapter well-suited for setup of and access to its POS registers. Figure 21.3 shows the assignment of this 8-bit register.

The three least-significant bits define the selected slot or adapter. A set *adapter setup* bit activates this adapter for a setup. The $\overline{\text{CDSETUP}}$ signal for a slot *n* is thus activated, and the adapter is ready for a setup.

Example: `Activate adapter in slot 3 (note: the slots are enumerated 1 to 8 but the slot selection with 0 to 7).`

```
MOV al, 0000 1010b  ; slot select=2, setup active
OUT 096h, al        ; write register
```

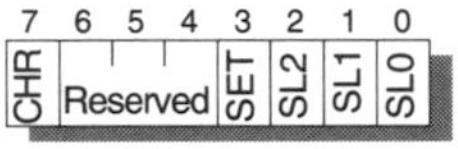


```
CHR: channel reset
     0=no reset             1=reset all adapters
res: reserved (=0)
SET: adapter setup
     0=normal mode          1=setup mode
SL2–SL0: adapter/slot select
     000=slot 1   001=slot 2   010=slot 3   ...   111=slot 8
```

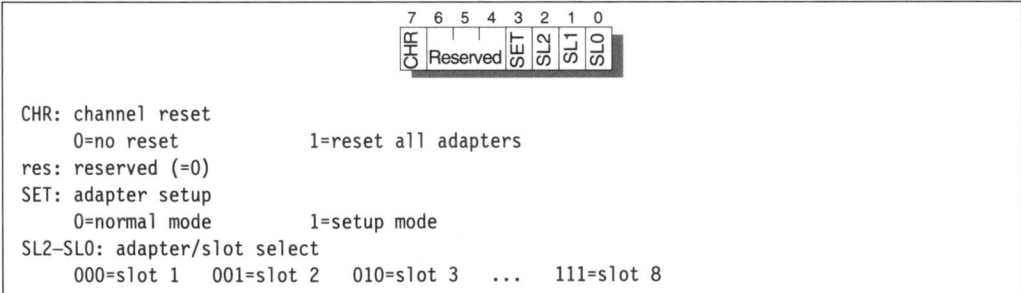

Figure 21.3: Adapter activation/setup register (port 096h).

Now you can access the POS registers of the selected adapter card and configure the adapter or read the channel check bit.

If the *channel reset* bit is set in register 096h, the CHRESET signal is activated in the microchannel and *all* adapters are reset. Thus in the setup mode, channel reset must always be equal to 0.

After completion of the configuration the *adapter activation* bit in POS register 2 must be set to enable normal functioning of the adapter. This only refers to the adapter's logic. Write the value 00h into the adapter activation/setup register afterwards to enable the adapter ($\overline{\text{CDSETUP}}$ rises to a high level). This only refers to driving the adapter.

Besides the adapters, the motherboard also comprises various setup registers which may be activated by means of the motherboard activation/setup register at I/O address 094h. Figure 21.4 shows the structure of this register.

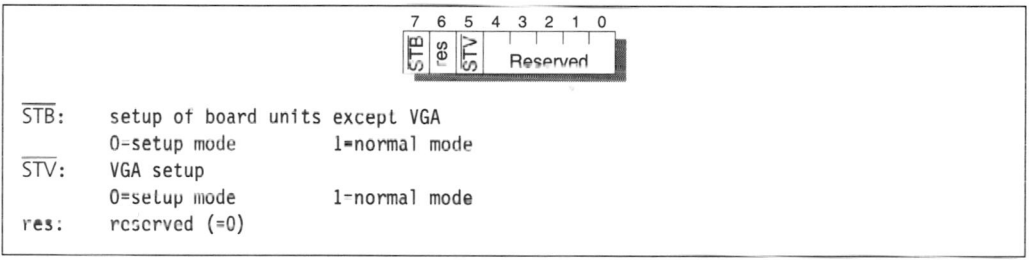

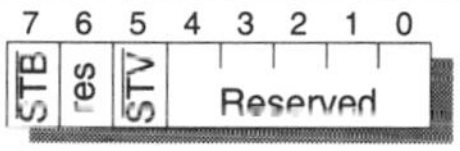

$\overline{\text{STB}}$:	setup of board units except VGA	
	0=setup mode	1=normal mode
$\overline{\text{STV}}$:	VGA setup	
	0=setup mode	1=normal mode
res:	reserved (=0)	

Figure 21.4: Motherboard activation/setup register (Port 094h).

If you clear the $\overline{\text{STV}}$ bit (set equal to 0) then you can configure the VGA option bytes. With a value of 1 in this register the VGA operates normally. To the board units belong the VGA, RAM, floppy controller, and serial and parallel interfaces. If the $\overline{\text{STB}}$ bit is set equal to 0 then you can access POS registers 2 and 3 of the motherboard units and configure them. As is the case with adapters, these POS registers are present at I/O addresses 102h and 103h. The structure of POS register 2 is shown in Figure 21.5. POS register 3 serves to configure the RAM, and is very model-dependent. Thus, only POS register 2 is described in further detail here. Information concerning POS register 3 can be found in the technical reference manual for your PS/2. For all other users, this information is of no value.

In extended mode the parallel port can be operated bidirectionally. The remaining bits are self-evident.

The adapter activation/setup register (port 096h) structure ensures that you can only activate a single slot for a setup, thus setup conflicts on the adapters are impossible. However, note that you may put an adapter and the motherboard simultaneously into the setup mode. This inevitably leads to problems, and damage to chips may even occur. Therefore, be careful when programming the setup!

As was the case for EISA, every MCA product comes with a configuration disk which holds a file containing the necessary information. This file is called the *adapter description file* (*ADF*). The filename has the format «@iiii.adf», where iiii is the four-digit adapter identification number in hexadecimal notation. Like EISA, the ADF also uses a configuration language that reminds us of CONFIG.SYS commands.

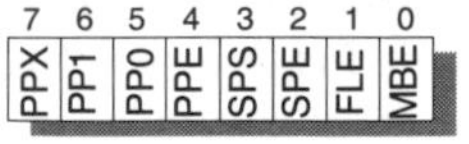


```
PPX: extended mode of the parallel port
     0=no extended mode (standard)   1=extended mode
PP1, PP0: parallel port select
     00=LPT1 (standard)   01=LPT2   11=LPT3
PPE: parallel port enable
     0=disabled           1=enabled (standard)
SPS: serial port select
     0=COM1 (standard)    1=COM2
SPE: serial port enable
     0=disabled           1=enabled (standard)
FLE: floppy controller enable
     0=disabled           1=enabled (standard)
MBE: motherboard unit enable (except VGA)
     0=disabled           1=enabled (standard)
```

Figure 21.5: Motherboard POS register 2 (Port 102h).

21.9 On-Board VGA and External Graphics Adapters

A main emphasis of the PS/2 concept is the integration of many units on the motherboard which previously have been located on separate adapter cards in a bus slot. To these units belong, for example, the serial and parallel interface, and especially the *video graphics array (VGA)*. All these units are accessed by means of the *local channel* or the *peripheral standard bus*. The VGA is functionally identical to (and also available as) the *video graphics adapter* (*VGA*) for AT and EISA computers. Original VGA (that is, the video graphics *array*) is integrated on the PS/2 motherboard, but the video graphics *adapter* is implemented as an adapter for a bus slot. Thus, a PS/2 computer with an integrated VG array needs significantly fewer slots than an AT or EISA computer.

For some users even the video graphics array with a resolution of 640*480 pixels and 256 colours is not sufficient. In particular, high-resolution graphics applications like CAD need more powerful adapters. These adapters may be inserted into a bus slot, of course, but the only problem is that the VGA on the motherboard is still present and must be disabled for correct operation of the new adapter. Removing the VGA is naturally impossible. Instead, IBM had a more elegant idea. One MCA slot in every PS/2 comprises a so-called *video extension* (see Figure 21.6). An MCA graphics adapter must always be inserted into this slot to service the graphics signals. By pulling some of these signals to a low level, the inserted adapter can deactivate parts of the on-board VGA and generate the corresponding signals itself. For this purpose, the connected monitor need not even be plugged in differently (if it accepts the new video mode, of course); it is still driven by the same plug of the PS/2. Internally, though, the change can be immense. For example, the high-resolution 8514/A adapter with a dedicated graphics processor pulls the ESYNC, EDCLK and EVIDEO signals to a low level. Then it generates its own synchronization, pixel clock and colour signals for the monitor which it transfers by means of the contacts HSYNC, VSYNC, BLANK, DCLK and P0–P7 to the motherboard's logic to drive the monitor. Thus, the on-board VGA is more or less disabled and the monitor cut off. Only the DAC is still running, converting the digital video data P0–P7 to an analogue signal for the monitor. All control and pixel signals come from the 8514/A.

21.10 PS/2 Model 30

The PS/2 Model 30 occupies a special position. It is actually a hidden XT with the outward appearance of a PS/2 case. The model 30 thus has no microchannel, but instead the old XT bus. The only advantage is that the model 30 is already prepared for the 1.44 Mbyte floppy and hard disk drives, and thus also has a much more modern BIOS.

21.11 The MCA Slot

After deciding to throw the AT concept overboard, IBM was of course free to redesign the layout of the bus slots. Also, for a PS/2 there should be 8-bit adapters (for example, parallel interface adapters), 16-bit adapters for models 50 and 60 with 80286 or i386SX processors, and 32-bit adapters (for example, fast ESDI controllers for the PS/2 models with i386 or i486 CPUs) Thus, 8-, 16- and 32-bit slots are required, with the 8-bit slot already implementing all the important control lines. The result is the MCA slot with various slot extensions, as shown in Figure 21.6.

The kernel of the MCA slot is the 8-bit section with its 90 contacts. Unlike EISA, the MCA slot only has contacts on a single layer, but they are much narrower and every fourth contact of a row is grounded or at the power supply level. The ground and supply contacts on both sides are shifted by two positions so that, effectively, every second contact pair has a ground or supply terminal. By the defined potential of these contacts, the noise resistance is significantly better than on an AT.

The AT had up to 31 succeeding signal contacts without any interposed ground or supply contacts. With the EISA slot, the noise sensitivity is slightly reduced because the lower EISA contact row has significantly more such contacts than the AT section of the EISA slot.

Besides the 8-bit section there are various extensions: the 16-bit section for 16-bit MCA adapters; the 32-bit section for 32-bit MCA adapters; the video extension for additional graphics adapters; and the matched-memory extension for memories with a higher access rate. The 16-bit PS/2 models do not have any 32-bit extensions, of course. Because of the narrow contacts, the MCA slot is nevertheless quite compact, although it holds up to 202 contacts.

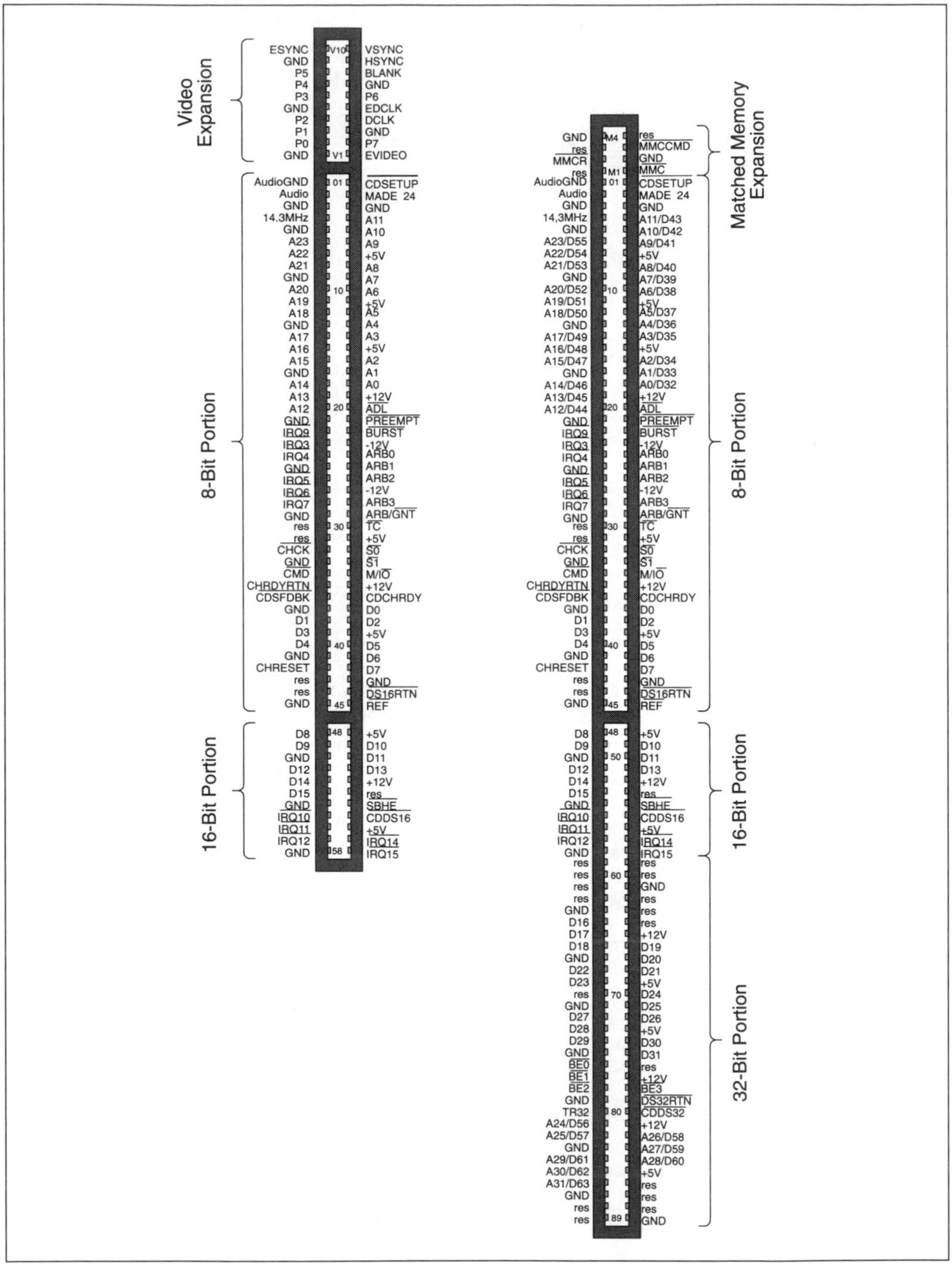

Figure 21.6: The MCA slot.

21.12 MCA Signals

This section discusses the MCA contacts and the meaning of the signals which are supplied or applied.

Because the microchannel supports busmasters on external adapters without any restriction, all connections are bidirectional. To show the data and signal flow more precisely, I have assumed for the indicated transfer directions that the CPU (or another device on the motherboard) represents the current busmaster. The enumeration follows the original IBM convention; *l* indicates the (according to the figure) left contact, and *r* the right contact. The MCA connections are grouped corresponding to their functions.

Video Extension

BLANK (I)
Terminal V8r
A high-level signal from the inserted adapter blanks the screen.

DCLK (I)
Terminal V4r
The data clock signal from the inserted adapter supplies the pixel clock for the DAC.

EDCLK (I)
Terminal V5r
A low-level enable DCLK signal from the inserted adapter cuts the VGA on the motherboard off from the pixel clock line to the video DAC. Instead, the DAC uses the clock signal DCLK from the inserted adapter.

ESYNC (I)
Terminal V10l
A low-level enable synchronization signal from the inserted adapter causes the VGA on the motherboard to be cut off from the three synchronization signals VSYNC, HSYNC and BLANK.

EVIDEO (I)
Terminal V1r
A low-level enable video signal from the inserted adapter cuts off the VGA on the motherboard from the palette bus. Using this, the inserted adapter can supply the video data P7–P0.

HSYNC (I)
Terminal V9r
A high-level horizontal synchronization pulse from the inserted adapter causes a horizontal synchronization, that is, a horizontal retrace of the electron beam.

P7–P0 (I)
Terminals V2l–V4l, V6l–V8l, V2r, V6r
These eight signals form the binary video data for the video DAC (*digital to analogue converter*) on the motherboard, which then generates the analogue signal for the monitor. By means of the eight bits P7–P0, the 256 simultaneously displayable colours of the VGA can be encoded.

VSYNC (I)
Terminal V10r
A high-level vertical synchronization pulse from the inserted adapter causes a vertical synchronization, that is, a vertical retrace of the electron beam.

Matched Memory Extension

$\overline{\text{MMC}}$, $\overline{\text{MMCCMD}}$, $\overline{\text{MMCR}}$ **(O, O, I)**
Terminals M1r, M3r, M2l
These three signals control the so-called matched-memory cycles. To carry out a matched memory cycle the bus controller activates the matched-memory cycle signal $\overline{\text{MMC}}$. If the addressed unit supports this cycle type, it returns an active matched-memory cycle return signal $\overline{\text{MMCR}}$ with a low level. Instead of $\overline{\text{CMD}}$ of the normal cycle, here the MMC command signal $\overline{\text{MMCCMD}}$ is used for controlling the bus transfer.

8-Bit, 16-Bit and 32-Bit Section

14.3 MHz (O)
Terminal 4l
This signal is the 14317180 Hz clock signal for timers and other components.

A31–A0 (O)
Terminals 6l–8l, 10l–12l, 14l–16l, 18l–20l, 81l–82l, 84l–86l, 4r–6r, 8r–10r, 12r–14r, 16r–18r, 82r–84r
These 32 connections form the 32-bit address bus of the microchannel.

$\overline{\text{ADL}}$ **(O)**
Terminal 20r
A low-level address latch signal indicates that a valid address is present on the microchannel, and activates the address decoder latches.

ARB0–ARB3 (I/O)
Terminals 24r–26r, 28r
These four arbitration signals indicate (in binary-encoded form) which of the maximum 16 possible busmasters has won the bus arbitration and gets control of the system bus.

ARB/$\overline{\text{GNT}}$ (O)
Terminal 29r
If this arbitration/grant connection is on a high level, an arbitration cycle is in progress. If ARB/$\overline{\text{GNT}}$ falls to a low level the arbitration signals ARB0–ARB3 are valid and indicate the new busmaster.

Audio, AudioGND (I, I)
Terminals 1l, 2l
These two connections supply the tone signal and the accompanying tone signal ground to the motherboard. An adapter is thus able to use the speaker logic of the motherboard. The adapter applies the tone signal which the system speaker outputs to the connection Audio.

$\overline{\text{BE0}}$–$\overline{\text{BE3}}$ (O)

Terminals 76l–78l, 78r

These four byte enable signals indicate on which byte of the 32-bit data bus data is transferred. They correspond to the address bits A0 and A1, therefore. The signals come directly from the CPU. $\overline{\text{BE0}}$ refers to the least significant byte D0–D7 of the data bus, $\overline{\text{BE3}}$ the high-order byte D24–D31.

$\overline{\text{BURST}}$ (O)

Terminal 22r

A low-level signal instructs the bus system to carry out a burst cycle.

$\overline{\text{CDDS16}}$ (I)

Terminal 55r

The inserted adapter card applies a high-level signal to this card data size 16 connection to indicate that it is running with a data width of 16 bits. Then the bus controller operates accordingly.

$\overline{\text{CDDS32}}$ (I)

Terminal 80r

If the inserted adapter card applies a low-level signal to this card data size 32 connection, it has a data width of 32 bits.

$\overline{\text{CDSETUP}}$ (O)

Terminal 1r

An active (low) card setup level instructs the addressed adapter to carry out a setup.

$\overline{\text{CDSFDBK}}$ (I)

Terminal 36l

An active (low) card select feedback level indicates that the addressed adapter card is ready. $\overline{\text{CDSFDBK}}$ is the return signal for the adapter selection.

$\overline{\text{CHCK}}$ (i)

Terminal 32l

Via this channel check contact the adapter cards apply error information to the motherboard to indicate, for example, a parity error on a memory expansion adapter, or a general error on an adapter card.

CHRDY (i)

Terminal 36r

A high-level signal at this channel ready connection indicates that the addressed unit is ready, that is, has completed the intended access. Thus this contact transfers the ready signal from addressed devices on an adapter card. If CHRDY is low the processor or DMA chip extends the bus cycles; it inserts one or more wait states.

CHRDYRTN (i)

Terminal 35l

A high channel ready return level as the return signal from the addressed device indicates that the I/O channel is ready.

CHRESET (O)
Terminal 42l
A high level at this channel reset connection resets all adapters.

$\overline{\text{CMD}}$ (O)
Terminal 34l
If the command signal $\overline{\text{CMD}}$ is active (that is, low), the data on the bus is valid.

D0–D31 (I/O)
Terminals 38l–40l, 48l–49l, 51l–53l, 64l–66l, 68l–69l, 72l–74l, 37r–39r, 40r–42r, 49r–51r, 66r–68r, 70r–72r, 74r–75r
These 32 connections form the 32-bit data bus of the microchannel.

$\overline{\text{DS16RTN}}$ (I)
Terminal 44r
A data size 16 return signal with a low level from the addressed device indicates that the device is running at a data bus width of 16 bits. The bus controller thus splits 32-bit quantities into 16-bit portions, and combines two 16-bit items into a single 32-bit quantity.

$\overline{\text{DS32RTN}}$ (I)
Terminal 79r
A data size 32 return signal with a low level indicates that the addressed device is running at the full data bus width of 32 bits.

$\overline{\text{IRQ3}}$–$\overline{\text{IRQ7}}$, $\overline{\text{IRQ9}}$–$\overline{\text{IRQ12}}$, $\overline{\text{IRQ14}}$, $\overline{\text{IRQ15}}$ (I)
Terminals 22l–24l, 26l–28l, 55l–57l, 57r–58r
These 11 interrupt request connections are available for hardware interrupt requests from peripheral adapters. The microchannel operates with level-triggered hardware interrupts. IRQ0 (system clock), IRQ1 (keyboard), IRQ2 (cascading according to the second AT PIC), IRQ8 (real-time clock) and IRQ13 (coprocessor) are reserved for components on the motherboard, and therefore do not lead into the bus slots.

MADE 24 (O)
Terminal 2r
A high-level memory address enable 24 signal activates the address line A24.

M/$\overline{\text{IO}}$ (O)
Terminal 34r
A high-level memory/IO signal indicates a memory cycle; a low-level signal an access to the I/O address space.

$\overline{\text{PREEMPT}}$ (I)
Terminal 21r
A low-level signal issues an arbitration cycle for passing the bus to various busmasters. External busmasters activate $\overline{\text{PREEMPT}}$ to request control of the bus.

$\overline{\text{REF}}$ (O)

Terminal 45r

The refresh signal is at a low level if the motherboard is currently executing a memory refresh. With this signal, the dynamic memory on adapter cards (for example, the video RAM) can also be refreshed synchronous to main memory. Thus the adapter does not need its own refresh logic and no additional time is wasted for refreshing DRAM on the adapters. The $\overline{\text{REF}}$ signal indicates that the address bus has a row address for the refresh.

$\overline{\text{S0}}$, $\overline{\text{S1}}$ (O; O)

Terminals 32r–33r

These two contacts transfer the corresponding status bits of the microchannel.

SBHE (O)

Terminal 54r

A high-level system byte high enable signal indicates that the high-order data bus byte D8–D15 of the 16-bit microchannel section transfers valid data.

$\overline{\text{TC}}$ (O)

Terminal 30r

A low-level signal at this terminal count pin indicates that the counter of the active DMA channel has reached its terminal value and the DMA transfer is complete.

TR32 (I)

Terminal 80l

A high-level translate 32 signal indicates that the external busmaster is a 32-bit device and drives $\overline{\text{BE0}}$–$\overline{\text{BE3}}$ instead of SBHE.

For the extension of the standard MCA specification and the 32-bit streaming data procedures to 64-bit SDPs the address contacts A0–A31 are used for data transfer and mapped onto the 32 high-order data bits D32–D63.

All other contacts are reserved (res), are grounded (GND), or transfer supply voltages for chips (+5 V, –5 V) and interfaces or drives (+12 V, –12 V).

22 32 Bits and More – The Local Bus

For many PC owners, Chapters 20 and 21 must have been a great disappointment – even EISA bus and microchannel, as high-end solutions for the personal computer, run in a 50 MHz i486 with only a miserable 8 MHz and 10 MHz, respectively. This is far too slow for quick screen rewrites in a graphic oriented operating system or system interface such as Windows. Even a small dialogue window with 512*384 points, which only covers a quarter of the screen surface in a high resolution mode, consists of 192k pixels. Thus, in 256 colour mode, 192 points on the screen must first be saved and then rewritten, corresponding to 384 kbytes of screen data. However, the screen memory can only be rewritten if the graphic control chip on the graphic adapter is not performing a read access. This is usually only the case during horizontal and vertical returns; the 384 kbytes must, therefore, be transferred in the relatively short return time window. In a VGA card, a complete line scan including a horizontal return takes about 25 μs, the horizontal return itself approximately 4 μs. This means that the line return takes approximately a seventh of the time required by a horizontal scan. The transfer of the 384 kbytes in a 16-bit ISA system, therefore, realistically requires approximately a third of a second. This is clearly noticeable by the user. The refresh time of the screen memory is not even included in the calculation.

One solution to this problem is offered by graphic adapters containing a graphics processor, such as the TIGA or 8514/A. Another similar solution – especially when you consider the substantially higher clock frequencies of processors in comparison to bus clock speeds – is to drive the graphic system bus at the same frequency as the CPU. The local bus attempts to do just that. The first local buses located on motherboards were, therefore, nothing more than a fast interface to the display memory, so that the CPU data could be transferred far quicker than in a normal system with a standard expansion bus. Naturally, the concept can also be applied to other equipment requiring higher transfer rates. One such example would be a fast hard disk with an integrated cache memory. This leads to another problem: host adapters or controllers for hard disks are usually constructed as plug-in cards which are inserted into a bus slot. To begin with there was no standard, so for this reason the local bus slot can differ greatly from motherboard to motherboard. To rectify this incompatibility problem, Intel developed the *PCI bus* (*Peripheral Component Interconnect*) and the VESA committee has developed the *VL bus*. They have been introduced independently of one another as local bus standards.

I would also like to mention that EISA and microchannel have recognized the threat that local bus systems represent. For this reason, the EISA specification has been extended to include the EMB (Enhanced Master Burst) cycle with a data bus width of 64 bits (EMB-66) and, additionally, the effective bus frequency has been doubled to a maximum of 16 2/3 MHz (EMB-133). Even microchannel has been improved, with a 64-bit streaming data procedure and a doubled clock cycle of 20 MHz, giving a maximum transfer rate of 160 Mbytes/s – the same as the 64-bit VL bus at 50 MHz. Whether these extensions actually represent a threat to local bus systems, or only increase the number of possible bus systems available, remains to be seen. Nevertheless, PCI can reach a transfer rate of 266 Mbytes/s which, of course, can only be achieved in perfect conditions. In the 80x86 processor family, only the Pentium achieves a similar or higher rate. However, PCI, as a processor independent bus system, should also serve the Alpha from DEC, for example (the Alpha version 21066 already includes a PCI interface on the processor chip). Currently, 266 Mbytes/s appears to be an enormous transfer rate. One should, however, not forget that not so long ago (almost 15 years) 640 kbytes of memory was considered as entirely sufficient and satisfactory for the next ten years. The consequences of this erroneous evaluation can now be found in their millions, including, perhaps, on your desk.

22.1 Peripheral Component Interconnect (PCI)

Today, PCI represents a high-end solution for powerful personal computers and workstations. As an introduction, I would like to list a few characteristics of this Intel-initiated bus system.

- coupling of the processor and expansion bus by means of a bridge,
- 32-bit standard bus width with a maximum transfer rate of 133 Mbytes/s,
- expansion to 64 bits with a maximum transfer rate of 266 Mbytes/s,
- supporting of multi-processor systems,
- burst transfers with arbitrary length,
- supporting of 5 V and 3.3 V power supplies,
- write posting and read prefetching,
- multimaster capabilities,
- operating frequencies from 0 MHz to a maximum of 33 MHz,
- multiplexing of address and data bus reducing the number of pins,
- supporting of ISA/EISA/MCA,
- configuration through software and registers,
- processor independent specification.

22.1.1 PCI Bus Structure

An essential characteristic of the PCI concept is the strict decoupling of the processor's main memory subsystems and the standard expansion bus. You can see the structure of the PCI bus in Figure 22.1.

The *PCI bridge* represents the connection between the subsystems of the processor's main memory and the PCI bus. For the user, bridges are generally an invisible interface between two bus systems (and also networks). All of the PCI units (also known as *PCI agents*) are connected to the PCI bus, for example, a SCSI host adapter, a LAN adapter, an I/O unit and a graphic adapter (see Figure 22.1). Contrary to the VL bus, these units should, as far as possible, be integrated onto the motherboard, but they are mostly constructed as adapters. In total, a maximum of three slots are provided for PCI units; for example, two slots can be used for an audio and motion video unit. Motion video concerns moving pictures, which require a staggering number of complicated calculations. For this reason, the corresponding PCI unit is often very large, making integration impossible. The audio/video extensions should make the PCI bus most suitable for future multimedia applications. The interface to the expansion bus is a third type of PCI unit. This means that the standard expansion bus – whether ISA, EISA, microchannel or another bus system – can be considered here as a PCI unit. In this way, in principle, every bus system can be integrated, enabling the PCI bus to be connected at a later date. In total, it is possible to connect the PCI bus with up to ten PCI units. In Figure 22.2 you can see a typical layout of a PCI bridge.

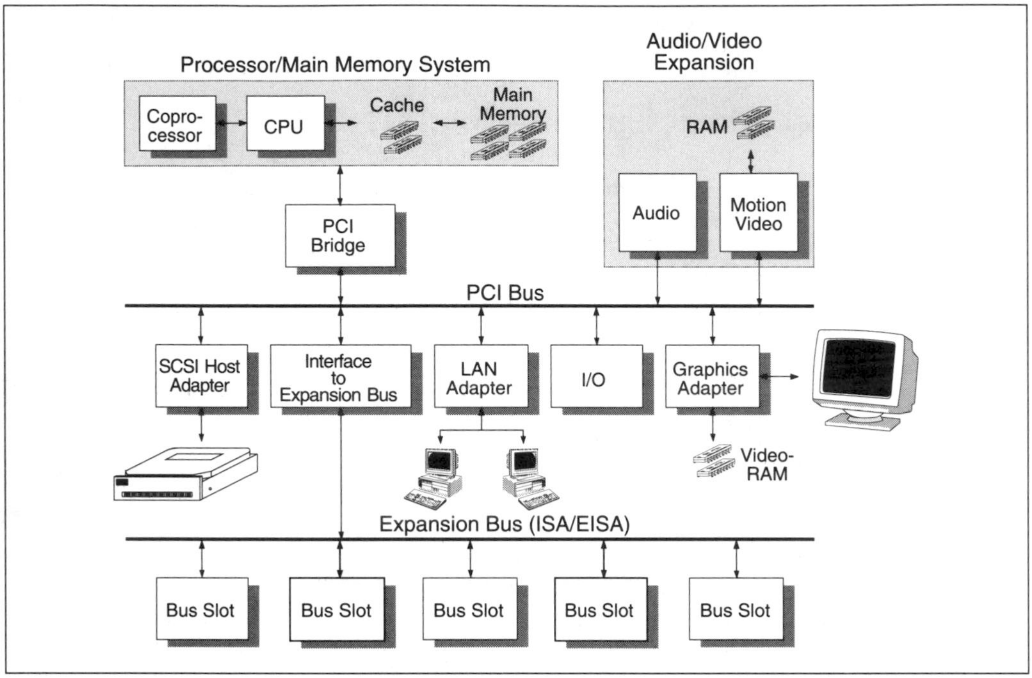

Figure 22.1: The PCI bus.

The local bus to the host CPU, or to a PCI bridge located nearer to the host CPU, is known as the *primary bus*. The PCI bus to the PCI units, or to a further PCI bridge, is known as the *secondary bus*. The register of the configuration address area stores the configuration data. The prefetch buffers read in data as a reserve, if a read access has been previously performed and it is possible that further data accesses may be required. In a similar way, the posting buffers temporarily store write data in order to pass it on to the addressed bus later.

The PCI bus and its bus cycles use a multiplexing scheme in which the lines are alternately used as address and data lines. This saves on the number of lines required, but two to three clock cycles are now required for a single transfer, as the address is transferred in the first cycle, write data in the second, and read data in the third. For this reason, the maximum data transfer rate is only 66 Mbytes/s (write access) and 44 Mbytes/s (read access), with a 32-bit bus width. In addition, the PCI bus also includes a very powerful burst mode in which the address is only transferred once. Then, the sender and receiver increase the amount of data transferred for the address with each clock cycle because the address is always implicitly known. With burst mode, any number of transfer cycles can be performed. The maximum data transfer rate in burst mode increases to 133 Mbytes/s with a 32-bit data bus and 266 Mbytes/s with a 64-bit data bus. Whether or not the addressed PCI units can keep up with this is, of course, another matter.

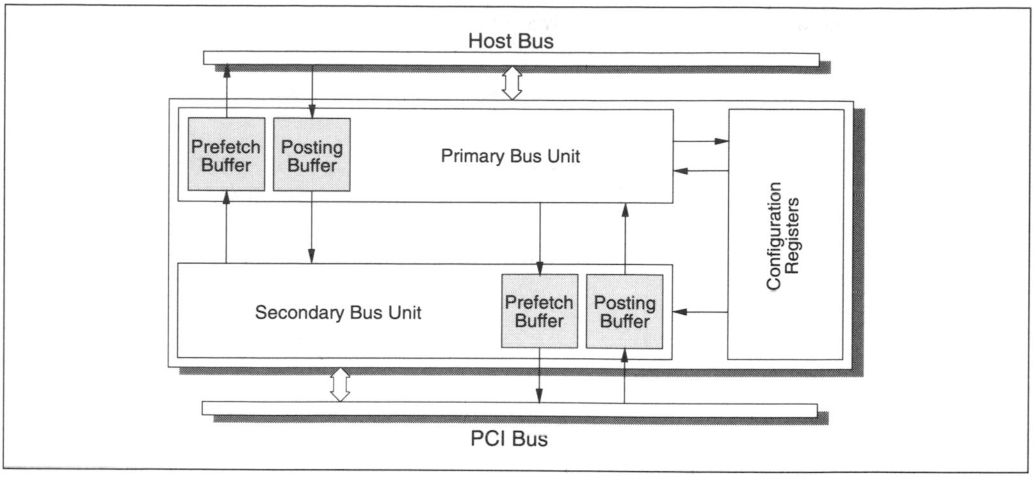

Figure 22.2: Typical layout of a PCI bridge.

An essential characteristic of the PCI bridge – and here lies the main difference to all other bus systems – is that it independently forms burst accesses. This means that the PCI bridge independently joins together incoming single transfer read and write operations to form burst accesses if the addresses of the individual accesses sequentially follow one another. This is also the case, for example, with a 32-bit bus, if the CPU communicates with the double-word addresses DW0–DW1–DW3–DW4–DW5 one after the other. Note that DW2 is not called up. PCI solves this problem elegantly, in that the bridge produces the burst DW0–DW1–DW2–DW3–DW4–DW5 and simply deactivates all $\overline{BEx}$ signals for DW2, in order to indicate that no data will be transferred.

For this purpose, extensive and intelligent read and write buffers are included in the bridge. Even the i486-50 with 100 Mbytes/s has, in single transfer mode, a bus bandwidth greatly exceeding the transfer rate of the PCI bus in single transfer mode. Thus, without PCI burst mode, the PCI bus would again be the hold up. The PCI bridge solves this problem, where possible, in that it joins together these single accesses to form a PCI burst. An example would be an access to the video RAM in order to open a window (write access) or to save the contents of the window (read access). Both tasks are performed conventionally (without a graphic processor) by the CPU, which performs multiple single transfers with sequential addresses. Single transfers are performed because the video RAM typically represents a non-cachable area of the memory address range and, thus, cannot be addressed by CPU burst cycles. This is reserved for cache line fills or write-backs (Pentium). The PCI bridge can independently recognize that the single transfers have sequential addresses and can join these single transfers together to form a burst. In this way, the PCI bus bandwidth at 32 bits is increased to 133 Mbytes/s, thus PCI is no longer the bottleneck. Pentium single transfers are also fully served by such bursts because, during single transfers, only 32 bits of the 64-bit address bus are used. At 66 MHz, this gives a maximum Pentium bus bandwidth of 133 Mbytes/s. The maximum rate in 64-bit pipelined burst mode at 528 Mbytes/s clearly surpasses the PCI maximum rate (266 Mbytes/s at 64-bit), but was developed mainly for the reloading or writing back of cache lines in an L2-cache; the PCI bus was not taken into consideration.

In addition to the memory and I/O address areas already known from the 80x86 CPUs, PCI also includes a third area, namely the configuration address area. It is used for accessing the configuration register and the configuration memory of each PCI unit. A configuration memory of 256 bytes is provided for each unit.

The decoupling of processor memory subsystems and the PCI bus through the PCI bridge is strong enough to allow the bridge and CPU to operate in parallel, providing that the CPU is not currently addressing a PCI unit. In this way, for example, it is possible to exchange data between two PCI units via the PCI bridge, while the CPU is only addressing the applicable memory to perform a program.

22.1.2 Bus Cycles

The PCI bridge is considerably more intelligent than an ISA/EISA or MCA bus controller. It switches CPU accesses through to the addressed PCI unit, or «filters» such accesses to optimally address the unit (through the PCI bridge). PCI currently recognizes 12 types of access which are differentiated by the four command signals C/$\overline{\mathrm{BE3}}$–C/$\overline{\mathrm{BE0}}$ (the command and byte-enable signals are multiplexed). The transfer types are (the level of the command signals C/$\overline{\mathrm{BE3}}$–C/$\overline{\mathrm{BE0}}$ are shown in parentheses):

- INTA sequence (0000),
- special cycle (0001),
- I/O read access (0010),
- I/O write access (0011),
- memory read access (0110),
- memory write access (0111),
- configuration read access (1010),
- configuration write access (1011),
- memory multiple read access (1100),
- dual addressing cycle (1101),
- line memory read access (1110),
- memory write access with invalidation (1111).

Every transfer begins with an address phase, during which the address/data pins ADx transfer the address and the C/$\overline{\mathrm{BEx}}$ pins transfer the instruction code. One or more data phases follow this phase, during which the same address/data pins ADx transfer data and the C/$\overline{\mathrm{BEx}}$ pins transfer the byte-enable signals. In a burst cycle, multiple data phases can follow a single address phase. In PCI terminology, the requesting PCI unit is known as the *initiator* (ISA/EISA/MCA: busmaster), and the addressed PCI unit as the *target* (ISA/EISA/MCA: slave). Every transfer starts with the activation of the $\overline{\mathrm{FRAME}}$ signal. The target indicates its readiness with an active $\overline{\mathrm{TRDY}}$ signal (target ready). An active $\overline{\mathrm{TRDY}}$ during a write access indicates that the target can take the data from the lines AD31–AD0 (32 bits) or A63–A0 (64 bits) respectively, in a read access, that the addressed data has been sent on the lines AD31–AD0 or A63–A0, respectively. Thus, $\overline{\mathrm{TRDY}}$`s function corresponds to the $\overline{\mathrm{READY}}$ and $\overline{\mathrm{BREADY}}$ signals known from the 80x86 CPUs. In addition, the initiator must also indicate its readiness to the PCI bridge, namely through an active $\overline{\mathrm{IRDY}}$ signal (initiator ready). An active $\overline{\mathrm{IRDY}}$ during a write access indicates that the initiator has sent the write data on the lines AD31–AD0 or A63–A0, respectively. In a read access, $\overline{IRDY}$ indicates that it takes the addressed data from the lines AD31–AD0 or A63–A0, respectively.

The PCI bridge can, in this way, almost function as a fast buffer between the initiator and the target, thus synchronizing the two PCI units. Only in this way is it possible for the bridge to convert CPU single accesses into a PCI burst. With the help of $\overline{IRDY}$ and $\overline{TRDY}$, the PCI bridge can also perform write posting and read prefetching. During *write posting*, the CPU first writes the data at a much higher speed (faster than the PCI bus can currently pass it on) to a buffer. The $\overline{READY}$ signal is essential for this transfer in the 80x86. The posting buffer then transfers the data to the addressed PCI unit. For this, $\overline{IRDY}$ and $\overline{TRDY}$ are necessary. If, for whatever reason, the PCI bus can pass on the data faster than the CPU can supply it, the PCI bridge deactivates the $\overline{IRDY}$ signal to inform the target that the transfer has not yet finished, and that the bridge is waiting for the CPU. During *read prefetching*, the PCI bridge reads data from the target faster than necessary and stores it in a prefetch buffer; it then passes the data on to the CPU later. If the prefetch buffer is full because the data has not been collected quickly enough, then the bridge must deactivate the $\overline{IRDY}$ signal to inform the target that it should not deliver any more data. Naturally, $\overline{IRDY}$ and $\overline{TRDY}$ can also be used to exchange data between two PCI units without affecting the CPU (for example, if data from a hard disk with a PCI adapter has to be written directly to the video RAM on a different PCI graphic card to recreate a window).

The initiator ends or interrupts the transfer by deactivating $\overline{FRAME}$. The target can also stop the transfer by activation of the $\overline{STOP}$ signal; this leads to a so-called *target abort*. I would briefly like to discuss the bus transfer types in the following section.

INTA sequence

During an INTA, an interrupt controller is implicitly addressed, that is, without explicitly sending out an I/O or memory address (the applicable controller recognizes the INTA sequence independently and automatically reacts to it). In the data phase, it transfers the interrupt vector through the ADx lines.

Special cycle

A special cycle can be used to transfer information to all PCI agents, for example, on the operating condition of the processor. The least significant ADx word AD15–AD0 delivers an information code corresponding to Table 22.1. The x86 specific codes correspond to the codes for the i486 and Pentium special cycles such as Flush, INTA, etc., and are sent out with the least ADx word AD31–AD16.

AD15–AD0	Information
0000h	processor shutdown
0001h	processor halt
0002h	x86 specific code
0003h to ffffh	reserved

Table 22.1: Information codes for the PCI special cycle

I/O read access

This access reads data from a PCI unit in the I/O address area. The addresses ADx define a byte address, that is, AD1 and AD0 must also be decoded because, in the PCI address area, both 8-bit and 16-bit ports could be available. The access usually consists of an address and a data phase.

I/O write access

This access transfers data to a PCI agent in the I/O address area. Here also, the addresses ADx define a byte address. The access most often consists of an address and a data phase.

Memory read access

The memory read access addresses a PCI unit in the memory address area and reads data from this agent. A read prefetch buffer is useful in supporting the read access and can increase its speed. The addresses ADx define a double word address, that is, AD1 and AD0 need not be decoded. Instead, the byte-enable signals $\overline{\text{BEx}}$ indicate which groups of the 32-bit or 64-bit data bus contain valid values. The access usually encompasses an address and a data phase.

Memory write access

This access addresses a PCI agent in the memory address area and transfers data to it. Write posting usually increases the speed of the write operation considerably, because the initiator only has to wait for a return signal from the posting buffer and not from the target. As in the memory read access, the addresses ADx define a double word address, that is, AD1 and AD0 need not be decoded, but the byte-enable signals $\overline{\text{BEx}}$ must. The access usually consists of an address and a data phase.

Configuration read access

PCI uses this access to address the configuration address area of the respective PCI unit. Here, IDSEL is activated to select the unit. Address bits AD7–AD2 indicate the addresses of the double words to be read in the configuration address area of the unit; AD1 and AD0 are equal to 0. AD10–AD8 are also used for selecting the addressed unit in a multifunction unit. All other ADxs have no significance. The access most often consists of an address and a data phase.

Configuration write access

This access is the counterpart to the configuration read access, the only difference being that the initiator writes data into the configuration address area of the target. The addressing is accomplished as in the configuration read access. The access usually encompasses an address and a data phase.

Memory multiple access

This access represents an extension to the line memory read access (and therefore, naturally, of the normal memory read access) and indicates to the target that the initiator (busmaster) wishes to read more than a complete cache line, or a correspondingly sized data block, from the memory without caching. The access is mainly beneficial for long sequential memory accesses, for example, if a large part of the video RAM corresponding to a window is to be saved. Thus, the access consists of one address phase and multiple data phases until $\overline{\text{FRAME}}$ is deactivated by the initiator.

Dual addressing cycle

This cycle is used to transfer a 64-bit address to a PCI unit, which only contains a 32-bit address/data path. Normally, the 64-bit address would be transferred through the 64-bit address/data path in a single clock cycle. However, if only a 32-bit address/data path is available, the 64-bit address must be split into a least significant 32-bit address (first addressing cycle) and a most significant 32-bit address (second addressing cycle). The dual addressing cycle serves for this purpose. In the first addressing cycle, the PCI bridge initiates a dual addressing cycle and transfers the least significant 32-bit address, in the second addressing cycle it initiates another cycle and transfers the most significant 32-bit address. The target then joins the 64-bit address back together. Thus, only in the second addressing cycle is it determined whether the access is a simple read access or an I/O access etc. Note that even PCI agents which support the 64-bit PCI data bus AD63–AD0 need not necessarily also handle 64-bit addresses (as an example, the Pentium contains a 64-bit data bus, but only has a 32-bit address area). On the other hand, a PCI unit may support 64-bit addressing, but may only contain a 32-bit data bus (such as a memory mapped register).

Line memory read access

This access represents an extension to the normal memory read access, but does not contain as many data transfers as the memory multiple access. The instruction informs the target that the initiator wishes to read more than two 32-bit data blocks from the memory, typically to the end of a cache line. This access is also mainly beneficial for long sequential memory accesses. Thus, the access consists of one address phase and multiple data phases until $\overline{\text{FRAME}}$ is deactivated by the initiator.

Memory write access with invalidation

This access represents the counterpart to a line memory read access or a memory read access. Through a memory write access with invalidation, the initiator indicates that a minimum of one complete cache line should be transferred. In this way, the content of the main memory is then automatically more up to date than the content of the cache, so that the applicable line can also be invalidated; thus, a write-back is bypassed. The cache line size is defined in a configuration register of the master that sent out the cache line write-back. If a value of a subsequent cache line is to be written with this access, the complete cache line must be transferred, or a simple memory write access must be performed.

The PCI specification recommends the use of different read access modes to the memory in accordance with Table 22.2, depending on whether or not a register for the cache line size is implemented in the busmaster.

With register for cache line size	
quantity of data to be transferred	mode
half cache line or less	memory read access
half to three cache lines	line memory read access
more than three cache lines	memory multiple access
Without register for cache line size	
quantity of data to be transferred	mode
two transfers or less	memory read access
three to twelve data transfers	line memory read access
more than twelve data transfers	memory multiple access

Table 22.2: Use of the PCI block access modes

For extensive sequential write accesses, the memory write access with invalidation should be used as far as possible. However, a register for the cache line size is required for this in the initiator.

Note that for memory accesses, address bits AD1 and AD0 are not decoded for the addressing. PCI always addresses double words; the active bytes within a double word are then given by $\overline{\text{BEx}}$. AD1 and AD0, however, are not without purpose; they are very important for setting the addressing sequence. For all burst accesses, PCI makes a distinction between linear and toggle incrementations of the addresses: linear incrementation (AD1=AD0=0) means that all addresses follow one another sequentially; toggle incrementation (AD1=0, AD0=1) means that the addresses follow in the style of a cache line fill, for instance they are interleaved as in the Pentium, and thus do not follow one another sequentially.

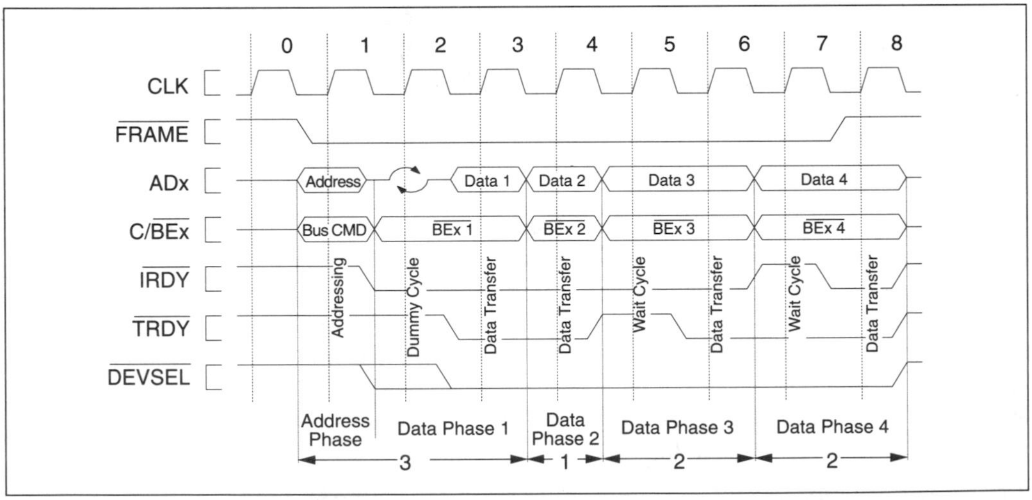

Figure 22.3: The PCI read transfer burst. Contrary to the optimum 3-1-1-1-... burst, a 3-1-2-2 burst is shown, whereby in the first instance an inactive $\overline{\text{TRDY}}$, and in the second instance an inactive $\overline{\text{IRDY}}$, requests a wait state. The addressed PCI unit reacts with an active $\overline{\text{DEVSEL}}$ signal, if it has identified itself as the target of the PCI transfer. The transfer (3-1-2-2 burst) is ended by the deactivation of $\overline{\text{FRAME}}$.

In Figure 22.3 you can see the flow of the most important signals for a typical PCI read access. Note that the first clock cycle after the address phase is used to switch the transfer direction of the multiplexed PCI address/data bus. During the address phase, the ADx pins deliver a value (the address), while during the data phase they receive a value (read data). As in the 8086/88, with its multiplexed address/data bus, a dummy cycle is required for the change in direction. Thus, the first value can be transferred in the third PCI clock cycle at the earliest. The PCI read transfer burst is, therefore, most economically performed (no wait states) as a 3-1-1-1-... burst.

A typical PCI write access is performed in a similar way. It is also initiated by the activation of $\overline{\text{FRAME}}$. In Figure 22.4, the flow of the most important signals is shown. Here, contrary to a read access, the multiplexed PCI address/data bus need not be switched. The data phase can follow immediately after the address phase, without the need for a dummy cycle. Thus, the first value can be transferred in the second PCI clock cycle. The PCI read transfer burst is most economically performed (no wait cycles) as a 2-1-1-1-... burst.

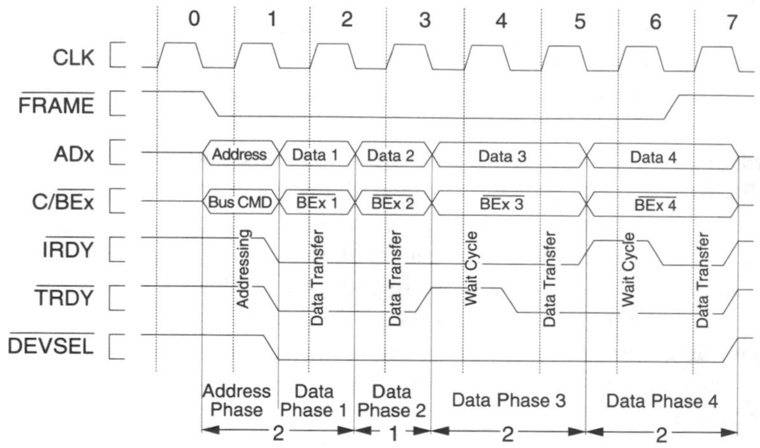

Figure 22.4: The PCI write transfer burst. Contrary to the optimum 2-1-1-1-... burst, a 2-1-2-2 burst is shown, whereby in the first instance an inactive $\overline{TRDY}$, and in the second instance an inactive $\overline{IRDY}$, requests a wait cycle. The addressed PCI unit reacts with an active $\overline{DEVSEL}$ signal, if it has identified itself as the target of the PCI transfer. The transfer (2-1-2-2 burst) is ended by the deactivation of $\overline{FRAME}$.

22.1.3 Bus Arbitration

PCI bus arbitration is performed separately for each access, that is, a busmaster cannot hold up the PCI bus between two accesses. This may occur with EISA and MCA. For this reason, a PCI burst, which in the sense of bus arbitration represents a single access, can extend over any number of transfer cycles. However, this single arbitration does not impair the transfer bandwidth of the PCI bus because the arbitration is «hidden» behind the active bus; a *hidden arbitration* takes place. This means that the arbitration is already being performed if the active bus access is still running. In this way, no PCI bus cycles are required for the arbitration.

PCI includes two control signals for arbitration: $\overline{REQ}$ and $\overline{GNT}$. Each busmaster has its own request and grant signal, which are intercepted and used by a central arbitration logic. However, the PCI specification does not lay down a model for the arbitration; this is a task for the system designer. Usually, a model corresponding to the CACP from microchannel, or the bus arbitrators from EISA are used. The PCI specification only requires that a PCI busmaster must activate the $\overline{REQ}$ signal to indicate a request for the PCI bus, and the arbitration logic must activate the $\overline{GNT}$ signal so that the requesting master can gain control of the bus. The busmaster must then begin a bus transfer within 16 CLK cycles, otherwise a time overrun error occurs.

22.1.4 DMA

If you look at the layout of the PCI slots (Section 22.1.9) and the specific PCI signals (Section 22.1.11), you can see that contrary to ISA/EISA and microchannel, no Direct Memory Access (DMA) is implemented. The «normal» DREQx and DACKx signals known from the PC are missing. At first, this may appear as a backward step because, above all in EISA and MCA PCs, the transfer of large quantities of data from peripheral devices to the main memory, and vice versa, can be performed very quickly via a DMA (even though PC manufacturers very rarely use this channel). The busmaster concept (not only in PCI, but also EISA and microchannel) actually makes direct memory accesses superfluous. The DMA controller is usually located on the motherboard, but typically controls an I/O unit located on an adapter (such as the hard disk controller). In this way, the data transfer is triggered, for example, by the DREQ signal (single transfer mode). However, the necessary bus control signals (such as $\overline{IOW}$, $\overline{MEMR}$, etc.) are produced by the DMA controller (as busmaster) itself, that is, the CPU is not involved with the data transfer. Stated another way, you could regard the combined efforts of the (busmaster) DMA controller and of the trigger signal DREQ as a busmaster function of the adapter, where the busmaster chip is generally located on the motherboard where the bus control signals are produced, while the adapter uses this second busmaster in addition to the CPU through its DREQ signal. A single busmaster chip on the adapter itself makes this somewhat complicated procedure superfluous. The adapter busmaster can now produce all of the bus control signals itself and, thus, can address the I/O and memory address area in any number of ways. However, this requires bus arbitration by means of the expansion bus (or the slots), because with the DMA, only the arbitration between the CPU and the DMA controller is performed on the motherboard. Thus, the use of an external busmaster is more flexible and efficient than the DMA, but makes a more complicated arbitration necessary. It is, of course, possible that the external busmaster located on the adapter is a form of DMA controller which quickly exchanges data between the main memory and the adapter. The busmaster concept is, therefore, more generally understood than the Direct Memory Access, but DMA is only part of the busmaster concept.

22.1.5 Interrupts

Only optional interrupts are included in the PCI specification; they should be level-triggered and active-low. One interrupt line, $\overline{INTA}$, is assigned to each PCI unit. Only multifunctional units can also use the other three interrupt lines $\overline{INTB}$, $\overline{INTC}$ and $\overline{INTD}$. The PCI interrupts are

formed in the CPU PCI bridge like the interrupt requests IRQx of the AT architecture. This usually occurs in a flexible way with help from the setup in the computer BIOS. Depending on which slot a PCI IDE hard disk adapter is installed in, the corresponding interrupt $\overline{\text{INTA}}$ for *this* slot must be set to the IRQ14 of the AT architecture. The $\overline{\text{INTA}}$ of a different slot (with, for example, a LAN adapter) can then be set to a different AT IRQx, for instance, IRQ11. Thus, for a single function PCI unit, only one interrupt (namely $\overline{\text{INTA}}$) is available for each slot; whereas for a multifunction agent, one to four are available ($\overline{\text{INTA}}$ to $\overline{\text{INTD}}$). The actual IRQ activated by the PCI interrupt is set by software configuration. In this way, the inflexible setting of the IRQs, as in the AT architecture and also EISA/MCA, is no longer applicable. In addition, fewer contacts are needed – ISA/EISA/MCA slots contain 11 contacts without an increase in functionality. In a typical ISA/EISA/MCA adapter, ten contacts are not utilized; in a typical PCI adapter only three are not used (with which the adapter activates more than just an IRQ).

22.1.6 I/O Address Space

According to its specification, the PCI bus supports a 32-bit and also a 64 bit I/O address area. However, this only applies to true PCI units. You cannot reach an address greater than 64k with an 80x86 CPU because these processors can only produce 16-bit I/O addresses. The ports in a personal computer with a PCI bus are all located below 64k; the usage and address of each port have not changed when compared to ISA/EISA and MCA, depending on whether your PC is based on the AT, EISA or PS/2 architecture, or a standard expansion bus with either ISA/EISA or microchannel. ISA/EISA/MCA and PCI can, and should, be available alongside each other as PCI and the expansion bridge make this possible. You will find all of the valid I/O addresses and their corresponding usage in Chapters 19 (ISA), 20 (EISA) and 21 (MCA).

PCI stores two PCI registers in an I/O address area, which in EISA are reserved for the motherboard. These two 32-bit registers CONFIG_ADDRESS and CONFIG_DATA are used for accessing the configuration address area and are located at the addresses 0cf8h (ADDRESS) and 0cfch (DATA). If you wish to read or write a double word in the configuration area of a PCI unit, you must transfer the corresponding address to the CONFIG_ADDRESS register first. A write to the CONFIG_DATA register transfers the value to the specified location in the configuration address area of the addressed unit; a read transfers the value from this location. You can see the layout of the address registers in Figure 22.5.

If you set the *ECD* bit, the bridge carries out a configuration cycle for the I/O address 0cfch (corresponding to CONFIG_DATA). If the ECD bit is not set, a normal I/O cycle is performed which does not reach the configuration address area; it is switched through to the normal I/O address area. The *bus* entry stores the number of the PCI bus in a hierarchically structured system containing a maximum of 256 PCI buses. Such a hierarchically structured PCI bus system can be implemented by PCI–PCI bridges. *Unit* selects one of 32 possible PCI agents, *function* one of a maximum of eight functions within a PCI multifunction unit. Then, *register* addresses one of 64 possible Dword entries in a specified configuration address area. *Type* is used to inform the bridge whether it is connected to the addressed unit (type=0), and that after decoding of the unit and function entries it should send out a configuration cycle. If type equals 01b, then the unit is connected to the bridge and the bridge copies the contents of

CONFIG_ADDRESS, unchanged, to the address/data bus. An access to the configuration address area through the two registers CONFIG_ADDRESS and CONFIG_DATA is known as *configuration mechanism #1*. In this way you can also instruct a PCI bridge to send out a special cycle in which the PCI bridge is specified in the address register for the bus entry, the entries for unit and function are written with a series of 1s and the register entry is written with a series of 0s. The next access to the data register then initiates a special cycle, where AD31–AD0 transfer the data register value.

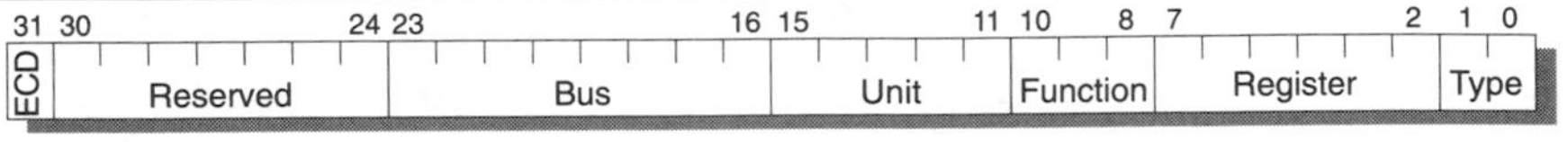

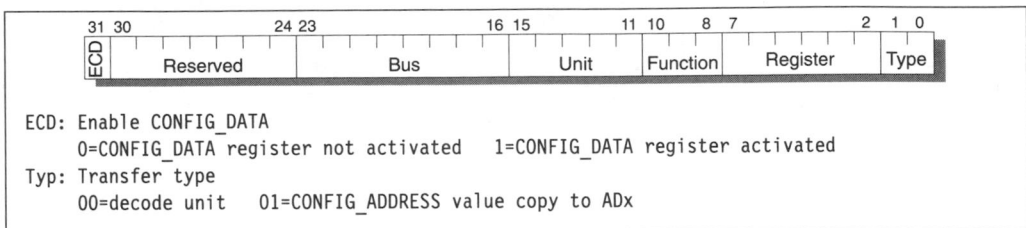

```
ECD: Enable CONFIG_DATA
     0=CONFIG_DATA register not activated    1=CONFIG_DATA register activated
Typ: Transfer type
     00=decode unit   01=CONFIG_ADDRESS value copy to ADx
```

Figure 22.5: The CONFIG_ADDRESS register.

In addition, there is also a *configuration mechanism #2*, but this is only provided for PC systems (as a processor-independent bus system, PCI can also be used in the Alpha or PowerPC, for example). Here, the PCI configuration area of a PCI unit is mapped into a 4k I/O address range between c000h and cfffh. This is achieved by using the activation register CSE (Configuration Space Enable) for the configuration area at the port address 0cf8h; you can see the structure in Figure 22.6, together with the layout of the forward register.

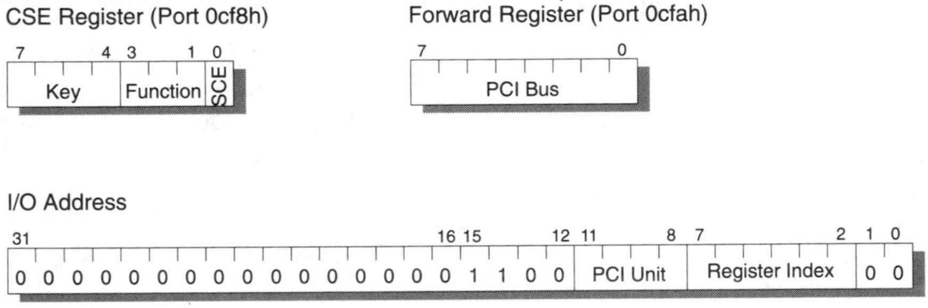

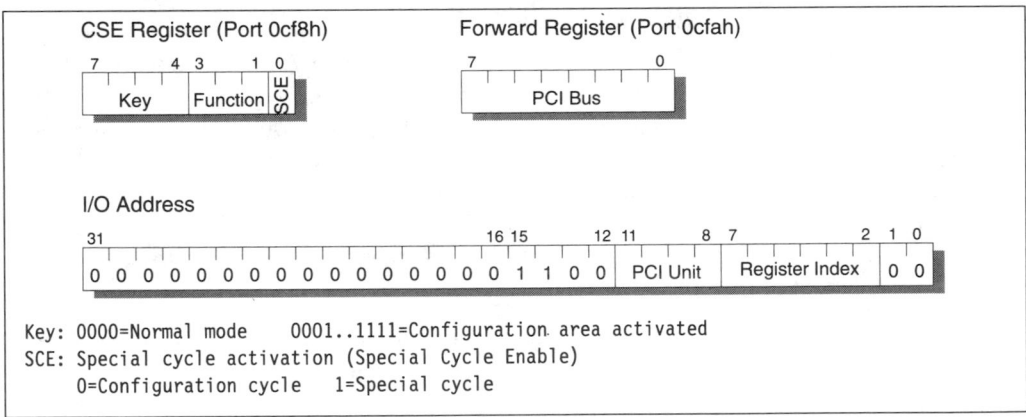

```
Key: 0000=Normal mode     0001..1111=Configuration area activated
SCE: Special cycle activation (Special Cycle Enable)
     0=Configuration cycle   1=Special cycle
```

Figure 22.6: Activation register, forward register and I/O address for the configuration area.

A value other than zero for *key* activates the mapping of the configuration area, that is, all I/O accesses with an address between c000h and cfffh initiate a configuration cycle. Otherwise, the I/O accesses to the 4k range between c000h and cfffh would be performed as normal I/O cycles. The *PCI bus* entry in the forward register at the port address 0cfah indicates the PCI bus for which the configuration cycle should be performed. A value of 00h means, for example, the bus immediately after the host bridge. Now, if you write a value to the 4k I/O range between c000h and cfffh, the address bits AD11–AD8 give the I/O address of the PCI unit, the *function* entry in the CSE register gives the function number within this PCI unit (if it represents a multifunction unit), and the address bits AD7–AD2 give the I/O address of the register index (or the Dword register offset). The two address bits AD1 and AD0 of the I/O address are ignored (it is better to set them to 00), address bits AD31–AD12 are equal to 0000ch or 0000 0000 0000 0000 1100.

In addition to these direct accesses to the configuration area of a PCI unit through the I/O ports, personal computers with a PCI bus, in general, also have an interface available through the BIOS interrupt 1ah. Its standardized functions are detailed in Section 22.1.9. First, however, we shall look at the layout of the configuration address area.

22.1.7 Configuration Address Space

A configuration area of 256 bytes is provided for every PCI unit (and every separate function in a multifunction unit), thus there are 64 *registers* for each 32 bits. A fixed *header* of 64 bytes is located at the start, which is predefined for each unit with this structure. The use of the remaining 192 bytes depends upon each individual PCI unit. The configuration software for such a unit then recognizes the use of this range. Figure 22.7 shows the layout of the configuration area and that of the header.

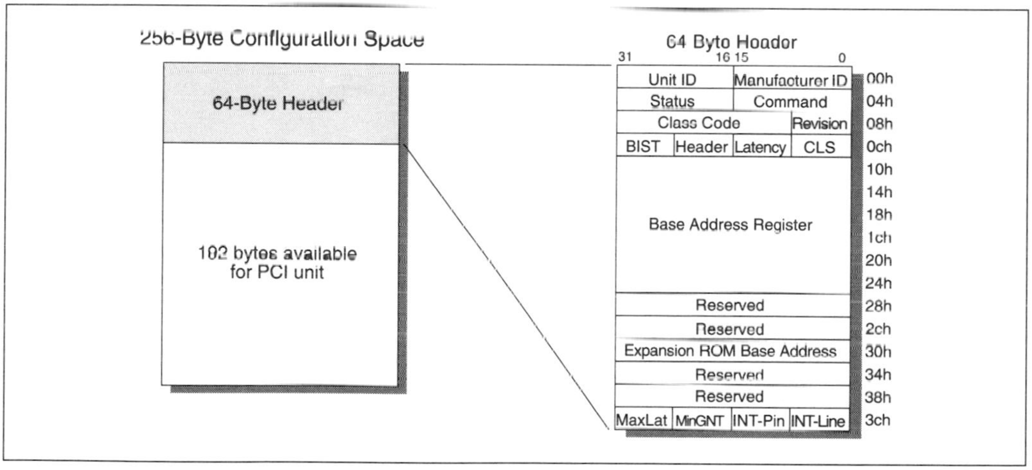

Figure 22.7: 256-byte configuration area and 64-byte header.

Authentic values for *unit ID* are between 0000h and fffeh; the value ffffh indicates that a PCI unit is not installed. In this way, the start routine of the PCI BIOS can identify all of the PCI units. The entries in the configuration area follow the little-endian format. The header itself is divided into two sections: the first 16 bytes (00h to 0fh) are the same for all PCI units; the layout of the subsequent 48 bytes can vary for different PCI units. These layouts are differentiated by the *header* entry (offset 0eh). Currently, only a single header type is defined (header=00h), namely that you can see in the figure between offsets 10h and 3fh. The most significant header bit 7 indicates whether the unit is multifunctional (bit 7=1) or single function (bit 7=0). Note that the PCI specification only requires that the manufacturer ID, unit ID, command and status entries are available. The *manufacturer ID* is allocated by PCI SIG (the governing body that produced the PCI standard). However, *unit ID* and *revision* are inserted by each manufacturer.

Basic code	**Meaning**	**Subcode**	**Meaning**
00h	Unit was produced before the class code definition was defined	00h	All previous units except VGA
		01h	VGA
01h	Controller for mass storage	00h	SCSI controller
		01h	IDE controller
		02h	Floppy controller
		03h	IPI controller
		80h	Other controller
02h	Network controller	00h	Ethernet
		01h	Token ring
		02h	FDDI
		80h	Other controller
03h	Video controller	00h	VGA
		01h	XGA
		80h	Other controller
04h	Multimedia unit	00h	Video
		01h	Audio
		80h	Other unit
05h	Memory controller	00h	RAM
		01h	Flash memory
		80h	Other controller
06h	Bridge	00h	Host
		01h	ISA
		02h	EISA
		03h	MCA
		04h	PCI-PCI
		05h	PCMCIA
		80h	Other bridge
07h–eh	Reserved		
ffh	Uit does not belong to any class 00h–feh	none	

Table 22.3: Basic and sub-class codes

The *class code* indicates the type of PCI unit. For this, the field is sub-divided into three 1-byte sections. The most significant byte (at the offset 0bh) indicates the basic class code, the middle byte (at the offset 0ah) indicates the sub-class code, and the least significant byte (at the offset u09h) delivers a programming interface for the applicable unit. The authentic basic and sub-class codes are shown in Table 22.3.

For many previously defined basic and sub-class codes, clearly defined programming interfaces already exist (such as VGA or SCSI), so that here no programming interface through the least significant byte (at the offset 09h) of the class code entry is required. For all other units, no such programming interface has been defined. For this reason, all detailed classes have the entry 00h in the programming interface field. The *instruction* entry in the header makes it possible to control the unit, that is, how it reacts to PCI cycles. Figure 22.8 shows the structure of this entry. If you write the value 0000h to the instruction register, you deactivate the applicable PCI unit; then, it will only react to a configuration cycle.

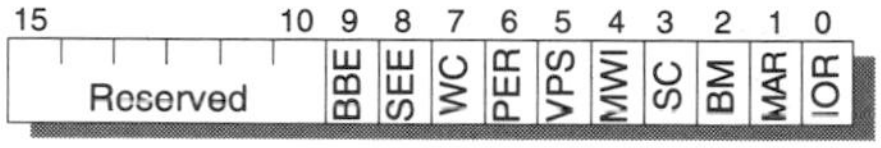

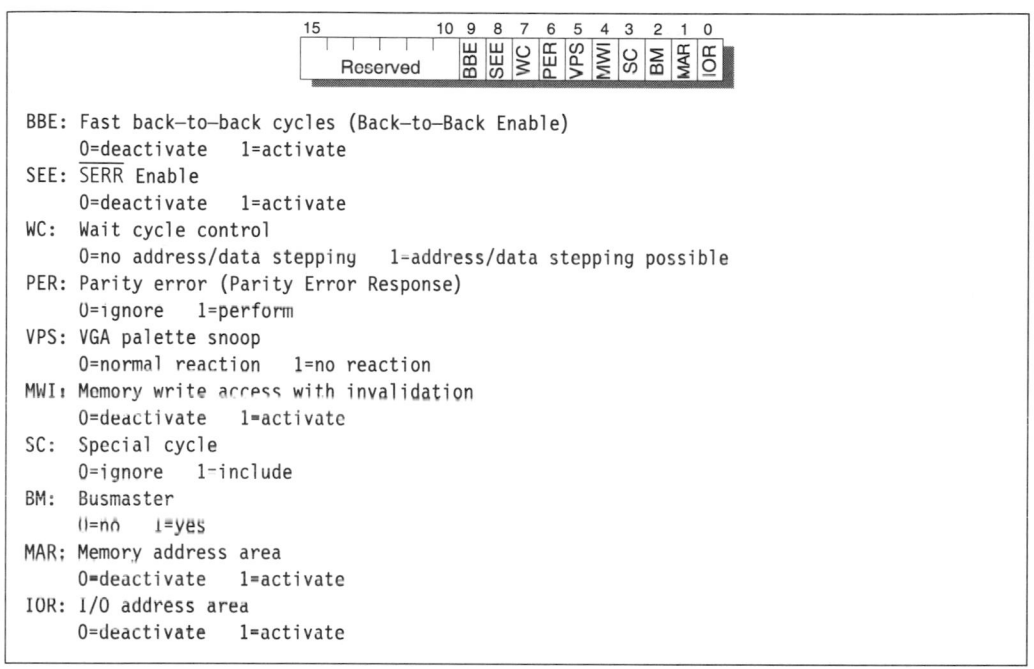

```
BBE: Fast back-to-back cycles (Back-to-Back Enable)
     0=deactivate   1=activate
SEE: SERR Enable
     0=deactivate   1=activate
WC:  Wait cycle control
     0=no address/data stepping   1=address/data stepping possible
PER: Parity error (Parity Error Response)
     0=ignore   1=perform
VPS: VGA palette snoop
     0=normal reaction   1=no reaction
MWI: Memory write access with invalidation
     0=deactivate   1=activate
SC:  Special cycle
     0=ignore   1=include
BM:  Busmaster
     0=no   1=yes
MAR: Memory address area
     0=deactivate   1=activate
IOR: I/O address area
     0=deactivate   1=activate
```

Figure 22.8: Instruction register.

A set *BBE* bit enables so-called fast «back-to-back» cycles for different targets. In this way, fewer dummy cycles are required between two PCU bus transactions. The *SEE* bit activates (SEE=1) or deactivates (SEE=0) the driver for the SERR signal. Should the system control also be informed of address parity errors, both SEE and PER must be set. The *WC* bit must be set for PCI units which perform address/data stepping. Address/data stepping means that not all necessary address/data signals are activated at one time. To reduce the load on the internal driver during activation of the lines, they are gradually set to a high level by means of blocks over a number of clock cycles. With this, the PCI units must wait a short time until all of the potentials have stabilized. If the PER bit is set, the PCI unit will react to a parity error; with a reset PER bit, all parity errors are ignored. By setting the VPS bit, you instruct a VGA compatible PCI unit to ignore all accesses to the palette register. If VPS=0, the unit will react normally. A set MWI bit permits the unit to send out a memory write access with invalidation; if MWI is reset, it must use a normal memory write access instead. By resetting *SC*, you can instruct the unit to ignore all special cycles; if SC=1, then the unit will also recognize special cycles, and will react accordingly to them. If a unit should operate as a busmaster, you must set the *BM* bit. When *MAR* is set, the unit will react to an access of the memory address area, with a set *IOR* bit, it will react to I/O cycles. In addition to the instruction register, a status register is also provided; it indicates the status of the applicable unit for a PCI operation. The layout of the register is given in Figure 22.9.

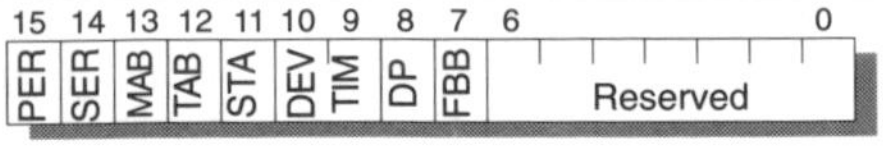

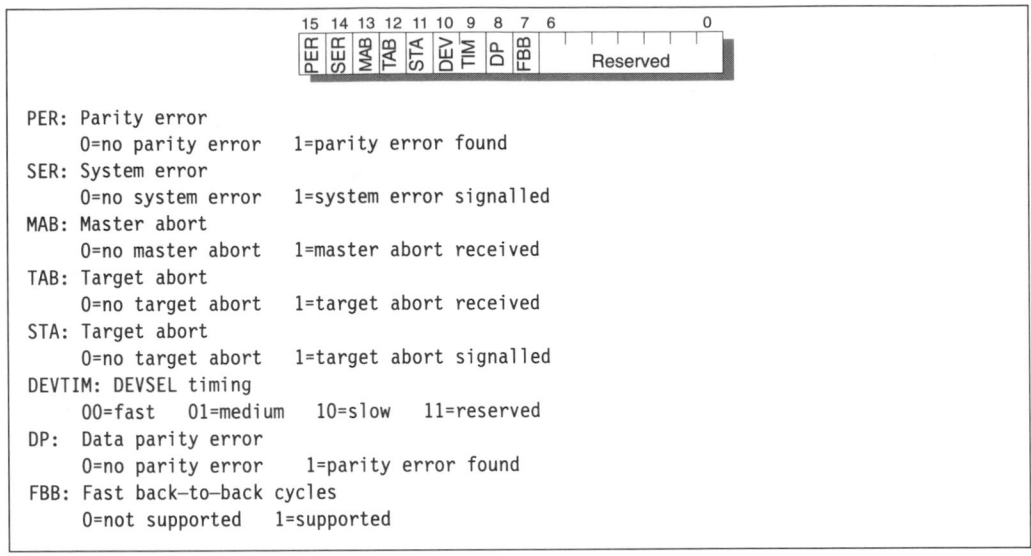

```
PER: Parity error
     0=no parity error   1=parity error found
SER: System error
     0=no system error   1=system error signalled
MAB: Master abort
     0=no master abort   1=master abort received
TAB: Target abort
     0=no target abort   1=target abort received
STA: Target abort
     0=no target abort   1=target abort signalled
DEVTIM: DEVSEL timing
     00=fast   01=medium   10=slow   11=reserved
DP:  Data parity error
     0=no parity error    1=parity error found
FBB: Fast back-to-back cycles
     0=not supported   1=supported
```

Figure 22.9: Status register.

If the unit discovers a parity error it sets the *PER* bit. The *SER* bit is set if the unit activates the $\overline{\text{SERR}}$ signal. If a unit operating as a busmaster stops a transaction, it must set the *MAB* bit. This is similar for *TAB*, except that here, the target has stopped the operation. MAB and TAB are set by the busmaster. *STA*, on the other hand, is set by a unit operating as the target if it has initiated a target abort. The two *DEVTIM* bits set the time characteristic for the $\overline{\text{DEVSEL}}$ signal. The *DP* bit is only implemented for the busmaster, and is set if $\overline{\text{PERR}}$ is activated, the unit is operating as a busmaster, and the PER bit is set in the instruction register. Finally, the *FBB* bit implemented for targets indicates whether the target supports fast back-to-back cycles (FBB=1) or not (FBB=0).

The header entry *CLS* (cache line size) defines the cache line size of the system in units of 32 bytes. It is necessary, for example, for the memory write access with invalidation instruction. The *latency* entry indicates how long a PCI bus operation can take: the effective time span amounts to the latency+8 PCI clock cycles. The most significant bit in the *BIST* (Built-In Self-Test) register indicates whether the unit can carry out a self-test (bit 7=1). If that is the case, you can issue BIST by writing the value 1 to bit 6. BIST then returns a termination code to the four least significant BIST bits 3–0. Any value other than zero indicates an error. The header entry *INT-line* in an AT PC indicates which hardware interrupt line IRQx is connected to the interrupt pin of the unit or function. The values 0–15, corresponding to IRQ0–IRQ15, are valid. The interrupt routing logic of the PCI bridge then activates the corresponding input of the PIC. Which interrupt pin the unit or function actually uses is defined by the *INT pin*: a value of 1 means $\overline{\text{INTA}}$, a value of 2 $\overline{\text{INTB}}$, etc. If the unit does not use interrupts, you must enter the value 0. The two read-only registers *MinGNT* and *MaxLat* give the minimum and maximum latency values required by the manufacturer of the PCI unit, so that the unit can optimally use the PCI bus. Adapter and PCI units frequently contain an I/O or memory area, which they use, for example, for storing data, program execution, etc. With the help of the *base address register(s)*,

PCI now allows these I/O and memory areas to be arranged in any I/O or memory address area. In Figure 22.10, you can see the structure of the base address register for a 32/64-bit memory base and a 32-bit I/O Base. The memory address area can contain 32 or 64 bits, depending on the implementation; the I/O address area, however, always has only 32 bits (of which the 80x86 CPUs still only use the least significant address word AD15–AD0).

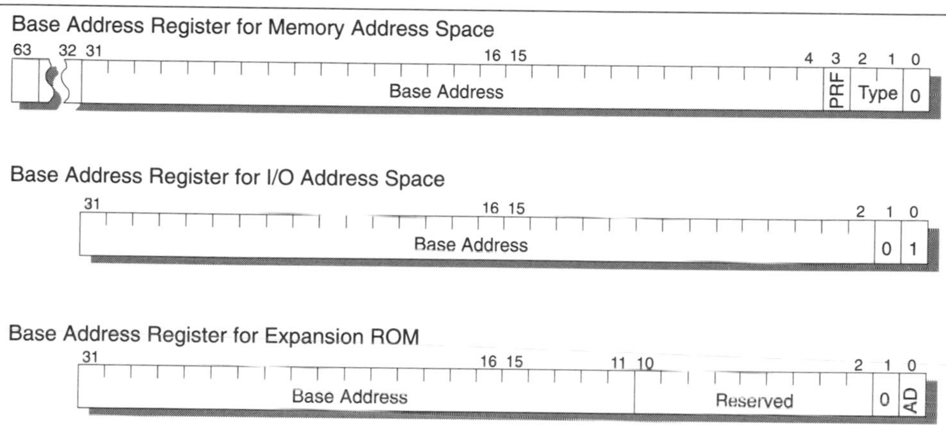


```
PRF:  Prefetching
      0=not possible   1=prefetching possible
Type: Positioning type
      00=any 32-bit address   01=less than 1M
      10=any 64-bit address   11=reserved
AD:   Address decoding and expansion ROM
      0=deactivated   1=activated
```

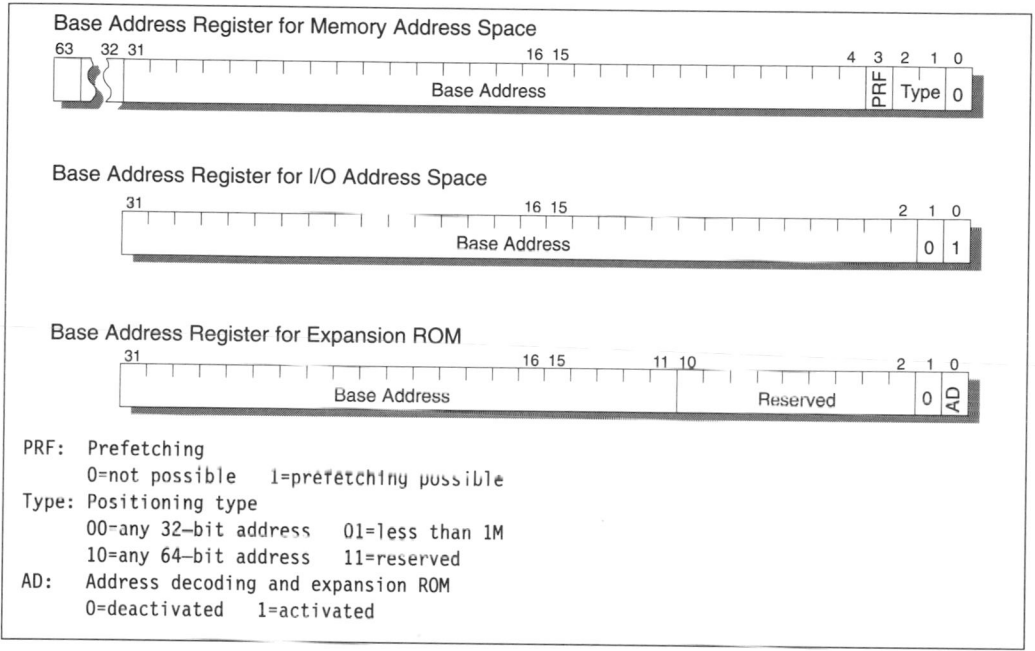

Figure 22.10: Base address register for memory and I/O ports, and also expansion ROM base address.

Bit 0 differentiates a memory base address (bit 0=0) from an I/O base address (bit 0=1). Depending on the size of address, three to six base addresses are possible, the corresponding entry in the header contains 24 bytes. First I would like to explain the entry for a memory base. To be able to perform a remapping of an address area, the POST routine must naturally know how large the area to be formed should be. For this purpose, all bits in the applicable base register which, in practice, represent an offset within the address area to be formed, are hard-wired with the value 0. The POST routine can then simply determine the size of the area, whereby it writes the base address with a series of 1s and then reads back the base address value. All bits which return the value 0 are located within the address area to be formed; all bits set to 1 should be affected by the remapping. If, for example, bits 15 to 4 return the value 0 and the bits 31 (or 63) to 16 return the value 1, the area to be mapped encompasses 64 kbytes, because the 16 least significant bits can address 2^{16} bytes=64 kbytes (the four least significant bits 3–0 cannot be changed, but are included for determining the size of the area). The remapping is performed, whereby the POST routine overwrites the address bits which returned the value 1 with the required base address. As you can see, the remapping is performed in blocks of 16 bytes, 32 bytes, 64 bytes, ..., 1 kbyte, 2 kbyte, etc. As the base address entry in the header can include a number of base addresses, it also enables a fragmented remapping to be realized. If the *PRF* bit is set, the unit permits prefetching, that is, the bridge can read data in advance from the unit into a buffer without disturbing the unit or causing detrimental side-effects to occur. The 2-bit *type* entry indicates the address area where the mapping can be performed. The value 00b means that a 32-bit register can be mapped anywhere in the 32-bit address area; the value 10b has a similar meaning, only here the register and the address area each contain 64 bits. The value 01b is provided for 32-bit registers which must be formed in a 20-bit address below 1 M.

The remapping for I/O addresses is achieved in a similar way, except that here only the two least significant bits 1 and 0 remain unchanged (bit 0=1 indicates that mapping in an I/O address area will be carried out). Thus, I/O address areas can be mapped in units of 2 bytes, 4 bytes, etc. A remapping of 2 bytes usually means that a single 32-bit I/O port will be placed in a suitable position in the I/O address area.

As the last entry in the header, you will also find the *expansion ROM base address*. With this, you can shift a ROM expansion to any position in a 32-bit memory address area. The remapping is achieved in exactly the same way as for a 32-bit base address, only here the 21 most significant bits are provided for the remapping. Thus, ROMs can occur and be remapped in units of 2 kbytes, 4 kbytes, etc. By setting *AD*, you activate the expansion ROM, that is, addresses are decoded; the value zero deactivates the ROM expansion. In this way, a PCI unit can operate with or without a ROM expansion selected. Only if AD is set does the remapping address in bits 32–11 have any significance.

22.1.8 PCI-Specific BIOS Routines

You can comfortably access the configuration address area with ten functions of the BIOS interrupt 1ah. They are listed in the following section along with brief explanations.

- **PCI BIOS available?**

The function determines whether or not a PCI BIOS is available.

Register	Call value	Return value
AH	b1h	00h=available, 01h–ffh=not available[1)]
AL	01h	Configuration mechanism, special cycles[2)]
BH		Version (main level)
BL		Version (sub level)
CL		Number of the last PCI bus in the system
EDX		String "PCI " ('P' in DL, 'C' in DH etc.)
Carry		Status: 1=no PCI BIOS1)

[1)] PCI BIOS only available, if EDX also equals "PCI"

[2)] Bit 0=1: configuration mechanism #1, bit 1=1: configuration mechanism #2, bit 4=1: special cycle through configuration mechanism #1, bit 5=1: special cycle through configuration mechanism #2

– **PCI unit search**

The function determines, by means of the unit and manufacturer identification, and also an index N, the PCI address of the unit, that is, bus number, unit number and function number of the Nth unit which fulfils the search criteria.

Register	Call value	Return value
AH	b1h	Result code in accordance with Table 22.4
AL	02h	
BH		Bus number
BL		Bits 7..3: unit, bits 2..0: function
CX	Unit	
DX	Manufacturer	
SI	Index	
Carry		1=error, 0=o.k.

PCI class code search

The function determines, by means of a specific class code, the PCI address of the Nth unit which contains this class code.

Register	Call value	Return value
AH	b1h	Result code in accordance with Table 22.4
AL	03h	
BH		Bus number
BL		Bits 7..3: unit, bits 2..0: function
ECX	Class code	
SI	Index	
Carry		1=error, 0=o.k.

– **Initiate special cycle**

The function sends out a special cycle to a specific PCI bus in the system. The 32-bit value in EDX is sent on the address/data bus ADx during the data phase.

Register	Call value	Return value
AH	b1h	Result code in accordance with Table 22.4
AL	06h	
BH	Bus number	
EDX	Data	
Carry		1=error, 0=o.k.

– **Configuration byte/word/double word read**

The three functions read a byte (8 bits), word (16 bits) or double word (32 bits) from the configuration area of a PCI unit.

Register	Call value	Return value
AH	b1h	Result code in accordance with Table 22.4
AL	08h (byte), 09h (word), 0ah (Dword)	
BH	Bus number	
BL	Bits 7..3: unit, bits 2..0: function	
CL/CX/ECX	Read byte, word, Dword	
DI	Register number	
Carry	1=error, 0=o.k.	

– **Configuration byte/word/double word write**

The three functions write a byte (8 bits), word (16 bits) or double word (32 bits) into the configuration area of a PCI unit.

Register	Call value	Return value
AH	b1h	Result code in accordance with Table 22.4
AL	0bh (byte), 0ch (word), 0dh (Dword)	
BH	Bus number	
BL	Bits 7..3: unit, bits 2..0: function	
CL/CX/ECX	Write byte/word/Dword	
DI	Register number	
Carry		1=error, 0=o.k.

All functions return a result code in register AH. The five possible PCI BIOS result codes are listed in Table 22.4.

Code	Meaning
00h	Successful completion
81h	Function not supported
83h	Invalid manufacturer identification
86h	Unit not found
87h	Invalid register number

Table 22.4: PCI BIOS result codes

22.1.9 PCI Slots

PCI frees itself not only from ISA – as microchannel did a few years previously – but with its slot geometry and contact layout, it is entirely independent from all existing bus systems. Only the dimensions of the slots bring microchannel to mind. PCI is laid out for an address and data bus width of 32 bits without compromise; you are wasting your time looking for 8-bit and 16-bit segments. Instead, an expansion increase to 64 bits is planned. You can see the construction and signal layout of a PCI slot in Figure 22.11. The multiplexing scheme for the data and address bits can clearly be seen. In total, a maximum of three PCI slots can be available. However, as each slot can be filled by a PCI adapter containing a number of functional units and, in addition, PCI units can also be included on the motherboard, the quantity of possible PCI devices is not restricted to three. With a PCI clock speed of 33 MHz and the high current driving capabilities which adapters request compared to on-board units, more than three external adapters would overload the PCI components, or would become too error-prone.

The 32-bit section contains 124 contacts, of which, however, only 120 are actually used. The remaining four contacts are blocked by a code bridge. Due to the different slots, PCI takes into account the technical developments initiated for the 3.3 V technology used in power saving notebooks or green PCs. In this way, the power consumption in a CMOS circuit can be halved. This is because the power consumption is proportional to the square of the supply voltage. Some highly integrated circuits go one stage further, and can no longer even tolerate the normal 5 V supply, because their internal structure (above all, the channel width of the MOSFETs) would burn. A further PCI demand with respect to lower power consumption is that every PCI unit must operate with a clock between 0 Mhz and 33 MHz. In this way, for example, the clock signal can be switched off (0 MHz) to reduce the power consumption by more than 99.9%.

The two *present* contacts $\overline{\text{PRSNT1}}$ and $\overline{\text{PRSNT2}}$ are individually, or jointly, connected to ground or left open by an installed PCI adapter, in order to indicate that an adapter is installed and what its power consumption is. If no adapter is installed, then both contacts naturally remain open. The possible configurations are shown in Table 22.5.

$\overline{\text{PRSNT1}}$	$\overline{\text{PRSNT2}}$	Meaning
open	open	no adapter installed
GND	open	adapter with max. 25 W power consumption
open	GND	adapter with max. 15 W power consumption
GND	GND	adapter with max. 7.5 W power consumption

Table 22.5: Present contacts

The pins identified as *I/O* represent special supply pins for a universal adapter, which can be operated with both 5 V and 3.3 V. Such adapters can be inserted into any slot. Note that in addition to the special +5 $V^{I/O}$ and +3.3 $V^{I/O}$ pins, the usual +5 V (5 V slot) and normal 3.3 V pins (3.3 V slot) also exist.

The 64-bit section is separated from the 32-bit part by a coding bridge. It is optional and stores the most significant double word of a quad word value or a quad word address. Note that the control and status pins $\overline{\text{REQ64}}$ and $\overline{\text{ACK64}}$ for the activation of the 64-bit extension are included in the 32-bit part. Due to the fact that the contacts are close together, the 64-bit PCI slot is very compact, despite its total of 188 contacts. The address/data multiplexing reduces the quantity of contacts, even with the 64-bit slot, to less than that in a microchannel slot (maximum of 202 pins).

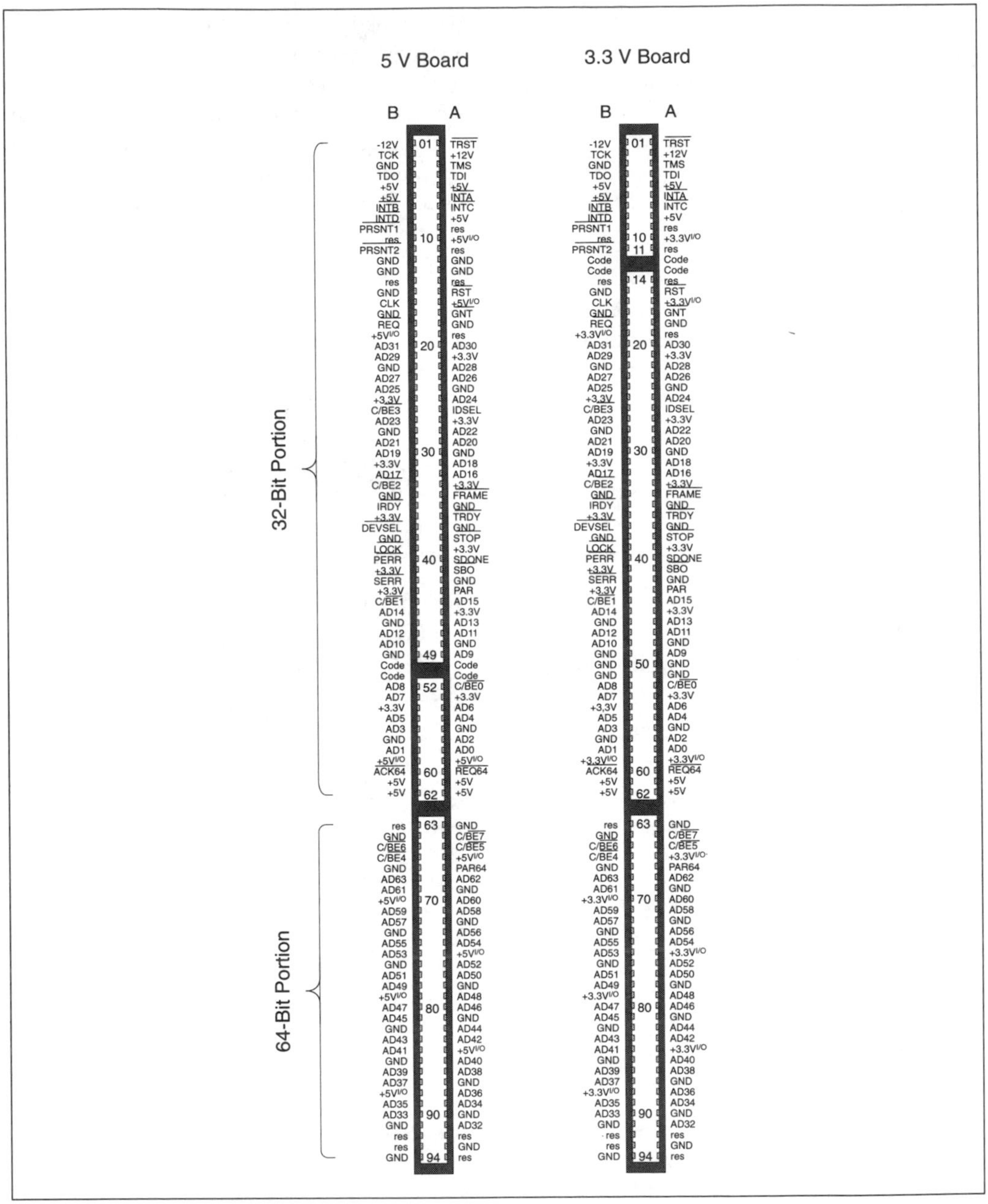

Figure 22.11: The PCI slots. PCI defines two different slot geometries for 5 V, 3.3 V and universal adapter (for 3.3 V and 5 V). They are differentiated by different code bridges so that an adapter cannot be incorrectly installed. In addition, a 64-bit segment is provided.

In addition to the 64-bit extension, a few signals in the standard 32-bit slot are also optional. It is not absolutely necessary for them to be implemented in order to comply with the PCI specification. The required and the optional pins and signals are listed in Table 22.6.

Required:
AD31–AD0, C/$\overline{BE3}$–C/$\overline{BE0}$, PAR, $\overline{FRAME}$, $\overline{TRDY}$, $\overline{IRDY}$, $\overline{STOP}$, $\overline{DEVSEL}$, IDSEL,
$\overline{PERR}$, $\overline{SERR}$, $\overline{REQ}$, $\overline{GNT}$, CLK, $\overline{RST}$

Optional:
AD63–AD32, C/$\overline{BE7}$–C/$\overline{BE4}$, PAR64, $\overline{REQ64}$, $\overline{ACK64}$, $\overline{LOCK}$, $\overline{INTA}$, $\overline{INTB}$, $\overline{INTC}$,
$\overline{INTD}$, $\overline{SBO}$, SDONE, TDI, TDO, TCK, TMS, $\overline{TRST}$

Table 22.6: Required and optional PCI pins and signals

With a so-called *shared slot* you will find an ISA, EISA or microchannel slot along the PCI slot. A true ISA/EISA/MCA adapter would normally be inserted in the ISA/EISA/MCA part of a shared slot, or a true PCI adapter would be inserted in the PCI part of the same slot. These shared slots should allow the number of slots to be reduced to a minimum and, in this way, permit ISA/EISA/MCA adapters to be used without increasing the space required (which is necessary for building very compact notebooks or portables). Thus, PCI has learnt from IBM's experiences with microchannel.

22.1.10 PCI Adapters

PCI includes three different types of boards, namely 5 V, 3.3 V and the universal board. The 5 V boards have a recess at the pin positions A50/B50 and A51/B51, thus they only fit into 5 V slots. In a similar way, the 3.3 V adapter has a recess at the pin positions A12/B12 and A13/B13. As the universal board can be installed in both 5 V and 3.3 V slots, two recesses are provided, namely at A50/B50, A51/B51 (5 V coding) and A12/B12, A13/B13 (3.3 V coding).

PCI adapters which do not support the JTAG boundary scan test must short-circuit their TDO and TDI pins. Frequently, a single scan path is implemented across the complete motherboard and the PCI slots. This makes checking simpler because only a single input and a single output are necessary. If TDO and TDI are not connected together in an adapter without the JTAG test, the scan path is interrupted.

22.1.11 PCI Signals

Here, I would like to list the PCI contacts and explain the meaning of their corresponding signals. As PCI supports busmasters located on PCI adapters in the same way as EISA and microchannel adapters do, all pins are bidirectional. To make the data and signal flow clearer, I have assumed that the CPU (or another unit on the motherboard) represents the current busmaster for the given transfer direction. The pins are divided into their corresponding 32-bit and 64-bit groups, and are listed alphabetically.

Standard 32-bit Section

$\overline{\text{ACK64}}$ (I/O)
Pin B60

An active acknowledge 64-bit transfer signal with a low level indicates that the PCI unit has identified itself as the target for the current bus cycle, and that it can perform the requested 64-bit transfer.

AD31–AD0 (I/O)
Pins A20, A22–A23, A25, A28–A29, A31–A32, A44, A46–A47, A49, A54–A55, A57–A58, B20–B21, B23–B24, B27, B29–B30, B32, B45, B47–B48, B52–B53, B55–B56, B58

The 32 address and data pins form the multiplexed PCI address and data bus. Each PCI bus operation consists of an addressing phase, during which the pins AD31–AD0 transfer an address, and one or more data phases where data is transferred.

C/$\overline{\text{BE3}}$–C/$\overline{\text{BE0}}$ (I/O)
Pins A52, B26, B33, B44

The bus command and byte-enable signals are transferred on these four pins. Like AD31–AD0, they form a multiplexed bus. During the addressing phase, the signals C/$\overline{\text{BE3}}$–C/$\overline{\text{BE0}}$ indicate the type of bus cycle. With this, the possible combinations of C/$\overline{\text{BE3}}$–C/$\overline{\text{BE0}}$ have the following meaning:

```
(0000) INTA sequence        (1000) Reserved
(0001) Special cycle        (1001) Reserved
(0010) I/O read access      (1010) Configuration read access
(0011) I/O write access     (1011) Configuration write access
(0100) Reserved             (1100) Memory multiple access
(0101) Reserved             (1101) Dual addressing cycle
(0110) Memory read access   (1110) Line memory read access
(0111) Memory write access  (1111) Memory write access with invalidation
```

During the data phase, the byte-enable signals $\overline{\text{BE3}}$–$\overline{\text{BE0}}$ define which bytes of the 32-bit data bus transfer authentic values. Note that between the valid bytes «gaps» can occur (for example, the combination $\overline{\text{BE3}}$ = 0, $\overline{\text{BE2}}$ = 1, $\overline{\text{BE1}}$ = $\overline{\text{BE0}}$ = 0 is valid).

CLK (O)
Pin B16

The pin gives the PCI clock signal for all PCI operations. In accordance with the specification, it has a frequency of between 0 MHz and 33 MHz.

$\overline{\text{DEVSEL}}$ (I/O)
Pin B37

An active device select signal with a low level indicates that the decoding logic has identified the applicable PCI unit as the target of a bus operation.

$\overline{\text{FRAME}}$ (I/O)
Pin A34

The $\overline{\text{FRAME}}$ signal is sent by the active PCI master. The reduction of $\overline{\text{FRAME}}$ to a low, that is, active, level starts the addressing phase. The master deactivates $\overline{\text{FRAME}}$ again, to indicate the last data phase of a bus operation.

$\overline{\text{GNT}}$ (O)
Pin A17

An active grant signal with a low level indicates to the corresponding unit that the arbitration logic has handed over the bus, and that it can now use the PCI bus as the master. Each master has its own $\overline{\text{GNT}}$ input.

IDSEL (O)
Pin A26

The initialization device select signal is used as a chip select signal during the accessing of the configuration address area, to determine the unit to be configured and to address it.

$\overline{\text{INTA}}$, $\overline{\text{INTB}}$, $\overline{\text{INTC}}$, $\overline{\text{INTD}}$ (I, I, I, I)
Pins A6–A7, B7–B8

Every PCI functional unit can issue a maximum of four hardware interrupts by means of a low level signal at these pins. A single function unit can only activate $\overline{\text{INTA}}$, a multifunction unit can also activate $\overline{\text{INTB}}$ to $\overline{\text{INTD}}$, depending on the requirements and layout. Hardware interrupts are level-triggered with an active low level. For a PC, $\overline{\text{INTA}}$ to $\overline{\text{INTD}}$ of the respective units are associated with the hardware interrupts IRQ0 to IRQ15 on compatibility grounds.

$\overline{\text{IRDY}}$ (I/O)
Pin B35

The initiator ready signal indicates that the initiator (busmaster) is ready, and that it can complete the current data phase. For a write access, the initiator activates the $\overline{\text{IRDY}}$ signal, to show that the data on the bus is valid. For a read access, $\overline{\text{IRDY}}$ indicates that the initiator can take the read data. Thus, $\overline{\text{IRDY}}$ corresponds to the processor $\overline{\text{READY}}$ signal, except that it is sent out by the initiator (master) and not the target (slave). Only if $\overline{\text{IRDY}}$ and $\overline{\text{TRDY}}$ are active at the same time is the data phase actually completed.

$\overline{\text{LOCK}}$ (I/O)
Pin B39

An active $\overline{\text{LOCK}}$ signal with a low level defines an atomic access which extends over a number of bus operations. Accesses to non-locked elements can still be performed, that is, $\overline{\text{LOCK}}$ only blocks accesses to the PCI element and does not completely block the PCI bus for other accesses. The $\overline{\text{LOCK}}$ signal of the 80x86 CPUs, on the other hand, blocks the whole local CPU bus, and thus the transfer to another master.

PAR (I/O)
Pin A43

The parity pin transfers a parity bit so that even parity is achieved across AD31–AD0 and C/$\overline{\mathrm{BE3}}$–C/$\overline{\mathrm{BE0}}$, that is, the quantity of all 1s in AD31–AD0, C/$\overline{\mathrm{BE3}}$–C/$\overline{\mathrm{BE0}}$ and PAR is even.

$\overline{\mathrm{PERR}}$ (I/O)
Pin B40

For all PCI operations, with the exception of special cycles, an active parity error signal with a low level indicates that a data parity error has occurred.

$\overline{\mathrm{PRSNT1}}$, $\overline{\mathrm{PRSNT2}}$
Pins B9, B11

The two present contacts $\overline{\mathrm{PRSNT1}}$ and $\overline{\mathrm{PRSNT2}}$ are individually, or jointly, set to ground or left open by an installed PCI adapter to indicate that an adapter is installed and what its power consumption is (Table 22.5).

$\overline{\mathrm{REQ}}$ (I)
Pin B18

An active request signal with a low level indicates to the arbitration logic that the applicable unit wishes to use the bus as the master. Each master has its own $\overline{\mathrm{REQ}}$ output.

$\overline{\mathrm{REQ64}}$ (I/O)
Pin A60

An active request 64-bit transfer signal with a low level indicates that the current busmaster wishes to perform a 64-bit transfer.

$\overline{\mathrm{RST}}$ (O)
Pin A15

An active reset signal with a low level resets all connected PCI units.

$\overline{\mathrm{SBO}}$ (I/O)
Pin A41

An active snoop backoff signal with a low level at this pin indicates an inquiry hit to a modified cache line. $\overline{\mathrm{SBO}}$, together with SDONE, supports a write-through or write-back cache which is located in the area of the PCI bridge and lies within the CPU address area.

SDONE (I/O)
Pin A40

An active snoop done signal with a high level shows that the current inquiry cycle has been completed.

$\overline{\text{SERR}}$ (I/O)
Pin B42

For all PCI operations, an active system error signal with a low level indicates an address parity error for special cycles, or another serious system error.

$\overline{\text{STOP}}$ (I/O)
Pin A38

By an active $\overline{\text{STOP}}$ signal with a low level, the target of a master (initiator) indicates that the master should stop the current operation (target-abort).

TCK, TDI, TDO, TMS, $\overline{\text{TRST}}$ (I, O, O, O, O)
Pins A1, A3, A4, B2, B4

These five pins form the interface for the JTAG boundary scan test in accordance with IEEE 1149.1. Through TDI (Test Data Input), test data or test instructions are input and through TDO (Test Data Output), output, synchronous to TCLK (test clock). An active TMS (Test Mode Select) signal activates the TAP control, an active $\overline{\text{TRST}}$ (test reset) resets them.

$\overline{\text{TRDY}}$ (I/O)
Pin A36

The target ready signal indicates that the addressed PCI unit (the target) is ready and that the current data phase can be completed. During a write access, the target activates $\overline{\text{TRDY}}$, to indicate that it can take the write data. For a read access, $\overline{\text{TRDY}}$ shows that the target now has the read data ready. Thus, $\overline{\text{TRDY}}$ corresponds to the processor $\overline{\text{READY}}$ signal. Only if $\overline{\text{TRDY}}$ and $\overline{\text{IRDY}}$ are active at the same time is the data phase actually completed.

64-bit Expansion

AD63–AD32 (I/O)
Pins A68, A70–A71, A73–A74, A76–A77, A79–A80, A82–A83, A85–A86, A88–A89, A91, B68–B69, B71–B72, B74–B75, B77–B78, B80–B81, B83–B84, B86–B87, B89–B90

The 32 address and data pins form the expansion of the multiplexed PCI address and data bus to 64 bits. Every PCI bus operation consists of an addressing phase, during which the pins AD63–AD32 transfer an address, providing $\overline{\text{REQ64}}$ and a DAC command are active; otherwise, AD63–AD32 are reserved. During the data phase(s) the most significant double word of a 64-bit quad word are transferred through AD63–AD32, if $\overline{\text{REQ64}}$ and $\overline{\text{ACK64}}$ are both active.

C/$\overline{\text{BE7}}$–C/$\overline{\text{BE4}}$ (I/O)
Pins A64–A65, B65–B66

The bus command and byte-enable signals are similar to C/$\overline{\text{BE3}}$–C/$\overline{\text{BE0}}$ and are transferred through these four pins. Thus, they form a multiplexed bus. During the addressing phase, signals C/$\overline{\text{BE7}}$–C/$\overline{\text{BE4}}$ indicate the bus type in a similar way to C/$\overline{\text{BE3}}$–C/$\overline{\text{BE0}}$ (refer to the appropriate section). In the data phase, the byte-enable signals $\overline{\text{BE7}}$–$\overline{\text{BE4}}$, together with $\overline{\text{BE3}}$–$\overline{\text{BE0}}$, define which bytes of the 64-bit data bus transfer authentic values.

PAR64 (I/O)
Pin A67
The parity pin transfers a parity bit so that even parity is achieved through AD63–AD32 and $C/\overline{BE7}$–$C/\overline{BE4}$.

22.2 VESA Local Bus VLB

The VESA local bus, or VLB for short, has been designed as much more of a local bus than its later competitor, the PCI. It is directly connected to the local CPU bus of a i386, i486 or Pentium (from specification 2.0 onwards). In this way, it uses bus cycles that are largely the same as those of the 80x86 processors. Note, however, that the cycles even within the 80x86 family can vary, for example, the i386 does not include a burst cycle. To begin with, I would like to introduce a few of the distinguishing features of this bus system:

- no decoupling of processor and expansion bus,
- other bus systems can be connected through their own bridge,
- VLB runs with the bus frequency of the processor: maximum 66 MHz on-board or 40 MHz (specification 1.0) and 50 MHz (specification 2.0) in a slot,
- 32-bit standard bus width with a maximum 133 Mbytes/s (specification 1.0) and 160 Mbytes/s (specification 2.0) transfer rate,
- expansion to 64 bits with a maximum 267 Mbytes/s transfer rate (specification 2.0),
- burst transfers of up to four cycles maximum,
- multimaster capabilities,
- only a single host CPU,
- separate address and data lines for simultaneous transfers of address and data bytes,
- combined VLB/ISA slots,
- processor dependent specification for the 80x86 family,
- supporting of dynamic changes of the clock frequency,
- simpler and therefore cheaper solution than PCI, but in end effect somewhat less powerful,
- maximum of three VL busmasters in addition to the VL bus controller of each VLB subsystem,
- supporting of write-back caches.

22.2.1 VLB Bus Structure

You can see the concept layout of the VL bus system in Figure 22.12. As in the PCI bus, the VL bus is situated between the processor and memory system and the standard expansion bus. From the illustration, you can clearly see that the VL bus is not so strictly decoupled from the processor system on the one side and the standard expansion bus on the other, as in PCI. The VL bus can include up to three VL bus units, which can be inserted in the corresponding VL slots on the motherboard. In Figure 22.12, you can schematically see the layout of a system using a VL bus. The VLB subsystem is controlled by a VL bus controller, which generates all the necessary address, data and control signals for the local bus, or acts on them accordingly.

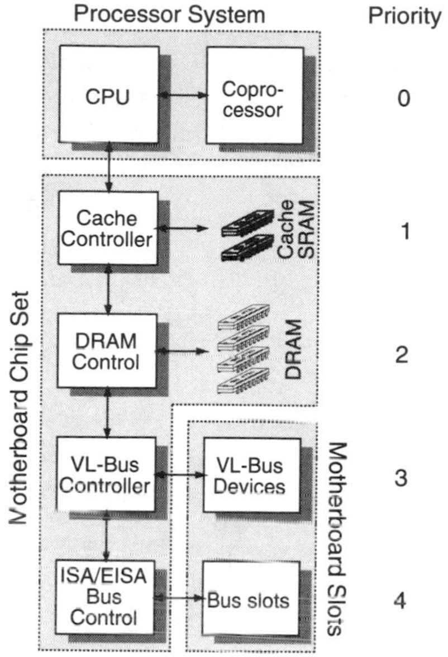

Figure 22.12: The VL bus.

Like the microchannel slots, the VL slots have a 116 pole mounting (however, four are used for the coding bridge). The main difference is that each VLB slot lies 5 mm behind the slot of a standard expansion bus. In this way, a VL bus adapter can not only use the signals and contacts of the VL bus, but with the corresponding geometry, it can also use the standard slot, if necessary. As in the PCI bus, the standard bus width is 32 bits, but it can be halved to 16 bits. For this, the addressed VL unit must set the $\overline{\text{LBS16}}$ (*Local Bus Size 16*) signal to a low level. With the new specification 2.0, an expansion of the VL bus to 64 bits is planned. For this, a further 37 signals are necessary, which must be transferred through the existing contacts (multiplexing). A VLB unit can request a 64-bit cycle using the $\overline{\text{LBS64}}$ signal.

The VL bus runs at the external clock frequency of the CPU. Thus, i386SX/DX, i486SX/DX and i486DX2 processors supply the VL bus with differing frequencies. The VL bus is laid out in such a way that it can be operated with a maximum of 66 MHz. However, this is only possible if no local bus slots are included and the VL units are integrated directly onto the motherboard. Damping, signal reflections and the capacity of the VL bus slot impede such a high frequency. For this reason, using expansion slots, the VL bus runs with a maximum of 50 MHz – even this is six times that of EISA. In too highly clocked CPUs, a frequency divider reduces the clock speed supplied. This also applies to i386 CPUs, because the VL bus runs with a 1x-clock speed and all 386s are supplied with a 2x-clock signal.

The integrated bus buffer of the VL bus makes it possible to perform write accesses to VL units at 33 MHz without wait cycles; like the PCI bus, the VESA local bus also carries out write posting. During read accesses, these buffers do not give any advantage, therefore read accesses are always accomplished with a wait state. The VL bus specification also makes provision for a burst mode, like that of the i486, and so implements the necessary control signals $\overline{BRDY}$ and $\overline{BLAST}$. In specification 1.0, only a read burst was implemented (because the i486 can also only use burst mode for cache line fills). The new specification 2.0 also makes it possible for continual write operations to be performed using a burst. This is mainly included for CPUs or L2-caches that use a write-back strategy. In this way, the shortest write burst thus runs 2-1-1-1 (maximum of four transfers, no wait cycles; note that the i486 cannot perform a write burst). The theoretical data transfer rate with a data bus width of 32 bits at 50 MHz (the maximum for VL slots) during a write is thus 32 bits$*50*10^6$ s^{-1} $*4/5$ = 160 Mbytes/s. For the first transfer of a read operation an additional wait cycle is necessary; the burst thus runs 3-1-1-1 and the data transfer rate sinks to 133 Mbytes/s. An expansion to 64 bits gives almost twice the rate, namely 267 Mbytes/s for a write burst and 222 Mbytes/s for a read burst. The multiplexing of the most significant data double word prevents a true doubling of the bus bandwidth. Naturally, VL units can also request additional wait cycles, for instance, if no access to the video RAM is currently possible due to a memory refresh of the adapter, or the electron beam does not perform a return. For this purpose, the VL bus includes the two signals $\overline{LRDY}$ (*local bus ready*) and $\overline{BRDY}$ (*burst ready*).

Logically, the three possible VL units are sub-divided into a so-called *Local Busmaster* (*LBM*) and a *Local Bus Target* (*LBT*). An LBM can – as in an EISA or MCA busmaster – independently take control of the VL bus and initiate a data transfer. An LBT, on the other hand, is not capable of doing this, and only controls the VL bus during the data transfer; it cannot produce any bus signals itself (except $\overline{LRDY}$). The transfer of the bus control is accomplished by the VL bus controller, which is usually integrated on the motherboard and performs arbitration in a similar way to that in the EISA or microchannel. The different units on the motherboard and in the slots are assigned different priorities. If a unit with a high priority has control of the bus, a unit with a lower priority cannot take over control. In addition to the VL bus controller, three other VL busmasters are provided. Naturally, more VLB subsystems can be integrated onto a single motherboard. The quantity of slots and external busmasters increases accordingly.

22.2.2 Bus Cycles

If the CPU (or a VL busmaster) addresses a unit to perform a bus cycle, the addressed VLB unit has a maximum of 20 ns to react and to activate its corresponding $\overline{LDEV}$ (*local device*) signal. This is an indication to the VL bus controller that the requested bus cycle can be performed. In total, eight types of access are possible which, in the case of the 80x86 CPUs, can be differentiated by the control signals M/$\overline{IO}$ (memory/IO), D/$\overline{C}$ (data/command) and W/$\overline{R}$ (write/read):

- INTA sequence (000)
- Instruction fetching (100)
- Halt/special cycle for i486 (001)
- Halt/shutdown for i386 (101)
- I/O read access (010)
- Memory read access (110)
- I/O write access (011)
- Memory write access (111).

The type of special cycle for an i486, and also the differentiation between a halt and a shutdown cycle in an i386, is achieved with the byte-enable signals $\overline{\text{BEx}}$ in exactly the same way as in the applicable CPU. The VL bus cycles for single transfers and INTA sequences follow exactly the same rules and phases as for an i386 or i486 CPU. Details concerning this can be found in Sections 4.2 and 10.7. Therefore, here I would only like explain the VLB burst cycles. I should also mention that all I/O accesses to an ISA busmaster are switched through to the VL bus, but are always performed as only 8-bit accesses.

Burst Cycles

Every burst cycle is initiated by an address phase, during which address pins A31–A2 transfer an address and the $\overline{\text{BEx}}$-pins all send out a signal with a low level. $\overline{\text{BLAST}}$ is held at a high level until the last data transfer has begun. The VL bus uses a burst cycle corresponding to the i486 read burst. This was also the only possible burst for VLB boards according to specification 1.0. The addressed unit returns an active $\overline{\text{BRDY}}$ for every data transfer. A maximum of 16 bytes, that is, four double words, can be transferred in a burst. Then, one or more data phases follow the address phase, during which the data pins Dx transfer data and the $\overline{\text{BEx}}$ pins transfer the byte-enable signals. An active $\overline{\text{BRDY}}$ during a read access indicates that the target has transferred the data on lines D31–D0 (32 bits). Thus, in its function, $\overline{\text{BRDY}}$ corresponds to $\overline{\text{BRDY}}$ known from the i486 CPU. The VLB read transfer burst is best performed (no wait cycles) as a 3-1-1-1 burst.

In specification 2.0, VESA has also specified a burst write transfer. It is carried out in exactly the same way as a burst read transfer except, naturally, in the other direction. In addition to the address on A31–A2, the initiator also sends out data on D31–D0. By using the bus buffer of the VL bus, write posting can be performed so that in most suitable cases a 2-1-1-1 burst occurs. Otherwise, the burst cycles of the VL bus are not especially interesting; they follow the same signal sequence as in the i486 burst mode (you can find all important details in Section 10.7.1).

If a VLB master wishes to stop burst cycles, it must set the $\overline{\text{BLAST}}$ signal to a low level immediately after activation of $\overline{\text{ADS}}$. The target will then only perform single transfers.

16-bit Transfers

Only address signals A31–A2 and byte-enable signals $\overline{\text{BE3}}$–$\overline{\text{BE0}}$ end in the VLB slots. The i386SX CPU with a 16-bit data bus, on the other hand, has signals $\overline{\text{BLE}}$ (Bus Low Enable) and $\overline{\text{BHE}}$ (Bus High Enable) and address bus bit A1. To produce byte-enable signals $\overline{\text{BE3}}$–$\overline{\text{BE0}}$ in the VLB slots from the CPU signals $\overline{\text{BLE}}$, $\overline{\text{BHE}}$ and A1, the VL bus controller for an i386SX system must perform the following logic combinations (or equivalent):

$\overline{\text{BE0}}$=A1 OR $\overline{\text{BLE}}$
$\overline{\text{BE1}}$=A1 OR $\overline{\text{BHE}}$
$\overline{\text{BE2}}$=$\overline{\text{A1}}$ OR $\overline{\text{BLE}}$
$\overline{\text{BE3}}$=$\overline{\text{A1}}$ OR $\overline{\text{BHE}}$

(Note: $\overline{\text{A1}}$ corresponds to the negative value of A1.)

In addition, the i386 and also the i486 can be operated with a width of 16-bits. Note, however, that the i486 does not perform write data duplication of the most significant data word (D31–D16) in the least significant data word (D15–D0) of the second 16-bit part-cycle. In addition, the i486 CPU always reads in the most significant data word through data lines D31–D15, and not like the i386 through D15–D0, if a 32-bit access is split into two 16-bit accesses using $\overline{\text{LBS16}}$ (VL bus) or $\overline{\text{BS16}}$ (i386/i486). The VL bus controller must handle the differences in behaviour of the two processors accordingly.

64-bit Transfers

In specification 2.0, an optional expansion of the VL data bus to 64 bits is also included, without the need to enlarge the VLB slot or to increase the quantity of contacts.

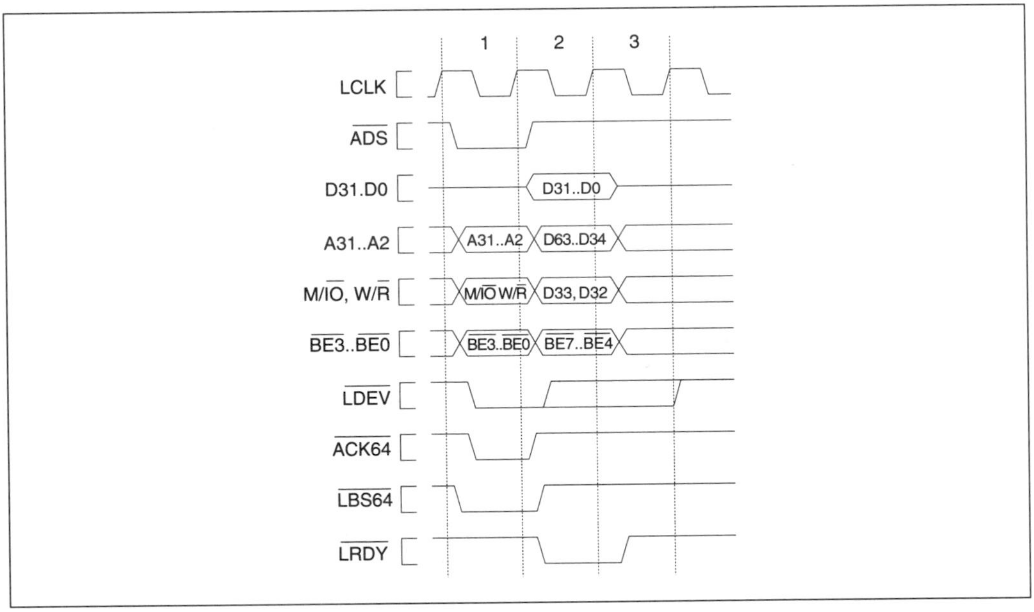

Figure 22.13: The 64-bit VLB single write transfer. The illustration shows an optimum write transfer which consists of an addressing phase (1) and a data phase (2).

The expansion is achieved by multiplexing the additional data and control signal pins required with already existing pins (see Figure 22.15). The 64-bit transfer should, above all, aid burst cycles (the multiplexing and the associated lengthening of a single transfer cycle would almost reabsorb the gain from the wider bus). I would like to use two illustrations to explain the multiplexing system and the sequence of 64-bit transfers: Figure 22.13 shows a 64-bit single write transfer, Figure 22.14 a 64-bit burst read cycle.

For a 64-bit single write transfer, the address and control signals are first sent out on the bus and the VLB controller activates the address strobe signal $\overline{\text{ADS}}$. Then, the controller sends out the request signal $\overline{\text{LBS64}}$ with a low level to indicate to the target that a 64-bit transfer should be performed. The addressed target intercepts the request and reacts with an $\overline{\text{LDEV}}$ signal to indicate to the VL bus controller that it has recognized itself as the target of the cycle. The target also sends back an active $\overline{ACK64}$ if it can perform a 64-bit transfer. That is the case here. The write data is prepared at the start of the second LCLK. For this, the VLB controller sends out the least significant double word D31–D0 on the data bus. In addition, A31–A2, M/$\overline{IO}$, W/$\overline{R}$ and $\overline{BE3}$–$\overline{BE0}$ are invalidated and, in their place, the most significant data double word D63–D32 and also the corresponding byte-enable signals $\overline{BE7}$–$\overline{BE4}$ are provided. The target takes the 64 bits and returns an $\overline{LRDY}$ (and an $\overline{RDYRTN}$ also) in order to complete the single transfer cycle. Here, the entire operation has taken two LCLK cycles and, thus, represents the quickest possible single transfer of the VL bus. If the 64 bits were to be transferred in two separate 32-bit cycles, four LCLK cycles would be necessary. For this reason, the transfer rate for single transfers in 64-bit mode increases by a factor of two. With slower chips, or a very high CPU clock frequency, the addressing phase and also the data phases can take longer (wait states); the transfer bandwidth is then clearly lower.

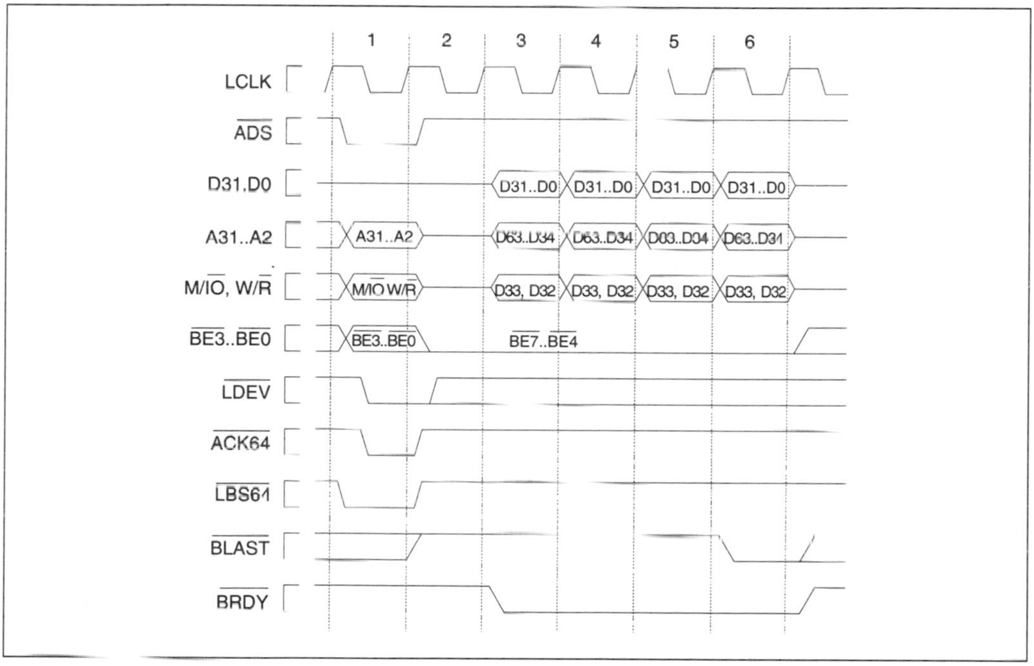

Figure 22.14: The 64-bit VLB read transfer burst. The illustration shows an optimum read burst which consists of an addressing phase (1), a phase (2) for the changing of transfer direction on the address and control bus, and also four data phases (3–6).

A burst cycle in 64-bit mode is initiated in the same way as a single transfer cycle. In the 64-bit VLB read transfer burst shown in Figure 22.14, the VLB controller first sends out the address, control and corresponding $\overline{BE3}$–$\overline{BE0}$ signals. At the start of the second LCLK cycle, in addition to $\overline{BE3}$–$\overline{BE0}$, the byte-enable signals $\overline{BE7}$–$\overline{BE4}$ for the most significant double word D63–D32 are also prepared. They are always at a low level, because this is after all a burst cycle. Only in the last transfer is it possible for one $\overline{BEx}$ or more to also have a high level. The second LCLK cycle is required for the change in direction of the transfer on the combined address/data bus

A31–A2, M/$\overline{\text{IO}}$ and W/$\overline{\text{R}}$, so that data can be read after the address has been given out. Thus, the read data is transferred at the start of the third LCLK cycle at the earliest. The VLB controller indicates that it wishes to perform a burst, in that it pulls the $\overline{\text{BLAST}}$ signal to a high level before the target reacts with the activation of $\overline{\text{LDEV}}$ and $\overline{\text{ACK64}}$. The target shows, by returning the $\overline{\text{BRDY}}$ signal in place of $\overline{\text{LRDY}}$, that it can perform the required burst. Directly before the sending back of the last $\overline{\text{BRDY}}$ signal, the VL bus controller decreases the $\overline{\text{BLAST}}$ signal to a low level to complete the burst. The complete read burst in this particular case has taken six LCLK cycles. Here also, under optimum conditions (a 3-1-1-1 read burst with an addressing and direction changing phase each of only one LCLK clock cycle) a doubling of the transfer bandwidth is possible, as compared to that of a normal 32-bit VL data bus.

Supporting of Write-Back Caches

Specification 1.0 only included the supporting of write-through caches in the VLB system. It is then always necessary to activate the snoop signal $\overline{\text{LEADS}}$ (local external address strobe), if a read or I/O cycle occurs. In this way, a snoop cycle is automatically initiated for all except the currently active busmaster. In specification 2.0, the supporting of write-back caches is now also included. Thus, inquiry cycles must also be performed for write accesses, but not for I/O cycles (because otherwise it is possible for an unnecessary write-back to be sent out, even though the address of a unit in the non-cachable I/O address area is indicated). The $\overline{\text{WBACK}}$ signal is used for this. An active $\overline{\text{WBACK}}$ signal with a low level indicates that the inquiry cycle sent out with a read or write access to a cachable memory address area has resulted in a hit of a modified line of a write-back cycle in an external cache (this is not necessary for non-cachable sections or areas that do not support a write-through strategy). The external cache could be the L1 cache of a different busmaster (for example, the CPU, if the current busmaster is not the CPU) or the L2-cache of a cache subsystem.

If the VL bus controller activates the $\overline{\text{WBACK}}$ signal, the access of the active busmaster must be interrupted so that the modified line can be written back to the main memory first. The VLB controller then disconnects the current busmaster from the VL bus (backoff) and informs the CPU of the role of the active busmaster. The CPU can now write back the modified line. Finally, the VL bus controller takes away control of the VL bus from the CPU and returns it back to the previously interrupted busmaster. The re-activated busmaster repeats the same bus cycle which previously led to the inquiry hit in the CPU cache. Now, $\overline{\text{WBACK}}$ is no longer activated because the applicable cache line has been written back. Naturally, in addition to an L1 CPU cache, an L2-cache with a write-back strategy and a corresponding design can lead to the activation of $\overline{\text{WBACK}}$ and, therefore, initiate the operation described.

22.2.3 Bus Arbitration

The VL bus supports up to three Local Busmasters (LBM). The arbitration protocol is very simple: control of the VL bus is handed over in accordance with a set priority; the arbitration signals $\overline{\text{LREQ<x>}}$ and $\overline{\text{LGNT<x>}}$ are used for this purpose. One $\overline{\text{LREQ}}/\overline{\text{LGNT}}$ pair is included in every VLB slot <x>. An LBM with a high priority can snatch control of the bus from an LBM with a lower priority, but not the other way around. If an LBM wishes to take control of the bus, it activates its $\overline{\text{LREQ}}$ signal. If no LBM with a higher priority currently has control, then the VLB controller reacts with a $\overline{\text{LGNT}}$ and so hands over control of the bus. To make the bus available again, the currently active LBM deactivates its $\overline{\text{LREQ}}$ signal and the bus control confirms this, in that it also increases the $\overline{\text{LGNT}}$ signal to a high level.

If an LBM wishes to take control of the bus while another bus controller has control, it must also activate its $\overline{\text{LREQ}}$ signal first. It is then decided whether the new requesting LBM has a higher priority than the currently active LBM. If this is not the case, the VLB controller denies the transfer request and keeps the $\overline{\text{LGNT}}$ signal inactive. If, on the other hand, the new requesting LBM has a higher priority, then the VLB controller deactivates the corresponding $\overline{\text{LGNT}}$ signal to indicate to the currently active LBM that it must hand over control of the bus. The active LBM finishes the current operation and deactivates its $\overline{\text{LREQ}}$ signal. The way is then clear for transferring control of the VL bus to the requesting busmaster with a higher priority and so the VLB controller activates the corresponding $\overline{\text{LGNT}}$ signal. If the new master has finished its activities and has deactivated its $\overline{\text{LREQ}}$ signal, the VLB controller can hand back control of the bus to the previously interrupted LBM.

22.2.4 DMA

If you consider the layout of the VLB slots (Section 22.2.7) and the specified VLB signals (Section 22.2.9), you can see that here also, as in the PCI, no Direct Memory Access (DMA) is provided. The main difference to PCI is the fact that a VLB adapter usually uses an ISA or EISA slot as well and, therefore, also uses the (E)ISA control signals (incidentally, in the case of VLB, this also justifies the title «local bus»). VLB adapters generally include the signals DREQx and DACKx. Thus, a DMA access in the style of an AT or EISA PC is still possible. However, it is then carried out by the (E)ISA bus and *not* the VL bus, with all limitations regarding the data transfer rate, etc. Naturally, a VLB unit located in the memory address area of the CPU or the DMA controller can represent the target of a DMA transfer which is controlled by the DMA controller on the motherboard, or a busmaster on an expansion card. This, however, has nothing to do with the VL bus; it only concerns the addressing of a unit in the memory address area (which can be achieved equally as well through the (E)ISA bus). If a VLB unit uses only the VL bus to perform a data transfer, then it must represent a VL busmaster which can fully control the VL bus. This strategy normally permits a far greater data transfer rate than the classic DMA technique, because the VL busmaster can use the wide (32 bits or even 64 bits) and fast (up to 50 MHz in the slots) VL bus in burst mode. The necessary bus arbitration is performed by means of a VL bus controller as in PCI. Thus, in the VL bus also, the concept of the direct memory access is replaced by the more flexible, and more powerful, external busmaster principle.

22.2.5 Interrupts

Only a single interrupt pin is included in the VLB specification, namely IRQ9. It is level triggered, active at a high level and is directly connected to IRQ9 of the (E)ISA bus.

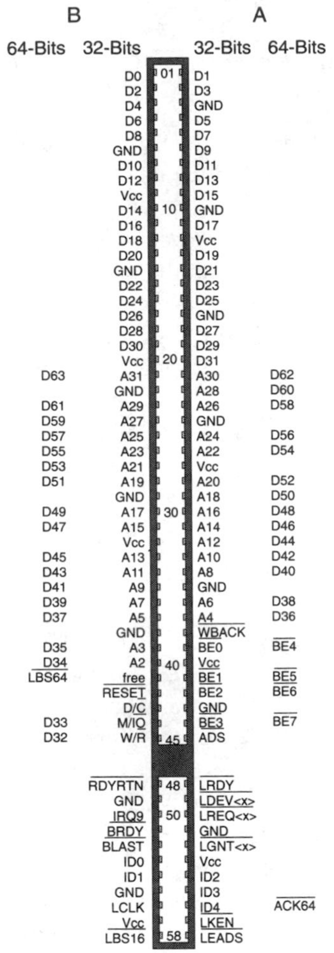

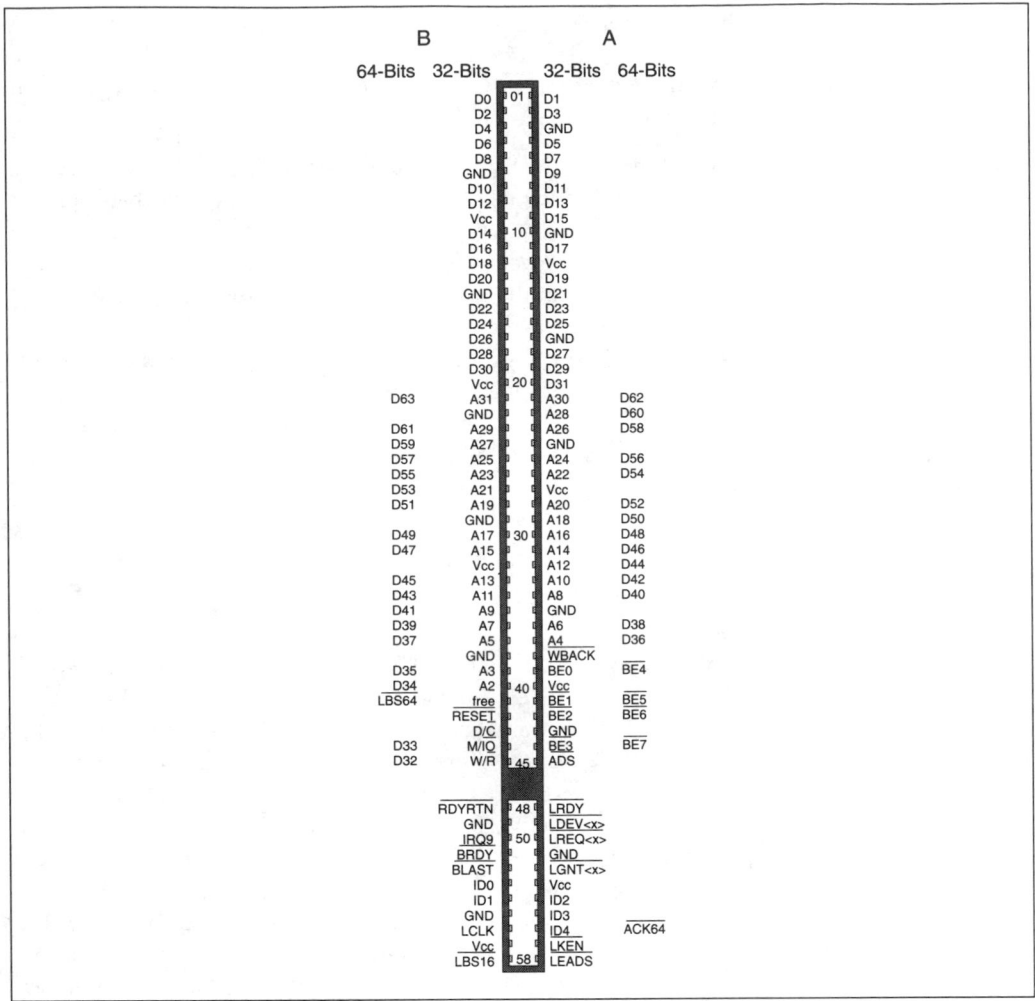

Figure 22.15: The VLB slots.

If the VL bus is integrated into a microchannel system, then the VLB IRQ9 is connected to the MCA $\overline{\text{IRQ9}}$ through an inverter. Normally, the VLB adapter also uses the existing ISA, EISA or MCA slot, so that sufficient interrupt lines are available. It is, of course, theoretically possible for a manufacturer to deliver a pure VLB adapter without contacts for the (E)ISA bus or microchannel. For such *stand-alone VLB adapters,* you do not need to concern yourself about whether they are used in an (E)ISA or a microchannel system – after all, the VLB part is always the same. The only problem is that along with the standard slot, the interrupt pins also disappear. For this reason, the VLB specification includes the Interrupt IRQ9, to give stand-alone adapters at least one possible hardware interrupt.

22.2.6 I/O Address Space

As a local bus for i386/i486 and Pentium CPUs, in accordance with its specification, the VL bus supports a 64k I/O address area with 8-, 16- or 32-bit ports. In general, because the VL bus represents the expansion of an ISA/EISA or MCA system, the affected ports also have the corresponding registers. You will find all valid I/O addresses and the corresponding layout in Chapters 19 (ISA), 20 (EISA) and 21 (MCA). The VLB specification does not provide a set configuration register at a clearly predefined I/O address. Often, however, such registers are available depending on the manufacturer, so that in the setup, for example, you can input the quantity of VLB wait states or the VLB clock frequency. Also note that unlike PCI, no special VLB BIOS is provided, thus, the VL bus is designed as a local system for an IBM-compatible personal computer with an 80x86 processor.

22.2.7 VLB Slots

As already explained, the VL slots have a 116-pole standard microchannel mounting. Each lies behind a standard expansion bus slot so that a VL bus adapter can also use the signals and contacts of the standard slots (and this usually enables them to have access to the hardware interrupts). In the new specification 2.0, with its expansion of the VL bus to 64 bits, the 37 new signals necessary are multiplexed with the address signals through the existing contacts. You can see the geometry and layout of the VLB slots in Figure 22.15.

The quantity of VLB slots is only restricted by their load capacity. For this reason, it is not absolutely necessary for a VLB system to actually include slots. The VLB units can also be integrated onto the motherboard. However, this solution would, certainly in most cases, run contrary to the target of greater flexibility. Usually, a VLB subsystem with a maximum of 40 MHz would include two or three VLB slots, a VLB subsystem operating with the full 50 MHz would contain one or two slots.

22.2.8 VLB Adapters

The VL bus is mainly sold as an expansion of ISA motherboards. In this way, the flexibility of the ISA bus is retained. The 16-bit data bus is completely sufficient for most applications (such as serial and parallel interfaces, floppy drives, etc.). Only the few units with a very high transfer rate (like graphic adapters, hard disks) are served by the faster VL bus. For this reason, you get very good value for money in the form of a flexible (ISA) but nevertheless fast (VL bus) system. The VESA local bus is also a very good compromise between technical and financial restraints and a higher transfer speed.

So that a VLB adapter can use both the ISA (or EISA/MCA also) and the VLB part of a slot, two distinct contact strips are normally included. The somewhat «larger» strip with considerably thicker contacts represents the ISA part, the filigree contacts represent the VLB section. If you have an adapter for a VLB/MCA slot in front of you, the two contact strips appear similar (because the VLB slot still represents a standard MCA slot with respect to the contact geometry). Differently coded bridges, however, prevent the incorrect installation of such an adapter.

Contrary to PCI, VLB does not require a different type of board. Despite this, for example, it is possible to use energy saving adapters which operate internally with 3.3 V. It is only necessary for all the signal levels and signal flows to satisfy the VLB specification. A JTAG boundary scan test is also not provided, and so no pins are implemented for it.

22.2.9 VLB Signals

Here, I would like to explain the VLB contacts and the meaning of their corresponding signals. As VLB, like PCI, supports busmasters on the VLB adapters, all pins are bidirectional. To show the data and signal flows more clearly, I have assumed that the CPU (or another unit on the motherboard) represents the current busmaster for the given transfer direction. The pins are listed alphabetically in 32-bit and 64-bit groups. Note that, contrary to PCI, no physically separate 64-bit section is provided. In its place, the necessary signals are multiplexed with the address signals A31–A2, $M/\overline{IO}$, $W/\overline{R}$, ID4 and $\overline{BE3}$–$\overline{BE0}$. In addition, a VLB adapter can also use the ISA or EISA signals of the corresponding ISA or EISA adapter.

Standard 32-Bit Section

A31–A2 (O)
Pins A21–A23, A25–A26, A28–A34, A36–A37, B21, B23–B28, B30–B31, B33–B37, B39–B40
These 30 address pins form the VLB address bus. Each VLB operation (single or burst transfer) starts with an addressing phase during which the pins A31–A2 transfer an address. The VLB does not support parity formation for the address bus.

$\overline{ADS}$ (O)
Pin A45
By an active address strobe signal with a low level, the VL bus control indicates the start of a bus cycle. A31–A2 then lead with a valid address.

$\overline{BE3}$–$\overline{BE0}$ (O)
Pins A39, A41–A42, A44
The byte-enable signals are transferred on these four pins. An active BEx signal with a low level indicates that the corresponding eight data lines will deliver a valid byte.

$\overline{BLAST}$ (O)
Pin B52
An active burst last signal with a low level indicates that the current burst cycle will be completed with the next $\overline{BRDY}$ signal, that is, the current transfer is the last transfer of a VLB burst.

$\overline{BRDY}$ (I)
Pin B51
The burst ready signal ends the current burst transfer. To complete the whole burst cycle consisting of an addressing phase and four subsequent data phases, $\overline{BLAST}$ must also be active.

The $\overline{\text{LRDY}}$ signal is provided for single transfer cycles, thus VLB carries out an i486-compatible burst.

D31–D0 (I/O)

Pins A1–A2, A4–A9, A11, A13–A16, A18–A20, B1–5, B7–B8, B10–B13, B15–B19

These 32 address pins form the VLB data bus. The byte-enable signals set which of the four data bytes in a data transfer actually transfer valid values. VLB does not support parity formation for the data bus.

ID4–ID0 (O)

Pins A54–A56, B53–B54

These five pins send identification signals to the VLB targets to establish the type and speed of the CPU, and also the burst capabilities and the possible bus width (16 to 64 bits). They are typically sensed immediately after a reset; the BIOS or the VL bus controller of the VLB subsystem are configured accordingly. The signals on ID4–ID0 have the following meanings:

Burst capabilities and bus width:

ID0	ID1	ID4	CPU	Burst capability	Bus width
0	0	0	Reserved	Reserved	Reserved
0	0	1	Reserved	Reserved	Reserved
0	1	0	i486	Burst possible	16, 32 bits
0	1	1	i486	Read burst	16, 32 bits
1	0	0	i386	No burst	16, 32 bits
1	0	1	i386	No burst	16, 32 bits
1	1	0	Reserved	Reserved	Reserved
1	1	1	i486	Read/write burst	16, 32, 64 bits

Wait states for write accesses:

ID2	Wait cycle
0	Minimum of one wait cycle
1	No wait cycles

CPU clock speed:

ID3	Frequency
0	>33.3MHz
1	<=33.3MHz

IRQ9 (I)

Pin B50

This pin operates as a level-triggered interrupt pin with an active high level. It is directly connected to IRQ9 of the ISA bus. IRQ9 is also provided to enable adapters to issue hardware interrupts, which the corresponding ISA or EISA slot and its signals do not use. Usually, VLB adapters issue interrupts through the ISA or EISA contact strips.

$\overline{\text{LEADS}}$ (O)

Pin A58

If a unit performs a cache invalidation cycle on the CPU, it activates the local external address strobe signal. Every VL busmaster (that is, not the CPU) sets $\overline{\text{LEADS}}$ to a low (active) level, if it performs a memory access. In this way, an invalidation cycle is automatically initiated. As a result, the CPU can react with an active $\overline{\text{WBACK}}$ signal if the inquiry has led to a hit of a modified line in the write-back cache. The CPU then immediately issues a write-back cycle and the VL busmaster must wait for the completion of the write-back operation.

$\overline{\text{LBS16}}$ (I)
Pin B58
If the addressed VLB target operates with a width of only 16 bits, it must activate the local bus size 16 signal. The VL bus controller then performs the corresponding number of 16-bit accesses in place of the fewer 32-bit accesses.

LCLK (O)
Pin B56
This pin indicates the local clock speed for all VLB transfers. According to the specification, it is a maximum of 66 MHz in the case of an on-board unit and 50 MHz in the case of a slot. If the CPU is supplied with a 2x-clock cycle (like an i386DX/SX, for example), then PCLK must be divided by two in order to produce LCLK. LCLK always represents a 1x-clock signal.

$\overline{\text{LDEV<x>}}$ (I)
Pin A49
If a VLB target recognizes that it represents the target of the current address (and M/$\overline{\text{IO}}$), it activates the local device signal to inform the VL bus controller that it is the target. Only if a target actually activates $\overline{\text{LDEV}}$ does the VL bus controller send the associated cycle on the VL expansion bus.

$\overline{\text{LRDY}}$ (I)
Pin A48
The local ready signal indicates that the target of a cycle has completed the request. $\overline{\text{LRDY}}$ is only used for single transfer cycles, the separate signal $\overline{\text{BRDY}}$ is provided for burst cycles. Thus, VLB performs i486-compatible bursts.

$\overline{\text{LREQ<x>}}$, $\overline{\text{LGNT<x>}}$ (I, O)
Pin A50, A52
If a VL busmaster in slot x requests control of the VL bus, it activates the local request signal. If the VL bus controller can hand over control of the VL bus to the requesting busmaster after an arbitration phase, it reacts by sending out the corresponding active local bus grant signal with a low level.

M/$\overline{\text{IO}}$, D/$\overline{\text{C}}$, W/$\overline{\text{R}}$ (O, O, O)
Pins B44, B45, B43
The signals Memory/IO, Data/Command and Write/Read indicate the type of bus cycle. With this, the possible combinations of M/$\overline{\text{IO}}$, D/$\overline{\text{C}}$ and W/$\overline{\text{R}}$ have the following associated meanings:

(000)	INTA sequence (100)	(100)	Instruction fetching
(001)	Halt/special cycle (i486)	(101)	Halt/shutdown (i386)
(010)	I/O read access (110)	(110)	Memory read access
(011)	I/O write access (111)	(111)	Memory write access

For an i486-compatible VL bus cycle, the byte-enable signals $\overline{\text{BE3}}$–$\overline{\text{BE0}}$ also indicate the type of special cycle as in the i486. This is similar to the halt/shutdown condition of an i386-compatible bus cycle.

$\overline{\text{RDYRTN}}$ (O)
Pin B48
The VLB controller transfers the ready return signal at this pin to all VL busmasters and VL targets. $\overline{\text{RDYRTN}}$ indicates that a VLB cycle has been completed. For VLB frequencies over 33 MHz, $\overline{\text{RDYRTN}}$ can precede the $\overline{\text{LRDY}}$ signal by one LCLK cycle (in this context, note the local bus setup in the BIOS).

$\overline{\text{RESET}}$ (O)
Pin B42
An active reset signal with a low level resets all connected VLB units.

$\overline{\text{WBACK}}$ (O)
Pin A38
The write-back signal is produced by the VLB controller and instructs a VL busmaster to interrupt the current bus cycle. In this way, snooping cycles are supported which lead to a hit in one of the caches in a multi-cache system initiating a write-back cycle.

64-bit Expansion

Contrary to the PCI local bus, no separate 64-bit expansion is provided in the VESA local bus. The expansion of the data bus to 64 bits included in specification 2.0 is achieved by multiplexing the most significant data double word D63–D32 on the existing address pins A31–A2 and also M/$\overline{\text{IO}}$ and W/$\overline{\text{R}}$.

$\overline{\text{ACK64}}$ (I)
Pin A56
An active acknowledge 64-bit transfer signal with a low level indicates that the addressed VLB target can perform the requested 64-bit transfer.

$\overline{\text{BE7}}$–$\overline{\text{BE4}}$ (O)
Pins A39, A41–A42, A44
These byte-enable signals are, like $\overline{\text{BE3}}$–$\overline{\text{BE0}}$, transferred on these four pins. In a similar way to $\overline{\text{BE3}}$–$\overline{\text{BE0}}$, the byte-enable signals $\overline{\text{BE7}}$–$\overline{\text{BE4}}$ indicate which bytes of the most significant DW section of the 64-bit data bus transfer authentic values.

D63–D32 (I/O)
Pins A21–A23, A25–A26, A28–A34, A36–A37, B21, B23–B28, B30–B31, B33–B37, B39–B40, B43, B44
These 32 data pins form the expansion of the data bus to 64 bits. $\overline{\text{LBS64}}$ and $\overline{\text{ACK64}}$ must both be active before a 64-bit transfer can be performed.

$\overline{\text{LBS64}}$ (O)
Pin B41
The VL bus controller or the active VL busmaster activates the local bus size 64 signal, in order to indicate to the target that it wishes to perform a 64-bit transfer.

22.3 Typical Local Bus Units

As already explained, the local bus is targeted at units which require, or which must send, large quantities of data quickly. Above all, this affects graphic adapters and hard disks. Currently, these are also the only local bus devices available. Graphic adapters with a local bus interface are substantially quicker than ISA adapters without dual-port memory or graphic processors. In Section 32.6, you will find a comparison of the different concepts for accelerating the formation of a picture. Powerful hard disk drives are further candidates for local bus units. With their cache memory, they achieve data transfer rates comparable to EISA and MCA systems, or even exceed them. This, above all, applies to host adapters with a local busmaster which, independently and with a higher speed, control the local bus in burst mode. A PIO access through the CPU is, naturally, much slower. Also the trend towards more and more powerful LANs with transfer rates of 100 Mbits/s or greater make such adapters future candidates for the local bus.

22.4 Bottlenecks in Local Bus Systems

Many proud owners of new local bus systems are frequently upset by the performance of their systems, especially if they have previously worked on an EISA system. Often, no performance gain is noticed, mainly with respect to hard disks. Here, we are evidently often confronted with a «bottleneck» in the system. In the case of hard disks, this can be due to the method of data transfer or a lower quantity of sectors for each cylinder, for example. In the following section, I have briefly made reference to concepts which occur in connection with hard disks. In Section 28 you will find a more comprehensive explanation of these concepts. In Section 32.6, the advantages and disadvantages of local bus and graphic processors are discussed.

There are several possibilities for the transfer of data to and from the controller: DMA, PIO (programmed I/O) and busmaster. Only PIO and busmaster apply to adapters with a local bus interface, because a data transfer using DMA only operates with the maximum data throughput of the DMA system which, for an ISA system, is in the region of 1 Mbyte/s. A PIO cycle, however, requires a minimum of two expansion bus cycles and two memory bus cycles because, in the example of a controller–main memory transfer, the following cycles occur: output of the I/O address and reading of the data from the controller (expansion bus), as well as output of the memory address, and output of the data to the main memory (memory bus cycle). For this, EISA controllers which transfer the data with the help of the DMA burst mode C require only a single EISA clock cycle. With a local bus, even if all units can react without wait states, at least 33 MHz as the clock frequency are necessary to achieve the same transfer rate. Only cache SRAM is capable of this; all other components, such as the DRAM chips of the main memory, the I/O registers of the adapters, etc., insert wait states. At 8 MHz, on the other hand, the EISA bus has no such problems; the transfer rate in EISA systems is, thus, frequently even greater than that of local bus systems. One possible solution is the SCSI host adapter (very expensive), which includes a busmaster. This external busmaster can take control of the local bus following an arbitration phase, and can then shovel the data directly into the main memory using burst mode. Expensive busmaster adapters such as these even surpass EISA busmaster adapters, because here the higher clock frequency of the local bus comes into play. Such busmaster adapters are not available for the IDE interface, because the AT bus does not support external busmasters in the required way; for EISA, on the other hand, SCSI busmaster adapters have been standard for quite some time.

The higher transfer rates of busmaster adapters for the local bus, as compared to EISA, unfortunately only apply if the data is available in the on-board cache of the hard disk controller or disk drive. With larger quantities of data, the drive must reload data from the disk into the cache before further bytes can be transferred to the main memory, or the drive must save data to the disk before further data can be transferred from the main memory to the drive. This is often the case, for example, when calling up a program or saving a large graphics file. In both cases, the transfer rate is now limited (whether ISA, EISA, MCA or local bus) to the speed at which the data can pass through the read/write head of the drive. With the currently typical 50–60 sectors per track, and 3600 to 5400U/min, this is only 1.5–2.6 Mbytes/s. In many cases, even an ISA system with a cache controller can achieve this.

Every hard disk controller includes a more or less powerful CPU to control the drive on the one hand, and to manage the on-board cache (if available) on the other. If a manufacturer attempts to use an installed ISA controller with a local bus interface, the CPU cache (which was sufficient for ISA) can quickly become overworked. This, naturally, reduces the data transfer rate. Therefore, during the introduction phase of the local bus into actual computer applications, the performance values of the new local bus adapters were only slightly better than the classic adapters, if at all. Simply to swap the interface was not sufficient. The insides of the basic adapter were specifically designed for the ISA bus and so, for cost reasons, every manufacturer was reluctant to install more powerful (and thus more expensive) chips onto the board than the (ISA) interface to the system bus could actually handle (for example, many cache controllers of disk drives operate with the quite antiquated 80186/188 CPU). If you then replace the ISA interface with a local bus interface, the situation is reversed: now the interface is no longer the bottleneck, instead it is the circuits of the adapter itself which were designed for its predecessors. As the two were balanced out (the circuits delivered or accepted the data with the same speed as the interface), the effect on the performance was negligible. For example, ISA graphic adapters with VRAM have long since outperformed local bus graphic adapters with DRAM. In the meantime, however, this situation has changed considerably; local bus adapters are, in most cases, clearly more powerful than their EISA or MCA competitors, and even use 32-bit chips. The first graphic adapters with 64-bit chips are currently coming onto the market.

Part 4
Support Chips – Nothing Runs Without Us

Peripheral and support chips belong together, and are components that support the processor for certain tasks. These chips are far less flexible than the processor, but carry out the allocated jobs at higher speed and independent of the CPU. Support chips are usually developed in close relation to a certain processor, or at least to a processor family. Together, the processor and support chips are often called a *chip set*. The following sections discuss the most important support chips used in PCs. However, because of the enormous advance in microelectronics, several of the separately described components are today usually integrated into a single chip. Therefore, don't be surprised if you can't, for example, find a chip labelled 8259A. It will be integrated as a functional unit into one of the ICs on the motherboard. These support components integrated into a single chip, though are accessed and programmed in the same way as described below in connection with the original Intel chips.

23 Hardware Interrupts and the 8259A Programmable Interrupt Controller

Several components are present in PCs that only require a service by the processor from time to time. This includes the serial interface, where characters from a modem arrive asynchronously (hence the chip is also called a UART). Moreover, the time period between two successive characters or character blocks may be quite long. For this reason, the processor is often occupied by executing a program while the incoming characters are first collected in the background so as to be available for processing later.

23.1 Interrupt-Driven Data Exchange and Polling

If the PC expects characters to arrive at the serial interface, there are two principal possibilities for collecting them:

- the serial interface is regularly examined to see whether a complete character has arrived;
- the serial interface itself indicates that it has received a complete character.

In the first case the strategy is called *polling*. The disadvantage of this method is obvious: the processor is heavily occupied with the polling process so that execution of the foreground program proceeds slowly. Additionally, the extensive polling routine must be integrated into the program, which leads to more code and a worse performance. If the characters are arriving very quickly, the time period between two pollings may be longer than the interval between two incoming characters; data is thus lost.

The other possibility is usually realized by a hardware interrupt. The strategy is then called *interrupt-driven data exchange* or interrupt-driven communication. In this case, the serial interface activates an IRQ signal to inform the processor that a complete character has been received and is ready for transfer to the CPU. In the PC this signal is transmitted to the 8259A programmable interrupt controller (PIC), a support chip that issues an interrupt request to the processor. As the CPU in this case knows that a character is available, the interrupt handler only needs to read the character from the serial interface. The periodic examination as to whether a character is available is no longer required, thus the program overhead for servicing the serial port is less, and the performance increases. With interrupt-driven data exchange significantly higher transfer rates can therefore be achieved without lowering the execution speed of the foreground program.

Potential candidates for interrupt-driven communication, besides the serial interface, are all those components that exchange data with the main memory:

- the parallel interface;
- the floppy/hard disk controller;
- network adapter;
- the keyboard.

Also the hard disk, for example, may need quite a long time (in computer terms, of course) to position the read/write head and to read certain data. While this is carried out the computer doesn't have to wait, but can carry out other tasks. Once the drive has read the data from disk, the controller activates the interrupt signal to cause the processor to service the hard disk again. By using interrupts instead of polling, the performance and reliability of a computer system are increased.

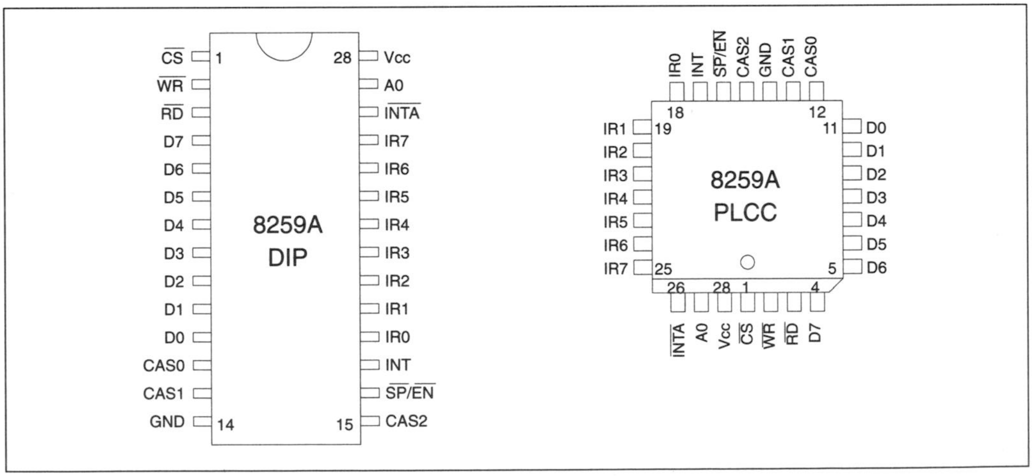

Figure 23.1: 8259A PIC pin assignment.

As the processor usually only has a single interrupt input but in the PC several units for interrupt-driven data exchange are present, the 8259A PIC is implemented to manage them. The 8259A PIC is connected between the interrupt-requesting components and the processor, that is, the interrupt requests are first transferred to the PIC, which in turn drives the interrupt line to the processor. Figure 23.1 shows the pin assignment of this chip.

23.2 8259A Connections and Signals

The 8259A comes in two package types, that is, as a dual in-line package and as a plastic leaded chip carrier. In the following, the pins and signals applied or provided are outlined.

A0 (I)
Pin 27

A0 is used together with $\overline{CS}$, $\overline{WR}$ and $\overline{RD}$ to distinguish among various commands from the CPU and provide status information to the CPU.

CAS0–CAS2 (O)
Pins 12, 13, 15

With these cascade line connections, and the accompanying signals, several PICs can be cascaded. Usually, a hierarchical structure of one master PIC and up to eight slave PICs is the result. The master PIC selects one of these $2^3=8$ slave PICs via lines CAS0–CAS2. Thus, CAS0–CAS2 form something like a local PIC address bus.

$\overline{CS}$ (I)
Pin 1

If this chip select pin is at a low level, the CPU can read data from or write data to the internal 8259A registers by means of the data bus D7–D0 and the signals $\overline{RD}$ and $\overline{WR}$. Thus the $\overline{CS}$ signal enables the PIC for read and write processes. For managing and servicing interrupts, the $\overline{CS}$ signal has no meaning.

D7–D0 (I/O)
Pins 4–11

These eight pins form the bidirectional data bus (to/from the CPU), through which the CPU can write to or read data from internal registers. The number of the interrupt vector to be called is also transferred via D7–D0.

INT (O)
Pin 17

If a valid interrupt request is issued by a peripheral via lines IR0–IR7, the INT signal rises to a high level. INT is directly connected to the INTR input of the processor.

$\overline{INTA}$ (I)
Pin 26

This interrupt acknowledge pin is connected to the processor's $\overline{INTA}$ pin, through which the CPU outputs $\overline{INTA}$ pulses to carry out an interrupt acknowledge sequence for transferring the interrupt vector concerned.

IR0–IR7 (I)
Pins 18–25

These interrupt request pins are connected to those peripherals which request an interrupt. One pin may be connected to only one peripheral at most. To issue a hardware interrupt the peripheral concerned raises its IRQ output, and thus the connected IRx pin, to a high level. The input IR0 has the highest and IR7 the lowest priority. A single 8259A PIC can service a maximum of eight different peripherals. By cascading, as is the case in the AT, however, up to 64 devices can be managed, and up to 64 interrupt levels can be realized.

$\overline{RD}$ (I)
Pin 3

If this read pin is supplied with a low-level signal, the 8259A outputs data onto the data bus, that is, the CPU can read data from the internal PIC registers.

$\overline{SP/EN}$ (I(O)
Pin 16

Depending on the 8259A operation mode (buffered or unbuffered), the meaning of the signal at this slave program/enable buffer pin differs. In buffered mode the connection outputs a signal $\overline{EN}$ to control the external buffer. In unbuffered mode the pin recives a signal $\overline{SP}$, which indicates whether the 8259A is to be operated as a master PIC ($\overline{SP}=1$) or a slave PIC ($\overline{SP}=0$).

$\overline{WR}$ (I)
Pin 2

(Write) If this pin is supplied with a low-level signal, the 8259A accepts data from the data bus, that is, the CPU can write data into the internal PIC registers.

Vcc
Pin 28
This pin is always supplied with the supply voltage (usually +5 V).

GND
Pin 14
This pin is supplied with the ground potential (usually 0 V).

23.3 Internal Structure and Interrupt Acknowledge Sequence

Figure 23.2 shows the internal structure of the 8259A programmable interrupt controller.

To detect and manage the interrupt requests of peripherals, three registers are available in the 8259A: interrupt request register (IRR); in-service register (ISR); and interrupt mask register (IMR). The eight interrupt lines IR0–IR7 are connected to the IRR. Each of the three registers is eight bits wide, where every bit corresponds to one of the lines IR0–IR7 (see Figure 23.3).

To issue an interrupt request the peripheral concerned raises the signal at one of the corresponding pins IR0–IR7 to a high level. The 8259A then sets the accompanying bit in the interrupt request register. In the IRR all devices for which an interrupt request is currently pending are memorized. As it is possible for several peripherals to issue a hardware interrupt simultaneously, and therefore several bits may also be set in the IRR simultaneously, the priority encoder passes only the highest priority bit.

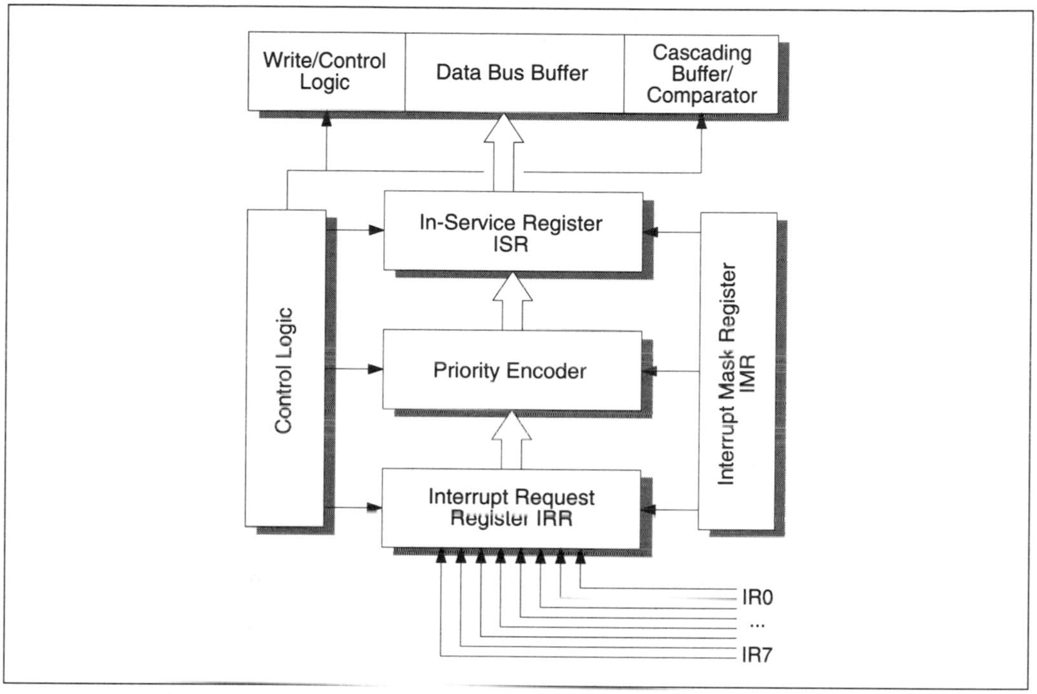

Figure 23.2: Internal structure of the 8259A PIC.

At the same time, the PIC activates its output INT to inform the processor about the interrupt request. This starts an *interrupt acknowledge sequence*. If the IE flag in the processor's flag register is set, then the CPU responds with the output of a first $\overline{\text{INTA}}$ pulse to the $\overline{\text{INTA}}$ input of the 8259A. The priority encoder now transfers the highest priority bit to the in-service register (ISR), and clears the corresponding bit in the IRR. The set bit in the ISR indicates which interrupt request is currently serviced (is *in-service* now). The processor outputs a second $\overline{\text{INTA}}$ pulse to instruct the 8259A to put the 8-bit number of the interrupt handler onto the data bus D7–D0. This 8-bit number consists of the three least significant bits of the number of the set bit in the ISR (see Figure 23.4).

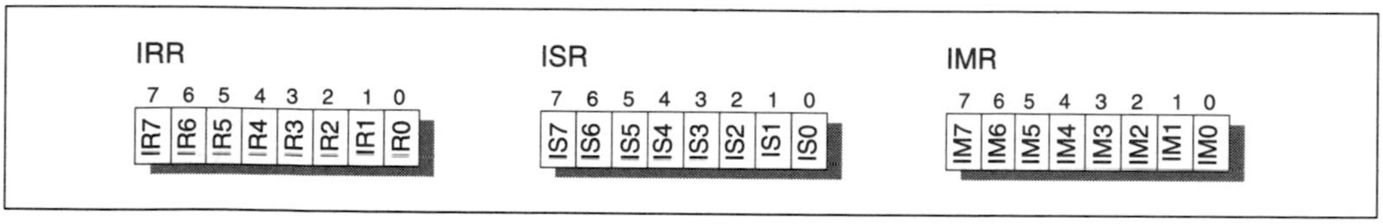

Figure 23.3: IRR, ISR and IMR.

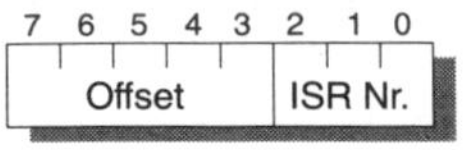

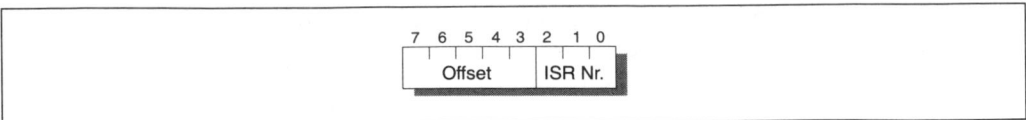

Figure 23.4: The interrupt number. The five most significant bits are determined by the programmable offset, the three least significant bits by the number of the set bit in the ISR.

The five most significant bits can be programmed appropriately as an offset upon initializing the PIC (see below). The CPU reads the 8-bit number and calls the corresponding interrupt handler. If the 8259A is operating with automatic interrupt completion (in the so-called AEOI mode), the acknowledge sequence is completed and the ISR bit is reset. If, on the other hand, the 8259A is not operating in AEOI mode, it is the responsibility of the interrupt handler to issue an EOI command (end of interrupt) to the PIC. The set ISR bit is thus cleared manually. The various operation modes can be programmed via software.

In both cases, the 8259A is now ready to process the next hardware interrupt request (if another bit is set in the IRR). For this purpose, the priority encoder transfers the bit with the next lowest priority from the IRR into the ISR, and the described interrupt acknowledge sequence is repeated.

If a request of a higher priority occurs during the course of the $\overline{INTA}$ cycle or the servicing of an interrupt request, the 8259A completes the current $\overline{INTA}$ cycle and then services the new interrupt of higher priority.

The following actions are carried out for an interrupt request by a peripheral:

- One of the interrupt request lines IR0–IR7 is raised to a high level and thus the corresponding bit in the IRR is set.
- The 8259A detects this signal and responds with an INT signal to the processor.
- The CPU receives the INT signal and outputs a first $\overline{INTA}$ pulse if the IE flag is set.
- With the receipt of the first $\overline{INTA}$ signal from the CPU the highest priority bit in the IRR register is cleared, and the corresponding bit in the ISR register is set.
- The processor outputs a second $\overline{INTA}$ pulse and thus causes the 8259A to put an 8-bit pointer onto the data bus. The CPU reads this pointer as the number of the interrupt handler to call.
- In the AEOI mode the ISR bit is automatically reset at the end of the second $\overline{INTA}$ pulse. Otherwise, the CPU must issue an EOI command to the 8259A when executing the interrupt handler to manually clear the ISR bit.

Example: The serial interface COM1: in the XT is connected to IRQ4 corresponding to the 8259A IR4 line. The programmed offset is equal to 7. If COM1 issues an interrupt request then pin IR4 of the PIC is set to a high level and the IRR4 bit in the IRR is set. The priority encoder sets bit IS4 in the ISR and clears the bit IR4 in the IRR. During the course of the following interrupt acknowledge sequence, the 8259A outputs the value 8(offset)+4(IS4) = 12 (0ch) as the interrupt vector number. Thus the processor calls interrupt handler 0ch. During the course of servicing the interrupt the processor passes an EOI command to the 8259A, and the IS4 in the ISR is reset.

To be able to mask a certain interrupt request the interrupt mask register (IMR) is implemented. A set bit in this register masks all the interrupt requests of the corresponding peripheral, that is, all requests on the line allocated the set bit are ignored; all others are not affected by the masking.

Thus, the PIC 8259A not only activates the processor's IRQ input and manages the hardware requests according to their priority, but also, during the course of the interrupt acknowledge sequence, passes the number of the interrupt handler to be called.

23.4 Cascading

One characteristic of the 8259A is its *cascading* capability. For this at least two PICs are required, which form two levels: the first is formed by a master PIC, the second by 1–8 slave PICs. With this configuration interrupt requests of more than eight peripherals can be managed. Figure 23.5 shows the wiring of two 8259As as master and slave PIC, as is the case in an AT or PS/2.

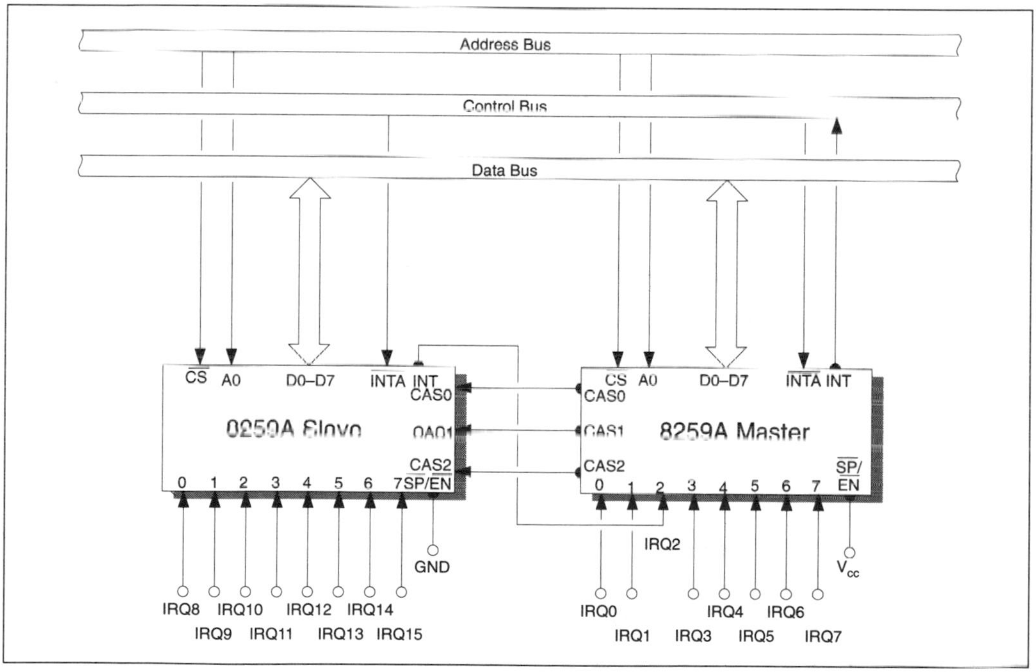

Figure 23.5: Cascading the 8259A PICs. The 8259A PICs can be cascaded so that a maximum of 64 interrupt levels is available. For this purpose, the INT output of the slave is connected to one IR input of the master, and signals CAS0–CAS2 are used for information interchange.

To realize cascading the INT output of the slave PIC is connected to one of the IR inputs of the master PIC. In the AT or PS/2, the interrupt request signal of the slave is applied to input 2 of the master PIC. The PC literature established the name IRQ0–IRQ7 (master) and IRQ8–IRQ15 (slave) for the various interrupt channels and PIC connections (Figure 23.5). Thus the slave's

INT output is redirected to IRQ2 of the master. Only the INT output of the master is connected to the INTR input of the processor via the control bus. The pins $\overline{CS}$, A0, $\overline{INTA}$ and D0–D7 are connected to the address, control and data bus, as is the case for a single-PIC configuration. Additionally, the connections CAS0–CAS2 of the master and slave are wired. The master PIC uses CAS0–CAS2 as outputs, the slave PIC, however, as inputs. This means that the master PIC supplies control signals and the slave receives them.

With a high-level signal (Vcc) at the $\overline{SP}/\overline{EN}$ pin, the 8259A is operated as a master and by a low-level signal as a slave. For a master, $\overline{SP}/\overline{EN}$ is therefore usually fixed to the supply voltage, and for a slave this pin is grounded. This is in general already carried out during manufacturing by soldering the pin to a corresponding supply line.

The processing of an interrupt request of a peripheral is dependent upon whether the request is running through the slave PIC or is directly managed by the master. If one of the devices connected to IRQ0, IRQ1 or IRQ3–IRQ7 requests an interrupt, the same steps as described above are carried out.

However, if the request is running over one of the lines IRQ8–IRQ15 (that is, via the slave PIC), additional steps are required:

- One of the interrupt request lines IRQ8–IRQ15 is raised to a high level, and thus the corresponding bit in the IRR of the slave PIC is set.
- The 8259A slave detects this, and responds with an INT signal to the master PIC.
- The master PIC receives the INT signal via connection 2 (IRQ2); thus bit 2 is set in the master's IRR.
- The 8259A master detects this, and responds with an INT signal to the processor.
- The CPU receives the INT signal and outputs the first $\overline{INTA}$ pulse if the IE flag is set. At the same time the master PIC activates the signals CAS0–CAS2 to address the slave PIC which manages the interrupt.
- Upon receipt of the first $\overline{INTA}$ signal from the CPU, the highest priority bit in the IRR register of the master and slave PIC is cleared, and the corresponding bits in the ISR registers are set.
- The processor outputs a second $\overline{INTA}$ pulse, and causes the slave 8259A to put an 8-bit pointer onto the data bus. The CPU reads this pointer as the number of the interrupt handler to call.
- In AEOI mode the ISR bits in the master and slave are automatically reset at the end of the second $\overline{INTA}$ pulse; otherwise, the CPU must output two EOI commands during the course of executing the handler (one to the master PIC and the other to the slave PIC) to clear the ISR bits manually.

If the 8259A is not operating in AEOI mode, then the interrupt handler needs to know whether the interrupt request is managed by the master alone or by the master–slave pair, because in the latter case two EOI commands are required. Thus, servicing a hardware interrupt depends to a great extent on the architecture forming the base of the computer. For this reason, the BIOS usually has all the necessary instructions for the appropriate handling of such requests. A programmer should therefore complete his/her own handler for hardware interrupts by chaining to the original routine instead of to their own EOI sequence.

Redirecting the INT signal from the slave's INT output to the IRQ2 input of the master leads to a shift in the priorities of the corresponding interrupt requests. As input 2 of the master has a higher priority than inputs 3–7, all interrupt requests running through the slave push their way to the front. Thus the priority in descending order is as shown in Table 23.1.

Master	Slave	Priority	PC/XT	AT/PS/2
IRQ0		highest	timer 0	timer 0
IRQ1			keyboard	keyboard
IRQ2			reserved	slave PIC
	IRQ9			reserved*)
	IRQ10			reserved
	IRQ11			reserved
	IRQ12			reserved
	IRQ13			coprocessor 80287/i387
	IRQ14			hard disk controller
	IRQ15			reserved
IRQ3			COM2	COM2
IRQ4			COM1	COM1
IRQ5			hard disk controller	LPT2
IRQ6			floppy controller	floppy controller
IRQ7		lowest	LPT1	LPT1

*) An IRQ9 leads to the call of the interrupt handler for IRQ2 (redirection of IRQ9 to IRQ2).

Table 23.1: IRQ Priorities (in descending order)

With one master and one slave 8259A PIC a maximum of 15 peripherals or interrupt channels can be handled. The IRQ2 channel is reserved for redirecting the INT signal from the slave. This 2-level cascading model can be expanded to 64 channels at most. In this case, the INT outputs of the eight slave PICs are connected to the eight inputs of the master PIC, all interrupt requests running through the slaves. For the PC, including the PS/2 and EISA models, the 15 interrupt channels that can be realized with one master and one slave are sufficient. Usually, you therefore find two chips at most. Because of the technical advances in integration, these two PICs are often integrated into a single *system controller*, together with other control chips such as DMA, timer and real-time clock. Structure and functionality, though, remain the same.

23.5 Initialization and Programming

For a defined operation the 8259A needs to be initialized first. This is carried out by the four *initialization command words* (*ICW*) ICW1–ICW4. Using the three *operation command words* (*OCW*) OCW1–OCW3 the 8259A PIC is instructed to operate in various modes to handle the interrupt requests. In the following description, however, the programming is only discussed for use in a PC. Other operation modes for use with the MCS–80, 85 and other systems are not described.

For accessing the 8259A registers two ports are available for the master and slave. The PIC in the PC/XT, as well as the master in the AT and PS/2, is accessed via ports 020h and 021h, and the slave PIC in the AT and PS/2 via ports 0a0h and 0a1h. Table 23.2 lists the addresses as well as the read and write data for these registers.

I/O address IRQ0–IRQ7[1]	**I/O address IRQ8–IRQ15**[2]	**Read data**	**Write data**
020h	0a0h	IRR	ICW1
		ISR	OCW2
		interrupt vector	OCW3
021h	0a1h	IMR	ICW2
			ICW3
			ICW4
			OCW1

[1] valid for PC/XT and the master PIC in the AT and PS/2.
[2] valid for slave in the AT and PS/2.

Table 23.2: 8259A PIC I/O Addresses and I/O Data

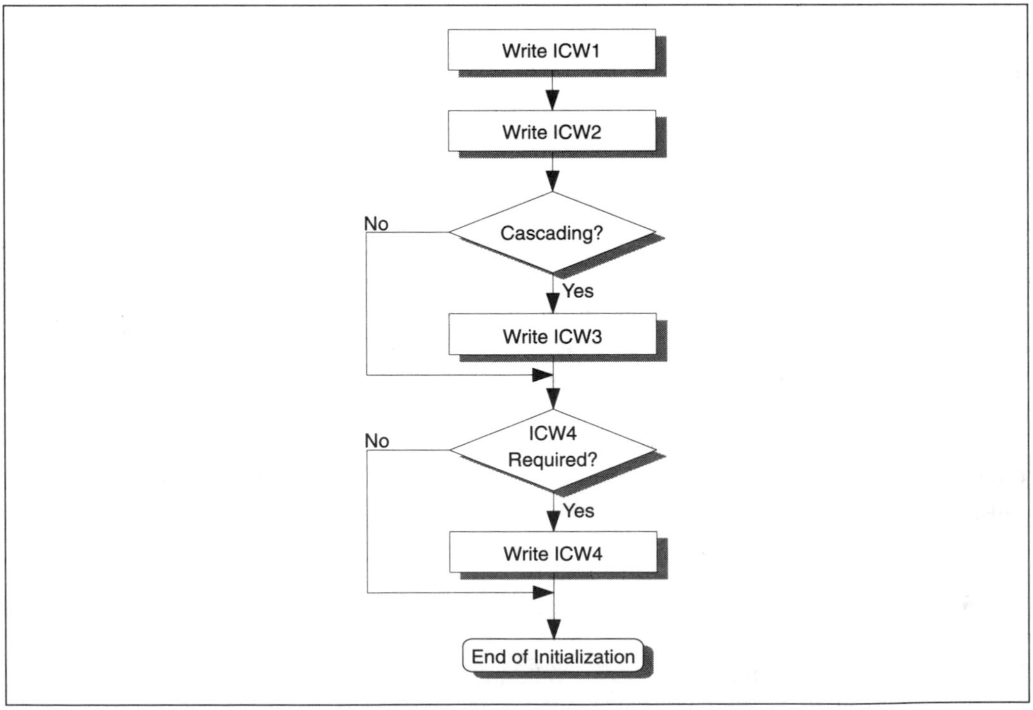

Figure 23.6: Initializing the 8259A PIC. Initializing the PIC is carried out by two to four initialization command words ICWx, depending upon the chosen operation mode.

The initialization of an 8259A PIC is started by outputting the initialization command word ICW1 via port 020h (master) or 0a0h (slave). Thus the PIC recognizes that an initialization has begun, and resets the internal registers to default values. Figure 23.6 shows a flowchart for initializing the 8259A.

After starting initialization by writing ICW1, the CPU supplies the initialization command word ICW2 via port 021h (master) or 0a1h (slave). If cascaded PICs are employed in the system, the processor also writes ICW3. If only one PIC is implemented, as in the PC/XT, this is not necessary. An entry in ICW1 indicates whether the PIC requires the information supplied by ICW4. If this is the case, the CPU also supplies the ICW4 word. Thus, the PIC initialization is completed with at least two and a maximum of four initialization command words.

In the following, the formats of the four ICWs is described (Figure 23.7).

Bits D7–D5 and D2 in ICW1 are equal to 0 and bit D4 is equal to 1. By means of the *LTIM* bit, the PIC is instructed to operate with either edge or level triggering. With an edge-triggered operation an interrupt request is indicated by a *transition* of the signal at the corresponding IR input from low to high. If level triggering is enabled then the interrupt request is indicated solely by a high *level*. In the PC/XT and AT, the PICs operate with edge triggering only. In PS/2 and EISA computers, level triggering can also be employed. The *SNGL* bit determines whether only a single PIC (as in the PC/XT) or at least two cascaded PICs (as in the AT and PS/2) are used. If cascaded PICs are present in addition to ICW1 and ICW2, ICW3 must be also specified. Thus with SNGL the PIC recognizes whether ICW3 is passed after transfer of ICW1 and ICW2. If *IC4* is set, then the PIC knows that later additional information is passed with word ICW4.

Bits *Off7–Off3* in ICW2 define the offset of the interrupt vector, which is passed to the CPU during the course of an interrupt acknowledge sequence. The remaining three bits of the interrupt vector number are specified implicitly by the number of the serviced request.

The meaning of the bits in the initialization word ICW3 differs from master to slave. For the master a cleared bit *S7–S0* indicates that the corresponding IR line is connected to a peripheral that is able to issue an interrupt request directly, or that line is free. A set bit, on the other hand, shows that the corresponding input is connected to the INT output of a slave PIC. For a slave PIC the three least significant bits *ID2–ID0* define the number of the master's IR input to which the slave concerned is connected. During the course of an INTA sequence the slave PICs compare their identification number (defined by means of ID2–ID0) with the number that the master PIC outputs via lines CAS2–CAS0. Only the slave PIC whose identification number matches CAS2–CAS0 responds with the output of the number of the interrupt vector to be called.

The 8259A PIC expects the transfer of ICW4 only if this is explicitly defined in ICW1. Usually, the PICs in the PC operate in the normal *nested mode*. This means that the interrupt requests managed by the PIC are structured hierarchically in the above mentioned way, that is, the request via IR line 0 has the highest priority, that via IR line 7 the lowest. Thus the interrupts are serviced according to their priority, and not according to their occurrence. For very large systems with many interrupt channels this mode can be modified by setting the *SFNM*. This prevents a slave PIC from blocking interrupt requests of a higher priority in the slave PIC while being serviced by the master. But the PC doesn't use this capability; it is only important for large computer systems. If the *BUF* bit is set then the PIC is operating in buffered mode. The $\overline{SP}/\overline{EN}$ pin is not used as input to distinguish master and slave, but as an output for activating external buffers. This is necessary for large computer systems with a power-consuming system bus; the PC doesn't use this option. In buffered mode the $\overline{SP}/\overline{EN}$ pin is no longer available for distinguishing master and slave. In this case, the operation mode as a master or slave is not defined by fixing the $\overline{SP}/\overline{EN}$ potential on Vcc (master) or GND (slave), but by programming the *M/S* bit. A set M/S bit indicates that the PIC concerned is operating as a master. If the 8259A is operated in unbuffered mode then M/S has no meaning.

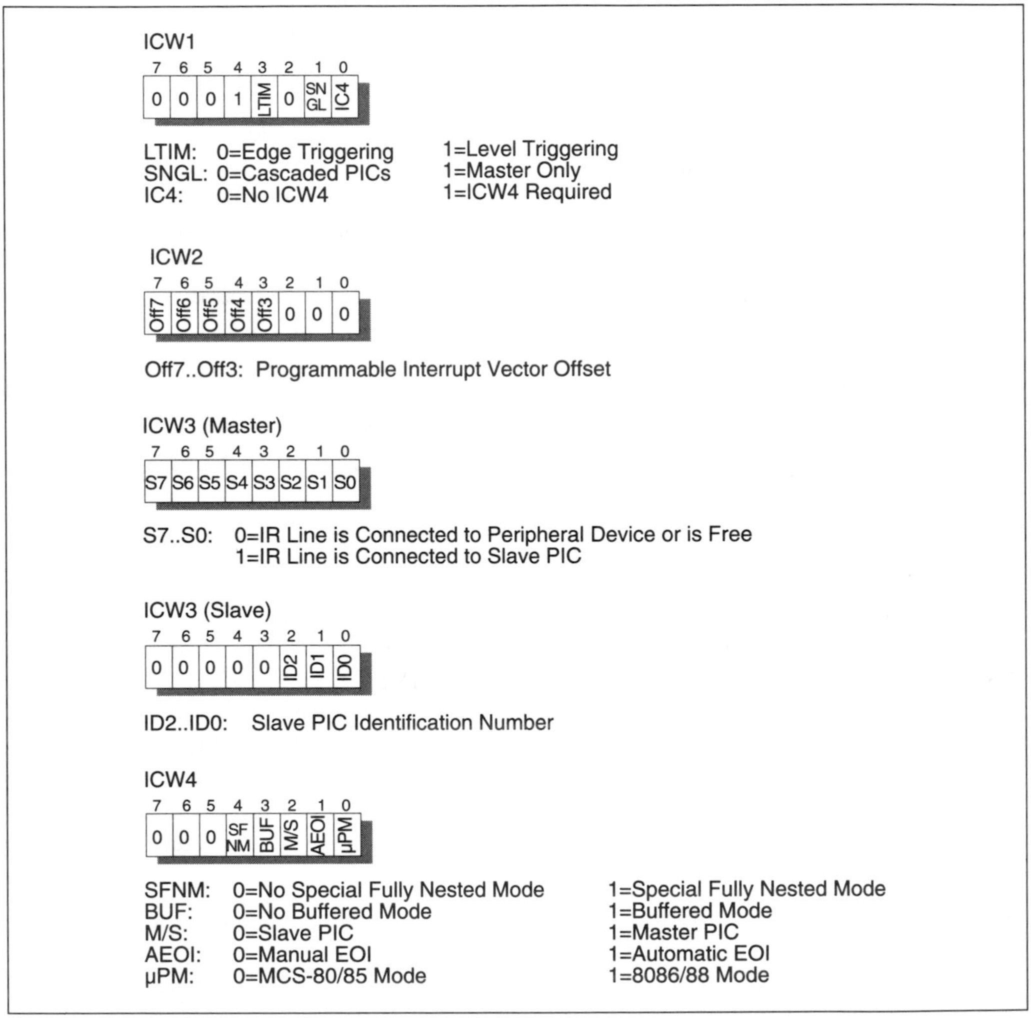

Figure 23.7: ICW formats.

By means of *AEOI* you can determine whether the PIC completes the interrupt acknowledge sequence with an automatic end-of-interrupt (EOI) or expects the transfer of an EOI command by the processor. With a set AEOI bit completion is carried out automatically after the second INTA signal from the CPU. Thus the ISR bit is cleared automatically. Finally, the *μPM* (microprocessor mode) bit defines whether the PIC is installed in a system with an 8086/88 processor (μPM=1) or in an MCS–80/85 system. In 8086/88 systems the PIC passes the 8-bit number of the interrupt handler to call. For this two $\overline{\text{INTA}}$ pulses from the CPU are required. In an MCS-80/85 system, however, the 8259A supplies the 16-bit address of the interrupt vector directly, and needs three $\overline{\text{INTA}}$ pulses for this.

Example: `Initializing master and slave PIC in the AT.`

ICW1 for Master and Slave

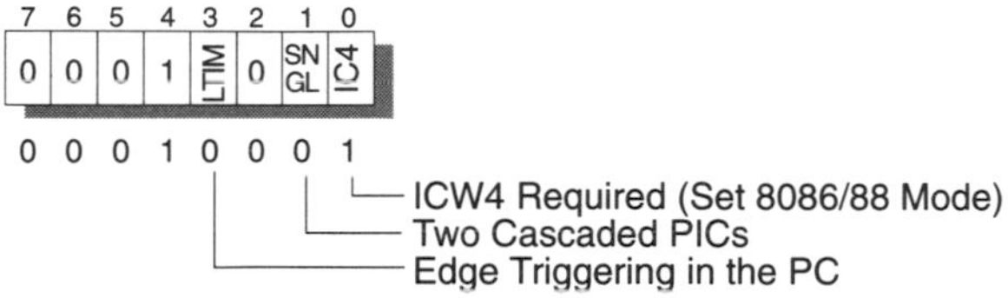


```
MOV al, 11h    ; load 00010001b=11h into accumulator
OUT 20h, al    ; output ICW1 via port 020h to master and start master initialization
OUT a0h, al    ; output ICW1 via port 0a0h to slave and start slave initialization
```

ICW2 for Master

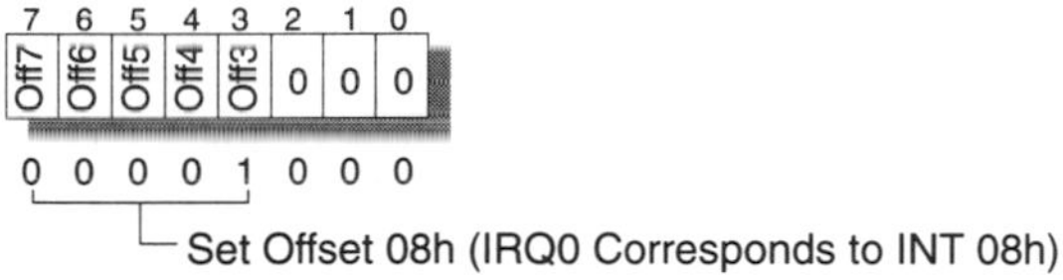

ICW2 for Slave

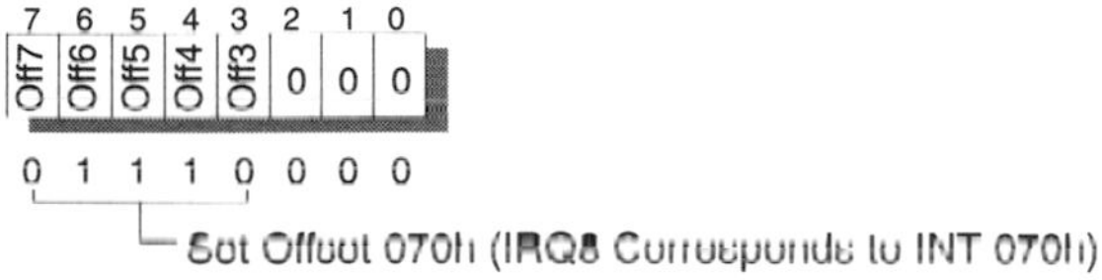


```
MOV al, 08h    ; load 00001000b=08h into accumulator
OUT 21h, al    ; output ICW2 via port 021h to master
MOV al, 070h   ; load 01110000b=070h into accumulator
OUT a1h, al    ; output ICW2 via port 0a1h to slave
```

ICW3 for Master

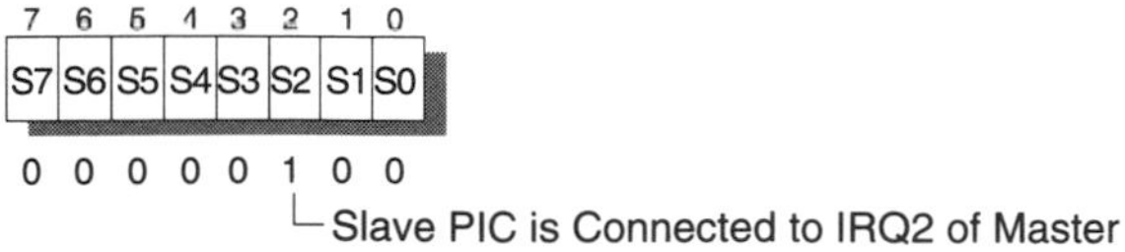


```
MOV al, 04h    ; load 00000100b=04h into accumulator
OUT 21h, al    ; output ICW3 via port 021h to master
```

ICW3 for Slave

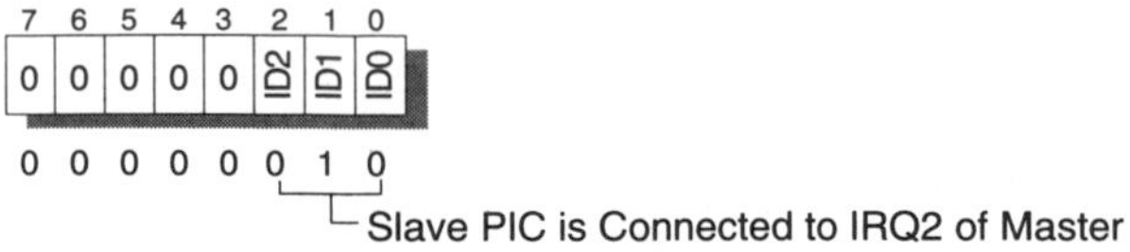

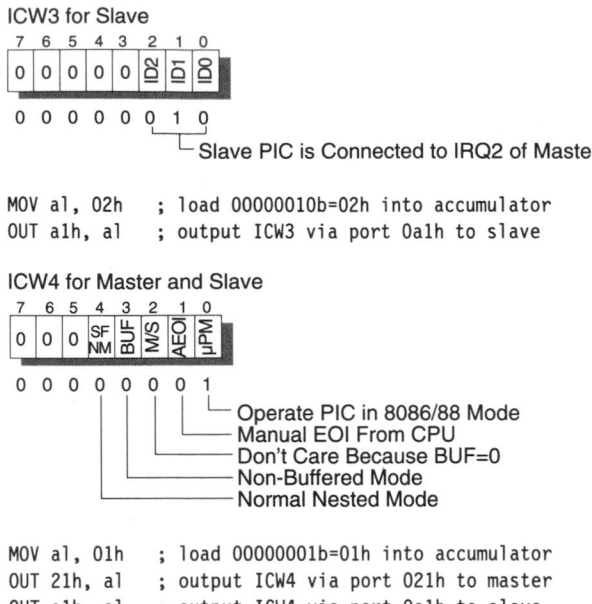

```
MOV al, 02h    ; load 00000010b=02h into accumulator
OUT a1h, al    ; output ICW3 via port 0a1h to slave
```

ICW4 for Master and Slave

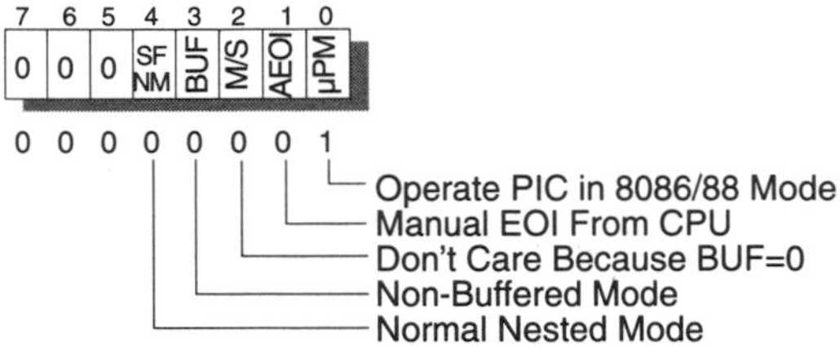


```
MOV al, 01h    ; load 00000001b=01h into accumulator
OUT 21h, al    ; output ICW4 via port 021h to master
OUT a1h, al    ; output ICW4 via port 0a1h to slave
```

After this initialization the PIC can manage and service interrupt requests from various peripherals. Using the OCWs, additional commands can be passed to the 8259A during operation to set up various operating modes. Figure 23.8 shows the format of the three OCWs.

OCW1 masks certain IR lines. If one of the bits *M7–M0* is set, then this masks the corresponding interrupt request.

Example: `Mask timer interrupt.`

The timer interrupt updates the internal DOS system clock and is applied to the master PIC via IRQ0. The following C program fragment (Microsoft C 5.10) outputs the current time. After the first key hit the timer interrupt is masked and the clock stops. Upon the second keyboard operation, masking is cancelled and the clock continues to run.

```
#include <dos.h>
#include <graph.h>

void displaytime(void);

main()
{
  displaytime();       /* display time */
  outp(0x21,0x01);     /* disable timer interrupt */
  displaytime();       /* display time */
  outp(0x21,0x00);     /* enable timer interrupt */
  displaytime();       /* display time */
  exit(0);
}
```

```
void displaytime(void)
{
  struct dostime_t time;

  for (;;) {
    _dos_gettime (&time);  /* read time via DOS */
    /* display time in the middle of the screen */
    _settextposition (13,35),printf("%i:%i:%i:%i",
                                time.hour,time.minute,time.second,time.hsecond);
    if (kbhit()) {  /* check for keyboard hit */
      getch();
      break;
    }
  }
  return;
}
```

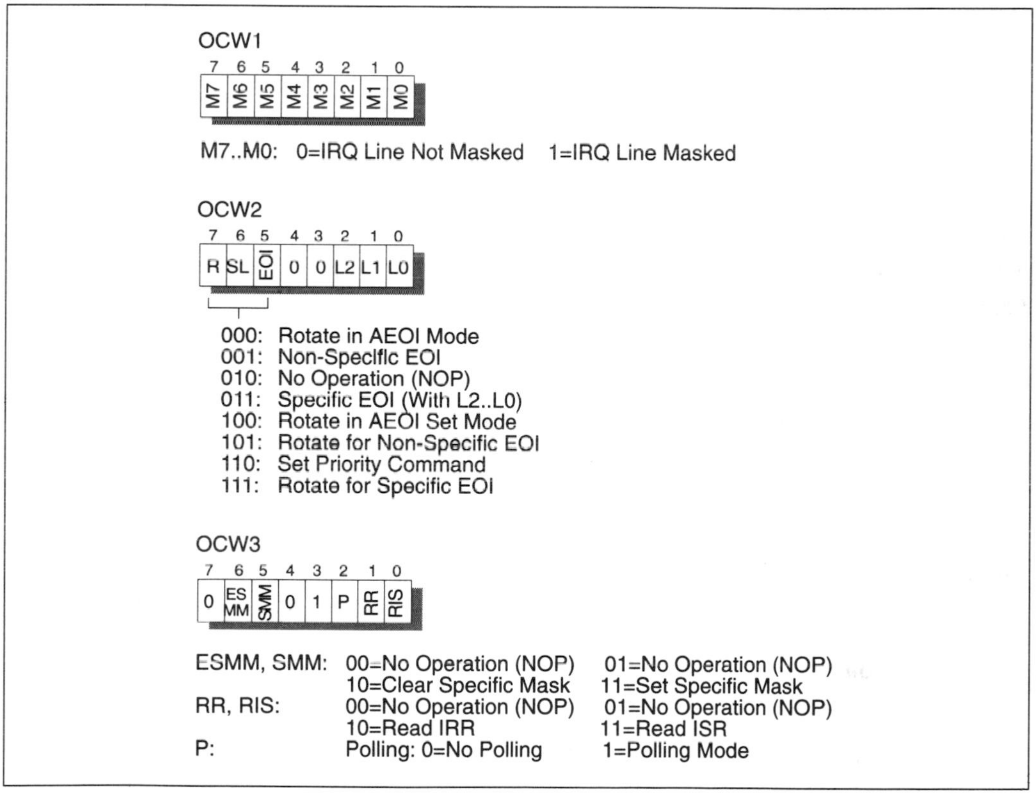

Figure 23.8: OCW formats.

The three high-order bits *R*, *SL* and *EOI* control the rotating and EOI modes. If, unlike the PC with its hierarchical structure, peripherals with the same priority are installed, then the PIC carries out servicing in the order of the occurring interrupt requests. This «rotating» servicing, together with the EOI mode, can be programmed via R, SL and EOI. For rotating service it may be that the PIC «forgets» which IR level has currently been serviced. To reset the set ISR bit the CPU has to issue a specific EOI command. In this case, the three least significant bits *L2–L0* indicate the ISR bit to be reset.

Example: `Reset ISR bit 5 in master PIC with a specific EOI command.`

```
MOV al, 66h  ; load 01100101b=66h into accumulator
OUT 20h, al  ; output OCW2 via port 020h to master
```

In the PC the PIC generally operates in nested mode, that is, a hierarchical servicing of the interrupt requests is carried out. Resetting the ISR bit is executed by means of an unspecific EOI command.

Example: `Resetting the ISR bit after servicing a coprocessor interrupt IRQ13 according to the IR line 5 in the slave PIC and IR line 2 in the master PIC (observe cascading!).`

```
MOV al, 20h  ; load 00100000b=020h into accumulator
OUT a0h, al  ; output unspecific EOI command to slave PIC
OUT 20h, al  ; output unspecific EOI command to master PIC
```

If a certain interrupt request is in-service (that is, the corresponding bit in the ISR is set), all interrupts of a lower priority are disabled because the in-service request is serviced first. Only an interrupt request of a higher priority pushes its way to the front immediately after the $\overline{INTA}$ sequence of the serviced interrupt. In this case the current $\overline{INTA}$ sequence is completed and the new interrupt request is already serviced before the old request has been completed by an EOI. Thus interrupt requests of a lower priority are serviced once the processor has informed the PIC by an EOI that the request has been serviced. Under certain circumstances, it is favourable to also enable requests of a lower priority. This applies, for example, to a dynamic change of the priority structure during the course of executing an interrupt routine. For this purpose, the *ESMM* and *SMM* bits in OCW3 are implemented. They enable (ESMM=1, SMM=1) and disable (ESMM = 1, SMM = 0) the so-called *special mask mode*. If a bit in the OCW1 is set in this mode (thus the corresponding interrupt input is masked), all further requests of this level are disabled and all other requests of a higher *and* lower priority are enabled. In the special mask mode the interrupt requests can be masked or enabled individually.

The *RR* (read request) and *RIS* (read in-service) bits read the PIC status, and determine the requested (IRR) and currently serviced (ISR) interrupts. If you want to read the IRR status then you have to first output an OCW3 with a set RR bit via the port 020h (master) or 0a0h (slave). Afterwards, you can read the IRR byte through the same port. Determining the ISR status is carried out in the same way.

Example: `Determine all interrupt requests currently serviced by the master.`

```
MOV al, 09h  ; load 00001010b=0ah into accumulator
OUT 20h, al  ; output OCW3 to master
IN al, 20h   ; read ISR into accumulator
```

Besides the IRR and ISR, the mask register IMR can also be read. This is carried out by a simple IN instruction to the port 021h (master) or 0a1h (slave). In this case, no read command via an OCW is required.

Example: `Read mask status of slave PIC.`

```
IN al, alh  ; read mask byte into accumulator
```

If the CPU passes the PIC an OCW3 with a set bit *P*, then the PIC operates in polling mode. The 8259A interprets the next read instruction of the processor as an acknowledge signal, and sets the corresponding bit in the ISR if a valid interrupt request of a peripheral is pending. Additionally, the PIC determines the priority level of the request, and at the same time outputs a byte with the following format onto the data bus, which is read by the CPU:

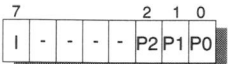

7					2	1	0
I	-	-	-	-	P2	P1	P0

If a valid interrupt request is pending, then *I* is equal to 1, otherwise equal to 0. The three least significant bits *P2–P0* indicate the level of the request of highest priority. If the PIC is investigated by polling and not by means of an automatic $\overline{\text{INTA}}$ sequence, then the INT output of the PIC must not be connected to the processor. Instead, the CPU polls the PIC(s) periodically, as already mentioned. Therefore, even more than 64 interrupt levels can be realized (but with the described disadvantages, of course). As the INT output of the PIC is no longer connected to the processor, the 8259A can also be combined with other processors such as the 8086/88 and MCS–80/85 systems.

23.6 Masking the NMI

The NMI also belongs to the interrupts issued by hardware. Unlike the interrupt requests IRQx, an NMI is not fed over the 8259A PIC but is directly supplied by the processor via the NMI pin. A high-level signal at this connection gives rise to an interrupt 2 immediately after the current instruction has been completed. The NMI can neither be masked by the CLI instruction nor via the IMR in the 8259A PIC. It is always enabled and has the highest priority among all hardware interrupts.

The NMI is issued in the PC by the parity checking module of the memory controller. If the module detects a parity error upon reading a byte from main memory, it raises the NMI signal to a high level. On the screen appears a message reporting the parity error. Some new ATs have a second timer chip, the so-called failsafe timer, which periodically issues an NMI to avoid a «hang» of the computer if the IRQs are masked.

But during the boot procedure a serious problem now arises. The boot routine first has to initialize all the chips and memory, and to set up the interrupt vector table. For the IRQs this gives rise to no problems; a simple CLI instruction disables all interrupt requests. If the parity check module or the failsafe timer is in an undefined state, and if one of them issues an NMI, then the processor calls the as yet uninitialized handler for interrupt 2, as the NMI is not masked by the CLI instruction. But the interrupt vector table holds only a non-initialized value (that is, a wild pointer), which points to an unknown location. You can surely imagine that the PC will already have crashed in the boot process.

To disable the NMI for initialization, each PC has an a NMI mask register. Figure 23.9 shows the signal path between parity module, failsafe timer and processor via the NMI mask register. In the PC/XT it is controlled by bit 7 of port a0h. Starting with the AT, bit 7 of port 70h carries out this job. If the bit is set, the NMI is masked. If the bit is cleared, the hardware can issue an NMI. Note that in the AT the address register for the CMOS RAM and the real-time clock are also located at port address 70h (see Section 26.3). If you want to alter the NMI mask bit then you need to read the port first. Now you can set or clear bit 7 and write back the byte with unchanged bits 0–6.

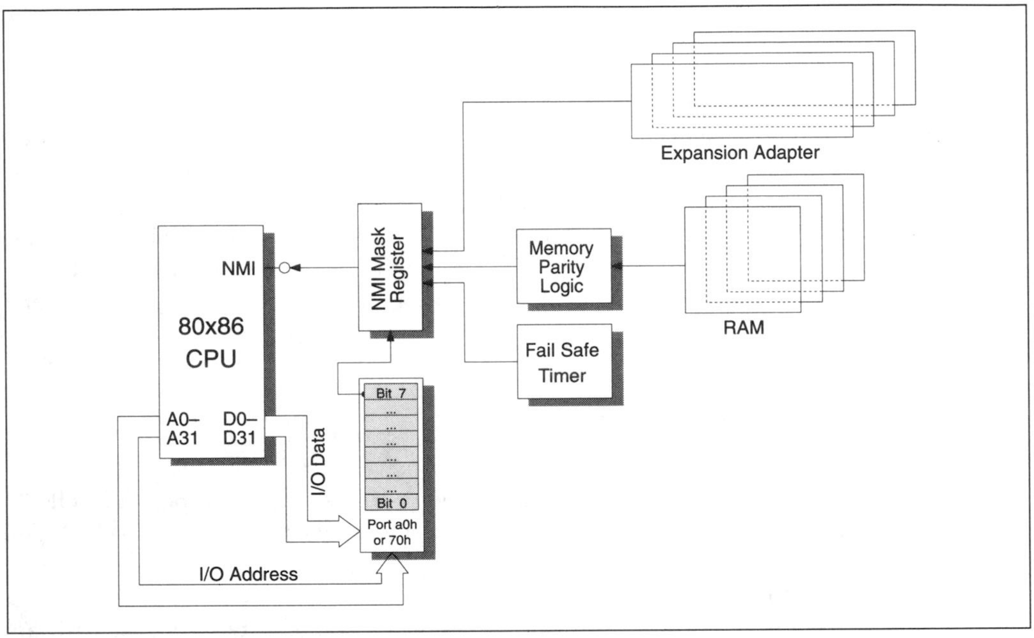

Figure 23.9: NMI and NMI mask register. The NMI issued by extension adapter cards, memory parity logic or the failsafe timer can be disabled by means of the NMI mask register. The register is controlled by bit 7 of port a0h (PC/XT) or 70h (AT).

Example: Disable and enable the NMI in the AT; by calling **nmi mask** the NMI is disabled, by calling **nmi unmask** it is enabled.

```
/* nmi.c */
main(argc, argv)
int argc;
char *argv;

{ int i;

  if (strcmpi(argv[1], "mask") != 0) {              /* check whether disable */
    if (strcmpi(argv[1], "unmask") != 0) {          /* check whether enable */
      printf("\n\nInvalid Argument %s", argv[1]);   /* no valid argument */
      exit(1);                                      /* exit with ERRORLEVEL 1 */
    }
```

```
    else {                                      /* enable NMI */
      i = inp(0x70);                            /* read byte of port 70h */
      i = i & 0x7f;                             /* clear bit 7 */
      outp(0x70, i);                            /* write back byte to port 70h */
      printf("\n\nNMI enabled !!\n\n");         /* display message */
    }
  }
  else {                                        /* disable NMI */
    i = inp(0x70);                              /* read byte of port 70h */
    i = i | 0x80;                               /* set bit 7 */
    outp(0x70, i);                              /* write back byte to port 70h */;
    printf("\n\nNMI masked !!\n\n");            /* display message */
  }
  exit(0);                                      /* exit with ERRORLEVEL 0 */
}
```

You can easily test the consequences of masking the NMI. Disable the memory refresh by an extremely low refresh rate, or by deactivating counter 1 in the 8253/8254 PIT (see Chapter 24). After a short time the PC displays a memory parity error. If you additionally disable the NMI first by means of the command *nmi mask* and disable the memory refresh afterwards, then your computer crashes without displaying any message. Also here, parity errors have occurred and the hardware (the memory check module) has attempted to issue an NMI. But this NMI could not reach the CPU as the NMI mask register is locked. At some time the processor reads one or more destroyed (because they were not refreshed) bytes into the prefetch queue and hangs itself up. Don't worry; at the next hardware reset the ROM BIOS enables the NMI and the memory refresh correctly again.

23.7 Remarks About Powerful Multiprocessor Interrupt Subsystems

It is obvious that the performance of microprocessors cannot continue to be increased limitlessly (surely by several orders of magnitude, but not without any limitation). Moreover, several well-tested processors that have been on the market for a longer time are often more powerful together, and even cheaper, than a single high-end product. Both aspects lead to multiprocessor systems to enhance computation performance. In addition to the already mentioned problems with the coordination of instruction execution in the individual processors (interlocks) and memory consistency problems, the interrupt subsystem is one of the bottlenecks in the system. That's especially true in Personal Computers, as usually a very old chip handles the hardware interrupt requests – the above discussed 8259A which is more than 15 years old, for instance. In addition to its 8 MHz clock and 8-bit registers, it is unsuited for use in multiprocessor systems (which are also, of course, multi-interrupt systems). The significance of the interrupt subsystem for performance is apparent from the fact that (according to Intel) for a typical file server (which has to execute a considerable number of interrupts, the result of a continuous flow of requests from the work place), there is a performance gain of 8% achieved purely by using the 82489DX instead of the 8259A. This shows once again that a computer is a system and not only a CPU with some unimportant support chips.

Therefore, after more than ten years, Intel has developed a replacement for the ageing PIC 8259A: the *Advanced Programmable Interrupt Controller APIC 82498DX*. It is available at a maximum of 50 Mhz, and is typically used at 33 MHz. All internal registers are now a minimum of 32 bits wide. While common PC systems usually access the 8259A through I/O ports, the 82489DX is located in the memory address space (though with some decoders it could also be addressed with IN and OUT).

23.7.1 APIC 82489DX Structure and Function

During development of the APIC architecture, the aim was to have flexible management and distribution of interrupt requests to the CPUs in a multiprocessor system. In a multiprocessor system, it is not necessary for an interrupt source to always be handled by the same CPU. To this end, each 82489DX integrates a *local interrupt unit* and an *I/O interrupt unit*. In Figure 23.10 you can see the internal structure of the APIC. In addition to both of the previously mentioned interrupt units, a 32-bit timer, a JTAG test logic and a bus and system control unit are also available.

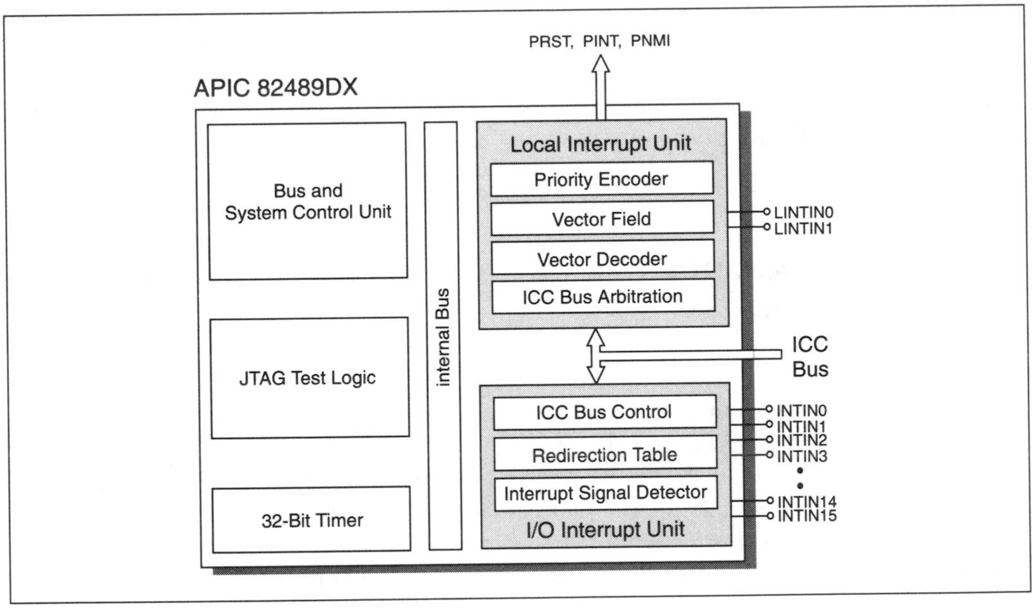

Figure 23.10: Internal Structure of the APIC 82489DX.

The local interrupt unit is connected via the PRST, PINIT and PNMI pins to the applicable Pentium chip. It can accept two local interrupts via LINTIN0 and LINTIN1, which are always passed to the local processor. In comparison, the interrupt requests to the I/O interrupt unit, which arrive via all 16 interrupt pins INTIN15–INTIN0, are redirected to the local interrupt unit of another APIC with the help of a redirection table and the *ICC bus* and, thus, to an external processor. The priority sequence of all 16 interrupt pins is entirely optional; even an NMI can be managed via the APIC.

The whole idea behind interrupt redirecting is that a processor is not interrupted when executing a higher priority task. Instead, the interrupt is redirected to a processor with a task of a lower priority, where it becomes an interrupt. The priority of the currently active task in each processor is determined for the local processor by an input in the task priority register of the 82489DX. This task is typically undertaken by the operating system, that is, during a task switch and, in addition to other proceedings, the task priority register is also loaded with an appropriate value. In this way, the task priority can be altered dynamically. With dynamic assignments, all installed APICs search via the ICC bus for the processor which executes the task with the lowest priority.

To carry out this distribution, and to enable inter-APIC communication, an ICC bus is implemented. It consists of four lines for arbitration and message signals, as well as a clock line. In addition to the system bus, the ICC bus forms an independent interrupt bus for communication of the APICs without occupying the system bus. The redirecting of the interrupt is executed with the aid of so-called *messages*. Thus, the ICC protocol is a high-level protocol.

23.7.2 Multi-APIC Systems and the ICC Bus

It is normal in a multiprocessor system for each CPU to be allocated its own APIC. Thus, the local interrupt unit of each 82589DX is connected to the local CPU, and the I/O interrupt unit with I/O devices. This setup is shown in Figure 23.11.

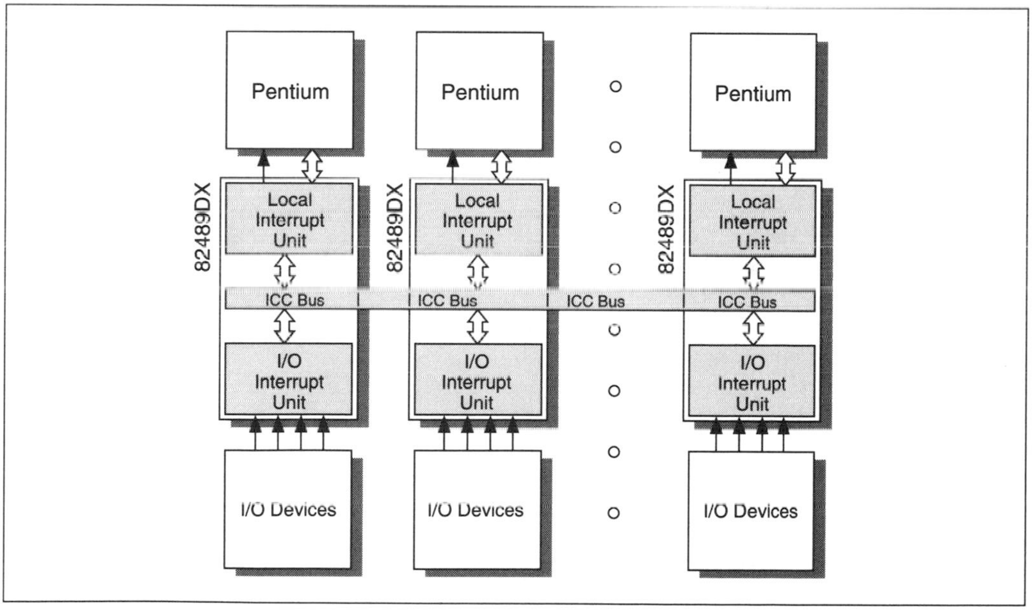

Figure 23.11: Multi-APIC system with communication via the ICC bus.

Two procedures are available for choosing the target processor (which will actually be interrupted) of an interrupt request: fixed and lowest priority mode: in *fixed mode*, all requests which fulfil the target requirements are supplied to the APICs; in *lowest priority mode*, all APICs together search for the 82489DX whose local processor is executing the task with the lowest priority. During the interrupt allocation, all APICs communicate via the ICC bus, where another identification is allotted to each APIC.

To transfer a message, the ICC bus must first execute an arbitration. During this, the APIC with the lowest priority is determined. Subsequently, the message is transferred which includes the target mode, control bits, vector, target and a checksum. The local interrupt unit of the target APIC has now received all the necessary information, and can interrupt its local processor in order to service the interrupt.

Another feature of the 82489DX as compared to the 8259A is the so-called *inter-processor interrupt*. It is issued if a local CPU writes to the interrupt command register in the local unit of the allocated 82489DX. This command register records the same information as a redirection input. Directly after the write, the local interrupt unit outputs an interrupt message to the ICC bus, which is taken on by the target APIC. The local unit then issues an interrupt to the local processor. Thus, a task in a multiprocessor system (the operating system kernel, for example) can control execution of the parallel tasks in the other processors.

24 8253/8254 Programmable Interval Timer

Every programmer is sometimes confronted with the problem of implementing certain delays into a program, for example to move a point slowly on-screen. Often, «dummy» loops of the following form are employed:

```
FOR I=0 TO 1000:NEXT I
```

But such delay loops have a significant disadvantage: they rely on the processor speed. The delay time can therefore be very different on a 50 Mhz i486 and on the ancestor 4.77 Mhz 8088 (namely by a factor of 100). Old computer games in particular make use of such loops, and the result is well known: while it is possible to «fly» on a PC with a 4.77 MHz 8088 with a flight simulator with no problems, the plane has crashed on a 50 MHz i486 before the pilot can operate a single key.

But the problem of generating exactly defined time intervals also occurs in the system itself. DOS, for example, provides the time and date for every file, and the control of electric motors in floppy drives requires exactly defined signals. In both cases, time intervals defined by means of program loops are not suitable. Thus, the PC's designers have implemented one (PC/XT and most ATs) or sometimes two (some new ATs or EISA) *programmable interval timers (PITs)*.

24.1 Structure and Functioning of the PIT 8253/8254

The PIT generates programmable time intervals from an external clock signal of a crystal oscillator that are defined independently from the CPU. The 8253/8254 is a very flexible PIT and has six operation modes in all. Figure 24.1 shows a block diagram of the 8253/8254's internal structure.

The 8253/8254 comprises three independently and separately programmable counters 0–2, each of which is 16 bits wide. Every counter is supplied with its own clock signal (CLK0–CLK2), which serves as the time base for each counter. In the original PC a 14317180 Hz crystal provided the base clock which was divided by three to generate the 4.77 MHz clock signal for the processor. Further dividing by four leads to a signal with about 1.193180 MHz, which is applied to the three inputs CLK0–CLK2 of the 8253/8254 as the clock signal. In the PC, each of the three independent counters therefore runs with the same time base of 0.838 μs. Also today's PCs with processor clock frequencies between 4.77 MHz and 66 MHz have an oscillator that provides this 1.19318 MHz for the PIT(s).

To enable or trigger (see the section about 8253/8254 counting modes) a counter a gate signal GATE0–GATE2 is applied. Depending upon the counting mode, the counter concerned is activated by a transition low–high or a high level of the GATEx signal. Via the corresponding outputs OUT0–OUT2 the counter outputs a signal. Also, the shape of the output signals depends upon the counter's mode.

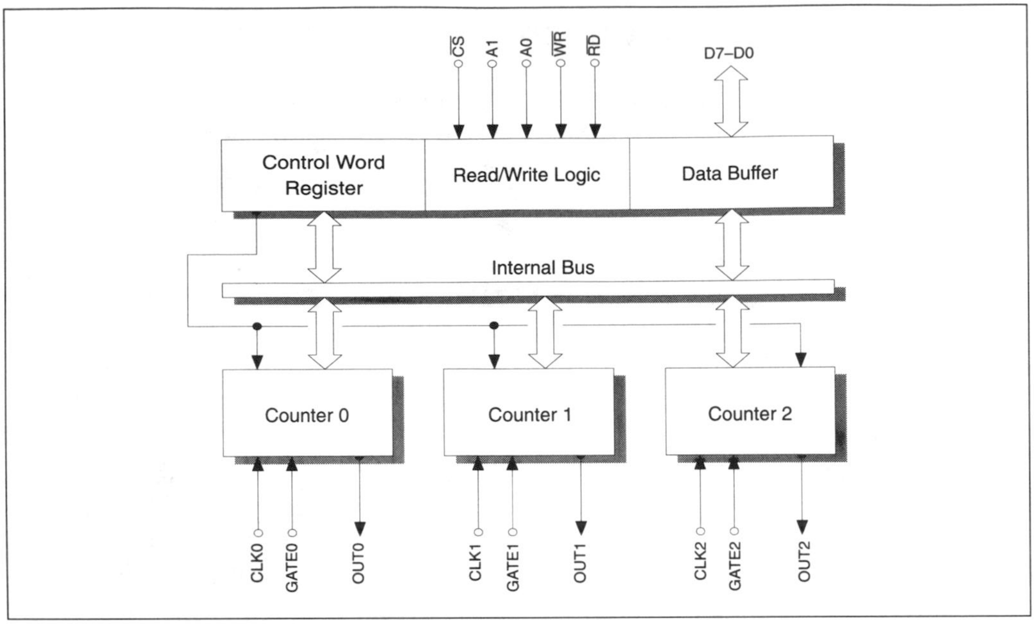

Figure 24.1: Structure of the 8253/8254 PIT. The timer chip comprises three independently operating counters 0–2, which are supplied separately with clock and control signals.

The data bus buffer together with the control/write logic reads and writes data from and to the PIT. The control register loads the counters and controls the various operation modes. Certain time intervals and signal shapes at outputs OUT0–OUT2 can thus be set. The counters may be read or written, but the control register is write-only. The 8254 also implements an additional command to read the control register (the read-back command).

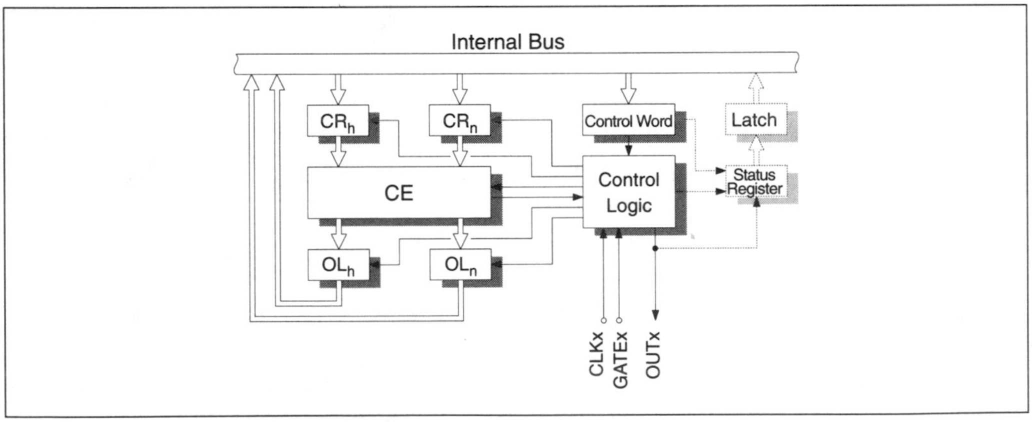

Figure 24.2: Internal structure of a PIT counter.

Figure 24.2 shows the internal structure of a counter. The central part is the counting element (CE), in which the counting process is carried out. The programmable control register defines the operation mode of the control logic, which in turn controls the counting element (CE), the high-order and low-order output latches OL_h, OL_n as well as the high-order and low-order count registers CR_h, CR_n. The 8254 additionally implements a status latch by means of which (and the read-back command) the 8254 outputs status information. When the CPU writes count values, the passed bytes are transferred into the count registers CR_h and CR_n first. Afterwards, the control logic transfers the two bytes simultaneously into the 16-bit counting element.

24.2 8253/8254 Terminals and Signals

8253 and 8254 coincide in their pin assignments and the meaning of the applied and output signals. The only difference between them is that the 8254 implements an additional command for reading the programmed status (read-back command). Figure 24.3 shows the pin assignment for the 8253/8254.

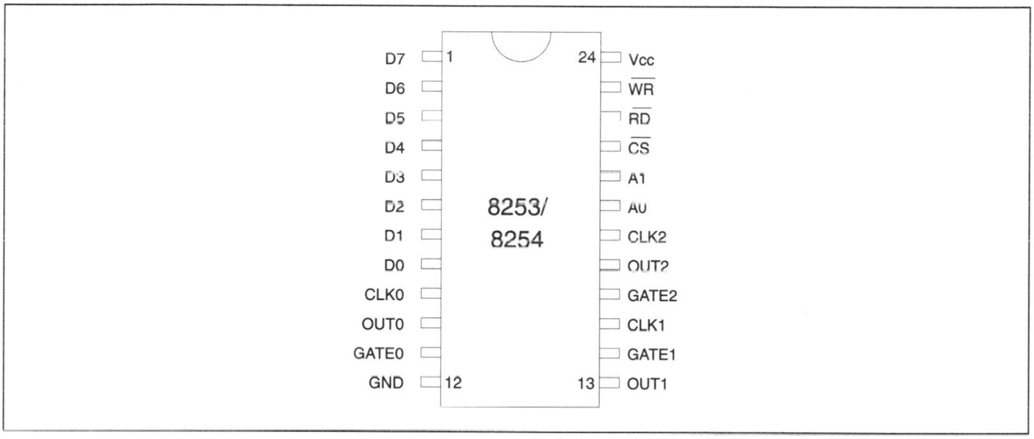

Figure 24.3: 8253/8254 pin assignment.

A0, A1 (I)
Pins 19, 20

The signals at these address pins indicate the number of the counter or the control register that the CPU accesses for data reading or writing. A0 and A1 are usually connected to the address bus of the system. The possible combinations of (A1, A0) have the following meanings:

```
(10)  counter 2
(11)  control register
(01)  counter 1
(00)  counter 0
```

CLK0, CLK1, CLK2 (I, I, I)
Pins 9, 15, 18
These pins are supplied with the clock signals for the counters 0, 1 and 2, respectively.

$\overline{\text{CS}}$ (I)
Pin 21

If this chip select pin is on a low level, the CPU can read data from or write data to the internal 8253/8254 registers via the data bus D7–D0 using the $\overline{\text{RD}}$ and $\overline{\text{WR}}$ signals. Thus the $\overline{\text{CS}}$ signal enables the PIT for read and write processes. For the counting operation and the signals supplied by the PIT, $\overline{\text{CS}}$ has no meaning.

D7–D0 (I/O)
Pins 1–8

These eight connections form the bidirectional data bus through which the 8253/8254 receives and provides data and instructions from or to the CPU.

GATE0, GATE1, GATE2 (I, I, I)
Pins 11, 14, 16

These pins are supplied with the gate signals for the counters 0, 1 and 2, respectively, to enable the counters.

OUT0, OUT1, OUT2 (O, O, O)
Pins 10, 13, 17
These connections supply the output signals of the counters 0, 1 and 2, respectively.

$\overline{\text{WR}}$ (I)
Pin 23

If the signal at this write pin is at a low level, the CPU writes data into the internal 8253/8254 registers via the data bus D7–D0.

$\overline{\text{RD}}$ (I)
Pin 22

If the signal at this read pin is at a low level, the CPU can read data from the internal 8253/8254 registers via the data bus D7–D0.

Vcc
Pin 24
The supply voltage (usually +5 V) is applied to this pin.

GND
Pin 12
The ground potential (usually 0 V) is applied to this pin.

24.3 Programming the 8253/8254

You may program the 8253/8254 PIT by first writing one control word via port 043h into the control register, and then one or two data bytes via the port of the intended counter. If the control register is loaded once, the counters may be overwritten with other values without accessing the control register again. Counting mode and format remain the same. Table 24.1 lists the port addresses of the various registers.

Port (1st PIT)	Port (2nd PIT)	Register	Access type
040h	048h	counter 0	read/write
041h	049h	counter 1	read/write
042h	04ah	counter 2	read/write
043h	04bh	control register	write-only

Table 24.1: 8253/8254 register ports in a PC

The 8253 control register is write-only; no data can be read. For the 8254 a new command is available, the read-back command, with which certain control information can be determined. Programming one of the three 8253/8254 counters is begun by writing a control word via port 043h (1st PIT) or 04bh (2nd PIT). Figure 24.4 shows the control word format.

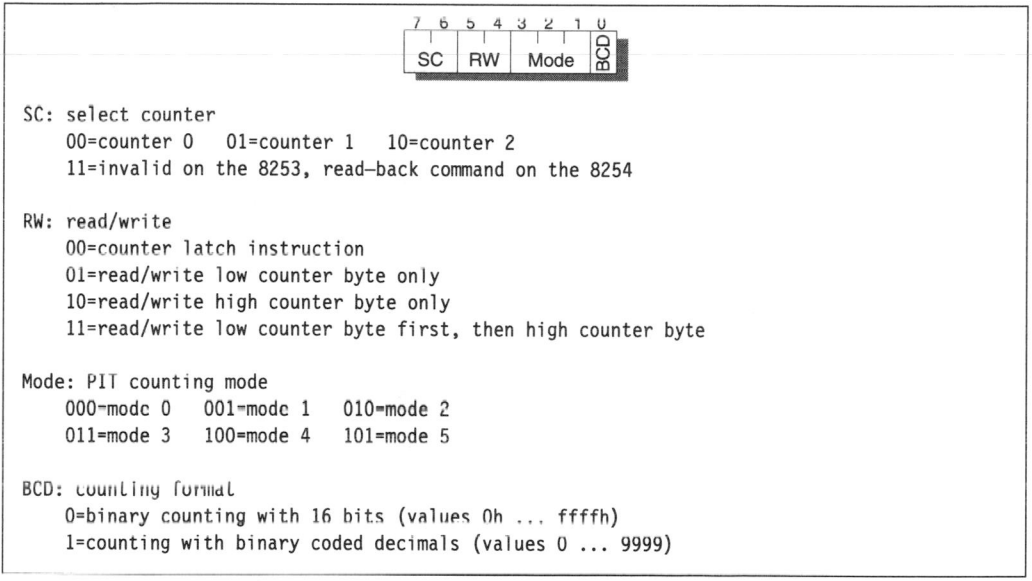

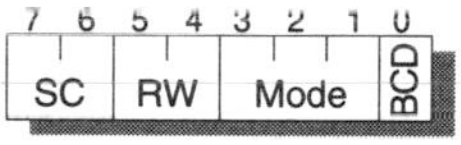


```
SC: select counter
    00=counter 0   01=counter 1   10=counter 2
    11=invalid on the 8253, read-back command on the 8254

RW: read/write
    00=counter latch instruction
    01=read/write low counter byte only
    10=read/write high counter byte only
    11=read/write low counter byte first, then high counter byte

Mode: PIT counting mode
    000=mode 0   001=mode 1   010=mode 2
    011=mode 3   100=mode 4   101=mode 5

BCD: counting format
    0=binary counting with 16 bits (values 0h ... ffffh)
    1=counting with binary coded decimals (values 0 ... 9999)
```

Figure 24.4: 8253/8254 control word.

24.4 Writing Count Values

To start a counter or load it with new values, you must first output a control word in which you define the intended counter, number and type of the byte to write, the counting mode of the counter concerned, and the counting format.

The *SC* bits determine the counter to which the following entries refer. The combination SC=11b is invalid on the 8253. On the 8254 this issues a read-back command for reading the control register (see below). With *RW* bits you indicate which (low-order or high-order) and how many counter bytes you are going to write. If you specify that only the low-order or high-order byte is to be written, then you can also only read the low-order or high-order counter byte in a later read access. But the 8253/8254 is, nevertheless, operating as a 16-bit counter internally, that is, a high-order counter byte 10 doesn't mean a count value of 10 but 256*10=2560. The counter latch command is important only for reading a counter. With the three *mode* bits you define the counting mode of the counter selected via SC (details concerning the counting modes are given in the next section). Finally, the *BCD* bit determines the counting format. With a set BCD bit the counter operates with binary coded decimals, thus the range of values from 0 to 9999 is available. If BCD is equal to 0 then the counter performs a binary operation with 16 bits, and the counting range is 0 (0h) to 65 535 (ffffh). According to RW bits you need to write either the low-order, the high-order, or both into the counter after passing the control word. With the combination RW=01b (write low-order byte only) you provide the low-order byte via the port of the corresponding counter.

According to the control word, the control logic recognizes that only the low-order byte will be passed and sets the high-order byte in CR_h automatically to 0. The same applies to the combination RW=10b (write high-order byte only). In this case, the control logic sets the low-order byte in CR_n automatically to 0. If RW=11b, then you first need to write the low-order byte and then the high-order byte by means of two OUT instructions. The control logic transfers the byte received first into the CR_n register and that received second into the CR_h register. For small counting values or counting values that are a multiple of 256, it is therefore sufficient to pass the low-order or high-order counter byte. You can then save one OUT instruction. This is important if you are generating ROM code, as here the available storage capacity is usually rather limited.

Example: Counter 2 shall output a square wave signal (mode 3) with a frequency of 10 kHz; the CLK frequency in the PC is 1.19318 MHz, thus the divisor has to be equal to 119. For this the low-order counter byte of counter 2 is sufficient; the high-order one is automatically set to 0.

```
MOV al, 01010110b ; load accumulator with the corresponding control word
OUT 43h, al       ; write control word via port 43h into the control register of first PIT
                  ; frequency shall be 10kHz, CLK frequency equal 1.19318MHz → divisor 129
MOV al, 119       ; load low-order byte of counting value into accumulator
OUT 42h, al       ; write counting value into 2nd PIT
```

The maximum loadable count value is not ffffh (binary counting) or 999 (BCD counting), but 0. Upon the next CLK pulse the counter concerned jumps to ffffh or 9999, respectively, without resulting in any action. Once the value is decreased to 0 again, it outputs a signal according to the programmed mode at the OUTx pin. Thus the value 0 corresponds to 2^{16} for binary counting and 10^4 for counting with BCDs.

24.5 Reading Count Values

Two options for reading a counter are available on the 8253, and three on the 8254:

- direct reading by means of one or two IN instructions;
- counter latch command;
- read-back command (8254 only).

When reading a counter you should not use the first option but transfer the current state of the counting element (CE) into the output latches OL_h and OL_n, and latch there using the counter latch or read-back command. Latch OL_h then holds the high-order byte, and latch OL_n the low-order byte of the counting element. One or two successive IN instructions for the port address of the counter concerned then read these latches. If only the low-order (RW=01b) or high-order byte (RW=10b) was written when the counter was loaded with the initial counting value, then read the current counting value of the initially written byte by a single IN instruction. A succeeding IN instruction fetches the non-latched value of the low-order or high-order counter byte at the time of the IN instruction and not the corresponding second byte of the 16-bit counting element. This is only possible if you have previously written the low-order as well as the high-order counter byte. In this case you need to read the current counter value by means of two IN instructions. The PIT returns the low-order byte of the 16-bit counter with the first IN instruction, and then the high-order byte with the second IN instruction.

The processor doesn't access the counting element (CE) directly, only the output latches. If the content of CE has been transferred once by a counter latch command into the output latches, then this value is held there until the PU executes one or two IN instructions, or until the corresponding counter is reprogrammed. Successive counter latch commands are ignored if the output latches haven't been read before. The counting element, however, also continues to count after a counter latch command; the counter latch makes only a «snapshot» of the counting element CE. If you read the counter in the mode RW=00b directly without the counter latch command by means of two IN instructions, then the counter value may have changed already when you issue the second IN instruction. Thus the high-order byte of the counting element CE read second doesn't fit the low-order byte read first. The determined values do not coincide with the actual values. As an interrupt or a memory refresh may occur between two successive IN instructions, for example, the period between the execution of two IN instructions is not predictable. Therefore, you should always issue a counter latch command or determine the counter value by means of a read-back command. Figure 24.5 shows the format of the control word for the counter latch command.

To determine the current counter value you have to output a counter latch command for the counter to read via ports 043h or 04bh. According to the programmed mode, you issue one or two IN instructions for the counter concerned afterwards. But ensure that in all cases the counter has been programmed with one or two bytes before. The read 8-bit or 16-bit value then indicates the current counter value at the time of the counter latch command in the programmed counting mode (binary or BCD). If the thus determined 8-bit value is the high-order counter byte, then you need to multiply it (at least in your head) by 256 to get the «real» value that the counting element CE in the PIT uses.

7	6	5	4	3	2	1	0
SC		0	0	X	X	X	X

SC: counter to latch
X: values without any meaning, use X=0 for compatibility

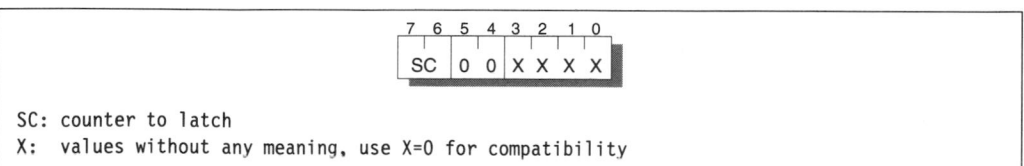

Figure 24.5: Counter latch command format.

Example: Determine value of counter 2; the counter has initially been loaded with low-order and high-order bytes.

```
MOV al, 10000000b ; load counter latch command for counter 2 into al
OUT 43h, al       ; output counter latch command to control register
IN al, 42h        ; read low-order counter byte into al
IN ah, 42h        ; read high-order counter byte into ah
                  ; thus ax=ah.al contains the current 16-bit counter value
```

The first IN instruction transfers the low-order byte of the counting element (CE), which is held by the latch CL_n into the least significant byte al of the accumulators ax; the second IN instruction loads the high-order byte held by the latch CL_h into the most significant accumulator byte ah. Thus, ax contains the 16-bit counter value after the two INs.

Unfortunately, there is no possibility of determining the initial value of a counter directly. This would be useful, for example, for investigating the refresh rate of counter 1. The only option is to read the counter concerned often, and to regard the maximum read value as the initial value. Another disadvantage is that on the 8253 the programmed counting mode cannot be determined. However, the interpretation of the read counter value is very different depending upon whether the counter operates with binary or BCD numbers. Further, it cannot be determined whether the counter has been loaded with a low-order and a high-order byte or only with one of them. This is necessary, though, to determine the counting rate of a PIT that is programmed in an unknown way. Without knowing the counting mode you can only speculate when interpreting the read values.

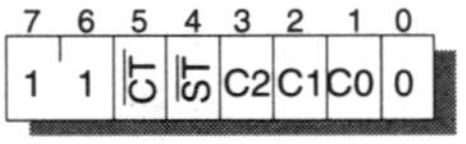

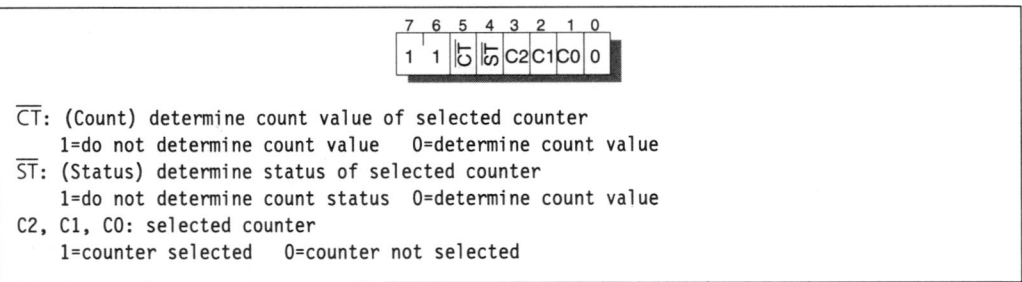

$\overline{CT}$: (Count) determine count value of selected counter
  1=do not determine count value 0=determine count value
$\overline{ST}$: (Status) determine status of selected counter
  1=do not determine count status 0=determine count value
C2, C1, C0: selected counter
  1=counter selected 0=counter not selected

Figure 24.6: Read-back command format.

The newer PIT model, the 8254 (used first with the AT), implements the possibility of also reading the counter's mode by means of a read-back command as a significant advance. Additionally, with the read-back command you can determine the current counter value. You issue the read-back command via the control register (ports 43h or 04bh). Figure 24.6 shows the format of this new 8254 command.

The two most significant bits define the read-back command with their value 11b (compare with Figure 24.4). $\overline{CT}$ indicates that the value and $\overline{ST}$ that the counting mode of a counter is to be determined. Note that $\overline{CT}$ and $\overline{ST}$ are complementary signals, which issue the intended action if you set the bit concerned to 0, and not 1 as usual. The bits *C0–C2* define the counter whose value or mode is to be determined.

With the read-back command you can issue several counter latch commands in parallel by indicating several counters simultaneously with the bits C0–C2. The 8254 then behaves as if you had issued several counter latch commands (Figure 24.5) individually, and transfers the individual CE values into the latches CL_n and CL_h of each counter. All successive counter latch commands, whether issued by its own counter latch or a further read-back command are ignored if the counter concerned hasn't been read by one or two IN instructions.

It is also possible to determine the value as well as the mode of a counter by means of the read-back command. If you only want to determine the value of a counter then set $\overline{CT}=0$ and $\overline{ST}=1$. In this case the read-back command is equivalent to one (if you set only one single Cx=1; x=0, 1, 2) or more counter latch commands (if you set several Cx=1). For the number and interpretation of the IN instructions the same applies as for a normal counter latch command.

If, however, you want to determine the programmed mode of a certain counter, then set $\overline{ST}=0$ and $\overline{CT}=1$. Also, in this case, it is possible to select several counters simultaneously. You only need to set several Cx to 1. The read-back command latches the current mode and supplies a status byte at the port address of the counter(s) concerned. You can fetch this status byte with an IN instruction. If you issue a new read-back command to determine the mode without having read out the counter concerned in advance, then this second command is ignored. The latches further contain the mode at the time of issuing the first command. Figure 24.7 shows the status byte format.

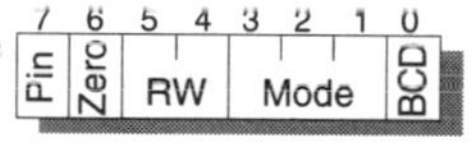

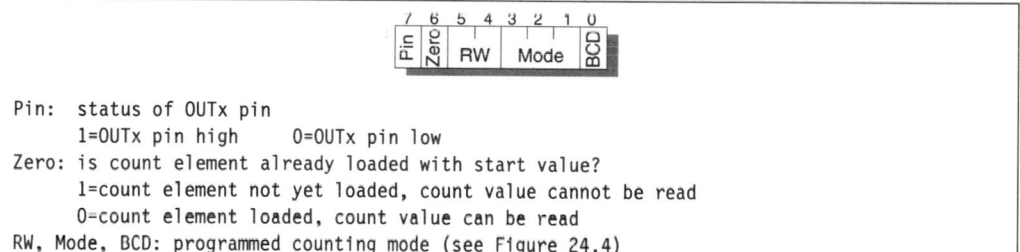

```
Pin:  status of OUTx pin
      1=OUTx pin high     0=OUTx pin low
Zero: is count element already loaded with start value?
      1=count element not yet loaded, count value cannot be read
      0=count element loaded, count value can be read
RW, Mode, BCD: programmed counting mode (see Figure 24.4)
```

Figure 24.7: Status byte format.

The *Pin* bit indicates the current status of the concerned counter's OUTx pin. If Pin=1 then the counter provides a high-level signal (+5 V), otherwise it supplies a low-level signal (0 V). The bit *Zero* shows whether the last written counter value has already been transferred to the counting element CE by latches CR_n and CR_h. Depending upon the programmed counting mode, this may last some time. Not before Zero=0 is it meaningful to read back the counter value. Before this the PIT returns a value that further reflects the old state. The remaining six bits RW, Modus and BCD return the values with which they have been loaded for the counter concerned during the last write of the control register (Figure 24.4). Thus you can determine, for example, whether you need to read the low-order or high-order byte with a single IN instruction only, or whether you must issue two IN instructions to get the current value of a counter.

Example: `Determine counting mode of counter 0.`

```
MOV al, 11100010b ; load accumulator with read–back command for mode: CT=1, ST=0
OUT 43h, al       ; output read–back command to control register
IN  al, 40h       ; get mode via port of counter 0
```

It is assumed that the status byte in the accumulator al has the value 00110100b. Thus the OUT pin is on a 0 V level, the counter has been already loaded with the latest passed value, the low-order and high-order bytes are used, the counting mode is equal to 2, and the counting proceeds in a binary fashion with 16 bits. This mode is used, for example, to issue the interrupt 08h that updates the internal system clock.

In the read-back command you may also combine the determination of counter mode and value. Set $\overline{CT}$ as well as $\overline{ST}$ to 0 in this case. All counters specified by means of C0–C2 then return information concerning the counting mode and the current count value. With the first IN instruction referring to a selected counter you get the status byte; with the second or second and third IN instructions, the PIT returns the low-order and/or high-order byte of the currently latched counter value. All further IN instructions pass non-latched counter values as they are taken from the counting element (CE) but no more status bytes. Ensure that all counters selected with bits C0–C2 are read completely by means of two or three IN instructions; otherwise, further counter latch or read-back commands may be ignored.

If you output a counter latch command and later a read-back command to determine the counting mode without having read the counter value before, then the PIT first supplies the status byte with the first IN instructions and only afterwards the byte(s) that indicate the counter value. Thus the order of passing latched bytes is always the same. If you have read the counting value in advance of the read-back command, then the IN instruction after the read-back command of course returns the latched status byte.

24.6 8253/8254 Counting Modes

The 8253/8254 recognizes six different counting modes in all. Further, the PIT can count in binary or in binary coded decimals. Figure 24.8 shows the signals that are supplied by the OUTx connection in each mode, as well as the meaning of the trigger signals at the GATEx input.

In the following the various operation modes are briefly explained. In all modes the PIT counts from initial count values down to lower values. If you newly write the control register, then the control logic is immediately reset and the output OUT of the counter concerned is reset to a defined initial state.

You may write new counting values into one of the counters at any time, but you have to observe the last programmed mode (low-order and/or high-order counter byte, etc.). The new values, however, become effective at different times in the various modes. If a counter has reached the value 0, then it does not stop to count in the non-periodical modes 0, 1, 4 and 5, but continues with ffffh (BCD=0) or 9999 (BCD=1). The OUT pin, however, is not reset, and the counting operation only occurs internally without any external consequences.

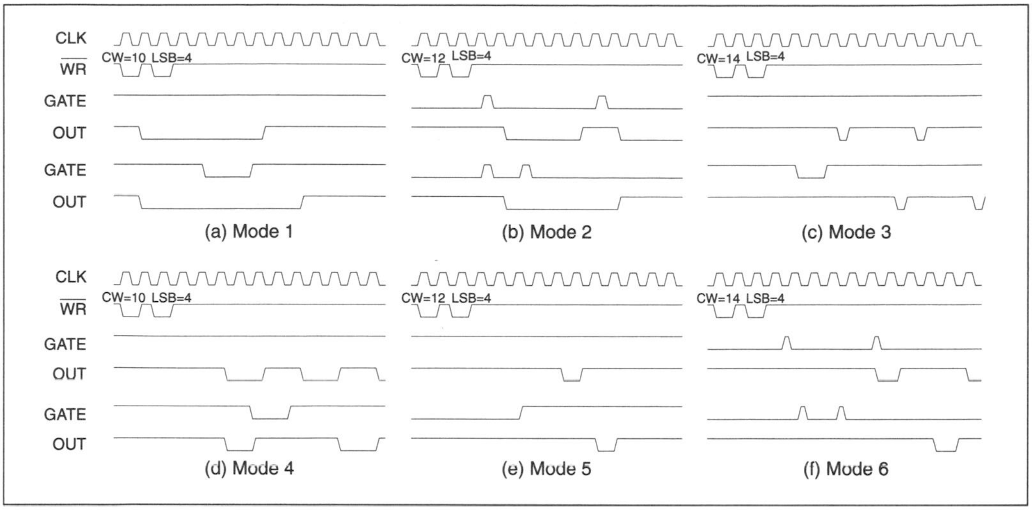

Figure 24.8: 8253/8254 operating modes.
(a) Mode 0: interrupt on terminal count; (b) Mode 1: programmable monoflop; (c) Mode 2: rate generator; (d) Mode 3: square-wave generator; (e) Mode 4: software triggered pulse; (f) Mode 5: hardware triggered pulse;

In some modes the GATE signal executes the counting operation: if GATE=1 then the 8253/8254 continues counting, otherwise it keeps the current value without any change. In other modes a low-high transition or a high level at the GATE input starts the counting operation; the GATE pulse acts as a trigger. Even if GATE then returns to a low level, the counter continues to work. The entity N in the following description names the initial counter value.

Mode 0 (Interrupt on Terminal Count)

After the control register and the initial count value have been written, the counter is loaded upon the next CLK pulse. The OUT pin is on a low level (0 V) at the start of counting. If the counter reaches the value 0, then OUT rises and remains on a high level (+5 V) until a new count value or a new control word for mode 0 is written. If GATE=1 the counter concerned counts down; if GATE=0 the count value is kept.

If a new count value is written into a counter it is loaded upon the next CLK pulse, and the counter continues the counting operation with the newly loaded value. Also, if GATE=0 the counter can be loaded, but the counting operation doesn't start until GATE rises to a high level.

Mode 0 is mostly used to issue a hardware interrupt after the elapse of a certain time period. The PC uses mode 2 for the periodic timer interrupt as mode 0 is not periodic.

Mode 1 (Programmable Monoflop)

After writing the control register and the initial count value, the output OUT is on a high level (+5 V) for the moment. A trigger (transition low–high) at the GATE input loads the counter. Upon the next CLK pulse, OUT drops to a low level (0 V) and remains at that level until the counter has reached the value 0. Then OUT rises to a high level. Not until one CLK pulse after the next trigger does OUT fall again to a low level. Thus, in mode 1 the PIT generates a triggered one-shot pulse with a duration of N CLK cycles and a low level.

If another trigger pulse appears during the course of a count operation (that is, while OUT is at a low level), the PIT reloads the counter with the initial value. Thus the OUT pin is at a low level N CLK cycles after the last trigger pulse. Unlike mode 0, the PIT can be triggered in this mode.

If you write a new count value while the PIT is counting in mode 1, the new value is not effective for the current process. Not until the next trigger pulse at the GATE input is the new count value transferred to the counter. The trigger pulse can occur, of course, when the PIT has not yet completed the current counting operation. The single pulse with a low level lasts in this case until the PIT has counted the new count value down to 0.

Mode 2 (Rate Generator)

After the control word and the initial count value N have been loaded, the PIT starts counting upon the next CLK pulse. As soon as the counter reaches the value 1, OUT drops to a low level for one CLK cycle. Thus the 8253/8254 generates a short peak pulse. Afterwards, the initial count value is automatically reloaded and the PIT restarts the same counting operation again; mode 2 is therefore periodic. The distance of two OUT pulses is N CLK cycles long.

A signal GATE=1 enables (and a signal GATE=0 disables) the counter. If GATE drops to a low level during the counting operation and rises to a high level later, the PIT loads the initial count value at the rise and starts counting. Thus the 8253/8254 can be triggered by a hardware pulse in mode 2. On the other hand, the PIT starts immediately after writing the last data byte. With an active GATE the PIT can therefore also be triggered by software, that is, by the last write access.

Mode 2 is used for counter 2 in the PC for the periodic timer interrupt. The low–high transition during the rise of signal CLK0 issues a hardware interrupt IRQ0 corresponding to INT 08h via the 8259A PIC. The count value must not be equal to 1.

Mode 3 (Square-Wave Generator)

Mode 3 generates a periodic square-wave signal with a period of N CLK cycles. Initially, OUT is at a high level. If half of the N CLK cycles have elapsed, then OUT drops to a low level. After the counter has reached the value 0, OUT again rises to a high level, and the initial value N is reloaded into the counter. Mode 3 is therefore periodically like mode 2. But unlike mode 2, the low phase of the OUT pin lasts N/2 CLK cycles, not only a single CLK cycle. If GATE=1 the counter is operating; if GATE=0 it is stopped. A drop of GATE to a low level while the OUT pin is also on a low level immediately raises OUT to a high level. A rise from a low to a high level at the GATE input (trigger pulse) loads the counter with the initial count value and starts the counting operation. Thus the PIT can be synchronized by hardware in mode 2. After the control register and the initial count value have been written, the 8253/8254 loads the counter upon the next CLK pulse. Thus, the PIT can also be synchronized by software.

A new count value supplied during the course of an active counting operation doesn't affect the current process. At the end of the current half cycle the PIT loads the new value.

The length of the low and high states differs for odd and even values of N. As a CLK cycle defines the smallest possible time resolution, no time periods with half the CLK cycle length can be generated. With an odd N the OUT pin is initially at a high level. The PIT loads the value N–1 (that is, an even number) into the counter, and begins to decrement this value (in steps) by two. Once the CLK pulse after the counter has reached a value of 0, the potential at OUT drops to a low level and the counter is reloaded with N–1. This value is decremented (again in steps) by two. If the value of 0 is reached, then OUT rises to a high level and the whole process is repeated. Thus the signal at the OUT pin is at a high level for (N + 1)/2 CLK cycles and at a low level for (N–1)/2 CLK cycles, that is, the signal is low somewhat longer than it is high.

With even N values, N is loaded unaltered into the counter and decremented in steps by two. If the value 0 is reached, then OUT drops to a low level and the initial value N is reloaded immediately. After the counter has counted downwards in steps of two, OUT rises again to a high level and the whole process is repeated. Thus, even with N values, the phases with high and low levels are equal in time. In both cases, the period of the square-wave signal lasts N CLK cycles. The initial value must be at least equal to 2.

The generated square-wave signal can be used, for example, to transmit data via serial interfaces. The PIT then operates as a baud rate generator. In the PC, counters 1 and 2 are operated in mode 3 to drive the memory refresh and the speaker, respectively.

Mode 4 (Software-Triggered Pulse)

Initially, OUT is at a high level. If the counter has reached the value 0, then OUT drops to a low level for one CLK cycle and rises again to a high level afterwards. If GATE is at a high level the counter is operating; if GATE=0 it is disabled. Thus the triggering is carried out by software as the PIT starts counting after the control register and initial count values are written. Because the counter is loaded upon the first CLK pulse after writing and doesn't start counting until the next CLK cycle, OUT drops (if GATE=1) to a low level N+1 CLK cycles after the write process. Unlike mode 2, the PIT doesn't operate periodically in mode 4. Only a newly written count value triggers the counter again.

If you write a new count value while a counting operation is active, the PIT loads the new value upon the next CLK cycle and continues counting, starting with the new initial value. Thus the 8253/8254 is retriggerable in mode 4 by means of software.

Mode 5 (Hardware-Triggered PULSE)

The pulse form at the OUT pin coincides with that in mode 4. But the triggering is carried out with a low–high transition of GATE. By means of this, the PIT loads the initial count value into the counter upon the next CLK cycle, and the counting process starts. If the value 0 is reached, OUT drops for a single CLK cycle to a low level, and immediately afterwards rises to a high level again. Thus, OUT drops to a low level N + 1 CLK cycles after a trigger pulse at the GATE input. If a trigger pulse occurs during a counting operation, the PIT reloads the initial value into the counter and continues counting with the initial value. Thus in mode 5 the 8253/8254 can be triggered by hardware.

If you write a new count value during the course of an active counting operation then this operation is not affected. Only after the next trigger pulse does the PIT load the new initial value.

In the following sections the application of the various counters in the PC are discussed.

24.7 System Clock

DOS and other operating systems use a system clock for the internal management of date and time. Using this system, the clock date and the time of the last change of directories and files are determined, alarms are issued at a certain time, etc. Besides this system clock, most PCs also have a so-called real-time clock. Unlike the PITs and the connected system clock, the real-time clock runs even if the computer is switched off. The PC queries the clock during the boot process, so you no longer need to input the date and time at power-up. Details on the real-time clock and the allocated CMOS RAM are discussed in Section 26.4.

All programming languages available for the PC implement functions to read this internal system clock. The instructions are, for example, TIMER in BASIC, _dos_gettime in C, or the direct call of INT 21h, function 2ch. This system clock is realized by counter 0 of the first (or only) 8253/8254 PIT, the 8259A PIC and the handler routines for the interrupts 08h and 1ch. Figure 24.9 shows a scheme for this.

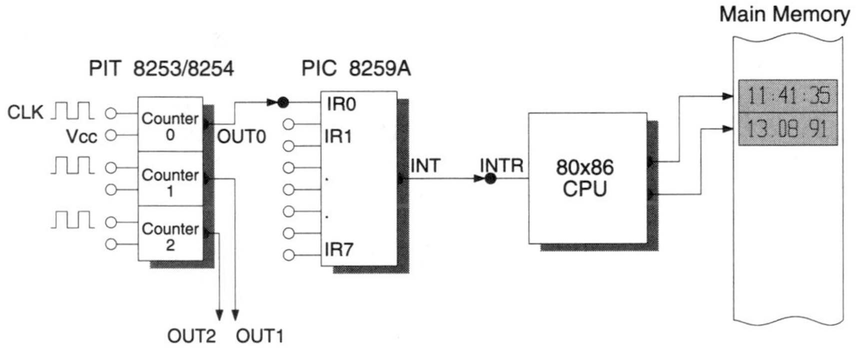

Figure 24.9: Scheme of the internal system clock. The counter 0 periodically issues a hardware interrupt via IRQ0 so that the CPU can update the DOS system clock.

The output OUT0 of counter 0 in the 8253/8254 PIT is connected to the input IR0 (corresponding to IRQ0) of the first (or only) 8259A PIC. The counter 0 operates in mode 2 (rate generator) with periodic binary counting. The CLK0 input is connected to an oscillator's output in the same way as CLK1 and CLK2, which provides a frequency of 1.19318 MHz. The GATE0 input is soldered to the supply potential Vcc = + 5 V so that counter 0 is always enabled. The initial count value is equal 0h or 2^{16}, that is, the PIT outputs a peak pulse exactly 1.19318 MHz/65536=18.206 times per second. The transition from low-high at the end of the pulse issues a hardware interrupt in the 8259A PIC, which operates in the edge-triggered mode. In Section 23.5 the values of the PIC registers upon initialization are indicated.

An interrupt request on IR0 leads via the accompanying acknowledge sequence between PIC and 80x86 processor to an interrupt 08h. The allocated handler updates the system clock, which is a simple DOS-internal data structure, 18.206 times per second. Further, the handler calls interrupt 1ch by explicitly executing the INT 1ch instruction. This 1ch interrupt is called the user exit of the timer interrupt IRQ0. Afterwards, the handler of interrupt 08h completes the hardware interrupt by passing an EOI command to the PIC. Table 24.2 shows the structure of the BIOS data area as far as the DOS system clock is concerned.

Address	Size	Contents	Meaning
40:6c	word	low timer count	number of timer pulses
40:6e	word	high timer count	since 0:00 a.m.
40:70	byte	timer overflow flag	1=24h-boundary passed

Table 24.2: BIOS data area for the DOS system clock

Usually, the interrupt vector of interrupt 1ch points to a simple IRET instruction. But a programmer can redirect the entry in the interrupt vector table to his/her own routine, which is called 18.2 times per second. It is preferable to use the user exit 1ch instead of the system interrupt 08h. Popular applications are the periodic activation of TSR programs, which check the status of floppy or hard disk drives to read data. One example of such programs is the DOS command (and program) PRINT. Section 26.1 briefly describes the cooperation of timer interrupt IRQ0 and the PIT counter 2 to output tone sequences in the background independently of the CPU.

Example: The program shall display the time according to the internal system clock; after the first keyboard hit the clock is accelerated by a factor of eight; upon the second keyboard hit the clock is updated normally.

```
main()
{
  displaytime();      /* display time in upper left corner and wait for first keyboard hit */

  /* accelerate by factor 8 */
  outp(0x43,0x34);    /* output control word 00110100b */
  outp(0x40,0x00);    /* low-order counter byte */
  outp(0x40,0x20);    /* high-order counter byte */
  displaytime();      /* display fast running time and wait for second keyboard hit */

  /* time with normal speed */
  outp(0x43,0x34);    /* output control word 00110100b */
  outp(0x40,0x00);    /* low-order counter byte */
  outp(0x40,0x00);    /* high-order counter byte */
  displaytime();      /* display normal running time */
```

```
  exit(0);
}

void displaytime(void)
{ struct dostime_t time;

  for (;;) {
    _dos_gettime (&time);         /* get time */
    /* display time in the format hour:minute:second:100th second */
    _settextposition (1, 1), printf("%i:%i:%i:%i          ",
      time.hour,time.minute,time.second,time.hsecond);
    if (kbhit()) {    /* return on keyboard hit */
      getch();
      return;
    }
  }
}
```

```
Note: The output of control word 00110100b via port 0x43 to the control register is not
absolutely necessary as the defined mode need not be altered; it is sufficient to supply the
low-order and high-order counter bytes via port 0x40.
```

Instead of mode 2, the PIT counter 0 may also be operated in mode 3, because in this case the transition from low–high of the square-wave signal also issues a hardware interrupt via the 8259A PIC. In this case, the control word 00110100b has to be changed to 00110110b. As the other 8253/8254 modes 0, 1, 4 and 5 are not periodic, the internal clock stops if you operate the PIT in one of these modes. Try it if you like. Later, after a boot process by means of Ctrl-Alt-Del, the BIOS sets up the original mode again.

24.8 Memory Refresh

Besides the periodic activation of the hardware interrupt IRQ0, the PIT is also used in the PC for refreshing dynamic main memory regularly. For this purpose, PC designers have reserved counter 1, which instructs all 18 CLK cycles on a DMA chip to carry out a dummy read cycle. In the course of this dummy cycle, data is read from memory onto the data bus and the address buffers, and address decoders and sense amplifiers in the memory chips are activated to refresh one memory cell row. But the data is not taken off the data bus by a peripheral. Upon the next bus cycle it disappears. Details concerning the refreshing of dynamic memory chips (DRAMs) are discussed in Section 17.1.4. Here I want to explain the use of counter 1 in the 8253/8254 PIT. Figure 24.10 shows the principal connection of timer and DMA chip for memory refresh.

Counter 1 is operated in mode 3 (square-wave generator) with a count value of 18 (12h). Only the low-order counter byte is loaded (RW=01b), that is, the PIT generates a square-wave signal with a frequency of 1.19318 MHz/18=66288 Hz. Thus, counter 1 issues a dummy read cycle every 15 μs by means of the rising edge of the generated square-wave signal. The read cycle refreshes the memory. By means of the read-back and/or counter latch command, you may determine the refresh rate of your PC. Usually, you should obtain the same value as indicated above, but as the memory refresh is very hardware-dependent, other values are also possible.

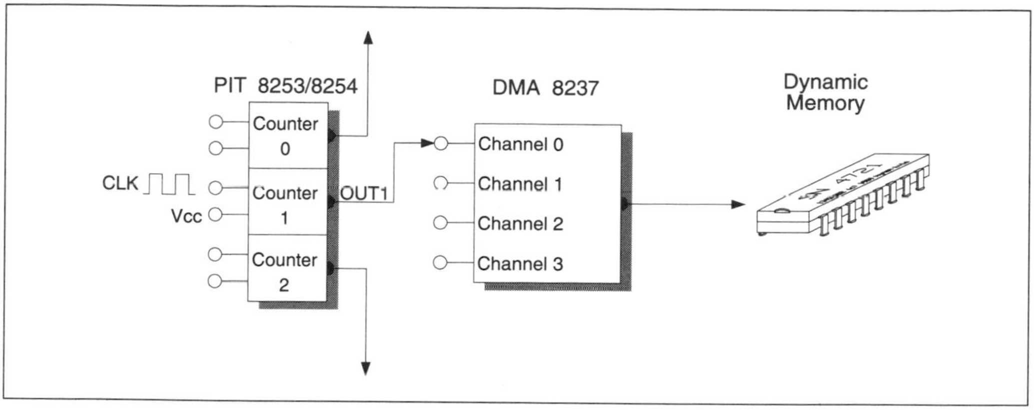

Figure 24.10: Connection of timer and DMA chip for the memory refresh. The counter periodically activates channel 0 of the 8237A DMA chip, which carries out a dummy read cycle to refresh the DRAM memory.

System designers usually lay out the memory refresh rather carefully, that is, the memory is refreshed more often than is really necessary. The so-called *refresh overhead* (that is, the proportion of memory accesses which are caused by the refresh) can reach 10% and more. Modern and very «tight» memory chips in particular require a refresh much less frequently than older models. You may decrease the refresh rate of your PC and gain up to 5% more data throughput without degrading the reliability. Data losses because of too low a refresh rate give rise to parity errors upon reading main memory. A corresponding message then appears on the screen. Therefore, do not set the refresh rate too low. Also, modern refresh concepts such as CAS-before-RAS or hidden refresh decrease the refresh overhead drastically. Unlike a lower refresh rate, however, they do not deteriorate the reliability. The reason for the decreased overhead is an improvement in the refresh method; for example, neither CAS-before-RAS nor hidden refresh require a dummy read cycle of the DMA controller together with the accompanying bus arbitration, because the refresh is controlled by the DRAM chip itself. If your BIOS offers the possibility of using CAS-before-RAS or hidden refresh instead of RAS-only refresh, then you should take advantage of this extra 5% of performance.

Example: The following listing contains a program that sets up the refresh rate of your PC. The call is carried by means of "refresh <count>" where count indicates the number of CLK cycles after which the PIT shall request a memory refresh by means of the generated square wave. On the PC this value is normally equal to 18. With the program you can set values between 2 and 255 as only the low-order counter byte is loaded.

```
main(argc, argv)  /* program called refresh.c */
int argc;
char *argv;
{ int count;

  if (argc < 2) {                        /* no argument is passed, exit with ERRORLEVEL 2 */
    printf("\n\nArgument is missing!\nFormat:  refresh <count>\n\n");
    exit(2);
  }

  count=atoi(argv[1]);
```

```
  f (count < 0x02 || count > 0xff) {  /* invalid argument, exit with ERRORLEVEL 1 */
    printf("\n\nInvalid value %d !!\n\n", count);
    exit(1);
  }

  /* set new refresh rate */
  outp(0x43, 0x56);                   /* 01010110b, output only LSB */
  outp(0x41, count);                  /* write refresh counter value */

  printf("\n\nNew refresh value %d set.\n\n", count);
  exit(0);
}
```

The example program listed loads only the low-order byte of counter 1. The counter values are therefore limited to the range between 2 and 255. You are, of course, free to program an extension with which you can also set higher initial values. For this purpose, however, you must also use the high-order byte and load the control register with the value 01010110b instead of 01110110b, and then pass the low-order as well as the high-order byte. With high-quality chips, refresh count values of up to 1000 can be achieved without the occurrence of parity errors.

You are really free to experiment; set various refresh values and check their effects on computer performance using benchmark programs. The effect is not very significant, but you get some feeling for the «buttons» to turn to in a computer so that the performance is enhanced. After all, ten times 5% is 50%! But for permanent operation you should proceed carefully. What's the gain of 0.1% performance enhancement if your PC crashes when you are editing an important text or program? And this danger is always present while doing such experiments.

24.9 The Speaker

Counter 2 of the first (or only) PIT is dedicated to the tone frequency generation for the installed speaker. You may generate various frequencies with it. How this is carried out and which points you must observe are described in Section 26.1.

24.10 Failsafe Timer

Some newer ATs incorporate a second 8254 PIT, but only counter 0 of this PIT is used, the others usually being free. The counter's output OUT0 is connected to the NMI input of the processor via some circuitry. (See Figure 24.11 on this subject.)

A signal rise from low–high at the OUT0 pin generates a non-maskable interrupt. This is useful if all hardware interrupts are intentionally blocked, or because of a program error which leads to an incorrect CLI instruction or interrupt masking in the PICs, and the computer is looping. Then the PC responds neither to a keyboard hit nor to another external request, except a hardware reset – the computer hangs. Only the NMI issued by the second PIT can «free» the CPU, hence the name failsafe timer. Especially for multitasking systems such as OS/2 or UNIX, such a last resort is useful if, despite all the care taken and the use of protected mode, a program error hangs up the computer and all other tasks are affected. While developing an operating system this happens frequently, and the system programmer will certainly be very thankful for the presence of such a failsafe device.

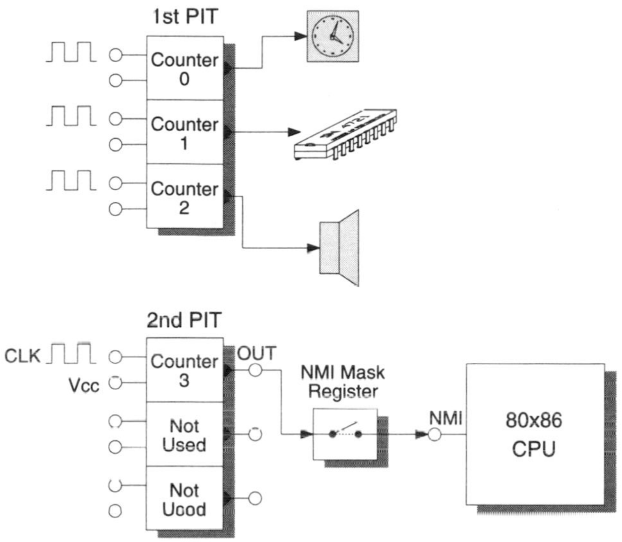

Figure 24.11: Failsafe timer wiring. Counter 3 is used as the failsafe timer which issues an NMI via the NMI mask register as soon as a certain time period has elapsed.

The NMI handler (interrupt 2) can, of course, determine whether the source of the interrupt is counter 0 of the second PIT or a parity error when data is read from a memory chip. In the latter case, a serious hardware malfunction has occurred. The PC must be shut down immediately, or at least as quickly as possible to avoid extensive data loss or damage.

25 DMA Chip 8237A – A Detour Highway in the PC

Besides the CPU, the PC has another chip that accesses the main memory or peripherals on its own – the 8237A DMA controller chip. Compared with access via the CPU, direct memory access was already placed in the background in the AT, probably because IBM was unable to make up its mind and implement a fast-clocked 16-bit DMA chip. Instead, the Stone Age era chips of the PC/XT are also used here. Only with EISA and MCA has DMA become interesting again because of the 32-bit chip employed. But first let us see what's hiding behind the often neglected and seemingly obscure term DMA.

25.1 Direct Memory Access with Peripherals and Memory

Powerful computers with a multitasking operating system in particular use the DMA concept to free the CPU from simple but time-consuming data transfers. The *DMA chip* or *DMA controller* establishes a second path between the peripheral and main memory in a computer system. Figure 25.1 shows the principles of the direct memory access concept.

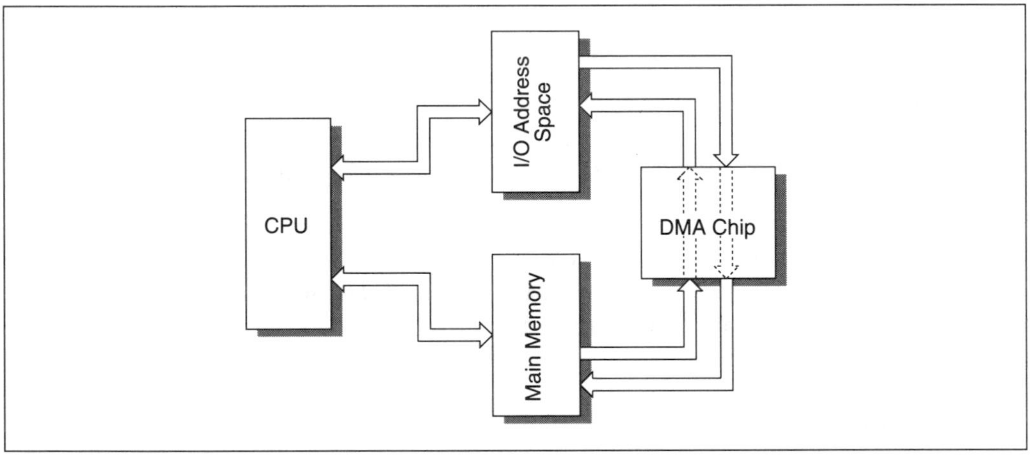

Figure 25.1: DMA. During the course of a DMA cycle, a peripheral can exchange data with the main memory without any intervention from the CPU.

The CPU transfers data from a peripheral into an internal register, and from this register into the main memory. Of course, the transfer can also be carried out in the opposite direction. The arrows in Figure 25.1 indicate that this is a 2-step process, where an internal CPU register is always involved. If a large data block is to be transferred, the CPU can be occupied for quite a long time with this rather trivial job.

Remedial action uses the DMA chip, which establishes a second data path between the peripheral and main memory. The data transfer is not carried out via an internal register of the DMA chip, but immediately via the data bus between the peripheral and main memory. The DMA controller outputs only the address and bus control signals, thus the peripheral can access main memory directly for a read or write – hence the reason for the name DMA. The CPU is therefore freed from data transfers, and can execute other processes.

The peripherals are usually allocated a *DMA channel*, which they activate by means of a *DMA request signal* (*DREQ*). The DMA chip responds to this request and carries out data transfer via this channel. This is useful, for example, when reading a sector from disk: the CPU initializes the DMA controller in a suitable manner and issues the corresponding FDC (Floppy Disk Controller) command. The FD (Floppy Disk) controller moves the read/write head to the intended sector, and activates the read head and the DMA controller. Then the DMA controller transfers the sector data into a buffer in the main memory. By means of a hardware interrupt, the FD controller informs the CPU about the completion of the command. The whole process between outputting the command to the FDC and the hardware interrupt from the FDC is carried out by the FDC and the DMA controller without any intervention from the CPU. Meanwhile, the processor has, for example, calculated the shading of a drawing or the makeup of a page to be printed.

Some DMA chips (for example, the 8237A used in PCs) additionally implement a transfer within main memory, that is, copying a data block to another memory address. Because of the very powerful i386, i486 and Pentium processors with their 32-bit data bus and the repeatable string instruction REP MOVSW, this capability is rarely used.

25.2 Standard 8237A DMA Chip

The Personal Computer normally uses the 8237A or a compatible chip. Also, advanced EISA/MCA or Local-Bus PCs follow the original DMA architecture designed for the PC/XT and AT. Thus, the following discussion is valid even today – even when the discrete 8237A chip has been part of a highly integrated system controller for a long time. Neither port addresses nor the logical structure are affected by that.

25.2.1 8237A Connections and Signals

The original 8237A comes in a 40-pin DIP. Its pin assignment scheme is shown in Figure 25.2. As is the case for other chips, too, the DMA controller is often integrated together with other functional units (like the 8259A PIC or the 8253/8254 PIT) into a single LSI chip.

A0–A3 (I/O)
Pins 32–35
These four connections form a bidirectional address nibble. In the 8237A's standby state the CPU addresses internal 8237A registers. If the 8237A is active then the four low-order address bits are supplied by A0–A3.

A4–A7 (O)
Pins 37–40
These four connections provide four address bits if the 8237A is active. In the standby state they are disabled.

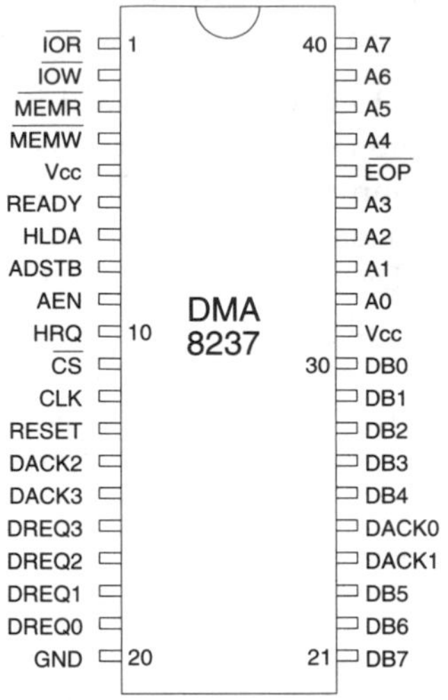

Figure 25.2: 8237A pin assignment.

ADSTB (O)
Pin 8
The address strobe signal is used to fetch the high-order address byte A8–A15 into an external DMA address latch. The 8237A activates ADSTB if the high-order address byte A8–A15 is available on the data bus DB0–DB7.

AEN (O)
Pin 9
The 8237A provides an address enable signal at this pin to activate the external DMA address latch. If AEN is at a high level, the DMA address latch puts the stored address as address bits A8–A15 onto the address bus. AEN can also be used to disable other bus drivers that generate address bits A8–A15 on their own, or to deactivate peripheral components.

CLK (I)
Pin 12
This input is supplied with the DMA clock signal. In the PC the DMA chips usually run at 4.77 MHz, and sometimes at 7.16 MHz.

$\overline{\text{CS}}$ (I)
Pin 11
The CPU activates the chip select signal $\overline{\text{CS}}$ to get an access to the internal 8237A registers if command and data bytes are to be read or written. The data exchange with the CPU is then carried out via the data bus DB0–DB7. During DMA transfers, the $\overline{\text{CS}}$ input is disabled by the 8237A both internally and automatically.

$\overline{\text{DACK0}}$–$\overline{\text{DACK3}}$ (O)

Pins 25, 24, 14, 15

An active DMA acknowledge signal $\overline{\text{DACKx}}$ indicates that the DMA channel concerned is enabled and the corresponding peripheral that issued a DMA request via DRQx is now serviced. Only a single $\overline{\text{DACKx}}$ can be active at a time. The 8237A activates a line $\overline{\text{DACKx}}$ only once it has taken over control of the local bus by means of HRQ and HLDA. The signal polarity (active-low or active-high) can be individually programmed with the mode register.

DB0–DB7 (I/O)

Pins 30–26, 23–21

These eight pins form the bidirectional 8237A data bus for read and write accesses to internal registers or during DMA transfers. In DMA cycles the high-order eight bits of the DMA address are output to DB0–DB7 and latched into the external DMA address latch with ADSTB. During the course of memory–memory transfers, the data byte to be transferred is first loaded into the internal temporary register (memory–DMA half cycle), and then output again by the temporary register via DB0–DB7 (DMA–memory half cycle).

DREQ0–DREQ3 (I)

Pins 19–16

An active DMA request signal DREQx from a peripheral indicates that the device concerned requests a DMA transfer. For example, a floppy controller may activate a DREQx line to carry out the transfer of read data into main memory. Usually, DREQ0 has the highest and DREQ3 the lowest priority. A corresponding $\overline{\text{DACKx}}$ signal from the 8237A acknowledges the request. Also, the polarity of these signals (active-low or active-high) can be individually programmed by means of the mode register.

$\overline{\text{EOP}}$ (I/O)

Pin 36

The end-of-process signal at this bidirectional connection indicates the completion of a DMA transfer. If the count value of the active 8237A channel reaches the value 0, then the 8237A provides an active $\overline{\text{EOP}}$ signal with a low level to inform the peripheral about the termination of the DMA transfer. On the other hand, the peripheral may also pull $\overline{\text{EOP}}$ to a low level to inform the DMA chip about the early termination of the DMA transfer. This is the case, for example, if a buffer in the peripheral that requested the DMA service has been emptied by the 8237A and all data has been transferred to main memory. By the internal as well as the external $\overline{\text{EOP}}$ condition, the TC bit in the status register is set, the corresponding request bit is reset, and the DMA transfer terminated.

HLDA (I)

Pin 7

The hold acknowledge signal HLDA from the CPU or another busmaster informs the DMA chip that the CPU has released the local bus, and that the 8237A is allowed to take over control to carry out a data transfer.

HRQ (O)
Pin 10
With the hold request signal HRQ, the 8237A DMA chip requests control of the local bus from the CPU or another busmaster. The CPU responds with an HLDA signal. The 8237A activates HRQ if a non-masked DRQx signal or a DMA request by software occurs.

$\overline{\text{IOR}}$ (I/O)
Pin 1
In the 8237A standby state, the CPU reads an internal register of the DMA chip by pulling the I/O read signal $\overline{\text{IOR}}$ to a low level. If the 8237A is active and controls the data and address bus, then an active $\overline{\text{IOR}}$ signal indicates that the DMA chip is reading data from a peripheral via a port address. The $\overline{\text{IOR}}$ signal can be active during a write transfer (peripheral–memory).

$\overline{\text{IOW}}$ (I/O)
Pin 2
In the 8237A standby state the CPU writes data into an internal register of the DMA chip by activating the I/O write signal $\overline{\text{IOW}}$. If the 8237A is active and controls the data and address bus, then an active $\overline{\text{IOW}}$ signal indicates that the DMA chip is currently writing data to a peripheral via a port address. The $\overline{\text{IOW}}$ signal can be active during a read transfer (memory-peripheral).

$\overline{\text{MEMR}}$ (I/O)
Pin 3
The 8237A uses the memory read signal $\overline{\text{MEMR}}$ to inform the bus control that data is being read from main memory. The $\overline{\text{MEMR}}$ signal can be active (that is, low) during a read transfer or a memory–memory transfer.

$\overline{\text{MEMW}}$ (I/O)
Pin 4
The 8237A uses the memory write signal $\overline{\text{MEMW}}$ to inform the bus control that data is being written into main memory. The $\overline{\text{MEMW}}$ signal can be active (that is, low) during a write transfer or a memory–memory transfer.

READY (I)
Pin 6
Slow memories or peripherals may activate the input signal READY to extend the 8237A read and write cycles. The 80x86 processors use the same strategy during accesses to main memory and peripherals.

RESET (I)
Pin 13
By means of a high-level RESET signal, the 8237A is reset.

Vcc
Pins 5, 31
This pin is supplied with the supply voltage (usually +5 V).

GND
Pin 20
This pin is grounded (usually 0 V).

25.2.2 Internal Structure and Operation Modes of the 8237A

The 8237A is, despite its limited functions, a rather complex chip, which has 27 internal registers with a width between four and 16 bits. Table 25.1 lists all registers and their widths. The 8237A has four independently working DMA channels 0–3, so the base and current registers are implemented four times.

Register name	Register width	Number of registers
base address register	16 bits	4
base count register	16 bits	4
current address register	16 bits	4
current count register	16 bits	4
temporary address register	16 bits	1
temporary count register	16 bits	1
status register	8 bits	1
command register	8 bits	1
intermediate register	8 bits	1
mode register	6 bits	4
mask register	4 bits	1
request register	4 bits	1

Table 25.1: 8237A internal registers

The temporary registers hold the corresponding values for the currently active channel during the course of executing a DMA function. Only one channel may be active at any time, so one temporary register is sufficient for all four channels. By means of the status register you may read information concerning the current 8237A status; the remaining registers are for programming the DMA controller. Figure 25.3 shows the 8237A's internal structure.

The 8237A has two different priority modes for servicing arriving DMA requests: *fixed priority* and *rotating priority*. With fixed priority channel 0 is assigned the highest and channel 3 the lowest priority. This means that requests on channel 0 are always serviced, but on channel 3 they are serviced only if no other channel is active. With rotating priority the DMA requests are serviced in the order of their occurrence. Afterwards, the currently serviced channel is assigned the lowest priority level.

From Table 25.1 you can see that the count value registers are 16 bits wide. Thus the 8237A can carry out a maximum of 64 k transfers before a wrap-around of the count register occurs. How many bytes these 64 k transfers correspond to depends upon the connection of the 8237A to the computer's data and address bus. How the DMA chip is used in the PC architecture is described in Part 3. The CPU writes a value into the count register which defines the number of DMA transfers of the channel concerned. The 8237A terminates the DMA transfer for the active channel when the count register wraps from 0000h to ffffh. Because, after every transfer, the count register is decreased by one, the actual number of DMA transfers is equal to the value written by the CPU plus one. Thus, 64 k transfers can be carried out if you initially load the count register with the value ffffh.

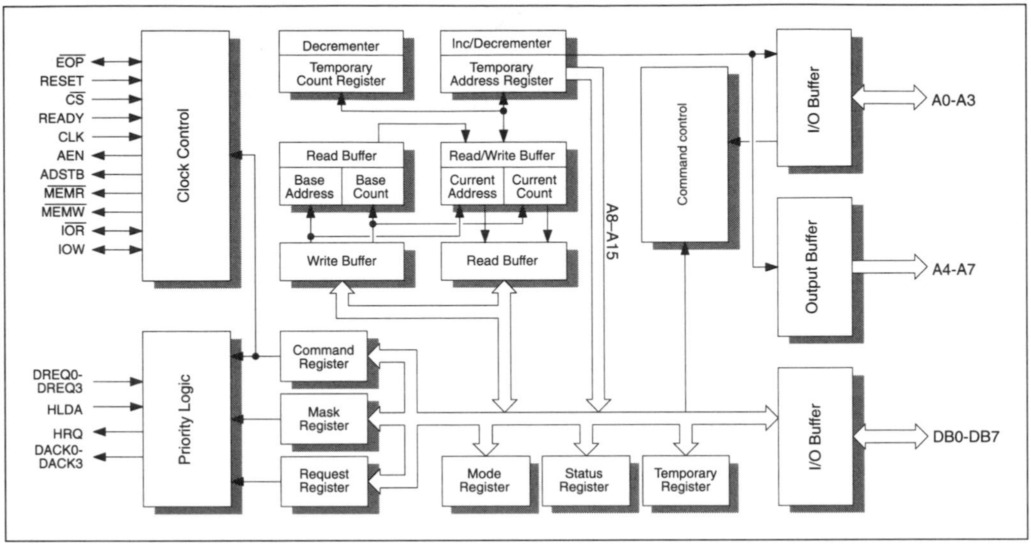

Figure 25.3: The 8237A DMA controller.

As soon as the count register reaches the value ffffh, this is called a *terminal count (TC)*. The end of the transfers is only reached upon a TC or an external $\overline{EOP}$ but not if the DREQ signal is disabled in a demand transfer.

If you look at the 8237A pin assignment in Figure 25.2 and compare it to Table 25.1, you can see that the 8237A address registers are 16 bits wide but the 8237A address bus comprises only eight bits A0–A7. To save terminals and to accommodate the 8237A in a standard DIP with 40 pins, the designers intended to have an external *DMA address latch* which holds the high-order address byte A8–A15 of the address registers. However, only a 16-bit address space is thus accessible – too little for a PC. For the complete address a so-called *DMA page register* is additionally required, which holds the address bits beyond A15. Figure 25.4 shows this schematically for the 24-bit AT address bus, which serves the complete 16 Mbyte address space of the 80286.

The DMA address latch is an external chip loaded by the 8237A with the high-order address byte in the address register. For this purpose, the 8237A puts address bits A8–A15 onto data bus DB0–DB7 and activates the ADSTB signal. The DMA address latch then fetches and latches the 8-bit address onto the data bus. Thus the DMA chip need only provide the low-order address byte via its address bus A0–A7.

The DMA page register, on the other hand, is loaded by the CPU and accommodates the address bits beyond A15. Each channel has its own page register, which is activated according to the active DMA channel. In a PC/XT with its 20-bit address bus, only a 4-bit page register is therefore necessary, but an AT with a fully equipped 16 Mbyte memory requires an 8-bit register. Motherboards with i386, i486 and Pentium processors that support a physical DMA address space of more than 16 Mbytes have an additional DMA page register for every channel, which holds the necessary address bits A24 and beyond. Figure 25.5 shows the scheme for DMA addressing.

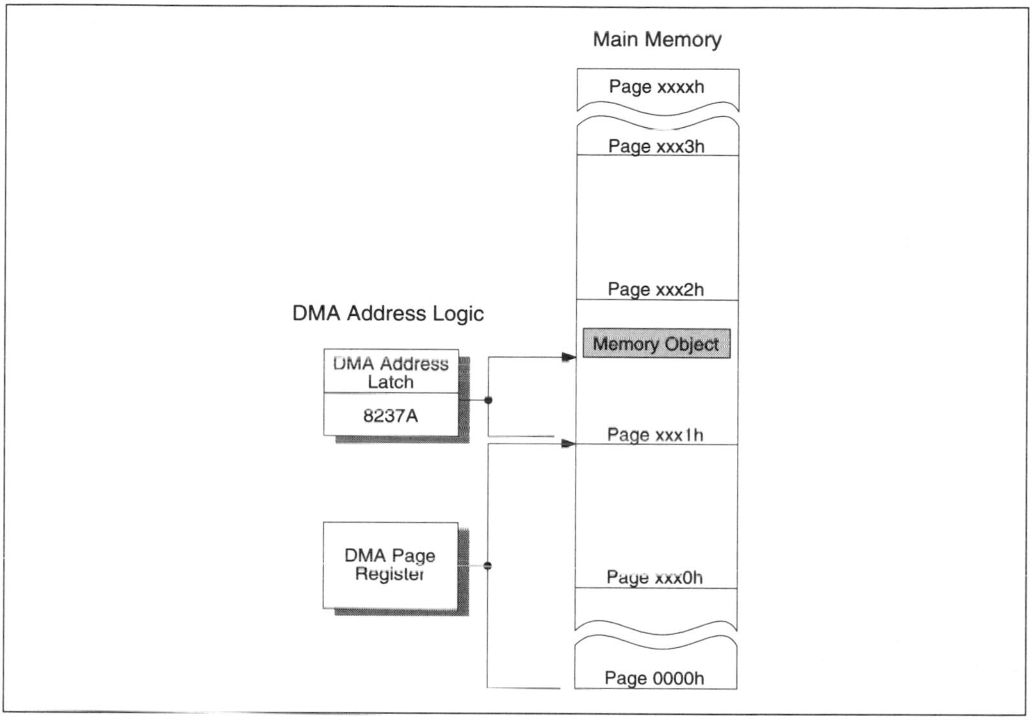

Figure 25.4: Address generation with 8237A, DMA address latch and DMA page register. The DMA page register supplies the number of the corresponding 64 kbyte page. The DMA address latch holds the high-order address byte and the 8237A address register the low-order address byte within that DMA page.

Because of the addressing structure with DMA page registers, the address space is physically divided into pages (or segments, if you like) of 64 kbytes each for 8-bit channels 0–3, or into pages of 128 kbytes each for 16-bit channels 5–7. Thus the page size is 64 kbytes for 8-bit channels 0–3 and 128 kbytes for 16-bit channels 5–7. Within these pages, the DMA address latch and the address bits A0–A7 from the 8237A indicate the offset. The DMA address cannot go beyond the current page. If for instance, you write the base address ff00h into the address register and the value 0fffh into the count register (that is, you want to transfer 4 kbytes via a DMA channel) then the address register wraps around from ffffh to 0000h during the course of this transfer. The DMA transfer is not completed by this, of course, as the count register further holds the value 0f00h. The rest of the data is therefore written to the beginning of the DMA page. This wrap-around of the address register is called a *DMA segment overflow*. Thus when programming a DMA transfer, you must always ensure that all data to be transferred can be accommodated contiguously in the remaining section of the DMA page. The DMA chip doesn't report any message if a DMA overflow occurs.

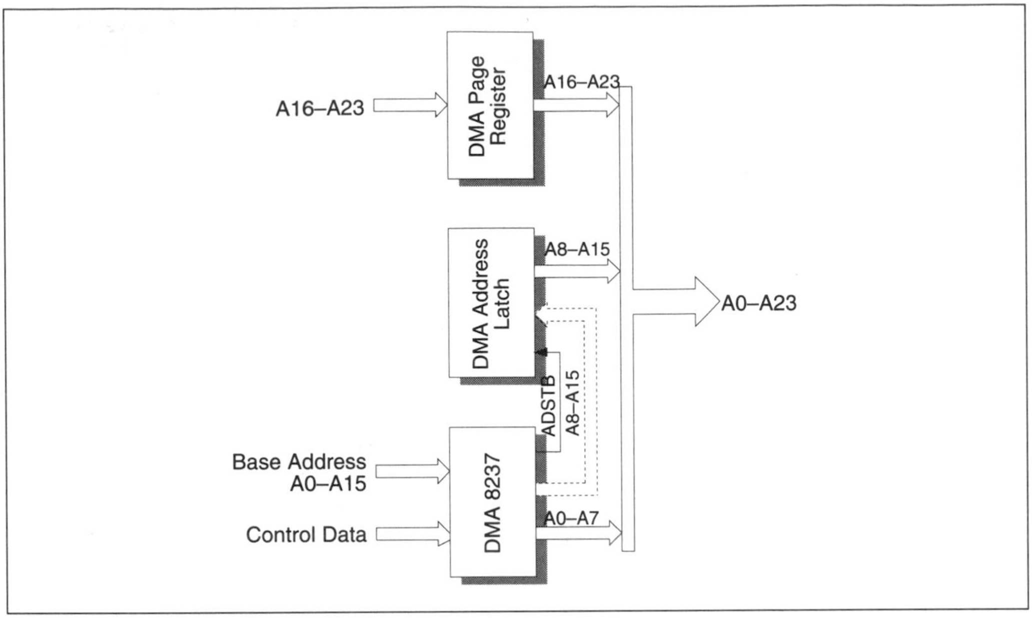

Figure 25.5: DMA addressing.

The 8237A Standby Mode

If the 8237A is in standby mode it checks with every clock cycle whether the $\overline{CS}$ signal is active and the CPU is trying to access one of its registers. If $\overline{CS}$ is active (that is, on a low level), the 8237A enters the programming state and waits for addresses and, eventually, data from the CPU to write them into the corresponding register, or to provide data from the addressed register to the CPU. Address lines A0–A3 determine the register selected. To be able to read from and write to the 16-bit 8237A registers via the 8-bit data bus DB0–DB7, the 8237A uses an internal flip-flop for switching between low-order and high-order data bytes. If you attempt to read or write a 16-bit register you must reset this flip-flop first, and then read or write the least significant and then the most significant data byte. (Details on programming the 8237A are discussed in Section 25.5.)

In the standby mode, the 8237A further samples its DREQ inputs upon every clock cycle to determine whether a peripheral has issued a DMA request. If the corresponding DMA channel is not masked internally then the DMA chip outputs a request for the local bus to the CPU via the HRQ pin to take over control of the local bus. After the CPU has responded with an HLDA signal and has released the bus, the requesting 8237A enters the active mode to carry out a DMA service. Depending upon the programming, it is able to operate in four different modes, explained now in brief.

Single Transfer

In this mode the 8237A carries out only a single transfer. The count register is decremented by one and the address register, depending upon the programmed state, is also decremented or incremented by one. If the count register reaches the value ffffh, starting from 0000h, then the 8237A internally issues a TC and with a corresponding programmed state also an autoinitialization of the DMA chip.

With this mode you can also move a whole block of sequentially ordered data. Unlike the block transfer mode, though, you have to start every data transfer individually by a signal DREQ or a set bit on the request register. As compensation for this restriction, however, the CPU can again get control of the local bus between two transfers.

The single transfer mode is used in the PC for transferring a data sector from the floppy disk drive into the main memory. For this purpose, the CPU has to load the count register with the value 511 (512 bytes to transfer) and the address and page register with the buffer address in the main memory. The floppy controller activates the DREQ2 line with every decoded data byte from the floppy disk to issue a single transfer cycle. After transferring 512 bytes into main memory, a wrap-around in the count register occurs, and a TC is generated. The 8237A then terminates the DMA transfer.

Block Transfer

This mode causes the 8237A to continuously transfer data after acknowledging the DREQ request and the output of $\overline{\text{DACK}}$. For this purpose, the count register is decremented by one upon each transfer, and the address register (depending upon the programmed state) decremented or incremented until a TC or an external $\overline{\text{EOP}}$ occurs. A TC is present if the count register reaches the value ffffh, starting from 0000h. With a correspondingly programmed state an autoinitialization is carried out.

Demand Transfer

In demand transfer mode the 8237A carries out data transfer continuously until a TC or an external $\overline{\text{EOP}}$ occurs, or the peripheral deactivates DREQ. Thus the demand transfer differs from the block transfer in that disabling DREQ also leads to interruption of the data transfer. In block transfer mode this has no consequences. Moreover, in demand transfer mode the data transfer continues at the location of the interruption if the peripheral activates DREQ again. Demand transfer mode is of some importance in the PC, as the bus slots don't have a connection for $\overline{\text{EOP}}$ through which a peripheral might indicate the end of the data transfer to the DMA chip. Disabling DREQ only leads to an interruption, not to the transfer's termination. Autoinitialization is therefore not carried out. This is only possible by means of a TC or an external $\overline{\text{EOP}}$.

Cascading

One characteristic of the 8237A is its capability for cascading. The number of DMA channels can thus be extended, similar to the 8259A PIC and its interrupt channels. Unlike the PIC the extension with the 8237A works to any depth. Figure 25.6 shows a scheme for this cascading capability.

Cascading is carried out by connecting one channel's DREQ and $\overline{\text{DACK}}$ of a DMA chip of a higher level with HRQ and HLDA, respectively, of a DMA chip of a lower level. Normally, an

8237A takes control of the local bus by means of HRQ and HLDA when it receives a DMA request via DREQ. With the cascading scheme, however, a DMA request to a second level DMA chip (the *slave*) leads to a DMA request to the DMA chip of the first level (the *master*), as the slave's HRQ signal is passed to the DMA chip of the first level via the DREQ input. The master takes control of the local bus by means of HRQ and HLDA, and activates its output $\overline{DACK}$, which is connected to the input HLDA of the DMA slave. Thus the DMA slave interprets the $\overline{DACK}$ signal from the master as an HLDA from the CPU. Cascading therefore leads the control signals HRQ and HLDA through master and slave. The figure shows further that the cascading scheme is extendable up to any level. The AT uses one slave and one master. The slave is connected to channel 0 of the master, thus the slave channels have a higher priority than the master's channels. Channel 0 of the AT's master is usually denoted as DMA channel 4.

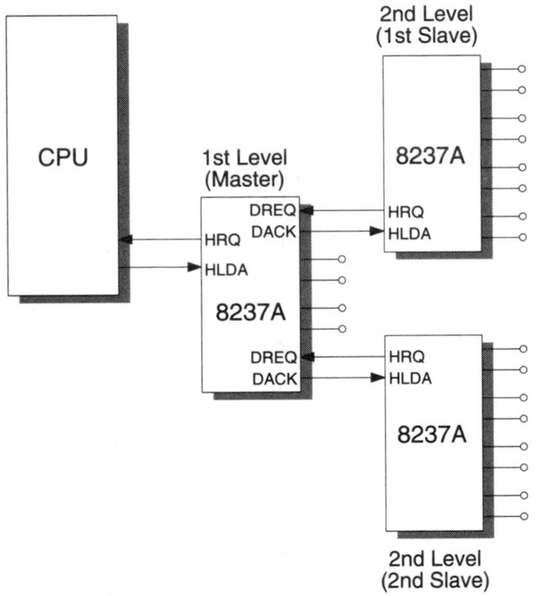

Figure 25.6: 8237A cascading. The 8237A DMA chips can be cascaded up to any level. For this purpose, the HRQ and HLDA of a slave must be connected to the master's DREQ and DACK.

Besides the connections shown, the master channel concerned needs to be programmed in cascading mode to realize cascading. It is then only used for passing the control signals from the DMA slave, and doesn't provide any address or control signals for the bus.

The three transfer modes (single, block and demand) can carry out four transfer types, each of which differs in the source and target of the transfer. The following discusses these four transfer types.

Read Transfer

In read transfer, data is transferred from main memory to an I/O device, thus from memory to the I/O address space. For this purpose, the 8237A uses the $\overline{\text{MEMR}}$ and $\overline{\text{IOW}}$ signals. By activating $\overline{\text{MEMR}}$, data is read from memory onto the data bus. The data on the data bus is transferred to the I/O device by activating $\overline{\text{IOW}}$. Figure 25.7 shows a signal diagram for a read transfer.

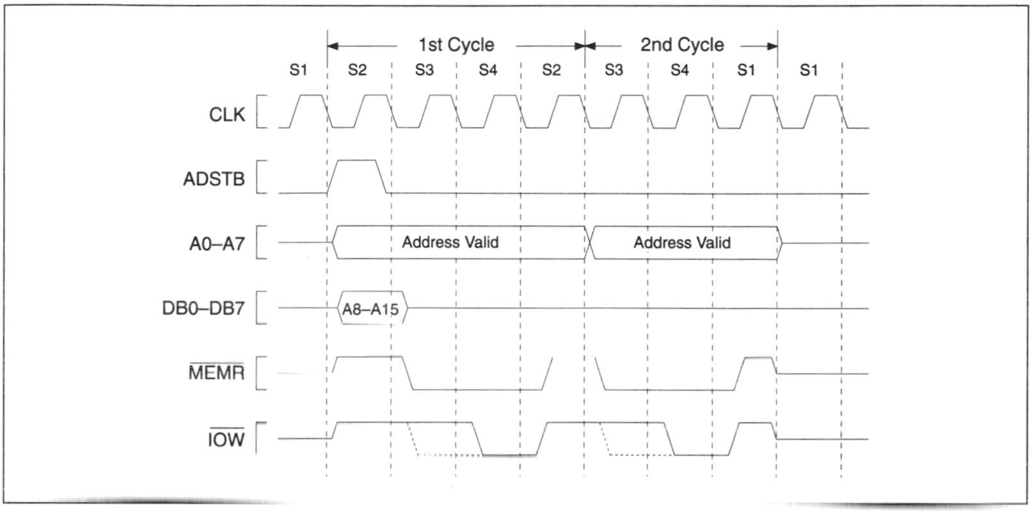

Figure 25.7: Read transfer.

During the course of the shown read transfer, the 8237A initially outputs the high-order address byte of the memory address via the data bus DB0–DB7, and activates ADSTB to latch address bits A8–A15 onto the DMA address latch. At the same time, the low-order address byte of the memory address is output via address lines A0–A7. Activating $\overline{\text{MEMR}}$ to a low level causes the memory subsystem to read data from memory, and to put it onto the system data bus. The memory buffer (see Figure 4.2) latches the read data and keeps it stable on the system data bus. By activating $\overline{\text{IOW}}$ the peripheral is advised to fetch the data on the system data bus into its I/O buffer (see Figure 4.8). The peripheral takes the data directly off the system data bus. No temporary storage in the temporary register of the 8237A is carried out.

As you can see from the figure, the 8237A doesn't generate any I/O address for the peripheral. The peripheral is only accessed via the assigned lines DREQx and $\overline{\text{DACKx}}$, while the other peripherals in the I/O address space are disabled, for example, by the active AEN signal from the DMA chip. Now only the intended device responds to the 8237A control signal. Figure 25.7 shows further that one DMA cycle lasts for four DMA clock cycles. If a slow memory or I/O device is addressed, one or more wait cycles may be inserted between S2 and S3, or between S3 and S4. The DMA cycle is then extended accordingly.

The high-order address byte A8–A15 need not be output during each DMA cycle, but only if the high-order address byte really changes. This occurs only every 256 bytes. In the second cycle of the figure, phase S2 is therefore missing, so only three clock cycles are required for a single DMA cycle. This means a time saving of 25% in the end.

Write Transfer

The write transfer is, so to speak, the opposite of the read transfer. Data is transferred from an I/O device into main memory, that is, from the I/O to memory address space. The 8237A uses the $\overline{IOR}$ and $\overline{MEMW}$ signals for this purpose. By activating $\overline{IOR}$, data is read from the I/O device onto the data bus. The data is then transferred to memory by an active $\overline{MEMW}$. The signal diagram in Figure 25.7 is also valid for a write transfer if you replace $\overline{MEMR}$ by $\overline{IOR}$ and $\overline{IOW}$ by $\overline{MEMW}$. The DMA cycle is four clock cycles long if the high-order address byte needs to be supplied to the DMA address latch, otherwise it is three clock cycles. If the DMA chip has to insert wait cycles because of slow memories or I/O devices, the DMA cycle is extended accordingly.

Verify Transfer

Verify transfer is merely a pseudo-transfer as the 8237A operates internally in the same way as in a read or write transfer, therefore it generates addresses and responds to $\overline{EOP}$ and other signals but doesn't provide any I/O and memory control signals such as $\overline{IOR}$, $\overline{IOW}$, $\overline{MEMR}$, $\overline{MEMW}$, etc. externally. Thus the verify transfer serves only for internal 8237A checking to determine whether the addressing and control logic are operating correctly. With a real verification of data this has nothing to do.

Memory–Memory Transfer

With memory–memory transfer the 8237A may move a complete data block from one address area in the main memory to another. However, this type of transfer is only available for channels 0 and 1; channels 2 and 3 only carry out the three transfer types indicated above. Channel 0 determines the source and channel 1 the destination of the data transfer. For memory–memory transfer, the temporary register is important because it accommodates the data byte read from the source area in the main memory before it is written to another location in main memory via channel 1. The memory–memory transfer is issued by a software request for channel 0, because an external DMA request with DREQ0 is not possible here. As usual, the 8237A requests control of the local bus by means of HRQ and HLDA. The memory–memory transfer is generally terminated by a TC of channel 0 or 1 if the count register reaches the value ffffh, starting with 0000h. The 8237A responds in memory–memory transfer to an external $\overline{EOP}$ signal. Through this, external diagnostic hardware, for example, may terminate the DMA transfer if the source or destination address becomes of a certain value. Figure 25.8 shows a signal diagram for a memory–memory transfer.

During the first half cycle the DMA chip reads the data byte into the temporary register by first providing the high-order address byte A8–A15 on DB0–DB7. The address byte is then loaded into the DMA address latch by activating ADSTB. At the same time, the 8237A outputs the low-order address byte via A0–A7, and activates $\overline{MEMR}$ to read out the data byte onto the system data bus. The 8237A fetches the data, via DB0–DB7, into its temporary register. The next half cycle then writes the data byte held by the temporary register to a new address in main memory. To carry out this process, the 8237A first writes the high-order address byte into the DMA address latch and puts the data byte via DB0–DB7 onto the system bus afterwards. The following activation of $\overline{MEMW}$ instructs the memory to write the data byte to the corresponding address. Thus the memory-memory transfer is complete. As can be seen from Figure 25.8, such a transfer requires eight DMA clock cycles.

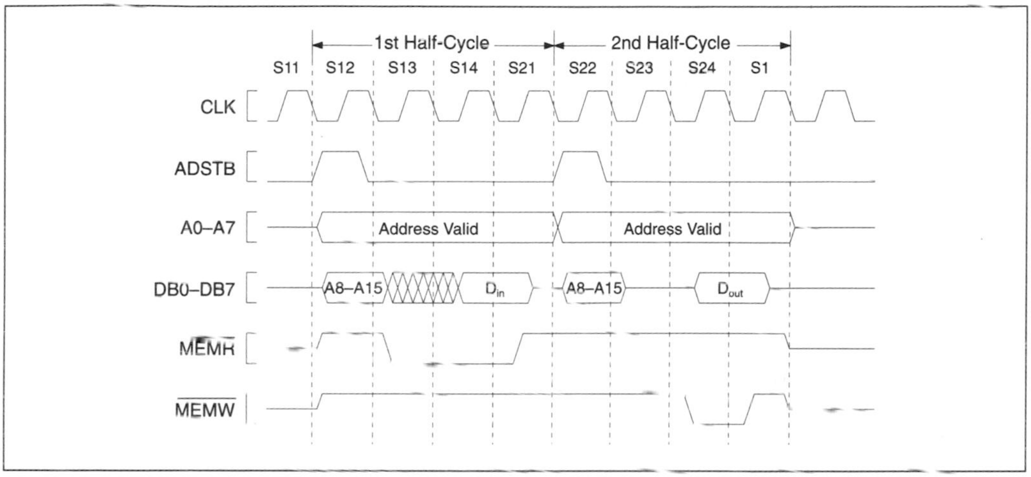

Figure 25.8: Memory–memory transfer.

Note that CLK indicates the DMA clock and not the CPU clock. Even in i386 systems with 33 MHz, the DMA chip usually runs at 4.77 MHz. Thus a memory–memory transfer lasts for about 1680 ns. If we assume a 70 ns main memory with about 120 ns cycle time and three CPU clock cycles for the execution of one i386 MOVS instruction, then the transfer of one word via the CPU lasts only 330 ns. This is five times faster. If we further take into account that the i386 can transfer 32 bits all at once, but the 8237A only eight, then the i386 transfers data from memory to memory 20 times faster than the 8237A.

As a feature, channel 0 can be programmed to keep the same address during the course of the whole memory–memory transfer. The 8237A then carries out a memory block initialization. The size of this block is defined by the count value in the count register of channel 1.

Compressed Mode

For fast memories and I/O devices the 8237A may be programmed so that it carries out a compressed mode. The transfer time is then compressed to two DMA clock cycles. Figure 25.9 shows a signal diagram for the compressed mode.

As you can see, cycle S3 is missing. It extends the read pulse with slower memories and I/O devices so that the addressed unit has enough time to provide the data. With modern devices this is no longer required, and S3 can be dropped. Note that the 8237A runs only at 4.77 MHz in the PC. Every device as slow as the 8237A can easily follow, but after 256 bytes at most an additional cycle S1 is required, because a new high-order address byte for the DMA address latch must then be supplied via DB0–DB7.

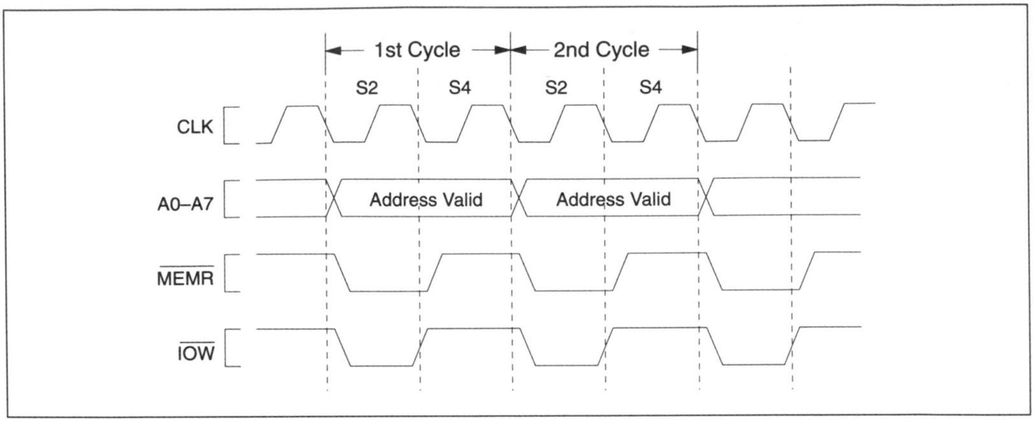

Figure 25.9: Compressed mode.

The compressed mode is only implemented for read and write transfers. For a memory–memory transfer the compressed mode is not possible, although today's RAM chips are among the fastest components in a PC.

Autoinitialization

The individual 8237A channels may be programmed so that they initialize themselves to the initial values after a TC or $\overline{EOP}$ automatically. For this purpose, the current address register and the current count register are loaded with the values from the base address register and the base count register. The base address register and base count register are not accessible, but are loaded during the course of a write to the current address register and the current count register by the CPU with the same values. The base address register and base count register are not altered by the following DMA cycles, and hold the initial values even after an $\overline{EOP}$ from which the current address register and the current count register are restored during autoinitialization. Afterwards, the 8237A channel concerned is again ready for a DMA transfer.

Autoinitialization is used if data quantities of the same size are always to be transferred to a fixed buffer in the main memory, or from the main memory. This can be the case, for example, when reading a sector from a floppy disk into the main memory. Here it would be sufficient to program the DMA chip once. For all succeeding sector transfers, the chip initializes itself again and again.

25.2.3 Programming the 8237A

For programming the 8237A five control registers are available. Additionally, you can determine the 8237A's current state by a status register. From the temporary register you may read the last transferred data byte of a memory–memory transfer. Table 25.2 lists the I/O addresses of the registers concerned. Note that the PC/XT only has the DMA 1 chip.

DMA 1[1]	DMA 2[2]	Read (R) Write (W)	Register name
08h	d0h	R	status register
08h	d0h	W	command register
09h	d2h	W	request register
0ah	d4h	W	channel mask register
0bh	d6h	W	mode register
0dh	dah	R	intermediate register
0fh	deh	W	mask register

[1] master in PC/XT, slave in AT
[2] master in AT

Table 25.2: I/O addresses of control and status register

The read-only status register provides some information on the current state of the individual channels in the 8237A. Figure 25.10 shows the structure of this register.

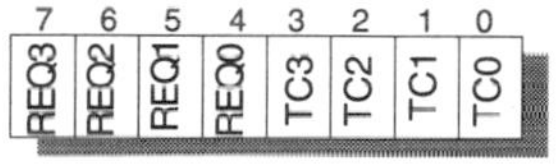


```
REQ3–REQ0: DMA request for channels 3 to 0 or 7 to 4
           1=DMA request    0=no DMA request

TC3–TC0:   terminal count for channel 3 to 0 or 7 to 4
           1=TC reached, transfer complete    0=status register read or cancelled
```

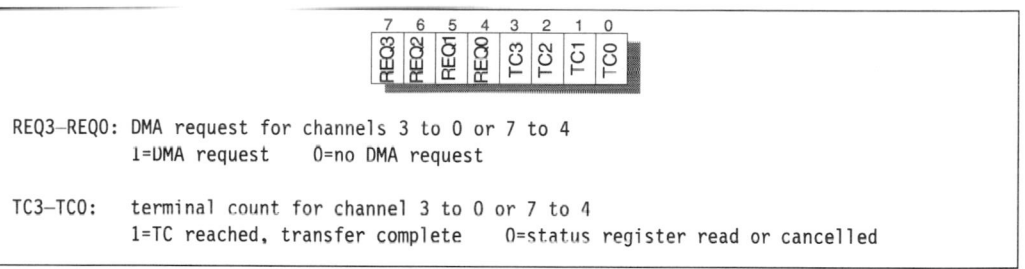

Figure 25.10: Status register (08h, d0h).

The four high-order bits *REQ3–REQ0* indicate whether a request is pending via a DREQx signal for the channel concerned. Bits *TC3–TC0* show whether the 8237A has reached a terminal count of the corresponding channels according to a transition from 0000h to ffffh of each count register. If you read the status register, the four bits TC3–TC0 are automatically cleared.

Before programming an 8237A channel you should disable the whole chip, or at least the channel to be programmed. According to Murphy's law, no DMA request for this channel occurs all year – until you try to program it! If a DMA request occurs, for example after programming the low-order address register byte, then the 8237A immediately responds to the request and carries out the DMA transfer with the new low-order and the old high-order address byte. You can surely imagine what this means. Once the catastrophe is complete, the 8237A enters program mode again and the CPU can write the high-order address byte – if it is really able to do this any more. You may disable the complete DMA controller with the COND bit in the control register. An individual channel can be masked by means of the channel mask or the mask register. Figure 25.11 shows the command register.

With the *DAKP* bit you can determine the active level of the $\overline{\text{DACK}}$ signals. If DAKP is cleared, then the 8237A provides a low-level signal at the $\overline{\text{DACKx}}$ pin if it is servicing a DMA request via DRQx; otherwise, the pin outputs a high-level signal. With a set DAKP bit the 8237A supplies a high-level signal at the $\overline{\text{DACKx}}$ if it is servicing a DMA request via DRQx, otherwise a low-level signal is supplied. The standard setup after a reset is a cleared DAKP bit, which is also used by the PC. Thus, $\overline{\text{DACK}}$ signals are always active-low in the PC. The *DRQP* bit has a similar effect. With this bit you can define the active level that the 8237A assigns to the DMA request signals. A cleared DRQP bit means that the 8237A interprets a high level at its DRQx input as a DMA request for the channel x concerned. With a set DRQP bit, on the other hand, the 8237A issues a DMA transfer if a high-level signal is supplied. Thus DRQP and DAKP behave in opposite ways. The standard setup after a reset is a cleared DRQP bit, which is also used in the PC. DRQ signals are therefore always active-high in the PC.

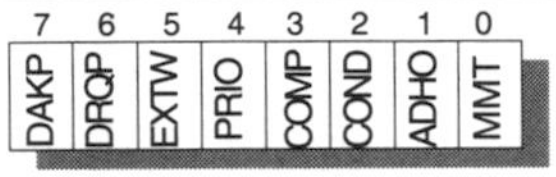

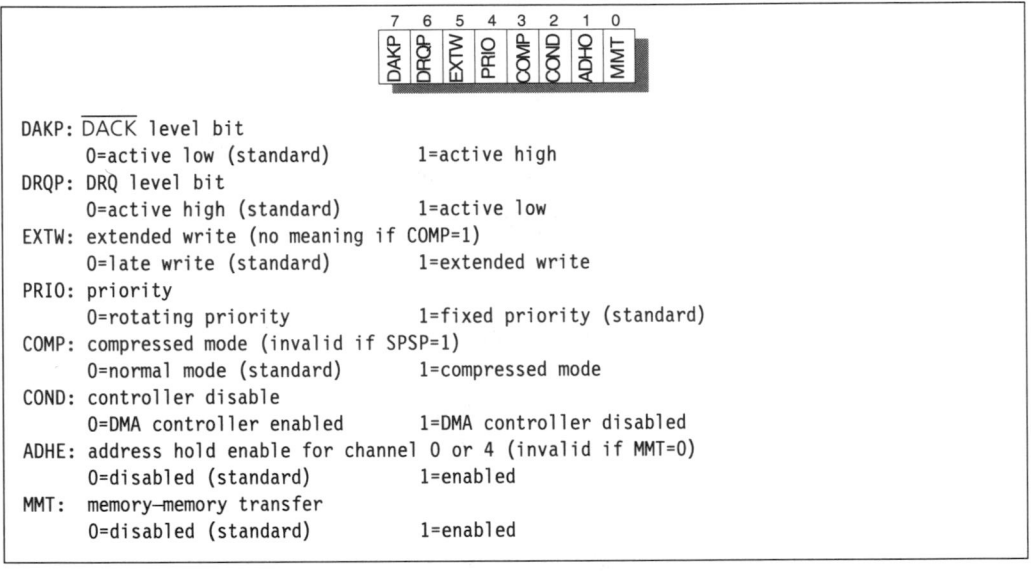

```
DAKP: DACK level bit
      0=active low (standard)        1=active high
DRQP: DRQ level bit
      0=active high (standard)       1=active low
EXTW: extended write (no meaning if COMP=1)
      0=late write (standard)        1=extended write
PRIO: priority
      0=rotating priority            1=fixed priority (standard)
COMP: compressed mode (invalid if SPSP=1)
      0=normal mode (standard)       1=compressed mode
COND: controller disable
      0=DMA controller enabled       1=DMA controller disabled
ADHE: address hold enable for channel 0 or 4 (invalid if MMT=0)
      0=disabled (standard)          1=enabled
MMT:  memory–memory transfer
      0=disabled (standard)          1=enabled
```

Figure 25.11: Command register (08h, d0h).

The *EXTW* bit controls the length of the write pulse $\overline{\text{IOW}}$ or $\overline{\text{MEMW}}$ during a DMA transfer. With a set EXTW bit the write pulse will already have started one DMA clock cycle earlier during DMA phase S3; thus it is longer. You can see this in Figure 25.7: the broken line indicates an extended write, and the solid line a late write. In compressed mode (that is, with a set COMP bit), the value of EXTW is immaterial as the S3 cycle is missing. With the *PRIO* bit you may set up the priority strategy that the 8237A uses to service incoming DMA requests. After a reset, PRIO is set so that the 8237A uses fixed priority with the order 0, 1, 2, 3. A set *COMP* bit advises the 8237A to carry out compressed clocking where phase S3 is missing. Memory–memory transfers do not allow compressed mode – a relic of memory access times of 200 ns and more.

Using the *COND* bit you can disable the DMA controller completely. It doesn't respond to any DMA requests but must always be kept in programming mode. Thus the 8237A can only accept commands, and enables the CPU to access its internal registers.

The *AHDE* bit is important for memory–memory transfers. With a set AHDE bit the 8237A keeps the value in the address register of channel 0 unchanged; only the address register of channel 1 is continuously increased or decreased. A whole memory block can thus be initialized with the value to which the channel 0 address register points. If AHDE is cleared, a real memory–memory transfer of a complete data block is executed. The value of AHDE is only effective with a set MMT bit.

With a set *MMT* bit the 8237A enters memory–memory transfer mode. Note that only a few motherboards support this transfer mode. For the memory–memory transfer only channels 0 and 1 are available. Channel 0 defines the source and channel 1 the target of the transfer. All other modes are defined via the mode register (Figure 25.12).

Example: `Setup level, priority etc. for DMA 1 and enable DMA 1.`

```
OUT 08h, 10h  ; output 00011000b to command register of DMA 1:
              ; DACK: active-low, DRQ: active-high, late write, priority: fixed
              ; clocking mode: compressed, DMA 1: enabled,
              ; address hold: disabled, memory-memory: disabled
```

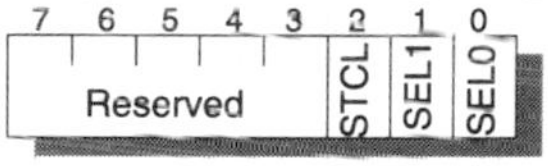


```
reserved: normally equal 0
STCL: set/clear request bit
      1=set      0=clear
SEL1, SEL0: channel select
      00=channel 0/4   01=channel 1/5   10=channel 2/6   11=channel 3/7
```

Figure 25.12: Request register (09h, d2h).

Besides a hardware DMA request via the DRQx signals, you also have the option to start a DMA transfer by a software command. The 8237A behaves in the same way as if activated by a DRQx. DMA requests by software are imperative for memory–memory transfers, as the memory subsystem is unable to provide a DRQx signal for initiating the data transfer. The request of a DMA transfer is carried out with the request register (Figure 25.12). Bits *SEL1, SEL0* determine the channel for which the request is to be issued. The *STCL* bit defines whether the accompanying request bit is to be set or cleared. If no further DMA requests are currently active, or of a high priority, then setting the request bit immediately leads to a DMA transfer. The request is otherwise queued according the programmed priority strategy. You may remove a DMA transfer not yet initiated from the queue by clearing the corresponding request bit.

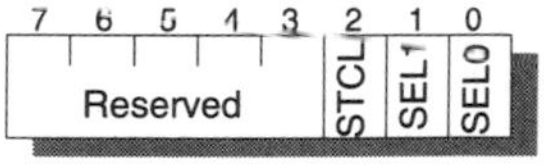


```
reserved: normally equal 0
STCL: set/clear mask bit
      1=mask     0=clear
SEL1, SEL0: channel select for mask bit
      00=mask bit for channel 0/4   01=mask bit for channel 1/5
      10=mask bit for channel 2/6   11=mask bit for channel 3/7
```

Figure 25.13: Channel mask register (0ah, d4h).

Example: `Issue DMA request for channel 6.`

```
OUT d2h, 06h  ; output 00000110b (res=0, STCL=1, SEL1/SEL0=10)
              ; to request register
```

The channel mask register (Figure 25.13) masks a single channel. With the related mask register, on the other hand, you can mask or release several channels all at once. Bits *SEL1, SEL0* define the channel to be masked or released. STCL determines whether this channel is to be masked or released.

Example: `Mask channel 1 of DMA 1.`

```
MOV 0ah, 05h  ; write 00000101b into channel mask register
              ; (res=0, STCL=1, SEL1/SEL0=01)
```

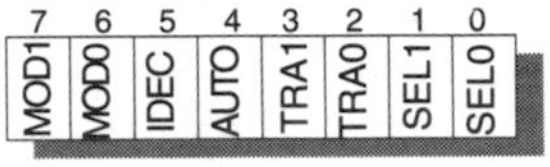


```
MOD1, MOD0: mode select
        00=demand    01=single    10=block    11=cascade
IDEC:   address increment/address decrement
        0=increment           1=decrement
AUTO:   autoinitialization
        0=inactive            1=active
TRA1, TRA0: transfer mode (invalid if MOD1,MOD0=11)
        00=verify    01=write    10=read    11=invalid
SEL1, SEL0: channel select
        00=channel 0/4    01=channel 1/5    10=channel 2/6    11=channel 3/7
```

Figure 25.14: Mode register (0bh, d6h).

With the mode register (Figure 25.14) you may set the operation mode and the transfer type of an 8237A channel. Bits *MOD1, MOD0* define the operation mode of the channel concerned; demand, single and block transfer as well as cascading are available, though in cascading mode the following bits are of no meaning. With *IDEC* you can define whether the address register is to be increased or decreased after each data transfer. *AUTO* activates or disables the autoinitialization of the 8237A for one channel. If you haven't selected cascading mode by means of MOD1, MOD0, then you must now define the transfer mode with *TRA1, TRA0. SEL1, SEL0* determine the 8237A channel for which the definitions by means of bits 7–2 hold.

Example: `Configure channel 2 of DMA 2.`

```
MOV d6h, b6h  ; load 1011 0110b into mode register of DMA 2
              ; mode: block transfer, address decrementing, autoinitialization: enabled
              ; transfer mode: write (peripheral → memory), channel: 2
```

As already mentioned, you have the option of masking or releasing several channels all at once using the mask register (Figure 25.15). Bits *STC3–STC0* indicate whether the corresponding mask bit is set and whether the DMA request for the channels concerned is masked, or whether the mask bit is cleared and the channel released.

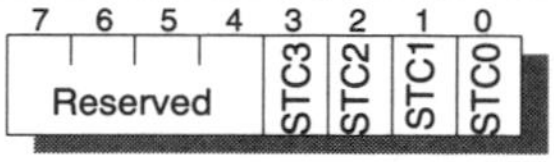

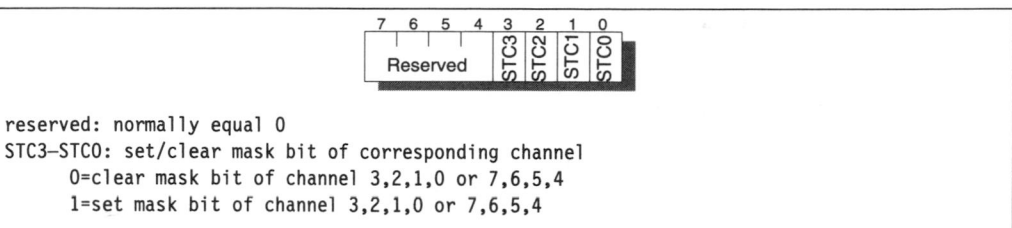

```
reserved: normally equal 0
STC3–STC0: set/clear mask bit of corresponding channel
      0=clear mask bit of channel 3,2,1,0 or 7,6,5,4
      1=set mask bit of channel 3,2,1,0 or 7,6,5,4
```

Figure 25.15: Mask register (0fh, deh).

Example: `Release channels 0 and 1 of DMA 1, mask channels 2 and 3.`

```
MOV 0fh, 0ch  ; write 00001100b into mask register
              ; (res=0, STC3=1, STC2=1, STC1=0, STC0=0)
```

The 8237A implements three additional commands, but they are programmed as an output to a register. This means that you have to execute an OUT command with any data byte to the corresponding address to issue the command. By decoding the address bits A0–A3, the 8237A recognizes that a command and not a data write to a register has occurred. The data byte passed by the OUT instruction is ignored. Table 25.3 lists the three additional commands.

DMA 1[1]	DMA 2[2]	Command
0ch	d8h	reset flip-flop
0dh	dah	master clear
0eh	dch	clear mask register

[1] master in PC/XT, slave in AT
[2] master in AT

Table 25.3: DMA commands

You need the command *reset flip-flop* to reset the internal flip-flop in the 8237A if you want to write to a 16-bit register. Afterwards, you pass the low order and then the high order data byte. Without the command the flip-flop may be in an unpredictable state, and low- and high-order data bytes are possibly interchanged.

Example: `Reset flip-flop of DMA 1.`

```
OUT d8h, al        ; output any value to port d8h
                   ; → command "reset flip-flop" executed
```

The *master clear* command has the same effect as a hardware reset of the 8237A. Command, status, request and temporary registers are cleared, and the flip-flop is reset.

Example: `Reset DMA 1 with master clear.`

```
OUT 0dh, al       ; output any value to port 0dh
                  ; → command "master clear" executed
new_init          ; reinitialize DMA 1 now
```

The *clear mask register* command clears the mask bits of all four channels in the 8237A, and all channels are released for accepting DMA requests.

Example: `Release mask bits in DMA 2.`

```
OUT dch, al          ; output any value to port dch
                     ; → command "clear mask register" executed
```

The above listed control registers control the operation of the 8237A. To carry out one concrete DMA transfer you must additionally initialize the address, count value and DMA page registers with appropriate values. Table 25.4 lists the I/O addresses of the address and count registers for chips DMA 1 and DMA 2.

DMA 1[1]	DMA 2[2]	Register name
00h	c0h	address register channel 0/4
01h	c1h	count register channel 0/4
02h	c2h	address register channel 1/5
03h	c3h	count register channel 1/5
04h	c4h	address register channel 2/6
05h	c5h	count register channel 2/6
06h	c6h	address register channel 3/7
07h	c7h	count register channel 3/7

[1] master in PC/XT, slave in AT
[2] master in AT

Table 25.4: Address and count register I/O addresses

Note that only the AT has two cascaded DMA chips. The PC/XT has only a DMA 1. Before you write one of these 16-bit registers you first need to reset the internal flip-flop by means of the *reset flip-flop* command.

Example: `Set address register of channel 6 to 1080h and write count value 0100h into the corresponding count register.`

```
OUT d8h, al          ; output any value to port d8h
                     ; → command "reset flip-flop" executed
OUT c4h, 80h         ; output low-order address byte to channel 6 of DMA 2
OUT c4h, 10h         ; output high-order address byte to channel 6 of DMA 2
OUT d8h, al          ; output any value to port d8h
                     ; → command "reset flip-flop" executed again
OUT c5h, 00h         ; output low-order counter byte to channel 6 of DMA 2
OUT c4h, 01h         ; output high-order counter byte to channel 6 of DMA 2
```

For completely initializing a DMA transfer you must additionally load the page register of the channel concerned with the page address of the source and destination in the main memory. Table 25.5 lists the I/O addresses of the page registers.

Note that in the PC/XT channels 0 and 1 are assigned the same physical page register. Therefore, you access the same physical register via the two different I/O addresses 87h and 83h. On the AT the page register for channel 4 – which is used for cascading – is the page address for memory refresh.

Port	Page register	Port	Page register
87h	channel 0	8fh	channel 4 (refresh)
83h	channel 1*)	8bh	channel 5
81h	channel 2	89h	channel 6
82h	channel 3	8ah	channel 7

*) PC/XT only: simultaneously channel 0

Table 25.5: Page register I/O addresses

25.2.4 Example: Initialize DMA 1, Channel 2 for Floppy Data Transfer

The following program example initializes channel 2 of DMA 1 for a write transfer to transfer one floppy disk sector with 512 bytes from the controller into main memory. The segment and offset of the read buffer are passed in the registers ES:BX. A check whether a DMA segment overflow might occur is not carried out. The DMA transfer is initiated by a DREQ2 from the floppy disk controller. The program code can be part of a routine by which the CPU drives the floppy controller to transfer one sector with a read command. If several sectors are to be transferred in succession, then the value in the count registers must be increased accordingly.

```
;************************************************************************************
;** ES: buffer segment      ssss ssss ssss ssss                                    **
;** BX: buffer offset       oooo oooo oooo oooo                                    **
;**                                                                                **
;** base address:      ssss ssss ssss ssss 0000                                    **
;**                  +      oooo oooo oooo oooo                                    **
;**                 ______________________________                                 **
;**                    pppp hhhh hhhh 1111 1111                                    **
;**                                                                                **
;** pppp: entry for the DMA page register                                          **
;** hhhh hhhh: high order byte for the DMA address register                        **
;** 1111 1111: low-order byte for the DMA address register                         **
;************************************************************************************

dma1_disable:       ; disable DMA 1
OUT 08h, 14h        ; output 0001 0100b to command register to disable and initialize the 8237A
                    ; (DACK: active low, DRQ: active high, late write, priority: fixed,
                    ; clocking: normal, controller: disabled, address hold: disabled,
                    ; memory-memory: disabled)

mode:               ; set up DMA mode for channel 2
OUT 0bh, 56h        ; output 0101 0110b to mode register
                    ; (mode: single transfer, address incrementation, no autoinitialization,
                    ; transfer mode: write, channel: 2)

split_address:      ; split address in ES:BX into pppp hhhh hhhh 1111 1111
```

```
MOV ax, es           ; load segment ssss ssss ssss ssss of read buffer into ax
MOV cl, 04h          ; load count value into cl
SHL ax, cl           ; shift left four times → result ssss ssss ssss 0000
ADD ax, bx           ; add offset → ax contains hhhh hhhh llll llll
JC carry             ; carry is set → jump to carry

no_carry:
MOV bx, es           ; load segment ssss ssss ssss ssss of read buffer into bx
MOV cl, 04h          ; load count value into cl
SHR bh, cl           ; shift right bh four times → bh contains
                     ; high-order bits ssss of buffer segment as pppp
JMP buffer_address ; proceed with output of buffer address

carry:
MOV bx, es           ; load segment ssss ssss ssss ssss of read buffer into bx
MOV cl, 04h          ; load count value into cl
SHR bh, cl           ; shift right bh four times → bh contains high-order bits ssss
                     ; of buffer segment
ADC bh, 00h          ; add carry

buffer_address:      ; output address to 8237A and page register
OUT 0ch, al          ; reset flip-flop
OUT 04h, al          ; output low-order address byte nnnn nnnn to address register
MOV al, ah           ; load high-order address byte hhhh hhhh into al
OUT 04h, al          ; output high-order address byte hhhh hhhh to address register
MOV al, bh           ; load page value pppp into al
OUT 81h, bh          ; load page register with pppp

count_value:         ; load count register with value 511 → 512 bytes are transferred
OUT 0ch, al          ; reset flip-flop
OUT 05h, ffh         ; load low-order byte 255 of count value into count register
OUT 05h, 01h         ; load high-order byte 1 of count value into count register

channel_unmask:      ; release eventual channel masking
OUT 0ah, 02h         ; output 0000 0010b → release channel 2

dma1_enable:         ; enable DMA 1
OUT 08h, 10h         ; output 0001 0000b to command register to enable 8237A again
                     ; (DACK: active-low, DRQ: active-high, late write, priority: fixed
                     ; clocking: normal, controller: enabled, address hold: disabled,
                     ; memory-memory: disabled)
```

Alternatively, you may also mask only the channel concerned of the first DMA controller 1. All other channels remain enabled during the initialization of channel 2. Some 386 memory drivers need one or more DMA channels of the first DMA controller to access extended memory. Masking the controller, especially for a longer time period, may lead to the crash of these drivers.

25.2.5 DMA Cycles in Protected and Virtual 8086 Mode

If you want to initialize and execute a DMA transfer in protected or even virtual 8086 mode with active paging, you are confronted with many problems; in most cases, the task crashes immediately after the DMA transfer. The addresses that the 8237A, the DMA address latch, and the DMA page register provide are physical addresses. If you try to load one of these registers with a segment descriptor, the address points somewhere, but certainly not to the intended location. In virtual 8086 mode the situation doesn't get any better. Even if you succeed in eliciting the linear address from the segment descriptor, this doesn't help if paging is active. The linear address is completely replaced by the paging mechanism and the page concerned will possibly have been swapped by the operating system a long time before. The DMA controller realizes nothing, of course, as it is only running in a real mode and doesn't understand the CPU's segmentation and paging mechanisms.

In the environment of a protected mode operating system or virtual 8086 monitor, application programs have no chance of initiating a DMA transfer on their own. This is the job of the operating system only. All attempts to write the DMA registers by OUT instructions are intercepted by an exception if the IOPL flag isn't privileged enough, or the I/O port is protected by means of the I/O permission bit map. A DMA transfer is not a trivial job, especially when paging is enabled, even for the operating system or the virtual 8086 monitor, as the DMA controller overwrites the physical memory contents mercilessly without any care for the protection mechanisms of the protected mode. Therefore an incorrectly initialized DMA chip may overwrite protected memory locations even in protected mode. This inevitably gives rise to a crash of the task concerned immediately, or of the complete computer system.

26 Other Peripheral Chips and Components

In addition to those support chips already discussed which carry out major tasks in a Personal Computer (a PC without an interrupt controller is unthinkable), there are some other components. These are, for example, the speaker, the PPI 8255 (this chip is frequently installed on multi-I/O adapters for driving external devices), and the CMOS RAM as the long-term memory of your PC.

26.1 About Tones and Sounds – The Speaker

During the course of each boot process, your PC outputs (hopefully) a good-tempered beep to signal that everything is OK. The installed speaker can also provide tones of various frequencies and duration, from a short glottal stop to a continuous nerve-racking squealing tone. In the following sections the two principal possibilities for driving the speaker and playing tone sequences in the background independently of the CPU are discussed. The key for operating the speaker is counter 2 of the 8253/8254 timer chip (see Chapter 24), as well as bits 0 and 1 of port B in the 8255 PPI chip (see Section 26.2). Figure 26.1 shows a diagram of the connections between PIT, port B and the speaker.

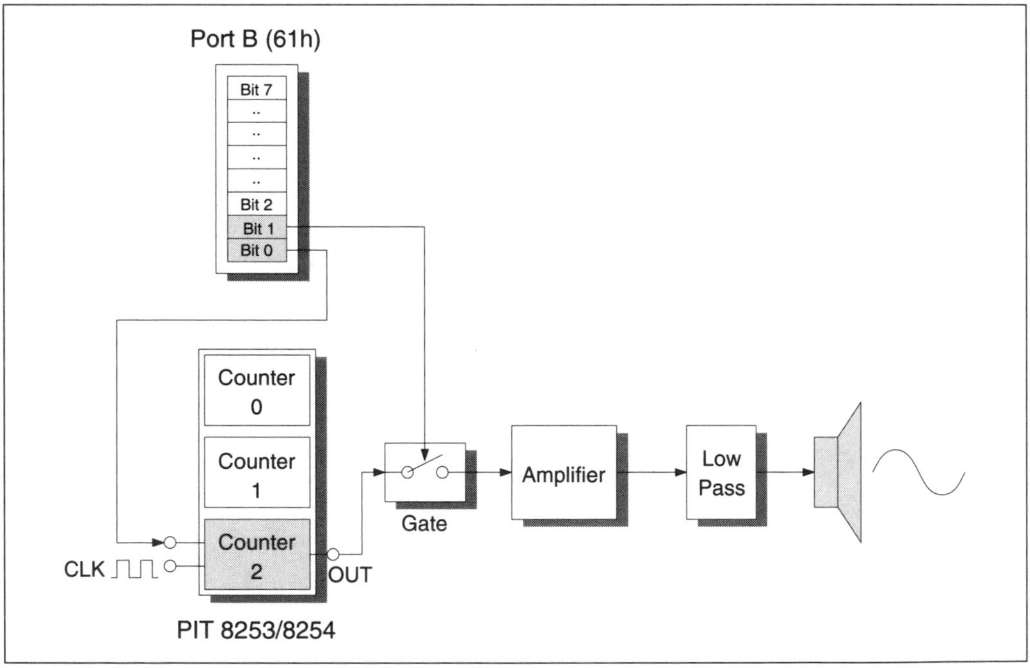

Figure 26.1: PIT, port B and speaker. Bit 0 of Port B controls the GATE input of counter 2, and bit 1 the gate that transmits the clock signal from counter 2 to the speaker.

To generate a stable tone, the output OUT of counter 2 in the 8253/8254 PIT is connected via a gate to the amplifier that drives the speaker. The low-pass filter suppresses the tones that are too high for the speaker. Like all other clock signal inputs, the PIT's CLK2 input is also connected to the 1.19318 MHz oscillator. To generate a tone, two possibilities are now available:

- directly driving the speaker by means of counter 2 in the 8253/8254;
- periodic activation of the amplifier with the CPU.

The first possibility is better and more direct, as the PIT carries out tone generation without any intervention from the CPU. The processor is only needed to set the tone frequency and to activate or disable the speaker. Thus the processor is free to do other jobs while the speaker is generating a tone. But don't demand high standards from the tone quality of the speaker; neither the installed amplifier nor the speaker belong to the HiFi class! For generating tones and the sounds of various instruments, synthesizer adapters (especially for multimedia applications) are now available on the market.

The audible range of tones lies between about 16 Hz and 16 kHz. Frequencies above and below this range are called infra- or supersonic: Your PC's amplifier is probably unable to generate such tones. The basis for the music scale is the so-called concert pitch A, with a frequency of 440 Hz. The scale of all octaves is deduced from this single concert pitch A. The tone A of the next lowest or next highest octave has half or twice the frequency. This applies analogously to all other tones. Table 26.1 lists the frequencies for all twelve half tones of the eight octaves. Only very modern composers use tones that are beyond the 8th octave.

Tone	Octave 1	Octave 2	Octave 3	Octave 4	Octave 5	Octave 6	Octave 7	Octave 8
C	16.4	32.7	65.4	130.8	261.6	523.3	1046.5	2093.0
C#	17.3	34.7	69.3	138.6	277.2	554.4	1108.8	2217.5
D	18.4	36.7	73.4	146.8	293.7	587.3	1174.7	2349.3
D#	19.5	38.9	77.8	155.6	311.1	622.3	1244.5	2489.0
E	20.6	41.2	82.4	164.8	329.6	659.3	1328.5	2637.0
F	21.8	43.6	87.3	174.6	349.2	698.5	1396.9	2793.8
F#	23.1	46.3	92.5	185.0	370.0	740.0	1480.0	2960.0
G	24.5	49.0	98.0	196.0	392.0	784.0	1568.0	3136.0
G#	26.0	51.9	103.8	207.7	415.3	830.6	1661.2	3322.4
A	27.5	55.0	110.0	220.0	440.0	880.0	1760.0	3520.0
A#	29.1	58.3	116.5	233.1	466.2	923.3	1864.7	3729.3
B	30.9	61.7	123.5	247.0	493.9	987.8	1975.5	3951.1

Table 26.1: The eight octaves of music

Music scale and octaves are based on the geometric mean, that is, the frequency of each tone is the geometric mean of the adjacent tones in the row as well as column directions. For example, concert pitch A: frequency 440 Hz; adjacent tones 220 Hz, 880 Hz and 415.3 Hz, 466.16 Hz; geometric mean in both cases $\sqrt{(220*880)}=\sqrt{(415.3*466.16)}=440$ Hz. Stated differently, from one octave to another the frequencies increase by a factor of two, and within the same octave by a factor of $12\sqrt{(2)}=1.05946$. All tones are thus defined unambiguously. Of course, there are also tones of other frequencies, but an orchestra working with such tones sounds out of tune (or like

Stockhausen!) After this short journey into the higher spheres of music, let's now turn back to the programming of our trivial PC speaker.

26.1.1 Direct Activation via the 8253/8254 PIT

For generating a tone only PIT mode 3 is applicable, that is, the timer chip generates a periodic square-wave signal. The other periodic mode 2 is not suitable as it only generates peak pulses with a width of 0.838 μs. The membrane of the speaker cannot follow this fast pulse, and the speaker remains quiet. To generate a square wave with the intended frequency you must put the PIT into counting mode 3 using a control word, and write one or two counter bytes afterwards. Note that the initial count value acts as a divisor, that is, the higher the value the lower the generated frequency.

Example: `Counter 2 shall generate a square wave of 440 Hz; thus the counter value (equal divisor) is 1,193,180 Hz/440 Hz = 2712.`

```
MOV al, 10110110b ; counter 2, low-order and high-order counter byte, mode 3, binary counting
out 43h, al       ; write control register
mov al, 152       ; transfer low-order counter byte into al
out 42h, al       ; output low-order counter byte
mov al, 10        ; transfer high-order counter byte into al
out 42h, al       ; output high-order counter byte
                  ; now counter 2 generates a square-wave signal with 440Hz
```

Even if you generate a square-wave signal with the exact frequency of the concert pitch A (440 Hz), the result sounds somewhat different. Table 26.1 refers to pure sine oscillations; but the square wave with 440 Hz also contains, besides the 440 Hz sine signal, many other frequencies of various intensities. We as humans mainly perceive the strongest component (thus the 440 Hz), but the other additions appear as the tone «colour». Depending upon the instrument (violin, saxophone, PC speaker), the frequency and intensity of the additional tones are different, and actually characterize the sound of an instrument. Synthesizers and electronic organs use this effect to imitate various instruments by emphasizing certain additional tones.

With our PIT we are unfortunately limited to the generation of a simple tone. To cause the 8253/8254 to count in mode 3, the GATE input must be at a high level. For this purpose, bit 0 in port B of the 8255 chip is used. Port B can be accessed by port address 61h. If the value of this bit is equal to 1, then a high-level signal is applied to GATE2 and the PIT is enabled, otherwise a low-level signal is supplied and the counter is stopped. But activating the GATE input is not sufficient; a further gate is connected between PIT and the amplifier, controlled by bit 1 of port B. Only if this bit is equal to 1 is the square wave signal actually transmitted from counter 2 of the 8253/8254 to the amplifier, which in turn drives the speaker.

To generate a tone you therefore have to carry out the following steps:

- operate counter 2 of the 8253/8254 in mode 3 with the intended frequency;
- activate the GATE input of counter 2 by means of a set bit 0 in port B (port address 61h); and
- turn on the gate by means of a set bit 1 in port B.

Example: To cause the speaker to actually output the 440 Hz tone in the above-indicated example, bits 0 and 1 in port B must additionally be set.

```
IN al, 61h        ; read old value of port B first
OR  al, 00000011b ; set bits 0 and 1, bits 2 to 7 remain unchanged
OUT 61h, al       ; output byte with set bits 0 and 1 to port B
```

Now the speaker constantly outputs a tone with a frequency of 440 Hz. The tone generation is carried out without any intervention of the CPU. You may call another program, but the speaker goes on sounding. A remedy is not possible until you reach the next example.

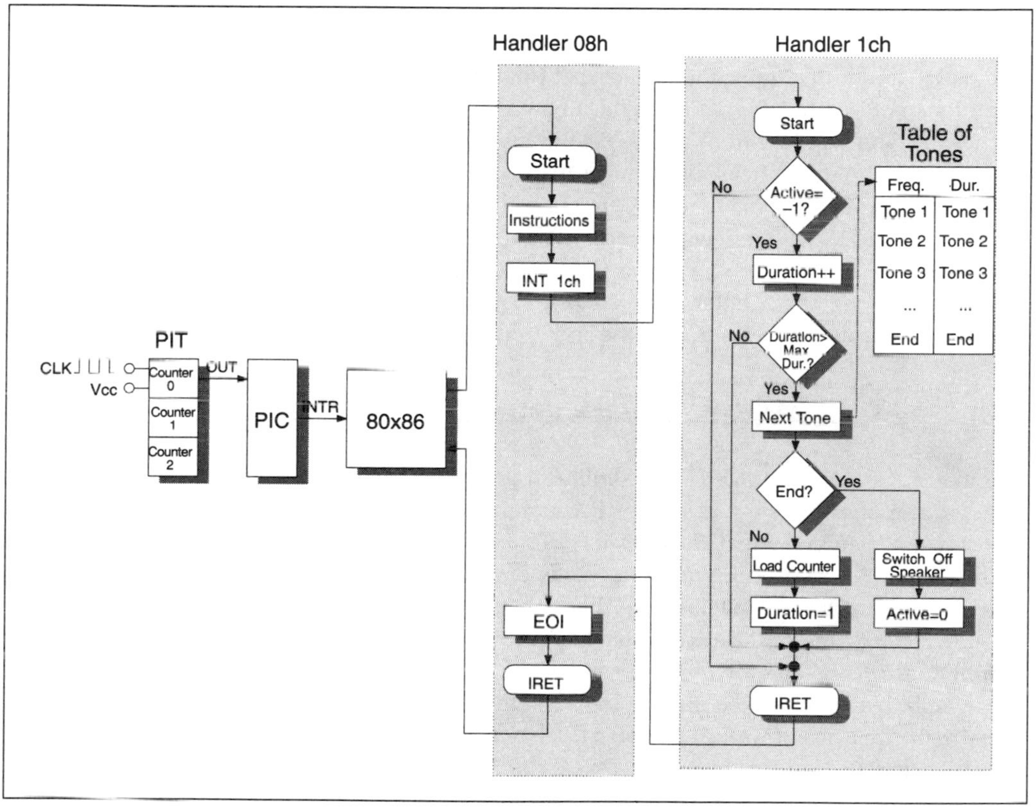

Figure 26.2: Tone sequences in the background.

If you set only bit 0 in port B, but not bit 1, then the PIT generates the intended square-wave signal but this is not transmitted to the amplifier and the speaker remains quiet. However, if you have set bit 1 in port B but not bit 0, then the gate is turned on but there is no signal from the PIT and the speaker again remains quiet. You may load the PIT with a new count value at any time, and the speaker then outputs a tone with an accordingly altered frequency.

Example: Switch off the speaker.

```
IN al, 61h          ; read old value of port B first
AND al, 11111100b ; clear bits 0 and 1, bits 2 to 7 remain unchanged
OUT 61h, al         ; output byte with cleared bits 0 and 1 to port B, speaker is switched off
To make the speaker quiet it is sufficient to clear one of the two bits 0 and 1.
```

In connection with the user exit 1ch of the periodic timer interrupt, the tone generation via the PIT is particularly powerful. Long tone sequences with tones of various durations can be played in the background while the CPU is executing another program. To achieve this a new handler for interrupt 1ch is required, which is called 18.2 times per second. Figure 26.2 shows a scheme for this.

The new handler determines with each call (that is, every 55 ms) whether the currently generated tone is to be terminated and which new tone the speaker needs to output. The handler fetches the data required from a table held in memory, where the frequencies and the duration (as the number of timer ticks) of the tones to be output are stored. Thus the CPU is taken up for a short time only every 55 ms to determine the end of the currently output tone, and to reprogram the PIT with a new frequency. The rest of the time it can process other tasks. If the stored table is extensive enough, the PC may play a complete symphony in the background while you are writing a letter, for example. Commands such as PLAY in BASIC use such a strategy to output tone sequences in the background.

26.1.2 Periodic Activation by the CPU

Another but not very powerful possibility to generate tones is the periodic activation of the speaker amplifier by the CPU. Even if counter 2 in the 8253/8254 PIT is not operating, or possibly not even in mode 3, the output OUT2 provides a voltage. This can be on a low (0 V) or high level (+5 V), depending upon the mode or signal at the GATE input. If you transmit this voltage to the amplifier via the gate that is turned on by means of bit 1 of port B, then the amplifier drives the speaker. As the signal provided by the counter is constant in time, the amplifier also generates a constant output signal. The speaker's magnet pulls or pushes away the membrane according to the polarity of the output signal. Afterwards, the membrane remains in this position until the signal from the amplifier is switched off. The membrane shoots back to the rest location.

If the amplifier turning on and off is repeated within short time intervals, the speaker outputs a tone with the frequency of this turning on and off. In other words, you may generate a tone with a certain frequency by setting and clearing bit 1 in port B in the phase of this frequency.

Example: Generate a tone by turning on and off the amplifier; program tone.c: called by "tone <count>".

```
main(argc, argv)
int argc;
char *argv;

{ int i, count;
```

```
  count=atoi(argv[1]);       /* determine passed count value */

  while (!kbhit()) {         /* keyboard hit terminates tone generation */
                             /* enable amplifier */
    i=inp(0x61);             /* read old byte from port B */
    i=i | 0x02;              /* set bit 1 */
    outp(0x61,i);            /* write byte with set bit 1 to port B */

    for (i=0;i<count;i++);   /* wait for count loops */
                             /* disable amplifier */
    i=inp(0x61);             /* read old byte from port B */
    i=i & 0xfd;              /* clear bit 1 */
    outp(0x61,i);            /* write byte with cleared bit 1 to port B */
  }

  getch();
  exit(0);
}
```

The disadvantages of this method are obvious. First, the CPU is permanently occupied by the tone generation, thus speaker operation in the background is impossible. Second, the frequency of the generated tone cannot be set up precisely as the clock frequency of the CPU is different in different PCs, and the CPU may be interrupted unpredictably by interrupts. To add a «click» to keyboards without such an in-built mechanical sound (as, for example, the Compaq keyboards), some manufacturers employ a similar method. If you are pressing a key you issue a hardware interrupt 09h whose handler fetches the character according to the depressed key into the keyboard buffer. Moreover, the handler may set bit 1 in port B for a short time. You perceive the speaker's turning on and off as a short click. The advantage compared to normal «click», keyboards is that you hear a click only if a character is actually passed. Older keyboards which have been in use for a long time may very often click without closing a corresponding contact in the scan matrix and passing a character to the PC's keyboard interface.

Example: `Click on keyboard hit; keyb_echo.c generates a click sound upon every key hit.`

```
main()

{ int i;

  for (;;) {
    while (!kbhit());        /* click tone upon keyboard hit */
    getch();                 /* abort when Ctrl-C or Ctrl-Break */

    i=inp(0x61);             /* enable amplifier */
    i=i | 0x02;              /* by setting bit 1 */
    outp(0x61,i);            /* in port B */

    for (i=0;i<50;i++);      /* wait for 50 loops */

    i=inp(0x61);             /* disable amplifier */
    i=i & 0xfc;              /* by clearing bit 1 */
    outp(0x61,i);            /* in port B */
  }
  exit(0);
}
```

26.2 The 8255 Programmable Peripheral Interface

The 8255 PPI chip is only present in the PC/XT to establish a connection between CPU and various other components, such as the keyboard, the DIP switches for the configuration settings, and the NMI mask register.

26.2.1 PPI 8255 Terminals and Signals

The 8255 has 24 I/O pins in all, divided into three groups of eight pins each. The groups are denoted by port A, port B and port C, respectively. The PPI usually comes in a 40-pin DIP or 44-pin PLCC package. Figure 26.3 shows the pin assignment scheme of the 8255.

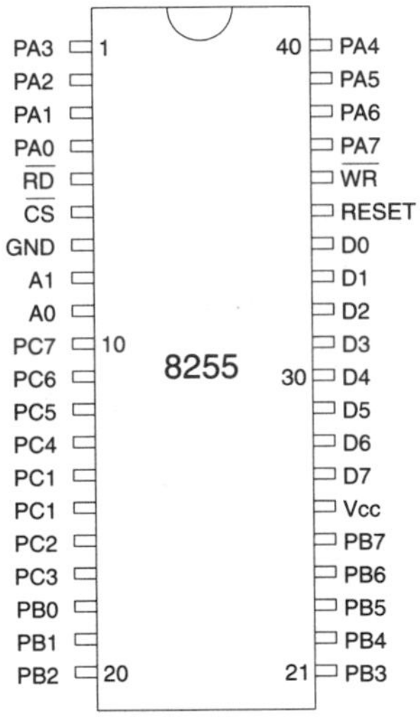

Figure 26.3: PPI 8255 connections.

A1–A0 (I)
Pins 8, 9

The address signals at these pins, together with $\overline{RD}$ and $\overline{WR}$, select one of the three ports of the control word register. The possible combinations of (A1 A0 $\overline{RD}$ $\overline{WR}$) have the following meanings:

```
(0001)  port A → data bus (read)
(0101)  port B → data bus (read)
(1001)  port C → data bus (read)
(1101)  control word → data bus (read)
(0010)  data bus → port A (write)
(0110)  data bus → port B (write)
(1010)  data bus → port C (write)
(1110)  data bus → control word (write)
```

$\overline{\text{CS}}$ (I)
Pin 6
If this chip select pin is at a low level, the CPU can read data from or write data to the internal 8255 registers, or access the I/O pins of the ports A, B and C by the $\overline{\text{RD}}$ and $\overline{\text{WR}}$ signals. Thus the $\overline{\text{CS}}$ signal enables the PPI for read and write processes.

D7–D0 (I/O)
Pins 27–34
These eight connections form the bidirectional data bus through which the 8255 receives data and commands from or outputs them to the CPU.

PA7–PA0 (I/O)
Pins 37–40, 1–4
These eight pins form port A. The lines lead to a data output latch/buffer and a data input latch, which are each eight bits wide.

PB7–PB0 (I/O)
Pins 25–18
These eight pins form port B. The lines lead to a data output latch/buffer and a data input buffer, which are each eight bits wide.

PC7–PC4 (I/O)
Pins 10–13
These four pins form the high-order nibble of port C. The lines lead to a data output latch/buffer and a data input buffer, which are each four bits wide.

PC3–PC0 (I/O)
Pins 17–14
These four pins form the low-order nibble of port C. The lines lead to a data output latch/buffer and a data input buffer, which are each four bits wide.

$\overline{\text{RD}}$ (I)
Pin 5
If the signal at this read pin is at a low level, the CPU can read data from the 8255 PPI via the data bus D0–D7.

RESET (I)
Pin 35
If the signal at this pin is at a high-level, the control register is cleared and the pins of all ports attain a level «1» (high).

$\overline{\text{WR}}$ (I)
Pin 36
If the signal at this write pin is at a low level, the CPU can write data into internal 8255 registers via the data bus D0–D7.

Vcc
Pin 26
This pin is supplied with the supply voltage (usually +5 V).

GND
Pin 7
This pin is grounded (usually 0 V).

26.2.2 8255 PPI Structure and Operating Modes

As the name PPI already indicates, the 8255 is programmable in three different modes:

- mode 0: simple unidirectional input/output without handshake;
- mode 1: unidirectional input/output with handshake via a nibble of port C;
- mode 2: bidirectional input/output via port A with handshake via the high-order nibble of port C.

Thus a very flexible chip for I/O purposes is available for computer designers. Figure 26.4 shows a diagram of its internal structure.

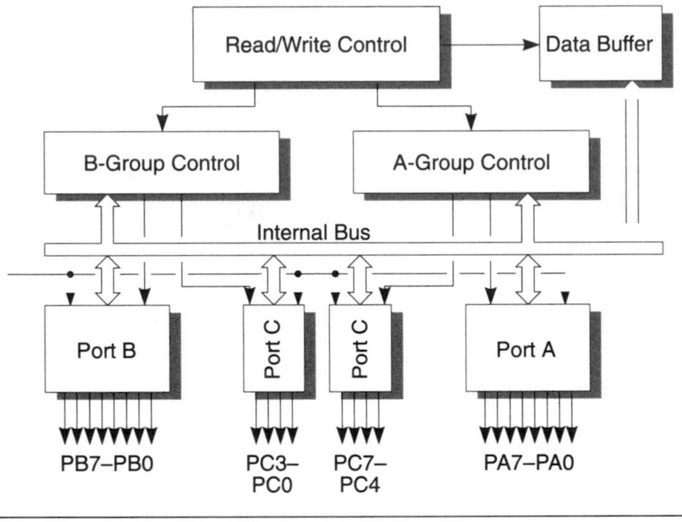

Figure 26.4: 8255 internal structure. The 8255 PPI has three ports A to C which can be programmed individually.

Ports A, B and C are combined into two groups A and B. For this purpose, port C is divided into two sections, a high-order nibble PC7–PC4 and a low-order nibble PC3–PC0. The A-group controls the eight I/O pins PA7–PA0 of port A, as well as the four high-order pins PC7–PC4 of port C; the B-group controls the eight I/O pins PB7–PB0 of port B and the four low-order pins PC3–PC0 of port C.

Port A has an 8-bit data output latch/buffer and an 8-bit input latch/buffer; port B has a data input/output latch/buffer; and port C an 8-bit output latch/buffer, as well as an 8-bit input buffer. Port C doesn't have a latch for the input. It can be divided into two 4-bit ports, which may be used for outputting control signals and inputting status information for ports A and B.

Ports A, B and C may be operated separately or in the A and B combination with the high- and low-order nibble of port C, respectively. For example, port A can be programmed for a bidirectional input and output of data to a controller with handshake and interrupt-driven data exchange, while port B in mode 0 only observes the switching states of simple DIP switches. If you change the mode of a port then the output register of the pins concerned is reset to «1». The following briefly discusses the three modes.

Mode 0

Depending upon the programming for input or output, the data is simply read from or written to the port concerned. In this mode ports A and B, as well as the high- and low-order nibbles of port C, can be defined independently as input or output pins. Thus, the 8255 has two 8-bit and two 4-bit ports in this mode. In the PC/XT all three ports are operated in mode 0.

Mode 1

The data may be input or output in cooperation with handshake signals. In mode 1 ports A and B use the pins of port C to output the handshake signals. Ports A and B are themselves employed for the input and output of 8-bit data. Pins PC3 and PC0 provide interrupt request signals for ports A and B, respectively, if corresponding handshake signals have been received. An interrupt-driven data exchange can thus be realized with mode 1. As this 8255 capability is not used in the PC/XT and a description is only of interest for hardware developers, this mode 1 option is not described in further detail here. We shall meet interrupt-driven data exchange with handshake signals in connection with the serial and parallel interface.

Mode 2

Mode 2 is only available for Port A together with the high-order nibble of port C. In mode 2 data may be input and output; a bidirectional transfer takes place. The direction of the data flow must be inverted in certain circumstances. This is carried out by means of handshake signals, as is the case with mode 1. Further, the 8255 can also provide an interrupt request signal in mode 2 to issue a hardware interrupt. By means of mode 2, a very complex bidirectional data exchange can be realized.

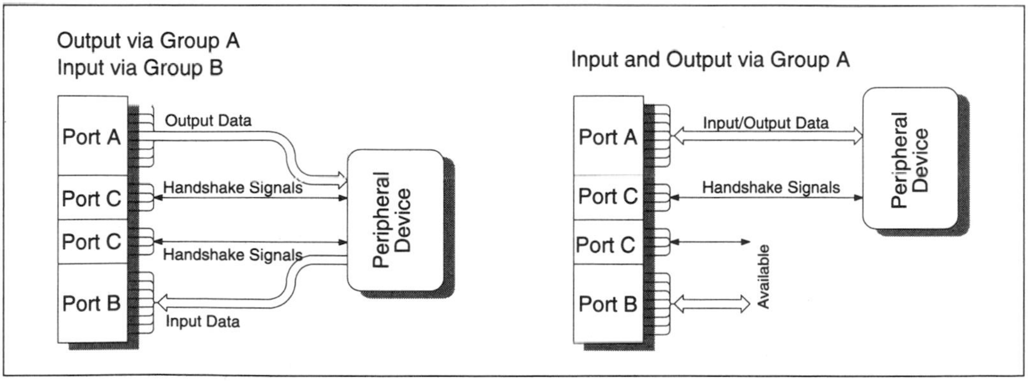

Figure 26.5: Duplex connection with an 8255.

One feature of the 8255 is its capability to combine modes 0, 1 and 2 for different ports. For example, you can program groups A and B in mode 1 for output and input, respectively, and connect them to the same peripheral (Figure 26.5). Thus, you get a duplex connection between the 8255 and the peripheral. Of course, you may also realize such a bidirectional connection with port A in mode 2, but here the transfer direction must be switched according to the requirements. As a compensation, port B is available for another application.

26.2.3 Programming the 8255 PPI

Mode programming of the individual ports is carried out with a control word. You can access the control word register in the PC/XT at the port address 63h, and the three ports A, B and C with the port addresses 60h, 61h and 62h, respectively.

The ports programmed for output may be written by a simple OUT or read by an IN instruction. On the other hand, all ports programmed for input can only be read, not written. All write attempts to these ports are ignored.

Example: `Read port B.`

```
IN al, 61h  ; read port B into accumulator al
```

Example: `Write port A.`

```
MOV al, byte_value ; transfer byte_value into accumulator al
OUT 60h, al        ; write byte_value into port A; if port A is programmed
                   ; for input only then byte_value is ignored
```

For port C you have the option to set bits (and thus pins) individually to «1», or to reset to «0» by means of a control word. Also, in this case, the write commands via the control words are ignored if the port concerned is programmed for input only. Figure 26.6 shows the format of the control word.

A mode control word for setting the operation modes of ports A, B and C comprises a set bit 7 (*D7*) to distinguish this control word from a set or reset command for a single pin of port C. The three low-order bits *D2–D0* refer to the mode of group B, which consists of port B and the low-order nibble of port C. Port B and pins PC3–PC0 can be programmed separately for input or output. As for port B, only modes 0 and 1 are available – the single bit D2 is sufficient for defining the mode.

Bits *D6–D3* concern group A, which is port A and the high-order nibble of port C. Also in this case, port A and pins PC7–PC4 may be separately programmed for input and output. Besides modes 0 and 1, mode 2 with bidirectional data flow is also available for port A. For the determination of the mode, bits D5 and D6 are reserved. You may read or write the control word in the PC/XT via port address 63h. If the control word is read then *D7* is always equal to 1 as it provides mode control word information. You may thus determine the PPI's operating mode.

Example: `Operate all ports in mode 0; use ports A and C for data input, port B for signal output.`

```
OUT 63h, 9ch ; output control word 10011100b
```

Example: `Determine operation mode of ports A, B and C.`

```
IN al, 63h   ; read operation mode byte into accumulator al
```

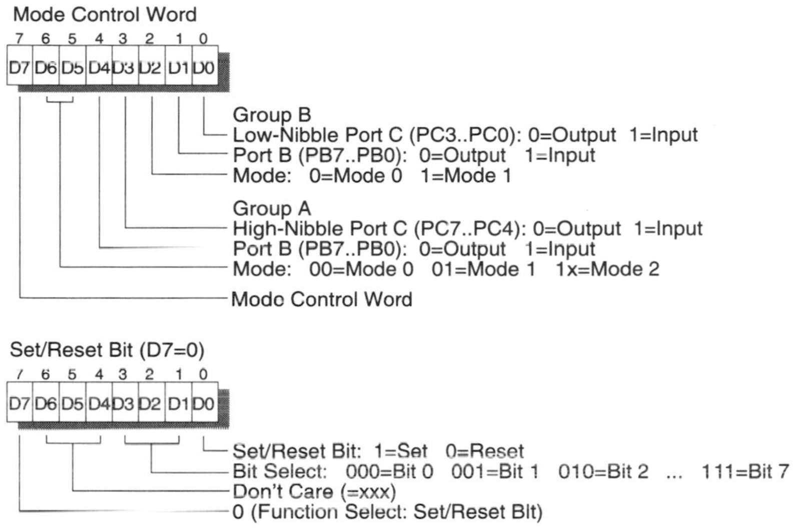

Figure 26.6: 8255 control word format.

If bit D7 in the control word is cleared (that is, equal to 0), the 8255 handles the passed byte as a set or reset command for an individual pin or individual bit of port C. Note that pins and bits can be set or reset only if the nibble to which the bit concerned belongs is operated in output mode by a mode control word; otherwise, the 8255 ignores the command. Bits D3–D1 form a 3-bit number, which defines the bit to set or reset. D0 indicates whether the selected bit is to be set to 1 or reset to 0.

Example: `Set bit 5 corresponding to pin 5 of port C to 1.`

```
OUT 63h, 0bh  ; set bit 5 of port C by means of the control word 00001011b
```

Being able to set individual bits (and therefore pins) of port C is especially useful if port C is used for exchanging handshake signals in modes 1 and 2.

26.2.4 Port Assignment in the PC/XT

The 8255 PPI is used in the PC/XT to establish a connection to various components. The following figures show the port addresses of ports A, B, C and the 8255 control register, as well as the assignment of the ports in the PC/XT. Ports A, B, C may be read by a simple IN instruction and written by means of an OUT instruction if they are programmed for input and output, respectively. In the PC/XT, all three ports are operated in mode 0, that is, unidirectional input/output without handshake. Ports A and C are read-only; port B is write-only.

```
MB:  make/break code
     1=key pressed (make-code)      0=key released (break-code)
Scancode:  scancode of key

FL1, FL0: number of installed floppy drives (if FLP=1)
          00=1 drive        01=2 drives
          10=3 drives       11=4 drives
GR1, GR0: type of primary graphics adapter
          00=adapter with own BIOS (EGA, VGA etc.)
          01=CGA with 40 characters/line   10=CGA with 80 characters/line
          11=monochrome (MDA, Hercules) or several graphics adapters
MM1, MM0: main memory on the motherboard
          00=16kbyte   01=32kbyte    10=48kbyte    11=at least 64kbyte
x87:      Coprocessor 80x87
          1=installed                0=not installed
FLP:      floppy drive
          1=at least one installed   0=none installed
```

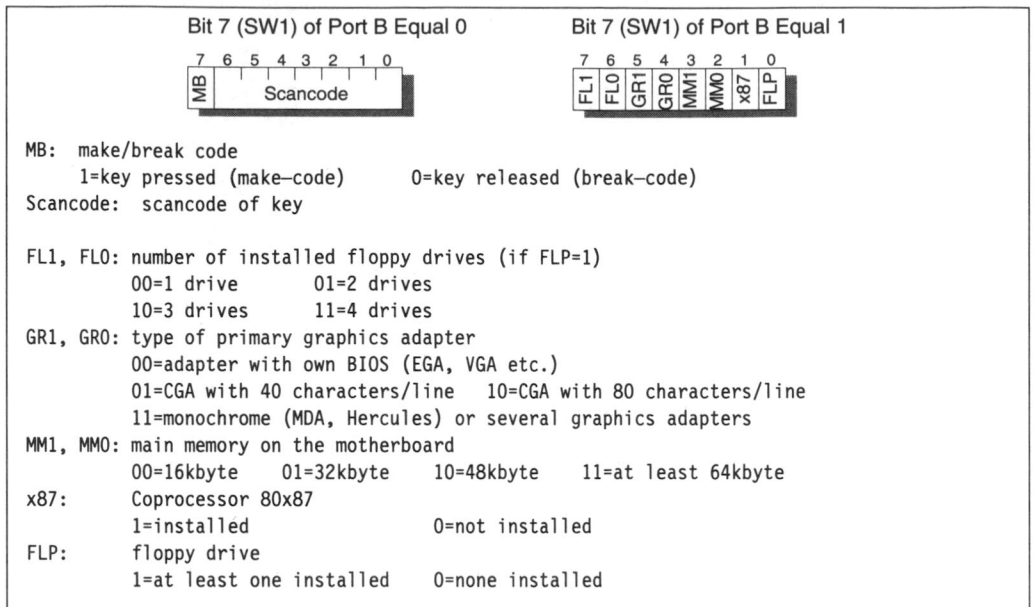

Figure 26.7: Port A (Port address 60h).

Port A has two main functions. If bit 7 of port B is equal to 0, then the keyboard is accessible via port A (Figure 26.7, left). Bit 7, after a keyboard interrupt 09h via IRQ1, indicates whether the key has been depressed (bit 7 equal to 1, «make-code») or released (bit 7 equal to 0, «break-code»), and the seven low-order bits contain the scan code of the key concerned. The keyboard is described in detail in Chapter 31.

If bit 7 of port B is equal to 1, the state of the DIP switches with the configuration settings can be read (Figure 26.7, right). Note that the assignment of port A coincides with the structure of the device byte (20, 14h) in the CMOS RAM. However, the bits *MM1* and *MM0* are reserved there; in port A they indicate the amount of main memory installed on the motherboard. Through bits *MM6–MM2* of port C you may also determine the number of 32 kbyte blocks of main memory on the motherboard installed in addition to the memory indicated by bits MM1 and MM0. Bits *FL1* and *FL0* indicate the number of floppy drives installed if the *FLP* bit is set. Through bits *GR1* and *GR0* you may determine the type of graphics adapter installed. Finally, bit *x87* indicates whether or not a coprocessor is installed.

Example: Determine whether a coprocessor is installed according to the DIP switches (bit SW1 of port B assumed as 1).

```
IN  ah, 60h   ; transfer configuration byte of port A DIP switch to ah
AND ah, 02h   ; check whether bit 1 (x87) is set
```

Note that the values of the port A bits reflect the position of the DIP switches. If the switches are positioned incorrectly, then the bits also indicate an incorrect configuration, of course. The same applies to the CMOS RAM in the AT. The system is unable to determine the configuration on its own, but relies on the configuration settings according to the DIP switches or CMOS RAM during the boot process.

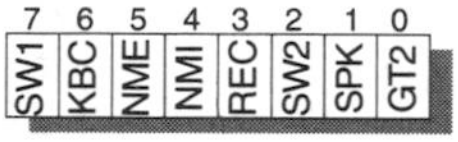


```
SW1:  read configuration switch block SW1 or keyboard byte
      0=read configuration    1=read keyboard byte
KBC:  keyboard clock
      0=disabled              1=enabled
NME:  NMI on error on expansion adapter card
      0=enabled               1=disabled
NMI:  memory parity check of main memory
      0=enabled               1=disabled
REC:  motor of cassette recorder
      0=on                    1=off
SW2:  configuration switch block SW2
      0=read DIP switch 5 via bit 0 of port C
      1=read DIP switches 0 to 3 via bits 0 to 3 of Port C
SPK:  supply counter 2 signal of PIT 8253
      0=to cassette recorder
      1=to speaker (enable speaker)
GT2:  drive counter 2 of PIT 8253
      0=disable counter 2 (GATE2=low)   1=enable counter 2 (GATE2=high)
```

Figure 26.8: Port B (port address 61h).

Port B (Figure 26.8) of the 8255 is programmed in output mode, and controls certain PC/XT registers. As already mentioned, bit *SW1* indicates whether the configuration settings or the keyboard byte can be read via port A. By means of bit *KBC*, you may deactivate or enable the clock signal for the keyboard. The keyboard is locked or released by this. Bits *NME* and *NMI* enable or disable the checking of extension adapters, for example the graphics adapter or the parity check function for main memory. The first PC came with a cassette recorder. By means of *REC* you can control its motor (an anachronism). The *SW2* bit indicates whether DIP switch 5 or DIP switches 0–3 of the second switch block can be read via port C. The *SPK* bit controls whether the output signal of the 8253 counter 2 is supplied to the cassette recorder or the speaker. Finally, the *GT2* drives the GATE input of the second counter in the 8253 PIT to enable or disable its counting function.

Example: `Enable parity checking on the motherboard.`

```
IN  al, 61h  ; transfer byte from port B to al
OR  al, 10h  ; set bit 4 (NMI)
OUT 61h, al  ; transfer byte to port B
```

Like port A, port C (Figure 26.9) is also programmed as an input channel in the PC/XT. The *PAR* and *EXT* bits indicate whether an NMI is issued after a parity error in main memory or an error on an expansion adapter. The handler determines the source of the NMI using these bits and proceeds accordingly. With *TIM* you can read the current state of the output OUT2 of counter 2 in the 8253 timer chip. The *CSR* bit indicates the level of the signal from the cassette recorder.

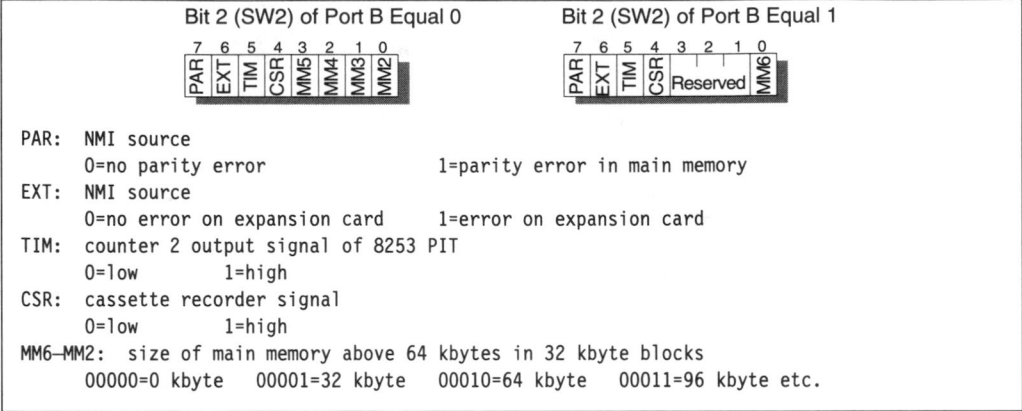

```
PAR:  NMI source
      0=no parity error              1=parity error in main memory
EXT:  NMI source
      0=no error on expansion card    1=error on expansion card
TIM:  counter 2 output signal of 8253 PIT
      0=low        1=high
CSR:  cassette recorder signal
      0=low        1=high
MM6–MM2:  size of main memory above 64 kbytes in 32 kbyte blocks
      00000=0 kbyte   00001=32 kbyte   00010=64 kbyte   00011=96 kbyte etc.
```

Figure 26.9: Port C (port address 62h).

If bit SW2 of port B is cleared, you can read the four low-order bits of a 5-bit number via *MM5–MM2*. If you set bit SW2 of port B then you can read the most significant bit of this number via *MM6*. The 5-bit number MM6–MM2 indicates the memory installed on the motherboard beyond 64 kbytes in 32 kbyte blocks.

26.3 CMOS RAM and Real-Time Clock

The old PC/XTs had several small DIP switches (sometimes mockingly called mice pianos), by means of which the user had to set the configuration of the computer. The configuration information includes the number and type of floppy drives, graphics adapter, base memory, etc. As a PC is a «personal» computer, the configurations can be very different. Because of the nearly infinite number of hard disks with different geometries (number of heads, tracks, sectors) a configuration setting by means of DIP switches is now ruled out. Another big disadvantage was the lack of a real-time clock. After every boot process the PC initialized itself to 1.1.1980, 0:00 o'clock. The user first had to input the current date and time via the DOS commands DATE and TIME. As the first PC was shipped after that date, all PCs (and therefore also DOS, by the way) don't know any earlier time than 1.1.1980, 0:00 o'clock; DOS manages all times relative to this time and date.

IBM recognized this inadequacy and installed a real-time clock as well as CMOS RAM, beginning with the successor to the PC/XT, the AT. These two elements are supplied by an accumulator or an in-built battery once the PC is switched off. Instead of CMOS RAM you will often see the name *NVR* (non volatile RAM). This indicates that the data in this memory is kept even after the power is switched off. The real-time clock is independent of the CPU and all other chips (also the 8253, 8254 PIT for the internal system clock) and keeps on updating the time and date in the background. The CMOS RAM holds the configuration data, which had to be set by means of DIP switches on the PC/XT. The ROM BIOS reads the real-time clock and the CMOS RAM during the boot process, and thus determines the current configuration as well as time and date. The TIME and DATE commands for setting time and date are now obsolete. The CMOS RAM and real-time clock are integrated in a single chip, the Motorola MC146818, or compatible. In most of today's PCs, this chip is already installed on the motherboard (or the processor card in modular machines). With a separate clock adapter card you can also equip an older PC model with this chip. If your computer has a very old BIOS that is not designed for an access to the real-time clock and CMOS RAM, this clock adapter is not very useful. You should replace the ROM or EPROM chips with the old BIOS with a newer version. For buffering, small batteries or accumulators are largely used. Accumulators are usually soldered to the board; batteries are held in a socket. The power consumption by the CMOS RAM and the real-time clock is so low that usually it plays no role in the lifetime of the batteries or accumulators. Instead, the life is determined by the self-discharge time of the accumulator or battery, and is about three years (with lithium batteries up to ten years).

26.3.1 MC146818 Structure and Programming

The accumulator or the battery supplies the following elements with power if the PC is switched off (see Figure 26.10):

- the CMOS RAM with the configuration settings as well as time and date, which are periodically updated by the real-time clock;
- the real-time clock.

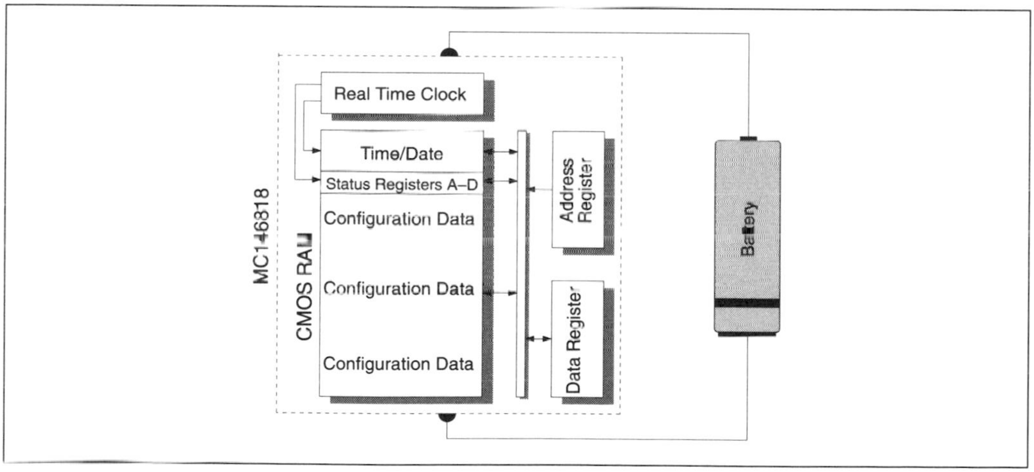

Figure 26.10: Technical structure of the MC146818. The MC146818 has a real-time clock and 64 bytes of battery-buffered RAM. The MC146818 can be programmed by an address and a data register.

The CMOS RAM in the MC146818 usually has 64 individually accessible bytes of memory. Some chips have more than these 64 bytes, especially if the data of an extended setup has to be stored. The meaning of the additional bytes, however, is no longer standardized. Of these 64 bytes, the first 14 (addresses 00h to 0dh) are reserved for the time and date, as well as the control and status registers of the real-time clock. The remaining 50 bytes hold information concerning the PC's configuration. Table 26.2 shows the memory configuration of the CMOS RAM.

Byte	Address	Contents
0	00h	second*)
1	01h	alarm second*)
2	02h	minute*)
3	03h	alarm minute*)
4	04h	hour*)
5	05h	alarm hour*)
6	06h	day of week*)
7	07h	day of month*)
8	08h	month*)
9	09h	year*)
10	0ah	status register A
11	0bh	status register B
12	0ch	status register C
13	0dh	status register D
14	0eh	diagnosis status
15	0fh	shutdown status
16	10h	type of floppy drives
17	11h	reserved
18	12h	type of hard disk drives
19	13h	reserved
20	14h	device byte
21	15h	base memory (low byte)
22	16h	base memory (high byte)
23	17h	extended memory (low byte) according to SETUP
24	18h	extended memory (high byte) according to SETUP
25	19h	extension byte 1st hard disk
26	1ah	extension byte 2nd hard disk
27–31	1bh–1fh	reserved
32–39	20h–27h	parameter hard disk type
40–45	28h–2dh	reserved
46	2eh	check sum (low byte)
47	2fh	check sum (high byte)
48	30h	extended memory (low byte) according to POST
49	31h	extended memory (high byte) according to POST
50	32h	century*)
51	33h	setup informations
52	34h	reserved
53–60	35h–3ch	parameter hard disk type
61–63	3dh–3fh	reserved

*) usually binary coded decimals (1 byte)

Table 26.2: CMOS-RAM memory configuration

Note that all time and date information is usually held as binary coded decimals. You may alter this standard encoding with status register B (Figure 26.11). If the real-time clock is running in

12-hour mode (set with status register B, see Figure 26.11), then a.m. and p.m. are distinguished by bit 7 in the entry hour or alarm hour: a cleared bit indicates a.m., a set bit p.m. DOS usually sets the time format and therefore also this bit according to the country information in CONFIG.SYS (COUNTRY=xxx). The range of values for a.m. is therefore $01–$12 and $81–$92 for p.m. (The dollar sign indicates binary coded decimal numbers.)

Example: `39 (= 27h) in byte 2/address 02H (minute) leads to 27 minutes.`

All other information is binary encoded. The quantities comprising two bytes are stored in little endian format.

Example: `Base memory.`

```
80H (= 128) in byte 21/address 15h
02H (= 2) in byte 22/address 16h
leads to 2*256 + 128 = 640 (kbyte) base memory
```

Besides the normal time and date function, the chip also has an in-built daylight saving function (activated via status register B, see Figure 26.11), as well as a function for determining the day of the week or month. The AT doesn't use these functions, however. For compatibility reasons, DOS determines the day of the week according to its own algorithm, as the PC/XT didn't incorporate such a chip. In the PS/2, the bytes 19h–31h (25d–49d) are assigned differently, that is, the configuration register values for the adapters in slots 0–3. Table 26.3 shows this assignment.

Byte	Address	Content
25	19h	adapter ID for slot 0 (LSB)
26	1ah	adapter ID for slot 0 (MSB)
27	1bh	adapter ID for slot 1 (LSB)
28	1ch	adapter ID for slot 1 (MSB)
29	1dh	adapter ID for slot 2 (LSB)
30	1eh	adapter ID for slot 2 (MSB)
31	1fh	adapter ID for slot 3 (LSB)
32	20h	adapter ID for slot 3 (MSB)
33	21h	POS-2 configuration byte for slot 0
34	22h	POS-3 configuration byte for slot 0
35	23h	POS-4 configuration byte for slot 0
36	24h	POS-5 configuration byte for slot 0
37	25h	POS-2 configuration byte for slot 1
38	26h	POS-3 configuration byte for slot 1
39	27h	POS-4 configuration byte for slot 1
40	28h	POS-5 configuration byte for slot 1
41	29h	POS-2 configuration byte for slot 2
42	2ah	POS-3 configuration byte for slot 2
43	2bh	POS-4 configuration byte for slot 2
44	2ch	POS-5 configuration byte for slot 2
45	2dh	POS-2 configuration byte for slot 3
46	2eh	POS-3 configuration byte for slot 3
47	2fh	POS-4 configuration byte for slot 3
48	30h	POS-5 configuration byte for slot 3
49	31h	POS-2 configuration byte for motherboard

Table 26.3: CMOS RAM configuration in the PS/2

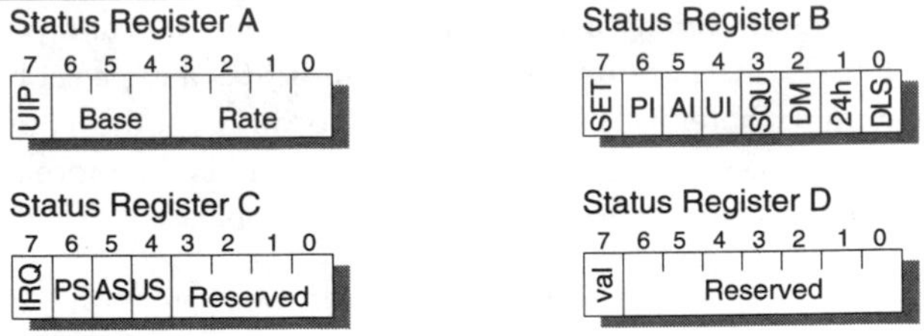

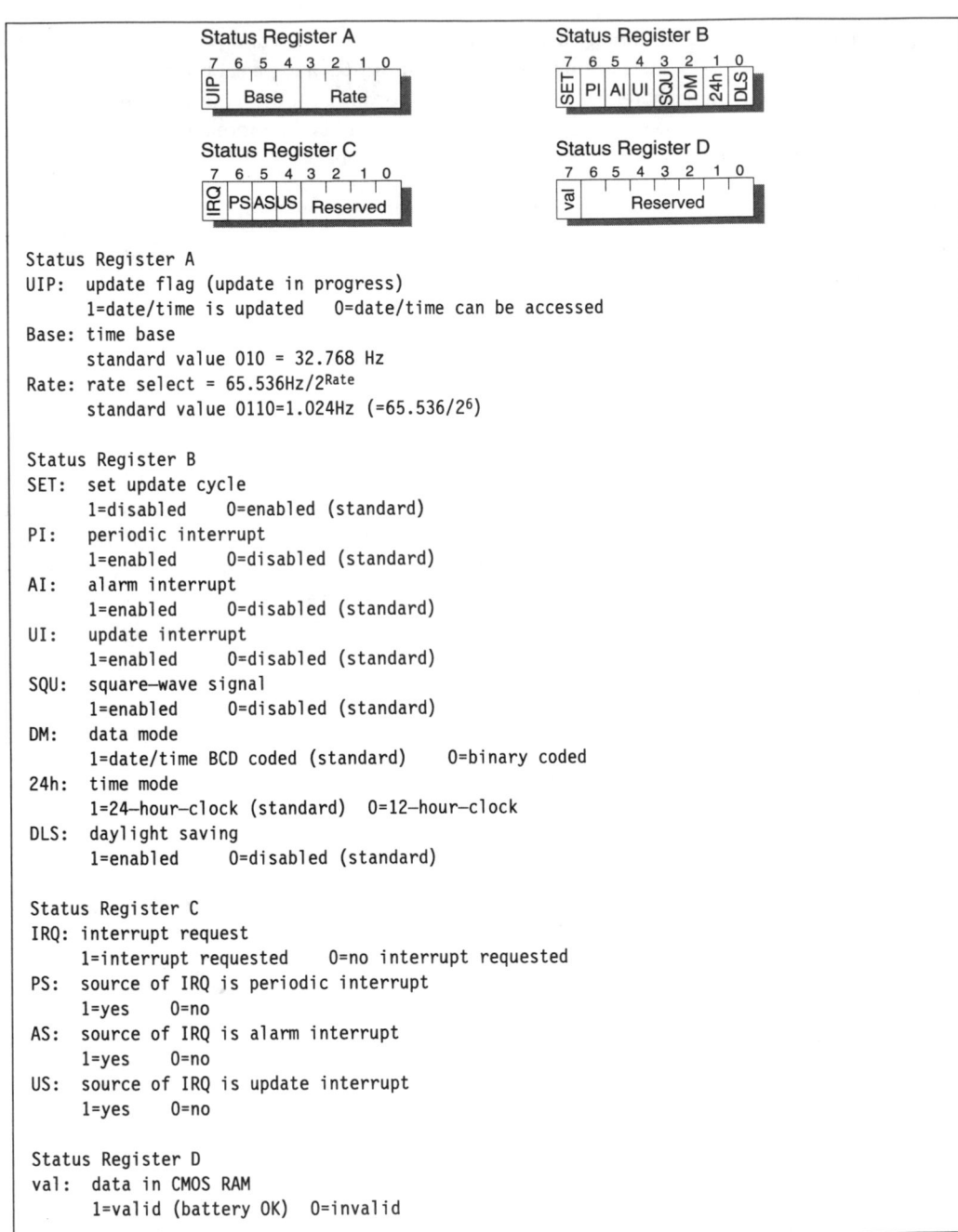

Status Register A
UIP: update flag (update in progress)
  1=date/time is updated 0=date/time can be accessed
Base: time base
  standard value 010 = 32.768 Hz
Rate: rate select = 65.536Hz/2^{Rate}
  standard value 0110=1.024Hz (=65.536/2^6)

Status Register B
SET: set update cycle
  1=disabled 0=enabled (standard)
PI: periodic interrupt
  1=enabled 0=disabled (standard)
AI: alarm interrupt
  1=enabled 0=disabled (standard)
UI: update interrupt
  1=enabled 0=disabled (standard)
SQU: square-wave signal
  1=enabled 0=disabled (standard)
DM: data mode
  1=date/time BCD coded (standard) 0=binary coded
24h: time mode
  1=24-hour-clock (standard) 0=12-hour-clock
DLS: daylight saving
  1=enabled 0=disabled (standard)

Status Register C
IRQ: interrupt request
  1=interrupt requested 0=no interrupt requested
PS: source of IRQ is periodic interrupt
  1=yes 0=no
AS: source of IRQ is alarm interrupt
  1=yes 0=no
US: source of IRQ is update interrupt
  1=yes 0=no

Status Register D
val: data in CMOS RAM
  1=valid (battery OK) 0=invalid

Figure 26.11: Formats of status registers A to D.

For supervising and programming the MC146818 the four status registers A to D are of importance. Using these you can define the chip's operation mode. Figure 26.11 shows the format of these bytes.

The MC146818 updates the clock every second by updating bytes 0, 2, 4, 6, 7, 8, 9 and 50 of the CMOS RAM. While this update is in progress, bytes 0–9 cannot be accessed; an access provides possibly meaningless values. Thus the MC146818 sets the *UIP* bit in status register A to indicate this update process. Bits *Base* define the time base that the real-time clock uses. In the AT the value 010b is set as standard. It provides a time base of 32768 Hz. Other values may accelerate or slow down the real-time clock. Using the four bits *Rate* you can define the rate of the square-wave signal or the periodic interrupt (see below). The values may be in the range between 0011 and 1111. With the relation

$$\text{frequency} = 65\,536\ \text{Hz}/2^{\text{Rate}}$$

rates between 8192 Hz (cycle time 122 μs) and 2 Hz (500 ms) are possible. *Rate* denotes the value of the rate select bits. The AT initializes the rate select to 0110b corresponding to 1024 Hz ($=65\,536/2^6$) or a cycle time of 976.56 μs as standard. An entry 0000b disables the rate generator. The two functions 83h and 86h of interrupt INT 15h use the 1024 Hz clock for determining wait intervals (see below).

Using the *SET* bit in the status register you can disable the update of the time and date bytes in the CMOS RAM. Thus you may initialize the MC146818 first and start the clock afterwards. The chip can not only serve as a real-time clock and an NVR, but can also generate a square-wave signal. The frequency of this signal is defined by the rate select bits in status register A. In the PC, the MC146818 output is not used, however, so that this capability is of only a theoretical nature as long as you don't fetch your soldering iron and use the square-wave output for your private purposes! The date and time values stored in CMOS RAM are usually held in BCD format, as already mentioned. The *DM* bit also advises the MC146818 to store all date and time values with binary encoding. But be careful: all DOS and BIOS functions assume the BCD format. Moreover, you are free to select a 12- or 24-hour clock. The *24h* bit switches the real-time clock between these two modes. Note that in the case of a 12-hour clock the most significant hour bit is set for all hours after noon (p.m.). Thus the hour counting runs from $81 to $92.

Using the most significant hour bit, you may distinguish between a.m. and p.m. The *DLS* bit enables the daylight saving function of the MC146818, but the PC makes no use of it.

Bits *PI*, *AI* and *UI* enable various interrupt requests. A set PI bit leads to a periodic interrupt request with a rate defined by the rate bits in status register A. The MC146818 then behaves like counter 0 of the PIT, which updates the internal system clock. The AI bit activates the C146818's alarm function. Upon every update of the time entries, the chip checks whether the updated time coincides with the alarm time held by bytes 1, 3 and 5. If this is true, the MC146817 issues an alarm interrupt. If you have set bit UI, then after every completed update of time and date in the CMOS RAM an interrupt request occurs. This is called the update interrupt.

The interrupt signal output of the MC146818 is connected via IRQ8 to the slave 8259A PIC in the AT. Thus all three sources lead to the same interrupt, namely interrupt 70h. Similar to the timer interrupt 08h via IRQ0, the handler of interrupt 70h calls a further interrupt as the user exit, namely interrupt 4ah. Usually, the handler consists of a simple IRET instruction, but you are free to redirect it to your own routine which, for example, tells you by the wail of a siren through the speaker and a pop-up window that it's time to have a cup of coffee.

Thus the handler of interrupt 70h or 4ah has to respond differently according to the interrupt source. If the periodic interrupt request is interpreted as an alarm interrupt, the user is unable to enjoy his or her computer (or life) anymore. To avoid such misunderstandings, status register C is helpful. It serves to determine the source of an interrupt request. The *IRQ* bit as an interrupt flag indicates whether the MC146818 has issued an interrupt request at all. If IRQ is set then bits *PS, AS* and *US* show whether a periodic, alarm or update interrupt has occurred. If several interrupt requests are allowed by means of several set enable bits in status register B, then they may, of course, be issued concurrently. In this case, several of the bits PS, AS and US are also set. The handler has to decide which request is serviced first.

The MC146818 has a function that permanently observes the charge state of the battery or accumulator. If the voltage drops below a critical value once, this function sets the *val* bit in status register D to indicate that the stored data is possibly invalid. The BIOS checks status register D in the course of the boot process to detect such a power break, and to display an appropriate message eventually.

Note that the time and date bytes 0–9, as well as the four status registers, are not accessible during an MC146818 update cycle (bit UIP in the status register A). However, you may always read and write the configuration bytes (described in the following) as only the setup program accesses them and not the real-time clock.

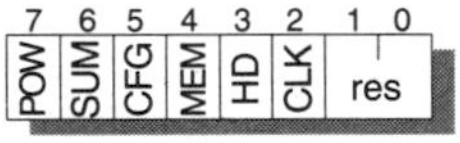


```
POW:  MC146818 power supply
      1=temporary interrupted       0=OK
SUM:  checksum test
      1=OK                          0=check sum incorrect
CFG:  configuration
      1=invalid                     0=OK
MEM:  evaluated memory size
      1=different from entry        0=OK
HD:   hard disk
      1=controller or drive initialization failed     0=OK
CLK:  time
      1=valid                       0=OK
```

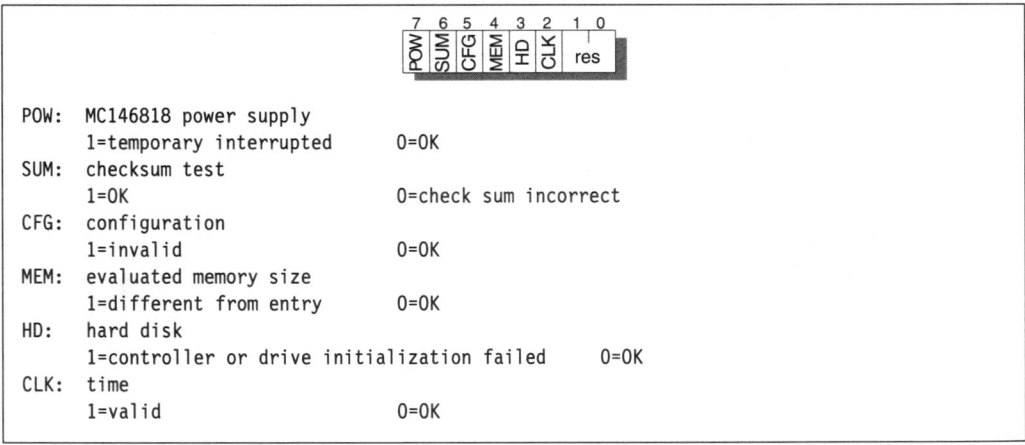

Figure 26.12: Diagnostics status byte (14, 0eh).

In the diagnostics status byte (see Figure 26.12) the POST routine of the BIOS stores certain check results that the PC carries out during the boot process. As already mentioned, the MC146818 sets bit val in status register D if the voltage of the battery or accumulator has once dropped below a certain minimum value. The BIOS reads this entry during the course of the boot process, and sets or clears the *POW* bit in the diagnosis status byte. In bytes 46 and 47 the BIOS stores a checksum, which is formed for bytes 16–45 (see Figure 26.21). During the course of the boot process, the PC determines whether the stored checksum coincides with the newly calculated one, and sets (checksum OK) or clears (checksum false) the *SUM* bit. Note that it is not the MC146818 but the BIOS that calculates the checksum. If you alter one of bytes 16–46 then you have to recalculate the checksum and store it in bytes 46–47. If you don't do this the BIOS displays a CMOS checksum error upon the next boot process. While booting, the BIOS further checks first whether the indicated configuration is consistent, and second, whether it coincides with the controllers, etc. actually present. The result of this check is stored in the *CFG* bit. The *MEM* bit indicates whether the POST routine has determined the same memory size as you have entered via the setup program. During the course of the boot process, the BIOS attempts to initialize all controllers. According to bit *HD* you may recognize whether or not this process was successful for hard disk drive C:. Finally, the *CLK* bit shows whether the current time is correct or invalid (indicates, for example, 12:78 o'clock).

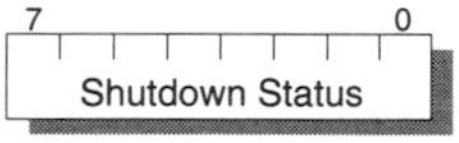


```
Shutdown Status: reset information
   00h=normal system reset    01h=initialization for real mode
   04h=JMP to bootstrap
   05h=output EOI to PIC, clear keyboard, JMP with far pointer at 40:67h
   06h=JMP with far pointer at 40:67h without EOI
   07h=return to INT 15h, function 87h "move block in extended memory"
   08h=return to POST memory test
   09h=return to INT 15h, function 87h "move block in extended memory"
   0ah=JMP with far pointer at 40:67h without EOI
   0bh=IRET via far pointer at 40:67h
   0ch=return via far pointer at 40:67h
```

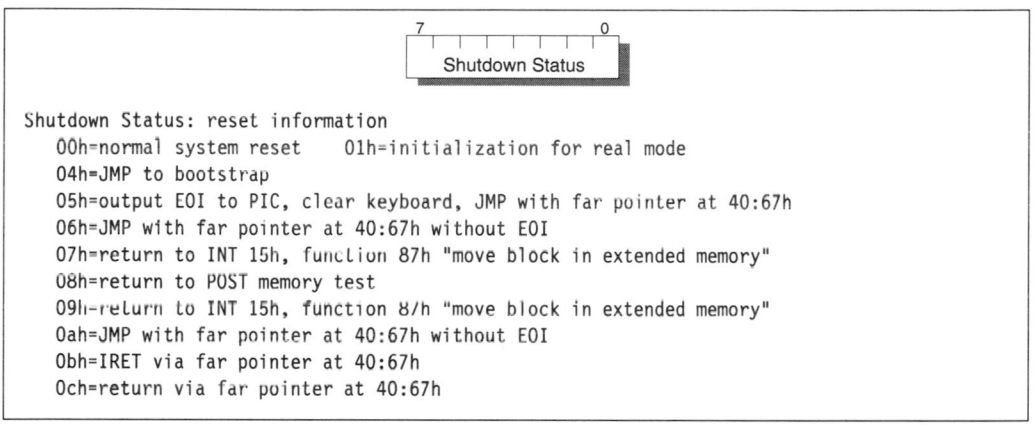

Figure 26.13: Shutdown status byte (15, 0fh).

During a processor reset the shutdown status byte (see Figure 26.13) is loaded with a value that provides some information about the cause of the reset during the course of the following boot process. A value 00h of *Shutdown Status* bits indicates a normal reset to the BIOS which, for example, was issued by the user through the reset button. The 80286 cannot be switched back from protected to real mode, unlike the i386 and following chips; this is only possible by a processor reset. Programs such as SMARTDRV.SYS or RAMDRIVE.SYS, which access extended memory in protected mode, therefore set the shutdown status byte to a value of 09h to inform the BIOS that no «real» reset has occurred, and that only a switch back to the real mode should be carried out.

Byte 16 in the CMOS RAM (see Figure 26.14) indicates the type of the first (high-order nibble) and second (low-order nibble) floppy drive. The values 0101 to 1111 are reserved for future types of floppy drives.

Similarly, byte 18 holds the hard disk drive types (see Figure 26.15). The high-order nibble indicates the type of the first, and the low-order nibble the type of the second hard disk. Thus, a maximum of 16 possibilities is available for every drive (including 0 for none).

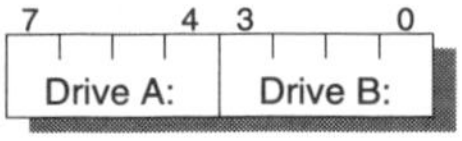


```
Drive A: type of first floppy drive (A:)
Drive B: type of second floppy drive (B:)
    0000=not installed          0001=5 1/4" 360 kbyte
    0010=5 1/4" 1.2 Mbyte       0011=3 1/2" 720 kbyte
    0100=3 1/1" 1.44 Mbyte      0101–1111=reserved
```

Figure 26.14: Floppy drive types (16, 10h).

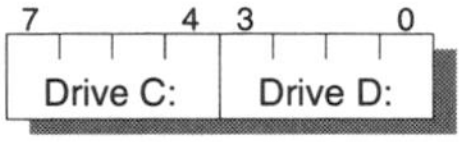


```
Drive C: type of first hard disk (C:)
Drive D: type of second hard disk (D:)
    0000=not installed      0001–1110=type 1 ... 14
    1111=type 16 ... 255 according to hard disk extension bytes
```

Figure 26.15: Hard disk drive types (18, 12h).

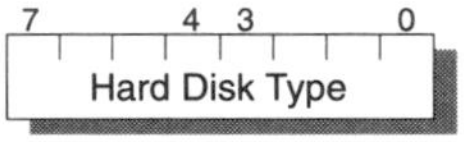

Figure 26.16: Hard disk extension byte (25, 19h and 26, 1ah).

In view of today's variety of hard disks, this is, of course, not sufficient. The value 15 (=0fh) is therefore reserved as «extended». If this value is stored for one of the drives, then the actual type byte is stored at address 19h (first hard disk) or 1ah (second hard disk). The format of this hard disk extension byte is shown in Figure 26.16. The number indicated by the high-order or low-order nibble in the hard disk drive byte or in the hard disk extension byte serves as an index into a BIOS parameter table, which holds the geometry of the hard disk concerned. These BIOS tables may differ from manufacturer to manufacturer; the only solution is to look at the manual.

Many BIOS chips allow a user-defined hard disk type. This is necessary if you have a hard disk with an exotic geometry, or a recently developed one whose parameters were unknown when the BIOS was programmed. From the viewpoint of BIOS and the operating system, PCs are designed as standard for operation with a maximum of two physical hard disks. In most cases, hard disk types 48 and 49 are reserved for freely definable types. In CMOS RAM two parameter blocks are implemented for them (see Figure 26.17). The block has eight bytes each, starting at bytes 32 and 53, respectively. The meaning of the corresponding entries is described in Section 28.3. Note that older BIOS versions, in particular, don't have the option to define an exotic drive geometry, and therefore neither the structure shown in Figure 26.17 nor the block addresses are strictly standardized. Fortunately, most BIOS manufacturers obey the above mentioned convention.

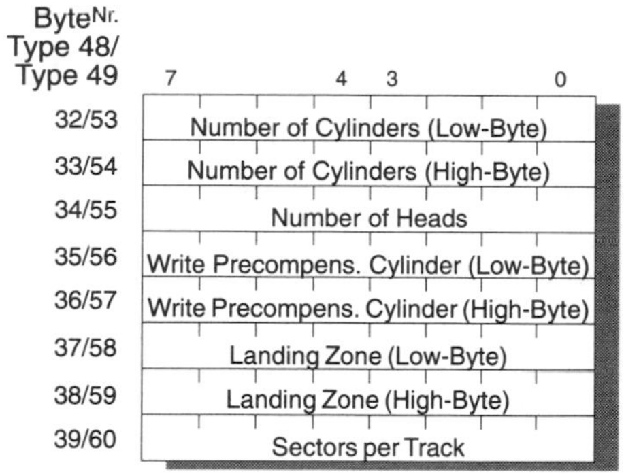

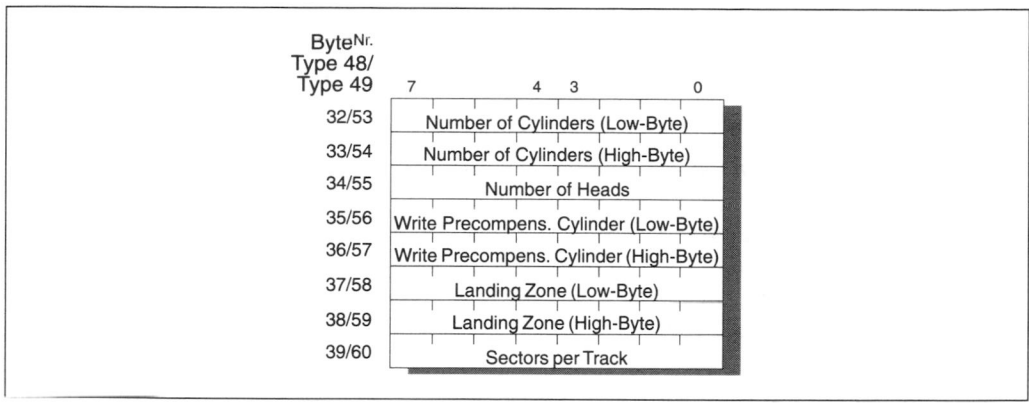

Figure 26.17: Hard disk drive parameter block for types 48 and 49 (32, 20h and 53, 35h).

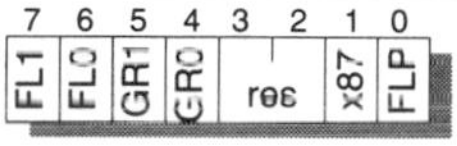


```
FL1, FL0: number of floppies installed (if FLP=1)
          00=1 drive        01=2 drives
GR1, GR0: type of primary graphics adapter
          00=adapter with own BIOS (EGA, VGA etc.)
          01=CGA with 40 characters/line   10=CGA with 80 characters/line
          11=monochrome (MDA, Hercules)
x87:      coprocessor 80x87
          1=installed                      0=not installed
FLP:      floppy drive
          1=at least one installed         0=none installed
```

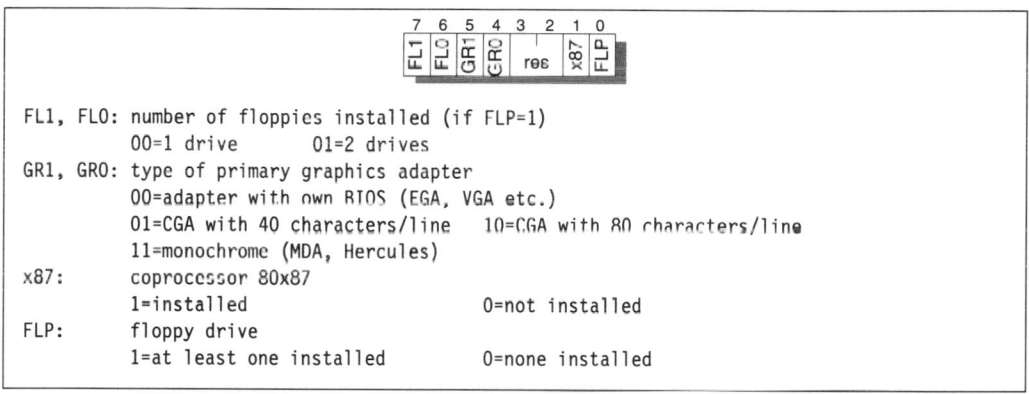

Figure 26.18: Device byte (20, 14h).

In the device byte (see Figure 26.18) the setup program stores data concerning certain components of the PC. The bits *FL1, FL0* indicate the number of floppy drives installed if the *FLP* bit is set; otherwise, the entry has no meaning. Bits *GR1, GR0* define the type of the primary graphics adapter. Modern adapters with their own BIOS, such as EGA or VGA, are characterized by an entry 00b. Finally, the *x87* bit indicates whether a coprocessor is installed.

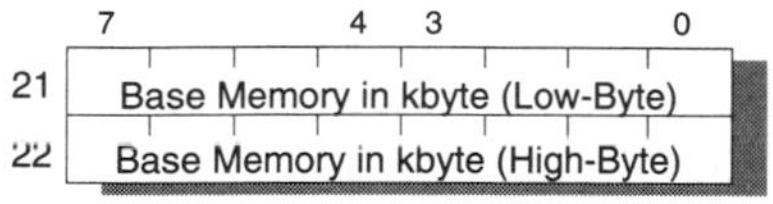

Figure 26.19: Base memory (21, 15h and 22, 16h).

The two base memory bytes (see Figure 26.19) indicate the amount of installed base memory in kbytes as a 16-bit number in Intel format.

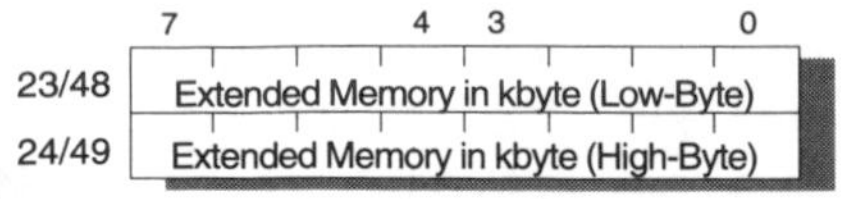

Figure 26.20: Extended memory as stored and determined by BIOS (23, 17h and 24, 18h or 48, 30h and 49, 31h).

In the setup program you normally also have to enter the size of extended memory. The program stores this value in the two extended memory bytes 23 and 24, which indicate the size of extended memory as the two base memory bytes in kbytes as a 16-bit number in Intel format (see Figure 26.20). During the course of the boot process, the POST routine of the BIOS checks how large the extended memory actually is, and stores the resulting value in extended memory bytes 48 and 49. If the two values of stored and checked extended memory don't match, then either you have entered a wrong number, the CMOS RAM has suffered a power break, or the memory chips are faulty.

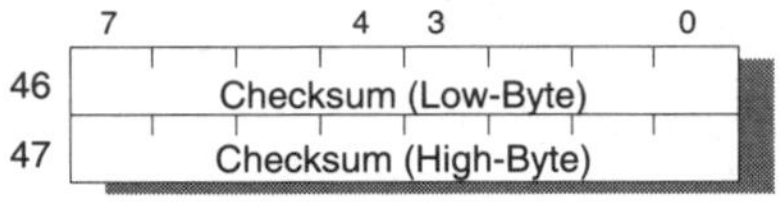

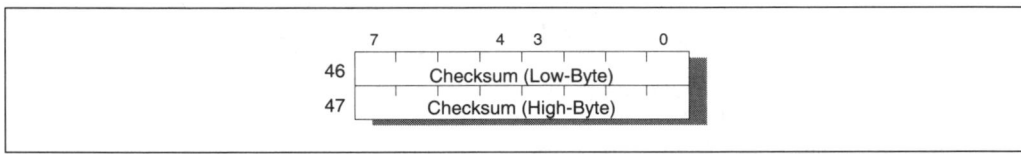

Figure 26.21: Checksum (46, 2eh and 47, 2fh).

Bytes 46 and 47 of the CMOS RAM hold the checksum of bytes 16–45 (see Figure 26.21). This is determined by simply adding the values of bytes 16–45, and is stored by the BIOS as a 16-bit number in Intel format.

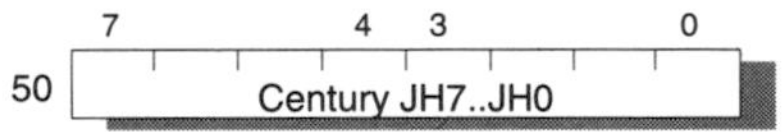

Figure 26.22: Century byte (50, 32h).

Byte 50 holds the century, usually in the BCD format (see Figure 26.22). By means of the DM bit in status register B, you can also define the binary coded format. Note that in byte 9 of the CMOS RAM only the decade and the year can be accommodated, not the century.

In the reserved bits and bytes some BIOS (the AMI BIOS, for example) store very hardware-dependent information, for example the clock speed of the processor, the size of the BIOS ROM, the size of the data bus, shadowing of ROM code, or caching. The use of the individual bits and bytes is not standardized in these cases so you should not attempt to use reserved bits and bytes for your own purposes, or to alter them in any way. Be aware that the entries in battery-buffered CMOS RAM are very long lived. Even a power-down and rebooting doesn't free you from faulty entries in the CMOS RAM, which let your brand new 50 MHz i486 PC with disabled caching, shadowing and paging/interleaving appear to be a slow XT. You can access the bytes described in CMOS RAM and the four control registers A to D in two ways:

- with limited capability (only date/time and alarm) via the BIOS interrupt 1ah (see Appendix E).
- complete, by means of the address and data registers at ports 70h and 71h.

26.3.2 Access via the BIOS

Eight functions are available for the BIOS interrupt 1ah. The first two refer to the DOS-internal system clock; the other six to the real-time clock. You can thus set and clear time and date as well as set and clear an alarm time. The access via BIOS is therefore rather limited. Configuration data can neither be read nor written. Also, the other MC146818 functions, such as the periodic interrupt or generation of the square-wave signal, are not programmable. This is only possible by directly accessing the accompanying ports.

Example: `Set time to 12.45 o'clock without daylight saving.`

```
mov ah, 03h  ; function 03h
mov cl, 45h  ; 45 minutes
mov ch, 12h  ; 12 hours
mov dl, 00h  ; no daylight saving
mov dh, 00h  ; 0 seconds
int 1ah      ; set time via interrupt 1ah
```

Appendix E gives a list of all possible functions of interrupt 1ah as far as they refer to the real-time clock. Note that passing the date and time values to or from the interrupt 1ah is carried out using binary coded decimals. If the interrupt handler is unable to read the data concerned from or write it into the CMOS RAM as the MC146818 currently updates the date and time, then the carry flag is set and the values passed in the registers are meaningless.

With DOS commands DATE and TIME you can read and set the internal system clock. The real-time clock is not affected by this before DOS version 3.30. Before DOS 3.30, the system date and time are newly set, but the real-time clock is not accessed and updated. After the next boot process the system clock therefore shows the old settings again.

Besides the programming of date and time you may further use the functions 83h and 86h of interrupt 15h to set certain time intervals until an action occurs. With function 83h, the program execution is continued and a user-defined bit in the main memory is set after the wait time has elapsed. Function 86h, on the other hand, suspends program execution until the set time interval has elapsed, and therefore a real wait is carried out. Both functions are also to be found in Appendix E.

26.3.3 Access via Address and Data Register

For an access via the address and data registers ports 70h (address register) and 71h (data register) are used. Note that data bit 7 of port 70h controls the NMI mask register. Never alter its value, but read the byte from port 70h first and overwrite only the five low-order bits, which are sufficient for addressing the 64 bytes in the CMOS RAM. To read or output a data byte proceed as follows:

- fetch the old byte via port 70h and output the address of the data byte to access using the five low-order bits;
- read or write the thus accessed data byte via port 71h.

Example: Read hard disk drive type.

```
IN  al, 70h    ; read old byte from port 70h
AND al, e0h    ; clear the five low-order bits
OR  al, 12h    ; load accumulator al with address of byte 18,
               ; bit 7 remains unchanged;
OUT 70h, al    ; write address of byte 18 into address register
IN  al, 71h    ; read drive type into accumulator
```

The byte read in the example then contains the type of both hard disks.

Example: Determine the base memory size.

```
IN  al, 70h  ; read byte from port 70h
AND al, e0h  ; clear five low-order bits
OR  al, 16h  ; load address of high-order base memory byte into al
OUT 70h, al  ; output address to the MC146818 address register
IN  al, 71h  ; read high-order base memory byte
MOV ah, al   ; transfer high-order base memory byte into ah
IN  al, 70h  ; read byte from port 70h
AND al, e0h  ; clear five low-order bits
OR  al, 15h  ; load address of low-order base memory byte into al
OUT 70h, al  ; output address to the MC146818 address register
IN  al, 71h  ; read low-order base memory byte,
             ; thus ax=ah.al contains the size of base memory in kbytes
```

If you alter an entry then ensure that the CMOS RAM holds a checksum of the configuration bytes 10h to 2dh in bytes 46 and 47. Thus you also have to recalculate and write the checksum. During the course of the boot procedure the ROM BIOS checks whether configuration data and checksum conform. If this is not the case, the BIOS displays a message indicating that a CMOS RAM error has occurred and refuses to boot. This prevents the operating system from being configured incorrectly in the course of the boot process, and from damaging data or even hardware components because of a configuration error.

You may, of course, also program all functions accessible via BIOS interrupt 1ah via the ports. For setting an alarm time, for example, you have to write byte 1 (alarm second), 3 (alarm minute), and 5 (alarm hour) according to the intended alarm time and the data mode set in status register B. Further, you must enable the alarm interrupt using bit AI in status register B.

26.3.4 Extended CMOS RAM

EISA/MCA and Local Bus PCs have a further battery-buffered NVR besides the conventional CMOS RAM. The EISA standard demands an extended CMOS RAM of at least 4 kbytes, and PS/2 an extended CMOS RAM of 2 kbytes (if more than four MCA slots are present). Its exact size will be found in your manual.

You may access the data in the extended CMOS RAM of an EISA PC through the CMOS RAM page register at port address 0c00h and the I/O port access registers at 0800h–08ffh. The I/O port access registers provide a 256-byte window into the extended EISA CMOS RAM; you select the CMOS page number with the page register.

Example: Read byte 745 of the extended EISA CMOS (745d=2e9h).

```
MOV al, 2      ; load page number (high-order address byte) into accumulator al
MOV dx, 0c00h  ; load I/O address of CMOS RAM page register into dx
OUT dx, al     ; output page number to CMOS RAM page register
MOV dx, 08e9h  ; load I/O addresse of I/O access registers for byte 745 into dx (base 0800h +
               ; offset e9h=233d)
IN al, dx      ; read byte 745 (2*256+233) via data port 76h into accumulator al
```

On a PS/2, you can address the data in the extended CMOS RAM through the two address ports 74h (low-order address byte) and 75h (high-order address byte), and read or write the addressed byte via port 76h. Unlike the normal CMOS RAM, you need two bytes for addressing because you can access only 256 bytes with a 1 byte address.

Example: Overwrite byte 1186 in the extended CMOS RAM with a value of 76.

```
MOV al, 162  ; load low-order address byte into accumulator al
OUT 74h, al  ; output low-order address byte via port 74h
MOV al, 4    ; load high-order address byte into accumulator al
OUT 75h, al  ; output high-order address byte via port 75h
MOV al, 76   ; load data byte into accumulator al
OUT al, 76h  ; write value 76 through data port 76h into byte 1186 of extended PS/2 CMOS RAM
```

The extended PS/2 CMOS RAM implements a 35-byte entry for every slot, having the following structure:

Offset	Size	Entry
00h	1 word	adapter ID
02h	1 byte	number of used POS registers
03h	1 byte	POS-2 configuration byte
04h	1 byte	POS-3 configuration byte
05h	1 byte	POS-4 configuration byte
06h	1 byte	POS-5 configuration byte
07h–22h	28 bytes	reserved

These entries are contiguous for each slot, that is, the entry for slot 0 starts at offset 00h, the entry for slot 1 at offset 23h (=35d), etc. The bytes 0fch–7ffh are reserved.

Part 5
Mass Storage

27 Floppies and Floppy Drives

27.1 Ferromagnetism and Induction – The Basis of Magnetic Data Recording

Pure magnetic fields in a vacuum which are generated, for example, by an electromagnet can be physically described quite easily. The situation becomes more complicated if metals or ceramics are introduced into the field, as such substances alter the magnetic field. Depending upon the strength and sign of the interaction we can distinguish three kinds of magnetism: diamagnetism, paramagnetism, and ferromagnetism. The latter is that used in most technical applications and in all magnetic data recordings (audio tape, magnetic card, floppy or hard disk).

27.1.1 Diamagnetism and Paramagnetism

All substances are diamagnetic in principle, but this effect is obscured by the frequent presence of paramagnetism. If a diamagnetic substance such as hydrogen or silver is introduced into a magnetic field, the substance weakens the magnetic field slightly (typically by 0.000001% to 0.05%). Pure diamagnetism occurs only in substances that don't have unpaired electrons, for example rare gases or metal salts. The distinctive characteristic of diamagnetism when compared to paramagnetism and ferrormagnetism is that it is completely temperature-independent.

Most atoms have at least one unpaired electron in their shell; thus paramagnetism occurs. If one introduces a paramagnetic substance, for example aluminium or liquid oxygen, into a magnetic field then this substance strengthens the magnetic field already present by 0.00001% to 0.05%. The reason for this effect is the alignment of the atoms by the external magnetic field. The lower the temperature the stronger this effect becomes, as the temperature movement of the atoms disturbs the alignment with a rising temperature.

Diamagnetism and paramagnetism have the common characteristic that the amount of magnetization is dependent upon the existence of an external magnetic field. The external field gives rise to a magnetic effect which weakens (diamagnetism) or strengthens (paramagnetism) the already existing magnetic field. If the external magnetic field is switched off, then the substances's own magnetization vanishes. Thus diamagnetic and paramagnetic substances do not generate their own permanent magnetic field, and are therefore unsuitable for the long-term recording of data.

27.1.2 Ferromagnetism

Of significant technological importance are ferromagnetic substances, the best-known of which is iron. In these materials microscopically small areas of billions of atoms, the so-called *domains*, are completely magnetized (see Figure 27.1). However, as these areas are usually aligned statistically, their effect is compensated for macroscopically and the substance seems to be unmagnetized to the exterior.

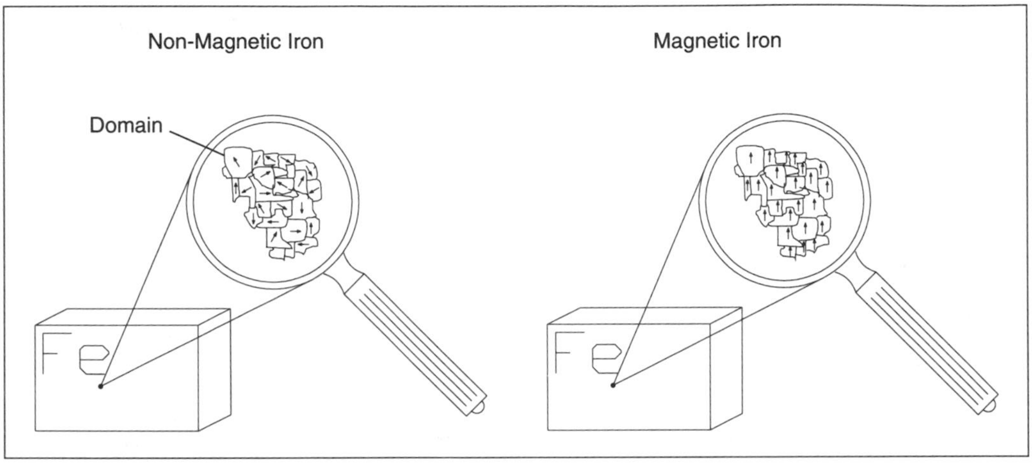

Figure 27.1: Ferromagnetic material. In unmagnetized iron the domains are oriented statistically; in magnetized iron the magnetic fields of the domains point uniformly in one direction.

If we introduce a ferromagnetic body into a magnetic field then (nearly) all domains align to the external field, and can amplify the field a million times (see Figure 27.1). Therefore, iron is used as the core for transformers, for example. The field, which is generated by the primary coil, is amplified by the iron core and induces a strong voltage in the secondary coil. The efficiency thus rises. You can see a similar effect with knives and forks made of iron, or steel scissors. If you always put them into the drawer in the same position, the earth's steadily present magnetic field magnetizes the knives and forks, and these attract other iron objects such as pins.

For data recording another characteristic of ferromagnetic substances is significant: so-called *remanence*. This is where ferromagnetic substances remain magnetic even after the external magnetic field has been «switched off». Diamagnetic and paramagnetic substances, on the other hand, lose their magnetization completely after the external magnetic field has been switched off. Figure 27.2 shows the relationship between external magnetic field H and the magnetization M of the ferromagnetic material.

With an increasing external magnetic field H, the magnetization M also rises, and sometimes reaches a saturation value J_S, which cannot be exceeded – the so-called *saturation magnetization*. Above all, domains cannot be aligned in the end. If the external magnetic field is weakened then the magnetization also decreases again, but by a smaller amount than that by which it rose during the rise of the magnetic field. If the magnetic field reaches the value 0 (that is, the external field is switched off), some magnetization remains, which is called *remanence* or *remanent magnetization*. Once a certain magnetic field of the opposite direction has been applied, the remanent magnetization also vanishes. The strength of this opposite field required for complete demagnetization is called *coercivity* or *coercitive force*. Finally, the ferromagnetic material attains a magnetization with a further rising field strength, which is opposite to the previous maximum magnetization, but has the same absolute value. If we decrease the external magnetic field again, and finally change its direction, then the magnetization follows a curve that is symmetric to the former change of magnetization. The complete curve is called a *hysteresis loop*. We say that ferromagnetic materials show a hysteresis because the magnetization is not only dependent upon the external magnetic field, but also upon the past history of the body. The generation of domains and the strong magnetization compared to paramagnetism is based on quantum-physical laws, which give rise to a strong magnetic coupling of adjacent atoms and molecules in a solid.

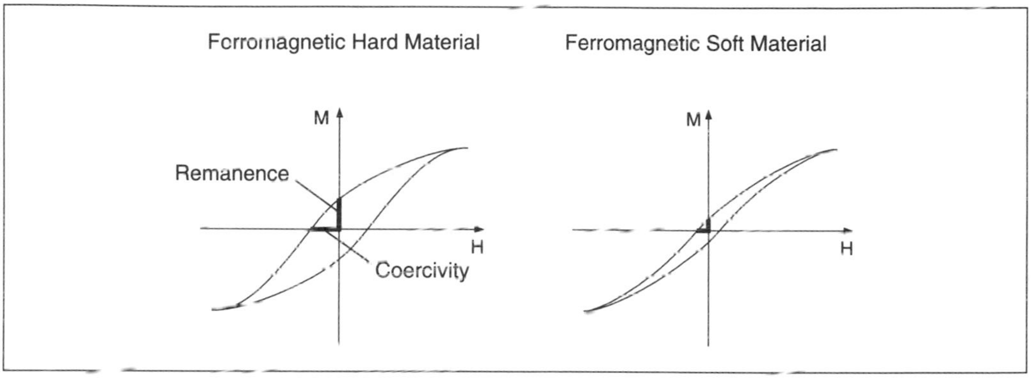

Figure 27.2: Hysteresis loop. A magnetically hard ferromagnetic material has a high remanence and coercivity, and thus the hysteresis is distinct. For a magnetically soft ferromagnetic material, on the other hand, the two curves nearly meet.

With certain additives and manufacturing methods, ferromagnetic materials can be formed which show a distinct hysteresis, that is, strong remanence and high coercivity. Such materials are called *magnetically hard*. *Magnetically soft* materials with low hysteresis, on the other hand, show a weak remanence and low coercivity.

The hysteresis properties of ferromagnetic substances are decisive for recording. Usually, one bit is represented by an area homogenously magnetized in a certain direction. This area must be at least as large as one domain. The magnetic field for magnetizing the area is mostly generated by a small electromagnet in a read/write head of the floppy or hard disk drive. Thus the domains within the area align according to the generated magnetic field and a «1» is written. By inverting the polarity of the magnetic field the domains are also aligned, but in another direction; thus a «0» is stored.

From the hysteresis loop it is apparent that for aligning the domains or overwriting old values at least a magnetic field with the strength of the coercivity is required. The data itself is stored by a magnetization with the amount of the remanence. Thus magnetically hard substances hold the data more strongly as their remanence is larger. But you need a stronger write field to generate the coercive force necessary for magnetization. Adjacent domains magnetized in opposite directions may affect each other, and demagnetize each other in the extreme. If one attempts to pack as much data as possible onto a magnetic data carrier (which, of course, become more adjacent), then one needs magnetically harder substances than with a low packing density. The $5^1/_4$" disks with a 1.2 Mbyte capacity are therefore coated with magnetically harder substances than the $5^1/_4$" disks of only 360 kbyte capacity. The accompanying 1.2 Mbyte drives generate stronger magnetic fields to format and write the 1.2 Mbyte disks. If you format a magnetically soft 360 kbyte disk in a 1.2 Mbyte drive now, the tracks may be magnetized to an amount for which a 360 kbyte drive that generates a correspondingly lower field for the soft 360 kbyte disks is unable to provide the required coercive force. You may read floppies which have been formatted and written in a 1.2 Mbyte drive, but not reformat them nor overwrite the data held on them. Only after several attempts may reformatting or overwriting happen – perhaps.

Another characteristic of ferromagnetic substances is the existence of a sharply defined temperature, the so-called *Curie temperature* T_c, or *Curie point*. Up to this temperature ferromagnetica behave in the described manner. But if, for example, iron is heated above 774°C (its Curie point), then the ferromagnetism suddenly vanishes and the iron behaves like a paramagnetic substance with a much lower magnetization. This property is used in magneto-optical drives and with magneto-optical data carriers. Section 28.8.3 gives more information on this.

The technically most important ferromagnetic materials are iron, cobalt, nickel, and their alloys. Table 27.1 lists the most important ferromagnetic materials, together with their Curie temperature T_c and saturation magnetization J_s.

	T_c [°C]	J_s [Tesla]
Iron (Fe)	770	2.15
Cobalt (Co)	1121	1.76
Nickel (Ni)	358	0.68
Gadolinium	20	2.52
$Fe_{65}Co_{35}$	920	2.45
MnBi*)	360	0.78

*) Manganese–Bismuth alloy

Table 27.1: Ferromagnetic materials

27.1.3 Induction

So far we have only got to know the basics of long-term data storage, but not how such magnetizations can be generated and how the data can be restored from them. It is generally known that an electric current generates a magnetic field. If a constant current is flowing through a coil then a constant magnetic field is generated, and the coil serves as an electromagnet. By means of tiny coils, domains may be aligned permanently in a ferromagnetic material and therefore – they hold data.

For detecting the aligned magnetic areas another effect of electrodynamics is used, *induction*. This denotes the phenomenon where a changing magnetic field generates a voltage. Thus if one introduces a coil into a changing magnetic field then the induction gives rise to an electrical voltage. Remarkably, in this case only the change of the magnetic field leads to a voltage, but not the magnetic field itself. On the contrary, a constant current generates a constant magnetic field or, stated differently, an altering current leads to an altering magnetic field. Exactly these two effects are used in a transformer: the alternating current in the primary coil generates a changing magnetic field, which induces a voltage in the secondary coil by means of electromagnetic induction. This induced voltage oscillates with the same frequency as the current in the primary coil changes.

But this means that a homogenously magnetized ferromagnetic material cannot induce any voltage. If a coil is moved over such a body, no voltage is generated and no (data) signal appears. Once the ferromagnetic material has alternately magnetized areas, the magnetic field also changes in the course of the coil movement and thus generates a voltage that can be detected and amplified as a data signal. Thus for data recording, it is not a homogenous magnetization of floppies, hard disks or magnetic tapes that is required, but the formation of alternately aligned areas.

27.2 Structure and Functioning of Floppies and Floppy Drives

You probably already know the principle of an audio tape. A motor moves the tape over a recording head, which detects the information stored on the tape or writes new information onto it. Usually, music or other sound forms the information, which is output by a speaker or input by a microphone. Instead of music, every other kind of «information» can also be recorded onto the magnetic tape, for example programs or data for a computer. Magnetic tapes play an important role as an inexpensive medium for archiving data. In the field of PCs they are mainly found in the form of streamer cartridges, where the tape is installed in a case. Mainframes, on the other hand, mainly use magnetic tape reels which are handled without a case.

You have surely experienced the big disadvantage of magnetic tapes: if you want to hear a song again from the beginning or to skip it, you have to wind the tape forwards or backwards. The same applies, of course, in the field of computers. Earlier and simpler home computers only had a cassette recorder and no floppy drive. Loading a program mostly became a trial of your patience. Thus magnetic tapes are unsuitable as online mass storage, at least for more powerful computer systems, but in view of the costs unbeatable for extensive backups.

The spooling of the magnetic tape gives rise to a very long *access time*, which is defined as the time interval between an access demand and the delivery of the data. To shorten the access time, floppies and hard disks were developed. Figure 27.3 shows the structure of common $5^1/_4$" and $3^1/_2$" floppy disks.

Instead of a long and thin magnetic tape, a floppy disk consists of a flexible, circular plastic disk coated with a ferromagnetic material. To protect this data carrier from dirt and damage, the actual floppy is housed in a protective envelope or a plastic case. In the PC field today you will only find $5^1/_4$" floppies with a capacity of 360 kbyte and 1.2 Mbyte, and the newer $3^1/_2$"

floppies with a capacity of 720 kbytes and 1.44 Mbytes. All of these floppies are double-sided; thus data is recorded on both sides. For DOS 1.x (and the original PC) single-sided floppies with a capacity of 160 or 180 kbytes were available, but they have vanished completely from the market together with their single-sided drives. Finally, the real dinosaurs were the 8" floppies, which also don't have any role in today's PCs. However, some internal DOS and BIOS structures support these floppy monsters for compatibility reasons.

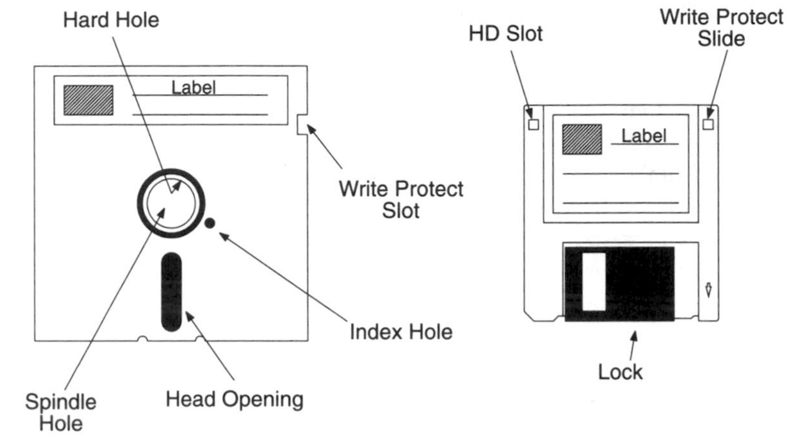

Figure 27.3: Floppy disks.

The $5^1/_4$" floppies are housed in a flexible envelope so that you can only see a small part of the actual data carrier through the opening for the read/write heads. Never touch the data carrier through this opening – even tiny dirt and fat particles make the floppy unusable, and the data gets lost.

To store data on or read data from the floppies you have to insert them into a floppy drive (see Figure 27.4). In the case of a $5^1/_4$" floppy a central mounting awl which is connected to the spindle of the drive motor takes up the floppy by means of the *spindle hole*. High-quality $5^1/_4$" floppies therefore have a *hard hole*. The more compact $3^1/_2$" floppy, on the other hand, has a gap in the metal disk. When such a floppy is inserted into a drive, the spindle meshes with this gap and locking the drive is unnecessary. Moreover, the envelopes of $5^1/_4$" floppies and the floppies themselves have an *index hole* that establishes an origin similar to the meridian on a globe. If you pick up a floppy the data carrier is probably rotated so you see only the data carrier's surface through the index hole in the envelope. If you carefully rotate the data carrier using the spindle and hard holes, then a small hole appears – the index hole of the data carrier.

With the *write protect hole* you can prevent data on the floppy disk from being erroneously overwritten. You only need to cover the hole with adhesive tape. All floppy drives have a photosensor assembly inside which senses this hole. If it is closed then the drive denies any write access to the inserted floppy. This denial is carried out on a hardware level and thus cannot be bypassed with a software command – a very reliable protection against computer viruses. For this reason, some manufacturers supply the original floppies of operating systems or application programs on floppies in envelopes that don't have any hole. Thus the data cannot be altered in any way – or at least as long you don't take a knife to one!

Because of the spindle hole, the index hole and the opening for the read/write heads, $5^1/_4$" floppies are subject to dirtying. You should therefore keep them in a clean and dust-free place, and avoid touching the actual data carrier. Even your just cleaned hand has enough fat particles to damage the surface. Furthermore, you must never write anything onto labels stuck to the floppies using a hard pen (for example, a ballpoint pen or pencil) as the data carrier can be damaged through the thin protective envelope. Labels must be written before sticking them onto the floppy (even if the author himself doesn't always proceed according to these well-intended hints!).

In comparison, the newer $3^1/_2$" floppies are far better protected. This is necessary because of the higher data recording density. The floppies are accommodated in a stiff and stable plastic case, where the opening for the read/write heads is protected by a bolt. Once you insert the floppy into the drive, the drive's mechanism moves the bolt aside. You are free to try this by hand, but don't touch the data carrier here. Instead of the spindle hole the $3^1/_2$" floppy has a central metal disk with two slots: one for the motor spindle and one as the substitute for the index hole. Unlike the $5^1/_4$", here the floppy is not taken up by a mounting awl, but the specially formed motor spindle meshes directly with the slot. The second slot indicates the origin, in the same way as the former index hole. $3^1/_2$" floppies need not be locked manually in the drive, as is the case for $5^1/_2$" floppies. This is carried out by the drive mechanism automatically. The $3^1/_2$" floppies can be write-protected much more easily than their predecessors. Instead of the write protect hole they have a small *write protect slide* with which you can cover the case's hole. But note that $3^1/_2$" floppies, unlike the $5^1/_4$", are write protected if the hole is opened. Some manufacturers thus supply their software on write-protected $3^1/_2$" floppies, which lack the write protect slide.

The $3^1/_2$" floppies with a capacity of 1.44 Mbytes further have an *HD notch* to tell the floppy drive that a high-density or short HD-floppy is inserted. The problems that arise if 360 kbyte floppies are formatted or written in a 1.2 Mbyte drive can thus be avoided. As the two floppy types have an identical diameter, the data density of 1.2 Mbyte floppies must be higher, of course. Thus the magnetized areas are closer together and a higher coercivity of the magnetic coating is required to hold the data permanently. Thus, 1.2 Mbyte drives must therefore generate a stronger magnetic field to write onto the floppies, as is the case in 360 kbyte drives. As a consequence, the 360 kbyte floppies are magnetized during writing or formatting to an amount such that 360 kbyte drives have no chance of deleting the data again. The situation is similar with 720 kbyte and 1.44 Mbyte capacity $3^1/_2$" floppies. For the lower data density on 720 kbyte floppies a lower field strength is also required. Therefore, $3^1/_2$" drives have a sensor which probes the HD notch of the floppy. If you have inserted a 1.44 Mbyte floppy then the floppy drive increases the write current to generate a stronger magnetic field. If no HD notch is present (that is, you have inserted a 720 kbyte floppy), then the drive operates with a reduced write current and an accordingly weaker magnetic field. Thus, $3^1/_2$" drives adapt their magnetic field to the floppy type used. Problems such as those described for the older 360 kbyte and 1.2 Mbyte floppies and drives therefore don't occur here.

The drive motor rotates the inserted floppy at 300 rotations per minute for 360 kbyte floppies, or 360 rotations per minute for all other floppy types. This means that one rotation is completed every $^1/_5$ or $^1/_6$ second. For recording and restoring data a read/write head is additionally required, which is located at the end of an access arm. Figure 27.4 shows the scheme for a floppy drive with motor, floppy and access arm.

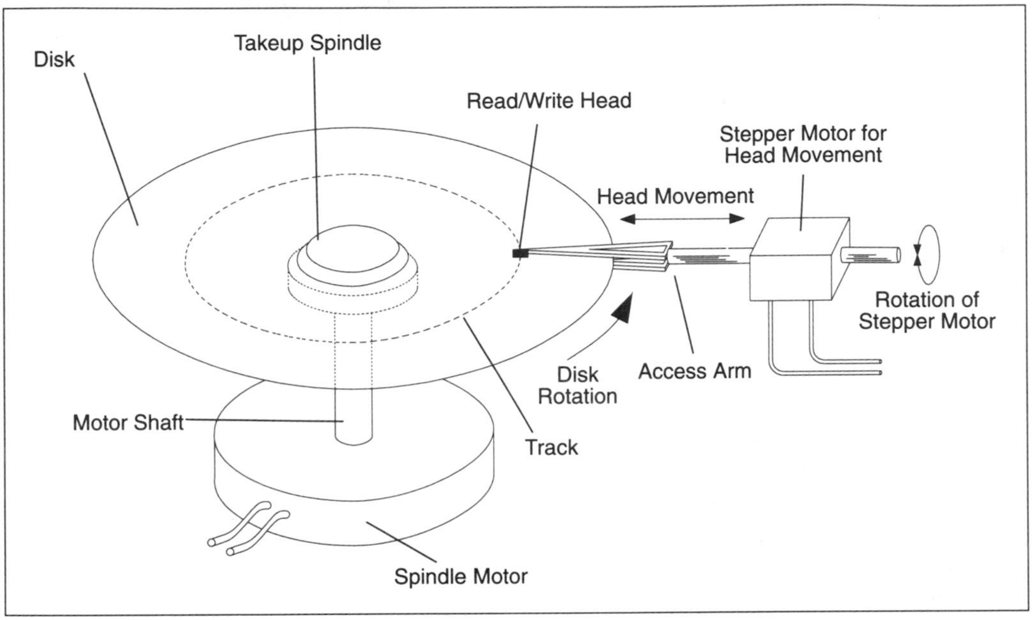

Figure 27.4: Floppy drive.

Today's common double-sided drives for double-sided floppies have two read/write heads mounted, however, on the same access arm, and they therefore cannot be moved independently, but are activated separately. The access arm is mostly moved by means of a stepper motor that drives a gear, which in turn converts the motor rotation into a linear movement of the access arm. Older models sometimes use a metal band to move the read/write heads along a rail. To move the heads to a certain position the electronic equipment of the floppy drive controls the stepper motor according to the instructions from the floppy controller, so that it carries out a certain number of angular steps. Therefore, no feedback control is carried out here. If you insert the floppy incorrectly the head may not find the addressed data, as the angular position of the stepper motor during the course of recording doesn't coincide with the stepper motor position for data reading.

Thus the one-dimensional movement of the magnetic tape past the read/write head has been converted to a two-dimensional movement; namely, the rotation of the data carrier and the linear movement of the read/write head. You may imagine a floppy disk as a rolled-up magnetic tape. On the floppy, certain data is accessible in the most disadvantageous case within one rotation of the data carrier and a complete linear movement of the access arm. One single rotation is carried out within 170–200 ms, the complete linear movement of the head typically within 200 ms. Thus 200 ms is required at most to access a data byte. With the magnetic tape you have to spool the complete tape in the most disadvantageous case, and this usually lasts longer than 200 ms. Another advantage of the floppy compared to magnetic tape is that the floppy can be removed from the drive at any position of the data carrier and the heads. Magnetic tapes, on the other hand, must be completely spooled onto a spool. Only tape cartridges are an exception.

Up to now we have only got to know the access to certain positions on the data carrier but not how the data is read or written. The basis is formed by ferromagnetism, induction, and the presence of read/write heads. Recording and restoring data is carried out only at the position of the read/write heads. Figure 27.5 shows a sectional view through a read/write head, located above the floppy.

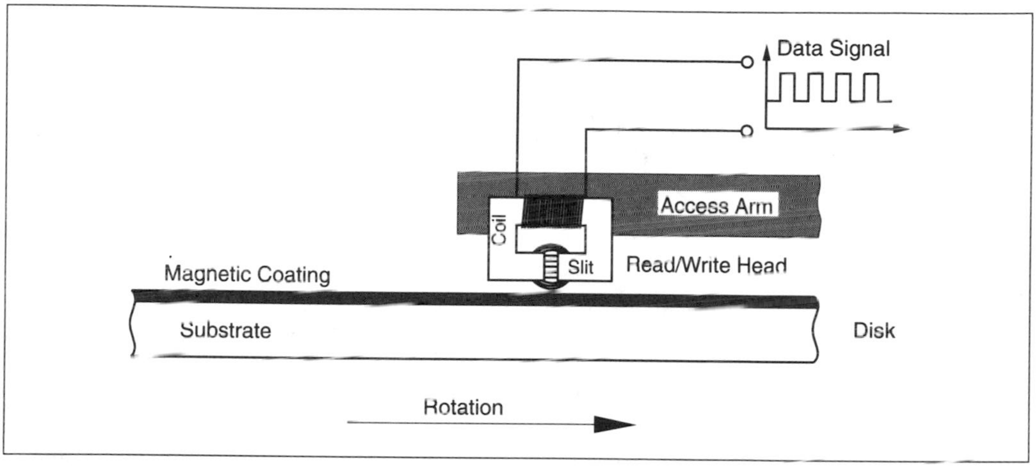

Figure 27.5: Read/write head and floppy disk. The read/write head has a coil that generates the magnetic field. The field comes out of the slit and magnetizes the coating of the disk.

Section 27.1 stated that an external magnetic field aligns the domains in a ferromagnetic material, and these domains keep their orientation even after the external magnetic field has been switched off. This effect is used for recording data. The read/write head is mainly formed of a small electromagnet with an iron core which has a tiny slit. The magnetic field lines of the electromagnet emanate from this slit during the write process, and magnetize small areas of the data carrier's coating. Depending upon the alignment of the domains, a 1 or a 0 can be represented at the location concerned.

The floppy, coated with an iron or cobalt compound, rotates below the read/write head so that the drive controller sends a short current pulse through the electromagnet of the head at a suitable moment to set up a magnetic field with the intended direction. Thus it is necessary to coordinate the rotation of the data carrier, the linear position of the access arm, and the timing of the write pulse in such a way that a defined bit can be written as the magnetization of a tiny area at any location. If several data bits are to be written in succession then the drive controller supplies a pulse stream to the read/write head in phase with the data recording, which leads to the recording of all data bits. The size of the slit and the distance between head and data carrier have a major influence on the recording density. The smaller the slit the smaller also the area of emanating field lines, and thus the area on the data carrier surface which is affected by these field lines. A small slit may thus lead to a higher data density. On the other hand, the magnetic field expands more and more with the distance from the slit. The further away the head is from the data carrier, the larger the affected area therefore becomes. Thus a small distance between head and floppy also supports a high recording density. Floppy drives and especially hard disk drives with a high capacity thus have a small read/write head with a tiny slit located as far away as possible from the data carrier.

In floppy drives the read/write head touches the floppy's surface through the force of a spring, and therefore rubs; the distance between head and data carrier is virtually zero. The floppies thus wear out in time, although the magnetic coating is further covered by a teflon layer or similar mechanically resistive material. The wearing out is limited, though, because of the low rotation speed and the fact that the data carrier is only rotated by the drive motor during the course of a data access. In the case of fast and permanently running hard disk drives, however, a head rubbing would rapidly lead to damage of the mechanical coating, and thus to a data loss. In hard disks the head, therefore, doesn't touch the data carrier's surface. You will find additional information about this subject below.

When reading recorded data the coil in the read/write head takes up the field lines of the magnetized data carrier surface which penetrate through the slit. Because of the floppy's rotation, alternating magnetizations of the data carrier's surface give rise to a variable magnetic field, which induces a voltage in the coil. The voltage reflects the data previously written. Initially, we get a stream of electric signals that are converted into a bit stream by the electronic equipment of the drive and the floppy controller. To read a certain value the controller moves the head to a certain location and drives the motor. When the intended data appear below the read/write head the controller turns on a gate to transfer the induced data signals to an amplifier. Thus data reading, a precise coordination of rotation, linear movement and the timing of gate opening is also required. For obvious reasons, floppy drives are denoted as *drives with removable data carrier*. In this respect they differ from hard disk drives. However, the removability of the floppies is paid for with a significant data security disadvantage, as dust, fingerprints and other dirt can hardly be avoided over the course of time. Because of the floppy's rotation, this dirt acts as a scouring powder, the coating is damaged or destroyed, and data gets lost. The high-capacity $3^1/_2$" floppies are therefore housed in a much better protective case than was the case for the $5^1/_4$" floppies. Meanwhile, floppy drives and floppies with a capacity of up to 20 Mbytes have come onto the market. The recording density, increased by one magnitude, requires a further enhanced protection against dirt. Thus these floppies usually come in a hermetically sealed case. Such data carriers are more accurately called moving head disks rather than floppies, as in view of their capacity and technology they are located somewhere between floppies and hard disks.

27.3 Physical Organization of Floppies

If you cut open the protective envelope of a floppy disk then you hold the actual data carrier in your hand: a completely structureless circular disk. The sections above mentioned that the read/write head can be placed above every location of the floppy by means of the floppy rotation and movement of the access arm. But for a correct and reliable management of the written data, additionally a minimum data carrier organization is required.

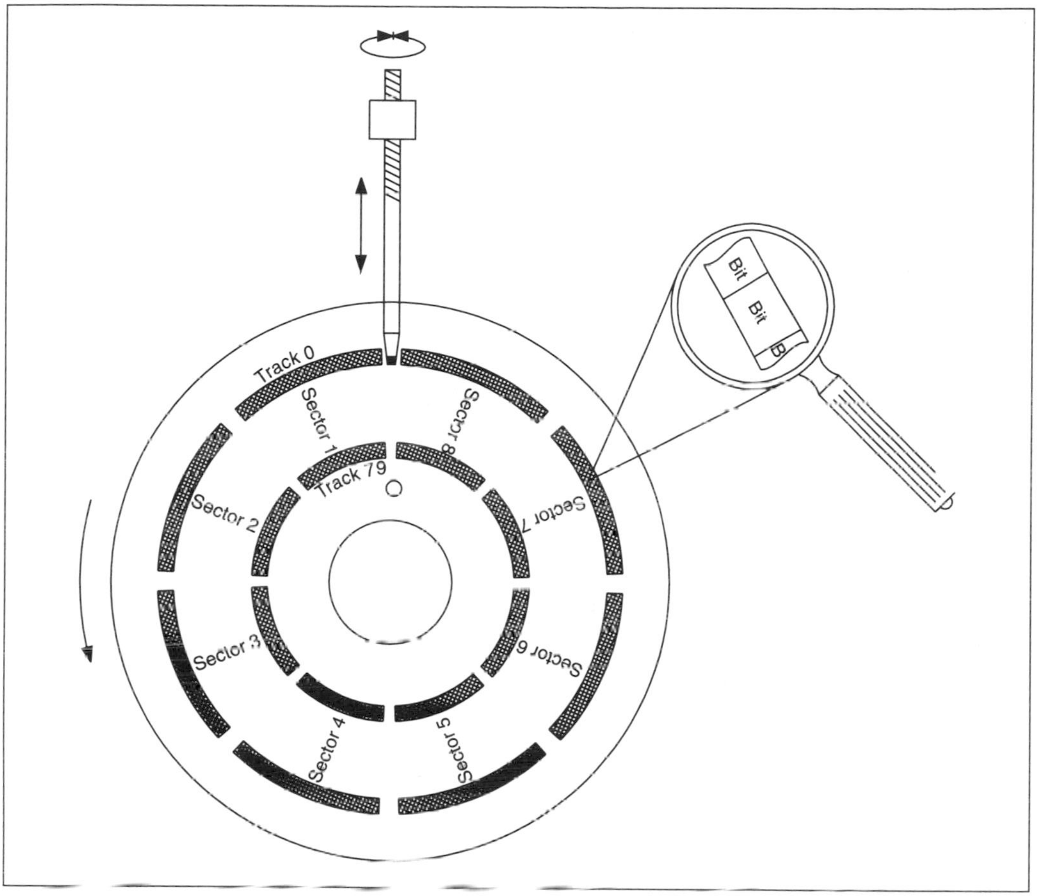

Figure 27.6: Tracks, cylinders and sectors. Every floppy disk is organized into tracks, which in turn are divided into sectors. Within one sector the bit is the smallest data unit.

Let us look at the track that a read/write head follows when viewed from the rotating data carrier. With fixed radial position of the head (that is, fixed position of the access arm) this is a circle. Its midpoint is the spindle of the drive motor. Imagine a felt-tip pen mounted on the access arm instead of the read/write head. If the radial position of the felt-tip pen is altered because of a rotation of the stepper motor, then the read/write head describes another circle with a different diameter. What's better than to take such «circles» for organizing the floppy? They are now called *tracks* which are assigned a number (Figure 27.6). Usually, the counting starts at the outermost track (that is, the circle of largest radius) with the number 0, and proceeds to the inner ones. Between the tracks there are narrow areas that are not magnetized so the tracks can be distinguished unambiguously. Today's commonly used floppies have between 40 and 80 tracks; high-capacity hard disks have up to 2000.

With double-sided floppies and hard disks which usually comprise more than one disk, more than one read/write head is also installed. Each of these heads describes its own track called a *cylinder*. Imagine a hollow cylinder for this purpose, which intersects the floppy or all of the disks. The lines of intersection with the disk surfaces define circles or tracks of equal radius. Thus the individual tracks of a cylinder are further distinguished by the *head* to which they belong. Generally, the head counting starts with the value 0. With single-sided floppies you don't have to distinguish cylinder and track, of course.

But in connection with the track we again get similar problems as with the floppy: where is the beginning of a circle? Answer: nowhere! (This seems to be a very deep and philosophical problem, indeed.) If we look at a 1.2 Mbyte floppy with 80 tracks then we realize that every track can (roughly) accommodate 7680 bytes.

The tracks are therefore further divided, into so-called *sectors*. These sectors are enumerated in the same way as the tracks or cylinders. The beginning of every sector of a track is indicated to the drive by means of the index hole if $5^1/_4$" floppies are used. In the case of $3^1/_2$" floppies, the fixed position of the notch in the central metal plate, and in the case of hard disks a certain magnetic pattern on the disk, indicates the beginning of the first sector (or the track/cylinder). In front of every sector a so-called *address mark* is present, which indicates the number of the current track and sector. The actual data area of a sector is characterized by a *data mark*. Floppies have 8 to 18 and hard disks up to 60 or 70 sectors per track. With DOS and most other PC operating systems such as OS/2 or UNIX/XENIX, the data area of a sector usually comprises 512 bytes. DOS further groups one or more sectors logically into a so-called *cluster* or *allocation unit*. (More about this subject in the following sections.) Table 27.2 lists the parameters for the most common floppy types.

Disk	Tracks	Sectors/ track	Cluster size [sectors]	Track width [mm]	Sectors total
$5^1/_4$" 360 kbyte	40	9	2	0.330	720
$5^1/_4$" 1.2 Mbyte	80	15	1	0.160	2400
$3^1/_2$" 720 kbyte	80	9	2	0.115	1440
$3^1/_2$" 1.44 Mbyte	80	18	1	0.115	2880

Table 27.2: Floppy disk parameters

The address and data marks as well as certain synchronization patterns occupy storage area on the data carrier. Thus the formatted capacity of floppies and hard disks is lower than the unformatted capacity. Pay attention to this fact when buying one. Some manufacturers and dealers like to cheat, especially with hard disks. They sometimes specify the unformatted capacity to lead you to believe in a higher storage capacity. The $5^1/_4$" HD floppies, for example, have an unformatted capacity of 1.6 Mbytes, but after formatting only 1.2 Mbytes remain. The remarkable 400 kbyte difference is used for address and data marks, synchronization patterns, and other data for the controller. Data carriers are not only characterized by their capacity.

More meaningful are the number of tracks per inch *(TPI)* and the number of bits per inch *(BPI)*. Table 27.3 lists these and other quantities for the most common floppy types. The $5^1/_4$" quad-density floppy was not used in the PC domain, but is present in the market and is mainly employed in 360 kbyte drives instead of the usual double-density floppy.

Disk type	**Capacity**	**TPI**	**BPI [oersted]**	**Coercivity**
$5^1/_4$" double density	360 kbyte	48	5,876	300
$5^1/_4$" quad density	720 kbyte	96	5,876	300
$5^1/_4$" high density	1.2 Mbyte	96	8,646	600
$3^1/_2$" double density	720 kbyte	135	8,717	300
$3^1/_2$" high density	1.44 Mbyte	135	17,434	600

Table 27.3: Physical disk parameters

Perhaps you have wondered why new floppies have to be formatted before they can be used. The answer is very easy: during the course of formatting, magnetic patterns are written onto the floppy or hard disk which indicate the tracks, cylinders and sectors. This is denoted as *low-level formatting*. In so-called *high-level formatting* only preparations for logical data organization are carried out (details are discussed in Section 27.4). Once this formatting process is complete, it is possible to read and write data by means of the described addressing scheme. Addressing via these *physical sectors* is used by the BIOS and IO.SYS or IBMBIOS.SYS as the component of DOS closest to the hardware. DOS itself, and many other operating systems, map the physical addressing onto a logical addressing by means of *logical sectors* (details on this subject are discussed in Section 27.4.1).

With floppies the DOS command *FORMAT* carries out the job of forming tracks and sectors. It writes the value 0f6h corresponding to the character «÷» 512 times into every data sector. Therefore you don't need a special low-level formatting program here. The situation changes if a hard disk is involved. Here, FORMAT only sets up the logical structure of the data carrier but doesn't form any tracks or sectors. This is only possible by means of specialized formatting programs, for example DiskManager by Ontrack.

27.4 Logical Organization of Floppies and Hard Disks with DOS

This section discusses the logical organization of data at a system level. Knowledge of file and directory commands on a user level (for example DIR, COPY, DEL, MKDIR, CHDIR, etc.) is required. The logical organization of floppies and hard disks differs only in that hard disks additionally have a partition table. For the technical structure this is insignificant, however, so the data organization for floppies and hard disks is discussed together in the following sections.

27.4.1 Logical Sectors

As already mentioned, the BIOS uses physical sectors for organizing data. But DOS and many other operating systems employ a different scheme of so-called *logical sectors*. For this purpose the physical sectors are assigned a serial number, which starts with the value 0. Thus the scheme is: assign the first physical sector (that is, the sector with the physical «address» cylinder 0, head 0, sector 1) the logical sector number 0. Now the sectors of side 0 are counted. Afterwards, we continue with side 1 or head 1, respectively. This scheme is continued until the last side is reached. If we do the counting similarly with the next track, then every physical sector is assigned a continuous number, namely the logical sector number.

Example: Double-sided floppy with 80 tracks and 18 sectors per track according to a 3 $^1/_2$" floppy with 1.44 Mbyte capacity.

```
physical sector                     logical sector
head 0, track 0, sector 1           0
........................            .....
head 0, track 0, sector 18          18
head 1, track 0, sector 1           19
........................            .....
head 1, track 0, sector 18          36
........................            .....
head 0, track 1, sector 1           37
........................            .....
........................            .....
head 1, track 79, sector 18         2879
```

The floppy comprises 2880 sectors with 512 bytes each in total; this leads to a storage capacity of 1.44 Mbyte.

The above described mapping of physical sectors onto logical sectors with a continuous number is only valid for floppies. Hard disks have another characteristic, explained in the next section as a short leap ahead to hard disks.

Of significance for applications programmers who only use DOS functions is that the logical sectors are the smallest data entity on floppies and hard disks addressable with DOS. Only logical sectors may be accessed directly, and they are always read or written as a whole. With DOS, therefore, only logical (no physical) sectors are accessible. That is important if you have installed OS/2 or XENIX besides DOS on your hard disk.

27.4.2 The Partition

As already mentioned, other operating systems for microcomputers are on the market besides DOS. OS/2 and UNIX/XENIX are the most common. In hard disks the control electronics and the mechanics are usually much more expensive than the data carrier itself. Thus it is best to use only one high-capacity hard disk for several operating systems instead of allocating each operating system its own hard disk drive. Further, the controller hardware and the BIOS are normally only able to manage a limited number of drives. One problem that now occurs is that the data structures of DOS and XENIX are completely incompatible. Thus you must allocate every operating system its own section of the hard disk which is exclusively used and managed by each operating system. Such a section is called a *partition* (Figure 27.7).

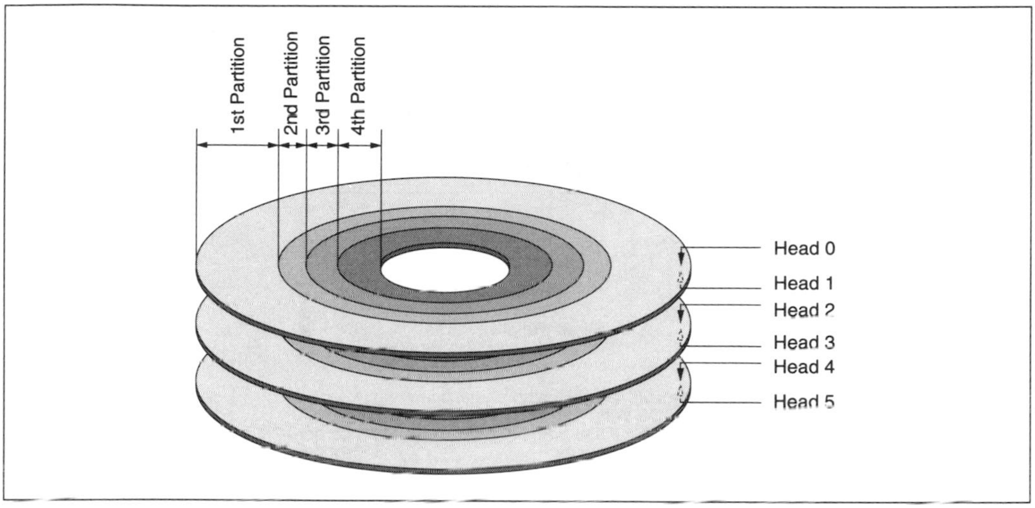

Figure 27.7: Partitions. A hard disk is divided into partitions, which generally start and end at cylinder boundaries.

Microchips are not clairvoyant, and thus the information as to whether several operating systems are present and how extensive the allocated partitions eventually are must be stored somewhere. This information is specific for a certain hard disk, and therefore it is best to write it onto the hard disk itself. You may then remove the hard disk from your PC and install it in your friend's PC without the need to reconfigure the partitions again. If you were to store the partition information in CMOS RAM, on the other hand, then you would have to reconfigure your CMOS RAM, as well as that in your friend's PC.

For storing the partition information a unique location which is definitely present on every hard disk is chosen: head 0, track 0, sector 1. This is the first physical sector of the hard disk. Hard disks may be different in size and thus may have any combination of heads, tracks and sectors. The last sector on the disk is therefore ruled out as its head, track, and sector address varies from disk to disk. Thus in the first physical sector, the so-called *partition sector*, the information about the individual partition(s) is stored by means of *partition entries* in a *partition table*.

Floppies, on the other hand, have no partition table as nothing can be saved because of their low capacity when compared to hard disks, and the data carrier can also be removed. Together with suitable drivers, you may use the same floppy drive for various operating systems. Only the form of organizing the data on the floppies differs. Floppies written with UNIX may be read with DOS, but the information is as clear as mud to DOS, which issues a corresponding error message.

Figure 27.8 shows the structure of a partition sector, partition table and partition entry. The partition table is 64 bytes long, and can accommodate four partitions at most, held in inverse order.

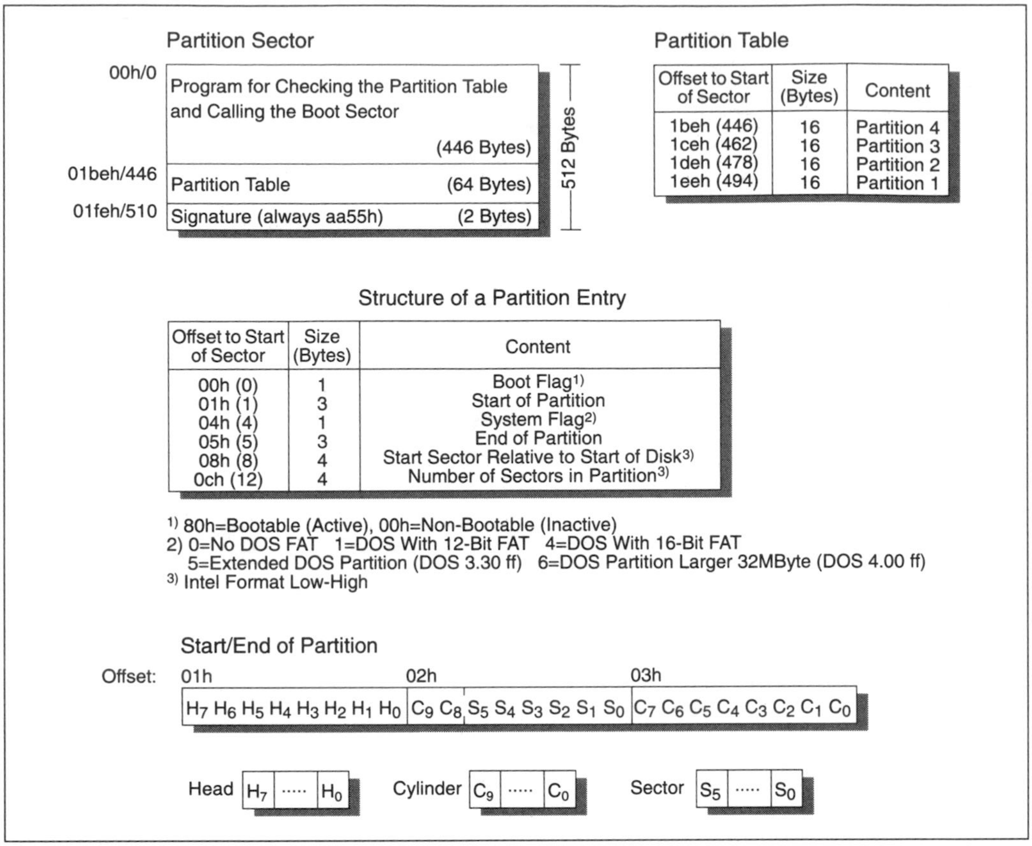

Partition Table

Offset to Start of Sector	Size (Bytes)	Content
1beh (446)	16	Partition 4
1ceh (462)	16	Partition 3
1deh (478)	16	Partition 2
1eeh (494)	16	Partition 1

Structure of a Partition Entry

Offset to Start of Sector	Size (Bytes)	Content
00h (0)	1	Boot Flag[1)]
01h (1)	3	Start of Partition
04h (4)	1	System Flag[2)]
05h (5)	3	End of Partition
08h (8)	4	Start Sector Relative to Start of Disk[3)]
0ch (12)	4	Number of Sectors in Partition[3)]

1) 80h=Bootable (Active), 00h=Non-Bootable (Inactive)
2) 0=No DOS FAT 1=DOS With 12-Bit FAT 4=DOS With 16-Bit FAT
5=Extended DOS Partition (DOS 3.30 ff) 6=DOS Partition Larger 32MByte (DOS 4.00 ff)
3) Intel Format Low-High

Figure 27.8: Partition sector, partition table and partition entry.

Besides the partition table the partition sector contains a small program with a maximum of 446 bytes, as well as the 2-byte signature 0aa55h. Upon power-up of the PC, the BIOS calls the partition sector program, which checks the internal consistency of the entries in the partition table, and then the bootstrap loader in the boot sector (see below). If the partition table is damaged or inconsistent, the program issues an error message and terminates the load process. Hard disks with a damaged partition sector are completely unusable as no information as to where each partition starts and ends is available to the operating system.

The partition table holds the entries for a maximum of four partitions. They specify the physical start and end sectors of each partition in a compressed 3-byte format (Figure 27.8, bottom). From the format you can see that such a partition table can only manage hard disks with up to 256 heads, 1024 cylinders and 64 sectors per track. The 256 heads haven't been reached up to now for any drive, but some high-capacity hard disks already have more than 1024 cylinders and the number of sectors per track is meanwhile getting closer to 64. Features that the controllers implement to solve these problems are discussed below.

Because of the partition table's structure, a hard disk may have up to four partitions. If several operating systems are installed in separate partitions on disk, then the PC must be able, in the course of the boot process, to determine which of the various systems is to be loaded. The boot indicator solves this problem. An entry 80h indicates a bootable active partition, an entry 00h a non-bootable inactive partition. The small program at the beginning of the partition sector determines during the boot where the bootable partition is located, and then activates its load routine. The system indicator shows which file system with or without FAT is present on disk. The use and meaning of FAT is described below.

```
Example: end of partition at 04 a2 60
    head:      04h = 4 decimal
    cylinder: a2h = 10100010b
               60h = 01100000b
               adding the two most-significant bits 10 of a2h to 60h
               leads to 1001100000b= 260h = 608
    sector:    the six low-order bits of a2h give 100010b = 22h = 34
End of partition therefore at head 4, cylinder (track) 608, sector 34.
```

The mapping of physical onto logical sectors (described in the preceding section) is now carried out within the partition: the first sector of the partition is assigned the logical sector number 0. Afterwards, a mapping of physical sectors onto logical ones is carried out in the same way as on the floppies until the last sector (characterized by head, track, sector in the partition table) of the partition concerned is reached. Broadly speaking, one could say that the partition table divides the hard disk into smaller «floppies» so that each operating system is only able to access the floppy assigned. Some mainframe operating systems (for example VMS) divide the storage capacity of disks into such «virtual» disks, which are then available to a single user. But unlike PC partitions, the operating system itself has complete access to all data.

Modern hard disks can be very large (Seagate's model ST83050K reaches a formatted capacity of 2.84 Gbytes). Versions of DOS up to 3.30, however, use only a 16-bit number internally to indicate the logical number of the intended sector for a disk access. By means of these 16 bits, a maximum of 65536 different numbers can be represented. The sector size of 512 bytes thus leads to partitions which hold 512 bytes*65536=33554432 bytes=32 Mbytes at most. This is the magic *32-MB-boundary* for DOS partitions. Starting with DOS 3.30, an advance was made which enabled DOS partitions of more than 32 Mbytes, but these partitions had to be divided into so-called *virtual drives* with a maximum size of 32 Mbytes each. Within these virtual drives DOS continued to deal with 16-bit sector numbers. To this number is added a number that indicates the offset of the virtual drive within the partition. Thus the effective size of files is further restricted to 32 Mbytes. DOS 4.00 and all higher versions actually break through this boundary, and continuous partitions of 512 Mbytes at most are possible.

It is also important that DOS can only access the logical sectors within the partition. Physical sectors located outside the DOS partition can only be accessed by means of the BIOS, or by directly programming the controller. This protects the data of other operating systems against program errors from DOS programs. Be careful if you attempt to access floppies or hard disks via the BIOS or even directly by means of the controller hardware. Erroneously overwritten sectors in other partitions can give rise to very serious trouble.

27.4.3 The Boot Sector

You may know that there are bootable system disks as well as non-bootable disks. In connection with the partition table we also learned that bootable partitions and non-bootable partitions exist as well. Moreover, you can, for example, format, write and read floppies with a capacity of 160, 320 and 360 kbytes and 1.2 Mbytes in a $5^1/_4$" HD drive. Thus DOS and BIOS must be able to detect the data carrier type in some way.

The key to this is the *boot sector* or *boot record*. It occupies the first sector of a floppy (head 0, track 0, sector 1) or partition, that is, the start sector of the partition. Figure 27.8 shows the structure of the boot sector.

Offset	Contents	Size
00h/0	e9xxxxh or ebxx90h[1)]	(3 Bytes)
03h/3	OEM Name and Number	(8 Bytes)
0bh/11	Bytes per Sector	(2 Bytes)
0dh/13	Sectors per Allocation Unit (Cluster)	(1 Byte)
0eh/14	Reserved Sectors (for Boot Record)	(2 Bytes)
10h/16	Number of FATs	(1 Byte)
11h/17	Number of Root Directory Entries	(2 Bytes)
13h/19	Number of Logical Sectors	(2 Bytes)
15h/21	Medium Descriptor Byte[2)]	(1 Byte)
16h/22	Sectors per FAT	(2 Bytes)
18h/24	Sectors per Track	(2 Bytes)
1ah/26	Number of Heads	(2 Bytes)
1ch/28	Number of Hidden Sectors	(2 Bytes)
1eh/30	Program for Loading the Operating System (DOS)	

1) e9h is the machine code for a Near Jump, xxxxh refers to the entry point of the operating system loader at offset 1eh/30 (DOS 2.x)
ebh is the machine code for a Short Jump, xxh refers to the entry point,
90h is the machine code for NOP (DOS 3.x and above)

2) probably no longer valid with DOS 2.x and above, refer to Table 27.4

Figure 27.9: Boot sector.

Like the partition table of a hard disk, the boot sector is also present at an unambiguously defined location which exists on all floppies or partitions. Thus DOS and BIOS can address and read the boot sector without knowing the exact data carrier type.

As you can see in Figure 27.9, all important disk and partition parameters are located between offsets 0bh and 1eh. This area is also called the *medium descriptor table*. Most entries are self-evident, so only the most important are discussed here. Terms such as cluster and FAT are explained below.

The eight bytes of the *OEM name* contain an identity that characterizes the manufacturer and version of the operating system, for example *MSDOS4.0*. The *reserved sectors* specify the number of sectors allocated to the boot record. Usually, a value of 1 is held as the loader routine normally doesn't need more than the 488 bytes which are available after these configuration entries. Essential for determining the floppy type is the medium descriptor byte at offset 15h. The BIOS and DOS can determine the disk type with this entry (Table 27.4 shows the currently valid entries), but the medium descriptor byte is not always unambiguous so you should rely on the detailed structure as it is held by the medium descriptor table. Because of the various geometries of hard disks on the market, only the single value 0f8h is used for the medium descriptor byte to characterize a hard disk. As a hard disk cannot be removed as easily as a floppy, this is sufficient. The exact hard disk drive parameters are stored in the CMOS RAM. Alternatively, the hard disk controller may have its own BIOS which is precisely informed about the hard disk type. Details concerning the extraordinarily powerful concept of such BIOS extensions are discussed in the chapter about hard disks.

Byte	**Medium**					**DOS version**
0f8h	hard disk					2.00
0f0h	3 1/2"	double sided	18 sectors	80 tracks	1.44 Mbyte	3.20
0f9h	3 1/2"	double sided	9 sectors	80 tracks	720 kbyte	3.20
0f9h	5 1/4"	double sided	15 sectors	80 tracks	1.2 Mbyte	3.00
0fah	5 1/4"	single sided	8 sectors	80 tracks	320 kbyte	1.00
0fah	3 1/2"	single sided	8 sectors	80 tracks	320 kbyte	1.00
0fbh	5 1/4"	double sided	8 sectors	80 tracks	640 kbyte	1.00
0fbh	3 1/2"	double sided	8 sectors	80 tracks	640 kbyte	1.00
0fch	5 1/4"	single sided	9 sectors	40 tracks	180 kbyte	2.00
0fdh	5 1/4"	double sided	9 sectors	40 tracks	360 kbyte	2.00
0fdh	8",	double sided	26 sectors	77 tracks	1.96 Mbyte	1.00
0feh	5 1/4"	single sided	8 sectors	40 tracks	160 kbyte	1.00
0feh	8",	single sided	2 sectors	77 tracks	77 kbyte	1.00
0feh	8",	single sided	6 sectors	77 tracks	231 kbyte	1.00
0feh	8",	single sided	8 sectors	77 tracks	308 kbyte	1.00
0ffh	5 1/4"	double sided	8 sectors	40 tracks	320 kbyte	1.10

Table 27.4: Medium descriptor byte

The first three bytes and the loader program at offset 1eh determine whether the floppy is bootable or not. If you boot your PC from a floppy, the BIOS start routine branches to the first three boot sector bytes at offset 00h and calls them as a program code. These three bytes contain a near jump (DOS 2.xx) to the start address of the loader program. Starting with DOS 3.00, the BIOS finds a short jump to the start address as well as a NOP instruction.

The loader program in the boot sector then checks whether system files IO.SYS and MSDOS.SYS (in the case of MS-DOS) or IBMBIOS.SYS and IBMDOS.SYS (in the case of PC-DOS) are present on disk. For all other operating systems the same applies. If the loader program finds the required system files, then these files and thus DOS (or another operating system) are loaded into the main memory. The computer now boots from floppy disk. If the system files are missing, the loader routine issues a message No system disk!

If you instead boot from the hard disk (more exactly, from the active partition of the hard disk) then the BIOS start routine branches to the program at offset 00h in the partition sector first (Figure 27.8). This program now investigates the partition table and determines the bootable partition. The rest of the load process is carried out in the same way as with a floppy disk, that is, a jump to the first three boot sector bytes occurs and the boot process proceeds as described above. Your PC is thus booted from hard disk. The boot record may comprise several sectors in principle, for example, if an extensive program for loading the operating system is required. In this case only the entry at offset 0eh for the reserved sectors needs to be higher.

The boot sector of every floppy or partition contains the program for loading DOS regardless of whether the floppy or partition is bootable or not. Only the loader program in the boot sector determines whether the required system data is actually present on disk or in the partition. DOS builds up the boot sector automatically during the course of the formatting process by means of the DOS command FORMAT. The same applies to hard disks.

27.4.4 The Root Directory

By means of the entries in the boot sector, DOS knows how large the storage capacity of the floppy or partition is, and how many tracks, sectors per track and bytes per sector are present. A file management system, however, cannot be established yet. Every floppy or partition with DOS has two further fixedly defined sections besides the boot sector and the partition table: the root directory, which you meet as «\» on the user level, and the file allocation table (FAT).

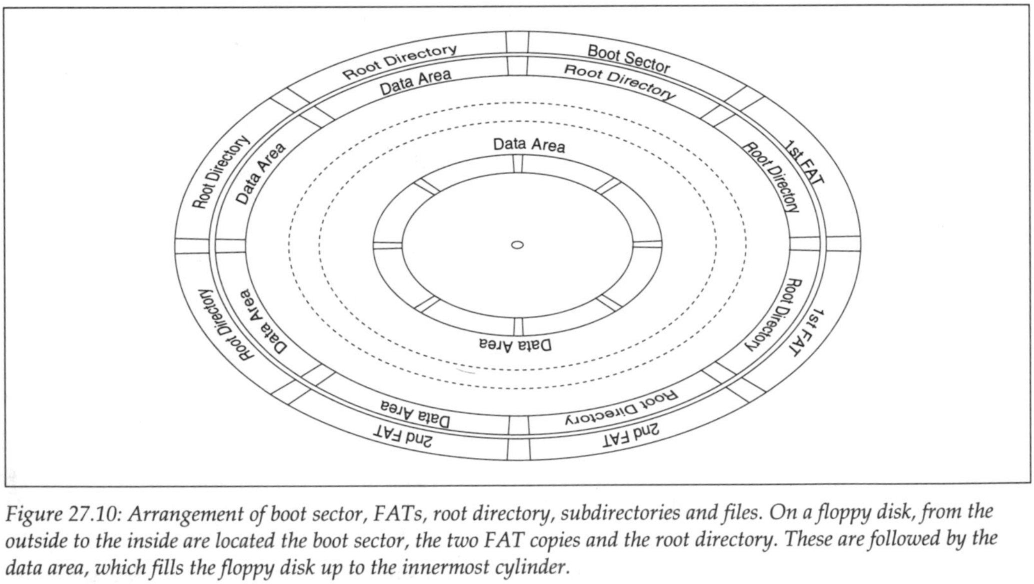

Figure 27.10: Arrangement of boot sector, FATs, root directory, subdirectories and files. On a floppy disk, from the outside to the inside are located the boot sector, the two FAT copies and the root directory. These are followed by the data area, which fills the floppy disk up to the innermost cylinder.

For file management with DOS it is necessary that the operating system knows the beginning of the data storage area. For this purpose the *root directory* is implemented, starting immediately after the boot sector and the FATs (see Figure 27.10).

If you look at the boot sector's structure in Figure 27.9, you will see that the position of the root directory is unambiguously determined by the entries in the boot sector. The root directory holds the necessary information on location, size, date and time of the last change of the files and subdirectories, as well as certain attributes in the form of a *directory entry*. Figure 27.11 shows the structure of such a 32-byte entry.

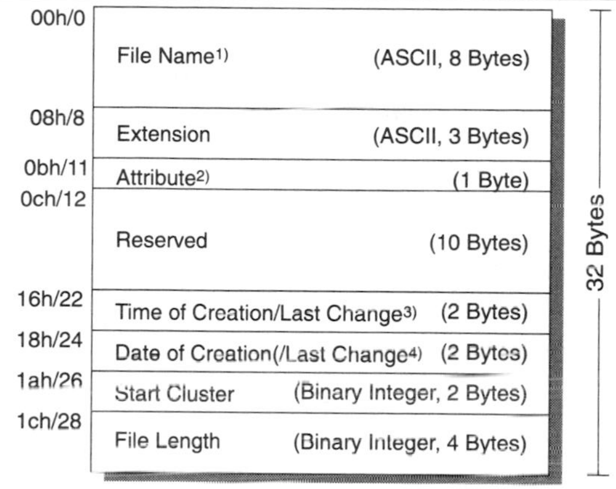

All numbers are stored in Intel format Low–High.

1) values of the first character with special meaning:
   00h=entry was never in use
   05h=first character of file name is σ (e5h=229)
   e5h=entry (that is file/directory) is deleted
   2eh=entry is a directory (if second byte also equal 2eh), thus the start cluster points to the parent directory (..)

2) see Figure 27.12

3) coded as binary unsigned integer

4) coded as binary unsigned integer

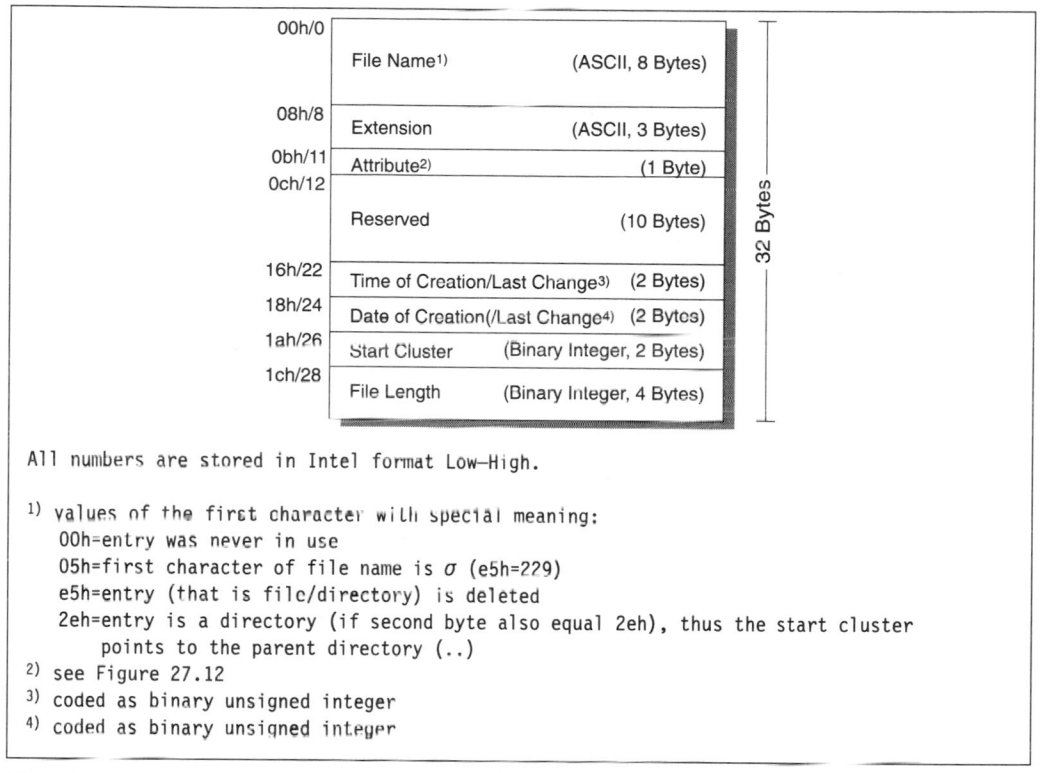

Figure 27.11: Structure of root directory and subdirectories.

The first two entries *file name* and *extension* are held in the same form as they are provided on the user level, but note that the two entries are not separated by a point from each other. Only the application program or DOS commands such as DIR insert the point for an output on-screen. Concerning the first byte of the file name, four values are reserved. If the first byte has the value 00h then the directory entry has never been used before. If the first byte is equal to e5h, which corresponds to the character σ (ASCII 229), then the directory entry concerned has been erased by a DEL or ERASE command if it pointed to a file, or by a MKDIR command if the entry pointed to a subdirectory. A value 05h for the first byte indicates that the first file name character should be σ. This character cannot be stored in this simple form as it defines an erased and therefore invalid entry. The value 2eh corresponding to the character «.» symbolizes a directory and the entry points to the directory which holds the entry itself. The DIR command displays this entry as «. <DIR>». If the second byte in the entry is also equal to 2eh (that is, the file name is «..»), then the start cluster points to the beginning of the next higher directory, the so-called *parent directory*. This is necessary to travel up the hierarchy to the next highest directory level by means of the command «CD..».

Time and *date* indicate the time and date, respectively, of the last alteration of the directory or file concerned. Overwriting data, extending files, and the creation of a directory (with MKDIR) or file lead to an alteration. The time is encoded as an unsigned integer in the format *time=2048*hours+32*minutes+seconds/2*. The date, too, is stored as an unsigned integer, but in the format *date=512*(year-1980)+32*month+day*. The date counting of DOS is always relative to 1.1.1980. This actually is no restriction, as the PC and DOS came into the market after this date, and therefore there can't be any files and directories generated on a PC before this date.

Example: `19 o'clock, 17 minutes, 32 seconds lead to`
`2048 * 19 + 32 * 17 + 32/2 = 38,472d = 9a30h`

Example: `October 3rd, 1991 is encoded as`
`512 * 11 + 32 * 10 + 3 = 5955d = 1743h`

The *start cluster* entry specifies the beginning of the file or subdirectory, and the *file size* entry the length of the file. The *attribute* characterizes the type of the directory entry. The values used are listed in Figure 27.12.

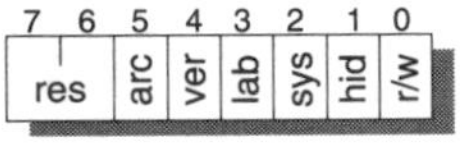


```
arc:   archive bit
       1=file/directory to be archived   0=not to be archived
dir:   directory bit
       1=entry characterizes subdirectory   0=file
lab:   volume label
       1=volume label  0=normal directory entry
sys:   system file
       1=system file   0=normal file
hid:   hidden file
       1=hidden        0=not hidden
r/w:   read-only file
       1=read only     0=readable and writeable
res:   reserved
```

Figure 27.12: Attributes.

Read-only files or directories with a set *ver* bit cannot be overwritten by DOS; DOS denies any write access and returns an error code. The erasure of the file or subdirectory is also an overwriting process. Thus you have to reset the attribute of a read-only file to 0 before you can erase it by means of DEL or ERASE. If a file or subdirectory is hidden (that is, bit *hid* is equal to 1), then the DOS command DIR doesn't display the file or subdirectory. With DOS the two system files IO.SYS and MSDOS.SYS are always hidden and are not displayed by DIR. But utilities such as Norton Commander or PCTools can list such files and subdirectories. The attribute *sys* characterizes system files to distinguish them from normal application files. Using the DOS command LABEL you may assign a name of eleven characters at most to a floppy or hard disk.

The eleven label characters are stored in the file name and extension fields of an entry in the root directory. The attribute *lab* informs DOS that this entry doesn't point to a file or subdirectory but contains the volume label. If the directory bit *dir* is set, then the directory entry concerned doesn't point to a file but a subdirectory which is one level below in the hierarchically structured DOS file system. The *arc* bit controls the backup and archiving of data. Programs such as BACKUP investigate this bit and eventually backup only those files and directories whose arc bit is set. At the same time, the arc bit is reset to 0. During the course of a write access to a file, the DOS file functions activate the arc bit automatically. This means that files with a set arc bit have been altered since the last backup. You are free to set several attributes concurrently as there are, for example, hidden and read-only system files. But ensure that the set attributes are consistent. For example, it is impossible for an entry to represent a subdirectory and a volume label simultaneously.

From Figure 27.11 you can see that the length of each entry is 32 bytes. But with DOS the logical sector derived from the physical sector of 512 bytes is the smallest readable and writeable unit, as only complete sectors can be read and written, not individual bytes. Thus the size of the root directory is always chosen so that the root directory ends on a sector boundary, otherwise storage capacity would be wasted. The boot sector entry at offset 11h, containing the number of root directory entries, is therefore always a multiple of 16. Table 27.5 lists the number of root directory entries for various floppy and hard disk formats.

Floppy disk	Root directory entries
5 1/4" 360 kbyte	112 (7 sectors)
5 1/4" 1.2 Mbyte	224 (14 sectors)
3 1/2" 720 kbyte	112 (7 sectors)
3 1/2" 1.44 Mbyte	224 (14 sectors)
hard disk	512 (32 sectors)

Table 27.5: Number of root directory entries

If you recall a complete directory by means of the DOS command DIR, you see that most data is larger than one sector of 512 bytes. Thus it is advantageous to combine several sectors into larger groups called *cluster* or *allocation units*. Clusters are therefore of a larger granularity than sectors. The number of sectors grouped into one cluster is stored at offset 0dh in the boot sector (Figure 27.9) of the floppy or hard disk concerned. One cluster consists of two sectors on a 360 kbyte floppy, of one sector on a 1.2 Mybte or 1.44 Mbyte floppy, and usually of four sectors on a hard disk. Thus, for example, two sectors are assigned to the first cluster on a 360 kbyte floppy, the next two sectors to the second cluster, etc. Other values are possible. If you write your own formatting program you are free to combine, for example, 16 sectors into one cluster. But remember to adapt the boot sector entry accordingly. DOS understands this cluster grouping, too, and operates accordingly.

Note that the directory entry indicates the number of the start *cluster* and not that of the start *sector* of a file or subdirectory. Every file or subdirectory is allocated a certain number of clusters by the file management routines of the operating system (hence the name allocation unit), which is sufficient to accommodate the complete contents of the file or subdirectory.

Note also that the root directory can only accommodate a limited number of entries, independent of the size of files and subdirectories, as its position and length is unambiguously and fixedly determined by the boot sector entries. If DOS reports that the floppy or hard disk is full, although according to DIR a lot of storage capacity is unused, then you have probably exhausted the root directory's capacity and DOS is unable to generate any new files or subdirectory entries in the root directory.

The root directory forms the origin of the *hierarchical file system* of DOS. This means the hierarchical grouping of subdirectories and files in each directory. As you can see from Figure 27.10, the root directory is the last static (that is, fixedly defined) area on the floppy or hard disk partition. All the remaining storage is available for dynamic allocation to subdirectories and files; it forms the so-called *data area*. In the data area, DOS carries out the grouping of sectors into clusters. The cluster counting starts with 2 – the reason for this is discussed in the following section on FAT. This means that, for example, on a hard disk with four sectors per cluster, the first four sectors of the data area form cluster 2, the next four cluster 3, etc.

Besides the boot sector and FAT, during the course of the format process FORMAT also generates the root directory as an empty directory without file or subdirectory entries. Once subdirectories are generated by MKDIR or files are opened (for example, in BASIC with the command OPEN TXT_FILE FOR OUTPUT AS #1), the root directory can be filled step by step.

27.4.5 The Subdirectories

With the MKDIR command you can generate subdirectories, for which DOS prepares a directory entry in the root directory. File name and extension define the name of the subdirectory, and the attribute is set to characterize the entry as a subdirectory. Like the root directory, subdirectories accommodate files and further subdirectories (that is, sub-subdirectories). For this purpose, a cluster is allocated that holds directory entries for the files or sub-subdirectories. The start cluster in the root directory points to this allocated cluster.

The first two directory entries in a subdirectory are generated by the MKDIR command. One entry points to the subdirectory itself (namely «.» if you issue DIR), and the second to the directory («..») one level above in the hierarchy, thus to the root directory in the case concerned. Therefore, the DOS command CHDIR .. moves up one level in the directory tree. For this purpose, the start cluster in this entry points to the beginning of the parent directory above. An entry 0 means that the root directory is the parent directory, that is, the current subdirectory is a first-order subdirectory.

A sub-subdirectory is generated in the same way. DOS prepares a directory entry in the subdirectory with the name of the sub-subdirectory as the file name and extension, and sets the directory attribute. Furthermore, the operating system allocates a cluster which accommodates the directory entries of the sub-subdirectory. Again, the MKDIR command generates the two first entries automatically. Figure 27.13 shows this scheme for the logical connection of the individual directories and files in a graphical manner. A further «diving» into the directory hierarchy or the directory tree is carried out analogously. Thus you are free to generate sub-sub-...-subdirectories as long as the complete access path drive:\sub\sub\...\subdirectory, including the drive's name and the backslashes, doesn't exceed 64 bytes.

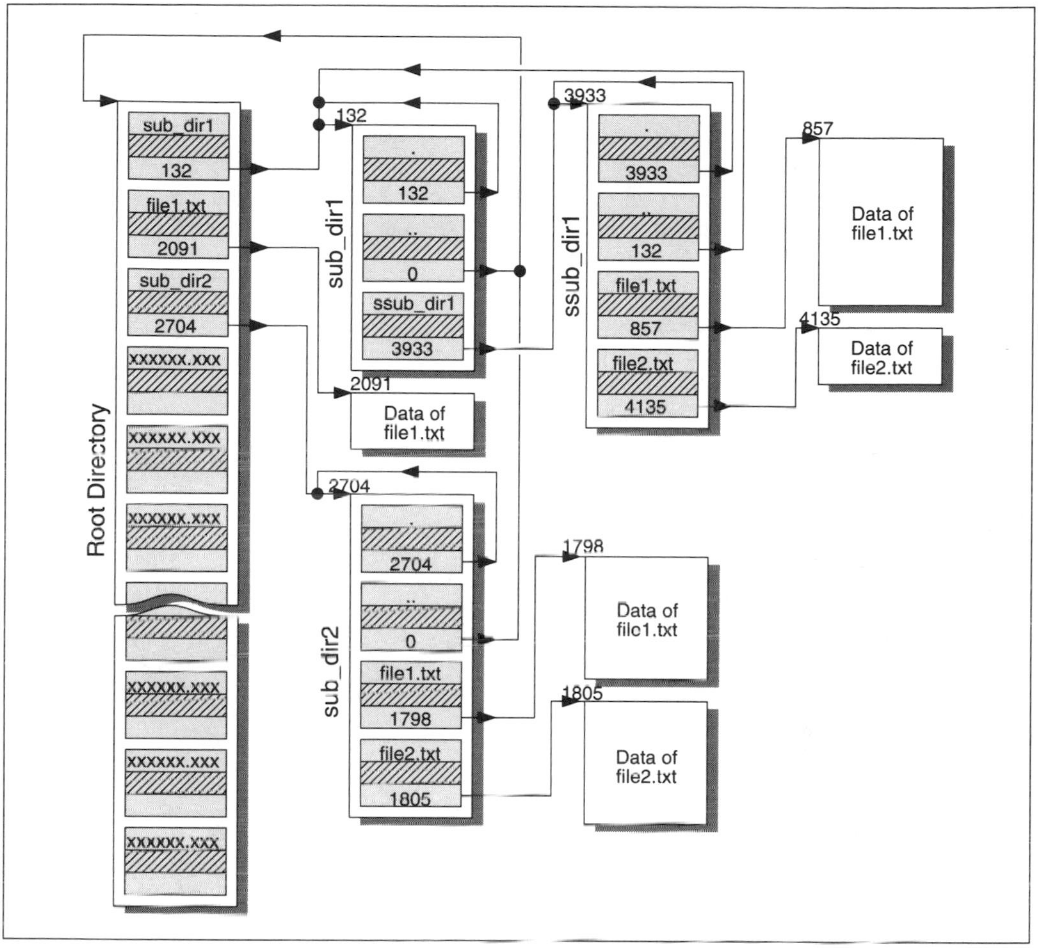

Figure 27.13: The logical connection of subdirectories.

The FORMAT command generates the boot sector, the FAT, and the root directory automatically. But subdirectories as dynamically allocated file structures must be prepared manually by means of the MKDIR command. Also, application programs, of course, can generate or erase subdirectories by means of certain DOS functions.

27.4.6 The File Allocation Table (FAT)

It has already been mentioned that the files and subdirectories are allocated a cluster whose number is stored in the directory entry as the start cluster. A cluster usually has between one and four sectors, that is, a maximum of 2048 bytes. Many files are much longer, and these

2048 bytes are not enough even for short letters. But how does DOS succeed in handling large files?

The key to its strategy is the already mentioned *file allocation table (FAT)*. The FAT is located between the boot sector and the root directory (Figure 27.10), and is automatically generated during the course of the format process (Figure 27.14). The FAT plays a central role in data management. Any destruction of the FAT or part of it immediately leads to a complete or partial data loss. Thus every floppy or hard disk usually holds two or more FAT copies. The actual number is stored at offset 10h in the boot sector. Beginning with offset 16h, you find the FAT size in units of sectors. If you write a value higher than 2 for this word, then DOS manages all FAT copies automatically without any intervention from you or a program.

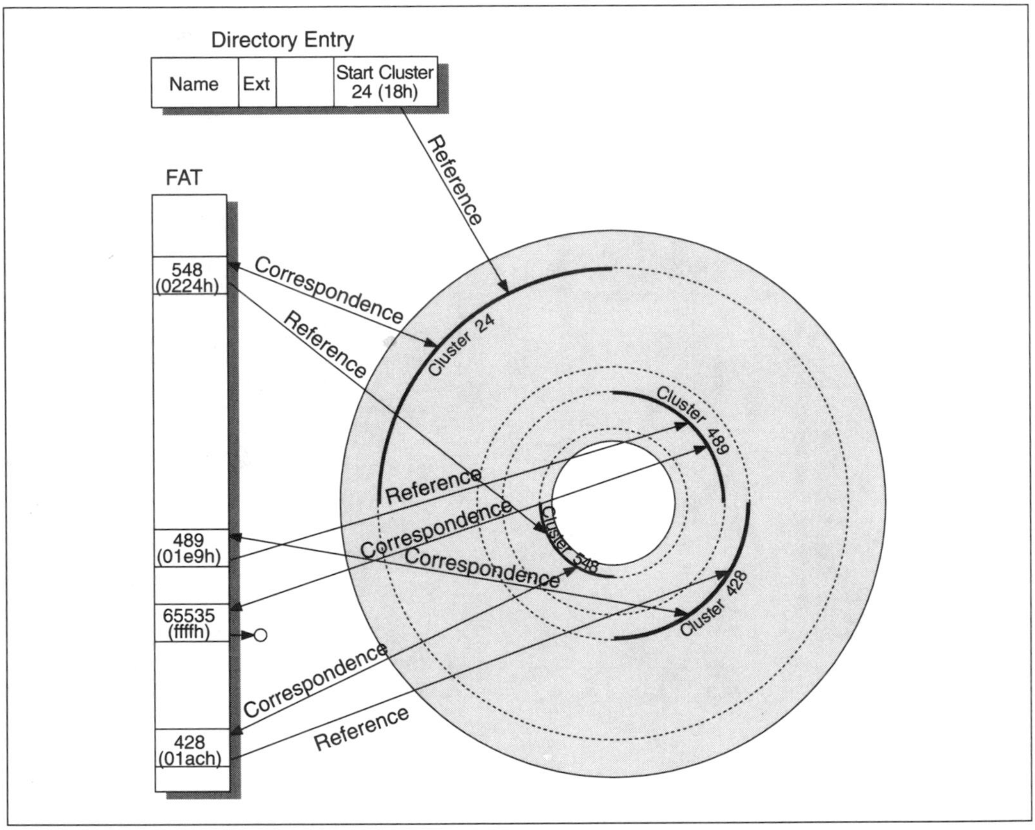

Figure 27.14: FAT. Every cluster is allocated a FAT entry, and every FAT entry points to the next cluster in the chain.

For all FATs two formats are available: 12- and 16-bit. In the first case, every cluster is assigned a 12-bit number (in the latter case a 16-bit number), enumerated starting with 0. The two first entries (that is, 0 and 1) are reserved, and are occupied by a copy of the medium descriptor byte (Table 27.5) as well as two bytes (12-bit FAT) or three bytes (16-bit FAT) with the value 0ffh. Starting with FAT entry number 2, the clusters are assigned to the cluster numbers in a definite and irreversible manner: cluster number 2 is assigned to FAT entry number 2, cluster number 3 is assigned to FAT entry number 3, etc. Thus the cluster enumeration starts with 2 and not with 0.

For example, DOS has to allocate seven clusters to a 14 kbyte file if the cluster size is four sectors, that is, 2048 bytes or 2 kbytes. In the directory entry, however, only the start, namely the first cluster of the file, is stored. Thus some information is missing as to where the file is continued, that is, a pointer to the 2nd to 7th clusters. This job is carried out by the FAT. Table 27.6 lists the meaning of the various FAT entries.

12 bit FAT	16 bit FAT	Meaning
000h	0000h	free
ff0h–ff6h	fff0h–fff6h	reserved
ff7h	fff7h	bad sector, unusable for allocation
ff8h–fffh	fff8h–ffffh	end of cluster chain, last cluster of file/directory
xxxh	xxxxh	next cluster of file/directory

Table 27.6: FAT entries of 12 and 16 bit FATs

Of significance for the allocation of clusters are the values xxxh and xxxxh, respectively. They specify the number of the cluster which accommodates the following section of the file or directory. If the file occupies only two clusters (that is, the file is not larger than 4096 bytes) then the FAT entry assigned to the cluster containing the second file section has a value between ff8h and fffh or fff8h and ffffh, respectively. If the file or directory is even larger, then this chaining is continued until DOS has allocated sufficient clusters to accomodate all file or directory sections. This accounts for the name file allocation table. In the example indicated, six references to clusters with their following sections as well as a value fff8h to ffffh are therefore required. The result is a so-called *cluster chain* (see Figure 27.15). Note that the cluster chain is only forward-directed. All FAT entries only point to the next cluster, never to the preceding one, that is, no back-links are stored. Thus the cluster chain can only be scanned in a forward direction.

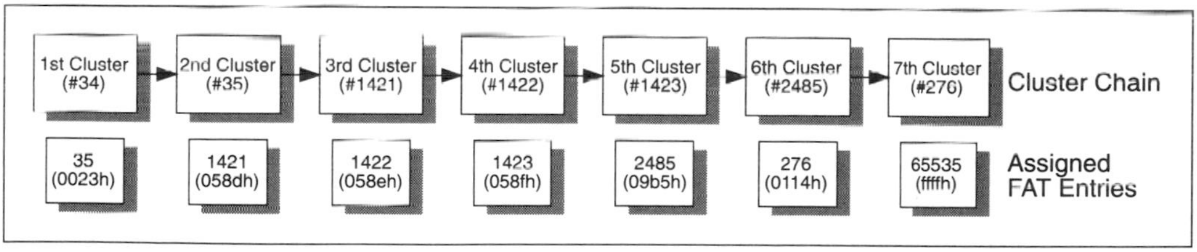

Figure 27.15: Cluster chain.

After the formatting process by means of FORMAT, all FAT entries except the first three or four bytes have the value 00h. This means that in the corresponding clusters neither files nor directories are stored.

The same applies, of course, to erased files or directories. If you delete a file with DEL or ERASE or a directory with RMDIR, then the first character in the corresponding directory entry is overwritten with the value 229 (the character σ). Then, DOS resets all FAT entries of the cluster chain belonging to the file or directory to the value 000h or 0000h. Thus, the «physical» contents of a file are not erased, as only the first character in the directory entry and the FAT entries are overwritten, but the logical structure of the file or directory is invalidated. The advantage of this strategy is that the erasure process proceeds very quickly. Only the directory and FAT entries have to be overwritten with the erase character σ or deleted, respectively, but not the complete file. If you delete, for example, a 10 Mbyte file at a cluster size of four sectors, DOS has to overwrite (instead of the 10 Mbytes of the file) only about 10 kbytes in the FAT and one byte in the directory entry. This is 1/1000 of the file size. The second advantage is that erroneously deleted files and directories can sometimes be conjured up by means of certain restore programs, such as Norton Utilities or PCTools. But this is only successful if the programs can reconstruct the former logical structure. The use of 16- and 12-bit FATs is now discussed, together with two examples:

Example: 16-bit FAT
Assume that the first 16 bytes of the file allocation table of a hard disk are as follows: f8 ff ff ff 03 00 04 00 05 00 ff ff b1 05 01 a9.
f8 is the medium descriptor byte of the hard disk (see Table 27.4); ff ff ff are the three fill bytes. The first cluster has the number two, to which the directory entry **start cluster** for a file or directory points. To determine the next cluster of the chain DOS must read the FAT entry for cluster 2; here it is equal 03 00. Note that the CPU also stores all FAT values in the Intel format low-high. Thus you have to interchange the two bytes to get the actual value; this leads to 0003h. The following cluster of the chain therefore has the number 3. Now DOS determines the value of the FAT entry 3; it is equal 0004h. Thus the cluster chain doesn't terminate with cluster 3 yet, but continues with cluster 4. If you proceed in the manner described you will get the cluster chain 2 → 3 → 4 → 5. The 5th FAT entry now has the value ffffh; thus the cluster chain terminates with cluster 5 and the end of the file is reached. The file concerned therefore occupies four clusters in total. The FAT entries b1 05 and 01 a9 already belong to another cluster chain.

Example: 12-bit FAT
Assume that the first 16 bytes of the file allocation table of a hard disk are as follows: f0 ff ff 03 40 00 05 60 00 07 80 00 ff 0f 00 00.
f0 is the medium descriptor byte, here of a double-sided 3 $^1/_2$" floppy with 18 sectors per track (see Table 27.4); ff ff are the two fill bytes. After them the assignment of FAT entries and clusters starts. We have to deal with a 12-bit FAT; therefore we have to combine every 12 bits corresponding to 1 $^1/_2$ bytes into one number. Unfortunately, this complicates the evaluation of the cluster chain somewhat. It is best to proceed as if the FAT bytes are to be combined as groups of three each (at least in mind). Thus we have to form pairs of FAT entries. For clusters 2 and 3 we get the three-group 03 40 00 by this process. The first 1 $^1/_2$ bytes or 12 bits in "natural" order form the FAT value for the cluster 2, the second 1 $^1/_2$ bytes the FAT entry for cluster 3. Be careful also in this case: the bytes are present in Intel format. Thus for cluster 2 we get the value 40 03 from which only the 12 **low**-order bits are significant. The FAT entry is therefore equal to 003h and points to cluster 3. For this cluster we get the value 00 40 according to the above described scheme. Here only the 12 **high**-order bits are significant as the 0 in 40 has already been "used" for cluster 2. The FAT entry for cluster 3 has the value 4. If we proceed in the manner indicated then we get the cluster chain 2 → 3 → 4 → 5 → 6 → 7 → 27. The 8th entry has the value fffh, thus the end of the chain is reached. The file concerned therefore occupies seven clusters in total. Further, it is interesting that the 9th entry has the value 000h, that is, the allocated cluster is free and can be allocated by DOS for a newly generated file.

In the two examples described the clusters are contiguous but this is not required. Instead, it is actually a strength of the FAT concept that the chaining also works if the clusters are spread out irregularly. The cluster chain in the first example could also be 2→3→3256→5→28 without DOS losing the thread. Such files are called *fragmented*. The FAT entries then ensure that the successive sections of a file or directory remain chained.

But the fragmentation can give rise to some very unpleasant consequences for restoring deleted files or directories. Restore programs overwrite the erase indicator σ in the directory entry according to your inputs with the first character of the file or directory name again, and attempt to rebuild the cluster chain automatically or with your help. This only works, of course, if the cluster has been stored successively, or if you know the chaining. With extensively fragmented files all attempts to restore the original data are hopeless. An example: there are more than 3.6 million possibilities for arranging ten clusters. If we take into account that one cluster on a hard disk has four sectors then these ten clusters correspond to a maximum file size of only 20 kbytes. In the case of the above-mentioned 10 Mbyte file, the number of possibilities for arranging the required 5000 clusters largely exceeds the number of all atoms in the universe!

The characteristic that the clusters of a file need not be successive is essential if files are altered later. If, for example, you enlarge the file of the first example (which has five clusters) by a further 2 kbytes, then it is impossible to use the following 6th cluster. This cluster is already occupied by another file or directory as the corresponding FAT entry is equal to b1 05 and not 00 00. If, for example, cluster 839 is free (that is, the corresponding FAT entry has the value 00 00), then the new data can be written onto this cluster. The FAT entry 6 gets the value 839d = 0343h, or 43 03 in Intel format. Cluster 839 forms the end of the chain; thus it is assigned the value ff ff. In this way, DOS need not shift any cluster to accommodate extensions. The shortening of files is carried out analogously in the opposite direction.

The above sections make it clear that the FAT is an essential instrument for allocating files. Without FAT it would be impossible to determine the cluster of the next file or directory section if they are fragmented. Therefore, the FAT is usually present in the form of two copies (the precise number of copies is stored in the floppy or hard disk partition's boot sector). The system indicator in the partition table indicates whether you will find a 12- or 16-bit FAT. With a 12-bit FAT, 4077 clusters can be accommodated after subtracting the reserved and unused values; with a 16-bit FAT this rises to 65 517.

27.4.7 The Files

On a user level the directories only support you for organizing and managing large amounts of data. The actual information is held in the files, which may accommodate texts, business data, programs, and many other types depending upon their usage. The order of the information (that is, the data in the files) follows the route determined by the programmer. This order is not interesting, for DOS as the operating system and you as the user are not confronted with the data structure. If you output a relational data set by means of the DOS command TYPE on-screen, you may be surprised at the strange form in which the data that you normally put on-screen by means of the database program appears.

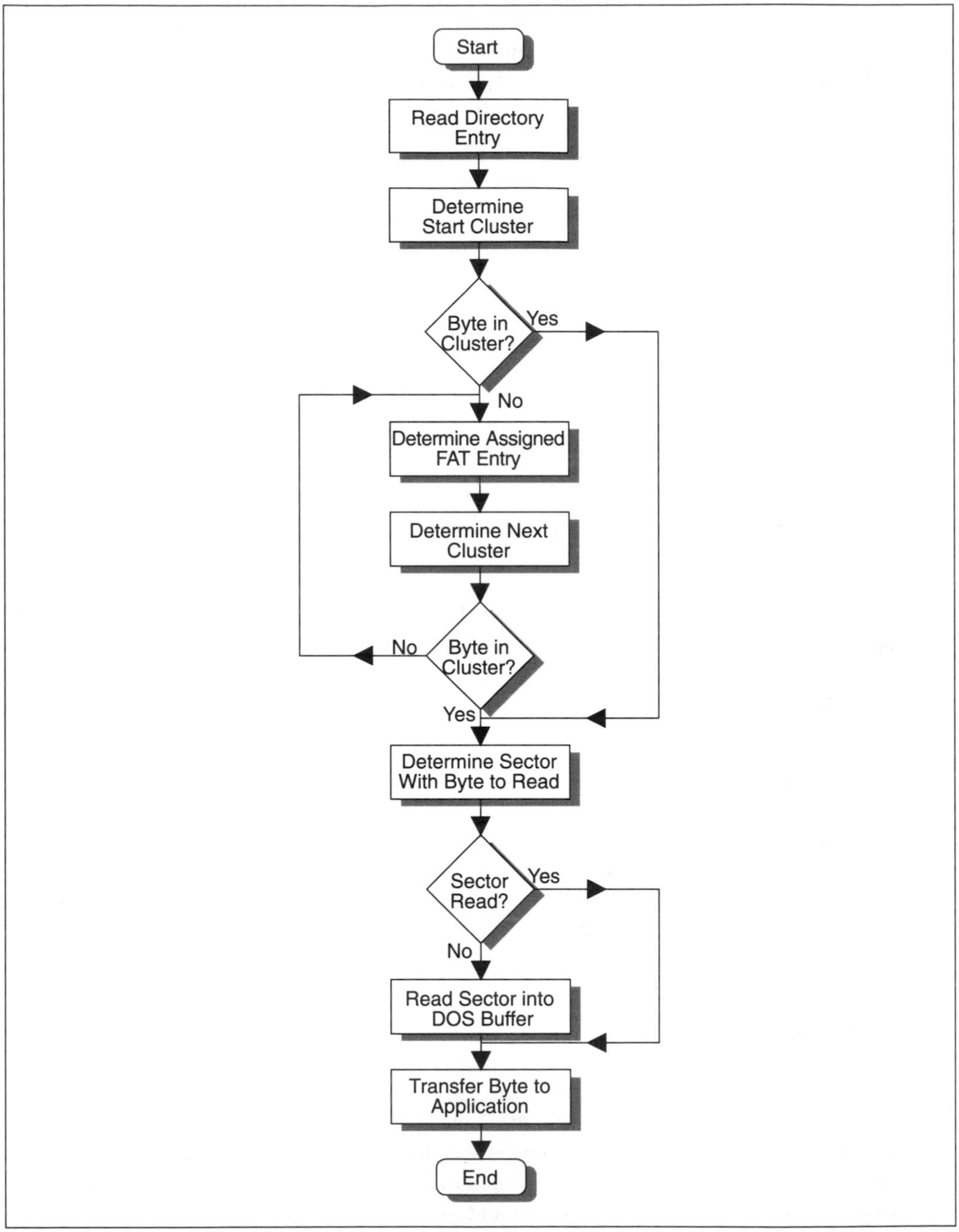

Figure 27.16: Reading a byte from disk.

Also, for every such file which uses its own data format, DOS generates a directory entry in the corresponding directory containing the start cluster of the file as well as its size. If the file is smaller than one cluster, then the start cluster accommodates the whole file and DOS sets the accompanying FAT entry to a value between ff8h and fffh (12-bit FAT) or fff8h and ffffh (16-bit FAT). If the file is larger than one cluster, then DOS distributes it in portions of one cluster to free clusters. The corresponding FAT entries are filled in such that they form a cluster chain according to the above-indicated scheme.

Under various circumstances it is possible that a file doesn't occupy the last cluster completely; it would only do so if its size is a multiple of the cluster size. Thus it is necessary to specify the file size in the directory entry. By this means, DOS is able to determine how many bytes of the last cluster are actually occupied by the file. Remember that DOS can only read and write complete sectors and allocate storage capacity in units of complete clusters because of the physical data carrier's organization into 512-byte sectors. The remaining cluster bytes are not taken into account, and can have any value. If DOS uses a cluster for a directory then it sets all cluster bytes to 0. This indicates that the directory entries are free and can be used for managing new files and subdirectories. Thus a file or directory may occupy more bytes on a floppy or hard disk than it actually comprises.

If you want to read a complete file into a word processing program, then DOS determines, according to the corresponding directory entry, the start cluster first, and reads the sectors as far as is necessary. If the file size is more than one cluster, the operating system evaluates the following clusters in the chain by means of the FAT. DOS reads the sectors until it detects an *end of the chain* entry in the FAT.

If a program attempts to read a byte or a record (for example, by the BASIC command GET #1, 1, A$), then DOS first determines in which logical sector the byte or record is located. For this the directory entry as well as the FAT is used. Afterwards, DOS reads the whole sector and determines the byte or record within the buffer that now contains the sector concerned. You may define the number of such buffers by means of the CONFIG.SYS command FILES=xx. This read procedure is shown in Figure 27.16.

DOS thus always converts any read or write access to a byte or record into an access to a certain cluster and the reading or writing of a complete sector. If you alter a byte or record by overwriting, then DOS reads the complete sector first, modifies the byte or record, and writes the complete sector back to the disk.

27.4.8 DOS Version Differences

You may have recognized that the directories and the underlying hierarchical structure of the file system are especially useful for organizing larger amounts of data. But the first IBM PC was only equipped with a simple cassette recorder and a single-sided 160 kbyte floppy drive at most. Therefore, the Stone Age DOS version 1.00 had no means of generating directories. Microsoft's DOS developers took over the concept of the *file control blocks* from CP/M (the successful *control program for microcomputers*) for the older 8-bit processors which didn't have any subdirectories. Because of the low storage capacity of the drives at that time, subdirectories weren't necessary; 20 files can be managed readily without any problems.

With DOS version 2.00 Microsoft introduced the concept of subdirectories. At the same time the more modern concept of so-called *handles* was implemented, which was already known from the XENIX system. Here the operating system assigns a unique number to an opened file for its internal management. The BASIC command OPEN TXT_FILE FOR RANDOM AS #1, for example, uses the handle «1» for the internal management of TXT_FILE. Application programs may access DOS system functions by calling interrupt INT 21h. The calling programs usually pass the parameters in the processor registers so that you must load certain registers with appropriate values before the call. DOS was designed for the 8086/8088 16-bit processors. Moreover, the sacred cow of compatibility should not be slaughtered, so DOS needs to be compatible not only on an 80286 but even on the advanced 32-bit i386 and i486 processors. Thus 16-bit numbers at most are available. The logical sectors, too, are managed by DOS with such a 16-bit number so that a maximum of 65536 sectors of 512 bytes each can be accessed. Thus partitions can have a size of 32 Mbytes at most with DOS 2.00 to 3.20. With DOS 3.30 the simultaneously manageable amount of data on hard disks is also limited to 32 Mbytes. Only the complete DOS partition comprising several such logical drives can exceed the 32 Mbyte border. One might denote these logical drives by the term «subpartitions».

With DOS 4.00 Microsoft cancelled this limitation. The technical advances as well as competing and MS-DOS-compatible operating systems such as DR-DOS made this step unavoidable. Now DOS partitions can be of nearly any size; their logical sectors are managed by a 32-bit number. Today the limitation arises from the fact that a 16-bit FAT can only serve 65517 clusters. With the usual grouping of four sectors (2 kbytes) into one cluster the data area is now limited to about 128 Mbytes. One possibility for getting larger partitions is to combine more sectors into a single cluster. This is possible up to 16 sectors per cluster. The maximum partition size is now about 512 Mbytes. Other operating systems (for example, OS/2) are free of such DOS limitations.

Besides MS-DOS and PC-DOS, several other operating systems exist (for example, Compaq DOS or DR-DOS) whose functions are compatible with MS-DOS. Some versions of these third-party operating systems have supported DOS partitions of more than 32 Mbytes for a long time, but their structures are often incompatible with MS-DOS 4.00 and higher versions. They also write a different value to the system indicator in the partition table from the original DOS. MS-DOS classifies such partitions as non-DOS partitions, and ignores them. With MS-DOS, which you may boot from a floppy, for example, you cannot access the data in such hard disk partitions.

27.4.9 Other File Systems

Besides DOS there are a lot of other operating systems. For PCs especially, OS/2 and in the future also Windows NT are of importance. Both support the FAT system used by DOS, but their increased performance requires a renovated and enhanced file system. Even the extension to partitions of up to 512 Mbytes storage capacity which has been introduced with DOS 4.00 is not enough for the future. The conceptual weak points of the FAT system concerning the fixed root directory size, the structure of the directory entries with a limited file name size of eleven characters at most, as well as the lack of any access protection, make the traditional DOS file system unsuitable for powerful, future-oriented operating systems.

Thus, with OS/2 a new file system was introduced, the so-called *high performance file system (HPFS)*. The characteristic features of HPFS are the division of a large hard disk into so-called data bands, the much more flexible arrangement of directories and files, a more efficient management strategy for free clusters, the use of sectors instead of clusters as the smallest allocation unit, a flexible length of the directory entries with 32 to 286 characters, file names up to 255 characters, and the implementation of so-called extended attributes with a size of up to 64 kbytes. In particular, the extended file names and attributes significantly help the user. Names like ANSL92_1.TXT become obsolete; now you can write ANALYSIS_SALES_1992 _VERSION_1.TXT. This file name is clear enough so that you know what's in the file even two years later. Moreover, the directory entry holds not only the date and time of the generation or last alteration, but also the date and time of the last read access. One disadvantage of the FAT system is that it is a single-chained list, that is, every entry only points to the following entry. The preceding entry can only be determined by scanning the list from the beginning again, and counting the entries. HPFS is much more powerful in this respect: all file operations proceed much faster with HPFS, a gain which is reached without any improved drive access time.

Despite all the advantages of HPFS the shortcoming remains the fact that the file system doesn't implement a protection for sensitive data. Because of the strong advance of data networks and the possibility that even unauthorized personnel can get access to the file system, such protection is becoming more and more important. To reach a higher security level, Windows NT therefore implements a further improved file system with the name *NT file system (NTFS)*. The DOS FAT system and HPFS, however, are still supported.

Mass storage such as floppies and hard disks belong to the system resources of a computer, and therefore are protected in a multitasking environment against a direct access by an application. Thus with OS/2 and Windows NT you may not readily access allocation tables, directory entries, etc. any longer. The operating system cannot allow a bypassing of its protection mechanisms without losing control of the system resources. Additionally, the logical structures are more complicated than with the DOS FAT system. If you intend to program drivers or other system near routines, you should consult a detailed manual about the various file systems.

It is important that the *physical organization* of floppies and hard disks remains unaltered even with these advanced file systems. All data carriers are organized by means of sectors, tracks and cylinders. Only the *logical organization* (that is, the strategy of storing and addressing data) has been changed.

27.5 System Configuration PC–Controller–Drive

The PC cannot read or write a single byte directly, but always has to process a complete sector, that is, the sector is the smallest addressable unit on a floppy or hard disk. To read a certain byte or bit within a byte the CPU indicates the intended cylinder first, then the required read/write head (thus the track concerned) and finally the sector with the byte to be read. The drive moves the read/write head to the corresponding cylinder and enables the indicated head. When the sector concerned appears below the enabled head, the controller turns on the transfer gate, reads the complete sector (512 bytes), and transfers the data into main memory. Then the CPU only needs to specify the location or the number of the byte within the 512-byte sector in memory to read it.

27.5.1 Controllers and Drives

Between the CPU and the floppy drive is a *floppy drive controller* which supports the CPU for accessing floppies. Figure 27.17 shows the scheme for the connection of CPU and floppy drive.

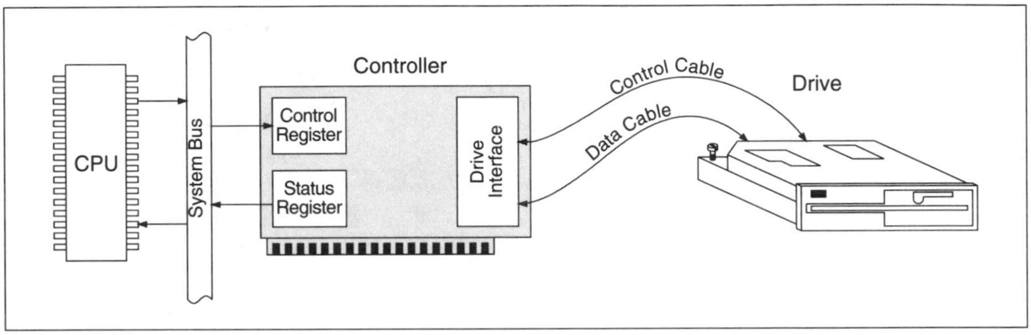

Figure 27.17: CPU–controller–drive connection. The controller is located between CPU and drive.

The floppy controller is usually located on a separate adapter card inserted into one of the bus slots. Today, often a so-called *combicontroller* is used, which can manage two hard disks as well as two floppy drives. If you have an AT-bus hard disk and the hard disk interface is already integrated on the motherboard, then it is possible that the floppy controller is also implemented on the motherboard. Then you don't need your own floppy controller any more, but may connect the floppy drive(s) immediately with the motherboard.

In principle, you are free to install more than one floppy controller in your PC, for example, to control various floppy drives such as 360 kbytes, 1.2 Mbytes and 1.44 Mbytes, or a streamer. As peripherals, floppy controllers are programmed via registers, which are accessable via port addresses. If you install two standard controllers then these controllers usually disturb each other, as several registers are present at the same port address. Most controllers can therefore be configured as a primary or secondary adapter. In the first case, the base address of the control and data registers is equal to 3f0h, and to 370h in the latter case. If you want to access the floppy drives on a pure hardware level, you must select the base address 3f0h for the first controller and the base address 370h for the second.

An access via the BIOS or DOS, on the other hand, is rather disappointing in most cases. The second controller and the connected drives seem to be dead; they don't respond to any command. The reason is that most BIOS versions and DOS support a primary but not a secondary adapter. In this way you can disable, for example, the floppy controller on a combicontroller by simply configuring it as a secondary adapter. This is useful if compatibility problems occur and you have to employ a separate floppy controller.

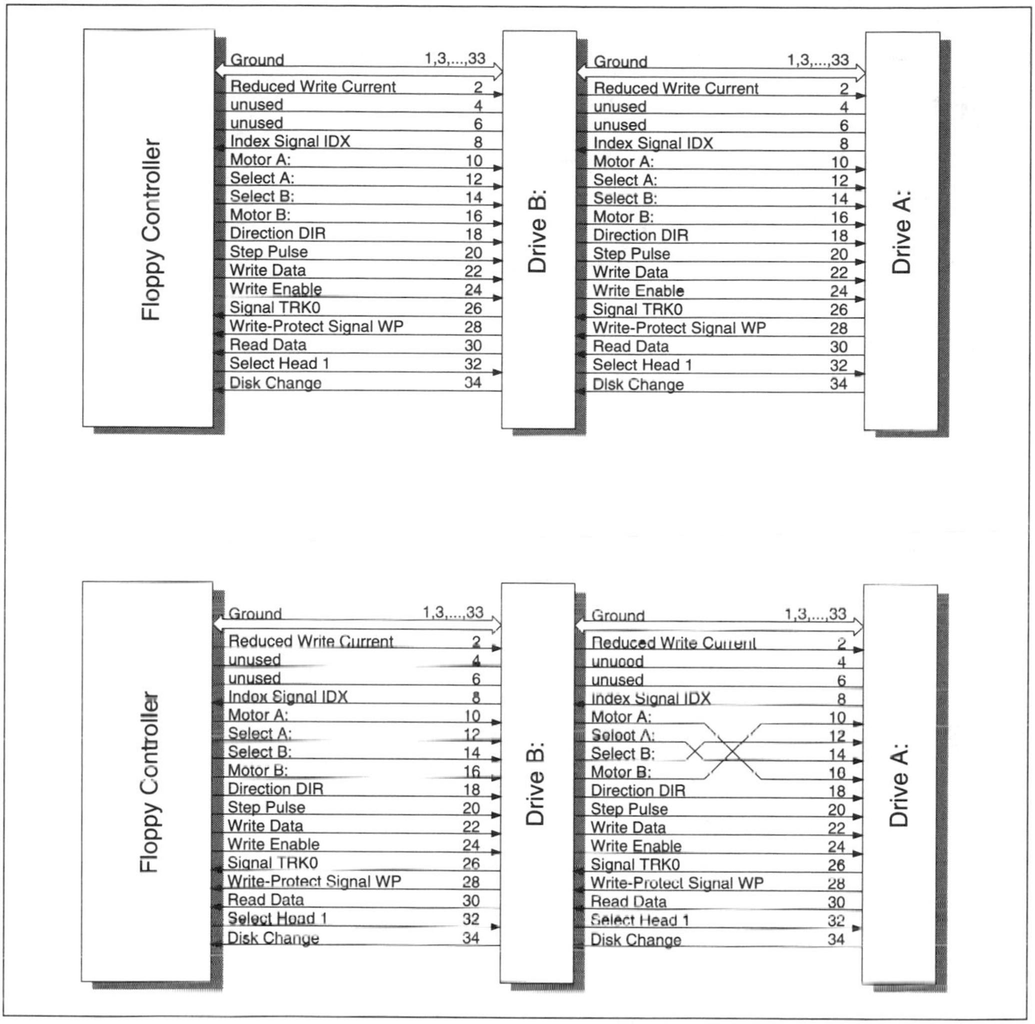

Figure 27.18: Interface cable. With a normal floppy disk cable up to two drives can be connected. If you are using a cable with twisted wires 10 to 16, drives A: and B: can both be configured as drive select 1.

The floppy drive is powered via the usual four-pole supply cable and the controller via the bus slot contacts. For $3^1/_2$" drives it is possible that a smaller supply plug is required. Modern power supplies therefore have cables with branching supply lines on which such small plugs are mounted. If your PC case doesn't allow you to install the small $3^1/_2$" drives readily and you have to insert the drive into a $5^1/_4$" frame first, this is not a problem as the larger frames are prepared for the large plug.

The connection between floppy drive and controller is established by a 34-pole flat cable which you must put onto the controller on one side and the drive on the other. Thus such cables have a plug for the controller and two plugs in most cases for up to two floppy drives. $3^1/_2$" drives often have contacts for which you need an additional adapter. Figure 27.18 shows the assignment scheme of the plugs and the signals on the individual wires of the interface cable.

There are 34-pole interface cables where wires 10 to 16 are twisted. If you use such a twisted cable it is easier to configure the floppy drives (details are given in the next section). From Figure 27.18 you can see that all control signals for activating the drives, return signals for disk change, to read and write data to and from the controller, etc. are transferred via the interface cable. One ground line with an odd number is always located between two signal lines of an even number, to avoid any influence of the signals on each other.

27.5.2 Drive Configuration

When you buy a blank drive you must configure the drive so that BIOS and DOS can access it correctly. You may install several floppy drives in your PC, so the operating system has to know how many there are and which drives are present at which address. For this purpose most drives have one or more jumpers:

- drive select jumper;
- termination resistor;
- jumper for disk change and ready;
- jumper for floppy type identification.

Via the interface cable, select signals for activating a drive are transferred. The floppy drives respond to these select signals by passing or accepting data. For this purpose it is necessary to identify every drive uniquely to achieve a unique activation. This is carried out by means of the drive select jumper. On the back side of the drive you will find a pin row with four or eight contact pairs in most cases, denoted *DS* (*drive select*). The individual floppy drives in the system are assigned a number, depending upon the drive, which begins with 0 or 1, running up to 8 at most. Near the contact pairs you will therefore see the symbols DS0–DS7 or DS1–DS8. If you short-circuit a contact pair by means of the jumper, you assign the drive concerned a corresponding number. Note that you may configure the drive as A: if you short-circuit the contact pair with the lowest DS number, that is, DS0 or DS1 depending on which number the counting starts with. You configure your floppy drive as B: analogously if you short-circuit the contact pair with the next highest DS number.

Take note of whether you are using an interface cable with twisted wires 10 to 16, or not. With a non-twisted cable you must configure drives A: and B: in the manner indicated above. Whether you connect drive A: to the plug in the middle or at the end of the cable is insignificant if you use a non-twisted interface cable. You only have to note the terminating resistor (see below). The activation of the drives is carried out exclusively and correctly by the signals motor A:, select A:, select B:, motor B:.

The situation changes if you use an interface cable with twisted wires. In this case you must configure *both* drives A: and B: by means of the drive select jumper as drive B:, that is, short-circuit the contact pair with the second lowest number. Furthermore, the plug in the middle of the cable must be connected to drive B: and the plug at the end of the cable to drive A:. IBM (and other manufacturers) use cables with twisted wires so that the drives can be configured by the manufacturer as B: as standard, and the client doesn't need to carry out the configuration as drive A: or B: on his own as is required in the case of untwisted cables. Therefore, it is possible to install a standard configured floppy drive without any drive configuration.

By twisting the wires 10 to 16, the motor and select signals for A: and the corresponding signals for B: are interchanged (see Figure 27.18, bottom). If the controller selects drive B: by means of the signals motor B: and select B:, then drive B: in the middle is accessed because it is configured as drive B: and the signals are not interchanged. As the interface cable is continuous the same select signals are also transferred to drive A:, which is also configured as B:. But because of the twisted wires the signals motor B: and select B: appear as motor A: and select A:, that is, they appear at the plug contacts for these A: signals. If the controller enables, on the other hand, drive A: using the signals motor A: and select A:, then drive B: ignores this selection because it is configured as drive B:. Because of the twisted wires, the signals motor A: and select A: appear at the plug for drive A: as signals motor B: and select B:. Drive A: has been configured as B: as is the case for drive B:, however, and accepts the two enable signals and responds to them.

The same effect is achieved if you configure the two floppy drives as A: and if you connect drive A: to the middle and drive B: to the plug at the end of the interface cable. The remaining control, return, and data signals are transferred in an unaltered manner via the untwisted wires and are always available for both drives simultaneously.

But you always have to pay attention to another configuration: the terminating resistor. In the controller such a terminating resistor is already installed, therefore you only have to configure the drives accordingly. The terminating resistor is mostly formed by a ten pole plug inserted into a corresponding jack. To determine where this resistor is located on your drive consult the data sheet that you received with the drive (or not?). As the name indicates, the resistor must be present at the end (termination) of the interface cable, that is, on the last drive connected to the cable. As you can see from Figure 27.18, this is always drive A:. If you have additionally installed a drive B:, then remove the terminating resistor from it and store it in a safe place. You need the terminating resistor again if you remove drive B: later and want to install it as drive A: in another PC.

Some drives have an integrated terminating resistor that can be activated or disabled by means of a simple jumper. Some modern drives use another method called *distributed terminations*. Here every drive has its own terminating resistor so that the terminating resistors of all connected drives contribute to the actual terminating resistor. Thus, resistors to be installed or enabled separately are no longer required. If you don't find any terminating resistor or jumper for enabling it even after carefully investigating the drive, then you have possibly got such a drive, and you can install it without any further action.

The purpose and meaning of this terminating resistor are obscure for most users, therefore some notes on this subject are in order. Between the drives and the floppy controller a fast and busy exchange of data signals takes place, which run as very short electromagnetic pulses through the interface cable. But such pulses have the unpleasant property of being reflected at the end of the cable, and therefore generating an echo which returns to the transmitter of the pulse. You can observe the same effect in the mountains, too, if you give a cry and the echo returns from the opposite rock face after a few seconds. A strong echo on the signal lines between controller and the drive disturbs the functioning of the electronics, or even damages them because of signal interference. Thus echos should be avoided as far as possible. This is carried out with a trick. For physical reasons, the terminating resistor simulates an infinitely long interface cable. This means that for the transmitter of the pulse the cable continues infinitely beyond the receiver. Now it takes an infinite time before the echo returns from the end of the infinite cable. In other words, no echo and thus no interference occurs. If you are in London then you will also wait *ad infinitum* for an echo from the Alps!

By means of the disk change and ready jumper on some drives you may set whether the drive is to indicate a disk change via line 34 of the interface cable. This function was used starting with the AT. The PC and XT ignore the signal on line 34. Every time you open the drive's door the signal level rises to «1». The AT controller detects the level change and sets an internal bit. Now the BIOS can determine whether a disk change has occurred since the last access. If this is the case, then the internal DOS buffers that still contain information concerning the previous access must be updated using a new access to the data volume. Without a disk change the internal DOS buffers may be used, and the access is carried out much more quickly. In the PC and XT this function is not implemented: DOS always accesses the disk even if it hasn't been removed. Some controllers further handle a ready signal from the drive. This is usually not used in the PC. As the floppy drives of the same type and model are also used in other computers, some drives implement this function; by means of the jumper(s), in most cases you can choose between a no disk change and a ready function.

Note that a drive with a standard ready signal (SR signal) may give rise to some problems in an AT. The SR signal is also passed via line 34, but always provides the opposite level of the disk change signal. «1» indicates that the drive is ready, that is, the flap is closed. Interpreted as a disk change signal this means that the floppy has been changed. That's not a tragedy yet. The AT access then always accesses the floppy instead of using the internal buffers, and the access proceeds more slowly. The situation becomes more critical if you open the flap and remove the floppy. Now the SR signal drops to «0» to indicate that the drive is not ready. But the AT interprets this signal as if no disk change had occurred, and reads the internal DOS buffer. This may give rise to strange behaviour: you have listed the directory by means of DIR, opened the drive flap, removed the floppy and called DIR again. Although you hold the floppy in your hand, the AT goes on displaying the same «ghost» directory without grumbling. You can only use such a drive in an AT if you disconnect line 34 from the drive and fix it at a potential of +5 V indicating «1». The AT then always assumes that a disk change has occurred and always reads the data from disk.

Some ATs with an older BIOS version that doesn't interpret the disk change signal correctly demonstrate other awkward behaviour. Many manufacturers of large program packets thankfully began to supply a reasonable installation program with their software. Today's program packets often need a storage capacity far beyond 1 Mbyte, that is, the programs come on a whole packet of floppies. Some installation procedures now use the disk change signal by means of function 16h of the BIOS interrupt INT 13h to determine whether the user actually has inserted the next floppy before they proceed with the installation. But if the drive doesn't provide a correct signal then the installation procedure denies continuation of the installation process, and keeps asking you for the next floppy after you have inserted the first one. This next floppy has been in the drive for half an hour now, but the installation program doesn't copy or install any further files. Even opening and closing the flap isn't successful, only a new drive or the soldering iron (admittedly a rather radical solution...).

Some $3^1/_2$" drives further have a jumper for enabling the identify floppy type function. The jumper enables a mechanism on 1.44 Mbyte drives which detects the HD signature on the right side of a 1.44 Mbyte floppy (see Figure 27.3) to enhance the field strength of the write field.

27.6 Recording Formats and CRC

Up to now we have only learned that data is written in tracks and sectors onto the disk. How these tracks and sectors appears in detail (that is, «looking through a microscope») is discussed in the following sections.

27.6.1 Sector Layout

Figure 27.19 shows the format of a floppy track in IBM format for MFM and FM encoding. Details concerning these two recording formats are discussed in the following sections.

Here I want to explain only the MFM format as it superseded the FM format completely. As you see, a sector accommodates not only the 512 data bytes but the tracks and sectors have many additional bytes for addressing and synchronization. A track always starts with *GAP 4A*. This gap contains 80 bytes of value 4eh, which can also be found in all other gaps. A floppy indicates the beginning of a track by means of the index hole, but its position is far less precise for exactly determining the beginning. Two data bits are separated on a $5^1/_4$" floppy with 15 sectors per track by about 2 μm only, and such precision can't be achieved with a hole of 1 mm in diameter. The pattern of the 80 4eh bytes informs the controller about the beginning of the track and gives it enough time for its electronics to be able to respond to the beginning of the track. The next 12 bytes *SYNC* with the value 00h synchronize the decoder elements in the controller with the floppy's rotation. The individual bits are passing below the read/write head, and they generate a pulse pattern for the controller through electromagnetic induction. Thus the controller must adapt itself to the clocking of this pattern, as minor rotation variations cannot be avoided. All synchronization patterns on the disk comprise a 12-byte chain with the value 00h. The four bytes of the *index address mark (IAM)* inform the controller that now the sectors of the track are following. Immediately afterwards, another gap appears, *GAP 1*. The IAM consists of three bytes of value a1h and a fourth byte of value fch which identifies the address mark as an index address mark. The IAM characterizes the beginning of the track far more precisely than the index hole in the floppy. As you will see below, the track contains further address marks.

After this track start, which already occupies 146 bytes, the sector area begins. Every sector contains ten sections; the first is a synchronization pattern SYNC consisting of 12 bytes of value 00h in the same way as for the start of the track. SYNC is followed by the *ID address mark (IDAM)*, which indicates the start of the identification field for the sector concerned. The IDAM has three bytes a1h and one byte feh. After the ID address mark the controller finds the *sector identification (ID)*. It identifies the sector concerned in the format track–head–sector–sector size.

When you are formatting a floppy (see Section 27.7.3) you have to supply a format buffer for every track to be formatted which contains exactly this information. The controller calculates from the four IDAM bytes and the sector identification ID a CRC check value in the course of formatting, and stores it in the two bytes of the *CRC* section. *Cyclic redundancy check* (CRC) undertakes consistency checking of data (similar to parity checking) but CRC is much more powerful.

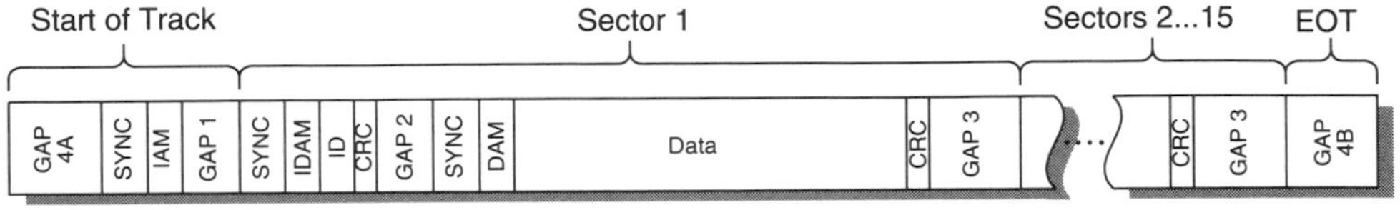


```
MFM sector format                     FM sector format
start of track                        start of track
GAP 4A: 80 byte 4eh                   GAP 4A: 40 byte ffh
SYNC:   12 byte 00h                   SYNC:    6 byte 00h
IAM:     4 byte c2h c2h c2h fch       IAM:     1 byte fch
GAP 1:  50 byte 4eh                   GAP 1:  26 byte ffh

sector                                sector
SYNC:   12 byte 00h                   SYNC:    6 byte 00h
IDAM:    4 byte a1h a1h a1h feh       IDAM:    1 byte feh
ID:      4 byte tr hd sc sz*)         ID:      4 byte tr hd sc sz*)
CRC:     2 byte CRC value             CRC:     2 byte CRC value
GAP 2:  22 byte 4eh                   GAP 2:  11 byte ffh
SYNC:   12 byte 00h                   SYNC:    6 byte 00h
DAM:     4 byte a1h a1h a1h fbh       DAM:     1 byte fbh
      or 4 byte a1h a1h a1h f8h       or 4 byte f8h
Data: 512 data byte                   Data: 512 data byte
CRC:     2 byte CRC value             CRC:     2 byte CRC value
GAP 3:  80 byte 4eh                   GAP 3:  40 byte ffh

EOT                                   EOT
GAP 4B:  xx byte 4eh                  GAP 4B:  xx byte ffh

*) the four bytes identify the corresponding sector in the format
track-head-sector-sector size
```

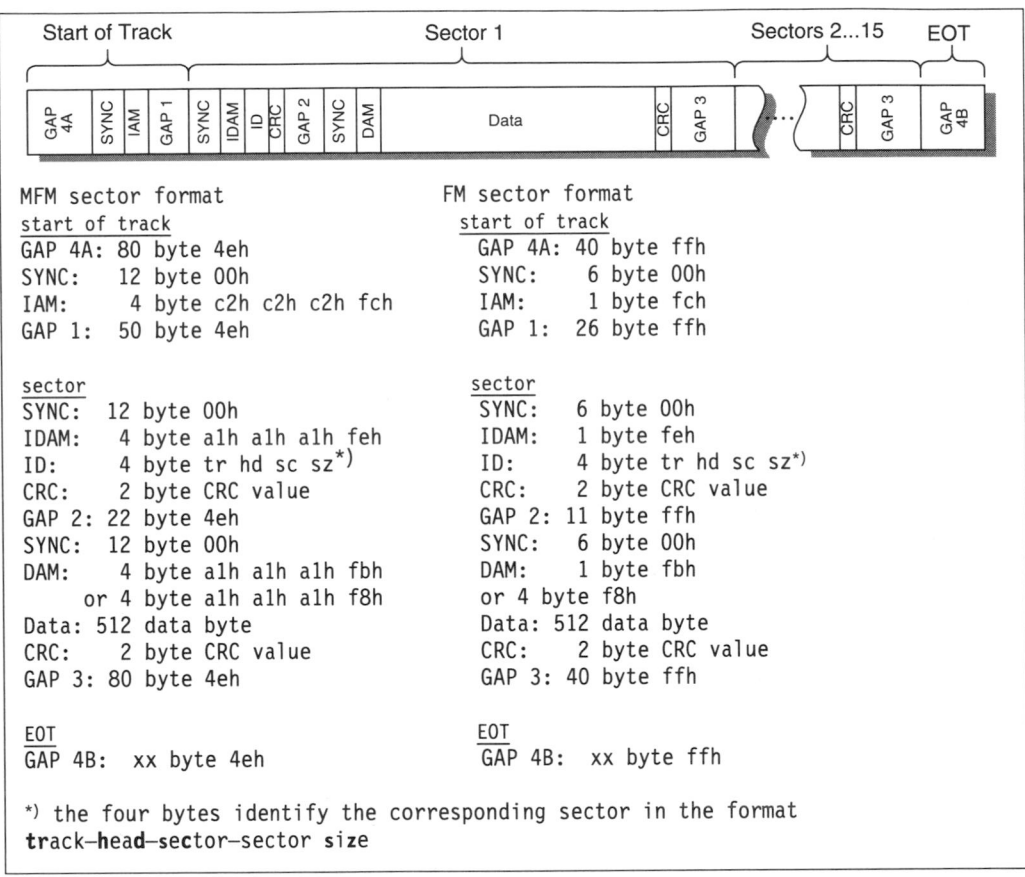

Figure 27.19: Track layout.

The CRC section is followed by another gap, *GAP 2*, with 22 bytes. GAP 2 is necessary as the controller must first calculate a CRC check value from the read bytes IDAM, ID and CRC, and compare to this calculated value with the stored one. This lasts a certain time, and without the gap the values that come after it would have already passed below the head. After GAP 2 another synchronization field SYNC appears to enable resynchronization of the controller with the disk rotation after the CRC calculation. The *data address mark (DAM)* finally indicates the beginning of the sector data area *data*. It comprises 512 bytes which you write as the physical sector onto the data carrier. But besides the standard 512 bytes, other sizes for the sector data area are also possible, which you may define during the formatting process of the track. Valid sizes are 128, 256, 512 bytes up to 16 kbytes. Large values may give rise to difficulties in synchronization, as the controller must operate during reading or writing a sector for a long time without any synchronization pattern SYNC. With small sector sizes you waste storage capacity, because the controller generates the above-mentioned and the following data sections for every large or small sector on disk. As was the case for IDAM and ID, the controller also calculates a CRC check value for the sector data area and stores it in *CRC* behind the field data. During the course of reading a sector, the check value is calculated again and the controller compares the calculated and stored values. At the termination of a sector you find another gap, *GAP 3*. Thus a sector not only comprises 512 bytes, but may grow up to 654 bytes because of all the marks that are automatically generated by the controller. If you look at Figure 27.19 you will readily see why the formatted capacity is lower than the unformatted.

GAP 3 has a special job. As the recording of data is a rather delicate procedure and needs to be carried out very precisely, GAP3 serves as an elastic buffer between two sectors. If a drive has elongated a sector because of thermal deformation, rotation variations, or incorrect timing of the write signals (like a rubber band), then GAP 3 prevents the data of the sector concerned from overlapping with the data of the next sector and damaging them. Such an elongation can be caused, for example, if the rotation rate of the floppy disk increases suddenly due to reduced friction. But the controller assumed a certain rotation rate in advance by means of SYNC before DAM. The controller keeps this rotation rate throughout the complete sector. Thus the increased rotation rate leads to a slight elongation of the sector data area, which may be up to 5%. This is, technically speaking, not a serious value. Instead, it shows the power and flexibility of modern microchips.

The other sectors of the track now follow the sector described. After 8 to 18 sectors in total, one rotation is complete and the controller detects a number of bytes of value 4eh located as *GAP 4B* between the end of the track (EOT) and the start of the track. Their number is not exactly defined. Instead, GAP 4B serves as an elastic buffer between the end and the beginning of the track, as was the case for GAP 3 between the individual sectors.

27.6.2 FM and MFM

The described track and sector layout only defines the number and value of the individual data bytes, but not how they are brought onto the floppy surface as magnetizations of the ferromagnetic coating. The information is written as a continuous bit stream onto the surface. For floppies, two recording methods exist: FM and MFM. In the following sections these two methods are briefly explained. As the MFM method enables twice the information density with the same recording density, only the MFM method is used today. For compatibility reasons, all floppy controllers still support the older FM recording (or encoding) format. Figure 27.20 shows the encoding of the byte 01101001 in FM and MFM format.

The data bits are stored in a so-called *bit cell*. A bit cell is a certain section on the floppy's surface which accommodates a single bit. For the FM recording format, every bit cell is divided into two half cells which hold a *clock bit* and a *data bit*, respectively. Remember that only a flux change in the magnetic data carrier medium is able to generate a signal. Thus every pulse is generated by a flux change (usually a reversal of the magnetization), and therefore a set clock or data bit must comprise a reversal. The granularity of the magnetic recording medium and the size of the read/write head limit the size of such a bit cell (towards smaller sizes). Typical values for the size of a bit cell are about 1 μm to 3 μm for floppies.

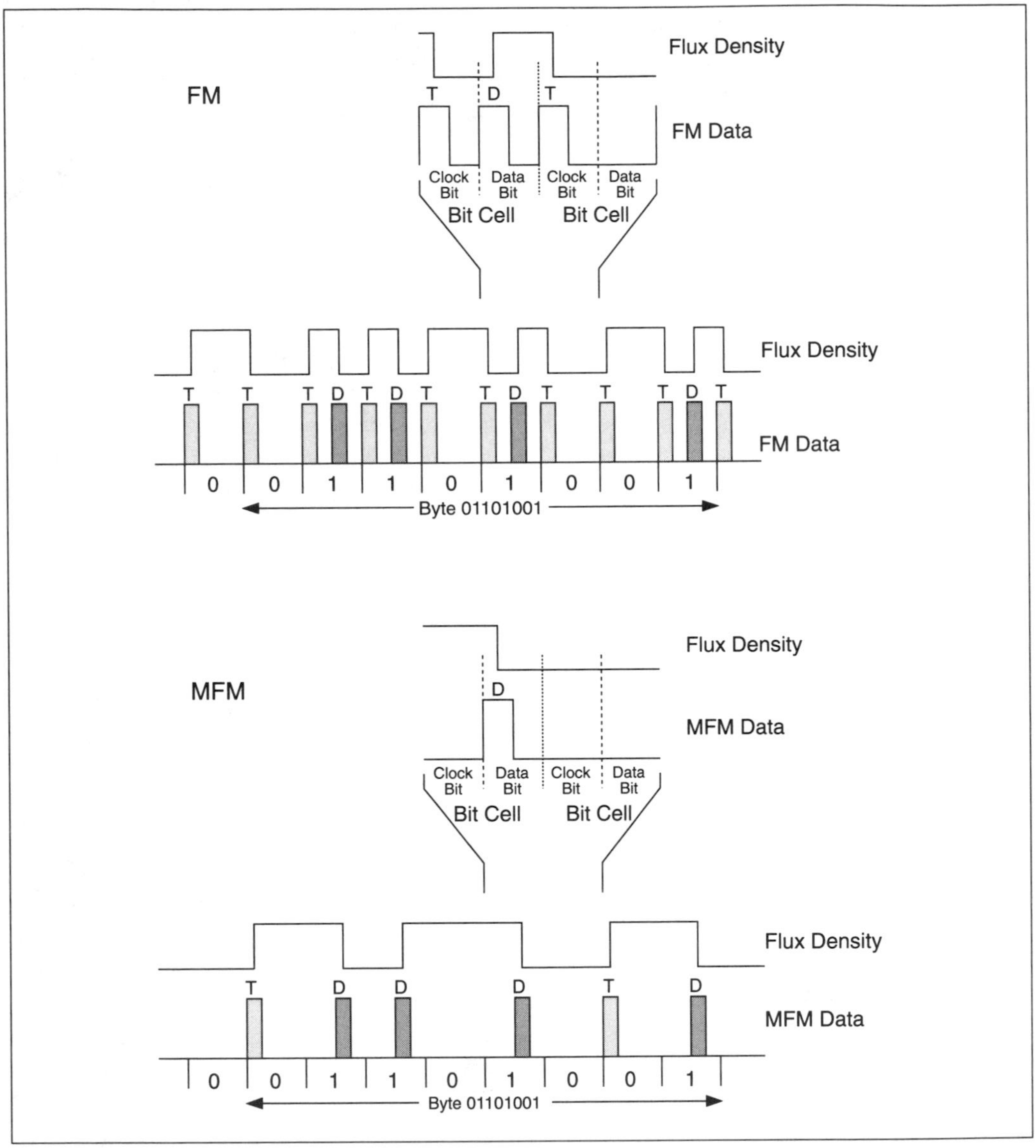

Figure 27.20: FM and MFM format of byte 01101001.

Characteristic of the FM format is that every bit cell contains a set clock bit. The actual information stored in the clock bits appears between two successive clock bits as an active or inactive signal, corresponding to a value of 1 or 0, respectively. Thus, writing data in the FM encoding format is very easy. You only need a clocked counter that outputs a clock pulse for all odd count pulses, and for all even clock pulses supplies a pulse to the read/write head if the value of the bit to write is equal to 1, or no pulse if the value concerned is equal to 0.

Also, restoring the data bits is very easy. A read signal logic equipment detects the clock bits and determines whether an active signal according to a set bit or an inactive signal corresponding to a bit value of 0 appears between two successive clock bits. Thus the FM method operates quite simply and reliably, but the information density on the data carrier is not very exciting. The MFM method increases the density by a factor of two without the need to raise the density of the clock and data bits. Figure 27.20 shows the same data byte as it is written with MFM encoding format onto the data carrier. It is obvious at once that the number of clock bits is much smaller, and the distance between two active bits is much larger than is the case for the FM method. The reason for this is the encoding rule for MFM data recording:

- A clock bit is only written if the preceding as well as the current bit cell doesn't have a set data bit.
- A data bit is always written if it is equal to 1.

For encoding data in the MFM format, not only the current data bit is taken into account, as is the case with the FM method, but also the preceding data bit. Thus the value stored in a bit cell is the result of two successive data bits. Accordingly, the electronic equipment for executing this encoding, and especially for restoring the data, is much more complicated (and expensive). As a compensation, fewer active bits must be written into the bit cells. With the FM method every bit cell has a set clock bit; with the MFM method active clock bits only occur if at least two data bits of value 0 are successive. As you may see from Figure 27.20, the result is that the distance between two successive active bits, regardless of whether clock or data bits and thus the distance between two successive flux changes, is at least as large as one bit cell and at most as large as two bit cells. On the contrary, the distance between two active bits with the FM method is as large as half a bit cell at least and a whole bit cell at most. In other words, the bit cells can be made half as large without increasing the bit and flux change rate compared to the FM encoding method. Thus the information density now becomes twice as large as with the FM method, and this is achieved without increasing the flux change density on the data carrier surface. The additional expenditure affects only the encoding and decoding electronics of the controller, a problem which modern microelectronics can solve without problems and very reliably.

The method for restoring the original data from the MFM data is quite interesting, and is important for understanding the error recovery strategies of hard disk controllers. Therefore, how the controller decodes the MFM data from the flux changes on the data carrier by means of various clock signals is explained. Figure 27.21 shows the scheme for restoring data byte 01101001 from the MFM data of Figure 27.20 (bottom).

Figure 27.21 (top) shows the flux density with the flux changes for inducing a voltage pulse in the read/write head. Note that every flux change gives rise to a pulse, but a regular magnetization doesn't generate any voltage. The read/write head continuously detects the signals and transfers them to two gates: a data and a clock gate. The data gate is supplied with a data clock signal so that the high signal levels form a periodically opened *data window*. The data gate then simply turns on and lets the signals pass. In the same way, a clock signal is supplied to the clock gate, but this clock signal is shifted in phase against the data clock signal by 180°. The high levels of the clock signal define a periodically opened *clock window*. The clock gate then simply turns on and lets the signals pass. The phase shift is chosen so that the signal, because of a flux change, can pass the data gate if it is a data bit. The signal, on the other hand, passes through the clock gate if it is a clock bit. As you can see from Figure 27.21, the data gate provides the originally encoded data bits and the decoding process has been carried out. The clock bits running through the clock window keep the synchronization if the data bits are equal to 0, and therefore no data signals appear at the data gate. With set data bits the MFM decoder uses the data bits to keep the synchronization. This is important if many set bits are arriving in succession, for example 512 bytes of value ffh.

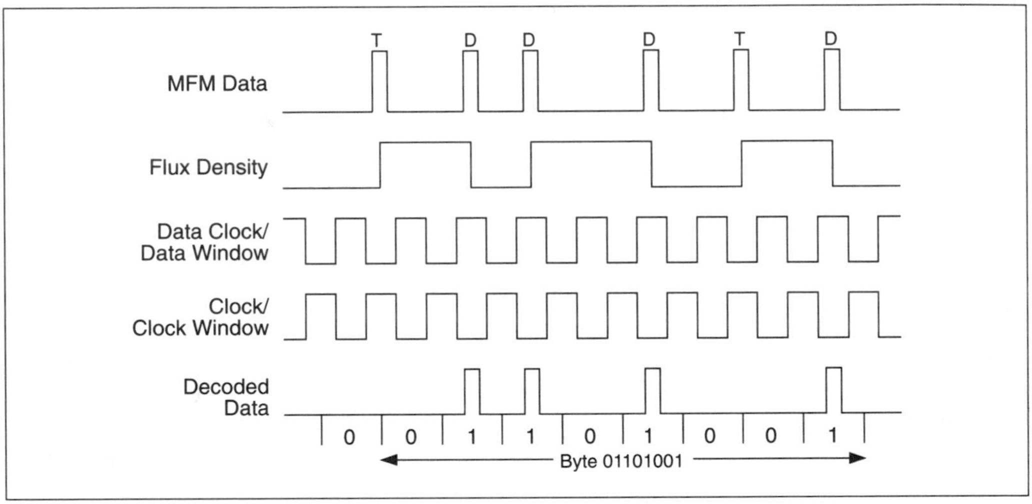

Figure 27.21: Decoding MFM data.

The most delicate point with MFM recording is that synchronization becomes more difficult because of the partially missing clock bits. As already mentioned, a clock bit only appears if at least two bits of value 0 are successive. For this reason, the synchronization fields of the tracks and sectors all have the value 00h (see Figure 27.19). Floppies used for the MFM method are formatted with longer synchronization fields than is the case with FM floppies. If the MFM method is used, then the SYNC fields typically comprise 12 bytes; with the FM method, on the other hand, they are only 6 bytes long (see Figure 27.19). Also, the values for IAM, IDAM and DAM in the sector format generate bit patterns with the MFM method that can easily and reliably be decoded by the controller to identify the corresponding bit sequences as address marks.

27.6.3 CRC – Nothing Can Hide From Me

The CRC fields have a mysterious feel as one usually doesn't get any information other than that they can detect data errors very efficiently. In the following sections the veil will be lifted. You may know the method of checking, by means of a so-called *parity bit*, whether or not a transmitted character has arrived correctly. For this purpose, transmitter and receiver have to agree upon whether the parity is to be odd or even. If you want to transfer the basic principle to other check methods then you can see that a check value (the parity bit in the case of the parity check) and a checking rule (in the case of the parity check the agreement as to whether an odd or even parity should be generated and how it is determined) are required. The analogous rules of the CRC check indicate that a 16- or 32-bit check value must be formed by dividing the value by a divisor, and that this has to be carried out by means of modulo-2 division. First, a few words on modulo-2 division.

Usually, a larger value DIVIDEND is divided by a smaller value DIVISOR by taking into account as many places of the dividend as the divisor has, and determining how often the divisor is included in the dividend. Afterwards, this multiple is subtracted from the places used. Now the next lower place of the dividend is added on the right side of the subtraction result. The division is continued accordingly. Finally, we get the quotient and a remainder:

```
DIVIDEND ÷ DIVISOR = QUOTIENT + REMAINDER
```

For dividing binary numbers only the subtraction is required, as one immediately recognizes whether the divisor is larger or smaller than the partial dividend.

Example: a209h ÷ 9bh (1010 0010 0000 1001b ÷ 1001 1011b or 41.481d ÷ 155d); numbers pulled down step by step are represented in bold face.

```
1010001000001001 ÷ 10011011 = 100001011 + 1100000
10011011
 00001110
 00000000
  00011100
  00000000
   00111000
   00000000
    01110000
    00000000
     11100001
     10011011
      10001100
      00000000
      100011000
       10011011
        11111011
        10011011
         1100000
```

Thus the quotient is 100001011b=10bh=267d, the remainder 1100000b=60h=96d.

In the example indicated the division has been carried out step by step by means of «normal» subtraction. Here, normal means that the subtraction follows the rules you learnt at school. A carry occurs if a digit of the subtrahend is larger than the corresponding place of the minuend. For CRC calculations this normal arithmetic is not used, but the so-called *modulo-2 arithmetic*. Here the subtractions are no longer carried out in the normal way, but XOR values (see below) of minuend and subtrahend are evaluated. In the same way, the addition is also carried out by XORing the individual places of the two summands. Addition and subtraction are therefore identical, and provide identical results. At a first glance this seems to be contradictary, as addition and subtraction usually behave in an opposite way. But it is exactly this that is very interesting from a mathematical view. Additionally, the technical realization of the modulo-2 arithmetic is much easier than that of normal arithemtic, as no carries need to be taken into account. With ordinary addition and subtraction, every place of the sum or difference is the result of the corresponding places of the two summands or minuend and subtrahend *as well as* of a possible carry. The modulo-2 arithmetic can therefore be realized by means of simple XOR gates and registers. Thus the electronic circuitry operates much faster than with conventional arithmetic. This is very advantageous for time-critical applications, to which the online evaluation of CRC checksums during the course of reading from or writing to floppies and hard disks also belongs.

The name XOR means that the result of two values is evaluated by means of an exclusive-or operation. The logical XOR operation thus corresponds more to our «common OR» than the ordinary logical OR. The result of an XOR operation is true (equals 1) if either the first or the second value is true. Table 27.7 shows the truth table for this operation.

0 XOR 0 = 0
0 XOR 1 = 1
1 XOR 0 = 1
1 XOR 1 = 0

Table 27.7: XOR truth table

Division with modulo-2 arithmetic is carried out in the same way as ordinary division, but instead of the successive normal differences modulo-2 differences are formed, that is, the bit by bit XOR values.

Example: as in the example above a209h ÷ 9bh (1010 0010 0000 1001b ÷ 1001 1011b or 41.481d ÷ 155d); numbers pulled down step by step are represented in bold face.

```
1010001000001001 ÷ 10011011 = 101111011 + 1101100
10011011
 01110010
 00000000
  11100100
  10011011
   11111110
   10011011
    11001010
    10011011
     10100011
     10011011
      01110000
      00000000
      111000000
       10011011
        11110111
        10011011
         1101100
```

Thus the quotient is 101111011b or 17bh or 379d, the remainder is equal to 1101100b or 6ch or 108d.

The quotient and the remainder differ from the result above. But before you say that this result is now wrong, remember that the values have been generated by a completely different calculation rule than we are accustomed to in our everyday life. The calculation process and the results are denoted by the same terms only for reasons of analogy. If you try on your own to calculate the quotient and remainder of two binary numbers, then you will readily realize that the division with modulo-2 arithmetic is much easier and therefore also much faster, as no error-prone carries must be handled. The same applies, of course, to the electronic circuitry for executing the divisions. Thus it is not surprising that mathematicians looked for meaningful ways in which to apply this simpler kind of arithmetic to checksum calculations. One result of this search is CRC.

Of course, for modulo-2 arithmetic the above-mentioned expression DIVIDEND ÷ DIVISOR = QUOTIENT + REMAINDER also holds, but the values for QUOTIENT and REMAINDER differ for modulo-2 arithmetic from the above evaluated results. In both cases, however, it is true that QUOTIENT and REMAINDER say more about DIVIDEND than a simple parity bit is able to do.

For CRC checksums, therefore, the remainder of a modulo-2 division of the value to be checked by a fixed divisor is calculated. The quotient is not suited for that, as its length is dependent upon the value of the dividend, and thus varies significantly according to the number and value of the data bytes for which the CRC check value is to be calculated. The remainder, on the other hand, is always equal to DIVISOR – 1 at most. If it were to be larger then the remainder could again be divided by the divisor at least once. Thus the length of the divisor in bits determines the length of the CRC checksum. In computers, a 17-bit divisor is usually used for ordinary and a 33-bit divisor for more critical applications. The divisors are called the *generators* of the CRC, as they generate the CRC checksums. The 17- and 33-bit generators lead to 16- and 32-bit CRC values, respectively. The evaluation of CRC checksums can be carried out by means of hardware, but you are free to execute the CRC calculations by software, too (for example, if you want to carry out a data communication via the serial interface and to check the transferred data in more detail, as this is possible with a simple parity bit).

The power of CRC checksums for detecting data errors is enormous. For a 16-bit CRC-CCITT (described below) the following holds:

– single bit errors:	100%
– double bit errors:	100%
– errors with an even number of bits:	100%
– burst errors less than or equal 16 bits:	100%
– burst errors with 17 bits	99.9969%
– all other burst errors:	99.9984%

The parity check, on the other hand, may fail with two erroneous bits, for example if the two erroneous bits have been complemented compared to the original ones. The relatively simple calculation on the one hand and the enormous power on the other have positioned CRC checksums as an instrument for error checking. They are not only used for floppies and hard disks but also for data communication, for example. Here, mainly 17-bit generators are used which lead to 16-bit checksums. Generally, the following are employed:

- 10001000000100001: the value (11021h or 68,665d) has been defined by the CCITT; thus the CRC result is often called CRC-CCITT;
- 11000000000000101: the value (11005h or 68,637d) is used by IBM for its BYSYNC data communications protocol.

The first generator is somewhat more powerful for detecting errors than the second used by IBM. The CCITT generator is employed by floppy controllers for calculating the CRC checksum in the sectors.

To carry out data checking using CRC values, the data transmitter must evaluate the CRC values from the data bytes and additionally transfer them to the data bytes. The receiver detects the data bytes, determines a CRC checksum from them by applying the same rule, and then? One would expect, of course, that the receiver compares the calculated CRC value with the received value. If they coincide then the data bytes are correct with a probability of at least 99.9969%. This strategy is also possible, of course, and successful.

A better option uses the special properties of the modulo-2 arithmetic and the CRC codes. If you look at the sector layout of Figure 27.19 then you can see that, for example, the 512 data bytes and the two CRC bytes are in succession. Thus, 514 bytes are transferred to the controller in succession, which then have to be split by the CRC logic into 512 data bytes for calculating the CRC checksum as well as two received CRC bytes. But it is easier to combine the two CRC bytes and the 512 data bytes into a single 514-byte value, and to carry out the CRC calculation with these 514 bytes. For this purpose the 512 data bytes need to be extended by two 0-bytes at the right-hand side *before* the CRC calculation. Thus the data bytes are extended by two bytes of value 0 at that position in the 514-byte block where the CRC bytes are to be placed. This corresponds to a multiplication by 65536 and the quotient also increases by this factor. The CRC check value is now calculated by means of these 514 bytes, which have the two 0-bytes at the right-hand side.

One feature of the CRC calculation with modulo-2 arithmetic is that the CRC value of these 514 bytes is exactly equal to 0 if the CRC value calculated before from the 512 data bytes plus the two 0-bytes coincides with the two received CRC bytes. Fantastic, isn't it? The same applies, of course, to 32-bit CRC values. You only have to fill the data bytes on the right-hand side with 32 0-bits in advance of calculating the CRC value that is to be written onto disk.

For data exchange with a CRC check, transmitter and receiver therefore proceed as follows:

- The transmitter extends the data bytes on the low-order side by that number of 0-bytes which corresponds to the intended number of CRC bytes. The transmitter then determines a CRC value from the data bytes plus the 0-bytes, and transmits the data bytes as well as the CRC value as a continuous data stream.

- The receiver regards the received data (which comprise the data bytes as well as the CRC value) as a continuous data block, and determines a CRC value for the whole block. If this CRC value is equal to 0 then the calculated and the received CRC checksum coincide; otherwise, a data error has occurred.

The scheme is valid for data communication, for example, and also for the CRC checksums on disk, of course. The controller calculates the accompanying CRC values while writing the data onto disk, and puts them after the sector data. During the course of reading a sector, the controller handles the sector data plus the CRC bytes as a continuous data block, and calculates its CRC checksum. If this sum is equal to 0, then the 512 data bytes are correct.

Example: `The four data bytes a2 50 b9 09h corresponding to 10100010010100001011100100001001 shall be transmitted; the CRC checksum is calculated with the CCITT generator 10001000000100001.`

```
CRC checksum of the four data bytes only:
10100010010100001011100100001001 ÷ 10001000000100001 = 1010100011001001 remainder
1001100011100000
quotient a8c9h, remainder=CRC checksum 98e0h
CRC checksum of the four data bytes plus two 0-bytes:
101000100101000010111001000010010000000000000000 ÷ 10001000000100001
= 10101000110010011001000111101100 remainder 0110110001101100
quotient a8c991ech, remainder=CRC checksum 6c6ch
The quotient has increased by two bytes because of the extension from four to six bytes. The
four data bytes a250b909h, as well as the two CRC bytes 6c6ch, are transmitted; thus the data
block is a250b9096c6ch or 101000100101000010111001000010010110110001101100b.
CRC checksum of the four data bytes plus two CRC bytes, that is, of data block a250b9096c6ch:
101000100101000010111001000010010110110001101100 ÷ 10001000000100001
= 10101000110010011001000111101100 remainder 0000000000000000
quotient a8c991ech, remainder=CRC checksum 0000h
The CRC checksum 0000h indicates that the four data and two CRC bytes are consistent; the
quotient is equal to the above indicated value.
```

But the CRC and the even more powerful *ECC codes* (*error correcting codes* or *error checking and correcting*) are not only used for magnetic data recording with floppy or hard disk drives. ECC codes are, in principle, CRC codes whose redundancy is so extensive that they can restore the original data if an error occurs that is not too disastrous (for example, a burst error with eleven destroyed data bits). Very fail-safe RAM memory systems also use them.

Usually, the control logic of the main memory in a PC only checks whether the parity of every stored data byte is consistent with the stored parity bit. There are memory controllers available that store a CRC or ECC value instead of the parity bit, and which are therefore able to detect (CRC) or even correct (ECC) a memory data error. One example of such a memory controller with embedded ECC logic (sometimes also called EDC logic for *error detecting and correcting*) is AMD's AM29C660. The controller is able, for example, to repair soft errors in DRAM chips caused by natural radioactivity in the air or tiny amounts of radioactive substances in the chip substrate (for example, thorium). The ionizing effect of the emitted α-rays causes additional charges in the charge storage area of a DRAM memory cell, and thus distorts the held value.

27.6.4 For Freaks Only – Some Amazing Features of CRC Codes

The following sections briefly present the mathematical background of CRC codes. At the beginning we started with the expression

```
data = quotient * divisor + remainder
```

With modulo-2 arithmetic the ordinary + must be replaced by the modulo-2 plus ++:

```
data = quotient * divisor ++ remainder
```

This expression doesn't exhibit any exciting feature yet; but after a modulo-2 addition of the remainder, on both sides we get

```
data ++ remainder = quotient * divisor ++ remainder ++ remainder
```

If two identical values (here remainder) are added by means of modulo-2 arithmethic, then a 0-bit always meets a 0-bit and a 1-bit a 1-bit. According to the truth table for the XOR operation, all matching sum bits are set to 0. Thus the result is equal to 0. We then get the following expression:

```
data ++ remainder = quotient * divisor
```

or in a rearranged form

```
           data ++ remainder
quotient = ─────────────────
                divisor
```

This doesn't mean anything, but with a modulo-2 addition of the remainder (that is, the CRC checksum) the result of the addition can be divided by the divisor without any remainder. Thus the remainder is equal to 0 with this division.

If you meet CRC checksums, in most cases the generator used to calculate the CRC checksums is indicated. Without knowing the generator you are not able to check the data block for consistency, of course. But the generator appears on the data sheets for controllers or communication protocols, in most cases as a polynomial. The *generator polynomial* of CRC-CCITT, for example, is $x^{16}+x^{12}+x^5+1$, and that of CRC-16 $x^{16}+x^{15}+x^2+1$.

The assignment of generator polynomials and binary divisors for modulo-2 division is very simple:

- The exponent of the each polynomial term indicates the position of the corresponding bit in the divisor.
- All terms which correspond to a divisor bit of 0 are neglected.

Example: CRC–CCITT $x^{16}+x^{12}+x^5+1$ means
$1*x^{16}+0*x^{15}+0*x^{14}+0*x^{13}+1*x^{12}+0*x^{11}+0*x^{10}+0*x^9+0*x^8+0*x^7+0*x^6+1*x^5+0*x^4+0*x^3+0*x^2+0*x^1+1*x^0$
thus the binary divisor is equal to 10001000000100001

CRC–16 $x^{16}+x^{15}+x^2+1$ means
$1*x^{16}+1*x^{15}+0*x^{14}+0*x^{13}+0*x^{12}+0*x^{11}+0*x^{10}+0*x^9+0*x^8+0*x^7+0*x^6+0*x^5+0*x^4+0*x^3+1*x^2+0*x^1+1*x^0$
thus the binary divisor is equal to 11000000000000101

The deeper reason for this assignment is that the modulo-2 division can be put down to the division of polynomials with binary coefficients, that is, coefficients that may only have the values 0 and 1. In a strict mathematical treatment of CRC codes (with which I don't want to torture you), such polynomials are used. Which generator polynomials and thus which divisors are especially suited to maximize the error detection properties is not a trivial mathematical question. But characteristic of all generator polynomials is that the power x^0 (that is, the summand 1) must always be present.

Strictly speaking, CRCs are not only checksums but codes that serve to encode information. The fact that the codes incorporate redundant information makes them so valuable for error checking. Redundant information means that some part of the information can be determined along with the rest of the information. This also applies to parity: the parity bit can be determined from the other bits, that is, the data bits. Also, the ASCII code serves (as the name already implies) for encoding information, but it is not redundant as each of the 256 different codes is assigned exactly one character, that is, a single piece of information. All of the eight ASCII bits are needed, and no bit is left for any redundant information. Thus with a redundant code there are always fewer codewords than would be possible because of the number of available bits. Eight data bits plus one parity bit enable 512 different code words, on the one hand; but only 256 are actually used and valid – those whose parity bit is consistent with the corresponding data bits (that is, all code words with odd *or* even parity, but not both).

The same applies to the CRC codes. Here the generator polynomials generate the various CRC codes. Let's look at the following example for a generator polynomial: x^3+x^2+1. This means a generator of 1101. Thus the generator polynomial has four digits. The degree of the polynomial (that is, the highest power) is denoted by m; thus the length of the accompanying polynomial is m+1. Using the generator polynomial, the code words are generated in two steps.

In the first step, code words longer than m+1, containing only zeros except for the generator, and formed by cyclic shifts of the generator, are formed. No 1s may go beyond the beginning or end of the word. The code words must be longer than the generator, as they don't carry any information otherwise. Let's assume codewords with a length of six. With the generator 1101 only the basic words 001101, 011010 and 110100 are possible. With 101001 the leading 1 would go beyond the beginning and be added at the end again; but this is not allowed according to the rule indicated above.

In the second step, all further code words are formed by means of modulo-2 addition. We get eight code words in total: 001101, 011010, 110100, 010111, 111001, 101110, 100011, 000000. Thus the code of length 6 according to the generator 1101 comprises eight valid code words. By means of six bits, $2^6=64$ code words can otherwise be represented. The remaining 56 code words are invalid. The generated code is therefore highly redundant. The probability that a statistically constructed 6-bit word represents a code word of this special CRC code is only 1:8.

If the degree of the generator polynomial is increased from three to a higher value, the redundancy also rises further. The probability that a statistically constructed code word is a valid code word of a CRC code generated by a polynomial of degree m is equal to $^1/_{2^m}$, in general. Stated differently: the probability that a statistically generated code word is detected to be erroneous is equal to $1-1/2^m$. All damaged data bytes on a floppy represent such statistical code words, as the alteration of the data bytes is unpredictable and thus completely statistical. Any error is detected by the CRC logic of a floppy controller employing the CRC-CCITT generator $x^{15}+x^{12}+x^5+1$ with a probability of $1-1/2^{16}=0.999984$ or 99.9984%. The value coincides with the above indication. Some statistical code words generated by an unpredictable change of part of a valid code word (for example, by a simple bit error) can be detected with an even higher probability. For storing data onto disk or communication with CRC checksums one therefore generates valid code words (according to the CRC rules indicated above) which are written onto disk or transmitted to the receiver. During the course of checking the inner consistency of data and the CRC value, an important property of valid code words with ECC codes comes in useful: a code word is valid if it can be divided by the generator of the CRC code without a remainder. For example, the above-indicated 6-bit code words generated by generator 1101 can be divided by generator 1101 without a remainder. For all other 6-bit values, such as 111111, this is not true. Remember that the CRC check was successful if, for a modulo-2 division of the data block made up of the data bytes and the CRC value, the remainder is equal to 0. Thus the addition of the CRC sum to the actual data always generates a valid code word. In other words: in a CRC check (for example, in floppy drives) the CRC logic investigates whether the 514-byte data blocks made up of 512 data bytes and two CRC bytes represent valid code words or not. Mathematics and computer science are therefore no mystery at all.

The cyclic shifts during the course of generating the code words from the generator, as well as the fact that the code words contain redundant information, lead to the name CRC or cyclic redundancy codes. Also, the seemingly very trivial parity compared to the CRC codes represents a cyclic code. If you use the generator polynomial x+1 you may generate all code words with an even parity. As the degree of the generator polynomial is equal to 1 the probability of detecting a statistical error by means of the parity bit according to the formula indicated above is $1-1/2^1={}^1/_2$. Statistically generated code words are therefore detected in only half of all cases.

27.7 Programming Floppy Drives – Access Levels and Compatibility

The following sections discuss the various interfaces to floppy drives and controllers. Unfortunately, minor repetitions of subjects already covered by Chapter 1 are unavoidable. Appendices F and G summarize the most important functions.

27.7.1 Application Programs

If you access a file as a user of, for example, dBASE or Word then you usually select a program function and mark the intended file or input its name manually. You don't get to know the characteristics that distinguish your PC from a home or supercomputer: as the user you are only confronted by the user shell of each program. If this shell is ported to other machines and systems, then you don't see any difference between a slow XT and a terrifically fast Cray Y-MP3, the current top dog computer for computer freaks and serious scientific applications. The hardware-near characteristics remain hidden. Thus application programs define the highest access level to floppies and hard disks (see Figure 1.27 in Chapter 1).

27.7.2 High-Level Languages and Operating Systems

However, application programs have to be programmed in some way; they don't arrive on their own, unfortunately. Application programmers use so-called *high-level languages* in most cases (for example, C, Pascal, BASIC or COBOL). Some program packages such as Lotus 1-2-3 are also written in hardware-near assembler, but the maintenance of the program code gets rather difficult then. High-level languages or the function libraries of C and assembler usually have more or less extensive file and directory functions which enable a high-level access to floppies and hard disks without the need to handle the underlying technical characteristics. System programmers who supply these functions can tell you a thing or two about that! By means of the functions mentioned you may access files and the directory concerned via its usual name, read and write records or lines of data, etc. By combining several of these functions you may construct a more complex function, for example loading a long piece of text or storing an altered entry in a database. As the classification of DOS as an *operating system* already indicates, it is responsible for the operation of the PC and therefore for managing the data and directories, the input and output of characters via the keyboard and monitor, the provision of date and time, etc. Application programs should not rely on direct hardware accesses to try to bypass the operating system. This works well with DOS (provided your programs are free of bugs), but with a more powerful operating system such as OS/2 or UNIX/XENIX the protected mode system aborts the application in most cases, as such a strategy is an obvious violation of the protection mechanisms.

The compilation of high-level languages on certain computers (in our case the PC) must therefore rely on the capabilities and the functions of the operating system. ANSI-C as a reasonably standardized language appears very similar to a PC programmer and a programmer using the above cited CRAY Y-MP3, but the generated codes have nothing to do with each other. In view of the multiprocessor architecture and the several hundred times higher processing speed of the CRAY, this seems to be evident. But let's turn back to DOS now.

DOS supplies three interrupts for disk-oriented functions, that is, interrupts 25h and 26h as well as the *function distributor* interrupt 21h. By means of interrupts 25h and 26h you may read and write logical sectors within the DOS partition. Thus you have a low-level access to the DOS data organization, namely the boot sector, the FATs, the root directory, and the subdirectories. The partition table is outside the DOS partition and remains unreachable even with the help of interrupts 25h and 26h. For application programmers who don't deal with the file organization on an operating system level, the file and directory functions of the INT 21h are much more comfortable. They provide the basis for processing and managing data by means of the commands and subroutine libraries of high level languages or assembler. You can, of course, achieve the same results by means of an access to the logical sectors via interrupts 25h and 26h. As DOS always converts any data access into an access to logical sectors via INT 25h and INT 26h, and then into an access to a physical sector via the BIOS, you would be building your own operating system functions, functions which Microsoft has already incorporated into DOS! The data-oriented functions of INT 21h have the further advantage that you don't have to pay attention to DOS-internal changes of the file and directory structure among various DOS versions. For example, you access data with DOS 5.00 by means of INT 21h in the same way as you do with DOS 3.00. However, the situation changes as far as interrupts 25h and 26h are concerned. The extension of the DOS area to more than 64k sectors also required a change in accessing the logical sectors by means of INT 25h and INT 26h. Before DOS 4.00 came onto the market the application passed the number of the intended sector in a 16-bit register. Starting with DOS 4.00, this is carried out by a pointer to a 32-bit data structure in main memory, which holds the number of the intended sector. This is characteristically for the «small operating system» DOS, as mainframes don't allow any access to the internal data structure of the mass storage by an application – this is the exclusive right of the system programs and the operator who controls the machine. Section 27.8 describes the data access by means of interrupts INT 21h, INT 25h and INT 26h in more detail.

The DOS functions more or less form a translator between the application programs and the PC hardware. DOS programs have to run correctly on such different machines as a Stone Age PC with an 8088 processor, a 4.77 MHz clock rate and an 8 bit data bus and, on the other hand, on an i486 machine with a 32-bit EISA bus and a 50 MHz clock rate. This really is a hard job. To adapt DOS to such very different computers it is divided into three parts (see Figure 1.28 in Chapter 1).

From Chapter 1 you know that the part of DOS with which you are confronted as a user is called the *command interpreter COMMAND.COM*. COMMAND.COM outputs the well-known and infamous prompt C:\>, processes internal DOS commands such as DIR, and calls application programs. Even COMMAND.COM relies on DOS functions in the same way as application programs for inputting and outputting characters as well as for loading and executing programs. These functions are embedded in the second part, called *MSDOS.SYS* (or *IBMDOS.SYS* if you are working with IBM's PC-DOS). In this part you also find the routines for handling interrupts 21h, 25h, and 26h. For adapting to various hardware environments, DOS further has a third part called *IO.SYS* or *IBMBIOS.SYS*. Computer manufacturers such as Compaq, Tandon and others adapt this part to the characteristic behaviour of their computers to ensure correct operation. IO.SYS contains specific code for accessing the drives and graphics adapters of these manufacturers. But you may also operate 100% IBM-compatible PCs from Taiwan with the «normal» DOS, without the need of special adaptations to the machine. Unfortunately, there is at least one crash per day between 99.99% and 100% compatibility.

The adaptation of IO.SYS to various hardware environments is made as compatible as possible. Of course, it is always possible to program a certain computer in the intended manner; but if your program has to run without any change on several computers then the PCs have to be compatible. This actually is, besides the open architecture, the reason for the PC's success. As an off-the-peg suit is cheaper than a made-to-measure suit, of course, individually programmed word processing systems would be impossibly expensive. The comparison with the made-to-measure suit is also correct in another sense. No program fulfils exactly your requirements, only the average ones. Application programmers must rely on the operating system functions. In this sense, all DOS versions are compatible. A later version is always able to carry out what a former was able to do. But be careful: the inverse doesn't hold! Remember that with DOS 2.00 directories, with DOS 3.00 network functions, and with DOS 4.00 partitions of more than 32 Mbyte capacity were introduced. MSDOS.SYS and IO.SYS are located on floppies and hard disks as hidden system files immediately after the root directory. Using the «hidden» attribute prevents MSDOS.SYS and IO.SYS from being deleted erroneously. DIR doesn't display the files IO.SYS and MSDOS.SYS; this is only possible with tools such as Norton Commander or PCTools.

27.7.3 BIOS and Registers

With IO.SYS or IBMBIOS.SYS we are already much nearer the hardware level than with an application program. The software at the lowest level that can be accessed by a program is formed by the *BIOS* (basic input/output system). As the name indicates, the routines of the BIOS implement an interface for inputting and outputting data or accessing and investigating peripheral hardware devices; graphics adapter, parallel and serial interface, EMS expansion adapters as well as (what else?) floppy and hard disk controllers, which in turn control the drives belonging to them.

Each of these peripherals has its own dedicated BIOS interrupt. In the case of floppy and hard disk drives, this is interrupt INT 13h. Section 27.9 and Appendix F discuss its functions. INT 13h exclusively works with physical sectors; thus we are already on the level of the physical data carrier organization and the partition table becomes accessible. For calling and executing the BIOS functions, a *de facto* standard has been established which orients to the assumptions of IBM BIOS. Among all DOS parts only IO.SYS accesses the BIOS, thus such a standard would not necessarily be required as IO.SYS, as the very hardware-dependent part of DOS, can always be adapted to every BIOS. Because of the standardization of the BIOS functions, even an application programmer can call BIOS functions and be sure in most cases that the called function will be carried out correctly on another PC.

As you already know, the ports form the interface to peripherals such as the controller and graphics adapters, and access their control and data registers. Note that most peripherals have a (more or less) complex microprocessor that often has its own BIOS. Thus powerful peripherals more or less form their own «computer» in the PC, to which you pass commands via the ports. As different controllers from different manufacturers for different floppy or hard disk drives with different encoding formats can also have very different ports and a different «command set», direct programming by means of the registers or ports is out of the question. Direct programming gives rise to maximum performance and maximum control of the hardware, but porting the program to another PC (which may even have the same name) often fails because of minor but nevertheless decisive differences in hardware. The BIOS offers a good compromise between performance and control on the one hand, and compatibility on the other. Unlike DOS, it is always tailored especially for the actual computer type. The functions of INT 13h (for example, move head) are passed to the floppy controller via the corresponding port as a suitable «command sequence». Unfortunately, DOS gives hardly any possibilities for programming the serial and parallel ports, or even the graphics adapter, so that they are suitable for powerful applications. If you want to employ, for example, the features of EGA and VGA adapters, or even those of the new graphics adapters with fast graphics processors, then you are forced to use BIOS functions. The same applies for accesses to data beyond the DOS partition (for example, the partition table). Here only a direct call of BIOS functions solves the problem. As already mentioned, nearly all BIOS interrupts have become *de facto* standards today. This means that in modern PCs the BIOS functions of all manufacturers carry out the same functions, thus compatibility generally holds right down to the BIOS level.

27.8 Programming Floppy Drives – Access via DOS

DOS provides three interrupts (25h, 26h and 21h) for access to floppy and hard disks. Interrupts 25h and 26h form the lower level as you may address logical sectors directly by means of them. But note that a direct access to logical sectors may lead to disastrous results in the case of an access error. For example, incorrect FAT entries destroy the logical structure of the file system, and make the data completely inaccessible. Figure 27.22 shows the call and return formats for the interrupts INT 25h for reading and INT 26h for writing a logical sector. By means of these interrupts you may read or write several successive sectors all at once. For hard disks a new call format via parameter blocks was introduced with DOS version 4.00 to access sectors with a number beyond 65535, but this applies only to hard disks, as 65536 sectors with 512 bytes each correspond to 32 Mbytes of data. Further details about this format are discussed in Section 28.4.1.

Partitions up to 32Mbytes or 65,536 Sectors

INT 25h – Read One or More Logical Sectors

Register	Call Value	Return Value
AL	Drive Number[1]	
AX		Error Code[2]
CX	Number of Sectors	
DX	First Sector	
BX	Read Buffer Offset	
DS	Read Buffer Segment	
Carry		Error if <> 0

INT 26h – Write One or More Logical Sectors

Register	Call Value	Return Value
AL	Drive Number[1]	
AX		Error Code[2]
CX	Number of Sectors	
DX	First Sector	
BX	Write Buffer Offset	
DS	Write Buffer Segment	
Carry		Error if <> 0

[1] 00h=Drive A:, 01h=Drive B: etc. [2] see Table 27.8

Figure 27.22: INT 25h and INT 26h formats.

Note that interrupts 25h and 26h leave a status byte on the stack after a call that you must remove (and use) with a POP instruction. If the intended sector cannot be read or written for some reason, then DOS sets the carry flag and returns an error code in register AX. The code specifies the cause for the failed read or write attempt. Table 27.8 lists the valid error codes.

Code	Error
01h	invalid command
02h	incorrect address mark
04h	sector not found
08h	DMA overflow
10h	CRC or ECC error
20h	controller error
40h	seek error
80h	drive not ready

Table 27.8: INT 25h and INT 26h error codes

Example: `read logical sector 519 with INT 25h from floppy in drive B: (programming language: C)`

```
unsigned char far buffer[512];
void read_log_sector_519(void)
{ union REGS inregs, outregs;
  struct SREGS segregs;

  inregs.h.al=0x01                          /* drive B: */
  inregs.x.cx=0x0001                        /* read only one sector */
  inregs.x.dx=0x0207                        /* first sector is 519 */
```

```
  inregs.x.bx=FP_OFF(buffer)                 /* transfer offset of buffer to bx */
  segregs.ds=FP_SEG(buffer)                  /* transfer segment of buffer to ds */
  int86x(0x25, &inregs, &outregs, &segregs)  /* call interrupt, sector is transferred
                                                to buffer */
  if ((outregs.x.cflag & 0x01) == 0x01) {    /* check whether carry is set */
    printf("\nerror code: %x", outregs.x.ax); /* display error code */
  }
}
```

Example: write logical sector 1482 with INT 26h onto floppy in drive A: (programming language: C)

```
unsigned char far buffer[512];
void write_log_sektor_1482(void)
{ union REGS inregs, outregs;
  struct SREGS segregs;

  inregs.h.al=0x00                           /* drive A: */
  inregs.x.cx=0x0001                         /* write only one sector */
  inregs.x.dx=0x05ca                         /* first sector is 1482 */
  inregs.x.bx=FP_OFF(buffer)                 /* transfer offset of buffer to bx */
  segregs.ds=FP_SEG(buffer)                  /* transfer segment of buffer to ds */
  int86x(0x26, &inregs, &outregs, &segregs)  /* call interrupt, sector is written
                                                from buffer */
  if ((outregs.x.cflag & 0x01) == 0x01) {    /* check whether carry is set */
    printf("\nerror code: %x", outregs.x.ax); /* display error code */
  }
}
```

If you want to write, for example, byte 6294 of the file TEXT.TXT in directory \S_DIR\SS_DIR\SSS_DIR by means of interrupt INT 26h, then this would be very cumbersome (but not impossible, of course). First you have to look for S_DIR in the directory entries of the root directory by reading the corresponding sector with INT 25h. Then the start cluster of S_DIR must be read; eventually, an access to the FAT via INT 25h is required to determine the accompanying cluster chain. In S_DIR you have to look for the directory entry for SS_DIR analogously, etc. until you have found the entry for TEXT.TXT in SSS_DIR. With the start cluster in the directory entry and the corresponding cluster chain, which you determine by means of the FAT, you have to determine the logical number of the 13th sector of TEXT.TXT. The 6294th byte is located in the 13th sector of the cluster chain, as one sector is able to hold 512 bytes. Now you must read this sector by means of INT 26h into a 512-byte buffer, alter the byte with the number 150 as intended, and write the whole sector by means of INT 26h back to disk again. To update the date and time marks in the directory entry of TEXT.TXT, the sector with the directory entry must be read, altered, and stored. If you want to enlarge the file by the write process then you first need to look for one or more free clusters and mark them appropriately in the FAT. You can see that interrupts INT 25h and INT 26h are only interesting for programming tools or for computer freaks who really want to know every detail. But they are completely unsuitable for file-oriented programming of applications.

With the file-oriented functions of INT 21h, DOS offers an essential simplification in the tasks of searching, reading and writing sectors, updating date, time and file size, and allocating free clusters. As a user or application programmer you therefore do not need to keep struggling with multiple sector accesses and the organization structure of the data with DOS. Instead, DOS internally converts every file or directory access into sector accesses as described above.

A significant alleviation of INT 21h is that you may access files with the common name drive:path\filename.ext. Moreover, an access to certain bytes or records is possible by indicating the position relative to the beginning of the file or relative to the location of the last write or read process. Thus, DOS defines something like a «cursor» within an opened file, indicating the location of the read and write accesses. Table 27.9 lists the most important file and directory functions of INT 21h, but a detailed description would go far beyond the scope of this book.

Number	Function	DOS version
39h	create subdirectory	2.00 ff.
3Ah	delete subdirectory	2.00 ff.
3Bh	change directory	2.00 ff.
3Ch	create file	2.00 ff.
3Dh.	open file	2.00 ff.
3Eh	close file	2.00 ff.
3Fh	read file (device)	2.00 ff.
40h	write file (device)	2.00 ff.
41h	delete file	2.00 ff.
42h	move file cursor	2.00 ff.
43h	set/read file attribute	2.00 ff.
45h	duplicate handle	2.00 ff.
46h	adapt handle	2.00 ff.
47h	determine current directory	2.00 ff.
4Eh	find first directory entry	2.00 ff.
4Fh	find next directory entry	2.00 ff.
56h	rename file	2.00 ff.
57h	set/read date/time of file	2.00 ff.
5Ah	create temporary file	3.00 ff.
5Bh	create new file	3.00 ff.
67h	determine max. handle number	3.30 ff.
68h	forced write of DOS buffers	3.30 ff.

Only the handle-oriented functions are listed since FCB-oriented functions are internally converted by DOS into handle-oriented functions.

Table 27.9: INT 21h file and directory functions

Originally, DOS was designed as a successor of CP/M for the 16-bit 80x86 microprocessor family. In the first DOS version 1.00, the designers therefore used the concept of *file control blocks (FCB)* for file management. But CP/M's FCBs have a serious disadvantage: they don't allow any directory structure, and all files are, so to speak, located in the root directory. DOS 2.00 (according to Bill Gates, the first «real» DOS) replaced this outdated concept by so-called *handles*. While opening a file in any directory using the function 3Dh of INT 21h, DOS (or more precisely, the INT 21h) provides a number, namely the handle, which unambiguously characterizes the opened file.

Instead of the nearly infinite litany drive:path\filename.ext you only have to pass this number to DOS to access data in an opened file or to extend the file. The rest of the work is done by the operating system for you. DOS searches the relevant sectors, reads them into the transfer buffer, transfers the intended byte or the intended record to the user program, writes the byte or record after the alteration back to the transfer buffer, writes the buffer as a sector onto the disk, eventually allocates a new cluster in the FAT, and finally updates date, time, archive attribute and file size in the directory entry when closing the file. Note that it does not update the directory entries until the file is closed. If you switch off the PC with opened files or issue a boot process (by means of Ctrl-Alt-Del), then DOS may possibly leave an erroneous directory entry and CHKDSK reports lost clusters or allocation errors.

27.9 Programming Floppy Drives – Access via BIOS Interrupt INT 13h

It has already been mentioned above that the BIOS is usually the level nearest the hardware where compatibility among various computers can still be expected for an access to floppy and hard disk drives. The access is carried out via the functions of interrupt INT 13h, listed in Appendix F. Note that for floppy drives only the six first functions 00h–05h are available. Most functions with a higher number are exclusively dedicated to hard disks. Starting with the AT, the BIOS additionally recognizes functions 15h–18h. Some modern BIOS versions also support function 08h for determining the parameters of the floppy drive concerned. In the PC/XT BIOS this function was not implemented for floppies.

The following sections briefly discuss the functions for floppy drives. The precise call and return parameters are listed in Appendix F. The called interrupt handler checks the validity of most of the parameters passed in the registers, and carries out the function requested. Note that the BIOS counting for the floppy drives starts with 00h corresponding to A: with DOS. For hard disks, bit 7 of the drive's number is additionally set so that the first hard disk has the BIOS number 80h.

If the BIOS has completed the requested function, it passes an indicator in the carry flag as to whether or not the operation was successful. If the carry flag is set (=1) then an error has occurred and the register ah contains an error code. Appendix F.2 lists the possible error codes and their meaning. However, note that not all codes are valid for both floppies and hard disks. For example, a hard disk may not be write-protected by hardware; the corresponding error message is senseless for a hard disk.

The most important INT 13h functions are:

- function 00h – initialize drive
- function 01h – read status of last operation
- function 02h – read sector(s)
- function 03h – write sector(s)
- function 04h – verify sector(s)
- function 05h – format track
- function 08h – determine drive parameters
- function 15h – determine DASD type

- function 16h – determine disk change (AT only)
- function 17h – determine floppy format (AT only)

The 04h (verify sector) function shows somewhat mysterious behaviour. According to all the available information, this function compares one or more sectors on disk with the contents of a verification buffer in the main memory. But no controller actually does this, so I'm of the opinion that the function code is only implemented for reasons of compatibility with the original PC BIOS, and the BIOS doesn't carry out a real comparison. Instead, the controller seems to check only whether the CRC or ECC bytes are correct.

Using two examples, I want to briefly explain the use of INT 13h functions. The function calls and their formats are described in Appendix F.

Function 02h – Read Sector(s)

Example: Read sector 1 of track 0, head 0 of the floppy in drive B:; this sector contains the boot record of the floppy (assembler MASM 5.1).

```
buffer DB 512 DUP (?)       ; provide read buffer with 512 bytes (=1 sector)
mov ah, 02h                 ; function 02h (read sector)
mov dl, 01h                 ; second floppy drive B:
mov dh, 00h                 ; head 0
mov ch, 00h                 ; track 0
mov cl, 01h                 ; sector 1
mov al, 01h                 ; read only one sector
mov es, SEG buffer          ; segment address of read buffer
mov bx, OFFSET buffer       ; offset address of read buffer
int 13h                     ; read sector by means of interrupt 13h into buffer
```

Function 05h – Format Track

Example: format one track of a floppy with 15 sectors/track in drive A:

```
struct format_buffer {                          /* define format buffer structure */
  unsigned char track;
  unsigned char side;
  unsigned char sector;
  unsigned char bytes;
};

/*=====================================*/
/* format floppy with 15 sectors/track */
/*=====================================*/

format_track(track, side)
int track, side;
{ union REGS inregs,outregs;
  struct SREGS segregs;
  struct format_buffer far *form_buffer;
  int i;

  form_buffer = (struct format_buffer far *)_fmalloc(60);  /* generate format buffer */
```

```
  for (i=0; i<15; i++) {                    /* configure format buffer */
    form_buffer[i].track = track;
    form_buffer[i].side = side;
    form_buffer[i].sector = i;
    form_buffer[i].bytes = 2;               /* 512 bytes/sector */
  }

  inregs.h.ah=0x05;                         /* function 0x05 */
  inregs.h.dl=0x00;                         /* floppy drive A: */
  inregs.h.dh=side;
  inregs.h.ch=track;
  inregs.h.al=0x0f;                         /* 15 sectors/track */
  segregs.es=FP_SEG(form_buffer);
  inregs.x.bx=FP_OFF(form_buffer);
  int86x(0x13,&inregs,&outregs,&segregs);   /* issue interrupt */

  if ((outregs.x.cflag & 0x01) == 0x01) {   /* check whether error occurred */
    printf("\nerror: %x", outregs.h.ah);
  }

  _ffree(form_buffer);
}
```

During the course of an access to disk on a BIOS level, you alone are responsible for intercepting errors. The succinct error message «(a)bort, (r)etry, (i)gnore», well-known from DOS, is not output by the BIOS. If, for example, a non-recoverable read error occurs in a read access, then the BIOS function returns to the calling program with a set carry flag, and the register ah contains the value 10h as an error indicator for *read error*. If you don't carry out an error check immediately after returning from the BIOS interrupt, your program may use incorrect data, namely that which was already in the read buffer before the call was issued. In the best case, your PC now processes gibberish. Under the worst circumstances, data may now be destroyed; for example, if your program erroneously determines a «free» location on disk because of an incorrectly read FAT sector and writes another data sector to this place. Also, always make sure that the read or write buffer is of a sufficient size to accommodate all read sectors or data to be written.

Besides the above indicated examples, you can also read, write or verify several sectors at once. You only have to pass to the INT 13h the number in register al. But be careful: some BIOS variants don't support function calls that span more than one cylinder.

In a more technical view, this means that most BIOS variants are able to switch among several heads, but don't move the read/write head to another track. If you try, for example, to read more than 30 sectors all at once from a double-sided floppy with 16 sectors per track, then you surely pass a cylinder boundary. If your read attempt doesn't start at sector 1, head 0 of a cylinder, then you pass the cylinder boundary even earlier, of course. Depending upon the BIOS type, the BIOS can behave unpredictably. For example, users of PC-DOS have had such experiences: this DOS version doesn't worry about passing cylinder boundaries, and on some PCs this leads to a system crash whose cause isn't immediately apparent; or the word processor seems to have a bug as the text previously written onto disk later has utterly confused contents which suddenly appears normal on-screen after a further attempt to load the text.

The behaviour described is called a *multi-track problem*. If you intend to use the BIOS interrupt INT 13h for programming your floppy drives, you should always check for maximum compatibility and operation reliability before you call a BIOS function that passes a cylinder boundary. Another possibility is to always process only a single sector. Of course, you never pass a cylinder boundary then. But reading many individual sectors is much slower than handling complete cylinders. It's up to you which strategy you use as the programmer: real problems sometimes favour this strategy and sometimes the other. Table 27.10 lists all the sections of the BIOS data area that concern floppies and floppy operations.

Address	Size	Structure 76543210	Content	Meaning
40:10	byte	xx	installed hardware	number of installed floppies if bit 0 is equal to 1 (00=1, 01=2, 10=3, 11=4)*)
		1		floppy installed
40:3e	byte	1	calibration status floppy drives	interrupt requested
		xxx		reserved (=0)
		1		calibrate DR3*)
		1		calibrate DR2*)
		1		calibrate DR1
		1		calibrate DR0
		76543210		
40:3f	byte	x	motor status floppy drives	1=write/format 0=read/verify
		1		reserved
		xx		selected drive (00=A, 01=B, 10=C, 11=D)1)
		1		motor DR3 on*)
		1		motor DR2 on*)
		1		motor DR1 on
		1		motor DR0 on
40:40	byte		time-out value of drive motors	value in timer-ticks
40:41	byte	1	status of last floppy operation	drive not ready
		1		seek error
		1		general controller error
		xxxxx		error code: 01h=invalid function number 02h=address mark not found 03h=write protection 04h=sector not found 06h=disk change 08h=DMA overflow 09h=DMA segment error 0ch=invalid media type 10h=CRC error
40:42	7byte		result status	max. 7 result status bytes of floppy controller

Table 27.10: BIOS data area for floppy drives.

Address	Size	Structure 76543210	Content	Meaning
40:8b	byte	xx	transfer rate controller	rate last set (00=500kbit/s, 01=300kbit/s, 10=250kbit/s, 11=reserved)
		xx		step rate
		xx		transfer rate (00=500kbit/s, 01=300kbit/s, 10=250kbit/s, 11=reserved
		xx		reserved,
40:94	byte		current track drive 0	
40:95	byte		current track drive 1	

*) The Personal Computer only supports two floppy drives.

Table 27.10: cont.

27.10 Programming Floppy Drives – Direct Access via Registers

The most immediate control of the floppy controller and connected drives you have is through the controller's control and data registers. The following discusses how a floppy controller is constructed, and how it carries out certain actions.

27.10.1 Structure and Functioning of a Floppy Controller

Figure 27.23 shows a simple block diagram of a controller with an SA–450 interface, which is used in most PCs. The SA–450 interface was developed by Shugart Associates in the 1970s, and taken over later by IBM for the PC. Since that time, all PC floppy drives have worked with this interface. Note that the interface specification only defines the layout and the signals of the connections, but not its shape. $3^1/_2$" drives can eventually have a completely different plug so that you may need an adapter to connect a $3^1/_2$" drive to your floppy controller.

To communicate with the rest of the PC the controller needs access to the bus. This is established via the PC interface, which is also present in a similar form on all other adapter cards. The C interface accepts data as commands or write data from the bus, and transfers data as status or read data to the bus. The controller has a buffer that holds one or more bytes to be transferred from the drive to main memory, or vice versa. Unlike hard disk controllers, the floppy controller has no sector buffer, in most cases, which accommodates a complete sector of data plus the accompanying CRC or ECC bytes.

A floppy controller is quite a powerful peripheral device which has to carry out far more extensive control tasks than, for example, the parallel interface. The controller therefore usually has its own microprocessor with a program ROM. In the case of your PC's floppy controller, this is usually the NEC μPD765 or compatible. The AT can also incorporate an Intel 82072A and the PS/2 an 82077A. μPD765 and the program ROM together form a so-called *microcontroller*, which handles a main part of the control job. The microprocessor controls the individual components on the controller adapter and partially the electronics on the drives according to the program in the ROM. The μPD765 can encode data in the FM and MFM recording formats. Nearly all of today's floppy drives use the MFM method, however. As the μPD765 is an older but nevertheless powerful chip, the FM method is still integrated. The differences between FM and MFM are not serious enough to warrant two fundamentally different chips. Because all floppy drives in the PC only work with the MFM method, all further values for recording density, data transfer rate, etc. refer to MFM encoding. You get the corresponding values for FM by dividing the MFM values by two, as the recording density for MFM is twice as large as for FM.

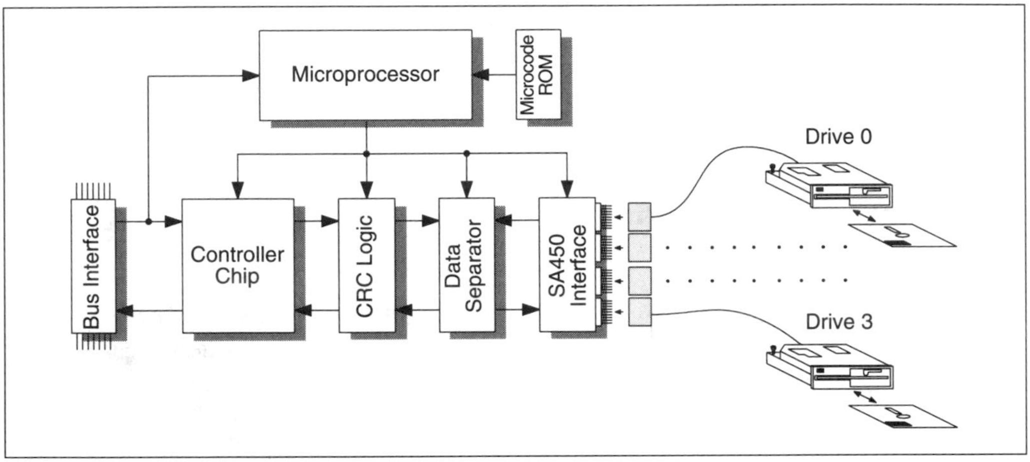

Figure 27.23: Block diagram of a floppy controller.

The main part of the drive control is carried out by the *storage controller*. It does the heavy labour and controls, for example, the read and write functions, converts parallel data from the CPU into serial data for recording on disk (and vice versa), and executes the CRC check of the read data. The bus actually transmits the data in byte or word format with eight or 16 bits. But on the floppy disk the data is present as a continuous bit stream. Individual bits according to the magnetized areas passing below the read/write head, but not complete bytes, follow each other. All data for or from the floppy run through this storage controller. The *data separator* or *data synchronizer* carries out the encoding into FM or MFM data, which is then transferred to the drive for recording on disk. Furthermore, the data is synchronized according to the FM or MFM encoding format, and address marks for the sectors are generated or read. The feedback signals from the drives enable the microcontroller to respond to the dynamic behaviour of the electronic elements and the drives.

In a data write the data therefore goes through the following data path:

- the data is transferred from the bus into the bus interface;
- the storage controller determines the CRC bytes, converts the parallel submitted data into serial data, and formats it in a suitable manner;

- the data separator converts this regular serial data stream into a data stream according the FM or MFM recording format, and generates an address mark;
- the SA–450 interface transfers the encoded data stream to the floppy drive;
- the drive's read/write head writes the encoded data stream as tiny magnetized areas onto the disk's surface.

All components are continuously controlled by the microcontroller on the floppy adapter. To read data from a floppy disk the microcontroller inverts the above indicated course of events. It detects the address marks and reads the sector concerned. The data separator separates the data and clock signals (hence the name separator). Note that FM and MFM refer only to the encoding method, and not the interface between controller and drive. There are MFM drives that you cannot connect to your MFM floppy controller, as the interface between them doesn't follow the SA–450 standard.

I would like to mention that because of the advances in miniaturizing electronic components over the past ten years, today several components are often integrated on a single chip. Thus you will rarely find more than two chips on your floppy controller or combicontroller. All functions of μPD765, program ROM, storage controller, etc. are now integrated into one or two chips, but the functions remain the same. The same applies (fortunately) to the command set of the microcontroller. In the AT and PS/2 the registers and some of the commands have been extended.

27.10.2 Configuration of a PC Floppy Controller

So far we have got to know the principal structure and data flow in a controller. The following sections discuss the configuration and programming of the floppy controller in connection with an example, namely the reading of one sector. You can access the control and data registers on a PC/XT by means of three, on the AT by four and on the PS/2 by five ports.

	Primary	**Secondary**	**Write (W) Read(R)**
base address	3f0h	370h	
status register A (PS/2)	3f1h	371h	R
status register B (PS/2)	3f1h	371h	R
digital output register DOR	3f2h	372h	R/W
main status register	3f4h	374h	R
data rate select register (PS/2)	3f4h	374h	W
data register	3f5h	375h	R/W
digital input register DIR (AT)	3f7h	377h	R
configuration control register (AT)	3f7h	377h	W
DMA channel	2	2	
IRQ	6	6	
INTR	0eh	0eh	

Table 27.11: Floppy controller port addresses and configuration data

Table 27.11 lists all the important information concerning configuration and port addresses. The base addresses differ depending upon whether you have configured the controller as a primary or secondary adapter. The PS/2 model 30 differs slightly in its port assignment from all other PS/2 machines, because it follows the XT's architecture.

All floppy controllers use DMA channel 2 to transfer data between the controller and main memory during the course of a read or write. After completing a command the controller issues a hardware interrupt via IRQ6 during the so-called result phase (see below). The interrupt is serviced by the interrupt handler 0eh, but you are free to configure the controller in another way.

27.10.3 Floppy Controller Registers

The digital output register can only be written. It controls the drive motors, selects a drive, and resets the controller. Figure 27.24 shows the structure of this register.

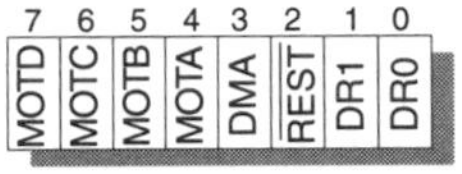


```
MOTD, MOTC, MOTB, MOTA:  motor control for floppy drive D, C, B, A
          1=start motor        0=stop motor
DMA:      DMA and IRQ channel
          1=enabled            0=disabled
REST:     controller reset
          1=controller enabled 0=execute controller reset
DR1, DR0: drive select
          00=drive 0 (A)   01=drive 1 (B)   10=drive 2 (C)   11=drive 3 (D)
```

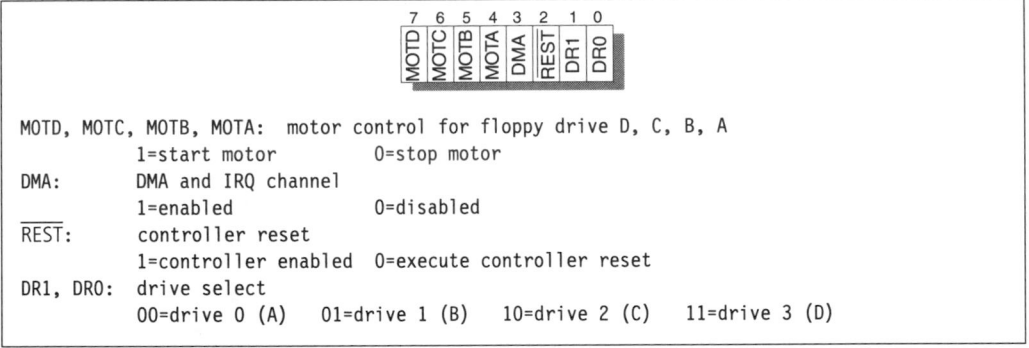

Figure 27.24: Digital output register.

Using the *MOTD–MOTA* bits you can turn the motors of drives D to A on and off. A set bit activates the corresponding spindle motor. The *DMA* bit enables the DMA and IRQ channels on the controller, through which it issues a data exchange between controller and main memory as well as a hardware interrupt request to the CPU. But this only applies to the PC/XT and AT; on a PS/2 this bit has no effect – the data transfer is always carried out by means of DMA. With a set $\overline{\text{REST}}$ bit the floppy controller is enabled to accept and execute commands. If $\overline{\text{REST}}$ is equal to 0, then the controller ignores all commands, including the motor activations via the digital output register; it carries out an internal reset of all registers except the POR. With the *DR1, DR0* bits you select the drive you want to access. A μPD765 can manage up to four floppy drives A: to D:.

The main status register is read-only and contains the status information of the floppy controller. Don't confuse this register and status registers ST0–ST3 that contain the status information concerning the last executed command, and which you may read via the data register. Figure 27.25 shows the structure of the main status register. Unlike the data register, the main status register can always be read, even if the controller is currently executing a command and, for example, is placing the head above a certain track.

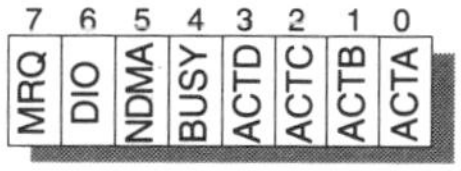


```
MRQ:    main request
        1=data register ready      0=data register not ready
DIO:    data input/output
        1=controller → CPU          0=CPU → controller
NDMA:   non-DMA mode
        1=controller not in DMA modes  0=controller in DMA mode
BUSY:   instruction (device busy)
        1=active                   0=not active
ACTD, ACTC, ACTB, ACTA:  drive D, C, B, A in positioning mode
        1=active                   0=not active
```

Figure 27.25: Main status register.

If the *MRQ* bit is set, the data register can receive or provide commands and data from and to the processor. Using *DIO*, the controller indicates whether it expects data from the CPU or whether it wants to hand over status information to it. If the *NDMA* bit is set, the floppy controller doesn't operate in DMA mode, that is, it doesn't transfer data via DMA channel 2 to or from main memory. The data transfer is carried out by means of a read or write command to the data register. The controller then always issues a hardware interrupt with every expected data byte or every data byte that is being supplied. If you find a set *BUSY* bit then the controller is currently executing a command. According to bits *ACTD–ACTA*, you can determine which drive is currently positioning the read/write heads.

The data register is eight bits wide, and is actually a whole stack of registers. Newer, powerful floppy controllers such as Intel's 82077A have a 16-byte FIFO memory instead of a simple data register, which accelerates the data throughput and doesn't subject the response time of the main system (that is, CPU and DMA) to the rather strict range of the μPD765. Controller commands are one to nine bytes long. According to the first command byte, the controller recognizes how many bytes the command concerned comprises. Therefore, you do not need to index the registers of the stack by means of an index register, as is the case, for example, with the video controller MC6845. The controller automatically transfers the command bytes for the data register internally to the corresponding command registers to carry out the command concerned. The controller's command formats are listed in Appendix G.

In the AT and PS/2, the digital input register (DIR) and the configuration control register are additionally available at port addresses 3f7h and 377h, respectively. But note that the register assignment differs among AT, model 30 and all other PS/2 models (see Figure 27.26). With these registers you can detect a disk change, determine the data transfer rate between controller and drive, and investigate the DMA mode of the controller.

The detection of a disk change was implemented in the AT to accelerate the access to floppies. If you don't change the floppy between two successive DIR commands, then DOS fetches the sector with the directory entries from an internal DOS buffer in main memory for the second call, but doesn't reread the sector concerned from disk. This is carried out much faster, but only if you did not change the floppy in the meantime. The PC/XT doesn't support the disk change function, but DOS always reads the sector concerned from disk. Thus the AT carries out floppy access much faster on average than the PC/XT.

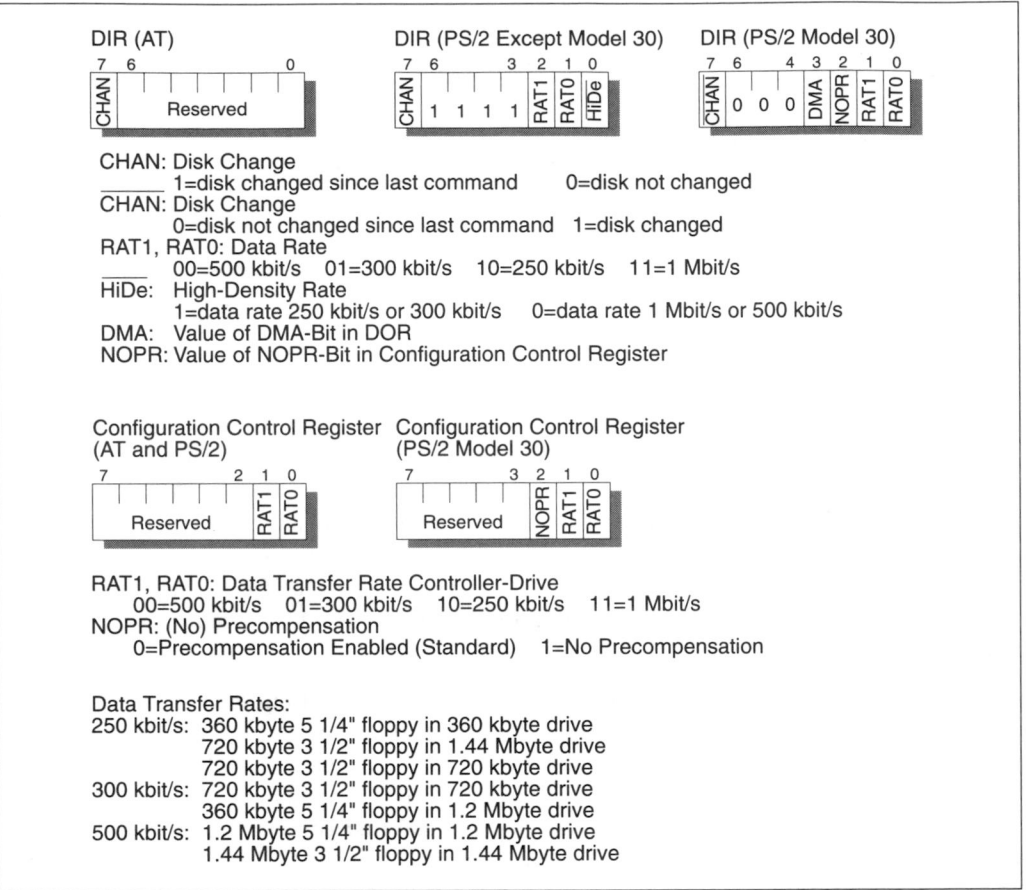

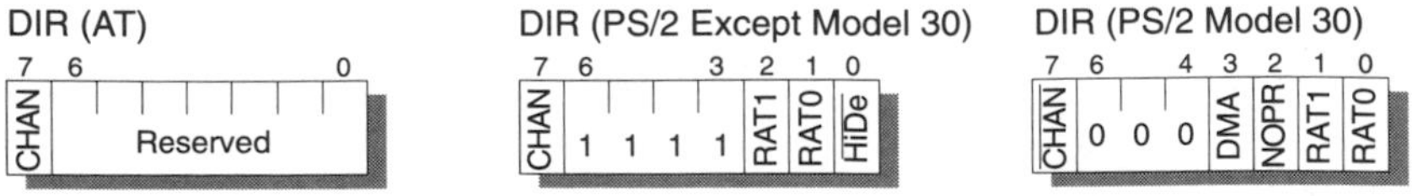

CHAN: Disk Change
1=disk changed since last command 0=disk not changed
$\overline{CHAN}$: Disk Change
0=disk not changed since last command 1=disk changed
RAT1, RAT0: Data Rate
00=500 kbit/s 01=300 kbit/s 10=250 kbit/s 11=1 Mbit/s
$\overline{HiDe}$: High-Density Rate
1=data rate 250 kbit/s or 300 kbit/s 0=data rate 1 Mbit/s or 500 kbit/s
DMA: Value of DMA-Bit in DOR
NOPR: Value of NOPR-Bit in Configuration Control Register

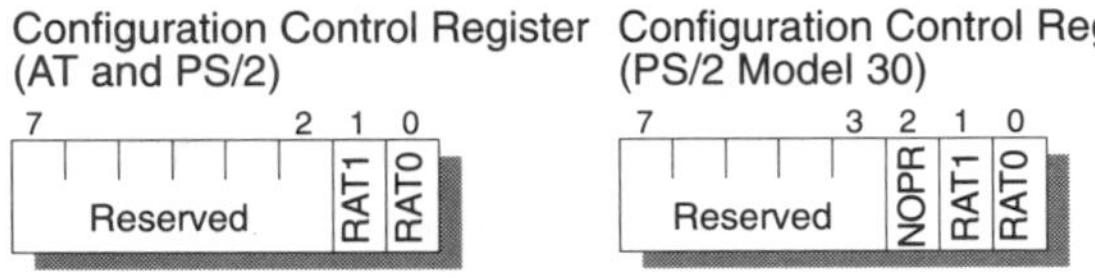

RAT1, RAT0: Data Transfer Rate Controller-Drive
00=500 kbit/s 01=300 kbit/s 10=250 kbit/s 11=1 Mbit/s
NOPR: (No) Precompensation
0=Precompensation Enabled (Standard) 1=No Precompensation

Data Transfer Rates:

250 kbit/s: 360 kbyte 5 1/4" floppy in 360 kbyte drive
720 kbyte 3 1/2" floppy in 1.44 Mbyte drive
720 kbyte 3 1/2" floppy in 720 kbyte drive

300 kbit/s: 720 kbyte 3 1/2" floppy in 720 kbyte drive
360 kbyte 5 1/4" floppy in 1.2 Mbyte drive

500 kbit/s: 1.2 Mbyte 5 1/4" floppy in 1.2 Mbyte drive
1.44 Mbyte 3 1/2" floppy in 1.44 Mbyte drive

Figure 27.26: DIR and configuration control register.

Additionally, the HD drives and the accompanying floppies introduced with the AT require a much higher data transfer rate between controller and drive, as the number of revolutions has increased from 300–360 revs/min and, on the other hand, the number of sectors per track has risen to 15 with a 1.2 Mbyte floppy (and even 18 with a 1.44 Mbyte floppy). With an effective sector length of 654 bytes plus 146 bytes for the start of the track, as well as nine sectors per track for a $5^1/_4$" floppy with a capacity of 360 kbytes, the amount of data passing below the read/write head reaches about 250 kbits/s. If you insert the same floppy into a 1.2 Mbyte drive with 360 revs/min, then the data transfer rate increases to 300 kbits/s. The increase of the sector number up to 18, together with the higher rotation speed of 360 revs/min, leads to a data transfer rate of 500 kbits/s for a 1.44 Mbyte floppy. Depending upon the drive you connect to an AT floppy controller and which floppy you are using in such a drive (360 kbyte floppy in an HD drive, for example), you need to program the floppy controller for the respective data transfer rate. This is carried out by the configuration control register at port address 3f7h or 377h. The structure of DIR and the configuration control register is shown in Figure 27.26.

With the *CHAN* or $\overline{\text{CHAN}}$ (PS/2 model 30) bit you can determine a disk change. If CHAN is set then the data medium has possibly been changed since the last access. Note that the meaning of $\overline{\text{CHAN}}$ on a PS/2 model 30 is inverted compared to all other computers. With the two *RAT1, RAT0* bits and the help of the configuration control register, you can program the data transfer rate between controller and drive. The selected rate can be determined by the DIR. Note that not all AT controllers and drives support a data transfer rate of 1 Mbit/s. On all PS/2s except model 30, you can determine via $\overline{\text{HiDe}}$ whether the controller has set up the high-density rate of 500 kbit/s or 1 Mbit/s. On a PS/2 model 30, the *DMA* and *NOPR* bits additionally indicate the values of the corresponding bits in the DOR and configuration control register, respectively.

The bit NOPR on a PS/2 model 30 controls the activation of the so-called precompensation; the standard value is 0.

On a PS/2 there are two more status registers A and B. But note also that here the structure of the two registers differs between model 30 and all other PS/2 models. Figure 27.27 shows the structure of the status registers A and B.

From the two status registers A and B you can read the status of the control lines between floppy controller and floppy drive on a PS/2. The register bits $\overline{\text{DRV2}}$, $\overline{\text{TRK0}}$, $\overline{\text{INDX}}$, $\overline{\text{WP}}$ and RDAT directly indicate the status of the corresponding data lines. But in the case of status registers A and B, note the different bit values between model 30 and all other PS/2 models.

27.10.4 Floppy Controller Commands and Command Phases

On the μPD765 15 different commands are available. The PS/2 implements some further commands oriented to the hard disk controllers. All commands proceed according to three phases:

- command phase: the controller is activated and the CPU passes the command;
- data phase: the controller searches one or more sectors and transfers the data to or from the PC if required;
- result phase: the controller issues an interrupt and provides status information concerning the last executed command.

In the following sections I want to discuss the three command phases using an example concerning the reading of one sector into main memory.

If you are programming a command that gives rise to a data transfer between main memory and controller, you must set up the DMA controller before activating the command so that the DMA controller transfers the data correctly after DRQ2 is activated. Depending upon the number of sectors to be transferred, you therefore have to provide a buffer in main memory which is able to accommodate the data. The DMA base address must point to the beginning of the buffer, and the count direction must be set for counting up. After DRQ2 has been activated by the controller, the DMA controller responds with a $\overline{\text{DACK2}}$ and transfers the data from the buffer to the controller, or vice versa. A program example for this is provided in Section 25.2.4 which discusses the 8237A DMA controller.

Status Register A (PS/2)

7	6	5	4	3	2	1	0
INTP	$\overline{DRV2}$	STEP	$\overline{TRK0}$	HDSL	$\overline{INDX}$	$\overline{WP}$	DIR

INTP: Interrupt Pending
0=interrupt signal inactive 1=active
$\overline{DRV2}$: 0=2 drives connected
1=one drive only
STEP: Stepper Pulse
0=no pulse 1=pulse is submitted
$\overline{TRK0}$: Track 0
0=head not above track 0 1=head above track 0
HDSL: Head Select
0=head 0 1=head 1
$\overline{INDX}$: Index Mark
0=detected 1=not detected
$\overline{WP}$: Write Protection
0=disk write-protected
1=not write-protected
DIR: Direction of Head
0=outwards (to smaller cylinder numbers)
1=inwards (to higher cylinder numbers)

Status Register A (PS/2 Model 30)

7	6	5	4	3	2	1	0
INTP	DRQ	STEP	TRK0	$\overline{HDSL}$	INDX	WP	$\overline{DIR}$

INTP: Interrupt Pending
0=interrupt signal inactive 1=active
DRQ: DMA Request
0=not active 1=active
STEP: Step Pulse
0=pulse is submitted 1=no pulse
TRK0: Track 0
0=head above track 0 1=head not above track 0
$\overline{HDSL}$: Head Select
0=head 1 1=head 0
INDX: index mark
0=not detected 1=detected
WP: Write Protection
0=disk not write-protected
1=disk write-protected
$\overline{DIR}$: Head Direction
0=inwards (to higher cylinder numbers)
1=outwards (to smaller cylinder numbers)

Status Register B (PS/2)

7	6	5	4	3	2	1	0
1	1	DS0	WDAT	RDAT	WE	MOT1	MOT0

DS0: Drive Select
0=other drive 1=drive 0
WDAT: Write Data
0=no data write
1=data are transferred to drive
RDAT: Read Data
0=no data read
1=data are transferred by drive
WE: Write Enable
0=head reads data
1=head is activated for write
MOT1, MOT0: motor of drive 1 and drive 0 respectively
0=switched off 1=switched on

Status Register B (PS/2 Modell 30)

7	6	5	4	3	2	1	0
$\overline{DRV2}$	$\overline{DS1}$	$\overline{DS0}$	WDAT	RDAT	WE	$\overline{DS3}$	$\overline{DS2}$

$\overline{DRV2}$: 0=two drives connected
1=only one drive connected
$\overline{DS1}$: Drive Select
0=drive 1 selected 1=not selected
$\overline{DS0}$: Drive Select
0=drive 0 selected 1=not selected
WDAT: Write Data
0=no data write
1=data are transferred to drive
RDAT: Read Data
0=no data read
1=data are transferred by drive
WE: Write Enable
0=head reads data
1=head enabled for write
$\overline{DS3}$: Drive Select
0=drive 3 selected 1=not selected
$\overline{DS2}$: Drive Select
0=drive 2 selected 1=not selected

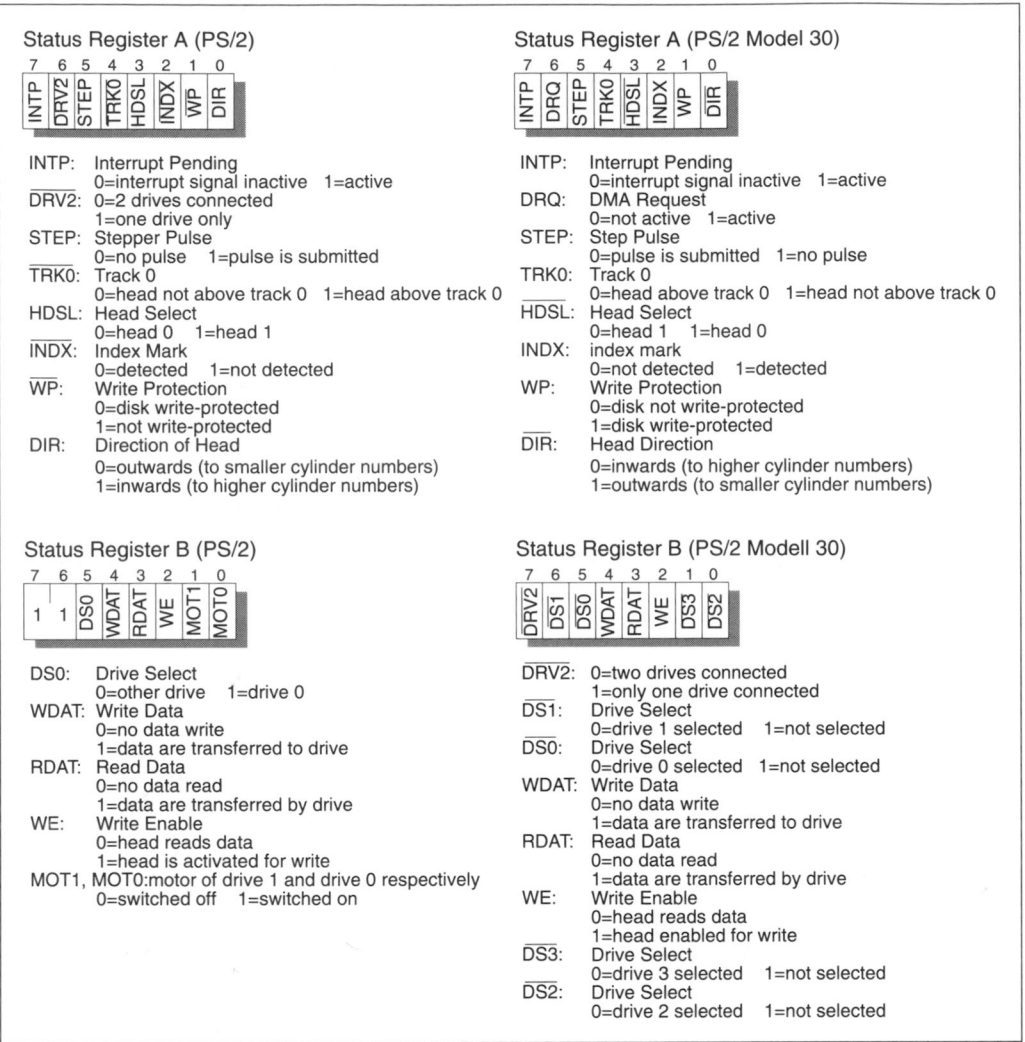

Figure 27.27: Status registers A and B (Port 3f1h or 371h, read-only).

Command Phase

The command phase is issued by activating the floppy controller via the digital output register (DOR), and selecting the intended drive. As in the PC many floppy drive operations issue an interrupt after command completion, and the data transfer is carried out via the DMA chip, you should also set the DMA bit in the DOR. If you want to access not only the controller but also the floppy, then you have to start the corresponding drive motor by means of a set MOTx bit (x=A, B, C, D).

Example: issue command phase (assembler MASM 5.1)

```
mov dx, 3f2h          ; load port address into dx
out dx, 1ch           ; output 0001 1100 (MOTA=1, DMA=1, AKTV=1, LW1/LW0=00) to DOR
```

```
(C, Microsoft C5.1)
outp (0x3f2, 0x1c); /* output 0001 1100 (MOTA=1, DMA=1, AKTV=1, LW1/LW0=00) to DOR */
```

The controller now expects the supply of a command via the data register. Appendix G summarizes all commands. In the following section I therefore want to discuss only the command for reading one sector; its format is shown in Figure 27.28. Nine command bytes are required in total. Note that the controller accepts a command byte only if the MRQ bit in the main status register is set; otherwise the controller ignores the passed command byte and gets into a muddle. Thus you have to read the main status register before passing a command byte, and check whether the MRQ bit is set. A fast CPU can pass the command bytes much faster than the rather slow floppy controller is able to accept and transfer them to the corresponding internal register according to the command selected.

With the *M* bit you may also instruct the μPD765 to carry out the same command for the other track. The controller then not only reads the sector(s) concerned on one side of the floppy, but also that on the other. As, during the course of the data transfer for the first sector, the DMA controller continuously counts up the target address, the sector read later doesn't overwrite the previously read data but is appended to the data of the first sector. Thus you can read several sectors all at once with this command. Such multitrack operations are also available for other commands, for example writing sectors, reading tracks, etc. With the *F* bit you determine the encoding format. The PC exclusively uses the MFM method for floppies; thus the F bit must be set, otherwise the controller cannot read the data correctly, or it writes them onto disk in a format which is not understandable for other functions. If you set the skip bit *S*, the controller ignores deleted data address marks and skips the accompanying sectors. If, on the other hand, the controller detects a deleted data address mark with the S bit cleared, it aborts the current command and returns an error message. You may access data with a deleted address mark only by means of the two commands *read deleted data* (opcode MFS01100) and *write deleted data* (opcode MF001001). These functions are also listed in Appendix G. The remaining five bits 00110 in the first command byte represent the opcode for *read sector*. From 00110 the controller recognizes that eight additional command bytes will follow.

The *HD* bit informs the controller about the intended head. As floppy drives only have two heads with the numbers 0 and 1, one bit is sufficient. Note that HD always coincides with the head address in byte 3. With *LW1, LW0* you select one of the four possible drives connected to the controller. *Cylinder, head* and *sector number* are self-evident, I think.

The *sector size* entry informs the controller about how many bytes it can expect in the addressed sector, and therefore how many it has to transfer into main memory. The value 2, indicating 512 bytes per sector, is used as standard. *Track length/max. sector number* indicates the number of the last sector in the track or cylinder (that is, the length of a track in sectors), or the maximum sector number for which the command is to be carried out. The controller executes all commands by starting with that sector which is determined by the cylinder, head and sector numbers. If it has carried out the command for this start sector, it reads the next sector and transfers it into main memory. The controller continues with this operation until it has read and transferred the sector indicated by the entry track length/max. sector number. If you specify a sector here which is no longer present in the track, the controller attempts to read a sector which would be located beyond the end of the track. This, of course, doesn't work, and the controller aborts the command with an error code. If you specify the same value as in the entry sector number, then the controller reads only one sector.

Bit / Byte	7	6	5	4	3	2	1	0
0	M	F	S	0	0	1	1	0
1	x	x	x	x	x	HD	LW1	LW0
2	Cylinder							
3	Head							
4	Sector Number							
5	Sector Size							
6	Track Length/Max. Sector Number							
7	Length of GAP3							
8	Data Length							

```
M:   multi-track operation
     1=execute cylinder operation    0=execute single track operation
F:   FM or MFM recording method
     1=MFM                 0=FM
S:   skip mode
     1=skip deleted data address mark     0=do not skip
HD:  head number (always equal head address in byte 3)
DR1, DR2:  drive
     00=drive 0 (A)   01=drive 1 (B)   10=drive 2 (C)   11=drive 3 (D)
cylinder, head, sector number:  address of sector to be read
sector size: 0=128byte   1=256byte   2=512byte   3=1024byte   ...   7=16kbyte
track length/max. sector number:  number of sectors per track or max. sector number, for
which the instruction is to be executed
length of GAP 3:  standard=42, min.=32
data length:      length of data to be read in byte (only valid, if sector size=00, else
always equal ffh)
```

Figure 27.28: Sector read.

A further possibility to abort the reading of sectors before the end of the track is reached is to supply the controller with a TC (terminal count) signal from the DMA controller. The programmed DMA chip always activates this signal if its count value has been decremented to 0. If you only want to read a single sector and select DMA for the data transfer, then you have to specify a count value that corresponds to the sector size of, generally, 512 bytes. Because of the TC signal generated after the transfer of 512 bytes, the sector read command is aborted. The opposite applies, of course, if you want to transfer two or more sectors into main memory.

With the *length of GAP 3* byte you inform the controller about the length of GAP 3 as it is to be used for data reading. The value for reading and writing data is different from that for formatting the drive. For formatting the PC uses a GAP-3-length of 80 bytes for a $5^1/_4$" drive, and 84 bytes for a $3^1/_2$" drive, as standard. For a read or write access, only 42 bytes and 27 bytes, respectively, are used. Some $5^1/_4$" drives may only use a value of 32 for reading or writing, thus these values are not defined very strictly. Remember the meaning of GAP 3 as described in Section 27.6: because of rotation variations and timing deviations of the write pulses, the actual length of a sector may vary. GAP 3 then serves as a buffer. If you overwrite an already formatted sector which has been elongated because of a slightly increased rotation speed during the course of the fomatting process with new data, and the rotation speed is somewhat lower than in the formatting process because of an increased friction, then the controller has already written the sector up to the last CRC field onto disk before GAP 3 begins. In the next read process, the controller becomes confused, as it expects only the values 4eh of GAP 3 and not the actually overwritten old data. Thus the sector cannot be read without an error.

The controller therefore also writes a GAP 3 onto disk with every write process even after the floppy has been formatted. This ensures that on a slower rotating floppy the formerly held data is also overwritten, and cannot cause any distortion. Let us assume the inverse case. During formatting the rotation speed was somewhat too low and the sector has therefore been compressed. If the floppy is now rotating faster in the course of writing a sector, then the last CRC data of the sector already overlaps GAP 3. If the controller additionally writes all the 80 bytes of GAP 3 onto disk, then it damages the beginning of the next sector as the end of GAP 3 overlaps SYNC or even IDAM of the next sector. You can see that it is necessary, on the one hand, to write GAP 3 additionally to the write data onto disk with every write process but, on the other hand, this GAP 3 may not be as long as for formatting the floppy. A reasonable value for its length is therefore about half the formatting length of 80 or 84 bytes. Thus the floppy drives in the PC use the value 42 for a $5^1/_4$" drive and 27 for a $3^1/_2$" drive as standard. Newer and more reliably controlled $5^1/_4$" drives don't need more than 32 bytes, though. It is more important to specify the length of GAP 3 for a formatting or write process, and less so for reading data.

If the number of bytes per sector is defined as 00, corresponding to 128 bytes per sector, then you inform the controller by means of *data length* about the actual number of bytes you want to read. If the actual data length for writing data is less than the sector size of 128 bytes, then the remaining bytes are all filled with zeroes. For calculating the CRC checksum, these fill bytes are also used. The PC employs a sector size of 512 bytes as standard, so the command byte *data length* is without meaning. But you must nevertheless pass a value as the controller expects nine command bytes for the command *read sector*. It will not start the programmed command until you have passed the 9th byte. Use the value ffh in this case.

Example: read sector 12, head 1, track 40 of the 1.2 Mbyte floppy in drive B:; the DMA controller programming required in advance is described in Chapter 7.3.6 (programming language: Microsoft C 5.1).

```
main()
{ unsigned char opcode[9];
  int index;

  outp(0x3f2, 0x2d); /* enable motor B:, controller, DMA and IRQ */

  opcode[0]=0x46;     /* 0100 0110, no multitrack operation (M=0), MFM (F=1), no skip mode
                         (S=0) */
  opcode[1]=0x05;     /* 0000 0101, head 1, drive B (01) */
  opcode[2]-0x28;     /* cylinder (track) 40 */
  opcode[3]=0x01;     /* head 1 */
```

```
  opcode[4]=0x0c;      /* sector 12 (0ch) */
  opcode[5]=0x02;      /* 512 bytes per sector */
  opcode[6]=0x0f;      /* 1.2 Mbyte floppy, thus maximum 15 (0fh) sectors per track */
  opcode[7]=0x2a;      /* 42 (2ah) bytes for Gap 3 */
  opcode[8]=0x00;      /* data length insignificant as 512 bytes per sector */

  for (index=0; index<9; index++) {
    write_controller(opcode[index]);  /* pass command byte to controller */
  }

  outp(0x3f2, 0x00); /* disable motor B:, controller, DMA and IRQ */
  exit(0)
}

void write_controller(command_byte)
unsigned char command_byte;
{ int mrq;

  for ( ; ; ) {                     /* wait until controller is ready */
    mrq=inp(0x3f4) && 0x80;         /* determine status of MRQ */
    if (mrq==0x80) {                /* check whether controller is ready */
      outp(0x3f5, command_byte);    /* output command byte to data register */
      return;                       /* return to main program */
    }
  }
}
```

The controller decodes the received command bytes and proceeds to the data phase if the input command bytes are consistent and data is to be transferred. If the input command bytes are inconsistent, however, then the controller jumps directly to the result phase. Thus the command phase is completed and the PC waits for a hardware interrupt from the controller, which indicates that the command has been completed. In a multitasking environment, the CPU can meanwhile carry out other tasks.

Data Phase

After the last command byte has been passed, the controller waits (in the discussed example) until the head-load time has elapsed and then lowers the read/write head onto the disk. Afterwards, head and controller start to read the ID address marks from the rotating floppy. If the controller detects an ID address mark that coincides with the programmed sector address, then the controller reads the data area of the sector and the CRC checksum and transfers the data into main memory. If this process has finished, the controller increments the sector address and reads the next sector. This process continues until the controller receives a TC signal from the DMA chip, or the controller issues an implicit TC signal as the end of the track is reached, or the data cannot be transferred into main memory quickly enough, or the sector with the programmed maximum sector number has been read and transferred. After completing the read process, the read/write head remains on the data carrier until the head-unload time has elapsed. If the CPU issues another command within this time period, the heads are already on the floppy and the head-load time is saved. Thus the data access is carried out more quickly.

If the controller receives two IDX pulses via the IDX line from the drive without having detected the programmed ID address mark in the meantime, it sets the interrupt code IC1, IC0 to a value of 01, indicating an abnormal command termination. Additionally, the controller sets the

ND bit in status register 1 to indicate that it hasn't found the programmed sector. A twice repeated IDX pulse thus means only that the index hole of the floppy disk has passed the drive's photosensor assembly twice, or that the controller has detected the index address mark (IAM) at the start of the track twice, and therefore the floppy has carried out at least one complete rotation.

During the course of the command phase, direct action by the CPU is required as it must activate the controller and pass the command bytes. But in the data phase, controller and floppy drive work undependently as the head positioning, searching for the selected cylinder, the physical reading or writing and all other controller and drive processes are carried out without any intervention from the CPU. Even transferring the data of a read sector or sector to be written proceeds without any CPU activity. The DMA controller, programmed in advance, carries out this job alone, but you must set the DMA bit in the digital output register for this purpose so that the controller actually generates the DRQ2 and IRQ6 signals. Additionally, the NDM bit in the second byte of the *specify drive parameters* command must be cleared to enable the DMA transfer capability in the controller. In a data read process the controller first reads the data from the floppy, and then enables the DRQ2 signal to issue a data transfer via channel 2 of the DMA controller. During the course of a data write, the controller activates the DMA control to transfer data from main memory to the controller via DMA channel 2, and writes the sector data together with the self-generated control data, for example the GAPs, IDAM, CRC, etc. onto disk.

If you have programmed a command that moves data, then the DMA chip cuts off the CPU from main memory and takes over control of the data and address bus. During the course of data transfer via the DMA controller, the CPU can continue to execute instructions which don't require a memory access, for example the multiplication of two register values. This means that the moving of large amounts of data is not carried out via the CPU.

OS/2 or UNIX/XENIX, as multitasking operating systems, enable the concurrent execution of several programs or, in the case of UNIX/XENIX, even the servicing of several users. As a processor can carry out a lot of work within the 100 ms that a floppy drive needs on average to address the intended sector, it is a waste of time to wait for the completion of the sector search and the transfer of data. Instead, the processor passes the controller the corresponding command (for example, read sector), and prepares a channel of the DMA controller for data transfer between controller and main memory. The floppy controller and the floppy drive then work autonomously and read a sector. The DMA controller transfers the sector data to the location in main memory determined in advance. The CPU is not burdened with this process at all, but can execute other tasks. Once the command has been completed the controller issues a hardware interrupt to get the attention of the CPU and operating system again. This is not the case with DOS, because as a single-tasking operating system no other programs execute concurrently.

However, there are other possibilities for the transfer of data between main memory and controller: interrupt-driven data exchange and polling. For interrupt-driven data exchange you must set the NDM bit in byte 2 of the *specify drive parameters* command and the DMA control bit in the POR to a value of 1. As standard, NDM is cleared so that the controller transfers the data to or reads it from main memory by means of DMA. If a data byte in the data register is ready for output, or if the controller needs another data byte from main memory, it issues an interrupt request via IRQ6, but no DRQ signal for a DMA request. The interrupt handler of interrupt 0eh must then be able to determine the cause of the interrupt and to transfer the data byte from the controller to main memory or vice versa. According to bits IC1, IC0 and SE in status register ST0, the handler can determine the cause of an interrupt (see Table 27.12).

SE	IC1/0	Interrupt source
0	11	polling
1	00	normal termination of seek or calibration command
1	01	abnormal termination of seek or calibration command

Table 27.12: Interrupt sources

For data transfer the CPU reads the data byte with an IN instruction from the data register of the controller, and writes it into main memory using a MOV instruction. If data is to be transferred from main memory to the controller, then the CPU reads a data byte with a MOV instruction from main memory and writes it with an OUT instruction into the controller's data register. Note that the controller also issues an interrupt upon entering the result phase (after completing the data phase), if you are programming such a handler for interrupt 0eh. The second interrupt is used to inform the main system about the command's completion, and to indicate that status data is available in the status registers.

If you want to carry out the data transfer using polling you must additionally clear the DMA bit in the POR to disable the IRQ drivers in the controller. Then the floppy controller doesn't generate an IRQ or a DRQ signal. The only possibility of determining whether data is available in the data register, or is to be transferred into it, is a periodic investigation of the MRQ bit in the main status register. If MRQ is set then the controller expects the transfer of a byte or the reading of its data register. If the DIO bit in the main status register is set, the controller wants to provide data to the CPU. With a cleared DIO bit, it expects data from the CPU. The polling program has to determine whether the data consists of command bytes, read data, write data, or status bytes. Although the timing problems are serious enough with interrupt driven data exchange, they become virtually unsolvable in polled operation of several powerful drives connected to the one controller. The data register will not wait until the end of time, of course, for a service by the CPU, which additionally is carrying out other tasks such as supervising the hard disk drives, the timer chips, and the execution of the foreground program. Thus, data exchange using DMA is surely the best solution. In all Personal Computers it is carried out via DMA channel 2.

After the completion of the transfer the data phase is finished, and the controller now proceeds to the result phase to inform the host of success or failure using appropriate status information.

Result Phase

At end of the data phase, or if you have programmed a command that doesn't have a data phase such as *check drive status*, the controller issues a hardware interrupt. The CPU then recognizes that the command has been completed, and that result status bytes are available in the data register.

The floppy controller has four status registers ST0–ST3 in all, which you may extract in this order from the data register. The exact number of status registers with a status byte depends upon the command concerned. Appendix G lists the number and type of the status bytes for every command. Additionally, the data register provides some information about the head, drive, etc. of the last processed sector (you will also find this information in Appendix G). The structure of the four status registers is shown in Figure 27.27.

	7 ... 0
0	ST0
1	ST1
2	ST2
3	Cylinder
4	Head
5	Sector Number
6	Sector Size

ST0, ST1, ST2: status register 0...2
cylinder, head, sector number: address of sector last read
sector size: 0=128 bytes 1=256 bytes 2=512 bytes ... 7=16 kbytes

Figure 27.29: Status and result bytes of «read sector» command.

The following discusses the status and result bytes of the example command *read sector*. This command provides seven status and result bytes during the course of the result phase, and these are shown in Figure 27.29.

The seven result bytes can be read via the data register by an IN instruction. As is the case for writing the command bytes, here also you have first to check whether the data register is ready. The following example shows this procedure.

Example: Read sector 12, head 1, track 40 of the 1.2 Mbyte floppy in drive B:; DMA controller programming required in advance is described in Section 25.2.4 (programming language: Microsoft C 5.1).

```
main()
{ unsigned char st0, st1, st2, cylinder, head, sector, byte_per_sector;

  st0=read_controller();             /* read result byte st0 from controller */
  st1=read_controller();             /* read result byte st1 from controller */
  st2=read_controller();             /* read result byte st2 from controller */
  cylinder=read_controller();        /* read cylinder concerned from controller */
  head=read_controller();            /* read head concerned from controller */
  sector=read_controller();          /* read sector concerned from controller */
  byte_per_sector=read_controller(); /* read sector size from controller */

  exit(0)
}

unsigned char read_controller(void)
{
int mrq;
```

```
  unsigned char result-byte;

  for ( ; ; ) {                    /* wait until controller is ready */
    mrq=inp(0x3f4) && 0x80;        /* determine status of MRQ */
    if (mrq==0x80) {               /* check whether controller is ready */
      intp(0x3f5, result_byte);    /* output command byte to data register */
      return(result_byte);         /* return result byte */
    }
  }
}
```

Now the corresponding bytes contain the status ST0–ST2 of the read command. According to ST0–ST2, you may determine whether the command was executed correctly, and if not, analyse the reasons for a failure. The interrupt handler for IRQ6 corresponding to interrupt 0eh of the BIOS stores the maximum of seven status bytes for a floppy operation in the seven bytes at address 0040:0042 and above. Note that you must read out all completion status bytes from the status register before the controller is ready to accept and execute a new command. This also applies if the status registers ST0–ST3 indicate a failure.

27.10.5 Specify Drive Parameters

Before you can read or write data you have to set up some drive parameters that directly affect the electromechanical behaviour of the read/write heads using the controller command *specify drive parameters*. As an addition to the above discussed example, I therefore want to describe the technical background of this command. Figure 27.30 shows its format.

The *step rate time* entry determines the time interval between two pulses to the stepper motor of the floppy drive. Each pulse leads to a certain rotation of the motor and thus to a certain movement of the read/write head (usually to the adjacent track). Thus, by means of the step rate time entry, you can influence the drive's access time. If you specify a value that is too small then the stepper motor will have already received the next step pulse before it can respond to the last one. As in floppy drives, access to the tracks is solely controlled by the number of step pulses to the stepper motor of the read/write head (starting from track 17, 20 pulses, for example, lead to track 37); seek errors are the consequence, and the controller responds with a read/write error.

The two entries *head-load time* and *head-unload time* control the loading and unloading of the read/write head onto and from the disk. The value for head-load time defines the time interval that the μPD765 waits before it instructs the floppy drive to load the read/write head onto the data carrier. Waiting is necessary to give the head and access arm enough time to settle down (that is, to damp all oscillations) after an access movement. Any radial movement of the head, and therefore damage to the data carrier, can thus be prevented. With the head-unload time entry you control the time interval that the controller waits before it instructs the drive to unload the head from the data carrier after a read or write access. If the controller were to unload the heads immediately after an access, then no continuous reading or writing of successive sectors would be possible. The time required for unloading and then reloading the heads is longer than the time interval until the next sector appears below the head. With a head-unload time different from zero, the drive is therefore able to read or write a complete track or a complete cylinder. Once this process is complete, the heads are unloaded and possibly moved to another cylinder. The *NDM* bit defines whether a DMA channel (NDM=0) or interrupt-driven data exchange is employed. The PC always uses DMA channel 2 for data transfer, thus NDM is always equal to 0 here. Note that in the AT and PS/2 the effective values for step rate time, head-unload time, and head-load time are also dependent upon the programmed data transfer rate as well as on the entries in the command bytes. With a PC/XT floppy controller this rate is always set to 250 kbits/s, thus the effective values are only determined by the command bytes here. The BIOS stores these values (as well as others) in the floppy parameter table (see Appendix F.5). The entry of the pseudo-interrupt vector 1eh points to the beginning of this table.

Call Format

Bit / Byte	7	6	5	4	3	2	1	0
0	0	0	0	0	0	0	1	1
1	Step Rate Time				Head Unload Time			
2	Head Load Time							NDM

NDM: Non-DMA Mode
0=DMA enabled 1=DMA disabled

Step Rate Time [ms]

Entry	Data Transfer Rate 1M	500k	300k	250k
0h	8,0	16	26,7	32
1h	7,5	15	25,0	30
2h	7,0	14	23,3	28
...	...	...	...	
eh	1,0	2	3,3	4
fh	0,5	1	1,7	2

Head Unload Time [ms]

Entry	Data Transfer Rate 1M	500k	300k	250k
0h	128	256	426	512
1h	8	16	26,7	32
2h	16	32	53,5	64
...	...	...	...	...
eh	112	224	373	448
fh	120	240	400	480

Head Load Time [ms]

Entry	Data Transfer Rate 1M	500k	300k	250k
0h	128	256	426	512
1h	1	2	3,3	4
2h	2	4	6,7	8
...	...	...	...	...
eh	126	252	420	504
fh	127	254	423	508

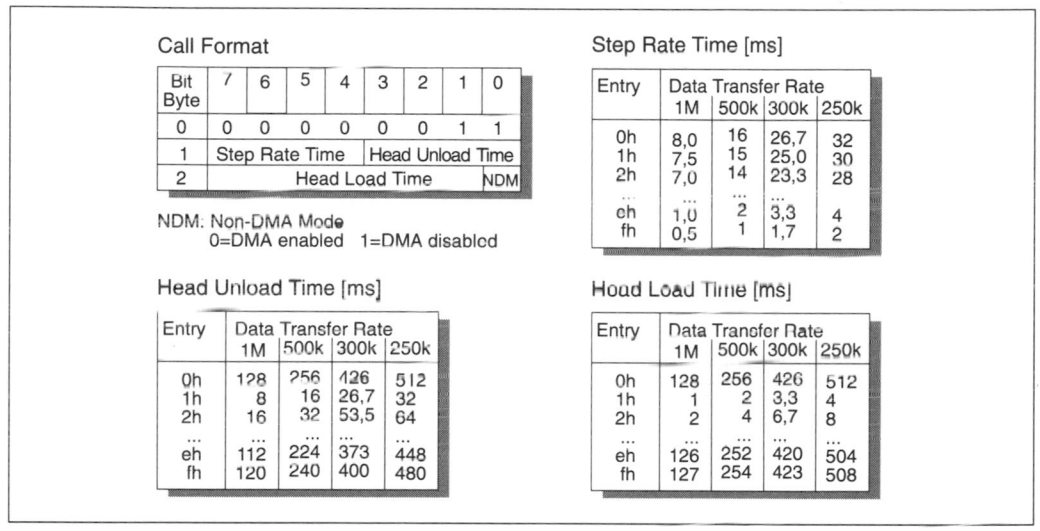

Figure 27.30: Specify drive parameters.

Finally, a few words on reading, writing, and formatting 360 kbyte floppies in 1.2 Mbyte drives. As you know, it is not only possible to read and write a 360 kbyte floppy with 40 tracks and nine sectors per track in an HD drive with a capacity of 1.2 Mbytes, but also to format it. While it is quite easy for you to set up the controller to a track length of nine sectors, by means of the *track length* entry, for example, in the *read sector* command of the above mentioned example, there is no possibility of reducing the number of tracks from 80 to 40. The problem must thus be bypassed. During the course of a read, write, or formatting process, only every second track is accessed. To format a 360 kbyte floppy in a 1.2 Mbyte drive you therefore have to generate tracks 0, 2, ..., 78. In the same way, the drive must access tracks 0, 2, ..., 78 for data reading and writing. DOS and the BIOS do this for you if you remain at their level. For programming a direct access to the floppy controller by means of its registers, you thus have to pay attention to many critical technical details. Determining whether the machine is a PC/XT, AT, PS/2 model 30 or another PS/2 machine is a really difficult job. The fixed installed BIOS need not worry about determining the computer type, as it knows it in advance. Therefore, this BIOS can be tailored for the PC as the programmer knows in which computer the ROM chips are to be installed.

27.10.6 Error Recovery Strategy

Unlike the hard disk controllers, floppy controllers don't have an in-built error recovery strategy. If a read or write error has occurred you should repeat the read or write attempt at least twice to exclude an unintended start delay of the spindle motor as a possible reason. If this doesn't help, or if a seek error has occurred, then it is best to recalibrate the drive. For this purpose, move the head back to track 0 and repeat the access. Sometimes, the tolerance may be so high that the read/write head reaches the edge or even the middle of two adjacent tracks. This is especially the case if the drive has carried out multiple relative seeks, or seeks over a large distance (from track 0 to track 70, for example). The signals from the address marks are no longer strong enough for the controller to determine the position correctly. Unlike hard disk drives, floppy drives operate with an open-loop positioning scheme, that is, the positioning electronics don't receive any feedback signals to indicate the current location of the head.

28 Hard Disk Drives

Many PC users see the hard disk as the most important and valuable part of their computer. This is justifiable if no data backup is made and all the past three years' work is on the hard disk. Besides the memory chips and processors, hard disks have been the subject of much development towards higher and higher capacities (with steadily falling prices) in the past ten years. Remember that the first hard disk for the XT (with its exciting capacity of 10 Mbytes!) cost more than $3,000 when introduced; an access time of more than 100 ms was included in this price. If you wanted to spend $3,000 on a hard disk today you'd have trouble in getting hold of one!

In spite of the low price, some dealers continue to sell their i386s with a 40 Mbyte hard disk and Windows. As everyone knows graphics, and therefore also graphics-oriented shells, occupy a large amount of storage, so 40 Mbytes are only enough for an older 80286 without Windows. When you buy a new PC, multiply the estimated storage requirements by at least three. In less than a year, your disk will be full (this is a tip based on my own long-suffering experiences!). If installing Windows and a graphics application such as CorelDRAW!, then 100 Mbytes at least are required.

Another common name for the hard disk drive is the *winchester drive*, for historical reasons: in the 1960s IBM introduced a cupboard-sized disk drive with an overall capacity of 60 Mbytes onto the market. 30 Mbytes were installed, and the other disk (also with 30 Mbytes) could be removed and changed. You may have seen pictures where this cooking-pot-sized 30 Mbyte disk pack is screwed onto the drive spindle. As an abbreviation, the drive was also called a 30–30 (30 Mbytes installed and 30–30 Mbytes removable storage capacity). John Wayne fans may remember that he always had his Winchester 30 ready! Thus the mental leap to calling the 30–30 drive a Winchester was not too far. This has nothing to do with guns, of course, but the term has remained until today, and is particularly used in the field of mainframes as «insider» slang.

The advances made in the past decade can be seen by the fact that Seagate's ST506 drive, introduced onto the market in 1980 with its $5^1/_4$" disks, only had a capacity of 5 Mbytes, but nevertheless required full height. The ST412 successor already had a capacity of 10 Mbytes. (By the way, the name ST506/412 interface comes from these drives.) With its four heads and 17 sectors per track the ST412 had only 150–300 cylinders. Today's powerful IDE, ESDI and SCSI models have up to 70 sectors per track, and 2000 cylinders with a disk size between 2" and $3^1/_2$". Advanced interface concepts that take into account the advancing development of microelectronics and encoding methods therefore became absolutely necessary. In the following sections, information concerning the ST506/412 standard and also the more advanced concepts such as IDE, ESDI and SCSI are discussed.

28.1 Structure and Functioning of Hard Disk Drives

28.1.1 The Head-Disk Assembly (HDA)

The differences between floppy drives and hard disks are, in terms of principle, not very significant, but the latter are far more powerful. Also, in a hard disk drive the actual data carrier is a stiff rotating disk, unlike flexible floppies. The data is organized in tracks and sectors, as is the case for floppies, while access to data is also carried out by read/write heads moved by an actuator. But the mechanical equipment and the control of hard disk drives is far more elaborate so as to achieve the larger capacity and higher performance. Figure 28.1 shows the interior of a hard disk. For the figure, the cover of the *head-disk assembly (HDA)* has been removed, but *never* do that on your own; you have to scrap your hard disk afterwards and all the stored data is lost. I recommend that nosy users go to a computer exhibition and admire the drives under glass at the stands of hard disk manufacturers, or otherwise open an old and no longer used drive.

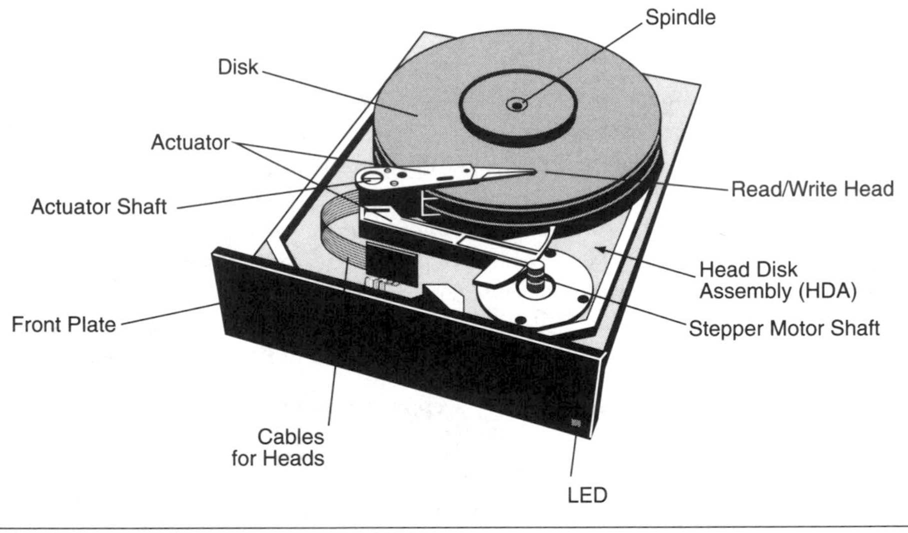

Figure 28.1: Hard disk drive.

The HDA consists of all mechanical and electronic components, which have to be specially protected against external dirt. Disks, heads, actuator and drive spindle belong to the HDA. The electronic controller, however, is located on a board at the drive peripheral. The rotation speed of the hard disk's spindle motor is stabilized by a feedback control circuit so the disks rotate with a constant speed of about 3600 revolutions per second. The control circuit reduces the revolution variations to about ±0.3%, and on high-quality drives to even ±0.1%. This means that the data carrier of a hard disk moves ten times faster than a floppy. Even the simplest drives accommodate 17 sectors per track, and powerful high-end drives have up to 70. Together with the increased rotation speed, this gives rise to 80 times the data amount which passes per second below the head compared to an old 360 kbyte floppy. Thus, drive and controller electronics need to be much more powerful than for floppy drives.

While you can insert a floppy disk with two sides at most into a floppy drive, most hard disk drives accommodate two to eight disks. Only very small 2" hard disk drives for notebooks have one (high-capacity) disk. As every disk has two sides, between four and 16 heads are required, located at the end of an access arm as is the case for the floppy drive. All heads are fixed to the same *actuator*, and are in moved in common by it. Thus the heads interpose the disks in the form of a comb or pincers. Figure 28.2 shows this in a graphical manner.

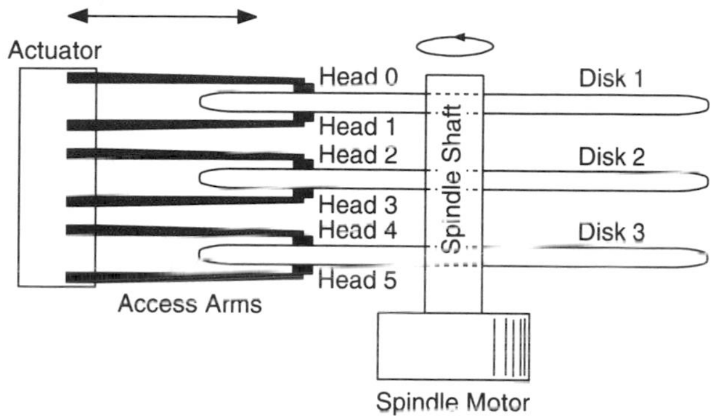

Figure 28.2: Heads and disks. Each disk surface is allocated a head, which is fixed to the end of an access arm. All arms and heads are moved in common and simultaneously by a single actuator.

As is the case for floppy drives, usually one head is active at most to read or write data. Only extremely powerful models activate several heads simultaneously to increase the data rate. The actuator is operated by a stepper or linear motor. The latter is also often called a *voice coil actuator*. Both carry out positioning of the heads above the track or cylinder concerned. Details on disks, heads, and actuators are given below.

Most hard disks come with a front plate that usually accommodates an LED. Every time the controller accesses the drive to read or write data or to move the heads, only this diode lights up. You can remove this front plate without any problems if the drive doesn't fit into your PC's case with it.

The Disk

Today's hard disk drives usually come with a disk size of $5^1/_4$" or $3^1/_2$". The smaller disks have the advantage that the heads don't need to be moved so far, thus smaller actuators and spindle drivers are sufficient, and the head positioning time is shorter. Additionally, smaller drives are usually quieter. With some larger and, especially, older hard disks you have the impression that a coffee grinder is working in your PC and not a high-tech product! For small notebooks, 2" drives are also available, and even midgets of only one inch in diameter exist (with a comparably incredible storage capacity). On the other hand, you can also buy hard disk drives with 8" or even 14" disk diameters, but they are largely used for mainframes.

To accommodate data in the form of tiny magnetizations, at least the surface of the disks must be magnetizable. Today, aluminium alloys are mainly used as the disk material, as they are light but nevertheless mechanically stable. The low mass of the aluminium disks compared to disks made of iron, for example, and therefore the low inertia, gives rise to the fact that the operational revolution speed is reached more quickly after power-up. This is especially important for hard disks that are switched off regularly to save power in laptops and notebooks, and which must be accelerated again if an access is required.

A magnetizable coating (the data medium) is deposited on the aluminium carrier. The high bit density when compared to floppies requires magnetically hard substances; usually, cobalt or certain ferroceramics are therefore employed. For coating the aluminium disks there are two main methods. With the *ferrite coating* a solvent with the ferrite is squirted near to the disk's centre and the disk itself is rotated at a high speed. By means of centrifugal force, the solvent and therefore also the ferrite material moves towards the circumference. After the solvent has vaporized, an only 1–2 μm thick and regular ferrite layer remains on the alumium carrier. Afterwards, the ferrite layer is hardened or a very thin but hard protective layer is deposited on it. Finally, the disk is polished so that even the smallest unevenness which might disturb the head passing above it vanishes. Because of the ferrite material, the disk becomes a russet or brown colour. This colour is an unambiguous hint that the disk has been coated with a ferrite material. The method is used for disks of a low to medium data density.

For disks with more than 20 Mbytes capacity per disk side, the magnetic layer is deposited by galvanization or by sputtering. You may also find the *galvanization method* with chromium-plated car bumpers or for pieces of jewellery. The object to be galvanized is immersed in a salt solution containing ions of the material with which the object is to be coated. If a negative voltage is applied to the object to be galvanized, the metal ions move to it, are discharged there, neutralized to atoms, and deposited regularly on the object. Thus, for example, car bumpers can be coated with chromium, copper jewellery with gold, and the aluminium disk for a hard disk drive with cobalt. The result is a hard, regular cobalt layer with a thickness of only 0.1–0.2 μm. This corresponds to only a few hundred atom layers. The thickness can be controlled easily by the galvanization current and the time of the galvanization process.

In *sputtering* the metal with which the carrier is to be coated is atomized by ion irradiation in a vacuum. The atoms move to the object to be coated (here the aluminium disk), and deposit there as a very regular and hard layer with a thickness of 0.05–0.2 μm. Also, in this case, the thickness can be easily controlled by means of the ion irradiation strength and the sputtering time.

Afterwards, a thin graphite layer is deposited to protect the magnetic medium against mechanical damage. A hard disk coated by means of galvanization or sputtering shines like a mirror, and is more resistant to a head-crash (that is, an unintentional hard bouncing of the heads onto the disk while the disk is rotating) than ferrite-coated disks.

Usually, the data bits are recorded in a linear way, thus the magnetizations lie within the disk plane. If you imagine the magnetization for a data bit as a bar magnet, then this means that the bar magnet is either aligned to the track direction or in an opposite direction to it, depending upon the bit value. Besides this method there also exist hard disks with *vertical recording*. Here the «bar magnets» are no longer collinear to the track, but instead are perpendicular or vertical to the aluminium disk. Thus the recording takes place into the depth of the data carrier medium and much higher bit densities can be achieved. But today, hard disks with horizontal recording are largely used.

The number of flux changes that can be accommodated is decisive for the capacity of a disk. Remember that only the change of the magnetization (a flux change) may generate a signal in the read/write heads. The number of flux changes is indicated as *FCI* (Flux Changes per Inch). Note that the bit density *(BPI)* not only depends upon the maximum number of flux changes FCI, but also on the encoding method used. On RLL hard disks the number of flux changes is about 50% *lower* than the number of BPI. The RLL encoding method is so powerful that a bit can be encoded with less than a single flux change. In contrast, the very old FM method requires two flux changes for every bit, namely one for the clock and one for the data signal. Without increasing the mechanical quality of a disk (which is expressed by FCI), just the use of another recording method raises the storable data amount by a factor of three. The disk remains the same; only the electronics used become more complex because of the more extensive encoding method. Details concerning RLL are discussed below.

The Heads

As is the case for floppy drives, the read/write heads write data onto disk as tiny magnetizations, or detect these magnetizations as data bits. But the significantly higher bit density on hard disks requires new technologies when compared to floppy drives. As already seen in Figure 28.2, for every disk side a dedicated head is available, but all heads are moved in common by a single actuator. The smaller the heads, the tinier the magnetizations can get. A small head also means a low mass, and therefore low inertia. Thus the heads may be positioned more quickly.

For generating and detecting small magnetization areas on the data carrier, it is necessary that the heads are at a distance which is as small as possible above the disks. Figure 28.3 shows the reason.

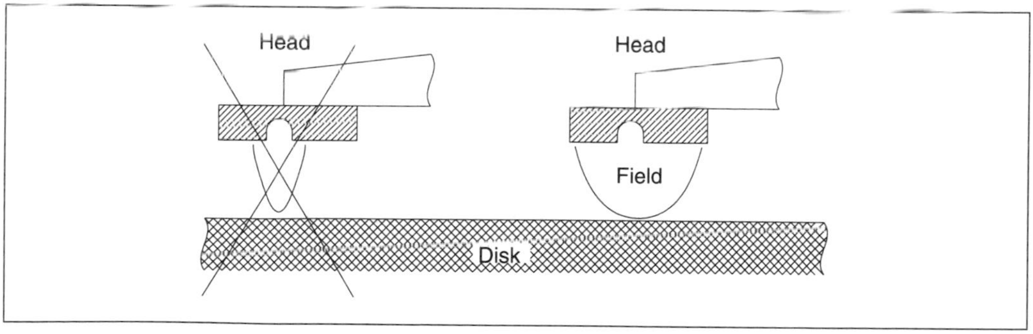

Figure 28.3. Head-disk distance and size of the magnetized region. The magnetic field is not emanating from the slit in a certain direction, but more likely in a half circle form. Thus the distance between head and disk determines the elementary magnetizing region.

The magnetic field generated by the read/write head may not be focused as is shown in Figure 28.3 (left side). Instead, it spreads out nearly hemispherically with a slight vertical concentration towards the disk (Figure 28.3, right side). You can see that the horizontal size of the magnetic field on the disk surface is about the same as the distance between head and disk, but the size of the magnetic field directly determines the smallest region of the medium that can be magnetized in one direction, that is, one bit. This means that the recording density can be increased solely by a reduced head/disk distance. Therefore, one tries to make the heads as small as possible, and also to position them as near to the disk as possible. Of course, the magnetic medium must also be sufficiently fine-grained so that the domains don't get larger than one of these elementary bits.

Presently, there are two main head technologies: ferrite heads and thinfilm heads. The *ferrite heads* are low-cost and reliable members of the older head generation. They generate the magnetic field by means of a coil with a ferrite core, as already described in connection with floppy drives. The heads act as a simple conventional electromagnet. The winding, however, may not be miniaturized to any extent, so the size of the ferrite heads is limited towards smaller sizes. Because of the rather heavy ferrite core, ferrite heads are of a higher mass than the thinfilm heads. The power expenditure of the actuator becomes larger. Therefore, today ferrite heads are still employed, but only for hard disks in the lower and middle capacity ranges (up to about 10 Mbytes per disk side).

The modern concept of *thinfilm heads* is virtually a waste product of microelectronics and its manufacturing methods. Semiconductor chips are formed by depositing and etching various layers. What better, therefore, than also to apply this reliable technique to the read/write heads of a hard disk drive. Here the heads are no longer formed by winding a wire around a ferrite core, but by means of various thin layers. The result is a microscopically small and very light head which is, nevertheless, able to generate a rather strong magnetic field. Because of the low distance between head and disk the field generated by the head need not be as strong as is the case for the ferrite heads. Thus, in the data medium the thinfilm heads generate a sufficiently strong field to magnetize the cobalt domains.

When the drive is switched off the heads rest on the disk. Most of today's drives «park» their heads on a track reserved for this purpose which is not in use for data recording. This prevents the heads from scratching off the coating in areas occupied by stored data during acceleration at power-up. When the spindle motor starts the disk rotation, they take up the surrounding air similar to a ventilator, and an air stream occurs. This air stream is strong enough to generate an air cushion above the disk, thus the heads take off from the disk surface and ride a microscopic distance from the disk's surface on this air cushion without actually touching the disk. Typical distances are 1 μm for ferrite heads and 0.2–0.5 μm in the case of thinfilm heads. Figure 28.4 shows a comparison between the size of a thinfilm head, its distance from the disk, a human hair, and various dirt particles.

The disk-head distance is mainly dependent upon the head shape. According to their aerodynamic properties, they fly quite high. Thus a hard disk can be operated in a vacuum only with some difficulties, as the springy air cushion between head and disk is missing. The thickness of the cushion is, by the way, dependent upon the air pressure: the lower the pressure the thinner the cushion gets. Thus on a high mountain the heads fly lower than at the coast. This is one reason why data sheets for hard disks contain an entry for the hard disk's operation range concerning altitude. If Reinhold Messner intends to take a notebook up Mt Everest (which seems improbable), he would be very surprised. Because of the low air pressure of less than 400 mbar, the air cushion is so thin that the heads permanently touch the disk's surface, and the stored data is destroyed within a short time.

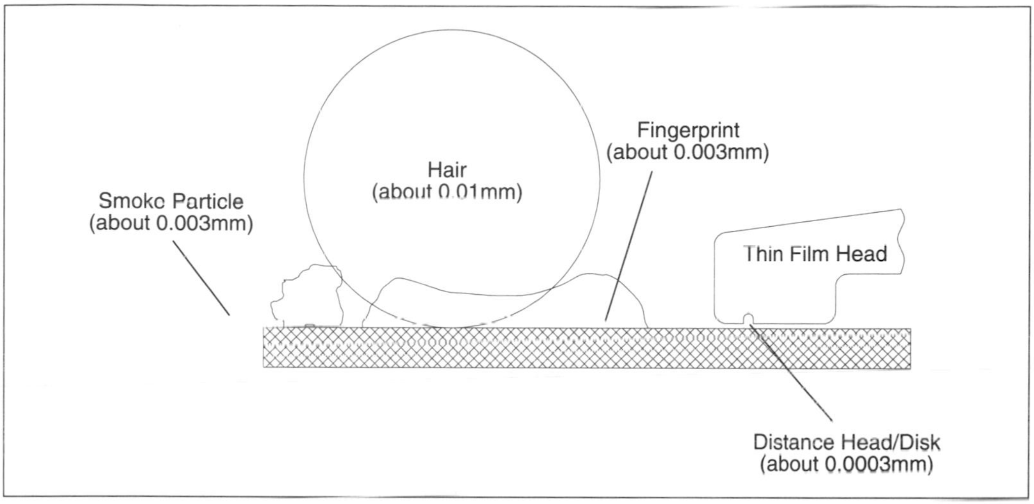

Figure 28.4: Comparison of various typical sizes of the head, its distance from the disk, and various dirt particles.

Actuators with a Stepper or Linear Motor

As already mentioned, the read/write heads are moved in common by an actuator. An actuator means all mechanical components necessary for the head's movement. Presently, actuators with a stepper or linear motor are used.

Figure 28.1 shows an *actuator with a stepper motor*. In the figure you can only see the spindle of the stepper motor, however. As is the case with the floppy drive, the stepper motor in hard disk drives is also rotated step by step in one or other direction by means of stepper pulses. These steps are fixed, and mean a fixed alteration of the motor spindle's angular position. Intermediate rotation angles are impossible: if, for example, the stepper motor can make a complete rotation with 180 steps, then this means that every stepper pulse turns the motor spindle by 2°. Thus only angular positions of 0°, 2°, 4°,... 358° can be realized; an intermediate position of, for example, 3° is not possible. The rotation of the motor spindle is transferred onto the actuator by friction. In Figure 28.1, the actuator can rotate around the actual axis. The stepper motor rotation is transferred to the arc-like actuator element, and the actuator rotates around the actuator axis. Thus the heads fixed to the actuator end are moved radially, and a head positioning occurs. By rotating the motor step by step, the actuator and thus the heads are also moved step by step. Usually, one motor step corresponds to a movement of the heads one track inwards or outwards.

It is characteristic of actuators with a linear motor that no feedback between the actuator's position and the stepper motor is implemented. If the motor has to move the heads from track 0 to track 219, for example, then the motor control simply provides 219 stepper pulses. Upon each pulse the motor is rotated one step, and thus the head moves one track. After 219 stepper pulses the head reaches track 219. That this doesn't work very exactly and reliably seems to be obvious. On floppy drives with a track width of at least 0.1 mm, problems seldom occur: such precision can be governed very easily. But even on simple hard disk drives with a stepper motor (for example, the formerly widely used Seagate ST225 with its 615 tracks), the track width reaches only 1/10 of that for floppies. Such a positioning precision can just be reached with a stepper motor. For the smaller $3^1/_2$" disks with more than 1000 tracks, the stepper motor is not suitable because of its poor positioning precision.

For an exact positioning of the heads, not only the precision but also the reproducibility is decisive, that is, a reliable repeatability of the head positioning to the same track – and this is the main problem for actuators with a stepper motor. The coupling between stepper motor spindle and actuator is done via the friction between the spindle and the arc-shaped element. Although the spindle is usually coated with a gum or plastic layer to keep the slippage as low as possible, it may be that the actuator temporararily slides on the stepper motor spindle, especially during large actuator accelerations. But now the strict correspondence of rotation angle and actuator position is lost, and positioning errors occur because the heads are moved to the wrong tracks, or at least to the edges of the tracks. This problem may be solved quite easily by returning the actuator to the abut position corresponding to track 0. For this purpose, the *recalibrate drive* command is used. The abutting actuator position is assigned to track 0, and the actuator control then restarts track and pulse counting.

A much more unpleasant problem concerning stepper motor actuators is heat deformation. Assume the following situation. Immediately after power-up you format your hard disk. All drive components are cold at that time. Thus upon every step pulse you generate the next track. After your PC has been operating for several hours, suddenly positioning and read errors occur. The reason is simply the heat deformation of the mechanical components. For example, the actuator enlarges with rising temperature, and therefore the arm between the actuator spindle and head gets longer. This means that the amount of the head's track-to-track movement becomes slightly larger than the actual track distance generated in advance by formatting with a cold actuator. Although the heat deformations are very low, and the manufacturers try to compensate for these deformations by certain material combinations, they are sufficient to make at least cylinders with a higher number inaccessible. If, on the other hand, you format your hard disk in a warm state, the PC may report positioning errors during power-up when all mechanical components are still cold. You can't even boot your PC then! You don't recognize many access failures directly as the controller carries out an in-built error recovery routine in the background which comprises seek retries and other procedures. Even then you may recognize access failure only indirectly by a nearly infinite access time for storing a short letter or the loud workings of the actuator motor and the drive mechanics.

The deeper cause for such failures is that no feedback between the head position and the motor control is implemented. The motor control passes the motor the seemingly required number of step pulses, and the stepper motor positions the head on the off-chance. If the head is located between two tracks, then an access is impossible, although only a further movement of half a track would be required.

Another disadvantage of hard disks with a stepper motor is that the manufacturers didn't implement an automatic head parking device, as these are low-cost models. The automatic head parking device moves the actuator into a transport position by means of a spring. In operation, the stepper motor exceeds the spring force to move the head accordingly. Some drives use the spindle motor as a generator that generates a sufficiently strong current pulse by means of the remaining rotation to move the actuator into the parking position when the drive is switched off.

Without a parking device the heads touch down onto tracks that usually contain data. At power-up the heads which are at rest scratch the disk's surface until the air cushion is strong enough to lift the heads. This is not very serious if you leave your PC in the same place all the time without moving it, but the missing automatic parking may give rise to a medium-sized disaster if you take your PC home in your car and you drive into a pothole. The shock of the hard heads onto the smoother disk may possibly destroy a data sector in that case. Manufacturers generally indicate the maximum allowed accelerations on the data sheets for their drives in g (which means the earth's gravitational acceleration of 9.805 m/s^2). Any shock that exceeds the limit in operation or switched-off state may give rise to serious damage. But the accelerations and shock forces actually occurring can hardly be estimated.

Fortunately, many PC manufacturers deliver a floppy disk with the setup program and a park routine for moving the hard disk heads to a safe location. If you are not sure whether your hard disk has an autopark device, then call the program in advance of each transportation. The programs are usually called *park*, *diskpark*, or something like this. It is also recommended that you call the program every time before you switch off the PC. You can recognize hard disks that park their heads automatically at power-down by a short scratch or knock, which indicates the positioning of the heads in their parking position.

High-quality hard disk drives use a linear motor instead of the stepper motor. Additionally, a control circuitry is implemented which compares the current head position to the intended one. Thus the read/write heads are always positioned above the correct track. According to the operation principle, two types of actuators with a linear motor (also called voice-coil actuators) can be distinguished (see Figure 28.5): linear and rotating.

The operation principle of such a voice-coil actuator is similar to that of the membrane drive in a speaker. A coil surrounds a permanent magnet or moves between two permanent magnets. If a current flows through the coil then a magnetic field occurs which is, depending upon the current direction, parallel to the field of the permanent magnet, or antiparallel to it. In the first case, the coil is pushed away; in the latter it is attracted. This leads to a linear movement of the coil, and thus of the actuator, which is connected to the coil. By means of a speedy electronic control of the coil current, coil and actuator can thus be moved and positioned along the permanent magnet.

With the linear voice-coil actuator the coil moves on two rails in a linear direction. The head at the actuator's end is directly moved in the same way as the actuator coil and radially shifted relative to the disk. Even rather low current pulses in the coil generate remarkable magnetic forces and actuator accelerations. Therefore, more and more the *rotating voice-coil actuator* is used as standard. Here the actuator is held in rotation around the actuator axis similar to the stepper motor actuator. On one end the read/write heads are mounted; at the other is the coil that carries out an arc-shaped movement in or around an arc-shaped permanent magnet. Because of a larger arm length between actuator axis and head compared to the distance of actuator axis and coil, a short coil movement is converted to an extensive head movement. This is favourable as the coil and the thus connected actuator part are rather heavy, and therefore inert, especially compared to the tiny thinfilm heads. In this way, a modest movement of the massive parts with a low power expenditure can be converted to a fast positioning movement of the heads. Thus the rotating actuator type allows shorter positioning times at a lower power consumption by the coil.

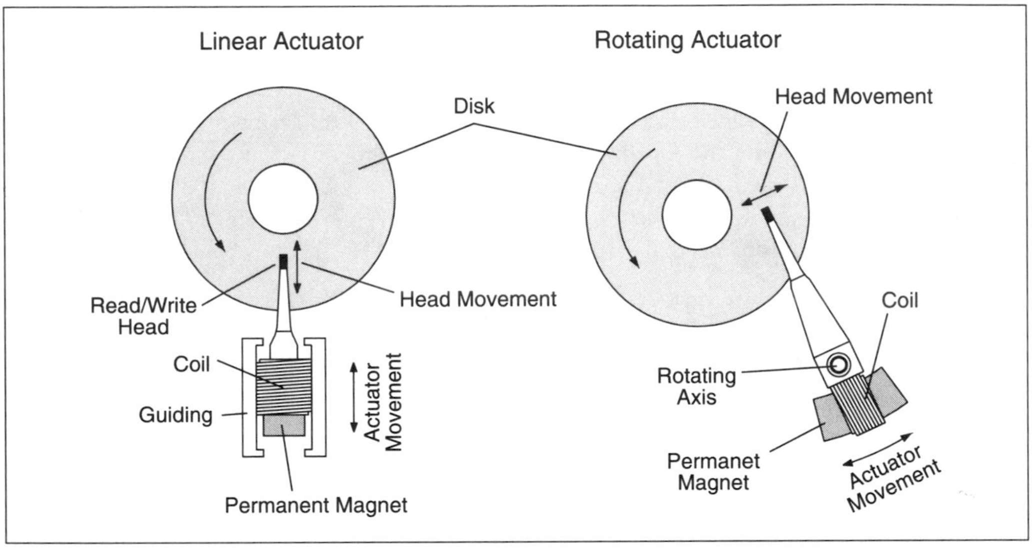

Figure 28.5: Actuator with a linear motor.

Unfortunately, the linear motor described has a significant disadvantage compared to the stepper motor: the positionings are not absolute. A short current pulse in the coil moves the actuator, but by how much can't be precisely predicted. Moreover, the magnetic fields generated by the coil slightly alter the magnetic properties of the permanent magnet. One has to choose another strategy and implement an active feedback loop that always leads to an absolute position of the read/write head and the actuator.

This is carried out by so-called *servo tracks* and a *servo head* (also called *index tracks* and *index head*, respectively). Perhaps you have been surprised by the fact that some hard disks have an odd number of heads. Why didn't the engineers simply add another head to use the last remaining disk side, as all other parts are already present? The answer is simple: the head is actually present but is dedicated to detecting the servo tracks, and is therefore part of the feedback loop for the head positioning. At the manufacturer's site the seemingly unused disk side is provided very precisely with the servo tracks. Their only job is to implement a reference for head positioning.

When the drive attempts to access a certain track, the servo head is positioned above the servo track concerned. Thus, all other read/write heads that are intended for data recording are also located at this track. As the user you cannot alter the servo tracks. Also, all low-level formatting programs orient according to these servo tracks, and generate the data tracks on all disks at the same radial position as the servo tracks. If the drive attempts to position the head above a certain track, then the drive control energizes the coil of the linear motor and the servo head permanently detects the number of that track which is currently present below the servo head. When the servo head has reached the intended track, the drive aborts this rough positioning, turns off the current, and carries out a fine positioning. For this purpose, the servo head is moved forwards and backwards in tiny steps by means of small current pulses until the signal from the servo track is maximal. Therefore, the head is exactly in the middle of the track concerned.

It is obvious that positioning with a servo head and servo tracks is much more precise and especially temperature-independent. However, the feedback of the servo signal to the drive control requires more electronic equipment. Furthermore, the precise generation of the servo tracks is complicated. High-capacity hard disk drives with a linear motor and servo tracks are therefore much more expensive than their stepper motor counterparts. With a capacity of more than 20 Mbytes per disk side, such a technology cannot be avoided any longer. Here I also want to mention that higher-capacity drives for mainframes and supercomputers exist, which carry out the servo track detection optically. The principle is similar to that of a CD player or CD ROM drive, where a laser beam with a diameter of only about 1 μm scans the disk surface and provides information on the servo tracks to the drive control. The magnetic read/write heads can thus be positioned with an even higher precision than is possible with magnetic servo tracks and magnetic servo heads. However, don't confuse this method with optical drives; the data recording and restoring is carried out in a purely magnetic and not an optical manner.

Air Filtering and Ventilation

All hard disk drives have an air filter. This filter serves not for filtering the air from outside which penetrates into the HDA, but for internally filtering the air already in the case. An air exchange with the environment takes place only to a small degree if the air pressure is changing. Figure 28.6 shows a scheme for the air circulation in a hard disk drive.

To avoid the HDA being blown up by a low environmental pressure or being pressed by a high air pressure, every case has a ventilation slit which leads to an air filter. Depending upon the environmental pressure, air can penetrate from or escape to the outside via the air filter. This is essential: if you take a $5^1/_4$" hard disk onto an aeroplane with a pressurized cabin you would expose the cover to a force which is higher than 100 pounds! I don't think you would ever wish to put such a heavy load on your hard disk. But it could become worse: in an aeroplane without a pressurized cabin your hard disk would really explode!

The air filter of a hard disk drive largely serves to filter the air already in the HDA. Because of slight head touches onto the disk or general wear-out of the rotating elements, microscopic dirt particles are formed, but they still are large enough to act as a scouring powder if they come between the head and the disk. The rotating disks therefore take up the air and generate an air circulation. The air filter is located within the streaming area of this circulation and filters off these small particles.

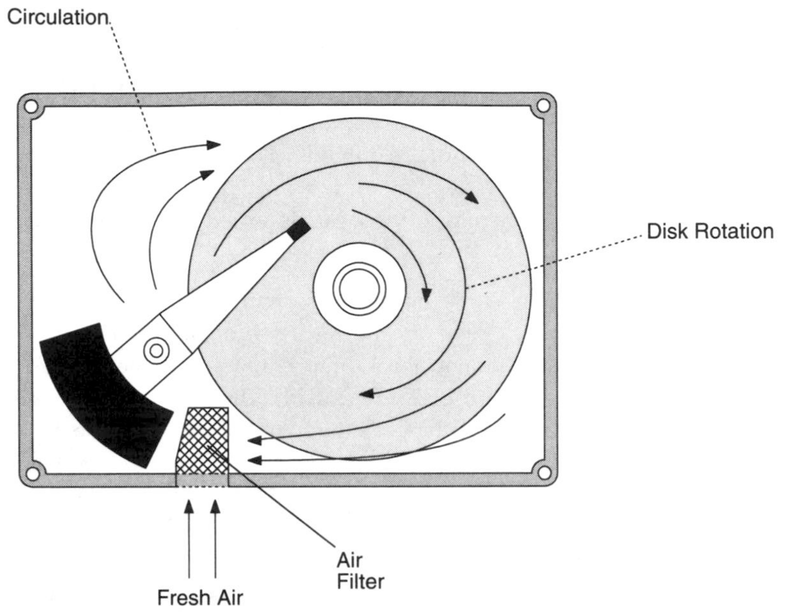

Figure 28.6: Air circulation in a hard disk drive. The disk rotation takes up the air in the drive; because of this a circulation stream is generated.

The air exchange with the environment is usually insignificant, and the internal wear-out is small. Thus the air filters of hard disks are designed as permanent filters that don't need to be replaced by you. This is completely different with large disk drives for mainframes, the so-called disk-packs. Here air is intentionally pressed through the whole drive to blow out all the dirt which has entered the drive during a disk change. This air must be filtered, of course, and because of the extensive air stream the filters have to be regularly replaced.

28.1.2 Interleaving

During reading or writing, the intended sector passes below the head because of the floppy or disk rotation and the controller enables the read/write head. Then the sector data is written into or read from the controller's sector buffer. If, for example, more data is to be read, then the data of the just read sector must be transferred into the main memory of the PC before the sector buffer can be filled with the data of the next sector. The controller-internal sector buffer usually has only a capacity sufficient for one sector plus the additional redundancy bytes. To be able to read the next sector, this sector data must be transferred within that short time interval which corresponds to the passage of the gap between the two sectors below the head. Only very fast ATs with a powerful controller succeed in doing this. On old XTs or on slow hard disk controllers, the new sector has already passed partially below the head by the time the sector buffer is ready to accommodate the new one. Thus the CPU must wait for a complete disk revolution before the new sector again appears below the read/write head. On a hard disk running at about 3600 rpm, this lasts about 16 ms. If you want to read a small file with 100 kbytes of data corresponding to 200 sectors, the read process would last for 200*16ms=3.2 seconds. This is too long, of course, and makes a nonsense of the high transfer rate of the hard disks.

The solution to these problems is called *interleaving*. Here the sectors are not positioned successively, as is the case for floppies, but they are shifted by one or more sectors. Figure 28.7 shows the scheme. The amount of sector shifting is indicated by the *interleave factor*. A factor of three, for example, means that the sector with the next successive number N+1 is the third sector after the sector numbered N. One could also say that two sectors come between two successively enumerated sectors. For a hard disk with N sectors per track, interleave values between one (which means no shifting) and N–1 are allowed. Between two successively enumerated sectors, zero to N–2 sectors are located.

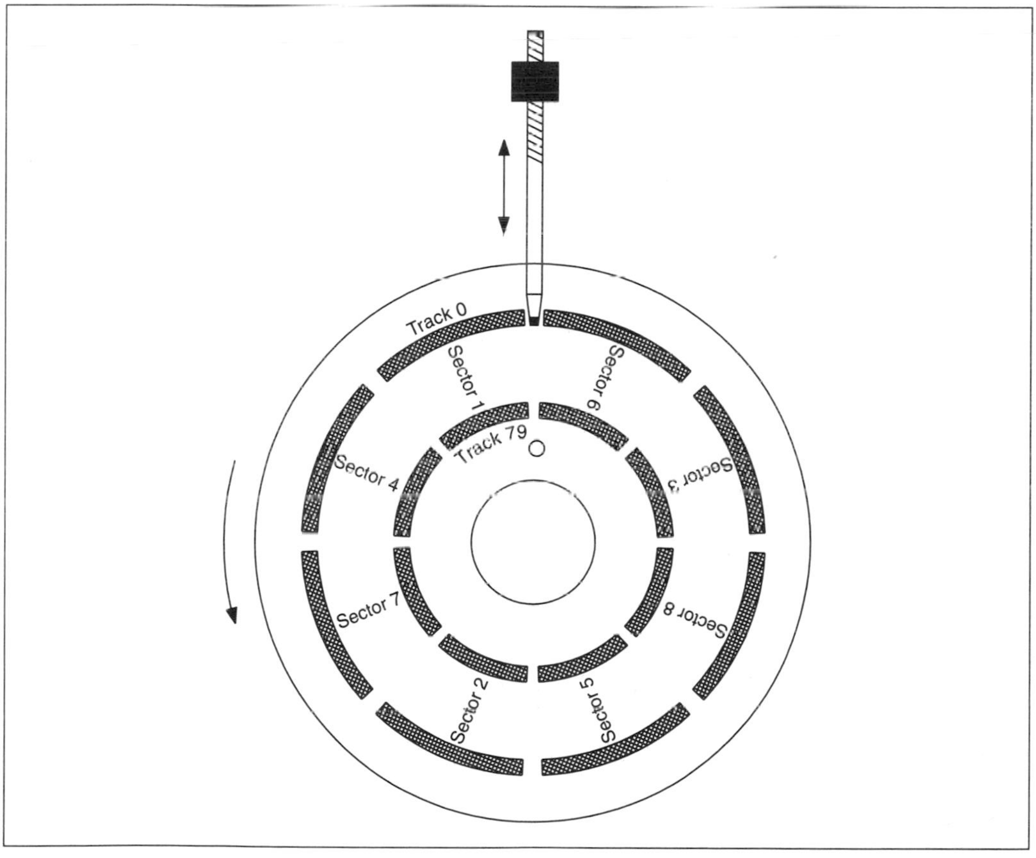

Figure 28.7: Interleaving doesn't position the sectors successively; instead they are shifted according to the interleave factor.

The effect of interleaving is readily explained. When two successively enumerated setors are to be read, then controller and system bus have enough time to transfer the data in the sector buffer into main memory before the next sector appears below the read/write head. On the XT the interleave factor was equal to 6; on the AT equal to 3; and on the PS/2 machines only one (that is, no interleaving). Turbo ATs or i386/i486 machines can also have an interleave factor of one. Floppies are always handled with an interleave factor of one, as their data transfer rate doesn't inconvenience even a 4.77 MHz PC. Additionally, floppy drives transfer the sector data more or less online into main memory without temporary storage in a sector buffer. On hard disks this is not possible, as they not only carry out a CRC-check by means of their redundancy bytes, but they can even correct the data by additional ECC-bytes. However, this correction can only be carried out when all bytes have been read into the sector buffer; otherwise, an erroneous byte may already have been transferred to main memory when the ECC logic is just detecting the error by means of the previously read ECC bytes. Details on this subject are discussed below.

It is important that the interleave factor of a hard disk is defined during the course of the low-level formatting procedure. You may determine the optimum interleave value only by testing. For this purpose, you start to format your disk with a large value and check the data transfer rate. But note that too small a value has more fatal consequences than too large a value. With too large a value the controller waits longer for the next sector than is required. The time may be in the range for the passage of two sectors but in the case of too low a value the sector has just disappeared and the controller must wait nearly one complete revolution (that is, N–1 sectors) until the intended sectors appear again. You may ascertain this on your own: while the transfer rate rises slowly up to a maximum value with a decreasing interleave value at first, the rate sharply drops to the worst value you can get after the interleave value falls below the optimum value. Some programs (for example, Spinrite) carry out such a check automatically, and determine the optimum value for your system.

While you get hardly any problems on conventional ST506/412 hard disks if you carry out low-level formatting and determine the interleave value by means of a special formatting program such as DiskManager or Spinrite, this is usually not possible with the modern IDE or SCSI drives. As a compensation, these disks are usually preformatted with an interleave value of one. High-performance hard disks may have up to 70 sectors per track today and, nevertheless, operate with an interleave factor of one. This is possible because a cache memory is implemented on them, which can accommodate a complete track, or even more. Thus the data is first written from disk into the sector buffer, and during the course of a disk revolution, the sectors of one track are written into the cache memory. The host system can now read the cache memory at its leisure. Here, too low an interleave value no longer plays a role.

28.1.3 Controller and Interfaces

For the driving head and actuator you need a controller to carry out the commands from the CPU, as well as the encoding and decoding of data. Figure 28.8 shows a schematic block diagram for the controller–drive combination.

The bus interface establishes the connection of the controller to the PC. Read and write data for the drive as well as command data for the controller are exchanged via the interface. The controller itself consists of a microprocessor for controlling the drive interface and the controller-internal logic elements. For this purpose, a machine program is stored in the microcode ROM that the microprocessor uses. The data which is to be written into or read from a sector is held by the sector buffer, which always accommodates one complete sector. The interface to the drive can be formed very differently depending upon whether it is an ST412/506, ESDI, or embedded controller. Embedded controllers are integrated (embedded) on the drive, and exclusively control this single drive. On the other hand, ST412/506 and ESDI controllers can be connected to virtually any ST412/506 and ESDI drive, respectively. The drive interface supplies the connected drive with all the required control and data signals, and also accepts the corresponding return and data signals from the drive.

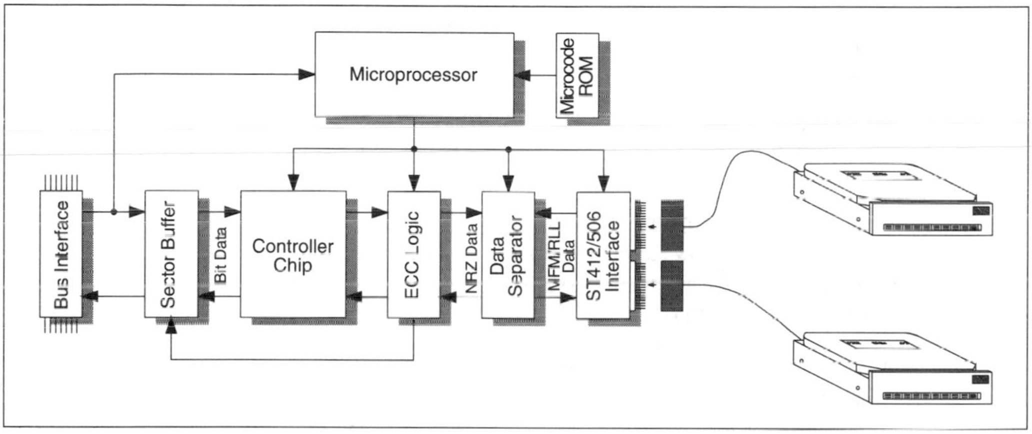

Figure 28.8: Controller and drive.

Let's discuss the principal functioning of a hard disk controller in relation to a read process. To read one sector the CPU passes a command block that has several command and parameter bytes to a register in the PC interface. The controller's microprocessor detects the command block and interprets the codes. The controller carries out the relevant command (here reading one sector) under the control of the program in microcode ROM. For this purpose, it drives the drive interface to position the drive's head above the intended track by means of precise stepper pulses. The drive head now continuously reads the signals passing below the head, and transfers the corresponding signals via the drive interface to the data separator. Depending upon the recording method, the data separator converts the MFM or RLL encoded data into an intermediate format called *NRZ* (non-return to zero). The microprocessor determines, by means of the programmable storage controller, whether an address mark, a gap, or another field is currently passing below the head. If the microprocessor has detected an address mark, then it determines whether track and sector numbers coincide with the intended values. If the track number is not as intended, then it directs the drive to carry out another positioning; if only the sector number doesn't coincide, the microprocessor simply waits for the next address mark. If the sector number becomes equal to that intended, the controller opens the read gate and accepts the read data from disk (and converted to NRZ data by the data separator). The completely decoded data is then transferred into the sector buffer.

At the same time, the ECC circuitry checks whether the sector data conforms to the ECC bytes. If this is not the case, then the data is corrected by means of the ECC bytes. Unlike floppy controllers, which because of their CRC bytes are only able to check whether the data is correct, hard disk controllers can not only check for errors but even correct them with their ECC (error correcting code) bytes as long as the error is not too serious. The principle behind the ECC codes is similar to that of the CRC checksums, but more complex generator polynomials are used. Correspondingly adapted circuits recover the original data bytes from the erroneous data and ECC bytes. A hard disk controller with an ST412 interface usually uses a 4-byte ECC with the generator polynomial

$$ECC = x^{32}+x^{28}+x^{26}+x^{19}+x^{17}+x^{10}+x^{6}+x^{2}+1$$

Powerful hard disks with RLL encoding also employ longer ECC codes, with up to six or even eight bytes. But even with a 4-byte ECC, burst errors up to eleven bits can be corrected.

If the read data in the sector buffer is held in a correct or corrected form, then it may be transferred into the main memory. XT controllers use DMA channel 3 for this purpose. Thus, similar to floppy drives, a data transfer by means of the DMA chip takes place. On the other hand, the AT controller uses interrupt-driven data exchange with IN and OUT commands. For this purpose, the controller issues a hardware interrupt via IRQ14 after the sector has been read into the sector buffer. Now the handler transfers all 512 read data bytes from the sector buffer into main memory via programmed I/O.

When writing a sector the process is inverted. First, the 512 data bytes to be written are transferred from main memory to the sector buffer. The controller then carries out the positioning of the head and the search for the correct track and the intended sector in the same way as was the case for data reading. If the microprocessor has detected the address mark of the correct sector by the signals from the read/write head, it opens the write gate and continuously transfers the data via the storage controller. The storage controller now generates data address marks and other gap information, calculates the ECC bytes, converts the sector data into the NRZ format, and transfers the NRZ data stream to the data separator. In the data separator the encoding to MFM or RLL data is carried out, and this the data separator then transfers to the drive and thus to the activated read/write head via the drive interface. The head writes the data signals arriving from the data separator, without any further alterations, onto disk. If all address marks, sector data, and gaps have been written then the write process is complete, and the microprocessor may detect and process the next command.

A legitimate question is why IBM has implemented a second DMA chip in the AT, but unlike the XT doesn't use the DMA controller for data transfer between controller and main memory. The reason may possibly be that the AT with its 80286, and in particular the i386 and i486 PCs with an ISA bus, can carry out much faster data transfer using the IN, OUT and MOV commands than relatively low-clocked (4.77 MHz or 5 MHz) 8-bit DMA chips. Only in the environment of a multitasking operating system might the DMA transfer be more advantageous to free the CPU from such boring jobs. The PS/2 has thus been designed for multitasking operation.

Some magnetic media show the unpleasant property that a slight movement of the magnetized areas, and thus of the stored data bits, occurs if the magnetized areas are very close together. These *bit-shiftings* therefore occur only on the inner cylinders with high cylinder numbers, and further also depend upon the magnetization patterns on the disk. This means that the shifting only occurs for certain bit sequences. These critical bit sequences are well-known and can thus be handled by so-called *write-precompensation*. For this purpose, certain bits are written onto the disk slightly earlier or later, depending on the preceding and following bit, as this would actually be correct according to the encoding method used. The precompensation logic thus investigates online the data stream running to the drive for critical bit patterns, and delays or accelerates the corresponding signals. The time values for delay or acceleration for a hard disk with 17 sectors per track are in the range of 12–15 ns, that is, about 6% of an MFM bit cell. But note that many hard disks don't require a precompensation. Embedded controllers handle this problem without your intervention, as they are designed for each drive and therefore know its behaviour best. For some other hard disks you have to enter the start cylinder of the precompensation in the setup.

Another possibility for handling these bit shiftings is to reduce the write current for the inner cylinders with the closely adjacent data bits. You will therefore find, in the setup for your hard disk controller if it is not directly fixed on the drive, a *reduced write current* entry. By this reduction the data bits on the disk are not magnetized so strongly, and therefore affect each other less; the bit shifting is suppressed. Also, for this quantity you will find an entry in the setup where you have to enter the start cylinder at which the write current is to be reduced. A value that is larger than the maximum hard disk cylinder means in both cases that no precompensation and no reduced write current, respectively, is present, because the start cylinder cannot be reached.

Which of the components shown in Figure 28.8 is actually present on the controller adapter or the drive depends upon the interface standard and the actual implementation used. The widely used controllers with an ST412/506 interface accommodate all components from the bus to the drive interface on a separate controller board. The drives themselves are connected to the controller via the ST412/506 interface. Characteristic of this interface is that the read and write data runs via the physical connection controller–drive already in MFM or RLL-encoded form, and therefore as an asynchronous signal pattern. Further details are discussed in Section 28.4.

In ESDI systems the data separator is already integrated on the drive. Between drive and controller only the synchronous NRZ data is exchanged, thus raising the maximum achievable data transfer rate. Finally, controller and drive form a unit in IDE and SCSI systems. The connection to the PC bus is carried out by a host adapter which, in principle, is only an extended PC bus interface in the form of a small adapter board. Every manufacturer is free to implement the connection between controller and drive in any form.

28.1.4 Capacity, Data Transfer Rate and Reliability

Manufacturers and dealers like to shower their clients with a lot of catchwords and accompanying data to show their products in the most favourable light. Lies are seldom told, but leaving out some background information may give rise to a wrong impression. The following sections therefore investigate some of the frequently recited and «decisive» properties of hard disks.

Storage Capacity

The first characteristic of a hard disk is, of course, the *storage capacity*. Here, four different combinations are possible, which differ in their amount by nearly one quarter (!), but nevertheless refer to the same hard disk on which you can store the same number of bytes in all four cases. A popular cheat is to indicate the unformatted capacity. As you already know from the floppies, the controller generates several address fields and gaps apart from the data area, thus the formatted capacity is about 20% less, on average. Therefore, note whether the manufacturer or dealer indicates the (unformatted) gross or the (formatted) net capacity. As a user only the formatted data capacity is decisive for you, of course. Depending on the formatting parameters and the sector size, the formatted capacity may vary only slightly. In the PC today, only hard disks with a sector size of 512 bytes are used, so that the formatted capacity enables a better comparison of various hard disks.

A further possibility to make the capacity of a hard disk appear to be larger without being dishonest is to indicate the capacity not in Mbytes but miobytes (million bytes). Remember that 1 kbyte is 1024 bytes, not 1000 bytes. In the same way, 1 Mbyte is equal to 1024*1024=1 048 576 bytes and not 1 000 000 bytes – a remarkable difference of 5%. If you buy a hard disk with an unformatted capacity of 100 miobytes, which is already a reasonable size, you will not be able to accommodate more data than your friend who got one with a net capacity of 80 Mbytes.

Access Time

Another popular quantity, especially at the time of hard disk dinosaurs, is the *access time*. But which one is meant? There are four different access times: track–track, positioning, random, or full-stroke. The first time indicates the time interval that the actuator requires to move the head from the current to an adjacent track. The value includes the so-called *settle time*. When actuator and head are accelerated by the actuator motor and decelerated shortly before the destination track, they tend to oscillate. Once this oscillation has been dampened (that is, the head has settled), the head can access the track correctly. Typical values for track–track access times are about 2.5–5 ms today. A small value for this access time is important, as most data is held by successively enumerated sectors. If the capacity of one cylinder is exhausted, then the file continues on the next cylinder. Thus the head must be moved by one track. Finally, after optimization with a disk optimizer (for example, Compress or Speed Disk), the directories are also grouped so that often only a few track movements are necessary to access all the data in a directory. Thus a low track–track access time is favourable.

The *average positioning time* indicates the time interval required on average to move the head from the current track to a randomly selected destination track. This time indication includes the head settle time, but not the so-called *latency*. When you attempt to access a certain sector of the disk by a controller command, then the drive must position the head above the intended track first. But now the sector is usually not accessible yet. Only in a few rare cases will the sector appear below the read/write head immediately after the head settlement. However, it may also be that the intended sector has just passed and the controller must wait for one complete revolution. On average this wait time or latency is just the time interval required for half a disk revolution. As all hard disks rotate at 3600 rpm, the latency is usually equal to 8.3 ms. Stone Age hard disks and modern ESDI disks don't differ here. The latency becomes especially dominant on drives with low positioning times. For high-performance hard disks with a low access time, the manufacturers have therefore increased the revolution rate up to 6000 rpm. Thus, the average latency decreases to 5 ms. As a welcome side-effect, the internal data transfer rate is also improved because now more sectors pass per time unit below the read/write heads.

Positioning time and latency together lead to the *random* or *average access time*. This is the time required for a random access to a certain sector, thus the average time for a completely random head movement from the current track to the destination, and the wait until the sector concerned appears below the head after the elapse of the latency time. The old and formerly widely used ST225 drive required 65 ms; typical values today are between 12 ms and 28 ms. A low average access time is important if you work with many applications that use randomly distributed data or contain index data for searching the data actually required. Spreadsheets and database programs belong to this group. To locate one byte in a database, several disk accesses and therefore accompanying head movements may be required. A low access time is then very important.

Also, the interpretation of the average access time requires some care. There is an elegant possibility to reduce this time remarkably: disk caches. These are cache memories integrated on the drive or controller which can accommodate a complete track or individual sectors before the track or sector data is transferred into main memory, or the data delivered by the main memory is written onto disk. The access to disk caches is, of course, very fast; the access times are significantly below 1 ms. However, the average mechanical access time remains the same, and is further composed of the average (mechanical) positioning time as well as the latency. Sequential disk accesses in particular are significantly accelerated by the disk cache. Some manufacturers assume, rather arbitrarily, that 40% of all accesses are sequential with the cache access time, 40% are random accesses with the average mechanical access time, and 20% are write accesses, also with the average mechanical access time, for example. The weighted average is thus equal to 40% * cache access time + 60% * average mechanical access time. Together with an average mechanical access time of 20 ms, an average access time of 12 ms is the result – a value which looks rather good. I want to leave judgement as to the 40%–40%–20% distribution up to you. Always ask when you buy a hard disk drive whether the access time with cache or only with the mechanical access time is indicated. A disk with a 30% longer mechanical access time usually leads to better system performance than its counterpart which achieves the shorter access time only with the help of a cache. That is especially true for PCs with an i386 processor or above which carries out demand paging and, thus, continuously swaps data onto the hard disk, or reads data from there. Here, a low mechanical (!) access time is decisive. What's the gain of a 64 kbyte disk cache if a 16 Mbyte main memory is available, and even this capacity is not sufficient so that the processor has to swap pages which certainly are larger than 64 kbyte (corresponding to about 0.4% of the 16 Mbyte main memory).

The disk caches become really effective starting at a size beyond 1 Mbyte. The corresponding cache controller for hard disks speeds up, for example, link processes remarkably, as during the course of these processes many library files must be opened and closed. A real alternative for i386/i486 computers with a large main memory are software caches that emulate a disk cache in main memory. Programs like SmartDrive, DiskCache, etc. belong to this class. On fast-clocked i386/i486 PCs these software caches are even faster, as a lot of data is already present in the fast accessible main memory, and need not be fetched from the controller cache via the slowly clocked PC system bus. But the significant disadvantage is that a hang-up of the PC because of a system failure also leads to a loss of the data just written onto the «disk» if it was temporarily stored in the cache and the hang-up occurred before it was written onto disk. Only a write-through strategy can avoid this problem, but this is very unfavourable if programs swap data blocks as the cache now has virtually no effect. Hardware caches on the controller are not affected by such system crashes. Their logic is separated from the main system, and even works when the PC has already hung-up. You should only wait for a few seconds after the last write access before you switch off your PC and turn off the current supply for the cache before all cache data has been written, or force a cache flush (with smartdrv /c, for example).

Besides these access times, manufacturers often also indicate the *full-stroke time*. This is the time required to move the head from track 0 to the track with the maximum cylinder number, or vice versa. The value is significant for an access to data which is very far away from each other. Such very strongly fragmented data can appear with DOS, for example, if you extend an old file and nearly all clusters up to the end of the disk are already occupied by other files and directories. DOS then allocates a sector on a track in the very innermost part of the disk for the additional data. Thus the heads must be moved quite far.

Data Transfer Rate

Another way of showing certain hard disks in a more favourable light by insufficient explanation is the *data transfer rates*. They generally refer to the quotient from the transferred amount of data and the time required for this. If you are leaving the City of London on Friday afternoon at 4 p.m. to go in your Lotus to Bournemouth for the weekend, you surely don't tell your friends that you drove to Bournemouth at a speed of 150 mph only because it was possible to go at this speed for a few miles because the traffic jam cleared for a short time! For a distance of about 150 miles you need at least three hours on a Friday afternoon! But this doesn't hinder some hard disk manufacturers (like some printer manufacturers) from indicating data transfer rates which are as realistic as the above car journey! By the term data transfer rate I would understand a value with which a realistic (that is, medium-sized) file is transferred from the drive into main memory. All other definitions may also be correct in the strict context for which they are defined, but for practical use they often don't tell you anything.

Three components mainly contribute to the transfer rate: disk-controller transfer, processing in the controller, and controller–main memory transfer. The first part, the so-called *internal transfer rate*, is limited by the number of bytes passing below the read/write head every second, and is given, in general, by the following expression:

$$\text{internal data transfer rate} = \frac{\text{sectors/track} * \text{bytes/sector} * \text{rpm}}{\text{interleave}}$$

With 17 sectors per track at 3600 rpm, this value (together with the address fields, gaps, etc.) reaches about 600 kbytes/s. This actually corresponds to the 5 Mbits/s specification for the ST412 interface of MFM-encoded data. The controller separates all bytes which don't belong to the sector data field, thus only about 510 kbytes remain. First, these 510 kbytes/s are only valid for a single sector; we ought to write 512 bytes/980 μs as one sector comprises 512 data bytes and the sector together with all address fields and gaps passes within about 980 μs below the head. Now the data is in the sector buffer and has to be further transferred into main memory. If the controller and main system are fast enough to carry out this job before the next sector appears (that is, with an interleave of 1:1), then this transfer rate remains the same for the complete track. The transfer rate is effectively equal to 510 kbytes/s. But with an interleave factor of two, already two complete revolutions are required to transfer all the data of a track into main memory. Thus the transfer rate reduces to 255 kbytes/s. On an XT the interleave of 6:1 used leads to a ridiculous transfer rate of only 85 kbytes/s; a value which is nearly reached by a 1.2 Mbyte drive. On the other hand, a modern high-performance hard disk with 70 sectors/track, 6000 rpm and interleave 1:1 reaches an internal transfer rate of nearly 3.5 Mbyte/s. But note that even this value does not exhaust the transfer rate on a SCSI bus. Therefore, the widespread bus or host adapter tests only very rarely check the performance of, for example, a SCSI host adapter with a PCI interface, but determine the internal transfer rate of the connected drive.

The processing time in the controller is usually very short, as the CRC and ECC checking and the ECC correction is carried out within a very short time. The processing time thus only slightly affects the transfer rate.

But the transfer rate between the controller and main memory via the PC system bus is, during the short time interval until the next sector appears and within which all the sector data must be transferred from the controller into main memory, significantly larger, of course. The distance between two sector data fields is only 100 μs. Thus, the transfer rate into main memory must be equal to 512 bytes/100 μs, or about 5 Mbytes/s! The PC system bus must therefore be able to handle at least such a rate so that an interleave value is possible. ISA and EISA buses only run at a frequency of 8.33 MHz at most, according to their specification. Together with a width of 16 bits for the ISA and 32 bits for the EISA bus, the data transfer rate of the bus system is thus limited to a maximum of 8.33 Mbytes/s and 16.67 Mbytes/s, respectively, as the processor requires two bus clock cycles for one bus cycle. Only the burst mode of the EISA bus with an i486 processor or the DMA mode C enables a doubled transfer rate of 33.3 Mbytes/s for a short time. Therefore, already the RLL-encoded data with an ST412 interface and 26 sectors per track exhausts the ISA bus capacity. Don't think that your PC doesn't operate well if your hard disk test program reports a transfer rate not very much above 800 kbytes/s, even with the brand new high-performance controller. The transfer rate between two sectors is much higher and needs the complete ISA bus capacity. An average value over long time intervals always smears out peak values completely.

Now it becomes clear why high-capacity drives with up to 70 sectors per track and an interleave of 1:1 have a disk cache (or at least a track instead of a sector buffer). The cache operates much faster than the transfer via the ISA or EISA bus and can therefore accommodate a complete track. The transfer into main memory via the PC bus can be carried out continuously, and the transfer capacity of 8.33 Mbytes/s or 16.67 Mbytes/s can be used for a longer time than the 100 μs between two sectors in the case of MFM-encoded disks with an ST412 interface. With a low number of sectors per track, the number of passing sector data bytes (and with a high number of sectors per track, the transfer capabilities of the ISA or EISA bus) limits the transfer rate; only the local bus or busmaster adapters in EISA burst mode can stand nearly any amount of data from the drives. The buffering between the two asynchronously operating system elements, hard disk and PC system bus, raises the transfer rate remarkably. Also, here it becomes obvious that the performance of a complete system is governed by the performance of the weakest member. The disk cache on the drive thus serves mainly for enhancing the data transfer rate, and not for reducing the access time. But up to now, the access time has been valid as the exclusive performance characteristic and sacred cow, for hard disk manufacturers tend to gloss over the access time of their hard disks by means of the cache instead of emphasizing the much more important function for the transfer rate.

You may determine the various access times and data transfer rate by means of a hard disk test program such as the CORETEST. Disable any software cache for this purpose to avoid any distortion of the transfer rate. With an active software cache you get values only concerning the data transfer capacity of your system bus and the performance of the cache driver.

Benchmark programs for determining the data transfer rate usually only read the same data block repeatedly. If this block is no larger than the on-board cache then the drive must read the data from the disk only once. All further accesses refer solely to the FATS cache. You thus only investigate the transfer rate from cache–main memory, that is, the performance of the connection. If the size of the data block exceeds the storage capacity of the controller cache, then the data transfer rate is brought to its knees; in some cases it can be decreased by a factor of ten! You can recognize this clearly when you are looking at the frequently shown data transfer diagrams in computer magazines. Large files, and also small files or file fragments that can be readily accommodated by the cache but have to be fetched first, are transferred only at this significantly lower transfer rate.

Reliability and MTBF

As a user of hard disks, the drive's reliability is of particular importance. Where is the gain if you access data within 15 ms and this data can theoretically be transferred with a rate of 1 Mbytes/s, but your drive is out of order because of a hardware failure? Manufacturers therefore generally indicate some reliability information. The time interval between two complete failures of the drive which requires some repair is described by *MTBF* (Mean Time Between Failures). The MTBF must be interpreted as follows: if we assume a plurality of identical drives, then on average one failure occurs within the MTBF. Thus MTBF is a statistical quantity, and statistical quantities have to be handled with care. For this reason some astronomical values for MTBF are discussed in brief here. I have already seen MTBF values of 150000 hours, which is more than 17 (!) years of uninterrupted 24-hour operation. To get a trustworthy average value for the MTBF one would have to operate a plurality of identical drives for a much longer time than the MTBF indicates. How is it possible otherwise to indicate a time average value if the test time is much below this? With an MTBF of 17 years this is, of course, impossible, as the drive would be outdated long before reaching the MTBF test time. Instead, manufacturers make certain assumptions and elaborate statistical failure models that rely on experience with other and older drives. Afterwards, a test is carried out that may stretch over six months. From the failure rate in this time interval and the comparison with the failure rate of older drives for which some experience values exist, one extrapolates the MTBF for the investigated drive. The manufacturers prefer, of course, a linear dependency, but this doesn't correctly reflect the technical behaviour in all cases. For example, the failure rate of a car rises remarkably with its age. With a linear extrapolation of the failure rate, within the first two years each car would become at least (statistically) 30 years old. Thus be careful when interpretating the MTBF values. It's better that you rely on well-informed (!) consultants, who may provide you with global experience and no statistical average values.

Besides a complete failure which is characterized by the MTBF, there are other ordinary and more or less troublesome read and positioning errors. Write errors are not detected by the drive in most cases. They manifest themselves only by later read errors. On average, the number of recoverable read errors for good hard disks is about 1 per 10^{10} read bits. Note that the error rate is indicated as *error per read bits* but a read access is always carried out sector by sector with 512 bytes and eight bits per byte. Converted to the number of read accesses, a value 4000 times larger arises. The number of recoverable read errors then reaches 1 per $2*10^6$ read accesses; a value which no longer looks as trustworthy as the one indicated above. Performance and reliability infomation should therefore always be investigated precisely. But nevertheless, the above indicated value is quite good. You may read 1 Gbyte of data before a recoverable read error occurs, but as a user you don't recognize such an error because the ECC bytes correct it. Only the BIOS detects the ECC correction and sets a corresponding indicator. Much more troublesome are the non-recoverable read errors. A typical rate for a high-quality drive is 1 error per 10^{14} read bits or 1 failure per $2*10^{10}$ read commands. But such errors characterize only the so-called *soft errors*. They assume error-free working mechanics and a damage-free disk surface. Mechanical damage because of natural wear-out or a head crash, as *hard errors*, increase the error rate by several powers of ten. The most likely failure reason is an incorrect head positioning. The rate of such *seek errors* is about 1 per 10^6 positionings with linear motors. Stepper motors show an error rate that is about ten times higher. All these values seem to be rather good, but take into account the fact that the heads of hard disks must be moved frequently and quickly – one million head movements are reached within a short time. But as a compensation, the error recovery strategies built into the controller handle such positioning errors automatically. For example, in most cases it's sufficient to move the head back to track 0 to recalibrate the drive and then repeat the positioning. Generally speaking, today's hard disks are very reliable devices if you handle them with care.

28.1.5 BIOS Configuration

This section discusses the BIOS setup configuration for all presently used interface standards.

First, a few words about hard disk entries in the BIOS entries. If you're using an ST412/506 controller that can be accessed by the on-board BIOS of the AT and which does not have its own BIOS, you usually have to define the drive geometry with the setup program. Normally, one of the entries available in the BIOS fits your drive. If this is not the case, then most PCs allow you to enter the geometry parameters using a user-definable entry. Consult the data sheet of your hard disk drive for this purpose. There you will find the number of tracks, heads and sectors per track. Furthermore, the sheets also indicate where the write precompensation and the reduced write current starts. If the data sheet doesn't contain any information about them, then always enter a value that is higher than the maximum cylinder number to disable the precompensation and the reduced write current. If read errors occur, especially with high cylinder numbers, it's best then to enter about 2/3 of the maximum cylinder number.

On new IDE hard disks, which can be directly accessed by the AT BIOS as the ST412/506 controller, the precompensation and reduced write current entries are without meaning. The embedded controllers of these drives are best adapted to the hard disks concerned. Whether and in which way, for example, the precompensation is carried out is hidden from you. The controller does this internally. On the other hand, you usually have to enter the drive geometry into the setup table as the IDE hard disk appears to the system. Always consult the data sheet of your hard disk and obey the manufacturer's indications of the physical geometry with various zones. Some IDE drives are intelligent enough to use any geometry indicated by you, as long as the resulting number of sectors doesn't exceed the number of sectors physically present on the drive.

ESDI and SCSI hard disks cannot be accessed by the AT BIOS directly, as their register assignment isn't compatible with the AT bus standard. Such hard disks have a BIOS extension on the controller or host adapter which replaces the former INT 13h interrupt and carries out all hard disk functions. As more or less intelligent drives, these hard disks identify their geometry to the controller and BIOS by an identify command. You should therefore not enter any value in the BIOS setup for them, but indicate that no hard disk is present. If you use, for example, a SCSI hard disk as drive C: then you must enter for the first hard disk in the setup that no drive is present; otherwise, you may provoke a conflict between the controller and the system BIOS. With the BIOS extension engagement, during the course of booting, the ESDI and SCSI drives are integrated into the system, and you may access the hard disks with no problem. Today, Windows NT and OS/2 hardly have any problems in accessing most of the SCSI adapters and SCSI drives; the necessary drivers are already part of the operating system.

28.2 Recording Formats, Low-Level Formatting and Bad-Sector Mapping

This section discusses the «low-level properties» of hard disk drives and controllers. Here, I want to present a new and very powerful recording or encoding method, RLL. Moreover, you will gain an insight into the various tasks and strategies of the controller for managing hard disks.

28.2.1 MFM and RLL

The use of MFM instead of FM already leads to a significant increase of the data density BPI without the need to enhance the flux change density FCI. Thus it's not surprising that the developers of hard disks searched for other ways in which to realize higher and higher storage capacities. One way to achieve this is the *RLL method* which seems to be surrounded by even more mystery than the MFM method. RLL is the abbreviation for *run length limited*. This means that the number of zero bits between two set bits is limited. With the MFM method this is not the case. You may fill a 512-byte sector with 4096 zero bits with no problem. With the MFM method only clock but no data bits are then recorded. This is already the main difference to RLL: the MFM method records a clock bit if two zero bits occur in succession. The RLL method, on the other hand, gets along without any clock bit. The RLL logic determines, solely from the time interval between two set bits, how many zero bits were interposed. Because of synchronization problems, rotation variations, etc., which give rise to a variation of the period between the zero bits, this doesn't work for all numbers of zero bits. Therefore, their number is limited (hence the name RLL) to avoid the RLL logic losing the beat.

With the most widely used RLL method there are, by definition, at least two and at most seven zero bits between two set bits. The method is therefore called *RLL 2,7*. But now a problem arises: a 16-bit integer with the value 0 consists of 16 zero bits. That's too much for RLL. The data bits must therefore be re-encoded so that at least two and at most seven zero bits are in succession. Table 28.1 shows the encoding table for RLL 2,7.

data bit	RLL 2,7 code
000	000100
10	0100
010	100100
0010	00100100
11	1000
011	001000
0011	00001000

Table 28.1: RLL 2,7 encoding

You can see that data bit groups of different lengths are encoded into RLL codes also of different lengths. In the RLL codes a maximum of four zero bits is in front and a maximum of three zero bits behind a 1. Thus seven zero bits at most can meet. Furthermore, behind every 1 at least two zero bits occur. Therefore, between two 1s there are always at least two zero bits and the requirements for RLL 2,7 are fulfilled.

From Table 28.1 you can also see the disadvantage of the RLL method: the RLL codes are much longer than the data bit groups by a factor of two. We now discuss, in connection with Figure 28.9, why RLL enables a higher data density BPI with the same flux change density FCI.

In Figure 28.9, the same data byte 01101001 as in Figure 8.20 is encoded in RLL format. I have assumed the first bit of the following data byte to be equal to 0. From Table 28.1 you can deduce that the RLL code for the nine data bits 01101001 | 0 is as follows: 001000100100100100. Figure 28.1 (bottom) shows the data and (above) the flux density, as well as flux changes, for the case where the RLL code is recorded by the MFM method. The MFM flux density also comprises, besides the set RLL bits, clock bits if two zero bits are in succession.

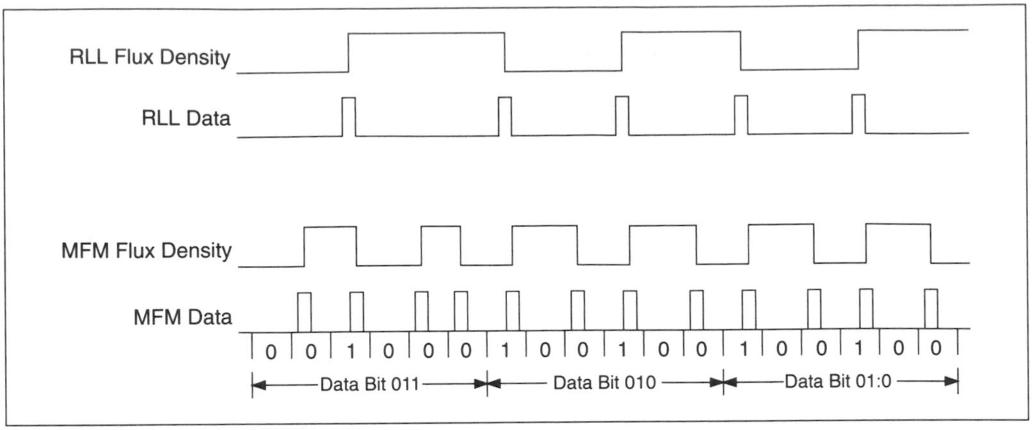

Figure 28.9: The RLL 2,7 encoding method.

The RLL method, on the other hand, records only the set RLL bits. According to the RLL code 001000100100100100, these are only of four set bits. In data reading the zero bits in-between are generated by the RLL logic purely from the time delay between two set RLL bits and added to the 1-bits. For recording the nine data bits by means of the MFM method, twelve flux changes are required; with the RLL method, on the other hand, only five flux changes are necessary. A precise mathematical analysis of the RLL method shows that in the statistical average the MFM method requires three times the flux changes for data recording compared to the RLL method. With the same packaging density of flux changes, three times more data can thus be accommodated by means of the RLL method compared to MFM.

But as already mentioned, the RLL codes are unfortunately twice as long as the data bit groups so that the three times higher packaging density is halved again by the twice as long RLL codes. As the net gain a factor of 1.5 remains, or stated differently: with the RLL method, 50% more data can be accommodated on the disk than is possible with MFM. On average, thus only two flux changes are required for recording three data bits. As was the case for the replacement of the FM by the MFM method, this data density increase is achieved largely by nothing as the flux change density, and thus the quality of the disk and read/write head, need not be improved. The enhancement is exclusively packed into the encoding method, and therefore into the RLL logic of the controller.

But the RLL logic becomes significantly more complicated than the electronics for encoding and decoding by means of the MFM method. The difficulties arise in that the code words are comprised of between four and eight RLL bits. With the MFM method the code word length was uniformly equal to one bit. If the RLL logic gets into a muddle even only for a single RLL bit, then burst errors of up to five data bits are the result. Thus, RLL controllers must have a much more powerful ECC logic to be able to correct such errors reliably. High-quality RLL controllers therefore use a 6-byte instead of a 4-byte ECC code.

An RLL controller has not yet finished its work with the decoding of the flux changes to RLL data, but additionally it has to convert the RLL data into the actual data bits. This contrasts with an MFM controller where the bit stream behind the data gate can be directly used as a serial data stream. The same applies, of course, to data writing when the data stream to be written has to be converted into RLL data first, and then the RLL data must be encoded into flux changes according to the set RLL bits.

Besides the described and proved RLL 2,7 method there exist further RLL methods, called *advanced RLL (ARLL)*. Examples are the RLL 1,7 and the RLL 3,9 method. In both cases, the encoding overhead for the data bit groups into RLL code is much higher and, in addition, the larger number of zero bits between two set RLL bits makes great demands on the stability of the RLL electronics. With ARLL a data density increase of up to 90% compared to MFM can be realized, so that a single flux change encodes nearly two data bits.

28.2.2 High-Level Formatting of Hard Disks with FORMAT

Unlike floppies, for hard disks the FORMAT command doesn't generate any tracks or sectors. During the course of *high-level formatting* with FORMAT, only the logical structure of the partition concerned is established. The generation of the boot sector, the two FAT copies, and the root directory belong to this process. All entries in the FAT are set to 00h to indicate that the partition is free of data. In particular, the sectors of the subdirectories and files are not overwritten with a certain data pattern. On hard disks you can only format individual partitions, but not the complete hard disk with FORMAT. Thus you must first partition the hard disk and generate the partition table by means of *FDISK*, or another suitable program. The FORMAT command itself doesn't affect the partition table, but only reads the information stored there to determine the beginning and size of the partition to be formatted, and to carry out the formatting accordingly.

Reformatting hard disks with FORMAT only erases their logical structure, similar to the DEL and RMDIR commands. Physically, the data is still present. Some utilities (for example, PCTools or Norton Utilities) can then even recover an erroneously formatted hard disk partition. Because of the destruction of more than a single file (as is the case with DEL) or a single subdirectory (with RMDIR), the reconstruction of the original directory and file structure is much more complicated here. If the original directories and files were fragmented, then even these tools have no chance. Therefore, resident programs exist that intercept all hard disk operations and store the logical structure of the hard disk in certain sectors reserved for this purpose. One example is the MIRROR program of PCTools. The accompanying recovery program recognizes the reserved sectors, and because with high-level formatting only the logical structure of the hard disk, but not the data itself, has been destroyed the program can recover the logical structure of the hard disk from the information held in the reserved sectors.

Unlike low-level formatting, you don't have the opportunity to replace damaged sectors and tracks with FORMAT. When FORMAT detects a damaged sector, the corresponding cluster is simply marked as *bad*. But a single hard disk cluster usually has eight sectors with DOS 2.xx and four sectors with DOS 3.00 and above. Thus, FORMAT wastes between three and seven intact sectors when marking a cluster as bad. The low-level formatting, together with the bad-sector mapping, solves the problem of defect sectors much more intelligently. Details are given in the following section.

28.2.3 Low-Level Formatting and Bad-Sector Mapping

To emboss tracks and sectors on a hard disk you have to carry out a low-level format. But note that most hard disks come in a preformatted form already.

Advice: **Generally, you must not reformat intelligent drives with an embedded controller that carries out translating, such as IDE drives.**

The usual formatting programs such as DiskManager or Spinrite are overtaxed with the various recording zones of the drives and the translating which the controller carries out. The only effect they have is that they probably destroy the drive structure. This especially applies to AT bus hard disks, as they can be accessed by the utilities in the same way as the ST412/506 hard disks. With the ST412/506 this works excellently as the programs are particularly tailored for this kind of drive and controller. But the AT bus interface is only register-compatible; the internal conversion in the drives differs significantly from the ST412/506 drives, as every AT bus hard disk has it own controller. AT bus drives and others (for example, SCSI) may only be formatted with specially adapted programs. As the user you should not try to do this on your own.

The first job of the low-level fomatting procedure is to generate tracks and sectors. This is carried out by positioning through rotation steps of a stepper motor, which moves the head from track to track, or by orienting the data tracks according to the servo tracks on the servo disk on drives with a linear motor. After every positioning the head writes the passed track format data onto the data carrier according to the commands from the controller. Figure 28.10 shows the typical layout of a hard disk track of ST412/506 drives for MFM and RLL encoding.

The fields of the sectors and the track are essentially the same as those on floppies. Therefore, only the significant differences are discussed. First, the gaps between the sectors as well as between the end and start of the track are smaller. This is possible as the rotation of the hard disk is stabilized by means of an electronic feedback loop, and the rotation variations are lower because of the missing friction between head and disk. Gaps acting as «speed buffers» between the individual sectors are therefore virtually unnecessary. Additionally, hard disks don't have an index hole like the floppies to mark the beginning of the track. On hard disks this is carried out exclusively by an *index address mark (IDAM)*, which indicates the beginning of the track and activates the index signal line *IDX* to the controller. The value for the fields differs only a little between MFM and RLL. Only the address marks have different identifiers.

Of significance for establishing the bad-sector mapping are the *ID fields*. They have four bytes, and at first specify the number of the cylinder, head and sector. The two most significant bits of the 10-byte cylinder number are always stored as high-order bits of the sector number. Unlike the format of a floppy track, the 4th byte doesn't contain any information concerning the sector size, but the sector flag. Table 28.2 shows the structure of the sector flag.

Thus a set bit 0 indicates that the sector concerned is damaged. Bit 1 characterizes the track to which the sector belongs as defective and no alternative track is assigned. A set bit 2 indicates that the track is defective but the controller has assigned an alternative track. The identification of the alternative track is stored in the ID field of the sectors, that is, the three bytes sc hd sc in the ID field don't characterize the current track, but define the alternative track.

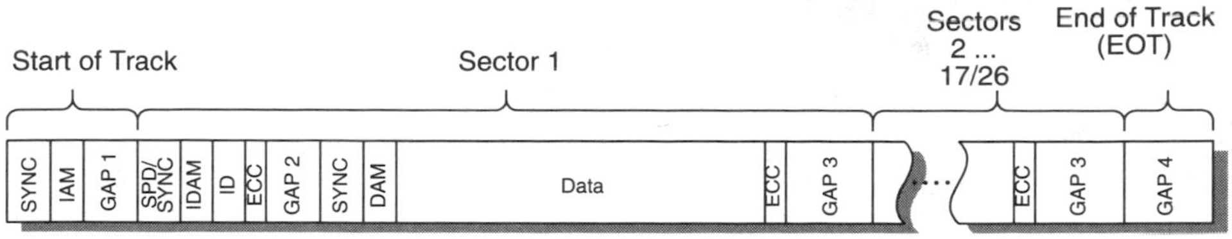


```
MFM sector format
beginning of track
SYNC:   10 byte 00h
IAM:     2 byte a1h fch
GAP 1:  11 byte 4eh

sector
SPD:     7 byte 4eh
SYNC:   10 byte 00h
IDAM:    2 byte a1h feh
ID:      4 byte cy hd sc fl*)
ECC:     4 byte ECC value
GAP 2:   5 byte 00h
SYNC:   10 byte 00h
DAM:     2 byte a1h f8h
data:  512 data byte
ECC:     4 byte CRC value
GAP 3:  15 byte 00h

EOT
GAP 4:    ca. 56 byte 00h
```

```
RLL sector format
beginning of track
SYNC:   11 byte 00h
IAM:     2 byte a1h fch
GAP 1:  12 byte ffh

sector

SYNC:   10 byte, 00h
IDAM:    2 byte 5eh a1h
ID:      4 byte cy hd sc fl*)
ECC:     4 byte ECC value
GAP 2:   5 byte 00h
SYNC:   11 byte 00h
DAM:     2 byte 5eh a1h
data:  512 data byte
ECC:     4 byte ECC value
GAP 3:   3 byte 00h and 17 byte ffh

EOT
GAP 4:    ca. 93 byte 00h
```

*) the four bytes identify the corresponding sector in the format **cy**linder–**head**–**sec**tor–sector **flag**

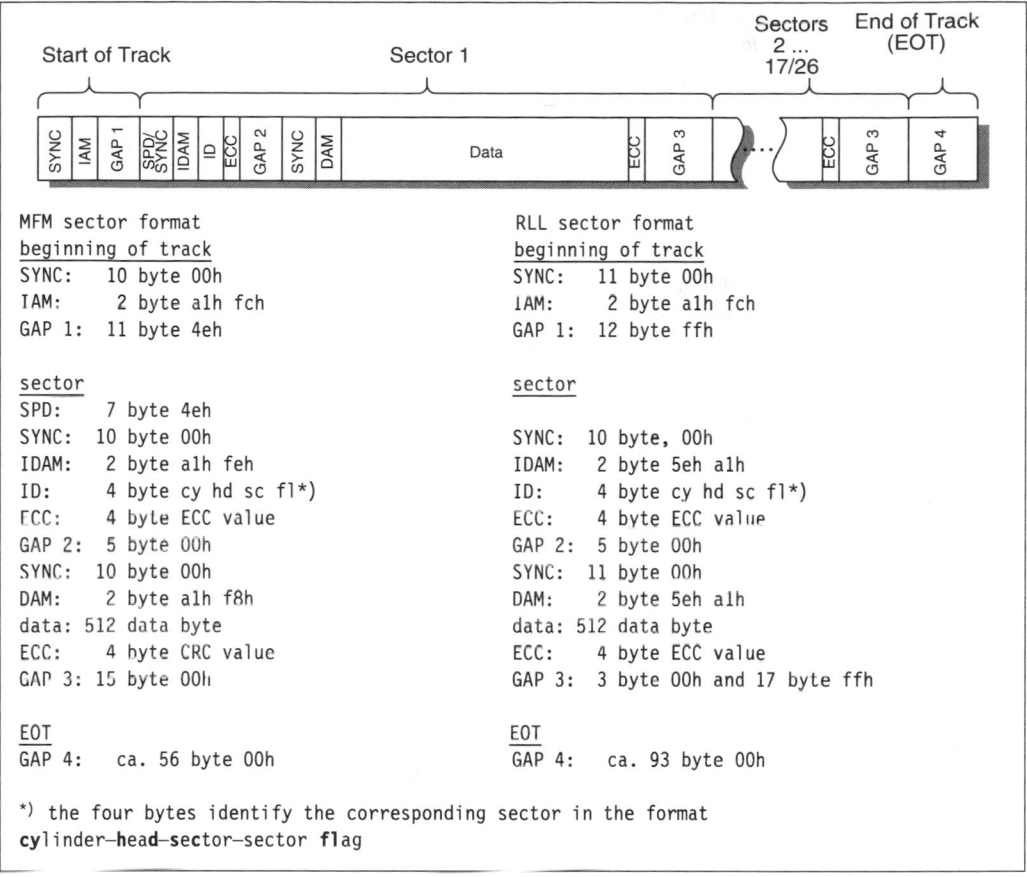

Figure 28.10: Layout of a hard disk track.

Bit	Meaning
0	bad sector
1	bad track without reassignment
2	track ID points to alternative track
3	alternative track
4–7	reserved

Table 28.2: Sector flag structure

If bit 3 in the sector flag is set, this means that the track concerned represents an alternative track and has been assigned to a defective track as a substitute. Finally, bits 4–7 are reserved.

The reason for the bad-sector mapping is that absolutely error-free disk surfaces can only be manufactured with difficulty. Even a microscopic defect of the medium destroys a data bit and makes the accompanying sector unusable. The manufacturers therefore check their disks intensively for several hours, thus detecting defective spots that would not give rise to any problems in normal operation. You get such a *manufacturer defect list* for every drive. The list specifies the error location in the format cylinder, head, sector. The defect list usually comes as a data sheet, or the defects are listed on a label attached to the drive's case. Even if such a defect list contains several dozens of error locations, this is not very serious as the bad-sector mapping removes them. This works as follows.

If the controller detects a defect on the disk according to the two defect lists (see below) that only affects a single sector of the track, the controller simply shifts the sectors slightly so that the error is now outside the sector (or between two sectors, or at the beginning and end of the track). Thus the error no longer disturbs the data in the track. This process is called *sector slipping*. Not a single byte of the storage capacity gets lost through this.

Alternatively, the controller can mark the sector concerned as bad by setting bit 1 in the sector flag. But here the storage capacity is reduced by one sector. Some controllers format a normally unused spare sector in addition to the usual 17 or 26 sectors per track for ST412/506 hard disks. This sector can be employed instead of the marked sector. In this case, no storage capacity gets lost even if one sector is marked as bad. Thus, errors that only affect one single sector can easily be recovered.

The situation becomes more complicated if a medium's errors affect more than one sector. Such damage can no longer be handled within the track. The controller marks the complete track as bad by setting bit 2 in the sector flag of all sectors in the track. By doing this, the track is marked as bad. Furthermore, the controller assigns an alternative track, beginning with the highest cylinder.

The identification cy hd sc fl of this alternative track is stored in the ID fields of all sectors of the damaged track. When a controller command addresses the bad track, the controller recognizes, according to the sector flag, that the complete track is marked as bad and is assigned an alternative track. It reads the identification of the alternative track from the ID field and moves the head to the alternative track. Thus the controller carries out another positioning; all accesses to the defective track are diverted to the alternative track. The alternative track itself is defined as an alternative track by a set bit 3 in the sector flag of all sectors in the track. Such alternative tracks are no longer available for a normal access, that is, direct addressing by the «actual» track number.

It is less favourable to mark a defective track as bad solely by setting bit 1. The controller thus detects that the track is damaged and cannot be used anymore, but no alternative track has been assigned. A «hole» therefore appears in the address space of sectors and tracks.

The capacity of the hard disk is reduced if a defective track is assigned an alternative track, but you get the advantage that the whole continuously formatted area is now error-free. In this way we get something like a «sector address space» which is continuous and free of holes, that is, damaged sectors or tracks. It is thus much easier to manage such a seemingly error-free area, even if some accesses are diverted to other tracks, than to handle a plurality of defect sectors. Then the hard disk always comprises 17 or 26 sectors per track, and not, for example, 17 sectors in this track, only 14 in another, 16 in the next, etc. As most medium errors are only very small today, and mainly affect only a single sector, the controller has to replace a complete track only in a very few cases. Normally, sector slipping is sufficient to repair the defect.

Controllers that carry out such a bad-sector mapping usually reserve the first physical cylinder of the connected hard disk for their own purposes. This cylinder is assigned the number –1 (that is, a negative number) so that only the controller can access the information stored there. Using the normal controller commands, such as read sector, this cylinder cannot be accessed. The lowest possible cylinder number 0 already addresses the second physical cylinder. Thus the partition table and other important areas are not shifted logically. Some manufacturers write the manufacturer defect list and the geometry information concerning the drive onto cylinder –1 before the hard disk is shipped. The geometry information is very important for autoconfiguring controllers (see Section 28.2.5 for details). Table 28.3 shows the layout of the controller cylinder –1.

Sector Number	Track 0	Track 1
1	geometric information (1st copy)	geometric information (3rd copy)
2	geometric information (2nd copy)	geometric information (4th copy)
3–8	reserved	reserved
9–10	manufacturer defect list (1st copy)	reserved
11–12	manufacturer defect list (2nd copy)	reserved
13–14	known defects (1st copy)	reserved
15–16	known defects (2nd copy)	reserved
17	reserved	reserved

Table 28.3: Controller cylinder layout

From the first physical cylinder only the first two tracks corresponding to heads 0 and 1 are used, as every hard disk at least has these two tracks. The geometry information is stored in four identical copies for redundancy purposes. If one copy is destroyed then the controller can access the other three. The manufacturer defect list is also present as two identical copies in sectors 8 and 9 as well as 10 and 11. The structure of this list is shown in Table 28.4. In the same way, the list of known defects is also stored twice; its structure is shown in Table 28.5.

Byte	Contents	
0–1	signature 0beedh of manufacturer defect list	
2–4	reserved	
5–6	bad cylinder or ffh for end of list	1 defect entry
7	bad head	1 defect entry
8–9	number of bytes from IDAM up to defect	1 defect entry
10–509	max. 100 more defect entries	
510–511	reserved	

Table 28.4: Manufacturer defect list structure

The manufacturer defect list is (as the name implies) written by the manufacturer onto track 0 after checking the hard disk. The list can accommodate up to 101 entries, and is closed by an entry ffffh for the section defective cylinder. The entries characterize the defects by indicating the cylinder, head and number of bytes located between the index address mark IDAM at the beginning of the track, and the defect itself. The controller uses this defect list during the course of formatting to carry out sector slipping or to assign an alternative track.

Byte	Contents	
0–1	signature 0fabeh of list of known defects	
2–4	reserved	
5–6	bad cylinder or ffh or end of list	1 defect entry
7	bad head	
8	first bad physical sector	
9	second bad physical sector (or ffh if not present)	
10–509	max. 100 more defect entries	
510–511	reserved	

Table 28.5: Structure of the grown defect list

The *grown defect list* is generated and extended during the course of the formatting procedure by the controller or by explicit controller commands for assigning alternative sectors or tracks. Unlike the manufacturer defect list, the defects are characterized by the values for cylinder, head and sector number. Both lists together indicate all known defects on the hard disk, and the controller uses them during the course of a formatting process to carry out the bad-sector mapping and the assignment of alternative tracks automatically and independently. Note that this remapping is carried out by the hard disk controller's microcode, and not by the CPU.

For characterizing defective tracks and sectors, and for assigning alternative tracks, three commands are usually available for an ST412/506 controller:

- *Format defective track* (opcode 07h): this command formats a track and sets bit 1 in all sector flags of the track to mark the track as defective. An alternative track is not assigned by this command.
- *Reassign sector* (opcode 09h): the sector is added to the grown defect list so that each subsequent formatting procedure attempts to repair the sector defect by means of sector slipping or by assigning an alternative sector within the track. If the track already has a defective sector, then any subsequent formatting process marks the whole track as bad and assigns an alternative track.
- *Reassign alternative track* (opcode 11h): this command marks a track as defective and explicitly assigns a certain other track as the alternative track. Unlike the above indicated command, the reassignment is therefore carried out at once, and not during the course of the next formatting process.

Special formatting programs are unnecessary for IDE or SCSI drives, as a later reformatting only improves the interleaving or carries out a bad-sector mapping of bad sectors with the grown defect list. The first aim is irrelevant, as all IDE and SCSI drives are always preformatted with an interleave of 1:1. Furthermore, the controllers of these drives are intelligent enough to carry out a dynamic bad-sector remapping. This means that the controller marks a sector or track as bad, and reassigns an alternative sector or track automatically and on its own if it has detected a persistent read error. Such errors usually indicate damage to the data carriers at the corresponding location.

28.2.4 Error Recovery Strategies

Because of the extremely high data density of the hard disks, even on high-quality drives, read and seek errors frequently occur. But drive manufacturers have taken into account such errors by implementing certain error recovery procedures in the controller. Head crashes that don't destroy a sector completely, but only give rise to some problems for a data read, can be diminished somewhat by this. Finally, the hard disk medium demagnetizes itself slowly but continuously. If a sector is only read for a long time but never written, as is the case, for example, for the boot sector, then after several years demagnetization may be rather serious. At first, only recoverable read errors occur, which can be overcome by the implemented error recovery procedure. Later, though, the whole sector becomes inaccessible. An early reading and rewriting of the sector's contents may counteract such data losses. Elaborate hard disk test programs such as HDTEST or DiskTechnician may determine such sneaking demagnetization, and repair it simply by rewriting the sector's contents.

The following sections discuss which extensive procedures the controller carries out for error recovery in order to be able read the data anyway. The procedures are enabled on the XT controller, for example, using the 5th command byte in a 6-byte command block, and on the AT bus controller by a set R bit in the command code (see Section 28.6.4). The procedures that a controller actually carries out depend upon the microcode which controls the controller's microprocessor, and thus on the manufacturer and the controller model. Therefore, a typical error recovery procedure which is used, for example, by the ST412/506 hard disk controllers ST11x and ST21x is discussed.

The procedures differ depending upon whether an error has occurred while reading a data or address field of a sector. The controller cannot detect a positioning error absolutely, but only by comparing the entries in the ID field of the sector with the intended ones. If the two cylinder numbers don't coincide then a positioning error has occurred. The same applies to errors in the data area. If the sector area has been damaged, for example, by a head crash, then the controller is unable to detect this reason directly. Instead, it accepts further signals from the head and decodes them according to the recording method. From the damaged sections it gets only confusing information which is decoded in the same way at first. Using the ECC bytes, the controller can then, however, recognize that part of the sector which contains invalid data. Whether the reason for this is a head crash, a former write error or a sneaking demagnetization, the controller is not able to determine. For the outcome (erroneous data), this is, of course, insignificant.

If the controller has detected an error in the data area because of some inconsistencies between the sector data and the ECC bytes, it proceeds as follows. If an attempt is successful (that is, the sector concerned can be read without any error), then the controller terminates the procedure and transfers the data into main memory.

- Read sector eight times: the controller repeats the read attempt up to eight times without applying an ECC correction. If the failure reason is only a synchronization problem or too extensive a rotation variation, then the first retry is successful in most cases.
- Shoe shining: the controller first moves the head back to track 0, then to the track with the maximum cylinder number, and finally positions the head above the track with the addressed data sector again. Errors can thus be recovered which result from a tiny mispositioning of the head, that is, the head is at the side and not in the middle of the track, so that certain data signals are too weak.
- Reread sector and carry out ECC correction: if the error can be recovered only by means of the ECC bytes, then the controller corrects the data, and sets an indicator in the status byte that shows a recoverable ECC error has occurred. Minor write errors or damage because of weak head crashes can thus be recovered.
- Read the sector six times shifting the data and clock window: the controller attempts to read the sector but shifts the data as well as the clock window (see Section 27.6.2) by +1.5%, +6%, +7.5%, 1.5%, –6% and (at the last attempt) –7.5%. Errors caused by bit shifting with missing precompensation can thus be recovered.
- Microstepping and reading the sector eight times without ECC correction: the controller moves the head in tiny steps and tries to read the sector without applying any ECC correction eight times. Therefore, errors because of small deviations of the track from the originally defined position can be recovered. The reasons are mostly heat deformations and temperature differences between formatting and the read process. Drives with a stepper motor are particularly affected by this.
- Microstepping and reading the sector eight times with ECC correction: the controller moves the head in tiny steps and attempts to read the sector while carrying out an ECC correction eight times.

Thus, the six procedure steps carry out up to 31 (!) read accesses before the controller finally gives up and indicates a non-recoverable read error to the host. This has many advantages, but also a few disadvantages. One advantage is that because of the extensive recovery attempts the controller can nearly always restore the data if the errors and damage are only minor. The disadvantage is that neither you, DOS nor the BIOS recognize nearly complete failures, as such. Only a lasting and in most cases also loud head activity points to such dangers. Errors because of minor damage, a sneaking demagnetization, or the mechanical wear of the drive are hidden until the catastrophe occurs. Some elaborate hard disk test programs such as HDTEST and DiskTechnician can detect such errors, which are normally corrected by the controller early enough, and take precautions or display some warning.

I particularly want to point out that CHKDSK is not able to detect such failures in any way. CHKDSK checks only the logical structure of the disk, that is, the consistency of directories and FAT. Also, many other hard disk test programs (for example, DiskTest of Norton Utilities) read the sectors only on a DOS or maybe BIOS level. In both cases, the error recovery procedures of the controller are enabled and the programs detect (following the 31 failed attempts) that something is wrong with the drive. This cannot be called a precaution by any stretch of the imagination. Another source of errors is positioning failures (also called seek errors), which particularly occur on drives with a stepper motor or old and mechanically worn drives. The controller recognizes them according to a missing or incorrect ID address mark:

- No ID address mark found: recalibrate drive and reseek. In most cases the cause is a head positioning between two tracks or a non-formatted drive.
- Wrong ID address mark found: recalibrate drive four times and reseek.

Thus persistent seek errors are reported faster than data errors, but they can usually be recovered more quickly by means of a drive recalibration as they are independent of the data carrier. Note that intelligent drives with an embedded controller often carry out a dynamic bad-sector remapping: after a persistent read error these controllers mark the sector concerned, or the whole track, as bad and reassign an alternative sector or track automatically and on their own. The whole process is executed without your intervention or any command from DOS or the BIOS.

28.2.5 Autoconfiguration

One problem when installing a new hard disk is adjusting the correct drive parameters in the BIOS setup. Besides the drive geometry (that is, the number of cylinders, heads and sectors per track) you additionally need to know the start cylinder for the write precompensation, for example, and to select the corresponding entry in the setup. But that's not sufficient. A drive that has come onto the market after the BIOS has been programmed can have a geometry that hasn't been implemented. A maximum of 271 different disks can be held in CMOS RAM if we take into account the 15 regular and 256 extended entries, but integrating 271 different parameter tables into a ROM is a pure waste of storage capacity. Some manufacturers of compatible PCs have therefore reserved a free definable entry, because at some time the number of possible parameter values becomes too large for the BIOS ROM or the CMOS RAM. But as the user, you have to know the geometry of your drive exactly to be able to employ this user-specific entry.

IBM and other manufacturers had a better idea; autoconfiguring controllers and drives. On these hard disks the geometry information is stored in the first physical cylinder. All information required is held by sectors 1 and 2 of tracks 0 and 1 in the form of four identical copies (Table 28.3). Table 28.6 shows the structure of these four geometry sectors.

Byte	Contents
0–1	signature 0dabeh of geometric information
2–3	number of cylinders
4	number of heads
5	number of sectors per track
6–7	reserved
8	interleave factor
9	BIOS flag byte
10	number of cylinders for alternative tracks

Table 28.6: structure of geometric information

Byte	Contents
11	reserved
12–13	start cylinder of write precompensation
14–20	manufacturer's name (ASCII)
21–39	product name
40–511	reserved

Table 28.6: cont.

The information starts with the signature 0dabeh so the controller can be sure that the sector concerned actually holds geometric information, and doesn't erroneously interpret some data bytes. As you can see from Table 28.6 all the required parameters are stored. Thus the controller only needs to read the first physical drive sector at power-up to determine the correct drive parameters.

28.3 Integrating Exotic Drives and Translating

If you look at the market for hard disk drives you'll see that a virtually infinite variety of different drive geometries exists. But BIOS and DOS need to know precisely how many sectors per track, cylinders and heads the installed hard disk has to access it correctly. The PC implements two possibilities for integrating non-standardized drives: function 09h of INT 13h, and BIOS extensions.

28.3.1 BIOS Interrupt 13h, Function 09h – Set Drive Parameters

In the CMOS RAM you store information concerning the hard disk type by selecting the corresponding hard disk type with the setup program. Then the BIOS looks for the accompanying drive parameters which are stored in an internal BIOS table. Perhaps you have already noticed that most setup programs also have, besides many «in-built» hard disks one free entry that you can fill with the number of heads, cylinders, etc. of your drive, that is, all those parameters which unambiguously characterize your hard disk. But how does the BIOS process such an entry? The key is the function 09h *set drive parameters* of interrupt 13h as well as interrupts 41h and 46h that point to parameter tables. In this way you can also integrate quite exotic hard disks into your system.

The entries for interrupts 41h and 46h in the interrupt table, however, don't point to a handler (that is, executable program code) which can be called by means of an INT instruction; the instruction INT 41h would lead to a system crash immediately. Instead, the addresses segment:offset point to two tables with the user-defined geometry parameters of the hard disks concerned. Interrupt 41h is reserved for the first hard disk, interrupt 46h for the second. The tables have 16 bytes, and are called *hard disk parameter tables*. Figure 28.11 shows the structure of these tables.

The entries *number of cylinders* and *number of heads* define the geometry. After formatting, the number of sectors per track is unambiguously defined by the generated address marks so that this information is not required. The values for *start cylinder of reduced write current* and *start cylinder of precompensation* control the write current and the precompensation (see Section 28.1.3). The *maximum ECC data burst length* defines the length of burst errors which can be corrected using the ECC code used. Usually, this value is equal to 11. The *control byte* determines the controller's behaviour in the case of an error. With the three *time-out* values you inform the BIOS when, depending upon the process concerned, it should report a time-out error. The last four bytes of the table are reserved, and should always be set to 0.

XT-Controller

Offset	Entry	Size
00h	Number of Cylinders	(Word)
02h	Number of Heads	(Byte)
03h	Start Cylinder of Reduced Write Current	(Word)
05h	Start Cylinder of Precompensation	(Word)
07h	Max. ECC Burst Length	(Byte)
08h	Control Byte[1]	(Byte)
09h	Standard Time-out Value[2]	(Byte)
0ah	Time-out Value for Formatting[2]	(Byte)
0bh	Time-out Value for Drive Check[2]	(Byte)
0ch	Reserved	(4 Bytes)
0fh		

[1] Bit 0..2: Drive Option
Bit 3..5: Null
Bit 6: ECC Retries Disabled
Bit 7: Seek Retries Disabled
[2] in Timer Ticks

AT-Controller

Offset	Entry	Size
00h	Number of Cylinders	(Word)
02h	Number of Heads	(Byte)
03h	Reserved	(Word)
05h	Start Cylinder of Precompensation	(Word)
07h	Reserved	(Byte)
08h	Control Byte[1]	(Byte)
09h	Reserved	(3 Bytes)
0ch	Landing Zone for Head Parking	(Word)
0eh	Number od Sectors per Track	(Byte)
0fh	Reserved	(Byte)

[1] Bit 0..2: Reserved
Bit 3: 1=more than 8 Heads
Bit 4: Reserved
Bit 5: 1=Defect List at MaxCylinder+1
Bit 6: ECC Retries Disabled
Bit 7: Seek Retries Disabled

Figure 28.11: Hard disk parameter table.

During the course of a call to function 09h of interrupt INT 13h, the handler reads the address corresponding to interrupt 41h or 46h and determines the entries in the tables. For all accesses to the first or second hard disk, the BIOS then uses the geometries as they are indicated in the tables. If you replace the addresses stored in the interrupt table for interrupts 41h and 46h by the addresses in your own tables, you can integrate hard disks with nearly any geometry into the system. But this, of course, is only possible if controller and hard disk use the same recording method (for example MFM or RLL 2,7) and the same interface format as the ST412/506, AT-Bus, etc. Otherwise, the combination is impossible for physical reasons.

To integrate an exotic hard disk into your system so that the BIOS and DOS are able to access it, you must therefore first generate the corresponding hard disk parameter table, store the address of that table in the entry for interrupt 41h or 46h in the interrupt table, and then call function 09h of interrupt INT 13h. Also, the BIOS start routine does the same when initializing the hard disks. It reads the hard disk parameters from the CMOS RAM and generates one or two tables for INT 41h or INT 46h using this information, depending upon how many drives are installed. Afterwards, the start routine calls function 09h of INT 13h and the drive parameters are now available to the system.

Inversely, you can also determine the parameters of a connected hard disk by function 08h of INT 13h, for example, when you attempt to check whether the BIOS has carried out the integration correctly. Format and return values of this function are indicated in Appendix F.

28.3.2 BIOS Extensions and Booting

The execution of an INT 13h function for an MFM-encoded disk with an IDE interface can be very different from that for an SCSI hard disk with the SCSI command set defined by ANSI. If you replace your old MFM disk by a modern SCSI disk, then you would also need to replace the BIOS. But the PC's designers had a better idea to avoid such problems, one which is more suited for the open concept of the PC: so-called *BIOS* or *ROM extensions*.

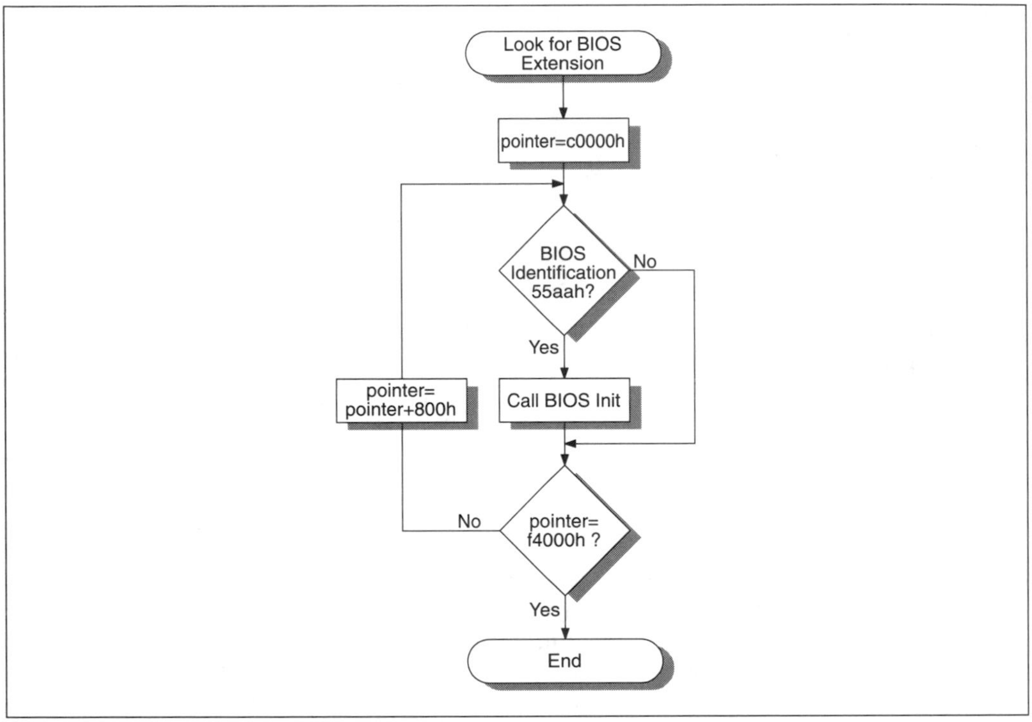

Figure 28.12: Integrating a BIOS extension.

As you know, the PC and XT didn't have a hard disk as a standard; only the AT was already prepared for such a drive. Thus the PC/XT BIOS doesn't implement any INT 13h functions for hard disks, only floppy drive functions. At the time when the AT came onto the market, the ST412/502 interface was the measure to live up to. Thus in the AT BIOS the access to such a hard disk with an AT bus interface is already implemented. If you attempt to expand a PC/XT with a hard disk you must use a controller with its own hard disk BIOS; for the AT, a controller without BIOS is sufficient. Without a BIOS extension the PC/XT ignores all hard disk accesses; controller and drive thus seem to be dead.

Now you can see why BIOS functions are called by interrupts: to replace the former routines stored in the old BIOS by the new ones of the BIOS extension, only the interrupt address has to be altered so it points to the BIOS extension. This *interception* is carried out during the course of the boot process. As you know, all ROM chips with the BIOS are located between the segment addresses c000h and ffffh. The area above f600h is reserved for the standard BIOS with startup routines. To additionally detect installed BIOS extensions, the startup routine scans the segment area between c000h and f5ffh in steps of 2 kbytes during system initialization. This searching for BIOS extensions and their initialization is shown in Figure 28.12.

Note that BIOS extensions always begin with the identifier 55aah. If the initialization routine detects such an identifier then the BIOS extension is initialized. Figure 28.13 shows the structure of this 4-byte header of BIOS extensions.

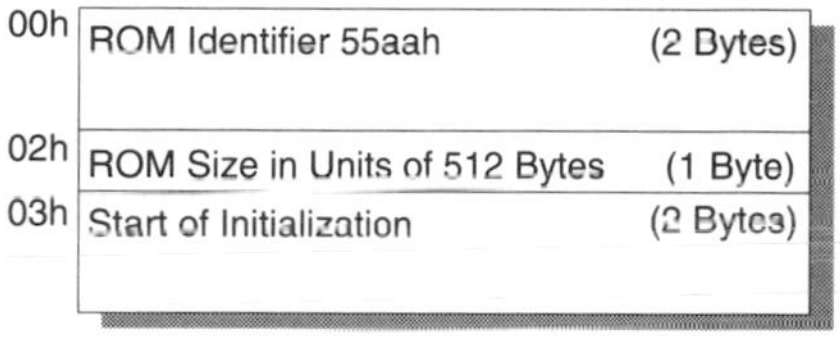

Figure 28.13: BIOS identifier.

The first two bytes accommodate the ROM BIOS identifier 55aah. The following byte specifies the size of the ROM extension in units of 512-byte blocks. Finally, the 4th and 5th bytes hold the start address of the initialization routine for the BIOS extension as an offset relative to the ROM beginning. Note that according to the IBM standard the sum of all bytes in the ROM extension, determined by the number of the 512-byte blocks in the BIOS identifier, must be equal to 0. Thus every ROM extension has at least one check byte so that the sum actually has a value of 0.

Example: Scan ROM area from segment c000h to f400h and call initialization routine if present (language: Microsoft C 5.10).

```
main()
{ unsigned char far *rom_pointer;
  void far *init_pointer();
  unsigned char sum, blocks;

  rom_pointer = 0xc0000;                  /* initialize rom_pointer to beginning of ROM area */
  while(rom_pointer < 0xf6000) {          /* scan while rom_pointer is in the range between */
                                          /* c000:0000 and f400:1fff */
    if ((int) *rom_pointer == 0x55aa) {   /* check for BIOS identifier */
     blocks = *(rom_pointer+2)            /* determine number of 512-byte blocks */
     sum = checksum(rom_pointer, blocks); /* check whether checksum is equal to 0 */
     if (sum == 0) {                      /* yes, checksum is equal to 0 */
       init_pointer = rom_pointer+3;      /* load start address of initialization routine */
       init_pointer();                    /* call initialization routine */
     }
    }
    rom_pointer = rom_pointer+0x800;      /* next block 2 kbytes later */
  }
```

```
  exit(0);                              /* end */
}

unsigned char check_sum(rom_pointer, blocks)
  unsigned far *rom_pointer;
  unsigned char blocks;

{  unsigned char sum, blocknr;
   unsigned int index;

   sum=0                                             /* initialize sum */
   for (blocknr = 0; blocknr < blocks; blocknr++) {  /* scan all blocks */
     for (index = 0; index < 512; index++, rom_pointer++) { /* block size equal to 512 bytes */
       sum = sum + *rom_pointer;                     /* form checksum, ignore carry */
     }
   }
   return(sum);                                      /* return checksum */
}
```

The initialization routine of the BIOS extension now executes an initialization, which refers to the BIOS extension itself and the peripherals which the extension is to serve. The initialization routine completes the integration of the BIOS extension by detouring one or more interrupts to routines that are part of the BIOS extension. All BIOS extensions on hard disk controllers detour, for example, the existing INT 13h for floppy drives integrated into the BIOS on the motherboard to interrupt 40h. If a program issues an interrupt 13h then the BIOS first checks whether a request to a hard disk or a floppy drive has occurred. If the program wants to access a hard disk then the BIOS extension proceeds with the execution of the intended routine; otherwise it branches to interrupt 40h, which now carries out the function for the floppy drive concerned.

By means of the engagement of BIOS extensions the standard routines of the BIOS on the system board have been replaced by the new routines of the BIOS extension on the new controller. According to this scheme, the BIOS extension of, for example, an SCSI host adapter replaces INT 13h of the system BIOS in an AT. Therefore, you may access an SCSI hard disk drive using INT 13h in the conventional manner. With the help of a suitable BIOS extension, a tape drive can also be programmed as a floppy drive, for example. The engaged BIOS routines convert the commands for hard disk or floppy drives into commands for tape drives.

By means of function 08h of interrupt 13h you can determine the format of the hard disk in which it appears to the system. This is particularly important for high-capacity hard disks with more than 1024 tracks, or a variable number of sectors per track. Such hard disks appear to the system with a completely different geometry to that which the drive actually has. The 08h function converts the «hard disk» drive into a transparent peripheral.

Example: My SCSI hard disk with 105 Mbytes storage capacity comprises physically six heads, an outer group with 831 cylinders, and 35 sectors per track, as well as an inner group with 188 cylinders and 28 sectors per track. But to the BIOS and the user the drive appears as a hard disk with 12 heads, 1005 cylinders and 17 sectors per track.

But the BIOS extension is not only effective when installing a new hard disk drive. It is a very general and therefore also a very powerful concept. For example, the BIOS extension on EGA and (S)VGA adapters replaces the INT 10h of the standard BIOS to make the specialized and powerful functions of these graphics adapters available to the system. The BIOS on the motherboard recognizes only the simple, and for programmers, not very exciting functions of the monochrome and CGA adapters. On the other hand, EGA and (S)VGA boards support many functions on a hardware base (for example, scrolling of the screen contents or zooming of several sections). With older adapters these functions had to be programmed by software, and were thus quite slow. Very new graphics adapters with a graphics processor or a video RAM of more than 128 kbytes cannot be accessed conventionally. They need their own BIOS, as the interface to the PC system bus is incompatible with conventional adapters. The open and powerful concept of BIOS extensions enables the integration of such graphics adapters into a PC without any problems. As long as you remain on a BIOS level, no difficulties arise; the BIOS extension handles all the problems. That is, of course, no longer the case if you program the adapter directly using the registers. For graphics adapters, *de facto* standards are not yet established to the same extent as is the case for floppy and hard disk controllers concerning addresses and the meanings of the registers. BIOS extensions for hard disks usually start at address c800:0000, those for graphics adapters at c000:0000. In most cases, you can alter the start address of ROMs extensions by means of a jumper on the adapter board. This is useful if two ROMs disturb each other. Meanwhile, the drivers are often provided on disk, and are no longer integrated as a ROM extension. For DOS, they must be integrated as *DEVICE=xx* or as a TSR program.

It is not impossible that certain BIOS variants are more powerful than others. Particularly with new technical developments, it takes some time for a standard to become established. For example, all 8086/88 machines don't recognize an interrupt 15h/function 89h for switching the processor into protected mode, as the 8086/88 CPU is not capable of this. If you attempt to detect by software whether a BIOS supports certain functions, this can get quite laborious and error-prone. Depending upon the quality of the BIOS, it returns an error message, the registers are not changed, or the registers are filled with unpredictable values.

As already mentioned, compatibility on a register level among various interface and drive specifications is very rare. But within a certain type the controllers and floppy/hard disk drives fortunately get along with one another, in most cases. You may, for example, connect a no-name controller with an ST412 interface for RLL drives to an NEC RLL hard disk with an ST412 interface without problems, and access it by means of the AT system BIOS.

28.3.3 Translating and Zone Recording

You may know that the circumference of a circle rises with increasing radius. Applied to hard disks, this means that the length of a track gets larger the lower the cylinder number is, because the outermost cylinder with the largest diameter is assigned the number 0 and the innermost cylinder with the smallest diameter has the highest possible number.

But now the number of bytes per track is dependent upon the length of the track, that is, the circumference of the cylinder, and thus the cylinder number. It seems absurd to fill the large outer cylinders only with the same number of sectors as the smaller inner ones: the outer sectors would be elongated by this. To use the storage capacity of a disk best it would be more favourable, therefore, to raise the number of sectors per cylinder with increasing cylinder diameter. However, this gives rise to the fact that the fixed number of sectors per track must be given up. Accordingly, the BIOS functions become more complicated as you must additionally know for every hard disk how many sectors each cylinder accommodates.

Thus, simpler unintelligent drives without their own controller are content with a fixed number of sectors per track throughout the whole disk. High-quality and intelligent drives such as SCSI and AT bus hard disks, on the other hand, carry out such a conversion. These drives have their own controller which is fixed to the drive and is no longer inserted as an additional board into a bus slot. The connection to the host is established by a so-called *host adapter*, which is often but erroneously called a controller. The controller now knows which track accommodates how many sectors; but to the user the disk appears on a BIOS level homogenously with a fixed number of sectors per track. This means that the controller converts the indicated values for head, cylinder, sector of a BIOS call into the actual values for head, cylinder, sector on the hard disk without any external intervention. This process is completely hidden from the user. Usually you can't affect this *translation* even on a register level, but some IDE hard disk drives allow a variable translation.

In practice, a hard disk is usually divided into an inner and an outer zone which each have a fixed number of sectors per track. Thus the number of sectors per track changes only from zone to zone, and not from track to track. This is called *zone recording*.

Because of the extensive translation, the logical format used by the BIOS has virtually nothing to do with the actual physical format. But this seems to be more complicated than it really is. A controller separated from the drive, as was usual a few years ago, must of course be able to control many different drives. But a controller that is integrated into the drive's case can best be adapted to this single hard disk on which it is mounted. The rapidly falling prices in the field of microelectronics now means that every hard disk has its own controller without raising the costs too much.

But the BIOS (and also you as the programmer) want to know, of course, with which geometrical format you can now access the hard disk. For this purpose, function 08h *determine drive parameters* of interrupt INT 13h is also implemented. The function returns the geometric parameters that you can use for accessing the hard disk. The function call is carried out by the BIOS on the host adapter of the intelligent hard disk which has intercepted the already existing interrupt 13h at power-up.

When you look at the hard disk functions of INT 13h in Appendix F, you can see that the cylinder number has only 10 bits. Only 1024 cylinders can thus be represented, while powerful ESDI or SCSI drives accommodate far more cylinders. The ESDI interface is designed for up to 4096 cylinders as standard. With translation, the BIOS can be altered in such a way that 4096 cylinders can actually be accessed. For this purpose, translating increases the virtual head number until the cylinder number has been decreased to 1024 or less. The increase of the head number together with the decrease of the cylinder number keeps the drive capacity constant, and makes it possible for the physical cylinders beyond 1024 to be accessed via the BIOS in the same format as before.

Another note on translation and the formatting of hard disks. During the course of a low-level formatting the controller generates sectors and tracks on the data carrier. Depending upon the translation and the boundary between the areas of different sector numbers per track, different formatting parameters must be passed to the controller. The conversion of BIOS sectors and the physical sectors on disk within the controller does not depend on any rule from the hard disk used: there is no standard which determines how many sectors per track must be generated up to which track, etc. If you now try to format such a hard disk by means of direct register commands, then you will usually cause chaos, but nothing more. SCSI and IDE hard disks therefore always come preformatted, and can be successfully reformatted on a low level by the user only in some rare cases. Even professional utilities such as DiskManager, Spinrite or Norton Utilities usually assume a fixed format. These very popular and useful utilities for conventional hard disks cannot be employed here. It's best to refrain from such formatting attempts if you are not absolutely (really 100%) sure that you know everything about the translating of your hard disk, and you are also absolutely sure that your formatting routine is free of any bugs.

Also, be somewhat sceptical when interpreting benchmark results concerning, for example, the access time of a hard disk whose controller carries out translation. In many head positionings the logical head only «moves» one track but the physical one remains on the same track. On the other hand, it is also possible that the physical head is moved although the program accesses only a single logical track, for example to read a complete track. The access times and transfer rate determined may therefore differ from the actual properties of the investigated drive.

28.4 Access via DOS and the BIOS

The variety of hard disk interfaces unavoidably gives rise to incompatibilities. Here the hierarchical access scheme DOS–BIOS–register comes to the rescue again, because you can access logical sectors by the two DOS interrupts 25h and 26h, and physical sectors via the BIOS interrupt 13h, without the need to take the interface actually used into account in detail. Of course, you achieve a higher execution speed with direct register programming, and you can further use the features of the interface concerned which are not accessible with the BIOS. The BIOS standard functions orient to the first XT and AT models, and cannot, in the nature of things, cope with the much more advanced ESDI, IDE or SCSI interfaces. For programs that are to be executed on as many PCs as possible and have to be compatible (unfortunately reduced to a common denominator), the DOS interrupts 25h and 26h as well as the BIOS interrupt 13h are indispensable.

28.4.1 DOS Interrupts 25h and 26h

With the DOS interrupts 25h and 26h (already presented in Chapter 8 in connection with floppy drives), you can read and write the logical sectors within the DOS partition. Thus you may access all data areas, including the boot sector and the FAT. The partition table as well as other partitions, however, remain unreachable. The calling procedure for the two interrupts in the case of sectors with numbers lower than 65536 is the same as already discussed in this chapter.

But with DOS 4.00 a new calling format was introduced to serve partitions comprising more than 65536 sectors or 32 Mbytes. Figure 28.14 shows the two calling formats with and without the new parameter block.

Partitions up to 32 Mbytes or 65,536 Sectors

INT 25h – Read One or More Logical Sectors

Register	Call Value	Return Value
AL	Drive Number[1)]	
AX		Error Code[2)]
CX	Number of Sectors	
DX	First Sector	
BX	Offset Read Buffer	
DS	Segment Read Buffer	
Carry		Error if <> 0

INT 26h – Write One or More Logical Sectors

Register	Call Value	Return Value
AL	Drive Number[1)]	Error Code[2)]
AX		
CX	Number of Sectors	
DX	First Sector	
BX	Offset Write Buffer	
DS	Segment Write Buffer	Error if <> 0
Carry		

1) 00h=Drive A:, 01h=Drive B: etc. 2) see Table 28.7

Partitions Larger Than 32 Mbytes or 65,536 Sectors

INT 25h – Read One or More Logical Sectors

Register	Call Value	Return Value
AL	Drive Number[1)]	
AX		Error Code[2)]
CX	0ffffh	
DX		
BX	Offset Parameter[3)]	
DS	Segment Parameter[3)]	
Carry		Error if <> 0

INT 26h – Write One or More Logical Sectors

Register	Call Value	Return Value
AL	Drive Number[1)]	
AX		Error Code[2)]
CX	0ffffh	
DX		
BX	Offset Parameter[3)]	
DS	Segment Parameter[3)]	
Carry		Error if <> 0

1) 00h=Drive A:, 01h=Drive B: etc. 2) see Table 28.7

3) Parameter Block

First Sector	(4 Bytes)
Number of Sectors	(2 Bytes)
Address of Read/ Write Buffer	(4 Bytes)

Figure 28.14: INT 25h and INT 26h calling formats.

When using interrupts 25h and 26h, note that they leave a status byte on the stack that you must remove with a POP instruction. If the intended sector cannot be read or written for some reason, then DOS sets the carry flag and returns an error code in register ax, indicating the cause of the failed read or write attempt. Table 28.7 lists the valid error codes.

The following sections discuss only the extended function call via the new parameter block for accessing sectors with a number beyond 65 535. The conventional calling format is discussed in Chapter 27. According to an entry ffffh in the register cx, DOS 4.00 and above recognizes that the extended calling format is to be used. The calling program must pass the offset and segment of the parameter block in the registers bx and ds for this purpose. The parameter block defines the first sector, the number of sectors, and the address of the read or write buffer for these sectors. With the conventional format these quantities are passed by registers cx, dx, bx and ds. Now the use of the extended form is explained using an example.

Code	Error
01h	invalid command
02h	incorrect address mark
04h	sector not found
08h	DMA overflow
10h	CRC or ECC error
20h	controller error
40h	seek error
80h	drive not ready

Table 28.7: INT 25h and INT 26h error codes

Example: Read three sectors beginning with sector 189,063 from hard disk C: (language: Microsoft C 5.10).

```
type parm_block {
  unsigned long start_sector;
  unsigned num_of_sectors;
  char far *buffer;
}

main()
{
  union REGS inregs, outregs;
  struct SREGS segregs;
  struct far parm_block p_block;

  /* construct parameter block */
  p_block.start_sector = 189063;
  p_block.num_of_sectors = 3;
  p_block.buffer = (char far *) _fmalloc(1536);  /* buffer for three sectors */

  /* call function */
  inregs.h.al = 0x02;                           /* drive C: */
  inregs.x.cx = 0xffff;                         /* extended calling format */
  inregs.x.bx = FP_OFF(p_block);                /* transfer parameter block offset into bx */
  segregs.ds = FP_SEG(p_block);                 /* transfer parameter block segment into ds */
  int86x(0x25, &inregs, &outregs, &segregs);    /* call interrupt, sectors are read into */
                                                /* p_block.buffer */

  if ((outregs.x.cflag & 0x01) == 0x01) {       /* check whether carry is set */
    printf("\nError code: %x", outregs.x.ax);  /* display error code */
    exit(1);                                    /* abort with ERRORLEVEL 1 */
  }
  ....................................          /* process read sectors */

  exit(0);
}
```

28.4.2 Hard Disk Functions of BIOS Interrupt 13h

This section briefly discusses the most important functions of INT 13h that you haven't already met in connection with the floppy drives, or which differ significantly from that case. All functions are summarized in Appendix F.

When the BIOS has completed the requested function it indicates (by means of the carry flag) whether the operation could be carried out successfully. If the carry flag is set (CF=1) then an error has occurred and register ah contains the error code. You will find all possible error codes and their meaning in Appendix F.2. Note that not all codes are valid for both floppy and hard disk; because of their more elaborate intelligence, hard disk controllers can classify the errors in more detail.

Note also that for the hard disk functions the two most significant bits of the sector register cl represent the two most significant bits of a 10-bit cylinder number which is composed of the two cl bits mentioned and the eight bits of the cylinder register ch. Thus you may access a maximum of 1024 cylinders by means of the BIOS.

You must *never* call any of functions listed below which refer to the formatting of a track or whole drive if you use an embedded controller or a drive which carries out translation. By doing this you would only disturb the internal management of the tracks and the translation, or even the bad-sector mapping of these intelligent drives. I cannot to predict the consequences for every drive, but take into consideration that a logical track as you can access it via the BIOS may possibly be only part of a physical track, or may be distributed over two tracks or even two cylinders. If you attempt to format such a partial track or a divided track, then this can only fail, of course.

Function 05h – Format Track or Cylinder

Unlike floppy drives, in the case of hard disks the interleave is also of importance. You may adjust the interleave factor using the format buffer. It successively contains the track, head, sector number and sector size entries in the same way as they are written into the address field of the sector concerned of an ST412/506 hard disk. Note that you can only format a complete track, not individual sectors. The BIOS passes the controller the entries in the format buffer for every sector to format. If you don't count up the sector number by one from entry to entry, but arrange it in such a way that it corresponds to the intended interleave value, then you also achieve a corresponding sector shift (that is, interleaving) on the hard disk. Thus you may alter the interleave value for a track without any major problems, for example to determine the optimum interleave factor.

Advice: **if you own an already preformatted hard disk that carries out translation then you must never call this function.**

The drive may behave completely unpredictably, especially if you alter the interleave value. The number of sectors per track with which the drive appears to the system, and therefore to your program, has nothing to do with the drive's actual geometry. If you attempt to format a certain (logical) track with function 05h you may refer to some unintended location on the disk or even cross a cylinder boundary. You can imagine that you would cause confusion.

Example: Format track 0 of the first hard disk with interleave 3 (language: Microsoft C 5.10).

```
type format_buffer {
  unsigned char cyl;
  unsigned char head;
  unsigned char sector;
  unsigned char byte_p_sector;
}

struct far format_buffer f_buffer[17];  /* format buffer for 17 sectors */
int sector;

/* construct format buffer */
for (sector = 0; sector < 17; sector++) {
  f_buffer[sector].cyl = 0;                /* cylinder 0 */
  f_buffer[sector].head = 0;               /* track 0 */
  f_buffer[sector].byte_p_sector = 0x02;   /* 512 bytes per sector */
}
/* set interleave 3:1 */
f_buffer[0].sector = 0, f_buffer[1].sector = 6, f_buffer[2].sector = 12;
f_buffer[3].sector = 1, f_buffer[4].sector = 7, f_buffer[5].sector = 13;
f_buffer[6].sector = 2, f_buffer[7].sector = 8, f_buffer[8].sector = 14;
f_buffer[9].sector = 3, f_buffer[10].sector = 9, f_buffer[11].sector = 15;
f_buffer[12].sector = 4, f_buffer[13].sector = 10, f_buffer[14].sector = 16;
f_buffer[15].sector = 5, f_buffer[16].sector = 11;

inregs.h.al = 17;                  /* 17 sectors per track */
inregs.h.ch = 0x00;                /* cylinder 0 */
inregs.h.dh = 0x00;                /* Head 0 according to track 0 */
inregs.h.dl = 0x80;                /* first hard disk */
segregs.es = FP_SEG(f_buffer);     /* segment address of format buffer */

for (sector = 0; sector < 17; sector++) {
  inregs.h.ah = 0x05;                     /* function 05h */
  inregs.h.cl = sector;
  inregs.x.bx = FP_OFF(f_buffer);         /* offset address of format buffer */
  int86x(0x13, &inregs, &outregs);        /* format sector by means of interrupt 13h */
  f_buffer++;                             /* next entry in format buffer */
}
```

Function 06h – Format and Mark Bad Track

This function manages bad tracks within the frame of the bad-sector mapping if the track has more than one defect sector, and thus the whole track is unusable. The 06h function writes address marks onto the track whose flags indicate a defective track. The controller then skips this track for data recording and assigns an alternative track automatically. The function can be employed only for ST412/506 controllers and drives. Intelligent hard disks with an embedded controller and translation carry out the bad-sector mapping automatically. Unlike function 05h, you may pass the interleave value directly via register ah. You don't need a format buffer; no rearrangement of the sector numbers in that buffer according to the interleave value is therefore required.

Advice: **never use this function if your drive has its own controller or carries out translation.**

The BIOS track length doesn't coincide with the physical track length if translation is in force. Therefore, you would only mark part of the track as bad, or two partial tracks if a cylinder boundary is crossed. What your controller does with your drive in this case is unknown.

Example: `Mark bad drive 80h, cylinder 951, head 2 with interleave 2.`

```
inregs.h.al = 2;                  /* interleave 2 */
inregs.h.ch = 183;                /* 8 low-order cylinder bits */
inregs.h.dh = 2;                  /* head 2 */
inregs.h.dl = 0x80;               /* first hard disk */
for (sector = 0; sector < 17; sector++) {
  inregs.h.ah = 0x06;             /* function 06h */
  inregs.h.cl = 0xc0 + sector;    /* 2 high-order cylinder bits plus 6 sector bits */
  int86x(0x13, &inregs, &outregs); /* mark track by means of interrupt 13h */
}
```

Function 07h – Format and Mark Drive

This command formats the complete drive, from the start cylinder indicated up to the physical end of the drive. For the formatting process, the interleave value passed in register al is used. Set the head and sector number in registers cl and dh to a value of 0 so that the formatting procedure starts at the beginning, and not in the middle of the start cylinder.

Example: `Format drive 81h beginning with cylinder 100 (interleave=3).`

```
inregs.h.ah = 0x07;              /* function 07h */
inregs.h.al = 3;                 /* interleave 3 */
inregs.h.ch = 100;               /* 8 low-order cylinder bits */
inregs.h.cl = 0;                 /* 2 high-order cylinder bits plus sector 0 */
inregs.h.dh = 0;                 /* head 0 */
inregs.h.dl = 0x81;              /* second hard disk */

int86x(0x13, &inregs, &outregs); /* format drive */
```

Advice: **never use this function if your drive has its own controller or carries out translation.**

Functions 08h (determine drive parameters) and 09h (set drive parameters) are discussed in Section 28.3. The following INT 13h functions are described in Appendix F:

- function 08h – determine drive parameters
- function 09h – set drive parameters
- function 0ah – read extended sectors
- function 0bh – write extended sectors
- function 0ch – seek
- function 0dh – hard disk reset
- function 0eh – read sector buffer
- function 0fh – write sector buffer
- function 10h – check drive ready
- function 11h – recalibrate drive
- function 19h – park read/write heads

The functions *12h – check controller RAM* and *13h – controller diagnostics* listed in Appendix F are not implemented for all BIOS variants. Table 28.8 shows the BIOS data area as far as hard disks and hard disk operations are concerned.

Address	Size	Structure 76543210	Contents	Meaning
40:74	byte		status of last hard disk operation	see Appendix F.2
40:75	byte		number of installed hard disks	
40:76	byte		control byte of hard disk	
40:77	byte		offset address of hard disk port	
40:8c	byte	.....0..	status of hard disk controller	command phase
		......0.		controller transmits data
		..1.....		IRQ of controller
		...1....		DRQ of controller
		....1...		controller selected (active)
		.....1..		data phase
		......1.		controller receives data
		1		controller ready
40:8d	byte		error code of hard disk controller	see Table 28.9
40:8e	byte	......1.	IRQ/DMA control of hard disk controller	IRQ enabled
		1		DMA enabled

Table 28.8: BIOS data area for hard disks

The controller error codes differ from the error codes which are returned by the BIOS. Table 28.9 shows the valid controller error codes.

Code	Description
00h	no error
02h	no seek signal
03h	write error
04h	drive not ready
06h	track 0 not found
10h	ECC error in ID field
11h	ECC error in data field
12h	no ID address mark found
13h	no data address mark found
14h	no ID field
15h	seek error
16h	internal controller error
17h	DMA error
18h	correctable data error
19h	bad track without alternative track
1ah	error reading data
1bh	error writing data
1ch	alternative track not marked
1dh	squencer error
1eh	invalid access to alternative track
20h	invalid opcode

Table 28.9: Controller error codes

Code	Description
21h	invalid logical block address
22h	invalid parameter
23h	overflow of defect list
30h	error in sector buffer
31h	ROM check error
33h	internal microprocessor error

Table 28.9: cont.

Finally, I want to mention that the BIOS detours all floppy calls internally to interrupt INT 40h if a hard disk is installed, or if a hard disk BIOS replaces INT 13h during the course of the boot process. For this purpose, the interrupt vector of INT 13h is moved to INT 40h. This causes the handler of INT 13h always to check first whether the request refers to a hard disk or a floppy drive. In the first case, the function call is processed within that handler. In the latter case, the handler issues (via instruction INT 40h) another software interrupt. The INT 40h handler comprises all necessary routines to serve the function call for a floppy drive.

28.5 ST412/506 and ESDI

The interface most widely in use is still the ST412/506, but it is more and more being superseded by the IDE or AT bus. Because of the close relationship between ESDI and ST412/506, both are discussed. An extensive description of every detail would go beyond the scope of this book.

28.5.1 ST412/506 Interfaces and the Connection Between Drive and Controller

The name ST412/506 interface has a historical background. Seagate introduced the ST506 system in 1980 with a storage capacity of 5 Mbytes and a strictly defined interface to the controller. One year later, in 1981, the successor model ST412 system with a storage capacity of 10 Mbytes and a slightly altered interface came onto the market. The interface concept was adapted by IBM for the PC and is known today as the ST412/506 interface.

For the transfer rate between drive and controller the ST412/506 standard *requires* a value of 5 Mbits/s for MFM encoding and 7.5 Mbits/s for RLL encoding. These values must not be understood as a minimum specification but as an «exact» specification. The 5 Mbits/s and 7.5 Mbits/s, respectively, also contain, besides the actual data bit, address marks, CRC and ECC bytes, as well as gap bits.

With a sector length of about 575 bytes, MFM-encoded hard disks with an ST412/506 interface can thus accommodate 17 sectors and RLL-encoded hard disks 26 sectors per track. An increase of the sector density, which is technically quite easy today, would be a Pyrrhic victory as the required transfer rate of 5 Mbits/s or 7.5 Mbits/s doesn't allow any more sectors. The only solution is the use of another interface such as ESDI, IDE or SCSI.

Although ST412/506, strictly speaking, only defines the interface between drive and controller, but doesn't make any assumption for the integration of controller and drive into the PC system, the following configuration has been established. The controller is located on a separate adapter card which is inserted into a bus slot; a maximum of two hard disk drives are connected to the controller by a control and data cable. The controller adapter card establishes a connection to the PC bus simultaneously; a host adapter is not required here. Many ST412/506 controllers also accommodate a floppy controller besides the hard disk interface; they are then called a *combicontroller*. Unlike floppies, where the connection between drive and controller was effected by a single flat conductor cable, in the hard disk system the control and data signals run through separate cables. The wider cable with 34 wires is the control cable, and the narrow one with only 20 wires the data cable. Figure 28.15 shows the assignment of the corresponding wires.

You can connect a maximum of two hard disks with the control cable. On the other hand, for every hard disk its own data cable is necessary. Note also that for hard disks control cables which have twisted wires between the plug in the middle and the end of the cable (similar to the cable for floppy drives) do exist. But unlike floppies, wires 25–29 are twisted here. Therefore, don't mix the control cables for hard disks and for floppy drives; the cables for floppy drives have twisted wires 10–16. From Figure 28.15 you can see that the control cable for the ST412/506 interface is designed for up to four drives. But on the PC, the signals *drive select 3* and *drive select 4* are not used, so you may connect a maximum of two hard disks. Among all hard disk interfaces used on the PC, the ST412/506 is the least «intelligent». It is a pure signal interface, thus the controller is unable to pass any command to the drive. The drive itself accommodates only the control circuitry for stabilizing the disk rotation and the head positioning. All other control functions are carried out by the controller itself, for example interpretation of the commands from the PC system, the encoding and decoding of the read and write data, the generation of address marks, etc. This means that the controller passes the drive the write data immediately in the form the head writes them onto disk. In the drive itself, neither a synchronization of the signals nor any improvement in the pulse forms of the write pulses is carried out.

ST412/506 controllers and drives were used first in the XT, and later also in the AT. Because the XT BIOS was not designed as standard for the support of hard disks, all XT controllers must have their own BIOS with the hard disk functions of INT 13h. The start address of this BIOS extension is usually c8000h. The AT, on the other hand, supported hard disks from the first day, and the required routines are already implemented in the system BIOS at address f0000h. But there are other differences between XT and AT controllers with an ST412/506 interface:

- The XT controller uses DMA channel 3 for transferring data between sector buffer and main memory; in the AT, on the other hand, the BIOS carries out a programmed I/O by means of the port instructions IN and OUT without using any DMA channel.
- The XT controller employs IRQ5 for issuing a hardware interrupt, the AT controller IRQ14.
- The XT controller is accessed via the XT task file, the AT controller via the AT task file; the register assignment and addresses of these two task files are incompatible; drivers for XT hard disk controllers with an ST412/506 interface cannot be used for an AT controller.

– The commands for an XT controller always consist of a 6-byte command block to a single register; the AT controller, on the other hand, is programmed by means of single command bytes to several individual registers.

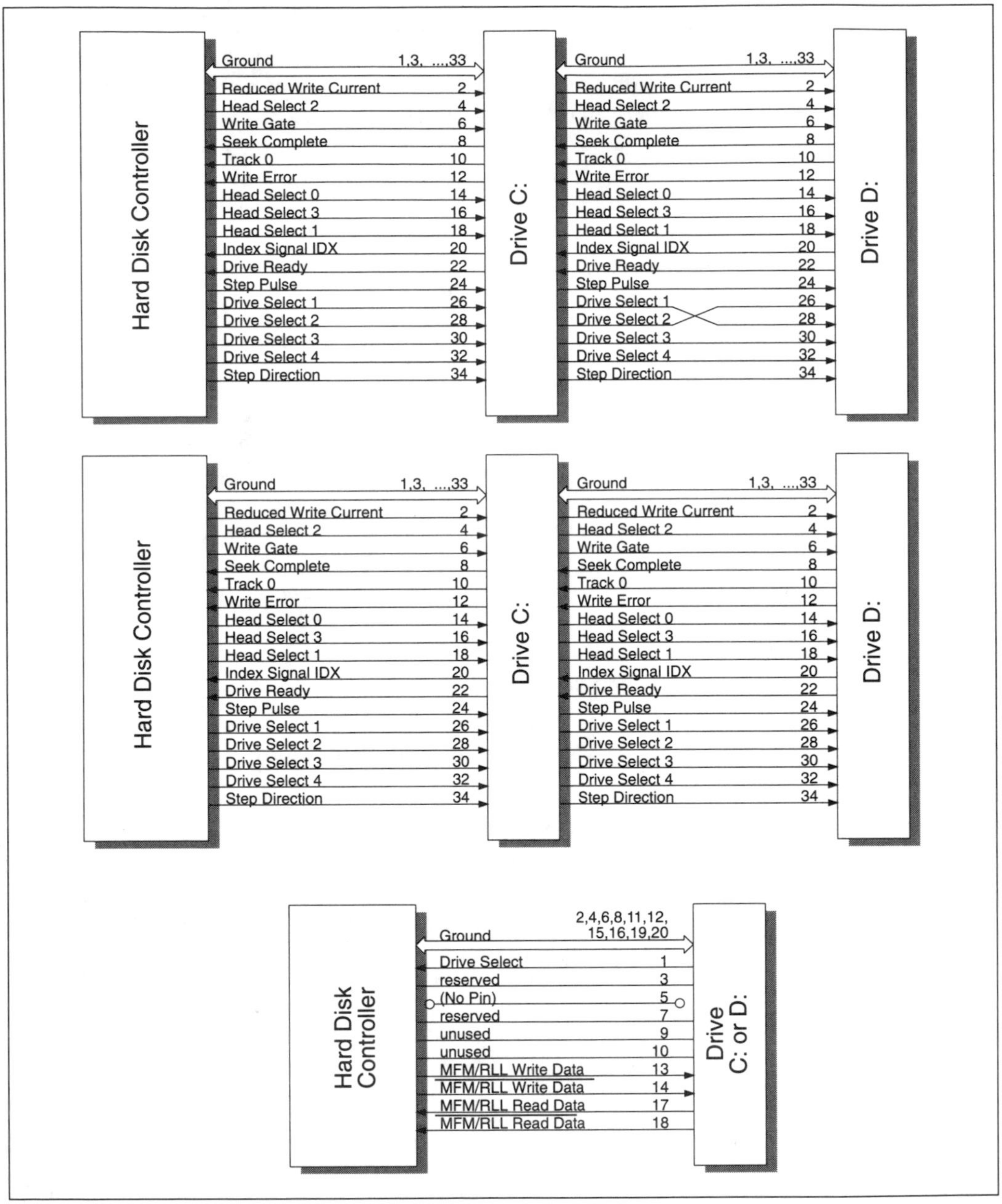

Figure 28.15: ST412/506 interface control and signal cable. The drives are connected to the controller with a control cable with 34 wires, and a data cable with 20 wires.

You will find a detailed description of the AT bus interface in Section 28.6. Today, XT hard disk controllers have nearly vanished from the market (as is the case for the XT itself). Therefore, the XT task file is not discussed in detail.

28.5.2 Connecting and Configuring ST412/506 Hard Disk Drives

One remark in advance: all plugs and cable connectors are identical for MFM and RLL hard disks with an ST412/506 interface; thus you can connect, for example, an RLL disk to an MFM controller. But the different transfer rates of 5 Mbits/s and 7.5 Mbits/s, as well as the different design of the electronics for MFM and RLL, lead to frequent read, write and seek errors. If you connect an MFM disk to an RLL controller, then this works even worse as the drive responds far too slowly to the RLL data pulses from the controller. In some unfavourable cases, electric equipment may be damaged because of the extensive design differences. Thus you may operate MFM hard disks only with an MFM controller, and RLL hard disks only with an RLL controller; mixtures between RLL and MFM are *never* allowed.

The connection of ST412/506 hard disks by means of the control cable to the controller is carried out in the same way as with floppy drives. You must connect the first hard disk to the end of the control cable, an eventual second hard disk to the connector in the middle. If you are using a control cable without twisted wires, then configure drive C: as *drive select 0* and drive D: as *drive select 1* by means of the corresponding jumpers on the drives. If you are using a control cable with twisted wires then you may configure both hard disks as *drive select 1*, as was the case for floppy drives. Because of the exchange of the select signals, the intended disk is always enabled. Don't forget, too, to remove the terminating resistor (if present) from drive D: in the middle. Finally, connect the data cable with the data connection of the drive and the data connector on the controller. The ST412/506 hard disk system is now configured correctly.

You will see that the data cables are normally much shorter than the control cables. The reason is that long cables are very sensitive to external noise as no shielded wires are used for the connection of drive and controller. The data runs at 5 Mhz between drive and controller, a range in which some other internal components of the computer are active (for example, the 4.77 MHz signal for the processor or the 8 Mhz bus clock). But external noise sources such as short-wave transmitters emit electromagnetic waves in this frequency range. The data cable as an antenna may receive these signals. By shortening the cable the antenna effect, and thus the influence of noise on the sensitive MFM and RLL signals, will be reduced. But this is hardly possible at higher frequencies or data transfer rates. Thus ESDI as the immediate successor of ST506/412 follows another concept.

28.5.3 The ESDI Interface

ESDI was conceived by Maxtor in 1983 as a powerful and intelligent successor to the ST412/506 interface. The main problem of the long transfer distances between hard disk and data separator was solved, in that ESDI already integrates the data separator on the drive. Thus, the asynchronous MFM or RLL data which gives rise to read and write errors if minor signal distortion occurs must not be transferred between drive and controller. Instead, synchronous NRZ data run through the cables, which are much more resistent against such signal alterations. The ESDI cables may be up to 3 m long.

ESDI is designed for a transfer rate of up to 24 Mbits/s between drive and controller; typically 10-15 Mbits/s are achieved. A sector density of 34 sectors per track and interleave 1:1 leads to a maximum data transfer rate between drive and main memory of 1020 kbytes/s. ESDI hard disks are therefore high-end drives; for data encoding the RLL method is mainly used. Furthermore, an ESDI controller is intended for connecting up to seven ESDI drives, and may access hard disks with a maximum of 64 heads in four groups of 16 heads each, as well as a maximum of 4096 cylinders. The controller of its predecessor interface (ST412/506), on the other hand, only allowed a maximum of 16 heads and 1024 cylinders.

An ESDI controller may also pass complete commands which are decoded and executed by the drive. Therefore, it's obvious that an ESDI controller cannot be supported by the AT-BIOS; every ESDI adapter has its own BIOS extension with the hard disk functions of INT 13h and internal diagnostics and configuration routines for serving the connected ESDI drives. Although the ESDI controller may also pass complete commands, the generation of address marks, synchronization pattern, and the decoding of the NRZ into parallel bit data for the PC system bus is carried out by the controller. Thus an ESDI controller is neither a pure controller which takes over *all* control functions, nor a host adapter which solely establishes a connection to the system bus; instead, it is something like an intermediate product between controller and host adapter.

The following sections briefly discuss the ESDI signals and commands. The connection between ESDI controller and the drives is established, similar to the ST412/506 interface, by means of a common 34-wire control cable and an individual 20-wire data cable for every drive. To the ESDI control cable up to seven drives can be connected. Figure 28.16 shows the assignment of the control and data cable.

The controller selects one of the 16 heads with numbers 0–15 from a group of 16 heads by means of the lines $\overline{\text{head select } 2^3}$ to $\overline{\text{head select } 2^0}$. Note that the signals are complementary; for example, head 15 is selected by the signal combination 0000. ESDI drives may have up to four such groups, that is 64 heads. A certain group is selected by the command *select head group* (see below). The lines for the head select determine the head within the selected group. In a similar way, the controller can select one of the seven possible drives by means of the signals $\overline{\text{drive select } 2^2}$ to $\overline{\text{drive select } 2^0}$. These signals are also active low (complemented); thus drive 1 is selected by the signal combination 110. The signal combination 111 corresponding to drive address 0 means that the controller has currently not selected any drive. The two control signals $\overline{\text{write gate}}$ and $\overline{\text{read gate}}$ control the activation of the write and read gate in the selected drive so that data can be written by the controller onto or read from the data carrier. $\overline{\text{Index signal IDX}}$ indicates that the beginning-of-track mark has just passed below the head. The $\overline{\text{drive ready}}$ signal shows that the addressed hard disk is rotating at the indended rpm and is read to execute commands.

The other signals implement the protocol for the command transfer to the selected drive and the return of status data from the addressed hard disk. The two signals $\overline{\text{ACK}}$ (acknowledge) and

REQ (request) form the handshake signals for an ordered transfer of command and status data between controller and drive. The transfer is carried out in two cases:

- The controller passes a command to the selected drive; commands are always transferred via the line command data as a serial stream of 16 command bits plus one parity bit so that odd parity occurs; the handshake signals serve to agree on a correct course for this serial data transfer.
- The drive transfers status or configuration data to the controller; after a corresponding command the drive returns 16 status bits plus one parity bit (odd parity) via the line configuration/status data, which indicates the configuration of the addressed drive or the status of the last command.

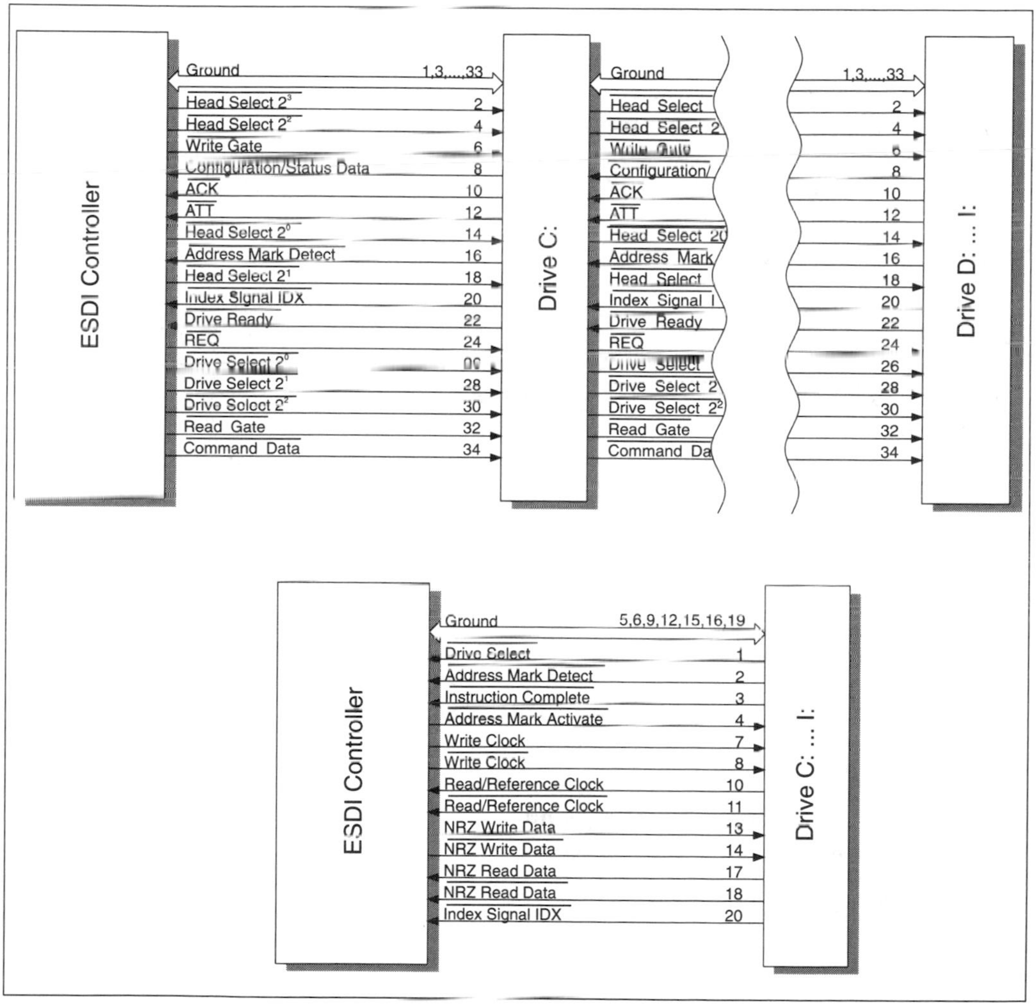

Figure 28.16. The ESDI cable. The drives are connected to the controller by means of a control cable with 34 wires and a data cable with 20 wires. Up to seven ESDI drives can be connected to a single ESDI controller.

Don't confuse this data transfer with the transfer of NRZ data between drive and controller via the data cable. The NRZ data is decoded in the controller, and is data that has been read from the hard disk or which is to be written onto it. On the contrary, the exchange of command, configuration and status data is carried out via the control cable, and the transferred data is neither written onto nor read from the disk. It is used exclusively by the hard disk control, or generated by this control for the controller.

The ATT (attention) signal is activated by the drive if an error occurs and the controller is to read the command status via the line configuration/status data. Finally, the signal address mark found indicates that the hard disk control has detected an address mark. The NRZ data now following on the data cable thus indicates the corresponding address.

The transfer of the read and write data from or to the addressed drive is carried out similar to ST412/506 via a separate data cable. But ESDI occupies far more wires with a signal. As is the case for ST412/506, the drive select signal indicates that the drive to which the data cable concerned is connected has been selected by the controller by means of the control lines drive select 2^x. Accordingly, the address mark found signal shows that the drive has detected an address mark and the following NRZ data represents address data. By means of the signal activate address mark the drive is instructed to write the NRZ data passed afterwards as an address mark onto the data carrier. Index signal IDX indicates that the beginning-of-track mark has just passed below the head. When the drive has completed a command, it activates the line command complete to inform the controller that it can now read status data from the drive.

The other signals and lines of the data cable synchronize and transfer the NRZ data from or to the drive, and are always passed as complementary signals. The *NRZ write data* is transferred from the controller to the drive to write them onto the data carrier. On the contrary, during the course of a read process the drive transfers *NRZ read data* to the controller. The drive generates the *read/reference clock* to define the data transfer rate. ESDI, unlike ST506/412, doesn't fix the transfer rate to a certain value, but implements three different classes instead: transfer rate lower than 5 Mbits/s, between 5 Mbits/s and 10 Mbits/s and above 10 Mbits/s. Depending upon the requested class the connected controller must be more or less powerful. The drives can identify their transfer rates, corresponding to one of the classes, to the controller by means of a command. Usually, the BIOS extension on the ESDI adapter carries out this job to check whether the controller can service the connected drive or whether their transfer rate is too high. The read/reference clock then determines the transfer rate exactly. For this reason, the number of sectors per track is not so strictly defined with ESDI hard disks as is the case with the 17 or 26 sectors for the ST412/506 interface. ESDI disks usually have 34 sectors per track which corresponds to a transfer rate of about 10 Mbits/s. But high-end ESDI drives can accommodate up to 70 sectors per track if the connected controller can stand a transfer rate of 20 Mbits/s. Originally, ESDI was intended for a transfer rate of 15 Mbits/s at most, but this maximum value has recently been increased up to 24 Mbits/s. Only SCSI, with a maximum of 6 Mbytes/s equal to 48 Mbits/s in synchronous mode, provides an even higher data transfer rate. But note that all these values only refer to the transfer between controller and hard disk: they don't say anything about the speed at which the data can be shovelled into or out of main memory, however. All the remarks of Section 28.1.4 are also valid for ESDI. The controller further generates the write clock from the read/reference clock, which determines at which speed the controller transfers the write data to the drive. Thus the term *reference clock* is quite correct. Unlike the read/reference clock, the write clock need not be active all the time; it is sufficient if the controller drives this line during write processes.

You can see that the ESDI interface between controller and drive is a mixture of a low-level interface because of the physical signals $\overline{\text{head select }2^3\text{–}2^0}$, $\overline{\text{drive select }2^2\text{–}2^0}$, $\overline{\text{ACK}}$, $\overline{\text{REQ}}$, etc., and a high-level interface because of the command and status codes. The ST412/506, on the other hand, is a purely physical interface, which is only realized by means of electrical signals; and SCSI is a high-level interface, as the complete drive control including drive selection is carried out with logical commands.

28.5.4 ESDI Commands and Configuration Data

The 16-bit ESDI commands appear in two formats, depending upon whether the controller passes command parameters. Figure 28.17 shows the ESDI command format.

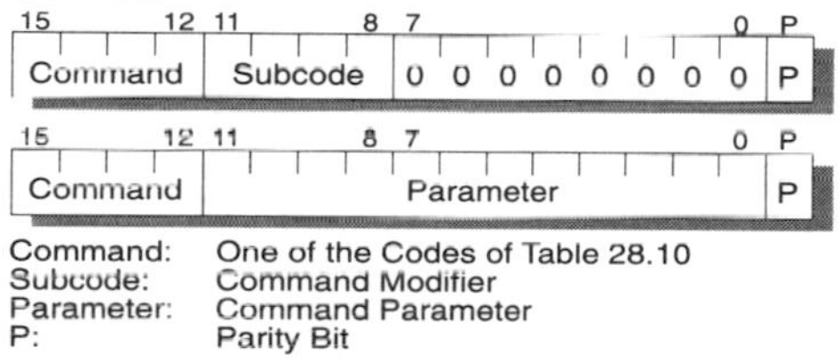

Figure 28.17: ESDI command data word.

Note that in addition to the 16 command bits a parity bit P is passed to generate odd parity. The following sections list the ESDI commands in brief to give an impression of the intelligence of this advanced interface. I have neglected an extensive description of every individual command in favour of the IDE and SCSI interface. Table 28.10 shows all the commands, as well as the accompanying command codes.

Command code	Subcode	Parameter	Command name
0 0 0 0	no	yes	seek head
0 0 0 1	no	no	calibrate drive
0 0 1 0	yes	no	request sense
0 1 0 0	yes	no	request configuration
0 1 0 1	no	yes	select head group
0 1 1 0	yes	no	control drive
0 1 1 1	yes	no	set data sense offset
1 0 0 0	yes	no	set track offset
1 0 0 1	no	yes	start diagnostics
1 0 1 0	no	yes	set byte/sector
1 1 1 0	no	yes	set configuration
others	–	–	reserved

Table 28.10: ESDI commands and command codes

According to the listed ESDI commands, you can clearly see that the ESDI controller is neither a pure controller, because it passes high-level commands (for example, *seek head* to the drive) and doesn't control the positioning itself by means of stepper pulses, nor a host adapter because, for example, no command *read sector* is implemented. To read a sector the ESDI controller must first transfer a seek-head command, and afterwards a parameter which indicates the intended track to the ESDI drive. When the drive has activated the line command complete on the data cable to indicate completion of the seek command then it is the job of the controller to observe the lines address mark found and NRZ read data to detect the address mark of the intended sector first, to filter the sector data out of the NRZ data stream, and to transfer it into the sector buffer afterwards. Thus the head positioning is carried out by means of a command, as is the case with a host adapter. The following sector data read, though, is executed in the same way as with a conventional controller. ESDI thus achieves much higher performance data than an ST412/506 drive, but is nowhere near as flexibile as the SCSI.

To give you an impression of what configuration data ESDI drives provide for a struggling system programmer, I have listed in Table 28.11 the configuration word that is transferred to the controller as a 16-bit word plus parity by the drive via the line configuration/status data. For this purpose, the controller must pass a *request sense* command with the subcode 0000b to the drive. This configuration word is called a *general configuration word*.

Bit	Meaning
0	1=sectors hard-sectored by byte pulses from controller
1	1=sectors hard-sectored by drive, sector pulses from drive
2	1=sectors soft-sectored by controller with address marks, address mark pulses from drive
3	0=drive uses MFM encoding 1=drive uses other encoding method (usual RLL)
4	1=head switch time > 15 μs
5	1=drive supports control of spindle motor for motor switch off/on
6	1=hard disk drive (non-removable volume)
7	1=drive with removable volume
8	1=data transfer rate < 5 Mbits/s
9	1=data transfer rate between 5 Mbits/s and 10 Mbits/s
10	1=data transfer rate > 10 Mbits/s
11	1=rotation deviation > ±0.5%
12	1=drive supports data sense offset
13	1=drive supports track offset
14	1=GAP 3 necessary to compensate rotation deviation
15	0=magnetic disk drive 1=no magnetic disk drive

Table 28.11: General configuration word

Table 28.12 further lists the *special configuration words* that the drive transfers to the controller if the subcode in the command word differs from 0000b. The drive returns the configuration data in the same way as above, as a 16-bit word plus parity bit via the line configuration/status data to the controller.

From Tables 28.11 and 28.12 you can easily recognize that an ESDI drive can identify its geometry and formatting parameters to the system in a very detailed way. The nearly infinite variety of drive entries in the AT setup is now obsolete. If you install an ESDI controller with its own BIOS and ESDI drives, then the BIOS routines determine the geometry and all other important drive parameters on their own, and initialize the system accordingly. Thus ESDI systems are self-configuring, as is the case for SCSI drives.

Subcode	Meaning
0001	number of fixed drive cylinders
0010	number of removable drive cylinders
0011	number of heads bit 15–8: removable heads; bit 7–0: fixed heads
0100	min. number of unformatted bytes per track (hard-sectored drives only)
0101	actual number of unformatted bytes per track (hard-sectored drives only)
0110	sectors per track (hard-sectored drives only) bit 15–8: reserved; bit 7–0: sectors per track
0111	min. number of bytes in intersector gap ISG bit 15–8: ISG bytes after index or sector pulse bit 7–0: byte per ISG
1000	min. number of bytes per PLO synchronization field bit 15–8: reserved; bit 7–0: byte per PLO field
1001	number of words of manufacturer-own status bit 15–4: reserved; bit 3–0: number of words
1111	manufacturer identification
others	reserved

Table 28.12: Special configuration word

28.5.5 Connecting and Configuring ESDI Hard Disk Drives

For the connection of ESDI hard disks in principle the same rules as for an ST506/412 drive apply. First you must configure the drives, that is, adjust their ESDI address. This is carried out by a *drive select jumper* with which you assign the drive a number. The drive concerned then responds to a corresponding address $\overline{\text{drive select } 2^x}$ on the control cable and becomes active. Also, make sure that you don't assign an address twice, and thus give rise to an address conflict. Because of the different uses of the cable wires and the binary encoding of the drive address on the control cable, no cables with twisted wires are available for ESDI to free you from this drive configuration. With ESDI you always need to assign every drive an ESDI address. On the contrary, it is insignificant here which plug of the control cable you connect with which ESDI drive. You only have to remove the terminating resistor (if present) from all except the last drive to terminate the control cable.

Also ensure that you actually connect the data cable of a drive to the corresponding plug on the controller when installing the data cable. Unlike the ST412/506, ESDI can manage up to seven drives, so you have much more opportunity to mix the cables. There is nothing else to do for configuring the system. By means of the BIOS extension on the ESDI controller and the in-built intelligence of the ESDI drives, you don't even need to adjust the BIOS setup. Simply enter *no drive* in the setup to avoid any conflicts between the system BIOS and the BIOS extension. During the course of the boot procedure, the ESDI BIOS intercepts interrupt 13h automatically, and all programs may access the ESDI hard disk(s) without any problem.

28.6 Drives with IDE, AT Bus or ATA Interface

Recently, a new hard disk interface standard was established for PCs which is overtaking the ST412/506 standard more and more: the so-called *IDE* or *AT bus* interface. IDE is the abbreviation for *intelligent drive electronics* – an indication that the connected drives are intelligent on their own. With the conventional controller-hard disk combination, the drive itself has only those electronic elements required to drive the motors and gates of the drive. The more extensive control for executing commands (for reading a sector, for example, a head seek, the reading of the encoded signals, the separation of data and clock signal, the transfer into main memory, etc. must be carried out) is taken over by the electronic equipment on a separate adapter, that is, the hard disk controller. Thus the drive itself is rather «stupid». A further disadvantage of this solution is that the still encoded signals must run from the drive via the data cable to the controller to be decoded there. The transfer path worsens the signals; a high data transfer rate between drive and controller fails because of the relatively long signal paths. Further, the exploding market for hard disk drives gave rise to a nearly infinite variety of drive geometries and storage capacities, so that a separate controller (which possibly comes from a third-party manufacturer) is simply overtaxed to serve all hard disk formats.

The falling prices for electronic equipment during the past few years, in parallel with a remarkable performance enhancement, gave a simple solution: modern and powerful hard disk drives already integrate the controller, and it is no longer formed by a separate adapter card. The signal paths from disk to controller are thus very short, and the controller can be adapted in an optimized way to the hard disk it actually controls. The IDE and SCSI interfaces follow this method of integrating drive and controller into a single unit. But SCSI has another philosophy in other aspects; details concerning SCSI are discussed in the next chapter. ESDI, as a middle course, integrates the data separator on the drive but the rest of the controller (for example, the sector buffer and drive control) is still formed on a separate adapter.

The IDE interface (discussed in the following sections) lies, in view of its performance, between the conventional solution with a separate controller and an ST412/506 interface to the drive on the one side, and the SCSI and ESDI hard disks as high-end solutions on the other.

At the end of 1984, Compaq initiated the development of the IDE interface. Compaq was looking for an ST506 controller which could be directly mounted onto the drive and connected to the main system by means of simple circuitry. In common with hard disk manufacturers such as Western Digital, Imprimis and Seagate, the AT bus interface arose in a very short time. Too many cooks spoil the broth, and so in the beginning incompatibilities were present everywhere. To take remedial action several system, drive and software manufacturers founded an interest group called CAM (common access method), which elaborated a standard with the name ATA (AT attachment) in March 1989. Besides other properties, the command set for IDE drives was also defined. As well as the eight commands with several subcommands already present on the AT controller, 19 new commands were added, which mainly refer to the drive control in view of low power consumption. For example, the sleep command for disabling the controller and switching off the drive if no access has been carried out for a while is one of these. Appendix H lists all the necessary and optional commands. Today, all manufacturers orient to this specification, so that incompatibilities are (nearly) a thing of the past. You may use the terms AT bus,

IDE and ATA synonymously. An extension to the standard with a higher transfer rate, and also to drives with removable mediums (especially CD-ROM), is presently in preparation, and will be called *Enhanced IDE*; this seems to be a response to the triumph of SCSI. However, more flexibility and higher performance isn't at all bad for IDE either.

28.6.1 The Physical CPU–Drive Interface

IDE is a further development of the AT controller with an ST506 interface so that the AT bus hard disks orient to the register set and the performance of such hard disks. Thus, IDE is a logical interface between system and hard disk, and accepts high-level commands (for example, read sector or format track). ESDI and ST412/506, on the other hand, are physical interfaces between controller and drive and refer, for example, to the control signals for the drive motors to move the head to a certain track. As with IDE the controller and hard disk form an inseparable unit, it is the job of every manufacturer to design the control of the drive and the transfer of the data. The definition of a physical interface is therefore obsolete.

The physical connection between the AT bus in the PC and the IDE interface of the drives (or better, the controllers on the drives) is established by a so-called *host adapter*. The motherboard plays the role of host here. The host adapter accommodates only a few buffers and decoder circuits, which are required to connect the IDE drives and the AT system bus. Newer motherboards already integrate these host adapters, otherwise they need a separate adapter card which is inserted into a bus slot. Many host adapters further have a floppy controller so that they are often called an AT bus controller. That's not correct as the controller is located immediately on the board of the drive; the adapter only establishes the connection between the drive and system bus. To the system and you as a programmer, the AT bus drives appear to be the usual controllers and drives with an ST412/506 interface which had been operating in your PC up to now. Thus AT bus drives can be accessed by the routines of INT 13h implemented in the conventional AT BIOS. Unlike ESDI or SCSI hard disk drives, no BIOS extension is required.

For connecting the drives, only a single 40-wire flat conductor cable is used, with which you connect the host adapter and the drives. The IDE interface can serve a maximum of two drives, one of which must be the master, and the other the slave (adjust the jumper or DIP switch accordingly). The master drive is assigned address 0, the slave address 1. Table 28.13 lists the assignment of the 40 wires and the signals running on them.

Pin 20 of the cable is locked to avoid a misinsertion of the plug. Most of the 40 IDE lines are grounded or can be directly connected to the AT system bus. This explains the name AT bus interface. Between host adapter and IDE drive there are only five signals, $\overline{\text{CS1Fx}}$, $\overline{\text{CS3Fx}}$, SPSYNC, $\overline{\text{DASP}}$ and $\overline{\text{PDIAG}}$, which control the IDE drives and are not connected to the AT bus. The two first signals $\overline{\text{CS1Fx}}$ and $\overline{\text{CS3Fx}}$ are chip select signals generated by the host adapter to select the register group with the base address 1f0h or the register group with the base address 3f0h. The meaning of the accompanying registers is described below.

With the spindle synchronization signal SPSYNC the spindle motor rotation of master and slave can be synchronized. This is advantageous if, for example, drive arrays are formed or a mirroring is carried out. But many IDE drives don't implement this, and the SPSYNC pin is not used.

IDE signal	Pin	Signal meaning	AT signal	Signal direction
RESET	1	reset drives	RESET DRV[1)]	host→drive
GND	2	ground	—	—
DD7	3	data bus bit 7	SD7	bidirectional
DD8	4	data bus bit 8	SD8	bidirectional
DD6	5	data bus bit 6	SD6	bidirectional
DD9	6	data bus bit 9	SD9	bidirectional
DD5	7	data bus bit 5	SD5	bidirectional
DD10	8	data bus bit 10	SD10	bidirectional
DD4	9	data bus bit 4	SD4	bidirectional
DD11	10	data bus bit 11	SD11	bidirectional
DD3	11	data bus bit 3	SD3	bidirectional
DD12	12	data bus bit 12	SD12	bidirectional
DD2	13	data bus bit 2	SD2	bidirectional
DD13	14	data bus bit 13	SD13	bidirectional
DD1	15	data bus bit 1	SD1	bidirectional
DD14	16	data bus bit 14	SD14	bidirectional
DD0	17	data bus bit 0	SD0	bidirectional
DD15	18	data bus bit 15	SD15	bidirectional
GND[2)]	19	ground	—	—
	20	pin 20 mark	—	—
DMARQ[3)]	21	DMA request	DRQx	drive→host
GND	22	ground	—	—
$\overline{\text{DIOW}}$	23	write data via I/O channel	$\overline{\text{IOW}}$	host→drive
GND	24	ground	—	—
$\overline{\text{DIOR}}$	25	read data via I/O channel	$\overline{\text{IOR}}$	host→drive
GND	26	ground	—	—
IORDY[3)]	27	I/O access complete (ready)	IOCHRDY	drive→host
SPSYNC	28	spindle synchronization	—	drive→drive
$\overline{\text{DMACK}}$[3)]	29	DMA acknowledge	$\overline{\text{DACKx}}$	host→drive
GND	30	ground	—	—
INTRQ	31	interrupt request	IRQx	drive→host
$\overline{\text{IOCS16}}$	32	16 bit transfer via I/O channel	$\overline{\text{I/OCS16}}$	drive→host
DA1	33	address bus 1	SA1	host→drive
$\overline{\text{PDIAG}}$	34	passed diagnostic from slave	—	drive→drive
DA0	35	address bus 0	SA0	host→drive
DA2	36	address bus 2	SA2	host→drive
$\overline{\text{CS1Fx}}$	37	chip select for base addr. 1f0h	—	host→drive
$\overline{\text{CS3Fx}}$	38	chip select for base addr. 3f0h	—	host→drive
$\overline{\text{DASP}}$	39	drive active/slave present	—	drive→host
GND	40	ground	—	—

1) inverted signal of AT bus signal

2) pin locked to prevent incorrect insertion of plug

3) optional

Table 28.13: IDE interface cable layout

The two signals $\overline{\text{DASP}}$ (drive active/slave present) and $\overline{\text{PDIAG}}$ (passed diagnostic) return acknowledge signals by the slave to the master during the course of initialization. Also, these signals are not implemented in many older IDE models manufactured before the ATA standard became effective. That's not very serious; only some diagnostics routines are not always executed correctly. If your diagnostics software reports some obscure errors, although your drives have been running error-free for several months, then the reason may be the lack of one or both signals.

An optional but, nevertheless, important signal is IORDY. With a low level a drive can inform the CPU that it requires additional clock cycles for the current I/O cycle, for example, for reading the sector buffer or transferring the command code. The CPU then inserts wait states. But many IDE drives don't use this signal, and always fix the corresponding line at a high level.

For performance enhancement the IDE standard defines two more signals, which were not to be found on an ST506 controller in the original AT: DMARQ (DMA request) and $\overline{\text{DMACK}}$ (DMA acknowledge). In the AT, the data exchange between main memory and the controller's sector buffer was not carried out via a DMA channel, as was the case on the PC/XT, but by means of the CPU; a so-called *programmed I/O (PIO)* is executed. If, for example, a sector is to be read, then the sector data read into the sector buffer is repeatedly transferred via the data register into a CPU register by an IN instruction, and from there into main memory by a MOV instruction, until the sector buffer is empty. Thus the AT controller didn't carry out a DMA transfer, and therefore didn't provide any DMA control signals. As with modern and powerful DMA chips, the transfer rate between sector buffer and main memory is much higher (a factor of two can readily be achieved) and the development of multitasking systems like OS/2 request a relief from such «silly» data transfer operations, the two optional DMA control signals are implemented in the new IDE standard. Some AT bus hard disks can be instructed by a software command or a jumper to use a DMA channel instead of PIO for exchanging data between sector buffer and main memory. But as the programmer, you must then take into account the preparations for carrying out such a DMA transfer.

The integration of the controllers on the drives makes it possible to integrate more intelligence into the hard disk control. To this belongs, for example, intelligent retries if an access has failed. It is especially important that many IDE drives carry out an automatic *bad-sector remapping*. Usually, you can mask defective sectors and cylinders during the course of a low-level formatting process via the defect list, and use error-free alternative sectors and tracks instead. But if, after such a low-level formatting, a sector or track is damaged, the mapping is no longer possible and the sector is lost for data recording. This becomes fiendish, especially in the case of sneaking damage. The controller then always needs more retries to access the sector concerned correctly. Using the in-built retry routine, the operating system seldom recognizes anything about this as the data is read or written correctly after several retries. But at some time the point is reached where even the retry routine is overtaxed, the sector is completely inaccessible, and all data is lost. Many IDE drives are much more clever: the controller reserves several sectors and tracks of the hard disk for later use during the course of bad-sector remapping. If the controller detects several failed accesses to a sector, but finally leads to a correct data access, then the data of the sector concerned is written into one of the reserved spare sectors and the bad sector is marked. Afterwards, the controller updates an internal table so that all future accesses to the damaged sector are diverted to the reserved one. The system, or you as its user, doesn't recognize this procedure. The intelligent IDE drive carries out this remapping without any intervention, in the background.

The emergence of battery-powered laptops and notebooks gave rise to the need for power-saving drives. In a computer, powerful hard disks are one of the most power-consuming components, as they require strong current pulses for fast head seeks, and unlike floppy drives the hard disks are continuously running. Most specialist drives for portable computers can be switched off or disabled by software commands to minimize power consumption. Also, for the IDE hard disks according to the ATA standard such commands are optionally implemented. In the order of decreasing power consumption such hard disks can be operated in the active, idle, standby and sleep modes. Of course, it takes the longest time to «awaken» a drive from sleep into the active state. For this purpose the disk has to be accelerated from rest to the operation rpm, the head must be positioned, and the controller needs to be enabled.

28.6.2 Features of IDE Hard Disk Drives

Intelligent drives with an embedded controller, the most powerful among all IDE hard disks, carry out a translation from logical to physical geometry. The high recording density allows drives with up to 50 sectors per track in the outer zone with a large radius. IDE hard disks run virtually exclusively with an interleave of 1:1. To reduce the average access time of the drives, some hard disks are equipped with a cache memory which accommodates at least two tracks, in most cases. Even if your PC is unable to stand an interleave value of 1:1 as the transfer via the slowly clocked AT bus is not fast enough, this is not a disaster. Because of the 1:1 interleave, the data is read very quickly into the controller cache which is acting as a buffer. The CPU fetches the data from the cache with the maximum transfer speed of the AT bus. An interleave value which is adjusted too low, therefore, has no unfavourable consequences as it would do without the cache.

For high-capacity IDE hard disks, the RLL encoding method is mainly used; simpler ones may also use the MFM method. High performance IDE drives enable data transfer rates between drive and main memory of up to 1 Mbyte/s; a value which comes near the top of the practical values of SCSI and ESDI. On average, transfer rates of more than 1 Mbyte/s are realistic for usual IDE drives. Thus they are located between the older ST412/506 controllers and the high-end SCSI and ESDI solutions. The simpler interface electronics of the IDE host adapter and the support of the AT bus drives by the AT's on-board BIOS make it appear that the IDE hard disks are a rather good solution for Personal Computers in the region of medium performance.

An IDE interface manages a maximum of two drives. As long as the connected drive meets the IDE interface specification, the internal structure of the drive is insignificant. For example, it is possible to connect a powerful optical drive by means of an IDE interface. Usually, one would select an SCSI solution as this is more flexible in a number of ways than the AT bus.

One restriction of IDE is the maximum cable length of 18" (46 cm); some manufacturers also allow up to 24" (61 cm). For larger systems which occupy several cabinets, this is too little, but for a Personal Computer even in a large tower case it is sufficient. These values are part of the IDE standard. Thus, it is not impossible that the cables may be longer; but the IDE standard does not guarantee this.

Another disadvantage is that (especially older) but even also some present implementations of the IDE standard don't operate absolutely error-free in view of the signal timing. With an unfavourable combination of drive, host adapter and driver it may be (for example, with network software running in protected mode) that the IDE drive doesn't respond to instructions from the processor quickly enough. The consequences are rather unnerving, with unpredictable crashes during the course of an access to the IDE drives, even though no problems had occurred before with an ST412/506 controller. Thus IDE is not identical to an ST506 AT controller, but is a new product. Because of the market development during the past three years, and the attempts to form a clearly defined and obligatory standard, such problems are now vanishing more and more.

28.6.3 The AT Task File

The CPU accesses the controller of the IDE hard disk by means of several data and control registers, commonly called the *AT task file*. The address and assignment of these registers is identical to that of the hard disk controller with an ST506 interface in the IBM AT, but note that the registers are not compatible with the XT task file, or other interfaces such as ESDI or SCSI. The AT task file is divided into two register groups with port base addresses 1f0h and 3f0h. The following sections describe the registers of the AT task file and their meaning in more detail. Table 28.14 lists all the registers concerned.

The data register, which is the only 16-bit register of the AT task file, can be read or written by the CPU to transfer data between main memory and the controller. The original AT interface supported only programmed input/output via registers and ports, but no data transfer by means of DMA. The reading and writing is carried out in units of 16 bits; only the ECC bytes during the course of a read-long command are passed byte by byte. In this case, you must use the low-order byte of the register. Note that the data in the data register is only valid if the DRQ bit in the status register is set.

Register	Address [bit]	Width Write(W)	Read (R)
data register	1f0h	16	R/W
error register	1f1h	8	R
precompensation	1f1h	8	W
sector count	1f2h	8	R/W
sector number	1f3h	8	R/W
cylinder LSB	1f4h	8	R/W
cylinder MSB	1f5h	8	R/W
drive/head	1f6h	8	R/W
status register	1f7h	8	R
command register	1f7h	8	W
alternate status register	3f6h	8	R
digital output register	3f6h	8	W
drive address	3f7h	8	R

Table 28.14: The AT task file

The CPU can only read the error register; it contains error information concerning the last active command if the ERR bit in the status register is set and the BSY bit in the status register is cleared; otherwise, the entries in the error register are not defined. Note that the meaning of this register differs for the diagnostics command. Figure 28.18 shows the structure of the error register.

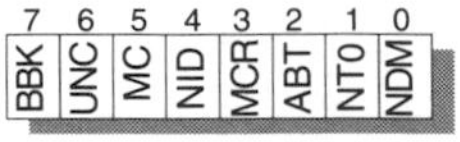


```
BBK:  1=sector marked as bad by host     0=no error
UNC:  1=uncorrectable data error         0=no or correctable data error
NID:  1=ID mark not found                0=no error
ABT:  command abort
      1=command aborted                  0=command executed
NT0:  1=track 0 not found                0=no error
NDM:  1=data address mark not found      0=no error
x:    unused

Enhanced IDE only:
MC:   1=medium changed     0=medium not changed
MCR:  1=medium change required  0=no medium change required
```

Figure 28.18: Error register (1f1h).

A set *NDM* bit indicates that the controller hasn't found a data address mark on the data carrier. If *NT0* is set this means that after a corresponding command the drive was unable to position the read/write head above track 0. If the controller had to abort execution of the active command because of an error, the *ABT* bit is set. If the *NID* bit is equal to 1, the controller was unable to detect the ID address mark concerned on the data carrier. A set *UNC* bit shows that an uncorrectable data error has occurred; the data is invalid even after applying the ECC code. If *BBK* is equal to 1 then the CPU has earlier marked the sector concerned as bad; it can no longer be accessed.

For supporting drives with removable volumes, enhanced IDE implements the (formerly reserved) MC and MCR bits. A set *MC* bit indicates that the volume in the drive has been changed, thus it corresponds to the disk change bit of the floppies. A set MCR bit shows that the user has requested a medium change, for example, by operating the eject key. The system must complete all running accesses and send a pulse or command to the drive to actually eject the volume.

The precompensation register (1f1h) is only implemented for compatibility reasons with the AT task file of the original AT. All data passed by the CPU is ignored. The intelligent IDE hard disk drives with an embedded controller process the precompensation internally without any intervention by the CPU.

The sector count register (1f2h) can be read and written by the CPU to define the number of sectors to be read, written or verified. If you pass the register a value of 0, then the hard disk carries out the command concerned for 256 sectors, and not for 0 sectors. After every transfer of a sector from or into main memory, the register value is decreased by one. Thus the register's contents, which can be read by an IN instruction, indicates the number of sectors still to be read, written or verified. Also, during the course of a formatting process, the controller decrements the register value. Note that the meaning of the register differs somewhat for the command *set drive parameters*.

The sector number registers (1f3h) specifies the start sector for carrying out a command with disk access. After processing every sector the register contents is updated according to the executed command. Thus the register always indicates the last processed sector independently of whether the controller was able to complete the concerned command successfully or not.

The two registers cylinder MSB (1f5h) and cylinder LSB (1f4h) contain the most-significant (MSB) and least-significant byte (LSB) of the 10-bit cylinder number. The two most-significant bits are held by the register cylinder MSB, the eight least-significant ones by the register cylinder LSB. The six high-order bits of register cylinder MSB are ignored, thus the registers are able to represent cylinder numbers between 0 and 1023, as is also the case for the original AT. Because many IDE hard disks carry out a translation, the physical cylinders of the hard disk are not limited to this range. The physical drive geometry is then converted into a logical one, which has a maximum cylinder number of 1023. After processing of each sector, the contents of both registers are updated, thus the registers always indicate the current cylinder number. Some IDE drives and especially hard disk corresponding to the enhanced IDE standard, also use the six high-order bits in the MSB cylinder register 1f5h. Therefore, a total of 65 535 cylinders can be addressed at the most.

By means of the registers drive/head (1f6h) you can determine the drive for which the command concerned is to be carried out. Furthermore, head defines the start head with which the disk access begins. Figure 28.19 shows the format of this register.

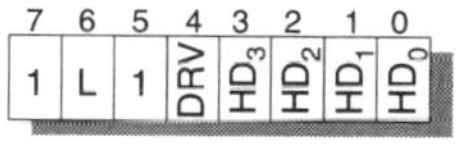


```
DRV: drive
     1=slave     0=master
HD3–HD0:  head number (binary)
     0000=head 0   0001=head 1   0010=head 2   ...   1111=head 15

Enhanced IDE only:
L:   1=LBA mode    0=CHS mode
```

Figure 28.19: Drive/head register (1f6h).

The three most-significant bits always have value of 101b. The *DRV* bit defines the addressed drive, and the bits *HD3–HD0* specify the number of that head with which the command concerned starts to execute. A maximum of 16 heads can therefore be accessed. IDE drives which can carry out a logical block addressing (LBA), additionally implement the *L* bit. If L equals to 1, LBA is enabled for the present access.

The status register (1f7h) can only be read by the CPU, and contains status information concerning the last active command. The controller updates the status register after every command, or if an error occurs. Also, during the course of a data transfer between main memory and controller, the register is updated to carry out handshaking. If the CPU reads the status register an eventually pending interrupt request (via IRQ14 in the PC) is cancelled automatically. Note that all bits of this register except BSY and all registers of the AT task file are invalid if the BSY bit is set in the status register. Figure 28.20 shows the structure of the register.

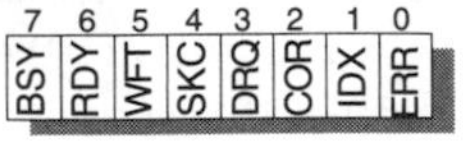


```
BSY:  busy
      1=drive is busy              0=drive not busy
RDY:  ready
      1=drive is ready             0=drive not ready
WFT:  write fault
      1=write fault                0=no write fault
SKC:  head positioning (seek)
      1=complete                   0=in progress
DRQ:  data
      1=can be transferred         0=no data access possible
CORR: correctable data error
      1=data error                 0=not data error
IDX:  disk index
      1=disk index has just passed 0=disk index did not pass
ERR:  error
      1=error register contains error information
      0=error register does not contain error information
```

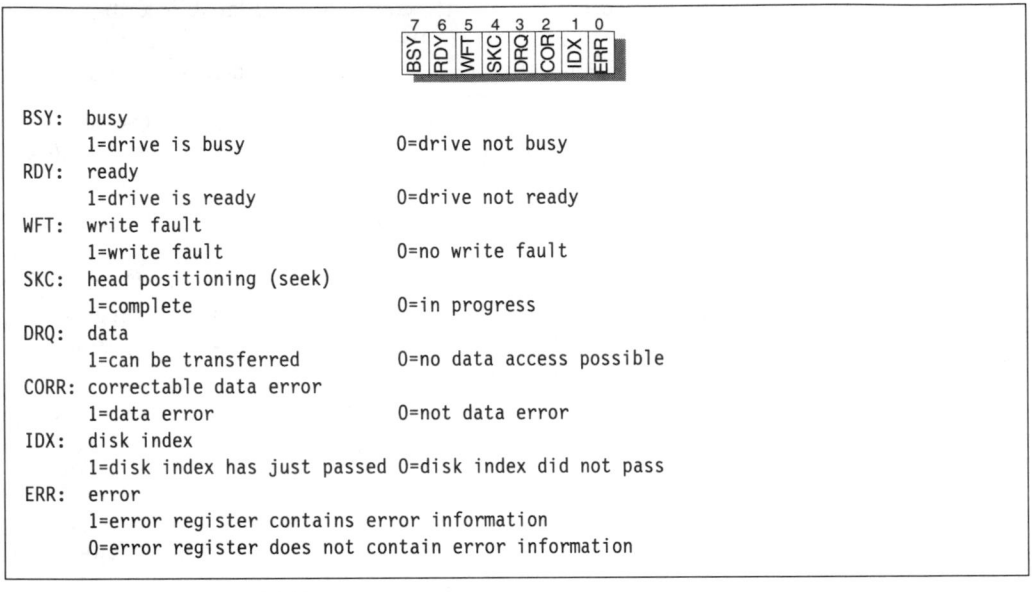

Figure 28.20: Status register (1f7h).

The *BSY* bit is set by the drive to indicate that it is currently executing a command. If BSY is set then no registers may be accessed except the digital output register. In most cases you get any invalid information; under some circumstances you disturb the execution of the active command. A set *RDY* bit shows that the drive has reached the operation rpm value and is ready to accept commands. If the revolution variations of the spindle motor are beyond the tolerable range, for example because of an insufficient supply voltage, then the controller sets the RDY bit to 0. A set *WFT* bit indicates that the controller has detected a write fault. If the *SKC* bit is equal to 1, then the drive has completed the explicit or implicit head positioning. The drive clears the SXC bit immediately before a head seek. A set *DRQ* bit shows that the data register is ready for outputting or accepting data. If DRQ is equal to 0 then you may neither read data from the data register nor write data into it. The controller sets the *CORR* bit to inform the CPU that it has corrected data by means of the ECC bytes. Note that this error condition doesn't abort the reading of several sectors. Upon the passage of the track beginning below the read/write head of the drive, the controller sets the *IDX* bit for a short time. If the *ERR* bit is set, the error register contains additional error information.

The command register (1f7h) passes command codes; the CPU is only able to write to it. The command register is located at the same port address as the read-only status register. The original AT has eight commands in total with several variations. The new IDE standard additionally defines some optional commands, but I want to restrict the discussion to the requested command set which is already implemented on the IBM AT. The execution of a command starts immediately after you have written the command byte into the command register. Thus you have to pass all other required data to the corresponding registers before you start the command execution by writing the command byte.

Command	SC	SN	CY	DR	HD
calibrate drive				xx	
read sector	xx	xx	xx	xx	xx
write sector	xx	xx	xx	xx	xx
verify sector	xx	xx	xx	xx	xx
format track			xx	xx	xx
seek head			xx	xx	xx
diagnostics					
set drive parameters	xx			xx	

SC: sector count SN: sector number CY: cylinder MSB and LSB
DR: drive (in register drive/head)
HD: head (in register drive/head)
xx: parameter necessary for corresponding command

Table 28.15: Command parameter registers

Table 28.15 lists the requested IDE commands as well as the parameter registers that you must prepare for the corresponding commands.

Besides the status register under the port address, additionally an alternate status register is implemented at I/O address 3f6h. It has the same structure as the normal status register, and contains the same information. The only difference between them is that a read-out of the alternate status registers doesn't cancel a pending interrupt request via IRQ14.

Under the same port address 3f6h you also find the digital output register DOR; the CPU is only able to write to it. The DOR defines the controller's behaviour; its structure is shown in Figure 28.21.

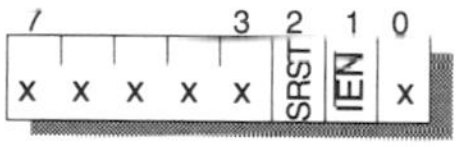

SRST: system reset
1=reset all connected drives 0=accept command
$\overline{\text{IEN}}$: interrupt enable
1=IRQ14 always masked 0=interrupt after every command

Figure 28.21: Digital output register (3f6h).

If you set the *SRST* bit you issue a reset for all connected drives. The reset state remains active until the bit is equal to 1. Once you clear the SRST bit again, the reset drives can accept a command. With the $\overline{\text{IEN}}$ bit you control the interrupt requests of the drives to the CPU. If $\overline{\text{IEN}}$ is cleared (that is, equal to 0) then an interrupt is issued via IRQ14 after every command carried out for one sector, or in advance of entering the result phase. If you set $\overline{\text{IEN}}$ to 1 then IRQ14 is always masked and the drives are unable to issue an interrupt. In this case, the CPU may only supervise the controller by polling.

With the read-only drive address register (3f7h) you may determine which drive and which head are currently active and selected. Figure 28.22 shows the structure of this register.

```
WTGT:     write gate
          1=write gate closed   0=write gate open
HS3-HS0:  currently active head as 1'complement
DS1, DS0: currently selected drive
```

Figure 28.22: Drive address register (3f7h).

If the $\overline{\text{WTGT}}$ bit is cleared (that is, equal to 0), the write gate of the controller is open and the read/write head is currently writing data onto disk. The bits $\overline{\text{HS3}}$–$\overline{\text{HS0}}$ indicate the currently active head as 1'complement. Similarly, the bits $\overline{\text{DS1}}$ and $\overline{\text{DS0}}$ determine the currently selected drive.

28.6.4 IDE Interface Programming and Command Phases

The programming and execution of the commands for an IDE interface proceed similar to a floppy controller or other hard disk interface in three phases:

- Command phase: the CPU prepares the parameter registers and passes the command code to start the execution.
- Data phase: for commands involving disk access, the drive positions the read/write heads and eventually transfers the data between main memory and hard disk.
- Result phase: the controller provides status information for the executed command in the corresponding registers, and issues a hardware interrupt via IRQ14 (corresponding to INT 76h).

The controller's command and register are written and read by the CPU via ports, but unlike the PC/XT, the IBM AT and all compatibles don't use the DMA controller for transferring the sector and format data between main memory and controller. Instead, this data transfer is also carried out by *programmed I/O* via CPU and data register. This means that the CPU writes sector and format data into or reads them from the data register in units of 16 bits. Only the ECC bytes are read and written in 8-bit portions via the low-order byte of the data register. To synchronize CPU and controller for a data exchange, the controller issues a hardware interrupt at various times via IRQ14:

- Read sector: the controller always enables IRQ14 when the CPU is able to read a sector, eventually together with the ECC bytes, from the sector buffer. Unlike all other commands, this command doesn't issue an interrupt at the beginning of the result phase, thus the number of hardware interrupts is the same as the number of read sectors.

- Write sector: the controller always activates IRQ14 when it expects sector data from the CPU. Note that the first sector is transferred immediately after issuing the command, and the controller doesn't issue an interrupt for this purpose. Furthermore, the controller activates, via IRQ14, a hardware interrupt at the beginning of the result phase. Thus the number of hardware interrupts coincides with the number of written sectors.
- All other commands: the controller issues a hardware interrupt via IRQ14 at the beginning of the result phase.

The interrupt handler for INT 76h corresponding to IRQ14 in the PC must therefore be able to determine whether the controller wants to output data, is expecting it or whether an interrupt has occurred which indicates the beginning of a result phase. If you intend to program such a handler, use the status and error register to determine the interrupt source. The IRQ14 controller is disabled as soon as the CPU reads the status register (1f7h). If IRQ14 remains active, you must read the status information via the alternate status register (3f6h).

Note for your programming that the controller of the addressed drive starts command execution immediately after the CPU has written the command code into the command register. Thus you have to load all necessary parameter registers with the required values before you start command execution by passing the command code.

AT Task File Register		Bit 7	6	5	4	3	2	1	0
Command	(1f7h)	0	0	1	1	0	0	L	R
Sector Count	(1f2h)	Number of Sectors to Write							
Sector Number	(1f3h)	S_7	S_6	S_5	S_4	S_3	S_2	S_1	S_0
Cylinder LSB	(1f4h)	C_7	C_6	C_5	C_4	C_3	C_2	C_1	C_0
Cylinder MSB	(1f5h)	0	0	0	0	0	0	C_9	C_8
Drive/Head	(1f6h)	1	0	1	DRV	HD_3	HD_2	HD_1	HD_0

```
L: long
   1=with ECC bytes    0=without ECC bytes
R: retry
   1=carry out retry procedure    0=no retry procedure
sector count: number of sectors to be written onto disk
S7-S0:     sector number (start sector)
C9-C0:     cylinder number (start cylinder)
DRV:       drive
           1=drive 1    0=drive 0
HD3-HD0:   head
           1111=head 15    1110=head 14   ...   0000=head 0
```

Figure 28.23: Write sector command.

Appendix H lists all requested controller commands for the IDE interface, and the three optional commands for identifying the controller as well as reading and writing the sector buffer. As an example one command is discussed here in more detail: write four sectors beginning with cylinder 167, head 3, sector 7 with ECC bytes. The format for this command is shown in Figure 28.23.

If the *L* bit is set then the four ECC bytes are also supplied by the CPU and not generated internally by the controller. The ECC logic then doesn't carry out an ECC check. For a single sector you therefore have to pass 516 bytes. If L is equal to 0 then this means a normal write command. The CPU only passes the 512 data bytes, and the controller generates the four ECC bytes internally and writes them, together with the data bytes, onto disk. The *R* bit controls the internal retry logic of the controller. If R is set, then the controller carries out an in-built retry procedure if it detects a data or address error during the course of the command execution. Only if these retries are also unsuccessful does the controller abort the command and return an error code. If R is cleared, the controller aborts the command immediately without any retry if an error has occurred.

With *sector count* you may determine the number of sectors to be written onto disk. Possible values are between 0 and 255; a value of 0 writes 256 sectors onto disk. The sector numbers *S7–S0* indicate the number of the start sector to be written first. If the number of sectors to write is larger than 1, the controller automatically counts up the sector number until it detects the end of the track. Afterwards, it proceeds with the next head, and eventually with the next cylinder, until all sectors have been written or an error occurs. The values *C9–C0* of the cylinder number define the start cylinder for the write process. The two bits C_9 and C_8 represent the two most significant bits of the 10-bit cylinder number. Using *DRV* you can select one of the two drives, and with HD_3–HD_0 the head of the drive for which the command is to be carried out.

Immediately after the command byte has been written, the controller starts the command execution, that is, the data phase. It sets the BSY bit in the status register to indicate that it has decoded the command and prepared the sector buffer for accommodating the 512 data bytes, as well as the four ECC bytes. If this is finished, the controller clears the BSY bit and sets the DRQ bit in the status register to inform the CPU that it now expects the sector data. The CPU first transfers the 512 data bytes word by word, and afterwards the four ECC bytes byte by byte. If all 516 sector bytes have been passed the controller sets the BSY bit again and clears the DRQ bit. Now it begins to write the data onto disk.

If the first sector has been written then the controller issues an interrupt 76h via IRQ14. The handler concerned now transfers the 516 bytes of the following sector data via the data registers to the controller in the same manner as described above. This process is repeated four times until all four sectors, together with their ECC bytes, have been written.

Example: `Write four sectors starting with cylinder 167, head 3, sector 7 together with ECC bytes onto master drive (language: Microsoft C 5.10).`

```
unsigned int word_buffer[1024];
unsigned char byte_buffer[16];
unsigned int *word_pointer;
unsigned char *byte_pointer;
int int_count;

main()
{ int word_count, byte_count;
  void far *old_irq14;
```

```
  word_pointer = &word_buffer;         /* initialize */
  byte_pointer = &byte_buffer;         /* pointer    */

  init_buffers();                      /* initialize buffer */

  old_irq14=_dos_getvect(0x76);        /* set new interrupt  */
  _dos_setvect(0x76, new_irq14());     /* for IRQ14          */

  while((inp(0x1f7) & 0x80) == 0x80);  /* wait until BSY in status register is cleared */
  outp(0x1f2, 0x04);                   /* register sector count: 4 sectors */
  outp(0x1f3, 0x07);                   /* register sector number: 7 */
  outp(0x1f4, 0xa7);                   /* register cylinder LSB: 167 */
  outp(0x1f5, 0x00);                   /* register cylinder MSB: 0 */
  outp(0x1f6, 0xa3);                   /* register drive/head: DRV=0, head=3 */
  outp(0x1f7, 0x33);                   /* register command: opcode=001100, L=1, R=1 */

  /* write first sector (512 data bytes + 4 ECC bytes */
  while((inp(0x1f7) & 0x80) == 0x80 || (inp(0x1f7) & 0x08) != 0x08);  /* wait until BSY in
                                                  status register is cleared and DRQ is set */
  word_pointer = word_buffer;          /* initialize pointer */
  for (word_count = 0; word_count < 256; word_count++, word_pointer++) {
    outpw(0x1f0, *word_pointer);       /* transfer 256 words = 512 data bytes */
  }

  byte_pointer = byte_buffer;          /* initialize pointer */
  for (byte_count = 0; byte_count < 4; byte_count++, byte_pointer++) {
    outp(0x1f0, *byte_pointer);        /* transfer 4 ECC bytes */
  }

  int_count=0;                         /* initialize interrupt count */

  while (int_count < 4);               /* wait until all four sectors are transferred */
  _dos_setvect(0x76, old_irq14());     /* set old IRQ14 */

  status_check();                      /* check status information and determine error code*/

  exit(0);
}

void interrupt far new_irq14()
{ int word_count, byte_count;

  int_count++;

  if (int_count < 4) {                 /* ignore interrupt at the beginning of result phase */
    for (word_count = 0; word_count < 256; word_count++, word_pointer++) {
      outpw(0x1f0, *word_pointer);     /* transfer 256 words = 512 data bytes */
    }
    for (byte_count = 0; byte_count < 4; byte_count++, byte_pointer++) {
      outp(0x1f0, *byte_pointer);      /* transfer 4 ECC bytes */
    }
  }
  return;
}
```

In the example, the handler for IRQ14 serves only for transferring the data; a more extensive function, for example for determining the interrupt source, is not implemented. The 2048 data bytes in 1024 data words as well as the 16 ECC bytes must be suitably initialized. This is not carried out here because of the lack of space. Furthermore, the procedure status_check() for checking the status information is not listed in detail.

Upon the last interrupt the result phase is entered. Figure 28.24 shows the task file registers that contain valid status information after the command has been completed. The entries in the error register are only valid if the ERR bit in the status register is set and the BSY bit is cleared.

AT Task File Register		Bit 7	6	5	4	3	2	1	0
Error	(1f1h)	NDM	NTO	ABT	x	NID	x	UNC	BBK
Sector Count	(1f2h)	Number of Sectors Written							
Sector Number	(1f3h)	S_7	S_6	S_5	S_4	S_3	S_2	S_1	S_0
Cylinder LSB	(1f4h)	C_7	C_6	C_5	C_4	C_3	C_2	C_1	C_0
Cylinder MSB	(1f5h)	0	0	0	0	0	0	C_9	C_8
Drive/Head	(1f6h)	1	0	1	DRV	HD_3	HD_2	HD_1	HD_0
Status	(1f7h)	BSY	RDY	WFT	SKC	DRQ	COR	IDX	ERR

```
NDM:  1=data address mark not found      0=no error
NTO:  1=track 0 not found                0=no error
ABT:  instruction abort
      1=instruction aborted              0=instruction executed
NID:  1=ID mark not found                0=no error
UNC:  1=not-correctable data error       0=no or correctable data error
BBK:  1=sector marked bad by host        0=no error
DRV:  drive
      1=slave    0=master
```

C_9–C_0, S_7–S_0, HD_3–HD_0: sector identification of last written sector

Figure 28.24: Result phase of «Write Sector» instruction.

According to the sector identification, you can determine the last written sector or the sector which gave rise to the command abortion. The *sector count* register specifies the number of sectors still to be written, that is, a value of 0 if the command has been terminated without any error.

28.6.5 Enhanced IDE

The main advantage of IDE over SCSI is the very simple structure of the host adapter for disk drives using this interface. In fact, the host adapter just switches the AT bus of the PC through to the IDE drive controller. A complicated converting of the signals, or the independent performing of (SCSI) bus cycles, is not necessary. For this reason, IDE adapters and IDE disk drives, for a while, clearly had a price advantage, and so kept their nose in front. Not surprisingly, this has changed in the meantime. On the one hand, both SCSI disk drives and SCSI host adapters have become much better value for money (the price advantage of many IDE boards is purely the result of lower performance and, thus, cheaper drives). On the other hand, the integration of an interface designed for an AT bus into an MCA or local bus system means increased complexity and, therefore, a higher price. So as not to give the advantage to SCSI, the specification has been expanded, and the result is enhanced IDE.

Enhanced IDE is characterized by two essential points: the supporting of disk drives with removable data volume devices; and a higher transfer rate between the host and the disk drive.

The former is achieved with a few new instructions such as medium exchange confirmation (0dbh), secure drive shutter (0deh), release drive shutter (0dfh), and also the MC and MCR bits in the cylinder registers (1f4h/1f5h). In addition, a high-level protocol is planned so that the host adapter can communicate with the disk drive; the SCSI model is easy to spot. Furthermore, it should be possible to connect more than two disk drives to an IDE adapter. For this, a second IDE task file is provided at 170h–177h and 376h–377h, but which should only serve disk drives with a removable data volume device.

The requirement for more performance affects not only the data transfer rate itself (here, the PIO and DMA modes, if available, prove themselves to be bottlenecks), but also the maximum capacity of the IDE hard disk. The most frequently used (and targeted at AT) CHS procedure for addressing a sector (Cylinder Head Sector) limits the capacity to 504 Mbytes (cylinder 1024, head 16, sector 63). The IDE standard itself (that is, the layout of the registers), with 255 sectors per track and a maximum of 65536 cylinders, would still permit 127.5 Gbytes. As a solution, enhanced IDE offers Logical Block Addressing (LBA), similar to SCSI. The disk drive then appears as a continuous medium with sequential blocks. The quite laborious addressing of data by converting it into cylinder, head and sector is no longer necessary as the disk drive controller accomplishes this automatically. This means no additional workload, because the controller must convert the logical into a physical geometry anyway. To activate LBA for an access, you must set the L bit in the disk drive/head register at 1f6h (Figure 28.19). From the 127.5 Gbyte maximum capacity of IDE, more than 7.8 Gbytes remains available for use by the BIOS. During booting, the BIOS uses the identify drive instruction to determine the capacity, but can only cope with a maximum of 1024 cylinders (in place of the 65536 offered by enhanced IDE). Only special drivers can bypass this limitation and allow the full 127.5 Gbytes to be used.

With enhanced IDE, the transfer rate should be greatly increased over that possible in current EISA and local bus systems. For this, a new PIO mode #3 is provided which should (theoretically) perform a transfer in 120 ns. With a 16-bit data bus width to the disk drive, this produces a maximum transfer rate of 16.6 Mbytes/s. The also accelerated DMA block mode #1 transfers a 16 bit data packet within 150 ns; the transfer rate achieved is 13.3 Mbytes/s. Both values, as continuous transfer rates from hard disks, cannot yet be achieved, so there is still a little breathing space in the IDE standard for a few years yet to come.

28.7 SCSI

A very flexible and powerful option for connecting hard disks to a PC is SCSI (*small computer systems interface*). The term itself indicates that SCSI is intended for the PC and other small systems (for example, workstations or the Mac). However, the characterization of PCs and workstations as «small» has changed, at least as far as MIPS numbers are concerned, since the Pentium has been on the market. SCSI was derived from the SASI interface of Shugart

Associates (Shugart Associates systems interface). SCSI comes with a somewhat older standard SCSI-I, which is not strict enough in some aspects, resulting in compability problems when implementing SCSI-I. The new standard SCSI-II determines the properties more precisely, and additionally defines some more commands and operation modes. SCSI follows a different philosophy to those hard disk interfaces already discussed; this section gives more information on this subject.

28.7.1 SCSI Bus and Connection to the PC

SCSI defines a bus between a maximum of eight units, as well as the protocol for data exchange among them. Such SCSI units may be hard disks, tape drives, optical drives, or any other device that fulfills the SCSI specification. Thus, SCSI drives are intelligent, as are the IDE hard disks; the unit's controller is always integrated on the drive. For connection to the PC a *SCSI host adapter* is required, which establishes the connection to the PC's system bus similar to the IDE interface. The host adapter itself is also a SCSI unit, so that only seven «free» units remain. Unlike an IDE host adapter, the SCSI host adapter is thus rather complex, as it must recognize all the functions of the SCSI bus and be able to carry them out. But the advantage is that SCSI is not limited to the AT bus. There are also host adapters for EISA or the Mac. The enormous data transfer rate as well as the high-end performance of the SCSI hard disks doesn't suggest its use in a PC/XT, however. With an accordingly adapted host adapter the same SCSI devices can also be integrated into workstations or an Apple. The Mac has a SCSI interface as standard to connect up to seven external SCSI devices. Apple thus elegantly bypasses its lack of flexibility compared with the IBM-compatible PCs.

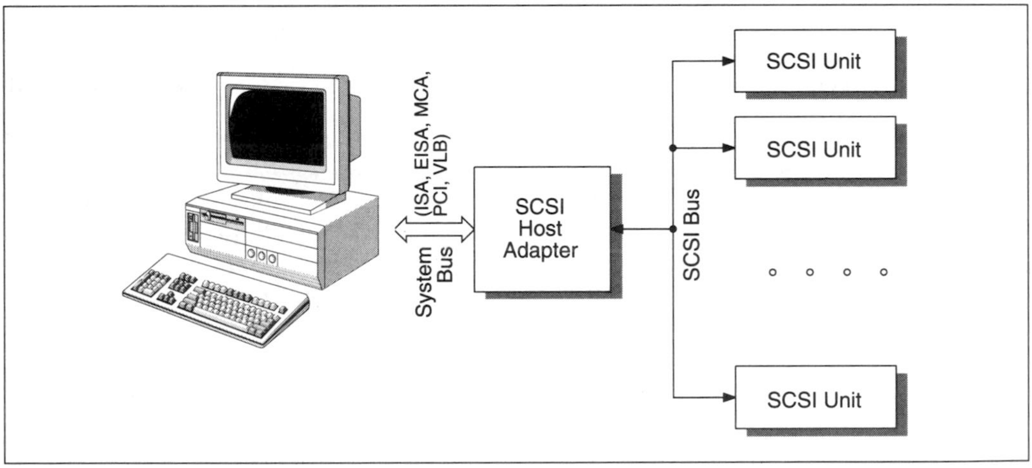

Figure 28.25: SCSI bus and PC integration. The SCSI bus is connected to the PC system bus by a SCSI host adapter. Up to seven SCSI units can be served.

Thus the SCSI bus serves only for a data exchange among the SCSI units connected to the bus. A maximum of two units may be active and exchange data at any one time. The data exchange can be carried out between host adapter and a drive, or (as a special feature of SCSI) also between two other SCSI devices (for example, a tape drive and a hard disk). It is remarkable that this data exchange is carried out without the slightest intervention from the CPU; the SCSI drives are intelligent enough to do this on their own. Figure 28.25 shows a scheme of the SCSI bus in the case of integrating SCSI into a PC.

Every SCSI unit is assigned a SCSI address, which you can set by a jumper on the drive. Addresses in the range 0–7 are valid; according to the SCSI standard, address 7 is reserved for a tape drive. The address is formed by bytes where the least significant bit 0 corresponds to the address or SCSI-ID 0, and the most significant bit 7 to the address or SCSI-ID 7. SCSI addresses are transferred via the data section of the SCSI bus (see Table 28.16).

But don't confuse the SCSI address or SCSI-ID with the logical unit number (LUN). Every target can accommodate up to eight logical units, which you identify in a SCSI command with the LUN. An example of this would be a SCSI controller which serves several drives. The controller establishes the connection to the SCSI bus, and further carries out all control functions. Thus the controller is the target. Additionally, the target is assigned several drives (the logical units), which are distinguished by the LUN. Today, external SCSI controllers are rare; most hard disks and also other drives integrate the SCSI controller directly. If you attempt to access such a hard disk you always have to set LUN to a value of 0, as the drive is the first and only logical unit of the target.

Be careful not to cause an address conflict between two drives. The controller of a drive determines its SCSI address at power-up, and then responds to commands that concern this SCSI address. As the host adapter is a SCSI unit, too, with a corresponding SCSI address, several host adapters may access the same SCSI bus. In this way, it is possible for several PCs to share a common SCSI bus, and thus the same drives. They can exchange data via the host adapters without the need for the usual network. Unfortunately, the SCSI bus is restricted to a length of 6 m; a value which is still quite high when compared to the IDE cables with their maximum of about 0.5 m.

The connection between SCSI units is established by means of a 50-wire flat conductor cable with 50-pole plugs. You may also see cables with 25 twisted cable pairs; here one ground line is always twisted around one signal line, similar to Centronics cables. Table 28.16 shows the assignment of the lines and plug pins.

Like all other bus systems for connecting drives (floppy, hard disk, etc.), the SCSI bus must also be terminated by a resistor. This is carried out by removing or disabling the terminating resistor on all but the last drive on the bus. Most SCSI host adapters have a jack for connecting external SCSI devices (typically a scanner, an external SCSI hard disk, or a WORM). Usually the host adapter is one end of the bus and, thus, also incorporates a terminating resistor. If you connect one or more external SCSI devices to the external jack, and if at least one more internal device is present, you must remove or disable the terminating resistor of the host adapter, because now the adapter no longer forms the end of the SCSI bus. Instead, the SCSI bus is guided through the host adapter. Generally speaking, the terminating resistors must always be present at both ends of the bus. Dependent upon the configuration, one of these ends is formed by the host adapter, the last internal SCSI device or the last external device. For the earlier adapters

(ST412/506, ESDI and IDE), external devices have not been allowed; there the host adapter or controller always forms one of the two ends of the bus.

Signal	Pin	Meaning			
GND	1	ground	TERMPWR	26	termination
$\overline{\text{DB(0)}}$	2	data bit 0	GND	27	ground
GND	3	ground	GND	28	ground
$\overline{\text{DB(1)}}$	4	data bit 1	GND	29	ground
GND	5	ground	GND	30	ground
$\overline{\text{DB(2)}}$	6	data bit 2	GND	31	ground
GND	7	ground	$\overline{\text{ATN}}$	32	attention
$\overline{\text{DB(3)}}$	8	data bit 3	GND	33	ground
GND	9	ground	GND	34	ground
$\overline{\text{DB(4)}}$	10	data bit 4	GND	35	ground
GND	11	ground			
$\overline{\text{DB(5)}}$	12	data bit 5			
GND	13	ground			
$\overline{\text{DB(6)}}$	14	data bit 6			
GND	15	ground	$\overline{\text{BSY}}$	36	busy
$\overline{\text{DB(7)}}$	16	data bit 7	GND	37	ground
GND	17	ground	$\overline{\text{ACK}}$	38	acknowledge
$\overline{\text{DB(P)}}$	18	parity bit	GND	39	ground
GND	19	ground	$\overline{\text{RST}}$	40	reset
GND	20	ground	GND	41	ground
GND	21	ground	$\overline{\text{MSG}}$	42	message
GND	22	ground	GND	43	ground
GND	23	ground	$\overline{\text{SEL}}$	44	select
GND	24	ground	GND	45	ground
1)	25	–	$\overline{\text{C/D}}$	46	command/data
			GND	47	ground
			$\overline{\text{REQ}}$	48	request
			GND	49	ground
			$\overline{\text{I/O}}$	50	I/O

1) no connection

Table 28.16: SCSI interface cable layout

As you can see from Table 28.16, eight data bits $\overline{\text{DB(0)}}$–$\overline{\text{DB(7)}}$ together with one parity bit $\overline{\text{DB(P)}}$ and nine control signals are transferred. The SCSI logic generates the parity bit automatically if the unit supports parity; this is not always the case. Using a jumper, you can often determine whether the parity bit should be generated and checked. All signals are active low. TERMPWR drains surplus charges and damps the SCSI bus. Although the data bus has only eight bits, SCSI is designed for a data transfer rate of up to 4 Mbytes/s in asynchronous and 10 Mbytes/s in synchronous (fast) mode. In asynchronous mode, handshake signals are used for data exchange; in synchronous mode the data transfer is carried out with the handshake signals as clock signals, which leads to a higher transfer rate. But note that not all SCSI units support the synchronous mode. Only in the drives orienting to the SCSI-II standard is the synchronous mode implemented. Moreover, the indicated data transfer rates refer only to the SCSI bus. At which speed the data is passed from or into the PC's main memory via the PC system bus is another question, and it is not determined by the SCSI transfer rates. The overall transfer rate essentially depends upon the quality of the host adapter and the firmware in the adapter's ROM BIOS; a realistic value is 5 Mbyte/s at most. Also, it is decisive, of course, at which speed the data can be read from disk or tape. The principle of the data transfer on a SCSI bus is shown in Figure 28.26.

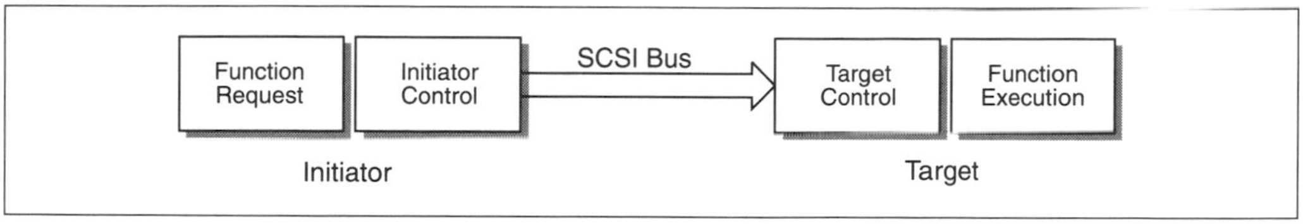

Figure 28.26: Data transfer on the SCSI bus.

Any SCSI unit can carry out the function of an *initiator* and take control of the SCSI bus by means of control signals. With a SCSI address the initiator activates a certain unit called the *target* which carries out certain funtions. It is of further importance that the initiator occupies the SCSI bus only for command and data transfer, otherwise the bus is free and can be used by other SCSI units. This also applies if the target unit carries out a command (for example, reading a block), and during this time doesn't require a connection to the initiator. Following the command execution, the target unit establishes the connection to the initiator again and transfers the data. The control of the bus is executed by the following control signals:

- $\overline{\text{BSY}}$ (busy): the signal indicates whether the bus is currently busy.
- $\overline{\text{SEL}}$ (select): the signal is used by the initiator to select the target device; on the contrary, the target may also use SEL to re-establish the connection to the initiator after a temporary release of the bus control.
- $\overline{\text{C/D}}$ (control/data): the signal is exclusively controlled by the target, and indicates whether control information or data is present on the SCSI bus. An active signal (with a low level) denotes control information.
- $\overline{\text{I/O}}$ (input/output): the signal is exclusively controlled by the target device, and indicates the direction of the data flow on the data bus relative to the initiator. An active signal (with a low level) means a data transfer to the initiator.
- $\overline{\text{MSG}}$ (message): the signal is activated by the target during the message phase of the SCSI bus.
- $\overline{\text{REQ}}$ (request): the signal is activated by the target unit to indicate the handshake request during the course of a $\overline{\text{REQ}}/\overline{\text{ACK}}$ data transfer.
- $\overline{\text{ACK}}$ (acknowledge): the signal is activated by the initiator to indicate the handshake acknowledge during the course of a $\overline{\text{REQ}}/\overline{\text{ACK}}$ data transfer.
- $\overline{\text{ATN}}$ (attention): an initiator activates the signal to indicate the attention condition.
- $\overline{\text{RST}}$ (reset): an active signal resets all connected SCSI devices.

You may already recognize that an extensive activation and deactivation procedure with a data transfer by means of handshake signals is carried out. The following sections discuss the various phases of the SCSI bus, but note that they are only of importance during the course of a data transfer via the SCSI bus. The CPU access to a SCSI device is only affected by this indirectly, as the SCSI logic implemented in the host adapter detects the various bus phases and generates the corresponding control signal automatically. The SCSI bus recognizes eight bus phases in total:

- bus-free
- arbitration
- selection
- reselection
- command
- data
- message
- status.

The last four bus phases (command, data, message and status) together are also called the information transfer phase.

Bus-Free Phase

This bus phase indicates that no SCSI unit is currently using and controlling the bus, thus the SCSI bus may be taken over by any connected SCSI unit. This phase is effective when both $\overline{\text{SEL}}$ and $\overline{\text{BSY}}$ are disabled (high).

Arbitration Phase

In this bus phase a SCSI unit may take control of the bus so that the unit acts as an initiator or target for a bus operation. For this purpose the following procedure is carried out:

- The SCSI bus must be in the bus-free phase as otherwise no unit except the active one is able to take control of the bus; thus $\overline{\text{BSY}}$ and $\overline{\text{SEL}}$ are both active.
- The unit activates $\overline{\text{BSY}}$ and puts its SCSI-ID onto the data bus.
- After a short arbitration delay, the unit investigates the data bus. If another SCSI-ID with a higher priority is active (that is, with a higher SCSI-ID number than its own), then the unit is not allowed to take control of the bus. If this is not the case, then the unit may control the bus; it has won the arbitration and activates $\overline{\text{SEL}}$.
- After a short bus-clear delay, the SCSI unit is now able to control the SCSI bus and change the bus signals.

Selection Phase

In this phase an initiator selects a target unit and advises the target to carry out certain functions (for example, reading and writing data blocks). During the selection phase, the $\overline{\text{I/O}}$ signal is inactive to distinguish this phase from the reselection phase of a target. The initiator now outputs the OR-value of its SCSI-ID and the SCSI-ID of the target onto the data bus. Therefore, the two data bits which characterize initiator and target are active.

The thus addressed target must now detect that it has been selected by an initiator and activate $\overline{\text{BSY}}$ within a certain time period. If this doesn't happen, then the selection phase has failed and the initiator deactivates $\overline{\text{SEL}}$; the SCSI bus enters the bus-free phase. As the initiator has also output its own SCSI-ID besides the target-ID onto the data bus, the target unit is able to identify the initiator. This is important so that the target unit, after a bus-free phase, can activate the correct initiator in the following reselection phase.

Reselection Phase

With the reselection phase a target may re-establish the connection with the original initiator to continue the interrupted operation. This is the case, for example, if a host adapter issues a read command to a target drive. Head positioning and reading the sector concerned takes up to 40 ms, even on fast hard disks; this is a very long time for a computer. Therefore, the target unit releases the SCSI bus and carries out head positioning and reading on its own, but remembers the initiator's SCSI-ID. Thus a bus-free phase occurs, which other devices may use to exchange data. If the target drive has completed the read operation, then it re-establishes the contact to the original initiator by means of a reselection phase and transfers the read data.

The reselection phase proceeds similar to an arbitration and selection phase. The target unit takes over the SCSI bus in an arbitration phase of the SCSI bus, activates $\overline{\text{BSY}}$, $\overline{\text{SEL}}$ and then the $\overline{\text{I/O}}$ signal to identify the phase as a reselection phase and itself as the target. Afterwards, the target outputs its own SCSI-ID and that of the original initiator. The initiator detects that it is selected, and sets up the connection to the target again; now the data exchange can start.

During the course of the four information transfer phases command, data, message and status, phase data and control information are transferred via the data bus. The signals $\overline{\text{C/D}}$, $\overline{\text{I/O}}$ and $\overline{\text{MSG}}$ are used to distinguish the individual transfer phases. If $\overline{\text{I/O}}$ is active, then information is transferred from the target to the initiator, otherwise the data transfer proceeds in the opposite direction. Each data transfer in one of these four phases is carried out by handshake. The transmitter puts the data onto the data bus $\overline{\text{DB(0)}}$–$\overline{\text{DB(7)}}$, and eventually the parity information onto $\overline{\text{DB(P)}}$, and activates $\overline{\text{REQ}}$ to indicate the validity of the data to the receiver. The receiver fetches the data and activates $\overline{\text{ACK}}$ afterwards to inform the transmitter that the data has been accepted. As a result, the transmitter deactivates $\overline{\text{REQ}}$. Now the receiver also negates the signal $\overline{\text{ACK}}$ (that is, both handshake signals are deactivated), and the next transfer of a data byte by means of a handshake can be carried out.

It is important here that the target unit controls the three signals $\overline{\text{C/D}}$, $\overline{\text{I/O}}$ and $\overline{\text{MSG}}$. The initiator, though, may request a message-out phase by activating $\overline{\text{ATN}}$. Table 28.17 shows the connections between the $\overline{\text{MSG}}$, $\overline{\text{C/D}}$ and $\overline{\text{I/O}}$ signals on the one hand, as well as the phase and transfer directions on the other.

$\overline{\text{MSG}}$	$\overline{\text{C/D}}$	$\overline{\text{I/O}}$	Phase	Transfer direction
0	0	0	data-out	initiator→ target
0	0	1	data-in	target→ initiator
0	1	0	command	initiator→ target
0	1	1	status	target→ initiator
1	0	0	invalid	–
1	0	1	invalid	–
1	1	0	message-out	initiator→ target
1	1	1	message-in	target→ initiator

Table 28.17: SCSI bus phases

Command Phase

In the command phase the addressed target may request command data from the initiator. For this purpose, the target unit activates the $\overline{\text{C/D}}$ signal and deactivates the $\overline{\text{MSG}}$ and $\overline{\text{I/O}}$ signals. The initiator now transfers the command data.

Data Phase

During the course of the data phase, the target may instruct the initiator to transfer data to the target (the data-out phase), or it can provide data for the initiator (the data-in phase).

Message Phase

In the message phase, the target may advise the initiator to transfer messages to the target (the message-out phase), or it can provide messages for the initiator (the message-in phase).

Status Phase

During the course of the status phase, the target supplies status information to the initiator.

Besides the control signals for issuing the various phases, there are the two further signals, $\overline{\text{ATN}}$ (attention) and $\overline{\text{RST}}$ (reset). With $\overline{\text{ATN}}$ the initiator informs the target that it intends to pass a message. The target fetches the message with a message-out phase. However, the target can transfer a message simply by issuing a message-in phase; only the initiator uses the attention signal. When a SCSI unit activates the $\overline{\text{RST}}$ signal, all units are separated from the SCSI bus, all operations are aborted, and the units are set to a defined state.

According to the SCSI specification every initiator implements two sets of three pointers each, called the *current pointers* and the *saved pointers*, respectively. The current pointers point to the next command, data and status byte which are to be transferred between the initiator and the target. They are used by the target currently connected to the initiator. As the connection between initiator and target can be interrupted during an active command and re-established later (reselection phase), the saved pointers are also of further importance. For every active command there is in fact a set of saved pointers, independently of whether the corresponding connection between initiator and target is currently established. The saved command pointer points to the beginning of the command block for the active command, and the saved status pointer to the beginning of the status area of the active command. The pointers are usually realized by means of registers, which accommodate the corresponding pointer values.

At the beginning of every command the saved data pointer refers to the beginning of the data area until the target unit passes the initiator a message *save data pointer*. Upon this instruction, the initiator shifts the current data pointer into the saved data pointer. Inversely, the target may load the active pointer with the saved pointer by passing the initiator the message *restore pointer*. If a SCSI unit is separated from the bus, only the saved pointers are kept; the active ones are reloaded with new values upon connection with another unit. If the separated SCSI unit is reconnected to the initiator by a reselection phase, then the current pointers are restored from the saved ones. Messages coordinate the connection of the various SCSI units, and pass status information indicating the state of the currently active commands. Thus the protocol of the SCSI bus comprises the physical control signals as well as the logical messages. On the other hand, the commands of the command phase issue certain operations of the SCSI target unit and do not determine the connection of initiator and target. It is only essential for the SCSI units to support the message *command complete* (00h); all other messages are optional.

An initiator informs the target that it also supports the other messages by activating the $\overline{\text{ATN}}$ signal in the course of the selection phase before $\overline{\text{SEL}}$ is activated and $\overline{\text{BSY}}$ is disabled. Then the first message of the initiator to the target after the selection phase is the identification, in the same way as the target must pass the initiator this message after a reselection phase. The SCSI standard defines the following messages:

- Command complete (00h): the target passes the initiator this message in a message-in phase to indicate whether or not a command or a linked command has been completed successfully, and status information has been transferred to the initiator during the course of a status phase. After transferring this message, the target enters the bus-free phase.
- Extended message (01h, xxh): the extended message indicates that further message codes are following. The second xxh byte determines how many bytes are following after xxh. Usually, the first byte after xxh defines the message subcode.
- Save data pointer (02h): the target passes the initiator this message to instruct it to save the current data pointers for the currently connected SCSI unit in the saved data pointers.
- Restore data pointers (03h): the target passes the initiator this message to instruct it to restore the current data pointers from the saved ones.
- Separate (04h): the target passes the initiator this message to indicate that the target is going to interrupt the current connection, that is, to deactivate $\overline{\text{BSY}}$. Later, a new connection is required by means of the reselection phase to complete the command successfully.
- Error at initiator (05h): the message indicates that the initiator has detected an error.
- Abortion (06h): the initiator transfers this message to the target to advise it to abort the current operation, to delete the current data and status information, and to enter the bus-free phase.
- Message rejected (07h): this message can be supplied by the initiator or the target to indicate that the last received message was invalid, or is not implemented in the SCSI unit.
- No operation (08h): the message has no result.
- Message parity error (09h): the message received before shows a parity error.
- Linked command complete (0ah): the target outputs the message to the initiator to indicate that a linked command has been completed, and that status information has been transferred to the initiator during the course of a status phase.
- Linked command with flag complete (0bh): the target outputs the message to the initiator to indicate that a linked command with a set flag has been completed, and that status information has been transferred to the initiator during the course of a status phase.
- Reset bus unit (0ch): the message is passed to the target by the initiator to reset the target.

- Abort tag process (0dh): the message instructs the target to abort the active tag process of a queue. Unlike the message 0eh, here only the currently active process is aborted.
- Clear queue (0eh): this message instructs the target to abort all tag processes of a queue.
- Terminate I/O process (11h): the message instructs the target to terminate (not to abort) the active I/O process as fast as possible.
- Single queue tag (20h): the assigned process can be inserted into the queue by the target at any location. Thus, the target is able to optimize the execution of several initiator requests. The order of such processes can be changed even after the insertion into the queue.
- Tag as queue head (21h): the message instructs the target to insert the assigned process at the beginning of the queue, that is, the process has highest priority and is started as soon as the current process has been terminated or interrupted.
- Ordered queue tag (22h): the assigned process is inserted by the target into the queue and is executed exactly at that location. The order of such processes cannot be changed after the insertion into the queue.
- Ignore wide rest (23h): even if wide mode is active, sometimes the target or initiator does not transfer parameter lists or data as a multiple of two and four bytes, respectively. The receiver must ignore part of the wide SCSI bus. This is achieved by this message.
- Identify (80h to ffh): the message is output by the initiator or target for its own identification. Bit 7 of the message is always set to characterize it as an identification. The remaining seven bits contain the identification code (see Figure 28.27).

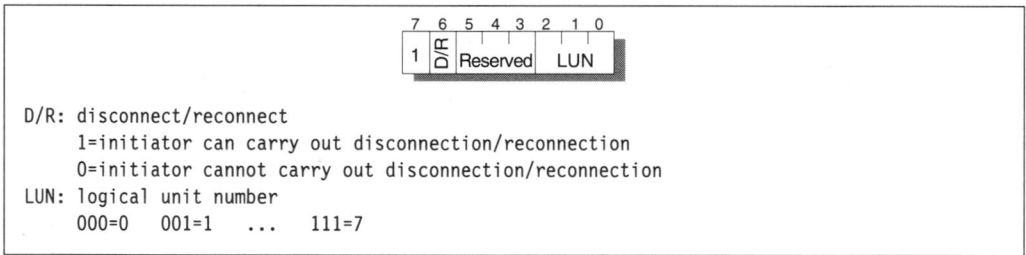

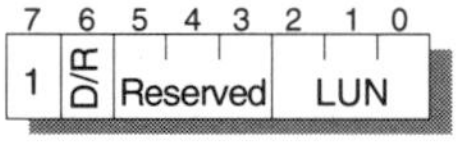


```
D/R: disconnect/reconnect
     1=initiator can carry out disconnection/reconnection
     0=initiator cannot carry out disconnection/reconnection
LUN: logical unit number
     000=0   001=1   ...   111=7
```

Figure 28.27: Identification code.

Additional to the listed messages, SCSI-II implements the following extended messages:

- Change data pointer (01h, 05h, 00h): two more bytes follow after the message subcode 00h; they are added to the current data pointer value.
- Request synchronous mode (01h, 03h, 01h): with this message, a SCSI unit is able to indicate that it wants to use synchronous data transfer. The bytes following after the subcode 01h determine the transfer time (in multiples of 4 ns) and the REQ/ACK delay. Only if the partner also responds with this message is the synchronous mode actually enabled.
- Request wide mode (01h, 02h, 03h): with this message (subcode 03h), a SCSI unit indicates that it wants to use 16- or 32-bit transfer (4th message byte equal to 01h and 02h, respecti-

vely). The partner also responds with such a message, and indicates its own width capability. The lesser of the capabilities is used.

Besides the messages the target also transfers a status code to the initiator once a command has been completed. Figure 28.28 shows the structure of this status byte.

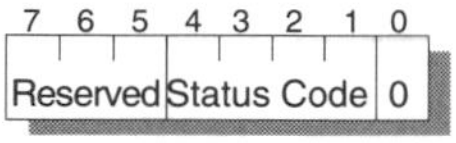


```
Status code: 0000=o.k.     0001=check status     0100=busy
             1000=intermediate status/o.k.       1100=reservation conflict
```

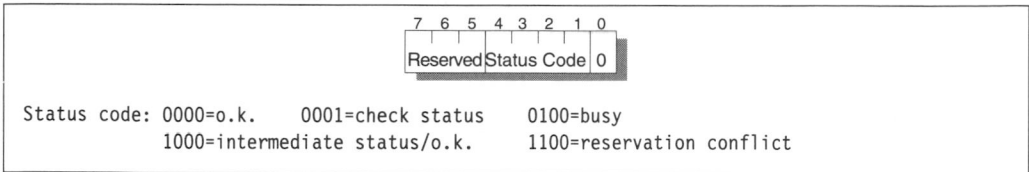

Figure 28.28: Status code.

The code 0000 indicates that the SCSI unit has executed the command successfully. If a *check status* code is output then an error, an exception, or an abnormal command termination has occurred. You should use the command request sense to determine the cause of this condition. If the target is busy, the status code 0100 is passed. If a linked command is active, the target passes the status code 1000 for every completed individual command except the last one. Thus the status code 1000 confirms the link and takes care that the command sequence is not interrupted. If an error occurs, the status code 0001 is supplied and the linked command is aborted. Finally, a code 1100 means a reservation conflict, that is, a SCSI device has attempted to access a logical unit that is already reserved for another SCSI unit.

Messages are usually not accessible for you as the programmer; they only coordinate the SCSI units among themselves. You can see that SCSI defines a high-level protocol that is not only based on physical signals but also on logical messages. SCSI is therefore very flexible; but presently there is a lack of a strictly defined standard for connecting the SCSI bus to the system bus of a PC. All users of an operating system or an operating system extension (for example, UNIX, OS/2 or Windows) running at least partially in protected mode could tell you a thing or two about that! The problem here is not the SCSI standard, but the appropriate programming of the host adapter to get an access.

The following two sections therefore discuss the programming of the SCSI host adapters ST01 and ST02. With these you may transfer data via the SCSI bus to or from your PC's main memory to access, for example, SCSI hard disks or tape drives.

28.7.2 Memory-Mapped I/O and SCSI Task File of Host Adapters ST01 and ST02

The two host adapters only differ in that the ST02 additionally has a floppy controller for a maximum of two drives; the ST01 does not. All SCSI functions of these host adapters are identical. If, in the following, the host adapter is discussed then the information concerned is also valid for the ST02. The adapters come in two versions, each with an 8 kbyte or a 16 kbyte BIOS. The following description is restricted to an ST01 with an 8 kbyte BIOS. For the other adapter and BIOS sizes the analogous information applies. You can configure the adapters by means of a jumper so that they issue a hardware interrupt via IRQ3 or IRQ5 if another SCSI unit activates the SEL line of the SCSI bus, for example the target for reselecting the initiator.

Both host adapters operate with so-called *memory-mapped I/O* to allow an access to their internal control and status registers. With memory-mapped I/O the registers concerned are located in the normal memory address space of the CPU; thus they are accessed with common memory commands (for example, MOV). With *I/O-mapped I/O*, on the other hand, the registers are addressed via port addresses (that is, IN and OUT instructions); the registers are located in the CPU's I/O address space. It seems to be impossible at first glance to access a control register by means of a memory command. But remember that the access to a memory chip is carried out in the same way as that to the I/O address space by means of electrical signals. And these signals don't care whether the transistor of a memory cell or the transistor of a register is on the end of the line. Apple Macs, for example, use only memory-mapped I/O, while on the PC most register accesses are carried out by means of I/O-mapped I/O because of Intel's processor architecture and the powerful I/O protection mechanisms in protected mode.

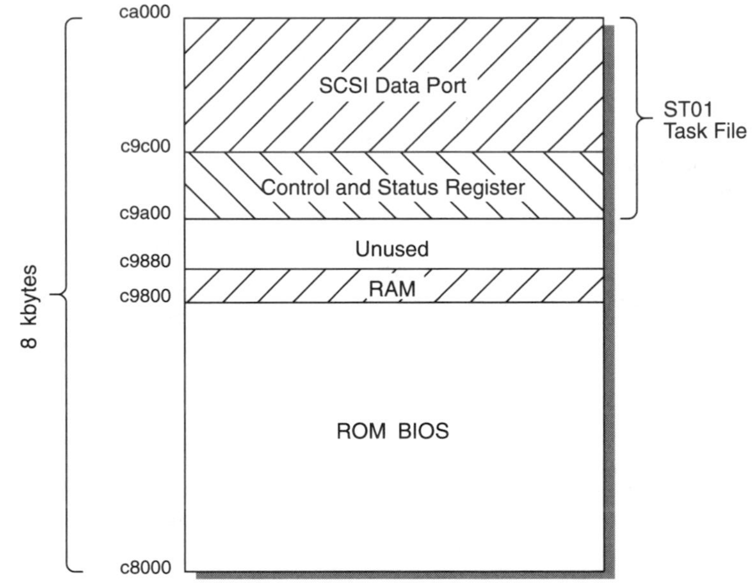

Figure 28.29: Memory organization of an ST01 with 8 k bytes ROM BIOS.

Besides a ROM BIOS with the INT 13h routines and internal diagnostics and initialization programs, the host adapter has a control and status register as well as a SCSI data port and static RAM, which are all in a continuous address area. As is the case for most adapters with their own BIOS, you may also select the start address by means of a jumper on the ST01. The following description therefore uses that value as the base address, where usually the ROM BIOS of a hard disk controller begins (namely c8000h or segment c800h). Figure 28.29 shows the corresponding address organization for an ST01 with 8 kbytes of ROM BIOS. Thus all addresses of BIOS, registers, and RAM are located within a range of 8 k.

Between the addresses c8000h and c9800h there is the ROM BIOS comprising a maximum of 6 kbytes of code and data. The 128 bytes above are occupied by the RAM, which is used by the BIOS routines for temporarily storing data. Thus the ST01 adapter doesn't use any system memory for executing its in-built routines. You can, of course, read and write this adapter RAM on your own, but the results cannot be predicted. The control and status register area starts at c9a00h and comprises 512 bytes. Finally, the 1024 bytes at c9c00h accommodate the SCSI data port for transmitting and receiving data from the SCSI bus. Note that you must not move the area of the control and status register and the SCSI data port by shadowing into RAM, although they are located in the ROM address area. The registers are physically present at this address. If the addresses are detoured during the course of shadowing, then memory chips are present at these addresses and not the required adapter registers (remember that memory-mapped I/O is used here).

If you carry out a write process with an address between c9a00h and c9bffh, you automatically write the control register. If you read data from the same address range (for example, by an instruction *MOV memory, register*), you automatically read the status register. Thus for an access to these two adapter registers the nine least significant address bits are not decoded. The same applies for the SCSI data port through which you may read or write data bytes from or onto the SCSI bus. A read or write access to the address range between c9c00h and cbfffh leads directly to an access to the data bits of the SCSI bus; here the ten least significant address bits are not decoded. The advantage is that you can rapidly read or write a complete data block using the string instructions and the prefix *REP* without the need to initialize the address for every byte. The structure of the control register is shown in Figure 28.30, that of the status register in Figure 28.31.

7	6	5	4	3	2	1	0
SCSI ENAB	INTR ENAB	PAR ENAB	ARB STRT	SCSI ATTN	SCSI BUSY	SCSI SEL	SCSI RST

```
SCSI ENAB: SCSI bus enable
           1=SCSI bus drivers of host adapter enabled   0=disabled
INTR ENAB: interrupt enable
           1=interrupt is issued when SEL line active
           0=interrupt disabled
PAR ENAB:  SCSI parity
           1=generate and check parity bit          0=not parity check
ARB STRT:  SCSI arbitration
           1=start arbitration, ARB line of SCSI bus active (low)
           0=inactive (high)
SCSI ATTN: SCSI attention
           1=ATN line of SCSI bus active (low)      0=inactive (high)
SCSI BUSY: 1=BSY line of SCSI bus active (low)      0=inactive (high)
SCSI SEL:  SCSI selection
           1=SEL line of SCSI bus active (low)      0=inactive (high)
SCSI RST:  SCSI reset
           1=reset all SCSI units
```

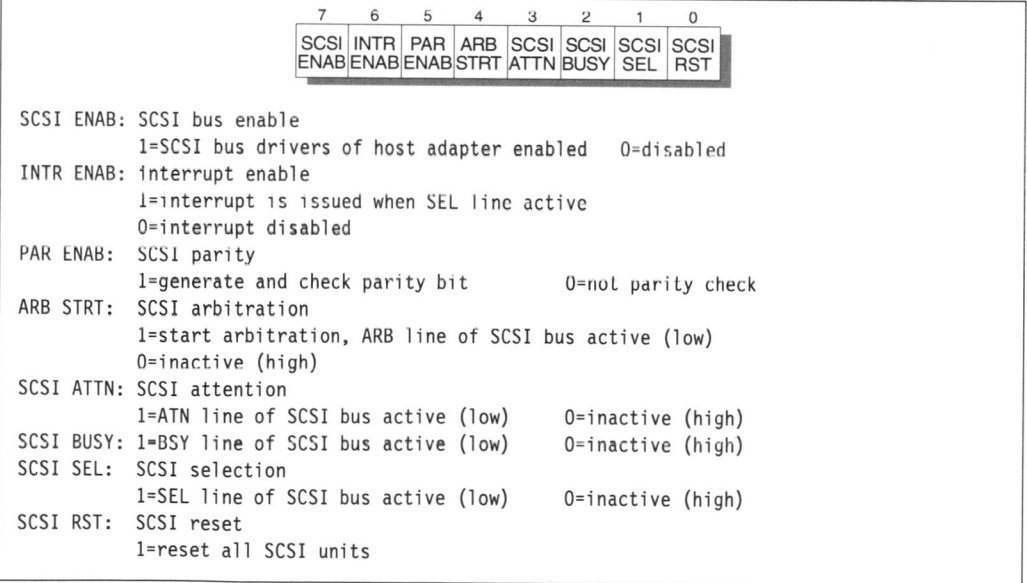

Figure 28.30: ST01 control register (c9a00h to c9bffh).

Using the control register you may control certain control lines of the SCSI bus directly, besides adapter activation. The *SCSI ENAB* bit advises the host adapter to drive the data bits of the SCSI bus to output data. The same is carried out implicitly when you start an arbitration phase with ARB STRT; the host adapter as the initiator then puts its SCSI-ID onto the SCSI bus. If the *INTR ENAB* bit is set, the host adapter issues an interrupt via IRQ3 or IRQ5 if another SCSI unit activates the SEL line of the SCSI bus. The handler serves a reselection phase of a previously addressed target or completes an arbitration phase. *PAR ENAB* enables the parity generator on the host adapter so that it generates a parity bit upon every data transfer to a target. The *ARB STRT* bit starts an arbitration phase of the host adapter to establish a connection to a target. The remaining four bits *SCSI ATTN*, *SCSI BUSY*, *SCSI SEL* and *SCSI RST* directly control the signals on the corresponding lines of the SCSI bus. A set bit leads to an activated SCSI line, that is, to a low level.

Example: `Reset all SCSI units by means of an active RST line.`

```
MOV ax, c800h;        ; load control register segment via
MOV es, ax            ; ax into extra segment register es
MOV ES:[1b00], 01h    ; output set SCSI RST bit via an
                      ; address between c9a00h and c9bffh
```

7	6	5	4	3	2	1	0
ARB CMPL	SCSI PARF	SCSI SEL	SCSI REQ	SCSI C/D	SCSI I/O	SCSI MSG	SCSI RST

```
ARB CMPL:  arbitration complete
           1=host adapter took over control of SCSI bus
SCSI PARF: SCSI parity error
           1=parity error when reading data    0=no parity error
SCSI SEL:  SEL line status of SCSI bus
           1=selection phase
SCSI REQ:  REQ line status of SCSI bus
           1=request in REQ/ACK handshake
SCSI C/D:  C/D line status of SCSI bus
           1=command phase      0=data-out or data-in phase
SCSI I/O:  I/O line status of SCSI bus
           1=in phase           0=out phase
SCSI MSG:  MSG line status of SCSI bus
           1=message phase
SCSI RST:  RST line status of SCSI bus
           1=reset all SCSI units
```

Figure 28.31: ST01 status register (c9a00h to c9bffh).

The status register, which is located in the same address area as the control register, reads status information concerning host adapter operations and the signals on SCSI control lines (see Figure 28.31).

If the *ARB CMPL* bit is set then the SCSI host adapter has completed the arbitration phase and taken over control of the SCSI bus as the initiator. Now you can transfer a command block via the SCSI data port to the SCSI bus and thus to the target. If a parity error occurs during the course of a read process then the adapter sets the *SCSI PARF* bit. All other bits *SCSI SEL, SCSI REQ, SCSI C/D, SCSI I/O, SCSI MSG* and *SCSI RST* directly indicate the status of the corresponding control lines of the SCSI bus. According to this information, you may determine whether the target, for example, expects data or attempts to output a message to the initiator, that is, the host adapter. It is up to you to handle the corresponding situations by suitably programming the SCSI data port and the control register according to the SCSI protocol.

Example: `read status register`

```
MOV ax, c800h;       ; load control register segment via
MOV es, ax           ; ax into extra segment register es
MOV ah, ES:[1a90]    ; read status byte from status register via
                     ; an address between c9a00h and c9bffh into ah
```

The SCSI host adapter frees you from carrying out a REQ/ACK handshake; the ST01 generates the corresponding control signals automatically. For example, to transfer a 512-byte block during the course of a *write block* command to the target, you only need to write a corresponding data byte 512 times into the data port. The host adapter's logic generates all the control signals required such as *I/O CH RDY* and *0WS* for the PC system bus to confirm receipt of the data byte to the CPU, and to instruct the CPU to insert wait states if necessary. Thus the control signals REQ of the SCSI bus and MEMW and MEMR of the PC system bus are synchronized. Moreover, the adapter also generates the REQ signals for the SCSI bus and waits for the ACK signal from the target to carry out a handshake for the data byte transfer to the target. You access the data bits of the SCSI bus via the SCSI data port between addresses c9c00h and cbfffh. When you attempt to output a data byte, for example of a command, parameter block, message or data block to the target, you always need to write the byte into the data port. If you want to read a byte, for example of a status message or data block, from the SCSI bus, you must read the byte from the data port.

Because of the extensive size of the data port with its 1024 bytes, you may, for example, write a 512-byte data block using the string instruction MOVSB together with the prefix REP, and loading the value 512 into the count register CX. Now the CPU can transfer a complete block from a buffer in the main memory to the SCSI bus, and thus to the target, all at once. The same procedure can be carried out, of course, in the opposite direction. By the same instruction, you may read 512 data bytes from the SCSI bus and transfer them into a buffer in the main memory. Because of the REP prefix, source and destination addresses are counted up or down in the same way, according to the value of the direction flag. If you suitably initialize the start address for the SCSI data port, then the address doesn't pass beyond the value c9fffh and you are always accessing the data port.

Example: `transfer 512 data bytes from a buffer in main memory via the SCSI data port to the SCSI bus`

```
buffer DB 512 DUP (?)  ; provide a buffer with 512 bytes (1 data block)
..................     ; initialize buffer with suitable data
MOV ax, c800h;         ; load SCSI data port segment via
MOV es, ax             ; ax into extra segment register es
MOV di, 1c00h          ; initialize destination index to the beginning of SCSI data port
MOV si, OFFSET buffer  ; load buffer offset into source index
```

```
MOV CX, 200h           ; transfer 512 bytes
CLD                    ; clear direction flag, address counting to higher addresses
MOVSB                  ; transfer 512 bytes from buffer to SCSI data port
```

The host adapter handles all requests for CPU wait cycles, as well as the generation and detection of the handshake signals.

Another popular SCSI host adapter is constructed very similarly: Future Domain's TMC950. Here, the SCSI data port begins at offset 1e00h and comprises 512 bytes. The control and data registers occupy the area between offsets 1c00h and 1dffh, and the internal RAM occupies the offsets between 1800h and 18ffh.

28.7.3 Programming and Command Phases

The SCSI-II standard defines ten device classes that have quite different commands and functions. As a detailed discussion of all SCSI classes and commands would obviously go beyond the scope of this book (the original literature comprises about 600 pages), the following details mainly the class of hard disks; Appendix H.2 summarizes commands and parameters for that class. In Table 28.18 you will find the ten SCSI-II classes as they are returned by an inquiry command.

Class code	Device
00h	hard disk
01h	tape drive
02h	printer
03h	processor device
04h	WORM
05h	CD-ROM
06h	scanner
07h	optical storage
08h	media changer
09h	communication device
0ah–1fh	reserved

Table 28.18: SCSI-II classes

Unlike previous hard disk interfaces (for example, ST412/506 and IDE), SCSI doesn't deal with tracks and sectors, but regards the complete storage capacity of a hard disk as a continuous list of data blocks with a fixed size. In view of the logical structure, these data blocks are similar to the logical sectors of DOS, which are assigned a logical sector number between 0 and ∞. How a SCSI unit manages this list appearing on the SCSI level internally is the exclusive job of the intelligent controller. On hard disks the logical block number is converted into tracks and sectors, often using zone recording. A SCSI tape drive, on the other hand, can use the logical block numbers in a virtually unaltered form, as on the magnetic tape the data blocks are in succession.

On a PC running under DOS an enormous conversion process is carried out between logical and physical structures:

- the logical DOS sectors must be converted into cylinder, head and sector for INT 13h;
- INT 13h must convert the values for cylinder, head, and sector into a logical block number for the SCSI host adapter;
- the addressed hard disk drive converts the logical block number into a value comprising the physical cylinder, head, and sector, of the SCSI drive.

Thus it is not surprising that every SCSI host adapter has its own BIOS extension to establish the connection between system and SCSI bus, and to carry out the conversion of the physical sectors of INT 13h into logical block numbers for SCSI. The BIOS extension identifies the drive geometry via function 09h of INT 13h to the system. Register addresses and meanings, as well as the programming schemes for the various host adapters, don't coincide in most cases with any known programming interface, for example the AT task file. Until a short time ago, the lack of a standard for programming the host adapters was a significant deficit of SCSI. Meanwhile, however, two commonly used drivers with a standardized programming interface are available with ASPI and CAM. They, in turn, access the host adapter register in a hardware-dependent manner. On IDE this was never a problem, as the AT task file known from the IBM AT was simply taken.

For a PC with DOS even the lack of a defined programming interface to the host adapters was not yet a serious problem, as the host adapters are equipped with an extension ROM for the BIOS routines for INT 13h. The BIOS extension intercepts the INT 13h during the course of the boot process, and replaces the standard routines that are incompatible with the host adapter. But with operating systems running in protected mode (for example, OS/2 or UNIX/XENIX), enormous problems arise. The shipped ROM code is largely only executable in real mode, but cannot support the protected mode operating system. For this reason you always get problems with adapters that have their own BIOS extensions when installing them in a computer running under OS/2 or UNIX/XENIX, if the operating system does not support that adapter on a register level. Only PS/2 machines with advanced BIOS implement a BIOS running in protected mode. Therefore, the BIOS is also loaded from disk, and not just the operating system, if you are using OS/2 on an IBM-compatible PC. If this BIOS doesn't support the installed adapter (and this applies not only to hard disk controllers but to all other adapters, too), then the adapter is not operating correctly, or the BIOS extension prevents you from working in protected mode.

Also, the lack of a defined programming interface to the host adapter means that instead of the ROM code the operating system cannot be equipped with a universal driver, which can access all SCSI drives according to the SCSI specification. As long as the boot routine is running in real mode, the system data can be read from the SCSI drive to boot the computer. But at that moment when the initialization routine switches the processor into protected mode, the hard disk becomes «dead» as the real-mode BIOS denies the access when the hard disk is addressed, or hangs up the PC. Such problems cannot occur with IDE or ESDI hard disks, as they are programmed via registers. These registers, though, are located in the I/O address space for which even in protected mode no address transformation is carried out: only the access rights are checked by the operating system. Therefore, the system can manage its own accesses, and problems hardly ever arise.

At the end of every command the target (that is, the drive) returns a status byte to the initiator (the host adapter). If this byte indicates an error condition, then you should investigate the cause using the *request sense* command. With a single byte the cause cannot be described exactly enough, and the SCSI host adapter doesn't implement a status register with error information, as was the case, for example, for IDE.

The SCSI commands follow a strict scheme. The first command byte always contains the command code, the second the number of the addressed target, and the third a control byte. SCSI commands always have six, ten or twelve bytes. The 10- and 12-byte commands are denoted as extended. The command code is divided into a 3-bit group code and a 5-bit code with the command within that group (see Figure 28.32).

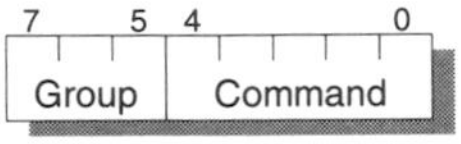


```
Group: 0=6-byte command    1=10-byte command   2,3,4=reserved
       5=12-byte command   6,7=reserved

Command: 0-31: command code
```

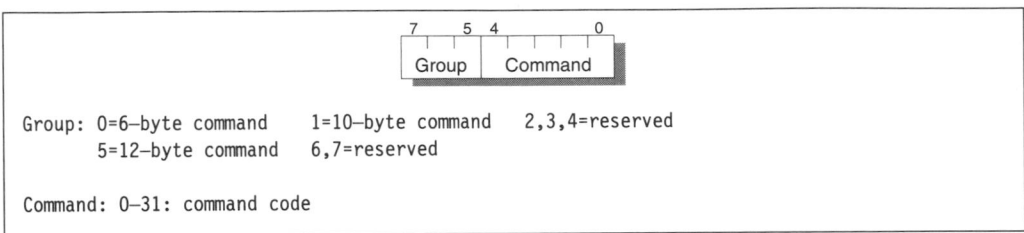

Figure 28.32: Command byte structure.

The structure of the command byte gives rise to eight different command groups; only four of them (0, 1, 2 and 5) are currently in use. The five command bits allow 32 commands per group; thus a maximum of 256 different commands is possible. You must set all reserved bits of the command codes to a value of 0. Figure 28.33 shows their structure.

The first byte of the command block represents the command code, consisting of the 3-bit group and the 5-bit command. The logical unit number *(LUN)* specifies the address of the logical unit to access within the target. For drives with an embedded controller this is always equal to 0. The logical block address *(LBA)* has 21 bits for a 6-byte command and 32 bits for a 10-byte or 12-byte command. It indicates the number of the intended data block. Thus, with a 6-byte command you can access a maximum of 2 M blocks and with a 10-byte or 12-byte command a maximum of 4 G blocks. For hard disks where one block usually corresponds to a 512-byte sector, a 6-byte command is sufficient in most cases. You can then access 1 Gbyte of data. If you set the *REL* bit for relative addressing then the block address is relative to the block referred to in the previous process. The block address is interpreted in this case as the 2'complement of a signed number. Most SCSI units and hard disks, though, don't support relative addressing. Note that this option is missing on 6-byte commands.

The *transfer length* specifies the amount of data to be transferred. Usually, this is the number of intended blocks, but some commands also use the number of bytes. Details on this subject are discussed in Appendix H, together with a list of all SCSI commands. Six-byte commands with a byte for the transfer length allow the transfer of a maximum 256 blocks, where a value of 0 means that 256 blocks are transferred. Thus you can read or write up to 256 blocks all at once, for example. On an IDE interface this means a multisector transfer. With the use of a 10-byte command, which reserves two bytes for the transfer length, up to 65535 blocks may be transferred with a single command. A value of 0 here really means that no block is transferred. Even larger is that amount with a 12-byte command; here, four bytes are reserved for the transfer length, corresponding to 4 G data blocks. Thus, SCSI commands are very powerful; the 65535 sector blocks of a 10-byte command with 512 bytes each corresponds to nearly 32 Mbytes of data, after all! Thus you may transfer, for example, a complete DOS partition (before version 3.30) by means of a single SCSI command. The 4 G data blocks with 512 bytes each should also be enough for the future graphic interfaces according to SCSI-III.

6-Byte Command

Bit / Byte	7	6	5	4	3	2	1	0
0	Command Code							
1	LUN			LBA (MSB)				
2	Logical Block Address							
3	Logical Block Address (LSB)							
4	Transfer/Allocation/Parameter Length							
5	Control Byte							

10-Byte Command

Bit / Byte	7	6	5	4	3	2	1	0
0	Command Code							
1	LUN			Reserved				REL
2	Logical Block Address (MSB)							
3	Logical Block Address							
4	Logical Block Address							
5	Logical Block Address (LSB)							
6	Reserved							
7	Transfer/Allocation/Parameter Length							
8	Transfer/Allocation/Parameter Length							
9	Control Byte							

12-Byte Command

Bit / Byte	7	6	5	4	3	2	1	0
0	Command Code							
1	LUN			Reserved				REL
2	Logical Block Address (MSB)							
3	Logical Block Address							
4	Logical Block Address							
5	Logical Block Address (LSB)							
6	Transfer/Allocation/Parameter Length							
7	Transfer/Allocation/Parameter Length							
8	Transfer/Allocation/Parameter Length							
9	Transfer/Allocation/Parameter Length							
10	Reserved							
11	Control Byte							

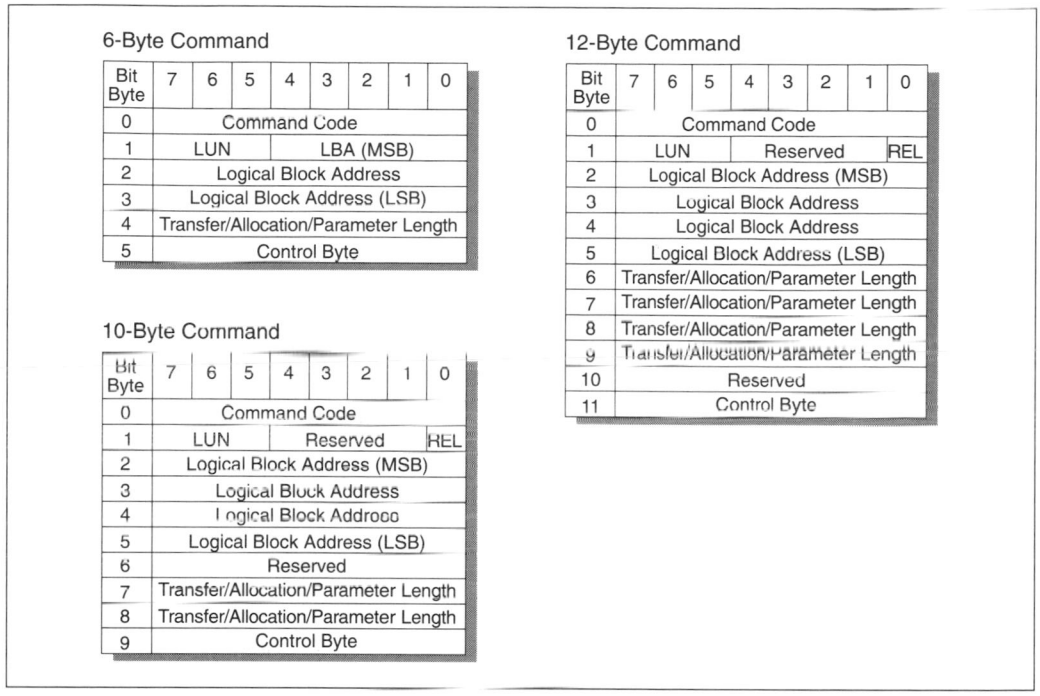

Figure 28.33: Structure of the 6-, 10- and 12-byte commands.

The *parameter list* entry usually indicates the number of bytes transferred during the data out phase of a command as a parameter list to the target. This applies, for example, to the *mode select* command.

If you issue a command used for returning sense data such as request sense or inquiry, then you need to enter in the *allocation length* field the number of bytes that the initiator is to receive from the target. The target terminates the transfer of the sense data when the value indicated in the field allocation length is reached. If the value is higher than the number of transferred sense bytes, then the target terminates the data-in phase earlier. The remaining bytes are not defined.

Every command block is terminated by a control byte, which mainly controls the linking of several commands. Figure 28.34 shows its format.

The two most significant bits *manufac* are available for the manufacturers of SCSI units; their value is ignored by the target. The four reserved bits must be set to 0. If the link bit *L* is set, then the initiator requests a command link. The target then returns only an intermediate status after completing a command, and requests the next command. The connection is not interrupted (as is the case for individual commands) and re-established by means of a bus-free and a selection phase, but remains effective so that the initiator can pass the next command block at once. Closely related to the link bit is the flag bit *F*. If L is cleared then F should also be equal to 0. With an enabled link a cleared flag bit F indicates that the target passes the initiator a message *linked command complete* after successfully completing a partial command. If the flag bit is set then a message *linked command with flag complete* is transferred instead.

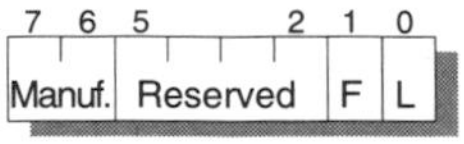


```
Manuf.:    manufacturer (insignificant)
reserved:  0
F:     flag
       1=message "linked command with flag complete" output
       1=message "linked command complete" output
L:     link
       1=command link       0=no command link
```

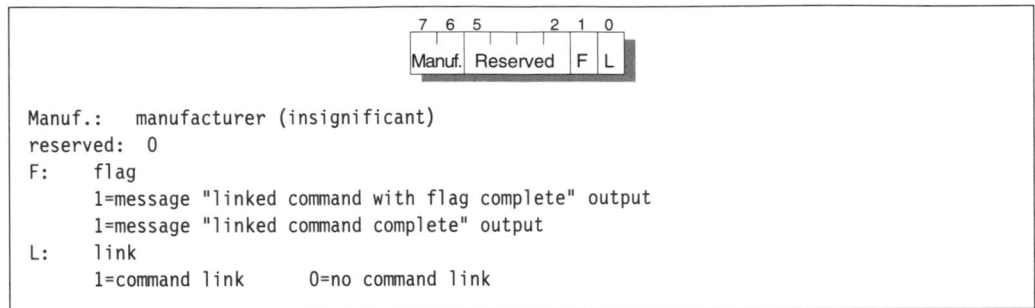

Figure 28.34: Control byte structure.

You start a command execution by transferring a 6-, 10- or 12-byte command block to the target. Some commands additionally require a parameter list, which is transferred during the course of a data-out phase. If you employ the ST01 then you must therefore proceed as follows:

- Clear the SCSI ENAB bit in the control register and set SCSI ENAB to activate the SCSI bus; write the SCSI-ID of the host adapter into the SCSI data port, and start an arbitration phase of the host adapter by means of the ARB STRT bit in the control register.
- Observe the ARB CMPL bit in the status register to determine the end of the arbitration phase, and to confirm that the host adapter has gained control of the SCSI bus.
- Issue a selection phase to select the intended target by activating the SEL line with the SCSI SEL bit of the control register, and by outputting the target's SCSI-ID via the SCSI data port.
- Observe the SCSI BSY bit in the status register afterwards to determine whether the addressed target has responded to the selection phase and has taken control of the bus.
- Observe the SCSI C/D, SCSI MSG and SCSI I/O bits in the status register to determine the beginning of a command phase; for this purpose, SCSI MSG and SCSI I/O must be cleared, but SCSI C/D must be set.
- Transfer the six or ten command bytes of the command block via the SCSI data port to the target to start command execution.
- If, additionally, a parameter list has to be transferred for the command concerned (mode select, for example), then observe the bits SCSI MSG, SCSI C/D and SCSI I/O to determine the beginning of a data-out phase (SCSI MSG, SCSI C/D and SCSI I/O cleared), and provide the parameter list via the SCSI data port.

- If a command (write block, for example) requires the transfer of a data block, then observe the SCSI MSG, SCSI C/D and SCSI I/O bits to determine the beginning of a data-out phase (SCSI MSG, SCSI C/D and SCSI I/O cleared), and provide the data block via the SCSI data port.
- If a command (read block, for example) returns a data block to the initiator (that is, the host adapter), then observe the bits SCSI MSG, SCSI C/D and SCSI I/O to determine the beginning of a data-in phase with cleared bits SCSI MSG, SCSI C/D and set bit SCSI I/O, and to fetch the data block via the SCSI data port.
- Observe SCSI MSG, SCSI C/D and SCSI I/O bits in the status register to determine the beginning of a status phase when SCSI MSG is cleared and SCSI C/D and SCSI I/O are set; the status byte is read via the SCSI data port.
- Observe the SCSI MSG, SCSI C/D and SCSI I/O bits in the status register to determine the beginning of a message-in phase (SCSI MSG, SCSI C/D and SCSI I/O are set), and to fetch the message via the SCSI data port.

You can see that the data exchange via host adapter and the SCSI bus is a rather extensive operation. All the details concerning correct programming of the host adapters would go far beyond the scope of this book. I have no other choice than to refer the SCSI freaks among you to the original literature on this subject. I hope, nevertheless, that the basic concepts and idea behind the very powerful and flexible SCSI interface have become somewhat clearer now. Consider that you can, by means of SCSI, integrate hard disks, tape drives, optical drives, and all the other revolutions that will surely arise in the future into your PC without the need of a hardware adapter or memory-eating driver for every single device. A general interface standard gives rise to an enormous flexibility but the concrete programming, unfortunately, becomes somewhat ponderous.

More powerful SCSI host adapters than the ST01 and ST02 implement a major portion of the SCSI bus control, which has to be programmed explicitly on an ST01 or ST02, by means of a processor, which is in turn controlled by firmware or exclusively by means of hardware, that is, an ASIC. The data exchange between host adapter and drive is then carried out very quickly. EISA SCSI host adapters often transfer the data from the host adapter by means of an EISA DMA channel operating in burst DMA mode C at the full width of 32 bits. Such SCSI systems achieve the highest transfer rates of up to 10 Mbytes/s if the host adapter has an on-board cache. But the 10 Mbytes/s refers only to the pure DMA transfer, that is, the path host–adapter–cache to main memory, or vice versa. The transfer rates on the SCSI bus are significantly lower but, nevertheless, impressive (up to 4 Mbytes/s).

28.7.4 ASPI

As already explained, the greatest problem concerning SCSI host adapters is the lack of a binding standard for a programming interface. With its help, it should be possible to send SCSI instructions, data and parameters to a SCSI target, or to receive data and parameters from a target, in a simple way. In the meantime, however, two *de facto* standards have been produced, namely the *Common Access Method (CAM)* from ANSI and the *Advanced SCSI Programming*

Interface (ASPI) from Adaptec. In the following section, I would briefly like to introduce the basics of ASPI.

Normally, ASPI is a driver which is loaded during start-up of your PC. You can use the ASPI functions (Table 28.19) as they are stored in the stack segment and offset (in this sequence) of a *SCSI Request Block (SRB)*. Before the call, the SRB contains all other important information for the requested function and, after the request has been performed, it contains the applicable data from ASPI or the SCSI target. The structure of the first eight SRB bytes is the same for all ASPI functions. Then, you must perform a far call to the entry point of the ASPI driver. In DOS you can determine this entry point using INT 21h, function 44h (communication with device drivers), sub-function 02h (read control code). For this you must first open the ASPI driver with the help of the ASPI driver *SCSIMGR$* and use the returned DOS handle as the AL value for INT 21h, function 4402h.

Code	Function
00h	Host adapter inquiry
01h	Determine unit type
02h	Perform SCSI instruction
03h	Interrupt SCSI instruction
04h	Reset SCSI unit
05h	Set parameters for host adapter
06h	Reserved for target mode
07h–7fh	Reserved for expansions
80h–ffh	Reserved for manufacturer

Table 28.19: The ASPI functions

As an example, I would like to explain the usage of the *perform SCSI instruction* ASPI function. In Table 28.20 you can see the layout of the SRB for this function. From the complete SRB for this ASPI function, bytes 00h, 02h–17h, 1ah–40h+l2–1 are the input values, and the bytes 01h, 18h–19h, 40h+l2–40h+l2+l1–1 are the returned values. The completion of the ASPI function call is identified by a status value other than 00h (byte 01h). In Table 28.21 you will find all the valid status values for the ASPI functions.

Byte	Content
00h	02h (perform SCSI instruction)
01h	Status
02h	Host adapter number
03h	Bit 0: POST, Bit 1: link, Bit 2..3: direction, Bit 3..5: reserved
04h–07h	Reserved
08h	ID of target
09h	LUN
0ah–0dh	Size of the data buffer
0eh	Extent of sense data in byte (l1)
0fh–12h	Segment:Offset of the data buffer
13h–16h	Segment:Offset of the SRB link
17h	Extent of SCSI instruction in byte (l2)

Table 28.20: Layout of the SRB for the ASPI function perform SCSI instruction

Byte	Content
18h	Status of host adapter
19h	Target status
1ah–1dh	Segment:Offset of POST
1eh–3fh	Reserved
40h–40h+l2-1	SCSI instruction
40h+l2..40h+l2+l1-1	Sense data

Table 28.20: cont.

Status value	Meaning
00h	Function is currently being performed (ASPI in progress)
01h	Function successfully completed
02h	Function interrupted by host instruction
03h	SCSI command cannot be interrupted
04h	General failure
80h	Invalid SRB format
81h	Invalid host adapter specified
82h	SCSI target not found

Table 28.21: Status value of the ASPI functions

To call up the ASPI function with the required SCSI instruction, you must first prepare a buffer for the SRB itself, and then a sufficiently large data buffer (for example, if you wish to read or write a disk drive block). Finally, the SRB fields are initialized (you will find the meaning of the entries in Appendix H.3). The call is then simply accomplished in the following way (address of the SRB: SRB_seg:SRB_off, jump address from ASPI: ASPI_ptr=ASPI_seg:ASPI_off):

```
ASPI_start:           ; ASPI function call
mov ax, SRB_seg       ; Load segment from SRB into accumulator ax
push ax               ; Put segment value on the stack
mov ax, SRB_off       ; Load offset from SRB into accumulator ax
push ax               ; Put offset value on the stack
call ASP_ptr          ; Far call to the ASPI jump point
pop ax                ; Get SRB offset from the stack
pop ax                ; Get SRB segment from the stack

SRB_check:            ; Check whether ASPI function has been completed
mov bx, SRB_seg       ; Load segment from SRB into bx
mov es, ax            ; Load segment from SRB into extra segment es
mov bx, SRB_off       ; Load offset from SRB into bx
check_start:          ; Begin the checking
mov al, [es:][bx+1]   ; Load status byte in SRB into al
or al, 00h            ; Compare al with value 00h
JZ check_start        ; Check again if al equals zero
```

SRB_check is used to interrogate the status byte in the SRB until a value other than 0 occurs. This is the indication that the requested SCSI function has been performed. The status byte in the SRB then contains an end code (see Appendix H.3), the sense data in the SRB (byte 40h+l2..40h+l2+l1–1) and the sense code from the SCSI adapter.

ASPI supports SCSI instruction chains by «linking» a number of SRBs. The 4 bytes *Segment:Offset* of the *SRB link* (Bytes 13h..16h) entry are used for this. It refers to the SRB of the next instruction in a chain. To actually activate the SRB linking, you must set the link bit in byte 3. This applies to all except the last SRB in a chain. As soon as an addressed target sends back the *linked command complete* status code, execution of the next instruction in the chain commences, that is, the following SRB is performed.

If you set the *POST* bit 0 in the SRB, ASPI carries out a so-called *Posting* and, after execution of the SCSI instruction, jumps to the far address stored in bytes 1ah–1dh You can use the call in addition to checking the status code in SRB, for example, as an alternative method of identifying the completion of an ASPI function. A further use would be the processing of SCSI results, such as the evaluation of sense data. Immediately following the call-up of the POST routine, the 4 byte return jump address (Segment:Offset) for ASPI, and a 4 byte SRB pointer (Segment:Offset) for the SRB which is currently being performed are stored on the stack.

28.7.5 Other Standardized SCSI Programming Interfaces

For a complete picture, I would like to introduce two additional standardized programming interfaces for access to the SCSI bus: the *Common Access Method (CAM)* and *TARGA*. Due to the lack of space (a detailed specification for ASPI, CAM and TARGA could quite easily fill a book of its own), I will have to limit the explanation to those functions that are implemented and a few general details.

Common Access Method (CAM)

Like ASPI, CAM operates with the help of a data structure in the memory, the *CAM Control Block (CCB)*, corresponding to the SRB from ASPI. The CCB contains all important information for performing the instruction, and keeps a buffer ready for the returned data (depending on the function). You will find the specific CAM instructions in Table 28.22.

Code	Function
00h	No operation (NOP)
01h	Perform SCSI I/O function
02h	Determine unit type
03h	Scan SCSI path
04h	Release SIM queue
05h	Set asynchronous reply
06h	Set unit type
07h–0fh	Reserved
10h	Interrupt SCSI command
11h	Reset SCSI bus
12h	Reset SCSI unit
13h	Interrupt I/O operation
14h–1fh	Reserved
20h	Sense unit

Table 28.22: The CAM instructions

Code	Function
21h	Perform unit request
22h–2fh	Reserved
30h	Activate LUN
31h	Perform target I/O
32h–7fh	Reserved
80h–ffh	Manufacturer dependent

Table 28.22: cont.

Register	Call value	Return value
AH		Error code*)
AX	8100h	
BX	CCB-Offset	
ES	CCB-Segment	

*) 00h=o.k., 01h=invalid CCB address

Table 28.23: Call format of INT 4fh, function 8100h – transfer CCB to CAM driver

Register	Call value	Return value
AH		Error code1)
AX	8200h	
CX	8765h	9abch2)
DX	cba9h	5678h2)
ES:DI		Far pointer to "SCSI_CAM"2)

1) 00h=CAM driver installed
2) Only if CAM driver is installed (AH=00h)

Table 28.24: Call format of INT 4fh, function 8200h – installation check for a CAM driver

Contrary to ASPI, a CAM function is not activated by a far call to the jump point of the driver, but by calling up INT 4fh, function 8100h. You can see the format of the call in Table 28.23.

Using the function 8200h of INT 4fh, you can determine whether or not a CAM driver is installed. Table 28.24 shows the format of the call.

TARGA

TARGA is a manufacturer-independent SCSI unit driver which, like INT 13h, is constructed as an interrupt interface. This means that all function calls using interrupt INT 78h will be performed, and all parameters in the processor registers will be transferred. Thus, TARGA has no data structure in memory, unlike CAM and ASPI. All of the TARGA functions are listed in Table 28.25.

Code in AH	Function
00h	Set I/O port
01h	Determine I/O port
02h	Set DMA channel
03h	Determine DMA channel
04h	Set SCSI unit number
05h	Determine SCSI unit number
06h	Set/reset early return mode
08h	Adapter self-test
09h	Reset SCSI bus
10h	Send SCSI command
11h	Send SCSI command and receive data (PIO)
12h	Send SCSI command and transfer data (PIO)
13h	Send SCSI command and receive data (DMA)
14h	Send SCSI command and transfer data(DMA)
15h	Finish data transfer (DMA)

Table 28.25: Functions of TARGA interrupt 78h

28.7.6 Different SCSI Standards

Finally, I would like to bring together the attributes and expansions of each of the different SCSI standards.

SCSI-I

SCSI as a standard was born with the (subsequently named) SCSI-I specification. It was originally only an interface for disk drives. Many things remained somewhat vague, and so compatibility problems were still the order of the day. However, SCSI-I did implement a synchronous transfer rate as an option. As the instructions from each equipment manufacturer were at first given too much freedom for the actual implementation (far too much in fact), a standardization was achieved with the *Common Command Set (CCS).* CCS is an extension to SCSI-I, and is not an actual SCSI standard itself. SCSI-I contains only an 8-bit SCSI bus; the transfer rate in asynchronous mode is a maximum of approximately 4 Mbytes/s, or in optional synchronous mode 7 Mbytes/s.

SCSI-II

SCSI-II represents a great step towards an equipment-independent and, therefore, very flexible bus interface. Not only are the instructions and parameter lists clearly defined, and the synchronous mode laid down as compulsory, but in addition, ten classes of equipment with their corresponding required and optional instructions have been defined. In this way, such different equipment as hard disks, CD-ROMs, magneto-optical disk drives, scanners, streamers, media-changers (the good old Juke Box), printers, communication equipment and general SCSI processor systems like a host adapter can be connected and controlled. Thus, SCSI-II is the first «true» SCSI (if you consider the original intention). The two subsequent standards are also embedded into SCSI-II.

Fast SCSI

With Fast SCSI, the maximum clock frequency in synchronous mode is increased to 10 MHz: with an 8-bit SCSI bus, this corresponds to a data transfer rate of 10 Mbyte/s. Note, however, that the SCSI instructions and also the messages, as previously, are transferred asynchronously.

Wide SCSI

In the age of 32- and 64-bit EISA/MCA and local bus systems, the eight bits of the SCSI data bus appear quite modest. Not surprisingly, the width of the SCSI bus has also been increased to 16 or even 32 bits. It is, of course, much easier to expand the bus width than to increase the bus frequency. The relatively long SCSI cables set the frequency limits, not the quantity of parallel lines (ignoring the additional electronic complexity). To be able to use the additional data bits as well, a further so-called *B-cable* is necessary. It transfers the most significant data byte (16-bit SCSI bus) of a 16-bit word, or the three most significant data bytes (32-bit SCSI bus) of a 32-bit double word. At present, only wide SCSI devices with a 16-bit SCSI bus are available commercially. Table 28.26 shows the layout of this 68-pole B-cable.

Wide and normal SCSI devices can be operated on the same SCSI bus. During a message phase (asynchronous 8 bit), the initiator and the target negotiate as to whether an asynchronous or synchronous, normal or fast mode, 8-, 16- or 32-bit transfer should be performed. A faster or slower mode is selected depending on the performance capabilities and the actual implementation of the applicable SCSI units. Fast and wide modes can be simultaneously active; the maximum transfer rate at 10 MHz and with a 32-bit width then increases to 40 Mbyte/s. This is a very respectable rate for an external bus.

Signal	Pin	Meaning	Signal	Pin	Meaning
GND	1	Ground	GND	35	Ground
GND	2	Ground	$\overline{\text{DB(8)}}$	36	Data bit 8
GND	3	Ground	$\overline{\text{DB(9)}}$	37	Data bit 9
GND	4	Ground	$\overline{\text{DB(10)}}$	38	Data bit 10
GND	5	Ground	$\overline{\text{DB(11)}}$	39	Data bit 11
GND	6	Ground	$\overline{\text{DB(12)}}$	40	Data bit 12
GND	7	Ground	$\overline{\text{DB(13)}}$	41	Data bit 13
GND	8	Ground	$\overline{\text{DB(14)}}$	42	Data bit 14
GND	9	Ground	$\overline{\text{DB(15)}}$	43	Data bit 15
GND	10	Ground	$\overline{\text{DB(P1)}}$	44	Parity for DB8–DB15
GND	11	Ground	$\overline{\text{ACKB}}$	45	Acknowledge B cable
GND	12	Ground	GND	46	Ground
GND	13	Ground	$\overline{\text{REQB}}$	47	Request B cable
GND	14	Ground	$\overline{\text{DB(16)}}$	48	Data bit 16
GND	15	Ground	$\overline{\text{DB(17)}}$	49	Data bit 17
GND	16	Ground	$\overline{\text{DB(18)}}$	50	Data bit 18
TERMPWR	17	Termination	TERMPWR	51	Termination
TERMPWR	18	Termination	TERMPWR	52	Termination
GND	19	Ground	$\overline{\text{DB(19)}}$	53	Data bit 19
GND	20	Ground	$\overline{\text{DB(20)}}$	54	Data bit 20

Table 28.26: The layout of the 68-pole B-cable

Signal	Pin	Meaning	Signal	Pin	Meaning
GND	21	Ground	$\overline{\text{DB(21)}}$	55	Data bit 21
GND	22	Ground	$\overline{\text{DB(22)}}$	56	Data bit 22
GND	23	Ground	$\overline{\text{DB(23)}}$	57	Data bit 23
GND	24	Ground	$\overline{\text{DB(P2)}}$	58	Parity for DB16–DB23
GND	25	Ground	$\overline{\text{DB(24)}}$	59	Data bit 24
GND	26	Ground	$\overline{\text{DB(25)}}$	60	Data bit 25
GND	27	Ground	$\overline{\text{DB(26)}}$	61	Data bit 26
GND	28	Ground	$\overline{\text{DB(27)}}$	62	Data bit 27
GND	29	Ground	$\overline{\text{DB(28)}}$	63	Data bit 28
GND	30	Ground	$\overline{\text{DB(29)}}$	64	Data bit 29
GND	31	Ground	$\overline{\text{DB(30)}}$	65	Data bit 30
GND	32	Ground	$\overline{\text{DB(31)}}$	66	Data bit 31
GND	33	Ground	$\overline{\text{DB(P3)}}$	67	Parity for DB24–DB31
GND	34	Ground	GND	68	Ground

Table 28.26: cont.

SCSI-III

Currently, the follow-on specification for the very successful SCSI-II standard is in the planning stage. Protocols for the supporting of serial interfaces, multi-host systems and also fibre optic lines and graphic units are planned. In addition to an increase in the data transfer rate (fibre optics), new classes of equipment are also expected.

28.8 Optical Mass Storage

For several years (and especially since the appearance of the CD in the audio and video fields) a triumphant progress has been predicted for optical mass storage. But as with all great prophesies – the reality is usually far more leisurely (fortunately, if we consider the daily end-of-the-world' prophesies!). The fact that optical mass storage hasn't already superseded magnetic media, and especially hard disks, is largely due to two reasons: the storage capacity of the hard disks has increased remarkably in the past five years, and further, rewriteable and high-capacity optical data carriers have been under development for years, or very expensive.

Today most optical drives have a SCSI interface. Only a short time ago, manufacturers often used their own interface so that in addition to the drive, an adapter for the bus slot also had to be provided. You may access the data on the optical mass storage, in principle, in the same way as that on a SCSI hard disk. Thus, there are three possibilities in total:

- INT 21h file and directory function: for that purpose, most drives or controllers/host adapters come with a driver (for CD-ROMs it is usually called MSCDEX.SYS – Microsoft's CD-ROM driver).
- ASPI interface: through the ASPI functions you can issue SCSI commands to access the volume in the optical drive.

- Programming the host adapter directly: this is only possible if you know the adapter very well; for example, you know the memory or I/O addresses of the control, status and data registers.

Because programming an optical drive with a SCSI interface is (except for the different SCSI device class and the assigned commands) not very different from programming a hard disk drive, this is not detailed here. If you use INT 21h, the differences between CD-ROMs, hard disks and other drives disappear completely. The following sections, therefore, discuss only the structure and function of the presently most widely used optical mass storage in brief.

28.8.1 CD-ROM

The common CD is well-suited as a read-only memory for extensive amounts of data. Even the music held in digital form on CDs is nothing more than a certain kind of information, after all. The high storage capacity of the CD and the well-tested techniques of the optical and mechanical components make the CD-ROM a reasonable alternative for data which is very extensive and will not be altered. To this group of data belong, for example, large program and data packs; Windows applications in particular come with a box full of floppies, which significantly contributes to the price. The difference between a CD player and a CD-ROM drive is not very extensive. Only a data interface for transferring data to the PC system bus and a very poor control interface so that the CPU has the opportunity to access certain data with software commands have been added. The interface is accessed by means of a suitable driver. With the driver a CD-ROM drive can be integrated into a PC system without any major problems. Further, CD-ROM drives are quite cheap; you can get high-quality drives for less than $500. Most drives have a SCSI interface, or can be directly connected to the floppy controller, but SCSI offers higher flexibility and more power. The disks typically have a capacity of 300 Mbytes or more. As is the case for all optical drives (this applies to WORMs as well as magneto-optical drives, too), the data transfer rate of a maximum of 150 kbytes/s and the access time of about 50 ms are not very exciting.

Especially for multimedia PCs, which enable the concurrent input, processing and output of data, the generation and output of visual information (for example, pictures that are part of an encyclopedia), as well as the input, processing and output of audio information (for example, speech and music), a certain variant of the CD-ROM has been developed, *CD-I (CD-interactive)*. CD-I supplies a significantly improved and more powerful programming interface to the actual computer so that the enormous amounts of data on a CD can be managed in a better way. Which multimedia capabilities are rapidly arising you may recognize, for example, by the fact that recently PC adapter cards with an integrated TV receiver have come onto the market. With a suitable driver and Windows you can watch the news in one window while you are working in another.

The operating principle of CD-ROM is quite easy, and corresponds largely to that of a conventional CD player (see Figure 28.35). Inside the drive a small semiconductor laser emits a very thin laser beam with a wavelength of about 850 nm. The beam is invisible, therefore, as the wavelength is in the near-infrared. Via an optical mirror assembly, which is precisely moved with some control elements, the laser beam is focused onto the surface of the CD-ROM disk.

The disk usually accommodates the information in the form of small depressions. If the laser beam hits such a dip then the beam is not back-reflected in a well-directed way, as is the case between the dips, but is instead scattered. Thus the back-reflection intensity is much lower if the beam hits such a depression. (You see the same effect in connection with a mirror and a rough wall: although the amount of reflection of the mirror is not significantly higher than that of a white wall, you are dazzled by the sun reflected by the mirror but not by the white wall.) In the drive a sensor detects the intensity of the back-reflected beam, which varies according to the passing dips (that is, according to the information bits), and thus converts this variation into a data bit pattern.

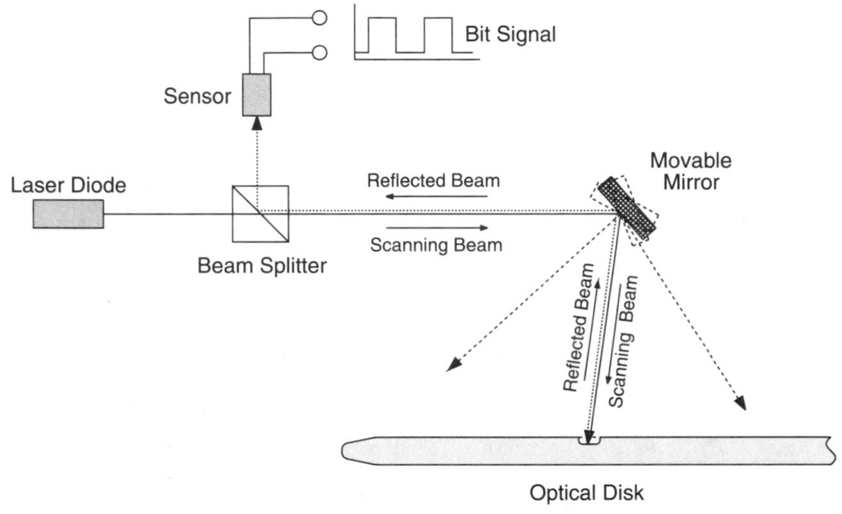

Figure 28.35: CD-ROM. A precisely focused laser beam emitted by a laser diode is radiated onto the surface of an optical disk by an optical assembly with a movable mirror. The intensity of the back-scattered beam is detected by a sensor, which converts the optical signal into a bit signal.

Unlike floppies and hard disks, the information is not arranged in concentric circles (the tracks) but as a single spiral from the beginning of the disk up to its end. This spiral is further divided into data portions, but these units are assigned a certain amount of (play) time and not a fixed number of bytes. Thus, CD-ROM cannot deny that it has been developed from the CD player. After all, music is usually output as a continuous stream of tones from the beginning to the end; an organization according to tracks and sectors is therefore unnecessary.

CDs are well-suited for the mass distribution of large amounts of data. At first a master-CD made of copper or another stable material is formed by depositing a photoresist on it, writing the information by means of a laser beam, and thus exposing certain locations. These exposed locations of the photoresist are removed and the disk is then etched so that part of the carrier material is removed at the exposed locations. Thus we get a disk that already contains dips at the right positions. Afterwards, a reverse disk is formed which contains the information as tiny bumps instead of dips. By pressing, a positive disk can be formed easily. For this purpose, a blank CD is put on the reverse disk and they are pressed together under high pressure. The bumps of the reverse disk form dips in the blank CD and a CD for CD-ROM is complete. For protection purposes, the disk is afterwards coated with an infrared-transparent layer.

In principle, dips are not essentially required for recording. Two different reflection types are sufficient, no matter how they are achieved. These may, for example, be two different phases (crystalline or amorphous) or two different magnetizations of the carrier's surface. The first method is used for WORMs, the latter for magneto-optical drives. (More about these in the following sections.) The main disadvantage of CD-ROM cannot be overlooked: the information held must be burnt-in during the manufacturing process. As the user you can't extend the stored data. Therefore, a first advance are the WORMs.

28.8.2 WORM

WORM has nothing to do with worms either in the biological or in the computer sense, but is simply the abbreviation for *write once, read many* (times). You may write on the WORM data carrier once and read it in principle until the end of time. Thus WORMs are well-suited for archiving large amounts of data (for example, the correspondence of legal chambers or the credit transfers of banks). The stability of the written information is good, and remains readable for a longer time than on magnetic data carriers.

In addition to a sense laser beam, a WORM drive has a second, the so-called write laser beam, which is much more intensive than the sense laser beam. If information is written then the write laser generates a short but, nevertheless, very powerful laser pulse. Depending upon the structure and surface, the coating at the hit location vaporizes and exposes the surface of the data carrier itself, located below. This surface has a different reflection coefficient from the vaporized data carrier coating. Alternatively, the coating of the data carrier or the data carrier itself may only be melted at the location concerned, but not vaporized. At the end of the write laser pulse, the melted coating cools down very rapidly and solidifies in an amorphous form, that is, without any regular arrangement of the atoms. This amorphous form usually has a different reflection coefficient from the previously present crystalline or polycrystalline coating. In both cases, another intensity of the sense laser beam is reflected which the sensor converts into a corresponding bit signal. Thus reading is carried out similar to the CD-ROM.

The disadvantage of WORMs is that the information, once written, cannot be erased. If you alter a single bit in an allocation unit, the complete allocation unit must be rewritten at another location. Thus WORMs are only suitable for archiving data that is hardly altered later. WORM data carriers achieve storage capacities of up to 500 Mbytes per disk side (that is, ten times more than a current high-end hard disk). But as is the case for CD-ROMs, you pay for the high capacity with a poor transfer rate of typically 150 kbytes/s and an average access time of 50 ms.

28.8.3 Magneto-Optical Drives

The only optical drives with erasable and rewriteable data carriers that have made the leap from development onto the market are magneto-optical drives. They use the influence of a magnetic field onto the polarization of an electromagnetic wave. Light and infrared beams are a form of electromagnetic radiation, as radio or radar waves are. Normal light is depolarized and the electrical as well as the magnetic field of the wave can have any direction perpendicular to the beam direction.

In polarized (or better, linearly polarized) light, the electric field of the wave only points in one direction, perpendicular to the propagation direction (see Figure 28.36). In the same way the magnetic field of the wave also points solely in a certain direction, the so-called *polarization direction*, which is perpendicular to the electric field as well as the propagation direction. The light of a laser, for example, is always polarized in a certain direction. A *polarization filter* only lets a polarized wave with certain polarization direction pass, but no light polarized perpendicularly thereto. Thus polarization filters can be used for determining the polarization direction: if the detector behind the polarization filter detects some light, it is polarized according to the filter direction; if the polarization filter doesn't let any light pass, it is polarized perpendicular to the filter direction.

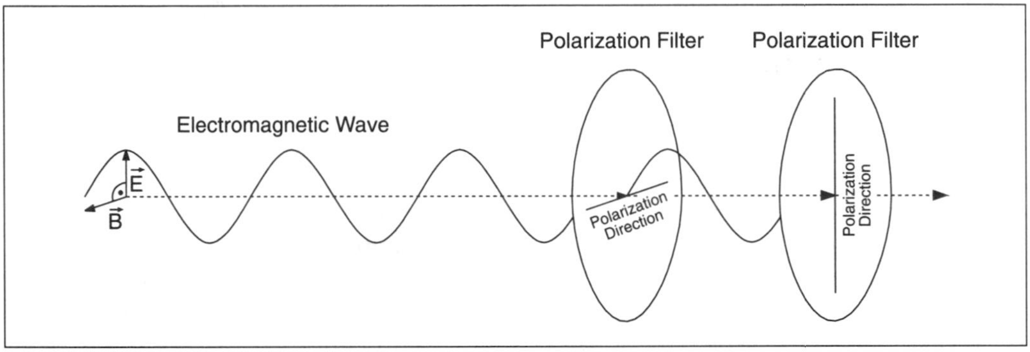

Figure 28.36: Polarization and polarization filter. An electromagnetic wave (for example, light) consists of a periodically changing field E and a periodically changing magnetic field B. The direction of B is called the polarization. Polarization filters only let pass waves whose polarization meets the polarization direction of the filter.

When an electromagnetic wave passes through a body located in a magnetic field, the external magnetic field affects the electromagnetic field of the wave and turns the electrical and magnetic field of the wave, that is, its polarization direction. This phenomenon is called the *Faraday effect*. The same applies to the reflection at the surface of a magnetized substance. The magnetic field generated by the magnetization of the substance turns the polarization direction of the reflected wave relative to the incoming one. The direction of the polarization turn depends upon the magnetization direction of the substance.

Magneto-optical drives now use the Faraday effect to record data. This works as follows: a magneto-optical disk at first has a uniformly magnetized coating made of a ferromagnetic lanthan-alloy. When the polarized laser beam hits the surface, the polarization direction of the reflected beam is turned according to the magnetization of the surface. A polarization filter serves as an analyser for the polarization direction of the back-reflected beam, and the sensor behind the filter detects the intensity passed through the polarization filter (see Figure 28.37).

If a bit is to be written onto disk, then a short but intensive write pulse from the laser heats up the surface at the corresponding location above the *Curie-point* T_C. As you know from Chapter

27, the magnetization of the ferromagnetic disk coating vanishes completely. At the same time, an electromagnet generates a magnetic field whose direction depends on the value of the bit to write; for a «1» the magnetic field is opposite to that for a «0». The direction of this magnetic field now determines the direction in which the elementary magnets (domains) of the heated spot orient when they are again cooled down below the Curie-point. Thus the value of the written bit is also decided. The coating freezes the direction of the magnetic field more or less at the time of writing; thus the writing of a bit is complete.

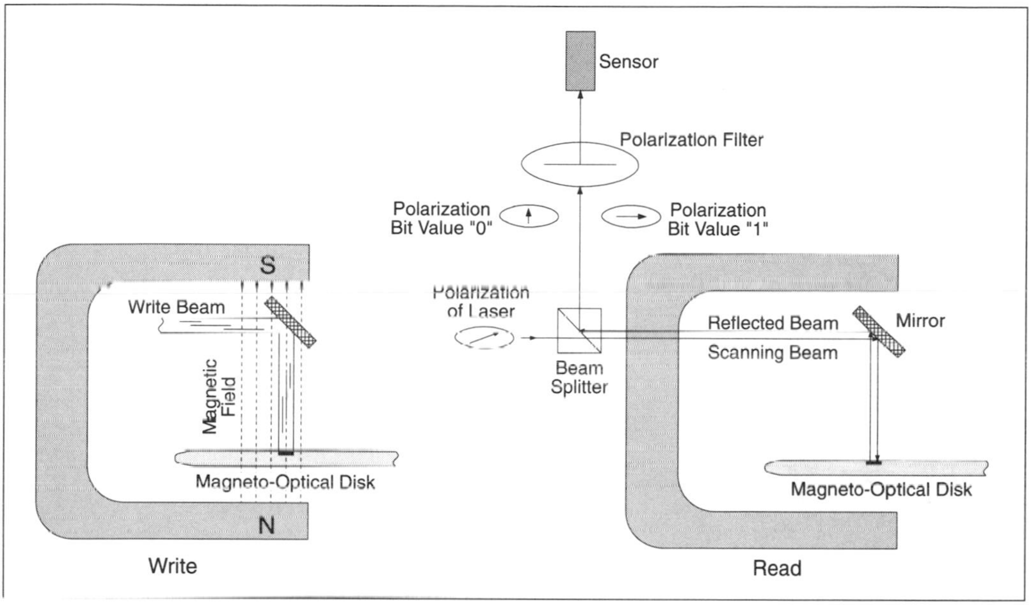

Figure 28.37: Magneto-optical disk. When writing data an intensive write beam warms up the surface of the disk. Under the influence of an external magnetic field, this spot cools down and magnetizes according to the external magnetic field. When reading data the external magnetic field is switched off and a weak sensing beam scans the disk. A sensor determines the magnetization direction of the disk with a polarization filter.

When reading a bit the laser beam scans the surface of the disk and the polarization system detects the direction of the polarization turn for the reflected beam. If the laser beam hits the above written bit, then the direction of the polarization turn for the reflected beam is dependent upon the magnetization direction of the surface coating. For example, the polarization direction for a «0» is turned to the left, and for a «1» turned to the right. In the first case, for example, no light can pass through the polarization filter, and the sensor detects a bit of value «0». In the latter case, the full intensity of the reflected beam reaches the sensor, and it detects a bit of value «1». Thus the information is also held here in the form of a tiny magnetization; but unlike a hard disk, the localization of a certain bit on the disk is carried out by means of a laser beam, that is, in an optical way.

By warming up the relevant spot later, and with a corresponding direction of the magnetic field generated by the electromagnet, the written bit can be erased again without any problem. Multiple write processes are thus possible, but presently their total number doesn't reach the possible number of erasures for pure magnetic disks. The stability of the written information is somewhere between 10 and 25 years. Also, magneto-optical drives pay for their high storage capacity with a comparably poor transfer rate for high-performance drives of significantly less than 1 Mbyte/s and an average access time of typically 50 ms. But you should consider that a magneto-optical disk accommodates up to 30000 (!) tracks. The enormous capacity of the optical data carriers is thus not achieved by increasing the bit density bpi, but mainly by raising the track density tpi – a hint that optical systems with mirrors which only need to position a completely massless and inertless laser beam operate much more exactly than magnetic ones. Compared to a laser beam, they have to move a very heavy read/write head.

Part 6
Externals and Peripherals

29 Interfaces – Connection to the Outside World

The chapter title already outlines the purpose of interfaces; to establish a connection with the rest of the world. The original concept of the PC was to supply users with their own complete computer system. But even in this case interfaces are required – for example, to connect a printer or plotter. You can break the isolation of an autonomous PC from its environment by installing a serial interface and a modem or network adapter; your PC becomes an intelligent telecommunications device with local computing power.

Generally, the term «interface» characterizes a hardware or software unit that establishes a connection between two (in most cases) different units. The following chapters discuss components that are usually called the interfaces of a PC. In particular, the parallel and serial interfaces, as well as network adapters, belong to this group.

29.1 Parallel Interface

Every PC is equipped with at least one parallel and one serial interface. Unlike the serial interface, for which a lot of applications exist, the parallel interface ekes out its existence as a wallflower, as it's only used to serve a parallel printer. Which undreamt-of possibilities the parallel interface can further offer are discussed in Section 29.1.4. But let's first turn to the «standard job» of parallel interfaces.

29.1.1 Printing

BIOS and DOS can usually serve up to four parallel interfaces in a PC, denoted LPT1, LPT2, LPT3 and LPT4 (for *line printer*). The abbreviation PRN (for printer) is a synonym (an alias) for LPT1; all commands with the target PRN are equivalent to commands with the target LPT1. The interface name already indicates the job of the parallel interface: to access a printer. (Whether you actually connect a printer to the interface is another question, of course.) Also, a robot which you program using the first parallel interface, for example, has the «address» LPT1.

The connection between interface and parallel printer is carried out by a Centronics cable. Centronics succeeded in the 1970s as the first printer manufacturer to establish a clearly defined interface standard for printers. Until then printing was its own science! Usually, a Centronics cable has 36 wires, and thus also 36 pins or contacts. 18 wires serve as ground lines and are twisted around the corresponding signal wire to provide at least a minimum of shielding and a simple protection against signal crosstalk. This still holds for the printer's cable connector; it has a two-sided contact strip with 36 contacts in total. Figure 29.1 shows the plugs on the side of the printer and PC, respectively.

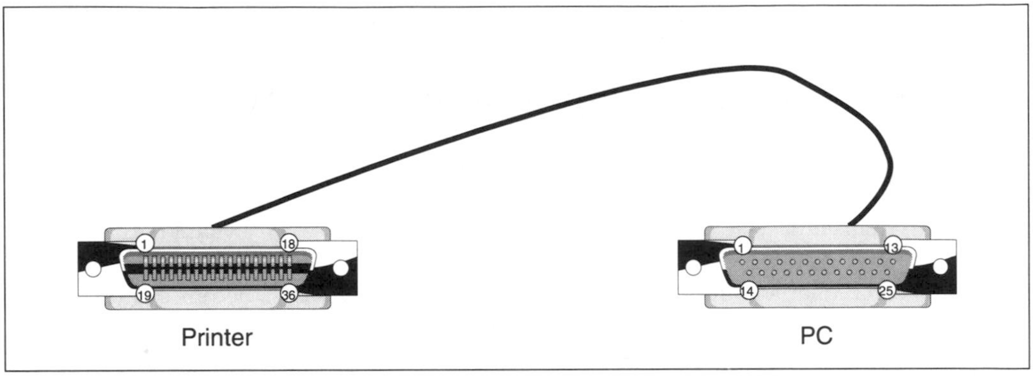

Figure 29.1: Centronics plug.

For the transfer of data and control signals to the printer only half (18) of the contacts are required. IBM therefore used only 25 contacts on the side of the PC instead of 36 to reduce the plug size (and to decrease the cost). The other ground lines required can easily be formed by internally splitting a ground line; the number of contacts is reduced and the plugs get smaller (and cheaper, of course). Because of the smaller jack and plugs, more interfaces can be implemented within the same installation space. An interface board usually has a jack each for the parallel and serial interfaces additionally implemented on the board on its reverse. When using an original Centronics plug, only a single jack would be possible.

The connection of a printer is very easy: you only have to connect the corresponding plugs on the cable ends to the jacks of the printer and PC. Confusion is impossible because of the different shape. But make sure that you don't try a similarly formed but otherwise incompatible jack, such as the connection for an external floppy drive or the SCSI bus.

Note also that the length of cable may not exceed 5 m, as otherwise data transfer errors occur and the cable sometimes seems to slur the data. The specification of the parallel interface and the structure of the Centronics cable doesn't allow large distances, unlike the serial interface and the serial data transfer. If you insist on operating a printer in your cellar (because of the noise, perhaps) which is 20 m away from your computer desk then you have no choice but to use the serial interface. This allows distances of up to 200 m but the serial data transfer is about ten times slower.

29.1.2 Printing Via DOS

In most cases you can print text and other data with no problem using the application program concerned. Usually, you only need to select the corresponding menu item. However, ensure that the printer is actually installed at the relevant interface!

Another possibility for printing data via DOS is the DOS commands COPY, PRINT and TYPE. With COPY file PRN, for example, you print the file on the first parallel printer. The same effect is achieved with PRINT file /d:PRN. Finally, you have the opportunity to input TYPE > PRN using the TYPE command and redirection to PRN. A detailed description of these commands is included in your DOS manual. The principle behind the use of PRN as something like a «file» is that DOS manages all units, whether they be a hard disk, a floppy, the screen, or here the parallel interface, by a device driver. The power of this concept is that the driver's interface to DOS is the same for all units, thus DOS can access a file on an optical disk in the same way as a parallel interface and pass data. DOS doesn't care whether you input on a COMMAND.COM-level C:\> the command `COPY file a:new_file` or `COPY file PRN`. DOS recognizes, from the (reserved) name PRN, that the target is the first parallel interface, not a file on the standard drive. Further reserved device names are LPT1–LPT4, COM1–COM4, CON and AUX. (See your DOS manual for further details.)

Programmers further have the opportunity to print data using the DOS function interrupt INT 21h. For this purpose, the two following functions are implemented; their call format is indicated in Appendix I.

Function 05h printer output:

This old 05h function dates from the CP/M era, and outputs one character to PRN; LPTx can't be accessed. If a printer error occurs then DOS calls INT 24h as the hardware error handler.

Example: `print character 'a' on PRN.`

```
MOV ah, 05h    ; load function number into ah
MOV dl, 'a'    ; load ASCII code of 'a' into dl
INT 21h        ; call DOS interrupt
```

Function 40h write file/device:

This function uses the more modern concept of handles, and outputs a whole string. Note that the DOS device PRN is assigned handle 4 as standard. All other devices LPTx must be opened in advance with the 3dh function *open file/device* for a write access (that you are not able to read anything from the printer by means of function 3fh seems to be obvious). For PRN this is not necessary; but jokers readily have the opportunity to let PRN disappear from the scene by means of a function call 3eh, *close file/device*. A future call of function 40h with the target handle 4 corresponding to PRN fails.

Example: `print character 'a' on PRN.`

```
buffer DB 1 DUP('a')  ; load buffer with byte 'a'
MOV ah, 40h           ; load function number into ah
MOV bx, 04h           ; load handle 4 for PRN into bx
MOV cx, 01h           ; write one character
MOV dx, OFFSET buffer ; load offset of buffer into dx
                      ; segment of buffer already in ds
INT 21h               ; function call
```

The main advantage of function 40h is that you can output a whole string quite easily, and get an error code in register ax. As is usual for such high-level functions, you cannot, for example, determine the status of the parallel interface and the connected printer. This is only possible using the BIOS.

29.1.3 Printing Via BIOS Interrupt INT 17h

Another possibility for accessing the parallel interface is the three functions of BIOS interrupt 17h. With function 00h you can output a character similar to the 05h function of INT 21h; the 01h function initializes the interface and printer, and function 02h determines the current status. Every function provides a status byte in the ah register. Its structure is shown in Figure 29.2.

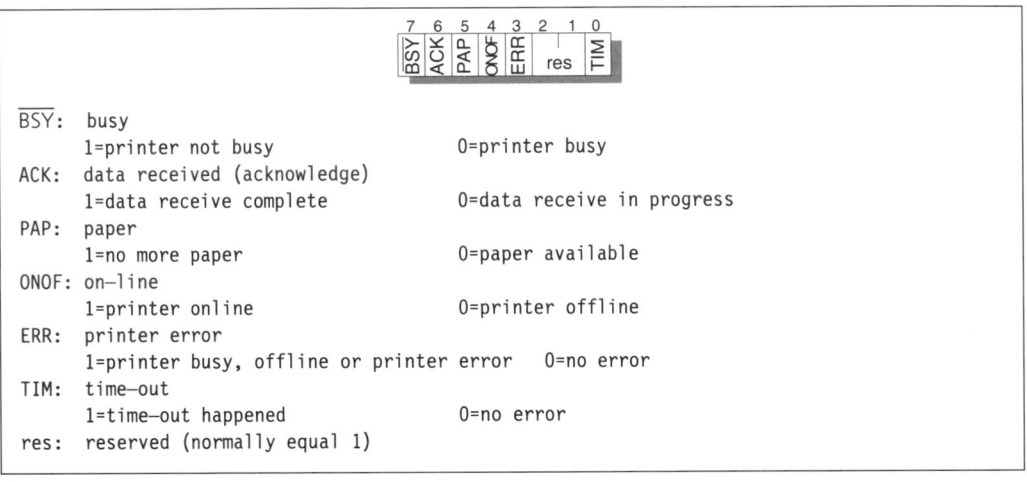

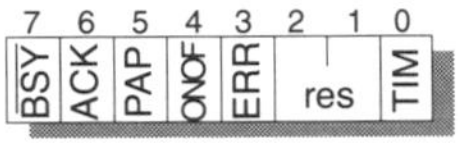


```
BSY:  busy
      1=printer not busy                 0=printer busy
ACK:  data received (acknowledge)
      1=data receive complete            0=data receive in progress
PAP:  paper
      1=no more paper                    0=paper available
ONOF: on-line
      1=printer online                   0=printer offline
ERR:  printer error
      1=printer busy, offline or printer error   0=no error
TIM:  time-out
      1=time-out happened                0=no error
res:  reserved (normally equal 1)
```

Figure 29.2: Printer status byte.

If $\overline{BSY}$ is set (=1) then the printer accepts further data; it is not busy. The printer itself signals, via a set *ACK* bit, that it has received a character correctly, and can receive further data bytes. If no more paper is available in the printer then the *PAP* bit is set. The *ONOF* checks whether the printer concerned is on or offline, perhaps because of an erroneously operated printer key, a paper or another error, or it is even switched off. The *ERR* bit is always set if an error has occurred in the printer, for example because of exhausted paper, a stuck printing head, or an error during the course of data transfer. You may define a time-out value for the printer or parallel interface (as a standard, 20 s are set). If the printer is not ready (bit $\overline{BSY}$) or if the BIOS doesn't receive an ACK signal after the lapse of this time interval, then the BIOS sets the *TIM* bit. On a DOS level you have the opportunity to set an infinite time-out value by the command MODE LPTx ,,P. The system always retries the data transfer after a time-out value.

The values of the individual bits in the printer status byte, except ACK and ERR, reflect the status of the corresponding lines or pins. A bit value of 1 corresponds to a high signal level of about +5 V, a bit value of 0, on the other hand, to a signal level of about 0 V. With ACK and FEH the situation is inverted; a value of 1 corresponds to a high, a bit value of 0 to a low signal level. With the exception of the TIM bit, the printer status byte indicates the contents of the parallel interface concerned; but ACK and FEH are inverted by the BIOS. Further information on the status register and the signals is presented in Section 29.1.5.

Use function 00h of the BIOS interrupt 17h for outputting a character to a printer. But also note that other devices may be connected to a parallel interface. Meanwhile, programs exist through which you may exchange data between two computers via the parallel interface, but these programs directly access the interface registers; a data output by means of BIOS interrupt 17h doesn't succeed in most cases.

Example: `output character 'a' via the BIOS to the first parallel printer.`

```
MOV ah, 00h    ; load function number 00h into ah
MOV al, 'a'    ; print character 'a'
MOV dx, 00h    ; transmit character to LPT1
INT 17h        ; call interrupt
```

Before you can use a parallel interface to output a character, for example after booting, you first need to initialize the interface. Depending upon the printer type, the printer may also carry out an initialization. You may also reset the printer by passing an explicit initialization command. The 01h function, on the other hand, issues an initialization by activating a signal on the interface cable while the reset command is passed over the eight data lines as a normal print character, and interpreted by the printer as a command code and not as a character to be printed.

Example: `initialize second parallel printer.`

```
MOV ah, 01h    ; load function number 01h into ah
MOV dx, 01h    ; initialize LPT2
INT 17h        ; call interrupt
```

You get the status byte with every command in register ah. Through the 02h function of interrupt 17h you also have the opportunity to determine the status without any further action. This is advantageous, for example, if you want to detect in advance whether the printer is ready.

Example: `determine status of the third parallel printer.`

```
MOV ah, 02h    ; load function number 02h into ah
MOV dx, 02h    ; determine status of LPT3
INT 17h        ; call interrupt
```

The BIOS interrupt 17h thus returns more status information concerning the corresponding parallel interface than DOS functions 05h and 40h. Of significance for precisely detecting the cause of a printer error is function 02h. But you don't get ultimate control over the function capabilities of the parallel interface until you have programmed the registers directly. The strategy and the exciting capabilities of the parallel interface beyond plain printing on a parallel printer are discussed in the following sections.

Table 29.1 lists all the relevant sections of the BIOS data area as far as the parallel interface is concerned. The base addresses indicate the beginning of the three interface registers (see Section 29.1.5). By altering the time-out values you can determine how long the BIOS should try to access the printer concerned before a time-out error is reported. Finally, the *installed hardware* byte indicates how many parallel interfaces are present in your system. The startup routine of the BIOS determines the base addresses and the number of interfaces present during the course of booting and writes the corresponding values to the BIOS data area.

Address	Size	Structure 76543210	Contents	Meaning
40:08	word		base address LPT1	
40:0a	word		base address LPT2	
40:0c	word		base address LPT3	
40:0e	word		base address LPT4	
40:11	byte	xx......	installed hardware	number of parallel interfaces (00=0, 01=1, 10=2, 11=3)
40:78	word		time-out LPT1	time-out value in seconds
40:79	word		time-out LPT2	time-out value in seconds
40:7a	word		time-out LPT3	time-out value in seconds
40:7b	word		time-out LPT4	time-out value in seconds

Table 29.1: BIOS data area and parallel interface

29.1.4 Structure, Function and Connection to Printers

The parallel interface demonstrates a quite simple structure, as it is normally used in a PC only for data output to a printer. Figure 29.3 shows a block diagram of this interface.

Connection to the PC system bus is established as usual by a PC interface. Note that the interface adapter cards have only an 8-bit data bus and thus will run even in an ISA or EISA computer with a width of eight bits. This is sufficient, as data is always passed to printers in units of eight bits, and the internal registers of the interface are only eight bits wide. The address decoder decodes address bits A0–A9 if one of the $\overline{IOR}$ and $\overline{IOW}$ signals is enabled to determine whether the interface, and eventually which register, is selected. The control supervises all input and output operations of the registers, and thus of the whole interface.

The central part of the parallel interface is the 8-bit data register, which can be read and written by the CPU (that is, it is bidirectional). The CPU passes the data register the data bytes for the printer. If the processor reads out the data register then it gets the OR-value of the last written byte and the signals which are externally applied to interface pins 2–9. Usually, a printer doesn't drive lines 2–9 onto a high level, so that an IN instruction referring to the data register simply returns the last written value. The situation changes if an external device drives the lines concerned onto a high level. The high level then overwrites a possible 0 bit in the data register, and you get the corresponding OR-value. If you write a 0-byte into the data register in advance of an IN instruction, then this instruction always supplies the signal levels at pins 2–9. You may thus realize, for example, a data exchange with another parallel interface, that is, another PC (see below). If you only want to access a printer (the standard job of the parallel interface), then you simply need to load the data register with the value to be passed.

The status register reflects the current status of the connected printer, which returns status values to the interface via various lines (see Table 29.2). The CPU can only read the status register (it is unidirectional). Using the control register, you may determine the behaviour of the interface, as well as control the printer, via several control signals. The control register can be read and written, and serves particularly to control data transfer to the printer. You can configure the interface so that the IRQ logic issues a hardware interrupt request as soon as the printer is ready to accept another character. The next section discusses further details concerning programming the interface in more detail.

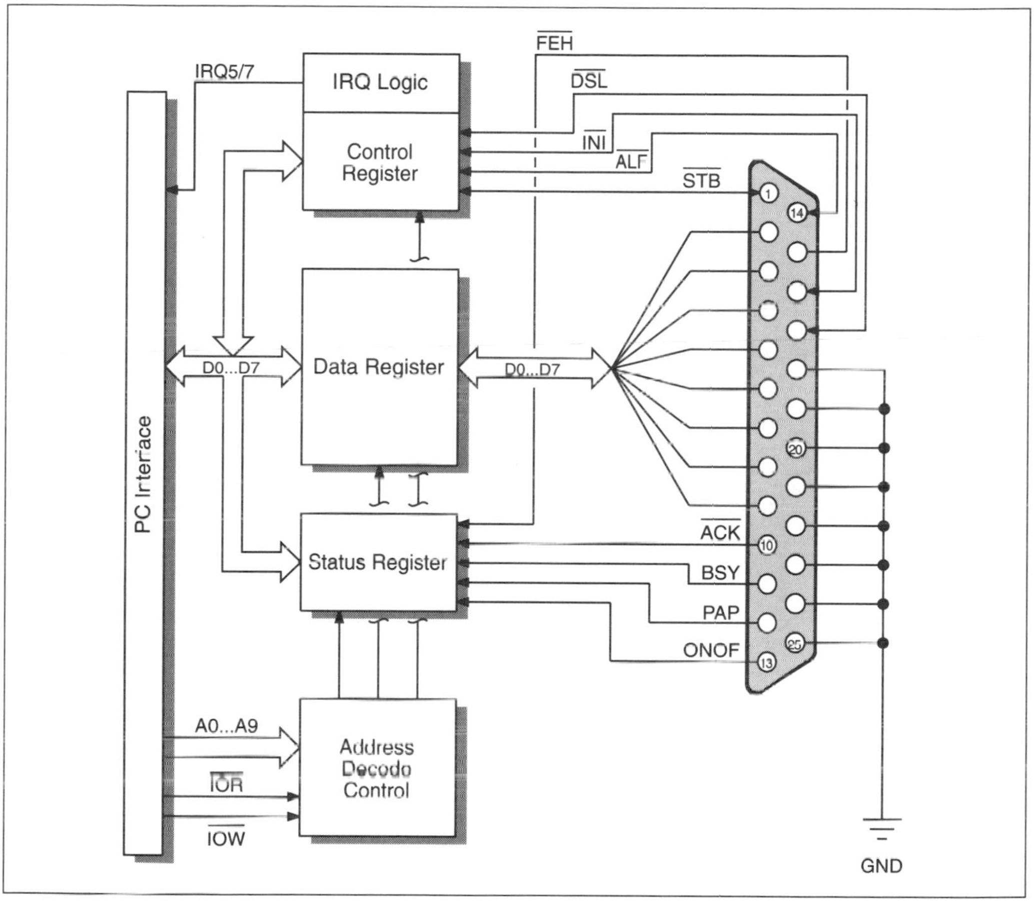

Figure 29.3: Block diagram of the parallel interface.

The connection to the printer is established with a Centronics cable. Table 29.2 lists the assignment and the signals on the pins and plug contacts.

Most printers fix the $\overline{\text{DSL}}$ signal internally to ground, that is, the printer is always selected. In older systems, the CPU was able to select or deselect the printer explicitly by this signal. The eight data pins D0–D7 transfer a data byte to the printer; but you may also receive data if the circuitry of the interface is implemented bidirectionally. By means of lines $\overline{\text{STR}}$, $\overline{\text{ALF}}$ and $\overline{\text{INI}}$, the printer is controlled by the CPU and the interface. A transition of the $\overline{\text{STR}}$ (strobe) signal from a high to a low level instructs the printer to accept the data byte on lines D0–D7 as the data byte to be transferred. With a low level of connection $\overline{ALF}$ the printer carries out an automatic line feed after every printed line. Finally, a transition of the signal $\overline{INI}$ from a high to a low level gives rise to an initialization of the connected printer if it supports the $\overline{INI}$ signal.

25 pin	36 pin	Signal	Description
1	1	$\overline{STR}$	low signal level transmits data to printer
2	2	D0	data bit 0
3	3	D1	data bit 1
4	4	D2	data bit 2
5	5	D3	data bit 3
6	6	D4	data bit 4
7	7	D5	data bit 5
8	8	D6	data bit 6
9	9	D7	data bit 7
10	10	$\overline{ACK}$	low level indicates that printer received one character and is able to receive more
11	11	BSY	high level of signal indicates – character received – printer buffer full – printer initialization – printer offline – printer error
12	12	PAP	high level indicates out of paper
13	13	OFON	high level indicates that printer is online
14	14	$\overline{ALF}$	auto line feed; low level indicates that printer issues line feed automatically
15	32	$\overline{ERR}$	low level indicates – out of paper – printer offline – printer error
16	31	$\overline{INI}$	low level initializes printer
17	36	$\overline{DSL}$	low level selects printer
18–25	19–30, 33	ground	ground 0 V
—	16	0V	—
—	17	case	protective ground of case
—	18	+5V	—
—	34, 35	—	unused

Table 29.2: Layout and signals of 25 and 36 pin plugs

The other control signals are usually passed by the printer to the interface, and indicate the printer's current state. If the CPU attempts to transfer a byte to the printer by activating $\overline{STR}$, then the printer responds with the activation of the $\overline{ACK}$ signal to acknowledge reception. It pulls $\overline{ACK}$ to a low level to indicate that the interface is allowed to pass further data. An activated BSY signal indicates that the printer is currently busy and cannot receive any character. If the printer is out of paper then it raises the PAP signal to a high level. When you are switching the printer online it enables the ONOF signal. You can try this if you like, and read the printer's status by means of function 02h of the BIOS interrupt 17h. Finally, the $\overline{ERR}$ signal indicates, with a low level, that an error has occurred; for example, the printing head is stuck.

Note that not all listed signals are actually supported by all printers. In particular, the $\overline{INI}$ and $\overline{DSL}$ signals are not used often. Furthermore, the parallel interface inverts some signals internally. The meaning of a signal and the accompanying register bit is then inverted; therefore, pay attention!

29.1.5 Programming the Registers Directly

The parallel interface has three registers with which you can transfer data and control the printer as well as the interface. The base address of the registers for all interfaces LPT1–LPT4 is stored in the BIOS data area (see Table 29.1). The data register (Figure 29.4) is located at offset 00h, the status register (Figure 29.5) at offset 01h and the control register (Figure 29.6) at offset 02h. Generally, the base address of LPT1 is 378h and that of LPT2 278h. The parallel interface on a Hercules or monochrome adapter card starts at 3bch, but may still represent LPT1. Further, 2bch can be used as a fourth possibility, so the registers can serve a maximum of four parallel interfaces. During the course of booting, the BIOS checks in the I/O address order 3bch, 378h, 278h and 2bch whether a parallel interface is physically present at the corresponding I/O addresses, and assigns those actually found the names LPT1, LPT2, etc. in succession. But some BIOS variants support only two parallel interfaces, and don't recognize any others. A configuration check by means of the BIOS interrupt INT 11h then returns only two installed parallel interfaces, even though you have installed four, for example. The following sections discuss the meaning of the registers in more detail.

	7	6	5	4	3	2	1	0
Printer Signal	D_7	D_6	D_5	D_4	D_3	D_2	D_1	D_0
Pin Number	9	8	7	6	5	4	3	2

D7–D0: data bit 7–0

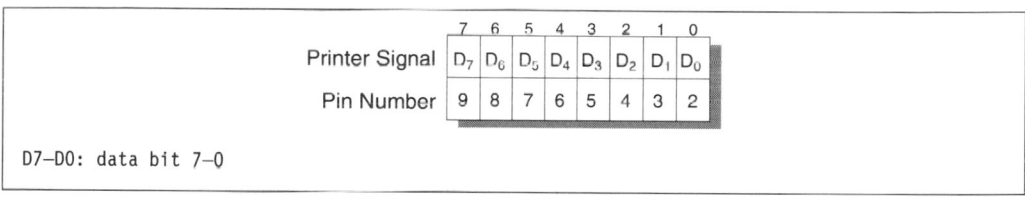

Figure 29.4: Data register (bidirectional, offset 00h).

The data register is eight bits wide, and accommodates the data bits to be transferred. You may read and write this register simply by using an IN or OUT instruction.

	7	6	5	4	3	2	1	0
Printer Signal	$\overline{BSY}$	$\overline{ACK}$	PAP	OFON	$\overline{ERR}$	x	x	x
Pin Number	11	10	12	13	15	–	–	–

$\overline{BSY}$: busy
1=printer not busy 0=printer busy, offline or error
$\overline{ACK}$: acknowledge
1=data transfer in progress 0=data transfer to printer complete
PAP: paper
1=no more paper 0=paper available
OFON: offline or online
1=printer online 0=printer offline
$\overline{ERR}$: printer error
1=no error 0=printer error
x: unused (normally equal 1)

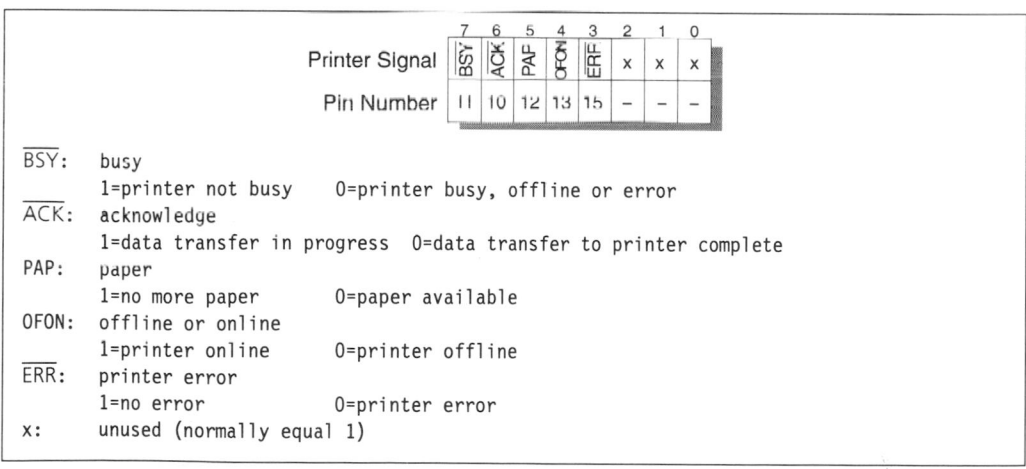

Figure 29.5: Status register (read-only, offset 01h).

The status register is read-only, and returns control information from the printer. Upon a cleared $\overline{BSY}$ bit the printer is currently busy (that is, the printer buffer is full), a character transfer is in progress, or the printer carries out an initialization. The interface may not transfer another character, but has to wait until the $\overline{BSY}$ bit is set. The $\overline{ACK}$ bit, together with the STR bit of the control register (see Figure 29.6), is of significance for a correct data transfer. If the interface has transferred a data byte to the printer, then the printer activates the $\overline{ACK}$ line to acknowledge receipt of the character. Accordingly, the $\overline{ACK}$ bit in the status register is cleared. If $\overline{ACK}$ is set, this shows the printer is still occupied with the reception (if $\overline{BSY}$ is cleared simultaneously), or that the previous character transfer was a long time ago (with a set $\overline{BSY}$ bit). To determine whether the printer is ready to receive data, you must therefore use $\overline{BSY}$, and for the character transfer itself the $\overline{ACK}$ bit.

If the printer is out of paper the *PAP* bit is set to 1. At the same time, the *OFON* bit is cleared and the $\overline{ERR}$ bit is set to indicate this error, and to tell you the printer is now offline. By investigating the OFON bit you can therefore determine whether the printer is online at all, for example, in the case of a time-out error.

	7	6	5	4	3	2	1	0
Printer Signal	x	x	x	IRQ	DSL	$\overline{INI}$	ALF	STR
Pin Number	–	–	–	–	17	16	14	1

```
x:   unused (normally equal 1)
IRQ: hardware interrupt request
     1=enabled                          0=disabled
DSL: printer select
     1=printer selected                 0=printer not selected
INI: printer initialization
     1=printer is operating normal      0=carry out initialization
ALF: automatic line feed
     1=automatic line feed by printer   0=line feed by host
STR: strobe
     1=transfer data to printer         0=no data transfer
```

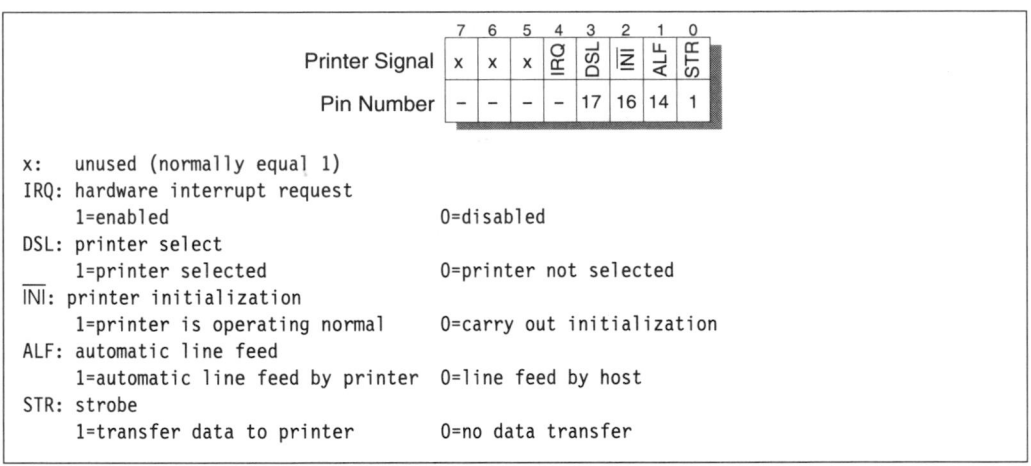

Figure 29.6: Control register (bidirectional, offset 02h).

The control register controls the printer behaviour and the generation of hardware interrupts by the parallel interface. If the *IRQ* bit is set, then the interface issues a hardware interrupt via IRQ5 (LPT2) or IRQ7 (LPT1) corresponding to INT 0dh and INT 0fh, respectively, if a transition of the $\overline{ACK}$ signal from a high to a low level occurs. Thus an interrupt occurs exactly when the printer acknowledges receipt of the character. The accompanying handler can then transfer the next character to the ready printer. But the PC BIOS doesn't usually use this interrupt-driven data transfer, but simply investigates the $\overline{ACK}$ bit to detect the acknowledgement by the printer. With the IRQ bit you can, for example, implement an interrupt driven and bidirectional data exchange via the parallel interface. Details on this subject are discussed in the following section.

Note that the IRQ channel of the interface is usually set by a jumper or DIP switch. In the case of polling by the BIOS, this is insignificant as an interrupt never occurs. But if you program a handler, for example for the IRQ channel of LPT1 to realize a hardware-driven data transfer in the background, you must ensure that IRQ7 is actually used for the LPT1 board. The situation gets even more complicated if all four possible parallel interfaces can issue an interrupt. As only two IRQ channels, and therefore also only two handlers, are available, the interrupt handler must be able, for example by reading the status bits, to determine which interface has actually issued the interrupt request.

Printers that strictly orient to the Centronics standard must be explicitly activated by setting the *DSL* bit. On IBM-compatible parallel printers the corresponding line is not used, and the printer is always enabled when you switch it on or press the online button. A cleared $\overline{\text{INI}}$ bit gives rise to a printer initialization. You also achieve the same effect on most printers by passing an explicit reset command; the only difference here is that an electrical signal of the interface, and not a command code, is used. If you set the *ALF*, the printer carries out an automatic line feed after printing each line.

For the data transfer to printers besides $\overline{\text{ACK}}$ the *STR* bit is also of significance. A set STR bit generates a short *strobe pulse* that instructs the printer to accept the signals on the data lines, according to the data register, as the transfer data. Thus, STR clocks the data transfer from the interface to the printer. Note that setting the STR bit only gives rise to a single strobe pulse. If you want to pass another data byte it is not, therefore, sufficient only to load the data register. Additionally, you must clear and set the STR bit again to generate a strobe pulse. The following example illustrates the strategy for printing a character out to a printer by directly programming the interface registers:

Example: routine for outputting a character to printer LPT1 (language: Microsoft C 5.10); the routine returns with an error code.

```
int parall_output(char character)
{
  int i, code;

  for (i = 0; i < TIMEOUT_COUNT; i++) {  /* wait until printer no more busy */
    code = inp(0x379);                   /* read status register */
    if ((code & 0x80) == 0x80) break;    /* check whether BSY bit is set */
  }
  if (i == TIMEOUT_COUNT) return (1);    /* BSY timeout error, error code 1 */

  outp(0x378, (int) character);          /* load data register */

  code = inp(0x37a);                     /* read control register */
  code = code | 0x01;                    /* set STB bit */
  outp(0x37a, code);                     /* strobe high */

  for (i = 0; i < STROBE_WAIT) ;         /* wait a short time */
  code = inp(0x37a);                     /* read control register */
  code = code & 0xfe;                    /* clear STB bit */
  outp(0x37a, code);                     /* strobe low, data are transferred */

  for (i = 0; i < TIMEOUT_COUNT; i++) {  /* wait for ACK from printer */
    code = inp(0x379);                   /* read status register */
    if ((code & 0x40) == 0x00) break;    /* check whether ACK bit is cleared */
  }
```

```
  if (i == TIMEOUT_COUNT) return (2);      /* ACK timeout error, error code 2 */

  return(0);                               /* character passed correctly, error code 0 */
}
```

If you compare the meaning of the bits in the control and status registers with the assignment of the corresponding lines, then you see that the bits $\overline{\text{BSY}}$, DSL, ALF and STR are inverted compared to their corresponding signals. Thus the parallel interface inverts the signals at pins 11, 17, 14 and 1, respectively. Why especially these signals are inverted I don't know, but maybe you have a good idea?

29.1.6 More About LPTx – General Interface Assignment

All the descriptions above only refer to the use of the parallel interface for accessing a parallel printer. For example, the receiving interface inside the printer is responsible for pulling the $\overline{\text{ACK}}$ signal to a low level if the printer has received the character correctly. But, of course, you are free to connect any other device to the parallel interface, too; for example, a small robot. This robot doesn't need to generate an active-low signal $\overline{\text{ACK}}$ in any way when data has been transferred. Instead, the 12 pins 1–9, 14, 16 and 17 are available to you without restriction for output and the 17 pins 1–17 for fetching signals. Thus the parallel interface is very flexible, and you have the opportunity to use it in some way which differs significantly from its very limited use as a printer interface.

To access an external device connected to the parallel interface, you need to know what conseqences a set or cleared bit in the data or control register for the signals at the corresponding pins has, and which signal level a set or cleared bit in one of these three registers means. Exactly these points are discussed in the following sections. Some precautions are demanded as the parallel interface inverts several signals before they are output at or read from the corresponding pin. This applies (as already mentioned) for pins 1, 11, 14 and 17.

	7	6	5	4	3	2	1	0
Pin Signal	P_9	P_8	P_7	P_6	P_5	P_4	P_3	P_2

P9–P2: signal level at pins 9–2 (0=low, 1=high)

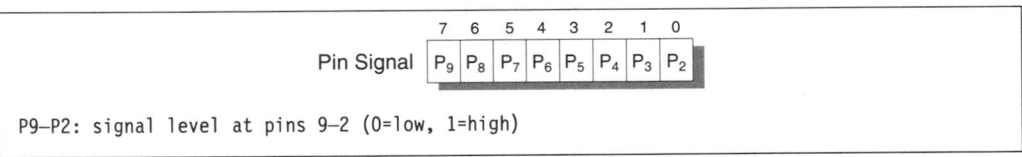

Figure 29.7: Data register (bidirectional, offset 00h).

The eight bits of the bidirectional data register (Figure 29.7) correspond to the pins with numbers 9–2. The assignment of bit value and signal level is not inverted, that is, a set bit corresponds to a high-level signal of about +5 V. Ensure, when reading the register value, that the value of a bit is determined by OR-ing the last written bit and the level of the applied signal. If you want to determine the «pure» pin signal, then you must first set the register bit to 0; afterwards, you may determine the signal level at the accompanying pin correctly. The same also applies for all bidirectional registers. (One reader reports that his interface returns the AND value of the last written bit and the signal level; all parallel interfaces tested, however, return the OR value.)

	7	6	5	4	3	2	1	0
Pin Signal	$\overline{P_{11}}$	P_{10}	P_{12}	P_{13}	P_{15}	x	x	x

P10–P15: signal level at pins 10–15 (0=low, 1=high)
$\overline{\text{P11}}$: inverted signal level at pins 10–15 (0=high, 1=low)

Figure 29.8: Status register (read-only, offset 01h).

The status register (Figure 29.8) is read-only, even for a general use of the parallel interface. The three low-order register bits are not used and usually provide a value of 1. The four most significant bits 3–6 indicate the signal levels at pins 15, 13, 12 and 10 in non-inverted form. On the other hand, the interface inverts the signal level at pin 11, that is, a set bit $\overline{\text{P11}}$ corresponds to a low, a cleared bit to a high signal level.

	7	6	5	4	3	2	1	0
Pin Signal	x	x	x	IRQ	$\overline{P_{17}}$	P_{16}	$\overline{P_{14}}$	$\overline{P_{1}}$

IRQ: hardware interrupt request
1=enabled 0=disabled
$\overline{\text{P17}}$, $\overline{\text{P14}}$, $\overline{\text{P1}}$: inverted signal level at pins P17, P14, P1 (0=high, 1=low)
P16: signal level at pin P16 (0=low, 1=high)

Figure 29.9: Control register (partially bidirectional, offset 02h).

The control register (Figure 29.9) is partially bidirectional. The IRQ bit has a meaning only for write accesses; you can use it for defining whether the interface is to issue a hardware interrupt via IRQ5 or IRQ7 if the signal at pin 10 (see status register) drops from a high to a low level. Reading the IRQ bit always returns the last written value. The three most significant bits are not used, and return a value of 1 during the course of a read access. The four low-order bits of the register, on the other hand, are bidirectional. But note that only the bit P16 corresponding to pin 16 is not inverted. The other three bits indicate the inverted ones of the signals at pins 17, 14 and 1 when read. If you are writing some values then the interface sets the signal levels at these pins so that they appear inverted compared to the bit values in the control register.

Another possible application of the parallel interface is the control of an external device. Suitable signal levels at the programmable output pins then drive the device accordingly. Via the input pins, the device can also return information to the PC. With a soldering iron and some skill you can, for example, construct a computer-controlled irrigation plant for your garden where the parallel interface controls magnetic valves and pumps to irrigate the garden, depending upon signals that humidity and sunshine sensors apply to the input pins.

A somewhat more serious application is the exchange of data between two computers via the parallel interface. This works much faster than by means of a serial interface, as the data is transferred in portions of one byte and not only of a single bit (if you use only one of the output lines for transferring control information then you may even transfer eleven bits at a time). Besides the continuous access to another computer, this data exchange is advantageous particularly if no data exchange by means of floppies is possible, for example because the floppy sizes are incompatible. Figure 29.10 shows a scheme for a possible data transfer via the parallel interface.

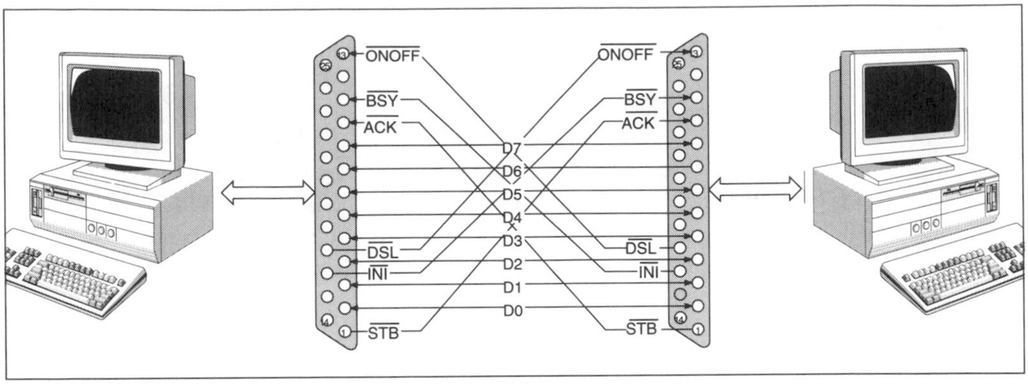

Figure 29.10: Data exchange via the parallel interface. For a data exchange, several control and status lines must be interchanged to enable a handshake.

As you can see from Figure 29.10, data pins 2–9 of the two interfaces are connected to each other, and pins 1 ($\overline{STB}$), 17 ($\overline{DSL}$) and 16 ($\overline{INI}$) are connected crossways to pins 10 ($\overline{ACK}$), 13 (ONOFF) and 11 (BSY). The data exchange proceeds as follows:

1. The transmitter raises line 17 ($\overline{DSL}$) to a high level by clearing bit $\overline{P17}$ in the control register to indicate that it wants to transfer data to the receiver.

2. The receiver detects this selection by means of the set bit P13 in the status register, and activates the line $\overline{INI}$ by setting bit P16 in the control register.

3. The transmitter detects this acknowledgement by the receiver through the cleared bit P11 in the status register; the connection is therefore established, the roles as transmitter and receiver are unambiguously defined, and the transmitter is now able to transfer data to the receiver.

4. The transmitter loads the character to be transmitted into the data register and lowers the potential of the $\overline{STB}$ line by means of a set bit $\overline{P1}$ in the control register to a low level, and clears the bit $\overline{P1}$ afterwards to raise the potential of the line $\overline{STB}$ to a high level again. Because of the short pulse, the data transfer is started and an IRQ is issued in the receiver.

5. The called IRQ handler of the receiver reads the data register and thus the transmitted data, and transfers it into a buffer in main memory.

6. Afterwards, the receiver lowers the potential of the $\overline{STB}$ line by means of a set $\overline{P1}$ bit on the control register to a low level, and clears the $\overline{P1}$ bit to raise the potential of the $\overline{STB}$ line again to a high level. This short pulse acknowledges the reception of the data and issues an IRQ in the transmitter.

7. The called IRQ handler of the transmitter returns control to the transfer program, which repeats steps 4–6 until all data has been transferred.

8. The transmitter disconnects itself by setting bit $\overline{P17}$ in the control register.
9. The receiver responds to the disconnection by clearing bit P16 in the control register; now the roles as transmitter and receiver can be distributed again.

Steps 1–9 outline the data transfer only, of course. For the receiver's response to the selection by the transmitter or the acknowledgement by the receiver, several check steps for determining time-out errors should additionally be implemented. With the remaining pins 12, 14 and 15, for example, an additional error signal, an attention signal (if the receiver has important data ready for the transmitter), or other status information may be transmitted. Clever programming of the steps required enables a data transfer rate of more than 100 kbytes/s. Not very exciting when compared to «real» networks, but nevertheless significantly more than via a serial interface. The main disadvantage, though, is that the connection length must not exceed 5 m. Additionally, you are forced to fetch your soldering iron to form the necessary wirings.

29.2 Serial Interface

Besides the parallel interface for accessing parallel printers, the serial interface is of great importance on a PC because of its flexibility. Various devices such as a plotter, modem, mouse and, of course, a printer can be connected to a serial interface. The structure, functioning and programming of the serial interface are the subject of the following sections.

29.2.1 Serial and Asynchronous Data Transfer

We have already met parallel data transfer in the previous section. Characteristic of parallel data transfer is that the bits of a data byte, and eventually a parity bit, are transmitted in parallel, that is, simultaneously via a plurality of data lines. Thus for a data byte and a parity bit, nine data lines are required. In a serial data transfer the individual data bits and the eventual parity bit are, however, transferred successively, that is, in a serial manner via a single data line. One objection to this might be that the parallel interface also passes the data bytes successively (that is, serially) when printing a large document. But the difference is that in a parallel data transfer the individual data units (that is, the data bytes) are transmitted as a whole, while the serial data transfer splits even the data units into single bits and transfers them bit by bit.

Synchronous and Asynchronous Transfer

The serial data transfer is further distinguished according to whether the data exchange is carried out synchronously or asynchronously. The difference is quite simple: in a synchronous transfer one or more additional signals are transmitted, which indicate when the next bit is valid on the data line. These signals may be formed by clock signals of a clock signal source or by handshake signals of the form *request* and *acknowledge*. The main advantage of synchronous transfer is that the receiver responds to various clock rates, as long as its maximum frequency is not exceeded. For this purpose it simply detects, for example, the low–high transition of the clock signal.

In contrast, in an asynchronous data transfer the data bits themselves accommodate a minimum of synchronization information; receiver and transmitter must operate at the same clock frequency here. The embedded synchronization information comprises a so-called *start bit*, which indicates the beginning of a data unit, and at least one *stop bit*, which indicates the end of the data unit concerned. If the parity information (which is also frequently used for a parallel data transfer) is taken into account, too, then a *serial data unit (SDU)* consists of a start bit, the data bits, eventually one parity bit, and at least one stop bit. Thus, compared to the synchronous serial data transfer we have an overhead because of the start and stop bits here.

Parity and Baud Rate

The parity is a simple and, unfortunately, also a poor protection against transmission errors. Parity can only detect single-bit errors reliably; burst errors with several disturbed bits are not detected with a probability of 50%. Thus the parity is only suitable for short and less error-prone transfer paths; for other applications, CRC codes are much more reliable, but are more complicated to calculate. The advantage of parity is that nearly all serial interface chips support the generation and checking of parity bits on a hardware level. Five different parities in total are distinguished:

- no parity: no parity bit is embedded at all.
- even parity: the parity bit is set so that in the data bits and the parity bit together an even number of 1s appears.
- odd parity: the parity bit is set so that in the data bits and the parity bit together an odd number of 1s appears.
- mark: the parity bit is always set to a value of 1.
- space: the parity bit is always set to a 0.

At this point, a few remarks are needed on the apparently pointless parities mark and space. Mark and space are actually suitable only for detecting errors in the parity bit itself. When an SDU with a cleared or set parity bit arrives, and a mark or space parity should actually be valid, an error of the parity bit has occurred. This doesn't say anything about whether the data bits are correct or not, of course. Inversely, the data bits can be destroyed, but the receiver doesn't notice that at all if the parity bit is OK. But nevertheless mark and space are frequently used, and I don't know why: perhaps you have a good idea (if so, please tell me)! Mark and space are thus only of minor value. Leave out the parity in this case, although no parity seems to be less reliable than the parities mark and space (but this only *seems* to be).

Another measure in connection with serial data transfer which frequently gives rise to misunderstandings is the *baud rate*. Named after the French mathematician J.M.E. Baudot, it means the number of signal changes of a transfer channel per second. As for the usual serial interfaces, the signal changes are equidistant in time and a very simple binary data encoding is carried out (a logical high level equal to mark corresponds to a «1», a logical low level equal to space to a «0»), the baud rate here is equal to the number of transferred *bits per second (bps)* if one also includes the start, parity and stop bits. For more powerful encodings, and by using data compression methods, the data rates (in bps) may exceed the baud rate significantly.

SDU and Serialization

Before an asynchronous serial data transfer between two devices can take place, transmitter and receiver must be set up to the same formats. To the format belong the number of data bits, whether and eventually which parity is to be established, as well as the number of stop bits. Valid specifications for the number of data bits are five, six, seven, and eight. If you choose five data bits the serial interface chip in your PC automatically adds 11/2 stop bits. This means that the active-time of the stop bit is as long as 11/2 bits; otherwise you may choose one or two stop bits. Moreover, you must set the baud rate for transmitter and receiver to the same value. As an example, Figure 29.11 shows an SDU with one start bit, seven data bits, odd parity and one stop bit. Note that the start bit always has a value of 0 corresponding to space and the stop bit(s) is (are) always equal to 1 corresponding to mark.

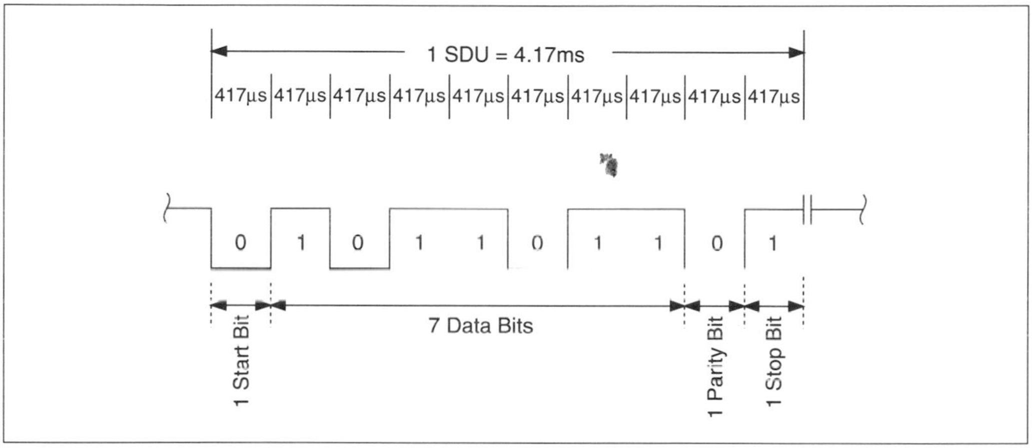

Figure 29.11: SDU. The serial data unit shown has one start bit, seven data bits, one parity bit, and one stop bit. At the selected baud rate of 2400, each bit is transferred within 417 µs.

But how is the SDU generated inside the interface, and output or received, and the received SDU separated into its components? Figure 29.12 shows a scheme for generating the SDU. The interface chip has a transmitter hold register for transmitting data, which first fetches the data bytes from the CPU. According to the selected data format, the SDU logic puts the start bit in front of the set number of data bits, eventually calculates the parity bit, and appends it together with the set number of stop bits to the data bits. The thus formed SDU is transferred into the transmitter shift register. The transmitter shift register is now operated by a clock source according to the phase of the baud rate, and thus provides (beginning with the start bit and the least significant data bit) the individual bits of the SDU at its serial output. For this purpose, the AND-value of the clock signal and the current least significant SDU bit at the output of the transmitter shift register are formed. The operation mode of the transmitters causes first the low-order and then the high-order data bits to be supplied. If no further data is to be output, the chip provides a mark signal (that is, a level corresponding to a logical «1»), and drives the transmission line to a logical high level.

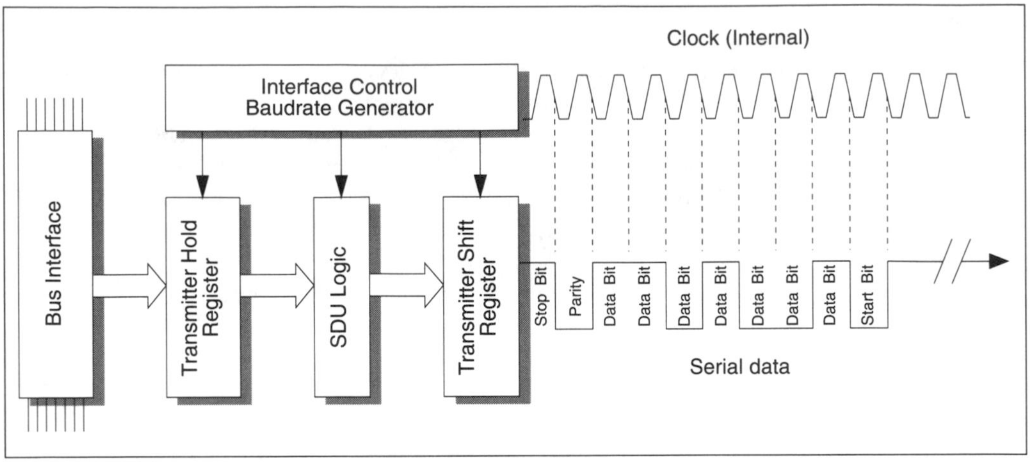

Figure 29.12: Transmitting an SDU.

The reception of an SDU proceeds inversely. The start bit with a logical value of 1 corresponding to space is an unambiguous signal for an incoming SDU, as the reception line is usually held on mark by the transmitter. Thus the start bit acts as a trigger pulse, and starts the receiver in the serial interface chip. The SDU bits are loaded into the receiver shift register according to the phase of the setup baud rate. This means that in the receiver shift register first the low-order and then the high-order data bits arrive. The receiver logic separates start bit, parity bit (if present) and the stop bit(s) from the received SDU bits, eventually calculates the parity of the received bits, and compares it to the setup parity. Afterwards, the extracted data bits are transferred into the receiver buffer register from which they may be read out as the received data byte by the CPU. This reception scheme is illustrated in Figure 29.13.

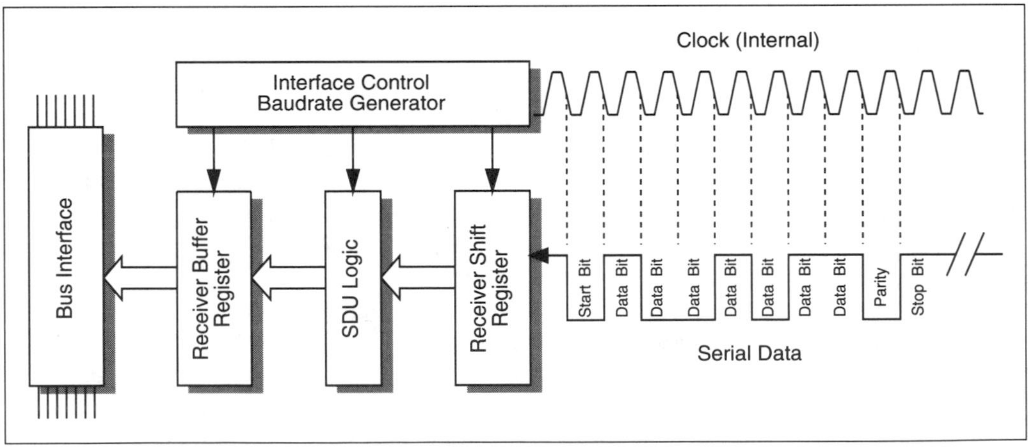

Figure 29.13: Receiving an SDU.

From the description of the transmission and reception process, it can be readily seen that transmitter and receiver must be set to the same baud rate. Additionally, the set data formats (that is, number of data bits, parity and number of stop bits) must also coincide, otherwise the receiver may reassemble possibly a different byte from that which the transmitter was passed for transmitting. Upon reception of an SDU, various errors may occur, discussed briefly in the following:

- Framing error: if the receiver has detected an invalid stop bit then the received SDU doesn't fit into the «frame» that the setup data format and the setup baud rate define. Thus the receiver has detected a framing error.
- Break error: if the reception line is at a logical low level (corresponding to space) for a longer time than an SDU usually lasts then the receiver assumes that the connection to the transmitter is broken, as the transmitter usually drives the line to a logical high level as long as no data is transferred.
- Overrun error: if data is arriving in the receiver faster than it is read from the receiver buffer register by the CPU, then a later received byte may overwrite the older data not yet read from the buffer. This is called an overrun error.
- Parity error: if none of the above indicated errors has occurred and the SDU has been received seemingly in a correct form, a parity error may still be present, that is, the calculated parity doesn't coincide with the set one. The reason is either damage to the SDU in the course of the transmission (for example by noise), or a different setup for the parity at the transmitter's and the receiver's sites.

29.2.2 RS-232C Interface

Most PC interfaces for serial data exchanges follow the RS-232C standard of the EIA (**E**lectronic **I**ndustries **A**ssociation, the publisher of the RS-232C specification). In Europe you will often find the term V.24, which is identical to RS-232C, but published by the CCITT. (The following uses RS-232C.) The standard defines the mechanical, electrical, and logical interface between a data terminal equipment (DTE) and a data carrier equipment (DCE). The DTE is usually formed by a computer (in our case, the PC), and the DCE by a modem. The RS-232C standard defines 25 lines between DTE and DCE, and thus a 25-pin plug. Most are reserved for a synchronous data transfer. To remain on the chosen path of the *PC*, the discussion is restricted to its typical use in a Personal Computer: this is serial, asynchronous data exchange. For this purpose, only eleven of the RS-232C signals are required. Furthermore, IBM defines a 9-pin connection for its serial interface, where two of the usually present RS-232C lines are missing. Table 29.3 shows the corresponding assignments and signals for 25- and 9-pin plugs.

On the 9-pin connector the protective ground and the signal for the data signal rate are missing, but the remaining nine signals are sufficient for a serial asynchronous data exchange between a DTE and a DCE in accordance with the RS-232C standard. The pins 3/2 and 2/3 transfer the data signals; the rest of the connections are intended for the control signals.

For controlling the data transfer between DTE and DCE the five control signals RTS (request to send, pin 4/7), CTS (clear to send, pin 5/8), DCD (data carrier detect, pin 8/1), DSR (data set ready, pin 6/6) and DTR (data terminal ready, pin 20/4) are decisive. The meaning of the signals and their use is as follows (note that the computer forms the DTE and the modem is the DCE; the receiver of the data may be far away, for example, a modem in China):

25 pin	9 pin	Signal	Direction	Description
1	—	—	—	protective ground
2	3	TD	DTE→DCE	transmitted data
3	2	RD	DCE→DTE	received data
4	7	RTS	DTE→DCE	request to send
5	8	CTS	DCE→DTE	clear to send
6	6	DSR	DCE→DTE	data set ready
7	5	—	—	signal ground (common)
8	1	DCD	DCE→DTE	data carrier detect
20	4	DTR	DTE→DCE	data terminal ready
22	9	RI	DCE→DTE	ring indicator
23	—	DSRD	DCE↔DTE	data signal rate detector

Table 29.3: Layout and signals of 25 and 9 pin plugs

RTS (Request to Send)

This signal from the DTE instructs the DCE to prepare for a data transfer from the DTE to the DCE. Thus the DTE signals to the DCE that it intends to output data that is to be accepted by the DCE. The DCE activates its carrier frequency to transmit data to the target.

CTS (Clear to Send)

This signal from the DCE indicates to the DTE that the DCE is ready to accept data from the DTE. The DCE usually activates the CTS signal as a response to an activation of the RTS signal from the DTE. If the DCE has activated the signal, the DTE can begin to output data.

RTS and CTS distribute the roles of the two communication partners as transmitter and receiver for a half-duplex connection, and switch the two partners between transmitting and receiving. Thus RTS and CTS form something like handshake signals.

DCD (Data Carrier Detect)

The DCE activates the DCD signal if it has detected the carrier signal from the transmission target and the connection is going to be set up. DCD remains active while the connection remains established. In the half-duplex mode, only the receiving DCE outputs an active DCD signal.

DSR (Data Set Ready)

The DCE (usually a modem) informs the DTE by an active DSR signal that it is switched on, has completed all preparations for a connection to the target, and can communicate with the DTE. Data set generally denotes an external data terminal equipment.

DTR (Data Terminal Ready)

The signal from the DTE indicates the general readiness of the DTE, and is usually activated at power-up of the DTE. The DCE may be connected to the line afterwards, but DTR doesn't explicitly instruct this connection; this is carried out by RTS. If the connection between DTE and DCE is established once, then DTR must remain active throughout the whole connection time. Thus DTR and DSR are responsible for *establishing the connection*; RTS and CTS, on the other hand, are responsible for the *data transfer* (and the transfer direction in the case of a half-duplex connection). Without an active DTR signal the RTS and CTS signals have no effect; the DCE doesn't respond in any way to the control signals, and doesn't output or accept data. Thus DTR represents something like a «main switch». Deactivating DTR or DSR breaks the connection, but note that RI works independently of DTR; a modem may activate the RI signal even if DTR is not active.

The RI (ring indicator) signal informs the DTE that a ring has occurred at the DCE. This is the case, for example, if an external computer system calls the modem via the telephone line as it wants to set up a connection to your PC. If you operate a public database then your clients may dial your database via the telephone network and fetch data.

The 25-pin connector may additionally transmit a DSRD (data signal rate detector; pin 23) signal which allows switching between two different baud rates. The signal can be passed between the DTE and DCE in both directions, thus it is possible, for example, that the DTE instructs the DCE to select a high baud rate or that the DCE informs the DTE about the baud rate of the transmission channel. The use of the five indicated control signals differs depending upon the connection type. The following sections discuss the meaning and use of the control signals for a simplex, half-duplex, and full-duplex connection.

Simplex Connection

In principle, there are two possibilities here: data transfer from the DTE to the DCE, or vice versa. In the first case, only the DTE transfers data to the DCE via the TD line. The RD line is not connected. The DCE doesn't use RTS or the DTE holds the RTS signal active all the time. In the same way, the DTE doesn't use the return signal CTS from the DCE, or the DCE holds CTS constantly on an active level. The DCE always outputs an inactive DCD signal as it can only receive data from the DTE and transfer it to the destination, but cannot receive a data carrier signal from the destination. DSR is either always active or is activated when the destination is called. By means of DTR, the DTE can indicate to the DCE that it is ready for operation as usual and may activate or disable the DCE. The RI signal has virtually no meaning with this simplex connection, because normally the transmitter calls the receiver. Nevertheless, it is possible that the target via the DCE requests the DTE by means of RI to transfer data. One example for such a simplex connection is the access of a serial printer via the serial interface. Then the printer responds with a return signal (via DSR, for example) only to control the data transfer so that its internal buffer doesn't overflow.

In the latter case, however, only the DCE transfers data to the DTE via the RD line. The TD line is not connected. The DCE doesn't use RTS either, or the DTE holds the RTS signal active all the time. In the same way, the DTE doesn't use the return signal CTS from the DCE, or the DCE holds CTS constantly at an active level. The DCE may output an active DCD signal as it can detect a carrier signal from an external device and transfer data to the DTE. DSR is either always active or is activated when the external device gets ready. By means of DTR, the DTE can indicate that it is ready for operation, and it can activate or disable the DCE as usual. The RI signal has a meaning again, as the external device may call the DTE via the DCE.

Half-Duplex Connection

On a half-duplex connection both the DTE and the DCE can operate as receiver and transmitter, but only one data line is available, which is alternately used by the DTE and DCE. The TD and RD lines thus output and receive data, respectively, in a strictly ordered manner. For assigning the roles as receiver and transmitter between the DTE and DCE, the handshake control signals RTS and CTS are used. If the DTE device wants to act as a transmitter, then it activates the RTS signal and waits for an acknowledgement of the other DCE device by means of the CTS signal. Now data can be exchanged while the DTE is acting as the transmitter and the DCE as the receiver, otherwise the DCE may operate as a transmitter and the DTE as a receiver. The DCE can output an active DCD signal because the data transfer may be carried out to the DTE. DSR is either active or activates when the target is called. The DTR signal indicates (as usual) the operation readiness of the DTE, and enables or disables the DCE. In a half-duplex connection, the transfer direction can be switched by means of the RTS and CTS signals; also, the RI signal is of importance again, to inform the DTE that an external device wants to establish a connection to the DTE via the DCE. The output and reception of data is then controlled by means of RTS and CTS (in a somewhat ponderous way, however). Figure 29.14 shows the course of the signal levels for a connection of DTE and DCE in time.

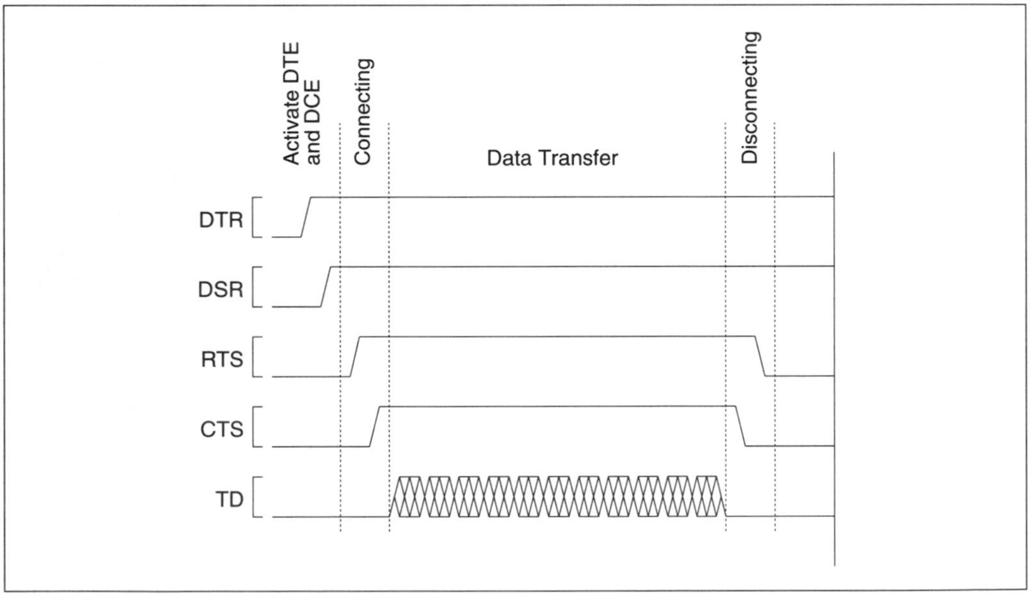

Figure 29.14: The course of the signal levels in the case of a connection between DTE and DCE.

Full-Duplex Connection

Most microcomputer modems are full-duplex, and transfer data in both directions simultaneously; thus DTE and DCE act simultaneously as receiver and transmitter. Whether physically two data lines are actually present or only two separate logical channels exist is insignificant. It is important that neither of the two transmitters (and simultaneously receivers) needs to wait for transmission enabling by its partner. The RTS and CTS signals thus are without meaning: RTS is usually not used, or is always active as CTS. Further, the DSR signal is also enabled all the time on most modems, but on other DCEs, DSR may be active only if the preparations for calling the destination device are completed. The signal is normally activated by the DCE only if it has detected a carrier signal from the destination device. Also in this case, the DTR signal acts as a main switch, and RI indicates that an external device wants to establish a connection with the DTE via the DCE. A full-duplex connection is very comfortable, as you as the programmer do not need to pay attention to the roles of receiver and transmitter, that is, you may keep the RTS signal active all the time while ignoring the CTS and DSR signals.

Figures 29.15a–f show an example for the various activations of the control signals if an incoming call reaches your PC via a full duplex modem.

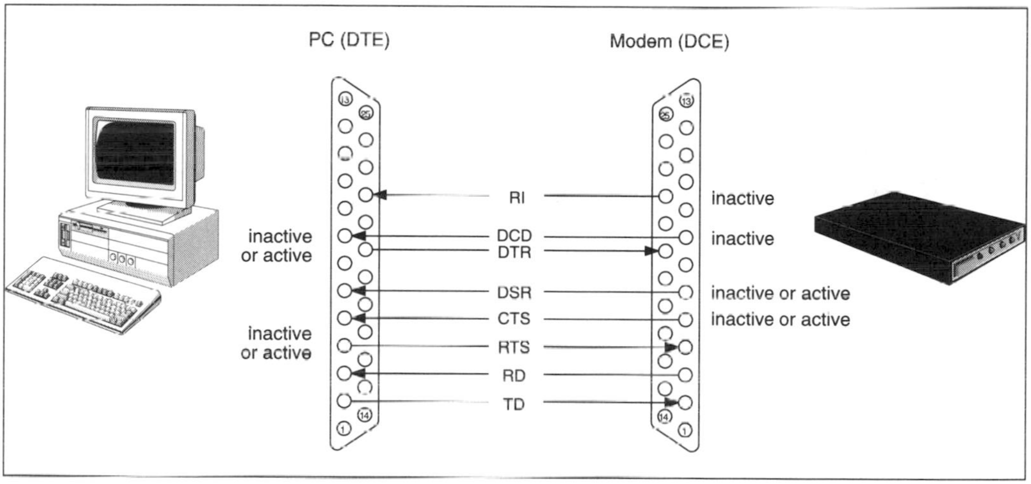

Figure 29.15 (a): Stand-by condition of PC (DTE) and modem (DCE).

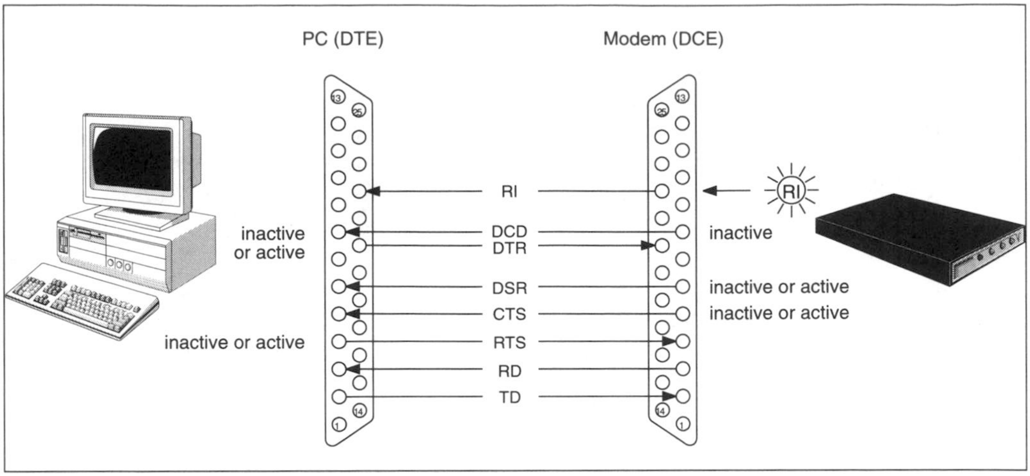

Figure 29.15 (b): An external unit attempts to call the PC via the modem; the modem activates signal RI each time the external unit is ringing.

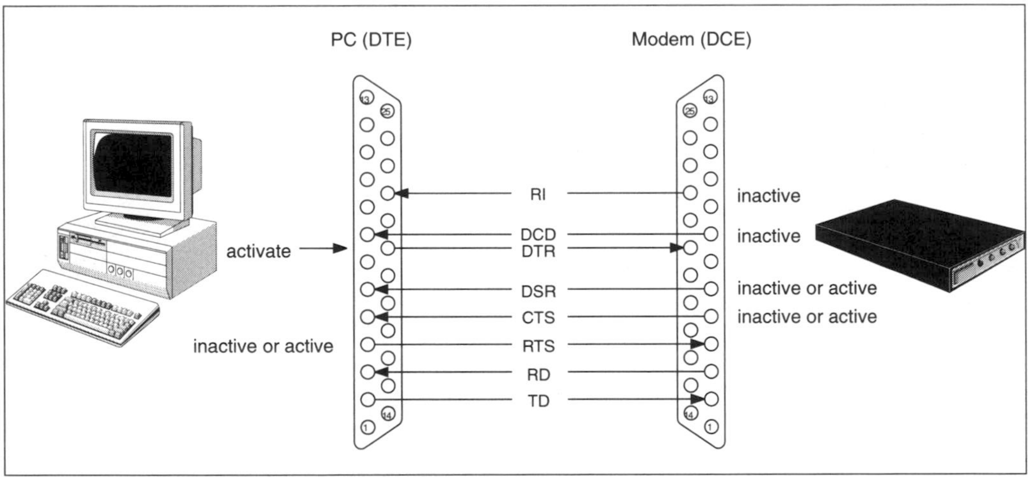

Figure 29.15 (c): The PC detects RI and activates DTR to show its ready state and to activate and instruct the modem to accept the incoming call; also, the modem has to establish a connection to the calling unit.

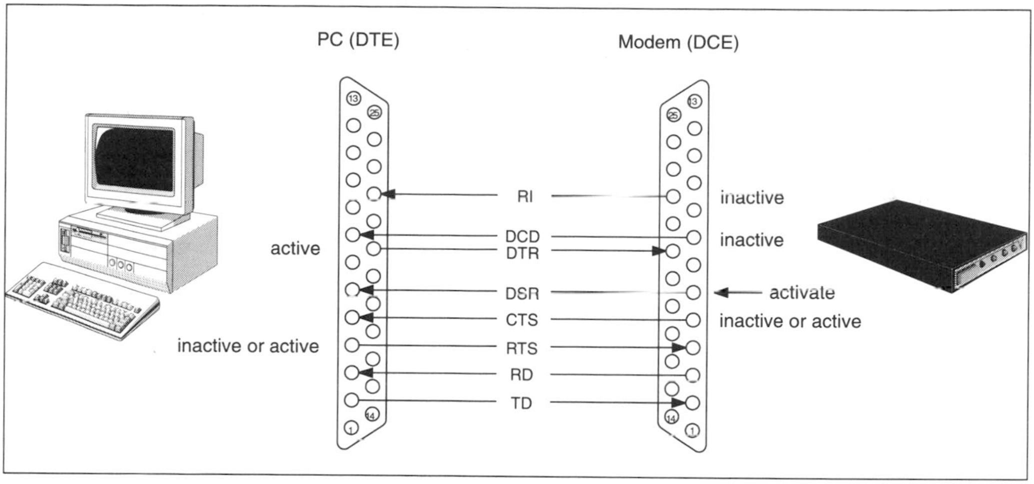

Figure 29.15 (d): After the modem has completed all preparations, it activates signal DSR and begins to build up the connection to the calling unit.

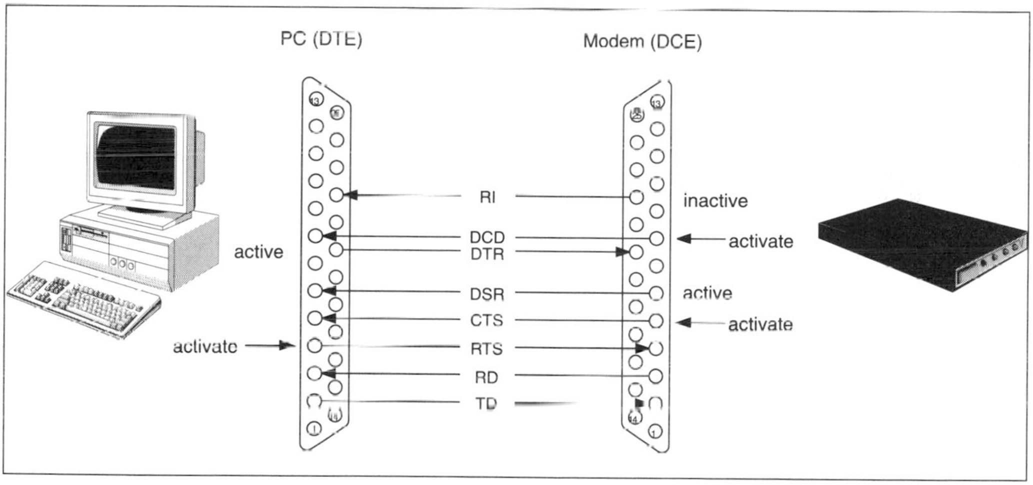

Figure 29.15 (e): If the connection between modem and calling unit is established, the modem activates signal DCD to inform the PC that the connection is usable, and the PC is allowed to transmit or receive data. The PC activates RTS to output data, that is, to carry out a bidirectional data exchange. The modem responds with CTS to indicate that it is ready to accept the transmission data from the PC.

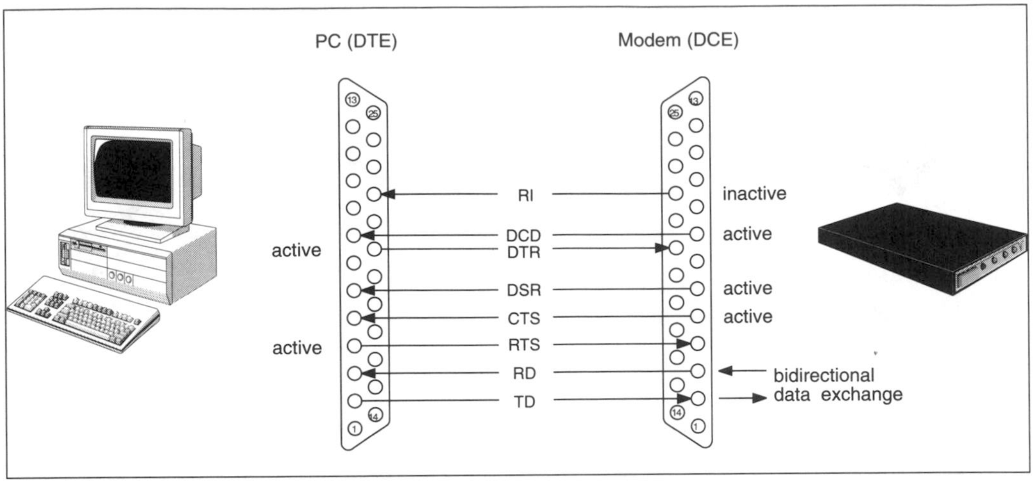

Figure 29.15 (f): The PC outputs data to the calling unit via the modem or accepts data from this unit until the connection is broken by deactivating DCD, DSR or DTR.

RS-232C Logic Levels and Transfer Rates

Unlike the logic signals normally used on a PC, the RS-232C signals are bipolar. This means that a level of 0 V (which corresponds to GND) doesn't indicate a logical low level but a negative voltage value. Thus a «1» is represented by positive voltage relative to ground, and a «0» as a negative voltage. For output signals, the voltage value for a «1» is between +5 V and +15 V, and for a «0» between –5 V and –15 V. Concerning input signals, a «1» is represented by a voltage between +3 V and +15 V, and a «0» by a voltage between –3 V and –15 V. These values are called *EIA signal levels*. The rather extensive voltage range and the relatively high maximum voltage ±15 V enables a noise-free signal transmission even over large distances. The parallel interface represents a «1» by a voltage of about +5 V and a «0» by a voltage of 0 V. Thus the difference between «0» and «1» may be up to six times larger on an RS-232C interface than on a parallel interface. As the power supplies in Personal Computers provide a voltage level of ±5 V and ±12 V only, the installed serial interface here supplies only voltages up to ±12 V.

The RS-232C standard allows a transfer rate up to 20000 baud according to its specification. But the interface chips in the PC enable up to 115200 baud if the cables between DTE and DCE don't get too long. An even higher value is impossible, because the UART 8250/16450/16550 used cannot generate higher baud rates.

29.2.3 Connection to Printers and the Zeromodem

From the above description of the serial interface you can see that RS-232C is unambiguously directed to a modem as the DCE. This modem is then usually connected to a destination modem, which in turn connects to another computer (not necessarily to a PC, but perhaps to a Cray, for example). The interface is therefore also called a *communications port*.

If you connect a serial printer or another PC peripheral with a serial interface (for example, a plotter) to your RS-232C, then the peripheral represents a DTE but not a DCE. This DTE is therefore formed by a printer controller. The DCD and RI signals on the PC's side are meaningless, and also for most other signals other interpretations hold. Figure 29.16 shows a typical connection between the serial interface of a PC and your printer.

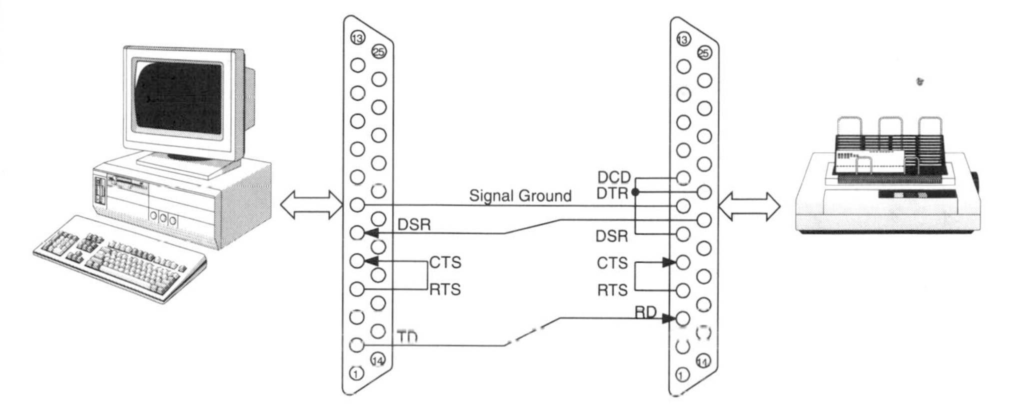

Figure 29.16: The connection between the serial interface and a printer. As a printer is not a DCE, various control and status lines have to be connected or interchanged to emulate the behaviour of a DCE.

The transmission data of the PC become the received data of the printer. Thus, serial printer cables connect the TD line from the PC to the RD pin of the printer plug. On the PC's side, RTS and CTS are connected to each other so that a transmission request from the PC immediately enables the transmission. Printers cannot output data; therefore we are confronted with the prime example for a simplex connection from the PC to the printer. Because of its RS-232C compatibility, the printer as the DTE refuses to print anything as long as no active signal is present at the inputs CTS, DSR and DCD. This problem is readily solved by connecting RTS with CTS and DTR with DCD and DSR. Thus, activating RTS immediately gives rise to an activation of CTS, and that of DTR to an activation of DCD and DSR.

But the main problem here is that the PC can transmit data much faster than the printer can print it, that is, the internal printer buffer gets full. On the parallel interface this problem is easily solved as the printer activates the BUSY signal, thus informing the PC that it can't accept data temporarily. Unlike this, the serial interface is not directed to serving a printer. Only a trick can help to solve the problem: the printer uses, for example, pin 19 (not used for asynchronous data exchange) to output a «buffer-full signal». On the PC's side, the connection DSR would provide an input for this signal, as according to the RS-232C standard the DSR signal from the DCE tells the DTE whether the target is ready to accept data. If the printer buffer is full, the printer simply disables the handshake signal at pin 19, and the DTE knows that temporarily no additional data can be transferred. If enough room is available in the buffer again, the printer enables the signal once more; the «data set» is ready, and the PC may transfer further data to the printer.

Warning: most but unfortunately not all printers with a serial interface provide such a buffer-full signal at pin 19. If your printer stubbornly refuses to print something even though you have connected it to the correct interface and the connection is OK, then the cause may be a different use of the RS-232C pins and signals. Consult the printer handbook or use a printer cable that the printer manufacturer supplies together with the printer concerned. Thus, cables for connecting a printer with the serial interface are *never* RS-232C interface cables. If you want to connect a «real» RS-232C DCE to your PC you must not use a printer cable but a standard RS-232C cable.

Another non-standard but, nevertheless, interesting application of the serial interface is the connection between two computers to exchange data. Directly connecting them by means of the conventional serial interface cables is impossible, of course, because both interfaces are configured as a DTE; not even the plug fits into the jack of the second PC. Another problem is that, for example, TD meets TD, RD meets RD, DTR meets DTR, etc. This means that outputs are connected to outputs and inputs to inputs. With this no data transfer is possible, of course. As both computers are of the same type, only another trick solves the problem. Figure 29.17 shows the scheme for such a zeromodem.

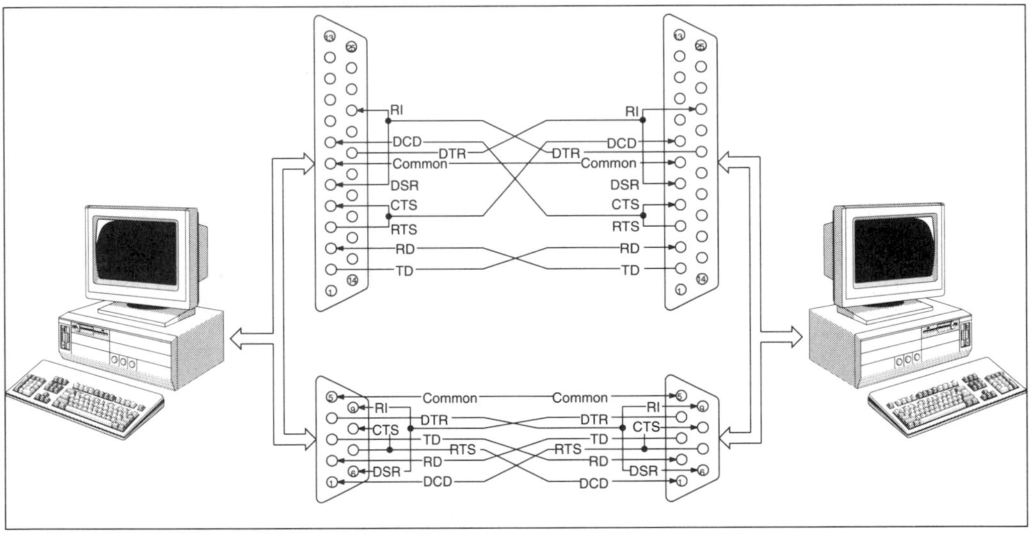

Figure 29.17: A zeromodem serves for data exchange between two DTEs, and therefore the interconnection is rather complicated.

The transmission data of the PC represents the received data of the other computer, of course. Thus it is required to twist the TD and RD lines. In this way, the transmission data of one PC becomes the received data of the other, and vice versa. Also, on a normal RS-232C connection between a DTE and a DCE, the transmission data of the DTE is the received data of the DCE, and vice versa. But there no crossing of the lines is required, as the DCE interface internally processes the data arriving on TD as received data and outputs the transmission data onto the RD line. But here we have to handle two DTEs, and not the combination DTE/DCE.

The other signals comply with the RS-232C standard for the control signals of a data transfer. When you look at Figure 29.17 you see that the activation of RTS to begin a data transfer gives rise to an activation of CTS on the same DTE, and to an activation of DCD on the other DTE. Via this a data transfer connection is simulated as it usually happens, for example, between a DCE and an external device. Furthermore, an activation of DTR leads to the rise of DSR and RI on the other DTE so that a «call» is registered there. By means of the interconnection shown in Figure 29.17, for every DTE it is simulated that a DCE is on the end of the line, although a connection between two DTEs is actually present.

In principle, it would be sufficient to connect one control output of the DTE (for example, RTS) with one control input of the other DTE (for example, CTS), and to cross the data lines. The two programs which serve the DTEs on both sides must only be structured accordingly to detect when the destination DTE is ready to receive data. But the advantage of the connection shown in Figure 29.17 is that the control signals strictly comply with the RS-232C requirements. Thus the zeromodem can be operated with standard DOS or standard BIOS functions, while otherwise a specialized program would be necessary. One prime example for this are mice connected to a serial interface. For integrating them into the PC system, you need a certain mouse driver as the mouse electronics doesn't meet the RS-232C specification in any form. For signal transfer the mouse only uses the RD line. All other lines are usually disabled (that is, they are on a low level). But this level corresponds to a voltage of –12 V for the DTR and RTS line, which the mouse uses as its power supply. Thus here the RS-232C control lines are used for supplying a peripheral with energy. That this doesn't comply with the RS-232C specification at all seems to be obvious; the mouse cannot be accessed either by DOS or by the BIOS, but only by direct register programming.

By means of a zeromodem you can always use the neglected DOS command CTTY, for example, to control a second PC from your desk. If you input the CTTY COM1 command on the second PC then this computer reads all commands from the first serial interface and outputs all data to COM1 instead of the first serial interface. In other words, COM1 becomes the standard input/output device. But programs which bypass DOS and access, for example, the keyboard buffer or the video memory directly don't work correctly any more. However, you may work with the usual DOS commands such as DIR or COPY on a second PC by means of a zeromodem and CTTY. You will only get a return message if your first computer accepts data from the serial interface and can display them (for example, in a dedicated window), otherwise your serial interface slurs the message arriving from the second PC. Special programs such as PC Anywhere or the Remote Access Service of Windows NT provide a solution to this problem by redirecting all video accesses to the serial interface, and by expecting all inputs from the serial interface instead of from the keyboard or mouse.

29.2.4 Access Via DOS

Unfortunately, the access possibilities to the serial interface are rather limited with DOS. By means of the DOS interrupt 21h, you may not even initialize the interface, for example, and set up the baud rate. On a DOS level, this is only possible with the external command MODE (consult your DOS manual), which uses a call to the BIOS interrupt 14h. With DOS you can only output a single character via the serial interface or read one, for example, to output a character on the printer, to draw on a plotter, or to receive data from a modem.

DOS manages the serial interface in the same way as the parallel interface, by means of a device driver. Thus you can also access COM1–COM4 like every other DOS device and, for example, print a file with the internal DOS command COPY file.txt COM1 on a printer connected to the first serial interface. If you have connected a modem via COM1 then you may «copy» the file «file.txt» to a PC in New Zealand, for example. COM1 belongs to the reserved device names, as is the case for LPT1 to LPT4, COM2–COM4, CON and AUX. (Consult your DOS manual for details.)

As a programmer you may further use the DOS function interrupt INT 21h to output data via the serial interface, or to receive data from it. Don't be too demanding as to the performance of the serial interface with DOS. Because of the enormous program overhead, you may achieve only up to 2400 or maybe 4800 baud even on fast ATs if the data transfer is to be carried out error-free. A direct programming via registers, on the other hand, enables up to 115 200 baud. For serial interfaces four functions are available (listed in Appendix I.2). These are:

- **Function 03h – read character from the serial interface.**

  Example: `read one character from AUX by means of function 03h.`

```
MOV ah, 03h   ; load function number into ah
INT 21h       ; call DOS interrupt, character is read into al
```

- **Function 04h – output character via the serial interface.**
- **Function 3fh – read file/device.**
- **Function 40h – write file/device.**

The main advantage of the functions 3fh and 40h is that you can easily read or output a whole string, and that you get an error code in the ax register. As usual for such high-level functions, you don't have the opportunity, for example, to determine the status of the serial interface, or that of the connected modem or printer. This is only possible via the BIOS.

29.2.5 Access Via the BIOS

Another possibility for accessing the serial interface is the functions of BIOS interrupt 14h. Via function 00h, you may initialize the serial interface and set up the data format as well as the transfer rate, for example. The new functions 04h and 05h, beginning with the PS/2 BIOS and BIOS variants of most compatible PCs, further allow you to extend initialization as well as directly access the modem control register (see Section 29.2.6). By means of the functions 01h and 02h, you can output and receive a character, respectively. With the function 03h the status of the serial interface concerned can be determined.

Every function returns a transfer status byte in the ah register. Some functions also supply a modem status byte in the al register. Figure 29.18 shows their structures.

For the DCE or serial interfaces you may define a time-out value (20 s are set up as a standard), which the BIOS uses to determine how long at most to wait for a response. If no connection can be established, or if no character can be output or received within this interval time, then the

Transmission Status Byte

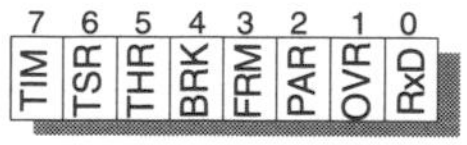

TIM:	time-out	
	1=time-out error	0=no error
TSR:	transmitter shift register	
	1=free	0=bus
THR:	transmitter hold register	
	1=free	0=busy
BRK:	break of transfer path	
	1=occurred	0=no break
FRM:	framing error	
	1=occurred	0=no framing error
PAR:	parity error	
	1=occurred	0=no parity error
OVR:	overrun error	
	1=occurred	0=no overrun error
RxD:	received data	
	1=ready	0=no data received

Modem Status Byte

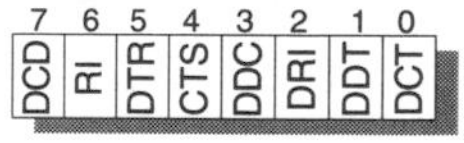

DCD:	data carrier detect	
	1=detected	0=not detected
RI:	ring indicator	
	1=detected	0=not detected
DTR:	data terminal ready	
	1=ready	0=not ready
CTS:	clear to send	
	1=ready	0=not ready
DDC:	delta DCD	
	1=detected	0=not detected
DRI:	delta RI	
	1=detected	0=not detected
DDT:	delta DTR	
	1=detected	0=not detected
DCT:	delta CTS	
	1=detected	0=not detected

Figure 29.18: Transmission status and modem status byte.

TIM bit is set. On a DOS level you have the opportunity to set an infinite time-out interval by means of the command `MODE COMx ,,P`. The remaining seven bits, TSR to EMP, define the current status of the interface and the signals concerned, respectively. If the *TSR* bit is set then the transmitter shift register is empty, but with a set *THR* bit only the hold register, which accommodates the next character to be output, is empty. If the interface detects a break of the connection between DCE and DTE, then the *BRK* bit is set. A general framing error gives rise to a set *FRM* bit. The cause may be a different baud rate of the transmitter and receiver, so that the receiver receives, for example, more signal bits than should be present according to the SDU format definition. A parity error is indicated by a set *PAR* bit, and an overrun error by means of a set *OVR* bit. An overrun error only occurs if the data is arriving more quickly at the interface than the CPU is able to read it from the receiver buffer. If received data is available that has been assembled by the interface into a complete data byte, then the *RxD* bit is set to inform the CPU that it may fetch the next data byte.

The values of the individual bits in the transfer status byte, except TIM, reflect the value of the corresponding bit in the serialization status register. Further information concerning the serialization status register and the meanings of the individual bits are discussed in Section 29.2.6. The modem status byte finally represents, in an unaltered form, the contents of the modem status register. This register is discussed in detail in Section 29.2.6.

Among all seven functions of the BIOS interrupt 14h, only the initialization of the serial interface, the determination of the interface status and reading one character from a serial interface are discussed here. The meaning and programming of the other functions is obvious.

Before you can use a serial interface (for example, after booting the PC for outputting a character or reading a data byte), you have to initialize it. This is carried out by function 00h and the transfer of a status byte which unambiguously defines the configuration of the interface. Figure 29.19 shows the format of this parameter byte.

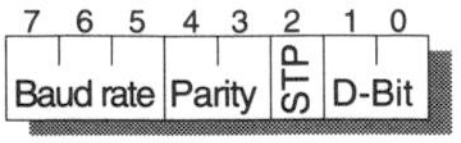

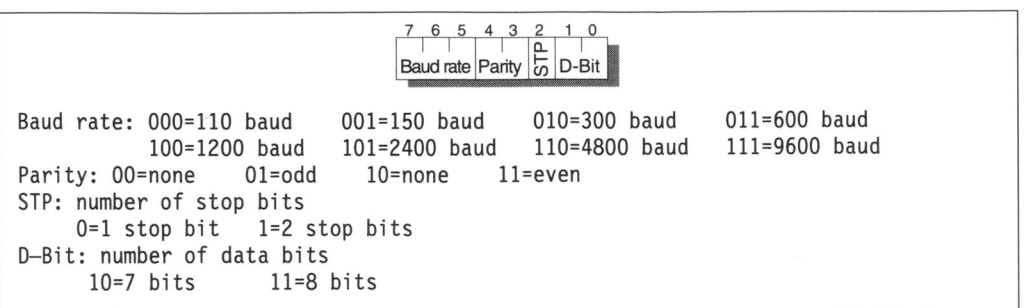

```
Baud rate: 000=110 baud     001=150 baud     010=300 baud     011=600 baud
           100=1200 baud    101=2400 baud    110=4800 baud    111=9600 baud
Parity: 00=none     01=odd     10=none     11=even
STP: number of stop bits
     0=1 stop bit   1=2 stop bits
D-Bit: number of data bits
      10=7 bits       11=8 bits
```

Figure 29.19: Parameter byte.

The three most significant *baud rate* bits define the baud rate. With function 00h you may set up a maximum baud rate of 9600 baud; by the extended function 04h (see Appendix I.2), up to 19200 baud are possible. Direct programming via registers, on the other hand, enables up to 115200 baud. The two *parity* bits determine the parity for the data transfer; the function 04h additionally allows the parities mark and space. The *STP* bit defines the number of stop bits. Finally, the two *D-Bits* define the number of data bits; valid entries are seven or eight data bits. But by means of the 04h function you are also free to set five or six data bits. Generally, the 04h function reflects the register values of the interface chip UART 8250/16450/16550 far more directly than the 00h function. Details on this are discussed in Section 29.2.6.

Example: `Initialize COM2 with 4800 baud, even parity, 2 stop bits, 7 data bits.`

```
MOV ah, 00h    ; load function number 00h into ah
MOV al, deh    ; parameter byte 11011110b
MOV dx, 01h    ; COM2
INT 14h        ; call interrupt
```

The transfer status byte is returned in register ah with every command, the modem status byte, on the other hand, only with function 00h. With function 03h of interrupt 14h you have the opportunity to determine both status bytes without any further action. This is advantageous, for example, if you want to determine in advance whether a modem or plotter is ready for operation.

Example: `determine status of first serial interface.`

```
MOV ah, 03h    ; load function number 03h into ah
MOV dx, 00h    ; determine status of COM1
INT 14h        ; call interrupt
               ; transfer status is returned in ah, modem status in al
```

Thus the BIOS interrupt 14h already returns much more status information concerning the corresponding serial interface and the connected devices than the DOS functions 03h, 04h, 03fh and 40h. Of interest is function 03h, for example, to determine the cause of an interface failure.

But only directly programming the registers allows ultimate control over the interface, and the use and optimization in view of its non-standard applications.

Via BIOS interrupt 14h you may also read one character from the serial interface. For this purpose, the function 02h waits until either a character has arrived or the time-out value has elapsed. Of importance concerning the performance of function 02h is that for *every* character the BIOS establishes the connection to the connected device strictly according to the RS-232C standard, via RS-232C control signals CTS, RTS, DSR and DTR, and disconnects afterwards. This, of course, affects the transfer rate enormously, so you may hardly achieve more than 19200 baud using the BIOS functions. Also in this case, a direct register access provides much higher rates for well-trained programmers, which may reach the hardware limit of 115200 baud without the CPU being occupied only by the serial interface.

Example: `read one character by means of the BIOS from COM3.`

```
MOV ah, 02h    ; load function number 02h into ah
MOV dx, 02h    ; fetch character from COM3
INT 14h        ; call interrupt
               ; function waits and returns character in register al
```

Table 29.4 lists all the important sections of the BIOS data area for the serial interface. The base addresses indicate the beginning of the interface registers (see Section 29.2.6). By altering the time-out values you can determine how long the BIOS will try to access the DCE via the interface concerned before a time-out error is reported. Finally, the *installed hardware* byte specifies how many serial interfaces are installed in your system. The BIOS startup routine determines the base addresses and the number of interfaces during the course of booting and writes the corresponding values into the BIOS data area.

Address	Size	Structure 76543210	Contents	Meaning
40:00	word		base address COM1	
40:02	word		base address COM2	
40:04	word		base address COM3	
40:06	word		base address COM4	
40:11	byte	....xxx.	installed hardware	number of serial interfaces (000= 0, 001= 1, 010=2, 011=3, 100=4)
40:7c	word		time-out COM1	time-out value in seconds
40:7d	word		time-out COM2	time-out value in seconds
40:7e	word		time-out COM3	time-out value in seconds
40:7f	word		time-out COM4	time-out value in seconds

Table 29.4: BIOS data area and serial interface

29.2.6 The UART 8250/16450/16550

For the complex functions of the serial interface, such as the conversion of parallel data from the system bus into serial data at a certain baud rate, restoring the parallel data from the serial data, etc., you will find a single chip in your PC: the *UART 8250* or *UART 16450/16550* (UART is the abbreviation for *universal asynchronous receiver and transmitter*). The name already outlines the job and function of the chip. It acts as a programmable and thus «universal» receiver and transmitter for an asynchronous data transfer. The 8250 version was used in the PC/XT; starting with the AT and on all of today's interface adapter boards, the improved 16450 or 82450 are employed. The early 8250 version has a bug which leads to an interrupt after an interface access, although there is no reason for that (interrupt sources are discussed below). Known bugs are harmless, and these unfounded interrupts are ignored by the PC/XT BIOS. In the first successor, version 8250A, this bug was fixed; but now the PC/XT BIOS, which expected an unfounded interrupt, did not cooperate correctly with the 8250A. On the second successor, 8250B, the bug was fixed, but the 8250B issues an unfounded interrupt in the same way as the 8250 to retain compatibility. Here you can clearly see the strange effects the surge towards compatibility may produce: for compatibility reasons, a bug-free chip is deliberately equipped with the bug again. That's not very good if we consider that rail companies could equip all modern high-speed trains with steam engines for compatibility with R.L. Stevenson's first engine!

The 8250 enables a maximum transfer rate of 9600 baud. That makes it clear why the BIOS interrupt 14h allows only an initialization of maximum 9600 baud. The improved 16450 successor for the AT can stand up to 115200 baud, but the PS/2 BIOS allows, even by means of the extended initialization, only 19200 baud, as the INT 14h for servicing serial interfaces can hardly operate faster because of all the ponderous setups for every transferred or received character. You can achieve the 115200 baud only by means of direct register accesses. This subject is discussed as a main point in the following sections. For high-speed serial communication, some RS-232 adapters have a 16550 UART chip. It is the same as the 16450, but incorporates a FIFO buffer for incoming and outgoing data. That allows a better decoupling of the serial interface and handling by the operating system. If some characters are arriving faster than they can be fetched by the interrupt handler for that interface (for example, because the operating system is occupied by other time-critical tasks and has masked the IRQs), the FIFO simply stores those characters and hands them over to the system later. Thus, character overruns occur less frequently. Note that programming the 16550 is the same as for the 8250/16450. But now a short glance at the structure of the UART chips and their integration into the PC system.

Connection Scheme and EIA Line Drivers

The UART 8250/16450/16550 comes in a standard DIP case with 40 pins. Figure 29.20 shows the corresponding pin assignment. The following sections discuss the terminals, and briefly describe the meaning of the provided or output signals.

A2–A0 (I)
Pins 26–28

These three address or register select signals determine the register that the CPU accesses for reading or writing. Note that for an access to the divisor latch register the DLAB bit must additionally be set (see also Table 29.6).

$\overline{AS}$ (I)
Pin 25

An active address strobe signal $\overline{AS}$ with a low level indicates the validity of address signals A0–A2 and the chip select signals CS0–$\overline{CS2}$.

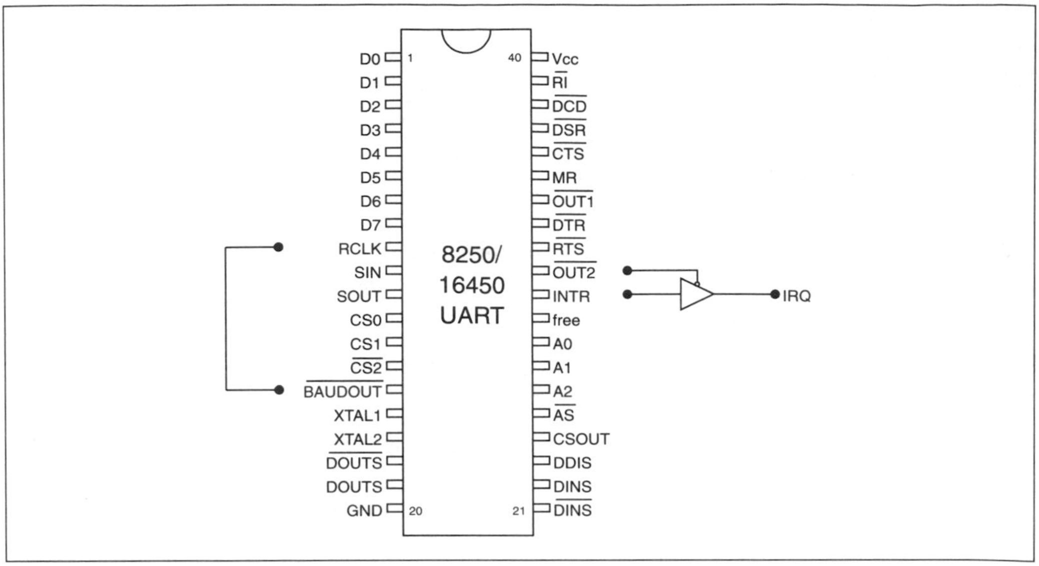

Figure 29.20: UART 8250/16450/16550 connections. The UART is the heart of a serial PC interface. Normally $\overline{BAUDOUT}$ and RCLK are connected to each other so that receiver and transmitter operate at the same baud rate. The INTR output is combined with $\overline{OUT2}$ by a logic gate.

$\overline{BAUDOUT}$ (O)
Pin 15

This pin outputs a signal with 16 times the frequency of the transmitter baud rate. If $\overline{BAUDOUT}$ is connected to RCLK, the receiver and transmitter operate at the same baud rate.

CS0, CS1, $\overline{CS2}$ (I, I, I)
Pins 12–14

(Chip Select x) If CS0 and CS1 are at a high level and $\overline{CS2}$ is at a low level, then the UART is selected by the CPU to transfer data to or from the CPU.

CSOUT (O)
Pin 24

If the signal at this chip select out connection is at a high level, the CPU has selected the UART using CS0, CS1 and $\overline{CS2}$.

$\overline{CTS}$ (I)
Pin 36

This clear to send terminal is supplied with an active-low signal according to the state of the CTS line.

D0–D7 (I/O)
Pins 1–8

These eight pins form the bidirectional data bus between CPU and 8250/16450/16550 through which data, control words and status information is transferred.

$\overline{\text{DCD}}$ (I)
Pin 38

This data carrier detect terminal is supplied with an active-low signal according to the state of the DCD line.

DDIS (O)
Pin 23

If the CPU is reading data from the UART then the level at this pin becomes low. Thus, for example, an amplifier between UART and the data bus can be switched off if the CPU doesn't read data.

$\overline{\text{DINS}}$, DINS (I, I)
Pins 21, 22

If $\overline{\text{DINS}}$ is on a low or DINS is on a high level, the CPU reads data or status words from internal registers of the UART.

$\overline{\text{DOUTS}}$, DOUTS (O, O)
Pins 18, 19

If $\overline{\text{DOUTS}}$ is supplied with a low or DOUTS with a high level, the CPU writes data or control words into internal registers of the UART.

$\overline{\text{DSR}}$ (I)
Pin 37

This data set ready terminal is supplied with an active-low signal according to the state of the DSR line.

$\overline{\text{DTR}}$ (O)
Pin 33

This data terminal ready terminal outputs an active-low signal according to the DTR bit in the modem control register.

INTR (O)
Pin 30

The UART raises this signal to a high level if it has detected an interrupt condition, and the bit concerned in the interrupt enable register is set.

MR (I)
Pin 35

If a high-level signal is applied to this master reset pin then the UART carries out a reset of all registers except the receiver buffer, the transmitter hold register, and the divisor latch register.

$\overline{\text{OUT1}}$ (O)
Pin 34

This pin can be freely programmed by the user.

$\overline{\text{OUT2}}$ (O)
Pin 31

This pin can be freely programmed by the user. In the PC $\overline{\text{OUT2}}$ is used as the master interrupt enable via a logic gate.

RCLK (I)
Pin 9

This receiver clock connection is supplied with 16 times the receiver baud rate.

$\overline{\text{RI}}$ (I)
Pin 39

This ring indicator terminal is supplied with an active-low signal according to the state of the RI line.

$\overline{\text{RTS}}$ (O)
Pin 32

The terminal outputs an active-low request to send signal according to the RTS bit in the modem control register.

SIN (I)
Pin 10

This serial-in pin is supplied with the serial input data.

SOUT (O)
Pin 11

This serial-out connection provides the serial transmission data.

XTAL1, XTAL2 (n/a)
Pins 16, 17

To these pins either an external crystal or an external oscillator is connected, which determines the UART's main reference frequency.

Vcc
Pin 40
This pin is supplied with the supply voltage (usually +5 V).

GND
Pin 20
This pin is supplied with the ground potential (usually 0 V).

The RS-232C control signals are output or processed by the UART 8250/16450/16550 in inverted form, and the serial data signals SIN and SOUT in normal form. Furthermore, the chip is supplied with a voltage Vcc of only +5 V so that an EIA level of ±12 V cannot be generated with the UART alone. For these reasons, so-called EIA line drivers are connected between UART and the transmission lines. They amplify the signals from or to the UART so that the EIA levels of ±12 V are available at the output. Additionally, the incoming signals are converted to 0 V or +5 V. The drivers are implemented as inverters so that on the 9-pin or 25-pin plug of the adapter signals are actually present which correspond to the bit values in the control and status registers. If you check the potentials at the RS-232C pins of your serial interface using a voltage meter, you will see that a logically low level of the control and status signals is represented by a voltage of about –12 V and a logically high level by a voltage of about +12 V. On the contrary, a voltage of –12 V on the TD and RD lines indicates a mark state of the serial data, and a voltage of +12 V a space state. Thus, SIN and SOUT are also guided through inverter circuits, but these signals are not output in a complementary form by the UART so that the difference described between control and status signals on the one hand and the serial data on the other arises.

When using the UART 8250/16450/16550 in the PC, the output signal $\overline{\text{OUT2}}$ is combined with the INTR output signal by a logic gate (see Figure 29.20, right side). In this way, the IBM engineers have implemented something like a master interrupt enable bit OUT2 in the modem control register (see Figure 29.27). If OUT2 is cleared then all interrupts of the UART are globally masked; if OUT2 is set, the individual interrupt sources are enabled. Thus the interrupt requests from the UART may be blocked during critical program sequences without destroying the interrupt mask.

Structure and Functioning

The UART 8250/16450/16550 has to carry out a lot of functions and is therefore a rather complex chip. Figure 29.21 shows a block diagram of its internal structure.

As a receiver and transmitter the UART has a receiver section (Figure 29.21, upper part) as well as a transmitter section (Figure 29.21, lower part). A feature of the 8250/16450/16550 is that the transmitter and receiver on the chip can be operated with different baud rates. The UART first generates from the main reference frequency (which is either supplied externally or formed internally by the crystal at inputs XTAL1 and XTAL2) the reference frequency for the baud rate by dividing the main reference frequency by the divisor, which is stored as a 16-bit value in the divisor latch register. The generated baud rate reference frequency is output as a complementary signal at the $\overline{\text{BAUDOUT}}$ pin. By further dividing the reference frequency by 16, the UART finally determines the transmission baud rate. In the PC, the main reference frequency is generated by an external oscillator, and is equal to 1.8432 MHz. The aim and object of this factor of 16 is discussed below.

Unlike this procedure, the receiver baud rate is generated externally and applied to the terminal RCLK as 16 times its intended value. If one connects the output $\overline{\text{BAUDOUT}}$ with the input

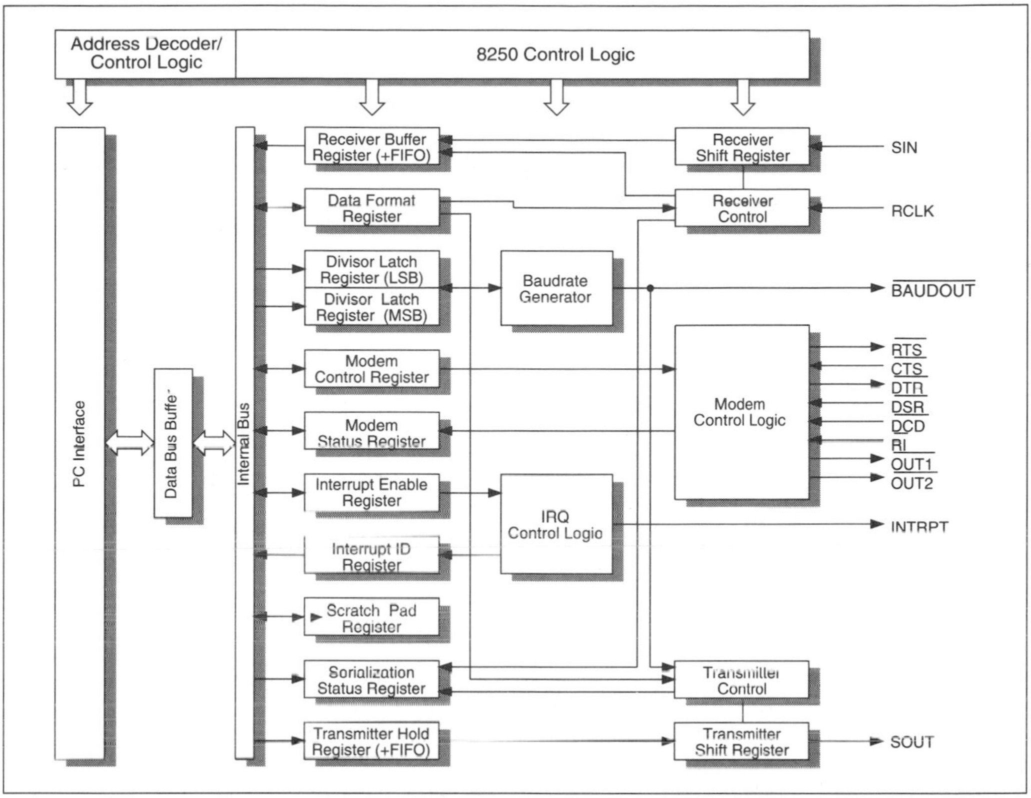

Figure 29.21: UART 8250/16450/16550 block diagram. Note that only the 16550 incorporates a FIFO buffer in the receiver buffer and transmitter hold registers.

RCLK, as is actually the case for the PC, then receiver and transmitter operate at the same baud rate. The separation of receiver and transmitter baud rate is advantageous, for example, if the data transfer is to be carried out at a high speed, but the return channel for control signals from the destination is operated at a significantly lower rate. Then it is possible to further process the $\overline{\text{BAUDOUT}}$ signals and, for example, to divide them by a factor of 100 before it is applied to the RCLK input. Alternatively, RCLK can also be supplied by an external oscillator, but as already mentioned, $\overline{\text{BAUDOUT}}$ is directly connected to RCLK in the PC (Figure 29.20, left side).

The receiver control detects and separates the start bit, parity bit (if present), and the stop bit(s) from the data bits arriving in the receiver shift register via the SIN input. The receiver control further controls the assembly of a data byte from the extracted serial data bits. If the receiver shift register has received all data bits, then the whole data byte is transferred to the receiver buffer register (8250/16450) or to a FIFO register in the receiver buffer register (16550). With a data length of eight bits no problems occur, but the situation becomes more difficult if the data has seven, six or even only five bits. The corresponding one, two or three high-order data bits are not defined in this case, and can take any random value. If you read data with a transfer length of less than eight bits from the receiver buffer register then you should mask the corresponding high-order data bit(s).

On the transmitter side, the transmitter shift register outputs the individual data bits at the programmed transmission baud rate at the SOUT output under the supervision of the transmitter control. The transmitter control automatically inserts the start bit, and eventually the parity bit and the stop bit(s) into the serial data stream. If the transmitter shift register is empty, then the control loads the data byte to be transferred next from the transmitter hold register (if available) into the transmitter shift register and outputs it via SOUT. If no transmission data is available in the transmitter shift register, then the transmitter control holds the SOUT output in the mark state.

The modem control logic provides and accepts the RS-232C control signals. The IRQ control logic detects the changes of the RS-232C control lines, the status of the receiver buffer and the transmitter hold register, the state of the line to the transmission partner, as well as possible transfer errors. Depending upon the programmed interrupt enable mask, the IRQ then raises the INTRPT output to generate a hardware interrupt, and writes the interrupt cause into the interrupt ID register. COM1 is usually assigned to IRQ4 and COM2 to IRQ3.

Baud rate generator, modem control logic, IRQ control logic and the receiver control can be configured and controlled by the two divisor latch registers accommodating the most significant (MSB) and the least significant (LSB) divisor byte, the modem control register, the interrupt enable register and the data format register. You may read the state of these chip groups via the modem status register, the interrupt ID register, and the data format register.

The data received can be fetched by a simple IN instruction from the receiver buffer register so that there is enough room for the next data byte. Similarly, you can write a data byte to transfer into the transmitter hold register via an OUT instruction. The data byte is automatically transferred to the transmitter shift register afterwards, and output via SOUT as a serial data stream. The 16450/16550 additionally implements a scratch-pad register which has no function in the UART but can be used as a temporary storage for a data byte. The value in the scratch-pad register has no effect on the 16450/16550's behaviour. All registers are connected to each other via an internal data bus and to the PC system bus by means of the data bus buffer. They can be read or written, respectively, with the port instructions IN and OUT.

If you add all of the registers you will get a total of eleven. To address them address bits A2–A0 are available, but they can encode only eight different registers. This problem is solved as follows: the most significant bit DLAB in the data format register (see Figure 29.26) indicates whether addresses 000b and 001b access the two divisor latch registers or the receiver buffer register. Moreover, an IN instruction referring to the 000b address automatically accesses the receiver buffer register, and an OUT instruction to this address writes the transmitter hold register. Thus, all eleven registers can be addressed.

Detecting the Start Bit and the Factor 16

The reliable detection of the start bit with which every SDU begins is a significant problem in connection with asynchronous data transfer. As you know, the value of the start bit is always equal to 0, that is, an SDU always starts with a decrease of the logic level from «1» to «0». With

Figure 29.22, which shows an SDU with one start bit, seven data bits, one parity bit for odd parity, and one stop bit, I want to discuss in detail the detection of the start bit and the associated factor of 16.

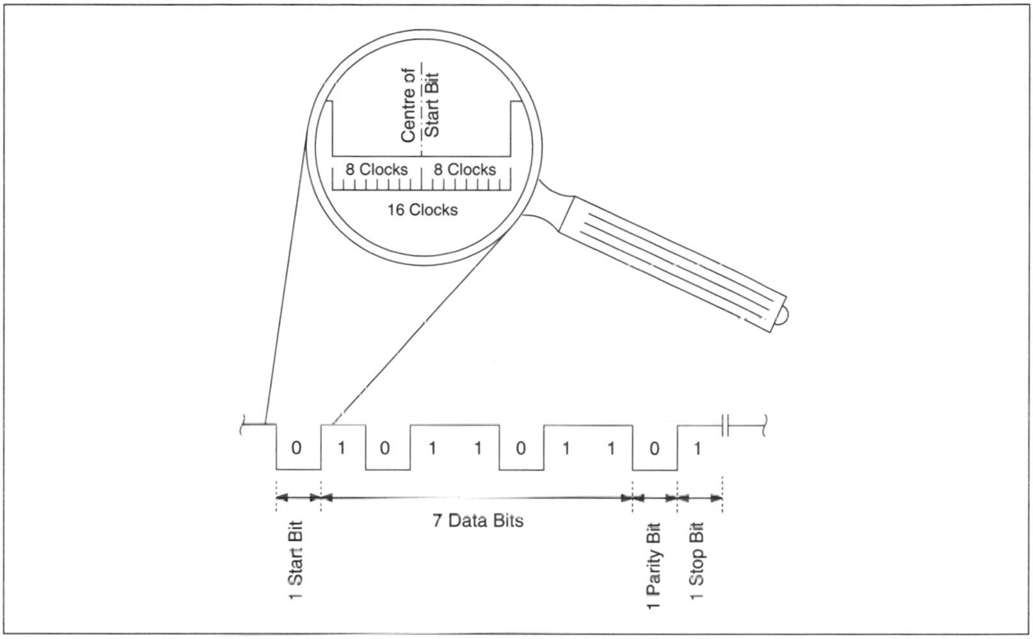

Figure 29.22: Detecting the start bit. The bits are sampled at a frequency 16 times the baud rate to enhance the reliability of data detection.

As already mentioned, the start bit begins with a drop of the logic level to «0», that is, a transition from mark to space. This drop serves as a trigger pulse for an internal circuit that starts the UART receiver. One would now expect the thus started circuitry to sample the arriving signal stream at regular time intervals corresponding to the programmed baud rate, so as to restore the bit values. From the figure it is apparent that this sampling of the individual bits should be carried out in the middle of every bit pulse to supply the best results. Put differently, the receiver should wait for 1½ bits after detecting the falling edge of the start bit before it samples the first data bit. Those of you who have seen the real signals of an incoming SDU on an oscilloscope would agree that the signal course shown in Figure 29.22 is somewhat idealized. In particular, the signal edges are often rather smeared out, and actually the first signal edge is decisive for detecting the start bit. Thus a strongly smeared edge, which may possibly reach to the middle of the start bit (and this can particularly happen for high baud rates), leads to significant problems for the subsequent detection of the data bits. Another problem is short spikes on the transmission line, which give rise to short pulses, and may lead the UART to believe in a start bit where none is actually present.

The problem can be solved in a simple but ingenious way: the serial data stream at the SIN terminal is not sampled at a frequency corresponding to the baud rate, but with a frequency 16 times higher. In other words, every individual SDU bit is sampled not once but 16 times, and the average value of all 16 samples leads to the value of the bit concerned. The individual bits can thus be restored even from heavily disturbed signals. But this strategy not only holds for the start bit, of course. Figure 29.22 shows an enlarged view of the start bit. When the signal drops to a level «0» a synchronization circuitry inside the UART is started by this trigger pulse. But the circuitry first waits for eight sample cycles; thus we are exactly in the middle of the start bit (at least theoretically). Even if the edge of the start bit is not very good, the middle of the start bit can be determined much more precisely than if we were simply to wait for a time interval corresponding to half an SDU bit. After eight sampling cycles (that is, in the middle of the start bit), where the signal should be expressed best, the synchronization circuitry detects the signal level again. If it is still on «0» then a real start bit has appeared and the synchronization circuitry starts the receiver, which samples the serial data stream with 16 times the baud rate now and determines the individual SDU bits. If, on the other hand, the signal level has already increased to «1» or nearly «1» again at the time of the second sampling in the middle of the start bit, then only a short noise pulse has occurred; the synchronization circuitry is reset and the receiver is not enabled. Thus the reference frequency 16 times higher than the baud rate increases the transfer reliability. Of course, other values such as eight or 32 are also possible in principle, but the UART 8250/16450/16550 always uses the factor of 16.

8250/16450/16550 Registers and Programming

The UART 8250 has ten control and status registers, and the 16450/16550 additionally has the scratch-pad register. All registers have successive addresses, and can be accessed by three address bits, that is, the offsets are in the range between 0–7. The base addresses of the UARTs and thus also of the registers are stored in the BIOS data area (see Table 29.4). Usually, you find the base addresses and IRQ assignments as indicated in Table 29.5.

On most interface adapter cards you may set up the base address and IRQ line with a jumper or DIP switch. Thus you might configure COM1 with IRQ4. As long as the handler for COM1 doesn't use an interrupt, this doesn't give rise to any problem. But some difficulties occur if you have installed a mouse on COM1 and you set up IRQ3 for COM1. The mouse driver knows to which COM interface the mouse is connected, and attempts to serve IRQ4 corresponding to INT 0ch. But there will never be any signal from COM1 because you have configured your interface with an incorrect IRQ, and the mouse seems to be dead. Some older BIOS versions further have problems managing more than two serial interfaces. It may be that COM3 and COM4 are not accessible, or can only be operated with polling. But polling is unsuitable, for example, for using the corresponding interface as a mouse port.

Interface	Base address	IRQ
COM1	3f8h	IRQ4
COM2	2f8h	IRQ3
COM3	3e8h	IRQ4*)
COM4	2e8h	IRQ3*)

*) or polling

Table 29.5: COMx base addresses and IRQ channels

Starting with the base address of the interface concerned, you additionally need the register offsets to actually address the various registers. Table 29.6 lists the information required.

Register	Offset	DLAB	A2	A1	A0
receiver buffer register transmitter hold register	00h	0	0	0	0
interrupt enable register	01h	0	0	0	1
interrupt identification register	02h	–	0	1	0
data format register (line control register)	03h	–	0	1	1
modem control register (RS-232 output)	04h	–	1	0	0
serialization status register (line status reg.)	05h	–	1	0	1
modem status register(RS-232 input)	06h	–	1	1	0
scratch-pad register	07h	–	1	1	1
divisor latch register (LSB)	00h	1	0	0	0
divisor latch register (MSB)	01h	1	0	0	1
DLAB=divisor latch access bit					

Table 29.6: UART 8250 register addresses

With offset 00h you can access both the receiver buffer and the transmitter hold register (Figure 29.23) assuming that the most significant DLAB bit in the data format register (see Figure 29.26) is cleared.

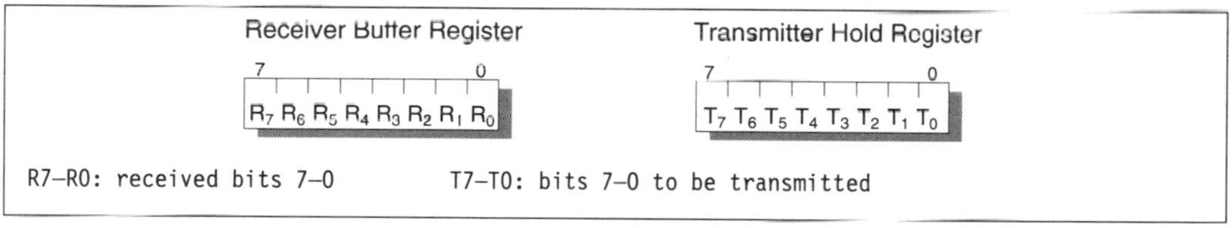

Figure 29.23: Receiver buffer and transmitter hold register (offset 00h).

After a serial data stream at the SIN input of the UART has been converted into a byte internally, the thus received byte is transferred into the receiver buffer register. The R_0 bit corresponds to the last received data bit. With an IN instruction you may now fetch the data byte. Note that possibly one or more high-order bits are not defined if you use a data length of less than eight bits, but an IN instruction, on the other hand, always reads one byte of eight bits. With a smaller data length you should always mask the high-order bits, that is, set to 0. By reading the receiver buffer register with IN you automatically empty the register so that it may accommodate the next data.

Example: `read receiver buffer register of COM1.`

```
MOV dx, 3f8h    ; load address of receiver buffer register into dx
IN al, dx       ; read contents of receiver buffer register into al
```

If you write a byte into the transmitter hold register using an OUT instruction, it is automatically transferred to the transmitter shift register and output as a serial data stream at SOUT.

Note that the T_0 bit is output first. The UART's transmitter control inserts start, parity, and stop bits automatically.

Example: write transmitter hold register of COM1 to output character 'a'.

```
MOV dx, 3f8h    ; load address of transmitter hold register into dx
MOV al, 'a'     ; load byte 'a' for output into al
OUT dx, al      ; write 'a' into transmitter hold register and output via SOUT
```

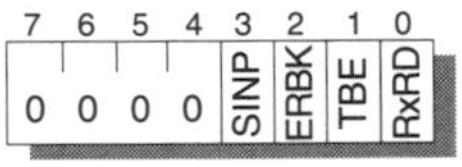


```
SINP:  RS-232 input
       1=interrupt on state-change of a RS-232 input line
       0=no interrupt
ERBK:  error & break
       1=interrupt on parity, overrun, framing error or BREAK
       0=no interrupt
TBE:   transmitter buffer empty
       1=interrupt on transmitter buffer empty    0=no interrupt
RxRD:  received data ready
       1=interrupt when one byte is ready in receiver buffer register
       0=no interrupt
```

Figure 29.24: Interrupt enable register (offset 01h).

As already mentioned, the UART 8250/16450/16550 issues a hardware interrupt request under certain circumstances. With the interrupt enable register (Figure 29.24) you may control the interrupt requests. The high-order nibble register is always equal to 0 and cannot be altered. If you set the *SINP* bit, then the UART activates its INTRPT line if the state of one of the RS-232C input signals $\overline{CTS}$, $\overline{DSR}$, $\overline{DCD}$ or $\overline{RI}$ changes. Thus, for example, a ringing $\overline{RI}$ signal can get attention via a hardware interrupt. If you set the *ERBK* bit then the UART issues an interrupt if the receiver control detects a parity, overrun, or framing error, or a break of the connection during the course of an incoming byte.

The two other bits *TBE* and *RxRD* communicate between CPU and UART in the case of a normal data transfer. If you set TBE then the UART issues an interrupt as soon as the data byte to be transmitted has been transferred from the transmitter hold register to the transmitter shift register, and the transmitter hold register can accommodate the character to be transmitted next. The RxRD bit has a similar function: if RxRD is set then the 8250/16450/16550 issues a hardware interrupt as soon as a complete data byte is available in the receiver buffer register, that is, the receiver control has assembled a data byte from the signals at SIN in the receiver shift register, and has transferred it into the receiver buffer register. You must fetch the data byte from the receiver buffer register, as otherwise an overrun error occurs with the next received data byte.

Example: issue interrupt upon an empty transmitter hold register, or if a data byte is available in the receiver buffer register for COM1, that is, set bits TBE and RxRD.

```
MOV dx, 3f9h    ; load address of interrupt enable register into dx
IN al, dx       ; read register into al
OR al, 03h      ; set TBE and RxRD
OUT dx, al      ; write register
```

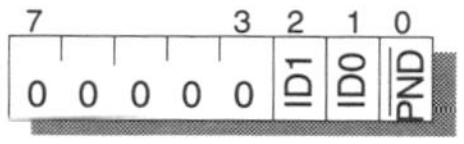


```
ID1, ID0: identify bit
     00=change of a RS-232 input signal (priority 3)
     01=transmitter buffer empty (priority 2)
     10=date received (priority 1)
     11=serialization error or BREAK (priority 0)
     0=highest priority   3=lowest priority
PND: pending bit
     1=no interrupt pending    0=interrupt pending, ID1 and ID0 identify source
```

Figure 29.25: Interrupt identification register (offset 02h).

With the interrupt identification register (Figure 29.25) you can determine, using an IN instruction, whether an interrupt is currently pending or not. An active interrupt is indicated by a cleared $\overline{PND}$ bit. This is especially useful if polling is used for the interface concerned, because you may readily determine, according to the $\overline{PND}$ bit, whether an interrupt is required; the two bits *ID1* and *ID0* then indicate the source of the interrupt request. Of course, you can only identify interrupts in the interrupt status register that you have enabled in advance by means of the interrupt activation register. Polling is also effective if the IRQ line is connected to the 8259A PIC, but the interrupt handler simply consists of an IRET instruction. You can use identification bits ID1 and ID0, for example, as index bits into a jump table to handle the interrupt cause.

The interrupt sources are assigned various priorities; level 0 corresponds to the highest priority, and level 3 to the lowest. Note that all interrupts of a lower priority are locked as long as an interrupt of a higher priority is pending. As long as, for example, a parity error (priority 0) has not been serviced, the RS-232C control signals may change to any extent, but no further interrupt is issued because of this change.

Interrupt source	**ID1**	**ID0**	**Clear pending interrupt by**
change of an RS-232C input signal	0	0	reading of RS-232C status register
transmitter hold register empty	0	1	writing data byte into transmitter hold register or reading interrupt identification register
data byte in receiver buffer register	1	0	reading data byte from receiver buffer register
receiver error or break	1	1	reading of serialization status register

Table 29.7: Clear pending interrupts

The handler must be able to actually clear a pending interrupt. The actions needed for this are shown in Table 29.7. As you can see, the interrupt can be cleared by reading the accompanying status register or receiver buffer register, or by writing the transmitter hold register. In the case of an interrupt because of an empty transmitter hold register, you have a choice between writing a new data byte into the transmitter hold register or reading the interrupt identification register. The reason is obvious: if you could clear the interrupt by writing the transmitter hold register only, then an endless data transmission would be the consequence. As you will usually read the interrupt identification register first after an interrupt has occurred to determine the interrupt source, an interrupt request because of an empty transmitter hold register has already been acknowledged by this.

Example: `determine whether an interrupt is pending for COM1 and jump to the handler according to the addresses in the jump table jp_tab.`

```
MOV dx, 3fah        ; load address of interrupt identification register into dx
IN al, dx           ; read register into al
TEST al, 01h        ; test PND bit
JNZ further         ; jump to further if PND is set

MOV bx, jp_tab[al] ; load D1, D0 as index for jump table jp_tab into bx
JMP bx              ; jump to the corresponding handler address

further:
....................................
```

```
DLAB: divisor latch access bit
      1=access to divisor latch
      0=access to receiver/transmitter registers and interrupt activation register
BRK:  BREAK
      1=on    0=off
Parity: 000=none   001=odd   011=even   101=mark   111=space
STOP: number of stop bits
      1=2 stop bits    0=1 stop bits
D-Bit: number of data bits
       00=5 data bits  01=6 data bits  10=7 data bits  11=8 data bits
```

Figure 29.26: Data format register (offset 03h).

Using the data format register (Figure 29.26) you may define the SDU format, and further determine whether an access with the offset addresses 00h and 01h accesses the receiver buffer/transmitter hold register and the interrupt enable register or the two bytes of the divisor latch register. If the divisor latch access bit *DLAB* is cleared, then an access with offset 00h leads to reading the receiver buffer register or writing the transmitter hold register. Moreover, the offset 01h addresses the interrupt enable register.

If you set bit *BRK* then the signal at the UART output SOUT is always held on the break state, that is, logical 0 corresponding to space. This also applies if you write a data byte into the transmitter hold register to output it via SOUT. Once you clear BRK again, data can be supplied via SOUT. Note that SOUT usually outputs a signal according to a logical 1 or mark if the transmitter shift register is empty, and the UART will not provide a serial data stream. Thus, a set BRK bit simulates a break of the connection for the receiver.

Using the three *parity* bits you can determine which parity (if any) the transmitter control generates for the data bytes. $Parity_0$ is sometimes called the parity enable bit, $parity_1$ the parity select bit, and $parity_2$ the forced-parity bit. With *STOP* you define the number of stop bits, and with *D-Bit* the number of data bits. Valid data lengths are five, six, seven, and eight data bits. Note that the UART 8250/16450/16550 automatically selects 1 ½ stop bits upon a data length of five bits. This means that the active phase of the stop bit lasts for 1 ½ times that of «normal» bits. Half a bit seems to be senseless.

With a set *DLAB* bit you can access the least significant (offset 00h) as well as most significant (offset 01h) byte of the divisor latch register. The divisor latch register is a 16-bit counter register, containing the divisor that the baud generator in the UART uses to generate the reference frequency. The baud rate rises by further dividing the reference frequency by the above described divisor 16. In general, the baud rate is therefore as follows:

$$\text{baud rate} = \frac{\text{main reference frequency}}{16*\text{divisor}} = \frac{\text{reference frequency}}{\text{divisor}}$$

In the PC a main reference frequency of 1.8432 MHz is usually used, generated by an external oscillator and applied to the two 8250/16450/16550 terminals XTAL1 and XTAL2 so that the following holds (main reference frequency = 1.8432 MHz, reference frequency=115200 Hz):

$$\text{baud rate} = \frac{115\ 200}{\text{divisor}}$$

Thus you can operate your UART in the PC with a maximum rate of 115200 baud if you write the value 1 into the divisor latch register. With one start bit, eight data bits, and one stop bit, this corresponds to a transfer rate of 10520 bytes per second. Thus the CPU has 86 μs at most to read the receiver buffer register if no overrun error occurs.

Example: `set COM1 to 300 baud; divisor = 384.`

```
MOV dx, 3fbh    ; load address of data format register into dx
IN al, dx       ; read data format register into al
OR al, 80h      ; set DLAB
OUT dx, al      ; write data format register
MOV dx, 3f8h    ; load address of divisor latch register (LSB) into dx
MOV al, 80h     ; load low-order divisor byte (128) into al
OUT dx, al      ; write divisor latch register (LSB)

INC dx          ; set up address of divisor latch register (MSB)
MOV al, 01h     ; load low-order divisor byte (256) into al
OUT dx, al      ; write divisor latch register (MSB)

MOV dx, 3fbh    ; load address of address of data format register into dx
IN al, dx       ; read data format register into al
```

```
AND al, 7fh     ; clear DLAB
OUT dx, al      ; write data format register
```

Note that the level of the output signals of the UART 8250/16450/16550 modem control logic and the values of the corresponding bits in the modem control register and the modem status register are complementary to each other. But the RS-232C output signals are further amplified by the EIA line drivers before they appear at the RS-232C terminal of your PC; moreover, the RS-232C input signals from the RS-232C connector of your PC have been amplified by these line drivers before they are applied to the UART terminals. As already mentioned, the EIA line drivers in your PC generally operate as inverters, so that the signal levels at the RS-232C connector of your PC correspond to the bit values in the modem control or modem status register; a set bit means a high signal level, a cleared bit a low signal level. Thus, in the following description, note whether the bit values, the signal levels at the UART terminal, or the signal levels at the RS-232C connector of your PC are meant.

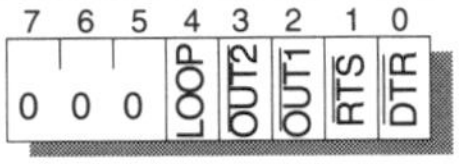

LOOP: loopback check
1=enabled 0=normal mode
$\overline{\text{OUT2}}$: general purpose output 2
1=enabled 0=disabled
$\overline{\text{OUT1}}$: general purpose output 1
1=enabled 0=disabled
$\overline{\text{RTS}}$: request to send
1=enabled 0=disabled
$\overline{\text{DTR}}$: data terminal ready
1=enabled 0=disabled

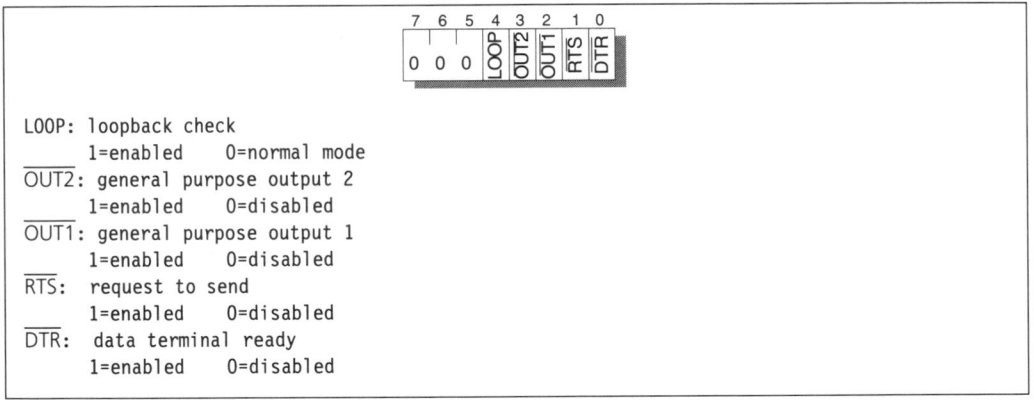

Figure 29.27: Modem control register (offset 04h).

The modem control register (Figure 29.27) supervises the UART modem control logic. The three most significant bits are not used; a reading access always returns a value of 0. By setting the *LOOP* bit you enable the feedback-loop check of the UART 8250/16450/16550. This is a special test and diagnostics mode implemented in the 8250/16450/16550, in which the four modem control logic outputs are internally connected to the RS-232C inputs of the modem control logic as follows: $\overline{\text{RTS}}$ to $\overline{\text{CTS}}$, $\overline{\text{DTR}}$ to $\overline{\text{DSR}}$, $\overline{\text{OUT1}}$ to $\overline{\text{RI}}$ and $\overline{\text{OUT2}}$ to $\overline{\text{DCD}}$. Moreover, the transmitter output SOUT is set to a logical 1 corresponding to mark, the receiver input SIN is cut off from the rest of the UART, and the transmitter shift register is directly connected to the receiver shift register. Thus, with a set LOOP bit you can test the modem control functions and the generation of interrupts in the UART, as well as the serializations in the transmitter shift register and the data assembly in the receiver shift register. If you write, for example, a data byte into the transmitter hold register, it is transferred to the transmitter shift register; eventually an interrupt «TBE» is issued upon an enabled interrupt; the serial data stream is directly transferred according to the format defined in the data format register into the receiver shift register and converted into a data byte there; the data byte is transferred into the receiver buffer register; and finally, an interrupt «RxRD» is issued if the interrupt enable register has been programmed accordingly. A comparison of the data byte that you have written into the transmitter hold register in advance with the byte that is now available in the receiver buffer register indicates whether the transmitter and receiver logic is operating correctly.

With a cleared LOOP bit the UART 8250/16450/16550 operates normally as a serial, asynchronous receiver and transmitter. The two bits OUT2 and OUT1 then control the logic level that the corresponding UART outputs provide: a set bit leads to a low, a cleared to a high level. Thus the bit values and signal levels at the UART output are complementary. Note that in the PC the output signal OUT2 is combined with the INTRPT signals by a logic gate; the OUT2 bit therefore acts as a master interrupt enable bit. You cannot mask the interrupt internally using OUT2 (that is, the corresponding bits in the interrupt identification register are set as usual), but using the logic gate you block transmission of the INTRPT signal to the 8259A PCI, and thus the generation of a hardware interrupt with a cleared OUT2 bit. OUT1, on the other hand, is not used in the PC.

The two bits RTS and DTR control the levels of the UART's RS-232C output signals $\overline{RTS}$ and $\overline{DTR}$ directly. A set bit leads to a low level at the UART outputs $\overline{RTS}$ and $\overline{DTR}$, respectively, and with the inverting line drivers to a high level of + 12 V at the RTS or DTR output of the PC's RS-232C connector.

Example: `set master interrupt bit to enable individual interrupts.`

```
MOV dx, 3fch    ; load modem control register address into dx
IN al, dx       ; read modem control register into al
OR al, 08h      ; set OUT2
OUT dx, al      ; write modem control register
```

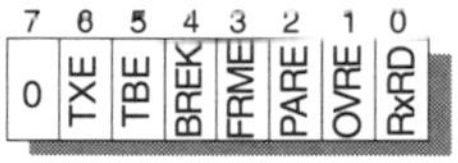


```
TXE:  transmitter empty
      1=no byte in transmitter hold register and transmitter shift register
      0=one byte in transmitter hold register or transmitter shift register
TBE:  transmitter buffer empty
      1=no byte in transmitter hold register   0=one byte in transmitter hold register
BREK: break
      1=detected                0=no break
FRME: framing error
      1=error                   0=no framing error
PARE: parity error
      1=error                   0=no parity error
OVRE: overrun error
      1=error                   0=no overflow error
RxRD: received data ready
      1=received data in receiver buffer register   0=no received data
```

Figure 29.28: Serialization status register (offset 05h).

The serialization status register (Figure 29.28) contains information on the status of the receiver and transmitter section in the UART 8250/16450/16550. The most significant bit is not defined, and always returns a value of 0. A set *TXE* bit indicates that the transmitter hold register and the transmitter shift register are empty. If TXE is equal to 0, then data is still present either in the transmitter hold register or in the transmitter shift register. If the *TBE* bit is set then the transmitter hold register is empty, otherwise a data byte is being held there.

The next four bits refer to the state of the connection and eventual reception errors. If the *BREK* bit is set, then the receiver logic has detected a break in the connection. This happens if SIN is on the space logic level for more than one SDU. A set *FRME* bit indicates a framing error, a set *PARE* bit a parity error, and a set *OVRR* bit an overrun error of the receiver buffer register. If the *RxRD* bit is set, then a data byte is available in the receiver buffer register. Thus you can use the serialization status register, for example, together with the interrupt identification register, to determine the cause of an error interrupt in detail, or to determine the UART status in polling mode even if the interrupts are masked.

Example: determine whether a data byte is available in the receiver buffer register and read the data byte if so.

```
MOV dx, 3fdh    ; load address of serialization status register into dx
IN al, dx       ; read serialization status registers into al
TEST al, 01h    ; test RxRD
JZ further      ; jump to further if RxRD is cleared
MOV dx, 3fdh    ; load address of receiver buffer register into dx
IN al, dx       ; read data byte in receiver buffer register into al
further:
   ..........
```

Using the modem status register (Figure 29.29) you can determine the status of the RS-232C input signals. The high-order nibble provides the current signal levels, and the low-order nibble gives information on the level change since the last register read. An IN instruction referring to the modem status register thus clears the low-order nibble register.

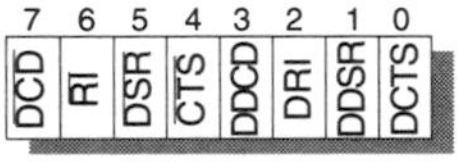

$\overline{\text{DCD}}$: data carrier detect
    1=DCD active   0=DCD inactive
$\overline{\text{RI}}$: ring indicator
    1=RI active   0=RI inactive
$\overline{\text{DSR}}$: data set ready
    1=DSR active   0=DSR inactive
$\overline{\text{CTS}}$: clear to send
    1=CTS active   0=CTS inactive
DDCD: delta data carrier detect
    1=DCD change since last read   0=DCD not changed
DRI: delta ring indicator
    1=RI change since last read   0=DCD not changed
DDSR: delta data set ready
    1=DSR change since last read   0=DSR not changed
DCTS: delta clear to send
    1=CTS change since last read   0=CTS not changed

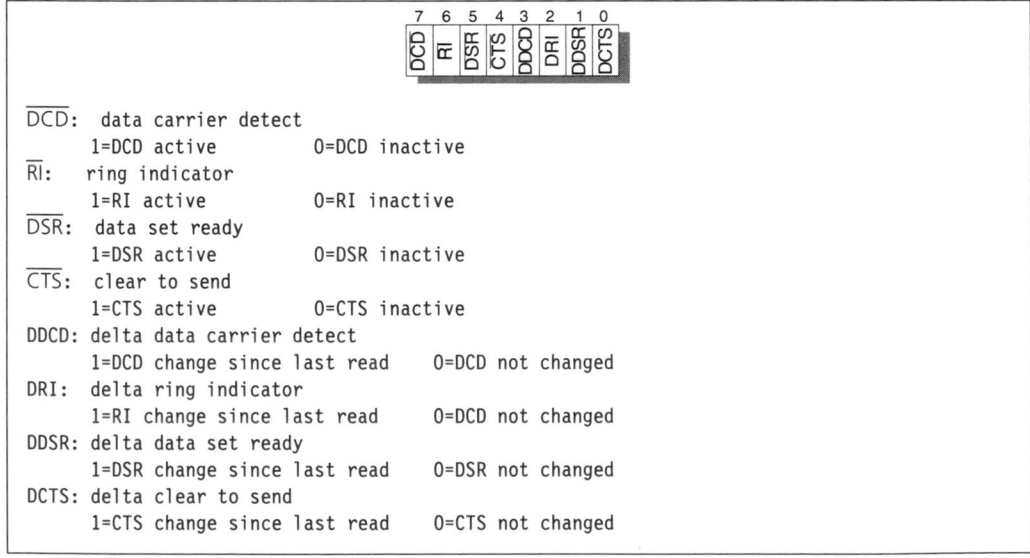

Figure 29.29: Modem status register (offset 06h).

The four bits $\overline{DCD}$, $\overline{RI}$, $\overline{DSR}$, and $\overline{CTS}$ indicate the signal levels at the UART input terminals $\overline{DCD}$, $\overline{RI}$, $\overline{DSR}$ and $\overline{CTS}$ directly; a set bit corresponds to a low signal level, a cleared bit to a high signal level. Note that the levels are inverted by the EIA line drivers. At the RS-232C connector of your PC, a set bit therefore corresponds to a high signal level of +12 V again, and a set bit to a low signal level of –12 V. If the *DCD* bit is set, then the modem has detected a carrier signal (or has simply set the DCD signal to a high level). If a call is arriving at the modem it raises the RI line to a high level and the UART sets the RI bit. Similarly, a set *DSR* bit signals that the modem is ready, and a set *CTS* bit that the UART is ready to output data to the modem.

The bits *DDCD*, *DRI*, *DDSR* and *DCTS* finally indicate whether the signals DCD, RI, DSR, and CTS at the RS-232C connector (or accordingly the DCD, RI, DSR, and CTS bits in the modem status register) have been altered since the last register read; a set DXXX bit means a bit change.

Example: `determine whether the DCD bit has changed, and eventually transfer a new DCD into the least significant bit of the al register.`

```
MOV dx, 3feh    ; load address of modem status registers into dx
IN al, dx       ; read modem status register into al
TEST al, 08h    ; test DeltaDCD
JZ further      ; jump to further if DeltaDCD is cleared
AND al, 80h     ; clear all bits except DCD
CLC             ; clear carry
RCL al          ; transfer DCD from most-significant al bit into carry
RCL al          ; transfer DCD from carry into least-significant al bit
further:
    ...........
```

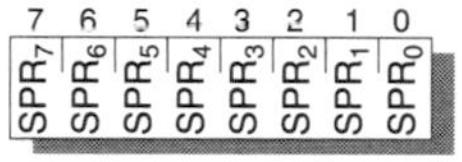

SPR_7–SPR_0: bit 7–0 in register

Figure 29.30: Scratch-pad register (offset 07h).

The scratch-pad register (Figure 29.30) is implemented only on the 16450/16550, and can be used as a 1-byte memory for temporary data, for example if you don't want to use the main memory in an IRQ handler. The values of the bits *SPR7–SPR0* don't affect the functioning and the behaviour of the UART 16450/16550 in any way.

29.3 Other Interfaces

29.3.1 IBM Adapter for Computer Games

A further and very simply structured interface is the adapter for computer games. Two joysticks with release buttons for machine guns, missiles and other pedagogically valuable toys can be connected. The structure and functioning of the adapter is quite simple (see Figure 29.31). You may access the adapter with IN and OUT instructions referring to port address 201h.

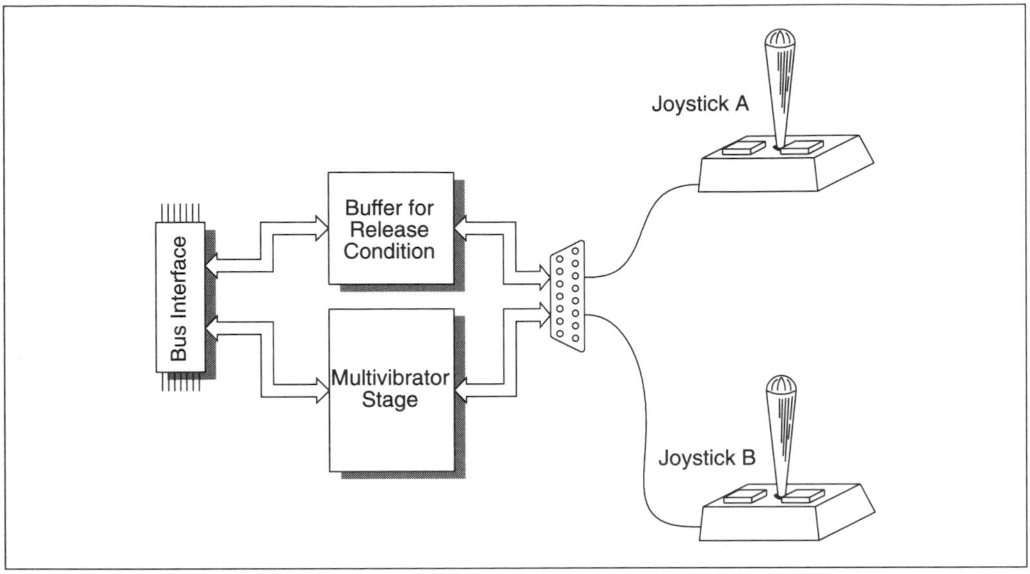

Figure 29.31: Structure of the game adapter. The game adapter has a buffer, in which the current release status of the joystick buttons is stored, and a multivibrator for determining the joystick position.

The adapter is connected to the PC system bus via only the eight low-order bits of the data bus, the ten low-order bits of the address bus, and the control lines $\overline{IOR}$ and $\overline{IOW}$. On the reverse the adapter has a jack with 15 contacts, to which a maximum of two game consoles can be connected. Some adapter cards also have two jacks so that joysticks can be connected individually. The assignment of the standard adapter connector is shown in Table 29.8.

Pin	Used for
2	1st button of joystick A (BA1)
3	X-potentiometer of joystick A (AX)
6	Y-potentiometer of joystick A (AY)
7	2nd button of joystick A (BA2)
10	1st button of joystick B (BB1)
11	X-potentiometer of joystick B (BX)
13	Y-potentiometer of joystick B (BY)
14	2nd button of joystick B (BB2)
1,8,9,15	supply voltage Vcc (+5 V)
4,5,12	ground GND (0 V)

Table 29.8: Layout of game adapter connector

Each of the two joysticks has two potentiometers with a resistance value between 0 Ω and 100 kΩ arranged perpendicular to each other, indicating the X and Y positions, respectively, of the joystick. Additionally, every joystick has up to two buttons. They are usually open, and the corresponding lines are pulled to a high level by the joystick's internal circuitry (see Figure 29.32).

7	6	5	4	3	2	1	0
BB2	BB1	BA2	BA1	BY	BX	AY	AX

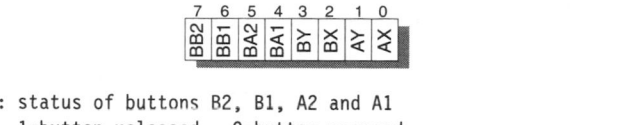

```
BB2, BB1, BA2, BA1: status of buttons B2, B1, A2 and A1
                    1=button released   0=button pressed
BY, BX, AY, AX:     multivibrator status according to the corresponding potentiometer
```

Figure 29.32: Game adapter status byte.

You can determine the *pressed* or *released* state of the buttons easily with an IN instruction referring to address 201h. The game adapter returns a data byte with the structure shown in Figure 29.32. The high-order nibble indicates the button's status. As the adapter doesn't use an IRQ line, and thus isn't able to issue an interrupt, you have to investigate the status byte regularly to determine the current status, that is, the game adapter operates only in polling mode.

Example: determine whether the 2nd button of joystick A has been operated.

```
MOV dx, 201h      ; load game adapter address into dx
IN al, dx         ; read status byte into al
TEST al, 20h      ; check whether BA2 is set
```

It is more ponderous to detect the current position of the joysticks; you must determine the current resistance value of the potentiometer concerned. The multivibrator element is implemented for this purpose. If you issue an OUT instruction referring to port address 201h with any output value, then a one-shot multivibrator in the multivibrator element is started. The values of the four low-order bits BY, BX, AY and AX in the status byte rises to 1. The one-shot multivibrator mainly has a capacitor, which is discharged via a 2.2 kΩ resistor on the adapter board and the corresponding joystick potentiometer. If the capacitor voltage is decreased below a certain threshold value by the discharge process, then the multivibrator outputs a 0 instead of a 1. Depending upon the potentiometer resistance value, this requires more or less time; the exact relation is as follows.

$$\text{time interval} = 24.2\ \mu s + 0.011\ \mu s * \text{resistance}[\Omega]$$

or

$$\text{resistance}[\Omega] = \frac{\text{time interval} - 24.2\ \mu s}{0.011\ \mu s}$$

Thus the time interval may be in the range between 24.2 µs for the potentiometer position 0 Ω, and 1124 µs corresponding to 100 kΩ. To determine the resistance value of the individual potentiometers you output any data byte to the 201h port first to start the one-shot multivibrator. The corresponding bit in the status byte rises to 1. Afterwards, you continuously determine (according to the status byte) whether the value of the bit corresponding to the potentiometer investigated has fallen to 0 by regularly reading port 201h. You may determine the time interval, for example, by reading counter 0 of the 8253/8254 PIT timer chips in advance of the first and after the last IN instruction. On counter 0 a wrap-around occurs only every 55 ms; thus the time interval corresponding to a potentiometer position is always significantly smaller than the cycle time of counter 0. Of course, you can load, for example, counter 2 of the PIT with appropriate count values and use counter 2 for determining the time interval. From this time interval and the above indicated relation, you can determine the resistance value and thus the joystick position.

Example: determine resistance value of the potentiometer AX corresponding to the X position of joystick A.

```
MOV dx, 201h      ; load game adapter address into dx
OUT dx, al        ; write any value to port 201h to start one-shot multivibrator

MOV al, 00h       ; load counter-latch command referring counter 0 into al
OUT 43h, al       ; output counter-latch command to PIT control register
IN al, 40h        ; read low-order counter byte into al
IN ah, 40h        ; read high-order counter byte into ah
                  ; thus ax=ah.al holds the current 16-bit counter value
MOV bx, ax        ; transfer counter value into bx

check_status:
IN al, dx         ; read status byte from port 201h
TEST al, 01h      ; check whether bit AX is still set
JZ check_status   ; if bit AX is set then check again

MOV al, 00h       ; load counter-latch command referring counter 0 into al
OUT 43h, al       ; output counter-latch command to PIT control register
IN al, 40h        ; read low-order counter byte into al
IN ah, 40h        ; read high-order counter byte into ah
                  ; thus ax=ah.al holds the current 16-bit counter value
MOV cx, ax        ; transfer counter value into cx
.............     ; determine counter difference from bx and cx and
                  ; thus time difference and resistance value
```

In principle, the game adapter can also be used for other purposes than the connection of a joystick. For example, you can measure resistance values in general, and you are not limited to the range 0–100 kΩ. Also, for example, the high-order nibble of the status byte could indicate the bell button state in your apartment if you take a soldering iron and connect the bell via the game adapter to your PC. Together with a speech synthesizer this may give rise to some funny experiences... but Figure 29.33 shows only the usual wiring for joysticks!

Starting with the AT and PS/2, you also have the opportunity to determine the status of the buttons as well as the multivibrator state using the BIOS instead of a direct register access. For this purpose, function 84h of INT 15h is implemented. Figure 29.34 shows the call format of this function.

The function carries out two different checks. If the DX register holds the value 00h upon the function call, the function determines only the button status and returns this in the high-order nibble of register al corresponding to Figure 29.32. If DX is set to a value of 01h, the function reads the state of the multivibrators and returns it in registers AX to DX.

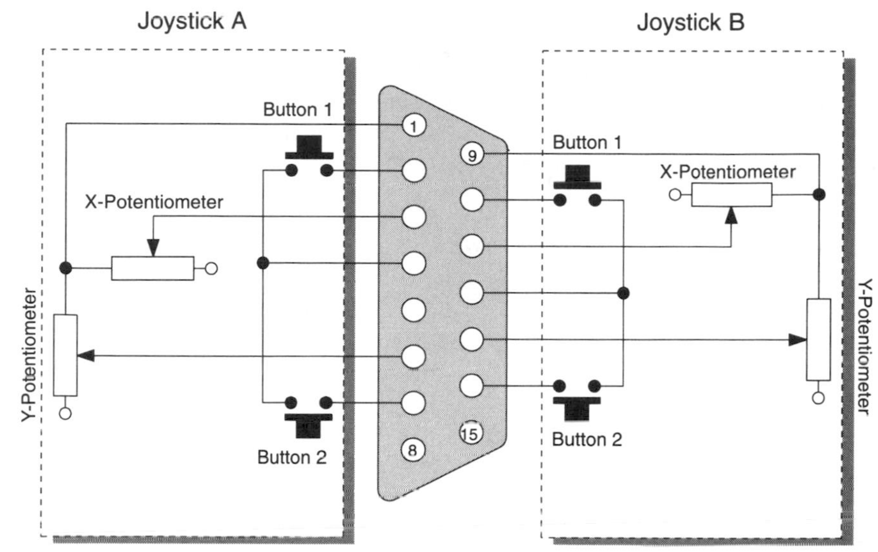

Figure 29.33: Joystick wiring.

Register	Call Value	Return Value
AH	84h	
AL		Button Status (Bit 7..4)
AX		AX-Value
BX		AY-Value
CX		BX-Value
DX	00h: Button Status 01h: Multivibrator Status	BY-Value
Carry		Error if <> 0

Figure 29.34: Calling format of INT 15h, function 84h.

29.3.2 Network Adapters

Network adapters are also interfaces in the narrower sense, because they establish a connection to other computers or peripherals (for example, a laser printer in the network). For connecting Personal Computers to each other, Ethernet has largely become established, on which, for example, Novell NetWare is built. If you want to connect your PC via a network to a larger computer system, for example a UNIX system or an AS/400, you will often meet IBM's Token Ring. Both networks are comparable in view of their performance. The various network standards will be discussed in Chapter 30 in brief; interested readers will find a large amount of specialized literature on this subject.

29.3.3 Datanets, Packet Switching and PAD Adapters

Parallel to the public telephone network, for several years there has been a pure data network, too, which has various names in different countries; for example, DATEX in Germany, or Datapac in Canada. Additionally, the telecoms or commercial datanets provide a gateway to the largest WAN in the world – the well-known *Internet*.

Initially, the Internet was built as a worldwide net (WAN) which should enable a data exchange between universities and research institutes. Meanwhile, nearly every PC user having a modem and a telephone line can have access to the Internet for little cost through commercial companies that provide a gateway to the Internet. In addition to the usual net servives such as e-mail and database access, newsgroups (user groups discussing thousands of subjects of interest) have emanated as a feature of the Internet. The Internet is looked upon as the communications platform of the worldwide 'computer freak' community. At the time of writing (mid-1994), about 20 million computers with a multiple of actual users are connected to this net. A more exact number cannot be determined because of the sometimes chaotic structure of the net (comparable to the world's street network which is extended and repaired all the time).

Unlike the telephone network which works in an analogue manner, large parts of the data networks were implemented for pure data transfer from the beginning. They are therefore much more reliable and also more powerful than the combination of a telephone and a network-modem (DATEX P10 reaches 48000 baud, while the telephone network doesn't reach much more than 4800 to 9600 baud without errors). Of course, in principle you are also free to transmit a conversation in binary-encoded form with CD quality, but the datanets are usually exclusively employed for worldwide data transfer. In many countries there are similar datanets, so you can exchange data with computer systems throughout the world in the same way as you talk with your friend in Australia via a telephone line.

Some datanets still operate with line switching, that is, your PC is connected to the destination computer by means of a line which is exclusively dedicated to it throughout the whole connection time. Thus you are occupying a line (for example, to a database) even if you are thinking which command you should input next. This is, of course, a pure waste, and very expensive especially if you have a connection to another continent via satellite. While you are thinking about the next command another communication member could be using the line without disturbing you.

For this reason, telecommunication companies have established so-called *packet-switching networks*. This means that all data and commands are transferred in the form of data packets after the destination has been called and the connection established. International datanets comply with the CCITT X.25 standard, which defines the calling procedure, transmission, and other network parameters. A data packet consists of the destination address and the data, and usually comprises 128 bytes. If you issue, for example, a read command referring to a database, then the command is first converted into one or more packets which are transferred to the destination via the network. Which route the packet takes (which line is used) is insignificant here; the transmission path can be very different from packet to packet. For example, it may be that your command packet is running via the path London – New York – Los Angeles – Stanford, but the second packet via the path London – Chicago – San Francisco – Stanford. The switching system must be able, of course, to handle problems; for example, depending upon the transmission time, the second packet may arrive in advance of the first one! But you nevertheless have the illusion that a data line is always reserved for you. The big advantage of packet switching is the much more efficient use of transmission paths, as the switching system is free to select the connection lines for every packet, and always uses a currently available physical line. These datanets thus operate with so-called *virtual connections*. The switching systems usually comprise a large computer with enormous storage capacity for transferring and temporarily storing the data packets. As the user you pay only for the number of transferred data packets if packet switching is effective, that is, the bill is calculated according to the amount of data (and, of course, the distance to the destination device). If you don't output or receive packets then you don't have to pay (or only a very low amount), even if the connection to the destination device is still established. With line switching, on the other hand, you have to pay according to the connection time because you occupy the line even if you don't accept or provide data.

Data networks often operate with normal modems that you can connect directly to the serial interface of your PC. With a suitable terminal program (and an account, of course) you are ready to exchange data via the public datanet now and access databases or mail boxes, etc.

Access to packet switching networks is not so easy, however, as the data that is to be output by your PC must first be converted into a suitable number of packets with corresponding addresses. The incoming data packets must also be separated into an address and actual data. This job is carried out by a so-called *PAD adapter* (packet assembler/disassembler, that is, a hardware device that assembles a transmission packet from the data and the address, or disassembles a data packet into address and data). The PAD adapter is connected to the modem, which transfers the data packet to the datanet or receives packets from the network; thus, the PAD forms a DCE. In most cases, you may access the PAD by means of suitably adapted terminal software and a serial interface on the PAD adapter. But some PAD adapters (for example, IBM's X.25 adapter) employ an interface chip other than the UART 8250, namely Zilog's Z80 SIO. It carries out many of the same functions as the 8250, but its register layout and addresses are incompatible with the 8250. When buying a PAD adapter, make sure that the terminal software is actually programmed for the adapter concerned; otherwise you remain separated from the (datanet) world. PADs are quite intelligent components, and implement commands that you may pass by means of the terminal program. You use these PAD commands to control the PAD's access to the data network or the disconnection of the destination device.

The calling of a destination device is as simple as using the telephone. If you have logged into the datanet (which is already carried out on some datanets with switching on the PC and the modem) you need only input the datanet number of the destination. Now the switching system establishes a connection to the destination (for example, a database). As soon as the (possibly virtual) connection is established, your PC behaves in the usual form as a terminal of the connected database (but which can be several thousand kilometres from the database).

The public datanet, with its higher reliability against noise, provides significant advantages compared to data exchange via the public telephone network, especially for users who regularly transfer large amounts of data over long distances, or who intend to use databases frequently. The higher base cost for a datanet account will pay for itself for all those who frequently use the datanet, because of the lower transfer costs.

29.3.4 Fax Adapter Cards

Another interesting interface for your PC are facsmile adapters, which are controlled by an appropriate fax program. They are usually normal modems, but equipped with some specialized hard- or software for fax communication. You don't need to print text or a drawing, go to the fax and insert the sheet into the fax machines; instead you instruct your fax modem directly on-screen to transmit the document to another fax device. For example, you may form a drawing including text with CorelDRAW! and export the result into a file; the fax program only needs to read the file, and provide corresponding fax data to the installed fax modem. This saves time and paper. If you already own a scanner you can also fax in the usual way by scanning in drawings and other documents and sending them via the fax program and the fax adapter.

For incoming faxes, your fax adapter doesn't print the documents on the very expensive thermopaper, but writes them into a file. Thus you may edit the fax, rotate or process it, or, for example, read it into your business graphics program. Also in this case you save paper, time and money.

29.4 Small but Universal – PCMCIA

The PCMCIA interface has recently become an extraordinarily successful standard. Although originally only intended as a memory expansion (standard 1.0), with the new specification 2.0, the credit card-sized cards are now also usable for a lot of I/O devices, such as fax modems, SCSI adapters or GPS (Global Positioning System) receivers with a PCMCIA interface. The specification is set-up and managed by the *Personal Computer Memory Card International Association*.

PCMCIA allows a card memory of a maximum of 64 Mbytes for so-called *Common Memory* and a maximum of 64 Mbytes for *Attribute Memory*, that is, the memory present on a single PCMCIA card may encompass up to 128 Mbytes – I presume that this should be enough for some years. For comparison: the entire 24-bit ISA address space holds only 16 Mbytes. With a PCMCIA memory card you can expand your notebook's memory considerably. Also, the installation of non-volatile memory (flash or battery-buffered SRAM memory, for example) is possible, for example, to install a quite high-capacity, external «drive» with removable volume on a solid-state basis (floppies as the most widely used drives with removable data volume have a maximum of no more than 2.88 Mbytes). With I/O cards beginning with specification 2.0, an I/O address space of 64k 8-bit ports is also available (or an equivalent of 16- and/or 32-bit ports).

Presently, specification 3.0 is under discussion; it will incorporate drives and, therefore, defines a larger slot. The PCMCIA interface should be manufacturer-independent and, moreover, free of the need for a specific hardware architecture in the computer system used. Thus, PCMCIA is intended for both the IBM-compatible PC and the Apple Macintosh.

29.4.1 Structure and Function

The PCMCIA interface provides a connection between a small *PC card*, or *PCMCIA card*, and a host PC. For this purpose, the host PC may have an adapter which connects the PC system bus (ISA/EISA/MCA/VLB/PCI) to the PCMCIA socket and incorporates the necessary control (*PCMCIA controller*). In the same way as your PC can have several serial (COM1–COM4) and parallel (LPT1–LPT3) interfaces on several adapters, it is also possible for several PCMCIA sockets (slots) to be installed on a Personal Computer with one or more PCMCIA sockets (slots) each. The sockets or slots hold the PC cards and have contacts for exchanging signals and providing supply voltages. Usually, the sockets perform power management to reduce power consumption of the PCMCIA interface as much as possible. This is particularly required in notebooks – one main segment for the use of the very compact PCMCIA interface.

The principal function of the PCMCIA interface and the inserted cards is quite simple: usually, in the main memory or I/O address space of the host system an address area (a so-called *window*) is defined, onto which a memory or I/O segment of the inserted card is mapped. An access to the host system's window then does not refer to the host system, but is redirected to the assigned PCMCIA slot and, thus, the inserted card. This is shown in Figure 29.35.

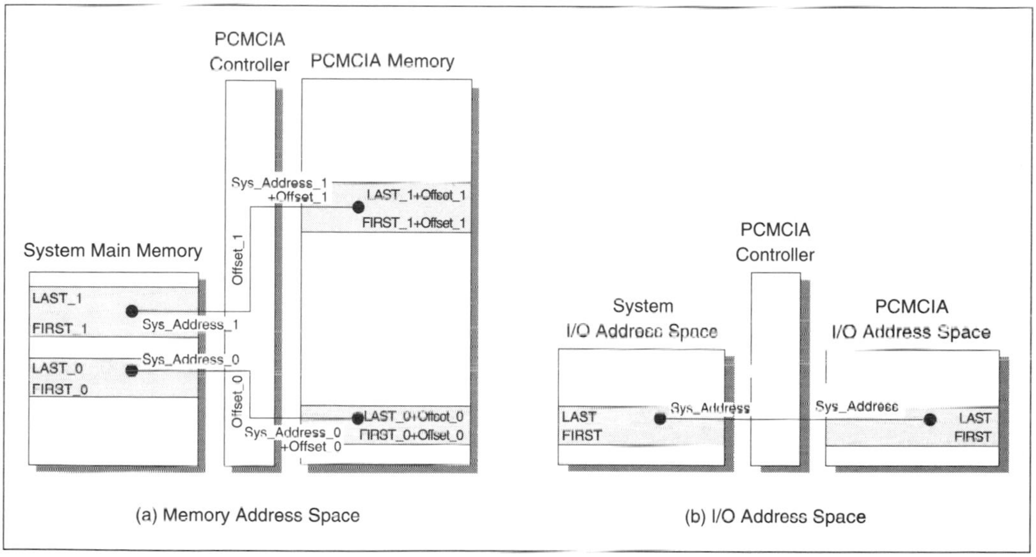

Figure 29.35: Function of the PCMCIA interface.

A window in system main memory is defined by two quantities: the beginning of the window or the address of the first window byte (*FIRST*), and the end of the window or the address of the last byte in the window (*LAST*). FIRST and LAST are held by a control register of the PCMCIA controller. If the system address *Sys_Address* (the address provided by the processor, cache controller, etc.) is between FIRST and LAST, the PCMCIA controller is activated and redirects this memory access to that PCMCIA socket for which the window is defined.

Additionally, the *card offset* is important for card memory addressing. It decides which memory location on the PC card is accessed physically by the system address. This offset is always provided in 2'complement representation, and added to the system address by the PCMCIA controller. Therefore, remapping of the PC card's address area between the physical card addresses *[FIRST+card Offset, LAST+Card Offset]* to the system address area *[FIRST, LAST]* is carried out. Because the card offset is given as a 2'complement, the offset can always be added even when a card memory area «below» the window in the system memory is to be accessed; the card offset is then only a negative number in 2'complement representation. Thus, in this area, a system address physically accesses a memory location on the inserted PCMCIA card.

The specification allows several such windows per socket or slot, and the usual PCMCIA controller makes use of that possibility. The windows can be configured independently (for example, regarding the access to common or attribute memory of the PCMCIA card, number of wait states, etc.). Accesses to main memory with a system address which is not within the window refer, of course, to the system main memory, and are not redirected to the PCMCIA slot. Additionally, each window can be subdivided into *pages* (if the PCMCIA controller is able to do that). If only one page is present, it encompasses the whole window. If several pages are formed, every page comprises 16 kbytes. Every page can have a different card offset, thus several «sub-windows» into the PCMCIA card's address space can be defined.

A quite cumbersome but nevertheless defined way in which to access the card memory goes through I/O ports and card registers, but you will rarely find such PCMCIA sockets and cards.

Specification 2.0 also intends to remap an I/O address area of the inserted PC cards onto the system I/O address area. Therefore, control and status registers on a PCMCIA card that, for example, integrates a fax modem are also accessible. In principle, this can also be achieved with memory-mapped registers, of course. In this case, however, we always need special drivers and, for example, a standard terminal program access which expects a UART 16450 at the COMx-usual I/O addresses is directed to nowhere. With the I/O cards we don't have this problem after configuring the PCMCIA slots: the card registers are simply remapped, for example, to the COM1-typical I/O addresses in the system's I/O address area. Such I/O windows do not implement pages and have byte granularity (memory windows: 4 kbytes). Additionally, there is no card offset; every port address in the window of the system I/O address space refers to the same port in the card I/O address space.

The PCMCIA interface can recognize many card status changes, for example battery warnings, insertion and removal of cards, etc. I/O cards can issue a hardware interrupt request to report incoming faxes, for example. Further, optional EDC generators (Error Detecting Code) are defined to ensure data integrity. With the write-protect switch on the PC cards you may prevent erasure or overwriting of stored data. You can configure or send a request to the PCMCIA interface by a direct access to the control and status registers of the installed PCMCIA controller, or through the socket and card service functions of the BIOS INT 1ah (functions 80h and above). Appendix M contains a detailed listing of the socket service functions (see also Section 29.4.3). Only the socket and card service functions are specified; every manufacturer can implement the registers as he chooses. Nevertheless, I will discuss the most important control registers of a typical PCMCIA controller (PCIC 82365SL) in Section 29.4.4. For compatibility reasons, you should prefer the socket or card services.

29.4.2 PCMCIA Contacts

In the following you will find all the contacts and signals of the PCMCIA interface according to specification 2.0. Note that standard 1.0 only dealt with memory cards, and the interface is configured as a pure memory interface upon power-up. Additionally the signals WAIT and RESET were not defined in specification 1.0 and, therefore, are marked as free. If you want to use these signals for an I/O card (define a combined memory/IO slot) you must configure the respective socket first.

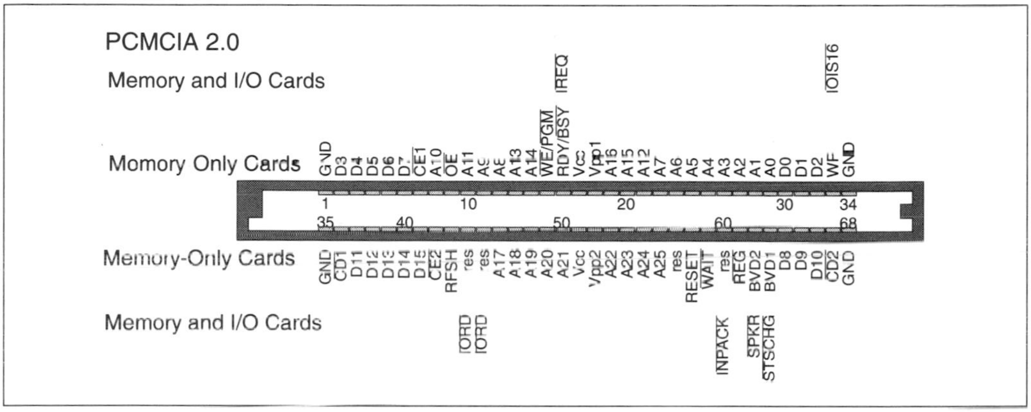

Figure 29.36: PCMCIA slot contacts according to PCMCIA 2.0.

First I want to discuss all the contacts and signals that have the same meaning for both pure memory sockets and memory/IO sockets. The contacts are listed alphabetically.

A25–A0 (O)

Contacts 8, 10–14,19–29, 46–50, 53–56

These 26 address contacts serve for addressing up to 64 Mbytes of memory or 64 k I/O ports (A15–A0; I/O cards only) on the inserted PCMCIA card.

$\overline{\text{CD1}}$, $\overline{\text{CD2}}$ (I)

Contacts 36, 67

These Card Detect contacts recognize whether a PCMCIA card is inserted or not. The adapter logic drives $\overline{\text{CD1}}$ and $\overline{\text{CD2}}$ to a high level if the socket is empty. If a card is inserted, it connects the card detect contacts with ground and pulls the signals to a low level. This level change indicates an inserted PC card.

$\overline{\text{CE2}}$, $\overline{\text{CE1}}$ (O)

Contacts 7, 42

These two Card Enable contacts serve for enabling the high-order ($\overline{\text{CE2}}$) and low-order ($\overline{\text{CE1}}$) part of the data bus D15–D0.

D15–D0 (I/O)

Contacts 2–6, 30–32, 37–41, 64–66

These contacts form the 16-bit data bus of the PCMCIA interface.

$\overline{\text{OE}}$ (O)
Contact 9

When data is to be read from a PCMCIA memory card, the PCMCIA controller pulls this Output Enable signal $\overline{\text{OE}}$ to a low level.

$\overline{\text{REG}}$ (O)
Contact 61

This Attribute Memory select or Register select signal is on a high level for all accesses to the common memory of the PCMCIA card through active $\overline{\text{WE}}$ or $\overline{\text{OE}}$ signals on a high level. When the attribute memory of the PCMCIA card is to be accessed, $\overline{\text{REG}}$ must be on a low level. I/O cards respond to $\overline{\text{IORD}}$ and $\overline{\text{IOWR}}$ only if $\overline{\text{REG}}$ is on a low level; thus, they actually carry out an I/O access for a low-level $\overline{\text{REG}}$ only.

RESET (O; from specification 2.0 on)
Contact 58

A signal with a high level at this contact resets the inserted PCMCIA card. RESET is implemented beginning with PCMCIA specification 2.0.

RFSH (O)
Contact 43

A high-level refresh signal instructs a refresh for a PCMCIA memory card.

$\overline{\text{WAIT}}$ (I; from specification 2.0 on)
Contact 59

When an inserted card cannot complete a memory or I/O access quickly enough, it pulls the signal at this contact to a low level. $\overline{\text{WAIT}}$ therefore serves to insert wait cycles. It is implemented beginning with specification 2.0.

$\overline{\text{WE/PRGM}}$ (O)
Contact 15

A low signal level at this Write Enable/Program contact determines the supply of write data by the slot to the inserted card.

Vpp1, Vpp2 (O)
Contact 18, 52

The two contacts supply programming voltages. They are usually higher than Vcc and serve flash memories, for example.

res
Contact 57
This contact is reserved.

Vcc (O)
Contacts 17, 51
The two contacts provide supply voltages for the inserted PCMCIA card.

GND
Contacts 1, 34, 35, 68
These contacts are grounded.
In the following, all contacts and signals implemented for pure memory sockets only are listed:

BVD2, BVD1 (I)
Contacts 62–63

The two Battery Voltage Detect contacts indicate the power state of the battery in a PCMCIA memory card. The signal combinations (BVD2, BVD1) have the following meanings:

(11) battery o.k.
(10) battery empty, data lost
(01) warning state, battery low, data not yet lost
(00) battery empty, data lost

RDY/$\overline{\text{BSY}}$ (I)
Contact 16
This Ready/Busy signal indicates whether the inserted card has already completed the previously issued write access (RDY/$\overline{\text{BSY}}$=1), or whether it is still occupied by this access (RDY/$\overline{\text{BSY}}$=0).

WP (I)
Contact 33
The Write Protect signal at this contact indicates the state of the write-protect switch of PCMCIA cards. A high WP level indicates a write-protected card.

res
Contacts 44–45, 60
These three contacts are reserved.

Finally, all contacts for combined memory and I/O slots are listed. To use the contacts in the described way, the socket must be configured first:

$\overline{\text{INPACK}}$ (I)
Contact 60

The inserted card acknowledges the transfer of a signal with a low-level Input Acknowledge signal $\overline{\text{INPACK}}$.

$\overline{\text{IORD}}$ (O)
Contact 44

Together with a low-level $\overline{\text{REG}}$ signal, a low-level I/O Read signal instructs the inserted card to carry out an I/O access and to return data to the socket.

$\overline{\text{IOWR}}$ (O)
Contact 45

Together with a low-level $\overline{\text{REG}}$ signal, a low-level I/O Write signal instructs the inserted card to carry out an I/O access and to fetch data from the socket.

$\overline{\text{IREQ}}$ (I)
Contact 16

This Interrupt Request signal is enabled by an inserted I/O card, that is, pulled down to a low level, to issue a hardware interrupt. An example for an I/O card which issues such a request is a PCMCIA modem which receives a call (RI active) and requests the host to service the incoming call.

$\overline{\text{SPKR}}$ (I)
Contact 62

The Speaker or Digital Audio contact receives audio data from the inserted card and forwards it to the system speaker.

$\overline{\text{STSCHG}}$ (I)
Contact 63

The Status Changed signal is enabled when the PCMCIA card status has changed.

$\overline{\text{IOIS16}}$ (I)
Contact 33

The signal at this contact (IO Port Is 16-Bit) is on a low level when the present I/O access addresses a 16-bit port.

29.4.3 Access with Socket Services of INT 1ah, Functions 80h–ffh

The socket services form the software interface nearest to the hardware for PCMCIA cards. Figure 29.37 shows the various layers.

The highest software interface to the PCMCIA slots is established by the *Card Services*. Their calling conventions are operating system dependent, and they process the requests of several processes (clients) under a multitasking operating system. In particular, they manage (share) the socket services among these competing processes to avoid access conflicts. For this purpose, the card services coordinate the access to PC cards, sockets and system elements for the clients. These are usually resident or transient drivers, system utilities and applications. The card services use the socket services to actually access a PCMCIA slot. Unlike the socket services (of which several can be present in the system simultaneously), there is only a single card service implementation per system at a time. Under certain circumstances, a client must be informed about a status change in the corresponding socket (for example, when the card has been removed and no further access is possible). Return messages, called *Events*, are responsible for this.

The socket services are also independent of the basic system architecture, and thus especially of the implemented processor registers and the calling conventions of the system. This is implemented by so-called *Processor Bindings*. In the case of the 80x86 architecture, the general-purpose and segment registers are used in the usual way for transferring parameters and a software interrupt (here: INT 1ah) is used for calling the functions. Note that socket services are not re-entrant (an error message BUSY is returned in this case). The card services handle this problem right from the start, so that a re-entrance problem cannot occur. You can easily determine whether a socket service is installed: you need simply call *function 80h – GetAdapterCount*. If you get the code *SUCCESS* and the signature 'SS' in the CX register, you can (virtually) be sure that at least one socket service is installed.

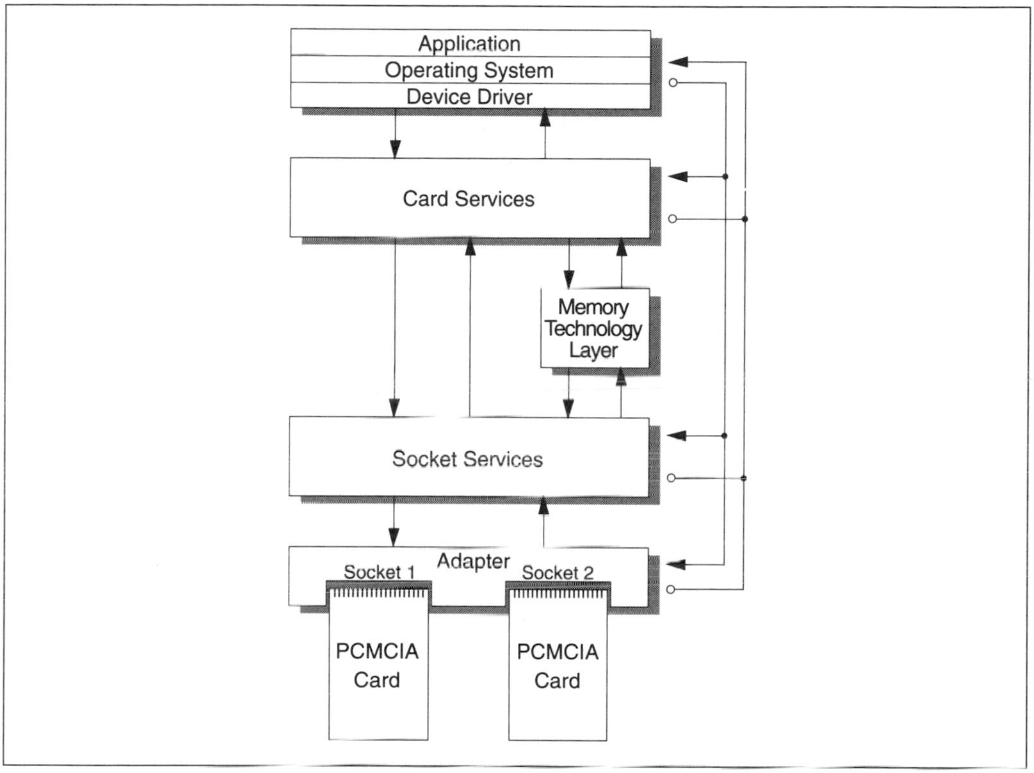

Figure 29.37: Various software layers of the PCMCIA interface.

Example: Determine whether a socket service is present.

```
MOV ah, 80h       ; load function number for GetAdapterCount
INT 1ah           ; call function
JC no_service     ; carry set -> error -> no service
CMP ah, 00h       ; determine whether SUCCESS
JNE no_service    ; ah contains error code <> 0 -> no SUCCESS -> no service
CMP CX, 'SS'      ; determine whether signature 'SS' in CX
JNE no_service    ; cx contains no 'SS' -> no service
service_installed:
                 ; return message that socket service is installed
no_service:
                 ; return message that no socket service is installed
```

The card services assume that the access behaviour of PCMCIA card memories corresponds to that of SRAM memories. For example, data can be individually read, written and erased (that is, overwritten with a standard value). This is not possible, for example, for flash memories, because here no individual cells can be overwritten, but only rows (pages), blocks or the complete chip. Reading data in the same way as with SRAM memories is, however, possible. To keep such technology-dependent procedures for writing and erasing data transparent for the card services, an additional software layer is defined between the card and socket services, if necessary – the so-called *Memory Technology Layer (MTL)*. It uses the socket services for all configuration-relevant accesses (defining windows and pages, for example). Only the access for erasing and writing data is carried out (as usual) directly, but with a programming algorithm which is adapted to the respective memory technology.

All levels of the software interfaces can, of course, be accessed directly in a more or less easy way (dependent on the operating system). For example, you can choose whether you want to use the socket or card services.

A detailed discussion of all socket services is given in Appendix M. Additionally, all card services are listed, but a detailed description of all of these functions would surely turn this book into a brick! Moreover, they form an operating system-near layer, and should therefore be part of a book called *PCMCIA Card Services for System Programmers*. I have therefore not detailed every card service function.

29.4.4 Access Through PCMCIA Controller Registers – An Example

As an example of memory and I/O window management on a hardware level by a PCMCIA controller, the most important registers of Intel's *PC Card Interface Controllers (PCIC) 82365SL* are discussed. Table 29.9 summarizes all PCIC registers; they are all 8-bits wide.

Register index	Register
00h	PCIC identification
01h	interface status
02h	power supply, RESETDRV
03h	interrupt control
04h	card status change
05h	configuration for card status change interrupt
06h	memory window enable
07h	I/O window control
08h/0ch	FIRST setup for I/O window 0/1 (low byte)
09h/0dh	FIRST setup for I/O window 0/1 (high byte)
0ah/0eh	LAST setup for I/O window 0/1 (low byte)
0bh/0fh	LAST setup for I/O window 0/1 (high byte)
10h/18h/20h/28h/30h	FIRST setup for memory window 0/1/2/3/4 (low byte)
11h/19h/21h/29h/31h	FIRST setup for memory window 0/1/2/3/4 (high byte)
12h/1ah/22h/2ah/32h	LAST setup for memory window 0/1/2/3/4 (low byte)

Table 29.9: Control and status registers of the PCIC 82365SL

Register index	Register
13h/1bh/23h/ 2bh/33h	LAST setup for memory window 0/1/2/3/4 (high byte)
14h/1ch/24h/ 2ch/34h	card offset setup for memory window 0/1/2/3/4 (low byte)
15h/1dh/25h/ 2dh/35h	card offset setup for memory window 0/1/2/3/4 (high byte)
16h	card detect, general control
17h	reserved
1eh	global control
1fh, 26h, 27h	reserved
2eh, 2fh	reserved
36h-3fh	reserved

The register indices are only valid for the first PCMCIA socket; you get the indices for the second socket managed by the same PCIC by adding the value 40h to the respective index (for example, 07h+40h=47h for the I/O window control of the second socket).

Table 29.9: cont.

The PCIC uses an indexing scheme to access the registers; the number of occupied ports is reduced by this. An index register at 3e0h and a data register at 3e1h is implemented. A certain register is, for example, written by writing the register index to the index port 3e0h first, and then writing the intended value to the data port 3e1h. The PCIC 82365SL can administer two sockets; thus all registers are implemented twice. The register indices for the second socket are evaluated by adding the value 40h to the register indices according to Table 29.9.

First I will explain the programming of memory windows. Figure 29.38 shows the structure of the enable register for memory windows (index 06h). To enable a window you must set the assigned MWx bit (for example, MW0 = 1 for window 0).

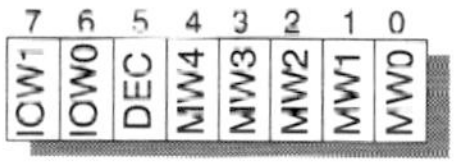

IOW1,IOW0: I/O Window 1/0 Enable
IOWx=1: I/O window x enabled   IOWx=0: I/O window x disabled
DEC: $\overline{\text{MEMCS16}}$ Decode A23–A12
DEC=1: $\overline{\text{MEMCS16}}$ generation from A23–A12   DEC=0: $\overline{\text{MEMCS16}}$ generation from A23–A17
MW4–MW0: Memory Window Enable
MWx=1: window x enabled   MWx=0: window x disabled

Figure 29.38: Address window enable register (06h/46h).

The setup of the FIRST address for window 0 is carried out through the register shown in Figure 29.39. Note that because of the 4 kbyte window granularity, the 12 low-order address bits A11–A0 are switched through to the PCMCIA card without any alteration; thus, no entries for A11–A0 are necessary.

```
DS:  Data Size
     1=16-bit data bus     0=8-bit data bus
OWS: 0 Wait State
     1=no additional wait states   0=additional wait states
SCR1, SCR0: Scratch Bits (not used by the PCIC)
A23-A12: Window Start Address A23-A12 in System Memory
```

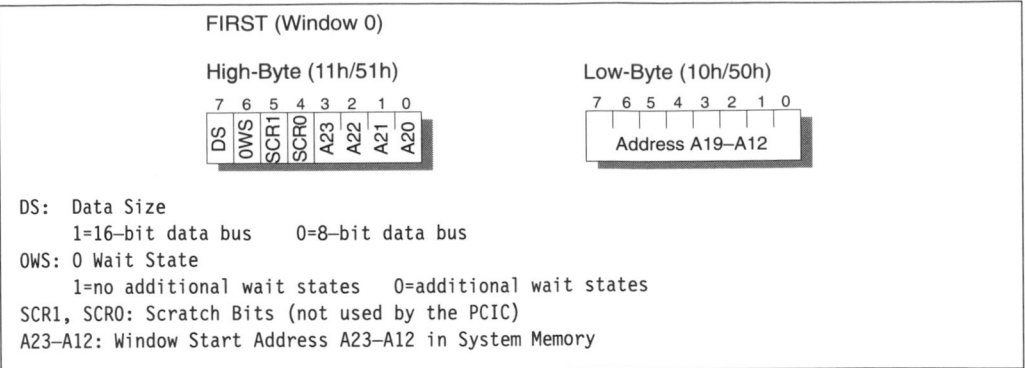

Figure 29.39: FIRST setup for memory window (11h/51h, 10h/50h).

You define the LAST address for window 0 in the same way with the help of the LAST setup registers (Figure 29.40). Thus, window 0 is defined in system memory. All accesses within that window are now redirected to the PCMCIA socket and access the inserted card.

```
WS1, WS0: Wait State
     00b=standard 16-bit cycle      01b=1 additional wait state
     10b=2 additional wait states   11b=3 additional wait states
A23-A12: last window address A23-A12 in system memory
```

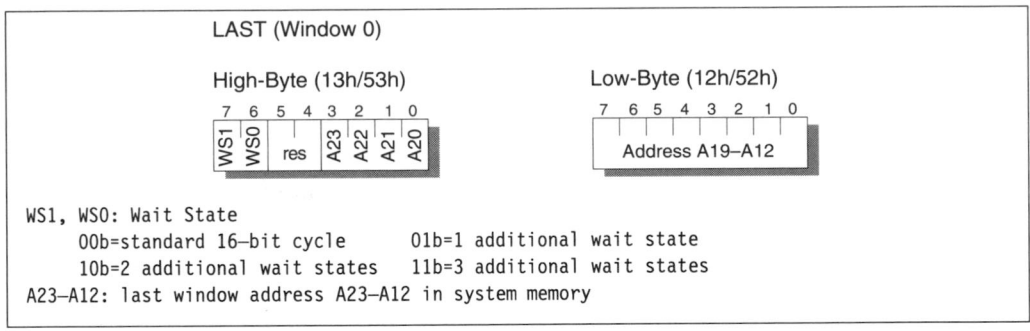

Figure 29.40: LAST setup for memory window (13h/53h, 12h/52h).

Which card address area is actually accessed with the so-defined window 0 depends upon the card offset for memory window 0. You can define the offset with the registers shown in Figure 29.41.

Example: A 512-kbyte window is defined in system memory between 4 M (address 400000h) and 4.5 M (47ffffh), which remaps the common card memory between 512 k (80000) and 1 M (fffff); 16-bit access, no additional wait states, standard 16-bit cycle; 2'complement of 0.5 M – 4 M = –3.5 M equal c80000h, no write protection.

```
FIRST:
MOV al, 00h       ; load low-byte of FIRST register to AL
OUT 3e0h, 10h     ; write index register with index 10h
OUT 3e1h, al      ; write data register

MOV al, c4h       ; load high-byte of FIRST register to AL (DS=1, OWS=1)
OUT 3e0h, 11h     ; write index register with index 11h
OUT 3e1h, al      ; write data register
```

```
LAST:
MOV al, 7fh         ; load low-byte of LAST register to AL
OUT 3e0h, 12h       ; write index register with index 12h
OUT 3e1h, al        ; write data register

MOV al, 04h         ; load high-byte of LAST register to AL (WSx=0)
OUT 3e0h, 13h       ; write index register with index 13h
OUT 3e1h, al        ; write data register

Offset:
MOV al, 80h         ; load low-byte of offset register to AL
OUT 3e0h, 14h       ; write index register with index 14h
OUT 3e1h, al        ; write data register

MOV al, 0ch         ; load high-byte of offset register to AL (WP=0, REG=0)
OUT 3e0h, 15h       ; write index register with index 15h
OUT 3e1h, al        ; write data register

Enable:
MOV al, 01h         ; load enable value to al (IOWx=0, DEC=0, MW4–MW1=0, MW0=1)
OUT 3e0h, 06h       ; write index register with index 06h
OUT 3e1h, al        ; write data register
```

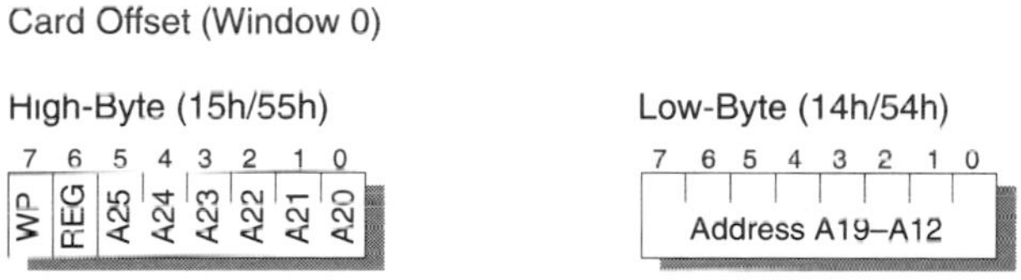

WP: Write Protection
1=window write-protected   0=window can be written
REG: $\overline{REG}$ Enable
1=access to attribute memory ($\overline{REG}$=low)   0=access to common memory ($\overline{REG}$=high)
A25–A12: offset A25–A12 in card memory (max. 64 Mbytes)

Figure 29.41: Card offset setup for memory window 0 (15h/55h, 14h/54h).

The definition of windows in the I/O address space is carried out in a similar way. Contrary to memory windows, I/O windows have a byte granularity so that a FIRST and a LAST entry is implemented for all 16 I/O address bits A15–A0. Further, there is no card offset; every port address in the window of the system's I/O address space points to the same port in the card I/O address space. The PCIC 82365SL allows two I/O windows, which are defined by the control register of Figure 29.42, as well as the FIRST and LAST registers (Figures 29.43 and 29.44), and which are enabled by the enable register (Figure 29.38).

The structure of the control register in Figure 29.42 is simple, and the entries are self-explanatory.

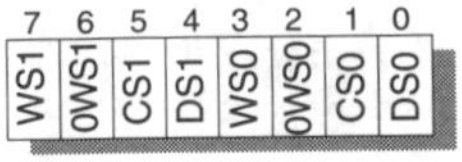

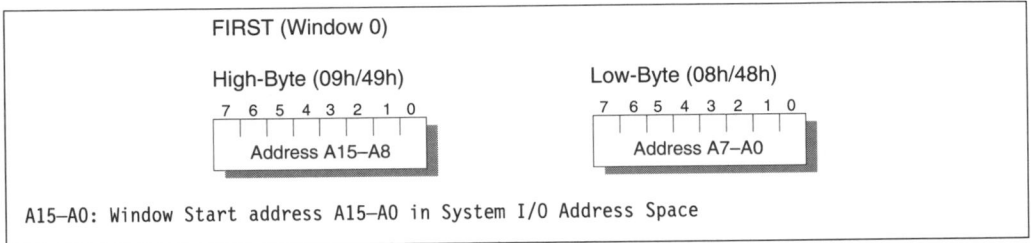

WS1, WS0: Wait States for Window 1, 0
    1=1 additional wait state for 16-bit access 0=no additional wait state
0WS1, 0WS0: Zero Wait States for Window 1, 0
    1=no additional wait state for 8-bit access 0=additional wait states
CS1, CS0: $\overline{\text{IOCS16}}$ Source
    1=$\overline{\text{IOIS16}}$ signal from PC card   0=data size bits DS1, DS0
DS1, DS0: Data Size
    1=16-bit data bus   0=8-bit data bus

Figure 29.42: Control register for I/O address windows (07h/47h).

A15–A0: Window Start address A15–A0 in System I/O Address Space

Figure 29.43: FIRST setup for I/O window 0 (09h/49h, 08h/48h).

The FIRST and LAST windows have the same meaning as their counterparts for memory windows.

A15–A0: Window End Address A15–A0 in System I/O Address Space

Figure 29.44: LAST setup for memory window 0 (0bh/4bh, 0ah/4ah).

Example: The port address range for COM1 (3f8h–3ffh) in the system I/O address area is redirected to the corresponding register address area of a PCMCIA card (which, for example, has a fax modem for COM1); I/O window 0, 8-bit I/O access, no additional wait states, $\overline{\text{IOCS16}}$ source are DSx bits.

```
FIRST:
MOV al, f8h      ; load low-byte of FIRST register to AL
OUT 3e0h, 08h    ; write index register with index 08h
OUT 3e1h, al     ; write data register

MOV al, 03h      ; load high-byte of FIRST register to AL
OUT 3e0h, 09h    ; write index register with index 09h
```

```
OUT 3e1h, al      ; write data register

LAST:
MOV al, ffh       ; load low-byte of LAST register to AL
OUT 3e0h, 0ah     ; write index register with index 0ah
OUT 3e1h, al      ; write data register

MOV al, 03h       ; load high-byte of LAST register to AL
OUT 3e0h, 0bh     ; write index register with index 0bh
OUT 3e1h, al      ; write data register

Control_Register:
MOV al, 00h       ; load control byte to AL
OUT 3e0h, 07h     ; write index register with index 07h
OUT 3e1h, al      ; write data register

Enable:
MOV al, 40h       ; load enable value to AL (IOW1=0, IOW0=1)
OUT 3e0h, 06h     ; write index register with index 06h
OUT 3e1h, al      ; write data register
```

30 Local Area Networks and Network Adapters

Network adapters represent the most «external» connection. They enable communication between greatly differing systems (personal computers, workstations, mainframes, etc.) across a network. Depending on the scale of the distance between them, they are identified as either *Local Area Networks (LANs)* or *Wide Area Networks (WANs)*. Ethernet and token ring are typical examples of the first kind. Above all, WANs have experienced a considerable up-surge with the *Internet*. They permit worldwide communications and data transfer in a matter of seconds. In this quite short section, however, I would like to limit myself to the essential characteristics of LANs.

30.1 Network Topologies

Over time, three different topologies for LANs have been developed: bus, ring and star topologies. These are also the three principles and methods for connecting the stations together. You can see the three network topologies in Figure 30.1.

In all three topologies, in general, the data is transferred in the form of varying sized packets. In addition to the actual useful data, they also contain frame data for identifying the beginning and end of the packet, checking or error correction code, and also the address of the target for the transfer, as a minimum. LANs (and also all high-performance WANs) make use of *packet switching*. Note that the individual stations of the LAN do not necessarily have to have the same task or the same layout. It is possible (and also usual) that a station represents a powerful printer, for example, which performs all the necessary printing tasks for all stations. The station would then be a *printer server*, because it provides the rest of the network with a printing service. The best known of all servers is, of course, the *file server*. Generally, it stores data in large data components (databases) and makes the information available to requesting stations; it also stores new data transferred from these stations. The actual development of LANs stems from the requirement to make the same data available for a number of stations (mainly PCs) that have, until now, been independent, and also to enable data exchange between them. Other servers, such as a *communications server*, are similar to *gateways*, offering an interface to other LANs, WANs or public communications services (Telefax, ISDN, etc.). The purpose of the network, however, is also to make a connection between all stations, and not just between the server and the station.

30.1.1 Bus Topology

With the *bus topology* shown in Figure 30.1, all stations have equal rights regarding the bus connection. Therefore, if a station wishes to transfer data, all connected processors can receive the packet. However, only the target of the transfer actually takes the data from the bus and, thus, from the network. For an error-free data transfer to occur, the station that wishes to transfer the data must first check whether the bus is free.

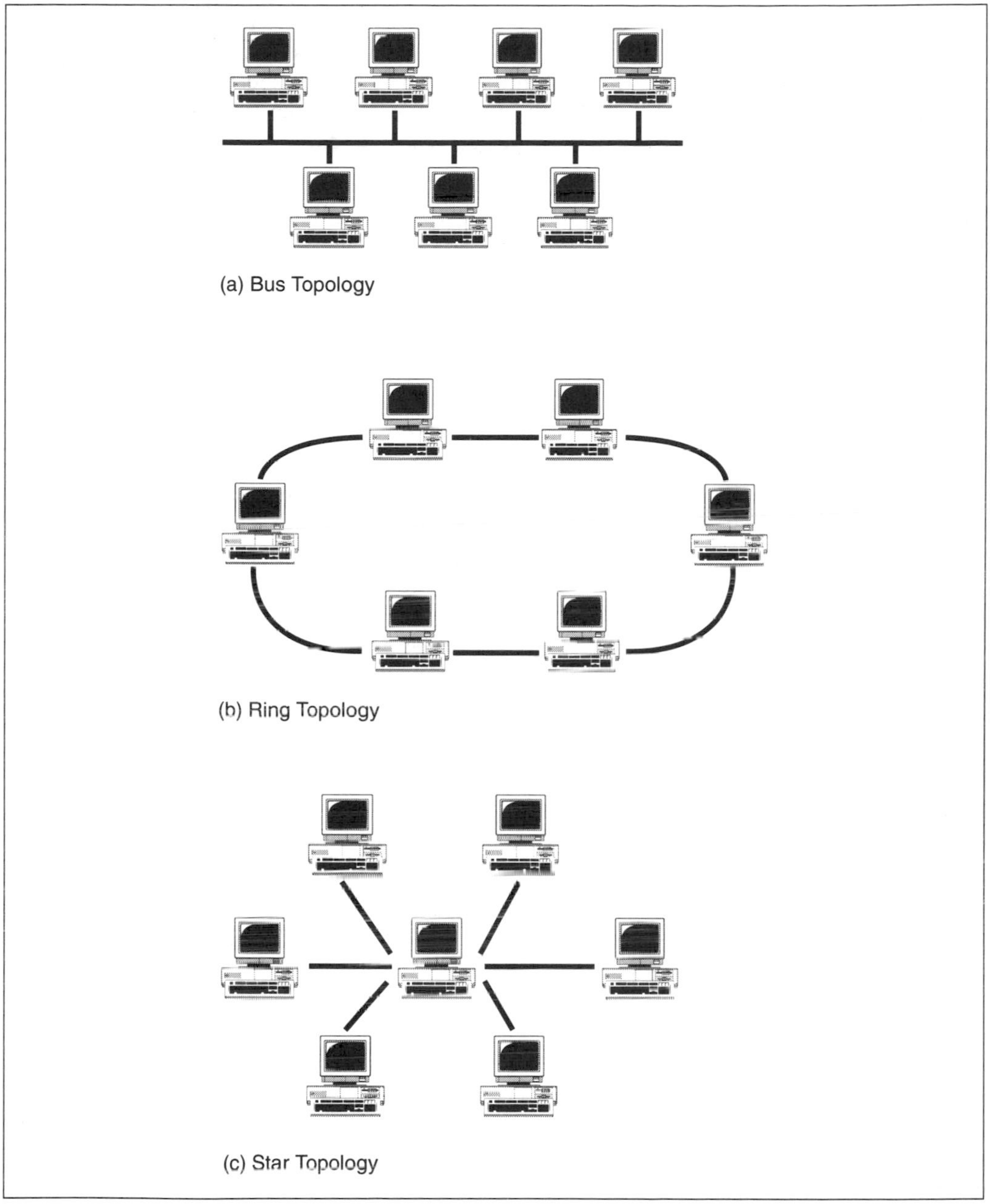

Figure 30.1: Network topologies for LANs: (a) Bus topology, (b) Ring topology, (c) Star topology.

If another station is currently using the network, then the new requesting station must wait. This limits the data throughput of the network, because a station can have an entirely unpredictable waiting time for a network access. In addition, the bus cannot be made any length you require. Ethernet, as the often used example of a LAN with a bus structure, is limited to 500 metres in length. A main advantage of the bus topology, on the other hand, is the simple method of extending the system; stations can usually be inserted into or removed from the network without the need to bring down the network. As in almost all bus systems (for example, SCSI), the bus must be terminated with resistors at both ends so that no signal reflections occur; any resulting echoes would create havoc with the LAN adapters.

30.1.2 Ring Topology

The *ring topology* differs from the bus topology mainly in that the two ends of the bus used here are simply joined together, thus forming a ring. Sometimes the ring is also formed by two anti-parallel connected buses; one bus then transfers data clockwise, the other counter-clockwise. Alternatively, a transfer on the bus can also be allowed in both directions. Both improve the integrity of the network. A station wishing to send data passes it on to the next station in the ring, which then checks whether the packet address is for itself or for another station. In the first instance, it takes the data from the bus. In the second instance, it simply passes the packet on to the next station unchanged. The CPU of the station is not strained by these receiving and passing on operations: the network adapter performs the address identification and the passing on to the next station in parallel to normal processor operation. Only if the data is to be taken from the network does it send an interrupt to the CPU or address the memory itself as the busmaster. The ring topology for a network is only seldom physically realized; in most instances a logical ring structure based on the physical bus or the subsequently described star structure is used instead. As an example, the token ring from IBM, a widely used LAN, has a logical ring structure but sometimes also has a physical star-shaped layout. In this way, the integrity of the network is increased, as a defective cable will generally only paralyse one station and not the whole ring.

30.1.3 Star Topology

The *star topology* is the simplest in terms of the structure and programming of the network operating system (but only for this). Here, all communication passes through the central server which, naturally, must have the corresponding performance capabilities. All connections between the stations also run through the central processor. In this case, it receives the data from the sending station, temporarily stores it (or a part of it at least), and then forwards it on to the receiver. Thus, peer-to-peer connections are not possible. The greatest disadvantage is that if the central processor goes down, the whole network is paralysed. The star topology is unsuitable for communication between stations of more or less similar performance. It dates from the time when the central processor was installed in a mainframe, where the stations consisted of a number of terminals with a lower performance or I/O stations. Then, the central processors were not only responsible for managing the network, but also for the actual data processing. Present-day LANs based on powerful PCs, on the other hand, have gone in the other direction; the data processing takes place in the stations and not in the central processor.

With a star topology, access to the network by individual stations can be achieved in two different ways. The stations can activate themselves and send requests to the central processor, which then controls the accesses in the most fair and equal way. This means, for example, that a station that has just transferred or received a data packet must make the network available to other stations, before it can again perform an access itself. A further method for controlling accesses is *polling*. Here, the central processor regularly asks all the connected stations if they wish to perform a network access. Here also, as in servicing hardware interrupts, polling is clearly the slower variant.

30.2 Access Procedure

Naturally, the individual stations of a network cannot access the network without restriction, and a few regulations are essential. In the following section, the essential access procedures which arise in association with LANs are presented.

30.2.1 CSMA/CD

Due to Ethernet, the so-called *CSMA/CD* (Carrier Sense Multiple Access/Collision Detection) procedure for the control of network accesses has become widely used. The name clearly identifies the strategy of the procedure. As only one line is available, only one station can give out data at a time (send). However, before station A can use the network, it must determine whether or not another station (B) is currently transferring data. For this, station A determines (senses) whether a carrier signal (Carrier) is active. If that is the case, station A must wait; otherwise it can immediately begin the data transfer. In some cases, it is quite possible that a further station (C) is also preparing to transfer data. It has checked the bus and has not found a carrier signal, because no station is currently sending out a data packet, or the data packet has not yet reached the station in question. Thus, stations A and C simultaneously begin sending out their data to be transferred, causing a multiple access. Without further preventive measures the result would be catastrophic: the data packets from both stations would disrupt and cancel each other out. Therefore, a collision must be recognized by the network (collision detection). For this purpose, using the CSMA/CD procedure, the sending station continues to monitor the network bus during the sending out of data, thus it receives its own output values from the network. If the logic determines that the data located on the network does not agree with the data sent out, then it interprets this as a collision and interrupts the output. At the same time, it sends out a *JAM signal* on the bus to inform the other stations of the collision. This causes all network nodes to stop sending data; the bus is then free. A counter is started with a randomly selected initial value in every station that wishes to send data. When the counter of a station reaches its end value, the station in question restarts its attempt to access the network. Thus, a further attempt to transfer data across the network is performed. The new network access by the station is usually successful, because it is unlikely that two counters reach their end values at the same time, thus causing a simultaneous access attempt due to the random start values. You already know the main reason why collisions can occur: the individual stations do not inform one another of their access attempts. Instead, a more or less passive monitoring of the condition of the network takes place. This is a relatively lengthy and drawn out operation, especially in extensive LANs with many stations, which greatly reduces the effective transfer rate of the network (in effect, the activation of the counter after a collision means that the bus remains inactive for a time which depends upon the corresponding random start value). Note that the normally given rates refer to a condition where a station can send data unhindered, thus *after* the station has already attempted an access. Near the load limits of the LAN, the data throughput can drop off very abruptly.

30.2.2 Token Passing

The core of the token passing procedure is the *token* – a data structure for controlling network operations. This free token runs continuously around the ring, passed from station to station. Token passing is the obvious procedure for a ring topology and, therefore, it is also known as the token ring procedure. In a manner of speaking, the token represents a permit for an access to the network: only the station (A) that currently holds the token may address the ring. With this, it identifies the token as in-use and passes it on, together with the data to be transferred, to the next station (B). This station recognizes that the token is in use and, therefore, that data will follow. Station B then checks the address of the data packet to determine whether it represents the target of the data transfer. If not, it passes both the token and the data, unchanged, on to the next station (C). On the other hand, if station B identifies itself as the target of the transfer, then it copies the data that has arrived into a buffer. In addition, it marks the data as received and passes it on, together with the token, to the next station (thus, the data sent is only copied by the receiver and not removed from the network). The token and the data packet are passed from station to station until they arrive back at the original sender, that is, station A. Then, by means of the packet marking, station A can see whether the data sent has actually been received by the target. If the sender receives the packet without it being marked, then a transfer error has occurred, such as the target processor being switched off or the connection being defective. The returning of the data back to the original sender A also enables the data to be checked to see if it has been corrupted during the transfer process. Then, station A deletes the data from the ring and, in every case (even if it wishes to transfer further data), passes on a *free token* to the next station. This allows the equal handling of all stations in a network, because the ring can only be used by a station for the transfer of a maximum of one data packet. Only when it next receives a free token can it use the network again and transfer further data. With CSMA/CD, on the other hand, the sending station is not interrupted.

30.2.3 Token Bus

The token bus has also attained a certain degree of importance. The physical topology of the basic network is formed by a bus (see Section 30.1.1). A logical ring structure with a modified token passing procedure is superimposed. For this purpose, every station in the network is assigned a number in a table which indicates the position of the applicable station in the logical ring. Logically, at a protocol level, a token and also a data packet (if necessary) are now transferred as in the token passing procedure. Physically, a station does not, however, pass on the token and packet to the next station in a physical ring. Instead, with the help of the previously mentioned table, it addresses the next logical station. In this way, the token and data are transferred across the bus. While the token passing procedure, in general, only uses a single transfer direction for the token and packet, here the token and data are transferred across the bus in both directions. In this way, logically sequential stations can have a very large distance between them, that is, sequential numbers in the table do not necessarily point to neighbouring stations on the bus. The advantage of the token bus procedure is that the advantages of token passing, such as the predictable access latency and the high degree of equal rights for all stations, can be combined together with the very simple and flexible topology of a bus. ARCNET from Data-Point is a good example of a logical ring that uses bus cabling.

30.3 Ethernet

Ethernet is currently the best known and most frequently installed LAN. It was developed in 1976 by Xerox, and uses a bus topology with coaxial cables, and also the CSMA/CD access procedure. The original transfer rate was not quite 3 Mbits/s; today 10 Mbits/s is standard. Ethernet is, therefore, one of the medium-speed LANs. There are two different versions of Ethernet, namely (the «true») *Thick Ethernet* and also *CheaperNet* or *Thin Ethernet*. Apart from a few variations with respect to the extent of the network, the main difference is simply the thickness of the cable (which gives it its name). The transfer rate in both cases is 10 Mbits/s – quite surprisingly here, cheaper does not mean slower. In the following, I would briefly like to describe the characteristics of thick and thin Ethernet.

30.3.1 Thick Ethernet

Thick Ethernet uses a (thick) standard coaxial cable which is coloured yellow, and so is also known as *yellow cable*. The maximum length of this cable must not exceed 500 m. The connections to the stations are achieved with a *transceiver* (*trans*mitter-re*ceiver*), whereby the length of the *drop-cable* between the transceiver and the station must not exceed 50 m. In a Personal Computer, the actual tying-in of the network is usually realized by a network adapter. Network adapters have a 15-pole D-sub socket at the rear for thick Ethernet. For reasons of signal flow, the stations and transceivers must be positioned a minimum of 2.5 m away from the yellow cable. In total, a maximum of 100 transceivers (and therefore a maximum of 100 stations) are permitted in an Ethernet line, that is, a yellow cable. However, the Ethernet LAN can be enlarged if you install a *repeater*. A repeater represents a connection between two «networked» Ethernet lines, thus two Ethernet LANs joined together. There are two types of repeater: local and remote. The maximum distance between two lines connected via a local repeater is 100 m; by using a remote repeater, on the other hand, a distance of up to 1000 m is possible. In the latter case, fibre optic cables are necessary for the repeater connections. Furthermore, a maximum of two such repeaters is possible (or stated another way: three Ethernet lines or yellow cables). For this reason, an Ethernet LAN is restricted to 300 stations and 1700 m, or 2500 m with a remote repeater. Only through the use of a gateway is a connection to another LAN possible (Ethernet or otherwise). In this way, in principle, networking knows no limits, except that at some point the distribution and transfer of data would collapse.

30.3.2 CheaperNet or Thin Ethernet

This Ethernet LAN uses a thinner and, therefore, cheaper BNC cable. Due to its simpler and more cost-effective installation, it is most frequently used inside buildings. Here, the connection to a station is not achieved through a transceiver, but by a simple BNC T-connector which is directly connected to the adapter card. It is not possible to use extension cables (do not, under any circumstances, attempt this!). The thinner cable only permits an Ethernet line of up to 185 m (as opposed to 500 m in «true» Ethernet), and a maximum of only 30 stations (instead of 100) can be connected together. There must also be a minimum of 0.5 m between two T-connectors. Apart from this, CheaperNet is identical to thick Ethernet with respect to transfer performance and functionality. In addition to the previously described 15-pole D-sub socket located at the rear, most Ethernet LAN adapters also have a connection for the BNC T-connector, and so can be used by both Thick and Thin Ethernet.

30.4 Token Ring

As already explained, the IBM token ring uses a logical ring structure, but also, at least in part, a physical star topology. For this, so-called *ring line distributors* or *concentrators* (sometimes they are also known as *Multi Station Access Units*, or *MSAUs*) are connected together in a physical ring. The stations themselves are then connected to these distributors in a physical star-shaped topology, but the logical ring structure remains intact. This concept, which may seem somewhat bewildering at first, is shown in Figure 30.2.

As you can see, at first only the ring line distributors (concentrators) are connected together in the form of a ring: the output RO (Ring Output) of a concentrator is connected to the input RI (Ring Input) of the next concentrator. From each of these concentrators there are lines to the associated stations. This physically conforms to a star topology, because each station is exclusively connected to the concentrator and not to another station. Nevertheless, through simple but intelligent activation of the concentrator, a ring structure is achieved.

Every concentrator contains eight connections for stations, not all of which need be used. Usually, a switch (mechanical relay) for every connection is located within the concentrator which, by means of a signal, knows whether a station is connected to the corresponding socket and if it is switched on. In a true ring structure, a switched off station would break the continuity of the ring. This problem is solved by the token ring concentrators in an intelligent way: a socket which is not connected to a switched-on station is simply short-circuited. You can see this in Figure 30.2. Even if the line between the concentrator and the station is damaged and no data can be transferred, the ring line distributor interprets this as a missing station and connects the corresponding contacts together. For this purpose, the applicable station checks the connection to the concentrator. Only if the connection is fully functioning does it send a so-called *phantom voltage*, which activates a relay in the concentrator and switches in the loop to the station. In this way, the station is integrated into the ring. Thus, the ring line distributor breaks open the star-shaped ring topology and permits the new station to be flexibly integrated into the ring, or an inactive station to be removed from the ring. Even though the connections from the concentrator to the stations are laid out in the form of a star, both the token and the data are nevertheless transported around the ring. A further advantage gained by using a concentrator is that stations can also be connected or removed while the system is in operation; it is not necessary to bring down and then restart the network.

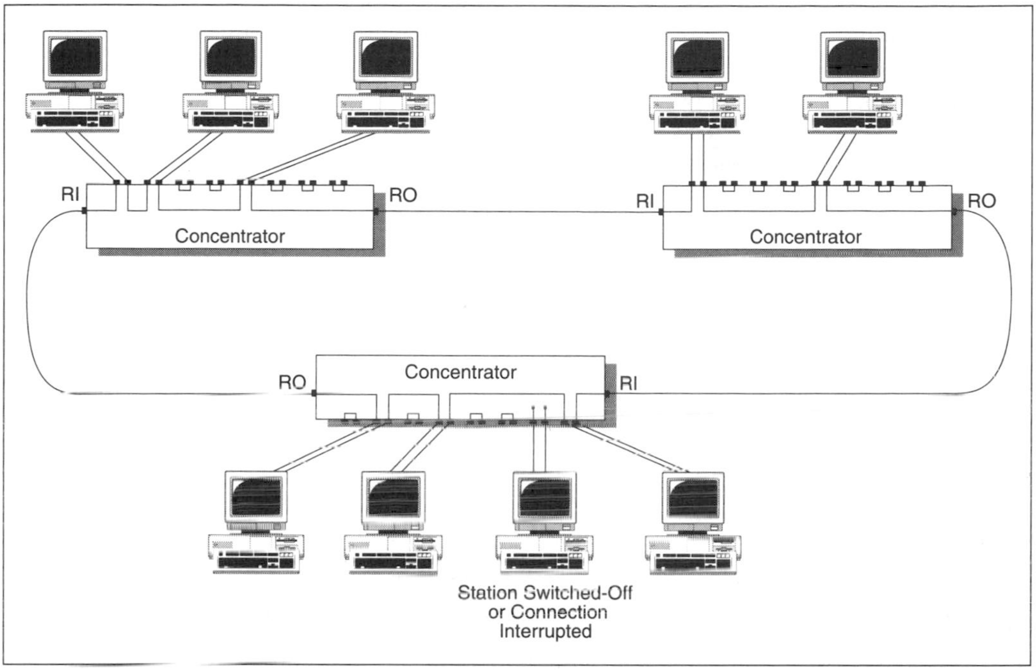

Figure 30.2: Structure of the IBM token ring.

The *lobe cable*, which is directly connected to the token ring adapter of a PC, can be a maximum of 2.5 m in length. The distance between the PC and the concentrator, on the other hand, is limited to a maximum of 100 m. For the remaining 97.5 m, for example from the ring line distributor to a network socket, a better protected cable must be used. The lobe cable only represents the connection between the socket and the PC itself. Without further amplification, the distance between two ring line distributors must not exceed 200 m. Using line amplifiers, the maximum distance can be increased to 750 m. If low damping fibre optic cables are used as the transfer medium, the concentrators can even be situated up to 2 km apart. A token ring can integrate up to 33 ring line distributors; in total, a maximum of 264 stations can be networked together in a ring. The IBM token ring is currently available with transfer rates of 4 Mbits/s and 16 Mbits/s. This is comparable to standard Ethernet, but here, however, with its collision-free operating methods and a more equal handling of all stations, the 16 Mbits/s token ring clearly leaves Ethernet behind when in actual operating situations. Note, however, that the bits for the token, receiver and sender address, etc. are also contained within the 4 Mbits/s and 16 Mbits/s. The effective useful data rates are then approximately 0.5 Mbytes/s and 1.8 Mbytes/s, respectively.

30.5 FDDI

In this last section, I would briefly like to delve into FDDI, a LAN at the higher end of the performance scale. In FDDI, or *Fibre Distributed Data Interface*, the transfer medium is quite obvious: fibre optics. FDDI represents a powerful further development of token ring, with a transfer capacity of up to 100 Mbits/s and a maximum length of between 100 and 200 km, for the networking of approximately 500–1000 stations. Here, the stations can be separated from one another by up to 2 km. The ring is formed by a two-veined gradient (of a distance less than 2 km) or mono-mode (distances up to 20 km) fibre optic cable. In accordance with ANSI recommendations regarding FDDI standardization, data transfer at 1300 nm takes place in the near-infrared range; here, the fibre optic cables have an especially low signal damping effect. The two-veined fibre optic cable should contain two rings: a *primary ring* and a *secondary ring*. Initially, the plan is to use the secondary ring only as a safety backup for the network (a so-called *backup ring*). In principle, however, the secondary ring could also transfer data in normal operation; the FDDI bandwidth would then be doubled. There are three classes of station defined for FDDI:

- A class: stations with four connections for fibre optic cables, that is, an input and output connection for both the primary and secondary rings. In this way, A stations can be installed directly into the ring.
- B class: stations with only two fibre optic connections, that is, only one input and one output connection. For this reason, B stations cannot be installed directly into the ring; instead they must be integrated into the ring via a concentrator (ring line distributor).
- C class: these stations correspond to the normal token ring concentrators and represent a single-veined connection to the B stations. Like the A stations, they contain four fibre optic connections and are installed directly into the ring.

Both A and C stations include a *station manager (STM)*. This is a combined hardware/software component which detects line errors between the stations and can act on them accordingly. If the STM discovers a connection error between A and C stations (which are located directly within the ring), then it automatically switches to the secondary ring. In a token ring, such a disruption has a fatal effect; the ring is broken and the network is paralysed. FDDI can also detect line errors to and from B stations. However, they cannot be rectified because there is no secondary line between the C concentrator and the B station. Then, like the ring line distributor in a normal token ring, the STM simply makes a bridge between the applicable B station and the C concentrator.

31 Keyboards and Mice

This chapter discusses the most common and most important input devices for PCs – the keyboard and the mouse.

31.1 The Keyboard

Despite all the «new-fangled» input devices such as the mouse, scanners, and voice input systems, the keyboard still plays the major role if commands are to be issued or data input to a computer. Well-trained typists can enter a lot of bytes/s, but we lesser mortals get minor muscle spasms after a few hours of intensive programming, or after writing a book manuscript using four fingers exclusively! How important the keyboard is can be seen, for example, because the computer refuses to load the system during booting if it doesn't recognize a keyboard. This is reasonable, of course: why run a computer that accepts neither commands nor data and continues to display C:\> until the end of time?

Depending upon whether you use a keyboard with American, British or some other language assignment, some control, shift or other keys may be named differently. Furthermore, in the literature you will sometimes find different names for the same key, for example the enter or CR keys. Therefore, Table 31.1 lists some different names for these keys. In the following I will only use the names given in the first column of Table 31.1

Key	Name	Alternative names
[↵]	enter key	CR key
[Strg]	control key (Ctrl)	
[Alt]	alternative key (Alt)	
	shift key (Shift)	
	shift-lock key	caps-lock
[↑]	cursor up	
[↓]	cursor down	
[←]	cursor left	
[→]	cursor right	
[Einfg]	insert (Ins)	
[Entf]	delete (Del)	
[Pos1]	cursor home (Home)	clear-home
[Ende]	end (End)	
[Bild↑]	page up (Pg Up)	
[Bild↓]	page down (Pg Dn)	
[S-Abf]	system request (S-Req)	

Table 31.1: Alternative key names

31.1.1 Structure and Functioning of Intelligent and Less Intelligent Keyboards

The keyboard and the accompanying keyboard interface, especially those for the AT and today's widely used MF II keyboard (multifunction keyboard), are more complex devices than they seem from the outside. Contrary to the widely held opinion, *every* keyboard has a keyboard chip, even the previous model of the less intelligent PC/XT keyboard with the 8048. The chip in the keyboard case supervises a so-called *scan matrix*, formed of crossing lines. At each crossing a small switch is located. If you press the key then the switch is closed. The microprogram of the keyboard chip is intelligent enough to detect a *pressing* of the keys. Bouncing is the phenomenon whereby the accompanying switch is first closed when a key is pressed, then the switch reopens and closes again. The reason for this behaviour is the sprung reaction force of the key switches. The chip must be able to distinguish such a fast bouncing from an intentional and slower double key press by the user.

Figure 31.1 shows a scheme for the principle structure of a keyboard and the accompanying keyboard interface in the PC.

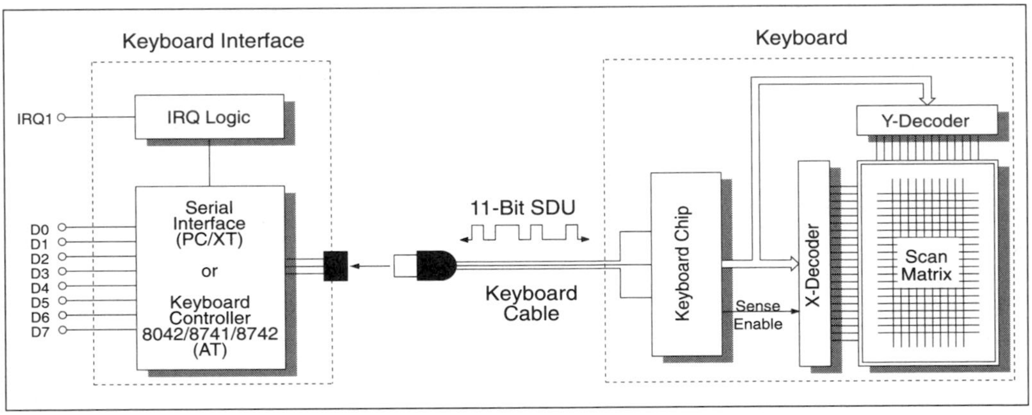

Figure 31.1: Structure of keyboard and keyboard interface.

The keyboard chip regularly checks the status of the scan matrix to determine the *open* or *closed* state of the switches. For this purpose, it activates successively and individually the X lines and detects from which Y terminal it receives a signal. By means of these X and Y coordinates, the newly pressed or released switch (that is, the newly pressed or released key) is unambiguously identified. The keyboard chip determines whether a key – and eventually which one – has been pressed or released, and it writes a corresponding code into a keyboard-internal buffer (details concerning these make and break codes are discussed in Section 31.1.2). Afterwards, the keyboard transmits the code as a serial data stream via the connection cable to the keyboard interface in the PC. Figure 31.2 shows the structure of the accompanying SDU for the data transfer, as well as the assignment of the keyboard jack on your PC.

The line *keyboard clock* transfers the data clock signal for the data exchange with the keyboard interface on the motherboard. Thus the transfer is carried out synchronously, unlike the UART

8250. Activating the signal *keyboard reset* on some interfaces gives rise to a keyboard initialization. Via the line *keyboard data*, the data is exchanged between the keyboard and the keyboard interface in the PC.

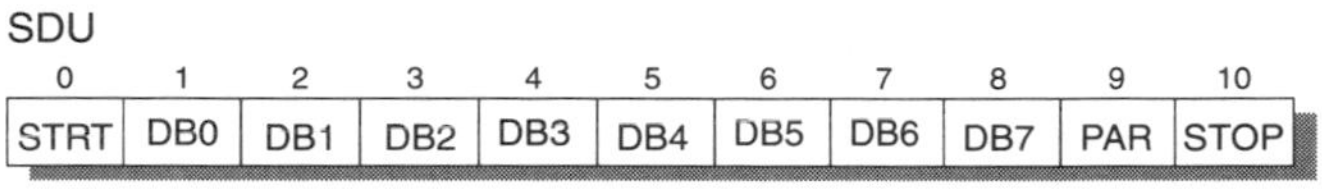

START: Start Bit (Always Equal 0)
DB0–DB7: Data Bits 0 to 7
PAR: Parity Bit (Always Odd Parity)
STOP: Stop Bit (Always Equal 1)

Contacts

Pin	Signal
1	Keyboard Clock
2	Keyboard Data
3	Keyboard Reset or Unused
4	Signal Ground
5	Vcc (+5V)
Shield	Protective Ground

Keyboard Connector

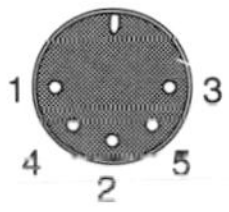

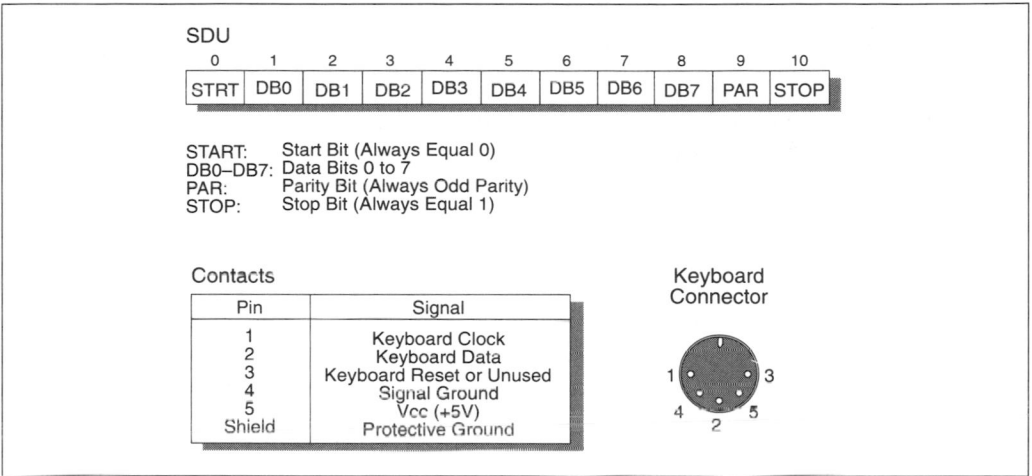

Figure 31.2: Keyboard SDU.

In a PC/XT the keyboard interface is essentially formed of a simple serial interface that only accepts the serial data stream from the keyboard. Here no data transfer to the keyboard is possible. The 8048 in the PC/XT keyboard is therefore not prepared to accept data from the keyboard interface in the PC. Thus the PC/XT keyboard cannot be programmed. Upon receipt of a code from the keyboard, the interface issues a hardware interrupt via IRQ1 corresponding to INT 09h, and provides the data at port B of the 8255 PPI.

In the AT, instead of the primitive serial interface a keyboard controller has been installed. In older ATs you will find the 8042 chip, in newer ones the 8741 or 8742 (or compatible) chip. Thus the keyboard interface became intelligent, and is able to do more than simply accept a serial data stream and issue an interrupt. The keyboard controller can be programmed, for example, to disable the keyboard. Moreover, a bidirectional data transfer between keyboard and keyboard controller is possible here; thus the keyboard controller can transfer data to the keyboard interface. The keyboard chip's microcode is therefore prepared for receiving control commands through which you may, for example, set the repetition rate of the keyboard. Details concerning the programming of the AT or MF II keyboards are discussed in Section 31.1.5. In IBM's PS/2 models an additional mouse port for a PS/2 mouse is integrated into the keyboard interface. A brief description of the PS/2 mouse interface is given in Section 31.2.4.

31.1.2 Scan codes – A Keyboard Map

You may have wondered how a keyboard with a British keyboard layout can be connected to a Taiwanese PC without the PC always mixing Chinese and English. The reason is quite simple: every key is assigned a so-called *scan code* that identifies it. For the scan code one byte is sufficient, as even the extensive MF II keyboards have a maximum of 102 keys. Only once the keyboard driver is effective is this position value converted into a character. Of course, this need not always be an ASCII code as, for example, for «F1» no ASCII code exists. Additionally, it is required that, depending upon the pressed SHIFT keys, various characters are output if you press, for example, the key «7»: without SHIFT you get the digit '7', with SHIFT the character '/', and with the ALT Gr-key pressed the bracket '{' is output. On the PC/XT keyboard the individual keys are simply enumerated continuously. The principle of key enumeration and scan codes has been kept for the AT and MF II keyboards; only some new keys were added and the layout changed so that some keys are shifted. Figure 31.3 shows the layouts of these keyboards, together with the scan codes assigned to the individual keys.

If you press a key (also a «silent» key such as Ctrl) then the keyboard first generates a so-called *make-code*, which is equal to the scan code of the pressed key, and transfers this make-code to the PC's keyboard interface. There a hardware interrupt INT 09h is usually issued via IRQ1 and the handler fetches the make-code from the keyboard interface. The handler routine processes the code differently, depending upon whether SHIFT (which can affect a following key press), a function or a control key such as HOME, or a normal key such as 'A', has been pressed.

Example: `press SHIFT first and afterwards 'C' without releasing SHIFT.`

```
transferred make-codes:  42 (SHIFT) and 46 ('C')
```

Note that here uppercase and lowercase is not distinguished. Only the keyboard driver combines the two make-codes into one ASCII code for the character 'C'. Further, a repetition function is implemented in every keyboard that continuously repeats and transfers the make-code of the pressed key to the keyboard interface so that you don't need, for example, to press and release the 'A' key 80 times if you want to fill a whole line with 'a'. On a PC/XT keyboard the repetition rate is fixed and equal to 10 characters/s; on AT and MF II keyboards you can program the rate with values between 2 and 30 characters/s.

If, on the other hand, you release a pressed key then the keyboard generates a so-called *break-code*, which is transferred to the keyboard interface in the same way as the make-code. Also in this case, the interface issues an interrupt INT 09h via IRQ1, and calls the handler of the keyboard driver. The break-code is simply the scan code with a set bit 7, that is, the most significant bit is equal to 1. Thus the break-code is equal to the make-code plus 128. According to the break-codes, the handler can determine that a key hasn't been pressed but released, and also which key has been released. In connection with a SHIFT key, the effect of the SHIFT key is cancelled for the following character. Now lowercase characters instead of uppercase characters are output again.

Example: `the keys SHIFT and 'C' of the above example are released in the opposite order.`

```
transferred break-codes:  174 (=46+128 corresponding to 'C') and 170 (=42+128 corresponding to
SHIFT)
```

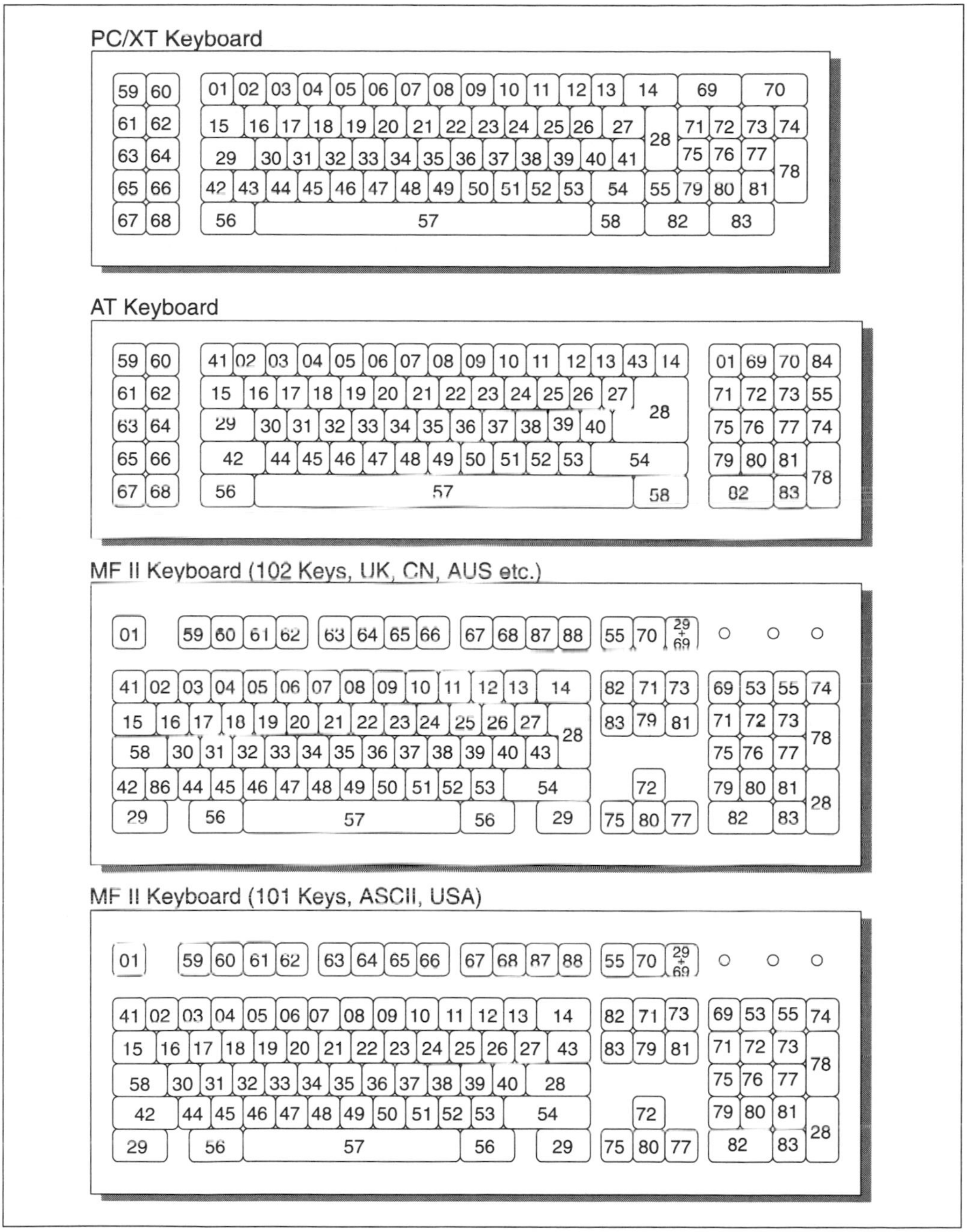

Figure 31.3: Scan codes of PC/XT, AT and MF II keyboards. The PC/XT keyboard has 83 keys with scan codes from 01 to 83. The AT keyboard additionally has a SysReq key. The MF II keyboard has several new control keys in separate blocks, and three LEDs to indicate the status of the shift keys.

Compared to the PC/XT keyboard, on the AT keyboard only the SysReq key with scan code 84 was added. All other keys were assigned the same make/break-codes as before, but some control keys are located at another place, and the numerical keypad was implemented as a separate block. Compatibility thus remains, even on the hardware level, as the only difference from the outside is the new SysReq key, and new components do not give rise to any incompatibility with older programs.

The situation becomes somewhat more complicated with the new MF II keyboard. This keyboard not only has a completely different layout (for example, the function keys are no longer arranged on the left-hand side but on the top), but it has been extended by the two function keys F11/F12 as well as separated control keys. On a PC/XT and AT keyboard the use of the numerical keypad with enabled NumLock is rather ponderous if the cursor has to be moved simultaneously. For this reason, IBM implemented the control keys on its extended or MF II keyboard in a separate control block between the alphanumerical and numerical keypads. Moreover, the keyboard has been extended by a second Ctrl and Alt key, as well as PRINT and PAUSE keys.

If these new keys (as is actually the case) are assigned the same scan code as the former keys with the same function, then a program cannot distinguish whether you have pressed, for example, the left or right Alt key. But with DOS this is of significance as, by means of the right Alt key (Alt Gr), you have access to the third keyboard level with characters {, [, etc. But for this purpose the new keys must differ from the former ones. A new scan code now gives rise to the problem that older programs that access the keyboard directly (for example, former versions of the BASIC interpreter) cannot detect and process the new keys. The engineers had (again) a good idea: if you press or release one of the new MF II keys then the precode byte e0h or e1h is output first, followed by the make or break-code. Make and break-codes thus remain the same compared to the former AT keyboards. The precode byte e1h is output if the PAUSE key is operated, the precode byte e0h for all other new keys of the MF II keyboard. Thus the keyboard driver can distinguish, for example, between the left and right Alt keys.

The MF II keyboard additionally attempts to imitate and behave like the AT keyboard. This means that the new control keys, whose equivalents are also present in the numerical keypad, output other make and break-code sequences if the NumLock function is enabled. With a disabled NumLock function you have to press only the intended control key.

Example: `cursor left with disabled NumLock function.`

```
make-break sequence: 4bh (cursor make) cbh (cursor break)
```

If, on the other hand, the NumLock function is enabled, then you have to press the SHIFT key first, and afterwards the intended control key, to avoid outputting a number because of the enabled NumLock function.

Example: `cursor left with enabled NumLock function.`

```
make-break sequence: 2ah (SHIFT make) 4bh (cursor make) cbh (cursor break) aah (SHIFT break)
```

To simulate the AT keyboard the MF II keyboard therefore outputs another make-break sequence if the NumLock function is enabled. If you press and release the key cursor left in the separate control block with the NumLock function disabled, then the MF II keyboard outputs the make-break sequence e0h 2ah e0h aah. The two precode bytes e0h in front of the actual scan code indicate that you have pressed a new key of the MF II keyboard. If you press the same cursor key with the NumLock function enabled, the chip in the MF II keyboard automatically generates the sequence e0h 2ah e0h 4bh e0h cbh e0h aah. The same applies, of course, for the other control keys.

Another special role is played by the PAUSE key. On the PC/XT and AT keyboard a program is paused by pressing Ctrl+NumLock. The MF II keyboard therefore supplies the following make-break sequence: e1h 1dh 45h e1h 9dh c5h. e1h characterizes the new MF II key, 1dh and 9dh are the make and break-code, respectively, for Ctrl, and 45h and c5h the make and break-code, respectively, for NumLock. Even if you keep the PAUSE key pressed the complete make-break sequence is output.

If you program a keyboard driver you have, in principle, every freedom to assign a scan code, depending upon the pressed shift keys, etc., a certain character. However, there is no effect if you remove the individual keys from the switches and rearrange them; even if you have arranged the keys in alphabetical order beginning in the upper left corner of your keyboard, the first key on the MF II keyboard will not return an 'a' but a '^', as before.

A keyboard driver uses an internal conversion table to assign the keyboard's scan codes an ASCII code, and thus a character, or to carry out certain functions. Using another conversion table, for example, a Spanish keyboard can easily be connected to a PC. The technical structure and the passed scan codes remain the same, but the keyboard driver converts them to another ASCII code. Also operating a shift-lock key such as NumLock is processed only by software: the driver sets an internal indicator that indicates the status and enables the LEDs with a certain command. Only on the MF II keyboard is an internal circuit really switched if the NumLock key is operated so that the keyboard actually outputs corresponding make-break sequences if you operate a control key in the separate control block. After a keyboard reset the NumLock function is always enabled. Every operation and the following switching of the internal circuit is registered by the keyboard driver via the issued interrupt, so that the BIOS-internal NumLock indicator always corresponds to the NumLock state of the keyboard – until you disable IRQ1 once, press the NumLock key, and reactivate IRQ1 again. The internal keyboard status and the NumLock indicator of the keyboard driver are then complementary.

31.1.3 Keyboard Access Via DOS

For accessing the keyboard seven functions of the DOS interrupt INT 21h are available: 01h, 06h, 07h, 08h, 0ah, 0bh, and 3fh. You will find a list containing the calling formats as well as the returned characters in Appendix J. Note that these functions don't access the keyboard itself, but only read and write a 32-byte buffer in the BIOS data area. Accordingly, they are inflexible and less powerful if you want to use the complete function palette of modern MF II keyboards. The first six keyboard functions are relics from the CP/M era, and always serve the standard input device only. If you make, for example, the printer at the serial interface COM1 erroneously the standard input device by using the redirection «program.exe < COM1», then you will wait until the end of time. Your printer is unable to output any character, and because of the redirection you have «disabled» the keyboard. The keyboard hits are registered and the characters are written into the keyboard buffer; DOS doesn't pass them to the program, but waits for a character from the printer. The only way out is the 3-finger input Ctrl-Alt-Del.

Significantly better is the 3fh function *(read file/device)*, which uses the concept of the handles. The standard input/output device is denoted by the reserved name *CON* (for console) with DOS, and is assigned the handle 0 as standard. We have already met the 3fh function, for example when reading a character from the serial interface. Thus you can see the power of handles in connection with device drivers: for an access to files, interfaces, and the keyboard, a single function is sufficient.

The functions of INT 21h differ in how they process an input character. In the so-called raw mode, which the functions 06h, 07h, 0ah as well as function 3fh (if configured accordingly) use, the control characters ^C, ^P, etc. are not processed accordingly, but simply passed to the calling program. But the functions 08h and 3fh correspondingly set up, on the other hand, interpret these control characters and, for example, call INT 23h for a program abortion if ^C was input.

Example: `buffered character input with a maximum of 80 characters (function 0ah; language: Microsoft C 5.10).`

```
char *ch_input(void)
{ char *buffer, *string;
  union REGS inregs, outregs;

  buffer = (char *) malloc(82);      /* provide buffer */
  *buffer=80;                        /* first byte indicates maximum number of characters */

  inregs.h.ah = 0x0ah;               /* function 0ah */
  inregs.x.dx = FP_OFF(buffer);      /* buffer offset; segment already in DS */
  int86(0x21, &inregs, &outregs);    /* call function */

  string = buffer + 2                /* pointer string to beginning of string */
                                     /* further: *buffer=80  *(buffer+1)=length of input string */
  return(string);                    /* return pointer to input string */
}
```

Consult Appendix J or a good DOS reference for details concerning the various DOS functions.

31.1.4 Keyboard Access Via the BIOS

The BIOS writes the characters passed by the keyboard into a temporary buffer called the *keyboard buffer*, which as standard starts at address 40:1e, has 32 bytes, and thus ends at address 40:3d. Every character is stored in the buffer as a 2-byte value whose high-order byte represents the scan code and whose low-order byte indicates the ASCII code. Thus the buffer can temporarily store 16 characters. All input characters are first accepted by the INT 09 (the handler of IRQ1), which determines the ASCII code from the scan code by means of a conversion table and writes both codes into the keyboard buffer afterwards.

Structure and Organization of the Keyboard Buffer

The keyboard buffer is organized as a ring buffer managed by two pointers. The pointer values are stored in the BIOS data area at addresses 40:1a and 40:1c (see Table 31.2). The write pointer indicates the next free write position in the keyboard buffer, where the character input next will be stored. The read pointer refers to the character in the keyboard buffer to be read first, that is, to the character that will be passed to a program next. Because of the ring organization it may be that the value of the read pointer is higher than that of the write pointer. In this case, all words between the read pointer and the physical end of the buffer at 40:3d, as well as the characters between the physical beginning of the buffer at 40:1e and the write pointer, are valid characters from the keyboard. However, all words between the write and the read pointer are empty, and may accept further characters from the keyboard.

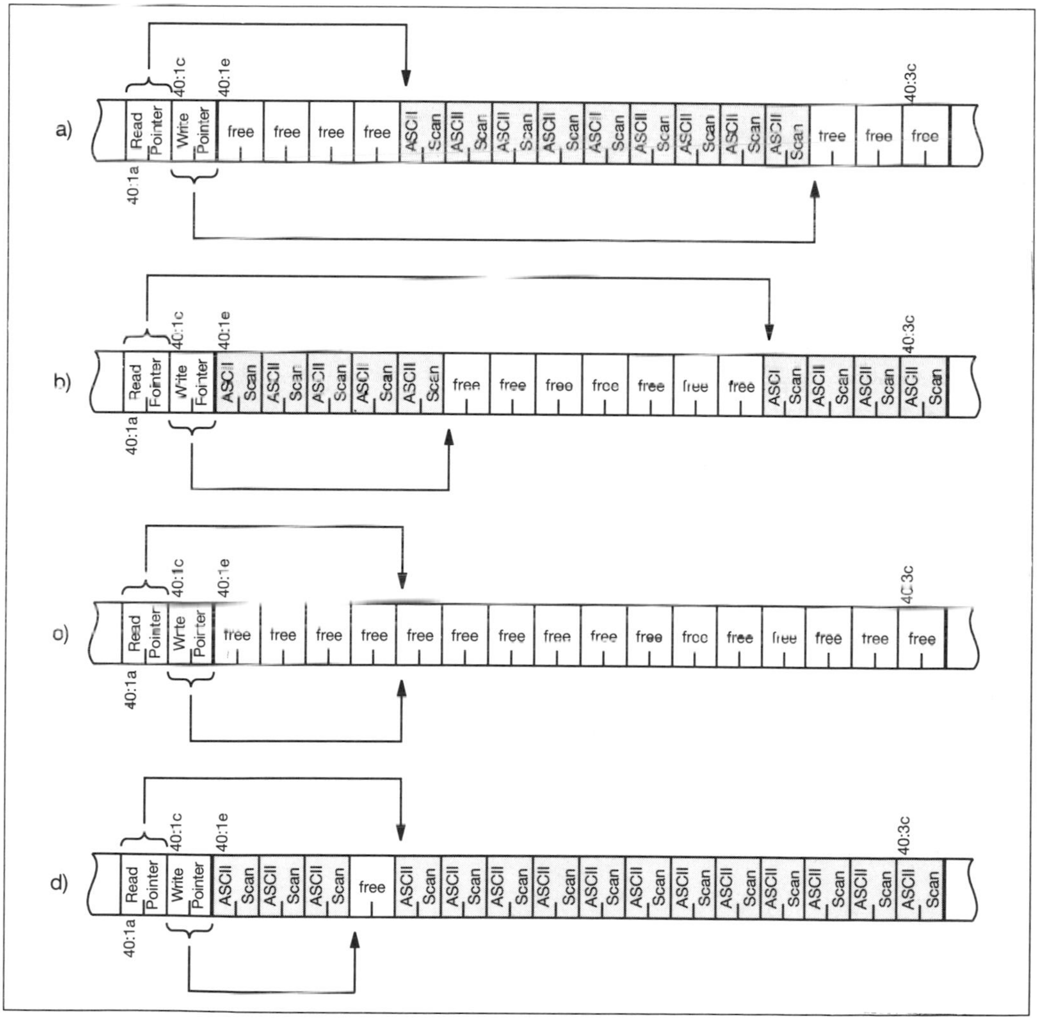

Figure 31.4: The ring organization of the keyboard buffer. (a) Normal, (b) wrap, (c) buffer empty, (d) buffer full.

From the buffer organization it is apparent that the keyboard buffer is empty if the beginning and the end of the buffer coincide. On the other hand, the buffer is full if the write pointer refers to the character that precedes the character to which the read pointer points. If you press a further key a short beep sounds. This means that the keyboard buffer has 32 bytes but because of its organization is only able to accommodate 15 characters with 2 bytes each. If one were to exhaust the full capacity of 16 characters with 2 bytes each, then the write pointer might refer to the same character as the read pointer, that is, read and write pointers coincide. But this is, as I have already mentioned, characteristic if the keyboard buffer is empty. Figure 31.4 shows this behaviour. Thus you can recognize an empty keyboard buffer simply by the fact that the values for the read and write pointers coincide while a full buffer is present if the write pointer refers to the character immediately preceding the character referred to by the read pointer.

Upon every keyboard hit the keyboard controller issues an interrupt 09h via IRQ1, which accepts the scan code of the character and converts it into an ASCII code if this is possible. Afterwards, scan code and ASCII code are written to that location in the keyboard buffer to which the write pointer refers, and the write pointer is updated to the next character position in the buffer. If you read a character using the BIOS functions discussed below the function passes the character referred to by the read pointer to the calling program and updates the read pointer. The character is thus logically removed from the buffer, although ASCII and scan code are still physically held by the buffer. A program can, of course, write back one character into the keyboard buffer by writing the character in front of the word which is referred to by the read pointer, and updating the read pointer accordingly. The written character is passed to a program in advance of the already stored characters. Alternatively, a character may also be written behind the already present characters, and the pointer is updated afterwards to point to the next location in the buffer. The thus written character is passed to a program once all characters present have been transferred.

Keyboard Status and BIOS Data Area

In the BIOS data area, besides the keyboard buffer and the pointers for the beginning and the end of the buffer, several bytes are also stored which indicate the keyboard's status. Table 31.2 indicates the use of the BIOS data area as far as the keyboard is concerned.

The bytes 40:17 and 40:18 refer to the keyboard status for the PC/XT and the AT keyboard. Because of several shift keys being present on the extended MF II keyboard, additional status bytes are required, for example to distinguish the left and right Alt key. This and other status information is held in bytes 40:96 and 40:97. With the words 40:80 and 40:82, DOS or another program can define an alternative keyboard buffer, which the BIOS then uses instead of the buffer starting at 40:1e. Note that the buffer address is limited to segment 0040h. The alternative buffer may exceed a size of 32 bytes, corresponding to 16 characters.

Address	Size	Structure 76543210	Content	Meaning
40:17	byte	1	first shift status byte	insert mode active
		1		shift lock mode active
40		1		NumLock mode active
		1		scroll active
		1		Alt key pressed
		1		Ctrl key pressed
		1		left shift key pressed
		1		right shift key pressed
40:18	byte	1	second shift status byte	insert key pressed
		1		shift lock key pressed
		1		NumLock key pressed
		1		scroll key pressed
		1		pause mode active
		1		SysReq key pressed
		1		left Alt key pressed
		1		left Ctrl key pressed
40:19	byte		alternative keyb. input	
40:1a	word		read pointer	points to character in buffer next to be read
40:1c	word		write pointer	points to next free location in buffer
40:1e	32 bytes		keyboard buffer	16 characters, but only 15 are used
40:80	word		begin of keyboard buffer	offset in segment 0040h
40:82	word		end of keyboard buffer	offset in segment 0040h
40:96	byte	1	keyboard status byte	ID code is read
		1		last character was ID code
		1		activate NumLock when reading ID and extended code
		1		MF II keyboard installed
		1		right Alt key pressed
		1		right Ctrl key pressed
		1		last code equal E0h
		1		last code equal E1h
40:97	byte	1	general keyboard status	error keyboard data
		1		LEDs are updated
		1		ACK sent back
		1		ACK received
		0		reserved
		x		shift LED: 1=on, 0=off
		x		NumLock LED: 1=on, 0=off
		x		scroll LED: 1=on, 0=off

Table 31.2: BIOS storage area and keyboard

Functions 4fh and 85h of BIOS Interrupt 15h

Starting with the AT, and on the PS/2, two functions have been implemented in the INT 15h system interrupt which are effective before the input character is written into the keyboard buffer. The handler of the hardware interrupt 09h corresponding to IRQ1, which accepts a character from the output buffer of the keyboard controller, internally calls the function 4fh of INT 15h for every character using the following instruction sequence. The function therefore forms a hook for the keyboard input. This is carried out as follows:

```
MOV ah, 4fh     ; load function number into ah
MOV al, scan    ; load scan code of key into al
STC             ; set carry flag
INT 15h         ; call interrupt 15h, function 4fh
```

Normally the handler for INT 15h, function 4fh consists of a simple IRET instruction. Thus the scan code in al remains unchanged, and INT 09h writes it together with the corresponding ASCII code into the keyboard buffer in the BIOS data area. But the situation becomes more interesting if you intercept INT 15h, function 4fh; now you can alter the passed scan code and fool the PC into recognizing an X for a U. For this purpose, you only have to load the al register with the new scan code 45 (corresponding to X) if a scan code 22 indicating U is passed during the call. The handler fragment of the following example carries out this process explicitly:

Example: `replace U (scan code 22) by an X (scan code 45).`

```
CMP ah, 4fh    ; check whether function 4fh is called
JNE further    ; other function, therefore jump
CMP al, 16h    ; check whether scan code is equal 22=16h
JNE return     ; return if scan code is not equal 22
MOV al, 2dh    ; load new scan code 45=2dh into al
return:
IRET
further:
 ...........   ; something else
```

A more serious application would be to replace the period in the numeric keypad of the MF II keyboard by a comma, which is the decimal sign in some languages (for example, German). But you have to carry out more checks to confirm that the user really has operated the period key in the numeric block, and not the Del key in the separate control block, with the same scan code but the precode byte 0eh.

Function 4fh of INT 15h can «slur» a character. For this purpose, you must simply clear the carry flag and return with a RET 2 command, or manipulate the carry flag on the stack before you issue an IRET instruction. (Remember that an INT instruction pushes the flags onto the stack, and that an IRET instruction reloads the flags from the stack into the flag register; see Section 3.6.1.) INT 09h then ignores the key hit and doesn't write any code into the keyboard buffer.

Another keyboard hook is the function 85h of INT 15h, which the handler of INT 09h calls if you press or release the SysReq key on an AT keyboard or Alt+SysReq on an MF II keyboard. The standard routine comprises a simple IRET instruction, and the keyboard driver normally ignores the key hit. But you may intercept the call, for example to open a window as a consequence of the SysReq hit, which allows an access to a resident program with system commands. Most pop-up programs (for example, Sidekick) don't use function 85h of INT 15h, but intercept INT 09h to supervise the keyboard before the handler of INT 09h processes the input character. A certain key combination (for example, Ctrl+Alt+F1) then gives rise to the activation of the TSR program. The reason for this strategy is that the PC/XT doesn't have a SysReq key, and thus the BIOS doesn't implement a call to INT 15h, function 85h. Actually, SysReq is aimed at use in a multitasking operating system to switch between various applications.

If the handler of INT 09h detects that you have operated the key combination *Ctrl-Break*, then it calls interrupt 1Bh. The BIOS initializes the accompanying handler to a simple IRET instruction so that Ctrl-Break is ignored. But DOS and application programs have the opportunity to install their own routine, and may intercept and process a Ctrl-Break accordingly. Note that Ctrl-C is intercepted only on a DOS level, and doesn't give rise to a call of INT 23h, but Ctrl-Break is intercepted on a BIOS level. With the entry BREAK=ON in *config.sys*, you instruct DOS to replace the simple IRET instruction by its own handler. Two further reserved key combinations recognized by the INT 09h are *Ctrl-Alt-Del* for a warm boot and *Print* or *Shift-Print* for printing the screen contents. With a Ctrl-Alt-Del the handler of INT 09h calls interrupt INT 19h *load bootstrap*; with Print INT 05h is issued.

Functions of BIOS Interrupt 16h

A much better keyboard control than the DOS functions is offered by the BIOS interrupt INT 16h, which provides eight keyboard functions. All functions of interrupt 16h are listed in Appendix J. In principle, you may determine the same values that the BIOS functions return (that is, scan code, ASCII code, and shift status) by directly accessing the keyboard buffer or the keyboard status byte in the BIOS data area. This way is much faster than via INT 16h, but you have to take care. Furthermore, you lose compatibility to a significant extent. Nearly all BIOS manufacturers comply with the formats indicated in Appendix J.

The functions 10h, 11h, and 12h have been implemented in the newer BIOS versions (since the end of 1985) to support the new function and control keys of the extended MF II keyboard. Usually, the BIOS functions return an ASCII value of 0 if a function or control key has been pressed, for example a cursor key, F1 or HOME.

Example: read character by means of INT 16h, function 00h; assume that key 'A' has been pressed.

```
MOV ah, 00h     ; execute function 00h, that is read character
INT 16h         ; issue interrupt
```

```
Result:  ah=30 (scan code for key 'A'); al=97 (ASCII code for 'a')
```

Example: read character by means of INT 16h, function 00h; assume that key 'HOME' in the separate control block of a MF II keyboard has been pressed.

```
MOV ah, 00h     ; execute function 00h, that is, read character
INT 16h         ; issue interrupt
```

```
Result:  ah=71 (scan code of key 'HOME'); al=00 (characterizes function and control keys which
is not assigned an ASCII code)
```

Thus, function 00h doesn't distinguish between the operation of a «normal» and the operation of a new function or control key of the MF II keyboard. But if you use function 10h for the extended keyboard instead of function 00h, then the interrupt returns an indicator e0h in the al register, which indicates the operation of an extended key.

Example: `read character by means of INT 16h, function 10h; assume that the key 'HOME' in the separate control block of a MF II keyboard has been pressed.`

```
MOV ah, 10h     ; execute function 10h, that is, read character
INT 16h         ; issue interrupt
```

```
Result:  ah=71 (scan code of key 'HOME'); al=e0 (indicator for a separate function or control
key of the MF II keyboard which is not assigned an ASCII code)
```

The only key that you cannot access even with the extended functions is the PAUSE key. This key is already intercepted by the handler of INT 09h (corresponding to IRQ1) and converted to an endless program loop. When you press another key the CPU leaves this loop and continues program execution.

On a PS/2 and some ATs you can set both the repetition rate at which the keyboard transfers characters if a key is kept pressed, as well as the delay until the first character repetition occurs, using function 03h of the BIOS interrupt 16h.

Example: `set a repetition rate of 20 characters/s and a delay of 500 ms.`

```
MOV ah, 03h   ; load function number 03h into ah
MOV bl, 04h   ; 20 characters/s
MOV bh, 01h   ; 500 ms delay
INT 16h       ; call function
```

31.1.5 Programming the Keyboard Directly via Ports

As already mentioned, you can program the AT and MF II keyboard similar to other peripheral devices. On the PC/XT keyboards this is not possible because this model doesn't implement a keyboard controller able to transfer commands and data to the keyboard. Here, all transfers proceed in one direction; only the keyboard transfers scan codes to the keyboard interface on the motherboard. Thus the following description focuses mainly on the AT and MF II keyboards. With PS/2 models you can also access the PS/2 mouse via the keyboard controller. Figure 31.5 shows the scheme for an AT, MF II or PS/2 keyboard controller with a mouse.

Registers and Ports

For directly programming the AT and MF II keyboards the two port addresses 60h and 64h are available. Using these you may access the input buffer, the output buffer and the control register of the keyboard controller. Table 31.3 lists the addresses of the corresponding registers. The PC/XT keyboard is only able to transfer the scan codes via port address 60h and to issue a hardware interrupt. Note that the SW1 bit in port A of the 8255 must be set for this purpose. The following descriptions refer exclusively to AT and MF II keyboards.

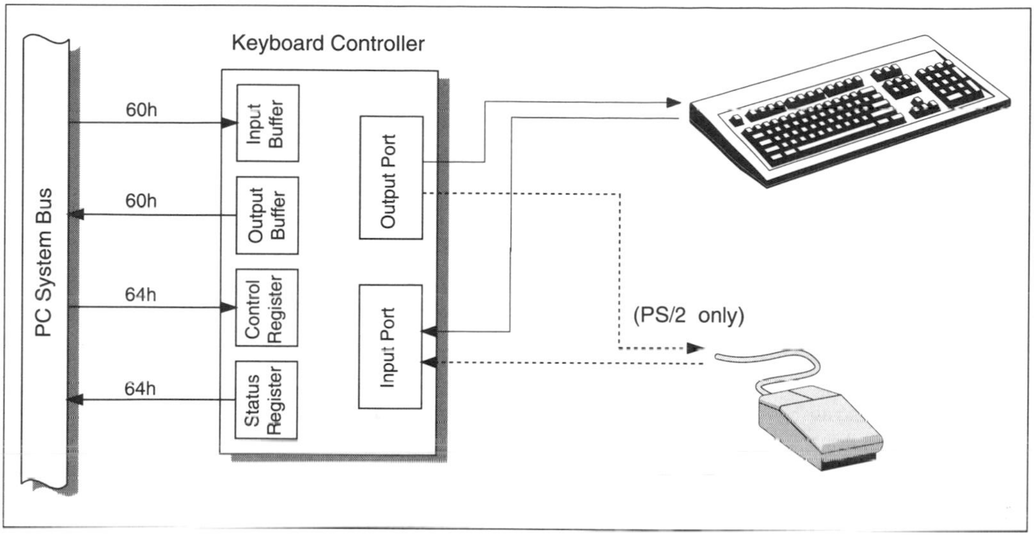

Figure 31.5: AT, MF II or PS/2 keyboard controller.

Port	Register	Read (R) Write (W)
60h	output buffer	R
60h	input buffer	W
64h	control register	W
64h	status register	R

Table 31.3: Keyboard controller registers

Using the status register you may determine the current state of the keyboard controller. The structure of the read-only status register is shown in Figure 31.6. You can read the status register by a simple IN instruction referring to the port address 64h.

The *PARE* bit indicates whether a parity error has occurred during the course of transferring the last SDU from the keyboard or the auxiliary device (beginning with PS/2). If *TIM* is set then the keyboard or mouse didn't respond to a request within the defined time period, that is, a time-out error occurred. In both cases, you should request the data byte once more using the controller command *Resend* (see below). The *AUXB* bit shows whether a data byte from the mouse is available in the output buffer. If *OUTB* is set, a data byte from the keyboard is available in the output buffer. When the CPU reads the byte from the output buffer, AUXB or OUTB, respectively, is cleared automatically. Before you read the output buffer using an IN instruction you should always check (according to OUTB or AUXB) whether or not the controller has already transferred a byte into the output buffer. This may take some time, for example if you carry out a keyboard self-test and wait for the result byte. The keyboard is unable to transfer another character via the input port to the keyboard controller before the CPU has read the last passed character from the output buffer. Inversely, the *INPB* bit indicates whether a character is still in the input buffer of the keyboard controller, or whether the CPU can pass another. The *C/D* bit shows whether the last written byte was a command byte that has been transferred by the CPU via the port address 64h, or a data byte that the CPU has written via the port address 60h. *KEYL* and *SYSF*, finally, indicate whether the keyboard is locked or not, and whether the self-test could be completed successfully.

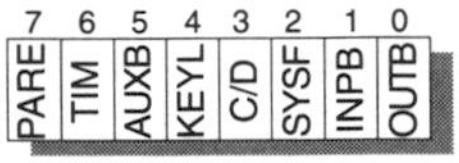

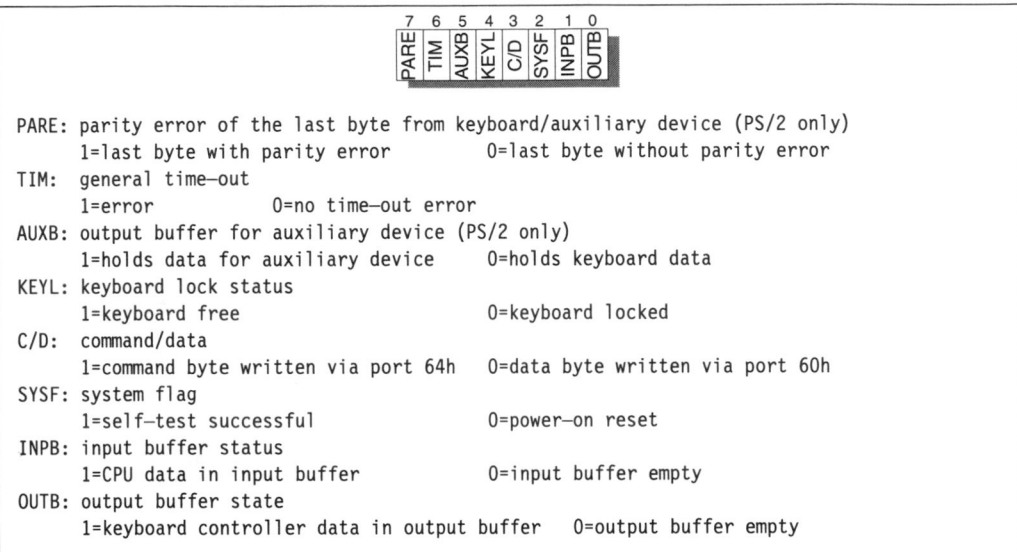

```
PARE: parity error of the last byte from keyboard/auxiliary device (PS/2 only)
      1=last byte with parity error        0=last byte without parity error
TIM:  general time-out
      1=error           0=no time-out error
AUXB: output buffer for auxiliary device (PS/2 only)
      1=holds data for auxiliary device    0=holds keyboard data
KEYL: keyboard lock status
      1=keyboard free                      0=keyboard locked
C/D:  command/data
      1=command byte written via port 64h  0=data byte written via port 60h
SYSF: system flag
      1=self-test successful               0=power-on reset
INPB: input buffer status
      1=CPU data in input buffer           0=input buffer empty
OUTB: output buffer state
      1=keyboard controller data in output buffer   0=output buffer empty
```

Figure 31.6: Status register (64h).

Example: `read status register.`

```
IN al, 64h  ; the IN instruction referring port address 64 transfers
            ; the contents of the status register into al
```

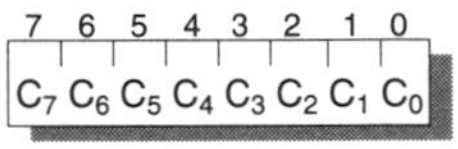

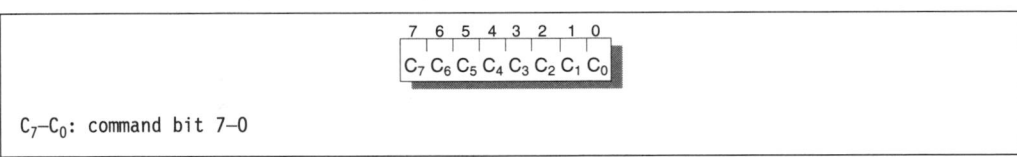

C_7–C_0: command bit 7–0

Figure 31.7: Control register (64h).

You access the write-only control register (Figure 31.7) by an OUT instruction referring to the port address 64h. The keyboard controller interprets every byte you pass in this way as a command. Note that commands for the keyboard are written via the input buffer, that is, by an OUT instruction with the keyboard command code referring to the port address 60h. Table 31.4 lists the commands valid for the keyboard controller.

Example: `disable keyboard.`

```
start:
IN al, 64h    ; read status byte
TEST al, 02h  ; check whether input buffer is full
JNZ start     ; some byte still in the input buffer
OUT 64h, adh  ; disable keyboard
```

`Note that afterwards you have no opportunity to input something via the keyboard; even Ctrl-Alt-Del doesn't work any more.`

Using the input and output buffer you can transfer data to the keyboard controller, as well as pass commands and data to the keyboard, and you can receive data from the keyboard controller or the keyboard itself. The structure of these two buffers is illustrated in Figure 31.8.

Code	Command	Description
a7h	disable auxiliary device	disables the auxiliary device
a8h	enable auxiliary device	enables the auxiliary device
a9h	check interface to auxiliary device	checks the interface to auxiliary device and stores the check code in the output buffer (00h=no error, 01h=clock line low, 02h=clock line high, 03h=data line low, 04h=data line high, ffh=no auxiliary device)
aah	self-test	the keyboard controller executes a self-test and writes 55h into the output buffer if no error is detected
abh	check keyboard interface	the keyboard controller checks the keyboard interface and writes the result into the output buffer (00h=not error, 01h-clock line low, 02h=clock line high, 03h=data line low, 04h=data line high, ffh=general error
adh	disable keyboard	disables the keyboard
aeh	enable keyboard	enables the keyboard
c0h	read input port	reads input port and transfers the data into the output buffer
c1h	read out input port (low)	reads bit 3–0 of input port repeatedly and transfers the data into bit 7–4 of status register until INPB in the status register is set
c2h	read out input port (high)	reads bit 7–4 of input port repeatedly and transfers the data into bit 7–4 of status register until INPB in the status register is set
d0h	read output port	reads output port and transfers the data into the output buffer
d1h	write output port	writes the following data byte into the output port
d2h	write keyboard output buffer	writes the following data byte into the output buffer and clears AUXB in the status register
d3h	write output buffer of auxiliary device	writes the following data byte into the output buffer and sets AUXB in the status register
d4h	write auxiliary device	writes the following data byte into the auxiliary device
e0h	read test input port	the keyboard controller reads its test input and writes T0 into bit 0 and T1 into bit 1 of output buffer
f0h–ffh	send pulses to output port	pulls low bits 3–0 of output port corresponding to low nibble 00h to 0fh of command for 6 ms

Table 31.4: Controller commands (AT, PS/2)

You may access the input buffer with an OUT instruction, referring to the port address 60h, if the INPB bit of the status register is cleared. Via the input buffer, data bytes are eventually transferred to the keyboard controller, which belong to a controller command issued in advance via port address 64h.

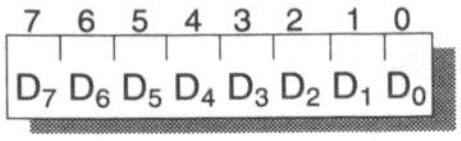

D_7–D_0: Data bit 7–0

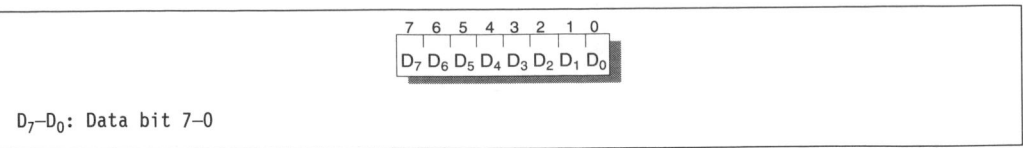

Figure 31.8: Input and output buffer (60h).

Example: `write byte 01h into the output port.`

```
OUT 64h, d1h     ; pass code for the controller command «write output port»
                 ; via the control register to the keyboard controller
wait:
IN al, 64h       ; read status register
TEST al, 02h     ; check whether input buffer is full
JNZ wait         ; input buffer full thus wait
OUT 60h, 01h     ; pass data byte 01h for the controller command
```

In the same way, you pass control commands to the keyboard by writing the code of the intended keyboard command into the input buffer of the keyboard controller. The keyboard controller then transfers the command byte to the keyboard, which in turn interprets and executes it. You will find a list of all keyboard commands and their interpretation in the next section.

The keyboard controller writes all data that the CPU has requested by means of a controller command into the output buffer. If you have pressed a key then the keyboard passes the scan code in the form of an SDU to the keyboard controller, which extracts the scan code byte and writes it into the output buffer. In both cases the keyboard controller issues (via IRQ1) a hardware interrupt corresponding to INT 09h if it has received a byte from the keyboard and written it into the output buffer. The handler of this hardware interrupt can then fetch the character by means of an IN instruction referring to the address 60h, determine the corresponding ASCII code, and put both into the keyboard buffer of the BIOS data area or process the return codes for ACK, etc. accordingly. Details concerning the transfer of scan codes are discussed below.

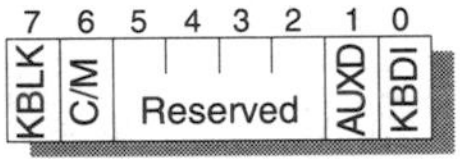

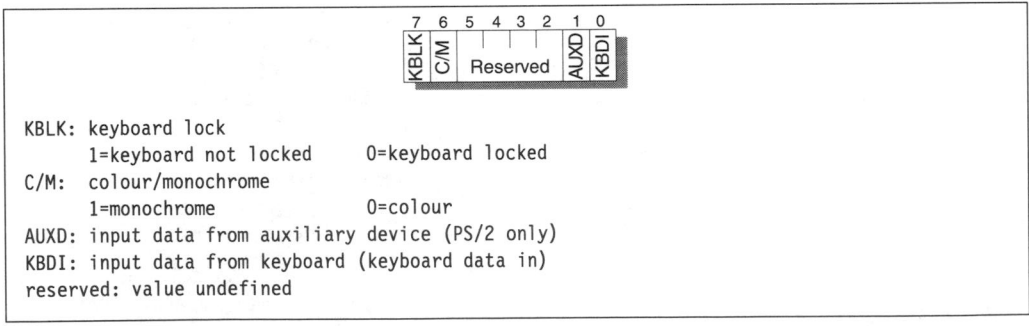

```
KBLK: keyboard lock
      1=keyboard not locked      0=keyboard locked
C/M:  colour/monochrome
      1=monochrome               0=colour
AUXD: input data from auxiliary device (PS/2 only)
KBDI: input data from keyboard (keyboard data in)
reserved: value undefined
```

Figure 31.9: Input port.

The input and output ports of the keyboard controller not only establish a connection to the keyboard or (in the case of PS/2) a mouse, but also control other gate chips in the PC or output status information from other devices. Don't confuse the input and output ports with the input and output buffers. Figure 31.9 shows the structure of the input port, Figure 31.10 that of the output port.

You can read the input port by passing the keyboard controller the command *read input port* via port 64h. The keyboard controller then transfers the contents of the input port to the output buffer, from which you may read the byte with an IN instruction referring to port 60h. The most significant *KBLK* bit indicates whether the keyboard is locked or not. On the first ATs, the user had to set a switch to inform the system about the installed graphics adapter type (colour or monochrome) for booting. The *C/M* bit indicates the corresponding switch position if your PC is still equipped with such a switch; otherwise this value is not defined, or provides the same information as is stored in the CMOS RAM. Using the two *AUXD* and *KBDI* bits you can read the serial data stream of the mouse (PS/2 only) and the keyboard.

Example: `read the input port.`

```
OUT 64h, c0h    ; output command «read input port» to keyboard controller
wait:
IN al, 64h      ; read status register of keyboard controller
TEST al, 01h    ; check whether byte is available in the output buffer
JZ wait         ; wait until byte is available
IN al, 60h      ; read input port byte from the keyboard
                ; controller's output buffer into al
```

```
KBDO: output data to keyboard
KCLK: keyboard clock
AUXB: output buffer of auxiliary device full (PS/2 only)
OUTB: output buffer full
ACLK: auxiliary device clock (PS/2 only)
AXDO: output data to auxiliary device (PS/2 only)
GA20: gate for A20
      1=on (A20 enabled)      0=off
SYSR: processor reset
      1=execute reset         0=no reset
```

Figure 31.10: Output port.

The output port of the keyboad controller not only supervises the keyboard via *KBDO* and *KCLK* bits (and on a PS/2 also the mouse via the *AXDO* and *ACLK* bits), but can additionally lock address line A20 of the 80286 and above via the *GA20* bit to emulate the 8086/88 address wrap-around. If you want to access the 64 kbytes of the high-memory area above the 1 Mbyte border, you must set bit GA20. HIMEM.SYS does this automatically when you access this storage area. As you know, you don't have the option on the 80286 to switch the processor back to real mode by simply clearing the PM flag. This is possible on the 80286 only by a processor reset, which must be carried out by hardware. For this purpose, the *SYSR* bit is implemented in the keyboard controller's output port. If you set SYSR to 1 then the 80286 carries out a processor reset. But the start routine of the AT BIOS recognizes (according to the shutdown status byte in the CMOS RAM) whether a boot process is in progress, or whether a program has issued a processor reset via SYSR to switch the 80286 back to real mode. In the latter case, the BIOS start routine returns control immediately back to the calling program, for example to the HIMEM.SYS or RAMDRIVE.SYS drivers which access extended memory to store and read data there. The *OUTB* and *AUXB* bits indicate whether the output buffers for the keyboard or the mouse (PS/2 only) are available.

Example: `issue processor reset.`

```
OUT 64h, d0h    ; output command «read output port» to keyboard controller
wait:
IN al, 64h      ; read status register of keyboard controller
TEST al, 01h    ; check whether byte is available in the output buffer
JZ wait         ; wait until byte is available
IN al, 60h      ; read output port byte from the keyboard
                ; controller's output buffer into al
OR al, 01h      ; set bit SYSR
OUT 64h, d1h    ; output command «write output port» to keyboard controller
OUT 60h, al     ; issue processor reset
```

Receiving Keyboard Characters

If you didn't issue a certain keyboard command for which the keyboard returns some data bytes, you will only receive the make and break codes according to the keys pressed or released. The keyboards have a small buffer memory, which usually holds about 20 bytes. Depending upon which keys you are operating, the buffer can therefore accommodate more or fewer key operations, as the scan code for a new MF II key occupies far more bytes than for the ordinary 'A' key, for example. If the internal keyboard buffer is overflowing because the CPU doesn't read data from the keyboard controller's output buffer (for example, if IRQ1 in the 8259A PIC is disabled), then the keyboard places the value 00h or ffh into the internal buffer to indicate the overflow condition. Table 31.5 shows the return codes of the keyboard.

Code	Meaning
00h	overflow error or
ffh	key error
41abh	keyboard ID of MF II keyboard
aah	BAT complete code
eeh	echo after echo command
fah	ACK
fch	BAT error
feh	resend request
1h–58h	make and break codes of keys

Table 31.5: Keyboard return codes

If the output buffer of the keyboard controller is empty (that is, bit OUTB in the status register is cleared), then the keyboard transfers a scan code (or return code) from the internal buffer as a serial bit stream to the keyboard controller. The controller in turn places the character into its output buffer, sets bit OUTB in the status register, and issues a hardware interrupt via IRQ1 (corresponding to INT 09h).

On a PC/XT keyboard the handler should first set the SW1 bit of port B so that port A really contains the scan code from the keyboard and not the data from the configuration DIP switches. As is the case for the other keyboards, the scan code can then be fetched by a simple IN instruction referring to the port address 60h. Thus the character has been removed from the output buffer so that the keyboard may pass the next scan code from its internal buffer.

The following example illustrates the principle of character passing between keyboard controller and the CPU. To disable IRQ1, bit 1 in the IMR of the 8259A PIC is masked. If you try this small program you may clearly see the amount of make and break codes the MF II keyboard generates for SHIFT and other keys if you operate one of the new MF II keys.

Example: `detect passed scan codes and display them on the screen until ESC is pressed.`

```
main()
{ int status, scan code;

  outp(0x21, 0x02);                   /* lock IRQ1 */
  for (;;) {                          /* endless loop for reading characters */
    for (;;) {                        /* wait until character is available in output buffer */
      status = inp(0x64);             /* read status register */
      if ((status & 0x01) == 0x01) break;  /* leave wait loop if character in output buffer */
    }
    scan code = inp(0x60);            /* read scan code from output buffer */
    printf("\t%d", scan code);        /* output scan code in tab-steps */
    if (code == 0x01) break;          /* leave endless loop if ESC is pressed */
  }
  outp(0x21, 0x00);                   /* release IRQ1 */
  exit(0);
}
```

Commands for the Keyboard

The AT and MF II keyboards implement several commands that you pass via the input buffer of the keyboard controller. But note that, for example, the command *turn on/off LEDs* is meaningless for an AT keyboard, as this keyboard doesn't have any LED. Table 31.6 summarizes all keyboard commands for the AT and MF II keyboard.

The following briefly discusses the most important commands. Generally, the keyboard returns an ACK corresponding to fah after every command except echo and resend. Every character from the keyboard to the controller issues an interrupt via IRQ1. Normally, the keyboard drivers process only codes between 0 and 127. Thus, ACK and all other return messages are slurred by the keyboard driver. Only if you suppress the generation of INT 09h, for example by masking IRQ1 in the IMR of the 8259A PIC, can you actually detect the return messages; otherwise the interrupt snatches away the return byte from you, as the keyboard controller issues the interrupt immediately after receiving the byte.

- **Turn On/Off the LEDs (edh):** After passing the command the keyboard responds with an ACK to the controller, aborts scanning the scan matrix, and waits for the indicator byte from the controller, which you must also pass to the controller via the input buffer. Figure 31.11 shows the structure of the indicator byte.

Code	Command	Description
edh	turn on/off LEDs	turns on/off the MF II keyboard LEDs
eeh	echo	returns a byte eeh
f0h	set/identify scan codes	sets one of three scan code sets and identifies the present scan code set
f2h	identify keyboard	identifies the keyboard (ACK=AT, ACK+abh+41h=MF II)
f3h	set repetition rate/ delay	sets repetition rate and delay of keyboard
f4h	enable	enables the keyboard
f5h	standard/disable	sets the standard values and disables the keyboard
f6h	standard/enable	sets the standard values and enables the keyboard
feh	resend	the keyboard transfers the last transmitted character once more to the keyboard controller
ffh	reset	executes an internal keyboard reset and afterwards the BAT

Table 31.6: Keyboard Commands (AT, PS/2)

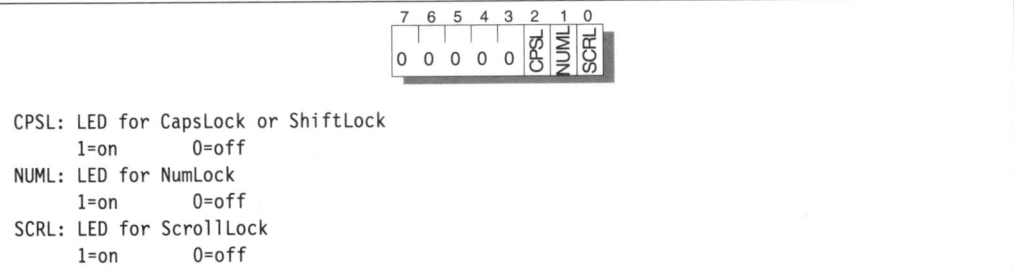

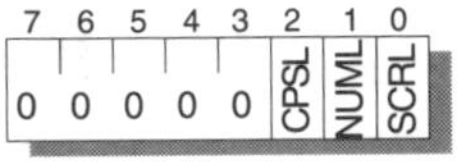


```
CPSL: LED for CapsLock or ShiftLock
      1=on       0=off
NUML: LED for NumLock
      1=on       0=off
SCRL: LED for ScrollLock
      1=on       0=off
```

Figure 31.11: Indicator byte.

Example: `switch on LED for NumLock, switch off all others.`

```
OUT 60h, edh   ; output command for turning on/off the LEDs
wait:
IN al, 64h     ; read status register
TEST al, 02h   ; check whether input buffer is empty
JNZ wait       ; input buffer full thus wait
OUT 60h, 02h   ; switch on LED for NumLock
```

- **Echo (eeh)**: this command checks the transfer path and the command logic of the keyboard. As soon as the keyboard has received the command it returns the same response byte eeh corresponding to an echo back to the keyboard controller.
- **Set/Identify Scan Codes (f0h)**: this command selects one of three alternate scan code sets of the MF II keyboard; 01h, 02h, and 03h are valid. The standard setup is the scan code set 02h. After outputting the command the keyboard responds with an ACK, and waits for the transfer of the option byte. The values 01h, 02h, and 03h select sets 1, 2, or 3; a value of 00h

instructs the keyboard to return, besides the ACK, another byte to the keyboard controller upon receiving the option byte which specifies the active scan code set.

- **Identify Keyboard (f2h)**: this command identifies the connected keyboard. A PC/XT keyboard without a controller doesn't respond in any way, that is, a time-out error occurs. An AT keyboard returns only an ACK, but an MF II keyboard returns an ACK followed by the two bytes abh and 41h, which are the low as well as high bytes of the MF II ID word 41abh.

Example: `identify keyboard.`

```
int keyb_ident(void)          /* function returns indicator:0=PC/XT, 1=AT, 2=MF II, 3=error */

{ int status, code, ret_code;

  outp(0x21,0x02);            /* lock IRQ1 */

  outp(0x60, 0xf2);           /* output command */

  timeout_wait();             /* wait loop for ACK */
  status=inp(0x64);           /* read status register */
  if ((status & 0x01) != 0x01) {
    ret_code=0;               /* no ACK from keyboard -> PC/XT keyboard */
  }
  else {
    code=inp(0x60);           /* fetch character */
    if (code != 0xfa) {       /* error */
      ret_code=4;
    }
    else {
      timeout_wait();         /* wait loop for 1st ID byte */
      status=inp(0x64);       /* read status register */
      if ((status & 0x01) != 0x01) {   /* no ID byte from keyboard -> AT keyboard */
        ret_code=1;
      }
      else {
        code=inp(0x60);       /* fetch 1st ID byte */
        if (code != 0xab) {   /* error */
          ret_code=5;
        }
        else {
          timeout_wait();     /* wait loop for 2nd ID byte */
          status=inp(0x64);   /* read status register */
          if ((status & 0x01) != 0x01) {   /* no 2nd ID byte from keyboard -> error */
            ret_code=6;
          }
          else {
            code=inp(0x60);   /* fetch 2nd ID byte */
            if (code != 0x41) {/* error */
              ret_code=7;
            }
            else {
              ret_code=2;
```

```
          }
        }
      }
    }
  }
 }
 outp(0x21,0x00);              /* release IRQ1 */
 return(ret_code);             /* return keyboard identifier */
}
```

- **Set repetition rate/delay (f3h)**: with this command you may set the repetition rate as well as the delay of an AT or MF II keyboard. After outputting the command the keyboard returns an ACK and waits for the data byte, which you may pass via the input buffer to the keyboard. Figure 31.12 shows the structure of the data byte.

Example: `set 30 characters/s and 150 ms delay`

```
int max_rate(void)   /* routine for maximum keyboard rate; return code: 0=o.k., -1=error */
{ int status, ret_code;

  outp(0x21,0x02);                /* lock IRQ1 */
  outp(0x60, 0xf3);               /* output command */
  timeout_wait();                 /* wait loop for ACK */
  status=inp(0x64);               /* read status register */
  if ((status & 0x01) != 0x01) {
    ret_code=-1;                  /* no ACK from keyboard -> error */
  }
  else {
    outp(0x60, 00h);              /* output data byte */
    ret_code=0;                   /* everything o.k. */
  }
  outp(0x21,0x00);                /* release IRQ1 */
  return(ret_code);               /* return code */
}
```

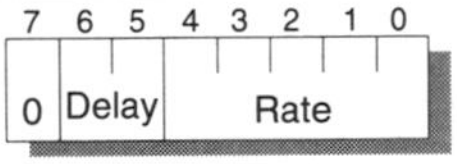

Delay: delay [ms]
00=250ms 01=500ms 10=750ms 11=1000ms
Rate: repetition rate [characters/s]

00000=30.0	00001=26.7	00010=24.0	00011=21.8	00100=20.0	00101=18.5	00110=17.1	00111=16.0
01000=15.0	01001=13.3	01010=12.0	01011=10.9	01100=10.0	01101=9.2	01110=8.5	01111=8.0
10000=7.5	10001=6.7	10010=6.0	10011=5.5	10100=5.0	10101=4.6	10110=4.3	10111=4.0
11000=3.7	11001=3.3	11010=3.0	11011=2.7	11100=2.5	11101=2.3	11110=2.1	10111=2.0

Figure 31.12: Repetition rate and delay.

- **Resend (feh)**: if an error has occurred during the course of transferring data between the keyboard and keyboard controller, you can instruct the keyboard with this command to pass the last character once again.
- **Reset (ffh)**: this command carries out an internal self-test of the keyboard. After receiving the command byte the keyboard first outputs an ACK for this purpose. The keyboard controller must respond by raising the data and clock line to the keyboard to a high level for at least 500 μs. Afterwards, the keyboard carries out the in-built BAT (basic assurance test). Upon the BAT's completion, it transfers a code aah (test passed) or fch (keyboard error) to the controller. You can set the data and clock line to a high level using bits 6 and 7 in the output port.

31.2 Mice and Other Rodents

For a long time, mice have been indispensable on Apple computers for using programs there. But on IBM PCs the mouse made its debut only once Windows came onto the market, as handling Windows with the usual keyboard and without a mouse is quite ponderous. On programs that allow an operation both by hotkeys and by a mouse, well-trained users work faster if they use only the hotkeys (that is, the keyboard) when selecting menu items. Thus, mice are surely not the ultimate solution, but they are at least very useful for graphics-oriented applications or drawing programs. Some mice can confidently be called rats if they exceed a weight of one pound or the required space for their movement is at least as large as your desk! In the following, however, we only discuss mice.

31.2.1 Structure and Function

A mouse is structured quite simply. The central part is a steel ball, coated with gum or plastic, which rotates as the mouse is moved. This movement is transmitted to two small rollers perpendicular to each other, which convert the mouse movement in the X and Y directions into a rotation of two disks, with holes. These disks alternately close or open a photosensor assembly when rotated, that is, the mouse is moved. Thus the number of interruptions and releases of the photosensor assembly is an unambiguous quantity for the amount of the mouse's movement in the X and Y directions, and the number of these interruptions and releases per second specifies the speed of this movement. Such mechanical mice are used most today.

A newer concept is the so-called optical mouse, where sensors on the bottom detect the mouse's movement on a specially patterned mouse pad. A special patterning is required so that the mouse's logic can determine the direction and speed; a normal mouse pad would only confuse the mouse.

All mice further have two or three buttons. Originally, Microsoft intended three buttons as the standard, but actually implemented only two on its own (Microsoft) mice. Many compatible mice therefore also only have two buttons. The information as to how far the mouse has moved and which buttons have been pressed or released is passed to the PC via a cable or an infrared beam.

31.2.2 Mouse Driver and Mouse Interface

Most mice are connected to the serial interface. Via the various control lines, the mouse is then supplied with energy; wireless infrared mice need a battery, of course. When you move your mouse or press or release a button, the mouse generally passes a mouse data packet to the interface, which in turn issues an interrupt. For handling this interrupt a *mouse driver* is needed, which intercepts the interrupt for the corresponding serial interface, reads the mouse data packet, and updates internal values that concern the current keyboard status as well as the mouse's position. Moreover, the mouse driver provides a software interface via mouse interrupt 33h for interpreting these internal values. You will find a list of all INT 33h functions in Appendix J.

The mouse driver is not only responsible for servicing the interface interrupt and providing the mentioned values, but also for moving the *mouse pointer* over the screen. This pointer seems to follow the mouse's movement. To clear up a common misconception: don't move the mouse pointer over the screen using the mouse itself; you only continuously issue interrupts when moving the mouse, during the course of which the amount of mouse movement is passed to the interface. The mouse driver detects these positional signals from the mouse and converts them into a movement of the mouse pointer on-screen. For this purpose, it deletes the mouse pointer at the current location, writes the old screen contents at this location again, reads the screen contents at the new location, and overwrites the location with the mouse pointer.

For the mouse driver you can choose from three options: hardware and software mouse pointer in text mode, as well as a graphics mouse pointer in graphics mode. You may define the type and shape of the mouse pointer by means of functions 09h and 0ah of INT 33h. The hardware mouse pointer is nothing more than the conventional cursor that the mouse driver moves on-screen according to the mouse's movements. For the software mouse pointer you can select any character; as a standard an inverted space character is defined. Thus in text mode the mouse pointer always has one character corresponding to a video memory word of two bytes (attribute and character code). The functions of INT 33h for reading the mouse pointer positions return the position in units of pixels, that is, in the case of a character box with 8*16 pixels for a VGA adapter, the X coordinate multiplied by the values 0, 8, 16, ... 472. You must first divide these quantities by the X dimension of the character box to determine the row and column of the mouse pointer in text mode.

The mouse pointer is not simply output on-screen, but combined bit by bit via the so-called screen and cursor masks of the mouse pointer with the video memory word at the mouse pointer's location:

```
new video memory word = (old word AND screen mask) XOR cursor mask
```

The combination is carried out in two steps. First, the mouse driver forms the AND value of the old video memory word and the screen mask. Thus, using the screen mask you can clear individual bits in the video memory word. Second, the XOR value of the AND result and the cursor mask is formed.

Example: `old word 'A' corresponding to ASCII code 41h with attribute 01h, thus old word is equal to 4101h; screen mask 4040h, cursor mask 0f1fh.`

```
new word = (4101h AND 4040h) XOR 0f1fh
         = (4000) XOR 0f1fh
         = 4f1fh

Resulting mouse pointer: character 4fh corresponding to '0', attribute equal to 1fh.
```

Thus, with the cursor mask you define the character and colour of the mouse pointer. Table 31.7 shows the combination table for this.

Screen bit	**Screen mask bit**	**Cursor mask bit**	**Resulting bit**
bit	0	0	0
bit	0	1	1
bit	1	0	bit (unchanged)
bit	1	1	$\overline{\text{bit}}$ (inverted)

Table 31.7: Combining screen bit, screen and cursor mask

You may clear, set, leave unchanged, or invert individual bits in the video memory word. Figure 31.13 shows the structure of the video memory word for a character in text mode. In Section 31.2.3 an example for using the screen and cursor mask is discussed.

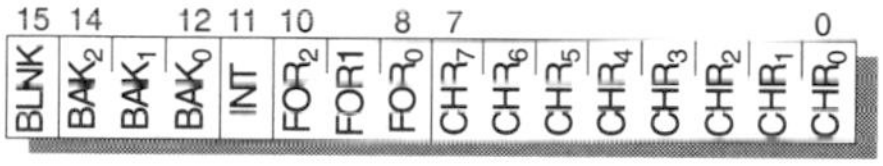

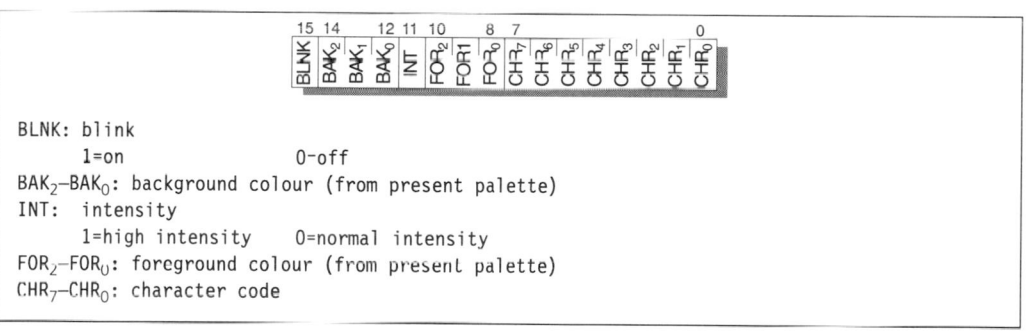

BLNK: blink
    1=on   0=off
BAK_2–BAK_0: background colour (from present palette)
INT: intensity
    1=high intensity   0=normal intensity
FOR_2–FOR_0: foreground colour (from present palette)
CHR_7–CHR_0: character code

Figure 31.13: Video memory word structure for a character in text mode.

In graphics mode the mouse pointer is represented similarly. Also in this case, the mouse driver first forms the AND value of the present screen bit and the screen mask, and afterwards the XOR value of this result and the cursor mask when displaying the mouse pointer. In graphics mode, one pixel is assigned one or more bits; if you are defining the mouse pointer you thus have to note the number of bits per pixel. Furthermore, the mouse pointer size here is always 16*16 pixels, and as standard an arrow is defined, which you may alter by means of function 09h. An example of this is discussed in the next section.

Many mouse drivers have problems with a Hercules card in graphics mode. The 720*348 resolution, differing from the geometry of standard IBM adapters, as well as the character box of 9*14 pixels, often gives rise to a phenomenon whereby the individual points of the graphics mouse pointer are widely spread over the whole screen, and therefore don't form a coherent mouse pointer.

Besides mice connected to a serial interface, there are further so-called bus mice which come with an adapter for a bus slot. They access the PC system bus directly, and therefore don't occupy a serial interface. The structure and functioning are largely the same as for conventional mice connected to a serial interface; INT 33h provides the same results. On the PS/2 the mouse was integrated into the system from the beginning, so that here, besides a keyboard connector, a connection for a PS/2 mouse is also implemented as standard.

31.2.3 Programming the Mouse

For programming and interrogating the mouse the functions of mouse interrupt 33h are available. INT 33h is a software interface to the mouse driver to determine the position of the mouse pointer and the number of «mouse clicks», as well as to define the shape and behaviour of the mouse pointer. Appendix J.2 lists all the functions of INT 33h. Only a few less obvious ones are discussed here because of the lack of space. To display the mouse pointer on-screen you always have to enable it with function 01h.

- **Function 09h – Define Mouse Pointer in Graphics Mode**: with this function you define the shape and behaviour of the mouse pointer in graphics mode. The screen and cursor mask are held in a buffer. The action point defines, relative to the upper left corner of the mouse pointer, which value is to be returned during the course of an inquiry referring to the mouse pointer's position. The mouse pointer always has 16∗16 pixels that must be covered by the screen and cursor mask. Thus, depending upon the screen mode and the number of colours used, a quite large buffer is necessary to accommodate the mask bits.

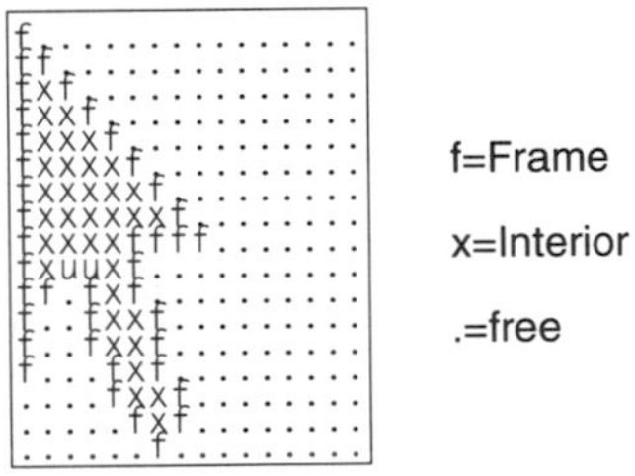

Figure 31.14: Arrow mask.

Example: `arrow pointer in the high-resolution VGA mode with 256 colours, that is, 1 byte per pixel.`

Figure 31.14 shows the mask for the arrow pointer which comprises frame, interior and free fields. The arrow pointer shall completely cover all underlying pixels, and in the free fields the background shall appear unaltered. For both the screen mask and the cursor mask, 256 bytes (16 characters ∗ 16 points/row) are required. Assume the colour of the frame to be ffh and that of the interior 88h. The action point shall be the upper left tip of the arrow. With the combination *(screen bit AND screen mask) XOR cursor mask*, the following values are required in the screen and cursor mask for the pixels u, x and . of the arrow pointer:

```
pixel           screen mask     cursor mask
u               00h             ffh
x               00h             88h
.               ffh             00h
```

Thus the buffer has the following contents:

```
00h ffh ffh ffh ffh ffh ffh ffh ffh ffh ffh ffh ffh ffh ffh ffh ffh ┐
00h 00h ffh ffh ffh ffh ffh ffh ffh ffh ffh ffh ffh ffh ffh ffh ffh │
00h 00h 00h ffh ffh ffh ffh ffh ffh ffh ffh ffh ffh ffh ffh ffh ffh │
00h 00h 00h 00h ffh ffh ffh ffh ffh ffh ffh ffh ffh ffh ffh ffh ffh │
00h 00h 00h 00h 00h ffh ffh ffh ffh ffh ffh ffh ffh ffh ffh ffh ffh │
00h 00h 00h 00h 00h 00h ffh ffh ffh ffh ffh ffh ffh ffh ffh ffh ffh │
00h 00h 00h 00h 00h 00h 00h ffh ffh ffh ffh ffh ffh ffh ffh ffh ffh │
00h 00h 00h 00h 00h 00h 00h 00h ffh ffh ffh ffh ffh ffh ffh ffh ffh ├─ screen mask
00h 00h 00h 00h 00h 00h 00h 00h 00h ffh ffh ffh ffh ffh ffh ffh ffh │
00h 00h 00h 00h 00h 00h ffh ffh ffh ffh ffh ffh ffh ffh ffh ffh ffh │
00h 00h ffh 00h 00h 00h ffh ffh ffh ffh ffh ffh ffh ffh ffh ffh ffh │
00h ffh ffh 00h 00h 00h 00h ffh ffh ffh ffh ffh ffh ffh ffh ffh ffh │
00h ffh ffh ffh 00h 00h 00h ffh ffh ffh ffh ffh ffh ffh ffh ffh ffh │
ffh ffh ffh ffh 00h 00h 00h 00h ffh ffh ffh ffh ffh ffh ffh ffh ffh │
ffh ffh ffh ffh ffh 00h 00h 00h ffh ffh ffh ffh ffh ffh ffh ffh ffh │
ffh ffh ffh ffh ffh ffh 00h ffh ffh ffh ffh ffh ffh ffh ffh ffh ffh ┘
ffh 00h 00h 00h 00h 00h 00h 00h 00h 00h 00h 00h 00h 00h 00h 00h 00h ┐
ffh ffh 00h 00h 00h 00h 00h 00h 00h 00h 00h 00h 00h 00h 00h 00h 00h │
ffh 88h ffh 00h 00h 00h 00h 00h 00h 00h 00h 00h 00h 00h 00h 00h 00h │
ffh 88h 88h ffh 00h 00h 00h 00h 00h 00h 00h 00h 00h 00h 00h 00h 00h │
ffh 88h 88h 88h ffh 00h 00h 00h 00h 00h 00h 00h 00h 00h 00h 00h 00h │
ffh 88h 88h 88h 88h ffh 00h 00h 00h 00h 00h 00h 00h 00h 00h 00h 00h │
ffh 88h 88h 88h 88h 88h ffh 00h 00h 00h 00h 00h 00h 00h 00h 00h 00h │
ffh 88h 88h 88h 88h 88h 88h ffh 00h 00h 00h 00h 00h 00h 00h 00h 00h ├─ cursor mask
ffh 88h 88h 88h 88h ffh ffh ffh ffh 00h 00h 00h 00h 00h 00h 00h 00h │
ffh 88h ffh ffh 88h ffh 00h 00h 00h 00h 00h 00h 00h 00h 00h 00h 00h │
ffh ffh 00h ffh 88h ffh 00h 00h 00h 00h 00h 00h 00h 00h 00h 00h 00h │
ffh 00h 00h ffh 88h 88h ffh 00h 00h 00h 00h 00h 00h 00h 00h 00h 00h │
ffh 00h 00h 00h ffh 88h ffh 00h 00h 00h 00h 00h 00h 00h 00h 00h 00h │
00h 00h 00h 00h ffh 88h 88h ffh 00h 00h 00h 00h 00h 00h 00h 00h 00h │
00h 00h 00h 00h 00h ffh 88h ffh 00h 00h 00h 00h 00h 00h 00h 00h 00h │
00h 00h 00h 00h 00h 00h ffh 00h 00h 00h 00h 00h 00h 00h 00h 00h 00h ┘
```

Function call to INT 33h, function 09h.

```
MOV ax, 09h          ; define function
MOV bx, 00h          ; upper left tip
MOV cx, 00h          ; upper left tip
MOV dx, SEG puffer   ; load buffer segment into dx
MOV es, dx           ; load segment into es
MOV dx, OFF puffer   ; load buffer offset into dx
INT 33h              ; call function
```

- **Function 0ah – Define Mouse Pointer in Text Mode**: this function defines the shape and behaviour of the mouse pointer in text mode. Thus the definition of the mouse pointer is much easier here than in graphics mode. You may choose from between a hardware mouse pointer (that is, the conventional cursor) and a software mouse pointer, for which you are free to select any character. If you choose a software mouse pointer then the video memory word of the character onto which the mouse pointer is mapped is combined with the screen and cursor mask as follows: *(video memory word AND screen mask) XOR cursor mask*. Therefore, the mouse pointer's colour as well as its character can change.

Example: bright, blinking software mouse pointer with colour 3 of the active palette of constant character.

```
MOV ax, 0ah     ; select function
MOV bx, 00h     ; software mouse pointer
MOV cx, 00h     ; screen mask (clear screen character completely -> constant character)
MOV dx, 8b02h   ; cursor mask (BLNK=1b, BAKx=000b, INT=1b, FORx=011b, CHRx=00000010b)
INT 33h         ; function call
```

Example: `software mouse pointer with scan lines between 3 and 8`

```
MOV ax, 0ah     ; select function
MOV bx, 01h     ; hardware mouse pointer
MOV cx, 03h     ; first scan line
MOV dx, 08h     ; last scan line
INT 33h         ; function call
```

- **Function 0ch – Define Call Mask for User-Defined Procedure:** with this function you can define a condition for which the mouse driver calls a user-defined procedure. An application program is thus always activated if, for example, you move the mouse or operate a mouse button. Thus a continuous inquiry is not necessary; the mouse gets attention on its own. The procedure is passed a mask in register ax according to the call mask in which the bit is set that gave rise to the procedure call. The bc, cx, and dx registers define the current button state and the mouse pointer position.

Example: `the mouse driver shall call the procedure mouse_handler if the mouse is moved or the left button is pressed.`

```
MOV ax, 0ch                   ; select function
MOV cx, 03h                   ; call mask (left button pressed, mouse moved)
MOV dx, OFF mouse_handler     ; load procedure offset into dx
MOV bx, SEGMENT mouse_handler; load procedure segment into bx
MOV es, bx                    ; load segment into es
INT 33h                       ; call function

mouse_handler   PROC   FAR
  ...............             ;
TEST ax, 01h                  ; check whether mouse has been moved
JNZ movement                  ; jump
TEST ax, 02h                  ; check whether left button pressed
JNZ button                    ; jump
  ...............
movement:
  ...............             ; process mouse movement
button:
  ...............             ; process button press
RETF                          ; far return to the mouse driver
END PROC
```

31.2.4 The PS/2 Mouse

In view of the success of graphics-oriented user shells (to which the OS/2 presentation manager also belongs), IBM has already implemented a mouse port into the keyboard controller of its PS/2 models. The mouse is generally denoted as the *pointing device* here. In principle, other pointing devices (for example, a trackball) can also be connected to the mouse port, as long as they comply with the PS/2 mouse interface. Because of the PS/2 mouse's interface integration, you can also access the PS/2 mouse via the keyboard controller ports 60h and 64h. The mouse passes the controller the data in the form of an 8-byte mouse data packet. Its structure is shown in Figure 31.15.

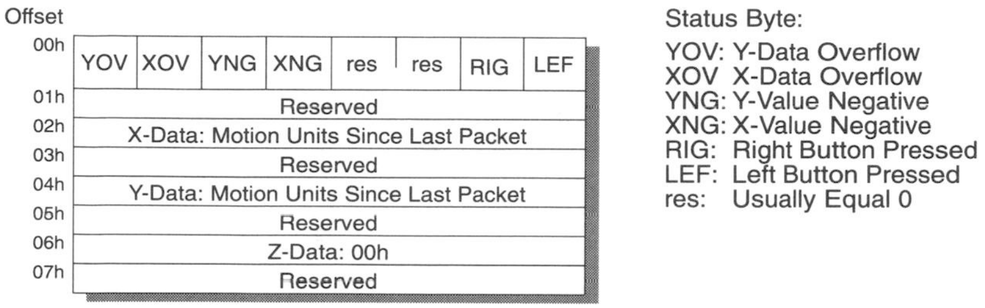

Figure 31.15: PS/2 mouse data packet.

The following discusses the mouse programming via the controller ports, as well as the new mouse functions of the PS/2 BIOS.

Programming the PS/2 Mouse Via Ports

To transfer data or commands to the mouse (or the auxiliary device in general) you must first pass the keyboard controller the command *write auxiliary device*, corresponding to the command code d4h. The following byte to the port address 60h is then transferred to the auxiliary device. If you write the command byte to port 60h, as you do for the keyboard, then the command is not transmitted to the mouse but the keyboard. Note that you don't instruct the keyboard controller permanently to transfer all data to the auxiliary device. The command code is only effective for the immediately following data byte to port 60h. Table 31.8 lists all valid command codes for the PS/2 mouse.

The PS/2 mouse can be operated in two different modes: *stream mode* and *remote mode*. In stream mode the mouse always passes data when you operate a mouse button or move the mouse a predefined distance. The programmable sample rate determines how often the mouse may transfer data to the controller per second at most. In remote mode, on the other hand, the mouse data is transferred only after an explicit request by the *read data* command, corresponding to code ebh. In both cases, the mouse writes data into the output buffer of the keyboard controller, which then issues a hardware interrupt corresponding to IRQ1. The interrupt handler determines (according to the AUXB bit in the status register of the keyboard controller) whether the output buffer contains keyboard or mouse data. The following briefly discusses the PS/2 mouse commands.

- **Reset Scaling (e6h):** this command resets the scaling factor to 1:1.
- **Set Scaling (e7h):** this command sets the scaling factor in stream mode to a value of 2:1, so that the X and Y values from the mouse are doubled. In remote mode the command has no effect.

Code	Command	Description
e6h	reset scaling	resets X-Y-scaling factor to 1:1
e7h	set scaling	sets X-Y-scaling to 2:1
e8h	set resolution	sets mouse resolution corresponding to following data byte (00h=1 count/mm, 01h=2 counts/mm, 02h=4 counts/mm, 03h=8 counts/mm)
e9h	determine status	supplies a 3-byte status: byte 3: sample rate byte 2: resolution byte 1:

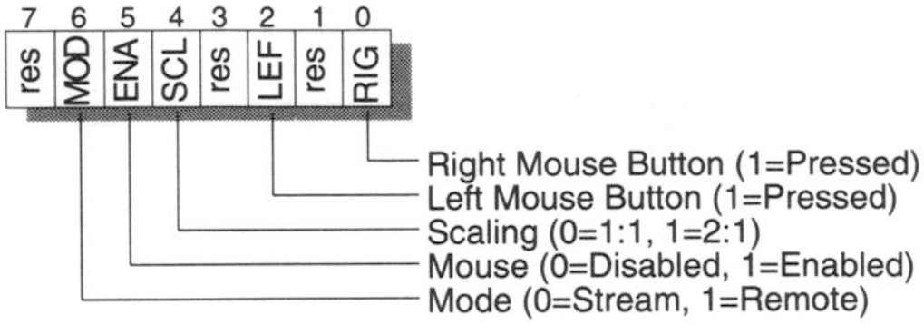

Code	Command	Description
eah	set stream mode	sets stream mode
ebh	read data	transfers a data packet from mouse to controller
ech	reset wrap mode	resets mouse from wrap mode to normal mode
eeh	set wrap mode	sets mouse to wrap mode
f0h	set remote mode	sets remote mode
f2h	indentify unit	supplies an identification code (00h=mouse)
f3h	set sample rate	sets sampling rate of mouse according to following data byte (0ah=10 samples/s, 14h=20 samples/s, 28h=40 samples/s, 3ch=60 samples/s, 50h=80 samples/s, 64h=100 samples/s, c8h=200 samples/s
f4h	enable	enables data transfer in stream mode
f5h	disable	disables data transfer in stream mode
f6h	set standard	initializes mouse with standard values (100 samples/s, scaling 1:1, stream mode, resolution 4 counts/mm, data transfer disabled)
feh	resend	mouse transmits the last transferred data packet to the controller once more
ffh	reset	executes an internal mouse test

Table 31.8: Commands for the auxiliary device mouse (PS/2)

Example: `set scaling.`

```
OUT 64h, d4h  ; command «write auxiliary device» for controller
wait:
IN al, 64h    ; read status register
TEST al, 02h  ; check whether input buffer is empty
JNZ wait      ; input buffer full, thus wait
OUT 60h, e7h  ; command «set scaling» for mouse
```

– **Set Resolution (e8h)**: with this command you can set the resolution of the mouse. The following values are possible: 00h=1 count/mm, 01h=2 counts/mm, 02h=4 counts/mm, 03h=8 counts/mm. After the command byte you must also write the data byte to port 60h.

Example: `resolution 4 counts/mm.`

```
OUT 64h, d4h  ; command «write auxiliary device» for controller
wait1:
IN al, 64h    ; read status register
```

```
TEST al, 02h  ; check whether input buffer is empty
JNZ wait1     ; input buffer full, thus wait
OUT 60h, e8h  ; command «set resolution» for mouse
wait2:
IN al, 64h    ; read status register
TEST al, 02h  ; check whether input buffer is empty
JNZ wait2     ; input buffer full, thus wait
OUT 60h, 02h  ; set resolution to 4 counts/mm
```

- **Determine Status (e9h)**: with this command you may determine the current mouse status. The status byte is passed in the controller's output buffer.
- **Set Stream Mode (eah)**: this command sets the mouse to stream mode.
- **Read Data (ebh)**: this command forces the transfer of a mouse data packet. The command is valid in stream as well as in remote mode. Moreover, in remote mode this is the only option for the CPU to receive data from the mouse.
- **Reset Wrap Mode (ech)**: this command resets the mouse to the normal operation mode.
- **Set Wrap Mode (eeh)**: this command sets the mouse to wrap or echo mode. In wrap mode the mouse returns every command or data byte which it receives from the controller back to the controller, except the commands *reset wrap mode* (code ech) and *reset* (code ffh).
- **Set Remote Mode (f0h)**: this command sets the mouse to remote mode. The mouse then transfers a data packet to the controller only after an explicit request via the *read data* (code ebh) command.
- **Identify Device (f2h)**: This command instructs the mouse to return an identification code to the controller's output buffer.
- **Set Sampling Rate (f3h)**: using this command you may set the sampling rate via a data byte, which is transferred to the mouse after the command code f3h via port 60h. The following values are possible: 0ah=10 samples/s, 14h=20 samples/s, 28h=40 samples/s, 3ch = 60 samples/s, 50h=80 samples/s, 64h=100 samples/s and c8h=200 samples/s.
- **Enable(f4h)**: this command enables data transfer if the mouse is in stream mode. In remote mode the command has no effect.
- **Disable (f5h)**: this command disables the data transfer if the mouse is in stream mode. In remote mode the command has no effect.
- **Set Standard (f6h)**: this command initializes the PS/2 mouse. The standard state is as follows:

```
sampling rate:  100 samples/s
scaling:        1:1
mode:           stream mode
resolution:     4 counts/mm
transfer:       disabled
```

- **Resend (feh)**: this command instructs the mouse to pass the controller the last data packet once again.
- **Reset (ffh)**: this command resets the mouse and carries out an internal self-test.

After the receipt of every valid command from the controller the mouse provides an ACK to acknowledge reception. This is not the case for the *reset wrap mode* (code ech) and *reset* (code ffh) commands. In both cases, the mouse doesn't output an ACK. Table 31.9 lists the valid mouse return codes.

Code	Meaning
00h	mouse identification
fah	ACK
feh	resend request

Table 31.9: Mouse return codes

The CPU must respond to a return code feh with the repeated transfer of the last command or data byte because a transmission error has occurred.

Programming via BIOS Interrupt 15h

In the PS/2 BIOS, eight subfunctions are implemented for interrupt INT 15h, function c2h which support the PS/2 mouse. Using these functions you may access the mouse in the same way as is possible via the controller ports. Appendix J.3 summarizes all the PS/2 mouse functions of the BIOS, so they are not all discussed in detail here.

Before you can use a PS/2 mouse and the accompanying BIOS routines, you have to specify the entry address of the driver which is to process the mouse data packet from the PS/2 mouse. You can do this using the subfunction *pass driver address* (subcode 07h) of INT 15h, function c2h. Afterwards, you must adjust the size of the mouse data packet by means of the subfunction *initialize mouse* (subcode 05h). Now mouse and BIOS are prepared so that you may activate the mouse with the subfunction *enable mouse* (subcode 00h).

When using the PS/2 BIOS routines, the mouse data transfer to a driver or an application proceeds as follows:

- The BIOS interrupt handler, corresponding to IRQ1, determines whether mouse or keyboard data is available, and pushes the one to eight bytes of the mouse data packet onto the stack.
- Afterwards, the BIOS executes a far call to the program.
- The called program processes the mouse data and returns to the BIOS routine with a far return using the BIOS return address held on the stack.

31.3 Trackball

The trackball is a space-saving alternative to the mouse, and is sometimes already integrated into the keyboard. With cheap and therefore low-resolution mice, the mouse pointer movement is similar to a mouse marathon on the desk! The structure of the trackball is like that of a mouse lying on its back, so that the ball is now on the top. To allow users with clumsy fingers to use the trackball, the ball is usually much larger than that of a mouse. On the trackball you are directly moving the ball, not indirectly via mouse movements. But the internal structure essentially remains the same; also here, the ball's movement is transmitted onto rollers, which in turn drive disks with holes for closing and opening photosensor assemblies. Connection of the trackball to the PC system is usually carried out via a serial interface and the trackball driver, which provides the same software interface as the mouse via INT 33h. Further discussion is not, therefore, necessary.

31.4 Digitizer or Graph Tablet

For CAD applications that need the very precise positioning of pointers on a high-resolution screen, so-called *digitizer tablets* are available on which you move a *cross-hair glass*. The digitizer tablets and glass form a unit, as is the case for an optical mouse and its mouse pad; they may not be operated separately. Below the surface of the tablet a very dense X-Y matrix made of thin wires is usually formed. The tablet processor successively sends short sense pulses through the X and Y wires by activating the first X wire and scanning all Y wires in succession with pulses, then activating the next X wire and successively sending a sense pulse through all Y wires, etc. The sense pulses give rise to a short pulse in the glass if it is exactly above the crossing of an X and Y wire through which a sense pulse is running simultaneously at that time. Through this pulse, and the time at which it occurred, the processor can then determine the position of the glass very precisely. The accompanying driver then locates the CAD cross-hair on the screen, or another pointer, accordingly.

The glass of the digitizer tablet usually has four buttons, with which certain reactions and actions of the CAD program are issued. Which actions occur is, of course, up to the programmer. For most CAD programs, the tablet comes with various templates that divide the tablet logically into a central part for positioning the cross-hair, and a peripheral section with certain function symbols. A button operation in the central area sets a point in most cases, while a button operation in the peripheral section calls the function above whose symbol the glass is currently located.

32 Graphics Adapters

This chapter mainly discusses graphics adapters. As you know, there is a virtually infinite variety of such adapters on the market, from the simple monochrome board that can only display text, up to high-resolution and rapid professional adapters for CAD applications, that incorporate dedicated graphics processors. A detailed discussion of all adapters is therefore far beyond the scope of this book, and probably impossible. For this reason, discussion is restricted mainly to the most widely used adapters, that is, the Hercules card as the low-cost beginner's model, and the VGA adapter as the colour model for Windows and other graphics-oriented applications.

32.1 Displaying Images on a Monitor and the General Structure of Graphics Adapters

The display of images (including text as well as graphics) on a computer monitor is similar to the method used in a conventional TV. Figure 32.1 schematically illustrates the generation of images on a *cathode ray tube (CRT)*.

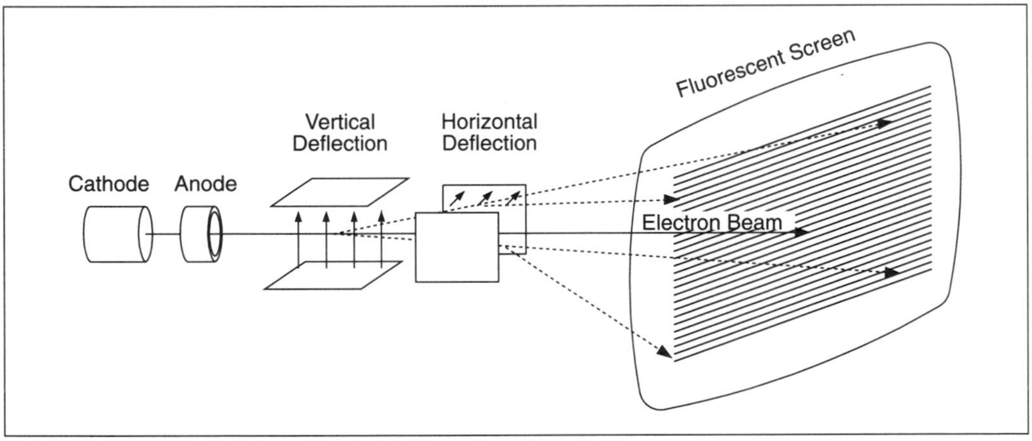

Figure 32.1: Displaying images on a monitor with a cathode ray tube. The electrons emitted by the cathode are accelerated by the anode and deflected in the deflection units. Afterwards, they hit and thus illuminate the fluorescent screen.

The screen's content is divided into many horizontal rows, where every row has a plurality of points, so-called *pixels* or *picture elements*. The tube is emptied so that the electrons emitted by the cathode (hence cathode ray tube) are rapidly accelerated by the electric field of the anode and hit the screen. This screen is coated with a fluorescent material that illuminates when the fast electrons hit it. The negatively charged electrons are deflected by electrical fields generated by electrical voltages at the deflection plates, thus forming so-called *scanlines*.

If the electron beam has reached the right-hand end of a row then it must return to the beginning of the next scanline; this is called a *horizontal retrace*. In the same way, the electron beam must return to the upper left corner when it has reached the lower right one; it carries out a *vertical retrace*.

To actually display an image consisting of many pixels the intensity of the electron beam is modulated accordingly. At the locations where a strong beam hits a bright pixel appears, and at positions hit by a less intensive beam, darker points are generated. Because of the persistence of the fluorescent layer, the points still emit light when the electron beam is already at another location, and because of the inertia of our eyes we get the impression that there is a steady image on the screen. With the electron beam just described, only monochrome or grey shaded images can be generated. These monitors usually have a fluorescent coating which emits green, amber, or white light.

If you attempt to display coloured images, three electron beams are required, each of which hits points on the screen surface lighting up in three different colours. Usually, coatings are used today that provide the three primary colours red, green, and blue. With these three primary colours all known colours can be generated by means of *additive colour mixing*. A white point, for example, results if all three colour elements of a pixel are illuminated at the same intensity. Thus, on colour monitors all three electron beams are modulated according to the image information, where the absolute beam intensity determines the brightness and the relative beam intensity the colour of the corresponding pixel.

You can imagine that the modulation of the electron beam as well as the horizontal and vertical retraces have to be synchronized so that, for example, the vertical retrace occurs exactly when the electron beam has reached the end of the last scanline with the pixel to be displayed last, and a horizontal retrace would be required anyway. Scanning of the screen is carried out line by line, therefore, and the image is displayed on the monitor in the same way. The graphics adapter has to provide the video signals required for the individual pixels (that is, the intensity and colour signal), as well as the synchronization signals for the horizontal and vertical retrace.

Example: on a VGA monitor with a resolution of 640*480 pixels, every line has 640 pixels and the image is generated by 480 scanlines. Thus, after 480 horizontal retraces a vertical retrace occurs. The image is built up 60 times per second, that is, a vertical retrace occurs every 16.7 ms.

For the VGA adapter at the resolution indicated, IBM specifies a video bandwidth of 25.175 MHz, which corresponds to the rate at which the pixels are written onto the screen. This means that every second more than 25 million points have to be be written, thus the video amplifiers of the monitor must operate very quickly. At even higher resolutions (today we already have a *de facto* standard of 1024*768 pixels) the video bandwidth rapidly rises up to 100 MHz; also, high-quality circuits and the tube itself become overtaxed with such frequencies, and only high-end CAD monitors can stand such rates. But there is a simple and quite cheap way out: *interlacing*. The interlacing method writes in two passes; first only those scanlines with an odd number are written, and in the second pass all those lines with an even number. The line frequency and thus the video bandwidth is halved, but the picture frequency (the number of vertical retraces) remains the same. This is necessary as the eye would recognize a halving of the image frequency as a flicker, but it can be tricked by alternately writing odd and even scanlines. Figure 32.2 shows the electron beam path in interlaced and non-interlaced modes. For a perfect image in the interlace mode, it is essential that the electron beam hits the screen's surface exactly between two scanlines of the previous pass. The precise adjustment is not very simple, so the image in interlaced mode is usually significantly worse than in non-interlaced mode.

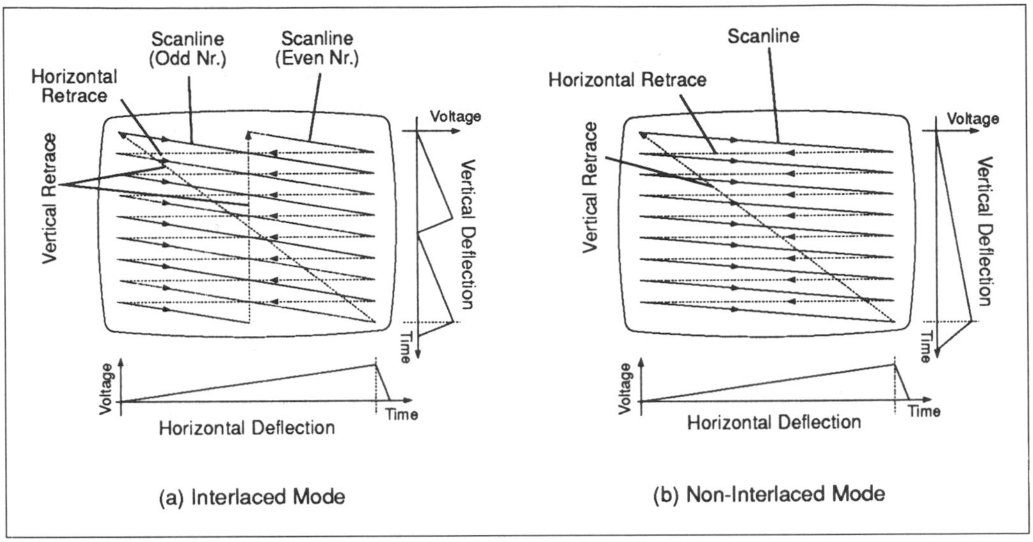

Figure 32.2: Interlaced and non-interlaced mode. (a) In interlaced mode, the scanlines with an odd number are first written, and then all scanlines with an even number. The voltage of the vertical deflection unit carries out two cycles for one complete image; (b) in non-interlaced mode the lines are written in succession.

If you think that the interlace display method is new then I must disappoint you. This method has been used since the start of the TV era to prevent the bandwidths of TV channels from going beyond all possible bounds. In Europe one TV image consists of 625 lines, separated into two partial images of 312.5 lines each. The partial images are transmitted 50 times per second, so that the TV effectively displays 25 complete images per second.

LCD and gas-plasma monitors generate the picture similar to a cathode ray tube, but here no electron beam forms the picture; instead the individual pixels are assigned elements that may be addressed in succession. Therefore, on these monitors the image is also generated line by line. Retraces don't play any role here, as the retrace can be carried out simply by an address change during the course of addressing the elements.

In their principal structure the graphics adapters don't differ significantly, despite all the differences concerning the capabilities of displaying colours and the various resolutions. Figure 32.3 shows a block diagram for the general structure of a modern graphics adapter.

The central part is the video controller or graphics control chip CRTC (cathode ray tube controller), which supervises the functions of the adapter and generates the necessary control signal. The CPU accesses the video RAM via the bus interface to write information that defines the text or graphics the monitor is to display. The CRTC continuously generates addresses for the video RAM to read the corresponding characters, and to transfer them to the character generator.

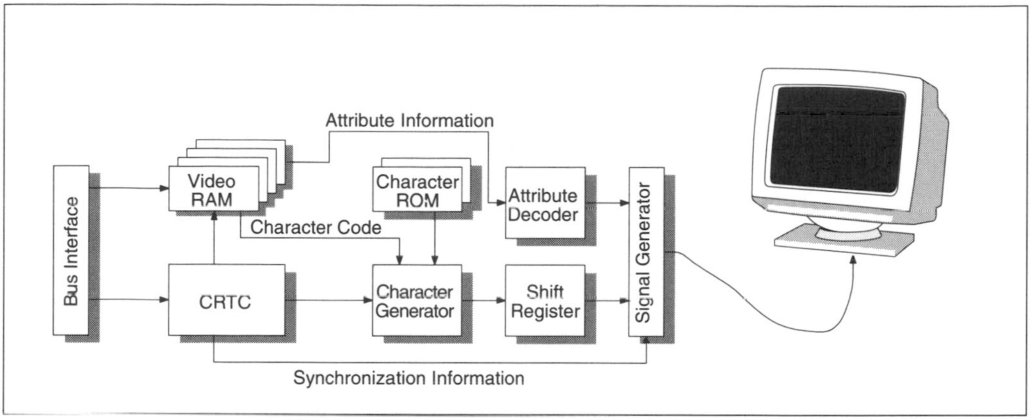

Figure 32.3: Block diagram of a graphics adapter.

In text mode the characters are usually defined by their ASCII codes, which are further assigned a so-called attribute. The attribute defines the display mode for the character concerned more precisely – for example, whether it is to be displayed in a blinking or inverted manner. The character ROM, for every ASCII code, holds a pixel pattern for the corresponding character. The character generator converts the character codes using the pixel pattern in the character ROM into a sequence of pixel bits, and transfers them to a shift register. The signal generator generates the necessary signals for the monitor, using the bit stream from the shift register, the attribute information from the video RAM and the synchronization signals from the CRTC. The monitor processes the passed video signals and displays the symbolic information in the video RAM in the usual form as a picture. The character information in the video RAM thus modulates the electron beam of the monitor through the intermediate stages of character ROM, character generator, shift register, and signal.

In graphics mode the information in video RAM is directly used for generating characters, that is, the entries don't define an index into the character ROM, but already represent the pixel pattern itself with the corresponding colour or grey scale information. Because of this, attribute information is no longer required; the signal generator generates from the bit values in the shift register the brightness and colour signals for the monitor.

32.2 Screen Modes and the 6845 Graphics Controller

Modern graphics adapters may be operated in two completely different (and incompatible) modes: text and graphics modes. Older display adapters such as IBM's monochrome display adapter (MDA) only allow pictures in text mode. Graphics adapters, on the other hand, can display free graphics with possibly very different resolutions. All of these functions are carried out under the control of the graphics controller. The following discusses the basic principles of text and graphics mode and presents a typical member of the graphics controller chips, Motorola's CRTC 6845.

32.2.1 6845 Video Controller

This video controller can be found as the original or compatible chip on nearly all graphics adapters (for example, the Hercules card). Exceptions are EGA/(S)VGA and graphics adapters with a dedicated graphics processor. The CRTC 6845 comes in a standard 40-pin DIP case; its connection scheme is shown in Figure 32.4.

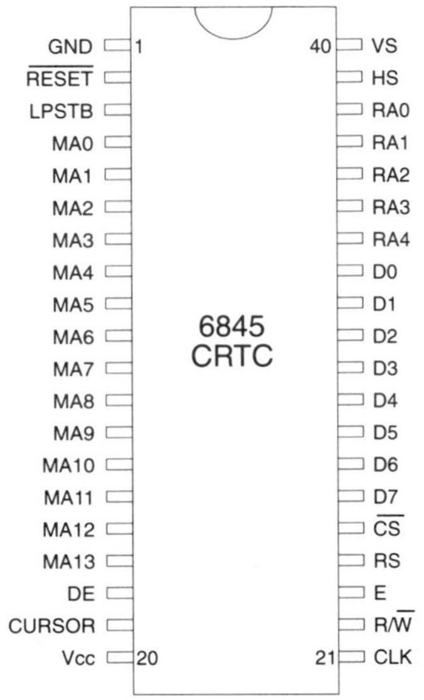

Figure 32.4: CRTC 6845 terminals.

The following briefly presents and discusses the terminals and signals of the 6845. Using the 6845 in text and graphics mode is described in Sections 32.2.2 and 32.2.3.

CLK (I)
Pin 21
The clock signal is used for synchronizing the 6845 monitor signals, and is usually equal to the rate at which the characters are displayed on screen.

$\overline{CS}$ (I)
Pin 25
A low-level signal at this chip select connection enables the 6845 for an access by the CPU.

CURSOR (O)
Pin 19
A high-level signal shows that the cursor position is currently scanned.

D0–D7 (I/O)
Pins 26–33
The eight terminals form the bidirectional data bus for an access by the CPU to the internal 6845 registers.

DE (O)
Pin 18
A high-level signal at this display enable pin indicates that the 6845 CRTC is currently providing address and control signals for the displayed region of the screen.

E (I)
Pin 23
A high-low transition of this enable signal activates the data bus, and serves as a clock pulse for the 6845 to read data from or write it into the internal registers.

HS (O)
Pin 39
At this horizontal synchronization terminal the 6845 outputs the signal for horizontal synchronization, and thus causes a horizontal retrace.

LPSTB (I)
Pin 3
(Light Pen Strobe) A pulse from the light pen instructs the 6845 to store the current address for the video RAM in the light pen register. The CPU reads this register and thus determines the position of the light pen on-screen.

MA0–MA13 (O)
Pins 4–17
These 14 memory address terminals provide the memory addresses for the video RAM. MA0–MA13 continuously increase with the line scanning to address the corresponding characters in video RAM successively.

RA0–RA4 (O)
Pins 34–38
These five row address connections specify the current scanline of a character in text mode. Thus, RA0–RA4 characters with a maximum of 32 scanlines can be displayed. In graphics mode RA0–RA4 is often combined with MA0–MA13 into a «large» address, and addresses, for example, the banks of the video RAM.

$\overline{\text{RESET}}$ (I)
Pin 2
A low-level signal at this pin resets the 6845.

RS (I)
Pin 24
A low-level register select signal (RS=0) selects the address register, and a high-level signal (RS=1) selects the 6845 data register for the next read or write access by the CPU.

R/$\overline{W}$ (I)
Pin 22
A high-level read/write signal means that the CPU reads internal 6845 registers; a low-level signal, on the other hand, means that the CPU writes an internal 6845 register.

VS (O)
Pin 40
At this vertical synchronization terminal the 6845 outputs the signal for vertical synchronization, and thus causes a vertical retrace.

Vcc
Pin 20
This pin receives the supply voltage (usually +5 V).

GND
Pin 1
This pin is earthed (usually 0 V).

Of particular importance for displaying texts and graphics on the monitor are the memory address MA0–MA13 and the scanline address RA0–RA4. The following sections discuss how the remaining hardware of a graphics adapter uses these address signals in text and graphics mode.

32.2.2 Character Generation in Text Mode

In text mode every character on-screen is assigned a word of two bytes in video RAM. The low-order byte contains the character code, the high-order byte the attribute. The signal generator on the graphics adapter then displays the character, depending upon the attribute byte value – for example, blinking, with high intensity, inversely, or with a certain colour. Figure 32.5 shows the structure of the video memory word.

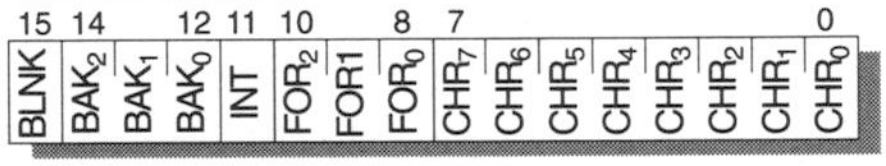

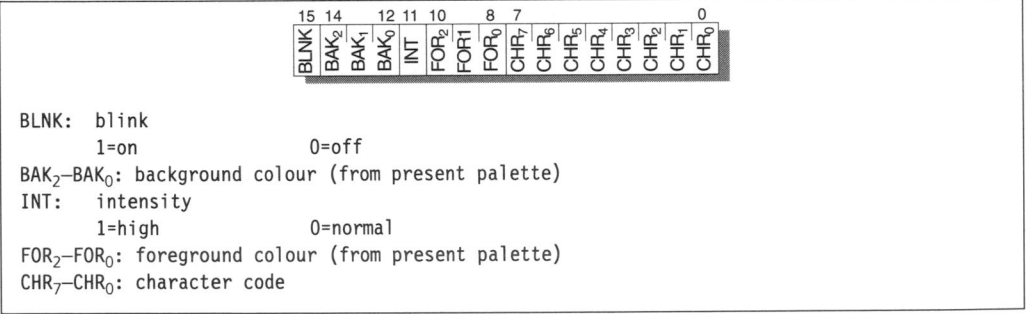

BLNK: blink
1=on 0=off
BAK_2–BAK_0: background colour (from present palette)
INT: intensity
1=high 0=normal
FOR_2–FOR_0: foreground colour (from present palette)
CHR_7–CHR_0: character code

Figure 32.5: Video RAM word structure for a character in text mode.

If the *BLNK* bit is set, the character concerned is displayed blinking. Depending upon the graphics adapter and its manufacturer, the character blinks at a rate of between 1 Hz and 3 Hz. The bits BAK_2-BAK_0 define the background colour of the character; eight different colours are possible. The actual colour not only depends on the value of the bits BAK_2–BAK_0, but also on the graphics adapter, the selected colour palette, whether a monochrome or colour monitor is used, and on the current resolution of the adapter. A set *INT* bit displays the character with a high intensity, that is, bright. The bits FOR_2–FOR_0 determine the character's foreground colour, as BAK_2–BAK_0 do for the background colour. Also here, the colour actually displayed depends upon the graphics adapter, the colour palette selected, whether a monochrome or colour monitor is used, and on the current resolution of the adapter. The eight low-order bits CHR_7–CHR_0 define the code of the displayed character, and serve as an index into the character table in character ROM, or into a character RAM containing the pixel pattern for the characters concerned.

In text mode, every text row is generated by a certain number of scanlines. The Hercules card, for example, uses 14 scanlines for one text row; every character is represented in text mode by a pixel block comprising a height of 14 scanlines and a width of nine pixels. As every character is separated by a narrow space from the next character, and every row by a few scanlines from the next row, the complete block is not occupied by character pixels. For the actual character a 7*11 matrix is available, the rest of the 9*14 matrix remains empty. Also in text mode, every alphanumerical character is displayed as a pixel pattern held in the character ROM or RAM. Figure 32.6 shows, for example, the pixel pattern for an «O» on a Hercules card as it appears on screen (Figure 32.6a).

```
    1       9             1      8
  1 000000000           1 00000000
    001110000             00111000
    011011000             01101100
    110001100             11000110
  5 110001100           5 11000110
    110001100             11000110
    110001100             11000110
    110001100             11000110
    011011000             01101100
 10 001110000          10 00111000
    000000000             00000000
    000000000             00000000
    000000000             00000000
 14 000000000          14 00000000

       (a)                   (b)
```

Figure 32.6: Pixel pattern 'O' in text mode. (a) on-screen; (b) in character ROM.

A «1» means that at the location concerned a pixel with the foreground colour is written, and a «0» that a pixel with the background colour appears. For technical reasons, only eight of the nine pixel columns are actually held in the ROM (Figure 32.6b). The 9th pixel column on the screen is formed for ASCII characters 0–191 and 224–255 by internally generating an empty column in the character generator, and for the block graphics characters with ASCII codes 192–223 by repeating the 8th column to generate the 9th one. The doubling of the 8th column to form the 9th is necessary so that for the horizontal graphics characters, no breaks appear between the individual characters. Thus, in the character ROM every pixel line of a character is eight bits, or exactly one byte, long. How many pixel lines a character comprises is defined by an entry in the 6845 control register *max. scanline*.

In the character ROM the pixel matrices for the 256 different characters are arranged so that the character code as the first index specifies the beginning of the character in ROM. The number of the current scanline for the character is then the second index or the offset, which determines the pixel line (that is, the byte) within the character.

The graphics adapter displays a character in text mode as follows. The 6845 outputs continuous addresses for the video RAM via MA0–MA13. The character in the upper left corner corresponds to the lowest address that the 6845 provides immediately after a vertical retrace. The adapter logic addresses the video RAM by means of this address, and fetches the character code and the attribute. The character code serves for the character generator as the first index into the character ROM. The line address is equal to 0 at this moment, that is, the 6845 addresses the first scanline of the character matrix. According to the timing of the video frequency, the bits of the pixel matrix are now transferred from the shift register to the signal generator. If the signal generator receives a «1» from the shift register, then it generates a video signal corresponding to the foreground colour of the character. If, on the other hand, a «0» arrives then it supplies a video signal corresponding to the background colour. The first scanline is thus displayed on the monitor according to the pixel matrices of the characters in the first text line.

When the electron beam reaches the end of the scanline, the 6845 activates the output HS to issue a horizontal retrace and a horizontal synchronization. The electron beam returns to the beginning of the next scanline. After every scanline (after every horizontal retrace) the 6845 increases the RA0–RA4. This line address forms the offset within the pixel matrix for the character to be displayed. Upon every scanline of the monitor a pixel line of the characters in the text row concerned is thus displayed on the monitor. This means that with the above indicated 9*14 pixel matrix for one character the first text row has been displayed after 14 scanlines. The line address RA0–RA4 returns to the value 0, the 6845 provides new addresses MA0–MA13, and the next text row is output in the same way. If the end of the last scanline is reached, the 6845 resets the address MA0–MA13 and the line address RA0–RA4 to the initial values and enables the output VS to issue a vertical retrace and a vertical synchronization. Exactly one picture has thus been formed on-screen. Because the screen image cannot persist, and as the CPU may overwrite the video RAM with new values, the screen must be refreshed within a short time interval (typically 50–70 Hz). The above-described procedure starts again.

EGA and (S)VGA hold the pixel patterns in a character RAM into which you can also load user-defined characters, and thus define your own characters. For this purpose, you have to fill the character RAM with appropriate pixel matrices. How this works in principle is discussed in Section 32.5.2.

Because of the 5-bit line address RA0–RA4, characters with a maximum height of 32 scanlines are possible. The 14-bit memory address MA0–A13 further enables the addressing of video memories up to 16 k words. In graphics mode, MA0–A13 and RA0–RA4 can be combined into one 19-bit address. The 6845 can then address a video memory of up to 512 k objects.

32.2.3 Character Generation and Free Graphics in Graphics Mode

In graphics mode the bytes in video RAM are no longer interpreted as a character code and attribute. Instead, they directly determine the intensity and colour of the corresponding pixel. The 6845 also outputs the memory addresses MA0–MA13, as well as the line addresses

RA0–RA4 in this case. How the hardware of the graphics adapter interprets these values for addressing the video memory depends upon the adapter card used, and may differ significantly. In most cases the video RAM is divided into several banks addressed by the line address RA0–RA4. The memory address MA0–MA13 then specifies the offset within each bank.

In graphics mode the data in the video RAM is directly transferred to the shift register and the signal generator; character ROM and hardware character generator don't play any role here, and are disabled. If you write, for example via the BASIC command `PRINT "A"`, the character «A» (ASCII 65) in graphics mode onto the screen, then BASIC doesn't write ASCII code 65 to the corresponding location in the video RAM but copies the pixel matrix for the character «A» to the corresponding location in the video RAM.

The power of the graphics mode is not displaying text, but the capability of drawing free graphics and lines. For this purpose, the program must write appropriate values to the corresponding locations in the display memory. A line, for example, is represented by a plurality of identical bit groups or bytes in the video RAM.

Depending upon the number of displayable colours, one pixel on the monitor is assigned more or fewer bits. Monochrome graphics requires only a single bit corresponding to bright (bit=1) or dark (bit=0) per pixel. Multicolour graphics usually assign several bits per pixel; on a VGA with 256 different colours, eight bits or one byte per pixel is required. Thus the storage capacity of the video RAM must increase rapidly with increasing resolution and the rising number of colours in the pictures. (S)VGA boards with a 1 Mbyte video RAM are therefore more or less the standard today; high-resolution graphics adapters for CAD applications may accommodate up to eight Mbtyes of video RAM.

32.2.4 General Video RAM Organization and Structure

The video RAM is organized differently, depending upon the operation mode and graphics adapter used. The following discusses in brief the usual organization. On graphics adapters with a video RAM up to 128 kbytes you may address the whole display memory via the CPU as the normal main memory. But if the video RAM gets larger, then it would overlap the ROM extensions at address c0000h and disturb them. Thus, EGA and (S)VGA boards with more than 128 kbytes of display RAM implement a switch that can be set by software to access various 128 kbyte windows into the much larger video RAM. How these switches are used is (with the exception of SVGA according to the VESA specification) not standardized, and is thus manufacturer-dependent. If you don't know the switch address and method, then there is nothing left but to use the BIOS.

RAM Organization in Text Mode

In text mode the video RAM is regarded as a linear array; the first word is assigned the character in the upper left corner, that is, the character in row 1, column 1. The second word then describes the character in row 1, column 2, etc. Depending upon the text resolution, a varying number of words is necessary to accommodate the whole screen's contents.

Example: the standard resolution of 25 rows with 80 characters each requires 2000 display memory words with two bytes each, thus a total of 4 kbytes of video RAM; high-resolution SuperVGA adapters with 60 rows of 132 characters each need 15 840 bytes.

You can see that the video RAM of most adapters is much larger than a single screen page requires. On an EGA or (S)VGA in text mode the video RAM is therefore divided into *pages*, which can accommodate a whole screen page. The size of the pages depends upon the screen mode and the maximum number of pages, plus, of course, the size of the video RAM. Figure 32.7 shows the division of the video RAM into pages in text mode.

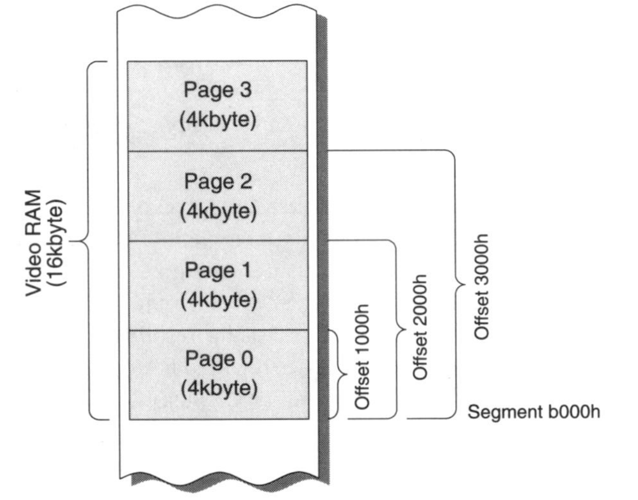

Figure 32.7: Video RAM in text mode divided into several pages.

The 6845 can be programmed so that it starts after a vertical retrace with a memory address MA0–MA13 different from 0. If the start address meets the beginning of a page, then several pages that are separated from each other can be managed in video RAM. Moreover, by altering the start address in the 6845 the pages can be switched rapidly. If the CPU changes the contents of a page that is currently not displayed, then the screen doesn't change. Thus you must distinguish between the active displayed page and the processed one. The PC's BIOS is prepared for managing up to eight pages; for each of them its own cursor is defined.

Example: the first and only page of the Hercules card begins at address b0000h. A blinking character 'A' shall be written into the upper left corner with the foreground colour 7 and the background 0 at a high intensity.

```
MOV ax, b000h        ; load ax with the segment address of the video RAM
MOV es, ax           ; transfer segment address into ES
MOV ah, f8h          ; load attribute 1111 1000 into ah
MOV al, 41h          ; load character code for 'A' into al
MOV es:[00h], ax     ; write attribute and character code into video RAM
```

In general, the address of the display memory word for the character in row i, column j of page k is given by the following equation:

```
address = video segment + page_size * k + 2 * characters_per_row * i + 2 * j
```

Video segment denotes the start address of the video RAM in the PC's address space, and *page_size* denotes the size of a page in the video segment (i, j and k start with 0).

RAM Organization in Graphics Mode

In graphics mode, the situation is more complicated. For example, on the Hercules card the video RAM is divided in graphics mode into four banks per page. The first bank accommodates the pixels for scanlines 0, 4, 8, ... 344, the second bank pixels for scanlines 1, 5, 9, ... 345, the third bank pixels for scanlines 2, 6, 10, ... 346, and the fourth bank pixels for scanlines 3, 7, 11, ... 347. The video RAM of the Hercules card in graphics mode has 64 kbytes, and is divided into two pages of 32 kbytes each. The resolution in graphics mode is 720*348 pixels; every pixel is assigned one bit. Thus 90 bytes are required per line (7120 pixels/8 pixels per byte). For the Hercules card, the address of the byte containing the bit corresponding to the pixel in line i and column j of page k is expressed by the following equation:

```
address(i,j,k) = b0000h + 8000h * k + 2000h * (i MOD 4) + 90 * INT(i/4) + INT(j/8)
```

b0000h characterizes the video segment, 8000h the size of a page, MOD 4 the modulo-4 division by 4, 2000h * (i MOD 4) the offset of the bank which contains the byte, INT the integer part of the corresponding division, 90 * INT(i/4) the offset of line i in the bank, and INT(j/8) the offset of column j in the bank. Figure 32.8 illustrates the division of the video RAM in various pages in graphics mode of the Hercules card.

You can see that addressing one pixel in the video RAM requires a quite extensive procedure. The above-indicated expression is, by the way, only valid on a Hercules card. On a CGA the video memory is divided in graphics mode into only two banks; on an EGA or (S)VGA the situation becomes even more complicated. Details are discussed in Section 32.6.

Access Conflicts

As just mentioned, the CPU can access the video RAM using a simple memory cycle. But besides the CPU, the logic on the graphics adapter also carries out an access to the video RAM according to memory addresses MA0–MA13 provided by the 6845. This may give rise, of course, to conflict if the CPU and the adapter logic address the same chip. The situation becomes particularly critical if the CPU attempts to overwrite an entry while the adapter is just reading it to display it on screen. Whether, finally, the old or the new value gets the upper hand is unpredictable. On the first PC graphics adapter, the CGA, no protection against a simultaneous access to video RAM by the CPU and the adapter logic was implemented; the result was the infamous CGA snow. The CPU access disturbs the read process by the adapter logic (especially in graphics mode) so seriously that the logic determines completely incorrect values, and on the screen bright points appear for a short time; the observer has the impression that snowflakes are blowing over his monitor!

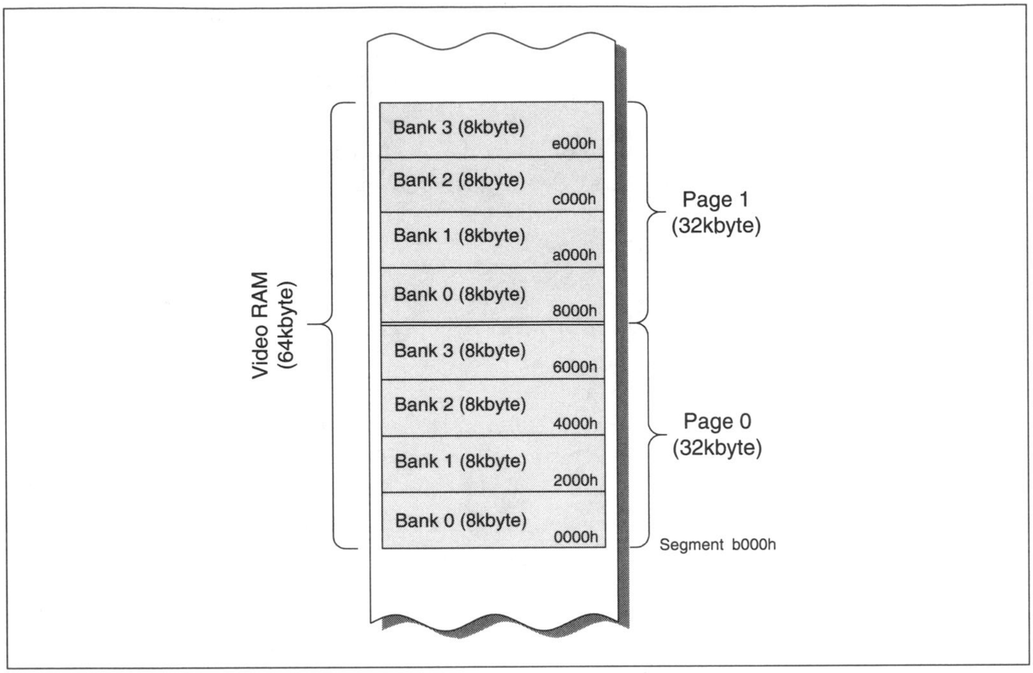

Figure 32.8: Hercules card video RAM splitting into several pages in graphics mode.

On more modern graphics adapters, the engineers have implemented a gate that blocks an access of the CPU to a video RAM bank if the adapter logic is currently reading the same bank. The CPU then inserts more or fewer wait cycles until access to the video RAM is possible. Depending upon the organization of the video RAM and the adjustment of the adapter to the PC system bus, many wait cycles may therefore occur. Benchmark programs that test the access to the display memory report up to 40 wait cycles on a fast 33 MHz Personal Computer. The only two time periods when the CPU has unlimited access to the video RAM (if the adapter doesn't carry out a refresh of its on-board DRAMs, however) are the horizontal and vertical retraces. During these retrace periods the adapter doesn't access the video RAM. The EGA/(S)VGA board and some other graphics adapters can be configured so that they activate IRQ2 at the beginning of a retrace period. The CPU is thus informed, via a hardware interrupt, that an access to the display memory is possible now without disturbing the screen picture.

The best solution of all these problems is to use *dual-port RAM*, which is often also called *VRAM (video RAM)*. Normal RAM chips have a single data port through which they accept write data and provide read data. Depending upon the organization of the RAM chips, one or more data pins are implemented for this port. Whether a read or write access to the RAM occurs, and thus whether the data port is acting as a read or write port, is determined by the DRAM controller via the RAM control signal $\overline{WE}$.

Dual-port RAM chips now have two data ports instead of a single switching data port, so that accesses of two different devices can be serviced concurrently without disturbing each other. On some dual-port memories the function of these two ports as a read and write port, respectively, is fixed. Via the first port, data is only output (read port), and via the second data is only accepted (write port). Some other dual-port memories implement the first port as a parallel and the other as a serial port. Via the first port, the data is input and output in parallel (parallel port), via the other exclusively in a serial manner (serial port). The serial port then provides (beginning with a start address) a certain number of internal memory cells synchronously to an external clock signal. By means of the parallel port, however, any memory cell can be accessed by means of an address. Such dual-port memories are especially suited for graphics adapters, as here the CPU carries out random accesses to the video RAM to read or write data, while the adapter logic is reading the memory in a more or less serial manner to display a row on the monitor.

32.2.5 The Hercules Card and Programming the 6845

With the Hercules card as an example, the programming of the 6845 CRTC for text and graphics modes is discussed in detail.

Advice: if you do not program the control register of the graphics adapter and the 6845 correctly and quickly enough, then your monitor or graphics adapter may be damaged. Carry out such programming only if you are sure that you haven't made any mistake.

During the course of a mode change, monitor and graphics adapter are more or less «up in the air», as far as the synchronization and video signals are concerned. Strong synchronization signals at the wrong time can damage the circuits or the monitor burns completely; therefore be careful!

Table 32.1 lists the I/O ports of the video system on the Hercules card. The I/O ports for the additionally implemented parallel interface are not specified, however.

Port	Register	Write (W) Read(R)
3b4h	6845 index register	W
3b5h	6845 data register	R/W
3b8h	mode control register	W
3b9h	set light pen flip-flop	W
3bah	status register	R
3bbh	reset light pen flip-flop	W
3bfh	configuration register	W

Table 32.1: Hercules card I/O port

For programming the display mode of the Hercules card, besides the 6845 registers, the mode control register, the status register and the configuration register are also important. The two «ports» 3b9h and 3bbh are not real I/O ports, but the addresses 3b9h and 3bbh represent command codes that give rise to the action indicated. To instruct the Hercules card according to these two commands, you simply need to issue an OUT instruction referring to the specified I/O addresses with any value. Figure 32.9 shows the structure of the write-only mode control register.

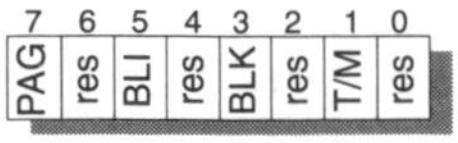

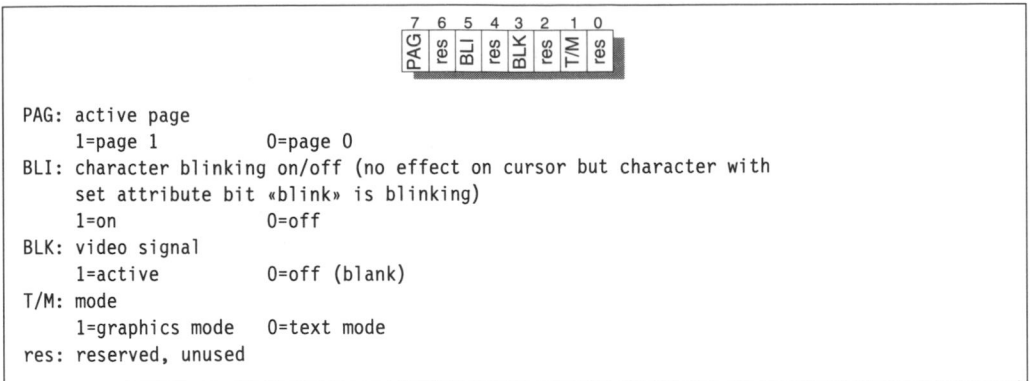

```
PAG: active page
     1=page 1            0=page 0
BLI: character blinking on/off (no effect on cursor but character with
     set attribute bit «blink» is blinking)
     1=on                0=off
BLK: video signal
     1=active            0=off (blank)
T/M: mode
     1=graphics mode     0=text mode
res: reserved, unused
```

Figure 32.9: The mode control register.

With the *PAG* bit you can define the active page to be displayed on-screen. Page 0 is located between addresses b0000h and b7fffh, and page 1 between b8000h and bffffh. Note that page 1 overlaps with the address area of the video RAM on a CGA. If you only use page 0 then you can install two graphics adapters in the same PC, that is, a Hercules card and a CGA. By setting the *BLI* bit you enable the blinking of characters that have a set blink attribute BLNK in the accompanying display memory word. The *BLK* bit determines whether the video signal from the Hercules card is actually transferred to the monitor. A set bit enables the screen display, a cleared one blanks the screen. Thus you can make a monitor safer with BLK by, for example, clearing bit BLK if no keyboard hit has occurred for more than three minutes. After operating any key BLK is set again and the previous picture appears again. This avoids character burn-in on the fluorescent layer of the tube.

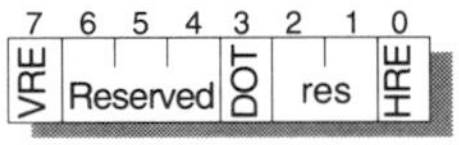

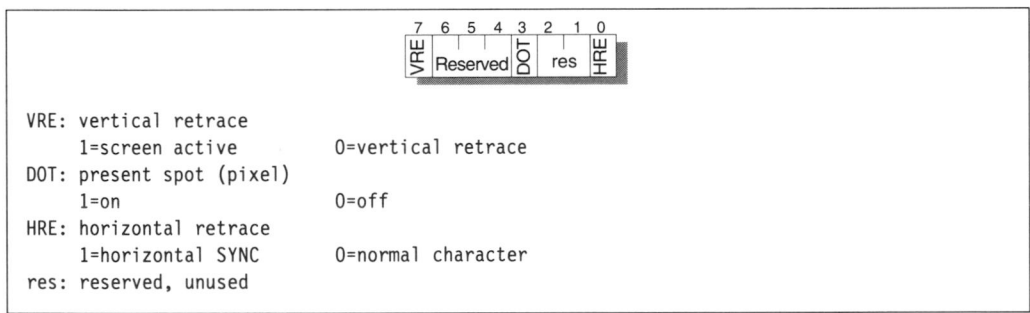

```
VRE: vertical retrace
     1=screen active        0=vertical retrace
DOT: present spot (pixel)
     1=on                   0=off
HRE: horizontal retrace
     1=horizontal SYNC      0=normal character
res: reserved, unused
```

Figure 32.10: The status register.

The *T/M* bit determines the operation mode of the Hercules card. If T/M is set the adapter operates in graphics mode; if T/M is cleared the Hercules card runs in text mode. But be careful: for changing the operation mode it is not sufficient only to clear or set T/M. Instead, you must additionally load the 6845 with parameters that are adjusted according to the intended operation mode. Table 32.3 lists the standard values for the 6845 register in text and graphics mode. The T/M bit in the mode control register mainly controls the character generator, the decoder logic, and the oscillator on the Hercules card, as the memory addresses MA0–MA13 and the line addresses RA0–RA4 output by the 6845 must be interpreted differently in graphics mode and text mode.

The status register of the Hercules card is read-only, and provides some information concerning the current adapter status. If the *VRE* bit is cleared, the monitor is currently executing a vertical retrace, that is, the 6845 has activated the vertical synchronization signal VS. Otherwise the electron beam is writing information onto the screen. The *DOT* bit indicates whether the electron beam is currently writing a bright (DOT=1) or a black point (DOT=0). Finally, you can determine, according to *HRE*, whether the monitor is currently carrying out a horizontal retrace, and the 6845 has activated the horizontal synchronization signal HS for this purpose. If HRE is cleared then a normal character is written onto the screen.

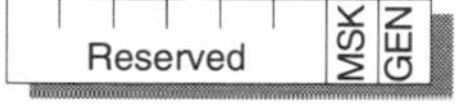

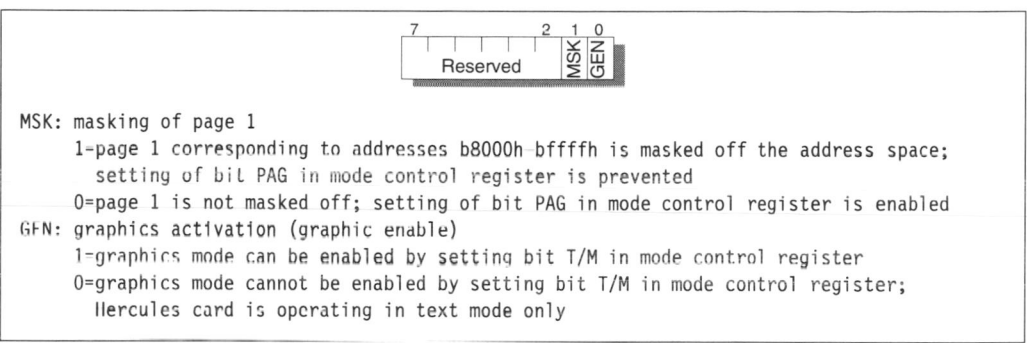

```
MSK: masking of page 1
     1=page 1 corresponding to addresses b8000h-bffffh is masked off the address space;
       setting of bit PAG in mode control register is prevented
     0=page 1 is not masked off; setting of bit PAG in mode control register is enabled
GEN: graphics activation (graphic enable)
     1=graphics mode can be enabled by setting bit T/M in mode control register
     0=graphics mode cannot be enabled by setting bit T/M in mode control register;
       Hercules card is operating in text mode only
```

Figure 32.11: The configuration register.

The write-only configuration register serves to avoid an erroneous switching into graphics mode, and to enable page 1 starting at address b8000h. If the *MSK* bit is set, then page 1 is physically masked off from the PC's address space. This is necessary, for example, if you have additionally installed a CGA on your system and want to use it concurrently with the Hercules card to display coloured graphics at a low resolution. Activating page 1 would give rise to certain disturbances of the CGA and Hercules card. With a cleared MSK bit, page 1 of the Hercules card can also be accessed. If you set bit *GEN*, you can switch between text and graphics mode by means of the T/M bit in the mode control register. If GEN is cleared, T/M has no effect on the operation mode of the adapter; it is always running in text mode, and thus emulates IBM's MDA (monochrome display adapter).

The main job when switching between text and graphics mode is the programming of the 6845. For adjusting all necessary parameters it comprises 19 registers; one index register and 18 control registers. To avoid a wide range being occupied in the I/O address space, the 6845 uses an indexed scheme for addressing its control registers. You first need to input the index of the intended register using the index register at port 3b4h before you access the 6845 control register concerned via the data register at port 3b5h. Table 32.2 lists all 6845 registers together with their indices.

Index	Register	R/W*)	Meaning
0	horizontal total	W	number of characters per line including SYNC minus 1
1	horizontal displayed	W	displayed characters per line
2	HSYNC position	W	position of character where HSYNC is issued
3	SYNC width	W	number of characters for HSYNC per line
4	vertical total	W	number of scanlines including line during vertical retrace minus 1
5	vertical adjust	W	number of scanlines additional to number of character lines
6	vertical displayed	W	number of displayed lines
7	VSYNC position	W	line where vertical retrace starts
8	interlace mode	W	non-interlaced, interlaced or interlaced/video mode
9	max scanline	W	number of scanlines per character line minus 1
10	cursor start	W	first scanline of cursor
11	cursor end	W	last scanline of cursor
12	start address (high)	W	start address of MA0-MA13
13	start address (low)	W	after vertical retrace
14	cursor (high)	R/W	offset of cursor position
15	cursor (low)	R/W	in video RAM
16	light pen (high)	R	offset of light pen position
17	light pen (low)	R	in video RAM

*) R=read, W=write

Table 32.2: 6845 data register indices on the Hercules card.

Notes to Table 32.2:

- For monochrome monitors the horizontal scan period is 54 μs corresponding to 18.43 kHz.
- The monitor has to be refreshed 50 times per second; the total number of character lines and scanlines has to be adapted to this value.
- The oscillator of the Hercules card generates in text mode a time base per character of 0.5625 μs corresponding to 1.778 MHz and in graphics mode a time base of 1.00 μs per character corresponding to 1.00 MHz.
- In text mode the character size is 9*14 pixels and in graphics mode 16*4 pixels.

The following presents the registers and the meaning of their entries in brief. All entry values specified in the example refer to the text mode of the Hercules card, with 25 rows of 80 characters each and a screen refresh rate of 50 Hz. The time base CLK in text mode is equal to 0.5625 μs per character, corresponding to 1.778 MHz.

Horizontal Total (Index 0)

This register defines the line frequency, that is, the frequency of HS. The line frequency is specified in units of character periods. If the 6845-internal character counter has counted up to the value that the register contains, then a new line begins. For one line all characters including HSYNC contribute.

Example: `97`

```
Upon the 97th character the new line begins; thus one line is scanned within
96*0.5625 μs = 54.0 μs, the line frequency is about 18.45 kHz.
```

Horizontal Displayed (Index 1)

This register contains the number of visible characters per row. With every character row the 6845 increments the memory address MA0–MA13 by this value, but keeps the address constant during a horizontal retrace. If the next scanline belongs to the same character row again, then MA0–MA13 is reset to the old value at the beginning of the row, that is, the value of this register is subtracted from the current memory address MA0–MA13. If, on the other hand, the next scanline already belongs to the next character row, then the memory address MA0–MA13 is not altered and is further incremented with every character after the horizontal retrace, that is, after HSYNC. The value in this register must be less than that in the register horizontal total. The less these two values differ, the more rapid is the horizontal retrace. Note that not all monitors can follow such a fast horizontal retrace; interference or even monitor damage may be the consequence.

Example: `80`
`Thus every row displays 80 characters.`

HSYNC Position (Index 2)

This register controls the position in the line where the 6845 activates the HS signal, and thus issues a horizontal retrace; it contains the position of the character concerned. The horizontal retrace may occur after the last displayed character of the line at the earliest, thus the value in this register is always at least equal to the value in the horizontal displayed register; additionally the sum of the register values HSYNC position and SYNC width is lower than the value in the horizontal total register. Increasing the register value gives rise to a left-shift of the screen picture, and vice versa.

Example: `82`
`The activation of HS and the horizontal retrace occurs with the 83rd character of the line. Thus one line comprises 80 displayed characters, one dummy character and 15 characters for the horizontal retrace, so that the horizontal retrace HSYNC requires a time period that corresponds to 15 characters, equal to 8.4375 µs.`

SYNC Width (Index 3)

This register determines the width, that is, the time period of the HS pulse for the horizontal retrace in units of character periods. The synchronization signal VS for the vertical retrace, on the other hand, is fixed to a time period which corresponds to 16 complete scanlines. The register may be loaded with values between 1 and 15 character periods to comply with the requirements of various monitors. A value of 0 means that no HS is provided.

Example: `15`
`The Hercules card provides an HS signal with a width of 15*0.5625 µs = 8.4375 µs. Thus HS is active for nearly the whole horizontal retrace, which lasts for 15 character periods.`

According to the values of the four registers indicated above, a line is displayed in the following manner. After a horizontal retrace the 6845 internally counts up the characters starting with 1, and continuously increases the memory address MA0–MA13 to actually output the number of displayed characters on the monitor. When as many characters have been output as are specified by the horizontal display register, then the 6845 stops counting up the memory address, but the beam continues to move. If the internal counting reaches the value in the HSYNC register position, then the 6845 activates the HS signal for the time period specified by the SYNC register width, and thus issues a horizontal retrace. As soon as the time corresponding to the characters indicated by the horizontal total register has passed, the 6845 begins to output the memory address for the next scanline.

Vertical Total (Index 4)

This register, together with the vertical total adjust register, defines the screen refresh frequency, that is, the frequency of VS. If we calculate the number of character rows necessary to keep a refresh frequency of exactly 50 Hz, for example, then we will get a value in most cases which comprises an integer and a fractional part. On many monitors the refresh rate is generated by means of the mains voltage frequency; in Europe we have 50 Hz, in North America 60 Hz. Thus the 6845 must adapt to this, and may enable the signal VS only at times which comply with the request for a refresh frequency of 50 Hz. For this purpose, this register determines the integer part of the above-mentioned value minus one. The fine-tuning corresponding to the fractional part is carried out by the next register, vertical total adjust.

Example: `25`
`The integer part corresponds to 26 character rows of 760 µs each.`

Vertical Total Adjust (Index 5)

This register carries out the fine-tuning corresponding to the above-mentioned fractional part and specifies that number of scanlines in addition to the total number of rows so that the request for a fixed refresh frequency for the vertical synchronization signal VS is fulfilled.

Example: `6`
`The Hercules card supplies 6 dummy scanlines in addition to the 26 character rows to fulfil the requested frequency of 50 Hz for the signal VS.`

Vertical Displayed (Index 6)

This register specifies the number of visible rows. Note that the register may only contain values that are less than or equal to the value in the vertical total register.

Example: `25`
`The Hercules card displays 25 visible rows.`

VSYNC Position (Index 7)

This register controls the position where the 6845 activates the VS signal, and thus issues a vertical retrace. It contains the position of the row concerned minus 1. The vertical retrace can be carried out after the last displayed row at the earliest. Thus the value in this register is always at least equal to the value in the vertical displayed register. Increasing the register value gives rise to a shift of the screen picture upwards, and vice versa.

Example: 25
The Hercules card issues a vertical retrace after 25 rows, that is, immediately after the beginning of the 26th row.

Interlace Mode (Index 8)

The 6845 can drive the monitor in interlaced and non-interlaced modes. For adjusting the modes the two low-order bits with the following meaning are used:

bit 1	bit 0	mode
0	0	non-interlaced
1	0	non-interlaced
0	1	interlaced
1	1	interlaced/video

Thus the 6845 carries out one non-interlaced mode as well as two different interlaced modes. Figure 32.12 shows the display of character «O» in both cases.

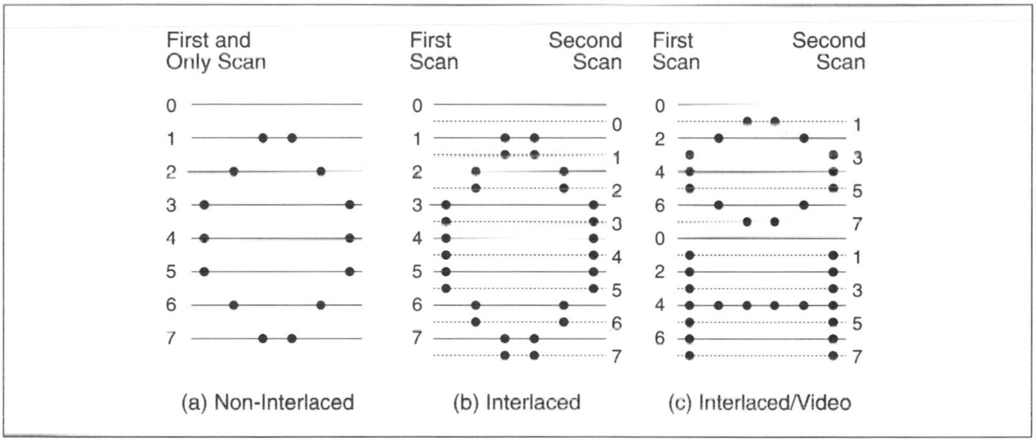

Figure 32.12: (a) Non-interlaced mode; (b) interlaced mode; (c) interlaced/video mode.

In interlaced mode (Figure 32.12b) the VS signal is delayed by half a scanline period, and the two passages of the electron beam write the same information. This enhances the readability of the characters but the character is not displayed at a higher resolution in principle. Also in interlaced/video mode (Figure 32.12c) the VS signal is delayed by half a scanline period, but the two electron beam passages write different information. As is apparent from the figure, the two passages display the odd and then the even-numbered scanlines of the character. The readability of the characters is thus not improved, but the monitor achieves a better resolution at the same bandwidth. The figure shows this by the «H» shown below the «O». For programming an interlaced mode you must pay attention to the following:

- The horizontal total register must contain an odd value.
- For the interlaced/video mode the max. scanline register must contain an odd value, that is, an even number of scanlines must be defined.

- For the interlaced/video mode the vertical displayed register must indicate a value equal to half of the actually required number of visible rows.
- For the interlaced/video mode the two registers cursor start and cursor end must both hold odd or even values.

Example: `2`
`The Hercules card uses non-interlaced mode.`

Max. Scanline (Index 9)

This register defines the number of scanlines per character row; the value is equal to the number of scanlines per character row, minus 1. Upon every scanline of a character row the line address RA0–RA4 is increased by one. Thus 32 scanlines for one character row can be realized at most by means of this 5-bit register. If the electron beam jumps to the next scanline which already belongs to the following character row, then the line address RA0–RA4 is reset to 0. In text mode, the line address serves to address the character's scanline in character ROM, and in graphics mode for addressing that bank in video RAM which contains the entry for the current scanline.

Example: `13`
`The character matrix in text mode comprises 14 scanlines.`

Cursor Start (Index 10)

This register determines the first scanline of the cursor and its behaviour. Bits 0–5 specify the start line, and bits 6 and 7 the behaviour as follows:

bit 6	bit 5	cursor behaviour
0	0	no blinking
0	1	cursor not displayed
1	0	blinking with 16*refresh rate
1	1	blinking with 32*refresh rate

The refresh rate is the time interval between two VS signals. Not all graphics adapters use bits 5 and 6 to define the cursor blinking. This may also be carried out by an external adapter logic and the CURSOR signal. This strategy synchronizes the cursor blink rate with the character blinking.

Example: `11`
`The cursor starts with scanline 11.`

Cursor End (Index 11)

This register defines the last scanline of the cursor.

Example: `12`
`The cursor ends with scanline 12, that is, comprises two scanlines (see example above).`

Start Address High/Low (Index 12/13)

This register pair, with its total of 14 bits (8 bits of the LSB register and 6 bits of the MSB register) defines the start address that the 6845 provides after a vertical retrace as the memory address MA0–MA13. It is thus possible to define several pages in video RAM. If a certain page is to be displayed on-screen, then you have to load the register pair start address with the offset of the intended page relative to the video segment. By altering the start address you can carry out very fast hardware scrolling.

Example: `0`

`The active page starts at offset 0.`

Cursor High/Low (Index 14/15)

The contents of the register pair, with a total of 14 bits (8 bits of the LSB register and 6 bits of the MSB register) defines the position of the cursor in video RAM. For a page change you must also alter the position of the cursor within this new page, relative to the beginning of the video segment. If the 6845 detects that the current memory address MA0–MA13 coincides with the entry in this register pair, then it displays the cursor on-screen and enables the CURSOR signal. But the cursor lines actually appear on screen only if the current scanline corresponding to the line address RA0–RA4 is within the range defined by the registers cursor start and cursor end: otherwise, the pixel pattern of the character underlying the cursor is output.

Example: `0`

`The cursor is located at the beginning of the video RAM, that is, in the upper left corner of the screen.`

Light Pen High/Low (Index 16/17)

The register pair with a total of 14 bits (8 bits of the LSB register and 6 bits of the MSB register) holds the internal 6845 memory address MA0–MA13 upon the rising edge of a signal applied to the input terminal LPSTB. Usually, this is a signal from a light pen that has detected the electron beam. Because of the signal propagation times and the consequent delays compared to the «real» light pen position, the values must be further corrected by software for one or two locations to the left.

Example: `40`

`Without correction the light pen is located in column 40 of row 1; after correcting the value, this corresponds to column 38 or 39 of row 1.`

Table 32.3 summarizes the standard values of the 6845 control register for text and graphics mode of the Hercules card. You can see that the values differ significantly. The reason is the completely different character generation and organization of the video RAM in text and graphics mode.

In text mode the adapter logic reads for every character (for every memory address MA0–MA13) two bytes from the video RAM: the character code as well as the attribute. The character code is used by the character generator as an index into character ROM containing the pixel matrices for the various characters. The 6845 specifies the scanline of each pixel matrix using the line address RA0–RA4. The attribute byte is transferred to the attribute decoder and the signal generator without any further intermediate stage. This gives rise to a displayed character box of 9*14 pixels per character (the register max. scanline contains an entry 13 for this purpose).

Register index	Text	Graphics	Register index	Text	Graphics
0	97	53	7	25	87
1	80	45	8	2	2
2	82	46	9	13	3
3	15	7	10	11	0
4	25	91	11	12	0
5	6	2	12	0	0
6	25	87	13	0	0

Table 32.3: Standard values for text and graphics mode

Also in graphics mode, the adapter logic fetches two bytes for every memory address MA0–MA13; but here every bit corresponds to exactly one pixel on-screen. Moreover, the video RAM is divided into four banks of 8 kbytes each for every page, which are addressed by the line address RA0–RA4. Thus a character that forms the definition base for the synchronization signals in graphics mode comprises 16*4 pixels. The time base for one character is therefore equal to 1 μs instead of the 0.5625 μs in text mode. Because of the significantly different form of the character matrix, altered entries in the 6845 control registers are also required. The number of displayed characters is therefore only equal to 45; with the character box width of 16 pixels, this corresponds exactly to 720 points on-screen, namely the horizontal resolution of the Hercules card. The number of displayed rows is a result of the smaller row's «thickness» of only four scanlines per character row – larger than in text mode – namely equal to 87. This corresponds to 87*4=348 scanlines, that is, the vertical resolution of the adapter in graphics mode. The max. scanline register contains the value 3, corresponding to four scanlines. Thus every line's address corresponds to one bank of the video RAM; the division into banks is now clear. The other register values, too, are adapted to the altered character format.

By changing the various register values you can therefore generate different screen formats. But remember that fixed-frequency monitors cannot always stand the programmed mode, and may be damaged by incorrect register values. Only the so-called multisync monitors, which can adjust to a very broad range of horizontal and vertical frequencies, carry out such experiments without being damaged.

32.3 Most Important Adapter Types and Their Characteristics

The following discusses the currently most important graphics adapters. Compatible adapters, particularly, usually have a nearly infinite number of display modes. The following list therefore mainly refers to the original adapters, and doesn't make any claim for completeness. Table 32.4 summarizes the possible standard video modes, together with the accompanying resolutions and the adapters required. As is the case for the other PC components, here also downward compatibility holds. For example, the EGA can carry out all CGA video modes, but not the new modes of the VGA.

Mode number	Mode type	Text lines	Text columns	Resolution	Colours	Pages	Adapter MDA	CGA	HGC	EGA	VGA
0	text	25	40	320*200	16	8		x			
0	text	25	40	320*350	16	8				x	
0	text	25	40	360*400	16	8					x
1	text	25	40	320*200	16	8		x			
1	text	25	40	320*350	16	8				x	
1	text	25	40	360*400	16	8					x
2	text	25	80	640*200	16	4		x			
2	text	25	80	640*350	16	4				x	
2	text	25	80	720*400	16	4					x
3	text	25	80	640*200	16	4		x			
3	text	25	80	640*350	16	4				x	
3	text	25	80	720*400	16	4					x
4	graphics	25	40	320*200	4	1		x		x	x
5	graphics	25	40	320*200	4	1		x		x	x
6	graphics	25	80	640*200	2	1		x		x	x
7	text	25	80	720*350	mono	1	x		x	x	
7	text	25	80	720*400	mono	8					x
–	graphics	25	80	720*348	mono	1			x		
13	graphics	25	40	320*200	16	8				x	x
14	graphics	25	80	640*200	16	4				x	x
15	graphics	25	80	640*350	mono	2				x	x
16	graphics	25	80	640*350	16	2				x	x
17	graphics	30	80	640*480	2	1					x
18	graphics	30	80	640*480	16	1					x
19	graphics	25	40	320*200	256	1					x

Table 32.4: Standard video modes

32.3.1 MDA – Everthing is Very Grey

he first PCs and XTs were equipped with IBM's MDA (*monochrome display adapter*). The MDA can only be operated in text mode. It is very interesting that IBM intended the MDA for professional use, but the graphics-capable CGA for home use. I think the reason was that the MDA has a character matrix of 9*14 pixels, but the CGA only one of 8*8 pixels. Table 32.5 lists the main adapter parameters.

The specified frequencies refer to the usual MDA use with a monochrome monitor of a fixed horizontal and vertical frequency. By altering the 6845 register values, other values may also be adjusted. At the respective port addresses the same 6845 registers are present as on the Hercules card. The MDA doesn't have its own BIOS, but is accessed via the system BIOS on the motherboard. The video RAM is organized linearly; every text character on the screen is assigned a word in video RAM which specifies character code and attribute.

	Text mode
video segment	b000h
size of video RAM	4 kbytes
screen pages	1
video controller	CRTC 6845
port addresses of 6845	3b0h–3bfh
character matrix	9*14
effective character size	7*9
resolution (pixels)	720*350
colours	mono
monitor control signals	digital
horizontal frequency*)	18.432 kHz
vertical frequency*)	50 Hz
video bandwidth*)	16.257 MHz
own BIOS	no

*) if connected to a standard monochrome monitor with fixed frequency

Table 32.5: MDA parameters

32.3.2 CGA – It's Getting to Be Coloured

The CGA (*colour graphics adapter*) was the first graphics-capable adapter from IBM (but with a very poor resolution of a maximum at 640*200 pixels). Just as bad is the representation of characters in text mode, as the character matrix consists of 8*8 pixels only. Table 32.6 summarizes the most important CGA parameters.

	Text mode	Graphics mode
video segment	b800h	b800h
size of video RAM	16 kbytes	16 kbytes
screen pages	4 ... 8	1
video controller	CRTC 6845	CRTC 6845
port addresses of 6845	3d0h–3dfh	3d0h–3dfh
character matrix	8*8	8*8
effective character size	7*7, 5*7	7*7, 5*7
max. resolution (pixels)	640*200	640*200
colours	16	4
monitor control signals	digital	digital
horizontal frequency*)	15.75 kHz	15.75 kHz
vertical frequency*)	60 Hz	60 Hz
video bandwidth*)	14.30 MHz	14.30 MHz
own BIOS	no	no

*) if connected to a standard colour monitor with fixed frequency

Table 32.6: CGA parameters

In text mode the video RAM is divided (depending upon the resolution) into eight (25 rows with 40 columns each) or four (25 rows with 80 columns each) pages of 2 kbytes or 4 kbytes each. Within the page concerned, the characters are addressed linearly. The CGA can display 16 different colours in text mode. Figure 32.13 shows the assignment of attribute bits and the displayed colour.

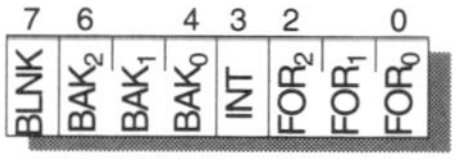

BLNK: character blinking
1=character is blinking 0=character is not blinking

BAK_2–BAK_0: background colour

000=black	001=blue	010=green	011=cyan
100=red	101=magenta	110=brown	111=white

INT, FOR_2–FOR_1: intensity and foreground colour

0000=black	0001=blue	0010=green	0011=cyan
0100=red	0101=magenta	0110=brown	0111=white
1000=grey	1001=light blue	1010=light green	1011=light cyan
1100=light red	1101=light magenta	1110=yellow	1111=bright white

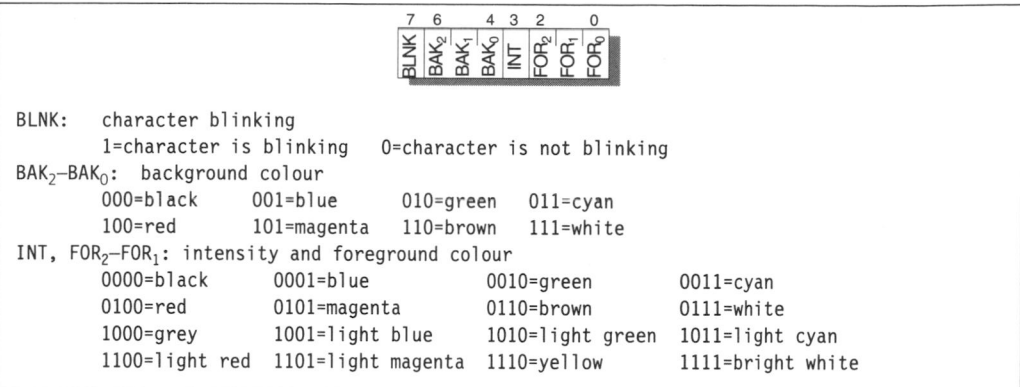

Figure 32.13: Attribute bits and corresponding colours in CGA text mode.

The CGA attribute decoder decodes the attribute byte and provides a corresponding RGBI signal (red-green-blue-intensity) to actually display the colour on the monitor. The colour and intensity of the pixels is therefore passed in a digital form to the monitor; you may only connect a digital RGB monitor to a CGA. The pixel colours in the three CGA graphics modes are generated differently. The mode control register at port 3d8h, and the colour select register at port 3d9h are decisive. Table 32.7 lists the CGA I/O ports.

Port	Register	Write (W) Read (R)
3d4h	6845 index register	W
3d5h	6845 data register	R/W
3d8h	mode control register	W
3d9h	colour select register	W
3dah	status register	R
3dbh	clear light pen flip-flop	W
3dch	set light pen flip-flop	W

Table 32.7: CGA I/O ports

The CGA is supported by the system BIOS routines on the motherboard in graphics mode, too, and therefore doesn't need any BIOS extension, unlike the EGA and (S)VGA. The system BIOS routines comprise, for example, the setting and reading of pixels, the set-up of various screen modes, and screen page management.

32.3.3 Hercules – The Non-Fitting Standard

The Hercules graphics card (HGC) in text mode emulates the MDA precisely; all parameters coincide. This also means, for example, that in text mode a video RAM of only 4 kbytes is available, although the Hercules card is equipped as standard with 64 kbytes. Unlike the MDA, it may also be operated in monochrome graphics mode, whose resolution corresponds to about the pixel resolution in text mode. Only the two last lines 348 and 349 are no longer displayed, but used already for the vertical retrace. The resolution incompatible with the CGA and the different register addresses are the reason why the Hercules card cannot be serviced by the motherboard's system BIOS. As this adapter, moreover, doesn't have its own BIOS either, a driver is required or the graphics programs must program the Hercules card directly. Earlier this gave rise to many problems. But meanwhile, the Hercules resolution became a *de facto* standard, supported by nearly all programs. Only some mouse drivers have difficulties in displaying the mouse pointer on a Hercules. Details on the adapter programming and the division of the video RAM in graphics mode are discussed in Sections 32.2 and 32.6. Table 32.8 summarizes all the main adapter parameters.

	Text mode	**Graphics mode**
video segment	b000h	b000h
size of video RAM	4 kbytes	64 kbytes
screen pages	1	2
video controller	CRTC 6845	CRTC 6845
port addresses of 6845	3b0h–3bfh	3b0h–3bfh
character matrix	9*14	9*14
effective character size	7*9	7*9
resolution (pixels)	720*350	720*348
colours	mono	mono
monitor control signals	digital	digital
horizontal frequency*)	18.432 kHz	18.432 kHz
vertical frequency*)	50 Hz	50 Hz
video bandwidth*)	16.257 MHz	16.257 MHz
own BIOS	no	no

*) if connected to a standard monochrome monitor with a fixed frequency

Table 32.8: Hercules adapter parameters

The second screen page starts at address b8000h, and thus overlaps with the CGA video RAM. On a Hercules card you have the option to block and mask the second page out of the CPU's address space. You can thus use two graphics adapters in a PC, a CGA and a Hercules with a blocked second page. Some debuggers use this to display the investigated code on one monitor and the current screen contents of the program on the other.

32.3.4 EGA – More Colours and a Higher Resolution

The really very poor graphics capabilities of the CGA (only suitable really in the children's room but not for the office), and the advance of business graphics, required an enhanced graphics adapter very soon. For this purpose, the CGA was extended to get an EGA. This adapter allows a maximum resolution of 640*350 pixels, and 16 colours out of a palette of 64 colours can be displayed simultaneously. I will discuss soon what the meaning of the somewhat dubious palette is, but let's first look at few useful but largely neglected features of the EGA:

– User-defined character sets: unlike MDA, HGC and CGA which operate with the fixed defined character sets in the ROM of the character generators, on an EGA you can define and load your own character matrices. Thus you are not limited to the characters defined by the BIOS.

- Two concurrently usable character sets: by redefining the blink bit 3 in the attribute byte (with function 10h, subfunction 03h of INT 10h) into a bit for distinguishing two character sets, you can display 512 different characters instead of 256 with an EGA. For this purpose, a 9-bit code composed of the 8-bit character code and the 1-bit «blink» code is used.
- Screen splitting: the screen can be split by hardware into two partial screens; the EGA displays information in them from two completely different video RAM locations.
- Video RAM division into several image layers: in the three new 16-colour EGA modes 13, 14, and 16, the image is divided into four layers which can be enabled or disabled by a simple register access. Some CAD programs use this multilayer technique to overlap several drawings by hardware.

Compatibility as the main and, often also cursed, maxim of PCs is also valid for EGA, of course: all CGA modes can also be carried out by the EGA. With the MDA's text mode, however, the EGA has some problems, as the requested resolution of 720*350 points corresponding to a character matrix of 9*14 pixels doesn't fit the internal EGA timing at all. But text modes 2 and 3 of the CGA are revamped to a resolution of 640*350 points corresponding to a character matrix of 8*14 pixels. This is nearly as good as the MDA text, and is additionally coloured (with 16 possible colours). The register addresses in CGA-compatible modes are equal to 3dxh; in pure EGA modes, on the other hand, they are equal to 3cxh. You will find these and other parameters given in Table 32.9.

	Text mode	**Graphics mode**
video segment	b800h	a000h
size of video RAM	64–256 kbytes	64–256 kbytes
screen pages	1 ... 8	1 ... 8
video controller	EGA–CRTC	EGA–CRTC
port addresses	3d0h–3dfh	3c0h–3dfh
character matrix	8*14, 8*8	8*14, 8*8
effective character size	7*9, 7*7	7*9, 7*7
resolution (pixels)	640*350	640*350
colours	16 of 64	16 of 64
monitor control signals	digital	digital
horizontal frequency	15.7–21.8 kHz	15.7–21.8 kHz
vertical frequency	60 Hz	60 Hz
video bandwidth	14.3–16.3 MHz	14.3–16.3 MHz
own BIOS	yes	yes

Table 32.9: EGA parameters

As a further feature, the EGA has its own BIOS which controls the adapter in the new modes, and is usually present in the CPU's address space starting at the segment address c000h. The system BIOS on the motherboard only supports MDA and CGA, as you know; thus the new operation modes cannot be set up by this BIOS as the EGA has a vast number of new registers which deal, for example, with the setup of the colour palette not implemented on the CGA. Table 32.10 summarizes the EGA I/O ports.

Port	Register	Write (W) Read (R)
3c0h	index/data register of attribute controller	W
3c2h	input status register 0	R
3c4h	sequencer index register	W
3c5h	sequencer data register	W
3cah	graphics position register 2	W
3cch	graphics position register 1	W
3ceh	graphics controller index register	W
3cfh	graphics controller data register	W
3b4h	CRTC index register	W
3b5h	CRTC data register	W
3bah	input status register 1	R
3d4h	CRTC index register	W
3d5h	CRTC data register	W
3dah	input status register 1	R

Table 32.10: EGA I/O ports

You can see that there is a large number of I/O ports and because of the three index/data register pairs, even more registers at these ports. Note that most of the registers are write-only. Thus the CPU is unable to determine the current video mode with its register values. With a detailed description of all EGA registers, a whole book could be filled; and this has actually already been done by others. Therefore, I restrict myself to the most important facts here.

With the CRTC index and data register you can access the registers of the CRTC chip. On an EGA you will find a controller that is improved compared to the 6845 and adapted to the special EGA's requirements.

The EGA, besides the usual monitor, also has an additional so-called feature connector. Using the feature connector an external device has the opportunity to affect the picture setup of the EGA and, for example, to provide its own clock signal: but I don't know of any important device that makes use of this.

The registers of the attribute controller are responsible for the displayed palette colours. On an EGA the attribute decoder can therefore be programmed to display various colours. The programmable sequencer controls the read-out of the video RAM and the conversion of the byte data into serial data for the generation of pixels on-screen. The CRTC provides the control signals for the monitor, as usual.

Despite its compatibility, the physical organization of the video RAM is very different between the EGA and the previous adapters. On an EGA the complete video RAM is divided into four parallel memory layers. This means that every one of these four layers starts at address a0000h; thus the four layers overlap. A write access to the byte address a0000h transfers the byte value into all four layers simultaneously. Under the control of the map mask and the read map select register, you may enable the various layers for a read or write process. How you may use these two registers is discussed in Section 32.6. Figure 32.14 shows a diagram for the four parallel memory layers described.

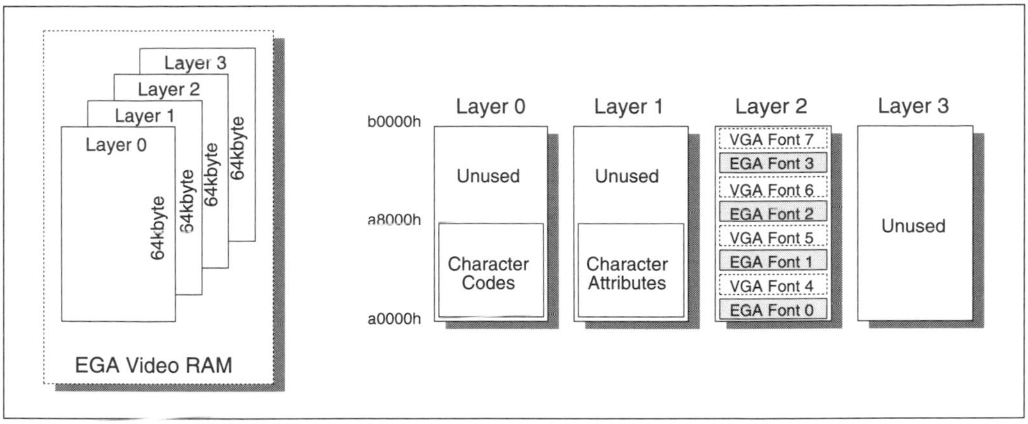

Figure 32.14: The EGA memory layers.

Although at a first glance this physical arrangement of the four layers appears strange, nevertheless, it does make sense: in the real mode address space of the PC the range between a0000h and bffffh is reserved for the graphics adapter. These 128 kbytes are far too little for a fully equipped EGA with 256 kbytes of display memory. Therefore, one has two possibilities:

- Divide the 256 kbytes into two or more banks, and switch between them with a programmable register; expanded memory follows a similar concept.
- Divide the 256 kbytes into two or more parallel layers, and enable or disable certain layers for an access.

The second possibility has a major advantage for a graphics adapter: if, for example, all layers are enabled in parallel for a write access, then writing one byte on an EGA, with its four parallel layers, gives rise to a simultaneous transfer of four bytes into all memory layers. If fewer layers are enabled, then the byte is transferred to correspondingly fewer memory layers. In the 16-colour EGA modes that assign one pixel four bits, the video RAM is organized in this way, in which every one of the four pixel bits is located in its own layer. By enabling or disabling the various layers, for example, three of the four pixel bits can be set or cleared at once. If one employs the first of the two methods indicated above, one would have to switch the banks more often. Furthermore, with parallel memory layers the adapter logic has to supply only a single byte address to fetch four bytes in a single cycle. Thus the graphics adapter requires fewer address lines and operates more quickly.

Figure 32.14 shows what information the four memory layers hold in text mode. Character codes and attributes are stored in the parallel layers 0 and 1. But how can compatibility with the RAM organization of the CGA be kept when it requires a linear array of code–attribute pairs? Very simply: the EGA has an address transfomation logic that connects layers 0 and 1 in such a way that they appear to the CPU in the usual manner, that is, in the order code_0 (layer 0), attribute_0 (layer 1), code_1 (layer 0), attribute_1 (layer 1), etc. But the adapter logic itself accesses the video RAM according to its physical organization, as parallel memory layers, when reading data for displaying it on the monitor.

A further significant difference compared to MDA, HGC and CGA is that on the EGA in text mode, part of the video RAM is reserved for the character generator; that is, the complete layer 2. There the character generator stores the character definition table for converting the character code into pixel patterns on-screen. RAM may be overwritten, of course, so that new character tables can be loaded, or the loaded ones can be altered. It's best to use the 10h function of INT 10h for this purpose. Details on this subject are given in Section 32.5.2. From Figure 32.14 it is apparent that on an EGA a maximum of four character definition tables can be installed; on a (S)VGA eight are possible.

On a CGA you may only choose from 16 colours. In text mode they are unrestrictedly available for the foreground, but in graphics mode you may choose from only four colours, each dependent upon the selected CGA palette; that is, only four of the 16 possible colours can be displayed simultaneously. The EGA also extends the number of simultaneously displayable colours to 16 in text mode. They can be selected from a palette of 64 different colours. This corresponds to the four foreground bits in the attribute of the text mode, or the four bits in the four memory levels in graphics mode.

For the colours actually displayed the palette register is decisive. It is connected between the «colour value» and the monitor driver (see Figure 32.15).

5	4	3	2	1	0
SRED	SGRE	SBLU	PRED	PGRE	PBLU

```
SRED: secondary red          PRED: primary red
      1=on      0=off              1=on      0=off
SGRE: secondary green        PGRE: primary green
      1=on      0=off              1=on      0=off
SBLU: secondary blue         PBLU: primary blue
      1=on      0=off              1=on      0=off
```

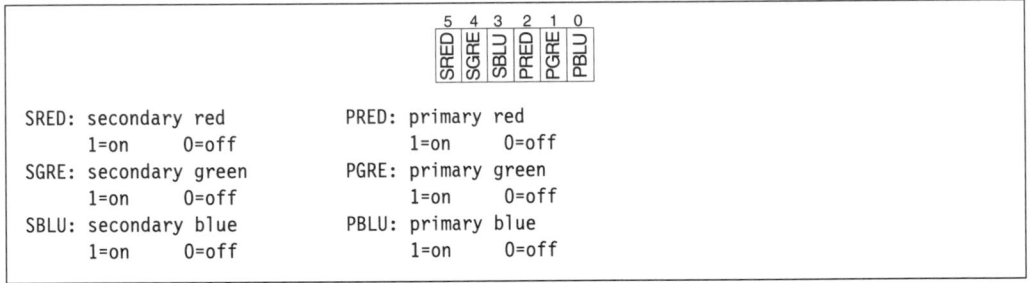

Figure 32.15: Colour generation with palette registers.

On the CGA the four colour bit values (for example, in the attribute byte in text mode) specify the colour to be displayed directly. On the EGA, however, the colour value points to one of 16 entries in the palette register. This entry finally determines the colour actually displayed. Every entry has six bits, and can therefore specify one of $2^6 = 64$ different colours. This happens as follows:

- The 64 colours are formed from all possible combinations of three primary and three secondary colours; the primary colours are much brighter than the secondary ones.
- A set bit in the palette register gives rise to an activation of the corresponding signal line to the monitor if the colour value of the current pixel or character points to the corresponding register.

It thus becomes apparent that on the EGA 64 different colours are possible using the six bits in the palette register, but with the four colour value bits only 16 different registers can be addressed. In the CGA-compatible video modes 4–6 with fewer than four bits per pixel, and thus fewer than 16 colour values, only the corresponding palette registers with the colour values 0–3 (modes 4 and 5) or 0 and 1 (mode 6) are addressed. The remaining palette registers are unused here. For changing the palette register entries the function 10h of INT 10h is available (see Section 32.5.2).

By altering the palette registers you can change the colour of the screen display instantaneously. The change affects all characters or pixels whose colour value points to the altered register; no change of the colour value itself is required for this. For example, you can program a seemingly rotating torus by outputting a circle or ellipse on-screen, which consists of line parts with alternating colour values. Now you only need to continuously switch the corresponding palette register entries and the observer gets the impression that the torus is rotating. The other possible strategy, to alter the colour values themselves, continuously requires much more programming overhead and execution time. The observer therefore gets the impression of a flickering torus.

32.3.5 VGA – Colours and More Colours

Starting with the PS/2, IBM introduced a new and, compared to the earlier models, significantly improved adapter: the *video graphics adapter* or the *video graphics array* (VGA). The main characteristic is not the resolution extended to 640*480 pixels, but the extension of the colour palette to 2^{18} = 262 144 different colours, from which a maximum of 256 can be displayed simultaneously. This, of course, is no longer possible with a digital colour signal to the monitor, as 18 colour signal lines would be required. VGA, therefore, outputs an analogue signal that drives an analogue monitor. With the 262 144 different colours very realistic images can be generated. VGA is equipped as standard with a display memory of 256 kbytes; newer VGA adapters even have a video memory with 1 Mbyte of RAM. They can display 1024*768 pixels with 256 different colours. Table 32.11 summarizes the main parameters of the standard VGA.

	Text mode	Graphics mode
video segment	b000h	a000h
size of video RAM	256 kbytes	256 kbytes
screen pages	1–8	1–8
video controller	VGA–CRTC	VGA–CRTC
port addresses of 6845	3b0h–3dfh	3b0h–3dfh
character matrix	9*16	9*16
effective character size	7*9	7*9
resolution (pixels)	640*480	640*480
colours	256	256
monitor control signals	analogue	analogue
horizontal frequency	31.5 kHz	31.5 kHz
vertical frequency	50–70 Hz	50–70 Hz
video bandwidth	28M Hz	28 MHz
own BIOS	yes	yes

Table 32.11: VGA parameters

For compatibility reasons, the VGA can carry out all CGA and EGA modes, and in contrast to EGA the VGA also recognizes the MDA text mode 7. The resolution in this mode is 720*400 pixels, corresponding to a character box of 9*16 points. This is 50 scanlines more in the vertical direction than the original MDA text mode. Of course, you are free to install your own character sets, too, as was the case on the EGA. But the VGA allows up to eight different character definition tables.

On the VGA all control registers can also be read, so that the CPU has the opportunity to determine the current video mode and the accompanying parameters and to store them for future use. The VGA BIOS implements the function 1ch which exclusively backs up and restores the video status. This is, for example, of importance for a multitasking operating system if the various programs frequently alter the video mode.

On the EGA the set bits in the palette registers give rise to an activation of the corresponding colour signal lines to the monitor. On a VGA this is no longer possible, but the colour generation is controlled by means of 256 registers in a video DAC (*digital-analogue converter*). Every register is divided into three groups of six bits each. The first bit group specifies the red, the second the green, and the third the blue contribution to the colour. Every primary colour can be added to the actual colour with $2^6=64$ shades; this leads to the 262144 different VGA colours. As only 256 video DAC registers exist, only 256 of these 256 k colours can be displayed simultaneously. You may access the DAC colour registers using function 10h of INT 10h, beginning with subfunction 10h.

The conversion of the colour values in the text attribute or the pixel values in graphics mode differs in the various modes. Figure 32.16a shows how the conversion of a colour value into a colour signal to the monitor is carried out if the VGA operates in text mode or a graphics mode (except VGA mode 19).

As is the case on the EGA, the colour value first selects one of 16 palette registers. Unlike the EGA, the palette registers don't determine the colours directly with their bits, but the value held by the selected palette register represents an index that selects one of the 256 video DAC colour registers. Then the selected DAC colour register determines the actual colour and the DAC provides an analogue signal to the monitor according to the 18-bit colour value stored there.

Also on a VGA, the palette registers are six bits wide so that $2^6=64$ video DAC registers may be addressed. The other 192 registers remain unreachable at first, but you can change this situation with the VGA's colour select register; it is available with index 14h via the index register 3c0h at data port 3c0h. The 256 video DAC registers are divided into four pages of 64 colours each, and the colour select register provides the address 0–3 of the currently enabled colour page. The value of the palette register then serves as an offset within such a colour page. The bits 2 and 3 of the colour select register specify the current colour page; all other bits are equal to 0. Four different colour pages can thus be managed.

Example: `enable colour page 2 corresponding to the DAC colour registers 128 to 191.`

```
OUT 3c0h, 14h  ; address colour select register
OUT 3c0h, 08h  ; select page 2 corresponding 00001000b (bit 3=1, bit 2=0)
```

But note that the VGA BIOS (except VGA mode 19) preloads only the first 64 DAC colour register with EGA-compatible colour values. If you want to use the other 192 colour registers, then you must load them with the intended values using function 10h of INT 10h.

In VGA mode 19 with its 256 different colours, the pixel values 0–255 select one of the 256 different DAC colour registers directly (see Figure 32.16b). The palette registers don't play any role here, but transfer the address values 0–15 to the video DAC unaltered. Address values 16–255 bypass the palette register in this mode in any case.

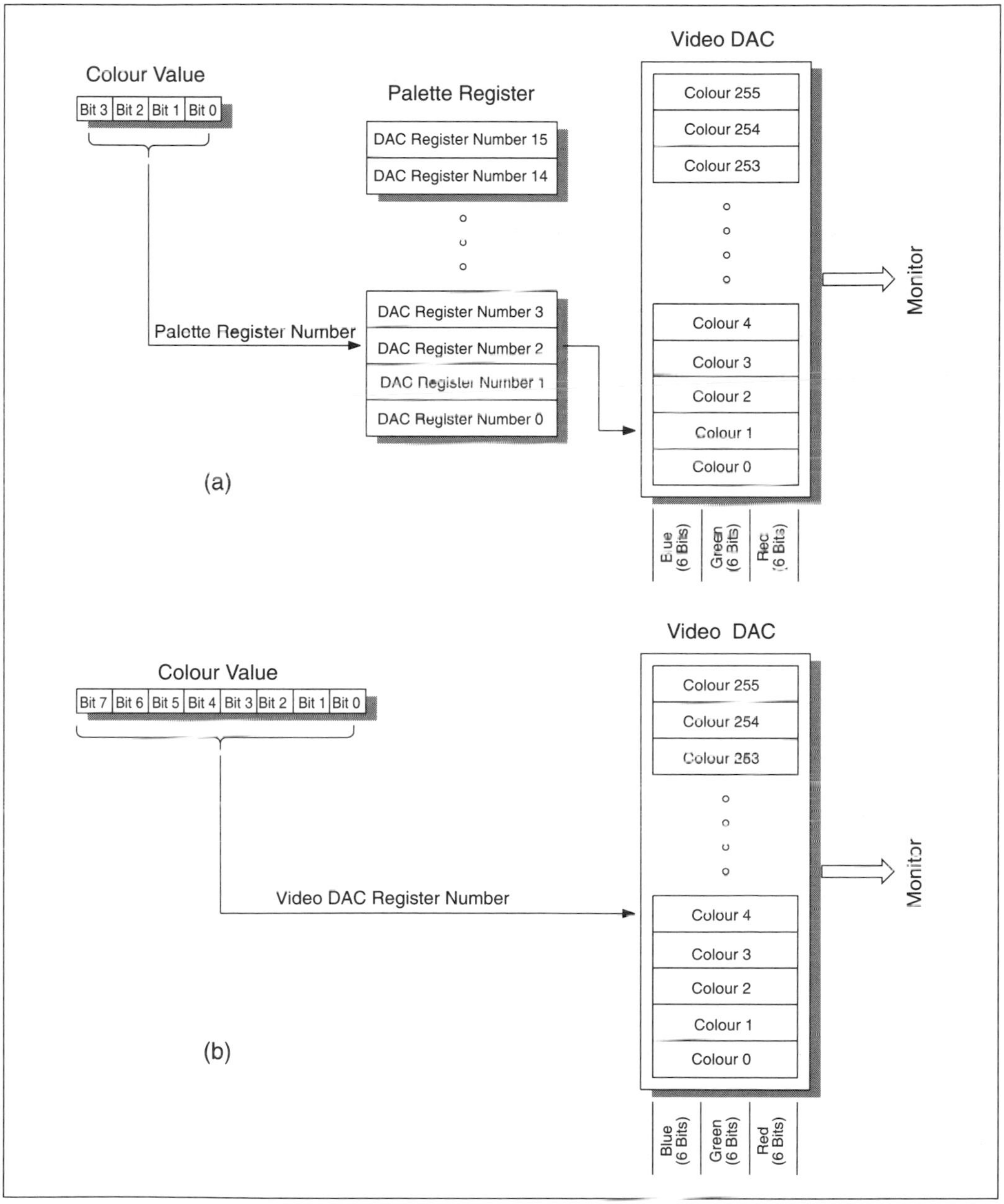

Figure 32.16: The colour generation with the video DAC registers. (a) Colour generation in text mode and graphics modes (except Mode 19); (b) colour generation in VGA Mode 19 with 256 colours.

32.3.6 VESA SVGA – High-Resolution Standard

The VGA standard according to IBM ends with a resolution of 640*480 pixels and a maximum of 256 from 64 k colours. Even a short time after the introduction of VGA cards onto the market, this was already inadequate. Ambitious manufacturers brought fast graphic adapters with a resolution of 1024*768 pixels, more colours and a 1 Mbyte video RAM or more to the market. While the principal functionality (the production of colours by the DAC register, or the linear arrangement of the pixels in the video memory with a quantity of bits corresponding to the selected depth of colour) has remained unchanged, incompatibility between high-resolution VGAs from different manufacturers has quickly developed, especially in two specific areas:

- Addressing the large video memory through the 64 k window after a0000.
- Setting of the resolution in text or graphic mode by the VGA BIOS.

After quite some time, VESA came up with the *Super VGA* standard to solve this problem. Here, the structure of the video RAM and the new SVGA BIOS functions are laid down. In the following section, I only wish to describe SVGA briefly, because the detailed specification has already been published (available from VESA), which includes details about the actual programmable interface for SVGAs (and also the subsequent accelerators and TIGA), and the graphic functions of Windows (NT) and OS/2. In effect, the ever increasing resolutions and depths of colours of the video adapters are initiated by the advances in operating systems with a graphic-oriented user interface. It is the responsibility of the adapter manufacturers to produce drivers for Windows (NT) and OS/2 – they know the peculiarities (and tricks) of their own adapters better than anyone. As a programmer, you should use the standard graphic adapter interface of the operating system, in order to prevent compatibility problems. You will find the main parameters of SVGA in Table 32.12.

	Text mode	**Graphic mode**
video segment	b000h	a000h
size of the video-RAM	1 Mbyte and more	1 Mbyte and more
screen pages	depending on video RAM	depending on video RAM
video controller	SVGA CRTC	SVGA CRTC
port addresses	3b0h–3dfh	3b0h–3dfh
character matrix	9*16 (typical)	9*16 (typical)
effective character size	7*9 (typical)	7*9 (typical)
resolution (pixel)	132*60 (max.)	1280*1024
colours	256	256 (24 Million max.)
monitor control signals	analogue	analogue
horizontal frequency	to 90 kHz	to 90 kHz
vertical frequency	50–90 Hz	50–90 Hz
video bandwidth	to 100 MHz	to 100 MHz
own BIOS	yes	yes

Table 32.12: Parameters of the SVGA

Addressing of the large video memory is solved in SVGA, as in VGA, by the bank structure of the video RAM. Each 64 kbyte or 128 kbyte segment is addressed with the help of a so-called *bank select register*. Its four least significant bits select the bank which is mapped into the window after a0000h. You will find more details concerning the direct addressing of the video memory in Section 32.6.

The second problem, namely the setting of the resolution in text or graphic mode with the VGA BIOS, is achieved by expanding the standard video modes to include the *super VGA video modes*. Currently, 13 new modes have been defined. Because manufacturer's of graphic adapters used the «highest» VGA mode 19 (320*200 pixels with 256 colours) at that time for the manufacturers own mode codes, VESA has assigned new SVGA modes with values greater than 100h. INT 10h has been expanded by the SVGA function 4fh; it forms the interface to the SVGA BIOS. You will find more details in Section 32.5.3.

32.3.7 8514/A and Windows Accelerator – One More Window

Even SVGA systems reach their limits at 256 colours and a resolution of 1024*768 pixels. Up until now, all graphic adapters have been quite dumb and could not produce graphic objects by themselves – this has solely been the responsibility of the CPU. As you already know, an EISA bus system, for example, operates at a maximum of 8.33 MHz, so even with a 50 MHz 486 CPU, the data can only be shovelled into the video RAM of the adapter at this speed. In addition, for the drawing of lines, circles, etc. the CPU must calculate all of the points itself, it must switch between the memory levels for EGA and VGA adapters, or the window in the SVGA address area, and it must also set the corresponding bits in the video RAM. Naturally, this takes ages – especially when measured against the calculation speed of modern processors. Thus, the obvious thing to do is to make the graphic adapter a little more intelligent so that it can produce lines, circles and other geometric shapes by itself.

The first example resulting from this train of thought was the 8514/A from IBM, which was closely followed by other accelerators (such as S3, Cirrus, Mach). As already mentioned, the continuing requirement for even greater resolution stems from graphic-oriented user interfaces (above all, Windows). For this reason, the accelerators are also frequently known as *windows accelerators*. Their (quite meagre) instruction sets have been especially tuned to the needs of Windows. In the meantime, a great number of such accelerators, with differing functions, have been released onto the market. For this reason, I only want to describe the basic working principles and the most frequently implemented graphic functions in the following section. In Figure 32.17, you can see the basic layout of an accelerator card.

While, with normal graphic adapters, up until SVGA, accesses by the video controller to the video memory (apart from switching the memory levels or blending in windows) were restricted to reading bit values for the representation of pixels on the monitor, the accelerator chip also controls the video RAM using a write methodology. In almost all cases, the three functions *line draw*, *square fill* and *bitblt* (bit blitting is used for quickly shifting a window) are provided for this. The great advantage is that the CPU only needs to transfer the start and end positions of a line, and its colour value. The accelerator chip then draws the required line itself, in that it writes the applicable bit values to the corresponding addresses in the video RAM. Naturally, the CPU can also access the video RAM directly and draw the line itself. For very short lines, under certain circumstances, this can also be done quicker than by using the accelerator chip because, here, one or more control and data registers must be addressed first.

For high-performance accelerator cards, the video memory is frequently constructed using dual-port VRAMs. In this way, both the CPU and the accelerator chip can access the video RAM, without them being disrupted when the CRTC reads data. Even when constructed with the more usual DRAMs, a great increase in speed is clearly possible, when compared to normal VGA cards, due to the fast integrated functions.

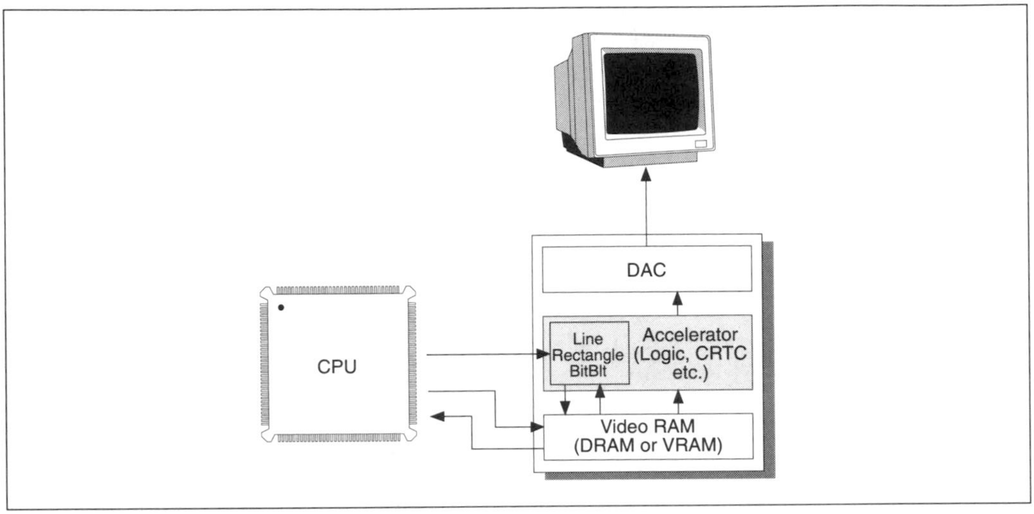

Figure 32.17: Basic layout of an accelerator card.

Note that although the accelerator chip of the adapter has a greater intelligence, the adapter still requires, among other things, a CRTC, a colour controller and a memory controller. Usually, however, these functions are already included as components on the accelerator card.

Today, accelerators typically contain a video memory of between 1 and 2 Mbytes for resolutions of at least 1024*768 points, and up to 16.7 million colours (TrueColor). If you can be satisfied with a somewhat smaller colour palette, resolutions of up to 1280*1024 pixels are easily possible. Only a few years ago, these values were limited to all but the most professional fields of CAD and image processing. For such resolutions, however, you need a minimum of a 17" (43 cm), or better still 20" (50 cm) monitor.

32.3.8 TIGA – Bigger, Better, Faster

At the higher performance and price end of the market for personal computers, you will find graphic adapters conforming to the TIGA (*Texas Instruments Graphics Architecture*) standard. These adapters use a pure-bred graphic processor which, in addition to simple arithmetic instructions, can also master complicated graphic instructions. In this way, it extends the performance of graphic subsystems considerably more than an accelerator such as the S3. Here, the CPU is very effectively relieved of all graphic tasks – the TMS 34010/020 not only performs individual graphic instructions such as the drawing of lines or the filling of squares, but it can also process complete programs and, in this way, independently produce complex graphical objects. A further advantage is that the CPU no longer has problems involving the organization of the video RAM – the graphic processor also takes over the management and organization of the video RAM. In Figure 32.18, you can see the typical layout of a TIGA adapter based on the TMS 34010/020 from Texas Instruments.

The central component of the adapter is the TMS 34010/020 graphic processor. It controls the entire operation of the adapter, such as the reading and writing of the video memory, and controlling the DAC for the graphical output to the monitor. In addition to the simple graphic instructions already known from the S3, however, the TMS 34010/020 can also perform complex logic and ALU instructions. The associated graphic programs are stored in a separate program memory. The CPU can load the routines that can be performed (such as for repeated drawing of a complicated object) into this program memory, which can then be performed by the graphic processor when required. Although the video RAM is usually implemented as dual-port VRAM, cheaper DRAMs are used for the program memory. The video memory is managed entirely by the TMS 34010/020 and, therefore, can no longer be accessed by the CPU. Due to the comprehensive possibilities for programming the graphic processors, this is also no longer necessary. As an example, you can load a routine into the program memory, which saves a window in another unused part of the video RAM. Then, the CPU does not need to read the content of the window from the video memory and save it in the main memory.

The correct interface for a TIGA adapter is, in almost all cases, represented by the driver supplied with Windows or OS/2 – apart from when you wish to program such a driver. Unfortunately, in this case I must refer you to the original programming handbook of the TMS 34010/020 due to lack of space.

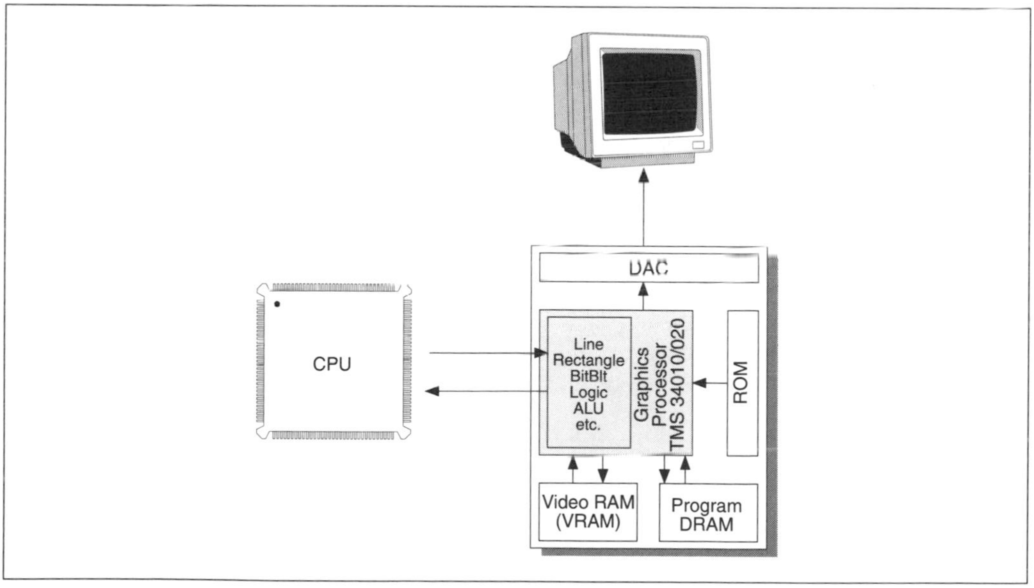

Figure 32.18: Basic layout of a TIGA adapter.

If you are of the opinion that the insertion of a graphic processor for the support of a CPU is a completely new concept, I must, unfortunately, disappoint you – your PC is teeming with such support processors. An old and very simple example is the FDC μPD765, which controls the floppy disk drive. In principle, the CPU could take over this task with the help of a number of registers and, for example, control the positioning of the write/read head in the disk drive over a specific track. The FDC does nothing more than perform a special microprogram in order to relieve the CPU of this task. Therefore, the CPU must – similar to the transfer of the end point coordinates of a line in the graphic processor – only provide the number of the required track. In defence of the graphic processors, it must be said that the programmer has much more influence over them than is possible in the μPD765. You can, for example, store complete programs in the graphic adapter, which can then be performed by the graphic processor. In this way, it is possible to support specific applications, such as CAD or business graphics, by using programs for the graphic processor.

A characteristic of graphic processors is their very high clock speeds – the TIGA-type adapter TMS 34020 operates at 60 MHz. Therefore, simple operations such as the filling of squares with a specific colour value are performed extremely quickly. However, you should not yet expect any miracles, especially in connection with Windows and other graphic oriented programs. The cause is mostly an insufficiently optimized adaptation – it would be far better to speak of an erroneous adaptation – of the programs to the capabilities of the graphic processors. A realistic average improvement in the output of high-resolution graphics would be a factor of around three. Many operations, such as the drawing of circles or the filling of squares, on the other hand, are performed up to ten times faster than is the case with a good VGA card.

32.4 Accessing the Screen via DOS

The response to this section's heading is very short and disappointing: pitiful. DOS doesn't implement a single function for accessing the adapter in graphics mode. Only in text mode are the usual CP/M-compatible and the handle functions of INT 21h available, which display text on the monitor. But you have no opportunity, for example, to specify the colour of the displayed characters with INT 21h.

Starting with DOS 4.00 you can slightly affect the screen's output using a somewhat enhanced MODE command. For example, you can adjust the number of text columns to 40 or 80, and on an EGA or VGA the number of lines to values between 25 and 50. Consult your DOS manual for further details on the MODE command.

To display text on the monitor you can use the DOS commands `COPY`, `TYPE` and `PRINT` on the COMMAND.COM level. DOS summarizes the keyboard and the monitor under the reserved device name CON (for console); a write access to CON is always transferred to the monitor, a read access from CON expects characters from the keyboard. You can therefore output text on-screen by selecting CON as the target for one of the above-mentioned commands. If you want to display the contents of the file output.txt on the monitor, you have the three following opportunities:

```
COPY output.txt CON
TYPE output.txt > CON
PRINT output.txt /D:CON
```

Instead of the second line you can also specify, of course, the usual command TYPE output.txt, as DOS directs the source of the TYPE command automatically to the standard output device corresponding to handle 1. This is usually the monitor. With TYPE output.txt > CON you redirect the output from the standard output device to CON, that is, normally from CON to CON.

As a programming freak you have some further options for outputting data using the function interrupt INT 21h. For this purpose, four functions are available (their calling formats are listed in Appendix K):

- function 02h – output on-screen;
- function 06h – direct character output;
- function 09h – string output;
- function 40h – write file/device.

The main advantage of function 40h is that you may output a whole string quite easily, and the function returns an error code in the ax register.

As DOS passes all the above-indicated function calls to the corresponding BIOS routines, you may use the functions in text as well as in graphics mode to display text. But now all capabilities for accessing the screen are exhausted. Setting and clearing individual pixels in graphics mode via DOS is impossible; only direct access to the BIOS graphics functions or even an immediate access to the video RAM and the graphics controller registers remains.

32.5 Accessing the Screen Via the BIOS

A much more powerful access to the graphics adapter compared to the DOS function interrupt INT 21h is offered by the BIOS interrupt INT 10h. Its functions serve, for example, to set the current video mode, which requires an extensive programming of the graphics controller. Furthermore, the INT 10h manages various screen pages automatically; you don't, therefore, need to know details of the video RAM's organization. Another significant advantage of BIOS functions over direct access to the video RAM is that you may specify points on-screen by their line and column coordinates. Thus the organization of the video RAM differing from adapter to adapter and mode to mode will only concern you if you attempt to access the video RAM directly.

Appendix K summarizes all the BIOS functions of INT 10h. The system BIOS on the motherboard has all the routines for the MDA and CGA adapters. The HGC in text mode emulates the MDA, and can therefore be accessed via the BIOS routines of the standard BIOS. But in graphics mode you have to read and write the video RAM directly to set and clear individual points. The HGC is incompatible with all IBM adapters in this mode. Meanwhile, nearly all compilers come with function libraries for programming the Hercules card.

The much more powerful EGA and VGA graphics adapters have their own BIOS so that you can use their improved and extensive capabilities. During the course of the boot process, the EGA/VGA BIOS intercepts INT 10h and replaces the handler by its own routine. The old INT 10h address is transferred into the interrupt vector table as INT 42h (the BIOS extension of hard disk controllers follows a similar strategy, as you know, which moves the old INT 13h of the system BIOS to INT 40h).

32.5.1 Graphics Routines of Standard BIOS

The system BIOS on the motherboard comprises all those functions required for accessing the MDA and CGA; Appendix K.2 lists them all. The corresponding functions are extended by the EGA/VGA BIOS to the advanced EGA/VGA operation modes, while the calling formats don't change. The EGA/VGA BIOS only allows a more extensive range of values, for example for positioning the cursor, which are adapted to the enhanced resolution.

One of the most important BIOS functions of INT 10h is function 00h for setting the video mode. As you have seen in Section 32.2 in connection with the quite simple 6845 graphics control chip, for a mode change many and sometimes very critical programming steps are required to load the 6845 registers with appropriate values. Function 00h carries out all of this dangerous work for you. However, you can emulate the other functions of INT 10h quite simply if you know the video RAM structure in detail.

Example: `setup graphics mode 6 with 640*200 pixels on the CGA.`

```
MOV ah, 00h     ; setup function 00h
MOV al, 06h     ; setup mode 6
INT 10h         ; call function
```

This simple 1-line code fragment gives rise to a rather extensive 6845 initialization by the BIOS and updates various parameters in the BIOS data area which characterize the current video mode. Table 32.13 lists the structure of the BIOS data area as far as the routines of INT 10h in the standard BIOS are concerned.

Note that the entries in the BIOS data area are correct only if you don't bypass the BIOS and program some 6845 registers directly, for example. Depending upon the adapter type and the resolution, the BIOS can manage up to eight different screen pages, each with its own cursor. Using function 05h, for example, you can display one of the eight pages and edit another page in the background with functions 02h, 03h, 08h, 09h, 0ah, 0ch, 0dh and 0eh. By switching the pages, animation effects can be achieved seemingly without any delay. All INT 10h functions are explained in detail in Appendix K.2, so they are not discussed here.

The last byte in the table actually already belongs to the DOS data area, and indicates the current status of INT 05h. The handler of INT 05h (the so-called *print-screen routine*) is called if you press the PRINT key, or SHIFT+PRINT. The routine then writes the current screen contents onto the printer. But this only works if the graphics adapter is running in text mode. In graphics mode, the routine simply reads the first 4000 bytes from the video RAM, interprets them as character code–attribute pairs, and outputs the seeming character codes on the printer. That you get nonsense if the CGA is operating in graphics mode (for example, if a circle is displayed on screen) seems to be obvious. Only after a call to the external DOS command GRAPHICS has installed a handler for INT 05h can the graphics contents be output on an IBM-compatible graphics printer.

Address	Size	Structure 76543210	Contents	Meaning
40:10	byte	..xx....	installed hardware	video adapter (00=EGA/VGA, 01=40*25 colour, 10=80*25 colour 11=80*25 monochrome)
40:49	byte		video mode	
40:4a	word		number of columns	
40:4c	word		size of active page	size in bytes
40:4e	word		offset of active page	
40:50	word		cursor position page 0	low=column, high=row
40:52	word		cursor position page 1	low=column, high=row
40:54	word		cursor position page 2	low=column, high=row
40:56	word		cursor position page 3	low=column, high=row
40:58	word		cursor position page 4	low=column, high=row
40:5a	word		cursor position page 5	low=column, high=row
40:5c	word		cursor position page 6	low=column, high=row
40:5e	word		cursor position page 7	low=column, high=row
40:60	word		cursor type	low=end scanline high=start scanline
40:62	byte		active page	low=column, high=row
40:63	word		6845 I/O port	03b4h=monochrome, 03d4h=colour
40:65	byte		mode control register	register value
40:66	byte		actual palette	actual palette value
40:100	byte		status print screen	00h=INT 05h not active 01h=INT 05h active, print screen in progress ffh=error

Table 32.13: BIOS data area of system BIOS (MDA, CGA)

32.5.2 Trouble Support – The EGA and VGA BIOS

A detailed description of all EGA/VGA BIOS functions would go far beyond the scope of this book. Therefore, only a few essential functions that can also be applied with some basic knowledge of the EGA/VGA features are discussed. Readers more interested in these subjects will find many books available which describe EGA/VGA programming precisely, particularly concerning the variety of EGA/VGA control registers and their meaning.

The EGA/VGA BIOS intercepts INT 10h during the course of the boot process and replaces the handler, which points to the motherboard's system BIOS using its own routine. The old handler is redirected to INT 42h, and all calls to INT 10h are redirected by the EGA/VGA BIOS to INT 42h if the EGA/VGA adapter is running in a strictly MDA or CGA-compatible mode. These are operation modes 0–7. Note that EGA and VGA may display text modes 0–3 and 7 with a different vertical resolution from MDA and CGA. You can adjust these vertical resolutions, and thus the height of the character matrix, using function 30h.

Moreover, the EGA and VGA BIOS additionally uses the storage location 40:84h to 40:88h in the BIOS data area and stores EGA/VGA-specific parameters there. Table 32.14 shows the structure of this EGA/VGA parameter area.

Address	Size	Structure 76543210	Contents	Meaning
40:84	byte		text rows–1	displayed text rows minus 1
40:85	word		character height	height of one character in scanlines
40:87	byte	x		video RAM not cleared at last mode setting
		xx		size of video RAM (00=64 kbyte, 01=128 kbyte, 10=192 kbyte, 11=256 kbyte)
		x		reserved
		x		EGA disabled
		x		BIOS has to wait for HSYNC
		x		EGA and monochrome monitor
		x		no cursor emulation
40:88	byte	xxxx		feature control bits (EGA only)
		xxxx		status of DIP switches

Table 32.14: BIOS data area of EGA/VGA BIOS extension

The EGA/VGA BIOS extension expands the already existing functions of INT 10h to the enhanced resolutions and the more extensive colour variety of the new adapters. It is thus possible, for example, to locate the cursor in text mode in line 30 if you are using the alphanumerical resolution 80*43. Most standard BIOS versions simply ignore such a function call. Additionally, the EGA/VGA BIOS has the following new functions with several subfunctions each:

- function 10h: accessing the palette and colour registers;
- function 11h: installing new character definition tables;
- function 12h: configuring the video subsystem;
- function 1ah: video combination;
- function 1bh: video BIOS function capabilities and status information (VGA only);
- function 1ch: save/restore video status (VGA only).

The following briefly discusses some functions and subfunctions that are not immediately self-evident.

Function 10h, Subfunction 03h – Enable/Disable Blink Attribute

Usually, bit 3 in the attribute byte of a character determines in text mode whether the character is to be displayed in a blinking (bit 3 set) or non-blinking (bit 3 cleared) manner. If you disable the meaning of this blink bit in the attribute byte (BL equal 0) using this function, then bit 3 selects one of two character sets that you have selected in advance using function 11h, subfunction 03h from four (EGA) or eight (VGA) possible character sets. If bit 3 in the attribute byte is cleared then the character code refers to the corresponding character in the primary character set. If, on the other hand, bit 3 in the attribute byte is set, then the character code points to the corresponding character in the secondary character set. Thus you can display 512 instead of 256 different characters; but the «blink capability» of the characters gets lost. The meaning of the bits 7–4 and 2–0 is not affected by this.

Example: disable blink attribute.

```
MOV ah, 10h     ; use function 10h
MOV al, 03h     ; use subfunction 3
MOV bl, 00h     ; disable blinking
INT 10h         ; call function
```

Function 11h – Interface to the Character Generator

This function implements 12 (EGA) or 15 (VGA) subfunctions for loading and activating character definition tables. Every table entry always has 32 bytes, where each byte corresponds to a scanline of the respective character even if the character matrix doesn't require 32 bytes per character (less than 32 scanlines, for example). In the EGA BIOS, two character definition tables for the two character matrices 9*14 and 8*8 are stored; the VGA BIOS additionally holds a character definition table for the character matrix 9*16. You can also load user-defined tables and thus display virtually any character in text mode.

If you load a table, using subfunctions 00h to 04h, which has a character height that differs from the current mode, then the graphics controller is not reprogrammed for the new character size. In the case of a larger character height than the current mode uses, the lower scanlines are simply cut off. But if the new character size is less than the former one, empty scanlines appear at the lower part, that is, the visible character distance gets larger. The EGA can hold four, the VGA eight different character tables in the character generator RAM. Thus you always need to specify the number under which the character definition table is to be stored when calling an installation subfunction.

Example: load 8*14 character definition table without reprogramming the CRTC.

```
MOV ah, 11h     ; use function 11h
MOV al, 01h     ; load 8*14 character table from ROM BIOS into character generator RAM
MOV bl, 03h     ; assign table the number 3
INT 10h         ; call function
```

Note that the loaded table doesn't become active until you explicitly enable it, by means of subfunction 03h, as the active character table. The same applies to functions 10h to 14h and 20h to 24h. You may specify a primary and a secondary character definition table. The secondary table only becomes active if you have disabled the blink attribute with function 10h, subfunction 03h. As standard, the table 0 forms the primary as well as the secondary character definition table.

Example: enable table 1 as the primary, table 7 as the secondary definition table.

```
MOV ah, 11h     ; use function 11h
MOV al, 03h     ; select subfunction character definition table
MOV bl, 2dh     ; enable tables 1 and 7 with 0010 1101b
INT 10h         ; call function
```

The example is valid only for a VGA, as the EGA can only hold four tables, and thus no table with number 7 exists. Subfunctions 10h to 14h, on the other hand, reprogram the video controller and thus adjust it to the new character height. The calling procedure for these functions doesn't differ from that for the functions 00h to 04h in any way.

Also in graphics mode you can install character definition tables using the subfunctions 20h to 24h. When outputting a character, the BIOS copies the corresponding table entry for the character into the video RAM and thus displays the corresponding pixel pattern. The subfunction 20h installs a 8*8 character definition table for codes 128–255, to which the pseudo-interrupt vector 1fh points. This is required in CGA-compatible mode, as in the system BIOS ROM no pixel patterns are stored for codes 128–255. You can install these patterns on a DOS level with the GRAFTABL command.

For every function group 0xh, 1xh and 2xh you have the opportunity to install its own character definition table. Happily, this is quite easy. You have only to note the fact that every character *always* occupies 32 bytes, as the maximum character height is 32 scanlines even if the actual character height has only eight or even fewer scanlines. Thus, each scanline of the character is represented by exactly one byte; a set bit means a pixel appearing with the foreground colour and a cleared one that the pixel has the background colour. A complete character set consists of 256 characters with 32 bytes each, that is, occupies 8 kbytes of memory. But you don't need to specify a whole set; instead, one or more characters are sufficient. If you define the number of an already loaded table upon the call to subfunctions 00h, 10h, or 21h, one or more table entries are overwritten, but the others remain unaltered. Thus you can specifically modify individual characters.

Example: for the ASCII code 128 (normally the character 'Ç') of the character set table 0 a rectangle shall appear in the 9*16 character matrix. The installation is carried out without reprogramming the CRTC.

```
The character matrix for the rectangle is as follows:
 scanline   pixel      byte value
       1    xxxxxxxx      ffh
            x000000x      81h
            x000000x      81h
            x000000x      81h
       5    x000000x      81h
            x000000x      81h
            x000000x      81h
            x000000x      81h
            x000000x      81h
      10    x000000x      81h
            x000000x      81h
            x000000x      81h
            x000000x      81h
            x000000x      81h
            x000000x      81h
      16    xxxxxxxx      ffh
```

No further scanlines have any set pixels, that is, the value of bytes 17–32 is equal to 00h. The 9th column is generated internally by the character generator; because the ASCII code is equal to 128 a blank column appears. Thus the buffer matrix has the following contents:

```
ffh 81h 81h 81h 81h 81h 81h 81h 81h 81h 81h 81h 81h 81h 81h ffh
00h 00h 00h 00h 00h 00h 00h 00h 00h 00h 00h 00h 00h 00h 00h 00h
```

The character matrix is installed as follows:

```
MOV bh, 20h             ; 32 bytes per table entry
MOV bl, 00h             ; complete table 0
MOV cx, 01h             ; install 1 character
MOV dx, 80h             ; install character starting with ASCII code 128
MOV bp, OFFSET matrix ; store character matrix offset in bp
MOV ax, SEG matrix      ; store character matrix segment in ax
MOV es, ax              ; load character matrix segment into es
MOV ah, 11h             ; use function 11h
MOV al, 00h             ; use subfunction 00h - install user-defined
                        ; character definition table
INT 10h                 ; call function
```

If you load the bh register in the above example with the value 16 instead of 32, the last 16 bytes of the buffer matrix can be omitted. In this case, the corresponding bytes in the character generator RAM are not overwritten, but remain unaltered. In an analogous manner you may install a complete character set; only the necessary work to set up the buffer becomes more extensive. The installation of one or more characters, or even a complete character set, by means of subfunctions 10h and 21h is carried out in the same way as described above.

You may use the installation of the user-defined character set, for example, to also display in text mode a small graphic in a window on-screen. If you reserve ASCII codes 128–255 for this purpose, then a graphics window of, for example, 16*8 text characters or 144*128 pixels is possible. This corresponds to a quarter of the screen in the CGA graphics mode with 320*200 points. To be able to actually output the graphics in text mode onto the screen, you must define a buffer in the main memory that you use like a virtual screen in which to store the pixel values for the character matrices. By installing this virtual screen as the character definition table in the character generator RAM, you can output simple graphics in text mode. If you work with a primary and a secondary character set and use more than 128 characters from the 512 possible, you can integrate quite complicated graphics without the need to use the more complicated and time-consuming graphics mode. The only disadvantage is that the 9th pixel column is generated by the character generator without any possibility of intervention.

Further, subfunction 30h is useful to determine the parameters and the storage location of the predefined ROM character tables in the EGA/VGA BIOS. You can thus, for example, read the predefined character matrices and alter them when defining new character definition tables.

Example: `determine parameter and storage location of 8*8 ROM table.`

```
MOV ah, 11h    ; use function 11h
MOV al, 30h    ; use subfunction 30h
MOV bh, 03h    ; select 8*8 ROM table
INT 10h        ; call function
```

After the call, cx contains the number of bytes per defined character, dl the number of scan-lines displayed on-screen for the corresponding character matrix, and es:bp points to the table in ROM.

Function 12h, Subfunction 20h – Select Alternate Print Screen Routine

Using this subfunction you can replace the standard handler for INT 05h by a routine that can serve the new EGA/VGA resolutions.

Example: enable new routine for printing the screen.

```
MOV ah, 12h    ; use function 12h
MOV bl, 20h    ; use subfunction 20h
```

Pressing **PRINT** or **SHIFT+PRINT** now calls the newly installed print routine.

Function 12h, Subfunction 31h – Load Standard Palette (VGA Only)

Using this subfunction you may determine whether the VGA is to load the standard palette or keep the current palette values when a graphic mode change by means of INT 10h, function 00h occurs. Normally, the palette registers are loaded with the standard values upon every mode change.

Function 1ch – Save/Restore Video Status (VGA Only)

One problem during the course of programming resident pop-up programs or graphics programs in a multitasking environment is that the activated program has virtually no opportunity to determine the current graphics status and restore it later. The reason is the many write-only registers of graphics adapters from CGA to EGA. Only on a VGA can all essential registers be read, and the VGA BIOS implements the 1ch function, with which you can save all important graphics parameters en bloc into a buffer and restore them later, also en bloc. As the number of parameters to be saved is not always the same you have to determine the size of the buffer required first by calling subfunction 00h.

32.5.3 Standard Extension – VESA SVGA BIOS

The new *SuperVGA video modes*, that is, the resolution in SVGA text and graphics mode, are setup with the SVGA BIOS. For that purpose, the standard video modes have been enhanced by 13 new SVGA modes. Because the manufacturers of graphics adapters had already occupied the area beyond the «highest» VGA mode 19 (320*200 pixels with 256 colours) with their own, manufacturer-dependent modes, VESA has assigned the new SVGA modes values beginning with 100h (see Table 32.15).

The SVGA video modes are selected with INT 10h, function 4fh, subfunction 02h; the call format is shown in Table 32.16.

The SVGA BIOS implements a function 4fh executing all eight SVGA functions; they are listed in Appendix K.4:

- INT 10h, function 4fh, subfunction 00h – get SVGA information
- INT 10h, function 4fh, subfunction 01h – get SVGA mode information
- INT 10h, function 4fh, subfunction 02h – set SVGA mode
- INT 10h, function 4fh, subfunction 03h – get SVGA mode
- INT 10h, function 4fh, subfunction 04h – save/restore SVGA video state
- INT 10h, function 4fh, subfunction 05h – CPU access to video RAM
- INT 10h, function 4fh, subfunction 06h – set logical length of scan line
- INT 10h, function 4fh, subfunction 07h – set beginning of SVGA display in video RAM

Of special importance is subfunction 00h because you can determine with the returned information how to access a non-standard SVGA directly.

Mode number	Mode type	Text lines	Text columns	Resolution	Colours
100h	graphics			640*400	256
101h	graphics			640*480	256
102h	graphics			800*600	16
103h	graphics			800*600	256
104h	graphics			1024*768	16
105h	graphics			1024*768	256
106h	graphics			1280*1024	16
107h	graphics			1280*1024	256
108h	text	60	80		
109h	text	25	132		
10ah	text	43	132		
10bh	text	50	132		
10ch	text	60	132		

Table 32.15: SVGA video modes

Register	Call value	Return value
AX	4f02h	
AH		status[1]
AL		support[2]
BX	mode accord. Table 32.15	

[1] 00h=o.k., 01h=error
[2] 4fh=function supported, other value=function not supported

Table 32.16: Call format of INT 10h, function 4fh, subfunction 02h

32.6 Help for Self-Help – Accessing the Video Memory Directly

Using BIOS INT 10h you can output characters in text mode and pixels in graphics mode in any colour at any location on the screen, but you won't break any records! To set a single point on-screen, the BIOS works very hard, but if you attempt to write a whole window onto the screen, or try to save one before it is overwritten by another, you have no choice but to access the video RAM directly. But now we have to pay for the fact that neither IBM nor Microsoft defined a reasonable standard for access to the PC's video system early enough. Fortunately, direct access to the display memory is not very complicated.

32.6.1 MDA

In MDA text mode with BIOS mode number 7, the 4 kbytes video RAM is organized as a linear array containing 2000 contiguous screen memory words attribute:character code for the 25 rows with 80 columns each. The character code forms the low-order, the attribute the high-order byte of the screen memory word. The video RAM starts at segment b000h; the character in the upper left corner is represented by the first word in the video RAM (as is the case for all video modes of all graphics adapters). Thus every character is encoded by two bytes, every row by 160 bytes (a0h bytes). The address of the screen memory word corresponding to the character in row i, column j (i=0 to 24, j=0 to 79) is given by the following expression:

```
address(i,j) = b0000h + a0h * i + 02h * j
```

32.6.2 CGA

The structure and organization of the video RAM on a CGA differ significantly between text and graphics mode.

Text Mode (Modes 0, 1, 2, 3)

In CGA text mode with mode numbers 0 and 1, the 16 kbytes of video RAM are divided into eight pages of 2 kbytes (800h bytes), each of which is organized as a linear array and contiguously accommodates the 1000 screen memory words attribute:character code for the 25 rows of 40 columns each. As is the case for all text modes, the character code forms the low-order and the attribute the high-order byte of every screen memory word. The video RAM on a CGA starts at segment b800h; the character in the upper left corner is represented by the first word of a page in the video RAM. Each character is encoded by two bytes, that is, every row by 80 bytes (50h bytes). The address of the screen memory word corresponding to the character in row i, column j of the page k (i=0 to 24, j=0 to 39, k=0 to 7) is given by the following expression:

```
address(i,j,k) = b8000h + 800h * k + 50h * i + 02h * j
```

In text modes 2 and 3, on the other hand, the 16 kbytes of video RAM are divided into four pages of 4 kbytes (1000h bytes), each of which is organized as a linear array and contiguously accommodates the 2000 screen memory words attribute:character code for the 25 rows of 80 columns each. Also here, the video RAM starts at segment b800h. Every character is encoded by two bytes, and every row by 160 bytes (a0h bytes.) The address of the screen memory word corresponding to the character in row i, column j of the page k (i=0 to 24, j=0 to 79, k=0 to 7) is given by the following expression:

```
address (i,j,k) = b8000h + 100h * k + a0h * i + 02h * j
```

Graphics Mode (Modes 4, 5, 6)

In graphics mode the video RAM is divided into two banks of 8 kbytes (2000h bytes) each. Bank 0 accommodates all scanlines with an even number, bank 1 all scanlines with an odd number. In graphics mode, only one page is available, which occupies the whole video RAM. The first bank has memory addresses b800:0000 to b800:1fffh, the second bank memory addresses b800:2000 to b800:3fffh. Figure 32.19 shows the division of the video RAM into banks for all three CGA graphics modes.

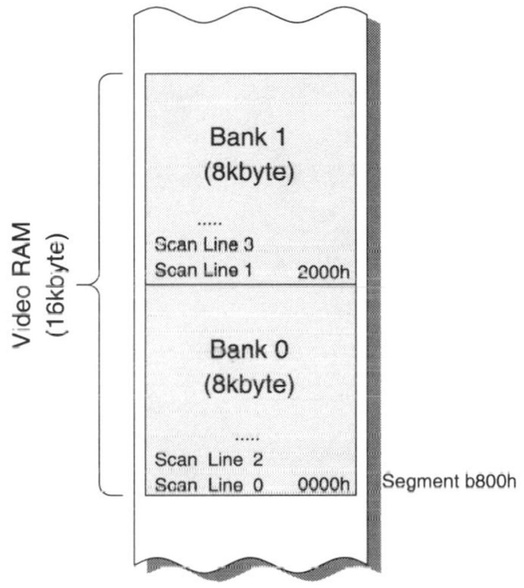

Figure 32.19: Video RAM bank structure for the three CGA graphics modes.

In the 4-colour modes 4 and 5, one pixel is assigned two bits to encode the four colours. Thus, one byte in video RAM is able to accommodate four pixels. The pixel with the higher number (that is, the pixel appearing more on the right of the monitor) is encoded by the low-order bits. The k-th byte accommodates pixels 4k, 4k+1, 4k+2 and 4k+3. Figure 32.20a shows this arrangement.

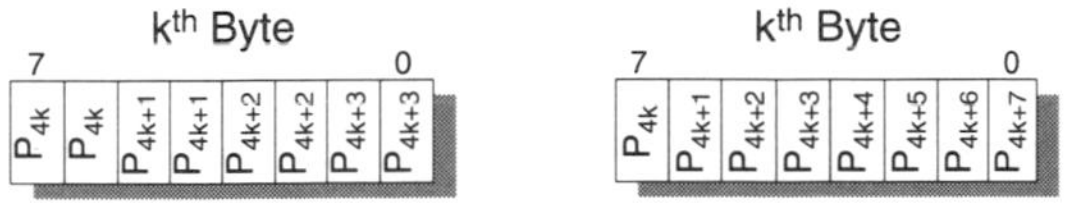

P_{4k}: pixel number 4k	P_{4k}: pixel number 4k	P_{4k+4}: pixel number 4k+4
P_{4k+1}: pixel number 4k+1	P_{4k+1}: pixel number 4k+1	P_{4k+5}: pixel number 4k+5
P_{4k+2}: pixel number 4k+2	P_{4k+2}: pixel number 4k+2	P_{4k+6}: pixel number 4k+6
P_{4k+3}: pixel number 4k+3	P_{4k+3}: pixel number 4k+3	P_{4k+7}: pixel number 4k+7

(a) low resolution modes 4 and 5 (b) high resolution mode 6

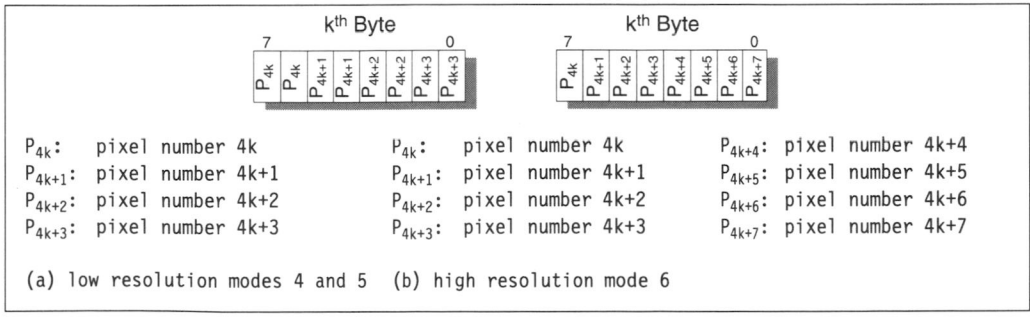

Figure 32.20: Pixel arrangement in the video byte of the CGA graphics modes.

Thus, in modes 4 and 5, 80 bytes (50h bytes) are required to encode one line (320 pixels/4 pixels per byte). The address of that byte which accommodates the pixel in line i and column j (i=0 to 199, j=0 to 319) is given by the following expression:

```
address(i,j) = b0000h + 2000h * (i MOD 2) + 50h * INT(i/2) + INT(j/4)
```

In high-resolution mode 6 («high» refers to the time when the first PC came onto the market) with only two colours, one pixel is assigned only one bit, that is, one video RAM byte can accommodate eight pixels. As is the case for the low-resolution mode, the pixels with a higher number are encoded by the low-order bits. Thus the k-th byte holds the pixels 4k, 4k+1, 4k+2, 4k+3, 4k+4, 4k+5, 4k+6, and 4k+7. Figure 32.20b shows this arrangement. In mode 6 also, 80 bytes (50h bytes) are necessary for one line (640 pixels/8 pixels per byte). The address of that byte which accommodates the pixel in line i and column j (i=0 to 199, j=0 to 639) is given by the following expression:

```
address(i,j) = b0000h + 2000h * (i MOD 2) + 50h * INT(i/2) + INT(j/8)
```

32.6.3 Hercules Graphics Card

On the Hercules card also, the structure and organization of the video RAM in text and graphics mode differs significantly.

Text Mode (Mode 7)

In text mode the Hercules card emulates the MDA precisely, so that all statements concerning the MDA apply to the Hercules card as well. Thus the address of the screen memory word corresponding to the character in row i, column j (i=0 to 24, j=0 to 79) is given by the following expression:

```
address(i,j) = b0000h + a0h * i + 02h * j
```

Graphics Mode

As already mentioned, the video RAM on the Hercules card is divided in graphics mode into four banks per page. The first bank accommodates the pixels for scanlines 0, 4, 8, ... 344, the second bank that for scanlines 1, 5, 9, ... 345, the third bank that for scanlines, 6, 10, ... 346, and the fourth bank that for scanlines 3, 7, 11, ... 347. The Hercules card video RAM in graphics mode has 64 kbytes, and is divided into two pages. The resolution is 720*348 pixels. Because of the monochrome display, every pixel is assigned one bit, thus 90 bytes are required per line (720 pixels/8 pixels per byte). The address of the byte which accommodates the pixel in line i and column j of page k (i=0 to 347, j=0 to 719, k=0 to 1) is given by the following expression:

```
address(i,j,k) = b0000h + 8000h * k + 2000h * (i MOD 4) + 90 * INT(i/4) + INT(j/8)
```

b0000h specifies the video segment, 8000h the size of one page (32 kbytes) and 2000h the size of one bank (8 kbytes). Figure 32.8 in Section 32.2.4 illustrates this division of the Hercules card's video RAM into pages if the graphics mode is active.

32.6.4 EGA

The EGA is downwards compatible with the CGA, so that all expositions concerning text modes 0–3 and graphics modes 4–6 apply here, too. In particular, the segment addresses and the division into screen pages, as well as RAM banks, remain the same in these modes.

Text Mode (Modes 0 to 3)

The character codes are stored in memory layer 0 and the accompanying attributes in memory layer 1 of the EGA video RAM. But the address transformation logic on the EGA board carries out a certain combination of the actually parallel storage layers, so that the organization and structure of the video RAM, as well as the address calculation, are identical for the CPU, as on a CGA. The EGA is unable to carry out MDA's text mode 7, however.

Graphics Mode (Modes 4–6 and 13–16)

The EGA can operate in CGA graphics modes 4–6 because of its downward compatibility. Also in this case, the address transformation logic on the EGA card carries out a combination of the actually parallel memory layers so that the organization and structure of the video RAM, as well as the address calculation, are identical to the CGA. On the other hand, nearly all parameters of the video RAM and its organization differ from the CGA if one of the EGA graphics modes 13–16 is effective. In all of these EGA modes, the video RAM begins at segment address a000h. Except for monochrome mode 15 every pixel can be displayed in 16 different colours from a palette of 64 colours. Thus four bits per pixel are required in modes 13, 14 or 16. Unlike CGA graphics modes, the video RAM is not divided into two banks here, but the pixels are contiguous in video RAM. The four bits per pixel are distributed to the four parallel memory layers of the EGA. Thus the address of one of these four bits per pixel not only comprises video segment and offset but additionally the memory layer. This is shown in Figure 32.21.

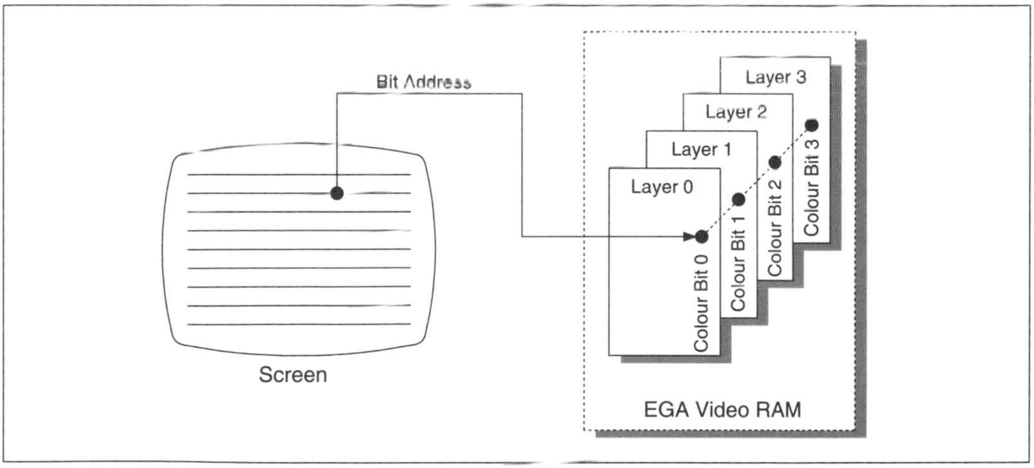

Figure 32.21: Distribution of the 4 bit/pixel to the memory layers in EGA modes 13, 14 and 16.

For the CPU the pixels follow one another bit by bit while every bit address is assigned four memory layers. Layer 0 accommodates bit 0 of the pixel concerned, layer 1 bit 1 of the pixel concerned, etc. To display pixels with all 16 possible colours on screen, you not only need to calculate the bit addresses, but additionally an access to the four memory layers is required. For this purpose, the EGA map mask register is implemented. It is addressed via the index port 3c4h with index 02h, and can be written via data port 3c5h. Figure 32.22 shows the structure of this map mask register.

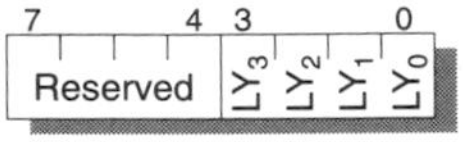


```
LY3–LY0: write access to layers 3 ... 0
         1=enabled              0=disabled
```

Figure 32.22: The map mask register (index 02h, index port 3c4h, data port 3c5h).

Using the map mask register you can enable several layers simultaneously for a write. A set one of the bits LY_3–LY_0 enables the corresponding layer. If you now carry out a write access to the corresponding bit address, then the value is transferred into one or more layers.

Example: `set bit 0 of the byte at address a000:0000h for the layers 0, 1 and 3.`

```
MOV ax, a000h    ; load video segment into ax
MOV es, ax       ; transfer video segment into es
MOV bx, 0000h    ; load offset 0000h into bx
OUT 3c4h, 02h    ; index 2 -> address map mask register
OUT 3c5h, 0bh    ; write 00001011b into map mask register
                 ; -> enable layers 0, 1 and 3
MOV [es:bx], 01h ; set bit 0 in layers 0, 1 and 3
```

For saving screen contents so that you can, for example, restore the original state after a window has appeared and then disappeared again, it is necessary to read the bit values of the four layers. For this purpose, the read map select register is implemented. It is addressed with index 04h via index port 3ceh, and can be written via data port 3cfh. Figure 32.23 shows the structure of the read map select register.

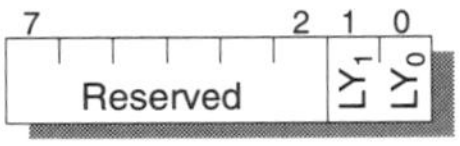


```
LY1, LY0: read access enabled for
          00=layer 0   01=layer 1   10=layer 2   11=layer 3
```

Figure 32.23: The read map select register (index 04h, index port 3ceh, data port 3cfh).

Unlike the map mask register, the read map select register enables access to only a single layer, as the four layers may actually hold different bit values. Therefore, reading all four layers simultaneously is impossible.

Example: `read byte at address a000:0000h for layer 2.`

```
MOV ax, a000h      ; load video segment into ax
MOV es, ax         ; transfer video segment into es
MOV bx, 0000h      ; load offset 0000h into bx
OUT 3ceh, 04h      ; index 4 -> address read map select register
OUT 3cfh, 02h      ; write 0000 0010b into read map select register
                   ; -> enable layer 2
MOV al, [es:bx]    ; load byte in layer 2 into al
```

Because of the distribution of the four bits per pixel to the four layers, the CPU has the impression that every pixel is assigned one bit in the address space. These four bits of one pixel are addressed by additionally specifying the layer via the map mask or the read map select register. Figure 32.24 shows the pixel bit arrangement in the screen byte for modes 13, 14 and 16.

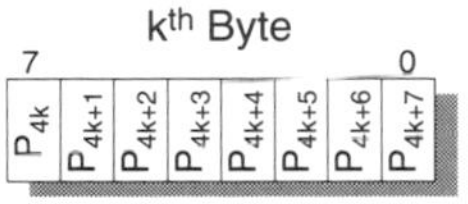

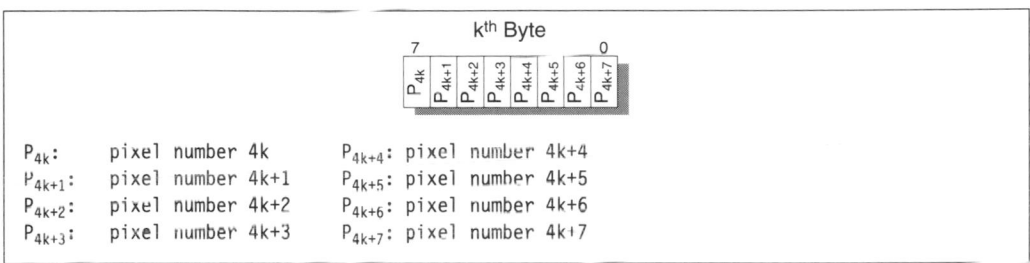

P_{4k}:	pixel number 4k	P_{4k+4}:	pixel number 4k+4
P_{4k+1}:	pixel number 4k+1	P_{4k+5}:	pixel number 4k+5
P_{4k+2}:	pixel number 4k+2	P_{4k+6}:	pixel number 4k+6
P_{4k+3}:	pixel number 4k+3	P_{4k+7}:	pixel number 4k+7

Figure 32.24: Distribution of the 4 bits/pixels to the memory layers in EGA graphics modes 13, 14 and 16.

In mode 13, 40 bytes (25h bytes) are required per line (320 pixels/8 pixels per byte). Every screen page comprises 8 bytes (2000h bytes). The address of the byte with the pixel in line i, column j of the screen page k (i=0 to 199, j=0 to 319, k=0 to 7) is therefore:

```
address(i,j,k) = a0000h + 2000h * k + 25h * j + INT (i/8)
```

Mode 14, with a higher resolution, requires 80 bytes (50h bytes) per line, corresponding to 640 pixels/8 pixels per byte. One screen page here comprises 16 kbytes (4000h bytes). The address of the byte with the pixel in line i, column j of the screen page k (i=0 to 199, j=0 to 639, k=0 to 3) is:

```
address(i,j,k) = a0000h + 4000h * k + 50h * j + INT (i/8)
```

In the best high-resolution EGA mode 16, every line also needs 80 bytes (50h bytes) per line (640 pixels/8 pixels per byte); each screen page comprises 32 kbytes (8000h bytes). The address of the byte with the pixel in line i, column j of the screen page k (i=0 to 349, j=0 to 639, k=0 to 1) is as follows:

```
address(i,j,k) = a0000h + 8000h * k + 50h * j + INT (i/8)
```

The EGA mode 15 drives a TTL monochrome monitor instead of the RGB monitors or extended EGA colour monitors usually employed with an EGA. This mode is something like an extended monochrome mode with the four monochrome intensities black, normal, bright and blinking. But note that although bright and blinking can be active, this mode is a graphics and not a text mode. Thus every pixel is assigned two bits, which are distributed to layers 0 and 2. Layers 1 and 3 are not used in this mode. This quite high resolution EGA monochrome mode 15 requires 80 bytes (50h bytes) per line corresponding to 640 pixels/8 pixels per byte. Every screen page comprises 32 kbytes (8000h bytes). The address of the byte with the pixel in line i, column j of the screen page k (i=0 to 349, j=0 to 639, k=0 to 1) is therefore:

```
address(i,j,k) = a0000h + 8000h * k + 50h * j + INT (i/8)
```

32.6.5 VGA

The VGA is downward compatible with the CGA, EGA, and MDA so that all expositions concerning text modes 0–3 and 7 as well as the graphics modes 4–6 and 13–16 are also valid. In particular, the segment addresses and the division into screen pages, as well as RAM banks, remain the same in these modes.

Text Mode (0–3, 7)

The character codes are stored in memory layer 0 and the accompanying attributes in memory layer 1 of the VGA video RAM, as is the case on the EGA. The VGA address transformation logic carries out a certain combination of the actually parallel storage layers so that the organization and structure of the video RAM, as well as the address calculation, are identical for the CPU, as on a CGA or MDA. Unlike the EGA, the VGA can also carry out MDA's monochrome text mode 7 with an enhanced resolution of 720*400 pixels corresponding to a character matrix of 9*16 pixels.

Graphics Mode (Modes 4–6, 13–19)

The VGA carries out CGA graphics modes 4–6 and EGA graphics modes 13–16 in the same way as on the original adapters. The organization and structure of the video RAM, as well as the address calculation, are identical to the CGA and EGA in these compatible modes.

Additionally, the VGA implements three new VGA modes: graphics modes 17, 18 and 19. VGA mode 17 serves mainly for compatibility to the graphics adapter of the PS/2 model 30, the MCGA (multi colour graphics array). The bits for the individual pixels are located only in layer 0–the three layers 1, 2 and 3 are not used. Every pixel is assigned one bit, that is, two colours may be displayed.

In VGA mode 17, 80 bytes per line (50h bytes) are required (640 pixels/8 pixels per byte). Every screen page comprises 40 kbytes (a000h bytes). The address of the byte with the pixel in line i, column j (i=0 to 479, j=0 to 639) is therefore:

```
address(i,j) = a0000h + 50h * j + INT (i/8)
```

In VGA mode 18 the four bits of a pixel are distributed to the four memory layers, as is the case for the EGA. For setting one pixel with the intended colour you must therefore additionally address the four layers besides the byte.

In the high-resolution VGA mode 18 with 16 different colours per line, 80 bytes (50h bytes) are also required (640 pixels/8 pixels per byte). Every screen page comprises 40 kbytes (a000h bytes). Thus the address of the byte with the pixel in line i, column j (i=0 to 479, j=0 to 639) is therefore:

```
address(i,j) = a0000h + 50h * j + INT (i/8)
```

In VGA mode 19 with 256 colours per pixel, the video RAM is again organized very simply as a linear array, in which one byte corresponds to one pixel. The byte value specifies the colour of the pixel. The bits are not distributed to various memory layers here. This mode requires 320 bytes (140h bytes) per line corresponding to 320 pixels/1 pixel per byte. The single screen page thus comprises 64 kbytes (10000h bytes), but only 64000 bytes are actually used. The remaining 1536 bytes remain free. The addres of the pixel in line i, column j (i=0 to 199, j=0 to 319) then is:

```
address(i,j) = a0000h + 140h * j + i
```

32.6.6 SVGA

SVGA is upwards compatible with CGA, EGA and VGA, so that all features used there remain unchanged here. In particular, the segment addresses and the splitting into monitor pages and video RAM banks remain the same in these modes.

Text Mode

Organization and layout of the video RAM, and calculation of character addresses and their attributes are, for the CPU, identical to VGA. Only the page in SVGA text mode, due to the expanded resolution to 132*60 characters, is correspondingly larger.

Graphic Mode (Modes 4–6, 13–19)

Due to its upwards compatibility, SVGA can perform CGA, EGA and VGA graphic modes unchanged. The organization and layout of the video RAM, and calculation of the addresses in these compatible modes, are identical to CGA, EGA and VGA, respectively. In the original SVGA modes, as in VGA mode 19, the video RAM is organized very simply as a linear byte field, in which a nibble (16 colours) or a byte (256 colours) corresponds to a pixel. The nibble or byte value indicates the colour of the point on the screen. Depending on the resolution, this mode requires up to 1280 bytes per line, or 1.25 Mbytes for each page (1280*1024 pixels with 256 colours). In mode 105h (1024*768 pixels with 256 colours), the offset of the byte with the pixel in line i, column j (i=0 to 767, j=0 to 1023) in video segment a000h would thus be:

```
Offset(i,j)=300h * j + i
```

For the last point of the screen (i=767, j=1023), together with the segment a000h, this already lies beyond 1 M, thus it covers the entire address area reserved for the system and the additional BIOS. In SVGA the problem is solved by the bank structure of the video RAM. Each 64 kbyte sized segment is addressed with the help of a so-called *bank select register*. You can see its layout in Figure 32.25. The four least significant bits *A19 A16* select the bank, which is blended into the 64 kbyte window after a000:0000h. Together with other words, A19–A16 represent the four most significant bits of a 20-bit address. In this way, up to 1 Mbyte of video RAM can be addressed. You can address the bank select register at port 3d5h, after you have selected it with the index 35h through the index port 3d4h.

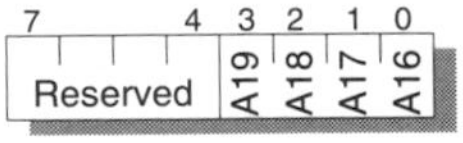

Figure 32.25: The bank select register of the SVGA.

Example: Select the bank 11h=1011b through the bank select register.

```
mov dx, 3d4h      ; Load the I/O address of the index port to dx
out dx, 35h       ; Write the index 35h into the index port, that is, select the bank select
                  ; register at the data port 3d5h
mov dx, 3d5h      ; Load the I/O address of the data port to dx
in al, dx         ; Read old value
and al, 11110000b ; A19–A16 reset, leave reserved bits unchanged
or al, 00001011b  ; A19–A16 set to 1011b, leave reserved bits unchanged
mov dx, 3d5h      ; Load the I/O address of the data port to dx
out dx, al        ; Write to the bank select register
```

As before, as many bits are assigned to a pixel as are necessary for the selected depth of colour. Originally (and strictly in accordance with VESA SVGA), only 256 different colours could be represented at the same time. Here, every pixel is assigned a byte. HighColor mode with 256k colours, and TrueColor mode with 16M colours, require 18 and 24 bits respectively for one pixel. They follow each other sequentially in the video RAM. Even with very large video memories (1 Mbyte and more), the video RAM is organized as a linear byte field, in which 64 kbyte or 128 kbyte sized windows are blended into the address area after a0000h (the standard video segment), as with expanded memory.

A further method of opening a window in the large video RAM after a000:0000h is provided by the subfunctions 01h and 05h of INT 10h, function 4fh (see Appendix K.4). The subfunction 01h indicates a buffer at offset 04h, into which units of this window can be shifted by subfunction 05h. With subfunction 05h, you can then select the start address of the window within the video RAM. It then appears at the usual video address a000:0000h in the CPU address area. Due to the combined efforts of a window granularity and a 16-bit window address in the granularity unit, almost any sized video RAM is possible. If you select the maximum video window size of 128 kbytes (17 address bits) between a000:0000h and b000:ffffh as granularity, then a video RAM of 8 Gbytes (33 address bits) is possible with the 64k window address in DX (16 address bits).

Example: In the CPU address area after a000:0000h, a window in the video RAM should be opened after the address 768k; the granularity is 1 kByte.

```
mov ax, 4f05h ; Transfer function code to ax
mov bh,00h    ; Set window address
mov dx, 30h   ; Window address in units of 1 kbyte (300h=768d)
int 10h       ; Call function through SVGA interrupt 10h
```

32.6.7 Accelerators

For accelerators, a direct access to the video memory is either not possible (original 8514/A modes), or unnecessary due to the existing graphic functions. The correct interface to the adapter is the supplied Windows or OS/2 driver. It takes advantage of the graphic accelerator functions. To date, no binding standard has been developed in the area of accelerators (due to the Windows driver interface at a software level, this is also unnecessary), so every BIOS and adapter manufacturer is free to do as he pleases – even when the same graphic accelerator is used. For this reason, a generalized overview regarding the programming of accelerators is not possible.

I would like to add that with an S3 adapter, you can access the video RAM in exactly the same way as is the case with SVGAs. Thus, here also, a bank select register is available at port 3d4h (index register; for bank select register: index 35h) and 3d5h (data register); with their help you can blend a 64 kbyte sized segment of the video RAM into the CPU address area after a0000h. As most accelerators are compatible with SVGA, naturally, you can also use the VGA and SVGA functions of the BIOS listed in Appendix K. As hardware-like software, these functions naturally make full use of the accelerators.

32.6.8 Summary

Table 32.17 lists together the segments and offsets the characters or pixels in row *rw*, column *cl* of the screen page *pg* in video RAM.

32.7 Graphics Processor Versus Local Bus

The two concepts of graphic adapters with graphic processors and local bus have the same target: to increase the speed of picture formation. Here the similarity ends. While a local bus should enable large quantities of data produced by the CPU to be transferred to the video RAM, graphic processors attempt to do exactly the opposite, namely to transfer only a few commands and parameters. They describe the content of the screen area which should be drawn. Here, the production of the large amounts of data necessary for the screen rewrite is performed on the adapter, the quantity of data to be transferred is typically reduced by a factor of 100, therefore, the transfer time is considerably less.

With the local bus concept, as before, the CPU must calculate the values for each pixel, and so it is constantly interrupted by operations such as the periodic timer interrupt, memory refreshing, mouse movement, etc. A relatively protracted task switch in a multitasking operating system such as OS/2 or Windows NT, for example, can slow down the sensitive picture formation. In addition, no intelligent CPU is necessary for the production of the pixel data, a simple but highly specialized and, therefore, faster chip can accomplish this just as well. Also with a local bus, the CPU is overloaded with quite trivial jobs, thus blocking more complicated calculations which require a higher intelligence. Although in the beginning many graphic adapters for local bus systems included an external 32-bit interface, they addressed the video RAM internally,

Mode	Segment	Offset	rw1)	cl2)	pg3)	Layers
0, 1	b800h	800h*pg + 50h*rw + 02h*cl	0–24	0–39	0–7	–
2, 3	b800h	1000h*pg + a0h*rw + 02h*cl	0–24	0–79	0–4	–
4, 5	b000h	2000h*(rw MOD 2) + 50h*INT(rw/2) + INT(cl/4)	0–199	0–319	0	–
6	b000h	2000h*(rw MOD 2) + 50h*INT(rw/2) + INT(cl/8)	0–199	0–639	0	–
7	b000h	a0h*rw + 02h*cl	0–24	0–79	–	–
13	a000h	2000h*pg + 25h*cl + INT (rw/8)	0–199	0–319	0–7	0–3
14	a000h	4000h*pg + 50h*cl + INT (rw/8)	0–199	0–639	0–3	0–3
15	a000h	8000h*pg + 50h*cl + INT (rw/8)	0–349	0–639	0–1	0, 2
16	a000h	8000h*pg + 50h*cl + INT (rw/8)	0–349	0–639	0–1	0–3
17	a000h	50h*cl + INT (rw/8)	0–479	0–639	–	–
18	a000h	50h*cl + INT (rw/8)	0–479	0–639	–	0–3
19	a000h	140h*cl + rw	0–199	0–319	–	–
100	a000h	280h*cl + rw	0–399	0–639	–	–
101	a000h	280h*cl + rw	0–479	0–639	–	–
102	a000h	190h*cl + rw	0–599	0–799	–	–
103	a000h	320h*cl + rw	0–599	0–799	–	–
104	a000h	200h*cl + rw	0–767	0–1023	–	–
105	a000h	400h*cl + rw	0–767	0–1023	–	–
106	a000h	280h*cl + rw	0–1023	0–1279	–	–
107	a000h	500h*cl + rw	0–1023	0–1279	–	–
HGCG4)	b000h	8000h*pg + 2000h*(rw MOD 4) + 90*INT(rw/4) + INT(cl/8)	0–347	0–719	0–1	–

1) line number
2) column number
3) screen page number
4) graphics mode of the Hercules card

Table 32.17: Addresses in video RAM

however, with only 16 or even 8 bits. The performance values were correspondingly disappointing. The reason was that manufacturers wanted to use the better known graphic chips available at the time, for instance the ET4000 from Tseng with its 16-bit technology. For ISA adapters it was fully sufficient, but when installed on a local bus graphic adapter it proved to be a restriction. In the meantime, it has been replaced by its 32-bit successor, the ET4000-W32, which makes full use of local bus advantages with a 32-bit width. Lastly, the computing speed of the CPU limits picture formation. As an example, not just repeated MOV instructions are necessary for the output of a square, but comparisons and conditional jump instructions are also necessary in order to define the borders of the square. The switching between different memory levels or banks also slows down the picture formation.

Graphic processors and also accelerators can relieve the CPU of much of the monotonous work. In order to produce a square filled with a uniform colour, for example, it is only necessary to fill a seemingly large area of the video RAM with a uniform data pattern. To this end, the CPU transfers only the coordinates of two corner points and the corresponding colour value. Due to very high clock speeds in such special processors (60 MHz and more), simple graphic patterns such as lines, squares and circles are produced very quickly. Here, any lower data transfer rate between the CPU and the graphic adapter does not play a significant role, because the graphic processor requires much longer to produce the pixel data than the data transfer to the graphic processor takes. Graphic processors first have a real advantage in multitasking operating systems, when task switches, refresh cycles of the main memory or hardware interrupts occur. While the CPU handles these requests, the graphic processor forms the picture in the background, undisturbed, and in parallel with the CPU operation.

A further problem is that the video RAM is only accessible during specific short time slots. The RAM chips on the adapter can only be either read or written to. If the CRTC chip of the adapter continuously reads the video RAM during the formation of a line, an access by the CPU is not possible even with a local bus. The processor must wait for the next line or screen return. For this, the adapter simply deactivates the RDY bus signal for as long as necessary, causing the CPU to insert the associated number of wait cycles. In principle, this also affects adapters with graphic processors. Only here, the accesses by the CRTC controller and the graphic processor can be co-ordinated such that the graphic processor, for example, writes to a RAM bank of the video memory which the CRTC controller is not currently reading for the formation of the current raster line. This is not possible with an external CPU, because the CPU does not know which address is currently being read and, therefore, which in principle are not accessible. Here also there is a clear advantage for adapters with graphic processors. A way around this problem is through the use of dual port memory in the video RAM. Here, the video memory is blocked during the refresh cycles; the reading of data by the CRTC controller no longer blocks the access. For this reason, an ISA graphic adapter with a dual port memory area is frequently as good as a local bus graphic adapter containing normal DRAM components in some benchmark tests. This, however, will change in future with the introduction of new 32-bit local bus graphic adapters.

The last, frequently neglected, but nonetheless deciding factor concerns the driver for a graphic adapter and how it is required to tie into the Windows or OS/2 system and represent a clearly defined programmable interface. While the programming of such a driver is quite simple for a few intelligent graphic cards (after all, only a very limited selection of adapter functions are available), the more intelligent accelerator cards have considerably higher requirements. For example, the programmer must weigh up whether or not it is worth making full use of the graphic functions of the accelerator chips for a specific function, or using the conventional (direct access) method using the video RAM. Thus, it is not surprising that the quality of the drivers supplied frequently varies, even though this point contributes to the overall performance by a factor of at least two

In summary, I am of the opinion that an installed graphic adapter should be intelligent enough to cope with the quantity of data being passed back and forth. For absolute high-end applications (CAD or picture processing at 1280∗1024 pixels in HighColor or even TrueColor mode), a graphics processor brings considerable relief to a CPU that is already heavily loaded down with «normal» calculations.

33 Multimedia

People have been talking about multimedia for a long time; however, until recently only demonstrations had been achieved, but no «real» applications (though the demonstrations were impressive). The main reason was the huge amount of data which has to be stored and processed. This requires powerful (and, of course, standardized) compression methods. Such methods have now become available, helping to push multimedia again. Together with increasingly powerful processors and storage devices, many multimedia applications can now be expected in a very short time. Our three main «communication channels», text, voice (audio) and visual recognition, are now united in the *Multimedia PC (MPC)*. Remarkably, the advance of electronic devices follows the same order as the development of the «classical» communication media: letter/book → telephone/radio → TV/video. In both cases, the reason is the enormously increasing amount of data implicit in every step. Only once the required technology was available at a reasonable price could the new medium be successful.

At present, the multimedia PC is suited particularly to imparting knowledge through, for example, encyclopedias or computer aided learning (CAL), and, of course, to highly animated computer games. Data input and output via spoken language is also possible, although some more work seems to be required to develop error-free devices. Apple has been engaged in the multimedia field for quite a long time – many Macs have been shipped as Multimedia Macs for a number of years.

In the following sections, I shall discuss the technological background in brief. A thorough examination of this interesting topic can be found in the specialist literature on multimedia.

33.1 Technological Background

In the following, I will look at multimedia as the complete unit of «written», audible and visual information. Stated differently, these three types of information are unified in a single data stream. For a multimedia encyclopedia which provides information, for example, about a certain musical composition, the data flow shown in Figure 33.1 would be typical.

A storage medium holds both the encyclopedia program and the encyclopedia data. Because of the immense amount of data, the CD (or MOD – modulo) is presently the only possible storage device that can be used. It holds the multimedia data in a compressed form, because otherwise the multimedia demonstration would terminate within a few minutes. The program controls the information's reproduction. It is executed by the program device of a central multimedia unit, usually the CPU of a multimedia PC. The data device serves mainly for decompressing the data. This can be done by the PC's CPU. Far more efficient, however, are specialized (and very quick) decompression chips or signal processors which are able, for example, to expand video data compressed according to the *MPEG* (*Motion Picture Expert Group*) standard in real time. If the CPU were to be loaded with this task as well, the multimedia output would begin to flag very soon. An example of such specialized chips and adapters is the SoundBlaster card, which generates and outputs sound. The width of the arrows in Figure 33.1 indicates the relative distribution of the amount of information between the program and data streams. Characteristic of multimedia is a very large amount of data (program parts are typically run through frequently so that the program's share of the execution time is higher than would be expected from the arrow width).

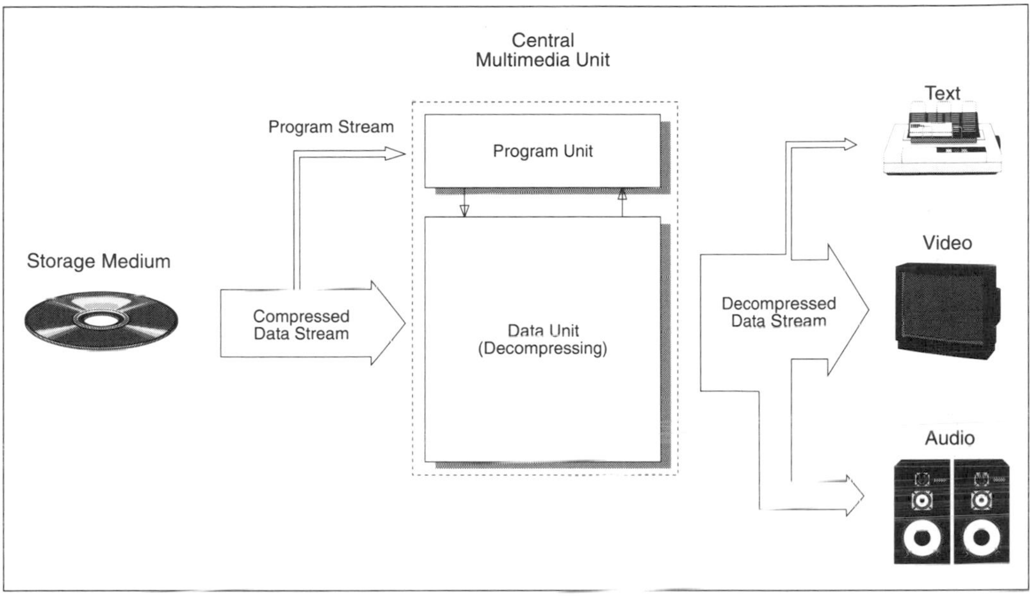

Figure 33.1: Multimedia data flow.

Fortunately, audio and video data is less sensitive to errors than programs. If a byte of a song stored on a CD is erroneous you will hardly notice it. The same applies to a pixel of a frame for motion video. But an erroneous program byte is disastrous; the MPC crashes and the multimedia demonstration is terminated at once. The data transfer rate of the data stream exceeds that of the program stream by some orders of magnitude. For that reason, the data stream is more compressed at the expense of reliability: an error rate of 10^{-8} is tolerable. The program stream is equipped with highly efficient error correcting means to reduce the error rate to less than 10^{-12}. A higher data reliability, of course, means more costly (and thus slower) decoding.

The data device then splits the decompressed data stream into three partial streams and supplies each of them to the relevant output device. The smallest data flow is required by the text output on a monitor or – as shown in Figure 33.1 – a printer. After all, we read more slowly than we are able to hear or look. Of course, text on a monitor is some kind of visual information, but in connection with multimedia, we mean motion video when we are talking about visual information. This requires a huge amount of information. The visual information of text on the monitor can be compressed efficiently because only a 1-byte ASCII code and a 1-byte attribute are necessary for every letter character (for a high-resolution graphic with 16*32 pixels of 256 colours, the pure graphical information encompasses 16*32 = 512 bytes!). The program which displays the respective character holds further information internally, namely the form of the character to be displayed. You may know from personal experience that in transmitting one page of text via a facsimile machine (which works in a graphical manner), despite a very efficient data compression method, ten to twenty times more data must be transferred as compared with email.

The second largest data stream is formed by the audio information. Stereo sound in CD quality at a sampling rate of 44.1 kHz with a depth of 16 bits already requires a bandwidth of 2*44.100*16 bits = 176.4 kbytes/s. This corresponds to about 40 DIN A4 pages completely filled with text, or reading for one hour. A very efficient compression method, which is based on the definition of the enveloping curve of a tone instead of the digitized course of the tone itself, is shown in Figure 33.2. This is used, for example, by the FM channels of the SoundBlaster card.

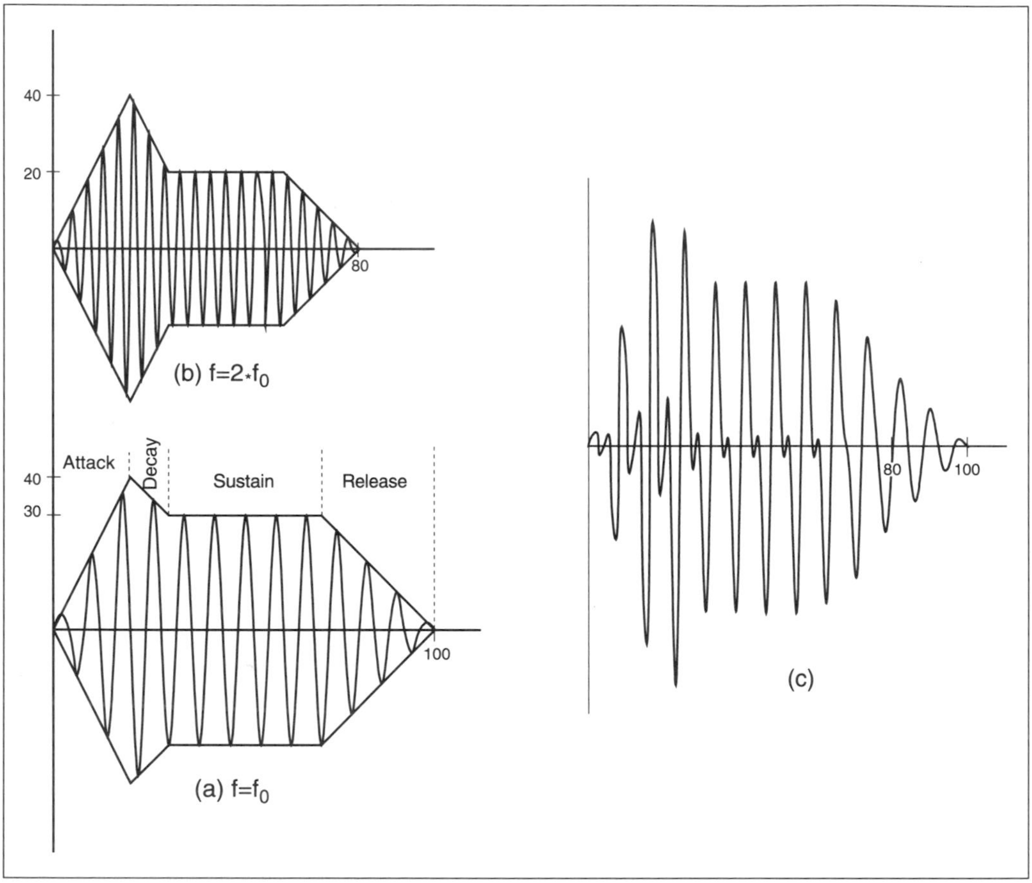

Figure 33.2: Envelope and superposition of sounds: (a) Sound with frequency f_0, amplitude=40, attack=20, decay=10, sustain=40, release=30, (b) sound with frequency $2*f_0$, amplitude=40, attack=20, decay=10, sustain=30, release=20, (c) superposition of (a) and (b).

Every sound is usually a linear superposition of an oscillation and its harmonics (oscillations with frequencies which are a multiple of the basic oscillation frequency); these basic oscillations and the harmonics have an amplitude and a damping characteristic for the musical instrument or voice. The combination of only a few oscillations with different amplitudes and dampings can produce a very complex course of the overall oscillation and, thus, the sound, although the course can be represented by only a few parameters. These are, according to Figure 33.2, attack, decay, sustain and release, in addition to frequency and amplitude. The audio synthesizer then generates a digital data stream from these few macro parameters, which in turn is converted into a voltage course by a DAC, and finally into audible sound in a speaker. The two «pure» sounds with frequencies f_0 (Figure 33.2a) and $2*f_0$ (Figure 33.2b) are combined and produce a tone (c). By the superposition of additional sounds, nearly any waveform can be generated. Figure 33.2 shows the course of a continuous sound; here, the sound is maintained until the release phase. For a descending sound, the decay phase is immediately followed by the release phase. The sustain value in both cases defines the amplitude of the signal where the decay phase ends. Continuous sounds are characteristic for wind or string instruments which are continuously operated (such as trumpets or violins); descending sounds, on the other hand, are characteristic of plucked string instruments (such as guitars).

Usually, we have to go the opposite way to determine, from a given waveform (for example, a human voice), a lot of «basic sounds» with courses shown in Figures 33.2(a) and 33.2(b). Their parameters are then stored instead of the sampling. You may ask how to solve this non-trivial problem. In principle, only an extensive calculation of higher mathematics is required – the so-called *Fourier Analysis* or *Fourier Transform*. With this process, the individual «contributions» of a tone can be determined.

An example will demonstrate the compression which can be achieved with such an envelope: at a 16-bit resolution for frequency and amplitude (which is more than enough) and an 8-bit depth of the other parameters, eight bytes are necessary for each sound. The superposition of ten different sounds usually leads to a very natural tone for one second. Thus, a total of 80 bytes is required. If we assume a sampling frequency of 22.05 kHz (significantly less than CD quality), 44 kbytes are necessary at a 16-bit depth. That is a factor of 500! Even if we need ten times more envelopes with various frequencies and amplitudes to improve the natural appearance of the sound, or for voice synthesis (which is far more complicated than synthesizing music), a compression factor of 50 is still achievable compared to the poor sampling at 22.05 kHz. The audio data stream is then comparable to ordinary text output (before decompression, of course).

A far more extensive amount of data is required for *motion video*: 25 complete pictures – so-called *frames* per second at a resolution of 1024*768 pixels and TrueColor (3 bytes per pixel) lead to 56.25 Mbytes/s. Stated differently: a CD with 682 Mbytes can hold a meagre 12 seconds of motion video (not to mention the impossibility of a transfer rate of 56.25 Mbytes/s with today's CD-ROM drives). A compression rate of at least 100 is therefore demanded.

Fortunately, motion video allows a high reduction of the data stream because the various frames are less different than would be expected because of the enormous amount of information contained in *one* single frame. When, for example, an object is moving in front of a fixed background, the content of the video RAM that represents the background only needs to be updated where the moving object is exposing or covering the background. Additionally, the moving object is hardly changing from frame to frame, because rotations or illumination changes only have a small effect from frame to frame. Moreover, large parts show a nearly homogeneous colour and brightness distribution. Therefore, it is only necessary to store the *image changes* from frame to frame, but not each frame itself. Additionally, the sharpness of transitions within a picture (for example, a dark object in front of a white wall) can be limited. This leads to a degradation of the contrast for fast-moving objects with sharp transitions, but this is hardly noticeable. The MPEG compression method, intended as a standard, makes use of that and other strategies (such as encoding of the colour and brightness values, which deviates from the normal red-green-blue distribution used in the computer field) to achieve a compression ratio of about 100. You can imagine that the decompression electronics must be extraordinarily quick to generate binary data for a video memory from such highly compressed data, which is additionally woven together with the audio and text information into a single data stream.

One further note in relation to the 25 frames in the era of the 100 Hz vertical frequency: for a completely untiring monitor image, at least 60 – 70 Hz are required, but this refers only to the *flicker* of the image. Even if the *image content* is altered to be much slower (with the 25 Hz indicated), the user has the impression of a constantly moving object. For that purpose, each frame is repeated, for example, two, three or four times before the next frame is displayed. By the continuous rewriting of the video memory for new frames, (intended) interpolations between the various frames occur, which contribute to the contiguous display of fast-moving objects. The method of displaying the same frame several times has been used for quite a long time in high-end TVs. The repetition frequency of 100 Hz is achieved by displaying the same frame a number of times, and produces a completely flicker-free image. Because the TV operates in an interlaced mode, 50 half-frames are displayed per second (60 half-frames in North America): this corresponds to exactly 25 (30) complete frames per second. The purpose of displaying 50 (60) half-frames per second is to obtain a reduction in screen flicker.

33.2 Programming

Programming the multimedia hardware components can be carried out, as usual, in various ways. The most straightforward method is direct access to the registers of the multimedia chips. This is (depending on the device) more or less standardized in some parts (for example, the FM channels of the SoundBlaster card have evolved as a *de facto* standard). Generally, the functions and register layouts vary considerably from manufacturer to manufacturer – multimedia is a very new field, after all, and a dominating company which could establish standards is (still) missing (compared with IBM ten years ago). Therefore, direct register access is useful only for programming the drivers of a superordinate operating system.

Multimedia applications demand «windows» for the various information channels of text, audio and video. The modern and graphic-oriented operating systems and user shells, for example Windows (NT) and OS/2, thus provide clearly defined programming interfaces to the multimedia devices supported (the so-called *Multimedia Managers*). Additionally, direct register accesses are not welcome, or are even forbidden, under these operating systems running in protected mode. Therefore, I must refer you to the programming manuals for these systems and their multimedia services. The specification of the multimedia services for Windows fills three books! As a quite simple but nevertheless interesting example, I will discuss the FM channels of the SoundBlaster card in the following section in brief, to introduce you to the world of multimedia programming.

33.3 An Example: The FM Channels of SoundBlaster

SoundBlaster from Creative Labs has evolved as a standard for sound adapters within a short time, mainly because of its reasonable price. In addition to the FM channels for sound generation discussed in the following, it usually has a *Digital Signal Processor* (*DSP*) for *sampling* tones input externally (for example, via a microphone), processing the signal course and outputting the processed sound. Various sound sources (CD, audio tape, microphone, etc.) can thus be mixed, processed and stored in a digital manner (and also output afterwards, of course). Further, the possibility of speech synthesis is also very interesting: that is, your computer reads (with a special program such as SBTALK) written text, or it can (again with a special program) understand spoken texts or commands – «real» multimedia (although image recognition will exceed the computing capacity of even modern PCs for some years).

Another important component of the SoundBlaster is the MIDI interface (*Musical Instrument Digital Interface*). This is mainly an asynchronous serial interface (similar to COMx) with a transfer rate of 31 250 baud. It is used for data exchange between various musical instruments (or, in general, sound sources). This interface is also called the MPU-401 UART (*MIDI Processing Unit*). Table 33.1 lists all the port addresses occupied by the SoundBlaster's components.

Port	Register
200h–207h	Joystick
2x0h*)	Index register of left channel
2x1h*)	Data register of left channel
2x2h*)	Index register of right channel
2x3h*)	Data register of right channel
330h	MIDI index register
331h	MIDI data register
388h	FM index register
389h	FM data register

*) x=2 (standard), 4, 6, 8 (base addresses therefore: 220h, 240h, 260h, 280h)

Table 33.1: SoundBlaster registers

The I/O addresses of the joystick port have the same structure as for the usual game adapter (see Section 29.3.1). The index and data registers for the left and right channels (stereo) refer to the programming of the DSP. The MIDI registers allow access to the MIDI interface; I will therefore not discuss these registers in detail. For an automatic playing of sound of every kind in the background (a must for multimedia), the SoundBlaster additionally integrates two timers similar to the 8253/8254 on the motherboard. Further, the adapter can request DMA transfers to relieve the CPU of continuous data transfers for «feeding» the DSP. But now let's turn to the programming of the SoundBlaster's FM channels.

33.3.1 Sound with Nine Channels

The FM channels can be operated in two different modes: sound with nine channels as well as sound with six channels and five percussions. In the following, I will mainly deal with sound with nine channels, and afterwards discuss the second FM mode in brief.

For programming the FM synthesizer, the index and data register at I/O addresses 388h and 389h are involved. You may already recognize that the SoundBlaster uses an indexing scheme for programming. This is necessary because a total of 18 generator cells for generating sound are available, which (combined into a pair each) form nine FM channels. The name FM (*Frequency Modulation*) characterizes the most important of the two possible sound generation types of SoundBlaster. More about that below.

Each generator cell has five registers for defining the sound properties. Their index offsets and layouts are summarized in Table 33.2. The index offsets are added to the base index of the generator cells (see Table 33.3) to evaluate the register index for a register of a certain cell.

Index offset	**Structure 76543210**	**Range of value**	**Content**
20h	x	0–1	tremolo (0=off, 1=on)
	x	0–1	vibrato (0=off, 1=on)
	x	0–1	envelope type (0=descending, 1=continuous)
	x	0–1	envelope shortening (0=off, 1=on)
	xxxx	0–15	multiplication factor
40h	xx	0–3	high-frequency damping (0=no, 1=3 dB per octave, 2=1.5 dB per octave, 3=6 dB per octave
	xxxxxx	0–63	damping factor
60h	xxxx	0–15	attack
	xxxx	0–15	decay
80h	xxxx	0–15	sustain
	xxxx	0–15	release
e0h	xx	0–3	waveform

Table 33.2: Registers of the generator cells

In the following, I will explain the meaning of the various register entries for the signal course. You can only switch the tremolo effect on or off. *Tremolo* means a variation of the sound *amplitude* (volume) at a frequency of 3.7 Hz. The situation with *vibrato* is similar; however, here the *frequency* of the sound varies at 6.4 Hz. The depths of tremolo and vibrato can be set through the channel register with index BDh (see Table 33.4). The entry *envelope type* refers to the form of the envelope. There are two different types: descending and continuous envelopes (see Figure 33.3).

The figure simultaneously defines the meaning of the values attack, decay, sustain and release. The larger the *attack* value (0–15), the faster the envelope ascends (the higher is the slope). *Decay* determines how quickly the envelope descends afterwards. The *sustain* value defines which value the envelope reaches during the course of the decay phase, that is, to which amplitude the envelope descends in the course of the decay. Here, a difference appears between a descending

(Figure 33.3a) and a continuous (Figure 33.3b) envelope: for a *descending envelope*, the decay phase is followed by the *release* phase immediately after the sustain value is reached. For a *continuous envelope*, the amplitude remains the same until the sound has been switched off through the corresponding channel register, that is, the release phase is delayed until the sound is switched off. For a descending envelope, on the other hand, the sound need not be switched off to remove the sound. That is the case automatically after the release phase. A high release value means (as usual) a quick descent of the envelope. The *envelope shortening* causes sound with a higher frequency to be shortened automatically (this is the case for some string instruments such as, for example, pianos or guitars).

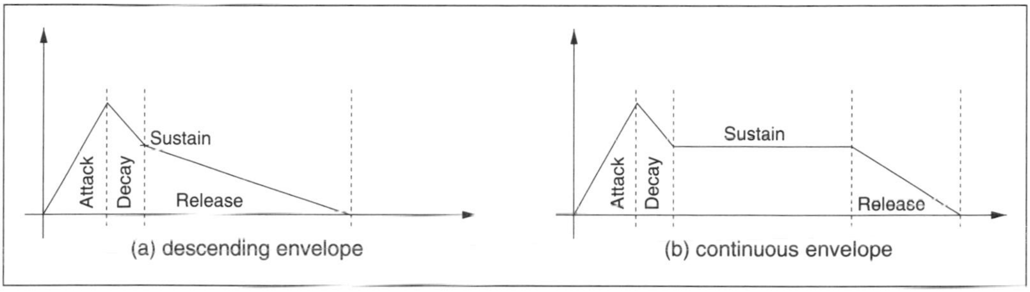

Figure 33.3: (a)Descending and (b) continuous envelope.

Another important entry which affects the frequency of the oscillation generated by the cell is the *multiplication factor*. It determines at which multiple of the base frequency (which is defined by the corresponding channel register) the signal of this generator cell oscillates. For factor values between 1 and 15, the frequency ratio is also equal to 1–15. The factor values 0 and 16 deviate from this rule: they correspond to frequency ratios of 0.5 and 15, respectively. The *high frequency damping* determines whether, and if so, to what extent the amplitude of higher frequencies is damped. You may have recognized that a (natural) musical instrument generates high sound at a considerably less volume than low frequencies.

The *damping factor* indicates to what extent the amplitude of the oscillation generated (or volume) will be damped compared to the maximum amplitude. The following relation holds:

damping = (0.75 * damping factor) dB or

amplitude = maximum amplitude * $10^{-0.75\text{*damping factor}}$

Note that the dB scale is logarithmic; doubling the damping factor leads to a lowering of the amplitude to $1/10^{0.75} = 1/5.6$. However, you will only hear a halving (roughly) of the volume because our ears have logarithmic sensitivity.

The last entry is the *waveform*. You can choose between four different signal courses, shown in Figure 33.4.

Waveform 0 is the common sine oscillation. Waveform 1 is produced from waveform 0 by neglecting all the negative parts of the sine oscillation; it is also called the *positive sine half-oscillation*. Waveform 2 is more or less the absolute of sine oscillation 0; all negative parts are «folded» to positive values. Finally, waveform 3 represents a saw-type oscillation. It is produced from waveform 2 simply by a descent of the signal at the vertex of each oscillation down to zero. These waveforms sound different, even at the same frequencies. With all this information you can now program the 18 generator cells. To actually output a sound via a channel, though, this channel must additionally be configured.

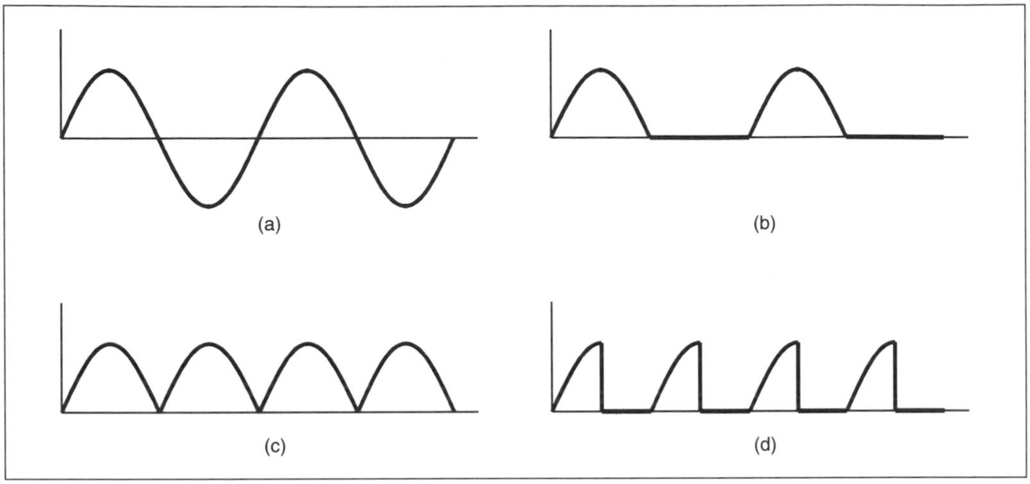

Figure 33.4: Waveforms of the SoundBlaster. (a) Sine oscillation, (b) positive sine half-oscillation, (c) pulsing oscillation, (d) saw-type oscillation.

Cell	Offset	Channel	Modulator/Carrier
0	00h	0	modulator
1	01h	1	modulator
2	02h	2	modulator
3	03h	0	carrier
4	04h	1	carrier
5	05h	2	carrier
6	08h	3	modulator
7	09h	4	modulator
8	0ah	5	modulator
9	0bh	3	carrier
10	0ch	4	carrier
11	0dh	5	carrier
12	10h	6	modulator
13	11h	7	modulator
14	12h	8	modulator
15	13h	6	carrier
16	14h	7	carrier
17	15h	8	carrier

Table 33.3: Base index of the generator cells and channels

Each channel can generate a sound; two generator cells are paired for this purpose. The first cell is called the *modulator cell*, the second the *carrier cell*. Table 33.3 lists the index offsets of the generator cells and the corresponding combination for one channel.

You can see that, unfortunately, the offsets are not linearly linked to the cell enumeration. The same applies to the assignment of two respective cells to one channel. For example, cell 6 with offset 08h forms the modulator, and cell 9 with offset 0bh the carrier for channel 3. If you want to use a channel, you must program both the modulator and the carrier cell which are assigned to the respective channel according to Table 33.3.

You program a register of a generator cell by transferring the register index (consisting of the base index and index offset) with OUT to the 8-bit index port 388h first. Then you must (again with OUT) write the 8-bit data value into data port 389h. Note that all SoundBlaster ports are write-only; a read access returns ffh.

```
Example: set up attack=12, decay=6 (index offset 60h) for channel 1, cell 1 (modulator) and 4
(carrier).

MOV ah, 61h     ; load index offset 60h + base index 01h to ah
MOV al, 388h    ; I/O address for index port
OUT al, ah      ; write index into index register
MOV ah, c6h     ; load attack 12=0ch and decay=06h to ah
MOV al, 389h    ; I/O address for data port
OUT al, ah      ; write attack and decay value into data register
```

Index	Structure 76543210	Content
axh*)	xxxxxxxx	frequency value (bits 7–0)
bxh*)	xx......	reserved
	..x.....	sound on/off (0=off, 1=on)
	...xxx..	octave
	xx	frequency value (bits 9–8)
bdh	x.......	tremolo depth (0=1 dB, 1=4.8 dB)
	.x......	vibrato depth (0=7/100, 1=14/100)
	..x.....	mode (0=9 FM channels, 1=6 FM channels with 5 percussions)
	...x....	bass drum
	....x...	snare drum
	.....x..	tom tom
	......x.	top cymbal
	x	hi hat
cxh*)	xxxx....	reserved
	....xxx.	feedback
	x	cell linking (0=FM, 1=addition)

*) x: base index of the channels: channel 0: x=0; channel 1: x=1; ...; channel 8: x=8.

Table 33.4: Channel registers.

Now only the channel registers are missing to program the channels and to actually generate sound. The channel registers of SoundBlaster are summarized in Table 33.4. Because two generator cells are required for one channel, the SoundBlaster has nine (18 cells/2) channels. The base indices of the channels are contiguous (for example, channel 0: base index 0; channel 1: base index 1; ...; channel 8: base index 8). For example, the frequency register of channel 3 is thus assigned index a3h.

Note that these channel registers represent one channel each, that is, two generator cells. Therefore, the entries affect the two cells of a channel together. Only one register bdh represents all channels.

You can set up the base frequency through two parameters: a 3-bit octave value for the octave range of the base frequency (the possible values 0–7 correspond to the octaves 1–8; see Section 26.1); and a 10-bit frequency value which allows tiny steppings within the same octave.

The base frequency thus generated is multiplied in two generators assigned to the channel by the respective multiplication factor. The result is the frequency of the oscillation which is produced by the generators. Because of the possibility of defining two different multiplication factors for the generators, you can determine nearly any frequency ratio and sound frequency.

Example: `octave=4 (corresponds to music octave 5), frequency value=577, multiplication factor=1 leads to a sound frequency of 440 Hz; this is exactly concert pitch A.`

You can switch the sound on or off through bit 5 in the register at index offset bxh. Bit 7 in the register with index BDh sets the tremolo depth; you can choose 1 dB or 4.8 dB. The same applies to bit 6, which determines the vibrato depth. Very important is the entry *mode*. If this bit is cleared (equal to 0), then the SoundBlaster operates with nine FM channels, that is, running in the operating state described in this section. If you set mode to 1, six FM channels and five percussions (bass drum, snare drum, tom tom, top cymbal and hi hat) are enabled; this mode is discussed in the following section.

The *feedback* entry defines the feedback strength of the output signal of the modulator cell to its input. A value of 0 means that there is no feedback; a value of 7 gives the strongest feedback. Note that this entry only affects the modulator cell of the channel; the output signal of a carrier cell is never fed back.

In connection with the last parameter, *cell linking*, we learn why two generator cells are always necessary for each channel. The output signals of these cells are combined in one of two ways. If the cell linking bit is cleared (equal to 0), the carrier signal is *frequency modulated* with the modulator oscillation (hence the name FM channels, carrier and modulator oscillation). In a mathematical sense, the following combination of carrier amplitude A_T, carrier frequency f_T, modulator amplitude A_M and modulator frequency f_M is carried out to produce the overall oscillation FM(t) (see also Figure 33.5):

$$FM(t) = A_T * \sin(2\pi * f_T * t + A_M * \sin(2\pi * f_M * t))$$

Incidentally, this combination is used for FM radio and television to transmit a useful signal (FM: music, speech; TV: image, tone) as error-free as possible via a carrier signal (ultra short wave, VHF and UHF). The receiver separates the modulator oscillation (which represents the useful signal) again, thus eliminating the carrier. The frequency of the modulator oscillation

(FM: music, speech with less than 20 kHz) is significantly lower than the carrier frequency (FM: about 100 MHz).

If the cell linking bit is set (equal to 1), however, then the carrier oscillation and the modulator oscillation are simply added. In a mathematical sense, the following simple combination is carried out:

$FM(t) = A_T * \sin(2\pi * f_T * t) + A_M * \sin(2\pi * f_M * t)$

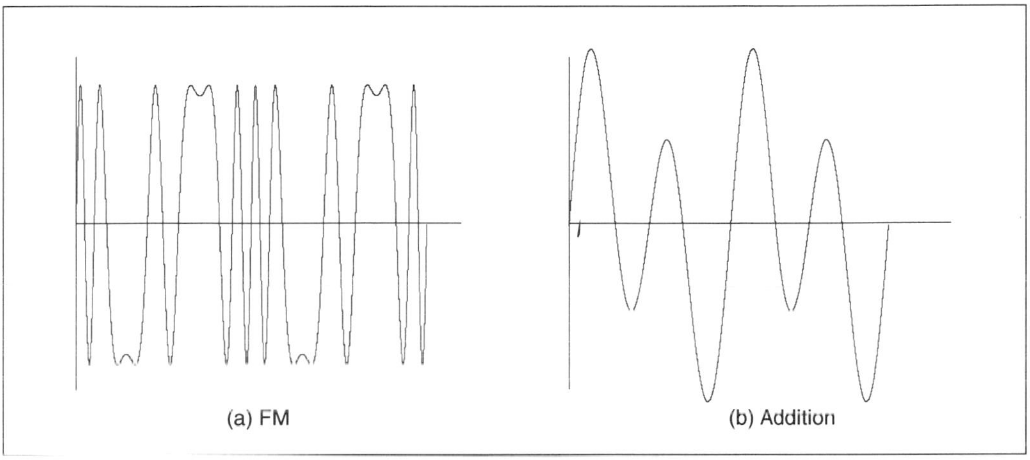

Figure 33.5: Cell linking for A_T=1, A_M=0.5, f_T=1, f_M=0.5 (arbitrary units). (a) Frequency modulation, (b) addition of waveforms.

Figure 33.5 shows the very different oscillation courses for frequency modulation and the simple addition of the carrier and modulator signals. For the example shown, it has been assumed that the carrier signal has twice the amplitude and twice the frequency of the modulator signal.

33.3.2 Sound with Six Channels and Five Percussions

One operating mode that is especially important for synthetic SoundBlaster music is sound generation with six FM channels and five percussion. You can switch between the 9-channel and 6-channel modes by means of the control register with index BDh (see Figure 33.6).

If you set the *RhM* bit, six FM channels and the five following percussions are enabled: bass drum, hi hat, tom tom, snare drum and top cymbal. Six generator cells are available for them, where the bass drum is supported by two cells. Table 33.5 lists the assignment of the cells to the percussion. Additionally, which channels are usually operated by these cells in the 9-channel mode is indicated.

The generator cells and channel registers for the six FM channels are programmed in exactly the same way as in the 9-channel mode, and they also have the same effect. The same applies for the cells of the percussion; however, despite programmable envelopes, etc., they generate oscillations which (approximately) correspond to each instrument. The best-simulated instrument of all is the bass drum, because it is generated by two cells (12 and 15); they are assigned to channel 6. Note that you always affect two instruments simultaneously when you are programming another channel register (that is, the hi hat and snare drum together, as well as the tom tom and top cymbal). After setting up the generator cells and channel registers, the percussions can be enabled individually. That is carried out with bits *BDr, SDr, Tot, TCy* and *HiH* in the percussion register at index BDh (see Figure 33.6).

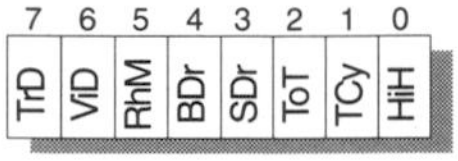


```
TrD: Tremolo Depth
     0=1 dB   1=4.8 dB
ViD: Vibrato Depth
     0=7/100   1=14/100
RhM: Rhythm Mode
     0=9 FM channels   1=6 FM channels and 5 percussions
BDr: Bass Drum
     0=off   1=on
SDr: Snare Drum
     0=off   1=on
ToT: Tom Tom
     0=off   1=on
TCy: Top Cymbal
     0=off   1=on
HiH: Hi Hat
     0=off   1=on
```

Figure 33.6: Percussion, vibrato and tremolo register (port BDh).

Percussion	**Cell**	**Channel**
bass drum	12+15	6 (modulator and carrier)
hi hat	13	7 (modulator)
tom tom	14	8 (modulator)
snare drum	16	7 (carrier)
top cymbal	17	8 (carrier)

Table 33.5: Generator cells of the percussion instruments

Example: enable 6-channel mode with bass drum and top cymbal (discard tremolo and vibrato depth).

```
MOV ah, 32h     ; value of percussion register (RhM=1, BDr=1, TCy=1)
MOV al, 388h    ; I/O address of index port
OUT al, bdh     ; output index of percussion register to index port
MOV al, 389h    ; I/O address of data port
OUT al, ah      ; write register value
```

Appendices

A ASCII and Scan Codes

A.1 ASCII Code

The following tables show the ASCII codes 0–127 and the extended ASCII codes 128–255. The values 0–31 are assigned control codes; they are therefore listed separately. Each code is indicated in decimal (dec) and hexadecimal (hex) form, together with the usually assigned character (chr).

Ctrl	dec	hex	char	code	
^@	0	00		NUL	Null Character
^A	1	01	▼	SOH	Start of Header
^B	2	02	-	STX	Start of Text
^C	3	03	♥	ETX	End of Text
^D	4	04	♦	EOT	End of Transmission
^E	5	05	♣	ENQ	Enquiry
^F	6	06	♠	ACK	Acknowledge
^G	7	07	.	BEL	Bell
^H	8	08	.	BS	Backspace
^I	9	09		HT	Horizontal Tabulation
^J	10	0A		LF	Line Feed
^K	11	0B		VT	Vertical Tabulation
^L	12	0C		FF	Form Feed
^M	13	0D		CR	Carriage Return
^N	14	0E		SO	Shift Out
^O	15	0F		SI	Shift In
^P	16	10	►	DLE	Data Link Escape
^Q	17	11	◄	DC1	Device Control 1
^R	18	12	↕	DC2	Device Control 2
^S	19	13	‼	DC3	Device Control 3
^T	20	14	¶	DC4	Device Control 4
^U	21	15	§	NAK	Negative Acknowledgement
^V	22	16	■	SYN	Synchronous Idle
^W	23	17	↨	ETB	End of Transmission Block
^X	24	18	↑	CAN	Cancel
^Y	25	19	↓	EM	End of Medium
^Z	26	1A	→	SUB	Substitute
^[	27	1B	.	ESC	Escape
^\	28	1C	∟	FS	File Separator
^]	29	1D	↔	GS	Group Separator
^^	30	1E	▲	RS	Record Separator
^_	31	1F		US	Unit Separator

dec	hex	char
32	20	
33	21	!
34	22	"
35	23	#
36	24	$
37	25	%
38	26	&
39	27	'
40	28	(
41	29	)
42	2A	*
43	2B	+
44	2C	,
45	2D	-
46	2E	.
47	2F	/
48	30	0
49	31	1
50	32	2
51	33	3
52	34	4
53	35	5
54	36	6
55	37	7
56	38	8
57	39	9
58	3A	:
59	3B	;
60	3C	<
61	3D	=
62	3E	>
63	3F	?

dec	hex	char
64	40	@
65	41	A
66	42	B
67	43	C
68	44	D
69	45	E
70	46	F
71	47	G
72	48	H
73	49	I
74	4A	J
75	4B	K
76	4C	L
77	4D	M
78	4E	N
79	4F	O
80	50	P
81	51	Q
82	52	R
83	53	S
84	54	T
85	55	U
86	56	V
87	57	W
88	58	X
89	59	Y
90	5A	Z
91	5B	[
92	5C	\
93	5D	]
94	5E	^
95	5F	_

dec	hex	char
96	60	'
97	61	a
98	62	b
99	63	c
100	64	d
101	65	e
102	66	f
103	67	g
104	68	h
105	69	i
106	6A	j
107	6B	k
108	6C	l
109	6D	m
110	6E	n
111	6F	o
112	70	p
113	71	q
114	72	r
115	73	s
116	74	t
117	75	u
118	76	v
119	77	w
120	78	x
121	79	y
122	7A	z
123	7B	{
124	7C	|
125	7D	}
126	7E	~
127	7F	⌂

dec	hex	char
128	80	Ç
129	81	ü
130	82	é
131	83	â
132	84	ä
133	85	à
134	86	å
135	87	ç
136	88	ê
137	89	ë
138	8A	è
139	8B	ï
140	8C	î
141	8D	ì
142	8E	Ä
143	8F	Å
144	90	É
145	91	æ
146	92	Æ
147	93	ô
148	94	ö
149	95	ò
150	96	û
151	97	ù
152	98	ÿ
153	99	Ö
154	9A	Ü
155	9B	¢
156	9C	£
157	9D	¥
158	9E	₧
159	9F	ƒ

dec	hex	char
160	A0	á
161	A1	í
162	A2	ó
163	A3	ú
164	A4	ñ
165	A5	Ñ
166	A6	ª
167	A7	º
168	A8	¿
169	A9	⌐
170	AA	¬
171	AB	½
172	AC	¼
173	AD	¡
174	AE	«
175	AF	»
176	B0	░
177	B1	▒
178	B2	▓
179	B3	│
180	B4	┤
181	B5	╡
182	B6	╢
183	B7	╖
184	B8	╕
185	B9	╣
186	BA	║
187	BB	╗
188	BC	╝
189	BD	╜
190	BE	╛
191	BF	┐

dec	hex	char
192	C0	└
193	C1	┴
194	C2	┬
195	C3	├
196	C4	─
197	C5	┼
198	C6	╞
199	C7	╟
200	C8	╚
201	C9	╔
202	CA	╩
203	CB	╦
204	CC	╠
205	CD	═
206	CE	╬
207	CF	╧
208	D0	╨
209	D1	╤
210	D2	╥
211	D3	╙
212	D4	╘
213	D5	╒
214	D6	╓
215	D7	╫
216	D8	╪
217	D9	┘
218	DA	┌
219	DB	█
220	DC	▄
221	DD	▌
222	DE	▐
223	DF	▀

dec	hex	char
224	E0	α
225	E1	ß
226	E2	Γ
227	E3	π
228	E4	Σ
229	E5	σ
230	E6	µ
231	E7	τ
232	E8	Φ
233	E9	θ
234	EA	Ω
235	EB	δ
236	EC	∞
237	ED	ϕ
238	EE	∈
239	EF	∩
240	F0	≡
241	F1	±
242	F2	≥
243	F3	≤
244	F4	⌠
245	F5	⌡
246	F6	÷
247	F7	≈
248	F8	°
249	F9	•
250	FA	·
251	FB	√
252	FC	^{n}
253	FD	^{2}
254	FE	■
255	FF	

A.2 Scan Codes UK

key	scan code		ASCII/extended			ASCII/extended with shift			ASCII/extended with ctrl			ASCII/extended with alt		
	dec	hex	dec	hex	char	dec	hex	char	dec	hex	char	dec	hex	char
ESC	1	01	27	1b		27	1b		27	1b		1	1	NUL
1 !	2	02	49	31	1	33	21	!				120	78	NUL
2 "	3	03	50	32	2	34	22	"	3	03	NUL	121	79	NUL
3 £	4	04	51	33	3	156	9c	£				122	7a	NUL
4 $	5	05	52	34	4	36	24	$				123	7b	NUL
5 %	6	06	53	35	5	37	25	%				124	7c	NUL
6 ^	7	07	54	36	6	94	5e	^	30	1e		125	7d	NUL
7 &	8	08	55	37	7	38	26	&				126	7e	NUL
8 *	9	09	56	38	8	42	2a	*				127	7f	NUL
9 (	10	0a	57	39	9	40	28	(				128	80	NUL
0)	11	0b	48	30	0	41	29	)				129	81	NUL
– _	12	0c	45	2d	–	95	5f	_	31	1f		130	82	NUL
= +	13	0d	61	3d	=	43	2b	+				131	83	NUL
BKSP	14	0e	8	08		8	08		127	7f				
TAB	15	0f	9	09		15	0f							
Q	16	10	113	71	q	81	51	Q	17	11	^Q	16	10	NUL
W	17	11	119	77	w	87	57	W	23	17	^W	17	11	NUL
E	18	12	101	65	e	69	45	E	5	05	^E	18	12	NUL
R	19	13	114	72	r	82	52	R	18	12	^R	19	13	NUL
T	20	14	116	74	t	84	54	T	20	14	^T	20	14	NUL
Y	21	15	121	79	y	89	59	Y	25	19	^Y	21	15	NUL
U	22	16	117	75	u	85	55	U	21	15	^U	22	16	NUL
I	23	17	105	69	i	73	49	I	9	09	^I	23	17	NUL
O	24	18	111	6f	o	79	4f	O	15	0f	^O	24	18	NUL
P	25	19	112	70	p	80	50	P	16	10	^P	25	19	NUL
[{	26	1a	91	5b	[	123	7b	{	27	1b				
] }	27	1b	93	5d	]	125	7d	}	29	1d				
ENTER	28	1c	13	0d		13	0d		10	0a		28	1c	NUL
ENTER 2)	28	1c	13	0d		13	0d		10	0a		28	1c	EXT
ctrl le	29	1d												
ctrl ri 1)	29	1d												
A	30	1e	97	61	a	65	41	A	1	01	^A	30	1e	NUL
S	31	1f	115	73	s	83	53	S	19	13	^S	31	1f	NUL
D	32	20	100	64	d	68	44	D	4	04	^D	32	20	NUL
F	33	21	102	66	f	70	46	F	6	06	^F	33	21	NUL
G	34	22	103	67	g	71	47	G	7	07	^G	34	22	NUL
H	35	23	104	68	h	72	48	H	8	08	^H	35	23	NUL
J	36	24	106	6a	j	74	4a	J	10	0a	^J	36	24	NUL
K	37	25	107	6b	k	75	4b	K	11	0b	^K	37	25	NUL
L	38	26	108	6c	l	76	4c	L	12	0c	^L	38	26	NUL
; :	39	27	59	3b	;	58	3a	:						
, @	40	28	44	2c	,	64	40	@						
¬ '	41	29	170	aa	¬	96	60	'						
shift le	42	2a												
# ~	43	2b	35	23	#	126	7e	~						
Z	44	2c	122	7a	z	90	5a	Z	26	1a	^Z	44	2c	NUL
X	45	2d	120	78	x	88	58	X	24	18	^X	45	2d	NUL
C	46	2e	99	63	c	67	43	C	3	03	^C	46	2e	NUL
V	47	2f	118	76	v	86	56	V	22	16	^V	47	2f	NUL
B	48	30	98	62	b	66	42	B	2	02	^B	48	30	NUL
N	49	31	110	6e	n	78	4e	N	14	0e	^N	49	31	NUL
M	50	32	109	6d	m	77	4d	M	13	0d	^M	50	32	NUL
, <	51	33	44	2c	,	60	3c	<						
. >	52	34	46	2e	.	62	3e	>						
/ ?	53	35	47	2f	/	63	3f	?						
/ 2)	53	35	47	2f	/	47	2f	/						
shift ri	54	36												
print scr	55	37	42	2a	*	INT 5h 4)						SysReq 5)		
* 2)	55	37	42	2a	*	42	2a	*	150	96	EXT	55	37	NUL
alt le	56	38												
alt ri 1)	56	38												
blank	57	39	32	20	SPC	32	20	SPC	32	20	SPC	32	20	SPC
CAPS–Lock	58	3a												

key	scan code		ASCII/extended			ASCII/extended with shift			ASCII/extended with ctrl			ASCII/extended with alt		
	dec	hex	dec	hex	char	dec	hex	char	dec	hex	char	dec	hex	char
F1	59	3b	59	3b	NUL	84	54	NUL	94	5e	NUL	104	5e	NUL
F2	60	3c	60	3c	NUL	85	55	NUL	95	5f	NUL	105	5f	NUL
F3	61	3d	61	3d	NUL	86	56	NUL	96	60	NUL	106	60	NUL
F4	62	3e	62	3e	NUL	87	57	NUL	97	61	NUL	107	61	NUL
F5	63	3f	63	3f	NUL	88	58	NUL	98	62	NUL	108	62	NUL
F6	64	40	64	40	NUL	89	59	NUL	99	63	NUL	109	63	NUL
F7	65	41	65	41	NUL	90	5a	NUL	100	64	NUL	110	64	NUL
F8	66	42	66	42	NUL	91	5b	NUL	101	65	NUL	111	65	NUL
F9	67	43	67	43	NUL	92	5c	NUL	102	66	NUL	112	66	NUL
F10	68	44	68	44	NUL	93	5d	NUL	103	67	NUL	113	67	NUL
NUM–Lock	69	45												
NUM–Lock 6)	69	45												
Pause 7)	69	45												
Scroll 6)	70	46												
home	71	47	71	47	NUL	55	37	7	119	77	NUL			
home 3)	71	47	71	47	EXT	71	47	EXT	119	77	EXT	151	97	EXT
cursor up	72	48	72	48	NUL	56	38	8						
cursor up 3)	72	48	72	48	EXT	72	48	EXT	141	8d	EXT	152	98	EXT
page up	73	49	73	49	NUL	57	39	9	132	84	NUL			
page up 3)	73	49	73	49	EXT	73	49	EXT	132	84	EXT	153	99	EXT
– 8)	74	4a	45	2d	–	45	2d	–						
cursor le	75	4b	75	4b	NUL	52	34	4	115	73	NUL			
cursor le 3)	75	4b	75	4b	EXT	75	4b	EXT	115	73	EXT	155	9b	EXT
5 8)	76	4c				53	35	5	143	8f	NUL			
cursor ri	77	4d	77	4d	NUL	54	36	6	116	74	NUL			
cursor ri 3)	77	4d	77	4d	EXT	77	4d	EXT	116	74	EXT	157	9d	EXT
+ 8)	78	4c	43	2b	+	43	2b	+	144	90	NUL	78	4e	NUL
End	79	4f	79	4f	NUL	49	31	1	117	76	NUL			
End 3)	79	4f	79	4f	EXT	79	4f	EXT	117	75	EXT	159	9f	EXT
cursor do	80	50	80	50	NUL	50	32	2	145	91	NUL			
cursor do 3)	80	50	80	50	EXT	80	50	EXT	145	91	EXT	160	a0	EXT
page do	81	51	81	51	NUL	51	33	3	118	76	NUL			
page do 3)	81	51	81	51	EXT	81	51	EXT	118	76	EXT	161	a1	EXT
ins 3)	82	52	82	52	NUL	48	30	0	146	92	NUL			
ins	82	52	82	52	EXT	82	52	EXT	146	92	EXT	162	a2	EXT
del 3)	83	53	83	53	NUL	44	2c	,	147	93	NUL			
del	83	53	83	53	EXT	83	53	EXT	147	93	EXT	163	a3	EXT
\	1)	86	56	92	5c	\	124	7c								
F11	87	57	133	85	EXT	135	87	EXT	137	89	EXT	139	8b	EXT
F12	88	58	134	86	EXT	136	88	EXT	138	8a	EXT	140	8c	EXT

1) alphanumeric block; MF II with precode byte 0eh only

2) numeric block; MF II with precode byte 0eh only

3) in separate control block of MF II

4) print screen via INT 05h with DOS

5) SysReq according to INT 15h, function 85h

6) MF II with precode byte e0h

7) MF II with precode byte e1h only

8) numeric block

A.3 Scan Codes USA

key	scan code		ASCII/extended			ASCII/extended with shift			ASCII/extended with ctrl			ASCII/extended with alt		
	dec	hex	dec	hex	char	dec	hex	char	dec	hex	char	dec	hex	char
ESC	1	01	27	1b		27	1b		27	1b		1	1	NUL
1 !	2	02	49	31	1	33	21	!				120	78	NUL
2 @	3	03	50	32	2	64	40	@	3	03	NUL	121	79	NUL
3 #	4	04	51	33	3	35	23	#				122	7a	NUL
4 $	5	05	52	34	4	36	24	$				123	7b	NUL
5 %	6	06	53	35	5	37	25	%				124	7c	NUL
6 ^	7	07	54	36	6	94	5e	^	30	1e		125	7d	NUL
7 &	8	08	55	37	7	38	26	&				126	7e	NUL
8 *	9	09	56	38	8	42	2a	*				127	7f	NUL
9 (	10	0a	57	39	9	40	28	(				128	80	NUL
0)	11	0b	48	30	0	41	29	)				129	81	NUL
–	12	0c	45	2d	–	95	5f	_	31	1f		130	82	NUL
= +	13	0d	61	3d	=	43	2b	+				131	83	NUL
BKSP	14	0e	8	08		8	08		127	7f				
TAB	15	0f	9	09		15	0f							
Q	16	10	113	71	q	81	51	Q	17	11	^Q	16	10	NUL
W	17	11	119	77	w	87	57	W	23	17	^W	17	11	NUL
E	18	12	101	65	e	69	45	E	5	05	^E	18	12	NUL
R	19	13	114	72	r	82	52	R	18	12	^R	19	13	NUL
T	20	14	116	74	t	84	54	T	20	14	^T	20	14	NUL
Y	21	15	121	79	y	89	59	Y	25	19	^Y	21	15	NUL
U	22	16	117	75	u	85	55	U	21	15	^U	22	16	NUL
I	23	17	105	69	i	73	49	I	9	09	^I	23	17	NUL
O	24	18	111	6f	o	79	4f	O	15	0f	^O	24	18	NUL
P	25	19	112	70	p	80	50	P	16	10	^P	25	19	NUL
[{	26	1a	91	5b	[	123	7b	{	27	1b				
] }	27	1b	93	5d	]	125	7d	}	29	1d				
ENTER	28	1c	13	0d		13	0d		10	0a		28	1c	NUL
ENTER 2)	28	1c	13	0d		13	0d		10	0a		28	1c	EXT
ctrl le	29	1d												
ctrl ri 1)	29	1d												
A	30	1e	97	61	a	65	41	A	1	01	^A	30	1e	NUL
S	31	1f	115	73	s	83	53	S	19	13	^S	31	1f	NUL
D	32	20	100	64	d	68	44	D	4	04	^D	32	20	NUL
F	33	21	102	66	f	70	46	F	6	06	^F	33	21	NUL
G	34	22	103	67	g	71	47	G	7	07	^G	34	22	NUL
H	35	23	104	68	h	72	48	H	8	08	^H	35	23	NUL
J	36	24	106	6a	j	74	4a	J	10	0a	^J	36	24	NUL
K	37	25	107	6b	k	75	4b	K	11	0b	^K	37	25	NUL
L	38	26	108	6c	l	76	4c	L	12	0c	^L	38	26	NUL
; :	39	27	59	3b	;	58	3a	:				39	27	NUL
, @	40	28	44	2c	,	64	40	@				40	28	NUL
¬ '	41	29	35	23	#	126	7e	~				41	29	NUL
shift le 1)	42	2a												
\ |	43	2b	95	5c	\	124	7c	|						
Z	44	2c	122	7a	z	90	5a	Z	26	1a	^Z	44	2c	NUL
X	45	2d	120	78	x	88	58	X	24	18	^X	45	2d	NUL
C	46	2e	99	63	c	67	43	C	3	03	^C	46	2e	NUL
V	47	2f	118	76	v	86	56	V	22	16	^V	47	2f	NUL
B	48	30	98	62	b	66	42	B	2	02	^B	48	30	NUL
N	49	31	110	6e	n	78	4e	N	14	0e	^N	49	31	NUL
M	50	32	109	6d	m	77	4d	M	13	0d	^M	50	32	NUL
, <	51	33	44	2c	,	60	3c	<						
. >	52	34	46	2e	.	62	3e	>						
/ ?	53	35	47	2f	/	63	3f	?						
/ 2)	53	35	47	2f	/	47	2f	/						
shift ri	54	36												
print scr	55	37	42	2a	*		INT 5h 4)						SysReq 5)	
* 2)	55	37	42	2a	*	42	2a	*	150	96	EXT	55	37	NUL
alt le	56	38												
alt ri 1)	56	38												
blank	57	39	32	20	SPC	32	20	SPC	32	20	SPC	32	20	SPC
CAPS–Lock	58	3a												

key	scan code		ASCII/extended			ASCII/extended with shift			ASCII/extended with ctrl			ASCII/extended with alt		
	dec	hex	dec	hex	char	dec	hex	char	dec	hex	char	dec	hex	char
F1	59	3b	59	3b	NUL	84	54	NUL	94	5e	NUL	104	5e	NUL
F2	60	3c	60	3c	NUL	85	55	NUL	95	5f	NUL	105	5f	NUL
F3	61	3d	61	3d	NUL	86	56	NUL	96	60	NUL	106	60	NUL
F4	62	3e	62	3e	NUL	87	57	NUL	97	61	NUL	107	61	NUL
F5	63	3f	63	3f	NUL	88	58	NUL	98	62	NUL	108	62	NUL
F6	64	40	64	40	NUL	89	59	NUL	99	63	NUL	109	63	NUL
F7	65	41	65	41	NUL	90	5a	NUL	100	64	NUL	110	64	NUL
F8	66	42	66	42	NUL	91	5b	NUL	101	65	NUL	111	65	NUL
F9	67	43	67	43	NUL	92	5c	NUL	102	66	NUL	112	66	NUL
F10	68	44	68	44	NUL	93	5d	NUL	103	67	NUL	113	67	NUL
NUM–Lock	69	45												
NUM–Lock 6)	69	45												
Pause 7)	69	45												
Scroll 6)	70	46												
home	71	47	71	47	NUL	55	37	7	119	77	NUL			
home 3)	71	47	71	47	EXT	71	47	EXT	119	77	EXT	151	97	EXT
cursor up	72	48	72	48	NUL	56	38	8						
cursor up 3)	72	48	72	48	EXT	72	48	EXT	141	8d	EXT	152	98	EXT
page up	73	49	73	49	NUL	57	39	9	132	84	NUL			
page up 3)	73	49	73	49	EXT	73	49	EXT	132	84	EXT	153	99	EXT
– 8)	74	4a	45	2d	–	45	2d	–						
cursor le	75	4b	75	4b	NUL	52	34	4	115	73	NUL			
cursor le 3)	75	4b	75	4b	EXT	75	4b	EXT	115	73	EXT	155	9b	EXT
5 8)	76	4c				53	35	5	143	8f	NUL			
cursor ri	77	4d	77	4d	NUL	54	36	6	116	74	NUL			
cursor ri 3)	77	4d	77	4d	EXT	77	4d	EXT	116	74	EXT	157	9d	EXT
+ 8)	78	4e	43	2b	+	43	2b	+	144	90	NUL	78	4e	NUL
End	79	4f	79	4f	NUL	49	31	1	117	75	NUL			
End 3)	79	4f	79	4f	EXT	79	4f	EXT	117	75	EXT	159	9f	EXT
cursor do	80	50	80	50	NUL	50	32	2	145	91	NUL			
cursor do 3)	80	50	80	50	EXT	80	50	EXT	145	91	EXT	160	a0	EXT
page do	81	51	81	51	NUL	51	33	3	118	76	NUL			
page do 3)	81	51	81	51	EXT	81	51	EXT	118	76	EXT	161	a1	EXT
ins 3)	82	52	82	52	NUL	48	30	0	146	92	NUL			
ins	82	52	82	52	EXT	82	52	EXT	146	92	EXT	162	a2	EXT
del 3)	83	53	83	53	NUL	44	2c	,	147	93	NUL			
del	83	53	83	53	EXT	83	53	EXT	147	93	EXT	163	a3	EXT
F11	87	57	133	85	EXT	135	87	EXT	137	89	EXT	139	8b	EXT
F12	88	58	134	86	EXT	136	88	EXT	138	8a	EXT	140	8c	EXT

1) alphanumeric block; MF II with precode byte 0eh only

2) numeric block; MF II with precode byte 0eh only

3) in separate control block of MF II

4) print screen via INT 05h with DOS

5) SysReq according to INT 15h, function 85h

6) MF II with precode byte e0h

7) MF II with precode byte e1h only

8) numeric block

B 80x86 Processor Machine Instructions

B.1 8086/88

AAA	*ASCII Adjust After Addition* Adjusts the result of a BCD addition.
AAD	*ASCII Adjust Before Division* Converts non-packed BCD to binary number.
AAM	*ASCII Adjust After Multiplication* Converts 8 bit binary number to non-packed BCD.
AAS	*ASCII Adjust After Subtraction* Converts the result of a subtraction to BCD.
ADC	*Add with Carry* Adds source operand, destination operand and carry flag.
ADD	*Add* Adds source and destination operand.
AND	*Logical AND* Bit by bit logical AND of two operands.
CALL	*Call Procedure* Calls a Procedure.
CBW	*Convert Byte to Word* Converts signed byte to signed word.
CLC	*Clear Carry Flag* Sets carry flag to zero.
CLD	*Clear Direction Flag* Clears direction flag for string instructions.
CLI	*Clear Interrupt Flag* Blocks out maskable interrupts.
CMC	*Complement Carry Flag* Complements the carry flag.
CMP	*Compare* Compares two operands.
CMPS *CMPSB* *CMPSW*	*Compare String* Compares two strings.

CWD	*Convert Word to Double* Converts signed word to signed double word.
DAA	*Decimal Adjust After Addition* Converts result of addition to packed BCD.
DAS	*Decimal Adjust after Subtraction* Converts result of subtraction to packed BCD.
DEC	*Decrement* Subtracts 1 from destination operand.
DIV	*Unsigned Divide* Divides destination operand by source operand.
ESC	*Escape* Supplies instruction and optional operand for coprocessor.
HLT	*Halt* Halts the processor.
IDIV	*Signed Divide* Divides signed destination operand by signed source operand.
IMUL	*Signed Multiply* Multiplies signed destination operand with signed source operand.
IN	*Input from Port* Transfers byte, word or double word (i386 and above) from port to accumulator.
INC	*Increment* Adds 1 to destination operand.
INT	*Interrupt* Issues a software interrupt.
INTO	*Interrupt on Overflow* Issues interrupt 4 if overflow flag is set.
IRET	*Interrupt Return* Returns control from interrupt handler to interrupted program.
JB/JNAE *JAE/JNB* *JBE/JNA* *JA/JNBE* *JE/JZ* *JNE/JNZ* *JL/JNGE* *JGE/JNL* *JLE/JNG*	

JG/JNLE
JS
JNS
JC
JNC
JO
JNO
JP/JPE
JNP/JPO — *Jump Conditionally*
Executes a jump dependent on a certain condition.

JCXZ
JECXZ — *Jump if CX is Zero*
Jumps if value of CX is equal zero.

JMP — *Jump Unconditionally*
Jumps always.

LAHF — *Load Flags into AH Register*
Transfers bits 0 to 7 into register AH.

LDS
LES — *Load Far Pointer*
Reads and stores the far pointer of source memory operand in a segment/register pair.

LEA — *Load Effective Address*
Calculates the effective address (offset) of the source memory operand.

LOCK — *Lock the Bus*
Locks out other processors from the bus.

LODS
LODSB
LODSW — *Load String Operand*
Loads a string from memory into accumulator.

LOOP — *Loop*
Returns repeatedly to a certain label and executes one or more loops.

LOOPE/LOOPZ
LOOPNE/LOOPNZ — *Loop if xxx*
Executes a loop conditionally.

MOV — *Move Data*
Copies the value of the source into the destination operand.

MOVS *MOVSB* *MOVSW*	*Move String Data* Copies a string from one memory area into another memory area.
MUL	*Unsigned Multiply* Multiplies two unsigned operands.
NEG	*Two's Complement Negation* Replaces the operand by its 2's complement.
NOP	*No Operation* Doesn't execute any process.
NOT	*One's Complement Negation* Replaces each operand bit by its complementary value.
OR	*Inclusive OR* Bit by bit logical OR of two operands.
OUT	*Output to Port* Transfers a byte, word or double word from the accumulator to a port.
POP	*Pop* Pops the last value off the stack and transfers it to the operand.
POPF	*Pop Flags* Transfers the last value on the stack into the flag register.
PUSH	*Push* Transfers the operand onto the stack.
PUSHF	*Push Flags* Transfers the flag register onto the stack.
RCL *RCR* *ROL* *ROR*	*Rotate* Rotates the bits of the operand.
REP	*Repeat String* Repeats the string instruction CX-times.
REPE *REPNE* *REPZ* *REPNZ*	*Repeat String Conditionally* Repeats the string instruction until the condition is true.

RET *RETF*	*Return from Procedure* Returns from a procedure to the calling program.
SAHF	*Store AH into Flags* Transfers AH into the bits 0 to 7 of the flag register.
SAL *SAR* *SHL* *SHR*	*Shift* Shifts the operand bits.
SBB	*Subtract with Borrow* Subtracts the source from the destination operand and additionally subtracts the carry flag.
SCAS *SCASB* *SCASW*	*Scan String Flags* Scans a string for a certain value.
STC	*Set Carry Flag* Sets carry flag to 1.
STD	*Set Direction Flag* Sets direction flag to 1.
STI	*Set Interrupt Flag* Sets interrupt flag to 1.
STOS *STOSB* *STOSW*	*Store String Data* Writes the accumulator value into a string.
SUB	*Subtract* Subtracts two operands.
TEST	*Logical Compare* Tests certain bits of an operand.
WAIT	*Wait* Halts the CPU until a corresponding signal from the coprocessor is received.
XCHG	*Exchange* Exchanges the value of two operands.

XLAT
XLATB — *Translate*
Translates a value from one encoding system into another encoding system.

XOR — *Exclusive OR*
Bit by bit exclusive OR of two operands.

B.2 80186/88

Only the new 80186/88 instructions are listed.

BOUND — *Check Array Bounds*
Checks whether a value is within the preset boundaries of an array.

ENTER — *Make Stack Frame*
Generates a stack frame for a local variable of a procedure.

INS
INSB
INSW — *Input from Port to String*
Transfers a string from a port into a string.

LEAVE — *High Level Procedure Exit*
Opposite to ENTER.

OUTS
OUTSB
OUTSW — *Output String to Port*
Transfers a string to a port.

POPA
POPAD — *Pop All*
Transfers the last eight values from the stack into the general-purpose registers.

PUSHA
PUSHAD — *Push All*
Transfers the general-purpose registers onto the stack.

B.3 80286

Only the new 80286 instructions are listed.

ARPL — *Adjust Requested Privilege Level (Privileged)*
Adjusts the requested privilege level.

CLTS	*Clear Task-Switched Flag (Privileged)* Clears the task-switched flag in the machine status word MSW.
LAR	*Load Access Rights (Protected Mode)* Loads the access rights of a selector into a certain register.
LGDT *LIDT* *LLDT*	*Load Descriptor Table (Privileged)* Loads the value of an operand into a descriptor table register.
LMSW	*Load Machine Status Word (Privileged)* Loads the value of a memory operand into the machine status word.
LSL	*Load Segment Limit (Protected Mode)* Loads the segment limit of a selector into a register.
LTR	*Load Task Register (Privileged)* Loads the value of an operand into the current task register.
SGDT *SIDT* *SLDT*	*Store Descriptor Table (Privileged)* Stores a descriptor table register in a certain operand.
SMSW	*Store Machine Status Word (Privileged)* Stores the machine status word in a memory operand.
STR	*Store Task Register (Privileged)* Stores the current task register in an operand.
VERR *VERW*	*Verify Read or Write (Protected Mode)* Verifies that a certain segment selector is valid and can be read or written.

B.4 i386

Only the new i386/i386SX instructions are listed.

BSF *BSR*	*Bit Scan Forward or Bit Scan Reverse* Scans the operand in forward or reverse direction to look for the first bit set (=1).

BT *BTC* *BTR* *BTS*	*Bit Test* Copies the value of a certain bit into the carry flag.
CDQ	*Convert Double to Quad* Converts signed double word into signed quad word.
CMPSD	*Compare String* Compares two strings.
CWDE	*Convert Word to Extended Double* Converts a signed word to a signed double word.
INSD	*Input from Port to String* Transfers a string from a port to a string.
IRETD	*Interrupt Return* Returns the control from an interrupt handler to the interrupted program.
LFS *LGS* *LSS*	*Load Far Pointer* Reads and stores the far pointer of the source memory operand in a segment/register pair.
LODSD	*Load String Operand* Loads a string from the memory into the accumulator.
MOVSD	*Move String Data* Copies a string from one memory area to another.
MOVSX	*Move with Sign-Extend* Copies an operand and extends its sign to 16/32 bits.
MOVZX	*Move with Zero-Extend* Copies an operand and extends its value with zeros.
OUTSD	*Output String to Port* Transfers a string to a port.
POPFD	*Pop Flags* Transfers the last value on the stack into the flag register.
PUSHFD	*Push Flags* Transfers the flag register onto the stack.
SCASD	*Scan String Flags* Scans a string for a certain value.

SETB/SETNAE
SETAE/SETNB
SETBE/SETNA
SETA/SETNBE
SETE/SETZ
SETNE/SETNZ
SETL/SETNGE
SETGE/SETNL
SETLE/SETNG
SETG/SETNLE
SETS
SETNS
SETC
SETNC
SETO
SETNO
SETP/SETPE
SETNP/SETPO — *Set Conditionally*
Sets the byte of the operand conditionally.

SHLD
SHRD — *Double Precision Shift*
Shifts the bits of an operand into another operand.

STOSD — *Store String Data*
Stores the value of the accumulator in a string.

B.5 i486

Only the new i486 CPU core instructions are listed.

BSWAP — *Byte Swap*
Swaps to bytes.

CMPXCHG — *Compare and Exchange*
Compares and exchanges source and destination operand dependent on the comparison result.

INVD — *Invalidate Cache*
Invalidates the entries in the on-chip cache.

INVPG — *Invalidate TLB Entry*
Invalidates the entries in the translation lookaside buffer of the paging unit.

WBINVD — *Write-Back and Invalidate Data Cache*
Writes the contents of the on-chip data cache back into main memory and invalidates the cache entries.

XADD — *Exchange and Add*
Exchanges and adds source register and destination register or memory operand and destination register and writes the result into the destination register.

B.6 Pentium

Only the new Pentium core instructions are listed.

CMPXCHG8B — *Compare and Exchange 8 Bytes*
The instruction compares the 8 byte value in EDX:EAX with the destination operand. If both are equal, then ECX:EBX is stored in the destination operand, otherwise the destination operand is loaded into EDX:EAX.

CPUID — *CPU Identification*
The instruction provides an identification in the EAX register which details the CPU model and additional information about the functions supported.

RDMSR — *Read Model Specific Register*
The instruction reads a model-specific register (such as test register, etc.) and stores its value in EDX:EAX.

RSM — *Resume from System Management Mode*
Resumes the execution of a task interrupted by an SMI and leaves System Management Mode.

WRMSR — *Write Model Specific Register*
The instruction writes a model-specific register (such as test register, etc.) with the value in EDX:EAX.

B.7 Pentium Instruction Pairing Rules

The following list summarizes which machine instructions can be paired internally by the Pentium and to what extent this is possible. U+V means that the instruction can be executed in both pipelines u and v; U alone means that the instruction can be paired with a (U+V) or V instruction, if it is in the u-pipeline, and the other can be executed in the v-pipe. Finally, V menas that the instruction can be paired with an (U+V) or U instruction, if it is in the v-pipeline, and the other can be executed in the u-pipe.

Instruction	Pairing
ADD	U+V
AND	U+V
CALL (immediate only)	V
CMP	U+V
DEC	U+V
INC	U+V
Jcc	V
JMP (immediate only)	V
LEA	U+V
MOV (general-purpose register and memory operands only)	U+V
NOP	U+V
OR	U+V
POP (register only)	U+V
PUSH (register only)	U+V
RCL (only one bit or immediate)	U
RCR (only one bit or immediate)	U
ROL (only one bit or immediate)	U
ROR (only one bit or immediate)	U
SAR (only one bit or immediate)	U
SHL (only one bit or immediate)	U
SHR (only one bit or immediate)	U
SUB	U+V
TEST (register–register, memory–register and immediate–EAX only)	U+V
XOR	U+V

Table B.1: Instruction pairing

Besides the indicated integer instructions, certain FPU instructions can also be paired in a restricted manner with the FXCHG instruction. FXCHG is always carried out in the v-pipeline, the paired instruction in the u-pipeline and the following stages of the FP-pipeline.

FABS
FADD/FADDP
FCHS
FCOM/FCOMP/FCOMPP
FDIV/FDIVP/FDIVR/FDIVRP
FLD (single/double, precision memory operand)
FLD ST(i)
FMUL/FMULP
FSUB/FSUBP/FSUBR/FSUBRP
FTST
FUCOM/FUCOMP/FUCOMPP

Table B.2: Floating-point instructions which can be paired with FXCHG

C 80x87 Processor Machine Instructions

Many 80x87 instructions have a format with or without WAIT. Instructions without WAIT are characterized by an N after the beginning F (for floating, that is, ESC instruction).

C.1 8087

F2XM1

2 to X minus 1
Calculates $y=2^{x-1}$ with $0 \le x \le 0.5$. x is taken from TOP and the result y is stored in TOP again afterwards.

FLD
FILD
FBLD

Load
Loads a value from memory or a register into a register.

FABS

Absolute
Converts the value in TOP to its absolute value.

FADD
FADDP
FIADD

Add/Add and Pop
Adds source and destination operand.

FCHS

Change Sign
Changes the sign of TOP.

FCLEX
FNCLEX

Clear Exceptions
Clears the exception flags, busy flag and bit 7 in the status word.

FCOM
FCOMP
FCOMPP
FICOM
FICOMP

Compare
Compares source with TOP.

FDECSTP

Decrement Stack Pointer
Decrements the pointer to the register (TOP) on top of the register stack.

FDISI
FNDISI

Disable Interrupts
Masks off all interrupts; only valid on the 8087, all other coprocessors ignore FDISI/FNDISI.

FDIV
FDIVP
FIDIV

Divide
Divides the destination by the source operand and stores the result in the destination operand.

FDIVR
FDIVRP
FIDIVR

Divide Reversed
Divides the source by the destination operand and stores the result in the destination operand.

FENI
FNENI

Enable Interrupts
Clears the IE flag in the control word and thus enables the interrupts; only valid on the 8087, all other 80x87 processors ignore FENI/FNENI.

FFREE
FREE

Free
Changes the tag entry of a register to empty without changing the register value.

FIADD
FISUB
FISUBR
FIMUL
FIDIV
FIDIVR

Integer Add/Subtract/Multiply/Divide
Carries out addition, subtraction, multiplication and division using integers.

FICOM
FICOMP

Compare Integer
Compares two integers.

FINCSTP

Increment Stack Pointer
Increments the pointer referring to the register (TOP) on top of the register stack.

FINIT
FNINIT

Initialize Coprocessor
Initializes the coprocessor and resets all registers and flags.

FLD
FILD
FBLD

Load
Converts the operand to the temporary real format and pushes it onto the register stack.

FFLD1
FLDZ
FLDPI
FLDL2E
FLDL2T
FLDLG2
FLDLN2

Load Constant
Loads +1, +0, π, $\log_2(e)$, $\log_2(10)$, $\log_{10}(2)$ and $\log_e(2)$, respectively, onto the register stack.

FLDCW

Load Control Word
Loads the control word from memory into the control register of the coprocessor.

FLDENV

Load Environment State
Loads the environment state from memory into the coprocessor. The environment state comprises control word, status word, tag word, instruction pointer and operand (data) pointer.

FMUL
FMULP
FIMUL

Multiply
Multiplies the source with the destination operand and stores the result in the destination operand.

FNOP

No Operation
Doesn't carry out any process.

FPATAN

Partial Arctangent
Calculates z = arctan (y/x). y is taken from register TOP, x from register TOP+1, x is popped off the stack and the result is stored in the new TOP (y).

FPREM

Partial Remainder
Calculates the partial remainder of TOP when divided by TOP+1, the result is stored in TOP.

FPTAN

Partial Tangent
Calculates y/x=tan(z); z is taken from register TOP; y is pushed into register TOP and x into register TOP–1.

FRNDINT

Round to Integer
Rounds broken TOP to an integer.

FRSTOR

Restore Saved State
Restores the coprocessor state from the data stored memory.

FSAVE
FNSAVE

Save Coprocessor State
Saves the current coprocessor state as a data array in memory.

FSCALE	*Scale* Scales with powers of 2 by calculating $y=y*2^x$. y is taken from TOP+1, y from register TOP. The result is stored in TOP.
FSQRT	*Square Root* Calculates the square root of TOP.
FST *FSTP* *FIST* *FISTP* *FBSTP*	*Store Real/Store Real and Pop/Store Integer/Store Integer and Pop/Store BCD and Pop* Writes the value in TOP in memory or a register.
FSTCW *FNSTCW*	*Store Control Word* Writes the control word into a memory operand.
FSTENV *FNSTENV*	*Store Environment State* Stores the coprocessor environment state in memory. The environment state comprises control word, status word, tag word, instruction and operand (data) pointer.
FSTSW *FNSTSW*	*Store Status Word* Writes the status word into a memory operand.
FSUB *FSUBP* *FISUB*	*Subtract* Subtracts the source from the destination operand and stores the difference in the destination operand.
FSUBR *FSUBPR* *FISURB*	*Subtract Reversed* Subtracts the destination from the source operand and stores the difference in the destination operand.
FTST	*Test for Zero* Compares TOP with +0.
FUCOM *FUCOMP* *FUCOMPP*	*Unordered Compare* Compares the source operand with TOP.

FWAIT — *Wait*
Halts the CPU operation until the coprocessor has completed the current process.

FXAM — *Examine*
Examines the contents of TOP and stores the result in condition code C3–C0 of the status word.

FXCH — *Exchange Registers*
Exchanges the contents of the destination register and TOP.

FXTRACT — *Extract Exponent and Mantissa*
Stores the exponential part of TOP in TOP and pushes the mantissa into TOP–1.

FYL2X — *Y log2(X)*
Calculates $z=y \log_2(x)$. x is taken from the register TOP and y from the register TOP+1; after a pop the result is stored in the new TOP.

FYL2XP1 — *Y log2(X+1)*
Calculates $z=y \log_2(x+1)$. x is taken from the register TOP and y from the register TOP+1; after a pop the result is stored in the new TOP.

C.2 80287

Only the new 80287 instructions are listed.

FSETPM — *Set Protected Mode*
Switches the 80287 into protected mode. The 80387 ignores this instruction as it handles addresses equally in real and protected mode.

C.3 80287XL and i387/i387SX

Only the new 80287XL/i387/i387SX instructions are listed.

FCOS — *Cosine*
Calculates the cosine of TOP.

FPREM1 — *Partial Remainder (IEEE)*
Calculates the remainder of TOP when divided by TOP+1 according to the IEEE standard; the result is stored in TOP.

FSIN — *Sine*
Calculates the sine of TOP.

FSINCOS — *Sine and Cosine*
Calculates the sine and cosine of TOP. The sine is stored in TOP and the cosine is pushed onto the register stack, i.e. into TOP–1.

C.4 i486

Only the new instructions of the i486 floating-point unit are listed.

FSTSW AX	*Store Status Word into AX* Stores the floating-point unit's status word in the accumulator of the CPU core.

C.5 Pentium

No FPU instructions have been added.

D Interrupts

D.1 PC Hardware Interrupts

Interrupt	PC/XT	AT and PS/2
08h	IRQ0 timer chip	IRQ0 timer chip
09h	IRQ1 keyboard	IRQ1 keyboard
0Ah	unused	IRQ2 slave 8259
0Bh	IRQ3 COM2	IRQ3 COM2
0Ch	IRQ4 COM1	IRQ4 COM1
0Dh	IRQ5 hard disk	IRQ5 LPT2
0Eh	IRQ6 floppy disk drive	IRQ6 floppy disk drive
0Fh	IRQ7 LPT1	IRQ7 LPT1
70h		IRQ8 real time clock
71h		IRQ9 redirected to IRQ2
72h		IRQ10 reserved
73h		IRQ11 reserved
74h		IRQ12 reserved
75h		IRQ13 coprocessor
76h		IRQ14 hard disk drive
77h		IRQ15 reserved

D.2 PC Software Interrupts

Interrupt	Description
5h	print screen[1)]
10h	BIOS video functions
11h	determine system configuration
12h	determine memory size
13h	floppy/hard disk drive functions
14h	serial interface
15h	cassette recorder (PC) or extended memory functions (AT)
16h	BIOS keyboard functions
17h	BIOS printer functions (LPTx)
18h	ROM BASIC
19h	load and execute bootstrap
1Ah	timer/real time clock functions
1Bh	program abortion[2)]
1Ch	timer interrupt (user exit)
1Dh	address of BIOS video parameter table
1Eh	address of BIOS floppy disk parameter table
1Fh	address of BIOS graphics character table

Interrupt	Description
20h	DOS program termination
21h	DOS system functions
22h	DOS program termination address
23h	DOS program abortion[3)]
24h	DOS handler for hardware errors
25h	read logical sectors (DOS)
26h	write logical sectors (DOS)
27h	terminate program resident (DOS)
28h	DOS idle (no file functions currently in progress)
29h	TTY output (DOS)
2Ah	critical section (DOS)
2Fh	DOS multiplexer
40h	redirected INT 13h for floppy drive functions
41h	address of parameter table for hard disk 0
42h	redirected INT 10h for video functions (EGA)
43h	address of EGA video parameter table
44h	address of the first 128 CGA graphics characters
46h	address of parameter table for hard disk 1
4Ah	alarm interrupt of real time clock (user)
50h	periodical/alarm interrupt (AT)
5Ah	cluster functions
5Bh	redirected INT 19h for PC cluster
5Ch	network functions
60h–67h	reserved for application programs

1) activated by PrScr or Shift PrScr
2) activated by Ctrl-Break
3) activated by Ctrl-C

D.3 80x86 Exceptions

Vector (hex)	Vector (dec)	Description	Type mode	Real in	Implemented
0h	0	division by zero	fault	yes	8086
1h	1	debug (trap flag or breakpoint register)	trap/fault	yes	8086/i386
3h	3	breakpoint through INT 3	trap	yes	8086
4h	4	overflow detection with INTO	trap	yes	8086
5h	5	BOUND	fault	yes	80186
6h	6	invalid opcode	fault	yes	8086
7h	7	coprocessor not present	fault	yes	8086
8h	8	double fault	abort	yes	80286
9h	9	segment overflow coprocessor	fault	yes	80286
Ah	10	invalid task state segment	fault	no	80286
Bh	11	segment not present	fault	no	80286

Vector (hex)	Vector (dec)	Description	Type mode	Real in	Implemented
Ch	12	stack exception	fault	yes	80286
Dh	13	general protection error	trap/ fault	yes	80286
Eh	14	page fault	fault	no	i386
Fh	15	reserved by INTEL	—	—	—
10h	16	coprocessor error	fault	yes	80286
11h	17	alignment errot	fault	no	i486
12h	18	machine check error	1)	yes	Pentium
13h–19h	19–31	reserved by INTEL	—	—	—
1ah–ffh	32–255	maskable interrupts	—	yes	8086
00h–ffh	0–255	software interrupts via INTn	—	yes	8086

1) dependant on Pentium model

Note: vector 02h is assigned the NMI.

E BIOS Clock Interrupt 1ah and Functions 83h/86h of INT 15h

- The functions 00h and 01h of INT 1ah are related to the DOS-internal system clock only, but not to the MC146818 real-time clock.
- The access to the real-time clock is carried out by functions 02h to 07h of INT 1ah.
- The functions 83h and 86h of INT 15h set time intervals.

E.1 BIOS Interrupt INT 1ah

Function 00h – Read Time Counter (DOS-Internal System Clock)

This function returns the number of timer ticks since 0:00 a.m. If more than 24 hours have elapsed since power-up, the value of AL is different from 0. In DX:CX the function returns the high and low timer values, respectively, at 40:6eh and 40:6ch in the BIOS data area and the timer overflow flag 40:70h in register AL. After a call to this function, the timer overflow flag will be cleared.

Register	Call value	Return value
AH	00h	
AL		24 hour indicator
CX		high count value
DX		low count value

Function 01h – Set Time Counter (DOS-Internal System Clock)

This function 00h sets the number of timer ticks since 0:00 a.m. The function stores the high and low timer values, respectively, which are passed in DX:CX into 40:6eh and 40:6ch in the BIOS data area and resets the timer overflow flag 40:70h.

Register	Call value	Return value
AH	01h	
CX	high timer count	
DX	low timer count	

Function 02h – Read Time (Real-time Clock)

This function reads the time from the real-time clock chip MC146818.

Register	Call value	Return value
AH	02h	00h
CL		minute*)
CH		hour*)
DH		second*)
Carry		error if < > 0

*) binary coded decimal

Function 03h – Set Time (Real-time Clock)

This function sets the time of the real-time clock chip MC146818.

Register	Call value	Return value
AH	03h	00h
CL	minute*)	
CH	hour*)	
DI	daylight saving (1–yes, 0–no)	
DH	second*)	
Carry		error if < > 0

*) binary coded decimal

Function 04h – Read Date (Real-time Clock)

This function reads the date from the CMOS RAM in the real-time clock chip MC146818.

Register	Call value	Return value
AH	04h	
CL		year*)
CH		century*)
DL		day*)
DH		month*)
Carry		error if < > 0

*) binary coded decimal

Function 05h – Set Date (Real-time Clock)

This function sets the date in the CMOS RAM of the real-time clock chip MC146818.

Register	Call value	Return value
AH	05h	
CL	year*)	
CH	century*)	
DL	day*)	
DH	month*)	
Carry		error if < > 0

*) binary coded decimal

Function 06h – Set Alarm Time (Real-time Clock)

This function sets the alarm time of the real-time clock chip MC146818. If the alarm time is reached, the MC146818 issues an interrupt 4ah. Before setting a new alarm time you have to clear an active alarm time via function 07h.

Register	Call value	Return value
AH	06h	
CL	minute*)	
CH	hour*)	
DH	second*)	
Carry		error if < > 0

*) binary coded decimal

Function 07h – Clear Alarm Time (Real-time Clock)

This function clears an active alarm time and has to be called before setting a new alarm time.

Register	Call value	Return value
AH	07h	
Carry		error if < > 0

E.2 Wait Functions 83h and 86h of BIOS Interrupt INT 15h

Function 83h – Set or Clear Wait Time Interval

If AL=00h this function sets the high bit of a byte in main memory at a user-defined address when the programmed time interval has expired. After a call to this function, the calling program continues at once. After expiry of the wait time interval, the real-time clock issues an interrupt. The wait time interval has to be specified in units of one microsecond, but because of the usually programmed real-time clock frequency of 1024 Hz the actual time resolution is about 976 μs, that is, 1/1024 Hz. If AL=01h the active wait time is disabled.

Subfunction 00h – Set Wait Time Interval

Register	Call value	Return value
AH	83h	00h
AL	00h	register B of MC146818
CX	time interval (high)[1]	
DX	time interval (low)[1]	
BX	offset of target byte[2]	
ES	segment of target byte[2]	
Carry		error if < > 0

1) in μs
2) bit 7 of target byte will be set after expiry of time interval

Subfunction 01h – Clear Wait Time Interval

Register	Call value	Return value
AH	83h	
AL	01h	

Function 86h – Wait Until Time Interval Has Elapsed

This function suspends execution of the calling program until the programmed time interval has elapsed. Afterwards, the program execution continues. The wait time interval must be specified in units of one microsecond, but because of the usually programmed real-time clock frequency of 1024 Hz, the actual time resolution is about 976 μs, that is, 1/1024 Hz.

Register	Call value	Return value
AH	86h	
CX	time interval (high)[1]	
DX	time interval (low)[1]	
Carry		error if < > 0

1) in μs

F BIOS Interrupt INT 13h

If you are using the BIOS Interrupt 13h, which is available for floppy drives as well as for hard disk drives, you should observe the following rules:

- With functions that refer to hard disk drives, bits 6 and 7 of the sector register CH represent bits 8 and 9 of a 10-bit cylinder number; the remaining eight bits of the cylinder number are passed in CH; therefore cylinder numbers 0–1023 are possible.
- For read, verify, or write operations you have to provide a buffer which is large enough to accommodate all sectors to be read, compared, or written.
- The drive count starts with 00h; for hard disk drives, additionally bit 7 is set so that here the drive number count starts with 80h.
- The error codes are returned in the AH register and simultaneously stored in the BIOS data area at 40:41h (floppy disk) and 40:74h (hard disk), respectively.

The first floppy drive A: has the drive number 00h, the second drive the number 01h. The first hard disk is assigned number 80h, the second number 81h. For every sector to be read, verified, or written you have to provide 512 bytes. To read three sectors, for example, a buffer comprising 1536 bytes is required. If you have to format four sectors, for example, you have to pass four format buffers.

F.1 The Functions

Function 00h – Initialize (Floppy/Hard Disk)

This function initializes the floppy controller and the drive and eventually aborts the current function. Upon completion of this function, controller and drive are in a well-defined state.

Register	Call value	Return value
AH	00h	error code[1)]
DL	drive[2)]	
Carry		error if < > 0

1) see F.2
2) floppy disk drives: 00h

Function 01h – Read Status (Error Code) of Last Floppy or Hard Disk Operation (Floppy/Hard Disk)

This function determines the termination status of the last hard disk or floppy drive operation. The status code returned in register ah has the same format as immediately after termination of an operation. The function is useful if you don't want to determine the status upon completion of an operation, and the content of ah with the status byte has already been destroyed by other instructions.

Register	Call value	Return value
AH	01h	error code[1]
DL	drive[2]	
Carry		error if < > 0

[1] see F.2
[2] floppy disk drives: 00h

Function 02h – Read Sectors (Floppy/Hard Disk)

One or more sectors are read from floppy/hard disk into the read buffer. The buffer must be large enough to accommodate all read sectors. If that is not the case, function 02h overwrites data in main memory, and a system crash is the result.

Register	Call value	Return value
AH	02h	error code*)
AL	number of sectors to read	
CH	track/cylinder	
CL	sector	
DH	head	
DL	drive	
ES	segment of read buffer	
BX	offset of read buffer	
Carry		error if < > 0

*) see F.2

Function 03h – Write Sectors (Floppy/Hard Disk)

This function writes one or more sectors from the write buffer in main memory onto the floppy or hard disk. The buffer contains all data to be written. Note that the data transfer is carried out with 512 byte blocks only. If your buffer is only partially filled with write data, function 03h transfers the other, unintended data onto disk, too, until all sectors programmed via the al register are written.

Register	Call value	Return value
AH	03h	error code*)
AL	number of sectors to write	
CH	track/cylinder	
CL	sector	
DH	head	
DL	drive	
ES	segment of write buffer	
BX	offset of write buffer	
Carry		error if < > 0

*) see F.2

Funcion 04h – Verify Sectors (Floppy/Hard Disk)

This function compares the contents of the verify buffer in main memory with the contents of one or more sectors on the floppy or hard disk, or determines whether one or more sectors can be found and read, and whether they return a valid CRC code. In the last case no data is compared.

Register	Call value	Return value
AH	04h	error code*)
AL	number of sectors to verify	
CH	track/cylinder	
CL	sector	
DH	head	
DL	drive	
ES	segment of verify buffer	
BX	offset of verify buffer	
Carry		error if < > 0

*) see F.2

Function 05h – Format Track or Cylinder (Floppy/Hard Disk)

This function formats the sectors of one track or one cylinder. On an AT you have to fix the medium type with function 17h or 18h first. For the formatting operation, a format buffer is necessary which contains the format information for every sector to format. If you want to fomat several sectors in one instance, the format buffer must be large enough to accommodate the format information for all sectors. The controller writes the information in the format buffer into the ID-field of the respective sector, and uses it to determine the correct sector afterwards when reading or writing data.

Register	Call value	Return value
AH	05h	error code[1)]
AL	number of sectors per track	
CH	track/cylinder	
CL	sector number	
DH	head	
DL	drive	
ES	segment of format buffer[2)]	
BX	offset of format buffer[2)]	
Carry		error if < > 0

1) see F.2
2) see F.4

Function 06h – Format and Mark Track Bad (Hard Disk)

This function marks a track with more than one bad sector entirely as bad so that this track is not used for further data recording. The function is only valid for an XT hard disk controller.

Register	Call value	Return value
AH	06h	error code[*)]
AL	interleave	
CH	cylinder	
CL	sector	
DH	head	
DL	drive	
Carry		error if < > 0

*) see F.2

Function 07h – Format Drive (Hard Disk)

This function formats the drive beginning with the specified start cylinder. The function is only valid for an XT hard disk controller.

Register	Call value	Return value
AH	07h	error code[*)]
AL	interleave	
CH	cylinder	
CL	sector	
DH	head	
DL	drive	
Carry		error if < > 0

*) see F.2

Function 08h – Determine Drive Parameters (Floppy Drive)

This function determines the geometric parameters of a floppy drive. The data are extracted from a BIOS table and reflect the geometry of the installed drive, but not that of the inserted data medium.

Register	Call value	Return value
AH	08h	error code[1]
BH		0
BL		drive type[2]
CH		number of cylinders – 1
CL		sectors per track – 1
DH		number of heads – 1
DL	drive	number of drives
ES		parameter table segment
DI		parameter table offset
Carry		error if < > 0

[1] see F.2
[2] 0=hard disk, 1=360 kbyte, 2=1.2 Mbyte, 3=720 kbyte, 4=1.44 Mbyte

Function 08h – Determine Drive Parameters (Hard Disk)

This function determines the geometric parameters of a hard disk drive.

Register	Call value	Return value
AH	08h	error code[1]
AL		0
CH		number of cylinders – 1
CL		sectors per track – 1
DH		numbers of heads – 1
DL	drive	number of drives
ES		parameter table segment
DI		parameter table offset
Carry		error if < > 0

[1] see F.2
[2] 0=hard disk, 1=360 kbytes, 2=1.2 Mbytes, 3=720 kbytes, 4=1.44 Mbytes

Function 09h – Specify Drive Parameters (Hard Disk)

This function specifies and adapts the geometric parameters of a hard disk drive. The respective parameters are stored in a table (see F.3) whose far address is hold by the pseudo-interrupt vectors 41h and 46h, respectively. After a call to this function, the BIOS uses the values stored in the respective table.

Register	Call value	Return value
AH	09h	error code[*]
DL	drive	number of drives
Carry		error if < > 0

[*] see F.2

Function 0Ah – Extended Read (Hard Disk)

This function reads one or up to 127 sectors together with their ECC check bytes from the hard disk into the read buffer in main memory. The controller's ECC logic does not carry out any ECC correction, but transfers the data as they are read from disk. You can then check whether the controller's ECC logic has calculated the ECC bytes correctly when writing the sector.

Register	Call value	Return value
AH	0Ah	error code[1]
AL	number of sectors to read	
CH	cylinder	
CL	sector	
DH	head	
DL	drive	
ES	read buffer segment[2]	
BX	read buffer offset[2]	
Carry		error if < > 0

[1] see F.2
[2] the read buffer must comprise 516 bytes for each sector to be read (512 sector bytes plus 4 check bytes)

Function 0Bh – Extended Write (Hard Disk)

This function writes one or up to 127 sectors together with their ECC check bytes from the write buffer in main memory onto the hard disk. The controller's ECC logic does not generate ECC bytes on its own, but writes the passed ECC bytes without any change into the ECC field of the sector. You can then, for example, generate intended and incorrect ECC data for checking the ECC function of the controller in a subsequent read operation.

Register	Call value	Return value
AH	0Bh	error code[1]
AL	number of sectors to write	
CH	cylinder	
CL	sector	
DH	head	
DL	drive	
ES	write buffer segment[2]	
BX	write buffer offset[2]	
Carry		error if < > 0

[1] see F.2

[2] the write buffer must comprise 516 bytes (512 sector bytes plus 4 check bytes) for each sector to be written; the check bytes are not calculated by the controller, but are written directly from the buffer

Function 0Ch – Seek (Hard Disk)

This function moves the read/write head to a certain track or cylinder and activates it.

Register	Call value	Return value
AH	0Ch	error code*)
CX	cylinder	
DH	head	
DL	drive	
Carry		error if < > 0

*) see F.2

Function 0Dh – Hard Disk Reset (Hard Disk)

This function resets the addressed drive.

Register	Call value	Return value
AH	0Dh	error code*)
DL	drive	
Carry		error if < > 0

*) see F.2

Function 0Eh – Read Buffer (Hard Disk)

This function transfers 512 bytes from the controller's sector buffer into the read buffer in main memory. No data is read from the volume. The function mainly checks the data path between controller and main memory.

Register	Call value	Return value
AH	0Eh	error code*)
DL	drive	
ES	read buffer segment	
BX	read buffer offset	
Carry		error if < > 0

*) see F.2

Function 0Fh – Write Buffer (Hard Disk)

This function transfers 512 bytes from the write buffer in main memory into the controller's sector buffer. No data is written onto the volume. The function mainly checks the data path between controller and main memory.

Register	Call value	Return value
AH	0Fh	error code*)
DL	drive	
ES	write buffer segment	
BX	write buffer offset	
Carry		error if < > 0

*) see F.2

Function 10h – Test Drive Ready (Hard Disk)

This function determines whether the hard disk is ready, and if not, determines the error status.

Register	Call value	Return value
AH	10h	error code*)
DL	drive	
Carry		error if < > 0

*) see F.2

Function 11h – Calibrate Drive (Hard Disk)

This function moves the read/write head to track 0. You can use this function, for example, for recalibrating the drive after a seek error. This is required especially for hard disk drives with a stepper motor.

Register	Call value	Return value
AH	11h	error code*)
DL	drive	
Carry		error if < > 0

*) see F.2

Function 12h – Check Controller RAM (Hard Disk)

This function checks the controller RAM, and investigates controller errors.

Register	Call value	Return value
AH	12h	error code*)
DL	drive	
Carry		error if < > 0

*) see F.2

Function 13h – Drive Diagnostics (Hard Disk)

The controller checks the drive and determines the error status, if necessary.

Register	Call value	Return value
AH	13h	error code*)
DL	drive	
Carry		error if < > 0

*) see F.2

Function 15h – Determine Drive/DASD Type (Floppy Drive, AT and PS/2 only)

This function investigates which kind of data volume the addressed drive uses (DASD=**D**irect **A**ccess **S**torage **D**evice). You can determine whether or not the drive recognizes a disk change, and how many 512 byte blocks or sectors the volume comprises. If the function has been completed successfully, the AH register contains a drive type indicator. Additionally, the two CX and DX registers hold the high and low-order word, respectively, of a 32-bit quantity, which indicates the number of data blocks or sectors on the volume.

Register	Call value	Return value
AH	15h	type[*]
DL	drive	
CX		data blocks/sectors (high-byte)
DX		data blocks/sectors (low-byte)
Carry		error if < > 0

[*] 00h=no drive installed, 01h=drive without connection for disk change
02h=drive with connection for disk change, 03h=hard disk

Function 16h – Determine Disk Change (Floppy Drive, AT and PS/2 only)

This function determines, via line 34 of the interface cable, whether the disk has been changed. For that purpose the BIOS reads an internal controller register.

Register	Call value	Return value
AH	16h	change flag[*]
DL	drive	
Carry		error if < > 0

[*] 00h=no change, 01h=invalid drive number, 06h=disk changed

Function 17h – Fix Floppy Disk Format (Floppy Drive)

This function fixes the controller-drive data transfer rate by means of the disk format. This is necessary, for example, to use a 360 kbyte floppy disk in a 1.2 Mbyte high density drive. A PC/XT BIOS supports 320/360 kbyte drives only, so that here this function is not required.

Register	Call value	Return value
AH	17h	type or error code[1]
AL	disk format[2]	
Carry		error if < > 0

[1] drive type or see F.2
[2] 1=320/360 kbyte disk in 320/360 kbyte drive
2=320/360 kbyte disk in 1.2 Mbyte drive
3=1.2 Mbyte disk in 1.2 Mbyte drive
4=720 kbyte disk in 720 kbyte drive

Function 18h – Fix Floppy Disk Format (Floppy Drive)

This function fixes the disk type for formatting. This is necessary, for example, to format a 360 kbyte floppy disk in a 1.2 Mbyte high density drive.

Register	Call value	Return value
AH	18h	type or error code[1)]
CH	number of tracks	
CL	sectors per track	
DL	drive number	
DI		parameter table offset[2)]
ES		parameter table segment[2)]
Carry		error if < > 0

1) 00h=no error, 0ch=medium unknown, 80h=no disk in drive
2) see F.5

Function 19h – Park Read/Write Heads (Hard Disk)

This function moves the read/write heads to a certain cylinder and parks them.

Register	Call value	Return value
AH	19h	error code[*)]
DL	drive	
Carry		error if < > 0

*) see F.2

F.2 Error Codes

Error code (AH value)	Meaning	Valid for Floppy	Valid for Hard disk
00h	no error	yes	yes
01h	invalid function number	yes	yes
02h	address mark not found	yes	yes
03h	disk write-protected	yes	no
04h	sector not found	yes	yes
05h	unsuccessful reset	no	yes
07h	erroneous initialization	no	yes
08h	DMA overflow	yes	no
09h	DMA segment overflow	yes	yes
10h	read error	yes	yes
11h	data read error, ECC correction successful	no	yes
20h	controller error	yes	yes
40h	track not found	yes	yes
80h	no drive response	yes	yes
BBh	BIOS error	no	yes
FFh	unknown error	no	yes

F.3 Hard Disk Drive Parameter Table

XT-Controller

Offset	Field	Size
00h	Number of Cylinders	(Word)
02h	Number of Heads	(Byte)
03h	Start Cylinder of Reduced Write Current	(Word)
05h	Start Cylinder of Precompensation	(Word)
07h	Max. ECC Burst Length	(Byte)
08h	Control Byte[1]	(Byte)
09h	Standard Time-out Value[2]	(Byte)
0ah	Time-out Value for Formatting[2]	(Byte)
0bh	Time-out Value for Drive Check[2]	(Byte)
0ch–0fh	Reserved	(4 Bytes)

[1] Bit 0..2: Drive Option
Bit 3..5: Null
Bit 6: 1=ECC Retries Disabled
Bit 7: 1=Seek Retries Disabled
[2] in Timer Ticks

AT-Controller

Offset	Field	Size
00h	Number of Cylinders	(Word)
02h	Number of Heads	(Byte)
03h	Reserved	(Word)
05h	Start Cylinder of Precompensation	(Word)
07h	Reserved	(Byte)
08h	Control Byte[1]	(Byte)
09h	Reserved	(3 Bytes)
0ch	Landing Zone for Head Parking	(Word)
0eh	Number of Sectors per Track	(Byte)
0fh	Reserved	(Byte)

[1] Bit 0..2: Reserved
Bit 3: 1=more than 8 Heads
Bit 4: Reserved
Bit 5: 1=Defect List at MaxCylinder+1
Bit 6: 1=ECC Retries Disabled
Bit 7: 1=Seek Retries Disabled

F.4 Format Buffer

Offset	Size	Contents
00h	byte	track of sector to format
01h	byte	head of sector to format
02h	byte	sector number
03h	byte	number of bytes per sector*)

*) 0=128, 1=256, 2=512, 3=1024

F.5 Floppy Disk Parameter Table

The parameter table is located in the DOS data area at address 50:22h.

Offset	Size	Content
00h	byte	first specification byte[1)]
01h	byte	second specification byte[2)]
02h	byte	number of timer pulses until drive motor is off
03h	byte	number of bytes per sector[3)]
04h	byte	sectors per track[4)]
05h	byte	gap length in byte[5)]
06h	byte	data length in byte[6)]
07h	byte	gap length for formatting[7)]
08h	byte	fill byte for formatting[8)]
09h	byte	head settle time after seek [ms][9)]
0Ah	byte	motor start time in 1/8 seconds

1) Bit 7..4: Step Rate [ms]

Entry	Data Transfer Rate 1 M	500 k	300 k	250 k
0h	8.0	16	26.7	32
1h	7.5	15	25.0	30
2h	7.0	14	23.3	28
...	...	...	...	...
eh	1.0	2	3.3	4
fh	0.5	1	1.7	2

Bit 3..0: Head Unload Time [ms]

Entry	Data Transfer Rate 1 M	500 k	300 k	250 k
0h	128	256	426	512
1h	8	16	26.7	32
2h	16	32	53.5	64
...	...	...	...	...
eh	112	224	373	448
fh	120	240	400	480

2) Bit 7..1: Head Load Time [ms]

Entry	Data Transfer Rate 1 M	500 k	300 k	250 k
0h	128	256	426	512
1h	1	2	3.3	4
2h	2	4	6.7	8
...	...	...	...	...
eh	126	252	420	504
fh	127	254	423	508

Bit 0: 0=Data Transfer Via DMA
1=Data Transfer Not Via DMA

3) 0=128, 1=256, 2=512, 3=1024
4) 08h=8 Sectors/Track, 09h=9 Sectors/Track
15h=15 Sectors/Track, 18h=18 Sectors/Track
5) 1bh for 1.2 Mbyte and 1.44 Mbyte, 2ah else
6) Don't Care, Mostly ffh
7) 50h for 360 kbyte/720 kbyte, 54h for 1.2 Mbyte
6ch for 1.44 Mbyte
8) Standard: f6h Corresponding to '÷'
9) Standard: 0fh

```
Data Transfer Rates:
250 kbit/s:   360 kbyte 5 ¼" floppy in 360 kbyte drive
              720 kbyte 3½" floppy in 1.44 Mbyte drive
              720 kbyte 3½" floppy in 720 kbyte drive
300 kbit/s:   720 kbyte 3½" floppy in 720 kbyte drive
              360 kbyte 5¼" floppy in 1.2 Mbyte drive
500 kbit/s:   1.2 Mbyte 5¼" floppy in 1.2 Mbyte drive
              1.44 Mbyte 5¼" floppy in 1.44 Mbyte drive
```

G Floppy Disk Controllers

G.1 The Commands

- The specifications cylinder, head, sector number, and sector size are called the *sector identification*.
- Before you can transfer a command byte or read a status byte in the result phase, you must read bit MRQ in the main status register to determine whether the data register is ready to receive or supply a byte.
- All command and status bytes are transferred via the data register (port 3f7h or 377h).
- The transfer of the read data or data to be written between main memory and controller is normally done via DMA; for this you have to program the DMA controller before the transfer of a command.
- Read and write commands concern all sectors from the start sector up to the end of the track; you can abort the read or write operation earlier by setting the count value of the DMA controller such that the DMA chip issues a TC signal after the desired number of sectors, or by setting the command byte *track length/max. sector number* to a value which indicates the last sector to be handled.
- If you set the multiple track bit *M* the controller executes the specified command not only for the programmed head but for the other head (i.e. for the opposite disk side) too; after the end of the track corresponding to the programmed head, the controller continues with the beginning of the track on the other disk side.
- After command completion the status registers ST0 to ST3 contain status information which helps you to confirm the correct execution of the command, or to determine the cause of an error.
- In advance of a read, write, or format operation, you first have to fix the drive format.
- The commands are divided into data transfer commands, control commands and extended commands, which are available on an AT or PS/2.

G.1.1 List of Valid Commands

- **Data transfer commands**
  read sector
  read deleted sector
  write sector
  write deleted sector
  read complete track
  format track

- **Control commands**
  read identification
  calibrate drive
  check interrupt status
  fix drive data
  check drive status
  seek
  invalid command
- **Extended commands**
  verify
  determine controller version
  seek relative
  register summary

G.1.2 Data Transfer Commands

Read Sector (x6h)

This command reads one or more sectors with a valid data address mark from disk and transfers the data into main memory.

Command Phase

Bit / Byte	7	6	5	4	3	2	1	0
0	M	F	S	0	0	1	1	0
1	x	x	x	x	x	HD	DR_1	DR_0
2	Cylinder							
3	Head							
4	Sector Number							
5	Sector Size							
6	Track Length/Max. Sector Number							
7	Length of GAP3							
8	Data Length							

```
M:            multi track operation
              1=carry out cylinder operation       0=carry out single track operation
F:            FM or MFM recording method
              1=MFM (standard)                    0=FM
S:            skip mode
              1=skip deleted data address marks  0=do not skip
HD:           head number (always equal head address in byte 3)
DR1, DR2:     drive
              00=drive 0 (A)   01=drive 1 (B)   10=drive 2 (C)   11=drive 3 (D)
cylinder, head, sector number:  address of first sector to read
sector size:       0=128 bytes   1=256 bytes   2=512 bytes   ...   7=16 kbytes
track length/max. sector number:   number of sectors per track or max. sector number, for which
                                   the command shall be carried out
length of GAP 3: standard value=42, minimal value=32 (5 1/4") or standard value=27 (3 1/2")
data length:     length of data to read in bytes (only valid if sector size=00), else equal ffh
```

Result Phase

	7 ... 0
0	ST0
1	ST1
2	ST2
3	Cylinder
4	Head
5	Sector Number
6	Sector Size

ST0, ST1, ST2: status register 0 to 2 (see G.2)
cylinder, head, sector number, sector size: sector identification according to Table G.1

Read Deleted Sector (xch)

This command reads one sector with a deleted data address mark from disk and transfers the data into main memory. Sectors with a correct data address mark cannot be accessed by means of this command.

Command Phase

Bit Byte	7	6	5	4	3	2	1	0
0	M	F	0	0	1	1	0	0
1	x	x	x	x	x	HD	DR_1	DR_0
2	Cylinder							
3	Head							
4	Sector Number							
5	Sector Size							
6	Track Length/Max. Sector Number							
7	Length of GAP3							
8	Data Length							

M: multi track operation
1=carry out cylinder operation 0=carry out single track operation
F: FM or MFM recording method
1=MFM (standard) 0=FM
HD: head number (always equal head address in byte 3)
DR1, DR0: drive
00=drive 0 (A) 01=drive 1 (B) 10=drive 2 (C) 11=drive 3 (D)
cylinder, head, sector number: address of first sector to read
sector size: 0=128 bytes 1=256 bytes 2=512 bytes ... 7=16 kbytes
track length/max. sector number: number of sectors per track or max. sector number, for which the command shall be carried out
length of GAP 3: standard value=42, minimal value=32 (5 1/4") or standard value=27 (3 1/2")
data length: length of data to read in bytes (only valid if sector size=00), else equal ffh

Result Phase

	7 ... 0
0	ST0
1	ST1
2	ST2
3	Cylinder
4	Head
5	Sector Number
6	Sector Size

```
ST0, ST1, ST2:  status register 0 to 2 (see G.2)
cylinder, head, sector number, sector size:  sector identification according to Table G.1
```

Write Sector (x5h)

This command transfers the data to be written from main memory to the controller, and writes one or more sectors with valid data address marks onto the disk.

Command Phase

Bit / Byte	7	6	5	4	3	2	1	0
0	M	F	0	0	0	1	0	1
1	x	x	x	x	x	HD	DR_1	DR_0
2	Cylinder							
3	Head							
4	Sector Number							
5	Sector Size							
6	Track Length/Max. Sector Number							
7	Length of GAP3							
8	Data Length							

```
M:   multi track operation
     1=carry out cylinder operation       0=carry out single track operation
F:   FM or MFM recording method
     1=MFM (standard)                    0=FM
HD:  head number (always equal head address in byte 3)
DR1, DR0:  drive
     00=drive 0 (A)   01=drive 1 (B)   10=drive 2 (C)   11=drive 3 (D)
cylinder, head, sector number:  address of first sector to write
sector size:       0=128 bytes   1=256 bytes   2=512 bytes   ...   7=16 kbytes
track length/max. sector number:   number of sectors per track or max. sector number, for which
                                   the command shall be carried out
length of GAP 3: standard value=42, minimal value=32 (5 1/4") or standard value=27 (3 1/2")
data length:     length of data to write in bytes (only valid if sector size=00), else equal ffh
```

Result Phase

	7 … 0
0	ST0
1	ST1
2	ST2
3	Cylinder
4	Head
5	Sector Number
6	Sector Size

```
ST0, ST1, ST2:  status register 0 to 2 (see G.2)
cylinder, head, sector number, sector size:  sector identification according to Table G.1
```

Write Deleted Sector (x9h)

This command transfers the data to be written from main memory to the controller, and writes one or more sectors onto disk. Simultaneously, the data address mark of the sector concerned is deleted so that this sector can be accessed only by the *read deleted sector* command.

Command Phase

Bit / Byte	7	6	5	4	3	2	1	0
0	M	F	0	0	1	0	0	1
1	x	x	x	x	x	HD	DR_1	DR_0
2	Cylinder							
3	Head							
4	Sector Number							
5	Sector Size							
6	Track Length/Max. Sector Number							
7	Length of GAP3							
8	Data Length							

```
M:   multi track operation
     1=carry out cylinder operation       0=carry out single track operation
F:   FM or MFM recording method
     1=MFM (standard)                    0=FM
HD:  head number (always equal head address in byte 3)
DR1, DR0:  drive
     00=drive 0 (A)   01=drive 1 (B)   10=drive 2 (C)   11=drive 3 (D)
cylinder, head, sector number:  address of first sector to write
sector size:      0=128 bytes   1=256 bytes   2=512 bytes   ...   7=16 kbytes
track length/max. sector number:   number of sectors per track or max. sector number, for which
                                   the command shall be carried out
length of GAP 3: standard value=42, minimal value=32 (5 1/4") or standard value=27 (3 1/2")
data length:     length of data to write in bytes (only valid if sector size=00), else equal ffh
```

Result Phase

	7 … 0
0	ST0
1	ST1
2	ST2
3	Cylinder
4	Head
5	Sector Number
6	Sector Size

```
ST0, ST1, ST2:  status register 0 to 2 (see G.2)
cylinder, head, sector number, sector size:  sector identification according to Table G.1
```

Read Track (x2h)

This command reads the data of one complete track, starting with the first sector after the index address mark (IDAM), sector by sector without attention to the logical sector number which is given in the ID address mark. The track is regarded as a contiguous data block, and multi-track operations are not allowed; the command is limited to one single disk side. The read operation starts as soon as a signal on the IDX line indicates the passing of the index hole, that is, the beginning of the track. Note that the available read buffer in main memory is large enough to accommodate all sectors of the track continuously. The sector specification in the command phase is ignored.

Command Phase

Bit Byte	7	6	5	4	3	2	1	0
0	0	F	S	0	0	0	1	0
1	x	x	x	x	x	HD	DR_1	DR_0
2	Cylinder							
3	Head							
4	Sector Number							
5	Sector Size							
6	Track Length							
7	Length of GAP3							
8	Data Length							

```
F:   FM or MFM recording method
     1=MFM (standard)                    0=FM
S:   skip mode
     1=skip deleted data address marks   0=do not skip
HD:  head number (always equal head address in byte 3)
DR1, DR0:  drive
     00=drive 0 (A)   01=drive 1 (B)   10=drive 2 (C)   11=drive 3 (D)
cylinder, head, sector number:  address of first sector to read, but sector number is ignored
here
sector size:      0=128 bytes   1=256 bytes   2=512 bytes   ...   7=16 kbytes
track length/max. sector number:   number of sectors per track or max. sector number, for which
                                   the command shall be carried out
length of GAP 3: standard value=42, minimal value=32 (5 1/4") or standard value=27 (3 1/2")
data length:     length of data to read in bytes (only valid if sector size=00), else equal ffh
```

Result Phase

Byte	7 … 0
0	ST0
1	ST1
2	ST2
3	Cylinder
4	Head
5	Sector Number
6	Sector Size

ST0, ST1, ST2: status register 0 to 2 (see G.2)
cylinder, head, sector number, sector size: sector identification according to Table G.1

Format Track (xdh)

This command formats one track. For each sector of the track to be formatted you have to provide a 4 byte format buffer which holds the sector identification of the corresponding sector (see Figure G.1). Note that you specify a sufficiently large and continuous format buffer for all sectors of the track. Before issuing the command you have to program the DMA control so that the controller can read the format buffer data successively via DMA channel 2. Alternatively you can transfer the format data by means of interrupt-driven data exchange; the controller issues a hardware interrupt before formatting each sector. The handler then may transfer the 4 byte format information for the sector to be formatted next. The formatting starts after the drive has indicated the beginning of the track by providing a signal on the line IDX at the time the index hole passes through the photosensor. The sectors are formatted continuously until the drive indicates again the passage of the index hole by a signal on the IDX line. For the formatting process the length of GAP is larger than is the case for reading or writing data. The bytes cylinder, head, sector number, and sector size don't have any meaning in the result phase here, but you have to read them out before you can program a new command.

Command Phase

Bit / Byte	7	6	5	4	3	2	1	0
0	0	F	0	0	1	1	0	1
1	x	x	x	x	x	HD	DR_1	DR_0
2	Sector Size							
3	Track Length							
4	Length of GAP3							
5	Fill Byte							

F: FM or MFM recording method
1=MFM (standard) 0=FM
HD: head number (always equal head address in byte 3)
DR1, DR0: drive
00=drive 0 (A) 01=drive 1 (B) 10=drive 2 (C) 11=drive 3 (D)
sector size: 0=128 bytes 1=256 bytes 2=512 bytes ... 7=16 kbytes
track length: number of sectors per track
length of GAP 3: standard value=80 (5 1/4") or 84 (3 1/2")
fill byte: byte to fill the sector's data area of the sectors (standard=0f6h corresponding to "÷")

Result Phase

	7 … 0
0	ST0
1	ST1
2	ST2
3	Cylinder
4	Head
5	Sector Number
6	Sector Size

ST0, ST1, ST2: status register 0 to 2 (see G.2)
cylinder, head, sector number, sector size: invalid values, but have to be read in advance of a new command

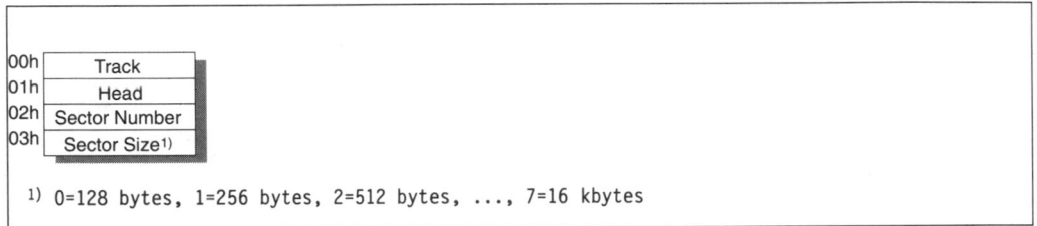

00h	Track
01h	Head
02h	Sector Number
03h	Sector Size[1)]

1) 0=128 bytes, 1=256 bytes, 2=512 bytes, ..., 7=16 kbytes

Figure G.1: Format buffer for one sector.

G.1.3 Control Commands

Read Sector Identification (xah)

This command reads the sector identification of the first ID address mark which the controller is able to detect. Thus you can determine the current position of the read/write head. If the controller cannot read any ID address mark between two pulses on the IDX line (that is, after a complete disk revolution), it issues an error message. The bytes cylinder, head, sector number and sector size in the result phase characterize the read sector identification.

Command Phase

Bit Byte	7	6	5	4	3	2	1	0
0	0	F	0	0	1	0	1	0
1	x	x	x	x	x	HD	DR_1	DR_0

F: FM or MFM recording method
1=MFM (standard) 0=FM
HD: head number (always equal head address in byte 3)
DR1, DR0: drive
00=drive 0 (A) 01=drive 1 (B) 10=drive 2 (C) 11=drive 3 (D)

Result Phase

	7 ... 0
0	ST0
1	ST1
2	ST2
3	Cylinder
4	Head
5	Sector Number
6	Sector Size

```
ST0, ST1, ST2:  status register 0 to 2 (see G.2)
cylinder, head, sector number, sector size:  sector identification read
```

Calibrate Drive (x7h)

This command moves the read/write head to cylinder 0. If a seek error occurred in the course of a sector access you can move the head to an absolute cylinder to calibrate the drive again. The command doesn't implement a result phase, but issues an interrupt after completion. Immediately afterwards you should use the command *check interrupt status* to determine the status information of the calibration operation.

The controller executes the command by setting the DIR signal to 0, passing the drive 79 step pulses at most, and checking the signal TRK0 of the drive after each step pulse. If the signal is active (that is, the head is on track 0), the controller sets bit SE in status register 0 and aborts the command. If the signal TRK0 is not active even after 79 step pulses, the controller sets bits SE and EC in status register 0 and terminates the command. To calibrate the drive you may have to issue several calibration commands. That's especially true for floppy drives which handle more than 80 tracks. After completion of the command you should always determine, by means of a command *check interrupt status,* whether the head is correctly positioned over track 0. After power-up a calibration command is necessary to initialize the head position correctly.

Command Phase

Bit / Byte	7	6	5	4	3	2	1	0
0	0	0	0	0	0	1	1	1
1	x	x	x	x	x	0	DR_1	DR_0

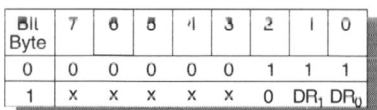

```
DR1, DR0:  drive
     00=drive 0 (A)   01=drive 1 (B)   10=drive 2 (C)   11=drive 3 (D)
```

Check Interrupt Status (x8h)

This command returns status information about the controller state in the result phase if the controller has issued an interrupt. Interrupts are issued:

- at the beginning of the result phase of the commands
  read sector
  read deleted sector
  write sector
  write deleted sector
  read track
  format track
  read sector identification
  verify
- after completion of the following commands without the result phase
  calibrate drive
  seek
  seek relative
- for data exchange between main memory and controller, when interrupt-driven data exchange is effective and the controller doesn't use DMA.

The command resets the interrupt signal and determines the source of the interrupt via status register ST0. If you issue the command and no interrupt is pending, the status register ST0 returns a value 80h corresponding to the message *invalid command.*

Command Phase

Bit Byte	7	6	5	4	3	2	1	0
0	0	0	0	0	1	0	0	0

Result Phase

	7 … 0
0	ST0
1	Current Cylinder

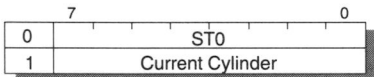

```
ST0:  status register 0 (see G.2)
current cylinder:  current position of read/write head
```

Fix Drive Data (x3h)

With this command you pass the controller mechanical control data for the connected drives. Note that the effective values are also dependent on the selected data transfer rate. With a PC/XT controller the values are fixed, because the data transfer rate cannot be programmed and doesn't vary in this case. The command doesn't have a result phase.

Command Phase

Bit / Byte	7	6	5	4	3	2	1	0
0	0	0	0	0	0	0	1	1
1	Step Rate				Head Unload Time			
2	Head Load Time							NDM

NDM: Non-DMA Mode
0=Data Transfer Via DMA
1=Data Transfer Not Via DMA

Step Rate [ms]

Entry	Data Transfer Rate 1 M	500 k	300 k	250 k
0h	8.0	16	26.7	32
1h	7.5	15	25.0	30
2h	7.0	14	23.3	28
...	...	...	...	...
eh	1.0	2	3.3	4
fh	0.5	1	1.7	2

Head Unload Time [ms]

Entry	Data Transfer Rate 1 M	500 k	300 k	250 k
0h	128	256	426	512
1h	8	16	26.7	32
2h	16	32	53.5	64
...	...	...	...	...
eh	112	224	373	448
fh	120	240	400	480

Head Load Time [ms]

Entry	Data Transfer Rate 1 M	500 k	300 k	250 k
0h	128	256	426	512
1h	1	2	3.3	4
2h	2	4	6.7	8
...	...	...	...	...
eh	126	252	420	504
fh	127	254	423	508

Check Drive Status (x4h)

In the result phase the command provides status information concerning the state of the connected drives.

Command Phase

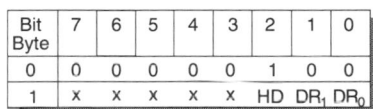

Bit / Byte	7	6	5	4	3	2	1	0
0	0	0	0	0	0	1	0	0
1	x	x	x	x	x	HD	DR_1	DR_0

```
HD:  head number
DR1, DR0:  drive
     00=drive 0 (A)   01=drive 1 (B)   10=drive 2 (C)   11=drive 3 (D)
```

Result Phase

	7 … 0
0	ST3

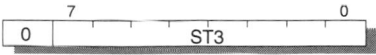

```
ST3:  status register 3 with drive information (see G.2)
```

Park Read/Write Head (xfh)

This command moves the read/write head to the park cylinder. For command execution the controller compares the current cylinder number with the programmed number, sets the direction signal (DIR) for the drive accordingly, and issues step pulses until both cylinder numbers coincide. The command has no result phase; you should therefore verify the head position immediately after command completion with the *check interrupt status* command.

Command Phase

Bit / Byte	7	6	5	4	3	2	1	0
0	0	0	0	0	1	1	1	1
1	x	x	x	x	x	HD	DR_1	DR_0
2	Cylinder							

```
HD:  head number
DR1, DR0:  drive
     00=drive 0 (A)   01=drive 1 (B)   10=drive 2 (C)   11=drive 3 (D)
cylinder:  cylinder where the head should be moved to
```

Invalid Command

If you specify an invalid opcode, the controller switches to a standby state and sets bit 7 of status register ST3. The same applies if you issue a *check interrupt status* command and no interrupt is pending.

Command Phase

Bit / Byte	7	6	5	4	3	2	1	0
0	Invalid Opcode							

Result Phase

	7 … 0
0	ST0

```
ST0:  status register 0 with entry 80h (see G.2)
```

G.1.4 Extended Commands

Verify (x16h)

This command reads one or more sectors with valid data address marks from disk, calculates the CRC check sum, and compares the calculated and the read CRC values to check the internal consistency of the data. The command therefore behaves like a read command without data transfer to main memory. Thus the command cannot be aborted by a TC signal from the DMA controller. On the other hand, you must set bit EC to «1» to issue an implicit TC signal when the count value *data length/verify sectors* is decremented to 0. *Data length/verify sectors* therefore indicates the number of sectors to be verified; a value 00h checks 256 sectors. If you set EC equal to 0, you should give *data length/verify sectors* a value of ffh.

Command Phase

Bit / Byte	7	6	5	4	3	2	1	0
0	M	F	S	1	0	1	1	0
1	EC	x	x	x	x	HD	DR_1	DR_0
2	Cylinder							
3	Head							
4	Sector Number							
5	Sector Size							
6	Track Length/Max. Sector Number							
7	Length of GAP3							
8	Data Length/Verify Sectors							

M: multi track operation
1=carry out cylinder operation 0=carry out single track operation
F: FM or MFM recording method
1=MFM (standard) 0=FM
S: skip mode
1=skip deleted data address marks 0=do not skip
EC: enable count value
1=command byte 8 specifies the number of sectors to verify
0=command byte 8 specifies the data length if sector size=00
HD: head number (always equal head address in byte 3)
DR1, DR0: drive
00=drive 0 (A) 01=drive 1 (B) 10=drive 2 (C) 11=drive 3 (D)
cylinder, head, sector number: address of first sector to verify
sector size: 0=128 bytes 1=256 bytes 2=512 bytes ... 7=16 kbytes
track length/max. sector number: number of sectors per track or max. sector number, for which the command shall be carried out
length of GAP 3: standard value=42, minimal value=32 (5 1/4") or standard value=27 (3 1/2")
data length/verify sectors: length of data to verify in bytes
(valid only if sector size=00) if EC=0 or
number of sectors to verify if EC=1

Result Phase

Byte	7 … 0
0	ST0
1	ST1
2	ST2
3	Cylinder
4	Head
5	Sector Number
6	Sector Size

ST0, ST1, ST2: status register 0 to 2 (see G.2)
cylinder, head, sector number, sector size: sector identification according to Table G.1

Determine Controller Version (x10h)

This command determines whether an extended controller which supports the extended commands is installed. A normal μPD765 regards the command code 00010000 as invalid opcode, and issues an error message.

Command Phase

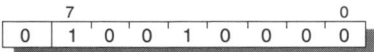

Bit Byte	7	6	5	4	3	2	1	0
0	0	0	0	1	0	0	0	0

Result Phase (only if an extended controller is installed)

	7							0
0	1	0	0	1	0	0	0	0

Seek Relative (1xfh)

This command moves the read/write head relative to the current cylinder. The command doesn't have a result phase.

Command Phase

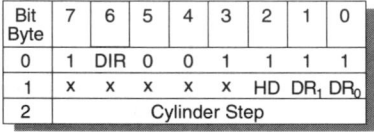

Bit Byte	7	6	5	4	3	2	1	0
0	1	DIR	0	0	1	1	1	1
1	x	x	x	x	x	HD	DR_1	DR_0
2	Cylinder Step							

```
DIR: step direction
     1=to inner (to larger cylinder numbers)
     0=to outer (to smaller cylinder numbers)
HD:  head number
DR1, DR0:  drive
     00=drive 0 (A)   01=drive 1 (B)   10=drive 2 (C)   11=drive 3 (D)
cylinder step:  number of cylinders to step
```

Register Dump(0fh)

This command reads internal controller registers, and provides their values in the result phase.

Command Phase

Bit Byte	7	6	5	4	3	2	1	0
0	0	0	0	0	1	1	1	1

Result Phase

Byte	7 … 4	3 … 0
0	Current Cylinder DR_0	
1	Current Cylinder DR_1	
2	Current Cylinder DR_2	
3	Current Cylinder DR_3	
4	Step Rate	Head Unload Time
5	Head Load Time	NDM (bit 0)
6	Number of Sectors/Track Length	

current cylinder DR_0, DR_1, DR_2, DR_3: cylinder where the read/write head is currently positioned

step time, head unload time, head load time: mechanical characteristics which are set by the command fix drive data

NDM: non-DMA mode
    1=DMA disabled 0=DMA enabled

number of sectors/track length: number of sectors per track

M	HD_{prog}	Last sector affected by command	Sector identification in the result phase Cylinder	Head	Sector	Sector size
0	0	before end of track	cyl_{prog}	HD_{prog}	sec_{prog}	siz_{prog}
0	0	end of track	cyl_{prog+1}	HD_{prog}	1	siz_{prog}
0	1	before end of track	cyl_{prog}	HD_{prog}	sec_{prog}	siz_{prog}
0	1	end of track	cyl_{prog+1}	HD_{prog}	1	siz_{prog}
1	0	before end of track	cyl_{prog}	HD_{prog}	sec_{prog}	siz_{prog}
1	0	end of track	cyl_{prog}	$\overline{HD}_{prog}$	1	siz_{prog}
1	1	before end of track	cyl_{prog}	$\overline{HD}_{prog}$	sec_{prog}	siz_{prog}
1	1	end of track	cyl_{prog+1}	$\overline{HD}_{prog}$	1	siz_{prog}

HD_{prog}: programmed head
sec_{prog}: programmed sector
$\overline{HD}_{prog}$: inverted value of HD_{prog} corresponding to opposite head
cyl_{prog}: programmed cylinder
siz_{prog}: programmed sector size

Table G.1: Sector identification in the result phase

G.2 Status Registers ST0 to ST3

The indicated status values are valid only if the corresponding status bit is set.

Status Register ST0

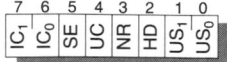

7	6	5	4	3	2	1	0
IC_1	IC_0	SE	UC	NR	HD	US_1	US_0

IC_1, IC_0: interrupt code

- 00=normal termination of controller command; the command was executed correctly and without any error
- 01=abnormal termination of the command; the controller has started the command execution but was not able to terminate it correctly
- 10=invalid command; the controller did not start command execution
- 11=abnormal termination by polling

SE: seek end

- The controller has terminated a seek or calibration command or has correctly executed a read or write command with implicit seek.

UC: unit check

- In a calibration command the TRK0 signal from the drive was not set after 79 step pulses, thus the head did not reach track 0 after 79 pulses.

NR: drive not ready

HD: currently active head

- 1=head 1 0=head 0

US_1, US_0: currently selected drive (unit select)

- 00=drive 0 (A:) 01=drive 1 (B:)
  10=drive 2 (C:) 11=drive 3 (D:)

Status Register ST1

7	6	5	4	3	2	1	0
EN	xx	DE	TO	xx	NDAT	NW	NID

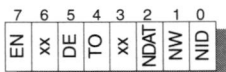

EN: end of cylinder

- The controller attempted to access a sector after the end of the track, that is, the last sector of the track. EN is set if, after a read or write command, no external or implicit TC signal is issued before the sector count exceeds the end of the track.

xx: bit unused; value always equal to 0

DE: data error

- The controller detected an error in the ID address field or the data field of a sector.

TO: time-out

- The controller did not receive a signal from the DMA controller or the CPU within the required time period.

NDAT: no data

- The controller cannot find the addressed sector in a *read sector* or *read deleted sector* command.
- The controller cannot read the ID address mark in a *read identification* command without error.
- The controller cannot determine the sector sequence in a *read track* command correctly.

NW: not writeable

- The write-protection signal of the drive is active, that is, the disk is write-protected while the controller is executing a write command.

NID: no address mark

- The controller did not find an ID address mark after two IDX pulses, that is, one complete disk revolution.
- The controller cannot find a data address mark DAM or a deleted data address mark DAM on the specified track.

Status Register ST2

7	6	5	4	3	2	1	0
xx	DADM	CRCE	WCYL	SEQ	SERR	BCYL	NDAM

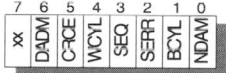

xx: bit unused; value always equal to 0

DADM: deleted address mark

- The controller detected a deleted data address mark DAM when executing a *read sector* command.
- The controller detected a valid data address mark DAM when executing a *read deleted sector* command.

CRCE: CRC error in data field

- The controller detected a CRC error in the data field of the sector.

WCYL: wrong cylinder

- The contents of the track address in the ID address mark differs from the track address in the controller.

SEQ: seek equal

- With a μPD765 the condition *seek equal* is fulfilled.
- Otherwise SGL is not used and is always equal to 0.

SERR: seek error

- With the μPD765 the controller did not find the corresponding sector when seeking on the cylinder.
- Otherwise SERR is not used and is always equal to 0.

BCYL: bad cylinder

– The track address in the ID address mark differs from the track address in the controller. The value is equal ffh and indicates a bad track with a physical error according to the IBM soft sector format.

NDAM: not data address mark DAM

– The controller cannot find a valid or deleted data address mark DAM.

Status Register ST3

The bits in the status register ST3 directly indicate the state of the control lines of the selected drive.

7	6	5	4	3	2	1	0
ESIG	WPDR	RDY	TRK0	DSDR	HDDR	DS1	DS0

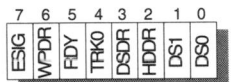

ESIG: error

– With a μPD765 the error signal of the drive is active, that is, an error has occurred.
– Otherwise ESIG is not used and is always equal to 0.

WPDR: write-protection

– The write-protection line is active, thus the inserted disk is write-protected.

RDY: ready

– With a μPD765 the ready signal of the drive is active, that is, the drive is ready.
– Otherwise RDY is not used and is always equal to 1, thus the drive is always ready.

TRK0: track 0

– The TRK0 signal of the drive is active, thus the head is above track 0.

DSDR: double sided drive

– The DSDR signal of the drive is active, thus the drive is double sided.

HDDR: head

– The bit indicates the status of the HDSEL signal of the drive: 1=head 1 active, 0=head 0 active.

DS1, DS0: drive select

– Both bits indicate the status of the select signals DS1 and DS0 of the drive: 00=drive 0 (A:), 01=drive 1 (B:), 10=drive 2 (C:), 11=drive 3 (D:).

H Hard Disk Drive Controllers

H.1 The IDE Interface Commands

- The specifications cylinder, head, sector number and sector size are called the *sector identification*.
- The data and status registers are together called the AT task file.
- Before you can access a register you have to determine whether the BSY bit in the status register (1f7h) is cleared.
- The transfer of a command byte to the command register (1f7h) starts the corresponding command; therefore you have to load the parameter registers with the necessary values in advance.
- All sector and format data is read and written via the data register (1f0h) by means of programmed I/O (PIO); a data exchange is only possible if the BSY bit in the status register is cleared and the DRQ bit is set.
- The DRQ bit remains set until the sector, format and, eventually, ECC data are completely read or written.
- Read and write commands can last across several sectors, starting with the start sector if the value in the sector number register (1f1h) is larger than 1; a value of 0 in this register means that the corresponding command is executed for 256 sectors.
- After command completion, the status register (1f7h) and, eventually, the error register (1f1h) contain status information, which enables you to confirm the correct execution of the command or to determine the reason for a malfunction or command abortion.
- If erroneous read data is correctable by the ECC bytes, the controller sets the CORR error bit in the status register (1f7h), but the command execution is not aborted.
- The sector identification after command completion or abortion indicates the last handled sector or the sector where the error occurred, respectively.
- Most IDE hard disks can be operated in native and translation mode: in native mode the logical drive geometry coincides with the physical geometry; in translation mode the translation logic of the controller translates the physical geometry to a completely different logical geometry.
- Be careful when using the format command because drives in translation mode can behave unpredictably if you program this command; the IDE hard disk comes preformatted with the best interleave factor; the dynamic bad sector remapping remaps defect sectors to good ones, and later reformatting of the drive is therefore unnecessary.
- The multiple sector commands *read sector* and *write sector* issue an interrupt 76h via IRQ14 before or after processing each sector.

- The result phase of each command starts with a hardware interrupt via IRQ14.
- The IDE interface supports two physical drives at most; the master (drive select 0) and the slave (drive select 1).
- For the IDE interface, the eight commands of the original AT are required; in H.1.4 you will find the additional optional commands that were introduced with the new IDE specification.

H.1.1 Summary of the Listed Commands

- required commands
  calibrate drive
  read sector
  write sector
  verify sector
  format track
  seek
  diagnostics
  set drive parameters
- optional commands
  read sector buffer
  write sector buffer
  identify drive

H.1.2 Required Commands

Calibrate Drive (1xh)

This command moves the read/write heads to cylinder 0. After issuing the command by transfering the command byte to the command register, the controller sets the BSY bit in the status register and moves the head to track 0. When the seek is complete the controller clears the BSY bit and issues a hardware interrupt via IRQ14. After a seek error, the command can be used to recalibrate the drive.

Command Phase

AT Task File Register	Bit 7	6	5	4	3	2	1	0
Command (1f7h)	0	0	0	1	x	x	x	x
Drive/Head (1f6h)	1	0	1	DRV	x	x	x	x

```
x:   values insignificant (recommendation: 0)
DRV: drive
     1=slave    0=master
```

Result Phase

AT Task File Register		Bit 7	6	5	4	3	2	1	0
Error	(1f1h)	x	NTO	ABT	x	NID	x	x	x
Cylinder LSB	(1f4h)	0							
Cylinder MSB	(1f5h)	0							
Drive/Head	(1f6h)	1	0	1	DRV	HD_3	HD_2	HD_1	HD_0
Status	(1f7h)	BSY	RDY	x	SKC	DRQ	x	x	ERR

```
NTO:  1=track 0 not found                     0=no error
ABT:  command abortion
      1=command aborted                       0=command completed
NID:  1=ID mark not found                     0=no error
DRV:  calibrated drive
      1=slave    0=master
HD3–HD0: active head (unchanged)
BSY:  busy
      1=drive busy  0=drive not busy
RDY:  ready
      1=drive ready       0=not ready
SKC:  seek
      1=complete          0=in progress
DRQ:  data request
      1=data can be transferred    0=no data access possible
ERR:  error
      1=error register contains additional error information
x:    unused, invalid
```

Read Sector (2xh)

This command reads 1–256 sectors according to the value in the *sector count* register; a value of 0 means 256 sectors. The first sector is specified by the sector number, cylinder MSB, cylinder LSB, and head registers. After transfer of the command code, the controller sets the BSY bit in the status register, and the addressed drive carries out an implicit seek, activates the corresponding read/write head, and reads the sector, eventually together with the ECC bytes, into the sector buffer. After the read of each sector the DRQ bit is set, and the controller issues a hardware interrupt 76h via IRQ14. The interrupt handler transfers the sector data into main memory. If all data words are transferred and at least one more sector is to be read, the controller sets the BSY bit again, clears DRQ and reads the next sector, etc. The sector identification is automatically updated, and always indicates the currently processed sector.

If a non-correctable data error occurs, the controller aborts the command and the sector identification defines the sector with the error. If the data error can be corrected by the ECC bytes, only the CORR bit in the status register is set, but the command is not aborted. If the long-bit L is set the controller executes a read-long command and the sector data, together with their ECC bytes, are read. In this case, the controller does not carry out an ECC check. DRQ is active until the last ECC byte is read by the host. The ECC data is transferred byte by byte, all other data is transferred word by word (16 bits).

Command Phase

AT Task File Register		Bit 7	6	5	4	3	2	1	0
Command	(1f7h)	0	0	1	0	0	0	L	R
Sector Count	(1f2h)	Number of Sectors to Read							
Sector Number	(1f3h)	S_7	S_6	S_5	S_4	S_3	S_2	S_1	S_0
Cylinder LSB	(1f4h)	C_7	C_6	C_5	C_4	C_3	C_2	C_1	C_0
Cylinder MSB	(1f5h)	0	0	0	0	0	0	C_9	C_8
Drive/Head	(1f6h)	1	0	1	DRV	HD_3	HD_2	HD_1	HD_0

L: long-bit
1=sector data and ECC bytes are read 0=only sector data are read
R: retry disable
1=automatic command retry is not executed
0=automatic command retry is executed
S_7–S_0: sector number
C_9–C_0: cylinder number (10-bit binary number)
DRV: drive
1=slave 0=master
HD_3–HD_0: head number (binary number)
0000=head 0 0001=head 1 0010=head 2 ... 1111=head 15

Result Phase

AT Task File Register		Bit 7	6	5	4	3	2	1	0
Error	(1f1h)	NDM	x	ABT	x	NID	x	UNC	BBK
Sector Count	(1f2h)	0*)							
Sector Number	(1f3h)	S_7	S_6	S_5	S_4	S_3	S_2	S_1	S_0
Cylinder LSB	(1f4h)	C_7	C_6	C_5	C_4	C_3	C_2	C_1	C_0
Cylinder MSB	(1f5h)	0	0	0	0	0	0	C_9	C_8
Drive/Head	(1f6h)	1	0	1	DRV	HD_3	HD_2	HD_1	HD_0
Status	(1f7h)	BSY	RDY	x	x	DRQ	COR	x	ERR

*) in the case of command abortion, the register indicates the number of sectors still to be read
NDM: 1=data address mark not found 0=no error
ABT: command abortion
1=command aborted 0=command completed
NID: 1=ID mark not found 0=no error
UNC: 1=uncorrectable data error 0=no or correctable data error
BBK: 1=sector marked bad by host 0=no error
C_9–C_0, S_7–S_0, HD_3–HD_0: sector identification of sector last read
DRV: drive
1=slave 0=master
BSY: busy
1=drive is busy 0=drive not busy
RDY: ready
1=drive ready 0=not ready
DRQ: data
1=can be transferred 0=no data access possible
COR: correctable data error
1=occurred 0=no data error
ERR: error

```
     1=error register contains additional error information
x:   unused, invalid
```

Write Sector (3xh)

This command writes 1–256 sectors according to the value in the *sector count* register onto disk. The first sector is specified by the sector number, cylinder LSB, cylinder MSB, and head registers. After the transfer of the command code, the controller sets the BSY bit in the status register, the addressed drive carries out an implicit seek and prepares the sector buffer for receiving the write data from main memory. Afterwards, the controller sets the DRQ bit and clears the BSY bit. The CPU now must transfer the sector data, eventually together with the ECC bytes, via the data register (1f0h) into the sector buffer. When the write data is transferred the controller clears the DRQ bit and sets the BSY bit again. Then the drive writes the data onto disk. If at least one more sector is to be written, the controller sets the DRQ bit, clears the BSY bit, and issues a hardware interrupt 76h via IRQ14. The interrupt handler now transfers the write data for the next sector from main memory to the data register, etc. The sector identification is automatically updated, and always indicates the current processed sector. After all sectors are written, the controller once again issues an interrupt via IRQ upon entering the result phase.

If a write error occurs, the controller aborts the command and the sector identification defines the sector with the error. If the long-bit L is set the controller carries out a write-long command, and the sector data together with the ECC bytes is written. In this case, the controller does not generate the ECC byte itself, but writes the transferred byte onto disk without any change. DRQ is active until the last ECC byte is transferred by the host. The ECC data is transferred byte by byte, all other data is transferred word by word (16 bits).

Command Phase

AT Task File Register	Bit 7	6	5	4	3	2	1	0
Command (1f7h)	0	0	1	1	0	0	L	R
Sector Count (1f2h)	Number of Sectors to Write							
Sector Number (1f3h)	S_7	S_6	S_5	S_4	S_3	S_2	S_1	S_0
Cylinder LSB (1f4h)	C_7	C_6	C_5	C_4	C_3	C_2	C_1	C_0
Cylinder MSB (1f5h)	0	0	0	0	0	0	C_9	C_8
Drive/Head (1f6h)	1	0	1	DRV	HD_3	HD_2	HD_1	HD_0

L: long bit
1=sector data and ECC bytes are written 0=only sector data are written

R: retry disable
1=automatic command retry is not executed
0=automatic command retry is executed

S_7–S_0: sector number

C_9–C_0: cylinder number (10-bit binary number)

DRV: drive
1=slave 0=master

HD_3–HD_0: head number (binary number)
0000=head 0 0001=head 1 0010=head 2 ... 1111=head 15

Result Phase

AT Task File Register		Bit 7	6	5	4	3	2	1	0
Error	(1f1h)	NDM	x	ABT	x	NID	x	x	BBK
Sector Count	(1f2h)	0*)							
Sector Number	(1f3h)	S_7	S_6	S_5	S_4	S_3	S_2	S_1	S_0
Cylinder LSB	(1f4h)	C_7	C_6	C_5	C_4	C_3	C_2	C_1	C_0
Cylinder MSB	(1f5h)	0	0	0	0	0	0	C_9	C_8
Drive/Head	(1f6h)	1	0	1	DRV	HD_3	HD_2	HD_1	HD_0
Status	(1f7h)	BSY	RDY	WFT	x	DRQ	x	x	ERR

```
*) in the case of command abortion, the register indicates the number of sectors still to be
written
NDM:  1=data address mark not found       0=no error
ABT:  command abortion
      1=command aborted                   0=command completed
NID:  1=ID mark not found                 0=no error
BBK:  1=sector marked bad by host         0=no error
C9-C0, S7-S0, HD3-HD0: sector identification of sector last written
DRV:  drive
      1=slave    0=master
BSY:  busy
      1=drive is busy     0=drive not busy
RDY:  ready
      1=drive ready       0=not ready
WFT:  write fault
      1=occurred                   0=no write fault
DRQ:  data
      1=can be transferred         0=no data access possible
ERR:  error
      1=error register contains additional error information
x:    unused, invalid
```

Verify Sector (4xh)

This command checks one or more sectors. The controller reads one or more sectors into the sector buffer and performs the ECC check, but doesn't transfer the read sector data to main memory. Therefore, the check is carried out based on the ECC bytes only; the written sector data is not compared with the data in an external buffer. At the beginning of the result phase, the command generates a hardware interrupt 76h via IRQ14. Between the individual sector checks no interrupts are issued.

Command Phase

AT Task File Register		Bit 7	6	5	4	3	2	1	0
Command	(1f7h)	0	1	0	0	0	0	0	R
Sector Count	(1f2h)	Number of Sectors to Verify							
Sector Number	(1f3h)	S_7	S_6	S_5	S_4	S_3	S_2	S_1	S_0
Cylinder LSB	(1f4h)	C_7	C_6	C_5	C_4	C_3	C_2	C_1	C_0
Cylinder MSB	(1f5h)	0	0	0	0	0	0	C_9	C_8
Drive/Head	(1f6h)	1	0	1	DRV	HD_3	HD_2	HD_1	HD_0

R: retry disable
1=automatic command retry is not executed
0=automatic command retry is executed
S_7–S_0: sector number
C_9–C_0: cylinder number (10–bit binary number)
DRV: drive
1=slave 0=master
HD_3–HD_0: head number (binary number)
0000=head 0 0001=head 1 0010=head 2 ... 1111=head 15

Result Phase

AT Task File Register		Bit 7	6	5	4	3	2	1	0
Error	(1f1h)	NDM	x	ABT	x	NID	x	UNC	BBK
Sector Count	(1f2h)	0*)							
Sector Number	(1f3h)	S_7	S_6	S_5	S_4	S_3	S_2	S_1	S_0
Cylinder LSB	(1f4h)	C_7	C_6	C_5	C_4	C_3	C_2	C_1	C_0
Cylinder MSB	(1f5h)	0	0	0	0	0	0	C_9	C_8
Drive/Head	(1f6h)	1	0	1	DRV	HD_3	HD_2	HD_1	HD_0
Status	(1f7h)	BSY	RDY	x	x	DRQ	COR	x	ERR

*) in the case of command abortion, the register indicates the number of sectors still to be verified
NDM: 1=data address mark not found 0=no error
ABT: command abortion
1=command aborted 0=command completed
NID: 1=ID mark not found 0=no error
UNC: 1=uncorrectable data error 0=no or correctable data error
BBK: 1=sector marked bad by host 0=no error
C_9–C_0, S_7–S_0, HD_3–HD_0: sector identification of sector verified last
DRV: drive
1=slave 0=master
BSY: busy
1=drive is busy 0=drive not busy
RDY: ready
1=drive ready 0=not ready
DRQ: data
1=can be transferred 0=no data access possible
COR: correctable data error
1=occurred 0=no data error
ERR: error
1=error register contains additional error information
x: unused, invalid

Format Track (50h)

This command formats one track of the hard disk. On most IDE drives the command can be used in native and translation modes, but the behaviour is rather different in these modes.

In native mode a low-level formatting of the addressed track is carried out. Immediately after you have passed the command byte, the controller sets the BSY bit and prepares the sector buffer for receiving the format data from the CPU. Then the controller clears the BSY bit, sets the DRQ bit, and waits for the transfer of 256 words with format data from the CPU. The CPU may now transfer the data via the data register (1f0h) to the sector buffer. The format data consists of two bytes for every sector of the track, where the low byte indicates the sector flag and the high byte the sector number. A sector flag 00h means a sector to format normally; a value 80h indicates a sector which has to be marked as bad. The format data is written into the format buffer with the low byte, that is, the sector flag, first. Note that the format buffer always has to contain 512 bytes, even if the number of sectors per track is less than 256. The remaining format bytes are ignored by the controller, but have to be transferred so that the controller sets the BSY bit and starts the format operation.

If the transfer of the format data is complete, the DRQ bit is cleared and the BSY bit is set. The controller now starts the format operation of the addressed track. After detecting the index pulse which indicates the physical beginning of the track, the ID fields of the sectors are rewritten and the sector data fields are filled with the byte values 6ch corresponding to the character «l». By means of the ID fields sectors or complete tracks can be marked as bad. After the formatting, the controller clears the BSY bit and issues a hardware interrupt 76h via IRQ14.

For a format operation in native mode you must therefore know the physical drive geometry very well. On a drive with zone recording, for example, it is absolutely necessary that you know all the borders of the individual zones and the number of sectors of each zone. You must transfer this number to the sector count register.

When formatting in translation mode the controller writes only the sector data filled with the byte values 6ch; the ID marks are not changed. That is actually not a real formatting operation, because the structure of the volume is not changed. For example it is not possible to adjust the interleave value by this. For the number of sectors per track in this case you have to specify the logical sector number per track; the borders of the zone recording are insignificant. With other values most controllers respond with an error message *ID mark not found* and abort the formatting operation. In some cases, the controller can do something unpredictable. Low level formatting of IDE hard disks in translation mode is therefore very critical, and the normally very useful tools such as DiskManager or PCTools are of no value. To overwrite all sectors with 512 bytes 6ch has the same effect as a format operation in translation mode.

Command Phase

AT Task File Register		Bit 7	6	5	4	3	2	1	0
Command	(1f7h)	0	1	0	1	0	0	0	0
Sector Number	(1f3h)	Number of Sectors per Track							
Cylinder LSB	(1f4h)	C_7	C_6	C_5	C_4	C_3	C_2	C_1	C_0
Cylinder MSB	(1f5h)	0	0	0	0	0	0	C_9	C_8
Drive/Head	(1f6h)	1	0	1	DRV	HD_3	HD_2	HD_1	HD_0

C_9–C_0: cylinder number (10-bit binary number)
DRV: drive
    1=slave 0=master
HD_3–HD_0: head number (binary number)
    0000=head 0 0001=head 1 0010=head 2 ... 1111=head 15

Result Phase

AT Task File Register		Bit 7	6	5	4	3	2	1	0
Error	(1f1h)	NDM	x	ABT	x	NID	x	x	x
Sector Number	(1f3h)	S_7	S_6	S_5	S_4	S_3	S_2	S_1	S_0
Cylinder LSB	(1f4h)	C_7	C_6	C_5	C_4	C_3	C_2	C_1	C_0
Cylinder MSB	(1f5h)	0	0	0	0	0	0	C_9	C_8
Drive/Head	(1f6h)	1	0	1	DRV	HD_3	HD_2	HD_1	HD_0
Status	(1f7h)	BSY	RDY	x	x	DRQ	x	x	ERR

NDM: 1=data address mark not found 0=no error
ABT: command abortion
    1=command aborted 0=command completed
NID: 1=ID mark not found 0=no error
C_9–C_0, S_7–S_0, HD_3–HD_0: sector identification of sector formatted last
DRV: drive
    1=slave 0=master
BSY: busy
    1=drive is busy 0=drive not busy
RDY: ready
    1=drive ready 0=not ready
DRQ: data
    1=can be transferred 0=no data access possible
ERR: error
    1=error register contains additional error information
x: unused, invalid

Seek (7xh)

This command moves the read/write heads to the programmed track and selects the addressed head. Immediately after transfer of the command code, the controller sets the BSY bit and executes the seek. If the seek is completed correctly, the controller clears the BSY bit, sets the SKC bit, and issues a hardware interrupt 76h via IRQ14. Note that the disk need not be formatted for carrying out the command correctly. In translation mode the passed logical cylinder number is converted to a physical cylinder number, and the head is moved to the physical cylinder.

Command Phase

AT Task File Register		Bit 7	6	5	4	3	2	1	0
Command	(1f7h)	0	1	1	1	x	x	x	x
Cylinder LSB	(1f4h)	C_7	C_6	C_5	C_4	C_3	C_2	C_1	C_0
Cylinder MSB	(1f5h)	0	0	0	0	0	0	C_9	C_8
Drive/Head	(1f6h)	1	0	1	DRV	HD_3	HD_2	HD_1	HD_0

C_9–C_0: cylinder number (10–bit binary number)
DRV: drive
  1=slave 0=master
HD_3–HD_0: head number (binary number)
  0000=head 0 0001=head 1 0010=head 2 ... 1111=head 15
x: unused, invalid

Result Phase

AT Task File Register		Bit 7	6	5	4	3	2	1	0
Error	(1f1h)	NDM	NTO	ABT	x	NID	x	x	x
Cylinder LSB	(1f4h)	C_7	C_6	C_5	C_4	C_3	C_2	C_1	C_0
Cylinder MSB	(1f5h)	0	0	0	0	0	0	C_9	C_8
Drive/Head	(1f6h)	1	0	1	DRV	HD_3	HD_2	HD_1	HD_0
Status	(1f7h)	BSY	RDY	x	SKC	DRQ	x	x	ERR

NDM: 1=data address mark not found 0=no error
NTO: 1=track 0 not found 0=no error
ABT: command abortion
  1=command aborted 0=command completed
NID: 1=ID mark not found 0=no error
C_9–C_0, HD_3–HD_0: track identification of sector where head is moved to
DRV: drive
  1=slave 0=master
BSY: busy
  1=drive is busy 0=drive not busy
RDY: ready
  1=drive ready 0=not ready
SKC: seek
  1=complete 0=in progress
DRQ: data
  1=can be transferred 0=no data access possible
ERR: error
  1=error register contains additional error information
x: unused, invalid

Diagnostics (90h)

This command starts the controller-internal diagnostics routine to check the controller electronics. The CPU can issue this command if the BSY bit is cleared. The RDY bit concerns only the drives, and is insignificant for the diagnostics command because only the controller and not the mechanical drives are checked. Note that the diagnostic information is returned in the error register (1f1h). The meaning of the individual error bits differs from the normal case;

furthermore, after the completion of the diagnostics command the ERR bit in the status register (1f7h) is always equal to 0. The seven low-order bits in the error register contain a binary diagnostics code for the master drive; the high-order bit indicates a summary error code for the slave drive.

Command Phase

AT Task File Register		Bit 7	6	5	4	3	2	1	0
Command	(1f7h)	1	0	0	1	0	0	0	0

Result Phase

AT Task File Register		Bit 7	6	5	4	3	2	1	0
Error	(1f1h)	SD	MD_6	MD_5	MD_4	MD_3	MD_2	MD_1	MD_0
Status	(1f7h)	BSY	x	x	x	DRQ	x	x	0

```
SD:       slave diagnostics code
          0=slave o.k. or slave not present
          1=error of slave in at least one diagnostics function
MD6–MD0: binary master diagnostics code
          1=master drive o.k.
          2=formatting circuit error in master drive
          3=buffer error in master drive
          4=ECC logic error in master drive
          5=microprocessor error in master drive
          6=interface circuit error in master drive
BSY:      busy
          1=drive is busy     0=drive not busy
DRQ:      data
          1=can be transferred          0=no data access possible
x:        unused, invalid
```

Set Drive Parameters (91h)

This command sets the logical geometry of the addressed drive. In the sector count register you specify the number of logical sectors per logical track, and in the drive/head register you specify the number of logical heads of the drive. In translation mode the translation logic of the controller then translates the logical geometry to the real physical geometry of the drive. In translation mode, the drive uses this logical geometry to carry out those commands involving a disk access. The number of logical cylinders of the drive is an automatic result of the request that the number of all logical sectors cannot be larger than the physical sectors actually present. A change of the logical geometry of a hard disk, where data is already stored, inevitably results in a complete data loss as the changed geometry destroys the logical structure of the file system.

Command Phase

AT Task File Register		Bit 7	6	5	4	3	2	1	0
Command	(1f7h)	1	0	0	1	0	0	0	1
Sector Count	(1f2h)	Number of Sectors per Track							
Drive/Head	(1f6h)	1	0	1	DRV	HD_3	HD_2	HD_1	HD_0

```
DRV: drive
     1=slave    0=master
```
HD_3–HD_0: number of logical heads of the drive

Result Phase

AT Task File Register		Bit 7	6	5	4	3	2	1	0
Status	(1f7h)	BSY	RDY	x	x	DRQ	x	x	x

```
BSY:  busy
      1=drive is busy     0=drive not busy
RDY:  ready
      1=drive ready       0=not ready
DRQ:  data
      1=can be transferred         0=no data access possible
x:    unused, invalid
```

H.1.3 Optional Commands

The following three commands are supported by most of the IDE hard disk drives, although they are optional commands and were not implemented in the original AT controller.

Read Sector Buffer (e4h)

This command reads out the contents of the controller's sector buffer. Immediately after you have passed the command code, the controller sets the BSY bit and prepares the buffer for a read operation by the CPU. Afterwards, the BSY bit is cleared, the DRQ bit is set, and the controller issues a hardware interrupt 76h via IRQ14. The CPU now can read the sector buffer and transfer the data to main memory. The command serves mainly for checking the data path between controller and main memory. You can use the command in self-programmed diagnostic routines to determine the source of drive faults.

Command Phase

AT Task File Register		Bit 7	6	5	4	3	2	1	0
Command	(1f7h)	1	1	1	0	0	1	0	0
Drive/Head	(1f6h)	1	0	1	DRV	x	x	x	x

```
DRV: drive
     1=slave    0=master
```

Result Phase

AT Task File Register		Bit 7	6	5	4	3	2	1	0
Status	(1f7h)	BSY	RDY	x	x	DRQ	x	x	x

```
BSY:  busy
      1=drive is busy     0=drive not busy
RDY:  ready
      1=drive ready       0=not ready
DRQ:  data
      1=can be transferred         0=no data access possible
x:    unused, invalid
```

Write Sector Buffer (e8h)

This command writes data into the controller's sector buffer. Immediately after passing the command code the controller sets the BSY bit and prepares the buffer for a write operation by the CPU. Afterwards, the BSY bit is cleared, the DRQ bit is set, and the controller issues a hardware interrupt 76h via IRQ14. The CPU can now transfer data from main memory to the sector buffer. The command serves mainly for checking the data path between controller and main memory. You can use the command in self-programmed diagnostic routines to determine the source of drive faults.

Command Phase

AT Task File Register		Bit 7	6	5	4	3	2	1	0
Command	(1f7h)	1	1	1	0	1	0	0	0
Drive/Head	(1f6h)	1	0	1	DRV	x	x	x	x

```
DRV: drive
     1=slave    0=master
```

Result Phase

AT Task File Register		Bit 7	6	5	4	3	2	1	0
Status	(1f7h)	BSY	RDY	x	x	DRQ	x	x	x

```
BSY:  busy
      1=drive is busy     0=drive not busy
RDY:  ready
      1=drive ready       0=not ready
DRQ:  data
      1=can be transferred         0=no data access possible
x:    unused, invalid
```

Identify Drive (ech)

This command reads parameters and other information from the addressed drive. Immediately after you have passed the command code, the controller sets the BSY bit, loads the information into the sector buffer, and prepares the buffer for a read operation by the CPU. Afterwards, the

BSY bit is cleared, the DRQ bit is set, and the controller issues a hardware interrupt 76h via IRQ14. The interrupt handler has to read all 256 data words of 16 bits each out of the sector buffer. The structure of the 512 byte information is shown in Table H.1.

Command Phase

AT Task File Register		Bit 7	6	5	4	3	2	1	0
Command	(1f7h)	1	1	1	0	1	1	0	0
Drive/Head	(1f6h)	1	0	1	DRV	x	x	x	x

```
DRV: drive
     1=slave    0=master
```

Result Phase

AT Task File Register		Bit 7	6	5	4	3	2	1	0
Status	(1f7h)	BSY	RDY	x	x	DRQ	x	x	x

```
BSY:  busy
      1=drive is busy     0=drive not busy
RDY:  ready
      1=drive ready       0=not ready
DRQ:  data
      1=can be transferred          0=no data access possible
x:    unused, invalid
```

Word[1)]	Meaning
00	configuration[2)]
01	number of physical cylinders
02	reserved
03	number of heads
04	number of unformatted bytes per physical track
05	number of unformatted bytes per sector
06	number of physical sectors per track
07–09	reserved for manufacturer
10–19	ASCII serial number
20	buffer type (01h=one-way, 02h=bidirectional, 03h=cache buffer)
21	buffer size/512
22	number of ECC bytes which are transferred in read/write-long operation
23–26	ASCII identification of controller firmware
27–46	ASCII model number
47	bit 0..7: number of sectors between two interrupts (multiple sector reads/writes only), bit 8..15: reserved
48	bit 0: 1=32-bit I/O, 0=no 32-bit I/O, bit 7..1: reserved
49	bit 0..7: reserved, bit 8: 1=DMA, 0=no DMA, bit 9: 1=LBA, 0=no LBA
50	reserved

Table H.1: Sector buffer identification information

Word[1]	Meaning
51	bit 0..7: reserved, bit 8..15: PIO cycle time (0=600 ns, 1=380 ns, 2=240 ns, 3=180 ns)
52	bit 0..7: reserved, bit 8..15: DMA cycle time (0=960 ns, 1=380 ns, 2=240 ns, 3=150 ns)
53	reserved
54	number of logical cylinders
55	number of logical heads
56	number of logical sectors per logical track
57–58	bytes per logical sector
59	bit 0..7: number of sectors between two interrupts, bit 8..15: reserved
60–61	sectors addressable in LBA mode
62	single DMA: bit 0..7=supported modes, bit 8..15=active mode
63	multiple DMA: bit 0..7=supported modes, bit 8..15=active mode
64–127	reserved
128–159	manufacturer
160–255	reserved

[1] 16-bit words

[2] bit structure:

0	reserved
1	1=hard-sectored drive
2	1=soft-sectored
3	1=RLL/ARLL format
4	1=head switch delay=15 μs
5	1=power-down mode implemented
6	1=hard disk
7	1=removable storage device drive (usually CD-ROM)
8	1=internal data transfer rate < 5 Mbits/s
9	1=5 Mbits/s < data transfer rate < 10 Mbits/s
10	1=data transfer rate > 10 Mbits/s
11	1=rotation deviation > 0.5% (notebook)
12–15	reserved

Table H.1: cont.

H.1.4 Optional IDE Commands

In the following table you will find all IDE commands, together with the hex command codes, which are optional according to the newest IDE interface specification.

Command	Command code
check for active, idle, standby, sleep	98 e5
identify drive	ec
idle	97 e3
idle immediate	95 e1
read sector buffer	e4

Command	Command code
read sector with DMA (with retry)	c8
read sector with DMA (without retry)	c9
read multiple sectors	c4
set features	ef
set multiple mode	c6
set sleep mode	99 e6
set standby mode	96 e2
standby immediate	94 e0
write sector buffer	e8
write sector with DMA (with retry)	ca
write sector with DMA (without retry)	cb
write multiple sectors	c5
write same sector	e9
write verification	3c
achnowledge medium change	db
lock drive door	de
unlock drive door	df
available for manufacturer	9a, c0–c3, 80–8f, f5–f
reserved	all other codes

H.2 SCSI Commands

- All *reserved* fields have to be set to 0.
- LSB characterizes the **l**east **s**ignificant **b**yte, MSB the **m**ost **s**ignificant **b**yte of a multiple byte quantity.
- The command codes are uniformly 6, 10 or 12 bytes long.
- A command is executed in the following phases: transfer of the command code from the initiator to the target in the command phase → transfer of the parameters and/or data from the initiator to the target in the data-out phase → transfer of the result data from the target to the initiator in the data-in phase → transfer of the status from the target to the initiator in the status phase → transfer of messages from the target to the initiator in the message phase.
- LUN indicates the logical unit within one target or one logical unit which is connected to the target. Examples are two hard disks (LUNs) which are connected to one SCSI controller (target).
- SCSI manages all drives by means of so-called *logical blocks* which are contiguous and equal in size. It is the job of the target to convert the logical block address, for example in the case of a hard disk, into physical cylinder, head, and sector numbers.
- The error codes are provided at two levels: as a status key which indicates the error group; and the status code with a detailed error description.

H.2.1 Summary of Listed Commands

Detailed are only the required and the most important optional SCSI commands for disk drives (hard disks). An extensive discussion of all SCSI device classes would go far beyond the scope of this book. If you are interested in programming scanners, CD-ROMs and other devices, I have to direct you to the (now widely available) specialized literature on these topics. For disk drives only 6 and 10 byte commands are available.

- 6-byte commands
  test unit ready (00h)
  rezero unit (01h)
  request sense (03h)
  format unit (04h)
  reassign blocks (07h)
  read (08h)
  write (0ah)
  seek (0bh)
  inquiry (12h)
  mode select (15h)
  reserve (16h)
  release (17h)
  mode sense (1ah)
  start/stop (1bh)
  send diagnostic (1dh)
- 10-byte commands
  read capacity (25h)
  read (28h)
  write (2ah)
  seek (2bh)
  write and verify (2eh)
  verify (2fh)
  read defect data (37h)
  write buffer (3bh)
  read buffer (3ch)
  read long (3eh)
  write long (3fh)
  change definition (40h)
  mode select (55h)
  mode sense (5ah)

The following table lists all SCSI-II commands for the ten device classes disk drive, tape drive, printer, processor device, WORM, CD-ROM, scanner, optical storage device, media changer and communication device. The column with the detailed SCSI commands is emboldened.

Command	Length[1]	Code	Class[2]									
			DD	TD	Pr	PD	WO	CD	Sc	OS	MC	Co
Test Unit Ready	6	00h	X	X	X	X	X	X	X	X	X	X
Rewind/Rezero Unit	6	01h	0	X	M	–	0	0	–	0	0	–
Request Sense	6	03h	X	X	X	X	X	X	X	X	X	X
Format/Format Unit	6	04h	X	–	0	–	–	–	–	0	–	–
Read Block Limits	6	05h	M	X	M	M	M	M	–	–	M	–
Reassign Blocks	6	07h	0	M	M	–	0	–	–	0	M	–
Read	6	08h	0	X	M	0	0	0	–	0	M	X
Write	6	0ah	0	X	X	X	0	0	–	0	M	X
Seek	6	0bh	0	–	0	–	0	0	–	0	M	–
Read Reverse	6	0fh	M	0	M	M	M	M	–	–	M	–
Write Filemarks/Synchronize Buffer	6	10h	M	X	0	M	0	M	–	–	–	–
Space	6	11h	M	X	M	M	M	M	–	–	–	–
Inquiry	6	12h	X	X	X	X	X	X	X	X	X	X
Verify	6	13h	M	0	M	M	M	M	–	–	–	–
Recover Buffered Data	6	14h	M	0	0	M	M	M	–	–	–	–
Mode Select	6	15h	0	X	0	–	0	0	0	0	0	0
Reserve	6	16h	X	X	X	–	X	X	X	X	0	–
Release	6	17h	X	X	X	–	X	X	X	X	0	–
Copy	6	18h	0	0	0	0	0	0	0	0	–	–
Erase	6	19h	M	X	M	M	M	M	–	–	–	–
Mode Sense	6	1ah	0	X	0	–	0	0	0	0	0	0
Load/Unload/Scan/Stop/Start	6	1bh	0	0	0	–	0	0	0	0	–	–
Receive Diagnostic Results	6	1ch	0	0	0	0	0	0	0	0	0	0
Send Diagnostic	6	1dh	X	X	X	X	X	X	X	X	X	X
Prevent/Allow Medium Removal	6	1eh	0	0	–	–	0	0	–	0	0	–
Set Window	10	24h	M	–	–	–	M	M	X	–	–	–
Get Window	10	25h	–	–	–	–	–	–	0	–	–	–
Read Capacity	10	26h	X	–	–	–	X	X	–	X	–	–
Read	10	28h	X	–	–	–	X	X	X	X	–	0
Write	10	2ah	X	–	–	–	X	–	0	X	–	–
Seek	10	2bh	0	0	–	–	0	0	–	0	0	–
Erase	10	2ch	M	–	–	–	–	–	–	0	–	–
Read Updated Block	10	2dh	M	–	–	–	0	–	–	0	–	–
Write and Verify	10	2eh	0	–	–	–	0	–	–	0	–	–
Verify	10	2fh	0	–	–	–	0	0	–	0	–	–
Search Data High	10	30h	0	–	–	–	0	0	–	0	–	–
Search Data Equal	10	32h	0	–	–	–	0	0	–	0	–	–
Search Data Low	10	33h	0	–	–	–	0	0	–	0	–	–
Set Limits	10	34h	0	–	–	–	0	0	–	0	–	–
Synchronize Cache	10	35h	0	–	–	–	0	0	–	0	–	–
Lock/Unlock Cache	10	36h	0	–	–	–	0	0	–	0	–	–
Read Defect Data	10	37h	0	–	–	–	–	–	–	0	–	–
Medium Scan	10	38h	–	–	–	–	0	–	–	0	–	–
Compare	10	39h	0	0	0	0	0	0	0	0	–	–
Copy and Verify	10	3ah	0	0	0	0	0	0	0	0	–	–
Write Buffer	10	3bh	0	0	0	0	0	0	0	0	0	0
Read Buffer	10	3ch	0	0	0	0	0	0	0	0	–	–
Update Block	10	3dh	–	–	–	–	0	–	–	0	–	–
Read Long	10	3eh	0	–	–	–	0	0	–	0	–	–

Command	**Length[1)]**	**Code**	**Class[2)]**									
			DD	**TD**	**Pr**	**PD**	**WO**	**CD**	**Sc**	**OS**	**MC**	**Co**
Write Long	10	3fh	0	–	–	–	0	–	–	0	–	–
Change Definition	10	40h	0	0	0	0	0	0	0	0	0	0
Write Same	10	41h	0	–	–	–	–	–	–	–	–	–
Read Sub-Channel	10	42h	–	–	–	–	–	0	–	–	–	–
Read Toc	10	43h	–	–	–	–	–	0	–	–	–	–
Read Header	10	44h	–	–	–	–	–	0	–	–	–	–
Play Audio	10	45h	–	–	–	–	–	0	–	–	–	–
Play Audio MSF	10	47h	–	–	–	–	–	0	–	–	–	–
Play Audio Track Index	10	48h	–	–	–	–	–	0	–	–	–	–
Play Track Relative	10	49h	–	–	–	–	–	0	–	–	–	–
Pause/Resume	10	4bh	–	–	–	–	–	0	–	–	–	–
Mode Select	10	55h	0	0	0	–	0	0	0	0	0	0
Mode Sense	10	5ah	0	0	0	–	0	0	0	0	0	0
Move Medium/Play Audio	12	a5h	–	–	–	–	–	0	–	–	X	–
Exchange Medium	12	a6h	–	–	–	–	–	–	–	–	0	–
Read	12	a8h	–	–	–	–	0	0	–	0	–	0
Play Track Relative	12	a9h	–	–	–	–	–	0	–	–	–	–
Write	12	aah	–	–	–	–	0	–	–	0	–	0
Erase	12	ach	–	–	–	–	–	–	–	0	–	–
Write and Verify	12	aeh	–	–	–	–	0	–	–	0	–	–
Verify	12	afh	–	–	–	–	0	0	–	0	–	–
Set Limits	12	b3h	–	–	–	–	0	0	–	0	–	–
Request Volume Address	12	b5h	–	–	–	–	–	–	–	–	0	–
Read Defect Data	12	b7h	–	–	–	–	–	–	–	0		–

1) length of SCSI command in bytes (6-byte, 10-byte, or 12-byte command)

2) DD=disk drive, TD=tape drive, Pr=printer, PD=processor device, WO=WORM, CD=CD-ROM, Sc=Scanner, OS=optical storage, MC=media changer, Co=communication device
X=requested, O=optional, M=manufacturer-specific

H.2.2 6-Byte Commands

Test Unit Ready (00h)

With this command you can determine whether the addressed target drive is ready. If so, the target completes the command with the status *everything o.k.* A *request sense* command returns only a *no status*. Note that the status key is valid only after an extended request sense command to determine the cause of a not-ready state of the addressed drive.

Bit / Byte	7	6	5	4	3	2	1	0
0	0	0	0	0	0	0	0	0
1	LUN			Reserved				
2	Reserved							
3	Reserved							
4	Reserved							
5	Reserved						F	L

```
LUN:  logical unit number 0 to 7
F:    flag
      1=return messages with flag, if L=1    0=messages without flag
L:    link
      1=linked commands                      0=single commands
```

Rezero Unit (01h)

This command moves the target back to the zero position, that is, mostly to the beginning of the drive. On a hard disk this means that the read/write heads are moved to track 0.

Bit / Byte	7	6	5	4	3	2	1	0
0	0	0	0	0	0	0	0	1
1	LUN			Reserved				
2	Reserved							
3	Reserved							
4	Reserved							
5	Reserved						F	L

```
LUN:  logical unit number 0 to 7
F:    flag
      1=return messages with flag, if L=1    0=messages without flag
L:    link
      1=linked commands                      0=single commands
```

Request Sense (03h)

This command instructs the target to return status data about the last executed command to the initiator. The target aborts the transfer of the status data if all available bytes have been transmitted to the initiator, or if the allocation length is exhausted. Note that the status data is only valid with a message *check status* for the preceding command as long as the target has not received any further command.

The target transfers status data to the initiator during the course of a data-in phase. The status data consist of an 8-byte header and additional status bytes in accordance with the preceding command and the error.

Only with a sufficient allocation length can you be sure that all status bytes are transferred by the target (specify a value of 255 here). Whether and, if so, how many additional status bytes the target transfers in an extended form depends upon the entry *additional status length* in byte 7 of the status data. Table H.2 shows an example for the status, where the physical location of the error is indicated. The returned status information is very extensive, so it is not detailed here.

Bit Byte	7	6	5	4	3	2	1	0
0	0	0	0	0	0	0	1	1
1	LUN			Reserved				
2	Reserved							
3	Reserved							
4	Allocation Length							
5	Reserved						F	L

```
LUN:  logical unit number 0 to 7
Allocation Length: number of bytes which the initiator reserves for the target's status data
      0=4 status bytes (SCSI-I)   0=0 status bytes (SCSI-II)
      1 ... 255: number of status bytes to transfer
F:    flag
      1=return messages with flag, if L=1    0=messages without flag
L:    link
      1=linked commands              0=single commands
```

Header

Bit Byte	7	6	5	4	3	2	1	0
0	VAL	Class			Error Code			
1	Segment Number							
2	FM	EM	ILI	res	Status Key			
3	Logical Block Address (MSB)							
4	Logical Block Address							
5	Logical Block Address							
6	Logical Block Address (LSB)							
7	Additional Status Length							

VAL:	valid 1=logical block address (byte 3–6) valid 0=LBA not valid
Class:	error class, for extended status class equal to 7
Error Code:	for extended status equal to 0
Status Key:	error group, see H.2.4
Logical Block Address:	identification of the block where the error occurred
Additional Status Length:	number of additional status bytes

Additional Status Bytes (Example)

Byte	Content	
8	Command Dependent	
9	Command Dependent	
10	Command Dependent	
11	Command Dependent	
12	Additional Status Code	
13	Extended Status Code	
14	FRU	
15	val	Status Code Dependent
16	Status Code Dependent	
17	Retries	
18	Physical Cylinder (MSB)	
19	Physical Cylinder (LSB)	
20	Physical Head	
21	Physical Sector	

Table H.2: Status

Format Unit (04h)

This command formats the whole drive by writing all ID and sector data fields. You must specify the block size and the geometric drive parameters, such as sectors per track, etc., in advance by a *mode select* command. If you do not, the target uses the same parameters as for a preformatted drive and the predetermined standard parameters for a non-formatted drive. Most SCSI hard disks contain a so-called manufacturer defect list, stored in one or more reserved tracks, which is managed by the controller. The target uses this list to correct the known defects by reassigning blocks. If you reformat a hard disk which has been in use for a long time, it may be possible that the function of the intelligent bad sector remapping has detected further defects and has repaired them by reassigning blocks in the background. Such defect entries are called a *grown defect list*, and are also stored in reserved tracks by the controller. In a format operation the initiator may further transfer additional defect parameters in a data-out phase. The data transferred by the initiator consist of a 4-byte header and zero or more 4-byte defect descriptors, whose structure is shown in Table H.4. The format command can be executed in one of three modes, which is determined by the bits *FMT* and *CMP* (Table H.3).

Bit Byte	7	6	5	4	3	2	1	0
0	0	0	0	0	0	1	0	0
1	LUN			FMT	CMP	Defect Format		
2	Reserved							
3	Interleave (MSB)							
4	Interleave (LSB)							
5	Reserved						F	L

```
LUN:  logical unit number 0 to 7
FMT:  format data                  ┐
CMP:  complete                     ├─ format mode, see Table H.3
Defect Form: defect list format  ──┘
Interleave:  interleave value
      0=standard value (normally equal 1)
      valid values: 1 to (sectors per track – 1)
F:    flag
      1=return messages with flag, if L=1    0=messages without flag
L:    link
      1=linked commands                 0=single commands
F:    flag
      1=return messages with flag, if L=1    0=messages without flag
L:    link
      1=linked commands                 0=single commands
```

FMT	CMP	Defect Format Bit 2 1 0	Com-mand	Description
0	x	x x x	P&G	Formatting with primary and grown defect list; no data-out phase with defect list from initiator.
1	0	0 x x	P&G&I	Formatting with primary, grown and defect list from initiator; data-out phase with defect list from initiator.
1	1	0 x x	P	Formatting with primary defect list only; grown defect list is ignored; no data-out phase with defect list from initiator.

Table H.3: FMT, CMP and defect list

Header

Byte	Content
0	Reserved
1	Reserved
2	Length of Defect List (MSB)
3	Length of Defect List (LSB)

The entry *length of defect list* indicates the total number of bytes in the following defect descriptors.

Descriptor

Byte	Content
0	Defect Block Address (MSB)
1	Defect Block Address
2	Defect Block Address
3	Defect Block Address (LSB)

Table H.4: Initiator defect list

Reassign Blocks (07h)

This command instructs the target to replace defect logical blocks by intact blocks in a certain area of the drive which is reserved for this pupose. The initiator passes to the target a defect list which contains the blocks to reassign. The defect blocks are thus mapped to intact blocks so that all further accesses are diverted to the intact blocks. The data in the defect blocks is lost. If the capacity of the drive is not sufficient to reassign all specified defect blocks, the command aborts with a *check status* and the error key is set to *medium error*. The target automatically adds all blocks reassigned by this command to the known defect list. The defect list, which is transferred in a data-out phase by the initiator, consists of a 4 byte header followed by one or more defect descriptors with a length of 4 bytes each. The structure of head and descriptor is shown in Table H.5.

Bit Byte	7	6	5	4	3	2	1	0
0	0	0	0	0	0	1	1	1
1	LUN			Reserved				
2	Reserved							
3	Reserved							
4	Reserved							
5	Reserved						F	L

```
LUN:  logical unit number 0 to 7
F:    flag
      1=return messages with flag, if L=1    0=messages without flag
L:    link
      1=linked commands              0=single commands
```

Descriptor

Byte	Content
0	Reserved
1	Reserved
2	Length of Defect List (MSB)
3	Length of Defect List (LSB)

The entry *length of defect list* indicates the total number of the bytes in the following defect descriptors.

Descriptor

Byte	Content
0	Defect Logical Block Address (MSB)
1	Defect Logical Block Address
2	Defect Logical Block Address
3	Defect Logical Block Address (LSB)

Table H.5: Header and descriptor of the defect list.

Read (08h)

This command instructs the target to read one or more blocks from the drive, and to transfer the data in a data-in phase to the initiator.

Bit Byte	7	6	5	4	3	2	1	0
0	0	0	0	0	1	0	0	0
1	LUN			LBA (MSB)				
2	Logical Block Address							
3	Logical Block Address (LSB)							
4	Transfer Length							
5	Reserved						F	L

```
LUN:  logical unit number 0 to 7
Logical Block Address:  number of block to read first
Transfer Length:        number of logical blocks to read
F:    flag
      1=return messages with flag, if L=1    0=messages without flag
L:    link
      1=linked commands                 0=single commands
```

Write (0ah)

This command instructs the target to receive one or more blocks from the initiator in a data-out phase, and to write them onto the medium.

Bit / Byte	7	6	5	4	3	2	1	0
0	0	0	0	0	1	0	1	0
1	LUN			LBA (MSB)				
2	Logical Block Address							
3	Logical Block Address (LSB)							
4	Transfer Length							
5	Reserved						F	L

```
LUN:  logical unit number 0 to 7
Logical Block Address:  number of block to write first
Transfer Length:        number of logical blocks to write
F:    flag
      1=return messages with flag, if L=1    0=messages without flag
L:    link
      1=linked commands                 0=single commands
```

Seek (0bh)

This command positions the target at the specified logical block. In the case of a hard disk, the read/write head is moved to the track which contains the corresponding block (sector).

Bit / Byte	7	6	5	4	3	2	1	0
0	0	0	0	0	1	0	1	1
1	LUN			LBA (MSB)				
2	Logical Block Address							
3	Logical Block Address (LSB)							
4	Reserved							
5	Reserved						F	L

```
LUN:  logical unit number 0 to 7
Logical Block Address:  number of the block where the target is to be positioned
F:    flag
      1=return messages with flag, if L=1    0=messages without flag
L:    link
      1=linked commands                 0=single commands
```

Inquiry (12h)

This command transfers target parameters to the initiator in a data-in phase. The inquiry parameters comprise a 5 byte header and additional information. The format is shown in Table H.6. The target aborts the data-in phase as soon as all target parameters have been transferred or the reserved bytes are exhausted. The additional information depends upon the type and manufacturer of the target, and typically indicates the manufacturer's name, the product name, the version number, and the serial number. Therefore the length of the additional information is manufacturer-dependent; SCSI host adapters use the *inquiry* command for initialization, and in many cases display the additional information on-screen during the course of the boot procedure.

Bit / Byte	7	6	5	4	3	2	1	0
0	0	0	0	1	0	0	1	0
1	LUN			Reserved				
2	Reserved							
3	Reserved							
4	Allocation Length							
5	Reserved						F	L

LUN: logical unit number 0 to 7
Allocation Length: number of bytes which are reserved by the initiator to receive the target parameters; a value of 0 means that no target parameters are transferred
F: flag
1=return messages with flag, if L=1 0=messages without flag
L: link
1=linked commands 0=single commands

Bit / Byte	7	6	5	4	3	2	1	0
0	Unit Type Code							
1	RMB	Reserved						
2	ISO		ECMA			ANSI		
3	AEN	TIO	Reserved	Data Format				
4	Additional Length							
5..6	Reserved							
7	rel	W32	W16	sync	Link	res	Que	SftR
8..15	Manufacturer (ASCII)							
16..31	Model (ASCII)							
32..35	Revision (ASCII)							
36..55	Manufacturer Dependent							
56..95	Reserved							
96..	Manufacturer Dependent							

Unit Type Code: 00h=LUN 0 7fh=else
RMB: removable medium bit
1=medium removable (e.g. tape drive, optical drive)
0=Medium not removable (e.g. hard disk)
ISO, ECMA, ANSI: revision level of the implemented standard according to ISO, ECMA or ANSI (00h=SCSI-I, 01h=SCSI-I with CCS, 02h=SCSI-II); most SCSI drives use the ANSI standard

Table H.6: Target parameters

AEN:	1=Unit supports asynchronous message transfer (processor devices only)
TIO:	1=target supports message *abort I/O process*
Data Format:	00h=SCSI-I, 01h=SCSI-I with CCS, 02h=SCSI-II
Additional Length:	number of following additional information bytes
rel:	unit supports relative addressing
W32/W16:	unit supports 32-bit and 16-bit wide SCSI, respectively
Sync:	unit supports synchronous transfer mode
Link:	unit supports linked commands
Que:	unit supports SCSI command queueing
SftR:	unit supports a soft reset
Manufacturer/Model/Revision:	ASCII string with this infomation

Table H.6: cont.

Mode Select (15h)

This command enables the initiator to set or alter the target parameters. The initiator transfers a list of mode parameters to the target in a data-out phase. The list comprises a 4 byte header which may be followed by a block descriptor and zero or more page descriptors. In Table H.7 you can see their formats. Each page descriptor holds information for the target concerning a certain function class, the descriptions of which are shown in Table H.8. The descriptors can be transferred in any order, and the target uses class-specific standard settings if no descriptor is passed for a class. Many parameters depend upon the drive type and the manufacturer, so that no generally valid statements are possible.

Bit / Byte	7	6	5	4	3	2	1	0
0	0	0	0	1	0	1	0	1
1	LUN			PF	Reserved			SP
2	Reserved							
3	Reserved							
4	Parameter List Length							
5	Reserved						F	L

LUN: logical unit number 0 to 7
PF: page format (ignored in most cases as the mode select parameters are always processed in page format)
1=page format
SP: save mode parameters (ignored in most cases as the mode select parameters are always stored by the target)
1=save parameters 0=do not save
Length of Parameter List: number of mode select data bytes
F: flagP 1=return messages with flag, if L=1 0=messages without flag
L: link
1=linked commands 0=single commands

Header

Byte	Content
0	Data Length
1	Medium Type
2	SCSI Unit Dependent
3	Block Descriptor Length

Data Length:	length of the complete parameter list
Medium Type:	00h=hard disk
Block Descriptor Length:	length of the following block descriptors in bytes

Block Descriptor

Byte	Content
0	Density Code
1	Number of Blocks (MSB)
2	Number of Blocks
3	Number of Blocks (LSB)
4	Reserved
5	Block Length (MSB)
6	Block Length
7	Block Length (LSB)

Density Code: medium density (00h=hard disk)

Page Descriptor Head

Bit / Byte	7	6	5	4	3	2	1	0
0	0	0	Page Code					
1	Page Length							
2	Page Code Dependent*)							
...	....							
n	Page Code Dependent*)							

*) see below
Page Code:
00h=operation parameters (dependent upon drive type and manufacturer)
01h=error recovery parameters
02h=disconnect parameters
03h=formatting parameters
04h=geometric parameters
05h=floppy disk parameters
06h=parameters for optical storage
07h=verify error parameters
08h=cache parameters
09h=parameters for peripheral unit
0ah=control parameters
0bh=medium type
0ch=parameters for zones of equal sector/track number (notch)
0dh=CD-ROM data parameters
0eh=CD-ROM audio parameters
10h=configuration parameters
11h=partition parameters 1
12h=partition parameters 2
13h=partition parameters 3
14h=partition parameters 4
1eh=drive geometry
1fh=function parameters
others=reserved
Page Length: length of the page (entries 0 to n) in bytes

Table H.7: Mode select parameters

Among the huge number of parameter pages, I will present some of them in the following by way of an example.

Disconnect Parameters (Page Code=02h, Page Length=0eh)

Byte	Content	
2	Buffer Fill Ratio	
3	Buffer Empty Ratio	
4	Max. Bus Idle Time (MSB)	
5	Max. Bus Idle Time (MSB)	
6	Min. Bus Idle Time (MSB)	
7	Min. Bus Idle Time (LSB)	
8	Max. Connect Time (MSB)	
9	Max. Connect Time (LSB)	
10	Max. Burst Length (MSB)	
11	Max. Burst Length (LSB)	
12	Reserved	DTDC
13	Reserved	
14	Reserved	
15	Reserved	

Buffer Fill Ratio: fill ratio for the buffer in units of 1/256, at which the target attempts for read processes to reconnect to the initiator

Buffer Empty Ratio: fill ratio for the buffer in units of 1/256, below which the target attempts for write processes to reconnect to the initiator

Max. Bus Idle Time: max. occupation time (in units of 100 μs) of the bus by the target without the need of executing a REQ/ACK sequence

Min. Bus Idle Time: min. time period (in units of 100 μs) which the target must wait after a bus occupation, before it issues a new bus arbitration

Max. Connect Time: max. occupation time (in units of 100 μs) of the bus by the target

Max. Burst Length: max. number of 512-byte blocks which the target can transfer in one instance

DTDC: data transfer disconnect control
00b=disconnection always possible, 01b=after data transfer initiation, do not free the bus until data transfer is complete, 10b=reserved, 11b=after data transfer initiation, do not free the bus until the command is complete

Formatting Parameters (Page Code=03h, Page Length=16h)

Byte	Content				
2	Tracks per Zone (MSB)				
3	Tracks per Zone (LSB)				
4	Spare Sectors per Zone (MSB)				
5	Spare Sectors per Zone (LSB)				
6	Spare Tracks per Zone (MSB)				
7	Spare Sectors per Zone (LSB)				
8	Spare Tracks per LUN (MSB)				
9	Spare Tracks per LUN (LSB)				
10	Sectors per Track (MSB)				
11	Sectors per Track (LSB)				
12	Bytes per Sector (MSB)				
13	Bytes per Sector (LSB)				
14	Sector Interleave (MSB)				
15	Sector Interleave (LSB)				
16	Track Interleave (MSB)				
17	Track Interleave (LSB)				
18	Cylinder Interleave (MSB)				
19	Cylinder Interleave (LSB)				
20	SSC	HSC	RMB	SRF	Reserved
21	Reserved				
22	Reserved				
23	Reserved				

Table H.8: Page Descriptors.

SSC: soft sector (1=drive with soft sector format)
HSC: hard sector (1=drive with hard sector format)
RMB: drive with removable medium
SRF: enumerate blocks surface by surface

Geometry Parameters (Page Code=04h, Page Length=16h)

Byte	Content
2	Number of Cylinder (MSB)
3	Number of Cylinder
4	Number of Cylinder (LSB)
5	Number of Heads
6	Start Cylinder Write Precomp. (MSB)
7	Start Cylinder Write Precompensation
8	Start Cylinder Write Precomp. (LSB)
9	Start Cylinder Red. Write Current (MSB)
10	Start Cylinder Reduced Write Current
11	Start Cylinder Red. Write Current (LSB)
12	Step Rate (MSB)
13	Step Rate (LSB)
14	Parking Cylinder (MSB)
15	Parking Cylinder
16	Parking Cylinder (LSB)
17	Reserved
18	Rotation Shift
19	Reserved
20	Drive Rotations (MSB)
21	Drive Rotations (LSB)
22	Reserved
23	Reserved

Table H.8: cont.

Reserve (16h)

This command reserves the corresponding logical unit for a SCSI device. This command, together with *release*, is the base for preventing access conflicts in systems with several initiators (host adapters). The command has two modifications: with a cleared PTY bit the logical unit is reserved for the initiator of the command; on the other hand, if PTY is set the unit is reserved for a third initiator, which is characterized by the SCSI ID. The complete logical unit and not just one block is affected by the reservation, which can only be cancelled by a release command of the corresponding initiator, by a reset message, or by a hardware reset.

Bit Byte	7	6	5	4	3	2	1	0
0	0	0	0	1	0	1	1	0
1	LUN			PTY	Unit ID			0
2	Reserved							
3	Reserved							
4	Reserved							
5	Reserved						F	L

```
LUN:   logical unit number 0 to 7
PTY:   1=reservation for a third initiator
       0=reservation for the current initiator
Unit ID:  SCSI ID of the third unit for which the LUN is reserved if PTY is set
F:     flag
       1=return messages with flag, if L=1    0=messages without flag
L:     link
       1=linked commands               0=single commands
```

Release (17h)

This command cancels the reservation of a logical unit for the initiator. If the unit has been reserved by a command from a third device the reservation can be cancelled only by a release command from the same initiator. For this the unit ID has to match the ID of the initiator that issued the reserve command before.

Bit Byte	7	6	5	4	3	2	1	0
0	0	0	0	1	0	1	1	1
1	LUN			PTY	Unit ID			0
2	Reserved							
3	Reserved							
4	Reserved							
5	Reserved						F	L

```
LUN:   logical unit number 0 to 7
PTY:   1=reservation for a third initiator
       0=reservation for the current initiator
Unit ID:  SCSI ID of the third unit for which the LUN was reserved if PTY is set
F:     flag
       1=return messages with flag, if L=1    0=messages without flag
L:     link
       1=linked commands               0=single commands
```

Mode Sense (1ah)

This command returns the medium and drive parameters of the target. By means of certain page parameter values, you can determine all changeable parameters and standard values for the parameters. The status data is transferred from the target to the initiator in a data-in phase. The status data comprises a 4 byte header followed by zero or more block descriptors, and eventually additional drive parameters. Their formats are shown in Table H.7. The structure of the pages is indicated in Table H.8.

Bit / Byte	7	6	5	4	3	2	1	0
0	0	0	0	1	1	0	1	0
1	LUN			res	DBD	Reserved		
2	PGP		Page Code					
3	Reserved							
4	Allocation Length							
5	Reserved						F	L

LUN: logical unit number 0 to 7
DBD: disable block descriptors
1=transfer pages only
PGP: returned page parameter values
00b=current values 01=changeable values
10b=standard values 11b=saved values
Allocation Length: number of bytes which are reserved by the initiator for the mode data
F: flag
1=return messages with flag, if L=1 0=messages without flag
L: link
1=linked commands 0=single commands

Start/Stop (1bh)

This command instructs the target to move the heads into transport position, or to move the heads out of this position. On many drives, additionally the spindle motor is switched off or on.

Bit / Byte	7	6	5	4	3	2	1	0
0	0	0	0	1	1	0	1	1
1	LUN			Reserved				IMM
2	Reserved							
3	Reserved							
4	Reserved							STR
5	Reserved						F	L

LUN: logical unit number 0 to 7
IMM: immediate
1=status is transferred immediately after the beginning of the command execution
0=status is transferred after command completion
STR: start
1=position head on track 0 or equivalent track
0=move head into transport position
F: flag
1=return messages with flag, if L=1 0=messages without flag
L: link
1=linked commands 0=single commands

Send Diagnostic (1dh)

This command instructs the target to execute a self-test. With the DvO and UnO bits you can avoid other units, or the addressed LUN itself, being affected by this test. Then, the self-test is only executed if the state of this (or these) unit(s) is not changed. The function returns a diagnostic page.

Bit Byte	7	6	5	4	3	2	1	0
0	0	0	0	1	1	1	0	1
1	LUN			PF	res	ST	DvO	UnO
2	Reserved							
3	Allocation Length							
4	Allocation Length							
5	Reserved						F	L

```
LUN:  logical unit number 0 to 7
PF    page format
      1=SCSI-II     0=SCSI-I
ST:   self-test
      1=issue self-test
DvO:  device off-line
      1=the target may execute the self-test, even if other LUNs are affected by this
UnO:  unit off-line
      1=the target may execute the self-test, even if the addressed LUN is affected by this
F:    flag
      1=return messages with flag, if L=1    0=messages without flag
L:    link
      1=linked commands                0=single commands
```

Diagnostic Page

Bit Byte	7	6	5	4	3	2	1	0
0	Page Code							
1	Reserved							
2	Allocation Length Beyond Byte #3 (MSB)							
3	Allocation Length Beyond Byte #3 (LSB)							
4..	Self-Test Information							

H.2.3 10-Byte Commands

Read Capacity (25h)

The target returns information concerning the drive's capacity to the initiator. There are two execution forms of the command: if the PMI bit is cleared, the command transfers the logical block address (LBA) and the block length of the last logical block on the drive. LBA in the command code has to be equal to 0 in this case. If the PMI bit is set, the target transfers the LBA and the block length of the last logical block after the LBA in the command, after which a significant delay in data transfer occurs. This can be a cylinder boundary which requires a repositioning of the head. The capacity information is transferred during the course of a data-in phase. Table H.9 gives the structure of the capacity information.

Bit / Byte	7	6	5	4	3	2	1	0
0	0	0	1	0	0	1	0	1
1	LUN			Reserved				rel
2	Logical Block Address (MSB)							
3	Logical Block Address							
4	Logical Block Address							
5	Logical Block Address (LSB)							
6	Reserved							
7	Reserved							
8	Reserved							PMI
9	Reserved						F	L

```
LUN:  logical unit number 0 to 7
rel:  1=relative block addressing
PMI:  partial medium indicator
      1=logical block address and block length of last block before a significant data transfer
      delay occurs
      0=logical block address and block length of last block
F:    flag
      1=return messages with flag, if L=1    0=messages without flag
L:    link
      1=linked commands               0=single commands
```

Capacity Information

Byte	Content
0	Logical Block Address (MSB)
1	Logical Block Address
2	Logical Block Address
3	Logical Block Address (LSB)
4	Block Length (MSB)
5	Block Length
6	Block Length
7	Block Length (LSB)

Table H.9: Capacity information

Extended Read (28h)

This command instructs the target to read one or more blocks from the drive, and to transfer the data in a data-in phase to the initiator. Unlike the normal reading of a block, here the logical block address comprises 32 bits and the transfer length 16 bits. Thus you can access volumes with a capacity of 4G blocks and read 64k blocks all at once.

Bit / Byte	7	6	5	4	3	2	1	0
0	0	0	1	0	1	0	0	0
1	LUN			DPO	FUA	Reserved		rel
2	Logical Block Address (MSB)							
3	Logical Block Address							
4	Logical Block Address							
5	Logical Block Address (LSB)							
6	Reserved							
7	Transfer Length (MSB)							
8	Transfer Length (LSB)							
9	Reserved						F	L

```
LUN:  logical unit number 0 to 7
DPO:  disable page output
      1=read data are not transferred into target cache
FUA:  force unit access
      1=target must read data from volume even if the block is available in the target cache
rel:  1=relative block addressing
Logical Block Address:  number of the first block to read
Transfer Length:        number of logical blocks to read
F:    flag
      1=return messages with flag, if L=1    0=messages without flag
L:    link
      1=linked commands             0=single commands
```

Extended Write (2ah)

This command instructs the target to receive one or more blocks in a data-out phase from the initiator, and to write them onto the medium. Unlike the normal writing of a block, here the logical block address comprises 32 bits and the transfer length 16 bits. Thus you can access volumes with a capacity of 4G blocks and write 64k blocks all at once.

Bit / Byte	7	6	5	4	3	2	1	0
0	0	0	1	0	1	0	1	0
1	LUN			DPO	FUA	Reserved		rel
2	Logical Block Address (MSB)							
3	Logical Block Address							
4	Logical Block Address							
5	Logical Block Address (LSB)							
6	Reserved							
7	Transfer Length (MSB)							
8	Transfer Length (LSB)							
9	Reserved						F	L

```
LUN:  logical unit number 0 to 7
DPO:  disable page output
      1=write data are not transferred into the target cache
FUA:  force unit access
      1=target must write data onto medium even if the block is available in the cache
rel:  1=relative block addressing
Logical Block Address:  number of the block to write first
Transfer Length:        number of logical blocks to write
F:    flag
      1=return messages with flag, if L=1    0=messages without flag
L:    link
      1=linked commands             0=single commands
```

Extended Seek (2bh)

This command moves the target to the specified logical block. In the case of a hard disk drive, the read/write head is positioned on that track which contains the corresponding block (sector). Unlike the normal seek, here the logical block address is 32 bits wide. Thus you can access volumes with a capacity of 4G blocks.

Bit / Byte	7	6	5	4	3	2	1	0
0	0	0	1	0	1	0	1	1
1	LUN			Reserved				
2	Logical Block Address (MSB)							
3	Logical Block Address							
4	Logical Block Address							
5	Logical Block Address (LSB)							
6	Reserved							
7	Reserved							
8	Reserved							
9	Reserved						F	L

```
LUN:  logical unit number 0 to 7
Logical Block Address:  number of the block where the drive is to be positioned
F:    flag
      1=return messages with flag, if L=1    0=messages without flag
L:    link
      1=linked commands                      0=single commands
```

Write and Verify (2eh)

This command instructs the target to write the data received from the initiator in a data-out phase onto the medium. Afterwards, the target has to verify whether the data has been written correctly. With the CHK bit you can choose between two different verify modes. With the CHK bit cleared the target verifies the write operation by comparing the written data with the data which has been transferred by the initiator before. If CHK is set, the target only performs a medium verification, that is, the target only checks whether the ECC bytes conform to the written data. If the verification leads to an error, the status key is set to compare error.

Bit / Byte	7	6	5	4	3	2	1	0
0	0	0	1	0	1	1	1	0
1	LUN			Reserved			CHK	0
2	Logical Block Address (MSB)							
3	Logical Block Address							
4	Logical Block Address							
5	Logical Block Address (LSB)							
6	Reserved							
7	Transfer Length (MSB)							
8	Transfer Length (LSB)							
9	Reserved						F	L

```
LUN:  logical unit number 0 to 7
CHK:  byte check
      1=verify by comparison     0=medium verification only via ECC
Logical Block Address: block to start write and verification with
Transfer Length: number of logical blocks to write and verify
F:    flag
      1=return messages with flag, if L=1    0=messages without flag
L:    link
      1=linked commands              0=single commands
```

Verify (2fh)

This command instructs the target to verify the data written onto the medium. Using the CHK bit, you can choose between two different verify modes. With the CHK bit cleared the target verifies the write operation by comparing the written data with data transferred by the initiator in a data-out phase. If CHK is set the target only performs a medium verification; the target only checks whether the ECC bytes conform to the written data. If the verification leads to an error, the status key is set to compare error. The command is similar to *write and verify*, but the data transferred with a cleared CHK bit are not written onto the medium.

Bit / Byte	7	6	5	4	3	2	1	0
0	0	0	1	0	1	1	1	1
1	LUN			Reserved			CHK	0
2	Logical Block Address (MSB)							
3	Logical Block Address							
4	Logical Block Address							
5	Logical Block Address (LSB)							
6	Reserved							
7	Verify Length (MSB)							
8	Verify Length (LSB)							
9	Reserved						F	L

```
LUN:  logical unit number 0 to 7
CHK:  byte check
      1=verify by comparison     0=medium verification only via ECC
Logical Block Address: block where to start verification
Transfer Length: number of logical blocks to verify
F:    flag
      1=return messages with flag, if L=1    0=messages without flag
L:    link
      1=linked commands              0=single commands
```

Read Defect Data (37h)

This command instructs the target to transfer the medium defect data stored on the medium to the initiator in a data-in phase. The defect data comprises a 4 byte header and (depending upon the P and G bits of the command) a defect list, or additionally a reassign list, which indicates the reassignment of the defect blocks. The reassign list is passed after the defect list. In this case, defect and reassign lists are separated by four bytes of value ffh. Table H.10 gives the corresponding formats.

Buffer Data Header

Byte	Content
0	Reserved
1	Reserved
2	Reserved
3	Reserved

Read Buffer (3ch)

This command instructs the target to transfer the indicated number of bytes in a data-in phase from its buffer memory to the initiator. The transferred read data comprises a 4-byte header and the read data itself. The header format is shown in Table H.12.

Bit Byte	7	6	5	4	3	2	1	0
0	0	0	1	1	1	1	0	0
1	LUN			Reserved				
2	Reserved							
3	Reserved							
4	Reserved							
5	Reserved							
6	Reserved							
7	Allocation Length (MSB)							
8	Allocation Length (LSB)							
9	Reserved						F	L

```
LUN:  logical unit number 0 to 7
Allocation Length:  max. number of data transferred by the target including header
      1=return messages with flag, if L=1    0=messages without flag
L:    link
      1=linked commands             0=single commands
```

Buffer Data Header

Byte	Content
0	Reserved
1	Reserved
2	Available Space (MSB)
3	Available Space (LSB)

Read Long (3eh)

This command reads one or more blocks together with the ECC bytes from the target and transfers them in a data-in phase to the initiator. No error check and error correction is carried out by the target by means of the ECC bytes.

Bit / Byte	7	6	5	4	3	2	1	0
0	0	0	1	1	1	1	1	0
1	LUN			DPO	FUA	Reserved		rel
2	Logical Block Address (MSB)							
3	Logical Block Address							
4	Logical Block Address							
5	Logical Block Address (LSB)							
6	Reserved							
7	Transfer Length (MSB)							
8	Transfer Length (LSB)							
9	Reserved						F	L

```
LUN:  logical unit number 0 to 7
DPO:  disable page output
      1=read data are not transferred into the cache
FUA:  force unit access
      1=target must read the data from medium even if the block is available in the cache
rel:  1=relative block addressing
Logical Block Address:  number of the block to read first
Transfer Length: number of logical blocks to read
F:    flag
      1=return messages with flag, if L=1    0=messages without flag
L:    link
      1=linked commands                0=single commands
```

Write Long (3fh)

This command instructs the target to receive one or more blocks together with the ECC bytes from the initiator in a data-out phase, and to write them onto the medium. The target doesn't generate the ECC bytes itself, but writes the data transferred by the initiator without any change onto the medium.

Bit / Byte	7	6	5	4	3	2	1	0
0	0	0	1	1	1	1	1	1
1	LUN			DPO	FUA	Reserved		rel
2	Logical Block Address (MSB)							
3	Logical Block Address							
4	Logical Block Address							
5	Logical Block Address (LSB)							
6	Reserved							
7	Transfer Length (MSB)							
8	Transfer Length (LSB)							
9	Reserved						F	L

```
LUN:  logical unit number 0 to 7
DPO:  disable page output
      1=write data are not transferred into the cache
FUA:  force unit access
      1=target must write data onto the medium even if the block is available in the cache
rel:  1=relative block addressing
Logical Block Address:  number of the block to write first
Transfer Length:        number of logical blocks to write
```

```
F:     flag
       1=return messages with flag, if L=1     0=messages without flag
L:     link
       1=linked commands                   0=single commands
```

Change Definition (40h)

This function switches a SCSI-II target to a behaviour according to an earlier SCSI specification.

Bit Byte	7	6	5	4	3	2	1	0
0	0	1	0	0	0	0	0	0
1	LUN			Reserved				
2	Reserved							S
3	res	SCSI Version						
4	Reserved							
5	Reserved							
6	Reserved							
7	Reserved							
8	Parameter List Length							
9	Reserved						F	L

```
LUN:   logical unit number 0 to 7
S:     save bit
       1=save changes
SCSI Version: 00h=unchanged, 01h=SCSI-I, 02h=SCSI-I with CCS, 03h=SCSI-II
Length of Parameter List: number of passed bytes (manufacturer-dependent)
F:     flag
       1=return messages with flag, if L=1     0=messages without flag
L:     link
       1=linked commands                   0=single commands
```

Mode Select (55h)

This command enables the initiator to set or alter the target parameters. The initiator transfers a list of mode parameters to the target in a data-out phase. The list comprises a 4 byte header which may be followed by a block descriptor and zero or more page descriptors. In Table H.7 you can see their formats. Each page descriptor holds information for the target concerning a certain function class, the descriptions of which are shown in Table H.8. The descriptors can be transferred in any order, and the target uses class-specific standard settings if no descriptor is passed for a class. Many parameters depend upon the drive type and the manufacturer, so that no generally valid statements are possible.

Bit / Byte	7	6	5	4	3	2	1	0
0	0	1	0	1	0	1	0	1
1	LUN			PF	Reserved			SP
2	Reserved							
3	Reserved							
4	Reserved							
5	Reserved							
6	Reserved							
7	Parameter List Length (MSB)							
8	Parameter List Length (LSB)							
9	Reserved						F	L

LUN: logical unit number 0 to 7
PF: page format (ignored in most cases as the mode select parameters are always processed in page format)
1=page format
SP: save mode parameters (ignored in most cases as the mode select parameters are always stored by the target)
1=save parameters 0=do not save
Length of Parameter List: number of mode select data bytes
F: flagP 1=return messages with flag, if L=1 0=messages without flag
L: link
1=linked commands 0=single commands

Mode Sense (1ah)

This command returns the medium and drive parameters of the target. By means of certain page parameter values, you can determine all changeable parameters and standard values for the parameters. The status data is transferred from the target to the initiator in a data-in phase. The status data comprises a 4 byte header is by zero or more block descriptors, and eventually additional drive parameters. Their formats are shown in Table H.7. The structure of the pages is indicated in Table H.8.

Bit / Byte	7	6	5	4	3	2	1	0
0	0	1	0	1	1	0	1	0
1	LUN			res	DBD	Reserved		
2	PGP		Page Code					
3	Reserved							
4	Reserved							
5	Reserved							
6	Reserved							
7	Allocation Length (MSB)							
8	Allocation Length (LSB)							
9	Reserved						F	L

LUN: logical unit number 0 to 7
DBD: disable block descriptors
1=transfer pages only
PGP: returned page parameter values
00b=current values 01=changeable values
10b=standard values 11b=saved values
Allocation Length: number of bytes which are reserved by the initiator for the mode data

```
F:   flag
     1=return messages with flag, if L=1    0=messages without flag
L:   link
     1=linked commands                 0=single commands
```

H.2.4 Status Key

Key	Meaning	Cause
0h	no status	no special status information necessary
1h	corrected error	last command completed successfully after recovery procedure of target
2h	not ready	drive cannot be accessed
3h	medium error	command aborted because of an uncorrectable error; cause probably bad medium
4h	hardware error	target detected an uncorrectable hardware-error of controller, drive, etc.
5h	invalid request	invalid parameter in command descriptor block or in the additional parameters
6h	attention/reset	reset occurred since the last selection by the initiator
7h	data protected	the data on the volume is protected against the current access
8h	blank check	unexpected access to certain parts of the medium
9h	reserved for manufacturer	(the manufacturer may use this code for own purposes)
ah	copy operation aborted	the copy operation between initiator and target has been aborted
bh	command aborted	the current command has been aborted
ch	equal	search command encountered data pattern
dh	volume overflow	the volume is full
eh	compare error	an error occurred during a verify operation
fh	reserved	

H.2.5 Additional Status Codes

Code	Meaning
00h	no status information
01h	no index or sector signal
02h	no seek signal
03h	write error
04h	drive not ready
05h	no response of LUN
06h	track 0 not found
07h	several units selected
08h	LUN error
09h	error in seek unit
0ah	error counter overflow

Code	Meaning
0ch	write error
10h	CRC or ECC error in ID
11h	uncorrectable read error of data blocks
12h	no address mark found in ID field
13h	no address mark found in data field
14h	no data record found
15h	seek error
16h	incorrect data synchronization
17h	recovered data after retries of target without ECC correction
18h	recovered data after ECC correction by target (without retries)
19h	error in the defect list
1ah	parameter overflow
1bh	error during synchronous data transfer
1ch	primary defect list not found
1dh	compare error
1eh	recovered ID after ECC correction by target
20h	invalid command code
21h	invalid logical block address LBA; address bigger than read drive capacity
22h	invalid function call
24h	invalid entry in command descriptor block
25h	invalid logical unit number LUN
26h	invalid entry in parameter list
27h	write protection
28h	medium change
29h	power-on or reset or bus-reset occurred
2ah	mode select parameters changed
2bh	copy process not possible
2ch	command linking not possible
2dh	overwrite error
2fh	command aborted by other initiator
30h	incompatible medium
31h	invalid format
32h	no spare sector available for defect sector
33h	incorrect tape length
36h	printer ribbon defect
39h	parameter cannot be saved
3ah	no volume inserted
3bh	medium error
3dh	invalid identify message
3eh	LUN not configured
3fh	changed operation conditions
40h	RAM error
41h	data path error
42h	power-on diagnostics error
43h	message error
44h	internal controller error
45h	error in selection or reselection phase

Code	Meaning
46h	unsuccessful software reset
47h	parity error of the SCSI interface
48h	initiator has detected an error
49h	invalid defect list
4ah	command phase error
4bh	data phase error
4ch	self-configuration of LUN failed
4eh	command overlap
50h	seek error during write
51h	erase error
52h	cassette error
53h	medium change error
54h	SCSI/host interface error
55h	system error
57h	directory not recoverable
59h	updated block read
5ah	condition change by user
5bh	usage counter error
5ch	drive spindle
60h	beam source error
61h	video error
62h	seek error of sense head
63h	end of data area
64h	invalid track mode
80h–ffh	reserved for manufacturer's own codes (for example error codes of the controller diagnostics routines)

H.3 ASPI Programming Interface

Adaptec's *Advanced SCSI Programming Interface* (*ASPI*) provides seven functions for making an access to the SCSI host adapter. Section H.3.1 summarizes these ASPI functions, together with the function codes.

H.3.1 ASPI Functions

Code	Function
00h	host adapter inquiry
01h	get device type
02h	execute SCSI command
03h	abort SCSI command
04h	reset SCSI device
05h	set host adapter parameters
06h	get disk drive information

H.3.2 SCSI Request Block

Usually, ASPI is present as a driver loaded when your PC is booted. You may use the seven ASPI functions listed in Section H.3.1 by placing the segment and offset (in this order) of a so-called *SCSI Request Block (SRB)* on the stack. The structure of the first eight SRB bytes is the same for all ASPI functions. The remaining bytes (if present) depend upon the ASPI function. In the following I will summarize the SRB structure for the each ASPI function (I=input parameter, O=output parameter).

Host Adapter Inquiry (00h)

This function provides information regarding the addressed host adapter.

Byte	Input/ Output	Content
00h	I	00h (host adapter inquiry)
01h	O	status (see H.3.3)
02h	I	host adapter number*)
03h		reserved
04h..07h		reserved
08h	O	number of installed host adapters
09h	O	SCSI ID of host adapter
0ah..19h	O	ASPI manager name
1ah..29h	O	host adapter name
2ah..39h	O	parameter, dependent upon adapter

*) 1st adapter: 0; 2nd adapter: 1, etc.

Get Device Type (01h)

This function returns information similar to the SCSI *inquiry* command.

Byte	Input/ Output	Content
00h	I	01h (get device type)
01h	O	status (see H.3.3)
02h	I	host adapter number*)
03h		reserved
04h..07h		reserved
08h	I	SCSI ID of target
09h	I	LUN
0ah	O	SCSI device class of target/LUN

*) 1st adapter: 0; 2nd adapter: 1, etc.

Execute SCSI Command (02h)

This function instructs the host adapter to execute the corresponding SCSI command.

Byte	Input/ Output	Content
00h	I	02h (execute SCSI command)
01h	O	status (see H.3.3)
02h	I	host adapter number[1)]
03h	I	bit 0: POST, bit 1: link, bit 2..3: direction[2)],
	I	bits 4..7: reserved
04h..07h		reserved
08h	I	ID of target
09h	I	LUN
0ah..0dh	I	data buffer size (allocation length)
0eh	I	size l1 of sense data in bytes
0fh..12h	I	segment:offset of data buffer
13h..16h	I	segment:offset of SRB link
17h	I	size l2 of SCSI command in bytes
18h	O	host adapter status[3)]
19h	O	target status[4)]
1ah..1dh	I	segment:offset of POST
1eh..3fh		depending upon operating system
40h..40h+l2-1	I	SCSI command
40h+l2..40h+l2+l1-1	O	sense data

1) 1st adapter: 0; 2nd adapter: 1, etc.

2) POST: 1=use POST routine, 0=SRB for sense request; link: 1=SRB link points to next SRB of an SRB chain, 0=no more SRB links; direction: 00b=determined by SCSI command, 01b=SCSI target->host, 10b=host->SCSI target, 11b=no data transfer

3) 00h=no error, 11h=no target response (time-out), 12h=data overflow/underflow, 13h=unexpected bus free phase, 14h=bus phase error of target, 15h..ffh=reserved

4) 00h=no target status, 02h=sense data available, 08h=addressed LUN busy, 18h=reservation conflict

Abort SCSI Command (03h)

This command attempts to abort the current SCSI command. Note that this command always returns a status o.k. in the allocated SRB, although the current command returns its status in its own SRB. Thus, the current command is successfully aborted only if the code 02h appears in the status field of its SRB (see Section H.3.3). Eventually, the abort attempt must be repeated.

Byte	Input/ Output	Content
00h	I	03h (abort SCSI command)
01h	O	status (see H.3.3)
02h	I	host adapter number[*)]
03h		reserved
04h..07h		reserved
08h..09h	I	offset of SRB for the command to be aborted
0ah–0bh	I	segment of SRB for the command to be aborted

*) 1st adapter: 0; 2nd adapter: 1, etc.

Reset SCSI Device (04h)

This command resets a certain SCSI device.

Byte	Input/ Output	Content
00h	I	04h (reset SCSI device)
01h	O	status (see H.3.3)
02h	I	host adapter number[1)]
03h		reserved
04h..07h		reserved
08h	I	target ID
09h	I	LUN
0ah..17h		reserved
18h	O	host adapter status[2)]
19h	O	target status[3)]

1) 1st adapter: 0; 2nd adapter: 1, etc.

2) 00h=no error, 11h=no target response (time out), 12h=data overflow/underflow, 13h=unexpected bus free phase, 14h=bus phase error of target, 15h..ffh=reserved

3) 00h=no target status, 02h=sense data available, 08h=addressed LUN busy, 18h=reservation conflict

Set Host Adapter Parameters (05h)

This function sets the parameters for a certain host adapter. The parameter values and their meanings depend upon the adapter.

Byte	Input/ Output	Content
00h	I	05h (set host adapter parameters)
01h	O	status (see H.3.3)
02h	I	host adapter number[1)]
03h		reserved
04h..07h		reserved
08h..17h	I	dependent upon the host adapter

1) 1st adapter: 0; 2nd adapter: 1, etc.

Get Disk Drive Information (06h)

This command instructs the addressed drive to transfer its parameters.

Byte	Input/ Output	Content
00h	I	06h (get disk drive information)
01h	O	status (see H.3.3)
02h	I	host adapter number[1)]
03h		reserved
04h..07h		reserved
08h	I	target ID
09h	I	LUN
0ah	O	drive flag[2)]
0bh	O	drive number for INT 13h[3)]
0ch	O	preferred head translation[4)]
0dh	O	preferred sector translation[4)]
0eh–17h		reserved

1) 1st adapter: 0; 2nd adapter: 1, etc.

2) bits 7..2: reserved, bits 1..0: 00b=drive cannot be accessed via INT 13h (access only via ASPI), 01b=drive can be accessed via INT 13h and is managed by DOS, 10b=drive can be accessed via INT 13h but is not managed by DOS, 11b=reserved

3) number (00h..ffh) which addresses the drive with INT 13h (only valid if drive flag equal to xxxxxx01b or xxxxxx10b)

4) preferred parameters drive heads and sectors per track for the translation of logical to physical geometry.

H.3.3 ASPI Status Codes

Status	Meaning
00h	ASPI in progress
01h	function completed successfully
02h	function aborted by host command
03h	SCSI command cannot be aborted
04h	general error
80h	invalid SRB format
81h	invalid host adapter specified
82h	SCSI target not found

I Access to Interfaces

I.1 Parallel Interface

To access the parallel interface four functions of DOS interrupt 21h and three functions of BIOS interrupt 17h are available.

I.1.1 DOS Functions

The functions are accessed by a call to DOS interrupt 21h.

Function 05h – Printing

This function transfers one character to the parallel interface PRN.

Register	Call value	Return value
AH	05h	
DL	ASCII code of character to print	
Carry		

Function 40h – Write File/Unit

This function transfers one or more characters from a buffer to the parallel interface. Usually, PRN is assigned handle 4, otherwise you must use the handle returned by function 3dh, *open file/device*.

Register	Call value	Return value
AH	40h	
AX		error code/byte number*)
BX	handle	
CX	number of bytes to write	
DX	write buffer offset	
DS	write buffer segment	
Carry		error if < > 0

*) system error code if carry is set, or the number of actually written bytes

I.1.2 BIOS Functions

The functions are accessed by calling BIOS interrupt 17h.

Function 00h – Output Character to Parallel Interface and Printer

This function outputs a character to the parallel interface.

Register	Call value	Return value
AH	00h	status[1)]
AL	character's ASCII code	
DX	interface/printer number[2)]	

[1)] see I.1.3
[2)] 0=LPT1=PRN, 1=LPT2, 2=LPT3, 3=LPT4

Function 01h – Initialize Parallel Interface and Printer

This function initializes the parallel interface and the connected printer.

Register	Call value	Return value
AH	01h	status[1)]
DX	interface/printer number[2)]	

[1)] see I.1.3
[2)] 0=LPT1=PRN, 1=LPT2, 2=LPT3, 3=LPT4

Function 02h – Determine Printer Status

This function determines the current status of the parallel interface and the connected printer.

Register	Call value	Return value
AH	02h	status[1)]
DX	interface/printer number[2)]	

[1)] see I.1.3
[2)] 0=LPT1=PRN, 1=LPT2, 2=LPT3, 3=LPT4

I.1.3 Printer Status Byte

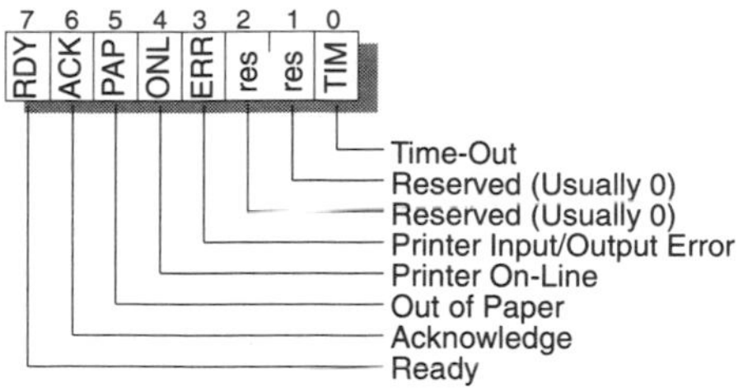

I.2 Serial Interface

For the serial interface four functions of DOS interrupt 21h and seven functions of BIOS interrupt 14h are available.

I.2.1 DOS Functions

The functions are accessed by a call to DOS interrupt 21h.

Function 03h – Read Character From the Serial Interface

This function reads one character from the serial interface COM1 corresponding to AUX.

Register	Call value	Return value
AH	03h	
AL		received character

Function 04h – Output Character Via the Serial Interface

This function outputs one character via the serial interface COM1 corresponding to AUX.

Register	Call value	Return value
AH	04h	
DL	ASCII code of character to output	
Carry		

Function 3fh – Read File/Device

This function reads one ore more characters from a serial interface into a buffer. Usually, AUX corresponding to COM1 is assigned handle 3, otherwise you must use the handle returned by the function 3dh, *open file/device*, for the interface concerned.

Register	Call value	Return value
AH	3fh	
AX		error code/byte number[*]
BX	handle	
CX	number of bytes to read	
DX	read buffer offset	
DS	read buffer segment	
Carry		error if < > 0

*) system error code if carry is set, or number of the bytes actually read

Function 40h – Write File/Device

This function outputs one or more characters from a buffer via a serial interface. Usually, AUX corresponding to COM1 is assigned handle 3, otherwise you must use the handle returned by the function 3dh, *open file/device*, for the interface concerned.

Register	Call value	Return value
AH	40h	
AX		error code/byte number[*]
BX	handle	
CX	number of bytes to write	
DX	write buffer offset	
DS	write buffer segment	
Carry		error if < > 0

*) system error code if carry is set, or number of the bytes actually written

I.2.2 BIOS Functions

The functions are accessed via a call to BIOS interrupt 14h.

Function 00h – Initialize Serial Interface

This function initializes the serial interface.

Register	Call value	Return value
AH	00h	transmit status[1]
AL	parameter byte[2]	modem status[3]
DX	interface number[4]	

1) see I.2.3
2) see I.2.5
3) see I.2.4
4) 0=COM1=AUX, 1=COM2, 2=COM3, 3=COM4

Function 01h – Output Character Via Serial Interface

This function outputs a character via the serial interface.

Register	Call value	Return value
AH	01h	transmit status[1]
AL	character	
DX	interface number[2]	

[1] see I.2.3
[2] 0=COM1=AUX, 1=COM2, 2=COM3, 3=COM4

Function 02h – Read Character Via Serial Interface

This function reads one character via the serial interface.

Register	Call value	Return value
AH	02h	transmit status[1]
AL		character
DX	interface number[2]	

[1] see I.2.3
[2] 0=COM1=AUX, 1=COM2, 2=COM3, 3=COM4

Function 03h – Determine Status of Serial Interface

This function determines the current status of the serial interface.

Register	Call value	Return value
AH	03h	transmit status[1]
AL		modem status[2]
DX	interface number[3]	

[1] see I.2.3
[2] see I.2.4
[3] 0=COM1=AUX, 1=COM2, 2=COM3, 3=COM4

Function 04h – Initialize Serial Interface Extended (PS/2 Only)

This function carries out an extended initialization of the serial interface. The function is available on the PS/2 only.

Register	Call value	Return value
AH	04h	transmit status[1]
AL	break setting	modem status[2]
BH	parity	
BL	stop bits	
CH	data bits	
CL	baud rate	
DX	interface number[3]	

[1] see I.2.3
[2] see I.2.4
[3] 0=COM1=AUX, 1=COM2, 2=COM3, 3=COM4

```
break setting: 00h=no break   01h=break
parity:     00h=none   01h=odd   02h=even   03h=mark   04h=space
stop bits: 00h=one stop bit    01h=two stop bits or 1 1/2 with 5 data bit
data bits: 00h=5   01h=6   02h=7   03h=8
baud rate: 00h=110 baud    01h=150 baud    02h=300 baud    03h=600 baud
           04h=1200 baud   05h=2400 baud   06h=4800 baud   07h=9600 baud
           08h=19200 baud
```

Function 05h, Subfunction 00h – Read Modem Control Register (PS/2 Only)

This function reads the modem control register of the serial interface. The function is available on the PS/2 only.

Register	Call value	Return value
AH	05h	
AL	00h	
BL		modem control register[1]
DX	interface number[2]	

[1] see I.2.6
[2] 0=COM1=AUX, 1=COM2, 2=COM3, 3=COM4

Function 05h, Subfunction 01h – Write Modem Control Register (PS/2 Only)

This function writes the modem control register of the serial interface. The function is available on the PS/2 only.

Register	Call value	Return value
AH	05h	transmit status[1)]
AL	01h	modem status[2)]
BL	modem control register[3)]	
DX	interface number[4)]	

1) see I.2.3
2) see I.2.4
3) see I.2.6
4) 0=COM1=AUX, 1=COM2, 2=COM3, 3=COM4

I.2.3 Transmit Status

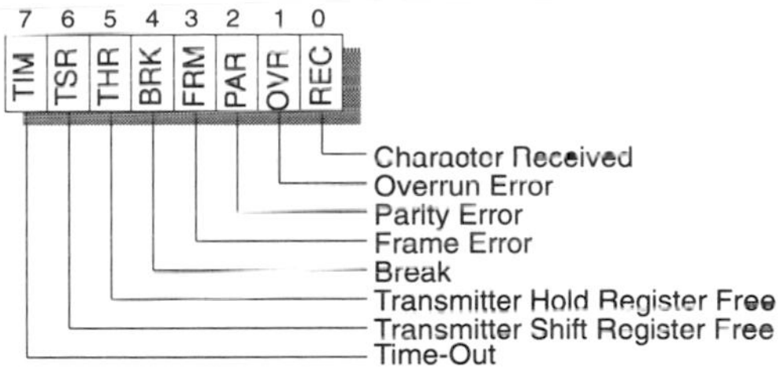

I.2.4 Modem Status

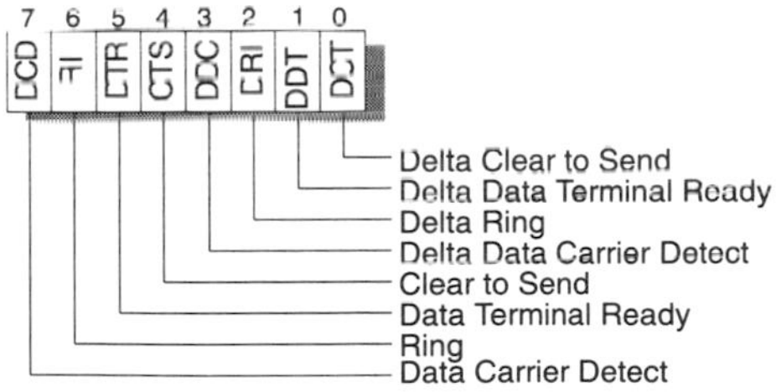

I.2.5 Parameter Byte

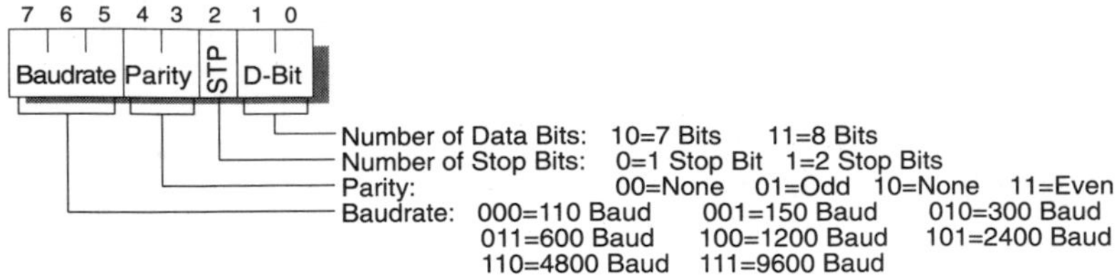

I.2.6 Modem Control Register

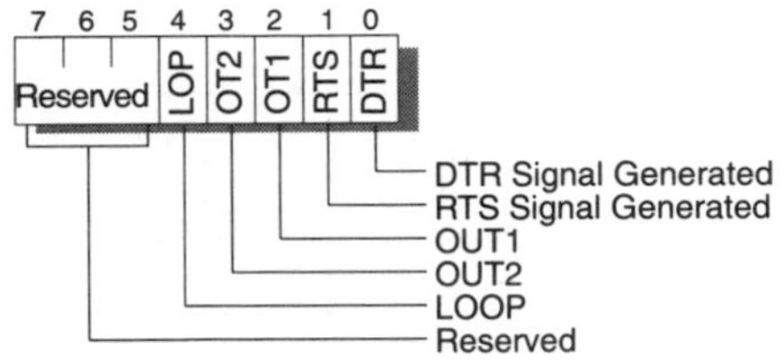

J Keyboard and Mouse Access

J.1 The Keyboard

- The seven DOS functions are accessed via a call to DOS interrupt 21h.
- The keyboard can be accessed directly by means of BIOS interrupt 15h.
- With many BIOS versions, the hardware interrupt handler 09h calls function 4fh of INT 15h and passes a scan code to the handler.
- If you press or release the SysReq key, the handler of interrupt 09h calls function 85h of INT 15h.

J.1.1 DOS Functions

Function 01h – Character Input With Echo

This function reads one character byte from the keyboard buffer and outputs the character via the standard output device at the same time. For non-ASCII characters like the function key, you have to call the function twice; the first call returns code 00h, the second call the scan code of the key.

Register	Call value	Return value
AH	01h	
AL		ASCII code

Function 06h – Character Input From Standard Input Device Without Check

This function attempts to read one character from the keyboard buffer, and doesn't wait for an available character. With non-ASCII keys like F1 the first call returns a code equal to 0, and the second call the scan code of the pressed key. The function reads the keyboard as long as it is the standard input device. If redirection like < file or < device is active, all characters are read from the file or device. Control characters like Ctrl-C are not interpreted, but only passed.

Register	Call value	Return value
AH	06h	
AL		ASCII code
DL	ffh	
zero		1=character read 0=no character available

Function 07h – Direct Character Input From Keyboard

This function attempts to read one character from the keyboard buffer and waits for an available character. With non-ASCII keys like F1, the first call returns a code equal to 0 and the second call the scan code of the key concerned. Unlike the 06h function, this function waits until a key is pressed if the keyboard buffer is empty. Control characters like Ctrl-C are not interpreted but only passed.

Register	Call value	Return value
AH	07h	
AL		ASCII code

Function 08h – Character Input From Standard Input Device With Check

This function attempts to read one character out of the keyboard buffer. The function waits until a character is available. With non-ASCII keys like F1, the first call returns a code equal to 0, and the second call the scan code of the pressed key. The function reads from keyboard as long as it is the standard input device. If redirection such as < file or < device is active, all characters are read from the file or device. Control characters like Ctrl-C are interpreted accordingly.

Register	Call value	Return value
AH	08h	
AL		ASCII code

Function 0ah – Buffered Character Input From Standard Input Device With Echo

This function reads a character string into a buffer. The input is terminated by pressing RETURN. Character codes except Ctrl-C (program abortion) and Ctrl-P (echo on printer) are passed with a preceding "^" (for example, Ctrl-R as ^R). The first byte of the buffer indicates the max. length of the input, and the second byte the actual length. Therefore, the buffer has to comprise max.length+2 bytes. The function reads from keyboard as long as it is the standard input device. If redirection such as < file or < device is active, all characters are read from the file or device.

Register	Call value	Return value
AH	0ah	
DX	buffer offset	
DS	buffer segment	

Function 0bh – Check Status of Standard Input Device

This function determines whether a character has been input via the standard input device. The function accesses the keyboard as long as it is the standard input device. If redirection such as < file or < device is active, all characters are read from the file or device.

Register	Call value	Return value
AH	0bh	
AL		00h=no character available ffh=one character available

Function 3fh – Read File/Device

This function reads one or more characters from the keyboard into a buffer. Usually, the keyboard (CON) is assigned handle 0.

Register	Call value	Return value
AH	3fh	
AX		error code/byte number*)
BX	handle	
CX	number of bytes to read	
DX	read buffer offset	
DS	read buffer segment	
Carry		error if < > 0

*) system error code if carry is set, or number of bytes actually read

J.1.2 BIOS Interrupt INT 16h

Function 00h – Read Next Character

This function reads the next character out of the keyboard buffer and updates the corresponding pointer. If the keyboard buffer is empty, the function waits for the next key.

Register	Call value	Return value
AH	00h	scan code
AL		ASCII code

Function 01h – Determine Buffer Status

This function determines the status of the keyboard buffer, and indicates whether a character is available. Unlike the function 01h, the keyboard pointer is not updated.

Register	Call value	Return value
AH	01h	scan code
AL		ASCII code
Zero		0=character available 1=no character available

Function 02h – Determine Shift Status

This function determines the status of the shift keys by checking the keyboard flag at 0040:0017.

Register	Call value	Return value
AH	02h	
AL		shift status*)

*) see J.1.4

Function 03h – Set Typing Rate and Delay (PS/2 and Some ATs)

This function sets the typing rate and the delay of the AT or MF II keyboard.

Register	Call value	Return value
AH	03h	
BL	typematic rate1)	
BH	delay2)	

1)	00h=30.0	01h=26.7	02h=24.0	03h=21.8	04h=20.0	05h=18.5	06h=17.1	07h=16.0
	08h=15.0	09h=13.3	0ah=12.0	0bh=10.9	0ch=10.0	0dh=9.2	0eh=8.5	0fh=8.0
	10h=7.5	11h=6.7	12h=6.0	13h=5.5	14h=5.0	15h=4.6	16h=4.3	17h=4.0
	18h=3.7	19h=3.3	1ah=3.0	1bh=2.7	1ch=2.5	1dh=2.3	1eh=2.1	1fh=2.0
2)	00=250 ms	01=500 ms	10=750 ms	11=1000 ms				

Function 05h – Write Character and Scan Code Back to Keyboard Buffer

This function writes an ASCII character and a scan code back to the keyboard buffer to emulate a key press.

Register	Call value	Return value
AH	05h	
AL		status*)
CH	scan code	
CL	ASCII code	

*) 00h=o.k. 01h=keyboard buffer full

Function 10h – Read One Character from Extended Keyboard

This function reads one character from the extended (MF II) keyboard. The function is similar to function 00h, but supports the codes of the extended keyboard, that is, for the codes of the new function and control keys a precode byte 0eh is passed instead of the value 00h. Thus the new keys can be distinguished from conventional ones.

Register	Call value	Return value
AH	10h	scan code
AL		ASCII code

Function 11h – Determine Buffer Status for the Extended Keyboard

This function determines the buffer status for the extended keyboard. This function is similar to function 01h, but supports the codes of the extended keyboard, that is, for the codes of the new function and control keys a precode byte 0eh is passed instead of the value 00h. Thus the new keys can be distinguished from the conventional ones.

Register	Call value	Return value
AH	11h	scan code
AL		ASCII code
Zero		0=character available
		1=no character available

Function 12h – Determine SHIFT Status of the Extended Keyboard

This function determines the status of the SHIFT keys by checking the keyboard flags at 0040:0017 and 0040:0018. The function corresponds to function 021h, but supports the additional SHIFT keys of the extended keyboard.

Register	Call value	Return value
AH	12h	2nd shift status byte[1)]
AL		1st shift status byte[2)]

[1)] see J.1.5
[2)] see J.1.4

J.1.3 BIOS Interrupt INT 15h

Function 4fh (AT and PS/2) – Keyboard Hook

The interrupt 09h calls this function if it receives a scan code from the keyboard. Normally, the function only clears the carry flag and executes a RET, but you can intercept the function and replace the scan code returned in AL by another code.

Register	Call value	Return value
AH	4fh	
AL	keyboard scan code	new scan code
Carry		0b (ignore key press) or
	1b	1b (process key)

Function 85h (AT and PS/2) – SysReq Hook

The interrupt 09h calls this function if you press or release SysReq on a PC/XT or AT keyboard, or if you press or release Alt+SysReq on an MF II keyboard. Normally, the function only sets AX to 00h and clears the carry flag. But you can intercept the function.

Register	Call value	Return value
AH	85h	00h
AL	00h (SysReq pressed) or 01h (SysReq released)	
carry		0b

J.1.4 First Shift Status Byte

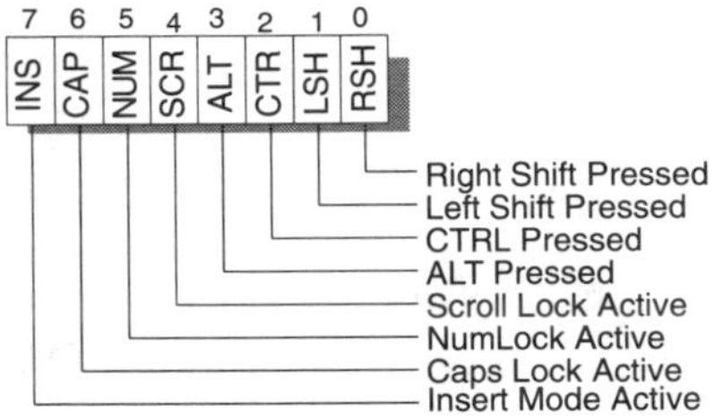

J.1.5 Second Shift Status Byte

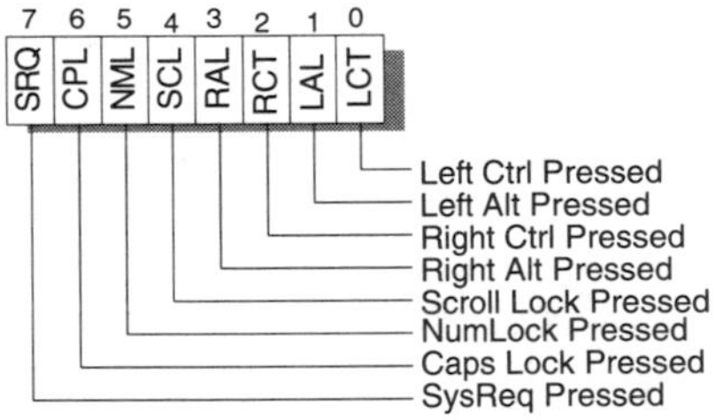

J.2 Mouse Interrupt 33h

Mouse and mouse driver can be accessed via mouse interrupt 33h.

J.2.1 Functions of INT 33h

Function 00h – Check Mouse Present

This function determines whether a mouse is present, and resets the mouse driver to its standard settings. In register BX the number of available mouse buttons is returned.

Register	Call value	Return value
AX	00h	status[1]
BX		mouse buttons[2]

[1] 0=mouse present; 1=no mouse present
[2] 2=two buttons (Microsoft); 3=three buttons

Function 01h – Display Mouse Cursor/Increment Cursor Flag

This function increments the cursor flag by one. The mouse cursor is displayed on-screen if the flag is equal to 0. Normally, the cursor flag has a value of –1.

Register	Call value	Return value
AX	01h	

Function 02h – Clear Mouse Cursor/Decrement Cursor Flag

This function decrements the cursor flag by one, and therefore clears the mouse cursor on the screen. The mouse cursor is displayed on-screen if the flag is equal to 0. Normally the cursor flag has a value of –1.

Register	Call value	Return value
AX	02h	

Function 03h – Determine Status of Mouse Buttons and Position of Mouse Cursor

This function determines the current status of the mouse buttons and the current position of the mouse cursor on-screen.

Register	Call value	Return value
AX	03h	
BX		button byte*)
CX		X-value of cursor position
DX		Y-value of cursor position

*) see J.2.2 (1=corresponding button pressed, 0=corresponding button released)

Function 04h – Set Mouse Cursor Position

This function sets the position of the mouse cursor on-screen.

Register	Call value	Return value
AX	04h	
CX	X-value of cursor position	
DX	Y-value of cursor position	

Function 05h – Determine Number of Mouse Button Clicks and Mouse Cursor Position

This function determines how often a certain mouse button has been pressed, and where the mouse cursor was on-screen at the time the last click occurred.

Register	Call value	Return value
AX	05h	button byte[1)]
BX	mouse button[2)]	count value[3)]
CX		X-value of cursor position
DX		Y-value of cursor position

1) see J.2.2 (1=corresponding button pressed, 0=corresponding button released)
2) 1=check left button, 2=check right button, 4=check middle button
3) number of clicks (0 to 32,767)

Function 06h – Determine Number of Mouse Button Releases and Mouse Cursor Position

This function determines how often a certain mouse button has been released since the last inquiry, and where the mouse cursor was on the screen at the time the last release occurred.

Register	Call value	Return value
AX	06h	button byte[1)]
BX	mouse button[2)]	count value[3)]
CX		X-value of cursor position
DX		Y-value of cursor position

1) see J.2.2 (1=corresponding button pressed, 0=corresponding button released)
2) 1=check left button, 2=check right button, 4=check middle button
3) number of releases (0 to 32,767)

Function 07h – Define Horizontal Borders for Mouse Cursor

This function defines the horizontal borders for the mouse cursor's movement. The mouse cursor cannot move outside them, even if the mouse is moved further. Thus, together with function 08h, you can define a window for the mouse cursor.

Register	Call value	Return value
AX	07h	
BX		
CX	left border	
DX	right border	

Function 08h – Define Vertical Borders for Mouse Cursor

This function defines the vertical borders for the mouse cursor's movement. The mouse cursor cannot move outside them, even if the mouse is moved further. Together with function 07h, you can define a window for the mouse cursor.

Register	Call value	Return value
AX	08h	
BX		
CX	upper border	
DX	lower border	

Function 09h – Define Mouse Cursor in Graphics Mode

This function defines the shape and behaviour of the mouse cursor in graphics mode. Screen and cursor mask are provided in this order in a buffer. The action point defines, relative to the upper left corner of the mouse cursor, which value is to be returned in an inquiry of the mouse cursor position.

Register	Call value	Return value
AX	09h	
BX	action point horizontal*)	
CX	action point vertical*)	
DX	mask buffer offset	
ES	mask buffer segment	

*) range of values: –16...+16

Function 0ah – Define Mouse Cursor in Text Mode

This function defines the shape and behaviour of the mouse cursor in text mode.

Register	Call value	Return value
AX	0ah	
BX	mouse cursor type[1]	
CX	screen mask[2]	
DX	cursor mask[3]	

1) 0=software mouse cursor, 1=hardware mouse cursor

2) software mouse cursor: screen mask code, hardware mouse cursor: first scan line of mouse cursor

3) software mouse cursor: cursor mask code, hardware mouse cursor: last scan line of mouse cursor

Function 0bh – Read Movement Counter of Mouse

This function reads the movement counter of the mouse and determines how far the mouse has been moved since the last function call. One count value is equal to one mickey, that is, 1/200" or 0.13 mm.

Register	Call value	Return value
AX	0bh	
CX		count value horizontal*)
DX		count value vertical*)

*) range of values: –32768 ... +32767

Function 0ch – Define Call Mask for User Procedure

This function defines the conditions for which the mouse driver calls a user-defined procedure via a far call.

Register	Call value	Return value
AX	0ch	
CX	call mask*)	
DX	procedure offset	
ES	procedure segment	

*)

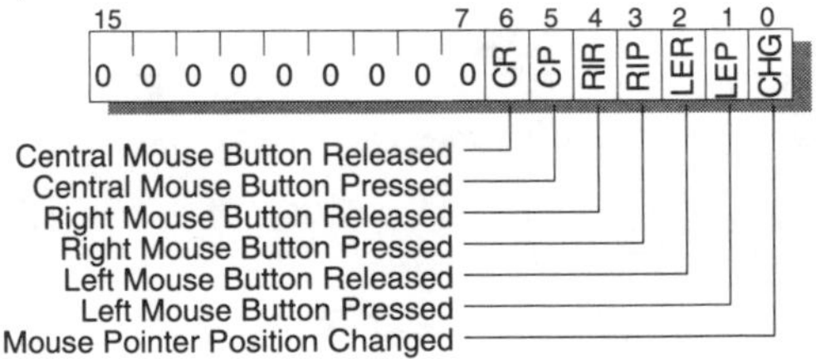

The procedure is passed the following parameters:

Register	Contents
AX	mask with set bit which led to the call
BX	current status of mouse buttons (see J.2.2)
CX	X-value of mouse cursor position
DX	Y-value of mouse cursor position

Function 0dh – Enable Light Pen Emulation

This function enables the light pen emulation of the mouse driver. The light pen is on the screen if the left and right mouse buttons are pressed.

Register	Call value	Return value
AX	0dh	

Function 0eh – Disable Light Pen Emulation

This function disables the light pen emulation of the mouse driver.

Register	Call value	Return value
AX	0eh	

Function 0fh – Define Mickey/Pixel Ratio

This function defines the number of mickeys per pixel. The horizontal standard value is equal to 8, the vertical equal to 16.

Register	Call value	Return value
AX	0fh	
CX	horizontal ratio*)	
DX	vertical ratio*)	

*) range of values: 1 ... 32,767

Function 10h – Disable Mouse Cursor Conditionally

This function defines the borders within which the mouse cursor is cleared from the screen. If the mouse cursor enters the defined window it will be cleared. For redisplaying the mouse cursor you must use function 01h.

Register	Call value	Return value
AX	10h	
CX	X-value of right border	
DX	Y-value of lower border	
SI	X-value of left border	
DI	Y-value of upper border	

Function 13h – Define Threshold Value for Double Speed

This function defines the threshold in mickeys/sec for which the mouse cursor is moved on-screen with double speed. The standard threshold value is equal to 64.

Register	Call value	Return value
AX	13h	
DX	threshold value	

J.2.2 Button Byte

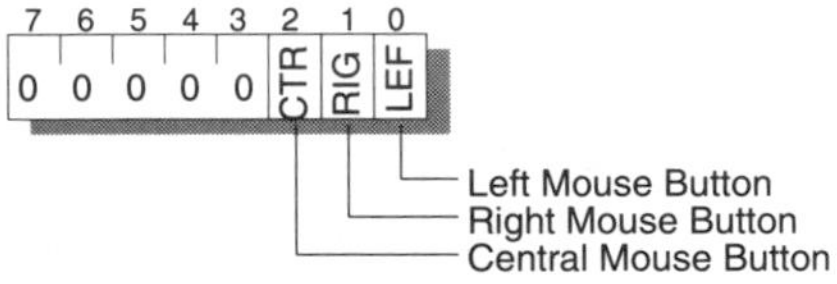

J.3 PS/2 Mouse Support via BIOS Interrupt INT 15h, Function c2h

- The PS/2 mouse support on a hardware level is carried out by subfunctions 00h to 07h of INT 15h, function c2h.
- Before using the routines you must pass the jump address of the mouse driver or the corresponding application program which handles the mouse packets to the BIOS via subfunction 07h – *pass driver address*. Afterwards, the mouse must be initalized via subfunction 05h – *initialize mouse*. Then the mouse can be enabled or disabled by subfunction 00h – *enable/disable mouse*.

J.3.1 Subfunctions of INT 15h, Function c2h

Subfunction 00h – Enable/Disable Mouse

This function enables or disables the mouse. Before activation the program must pass the address of the mouse driver or the program to the BIOS via subfunction 07h, and initialize the mouse with subfunction 05h.

Register	Call value	Return value
AH	c2h	status*)
AL	00h	
BH	00h enable mouse 01h disable mouse	
Carry		error if < > 0

*) see J.3.2

Subfunction 01h – Reset Mouse

This function resets the mouse.

Register	Call value	Return value
AH	c2h	status*)
AL	01h	
BH		mouse identification 00h
Carry		error if <> 0

*) see J.3.2

Subfunction 02h – Set Sample Rate

This function sets the sample rate for the mouse.

Register	Call value	Return value
AH	c2h	status[1]
AL	02h	
BH	sample rate[2]	
Carry		error if <> 0

1) see J.3.2

2) 00h=10 samples/s 01h=20 samples/s 02h=40 samples/s 03h=60 samples/s
04h=80 samples/s 05h=100 samples/s 06h=200 samples/s

Subfunction 03h – Set Resolution

This function sets the resolution of the mouse.

Register	Call value	Return value
AH	c2h	status[1]
AL	03h	
BH	resolution[2]	
Carry		error if <> 0

1) see J.3.2

2) 00h=1 unit/mm 01h=2 units/mm 02h=4 units/mm 03h=8 units/mm

Subfunction 04h – Determine Mouse Identification

This function determines the identification code of the connected mouse (or another connected device).

Register	Call value	Return value
AH	c2h	status*)
AL	04h	
BH		identification code
Carry		error if <> 0

*) see J.3.2

Subfunction 05h – Initialize Mouse

This function initializes the mouse and adjusts the size of the mouse data packet.

Register	Call value	Return value
AH	c2h	status[1]
AL	05h	
BH	data packet size[2]	
Carry		error if <> 0

[1] see J.3.2
[2] see J.3.3

Subfunction 06h – Extended Mouse Status

This function determines the extended mouse status and sets the X-Y-scaling factor of the mouse.

Register	Call value	Return value
AH	c2h	status[1]
AL	06h	
BH	function to execute[2]	
BL		first status byte[3]
CL		second status byte[3]
DL		third status byte[3]
Carry		error if <> 0

[1] see J.3.2
[2] 00h=determine status 01=scaling factor 1:1 02=scaling factor 2:1
[3] if equal to 00h on call

Subfunction 07h – Pass Driver Address

This function passes the BIOS the address of the PS/2 mouse driver.

Register	Call value	Return value
AH	C2h	status*)
AL	07h	
BX	offset address of driver or application program	
ES	segment address of driver or application program	
Carry		error if <> 0

*) see J.3.2

J.3.2 Status Byte

Status	Meaning
00h	no error
01h	invalid function call
02h	invalid input
03h	interface error
04h	resend necessary
05h	no device driver present

J.3.3 Mouse Packet on the Stack

The table below indicates the data on the stack where the BIOS pushes the mouse packet. The offsets are calculated relative to SP. The actual mouse packet therefore consists of a maximum of eight bytes of Z-data, Y-data, X-data, and status.

Offset	Size	Meaning
00h	dword	return address to BIOS
04h	word	Z-data (00h)
06h	word	Y-data: low byte=movement units since last packet
08h	word	X-data: low byte=movement units since last packet
0ah	byte	status byte:

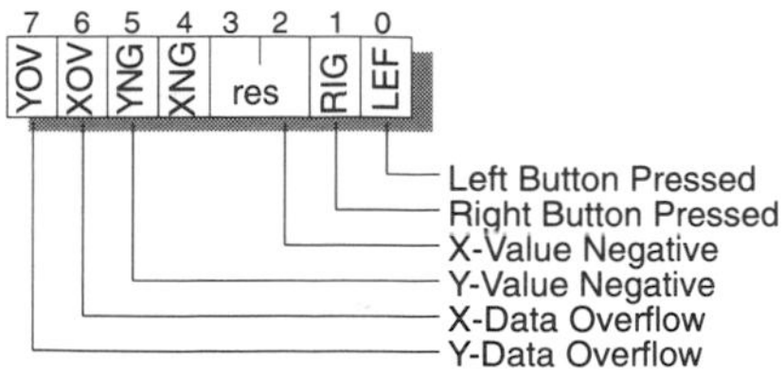

K Access to Graphics Adapters

- DOS functions are called via DOS interrupt 21h.
- The system BIOS comprises the standard functions for text and graphics mode of the graphics adapter.
- EGA and VGA have a BIOS extension with further powerful routines for adapter logic control, as well as character and graphics output in the new text and graphics formats.

K.1 DOS Functions

Function 02h – Character Output

This function outputs a character to the standard output device (usually CON). The character codes 07h (bell), 08h (backspace), 09h (tab), 0ah (line feed), and 0dh (carriage return) are interpreted as control characters, and the BIOS carries out a corresponding process.

Register	Call value	Return value
AH	02h	
DL	ASCII character code	

Function 06h – Character Output to Standard Output Device Without Check

This function outputs a character to the standard output device (usually CON). If redirection of the form < file or < device is in effect, all characters are output to the file or device. DOS control characters of the form Ctrl-C are not interpreted, but only transferred. But the character codes 07h (bell), 08h (backspace), 09h (tab), 0ah (line feed,) and 0dh (carriage return), which are recognized by the BIOS, are actually interpreted by the BIOS.

Register	Call value	Return value
AH	06h	
DL	ASCII character code	

Function 09h – String Output

This function outputs a complete string to the standard output device (usually CON). The string must be terminated by the character "$" (ASCII code 36). DOS control characters of the form Ctrl-C are not interpreted, but only transferred. But the character codes 07h (bell), 08h (backspace), 09h (tab), 0ah (line feed), and 0dh (carriage return), which are recognized by the BIOS, are actually interpreted by the BIOS.

Register	Call value	Return value
AH	09h	
DX	string offset	
DS	string segment	
AL		'$'

Function 40h – Write File/Device

This function outputs a string by means of a handle. The handle for the standard output device is equal to 1. If the standard output device is not CON anymore, and you still want to output one or more characters on-screen, you must open CON first with a call to function *open file/device* for a write access.

Register	Call value	Return value
AH	40h	
AX		error code/byte number*)
BX	handle (01h)	
CX	number of bytes to output	
DX	write buffer offset	
DS	write buffer segment	
Carry		error if < > 0

*) system error code if carry is set, or number of actual written bytes

K.2 BIOS Interrupt INT 10h – Standard Functions of the System BIOS

The listed functions are implemented in the system BIOS on the motherboard.

Function 00h – Set Video Mode

This function sets a certain video mode of the MDA and CGA by loading the mode and control registers of the grahics chip with appropriate values. After a call to the 00h function, the cursor is in line 0, column 0, the palette is reset to standard colours, and the screen is cleared.

Register	Call value	Return value
AH	00h	
AL	video mode*)	

*)

Mode no.	Mode type	Text lines	Text columns	Char. matrix	Resolution	Colours	Pages	Page size	Video segment	Adapter MDA	CGA
0	text	25	40	8*8	320*200	16	8	800h	b800h		x
1	text	25	40	8*8	320*200	16	8	800h	b800h		x
2	text	25	80	8*8	640*200	16	4	1000h	b800h		x
3	text	25	80	8*8	640*200	16	4	1000h	b800h		x
4	graphics	25	40	8*8	320*200	4	1	4000h	b800h		x
5	graphics	25	40	8*8	320*200	4	1	4000h	b800h		x
6	graphics	25	80	8*8	640*200	2	1	4000h	b800h		x
7	text	25	80	9*14	720*350	mono	1	1000h	b000h	x	

*) per video RAM layer

Function 01h – Set Cursor Size (Text)

This function sets the cursor size in text mode. If the value of the start scan line is more than the value of the end scan line, a divided cursor is displayed. If the values of the scan lines are out of the range given by the character box in the active video mode, no cursor is displayed. The cursor parameters are stored in the BIOS data area at 40:60h. The standard settings for a CGA are start scan line=6, end scan line=7 and for a MDA start scan line=11, end scan line=12.

Register	Call value	Return value
AH	01h	
CH	start scan line of cursor[1]	
CL	end scan line of cursor[2]	

[1] bit 7: reserved (=0); bit 6–5: 00=normal, 01=cursor not displayed
bit 4–0: start scan line of cursor
[2] bit 7–5: reserved (=0); bit 4–0: end scan line

Function 02h – Set Cursor Position (Text/Graphics)

This function sets the cursor position of the active screen page. The screen page need not be displayed; also, a hidden page can be addressed. In text mode, the text cursor appears at that location; in graphics mode the cursor remains invisible, but defines the coordinates where, for example, a point is to be set. The function stores the cursor coordinates at 40:50h.

Register	Call value	Return value
AH	02h	
BH	screen page	
DH	row	
DL	column	

Function 03h – Read Cursor Position (Text)

This function determines the cursor position of the active screen page. The screen page need not be displayed; also, a hidden page can be addressed. The function reads the cursor type from the BIOS storage area at 40:60h and the cursor coordinates at 40:50h.

Register	Call value	Return value
AH	03h	
BH	screen page	
CH		start scan line of cursor
CL		end scan line of cursor
DH		row
DL		column

Function 04h – Read Light Pen Position (Text/Graphics)

This function determines the position and status of the light pen. Nowadays, the light pen has been replaced by mouse and trackball.

Register	Call value	Return value
AH	04h	status1)
BX		pixel column (graphics mode)
CH		pixel line 0 to 199 (graphics mode)
CL		pixel line 0 to xxx2) (graphics mode)
DH		row (text mode)
DL		column (text mode)

1) 00h=switch of light pen open,
01h=switch closed, coordinates valid
2) for modes with more than 200 lines (xxx 200)

Function 05h – Select Screen Page (Text/Graphics)

This function specifies the active screen page, that is, the displayed screen page. The number of available screen pages depends upon the video mode and the graphics adapter used.

Register	Call value	Return value
AH	05h	
AL	screen page	

Function 06h – Scroll Window Up (Text/Graphics)

This function defines a window on-screen and scrolls the window contents up the number of specified rows. With AL=00h the window can be cleared. The blank rows appearing at the bottom of the window are filled with ' ' (blank) characters. These blank characters are assigned the attribute passed in register BH.

Register	Call value	Return value
AH	06h	
AL	number of rows to scroll	
BH	attribute of blank rows	
CH	upper row of window	
CL	left column of window	
DH	lower row of window	
DL	right column of window	

Function 07h – Scroll Window Down (Text/Graphics)

This function defines a window on-screen and scrolls the window content down the number of specified rows. With AL=00h the window can be cleared. The blank rows appearing at the top of the window are filled with ' ' (blank) characters. These blank characters are assigned the attribute which is passed in register BH.

Register	Call value	Return value
AH	07h	
AL	number of rows to scroll	
BH	attribute of blank rows	
CH	upper row of window	
CL	left column of window	
DH	lower row of window	
DL	right column of window	

Function 08h – Read Character/Attribute From Screen (Text/Graphics)

This function reads the character at the current cursor position. Eventually, you must locate the cursor at the desired position in advance with function 02h. In text mode the function returns not only the character code, but also the character attribute. In graphics mode, the character matrix at the specified cursor position is compared with the active character table to determine a character code. If the matrix pattern does not meet a character in the table, the function returns a code 00h.

Register	Call value	Return value
AH	08h	character attribute (text mode only)
AL		character code
BH	screen page	

Function 09h – Write Character/Attribute Onto Screen (Text/Graphics)

This function write a character, starting at the current cursor position, and repeats the process CX-times. The cursor position is not altered by this. In text mode BL specifies the attribute, and in graphics mode the foreground colour of the character to be written. If characters are written in graphics mode and bit 7 of BL is set, the character matrix of the character to be written is XOR-ed with the contents of the video RAM at that location.

Register	Call value	Return value
AH	09h	
AL	character code	
BH	screen page	
BL	character attribute or foreground colour	
CX	number if repetitions	

Function 0ah – Write Character Onto Screen (Text/Graphics)

This function write one character, starting with the current cursor position, and repeats the process CX-times. The cursor position is not altered by this. The character attribute at the concerned location is not modified. If characters are written in graphics mode and bit 7 of BL is set, the character matrix of the character to be written is XOR-ed with the contents of the video RAM at that location.

Register	Call value	Return value
AH	0ah	
AL	character code	
BH	screen page	
CX	number of repetitions	

Function 0bh – Set Colour Palette (Graphics)

This function sets the colours for medium resolution of the CGA. Depending upon the value of the BH register, the BL register has a different meaning. By modifying the palette the colour of the displayed screen can be changed instantaneously, and the user has the impression of a blinking screen.

BH=00h

Register	Call value	Return value
AH	0bh	
BH	00h	
BL	colour 0–31*)	

*) mode 4, 5: background colour equal to BL
mode 0, 1, 2, 3: margin colour equal to BL
mode 6, 11: foreground colour equal to BL

BH=01h

Register	Call value	Return value
AH	0bh	
BH	01h	
BL	palette*)	

*) 00h: palette = green (1), red (2), yellow (3)
01h: palette = cyan (1), magenta (2), white (3)

Function 0ch – Write Pixel Onto Screen (Graphics)

This function writes one pixel onto the screen at a desired location. Bit 7 of register AL serves as the inverting bit, i.e. the colour in AL is XOR-ed with the pixel currently located at the addressed location. If you write the pixel in the same manner again, it has disappeared from the screen. Thus objects can seemingly be moved on-screen.

Register	Call value	Return value
AH	0ch	
AL	colour	
BH	screen page*)	
CX	pixel column	
DX	pixel line	

*) only necessary if the video mode supports more than one page

Function 0dh – Read Pixel From Screen (Graphics)

This function reads one pixel at a certain location on the screen.

Register	Call value	Return value
AH	0dh	
AL		colour of read pixel
BH	screen page*)	
CX	pixel column	
DX	pixel line	

*) only necessary if the video mode supports more than one page

Function 0eh – Write in TTY Mode (Text/Graphics)

This function writes one character onto the screen while the screen behaves like a serial terminal from the system's point of view (therefore, TTY mode). This function does not display the four characters with codes 07h (bell), 08h (backspace), 0ah (line feed), and 0dh (carriage return), but executes a corresponding action. For example, a code 08h deletes the character left of the cursor and moves the cursor one position to the left. After each character the cursor is moved implicitly.

Register	Call value	Return value
AH	0eh	
AL	character code	
BH	screen page	
BL	foreground colour*)	

*) graphics mode only

Function 0fh – Determine Video Status (Text/Graphics)

This function determines the current video mode and video status.

Register	Call value	Return value
AH	0fh	number of columns from 40.4ah
AL		video mode from 40:49h
BH		active screen page from 40:62h

Function 13h – Write String (Text/Graphics)

This function writes a whole string onto the screen. The bits 0 and 1 of register AL determine the behaviour of the function. The string may contain character codes and character attributes alternately, or character codes only. In the second case, the attribute passed in register BL is used.

Register	Call value	Return value
AH	13h	
AL	function behaviour1)	
BH	screen page	
BL	character attribute2)	
CX	length of string without attributes	
DH	start cursor row	
DL	start cursor column	
BP	string offset	
ES	string segment	

1) bit 0: 1=cursor points to last written character after function call
0=cursor points to start after function call
bit 1: 1=string contains character codes and character attributes alternately
0=string contain character code only, the attribute is taken from BL; codes 07h (bell), 08h (backspace), 0ah (line feed), and 0dh (carriage return) are interpreted as control commands
2) graphics mode only

K.3 BIOS Interrupt INT 10h – Additional Functions of the EGA/VGA BIOS

- The functions listed are implemented in the BIOS extension of EGA and VGA adapters.
- The EGA and VGA BIOS redirects the start address of the handler for INT 10h of the system BIOS on the motherboard to INT 42h upon booting.

Function 00h – Set Video Mode

This function sets a certain video mode of the EGA and VGA by loading the mode and control registers of the grahics chip with appropriate values. High-resolution EGA and VGA adapter cards have plenty of resolution for text and graphics mode, which you can find in the manual of your adapter card. After a call to the 00h function, the cursor is in line 0, column 0, the palette is reset to standard colours, and the screen is cleared.

Register	Call value	Return value
AH	00h	
AL	video mode*)	

*) available video mode:

Mode no.	Mode type	Text lines	Text columns	Char. matrix	Resolution	Colours	Pages	Page size	Video segment	Adapter EGA	VGA
0	text	25	40	8*14	320*350	16	8	800h	b800h	x	
0	text	25	40	8*16	360*400	16	8	800h	b800h		x
1	text	25	40	8*14	320*350	16	8	800h	b800h	x	
1	text	25	40	8*16	360*400	16	8	800h	b800h		x
2	text	25	80	8*14	640*350	16	4	1000h	b800h	x	
2	text	25	80	9*16	720*400	16	4	1000h	b800h		x
3	text	25	80	8*14	640*350	16	4	1000h	b800h	x	
3	text	25	80	9*16	720*400	16	4	1000h	b800h		x
4	graphics	25	40	8*8	320*200	4	1	4000h	b800h	x	x
5	graphics	25	40	8*8	320*200	4	1	4000h	b800h	x	x
6	graphics	25	80	8*8	640*200	2	1	4000h	b800h	x	x
7	text	25	80	9*14	720*350	mono	1	1000h	b000h	x	
7	text	25	80	9*16	720*400	mono	8	1000h	b000h		x
13	graphics	25	40	8*8	320*200	16	8	2000h*)	a000h	x	x
14	graphics	25	80	8*8	640*200	16	4	4000h*)	a000h	x	x
15	graphics	25	80	8*14	640*350	mono	2	8000h*)	a000h	x	x
16	graphics	25	80	8*14	640*350	16	2	8000h*)	a000h	x	x
17	graphics	30	80	8*16	640*480	2	1	a000h	a000h		x
18	graphics	30	80	8*16	640*480	16	1	a000h*)	a000h		x
19	graphics	25	40	8*8	320*200	256	1	10000h	a000h		x

*) per video RAM layer

Function 10h – Set Palette Registers

This function sets the palette registers of EGA and VGA. With an EGA, 64 different colours are possible; with a VGA $2^{18}=262.144$.

Subfunction 00h – Set Individual Palette Registers (EGA/VGA)

This function updates the specified palette register in the attribute controller.

Register	Call value	Return value
AH	10h	
AL	00h	
BH	new register value	
BL	palette register	

Subfunction 01h – Set Overscan Register (EGA/VGA)

This function determines the overscan colour, that is, the border colour. The value in BH is transferred into the overscan register.

Register	Call value	Return value
AH	10h	
AL	01h	
BH	new register value	

Subfunction 02h – Set All Registers (EGA/VGA)

This function loads all 16 palette registers and the overscan register with values which are passed in a table. The bytes 0–15 of the table contain the new values for the registers 0–15, and byte 16 of the table holds the new value for the overscan register.

Register	Call value	Return value
AH	10h	
AL	02h	
DX	register table offset	
ES	register table segment	

Subfunction 03h – Enable/Disable Blink Attribute (EGA/VGA)

This function determines the value of bit 3 in the mode control register. If bit 3 is set, a character with a set blink attribute is displayed on the monitor in a blinking manner. If bit 3 is cleared the blink bit in the attribute has no effect; the character is always displayed non-blinking. In this case, bit 3 of the attribute byte selects one of two active character definition tables. Therefore, 512 instead of 256 characters are available.

Register	Call value	Return value
AH	10h	
AL	03h	
BL	blinking (1=on, 0=off)	

Subfunction 07h – Read Palette Register (VGA)

This function reads the value of the indicated palette register.

Register	Call value	Return value
AH	10h	
AL	07h	
BH		palette register value
BL	palette register	

Subfunction 08h – Read Overscan Register (VGA)

This function reads the value of the overscan register.

Register	Call value	Return value
AH	10h	
AL	08h	
BH		value of the overscan register

Subfunction 09h – Read All Registers (VGA)

This function reads all 16 palette registers and the overscan register into a table. Bytes 0–15 of the table contain the values of the registers 0–15, and byte 16 of the table holds the value of the overscan register.

Register	Call value	Return value
AH	10h	
AL	09h	
DX		register table offset
ES		register table segment

Subfunction 10h – Write Video DAC Colour Register (VGA)

This function writes new colour values into the specified video DAC colour registers. Only the six lower bits are significant. There are 256 video DAC colour registers.

Register	Call value	Return value
AH	10h	
AL	10h	
BX	colour register number	
CH	green value	
CL	blue value	
DH	red value	

Subfunction 12h – Write Block of Video DAC Colour Registers (VGA)

This function loads one block of video DAC colour registers with the values indicated in a table. All 256 colour registers can thus be written at one time. Only the six lower bits of each table entry are significant.

Register	Call value	Return value
AH	10h	
AL	12h	
BX	first register to write	
CX	number of registers	
DX	table offset*)	
ES	table segment*)	

*) table entry structure:

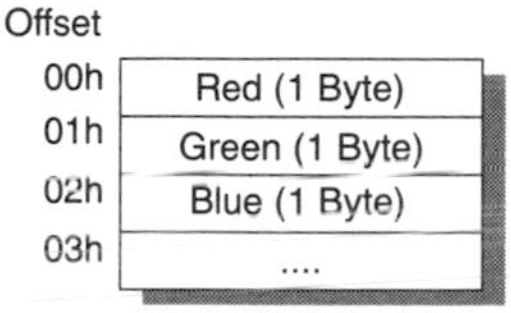

Subfunction 13h – Set Colour Select State of Attribute Controller (VGA)

This function sets the colour selection of the attribute controller. This is carried out by the colour select register and mode control register.

Register	Call value	Return value
AH	10h	
AL	13h	
BL	register selection*)	
BH	value of colour select register or bit 7	

*) 1=set colour select register, 0=set bit 7 of mode control register

Subfunction 15h – Read Video DAC Colour Register (VGA)

This function reads the value of the indicated video DAC colour register.

Register	Call value	Return value
AH	10h	
AL	15h	
BX	colour register number	
CH		green value
CL		blue value
DH		red value

Subfunction 17h – Read Block of Video DAC Colour Registers (VGA)

This function reads the values of a block of video DAC colour registers into a table. All 256 registers can thus be read at one time.

Register	Call value	Return value
AH	10h	
AL	17h	
BX	first register to read	
CX	number of registers	
DX	table offset*)	
ES	table segment*)	

*) table entry structure:

Offset	
00h	Red (1 Byte)
01h	Green (1 Byte)
02h	Blue (1 Byte)
03h	....

Subfunction 18h – Write Video DAC Mask Register (VGA)

This function loads the video DAC mask register with a new value.

Register	Call value	Return value
AH	10h	
AL	18h	
BL	new mask value	

Subfunction 19h – Read Video DAC Mask Register (VGA)

This function reads the video DAC mask register.

Register	Call value	Return value
AH	10h	
AL	19h	
BL		mask value

Subfunction 1ah – Read Colour Select Register of Attribute Controller (VGA)

This function reads the colour select register of the attribute controller.

Register	Call value	Return value
AH	10h	
AL	1ah	
BL		bit 7 of mode control register
BH		colour select register*)

*) bit 2 to 3, if BL=0; bit 0 to 3, if BL=1

Subfunction 1bh – Carry Out Grey Scale Mapping for a Block of Video DAC Colour Registers (VGA)

This function carries out a grey scale mapping for the colour values of a colour register block.

Register	Call value	Return value
AH	10h	
AL	1bh	
BX	first colour register	
CX	number of colour registers	

Function 11h – Interface to the Character Generator

This function serves as an interface to the character generator of the EGA and VGA. You may thus define your own character sets.

Subfunction 00h – Load User-Defined Character Definition Table for Text Mode (EGA/VGA)

This function loads a user-defined character definition table from the main memory into the character generator RAM. The character definition table holds the pixel pattern for each of the character codes. The video controller is not reprogrammed for an eventually new character height.

Register	Call value	Return value
AH	11h	
AL	00h	
BH	byte per defined character	
BL	table number in character generator RAM	
CX	number of defined characters	
DX	ASCII code of first defined character	
BP	offset of table in main memory	
ES	segment of table in main memory	

Subfunction 01h – Load 8*14 Character Definition Table From EGA/VGA ROM for Text Mode (EGA/VGA)

This function loads the 8*14 character definition table from EGA/VGA ROM into the character generator RAM. The character definition table holds the pixel pattern for each of the character codes. The video controller is not reprogrammed for an eventually new character height.

Register	Call value	Return value
AH	11h	
AL	01h	
BL	table number in character generator RAM	

Subfunction 02h – Load 8*8 Character Definition Table From EGA/VGA ROM for Text Mode (EGA/VGA)

This function loads the 8*8 character definition table from EGA/VGA ROM into the character generator RAM. The character definition table holds the pixel pattern for each of the character codes. The video controller is not reprogrammed for an eventually new character height.

Register	Call value	Return value
AH	11h	
AL	02h	
BL	table number in character generator RAM	

Subfunction 03h – Select Active Character Definition Table (EGA/VGA)

This function selects one of the loaded character definition tables in the character generator RAM for displaying characters on the monitor. With an EGA, bits 0 and 1 of the BL register determine the primary of four character tables, which is used if bit 3 of the character attribute is equal to 0. Bits 2 and 3 of register BL indicate the secondary character table, which the character generator uses if bit 3 of the character attribute is equal to 1. With a VGA, bits 0, 1, and 4 of the BL register determine the primary of eight character tables, which is used if bit 3 of the character attribute is equal to 0. Bits 2, 3, and 5 of register BL indicate the secondary character table, which the character generator uses if bit 3 of the character attribute is equal to 1. Bit 3 of the attribute byte determines the primary or scondary character tables only if you have disabled the blink attribute with INT 10h, function 10h, subfunction 03h.

Register	Call value	Return value
AH	11h	
AL	03h	
BL	value of character map select register*)	

*)

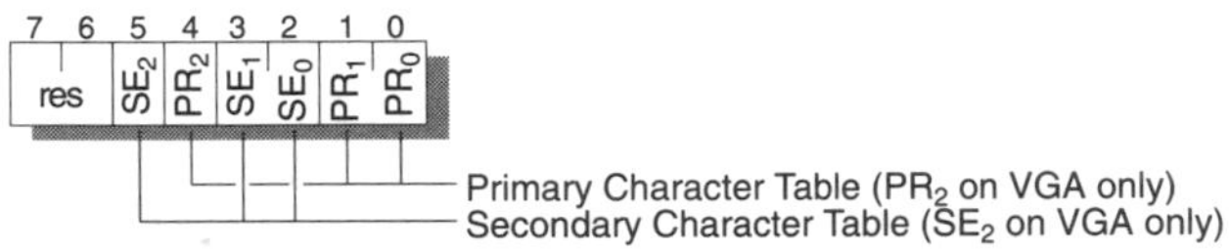

Subfunction 04h – Load 8*16 Character Definition Table From VGA ROM for Text Mode (VGA)

This function loads the 8*16 character definition table from VGA ROM into the character generator RAM. The character definition table holds the pixel pattern for each of the character codes. The video controller is not reprogrammed for an eventually new character height.

Register	Call value	Return value
AH	11h	
AL	04h	
BL	table number in character generator RAM	

Subfunction 10h – Load User-Defined Character Definition Table for Text Mode and Program CRT Controller (EGA/VGA)

This function loads the user-defined character definition table from main memory into the character generator RAM, and programs the CRT controller. The character definition table holds the pixel pattern for each of the character codes.

Register	Call value	Return value
AH	11h	
AL	10h	
BH	byte per defined character	
BL	table number in character generator RAM	
CX	number of defined characters	
DX	ASCII code of first defined character	
BP	offset of table in main memory	
ES	segment of table in main memory	

Subfunction 11h – Load 8*14 Character Definition Table From EGA/VGA ROM for Text Mode and Program CRT Controller (EGA/VGA)

This function loads the 8*14 character definition table from EGA/VGA ROM into the character generator RAM, and programs the CRT controller. The character definition table holds the pixel pattern for each of the character codes.

Register	Call value	Return value
AH	11h	
AL	11h	
BL	table number in character generator RAM	

Subfunction 12h – Load 8*8 Character Definition Table From EGA/VGA ROM for Text Mode and Program CRT Controller (EGA/VGA)

This function loads the 8*8 character definition table from EGA/VGA ROM into the character generator RAM, and programs the CRT controller. The character definition table holds the pixel pattern for each of the character codes.

Register	Call value	Return value
AH	11h	
AL	12h	
BL	table number in character generator RAM	

Subfunction 14h – Load 8*16 Character Definition Table From EGA/VGA ROM for Text Mode, and Program CRT Controller (VGA)

This function loads the 8*16 character definition table from VGA ROM into the character generator RAM, and programs the CRT controller. The character definition table holds the pixel pattern for each of the character codes.

Register	Call value	Return value
AH	11h	
AL	14h	
BL	table number in character generator RAM	

Subfunction 20h – Load 8*8 Character Definition Table From EGA/VGA ROM for INT 1fh in Graphics Mode (EGA/VGA)

This function loads the 8*8 character definition table from EGA/VGA ROM. The character definition table holds the pixel pattern for the character codes 80h to ffh (128 to 256) if the EGA/VGA carries out a CGA-compatible graphics mode.

Register	Call value	Return value
AH	11h	
AL	20h	
BP	offset of table in main memory	
ES	segment of table in main memory	

Subfunction 21h – Load User-Defined Character Definition Table for Graphics Mode (EGA/VGA)

This function loads the user-defined character definition table from main memory into the character generator RAM. The character definition table holds the pixel pattern for each of the character codes.

Register	Call value	Return value
AH	11h	
AL	21h	
BL	screen rows*)	
CX	bytes per defined character	
DL	screen rows (if BL=0)	
BP	offset of table in main memory	
ES	segment of table in main memory	

*) 0=DL valid, 1=14 screen rows, 2=25 screen rows, 3=43 screen rows

Subfunction 22h – Load 8*14 Character Definition Table From EGA/VGA ROM for Graphics Mode (EGA/VGA)

This function loads the 8*14 character definition table from EGA/VGA ROM into the character generator RAM. The character definition table holds the pixel pattern for each of the character codes.

Register	Call value	Return value
AH	11h	
AL	22h	
BL	screen rows*)	
DL	screen rows (if BL=0)	

*) 0=DL valid, 1=14 screen rows, 2=25 screen rows, 3=43 screen rows

Subfunction 23h – Load 8*8 Character Definition Table From EGA/VGA ROM for Graphics Mode (EGA/VGA)

This function loads the 8*8 character definition table from EGA/VGA ROM into the character generator RAM. The character definition table holds the pixel pattern for each of the character codes.

Register	Call value	Return value
AH	11h	
AL	23h	
BL	screen rows*)	
DL	screen rows (if BL=0)	

*) 0=DL valid, 1=14 screen rows, 2=25 screen rows, 3=43 screen rows

Subfunction 24h – Load 8*16 Character Definition Table From VGA ROM for Graphics Mode (VGA)

This function loads the 8*16 character definition table from VGA ROM into the character generator RAM. The character definition table holds the pixel pattern for each of the character codes.

Register	Call value	Return value
AH	11h	
AL	24h	
BL	screen rows*)	
DL	screen rows (if BL=0)	

*) 0=DL valid, 1=14 screen rows, 2=25 screen rows, 3=43 screen rows

Subfunction 30h – Determine Current Parameters of the Character Definition Table (EGA/VGA)

This function determines the current parameters of the indicated character definition table in EGA/VGA ROM.

Register	Call value	Return value
AH	11h	
AL	30h	
BH	character table*)	
CX		bytes per defined character
DL		screen rows
BP		offset of character definition table
ES		segment of character definition table

*) 0=content of INT 1fh, 1=content of 43h, 2=address of 8*14 ROM table
3=address of 8*8 ROM table, 4=address of second half of 8*8 ROM table
5=address of alternate 9*14 ROM table, 6=address of 8*16 ROM table,
7=address of alternate 9*16 ROM table

Function 12h – Configuration of Video Subsystem (EGA/VGA)

This function selects various configuration parameters for the EGA/VGA. Function 12h is often called alternate select.

Subfunction 10h – Determine Video Configuration (EGA/VGA)

This function determines the EGA or VGA configuration.

Register	Call value	Return value
AH	12h	
BL	10h	size of video RAM[1)]
BH		standard mode[2)]
CH		feature bits
CL		position of configuration switches

1) 0=64 kbytes, 1=128 kbytes, 2=192 kbytes, 3=256 kbytes
2) 0=colour, 1=monochrome

Subfunction 20h – Select Alternate Routine for Print Screen (EGA/VGA)

This function enables the alternate routine for print screen to support the new screen modes with more than 25 rows.

Register	Call value	Return value
AH	12h	
BL	20h	

Subfunction 30h – Set Scan Line Number for Text Mode (VGA)

This function defines the number of scan lines in text mode.

Register	Call value	Return value
AH	12h	
AL	scan lines*)	12h
BL	30h	

*) 0=200 scan lines, 1=350 scan lines, 2=400 scan lines

Subfunction 31h – Load Standard Palette (VGA)

This function defines whether the standard palette is to be loaded, or whether the current palette values should be kept if the video mode is changed by a call to INT 10h, function 00h.

Register	Call value	Return value
AH	12h	
AL	command code*)	12h
BL	31h	

*) 0=load standard palette, 1=do not load standard palette

Subfunction 32h – Control CPU Access to Video RAM and I/O Ports (VGA)

This function determines whether or not the CPU can access the video RAM and the corresponding I/O ports.

Register	Call value	Return value
AH	12h	
AL	command code*)	12h
BL	32h	

*) 0=access enabled, 1=access disabled

Subfunction 33h – Control Grey Scale Mapping (VGA)

This function determines whether or not the VGA carries out a grey scale mapping.

Register	Call value	Return value
AH	12h	
AL	command code*)	12h
BL	33h	

*) 0=enable grey scale mapping, 1=disable grey scale mapping

Subfunction 34h – Control Cursor Emulation (VGA)

This function determines whether or not the VGA is to carry out a cursor emulation. The BIOS then adjusts the start and end scan lines if the character size is changed (for example, by a change from 9*16 to 8*8 character matrix) so that the cursor keeps the same form. That is advantageous if, for example, you have defined the lines 14 and 15 as cursor scan lines for a 9*16 character matrix because these lines are nolonger valid for an 8*8 character matrix. Without cursor emulation the cursor would disappear from the screen.

Register	Call value	Return value
AH	12h	
AL	command code*)	12h
BL	34h	

*) 0=enable cursor emulation, 1=disable cursor emulation

Subfunction 36h – Enable or Disable the Monitor Control Signals (VGA)

This function enables or disables the monitor control signals by enabling or disabling the reading of the video RAM and transfer of the control signals to the monitor. A disable shortens the access time for several successive accesses to the video RAM.

Register	Call value	Return value
AH	12h	
AL	command code*)	12h
BL	35h	

*) 0=enable monitor control signals, 1=disable monitor control signals

Function 1ah – Video Combination (EGA/VGA)

Subfunction 00h – Determine Video Combination (EGA/VGA)

This function determines the current video combination of graphics adapter and monitor as it is set by means of the DIP switches of the adapter.

Register	Call value	Return value
AH	1ah	
AL	00h	1ah
BH		inactive combination*)
BL		active combination*)

*) see below

Subfunction 01h – Set Video Combination (EGA/VGA)

This function sets the current video combination of graphics adapter and monitor and stores the information in the BIOS data area.

Register	Call value	Return value
AH	1ah	
AL	01h	1ah
BH	inactive combination*)	
BL	active combination*)	

*) combination:

value	meaning
00h	no monitor connected
01h	MDA with monochrome monitor
02h	CGA with colour monitor
03h	reserved
04h	EGA with colour monitor
05h	EGA with monochrome monitor
06h	PGA (professional graphics adapter)
07h	VGA with analogue monochrome monitor
08h	VGA with analogue colour monitor
09h	reserved
0ah	MCGA with digital colour monitor
0bh	MCGA with analogue monochrome monitor
0ch	MCGA with analogue colour monitor
ffh	video system not recognized

Function 1bh – Determine Video BIOS Function Capabilities and Status Informations (VGA)

This function provides exhaustive information about the capabilities of your video BIOS by determining the VGA BIOS function capabilities and the corresponding status information, and storing them in a 64 byte buffer. After the function call, the buffer contains a pointer segment:offset to a 16 byte table with a description of the BIOS function capabilities, and to 60 bytes which describe the current video status.

Register	Call value	Return value
AH	1bh	
AL		1bh
BX	0	
DI	buffer offset	*)
ES	buffer segment	*)

*) buffer contents:

Offset	Size	Contents
00h	dword	address of table with BIOS function capabilities (segment:offset)
04h	byte	video mode
05h	word	number of displayed character columns
07h	word	length of displayed range of video RAM (in bytes)
09h	word	start address of upper left corner on monitor in video RAM
0bh	16 bytes	8 cursor positions (column:line) for 8 screen pages
1bh	byte	cursor end (scan line)
1ch	byte	cursor start (scan line)
1dh	byte	number of active screen page

1eh	word	I/O address of CRTC address register
20h	byte	value of mode select register (I/O address 3b8h/3d8h)
21h	byte	value of palette register (I/O address 3b9h/3d9h)
22h	byte	number of displayed character lines
23h	word	height of displayed character matrix in scan lines
25h	byte	code for active video combination
26h	byte	code for inactive video combination
27h	word	number of simultaneously displayed colours (monochrome: 0)
29h	byte	maximum number of screen pages
2ah	byte	number of scan lines: 0=200, 1=350, 2=400, 3=480
2bh	byte	character table if attribute bit 3 equal to 0 (VGA only)
2ch	byte	character table if attribute bit 3 equal to 1 (VGA only)
2dh	byte	general status information:

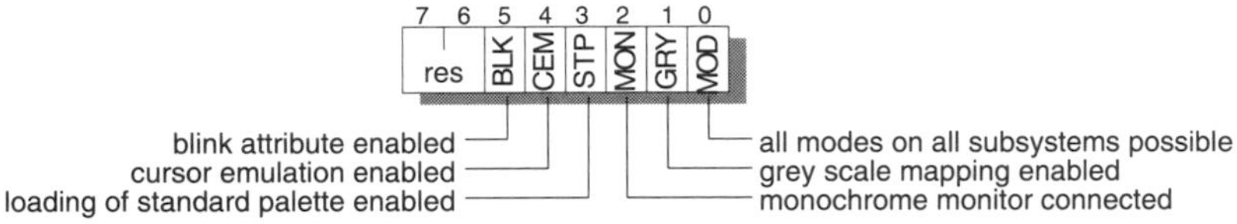

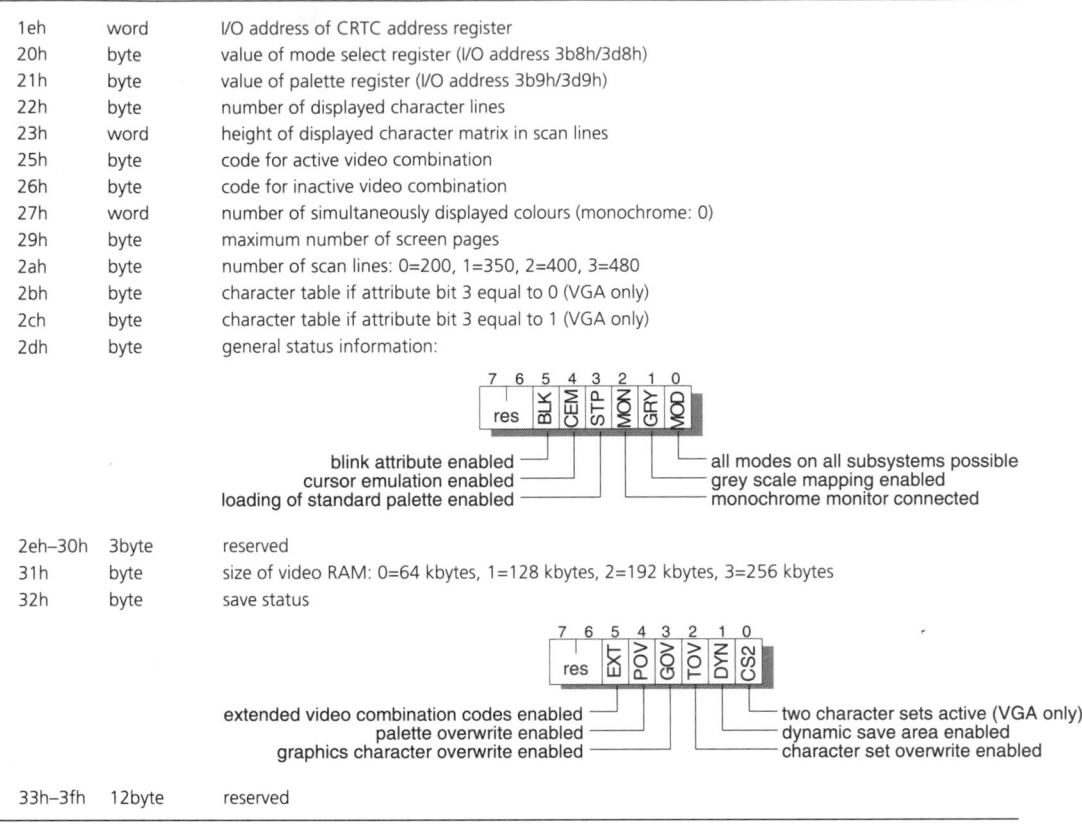

2eh–30h	3byte	reserved
31h	byte	size of video RAM: 0=64 kbytes, 1=128 kbytes, 2=192 kbytes, 3=256 kbytes
32h	byte	save status

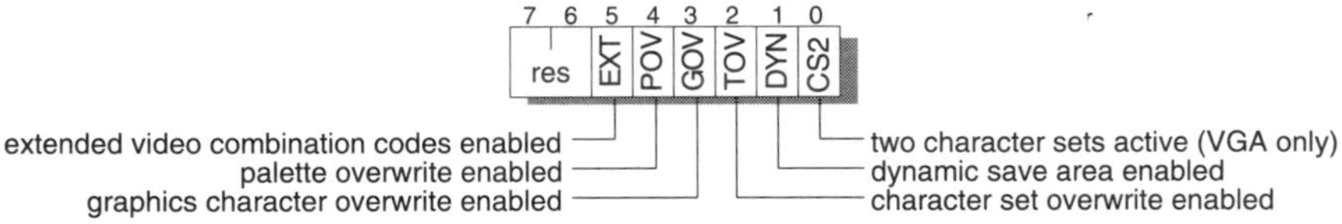

33h–3fh	12byte	reserved

Table of BIOS function capabilities

Offset	Size	Content
00h	byte	supported video modes

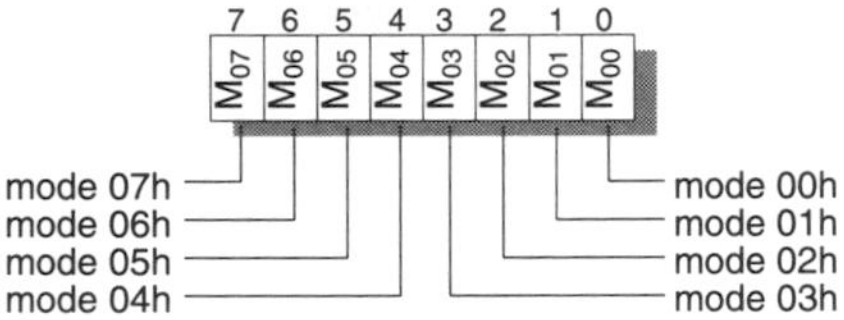

Offset	Size	Content
01h	byte	supported video modes

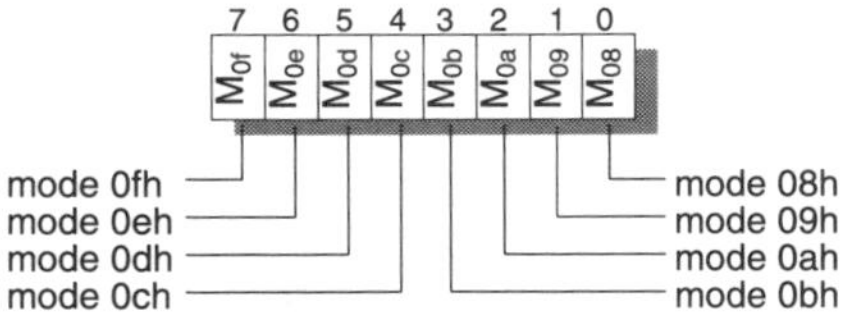

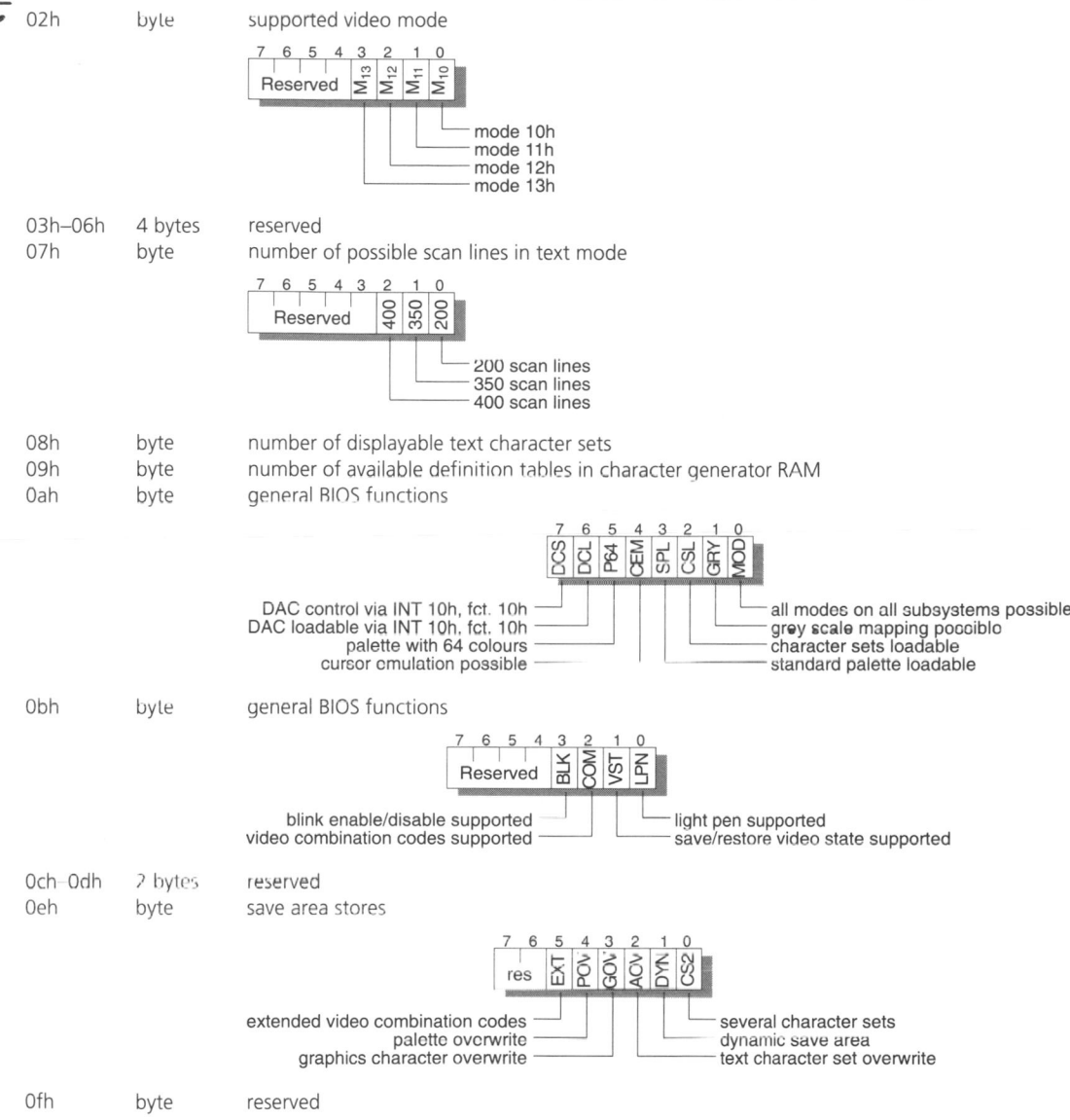

02h byte supported video mode

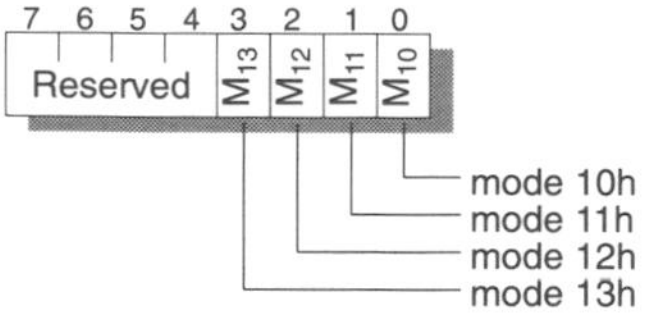

03h–06h 4 bytes reserved

07h byte number of possible scan lines in text mode

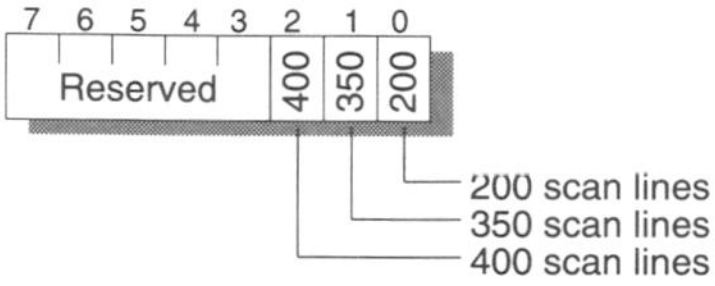

08h byte number of displayable text character sets

09h byte number of available definition tables in character generator RAM

0ah byte general BIOS functions

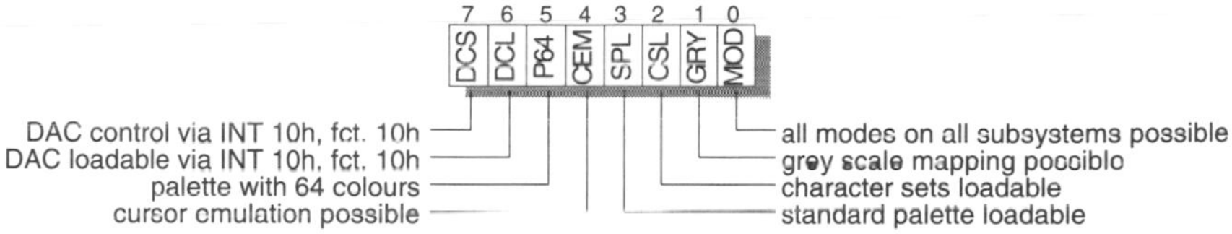

0bh byte general BIOS functions

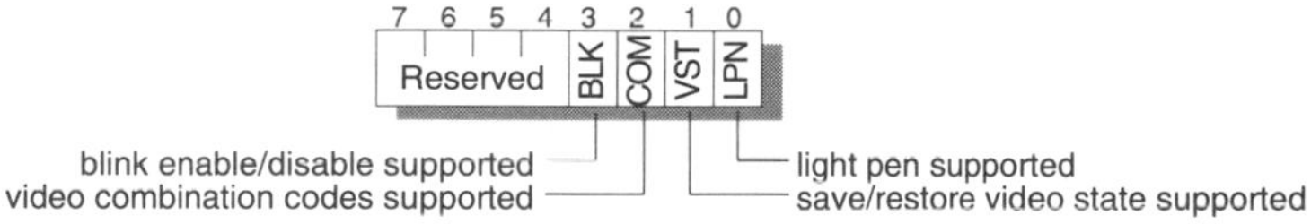

0ch–0dh 2 bytes reserved

0eh byte save area stores

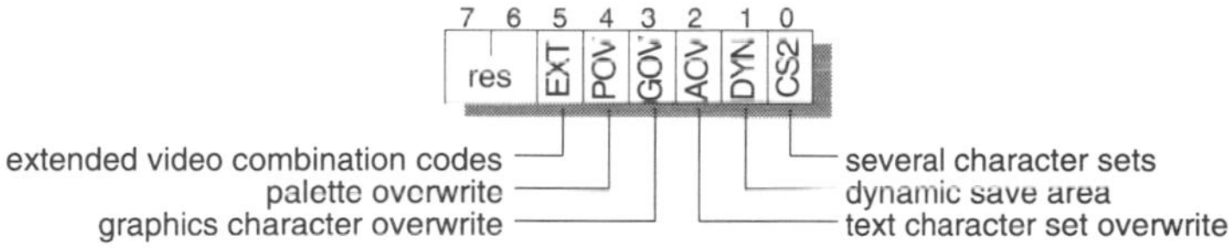

0fh byte reserved

Function 1ch – Save/Restore Video Status (VGA)

Subfunction 00h – Determine Size of Save/Restore Buffer (VGA)

This function returns the required size for the save/restore buffer to hold the specified status information.

Register	Call value	Return value
AH	1ch	
AL	00h	1ch
BX		buffer size in 64-byte blocks
CX	status information*)	

*)

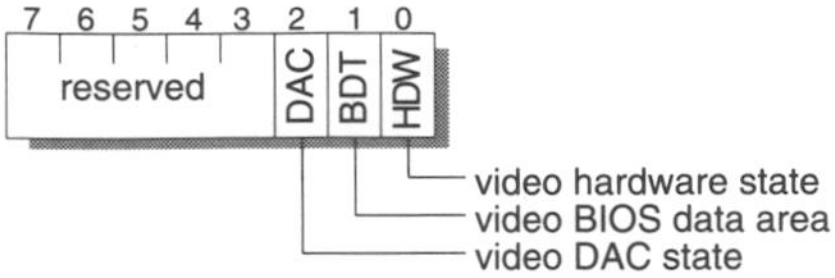

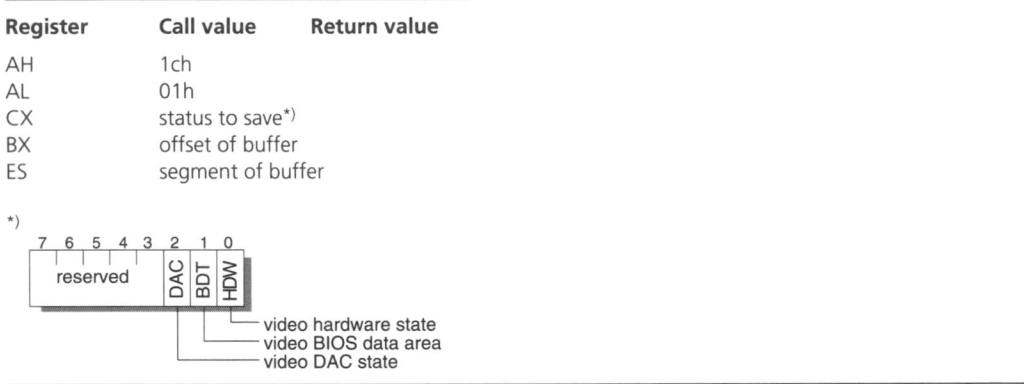

Subfunction 01h – Save Status (VGA)

This function saves the specified status in the save/restore buffer.

Register	Call value	Return value
AH	1ch	
AL	01h	
CX	status to save*)	
BX	offset of buffer	
ES	segment of buffer	

*)

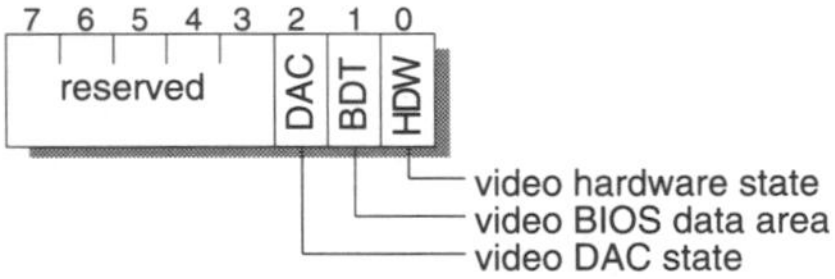

Subfunction 02h – Restore Status (VGA)

This function restores the specified status from the information in the save/restore buffer.

Register	Call value	Return value
AH	1ch	
AL	02h	
CX	status to restore*)	
BX	buffer offset	
ES	buffer segment	

*)

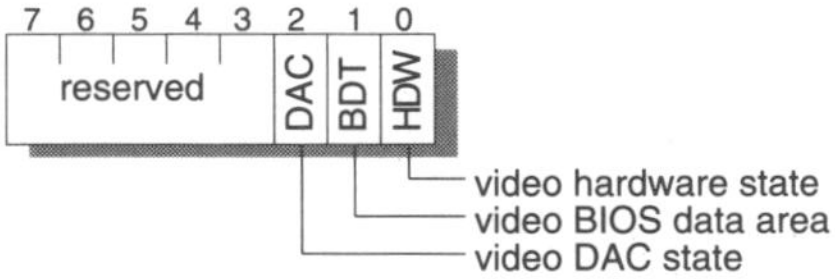

K.4 BIOS Interrupt INT 10h – Additional SVGA BIOS Functions

- The functions listed are located in the BIOS extension of SVGA adapters.
- The SVGA BIOS moves the entry point for the INT 10h handler of the system BIOS on the motherboard to INT 42h upon booting.
- The additional SVGA BIOS functions are accessed as subfunctions of function 4fh.

Function 4fh – Call SVGA BIOS Functions

Subfunction 00h – Determine SVGA Information

This function determines whether an SVGA BIOS is present, and if so, its current status.

Register	Call value	Return value
AH	4fh	status1)
AL	00h	4fh if function is supported
ES	segment of info buffer2)	
DI	offset of info buffer2)	

1) 00h=o.k., 01h=error
2) buffer structure:

Offset	Size	Content
00h	4 bytes	"VESA"
04h	word	version
06h	dword	far pointer to manufacturer's name
0ah	4 bytes	implemented functions
0eh	dword	far pointer to list of supported VESA and manufacturer video modes
12h	238 bytes	reserved

Subfunction 01h – Determine SVGA Mode Information

The function returns information regarding the SVGA modes in a 256 byte buffer.

Register	Call value	Return value
AH	4fh	status1)
AL	01h	4fh if function is supported
ES	segment of info buffer2)	
DI	offset of info buffer2)	

1) 00h=o.k., 01h=error
2) buffer structure:

Offset	Size	Content
00h	word	bit 0: 1=mode supported, bit 1: 1=optional information available at offset 12h, bit 2: 1=BIOS output supported, bit 3: 1=colour, 0=monochrome, bit 4: 1=graphics mode, 0=text mode, bits 5–15: reserved
02h	byte	A-window (bit 0: 1=A-window present, bit 1: 1=readable, bit 2: 1=writeable, bits 3–7: reserved)

03h	byte	B-window (bit 0: 1=B-window present, bit 1: 1=readable, bit 2: 1=writeable, bits 3–7: reserved)
04h	word	window granularity (smallest movability of windows in kbytes)
06h	word	window size in kbytes
08h	word	start segment of A-window
0ah	word	start segment of B-window
0ch	dword	far pointer to function for window positioning
10h	word	bytes per scan line
12h	word	display width in pixels (optional)
14h	word	display height in pixels (optional)
16h	word	width of character box in pixels (optional)
17h	word	height of character box in pixels (optional)
18h	word	number of memory planes
19h	word	number of bits per pixel
1ah	word	number of memory banks
1bh	word	memory model
1ch	word	bank size in kbyte

Subfunction 02h – Set SVGA Mode

This function sets one of the SVGA modes defined by VESA.

Register	Call value	Return value
AH	4fh	status*)
AL	02h	4fh if function is supported
BX	mode acc. to Table K.1	

*) 00h=o.k., 01h=error

Mode No.	Mode type	Text rows	Text columns	Resolution	Colours
100h	Graphic			640*400	256
101h	Graphic			640*480	256
102h	Graphic			800*600	16
103h	Graphic			800*600	256
104h	Graphic			1024*768	16
105h	Graphic			1024*768	256
106h	Graphic			1280*1024	16
107h	Graphic			1280*1024	256
108h	Text	60	80		
109h	Text	25	132		
10ah	Text	43	132		
10bh	Text	50	132		
10ch	Text	60	132		

Table K.1: SVGA video modes

Subfunction 03h – Determine SVGA Mode

This function determines the current SVGA mode.

Register	Call value	Return value
AH	4fh	status*)
AL	03h	4fh if function is supported
BX		mode acc. to Table K.1

*) 00h=o.k., 01h=error

Subfunction 04h – Save/Restore SVGA Video State

This function saves the state of the SVGA BIOS, or restores that state.

Partial Function 00h – Determine Required Buffer Size

Register	Call value	Return value
AH	4fh	status*)
AL	04h	4fh if function is supported
BX		number of required 64 byte blocks
DL	00h	

*) 00h=o.k., 01h=error

Partial Function 01h – Save Video State

Register	Call value	Return value
AH	4fh	status1)
AL	04h	4fh if function is supported
BX	buffer offset	
ES	buffer segment	
CX	flag2)	
DL	01h	

1) 00h=o.k., 01h=error

2) bit 0=save video hardware state, bit 1=save video BIOS data state, bit 2=save video DAC state, bit 3=save SVGA state

Partial Function 02h – Restore Video State

Register	Call value	Return value
AH	4fh	status[1)]
AL	04h	4fh if function is supported
BX	buffer offset	
ES	buffer segment	
CX	Flag[2)]	
DL	02h	

[1)] 00h=o.k., 01h=error

[2)] Bit 0=restore video hardware state, bit 1=restore video BIOS data state, bit 2=restore video DAC state, bit 3=restore SVGA state

Subfunction 05h – CPU Access to Video RAM

This function controls the access of the CPU to the video RAM by opening a window into the video RAM, or by reading its offset within the display memory. The CPU is then able to access the video RAM via the 64 kbyte address area located at address a0000h.

Partial Function 00h – Select Window Address Within Video RAM

Register	Call value	Return value
AH	4fh	status[1)]
AL	05h	4fh if function is supported
BH	00h	
DX	window address[2)]	

[1)] 00h=o.k., 01h=error

[2)] offset within video RAM in units of window granularities (see subfunction 00h)

Partial Function 00h – Determine Window Address Within Video RAM

Register	Call value	Return value
AH	4fh	status[1)]
AL	05h	4fh if function is supported
BH	01h	
BL		00h=A-window, 01h=B-window
DX		window address[2)]

[1)] 00h=o.k., 01h=error

[2)] offset within video RAM in units of window granularities (see subfunction 00h)

Subfunction 06h – Set/Determine Logical length of Scan Line

This function sets the length of a scan line in SVGA text mode, or determines this value. When you are setting that length, the value passed should be a multiple of the character box width.

Partial Function 00h – Set Length of Scan Line

Register	Call value	Return value
AH	4fh	status*)
AL	06h	4fh if function is supported
BL	00h	
CX	length in pixels	

*) 00h=o.k., 01h=error

Partial Function 01h – Determine Length of Scan Line

Register	Call value	Return value
AH	4fh	status*)
AL	06h	4fh if function is supported
BL	01h	
BX		bytes per scan line
CX		pixels per scan line
DX		max. number of scan lines

*) 00h=o.k., 01h=error

Subfunction 07h – Set/Determine SVGA Display Beginning in Video RAM

This function sets or determines the address of the pixel displayed in the upper left corner of the screen.

Partial Function 00h – Set Display Beginning

Register	Call value	Return value
AH	4fh	status*)
AL	07h	4fh if function is supported
BL	00h	
CX	first pixel of scan line	
DX	first scan line	

*) 00h=o.k., 01h=error

Partial Function 01h – Determine Display Beginning

Register	Call value	Return value
AH	4fh	status*)
AL	07h	4fh if function is supported
BL	01h	
BH		00h
CX		first pixel of scan line
DX		first scan line

*) 00h=o.k., 01h=error

L Functions 87h and 89h of Interrupt 15h

- Function 87h switches the processor to protected mode, moves a block of data so that extended memory is accessible, and resets the processor to real mode.
- Function 89h switches the processor to protected mode.

Function 87h – Move Block

This function moves a block of data in memory by switching the processor to protected mode, moving the block, and resetting the processor back to real mode. By means of this function, extended memory becomes accessible and data can be copied from standard memory to extended memory, and vice versa. The function moves the data in units of two bytes, or one word. In addition to the descriptors for source and target segments, the BIOS builds up the required four descriptors in the GDT. For this purpose the calling program has to reserve 48 bytes for a GDT with the entries needed. The source and target descriptors which comprise the entries segment limit (in bytes), base address and access rights (always equal to 93h) must be generated by the calling program. These have to be written into the 48 byte table at offset 10h and 18h, respectively. Note the differences between the 80286 and i386/i486/Pentium descriptors.

Register	Call value	Return value
AH	87h	1)
CX	number of words to copy	
SI	GDT offset2)	
ES	GDT segment2)	
carry		error if <> 0

1) 00h=move was successful, 01h= RAM parity error
02h=unexpected exception, 03h=error concerning address line A20
2) GDT structure:

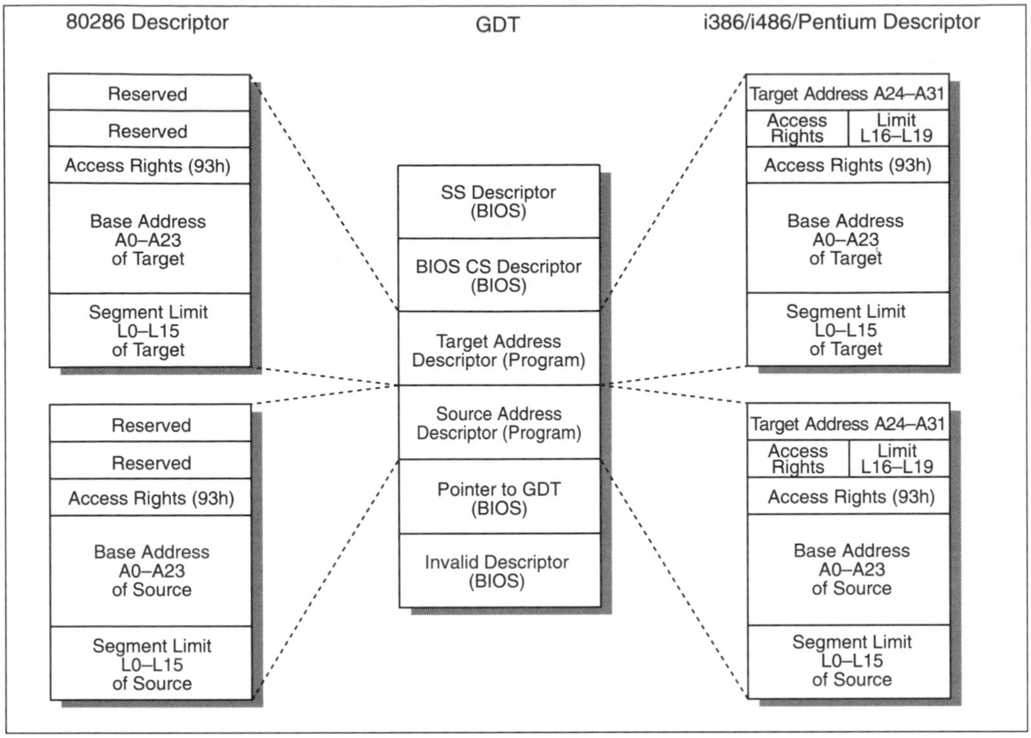

Function 89h – Switch to Protected Mode

This function switches the processor to protected mode and transfers the control to the code segment to which the GDT points. For this purpose, the GDT has to be built up in real mode by the calling program. The passed interrupt numbers for IRQ0 and IRQ8 are used to adjust the interrupt offsets of the 8259A PICs. Note that the processors 80286 and i386/i486/Pentium processors have different GDT formats. The function uses the entries in the GDT for initializing the IDTR and the SS register.

Register	Call value	Return value
AH	89h	*)
BH	interrupt number for IRQ0	
BL	interrupt number for IRQ8	
SI	GDT offset	
ES	GDT segment	
carry		error if <> 0

*) 00h=switch was successful, processor now in protected mode
ffh=switch was not successful, processor in real mode

M PCMCIA Socket Services

- The PCMCIA Socket Services are called with INT 1ah (functions 80h and above).
- INT 1ah also provides the interface for clock and date functions (DOS and Real-Time Clock).
- If the function returns with a set carry flag, an error has occurred and the ah register contains an error code.
- Reserved or undefined bits can be ignored when read, but must be set to a value of 0 when written.
- Section M.4 summarizes the PCMCIA Card Services.
- The window functions refer to the memory windows in the host's system memory.
- The page functions manage the offset within the PCMCIA card memory.

M.1 Function Groups

The socket services are subdivided into the following function groups.

- **Adapter Functions**
  Get Adapter Count (80h)
  Get Socket Service Info (83h)
  Inquire Adapter (84h)
  Get Adapter (85h)
  Set Adapter (86h)
  Get Vendor Info (9dh)
  Acknowledge Interrupt (9eh)
  Get/Set Prior Handler (9fh)
  Get/Set Socket Service Address (a0h)
  Get Access Offsets (a1h)
  Vendow Specific Function (aeh)

- **Socket Functions**
  Inquire Socket (8ch)
  Get Socket (8dh)
  Set Socket (8eh)
  Get Status (8fh)
  Reset Socket (90h)

- **Window Functions**
  Inquire Window (87h)
  Get Window (88h)
  Set Window (89h)
  Get Page (8ah)
  Set Page (8bh)

Error Detection Functions
Inquire EDC (95h)
Get EDC (96h)
Set EDC (97h)
Start EDC (98h)
Pause EDC (99h)
Resume EDC (9ah)
Stop EDC (9bh)
Read EDC (9ch)

M.2 The Functions

INT 1ah, Function 80h – GetAdapterCount

This function determines the number of installed socket service handlers and supported PCMCIA adapters in the system. CX returns the signature "SS" (Socket Service) if at least one handler is present. AL indicates the number of supported PCMCIA adapters (≥0).

Register	Call value	Return value
AH	80h	error code[1]
AL		number of PCMCIA adapters
CX		"SS"
Carry		error if <> 0

[1] see M.3

INT 1ah, Function 83h – Get Socket Service Info (GetSSInfo)

This function provides various items of information about a PCMCIA socket service handler.

Register	Call value	Return value
AH	83h	error code[1]
AL	adapter	'0'
BX		socket service revision[2]
CH		number of adapters supported by this socket service handler
CL		first adapter supported by this socket service handler
Carry		error if <> 0

[1] see M.3
[2] BCD

INT 1ah, Function 84h – InquireAdapter

This function returns information about a PCMCIA adapter in the system. The calling program must provide a buffer and store its size (without the first four bytes) in the entry (*buffer_length–4*) beginning at offset 00h. The socket service then returns at offset 02h the amount of information actually available. If that amount exceeds the buffer size, the information is truncated.

Register	Call value	Return value
AH	84h	error code[1]
AL	adapter	
BH		number of supported windows
BL		number of supported sockets
CX		number of EDC generators
(E)DI	buffer offset[2]	
ES	buffer segment[2]	
Carry		error if <> 0

1) see M.3

2) *Buffer structure:*

Offset	Size	Content
00h	word	buffer_size–4
02h	word	data size
04h	10 bytes	adapter table
0eh	word	number of power entries (num_ent)
10h	num_ent*(2 Bytes)	power entries

Adapter table:

Offset	Size	Content
04h	1 word	bit 0=1: indicators for write-protection, card lock, battery status, busy status and XIP status shared by all sockets of the adapter bit 0=0: indicators separately for each socket bit 1=1: power supply levels shared by all sockets bit 1=0: levels separately for each socket bit 2=1: data bus width equal for all adapter windows bit 2=0: data bus width adjustable separately for all adapter windows
06h	4 bytes	bit map of IRQ levels for active-high status change interrupt
0ah	4 bytes	bit map of IRQ levels for active-low status change interrupt

Power entry:

Offset	Size	Content
10h	1 byte	DC level in 1/10th of volt
	1 byte	bit 7=1: level for Vcc; bit 6=1: level for Vpp1; bit 5=1: level for Vpp2

INT 1ah, Function 85h – GetAdapter

This function returns the present adapter state.

Register	Call value	Return value
AH	85h	error code[1]
AL	adapter	
DH		adapter state[2]
DI		IRQ routing for status changes[3]
Carry		error if <> 0

[1] see M.3
[2] bit 0=1: power down; bit 0=0: enabled
bit 1=1: configuration information held; bit 1=0: information lost
[3] bit 6=1: IRQ for status change active-high; bit 7=0: IRQ active-low
bit 7=1: IRQ for status change enabled; bit 8=0: IRQ disabled

INT 1ah, Function 86h – SetAdapter

This function sets the adapter state.

Register	Call value	Return value
AH	86h	error code[1]
AL	adapter	
DH		adapter state[2]
DI		IRQ routing for status changes[3]
Carry		error if <> 0

[1] see M.3
[2] bit 0=1: power down; bit 0=0: enabled
bit 1=1: configuration information held; bit 1=0: information lost
[3] bit 6=1: IRQ for status change active-high; bit 7=0: IRQ active-low
bit 7=1: IRQ for status change enabled; bit 8=0: IRQ disabled
bits 4..0: IRQ level

INT 1ah, Function 87h – InquireWindow

This function provides information about a selected window. The calling program must supply a buffer and store its size (without the first four bytes) in the entry (*buffer_length–4*) beginning at offset 00h. The socket service then returns at offset 02h the actual amount of available information. If this amount exceeds the buffer size, the information is truncated.

Register	Call value	Return value
AH	87h	error code[1]
AL	adapter	
BH	window	
BL		window properties[2]
CX		socket (bit 0=socket 0 etc.)
(E)DI	buffer offset[3]	
ES	buffer segment[3]	
Carry		error if <> 0

1) see M.3

2) bit 0=1: window can map card memory into system memory
bit 1=1: window can map common card memory intp system memory
bit 2=1: window can map card I/O ports into system I/O address area
bit 7=1: window uses WAIT for wait states

3) *Buffer structure for memory window:*

Offset	Size	Content
00h	word	buffer_size–4
02h	word	data size
04h	13 bytes	window table

Table for memory window:

Offset	Size	Content
04h	1 word	bit 0=1: window base address programmable; bit 0=0: base address equal FirstByte bit 1=1: window size programmable, bit 1=0: size equal MinSize bit 2=1: window enable/disable without reprogramming bit 3=1: window can be programmed for 8-bit data bus bit 4=1: window can be programmed for 16-bit data bus bit 5=1: window base address must be an integer multiple of the window size bit 6=1: window size must be a power of 2 of ReqGran bit 7=1: card offsets must be specified in units of the window size bit 8=1: window can be subdivided into several pages bit 9=1: paging hardware shared by other windows, too bit 10=1: page enable/disable without reprogramming bit 11=1: page can be write-protected
06h	1 word	(FirstByte) window base address in system memory (usually a multiple of 4 kbytes)
08h	1 word	window end address in system memory (usually a multiple of 4 kbytes)
0ah	1 byte	(MinSize) min. window size (usually a multiple of 4 kbytes)
0bh	1 byte	max. window size (usually a multiple of 4 kbytes)
0ch	1 byte	(ReqGran) size of the window size unit as 2^{entry}
0dh	1 byte	alignment for window base address (as 2^{entry})
0eh	1 byte	alignment for card offset (as 2^{entry})
0fh	1 byte	slowest window access speed (01h=250 ns, 02h=200 ns, 03h=150 ns, 04h=100 ns)
10h	1 byte	quickest window access speed (01h=250 ns, 02h=200 ns, 03h=150 ns, 04h=100 ns)

Buffer structure for I/O windows:

Offset	Size	Content
00h	word	buffer_size–4
02h	word	data size
04h	11 bytes	window table

Table for I/O window:

Offset	Size	Content
04h	1 word	bit 0=1: window base address programmable; bit 0=0: base address equal FirstByte bit 1=1: window size programmable; bit 1=0: size equal MinSize bit 2=1: window enable/disable without reprogramming bit 3=1: window can be programmed for 8-bit data bus bit 4=1: window can be programmed for 16-bit data bus bit 5=1: window base address must be an integer multiple of the window size bit 6=1: window size a power of two of ReqGran bit 7=1: window supports INPACK bit 8=1: window supports I/O mapping as EISA bit 9=1: EISA I/O mapping ignored; bit 9=0: EISA I/O mapping enabled
06h	1 word	(FirstByte) window base address in system memory (usually a multiple of 4 kbytes)
08h	1 word	window end address in system memory (usually a multiple of 4 kbytes)
0ah	1 byte	(MinSize) min. window size (usually as a multiple of 4 kbytes)
0bh	1 byte	max. window size (usually as a multiple of 4 kbytes)
0ch	1 byte	(ReqGran) size of the window size unit as 2^{entry}
0dh	1 byte	number of address lines decoded by the window
0eh	1 byte	used for EISA I/O address decoding

INT 1ah, Function 88h – GetWindow

This function returns the present state of the indicated window.

Register	Call value	Return value
AH	88h	error code[1]
AL	adapter	
BH	window	
BL		socket
CX		window size[2]
DH		state[3]
DL		window access speed[4]
DI		window base[2]
Carry		error if <> 0

1) see M.3
2) I/O window: in bytes; memory window; in 4 kbytes
3) bit 0=1: card ports are mapped into system I/O address area; bit 0=0: card memory is mapped into system memory
bit 1=1: window active, mapping enabled
bit 2=1: 16-bit data bus width; bit 2=0: 8-bit data bus width
bit 3=1: memory window divided into 16-kbyte pages or I/O window uses EISA I/O mapping
bit 4=1: EISA I/O mapping enabled
4) (01h=250 ns, 02h=200 ns, 03h=150 ns, 04h=100 ns)

INT 1ah, Function 89h – SetWindow

This function sets the state of the window indicated.

Register	Call value	Return value
AH	89h	error code[1)]
AL	adapter	
BH	window	
BL	socket	socket
CX	window size[2)]	
DH	state[3)]	
DL	access speed[4)]	
DI	window size[2)]	
Carry		error if <> 0

1) see M.3
2) I/O window: in bytes; memory window; in 4 kbytes
3) bit 0=1: card ports are mapped into system I/O address area; bit 0=0: card memory is mapped into system memory
bit 1=1: window active, mapping enabled
bit 2=1: 16-bit data bus width; bit 2=0: 8-bit data bus width
bit 3=1: memory window divided into 16-kbyte pages or I/O window uses EISA I/O mapping
bit 4=1: EISA I/O mapping enabled
4) (01h=250 ns, 02h=200 ns, 03h=150 ns, 04h=100 ns)

INT 1ah, Function 8ah – GetPage

This function determines the present state of the addressed page. The returned offset indicates the card offset in 2'complement representation, which must be added to the system address to generate the address within the PCMCIA card.

Register	Call value	Return value
AH	8ah	error code[1)]
AL	adapter	
BH	window	
BL	page	
DL		page status[2)]
DI		offset[3)]
Carry		error if <> 0

1) see M.3
2) bit 0=1: card attribute memory mapped into system memory; bit 0=0: card common memory mapped into system memory
bit 1=1: page enabled
bit 2=1: page write-protected
3) in units of 4 kbytes

INT 1ah, Function 8bh – SetPage

This function sets the present state of the addressed page. The passed offset indicates the card offset in 2'complement representation, which is added to the system address to generate the address within the PCMCIA card.

Register	Call value	Return value
AH	8bh	error code[1)]
AL	adapter	
BH	window	
BL	page	
DL	page status[2)]	
DI	offset[3)]	
Carry		error if <> 0

[1)] see M.3
[2)] bit 0=1: card attribute memory mapped into system memory; bit 0=0: card common memory mapped into system memory
bit 1=1: page enabled
bit 2=1: page write-protected
[3)] in units of 4 kbytes

INT 1ah, Function 8ch – InquireSocket

This function provides information about the implemented functions of the addressed socket.

Register	Call value	Return value
AH	8ch	error code[1)]
AL	adapter	
BH		interrupt upon status change[2)]
BL	socket	
DH		callback upon status change[2)]
DL		supported indicators[3)]
(E)DI	buffer offset[4)]	
ES	buffer segment[4)]	
Carry		error if <> 0

[1)] see M.3
[2)] sources:
bit 0=1: write-protection
bit 1=1: card lock device
bit 2=1: card eject
bit 3=1: card insert
bit 4=1: BVD1 signal
bit 5=1: BVD2 signal
bit 6=1: RDY/BSY signal
bit 7=1: CDx signals

3) indicators:
bit 0=1: write-protection
bit 1=1: card lock device
bit 2=1: card eject
bit 3=1: card insert
bit 4=1: card lock
bit 5=1: BVDx signals
bit 6=1: RDY/BSY signal
bit 7=1: eXecute In Place active

4) *Buffer structure:*

Offset	Size	Content
00h	word	bit 0=1: memory-only interface
		bit 1=1: memory and I/O interface
02h	dword	bitmap of IRQ levels for an active-high status change interrupt
06h	dword	bitmap of IRQ levels for an active-low status change interrupt

INT 1ah, Function 8dh – GetSocket

This function provides information about the present state of the addressed socket.

Register	Call value	Return value
AH	8dh	error code[1]
AL	adapter	
BH		interrupt upon status change[2]
BL	socket	
CH		Vcc level
CL		Vpp level[3]
DH		status changes[2]
DL		indicator state[4]
DI		interface/IRQ[5]
Carry		error if <> 0

1) see M 3

2) activated interrupt sources and occurred status changes:
bit 0=1: write-protection
bit 1=1: card lock device
bit 2=1: card eject
bit 3=1: card insert
bit 4=1: BVD1 signal
bit 5=1: BVD2 signal
bit 6=1: RDY/BSY signal
bit 7=1: CDx signals

3) high-nibble: Vpp1; low-nibble: Vpp2

4) states:
bit 0=1: write-protection
bit 1=1: card lock device
bit 2=1: card eject
bit 3=1: card insert
bit 4=1: card lock
bit 5=1: BVDx signals
bit 6=1: RDY/BSY signal
bit 7=1: eXecute In Place active

5) bit 0..4: IRQ
bit 6=1: IREQ signal inverted (active-high IRQ); bit 6=0: IREQ signal not inverted
bit 7=1: IRQ enabled; bit 7=0: IRQ disabled
bit 8=1: memory-only interface
bit 9=1: memory and I/O interface

INT 1ah, Function 8eh – SetSocket

This function sets the present state of the addressed socket.

Register	Call value	Return value
AH	8eh	error code[1]
AL	adapter	
BH	status change interrupt[2]	
BL	socket	
CH	Vcc level	
CL	Vpp level[3]	
DH	status changes[2]	
DL	indicator state[4]	
DI	interface/IRQ[5]	
Carry		error if <> 0

1) see M.3
2) activated interrupt sources and occurred status changes:
bit 0=1: write-protection
bit 1=1: card lock device
bit 2=1: card eject
bit 3=1: card insert
bit 4=1: BVD1 signal
bit 5=1: BVD2 signal
bit 6=1: RDY/BSY signal
bit 7=1: CDx signals
3) high-nibble: Vpp1; low-nibble: Vpp2
4) states:
bit 0=1: write-protection
bit 1=1: card lock device
bit 2=1: card eject
bit 3=1: card insert
bit 4=1: card lock
bit 5=1: BVDx signals
bit 6=1: RDY/BSY signal
bit 7=1: eXecute In Place active
5) bit 0..4: IRQ
bit 6=1: IREQ signal inverted (active-high IRQ); bit 6=0: IREQ signal not inverted
bit 7=1: IRQ enabled; bit 7=0: IRQ disabled
bit 8=1: memory-only interface
bit 9=1: memory and I/O interface

INT 1ah, Function 8fh – GetStatus

This function returns the present status of various socket units.

Register	Call value	Return value
AH	8fh	error code[1]
AL	adapter	
BH		card status[2]
BL	socket	
DH		socket status[2]
DL		indicator state[4]
DI		interface/IRQ[5]
Carry		error if <> 0

[1] see M.3

[2] bit 0–1: write-protection
bit 1=1: card lock device
bit 2=1: card eject
bit 3=1: card insert
bit 4=1: BVD1 signal
bit 5=1: BVD2 signal
bit 6=1: RDY/BSY signal
bit 7=1: CDx signals

[3] high-nibble: Vpp1; low-nibble: Vpp2

[4] bit 4=1: card lock
bit 5=1: BVDx signals
bit 6=1: RDY/BSY signal
bit 7=1: eXecute In Place active

[5] bit 0..4: IRQ
bit 6=1: IREQ signal inverted (active-high IRQ); bit 6=0: IREQ signal not inverted
bit 7=1: IRQ enabled; bit 7=0: IRQ disabled
bit 8=1: memory-only interface
bit 9=1: memory and I/O interface

INT 1ah, Function 90h – ResetSocket

This function resets the addressed socket.

Register	Call value	Return value
AH	90h	error code[1]
AL	adapter	
BL	socket	
Carry		error if <> 0

INT 1ah, Function 95h – InquireEDC

This function provides information about the functional capabilities of the addressed EDC generator.

Register	Call value	Return value
AH	95h	error code[1]
AL	adapter	
BH	EDC	
CX		socket[2]
DH		EDC functions[3]
DL		EDC type[4]
Carry		error if <> 0

[1] see M.3
[2] bit 0=socket 0, bit 1=socket 1 etc.
[3] bit 0=1: unidirectional code generation
bit 1=1: bidirectional code generation
bit 2=1: EDC generation upon register (I/O) access
bit 3=1: EDC generation upon memory access
bit 4=1: EDC generation can be paused
[4] bit 0=1: 8-bit check code
bit 1=1: 16-bit SDLC check code (CRC)

INT 1ah, Function 96h – GetEDC

This function returns the present configuration of the EDC generator.

Register	Call value	Return value
AH	96h	error code[1]
AL	adapter	
BH	EDC	
BL		socket
DH		EDC functions[2]
DL		EDC type[3]
carry		error if <> 0

[1] see M.3
[2] bit 0=1: unidirectional code generation
bit 1=1: bidirectional code generation
[3] bit 0=1: 8-bit check code
bit 1=1: 16-bit SDLC check code (CRC)

INT 1ah, Function 97h – SetEDC

This function sets the present configuration of the addressed EDC generator.

Register	Call value	Return value
AH	97h	error code[1]
AL	adapter	
BH	EDC	
BL	socket	
DH	EDC functions[2]	
DL	EDC type[3]	
carry		error if <> 0

[1] see M.3
[2] bit 0=1: unidirectional code generation
bit 1=1: bidirectional code generation
[3] bit 0=1: 8-bit check code
bit 1=1: 16-bit SDLC check code (CRC)

INT 1ah, Function 98h – StartEDC

This function starts an EDC generator.

Register	Call value	Return value
AH	98h	error code[1]
AL	adapter	
BH	EDC	
carry		error if <> 0

[1] see M.3

INT 1ah, Function 99h – PauseEDC

This function pauses an EDC generator.

Register	Call value	Return value
AH	99h	error code[1]
AL	adapter	
BH	EDC	
Carry		error if <> 0

[1] see M.3

INT 1ah, Function 9ah – ResumeEDC

This function resumes a paused EDC generator.

Register	Call value	Return value
AH	9ah	error code[1]
AL	adapter	
BH	EDC	
Carry		error if <> 0

[1] see M.3

INT 1ah, Function 9bh – StopEDC

This function stops an EDC generator.

Register	Call value	Return value
AH	9bh	error code[1]
AL	adapter	
BH	EDC	
Carry		error if <> 0

[1] see M.3

INT 1ah, Function 9ch – ReadEDC

This function reads an EDC generator value.

Register	Call value	Return value
AH	9ch	error code[1]
AL	adapter	
BH	EDC	
CX		generator value
Carry		error if <> 0

[1] see M.3

INT 1ah, Function 9dh – GetVendorInfo

This function provides information about the vendor. The calling program must supply a buffer and store its size (without the first four bytes) in the entry (buffer_size–4) beginning at offset 00h. The socket service then returns at offset 02h the amount of actual information available. If this amount exceeds the buffer size, the information is truncated.

Register	Call value	Return value
AH	9dh	error code[1]
AL	adapter	
BL	info type[2]	
DX		version[3]
(E)DI	buffer offset[4]	
ES	buffer segment[4]	
Carry		error if <> 0

[1] see M.3

[2] presently only type 0 defined

[3] BCD format

[4] *Buffer structure:*

Offset	Size	Content
00h	word	buffer size – 4 (buf_siz–4)
02h	word	data size
04h	buf_siz-4	ASCIIZ string for vendor

INT 1ah, Function 9eh – AcknowledgeInterrupt

This function indicates which socket(s) of an addressed adapter has (have) experienced a status change.

Register	Call value	Return value
AH	9eh	error code[1]
AL	adapter	
CX		socket[2]
Carry		error if <> 0

[1] see M.3

[2] bit 0=socket 0, bit 1=socket 1, etc.

INT 1ah, Function 9fh – GetSetPriorHandler

This function determines (Get) the entry point of the previous handler for INT 1ah, or sets (Set) this entry point. It is thus possible, for example, to set the previous clock interrupt (INT 1ah, functions 00h–06h) and to remove the socket service from the handler chain.

Register	Call value	Return value
AH	9fh	error code[1]
AL	adapter	
BL	mode (0=Get, 1=Set)	
CX	handler segment (Set)	handler segment (Get)
DX	handler offset (Set)	handler offset (Get)
Carry		error if <> 0

[1] see M.3

INT 1ah, Function a0h – Get/Set Socket Service Address (GetSetSSAddr)

This function provides information about code and data for the socket service handler or passes data descriptors. The calling program must supply a buffer.

Register	Call value	Return value
AH	a0h	error code[1]
AL	adapter	
BH	mode[2]	
BL	subfunction[3]	
CX	data arrays[4] (Set)	data arrays[4] (Get)
(E)DI	buffer offset[5] (Set)	buffer offset[5] (Get)
ES	buffer segment[5] (Set)	buffer segment[5] (Get)
Carry		error if <> 0

[1] see M.3

[2] 00h=real mode, 01h=16:16 protected mode, 02h=16:32 protected mode, 03h=00:32 protected mode

[3] 00h=SS provides information about code and data in the buffer (Get)
01h=SS provides information about additional data in the buffer (Get)
02h=SS accepts an array with pointers to additional data in the buffer (Set)

[4] subfunction=00h: number of additional data areas (Get)
subfunction=01h: amount of information about additional data areas (Get)
subfunction=03h: number of pointers to additional data areas (Set)

[5] Buffer structure:

Subfunction=00h:

Offset	Size	Content
00h	dword	linear 32-bit base address of the code segment
04h	dword	code segment limit
08h	dword	offset of entry point
0ch	dword	linear 32-bit base address of the data segment
10h	dword	data segment limit
14h	dword	offset of data area

Subfunction=01h (one entry for each additional data segment):

Offset	Size	Content
00h	dword	linear 32-bit base address of the data segment
04h	dword	data segment limit
08h	dword	offset of data area

Subfunction=02h (one entry for each additional data segment):

Offset	Size	Content
00h	dword	32-bit offset
04h	dword	selector
08h	dword	reserved

INT 1ah, Function a1h – GetAccessOffsets

In a buffer, this function provides the offsets of an adapter-specific access routine to PCMCIA cards which allow an access to the card memory only through a register, that is, I/O ports (the usual method is mapping windows into the system memory). The calling program must supply a buffer.

Register	Call value	Return value
AH	a1h	error code[1]
AL	adapter	
BH	mode[2]	
CX	number of offsets[3]	
DX		number of offsets[4]
(E)DI	Offset buffer	
ES	Segment buffer	
Carry		error if <> 0

1) see M.3
2) 00h=real mode, 01h=16:16 protected mode, 02h=16:32 protected mode, 03h=00:32 protected mode
3) requested number of offsets
4) available number of offsets

INT 1ah, Function aeh – VendorSpecific

A call of this function leads in a defined way to a vendor-specific function. Vendors are allowed to implement the function in any way. With the exception of AH, AL and Carry, the use of all registers is vendor-specific, too.

Register	Call value	Return value
AH	aeh	error code[1]
AL	adapter	
Carry		error if <> 0

1) see M.3

M.3 Error Codes

Code	Name	Description
00h	SUCCESS	function completed successfully
01h	BAD_ADAPTER	invalid adapter address
02h	BAD_ATTRIBUTE	invalid attribute
03h	BAD_BASE	invalid base address of system memory
04h	BAD_EDC	invalid EDC generator
06h	BAD_IRQ	invalid IRQ level
07h	BAD_OFFSET	invalid PCMCIA card offset
08h	BAD_PAGE	invalid page
09h	READ_FAILURE	error while reading
0ah	BAD_SIZE	invalid size
0bh	BAD_SOCKET	invalid socket
0dh	BAD_TYPE	invalid window or interface type
0eh	BAD_VCC	invalid Vcc level index

Code	Name	Description
0fh	BAD_VPP	invalid Vpp1 or Vpp2 level index
11h	BAD_WINDOW	invalid window
12h	WRITE_FAILURE	error while writing
14h	NO_CARD	no PCMCIA card in the socket
15h	BAD_FUNCTION	invalid function
16h	BAD_MODE	mode not supported
17h	BAD_SPEED	invalid speed
18h	BUSY	socket or PCMCIA card busy

M.4 PCMCIA Card Services Summarized

- The Card Services provide a system-near interface for PCMCIA slots; calls to the card services are therefore system-dependent.
- For several processes in a system, the card services administer PCMCIA accesses to avoid access conflicts.
- For DOS in real mode (or real mode ROM BIOS), the card services are called through INT 1ah, function afh ([ah]=afh).

M.4.1 Card Services Functions

Code	Name	Description
00h	CloseMemory	closes a memory card area
01h	CopyMemory	copies data of a PCMCIA card
02h	DeregisterClient	removes a client from the list of registered clients
03h	GetClientInfo	provides information about a client
04h	GetConfigurationInfo	returns the configuration of a socket/PCMCIA card
05h	GetFirstPartition	returns information about the first partition of the card in a socket
06h	GetFirstRegion	returns information about the first region of the card in the socket
07h	GetFirstTuple	returns the first tuple of the specified type
08h	GetNextPartition	returns information about the next partition of the card
09h	GetNextRegion	returns information about the next region of the card
0ah	GetNextTuple	returns the next tuple of the specified type
0bh	GetCardServicesInfo	returns CS information (number of logical sockets, vendor etc.)
0ch	GetStatus	returns the present status of a PCMCIA card and the socket
0dh	GetTupleData	returns the content of the last passed tuple
0eh	GetFirstClient	returns the first client handle of the registered clients
0fh	RegisterEraseQueue	registers the erase queue of a client being serviced by the card services
10h	RegisterClient	registers a client for service by the card services
11h	ResetCard	resets the PCMCIA card in a socket
12h	MapLogSocket	maps a logical socket under card services to the physical adapter and socket values under socket services
13h	MapLogWindow	maps a window handle under card services to the physical adapter and window values under socket services

Code	Name	Description
14h	MapMemPage	maps a memory area of a PCMCIA card to a page in a window
15h	MapPhySocket	maps physical adapter and socket values under socket services to a logical socket under card services
16h	MapPhyWindow	maps physical adapter and window values under socket services to a window handle under card services
17h	ModifyWindow	modifies the attributes or access speed of a window
18h	OpenMemory	opens a memory card area
19h	ReadMemory	reads data from a PCMCIA card via a memory handle
1ah	RegisterMTD	registers a memory technology driver MTD
1bh	ReleaseIO	releases the previously requested I/O addresses
1ch	ReleaseIRQ	releases previously requested IRQs
1dh	ReleaseWindow	releases previously requested system memory block
1eh	ReleaseConfiguration	resets the socket configuration to memory-only interface
1fh	RequestIO	requests I/O addresses for a socket
20h	RequestIRQ	requets IRQ for a socket
21h	RequestWindow	request the mapping of a system memory block to a memory area of a PCMCIA card
22h	RequestSocketMask	requests callback upon a socket status change (event)
23h	ReturnSSEntry	returns the entry point into socket services
24h	WriteMemory	writes data via a memory handle onto a PCMCIA card
25h	DeregisterEraseQueue	removes a previously registered erase queue
26h	CheckEraseQueue	informs about new queue entries
27h	ModifyConfiguration	modifies a socket and PCMCIA card configuration
28h	RegisterTimer	registers a timer for issuing a callback (Events)
29h	SetRegion	sets the properties of a PCMCIA card area
2ah	GetNextClient	returns the client handle for the next registered client
2bh	ValidateCIS	validates the card information structure (CIS) of a PCMCIA card
2ch	RequestExclusive	requests the exclusive use of a PCMCIA card in a socket
2dh	ReleaseExclusive	releases the exclusive use of a card in a socket
2eh	GetEventMask	returns the bit map mask for issuing an event
2fh	ReleaseSocketMask	releases the previously defined event mask for a socket
30h	RequestConfiguration	configures the PCMCIA card in a socket
31h	SetEventMask	changes the event mask
32h	AddSocketServices	adds a new SS handler below the socket service level
33h	ReplaceSocketServices	replaces an existing socket service handler by a new one
34h	VendorSpecific	(vendor-dependent)
35h	AdjustResourceInfo	reads or adjusts the available resources
36h	AccessConfigurationRegister	accesses a PCMCIA configuration register

M.4.2 Events

Events are reported by the socket services to the clients. Usually, events are status changes of a socket or the inserted card.

Code	Event	Description
01h	BATTERY_DEAD	battery dead, data lost
02h	BATTERY_LOW	battery low, data still o.k.
03h	CARD_LOCK	mechanical lock has locked the inserted card
04h	CARD_READY	RDY/$\overline{\text{BSY}}$ signal has changed from busy to ready
05h	CARD_REMOVAL	card has been removed from a PCMCIA socket
06h	CARD_UNLOCK	mechanical lock has released the inserted card
07h	EJECTION_COMPLETE	card has been ejected from the socket by an automatic ejection device
08h	EJECTION_REQUEST	card should be ejected from the socket by an automatic ejection device
09h	INSERTION_COMPLETE	card has been inserted into the socket by an automatic insertion device
0ah	INSERTION_REQUEST	card should be inserted into the socket by an automatic insertion device
0bh	PM_RESUME	power management should power-up socket and card
0ch	PM_SUSPEND	power management should power-down socket and card
0dh	EXCLUSIVE_COMPLETE	client has been granted an exclusive access to a PCMCIA card
0eh	EXCLUSIVE_REQUEST	client attempts to get an exclusive access to a PCMCIA card
0fh	RESET_PHYSICAL	hardware reset for a PCMCIA card in a socket
10h	RESET_REQUEST	client has requested a hardware reset for a PCMCIA card in a socket
11h	CARD_RESET	hardware reset for the card in a socket completed
14h	CLIENT_INFO	client should return information
15h	TIMER_EXPIRED	timer expired
16h	SS_UPDATED	socket support via socket services has been changed
17h	WRITE_PROTECT	write-protect status for the PCMCIA card which is inserted in the socket has changed
40h	CARD_INSERTION	a PCMCIA card has been inserted
80h	RESET_COMPLETE	reset in the background complete
81h	ERASE_COMPLETE	erase in the background complete
82h	REGISTRATION_COMPLETE	registration in the background complete

M.4.3 Error Codes

Code	Name	Description
00h	SUCCESS	function completed successfully
01h	BAD_ADAPTER	adapter invalid
02h	BAD_ATTRIBUTE	attribute invalid
03h	BAD_BASE	system memory base invalid
04h	BAD_EDC	EDC generator invalid
05h	—	reserved
06h	BAD_IRQ	IRQ level invalid
07h	BAD_OFFSET	PCMCIA card offset invalid
08h	BAD_PAGE	page invalid
09h	READ_FAILURE	error while reading
0ah	BAD_SIZE	invalid size

Code	Name	Description
0bh	BAD_SOCKET	invalid socket
0ch	—	reserved
0dh	BAD_TYPE	window or interface type invalid
0eh	BAD_VCC	Vcc level index invalid
0fh	BAD_VPP	Vpp1 or Vpp2 level index invalid
10h	—	reserved
11h	BAD_WINDOW	window invalid
12h	WRITE_FAILURE	error while writing
13h	—	reserved
14h	NO_CARD	no PCMCIA card in socket
15h	UNSUPPORTED_FUNCTION	function not supported
16h	UNSUPPORTED_MODE	mode not supported
17h	BAD_SPEED	speed invalid
18h	BUSY	socket or PCMCIA card busy
19h	GENERAL_FAILURE	undefined error occurred
1ah	WRITE_PROTECTED	medium write-protected
1bh	BAD_ARG_LENGTH	function argument length invalid
1ch	BAD_ARGS	one or more function arguments invalid
1dh	CONFIGURATION_LOCKED	configuration already locked
1eh	IN_USE	resource already in use
1fh	NO_MORE_ITEMS	no more of the requested items
20h	OUT_OF_RESOURCE	no more resources
21h	BAD_HANDLE	handle invalid

Glossary

1"

Abbreviation for 1 inch; equals 2.54 cm.

14.318.180 Hz

This frequency forms the base clock in the PC/XT. Dividing by three generates the processor frequency of the 8086/88. For compatibility reasons, this frequency is still used today for the timer chips and the real-time clock after dividing by twelve.

16450/16550

The improved successor of the UART 8250. It is used in the AT and newer PC models, and enables a transmission rate of up to 115.200 baud. The 16550 additionally has a FIFO buffer.

38600DX/38600SX

An i386-compatible processor from Chips & Technologies with a new operating mode for reducing power consumption, the SuperState V Mode. The 38600SX has only a 16-bit data bus and a 24-bit address bus. Unlike the 38605DX/38605SX, no cache is implemented.

38605DX/38605SX

An i386-compatible processor from Chips & Technologies with an internal instruction cache and a new operating mode for reducing power consumption, the SuperState V Mode. The 38605SX has only a 16-bit data bus and a 24-bit address bus.

386SL

An Intel chip set which comprises the 386SL and the 82360SL I/O-subsystem. The 386SL integrates an i386 CPU, a cache controller and tag RAM, an ISA bus controller and a memory controller on a single chip. On the 82386SL a real-time clock, two timers with three channels each, a memory decoder, two DMA controllers, a parallel interface, two interrupt controllers, and two serial interfaces are integrated. With the 386SL chip set, very compact notebook ATs can be constructed.

386SLC

An i386-compatible processor from IBM with significantly increased performance compared to Intel's original. The 386SLC includes an internal 8 kbyte cache and is implemented in a power-saving static design. Currently, the 386SLC is not freely supplied, but reserved by IBM for its own products.

4.77 MHz

This frequency was the processor clock for the 8088/86 in the original PC/XT.

486DLC/486SLC

An i386-compatible and power-saving CMOS processor from Cyrix. Unlike its Intel counterparts, it incorporates an internal 1 kbyte cache, an enhanced processor kernel similar to the i486, and an internal power management unit for reducing power consumption. The SLC is the SX-model of the DLC with a 16-bit data bus and a 24-bit address bus.

640 kbyte boundary
In the PC the video RAM and various ROMs are located at the upper end of the real mode address space. They normally start at address a0000h. With DOS only the lower 640 kbytes of memory are available for operating system, drivers, and application programs.

6502
A common 8-bit microprocessor for CP/M, which was mainly used as the CPU in the legendary C64.

68000 family
A CISC processor family from Motorola, which is mainly used in Apple computers. They are the counterparts to the Intel 80x86 family.

6845
A graphics controller chip or CRTC, which is used in various forms in nearly all graphics adapters. Besides other jobs, it generates the control and synchronization signals for the monitor.

8042
A microchip used as a keyboard controller in the AT.

8048
A microchip used as a keyboard chip in PC/XT keyboards.

8080/85
A well-known 8-bit processor for CP/M, and the predecessor of the 8086/88.

8086
A 16-bit processor with 16-bit registers, a 16-bit data bus, and a 20-bit address bus. It is employed in the XT, and is the ancestor of the 80x86 family. The 8086 operates in real mode only. The address space comprises 1 Mbyte.

8088
A 16-bit processor with 16-bit registers, a 16-bit data bus, and a 20-bit address bus. It is used in the PC, and apart from the smaller data bus width is identical to the 8086.

80186/88
These processors are the successors to the 8086/88. Besides improved and extended instructions, an interrupt controller, a DMA chip and a timer chip are integrated on the 80186/88.

80286
The second generation of the 80x86 family. The 80286 represents a 16-bit processor with 16-bit registers, a 16-bit data bus, and a 24-bit address bus. With the 80286 protected mode was introduced, in which an address space of up to 16 Mbytes is enabled.

80287/80287XL
The mathematical coprocessor for the 80286. The 80287XL is improved compared to the normal 80287, and has all i387 functions.

80386/80386SX
Another name for i386DX/i386SX (see i386/i386SX).

80387/80387SX
Another name for i387/i387SX (see i387/i387SX).

80486/80486SX
Another name for i486DX/i486SX (see i486/i486SX).

80486DX2
Another name for i486DX2 (see i486DX2).

80487SX
Another name for i487 (see i487).

80586
A rather uncommon name for the Pentium.

8087
The mathematical coprocessor for the 8086/88.

80x86 family
The family of the downward-compatible 80x86 chips. Presently, the family comprises the 8086/88, 80186/88, 80286, i386/i386SX, i486/i486SX, and Pentium. They all are CISC processors with an extensive and microencoded instruction set.

82072A
A floppy disk controller for the AT.

82077A
A floppy disk controller for the PS/2 with a microchannel, and the successor to the 82072A.

82284
The clock generator for the 80286.

82288
The bus controller for the 80286.

8237A
An 8-bit DMA controller with four independently programmable DMA channels. In the PC/XT one such chip is present; in the AT two chips are cascaded so that seven DMA channels are available.

82450
A UART chip and improved successor to the 8250 for the AT.

82489DX
The Advanced Programmable Interrupt Controller (APIC) for supporting the Pentium and multiprocessor systems. It can operate up to 50 MHz and is the successor of the 8259A.

82491
An 256 kbit SRAM Module for an L2-cache with the 82496 cache controller.

82496
A cache controller for an L2-cache with 82491 SRAM modules. Its external interface is optimized for cooperation with the Pentium.

8250
A UART chip used in the PC/XT. There are several versions with the names 8250, 8250A, 8250B, and 8250C.

8253
A programmable interval timer (PIT) with three independent counters. The 8253 is used in the PC/XT and in many ATs.

8254
A programmable interval timer (PIT) with three independent counters, and the improved successor to the 8253. The 8254 is used in most ATs, and in EISA and microchannel PCs.

8255A
A programmable peripheral interface (PPI) with three 8-bit ports A, B, and C. Port C can be divided into two nibbles that extend ports A and B by four bits. The 8255A was used in the PC/XT for reading DIP switches and for transferring the scan codes from the PC/XT keyboard. The 8255A is not used in the AT any more.

8259A
A programmable interrupt controller (PIC) with eight different interrupt lines. In the PC/XT one such chip is used; in the AT two 8259As are cascaded so that here 15 different interrupt levels are available.

8284
The clock generator for the 8086/88 and 80186/88.

8288
The bus controller for the 8086/88 and 80186/88.

8514/A
An IBM graphics adapter with an in-built graphics processor.

8741
A microchip often used as a keyboard controller in the AT.

8742
A microchip often used as a keyboard controller in the PS/2.

ABIOS
Abbreviation for **A**dvanced **BIOS**. The ABIOS of the PS/2 comprises the BIOS routines for the PC operation in protected mode.

Abort
An exception which leads to an abortion of the task because it is not possible to recover from the exception. An abort typically occurs if the calling of a exception handler leads to another exception.

Access Time
The time period between the supply of an access signal and the output or acceptance of the data by the addressed subsystem. Examples are the access times for DRAMs, SRAMs, or hard disks.

Accumulator
A CPU register which is optimized for the execution of some instructions. In former processors the accumulator was the only register that could be used as the instruction destination, i.e. for providing the operation result.

ACK
Abbreviation for **ack**nowledge.

active-high
A signal is called active-high if a high potential level has the effect or shows the status which is indicated by the signal's name. For example, the 8086's READY signal is active-high because a high potential level indicates that the addressed unit is ready. On the other hand, a low level states that the unit is not ready yet.

active-low
A signal is called active-low if a low potential level has the effect or shows the status which is indicated by the signal's name. For example, the 8086's $\overline{RD}$ signal is active-low because a low potential level indicates that data is being read. On the other hand, a high level states that data is being written. Active-low signals are usually characterized by a cross bar ($\overline{RD}$), a preceding slanted line (/RD), a succeeding star (RD*), or in a few cases, by a succeeding tilde (RD~).

Actuator
Comprises all components of a drive necessary for positioning the read/write head. Normally, these are at least the access arm and the access motor.

Adapter Card
Also called an extension card or plug-in card. A board with electronic circuitry which is inserted into a bus slot to enhance the capabilities of the PC. Typical representatives are interface adapter cards, graphics adapter cards, and controller cards.

ADC
Abbreviation for **a**nalogue to **d**igital **c**onverter. An ADC converts an analogue signal into a predetermined number of bits, which represent the value of the analogue signal.

Address
A quantity which describes the location of an object. Specifically, an address is a word or a number that characterizes a storage location or a port.

Address Bus
A number of generally parallel lines that transmit an address.

Address Space
The number of objects that a CPU or another chip can address.

ALU
Abbreviation for **A**rithmetical and **L**ogical **U**nit. The ALU is part of a CPU, and executes the arithmetical and logical operations.

Am386DX/Am386SX
An i386-compatible processor from AMD with increased performance compared to Intel's original. The Am386SX only has a 16-bit data bus and a 24-bit address bus.

Am386DXL/Am386SXL
An i386-compatible processor from AMD with increased performance compared to Intel's original and a power-saving static design. The Am386SXL has only a 16-bit data bus and a 24-bit address bus.

Am386DXLV/Am386SXLV
The **L**ow-**V**oltage model of AMD's Am386DX/SX. The Am386DXLV operates at only 3.3 V, and therefore consumes 50% less power. The Am386SXLV has only a 16-bit data bus and a 24-bit address bus.

Am486DX/SX
AMD's 486DX-compatible and 486SX-compatible microprocessor, respectively.

Am486DXLV/SXLV
The **L**ow-**V**oltage model of AMD's Am486DX/SX. The Am486DXLV operates at only 3.3 V, and therefore consumes 50% less power.

Am486DX2
AMD's 486DX/2-compatible microprocessor with internal clock doubling.

AMD
Abbreviation for **A**dvanced **M**icro **D**evices. A US firm that produces microelectronic components such as processors, ASICs, RAM chips, etc. AMD became known through its Intel-compatible 80x86 and 80x87 processors, and it could win a considerable market share with its 386 clones.

Analogue
Without intermediate steps, continuously. An analogue signal, for example, can have continuous values without intermediate steps.

Analogue Monitor
A monitor for displaying text or graphics which is driven by an analogue signal. A VGA adapter would be an example of a graphics adapter that drives an analogue monitor.

ANSI
Abbreviation for **A**merican **N**ational **S**tandards **I**nstitute. An authority in the US that sets up technical standards. ANSI is comparable with the German DIN.

APIC
See 82489DX.

Arbitration
The transfer of control over a unit from the present holder of the control rights to another unit that wants to take over control. This is done by arbitration signals and an arbitration strategy.

Architecture
The overall concept for the design and structure of a computer or a computer system.

ARLL
Abbreviation for **A**vanced **RLL**. An RLL recording method which operates with a more complex encoding than RLL 2,7, and thus enables higher data densities. Compared to MFM, ARRL achieves an increase of up to 90%.

ASCII code
Abbreviation for **A**merican **S**tandard **C**ode for **I**nformation **I**nterchange. A 7-bit code that encodes 32 control characters for data transfer, and additionally 96 alphanumeric characters.

ASCIIZ string
A string that is terminated by the ASCII character \0, i.e. a null.

ASIC
Abbreviation for **A**pplication **S**pecific **IC**. An integrated circuit focused to a specific application. ASICs are often manufactured by gate arrays.

ASPI
Abbreviation for **A**dvanced **S**CSI **P**rogramming **I**nterface. A standardized software interface to SCSI devices. ASPI has been developed by Adaptec.

Assembler
A program that translates mnemonic code and symbolic addresses into machine code. Assemblers are the programming option which is closest to the machine and still accepts symbolic addresses and quantities.

Associative Memory
See CAM.

Asynchronous
Not corresponding to a phase or clock signal, or without a clock signal.

AT
1. Abbreviation for **A**dvanced **T**echnology.
2. The successor of the PC/XT with an 80286 CPU and 16-bit bus slots.

AT bus
The AT bus system with various support chips (DMA, PIC, PIT, etc.) and a 16-bit bus slot. The AT bus is strictly defined by ISA.

ATA
Abbreviation for **AT A**ttachment. A standard for mainly connecting hard disk drives to an AT bus; synonymous with IDE.

Attribute

1. A quantity which is added to another quantity, and which further defines the properties of this quantity.
2. The high byte of the video word which has information on the brightness, colour and background of the character to be displayed. The character code is stored in the low byte of the video word.

Autopark

A function of better quality hard disk drives which moves the actuator and the read/write heads into the park position upon switching off the drive. Any damage of the data medium can thus be prevented.

AUX

Abbreviation for **aux**iliary. With DOS synonymous with COM1, else generally an additional signal or an additional line.

Average Access Time

The average value for the time period between the output of an access instruction and the delivery of the data. The average access time is mainly used to characterize the speed of the positioning mechanism in hard disk drives and similar mass storages devices.

Bad Sector Mapping

The logical replacement of defective sectors or tracks by intact spare sectors or spare tracks when formatting the drive. This is done either by shifting the sectors within one track (sector slipping), or by diverting the accesses to the corresponding spare track if the defects are too serious. The capacity of the hard disk drive can thus be maintained in spite of defective spots. The bad sector mapping is carried out by the controller, and therefore transparent for BIOS, DOS and all other software.

BASIC

Abbreviation for **B**eginners **A**ll-purpose **S**ymbolic **I**nstruction **C**ode. A very simple structured programming language with easy to remember instruction names like »PRINT«. Very often, BASIC is implemented in the form of an interpreter, but nowadays there exist several powerful BASIC compilers which have some structural elements of C or Pascal.

Baud Rate

The number of state changes of a transmission channel per second. On binary data channels the baud rate is usually equal to the number of transmitted bits per second (bps).

BCD

Abbreviation for **B**inary **C**oded **D**ecimal. BCD encodes a decimal digit as a binary value of one byte. Example: BCD = 04h corresponds to decimal 4. BCD wastes a lot of storage because one byte is able to encode 256 different values, but BCD uses only ten (0–9) of them.

Bidirectional

In the case of a bidirectional transmission, data can be exchanged in either direction between the communication participants. Thus the two participants can serve both as a transmitter and a receiver.

Big Blue
Nickname for IBM, because IBM is a big business group and the company's emblem is blue.

Big Endian Format
In the big endian format the high bytes of a multiple-byte quantity are stored at lower addresses, and the low bytes are stored at higher addresses. Motorola's 68000 family uses the big endian format.

BIOS
Abbreviation for **B**asic **I**nput/**O**utput **S**ystem. The BIOS comprises the system programs for the basic input and output operations, and represents the software interface to the PC hardware. Typical BIOS functions are accesses to the floppy disk, hard disk drive, interfaces, and graphics adapters.

BIST
Abbreviation for **B**uilt-**I**n **S**elf-**T**est. A test function of microchips, implemented by hardware or microcode (or both). The BIST is typically carried out at power-up or through the RUNBIST command of the boundary scan test. It checks more or less all chip components and writes a check code into a register.

Bit
Abbreviation for **Bi**nary Digi**t**. A digit, number, or a value that can show only two different conditions. These are normally named 0 and 1 or 0 and L. Very often, the bit is also called the smallest information unit.

Bit Line
The line in the column direction of a memory cell array in a RAM or ROM to which the stored value of a selected memory cell is transferred. The bit line is usually connected to the source terminal of the selection transistor.

Blue Lightning
IBM's essentially i486SX-compatible processor with a 16 kbyte L1-cache and internal clock tripling.

BNC
A special plug form for transmitting high frequency signals. By means of an extensive shielding of the BNC plugs, a BNC connection is very noise-safe. Very high resolution graphics adapters and monitors are often connected via BNC plugs and jacks.

Board
A stiff card which comprises electronic elements and wiring for connecting them.

Booting
Loading the BIOS and the operating system into a computer. The booting is normally the result of the operations of BIOS, bootstrap, and operating system loader.

Bootstrap
A small program on a bootable disk or partition which controls and executes the loading of the operating system. The name bootstrap has a somewhat fairytale background: just as the

braggart Baron Münchhausen pulled himself out of the swamp by his own bootstraps, the computer also boots itself via the bootstrap.

Bouncing
The phenomenon whereby when pressing a key the corresponding switch first closes, then opens, and afterwards closes again. The reason for this is the elastic reacting force of the key switch, and therefore this is not an intentional double key pressing.

Boundary Scan Test
A test function according to the standard IEEE 1149.1 which, by means of test cells and a test path, enables the serial input and output of test data and results. The boundary scan test implements a certain test command set to perform various checks of connections and chips.

bpi
Abbreviation for **b**its **p**er **i**nch.

bps
Abbreviation for **b**its **p**er **s**econd.

Branch Prediction
A Pentium innovation for predicting branches and therefore for accelerating program execution. The branch prediction logic comprises a control unit and the branch trace buffer BTB. The BTB is a cache which holds, as the tag, the address of the instruction preceding the branch instruction. Further, it contains the target address of the jump as the cache data entry as well as some history bits. They provide statistical information about the frequency of each branch. The dynamic branch prediction algorithm attempts to predict the branches according to the instructions which the Pentium has executed in the past. If such a prediction is later verified as correct, then all instructions which have been loaded into the pipeline after the jump instruction are correct. The pipeline operation is continued without interruption. Thus, jumps and calls are executed within one clock cycle and in parallel to other instructions – if the prediction was right. Branch prediction is used for compatibility because the powerful concept of delayed branches cannot be applied in the Pentium: existing 80x86 code has not been optimized to take that into account.

Break-Code
See scan code.

Built-In Self Test
See BIST.

Burst Mode
A special high-speed mode for the transmission of larger data blocks in the form of an uninterrupted burst of smaller data units. For example, a cache line of 16 bytes can be transferred as a burst of four data units with 4 bytes each.

Bus
A number of generally parallel signal lines which transmit control, data, and address signals.

Bus Master
A device or chip that can control a bus autonomously. Examples are the CPU and DMA chips.

Bus Slot
A dual contact strip in a PC into which adapter cards can be inserted. The bus slot comprises the contacts for all necessary control, data, and address signals.

Byte
A group of eight bits.

C
A very flexible programming language which is very close to the machine, but comprises all elements of a high-level language. Characteristic of C is that there are almost no reserved names and commands. Instead, all sophisticated commands which are known from other languages are implemented in the form of function libraries.

Cache
A very fast intermediate memory between a fast CPU and a slower memory subsystem.

Cache Consistency
The property in a multi-cache system that in an access by any CPU to a cache, that cache always returns the correct value. This means that in the course of updating a cache entry in one cache, all other caches are informed about that modification. The MESI protocol supports cache consistency.

Cache Flush
Writing the cache contents into main memory or to another data medium. Cache flushes are necessary only for cache systems that do not support a write-through strategy.

Cache Hit
If a CPU in a computer system with a cache outputs an address to read data, and if the thus addressed data is already in the cache SRAM and doesn't have to be read out of the slow main memory but may be read out of the fast cache SRAM, this is called a cache hit. If this is not true and the addressed data is only in the main memory and not in the SRAM, this is called a cache miss.

Cache Miss
See cache hit.

CAD
Abbreviation for **C**omputer-**A**ided **D**esign. CAD concerns the drawing of plans and all associated jobs with the aid of a computer. CAD is applicable in mechanical and electrical engineering, and for architects or building engineers.

Call Gate
A data structure of protected mode which is defined by a descriptor. It provides a protected access to code of another privilege level.

CAM
Abbreviation for **C**ontents **A**dressable **M**emory; often called associative memory. CAM concerns a memory or memory chip in which the information is not addressed by means of an address, but via a part of the information itself, thus by part of the memory contents. The CAM thus associates further data with this partial information so that eventually a range of infor-

mation is addressed. Then the information can be ambiguous. CAMs are mainly used for cache systems.

CAS

Abbreviation for **C**olumn **A**ddress **S**trobe. A control signal for a DRAM memory chip, which instructs the chip to accept the address provided as the column address and to interpret the address accordingly.

CAS-before-RAS Refresh

In the CAS-before-RAS refresh the external memory controller holds the signal $\overline{\text{CAS}}$ on a low level for a predetermined time, before $\overline{\text{RAS}}$ drops also – thus the name CAS-before-RAS refresh. Upon this the internal refresh logic is enabled and carries out an internal refresh. The refresh address is generated internally by an address counter which is part of the refresh logic. Thus, the refresh is only triggered by the memory controller. The actual refresh is done by the DRAM chip itself.

CCITT

Abbreviation for **C**omité **C**onsultatif **I**nternationale de **T**élégraphique et **T**éléphonique, an international committee for telegraph and telephone. A suborganization of the UN which sets up international mandatory standards for telecommunication services. You can thus telephone Australia or Europe without any problems caused by incompatibilities between different telephone networks.

CCS

Abbreviation for **C**ommon **C**ommand **S**et. See Common Command Set.

CD-I

Abbreviation for **CD** **I**nteractive. A modification of CD-ROM with an improved (interactive) interface.

CD-ROM

Abbreviation for **C**ompact **D**isc **ROM**. An optical mass storage where the information is written onto a compact disc. The information cannot subsequently be changed. Typical capacities are 500 Mbytes per disc side.

Centronics

A US printer manufacturer which was the first to set up a standard for connecting a printer to a parallel interface. Today all parallel printers are connected via a Centronics cable to the PC's parallel interface.

Character Generator

An electronic circuitry on a graphics adapter which in text mode supplies an alphanumeric character according to the corresponding bit mask stored in ROM or RAM. Thus the character generator generates the pixels for displaying the character from the character code in the video RAM. In graphics mode, however, each pixel is individually stored in the video RAM.

Cheaper Net

This Ethernet LAN uses a thinner and thus cheaper BNC cable. Because of its easy and cheap installation, it has been very successful for networking within individual buildings. Here, the stations are not connected through a transceiver but a simple BNC T-piece. The thinner cable allows only 185 m per Ethernet track to which a maximum of 30 stations can be connected.

Chip
A fingernail-sized silicon plate with up to several million circuits and electronic elements.

Chip set
A group of integrated circuits for a certain job, for example to build an AT. A chip set integrates the function of many discrete elements, for example CPU, PIC, PIT, DMA, etc., on a small number of chips.

CISC
Abbreviation for **C**omplex **I**nstruction **S**et **C**omputer. Microprocessors that comprise a very extensive instruction set of 100 to 400 machine instructions. Characteristic of CISC is the micro-encoding of the machine instructions.

CMOS
Abbreviation for **C**omplementary **M**etal **O**xide **S**emiconductor. CMOS is a technology for semiconductor elements with very low power consumption. Generally, this is achieved by connecting one NMOS and one PMOS element.

COBOL
Abbreviation for **Co**mmon **B**usiness **O**riented **L**anguage. COBOL is a programming language which is specifically designed for banking and business applications.

Coercivity
That magnetic field which is necessary to demagnetize a completely magnetized ferromagnetic body.

COM1, COM2, COM3, COM4
The DOS name for the various serial interfaces in a PC. COM is derived from **com**munications port.

Combicontroller
A combination of floppy and hard disk controller on a single adapter card. Normally, one combicontroller manages two hard disk and two floppy disk drives.

Common Access Method
A standardized software interface to SCSI devices. CAM has been developped by ANSI.

Common Command Set
An ANSI extension to SCSI-I which defines standard (common) SCSI commands. The Common Command Set (CCS) has been replaced by SCSI-II.

Compiler
A program which translates the commands written in a high-level language such as C or Pascal into a series of machine instructions for the computer.

CON
The DOS name for keyboard and monitor. CON is derived from **con**sole. Formerly, the console was the »workstation« for the operator who controlled and supervised the computer.

Concentrator
See Token Ring.

Console
See CON.

Control Bus
A number of lines that transmit control information or control signals, generally in parallel.

Controller
1. An electronic device which controls and supervises the function of a peripheral; examples are the floppy disk controller, hard disk controller, LAN controller, etc.
2. An electronic device which executes a certain function; for example, a DMA controller.

Coprocessor
Also called processor extension. A microchip specially designed for a certain CPU to enhance or support the functions of that CPU. Examples are numerical coprocessors which enhance the capabilities of the CPU by calculating numerical expressions with floating-point numbers.

CP/M
Abbreviation for **C**ontrol **P**rogram for **M**icrocomputers. A simple operating system for 8-bit processors such as the 8080/85 or Z80. CP/M was the predecessor of DOS, therefore DOS still uses some concepts of CP/M (the FCBs, for example).

CPU
Abbreviation for **C**entral **P**rocessing **U**nit. The CPU is the heart of a computer, and is also often called the (central) processor. Examples are the Intel 80x86 family and the Motorola 68000.

CR
Abbreviation for **C**arriage **R**eturn. CR is an ASCII control character with the code 0dh, which leads to the carriage return of a serial printer or to a cursor movement to the beginning of the line.

CRC
Abbreviation for **C**yclic **R**edundancy **C**heck or Cyclic Redundancy Code. A family of redundant codes that can detect data errors very efficiently. Burst errors, for example, are detected with a probability of more than 99.99%. CRC is especially applied to data recording and data transfer.

CSMA/CD
Abbreviation for **C**arrier **S**ense **M**ultiple **A**ccess/**C**ollision **D**etection. A method for controlling the net access in a LAN. The name comes from the fact that a station attempting to send data has to sense first whether a carrier is active on the net. If several stations output data at the same time, a multiple access occurs. The effects would be disastrous: the data packets affect and destroy each other. Thus, such a collision must be detected by the net and handled appropriately (usually by aborting the data output). The best-known LAN using the CSMA/CD method is the Ethernet.

CTS
Abbreviation for **C**lear **T**o **S**end. With CTS a DCE indicates its transmission readiness, and that the DTE may transmit data to the DCE now.

CU
Abbreviation for **C**ontrol **U**nit. The CU is part of a processor or CPU and controls the ALU, registers, and other components.

Curie Point/Curie Temperature
The sharp defined temperature T_c where the ferromagnetic properties of a material disappear.

Cyrix
A US manufacturer of microelectronic components. Cyrix became famous with its 80x87-compatible coprocessors for the 80x86 family. Now Cyrix is also manufacturing 80x86-compatible microprocessors, especially power-saving models for portable PCs.

DAC
Abbreviation for **D**igital to **A**nalogue **C**onverter. A DAC converts a digital signal made of a certain number of bits into an analogue signal, which represents the value of these bits.

Data Bus
A number of lines that transfer data generally in parallel.

Data Communication Equipment
See DCE.

Data Medium
A device on which data can be durably stored. Examples are floppy disks, hard disks, magnetic tapes, and optical disks.

Data Terminal Equipment
See DTE.

DCD
Abbreviation for **D**ata **C**arrier **D**etect. With DCD a DCE informs a DTE that it has detected a data carrier signal from another DCE.

DCE
Abbreviation for **D**ata **C**ommunication **E**quipment. A device for transmitting data, generally a modem.

DD
Abbreviation for **D**ouble **D**ensity.

Descriptor
An 8-byte data block which describes a segment or gate in protected mode.

Diamagnetism
A form of magnetism which somewhat weakens the external magnetic field (typically by 0.000001% to 0.05%). Pure diamagnetism appears only in materials with paired electrons.

Die
The unbonded, unpacked and therefore unprotected processor or memory chip (that is, *the* chip).

Digital
With intermediate steps, discontinuously, divided in discrete steps. A digital signal, for example, can only reach certain values on a scale, but no intermediate values.

Digital Monitor
A monitor for displaying text or graphics which is driven by a digital signal. The HGC adapter is an example of a graphics card which drives a digital monitor.

DIN
Abbreviation for **D**eutsche **I**ndustrie **N**ormenausschuß or Deutsche Industrienorm. An organization which sets up obligatory technical standards in Germany.

DIP
Abbreviation for **D**ual **I**n-line **P**ackage. A package with contacts on the two opposite lateral sides.

DIP Switch
A small switch block in a DIP package which has several small switches. Jokingly often called a mice piano.

Display Memory
See video RAM.

DMA
Abbreviation for **D**irect **M**emory **A**ccess. Besides the CPU, DMA forms a second data channel between peripherals and main memory through which a peripheral can directly access the main memory without the help of the CPU and read or write data. In the PC, DMA is implemented by the 8237A DMA controller.

Domain
The elementary region of uniform magnetization in a ferromagnetic material.

DOS
Abbreviation for **D**isk **O**perating **S**ystem. The most-installed operating system for IBM-compatible PCs. DOS operates only in the 80x86 real mode.

Doping
The introduction of other atoms into a semiconductor to affect the electrical properties of it.

Double Word
A 4-byte quantity, therefore 32 bits.

dpi
Abbreviation for **d**ots **p**er **i**nch.

Drain
One conduction terminal of a field effect transistor.

DRAM
Abbreviation for **D**ynamic **RAM**. DRAM is a direct accessible memory (RAM) where the information is usually stored in the form of charges in a capacitor. Because all capacitors are

gradually discharged by leak currents, the storage capacitor and therefore the whole DRAM must be periodically refreshed, hence the name dynamic.

DRDOS
Abbreviation for **D**igital **R**esearch **DOS**. An MS-DOS compatible operating system from Digital Research.

Drive Array
A group of physically different drives combined into one logical drive. The storage capacity of the drive is thus increased, the average seek time is reduced, and the data transfer rate grows because the drives of the drive array operate in parallel.

Driver
A software or hardware unit for driving a software or hardware component. The driver usually has a clearly defined interface so that, for example, a program can access the device without the need to know the device's structure and functioning in detail.

DSR
Abbreviation for **D**ata **S**et **R**eady. Using DSR a DCE informs a DTE that it is in general ready.

DTE
Abbreviation for **D**ata **T**erminal **E**quipment. A device located at the end of a transmission line which provides or receives data. Examples are a PC, a telephone and a fax.

DTR
Abbreviation for **D**ata **T**erminal **R**eady. With DTR a DTE informs a DCE that it is in general ready.

Dual-Port RAM
A RAM chip which has two independent access ports to the memory cells in the RAM chip. Two devices can thus access the information in RAM without disturbing each other. Dual-port memories are mainly used for the video RAM of graphic adapters, where CPU and adapter logic access the display memory concurrently. Another application is their use as communication memory in a multiprocessor system, so that two or more processors can exchange data through this memory.

Duplex
The concurrent data transmission capability of a channel in both directions.

DWord
Abbreviation for **D**ouble **Word**. See double word.

EBCDIC Code
Abbreviation for **E**xtended **B**inary **C**oded **D**ecimal **I**nterchange **C**ode. An 8-bit character code corresponding to the ASCII code which is mainly used in IBM mainframes.

ECC
Abbreviation for **E**rror **C**orrecting **C**ode. Sometimes also called self-correcting code. A form of cyclic redundancy code where the redundancy is so extensive that errors can not only be detected but also corrected. The ECC codes are mainly applied to data recording on hard disk drives.

ECL
Abbreviation for **E**mitter **C**oupled **L**ogic. A certain family of logic circuits.

EEPROM
Abbreviation for **E**lectrically **E**rasable **PROM**. A programmable read-only memory which can be erased by a high-level voltage pulse. EEPROMs are mainly implemented with FAMOST technology.

EGA
Abbreviation for **E**nhanced **G**raphics **A**dapter. An IBM graphics adapter with, compared to CGA, enhanced resolution and more colours. Standard EGA comprises 640*400 pixels.

EIA
Abbreviation for **E**lectronic **I**ndustries **A**ssociation. A US organization which sets standards for the electronics industry.

EISA
Abbreviation for **E**xtended **ISA**. EISA defines a 32-bit extension for the ISA or AT bus to integrate the i386/i486 32-bit processors. EISA is downward-compatible with the XT and AT bus, therefore XT and ISA adapters can be used without any problems (theoretically).

EISA Master
A bus master which can carry out EISA bus cycles.

EISA Slave
A device which serves EISA bus cycles.

EMS Window
A 64 kbyte block in the address space of the PC between 640 k and 1 M which can be overlaid by four EMS pages with 16 kbytes each. The EMS window is therefore something like a window into the much larger address space of expanded memory.

ENIAC
Abbreviation for **E**lectronic **N**umerical **I**ntegrator **A**nd **C**alculator. One of the first fully electronic digital computers which ran with vacuum tubes. It was developed in the US from 1943–1946.

EPROM
Abbreviation for **E**rasable **PROM**. A programmable read-only memory that can be erased by irradiation of UV-light. EPROMs are mainly implemented with FAMOST technology.

ESC Instruction (Coprocessor)
All opcodes for the 80x87 numerical coprocessor start with the bit sequence 11011, corresponding to 27. This is the ASCII code for the character ESC, therefore they are called ESC instructions.

ESDI
Abbreviation for **E**nhanced **S**mall **D**evice **I**nterface. ESDI is an interface between a hard disk controller and a hard disk drive. ESDI was introduced by Maxtor in 1983 as the more powerful successor to the ST506/412 interface. The main characteristic of ESDI is that the data separator

no longer resides on the controller, but is integrated into the drive itself. ESDI is designed for data transfer rates up to 24 Mbits/s, equal to 3 Mbytes/s.

Ethernet
A local area network (LAN) developed by XEROX in 1976. It has a bus topology using the CSMA/CD access method. The data transfer rate reaches up to 10 Mbits/s. There are two Ethernet implementations: the «real» *Thick Ethernet* and the *CheaperNet* or *Thin Ethernet*. Besides some deviations regarding the net size, the difference, as the names show, is the thickness of the cables used. The maximum length of the so-called *Yellow cable*, to which the stations are connected through *transceivers*, may not exceed 500m. In a Personal Computer, integration into the net is usually accomplished by a network adapter. A maximum of 100 transceivers (and, thus, stations) is allowed per Ethernet track, that is, per Yellow cable. The Ethernet LAN can be extended when using a *repeater*.

EU
Abbreviation for **E**xecution **U**nit. That part of a CPU which actually executes the instructions under the control of the control unit (CU).

Exception
If an internal processor error occurs, the CPU issues an interrupt called an exception. The source of an exception can, for example, be a segment which is not present in memory, an unloaded page, a division by zero, a set breakpoint, or a protection error.

Expanded Memory
A memory system accessed by bank switching. More than 1 Mbyte of memory is thus available for the 80x86 in real mode. From expanded memory only that part which is within the EMS window can be accessed at a given time.

Extended ASCII Code
An 8-bit code whose codes from 0–127 meet the standard ASCII code. The codes 128–255 are allocated block graphics and other characters.

Extended Memory
The memory above 1 M. Extended memory, except the first 64 kbytes immediately above the 1 Mbyte boundary, can be accessed in protected mode only.

FAMOST
Abbreviation for **F**loating gate **A**valanche injection **MOS** **T**ransistor. A FAMOST has a floating gate that can be loaded with electrons by a high-level voltage pulse which leads to an avalanche break-through. The characteristic of the FAMOST is thus changed. FAMOSTs are mainly used for EPROMs, EEPROMs and flash memories.

Faraday Effect
The effect whereby the polarization of an electromagnetic wave (for example, light) is rotated if the wave passes a magnetized medium.

Fast SCSI
An increase of the maximum clock frequency of the SCSI bus in synchronous mode to 10 MHz. SCSI commands and messages are, however, still transferred asynchronously. See SCSI.

Fault
An exception recognized by the processor before it executes the erroneous instruction. Thus the return address for the exception handler points to that instruction causing the exception. Therefore, the processor automatically attempts after a return to re-execute the erroneous instruction. Typical faults are exceptions because of swapped pages. The exception handler fetches the missing page and, after a return, the former unsuccessful instruction accesses the now available data again without causing an exception.

FCB
Abbreviation for **F**ile **C**ontrol **B**lock. A data structure under CP/M which describes an opened file. With DOS the FCB is replaced by the more modern handle concept.

fci
Abbreviation for **f**lux **c**hanges per **i**nch.

FDC
Abbreviation for **F**loppy **D**isk **C**ontroller.

FDDI
Abbreviation for **F**iber **D**istributed **D**ata **I**nterface. A high-speed LAN with 100 MBits/s which uses optical fibres as the transfer medium. FDD is a powerful improvement of the Token Ring with a maximum length of 100–200 km and a total of 500 to 1000 stations. The two-core fibre provides two rings: a primary ring and a secondary ring, where the secondary ring is operated as a backup ring for reliability reasons.

Ferromagnetic Material
A material which shows ferromagnetic properties. Examples are iron, cobalt, nickel, or permanent magnets.

Ferromagnetism
The phenomenon whereby microscopic regions of a material, the so-called domains, are completely magnetized. If such a body is moved into a magnetic field, all domains straighten according to the external field and the body is magnetized. A feature of ferromagnetism is that this magnetization remains even if the external field is switched off.

FET
Abbreviation for **F**ield **E**ffect **T**ransistor. In a FET the control of the conductivity is carried out by an electrical field between the gate and source.

FIFO
Abbreviation for **F**irst-**I**n, **F**irst-**O**ut. FIFO memories are often used as buffers.

Flip-Flop
Also called a bistable multivibrator. An electronic circuit with two stably defined states that can be switched by a strong write pulse. Flip-flops are used as latches or SRAM memory cells.

Floppy Disk
A data carrier which consists of a circular disk made of a flexible material. The floppy disk is usually located in a protective envelope or a case. For the PC, 5¼" floppy disks with 360 kbytes

and 1.2 Mbytes storage capacity and 3½" floppy disks with 720 kbytes and 1.44 Mbytes of storage capacity are currently in use.

Floppy Disk Drive
A drive to read and write floppy disks with a drive motor, one or two read/write heads, and an access arm for positioning the heads.

FM
Abbreviation for **F**requency **M**odulation. A data encoding method for magnetic data carriers.

Full Stroke Time
The time a disk drive needs to move the read/write head from cylinder 0 to the cylinder with the maximum cylinder number.

G
Symbol for **G**iga (that is, one billion of a quantity), for example in 1 GW = 1 000 000 000 W. Note that 1 Gbyte usually means 2^{30} bytes = 1 073 741 800 bytes.

Gallium Arsenide
Abbreviated GaAs. A semiconductor material for extremely fast operating circuits.

Galvanization
The deposition of metals on a substrate by introducing the substrate into a solution with ions of the desired coating metal and applying a certain voltage.

Gate
The control terminal of a field effect transistor. By changing the gate voltage the conductivity of the transistor can be varied.

Gate Array
A microchip with a number of logic gates. To carry out a certain function the connection of the gates is determined by a mask after the last manufacturing step. The gate array can thus be adapted very easily to various jobs, because the function concerned affects only a single step of the manufacturing process. Today, gate arrays are mainly used for ASICs or highly integrated controller chips in the PC.

Gbyte
2^{30} bytes = 1 073 741 800 bytes; **not** 1 000 000 000 bytes.

GDT
Abbreviation for **G**lobal **D**escriptor **T**able. A table of 8-byte entries (the descriptors), which describe segments and gates in protected mode.

GDTR
Abbreviation for **G**lobal **D**escriptor **T**able **R**egister. A memory management register from the 80286 which holds the base address and the limit of the GDT in memory.

Global Descriptor Table
See GDT.

Global Descriptor Table Register
See GDTR.

Gradual Underflow
A floating point number that is different from zero, but which cannot be represented in normalized form any more.

Graphics Adapter
An adapter for a PC bus slot to display graphics and text on a monitor. Examples are CGA, HGC, EGA, VGA, 8514/A, and TIGA.

Graphics Control Chip
A microchip which generates all the necessary control and data signals to display text and graphics on a monitor.

Graphics Mode
A certain operating mode of a graphics adapter where each point on the screen is allocated one or more bits. Each picture element (pixel) can be addressed individually. The image is not restricted to a certain font, but any characters and graphics may be displayed. Text characters are written into the video memory in bit-mapped form, and are not generated by the hardware character generator.

Graphics Processor
A specialized microprocessor which processes graphics commands. The processor can thus draw, for example, lines and geometric objects with only the coordinates of a few characterizing points, without any intervention from the CPU. With a graphics processor the CPU is relieved from ordinary graphics tasks.

Half Duplex
The transmission of data in one direction where, however, the transmission direction can be switched. The two communication participants may therefore operate as receiver and transmitter alternately.

Handle
A number which DOS internally allocates to an opened file or device, for example the keyboard (handle 0).

Handshake
The beginning of a data or control signal transmission by a request signal and the acknowledgement of the data or control signal's delivery by an acknowledge signal.

Hard Disk/Hard Disk Drive
A drive for data recording which uses a stiff data carrier in the form of a fast rotating disk. The read/write heads of the drive are moved by a common actuator. Generally, hard disks are located in a case.

HD
1. Abbreviation for **h**ard **d**isk.
2. Abbreviation for **h**igh **d**ensity.

HDA

Abbreviation for **H**ead **D**isk **A**ssembly. That part of a hard disk drive which comprises the disks, the heads, and the actuator. Normally, the HDA is surrounded by a case, and the incoming air is filtered so that no pollution may penetrate into the HDA.

HDC

Abbreviation for **H**ard **D**isk **C**ontroller.

Hercules Card or Hercules Graphics Card

Abbreviated HGC. A monochrome adapter card with graphics capabilities for the PC. In text mode it is compatible with the MDA; in graphics mode it supports a resolution of 720*348 pixels.

HEX

Abbreviation for **hex**adecimal number.

HGC

Abbreviation for **H**ercules **G**raphics **C**ard.

Hidden Refresh

Here, the refresh cycle is «hidden» behind a normal read access. After a memory access the $\overline{\text{CAS}}$ is further kept at a low level, and only the $\overline{\text{RAS}}$ signal is toggled. The data read in the normal read cycle is provided by the DRAM chip while the refresh cycle is in progress. An address counter inside the DRAM generates the refresh address internally.

High-Level Formatting

The formatting of a data carrier or medium if only the logical structure of the file system is established, but no tracks and sectors are physically generated. For a hard disk, the command FORMAT carries out a high-level formatting only.

Host

Also called a central computer. A computer or computer element which represents the kernel of a computer system.

Host Adapter

An adapter card which establishes the interface between a host and an external bus. Examples are SCSI host adapters for the connection of a SCSI bus with SCSI drives or IDE host adapters for the connection of the AT bus with IDE drives to the PC system bus.

Hz

Symbol for Hertz. 1 Hz=1 period/s.

i386/i386SX

The third generation of the 80x86 family. The i386 has a 32-bit processor with 32-bit registers, a 32-bit data bus, and a 32-bit address bus. With the i386 the virtual 8086 mode was introduced. The physical address space comprises 4 Gbytes. The SX modification, i386SX, is internally identical to the i386, but has only a 16-bit data bus and a 24-bit address bus.

i387/i387SX

The mathematical coprocessor for the i386 and i386SX, respectively.

i486/i486SX
The fourth generation of the 80x86 family. The i486 has a 32-bit processor with 32-bit registers, a 32-bit data bus, and a 32-bit address bus. Further, it has an improved i387 coprocessor, a cache controller, and an 8 kbyte cache SRAM. The i486SX only lacks the coprocessor.

i486DX2
An i486 with internally doubled processor frequency, that is, the internal processor clock is twice the external clock supplied by the clock generator. The bus interface and therefore the bus cycles, on the other hand, run with the external clock only.

i486DX4
An i486DX whose on-chip PLL can double or triple the external clock frequency, or which can operate at $2\frac{1}{2}$ times the external clock; it reaches up to 100 MHz. Compared with the i486DX and i486DX2 its 4-way set-associative cache has been extended to 16 kbytes. An improved hardware multiplier additionally enhances the performance.

i486SL
See SL Enhanced i486.

i487SX
The upgrade for an i486SX. The i487SX not only supplies the coprocessor, but is a complete i486 CPU with on-chip cache, etc. If the i476SX is installed it disables the i486SX CPU and takes over its jobs, too.

i586
A rather uncommon name for the Pentium.

IC
Abbreviation for **I**ntegrated **C**ircuit. A circuit consisting of several electronic elements which is provided on a single carrier (substrate). DRAMs and microprocessors belong to the highest integrated ICs.

IDE
Abbreviation for **I**ntelligent **D**rive **E**lectronics. A standard for connecting intelligent hard disks or other drives with an embedded controller to the AT bus. The IDE interface is also called an AT bus or ATA interface.

IDT
Abbreviation for **I**nterrupt **D**escriptor **T**able. A table of 8-byte entries (the descriptors) which describe gates for handling interrupts in protected mode.

IDTR
Abbreviation for **I**nterrupt **D**escriptor **T**able **R**egister. A memory management register from the 80286 which holds the base address and limit of the IDT in memory.

IEEE
Abbreviation for **I**nstitute of **E**lectrical and **E**lectronics **E**ngineers; sometimes called IE^3 (I-triple-E). An engineering organization in the US which defines standards.

IIL
Abbreviation for Integrated Injection Logic; also called I^2L. A family of logic elements.

Induction
The phenomenon whereby a varying magnetic field generates an electrical field and thus a voltage. The magnitude of the voltage is proportional to the flux change of the magnetic field.

Inert Gas
A chemical gas which does not, or only weakly, react (that is, inert). Inert gases are helium, neon, argon, krypton, xenon, and the radioactive radon.

Inquiry Cycle
Also called snoop cycle. A bus cycle to a processor with an on-chip cache or to a cache controller to investigate whether a certain address is present in the applicable cache.

Instruction Pipelining
Generally, instructions show very similar execution steps; for example, every instruction has to be fetched, decoded and executed, and the results need to be written back into the destination register. With instruction pipelining the execution of every instruction is separated into more elementary tasks. Each task is carried out by another stage of an instruction pipeline (ideally in one single clock cycle) so that, at a given time, several instructions are present in the pipeline at different stages in different execution states. Thus, not every instruction is executed completely in one clock cycle, but one instruction is completed every clock cycle. If the pipeline is filled with instructions, then these two statements are equal.

Intel
An important US firm which manufactures microelectronic components, for example memory chips and processors. The most important processor family is the 80x86. Intel is regarded as the inventor of the microprocessor.

Interlock
If a stage in a pipeline needs the result or the system element of another stage which is not yet available, this is called an interlock. Interlocks arise, for example, if in the course of calculating a composite expression the evaluation of the partial expressions is still in progress. The requesting pipeline stage then has to wait until the other pipeline stage has completed its calculations.

Internet
A worldwide net (WAN) which initially should enable data exchange between universities and research institutes. Meanwhile, commercial companies (for example, CompuServe) provide a gateway to the Internet which can be accessed quite cheaply by nearly every PC user having a modem and a telephone line. As well as the usual net services such as, for example, e-mail and data base access, newsgroups (user groups discussing almost every possible subject of interest) have emanated as a particular feature of the Internet. The Internet is regarded as the communication platform for the worldwide computer freak community. At the time of writing (mid-1994), about 20 million computers with a multiple of actual users are connected to this net. A more exact number cannot be determined because of the net's sometimes chaotic structure.

Interrupt (Software, Hardware)
A software interrupt is issued by an explicit interrupt instruction INT; a hardware interrupt, however, is transmitted via an IRQ line to the processor. In both cases, the processor saves flags, instruction pointer and code segment on the stack, and calls a certain procedure, the interrupt handler.

Interrupt Descriptor Table
See IDT.

Interrupt Descriptor Table Register
See IDTR.

Interrupt Gate
A gate descriptor for calling an interrupt handler. Unlike a trap gate the interrupt gate clears the interrupt flag and therefore disables external interrupt requests.

Interrupt Handler
See interrupt.

I/O
Abbreviation for **I**nput/**O**utput.

I/O-Mapped I/O
With I/O-mapped I/O the registers of peripherals are accessed via the I/O address space, that is, ports.

IRQ
Abbreviation for **I**nterrupt **Req**uest. A line or signal which is activated by a peripheral to issue a hardware interrupt to the CPU.

ISA
Abbreviation for **I**ndustrial **S**tandard **A**rchitecture. A defined standard which has replaced the vague AT bus specification. ISA defines the bus structure, the architecture of CPU and support chips, and the clock frequency of the ISA bus.

ISA Master
A bus master which can carry out ISA bus cycles.

ISA Slave
A device which serves ISA bus cycles.

IU
Abbreviation for **I**nstruction **U**nit. A portion of the CPU which drives the execution unit.

Joystick
A stick with buttons frequently used for computer games.

k
Symbol for **k**ilo (that is, one thousand of a quantity), for example, in kW = 1000 W. Note that kbyte generally means 2^{10} bytes = 1024 bytes.

kbit
2^{10} bits = 1024 bits.

kbyte
2^{10} bytes = 1024 bytes.

Keyboard
An input device for computers. A keyboard is usually connected to a keyboard controller or a keyboard interface on the motherboard via a serial interface. The keyboard consists of a scan matrix, a keyboard chip and several keys. If a key is pressed the keyboard chip transmits a scan code to the computer, which unambiguously characterizes the pressed key.

kHz
1000 Hz = 1000 periods/s.

L1-Cache
The first level nearest the CPU in a hierarchical structured cache subsystem. The L1-cache is usually much smaller than a possibly present L2-cache and integrated on the same chip as the CPU itself. The L1-cache can typically be accessed within one processor clock cycle.

L2-Cache
Also called second-level cache. The second level of a hierarchical structured cache subsystem nearer the main memory. Between the CPU and main memory first the L1-cache and then the L2-cache are located. The L2-cache is typically ten to fifty times larger than the L1-cache. It is formed by several SRAM chips and an L2-cache controller.

LAN
Abbreviation for **L**ocal **A**rea **N**etwork. LANs are data networks which are restricted in space. Typical distances are less than 500 m. Mainly Ethernet and Token-Ring LANs are used.

Lanthanoide
Also called rare earth. Certain metallic chemical elements which show very similar chemical properties. There are 14 different lanthanoides; the element lanthanum gave the name for this element group.

Laser
1. Abbreviation for **L**ight **A**mplification by **S**timulated **E**mission of **R**adiation, a phenomenon of quantum physics.
2. Light sources which emit a sharply focused beam of high optical quality.

Latch
A circuit which largely consists of two antiparallel connected inverters. The latch holds (latches) data which has been written once, even after deactivating the external signal (data). The data writing is usually controlled by a clock signal.

Latency
The average time between the positioning of the read/write head and the appearance of the desired sector below the head. On average, this takes half a disk rotation. Hard disks with 3600 rpm therefore show a latency of 8.3 ms, and floppy disk drives with 360 rpm a latency of 83 ms.

LDT
Abbreviation for **L**ocal **D**escriptor **T**able. A table of 8-byte entries (the descriptors) which describe segments in protected mode. These segments are local for the task concerned.

LDTR
Abbreviation for **L**ocal **D**escriptor **T**able **R**egister. A memory management register from the 80286 that holds a selector, which in turn indicates the descriptor for the local descriptor table in the global descriptor table.

LF
Abbreviation for **L**ine **F**eed. LF is an ASCII control character with the code 0ah. LF leads to a line feed in a serial printer, or to a positioning of the cursor in the next line but the same column.

Little Endian Format
In the little endian format the high-bytes of a multiple byte quantity are stored at higher addresses, and the low-bytes are stored at lower addresses. Intel's 80x86 family uses the little endian format. When writing multiple byte entities in the usual way, with the highest order bit left and the lowest order bit right, the arrangement in memory seems to be exchanged.

Local Bus
A new bus system for the Personal Computer which operates with 32 bits and, unlike EISA, up to 50 MHz. Unfortunately, the local bus is not as universally applicable as the ISA, EISA, or MCA buses, but is currently only used for the integration of fast graphics adapters and hard disk controllers. There exist two new standards for the local bus: Intel's PCI and the VESA VL-bus.

Local Descriptor Table
See LDT.

Local Descriptor Table Register
See LDTR.

Local Network
See LAN.

Login
To announce oneself to a mainframe as a user. The login is usually carried out by a LOGON command, as well as inputting a user identification and password.

Low-Level Formatting
The formatting of a data carrier involving the generation of physical tracks and sectors, but not the logical structure of the file system. With FORMAT and a floppy disk you may carry out a low and high-level formatting simultaneously. With a hard disk drive, however, only high-level formatting is possible with FORMAT.

LPT1, LPT2, LPT3, LPT4
The DOS names for the various parallel interfaces in a PC. LPT is derived from **l**ine **p**rin**t**er.

LSB
Abbreviation for **L**east-**S**ignificant **B**it or **L**east-**S**ignificant **B**yte.

LSI
Abbreviation for **L**arge **S**cale **I**ntegration. This means the integration of 10 000 to 100 000 elements on a single chip.

μ
Symbol for micro, that is, one millionth of a quantity. Example: 1 μm = 0.000 001 mm.

M
Symbol for **M**ega, that is, one million of an unit as, for example, in MW = 1 000 000 W. Note that Mbyte usually means 2^{20} bytes = 1 048 576 bytes.

m
Symbol for **m**illi, that is, one thousandth of a quantity. Example: 1 mm = 0.001 m.

Magneto-Optical Drive
A writeable and erasable mass storage where the recording and reading of data is carried out by a laser beam, that is, in an optical manner. The information itself is written in the form of tiny magnetizations: the data medium has a ferromagnetic coating. Magneto-optical drives use the Curie point for writing and the Faraday effect for reading the information.

Mainframe
A very powerful computer which serves many users (up to 1000 or more), and which may execute several tasks in parallel.

Main Memory
That memory of a computer which stores the program and the data necessary for program execution, or which are processed by the program. Generally, the main memory is implemented with DRAM.

Make-Code
See scan code.

Mantissa
The number by which the power in scientific notation is multiplied to give the value of the expression. Example: $1.83*10^4$; 1.83 is the mantissa, 10 the base, and 4 the exponent of the number 18 300 in scientific notation.

Mark
A form of parity where the parity bit is always equal to 1 independently of the data value.

Machine Instruction
An instruction for a microprocessor which is decoded and interpreted by the processor without further modification or translation by software or hardware. Machine instructions consist of a variable-length sequence of bits that specify the operation type, the addressing scheme, the affected registers, etc. The machine instruction is the lowest level of processor instruction accessible by a programmer. Assembler and high-level language instructions are translated into machine instructions by the assembler and compiler, respectively.

Matrix
A generally two-dimensional arrangement of objects, for example numbers or memory cells. An individual object within the matrix is determined by specifying its line and column.

Mbit
2^{20} bits = 1 048 576 bits.

Mbyte
2^{20} bytes = 1 048 576 bytes.

MC146818
A CMOS RAM and real-time clock chip from Motorola which is contained in the AT and its successors as the original or a compatible chip.

Mega
See M.

Memory Bank
A group of memory chips which are accessed in common.

Memory-Mapped I/O
With memory-mapped I/O all registers of the peripherals are located in the normal address space, and thus are accessed via the normal memory instructions such as MOV.

MESI Protocol
A protocol for managing cache entries on a cache line base. This protocol is mainly used for multi-cache systems. The protocol assigns each cache line one of the states **M**odified, **E**xclusive, **S**hared or **I**nvalid. Transitions between the individual states are issued by read or write accesses to the cache lines.

MF II Keyboard
Abbreviation for **m**ulti**f**unction II keyboard. An extended and programmable keyboard which has separate blocks with control keys and LEDs to indicate the shift status of various keys.

MFM
Abbreviation for **M**odified **F**requency **M**odulation. An encoding method to record data on a magnetic data carrier with twice the data density of FM.

MHz
1 000 000Hz = 1 000 000 periods/s.

Mickey
1/200", that is, 1/200 inch (equal to 0.127 mm.)

Micro
See μ.

Microchannel
A modern bus system from IBM for PS/2 Personal Computers. The microchannel is designed for an 8- to 32-bit data and address bus, and the support of multitasking operating systems on a hardware level. Unlike EISA, the microchannel is incompatible with the PC/XT and ISA bus.

Microchip
A highly integrated circuit on a single substrate plate – the chip. More particularly, microchip means ICs with extensive logic, for example, microprocessors or DRAMs.

Microcoding or Microencoding
The encoding of machine instructions of a processor into a sequence of more elementary instructions to the instruction and execution unit in a CPU. The microcode is stored in the processor's microcode ROM and is not accessible to the programmer but is burnt-in during the course of manufacture.

Microprocessor
A microchip with high intelligence for the execution of instructions. Therefore, a microprocessor is programmable and the program is usually stored in a ROM or main memory.

MIPS
1. Abbreviation for **M**illion **I**nstructions **P**er **S**econd. MIPS indicates the number of instructions executed by a processor within one second, and sometimes serves as a (not very powerful) degree for the performance of the CPU.
2. Abbreviation for **M**icroprocessor without **I**nterlocked **P**ipeline-**S**tages. A RISC architecture where no interlocks occur between the pipeline stages. Well-known MIPS implementations are the R3000/4000/6000.

Mirroring
The simultaneous and identical recording of data on two different mass storage mediums, for example, hard disks. This prevents data being lost if one drive is damaged.

μm
Symbol for micrometer, that is, one millionth of a metre or 0.000 001 m.

MMU
Abbreviation for **M**emory **M**anagement **U**nit. The MMU is either part of a processor or integrated on a separate chip, and carries out the address transformations for segmentation and paging.

Mnemonics
Easy-to-remember abbreviations which characterize the machine instructions of a processor, and which are translated by an assembler according to the addressing scheme, the operands, etc. into machine instructions, for example, MOV.

Modem
Abbreviation for **mo**dulator/**dem**odulator. Modem means a device which modulates a carrier signal with a data signal and extracts the data signal from the modulated carrier signal, respectively. Data can thus be transmitted over a data network or radio network.

Monitor
1. A device for computers to display text and graphics.
2. A supervision program for a hardware or software unit. Example: virtual 8086 monitor; a system program to supervise the i386 and successive processors and one or more tasks in virtual 8086 mode.

MOS

Abbreviation for **M**etal **O**xide **S**emiconductor. A technology for manufacturing electronic components or integrated circuits which have a layer structure of the form indicated.

MOSFET

Abbreviation for **M**etal **O**xide **S**emiconductor **FET** (field effect transistor). A field effect transistor which has a control gate (metal), a substrate (semiconductor), and an isolating film (oxide) which separates gate and substrate.

Motherboard

Also called a mainboard. That board in a PC housing the central components such as CPU, main memory, DMA controller, PIC, PIT, etc., as well as the bus slots.

Motorola

An important US manufacturer of microelectronic components, for example, memory chips and processors. The most important Motorola processor family is the 68000. Presently, Motorola is very involved in the telecommunications field.

Mouse

A pointing device in the form of a small housing with two or three buttons. In the housing is embedded a ball, rotated by a movement of the mouse by the user. The rotation of the ball is detected by sensors, and a logic can determine the direction and amount of the movement. Optical mice don't have a ball, but only optical sensors that detect the mouse's movement over a special mouse pad.

Mouse Cursor

An object in the form of a cursor or an arrow which is moved on the screen seemingly in accordance with the mouse's displacement. The location of the mouse cursor on-screen can be evaluated by software.

μP

Abbreviation for microprocessor.

μPD765

The floppy disk controller chip in the PC/XT.

MSB

Abbreviation for **M**ost-**S**ignificant **B**it or **M**ost-**S**ignificant **B**yte.

MS-DOS

Abbreviation for **M**icro**s**oft-DOS, the DOS implementation from Microsoft.

MSI

Abbreviation for **M**edium **S**cale **I**ntegration. It characterizes the integration of 100 to 10000 elements on a single chip.

MSW

Abbreviation for **M**achine **S**tatus **W**ord. A 80286 control and status register for protected mode.

MTBF
Abbreviation for **M**ean **T**ime **B**etween **F**ailures. MTBF indicates the average value for the time period between two complete failures of the corresponding device. MTBF is mainly used to characterize the reliability of hard disk drives.

Multimedia PC
A PC which has various extensions to provide, receive and process information in the form of data, image and audio concurrently.

Multiplexer
A device which transfers the data of several input channels to a smaller number of output channels in a strictly defined way. Example: the 20-bit memory address of the 80286 is divided into two successive 10-bit packets (the row and the column address) by the DRAM controller; here the number of input channels is equal to 20, but the number of output channels is only equal to 10. The DRAM controller therefore represents a multiplexer, and the described multiplexing manner is called time-divisional multiplexing.

Multitasking
The concurrent execution of several tasks in a computer. Users have the impression that the tasks are executed in parallel; actually, the computer only switches between the tasks very quickly.

Multitasking Operating System
An operating system which can manage several tasks in a computer system simultaneously, activating them for a short time period and interrupting them again later. Examples are OS/2, UNIX, or mainframe operating systems such as VMS or BS2000.

n
Symbol for **n**ano (that is, one billionth of a quantity). Example: 1 nm = 0.000 000 001 m.

NAN
Abbr. for **N**ot **A** **N**umber. A floating-point number which is different from zero but doesn't meet the IEEE definitions for the representation of floating-point numbers in a computer.

Nano
See n.

Nanometre
One billionth of a metre, that is, 0.000 000 001 m.

Nanosecond
One billionth of a second, that is, 0.000 000 001 s.

NEC
A major Japanese manufacturer of electrotechnical and electronic devices (**N**ippon **E**lectric **C**ompany).

Netnode
A station in a network. Netnodes are, for example, workstations, switching computers, or printers.

Network
Transmission equipment with a server, netnodes and transmission devices which enable communication between individual network users.

Network Adapter
An adapter card enables the access to a network. Generally, you also need drivers and network software.

Nibble
A group of four bits, that is, half a byte.

Nibble Mode
A particular operation mode of DRAM memory chips where after supplying and decoding a row and a column address the $\overline{\text{CAS}}$ signal is toggled as a clock signal for data output. Thus, a maximum of four bits (one nibble) within one row can be addressed very fast in a serial manner. The row and column address provided defines the start of the data output. With each of a maximum of three successive $\overline{\text{CAS}}$ toggles an internal address counter is incremented and the next value is output. Unlike the serial mode only four bits can be output here; in serial mode, however, a maximum of one complete row (1024 and more) can be output.

nm
Abbreviation for nanometre, that is, one billionth of a metre, or 0.000 000 001 m.

NMI
Abbreviation for **N**on-**M**askable **I**nterrupt. A hardware interrupt request to a CPU which cannot be masked internally in the processor by a bit, but must be serviced immediately.

NMOS
Abbreviation for **N**-channel **MOS**. A technology for manufacturing MOS transistors where the channel conductivity is based on negative charged electrons.

Normalized Representation
In normalized floating-point number representation, it is assumed that the leading digit is always equal to 1. Because the leading digit is always known implicitly, it is omitted and the exponent is adjusted accordingly, so that the value of the number remains equal. The precision is thus increased by one digit without enlarging the number format.

NRZ
Abbreviation for **N**on-**R**eturn to **Z**ero. An encoding method for binary data where the signal for two successive 1's doesn't return to zero.

ns
Abbreviation for nanosecond, that is, one billionth of a second or 0.000 000 001 seconds.

NVR
Abbreviation for **N**on-**V**olatile **RAM**. A memory which doesn't lose its contents even after the power has been switched off.

Offset
The address within a segment, that is, the number of bytes from the beginning of the segment.

Operating System
Hardware-near software which controls and supervises the operation of a computer, establishes an interface between application programs and the hardware and file system, and which manages the various tasks.

OS/2
Abbreviation for Operating System/2. The multitasking successor to DOS for IBM-compatible personal computers.

Overdrive
An upgrade for i486DX/SX processors. See upgrade.

Overflow
The condition where the result of an arithmetic operation is too large for the reserved memory location. For example, the multiplication of two integers may cause an overflow if the destination register can only accept an integer, but the result is longer than 16 bits.

P5
The short form or development name for the i586/Pentium.

Packed BCD
Binary coded decimal numbers where each nibble of a byte encodes a decimal digit. Example: 72h=decimal 72. Packed BCD saves much storage area when compared to ordinary BCD.

PAD
Abbreviation for **P**acket **A**ssembler/**D**isassembler. A hardware or software device in a network with packet switching which generates one or more data packets with corresponding addresses from data to be transmitted, or reconstructs the entire information from such received packets.

Page
A section of an address space which is handled as a unit.

Page Directory
The first-order page table in a system with paging which holds the addresses of the second-order page table. The page directory is always in memory and is, unlike the second-order page tables, not swapped onto disk.

Page Mode
A particular operating mode of modern DRAM memory chips where after supplying and decoding a row address only the column address is changed further. In a similar way to the static column mode, data within one row can be addressed randomly. Upon application of a new column address the column address strobe signal $\overline{CAS}$ needs to be disabled for a short time and then activated again. This instructs the DRAM chip to fetch and decode the new address. In static column mode, on the contrary, the $\overline{CAS}$ signal need not be toggled in advance of providing a new column address. The duration of the page mode is limited, typically to 100 memory cycles. If the required data is located outside the page, then a lasting page change is necessary.

Page Table
A table which holds the addresses of the corresponding pages in a system where paging is effective. The first-order page table is called a page directory. Unlike the first-order page table, the second-order page tables can be swapped like ordinary pages.

Paging
1. Generally, the division of an address space into smaller units – the pages.
2. Demand paging: the swapping of pages in main memory onto an external mass storage if the data stored there are currently not needed by the program. If the CPU wants to access the swapped data, the whole page is transferred into memory again and another currently unused page is swapped. A much larger virtual address space than that actually present physically can thus be generated.

Palette
The total of all possible colours which a graphics adapter (for example, EGA or VGA) is able to display.

Parallel Interface
A PC interface which provides or receives data in the parallel form of one byte.

Paramagnetism
A form of magnetism where the external magnetic field is slightly enhanced (typically by 0.00001% to 0.05%). Paramagnetism appears in all materials with unpaired electrons.

Parity
A simple means of detecting errors in data recording or transmission. For that purpose, a data quantity is allocated a parity bit whose value is computed from the data bits. With even parity the number of 1's of all data and parity bits is even, thus the modulo-2 sum of all bits is equal to 0. With odd parity, however, the number of 1's is odd, thus the modulo-2 sum of all bits is equal to 1. In addition, mark and space parities exist.

Pascal
A common structured programming language.

PC
1. Abbreviation for **P**ersonal **C**omputer.
2. IBM's first personal computer with an 8088 processor and an 8-bit data bus.

PC-DOS
Abbreviation for **P**ersonal **C**omputer-DOS; IBM's DOS implementation.

PCI
Abbreviation for **P**eripheral **C**omponent **I**nterconnect. A local bus standard initiated by Intel having a bus width of usually 32 bits and operating at 33 MHz at the most. A 64-bit version is intended with the forthcoming standard 2.0. Characteristic of PCI is the decoupling of processor and expansion bus by means of a bridge. The transfer rate reaches 133 MBytes/s at 32 bits and 266 Mbytes/s at 64 bits; bursts are carried out with any length. Unlike the VL bus, PCI is specified processor-independent.

PCMCIA
Abbreviation for **P**ersonal **C**omputer **M**emory **C**ard **I**nternational **A**ssociation. An interface for credit card-sized adapters which are inserted into a PCMCIA slot. Specification 1.0 was intended only as an interface for memory extensions. With specification 2.0, I/O cards are also allowed (for example, fax modems); beginning with specification 3.0, even drives could be inserted into the (now double-sized) slot.

Pentium
Presently the most powerful member of the 80x86 family and successor to the i486. The outstanding characteristic is the superscalar architecture with the two integer pipelines u and v. They can execute so-called simple instructions in parallel, that is, complete two instructions within one clock cycle. Additionally, two separate L1-caches with 8 kbytes each for code and data are integrated which support the MESI protocol. An improved floating-point unit enhances the performance further.

Peripheral
A device or unit located outside the system's CPU/main memory.

PGA
Abbreviation for **P**in **G**rid **A**rray. A package where the terminals are provided in the form of pins at the bottom of the package.

Physical Address Space
The number of physically addressable bytes, determined by the number of address lines of a processor or the amount of installed memory.

PIC
Abbreviation for **P**rogrammable **I**nterrupt **C**ontroller. A chip for the management of several hardware interrupts and the ordered transfer of the requests to a CPU which usually has only one input for such an interrupt request. Thus the PIC serves as a multiplexer for hardware interrupts. In the PC you will find the 8259A.

PIO
Abbreviation for **P**rogrammed **I/O**. With PIO data are exchanged between the main memory and a peripheral not by means of DMA, but with IN and OUT instructions via the CPU.

Pipeline Stage
An unit or stage within a pipeline which executes a certain partial task. A pipeline for a memory access may include the four pipeline stages address calculation, address supply, reading the value and storing the value in a register. An instruction pipeline comprises, for example, the stages instruction fetch, instruction decode, execution and register write-back.

Pipelining
Starting the execution of a function of the next cycle before the function of the current cycle has been completed. For example, the 80286 provides the address for the next read cycle in advance of receiving the data of the current cycle. This is called address pipelining or pipelined addressing. Similarly, a processor can start the execution of parts of a complex instruction in an early pipeline stage before the preceding instruction has been completed in the last pipeline stage.

PIT
Abbreviation for **P**rogrammable **I**nterval **T**imer. A chip which outputs a pulse as soon as a programmed time period has elapsed. In the PC you will find the 8253 or its successor, the 8254.

Pixel
Short form of picture element; a point on a monitor. Usually the name pixel is only used in graphics mode. The pixel may be allocated one or more bits which define the colour and brightness of the picture element.

PLA
Abbreviation for **P**rogrammable **L**ogic **A**rray. A highly integrated chip with logic gates which is employed as an ASIC, and whose logic can be freely programmed during manufacturing or by the user. A PLA usually has a field of AND gates and a field of OR gates. By combining AND and OR, any logical combination can be realized. This is similar to the fact that all natural numbers can be generated with 0 and 1.

PLCC
Abbreviation for **P**lastics **L**eaded **C**hip **C**arrier. A package where the contacts are formed on all of the four sides.

PMOS
Abbreviation for **P**-channel **MOS**. A technology for manufacturing MOS transistors where the channel conductivity is based on positively charged holes.

Polarization
If the electric or magnetic field of an electromagnetic wave is oscillating in one direction only, the wave is linearly polarized. The direction of the magnetic field is called the polarization direction.

Polarization Filter
A device for separating the part of a certain polarization direction from an electromagnetic wave. Only that part whose polarization direction coincides with the polarization direction of the filter passes through the filter.

Port
An address in the 80x86 I/O address space. Usually, registers in peripherals are accessed via ports.

Positioning Time
The time period between an instruction to position the read/write head and the head being moved to the indicated track.

POST
Abbreviation for **P**ower-**O**n **S**elf **T**est. A program in ROM which detects and checks all installed components during power-on.

PPI
Abbreviation for **P**rogrammable **P**eripheral **I**nterface. A chip which establishes a connection to peripherals such as the keyboard or the DIP switches of the PC/XT. In the PC/XT you will find the 8255.

PQFP
Abbreviation for **P**lastics **Q**uad **F**latpack **P**ackage. A package where the contacts are formed on all four sides.

Prefetch Queue
A small intermediate memory in a CPU where the prefetcher stores the following instructions before the processor has executed the current instruction. The prefetch queue relieves the bus system, and predecodes the instructions in CISC processors.

PRN
The DOS name for the first parallel printer. PRN is synonymous with LPT1.

Process Computer
A small computer usually without a monitor and a keyboard for controlling machines such as automobile engines, robots, or chemical reactors.

Processor
An intelligent microchip which is highly programmable. Often used synonymously for CPU.

Program
A group of instructions to a CPU to process data or to control machines.

PROM
Abbreviation for **P**rogrammable **ROM**. A read-only memory where the stored data can be programmed during the last manufacturing step, or in the field by the user.

Protected Mode
An advanced operating mode from the 80286 on, where the access of a task to code and data segments and the I/O address space is automatically checked by processor hardware. The address generation in protected mode is incompatible with that in real mode. Thus real mode applications like DOS cannot be executed in protected mode.

PS/2
An IBM Personal Computer series with microchannel; conceived as the AT's successor.

RAM
Abbreviation for **R**andom **A**ccess **M**emory. In a RAM data can be directly and randomly read or written (that is, with any choice of the address).

RapidCAD
An i386/i387 upgrade with an i486 processor kernel (CPU and coprocessor), but without an on-chip cache.

RAS
Abbreviation for **R**ow **A**ddress **S**trobe. A control signal for a DRAM chip which instructs the chip to accept the address supplied as a row address, and to interpret it accordingly.

RAS-only-Refresh
A refresh method for DRAMs by performing a dummy read cycle in which the $\overline{RAS}$ signal is activated and the DRAM is supplied with a row address (the refresh address). However, the $\overline{CAS}$ signal remains disabled; a column address is not required. Internally the DRAM reads one

row onto the bit line pairs and amplifies the read-out data. But they are not transferred to the I/O line pair and thus to the data output buffer as the $\overline{CAS}$ signal is disabled. To refresh the whole memory an external logic or the CPU itself must apply all row addresses successively.

Read/Write Head
A magnetically activated component at the tip of an access arm in a floppy disk or hard disk drive. The read/write head writes data as tiny magnetic regions onto the data medium or reads the data from the medium.

Real Mode
An 80x86 operating mode where the segment value is just multiplied by 16 and the offset is added to generate the physical memory address. In real mode no access checks are carried out for the code and data segments and the I/O address space. All 80x86 CPUs up to the Pentium support the real mode for compatibility reasons.

Real-Time Clock
A chip that regularly updates time and date without any intervention from the CPU.

Reduced Write Current
In hard disk drives there may be so-called bit shifts on the inner cylinders which disturb the writing and reading of data. By reducing the write current on these cylinders, this effect can be prevented.

Register
1. Internal memories of a CPU whose contents can be loaded or modified by instructions or the CPU itself.
2. Components or intermediate memories of peripherals whose value issues a certain action in the device (control register), or whose value indicate the status of the device (status register). The registers are accessed either via ports (that is, the I/O address space (I/O-mapped I/O)), or via the ordinary address space (memory-mapped I/O).

Remanence
The remaining magnetization of a ferromagnetic body if the external magnetic field is switched off. Materials with a high remanence are called magnetically hard; materials with low remanence magnetically soft. The remanence is the basis of all magnetic data recording methods.

REQ
Abbreviation for **req**uest.

RGB
Abbreviation for **R**ed-**G**reen-**B**lue.

RI
Abbreviation for **R**ing **I**ndicator. With RI a DCE informs a DTE that an external unit wants to establish a connection for data transmission.

RISC
Abbreviation for **R**educed **I**nstruction **S**et **C**omputer. Microprocessors which have a significantly reduced instruction set compared to a CISC (typically less than 100 machine instruc-

tions). Characteristic of RISC is that the machine instructions no longer microcoded, but may be executed immediately without decoding. Well-known representatives of RISC processors are MIPS (microprocessor without interlocked pipeline stages) and SPARC.

RLL

Abbreviation for **R**un **L**ength **L**imited. A very efficient encoding method for hard disks or magneto-optical drives where the number of successive zeroes is restricted to a certain range. With RLL 2,7 at least two (but at most seven) zero bits may be in succession. No clock bits are therefore necessary, and the number of required flux changes is reduced to one third. A disadvantage is that the data to record must be re-encoded to fulfil the RLL condition. Therefore, RLL 2,7 allows a data density increase of only 50% compared to MFM. But note that this is achieved without any improvement of the magnetic quality of the disk; the gain is exclusively a consequence of the better encoding method. However, the data retrieval is much more complicated, and because of the burst susceptibility of RLL also more error-prone.

ROM

Abbreviation for **R**ead-**O**nly **M**emory. ROM characterizes a memory chip from which data that has been written in advance can be read but cannot be written in the field. The stored data is determined once, and cannot be modified afterwards (or only with some special equipment). The data stored in a ROM remains, even if the power is switched off.

ROM BIOS

The PC BIOS routines in the ROM on the motherboard.

RS 232C

A generally accepted standard for serial interfaces which defines the signal levels, the signal meanings, the plug layout, and the procedure to establish a connection between a DCE and a DTE.

RTC

Abbreviation for **R**eal-**T**ime **C**lock.

RTS

Abbreviation for **R**equest **T**o **S**end. With RTS a DTE tells a DCE that it wants to transmit data. The DCE then responds with a CTS.

S3

A graphics adapter with a graphics accelerator capable of carrying out simple graphics functions such as drawing a line, filling a rectangle, and bit blitting.

Scan Code

A code which characterizes the keys on a keyboard unambiguously. The scan code is transmitted as make-code to the keyboard interface or the keyboard controller on the motherboard when the key is pressed. If the key is released, the key transmits the same scan code with bit 7 set as a so-called break-code.

Scan Matrix

A matrix made of intersecting lines. In a keyboard small switches are located at these intersections which connect the matrix at these locations if the corresponding key is pressed. The pressed key can thus be determined. In a tablet the controller activates the individual lines in succession so that the position of the moving cross-hair glass may be detected.

Scanner
A reading device with a sensor row which scans an original document (for example, an image, a drawing or text) in a graphical manner and transmits the bit pattern to a computer.

Stepper Motor
A motor that rotates a fixed angle upon every step pulse. Intermediate positions are not possible.

SCSI
Abbreviation for **S**mall **C**omputer **S**ystems **I**nterface. SCSI is an instruction-oriented, high-level interface for external mass storage (for example, hard disk drives, tape drives or CD-ROM). The data transfer is usually carried out at a width of eight bits, with Wide SCSI at 16 or even 32 bits. SCSI interfaces are designed for data transfer rates up to 10 Mbytes/s in synchronous mode (Fast SCSI). SCSI-I standardized only a very small command set, which was enlarged with the Common Command Set. SCSI-II put this bus on a respectable basis, for example, ten SCSI device classes and the accompanying commands were defined, and the synchronous transfer mode (Fast SCSI), as well as the extension of the bus width to 16 and 32 bits (Wide SCSI), was specified. The future SCSI-III standard will define further device classes and commands, especially for graphics interfaces.

SCSI-I, SCSI-II, SCSI-III
See SCSI.

SDLC
Abbreviation for **S**ynchronous **D**ata **L**ink **C**ontrol. A protocol developed by IBM for synchronous data exchange. It is implemented by the SDLC adapter.

SDU
Abbreviation for **S**erial **D**ata **U**nit. The smallest data quantity which is provided by a serial interface or a UART. It comprises one start bit, the data bits, eventually one parity bit, and one, one and a half or two stop bits.

Segment
A section in memory which is described by a segment register or a segment descriptor. Within the segment the objects are addressed by an offset.

Sector Slipping
The shifting of the start of the sector within a hard disk track during the course of bad sector mapping to repair a small defect.

Selector
An index into a descriptor table to select the segment or gate which is described by the descriptor.

Serial Interface
A PC interface that provides or accepts data in serial form as the bits of an SDU.

Serial Mode
A particular high-speed mode of DRAM chips where after supplying and decoding a row and a column address only the $\overline{CAS}$ signal is toggled as a clock signal for data output. Unlike page and static column mode the data within one row can be addressed very quickly in a serial manner. The row and column address passed defines the start of the output. Upon each $\overline{CAS}$ toggle an internal address counter is incremented and the next value is output.

Server
A central computer in a network which manages the common data and supplies it to the workstations in the network. Usually, it controls access of the individual network nodes to peripherals such as printers or modems.

Shadowing
The transfer of ROM code into RAM, where the ROM is masked out of the address space and the RAM is overlaid by the initial ROM address region thereafter. All ROM accesses are now redirected to the faster operating RAM.

Silicon
Chemical symbol Si. A semiconductor which has attained an outstanding importance in microelectronics. By introducing impurity atoms (doping) such as arsenic or phosphorus, the electrical properties of silicon can be varied across a very wide range. Silicon is the main part of quartz (that is, ordinary sand), and is therefore available in unrestricted amounts.

SIMM
Abbreviation for **S**ingle **I**n-line **M**emory **M**odule. A form of memory module with a contact strip to insert the module into a slot like adapter cards.

Simple Instructions
A class of Pentium instructions which can be paired for simultaneous execution in the u- and v-pipes. The simple instructions are completely hardwired and therefore no intervention of microcode is required, thus they can usually be executed within one clock cycle. Examples of simple instructions are MOV, ALU, INC, DEC, PUSH, POP, LEA, JMP/Jcc near, CALL and NOP. ALU is synonymous for any arithmetic or logical instruction.

Simplex
The transmission of data in one direction where the transmission direction, unlike half duplex, cannot be switched. The role of the communication participants as transmitter or receiver is therefore fixed.

SIP
Abbreviation for **S**ingle **I**n-line **P**ackage. A form of memory module with a pin row.

SL Enhanced i486
An i486DX or i486SX with all essential properties such as, for example, 8 kbyte on-chip cache, additionally having various power-saving functions.

Slot
See bus slot.

SMM RAM
Abbreviation for **S**ystem **M**anagement **M**ode **RAM**. The memory accessible in SMM where the processor usually saves its register values upon entering the system management mode.

Snoop Cycle
See inquiry cycle.

Source
One conduction terminal of a field effect transistor.

Space
A form of parity where the parity bit is always equal to 0 independent of the data.

SPARC
A RISC architecture which includes, as a specific feature, a number of registers (up to 2048 or more), the ring-like organized register set. But a task or a routine is only allocated a register window of 32 registers. SPARC processors can carry out a task switch very quickly because only the register window has to be moved, and no storage of the task environment in memory is necessary (at least as long as the register set is not exhausted).

Sputtering
In sputtering a metal which is intended to coat a substrate is atomized in vacuum by ion irradiation. The atoms move to the substrate and are deposited as a very regular and hard coating.

SQFP
Abbreviation for **S**urface Mounted **Q**uad **F**latpack **P**ackage. A package for surface-mounting of chips with contacts on all four sides.

SRAM
Abbreviation for **S**tatic **RAM**. SRAM is a random access memory (RAM) where the information is usually stored as the state of a flip-flop. Because the circuit state of the flip-flop is not changed without a write pulse, an SRAM need not be refreshed as is the case with a DRAM. This is the reason for the name static.

SSI
Abbreviation for **S**mall **S**cale **I**ntegration. This means the integration of fewer than 100 elements on a single chip.

ST506/412
A physical interface between a hard disk controller and a hard disk drive. The standard requires a transfer rate of 5 Mbits/s for MFM encoding, and 7.5 Mbits/s for RLL encoding.

Start Bit
The first bit of an SDU which serves as a trigger for the receiver of the SDU.

Static Column Mode
A particular high-speed mode of DRAM chips where after supplying and decoding a row address only the column address is changed. In a similar way to page mode the data within one row can be addressed randomly and very quickly. Unlike page mode, however, in static column

mode the $\overline{CAS}$ signal need not to be toggled in advance of applying a new column address. The static column chip detects a column change automatically and decodes the new address even without the column address strobe signal $\overline{CAS}$.

Static Electricity
When rubbing two different materials (for example, a cat's fur on a glass stick) the separation of charges occurs. One body is charged with positive and the other with negative charges.

Stop Bit
The last bit of an SDU.

Streamer
A tape drive which mainly serves for archiving and the backup of hard disks. The hard disk data is »streamed« as an uninterrupted bit stream to the streamer.

Streaming Data Procedures
A particular high-speed mode of the micro-channel. The 32-bit SDP is identical to the i486 burst mode as far as the signal course is concerned (data transfer rate max. 40 Mbytes/s). A further increase is achieved with the 64-bit SDP. Here, the address is provided only in the first bus cycle; afterwards the data is transferred both via the 32-bit data bus and the 32-bit address bus, that is, at a width of 64 bits, the transfer rate reaches 80 Mbytes/s. Even more powerful is the extended 64-bit SDP. Here, the bus cycle is shortened from 100 ns to 50 ns; the further data transfer is carried out in the same way as for the normal 64-bit SDP. Thus, the transfer rate is doubled to 160 Mbytes/s.

String
A group of successive characters terminated by \0 (ASCIIZ), or whose length is stored in a string descriptor.

Strobe
A signal that instructs a device such as a DRAM or a latch to read another signal as an address.

Structure Size
The size of the elementary components of a microchip in its smallest extension, therefore usually the width of these components. Source, drain, and gate of MOSFETs, bit lines, etc., belong to the elementary components. The most highly integrated chips have structure sizes of less than 1 μm.

Substrate
The carrier of the microchip circuitry. On the substrate the transistors and connections are formed. In most cases, silicon is used as the substrate material which is doped to adjust the electrical properties as intended.

Super386
A family of i386-compatible Chips & Technologies (C&T) processors. It comprises the processors 38600DX, 38605DX, 38600SX, and 38605SX.

Superscalar architecture
A RISC processor architecture which may start more than one instruction in separate pipelines; for example, a comparison instruction in the ALU pipeline and a floating-point calculation in

the floating-point pipeline. Using this, and some skilful programming techniques, some instructions need less than one clock cycle for execution. Intel's Pentium and i860 and Motorola's MC88110 apply this superscalar principle.

SVGA
Abbreviation. for **S**uper**VGA**. A VESA standard for graphics adapter resolutions and screen modes beyond VGA.

Synchronous
Corresponding to a phase or clock signal, or with the use of a clock signal.

System Clock
A functional group in a PC (or another computer) which generally comprises a PIT, a PIC channel, and a data structure. The group is periodically activated by the PIT to automatically update the data structure so that it always indicates the current time and date. The system clock is part of the operating system. The operating system uses the system clock to provide all files and directories with a time and date mark.

System Management Mode
A particular operating mode of, for example, the Pentium. The system management mode SMM serves mainly for implementing a stand-by state in which the processor requires less power, for example, by switching off or at least reducing the processor clock. The SMM is usually issued by an external signal to a dedicated terminal and leads to an interrupt which reorders addressing of the usual memory or addresses a certain SMM memory. Typically, either all important register contents are saved in a non-volatile memory or the processor is constructed in such a way that it keeps all register values even after switching off the clock. Fast-clocked CMOS CPUs then gain a 99.99% reduction in power consumption.

T
Symbol for **T**era; (that is, one trillion of a quantity), for example in THz = 1 000 000 000 000 Hz. Note that Tbyte generally means 2^{40} bytes and not 10^{12} bytes.

Tag
The tag forms the most important part of a cache directory entry. By means of the tag the cache controller determines whether a cache hit or a cache miss occurs. The tag holds the tag address, that is, particular address bits of the assigned cache line.

Taken Branch
See branch prediction.

TARGA
A standard software interface to SCSI devices.

Task
Also called a process or job. A task is a called program loaded into memory which is managed by the operating system. The operating system activates the individual tasks periodically, and interrupts them. Each task has its own environment. The distinction between task and program is only significant with multitasking operating systems.

Task Register
See TR.

Task State Segment
A data structure in protected mode which describes one task.

Task Switch
Switching from one active task to another task which is currently interrupted. For this purpose the active task is interrupted, all important parameters are saved in the TSS, and the new and up to now inactive task is activated by the operating systm.

Tbyte
2^{40} bytes, **not** 1 000 000 000 000 bytes.

Terminal
1. A device for data input and output which has only a rather simple local logic and is usually connected via a serial interface to the computer. Terminals are employed in multi-user systems.
2. A connection of a chip, interface or other device for inputting or outputting signals or supply voltages.

Text Mode
An operating mode of a graphics adapter where only the characters of a certain character set can be displayed on the monitor. The pixels cannot be addressed individually. The pixels are generated by a hardware character generator.

TIGA
Abbreviation for **T**exas **I**nstruments **G**raphics **A**rchitecture (or **A**dapter). A graphics adapter with an in-built graphics processor.

Timer Chip
See PIT.

Token Bus
A LAN with a physical bus topology, but with a logical ring structure using a modified token passing method.

Token Passing
A method for controlling the net access in a LAN with ring topology where a data packet (the *token*) is always circulating in the ring. A station may only send data when it owns this token.

Token Ring
A LAN developed by IBM using a logical ring structure which is at least partially based on a physical star topology. For that purpose, so-called concentrators are connected with each other in a physical ring. The stations themselves are connected to these concentrators in the form of a physical star topology; the logical ring structure remains.

tpi
Abbreviation for **t**rack **p**er **i**nch.

TR
Abbreviation for **T**ask **R**egister. A memory management register from the 80286 onwards that contains a selector which in turn indicates the descriptor for the active TSS in the global descriptor table.

Trackball
A pointing device which is similar to a mouse lying on its back, and which has two or three buttons. The user rotates an embedded ball. By detecting the ball's rotation using sensors, the track ball logic can determine the direction and amount of the movement.

Track–Track Access Time
The time period necessary to move the read/write head from the current to the adjacent track.

Trap
An exception which is recognized by the processor after executing the instruction which leads to the exception condition. Thus, the return address for the exception handler points to the instruction immediately following on the instruction which caused the exception. A typical trap is the debug breakpoint exception. The exception handler activates the debugger, for example, to display the current register contents. After a return for restarting program execution the processor continues the interrupted task with the next instruction.

Trap Gate
A gate descriptor for calling an interrupt handler. Unlike the interrupt gate the trap gate doesn't clear the interrupt flag.

Triggering
The start or stop of a process by an external signal.

TSOP
Abbreviation for **T**hin **S**mall **O**utline **P**ackage. A very flat package with contacts on two sides. TSOP packages are mainly used for flash memories.

TSS
See task state segment.

TTL
Abbreviation for **T**ransistor-**T**ransistor **L**ogic. A family of logic elements.

Two's Complement
Also 2'complement. A representation of negative numbers where the negative number is generated by complementing all bits of the corresponding positive number and adding the value 1 afterwards.

UART
Abbreviation for **U**niversal **A**synchronous **R**eceiver and **T**ransmitter. A UART is an intelligent microchip for a serial interface which carries out the serialization of parallel data and the insertion of start, parity, and stop bits, or the parallelization of serial data and the separation of start, parity, and stop bits. Typical representatives are the 8250 and the Z80SIO.

ULSI
Abbreviation for **U**ltra **L**arge **S**cale **I**ntegration. This means the integration of more than 1 000 000 elements on a single chip.

Underflow
The condition where the result of an arithmetic operation is too small for the reserved memory location. That is possible, for example, if the divisor in the division of two single-precision real numbers is so big that the result can no longer be represented as a single-precision real number, but the result, however, is different from null. If the result is representable by a single-precision real number but not in normalized form, this is called a gradual underflow.

UNIX
A multitasking operating system for simultaneously serving several workstations. UNIX is manufacturer-independent, and therefore its importance for more powerful computers (workstations) has been growing in the past few years.

Upgrade
Unlike the coprocessor, the upgrade not only supplies an enhancement for floating-point operations, but also takes over the previous CPU's jobs. Therefore, an upgrade is a complete and usually much more powerful CPU. In the case of the i486SX, which lacks the coprocessor, the corresponding upgrade (the i487SX) supplies a coprocessor as well as a faster CPU.

u-Pipe
Abbreviation for u-pipeline.

u-Pipeline
One of the two Pentium integer pipelines. The u-pipeline can execute all integer instructions and more or less forms the «main pipeline».

USART
Abbreviation for **U**niversal **S**ynchronous and **A**synchronous **R**eceiver and **T**ransmitter. Unlike the UART, a USART additionally has a logic for serial data transmission.

VESA Local Bus
See VL Bus.

VGA
Abbreviation for **V**ideo **G**raphics **A**rray or **V**ideo **G**raphics **A**dapter. VGA was introduced by IBM with the PS/2 series as a successor for EGA. Unlike the other graphics adapters, VGA supplies an analogue signal. Therefore, 256 different colours from a palette of 262 144 ($=2^{18}$) colours may be displayed simultaneously.

Video Memory
See video RAM.

Video RAM
Also called video memory or display memory. In text mode the screen words, and in graphics mode the pixel values, are stored in video RAM. With most of the graphics adapters, the video RAM is divided into several pages. The graphics control chip then reads the video RAM continuously to display the written information as text or graphics on the monitor.

Virtual 8086 Mode
An advanced operating mode from the i386 where the access of a task to code and data segments and the I/O address space is automatically checked by the processor hardware. But the address generation with segment and offset is done in the same manner as in real mode. Real mode applications can thus be executed in a protected environment. With paging, several virtual 8086 tasks are possible in parallel.

VLB
Abbreviation for **VL B**us. See VL Bus.

VL Bus
VESA's local bus standard with a bus width of usually 32 bits operating up to 66 MHz (on-board only). An extension to 64 bits is intended for the standard 2.0. Unlike PCI, there is no decoupling of processor and expansion bus. The transfer rate reaches 160 Mbytes/s at 32 bits and 267 MBytes/s at 64 bits. Usually, VLB slots and (E)ISA slots are combined.

VLSI
Abbreviation for **V**ery **L**arge **S**cale **I**ntegration. This means the integration of 100 000 to 1 000 000 elements on a single chip.

VMS
Abbreviation for **V**irtual **M**achine **S**ystem. An operating system for DEC mainframes which operates using the concept of a virtual machine for each user.

Voice Coil Actuator
Also called linear motor. A driving device for the access arm of a hard disk drive where a permanent magnet on the access arm moves in a coil which is energized from a driver circuit. The access arm is thus moved by the magnetic action of a coil and permanent magnet in the same way as the membrane of a speaker.

v-Pipe
Abbreviation for v-pipeline.

v-Pipeline
One of the two Pentium integer pipelines. The v-pipeline can only execute so-called simple instructions, and is only used for the second instruction of an instruction pair (if instruction pairing is possible).

VRAM
Abbreviation for **V**ideo **RAM**. Specifically, dual-port RAM chips used for the video RAM of graphics adapters.

Way
The term way indicates the associativity of a cache. For a given set address the tag addresses of all ways are simultaneously compared with the tag part of the address provided by the CPU to determine a cache hit or miss. Thus, a data group which corresponds to a cache line can be stored at different locations, the number of which matches the number of implemented ways.

WE
Abbreviation for **W**rite **E**nable. A control signal for a RAM chip which indicates that the access is a write cycle and the RAM chip should store the data supplied at the specified address.

Weitek
A US firm which became known by its 80x87-compatible coprocessors for the 80x86 family. Many Personal Computers have a Weitek socket as well as the 80x87 socket for inserting a Weitek 80x87.

Wide Area Network
A data network which is not restricted in terms of distance. Typical distances are larger than 100 km. The scientific networks or the NASA data network for the supervision of missile starts and flight trajectories are wide area networks.

Wide SCSI
An extension of the SCSI bus width from eight to 16 or even 32 bits implemented with SCSI-II. See SCSI.

Word
Two bytes, that is, 16 bits.

Word Line
The line in the row direction within a memory cell array of a RAM or ROM which turns on the access transistors of one memory row or page. The word line is usually connected to the gate of the access transistors.

WORM
Abbreviation for **W**rite **O**nce, **R**ead **M**any (times). A WORM is usually an optical drive where the data carrier may be written by the user without any restriction. Unlike magneto-optical drives, here the data medium cannot be erased.

Wrap-around
If the address exceeds the maximum possible value, a wrap-around occurs because the highest order address bit cannot be put into the address register or onto the address bus. This applies to the 8086 if the segment register also holds the value ffffh and the offset register holds the same value ffffh. The result is the 20-bit address 0ffefh. The leading 1 is, as the 21st address bit, neglected, and the address jumps from a value at the top of memory to a value very near to the bottom of memory.

Write Allocation
If a cache miss for a write access occurs in a system with cache and main memory, that is, the address to be written is not located in the cache, then the cache carries out a cache line fill to read the corresponding data. Usually a cache line fill is executed only when a read miss occurs.

Write-Back
Also called copy-back. Write-back refers to a cache strategy where, when writing data, the data is merely written into the cache but not into main memory. The data writing into main memory is carried out only upon an explicit request (cache flush) or if a cache line was to be replaced.

Write Precompensation
On hard disks there may be bit shiftings in the inner cylinders with high cylinder numbers which disturb the reading and writing of data. By an intended shifting of the individual bits when writing data, this effect is prevented. This is called write precompensation.

Write-Through
Also write-thru. Write-through characterizes a cache strategy where the data is always written into main memory when data is written by the CPU. Therefore, the write-through is carried out through the cache system. Additionally, the data may be written into the cache SRAM but this is not necessary.

X-Bus
That part of the PC/XT/AT system bus which accesses the I/O ports on the motherboard, for example the registers of the PIC, PIT or the keyboard controller.

XENIX
Microsoft's UNIX implementation for Personal Computers.

XT
1. Abbreviation for extended technology.
2. The successor of the PC with an 8086 processor and an internal 16-bit data bus.

Z4
The first freely programmable digital computer from Konrad Zuse. It operated with an electro-mechanical relay.

Z80
A common 8-bit microprocessor for CP/M which was, for example, used in the well-known Sinclair.

Index

(BPI) 735
(E)ISA bus 547
(MPC) 1014
(PCI) 513
(S)VGA 965
(TLB) 254
(ZIF) socket 278
_dos_gettime 592
μ 1245
μm 1247
μPD765 714, 1248
0WS 472
1-bit adder 161
1-bit adder with carry 161
1-transistor 1 capacitor 395
1/2x, 2/5x or 1/3x clock 281
10-byte commands 822, 1105, 1121
12-byte commands 822
14.3 MHz 508
16-Bit AT architecture 461
16-bit checksums 697
16-bit devices 467
16-bit MCA adapters 505
16-bit memory 380
16-bit peripherals 468
16-bit ports 152, 266
16-bit section 505
16-bit transfers 543
16-colour EGA modes 983
16450 20, 872, 1217
16450/16550 872, 878
16550 873, 1217
168-pin PGA overdrive 277
169-pin overdrives 277
1 Mword * 1 bit organization 404
1x-clock 273
2-1-1-1 burst 255, 337
2-1-1-1-... burst 521
2-input OR 158
2-way interleaving 337, 408
2-way set-associative
  cache 216, 218
256 kword * 4 bit organization 404
28F010 flash memory 446
2x-clock 273
3-2-2-2 burst 256
3-way interleaving 409
3.3 V adapter 535
3 1/2" floppies 655, 656
32-bit full adder 161
32-bit MCA adapters 505
32-bit ports 152, 266
32-bit SDP 495
32-bit section 505
32-MB boundary 667
34-pole flat cable 685
360 kbyte floppies in 1.2 Mbyte drives 729
38600DX 1217
38600DX/38600SX 206
38600SX 1217
38605DX 1217
38605DX/38605SX 206
38605SX 1217
386SL 194, 196, 1217
386SLC 210, 1217
4-1-1-1 burst 340
4-way interleaving 409
4-way set-associative cache 215
4 Mbyte memory chip 392
4 Mbyte pages 330
486DLC 209, 276, 1217
486DLC3 294
486DX2 processors 273
486SLC 209, 1217
486SLC2 294
5 1/4" floppies 655, 656
5 V boards 535
51258 437
6-byte commands 1105, 1107
64-bit expansion 539, 553
64-bit SDP 495, 496, 511
64-bit transfers 544
64-bit VLB read transfer burst 545
64-bit VLB single write transfer 544
64 kbit chips 392
640 kbyte boundary 36, 1218
6502 1218
68000 39, 1218
6845 12, 454, 962, 964, 967, 1218
– data register 967
– data register indices 970
– graphics controller 962
– index register 967
– register values 977
– video controller 958
71h (data register) 647
8-bit channels 455, 467
8-bit peripherals 467, 468
8-bit PC/XT architecture 451
8-bit ports 152, 266
8-bit processor 372
8-bit section 505

8-way set-associative caches 216
8/16-converter 451
80186/88 383, 1039, 1218
80286 354, 461, 1039, 1218
– bus cycles and pipelining 362
– connections and signals 354
– gate descriptor 360
– gates 105
– general-purpose registers 358
– I/O address space 354
– memory management registers 358
– pinout 354
– protected mode 358
– protection for I/O address space 361, 362
– register contents after a reset 364
– registers 357, 358
– reset 364
– segment and access types 359
– segment descriptor 358, 359
– special cycles 362
– system segment types 360
– task gate 360
– task state segment 361
– TSS 360
– /80287 system configuration 371
80287 365, 461, 1049, 1218
– connections and signals 366
– control word 369
– exceptions 370
– number formats 365
– pin assignment 366
– port addresses 370
– reset 369
– structure and functioning 369
80287XL 365, 1049, 1218
80386 1219
80386SX 1219
80387 1219
80387SX 1219
8042 26, 921, 1218
8048 26, 920, 1218
80486 1219
80486DX2 1219
80486SX 1219
80487SX 1219
80586 1219
8080 372, 426
8080/85 1218
8086 372, 450, 1218
– bus cycle 378
– operating modes 376
– pinout 372
– real mode 377
– reset 381
8086/8087 system configuration 390
8086/88 450, 1034
– address wrap-around 937
– dummy read cycle 389
8087 365, 385, 450, 1045, 1219
– control word 388
– memory cycles 389
– number formats 385
– pin assignment 386
– status word 388
– structure and functioning 388
– tag word 389
8088 382, 450, 1218
– pin assignment 382
80x86 7, 39, 1219
– exceptions 1052
– processor machine instructions 1034
80x87 8, 171
– processor machine instructions 1045
82072A 714, 1219
82077A 714, 1219
82284 371, 1219
82288 1219
82288 bus controller 461
82357 ISP 478
82358 EBC 478
82360SL 194, 196, 199
– I/O-subsystem 1217
82365SL 904
8237A 599, 1219
– cascading 608
– connections and signals 599
– internal registers 603
– pin assignment 600
– standby mode 606
82389 174
82450 872, 1219
82489DX 575, 1219
82491 351, 1219
82495DX 352
82496 351, 1220
82498DX 576
8250 20, 872, 1220
8250/16450/16550 registers and programming 880
8250A 872, 1220
8250B 872, 1220
8250C 1220
8253 1220
– control register 583
8253/8254 465
– control word 583
– counting modes 588
– operating modes 589

– pin assignment 581
– PIT 457
– register ports 583
– terminals and signals 581
8254 1220
8255
– control word 633
– internal structure 630
– PPI 630, 453, 921
  – structure and operating modes 636
8255A 1220
8259A 452, 465, 557, 558, 1220
– connections and signals 559
– PIC I/O addresses 566
8284 1220
– clock generator 450
8288 1220
– bus controller 376, 390, 450
82C212 configuration registers 427
82C212 connections 413
82C212 DRAM organization 418
82C212 page/interleave memory controller 412
8514/A 505, 989, 1220
8741 921, 1220
8742 921, 1220
9-pin connection for serial interface 857
9th pixel column 961

A
Abbreviation 1236, 1262
ABIOS 115, 1220
– standard functions 118
Abort 1220
Abort SCSI command 1136
Abort tag process 814
Abort the reading of sectors before the end of the track 722
Abortion 813
Accelerator chip 989, 1011, 1012
Access an external device 850
Access arm 658
Access behaviour of PCMCIA card 903
Access conflicts 965
Access data with a deleted address mark 721
Access levels 33, 702
Access of the CPU to a video RAM 966
Access path 675
Access possibilities to the serial interface 867
Access procedure 913
Access time 9, 379, 398, 421, 655, 748, 833, 1221
Access to a double word 149
Access to graphics adapters 1162
Access to interfaces 1139
Access to SRAM memory cells 436
Access to the I/O address space 380
Access to the internal cache 233
Access to the second-level cache 220
Access transistor 396, 400, 434, 437
Access types 98
Access via Address and Data Register 647
Access via BIOS Interrupt INT 13h 709
Access via DOS 705, 773, 867
Access via the BIOS 647, 773, 868
Access width of the DMA channel 482
Accessed 100
Accessing the 8259A registers 566
Accessing the screen via DOS 992
Accessing the screen via the BIOS 993
Accessing the video memory 1001
Accumulator 55, 56, 1221
Acknowledge 853, 1209
Action point 946
Activate SuperState V mode 208
Activating a drive 686
Activation register 524
Active level of the DACK signals 613
Active mode 502
Active page 968, 1164, 1165
Active-high 1221
Active-low 1221
Actuator 733, 1221
Actuator with a linear motor 738, 740
Actuator with a stepper motor 737
Adapter activation 501, 502, 503
Adapter busmaster 522
Adapter card 1221
Adapter description file 503
Adapter functions 1195
Adapter port address 890
Adapter setup 502
Adapter types 976
ADC 1221
Additional status codes 1132
Additive colour mixing 955
Address 9, 48, 1221
– and count register I/O addresses 618
– buffer 141, 394, 399
– bus 9, 68, 458, 461, 1221
– generation in real mode 80
– generation with 8237A 605
– line A20 79, 937
– mark 662
– multiplexer 141, 452, 464
– of the display memory word 965
– of the mouse driver 1158
– parity error 297, 349
– phase 516
– pipelining 147, 238, 304, 335, 379

– sequence 338
– size prefix 91
– space 36, 1221
– translation with segmentation and paging 124
– window enable register 905
– wrap-around 228
Addresses in video RAM 1012
Addresses in virtual 8086 mode 128
Addressing 72, 426
Addressing schemes 73, 74
Addressing unit 47
Advanced BIOS 116, 464, 821, 1220
Advanced micro devices 1222
Advanced Programmable Interrupt Controller 576, 1219
Advanced RLL 757, 1223
Advanced SCSI Programming Interface 825, 1134, 1223
Advanced technology 461
Advantage of microprogramming 165
AEOI mode 562, 564
Affine 184, 369, 388
Air circulation in a hard disk drive 742
Air filtering 741
Alarm function 641
Alarm interrupt 641
Alias 100
Aligning the domains 653
Alignment check 249
Alignment error 249
Alignment exception 250
Allocation length 823
Allocation unit 662, 673
Alpha 318
Alternate Print Screen routine 1000
Alternate scan code sets of the MF II keyboard 940
Alternate status register 799
Alternative key names 919
Alternative track 758, 760
ALU 47, 1222
AM29C660 699
Am386DX 1222
Am386DX/Am386SX 204
Am386DXL 1222
Am386DXL/Am386SXL 204
Am386DXLV 1222
Am386DXLV/Am386SXLV 205
Am386SX 1222
Am386SXL 1222
Am386SXLV 1222
Am486DX/Am486SX 291
Am486DX/SX 1222
Am486DX2 291, 1222
Am486DXLV/Am486SXLV 291, 293, 1222
AMD 1222
AMD clones 290
AMD processors 204
AMD system management mode 292
American National Standards Institute 1222
American Standard Code for Information Interchange 1223
Amiga 15
Amorphous form 835
Analogue 1222
Analogue circuit 41
Analogue monitor 13, 985, 1222
Analogue signal 985
Analogue to digital converter 1221
AND and OR combination 157
AND 157, 158
ANMI 207, 208
ANSI 1222
APIC 576, 1219, 1222
Apple 806
– Macintosh 15, 39
Application of the parallel interface 851
Application programs 33, 88, 702
Application segment 98, 99, 359
Application Specific IC 1223
Applications for SMM 292
Arbitration 578
– cycle 498
– phase 810
– priorities in the PS/2 496
– protocol 546
– register 498
Architecture 1223
Archive bit 672
ARCNET 915
Arithmetical and Logical Unit 47, 1222
ARLL 757, 1223
Arrangement of boot sector, FATs, root directory, subdirectories and files 670
Arrow mask 946
AS 873
ASCII 43, 44, 925, 926, 1027, 1223
ASCIIZ string 44, 1223
ASIC 1223
ASPI 825, 826, 1134, 1223
ASPI functions 826, 1134
ASPI Programming Interface 1134
ASPI status codes 1138
Assembler 73, 1223
Associative addressing 217
Associative memory (CAM) 214, 1223
Associativity of a cache 1266
Associativity of the cache system 215

Asynchronous 1223
Asynchronous bus system 494
Asynchronous extended bus cycle 494
Asynchronous mode 808
Asynchronous operation of CPU and coprocessor 371
AT 1223
AT and MF II keyboards 922, 932
AT architecture 462
AT attachment 790, 1223
AT BIOS 754, 768, 791
AT bus 16, 18, 464, 790, 1223
AT bus frequencies 474
AT bus slots 470, 471
AT controller 746
AT DMA channels 468
AT hardware interrupt channels 465
AT keyboard 924
AT or ISA bus 463
AT port addresses 466
AT slots 463
AT task file 781, 795, 1089
AT timer channels 465
AT, MF II or PS/2 keyboard controller 932, 933
ATA 790, 1223
ATN 809
Attribute 672, 960, 1224
Attribute bits and corresponding colours 979
Attribute controller 982
AU 47
Audible range of tones 623
Audio 508
Audio tape 655
AudioGND 508
Auto halt power down mode 288
Auto idle power down mode 288
Autoconfiguration 765
Autoconfiguring controllers 761, 765
Autoinitialization 612
Automatic configuration 488, 501
Automatic end-of-interrupt 568
Automatic head parking device 739
Automatic interrupt completion 562
Automatic line feed 846, 849
Autopark 1224
Autopark function 31
AUX 1224
Auxiliary carry 61
Auxiliary device 949
Avalanche breakthrough 444
Average access time 749, 1224
Average positioning 748
AX 57

B

B class 918
B-cable 831
Back invalidation cycle 226
Back link 108
Background colour 960
Backoff 230
Backup ring 918
Backwards compatibility 56
Bad sector remapping 754, 758, 762, 793, 1110, 1224
Bank enable registers 430
Bank select register 988, 1009, 1010
Bank structure of the video RAM 1009
Banks 8, 408
Base 43, 167
Base address 93, 684, 847, 880
Base address LPT1 844
Base address of the EMS windows 431
Base address register for memory and I/O ports 529
Base address register(s) 528
Base addresses of the UARTs 880
Base bits 359
Base frequency 1024
Base index of the generator cells and channels 1022
Base memory 645
Base pointer 58
Base register 57, 74
BASIC 1224
Basic and sub-class codes 526
Basic assurance test 943
Basic class code 526
Basic components 1
Basic input/output system 705, 1225
Basic layout of a TIGA adapter 991
Basic layout of an accelerator card 990
Basic PC equipment 2
Basics of RISCs 166
Battery and accumulator 25
Battery-buffered RAM 637
Baud rate 21, 854, 870, 885, 1224
Baud rate generator 878
Baud rate reference frequency 876
Baudot 854
BCD 46, 61, 1224
BCD counting 584
BCD numbers 46
BCLK 491
BCLK stretching 478
Beginner's desktop PC 50
Berkeley concept 240
Bias generator 355

Biased exponent 167, 168
BiCMOS 160, 281
Bidirectional 1224
Bidirectional bus 142
Big Blue 1225
Big endian format 47, 1225
Binary 43
Binary coded decimals 46, 1224
Binary counting 584
Binary digit 1225
Binary system 43
BIOS 32, 35, 421, 452, 464, 704, 768, 1225
– access to extended memory 115
– Clock Interrupt 1ah 1054
– configuration 753
– counting for the floppy drives 709
– data area and parallel interface 844
– data area and serial interface 871
– data area for floppy drives 712
– data area for hard disks 779
– data area for the DOS system clock 593
– data area of EGA/VGA BIOS extension 996
– data area of system BIOS 995
– extension 1162
– extension of EGA and VGA adapters 771, 1170
– extension of SVGA adapters 1187
– extensions and booting 768
– functions 1140, 1142
– identifier 769
– interrupt 10h 993, 1163, 1170, 1187
– interrupt 13h 766, 1058
– interrupt 14h 868, 870, 1141, 1142
– interrupt 15h 1147, 1151
– interrupt 16h 1149
– interrupt 17h 1139, 1140
– interrupt 1ah 530, 647, 1054
– setup configuration 753
– setup program 412
– storage area and keyboard 929
– track length 778
Bipolar transistors 160
BIST 258, 332, 1225
Bistable multivibrator 434, 1236
Bit 43, 125, 1225
Bit cell 691
Bit density 735
Bit line 400, 1225
Bit line pairs 395, 399, 437
Bit-shiftings 747
Bits per inch (BPI) 663
Bits per second 854
Block descriptor 1115, 1130
Block diagram of a dynamic RAM 394
Block diagram of a flash memory 443
Block diagram of a floppy controller 714
Block diagram of a graphics adapter 957
Block diagram of a PC 6, 449
Block diagram of the parallel interface 845
Block transfer 607
Blue Lightning 276, 294, 1225
BNC 1225
BNC cable 13, 916
BNC T-connector 916
Board 1225
Boosting circuitry 444
Boot from a floppy 674
Boot from the hard disk 670
Boot record 668
Boot sector 668
Booting 847, 1225
Bootstrap 1225
Bottlenecks in local bus systems 554
Bouncing 1226
BOUND 85
Boundary scan path 264, 347
Boundary scan register 262
Boundary scan test 1226
Bpi 1226
Bps 854, 1226
Branch delay slots 244
Branch prediction 77, 308, 318, 1226
Branch taken message cycle 302
Branch Target Buffer 309, 318
Branch Trace Buffer 308, 318, 1226
Branch trace message cycle 299, 340, 350
Branch trace signals 299
Break error 857
Break of the connection 869
Break state 884
Break-code 634, 922, 1226
Breakpoint 65, 67, 85
– hits 298
– interrupt 62
– pins 298
Bridge 513
Bright pixel 955
BU 47
Buffer organization 928
Buffer-full signal 865, 866
Buffered character input 926
Buffered mode 568
BUFFERS 214
Built-In Self-Test 1225, 1226
BURST 509
Burst accesses 520
Burst capabilities and bus width 551
Burst cycle 220, 229, 255, 336, 479, 543
Burst errors 697

Burst mode 212, 216, 255, 542, 1226
Burst read cycle 336, 337
Burst transfer rate 256, 338
Burst write cycle 338, 543
Burst write-back cycle 341
Bus 1226
Bus arbitration 138, 473, 479, 496, 521, 546
Bus buffer of the VL bus 541
Bus controller 140, 377, 1219, 1220
Bus cycle 378, 516, 542
– for read access 142
– for write access 144
– with BCLK stretching 479
Bus frequency 475
Busmaster 455, 463, 473, 546, 1226
– adapter 497
– interface 478
Bus mice 27, 946
Bus slots 7, 451, 452, 457, 463, 470, 1227
Bus topology 910, 911
Bus unit 47
Bus-clear delay 810
Bus-free phase 810
BUSY 138, 177, 196, 355, 366, 386
Button byte 1158
Button status 892
BYPASS 265
Bypassing 240
Byte 1227
Byte granularity 90

C
C class 918
C concentrator 918
C64 1218
C8042CS 202
Cache 9, 299, 1227
– association 353
– buffer access 260
– consistency 221, 225, 1227
– controller 211, 1220
– directory 214, 215
– directory entry 214, 1262
– entry 215
– flush 213, 214, 247, 1227
– hit 212, 1227
– hit determination 217
– invalidation 213, 231, 551
– line 212, 216, 218
– line fill 212, 235, 299, 335
– line fill buffer 235
– line fill cycle 215, 231
– memory 9, 146, 434, 794
– memory entry 214
– miss 212, 219, 1227
– organization 214
– pages 218
– principle 211
– sectoring 352
– SRAM 211
– strategies 211, 251
– test data register TR3 259
– test status register TR4 260
– unit 211, 233
Caching 211
Caching at a page level 324
CACP 496
CAD 1227
CAD applications 953
Calibrate drive 1079, 1090
Call and return values of CPUID 285, 290, 335
Call gate 102, 103, 360, 1227
Call mask for user-defined procedure 948
Calling format of INT 15h, function 84h 893
CAM 216, 790, 825, 828, 1227
CAM Control Block 828
CAM driver 829
CAM instructions 828
Capacity 747, 833
Capacity information 1122
Capacity of a disk 735
Capture DR 265
Card Detect contacts 899
Card memory 896
Card offset 898
Card offset setup 907
Card Services 902, 1212
Carriage Return 1230
Carrier Sense Multiple Access/Collision Detection 913, 1230
Carry 60, 161
CAS (column address strobe) 393, 395, 410, 1228
CAS access time 398
CAS-before-RAS 403, 595, 1228
Cascading 563, 607
– scheme 608
Cases 4
Cassette recorder 18, 635, 636, 655
Cathode 954
CBIOS 116
CCB 828
CCITT 698, 857, 1228
– X.25 894
CCS 1228
CD player 17, 833
CD-I 833, 1228
CD-interactive 833, 1228
CD-ROM 17, 833, 834, 1228

– disk 833
Cell linking 1024, 1025
Cell types 399
Central arbitration control point 496
Central Processing Unit 7, 1230
Centronics 18, 1228
– cable 839, 845
– plug 840
– standard 849
Century byte 646
CESR 346
CGA 965, 978, 1002
– attribute decoder 979
– I/O ports 979
– parameters 978
– text mode 1002
CH 57
Change definition 1130
Channel 40
Channel mask register 615, 616
Channel registers 1023
Character code 960
Character definition tables 984, 986, 997
Character generation 962
Character generation in text mode 960
Character generator 13, 957, 984, 1228
Character matrix 962, 997
Character RAM 962
Character ROM 957
Character sets 997
Character transfer 848
Charge state of the battery or accumulator 642
CHCK 509
Cheapernet 915, 916, 1228, 1235
Check controller RAM 779
Check Drive Status 1081
Check Interrupt Status 1079
Check status 815
Checker 301
Checking of extension adapters 635
Checking the data path between controller and main memory 1064, 1065, 1100, 1101
Checksum 642, 646
Chip 1229
Chip sets 384, 557, 1229
Chips & Technologies 206
CISC 71, 165, 235, 1229
– processor 163
CKM 177, 365, 367
CL 57
Class code 526
Classes of station 918
CLC 61
CLD 62
Clear mask register 618
Clear pending interrupts 883
Clear queue 814
Clear to Send 858, 873, 1230
«Click» to keyboards 627
Clock bit 691
Clock frequencies 270
Clock gate 694
Clock generator 1219, 1220
Clock rates indicated on the chips 274
Clock signal for the keyboard 635
Clock tripled 280
Clock window 694
Clocked flip-flops 436
Clocking mode 367
Clones 192
Cluster 662, 673
Cluster chain 677
Cluster enumeration 677
Cluster size 677
CMC 61
CMD 491, 495, 510
CMOS 42, 1229
CMOS inverter 158, 159
CMOS RAM 24, 25, 453, 466, 485, 636, 637
– configuration in the PS/2 639
– page register 649
– memory configuration 638
COBOL 1229
Code 42
– cache 321
– optimization 345
– segment 59, 69
– words 701
COE 196
Coercive force 653
Coercivity 653, 1229
Cold boot 156
Colour generation with palette registers 984
Colour generation with the video DAC registers 987
Colour graphics adapter 978
Colour page 986
Colour palette 985
Column address strobe 393, 410, 414, 1228
Column decoder 398, 399
COM programs 73
COM1 880
COM1, COM2, COM3, COM4 1229
Combicontroller 14, 15, 684, 781, 1229
Combining screen bit, screen and cursor mask 945
Command block 782
Command byte structure 822

Command codes 798
Command complete 813
Command cycle 142
Command interpreter 34, 704
Command link 823
Command parameter registers 799
Command phase 720, 800, 812
Command register 614, 798
Command transfer 784
COMMAND.COM 35, 704
Commands for the auxiliary device mouse 950
Commands for the keyboard 939
Common access method 790, 825, 828, 1229
Common command set (CCS) 830, 1229
Common data area 117
Communication between CPU and 80287 370
Communication between i386 and i387 189
Communication via the ICC bus 577
Communications interface 7, 21
Communications port 864, 1229
Communications server 910
Compact disc 17
Comparators 218
Compatibility 771
Compatible mode 480
Compiler 1229
Complex instruction set computer 235, 1229
Compressed mode 611, 612
Compression 1017
Computer architecture 449
Computer-aided design 1227
COMx base addresses and IRQ channels 880
CON 12, 926, 1229
Concentrators 916, 1230
Concept of coprocessors 174
Concept of microprogramming 162
Concept of the four privilege levels 88
Concert pitch 623
Condition code 183
Conditional branch 319
CONFIG.SYS 214, 639, 681
CONFIG_ADDRESS 523
CONFIG_ADDRESS register 524
CONFIG_DATA 523
Configuration address area 514, 516, 523, 525
Configuration byte/word/double word read 531
Configuration byte/word/double word write 532
Configuration control register 717, 718
Configuration cycle 523
Configuration data 636, 647, 715
Configuration file 488
Configuration mechanism #1 524
Configuration mechanism #2 524
Configuration of a PC floppy controller 715
Configuration read access 518
Configuration register 549, 967, 969
Configuration settings 634, 635
Configuration write access 518
Conforming 101, 102
Connecting and configuring ESDI hard disk drives 789
Connecting and configuring ST412/506 hard disk drives 783
Connection between drive and controller 780
Connection between the serial interface and a printer 865
Connection of a printer 840
Connection of timer and DMA chip for the memory refresh 595
Connection scheme 873
Connection to printers and the zeromodem 864
Console 12, 926, 1229, 1230
Content Addressable Memory 216, 1227
Continuous envelope 1021
Continuous multistaged functions 117
Control and status registers of the PCIC 82365SL 904
Control and status registers on a PCMCIA card 898
Control bits for the i486 on-chip cache 248
Control bus 68, 461, 1230
Control byte structure 824
Control cable with twisted wires 783
Control cable without twisted wires 783
Control cells 263, 347
Control characters 44, 926, 1147, 1148, 1162
Control commands 1072, 1078
Control commands to the keyboard 936
Control of the bus 809
Control program for microcomputers 681, 1230
Control register 52, 63, 612, 847, 848, 851, 934, 986
Control register CR0 92, 248, 250, 322, 358
Control register CR3 249
Control register CR4 284, 325
Control register for level/edge triggering 483
Control register TR12 350
Control signals for arbitration 522
Control transfer 102
Control unit 47, 162, 180, 308, 1231
Control word 632
Control/event select register 326, 346
Controller 7, 15, 16, 684, 1230
Controller and drive 745
Controller and interfaces 744
Controller commands 717, 801, 935

Controller cylinder layout 761
Controller diagnostics 779
Controller error codes 779
Controller of the IDE hard disk 795
Controller's sector buffer 1064, 1065, 1100, 1101
Controller–drive data transfer rate 1067
Controllers with an ST412/506 interface 781
Conversion 176
Conversion logical and physical structures 820
Conversion table 925
Coprocessor 8, 167, 171, 1230
– emulation 64
– error 86, 115, 187, 370
– exception 184
– port addresses 189, 194
– segment overflow 114, 186, 370
COPY 841
Copy-back 212, 1267
Core memory 236
Core storage 165
Count register 55, 57
Counter 1 594
Counter latch command 584, 585
Counter mode 588
Counting element 580
Counting format 584
Counting mode of the counter 584
Counting starts at the outermost track 661
COUNTRY = xxx 639
CP/M machines 424, 681, 1230
CPL 87
CPU 7, 39, 52, 1230
– access rate 409
– and memory benchmarks 220
– bus 68
– clock speed 551
– identification 334
– register dump 343
CPU–controller–drive connection 684
CPUID 284, 289, 334
call and return values 286, 291, 337
CPURESET 198, 199
CR 1230
CR0 control register 55
CR3 register 108, 120
CR4 control register 326
CRC 689, 690, 691, 694, 1230
– checksum 697, 1082
– code 699, 1060
CRC–CCITT 698, 700
Cross-hair glass 953
CRTC (cathode ray tube controller) 956, 958, 1218
CRTC 6845 terminals 958
Crystalline or polycrystalline coating 835
CS 59, 559, 582, 600, 629, 958
CS82310 419
CSMA/CD 913, 1230
Ctrl-Alt-Del 931
Ctrl-Break 931
Ctrl-C 1148
Ctrl-P 1148
CTS 858, 873, 1230
CTTY 867
CU 47, 1231
Curie point 654, 836
Curie point/Curie temperature 1231
Curie temperature 654
Current adapter status 969
Current pointers 812
Current Privilege Level 87
CURSOR 958
Cursor end 974
Cursor flag 1153
Cursor high/low 975
Cursor mask 944
Cursor parameters are stored in the BIOS data area 1164
Cursor size in text mode 1164
Cursor start 974
CWE 196
CX 57
Cx486S 294
Cx486S2/50 294
Cx487S 294
Cycle time 398, 407
«back-to-back» cycles 527
Cyclic redundancy check 690, 1230
Cyclic redundancy code 1230, 1233
Cylinder 662
Cylinder boundary 711, 712
Cylinder LSB 797
Cylinder MSB 797
Cylinder number 761, 802, 1058
Cyrix 209, 1231
Cyrix clones 294

D

D/C 139, 232, 300, 552
DAC 1231
DAC colour register 986
DACK level bit 614
DAM 690
Damping factor 1021
Darker points 955
DASD 1066
Data 99
– address mark 690, 746, 796

– area 674
– backup 32
– bit 691, 870
– buffer 141
– bus 9, 68, 461, 1231
– cache 321
– Carrier Detect 858, 874, 1231
– carrier equipment 857
– carrier organization 661
– checking using CRC values 698
– Communication Equipment 1231
– exchange via host adapter and the SCSI bus 825
– exchange via the parallel interface 852
– flow inside the PC 6
– format register 884
– gate 693
– length 723
– mark 662
– medium 734, 1231
– packet 894
– parity fault 348
– phase 720, 724, 800, 812
– register 57, 717, 795, 847, 850, 1071
– registers ports 70h 647
– Segment 59, 99
– Segment (DS) 72
– separator 714, 745, 747
– Set Ready 858, 874, 1233
– signal rate 857
– signal rate detector 859
– swapper 478
– synchronizer 15, 714
– terminal equipment 857, 1231, 1233
– Terminal Ready 858, 874, 1233
– transfer 800, 859
– transfer between memory and coprocessor 390
– transfer commands 1071, 1072
– transfer on the SCSI bus 809
– transfer rate 336, 514, 542, 547, 717, 729, 747, 750, 794, 831, 833, 1070
– transfer via the parallel interface 852
– window 693
– write 399
Data-in phase 812
Data-out phase 812
Datanets, Packet Switching and PAD Adapters 894
DATE 636
Date stored 672
Daylight saving function 639, 641
DCD 858, 874, 1231
DCE 857, 1231
DD 1231
DDIS 874
DE 326, 959
Debug address registers 67
Debug extensions 331
Debug mode control register 346
Debug registers 63, 65, 298
Debug status registers 67
Debug trap bit 108
Debugging extension bit 326
Decimal 43
– numbers 43
Decoding MFM data 694
Decoding phase 238
Decoding time 162, 236
Decoding unit 162
Decoupling of processor memory subsystems and the PCI bus 516
Defect list 1126
Defect parameters 1110
Definition of windows in the I/O address space 907
Degree of the generator polynomial 701
Delay loops have a significant disadvantage
Delay slots 243
Delayed branch 243
Delayed jump 243
Demand paging 100, 749
Demand transfer 607
DEModulator 21
Denormalized operand 186
Density code 1116
Descending envelope 1021
Descriptor 1231
Descriptor privilege level 91
Descriptor type 98
Desktop case 4
Destination Index 59
Detecting a statistical error 702
Detecting the start bit 878, 879
Detection of bus interface errors 348
Detection of internal errors 348
Determination of the interface status 869
Determine a disk change 719
Determine buffer status 1149
Determine controller version 1084
Determine drive parameters 772
Determine status 951
– cache hits 217
– initial value of a counter 586
Deviations 313
Device byte 634, 645
Device classes 1105
Device driver 868
DEVSEL 536

DH 57
Diagnostic Page 1121
Diagnostics 1098
Diagnostics status byte 642
Diagram of a motherboard 9
Diamagnetic substance 651
Diamagnetism 651, 1231
Die 1231
Didactical example for intelligent memory controllers 415
Digit 43
Digital 1232
Digital circuit 41
Digital colour signal 985
Digital input register 717
Digital monitor 1232
Digital output register 716, 799
Digital signal processor 1019
Digital to analogue converter 1231
Digitizer 953
Digitizer tablets 953
DIN 393, 1232
DINS 874
DIP 1232
DIP switches 24, 453, 466, 634, 635, 1232
DIR 717, 718
Direct access storage device 1066
Direct access via registers 713
Direct activation via the 8253/8254 PIT 624
Direct Memory Access 10, 522, 598, 1232
Direct memory operand 74
Direct-mapped cache 216, 218
Direction 62
Directly programming the interface registers 849
Directory bit 672
Directory entry 671
Disable 951
Disable keyboard 935
Disadvantage of microencoding 164
Discharging the floating gate 442
Discrete or continuous multistaged model 116
Disk 733
– cache 749, 751
– cache in main memory 750
– change 717, 1066
– change signal 688
Disk–head distance 736
DiskCache 750
Diskpark 739
Diskpark.exe 32
Displacement 74, 76
Display coloured images 955
Display Memory 1232
Displaying images on a monitor 954
Distributed terminations 687
Dividing binary numbers 695
Division by zero 85, 186
Division with modulo-2 arithmetic 696
Divisor latch access bit 881, 884
Divisor latch register 876, 885
DL 57
DLAB 878, 881, 884
DLE 414
DMA 11, 499, 522, 547, 554, 598, 1232
– acknowledge 459, 601
– address latch 468, 600, 604
– addressing 606
– and IRQ channels on the controller 716
– architecture 454, 467, 480
– base address 720
– burst type C 481
– channel 599, 603, 725, 746
– chips 11, 598
– commands 617
– controller 383, 499, 598, 1071, 1219
– cycles in protected and virtual 8086 mode 620
– mode of the controller 717
– page of the 16-bit channels 469
– page register 604
– request 459, 601
– request signal 599
– segment overflow 605
– transfer by a software command 615
– type B 480
Documentation 30
Domains 652, 1232
Doping 1232
DOR 799
DOS 33, 1232
– components 34
– function interrupt 88
– functions 1139, 1141, 1147, 1162
– interrupts 25h and 26h 773
– memory organization 37
– system clock 593
– version differences 681
DOS-internal system clock 647, 1054
Double bit errors 697
Double fault 114
Double word 43, 1232
Double word boundary 148
Double-sided drives 658
Double-sided floppies 658
Dout 393
Dpi 1232
Drain 40
DRAM 11, 392, 1232

– accesses 419
– and EPROM control logic 419
– cell 401
– configuration register 431
– controller 399
– memory cell with a plane capacitor 400
– memory cell with trench capacitor 401
– organization 417
– refresh 402
DRD 415
DRDOS 1233
Drive address register 800
Drive arrays 791, 1233
Drive configuration 686
Drive controllers 14
Drive count 1058
Drive motor 658
Drive select 686, 781, 783, 789
Drive select jumper 686
Drive/head register 797
Driver 1233
Driver address 952, 1158
Driver for a graphic adapter 1013
Drives 684
Drives with removable data carrier 660
Drives with removable volumes 796
Drop-cable 915
DRQ level bit 614
DS 59, 686
DSP 1019
DSR 858, 874, 1233
DSRD 859
DT/R 376
DTE 857, 1233
DTR 858, 874, 1233
Dual addressing cycle 519
Dual in-line package 1232
Dual system 43
Dual-port RAM 399, 966, 1233
Dummy cell 399
Dummy read cycle 389, 402, 594, 1255
Dummy transfer, which refreshes 457
Duplex 1233
Duplex connection with an 8255 631
DWord 1233
DX 57
DX4 276
Dynamic assignments 577
Dynamic bad-sector remapping 765
Dynamic branch prediction 318
Dynamic BTB algorithms 319
Dynamic circuit design 204
Dynamic power consumption 159
Dynamic RAM 11, 392, 1232

E
E-mail 894
Earthing bracelet 4
EAX 56
EBCDIC code 44, 1233
EBP 58
EBX 57
ECC 746, 1233
– bytes 746, 763, 802
– bytes from the target 1128
– check 802
– check bytes 1063
– circuitry 746
– codes 699
– correction 764
– data burst length 767
– generator polynomial 746
– logic 802
Echo 940
ECL 42, 160, 1234
ECX 57
EDC generators 898
EDC logic 699
Edge triggering 483, 567
EDI 59
EDP 6
EDX 57
EEPROM 441, 1234
– storage transistor 442
Effect of interleaving 744
Effective address 74
Effective Privilege Level 87
Effective processor clock 367
Effects of branch prediction 319
EFI 198
EFLAG 55
EGA 965, 980, 1005, 1234
– and VGA BIOS 995
– I/O ports 981, 982
– map mask register 1006
– memory layers 983
– mode 1005, 1007
– parameters 981
EGA/VGA BIOS 994
EIA 857, 1234
– level 876
– line drivers 873, 876, 886
– signal levels 864
Eight octaves of music 623
EISA 477, 1234
– 16-bit device 492
– 32-bit device 492
– adapter cards 478, 488
– architecture 476, 477

- bus 18, 553
- bus buffer 478
- bus controller 478
- bus structure 477
- busmaster adapters 554
- busmaster status register 480
- busmasters 479
- chip set 478
- CMOS RAM 485
- DMA cycles 481
- DMA operating type A 480
- interrupt controller 482
- IRQ channels 482
- master 1234
- port addresses 484
- signals 491
- slave 1234
- slot 489, 490
- timer 484

EISA/MCA and Local Bus PCs 648
Electric shocks 5
Electrically erasable PROM 441, 1234
Electrically programmable ROM 439
Electromagnetic wave 835, 836
Electronic data processing 6
Electronic Industries Association 857, 1234
EM 64
Embedded controller 745
Emission of electromagnetic waves 273
Emitter-coupled logic 42, 1234
EMS 424
- adapter card 425
- base address register 431, 432
- extension register 432
- logic 426
- memory 38
- page 426
- page registers 433
- window 424, 1234, 1235

Emulate a key press 1150
Enable/Disable Blink Attribute 996
Encoding data in the MFM format 693
Encoding format 693
Encoding into FM or MFM data 714
Encoding of an INT instruction 83
End of interrupt 562
End of the chain 681
End of the track 691
Energy saving 160
Enhanced graphics adapter 980, 1234
Enhanced IDE 791, 796
Enhanced master burst cycle 479
Enhanced small device interface 1234
Enhancement-type field-effect transistor 41
ENIAC 1, 1234
Entering and leaving Virtual 8086 Mode 129
Entries in the EMS page register 433
Entry address of the driver 952
Entry point of the ASPI driver 826
Entry point of the BIOS start routine 155
Entry point of the SMM handler 343
Entry point of the start-up BIOS 364
Envelope and superposition of sounds 1016
Envelope type 1020
EOI command 562, 568
EOP 601
EOT 691
EPL 87
EPROM 419, 438, 439, 441, 1234
- accesses 419

Erasable PROM 441, 1234
Erase-verify 444
Erased files or directories 677
ERBK 882
ERROR 138, 178, 196, 203, 355, 367
Error checking and correcting 699
Error codes 1068, 1211, 1214
Error codes for INT 15h, function d8h 488
Error correcting code 699, 746, 1233
Error detected by the CRC logic 701
Error detecting and correcting 699
Error detection functions 1196
Error on an adapter card 459
Error on an expansion adapter 635
Error per read bits 753
Error recovery strategies 730, 763
Error register 796
ES 60
ESC instruction 1234
ESC instructions 181
ESDI 16, 745, 780, 1234
- adapter 784
- cable 784, 785
- command data 787
- commands 784
- control cable 784
- controller 784
- interface 783
- signals 784
- systems 747
- transfer rate 784

ESI 58
Establishing the connection 859
ET 65
Ethernet 893, 911, 915, 1235
Ethernet LAN 1228
EU 47, 1235
Even parity 854, 1252

Events 902, 1214
Exception 0 85
Exception 1 85
Exception 3 85
Exception 4 85
Exception 5 85
Exception 6 86
Exception 7 86, 186, 370
Exception 8 86, 114
Exception 9 114, 186, 370
Exception 10 114
Exception 11 114
Exception 12 86, 114
Exception 13 86, 115, 186, 370
Exception 14 125
Exception 16 86, 115, 187, 370
Exceptions 61, 80, 84, 1235
Exchange of data between two computers 851
Exclusive 221
Execute SCSI Command 1136
Execution of the SMM program 293
Execution time 78, 162, 236
Execution tracing 349
Execution unit 47, 164, 1235
Expand-down 99
Expanded memory 38, 424, 431, 1234, 1235
Expanded memory and memory mapping with the 82C212 425
Expanded Memory Specification 424
Expanded Memory System 424
Expansion ROM base address 529, 530
Exponent 167
Extended 64-bit SDP 495
Extended ASCII 44, 1027, 1235
Extended Binary Coded Decimal Interchange Code 1233
Extended CMOS RAM 485, 648
Extended commands 1072, 1082
Extended controller 1084
Extended EISA CMOS RAM 649
Extended initialization 872
Extended Instruction Pointer 59
Extended ISA 477, 1234
Extended memory 38, 79, 421, 426, 646, 1193, 1235
Extended mode register 481, 482
Extended PS/2 CMOS RAM 649
Extended Read 1122
Extended real mode 345
Extended Seek 1124
Extended Write 1123
Extension card 1221
Extension of the standard MCA specification 511
Extension Type 65
Extensions to Pentium Virtual 8086 Mode 329
External DOS commands 35
External graphics adapters 504
Extra segments 60

F

Fail-safe RAM memory systems 699
Fail-safe timer 484, 499, 574, 596
Fail-safe timer wiring 597
FAMOST 441, 1235
– memory cells 443
Far call via a gate and a segment descriptor 104
Faraday effect 836, 1235, 1245
Fast operating modes 405
Fast SCSI 831, 1235
FAT 675
– 12-bit 676
– 16-bit 676
– copies 676
Fault 84, 1236
Fax Adapter Cards 896
FCB 708, 1236
FCI 735, 1236
FDC PD765 992, 1236
FDDI 918, 1236
FDISK 757
Feature connector 982
Feedback-loop check of the UART 8250/16450/16550 886
FERR 231, 250, 301
Ferrite coating 734
Ferrite heads 736
Ferromagnetic material 652, 654, 1236
Ferromagnetism 651, 652, 1236
FET 1236
Fibre Distributed Data Interface 918, 1236
Field Effect Transistor 1236
Field oxide films 400
Field-Effect Transistor 39
FIFO 1236
FIFO register 877
File Allocation Table 675
File control blocks 681, 708, 1236
File name 671
File server 910
File size 672
File systems 682
File-oriented functions of INT 21h 707
Files 679
FILES = xx 681
Filling a cache line 256
First-In, First-Out 1236
Fix Drive Data 1080

Fixed mode 577
Fixed priority 603
Fixed-point numbers 167
Flag register 55
Flags 60
– of the i486DX4 283
Flap case 4
Flash BIOS 444
Flash control 444
Flash memories 443
Flash memory instructions 444
Flash memory structure 443
Flat memory model 90, 250
Flicker 1018
Flip-flop 434, 435, 1236
Flip-flop's stability 436
Floating gate 439
Floating gate avalanche injection MOS transistor 441, 1235
Floating return from protected mode 187
Floating set protected mode 187
Floating-point 167
Floating-point instructions 174, 1044
Floating-point pipeline 308, 315
Floating-point unit 253
Floppies 7, 14, 651
Floppy controller 781
– commands 720
– port addresses 715
– registers 716
Floppy disk controllers 1071, 1219, 1236
Floppy disk drives 14, 1237
Floppy Disk Parameter Table 1070
Floppy disk parameters 662
Floppy disks 15, 656, 1236
Floppy drive 14, 634, 651, 658, 1058
– controller 684
– types 643
Floppy type identification 686
Floppy, coated 659
FLPCS 201
FLT 194, 205
Fluorescent material 954
Flush acknowledge special cycle 340
Flush special cycle 256
Flux changes 735
Flux Changes per Inch 735
FM 691, 1020, 1237
– and MFM format 692
– channels of SoundBlaster 1019
– encoding 689
– format 689, 692
– sector format 690
FMT, CMP and defect list 1111
Folded bit line 401
Forced-parity bit 885
Foreground colour 961
FORMAT 663, 675, 757, 1239
Format and Mark Bad Track 777
Format and Mark Drive 778
Format buffer 776, 1060, 1069, 1077, 1096
Format buffer for one sector 1078
Format data 1096
Format defective track 762
Format information 1060
Format of a floppy track 689
Format operation in native mode 1096
Format Track 776, 1077, 1096
Format Unit 1110
Formats of status registers A to D 640
Formatted capacity 662, 691, 748
Formatting Gap-3 length 722
Formatting in translation mode 1096
Forward register 524
Forwarding 240
Fourier analysis 1017
Fourier transform 1017
FPU exceptions 254
Fragmentation 679
FRAME 537
Frame data 910
Frames 1017
Framing error 857, 869, 887, 888
FRC 332
FRCMC 301
Free graphics in graphics mode 962
Free token 914
Frequency doubling by edge triggering 274
Frequency Modulation 1020, 1024, 1237
Frictional electricity 5
FRSTPM 187
FS 60
FSETPM 187
Full-duplex connection 861
Full-stroke time 750, 1237
Function
– Buffered Character Input From Standard Input Device With Echo 1148
– Calibrate Drive (Hard Disk) 1065
– Call SVGA BIOS Functions 1187
– Character Input From Standard Input Device With Check 1148
– Character Input From Standard Input Device Without Check 1147
– Character Input With Echo 1147
– Character Output 1162
– Character Output to Standard Output Device Without Check 1162

– Check Controller RAM (Hard Disk) 1066
– Check Mouse Present 1153
– Check Status of Standard Input Device 1148
– Clear Alarm Time (Real-time Clock) 1056
– Clear Mouse Cursor/Decrement Cursor Flag 1153
– Configuration of Video Subsystem 1180
– Define Call Mask for User Procedure 1156
– Define Horizontal Borders for Mouse Cursor 1155
– Define Mickey/Pixel Ratio 1157
– Define Mouse Cursor in Graphics Mode 1155
– Define Mouse Cursor in Text Mode 1156
– Define Threshold Value for Double Speed 1158
– Define Vertical Borders for Mouse Cursor 1155
– Determine Buffer Status for the Extended Keyboard 1151
– Determine Disk Change (Floppy Drive, AT and PS/2 only) 1067
– Determine Drive Parameters (Floppy Drive) 1062
– Determine Drive Parameters (Hard Disk) 1062
– Determine Drive/DASD Type (Floppy Drive, AT and PS/2 only) 1066
– Determine Number of Mouse Button Clicks and Mouse Cursor Position 1154
– Determine Number of Mouse Button Releases and Mouse Cursor Position 1154
– Determine Printer Status 1140
– Determine Shift Status 1150
– Determine SHIFT Status of the Extended Keyboard 1151
– Determine Status of Mouse Buttons and Position of Mouse Cursor 1153
– Determine Status of Serial Interface 1143
– Determine Video BIOS Function Capabilities and Status Information 1183
– Determine Video Status 1169
– Direct Character Input From Keyboard 1147
– Disable Light Pen Emulation 1157
– Disable Mouse Cursor Conditionally 1157
– Display Mouse Cursor/Increment Cursor Flag 1153
– Drive Diagnostics (Hard Disk) 1066
– Enable Light Pen Emulation 1157
– Extended Read (Hard Disk) 1063
– Extended Write (Hard Disk) 1063
– Fix Floppy Disk Format (Floppy Drive) 1067
– Format and Mark Track Bad (Hard Disk) 1061
– Format Drive (Hard Disk) 1061
– Format Track 710
– Format Track or Cylinder (Floppy/Hard Disk) 1060
– Hard Disk Reset (Hard Disk) 1064
– Initialize (Floppy/Hard Disk) 1058
– Initialize Parallel Interface and Printer 1140
– Initialize Serial Interface 1142
– Initialize Serial Interface Extended 1144
– Interface to the Character Generator 1175
– Keyboard Hook 1151
– Move Block 1193
– Output Character to Parallel Interface and Printer 1140
– Output Character Via Serial Interface 1143
– Output Character Via the Serial Interface 1139, 1141
– Park Read/Write Heads (Hard Disk) 1068
– Printer output 841
– Printing 1139
– Read Buffer (Hard Disk) 1064
– Read Character From the Serial Interface 1141
– Read Character Via Serial Interface 1143
– Read Character/Attribute From Screen 1166
– Read Cursor Position 1165
– Read Date (Real-time Clock) 1055
– Read File/Device 1141, 1149
– Read Light Pen Position 1165
– Read Modem Control Register 1141
– Read Movement Counter of Mouse 1156
– Read Next Character 1149
– Read One Character from Extended Keyboard 1150
– Read Pixel From Screen 1168
– Read Sector(s) 710
Read Sectors (Floppy/Hard Disk) 1059
– Read Status (Error Code) of Last Floppy or Hard Disk Operation (Floppy/Hard Disk) 1058
– Read Time (Real-time Clock) 1055
– Read Time Counter (DOS-Internal System Clock) 1054
– Save/Restore Video Status 1185
– Scroll Window Down 1166
– Scroll Window Up 1165
– Seek (Hard Disk) 1064
– Select Screen Page 1165
– Set Alarm Time (Real-time Clock) 1056
– Set Colour Palette 1167
– Set Cursor Position 1164
– Set Cursor Size 1164
– Set Date (Real-time Clock) 1056
– Set Mouse Cursor Position 1154
– Set or Clear Wait Time Interval 1056
– Set Palette Registers 1170
– Set Time (Real-time Clock) 1055
– Set Time Counter (DOS-Internal System Clock) 1054

– Set Typing Rate and Delay 1150
– Set Video Mode 1163, 1170
– Specify Drive Parameters (Hard Disk) 1062
– String Output 1162
– Switch to Protected Mode 1194
– SysReq Hook 1152
– Test Drive Ready (Hard Disk) 1065
– Verify Sectors (Floppy/Hard Disk) 1060
– Video Combination 1182
– Wait Until Time Interval Has Elapsed 1057
– Write Buffer (Hard Disk) 1065
– Write Character and Scan Code Back to Keyboard Buffer 1150
– Write Character Onto Screen 1167
– Write Character/Attribute Onto Screen 1166
– Write File/Device 841, 1142, 1163
– Write File/Unit 1139
– Write in TTY Mode 1168
– Write Modem Control Register 1145
– Write Pixel Onto Screen 1168
– Write Sectors (Floppy/Hard Disk) 1059
– Write String 1169
Function distributor 703
Function of the PCMCIA interface 897
Function transfer table 117
Functional redundancy checking 332
Functioning of a hard disk controller 745
Functioning of an SRAM memory cell 434
Functioning of the AT DMA 468
Fuzzy logic 42
FXCHG 315, 317

G
Gallium-arsenide 41, 1237
Galvanization 734, 1237
Game adapter status byte 891
GAP 1 689
GAP 2 690
GAP 3 691
GAP 4A 689
GAP 4B 691
Gap information 746
Gas-plasma monitors 956
Gate 40, 101, 1237
Gate array 1237
Gate descriptors 103, 360
Gate oxide film 400
Gate signal 579
Gates 87, 89, 98, 360
Gateway 894, 910, 915
Gbyte 1237
GDT 358, 1237
GDTR 92, 1237
General configuration word 788
General protection error 86, 115, 186, 370
General-purpose registers 52, 55
Generate a tone 623, 624
Generate the various CRC codes 701
Generating the SDU 855
Generator cells 1026
Generator polynomial 700
Generators of the CRC 697
Geometric information 765
Geometric mean 623
Geometric parameters of a hard disk drive 1062
Geometry information 761, 765
Geometry of the EISA slots 489
Get Device Type 1135
Get Disk Drive Information 1138
Get Socket Service Info (GetSSInfo) 1196
Get/Set Socket Service Address (GetSetSSAddr) 1210
GetAccessOffsets 1210
GetAdapter 1198
GetAdapterCount 1196
GetEDC 1206
GetPage 1201
GetSetPriorHandler 1209
GetSocket 1203
GetStatus 1205
GetVendorInfo 1208
GetWindow 1200
Giga 1237
Global descriptor table 89, 94, 358, 1237
Global Descriptor Table Register 92, 1237, 1238
GNT 537
Gradient 918
Gradual underflow 172, 185, 1238
GRAFTABL 998
Granularity bit 90
Granularity of the magnetic recording medium 692
Graph tablet 953
Graphic instructions 990
Graphic processor 990, 1012
GRAPHICS 995
Graphics accelerator 1257
Graphics adapter 7, 11, 12, 634, 954, 1238
Graphics control chip 12, 956, 1218, 1238
Graphics mode 13, 957, 962, 963, 976, 1003, 1004, 1005, 1008, 1238
Graphics mouse pointer 944
Graphics processor 1011, 1238
Graphics routines of Standard BIOS 994
Graphite layer 734
Green PC 292, 342
Grey shaded 955
Group code 822

Grown defect list 762, 1110
GS 60

H
Half duplex 1238
Half-duplex connection 860
HALT 198, 199, 362
Halt auto restart 344
Halt condition 150
Handle 1238
Handle for the standard output device 1163
Handles 682, 708
Handshake 19, 811, 1238
Handshake control signals 860
Hard disk drive 7, 14, 731, 732, 1058
– controllers 1089
– parameter block 645
– parameter table 1069
– types 644
Hard disk entries in the BIOS 753
Hard disk extension byte 644
Hard disk functions of BIOS Interrupt 13h 776
Hard disk parameter table 767
Hard disks and flash memories 445
Hard errors 753
Hard hole 656
Hardware Debug Support 350
Hardware debugger 350
Hardware DMA request 615
Hardware elements for performance monitoring 346
Hardware integer multiplier 281
Hardware interrupts 83, 329, 537, 557, 800, 845
– channels 453
– INT 09h 922
– requests 61, 246, 311, 460
– via IRQ5 or IRQ7 851
Hardware multiplier 210, 238, 253
Hardware triggered pulse 589
Hardware-dependent information 646
Hardwired instructions 237
Hardwired logic 164
HD 1238
HD drives 718
HD notch 657
HD signature 689
HDA 732, 1239
HDC 1239
Head 662, 735
Head disk assembly 1239
Head group 784
Head technologies 736
Head-disk distance 735
Head-load time 724, 728
Head-unload time 724, 728
Header 525
Header and descriptor of the defect list 1112
Header of BIOS extensions 769
Heat deformation 738
Hercules 979
Hercules adapter parameters 980
Hercules card 945, 965, 967
– I/O port 967
– video RAM 966
Hercules graphics card 1004
HEX 1239
Hexadecimal numbers 45
Hexadecimal system 45
HGC 1239
Hidden arbitration 521
Hidden file 672
Hidden refresh 403, 1239
Hierarchical file system 674
High memory area 79
High-performance file system 683
High-density rate 719
High-level formatting 663, 757, 1239
High-level languages 35, 702
HighColor 1010
Highest privilege level 88
HIMEM.SYS 79, 937
History bits 318, 1226
HIT 301
Hit rate 216, 410
HITM 301
Hold register 869
Hook for the keyboard input 930
Horizontal Displayed 971
Horizontal Machine Code Format 241
Horizontal retrace 955, 959, 962, 969, 971
Horizontal synchronization 959, 962, 969
Horizontal Total 970
Host 16, 1239
Host adapter 16, 772, 791, 1239
Host Adapter Inquiry 1135
Hotkeys 943
HPFS 683
Hysteresis 434
Hysteresis loop 653
Hz 1239

I
I/O 809, 1242
– address 57
– address area 523
– address for the configuration area 524
– address space 136, 152, 484, 500, 523, 549
– address space protection via the IOPL Flag 111

– addresses of control and status register 613
– addresses of EISA page registers 481
– addresses of the AT page registers 470
– addresses of the PC/XT page registers 456
– addressing 153
– base address 529
– base address of the EMS page register 431
– channel 457, 470
– controller 153
– coprocessors 174
– cycles 154
– gate block 398
– instruction break 205
– instructions 131
– interrupt unit 576
– line pair 398
– map base 108, 112
– mapped I/O 152
– mapped input/output 152, 454, 466
– peripherals 395, 396
– permission bit map 112
– port access registers 649
– ports 500
– ports of the video system on the Hercules card 967
– Protection Level 62
– read access 518
– trap restart 344
– write access 518
i386 39, 1040, 1239
– bus cycle 154
– clones 203
– control registers 63
– debug registers 66
– gate descriptor 103
– Internal Self-Test 155
– memory management registers 67
– microprocessor 50
– pinout 136
– processor registers 51
– protected mode 86
– read cycles 143
– real mode 79
– register contents after a processor reset 155
– registers and their uses 55
– segment descriptor 90
– special cycles 150
– task state segment 108
i386/i387 system configuration 190
i386/i486 Compatible Pentium Virtual 8086 Mode 328
i386DX 192
i386SL 50
i386SX 192, 193, 1239
i386SX and i387SX terminals 193
i387 1239
– condition codes 183
– control word 184
– error status 182
– exceptions 185
– internal registers 182
– mathematical coprocessor 167
– memory cycles 189
– number formats 174, 175
– pinout 177
– register contents after a reset/FNINIT 191
– reset 191
– status word 183
– tag word 185
i387/i387SX 1049
i387SX 192, 1239
i486 227, 1042, 1050, 1240
– bus 254
– clones 290
– die 228
– eflag register 249
– I/O address space 266
– identification codes 278
– internal structure 233, 234
– on-chip cache 247
– page table entry 251
– pinout 227, 229
– pipeline 245
– protected mode 253
– real mode 252
– register contents after a processor reset 252
– reset 252
– special bus cycles 257
– TAP structure 263
– virtual 8086 mode 253
i486DX2 274, 1240
i486DX4 280, 1240
– ID code 287
– identification 284
– JTAG Boundary Scan Test 286
– pinout 282
i486SL 1240
– identification 289
i486SX 267, 1240
– ID code 270
– in PGA and PQFP packages 268
i487SX 267, 1240
i487SX pin assignment 271
i586 1240
i860 236
IAM 689
IBM adapter for computer games 889
IBM-compatible parallel printers 849

IBMBIOS.SYS 34, 704
IBMDOS.SYS 34, 704
IBT 302
IC 1240
ICC bus 576
ICC protocol 577
ICW 565
ICW formats 568
ID address mark 689, 796, 1078
ID code register 264, 287
ID fields 758
IDAM 689, 758
IDCODE 265
IDE 790, 1240
– cable length 794
– hard disk drives 754, 794
– host adapters 1239
– interface 790
– interface cable layout 792
– interface commands 1089
Identification code 814
Identification flag 283, 325
Identification information 264, 270, 348
Identification level 334
Identification of the i486DX4 284
Identify 814
Identify Device 951, 1101
Identify floppy type 689
Identify keyboard 941
Idle 794
IDSEL 537
IDT 106, 358, 1240
IDTR 81, 92, 1240
IDX 7[illegible]58
IEEE 1240
IEEE 1149.1 261, 347, 1226
IEEE formats 1170
IERR 302
Ignore wide rest 814
IIBEN 205
IIL 42, 1241
Immediate operand 74
Implementing AND (a) and OR (b) with MOSFETs 158
Implicit Instruction Pairing by CISC Microcode 315
Impurities 40
IMR 560, 563, 572
In-service 561
In-service register 560
Inclusion 225
Increase in performance in connection with an L2-cache 352
Index address mark 689, 758
Index head 740
Index hole 656
Index register 75
Index tracks 740
Indicator byte 940
Indirect memory operand 74
Induction 654, 655, 1241
Industrial Standard Architecture 475, 1242
Inert gas 1241
Infinite quantities 184
Infinite time-out value 842
Information density 693
Information transfer phase 810, 811
INIT 302
Initialization 332
– and programming 565
– command words 565
– of an 8259A PIC 567
– of the connected printer 846
– of the serial interface 869
– routine of the BIOS 770
Initialize coprocessor 369
Initialize the serial interface 868
Initialize the PS/2 mouse 951
Initializing a DMA transfer 618
Initializing the 8259A PIC 566
Initiate special cycle 531
Initiator 516, 809
Initiator defect list 1111
Initiator ready 516
Input and output ports of the keyboard controller 936
Input buffer 935
Input port 936
InquireAdapter 1197
InquireEDC 1206
InquireSocket 1202
InquireWindow 1198
Inquiry 1114
Inquiry cycle 209, 213, 222, 228, 257, 297, 300, 301, 322, 341, 1241
Inquiry hit 538
Inquiry misses 341
Insert mode 929
Inserting EMS windows into the address space 426
Installation check for a CAM driver 829
Installation subfunction 997
Installed graphics adapter type 937
Installed hardware 871
Instruction branch taken 302
Instruction cache 209
Instruction codes 47
Instruction encoding 73, 76

Instruction execution in the two integer pipelines u and v 314
Instruction fetch 52, 77
Instruction flow 70
Instruction pairing 317, 1044
Instruction pipelining 208, 210, 237, 238, 239, 311
Instruction pointer 55, 69
Instruction register 527
Instruction serialization 317
Instruction set for the 8086 372
Instruction Unit 47, 1242
Instructions of a pair must be simple 312
INT 13h functions 709
INT 15h
– Access to EISA System Information, Erase Configuration RAM 487
– Access to EISA System Information, Read Function Info 486
– Access to EISA System Information, Read Slot Info 485
– Access to EISA System Information, Write Configuration 487
INT 19h 156
INT 21h file and directory functions 708
INT 25h and INT 26h calling formats 706, 774
INT 25h and INT 26h error codes 706, 775
INT 42h 1170, 1187
INT 76h 801
INT instruction 81
INT signal of the 8087 391
INTA sequence 61, 517
INTB 537
INTC 537
INTD 537
Integer 45
Integer core 253
Integer pipelines u and v 308, 309, 310
Integrated circuit 1240
Integrated injection logic 42, 1241
Integrated microcontroller 383
Integrated system peripheral 478
Integrating a BIOS extension 768
Integrating drive and controller 790
Integrating exotic drives 766
Integration density of memory chips 401
Integration of the SRAM memory cell 434
Intel 1241
Intel debug ports 305
Intel notation 47
Intelligent drive electronics 790, 1240
Intelligent drives 16
Inter-processor interrupt 578
Interception 769
Interface cable 685, 686
Interface cable with twisted wires 686
Interface Programming and Command Phases 800
Interface to the Character Generator 997
Interfaces 2, 839
Interior of a PC 5
Interlaced mode 973
Interlaced/video mode 973
Interlacing 955
Interleave 776, 794
Interleave factor 743
Interleaving 408, 430, 431, 742, 743
Interleaving with page mode 409
Interlock 1241
Internal 82C212 structure 419
Internal DOS buffer 688, 717
Internal DOS commands 35
Internal frequency doubling 273, 274
Internal i387 structure 181
Internal Pentium bus buffers 341
Internal Pentium structure 307
Internal self-test 156, 252, 258, 264, 332, 951
– of the keyboard 943
Internal snooping 341
Internal structure 603
– of a PIT counter 580
– of the 386SL and 82360SL 195
– of the 8259A PIC 561
– of the APIC 82489DX 576
Internal system clock 641
Internal transfer rate 750
Internet 894, 910, 1241
Interpretation of the average access time 74[illegible]9
Interpretation of the linear address 121, 3[illegible]31
Interrupt 81, 1242
– 40h 770
– 4ah 642
– 70h 641
– acknowledge 84, 559
– Acknowledge Sequence 560, 561
– and trap gates 1[illegible]
– call 103
– controller [illegible]83, 383
– delay time 247
– Descriptor Table 106, 358, 1240, 1242
– Descriptor Table Register 81, 92, 1240, 1242
– enable 61
– enable register 882
– gate 1242
– handler 8[illegible]2, 106, 1242
– handler for IRQ6 728
– identification register 883
– INT 15h, function c2h 952
– INT 40h [illegible]780

– mask register 560, 563
– masking in the 8087 386
– number 562
– on terminal count 589
– or trap gate 103
– redirecting 577
– request 83, 84, 559, 560, 562, 1242
– request register 560
– routine 117
– source 642, 726
– sources priorities 883
– subsystem 482, 575
– tables in real and protected mode 107
– vector 81
– vector table 81, 334
Interrupt, trap, and task gates 360
Interrupt-driven communication 558
Interrupt-driven data exchange 557, 558, 725, 729, 746
Interrupt-driven data transfer 848
Interrupts 80, 103, 311, 499, 522, 547, 1051
– 25h and 26h 774
– 41h and 46h 766
– in real mode 82
– in virtual 8086 mode 132
Intersegment call 70, 102
Intersegment jump 70
INTRPT line 882
INV 303
Invalid command 1082
Invalid opcode 86
Invalid operation 186
Invalid task state segment 114
Invalidate data cache 247
Invalidation cycles 257
Invalidations 322
IO.CYC 24
IOPL flag 111, 361, 362
IOPL-sensitive instructions 112, 362
IRQ 83, 1242
– channels 482, 848
– control logic 878
– line 880
– priorities 565
IRQ2 at the beginning of a retrace period 966
IRR, ISR and IMR 560, 561
ISA 481, 1242
ISA bus 474, 476
ISA master 1242
ISA slave 1242
ISA standard 464
ISR 560
Issue an interrupt request 560
Issue an NMI via software 484
Issuing and executing a task switch 110
IU 47, 303, 1242
IU, IV and IBT during execution tracing 350
IV 303

J
JAM signal 913
Job 1262
Job of the parallel interface 839
Joystick 21, 29, 889, 890, 1242
– wiring 893
JTAG Boundary Scan Test 261, 269, 535, 550
JTAG control cells and assigned pin groups 264, 269, 286, 347
JTAG logic 262, 576
JTAG test bus 262
Jump 78

K
Kbit 1243
Kbyte 1243
Kernel 88
Keyboard 2, 26, 27, 919, 1147, 1243
– access via DOS 925
– access via the BIOS 926
– and mouse Access 1147
– BIOS data area 928
– buffer 926, 929, 1147, 1149
– buffer memory 938
– chip 920, 1218
– clock 920
– commands 940
– controller 466, 921, 932, 949, 1218, 1220
– controller registers 933
– data 921
– driver 26, 924, 925
– flags 1150, 1151
– hook 930
– interface 920
– reset 921
– return codes 938
– SDU 921
– status byte 929
Keyboard (CON) is assigned handle 1149
KHz 1243
Kilo 1242

L
L-address bus 463
L1-cache 220, 1243
L2-cache 220, 352, 1220, 1243
L2-cache subsystem 225, 351
LAN 7, 22, 910, 1235, 1243
Landmark Test 220

Lanthan-alloy 836
Lanthanoide 1243
Large-scale integration 1245
Large 4 Mbyte pages 330
Laser 1243
Laser beam 833
Latch 1243
Latency 528, 748, 1243
Layout and signals of 25 and 36 pin plugs 846
Layout and signals of 25 and 9 pin plugs 858
Layout of a hard disk track 758, 759
Layout of a PCI bridge 515
Layout of game adapter connector 890
Layout of the 68-pole B-cable 831
Layout of the bus slots 475
Layout of the SRB 826
LBA 797, 822
LBM 542, 546
LCD 956
LDT 101, 358, 1244
LDTR 92, 1244
LEADS 551
Least-significant bit 1245
Least-significant byte 1245
LEDs 925
Length of cable 840
Length of GAP 3 722
Level 483
Level-triggered hardware interrupts 510
LF 1244
Light pen 29, 1165
Light Pen High/Low 975
LIM EMS 4.0 424
Limit 90
Limit entry 359
Line address 962
Line feed 1244
Line fill buffer 259, 342
Line frequency 970
Line memory read access 519
Line printer 839
Line switching 894
Linear address 53, 119
Linear address space 120, 134
Linear incrementation 520
Linear motor 733, 739, 1266
Linearly polarized 836
Link bit 823
Linked command complete 813, 824
Linked command with flag complete 813
Little endian format 47, 1244
LMEGCS 415
LMSW 64
Load 176
Load bootstrap 931
Load elements 434
Load MSW 64
Load/store architecture 237, 241
Loader program 669
Loading and activating character definition tables 997
Loading and unloading of the read/write head 728
Loading the floating gate 441
Lobe cable 917
Local address bus 450, 462
Local area network 7, 910, 1235, 1243
Local Bus 512, 1011, 1244
Local bus arbitrator 497
Local Bus Target 542
Local Busmaster 542, 546
Local channel 504
Local data 59
Local data bus 451, 463
Local descriptor table 89, 101, 358, 1244
Local Descriptor Table Register 92, 1244
Local interrupt 576
Local interrupt unit 576
Local network 1244
Local repeater 915
Local variables 59
Logic gates 157
Logical 95
– address 119
– address space 54
– block address 822
– block addressing 797
– block number 820
– blocks 1104
– connection of subdirectories 675
– cylinder number 1097
– format 772
– geometry of the addressed drive 1099
– high level 137
– interface 791
– memory addressing 69
– organization 683
– organization of floppies and hard disks 663
– ring structure 912
– sector number 664
– sectors 663, 664, 705
– structure of SMM RAM 344
– structure of the disk 764
– unit 1104
– unit number 807, 822
Login 1244
Long real 169, 172
LOOP bit 886

Lotus Intel Microsoft expanded memory specification 424
Low-level formatting 663, 754, 757, 758, 773, 1244
Low-pass filter 623
Low-power 486DX 279
Low-power 486SX 273, 279
Low-power versions of i486DX/SX 279
Lowest priority mode 578
Lowest privilege level 88
LPSTB 959
LPT1 839
LPT1, LPT2, LPT3, LPT4 1244
LPT2 839
LPT3 839
LPT4 839
LPTx General Interface Assignment 850
LRU algorithm 321
LRU entry 216
LRU strategy 218
LSB 1245
LSI 1245
LUN 807, 822, 1104

M

Mac 806
Machine check address register 326
Machine check enable 326
Machine check exception 300, 351
Machine check type register 326, 349
Machine code 73
Machine instruction 1245
Machine Status Word 64, 92, 358, 1248
Machine-related information representation 42
Macroassembler 73
Magnetic field 3, 652
Magnetic tapes 655
Magnetically hard 653
Magnetically soft 653
Magnetizable coating 734
Magnetization 652
Magneto-optical disk 836, 837
Magneto-optical drives 835, 1245
Main memory 7, 8, 52, 1245
Main memory on the motherboard 634
Main reference frequency 876, 885
Main status register 716, 717, 1071
Mainframe 1, 1245
Make and break codes 938
Make-code 634, 922, 1245
Management and distribution of interrupt requests 576
Mantissa 167, 1245
Manufacturer 492
Manufacturer defect list 760, 761, 1110
Manufacturer ID 526
Map mask register 1006
Mapping a linear address onto a physical address 121
Mapping physical sectors onto logical sectors 664, 667
Mark 854, 1245, 1252
Mark state 876
Mask register 572, 617
Mask ROM 439
Mask-programmable ROMs 439
Masking the NMI 573
Mass storage 651
Master 563, 608, 791, 1090
Master clear 617
Master diagnostics code 1099
Master DMA channels 467
Master interrupt enable bit 876
Master PIC 465, 559, 563
Master-CD 834
Matched-memory cycles 494
Matched-memory extension 505
Math present 271
Mathematical coprocessor 1218
Matrix 1246
Max. Scanline 974
Maximum active time in page mode 432
Maximum active time period 407, 419
Maximum allocation time for external busmasters 497
Maximum loadable count value 584
Maximum mode 374, 375
Maxtor 783
Mbit 1246
Mbytes 748, 1246
MC146818 26, 637, 1054, 1246
MC146818 structure and programming 637
MCA
– adapters 501
– bus structure 494
– port addresses 500
– signals 507
– slot 505, 506
– timer 499
MCE 326
MCGA (multi colour graphics array) 1008
MDA 977, 1002
– parameters 978
– text mode 1002
Mean Time Between Failures 752, 1249
Mechanical access time 749
Mechanical mice 943
Medium and drive parameters of the target 1119

Medium descriptor byte 669
Medium descriptor table 668, 669
Medium scale integration 1248
Mega 1245, 1246
Memory 39
– access 136
– access time 144
– address 215, 960
– address bus 451, 463
– addressing in protected mode 97
– and I/O address areas 516
– bank 1246
– base address 529
– block initialization 611
– buffer 141, 452, 464
– cards 445
– cell array 394, 396, 443
– chips 392
– configuration registers 498
– controller 141, 195, 395
– controller for SRAM chips 437
– data bus 451, 463
– data error 699
– element of the cell 396
– enable register 429, 430
– enable registers for shadow RAM 429
– expansion card 10
– flip-flop 437
– images of instruction and data pointers 187, 188
– interleaving 408
– layers 1005
– management 93, 251
– management and control registers for i386 93
– management registers 63, 67, 92
– management unit 1247
– mapped I/O 152, 423, 815, 816, 1246
– mapping 424
– mapping logic 420
– mapping with shadowing enabled 423
– mapping without shadowing 422
– modules 8, 410
– multiple access 518
– operand 74
– organization 32, 36
– parity 464
– parity error 84
– read access 518
– refresh 11, 457, 467, 469, 497, 575, 594
– system 498
– Technology Layer 904
– transistors 434
– write access 518
– write access with invalidation 519
Memory–memory transfer 457, 469, 602, 610, 611, 614
MESI protocol 221, 225, 307, 321, 341, 352, 1246
MESI state 221, 321
MESI State Transitions 222
Message phase 812
Message rejected 813
Message-in phase 812
Message-out phase 812
Messages 577, 812
Metal Oxide Semiconductor 1248
MF II ID word 941
MF II keyboard 26, 466, 920, 922, 924, 1246
MF II keyboard, additional status bytes 928
MF II keys 924
MFM 691, 754, 1246
– sector format 690, 759
MHz 1246
Mice 27, 919, 943
Mickey 1246
Micro 1245, 1246
Micro instruction pointer 164
Microchannel 18, 476, 1246
Microchip 1247
Microcode ROM 156, 162
Microcoding or microencoding 1247
Microcomputer modems 861
Microcontroller 384, 714
Microencoding 162, 236
Microprocessor 1247
Microprogram 162
Microprogram memory 164
Microprogramming 157
Microstepping 764
MIDI interface 1019
MIDI Processing Unit 1019
Milli 1245
Minimum mode 374, 375
Miobytes 748
MIPS 1247
Mirroring 791, 1247
Misaligned accesses 335
Miscellaneous register 432
MKDIR 675
MMU 1247
Mnemonics 73, 1247
Mode 0 (Interrupt on Terminal Count) 589
Mode 1 (Programmable Monoflop) 589, 631
Mode 2 (Rate Generator) 590
Mode change 967
Mode control register 967, 968
Mode register 616
Mode select 1115, 1130
Mode select parameters 1116

Mode sense 1119, 1131
Model for the arbitration 522
Model-specific register 326, 327
Modem 2, 21, 857, 1247
– control logic 878, 886
– control register 886, 1146
– status 1145
– status byte 869
– status register 869, 886, 888
Modems 20
Modified 221
Modified frequency modulation 1246
Modified, Exclusive, Shared, Invalid 221
Modular board 7
MOdulator 21
Modulator/demodulator 1247
Modulo-2 arithmetic 695
Modulo-2 division 695, 697
Monitor 2, 11, 1247
Monitor coprocessor 64
Mono-mode 918
Monochrome 955
– display adapter 957, 977
– graphics 963
– monitor 977, 978
More than one floppy controller in your PC 684
MOS 1248
MOS transistor 158
MOSFET 39, 1248
Most-significant bit 1248
Most-significant byte 1248
Motherboard 7, 8, 1248
– activation/setup register 503
– POS register 2 504
Motion Picture Expert Group 1014
Motion video 1017
Motorola 1248
Mouse 2, 21, 27, 943, 1248
– cursor 1248
– data packet 949
– driver 27, 944
– interrupt 33h 944, 1152
– packet on the stack 1161
– pad 28
– pointer 27, 944
– pointer in graphics mode 946
– pointer in text mode 947
– pointer positions 944
– port 921, 949
– return codes 952
MP 64, 271
MPC 1014
MPEG 1014
MPU-401 UART 1019
MS-DOS 1248
MSB 1248
MSBIN Format 172
MSDOS.SYS 34, 672, 704
MSG 809
MSI 1248
MSW 64, 92, 358, 1248
MTBF 752, 1249
MTL 904
Multi Station Access Units 916
Multi-APIC system 577
Multi-cache system 225, 1227
Multi-track problem 712
MULTIBUS 377
Multicolour graphics 963
Multifunction II keyboard 1246
Multifunction keyboard 920
Multifunction unit 522, 537
Multimedia 1014
– data flow 1015
– Managers 1018
– PC 11, 1014, 1249
Multiple register files 242
Multiplexed data and address bus 377
Multiplexed DRAM address 115
Multiplexed PCI address and data bus 536, 539
Multiplexer 1249
Multiplexing 394, 541, 544
Multiplexing scheme 514, 533
Multiplication rate of the internal
PLL oscillator 281
Multiprocessor Interrupt Subsystems 575
Multiprocessor operation 140
Multiprocessor systems 221, 575
Multistaged processing 116
Multitasking 107, 360, 1249
Multitasking operating system 36, 86, 1249
Multitrack operations 721
Multivibrator element 891
Music scale 623
Musical Instrument Digital Interface 1019
MWE 416

N

N-channel field-effect transistor 40
N-channel MOS 1250
N-input AND 158
N-input OR 158
NAN 171, 1249
Nano 1249
Nanometre 1249
Nanosecond 1249
Native mode 1089
Native mode a low-level formatting 1096

Near call 102
Near jump 102
NEAT chips 404
NEC 1249
NEC CPU 450
Negative integers 44
Nested mode 567
Nested task 62, 108
Netnodes 22, 23, 1249
Network 1250
Network adapter 7, 22, 893, 910, 1250
Network topologies 910
Newsgroups 894
Nibble 43, 1250
Nibble Mode 407, 1250
NMI 83, 139, 198, 199, 232, 304, 356, 374, 452, 464, 573, 574, 1250
NMI mask register 574
NMOS 42, 1250
No coprocessor available 86, 186, 370
No operation 813
No parity 854
Non Maskable Interrupts 83
Non-correctable data error 1091
Non-interlaced mode 956, 973
Non-preemptive multitasking 111
Non-return to zero 745, 1250
Non-twisted cable 686
Non-volatile memory 896
Non-volatile RAM 636, 1250
Normalized representation 170, 1250
Not a number 171, 1249
Not limited 184
Not-taken branch 309, 319
NRZ 745, 1250
NRZ data 783
NRZ read data 786
NRZ write data 786
Ns 1250
NT file system 683
Number 43
– of available mouse buttons 1153
– of cylinders 766
– of heads 766
– of root directory entries 673
– of the interrupt handler 562
– of wait cycles 146
Numeric Unit 180
Numerical Instruction Set 385
NumLock function 924
NumLock LED 929
NumLock mode 929
NumLock state 925
NVR 636, 1250

O
Octaves 623
OCW 565
OCW formats 571
Odd parity 854, 1252
OEM name 668
Offset 52, 122, 1250
Offset of the interrupt vector 82, 567
On-board VGA 504
On-chip cache 220
On-chip code and data caches 321
On-chip floating-point 253
On-chip refresh 403
ONCE 198, 199
One time programmable 439
One-shot multivibrator 891
Opcode 76
Open the case 2
Operand 76
Operand size prefix 91
Operating modes and registers for controlling on-chip caches 322
Operating principle of CD-ROM 833
Operating system 32, 33, 95, 702, 703, 1251
Operating system functions 88
Operation code 76
Operation command words 565
Operation mode of the Hercules card 968
Operation modes 8237A 603
Operation of the 8237A 618
Optical disk 17
Optical drives have a SCSI interface 832
Optical mass storage 832
Optical mice 28, 943
Optimum interleave value 744
Optional commands 1090, 1100
Optional IDE commands 1103
OR gate 158
OR operation 157
Ordered queue tag 814
Organization of caches 212
OS/2 36, 682, 1251
OTPs 439
Out of paper 848
Output buffer 933, 936
– of the keyboard controller 938
Output data buffer 398
Output latches 581, 585
Output port 937
Outputting a character to a printer 843
Overdrives 276, 1251
Overflow 62, 186, 1251
– condition 938
– with INTO 85

Overlay files 489
Overrun error 857, 869, 887, 888
Overscan colour 1171
Own busmaster 478

P

P-channel field-effect transistor 40
P-channel MOS 1254
P5 1251
Package types 269
Packed BCDs 46, 1251
Packet assembler/disassembler 895, 1251
Packet switching 910
Packet-switching networks 894
PAD 1251
PAD adapter 895
Page 1251
– 1 of the Hercules card 969
– change 975
– descriptors 1115, 1117, 1130
– Directory 120, 249, 324, 330, 1251
– fault 125
– frame 120, 122
– granularity 90
– interleaved memory 146
– mode 405, 1251
– not present 120
– register 457, 468, 469, 481, 618
– register I/O addresses 619
– size extension 326
– table 120, 249, 324, 330, 1252
– table entry 122
Page-mode access time 407
Page/interleave mode 431
Paged/interleaved memory 409
Pages 120, 424, 898, 964, 965, 1002
Paging 118, 120, 1247, 1252
Paging and virtual 8086 mode 134
Paging bit 64
Paging control register 331
Paging enable 65
Paging exceptions 125
Paging function of the Pentium 329
Paging mechanism 120
Paging routine of the operating system 123
Paging Unit 65
Pairing rules 312
Palette 13, 961, 984, 1252
Palette colours 982
Palette register 984, 986
Parallel 967
Parallel interface 7, 18, 839, 1139, 1252
Parallel interface card 19
Parallel interface data register 844
Parallel printer 1255
Paramagnetic substance 651
Paramagnetism 651, 1252
Parameter byte 870, 1146
Parameter list 823
Parameter tables 766
Parameters of the SVGA 988
Parent directory 672
Parity 61, 854, 870, 885, 1252
– and baud rate 854
– bit 21, 694
– check 452, 695, 697
– checking module 573
– enable 305
– enable bit 885
– error 573, 857, 869, 887, 888
– error in main memory 635
– module 574
– select bit 885
Park Read/Write Head 1081
Park.exe 32
Parking device 739
Partition 664
Partition entries 665, 666
Partition sector 665, 666
Partition size 682
Partition table 665, 666, 757
Partition table's structure 666
Pascal 1252
Passive bus cycle 150
Path between processor and main memory 141
Path between processor and ports 153
Pause mode 929
PauseEDC 1207
PC 450, 1252
– Card Interface Controllers 904
– card, 897
– hardware interrupts 1051
– software interrupts 1051
PC-DOS 1252
PC/XT 18
– architecture 450
– BIOS 768
– bus slot 458
– DMA channels 455
– keyboard 921, 922, 939
– port addresses 454
– system bus 457
– the keyboard interface 921
– timer channel 453
PCI 1252
– adapters 535
– agents 513
– BIOS available 530

– BIOS result codes 532
– bridge 513
– burst 515
– bus structure 513
– class code search 531
– interrupts 522
– master 537
– read transfer burst 520
– signals 535
– slots 532, 534
– unit search 531
– units 513
– write access 521
– write transfer burst 521
PCI-specific BIOS routines 530
PCIC 904
PCMCIA 896, 1253
– Card Services 1212
– card 897
– contacts 899
– controller 897
– Controller Registers 904
– interface 897, 898
– slot 898, 899
– Socket Services 1195
PCMD 198
Peer-to-peer connections 912
Pentium 48, 295, 1043, 1050, 1253
– address pipelining 339
– block diagram 308
– bus 335
– compatibility 325
– die 295
– EFlags 325
– features 325
– I/O address space 351
– ID code 348
– initialization 332
– instruction pairing rules 1043
– JTAG Boundary Scan Test 347
– on-chip caches 320
– overdrive 277
– pinout 296
– pipelines 309
– protected mode 328
– real mode 327
– register contents after a reset or init 333
– register dump in SMM RAM 344
– reset 332
– signals for MESI transitions and inquiry cycles 324
– special cycles 340
– system management mode 342
– test functions 347
– virtual 8086 mode 328
Percussion 1025
– vibrato and tremolo register (port BDh) 1026
Performance monitoring 345
Periodic activation by the CPU 626
Periodic interrupt 641
Periodic timer interrupt 590
Peripheral Component Interconnect 513, 1252
Peripheral standard bus 504
Peripherals 2, 152, 557, 839, 1253
Persistence of the fluorescent layer 955
Personal Computer 1
Personal Computer Memory Card International Association 896, 1253
PG 65
PGA 136, 354, 1253
Phantom voltage 916
Phases of the SCSI bus 809
Photosensor assembly 943
Physical address 119
Physical address space 52, 120, 1253
Physical CPU–drive interface 791
Physical cylinder number 1097
Physical disk parameters 663
Physical drive geometry 1096
Physical format 772
Physical interfaces 791
Physical memory access 140
Physical memory addressing 136
Physical organization of floppies 660
Physical organization of floppies and hard disks 683
Physical organization of the video RAM 982
Physical sectors 663
Physical start and end sectors of each partition 666
PIC 1220, 1253
Picture elements 954
«piggyback board» 366
Pin grid array 136, 354, 1253
Pins 180
PIO 554, 793, 1089, 1253
PIO cycle 554
Pipeline 227
– interlocks 240
– stage 1253
– structure 309
Pipelined addressing 142, 147, 238
Pipelined cache line fills 339
Pipelines of the Pentium 335
Pipelining 363, 1253
PIT 1220, 1254
PIT, port B and speaker 622
Pixel arrangement in the video byte 1003

Pixel block 961
Pixel pattern 'O' in text mode 961
Pixels 954, 1254
PLA 1254
Plastic leaded chip carrier 354, 1254
Plastics quad flatpack package 1255
PLCC 354, 1254
PLL oscillator 281
PLOCK 232
Plotter 2
Plug-in card 1221
PM/IO 198
PMOS 1254
Pointing devices 27, 948, 1248
Polarization 836, 1254
– direction 836, 1254
– filter 836, 1254
Polling 557, 725, 726, 913
– mode 573
Port 57, 136, 629, 705, 1254
Port A 628, 629, 630, 634
Port addresses 932
Port assignment in the PC/XT 633
Port B 622, 628, 629, 630, 635, 921
Port C 628, 629, 630, 636
POS 501
POS register 501
Position of the cursor in video RAM 975
Position of the root directory 671
Positional system 43
Positioning failures 765
Positioning time 1254
Positioning with a servo head and servo tracks 741
POST 1254
POST routine of the BIOS 501, 642
Posting 828
Posting buffer 514, 517, 518
Potential course for a data read 397
Potential equalization 397
Potentiometer resistance value 891
Power consumption 39, 204
– of CMOS chips 205, 280
Power management mode 195
Power saving features 285
Power supply 29, 453, 466
Power-down mode 159, 269
Power-good signal 30
Power-on self test 1254
Power-saving drives 794
PowerPC 318
PPI 1220, 1254
PPI 8255 connections 628
PPI 8255 terminals and signals 628
PQFP 1255
Precharge circuit 395, 396
Precision 168, 171, 185
Precode byte 924, 1151
Precompensation 754, 767
– register 796
Preemptive multitasking 111
Prefetch buffer 319, 514
Prefetch queue 52, 69, 77, 150, 162, 234, 1255
Prefetcher 233
Prefetching 77
Prefix 76
Present contacts 533
Pressing 920
Primary bus 514
Primary or secondary adapter 716
Primary ring 918
PRINT 841, 931
Print-screen routine 994
Printer server 910
Printer status byte 842, 1141
Printers 18
Printing 839
Printing via BIOS Interrupt INT 17h 842
Printing via DOS 840
Priority 565
Priority modes for servicing arriving DMA requests 603
Priority strategy 614
PRIVATE 265
Privilege levels 86, 87
PRN 839, 1255
PRN handle 4 841
Probe data register 346
Probe mode 305, 350
Procedure call 78
Process 1262
Process computer 7, 1255
Processing models 116
Processing of an interrupt request of a peripheral 564
Processor 38, 1255
Processor bindings 902
Processor board 7
Processor cards 165
Processor clock 464
Processor derivatives 192
Processor extension 8, 174, 1230
Processor families 39
Processor identification number 156
Processor reset 155, 937
Processor ROM 236
Program 6, 99, 1255
Program a flip-flop 436

Program execution in system management mode 345
Program segments 100
Program-verify 444
Programmable control register 580
Programmable counters 579
Programmable event counters 346
Programmable interrupt controller 465, 1220, 1253
Programmable interval timer 465, 1220, 1254
Programmable keyboard 27, 466
Programmable logic array 1254
Programmable monoflop 589
Programmable option select 501
Programmable peripheral interface 1220, 1254
Programmable ROM 439, 1255
Programmable sample rate 949
Programmable storage controller 15, 745
Programmable time intervals 579
Programmed counting mode 586
Programmed I/O 554, 793, 800, 1089, 1253
Programming an interlaced mode 973
Programming an optical drive with a SCSI interface 833
Programming and command phases 820
Programming and erasing rate 444
Programming and interrogating the mouse 946
Programming floppy drives 702, 705, 709, 713
Programming interface to the host adapter 821
Programming a flip-flop state 435
Programming date and time 647
Programming memory windows 905
Programming one of the three 8253/8254 counters 583
Programming the 6845 967, 969
Programming the 8237A 612
Programming the 8253/8254 582
Programming the 8255 PPI 632
Programming the keyboard directly via ports 932
Programming the mouse 946
Programming the multimedia hardware 1018
Programming the PS/2 mouse 949
Programming time 441
Projective infinity 187, 388
Projective sense 369
PROM 1255
PROM programmer 441
Prompt 34
PROMs 438
Properties 171
Protected mode 38, 54, 354, 461, 1255
– exceptions 114
– virtual interrupt 326
– virtual interrupt bit 284
Protected virtual address mode 86, 354
Protection enable 64, 93
Protection mechanism for pages 124
Protection mechanism in protected mode 115
PS/2 985, 1255
– BIOS 872
– BIOS routines 952
– memory system 498
– Model 30 505
– mouse 946, 948
– mouse data packet 949
– mouse support via BIOS interrupt INT 15h, Function c2h 1158
– series 474
Pseudo LRU replacement strategy 219
Pseudo protection exception 80, 129
Pseudo-interrupt vector 1eh 729
Pseudo-interrupt vector 1fh 998
Pseudo-interrupt vectors 41h and 46h 1062
PUSH 71
PUSH ESP 72
PUSHA 71
PUSHF 71
PVI 284, 326

Q

Q8 412
Quantities of sets 219
Queue 814

R

R2000 236
R3000 236
R4000 236
RAM 8, 1255
– memory mapping 421
– organization in graphics mode 965
– organization in text mode 963
Random access memory 1255
Random access time 749
Random replacement 220
RapidCAD 1255
Rare earth 1243
RAS 393, 395, 412, 1255
– access time 398
– precharge cycle 432
– precharge time 397, 398, 406, 408
– staggering 420
– time-out counter 432
RAS-only refresh 402, 403, 420, 595, 1255
RAS/CAS recovery times 437
RAS-CAS delay 395
Rate generator 589

Rate select 641
RC 200
Read 1112
– buffer 1059, 1128
– burst 542
– capacity 1121
– character by means of INT 16h, function 00h 931
– data 951
– defect data 1125
– deleted sector 1073
– error 711
– identifier code 444
– in-service 572
– input port 937
– internal system clock 592
– long 1128
– map select register 1006
– memory 444
– one character from the serial interface 871
– one sector 745
– pointer 927
– port 967
– prefetch buffer 518
– prefetching 513, 517
– receiver buffer register of COM1 881
– request 572
– sector 800, 1072, 1091
– sector buffer 1100
– sector identification 1078
– status register 934
– time stamp counter 346
– track 1076
– transfer 602, 609
Read-back command 581, 583, 584, 586
Read-only file 672
Read-only memory 10, 1257
Read/reference clock 786
Read/write head 658, 659, 735, 1256
Read/write head and floppy disk 659
ReadEDC 1208
Reading a byte from disk 680
Reading a counter 584
Reading and writing data 395
Reading count values 584
Reading instructions 77
Reading one character from a serial interface 869
Real mode 38, 52, 53, 90, 1256
– debuggers 61, 65
Real-time clock 24, 25, 453, 466, 592, 636, 647, 1054, 1256
Reassign alternative track 762
Reassign blocks 1111
Reassign sector 762
Received data ready 882
Receiver baud rate 876
Receiver buffer 881, 884
– register 856, 877
Receiver control 877, 878
Receiver shift register 856, 877
Receiving an SDU 856
Receiving keyboard characters 938
Reception errors 888
Reception of an SDU 856
Recording formats 689, 754
Recovery routine 151
Recovery time 398
Redirecting the INT signal 565
Redirection 1147, 1148, 1162
– bit map 329
– table 576
Reduced instruction set 237
– computer 235, 1256
Reduced write current 747, 754, 767, 1256
Redundant code 701
Redundant information 701
Reference frequency 885
Refresh address 402, 1255
Refresh cycle for the DRAMs 417
Refresh logic 464
Refresh method 595
Refresh overhead 595
Refresh rate 974
Refresh request 497
Refresh the memory chips 420
Refresh types 403
Refreshed periodically 392
Refreshing 398
REG 900
Register 501, 1256
– bypassing 240
– dependencies 313
– dump 288, 293, 1084
– dump base 345
– file pointer 242
– files 237, 241
– indices 427
– operand 74
– ports 427
– set 1260
– stack 181
– values after a processor RESET 381
– values after RESET/FNINIT 370
– window 1260
Registers 35, 152, 704
– and ports 932
– drive/head 797

– of the generator cells 1020
Release 1119
Reliability 747, 752
Relocation 431
Remanence 652, 1256
Remanent magnetization 652
Remapping of an address area 529
Remote mode 949
Remote repeater 915
Removable data volume 14
Repeater 915, 1235
Repetition function 922
Repetition rate 922, 932
Repetition rate and delay 942
Replacement of cache lines 321
Replacement strategies 218
Representation 171
Representation of floating-point numbers 167
Request 853
Request block 117
Request register 615
Request Sense 1108
Request to Send 858, 875, 1257
Requested IDE commands 799
Requested Privilege Level 87
Requests of a lower priority 572
Required and optional PCI pins and signals 535
Required commands 1090
Reselection phase 810, 811
Resend 933, 943, 951
Reserve 1118
Reserved device names 841, 868
Reserved POS register bits 502
Reserved sectors 668
Reset all connected drives 799
Reset bus unit 813
Reset flip-flop 617
Reset scaling 949
Reset SCSI device 1137
Reset wrap mode 951
ResetSocket 1205
Resolution of the mouse 950
Resolutions 955
Restore data pointers 813
Restore pointer 812
Restoring the data bits 693
Restoring the MFM data 693
Result of the BIST check 332
Result phase 720, 726, 800, 804
Resume from system management mode 342, 345
ResumeEDC 1208
Return channel 877
Return codes of the keyboard 938
Return from system management mode 345
Rezero Unit 1108
RGB 1256
RGB monitors 13
RGBI signal 979
RI 859, 875, 1256
Ring buffer 927
Ring indicator 859, 875, 1256
Ring input 916
Ring line distributors 916
Ring organization of the keyboard buffer 927
Ring output 916
Ring topology 911, 912
RISC 235, 1256
– characteristics at a hardware level 237
– characteristics at a software level 242
– implementation 241
– principles 165, 235
– processors 166
RISC-I 237
RISC-II 237
RLL 754, 1257
– 1,7 757
– 2,7 755, 1257
– 3,9 757
– controller 756
– encoding 746
– logic of the controller 756
– method 755
– sector format 759
ROM 10, 438, 452, 464, 1257
– activation signal 430
– BIOS 10, 15, 816, 1257
– BIOS identifier 769
– configuration register 428
– extensions 768
Root Directory 670, 674
Rotating and EOI modes 571
Rotating priority 603
Rotating voice-coil actuator 740
Rotation speed of the hard disk 732
Row Address Strobe 393, 395, 412, 416, 1255
Row and a column address 394, 414
Row decoder 397, 399, 437
RPL 87
RS-232C 1257
RS-232C control signals 876
RS-232C interface 857
RS-232C logic levels 864
RS-232C output signals 886
RS-232C standard 21, 857, 864
Run length limited 755, 1257
RUNBIST 265, 287

S

S3 adapter 1011
Safe instruction recognition 316
Safe instructions 316
SAMPLE/PRELOAD 264
Sampling 1019
– rate 951
SASI 805
Saturation magnetization 652
Saturation voltage 41
Save data pointer 812, 813
Saved pointers 812
Saving screen contents 1006
SBO 538
Scaling factor 75
Scan code 26, 634, 921, 923, 926, 939, 1027, 1257
Scan matrix 26, 920, 1257
Scan line address 960
Scan lines 954, 961
Scan lines per character row 974
Scanner 1258
Scheme of the internal system clock 592
Scientific notation 167
Scoreboarding 240
Scratch-pad register 889
Screen mask 944
Screen modes 957
Screen splitting 981
Scroll 929
Scroll LED 929
SCSI 16, 805, 1258
– address 807
– bus 806
– bus and PC integration 806
– bus phases 811
– commands 822, 1104
– data port 816
– high-level protocol 815
– host adapter 806, 815, 1239
– instruction chains 828
– interface cable layout 808
– Request Block 826, 1135
– standard 813, 830
– Task File 815
– unit 807
SCSI-I 830
SCSI-I, SCSI-II, SCSI-III 1258
SCSI-ID 807
SCSI-II 830
– classes 820
– commands 1105
– standard 820
SCSI-III 832
SDLC 1258
SDU 854, 855, 920, 1258
– format 884
Searching for BIOS extensions and their initialization 769
Second-level cache 221, 233, 1243
Second-level page tables 122
Secondary adapter 684
Secondary bus 514
Secondary colours 984
Secondary ring 918
Sector buffer 713
– identification information 1102
Sector count 802
– register 796
Sector flag 1096
– structure 759
Sector identification 689, 1071, 1089
Sector identification in the result phase 1085
Sector layout 689
Sector number registers 797
Sector numbers 802
Sector read 722
Sector size 721
Sector slipping 760, 1258
Sectors 662
Seek 1097, 1113
Seek errors 728, 753, 765
Seek Relative 1084
Segment 1258
Segment descriptor 87, 89, 94
– base and limit 91
– cache register 95, 155, 364
Segment interleaving 53
Segment not available 114
Segment override 58, 75
– prefix 76
Segment registers 52, 55, 59
Segment selector 87, 94
Segmentation 1247
Segmentation in real mode 52
Segments 52
SEL 809
Select signals 686
Selection phase 810
Selector 1258
Selects a target unit 810
Self-correcting code 1233
Self-test 194, 332
Semiconductor laser 833
Semiconductor layer structure 400
Semiconductor memories 165, 236
Send diagnostic 1120
Sense amplifiers 398, 399
Sense laser beam 835

Separate 813
Serial and asynchronous data transfer 853
Serial data signals 876
Serial data unit 854, 1258
Serial interface 7, 20, 591, 853, 1141, 1258
Serial mode 408, 1259
Serial port 967
Serial printer 865
Serial-in 875
Serial-out 875
Serialization 855
Serialization status register 869, 887
Server 22, 23, 1259
Servo head 740
Servo tracks 740
Set 215
– address 214
– Drive Parameters 766, 1099
– Host Adapter Parameters 1137
– Remote Mode 951
– repetition rate/delay 942
– Resolution 950
– Scaling 949
– Stream Mode 951
– Wrap Mode 951
Set/Identify Scan Codes 940
SetAdapter 1198
SetEDC 1207
SetPage 1202
SetSocket 1204
Setting the video mode 994
Settle time 748
Setup erase/erase 444
Setup mode 502
Setup of the RAS/CAS delay 419
SetWindow 1201
Several pages in video RAM 975
Shadow RAM 421, 422
Shadowing 421, 422, 498
Shared sense amplifiers 401
Shared slot 535
SHIFT key 922
Shift LED 929
Shift lock mode 929
shift status 929
Shift Status Byte 1152
Shift-Print 931
Shifting the data and clock window 764
Shoe shining 764
Short real 169, 172
Shugart Associates 713, 805
– systems interface 806
Shutdown 362
– cycle 150
– state 363
– status byte 643
– status entry 358
Sign 61
Signal generator 963
Signal levels 475
Signal levels at the UART input terminals 889
Signal levels in the case of a connection between DTE and DCE 860
Signal path between CPU and memory 140
Signal's course in page mode 405
Signed integers 45
Silicon 1259
Silicon hard disks 443
SIMM 8, 410, 411, 1259
Simple instructions 1259
Simplex 1259
Simplex connection 859
Simulate the AT keyboard 924
Single bit errors 697
Single cycle machine instructions 238
Single function PCI unit 523
Single function unit 537
Single in-line memory module 1259
Single in-line package 1259
Single queue tag 814
Single step 85
Single transfer 606
Single transfer cycles 336
Single transfer mode 336
Single transfer write cycles 336
Single-staged processing 116
Singletasking operating system 35
Size of the magnetized region 735
Size of the ROM extension 769
SL Enhanced i486 287, 1259
SL Enhanced i486DX with 1x-clock 287
SL Enhanced i486DX with 2x-clock 289
SL Enhanced i486DX2 with 1/2x-clock 288
SL Enhanced i486SX with 1x-clock 288
SL Enhanced i486SX with 2x-clock 289
Slave 608, 791, 1090
Slave diagnostics code 1099
Slave DMA channels 467
Slave PIC 465, 559, 563
Sleep 794
Slots 7, 1259
Small computer systems interface 805, 1258
Small scale integration 1260
SmartDrive 750
SMARTDRV 214
SMM 206, 283, 288
– identification 345
– initialization values 343

– memory 206
SMM RAM 1260
SMM RAM Structure 343
Snoop cycle 1241, 1260
Snooping 221, 222, 224
Socket Functions 1195
Socket Services 902
Soft errors 699, 753
Soft reset 281
Software caches 213, 750
Software emulations 173
Software interface to the mouse driver 946
Software interrupts 81
Software layers of the PCMCIA interface 903
Software mouse pointer 944
Software triggered pulse 589, 591
Solid state hard disks 445
Sound with nine channels 1020
Sound with six channels and five percussions 1025
SoundBlaster registers 1019
Source 40, 1260
Source index 58
Sources of interrupts 84
Space 854, 1252, 1260
Space state 876
SPARC 236, 1260
Speaker 596, 622
Special bus cycles 150, 340
Special configuration words 788, 789
Special cycles 256, 362, 517
Special mask mode 572
Specific EOI 572
Specify Drive Parameters 728
Spindle hole 656
Spindle synchronization 791
Spiral 834
Split cycle 305
Split-memory option 498
Sputtering 734, 1260
SQFP 1260
Square-wave generator 589, 590
SRAM 392, 434, 1260
– access times 434
– cell structure 434
– memory cell 434
– module 1219
SS 59
SSI 1260
ST01 815, 824
– control register 817
– status register 818
ST02 815
ST412 780
ST412/506 745, 747, 780
– controller 753
– interface control and signal cable 782
ST506/412 1260
Stack 71, 104
– exception 86, 114
– overflow 72
– pointer 55, 71
Stack Segment 59, 71
Stacked capacitors 401
Stand-alone VLB adapters 548
Standard bus cycle 479, 494
Standard configured floppy drive 687
Standard input device 1148
Standard on-chip exception handler 185
Standard output device 1147, 1162
Standard palette 1000
Standard ready signal 688
Standard video modes 976, 977
Standard 32-bit Section 536
Standardized SCSI Programming Interfaces 828
Standby 794
Stanford concept 242
Star topology 911, 912
Start a command execution 824
Start Address High/Low 975
Start address in the 6845 964
Start address of the EMS window 425
Start address of the window within the video RAM 1010
Start bit 854, 880, 1260
Start cluster 672
Start command execution 801
Start cylinder for the write process 802
Start routine 117
Start sector 802
Start/Stop 1120
StartEDC 1207
Start the command execution 802
State of the connection 888
State of the multivibrators 892
Static column mode 1260
Static design 204
Static electricity 5, 1261
Static power consumption 159
Static RAM 392, 1260
Static-Column Mode 407
Station manager 918
Stations of the LAN 910
Status cycle 142
Status key 1132
Status latch 581
Status of the keyboard buffer 1149
Status of the RS-232C input signals 888

Status register 528, 612, 613, 727, 797, 798, 844, 847, 851, 933, 934, 967
Status Register ST0 1085
Status Register ST1 1086
Status Register ST2 1087
Status Register ST3 1088
Status registers A and B 719, 720
Status value of the ASPI functions 827
Step rate time 728
Stepper motor 737, 1258
Stepper pulses 737
Stop bit 854, 870, 1261
Stop clock condition 286
Stop Clock Mode 285, 287
Stop grant mode 287
Stop grant special cycle 282
StopEDC 1208
Storage capacities and access times of ROM chips 442
Storage capacity 17, 748, 760, 838
Storage capacity of memory chips 392
Storage controller 714
Storage transistor 440
Storage transistor with floating gate 440
Store MSW 64
Storing data onto disk 701
Storing of one bit 435
Stream mode 949
Streamer cartridge 17
Streamers 16, 17, 1261
Streaming data procedure 495, 1261
Strength of the magnetic field 3
String 44, 1261
– instructions 62
Strobe 19, 845, 1261
– pulse 849
Structure
– and contact assignment of a bus slot 458
– and functioning of hard disk drives 732
– and functioning of the PIT 8253/8254 579
– and organization of the keyboard buffer 927
– of a local area network 23
– of a microprocessor 49
– of a segment selector 87
– of keyboard and keyboard interface 920
– of root directory and subdirectories 671
– of the 6-, 10- and 12-byte commands 823
– of the 8253/8254 PIT 580
– of the Floating-Point Pipeline 315
– of the game adapter 890
– of the grown defect list 762
– of the IBM token ring 917
– of the MC146818 637
– of the Pentium floating-point unit 316
– of the video memory word 960
– size 392, 1261
Structure, function and connection to printers 844
Sub-class code 526
Subdirectories 674
Subfunction
– Carry Out Grey Scale Mapping for a Block of Video DAC Colour Registers 1175
– Clear Wait Time Interval 1057
– Control CPU Access to Video RAM and I/O Ports 1181
– Control Cursor Emulation 1182
– Control Grey Scale Mapping 1181
– CPU Access to Video RAM 1190
– Determine Current Parameters of the Character Definition Table 1180
– Determine Mouse Identification 1160
– Determine Size of Save/Restore Buffer 1185
– Determine SVGA Information 1187
– Determine SVGA Mode 1189
– Determine Video Combination 1182
– Determine Video Configuration 1180
– Enable or Disable the Monitor Control Signals 1182
– Enable/Disable Blink Attribute 1171
– Enable/Disable Mouse 1158
– Extended Mouse Status 1160
– Initialize Mouse 1160
– Load 8*14 Character Definition Table From EGA/VGA ROM for Graphics Mode 1179
– Load 8*14 Character Definition Table From EGA/VGA ROM for Text Mode 1175
– Load 8*14 Character Definition Table From EGA/VGA ROM for Text Mode and Program CRT Controller 1177
– Load 8*16 Character Definition Table From EGA/VGA ROM for Text Mode, and Program CRT Controller 1178
– Load 8*16 Character Definition Table From VGA ROM for Graphics Mode 1179
– Load 8*16 Character Definition Table From VGA ROM for Text Mode 1176
– Load 8*8 Character Definition Table From EGA/VGA ROM for Graphics Mode 1179
– Load 8*8 Character Definition Table From EGA/VGA ROM for INT 1fh in Graphics Mode 1178
– Load 8*8 Character Definition Table From EGA/VGA ROM for Text Mode 1176
– Load 8*8 Character Definition Table From EGA/VGA ROM for Text Mode and Program CRT Controller 1177
– Load Standard Palette 1181

– Load User-Defined Character Definition Table for Graphics Mode 1178
– Load User-Defined Character Definition Table for Text Mode 1175
– Load User-Defined Character Definition Table for Text Mode and Program CRT Controller 1177
– Pass Driver Address 1161
– Read All Registers 1172
– Read Block of Video DAC Colour Registers 1174
– Read Colour Select Register of Attribute Controller 1174
– Read Overscan Register 1172
– Read Palette Register 1172
– Read Video DAC Colour Register 1173
– Read Video DAC Mask Register 1174
– Reset Mouse 1159
– Restore Status 1186
– Save Status 1186
– Save/Restore SVGA Video State 1189
– Select Active Character Definition Table 1176
– Select Alternate Routine for Print Screen 1180
– Set All Registers 1171
– Set Colour Select State of Attribute Controller 1173
– Set Individual Palette Registers 1171
– Set Overscan Register 1171
– Set Resolution 1159
– Set Sample Rate 1159
– Set Scan Line Number for Text Mode 1181
– Set SVGA Mode 1188
– Set Video Combination 1182
– Set Wait Time Interval 1057
– Set/Determine Logical length of Scan Line 1190
– Set/Determine SVGA Display Beginning in Video RAM 1191
– Write Block of Video DAC Colour Registers 1173
– Write Video DAC Colour Register 1172
– Write Video DAC Mask Register 1174
Subfunctions of INT 15h, Function c2h 1158
Substrate 40, 400, 1261
Summary of protection mechanisms in protected mode 115
Super VGA 988, 1262
– video modes 989, 1000
Super386 1261
– pipelines 208
Superpipelined architecture 239
Superscalar 240, 295
SuperState V mode 206, 208, 1217
Supervisor 124, 250
Supply cable 685
Supply voltages in a PC 30
Support chips 466, 557
Support the PS/2 mouse 952
Surface mounted quad flatpack package 1260
SUS_STAT 198, 201
SVGA 965, 1009
– BIOS 1187
– video modes 1001, 1188
Swap routine 100
Swapping 95
Switch back to the real mode 644
Switching between text and graphics mode 969
Switching into protected mode 96
SYNC width 971
Synchronization circuitry 880
Synchronization signals 955, 957
Synchronous 1262
Synchronous and Asynchronous Transfer 853
synchronous bus system 477
Synchronous data link control 1258
Synchronous extended bus cycle 494
Synchronous mode 808
Synchronous operation of the 8086/88 and 8087 388
SysReq 924, 930
SysReq key 1147
System address bus 451, 463
System bus 10
System clock 592, 1262
System configuration PC Controller Drive 683
System controller 140, 565
System data bus 451, 463
System files 672
System management interrupt 206, 283
– active 283
System management mode 205, 206, 283, 285, 288, 342, 1262
– interrupt 342
– RAM 1260
System management RAM 306
System resources 683
System segment and gate types 101
System segments 98, 101, 360

T

T 660
T/C 460
Table indicator 89
Tablet 28
Tag 214, 1262
– address 214
– address comparator 218
– and memory entries for the i486 cache 247

– and memory entries of the Pentium caches 321
– as queue head 814
Taken branch 309, 319, 1262
Taking care of data 31
TAP controller 262
Tape drive 807
TARGA 828, 829, 1262
Target 516, 807, 809
Target abort 517
Target parameters 1114
Target ready 516
Task 88, 1262
– gate 107, 109, 361
– gate descriptor 109, 361
– priority 577
– priority register of the 82489DX 577
– Register 92, 358, 1263, 1264
– State Segment 101, 360, 1263
– switch 62, 64, 86, 109, 1263
Tasks in Virtual 8086 Mode 130
TBE 882, 887, 888
Tbyte 1263
Technical reference 31
Temporary 8-bit register of the 8237A 468
Temporary real 169
Temporary register 603, 610, 612
Tera 1262
Terminal count 604, 722
Terminate I/O process 814
Terminating resistor 686, 687, 783, 789, 807
TEST 374
Test control register TR5 260
Test data register TR7 259
Test functions 257
Test instruction set 264
Test registers 125, 126, 258, 326
Test Unit Ready 1107
Testing the on-chip cache 259
Testing the TLB 258
Texas Instruments Graphics Architecture 990, 1263
Text adapter 11
Text mode 12, 957, 961, 975, 983, 1002, 1004, 1005, 1008, 1009, 1263
Text row 962
Thick Ethernet 915, 1235
Thin Ethernet 915, 916, 1235
Thin small outline package 445, 1264
Thinfilm heads 736
THR 869
Threshold voltage 41, 440
TIGA 990, 1263
TIME 636
Time and date function 639
Time and date information 638
Time base for one character 976
Time base for the real-time clock 641
Time intervals 1054
Time is encoded 672
Time stamp counter 326, 346
Time stamp disable 326
Time-divisionally multiplexed address and data bus 373, 385
Time-out 842, 869, 933
– error 848
– LPT1 844
– routine 117
– value 868
TIMER 592
Timer 383
– chip 11, 1263
– interrupt 81
– overflow flag 1054
TLB 123, 253, 322
TMS 262, 269, 306, 539
TMS 34010/020 990
– graphic processor 991
Toggle incrementation 520
Token 1263
Token bus 914, 1263
Token passing 914, 1263
Token Ring 893, 916, 1263
Token ring procedure 914
Tone generation 623, 624
Tone sequences in the background 625
TOP 181
Tower 4
– cases 5
Tpi 1263
TR 92, 358, 1264
TR32 511
TR6 test command register 259
Track density tpi 838
Track instead of a sector buffer 751
Track layout 690
Track length 729
Track length/max. sector number 721
Track-track access times 748, 1264
Trackball 21, 28, 952, 1264
Tracks 661
Tracks per inch (TPI) 663
Tracks, cylinders and sectors 661
Transceiver 915, 1235
Transfer bandwidth 546
Transfer CCB to CAM driver 829
Transfer length 822
Transfer of data and control signals to the printer 840

Transfer of data to and from the controller 554
Transfer rate 142, 362, 479, 780, 786, 830, 831, 835, 838, 864, 915
– between controller and drive 719
– between the controller and main memory 751
– in EISA systems 554
– with an ISA 475
Transfer rates 558, 864
– of busmaster adapters for the local bus 555
Transfer status byte 870
Transfer types 516
Transferring the data of a read sector or sector to be written 725
Transformation logic on the EGA card 1005
Transistor–transistor logic 42, 1264
Translating 766, 771
Translation
– and the formatting of hard disks 773
– from logical to physical geometry 794
– logic of the controller 1099
– lookaside buffer 123, 251, 254, 322
– mode 1089, 1097
Transmission baud rate 876
Transmission status 869, 1145
Transmitter buffer empty 882, 887
Transmitter hold register 855, 869, 881, 884
Transmitter shift register 855, 869, 878
Transmitting an SDU 856
Trap 61, 85, 1264
Trap gate 1264
Tremolo 1020
Trench capacitor 402
Trigger pulse 880
Trigger signals at the GATEx input 588
Triggering 1264
Triple fault 64
Triple the internal clock 276
Tristate Test Mode 261, 333
TrueColor 990, 1010
TSS 101, 107, 360, 1264
– descriptor 109
TTL 42, 1264
– monochrome monitor 1007
Tunnel oxide 442, 443
TURBO 199
Turbo-ATs 474
Turbo-PC/XT 450
Turn on/off LEDs 939
Two's complement 44, 1264
TXE 887
TYPE 841
Type of descriptor 90
Typical local bus units 554
Typical SRAM cell 434

U

U-Pipe 1265
U-pipeline 303, 1265
UART 20, 21, 872, 1264
– register addresses 881
UART 8250/16450/16550 864, 871, 895
– block diagram 877
– connections 872
UART chip 1219, 1220
ULSI 1265
Ultra large-scale integration 1265
Unbonded Pentium chip 295
Underflow 185, 1265
Unformatted capacity 662, 748
Unformatted gross 748
Unit block 117
Unit ID 526
Unit memory cells 436
Units supported by the ABIOS 117
Universal asynchronous receiver and transmitter 872, 1264
Universal board 535
Universal Synchronous and Asynchronous Receiver and Transmitter 1265
UNIX 36, 1265
Unsigned integers 43
Unsigned long integers 43
Unspecific EOI command 572
Update DR 265
Update interrupt 641
Update Present connection 269
Upgrade connection 272
Upgrade principle 271
Upgrade socket layout 277
Upgrades 267, 276, 1265
Upper Memory Area 80
USART 1265
User 124
– exit 1ch 626
– exit of the timer interrupt IRQ0 593
– manual 30
– shell 34
User-defined character sets 980, 999
User-defined hard disk type 644
UV radiation 441

V

V-Pipe 1266
V-pipeline 303, 1266
V.24 857
V20 450
V30 450
Valid code words 702
VendorSpecific 1211

Ventilation 741
Verify 1082, 1125
Verify buffer in main memory 1060
Verify Sector 1094
Verify Transfer 610
Version register 428
Vertical Displayed 972
Vertical machine code format 241
Vertical recording 734
Vertical retrace 955, 960, 962, 969, 972
Vertical synchronization 960, 962, 969
Vertical Total 972
Vertical Total Adjust 972
Very Large-Scale Integration 1266
VESA Local Bus 540, 1265
VESA SVGA 988
VESA SVGA BIOS 1000
VGA 504, 985, 1008, 1265
– adapter card 11
– BIOS 986
– modes 986, 1008
– parameters 985
VI 283, 325
Vibrato 1020
Video bandwidth 955
Video controller 956
Video DAC (digital-analogue converter) 986, 1174
Video DAC colour registers 986
Video extension 505
Video graphics adapter 504, 985, 1265
Video graphics array 504, 985, 1265
Video memory 1265
Video memory word 944, 945
Video RAM 12, 957, 964, 1265, 1266
– bank structure 1003
– division into several image layers 981
– in text mode 964
– word 960
Video segment 965
Video signals 955
Video Status 1000
VIP 283, 325
Virtual 8086 mode 54, 62, 127, 1266
– extension 284, 326
Virtual 8086 monitor 128
Virtual 8086 tasks 127, 130
Virtual address space 95
Virtual connections 895
Virtual drives 667
Virtual interrupt flag 283, 325
Virtual interrupt pending flag 283, 325
Virtual machine 128
Virtual machine system 1266
Virtual mode 129
Virtual disks 667
Visible characters per row 971
VL bus 541, 1266
VL bus controller 546
VL busmaster 552
VL slots 541
VLB 540, 1266
– adapters 549
– BIOS 549
– bus structure 540
– signals 550
– slots 548, 549
– targets 551
VLSI 1266
VME 284, 326
VMS 667, 1266
Voice coil actuator 733, 739, 1266
VOLDET 282
Volume label 672, 673
VRAM (video RAM) 399, 966, 1266
VSYNC 508
– position 972

W

Wait cycles 431, 464
Wait functions 83h and 86h of BIOS Interrupt INT 15h 1056
Wait state logic 452
Wait states 145, 146, 212, 459
Wait states for write accesses 551
Waiting time for a network access 911
WAN 22, 894, 910
Warm boot 156
Watchdog timer 484, 499
Waveforms of the SoundBlaster 1022
Way 215, 1266
Weitek 1267
Wide area network 22, 910, 1267
Wide SCSI 831, 1267
Winchester drive 731
Window 897
Window functions 1195
Window in the large video RAM 1010
Windows Accelerator 989
Windows NT 682
Word 1267
Word boundaries 363, 380
Word count 360
Word line 395, 400, 1267
WORM 17, 835, 1267
Wrap-around 79, 297, 377, 432, 461, 603, 605, 1267
Write 1113

– allocation 1267
– and Verify 1124
– Back and Invalidate Data Cache 247
– buffer 213, 235, 342, 1127
– buffer in main memory 1059, 1065
– burst 542
– data duplication 151, 544
– Deleted Sector 1075
– enable 395
– laser beam 835
– Long 1129
– once policy 225
– once, read many 835, 1267
– pointer 927, 929
– port 967
– posting 513, 517, 518, 541, 543
– precompensation 1268
– protect hole 656
– protect slide 657
– pulse 836
– Sector 801, 1074, 1093
– Sector Buffer 1101
– sector command 801
– transfer 602, 610
– transmitter hold register of COM1 882
Write-allocate 212, 222
– strategy 213, 222
Write-back 212, 335, 1267
– buffers 342
– cache 213, 222, 546
– special cycle 257
– strategy 321
Write-enable 10
Write-posting 420
Write-precompensation 747
Write-protect switch 898
Write-through 212, 321, 1268
– cache 222, 546
– strategy 212, 247
Write-thru 1268
Writing a sector 746
Writing count values 583

X
X-address bus 451, 463
X-bus 1268
X-data bus 451, 463
X-Y-scaling factor 1160
X.25 adapter 895
XENIX 682, 1268
XOR gates 696
XOR operation 696
XOR truth table 696
XT 450, 1268
XT controllers 746, 781, 788
XT hard disk controller 1061
XT task file 781
XT/286 450

Y
Yellow cable 915, 1235

Z
Z4 49, 1268
Z80 426
Zero 61
Zero insertion force 278
Zeromodem 866
ZIF socket 279
Zilog's Z80 895
Zone recording 771, 772, 1096